The Cambridge Edition of the Poets

DRYDEN

EDITED BY

GEORGE R. NOYES

The Cambridge Poets

Edited by

BROWNING	HORACE E. SCUDDER
MRS. BROWNING	HARRIET WATERS PRESTON
BURNS	W. E. HENLEY
BYRON	PAUL E. MORE
CHAUCER	F. N. ROBINSON
DRYDEN	GEORGE R. NOYES
ENGLISH AND SCOTTISH }	HELEN CHILD SARGENT
POPULAR BALLADS }	GEORGE L. KITTREDGE
HOLMES	HORACE E. SCUDDER
KEATS	HORACE E. SCUDDER
LONGFELLOW	HORACE E. SCUDDER
LOWELL	HORACE E. SCUDDER
MILTON	HARRIS FRANCIS FLETCHER
POPE	HENRY W. BOYNTON
SCOTT	HORACE E. SCUDDER
SHAKESPEARE	W. A. NEILSON
SHELLEY	GEORGE E. WOODBERRY
SPENSER	R. E. NEIL DODGE
TENNYSON	WILLIAM J. ROLFE
WHITTIER	HORACE E. SCUDDER
WORDSWORTH	A. J. GEORGE

The Poetical Works

of

DRYDEN

A NEW EDITION
REVISED AND ENLARGED BY

GEORGE R. NOYES

HOUGHTON MIFFLIN COMPANY BOSTON

Cambridge Edition

The Riverside Press Cambridge

The Riverside Press

CAMBRIDGE · MASSACHUSETTS

PRINTED IN THE U.S.A.

PREFACE TO SECOND EDITION

THE Cambridge edition of Dryden was published in March, 1909; a second issue, with very slight revision, followed in September, 1916. Since 1916 more study has been given to Dryden and his period than during the whole century that followed the publication of Sir Walter Scott's great edition of Dryden's works in 1808. In the present, second edition of my own book I have tried to take account of recent investigations. In it (1) the Biographical Sketch of Dryden has been rewritten and expanded; (2) a few further poems, certainly or probably by Dryden, have been inserted; (3) many new notes have been added, correcting and amplifying the commentary contained in the issue of 1916; and (4) minor changes have been made throughout the volume.

On the whole I am not ashamed of my labors of long ago, although, for instance, I blush to have included in my book two poems that are certainly not by Dryden. See the new notes on the *Epilogue to Secret Love* (page 52) and on *Song VI* from *King Arthur* (page 267).

The new notes in this edition are largely concerned with minutiæ, such details as additional bibliographical information, more exact dating, and explanation of allusions. Most of this added material has been culled from other students of Dryden. To these writers I have striven to make my debt clear when I have merely repeated their statements without verifying them: such are the references by Mr. Hugh Macdonald to advertisements in London newspapers of Dryden's time. When, as is more frequently the case, I have verified the information given by other students in printed books or articles, I have usually been silent concerning the guides who set me on the right track, contenting myself with the present general expression of gratitude.

In this revision, as in my original editorial work, I have been aided by many friends. Yet only one name is found in both my lists of benefactors, that of my devoted wife, careful and exacting as she was forty years ago. Most of my other recent helpers are persons whom I know solely by correspondence, but to whom I am grateful beyond measure.

My original work was done mainly with the Dryden books in the Harvard College Library, now and then supplemented by those in other collections, notably that of Mr. Beverly Chew. I knew nothing about bibliography, but when I used early Dryden editions I gave elementary information concerning them. Hence the bibliographical details in my book proved of some value. The work of Mr. Hugh Macdonald and other students has now made them seem infantile.

Since 1909 several great Dryden collections have been assembled in the United States and made accessible to scholars. Probably the most remarkable among them are those of the William Andrews Clark Memorial Library in Los Angeles and the Henry E. Huntington Library in San Marino, California. To the librarian of the former library, Mr. Lawrence Clark Powell, and to the bibliographers of both those libraries, Mr. H. Richard Archer and Mr. Herman Ralph Mead, I am in debt for kindly aid far exceeding the limits of mere official courtesy. To officials of the Harvard College Library, the Yale University Library, the Folger Shakespeare Library, the Boston Public Library, the Bodleian Library, and the Christ Church Library at Oxford, I am also under important obligations.

To Mr. James M. Osborn of Yale University I am grateful for aid of the most varied sort. His indications (published in *Modern Philology*) of the Dryden holdings in ten

American libraries have simplified my own labors. He himself has constantly encouraged me in my work and has given me information concerning a long series of fussy details.

To Professors Mark Van Doren, Edward N. Hooker, C. L. Day, and Louis I. Bredvold, and to President R. G. Ham, I return thanks for permission to quote from books or articles written by them. To the Cambridge University Press I am indebted for permission to quote passages from the *Lectures on Dryden* by the late Professor A. W. Verrall; to the Oxford University Press for permission to quote from the essay "Shelley, Dryden, and Mr. Eliot," in *Rehabilitations and Other Essays*, by C. S. Lewis; to the Clarendon Press for permission to quote from *Some Authors*, by Sir Walter Raleigh; and to Messrs. J. M. Dent and Sons for permission to quote from *English Satire and Satirists*, by Hugh Walker. Professor C. E. Ward of Duke University has guided me to new information concerning Erasmus Henry Dryden and Professor Guy Montgomery of the University of California has aided me in certain features of my work.

Dr. Norman H. Oswald of the University of Oregon has generously allowed me to use some of the notes contained in his unpublished University of California dissertation, *The Satires of John Dryden: a Critical Edition*, 1946. My debt to him in my commentary on *Mac Flecknoe* is extremely important. He is preparing for early publication an annotated edition of that satire.

For numerous patent contradictions in the present volume, statements made on one page and corrected on a later, I am sorry. Owing to the necessities of the situation I have been unable to avoid them.

G. R. N.

BERKELEY, CALIFORNIA
April 12, 1949.

PREFACE TO FIRST EDITION

THE present edition of *Dryden's Poetical Works* seeks to justify its existence by a more complete collection of Dryden's writings than has hitherto been attempted in popular form, by a careful collation of the entire text with the original editions, by the chronological arrangement of its contents, and by the reprinting in the *Notes* of a considerable portion of Sir Walter Scott's commentary on Dryden.

This volume includes all Dryden's undoubted poetical works, both original and translated, except his dramas; and, with the exception of some hymns (see page 919), all that have been attributed to him with any show of reason. An apology is due for giving to a book that omits so important a division of the poet's writings as his dramas the title, *Dryden's Poetical Works*, but the inaccuracy may be defended by tradition. About half of Dryden's critical essays also appear in the volume.

Details as to the sources of the text may be found in the notes to the different poems. For only a very few minor pieces have I been obliged to rely on copies made at the British Museum or elsewhere. The text of Dryden's verse is reproduced without any omissions whatever ; from his prose only a few lines, in the commentary on Persius, are left unprinted. The labor of collation has resulted in the restoring of Dryden's own text in numerous passages, especially in the translation of Virgil and in the prose essays, that had later become corrupt. For new errors committed I make no apology, but I hope that they are not frequent. The textual notes are more extensive than in previous editions, and are generally [1] intended to include all variant readings (other than obvious misprints and insignificant differences of spelling) of all important early editions. It has seemed needless, however, to collate texts that were evidently mere publishers' reprints, such as the later editions of most of the dramas ; or, except in rare instances, to consider any editions published after Dryden's death. The changes of text made in modern editions are noted, as a rule, only when adopted here.

The chronological arrangement of the contents should give the reader a clearer conception of Dryden's literary development, and of his relation to the politics of his time, than the classified arrangement hitherto followed.

Sir Walter Scott's great edition of Dryden, not the least of his claims to fame, was first published in 1808, just one hundred years ago. His sketches of the men of the seventeenth century, and his critical remarks on Dryden's genius, not only have independent literary value, but show his wide and intimate acquaintance with the society and the politics of Dryden's time. Unfortunately he was as inaccurate and diffuse as he was genial and sympathetic. In attempting to correct and condense Scott's work, I hope that I have not entirely destroyed the charm of his style.

Capitals and punctuation in this edition are made to agree with modern standards. The problem of spelling, as is always the case in a popular edition of an old author, was very difficult. No satisfactory compromise can be made between a literal reproduction of the old editions, with all their aimless inconsistencies and irregularities, and complete conform-

---

[1] Some cases in which editions desirable for collation, though not for use as a basis for the text, were inaccessible to me are specified in the *Notes*. The most important are the second editions of *Miscellany Poems, Sylvæ*, and *Juvenal and Persius*.

ity with modern usage. In general, modern spelling has been adopted wherever the change was merely external, not affecting the pronunciation of a word: thus *critick* is made *critic ; buisy, busy ; chuse, choose ; boult, bolt ; humane kind, humankind ; suddain, sudden*. In *honour, honor*, and similar words, the latter form has been adopted, in conformity with American usage, though the early editions usually print *honour*. Participles and past tenses like *confessed, confess'd, confest ; mixed, mix'd, mixt*, are normalized to *confess'd, mix'd*, but an exception is made of *blest* and *curst* as participles.

On the other hand, spellings that apparently indicate peculiarities of English vocabulary or pronunciation in Dryden's time are retained: thus, *reek* [*rick*], *shew, breer* [*briar*], *thrid, laund* [*lawn*], *prease* [*press*], *whether* [*whither*], *then* [*than*]. Here also may be mentioned Dryden's variation between the forms *them, 'em*. By discarding such peculiarities, modern editions have altered the character of Dryden's language, disguising its kinship with Elizabethan English.

In cases that seemed in any way doubtful, the inconsistencies of the early editions have been retained, as in *salvage, savage ; indued, endued ; desart, desert*. Thus on pages 872 and 873 the spellings *elfs* and *elves* occur within a short distance of each other (lines 3 and 34). Some of these cases probably might better have been made consistent, but I preferred to err on the side of archaism.

Dryden's marks of contraction are retained, as in *pow'r, wand'ring, heav'n, th' immortal ;* these are important as emphasizing the regular flow of English verse in Dryden's time, which so often makes it seem mechanical to modern ears. But here, also, the irregularities of the old editions are followed, and except in a few special cases *power, wandering, heaven, the immortal*, are reproduced wherever they occur ; *wandring*, however, is transformed into *wand'ring*.

The same principles are followed for Latin names used by Dryden : thus *Hyarbas, Sergesthus* are not changed to *Iarbas, Sergestus ;* but *Mecœnas, Cytheron, Ptolomy* become *Mœcenas, Cithœron, Ptolemy*. In English proper names the spelling of the *Dictionary of National Biography* is usually adopted. The titles of French works referred to in the *Biographical Sketch* and the *Notes* are ordinarily given in the orthography of the original editions.

Any editor of a classic author must depend largely on the labors of his predecessors. Besides my use of Scott, I have taken much material from Malone and Christie, and from Professors Saintsbury, Ker, and Williams. To the last three gentlemen I am deeply grateful for their courteous permission to make full use of their work. (Professor Saintsbury has also kindly allowed me to use the text of the Scott-Saintsbury edition as a basis for collation of the *Virgil* and the *Discourse concerning Satire*.) Occasional debts to other scholars, notably Professors Collins and Firth, are acknowledged in the *Notes*. I hope, however, that my commentary contains original contributions that will be useful to students of Dryden.

This edition has been in preparation since the summer of 1901, during which time I have been almost continuously resident in California, distant from all large collections of Drydeniana. For this reason, and others as well, I am indebted more than most editors to the help of many friends. The authorities of the Harvard and Yale libraries have generously sent their treasures to me across the continent ; Mr. T. J. Kiernan and Mr. F. B. Dexter, of those libraries, have been particularly courteous in the prompt attention that they have given to my many requests. Mr. Beverly Chew, President of the Grolier Club of New York City, and Mr. Winston H. Hagen, a member of that club, loaned me from their private libraries rare editions of Dryden that were elsewhere inaccessible to me, and the officers of the Club granted me the use of their building while collating or copying those volumes.

To Mr. E. H. Wells, Curator of Modern English Literature in the Harvard Library, I am more deeply indebted than I can well express. His zeal and skill have made the Harvard collection of Drydeniana exceptionally complete, so that Cambridge is now almost as satisfactory a place as London for the editing of Dryden's works. In my own behalf, though until my labor of collating was nearly finished I was a total stranger to him, he has taken infinite and unselfish pains, answering each of my queries with the utmost fullness, and finally sending me a card catalogue, prepared with great detail, of the Harvard Dryden collection. Largely through his aid, the bibliographical information in this volume is, I think, somewhat more complete than in previous editions.

Professors G. L. Kittredge and F. N. Robinson of Harvard University have aided me in many ways, especially by advice in regard to the text of the volume, and Professor W. A. Neilson has helped me very greatly by looking up questions that have arisen during the reading of the proof and in the preparation of the *Notes*. Mr. C. J. Barr, Assistant Librarian of the John Crerar Library in Chicago, has generously aided me by the gift of a copy of his valuable unpublished *Bibliography of Dryden*. I am indebted also to Professors E. K. Rand and W. S. Ferguson of Harvard, Professor W. T. Brewster of Columbia, Professor B. O. Foster of Stanford, and to my colleagues, Professors H. Morse Stephens, W. A. Merrill, W. M. Hart, H. W. Prescott, and T. F. Sanford of the University of California, for assistance of various kinds. Some minor obligations are acknowledged in the *Notes*.

Finally, all my other debts for aid in this edition of Dryden are as nothing compared to that I owe my wife, whose name, as joint editor, might well have been added to my own. She has collated, as well as I myself, every piece in this volume, and has read with me every line of the proof. She has prepared the *Indexes*, and has borne the larger part of the labor of making the *Glossary* ready for the press. She has revised the *Biographical Sketch* and the *Notes*, giving me invaluable advice in regard to them, and has coöperated with me in other ways too numerous for mention here.

G. R. N.

BERKELEY, CALIFORNIA,
December 1, 1908.

TABLE OF CONTENTS

NOTE

*The design on the title page is purely decorative, not
suggested by an early picture of Will's Coffee-House.*

BIOGRAPHICAL SKETCH

I

John Dryden is the greatest and the most representative English man of letters of the last quarter of the seventeenth century. From the death of Milton in 1674 to his own in 1700 no other writer can compare with him in versatility and power; indeed, in the varied character of his work, as dramatist, satirist, controversialist, translator, and critic, he has few rivals in the entire history of English literature. Though he composed his most important original poems to serve some passing political purpose, he made them immortal by his literary genius. Half unconsciously he became the founder of a literary school that retained its preëminence for more than a hundred years after his death. Any account of his life should deal primarily with his writings and with the political events that gave the occasion for many of them; at the same time it should pay due heed to Dryden's own personality, which has not always been treated with the respect that it deserves. Dryden was by profession a writer, not a hero or prophet; he suffers by the inevitable comparison with his great contemporary Milton. Yet, beneath his superficial inconsistency he had a large general honesty and uprightness, and the fierce invective of his satires must not blind us to his kindliness. Though not an heroic figure and apparently not an exceptionally interesting personality, Dryden was a likable man who grew more genial as he advanced in years and became genuinely lovable in his old age.

Dryden's parents were landed gentry. His father, Erasmus Driden,[1] third son of Sir Erasmus Driden, baronet, married on October 21, 1630, Mary, daughter of the Reverend Henry Pickering, rector of Aldwincle All Saints, in Northamptonshire. John Dryden, the first of the fourteen children of this marriage, was born August 9 (old style), 1631,[2] according to tradition at the parsonage house of Aldwincle All Saints, the residence of his mother's parents, and was baptized five days later.[3] He was brought up under strongly Puritan influences, since both the Dridens and the Pickerings took the side of the Parliament in its conflict against Charles I. He was educated first at Westminster School in London, under the famous master, Dr. Busby, to whom he later sent his own sons; and next at Trinity College, Cambridge, where he matriculated in July, 1650, and where he took his bachelor's degree in January, 1654.

The Conclusion Book of Trinity College records that in July, 1652, Dryden was disciplined for "his disobedience to the vice master, and his contumacy in taking his punishment inflicted by him." A pleasanter glimpse of the young poet is given in a letter quoted by Mr. Christie: "Dryden . . . was reckoned a man of good parts and learning while in college: he had . . . read over and very well understood all the Greek and Latin poets. He stayed to take his bachelor's degree, but his head was too roving and active, or what else you'll call it, to confine himself to a college life; and so he left it and went to London into gayer company, and set up for a poet, which he was as well qualified for as any man." [4]

---

[1] The spelling of the name *Dryden*, like that of many other names, varied in the seventeenth century. Even the poet was not rigorously consistent in his usage.

[2] At 5h 33' 16" p. m. The date of Dryden's birth, of which formerly even the year was doubtful, is now known to a second from a horoscope preserved in the Bodleian Library. See articles in *Times Literary Supplement*, 1931, pp. 633, 664, 706, 730. Dryden believed in astrology.

[3] J. M. Osborn, *John Dryden: Some Biographical Facts and Problems* (New York, 1940), pp. 269, 270.

[4] *Select Poems by Dryden*, ed. Christie and Firth (Oxford, 1893), p. xvi.

While at school and college Dryden had made some trifling experiments in writing
verse.   At Westminster School he had translated, as "a Thursday-night's exercise,"
the *Third Satire of Persius*, and had completed "many other exercises of this nature," [1]
now lost.   He had also composed in honor of his deceased schoolmate, Lord Hastings,
an elegy that is still preserved.   In 1650 he prefixed a short complimentary poem to
Sion and Parnassus, a collection of religious poems by his friend John Hoddesdon.
Probably in 1653, at all events while he was still at Cambridge, he wrote a curious letter
to his cousin Honor Dryden, mingling verse and prose in a strain of conventional and
not too delicate gallantry.   (From this fantastic epistle, which indicates nothing more
than a college flirtation, some critics have strangely concluded that the young poet was
seriously in love with his cousin.)   These early pieces are full of extravagant conceits
of the school of Cowley, and show at the best only a boyish dexterity in copying a prevailing literary fashion.

In June, 1654, Dryden's father died, leaving to his eldest son landed property that
yielded about forty pounds a year, enough at that time to support a single man in decent
comfort.   On April 23, 1655, an entry in the Trinity College records indicates that
Dryden had forfeited a scholarship by not returning to the college.   So there is a reasonable probability that late in 1654 or early in 1655 Dryden, now his own master, left
Cambridge and went to seek his fortune in London. [2]

Dryden's life after his settlement in London may be conveniently divided into three
periods: the first ending in 1681, the second in 1688, and the third with his death in 1700.
In the first period, after a few occasional poems, Dryden chose the drama as the most
profitable field of literary work, and by his success in it became the leading English man
of letters of his time.   In 1681, having from a number of causes become thoroughly dissatisfied with his occupation as playwright, he turned to satire and controversial writing, both in prose and verse, and brought his consummate literary skill to the service of
the royal power and the Tory party.   By the Revolution of 1688 he was deprived of his
position as a court favorite, and thrown back upon his pen for support.   After some
attempts, only partially successful, to recover his position as a popular dramatist, he
found a congenial occupation as a translator of the Greek and Latin poets, and as a
modernizer of Chaucer.

II

When Dryden settled in London, his first patron was his own cousin, Sir Gilbert
Pickering, a favorite of Oliver Cromwell, who in December, 1657, summoned him to his
new House of Lords and about the same time appointed him lord chamberlain.   Pickering seems to have employed his kinsman as his "clerk" or secretary. [3]   Documents in the
Public Record Office show that a Dryden or Driden or Drayden, in all probability the
poet, was in the service of the Commonwealth government from some time previous to
April 9, 1657, to September 7, 1658, that is, four days later than the death of Cromwell. [4]

If report may be trusted, Dryden did not begin professional literary work until after

---

[1] See page 365.

[2] The date usually given is 1657 or 1658.   On 1657 see Christie, *Op. cit.*, p. xvii.   The year 1658 is supported by
the author of *The Medal of John Bayes*.   This man attributes to Dryden a story about his own stupidity "when he
came first to town, being a young raw fellow of seven and twenty."   But the same writer, whose poem was printed
in 1682, also calls Dryden a "cherry-cheeked dunce of fifty-three," showing that, though he knew much gossip
about the poet, most of it probably based on fact, he was no expert on chronology.   One of his bits of gossip is that
Dryden's departure from Cambridge was because he "saucily traduced a nobleman," and would have been expelled
but for his flight.

[3] *The Medal of John Bayes.*

[4] Osborn, *Op. cit.*, pp. 168–170.

the death of Cromwell, when he entered the employ of a bookseller and publisher named Henry Herringman, lived in his house, and "writ prefaces to books for meat and drink." [1] This assertion has been tested by an examination of books published by Herringman from 1656 to 1664, but with no conclusive results. Several of the books contain prefaces that *may* have been written by Dryden, "but in none is the evidence more than suggestive." [2] It is unlikely that Dryden's fees for such prefaces would have contributed largely to his support. Certain it is that Herringman became Dryden's publisher immediately after the Restoration, when in June, 1660, he printed *Astræa Redux*, and remained so until March, 1678, when he printed *All for Love*. It must be remembered that Dryden lived before the time when an author depended for his livelihood primarily on the sale of his books through regular trade channels. Dryden's literary income came mainly from patrons to whom he dedicated his books or for whom he wrote complimentary poems; from the presentation of his plays in the theater, where the author was entitled to the receipts from the third night's performance; from his share in the profits of the King's Company of players; and from his pension as poet laureate and historiographer royal. A change occurred only during his latest years, above all with the great subscription project of the translation of Virgil.[3]

It is surprising, considering his later copiousness and versatility, that Dryden wrote for publication no verse whatever between his brief complimentary poem, *To his Friend John Hoddesdon*, of 1650, and a fairly ambitious elegy, *Heroic Stanzas consecrated to the Glorious Memory of His Most Serene and Renown'd Highness Oliver, Late Lord Protector of this Commonwealth, &c., Written after the Celebration of His Funeral*, which was printed early in 1659 along with poems on Cromwell by Waller and Sprat. Herringman had planned to publish the poems by Dryden and Sprat along with one by Marvell, but for some unknown reason changed his mind. Another printer, William Wilson, took over the enterprise, but substituted for the poem by Marvell one by Waller that had already appeared.[4] Dryden in his elegy adopts the four-line stanza that Davenant had brought into prominence by his *Gondibert*. His style, simpler and more direct than in his earlier poems, shows the influence of the study of Davenant, and also, no doubt, of Denham and Waller. As a young, ambitious literary man, Dryden began his career by copying authors of established reputation. This imitative method he followed to some extent through his whole life, modifying and developing his own numbers by the constant reading of earlier poets. The critical faculty was always a prominent element in his genius. Yet in stanzas like that which concludes the poem, he already shows that vigorous, rapid verse which remains his distinguishing characteristic among English poets: —

> His ashes in a peaceful urn shall rest;
> His name a great example stands, to show
> How strangely high endeavors may be blest,
> Where piety and valor jointly go.
>
> (Page **7**, lines 145–148.)

---

[1] The authority once more is *The Medal of John Bayes*, which has the lines: —

> But he [Cromwell] being dead, who should the slave prefer,
> He [Dryden] turn'd a Journey-man t'a Bookseller;
> Writ Prefaces to Books for Meat and Drink,
> And as he [the bookseller] paid, he [Dryden] would both write and think.

On the word "Bookseller" there is the note, "Mr. *Herringman*, who kept him in his House for that purpose."

[2] Osborn, *Op. cit.*, pp. 170–183.

[3] Alexandre Beljame, in *Le Public et les hommes de lettres en Angleterre au dix-huitième siècle, 1660–1744* (Paris, 1883), traces the change in the financial basis of English literature between Dryden, who depended primarily on patrons and pensions, and Pope, who depended primarily on the public.

[4] Hugh Macdonald, *John Dryden: a Bibliography of Early Editions and of Drydeniana* (Oxford, 1939), pp. 3, 4.

At the Restoration of King Charles II in 1660, Dryden joined the Royalist party, and expressed his loyalty to the new government in three poems, *Astræa Redux*, and addresses, *To his Sacred Majesty*, and *To my Lord Chancellor*, written in the heroic couplet, and published in the years 1660, 1661, and 1662. The contrast between his earlier praise of Cromwell and the adulation of royalty in these poems is certainly offensive to a modern reader. But Dryden's change of heart, though emphasized by his ability to clothe his opinions with rhetorical, hyperbolic flourishes that pleased his contemporaries, and with a vigorous verse that still has a certain charm, merely reflected that of the majority of people about him. Nobody thinks of drawing up an indictment against the English nation for its inconstancy, and only Dryden's later eminence has caused him to be singled out for special censure. Henceforth Dryden will be a consistent member of the Tory party.

Dryden's change of politics had been accompanied by his forming new associations. He became intimate with the family of Thomas Howard, Earl of Berkshire, a loyalist noble, at least three of whose nine sons, Edward, Robert, and James, were dabblers in literature. With Sir Robert Howard, the sixth son, he began a friendship that lasted, despite an interruption caused by a quarrel on literary questions, until Sir Robert's death in 1698.[1] This alliance with a loyalist family was cemented by Dryden's marriage, on December 1, 1663, with the Lady Elizabeth, the youngest daughter of the house. The children of this union were three sons: Charles, born in 1666; John, born in 1667 or 1668; and Erasmus Henry, born May 2, 1669. Scandal, unsupported by any trustworthy evidence, reports that Dryden's wife was no better than she should be, and even that the poet was forced into marriage with her by her "brawny brothers."[2] Though it is needless to enter into the details of this somewhat unsavory subject, a few general remarks may throw light on the situation. The numberless sneers at marriage in Dryden's writings merely reflect the literary fashion of the time and prove nothing as to his own experience. More important is the fact that in the numerous letters that have been preserved Dryden refers only casually to his wife, and never with any expressions of affection. The family traditions that survived into the eighteenth century were unfavorable to the character and the personality of the Lady Elizabeth.[3] When in his later years the poet visited his country kinsfolk, his wife seems to have remained at home in London. Dryden's own character, at least in his early life, probably differed little if at all from that of the licentious young noblemen whose associate he was proud to proclaim himself. His intrigue with the actress Anne Reeve was a never-failing subject for jest from his opponents. On the other hand, both Dryden and his wife show in their letters a charming parental tenderness for their three sons. Perhaps Dryden's marriage may be dismissed as one of convenience, good or bad, which had at all events no disastrous results.

Dryden was never a denizen of Grub Street. He was the eldest son of a country gentleman and the grandson of a baronet; the earliest of the many satires on him, published in 1668,[4] terms him derisively "the squire." By his marriage to an earl's

---

[1] Some complimentary verses, prefixed to an edition of Howard's poems published in 1660, are the first token of this friendship.

[2] The chief attacks on the character of the Lady Elizabeth are contained in two scurrilous satires, *Satyr to his Muse, by the Author of Absalom and Achitophel*, and *The Tory-Poets, a Satyr*, both published anonymously in 1682, eighteen years after the date of the marriage. *The Medal of John Bayes*, a third anonymous satire of 1682, written by a man just as foul-mouthed as the authors of the other two pieces, but apparently more copiously informed than they, is totally silent on this matter. On the authorship of the three pieces see below, pp. xlv, xlvi.

[3] Osborn, *Op. cit.*, prints in full certain letters from which Malone derived his information about those traditions. See especially pp. 245, 246, 250.

[4] *A Letter from a Gentleman to the Honourable Ed. Howard Esq; Occasioned By a Civiliz'd Epistle Of Mr. Dryden's Before his Second Edition of his Indian Emperour*. The Hon. Edward Howard was a brother-in-law of Dryden. The title "squire" was presumably prompted by Dryden's own *Prologue to The Wild Gallant, Reviv'd*: see page 52.

daughter he improved his social position. Among the English nobility he soon gained a circle of friends and patrons, including some persons of the very highest rank. For instance he won the favor of the Duke of Monmouth (an illegitimate son of Charles II) and of his duchess, to whom in 1667 he dedicated *The Indian Emperor*, and to whom in *Absalom and Achitophel* (line 34) he gave the title of "the charming Annabel." Despite a shy and hesitating manner and a lack of brilliance in conversation, mentioned both by his detractors and by himself, Dryden must have had no small charm of personality.

By his marriage Dryden also advanced himself financially; he was, as Leslie Stephen has justly remarked,[1] "the least unworldly of all great poets." On February 27, 1662, "Dame Elizabeth Howard" had been granted by the government the sum of £3000, presumably in recognition of her father's services, to be paid at the rate of £250 quarterly, "beginning March 25 next." The actual payment of this grant was delayed, but began at some time between June 25, 1666, and August 21, 1667, and was completed on August 11, 1669. One may assume that Dame Elizabeth's husband profited by this; at all events, in October, 1667, the young man of letters was opulent enough to make a loan of £500 to King Charles himself, secured by the customs. On June 17, 1673, Lord Treasurer Clifford signed an order that this loan "be paid forthwith" with interest. It is somewhat surprising that Dryden should have been a person to whom King Charles II could apply for a loan; perhaps even more surprising that the king repaid the loan.[2] One may mention also that Dryden in 1692[3] describes himself as owning a "small fortune in Wiltshire," the county in which his father-in-law, the Earl of Berkshire, had his chief possessions; but it is impossible to say whether Dryden acquired this estate by his marriage or at some later date.

So Dryden could have lived in tolerable comfort as a gentleman of wit and sense and pleasure, modeling his existence on that of his monarch, "sauntering Charles," and his titled courtiers. He could have lived on the fringe of the English nobility, writing occasional poems, or even dramas, with no particular thought of profit, just as did his brothers-in-law Edward, Robert, and James Howard; or, to give more prominent illustrations, such nobles as John Wilmot, Earl of Rochester, and George Villiers, Duke of Buckingham. Literature was a favorite amusement for "the wits of either Charles's days." But Dryden was more than a wit; he had serious intellectual interests. He was a university graduate, of wide reading in Latin, French, and Italian as well as in English; and he was interested in science as well as in literature. He was an early member of the Royal Society, which had been organized about 1660, being "elected" a fellow of it on November 19, 1662, and "admitted" a week later. In his poem *To my Honor'd Friend, Dr. Charleton*, written in that year, he showed his pride in English scientific achievements. In *Annus Mirabilis*, written in 1666, he not only employed imagery based on science or scientific speculations (lines 5, 6, 65–68, 553–556), but inserted a direct apostrophe to the Royal Society (lines 657–664). It is true that his enthusiasm did not lead him to any financial sacrifices, for on February 26, 1665, he was reported delinquent in the payment of dues; and on October 29, 1666, he was dropped from membership in the Society: he had apparently not even paid his initiation fee.[4] But this delinquency — not without parallels in later centuries — does not alter the fact that Dryden "was interested in the Royal Society, understood its spirit, and recognized that he was like minded with it." [5] In 1664, in the dedication to his drama *The Rival Ladies*, he expresses

---

[1] In the *Dictionary of National Biography*.
[2] On these financial matters see C. E. Ward, "A Biographical Note on John Dryden," in *Modern Language Review*, xxvii (1932), 206–210; and "Some Notes on Dryden," in *Review of English Studies*, xiii (1937), 297, 298; and various references in *Calendar of State Papers, Domestic*, and *Calendar of the Treasury Books*.
[3] See dedication to *Cleomenes* (*Works*, ed. Scott-Saintsbury, viii. 217).
[4] Claude Lloyd, "John Dryden and the Royal Society," in *Publications of the Modern Language Association of America*. xlv (1930), 967–976.   [5] Bredvold, *Ibid.*, xlvi (1931), 957.

regret that the English do not have an Academy similar to that in France.[1] On December 7, 1664, the Royal Society voted to establish "a committee for improving the English language" and elected Dryden as one of the twenty-two members of it.[2] Dryden probably attended meetings of that committee.[3] Later, in 1679, when he dedicated *Troilus and Cressida* to "the Right Honorable Robert, Earl of Sunderland, Principal Secretary of State, one of His Majesty's Most Honorable Privy Council, etc.," he once more pleaded that a British Academy be established.[4] And in 1692 and 1693, as passages in his *Discourse concerning the Original and Progress of Satire* and his dedication of *Examen Poeticum* amply show, he still had the subject in mind.[5] One may also note, as a proof of the breadth of Dryden's ideals, a sentence that he wrote in 1674, as a part of his castigation of Settle: —

"A man should be learned in several sciences, and should have a reasonable, philosophical, and in some measure a mathematical head, to be a complete and excellent poet; and besides this, should have experience in all sorts of humors and manners of men; should be thoroughly skilled in conversation, and should have a great knowledge of mankind in general." [6]

Aside from his intellectual interests, Dryden had no small practical, business sense. He desired to make his way in the world, to have not only a comfortable but a large income. He was not a man with a mission; he had no new ideas with which to enrich mankind and no intense emotions that clamored for utterance. But he knew that he had a talent for writing, and he took up the profession of letters just as with different gifts he might have turned to medicine or law. He was ready to adopt whatever literary form seemed likely to be profitable, financially and socially. Had he lived in our own times he would probably have become a journalist, a career for which he was unusually adapted. But English journalism was still in a rudimentary state. In the years following the Restoration, the only branch of literature that promised steady and adequate remuneration was the drama; and to this, notwithstanding the fact that he felt little inborn talent for it, he soon turned his almost undivided attention.

Dryden's work for the stage falls into three fairly distinct divisions. After a period of apprenticeship and experiment, he won immense success as the chief writer of a new type of drama, the "heroic play"; his most famous work of this class is *The Conquest of Granada*, acted in the winter of 1670–71. Next, dissatisfied with the plays that had brought him popularity, he developed, after a new series of experiments, a type of tragedy that imitated the methods of dramatic construction used by Corneille and Racine, but the style and character-drawing of Shakespeare. His finest production of this sort is *All for Love*, acted in 1677. After *All for Love* Dryden adopted no new dramatic methods; he merely used anew devices of which he had already tried the effect.

In 1660 there was an immediate revival of the theater, which had almost ceased to exist in England on the suppression of stage-plays by Parliament in 1642. The traditions of the old drama survived, and one prominent writer, Sir William Davenant, connected the old time with the new. On the other hand, upon the return of the king and his followers from their exile in France, French fashions, and to a less extent French ideas,

[1] *Works*, ed. Scott-Saintsbury, ii. 134.

[2] O. F. Emerson, "John Dryden and a British Academy," in *Proceedings of the British Academy*, 1921–1923, pp. 46, 47.

[3] This may be inferred from Evelyn's letter to Pepys of August 12, 1689 (*Diary and Correspondence*, London, 1859, iii. 311). See Ella Theodora Riske in *Publications of the Modern Language Association of America*, xlvi (1931), 951, 952.

[4] *Works*, ed. Scott-Saintsbury, vi. 250, 251.   [5] See pages 320, 385, 386.

[6] From the postscript to *Notes and Observations on The Empress of Morocco*; see *Works*, ed. Scott-Saintsbury, xv. 406. This pamphlet was the joint composition of Dryden, Shadwell, and Crowne; but Malone and Scott are probably correct in attributing the postscript to Dryden.

became a potent influence in the new English drama, which, even more than that of the time of Charles I, depended on the court for support. Without attempting an elaborate analysis of the drama at the time Dryden began his career, we may distinguish in it at least five different types. (1) The English comedy of humor, descended from Ben Jonson. This deals primarily with the lower orders of society; it presents men and women marked by one predominant trait, or *humor*. (2) Comedy of manners, represented in the old drama, for example, by several plays of Beaumont and Fletcher and of Shirley. This deals primarily with the higher ranks of society, and depends for its effect largely on the reproduction of the superficial manners of cultivated circles. This type was soon strongly affected by French models, notably the works of Molière. (3) Comedy of intrigue, depending for its effect on an involved plot, full of unexpected turns of fortune. Some comedies of Shakespeare and of Beaumont and Fletcher, such for instance as *Twelfth Night*, approach this type. In the Restoration period, however, the type owed much to Spanish influence, both directly and through the French drama; "Spanish plots" became a recognized factor in English dramatic production. (4) Romantic tragedy, derived from the work of Beaumont and Fletcher. (5) Tragedy of the "classic" type, obedient to the rules of the Renaissance dramatic critics. This form of drama, though it was well known to the Elizabethan dramatists, had never become really popular on the English stage before the closing of the theaters. In France, however, after the appearance of Corneille's *Cid* in 1636, it won a decisive victory, and through the masterpieces of Corneille and Racine it powerfully affected the practice of the Restoration playwrights.

Fully as important as the direct influence of the French drama on the English was the influence of the dramatic rules just mentioned, which had been developed by a succession of Italian and French critics. Of them the most important were the famous three unities, of time, place, and action. The first prescribed that the time of action of a play should not exceed one day; the second, that the scene of action should remain unchanged, or at least not depart from the limits of a single city; the third, that each drama must have one central plot, to which all subordinate intrigues, if they existed, must directly contribute. These rules had been known to Elizabethan men of letters, but had exercised a vital influence on only one leading Elizabethan dramatist, Ben Jonson. After the Restoration, however, they won greater respect, because they were supported not only by the precepts of French critics, but by the practice of gifted French dramatists, chief among whom were Corneille, Molière, and Racine.

French literature made its influence felt on the drama in two more ways. In the first place, French tragedy was invariably written in rhymed verse. English dramatists, when they came to imitate this practice, could fortify themselves by occasional precedents in their own predecessors of "the former age." Again, the favorite prose fiction of the time was the French chivalrous romances of D'Urfé, La Calprenède, and Mlle. de Scudéry. These vast works, extending through some dozen volumes apiece, treat of the adventures of gallant knights and faithful ladies; their scene may be in ancient Greece or Persia, or in barbarian Turkey, but the sentiments expressed in them are those of elaborate, ceremonial gallantry, akin to the artificial etiquette of the French court. Love and honor are the foundation of every plot — in fact, the only emotions recognized by the heroes and heroines. Evidently, when such fictions were the favorite reading of English ladies and gentlemen, their spirit would soon make itself felt upon the stage.

Finally, Dryden's dramatic work will be greatly affected by the "heroic poem," or artificial epic, of which Tasso's *Jerusalem Delivered* is the best example. This literary form was a favorite subject of discussion in Dryden's time, and was regarded as "the greatest work which the soul of man is capable to perform." [1] The romances that have

[1] See *Dedication of the Æneis*, page 487.

just been mentioned are, in large measure, heroic poems told in prose, so that their influence coöperates with that of the heroic poem in the strict sense.

Dryden's work as a dramatist was essentially eclectic. He himself was by temper, as we have seen, a critic and a stylist rather than a creative artist, and in his criticism two currents may be distinguished. Keenly sensible to literary merit wherever he found it, he was a devoted admirer of Shakespeare, Beaumont and Fletcher, and Ben Jonson. On the other hand, through his logical, analytic, somewhat scholastic temperament, he recognized the power of the new French criticism, with its hard and fast rules of dramatic construction. Hence in his own dramatic work he constantly tried to combine elements which he had found effective in other dramatists, in a form which should not too far diverge from the dictates of the current dramatic criticism.

In *The Wild Gallant*, his first play, a comedy written in prose, Dryden united humor studies, imitated from Ben Jonson, with wit combats in the vein of the comedy of manners, following the lead of Fletcher and of Shirley. His drama is coarse and indecent. He constructed his plot with some regard to the three unities, so that his piece was primarily in the Jonsonian tradition.

The Wild Gallant, first acted at the Theater Royal on February 5, 1663, failed on the stage. Meanwhile, only four weeks earlier (on January 8), a comedy by Sir Samuel Tuke, *The Adventures of Five Hours*, an adaptation from the Spanish with an involved, truly Spanish plot, written in blank verse but with occasional passages of heroic couplets, and absolutely free from vulgarity, had been presented at the rival house, the Duke's Theater, and had won conspicuous success. Dryden promptly adjusted his sails to the popular breeze. In his next independent play, *The Rival Ladies*, probably first put on the stage about May, 1664, he laid his scene in Spain, constructed an elaborate "Spanish" plot, avoided indecency, and wrote in blank verse mingled with passages in heroic couplets. That is, he followed closely the methods of Sir Samuel Tuke.[1] *The Rival Ladies* is serious in tone, but has a happy ending. It was apparently mildly successful.

Dryden's work on *The Rival Ladies* was of less historical importance and of less significance for his own career than his collaboration with his brother-in-law Sir Robert Howard on *The Indian Queen*, a tragedy, or more strictly an "heroic play," written entirely in the heroic couplet, which was produced with great magnificence in January, 1664. Encouraged by the success of this piece, Dryden composed independently a sequel to it, *The Indian Emperor*, a drama of the same species, acted in the spring of 1665. These "heroic plays" are the one type of English drama in which Dryden excels all other writers; his succeeding works of the same sort are *Tyrannic Love* (1669), *The Conquest of Granada* (1670–71), and *Aureng-Zebe* (1675). Briefly, they aim to reproduce on the stage the effect of an heroic poem. They are all, like *The Indian Emperor*, written wholly in the rhymed couplet, which was then regarded as the most appropriate form for English epic poetry. Unlike other English tragedies of the time, they contain no comic underplot, and they usually have a happy ending. Their plots are frequently taken from the French romances. In character-drawing and diction they are powerfully affected both by the romances and by epic poetry. Love and chivalric honor are practically the only passions that animate their characters.[2] Yet these heroic plays do not assimilate the finer qualities of the French neoclassic drama: Mr. C. S. Lewis has

---

[1] The discussion of Dryden's dramatic methods here and later follows that in *The Sources of John Dryden's Comedies*, by Ned Bliss Allen (Ann Arbor, 1935).

[2] In the romantic plays of Beaumont and Fletcher signs of this conventional drawing of character had already begun to appear. But Professor J. W. Tupper, in his article, "The Relation of the Heroic Play to the Romances of Beaumont and Fletcher," in *Publications of the Modern Language Association*, xx (1905), 584–621, seems to overestimate the kinship between the two types that he discusses. Dryden also continued some of the conventions of the "Platonic drama" of Davenant, Suckling, and others. See K. M. Lynch, "Conventions of the Platonic Drama in the Heroic Plays of Orrery and Dryden," in *Publications of the Modern Language Association*, xliv (1929), 456–471.

concisely expressed the contrast by his words, "Where the *Cid* was brave, Almanzor [the hero of *The Conquest of Granada*] swaggers." [1] Their diction, high-flown, often bombastic, makes no pretense at realism; the spectators, like those at an opera in our own day, were expected to leave their common sense at home. Indeed, the plays as a whole, besprinkled with dances and songs, and decorated with scenery more elaborate than had hitherto been used for the regular drama in England, were themselves half operatic in their effect. By their tumult and bustle these plays continue the traditions of the English stage, with no regard for French decorum; in this respect they remind us of Marlowe's *Tamburlaine*. Their plots, however, are constructed with some outward regard for the rules of French dramatic criticism: in the two parts of *The Conquest of Granada* a whole series of battles is compressed within the space of two days. The heroic plays offend our twentieth-century taste by their bombast and artificiality; in their own time they pleased audiences French enough to relish artificial gallantry, English enough to love sound and fury.

Despite their observance of some neoclassic rules, the heroic plays were fundamentally romantic in tone. It would be hard to frame a definition of romanticism that should include *Marmion* and exclude *The Conquest of Granada*. They represent a far-away, distorted survival of medieval romance. They had no future before them, giving way before the tide of neoclassic rationalism and exerting no influence on the origin of the romantic movement towards the close of the eighteenth century. Yet it is interesting to note that Dryden, who more than any other single man became the founder of the neoclassic school in England, won his earliest triumphs in the theater by dramas of a distinctly romantic type.

By the success of *The Indian Emperor* in 1665 Dryden attained a prominent place among English dramatists, perhaps the first place except for the veteran Davenant, who died soon after, in 1668. Taught by the failure of *The Wild Gallant*, he abandoned the vein of Jonson, returning to humor studies only after a long interval, in *The Kind Keeper* (1678). But he was vigorously productive, not confining his work to heroic plays. Between *The Indian Emperor* and *Tyrannic Love* he produced a tragicomedy, *Secret Love* (March, 1667), and two comedies, *Sir Martin Mar-All* (August, 1667) and *An Evening's Love* (1668), and collaborated with Davenant on a debased version of Shakespeare's *Tempest* (1667). *Secret Love*, by its combination of a serious plot taken from *Le Grand Cyrus*, a famous romance by Mlle. de Scudéry, with a comic intrigue in part dependent on the same author, reminds one both of the heroic plays and of the romantic tragedies of Beaumont and Fletcher. *Sir Martin Mar-All* Dryden based on Molière's *L'Étourdi* and Quinault's *L'Amant indiscret*, but he did not follow his sources slavishly and he made important additions to them.[2] *An Evening's Love* he founded on Molière's *Le Dépit amoureux* and Thomas Corneille's *Le Feint astrologue*. In this last play and in the comic portions of *Secret Love* he continued his work in the comedy of manners, attempting to reproduce on the stage the atmosphere of Restoration aristocratic society. "In the main," it has been well said, "the invariable elements of the comedy of manners are the presence of at least one pair of witty lovers, the woman as emancipated as the man, their dialogue free and graceful, an air of refined cynicism over the whole production, the plot of less consequence than the wit, an absence of crude realism, a total lack of any emotion whatsoever." [3] These pairs of witty lovers have been rightly termed "Dryden's chief contribution to Restoration comedy." [4] This motif was later carried to perfection by Congreve in *The Way of the World* (1700).

[1] "Shelley, Dryden, and Mr. Eliot," in *Rehabilitations* (Oxford, 1939), p. 13.
[2] On the authorship of this play see pages xxxi, xxxii, below.
[3] Allardyce Nicoll, *A History of Restoration Drama* (ed. 2, Cambridge, England, 1928), p. 185.
[4] Allen, *Op. cit.*, p. 166.

During this first period of his career Dryden was not entirely occupied by work for the stage. In the spring of 1665 the plague broke out in London, so that on June 5 the king forbade "acting any more plays"; the theaters did not reopen until November, 1666.[1] Dryden was among the many thousands of persons who deserted the city owing to the pestilence. On November 10, 1666, he signed his preface to *Annus Mirabilis* "from Charlton in Wiltshire," the seat of his father-in-law the Earl of Berkshire, and his eldest son Charles was born there at some time in the same year; hence it is fair to assume that he spent most of his enforced exile at that place. During his absence from London he wrote not only *Annus Mirabilis*, the chief non-dramatic poem of his earlier years, but his chief critical work, *An Essay of Dramatic Poesy*.[2]

Dryden's *Essay of Dramatic Poesy*, like so many other of his works, is an occasional production, part of a literary controversy now thoroughly forgotten.[3] Samuel Sorbière, a Frenchman, had published at Paris in 1664 his *Relation d'un voyage en Angleterre* [*Account of a Trip to England*], in which, among other matters, he had made aspersions on the English drama, with its disregard of the unities. Thomas Sprat, the official spokesman of the Royal Society, had replied in 1665 with *Observations on Monsieur Sorbier's Voyage into England*, in which he vigorously defended English dramatic practices. Sir Robert Howard, Dryden's brother-in-law, in a preface published with *Four New Plays*, 1665, had also entered the controversy, naturally on the English side.[4] In his own *Essay*, a much longer and more elaborate discussion, Dryden attempts to lay down general principles of dramatic criticism, to defend English dramatists, both of the Elizabethan period and of his own time, and to justify his own dramatic methods. He dismisses in a rather casual fashion the drama of the Greeks and Romans, with which he was but superficially acquainted, as being little adapted to delight modern audiences, or to instruct modern dramatists. The older English drama he regards as the greatest in the world. At the same time, the principles of the French dramatists, he admits, are superior to those of the English, though their performance as a whole, owing to inadequate style and character-drawing, is inferior. In but one type of construction is the English theater manifestly superior to the French, in tragicomedy, which Dryden boldly exalts as "a more pleasant way of writing for the stage than was ever known to the ancients or moderns of any nation." This daring statement is at once a defense of Shakespeare and Beaumont and Fletcher, and a plea for Dryden's own practice in such plays as *Secret Love*. Further, in order to justify his belovèd heroic plays, Dryden gives a long argument in favor of the use of rhyme in the drama, in contrast to the general English tradition; and in defense of duels and battles and tumult in general on the stage, in contrast to the French theatrical decorum.

By his attitude toward Shakespeare in *An Essay of Dramatic Poesy* and later, Dryden showed himself in advance of his contemporaries, most of whom regarded Ben Jonson as the greater dramatist of the two. After a detailed study of this topic G. E. Bentley writes: "His [Dryden's] championing of Shakespeare in his essays and prefaces was probably the most important single influence in the burgeoning of Shakespeare's reputation after the Restoration." [5]

Dryden composed his *Essay of Dramatic Poesy* in the form of a neoclassic dialogue,

---

[1] Nicoll, *Op. cit.*, pp. 286, 287.

[2] See *Works*, ed. Scott-Saintsbury, xv. 277. The *Essay* was not entered on the *Stationers' Register* until August 7, 1667; the first edition is dated 1668.

[3] The following account depends on an article by Professor George Williamson, "The Occasion of *An Essay of Dramatic Poesy*," in *Modern Philology*, xliv (1946), 1–9. It is impossible here to enter into the details of the controversy.

[4] Howard's preface has been reprinted in *Dryden and Howard, 1664–1668*, edited by D. D. Arundell (Cambridge, England, 1929); and in Spingarn, *Critical Essays of the Seventeenth Century* (Oxford, 1908), vol. ii.

[5] *Shakespeare & Jonson: their Reputations in the Seventeenth Century Compared* (Chicago, 1945), i. 101.

making each of four speakers contribute to the development of its topic. At the present time the *Essay* is less interesting for its substance than for the style in which it is written. The critical dicta are for the most part borrowed from older authors, notably Scaliger, Ben Jonson, and, above all, Corneille. The style, easy, graceful, flowing, is a model of what good critical prose should be. In its combined dignity and simplicity, Dryden's prose — his "other harmony," as he later terms it [1] — has never been surpassed. Though he writes only a few years after Milton and Browne, his essays are so modern in their diction that they might seem, except for an occasional quaint phrase, the work of a great artist of our own day.

Annus Mirabilis, as Professor Hooker has recently demonstrated,[2] was also a skillful tract for the times. Not all Englishmen had been gratified by the restoration of Charles II. In 1661–62 three seditious pamphlets were published, under the titles *Mirabilis Annus, the Year of Prodigies; Mirabilis Annus Secundus; or, The Second Year of Prodigies;* and *Mirabilis Annus Secundus: or, the Second Part of the Second Years Prodigies*. They strove to show that various disasters and portents indicated God's displeasure with England. Many people also expected, because of Rev. xiii. 18, that the year 1666 would be critical for the nation. "Dryden's poem was a piece of inspired journalism." Dryden indicated that the fire of London and the war with the Dutch were not *judgments* upon the English, but *trials* of the people. The fire "was never allowed to touch the king's palace or his naval magazines," and was checked by the king's prayer. "The king himself is portrayed as a natural leader with a special genius in naval undertakings." "Conceived as a means to counter certain vague and superstitious terrors that filled the air, and in particular to oppose certain seditious tracts the effects of which, it was feared, would call the people forth to rebellion in times of disaster, *Annus Mirabilis* was developed as a plea that citizens should leave off their waywardness, pay their loyalty and obedience to their anointed leader, and vote him all the supplies which his purposes required. And the whole of it became an eloquent panegyric to trade, and a noble proclamation of Britain's manifest destiny."

Dryden had rapidly risen to eminence as a dramatist, critic, and poet. Charles II and his ministers were keenly aware of this and of the benefits that the royal government might derive from his services. On April 13, 1668, there was issued a "warrant for a grant to John Dryden of the Office of Poet Laureate, void by death of Sir Wm. Davenant." [3] Davenant, who had died only six days earlier, on April 7, had received no regular remuneration as poet laureate, and none was now assigned to Dryden. But on August 18, 1670, a patent was issued appointing Dryden poet laureate and historiographer royal, with a yearly pension of two hundred pounds, such pension "to begin att the feast of the Nativity of St. John Baptist next & Imediately after the death of the said Sir William Davenant": that is, on June 24, 1668. The office of historiographer royal had become vacant with the death of James Howell in 1666; Howell seems to have been a paid functionary. But Dryden was the first regularly appointed, official poet laureate. On July 2, 1677, his pension was increased to three hundred pounds.[4] There is no record that any definite duties were assigned to him, but his subsequent career certainly indicates that he was expected to give general support to government policies

---

[1] See page 741.

[2] "The Purpose of Dryden's *Annus Mirabilis*," by E. N. Hooker, in *Huntington Library Quarterly*, x (1946), 49–67. Passages enclosed in quotation marks in the text above are taken directly from that article.

[3] Professor C. E. Ward shows that Dryden's loan of five hundred pounds to Charles II (see page xxi, above) was apparently renewed on April 30, 1668, and wonders whether there may not be "a more than accidental connection" between the two dates ("Some Notes on Dryden," in *Review of English Studies*, xiii (1937), 297, 298).

[4] On this general subject see E. K. Broadus, *The Laureateship: a Study of the Office of Poet Laureate in England, with Some Account of the Poets* (Oxford, 1921). As regards Dryden this must be supplemented by L. I. Bredvold, "Notes on John Dryden's Pension," in *Modern Philology*, xxx (1933), 267–274. These writers give references to the original records that need not be repeated here.

by his literary skill. Beginning with 1670, Dryden's material prosperity seemed to rest on secure and lasting foundations.

Soon after his triumph with *The Conquest of Granada*, however, Dryden's position was vigorously assailed. The high-flown style, the exaggerated character-drawing, and the complicated plots of the heroic plays made them an easy mark for ridicule. In an effort to bring contempt on the whole type, George Villiers, Duke of Buckingham, aided by some other wits of the time, wrote the stinging farce of *The Rehearsal*, which was first acted in December, 1671. In this play, Mr. Bayes, a fashionable poet, who represents Dryden — the name is of course a gibe at Dryden's office as poet laureate, wearer of the bays — invites two gentlemen to attend a rehearsal of his new drama, which proves to be a mess of nonsense, concocted largely of parodies of Dryden's plays, especially *The Conquest of Granada*. Lacy, the actor who created the part of Mr. Bayes, was costumed to imitate Dryden, and was taught to mimic his tricks of speech and his halting manner of recitation. To modern readers the wit of this clever satire seems irresistible. But we must remember that it was presented by the King's Company of players, a company in which Dryden was a shareholder and which had produced and continued to produce his dramas, including *The Conquest of Granada*. The farce naturally raised a laugh at Dryden's expense, but it did him little serious harm. The King's Company would not have cared to present *The Rehearsal* if they had thought that it would diminish their income. Just as we can now enjoy Calverley's parodies of Browning, while still admiring their originals, so "gentlemen of wit and sense" in Dryden's time could applaud both *The Rehearsal* and *The Conquest of Granada*.

Perhaps Buckingham's attack deterred Dryden from immediately undertaking another heroic play. Just after *The Conquest of Granada*, but before *The Rehearsal* had been acted, he had written a tragicomedy, *Marriage à la Mode*, which combines a rather slight serious plot, founded on an episode in *Le Grand Cyrus*, with an excellent comic intrigue, mainly original, depicting the adventures of two pairs of his favorite witty lovers. This portion of the drama is Dryden's finest achievement in comedy of manners and, despite its flagrant immorality, still retains its daintily artificial charm. But his next play was a wretched tragedy, *Amboyna*, huddled up in haste to serve a political purpose and probably performed at some time in the first half of 1672. In this drama Dryden sought to inflame the English against the Dutch, with whom they were then at war, thus supporting a policy for which he later fiercely condemned Lord Shaftesbury.[1] Despite its lack of general literary merit, *Amboyna* (and notably its prologue and epilogue, which are printed in this volume) is interesting as the author's first attempt at political satire. This tragedy was followed by a comedy, *The Assignation*, a nondescript affair, partly comedy of manners, partly farce of a Molièresque tinge, with some scenes marked by dialogue in a serious, "heroic" tone, which was produced late in 1672 and failed on the stage.[2] In his dedication to the printed drama, published in June, 1673, Dryden hints that the failure was due in part at least to the actors and to a cabal of his enemies. *The Assignation* seems to have had better fortune on revival and to have become a stock play of the King's Company.[3]

More serious trouble than from Buckingham came upon the Laureate from Elkanah Settle, an author who is now totally forgotten except as the object of Dryden's satire,

[1] See page 112, line 175, and note.

[2] J. U. Rundle in an article on "The Source of Dryden's 'Comic Plot' in *The Assignation*," in *Modern Philology*, xlv (1947), 104–111, gives evidence that in this drama Dryden drew on Calderon, *Con quien vengo vengo*. In his preface to *An Evening's Love* Dryden implies that he could read Spanish, but does not say so directly. Though not prone to hide his own linguistic accomplishments, Dryden never quotes a single line of Spanish. The evidence from *The Assignation* is isolated and does not prove that he used the Spanish text of Calderon, a difficult author. He may have had before him an English manuscript translation.

[3] Downes, *Roscius Anglicanus*, ed. Knight (London, 1886), pp. 9–15.

but who for a time was the acknowledged boy wonder among English dramatists. Born in 1648, Settle while still a student at Oxford wrote an heroic play, *Cambyses*, which was the first piece acted by the Duke's Company on the reopening of their theater in 1666.[1] This he followed with a second heroic play, *The Empress of Morocco*, which was twice presented at court, probably for the first time in 1669.[2] The Earl of Mulgrave wrote the prologue for the first court performance and the Earl of Rochester for the second.[3] None of Dryden's dramas had received such honors and both the noble authors of prologues were among his patrons. The piece was acted at the Duke's Theater in July, 1673, and was published not later than the following November.[4] The printed drama was decorated with six "sculptures" or cuts, an unprecedented piece of magnificence. Dryden, who was not of a captious and jealous disposition, might have submitted with only inward vexation to all these triumphs of a younger poet. But in his Dedication of *The Empress of Morocco* to the Earl of Norwich, Settle inserted sneers at the failure of *The Assignation* and at Dryden's Dedication of the comedy to Sir Charles Sedley. He refers to Dryden, for instance, as "a fawning scribbler."[5] This was too much!

Stung to the quick, Dryden forgot his accustomed dignity and joined Shadwell and Crowne, his friends and fellow dramatists, in writing a scurrilous pamphlet, published in 1674, under the title, *Notes and Observations on The Empress of Morocco, or, Some Few Erratas to be Printed instead of the Sculptures with the Second Edition of that Play.*[6] In this they abuse Settle roundly as a foolish pretender to poetry, and hold up to contempt the plot, character-drawing, and style of his tragedy. Their usual method is to quote a few lines from *The Empress of Morocco*, and then, in a paragraph or two of mordant criticism, to point out their defects. To such an assault Settle had no difficulty in replying. He issued a pamphlet "contumaciously entitled," as Sir Walter Scott remarks, *Notes and Observations on The Empress of Morocco Revised; with some few erratas, to be Printed instead of the Postscript, with the Next Edition of The Conquest of Granada*, in which he subjects Dryden's favorite play to the same sort of petulant analysis. The outcome of the whole controversy is well stated by Scott in his biography of Dryden: —

"Dryden seems himself to admit that the principal difference between his heroic plays and *The Empress of Morocco* was that the former were good sense, that looked like nonsense, and the latter nonsense, which yet looked very like sense. A nice distinction, and which argued some regret at having opened the way to such a rival. . . . It was obvious that the weaker poet must be the winner by this contest in abuse; and Dryden gained no more by his dispute with Settle than a well-dressed man who should condescend to wrestle with a chimney-sweeper. The feud between them was carried no further, until, after the publication of *Absalom and Achitophel*, party animosity added spurs to literary rivalry."[7]

This personal discomfiture came at the same time as financial troubles that overtook the proprietors of the Theater Royal, the King's Company of actors, in which Dryden was a shareholder: of these troubles more will be said presently. It is, then, small wonder that Dryden undertook no new work for the theater during the years 1673 and 1674.

---

[1] *Ibid.*, p. 27.

[2] On Settle's whole career see F. C. Brown, *Elkanah Settle*, Chicago, 1910. Brown (p. 12, n. 5) quotes from Settle's Preface to *Ibrahim*, "*Morocco* . . . was acted in less than three years after *Cambyses*."

[3] There are two issues of *The Empress of Morocco*, 1673; the first issue attributes the first prologue to Lord Lumley, while the second issue attributes it to the Earl of Mulgrave.

[4] An entry in the Lord Chamberlain's Department of the Public Record Office (see Nicoll, *Op. cit.*, p. 310) mentions a performance on July 3, 1673, and this is more likely to have been the first acting of the play than a revival. The drama is listed in the number of the *Term Catalogues* licensed on November 24, 1673.

[5] Brown, *Op. cit.*, p. 54.   [6] See page 913.

[7] In Dryden, *Works*, ed. Scott-Saintsbury, i. 160, 161.

He was not a little disenchanted with the plays that had brought him fame, and was driven to form new ideals of style. In this he was assisted by three critical works that appeared in France during 1674: Rapin's *Reflexions sur la poétique*, Boileau's *Art poétique*, and Boileau's translation of the treatise of Longinus *On the Sublime*. The whole drift of these works, which Dryden undoubtedly read soon after their appearance in France, and for which he had a lively admiration, was against the extravagant "bladder'd greatness"[1] of the heroic plays, and in favor of chastened, refined character-drawing and diction.

To abandon entirely the heroic plays, however, would have been to confess defeat and discomfiture. Accordingly, in 1675, Dryden returned to his task and produced his *Aureng-Zebe*. This drama, though superficially resembling *The Conquest of Granada*, is in its nature more like a French tragedy than a typical heroic play. Dryden completely altered the historic background of his story, and constructed a plot modeled on the *Mithridate* of Racine.[2] But in drawing his characters he did not submit to the restraints of French etiquette, choosing rather as his models the heroes of Shakespeare. "The personages are imperial," to use Dr. Johnson's courtly phrase, "but the dialogue is often domestic, and therefore susceptible of sentiments accommodated to familiar incidents." In the prologue Dryden admits that: —

> he has now another taste of wit;
> And, to confess a truth, (tho' out of time,)
> Grows weary of his long-lov'd mistress, Rhyme.
> Passion 's too fierce to be in fetters bound,
> And nature flies him like enchanted ground.
> What verse can do, he has perform'd in this,
> Which he presumes the most correct of his;
> But spite of all his pride, a secret shame
> Invades his breast at Shakespeare's sacred name:
> Aw'd when he hears his godlike Romans rage,
> He, in a just despair, would quit the stage.
>   (Page 77, col. 1, lines 6–16.)

In the dedication to the play he makes more explicit his wish, at which he hints above, of retiring from dramatic writing.[3]

Thus we are not surprised to find that when Dryden, two years later, determined after all to resume writing for the stage, he composed a blank verse drama, in which he attempted a full synthesis of the form of the French classic drama with a character-drawing and style imitated from Shakespeare. In his *All for Love* he recast the old story of Antony and Cleopatra into the form of a French tragedy, laying the emphasis not on action, but on psychological analysis. He is no longer influenced by the mechanical rules of Corneille's *examens*, but by the spirit of Racine. On the other hand, each speech bears witness to his careful study of Shakespeare. The play is beyond doubt the finest of Dryden's dramatic works, and it contains some of his truest poetry; fresh from Shakespeare's *Antony and Cleopatra*, we can still read with intense pleasure Dryden's version of the story. With the possible exception of Congreve's *Mourning Bride*, *All for Love* is the happiest result of the French influence on English tragedy, an influence that continued in force, practically undisputed, until the rise of the romantic movement.

All for Love seems to have been acted in December, 1677. Meanwhile in August of that year there had appeared a book by Thomas Rymer, *The Tragedies of the Last Age, Considered and Examined by the Practice of the Ancients and by the Common Sense of All*

---

[1] For the phrase, compare page 515, col. 1.
[2] See Holzhausen, "Dryden's heroisches Drama," in *Englische Studien*, xv (1891), 14, 15.
[3] See page xl.

Ages, the most ambitious critical work that had been written in England since Dryden's *Essay of Dramatic Poesy,* to which, despite the interval of nine years that separated them, it was in some sense a reply. Rymer sent Dryden a copy of his volume; and Dryden described it, in a letter probably addressed to the Earl of Dorset, as "the best piece of criticism in the English tongue, perhaps in any other of the modern," adding, "If I am not altogether of his opinion, I am so in most of what he says." [1] The book may have been published in time to influence Dryden in the composition of *All for Love,* but this seems improbable. At all events it confirmed him in his altered point of view. Whereas Dryden, a superficial scholar but a practical dramatist who understood the taste of the British public, had dismissed the Greek theater as worthy of only senti- mental respect, and had exalted the Elizabethan drama as the greatest in all history, Rymer, a man of real though prejudiced erudition, with no sympathy whatever for popular taste, condemned the English tragedy of Shakespeare and his school as brutish, and exalted Æschylus, Sophocles, and Euripides as models to be imitated by all later playwrights. Unlike Dryden, Rymer has no independent literary taste; he does not judge of any play immediately, as it appeals to him; instead of this, he has certain fixed tests, derived from the classical school of criticism, by which he tries all the tragedies that he discusses. For him the plot is the main subject of consideration; to character- drawing and style he pays little attention. Repelled as Dryden was by many of Rymer's opinions, he could not help respecting the critic's learning, and admiring the strictly logical method — so akin to one side of his own mind — by which he reached his re- sults. On first reading Rymer's book, Dryden made some notes for a reply to it, which a happy chance has preserved to us.[2] "My judgment on this piece is this," he tells us, "that it is extremely learned, but that the author of it is better read in the Greek than in the English poets; that all writers ought to study this critique, as the best account I have ever seen of the ancients; that the model of tragedy he has here given is excellent, and extreme correct; but that it is not the only model of all tragedy, because it is too much circumscrib'd in plot, characters, etc.; and lastly, that we may be taught here justly to admire and imitate the ancients, without giving them the preference, with this author, in prejudice to our own country." He will not admit that the plot is of any such exclusive importance in tragedy as Rymer maintains, and makes a strong plea for English character-drawing and style. When *All for Love* was printed in March, 1678, he summed up his opinions thus in his Preface: "I have endeavored in this play to follow the practice of the ancients, who, as Mr. Rymer judiciously observed, are and ought to be our masters. . . . Yet, though their models are regular, they are too little for English tragedy, which requires to be built in a larger compass. . . . In my style, I have professed to imitate the divine Shakespeare; which that I might perform more freely, I have dis- incumbered myself from rhyme." [3]

In Restoration London there were only two licensed dramatic companies, the King's Company and the Duke's Company. All but two of the plays by Dryden so far men- tioned were acted by the King's Company. There were special circumstances con- nected with the two exceptions, *Sir Martin Mar-All* and *The Tempest,* both of which dramas came early in his career, in 1667. Dryden is said to have received from the

---

[1] *The Letters of John Dryden,* ed. Ward (Durham, North Carolina, 1942), pp. 13, 14. Rymer's reputation has fluctuated as violently as that of any English writer. Saintsbury comments thus concerning him: "It has been held proper, for some time, to shake the head of deprecation over Macaulay's 'the worst critic that ever lived.' . . . For once, though no Macaulayan, I venture to indorse my unimportant name on a dictum of Macaulay's. I have read several critics . . . but I never came across a worse critic than Thomas Rymer" (*A History of Criticism,* New York, 1902: ii. 391, 397). On the other hand T. S. Eliot terms him: "A critic of whom Dryden speaks highly, and of whom I should be tempted to speak more highly still" (*John Dryden: the Poet, the Dramatist, the Critic,* New York, 1932, p. 55).

[2] *Works,* ed. Scott-Saintsbury, xv. 378–392.   [3] *Ibid.,* v. 338, 339.

Duke of Newcastle a "bare translation" from Molière and to have developed it into
Sir Martin Mar-All, writing the title part with special reference to Nokes, a famous
comic actor of the Duke's Company.[1] In the *Stationers' Register* the play was entered
under the name of the Duke of Newcastle. The earliest editions are anonymous, Dryden's name, *without* that of the Duke of Newcastle, being added only in that of 1691.[2]
As for *The Tempest*, Dryden made that adaptation in collaboration with Davenant,
who had been the founder of the Duke's Company and who remained its chief member
until his death in 1668. In that year, 1668, if we may trust some lines in the prologue to
An Evening's Love,[3] which must be interpreted in connection with a legal document
that will be cited presently, Dryden seems to have contracted to furnish the King's
Company three new plays each year.

After *All for Love*, however, Dryden deserted the King's Company and gave his plays
to the rival house. *The Kind Keeper*, acted by the Duke's Company on March 11,
1678, is not, like *Marriage à la Mode*, for instance, a comedy of manners, "a comedy
of witty repartee, in which one situation is enough." It is rather "a comedy of intrigue, in which the rapid movement of the action and the varying of the situation are
all-important; the wit which grows out of these situations counts for little." [4] It is the
most indecent of Dryden's dramas, but one not wanting in the comic spirit. Its characters are "personified eccentricities," humor studies, not quick-witted members of
cultivated society. It was apparently intended for a more bourgeois audience than
those which had relished the high comedy of *Marriage à la Mode*. Similar plays, notably
those of D'Urfey, had been popular at the Duke's Theater.[5]

Next Dryden joined Nathaniel Lee, who also had been working exclusively for the
King's Company, in writing *Œdipus*, a new handling of a topic already treated by Sophocles, Seneca, and Corneille. This tragedy was acted by the Duke's Company, probably
in August, 1678.

Naturally the King's Company were far from pleased with Dryden's conduct. Their
side of the case is known from a document published by Edmond Malone in 1790.[6]
Charles Killigrew, the governor of the King's Theater, and four other members of the
King's Company, in a memorial apparently addressed to the lord chamberlain, allege:
(1) that Dryden had bound himself to write three plays a year for the Company and
in return had received a share and a quarter in the Company; (2) that he "received for
his share and a quarter three or four hundred pounds, *communibus annis* [in average
years]; but though he received the moneys, we received not the plays, not one in a
year"; (3) that when the playhouse burned down [on January 25, 1672] and debts were
incurred for building a new house, so that the value of the shares declined, "thereupon
Mr. Dryden complaining to the Company of his want of profit, the Company was so
kind to him that they not only did not press him for the plays which he so engaged to
write for them, and for which he was paid beforehand, but they did also, at his earnest
request, give him a third day for his last new play, called *All for Love;* and at the receipt
of the money of the said third day, he acknowledged it as a gift and a particular kindness of the Company"; (4) that "notwithstanding this kind proceeding Mr. Dryden
has now, jointly with Mr. Lee . . . written a play called *Œdipus* and given it to the
Duke's Company, contrary to his said agreement, his promise, and all gratitude, to
the great prejudice and almost undoing of the Company, they being the only poets
remaining to us." The petitioners conclude: "These things considered, if, notwithstand-

---

[1] Downes, *Op. cit.*, p. 28.   [2] Macdonald, *Op. cit.*, pp. 97–99.   [3] See page 57, lines 29–35.
[4] Allen, *Op. cit.*, p. 192.   [5] *Ibid.*, pp. 194–202.
[6] In *An Historical Account of the Rise and Progress of the English Stage*, printed with *The Plays and Poems of
William Shakespeare*, vol. 1, part 2, pp. 150, 151. He reprinted it in *The Critical and Miscellaneous Prose Works
of John Dryden*, 1800: I, 1, 73–75. Nicoll (*Op. cit.*, pp. 294, 295) reprints the document from Malone.

ing Mr. Dryden's said agreement, promise, and moneys freely given him for his said last new play, and the many titles we have to his writings, this play be judged away from us, we must submit."

This memorial certainly presents Dryden in a most unfavorable light. It is supported by the lines already mentioned in the prologue to *An Evening's Love*, 1668, and by the fact that in the ten years 1668 to 1677, inclusive, Dryden produced for the Theater Royal only nine plays.

Yet one must never judge of a lawsuit solely by the brief for the plaintiff. There is evidence that, though Dryden violated the letter of his contract, he had the equity of the case on his side. The members of the King's Company were not persecuted saints or disinterested philanthropists. The best expert on their history, after careful study of the legal records, says pungently: "Advancing age and (more disastrous still) dissension, greed, and bad management combined to bring about their downfall." [1] If Dryden's contract began in 1668, it had been in force for only four years before the fire of January 25, 1672, and during that time Dryden gave the Company four and probably five plays (*An Evening's Love, Tyrannic Love*, the two parts of *The Conquest of Granada*, and probably *Marriage à la Mode*), all of which were successful, so that the Company had reason to be satisfied with him: otherwise they themselves would have terminated the agreement. In the Restoration theaters plays had short runs. "Many plays died on the first night: the majority of the others saw no more than three consecutive performances. A few . . . may have seen upwards of a dozen nights, but they were exceptions." [2] Now *Tyrannic Love* is stated to have run "about fourteen days together" to crowded houses, so that the Company "received all that while about one hundred pounds per diem, whereas at other plays they are not wont usually to receive above forty or fifty pounds per diem." [3] One may doubt whether this drama had greater success than its more famous successor, *The Conquest of Granada*. A new play that ran for a fortnight was more than twice as profitable as one that ran for a week, since no expense for new scenery was involved for the second week. It is probable also that the petition cited exaggerates the amount paid annually to Dryden.[4]

After the fire of January, 1672, the King's Company, largely owing to financial mismanagement, fell into sad straits. The actors "did get very little profit by their acting," and in 1675 some of the most prominent of them gave repeated written notice "that they were minded to give over and desist from acting." Owing to this actors' strike performances ceased, but on February 14, 1676, the king issued orders that they be resumed. Under such circumstances it is obvious that Dryden derived little profit from his agreement, though after the fire he wrote *The Assignation, Amboyna*, and *Aureng-Zebe* for the King's Company, and though that Company had the rights to revivals of his earlier plays. He evidently furnished them with *All for Love* only on the stipulation that he have the receipts from the third day's performance, the usual fee for an author not working under a regular contract. After that he washed his hands of the King's Company; so likewise did Nathaniel Lee. The affairs of the Company went from bad to worse. "Barely six new plays were produced at the Theater Royal between 1678 and 1681." [5] "In April, 1682, the Theater Royal closed its doors." [6] The King's Company fused with the Duke's Company, or rather were absorbed by them, and in November, 1682, leased the new Theater Royal to Charles Davenant, the manager of the Duke's Company, for performances by the United Company.

The petition printed by Malone in 1790 has apparently disappeared from view; no

[1] Leslie Hotson, *The Commonwealth and Restoration Stage* (Cambridge, Massachusetts, 1928), p. 242.
[2] Nicoll, *Op. cit.*, p. 26.   [3] Hotson, *Op. cit.*, pp. 252, 253.   [4] *Ibid.*, p. 245.
[5] Nicoll, *Op. cit.*, p. 295.
[6] Hotson, *Op. cit.*, p. 270. This whole paragraph is based on Hotson, pp. 253–273, and documents there cited.

later writer speaks of seeing it. There is no reason for suspecting its authenticity, but Malone does not furnish wholly satisfactory information concerning it. He notes that the date and superscription are lacking, but he fails to state whether the signatures of Killigrew and the rest are in their own hands. The language of the memorial is unduly vague for a legal document, not citing the date of the contract with Dryden, the exact language of it, the precise sums paid him in successive years, or the names of the different plays furnished by him. It is peculiar that the members of the King's Company made no protest when Dryden gave *The Kind Keeper* to the Duke's Company, being aroused to action only by his second offense. One may suspect that the document is merely the preliminary, rough draft of a petition that Killigrew and his colleagues thought of presenting to the lord chamberlain, but did not actually so present. At all events, even if he received such a petition, the lord chamberlain took no action upon it; he did not hinder Dryden and Lee from giving *Œdipus* to the Duke's Company, or from giving further plays to it. In equity the King's Company had no case against the two dramatists.

Finally, it is obvious that if in 1678 Dryden had actually been guilty of rascally conduct as regards the King's Company, the memory of such conduct would still have been fresh and green among men of letters in 1681 and 1682. But in the whole spate of pamphlets that were leveled against Dryden as the author of *Absalom and Achitophel* and *The Medal*, there is not the slightest allusion to any such rascality.[1] Dryden's enemies seem to have raked up every available bit of scandal about him, going back even to his undergraduate days at Cambridge in their search for it, but they made no mention of his desertion of the King's Company.

Dryden's next drama, *Troilus and Cressida*, acted late in 1678 or early in 1679, was an adaptation of Shakespeare's tragedy of that name into a form less at variance with the French rules. In conformity with Restoration tragic conventions, which would not tolerate infidelity in a mistress, Dryden transformed the traditionally wanton Cressida into a faithful sweetheart of Troilus, just as he had similarly rehabilitated Cleopatra in *All for Love*. Sir Walter Scott comments quaintly on the matter: —

"Even the partiality of an editor must admit that, on this occasion, the modern improvements of Dryden show to very little advantage beside the venerable structure to which they have been attached. The arrangement of the plot is, indeed, more artificially [that is, artistically] modeled; but the preceding age, during which the infidelity of Cressida was proverbially current, could as little have endured a catastrophe turning upon the discovery of her innocence, as one which should have exhibited Helen chaste, or Hector a coward. In Dryden's time the prejudice against this unfortunate female was probably forgotten, as her history had become less popular. There appears, however, something too nice and fastidious in the critical rule, which exacts that the hero and heroine of the drama shall be models of virtuous perfection. In the most interesting of the ancient plays we find this limitation neglected, with great success." [2]

With *Troilus and Cressida* Dryden published (1679) an important essay, *The Grounds of Criticism in Tragedy*. In writing this treatise he borrowed much from the fashionable French critics of the time, Boileau (especially from his translation of Longinus), Rapin, and Bossu (a new French critic, whose *Traité du poëme épique* had appeared in 1675); and by the whole tenor of his argument he showed the strong influence that the ideas of the English theorist Rymer had had upon him. By a new dictum on tragicomedy, which was in striking contrast with his previous words in *An Essay of Dramatic Poesy*, Dryden here made plain his conversion to the classic point of view: —

---

[1] For an account of such pamphlets see Hugh Macdonald, "The Attacks on Dryden," in *Essays and Studies by Members of the English Association*, xxi (Oxford, 1936), 41–74. Macdonald treats of the same topic in the "Drydeniana" section of *John Dryden: a Bibliography*.

[2] Dryden, *Works*, ed. Scott-Saintsbury, vi. 243.

"Two different independent actions distract the attention and concernment of the audience, and consequently destroy the intention of the poet; if his business be to move terror and pity, and one of his actions be comical, the other tragical, the former will divert the people, and utterly make void his greater purpose. Therefore, as in perspective, so in tragedy, there must be a point of sight in which all the lines terminate: otherwise the eye wanders, and the work is false. This was the practice of the Grecian stage." [1]

After this time Dryden in his critical works remains true to the classic theory of the drama, of which he never questions the validity. Yet his very next play, *The Spanish Friar* (1680), is a patent tragicomedy, with "two different independent actions." This departure from his critical tenets, however, he excuses as a concession to English taste, instead of defending it on abstract grounds, as he would have done in his earlier years. *The Spanish Friar* was well received in its own time, and later remained the most popular of Dryden's plays, holding the stage for about a hundred years. The character of Friar Dominic, from whom the comedy derives its name, has more vitality than most of its author's creations.

The Spanish Friar is the last play that Dryden wrote during the period in which he worked primarily for the theater. His dramas, though they have appealed to fewer readers than some other branches of his manifold production, are of both historic and permanent interest. More than any other writer, Dryden represents the long conflict between the English tradition and the French influence. In comedy he did creditable work in all three of the prevailing types — comedy of humors, comedy of intrigue, and comedy of manners. Though surpassed in comic force by Etherege and Wycherley, perhaps even by Shadwell, he is broader in his range than any of the three. In tragedy he first developed an entirely new type of drama, the heroic play: and then, abandoning his own creation, he succeeded in naturalizing in England the French classic tragedy.

Dryden's dramatic experience was of immense benefit to his poetic technique. Compelled to address a popular audience, he purified his diction of the last remnants of the artificiality that is so prominent in his early work, and of which traces still remain in *Annus Mirabilis*. He developed, both in prose and in verse, a style marked above all by transparent clearness. In the heroic plays he often allowed his fluency to degenerate into bombast; later, while retaining his impetuous vigor, he acquired dignity and reserve. Through this constant practice in the technique of style, based on study of the Elizabethan and the French dramatists, Dryden gained the matchless skill that he afterwards showed in satire and controversy, when he turned from the description of dramatic types to portraits of living men and women; from disputes on nice points of love and honor to arguments on questions of theology.

Dryden's dramas give many proofs of the versatility of his genius. Readers of the present day, who know primarily his satires, his narrative poems, and his imposing ode, *Alexander's Feast*, may fail to realize that he was a favorite author of sprightly lyrics, sung by ladies and gentlemen in Restoration drawing rooms. But sixty-two of his songs, nearly all of them taken from his plays, are included in the song-books of the second half of the seventeenth century. He is there surpassed in popularity by only three writers, all of them now practically forgotten: D'Urfey (444 songs), Stanley (89 songs), and Motteux (65 songs).[2] Professor C. L. Day has done a service to Dryden's memory by gathering together his lyrics and printing them together with the musical settings composed for them.[3]

At some time during the most barren period of his long literary career, in 1673 or early in 1674, Dryden wrote *The State of Innocence*, an opera based on Milton's *Paradise*

---

[1] *Ibid.*, vi. 260, 261.

[2] These figures are based on *English Song-Books, 1651–1702: a Bibliography*, by Cyrus Lawrence Day and Eleanore Boswell Murrie (London, 1940).

[3] *The Songs of John Dryden*, Cambridge, Massachusetts, 1932.

Lost; the work was entered in the *Stationers' Register* on April 17, 1674, but was not printed until 1677. The stage directions in this opera indicate that it was intended for actual performance; [1] "it may have been written for the wedding festivities of the Duke of York and Mary of Modena" [2] in November, 1673. It was never actually brought on the stage, unless a representation at a puppet show in 1712 be counted. Though the piece is not devoid of literary merit, it is now remembered principally from an anecdote related by Aubrey: "John Dryden, Esq., Poet Laureate, who very much admires him [Milton] . . . went to him to have leave to put his *Paradise Lost* into a drama in rhyme. Mr. Milton received him civilly, and told him he would give him leave to tag his verses." [3] At this meeting surely the smaller man stands forth in the better light: Dryden in his own years of old age and tribulation would scarcely have answered a polite request with such crusty condescension.

Fairly early in his career Dryden became convinced that he had a talent for satire, nor did he keep that conviction a secret. At the close of *The Rehearsal* Mr. Bayes exclaims, in almost tearful vexation over the failure of his play: "The town! why, what care I for the town? I'gad, the town has used me as scurvily as the players have done; but I'll be revenged on them too: I will both lampoon and print 'em too, i'gad. Since they will not admit of my plays, they shall know what a satirist I am." Buckingham, or whoever wrote those words, was a prophet against his will. At some time before the close of the year 1678, by an attack on his fellow dramatist Shadwell, Dryden showed a new side of his genius.

Thomas Shadwell (*c.* 1641–1692) was a dramatist of entirely different tastes and temperament from Dryden. His talent lay in humor comedy; he was proud to proclaim himself a follower of Ben Jonson. He promptly made a reputation by his first play, *The Sullen Lovers*, acted at the Duke's Theater in 1668 and published in the same year. In the preface to that play he defended Jonson, "whom I think all dramatic poets ought to imitate," against Dryden's lack of due veneration in *An Essay of Dramatic Poesy;* mentioned authors who "strain love and honor to that ridiculous height that it becomes burlesque; and alluded to "the fine people" "in the plays which have been wrote of late," who, he said, were "most commonly a swearing, drinking, whoring ruffian for a lover, and an impudent ill-bred tomrig for a mistress." These were evident sneers at the heroic plays and at dramas of the type of *Secret Love.* Dryden retorted in his preface to *An Evening's Love* (1671), and so began a cold war of prefaces, conducted with diplomatic civility, the details of which need not be analyzed here.[4] Outwardly Dryden and Shadwell remained on good terms. In 1673 Shadwell, as far as one can judge with Dryden's full approval, made some operatic additions to the version of *The Tempest* by Dryden and Davenant. In 1674, as has been mentioned, Dryden, Shadwell, and Crowne joined in an attack on Settle. As late as 1678 Dryden wrote a prologue for Shadwell's comedy, *A True Widow,* first acted on March 21 of that year, but printed in 1679. In the preface to *All for Love,* published in March, 1678, Dryden alluded to Shadwell with no trace of animosity. (It is noteworthy, however, that Dryden never paid Shadwell any such public compliments as he bestowed from time to time on Etherege, Wycherley, Southerne, and Congreve.) But in that same year, 1678, when Shadwell published his *History of Timon of Athens* (an adaptation of Shakespeare),

---

[1] See R. D. Havens, *The Influence of Milton on English Poetry* (Cambridge, Massachusetts, 1922), p. 120; and M. Summers, in *Dryden, The Dramatic Works* (London, 1931, 1932), iii. 410.

[2] Macdonald, *John Dryden: a Bibliography,* p. 115.

[3] *Brief Lives,* ed. Clark (Oxford, 1898), ii. 72. On this meeting see Masson, *Life of John Milton* (London, 1880), vi. 708–712, 716, 717.

[4] See A. S. Borgman, *Thomas Shadwell* (New York, 1928), pp. 38–51; and D. M. McKeithan, "The Occasion of MacFlecknoe," in *Publications of the Modern Language Association,* xlvii (1932), 766–771. The present writer accepts McKeithan's suggestion concerning the occasion of Dryden's attack on Shadwell.

licensed for the press on February 18, he dedicated his work to the Duke of Buckingham and inserted the following passage in his dedication: —

"I am extremely sensible what honor it is to me that my writings are approved by your Grace, who in your own have so clearly shown the excellency of wit and judgment in yourself, and so justly the defect of 'em in others, that they at once serve for the greatest example and the sharpest reproof. And no man who has perfectly understood *The Rehearsal* and some other of your writings, if he has any genius at all, can write ill after it."

This was more than a mere expression of disagreement on literary matters; it was a direct personal insult to Dryden. And it was dangerous to insult John Dryden. Dryden was a pudgy little man, diffident and halting in his speech — but he knew how to write. He soon replied by writing *Mac Flecknoe*, the finest personal lampoon in the whole history of English literature, in which he held up to scorn both Shadwell's literary productions and his personality. Dryden evidently composed this masterpiece with no thought of publication, for the mere joy of the working, to give utterance to what was within him. He was following the example of noble authors such as his patrons Rochester, Mulgrave, and Dorset. If published, the piece could have brought him no money from a patron, little from a bookseller; and it might have caused him annoyance. It circulated in manuscript for four years, until in October, 1682, it was printed in an unauthorized edition. Dryden himself did not authorize its printing until 1684, and then without adding his name to it. He did not publicly acknowledge his authorship of it until 1692, in his *Discourse concerning Satire*.[1]

A poetaster and minor dramatist named Richard Flecknoe had recently died. Dryden represented Shadwell as the heir to Flecknoe's dullness; and, since Flecknoe was an Irishman, gave him the title Mac Flecknoe.[2] One may regret that Dryden's just resentment blinded his critical discernment. Shadwell's comedies do not deserve the wholesale condemnation that Dryden heaps upon them. Shadwell is coarse and vulgar, more so than Dryden himself. And, unlike Dryden, he does not write well; his diction lacks the elegance and polish which Dryden himself possessed and which he admired in Etherege, Wycherley, Southerne, and above all in Congreve. On the other hand Shadwell has fine talent for realistic observation and he has genuine humor in the modern as well as in the Jonsonian sense of the word. His best comedies have permanent value.[3] Shadwell could reply to Dryden with some justice and with a certain clumsy dignity: "Sure he goes a little too far in calling me the dullest, and has no more reason for that than for giving me the Irish name of Mack, when he knows I never saw Ireland till I was three and twenty years old, and was there but four months. . . . Had he staid till he had supplied the stage with more new humor then I have done, or till he had written a better comedy then *Epsom Wells* or *The Virtuoso* . . . he might with a better grace and more authority have pronounced me dull."[4] On the whole, however, Shad-

---

[1] See page 303. The year in which Dryden wrote *Mac Flecknoe* is known from a copy of a portion of the poem in Oldham's handwriting, dated 1678, preserved in the Bodleian Library. There are also two printed allusions to it earlier than October, 1682. See Macdonald, *Op. cit.*, pp. 28, 29, and references there given. In *Mac Flecknoe* Dryden mentions no works by Shadwell written later than 1678 and he makes no allusion to Shadwell's political opinions. Such reticence would have been well-nigh impossible in 1682. The description of Shadwell as "the true-blue Protestant poet" on the title-page of the 1682 edition of *Mac Flecknoe* comes from the printer, not from Dryden.

[2] Whether Dryden had any personal grievance against Flecknoe is not clear. In a volume of verse published in 1670 Flecknoe had given warm praise to Dryden: see note to page 134, line 3, on page 967. But Flecknoe *may* have been the author of the first attack on Dryden, the *Letter from a Gentleman to the Honourable Ed. Howard Esq.*, mentioned above as published in 1668; this is signed "R. F."

[3] Four of them are included in the Mermaid Series (London and New York, *c.* 1907), with an excellent introduction by George Saintsbury. There is a complete edition of Shadwell (London, 1927), edited by Montague Summers.

[4] In his dedication of *The Tenth Satyr of Juvenal, English and Latin*, 1687.

well's name, like that of Settle, is known in English literature primarily because he was the object of Dryden's satire.[1]

In 1678 Dryden seems to have quarreled with his publisher Herringman, to whom he devotes a contemptuous line in *Mac Flecknoe;* [2] in 1679 his *Troilus and Cressida* was "printed for Jacob Tonson," then a young and far from prominent bookseller. Tonson printed nearly all Dryden's later works, and owes to this fact no small portion of his fame as one of the chief English publishers.

Among Dryden's early patrons was John Wilmot, Earl of Rochester (1647–80). Rochester was the most drunken and lecherous member of a drunken and lecherous nobility; he was also the man of finest literary talent among that nobility. In 1673 Dryden dedicated *Marriage à la Mode* to Rochester in terms of graceful flattery, saying that he was not only indebted to Rochester for personal favors, but that he, like other "comic writers of our age," had copied from Rochester "the gallantries of courts, the delicacy of expression, and the decencies of behavior . . . with more success then if they had taken their models from the court of France." Later the two men quarreled. In his *Allusion to Horace, the Tenth Satire of the First Book,* the exact date of which is unknown, Rochester devotes a long passage to Dryden. He does not deny his talent: —

> But to be just, 'twill to his praise be found,
> His Excellencies more than faults abound,
> Nor dare I from his sacred Temples tear
> That Laurel which he best deserves to wear.

Nevertheless his reservations make a stronger impression than his praise: —

> And may not I have leave impartially
> To search and censure D[ryden's] Works, and try,
> If these gross faults his choice Pen does commit,
> Proceed from want of Judgement or of Wit?
> Or if his lumpish Fancy does refuse
> Spirit or Grace to his loose slatten muse? [3]

Dryden did not hesitate to reply in vigorous terms. In his preface to *All for Love,* published in March, 1678, he refers to "little zanies" who "are persecutors even of Horace himself, as far as they are able, by their ignorant and vile imitations of him; by making an unjust use of his authority, and turning his artillery against his friends." Continuing, he calls Rochester "this rhyming judge of the twelvepenny gallery, this legitimate son of Sternhold," an old translator of the Psalms whose name was a synonym for doggerel.[4]

The rupture between Dryden and Rochester was probably due to the fact that Rochester, apparently through pure fickleness, secured for Crowne rather than for the laureate Dryden the honor of writing a masque to be produced at court. The result was *Calisto,* presented early in 1675 by a combined troupe of "persons of quality" and professional actors.[5] However the quarrel may have originated, it was undoubtedly fostered by Dryden's intimacy with an enemy of Rochester, John Sheffield, Earl of Mulgrave (1648–1721), to whom he dedicated *Aureng-Zebe* in 1676. Mulgrave was a wealthy young noble of practical capacity, particularly in politics, and he had literary ambitions. At some time in the

---

[1] See page 143, lines 408–411.   [2] See page 135, line 105.

[3] *Collected Works,* ed. Hayward (London, 1926), p. 57. Rochester did not publish any of his works, so that it is often impossible to date them. Even the canon of his writings is more than usually uncertain. He was so noted for bawdy verse that various bawdy poems of which he was probably totally innocent were attributed to him.

[4] On Sternhold see also page 143, lines 402, 403; and page 168, line 456. Sternhold died in 1549; the version of the Psalms by Sternhold and Hopkins was added to the Book of Common Prayer in 1502.

[5] See note to *Epilogue . . . Calisto,* on pages 1052, 1053. The story that Rochester also favored Settle at the expense of Dryden lacks foundation: see Pinto, *Rochester* (London, 1935), pp. 114–117; Macdonald, *John Dryden: a Bibliography,* p. 206, n. 1.

second half of 1679 he wrote a fairly long poem (285 lines), casting ridicule on various noted persons, which in November of that year, under the title *An Essay upon Satire*, began to circulate in manuscript among the London wits.[1] Among the objects of his attack were Rochester and the royal mistresses, the Duchess of Portsmouth and Nell Gwyn. The poem of course was anonymous, but public opinion usually ascribed it to Dryden, who indeed may have aided Mulgrave in polishing his work. A couplet in the description of Rochester is certainly worthy of Dryden: —

> Mean in each action, lewd in every limb,
> Manners themselves are mischievous in him.

So likewise is a couplet in the passage devoted to the "beastly brace" of mistresses: —

> Was ever prince by two at once misled,
> False, foolish, old, ill-natur'd, and ill-bred?

In consequence of this satire Dryden suffered an assault on the evening of December 18, 1679, while returning home through Rose Street, Covent Garden. Luttrell in his *Brief Historical Relation of State Affairs*[2] gives a contemporary account of the matter: — "About the same time [the middle of December] Mr. John Dryden was sett on in Covent Garden in the evening by three fellowes, who beat him very severely, and on peoples comeing in they run away; 'tis thought to be done by order of the dutchesse of Portsmouth; she being abused in a late libell called an Essay upon satyr, of which Mr. *Dryden* is suspected to be the author."

A reward was offered in the newspapers for the detection of the perpetrators of this cowardly crime, but they were never brought to justice. Nor have modern scholars ascertained who hired them. Passages in two of Rochester's letters, both undated, have been thought to make his guilt certain. In one letter, obviously written in November, 1679, he states: "I have sent you herewith a Libel, in which my own share is not the least. . . . the author is apparently Mr. [Dryden], his Patron my [Lord Mulgrave] having a Panegerick in the midst."[3] A passage in another letter has been regarded as certain evidence that Rochester planned other than literary retaliation: — "You write me word, That I'm out of favour with a certain Poet, whom I have ever admir'd, for the disproportion of him and his Attributes: He is a Rarity which I cannot but be fond of, as one would be of a Hog that could fiddle, or a singing Owl. If he falls upon me at the Blunt, which is his very good Weapon in Wit, I will forgive him, if you please, and leave the Repartee to *Black Will*, with a cudgel."[4]

A recent analysis of this letter shows, however, that it cannot have been written later than the spring of 1678, and that it was probably written two years earlier, in the spring or early summer of 1676. Since Rochester seems to have ignored Dryden's aspersions on him of March, 1678, in the preface to *All for Love*, his letter can scarcely be connected with the assault on Dryden in December, 1679.[5] Dryden himself apparently did not think Rochester responsible for the crime. At all events his allusions to him after his death show no personal resentment.[6]

Such was the low state of English public morals that Dryden's misfortune created amusement rather than sympathy. Even Mulgrave, who had been the occasion of it,

---

[1] For the poem see pages 913–916. The notes give further information concerning it.

[2] Oxford, 1857, vol. i, p. 30.

[3] So in Rochester, *Op. cit.*, p. 263. But Pinto (*Op. cit.*, p. 199) says that the letter is dated November 21, 1679, and he does not bracket the first letter of Dryden's name. The autographs of the two letters are not preserved.

[4] *Ibid.*, p. 264.

[5] See J. Harold Wilson, "Rochester, Dryden, and the Rose-street Affair," in *Review of English Studies*, xv (1939), 294–301; also Pinto, "Rochester, Dryden, and the Duchess of Portsmouth," *Ibid.*, xvi (1940), 177, 178.

[6] See page 283, col. 1, last line, and the following passage; page 515, col. 1, near close; and page 744, col. 2, near top.

referred to the matter with no touch of indignation in his *Essay on Poetry*,[1] first published in 1682: —

> The Laureate here [in satire] may justly claim our praise,
> Crown'd by *Mac Flecknoe* with immortal bays;
> Tho' prais'd and punish'd for another's rhymes,
> His own deserve as great applause sometimes.

The Rose Alley Satire, as Mulgrave's poem came to be called, did not find its way into print until after the Revolution of 1688. The lines in it concerning "sauntering Charles" and his mistresses may well have deterred even the most piratical publisher from using it while Charles II or James II was on the throne. The earliest known printed text of it is in *The Fourth (and Last) Collection of Poems, Satyrs, Songs, &c.*, 1689, where it is attributed to "J. Dr——en Esq." It is also found, similarly attributed, in *Poems on Affairs of State*, 1697, and in later editions of that volume. But it occurs, ascribed to the Earl of Mulgrave, in *A New Collection of Poems Relating to State Affairs*, 1705. Finally, in a text revised by Pope, it found its way into the sumptuous and posthumous edition of *The Works of John Sheffield, Earl of Mulgrave, Marquis of Normanby, and Duke of Buckingham*, 1723. This inclusion should settle the question of authorship.

With Mulgrave, one may add, Dryden always remained on most friendly terms. In 1681 he introduced him into *Absalom and Achitophel* as "sharp-judging Adriel, the Muses' friend." [2] In 1697 he dedicated his translation of the *Æneid* to Mulgrave, now become Marquis of Normanby.[3] And in 1720 that noble, now Duke of Buckinghamshire, "rescued his country from the disgrace incurred by the long neglect of so great a poet [as Dryden], and defrayed the charge of a very plain and unexpensive monument to his memory in Westminster Abbey." [4]

III

Beginning dramatic work more from the pressure of circumstances than from natural inclination, Dryden had never been fully satisfied with his success in it. He felt that his talents fitted him for a higher calling than that of a mere popular playwright, exposed to insults and humiliation from unworthy antagonists. Of his disappointment and his ambition he tells us in the dedication to *Aureng-Zebe*, published in 1676: —

"I desire to be no longer the Sisyphus of the stage; to roll up a stone with endless labor, which, to follow the proverb, gathers no moss, and which is perpetually falling down again. I never thought myself very fit for an employment where many of my predecessors have excell'd me in all kinds; and some of my contemporaries, even in my own partial judgment, have outdone me in comedy. Some little hopes I have yet remaining, and those, too, considering my abilities, may be vain, that I may make the world some part of amends for many ill plays, by an heroic poem. Your Lordship [the Earl of Mulgrave] has been long acquainted with my design; the subject of which you know is great, the story English, and neither too far distant from the present age, nor too near approaching it. Such it is, in my opinion, that I could not have wish'd a nobler occasion to do honor by it to my king, my country, and my friends; most of our ancient nobility being concern'd in the action. . . . But the unsettledness of my condition has hitherto put a stop to my thoughts concerning it. As I am no successor to Homer in his wit, so neither do I desire to be in his poverty. I can make no rhapsodies, nor go a-begging at the Grecian doors, while I sing the praises of their ancestors. The times of Virgil

---

[1] See headnote, pages 913, 914.   [2] See page 120, line 877.   [3] See page 487.
[4] Malone, in *The Critical and Miscellaneous Prose Works of John Dryden* (London, 1800), I, 1, 385–388.

please me better, because he had an Augustus for his patron; and, to draw the allegory nearer you, I am sure I shall not want a Mæcenas with him."[1]

The subject to which Dryden refers was undoubtedly, as we know from his *Discourse concerning Satire*,[2] the story of the wars of the Black Prince in Spain. The lack of adequate patronage that prevented him from carrying out his cherished plan probably caused small loss to English literature.

Dryden's genius as a satirist was of more vital consequence. Inspired by indignation against Shadwell, Dryden had written his masterly *Mac Flecknoe* in a private, literary quarrel. Soon he had an opportunity to become a champion of the royal party in a political controversy of the highest importance.

In 1678 England had been thrown into a ferment by the "Popish Plot." During the next three years party strife became so intense that the country seemed on the verge of civil war. On the one side stood the Whigs, led by the Earl of Shaftesbury, who, using Catholic intrigues, real and pretended, as his pretext, sought to exclude the Catholic Duke of York from the throne in favor of the Duke of Monmouth. On the other side stood the Tories, led in reality by the king himself, who, aided by secret grants of money from France, strove to secure the succession for his brother, and indirectly did all in his power to favor the Catholic cause. The king, however, concealed his real objects so far as might be, seeking above all to gain time, and waited for a revulsion of popular feeling in his favor. This occurred in the spring of 1681. Charles summoned a new parliament (the fifth of his reign) to meet at Oxford, where he hoped that the members, free from the influence of the London populace, which was predominantly on the side of Shaftesbury, would be in a conciliatory mood. The king came to Oxford with an armed guard and many of the Whig members also came under arms.[3] At the opening of the session on March 21 Charles urged the House of Commons to accept some precautions against Catholicism less drastic than the exclusion of his brother from the succession. When the Commons proved obdurate, the king dissolved parliament on March 28 and the members peaceably dispersed. The king forthwith ordered the publication of a pamphlet (dated April 8), *His Majesties Declaration to all His Loving Subjects, Touching the Causes and Reasons that Moved Him to Dissolve the Two Last Parliaments.*

Public opinion outside of London now supported Charles II. The English people disliked the prospect of another civil war more than they feared the accession of a Catholic king. On July 2 Shaftesbury was arrested and sent to the Tower under a charge of high treason and on November 24 his case was brought before the grand jury of Middlesex. The Tory reaction endured during all the remainder of the reign of Charles II, enabling him to govern without convoking another parliament. When Charles II died on February 6, 1685, his brother James became king without opposition; and in his first parliament, which met on May 19, 1685, the House of Commons was Tory by an enormous majority.

The years of tumult that began with 1678 were marked by furious political propaganda on both the Tory and the Whig side. There was a whole flood of pamphlets, and even books, devoted to the questions of the day. Political periodicals began to appear; English party journalism was born.[4]

Despite the interest in public affairs that he had shown at the outset of his career, Dryden made no immediate contribution to this party strife. In fact his attitude on the issues involved was not at once apparent. At some time in 1681 a loyalist writer saw fit to satirize Dryden as a partisan of the Earl of Shaftesbury. It was a current Tory

---

[1] *Works*, ed. Scott-Saintsbury, v. 195, 196.   [2] See page 291.
[3] Dryden wrote the prologue for a play acted before the king at Oxford on March 19: see pages 903, 904.
[4] On this party literature and on Dryden's share in it see R. B. Long, "Dryden's Importance as a Spokesman of the Tories," in *Studies in English* (*University of Texas Publication No. 4126*), Austin, Texas, 1941.

joke that in 1674 Shaftesbury had been a candidate for the Polish throne, at the time when Jan Sobieski was actually elected king.[1] A pamphlet entitled, *A Modest Vindication of the Earl of Shaftesbury: In a Letter to a Friend concerning his being Elected King of Poland*, dated 1681,[2] represented that Shaftesbury, preparing to set forth for his new realm after his election, chose to take with him Dryden as his poet laureate and Shadwell as the laureate's deputy! Shaftesbury had selected Dryden for such distinction because of his "writing panegyrics upon Oliver Cromwell, and libels against his present master, King Charles II of England." The basis of the second part of this charge was presumably Dryden's alleged authorship of *An Essay upon Satire*, actually composed by Mulgrave.

Besides this, the tone of *The Spanish Friar* had been strongly anti-Catholic and Dryden had dedicated his drama to Lord Haughton, "a Protestant play to a Protestant patron." A later satire, *The Laureat*, published in 1687,[3] alleged that Dryden (or "Jack Squabbs"), angered by the loss of his pension and "still tacking round with every turn of state," changed sides, became a "True Blue Protestant" (that is, a Whig), and wrote *The Spanish Friar* as an attack on the court party.

These accusations are groundless. Dryden did not lose his pension until after the Revolution of 1688. Beginning with 1677, the royal treasury was in difficulties, so that payments even to ambassadors fell into arrears. Dryden, as poet laureate and historiographer royal, suffered along with other functionaries, receiving from 1677 through 1684 only about half the amount due him. He did not change sides. His *Spanish Friar* was anticlerical and anti-Catholic, but it was not specifically Whig. Most of the Tories were Protestants, just as were the Whigs, though they did not lay quite so much stress on the fact. From the Tory point of view the worst that can be said against Dryden is that he strove to write a play that should win popularity by its appeal to the prevailing anti-Catholic sentiment. The play contains (in act iv, sc. 2) a passage apparently satirizing a Whig mob. It also contains, to be sure (in the same scene), lines vigorously uncomplimentary to the Earl of Danby, a Tory leader who had been lord treasurer. But in 1678 Danby had been impeached by the House of Commons; and in 1680, when *The Spanish Friar* was first acted, he was a prisoner in the Tower. Though constantly protected by the king, he had in general lost the confidence of the Tories as well as of the Whigs. Thus during the years from 1677 to 1681 Dryden, as Professor Bredvold argues convincingly, had been "a firm, consistent, and loyal Tory." [4]

Dryden's first clear, printed proof of his Tory attitude during these troubled times seems to have been a prose pamphlet published anonymously, like most of the controversial literature of the period, in June, 1681: *His Majesties Declaration Defended in a Letter to a Friend: being an Answer to a Seditious Pamphlet called a Letter from a Person of Quality to his Friend concerning the Kings late Declaration touching the Reasons which Moved him to Dissolve the Two Last Parliaments at Westminster and Oxford*. This longwinded title explains itself by reproducing almost literally the title of a Whig production published somewhat earlier, to which it is one of two replies from the Tory side. External testimony, joined to the evidence of parallel passages from undoubted writings

---

[1] Dryden refers to this jest in *The Medal*. See page 126, col. 1, line 14, and note; and page 128, line 3.

[2] This pamphlet is reprinted in *Somers Tracts*, viii. 313–318. Some important passages are given in Dryden, *Works*, ed. Scott-Saintsbury, ix. 330, 331, 436–438: see also Macdonald, *John Dryden: a Bibliography*, p. 223.

[3] Reproduced in full in Dryden, *Works*, ed. Scott-Saintsbury, x. 105–107.

[4] See L. I. Bredvold, "Political Aspects of Dryden's *Amboyna* and *The Spanish Fryar*," in *Essays and Studies in English and Comparative Literature* (Ann Arbor, 1932), pp. 119–132; and "Notes on John Dryden's Pension," in *Modern Philology*, xxx (1933), 267–274. One must confess, however, that from a purely personal point of view Dryden's needless attack on Danby in *The Spanish Friar* contrasts disagreeably with his adulation of him in the dedication of *All for Love*. *All for Love* was published in March, 1678, and Danby was impeached in December of that year.

of Dryden, make it almost certain that Dryden wrote *His Majesties Declaration Defended;* the task may have been enjoined upon him because of his position as historiographer royal.[1]

Of far greater importance was *Absalom and Achitophel,* the finest of English political satires, a poem published — also anonymously — about November 17, 1681, just at the proper time for exciting popular feeling against Shaftesbury and thereby securing his indictment by the grand jury. Dryden was from the first known to be the author, though his name was not added to any of the editions of the poem issued during his lifetime. He publicly acknowledged the work in his *Discourse concerning Satire,* 1692.[2]

The practice of using a scriptural story as a vehicle for political satire had begun before the Civil War.[3] In 1627 a book by Nathaniel Carpenter, *Achitophel, or the Picture of a Wicked Politician,* was published in Dublin; it was soon reprinted in Oxford and London and by 1641 had gone through six editions. The book applied to local conditions, particularly to the machinations of the Catholics. Through it and later similar publications *Achitophel* became a familiar term of opprobrium, popular with the Puritans but used also by the Royalists; the Vulgate spelling *Achitophel* was generally employed instead of the *Ahitophel* of the Authorized Version. An *Absalom's Rebellion* appeared at Oxford in 1645. When Charles II was restored the comparison of him to David became a commonplace; Dryden himself uses it in *Astræa Redux.*[4] A published *Letter to His Grace the Duke of Monmouth, this 15th of July 1680, by a true lover of his person and the peace of the kingdom,*[5] likened Monmouth to Absalom. Finally, also in 1680, a prose pamphlet was printed, *Absalom's Conspiracy; or, The Tragedy of Treason,*[6] which covered in an elementary fashion the same ground as Dryden's poem. Dryden by his genius gave to a hackneyed theme in a now forgotten controversial literature an important place among English classics.

In his great satire the poet draws a matchless series of portraits of the politicians of the time, exalting the Tories and damning the Whigs. "The young man Absalom," weak and misguided, but full of fine qualities and good intentions, represents the Duke of Monmouth. Achitophel,

> For close designs, and crooked counsels fit;
> Sagacious, bold, and turbulent of wit: —
>
> (Page 111, lines 152, 153.)

the cunning counselor who seduced Absalom into rebellion, represents Shaftesbury himself. Of the other portraits the most famous is that of Zimri, Dryden's old enemy, the Duke of Buckingham. There is little plot to the poem; Dryden describes at great length a group of conspirators, who, after many preparations, take flight at the sound of the king's speech from the throne. The author really made the best of the material at his command: the actual conspirators accomplished nothing, being defeated by a change in public opinion that, without too great abuse of poetic license, Dryden could term the result of the king's own words.

The king's speech at the close of *Absalom and Achitophel* (lines 939–1025) raises serious questions. According to a note published by Tonson in 1716, "in the year 1680 Mr. Dryden undertook the poem of *Absalom and Achitophel,* upon the desire of King Charles the Second."[7] This is partially confirmed by Joseph Spence, who reports in his *Anec-*

---

[1] R. G. Ham, "Dryden as Historiographer-royal: the Authorship of *His Majesties Declaration Defended,* 1681," in *Review of English Studies,* xi (1935), 284–298; and Macdonald, *Op. cit.,* p. 167.

[2] See pages 303 and 313.

[3] R. F. Jones, "The Originality of *Absalom and Achitophel,*" in *Modern Language Notes,* xlvi (1931), 211–218.

[4] See page 8, line 79.

[5] Reprinted in *Somers Tracts,* viii. 216–219; see also Dryden, *Works,* ed. Scott-Saintsbury, ix. 199, 200.

[6] Reprinted in Dryden, *Works,* ed. Scott-Saintsbury, ix. 206–208.

[7] See page 137. The date 1680 is presumably a mere blunder for 1681.

dotes [1] that Pope told him "that King Charles obliged Dryden to put his Oxford speech into verse, and to insert it toward the close of his *Absalom and Achitophel.*" So one would expect, if this anecdote be true, that Dryden's lines would have the same general purport as the actual speech of the king at the opening of the Oxford parliament on March 21, 1681. That speech had been brief, stating merely that the king would continue to rule according to the laws of the land and that such an administration was as much his concern as that of any of his subjects; calling attention to the need for further prosecution of the Popish Plot, for the trial of the lords confined in the Tower, and for the more speedy conviction of Catholic recusants; but warning the members that they must adopt other measures against popery than the exclusion from the throne of his brother the Duke of York.[2] Dryden made the king stress the first two points and the warning against exclusion; but, now that the tide of opinion was running in the king's favor, he let him remain silent concerning further prosecution of the Popish Plot, the lords in the Tower, and Catholic recusants. Furthermore, he allowed King Charles to express his fatherly affection for his erring son the Duke of Monmouth; and he managed to insert in the king's speech passages that correspond to portions of *His Majesties Declaration*, issued after the dissolution of the Oxford parliament. Dryden's object was obviously a brief, attractive, epigrammatic statement of the royal position, not a paraphrase of either the Oxford speech or *His Majesties Declaration.*[3]

Absalom and Achitophel had a wide sale, seven London editions being published within two years, not to speak of two editions printed in Dublin. How much the satire affected public opinion one cannot tell, just as one cannot estimate the real importance of any single piece of political propaganda in our own time. The Whigs did not regard Dryden as the ablest writer against them; in particular, they thought him by no means so dangerous an opponent as Sir Roger L'Estrange.[4] Dryden was attacking Shaftesbury, a statesman whose influence had already begun to decline, yet his poem certainly had no influence on the actual course of events. Shaftesbury could still count on the affections of the citizens of London. The grand jury of Middlesex, selected by Whig sheriffs, refused to indict him. The earl's adherents celebrated his release by striking and circulating a medal, which gave Dryden the occasion for a second satire, *The Medal*, directed against the Whigs and their leader, published in March, 1682. This poem is marked in many parts by a vigor fully equal to that of *Absalom and Achitophel*, though it is far inferior to its predecessor in interest and variety.

Dryden had now rendered important services to the Tory government and had a right to expect a reward for them. Actually, however, he seems to have been in rather straitened circumstances during the last half-dozen years of the reign of Charles II. As we have seen, he was receiving only about half the pension due him as poet laureate and historiographer-royal, and after 1680 his income from the theater must have practically ceased. There is preserved a letter by Dryden, without date or superscription, but probably written about August, 1683, to Laurence Hyde, Earl of Rochester, the first lord of the treasury.[5] In it Dryden complains of "my extreame wants, even almost to arresting, & my ill health, which cannot be repaird without immediate retireing into

---

[1] Ed. 2, London, 1858, pp. 129, 130.

[2] The "Oxford speech" is printed in the *Journals of the House of Lords*, xiii. 745, 746. Considerable excerpts are given in the notes to the present volume.

[3] Mr. Godfrey Davies in an article on "The Conclusion of Dryden's Absalom and Achitophel," in *Huntington Library Quarterly*, x (1946), 69–82, regards Dryden's use of the Oxford speech as of small account and stresses his debt to *His Majesties Declaration*. Some details are given in the notes to the present volume.

[4] Long, *Op. cit.*, pp. 92–99.

[5] John Wilmot, Earl of Rochester, had died on July 26, 1680. Laurence Hyde (1641–1711), the second son of the Earl of Clarendon, an early patron of Dryden, was created Earl of Rochester on November 29, 1681. For the letter see *Letters*, ed. Ward, 1942, pp. 20–22.

the Country." He continues: "If I durst I wou'd plead a little merit, & some hazards of my life from the Common Enemyes, my refuseing advantages offerd by them, & neglecting my beneficiall studyes for the King's service: But I onely thinke I merite not to sterve. . . . I have three sonns growing to mans estate, I breed them all up to learning, beyond my fortune; but they are too hopefull to be neglected though I want. Be pleasd to looke on me with an eye of compassion; some small Employment wou'd render my condition easy. . . . Either in the Customes, or the Appeales of the Excise, or some other way; meanes cannot be wanting if you please to have the will. . . . In the meane time be pleasd to give me a gracious and speedy answer to my present request of halfe a yeares pention for my necessityes."

All this fails to touch the heart very deeply. It is the plea of a man not so well-to-do as he used to be. Whether the letter had any financial results is unknown.[1] At all events Dryden remained on good terms with Laurence Hyde, Earl of Rochester, to whom he dedicated *The Duke of Guise* in 1683 and *Cleomenes* in 1692. Rochester may have been responsible for the fact that the half-payments on Dryden's pension were at least made regularly.

Though Dryden's two masterly political satires brought him no wealth, they brought him plenty of assaults from Whig writers. Among such writers were Settle and Shadwell, with whom he had previously been at odds for purely literary reasons. Early in April, 1682, Settle published a reply to *Absalom and Achitophel* under the title, *Absalom Senior; or, Achitophel Transprosed;* in which the word *transprosed* alludes to a jest leveled at Mr. Bayes early in *The Rehearsal.* The poem, though crude and slipshod in style, is legitimate in tone and not unreadable. Through a different, fantastic application of Scripture, by which Absalom is made to represent the Duke of York and Achitophel the Earl of Halifax, Settle tries to turn the tables against the Tory party. Lacking fertility of expression, he often inserts in his work parodies of Dryden's own lines. In a prose address "To the Tories," which he prefixed to his satire just as Dryden prefixed an "Epistle to the Whigs" to *The Medal,* Settle alludes to Dryden as "so famous an author" and to himself as "a minor poet." In the poem itself he devotes to Dryden a long paragraph of clumsy abuse.

Shadwell's part in this billingsgate warfare is more problematic. Three anonymous verse pamphlets have been attributed to him: (1) *The Medal of John Bayes, a Satyr against Folly and Knavery,* (2) *Satyr to his Muse, by the Author of Absalom and Achitophel,* and (3) *The Tory-Poets, a Satyr.*[2] Since the three pamphlets were all published in 1682, it is *a priori* improbable that all three were written by Shadwell, or by any one man. No external evidence connects either the second or the third with Shadwell. In fact, in *Poems on Affairs of State, Part III,* 1698, *Satyr to his Muse* is said to be "written by a Person of Honour," and in Rochester's *Works,* 1707, it is ascribed to Lord Somers.[3] This evidence does not count for much in favor of Somers, but it does count against Shadwell.

For the rare pamphlet *The Tory-Poets* there is no contemporary attribution whatever; the piece was not reprinted until 1927. On internal evidence R. G. Ham has confidently ascribed it to Shadwell, writing: "It bears the obvious impress of Shadwell from its inevitable allusion to Ben Jonson in the choice and graded virulence of the attack."[4]

---

[1] It has been thought that it gained for Dryden a place as collector of customs. But the John Dryden who was appointed to that office on December 17, 1683, was not the poet, for that John Dryden had died before November 2, 1692. See C. E. Ward, "Was John Dryden Collector of Customs?" in *Modern Language Notes,* xlvii (1932), 246–249, and Bredvold, "Notes on John Dryden's Pension."

[2] All three pieces may be found in *The Complete Works of Thomas Shadwell,* ed. Summers (London, 1927), vol. v.

[3] Macdonald, *Op. cit.,* pp. 234, 321.

[4] "Shadwell and 'The Tory Poets.'" in *Notes and Queries,* clii (1927), 6–8.

The lampoon holds up to scorn not only Dryden, but Otway, D'Urfey, Aphra Behn, and Ravenscroft as well. Shadwell had known personal grounds of offense against Otway and D'Urfey; but, to quote Macdonald,[1] both these men "were obvious marks for any Whig writer." On the whole, in the absence of any external testimony, Shadwell's authorship of the piece cannot be regarded as established.

The Medal of John Bayes is another story. This satire, published about May 15, 1682, is said by Luttrell, an exceptionally well-informed contemporary witness, to be "by Thomas Shadwell, against Mr. Dryden, very severe"; and his testimony is confirmed by two less important contemporaries. The internal evidence of some parallel passages corroborates this external evidence.[2] So, although Dryden never directly attributes *The Medal of John Bayes* to Shadwell, as he does attribute *Absalom Senior* to Settle, *The Medal of John Bayes* was in all probability Shadwell's work.[3]

The Medal of John Bayes is not a general satire on the Tory party, but a long and filthy personal tirade against Dryden, written by a man who knew a good deal about him.[4] Among its least vulgar lines are the following, which are taken from its opening and closing pages: —

> How long shall I endure, without reply,
> To hear this Bayes, this hackney railer, lie?
>
> The fool uncudgel'd for one libel swells,
> Where not his wit, but sauciness excels;
> Whilst with foul words and names which he lets fly,
> He quite defiles the satire's dignity. . . .
> Methinks the ghost of Horace there I see,
> Lashing this cherry-cheek'd dunce of fifty-three.
>
> .   .   .   .
>
> Now farewell, wretched, mercenary Bayes,
> Who the king libel'd and did Cromwell praise.
> Farewell, abandon'd rascal, only fit
> To be abus'd by thy own scurrilous wit. . . .
> Pied thing! half wit! half fool! and for a knave, ⎫
> Few men, than this, a better mixture have;   ⎬
> But thou canst add to that, coward and slave. ⎭

It is no wonder that Dryden felt inclined to chastise his tormentors, although concerning Shadwell he was anticipated by a bookseller who, as has been mentioned, in October, 1682, published an unauthorized edition of his *Mac Flecknoe*, written four years earlier. Dryden's own retorts to Settle and Shadwell were inserted in *The Second Part of Absalom and Achitophel*, a poem by Nahum Tate, a minor poet of the Tory party, published in November, 1682. According to Tonson,[5] many persons had urged Dryden to write a sequel to his masterpiece; but Dryden, declining the task himself, "spoke to Mr. Tate to write one and gave him his advice in the direction of it." Tate's poem continues the account of English politics to September, 1682, when the king's partisans succeeded in procuring the election of Tory sheriffs.[6] This was a fatal blow to the Whigs. Shaftesbury, after making futile efforts to organize a rebellion, in November fled to Holland, where he died on January 21, 1683.

---

[1] *Op. cit.*, p. 235.

[2] See D. M. McKeithan, "The Authorship of *The Medal of John Bayes*," in *University of Texas Studies in English*, No. 12, 1932, pp. 92–97.

[3] The account of the evidence given above is incomplete. For a fuller discussion of the problem see Macdonald, *loc. cit.*, and Osborn, *John Dryden: Some Biographical Facts and Problems*, pp. 155–167; and other writers cited by them.

[4] Compare pages xviii–xx, above, and footnotes.   [5] See page 137.

[6] See page 152, lines 1131–1140, and notes.

One may conjecture that for two reasons Dryden was loth to undertake a second part of *Absalom and Achitophel.* His literary tact forbade him to publish a work which would be on similar lines to his first satire, but which, being concerned with minor persons and events, would necessarily be less brilliant. Besides that, he was busy with a new poem of his own, *Religio Laici.* Yet he contributed about two hundred verses to Tate's production, "besides some touches in other places." Of Dryden's lines the most striking are those devoted to Settle and Shadwell, whom he celebrates under the names of Doeg and Og: —

> Two fools that crutch their feeble sense on verse;
> Who, by my Muse, to all succeeding times
> Shall live, in spite of their own dogg'rel rhymes.
> (Page 143, lines 409–411.)

To Settle Dryden is comparatively gentle; he is almost genially contemptuous — and perfectly just. He merely calls him in excellently varied terms a senseless creature gifted with some command of English verse expression: —

> Doeg, tho' without knowing how or why,
> Made still a blund'ring kind of melody;
> Spurr'd boldly on, and dash'd thro' thick and thin,
> Thro' sense and nonsense, never out nor in;
> Free from all meaning, whether good or bad,
> And, in one word, heroically mad.
> (Page 143, lines 412–417.)

Since, except for a passing mention in 1683,[1] Dryden has now finished with poor Settle, it may be proper to insert here a word on that person's later career. Although in 1682 he was only thirty-four years old, Settle had already passed the meridian of his fame. Losing his popularity at court, he had taken up with the Earl of Shaftesbury. A man of no principle, during the Tory reaction he turned Tory; then at the Revolution he "celebrated the occasion by writing *A View of the Times. With Britain's Address to the Prince of Orange* (1689)."[2] After that he abjured politics, though in 1706 he published another Whig effusion.[3] He had some transient success as a dramatist, but in general sank lower and lower, composing "drolls" or farces for Bartholomew Fair. He became "city poet," being employed by different merchant companies to arrange pageants for the lord mayor's shows. Finally in 1718 he was admitted to the Charterhouse as "a poor brother," that is, a dependent on charity; he died there in 1724. "Such are the revolutions of fame," Dr. Johnson moralizes excellently,[4] "that the man, whose works have not yet been thought to deserve the care of collecting them" — and, one may add, very few of whose works have ever been reprinted since the date of his death — "might with truth have had inscribed upon his stone: *Here lies the Rival and Antagonist of Dryden.*"

Dryden's reply to Shadwell is of a different sort. In lines that repeat from *Mac Flecknoe* only by calling Shadwell dull, he now accuses him of political as well as literary sins. He inveighs against him as corpulent, drunken, poor, addicted to opium, and traitorous: —

> A double noose thou on thy neck dost pull,
> For writing treason, and for writing dull.
> (Page 144, lines 496, 497.)

Dryden is unjust to Shadwell's talents, but a reader forgets the injustice in admiration for the superb, full-mouthed invective. And if any man think Dryden merely malicious,

---

[1] In *The Vindication* [of *The Duke of Guise*]: see *Works*, ed. Scott-Saintsbury, vii. 205, 206.
[2] Brown, *Elkanah Settle*, p. 26.   [3] *Ibid.*, p. 34.   [4] *Life of Dryden.*

let him turn to *The Medal of John Bayes.* If Shadwell was the author of that libel, Dryden had ample cause for wrath.

Dryden's political satires are on the whole his finest achievement. He was a man of marvelous versatility, but as a narrative and lyric poet, as a dramatist, as an essayist, even as a personal satirist, he has had rivals or superiors. As a political satirist he stands pre-eminent among all English men of letters.

Though he had now definitely retired from dramatic work, Dryden accepted the aid of Nathaniel Lee in completing for the stage *The Duke of Guise,* a tragedy that he had begun more than twenty years before. In its finished form, this play is a political satire, directed against the Whigs. It was first acted late in 1682 and was published in February, 1683. Shadwell and a lawyer named Thomas Hunt directed pamphlet attacks against it and Dryden replied to them with a *Vindication,* issued in April, 1683. In these prose pamphlets both Shadwell and Dryden are temperate and restrained in expression. The circumstance need excite no surprise, for both men were writing under their own names and were appealing to reason, not emotion. Dryden's *Vindication* has none of the glitter of his verse. In prose Dryden is at his best in a kindly, appreciative style like that of *An Essay of Dramatic Poesy;* in a prose polemic he is not sufficiently keen and incisive.

There is a report that Dryden took vengeance on Shadwell in a more practical fashion than by literary satire. According to an item in the periodical *The Muses Mercury* for January, 1707, Shadwell told a "gentleman" whom he met in the theater on the first night of a revival of Fletcher's *Prophetess* for which Dryden had written the prologue — that is, at some time in May, 1690 — that "while Mr. Dryden was poet laureate he would never let any play of his [Shadwell's] be acted." [1] This tale as it stands is in flat contradiction to the facts, and it probably does not contain even a kernel of truth. Dryden became poet laureate on April 13, 1668; he was replaced by Shadwell on August 29, 1689. Shadwell's series of dramas began with *The Sullen Lovers* in May, 1668. His quarrel with Dryden occurred as early as 1678. His comedy *A True Widow* was probably acted toward the end of that year and was followed about September, 1679, by *The Woman Captain.* His next play, *The Lancashire Witches,* produced about September, 1681,[2] caused trouble for its Whig author by its alleged political satire. After this no new play by Shadwell was put on the stage for seven years, during the period of Tory reaction that had begun early in 1681, but except for the item in *The Muses Mercury* of 1707 there is no evidence that Dryden had anything to do with the matter. Dryden's office of poet laureate gave him no control whatever over the theater. Unlike Settle, Shadwell was no turncoat, so that his known Whig sympathies would be a barrier to his having further dramas produced; presumably he thought it useless even to write any. But in May, 1688, when the tide of public opinion was running strongly against James II, Shadwell won a striking triumph with his play *The Squire of Alsatia.* Though Dryden's opponents eagerly published all sorts of scandal against him, during his lifetime no man ever accused him of interfering with Shadwell's success as a dramatist. The solitary item in *The Muses Mercury* was published fourteen years after the death of Shadwell and six years after that of Dryden. It is probably pure fiction.

After his two great political satires Dryden came forward with a poem on a religious topic, *Religio Laici; or, A Layman's Faith,* published in the last week of November, 1682. One may profitably expand the title into "The Religion of an English Tory Layman."

Dryden's early verses, *To his Friend John Hoddesdon,* published when he was only nineteen, show a certain Puritan fervor. This evidently soon passed away, for the

---

[1] For further details see note to page 260 (*Prologue to The Prophetess*), on page 1066.

[2] See Nicoll, *A History of Restoration Drama,* p. 195. On Shadwell in general see Borgman, *Thomas Shadwell,* New York, 1928.

Heroic Stanzas consecrated to the memory of Cromwell, except for a sneer at Pope Alexander VII (lines 117–120) and except for the one word *piety* in their last line, pay no tribute to the religious side of the protector's character and career. In his following works, up to 1682, Dryden's references to religion [1] are mainly of a negative sort; he attacks Puritans, Catholics, and priests of all religions. His caustic phrases concerning persons whom he regards as hypocrites are not counterbalanced by any references to his own sincere faith. He shows no spirituality himself, nor any understanding of spirituality in others. The king's prayer in *Annus Mirabilis* (lines 1045–1080) is a formal effusion, with no religious fervor. Dryden does, however, show an interest in religious discussion. For instance St. Catherine, the heroine of his *Tyrannic Love*, argues ably against her tormentors, though she herself exhibits no genuinely religious elevation.

In Dryden's time, as Verrall remarks,[2] arguments on religion were a part of politics. When Dryden became involved in political controversy he grew more interested in the connection between politics and religion. In *The Medal* he denounces Catholics and Puritans not as hypocrites but as a menace to the English monarchy: —

> Whether the plotting Jesuit laid the plan
> Of murth'ring kings, or the French Puritan,
> Our sacrilegious sects their guides outgo,
> And kings and kingly pow'r would murther too.
>
> (Page 130, lines 201–204.)

In the "Epistle to the Whigs" that serves as preface to that poem he emphasizes the danger to the state inherent in the Calvinistic doctrine.

Politics, however, was not the only factor that had deepened Dryden's interest in religious questions, or at least in certain aspects of them. He had been deeply moved by his own reading and study. One must always remember that Dryden, though by no means a professional scholar or a profound thinker, had a quick, active mind, so that he appreciated and enjoyed scholarship and thought in other men. A French scholar, a Catholic priest named Richard Simon (1638–1712), had in 1678 published his *Histoire critique du Vieux Testament*, a work that is a landmark in the development of biblical criticism. Father Simon's main positions are thus summarized by Professor Bredvold: —

"The First Book is a history of the Hebrew text from the time of Moses; we learn that Moses could not have written all the books attributed to him, that we sometimes have in the Old Testament only abridgements of longer works now lost, that the manuscripts are all imperfect and there is no wholly reliable tradition for their interpretation, that readings are often doubtful, and the whole matter full of difficulties and obscurities. The Second Book points out the faultiness of all translations, from the Septuagint down to those made by Protestants." [3]

Simon's book was promptly suppressed on publication, but a few copies survived and the work reached England. Of it "an ingenious young gentleman" [4] named Henry Dickinson, a friend of Dryden, made an English translation which was published by Tonson late in 1681 or in January, 1682, so that it was going through the press at the same time as *Absalom and Achitophel*. Dryden read the book and was prompted by it to compose in honor of the translator his *Religio Laici*.[5]

[1] They have been collected by Pierre Legouis in an article, "La Religion dans l'œuvre de Dryden avant 1682," in *Revue anglo-américaine*, ix (1932), 383–392, 525–536.

[2] *Lectures on Dryden* (Cambridge, England, 1914), p. 2.

[3] L. I. Bredvold, *The Intellectual Milieu of John Dryden* (Ann Arbor, 1934), p. 99. This book is a careful study of Dryden's ideas and in particular of his religious point of view. In the text above the treatment of the latter topic is based upon it. Professor M. E. Hartsock also discusses Dryden's intellectual outlook in "Dryden's Plays: a Study in Ideas," in *Seventeenth Century Studies, Second Series*, edited by Robert Shafer, Princeton, 1937.

[4] See page 161, col. 2, at close.

[5] For further details concerning Dickinson and Tonson see C. E. Ward, "*Religio Laici* and Father Simon's History," in *Modern Language Notes*, lxi (1946), 407–412.

In *Religio Laici* Dryden discusses the question of the seat of authority in religion. When near the opening of his prose Preface he describes himself as "naturally inclined to scepticism in philosophy," he means almost the exact opposite of what an author contemporary with ourselves would suggest by the same words. He means that he is a Pyrrhonist, that he does not believe that human reason is capable of attaining ultimate truth. Hence he is at liberty to accept any doctrines whatsoever on grounds of revelation. So in the splendid opening lines of the poem itself he proclaims that not Reason but Revelation is man's true guide in religious matters: —

> Reveal'd Religion first inform'd thy sight,
> And Reason saw not, till Faith sprung the light.
> (Page 163, lines 68, 69.)

Rejecting Reason as a guide to religious truth, Dryden turns to Scripture. For Protestants this is the ultimate authority concerning the divine Revelation; but, as Father Simon has amply proved, it is an authority that has been subject to corruption. If then Scripture as we have it is untrustworthy, some men may assert that truth must be sought and found in Church tradition (line 281). Dryden longs for such "an unerring guide" (line 277): —

> Such an omniscient Church we wish indeed;
> 'T were worth both Testaments; and cast in the Creed.
> (Lines 282, 283.)

But Dryden does not believe that an infallible Church exists. The "partial Papists" (line 356) claim to be such a Church, but their claim is invalid, since they are merely a part of the Church, not the whole of it; and since at best they are only the handers-down of Scripture, without authority to interpret it. Their assumption has led to abuses, since in times of ignorance their clergy plied "a gainful trade" (line 371). Yet giving a faulty translation of a faulty text to the rabble for individual interpretation leads to worse abuses: —

> While crowds unlearn'd, with rude devotion warm,
> About the sacred viands buzz and swarm,
> The fly-blown text creates a crawling brood,
> And turns to maggots what was meant for food.
> (Lines 417–420.)

So Dryden subsides into a middle ground of compromise: men should accept the fundamental doctrines approved both by Scripture and by the Fathers, but —

> points not clearly known
> Without much hazard may be let alone.
> (Lines 443, 444.)

If Reason and the teaching of the Church conflict: —

> That private Reason 't is more just to curb,
> Than by disputes the public peace disturb.
> For points obscure are of small use to learn;
> But common quiet is mankind's concern.
> (Lines 447–450.)

In *Religio Laici* Dryden is far less opposed to the Papists than to the Puritans. He longs for an infallible Church that shall interpret an infallible Scripture to fallible men, yet he never claims that his own Mother Church, the Church of England, is thus omniscient. Later he will definitely adopt an authoritarian position and accept the Catholic Church as infallible. He will then write *The Hind and the Panther*, a work logically more consistent and emotionally more powerful than *Religio Laici*.

For a modern reader perhaps the most interesting passage in this poem is that (lines 168–223) in which Dryden refuses to believe that the heathen who die without hearing of Christ must be damned to everlasting punishment. The authorities, that "good old man" Bishop Athanasius among the number, will have it so; but the kindly, genial, albeit somewhat wayward English gentleman, who writes satires only to serve his political party, or when roused by insults from his personal enemies, cannot force his charity to accept their cruel verdict.

The easy, ambling style of *Religio Laici* is totally different from the swift, impetuous invective of *Absalom and Achitophel*. Dryden's model is now the *Epistles* of Horace, not the *Satires* of Juvenal. By his "unpolished, rugged verse" (line 453) — which he modestly likens to that of Tom Sternhold or Tom Shadwell — Dryden shows his wonderful versatility, a versatility which readers of to-day, unused to the couplet in its classic form, do not always fully appreciate.

Dryden might write a begging letter to Laurence Hyde, and he often dedicated his works to patrons in terms of fulsome flattery that grate upon our present taste. But he also strove to increase his income by hard, patient toil. During his dramatic period he had won a reputation as a writer of prologues and epilogues, and had turned many an honest penny by furnishing them for his friends' plays. He continued such work after he had himself practically abandoned dramatic composition. If an anecdote dating from 1742 may be trusted, he ordinarily received four guineas for a prologue, but in 1682 raised his price to six guineas.[1]

In 1680 Dryden made his first experiment in poetical translation, a sort of work that later became his chief means of support. He contributed three translations (including one done in partnership with Mulgrave) to a little volume published by Tonson, *Ovid's Epistles, translated by several hands*, and wrote the prose Preface to the book. Since another of the "several hands" was Settle, it is probable that Tonson, not Dryden, originated this small project and selected the collaborators. Dryden had all his life, as is proved by his notes to *Annus Mirabilis* and by numerous passages in his critical works, been an attentive reader of the Latin poets, so that this new occupation was much to his liking. His versions were sure to find a ready acceptance among a public accustomed by school training, and by the whole trend of contemporary criticism, to look on the Latin writers as the standards of literary taste.

In the seventeenth century poetical miscellanies were a favorite form of publication. They were ordinarily publishers' ventures, and frequently piratical, bringing no profit to the authors of the pieces contained in them. The volume of *Miscellany Poems* issued by Tonson in February, 1684, was a publisher's venture, but it was not piratical and it presumably brought profit to Dryden, who was the chief contributor to the book and who may have been consulted concerning the selection for it of poems other than his own. It opens with new editions of *Mac Flecknoe*, *Absalom and Achitophel*, and *The Medal*, all of course without the author's name, but authorized by him. It also contains many of Dryden's prologues and epilogues. Some of these possibly appeared here for the first time, but the matter is uncertain, since they may have been printed earlier on broadsides of which no copies have survived. Of work by Dryden certainly never before printed it includes only four short translations from Theocritus, Ovid, and Virgil, and a single song.

Encouraged by his success with *Miscellany Poems*, 1684, Tonson promptly undertook a similar book, which was published in January, 1685, under the title, *Sylvæ, or The Second Part of Poetical Miscellanies*. This collection differed from its predecessor by including only new work, mainly translations. Of it Dryden was consulting editor, as his correspondence with Tonson makes plain. Besides contributing a couple of songs,

[1] See headnote, page 122.

Dryden wrote a critical preface for the volume and translated long extracts from Lucretius and Virgil, and smaller selections from Theocritus and Horace: his versions have the place of honor in the book. In his attempts with the last two writers Dryden is not happy: Horace's exquisite urbanity and Theocritus' union of elegance with rusticity are both beyond his reach. With Lucretius he has better fortune: his version has much of the dogmatic force and dramatic intensity of the original.

At about the same time Dryden also produced some hack work in prose: a *Life of Plutarch* (1683), prefixed to a coöperative translation of *Plutarch's Lives*, and a translation of Maimbourg's *History of the League* (1684), executed by order of the king.

On February 6, 1685, Charles II died. Dryden lamented his dead master in *Threnodia Augustalis*, a poem in the irregular "Pindaric" verse made popular by Cowley. The work has some interest as Dryden's first experiment in the versification that he brought to perfection in *Alexander's Feast*. For the rest, few modern readers will be inclined to quarrel with Dr. Johnson's verdict: "It has neither tenderness nor dignity; it is neither magnificent nor pathetic. He seems to look round him for images which he cannot find, and what he has he distorts by endeavoring to enlarge them."

Just before the death of the king, Dryden had prepared an opera, *Albion and Albanius*, which was to celebrate the triumph of the brothers Charles and James over their Whig opponents. After a few changes, to suit altered circumstances, the work was produced for the first time on June 6, 1685, but ran for only six nights. Downes in *Roscius Anglicanus* [1] says that this was owing to "the nation being in a great consternation" at the landing of the Duke of Monmouth in the West. Whether this consternation or the poor quality of both the drama and the music was the real reason for the failure, is a question. Despite the slight literary merit of *Albion and Albanius*, the preface published with it is important for the understanding of the author's critical work. Nothing could be more repugnant than opera, with its numberless conventions offending against common sense, to the principles of the French criticism with which Dryden was now in hearty agreement. But, finding that opera would serve his turn, Dryden forsook for the moment the tenets which he elsewhere had defended so stoutly, and justified opera, against reason, by the argument for authority. The inventors of opera must give law to it, as Homer did to his successors in epic poetry. Dryden's passion for logic here yields to his talent for gratifying the taste of the passing moment.

The Catholic James II was now King of England. The new monarch soon made it plain that he would do all in his power to spread his own religion among his countrymen, and that he would show most favor to its adherents. Toward the close of this same year (1685) Dryden became a Catholic. [2] For this change of faith he has been repeatedly denounced — notably by Macaulay· and by Christie, brilliant and learned men but ardent anti-Tory partisans — as a hypocritical time-server. At the present day scarcely any student of Dryden would concur in this accusation.

In none of Dryden's writings is there the least sign of a genuinely religious temperament. He was emphatically a man of this world, kind-hearted, and, as things go, honest; he had no overmastering sense of spiritual problems and no inclination to make himself miserable by brooding on them. In our time he would either not have meddled in religious discussion at all, or he would have written as a freethinker, not attached to any church. In his own time such indifference was impossible; a man who took sides in politics must take sides in religion as well. The position which Dryden adopted in all sincerity, and which he constantly defended, has been already set forth in the discussion

---

[1] Ed. Knight (London, 1886), p. 40.

[2] Evelyn notes in his *Diary* for January 19, 1686: "Dryden, the famous play-writer, and his two sons . . . were said to go to mass." In *The Reasons of Mr. Bays Changing his Religion*, 1688, p. 21, Tom Brown writes in reference to Dryden, "some Three Weeks before your Conversion in 1685."

of *Religio Laici*. As his writings clearly demonstrate, Dryden had an ever-increasing regard for the principle of authority — in religion and in all other matters. In *Religio Laici* he had shown his yearning for an infallible Church and his distrust of Scripture as handed down and interpreted by fallible men. He was thus already far advanced on the way to accept the Catholic Church as an infallible authority. Without impulse from external circumstances, in the shape of a Catholic king and Catholic influences predominant at court, he might never have become a member of that Church: of this no man can be sure. At all events his change of faith was in the line of his own intellectual growth; it involved no violence to his inner nature, no sacrifice of intellectual honesty. Once he had recognized the element of the irrational in religious faith, he could find no difficulty in accepting all the dogmas of the Catholic Church. Specifically, as he tells us in *The Hind and the Panther*, he admitted that to accept the doctrine of the Trinity involved a sacrifice of the reason, yet he denounced the Socinians, who denied that doctrine, as the worst of heretics: —

> With greater guile
> False Reynard fed on consecrated spoil:
> The graceless beast by Athanasius first
> Was chas'd from Nice; then, by Socinus nurs'd,
> His impious race their blasphemy renew'd,
> And nature's King thro' nature's optics view'd.
> Revers'd, they view'd him lessen'd to their eye,
> Nor in an infant could a God descry:
> New swarming sects to this obliquely tend,
> Hence they began, and here they all will end.
> (Page 218, lines 52–61.)

Once Dryden had accepted the doctrine of the Trinity he could accept all the Catholic dogmas, and in particular that of transubstantiation, which in Dryden's England was the official, governmental *test* that set apart Catholics from members of the Church of England and from all Dissenters: —

> Good life be now my task: my doubts are done:
> (What more could fright my faith, than three in one?)
> Can I believe eternal God could lie   ⎫
> Disguis'd in mortal mold and infancy?   ⎬
> That the great Maker of the world could die? ⎭
> And after that trust my imperfect sense,
> Which calls in question his omnipotence?
> Can I my reason to my faith compel,
> And shall my sight, and touch, and taste rebel?
> (Page 219, lines 78–86.)

Dryden has sketched his own religious development in the following lines of *The Hind and the Panther*: —

> My thoughtless youth was wing'd with vain desires,
> My manhood, long misled by wand'ring fires,
> Follow'd false lights; and, when their glimpse was gone,
> My pride struck out new sparkles of her own.
> Such was I, such by nature still I am;
> Be thine the glory, and be mine the shame.
> (Page 219, lines 72–77.)

This passage, perhaps intentionally, is so vague that interpretations of it have varied.[1]

---

[1] For discussions of the problem see Scott, *Life of John Dryden* (in Dryden, *Works*, ed. Scott-Saintsbury, i. 255–263); Firth, in Dryden, *Stanzas on the Death of Oliver Cromwell*, etc. (ed. 5, Oxford, 1893), p. 283; and, most important, Bredvold, *The Intellectual Milieu of John Dryden*, pp. 108–117.

It may be reasonable to understand "vain desires" as referring to a period of boyish indifference to religion. Then "wand'ring fires" and "false lights" will allude to the Puritan period of Dryden's youth and "new sparkles" to his intellectual speculations after he had settled down, formally at least, as a member of the Church of England. For these sparkles he exchanged the clear light of authority and constant tradition that he found in the Catholic Church. Perhaps, without being too fantastic, we may apply the same passage to Dryden's literary development. In his early poems he followed the "false lights" of the school of Cowley; later he "struck out new sparkles of his own" in the bombastic tirades of the heroic plays; at last he adopted an ideal of chastened elegance of style, and of literary construction limited by exact rules, imposed by critical authority, which is in all essentials that of the school of Boileau. These doctrines he was unable to carry out consistently in practice, so that his later poems and plays show many departures from them. This partial failure he excused, somewhat inadequately, by the necessity of accommodating his productions to the taste of the British public; a writer to whom the new theories were fundamentally congenial would have been able to make the public taste bow to him.

Similarly, Dryden's conversion to Catholicism was sincere, but it was intellectual, not spiritual; he underwent no religious crisis comparable, for instance, to that of St. Paul or of Tolstoy. His change of faith made no decided change in his attitude towards life. "A sincere Catholic," as one of them has remarked, "need neither be a mystic nor even notably devout." [1] Dryden remained of the same coarse temperament as before; some late expressions of regret on his part at the looseness of his writings are due rather to the softening influence of age than to his new religious faith. But in that faith he remained steadfast despite all the trials of his later years. His wife shared his new religion and they reared their three sons as Catholics. Utterances in Dryden's letters testify to his absolute sincerity. For example on November 7, 1699, at a time when Whigs and Tories were more or less united in opposition to King William III and Dryden might hope for renewed kindness from the government, he wrote thus to his cousin Mrs. Steward: —

... the Court rather speaks kindly of me, than does any thing for me, though they promise largely: & perhaps they think I will advance, as they go backward: in which they will be much deceivd: for I can never go an Inch beyond my Conscience & my Honour. If they will consider me as a Man, who have done my best to improve the Language, & Especially the Poetry, & will be content with my acquiescence under the present Government, & forbearing satire on it, that I can promise, because I can perform it: but I can neither take the Oaths, nor forsake my Religion, because I know not what Church to go to, if I leave the Catholique; they are all so divided amongst them selves in matters of faith, necessary to Salvation: & yet all assumeing the name of Protestants. May God be pleasd to open your Eyes, as he has opend mine: Truth is but one; & they who have once heard of it, can plead no Excuse, if they do not embrace it. But these are things too serious, for a trifling Letter. [2]

Dryden gained no new offices or pensions as the price of his conversion to Catholicism. Under James II his pension of £300 a year seems to have been paid regularly, and on August 18, 1685, there was a payment of £150 for arrears up to September 29, 1681; but the later arrears that had accumulated under Charles II were apparently never adjusted. The process of confirming him as poet laureate and historiographer royal was initiated by a royal *warrant* on April 27, 1685, several months before his conversion, although his *patent* was not issued until March 4, 1686. The delay, for which there are close parallels, may be regarded as an accident of red tape rather than as pressure brought on Dryden to change his religion.[3] It is not likely that King James would have

[1] Walter Shewring, *Topics* (London, 1940), p. 26.   [2] *Letters*, ed. Ward, p. 123.
[3] Bredvold, "Notes on John Dryden's Pension."

dismissed from office a man who had been one of his constant partisans, even if that man had remained a member of the Church of England.

Dryden's conversion bore fruit in his longest original non-dramatic poem, *The Hind and the Panther*, published in May, 1687. According to tradition Dryden wrote it while visiting his Catholic patron Lord Clifford at his estate of Ugbrooke in Devonshire. "Among the herd of deer then in [Ugbrooke] Park was a fairly good proportion of white deer. The milk-white hind of the poem was probably no figment of the poet's imagination, but was very likely suggested by the sight of the white deer in the herd as they grazed on the hillsides of the Park."[1] The plot of this work is absurd enough: the gentle and inoffensive Hind, representing the Catholic Church, and the fierce yet beautiful Panther, representing the Church of England, discuss between them questions of controversial divinity; the debate ending, of course, in the triumph of the Hind. While arguing on the Catholic side, Dryden retained his intellectual independence; he took the position of the moderate Catholics and made a thinly veiled attack on a favorite adviser of King James, the Jesuit Father Petres.[2] And whatever one may think of the substance of the piece, its poetic style places it very high among Dryden's compositions. A certain emotional fervor fills the debate, very different from the dry, intellectual, detached tone of *Religio Laici*. More than this, in his address to the Deity, defending his own sincerity, Dryden rises to true pathos, even to sublimity: —

> What weight of ancient witness can prevail,
> If private reason hold the public scale?
> But, gracious God, how well dost thou provide
> For erring judgments an unerring guide!
> Thy throne is darkness in th' abyss of light,
> A blaze of glory that forbids the sight.
> O teach me to believe thee thus conceal'd,
> And search no farther than thyself reveal'd;
> But her alone for my director take,
> Whom thou hast promis'd never to forsake!
>
> (Pages 218, 219, lines 62–71.)

In consequence of his conversion Dryden was employed to defend, against Stillingfleet, a paper by Anne Hyde (the first wife of James II), announcing her adoption of Catholicism, which was published in 1686 by the command of the king. He also translated from the French the *Life of St. Francis Xavier* by the Jesuit Bouhours.

Only one more poem written by Dryden during the short reign of James II need here be mentioned. In *Britannia Rediviva* he celebrates the birth of a son to the king on June 10, 1688. This production, though written in the heroic couplet, is of essentially the same sort as *Threnodia Augustalis*: sentiments made to order, with far-fetched imagery, prevent it from having any value as literature.

At various times during the reigns of Charles II and James II Dryden had aspirations for academic preferment. In 1674, during the very heyday of his career as a dramatist, he put the following lines into the mouth of the actress who spoke one of his epilogues at Oxford: —

> Oft has our poet wish'd, this happy seat
> Might prove his fading Muse's last retreat:
> I wonder'd at his wish, but now I find
> He here sought quiet, and content of mind;
> Which noiseful towns and courts can never know,
> And only in the shades like laurels grow.[3]

---

[1] C. E. Ward, "Some Notes on Dryden," in *Review of English Studies*, xiii (1937), 5.
[2] See note to page 240, line 1713, on page 1065.   [3] See page 76, col. 1, lines 1–6.

Lines of similar purport conclude a prologue spoken at Oxford two years later.[1] And in 1693, looking back with half-serious, half-whimsical regret over his past life, Dryden wrote in his Dedication to *Examen Poeticum:* —

> 'T is a vanity common to all writers, to overvalue their own productions; and 't is better for me to own this failing in myself, than the world to do it for me. For what other reason have I spent my life in so unprofitable a study? Why am I grown old in seeking so barren a reward as fame? The same parts and application which have made me a poet might have rais'd me to any honors of the gown, which are often given to men of as little learning and less honesty than myself.[2]

Sneers, rumors, and some more substantial evidence show that Dryden's words were more than vague outbursts of personal feeling.[3]

In 1682 Settle in *Absalom Senior* asserts that Dryden was anxious to become provost of Eton College.[4] Two later satires and some early manuscript notes lend support to this story. Settle further alleges that to serve his interests Dryden would have consented to become "his own loath'd thing call'd *Priest.*" Ordination in the Church of England would indeed have smoothed the way for any man seeking the position at Eton. There are other stories that Dryden, despite the frequent anticlerical expressions in his writings, had thought of entering the priesthood, but towards the close of his life he denied all such charges in the preface to his *Fables.*[5] The only time at which the office of provost of Eton could have been open to him was between January 28, 1681, when Richard Allestree died, and February 24, when Zachary Craddock succeeded him. There is no solid evidence that Dryden was considered for the position and one may doubt whether he regarded himself as a serious candidate for it.

Of much more importance is the evidence connecting Dryden in 1687 with two Oxford colleges.[6] He was now a Catholic and might count on royal favor. Thomas James, the warden of All Souls College, died on January 5, 1687. Before January 18 the king had selected Leopold Finch as his successor, but a letter from Finch shows that he had regarded Dryden as a dangerous rival. Then on March 24 Henry Clerke, president of Magdalen College, died, and the fellows had to fill the office by election. "So the king sent a mandamus, requiring them to choose one Farmer, an ignorant and vicious person, who had not one qualification that could recommend him to so high a post, besides that of changing his religion. . . . The fellows . . . did upon this choose Dr. Hough, one of their body, who, as he was in all respects a statutable man, so he was a worthy and a firm man, not apt to be threatened out of his right." [7] The king through his Ecclesiastical Commission disallowed the election of Hough, but did not insist upon Farmer. Apparently James II at least *thought* of Dryden for the position. At all events a news letter of June 30, 1687, states: "A mandate is said to be gone down [to] Oxford for Mr. Dryden to go out Doctor of Divinity, and also that he will be made President of Magdalen College." After reflection, however, the king appointed Samuel Parker, a man

---

[1] See page 106, and note on page 1054.   [2] See page 382.

[3] On what follows see R. G. Ham, "Some Uncollected Verse of John Dryden," in *The London Mercury*, xxi (1929–30), 421–426; L. I. Bredvold, "Dryden and the University of Oxford," in *Modern Language Notes*, xlvi (1931), 218–224; Ham, "Dryden and the Colleges," *Ibid.*, xlix (1934), 324–332; Pierre Legouis, "Dryden and Eton," *Ibid.*, lii (1937), 111–114; J. A. W. Bennett, "Dryden and All Souls," *Ibid.*, lii (1937), 115, 116; J. R. Bloxam, *Magdalen College and King James II*, Oxford, 1886. Macdonald in his *Dryden Bibliography* summarizes the main results of the investigations.

[4] Settle does not mention Eton by name, but he describes the college unmistakably. Nor does he use the word *provost*, but he says that the poet aspired "To be no less than Lord of that blest Quire."

[5] See page 749, col. 1.

[6] There are statements that Dryden at about the same time was one of the men considered for the position of provost of Trinity College, Dublin. This matter, however, seems not worth discussing here.

[7] Burnet, *Op. cit.*, pp. 444, 445.

who was at heart a Catholic, though he held the office of Bishop of Oxford in the Church of England. When all but two of the fellows refused to accept Parker, they were expelled and Parker was installed president by force. Presumably as a sop to Dryden, James II on December 31 nominated his second son, John, to a fellowship at Magdalen. The younger John Dryden had finished his course at Westminster School in 1685 and had been elected to a studentship at Christ Church, Oxford; but his father apparently preferred to put him in charge of Obadiah Walker, the Catholic master of University College, as a private student.[1] The lad was duly admitted "actual fellow" on January 6, 1688, but his appointment was canceled by the visitor on the following October 25, when the Revolution was imminent. The Magdalen College affair was among the chief causes of public resentment against James II. Lovers of Dryden may rejoice that the great poet did not become directly concerned in it.

IV

The Revolution of 1688 brought ruin to all Dryden's financial prosperity. As a Catholic, he could not take the oaths required of all officeholders under William and Mary. Already an old man, he was deprived of his position as poet laureate and historiographer royal, which passed to his despised rival Shadwell.[2] This meant that he lost his pension of £300 a year, the greater part of his income. It did not mean that he was left entirely without means of support, for he still had his small estates in Northamptonshire and in Wiltshire. He could presumably have retired to the country — or perhaps even remained in London — and lived on in idleness though in cramped conditions.[3] But such a way of life did not at all appeal to John Dryden. He accepted his situation with dignity, making no attempt to conciliate the new government, but, except for a few petulant expressions, refraining from attacks on it; and he applied himself manfully to work for money. (He lived at a time, one must remember, when no English author had yet made a living solely by the sale of his books.) Had he died just before the Revolution, his name would survive as that of the greatest writer of the Restoration period, but his personality would not seem in the least remarkable. Twelve years of toil remained to him, years hampered by old age, by poverty, and by illness. By his performance during this period Dryden showed himself still the undisputed prince of English letters; his character, meanwhile, acquired an elevation in which it had hitherto been lacking, and commands our respect and admiration. "Dryden rose to his greatest in failure," as Sir Walter Raleigh justly remarks, "and impressed himself most on his contemporaries when he was a sick and overtoiled man. His triumph was a triumph of character; so that his works cannot stand to us for all that the living man meant to his own generation." [4]

Dryden's first impulse was to return to the writing of plays, by which he had won his early fame. Between the years 1689 and 1693 he produced *Don Sebastian*, *Amphitryon*, *King Arthur* (an opera), *Cleomenes* (with Southerne), and *Love Triumphant*. These dramas, notably *Don Sebastian*, contain work in no way inferior to that of the poet's earlier period, but they contribute no new elements of importance for the study of his

---

[1] Such at least is the probable inference of Malone, *Op. cit.*, I, 1, 421–423.

[2] Shadwell did not long enjoy the distinction, for he died in November, 1692. His successor as poet laureate was Nahum Tate, the author of *The Second Part of Absalom and Achitophel*, who had now turned Whig. Shadwell, be it said to his credit, had been as stanch in his political principles as Dryden himself.

[3] Thorn-Drury has called attention to an entry in the expense book of Thomas Howard, son of Sir Robert Howard, under January 16, 1691/2, "P^d Lady Elizabeth Driden in Charitye...005.00.00": see *Review of English Studies*, i (1925), 83. This isolated item, recording a payment by a nephew to an elderly aunt, is no proof that Dryden's wife was a pauper! Thomas Howard may have given the Lady Elizabeth the five pounds to distribute in charity or because of some sudden emergency, such as illness.

[4] "John Dryden and Political Satire," in *Some Authors* (Oxford, 1923), p. 159.

genius, and may be dismissed without further analysis. They did not suffice to reëstablish their author's reputation as the chief English dramatist; the last of them, indeed, was a complete failure.

In his skill as a translator Dryden found a surer resource. Encouraged by his success with shorter pieces, he now undertook, aided by colleagues whom he himself selected, a complete version of Juvenal and Persius, which appeared in October, 1692. He himself translated five of the sixteen satires of Juvenal, and the whole of Persius, and contributed an elaborate dedicatory preface, in which, following Casaubon, Heinsius, Dacier, and other critics, he gives an account of the rise of Roman satire and an analysis of its chief authors. In the next year, 1693, he translated three selections from Ovid's *Metamorphoses* and the episode of Hector and Andromache from the *Iliad*, and wrote a preface for a third miscellany volume, *Examen Poeticum*, published by Tonson. With Ovid, a writer of easy, rapid, somewhat rhetorical verse, Dryden had much in common. His powers of invective and of sententious moralizing also fitted him to be the translator of Juvenal and Persius; though his versions are far from literal, they well reproduce in English the vigorous declamation of the Roman satire. His coarseness of mind is unfortunately likewise prominent in these translations. His command of the ludicrous is illustrated by his handling of Cicero's unfortunate hexameter, quoted by Juvenal: —

> O fortunatam natam me consule Romam!

This Dryden transformed into the startling couplet: —

> Fortune foretun'd the dying notes of Rome:
> Till I, thy consul sole, consol'd thy doom.
> (Page 350, lines 190, 191.)

Near the close of 1693 Dryden began the greatest single task of his life, the translation of the complete works of Virgil, which occupied practically all his time for more than three years. He worked conscientiously, using various commentaries, though he relied mainly on the Delphin edition of Virgil.[1] What from a modern point of view seems less admirable, he kept before him various earlier translations of Virgil and did not scruple to take from them rhyme words and even whole lines, with slight alteration and sometimes no alteration at all.[2] His translation was published by subscription, and was issued from Tonson's press in a handsome folio volume, early in July, 1697. To aid Dryden, Addison furnished an *Essay on the Georgics*, and the arguments in prose for the whole work; Dr. Knightly Chetwood wrote the *Life of Virgil* and the *Preface to the Pastorals*. The volume was illustrated with the same engravings that had once adorned the work of Ogleby, a previous translator whom Dryden heartily despised, but the plates were touched up for the occasion, and each was decorated with the arms of a subscriber to the book. Though the contract between Dryden and Tonson has survived, and

---

[1] On this book see page 496, col. 2, and note; on the general topic see Bottkol, "Dryden's Latin Scholarship," in *Modern Philology*, xl (1942–43), 241–254. Dryden had loved Virgil all his life and had been much influenced by him. See his own marginal notes on *Annus Mirabilis* and various notes in the present volume, on *Mac Flecknoe*, *Absalom and Achitophel*, *The Hind and the Panther*, and other poems. The topic of Virgil's influence on Dryden is treated by R. A. Brower in two articles: "Dryden's Poetic Diction and Virgil," in *Philological Quarterly*, xviii (1939), 211–217, and "Dryden's Epic Manner and Virgil," in *Publications of the Modern Language Association*, lv (1940), 119–138. Near the close of the second article Brower remarks pertinently: "In certain passages and in certain poems of less grandiose pretensions, when the avowed purpose was to convey the impression of epic rather than the reality, Dryden found in the use of Virgilian allusions the surest means of giving to his verse 'the majestic turn of heroic poesy.'"

[2] This topic has been studied carefully for the *Georgics:* see H. M. Hooker, "Dryden's *Georgics* and English Predecessors," in *Huntington Library Quarterly*, ix (1945–46), 273–310. The results are summarised in note to page 418 (on pages 1068, 1069); see also note to page 469, line 357. Study of the *Æneis* would probably give similar results: see note to page 546, line 763 (on pages 1069, 1070). Such practices seem not to have been regarded as reprehensible in Dryden's time.

though there are frequent references to it in their correspondence, it is impossible to determine just how much the poet received for his labors. In *Spence's Anecdotes* Pope is quoted as saying that the sum was about £1200, and this figure is probably not far from the truth.[1] This estimate presumably includes gifts from patrons as well as payments by Tonson. This reward, though small in comparison with the profit of about £9000 that Pope received from his *Homer*, was good pay for a literary man in those days; in our time it might amount to about $45,000. Dryden often wrote to his publisher in a testy tone, once protesting, for example: "Upon triall I find all of your trade are Sharpers & you not more than others; therefore I have not wholly left you." [2] Despite such explosions, Dryden kept Tonson's friendship to the close of his life.

Despite many revolutions of public taste, Dryden's *Virgil* still remains practically without a rival as the standard translation of the greatest Roman poet; the only one that, like two or three versions of Homer, has become an English classic. It has, indeed, almost none of the grace and tenderness, or the high seriousness, of the Latin original, to which Wordsworth attained in large measure in his *Laodamia*. Thus the marvelous verse,

> Sunt lacrimæ rerum et mentem mortalia tangunt,

disappears entirely in Dryden's commonplace: —

> Our known disasters fill ev'n foreign lands:
> See there, where old unhappy Priam stands!
> Ev'n the mute walls relate the warrior's fame,
> And Trojan griefs the Tyrians' pity claim.
> (Page 530, lines 646–649.)

Wordsworth, on the other hand, catches the Virgilian spirit in the lines: —

> — Yet tears to human suffering are due;
> And mortal hopes defeated and o'erthrown
> Are mourned by man, and not by man alone,
> As fondly he believes.
> (Cambridge edition, page 527, lines 164–167.)

The last words of Virgil's warrior maiden Camilla have a laconic, truly Roman vigor and nobility: —

> Hactenus, Acca soror, potui: nunc vulnus acerbum
> conficit, et tenebris nigrescunt omnia circum.
> Effuge et hæc Turno mandata novissima perfer:
> succedat pugnæ Troianosque arceat urbe.
> Iamque vale.

Dryden renders the passage thus: —

> Acca, 't is past! he swims before my sight,
> Inexorable Death; and claims his right.
> Bear my last words to Turnus; fly with speed,
> And bid him timely to my charge succeed,
> Repel the Trojans, and the town relieve:
> Farewell! and in this kiss my parting breath receive.
> (Page 687, lines 1197–1202.)

These lines, through "Farewell!" are neutral, reasonably faithful to the original, not strikingly felicitous, but not bad. Then the added clause, "and in this kiss my parting

---

[1] The latest student of the problem sets down the figure cautiously as possibly "as much as £1000." See C. E. Ward, "The Publication and Profits of Dryden's *Virgil*," in *Publications of the Modern Language Association of America*, liii (1938), 807–812.

[2] *Letters*, ed. Ward, p. 80.

breath receive," wholly without warrant in the Latin, spoils the beauty of the passage. It is inappropriate to the character of Camilla, and is in the style not of Virgil but of the flamboyant heroic plays.

Dryden is least satisfactory in his treatment of the *Pastorals* and of those portions of the *Georgics* of which the charm, for modern readers, consists less in the subject matter than in the exquisite delicacy of the treatment, and the haunting melody of the rhythm. His *Æneid*, however, is a masterpiece of rapid narrative. The buoyant, flowing verse carries the reader forward with a glorious energy, and, at its best, has something of Virgil's own noble simplicity. The following passage, though deformed in one line by Dryden's fondness for antithesis, is a favorable example of his power: —

> She thus replied: "The chaste and holy race
> Are all forbidden this polluted place.
> But Hecate, when she gave to rule the woods, ⎫
> Then led me trembling thro' these dire abodes, ⎬
> And taught the tortures of th' avenging gods. ⎭
> These are the realms of unrelenting fate;
> And awful Rhadamanthus rules the state.
> He hears and judges each committed crime;
> Enquires into the manner, place, and time.
> The conscious wretch must all his acts reveal,
> (Loth to confess, unable to conceal,)
> From the first moment of his vital breath,
> To his last hour of unrepenting death.
> Straight, o'er the guilty ghost, the Fury shakes ⎫
> The sounding whip and brandishes her snakes, ⎬
> And the pale sinner, with her sisters, takes." ⎭
>   (Pages 603, 604, lines 758–773.)

At times the veteran satirist indulges his genius. The following triplet on **Drances** might be the portrait of a Whig leader: —

> Factious and rich, bold at the council board, ⎫
> But cautious in the field, he shunn'd the sword; ⎬
> A close caballer, and tongue-valiant lord. ⎭
>   (Page 678, lines 512–514.)

More than this, Dryden inserts into his translation certain sly attacks on the reigning English monarch. (He had resisted, by the way, Tonson's request that he dedicate the volume to William III, though, as Dryden wrote to his sons in Rome, Tonson had "prepared the book for it"[1] by having the engraver make the portrait of Æneas resemble that of the king.) In the following lines, describing criminals scourged by the Fury, the words in italics have no warrant in the Latin:[2] —

> Then they, who brothers' better claim disown,
> Expel their parents, *and usurp the throne.*
>   (Page 604, lines 824, 825.)

And the portraits of the rival kings of the bees, which are much altered and expanded from the original, are obviously meant to suggest James and William: —

> With ease distinguish'd is the regal race:
> One monarch wears an honest open face;
> Shap'd to his size, and godlike to behold,
> His royal body shines with specks of gold,

---

[1] *Letters*, ed. Ward, p. 93.
[2] The editor is here indebted to a writer in *Notes and Queries*, series II. vii. 168, and series II. x. 263.

> And ruddy scales; for empire he design'd,
> Is better born, and of a nobler kind.
> That other looks like nature in disgrace:
> Gaunt are his sides, and sullen is his face;
> And like their grisly prince appears his gloomy race.
>
> (Page 478, lines 137–145.)

Like his verse, Dryden's prose had ripened with the years. The opening sentences of his *Postscript to the Reader* of his *Virgil*, by their splendidly sonorous rhythm, united with an unassumingly simple structure, are among the most beautiful in English.[1] Of them Matthew Arnold exclaimed, "Here at last we have the true English prose, a prose such as we would all gladly use if we only knew how."[2]

A musical society in London had for some years maintained the custom of celebrating November 22, the Feast of Saint Cecilia, by a public performance of vocal and instrumental music. Dryden, in 1687, had written an ode for this occasion; he now, ten years later, furnished another and a greater one, *Alexander's Feast*. This fine ode, which stands at the head of English lyric poetry between Milton and Gray, is to-day by far the best known of Dryden's poems. Yet, familiar as *Alexander's Feast* has become by ceaseless reprinting in schoolbooks and anthologies, it may be doubted whether many readers appreciate its full excellence. Brought up on the traditions of Wordsworth, Shelley, and Keats, we instinctively expect in lyric poetry either the expression of elevated moral or philosophical ideas, of intense passion, or of a delight in sensuous beauty. Dryden gives us none of these, but a rapid series of flashlight pictures, each expressed in verse that by its music suggests the scene described. The poem is rather a narrative than a pure lyric. No English poem is more full of life and animation; few show a more youthful spirit than this ode by the weary satirist and dramatist of sixty-six.

Dryden's last years were cheered by the success of his *Virgil*, which reached a second edition within a few months after its first publication, and were saddened by the attacks of a few critics and rivals. To Milbourne, who assailed his *Virgil*, and Blackmore, who attacked his character, he paid comparatively little attention, judging correctly that their words would not affect public opinion. The case was different with Jeremy Collier, who in 1698 published his *Short View of the Immorality and Profaneness of the English Stage*, in which he arraigned the whole school of the Restoration dramatists, and Dryden chief among the number. To the charges Dryden manfully pleaded guilty, though he rightly accused Collier of exaggeration; and, somewhat lamely, excused his own sins in part by the general corruption of the times.[3]

The comparatively large profits of the *Virgil* did not free Dryden from the need of further exertion. He thought of undertaking a translation of the *Iliad*, and translated the first book "as an essay to the whole work."[4] But, perhaps deterred by a consciousness of his defective knowledge of Greek, he turned back to translate further selections from Ovid; to put into modern English some tales from Chaucer, whom he had long loved with a truly sympathetic insight; and to clothe in heroic verse three stories from Boccaccio, to whom he was led by his study of Chaucer. The result of this work, more congenial and more desultory than the long struggle with Virgil, was a volume published in 1700, entitled *Fables, Ancient and Modern*. These products of the poet's old age have an enduring charm. The harshness and asperity of the great satirist are gone; there remain a clear, melodious diction, and a frank, kindly spirit, which show Dryden to be a kinsman of Chaucer and of William Morris. Sorely battered by the storms of life, conscious that he had often played a part not worthy of his great powers, he appeared just before his death as "the idle singer of an empty day."

---

[1] See page 707.   [2] "The Study of Poetry," in *Essays in Criticism, Second Series*.
[3] See page 749.   [4] See page 740, col. 2.

Henry David Thoreau, a man who by nature was very different from Dryden and who perhaps never thought of Dryden from one year's end to the next, once wrote wisely in his *Journal:* —

"Some poets mature early and die young. Their fruits have a delicious flavor like strawberries, but do not keep till fall or winter. Others are slower in coming to their growth. Their fruits may be less delicious, but are a more lasting food and are so hardened by the sun of summer and the coolness of autumn that they keep sound over winter." [1]

For the *Fables* Dryden composed a preface that is the most graceful of his critical works. In writing of Chaucer he is fresh, independent, and personal; unhampered by tradition or by critical systems, one great poet pays tribute to another.

Tonson contracted to pay Dryden 250 guineas for the *Fables*, provided that they should contain at least 10,000 lines, and to increase this amount to £300 when a second edition should go to press. The sum of 250 guineas for 10,000 lines was at the rate of about sixpence a line, say a dollar a line to-day. Dryden gave Tonson good measure, 10,952 lines aside from the addresses to the Duchess of Ormond and to his own kinsman John Driden of Chesterton, the epitaph from *The Monument of a Fair Maiden Lady who Died at Bath and is There Interr'd, Alexander's Feast* (reprinted), and his prose preface. Tonson paid Dryden £268 15s (that is, 250 guineas) on March 24, 1698; and on June 11, 1713, paid £31 5s to his administratrix, making up the stipulated £300.[2] From his kinsman Dryden received "a noble present" [3] in return for his poem. Presumably the Duke of Ormond, to whom he dedicated the volume, and the family of the "fair maiden lady," Mary Frampton, were similarly generous.

Dryden passed away, after a short illness, on May 1, 1700. He died poor, apparently leaving no personal property of any account, but not neglected. Vanbrugh and other friends had prepared for his benefit a performance of Fletcher's *Pilgrim*, for which Dryden himself wrote a prologue and epilogue and some small additions, the last of his works. He is said to have died "on the third night of its representation." [4] He received a splendid funeral, and was laid to rest in the Poets' Corner of Westminster Abbey, near the graves of his first master, Cowley, and his last master, Chaucer.

Lady Elizabeth Dryden became insane soon after her husband's death, but survived him until 1714.[5] The three sons whom Dryden "bred up to learning" were all, according to their kinswoman Mrs. Creed, "fine, ingenious, accomplished gentlemen." [6] The eldest, Charles, studied at Westminster School and at Trinity College, Cambridge. He had some skill in both English and Latin verse. A Latin poem by him is included in *Sylvæ*, 1685, and at his father's invitation he translated the seventh satire of Juvenal for the *Juvenal and Persius* of 1692. At about that time he went to Rome, where he became chamberlain of the household of Pope Innocent XII.[7] He returned home in 1698 and in 1704 was drowned in an attempt to swim across the Thames.

The education of the second son, John, has already been mentioned. Like his elder brother, he contributed a translation, the fourteenth satire of Juvenal, to his father's volume of 1692. And he too went to Rome, where he died on April 16, 1703.[8] From

---

[1] *Journal* for April 8, 1854.   [2] Malone, *Op. cit.*, I, 1, 560, 561.
[3] *Letters*, ed. Ward, p. 135.   [4] See note to page 898, on page 1071.
[5] Malone, *Op. cit.*, I, 1, 395–398.   [6] *Ibid.*, pp. 399, 565.

[7] The date when Charles Dryden went to Rome is uncertain. In September, 1697, Dryden and his wife sent a letter to their sons in Rome (*Letters*, ed. Ward, pp. 92–96). Lady Dryden's part of it is addressed "Al Illustrissimo Sig^re Carlo Dryden, Camariere d'Honore A S.S." She writes: "He [her husband] expresses a great desire to see my deare Charlles: and trully I see noe reason why you should not both come together, to be a comfort to woon another, and to us both . . . for you doe but just make shift to Live wheare you are: and soe I hope you may doe heare: for I will Leaf noe ston unturnd to help my beloved sonns." See also Malone, *Op. cit.*, I, 1, 399–404.

[8] Osborn, *Op. cit.*, pp. 265, 266, following Historical MSS Commission, 1903, *Report on the MSS of the Duke of Buccleuch*, ii. 768.

Rome he sent to his father a comedy, *The Husband his Own Cuckold*, which was acted about 1695, with an epilogue by his father and a prologue by Congreve, and was published by Tonson in the next year, with a preface by his father.[1]

Dryden's third son, Erasmus Henry, was admitted as a scholar at the Charterhouse on February 5, 1683, on the nomination of Charles II, and on November 2, 1685, was "elected to the University."[2] Yet he did not attend either of the English universities, but studied at Douay and from October 25, 1690, to March 1, 1691, was at the Venerable English College in Rome.[3] He entered the Dominican Order and was ordained priest in 1694. In a letter of September, 1697, sent to their sons in Rome, both John and Elizabeth Dryden desire his prayers.[4] He was then "residing in the Convent of Saints John and Paul, on the Cœlian Hill, which Cardinal Howard had obtained for the English Dominicans." On November 16 of that year he was sent to the Convent of Holy Cross, at Bornhem in Belgium. "Here he was sub-prior until 1700, when he returned to England, to labor on the mission in Northamptonshire, his native county."[5] In an account book of his uncle, Erasmus Dryden, he is mentioned as "Captain Dryden," but "it is unlikely that he was an officer of the British army, for his name is not found in the army lists. Moreover, as a Roman Catholic he could not legally have held a commission after the Revolution of 1688, at which time he was only nineteen years old."[6] In *Spence's Anecdotes* Pope is quoted as saying that one of Dryden's sons was a captain in the pope's guards; the reference *may* be to Erasmus Henry. In May, 1710, Erasmus Henry inherited the title of baronet that had been conferred on his great-grandfather, but he died in the following December.

The letters that survive from Dryden's later years give pleasant glimpses — but only glimpses — of the old man's personality and his way of life. He was an affectionate father, encouraging his sons to do literary work and showing an honest pride in their humble endeavors to follow in his footsteps. In general he was a kindly critic, eager to aid younger writers by his counsel; his correspondence with William Walsh (1663–1708) shows him in a most favorable light, friendly and helpful without condescension. From mean literary jealousy, which so deformed Pope's character, he was comparatively free.[7] He was a welcome visitor at the country house of his good kinswoman Mrs. Steward, "Att Cotterstock Neare Oundle, In the County of Northampton," and he gratefully acknowledges her hospitality. In one letter he praises the dainties that Mrs. Steward has sent to him: "Not to name my self, & my wife, My Sonn Charles is the great Commender of your last receivd Present: who being of late somewhat indisposd, uses to send for some of the same sort, which we call heer Marrow Puddings, for his Suppers: but the tast of yours, has so spoyld his Markets heer, that there is not the least Comparison betwixt them." But in his next letter he confesses: "As for the rarities you promise, if beggars might be choosers, a part of a chine of honest bacon wou'd please my appetite more than all the marrow puddings; for I like them better plain; having a very vulgar stomach."[8]

When in London, Dryden wrote at home all the morning, dined with his family, then went to Will's Coffee-House, where he spent his evenings. His reign there as judge of wit is described in a well-known passage by Dr. Johnson: —

"Of the only two men whom I have found, to whom he was personally known, one told me that at the house which he frequented, called Will's Coffee-House, the appeal upon any literary dispute was made to him: and the other related that his armed chair,

---

[1] See page 416; also *Letters*, ed. Ward, p. 82.   [2] Malone, *Op. cit.*, I, 1, 425, 426.
[3] *Publications of the Catholic Records Society*, xl (1943), 111.   [4] *Letters*, ed. Ward, pp. 94, 95.
[5] Article in Joseph Gillow, *Literary and Biographical History, or Bibliographical Dictionary, of the English Catholics* (1885–1902), based on Catholic sources, in part unprinted.   [6] Osborn, *Op. cit.*, p. 242; Malone, *Op. cit.*, I, 1, 427.
[7] The following sentence, attributed to Tonson in *Spence's Anecdotes*, really (by the use of *even*) praises Dryden in contrast to other writers: "Even Dryden was very suspicious of rivals. He would compliment Crowne, when a play of his failed, but was cold to him if he met with success."   [8] *Letters*, ed. Ward, pp. 105, 106, 109, 110.

which in the winter had a settled and prescriptive place by the fire, was in the summer placed in the balcony, and that he called the two places his winter and his summer seat."

To this resort the boy Pope "prevailed with a friend to carry him," [1] that he might see the man whom later he always revered as his master, on the occasion that he describes in *Spence's Anecdotes:* "I saw Mr. Dryden when I was about twelve years of age — this bust is like him. — I remember his face well; for I looked upon him, even then, with the greatest veneration, and observed him very particularly."

In person Dryden was short and plump. In *The Rehearsal* he is termed "little Bayes" and Rochester tells us [2] that he had won the nickname "poet squab." But a portrait of him in his youth shows a handsome face, with marked intellectual distinction. He retained his rosy cheeks beyond middle life. In conversation he was not brilliant, being hampered by a shy and hesitating manner, which is mimicked by Mr. Bayes in *The Rehearsal*. Even his reading of his own verses was far from excellent. Spence quotes Pope as saying: "Dryden was not a very genteel man, he was intimate with none but poetical men. — He was said to be a very good man, by all that knew him." From Dennis, also through Spence, comes the information: "Dryden was generally an extreme sober man. For the last ten years of his life he was much acquainted with Addison, and drank with him more than he ever used to do; probably so far as to hasten his end."

All this fails to satisfy. We long for accounts that shall be more than glimpses, and we fail to find them. We know what sort of man Milton was; we are likewise well informed concerning Pope and Dr. Johnson. But Dryden's personality remains indistinct in the twilight, despite the fact that for forty years he was a prominent man in London literary circles and that for about two-thirds of that period he was recognized as the foremost English man of letters. His scanty correspondence is generally dull, containing few intimate passages such as those quoted above, nor as a rule are his works self-revealing. The external testimony concerning him, aside from casual bits of gossip, consists of attacks by writers who for personal or political reasons heartily disliked him, and an affectionate panegyric by his friend Congreve that will be cited below. There is no middle ground of reminiscence by men who knew him well; memoirs were not yet an important part of English literature.[3] The attacks vary in tone with the lapse of time. *The Rehearsal* (1671) treats Dryden with amused and amusing contempt as a man who could write smooth verse but who was personally nothing but a joke. Of the same nature is the testimony by Rochester (*c.* 1676) that has been quoted above.[4] After 1681 the attacks are of a different sort. Dryden's assailants show bitter hatred, accusing him of lechery, of greed, and of dishonesty; but they tacitly recognize that he is a man of vigor and power. The facts that we know confirm the impression of power, but refute most of the charges against him. They enable us to say that by nature Dryden was receptive, kindly, honest, and, though aware of his own skill in expression, modest. His mind was so hospitable to new ideas, and so ready to adapt its utterance to the needs of the moment, that at a first impression we are apt to regard him as a mere flatterer, hypocrite, and time-server. On further acquaintance we find him a kindly gentleman, like some of our personal friends, unconcerned with superficial consistency, distin-

---

[1] Note by Warburton: see *The Works of Alexander Pope,* ed. Elwin and Courthope, vol. vi, p. 15.
[2] In *An Allusion to Horace, the Tenth Satire of the First Book.*
[3] Sir Walter Scott, who knew Dryden and his period marvelously well, introduces into *The Pirate* a rustic bard who is supposed to have seen Dryden at Will's Coffee-House and to have listened to him, and who brags of the meeting incessantly and copiously. But, save for the well-invented phrase "glorious John," Scott fails to infuse life into his imaginary portrait. He had before him no satisfactory contemporary sketch on which to base it.
[4] See page xxxix.

guished among his fellow men of letters not so much by elevation of spirit as by ability to express finely his passing opinions. As he advances in age, his character grows more mellow, and his opinions mold themselves into the semblance of a system, of which the central element is respect for authority and tradition, in letters, in government, and in religion. The old man wins our respect by his open confession of past errors and of his liability to fall into fresh ones. He ends his life surrounded by friends, both old and new.

This short account of the life and character of John Dryden may well close with Congreve's portrait of his friend; a portrait that is flattering, but, we may trust, not untrue in any essential respect: —

He was of a nature exceedingly humane and compassionate, easily forgiving injuries, and capable of a prompt and sincere reconciliation with them who had offended him.

Such a temperament is the only solid foundation of all moral virtues and sociable endowments. His friendship, where he professed it, went much beyond his professions; and I have been told of strong and generous instances of it, by the persons themselves who received them, though his hereditary income was little more than a bare competency.

As his reading had been very extensive, so was he very happy in a memory tenacious of everything that he had read. He was not more possessed of knowledge than he was communicative of it. But then his communication of it was by no means pedantic, or imposed upon the conversation; but just such, and went so far as by the natural turns of the discourse in which he was engaged it was necessarily promoted or required. He was extreme ready and gentle in his correction of the errors of any writer who thought fit to consult him, and full as ready and patient to admit of the reprehension of others in respect of his oversight or mistakes. He was of very easy, I may say, of very pleasing access; but something slow, and as it were diffident in his advances to others. He had something in his nature that abhorred intrusion into any society whatsoever. Indeed it is to be regretted that he was rather blamable in the other extreme; for, by that means, he was personally less known, and consequently his character might become liable both to misapprehensions and misrepresentations.

To the best of my knowledge and observation, he was, of all the men that ever I knew, one of the most modest, and the most easily to be discountenanced in his approaches, either to his superiors or his equals.[1]

V

Dryden's reputation as a writer has been no more constant than that of other great masters. In his own time his commanding position was early recognized; even his assailants admitted his power. In the eighteenth century his fame even increased. Pope acknowledged him as his teacher. Gray in *The Progress of Poesy* described him as the successor to Milton: —

> Behold, where Dryden's less presumptuous car,
> Wide o'er the fields of glory bear
> Two coursers of ethereal race,
> With necks in thunder cloth'd, and long-resounding pace.

Dr. Johnson in his carefully developed comparison of Dryden and Pope decided "with some hesitation" that the older writer had the superior genius, but added quickly that "every other writer since Milton must give place to Pope." Thus when Sir Walter Scott wrote in 1808, at the close of his *Life of Dryden*, that Dryden left in English literature "a name second only to those of Milton and of Shakespeare," he was merely recording a received though conservative literary opinion. But even before Scott's time a reversal of opinion had begun with Joseph Warton's essay on Pope in 1756,[2] and this reversal triumphed with the rise of the romantic school. Though Byron loved

[1] Dedication to Congreve's edition of Dryden's dramas, reprinted in Dryden, *Works*, ed. Scott-Saintsbury, ii. 17, 18.

[2] Mark Van Doren, *John Dryden, a Study of his Poetry* (New York, 1946), p. 250.

Dryden's poetry, Keats studied and imitated his versification, and even Wordsworth admired his genius,[1] Dryden's reputation declined until it probably reached its lowest point during the Victorian period. To be sure, Matthew Arnold and Saintsbury, men of totally different critical schools, both paid tribute to his power, and the latter revised Scott's great edition of his works. Yet Dryden lost his hold on the public, probably having fewer readers than the more epigrammatic and more quotable Pope. The general tone of criticism towards him became condescending and negative; people questioned whether he was a poet at all. Despite the fact that he recognized merits in Dryden's work, Matthew Arnold was chief among the critics who condescended to him; also the fairest of them. He expressed his attitude most adequately in his essay on Thomas Gray: —

The difference between genuine poetry and the poetry of Dryden, Pope, and all their school, is briefly this: their poetry is conceived and composed in their wits, genuine poetry is conceived and composed in the soul. The difference between the two kinds of poetry is immense. They differ profoundly in their modes of language, they differ profoundly in their modes of evolution. The poetic language of our eighteenth century in general is the language of men composing *without their eye on the object*, as Wordsworth excellently said of Dryden; language merely recalling the object, as the common language of prose does, and then dressing it out with a certain smartness and brilliancy for the fancy and understanding. This is called "splendid diction." The evolution of the poetry of our eighteenth century is likewise intellectual; it proceeds by ratiocination, antithesis, ingenious turns and conceits. This poetry is often eloquent, and always, in the hands of such masters as Dryden and Pope, clever; but it does not take us much below the surface of things, it does not give us the emotion of seeing things in their truth and beauty. The language of genuine poetry, on the other hand, is the language of one composing with his eye on the object; its evolution is that of a thing which has been plunged in the poet's soul until it comes forth naturally and necessarily. This sort of evolution is infinitely simpler than the other, and infinitely more satisfying; the same thing is true of the genuine poetic language likewise. But they are both of them also infinitely harder of attainment; they come only from those who, as Emerson says, "live from a great depth of being."

This attitude sounds broad and plausible, but Mark Van Doren has pointed out that, through the notions that Arnold connects with his word "soul," it is really narrow.

"Soul" in Arnold suggests stoicism; stoicism suggests philosophic melancholy; philosophic melancholy suggests sentiment; a poem "conceived in the soul" suggests a poem conceived in spiritual pain. Arnold's touchstones, if not sentimental, did deal in pain, sad old memories, and death, an atmosphere which Dryden could hardly expect to survive. If there were to be no touchstones ringing with malice, disdain, or merriment, Dryden could lay no claim to a soul. He had not written his verse to "console" or "sustain" a bewildered generation of *fin de siècle* scholars. He had written to please hard-headed men of the world; he had labored to satisfy critics of poetry, not critics of souls. He had written genuine poetry, but he was not a Dante.[2]

In many of the highest qualities of a poet Dryden was certainly lacking. He expressed no great moral ideas or social aspirations; he had little intuitive knowledge of human nature, and no feeling for the beauty of the external world. "He is virtually barren of illuminating comments on human life which move a reader to take new account of himself."[3] He began serious work when he was no longer young, and he always regarded his art as primarily a means for making a living. His original poems, except his dramas, were all occasional productions, written not from any creative impulse, but to serve some passing purpose; they were devoted to courtly panegyric or to party warfare. Unlike Milton, Dryden found no high ideals and lofty aspirations among the men

[1] For Wordsworth's general verdict on Dryden, see page 1024.
[2] Van Doren, *Op. cit.*, pp. 256, 257.   [3] *Ibid.*, p. 37.

whom he served; nor was he a man, like Shelley, to revolt against the tendencies of his environment and create ideals and aspirations for himself. The only social cause to which Dryden gave utterance was loyalty, loyalty to the established order of Charles II and James II. Now loyalty is in general a noble quality, but its nobility varies somewhat with its object. To-day most of us respect the Englishmen who were disloyal to James II more than those who were loyal to him. Our respect is not unbounded even for men who were vociferously loyal to Charles II. We have most regard for Dryden in his latest years, when, at heart still loyal to James II, he glumly repressed his feelings and silently accepted the rule of William III.

As the portraits in *Absalom and Achitophel* amply prove, no man could *describe* character, in a certain way, better than Dryden. The central defect of his dramatic works is that they too are essentially descriptive. Dryden's men and women are figures made to order, after the pattern of previous writers, rather than living beings, created by the poet from his immediate sympathy with human nature. Their speeches are eloquent, often beautiful, but rarely do we find a phrase like Cleopatra's in *All for Love*, —

> And thus one minute's feigning has destroy'd
> My whole life's truth, —
> (Scott-Saintsbury edition, v. 415.)

which seems wrung from the speaker by real depth of feeling.

Taken as a whole, Dryden's dramas are perhaps the most important contribution to the English stage made by any author of the Restoration period. Yet an abyss separates his best comedy, *Marriage à la Mode*, from *The Way of the World*, by Congreve. In contrast to Dryden, Congreve can express character through conversation with a skill that rivals that of Shakespeare himself. And in tragedy *All for Love*, fine as it is, does not touch our emotions so powerfully as Otway's *Venice Preserved*. Dryden is without a superior only in the flamboyant heroic plays, a type of drama that lost its charm even during his own lifetime.

Some reservations are necessary even as to Dryden's *description* of character. If we contrast his figures in *Absalom and Achitophel* with those of Chaucer in his *Prologue*, we notice Dryden's insistence on abstract qualities and on abstract adjectives, in contrast to Chaucer's attention to personal appearance, even to the details of attire, as an index of character. Shaftesbury's person gave free scope for concrete description, but to it Dryden came no nearer than the following lines: —

> A fiery soul, which, working out its way, ⎫
> Fretted the pigmy body to decay, ⎬
> And o'er-inform'd the tenement of clay. ⎭
> (Page 111, lines 156–158.)

Seldom does Dryden give details like those in regard to Oates: —

> Sunk were his eyes; his voice was harsh and loud,
> Sure signs he neither choleric was nor proud:
> His long chin prov'd his wit; his saintlike grace
> A church vermilion, and a Moses' face.
> (Pages 117, 118, lines 646–649.)

Even here he is not content to let the details speak for themselves, but must point out the abstract qualities they denote. Contrast with this Chaucer's description of the Monk!

This tendency to the abstract rather than the concrete prepares us for the fatal weakness of all Dryden's attempts at the description of nature. Brought up in the country, he was nevertheless insensible to its beauty. Of his few passages of natural description, the following, from *The Indian Emperor*, is perhaps the most ambitious: —

> *Enter* CORTEZ *alone, in a nightgown.*
> All things are hush'd, as Nature's self lay dead;
> The mountains seem to nod their drowsy head;
> The little birds in dreams their songs repeat,
> And sleeping flowers beneath the night dew sweat.
> Even Lust and Envy sleep; yet Love denies
> Rest to my soul, and slumber to my eyes.
> (Scott-Saintsbury edition, ii. 360.)

These lines Wordsworth, who was a competent judge, condemned as "vague, bombastic, and senseless." [1] And, in a sentence of the dedication to the same play, Dryden proclaims his insensibility to the grander aspects of nature. "High objects, it is true," he tells us, "attract the sight; but it looks up with pain on craggy rocks and barren mountains, and continues not intent on any object which is wanting in shades and greens to entertain it."

In this fondness for abstraction Dryden is partly a follower of current poetic theories, which insisted on the generalizing, philosophic nature of poetry; partly true to his own temperament, which loved reasoning, in verse and out of it, at the expense of observation. His passion for ratiocination, which shows itself throughout his original works, from the fine-spun debates on love and honor in the heroic plays to the theological discussion in *The Hind and the Panther*, has given Dryden the reputation of a great and vigorous intellect. This reputation, which may have been increased by the blunt coarseness of his language, really a sign of a lack of delicacy rather than an indication of strength, is only partially deserved. Dryden originated no ideas, and in his analysis of old ones he was not profound. He seems often to gnaw at the rind of thought while others have reached the kernel. His arguments never become fused into a well-developed, coherent system; he excels primarily in expressing in clear, incisive, melodious language thoughts that he has borrowed from other men.

Concerning Dryden's frequent coarseness, which is not a mere matter of language but extends to ideas and is indeed a feature of his temperament, many critics have written copiously and justly. On this topic Mr. C. S. Lewis, after some pungent condemnation of *Sigismonda and Guiscardo*, speaks with drastic emphasis: "Dryden fails to be a satisfactory poet because being rather a boor, a gross, vulgar, provincial, misunderstanding mind, he yet constantly attempts those kinds of poetry which demand the *cuor gentil.*" [2]

Dryden's literary greatness then depends, in greater measure than that of almost any other of the very greatest English poets, upon his mastery of the technique of his art. Indifferent to the beauty of nature, he was keenly susceptible to beauty of style; he was a critic by instinct, an author by training. In his criticism, and in his prose style, we may discover some explanation of his power as a writer of verse.

In Dryden's criticism two elements are constantly contending for mastery. By his passion for logic, he was attracted to the contemporary French critics, who busied themselves primarily with literary theory and loved to prescribe hard and fast rules for the guidance of future authors. Through his own writings he did much to introduce their tenets, and still more their general methods of work, into England. Hence he is justly praised by Dr. Johnson in a celebrated passage: "Dryden may be properly considered as the father of English criticism, as the writer who first taught us to determine upon principles the merit of composition. Of our former poets, the greatest dramatist wrote without rules, conducted through life and nature by a genius that rarely misled

---

[1] *Essay, Supplementary to the Preface* of the Edition of 1815; see Cambridge edition, page 811.

[2] "Shelley, Dryden, and Mr. Eliot," in *Rehabilitations* (Oxford, 1939), p. 13. For similar opinions by Wordsworth and Scott see pages 1024, 1031.

and rarely deserted him. Of the rest, those who knew the laws of propriety had neglected to teach them." By *criticism*, Dr. Johnson here means *dogmatic criticism*. Yet Dryden was himself no dogmatist. Quite apart from his devotion to logical method, he had an instinctive sympathy with fine poetry wherever he found it; his appreciation was too catholic to be warped by compliance with any narrow critical creed. Hence, in contrast to Dr. Johnson, but with equal truth, Professor Ker can write: "The separate positive sentences of Dryden are of small account in his work as a critic. His virtue is that in a time when literature was pestered and cramped with formulas he found it impossible to write otherwise than freely. He is sceptical, tentative, disengaged, where most of his contemporaries, and most of his successors for a hundred years, are pledged to certain dogmas and principles."[1] Finally, though the historical point of view never became prominent in Dryden's writings, his sound common sense made him see that every author must be judged not simply by a fixed code of literary principles, but with some reference to the spirit of the times in which he lived. Thus, when he came to discuss a poet whom he understood and loved, his respect for literary theory simply saved him from waywardness and eccentricity. Though his discussion of general literary problems now seems crude and mechanical, Dryden's comments on individual writers are still full of inspiration; of Shakespeare and Chaucer he has left appreciations which in their way have never been surpassed.

Dryden clothed his critical works in a prose style that has been described once and for all by Dr. Johnson, whose manner is in quaint contrast to Dryden's own: —

Criticism, either didactic or defensive, occupies almost all his prose, except those pages which he has devoted to his patrons; but none of his prefaces were ever thought tedious. They have not the formality of a settled style, in which the first half of the sentence betrays the other. The clauses are never balanced, nor the periods modeled; every word seems to drop by chance, though it falls into its proper place. Nothing is cold or languid: the whole is airy, animated, and vigorous; what is little, is gay; what is great, is splendid. He may be thought to mention himself too frequently; but while he forces himself upon our esteem, we cannot refuse him to stand high in his own. Everything is excused by the play of images and the sprightliness of expression. Though all is easy, nothing is feeble; though all seems careless, there is nothing harsh; and though since his earlier works more than a century has passed, they have nothing yet uncouth or obsolete.

He who writes much will not easily escape a manner — such a recurrence of particular modes as may be easily noted. Dryden is always *another and the same;* he does not exhibit a second time the same elegances in the same form, nor appears to have any art other than that of expressing with clearness what he thinks with vigor. His style could not easily be imitated, either seriously or ludicrously; for, being always equable and always varied, it has no prominent or discriminative characters. The beauty who is totally free from disproportion of parts and features cannot be ridiculed by an overcharged resemblance.

Perhaps we can best explain the charm of Dryden's finest prose, that of his critical essays, by saying that it represents the ideal of cultivated literary conversation. The controversial style of his few political prose pamphlets is less admirable, being somewhat arid in tone and not approaching the energy of some later prose masters, such as Swift. Dryden's verse, which he employed for nearly all his important writing except his criticism, shows not only the author's perfect command of his material, but his careful study and deliberation. To the wonderful clearness which it shares with his prose, it adds that vigor of line and that rapidity of movement which are Dryden's distinguishing glory among the English poets.

[1] *Essays of John Dryden* (Oxford, 1900), vol. i, p. xv. Dryden's varying critical utterances have given rise to much discussion. Among the best treatments of the topic are W. E. Bohn, "John Dryden's Literary Criticism," in *Publications of the Modern Language Association*, xxii (1907), 56–139; John Harrington Smith, "Dryden's Critical Temper," in *Washington University Studies*, xii (1924–25), 201–220; Hoyt Trowbridge, "The Place of Rules in Dryden's Criticism," in *Modern Philology*, xliv (1946–47), 84–96.

In his all-pervading clearness, both in his single sentences and in the general conduct of his poems, Dryden is in sharp contrast to the Elizabethan poets, and still more to the school of Cowley, whose follower he had been in his youth. With him, clearness became as natural in verse as in prose; he aimed to be understood first of all, and would not let the search for more poetic qualities of style blind him to this first necessity. In this respect his dramas are far superior to those of Congreve; regarded merely as rapid narratives, thrown into the form of dialogue, they command very high praise. And shallow though the reasoning may be in *Religio Laici* or in *The Hind and the Panther*, the reader is at least seldom left with the slightest doubt as to the poet's meaning. This remarkable clearness of diction and of construction Dryden owed primarily to his passion for logic and to his familiarity with French literature and criticism. He left it as a precious legacy to the writers who followed him, down to the rise of the romantic school. It would be wrong to say that Dryden alone made clearness the distinguishing virtue — frequently, to be sure, at the expense of higher qualities — of all English poetry in the eighteenth century; but certainly he, as the teacher of Pope, deserves that praise more than any other one man.

Clearness Dryden could teach to his successors; he could not impart to them his vigor and his rapidity. The former is seen at its best in *Absalom and Achitophel* and *The Medal*, where each phrase is like the stroke of a hammer; the latter is the greatest excellence of his translations from Ovid, Virgil, and Chaucer, and reaches its highest point in *Alexander's Feast*. At first, in the heroic plays, this resonant declamation and this animated narrative were apt to degenerate into bombast; later they became the unaffected, apparently simple utterance of Dryden in verse, just as his graceful, conversational style was in prose. Here, though we cannot point to any one poet as his model, Dryden showed himself a follower of the great Elizabethans, rather than the founder of the Augustan school. He was himself fully conscious of his power: "I pretend to no dictatorship among my fellow poets," he writes in his *Dedication of the Æneis*, "since, if I should instruct some of them to make well-running verses, they want genius to give them strength as well as sweetness." [1] Pope, by emphasizing the pause at the close of each line, and still more that at the close of the couplet, made his verse more fit for a succession of epigrams than for the full-mouthed invective and impetuous narrative of which Dryden was the master. Pope's poems are like a string of beads and Dryden's like a firm, well-twisted cord.

Finally, Dryden's verse at its best, as in the opening lines of *The Hind and the Panther*, or the translation of the *Æneis*, has a rare musical quality. Accustomed to the elaborately varied verse forms of nineteenth century poets, and to the incessantly changing harmonies of blank verse, modern readers do not always appreciate Dryden's consummate mastery of his own versification. Within the apparently narrow limits of the heroic couplet, he could subtly vary his style to suit his subject; he could, as he boasted, be "unpolished" and "rugged" in *Religio Laici* and majestic in some portions of *The Hind and the Panther;* he could be "sweet" in translating Ovid, and reach severity in the nobler portions of Virgil.

What happened in the early years of the present century was well summarized by Sir Walter Raleigh in 1913: —

Whoever speaks to-day in praise of John Dryden speaks to a world that is far from being predisposed in its favour. The poetry of to-day has many kinds of excellence, but they are all remote from the excellence of Dryden. The Romantic movement was against him, though two of the greatest and most vigorous masters of Romance, Byron and Scott, were his devoted adherents and champions. Now that Romance, after a long reign, has fallen into a decline,

[1] See page 512.

the newer kinds of poetry take their cue from Donne and the metaphysicals whom Dryden supplanted. We are fanciful, decorative, conceited, mystical; we find no difficulty with the jewelled raptures of Francis Thompson or the vague ecstasies of Rabindranath Tagore. Women, whose voice in criticism counts for more than it did in Dryden's time, have no use for the glorious John. He still has his admirers, but they are dwindled to an old-fashioned quiet sect.[1]

Nevertheless the tide of critical opinion has been running in favor of Dryden. In 1907 Prosser Hall Frye printed a notable essay on him that has received too little attention.[2] In 1920 Mark Van Doren published *The Poetry of John Dryden*,[3] the most adequate appreciation of Dryden's literary genius that has ever appeared. He was seconded in 1921 by the pontifical T. S. Eliot, with *John Dryden*,[4] a brief essay which concludes, "He [Dryden] remains one of those who have set standards for English verse which it is desperate to ignore"; and in 1932 with a somewhat ampler treatment in *John Dryden: the Poet, the Dramatist, the Critic*. Meanwhile professional scholars had been turning fresh attention to the Restoration period in English literature and to Dryden as its greatest writer. More advance in the study of Dryden has been made since 1909, when the first issue of the present edition came from the press, than in the whole century previous to that date. And, though the matter is not easy to determine, criticism and scholarship seem to have won back for glorious John some of his popularity with the general public. Contemporary poetry and criticism, as Van Doren remarks with some regret,[5] "give no evidence of having benefited by the study of Dryden's art," but at least Dryden's admirers no longer speak of him in an apologetic tone.

Certainly Van Doren does not apologize for Dryden or condescend to him; he emphasizes his varied mastery of English poetic style: —

He is not for philosophers, plainly, or for laymen; he does not move the minds of the few or the hearts of the many. He has tempered not spirits but pens; . . . he is as much as Spenser a poet for poets. Not only in his own generation, or in the next, but in all that have succeeded he has stood on the shelves of writers and offered the stimulus of a style that is both musical and stout. Poets of widely varying complexions have made important use of him, never exactly reproducing him, for that is impossible even if desirable, but drawing from him the strength or the beauty they have seemed to need.[6]

And then Van Doren points out the debt owed to Dryden by many later poets, including Keats and Francis Thompson.

Another brilliant essay that shows the changed attitude towards Dryden is by Bonamy Dobrée, "Milton and Dryden: a Comparison and Contrast in Poetic Ideas and Poetic Method."[7] Dobrée remarks for example: "Milton made the language stiff and tortuous, even distorted, unusable in that form by other poets, as Keats was to discover, but Dryden made it miraculously flexible. Milton may be the greater poet of the two, but in this respect he injured our poetry, while Dryden conferred upon it the greatest possible benefit."

Yet for the Olympian verdict on Dryden perhaps we should turn back to the condescending Arnold, who after all was more catholic in his appreciation than many more glowing critics. Arnold termed Dryden "the puissant and glorious founder" of an age of prose and reason, an age whose writers are marked, above all else, by "regularity, uni-

---

[1] "John Dryden and Political Satire," in *Some Authors* (Oxford, 1923), pp. 156, 157.
[2] "Dryden and the Critical Canons of the Eighteenth Century," in *University Studies published by the University of Nebraska*, vol. vii, no. 1.
[3] A third edition appeared in 1946 under the title *John Dryden, a Study of his Poetry*. Quotations here are from this edition.
[4] In *Times Literary Supplement*, June 9, 1921; reprinted in *Homage to John Dryden*, London, 1924; and in *Selected Essays, 1917–1932*, London and New York, 1932.
[5] *Op. cit.*, p. viii.   [6] *Op. cit.*, pp. 257, 258.   [7] In *English Literary History*, iii (1936), 83–100.

formity, precision, balance." [1] If we make certain reservations, the verdict is eminently just and penetrating. Dryden lacked the higher qualities of imagination and insight, but he was regular and uniform only in his hatred of eccentricity and bad taste; he was precise in his aversion to vagueness, and to the substitution of mere harmonious sound for solid sense; he showed balance in his continual dependence on his critical judgment, in his reverent attitude — much like Arnold's own — towards the poets of former times, and towards the critical good sense of his own period. His puissance and his glory are, that despite his lack of creative originality, he made his verse so fit an image of his own active and receptive mind.

[1] "The Study of Poetry," in *Essays in Criticism, Second Series.*

EARLY POEMS

UPON THE DEATH OF THE LORD HASTINGS

[The following poem, Dryden's first published work, is one of a number of pieces composing a small volume entitled, *Lachrymæ Musarum, the Tears of the Muses, exprest in Elegies, written by divers persons of Nobility and Worth, upon the death of the most hopefull Henry, Lord Hastings, onely sonn of the Right Honourable Ferdinando, Earl of Huntingdon, Heir-generall of the high-born Prince George, Duke of Clarence, brother to King Edward the Fourth, collected and set forth by R. B.* London, 1649. (A second issue of the book, differing very slightly from the first, is dated 1650.) The young nobleman, who seems to have been worthy of the praises heaped upon him, was born, according to Collins's *Peerage of England,* on January 16, 1630, and died of the smallpox on June 24, 1649. Among the contributors to *Lachrymæ Musarum* were Denham, Marvell, Herrick, and Richard Brome, the last of whom is thought to have been the editor of the collection. Dryden's boyish elegy was written under the direct influence of Cowley, whom he later styles "the darling of my youth" (see p. 320, below); it is signed *Johannes Dryden, Scholæ Westm. Alumnus.* It was first reprinted in 1702, in the third edition of *Miscellany Poems, the First Part.*]

Must noble Hastings immaturely die,
The honor of his ancient family,
Beauty and learning thus together meet,
To bring a *winding* for a *wedding sheet?*
Must Virtue prove Death's harbinger? must she,
With him expiring, feel mortality?
Is death, sin's wages, grace's now? shall art
Make us more learned, only to depart?
If merit be disease; if virtue death;
To be good, not to be; who'd then bequeath   10
Himself to discipline? who'd not esteem
Labor a crime? study self-murther deem?
Our noble youth now have pretense to be
Dunces securely, ign'rant healthfully.
Rare linguist, whose worth speaks itself, whose praise,
Tho' not his own, all tongues besides do raise!
Then whom great Alexander may seem less,
Who conquer'd men, but not their languages.
In his mouth nations speak; his tongue might be
Interpreter to Greece, France, Italy.   20
His native soil was the four parts o' th' earth;
All Europe was too narrow for his birth.
A young apostle; and, (with rev'rence may
I speak 'it,) inspir'd with gift of tongues, as they.
Nature gave him, a child, what men in vain
Oft strive, by art tho' further'd, to obtain.
His body was an orb, his sublime soul
Did move on virtue's and on learning's pole:
Whose reg'lar motions better to our view,
Then Archimedes' sphere, the heavens did shew.   30
Graces and virtues, languages and arts,
Beauty and learning, fill'd up all the parts.
Heav'n's gifts, which do, like falling stars, appear
Scatter'd in others; all, as in their sphere,
Were fix'd and conglobate in 's soul: and thence
Shone thro' his body, with sweet influence;
Letting their glories so on each limb fall,
The whole frame render'd was celestial.
Come, learned Ptolemy, and trial make,
If thou this hero's altitude canst take: 40
But that transcends thy skill; thrice happy all,
Could we but prove thus astonomical.
Liv'd Tycho now, struck with this ray, which shone
More bright i' th' morn, then others' beam at noon,
He'd take his *astrolabe,* and seek out here
What new star 'twas did gild our hemisphere.
Replenish'd then with such rare gifts as these,
Where was room left for such a foul disease?

The nation's sin hath drawn that veil, which
    shrouds
Our dayspring in so sad benighting clouds.
Heaven would no longer trust its pledge;
    but thus   51
Recall'd it; rapt its Ganymede from us.
Was there no milder way but the smallpox,
The very filth'ness of Pandora's box?
So many spots, like *næves*, our Venus soil?
One jewel set off with so many a foil!
Blisters with pride swell'd, which thro' 's
    flesh did sprout,
Like rose-buds, stuck i' th' lily skin about.
Each little pimple had a tear in it,
To wail the fault its rising did commit: 60
Who, rebel-like, with their own lord at
    strife,
Thus made an insurrection 'gainst his life.
Or were these gems sent to adorn his skin,
The cab'net of a richer soul within?
No comet need foretell his change drew on,
Whose corpse might seem a *constellation.*
O, had he died of old, how great a strife
Had been, who from his death should draw
    their life?
Who should, by one rich draught, become
    whate'er
Seneca, Cato, Numa, Cæsar, were;   70
Learn'd, virtuous, pious, great; and have
    by this
An universal *metempsuchosis.*
Must all these ag'd sires in one funeral
Expire? all die in one so young, so small?
Who, had he liv'd his life out, his great fame
Had swoll'n 'bove any Greek or Roman
    name.
But hasty winter, with one blast, hath
    brought
The hopes of autumn, summer, spring, to
    naught.
Thus fades the oak i' th' sprig, i' th' blade
    the corn;
Thus without young, this Phœnix dies, new-
    born.   80
Must then old three-legg'd graybeards with
    their gout,
Catarrhs, rheums, achës, live three ages out?
Time's offal, only fit for th' hospital,
Or t' hang an antiquary's room withal!
Must drunkards, lechers, spent with sinning,
    live
With such helps as broths, possets, physic
    give?
None live, but such as should die? shall we
    meet

With none but ghostly fathers in the street?
Grief makes me rail: sorrow will force its
    way;
And show'rs of tears tempestuous sighs best
    lay.   90
The tongue may fail, but overflowing eyes
Will weep out lasting streams of elegies.
    But thou, O *virgin-widow*, left alone,
Now thy belov'd, heaven-ravish'd *spouse* is
    gone,
(Whose skilful sire in vain strove to apply
Med'cines, when thy balm was no remedy,)
With greater then Platonic love, O wed
His soul, tho' not his body, to thy bed:
Let that make thee a mother; bring thou
    forth   99
Th' *ideas* of his virtue, knowledge, worth;
Transcribe th' original in new copies; give
Hastings o' th' better part: so shall he live
In 's nobler half; and the great grandsire be
Of an heroic divine progeny;
An issue, which t' eternity shall last,
Yet but th' irradiations which he cast.
Erect no *mausoleums ;* for his best
Monument is his spouse's marble breast.

TO HIS FRIEND JOHN HODDES-DON, ON HIS DIVINE EPI-GRAMS

[This complimentary poem was prefixed to
a little volume entitled, *Sion and Parnassus, or
Epigrams on severall texts of the Old and New
Testament ; to which are added a Poem on the
Passion, a Hymn on the Resurrection, Ascen-
tion, and Feast of Pentecost, by John Hoddesdon,*
London, 1650; it is signed *J. Dryden of Trin.
C.* and headed *To his friend the Authour, on his
divine Epigrams.* A portrait of Hoddesdon as
a youth of about Dryden's years forms the
frontispiece to the volume. Dryden's verses
distinctly show the influence of the Puritan
atmosphere in which he was brought up.]

Thou hast inspir'd me with thy soul, and I
Who ne'er before could ken of poetry,
Am grown so good proficient, I can lend
A line in commendation of my friend.
Yet 't is but of the second hand; if aught
There be in this, 't is from thy fancy brought.
Good thief, who dar'st, Prometheus-like,
    aspire,
And fill thy poems with celestial fire:
Enliven'd by these sparks divine, their rays
Add a bright luster to thy crown of bays.   10

Young eaglet, who thy nest thus soon forsook,
So lofty and divine a course hast took
As all admire, before the down begin
To peep, as yet, upon thy smoother chin;
And, making heaven thy aim, hast had the
    grace
To look the Sun of Righteousness i' th' face.
What may we hope, if thou go'st on thus fast!
Scriptures at first; enthusiasms at last!
Thou hast commenc'd, betimes, a saint, go on,
Mingling diviner streams with Helicon.   20
That they who view what Epigrams here be,
May learn to make like, in just praise of thee.
    Reader, I've done, nor longer will withhold
Thy greedy eyes; looking on this pure gold
Thou 'lt know adult'rate copper, which, like
    this,
Will only serve to be a foil to his.

LETTER TO MADAME HONOR DRYDEN

[This letter was written by Dryden, while a student at Cambridge, to his cousin Honor Dryden, who was then about eighteen years old. She never married, and in her later years is said to have lived with her brother, John Driden of Chesterton, to whom our author, in 1699, addressed one of his best poetical epistles. See page 784, below.

This letter is now in the William Andrews Clark Memorial Library in Los Angeles. The text below strives to preserve its peculiarities as far as is possible in types.]

To the faire hands
  of Madame Honor Dryden
    these crave
      admittance.

Madame

If you have received the lines I sent by the reverend Levite, I doubt not but they have exceedingly wrought vpon you; for beeing so longe in a Clergy-mans pocket, assuredly they have acquired more Sanctity then theire Authour meant them. Alasse Madame for ought I know they may become a Sermon ere they could arrive at you; and believe it haveing you for the text it could scarcely proove bad, if it light vpon one that could handle it indifferently. but I am so miserable a preacher that though I have so sweet and copious a subject, I still fall short in my expressions And in stead of an vse of thanksgiveing I am allways makeing one of comfort, that I may one day againe have the happinesse to kisse your faire hand. but that is a message I would not so willingly do by letter as by word of mouth. This is a point I must confesse I could willingly dwell longer on, and in this case what ever I say you may confidently take for gospell. But I must hasten. And indeed Madame (Beloved I had almost sayd) hee had need hasten who treats of you; for to speake fully to every part of your excellencyes requires a longer houre then most persons have allotted them. But in a word your selfe hath been the best Expositor vpon the text of your own worth, in that admirable Comment you wrote vpon it, I meane your incomparable letter. By all thats good (and you Madame are a great part of my Oath) it hath put mee so farre besides my selfe that I have scarce patience to write prose. and my pen is stealing into verse every time I kisse your letter. I am sure the poore paper smarts for my Idolatry, which by wearing it continually neere my brest will at last bee burnt and martyrd in those flames of adoration it hath kindled in mee. But I forgett Madame, what rarityes your letter came fraught with besides words; You are such a Deity that commands worship by provideing the sacrifice: you are pleasd Madame to force mee to write by sending mee Materialls, and compell mee to my greatest happinesse. yet though I highly vallue your Magnificent presents, pardon mee if I must tell the world they are but imperfect Emblemes of your beauty; For the white and red of waxe and paper are but shaddowes of that vermillion and snowe in your lips and forehead. And the silver of the Inkehorne if it presume to vye whitenesse with your purer skinne, must confesse it selfe blacker then the liquour it containes. what then do I more then retrieve your own guifts? and present you that paper adulterated with blotts which you gave spotlesse?

For since t'was mine the white hath lost its
    hiew
To show t'was n'ere it selfe but whilst in you;
The Virgin Waxe hath blusht it selfe to red
Since it with mee hath lost its Maydenhead.
You (fairest Nymph) are waxe; oh may you
    bee
As well in softnesse so as purity;
Till fate and your own happy choise reveale
Whom you so farre shall blesse to make your
    Seale.
    Fairest Valentine the unfeigned
    wishe of yor humble Votary.
        Jo. DRYDEN.

Cambridge
  May the   d.

HEROIC STANZAS

CONSECRATED TO THE GLORIOUS MEMORY OF HIS MOST SERENE AND
RENOWN'D HIGHNESS OLIVER, LATE LORD PROTECTOR OF THIS COMMON-
WEALTH, &C. WRITTEN AFTER THE CELEBRATION OF HIS FUNERAL

[Cromwell died on September 3, 1658, and was buried with great pomp on November 23.
Dryden therefore wrote the following poem, his first important work, at the close of 1658, when
he was already in his twenty-eighth year. By his choice of stanza, and by his comparatively
simple style, he shows that he is now influenced by Davenant quite as much as by Cowley.

This poem was published twice in 1659: separately, with a title-page reading, *A Poem upon
the Death of his Late Highness Oliver, Lord Protector of England, Scotland, & Ireland, written by
Mr. Dryden. London, Printed for William Wilson;* and, with poems by Waller and Sprat, in a
volume entitled, *Three Poems upon the Death of his late Highnesse Oliver, Lord Protector of England, Scotland, and Ireland*, printed by the same publisher. General probability, confirmed by
one significant variation in text (see note on line 56), points to the separate edition as the original
one; the poem would be likely to appear first by itself rather than together with work by other
authors. In 1682 some enemies of Dryden reprinted the *Three Poems* volume, with a title-page
reading, *Three Poems upon the Death of the Late Usurper Oliver Cromwel.*

The above heading is taken from the original *Three Poems* volume, the text of which was
probably revised by Dryden from the earlier edition.]

I

AND now 't is time; for their officious haste,
  Who would before have borne him to the
      sky,
Like eager Romans, ere all rites were past,
  Did let too soon the sacred eagle fly.

II

Tho' our best notes are treason to his
      fame,
  Join'd with the loud applause of public
      voice;
Since Heav'n, what praise we offer to his
      name,
  Hath render'd too authentic by its
      choice.

III

Tho' in his praise no arts can liberal be,
  Since they, whose Muses have the highest
      flown,   10
Add not to his immortal memory,
  But do an act of friendship to their
      own.

IV

Yet 't is our duty, and our interest too,
  Such monuments as we can build, to
      raise;
Lest all the world prevent what we should
      do,
  And claim a title in him by their praise.

V

How shall I then begin, or where con-
      clude,
  To draw a fame so truly circular?
For in a round what order can be shew'd,
  Where all the parts so equal-perfect are?

VI

His grandeur he deriv'd from heav'n alone;
  For he was great ere fortune made him
      so: 22
And wars, like mists that rise against the
      sun,
  Made him but greater seem, not greater
      grow.

VII

No borrow'd bays his temples did adorn,
  But to our crown he did fresh jewels
      bring;
Nor was his virtue poison'd, soon as born,
  With the too early thoughts of being
      king.

VIII

Fortune (that easy mistress of the young,
  But to her ancient servants coy and
      hard)   30
Him, at that age, her favorites rank'd
      among,
  When she her best-lov'd Pompey did dis-
      card.

IX

He, private, mark'd the faults of others'
　　sway,
And set as sea-marks for himself to shun:
Not like rash monarchs, who their youth
　　betray
　　By acts their age too late would wish un-
　　　　done.

X

And yet dominion was not his design;
　　We owe that blessing not to him, but
　　　　Heaven,
Which to fair acts unsought rewards did
　　join;
　　Rewards that less to him than us were
　　　　given.　　　　　　　　　　　　40

XI

Our former chiefs, like sticklers of the war,
　　First sought t' inflame the parties, then
　　　　to poise:
The quarrel lov'd, but did the cause abhor;
　　And did not strike to hurt, but make a
　　　　noise.

XII

War, our consumption, was their gainful
　　trade:
　　We inward bled, whilst they prolong'd
　　　　our pain;
He fought to end our fighting, and assay'd
　　To stanch the blood by breathing of the
　　　　vein.

XIII

Swift and resistless thro' the land he pass'd,
　　Like that bold Greek who did the East
　　　　subdue,　　　　　　　　　　　　50
And made to battles such heroic haste,
　　As if on wings of victory he flew.

XIV

He fought secure of fortune as of fame;
　　Till, by new maps, the island might be
　　　　shown,
Of conquests, which he strew'd where'er he
　　came,
　　Thick as the galaxy with stars is sown.

XV

His palms, tho' under weights they did not
　　stand,
　　Still thriv'd; no winter could his laurels
　　　　fade:

Heav'n in his portrait shew'd a workman's
　　hand,　　　　　　　　　　　　　59
　　And drew it perfect, yet without a shade.

XVI

Peace was the prize of all his toils and care,
　　Which war had banish'd, and did now
　　　　restore:
Bologna's walls thus mounted in the air,
　　To seat themselves more surely then be-
　　　　fore.

XVII

Her safety, rescued Ireland to him owes;
　　And treacherous Scotland, to no int'rest
　　　　true,
Yet bless'd that fate which did his arms dis-
　　pose
　　Her land to civilize, as to subdue.

XVIII

Nor was he like those stars which only shine
　　When to pale mariners they storms por-
　　　　tend:　　　　　　　　　　　　70
He had his calmer influence, and his mien
　　Did love and majesty together blend.

XIX

'T is true, his count'nance did imprint an
　　awe;
　　And naturally all souls to his did bow,
As wands of divination downward draw,
　　And point to beds where sov'reign gold
　　　　doth grow.

XX

When past all offerings to Feretrian Jove,
　　He Mars depos'd, and arms to gowns
　　　　made yield;
Successful counsels did him soon approve
　　As fit for close intrigues, as open field. 80

XXI

To suppliant Holland he vouchsaf'd a
　　peace,
　　Our once bold rival in the British main,
Now tamely glad her unjust claim to cease,
　　And buy our friendship with her idol,
　　　　gain.

XXII

Fame of th' asserted sea, thro' Europe
　　blown,
　　Made France and Spain ambitious of his
　　　　love;

Each knew that side must conquer he would
    own;
  And for him fiercely, as for empire,
    strove.

XXIII

No sooner was the Frenchman's cause em-
    brac'd,
  Than the light Mounsire the grave Don
    outweigh'd: 90
His fortune turn'd the scale where it was
    cast;
  Tho' Indian mines were in the other laid.

XXIV

When absent, yet we conquer'd in his right:
  For tho' some meaner artist's skill were
    shown
In mingling colors, or in placing light;
  Yet still the fair designment was his own.

XXV

For from all tempers he could service draw;
  The worth of each with its alloy he knew,
And, as the confident of Nature, saw
  How she complexions did divide and
    brew.   100

XXVI

Or he their single virtues did survey,
  By intuition, in his own large breast,
Where all the rich *ideas* of them lay,
  That were the rule and measure to the
    rest.

XXVII

When such heroic virtue Heav'n sets out,
  The stars, like commons, sullenly obey;
Because it drains them, when it comes about,
  And therefore is a tax they seldom pay.

XXVIII

From this high spring our foreign conquests
    flow,
  Which yet more glorious triumphs do
    portend;   110
Since their commencement to his arms they
    owe,
  If springs as high as fountains may as-
    cend.

XXIX

He made us freemen of the continent,
  Whom Nature did like captives treat be-
    fore;

To nobler preys the English lion sent,
  And taught him first in Belgian walks
    to roar.

XXX

That old unquestion'd pirate of the land,
  Proud Rome, with dread, the fate of
    Dunkirk heard;
And trembling, wish'd behind more Alps to
    stand,
  Altho' an Alexander were her guard. 120

XXXI

By his command we boldly cross'd the line,
  And bravely fought where southern stars
    arise;
We trac'd the far-fetch'd gold unto the
    mine,
  And that which brib'd our fathers made
    our prize.

XXXII

Such was our prince; yet own'd a soul
    above
  The highest acts it could produce to
    show:
Thus poor mechanic arts in public move,
  Whilst the deep secrets beyond practice
    go.

XXXIII

Nor died he when his ebbing fame went
    less,
  But when fresh laurels courted him to
    live: 130
He seem'd but to prevent some new suc-
    cess,
  As if above what triumphs earth could
    give.

XXXIV

His latest victories still thickest came,
  As near the center motion does in-
    crease;
Till he, press'd down by his own weighty
    name,
  Did, like the vestal, under spoils decease.

XXXV

But first the ocean, as a tribute, sent
  That giant prince of all her watery
    herd;
And th' isle, when her protecting genius
    went,   139
Upon his obsequies loud sighs conferr'd.

XXXVI

No civil broils have since his death arose,
But faction now by habit does obey;
And wars have that respect for his repose,
As winds for *halcyons*, when they breed at
sea.

XXXVII

His ashes in a peaceful urn shall rest;
His name a great example stands, to
show
How strangely high endeavors may be blest,
Where piety and valor jointly go.

ASTRÆA REDUX

A POEM ON THE HAPPY RESTORATION AND RETURN OF HIS SACRED
MAJESTY CHARLES THE SECOND

Jam redit et Virgo, redeunt Saturnia regna. — VIRGIL.

[Charles landed at Dover on May 25, 1660, and Dryden's poem must have been composed soon
after that date. It was published in the same year by Herringman, who remained Dryden's
publisher until 1679. In 1688 this poem was reprinted for Herringman, in a quarto volume,
together with *To his Sacred Majesty*, *To my Lord Chancellor*, and *Annus Mirabilis*. There are
no significant variant readings. The present edition follows the text of 1660.]

Now with a general peace the world was
blest,
While ours, a world divided from the rest,
A dreadful quiet felt, and worser far
Then arms, a sullen interval of war:
Thus when black clouds draw down the
lab'ring skies,
Ere yet abroad the winged thunder flies,
An horrid stillness first invades the ear,
And in that silence we the tempest fear.
Th' ambitious Swede, like restless billows
toss'd,
On this hand gaining what on that he
lost,   10
Tho' in his life he blood and ruin breath'd,
To his now guideless kingdom peace be-
queath'd.
And Heaven, that seem'd regardless of our
fate,
For France and Spain did miracles create;
Such mortal quarrels to compose in peace,
As nature bred, and int'rest did encrease.
We sigh'd to hear the fair Iberian bride
Must grow a lily to the lily's side,
While our cross stars denied us Charles his
bed,
Whom our first flames and virgin love did
wed.   20
For his long absence Church and State did
groan;
Madness the pulpit, faction seiz'd the
throne;
Experienc'd age in deep despair was lost,
To see the rebel thrive, the loyal cross'd:

Youth, that with joys had unacquainted
been,
Envied gray hairs that once good days had
seen;
We thought our sires, not with their own
content,
Had, ere we came to age, our portion spent.
Nor could our nobles hope their bold at-
tempt,
Who ruin'd crowns, would coronets ex-
empt: 30
For when by their designing leaders taught
To strike at pow'r which for themselves
they sought,
The vulgar, gull'd into rebellion, arm'd;
Their blood to action by the prize was
warm'd.
The sacred purple then and scarlet gown,
Like sanguine dye, to elephants was shown.
Thus when the bold Typhoeus scal'd the
sky,
And forc'd great Jove from his own heaven
to fly,
(What king, what crown from treason's
reach is free,
If Jove and heaven can violated be?)   40
The lesser gods, that shar'd his prosp'rous
state,
All suffer'd in the exil'd Thund'rer's fate.
The rabble now such freedom did enjoy,
As winds at sea, that use it to destroy:
Blind as the Cyclops, and as wild as he,
They own'd a lawless salvage liberty,
Like that our painted ancestors so priz'd

Ere empire's arts their breasts had civiliz'd.
How great were then our Charles his woes,
    who thus
Was forc'd to suffer for himself and us! 50
He, toss'd by fate, and hurried up and
    down,
Heir to his father's sorrows, with his
    crown,
Could taste no sweets of youth's desired
    age;
But found his life too true a pilgrimage.
Unconquer'd yet in that forlorn estate,
His manly courage overcame his fate.
His wounds he took, like Romans, on his
    breast,
Which by his virtue were with laurels
    dress'd.
As souls reach heav'n while yet in bodies
    pent,
So did he live above his banishment.   60
That sun, which we beheld with cozen'd eyes
Within the water, mov'd along the skies.
How easy 't is, when Destiny proves kind,
With full-spread sails to run before the
    wind!
But those that 'gainst stiff gales laveering
    go,
Must be at once resolv'd and skilful too.
He would not, like soft Otho, hope prevent,
But stay'd and suffer'd Fortune to repent.
These virtues Galba in a stranger sought,
And Piso to adopted empire brought.   70
How shall I then my doubtful thoughts
    express,
That must his suff'rings both regret and
    bless!
For when his early valor Heav'n had
    cross'd,
And all at Worc'ster but the honor lost,
Forc'd into exile from his rightful throne,
He made all countries where he came his
    own;
And viewing monarchs' secret arts of sway,
A royal factor for their kingdoms lay.
Thus banish'd David spent abroad his time,
When to be God's anointed was his crime; 80
And, when restor'd, made his proud neigh-
    bors rue
Those choice remarks he from his travels
    drew.
Nor is he only by afflictions shown
To conquer others' realms, but rule his own:
Recov'ring hardly what he lost before,
His right indears it much; his purchase
    more.

Inur'd to suffer ere he came to reign,
No rash procedure will his actions stain.
To bus'ness ripen'd by digestive thought,
His future rule is into method brought; 90
As they who first proportion understand,
With easy practice reach a master's hand.
Well might the ancient poets then confer
On Night the honor'd name of *Counselor*,
Since struck with rays of prosp'rous fortune
    blind,
We light alone in dark afflictions find.
In such adversities to scepters train'd,
The name of *Great* his famous grandsire
    gain'd;
Who yet a king alone in name and right,
With hunger, cold, and angry Jove did
    fight;   100
Shock'd by a Covenanting League's vast
    pow'rs,
As holy and as catholic as ours:
Till Fortune's fruitless spite had made it
    known,
Her blows not shook but riveted his throne.
  Some lazy ages, lost in sleep and ease,
No action leave to busy chronicles:
Such, whose supine felicity but makes
In story *chasms*, in *epoches* mistakes:
O'er whom Time gently shakes his wings of
    down,   109
Till with his silent sickle they are mown.
Such is not Charles his too too active age,
Which, govern'd by the wild distemper'd
    rage
Of some black star infecting all the skies,
Made him at his own cost like Adam wise.
Tremble, ye nations, who, secure before,
Laugh'd at those arms that 'gainst our
    selves we bore:
Rous'd by the lash of his own stubborn
    tail,
Our lion now will foreign foes assail.
With *alga* who the sacred altar strows?
To all the sea-gods Charles an off'ring
    owes: 120
A bull to thee, Portunus, shall be slain,
A lamb to you, the tempests of the main:
For those loud storms that did against him
    roar
Have cast his shipwrack'd vessel on the
    shore.
Yet as wise artists mix their colors so,
That by degrees they from each other go:
Black steals unheeded from the neighb'ring
    white,
Without offending the well-cozen'd sight:

So on us stole our blessed change, while
   we
Th' effect did feel, but scarce the manner
   see.   130
Frosts that constrain the ground, and birth
   deny
To flow'rs that in its womb expecting lie,
Do seldom their usurping pow'r withdraw,
But raging floods pursue their hasty thaw.
Our thaw was mild, the cold not chas'd
   away,
But lost in kindly heat of lengthen'd day.
Heav'n would no bargain for its blessings
   drive,
But what we could not pay for, freely give.
The Prince of Peace would, like himself,
   confer
A gift unhop'd without the price of war: 140
Yet, as he knew his blessing's worth, took
   care,
That we should know it by repeated pray'r;
Which storm'd the skies, and ravish'd
   Charles from thence,
As heav'n itself is took by violence.
Booth's forward valor only serv'd to show
He durst that duty pay we all did owe:
Th' attempt was fair; but Heav'n's prefixed
   hour
Not come: so, like the watchful travelour
That by the moon's mistaken light did rise,
Lay down again, and clos'd his weary eyes.
'T was MONK whom Providence design'd to
   loose   151
Those real bonds false freedom did impose.
The blessed saints that watch'd this turning
   scene,
Did from their stars with joyful wonder
   lean,
To see small clues draw vastest weights
   along,
Not in their bulk, but in their order strong.
Thus pencils can by one slight touch restore
Smiles to that changed face that wept be-
   fore.
With ease such fond *chimœras* we pursue
As fancy frames for fancy to subdue;   160
But when ourselves to action we betake,
It shuns the mint like gold that chymists
   make.
How hard was then his task, at once to be
What in the body natural we see.
Man's architect distinctly did ordain
The charge of muscles, nerves, and of the
   brain,
Thro' viewless conduits spirits to dispense,

The springs of motion from the seat of sense.
'T was not the hasty product of a day,
But the well-ripen'd fruit of wise delay. 170
He, like a patient angler, ere he strook,
Would let them play a while upon the hook.
Our healthful food the stomach labors thus,
At first embracing what it straight doth
   crush.
Wise leeches will not vain receipts obtrude,
While growing pains pronounce the humors
   crude;
Deaf to complaints, they wait upon the ill,
Till some safe *crisis* authorize their skill.
Nor could his acts too close a vizard wear,
To scape their eyes whom guilt had taught
   to fear,   180
And guard with caution that polluted nest,
Whence Legion twice before was dispos-
   sess'd:
Once sacred house; which when they enter'd
   in,
They thought the place could sanctify a sin;
Like those that vainly hop'd kind Heav'n
   would wink,
While to excess on martyrs' tombs they
   drink.
And as devouter Turks first warn their souls
To part, before they taste forbidden bowls;
So these, when their black crimes they went
   about,
First timely charm'd their useless conscience
   out.   190
Religion's name against itself was made;
The shadow serv'd the substance to invade:
Like zealous missions, they did care pretend
Of souls in shew, but made the gold their end.
Th' incensed pow'rs beheld with scorn from
   high
An heaven so far distant from the sky,
Which durst, with horses' hoofs that beat
   the ground,
And martial brass, bely the thunder's sound.
'T was hence at length just vengeance
   thought it fit
To speed their ruin by their impious wit. 200
Thus Sforza, curst with a too fertile brain,
Lost by his wiles the pow'r his wit did gain.
Henceforth their fogue must spend at lesser
   rate
Then in its flames to wrap a nation's fate.
Suffer'd to live, they are like Helots set,
A virtuous shame within us to beget.
For by example most we sinn'd before,
And glass-like clearness mix'd with **frailty**
   bore.

But since reform'd by what we did amiss,
We by our suff'rings learn to prize our
    bliss: 210
Like early lovers, whose unpractic'd hearts
Were long the may-game of malicious arts,
When once they find their jealousies were
    vain,
With double heat renew their fires again.
'T was this produc'd the joy that hurried o'er
Such swarms of English to the neighb'ring
    shore,
To fetch that prize, by which Batavia made
So rich amends for our impoverish'd trade.
O had you seen from Scheveline's barren
    shore,
(Crowded with troops, and barren now no
    more,)   220
Afflicted Holland to his farewell bring
True sorrow, Holland to regret a king,
While waiting him his royal fleet did ride,
And willing winds to their low'r'd sails de-
    nied.
The wavering streamers, flags, and standart
    out,
The merry seamen's rude but cheerful
    shout;
And last, the cannons' voice that shook ⎤
    the skies,   ⎪
And, as it fares in sudden ecstasies,   ⎬
At once bereft us both of ears and eyes. ⎦
The Naseby, now no longer England's
    shame,   230
But better to be lost in Charles his name,
(Like some unequal bride in nobler sheets)
Receives her lord; the joyful London
    meets
The princely York, himself alone a freight;
The Swift-sure groans beneath great Gloc'-
    ster's weight.
Secure as when the halcyon breeds, with
    these
He that was born to drown might cross the
    seas.
Heav'n could not own a Providence, and
    take
The wealth three nations ventur'd at a
    stake.
The same indulgence Charles his voyage
    bless'd,   240
Which in his right had miracles confess'd.
The winds that never moderation knew,
Afraid to blow too much, too faintly blew;
Or out of breath with joy, could not enlarge
Their straighten'd lungs, or conscious of
    their charge.

The British Amphitrite, smooth and clear,
In richer azure never did appear;
Proud her returning prince to entertain
With the submitted fasces of the main.

And welcome now, *great monarch*, to your
    own;   250
Behold th' approaching cliffs of Albion:
It is no longer motion cheats your view,
As you meet it, the land approacheth you.
The land returns, and in the white it wears
The marks of penitence and sorrow bears.
But you, whose goodness your descent doth
    shew,
Your heav'nly parentage and earthly too;
By that same mildness which your father's
    crown
Before did ravish, shall secure your own.
Not tied to rules of policy, you find   260
Revenge less sweet then a forgiving mind.
Thus, when th' Almighty would to Moses
    give
A sight of all he could behold and live;
A voice before his entry did proclaim
Long-suff'ring, goodness, mercy, in his name.
Your pow'r to justice doth submit your
    cause,
Your goodness only is above the laws;
Whose rigid letter, while pronounc'd by
    you,
Is softer made. So winds that tempests
    brew,
When thro' Arabian groves they take their
    flight,   270
Made wanton with rich odors, lose their
    spite.
And as those lees that trouble it, refine
The agitated soul of generous wine:
So tears of joy, for your returning spilt,
Work out and expiate our former guilt.
Methinks I see those crowds on Dover's
    strand,
Who, in their haste to welcome you to
    land,
Chok'd up the beach with their still grow-
    ing store,
And made a wilder torrent on the shore;
While, spurr'd with eager thoughts of past
    delight,   280
Those who had seen you court a second
    sight;
Preventing still your steps, and making
    haste
To meet you often, wheresoe'er you pass'd.
How shall I speak of that triumphant day

When you renew'd th' expiring pomp of
   May !
(A month that owns an int'rest in your
   name:
You and the flow'rs are its peculiar claim.)
That star that at your birth shone out so
   bright,
It stain'd the duller sun's meridian light,
Did once again its potent fires renew,   290
Guiding our eyes to find and worship you.
   And now Time's whiter series is begun,
Which in soft centuries shall smoothly run:
Those clouds that overcast your morn shall
   fly,
Dispell'd to farthest corners of the sky.
Our nation, with united int'rest blest,
Not now content to poise, shall sway the
   rest.
Abroad your empire shall no limits know,
But, like the sea, in boundless circles flow.
Your much-lov'd fleet shall with a wide
   command   300
Besiege the petty monarchs of the land;
And as old Time his offspring swallow'd
   down,
Our ocean in its depths all seas shall drown.

Their wealthy trade from pirates' rapine
   free,
Our merchants shall no more advent'rers be;
Nor in the farthest East those dangers fear
Which humble Holland must dissemble
   here.
Spain to your gift alone her Indies owes,
For what the pow'rful takes not he be-
   stows: 309
And France, that did an exile's presence fear,
May justly apprehend you still too near.
At home the hateful names of parties cease,
And factious souls are wearied into peace.
The discontented now are only they
Whose crimes before did your just cause
   betray:
Of those your edicts some reclaim from sins,
But most your life and blest example wins.
O happy prince, whom Heav'n hath taught
   the way,
By paying vows, to have more vows to pay !
O happy age ! O times like those alone   320
By fate reserv'd for great Augustus' throne !
When the joint growth of arms and arts
   foreshew
The world a monarch, and that monarch *you*.

TO MY HONOR'D FRIEND SIR ROBERT HOWARD, ON HIS EXCELLENT POEMS

[This complimentary poem is inserted in a
volume entitled, *Poems, viz. 1. A Panegyrick
to the King. 2. Songs and Sonnets. 3. The
Blind Lady, a Comedy. 4. The Fourth Book
of Virgil. 5. Statius his Achilleis, with Annotations. 6. A Panegyrick to Generall Monck.
By the Honorable S*r* Robert Howard.* London,
Printed for Henry Herringman, 1660. It is
signed *John Driden*. It forms the first proof
of Dryden's intimacy with the family of
Thomas, Earl of Berkshire, father of Sir
Robert Howard and of the Lady Elizabeth
Howard, the poet's future wife.]

As there is music uninform'd by art
In those wild notes, which, with a merry
   heart,
The birds in unfrequented shades express,
Who, better taught at home, yet please us
   less:
So in your verse a native sweetness dwells,
Which shames composure, and its art excels.
Singing no more can your soft numbers grace

Then paint adds charms unto a beauteous
   face.
Yet as, when mighty rivers gently creep,
Their even calmness does suppose them
   deep;   10
Such is your Muse: no metaphor swell'd high
With dangerous boldness lifts her to the sky:
Those mounting fancies, when they fall
   again,
Shew sand and dirt at bottom do remain.
So firm a strength, and yet withal so sweet,
Did never but in Samson's riddle meet.
'T is strange each line so great a weight
   should bear,
And yet no sign of toil, no sweat appear.
Either your art hides art, as Stoics feign
Then least to feel, when most they suffer
   pain;   20
And we, dull souls, admire, but cannot see
What hidden springs within the engine be;
Or 't is some happiness that still pursues
Each act and motion of your graceful Muse.
Or is it fortune's work, that in your head
The curious net * that is for fan-   * *Rete*
   cies spread,   *mirabile.*
Lets thro' its meshes every meaner thought,

While rich ideas there are only caught?
Sure that 's not all: this is a piece too fair
To be the child of chance, and not of care.
No atoms casually together hurl'd   31
Could e'er produce so beautiful a world.
Nor dare I such a doctrine here admit,
As would destroy the providence of wit.
'T is your strong genius then which does
    not feel
Those weights would make a weaker spirit
    reel.
To carry weight, and run so lightly too,
Is what alone your Pegasus can do.
Great Hercules himself could ne'er do
    more,
Than not to feel those heav'ns and gods he
    bore.   40
Your easier odes, which for delight were
    penn'd,
Yet our instruction make their second end:
We 're both enrich'd and pleas'd, like them
    that woo
At once a beauty and a fortune too.
Of moral knowledge Poesy was queen,
And still she might, had wanton wits not
    been;
Who, like ill guardians, liv'd themselves at
    large,
And, not content with that, debauch'd their
    charge.
Like some brave captain, your successful pen
Restores the exil'd to her crown again;   50
And gives us hope, that having seen the
    days
When nothing flourish'd but fanatic bays,
All will at length in this opinion rest:
" A sober prince's government is best."
This is not all; your art the way has
    found
To make improvement of the richest
    ground,
That soil which those immortal laurels
    bore,
That once the sacred Maro's temples wore.
Elisa's griefs are so express'd by you,
They are too eloquent to have been true. 60
Had she so spoke, Æneas had obey'd
What Dido, rather then what Jove, had
    said.
If funeral rites can give a ghost repose,
Your muse so justly has discharged those,
Elisa's shade may now its wand'ring cease,
And claim a title to the fields of peace.
But if Æneas be oblig'd, no less
Your kindness great Achilles doth confess;

Who, dress'd by Statius in too bold a look,
Did ill become those virgin's robes he
    took.   70
To understand how much we owe to you,
We must your numbers with your author's
    view;
Then we shall see his work was lamely
    rough,
Each figure stiff, as if design'd in buff;
His colors laid so thick on every place,
As only shew'd the paint, but hid the face.
But as in perspective we beauties see,
Which in the glass, not in the picture, be;
So here our sight obligingly mistakes
That wealth which his your bounty only
    makes.   80
Thus vulgar dishes are by cooks disguis'd,
More for their dressing than their sub-
    stance priz'd.
Your curious notes * so search   * Annotations
    into that age,   on Statius.
When all was fable but the sacred page,
That, since in that dark night we needs
    must stray,
We are at least misled in pleasant way.
But what we most admire, your verse no less
The prophet than the poet doth confess.
Ere our weak eyes discern'd the doubtful
    streak
Of light, you saw great Charles his morn-
    ing break.   90
So skilful seamen ken the land from far,
Which shews like mists to the dull pas-
    senger.
To Charles your Muse first pays her duteous
    love,
As still the ancients did begin from Jove.
With Monk you end, whose name preserv'd
    shall be,
As Rome recorded Rufus'   * Hic situs est
    memory,*   Rufus, qui
Who thought it greater honor   pulso Vindice
    to obey   Imperium as-
His country's interest than the seruit non sibi
    world to sway.   sed patriæ.
But to write worthy things of worthy men,
Is the peculiar talent of your pen: 100
Yet let me take your mantle up, and I
Will venture in your right to prophesy.

" This work, by merit first of fame secure,
Is likewise happy in its geniture:
For, since 't is born when Charles ascends
    the throne,
It shares at once his fortune and its own."

TO HIS SACRED MAJESTY

A PANEGYRIC ON HIS CORONATION

[Charles II was crowned on St. George's Day, April 23, 1661. This poem was published in 1661 and reprinted in 1688: see note on *Astræa Redux*, p. 7, above. There are no significant variant readings. The present edition follows the text of 1661.]

In that wild deluge where the world was
    drown'd,
When life and sin one common tomb had
    found,
The first small prospect of a rising hill
With various notes of joy the ark did fill:
Yet when that flood in its own depths was
    drown'd,
It left behind it false and slipp'ry ground;
And the more solemn pomp was still de-
    ferr'd
Till new-born nature in fresh looks appear'd.
Thus, royal sir, to see you landed here,
Was cause enough of triumph for a year; 10
Nor would your care those glorious joys
    repeat,
Till they at once might be secure and great;
Till your kind beams by their continued stay
Had warm'd the ground, and call'd the
    damps away.
Such vapors, while your pow'rful influence
    dries,
Then soonest vanish when they highest rise.
Had greater haste these sacred rights pre-
    par'd,
Some guilty months had in your triumphs
    shar'd;
But this untainted year is all your own;
Your glories may without our crimes be
    shown. 20
We had not yet exhausted all our store,
When you refresh'd our joys by adding
    more:
As Heav'n, of old, dispens'd celestial dew,
You give us manna, and still give us new.
  Now our sad ruins are remov'd from
    sight,
The season too comes fraught with new
    delight;
Time seems not now beneath his years to
    stoop,
Nor do his wings with sickly feathers droop:
Soft western winds waft o'er the gaudy
    spring,
And open'd scenes of flow'rs and blossoms
    bring. 30

To grace this happy day, while you appear
Not king of us alone, but of the year.
All eyes you draw, and with the eyes the
    heart,
Of your own pomp yourself the greatest
    part:
Loud shouts the nation's happiness proclaim,
And heav'n this day is feasted with your
    name.
Your cavalcade the fair spectators view
From their high standings, yet look up to
    you.
From your brave train each singles out a
    prey,
And longs to date a conquest from your
    day. 40
Now charg'd with blessings while you seek
    repose,
Officious slumbers haste your eyes to close;
And glorious dreams stand ready to restore
The pleasing shapes of all you saw before.
Next, to the sacred temple you are led,
Where waits a crown for your more sacred
    head:
How justly from the Church that crown is
    due,
Preserv'd from ruin, and restor'd by you!
The grateful choir their harmony employ,
Not to make greater, but more solemn
    joy. 50
Wrapp'd soft and warm your name is sent
    on high,
As flames do on the wings of incense fly:
Music herself is lost, in vain she brings
Her choicest notes to praise the best of
    kings;
Her melting strains in you a tomb have
    found,
And lie like bees in their own sweetness
    drown'd.
He that brought peace, and discord could
    atone,
His name is music of itself alone.
Now while the sacred oil anoints your head,
And fragrant scents, begun from you, are
    spread 60

Thro' the large dome, the people's joyful
    sound,
Sent back, is still preserv'd in hallow'd
    ground;
Which in one blessing mix'd descends on
    you,
As heighten'd spirits fall in richer dew.
Not that our wishes do increase your store:
Full of yourself, you can admit no more;
We add not to your glory, but employ
Our time, like angels, in expressing joy.
Nor is it duty, or our hopes alone,
Create that joy, but full fruition: 70
We know those blessings which we must
    possess,
And judge of future by past happiness.
No promise can oblige a prince so much
Still to be good, as long to have been such.
A noble emulation heats your breast,
And your own fame now robs you of your
    rest:
Good actions still must be maintain'd with
    good,
As bodies nourish'd with resembling food.
You have already quench'd sedition's
    brand;
And zeal, (which burnt it,) only warms
    the land.   80
The jealous sects, that dare not trust their
    cause
So far from their own will as to the laws,
You for their umpire and their synod take,
And their appeal alone to Cæsar make.
Kind Heav'n so rare a temper did provide,
That guilt repenting might in it confide.
Among our crimes oblivion may be set;
But 't is our king's perfection to forget.
Virtues unknown to these rough northern
    climes
From milder heav'ns you bring, without
    their crimes;   90
Your calmness does no after-storms pro-
    vide,
Nor seeming patience mortal anger hide.
When empire first from families did spring,
Then every father govern'd as a king;
But you, that are a sovereign prince, allay
Imperial pow'r with your paternal sway.
From those great cares when ease your
    soul unbends,
Your pleasures are design'd to noble ends:
Born to command the Mistress of the Seas,
Your thoughts themselves in that blue em-
    pire please.   100
Hither in summer ev'nings you repair

To take the fraischeur of the purer air:
Undaunted here you ride when winter
    raves,
With Cæsar's heart that rose above the
    waves.
More I could sing, but fear my numbers
    stays;
No loyal subject dares that courage praise.
In stately frigates most delight you find,
Where well-drawn battles fire your martial
    mind.
What to your cares we owe is learnt from
    hence,
When ev'n your pleasures serve for our de-
    fense.   110
Beyond your court flows in th' admitted tide,
Where in new depths the wond'ring fishes
    glide:
Here in a royal bed the waters sleep;
When tir'd at sea, within this bay they
    creep.
Here the mistrustful fowl no harm sus-
    pects,
So safe are all things which our king pro-
    tects.
From your lov'd Thames a blessing yet is
    due,
Second alone to that it brought in you;
A queen, from whose chaste womb, or-
    dain'd by fate,   119
The souls of kings unborn for bodies wait.
It was your love before made discord cease:
Your love is destin'd to your country's
    peace.
Both Indies, (rivals in your bed,) provide
With gold or jewels to adorn your bride.
This to a mighty king presents rich ore,
While that with incense does a god implore.
Two kingdoms wait your doom, and, as you
    choose,
This must receive a crown, or that must
    lose.
Thus from your Royal Oak, like Jove's of
    old,
Are answers sought, and destinies fore-
    told: 130
Propitious oracles are begg'd with vows,
And crowns that grow upon the sacred
    boughs.
Your subjects, while you weigh the nations'
    fate,
Suspend to both their doubtful love or hate:
Choose only, sir, that so they may possess
With their own peace their children's hap-
    piness.

TO MY LORD CHANCELLOR

PRESENTED ON NEW YEAR'S DAY

[The person addressed in this poem is Edward Hyde, Earl of Clarendon, the greatest statesman of the earlier years of Charles the Second's reign. The poem was published in 1662 and
reprinted in 1688: see note on *Astræa Redux*, p. 7, above. There are only small variations
between the two copies; the 1662 text is the basis of the present edition.]

MY LORD,
WHILE flattering crowds officiously appear,
To give themselves, not you, an happy year;
And by the greatness of their presents prove
How much they hope, but not how well
 they love;
The Muses, who your early courtship boast,
Tho' now your flames are with their beauty
 lost,
Yet watch their time, that, if you have for-
 got
They were your mistresses, the world may
 not:
Decay'd by time and wars, they only prove
Their former beauty by your former love; 10
And now present as ancient ladies do,
That courted long, at length are forc'd to
 woo.
For still they look on you with such kind
 eyes,
As those that see the Church's sovereign rise;
From their own order chose, in whose high
 state
They think themselves the second choice of
 fate.
When our great monarch into exile went,
Wit and religion suffer'd banishment.
Thus once, when Troy was wrapp'd in fire
 and smoke,
The helpless gods their burning shrines for-
 sook; 20
They with the vanquish'd prince and party
 go,
And leave their temples empty to the foe.
At length the Muses stand, restor'd again
To that great charge which Nature did or-
 dain;
And their lov'd Druids seem reviv'd by fate,
While you dispense the laws and guide the
 State.
The nation's soul (our monarch) does dis-
 pense,
Thro' you to us his vital influence;
You are the channel where those spirits flow,
And work them higher, as to us they go. 30

In open prospect nothing bounds our eye,
Until the earth seems join'd unto the sky:
So in this hemisphere our utmost view
Is only bounded by our king and you;
Our sight is limited where you are join'd,
And beyond that no farther heav'n can find.
So well your virtues do with his agree,
That, tho' your orbs of different greatness
 be,
Yet both are for each other's use dispos'd,
His to inclose, and yours to be inclos'd. 40
Nor could another in your room have been,
Except an emptiness had come between.
Well may he then to you his cares impart,
And share his burden where he shares his
 heart.
In you his sleep still wakes; his pleasures
 find
Their share of bus'ness in your lab'ring
 mind:
So, when the weary sun his place resigns,
He leaves his light and by reflection shines.
 Justice, that sits and frowns where public
 laws
Exclude soft Mercy from a private cause, 50
In your tribunal most herself does please;
There only smiles because she lives at ease;
And, like young David, finds her strength
 the more,
When disincumber'd from those arms she
 wore.
Heav'n would your royal master should ex-
 ceed
Most in that virtue which we most did
 need;
And his mild father (who too late did find
All mercy vain but what with pow'r was
 join'd)
His fatal goodness left to fitter times,
Not to increase, but to absolve our
 crimes: 60
But when the heir of this vast treasure
 knew
How large a legacy was left to you,
(Too great for any subject to retain,)

He wisely tied it to the crown again:
Yet passing thro' your hands it gathers
　　more,
As streams, thro' mines, bear tincture of
　　their ore.
While emp'ric politicians use deceit,
Hide what they give, and cure but by a
　　cheat;
You boldly show that skill which they
　　pretend,
And work by means as noble as your end; 70
Which should you veil, we might unwind
　　the clue,
As men do nature, till we came to you.
And as the Indies were not found before
Those rich perfumes, which from the happy
　　shore
The winds upon their balmy wings con-
　　vey'd,
Whose guilty sweetness first their world
　　betray'd;
So by your counsels we are brought to view
A rich and undiscover'd world in you.
By you our monarch does that fame assure
Which kings must have, or cannot live
　　secure: 80
For prosp'rous princes gain their subjects'
　　heart,
Who love that praise in which themselves
　　have part.
By you he fits those subjects to obey,
As heaven's eternal monarch does convey
His pow'r unseen, and man to his designs
By his bright ministers the stars inclines.
　　Our setting sun from his declining seat
Shot beams of kindness on you, not of
　　heat;
And, when his love was bounded in a few,
That were unhappy that they might be
　　true, 90
Made you the fav'rite of his last sad times,
That is, a suff'rer in his subjects' crimes:
Thus those first favors you receiv'd were
　　sent,
Like Heav'n's rewards, in earthly punish-
　　ment.
Yet Fortune, conscious of your destiny,
Ev'n then took care to lay you softly by;
And wrapp'd your fate among her precious
　　things,
Kept fresh to be unfolded with your king's.
Shown all at once, you dazzled so our eyes,
As newborn Pallas did the gods surprise;
When, springing forth from Jove's new-
　　closing wound, 101

She struck the warlike spear into the
　　ground;
Which sprouting leaves did suddenly in-
　　close,
And peaceful olives shaded as they rose.
　　How strangely active are the arts of
　　peace,
Whose restless motions less than war's do
　　cease !
Peace is not freed from labor, but from
　　noise;
And war more force, but not more pains
　　employs:
Such is the mighty swiftness of your mind,
That, like the earth's, it leaves our sense
　　behind, 110
While you so smoothly turn and roll our
　　sphere,
That rapid motion does but rest appear.
For as in nature's swiftness, with the
　　throng
Of flying orbs while ours is borne along,
All seems at rest to the deluded eye,
(Mov'd by the soul of the same harmony,)
So carried on by your unwearied care,
We rest in peace, and yet in motion share.
Let Envy then those crimes within you see
From which the happy never must be free;
(Envy, that does with Misery reside, 121
The joy and the revenge of ruin'd Pride.)
Think it not hard, if at so cheap a rate
You can secure the constancy of Fate,
Whose kindness sent what does their malice
　　seem,
By lesser ills the greater to redeem.
Nor can we this weak show'r a tempest
　　call,
But drops of heat, that in the sunshine fall.
You have already wearied Fortune so, 129
She cannot farther be your friend or foe;
But sits all breathless, and admires to feel
A fate so weighty that it stops her wheel.
In all things else above our humble fate,
Your equal mind yet swells not into state;
But like some mountain in those happy
　　isles,
Where in perpetual spring young nature
　　smiles,
Your greatness shows: no horror to af-
　　fright,
But trees for shade, and flow'rs to court the
　　sight:
Sometimes the hill submits itself a while
In small descents, which do its height be-
　　guile; 140

And sometimes mounts, but so as billows
      play,
Whose rise not hinders but makes short our
      way.
Your brow, which does no fear of thunder
      know,
Sees rolling tempests vainly beat below;
And, (like Olympus' top,) th' impression
      wears
Of love and friendship writ in former years.
Yet, unimpair'd with labors or with time,

Your age but seems to a new youth to climb.
Thus heav'nly bodies do our time beget,
And measure change, but share no part of
      it.   150
And still it shall without a weight increase,
Like this new-year, whose motions never
      cease:
For since the glorious course you have begun
Is led by CHARLES, as that is by the sun,
It must both weightless and immortal prove,
Because the center of it is above.

POEMS WRITTEN BETWEEN 1662 AND 1665

[Dryden's career as a dramatist began with the production of *The Wild Gallant* early in 1663. From that time until the publication of *Absalom and Achitophel* in November, 1681, his work, with the relatively unimportant exceptions of *Annus Mirabilis* (1666), the translations from *Ovid's Epistles* (1680), and possibly a few songs, was exclusively concerned with the theater; and hence, since the text of the dramas is excluded from this volume, can be here represented only in the scantiest manner.]

TO MY HONOR'D FRIEND, DR. CHARLETON

ON HIS LEARNED AND USEFUL WORKS; AND MORE PARTICULARLY THIS OF STONEHENGE, BY HIM RESTOR'D TO THE TRUE FOUNDERS

[This epistle is prefixed to *Chorea Gigantum; or, The Most Famous Antiquity of Great Britain, vulgarly called Stoneheng, standing on Salisbury Plain, restored to the Danes: by Walter Charleton, Dr. in Physic, and Physician in Ordinary to His Majesty.* London, 1663. Dryden's poem follows another epistle by Sir Robert Howard. Charleton, who was a man of mark both as physician and author, here presents an argument against the architect Inigo Jones. His summaries of his adversary's theory, and of his own, are as follows:
"Mr. Jones his opinion, then, of the founders, antiquity, and design of Stonehenge, is: that it was a work of the Romans, built by them when they flourished here in greatest peace and prosperity . . . not as a sepulchral monument, but as a temple, and particularly consecrated to the imaginary deity of Cœlus, or Cœlum, from whence their superstitions belief derived the original of all things." (P. 17.)
" I am apt to believe that having then overrun the whole kingdom, except only Somersetshire, and encamping their main army in Wiltshire, for near upon two years together, and setting up their rest in a confidence to perpetuate their

newly acquired power; they [the Danes] imployed themselves, during that time of leisure and jollity, in erecting Stonehenge, as a place wherein to elect and inaugurate their supreme commander King of England." (P. 64.)
The censor's *imprimatur* in Charleton's volume is dated *11 Sept. 1662*, and the book was probably published before the close of that year, though dated in the following. Of this edition two issues are known, one of them lacking the above *imprimatur*. There are a few variant readings in Dryden's epistle as printed in the two issues; the text below is that of the issue without the *imprimatur*, which is probably the later. A reprint in *Poetical Miscellanies, the Fifth Part,* 1704, introduces further variants, which may possibly be due to Dryden himself. The poem is principally important as showing Dryden's early enthusiasm for natural science.]

THE longest tyranny that ever sway'd
Was that wherein our ancestors betray'd
Their free-born reason to the Stagirite,
And made his torch their universal light.
So truth, while only one supplied the state,
Grew scarce, and dear, and yet sophisticate;
Until 't was bought, like emp'ric wares, or
      charms,
Hard words seal'd up with Aristotle's arms.
Columbus was the first that shook his
      throne,
And found a temp'rate in a torrid zone: 10
The fev'rish air fann'd by a cooling breeze,

The fruitful vales set round with shady
    trees;
And guiltless men, who danc'd away their
    time,
Fresh as their groves, and happy as their
    clime.
Had we still paid that homage to a name,
Which only God and nature justly claim,
The western seas had been our utmost
    bound,
Where poets still might dream the sun was
    drown'd:
And all the stars that shine in southern skies
Had been admir'd by none but salvage eyes.
    Among th' asserters of free reason's
      claim,   21
Th' English are not the least in worth or
    fame.
The world to Bacon does not only owe
Its present knowledge, but its future too.
Gilbert shall live, till loadstones cease to
    draw,
Or British fleets the boundless ocean awe;
And noble Boyle, not less in nature seen,
Than his great brother read in states and
    men.
The circling streams, once thought but
    pools, of blood
(Whether life's fuel, or the body's food) 30
From dark oblivion Harvey's name shall
    save;
While Ent keeps all the honor that he gave.
Nor are *you*, learned friend, the least re-
    nown'd;
Whose fame, not circumscrib'd with Eng-
    lish ground,
Flies like the nimble journeys of the light;
And is, like that, unspent too in its flight.
Whatever truths have been, by art or
    chance,
Redeem'd from error, or from ignorance,
Thin in their authors, like rich veins of ore,
Your works unite, and still discover more. 40
Such is the healing virtue of your pen,
To perfect cures on books, as well as men.
Nor is this work the least: you well may
    give
To men new vigor, who make stones to live.
Thro' you, the Danes, their short dominion
    lost,
A longer conquest than the Saxons boast.
Stonehenge, once thought a temple, you
    have found
A throne, where kings, our earthly gods,
    were crown'd;

Where by their wond'ring subjects they
    were seen,
Joy'd with their stature, and their princely
    mien.   50
Our sovereign here above the rest might
    stand,
And here be chose again to rule the land.
    These ruins shelter'd once his sacred
    head,
Then when from Wor'ster's fatal field he
    fled;
Watch'd by the genius of this royal place,
And mighty visions of the Danish race.
His refuge then was for a temple shown;
But, he restor'd, 't is now become a throne.

PROLOGUE AND EPILOGUE TO THE WILD GALLANT AS IT WAS FIRST ACTED

[This, Dryden's first play, was produced on
February 5, 1663, as is evident from the *Prologue*, line 15, and from an entry in Evelyn's
Diary of that date. It was unsuccessful: see
note before the poem *To the Lady Castlemaine*,
p. 20, below. It was later revived, with some
changes by the author, probably in 1667, since
it was entered on the *Stationers' Register* for
publication on August 7 of that year (Malone,
I, 1, 69). The first edition, dated 1669, contains both the original prologue and epilogue
and those written for the revival. See p. 52,
below.]

PROLOGUE

Is it not strange to hear a poet say,
He comes to ask you how you like the
    play ?
You have not seen it yet ! alas ! 't is true;
But now your love and hatred judge, not you;
And cruel factions, brib'd by interest, come,
Not to weigh merit, but to give their doom.
Our poet therefore, jealous of th' event,
And (tho' much boldness takes) not confi-
    dent,
Has sent me whither you, fair ladies, too,
Sometimes upon as small occasions go,   10
And from this scheme, drawn for the hour
    and day,
Bid me inquire the fortune of his play.

[*The curtain drawn discovers two* ASTROLOGERS; *the*
  PROLOGUE *is presented to them.*

    First Astrol. [*Reads.*] A figure of the
heavenly bodies in their several apartments,

Feb. the 5th, half an hour after three after
noon, from whence you are to judge the
success of a new play call'd *The Wild Gal-
lant.*   18
2 Astrol. Who must judge of it, we, or
these gentlemen?——We'll not meddle
with it, so tell your poet. Here are in this
house the ablest mathematicians in Europe
for his purpose.
They will resolve the question ere they
    part.
1 Astrol. Yet let us judge it by the rules
    of art.
First Jupiter, the ascendant's lord dis-
    grac'd,
In the twelfth house, and near grim Saturn
    plac'd,
Denote short life unto the play.
2 Astrol.   Jove yet,
In his apartment Sagittary set,
Under his own roof, cannot take much
    wrong.   30
1 Astrol. Why then the life's not very
    short, nor long.
2 Astrol. The luck not very good, nor
    very ill.
Prolo. That is to say, 't is as 't is taken
    still.
1 Astrol. But, brother, Ptolemy the
    learned says,
'T is the fifth house from whence we judge
    of plays.
Venus, the lady of that house, I find
Is *peregrine:* your play is ill design'd;
It should have been but one continued song,
Or at the least a dance of three hours long.
2 Astrol. But yet the greatest mischief
    does remain,   40
The twelfth apartment bears the lord of
    Spain;
Whence I conclude, it is your author's lot,
To be indanger'd by a Spanish plot.
Prolo. Our poet yet protection hopes
    from you,
But bribes you not with anything that's
    new.
Nature is old, which poets imitate,
And for wit, those that boast their own es-
    tate,
Forget Fletcher and Ben before them
    went,
Their elder brothers, and that vastly spent:
So much, 't will hardly be repair'd again, 50
Not tho' supplied with all the wealth of
    Spain.

This play is English, and the growth your
    own;
As such, it yields to English plays alone.
He could have wish'd it better for your
    sakes,
But that in plays he finds you love mis-
    takes:
Besides, he thought it was in vain to
    mend
What you are bound in honor to defend,
That English wit, (howe'er despis'd by
    some,)
Like English valor, still may overcome.

EPILOGUE

The Wild Gallant has quite play'd out his
    game;
He's married now, and that will make him
    tame;
Or, if you think marriage will not reclaim
    him,
The critics swear they'll damn him, but
    they'll tame him.
Yet, tho' our poet's threaten'd most by
    these,
They are the only people he can please,
For he, to humor them, has shown to-day
That which they only like, a wretched
    play.
But, tho' his play be ill, here have been
    shown
The greatest wits and beauties of the
    town;   10
And his occasion having brought you here,
You are too grateful to become severe.
There is not any person here so mean
But he may freely judge each act and
    scene;
But if you bid him choose his judges then,
He boldly names true English gentlemen;
For he ne'er thought a handsome garb or
    dress
So great a crime to make their judgment
    less;
And with these gallants he these ladies
    joins,
To judge that language their converse re-
    fines.   20
But if their censures should condemn his
    play,
Far from disputing, he does only pray
He may Leander's destiny obtain:
Now spare him, drown him when he comes
    again.

TO THE LADY CASTLEMAINE, UPON HER INCOURAGING HIS FIRST PLAY

[In his preface to *The Wild Gallant* Dryden says that it had "but indifferent success in the action. . . . Yet it was receiv'd at court; and was more than once the divertisement of his Majesty, by his own command." This probably does not refer to the revival of 1667; but, in part at least, to a court performance on February 23, 1663, which Pepys attended, and which may well have been procured for Dryden by the influence of the Countess of Castlemaine, then at the height of her power as the favorite mistress of Charles II. This woman was born Barbara Villiers, daughter of William Villiers, second Viscount Grandison; in 1670 she was created Duchess of Cleveland. This poem was first printed in *Examen Poeticum*, 1693.]

As seamen, shipwrack'd on some happy
    shore,
Discover wealth in lands unknown before;
And, what their art had labor'd long in
    vain,
By their misfortunes happily obtain:
So my much-envied Muse, by storms long
    toss'd,
Is thrown upon your hospitable coast,
And finds more favor by her ill success,
Than she could hope for by her happiness.
Once Cato's virtue did the gods oppose;
While they the victor, he the vanquish'd
    chose: 10
But you have done what Cato could not do,
To choose the vanquish'd, and restore him
    too.
Let others still triumph, and gain their
    cause
By their deserts, or by the world's applause,
Let merit crowns, and justice laurels give,
But let me happy by your pity live.
True poets empty fame and praise despise,
Fame is the trumpet, but your smile the
    prize.
You sit above, and see vain men below
Contend for what you only can bestow;   20
But those great actions others do by chance
Are, like your beauty, your inheritance:
So great a soul, such sweetness join'd in
    one,
Could only spring from noble Grandison.
You, like the stars, not by reflection bright,
Are born to your own heav'n, and your own
    light;

Like them are good, but from a nobler
    cause,
From your own knowledge, not from na-
    ture's laws.
Your pow'r you never use but for defense,
To guard your own, or others' innocence: 30
Your foes are such, as they, not you, have
    made,
And virtue may repel, tho' not invade.
Such courage did the ancient heroes show,
Who, when they might prevent, would wait
    the blow;
With such assurance as they meant to say:
"We will o'ercome, but scorn the safest
    way."
What further fear of danger can there be?
Beauty, which captives all things, sets me
    free.
Posterity will judge by my success,
I had the Grecian poet's happiness,   40
Who, waiving plots, found out a better way;
Some god descended, and preserv'd the play.
When first the triumphs of your sex were
    sung
By those old poets, Beauty was but young,
And few admir'd the native red and white,
Till poets dress'd them up to charm the
    sight;
So Beauty took on trust, and did engage
For sums of praises till she came to age.
But this long-growing debt to poetry   49
You justly, madam, have discharg'd to me,
When your applause and favor did infuse
New life to my condemn'd and dying Muse.

PROLOGUE TO THE RIVAL LADIES

[This tragi-comedy, Dryden's first attempt at the poetic drama, was acted late in 1663 or early in 1664. It was entered on the *Stationers' Register* June 5, 1664 (Malone, I, 1, 57); two separate editions were printed in that year. No epilogue appears in any early edition.]

'T IS much desir'd, you judges of the town
Would pass a vote to put all prologues
    down:
For who can show me, since they first were
    writ,
They e'er converted one hard-hearted wit?
Yet the world's mended well: in former
    days
Good prologues were as scarce as now good
    plays.
For the reforming poets of our age,

In this first charge, spend their poetic rage:
Expect no more when once the prologue 's
 done;
The wit is ended ere the play 's begun. 10
You now have habits, dances, scenes, and
 rhymes;
High language often; aye, and sense, some-
 times.
As for a clear contrivance, doubt it not;
They blow out candles to give light to th'
 plot.
And for surprise, two bloody-minded men
Fight till they die, then rise and dance again.
Such deep intrigues you 're welcome to this
 day:
But blame yourselves, not him who writ the
 play;
Tho' his plot 's dull, as can be well desir'd,
Wit stiff as any you have e'er admir'd: 20
He 's bound to please, not to write well; and
 knows
There is a mode in plays as well as clothes;
Therefore, kind judges —

A second PROLOGUE *enters.*

2.   Hold; would you admit
For judges all you see within the pit ?
 1. Whom would he then except, or on
 what score ?
 2. All who (like him) have writ ill plays
 before;
For they, like thieves condemn'd, are hang-
 men made,
To execute the members of their trade.
All that are writing now he would disown,
But then he must except — ev'n all the town;
All chol'ric, losing gamesters, who, in spite,
Will damn to-day, because they lost last
 night; 32
All servants, whom their mistress' scorn
 upbraids;
All maudlin lovers, and all slighted maids;
All who are out of humor, or severe;
All that want wit, or hope to find it here.

PROLOGUE, EPILOGUE, AND
SONG FROM THE INDIAN EM-
PEROR

OR, THE CONQUEST OF MEXICO BY THE
SPANIARDS

[This, Dryden's first independent heroic
play, was acted late in 1664 or early in 1665.
It was entered on the *Stationers' Register*

May 26, 1665 (Malone, I, 1, 218), but was not
printed until 1667. It was a sequel to *The
Indian Queen*, a play written by Sir Robert
Howard with some assistance from Dryden :
see *Appendix I*, p. 903, below.]

PROLOGUE

ALMIGHTY critics ! whom our Indians here
Worship, just as they do the Devil, for fear;
In reverence to your pow'r I come this day
To give you timely warning of our play.
The scenes are old, the habits are the same
We wore last year, before the Spaniards
 came;
[Our prologue, th' old-cast too —
For to observe the new it should at least
Be spoke by some ingenious bird or beast.]
Now if you stay, the blood that shall be
 shed 10
From this poor play, be all upon your head.
We neither promise you one dance, or show,
Then plot and language they are wanting
 too;
But you, kind wits, will those light faults
 excuse;
Those are the common frailties of the Muse,
Which who observes, he buys his place too
 dear;
For 't is your business to be cozen'd here.
These wretched spies of wit must then con-
 fess
They take more pains, to please themselves
 the less.
Grant us such judges, Phœbus, we request, 21
As still mistake themselves into a jest;
Such easy judges, that our poet may
Himself admire the fortune of his play;
And arrogantly, as his fellows do,
Think he writes well, because he pleases
 you.
This he conceives not hard to bring about,
If all of you would join to help him out;
Would each man take but what he under-
 stands,
And leave the rest upon the poet's hands.

EPILOGUE

BY A MERCURY

To all and singular in this full meeting,
Ladies and gallants, Phœbus sends me
 greeting.
To all his sons, by whate'er title known,
Whether of court, of coffee-house, or town;

From his most mighty sons, whose confi-
dence
Is plac'd in lofty sound, and humble sense,
Ev'n to his little infants of the time,
Who write new songs, and trust in tune and
rhyme;
Be 't known, that Phœbus (being daily
griev'd
To see good plays condemn'd, and bad re-
ceiv'd)   10
Ordains your judgment upon every cause,
Henceforth, be limited by wholesome laws.
He first thinks fit no sonnetteer advance
His censure farther than the song or dance.
Your wit burlesque may one step higher
climb,
And in his sphere may judge all dogg'rel
rhyme;
All proves, and moves, and loves, and
honors too;
All that appears high sense, and scarce is
low.
As for the coffee wits, he says not much;
Their proper bus'ness is to damn the
Dutch: 20
For the great dons of wit —
Phœbus gives them full privilege alone,
To damn all others, and cry up their
own.
Last, for the ladies, 't is Apollo's will,
They should have power to save, but not to
kill:

For love and he long since have thought it
fit,
Wit live by beauty, beauty reign by wit.

SONG

I

Ah fading joy, how quickly art thou
past !
Yet we thy ruin haste.
As if the cares of human life were few,
We seek out new:
And follow fate, which would too fast pur-
sue.

II

See how on every bough the birds ex-
press
In their sweet notes their happiness.
They all enjoy, and nothing spare;
But on their mother Nature lay their
care:
Why then should man, the lord of all be-
low,   10
Such troubles choose to know,
As none of all his subjects undergo ?

III

Hark, hark, the waters fall, fall, fall,
And with a murmuring sound
Dash, dash upon the ground,
To gentle slumbers call.

ANNUS MIRABILIS

THE YEAR OF WONDERS, 1666

AN HISTORICAL POEM

CONTAINING

THE PROGRESS AND VARIOUS SUCCESSES OF OUR NAVAL WAR WITH HOLLAND,
UNDER THE CONDUCT OF HIS HIGHNESS PRINCE RUPERT, AND HIS GRACE THE
DUKE OF ALBEMARLE

AND DESCRIBING
THE FIRE OF LONDON

Multum interest res poscat, an homines latius imperare velint.
TRAJAN IMPERATOR *ad Plin.*

Urbs antiqua ruit, multos dominata per annos. — VIRG.

[*Annus Mirabilis* was licensed for the press on November 22, 1666, and was published in a
tiny octavo, date 1667, the title-page of which reads as above. Different copies of this edition
apparently show at least one variation in the text: see note on line 267. The poem was reprinted

in 1688 : see note on *Astræa Redux*, p. 7, above.   The present edition follows the text of 1688, which was apparently slightly revised by Dryden.

The *Verses to the Duchess* were later published by themselves in *Poetical Miscellanies, the Fifth Part*, 1704, and have since usually been printed as a separate poem.   They are here restored, at the cost of a slight violation of the chronological order, to the position in which Dryden chose to print them.   They were addressed to Anne Hyde, first wife of James, Duke of York (afterwards King James II), and daughter of the Earl of Clarendon, in whose honor Dryden had written his poem *To my Lord Chancellor* (see p. 15, above).]

TO THE

METROPOLIS OF GREAT BRIT-AIN,

THE MOST RENOWN'D AND LATE FLOUR-ISHING CITY OF LONDON, IN ITS REPRE-SENTATIVES THE LORD MAYOR AND COURT OF ALDERMEN, THE SHERIFFS, AND COMMON COUNCIL OF IT

As perhaps I am the first who ever presented a work of this nature to the metropolis of any nation; so it is likewise consonant to justice, that he who was to give the first example of such a dedication should begin it with that city, which has set a pattern to all others of true loyalty, invincible courage, and unshaken constancy.   Other cities have been prais'd for the same virtues, but I am much deceiv'd if any have so dearly purchas'd their reputation; their fame has been won them by cheaper trials than an expensive, tho' necessary war, a consuming pestilence, and a more consuming fire. To submit yourselves with that humility to the judgments of Heaven, and at the same time to raise yourselves with that vigor above all human enemies ; to be combated at once from above and from below, to be struck down and to triumph ; I know not whether such trials have been ever parallel'd in any nation : the resolution and successes of them never can be. Never had prince or people more mutual reason to love each other, if suffering for each other can indear affection.   You have come together a pair of matchless lovers, thro' many difficulties ; he, thro' a long exile, various traverses of fortune, and the interposition of many rivals, who violently ravish'd and withheld you from him : and certainly you have had your share in sufferings.   But Providence has cast upon you want of trade, that you might appear bountiful to your country's necessities ; and the rest of your afflictions are not more the effects of God's displeasure, (frequent examples of them having been in the reign of the most excellent princes,) than occasions for the manifesting of your Christian and civil virtues.   To you, therefore, this *Year of Wonders* is justly dedicated, because you have made it so.   You, who are to stand a wonder to all years and ages, and who have built yourselves an immortal monument on your own ruins.   You are now a Phœnix in her ashes, and, as far as humanity can approach, a great emblem of the suffering Deity.   But Heaven never made so much piety and virtue to leave it miserable.   I have heard, indeed, of some virtuous persons who have ended unfortunately, but never of any virtuous nation : Providence is engag'd too deeply, when the cause becomes so general.   And I cannot imagine it has resolv'd the ruin of that people at home which it has blest abroad with such successes.   I am therefore to conclude that your sufferings are at an end ; and that one part of my poem has not been more an history of your destruction, than the other a prophecy of your restoration.   The accomplishment of which happiness, as it is the wish of all true Englishmen, so is by none more passionately desir'd than by,

> The greatest of your admirers, and
> Most humble of your servants,
> JOHN DRYDEN.

AN ACCOUNT OF THE ENSUING POEM

IN A LETTER TO THE HONORABLE SIR ROBERT HOWARD

SIR,

I AM so many ways oblig'd to you, and so little able to return your favors, that, like those who owe too much, I can only live by getting farther into your debt.   You have not only been careful of my fortune, which was the effect of your nobleness, but you have been solicitous of my reputation, which is that of your kindness. It is not long since I gave you the trouble of perusing a play for me, and now, instead of an acknowledgment, I have given you a greater, in the correction of a poem.   But since you are to bear this persecution, I will at least give you the encouragement of a martyr ; you could never suffer in a nobler cause.   For I have chosen the most heroic subject which any poet could desire ; I have taken upon me to describe the motives, the beginning, progress, and successes, of a most just and necessary war : in it, the care, management, and prudence of our king ; the conduct and valor of a royal admiral, and of two incomparable generals ; the invincible courage of our captains and seamen ; and three glorious victories, the result of all. After this, I have, in the fire, the most deplorable, but withal the greatest, argument that can be imagin'd: the destruction being so swift, so sudden, so vast, and miserable, as nothing can parallel in story. The former part of this poem, relating to the war, is but a due expiation for my not serving my king and country in it. All gentlemen are almost oblig'd to it; and I know no reason we should give that advantage to the commonalty of England, to be foremost in brave actions, which the nobless of France would never suffer in their peasants. I should not have written this but to a person who has been ever forward to appear in all employments whither his honor and generosity have call'd him. The later part of my poem, which describes the fire, I owe first to the piety and fatherly affection of our monarch to his suffering subjects; and, in the second place, to the courage, loyalty, and magnanimity of the city; both which were so conspicuous, that I have wanted words to celebrate them as they deserve. I have call'd my poem *historical*, not *epic*, tho' both the actions and actors are as much heroic as any poem can contain. But since the action is not properly one, nor that accomplish'd in the last successes, I have judg'd it too bold a title for a few *stanzas*, which are little more in number than a single *Iliad*, or the longest of the *Æneids*. For this reason (I mean not of length, but broken action, tied too severely to the laws of history) I am apt to agree with those who rank Lucan rather among historians in verse, than epic poets: in whose room, if I am not deceiv'd, Silius Italicus, tho' a worse writer, may more justly be admitted. I have chosen to write my poem in *quatrains*, or *stanzas* of four in alternate rhyme, because I have ever judg'd them more noble, and of greater dignity, both for the sound and number, than any other verse in use amongst us; in which I am sure I have your approbation. The learned languages have certainly a great advantage of us, in not being tied to the slavery of any rhyme; and were less constrain'd in the quantity of every syllable, which they might vary with *spondæes* or *dactiles*, besides so many other helps of grammatical figures, for the lengthening or abbreviation of them, than the modern are in the close of that one syllable, which often confines, and more often corrupts, the sense of all the rest. But in this necessity of our rhymes, I have always found the couplet verse most easy, (tho' not so proper for this occasion,) for there the work is sooner at an end, every two lines concluding the labor of the poet; but in *quatrains* he is to carry it farther on, and not only so, but to bear along in his head the troublesome sense of four lines together. For those

who write correctly in this kind must needs acknowledge that the last line of the *stanza* is to be consider'd in the composition of the first. Neither can we give ourselves the liberty of making any part of a verse for the sake of rhyme, or concluding with a word which is not current English, or using the variety of female rhymes; all which our fathers practic'd: and for the female rhymes, they are still in use amongst other nations; with the Italian in every line, with the Spaniard promiscuously, with the French alternately; as those who have read the *Alarique*, the *Pucelle*, or any of their later poems, will agree with me. And besides this, they write in *Alexandrins*, or verses of six feet; such as amongst us is the old translation of Homer, by Chapman; all which, by length'ning of their chain, makes the sphere of their activity the larger. I have dwelt too long upon the choice of my *stanza*, which you may remember is much better defended in the preface to *Gondibert;* and therefore I will hasten to acquaint you with my endeavors in the writing. In general I will only say, I have never yet seen the description of any naval fight in the proper terms which are us'd at sea; and if there be any such in another language, as that of Lucan in the third of his *Pharsalia*, yet I could not prevail myself of it in the English; the terms of art in every tongue bearing more of the idiom of it than any other words. We hear indeed among our poets, of the thund'ring of guns, the smoke, the disorder, and the slaughter; but all these are common notions. And certainly as those who, in a logical dispute, keep in general terms, would hide a fallacy, so those who do it in any poetical description would veil their ignorance:

Descriptas servare vices operumque colores,
Cur ego, si nequeo ignoroque, poeta salutor?

For my own part, if I had little knowledge of the sea, yet I have thought it no shame to learn; and if I have made some few mistakes, 'tis only, as you can bear me witness, because I have wanted opportunity to correct them; the whole poem being first written, and now sent you, from a place where I have not so much as the converse of any seaman. Yet, tho' the trouble I had in writing it was great, it was more than recompens'd by the pleasure: I found myself so warm in celebrating the praises of military men, two such especially as the prince and general, that it is no wonder if they inspir'd me with thoughts above my ordinary level. And I am well satisfied that, as they are incomparably the best subject I have ever had, excepting only the royal family; so also, that this I have written of them is much better than what I have perform'd on any other. I have been forc'd to help out other arguments; but this has been bountiful to me: they have been low and barren of praise, and I have exalted them, and made them fruitful; but here — *Omnia sponte sua reddit justissima tellus.* I have had a large, a fair, and a pleasant field; so fertile that without my cultivating it has given me two harvests in a summer, and in both oppress'd the reaper. All other greatness in subjects is only counterfeit; it will not endure the test of danger; the greatness of arms is only real: other greatness burdens a nation with its weight; this supports it with its strength. And as it is the happiness of the age, so it is the peculiar goodness of the best of kings, that we may praise his subjects without offending him. Doubtless it proceeds from a just confidence of his own virtue, which the luster of no other can be so great as to darken in him; for the good or the valiant are never safely prais'd under a bad or a degenerate prince.

But to return from this digression to a farther account of my poem; I must crave leave to tell you, that as I have endeavor'd to adorn it with noble thoughts, so much more to express those thoughts with elocution. The composition of all poems is, or ought to be, of wit; and wit in the poet, or wit writing (if you will give me leave to use a school-distinction) is no other than the faculty of imagination in the writer, which, like a nimble spaniel, beats over and ranges thro' the field of memory, till it springs the quarry it hunted after; or, without metaphor, which searches over all the memory for the species or ideas of those things which it designs to represent. Wit written is that which is well defin'd, the happy result of thought, or product of imagination. But to proceed from wit, in the general notion of it, to the proper wit of an heroic or historical poem, I judge it chiefly to consist in the delightful imaging of persons, actions, passions, or things. 'T is not the jerk or sting of an epigram, nor the seeming contradiction of a poor antithesis, (the delight of an ill-judging audience in a play of rhyme,) nor the jingle of a more poor *paronomasia;* neither is it so much the morality of a grave sentence, affected by Lucan, but more sparingly us'd by Virgil; but it is some lively and apt description, dress'd in such colors of speech that it sets before your eyes the absent object as perfectly and more delightfully than nature. So then, the first happiness of the poet's imagination is properly invention, or finding of the thought; the second is fancy, or the variation, deriving, or molding of that thought, as the judgment represents it proper to the subject; the third is elocution, or the art of clothing and adorning that thought, so found and varied, in apt, significant, and sounding words: the quick-

ness of the imagination is seen in the invention, the fertility in the fancy, and the accuracy in the expression. For the two first of these, Ovid is famous amongst the poets; for the later, Virgil. Ovid images more often the movements and affections of the mind, either combating between two contrary passions, or extremely discompos'd by one: his words therefore are the least part of his care; for he pictures nature in disorder, with which the study and choice of words is inconsistent. This is the proper wit of dialogue or discourse, and consequently of the *drama*, where all that is said is to be suppos'd the effect of sudden thought; which, tho' it excludes not the quickness of wit in repartees, yet admits not a too curious election of words, too frequent allusions, or use of tropes, or in fine anything that shews remoteness of thought or labor in the writer. On the other side, Virgil speaks not so often to us in the person of another, like Ovid, but in his own: he relates almost all things as from himself, and thereby gains more liberty than the other, to express his thoughts with all the graces of elocution, to write more figuratively, and to confess as well the labor as the force of his imagination. Tho' he describes his Dido well and naturally, in the violence of her passions, yet he must yield in that to the Myrrha, the Biblis, the Althæa, of Ovid; for, as great an admirer of him as I am, I must acknowledge, that if I see not more of their souls than I see of Dido's, at least I have a greater concernment for them: and that convinces me that Ovid has touch'd those tender strokes more delicately than Virgil could. But when action or persons are to be describ'd, when any such image is to be set before us, how bold, how masterly are the strokes of Virgil! We see the objects he represents us with in their native figures, in their proper motions; but so we see them, as our own eyes could never have beheld them so beautiful in themselves. We see the soul of the poet, like that universal one of which he speaks, informing and moving thro' all his pictures:

—— Totamque infusa per artus
Mens agitat molem, et magno se corpore miscet.

We behold him embellishing his images, as he makes Venus breathing beauty upon her son Æneas:

—— lumenque juventæ
Purpureum, et lætos oculis afflarat honores:
Quale manus addunt ebori decus, aut ubi flavo
Argentum Pariusve lapis circundatur auro.

See his tempest, his funeral sports, his combat of Turnus and Æneas: and in his *Georgics*, which I esteem the divinest part of all his writings, the plague, the country, the battle of bulls, the labor of the bees, and those many other excellent images of nature, most of which are neither great in themselves, nor have any natural ornament to bear them up: but the words wherewith he describes them are so excellent, that it might be well applied to him, which was said by Ovid, *Materiam superabat opus:* the very sound of his words has often somewhat that is connatural to the subject; and while we read him, we sit, as in a play, beholding the scenes of what he represents. To perform this, he made frequent use of tropes, which you know change the nature of a known word by applying it to some other signification; and this is it which Horace means in his epistle to the Pisos:

Dixeris egregie, notum si callida verbum
Reddiderit junctura novum ——

But I am sensible I have presum'd too far, to entertain you with a rude discourse of that art which you both know so well, and put into practice with so much happiness. Yet before I leave Virgil, I must own the vanity to tell you, and by you the world, that he has been my master in this poem: I have follow'd him everywhere, I know not with what success, but I am sure with diligence enough: my images are many of them copied from him, and the rest are imitations of him. My expressions also are as near as the idioms of the two languages would admit of in translation. And this, sir, I have done with that boldness for which I will stand accomptable to any of our little critics, who, perhaps, are not better acquainted with him than I am. Upon your first perusal of this poem, you have taken notice of some words which I have innovated (if it be too bold for me to say refin'd) upon his Latin; which, as I offer not to introduce into English prose, so I hope they are neither improper, nor altogether unelegant in verse; and, in this, Horace will again defend me:

Et nova, fictaque nuper, habebunt verba fidem, si
Græco fonte cadant, parce detorta ——

The inference is exceeding plain: for if a Roman poet might have liberty to coin a word, supposing only that it was deriv'd from the Greek, was put into a Latin termination, and that he us'd this liberty but seldom, and with modesty; how much more justly may I challenge that privilege to do it with the same prerequisites, from the best and most judicious of Latin writers? In some places where either the fancy or the words were his, or any other's, I have noted it in the margin, that I might not seem a plagiary; in others I have neglected it, to avoid as well tediousness, as the affectation of doing it too often. Such descriptions or images, well wrought, which I promise not for mine, are, as I have said, the adequate delight of heroic poesy; for they beget admiration,

which is its proper object; as the images of the burlesque, which is contrary to this, by the same reason beget laughter; for the one shews nature beautified, as in the picture of a fair woman, which we all admire; the other shews her deform'd, as in that of a lazar, or of a fool with distorted face and antic gestures, at which we cannot forbear to laugh, because it is a deviation from nature. But tho' the same images serve equally for the epic poesy, and for the historic and panegyric, which are branches of it, yet a several sort of sculpture is to be us'd in them. If some of them are to be like those of Juvenal, *Stantes in curribus Æmiliani,* heroes drawn in their triumphal chariots, and in their full proportion; others are to be like that of Virgil, *Spirantia mollius æra:* there is somewhat more of softness and tenderness to be shewn in them. You will soon find I write not this without concern. Some, who have seen a paper of verses which I wrote last year to her Highness the Duchess, have accus'd them of that only thing I could defend in them; they said, I did *humi serpere,* that I wanted not only height of fancy, but dignity of words to set it off. I might well answer with that of Horace, *Nunc non erat his locus;* I knew I address'd them to a lady, and accordingly I affected the softness of expression, and the smoothness of measure, rather than the height of thought; and in what I did endeavor, it is no vanity to say I have succeeded. I detest arrogance; but there is some difference betwixt that and a just defense. But I will not farther bribe your candor or the reader's. I leave them to speak for me; and, if they can, to make out that character, not pretending to a greater, which I have given them.

VERSES TO HER HIGHNESS THE DUCHESS

ON THE MEMORABLE VICTORY GAIN'D BY THE DUKE AGAINST THE HOLLANDERS, JUNE THE 3D, 1665; AND ON HER JOURNEY AFTERWARDS INTO THE NORTH

MADAM,
WHEN for our sakes your *hero* you resign'd
To swelling seas, and every faithless wind;
When you releas'd his courage, and set free
A valor fatal to the enemy;
You lodg'd your country's cares within your breast,
(The mansion where soft love should only rest:)
And, ere our foes abroad were overcome,

The noblest conquest you had gain'd at
    home.
Ah, what concerns did both your souls
    divide !
Your honor gave us what your love de-
    nied: 10
And 't was for him much easier to subdue
Those foes he fought with, than to part from
    you.
That glorious day, which two such navies
    saw,
As each, unmatch'd, might to the world give
    law,
Neptune yet doubtful whom he should
    obey,
Held to them both the trident of the sea:
The winds were hush'd, the waves in ranks
    were cast,
As awfully as when God's people pass'd:
Those, yet uncertain on whose sails to
    blow,
These, where the wealth of nations ought
    to flow.   20
Then with the duke your Highness rul'd
    the day:
While all the brave did his command obey,
The fair and pious under you did pray.
How pow'rful are chaste vows ! the wind
    and tide
You brib'd to combat on the English side.
Thus to your much-lov'd lord you did con-
    vey
An unknown succor, sent the nearest way.
New vigor to his wearied arms you brought,
(So Moses was upheld while Israel fought)
While, from afar, we heard the cannon
    play,   30
Like distant thunder on a shiny day.
For absent friends we were asham'd to
    fear,
When we consider'd what you ventur'd
    there.
Ships, men, and arms, our country might
    restore,
But such a leader could supply no more.
With generous thoughts of conquest he did
    burn,
Yet fought not more to vanquish than re-
    turn.
Fortune and victory he did pursue,
To bring them, as his slaves, to wait on
    you.
Thus beauty ravish'd the rewards of fame,
And the fair triumph'd when the brave o'er-
    came.   41

Then, as you meant to spread another
    way
By land your conquests, far as his by
    sea,
Leaving our southern clime, you march'd
    along
The stubborn North, ten thousand Cupids
    strong.
Like commons the nobility resort,
In crowding heaps, to fill your moving
    court:
To welcome your approach the vulgar run,
Like some new envoy from the distant
    sun,
And country beauties by their lovers go,   50
Blessing themselves, and wond'ring at the
    show.
So when the newborn Phœnix first is seen,
Her feather'd subjects all adore their queen;
And, while she makes her progress thro'
    the East,
From every grove her numerous train 's in-
    creas'd:
Each poet of the air her glory sings,
And round him the pleas'd audience clap
    their wings.

And now, sir, 't is time I should relieve you
from the tedious length of this account. You
have better and more profitable employment
for your hours, and I wrong the public to detain you longer. In conclusion, I must leave
my poem to you with all its faults, which I
hope to find fewer in the printing by your
emendations. I know you are not of the number of those of whom the younger Pliny speaks:
*Nec sunt parum multi, qui carpere amicos suos
judicium vocant :* I am rather too secure of you
on that side. Your candor in pardoning my
errors may make you more remiss in correcting
them ; if you will not withal consider that they
come into the world with your approbation, and
thro' your hands. I beg from you the greatest
favor you can confer upon an absent person,
since I repose upon your management what is
dearest to me, my fame and reputation ; and
therefore I hope it will stir you up to make my
poem fairer by many of your blots ; if not, you
know the story of the gamester who married
the rich man's daughter, and when her father
denied the portion, christen'd all the children
by his surname, that if, in conclusion, they must
beg, they should do so by one name, as well as
by the other. But since the reproach of my
faults will light on you, 't is but reason I should
do you that justice to the readers, to let them
know, that if there be anything tolerable in
this poem, they owe the argument to your

choice, the writing to your encouragement, the
correction to your judgment, and the care of it
to your friendship, to which he must ever acknowledge himself to owe all things, who is,
        Sir,
    The most obedient, and most
        Faithful of your Servants,
                JOHN DRYDEN.
From Charlton in Wiltshire,
    Nov. 10, 1666.

ANNUS MIRABILIS

THE YEAR OF WONDERS, MDCLXVI

I

IN thriving arts long time had Holland
        grown,
    Crouching at home and cruel when
        abroad;
Scarce leaving us the means to claim our
        own;
    Our king they courted, and our merchants
        aw'd.

II

Trade, which like blood should circularly
        flow,
    Stopp'd in their channels, found its free-
        dom lost:
Thither the wealth of all the world did
        go,
    And seem'd but shipwrack'd on so base
        a coast.

III

For them alone the heav'ns   (a) *In eastern*
        had kindly heat;   *quarries,* &c.
    (a) In eastern quarries ripen-   Precious
        ing precious dew: 10 *stones at first*
For them the Ídumæan balm   *dens'd and har-*
        did sweat,   *den'd by the*
    And in hot Ceylon spicy for- *sun or subter-*
        ests grew.   *ranean fires.*

IV

The sun but seem'd the lab'rer (b) *Each wax-*
        of their year;   *ing,* &c.
    (b) Each waxing moon sup- *According to*
        plied her wat'ry store, *who think that*
To swell those tides, which *great heap of*
        from the line did bear *waters under*
    Their brim-full vessels to the *press'd into*
        Belgian shore.   *tides by the*
                                moon, towards
                                the poles.

V

Thus mighty in her ships stood Carthage
        long,
    And swept the riches of the world from
        far;
Yet stoop'd to Rome, less wealthy, but more
        strong;
    And this may prove our second Punic
        war.   20

VI

What peace can be, where both to one pre-
        tend?
    (But they more diligent, and we more
        strong)
Or if a peace, it soon must have an end;
    For they would grow too pow'rful were
        it long.

VII

Behold two nations then, ingag'd so far,
    That each sev'n years the fit must shake
        each land:
Where France will side to weaken us by
        war,
    Who only can his vast designs withstand.

VIII

See how he feeds (c) th' Ibe- (c) *Th' Iberian.*
        rian with delays,   *The Spaniard.*
    To render us his timely friendship
        vain: 30
And while his secret soul on Flanders preys,
    He rocks the cradle of the babe of Spain.

IX

Such deep designs of empire does he lay
    O'er them whose cause he seems to take
        in hand;
And, prudently, would make them lords at
        sea,
    To whom with ease he can give laws by
        land.

X

This saw our king; and long within his
        breast
    His pensive counsels balanc'd to and fro:
He griev'd the land he freed should be op-
        press'd,
    And he less for it than usurpers do.   40

XI

His gen'rous mind the fair ideas drew
    Of fame and honor, which in dangers lay;

Where wealth, like fruit on precipices, grew,
Not to be gather'd but by birds of prey.

XII

The loss and gain each fatally were great;
And still his subjects call'd aloud for war;
But peaceful kings, o'er martial people set,
Each other's poise and counterbalance are.

XIII

He, first, survey'd the charge with careful eyes,
Which none but mighty monarchs could maintain;   50
Yet judg'd, like vapors that from limbecs rise,
It would in richer showers descend again.

XIV

At length resolv'd t' assert the wat'ry ball,
He in himself did whole armadoes bring:
Him aged seamen might their master call,
And choose for general, were he not their king.

XV

It seems as every ship their sovereign knows,
His awful summons they so soon obey;
So hear the scaly herd when (d) Proteus blows,
And so to pasture follow thro' the sea.   60

(d) When Proteus blows or: Cæruleus Proteus ponti Armenta et magnas pascit sub gurgite phocas. — VIRGIL.

XVI

To see this fleet upon the ocean move,
Angels drew wide the curtains of the skies;
And Heav'n, as if there wanted lights above,
For tapers made two glaring comets rise;

XVII

Whether they unctuous exhalations are,
Fir'd by the sun, or seeming so alone,
Or each some more remote and slippery star,
Which loses footing when to mortals shown;

XVIII

Or one, that bright companion of the sun,
Whose glorious aspect seal'd our new-born king,   70

And now, a round of greater years begun,
New influence from his walks of light did bring.

XIX

Victorious York did first, with fam'd success,
To his known valor make the Dutch give place:
Thus Heav'n our monarch's fortune did confess,
Beginning conquest from his royal race.

XX

But since it was decreed, auspicious king,
In Britain's right that thou shouldst wed the main,
Heav'n, as a gage, would cast some precious thing,
And therefore doom'd that Lawson should be slain.   80

XXI

Lawson amongst the foremost met his fate,
Whom sea-green Sirens from the rocks lament:
Thus as an off'ring for the Grecian state,
He first was kill'd who first to battle went.

XXII

(e) Their chief blown up, in (e) The Admiral of Holland. air, not waves, expir'd,
To which his pride presum'd to give the law:
The Dutch confess'd Heav'n present, and retir'd,
And all was Britain the wide ocean saw.

XXIII

To nearest ports their shatter'd ships repair,
Where by our dreadful cannon they lay aw'd: 90
So reverently men quit the open air,
When thunder speaks the angry gods abroad.

XXIV

And now approach'd their fleet from India, fraught
With all the riches of the rising sun:
And precious sand from (f) southern climates brought,
(The fatal regions where the war begun.)

The attempt at Berghen.
(f) southern climates. Guinea.

XXV

Like hunted castors, conscious of their store,
 Their waylaid wealth to Norway's coasts
  they bring:
There first the North's cold bosom spices
  bore,
 And winter brooded on the eastern spring.

XXVI

By the rich scent we found our perfum'd
  prey,   101
 Which, flank'd with rocks, did close in
  covert lie;
And round about their murdering cannon
  lay,
 At once to threaten and invite the eye.

XXVII

Fiercer than cannon, and than rocks more
  hard,
 The English undertake th' unequal war:
Seven ships alone, by which the port is
  barr'd,
 Besiege the Indies, and all Denmark
  dare.

XXVIII

These fight like husbands, but like lovers
  those:
 These fain would keep, and those more
  fain enjoy;   110
And to such height their frantic passion
  grows,
 That what both love, both hazard to destroy.

XXIX

Amidst whole heaps of spices lights a ball,
 And now their odors arm'd against them
  fly:
Some preciously by shatter'd porc'lain fall,
 And some by aromatic splinters die.

XXX

And tho' by tempests of the prize bereft,
 In heaven's inclemency some ease we
  find:
Our foes we vanquish'd by our valor left,
 And only yielded to the seas and wind.

XXXI

Nor wholly lost we so deserv'd a prey; 121
 For storms, repenting, part of it restor'd:
Which, as a tribute from the Baltic sea,
 The British ocean sent her mighty lord.

XXXII

Go, mortals, now, and vex yourselves in vain
 For wealth, which so uncertainly must
  come:
When what was brought so far, and with
  such pain,
 Was only kept to lose it nearer home.

XXXIII

The son, who twice three months on th'
  ocean toss'd,   129
 Prepar'd to tell what he had pass'd before,
Now sees in English ships the Holland coast,
 And parents' arms in vain stretch'd from
  the shore.

XXXIV

This careful husband had been long away,
 Whom his chaste wife and little children
  mourn;
Who on their fingers learn'd to tell the day
 On which their father promis'd to return.

XXXV

(g) Such are the proud designs (g) *Such are,*
  of humankind,   *&c.* From
 And so we suffer shipwrack Petronius: *Si*
  everywhere!   *bene calculum*
Alas, what port can such a pilot *ponas, ubique*
  find,   *fragium.*
 Who in the night of fate must blindly
  steer!   140

XXXVI

The undistinguish'd seeds of good and ill,
 Heav'n, in his bosom, from our knowledge hides;
And draws them in contempt of human
  skill,
 Which oft for friends mistaken foes provides.

XXXVII

Let Munster's prelate ever be accurst,
 In whom we seek (h) the (h) *The Ger-*
  German faith in vain: *man faith.*
Alas, that he should teach the Tacitus saith
  English first,   of them: *Nul-*
 That fraud and avarice in *los mortalium*
  the Church could reign! *fide aut armis*
          ante Germanos
          esse.

XXXVIII

Happy, who never trust a stranger's will,
 Whose friendship's in his interest understood!   150

Since money giv'n but tempts him to be
    ill,
    When pow'r is too remote to make him
        good.

XXXIX

Till now, alone the mighty nations strove;
    The rest, at gaze, without the lists did
        stand:
And threat'ning France, plac'd   War declar'd
    like a painted Jove,   by France.
Kept idle thunder in his lifted hand.

XL

That eunuch guardian of rich Holland's
    trade,
    Who envies us what he wants pow'r
        t' enjoy;
Whose noiseful valor does no foe invade,
    And weak assistance will his friends de-
        stroy: 160

XLI

Offended that we fought without his leave,
    He takes this time his secret hate to
        show;
Which Charles does with a mind so calm
    receive,
    As one that neither seeks nor shuns his
        foe.

XLII

With France, to aid the Dutch, the Danes
    unite:
    France as their tyrant, Denmark as their
        slave.
But when with one three nations join to
    fight,
    They silently confess that one more
        brave.

XLIII

Lewis had chas'd the English from his
    shore,
    But Charles the French as subjects does
        invite: 170
Would Heav'n for each some Solomon re-
    store,
    Who, by their mercy, may decide their
        right!

XLIV

Were subjects so but only by their choice,
    And not from birth did forc'd dominion
        take,

Our prince alone would have the public
    voice;
    And all his neighbors' realms would de-
        sarts make.

XLV

He without fear a dangerous war pursues,
    Which without rashness he began be-
        fore:
As honor made him first the danger choose,
    So still he makes it good on virtue's
        score.   180

XLVI

The doubled charge his subjects' love sup-
    plies,
    Who, in that bounty, to themselves are
        kind:
So glad Egyptians see their Nilus rise,
    And in his plenty their abundance find.

XLVII

With equal pow'r he does two chiefs cre-
    ate,
    Two such as each seem'd   Prince Rupert
        worthiest when alone;   and Duke Al-
Each able to sustain a nation's bemarle sent to
    fate,   sea.
    Since both had found a greater in their
        own.

XLVIII

Both great in courage, conduct, and in
    fame,
    Yet neither envious of the other's
        praise;   190
Their duty, faith, and int'rest too the same,
    Like mighty partners equally they raise.

XLIX

The prince long time had courted Fortune's
    love,
    But once possess'd did absolutely reign:
Thus with their *Amazons* the *heroes* strove,
    And conquer'd first those beauties they
        would gain.

L

The duke beheld, like Scipio, with dis-
    dain,
    That Carthage which he ruin'd rise once
        more;
And shook aloft the fasces of the main,
    To fright those slaves with what they felt
        before.   200

LI

Together to the wat'ry camp they haste,
 Whom matrons passing to
  their children show:
Infants' first vows for them to
  heav'n are cast,
 And (i) future people bless
  them as they go.

(i) *Future peo-
ple. Examina
infantium fu-
turusque popu-
lus.* — PLIN.
JUN. in *Pan.
ad Traj.*

LII

With them no riotous pomp, nor Asian
  train,
 T' infect a navy with their gaudy fears;
To make slow fights, and victories but vain;
 But war, severely, like itself, appears.

LIII

Diffusive of themselves, where'er they pass,
 They make that warmth in others they
  expect;   210
Their valor works like bodies on a glass,
 And does its image on their men project.

LIV

Our fleet divides, and straight the Dutch
  appear,
 In number, and a fam'd
  commander, bold:
The narrow seas can scarce
  their navy bear,
 Or crowded vessels can their soldiers
  hold.

Duke of
Albemarle's
battle, first
day.

LV

The duke, less numerous, but in courage
  more,
 On wings of all the winds to combat flies:
His murdering guns a loud defiance roar,
 And bloody crosses on his flagstaffs
  rise.   220

LVI

Both furl their sails, and strip them for
  the fight,
 Their folded sheets dismiss the useless
  air:
(j) Th' Elean plains could
 boast no nobler sight,
When struggling champions
 did their bodies bare.

(j) *Th' Elean,*
&c. Where the
Olympic games
were cele-
brated.

LVII

Borne each by other in a distant line,
 The sea-built forts in dreadful order
  move:

So vast the noise, as if not
 fleets did join,
But (k) lands unfix'd and
 floating nations strove.

(k) *Lands un-
fix'd, from*
Virgil : *Credas
innare revul-
sas Cycladas,*
&c.

LVIII

Now pass'd, on either side they nimbly
  tack;
 Both strive to intercept and guide the
  wind: 230
And, in its eye, more closely they come
  back,
 To finish all the deaths they left behind.

LIX

On high-rais'd decks the haughty Belgians
  ride,
 Beneath whose shade our humble frigates
  go:
Such port the elephant bears, and so defied
 By the rhinoceros her unequal foe.

LX

And as the built, so different is the
  fight;
 Their mounting shot is on our sails design'd:
Deep in their hulls our deadly bullets light,
 And thro' the yielding planks a passage
  find.   240

LXI

Our dreaded admiral from far they threat,
 Whose batter'd rigging their whole war
  receives:
All bare, like some old oak which tempests
  beat,
 He stands, and sees below his scatter'd
  leaves.

LXII

Heroes of old, when wounded, shelter
  sought;
 But he, who meets all danger with disdain,
Ev'n in their face his ship to anchor brought,
 And steeple-high stood propp'd upon the
  main.

LXIII

At this excess of courage, all amaz'd,
 The foremost of his foes a while withdraw: 250

With such respect in enter'd Rome they
  gaz'd,
  Who on high chairs the godlike fathers
    saw.

LXIV

And now, as where Patroclus' body lay,
  Here Trojan chiefs advanc'd, and there
    the Greek;
Ours o'er the duke their pious wings dis-
  play,
  And theirs the noblest spoils of Britain
    seek.

LXV

Meantime his busy mariners he hastes,
  His shatter'd sails with rigging to restore;
And willing pines ascend his broken masts,
  Whose lofty heads rise higher than be-
    fore.   260

LXVI

Straight to the Dutch he turns his dreadful
  prow,
  More fierce th' important quarrel to de-
    cide:
Like swans, in long array his vessels show,
  Whose crests, advancing, do the waves
    divide.

LXVII

They charge, recharge, and all along the
  sea
  They drive, and squander the huge Bel-
    gian fleet.
Berkeley alone, who nearest danger lay,
  Did a like fate with lost Creüsa meet.

LXVIII

The night comes on, we eager to pursue
  The combat still, and they asham'd to
    leave: 270
Till the last streaks of dying day withdrew,
  And doubtful moonlight did our rage de-
    ceive.

LXIX

In th' English fleet each ship resounds with
  joy,
  And loud applause of their great leader's
    fame:
In fiery dreams the Dutch they still de-
  stroy,
  And, slumb'ring, smile at the imagin'd
    flame.

LXX

Not so the Holland fleet, who, tir'd and done,
  Stretch'd on their decks like weary oxen
    lie:
Faint sweats all down their mighty mem-
  bers run,
  (Vast bulks, which little souls but ill sup-
    ply.)   280

LXXI

In dreams they fearful precipices tread;
  Or, shipwrack'd, labor to some distant
    shore:
Or in dark churches walk among the dead;
  They wake with horror, and dare sleep no
    more.

LXXII

The morn they look on with unwilling eyes,
  Till from their maintop joyful news
    they hear   Second day's
Of ships, which by their mold battle.
  bring new supplies,
  And in their colors Belgian lions bear.

LXXIII

Our watchful general had dis-   (1) *His face,*
  cern'd from far   *&c. Spem*
This mighty succor, which   *vultu simu-*
  made glad the foe;   290   *lat, premit*
He sigh'd, but, like a father of *alto corde*
  the war,   *dolorem.* —
  (1) His face spake hope, while deep his VIRGIL.
    sorrows flow.

LXXIV

His wounded men he first sends off to shore,
  (Never, till now, unwilling to obey:)
They not their wounds, but want of strength
  deplore,
  And think them happy who with him can
    stay.

LXXV

Then to the rest: "Rejoice," said he, "to-
  day;
  In you the fortune of Great Britain lies:
Among so brave a people, you are they
  Whom Heav'n has chose to fight for such
    a prize.   300

LXXVI

"If number English courages could quell,
  We should at first have shunn'd, not met,
    our foes,

Whose numerous sails the fearful only
    tell:
    Courage from hearts, and not from num-
      bers, grows."

LXXVII

He said, nor needed more to say: with
    haste
    To their known stations cheerfully they
      go;
And all at once, disdaining to be last,
    Solicit every gale to meet the foe.

LXXVIII

Nor did th' incourag'd Belgians long de-
    lay,
    But bold in others, not themselves, they
      stood: 310
So thick, our navy scarce could steer their
    way,
    But seem'd to wander in a moving wood.

LXXIX

Our little fleet was now ingag'd so far,
    That, like the swordfish in the whale, they
      fought:
The combat only seem'd a civil war,
    Till thro' their bowels we our passage
      wrought.

LXXX

Never had valor, no, not ours, before
    Done aught like this upon the land or
      main,
Where not to be o'ercome was to do more
    Than all the conquests former kings did
      gain.   320

LXXXI

The mighty ghosts of our great Harries
    rose,
    And armed Edwards look'd, with anx-
      ious eyes,
To see this fleet among unequal foes,
    By which fate promis'd them their
      Charles should rise.

LXXXII

Meantime the Belgians tack upon our
    rear,
    And raking chase-guns thro' our sterns
      they send:
Close by, their fire-ships, like jackals, ap-
    pear,
    Who on their lions for the prey attend.

LXXXIII

Silent in smoke of cannons they come on:
    (Such vapors once did fiery Cacus hide:)
In these the height of pleas'd revenge is
    shown,   331
    Who burn contented by another's side.

LXXXIV

Sometimes, from fighting squadrons of each
    fleet,
    (Deceiv'd themselves, or to preserve
      some friend,)
Two grappling Ætnas on the ocean meet,
    And English fires with Belgian flames
      contend.

LXXXV

Now, at each tack, our little fleet grows
    less;
    And, like maim'd fowl, swim lagging on
      the main;
Their greater loss their numbers scarce
    confess,
    While they lose cheaper than the Eng-
      lish gain.   340

LXXXVI

Have you not seen, when, whistled from the
    fist,
    Some falcon stoops at what her eye de-
      sign'd,
And, with her eagerness the quarry miss'd,
    Straight flies at check, and clips it down
      the wind;

LXXXVII

The dastard crow, that to the wood made
    wing,
    And sees the groves no shelter can afford,
With her loud caws her craven kind does
    bring,
    Who, safe in numbers, cuff the noble
      bird ?

LXXXVIII

Among the Dutch thus Albemarle did fare:
    He could not conquer, and disdain'd to
      fly;   350
Past hope of safety, 't was his latest care,
    Like falling Cæsar, decently to die.

LXXXIX

Yet pity did his manly spirit move,
    To see those perish who so well had
      fought;

And generously with his despair he strove,
    Resolv'd to live till he their safety
        wrought.

XC

Let other Muses write his prosp'rous fate,
    Of conquer'd nations tell, and kings re-
        stor'd;
But mine shall sing of his eclips'd estate,
    Which, like the sun's, more wonders does
        afford.   360

XCI

He drew his mighty frigates all before,
    On which the foe his fruitless force em-
        ploys:
His weak ones deep into his rear he bore,
    Remote from guns, as sick men from the
        noise.

XCII

His fiery cannon did their passage guide,
    And foll'wing smoke obscur'd them from
        the foe:
Thus Israel safe from the Egyptian's pride,
    By flaming pillars, and by clouds did go.

XCIII

Elsewhere the Belgian force we did de-
        feat,
    But here our courages did theirs sub-
        due;   370
So Xenophon once led that fam'd retreat,
    Which first the Asian empire overthrew.

XCIV

The foe approach'd; and one, for his bold
        sin,
    Was sunk; (as he that touch'd the ark
        was slain:)
The wild waves master'd him and suck'd
        him in,
    And smiling eddies dimpled on the main.

XCV

This seen, the rest at awful distance stood;
    As if they had been there as servants
        set,
To stay, or to go on, as he thought good, 379
    And not pursue, but wait on his retreat.

XCVI

So Libyan huntsmen, on some sandy plain,
    From shady coverts rous'd, the lion
        chase:

The kingly beast roars out with
    loud disdain,
    (m) And slowly moves, un-
    knowing to give place.

    (m) The simile is Virgil's: *Vestigia retro improperata refert*, &c.

XCVII

But if some one approach to dare his force,
    He swings his tail, and swiftly turns him
        round;
With one paw seizes on his trembling horse,
    And with the other tears him to the
        ground.

XCVIII

Amidst these toils succeeds the
    balmy night;   389
    Now hissing waters the
    quench'd guns restore;
And (n) weary waves, with-
    drawing from the fight,
Lie lull'd and panting on the
    silent shore.

    (n) *Weary waves:* from Statius, *Sylvæ: Nec trucibus fluviis idem sonus: occidit horror Æquoris, antennis maria acclinata quiescunt.*

XCIX

The moon shone clear on the becalmed
    flood,
    Where, while her beams like glittering
        silver play,
Upon the deck our careful gen-
    eral stood,
    And deeply mus'd on the
    (o) succeeding day.

    (o) The third of June, famous for two former victories.

C

" That happy sun," said he, " will rise
        again,
    Who twice victorious did our navy see;
And I alone must view him rise in vain,
    Without one ray of all his star for me. 400

CI

" Yet like an English gen'ral will I die,
    And all the ocean make my spacious
        grave:
Women and cowards on the land may lie;
    The sea 's a tomb that 's proper for the
        brave."

CII

Restless he pass'd the remnants of the
        night,
    Till the fresh air proclam'd the morning
        nigh;
And burning ships, the martyrs of the fight,
    With paler fires beheld the eastern sky.

CIII

But now, his stores of ammunition spent,
　His naked valor is his only guard;　410
Rare thunders are from his dumb cannon
　　sent,
And solitary guns are scarcely　Third day.
　　heard.

CIV

Thus far had Fortune pow'r, here forc'd to
　　stay,
　Nor longer durst with virtue be at strife:
This, as a ransom, Albemarle did pay
　For all the glories of so great a life.

CV

For now brave Rupert from afar appears,
　Whose waving streamers the glad gen-
　　eral knows:
With full-spread sails his eager navy steers,
　And every ship in swift proportion grows.

CVI

The anxious prince had heard the cannon
　　long,　421
　And from that length of time dire *omens*
　　drew
Of English overmatch'd, and Dutch too
　　strong,
　Who never fought three days, but to pur-
　　sue.

CVII

Then, as an eagle, who with pious care
　Was beating widely on the wing for prey,
To her now silent *eyry* does repair,
　And finds her callow infants forc'd away;

CVIII

Stung with her love, she stoops upon the
　　plain,
　The broken air loud whistling as she
　　flies,　430
She stops and listens, and shoots forth
　　again,
　And guides her pinions by her young
　　ones' cries:

CIX

With such kind passion hastes the prince
　　to fight,
　And spreads his flying canvas to the sound;
Him, whom no danger, were he there,
　　could fright,
　Now, absent, every little noise can wound.

CX

As in a drought the thirsty creatures cry,
　And gape upon the gather'd clouds for
　　rain;
And first the martlet meets it in the sky,
　And with wet wings joys all the fea-
　　ther'd train.　·　·　440

CXI

With such glad hearts did our despairing
　　men
　Salute th' appearance of the prince's fleet;
And each ambitiously would claim the ken
　That with first eyes did distant safety
　　meet.

CXII

The Dutch, who came like greedy hinds
　　before,
　To reap the harvest their ripe ears did
　　yield;
Now look like those, when rolling thunders
　　roar,
　And sheets of lightning blast the stand-
　　ing field.

CXIII

Full in the prince's passage, hills of sand
　And dang'rous flats in secret ambush lay,
Where the false tides skim o'er the cov-
　　er'd land,　451
　And seamen with dissembled depths be-
　　tray.

CXIV

The wily Dutch, who, like fall'n angels,
　　fear'd
　This new *Messiah's* coming, there did
　　wait,
And round the verge their braving vessels
　　steer'd,
　To tempt his courage with so fair a bait.

CXV

But he, unmov'd, contemns their idle threat,
　Secure of fame whene'er he please to
　　fight:
His cold experience tempers all his heat,
　And inbred worth doth boasting valor
　　slight.　460

CXVI

Heroic virtue did his actions guide,
　And he the substance, not the appearance
　　chose;

To rescue one such friend he took more
    pride
Than to destroy whole thousands of such
    foes.

CXVII

But when approach'd, in strict embraces
    bound,
Rupert and Albemarle together grow;
He joys to have his friend in safety found,
    Which he to none but to that friend
    would owe.

CXVIII

The cheerful soldiers, with new stores sup-
    plied,
    Now long to execute their spleenful
    will;   470
And in revenge for those three days they
    tried,
    Wish one, like Joshua's, when the sun
    stood still.

CXIX

Thus reinforc'd, against the adverse fleet,
    Still doubling ours, brave Rupert leads
    the way:
With the first blushes of the Fourth day's
    morn they meet, battle
    And bring night back upon the new-born
    day.

CXX

His presence soon blows up the kindling
    fight,
    And his loud guns speak thick like angry
    men:
It seem'd as slaughter had been breath'd
    all night,
    And Death new pointed his dull dart
    again.   480

CXXI

The Dutch too well his mighty conduct
    knew,
    And matchless courage, since the former
    fight:
Whose navy like a stiff-stretch'd cord did
    shew,
    Till he bore in and bent them into flight.

CXXII

The wind he shares, while half their fleet
    offends
    His open side, and high above him shows:

Upon the rest at pleasure he descends,
    And, doubly harm'd, he double harms
    bestows.

CXXIII

Behind, the gen'ral mends his (p) *So glides,*
    weary pace   *&c. From Vir-*
And sullenly to his revenge *gil : Quum me-*
    he sails;   490 *diu nexus, ex-*
                           tremæque ag-
(p) So glides some trodden *mina caudæ*
    serpent on the grass, *Solvuntur; tar-*
And long behind his wounded *dosque trahit*
    volume trails.   *sinus ultimus*
                             orbes, &c.

CXXIV

Th' increasing sound is borne to either
    shore,
    And for their stakes the throwing nations
    fear:
Their passion double with the cannons' roar.
    And with warm wishes each man combats
    there.

CXXV

Plied thick and close as when the fight be-
    gun,
    Their huge unwieldy navy wastes away;
So sicken waning moons too near the sun,
    And blunt their crescents on the edge of
    day.   500

CXXVI

And now reduc'd on equal terms to fight,
    Their ships like wasted patrimonies show;
Where the thin scatt'ring trees admit the
    light,
    And shun each other's shadows as they
    grow.

CXXVII

The warlike prince had sever'd from the
    rest
    Two giant ships, the pride of all the
    main;
Which with his one so vigorously he press'd,
    And flew so home they could not rise
    again.

CXXVIII

Already batter'd, by his lee they lay;
    In vain upon the passing winds they call:
The passing winds thro' their torn canvas
    play,   511
    And flagging sails on heartless sailors
    fall.

CXXIX

Their open'd sides receive a gloomy light,
  Dreadful as day let in to shades below;
Without, grim Death rides barefac'd in
    their sight,
  And urges ent'ring billows as they flow.

CXXX

When one dire shot, the last they could
    supply,
  Close by the board the prince's mainmast
    bore:
All three now, helpless, by each other lie,
  And this offends not, and those fear no
    more.   520

CXXXI

So have I seen some fearful hare main-
    tain
  A course, till tir'd before the dog she
    lay;
Who, stretch'd behind her, pants upon the
    plain,
  Past pow'r to kill, as she to get away:

CXXXII

With his loll'd tongue he faintly licks his
    prey;
  His warm breath blows her flix up as she
    lies;
She, trembling, creeps upon the ground
    away,
  And looks back to him with beseeching
    eyes.

CXXXIII

The prince unjustly does his stars accuse,
  Which hinder'd him to push his fortune
    on;   530
For what they to his courage did refuse,
  By mortal valor never must be done.

CXXXIV

This lucky hour the wise Batavian takes,
  And warns his tatter'd fleet to follow
    home:
Proud to have so got off with (q) From
    equal stakes,   Horace: *Quos*
  (q) Where 't was a triumph *opimus Fallere*
    not to be o'ercome.   *et effugere*
                            est triumphus.

CXXXV

The general's force, as kept alive by fight,
  Now, not oppos'd, no longer can pur-
    sue:

[CXXXV cont.]

Lasting till Heav'n had done his courage
    right;
  When he had conquer'd, he his weakness
    knew.   540

CXXXVI

He casts a frown on the departing foe,
  And sighs to see him quit the wat'ry
    field:
His stern fix'd eyes no satisfaction show
  For all the glories which the fight did
    yield.

CXXXVII

Tho', as when fiends did miracles avow,
  He stands confess'd ev'n by the boastful
    Dutch;
He only does his conquest disavow,
  And thinks too little what they found too
    much.

CXXXVIII

Return'd, he with the fleet resolv'd to stay;
  No tender thoughts of home his heart
    divide;   550
Domestic joys and cares he puts away;
  For realms are households which the
    great must guide.

CXXXIX

As those who unripe veins in mines explore,
  On the rich bed again the warm turf lay,
Till time digests the yet imperfect ore,
  And know it will be gold another day:

CXL

So looks our monarch on this early fight,
  Th' essay and rudiments of great success;
Which all-maturing time must bring to
    light,
  While he, like Heav'n, does each day's
    labor bless.   560

CXLI

Heav'n ended not the first or second day,
  Yet each was perfect to the work de-
    sign'd:
God and kings work, when they their work
    survey,
  And passive aptness in all subjects find.

CXLII

In burden'd vessels first, with speedy care,
  His plenteous stores do season'd timber
    send:

Thither the brawny carpenters
    repair,
And as the surgeons of
    maim'd ships attend.   *His Majesty repairs the fleet.*

CXLIII

With cord and canvas from rich Hamburg
    sent,
  His navies' molted wings he imps once
    more;   570
Tall Norway fir, their masts in battle spent,
  And English oak, sprung leaks and
    planks, restore.

CXLIV

All hands employ'd, (r) the
    royal work grows
    warm: (r) *Fervet opus : the same similitude in Virgil.*
  Like laboring bees on a long summer's
    day,
Some sound the trumpet for the rest to
    swarm,
  And some on bells of tasted lilies play;

CXLV

With gluey wax some new foundations lay
  Of virgin combs, which from the roof
    are hung;
Some arm'd within doors upon duty stay,
  Or tend the sick, or educate the
    young.   580

CXLVI

So here, some pick out bullets from the
    sides,
  Some drive old oakum thro' each seam
    and rift:
Their left hand does the calking-iron guide,
  The rattling mallet with the right they
    lift.

CXLVII

With boiling pitch another near at hand,
  From friendly Sweden brought, the
    seams instops:
Which well paid o'er, the salt sea waves
    withstand,
  And shakes them from the rising beak in
    drops.

CXLVIII

Some the gall'd ropes with dauby marling
    bind,
  Or searcloth masts with strong tarpauling
    coats: 590

To try new shrouds one mounts into the
    wind,
  And one, below, their ease or stiffness
    notes.

CXLIX

Our careful monarch stands in person by,
  His new-cast cannons' firmness to ex-
    plore:
The strength of big-corn'd powder loves to
    try,
  And ball and cartrage sorts for every
    bore.

CL

Each day brings fresh supplies of arms
    and men,
  And ships which all last winter were
    abroad;
And such as fitted since the fight had
    been,
  Or new from stocks were fall'n into the
    road.   600

CLI

The goodly London in her gal-
    lant trim,   *Loyal London describ'd.*
  (The Phœnix daughter of the vanish'd
    old,)
Like a rich bride does to the ocean swim,
  And on her shadow rides in floating
    gold.

CLII

Her flag aloft, spread ruffling to the
    wind,
  And sanguine streamers seem the flood
    to fire:
The weaver, charm'd with what his loom
    design'd,
  Goes on to sea, and knows not to retire.

CLIII

With roomy decks, her guns of mighty
    strength,
  Whose low-laid mouths each mounting
    billow laves: 610
Deep in her draught, and warlike in her
    length,
  She seems a sea-wasp flying on the
    waves.

CLIV

This martial present, piously design'd,
  The loyal city give their best-lov'd king:

And, with a bounty ample as the wind,
Built, fitted, and maintain'd, to aid him
bring.

CLV

By viewing Nature, Nature's **Digression**
handmaid Art   **concerning**
Makes mighty things from **shipping and**
small beginnings grow: **navigation.**
Thus fishes first to shipping did impart
Their tail the rudder, and their head the
prow.   620

CLVI

Some log, perhaps, upon the waters swam,
An useless drift, which, rudely cut
within,
And hollow'd, first a floating trough be-
came,
And cross some riv'let passage did begin.

CLVII

In shipping such as this, the Irish *kern*,
And untaught Indian, on the stream did
glide:
Ere sharp-keel'd boats to stem the flood
did learn,
Or fin-like oars did spread from either
side.

CLVIII

Add but a sail, and Saturn so appear'd,
When from lost empire he to exile
went,   630
And with the golden age to Tiber steer'd,
Where coin and first commerce he did
invent.

CLIX

Rude as their ships was navigation then;
No useful compass or meridian known;
Coasting, they kept the land within their
ken,
And knew no North but when the Pole-
star shone.

CLX

Of all who since have us'd the open
sea,
Than the bold English none more fame
have won;
(s) Beyond the year, and out (s) *Extra*
of heav'n's high way,   *anni solisque*
They   make   discoveries *vias.* — VIRG.
where they see no sun.   640

CLXI

But what so long in vain, and yet unknown,
By poor mankind's benighted wit is
sought,
Shall in this age to Britain first be shown,
And hence be to admiring nations
taught.

CLXII

The ebbs of tides and their mysterious
flow,
We, as arts' elements, shall understand,
And as by line upon the ocean go,
Whose paths shall be familiar as the
land.

CLXIII

(t) Instructed ships shall sail (t) By a
to quick commerce,   **more exact**
By which remotest regions **measure of**
                           longitude.
are allied;   650
Which makes one city of the universe;
Where some may gain, and all may be
supplied.

CLXIV

Then, we upon our globe's last verge shall
go,
And view the ocean leaning on the sky:
From thence our rolling neighbors we shall
know,
And on the lunar world securely pry.

CLXV

This I foretell from your auspicious care,
Who great in search of God and Nature
grow;
Who best your wise Creator's **Apostrophe to**
praise declare,   **the Royal**
Since best to praise his works **Society.**
is best to know.   660

CLXVI

O truly Royal ! who behold the law
And rule of beings in your Maker's mind;
And thence, like limbecs, rich ideas draw,
To fit the level'd use of humankind.

CLXVII

But first the toils of war we must endure,
And from th' injurious Dutch redeem
the seas.
War makes the valiant of his right secure,
And gives up fraud to be chastis d with
ease.

CLXVIII

Already were the Belgians on our coast,
 Whose fleet more mighty every day became   670
By late success, which they did falsely
 boast,
 And now by first appearing seem'd to
  claim.

CLXIX

Designing, subtile, diligent, and close,
 They knew to manage war with wise de-
  lay:
Yet all those arts their vanity did cross,
 And, by their pride, their prudence did
  betray.

CLXX

Nor stay'd the English long; but, well sup-
 plied,
 Appear as numerous as th' insulting foe:
The combat now by courage must be tried,
 And the success the braver nation show.

CLXXI

There was the Plymouth squadron now
 come in,   681
 Which in the Straits last winter was
  abroad;
Which twice on Biscay's working bay had
 been,
 And on the midland sea the French had
  aw'd.

CLXXII

Old expert Allen, loyal all along,
 Fam'd for his action on the Smyrna
  fleet;
And Holmes, whose name shall live in epic
 song,
 While music numbers, or while verse
  has feet;

CLXXIII

Holmes, the Achates of the gen'rals' fight,
 Who first bewitch'd our eyes with Guinea
  gold,   690
As once old Cato in the Romans' sight
 The tempting fruits of Afric did unfold.

CLXXIV

With him went Sprag, as bountiful as
 brave,
 Whom his high courage to command had
  brought;

Harman, who did the twice-fir'd Harry save,
 And in his burning ship undaunted fought;

CLXXV

Young Hollis, on a Muse by Mars begot,
 Born, Cæsar-like, to write and act great
  deeds:
Impatient to revenge his fatal shot,
 His right hand doubly to his left succeeds.

CLXXVI

Thousands were there in darker fame that
 dwell,   701
 Whose deeds some nobler poem shall
  adorn;
And tho' to me unknown, they, sure, fought
 well,
 Whom Rupert led, and who were British
  born.

CLXXVII

Of every size an hundred fighting sail,
 So vast the navy now at anchor rides,
That underneath it the press'd waters fail,
 And with its weight it shoulders off the
  tides.

CLXXVIII

Now, anchors weigh'd, the seamen shout so
 shrill,
 That heav'n, and earth, and the wide
  ocean rings;   710
A breeze from westward waits their sails to
 fill,
 And rests in those high beds his downy
  wings.

CLXXIX

The wary Dutch this gathering storm foresaw,
 And durst not bide it on the English
  coast:
Behind their treach'rous shallows they withdraw,
 And there lay snares to catch the British
  host.

CLXXX

So the false spider, when her nets are
 spread,
 Deep ambush'd in her silent den does lie,
And feels far off the trembling of her
 thread,
 Whose filmy cord should bind the struggling fly;   720

CLXXXI

Then, if at last she find him fast beset,
  She issues forth, and runs along her loom:
She joys to touch the captive in her net,
  And drags the little wretch in triumph
    home.

CLXXXII

The Belgians hop'd that, with disorder'd
    haste,
  Our deep-cut keels upon the sands might
    run;
Or, if with caution leisurely were pass'd,
  Their numerous gross might charge us
    one by one.

CLXXXIII

But with a fore-wind pushing them above,
  And swelling tide that heav'd them from
    below,   730
O'er the blind flats our warlike squadrons
    move,
  And with spread sails to welcome battle
    go.

CLXXXIV

It seem'd as there the British Neptune
    stood,
  With all his hosts of waters at command,
Beneath them to submit th' (u) *Levat ipse*
    officious flood,   *tridenti,*
  (u) And with his trident *Et vastas ape-*
    shov'd them off the sand. *rit syrtes, &c.*
                              — Virg.

CLXXXV

To the pale foes they suddenly draw near,
  And summon them to unexpected fight;
They start like murderers when ghosts ap-
    pear,
  And draw their curtains in the dead of
    night.   740

CLXXXVI

Now van to van the foremost Second battle.
    squadrons meet,
  The midmost battles hast'ning up behind;
Who view, far off, the storm of falling
    sleet,
  And hear their thunder rattling in the
    wind.

CLXXXVII

At length the adverse admirals appear;
  (The two bold champions of each coun-
    try's right:)

Their eyes describe the lists as they come
    near,
  And draw the lines of death before they
    fight.

CLXXXVIII

The distance judg'd for shot of every
    size,
  The linstocks touch, the pond'rous ball
    expires: 750
The vig'rous seaman every porthole plies,
  And adds his heart to every gun he fires.

CLXXXIX

Fierce was the fight on the proud Belgians'
    side,
  For honor, which they seldom sought be-
    fore;
But now they by their own vain boasts were
    tied,
  And forc'd at least in shew to prize it
    more.

CXC

But sharp remembrance on the English
    part,
  And shame of being match'd by such a
    foe,
Rouse conscious virtue up in (v) *Possunt,*
    every heart,   *quia posse*
  (v) And seeming to be *videntur.* —
    stronger makes them so. Virg.

CXCI

Nor long the Belgians could that fleet sus-
    tain,   761
  Which did two gen'rals' fates, and
    Cæsar's bear:
Each several ship a victory did gain,
  As Rupert or as Albemarle were there.

CXCII

Their batter'd admiral too soon withdrew,
  Unthank'd by ours for his unfinish'd fight;
But he the minds of his Dutch masters
    knew,
  Who call'd that providence which we
    call'd flight.

CXCIII

Never did men more joyfully obey,
  Or sooner understood the sign to fly: 770
With such alacrity they bore away,
  As if to praise them all the States stood
    by.

CXCIV

O famous leader of the Belgian fleet,
  Thy monument inscrib'd such praise shall
    wear,
As Varro, timely flying, once did meet,
  Because he did not of his Rome despair.

CXCV

Behold that navy, which a while before
  Provok'd the tardy English close to fight,
Now draw their beaten vessels close to
    shore,
  As larks lie dar'd to shun the hobby's
    flight.   780

CXCVI

Whoe'er would English monuments survey,
  In other records may our courage know:
But let them hide the story of this day,
  Whose fame was blemish'd by too base a
    foe.

CXCVII

Or if too busily they will enquire
  Into a victory which we dis-
    dain;   (w) *Patron*
Then let them know, the Bel-   *saint:* St.
    gians did retire   James, on
  (w) Before the patron saint   whose day
    of injur'd Spain.   this victory
                                     was gain'd.

CXCVIII

Repenting   England   this   revengeful
    day   (x) *Philip's*
  (x) To Philip's manes did an   *manes:* Philip
    off'ring bring: 790   the Second of
England, which first, by lead-   Spain, against
    ing them astray,   whom the Hol-
  Hatch'd up rebellion to de-   landers, rebel-
    stroy her king.   ling, were
                                     aided by Queen
                                     Elizabeth.

CXCIX

Our fathers bent their baneful industry
  To check a monarchy that slowly grew;
But did not France or Holland's fate fore-
    see,
  Whose rising pow'r to swift dominion
    flew.

CC

In fortune's empire blindly thus we go,
  And wander after pathless destiny;
Whose dark resorts since prudence cannot
    know,   799
  In vain it would provide for what shall be.

CCI

But whate'er English to the blest shall
    go,
  And the fourth Harry or first Orange
    meet;
Find him disowning of a Burbon foe,
  And him detesting a Batavian fleet.

CCII

Now on their coasts our conquering navy
    rides,
  Waylays their merchants, and their land
    besets;
Each day new wealth without their care
    provides;
  They lie asleep with prizes in their nets.

CCIII

So, close behind some promontory lie   809
  The huge leviathans t' attend their prey;
And give no chase, but swallow in the
    fry,
  Which thro' their gaping jaws mistake
    the way.

CCIV

Nor was this all: in ports and roads remote,
  Destructive fires among whole fleets we
    send;   Burning of the
Triumphant flames upon the   fleet in the
    water float,   Vlie by Sir
  And outbound ships at home   Robert
    their voyage end.   Holmes.

CCV

Those various squadrons, variously de-
    sign'd,
  Each vessel freighted with a several load,
Each squadron waiting for a several wind,
  All find but one, to burn them in the road.

CCVI

Some bound for Guinea, golden sand to find,
  Bore all the gauds the simple natives
    wear;   822
Some, for the pride of Turkish courts de-
    sign'd,
  For folded *turbants* finest *Holland* bear.

CCVII

Some English wool, vex'd in a Belgian
    loom,
  And into cloth of spongy softness made,
Did into France or colder Denmark doom,
  To ruin with worse ware our staple trade.

CCVIII

Our greedy seamen rummage every hold,
  Smile on the booty of each wealthier
      chest;   830
And, as the priests who with their gods
      make bold,
  Take what they like, and sacrifice the rest.

CCIX

But ah ! how unsincere are all our joys !
  Which, sent from heav'n, like lightning
      make no stay:
Their palling taste the journey's length de-
      stroys,   Transit to the
  Or grief, sent post, o'ertakes Fire of
      them on the way.   London.

CCX

Swell'd with our late successes on the foe,
  Which France and Holland wanted power
      to cross,
We urge an unseen fate to lay us low,
  And feed their envious eyes with English
      loss.   840

CCXI

Each element his dread command obeys,
  Who makes or ruins with a smile or
      frown;
Who, as by one he did our nation raise,
  So now he with another pulls us down.

CCXII

Yet London, empress of the northern clime,
  By an high fate thou greatly (y) Quum
      didst expire: mare, quum
(y) Great as the world's, which tellus correp-
      at the death of time   taque regia
Must fall, and rise a nobler   Ardeat, &c.
      frame by fire.   — Ovid.

CCXIII

As when some dire usurper Heav'n provides
  To scourge his country with a lawless
      sway,   850
His birth perhaps some petty village hides,
  And sets his cradle out of fortune's way,

CCXIV

Till fully ripe his swelling fate breaks out,
  And hurries him to mighty mischiefs on;
His prince, surpris'd at first, no ill could
      doubt,
  And wants the pow'r to meet it when 't is
      known.

CCXV

Such was the rise of this prodigious fire,
  Which, in mean buildings first obscurely
      bred,
From thence did soon to open streets aspire,
  And straight to palaces and temples
      spread.   860

CCXVI

The diligence of trades and noiseful gain,
  And luxury, more late, asleep were laid:
All was the Night's, and in her silent reign
  No sound the rest of nature did invade.

CCXVII

In this deep quiet, from what source un-
      known,
  Those seeds of fire their fatal birth dis-
      close;
And first, few scatt'ring sparks about were
      blown,
  Big with the flames that to our ruin rose.

CCXVIII

Then, in some close-pent room it crept along,
  And, smould'ring as it went, in silence
      fed;   870
Till th' infant monster, with devouring
      strong,
  Walk'd boldly upright with exalted head.

CCXIX

Now, like some rich or mighty murderer,
  Too great for prison, which he breaks
      with gold;
Who fresher for new mischiefs does appear,
  And dares the world to tax him with the
      old;

CCXX

So scapes th' insulting fire his narrow jail,
  And makes small outlets into open air;
There the fierce winds his tender force
      assail,
  And beat him downward to his first re-
      pair.   880

CCXXI

(z) The winds, like crafty (z) Like craf-
      courtesans, withheld   ty, &c. Hæc
  His flames from burning, but arte tracta-
      to blow them more: virum, ut
And, every fresh attempt, he is illius ani-
      repell'd   mum inopia
  With faint denials, weaker than before. accenderet.

CCXXII

And now, no longer letted of his prey,
  He leaps up at it with inrag'd desire;
O'erlooks the neighbors with a wide survey,
  And nods at every house his threat'ning
    fire.

CCXXIII

The ghosts of traitors from the Bridge de-
    scend,
  With bold fanatic specters to rejoice; 890
About the fire into a dance they bend,
  And sing their sabbath notes with feeble
    voice.

CCXXIV

Our guardian angel saw them where he
    sate
  Above the palace of our slumb'ring king:
He sigh'd, abandoning his charge to fate,
  And, drooping, oft look'd back upon the
    wing.

CCXXV

At length the crackling noise and dreadful
    blaze
  Call'd up some waking lover to the sight;
And long it was ere he the rest could
    raise,
  Whose heavy eyelids yet were full of
    night.   900

CCXXVI

The next to danger, hot pursued by fate,
  Half-cloth'd, half-naked, hastily retire;
And frighted mothers strike their breasts,
    too late,
  For helpless infants left amidst the fire.

CCXXVII

Their cries soon waken all the dwellers
    near;
  Now murmuring noises rise in every
    street;
The more remote run stumbling with their
    fear,
  And in the dark men justle as they meet.

CCXXVIII

So weary bees in little cells repose;
  But if night-robbers lift the well-stor'd
    hive,   910
An humming thro' their waxen city grows,
  And out upon each other's wings they
    drive.

CCXXIX

Now streets grow throng'd and busy as by
    day:
  Some run for buckets to the hallow'd choir:
Some cut the pipes, and some the engines
    play;
  And some more bold mount ladders to
    the fire.

CCXXX

In vain; for from the East a Belgian wind
  His hostile breath thro' the dry rafters
    sent;
The flames impell'd soon left their foes be-
    hind,
  And forward with a wanton fury went. 920

CCXXXI

A key of fire ran all along the shore,
  (a) And lighten'd all the river (a) *Sigœa igni*
    with a blaze; *freta lata re-*
The waken'd tides began again *lucent. —*
    to roar, *VIRG.*
  And wond'ring fish in shining waters gaze.

CCXXXII

Old father Thames rais'd up his reverend
    head,
  But fear'd the fate of Simoeis would re-
    turn:
Deep in his *ooze* he sought his sedgy bed,
  And shrunk his waters back into his urn.

CCXXXIII

The fire, meantime, walks in a broader
    gross;
  To either hand his wings he opens wide:
He wades the streets, and straight he
    reaches cross,   931
  And plays his longing flames on th' other
    side.

CCXXXIV

At first they warm, then scorch, and then
    they take;
  Now with long necks from side to side
    they feed;
At length, grown strong, their mother-fire
    forsake,
  And a new colony of flames succeed.

CCXXXV

To every nobler portion of the town
  The curling billows roll their restless
    tide:

In parties now they straggle up and down,
  As armies, unoppos'd, for prey divide. 940

CCXXXVI

One mighty squadron, with a side-wind
    sped,
  Thro' narrow lanes his cumber'd fire
    does haste,
By pow'rful charms of gold and silver led,
  The Lombard bankers and the Change to
    waste.

CCXXXVII

Another backward to the Tow'r would go,
  And slowly eats his way against the
    wind;
But the main body of the marching foe
  Against th' imperial palace is design'd.

CCXXXVIII

Now day appears, and with the day the
    king,
  Whose early care had robb'd him of his
    rest: 950
Far off the cracks of falling houses ring,
  And shrieks of subjects pierce his tender
    breast.

CCXXXIX

Near as he draws, thick harbingers of
    smoke
  With gloomy pillars cover all the place;
Whose little intervals of night are broke
  By sparks that drive against his sacred
    face.

CCXL

More than his guards his sorrows made
    him known,
  And pious tears, which down his cheeks
    did show'r:
The wretched in his grief forgot their own;
  (So much the pity of a king has pow'r.)

CCXLI

He wept the flames of what he lov'd so
    well,   961
  And what so well had merited his love:
For never prince in grace did more excel,
  Or royal city more in duty strove.

CCXLII

Nor with an idle care did he behold:
  (Subjects may grieve, but monarchs
    must redress;)

He cheers the fearful, and commends the
    bold,
  And makes despairers hope for good
    success.

CCXLIII

Himself directs what first is to be done,
  And orders all the succors which they
    bring: 970
The helpful and the good about him run,
  And form an army worthy such a king.

CCXLIV

He sees the dire contagion spread so fast,
  That, where it seizes, all relief is vain;
And therefore must unwillingly lay waste
  That country which would, else, the foe
    maintain.

CCXLV

The powder blows up all before the fire:
  Th' amazed flames stand gather'd on a
    heap;
And from the precipice's brink retire,
  Afraid to venture on so large a leap. 980

CCXLVI

Thus fighting fires a while themselves con-
    sume,
  But straight, like Turks, forc'd on to win
    or die,
They first lay tender bridges of their fume,
  And o'er the breach in unctuous vapors
    fly.

CCXLVII

Part stays for passage, till a gust of wind
  Ships o'er their forces in a shining sheet:
Part, creeping under ground, their journey
    blind,
  And, climbing from below, their fellows
    meet.

CCXLVIII

Thus to some desert plain, or old wood-side,
  Dire night-hags come from far to dance
    their round;   990
And o'er broad rivers on their fiends they
    ride,
  Or sweep in clouds above the blasted
    ground.

CCXLIX

No help avails: for, *hydra*-like, the fire
  Lifts up his hundred heads to aim his way,

And scarce the wealthy can one half retire,
Before he rushes in to share the prey.

CCL

The rich grow suppliant, and the poor grow
proud;
Those offer mighty gain, and these ask
more:
So void of pity is th' ignoble crowd,
When others' ruin may increase their
store. 1000

CCLI

As those who live by shores with joy behold
Some wealthy vessel split or stranded
nigh,
And from the rocks leap down for shipwrack'd gold,
And seek the tempests which the others
fly:

CCLII

So these but wait the owners' last despair,
And what 's permitted to the flames invade:
Ev'n from their jaws they hungry morsels
tear,
And on their backs the spoils of Vulcan
lade.

CCLIII

The days were all in this lost labor spent;
And when the weary king gave place to
night, 1010
His beams he to his royal brother lent,
And so shone still in his reflective light.

CCLIV

Night came, but without darkness or re-
pose,
A dismal picture of the gen'ral doom;
Where souls distracted, when the trumpet
blows,
And half unready with their bodies come.

CCLV

Those who have homes, when home they do
repair,
To a last lodging call their wand'ring
friends:
Their short uneasy sleeps are broke with
care,
To look how near their own destruction
tends. 1020

CCLVI

Those who have none, sit round where once
it was,
And with full eyes each wonted room require;
Haunting the yet warm ashes of the place,
As murder'd men walk where they did
expire.

CCLVII

Some stir up coals, and watch the vestal fire,
Others in vain from sight of ruin run;
And, while thro' burning lab'rinths they re-
tire,
With loathing eyes repeat what they
would shun.

CCLVIII

The most in fields like herded beasts lie
down,
To dews obnoxious on the grassy floor;
And while their babes in sleep their sorrows
drown, 1031
Sad parents watch the remnants of their
store.

CCLIX

While by the motion of the flames they guess
What streets are burning now, and what
are near,
An infant, waking, to the paps would press,
And meets, instead of milk, a falling
tear.

CCLX

No thought can ease them but their sovereign's care,
Whose praise th' afflicted as their comfort sing:
Ev'n those whom want might drive to just
despair, 1039
Think life a blessing under such a king.

CCLXI

Meantime he sadly suffers in their grief,
Out-weeps an hermit, and out-prays a
saint:
All the long night he studies their relief,
How they may be supplied, and he may
want.

CCLXII

"O God," said he, "thou pa- King's prayer.
tron of my days,
Guide of my youth in exile and distress !

Who me unfriended brought'st by wondrous
ways,
The kingdom of my fathers to possess:

CCLXIII

" Be thou my judge, with what unwearied
care
I since have labor'd for my people's
good;   1050
To bind the bruises of a civil war,
And stop the issues of their wasting
blood.

CCLXIV

" Thou, who hast taught me to forgive the
ill,
And recompense, as friends, the good
misled;
If mercy be a precept of thy will,
Return that mercy on thy servant's head.

CCLXV

" Or, if my heedless youth has stepp'd
astray,
Too soon forgetful of thy gracious hand;
On me alone thy just displeasure lay,
But take thy judgments from this mourn-
ing land.   1060

CCLXVI

" We all have sinn'd, and thou hast laid us
low,
As humble earth from whence at first we
came:
Like flying shades before the clouds we
show,
And shrink like parchment in consuming
flame.

CCLXVII

" O let it be enough what thou hast done;
When spotted deaths ran arm'd thro'
every street,
With poison'd darts, which not the good
could shun,
The speedy could out-fly, or valiant meet.

CCLXVIII

" The living few, and frequent funerals
then,
Proclaim'd thy wrath on this forsaken
place;   1070
And now those few who are return'd again,
Thy searching judgments to their dwellings trace.

CCLXIX

" O pass not, Lord, an absolute decree,
Or bind thy sentence unconditional;
But in thy sentence our remorse foresee,
And, in that foresight, this thy doom re-
call.

CCLXX

" Thy threatings, Lord, as thine thou mayst
revoke;
But, if immutable and fix'd they stand,
Continue still thyself to give the stroke,
And let not foreign foes oppress thy
land."   1080

CCLXXI

Th' Eternal heard, and from the heav'nly
choir
Chose out the cherub with the flaming
sword;
And bade him swiftly drive th' approaching
fire
From where our naval magazins were
stor'd.

CCLXXII

The blessed minister his wings display'd,
And like a shooting star he cleft the
night;
He charg'd the flames, and those that disobey'd
He lash'd to duty with his sword of
light.

CCLXXIII

The fugitive flames, chastis'd, went forth
to prey
On pious structures, by our fathers
rear'd;   1090
By which to heav'n they did affect the way,
Ere faith in churchmen without works
was heard.

CCLXXIV

The wanting orphans saw with wat'ry eyes
Their founders' charity in dust laid low;
And sent to God their ever-answer'd cries,
(For he protects the poor, who made
them so.)

CCLXXV

Nor could thy fabric, Paul's, defend thee
long,
Tho' thou wert sacred to thy Maker's
praise;

Tho' made immortal by a poet's song,
And poets' songs the Theban walls could
raise.   1100

CCLXXVI

The daring flames peep'd in, and saw from
far
The awful beauties of the sacred choir;
But, since it was profan'd by civil war,
Heav'n thought it fit to have it purg'd by
fire.

CCLXXVII

Now down the narrow streets it swiftly
came,
And, widely opening, did on both sides
prey:
This benefit we sadly owe the flame,
If only ruin must enlarge our way.

CCLXXVIII

And now four days the sun had seen our
woes;
Four nights the moon beheld th' inces-
sant fire: 1110
It seem'd as if the stars more sickly rose,
And farther from the fev'rish north retire.

CCLXXIX

In th' empyrean heaven, (the blest abode,)
The Thrones and the Dominions pros-
trate lie,
Not daring to behold their angry God;
And an hush'd silence damps the tuneful
sky.

CCLXXX

At length th' Almighty cast a pitying eye,
And mercy softly touch'd his melting
breast:
He saw the town's one half in rubbish lie,
And eager flames drive on to storm the
rest.   1120

CCLXXXI

An hollow crystal pyramid he takes,
In firmamental waters dipp'd above;
Of it a broad extinguisher he makes
And hoods the flames that to their
quarry strove.

CCLXXXII

The vanquish'd fires withdraw from every
place,
Or, full with feeding, sink into a sleep:

Each household genius shews again his face,
And from the hearths the little Lares
creep.

CCLXXXIII

Our king this more than natural change
beholds;
With sober joy his heart and eyes
abound: 1130
To the All-good his lifted hands he folds,
And thanks him low on his redeemed
ground.

CCLXXXIV

As when sharp frosts had long constrain'd
the earth,
A kindly thaw unlocks it with mild rain;
And first the tender blade peeps up to
birth,
And straight the green fields laugh with
promis'd grain:

CCLXXXV

By such degrees the spreading gladness
grew
In every heart which fear had froze before;
The standing streets with so much joy they
view,
That with less grief the perish'd they
deplore.   1140

CCLXXXVI

The father of the people open'd wide
His stores, and all the poor with plenty
fed:
Thus God's anointed God's own place sup-
plied,
And fill'd the empty with his daily bread.

CCLXXXVII

This royal bounty brought its own reward,
And in their minds so deep did print the
sense,
That if their ruins sadly they regard,
'T is but with fear the sight might drive
him thence.

CCLXXXVIII

But so may he live long, that town to sway,
Which by his auspice they
will nobler make,   1150
As he will hatch their ashes by
his stay,
And not their humble ruins now forsake

*City's request
to the king
not to leave
them.*

CCLXXXIX

They have not lost their loyalty by fire;
  Nor is their courage or their wealth so
    low,
That from his wars they poorly would re-
    tire,
  Or beg the pity of a vanquish'd foe.

CCXC

Not with more constancy the Jews of
    old,
  By Cyrus from rewarded exile sent,
Their royal city did in dust behold,   1159
  Or with more vigor to rebuild it went.

CCXCI

The utmost malice of their stars is past,
  And two dire comets, which have scourg'd
    the town,
In their own plague and fire have breath'd
    their last,
  Or, dimly, in their sinking sockets frown.

CCXCII

Now frequent trines the happier lights
    among,
  And high-rais'd Jove, from his dark
    prison freed,
(Those weights took off that on his planet
    hung,)
  Will gloriously the new-laid works suc-
    ceed.

CCXCIII

Methinks already, from this chymic flame,
  I see a city of more precious mold,   1170
Rich as the town which gives
    the (b) Indies name,   (b) Mexico.
  With silver pav'd, and all divine with
    gold.

CCXCIV

Already, laboring with a mighty fate,
  She shakes the rubbish from her mount-
    ing brow,
And seems to have renew'd her charter's
    date,
  Which Heav'n will to the death of time
    allow.

CCXCV

More great than human, now, and more
    (c) august.   (c) Augusta,
  New-deified she from her the old name
  fires does rise: of London.

CCXCVI

Her widening streets on new foundations
    trust,   1179
  And, opening, into larger parts she flies.

CCXCVI

Before, she like some shepherdess did show,
  Who sate to bathe her by a river's side;
Not answering to her fame, but rude and
    low,
  Nor taught the beauteous arts of modern
    pride.

CCXCVII

Now, like a maiden queen, she will behold,
  From her high turrets, hourly suitors
    come:
The East with incense, and the West with
    gold,
  Will stand, like suppliants, to receive her
    doom.

CCXCVIII

The silver Thames, her own domestic flood,
  Shall bear her vessels like a sweeping
    train;   1190
And often wind, (as of his mistress proud,)
  With longing eyes to meet her face
    again.

CCXCIX

The wealthy Tagus, and the wealthier
    Rhine,
  The glory of their towns no more shall
    boast;
And Seine, that would with Belgian rivers
    join,
  Shall find her luster stain'd, and traffic
    lost.

CCC

The vent'rous merchant, who design'd more
    far,
  And touches on our hospitable shore,
Charm'd with the splendor of this northern
    star,
  Shall here unlade him, and depart no
    more.   1200

CCCI

Our pow'rful navy shall no longer meet,
  The wealth of France or Holland to in-
    vade;
The beauty of this town, without a fleet,
  From all the world shall vindicate her
    trade.

CCCII

And, while this fam'd emporium we pre-
    pare,
The British ocean shall such triumphs
    boast,
That those who now disdain our trade to
    share,
Shall rob like pirates on our wealthy coast.

CCCIII

Already we have conquer'd half the war,
And the less dang'rous part is left behind;

Our trouble now is but to make them
    dare,   1211
And not so great to vanquish as to
    find.

CCCIV

Thus to the eastern wealth thro' storms we
    go,
But now, the Cape once doubled, fear no
    more;
A constant trade-wind will securely blow,
And gently lay us on the spicy shore.

POEMS WRITTEN BETWEEN 1667 AND 1680

PROLOGUE, EPILOGUE, AND SONG FROM SECRET LOVE

OR, THE MAIDEN QUEEN

[Pepys saw "*The Maiden Queen*, a new play
of Dryden's," on March 2, 1667. The play
was entered on the *Stationers' Register* on
August 7 of that year (Malone, I, 1, 69); the
first edition is dated 1668. The epilogue
printed with the play was "by a person of
honor;" that given below is taken from *The
Covent Garden Drollery*, a small miscellany
published in 1672, which contains a large
number of prologues and epilogues, some of
them known to be by Dryden. This piece,
however, has been shown not to be his work:
see *Notes*, pp. 1048, 1049. The song is one
which the *Maiden Queen* "made of" her lover
Philocles and "call'd . . . *Secret Love*."]

PROLOGUE

I

HE who writ this, not without pains and
    thought
From French and English theaters has
    brought
Th' exactest rules by which a play is
    wrought:

II

The unities of action, place, and time;
The scenes unbroken; and a mingled chime
Of Jonson's humor with Corneille's rhyme.

III

But while dead colors he with care did lay,
He fears his wit or plot he did not weigh,
Which are the living beauties of a play.

IV

Plays are like towns, which, howe'er forti-
    fied   10
By engineers, have still some weaker side
By the o'er-seen defendant unespied.

V

And with that art you make approaches now;
Such skilful fury in assaults you show,
That every poet without shame may bow.

VI

Ours therefore humbly would attend your
    doom,
If, soldier-like, he may have terms to come
With flying colors and with beat of drum.

[*The* PROLOGUE *goes out, and stays while a tune is play'd,
after which he returns again.*

SECOND PROLOGUE

I had forgot one half, I do protest,   19
And now am sent again to speak the rest.
He bows to every great and noble wit; ⎫
But to the little Hectors of the pit   ⎬
Our poet's sturdy, and will not submit. ⎭
He 'll be beforehand with 'em, and not stay
To see each peevish critic stab his play:
Each puny censor, who, his skill to boast,
Is cheaply witty on the poet's cost.
No critic's verdict should of right stand
    good;
They are excepted all, as men of blood;
And the same law should shield him from
    their fury   30
Which has excluded butchers from a jury.
You 'd all be wits —
But writing 's tedious, and that way may fail;

The most compendious method is to rail;
Which you so like, you think yourselves ill
    us'd
When in smart prologues you are not
    abus'd.
A civil prologue is approv'd by no man;
You hate it as you do a civil woman:
Your fancy's pall'd, and liberally you pay
To have it quicken'd, ere you see a play;
Just as old sinners, worn from their de-
    light,   41
Give money to be whipp'd to appetite.
But what a pox keep I so much ado
To save our poet? He is one of you;
A brother judgment, and, as I hear say,
A cursed critic as e'er damn'd a play.
Good salvage gentlemen, your own kind
    spare;
He is, like you, a very wolf or bear.
Yet think not he 'll your ancient rights in-
    vade,
Or stop the course of your free damning
    trade;   50
For he, he vows, at no friend's play can sit,
But he must needs find fault to shew his
    wit.
Then, for his sake, ne'er stint your own de-
    light;
Throw boldly, for he sets to all that write:
With such he ventures on an even lay,
For they bring ready money into play.
Those who write not, and yet all writers
    nick,
Are bankrupt gamesters, for they damn on
    tick.

EPILOGUE

THE Prologue durst not tell, before 't was
    seen,
The plot we had to swinge *The Maiden
    Queen*;
For had we then discover'd our intent,
The fop who writ it had not giv'n consent.
Or the new peaching trick at least had
    shown,
And brought in others' faults to hide his
    own.
That wit he has been by his betters taught,
When he 's accus'd to shew another's fault.
When one wit 's hunted hard, by joint ⎤
    consent |
Another claps betwixt and does prevent 10 ⎬
His death, for many hares still foil the |
    scent.   ⎦

Thus our poor poet would have scap'd to-
    day,
But from the herd I singled out his play.
Then heigh along with me —
Both great and small, you poets of the
    town,
And Nell will love you, [f]or to run him
    down.

SONG

I

I FEED a flame within, which so torments
    me,
That it both pains my heart, and yet con-
    tents me:
'T is such a pleasing smart, and I so love it,
That I had rather die then once remove it.

II

Yet he for whom I grieve shall never
    know it;
My tongue does not betray, nor my eyes
    show it:
Not a sigh, nor a tear, my pain discloses,
But they fall silently, like dew on roses.

III

Thus to prevent my love from being cruel,
My heart's the sacrifice, as 't is the fuel: 10
And while I suffer this, to give him quiet,
My faith rewards my love, tho' he deny it.

IV

On his eyes will I gaze, and there delight
    me;
Where I conceal my love, no frown can
    fright me:
To be more happy, I dare not aspire;
Nor can I fall more low, mounting no
    higher.

PROLOGUE AND EPILOGUE TO THE WILD GALLANT, REVIV'D

[See note on p. 18, above.]

PROLOGUE

As some raw squire, by tender mother bred,
Till one and twenty keeps his maiden-
    head,
(Pleas'd with some sport, which he alone
    does find,

And thinks a secret to all humankind,)
Till mightily in love, yet half afraid,
He first attempts the gentle dairymaid.
Succeeding there, and led by the renown
Of Whetstone's Park, he comes at length to
    town,
Where enter'd, by some school-fellow or
    friend,
He grows to break glass windows in the
    end;   10
His valor too, which with the watch began,
Proceeds to duel, and he kills his man.
By such degrees, while knowledge he did
    want,
Our unfletch'd author writ a *Wild Gallant.*
He thought him monstrous lewd (I 'll lay
    my life)
Because suspected with his landlord's wife;
But, since his knowledge of the town be-
    gan,
He thinks him now a very civil man;
And, much asham'd of what he was be-
    fore,
Has fairly play'd him at three wenches
    more.   20
'T is some amends his frailties to confess:
Pray pardon him his want of wickedness.
He 's towardly, and will come on apace;
His frank confession shows he has some
    grace.
You balk'd him when he was a young be-
    ginner,
And almost spoil'd a very hopeful sinner;
But, if once more you slight his weak in-
    deavor,
For aught I know, he may turn tail for
    ever.

EPILOGUE

Of all dramatic writing, comic wit,
As 't is the best, so 't is most hard to hit,
For it lies all in level to the eye,
Where all may judge, and each defect may
    spy.
Humor is that which every day we meet,
And therefore known as every public street;
In which, if e'er the poet go astray,
You all can point, 't was there he lost his
    way.
But, what 's so common, to make pleasant
    too,
Is more than any wit can always do.   10
For 't is like Turks, with hen and rice to
    treat:

To make regalios out of common meat.
But, in your diet, you grow salvages:
Nothing but human flesh your taste can
    please;
And, as their feasts with slaughter'd slaves
    began,
So you, at each new play, must have a
    man.
Hither you come, as to see prizes fought;
If no blood 's drawn, you cry, the prize is
    naught.
But fools grow wary now; and, when they
    see
A poet eyeing round the company,   20
Straight each man for himself begins to
    doubt;
They shrink like seamen when a press comes
    out.
Few of 'em will be found for public use,
Except you charge an oaf upon each house,
Like the trainbands, and every man ingage
For a sufficient fool, to serve the stage.
And when, with much ado, you get him
    there,
Where he in all his glory should appear,
Your poets make him such rare things to
    say,
That he 's more wit than any man i' th'
    play;   30
But of so ill a mingle with the rest,
As when a parrot 's taught to break a
    jest.
Thus, aiming to be fine, they make a show,
As tawdry squires in country churches
    do.
Things well consider'd, 't is so hard to make
A comedy which should the knowing take,
That our dull poet, in despair to please,
Does humbly beg, by me, his writ of ease.
'T is a land tax, which he 's too poor to pay;
You therefore must some other impost
    lay.   40
Would you but change, for serious plot and
    verse,
This motley garniture of fool and farce,
Nor scorn a mode, because 't is taught at
    home,
Which does, like vests, our gravity become,
Our poet yields you should this play re-
    fuse:
As tradesmen, by the change of fashions,
    lose,
With some content, their fripperies of
    France,
In hope it may their staple trade advance.

~UE, EPILOGUE, AND ~ONGS FROM SIR MARTIN MAR-ALL

OR, THE FEIGN'D INNOCENCE

[This comedy is an adaptation of Molière's *L'Étourdi*. Downes states that the Duke of Newcastle gave Dryden a bare translation from Molière, which our poet adapted for the English stage. Pepys saw the play on August 16, 1667, when he terms it "the new play acted yesterday . . . made by my Lord Duke of Newcastle, but, as everybody says, corrected by Dryden." It was entered on the *Stationers' Register* June 24, 1668 (Malone, I, 1, 93), as the Duke's play, and published anonymously in that year. Dryden's name did not appear on the title-page until 1691.

The first song is printed also in *Westminster Drollery; or, a Choice Collection of the Newest Songs and Poems*, 1671.]

PROLOGUE

FOOLS, which each man meets in his dish
    each day,
Are yet the great regalios of a play;
In which to poets you but just appear,
To prize that highest which cost them so
    dear.
Fops in the town more easily will pass;
One story makes a statutable ass:
But such in plays must be much thicker
    sown,
Like yolks of eggs, a dozen beat to one.
Observing poets all their walks invade,
As men watch woodcocks gliding thro' a
    glade;   10
And when they have enough for comedy,
They stow their several bodies in a pie:
The poet 's but the cook to fashion it,
For, gallants, you yourselves have found
    the wit.
To bid you welcome would your bounty
    wrong;
None welcome those who bring their cheer
    along.

EPILOGUE

As country vicars, when the sermon 's
    done,
Run huddling to the benediction;
Well knowing, tho' the better sort may
    stay,
The vulgar rout will run unblest away:

So we, when once our play is done, make
    haste
With a short epilogue to close your taste.
In thus withdrawing we seem mannerly,
But when the curtain 's down we peep and
    see
A jury of the wits who still stay late,
And in their club decree the poor play's
    fate: 10
Their verdict back is to the boxes brought;
Thence all the town pronounces it their
    thought.
Thus, gallants, we like Lilly can foresee;
But if you ask us what our doom will
    be,
We by to-morrow will our fortune cast,
As he tells all things when the year is
    past.

SONGS

I

I

MAKE ready, fair lady, to-night,
    And stand at the door below;
For I will be there
To receive you with care,
    And to your true love you shall go.

II

THE LADY'S ANSWER

And when the stars twinkle so bright,
    Then down to the door will I creep;
To my love will I fly,
Ere the jealous can spy,
    And leave my old daddy asleep.

II

I

BLIND love, to this hour,
Had never, like me, a slave under his
    power.
    Then blest be the dart
    That he threw at my heart,
        For nothing can prove
A joy so great as to be wounded with love.

II

My days and my nights
Are fill'd to the purpose with sorrows and
    frights:
    From my heart still I sigh,
    And my eyes are ne'er dry;   10

So that, Cupid be prais'd,
I am to the top of love's happiness rais'd.

III

My soul's all on fire,
So that I have the pleasure to dote and de-
      sire:
Such a pretty soft pain
That it tickles each vein;
      'T is the dream of a smart,
Which makes me breathe short when it
      beats at my heart.

IV

Sometimes in a pet,
When I am despis'd, I my freedom would
      get;   20
But straight a sweet smile
Does my anger beguile,
      And my heart does recall;
Then the more I do struggle, the lower I
      fall.

V

Heaven does not impart
Such a grace as to love unto ev'ry one's
      heart;
For many may wish
To be wounded, and miss:
      Then blest be love's fire,
And more blest her eyes that first taught
      me desire.   30

PROLOGUE AND EPILOGUE TO THE TEMPEST

OR, THE ENCHANTED ISLAND

[This play was an adaptation and debase-
ment of Shakespeare, by Sir William Davenant and Dryden. It was first acted, as the
epilogue shows, in 1667. Pepys saw a first-
day production of *The Tempest*, undoubtedly
this version, on November 7 of that year. It
was not printed until 1670. The style of prologue and epilogue clearly shows them to be
the work of the younger adapter.]

PROLOGUE

As, when a tree's cut down, the secret root
Lives under ground, and thence new branches
      shoot;
So from old Shakespeare's honor'd dust, this
      day

Springs up and buds a new reviving play:
Shakespeare, who (taught by none) did first
      impart
To Fletcher wit, to laboring Jonson art.
He, monarch-like, gave those, his subjects,
      law;
And is that nature which they paint and
      draw.
Fletcher reach'd that which on his heights
      did grow,   9
Whilst Jonson crept, and gather'd all below.
This did his love, and this his mirth digest:
One imitates him most, the other best.
If they have since outwrit all other men,
'T is with the drops which fell from Shake-
      speare's pen.
The storm which vanish'd on the neigh-
      b'ring shore,
Was taught by Shakespeare's *Tempest* first
      to roar.
That innocence and beauty which did smile
In Fletcher, grew on this *Enchanted Isle.*
But Shakespeare's magic could not copied
      be;
Within that circle none durst walk but he. 20
I must confess 't was bold, nor would you
      now
That liberty to vulgar wits allow,
Which works by magic supernatural things;
But Shakespeare's pow'r is sacred as a
      king's.
Those legends from old priesthood were re-
      ceiv'd,
And he then writ, as people then believ'd.
But if for Shakespeare we your grace im-
      plore,
We for our theater shall want it more:
Who by our dearth of youths are forc'd
      t' employ
One of our women to present a boy;   30
And that's a transformation, you will say,
Exceeding all the magic in the play.
Let none expect in the last act to find
Her sex transform'd from man to woman-
      kind.
Whate'er she was before the play began,
All you shall see of her is perfect man.
Or if your fancy will be farther led
To find her woman, it must be abed.

EPILOGUE

GALLANTS, by all good signs it does appear
That sixty-seven's a very damning year,
For knaves abroad, and for ill poets here.

Among the Muses there's a gen'ral rot:
The rhyming Mounsieur and the Spanish
        plot,
Defy or court, all's one, they go to pot.

The ghosts of poets walk within this place,
And haunt us actors wheresoe'er we pass,
In visions bloodier than King Richard's
        was.   9

For this poor wretch he has not much to say,
But quietly brings in his part o' th' play,
And begs the favor to be damn'd to-day.

He sends me only like a sh'riff's man here,
To let you know the malefactor's near,
And that he means to die *en cavalier.*

For if you should be gracious to his pen,
Th' example will prove ill to other men,
And you'll be troubled with 'em all again.

PROLOGUE TO ALBUMAZAR, REVIV'D

[This play was written by Thomas Tomkis,
of Trinity College, Cambridge, where it was
acted March 9, 1615, on the occasion of a visit
by King James I. Pepys saw a revival of it,
doubtless that for which Dryden wrote this
prologue, on February 22, 1668. The prologue
is printed anonymously in the *Covent Garden
Drollery,* 1672; and with Dryden's name in
Miscellany Poems, 1684, from which this text
is taken.
    Since *The Alchemist* was acted in 1610, there
is no possible truth in Dryden's assertion in
lines 5–10.]

To say, this comedy pleas'd long ago,
Is not enough to make it pass you now.
Yet, gentlemen, your ancestors had wit;
When few men censur'd, and when fewer
        writ.
And Jonson, of those few the best, chose
        this,
As the best model of his masterpiece.
Subtle was got by our Albumazar,
That Alchymist by his Astrologer;
Here he was fashion'd, and we may sup-
        pose
He lik'd the fashion well, who wore the
        clothes.   10
But Ben made nobly his what he did mold;
What was another's lead becomes his gold:

Like an unrighteous conqueror he reigns,
Yet rules that well, which he unjustly gains.
But this our age such authors does afford,
As make whole plays, and yet scarce write
        one word;
Who, in this anarchy of wit, rob all,
And what's their plunder, their possession
        call;
Who, like bold padders, scorn by night to
        prey,
But rob by sunshine, in the face of day: 20
Nay, scarce the common ceremony use
Of: "Stand, sir, and deliver up your
        Muse;"
But knock the poet down, and, with a
        grace,
Mount Pegasus before the owner's face.
Faith, if you have such country Toms
        abroad,
'T is time for all true men to leave that
        road.
Yet it were modest, could it but be said,
They strip the living, but these rob the
        dead;
Dare with the mummies of the Muses play,
And make love to them the Egyptian
        way;   30
Or, as a rhyming author would have said,
Join the dead living to the living dead.
Such men in poetry may claim some part:
They have the license, tho' they want the
        art;
And might, where theft was prais'd, for
        Laureats stand,
Poets, not of the head, but of the hand.
They make the benefits of others' study-
        ing,
Much like the meals of politic Jack-Pud-
        ding,
Whose dish to challenge no man has the
        courage;
'T is all his own, when once h' has spit i'
        th' porridge.   40
But, gentlemen, you're all concern'd in
        this;
You are in fault for what they do amiss:
For they their thefts still undiscover'd
        think,
And durst not steal, unless you please to
        wink.
Perhaps, you may award by your decree,
They should refund; but that can never be.
For should you letters of reprisal seal,
These men write that which no man else
        would steal.

PROLOGUE, EPILOGUE, AND SONGS FROM AN EVENING'S LOVE

OR, THE MOCK ASTROLOGER

[Mrs. Pepys saw this "new play" by Dryden on June 19, 1668. It was entered on the *Stationers' Register* on November 20 of that year (Malone, I, 1, 93), but was not printed until 1671, when two slightly different editions appeared. The fourth song is printed also in *Westminster Drollery; or, a Choice Collection of the Newest Songs and Poems*, 1671.]

PROLOGUE

WHEN first our poet set himself to write,
Like a young bridegroom on his wedding-
   night
He laid about him, and did so bestir him,
His Muse could never lie in quiet for him:
But now his honeymoon is gone and past,
Yet the ungrateful drudgery must last,
And he is bound, as civil husbands do,
To strain himself, in complaisance to you;
To write in pain, and counterfeit a bliss
Like the faint smackings of an after-kiss. 10
But you, like wives ill-pleas'd, supply his
   want:
Each writing *Monsieur* is a fresh gallant;
And tho', perhaps, 't was done as well be-
   fore,
Yet still there 's something in a new amour.
Your several poets work with several tools:
One gets you wits, another gets you fools;
This pleases you with some by-stroke of
   wit,
This finds some cranny that was never hit.
But should these jaunty lovers daily come
To do your work, like your good man at
   home, 20
Their fine small-timber'd wits would soon
   decay:
These are gallants but for a holiday.
Others you had who oft'ner have appear'd,
Whom for mere impotence you have
   cashier'd:
Such as at first came on with pomp and
   glory,
But, over-straining, soon fell flat before
   ye.
Their useless weight with patience long was
   borne,
But at the last you threw 'em off with
   scorn.

As for the poet of this present night,
Tho' now he claims in you an husband's
   right, 30
He will not hinder you of fresh delight.
He, like a seaman, seldom will appear;
And means to trouble home but thrice a
   year:
That only time from your gallants he 'll
   borrow;
Be kind to-day, and cuckold him to-mor-
   row.

EPILOGUE

MY part being small, I have had time to-
   day
To mark your various censures of our play:
First, looking for a judgment or a wit,
Like Jews I saw 'em scatter'd thro' the pit;
And where a knot of smilers lent an ear
To one that talk'd, I knew the foe was
   there.
The club of jests went round; he who had
   none
Borrow'd o' th' next, and told it for his
   own.
Among the rest they kept a fearful stir
In whisp'ring that he stole th' Astrologer; 10
And said, betwixt a French and English plot
He eas'd his half-tir'd Muse, on pace and
   trot.
Up starts a *Mounsieur*, new come o'er and
   warm
In the French stoop, and the pull-back o'
   th' arm:
"*Morbleu*," *dit-il*, and cocks, "I am a rogue,
But he has quite spoil'd *The Feign'd Astro-
   logue*."
"Pox," says another, "here 's so great a stir
With a son of a whore farce that 's regular;
A rule, where nothing must decorum
   shock!
Damme 'ts as dull as dining by the clock. 20
An evening! Why the devil should we be
   vex'd
Whether he gets the wench this night or
   next?"
When I heard this, I to the poet went,
Told him the house was full of discontent,
And ask'd him what excuse he could in-
   vent.
He neither swore nor storm'd as poets do,
But, most unlike an author, vow'd 't was
   true;
Yet said, he us'd the French like enemies,

And did not steal their plots, but made 'em
   prize.
But should he all the pains and charges
   count   30
Of taking 'em, the bill so high would
   mount
That, like prize-goods, which thro' the
   office come,
He could have had 'em much more cheap
   at home.
He still must write, and, banquier-like, each
   day
Accept new bills, and he must break or pay.
When thro' his hands such sums must
   yearly run,
You cannot think the stock is all his own.
His haste his other errors might excuse,
But there's no mercy for a guilty Muse; 39
For, like a mistress, she must stand or fall,
And please you to a height, or not at all.

SONGS

I

I

You charm'd me not with that fair face,
   Tho' it was all divine:
To be another's is the grace
   That makes me wish you mine.

II

The gods and Fortune take their part,
   Who like young monarchs fight,
And boldly dare invade that heart
   Which is another's right.

III

First, mad with hope, we undertake
   To pull up every bar;   10
But, once possess'd, we faintly make
   A dull defensive war.

IV

Now, every friend is turn'd a foe,
   In hope to get our store;
And passion makes us cowards grow,
   Which made us brave before.

II

I

After the pangs of a desperate lover,
   When day and night I have sigh'd all in
      vain,

Ah what a pleasure it is to discover,
   In her eyes pity, who causes my pain.

II

When with unkindness our love at a stand
   is,
   And both have punish'd ourselves with
      the pain,
Ah what a pleasure the touch of her hand
   is,
   Ah what a pleasure to press it again!

III

When the denial comes fainter and fainter,
   And her eyes give what her tongue does
      deny,   10
Ah what a trembling I feel when I ven-
      ture,
   Ah what a trembling does usher my joy!

IV

When, with a sigh, she accords me the
      blessing,
   And her eyes twinkle 'twixt pleasure and
      pain,
Ah what a joy 't is, beyond all expressing,
   Ah what a joy to hear: "Shall we
      again?"

III

I

Calm was the even, and clear was the
   sky,
   And the new-budding flowers did spring,
When all alone went Amyntas and I
   To hear the sweet nightingal sing.
I sate, and he laid him down by me,
   But scarcely his breath he could draw;
For when with a fear, he began to draw
   near,
   He was dash'd with: "A ha ha ha ha!"

II

He blush'd to himself, and lay still for a
   while,
   And his modesty curb'd his desire; 10
But straight I convinc'd all his fear with a
   smile,
   Which added new flames to his fire.
"O Sylvia," said he, "you are cruel,
   To keep your poor lover in awe;"
Then once more he press'd with his hand
   to my breast,
   But was dash'd with: "A ha ha ha ha!"

III

I knew 't was his passion that caus'd all his
    fears,
And therefore I pitied his case;
I whisper'd him softly: "There 's nobody
    near,"
And laid my cheek close to his face: 20
But as he grew bolder and bolder,
    A shepherd came by us and saw,
And just as our bliss we began with a kiss,
    He laugh'd out with: " A ha ha ha ha ! "

IV

I

Damon.   CELIMENA, of my heart,
    None shall e'er bereave you:
If with your good leave I may
    Quarrel with you once a day,
I will never leave you.

II

Celimena. Passion 's but an empty name
    Where respect is wanting:
Damon, you mistake your aim;
    Hang your heart, and burn your
      flame,
If you must be ranting.   10

III

Damon.   Love as dull and muddy is
    As decaying liquor:
Anger sets it on the lees,
    And refines it by degrees,
Till it works it quicker.

IV

Celimena. Love by quarrels to beget
    Wisely you endeavor;
With a grave physician's wit,
    Who, to cure an ague fit,
Put me in a fever.   20

V

Damon.   Anger rouses love to fight,
    And his only bait is:
'T is the spur to dull delight,
    And is but an eager bite,
When desire at height is.

VI

Celimena. If such drops of heat can fall
    In our wooing weather;
If such drops of heat can fall,
    We shall have the devil and all
When we come together.   30

PROLOGUE, EPILOGUE, AND SONG FROM TYRANNIC LOVE

OR, THE ROYAL MARTYR

[This heroic play, by Dryden, was probably
acted early in 1669; it was entered on the
Stationers' Register on July 14 of that year
(Malone, I, 1, 94), and published in 1670. The
epilogue was spoken by Nell Gwyn, who acted
the part of the chaste princess Valeria. The
second edition (1672) was "review'd by the
author," but the reviewing did not affect
the text of the pieces here printed.]

PROLOGUE

SELF-LOVE, which never rightly understood,
Makes poets still conclude their plays are
    good,
And malice, in all critics, reigns so high,
That for small errors they whole plays de-
    cry;
So that to see this fondness, and that
    spite,
You 'd think that none but madmen judge
    or write.
Therefore our poet, as he thinks not fit
T' impose upon you what he writes for
    wit;
So hopes, that leaving you your censures
    free,
You equal judges of the whole will be: 10
They judge but half, who only faults will
    see.
Poets, like lovers, should be bold and
    dare;
They spoil their business with an over-
    care;
And he, who servilely creeps after sense,
Is safe, but ne'er will reach an excel-
    lence.
Hence 't is, our poet, in his conjuring,
Allow'd his fancy the full scope and swing.
But when a tyrant for his theme he had,
He loos'd the reins, and bid his Muse run
    mad:
And tho' he stumbles in a full career, 20
Yet rashness is a better fault than fear.
He saw his way; but in so swift a pace,
To choose the ground might be to lose the
    race.
They then, who of each trip th' advantage
    take,
Find but those faults which they want wit
    to make.

EPILOGUE

SPOKEN BY MRS. ELLEN, WHEN SHE WAS TO
BE CARRIED OFF DEAD BY THE BEARERS

[*To the Bearer.*] Hold, are you mad ?
    you damn'd confounded dog,
I am to rise, and speak the epilogue.
    [*To the Audience.*] I come, kind gen-
    tlemen, strange news to tell ye,
I am the ghost of poor departed Nelly.
Sweet ladies, be not frighted, I 'll be civil;
I 'm what I was, a little harmless devil:
For after death, we sprites have just such
    natures
We had for all the world, when human
    creatures;
And therefore I that was an actress here,
Play all my tricks in hell, a goblin there. 10
Gallants, look to 't, you say there are no
    sprites;
But I 'll come dance about your beds at
    nights.
And faith you 'll be in a sweet kind of taking,
When I surprise you between sleep and
    waking.
To tell you true, I walk because I die
Out of my calling in a tragedy.
O poet, damn'd dull poet, who could prove
So senseless ! to make Nelly die for love !
Nay, what 's yet worse, to kill me in the
    prime
Of Easter term, in tart and cheese-cake
    time !   20
I 'll fit the fop, for I 'll not one word say
T' excuse his godly out-of-fashion play:
A play, which if you dare but twice sit out,
You 'll all be slander'd, and be thought de-
    vout.
But farewell, gentlemen, make haste to me;
I 'm sure ere long to have your company.
As for my epitaph, when I am gone,
I 'll trust no poet, but will write my own:

Here Nelly lies, who, tho' she liv'd a slattern,
Yet died a princess, acting in St. Cathar'n. 30

SONG

I

AH how sweet it is to love !
Ah how gay is young desire !
And what pleasing pains we prove
When we first approach love's fire !
    Pains of love be sweeter far
    Than all other pleasures are.

II

Sighs which are from lovers blown,
Do but gently heave the heart:
Ev'n the tears they shed alone,
Cure, like trickling balm, their smart. 10
    Lovers when they lose their breath,
    Bleed away in easy death.

III

Love and time with reverence use,
Treat 'em like a parting friend:
Nor the golden gifts refuse,
Which in youth sincere they send:
    For each year their price is more,
    And they less simple than before.

IV

Love, like spring-tides full and high,
Swells in every youthful vein;   20
But each tide does less supply,
Till they quite shrink in again:
    If a flow in age appear,
    'T is but rain, and runs not clear.

PROLOGUES, EPILOGUES, AND SONGS FROM THE CONQUEST OF GRANADA BY THE SPANIARDS

[This, Dryden's most famous heroic play, is
divided into two parts, which seem to have
been presented on successive days. It was
first acted at some time between May 8, 1670,
when a son was born to Nell Gwyn, the chief
actress in the play, and February 20, 1671,
when it was entered on the *Stationers' Register*
(Malone, I, 1, 94). The first edition is dated
1672. The second song is printed also in
*Westminster Drollery ; or, a Choice Collection of
the Newest Songs and Poems*, 1671, under the
title, *A Song at the King's House* (the Theater
Royal). The first song is twice printed in
the same collection, once under the title, *A
Vision*, and once under the same title as the
other song.]

PROLOGUE

TO THE FIRST PART

SPOKEN BY

MRS. ELLEN GWYN

IN A BROAD-BRIMM'D HAT, AND WAIST-BELT

THIS jest was first of t'other house's making,
And, five times tried, has never fail'd of
    taking;

For 't were a shame a poet should be kill'd
Under the shelter of so broad a shield.
This is that hat, whose very sight did win ye
To laugh and clap as tho' the devil were
      in ye.
As then, for Nokes, so now I hope you 'll
      be
So dull, to laugh, once more, for love of
      me.
" I 'll write a play," says one, " for I have
      got
A broad-brimm'd hat, and waist-belt,
      tow'rds a plot."   10
Says t'other: " I have one more large than
      that."
Thus they out-write each other with a hat !
The brims still grew with every play they
      writ;
And grew so large, they cover'd all the
      wit.
Hat was the play; 't was language, wit, and
      tale:
Like them that find meat, drink, and cloth
      in ale.
What dulness do these mungril wits con-
      fess,
When all their hope is acting of a dress !
Thus, two the best comedians of the age
Must be worn out, with being blocks o' th'
      stage;   20
Like a young girl who better things has
      known,
Beneath their poet's impotence they groan.
See now what charity it was to save !
They thought you lik'd, what only you
      forgave;
And brought you more dull sense, dull
      sense much worse
Than brisk gay nonsense, and the heavier
      curse.
They bring old ir'n and glass upon the
      stage,
To barter with the Indians of our age.
Still they write on, and like great authors ⎫
      show;   ⎪
But 't is as rollers in wet garden grow 30 ⎬
Heavy with dirt, and gath'ring as they go. ⎭
May none, who have so little understood,
To like such trash, presume to praise
      what 's good !
And may those drudges of the stage, whose
      fate
Is damn'd dull farce more dully to trans-
      late,
Fall under that excise the State thinks fit

To set on all French wares, whose worst is
      wit.
French farce, worn out at home, is sent
      abroad;
And, patch'd up here, is made our English
      mode.   39
Henceforth, let poets, ere allow'd to write,
Be search'd, like duelists, before they fight,
For wheel-broad hats, dull humor, all that
      chaff
Which makes you mourn, and makes the
      vulgar laugh:
For these, in plays, are as unlawful arms,
As, in a combat, coats of mail and charms.

EPILOGUE

SUCCESS, which can no more than beauty
      last,
Makes our sad poet mourn your favors
      past:
For, since without desert he got a name,
He fears to lose it now with greater shame.
Fame, like a little mistress of the town,
Is gain'd with ease, but then she 's lost as
      soon:
For as those tawdry misses, soon or late,
Jilt such as keep 'em at the highest rate;
(And oft the lackey, or the brawny clown,
Gets what is hid in the loose-bodied gown,)
So, Fame is false to all that keep her long;
And turns up to the fop that 's brisk and
      young.   12
Some wiser poet now would leave Fame
      first,
But elder wits are like old lovers curst;
Who, when the vigor of their youth is spent,
Still grow more fond, as they grow impo-
      tent.
This, some years hence, our poet's case
      may prove;
But yet, he hopes, he 's young enough to
      love.
When forty comes, if e'er he live to see
That wretched, fumbling age of poetry,   20
'T will be high time to bid his Muse adieu:
Well he may please himself, but never you.
Till then, he 'll do as well as he began,
And hopes you will not find him less a
      man.
Think him not duller for this year's de- ⎫
      lay;   ⎪
He was prepar'd, the women were away; ⎬
And men, without their parts, can hardly ⎪
      play.   ⎭

If they, thro' sickness, seldom did appear, ⎫
Pity the virgins of each theater: 29 ⎬
For, at both houses, 't was a sickly year! ⎭
And pity us, your servants, to whose cost,
In one such sickness, nine whole months
    are lost.
Their stay, he fears, has ruin'd what he
    writ:
Long waiting both disables love and wit.
They thought they gave him leisure to do
    well;
But, when they forc'd him to attend, he
    fell!
Yet, tho' he much has fail'd, he begs, to-day,
You will excuse his unperforming play:
Weakness sometimes great passion does
    express;
He had pleas'd better, had he lov'd you
    less.   40

PROLOGUE

TO THE SECOND PART

THEY who write ill, and they who ne'er durst
    write,
Turn critics, out of mere revenge and spite:
A playhouse gives 'em fame; and up there
    starts,
From a mean fifth-rate wit, a man of parts.
(So common faces on the stage appear;
We take 'em in, and they turn beauties
    here.)
Our author fears those critics as his fate;
And those he fears, by consequence, must
    hate,
For they the traffic of all wit invade,   9
As scriv'ners draw away the bankers' trade.
Howe'er, the poet 's safe enough to-day,
They cannot censure an unfinish'd play.
But, as when vizard-mask appears in pit,
Straight every man who thinks himself a
    wit
Perks up, and, managing his comb with
    grace,
With his white wig sets off his nut-brown
    face;
That done, bears up to th' prize, and views
    each limb,
To know her by her rigging and her trim;
Then, the whole noise of fops to wagers go:
" Pox on her, 't must be she;" and:
    " Damme, no!" —   20
Just so, I prophesy, these wits to-day
Will blindly guess at our imperfect play;

With what new plots our Second Part is
    fill'd,
Who must be kept alive, and who be kill'd.
And as those vizard-masks maintain that
    fashion,
To soothe and tickle sweet imagination;
So our dull poet keeps you on with masking,
To make you think there 's something worth
    your asking.
But, when 't is shown, that which does now
    delight you
Will prove a dowdy, with a face to fright
    you.   30

EPILOGUE

THEY who have best succeeded on the
    stage
Have still conform'd their genius to their
    age.
Thus Jonson did mechanic humor show,
When men were dull, and conversation low.
Then comedy was faultless, but 't was
    coarse:
Cob's tankard was a jest, and Otter's
    horse.
And, as their comedy, their love was mean;
Except, by chance, in some one labor'd
    scene
Which must atone for an ill-written play.
They rose, but at their height could seldom
    stay.   10
Fame then was cheap, and the first comer
    sped;
And they have kept it since, by being dead.
But, were they now to write, when critics
    weigh
Each line, and ev'ry word, throughout a
    play,
None of 'em, no, not Jonson in his height,
Could pass, without allowing grains for
    weight.
Think it not envy, that these truths are
    told;
Our poet 's not malicious, tho' he 's bold.
'T is not to brand 'em, that their faults are
    shown,
But, by their errors, to excuse his own.   20
If love and honor now are higher rais'd,
'T is not the poet, but the age is prais'd.
Wit 's now arriv'd to a more high degree;
Our native language more refin'd and free.
Our ladies and our men now speak more wit
In conversation, than those poets writ.
Then, one of these is, consequently, true;

That what this poet writes comes short of
    you,
And imitates you ill, (which most he fears,)
Or else his writing is not worse than theirs.
Yet, tho' you judge (as sure the critics
    will)   31
That some before him writ with greater
    skill,
In this one praise he has their fame sur-
    pass'd,
To please an age more gallant than the
    last.

SONGS

I

THE ZAMBRA DANCE

I

BENEATH a myrtle shade,
Which love for none but happy lovers made,
I slept; and straight my love before me
    brought
Phyllis, the object of my waking thought.
Undress'd she came my flames to meet,
While love strow'd flow'rs beneath her feet;
Flow'rs which, so press'd by her, became
    more sweet.

II

From the bright vision's head
A careless veil of lawn was loosely spread:
From her white temples fell her shaded
    hair,   10
Like cloudy sunshine, not too brown nor
    fair;
Her hands, her lips, did love inspire;
Her every grace my heart did fire:
But most her eyes, which languish'd with
    desire.

III

" Ah, charming fair," said I,
" How long can you my bliss and yours
    deny ?
By nature and by love this lonely shade
Was for revenge of suff'ring lovers made.
Silence and shades with love agree;
Both shelter you and favor me: 20
You cannot blush, because I cannot see."

IV

" No, let me die," she said,
" Rather than lose the spotless name of
    maid ! "

Faintly, methought, she spoke; for all the
    while
She bid me not believe her, with a smile.
" Then die," said I: she still denied;
" And is it thus, thus, thus," she cried,
" You use a harmless maid ? " — and so she
    died !

V

I wak'd, and straight I knew,
I lov'd so well, it made my dream prove
    true: 30
Fancy, the kinder mistress of the two,
Fancy had done what Phyllis would not
    do !
Ah, cruel nymph, cease your disdain,
While I can dream, you scorn in vain —
Asleep or waking, you must ease my pain.

II

I

WHEREVER I am, and whatever I do,
    My Phyllis is still in my mind;
When angry, I mean not to Phyllis to go,
    My feet, of themselves, the way find:
Unknown to myself I am just at her door,
    And, when I would rail, I can bring out
        no more,
    Than: " Phyllis too fair and unkind ! "

II

When Phyllis I see, my heart bounds in my
    breast,
    And the love I would stifle is shown;
But asleep, or awake, I am never at rest, 10
    When from my eyes Phyllis is gone.
Sometimes a sad dream does delude my sad
    mind;
    But, alas ! when I wake, and no Phyllis
    I find,
How I sigh to myself all alone !

III

Should a king be my rival in her I adore,
    He should offer his treasure in vain:
O let me alone to be happy and poor,
    And give me my Phyllis again !
Let Phyllis be mine, and but ever be kind,
    I could to a desart with her be confin'd,
    And envy no monarch his reign.   21

IV

Alas ! I discover too much of my love,
    And she too well knows her own pow'r !

She makes me each day a new martyrdom
      prove,
And makes me grow jealous each hour:
But let her each minute torment my poor
      mind,
   I had rather love Phyllis, both false and
      unkind,
      Than ever be freed from her pow'r.

III

I

He. How unhappy a lover am I,
      While I sigh for my Phyllis in vain;
   All my hopes of delight
   Are another man's right,
      Who is happy, while I am in pain!

II

She. Since her honor allows no relief,
      But to pity the pains which you
         bear,
   'T is the best of your fate,
   (In a hopeless estate,)   9
      To give o'er, and betimes to despair.

III

He. I have tried the false med'cine in vain;
   For I wish what I hope not to win:
   From without, my desire
   Has no food to its fire;
      But it burns and consumes me within.

IV

She. Yet at least 't is a pleasure to know
      That you are not unhappy alone:
   For the nymph you adore
   Is as wretched, and more;
      And accounts all your suff'rings her
         own.   20

V

He. O ye gods, let me suffer for both;
      At the feet of my Phyllis I 'll lie:
   I 'll resign up my breath,
   And take pleasure in death,
      To be pitied by her when I die.

VI

She. What her honor denied you in life,
      In her death she will give to your
         love.
   Such a flame as is true
   After fate will renew,   29
      For the souls to meet closer above.

PROLOGUE SPOKEN THE FIRST DAY OF THE KING'S HOUSE ACTING AFTER THE FIRE

[The Theater Royal in Drury Lane was
burnt on January 25, 1672. (See FitzGerald :
A New History of the English Stage, 1882;
vol. i, p. 137.) The King's Company in their
distress moved to the old playhouse in Lincoln's Inn Fields, which had recently been
vacated by their rivals, the Duke of York's
Company, in favor of a new and gaudy theater
in Dorset Gardens ; on February 26 they gave
a performance of Beaumont and Fletcher's
Wit without Money, for which Dryden wrote
this prologue (Malone, I, 1, 76). The piece is
printed anonymously in *Westminster Drollery,
the Second Part*, 1672, and in *Covent Garden
Drollery*, 1672 ; and, with Dryden's name, in
Miscellany Poems, 1684, from which the present
text and heading are taken.]

So shipwrack'd passengers escape to land,
So look they, when on the bare beach they
      stand
Dropping and cold, and their first fear
      scarce o'er,
Expecting famine on a desart shore.
From that hard climate we must wait for
      bread,
Whence ev'n the natives, forc'd by hunger,
      fled.
Our stage does human chance present to
      view,
But ne'er before was seen so sadly true:
You are chang'd too, and your pretense to see
Is but a nobler name for charity.   10
Your own provisions furnish out our feasts,
While you the founders make yourselves the
      guests.
Of all mankind beside Fate had some ⎫
      care,   ⎪
But for poor Wit no portion did prepare: ⎬
'T is left a rent-charge to the brave and ⎪
      fair.   ⎭
You cherish'd it, and now its fall you mourn,
Which blind unmanner'd zealots make their
      scorn,
Who think that fire a judgment on the stage,
Which spar'd not temples in its furious rage.
But as our new-built city rises higher, 20 ⎫
So from old theaters may new aspire,   ⎬
Since Fate contrives magnificence by fire. ⎭
Our great metropolis does far surpass
Whate'er is now, and equals all that was:
Our wit as far does foreign wit excel,
And, like a king, should in a palace dwell.

But we with golden hopes are vainly fed,
Talk high, and entertain you in a shed:
Your presence here, for which we humbly
sue,   29
Will grace old theaters, and build up new.

PROLOGUE TO ARVIRAGUS, REVIV'D

SPOKEN BY MR. HART

[*Arviragus and Philicia*, a tragi-comedy by
Lodowick Carlell, was first published in 1639.
The revival may be dated soon after the retreat of the King's Company to the old house
at Lincoln's Inn Fields. This prologue was
first printed, with title as above, in *Miscellany
Poems*, 1684.]

WITH sickly actors and an old house too,
We 're match'd with glorious theaters and
new,
And with our alehouse scenes, and clothes
bare worn,
Can neither raise old plays, nor new adorn.
If all these ills could not undo us quite,
A brisk French troop is grown your dear
delight,
Who with broad bloody bills call you each
day,
To laugh and break your buttons at their
play;
Or see some serious piece, which we presume
Is fall'n from some incomparable plume; 10
And therefore, Messieurs, if you 'll do us
grace,
Send lackeys early, to preserve your place.
We dare not on your privilege intrench,
Or ask you why you like 'em. — They are
French.
Therefore some go with courtesy exceeding,
Neither to hear nor see, but show their
breeding;
Each lady striving to out-laugh the rest,
To make it seem they understood the jest.
Their countrymen come in, and nothing pay,
To teach us English where to clap the play:
Civil, igad ! our hospitable land   21
Bears all the charge, for them to understand:
Meantime we languish, and neglected lie,
Like wives, while you keep better company;
And wish for our own sakes, without a
satire,
You 'd less good breeding, or had more
good nature.

PROLOGUE FOR THE WOMEN WHEN THEY ACTED AT THE OLD THEATER IN LINCOLN'S INN FIELDS

[The title proves that this prologue was written between February 26, 1672, when the
King's Company began performances in the
old theater, and March 26, 1674, when they
opened their new house in Drury Lane. It
probably came near the beginning of this
period ; otherwise the jests in it would have
lost their savor. It was first printed in *Miscellany Poems*, 1684.]

WERE none of you gallants e'er driven so
hard,
As when the poor kind soul was under
guard,
And could not do 't at home, in some by-
street
To take a lodging, and in private meet ?
Such is our case: we can't appoint our
house,
The lovers' old and wonted rendezvous,
But hither to this trusty nook remove;
The worse the lodging is, the more the love.
For much good pastime, many a dear sweet
hug,
Is stol'n in garrets on the humble rug.   10
Here 's good accommodation in the pit;
The grave demurely in the midst may sit,
And so the hot Burgundian on the side
Ply vizard-mask, and o'er the benches stride:
Here are convenient upper boxes too   ⎫
For those that make the most triumphant ⎬
show;   ⎭
All that keep coaches must not sit below.
There, gallants, you betwixt the acts retire,
And at dull plays have something to ad-
mire;   19
We, who look up, can your addresses mark,
And see the creatures coupled in the ark:
So we expect the *lovers, braves,* and *wits ;*
The gaudy house with scenes will serve for
cits.

PROLOGUE AND EPILOGUE TO [SECRET LOVE, OR] THE MAIDEN QUEEN, WHEN ACTED BY THE WOMEN ONLY

[These two pieces are taken from *Covent
Garden Drollery*, 1672. They must be of
about the same date as the preceding prologue.
Though they were never printed under Dry-

den's name in his lifetime, there seems no
reason to doubt his authorship of them. The
above heading is due in part to Christie.]

PROLOGUE

SPOKEN BY MRS. BOUTEL

WOMEN like us (passing for men), you'll
 cry,
Presume too much upon your secrecy.
There's not a fop in town but will pretend.
To know the cheat himself, or by his friend.
Then make no words on 't, gallants, 't is e'en
 true,
We are condemn'd to look, and strut, like
 you.
Since we thus freely our hard fate con-
 fess,
Accept us these bad times in any dress.
You'll find the sweet on 't, now old pan-
 taloons
Will go as far as formerly new gowns;
And from your own cast wigs expect no
 frowns. 11
The ladies we shall not so easily please;
They'll say: "What impudent bold things
 are these,
That dare provoke, yet cannot do us right,
Like men with huffing looks that dare not
 fight!"
But this reproach our courage must not
 daunt:
The bravest soldier may a weapon want;
Let her that doubts us still send her gal-
 lant.
Ladies, in us you'll youth and beauty find,
All things, but one, according to your mind;
And when your eyes and ears are feasted
 here, 21
Rise up and make out the short meal else-
 where.

EPILOGUE

SPOKEN BY MRS. REEVES

WHAT think you, sirs, was't not all well
 enough?
Will you not grant that we can strut and
 huff?
Men may be proud; but faith, for aught I
 see,
They neither walk nor cock so well as we.
And for the fighting part, we may in time
Grow up to swagger in heroic rhyme;
For tho' we cannot boast of equal force,

Yet at some weapons men have still the
 worse.
Why should not then we women act
 alone, 9
Or whence are men so necessary grown?
Ours are so old, they are as good as none.
Some who have tried 'em, if you'll take
 their oaths,
Swear they're as arrant tinsel as their
 clothes.
Imagine us but what we represent,
And we could e'en give you as good con-
 tent.
Our faces, shapes, all 's better than you see,
And for the rest they want as much as we.
O would the highest powers be kind to us,
And grant us to set up a female house!
We'll make ourselves to please both sexes
 then, 20
To the men women, to the women men.
Here, we presume, our legs are no ill sight,
And they would give you no ill dreams at
 night.
In dreams both sexes may their passions
 ease;
You make us then as civil as you please.
This would prevent the houses joining too,
At which we are as much displeas'd as
 you;
For all our women most devoutly swear,
Each would be rather a poor actress here
Then to be made a Mamamouchi there. 30

PROLOGUE, EPILOGUE, AND SONGS FROM MARRIAGE À LA MODE

[The date of this lively comedy, by Dryden,
is fixed by the opening lines of the prologue,
which apparently "allude to the equipment of
the fleet which afterwards engaged the Dutch
off Southwold Bay, May 28, 1672" (Malone,
I, 1, 106). The play was printed in 1673.
The prologue and epilogue, and the second of
the two songs, were printed in the *Covent
Garden Drollery*, 1672; both songs appear also
in *New Court Songs and Poems, by R. V.,
Gent.*, 1672; and the second of them in *Westminster Drollery, the Second Part*, 1672.]

PROLOGUE

LORD, how reform'd and quiet are we grown,
Since all our braves and all our wits are
 gone!

Fop-corner now is free from civil war,
White-wig and vizard make no longer jar.
France, and the fleet, have swept the town
　　so clear
That we can act in peace, and you can
　　hear.
[Those that durst fight are gone to get re-
　　nown,
And those that durst not, blush to stand in
　　town.]
'T was a sad sight, before they march'd ⎫
　　from home,　　　　　　　　　　　⎪
To see our warriors in red waistcoats ⎬
　　come,　　　　　　　　　10 ⎪
With hair tuck'd up, into our tiring-room. ⎭
But 't was more sad to hear their last
　　adieu:
The women sobb'd, and swore they would be
　　true;
And so they were, as long as e'er they ⎫
　　could,　　　　　　　　　　　　　⎪
But powerful guinea cannot be withstood, ⎬
And they were made of playhouse flesh ⎪
　　and blood.　　　　　　　　　　　⎭
Fate did their friends for double use or- ⎫
　　dain;　　　　　　　　　　　　　⎪
In wars abroad they grinning honor gain, ⎬
And mistresses for all that stay maintain. ⎭
Now they are gone, 't is dead vacation here,
For neither friends nor enemies appear. 21
Poor pensive punk now peeps ere plays be-
　　gin,
Sees the bare bench, and dares not venture
　　in;
But manages her last half-crown with care,
And trudges to the Mall, on foot, for air.
Our city friends so far will hardly come,
They can take up with pleasures nearer
　　home;
And see gay shows and gaudy scenes else-
　　where;
For we presume they seldom come to hear.
But they have now ta'en up a glorious
　　trade,　　　　　　　　　30
And cutting Morecraft struts in masquer-
　　ade.
There's all our hope, for we shall show
　　to-day
A masking ball, to recommend our play;
Nay, to endear 'em more, and let 'em see
We scorn to come behind in courtesy,
We'll follow the new mode which they be-
　　gin,
And treat 'em with a room, and couch
　　within:

For that's one way, howe'er the play fall
　　short,
T' oblige the town, the city, and the court.

EPILOGUE

THUS have my spouse and I inform'd the
　　nation,
And led you all the way to reformation;
Not with dull morals, gravely writ, like
　　those
Which men of easy phlegm with care com-
　　pose —
(Your poets of stiff words and limber sense,
Born on the confines of indifference;)
But by examples drawn, I dare to say,
From most of you who hear and see the
　　play.
There are more Rhodophils in this theater,
More Palamedes, and some few wives, I
　　fear:　　　　　　　　　10
But yet too far our poet would not run;
Tho' 't was well offer'd, there was nothing
　　done,
He would not quite the woman's frailty
　　bare,
But stripp'd 'em to the waist, and left 'em
　　there:
And the men's faults are less severely
　　shown,
For he considers that himself is one.
Some stabbing wits, to bloody satire bent,
Would treat both sexes with less compli-
　　ment;
Would lay the scene at home; of husbands
　　tell,
For wenches taking up their wives i' th'
　　Mell;　　　　　　　　　20
And a brisk bout, which each of them did
　　want,
Made by mistake of mistress and gallant.
Our modest author thought it was enough
To cut you off a sample of the stuff:
He spar'd my shame, which you, I'm sure,
　　would not,
For you were all for driving on the plot:
You sigh'd when I came in to break the
　　sport,
And set your teeth when each design fell
　　short.
To wives and servants all good wishes lend,
But the poor cuckold seldom finds a friend.
Since, therefore, court and town will take
　　no pity,　　　　　　　　　31
I humbly cast myself upon the city.

SONGS

I

I

WHY should a foolish marriage vow,
Which long ago was made,
Oblige us to each other now,
When passion is decay'd?
We lov'd, and we lov'd, as long as we
  could,
Till our love was lov'd out in us both;
But our marriage is dead, when the plea-
  sure is fled:
'T was pleasure first made it an oath.

II

If I have pleasures for a friend,
  And farther love in store,   10
What wrong has he whose joys did end,
  And who could give no more?
'T is a madness that he should be jealous
  of me,
Or that I should bar him of another:
For all we can gain is to give ourselves
  pain,
When neither can hinder the other.

II

I

WHILST Alexis lay press'd
In her arms he lov'd best,
With his hands round her neck, and his
  head on her breast,
He found the fierce pleasure too hasty to
  stay,
And his soul in the tempest just flying away.

II

When Celia saw this,
  With a sigh and a kiss,
She cried: "O my dear, I am robb'd of my
  bliss!
'T is unkind to your love, and unfaithfully
  done,   9
To leave me behind you, and die all alone."

III

The youth, tho' in haste,
  And breathing his last,
In pity died slowly, while she died more
  fast;
Till at length she cried: "Now, my dear,
  now let us go;
Now die, my Alexis, and I will die too!"

IV

Thus intranc'd they did lie,
  Till Alexis did try
To recover new breath, that again he might
  die:
Then often they died; but the more they
  did so,
The nymph died more quick, and the shep-
  herd more slow.   20

A SONG

[This *Song* and the following *Answer* to it
are found in *Covent Garden Drollery*, 1672,
and *New Court Songs and Poems, by R. V.,
Gent.*, 1672, from the latter of which collections the following texts are taken. They were
never published under Dryden's name during his lifetime. A parody of the second
stanza of the *Song* appears in the third (1675)
and later editions of *The Rehearsal*. The *Key*
to that piece, published in 1704, states that
the song ridiculed was " made by Mr. Bayes
[Dryden] on the death of Captain Digby,
son of George, Earl of Bristol, who was a
passionate admirer of the Duchess Dowager of
Richmond, called by the author Armida: he
lost his life in a sea-fight against the Dutch,
the twenty-eighth of May, 1672." The *Song*
may probably be accepted as Dryden's work;
the *Answer* has not so strong evidence in its
favor, as it may easily be the work of an imitator.

Christie suggests that another song in the
same meter in *Covent Garden Drollery*, addressed to " dear Revecchia," may also be by
Dryden, in honor of his mistress Anne Reeve.
The piece is given below (see *Appendix I*,
p. 904) among *Poems attributed to Dryden*.]

I

FAREWELL, fair Armeda, my joy and my
  grief;
In vain I have lov'd you, and find no relief;
Undone by your virtue, too strict and severe,
Your eyes gave me love, and you gave me
  despair.
Now call'd by my honor, I seek with content
A fate which in pity you would not prevent:
To languish in love, were to find by delay
A death that's more welcome the speediest
  way.

II

On seas and in battles, in bullets and fire,
The danger is less than in hopeless desire; 10
My death's wound you gave me, tho' far
    off I bear
My fate from your sight, not to cost you a
    tear.
But if the kind flood on a wave should con-
    vey,
And under your window my body should
    lay,
The wound on my breast when you happen
    to see,
You 'll say with a sigh: " It was given by
    me."

THE ANSWER

I

Blame not your Armeda, nor call her your
    grief;
'T was honor, not she, that denied you relief;
Abuse not her virtue, nor call it severe;
Who loves without honor, must meet with
    despair.
Now prompted by pity I truly lament,
And mourn for your fall, which I could
    not prevent;
I languish to think that your blood should
    defray
The expense of a fate, tho' so noble a way.

II

On seas and in battles that you did expire
Was th' effect of your valor, not hopeless
    desire; 10
Of the fame you acquir'd I greedily hear,
And grieve when I think that it cost you
    so dear.
And when dismal fate did your body convey
By my window, your funeral rites for to pay,
I sigh that your fate I could not reverse,
And all my kind wishes I strew on your
    hearse.

PROLOGUE, EPILOGUE, AND
SONG FROM THE ASSIGNA-
TION

OR, LOVE IN A NUNNERY

[Ravenscroft, in his prologue to *The Careless Lovers*, produced in Lent, 1673, exults
over the failure of Dryden's comedy, *The Assig-*
nation as if it were a recent event. The play
was probably produced late in 1672. It was
entered on the *Stationers' Register* March 18,
1673 (Malone, I, 1, 107), and published in the
same year.]

PROLOGUE

Prologues, like bells to churches, toll you
    in
With chiming verse, till the dull plays be-
    gin:
With this sad difference, tho', of pit and
    pew,
You damn the poet, but the priest damns
    you.
But priests can treat you at your own ex-
    pense,
And gravely call you fools, without offense.
Poets, poor devils, have ne'er your folly
    shown,
But, to their cost, you prov'd it was their
    own;
For, when a fop 's presented on the stage,
Straight all the coxcombs in the town in-
    gage: 10
For his deliverance and revenge they join,
And grunt, like hogs, about their captive
    swine.
Your poets daily split upon this shelf:
You must have fools, yet none will have
    himself;
Or, if in kindness you that leave would
    give,
No man could write you at that rate you
    live;
For some of you grow fops with so much ⎫
    haste,   ⎪
Riot in nonsense, and commit such waste, ⎬
'T would ruin poets should they spend so ⎪
    fast.   ⎭
He who made this, observ'd what farces
    hit,   20
And durst not disoblige you now with wit.
But, gentlemen, you overdo the mode;
You must have fools out of the common
    road.
Th' unnatural strain'd buffoon is only tak-
    ing;
No fop can please you now of God's own
    making.
Pardon our poet, if he speaks his mind;
You come to plays with your own follies
    lin'd:
Small fools fall on you, like small showers,
    in vain;

Your own oil'd coats keep out all common
rain.
You must have Mamamouchi, such a fop
As would appear a monster in a shop: 31
He 'll fill your pit and boxes to the brim,
Where, ramm'd in crowds, you see your-
selves in him.
Sure there's some spell our poet never
knew,
In *hullababilah da*, and *chu, chu, chu*.
But *marabarah sahem* most did touch you;
That is: "O how we love the Mamamou-
chi!"
Grimace and habit sent you pleas'd away:
You damn'd the poet, and cried up the play.
    This thought had made our author more
uneasy,   40
But that he hopes I 'm fool enough to
please ye.
But here's my grief: tho' nature, join'd
with art,
Have cut me out to act a fooling part,
Yet, to your praise, the few wits here will
say,
'T was imitating you taught Haynes to play.

EPILOGUE

SOME have expected from our bills to-day,
To find a satire in our poet's play.
The zealous rout from Coleman Street did
run,
To see the story of the Friar and Nun;
Or tales, yet more ridiculous to hear,
Vouch'd by their vicar of ten pounds a year:
Of nuns who did against temptation pray,
And discipline laid on the pleasant way;
Or that, to please the malice of the town,
Our poet should in some close cell have
shown   10
Some sister, playing at content alone.
This they did hope; the other side did fear;
And both you see alike are cozen'd here.
Some thought the title of our play to blame:
They lik'd the thing, but yet abhorr'd the
name;
Like modest punks, who all you ask afford,
But, for the world, they would not name
that word.
Yet, if you 'll credit what I heard him say,
Our poet meant no scandal in his play;
His nuns are good, which on the stage are
shown,   20
And, sure, behind our scenes you 'll look
for none.

SONG

I

LONG betwixt love and fear Phyllis, tormented,
Shunn'd her own wish, yet at last she consented:
But, loth that day should her blushes discover,
    "Come, gentle night," she said,
    "Come quickly to my aid,
    And a poor shamefac'd maid
    Hide from her lover.

II

"Now cold as ice I am, now hot as fire,
I dare not tell myself my own desire;   9
But let day fly away, and let night haste her:
    Grant, ye kind powers above,
    Slow hours to parting love,
    But when to bliss we move,
    Bid 'em fly faster.

III

"How sweet it is to love, when I discover
That fire which burns my heart, warming
my lover!
'T is pity love so true should be mistaken;
    But, if this night he be
    False or unkind to me,
    Let me die, ere I see   20
    That I 'm forsaken."

PROLOGUE, EPILOGUE, AND SONGS FROM AMBOYNA

OR, THE CRUELTIES OF THE DUTCH TO THE ENGLISH MERCHANTS

[This worthless tragedy, the poorest of all
Dryden's dramatic works, must have been performed before the end of 1672, since in a
prologue included in *Covent Garden Drollery*
(p. 33), printed in that year, there is an unmistakable reference to it :

> But when fierce critics get them in their clutch,
> They 're crueler then the tyrannic Dutch ;
> And with more art do dislocate each scene
> Then in *Amboyna* they the limbs of men.

It was entered on the *Stationers' Register* June
26, 1673 (Malone, I, 1, 108), and published in
the same year.
Amboyna was written for a political purpose, to stir up the national feeling against the
Dutch, with whom England was then at war.

From this prologue and epilogue a bookseller concocted a *Satire upon the Dutch, written by Mr. Dryden in the year 1662*, which was first printed in *Poems on Affairs of State*, vol. iii, 1704; and was afterwards regularly included in editions of Dryden. Christie called attention to the imposture.]

PROLOGUE

As needy gallants in the scriv'ners' hands,
Court the rich knave that gripes their mort-
    gag'd lands,
The first fat buck of all the season 's sent,
And keeper takes no fee in compliment:
The dotage of some Englishmen is such,
To fawn on those who ruin them — the
    Dutch.
They shall have all, rather than make a war
With those who of the same religion are.
The Straits, the Guinea trade, the herrings
    too,
Nay, to keep friendship, they shall pickle
    you.   10
Some are resolv'd not to find out the cheat,
But, cuckold-like, love him who does the feat:
What injuries soe'er upon us fall,
Yet, still the same religion answers all:
Religion wheedled you to civil war,
Drew English blood, and Dutchmen's now
    would spare:
Be gull'd no longer, for you 'll find it true,
They have no more religion, faith — then
    you;
Interest 's the god they worship in their
    state;   19
And you, I take it, have not much of that.
Well monarchies may own religion's name,
But states are atheists in their very frame.
They share a sin, and such proportions fall,
That, like a stink, 't is nothing to 'em all.
How they love England, you shall see this
    day;
No map shews Holland truer then our play:
Their pictures and inscriptions well we
    know;
We may be bold one medal sure to show.
View then their falsehoods, rapine, cruelty;
And think what once they were, they still
    would be;   30
But hope not either language, plot, or art;
'T was writ in haste, but with an English
    heart:
And least hope wit; in Dutchmen that would
    be
As much improper, as would honesty.

EPILOGUE

A POET once the Spartans led to fight,
And made 'em conquer in the Muses' right:
So would our poet lead you on this day,
Showing your tortur'd fathers in his play.
To one well born th' affront is worse, and
    more,
When he 's abus'd and baffled by a boor:
With an ill grace the Dutch their mischiefs
    do,
They 've both ill nature and ill manners
    too.
Well may they boast themselves an ancient
    nation,
For they were bred ere manners were in
    fashion;   10
And their new commonwealth has set 'em
    free
Only from honor and civility.
Venetians do not more uncouthly ride,
Than did their lubber state mankind be-
    stride;
Their sway became 'em with as ill a mien,
As their own paunches swell above their
    chin:
Yet is their empire no true growth, but
    humor.
And only two kings' touch can cure the
    tumor.
As Cato did his Afric fruits display,
So we before your eyes their Indies lay: 20
All loyal English will, like him, conclude,
Let Cæsar live, and Carthage be subdued !

SONGS

I

EPITHALAMIUM

I

THE day is come, I see it rise,
Betwixt the bride's and bridegroom's eyes;
That golden day they wish'd so long,
Love pick'd it out amidst the throng;
He destin'd to himself this sun,
And took the reins, and drove him on;
In his own beams he dress'd him bright,
Yet bid him bring a better night.

II

The day you wish'd arriv'd at last,
You wish as much that it were past;   10
One minute more, and night will hide
The bridegroom and the blushing bride.

The virgin now to bed does go:
Take care, O youth, she rise not so:
She pants and trembles at her doom,
And fears and wishes thou wouldst come.

III

The bridegroom comes, he comes apace,
With love and fury in his face;
She shrinks away, he close pursues,
And prayers and threats at once does
    use.   20
She, softly sighing, begs delay,
And with her hand puts his away;
Now out aloud for help she cries,
And now despairing shuts her eyes.

II

THE SEA-FIGHT

Who ever saw a noble sight,
That never view'd a brave sea-fight!
Hang up your bloody colors in the air,
Up with your fights, and your nettings pre-
    pare;
Your merry mates cheer, with a lusty bold
    sprite,
Now each man his brindice, and then to the
    fight.
St. George, St. George, we cry,
The shouting Turks reply.
O now it begins, and the gun-room grows
    hot;
Ply it with culverin and with small shot;   10
Hark, does it not thunder? no, 't is the guns'
    roar,
The neighboring billows are turn'd into
    gore;
Now each man must resolve to die,
For here the coward cannot fly.
Drums and trumpets toll the knell,
And culverins the passing bell.
Now, now they grapple, and now board
    amain;
Blow up the hatches, they're off all
    again:
Give 'em a broadside, the dice run at
    all;
Down comes the mast and yard, and
    tacklings fall.   20
She grows giddy now, like blind Fortune's
    wheel,
She sinks there, she sinks, she turns up her
    keel,
Who ever beheld so noble a sight,
As this so brave, so bloody sea-fight!

PROLOGUE AND EPILOGUE TO THE UNIVERSITY OF OXFORD

SPOKEN BY MR. HART, AT THE ACTING OF THE SILENT WOMAN

[These are evidently the pieces to which Dryden refers in a letter to Lord Rochester, dated
1673 by Malone, from internal evidence: "I
have sent your lordship a prologue and epilogue which I made for our players, when they
went down to Oxford. I hear they have succeeded; and by the event your lordship will
judge how easy 't is to pass any thing upon an
university, and how gross flattery the learned
will endure" (Malone, I. 2, 11-13). Both
poems were first printed in *Miscellany Poems*,
1684.]

PROLOGUE

What Greece, when learning flourish'd,
    only knew,
Athenian judges, you this day renew.
Here too are annual rites to Pallas done,
And here poetic prizes lost or won.
Methinks I see you, crown'd with olives, sit,
And strike a sacred horror from the pit.
A day of doom is this of your decree,
Where even the best are but by mercy
    free:
A day, which none but Jonson durst have
    wish'd to see.
Here they, who long have known the use-
    ful stage,   10
Come to be taught themselves to teach the
    age.
As your commissioners our poets go,
To cultivate the virtue which you sow;
In your Lycæum first themselves refin'd,
And delegated thence to humankind.
But as embassadors, when long from home,
For new instructions to their princes come;
So poets, who your precepts have forgot,
Return, and beg they may be better taught:
Follies and faults elsewhere by them are
    shown,   20
But by your manners they correct their
    own.
Th' illiterate writer, empiric-like, applies
To minds diseas'd, unsafe, chance reme-
    dies:
The learn'd in schools, where knowledge
    first began,
Studies with care th' anatomy of man;
Sees virtue, vice, and passions in their
    cause,

And fame from science, not from fortune,
  draws.
So poetry, which is in Oxford made
An art, in London only is a trade.
There haughty dunces, whose unlearned
  pen   30
Could ne'er spell grammar, would be read-
  ing men.
Such build their poems the Lucretian way;
So many huddled atoms make a play;
And if they hit in order by some chance,
They call that nature, which is ignorance.
To such a fame let mere town-wits aspire,
And their gay nonsense their own cits ad-
  mire.
Our poet, could he find forgiveness here,
Would wish it rather than a *plaudit* there.
He owns no crown from those Prætorian
  bands,   40
But knows *that* right is in this senate's hands.
Not impudent enough to hope your praise, ⎤
Low at the Muses' feet his wreath he lays, ⎬
And, where he took it up, resigns his bays. ⎦
Kings make their poets whom themselves
  think fit,
But 't is your suffrage makes authentic wit.

EPILOGUE

No poor Dutch peasant, wing'd with all his
  fear,
Flies with more haste, when the French
  arms draw near,
Than we with our poetic train come down
For refuge hither, from th' infected town:
Heaven for our sins this summer has
  thought fit
To visit us with all the plagues of wit.
A French troop first swept all things in
  its way;
But those hot Monsieurs were too quick to
  stay:
Yet, to our cost, in that short time, we find
They left their itch of novelty behind.   10
Th' Italian merry-andrews took their
  place,
And quite debauch'd the stage with lewd
  grimace;
Instead of wit and humors, your delight
Was there to see two hobby-horses fight;
Stout Scaramoucha with rush lance rode in,
And ran a tilt at centaur Arlequin.
For love you heard how amorous asses
  bray'd,
And cats in gutters gave their serenade.

Nature was out of countenance, and each
  day
Some new-born monster shewn you for a
  play.   20
  But when all fail'd, to strike the stage
    quite dumb,
Those wicked engines call'd machines are
  come.
Thunder and lightning now for wit are
  play'd,
And shortly scenes in Lapland will be laid:
Art magic is for poetry profess'd;
And cats and dogs, and each obscener
  beast,
To which Egyptian dotards once did bow,
Upon our English stage are worshipp'd
  now.
Witchcraft reigns there, and raises to re-
  nown
Macbeth, the Simon Magus of the town, 30
Fletcher's despis'd, your Jonson out of
  fashion,
And wit the only drug in all the nation.
In this low ebb our wares to you are ⎤
  shown;   ⎮
By you those staple authors' worth is ⎬
  known;   ⎮
For wit's a manufacture of your own.   ⎦
When you, who only can, their scenes have
  prais'd,
We 'll boldly back, and say their price is
  rais'd.

PROLOGUE AND EPILOGUE

SPOKEN AT THE OPENING OF THE NEW
HOUSE, MARCH 26, 1674

[These pieces were first printed in *Miscellany Poems*, 1684. The *new house* was the theater in Drury Lane, built for the King's Company on designs by Sir Christopher Wren.]

PROLOGUE

A PLAIN-BUILT house, after so long a stay,
Will send you half-unsatisfied away;
When, fall'n from your expected pomp,
  you find
A bare convenience only is design'd.
You, who each day can theaters behold,
Like Nero's palace, shining all with gold,
Our mean ungilded stage will scorn, we
  fear,

And, for the homely room, disdain the cheer.
Yet now cheap druggets to a mode are ⎤
  grown, ⎟
And a plain suit, since we can make ⎬
  but one,   10 ⎟
Is better than to be by tarnish'd gau- ⎦
  dry known.
They who are by your favors wealthy
  made,
With mighty sums may carry on the trade:
We, broken bankers, half destroy'd by ⎤
  fire, ⎟
With our small stock to humble roofs ⎬
  retire: ⎟
Pity our loss, while you their pomp ad- ⎦
  mire.
For fame and honor we no longer strive,
We yield in both, and only beg to live:
Unable to support their vast expense,
Who build and treat with such magnifi-
  cence;   20
That, like th' ambitious monarchs of the
  age,
They give the law to our provincial stage:
Great neighbors enviously promote excess,
While they impose their splendor on the
  less.
But only fools, and they of vast estate, ⎤
Th' extremity of modes will imitate, ⎬
The dangling knee-fringe, and the bib- ⎦
  cravat.
Yet if some pride with want may be allow'd,
We in our plainness may be justly proud:
Our royal master will'd it should be so; 30
Whate'er he 's pleas'd to own, can need no
  show:
That sacred name gives ornament and grace,
And, like his stamp, makes basest metals
  pass.
'T were folly now a stately pile to raise,
To build a playhouse while you throw
  down plays,
Whilst scenes, machines, and empty operas
  reign,
And for the pencil you the pen disdain.
While troops of famish'd Frenchmen hither
  drive,
And laugh at those upon whose alms they
  live:
Old English authors vanish, and give place
To these new conqu'rors of the Norman
  race.   41
More tamely than your fathers you submit:
You 're now grown vassals to 'em in your
  wit.

Mark, when they play, how our fine fops ⎤
  advance ⎟
The mighty merits of these men of ⎬
  France, ⎟
Keep time, cry *Ben*, and humor the ca- ⎦
  dence.
Well, please yourselves; but sure 't is un-
  derstood
That French machines have ne'er done
  England good.
I would not prophesy our house's fate:
But while vain shows and scenes you over-
  rate,   50
'T is to be fear'd ——
That as a fire the former house o'erthrew,
Machines and tempests will destroy the new.

EPILOGUE

Tho' what our Prologue said was sadly ⎤
  true, ⎟
Yet, gentlemen, our homely house is ⎬
  new, ⎟
A charm that seldom fails with wicked ⎦
  you.
A country lip may have the velvet touch; ⎤
Tho' she 's no lady, you may think her ⎬
  such: ⎟
A strong imagination may do much. ⎦
But you, loud sirs, who thro' your curls
  look big,
Critics in plume and white vallancy wig;
Who lolling on our foremost benches sit,
And still charge first, the true forlorn of
  wit;   10
Whose favors, like the sun, warm where
  you roll,
Yet you, like him, have neither heat nor
  soul:
So may your hats your foretops never press,
Untouch'd your ribbonds, sacred be your
  dress;
So may you slowly to old age advance,
And have th' excuse of youth for igno-
  rance;
So may fop-corner full of noise remain,
And drive far off the dull attentive train;
So may your midnight scourings happy
  prove,
And morning batt'ries force your way to
  love;   20
So may not France your warlike hands re-
  call,
But leave you by each other's swords to fall,
As you come here to ruffle vizard punk,

When sober, rail, and roar when you are
drunk.
But to the wits we can some merit plead,
And urge what by themselves has oft been
said:
Our house relieves the ladies from the
frights
Of ill-pav'd streets, and long dark winter
nights;
The Flanders horses from a cold bleak road,
Where bears in furs dare scarcely look
abroad;   30
The audience from worn plays and fustian
stuff
Of rhyme, more nauseous than three boys
in buff.
Tho' in their house the poets' heads appear,
We hope we may presume their wits are
here.
The best which they reserv'd they now ⎤
will play, |
For, like kind cuckolds, tho' w' have not ⎬
the way |
To please, we 'll find you abler men who |
may.   ⎦
If they should fail, for last recruits we ⎤
breed |
A troop of frisking Monsieurs to suc-   ⎬
ceed: |
You know the French sure cards at time |
of need.   40 ⎦

PROLOGUE AND EPILOGUE TO
THE UNIVERSITY OF OXFORD,
1674

[The prologue below was first printed in
Miscellany Poems, 1684, with the heading
*Prologue to the University of Oxford, 1674.
Spoken by Mr. Hart. Written by Mr. Dryden.*
After it follows *Epilogue, Spoken by Mrs. Bou-
tell. Written by Mr. Dryden.* Six pages later
the same epilogue is reprinted, with insignifi-
cant variations of text, but headed *Epilogue to
Oxford: Spoken by Mrs. Marshal, Writ by Mr.
Dryden.* The latter text is here followed.]

PROLOGUE

SPOKEN BY MR. HART

POETS, your subjects, have their parts assign'd
T' unbend, and to divert their sovereign's
mind:

When tir'd with following nature, you think
fit
To seek repose in the cool shades of wit,
And, from the sweet retreat, with joy sur-
vey
What rests, and what is conquer'd, of the
way.
Here, free yourselves from envy, care, and
strife,
You view the various turns of human life:
Safe in our scene, thro' dangerous courts
you go,
And, undebauch'd, the vice of cities know. 10
Your theories are here to practice brought,
As in mechanic operations wrought;
And man, the little world, before you
set,
As once the sphere of crystal shew'd the
great.
Blest sure are you above all mortal kind,
If to your fortunes you can suit your
mind:
Content to see, and shun, those ills we
show,
And crimes on theaters alone to know,
With joy we bring what our dead authors
writ,
And beg from you the value of their wit: 20
That Shakespeare's, Fletcher's, and great
Jonson's claim
May be renew'd from those who gave them
fame.
None of our living poets dare appear;
For Muses so severe are worshipp'd here,
That, conscious of their faults, they shun ⎤
the eye,   ⎬
And, as profane, from sacred places fly, |
Rather than see th' offended God, and die. ⎦
We bring no imperfections but our own;
Such faults as made are by the makers
shown:
And you have been so kind, that we may
boast,   30
The greatest judges still can pardon most.
Poets must stoop, when they would please
our pit,
Debas'd even to the level of their wit;
Disdaining that which yet they know will
take,
Hating themselves what their applause must
make.
But when to praise from you they would
aspire,
Tho' they like eagles mount, your Jove is
higher.

So far your knowledge all their pow'r
   transcends
As what *should* be, beyond what *is*, extends.

EPILOGUE

SPOKEN BY MRS. MARSHALL

OFT has our poet wish'd, this happy seat
Might prove his fading Muse's last re-
   treat:
I wonder'd at his wish, but now I find
He here sought quiet, and content of mind;
Which noiseful towns and courts can never
   know,
And only in the shades like laurels grow.
Youth, ere it sees the world, here studies
   rest,
And age returning thence concludes it
   best.
What wonder if we court that happiness
Yearly to share, which hourly you pos-
   sess,   10
Teaching ev'n you, while the vex'd world
   we show,
Your peace to value more, and better
   know?
'T is all we can return for favors past,
Whose holy memory shall ever last,
For patronage from him whose care pre-
   sides
O'er every noble art, and every science
   guides:
Bathurst, a name the learn'd with rev'rence
   know,
And scarcely more to his own Virgil owe;
Whose age enjoys but what his youth de-
   serv'd,
To rule those Muses whom before he
   serv'd.   20
His learning, and untainted manners too,
We find, Athenians, are deriv'd to you:
Such ancient hospitality there rests
In yours, as dwelt in the first Grecian
   breasts,
Where kindness was religion to their
   guests.
Such modesty did to our sex appear,
As, had there been no laws, we need not
   fear,
Since each of you was our protector here.
Converse so chaste, and so strict virtue
   shown,
As might Apollo with the Muses own.   30
Till our return, we must despair to find
Judges so just, so knowing, and so kind.

EPILOGUE INTENDED TO HAVE BEEN SPOKEN BY THE LADY HENR. MAR. WENTWORTH, WHEN CALISTO WAS ACTED AT COURT

[This epilogue is by no means certainly the work of Dryden. It was first printed, without any ascription to Dryden, in *Miscellany Poems*, 1684, near the end of the volume, apart from the other prologues and epilogues, and just before the translation of Virgil's *Eclogues*, which is paged separately. It was evidently inserted in the volume as an afterthought; in the table of contents it is put out of its natural order, at the close of the list of prologues and epilogues. Dryden's name was first joined to the piece in 1702, in the third edition of *Miscellany Poems, the First Part.*

Calisto, or The Chaste Nymph, a masque by John Crowne, was presented at Court in 1675 by a company of ladies and gentlemen. The Lady Mary and the Lady Anne, daughters of the Duke of York, played the parts of Calisto and of her companion, Nyphe (see line 29 below); Lady Wentworth, afterwards mistress of the Duke of Monmouth, who himself was among "the persons of quality of the men that danced," represented Jupiter.]

As Jupiter I made my court in vain;
I'll now assume my native shape again.
I'm weary to be so unkindly us'd,
And would not be a god, to be refus'd.
State grows uneasy when it hinders love;
A glorious burden, which the wise re-
   move.
Now, as a nymph, I need not sue, nor try
The force of any lightning but the eye.
Beauty and youth more than a god com-
   mand;
No Jove could e'er the force of these with-
   stand.   10
'T is here that sovereign pow'r admits dis-
   pute;
Beauty sometimes is justly absolute.
Our sullen Catos, whatsoe'er they say,
Even while they frown and dictate laws,
   obey.
You, mighty sir, our bonds more easy
   make,
And gracefully, what all must suffer, take;
Above those forms the grave affect to wear;
For 't is not to be wise to be severe.
True wisdom may some gallantry admit,
And soften business with the charms of
   wit.   20

These peaceful triumphs with your cares
  you bought,
And from the midst of fighting nations
  brought.
You only hear it thunder from afar,
And sit in peace the arbiter of war.
Peace, the loath'd manna, which hot brains
  despise,
You knew its worth, and made it early
  prize:
And in its happy leisure sit and see
The promises of more felicity:
Two glorious nymphs of your one godlike
  line,
Whose morning rays like noontide strike
  and shine;   30
Whom you to suppliant monarchs shall dis-
  pose,
To bind your friends, and to disarm your
  foes.

PROLOGUE AND EPILOGUE TO AURENG-ZEBE

[This, the last of Dryden's rhymed heroic
plays, was acted in 1675, being entered on the
Stationers' Register on November 29 of that
year (Malone, I, 1, 115). It was published in
1676.]

PROLOGUE

OUR author, by experience, finds it true,
'T is much more hard to please himself than
  you;
And out of no feign'd modesty, this day
Damns his laborious trifle of a play:
Not that it 's worse than what before he writ,
But he has now another taste of wit;
And, to confess a truth, (tho' out of time,)
Grows weary of his long-lov'd mistress,
  Rhyme.   8
Passion 's too fierce to be in fetters bound,
And nature flies him like enchanted ground.
What verse can do, he has perform'd in this,
Which he presumes the most correct of his;
But spite of all his pride, a secret shame
Invades his breast at Shakespeare's sacred
  name:
Aw'd when he hears his godlike Romans
  rage,
He, in a just despair, would quit the stage;
And to an age less polish'd, more unskill'd,
Does, with disdain, the foremost honors
  yield.

As with the greater dead he dares not
  strive,
He would not match his verse with those
  who live: 20
Let him retire, betwixt two ages cast,
The first of this, and hindmost of the last.
A losing gamester, let him sneak away;
He bears no ready money from the play.
The fate which governs poets thought it fit
He should not raise his fortunes by his wit.
The clergy thrive, and the litigious bar;
Dull heroes fatten with the spoils of war:
All southern vices, Heav'n be prais'd, are
  here;
But wit 's a luxury you think too dear.   30
When you to cultivate the plant are loth,
'T is a shrewd sign 't was never of your
  growth;
And wit in northern climates will not blow,
Except, like orange trees, 't is hous'd from
  snow.
There needs no care to put a playhouse
  down,
'T is the most desart place of all the town:
We and our neighbors, to speak proudly,
  are,
Like monarchs, ruin'd with expensive war;
While, like wise English, unconcern'd you
  sit,
And see us play the tragedy of wit.   40

EPILOGUE

A PRETTY task ! and so I told the fool,
Who needs would undertake to please by
  rule:
He thought that, if his characters were good,
The scenes entire, and freed from noise and
  blood,
The action great, yet circumscrib'd by time,
The words not forc'd, but sliding into rhyme,
The passions rais'd and calm'd by just de-
  grees,
As tides are swell'd, and then retire to seas;
He thought, in hitting these, his bus'ness
  done,
Tho' he, perhaps, has fail'd in ev'ry one: 10
But, after all, a poet must confess,
His art 's like physic, but a happy guess.
Your pleasure on your fancy must depend:
The lady 's pleas'd, just as she likes her
  friend.
No song ! no dance ! no show ! he fears
  you 'll say
You love all naked beauties but a play.

He much mistakes your methods to de-
   light,
And, like the French, abhors our target
   fight,
But those damn'd dogs can never be i' th'
   right.
True English hate your Monsieurs' paltry
   arts,   20
For you are all silk-weavers in your hearts.
Bold Britons, at a brave Bear Garden fray,
Are rous'd; and, clatt'ring sticks, cry:
   " Play, play, play ! "
Meantime, your filthy foreigner will stare
And mutter to himself: " Ha, gens bar-
   bare ! "
And, gad, 't is well he mutters; well for
   him;
Our butchers else would tear him limb from
   limb.
'T is true, the time may come, your sons
   may be
Infected with this French civility;
But this in after-ages will be done: 30
Our poet writes a hundred years too soon.
This age comes on too slow, or he too fast;
And early springs are subject to a blast !
Who would excel, when few can make a test
Betwixt indiff'rent writing and the best ?
For favors cheap and common who would
   strive,
Which, like abandon'd prostitutes, you give ?
Yet scatter'd here and there I some behold
Who can discern the tinsel from the gold:
To these he writes; and, if by them allow'd,
'T is their prerogative to rule the crowd. 41
For he more fears, like a presuming man,
Their votes who cannot judge, than theirs
   who can.

EPILOGUE TO THE MAN OF MODE

OR, SIR FOPLING FLUTTER

[This comedy, by Sir George Etherege, was
acted and published in 1676. Dryden had a
hearty admiration for Etherege, as a writer of
genuine comic power: see his Letter to Sir
George Etherege, p. 214, below ; and Mac Flecknoe, lines 151–154, p. 136, below.]

MOST modern wits such monstrous fools
   have shown,
They seem'd not of Heav'n's making, but
   their own.

Those nauseous harlequins in farce may
   pass,
But there goes more to a substantial ass !
Something of man must be expos'd to view,
That, gallants, they may more resemble you.
Sir Fopling is a fool so nicely writ,
The ladies would mistake him for a wit;
And, when he sings, talks loud, and cocks,
   would cry:
" I vow, methinks he 's pretty company: 10
So brisk, so gay, so travel'd, so refin'd,
As he took pains to graff upon his kind."
True fops help nature's work, and go to
   school,
To file and finish God-A'mighty's fool.
Yet none Sir Fopling him, or him can call;
He 's knight o' th' shire, and represents ye
   all.
From each he meets he culls whate'er he
   can;
Legion 's his name, a people in a man.
His bulky folly gathers as it goes,
And, rolling o'er you, like a snowball grows.
His various modes from various fathers
   follow;   21
One taught the toss, and one the new
   French wallow:
His sword knot this, his crevat this design'd;
And this, the yard-long snake he twirls be-
   hind.
From one the sacred periwig he gain'd,
Which wind ne'er blew, nor touch of hat
   profan'd.
Another's diving bow he did adore,
Which with a shog casts all the hair before,
Till he with full decorum brings it back,
And rises with a water-spaniel shake. 30
As for his songs (the ladies' dear delight),
Those sure he took from most of you who
   write.
Yet every man is safe from what he fear'd;
For no one fool is hunted from the herd.

PROLOGUE TO CIRCE

[This tragedy, by Charles Davenant, son of
Sir William, was probably acted late in 1676
or early in 1677 ; the songs in Circe are
mentioned in the Term Catalogue for Easter
Term (May), 1677, the play itself in that for
Trinity Term (July) of the same year. Downes
terms Circe an opera ; it is in fact a spectacu-
lar heroic play, with many songs interspersed.
The prologue is extant in two forms, of which
the later (given first below) was printed in

Miscellany Poems, 1684, with the heading, *An Epilogue, written by Mr. Dryden*. The earlier form was printed with the play in 1677.]

WERE you but half so wise as y' are severe,
Our youthful poet should not need to fear:
To his green years your censures you would
   suit,
Not blast the blossom, but expect the fruit.
The sex that best does pleasure understand,
Will always choose to err on t'other hand.
They check not him that's awkward in de-
   light,
But clap the young rogue's cheek, and set
   him right.
Thus hearten'd well and flesh'd upon his prey,
The youth may prove a man another day. 10
Your Ben and Fletcher, in their first young
   flight,
Did no *Volpone*, no *Arbaces* write;
But hopp'd about, and short excursions
   made
From bough to bough, as if they were
   afraid,
And each were guilty of some *Slighted
   Maid*.
Shakespeare's own Muse her *Pericles* first
   bore;
The Prince of Tyre was elder than the Moor:
'T is miracle to see a first good play;
All hawthorns do not bloom on Christmas-
   day.
A slender poet must have time to grow, 20
And spread and burnish as his brothers do.
Who still looks lean, sure with some pox
   is curst;
But no man can be Falstaff-fat at first.
Then damn not, but indulge his stew'd
   essays,
Encourage him, and bloat him up with
   praise,
That he may get more bulk before he dies:
He's not yet fed enough for sacrifice.
Perhaps, if now your grace you will not
   grudge,
He may grow up to write, and you to judge.

[The Prologue printed in the first edition
agrees with the above for ten lines. It then
continues as follows:]

For your own sakes, instruct him when he's
   out;
You'll find him mend his work at every
   bout.

When some young lusty thief is pass-
   ing by,
How many of your tender kind will cry:
   " A proper fellow, pity he should die !
He might be sav'd and thank us for our
   pains:
There's such a stock of love within his
   veins."
These arguments the women may persuade,
But move not you, the brothers of the trade;
Who, scattering your infection thro' the
   pit,   20
With aching hearts and empty purses sit,
To take your dear five shillings' worth
   of wit.
The praise you give him in your kindest
   mood
Comes dribbling from you, just like drops
   of blood;
And then you clap so civilly, for fear
The loudness might offend your neighbor's
   ear,
That we suspect your gloves are lin'd
   within,
For silence sake, and cotton'd next the skin.
From these usurpers we appeal to you,
The only knowing, only judging few;   30
You, who in private have this play allow'd,
Ought to maintain your suffrage to the
   crowd.
The captive once submitted to your bands
You should protect from death by vulgar
   hands.

TO MR. LEE, ON HIS ALEX-
ANDER

[This poem was published in 1677, in *The Rival Queens, or The Death of Alexander the Great*, by Nathaniel Lee. The play is entered on the *Term Catalogue* for Michaelmas Term (November). For Lee Dryden had a warm regard, mixed with a trifle of condescension. In a letter to Dennis he writes: "I remember, poor Nat. Lee, who was then upon the verge of madness, yet made a sober and a witty answer to a bad poet, who told him it was an easie thing to write like a madman. 'No,' said he, 'it is very difficult to write like a madman, but it is a very easie matter to write like a fool'" (Malone, I, 2; 35, 36).]

THE blast of common censure could I fear,
Before your play my name should not appear;

For 't will be thought, and with some color too,
I pay the bribe I first receiv'd from you;
That mutual vouchers for our fame we stand,
And play the game into each other's hand;
And as cheap pen'orths to ourselves afford,
As Bessus and the brothers of the sword.
Such libels private men may well endure,
When states and kings themselves are not secure;
For ill men, conscious of their inward guilt,
Think the best actions on by-ends are built.
And yet my silence had not 'scap'd their spite;
Then, envy had not suffer'd me to write;
For, since I could not ignorance pretend,
Such worth I must or envy or commend.
So many candidates there stand for wit,
A place in court is scarce so hard to get:
In vain they crowd each other at the door;
For ev'n reversions are all begg'd before:
Desert, how known soe'er, is long delay'd;
And then, too, fools and knaves are better paid.
Yet, as some actions bear so great a name,
That courts themselves are just for fear of shame;
So has the mighty merit of your play
Extorted praise, and forc'd itself a way.
'T is here as 't is at sea; who farthest goes,
Or dares the most, makes all the rest his foes.
Yet, when some virtue much outgrows the rest,
It shoots too fast and high to be oppress'd;
As his heroic worth struck envy dumb,
Who took the Dutchman, and who cut the boom.
Such praise is yours, while you the passions move,
That 't is no longer feign'd, 't is real love,
Where nature triumphs over wretched art;
We only warm the head, but you the heart.
Always you warm! and if the rising year,
As in hot regions, bring the sun too near,
'T is but to make your fragrant spices blow,
Which in our colder climates will not grow.
They only think you animate your theme
With too much fire, who are themselves all phle'me.
Prizes would be for lags of slowest pace,
Were cripples made the judges of the race.
Despise those drones, who praise, while they accuse
The too much vigor of your youthful Muse.
That humble style which they their virtue make,
Is in your pow'r; you need but stoop and take.
Your beauteous images must be allow'd
By all, but some vile poets of the crowd.
But how should any signpost dauber know
The worth of Titian or of Angelo?
Hard features every bungler can command;
To draw true beauty shews a master's hand.

PROLOGUE AND EPILOGUE TO ALL FOR LOVE

OR, THE WORLD WELL LOST

[This, Dryden's finest tragedy, treats the familiar theme of Antony and Cleopatra in a style that owes much to the study of Shakespeare. It was probably acted in 1677, since it was entered on the *Stationers' Register* on January 31, 1678 (Malone, I, 1, 116), and published in the same year.]

PROLOGUE

WHAT flocks of critics hover here to-day,
As vultures wait on armies for their prey,
All gaping for the carcass of a play!
With croaking notes they bode some dire event,
And follow dying poets by the scent.
Ours gives himself for gone; y' have watch'd your time!
He fights this day unarm'd, — without his rhyme; —
And brings a tale which often has been told;
As sad as Dido's; and almost as old.
His hero, whom you wits his bully call,
Bates of his mettle, and scarce rants at all:
He 's somewhat lewd, but a well-meaning mind;
Weeps much, fights little, but is wondrous kind.
In short, a pattern, and companion fit,
For all the keeping Tonies of the pit.
I could name more: a wife, and mistress too;
Both (to be plain) too good for most of you:
The wife well-natur'd, and the mistress true.

Now, poets, if your fame has been his
     care,
Allow him all the candor you can spare. 20
A brave man scorns to quarrel once a day;
Like Hectors, in at every petty fray.
Let those find fault whose wit's so very
     small,
They've need to show that they can think
     at all;
Errors, like straws, upon the surface flow;
He who would search for pearls must dive
     below.
Fops may have leave to level all they can,
As pigmies would be glad to lop a man.
Half-wits are fleas; so little and so light,
We scarce could know they live, but that
     they bite.   30
But, as the rich, when tir'd with daily
     feasts,
For change, become their next poor ten-
     ant's guests,
Drink hearty draughts of ale from plain
     brown bowls,
And snatch the homely rasher from the
     coals;
So you, retiring from much better cheer,
For once, may venture to do penance here.
And since that plenteous autumn now is
     past,
Whose grapes and peaches have indulg'd
     your taste,
Take in good part, from our poor poet's
     board,
Such rivel'd fruits as winter can afford. 40

EPILOGUE

Poets, like disputants, when reasons fail,
Have one sure refuge left — and that's to
     rail.
Fop, coxcomb, fool, are thunder'd thro' the
     pit,
And this is all their equipage of wit.
We wonder how the devil this diff'rence
     grows,
Betwixt our fools in verse, and yours in
     prose:
For, 'faith, the quarrel rightly understood,
'T is civil war with their own flesh and
     blood.
The threadbare author hates the gaudy
     coat,
And swears at the gilt coach, but swears
     afoot: 10
For 't is observ'd of every scribbling man,

He grows a fop as fast as e'er he can;
Prunes up, and asks his oracle, the glass,
If pink or purple best become his face.
For our poor wretch, he neither rails nor ⎫
     prays;   ⎪
Nor likes your wit just as you like his ⎬
     plays;   ⎪
He has not yet so much of Mr. Bayes. ⎭
He does his best; and if he cannot please,
Would quietly sue out his *writ of ease.*
Yet, if he might his own grand jury call, 20
By the fair sex he begs to stand or fall.
Let Cæsar's power the men's ambition
     move,
But grace you him who lost the world for
     love!
Yet if some antiquated lady say,
The last age is not copied in his play;
Heav'n help the man who for that face
     must drudge,
Which only has the wrinkles of a judge.
Let not the young and beauteous join with
     those;
For, should you raise such numerous hosts
     of foes,
Young wits and sparks he to his aid must
     call;   30
'T is more than one man's work to please
     you all.

EPILOGUE TO MITHRIDATES,
KING OF PONTUS

[This tragedy, by Lee, was published in
1678, being licensed for the press on March 28.
The following epilogue is taken from the first
edition. Scott prints another epilogue, from a
broadside, but gives no proof that it is by Dryden.]

You 've seen a pair of faithful lovers die: ⎫
And much you care, for most of you will ⎪
     cry,   ⎬
'T was a just judgment on their con- ⎪
     stancy.   ⎭
For, Heav'n be thank'd, we live in such an
     age,
When no man dies for love, but on the
     stage:
And ev'n those martyrs are but rare in
     plays;
A cursed sign how much true faith decays.
Love is no more a violent desire;
'T is a mere metaphor, a painted fire.
In all our sex, the name, examin'd well, 10

Is pride to gain, and vanity to tell.
In woman, 't is of subtile int'rest made:
Curse on the punk that made it first a trade !
She first did wit's prerogative remove,
And made a fool presume to prate of love.
Let honor and preferment go for gold,
But glorious beauty is not to be sold:
Or, if it be, 't is at a rate so high,
That nothing but adoring it should buy.
Yet the rich cullies may their boasting
   spare;   20
They purchase but sophisticated ware.
'T is prodigality that buys deceit,
Where both the giver and the taker cheat.
Men but refine on the old half-crown way;
And women fight, like Swizzers, for their
   pay.

PROLOGUE, EPILOGUE, AND SONG FROM THE KIND KEEPER

OR, MR. LIMBERHAM

[In a chronological list of his plays which Dryden printed with *King Arthur* in 1691 (see Malone, I, 1; 56, 218, 219), this comedy is placed between *All for Love* and *Œdipus.* Hence it was probably acted early in 1678; though, perhaps because of its ill success on the stage, it was not published until late in 1679, when it is entered on the *Term Catalogue* for Michaelmas Term (November). The first edition is dated 1680. This play and *Œdipus* were both "printed for R. Bentley and M. Magnes;" Dryden had evidently quarreled with his former publisher Herringman, to whom a little later (1682) he devoted a sarcastic line (line 105) in *Mac Flecknoe.*]

PROLOGUE

TRUE wit has seen its best days long ago;
It ne'er look'd up, since we were dipp'd in
   show;
When sense in dog'rel rhymes and clouds
   was lost,
And dulness flourish'd at the actor's cost.
Nor stopp'd it here; when tragedy was
   done,
Satire and humor the same fate have run,
And comedy is sunk to trick and pun.
Now our machining lumber will not sell,
And you no longer care for heav'n or hell;
What stuff can please you next, the Lord
   can tell.   10

Let them, who the rebellion first began
To wit, restore the monarch, if they can;
Our author dares not be the first bold man.
He, like the prudent citizen, takes care
To keep for better marts his staple ware;
His toys are good enough for Sturbridge
   fair.
Tricks were the fashion; if it now be spent,
'T is time enough at Easter to invent;
No man will make up a new suit for Lent.
If now and then he takes a small pretense,
To forage for a little wit and sense,   21
Pray pardon him, he meant you no offense.
Next summer, Nostradamus tells, they say,
That all the critics shall be shipp'd away,
And not enow be left to damn a play.
To every sail beside, good Heav'n, be kind;
But drive away that swarm with such a
   wind,
That not one locust may be left behind !

EPILOGUE

SPOKEN BY LIMBERHAM

I BEG a boon, that, ere you all disband,
Some one would take my bargain off my
   hand;
To keep a punk is but a common evil;
To find her false, and marry — that 's the
   devil.
Well, I ne'er acted part in all my life,
But still I was fobb'd off with some such
   wife:
I find the trick; these poets take no pity
Of one that is a member of the city.
We cheat you lawfully, and in our trades;
You cheat us basely with your common
   jades.   10
Now I am married, I must sit down by it,
But let me keep my dear-bought spouse in
   quiet;
Let none of you damn'd Woodalls of the
   pit
Put in for shares to mend our breed, in wit:
We know your bastards from our flesh and
   blood,
Not one in ten of yours e'er comes to good.
In all the boys their fathers' virtues shine,
But all the female fry turn Pugs like
   mine.
When these grow up, Lord, with what ram-
   pant gadders
Our counters will be throng'd, and roads
   with padders !   20

This town two bargains has, not worth one
    farthing,
A Smithfield horse, and wife of Covent
    Garden.

A SONG FROM THE ITALIAN

By a dismal cypress lying,
    Damon cried, all pale and dying:
"Kind is death, that ends my pain,
    But cruel she I lov'd in vain.
The mossy fountains
    Murmur my trouble,
And hollow mountains
    My groans redouble:
Every nymph mourns me,
    Thus while I languish;   10
She only scorns me,
    Who caus'd my anguish,
No love returning me, but all hope
    denying."

By a dismal cypress lying,
    Like a swan, so sung he dying:
"Kind is death, that ends my pain,
    But cruel she I lov'd in vain."

PROLOGUE TO A TRUE WIDOW

[This comedy was by Thomas Shadwell.
Two speeches by Lump, in the first act, indicate that it was first acted on March 21, 1678.
It was first printed in the next year. After
his quarrel with Shadwell, Dryden gave this
same prologue to Aphra Behn for her tragi-
comedy *The Widow Ranter, or The History of
Bacon in Virginia*, published in 1690. The
present text is from the first edition of Shadwell's play.]

HEAV'N save ye, gallants, and this hopeful
    age!
Y' are welcome to the downfall of the
    stage:
The fools have labor'd long in their voca-
    tion;
And vice (the manufacture of the nation)
O'erstocks the town so much, and thrives so
    well,
That fops and knaves grow drugs and will
    not sell.
In vain our wares on theaters are shown,
When each has a plantation of his own.
His cruse ne'er fails; for whatsoe'er he
    spends,

There 's still God's plenty for himself and
    friends.   10
Should men be rated by poetic rules,
Lord, what a poll would there be rais'd
    from fools!
Meantime poor wit prohibited must lie,
As if 't were made some French commodity.
Fools you will have, and rais'd at vast ex-
    pense;
And yet, as soon as seen, they give offense.
Time was, when none would cry: "That oaf
    was me!"
But now you strive about your pedigree:
Bauble and cap no sooner are thrown down,
But there 's a muss of more than half the
    town.   20
Each one will challenge a child's part at
    least,
A sign the family is well increas'd.
Of foreign cattle there 's no longer need,
When w' are supplied so fast with English
    breed.
    Well! flourish, countrymen; drink, swear,
        and roar;
Let every freeborn subject keep his whore;
And, wand'ring in the wilderness about,
At end of forty years not wear her out.
But when you see these pictures, let none
    dare
To own beyond a limb or single share;   30
For where the punk is common, he 's a sot
Who needs will father what the parish got.

PROLOGUE AND EPILOGUE TO ŒDIPUS

[This tragedy, by Dryden and Lee, was
probably acted in August, 1678, since the
Woolen Act (30th Charles II cap. 3), mentioned in the last line of the prologue, went
into effect on the first of that month. It
was printed the next year. The prologue and
epilogue are without doubt by Dryden.]

PROLOGUE

WHEN Athens all the Grecian state did
    guide,
And Greece gave laws to all the world be-
    side;
Then Sophocles with Socrates did sit,
Supreme in wisdom one, and one in wit:
And wit from wisdom differ'd not in those,
But as 't was sung in verse, or said in prose.
Then, Œdipus, on crowded theaters,

Drew all admiring eyes and list'ning ears:
The pleas'd spectator shouted every line,
The noblest, manliest, and the best design !
And every critic of each learned age,   11
By this just model has reform'd the stage.
Now, should it fail, (as Heav'n avert our
    fear !)
Damn it in silence, lest the world should
    hear.
For were it known this poem did not please,
You might set up for perfect salvages:
Your neighbors would not look on you as
    men,
But think the nation all turn'd Picts again.
Faith, as you manage matters, 't is not fit
You should suspect yourselves of too much
    wit: 20
Drive not the jest too far, but spare this
    piece;
And, for this once, be not more wise than
    Greece.
See twice ! do not pellmell to damning fall,
Like true-born Britons, who ne'er think at
    all:
Pray be advis'd; and tho' at Mons you won,
On pointed cannon do not always run.
With some respect to ancient wit proceed;
You take the four first councils for your
    creed.
But, when you lay tradition wholly by,
And on the private spirit alone rely,   30
You turn fanatics in your poetry.
If, notwithstanding all that we can say,
You needs will have your pen'worths of
    the play,
And come resolv'd to damn, because you
    pay,
Record it, in memorial of the fact,
The first play buried since the Woolen Act.

EPILOGUE

WHAT Sophocles could undertake alone,
Our poets found a work for more than one;
And therefore two lay tugging at the piece,
With all their force, to draw the pond'rous
    mass from Greece;
A weight that bent ev'n Seneca's strong
    Muse,
And which Corneille's shoulders did refuse.
So hard it is th' Athenian harp to string !
So much two consuls yield to one just king.
Terror and pity this whole poem sway;
The mightiest machines that can mount a
    play: 10

How heavy will those vulgar souls be found,
Whom two such engines cannot move from
    ground !
When Greece and Rome have smil'd upon
    this birth,
You can but damn for one poor spot of
    earth:
And when your children find your judgment
    such,
They 'll scorn their sires, and wish them-
    selves born Dutch;
Each haughty poet will infer with ease,
How much his wit must underwrite to
    please.
As some strong churl would, brandishing,
    advance
The monumental sword that conquer'd
    France;   20
So you, by judging this, your judgments
    teach:
Thus far you like, that is, thus far you
    reach.
Since then the vote of full two thousand
    years
Has crown'd this plot, and all the dead are
    theirs,
Think it a debt you pay, not alms you give,
And, in your own defense, let this play live.
Think 'em not vain, when Sophocles is
    shown,
To praise his worth, they humbly doubt
    their own.
Yet, as weak states each other's pow'r as-
    sure,
Weak poets by conjunction are secure.   30
Their treat is what your palates relish most.
Charm ! song ! and show ! a murder and a
    ghost !
We know not what you can desire or hope,
To please you more, but burning of a pope.

PROLOGUE, EPILOGUE, AND
SONG FROM TROILUS AND
CRESSIDA

OR, TRUTH FOUND TOO LATE

[In this adaptation from Shakespeare Dryden transformed Cressida into a faithful and
unjustly accused maiden. The play was probably acted late in 1678, since it was entered on
the *Stationers' Register* April 14, 1679 (Malone,
I, 1, 119) and published late in the same
year, being entered in the *Term Catalogue*
for Michaelmas Term (November). This was

the first of Dryden's works to be " printed for
Jacob Tonson," who from this time on published nearly all his writings.]

PROLOGUE

SPOKEN BY MR. BETTERTON, REPRESENTING
THE GHOST OF SHAKESPEARE

SEE, my lov'd Britons, see your Shake-
  speare rise,
An awful ghost confess'd to human eyes !
Unnam'd, methinks, distinguish d I had
  been
From other shades, by this eternal green,
About whose wreaths the vulgar poets
  strive,
And with a touch their wither'd bays re-
  vive.
Untaught, unpractic'd, in a barbarous age,
I found not, but created first the stage;
And, if I drain'd no Greek or Latin store,
'T was that my own abundance gave me
  more.   10
On foreign trade I needed not rely,
Like fruitful Britain, rich without supply.
In this my rough-drawn play you shall be-
  hold
Some master-strokes, so manly and so
  bold,
That he who meant to alter, found 'em
  such,
He shook, and thought it sacrilege to
  touch.
Now, where are the successors to my
  name ?
What bring they to fill out a poet's fame ?
Weak, short-liv'd issues of a feeble age;
Scarce living to be christen'd on the
  stage !   20
For humor farce, for love they rhyme dis-
  pense,
That tolls the knell for their departed
  sense.
Dulness might thrive in any trade but
  this:
'T would recommend to some fat benefice.
Dulness, that in a playhouse meets dis-
  grace,
Might meet with reverence in its proper
  place.
The fulsome clench, that nauseates the ⎱
  town,   ⎰
Would from a judge or alderman go ⎬
  down,   ⎭
Such virtue is there in a robe and gown !

And that insipid stuff which here you⎱
  hate,   30   ⎰
Might somewhere else be call'd a grave ⎬
  debate;   ⎭
Dulness is decent in the Church and⎱
  State.   ⎰
But I forget that still 't is understood
Bad plays are best decried by showing
  good.
Sit silent then, that my pleas'd soul may
  see
A judging audience once, and worthy me;
My faithful scene from true records shall
  tell
How Trojan valor did the Greek excel;
Your great forefathers shall their fame
  regain,
And Homer's angry ghost repine in vain. 40

EPILOGUE

SPOKEN BY THERSITES

THESE cruel critics put me into passion,
For in their low'ring looks I read damna-
  tion:
Ye expect a satire, and I seldom fail;
When I 'm first beaten, 't is my part to
  rail.
You British fools, of the old Trojan stock,
That stand so thick one cannot miss the
  flock,
Poets have cause to dread a keeping pit,
When women's cullies come to judge of
  wit.
As we strow ratsbane when we vermin fear,
'T were worth our cost to scatter fool-bane
  here;   10
And, after all our judging fops were
  serv'd,
Dull poets too should have a dose reserv'd;
Such reprobates, as, past all sense of
  shaming,
Write on, and ne'er are satisfied with
  damning:
Next, those, to whom the stage does not
  belong,
Such whose vocation only is to song;
At most to prologue, when, for want of
  time,
Poets take in for journeywork in rhyme.
But I want curses for those mighty shoals
Of scribbling Chloris's and Phyllis' fools:
Those oafs should be restrain'd, during
  their lives.   25

From pen and ink, as madmen are from
    knives.
I could rail on, but 't were a task as vain
As preaching truth at Rome, or wit in
    Spain:
Yet to huff out our play was worth my
    trying;
John Lilburne scap'd his judges by defying:
If guilty, yet I 'm sure o' th' Church's
    blessing,
By suffering for the plot, without confess-
    ing.

SONG

I

Can life be a blessing,
    Or worth the possessing,
Can life be a blessing, if love were away?
    Ah, no! tho' our love all night keep us
        waking,
And tho' he torment us with cares all the
    day,
    Yet he sweetens, he sweetens our pains
        in the taking;
There 's an hour at the last, there 's an
    hour to repay.

II

In every possessing,
    The ravishing blessing,
In every possessing the fruit of our pain, 10
    Poor lovers forget long ages of anguish,
Whate'er they have suffer'd and done to
    obtain;
    'T is a pleasure, a pleasure to sigh and
        to languish,
When we hope, when we hope to be happy
    again.

PROLOGUE TO CÆSAR BORGIA, SON OF POPE ALEXANDER THE SIXTH

[This tragedy, by Nathaniel Lee, was probably acted in 1679. It is entered on the *Term
Catalogue* for Michaelmas Term (November)
of that year, though the first edition is dated
1680.]

Th' unhappy man, who once has trail'd a
    pen,
Lives not to please himself, but other men;
Is always drudging, wastes his life and
    blood,

Yet only eats and drinks what you think
    good:
What praise soe'er the poetry deserve,
Yet every fool can bid the poet starve.
That fumbling lecher to revenge is bent,
Because he thinks himself or whore is
    meant:
Name but a cuckold, all the city swarms;
From Leadenhall to Ludgate is in arms. 10
Were there no fear of Antichrist, or
    France,
In the best times poor poets live by chance.
Either you come not here, or, as you
        grace
Some old acquaintance, drop into the
        place,
Careless and qualmish with a yawning
        face:
You sleep o'er wit, and by my troth you
    may;
Most of your talents lie another way.
You love to hear of some prodigious tale,
The bell that toll'd alone, or Irish whale.
News is your food, and you enough pro-
    vide, 20
Both for yourselves, and all the world be-
    side.
One theater there is of vast resort,
Which whilom of Requests was call'd the
    Court;
But now the great Exchange of News 't is
    hight,
And full of hum and buzz from noon till
    night.
Upstairs and down you run, as for a race,
And each man wears three nations in his
    face.
So big you look, tho' claret you retrench,
That, arm'd with bottled ale, you huff the
    French;
But all your entertainment still is fed 30
By villains in our own dull island bred:
Would you return to us, we dare engage
To show you better rogues upon the stage.
You know no poison but plain ratsbane
    here;
Death 's more refin'd, and better bred else-
    where.
They have a civil way in Italy,
By smelling a perfume to make you die;
A trick would make you lay your snuff-
        box by.
Murder 's a trade — so known and practic'd
    there,
That 't is infallible as is the chair — 40

But mark their feasts, you shall behold
    such pranks;
The Pope says grace, but 't is the Devil
    gives thanks.

PROLOGUE TO THE LOYAL GENERAL

[This tragedy, by Nahum Tate, was probably
acted in 1679; it was published in 1680, being
entered on the *Term Catalogue* for Hilary
Term (February) of that year. Dryden's prologue was reprinted in the third edition (1702)
of *Miscellany Poems, the First Part*, where it
is called simply *A Prologue written by Mr.
Dryden.*]

IF yet there be a few that take delight ⎫
In that which reasonable men should |
    write,   ⎬
To them alone we dedicate this night. ⎭
The rest may satisfy their curious itch
With city gazettes, or some factious speech,
Or whate'er libel, for the public good,
Stirs up the Shrovetide crew to fire and
    blood !
Remove your benches, you apostate pit,
And take, above, twelve pennyworth of
    wit;
Go back to your dear dancing on the
    rope,   10
Or see what 's worse, the Devil and the
    Pope !
The plays that take on our corrupted stage,
Methinks, resemble the distracted age;
Noise, madness, all unreasonable things,
That strike at sense, as rebels do at kings !
The style of forty-one our poets write,
And you are grown to judge like forty-
    eight.
Such censures our mistaking audience
    make,
That 't is almost grown scandalous to take !
They talk of fevers that infect the brains, 20
But nonsense is the new disease that reigns.
Weak stomachs, with a long disease op-
    press'd,
Cannot the cordials of strong wit digest.
Therefore thin nourishment of farce ye
    choose,
Decoctions of a barley-water Muse:
A meal of tragedy would make ye sick,
Unless it were a very tender chick.
Some scenes in sippets would be worth our
    time;

Those would go down; some love that 's
    poach'd in rhyme;
If these should fail ——   30
We must lie down, and, after all our cost,
Keep holiday, like watermen in frost;
Whilst you turn players on the world's
    great stage,
And act yourselves the farce of your own
    age.

THE PROLOGUE AT OXFORD, 1680

[This prologue is here reprinted from *Miscellany Poems*, 1684. It was written for an
Oxford production of Lee's *Sophonisba, or
Hannibal's Overthrow*, a tragedy first published
in 1675 (see *Term Catalogue* for Michaelmas
Term (November), 1675; the edition is dated
1676), and appeared in an edition of that play
in 1681. This text varies somewhat from that
included in *Miscellany Poems*, which Dryden
probably revised for publication.]

THESPIS, the first professor of our art,
At country wakes sung ballads from a cart.
To prove this true, if Latin be no trespass,
Dicitur et plaustris vexisse poemata Thespis.
But Æschylus, says Horace in some page,
Was the first mountebank that trod the
    stage:
Yet Athens never knew your learned sport
Of tossing poets in a tennis court.
But 't is the talent of our English nation,
Still to be plotting some new reforma-
    tion;   10
And few years hence, if anarchy goes on,
Jack Presbyter shall here erect his
    throne,
Knock out a tub with preaching once a
    day,
And every prayer be longer than a play.
Then all your heathen wits shall go to pot,
For disbelieving of a Popish Plot:
Your poets shall be us'd like infidels,
And worst, the author of *The Oxford
    Bells :*
Nor should we scape the sentence, to de-
    part,
Ev'n in our first original, a cart.   20
No zealous brother there would want a
    stone,
To maul us cardinals, and pelt Pope Joan:
Religion, learning, wit, would be sup-
    press'd,

Rags of the whore, and trappings of the
    beast.
Scot, Suarez, Tom of Aquin, must go down,
As chief supporters of the triple crown;

And Aristotle's for destruction ripe;
Some say, he call'd the soul an organ-pipe,
Which, by some little help of derivation,
Shall then be prov'd a pipe of inspiration. 30

TRANSLATIONS FROM OVID'S EPISTLES

Vel tibi composita cantetur epistola voce :
Ignotum hoc aliis ille novavit opus. — OVID.

[The following translations, Dryden's first experiment in a sort of work which was later
to become his main occupation, were first published in a small octavo entitled, *Ovid's Epistles,*
translated by several hands [motto as above], London, 1680. It contains twenty-three pieces, the
epistles from Dido to Æneas and from Phyllis to Demophon appearing in two different translations. Among the contributors, besides Dryden, were Tate, Aphra Behn, Duke, Rymer, Otway,
Butler, and, queerly enough, Dryden's arch-enemy Settle. Lord Mulgrave appears only as col-
laborating with Dryden on the epistle from Helen to Paris.]

THE PREFACE TO OVID'S EPISTLES

THE life of Ovid being already written in
our language, before the translation of his
Metamorphoses, I will not presume so far upon
myself, to think I can add anything to Mr.
Sandys his undertaking. The English reader
may there be satisfied, that he flourish'd in the
reign of Augustus Cæsar; that he was extracted from an ancient family of Roman
Knights; that he was born to the inheritance
of a splendid fortune; that he was design'd to
the study of the law, and had made considerable progress in it, before he quitted that profession for this of poetry, to which he was
more naturally form'd. The cause of his banishment is unknown; because he was himself
unwilling further to provoke the emperor, by
ascribing it to any other reason than what was
pretended by Augustus, which was the lasciviousness of his *Elegies*, and his *Art of Love.*
'T is true, they are not to be excus'd in the
severity of manners, as being able to corrupt a
larger empire, if there were any, than that of
Rome : yet this may be said in behalf of Ovid,
that no man has ever treated the passion of love
with so much delicacy of thought, and of expression, or search'd into the nature of it more
philosophically than he. And the emperor
who condemn'd him had as little reason as
another man to punish that fault with so much
severity, if at least he were the author of a
certain epigram which is ascrib'd to him, relating to the cause of the first civil war betwixt
himself and Mark Anthony the triumvir, which
is more fulsome than any passage I have met
with in our poet. To pass by the naked familiarity of his expressions to Horace, which are
cited in that author's life, I need only mention

one notorious act of his, in taking Livia to his
bed, when she was not only married, but with
child by her husband then living. But deeds,
it seems, may be justified by arbitrary power,
when words are question'd in a poet. There
is another guess of the grammarians, as far
from truth as the first from reason : they will
have him banish'd for some favors, which,
they say, he receiv'd from Julia, the daughter
of Augustus, whom they think he celebrates
under the name of Corinna in his *Elegies:*
but he who will observe the verses which are
made to that mistress, may gather from the
whole contexture of them, that Corinna was
not a woman of the highest quality. If Julia
were then married to Agrippa, why should our
poet make his petition to Isis for her safe de-
livery, and afterwards condole her miscarriage ;
which, for aught he knew, might be by her
own husband ? Or, indeed, how durst he be so
bold to make the least discovery of such a
crime, which was no less than capital, especially committed against a person of Agrippa's
rank ? Or, if it were before her marriage, he
would surely have been more discreet than to
have publish'd an accident which must have
been fatal to them both. But what most confirms me against this opinion is, that Ovid himself complains that the true person of Corinna
was found out by the fame of his verses to
her : which, if it had been Julia, he durst not
have own'd ; and, besides, an immediate punishment must have follow'd. He seems himself more truly to have touch'd at the cause of
his exile in those obscure verses :

Cur aliquid vidi, cur noxia lumina feci ? &c.

Namely, that he had either seen, or was conscious to, somewhat which had procur'd him

his disgrace. But neither am I satisfied that this was the incest of the emperor with his own daughter: for Augustus was of a nature too vindicative to have contented himself with so small a revenge, or so unsafe to himself, as that of simple banishment; and would certainly have secur'd his crimes from public notice by the death of him who was witness to them. Neither have histories given us any sight into such an action of this emperor: nor would he (the greatest politician of his time), in all probability, have manag'd his crimes with so little secrecy, as not to shun the observation of any man. It seems more probable, that Ovid was either the confident of some other passion, or that he had stumbled by some inadvertency upon the privacies of Livia, and seen her in a bath; for the words:

Nudam sine veste Dianam

agree better with Livia, who had the fame of chastity, than with either of the Julias, who were both noted of incontinency. The first verses which were made by him in his youth, and recited publicly, according to the custom, were, as he himself assures us, to Corinna; his banishment happen'd not till the age of fifty: from which it may be deduc'd, with probability enough, that the love of Corinna did not occasion it. Nay, he tells us plainly, that his offense was that of error only, not of wickedness: and in the same paper of verses also, that the cause was notoriously known at Rome, tho' it be left so obscure to after ages.

But to leave conjectures on a subject so uncertain, and to write somewhat more authentic of this poet: that he frequented the court of Augustus, and was well receiv'd in it, is most undoubted: all his poems bear the character of a court, and appear to be written, as the French call it, *cavalièrement*. Add to this, that the titles of many of his *Elegies*, and more of his *Letters* in his banishment, are address'd to persons well known to us, even at this distance, to have been considerable in that court.

Nor was his acquaintance less with the famous poets of his age, than with the noblemen and ladies. He tells you himself, in a particular account of his own life, that Macer, Horace, Tibullus, Propertius, and many others of them, were his familiar friends, and that some of them communicated their writings to him; but that he had only seen Virgil.

If the imitation of nature be the business of a poet, I know no author who can justly be compar'd with ours, especially in the description of the passions. And, to prove this, I shall need no other judges than the generality of his readers; for all passions being inborn with us, we are almost equally judges, when we are concern'd in the representation of them. Now I will appeal to any man who has read this poet, whether he find not the natural emotion of the same passion in himself, which the poet describes in his feign'd persons? His thoughts, which are the pictures and results of those passions, are generally such as naturally arise from those disorderly motions of our spirits. Yet, not to speak too partially in his behalf, I will confess that the copiousness of his wit was such that he often writ too pointedly for his subject, and made his persons speak more eloquently than the violence of their passion would admit; so that he is frequently witty out of season; leaving the imitation of nature, and the cooler dictates of his judgment, for the false applause of fancy. Yet he seems to have found out this imperfection in his riper age, for why else should he complain that his *Metamorphoses* was left unfinish'd? Nothing sure can be added to the wit of that poem, or of the rest; but many things ought to have been retrench'd; which I suppose would have been the business of his age, if his misfortunes had not come too fast upon him. But take him uncorrected, as he is transmitted to us, and it must be acknowledg'd, in spite of his Dutch friends, the commentators, even of Julius Scaliger himself, that Seneca's censure will stand good against him:

Nescivit quod bene cessit relinquere;

he never knew how to give over, when he had done well; but, continually varying the same sense an hundred ways, and taking up in another place what he had more than enough inculcated before, he sometimes cloys his readers instead of satisfying them; and gives occasion to his translators, who dare not cover him, to blush at the nakedness of their father. This then is the allay of Ovid's writing, which is sufficiently recompens'd by his other excellencies: nay, this very fault is not without its beauties; for the most severe censor cannot but be pleas'd with the prodigality of his wit, tho' at the same time he could have wish'd that the master of it had been a better manager. Everything which he does becomes him; and, if sometimes he appear too gay, yet there is a secret gracefulness of youth which accompanies his writings, tho' the staidness and sobriety of age be wanting. In the most material part, which is the conduct, 't is certain that he seldom has miscarried; for if his elegies be compar'd with those of Tibullus and Propertius, his contemporaries, it will be found that those poets seldom design'd before they writ; and tho' the language of Tibullus be more polish'd, and the learning of Propertius, especially in his fourth book, more set out to ostentation; yet their common practice was to look no further before them than the next line; whence it will inevitably follow that they can drive to no certain point, but ramble from one subject to another, and conclude with somewhat which is not of a piece with their beginning :

> Purpureus, late qui splendeat, unus et alter
> Assuitur pannus,

as Horace says : tho' the verses are golden, they are but patch'd into the garment. But our poet has always the goal in his eye, which directs him in his race ; some beautiful design, which he first establishes, and then contrives the means which will naturally conduct it to his end. This will be evident to judicious readers in this work of his *Epistles*, of which somewhat, at least in general, will be expected.

The title of them in our late editions is *Epistolæ Heroidum*, the *Letters of the Heroines*. But Heinsius has judg'd more truly, that the inscription of our author was barely, *Epistles;* which he concludes from his cited verses, where Ovid asserts this work as his own invention, and not borrow'd from the Greeks, whom (as the masters of their learning) the Romans usually did imitate. But it appears not from their writers, that any of the Grecians ever touch'd upon this way, which our poet therefore justly has vindicated to himself. I quarrel not at the word *Heroidum*, because 't is us'd by Ovid in his *Art of Love :*

> Jupiter ad veteres supplex Heroidas ibat.

But, sure, he could not be guilty of such an oversight, to call his work by the name of *Heroines*, when there are divers men or heroes, as, namely, Paris, Leander, and Acontius, join'd in it. Except Sabinus, who writ some answers to Ovid's *Letters :*

> (Quam celer e toto rediit meus orbe Sabinus)

I remember not any of the Romans who have treated this subject, save only Propertius, and that but once, in his *Epistle of Arethusa to Lycotas*, which is written so near the style of Ovid, that it seems to be but an imitation ; and therefore ought not to defraud our poet of the glory of his invention.

Concerning this work of the *Epistles*, I shall content myself to observe these few particulars : first, that they are generally granted to be the most perfect piece of Ovid, and that the style of them is tenderly passionate and courtly ; two properties well agreeing with the persons, which were heroines and lovers. Yet, where the characters were lower, as in Œnone and Hero, he has kept close to nature, in drawing his images after a country life, tho', perhaps, he has romaniz'd his Grecian dames too much, and made them speak, sometimes, as if they had been born in the city of Rome, and under the empire of Augustus. There seems to be no great variety in the particular subjects which he has chosen ; most of the *Epistles* being written from ladies who were forsaken by their lovers ; which is the reason that many of the same thoughts come back upon us in divers letters ; but of the general character of women, which is modesty, he has taken a most becoming care ; for his amorous expressions go no further than virtue may allow, and therefore may be read, as he intended them, by matrons without a blush.

Thus much concerning the poet : whom you find translated by divers hands, that you may at least have that variety in the English, which the subject denied to the author of the Latin. It remains that I should say somewhat of poetical translations in general, and give my opinion (with submission to better judgments) which way of version seems to me most proper.

All translation, I suppose, may be reduc'd to these three heads :

First, that of metaphrase, or turning an author word by word, and line by line, from one language into another. Thus, or near this manner, was Horace his *Art of Poetry* translated by Ben Jonson. The second way is that of paraphrase, or translation with latitude, where the author is kept in view by the translator, so as never to be lost, but his words are not so strictly follow'd as his sense ; and that too is admitted to be amplified, but not alter'd. Such is Mr. Waller's translation of Virgil's *Fourth Æneid*. The third way is that of imitation, where the translator (if now he has not lost that name) assumes the liberty, not only to vary from the words and sense, but to forsake them both as he sees occasion ; and, taking only some general hints from the original, to run division on the groundwork, as he pleases. Such is Mr. Cowley's practice in turning two odes of Pindar, and one of Horace, into English.

Concerning the first of these methods, our master Horace has given us this caution :

> Nec verbum verbo curabis reddere, fidus
> Interpres ——
>
> Nor word for word too faithfully translate,

as the Earl of Roscommon has excellently render'd it. Too faithfully is, indeed, pedantically : 't is a faith like that which proceeds from superstition, blind and zealous. Take it in the expression of Sir John Denham to Sir Richard Fanshawe, on his version of the *Pastor Fido :*

> That servile path thou nobly dost decline,
> Of tracing word by word, and line by line.
> A new and nobler way thou dost pursue,
> To make translations and translators too ;
> They but preserve the ashes, thou the flame,
> True to his sense, but truer to his fame.

'T is almost impossible to translate verbally and well at the same time; for the Latin (a most severe and compendious language) often expresses that in one word, which either the barbarity, or the narrowness, of modern tongues cannot supply in more. 'T is frequent also that the conceit is couch'd in some expression, which will be lost in English.

Atque iidem venti vela fidemque ferent.

What poet of our nation is so happy as to express this thought literally in English, and to strike wit, or almost sense, out of it ?

In short, the verbal copier is incumber'd with so many difficulties at once, that he can never disentangle himself from all. He is to consider, at the same time, the thought of his author, and his words, and to find out the counterpart to each in another language; and, besides this, he is to confine himself to the compass of numbers, and the slavery of rhyme. 'T is much like dancing on ropes with fetter'd legs: a man may shun a fall by using caution; but the gracefulness of motion is not to be expected : and when we have said the best of it, 't is but a foolish task ; for no sober man would put himself into a danger for the applause of scaping without breaking his neck. We see Ben Jonson could not avoid obscurity in his literal translation of Horace, attempted in the same compass of lines : nay, Horace himself could scarce have done it to a Greek poet :

Brevis esse laboro, obscurus fio :

either perspicuity or gracefulness will frequently be wanting. Horace has, indeed, avoided both these rocks in his translation of the three first lines of Homer's *Odysses*, which he has contracted into two :

Dic mihi, musa, virum, captæ post tempora Trojæ
Qui mores hominum multorum vidit et urbes.

Muse, speak the man, who, since the siege of Troy,
So many towns, such change of manners saw.
EARL OF ROSC.

But then the sufferings of Ulysses, which are a considerable part of that sentence, are omitted :

Ὃς μάλα πολλὰ πλάγχθη :

The consideration of these difficulties in a servile, literal translation, not long since made two of our famous wits, Sir John Denham and Mr. Cowley, to contrive another way of turning authors into our tongue, call'd, by the latter of them, imitation. As they were friends, I suppose they communicated their thoughts on this subject to each other; and, therefore, their reasons for it are little different, tho' the practice of one is much more moderate. I take imitation of an author, in their sense, to be an endeavor of a later poet to write like one who has written before him, on the same subject: that is, not to translate his words, or to be confin'd to his sense, but only to set him as a pattern, and to write as he supposes that author would have done, had he liv'd in our age, and in our country. Yet I dare not say that either of them have carried this libertine way of rend'ring authors (as Mr. Cowley calls it) so far as my definition reaches. For, in the *Pindaric Odes*, the customs and ceremonies of ancient Greece are still preserv'd. But I know not what mischief may arise hereafter from the example of such an innovation, when writers of unequal parts to him shall imitate so bold an undertaking. To add and to diminish what we please, which is the way avow'd by him, ought only to be granted to Mr. Cowley, and that too only in his translation of Pindar ; because he alone was able to make him amends, by giving him better of his own, whenever he refus'd his author's thoughts. Pindar is generally known to be a dark writer, to want connection, (I mean as to our understanding,) to soar out of sight, and leave his reader at a gaze. So wild and ungovernable a poet cannot be translated literally ; his genius is too strong to bear a chain, and, Samson-like, he shakes it off. A genius so elevated and unconfin'd as Mr. Cowley's was but necessary to make Pindar speak English, and that was to be perform'd by no other way than imitation. But if Virgil or Ovid, or any regular intelligible authors are thus us'd, 't is no longer to be call'd their work, when neither the thoughts nor words are drawn from the original ; but instead of them there is something new produc'd, which is almost the creation of another hand. By this way, 't is true, somewhat that is excellent may be invented, perhaps more excellent than the first design ; tho' Virgil must be still excepted, when that perhaps takes place. Yet he who is inquisitive to know an author's thoughts, will be disappointed in his expectation. And 't is not always that a man will be contented to have a present made him, when he expects the payment of a debt. To state it fairly : imitation of an author is the most advantageous way for a translator to shew himself, but the greatest wrong which can be done to the memory and reputation of the dead. Sir John Denham, who advis'd more liberty than he took himself, gives this reason for his innovation, in his admirable preface before the translation of the *Second Æneid :* " Poetry is of so subtile a spirit, that, in pouring out of one language into another, it will all evaporate ; and, if a new spirit be not added in the transfusion, there will remain nothing but a *caput mortuum*." I confess this argument holds good against a literal translation ; but who defends it ? Imitation and verbal version are, in my opinion, the two extremes which ought to be avoided; and therefore, when I have propos'd the mean betwixt them, it will be seen how far his argument will reach.

No man is capable of translating poetry, who, besides a genius to that art, is not a master both of his author's language, and of his own; nor must we understand the language only of the poet, but his particular turn of thoughts and of expression, which are the characters that distinguish, and as it were individuate him from all other writers. When we are come thus far, 't is time to look into ourselves, to conform our genius to his, to give his thought either the same turn, if our tongue will bear it, or, if not, to vary but the dress, not to alter or destroy the substance. The like care must be taken of the more outward ornaments, the words. When they appear (which is but seldom) literally graceful, it were an injury to the author that they should be chang'd; but, since every language is so full of its own proprieties, that what is beautiful in one, is often barbarous, nay, sometimes nonsense, in another, it would be unreasonable to limit a translator to the narrow compass of his author's words: 't is enough if he choose out some expression which does not vitiate the sense. I suppose he may stretch his chain to such a latitude; but, by innovation of thoughts, methinks he breaks it. By this means the spirit of an author may be transfus'd, and yet not lost; and thus 't is plain that the reason alleg'd by Sir John Denham has no farther force than to expression: for thought, if it be translated truly, cannot be lost in another language; but the words that convey it to our apprehension (which are the image and ornament of that thought) may be so ill chosen as to make it appear in an unhandsome dress, and rob it of its native luster. There is, therefore, a liberty to be allow'd for the expression; neither is it necessary that words and lines should be confin'd to the measure of their original. The sense of an author, generally speaking, is to be sacred and inviolable. If the fancy of Ovid be luxuriant, 't is his character to be so; and if I retrench it, he is no longer Ovid. It will be replied that he receives advantage by this lopping of his superfluous branches; but I rejoin that a translator has no such right. When a painter copies from the life, I suppose he has no privilege to alter features and lineaments under pretense that his picture will look better; perhaps the face which he has drawn would be more exact, if the eyes or nose were alter'd; but 't is his business to make it resemble the original. In two cases only there may a seeming difficulty arise; that is, if the thought be notoriously trivial, or dishonest; but the same answer will serve for both, that then they ought not to be translated:

—— Et quæ
Desperes tractata nitescere posse, relinquas.

Thus I have ventur'd to give my opinion on this subject against the authority of two great men, but I hope without offense to either of their memories; for I both lov'd them living, and reverence them now they are dead. But if, after what I have urg'd, it be thought by better judges that the praise of a translation consists in adding new beauties to the piece, thereby to recompense the loss which it sustains by change of language, I shall be willing to be taught better, and to recant. In the mean time, it seems to me that the true reason why we have so few versions which are tolerable, is not from the too close pursuing of the author's sense, but because there are so few who have all the talents which are requisite for translation, and that there is so little praise, and so small encouragement, for so considerable a part of learning.

To apply in short what has been said, to this present work, the reader will here find most of the translations with some little latitude or variation from the author's sense. That of Œnone to Paris is in Mr. Cowley's way of imitation only. I was desir'd to say that the author, who is of the fair sex, understood not Latin. But if she does not, I am afraid she has given us occasion to be asham'd, who do.

For my own part, I am ready to acknowledge that I have transgress'd the rules which I have given, and taken more liberty than a just translation will allow. But so many gentlemen whose wit and learning are well known being join'd in it, I doubt not but that their excellencies will make you ample satisfaction for my errors.   J. DRYDEN.

CANACE TO MACAREUS

THE ARGUMENT

Macareus and Canace, son and daughter to Æolus, god of the winds, lov'd each other incestuously: Canace was deliver'd of a son, and committed him to her nurse, to be secretly convey'd away. The infant, crying out, by that means was discover'd to Æolus, who, inrag'd at the wickedness of his children, commanded the babe to be expos'd to wild beasts on the mountains; and, withal, sent a sword to Canace, with this message, that her crimes would instruct her how to use it. With this sword she slew herself; but, before she died, she writ the following letter to her brother Macareus, who had taken sanctuary in the temple of Apollo.

IF streaming blood my fatal letter stain,
Imagine, ere you read, the writer slain;
One hand the sword, and one the pen em-
    ploys,
And in my lap the ready paper lies.
Think in this posture thou behold'st me
    write:
In this my cruel father would delight.
O, were he present, that his eyes and
    hands
Might see and urge the death which he
    commands !
Than all his raging winds more dreadful,
    he,
Unmov'd, without a tear, my wounds
    would see.   10
Jove justly plac'd him on a stormy throne,
His people's temper is so like his own.
The North and South, and each contending
    blast,
Are underneath his wide dominion cast:
Those he can rule; but his tempestuous mind
Is, like his airy kingdom, unconfin'd.
Ah ! what avail my kindred gods above,
That in their number I can reckon Jove ?
What help will all my heav'nly friends af-
    ford,
When to my breast I lift the pointed
    sword ?   20
That hour which join'd us came before its
    time:
In death we had been one without a crime.
Why did thy flames beyond a brother's
    move ?
Why lov'd I thee with more than sister's
    love ?
For I lov'd too; and, knowing not my
    wound,
A secret pleasure in thy kisses found:
My cheeks no longer did their color boast,
My food grew loathsome, and my strength
    I lost:
Still ere I spoke, a sigh would stop my
    tongue;
Short were my slumbers, and my nights
    were long.   30
I knew not from my love these griefs did
    grow,
Yet was, alas, the thing I did not know.
My wily nurse, by long experience, found,
And first discover'd to my soul its wound.
" 'T is love," said she; and then my down-
    cast eyes,
And guilty dumbness, witness'd my sur-
    prise.

Forc'd at the last, my shameful pain I tell;
And, O, what follow'd we both know too
    well !
' When half denying, more than half con-
    tent,
' Embraces warm'd me to a full consent, 40
' Then with tumultuous joys my heart did
    beat,
' And guilt, that made them anxious, made
    them great.
But now my swelling womb heav'd up
    my breast,
And rising weight my sinking limbs op-
    press'd.
What herbs, what plants, did not my nurse
    produce,
To make abortion by their pow'rful juice ?
What medicines tried we not, to thee un-
    known ?
Our first crime common; this was mine
    alone.
But the strong child, secure in his dark
    cell,
With nature's vigor did our arts repel. 50
And now the pale-fac'd empress of the night
Nine times had fill'd her orb with borrow'd
    light:
Not knowing 't was my labor, I complain
Of sudden shootings, and of grinding pain:
My throes came thicker, and my cries in-
    creas'd,
Which with her hand the conscious nurse
    suppress'd.
To that unhappy fortune was I come,
Pain urg'd my clamors, but fear kept me
    dumb.
With inward struggling I restrain'd my
    cries,
And drunk the tears that trickled from my
    eyes.   60
Death was in sight, Lucina gave no aid;
And ev'n my dying had my guilt betray'd.
Thou cam'st, and in thy count'nance sate
    despair;
Rent were thy garments all, and torn thy
    hair:
Yet, feigning comfort, which thou couldst
    not give,
(Press'd in thy arms, and whisp'ring me to
    live:)
" For both our sakes," saidst thou, " pre-
    serve thy life;
Live, my dear sister, and my dearer wife."
Rais'd by that name, with my last pangs I
    strove:

Such pow'r have words, when spoke by
   those we love. 70
The babe, as if he heard what thou hadst
   sworn,
With hasty joy sprung forward to be born.
What helps it to have weather'd out one
   storm ?
Fear of our father does another form.
High in his hall, rock'd in a chair of state,
The king with his tempestuous council sate.
Thro' this large room our only passage lay,
By which we could the newborn babe con-
   vey.
Swath'd, in her lap, the bold nurse bore
   him out,
With olive branches cover'd round about;
And, mutt'ring pray'rs, as holy rites she
   meant, 81
Thro' the divided crowd unquestion'd went.
Just at the door, th' unhappy infant cried:
The grandsire heard him, and the theft he
   spied.
Swift as a whirlwind to the nurse he flies,
And deafs his stormy subjects with his
   cries.
With one fierce puff he blows the leaves
   away:
Expos'd the self-discover'd infant lay.
The noise reach'd me, and my presaging
   mind
Too soon its own approaching woes divin'd.
Not ships at sea with winds are shaken
   more, 91
Nor seas themselves, when angry tempests
   roar,
Than I, when my loud father's voice I
   hear:
The bed beneath me trembled with my
   fear.
He rush'd upon me, and divulg'd my stain;
Scarce from my murther could his hands
   refrain.
I only answer'd him with silent tears:
They flow'd; my tongue was frozen up
   with fears.
His little grandchild he commands away,
To mountain wolves and every bird of
   prey. 100
The babe cried out, as if he understood,
And begg'd his pardon with what voice he
   could.
By what expressions can my grief be
   shown ?
(Yet you may guess my anguish by your
   own)

To see my bowels, and, what yet was
   worse,
Your bowels too, condemn'd to such a
   curse !
Out went the king; my voice its freedom
   found,
My breasts I beat, my blubber'd cheeks I
   wound.
And now appear'd the messenger of
   death;
Sad were his looks, and scarce he drew his
   breath, 110
To say: " Your father sends you " — with
   that word
His trembling hands presented me a sword —
" Your father sends you this; and lets you
   know,
That your own crimes the use of it will
   show."
Too well I know the sense those words im-
   part:
His present shall be treasur'd in my heart.
Are these the nuptial gifts a bride re-
   ceives ?
And this the fatal dow'r a father gives ?
Thou god of marriage, shun thy own dis-
   grace,
And take thy torch from this detested
   place: 120
Instead of that, let furies light their
   brands,
And fire my pile with their infernal hands.
With happier fortune may my sisters wed;
Warn'd by the dire example of the dead.
For thee, poor babe, what crime could they
   pretend ?
How could thy infant innocence offend ?
A guilt there was; but, O, that guilt was
   mine !
Thou suffer'st for a sin that was not thine.
Thy mother's grief and crime ! but just
   enjoy'd,
Shown to my sight, and born to be de-
   stroy'd ! 130
Unhappy offspring of my teeming womb,
Dragg'd headlong from thy cradle to thy
   tomb !
Thy unoffending life I could not save,
Nor weeping could I follow to thy grave !
Nor on thy tomb could offer my shorn
   hair;
Nor show the grief which tender mothers
   bear !
Yet long thou shalt not from my arms be
   lost;

For soon I will o'ertake thy infant ghost.
But thou, my love, and now my love's de-
   spair,
Perform his funerals with paternal care:
His scatter'd limbs with my dead body
   burn;   141
And once more join us in the pious urn.
If on my wounded breast thou dropp'st a
   tear,
Think for whose sake my breast that wound
   did bear;
And faithfully my last desires fulfil
As I perform my cruel father's will.

HELEN TO PARIS

BY THE RIGHT HONORABLE THE EARL
OF MULGRAVE AND MR. DRYDEN

THE ARGUMENT

Helen, having receiv'd the foregoing epistle
from Paris, returns the following answer:
wherein she seems at first to chide him for
his presumption in writing as he had done,
which could only proceed from his low opinion of her virtue; then owns herself to be
sensible of the passion which he had express'd for her, tho' she much suspect his
constancy; and at last discovers her inclinations to be favorable to him: the whole letter
shewing the extreme artifice of womankind.

WHEN loose epistles violate chaste eyes,
She half consents, who silently denies.
How dares a stranger, with designs so vain,
Marriage and hospitable rights profane?
Was it for this, your fate did shelter find
From swelling seas, and every faithless
   wind?
(For tho' a distant country brought you
   forth,
Your usage here was equal to your worth.)
Does this deserve to be rewarded so?
Did you come here a stranger or a foe? 10
Your partial judgment may perhaps com-
   plain,
And think me barbarous for my just dis-
   dain.
Ill-bred then let me be, but not unchaste,
Nor my clear fame with any spot defac'd.
Tho' in my face there's no affected frown,
Nor in my carriage a feign'd niceness
   shown,
I keep my honor still without a stain,

Nor has my love made any coxcomb vain.
Your boldness I with admiration see;
What hope had you to gain a queen like
   me?   20
Because a hero forc'd me once away,
Am I thought fit to be a second prey?
Had I been won, I had deserv'd your
   blame,
But sure my part was nothing but the
   shame.
Yet the base theft to him no fruit did
   bear,
I scap'd unhurt by anything but fear.
Rude force might some unwilling kisses
   gain,
But that was all he ever could obtain.
You on such terms would ne'er have let me
   go;
Were he like you, we had not parted so. 30
Untouch'd the youth restor'd me to my
   friends,
And modest usage made me some amends.
'T is virtue to repent a vicious deed:
Did he repent, that Paris might succeed?
Sure 't is some fate that sets me above
   wrongs,
Yet still exposes me to busy tongues.
I 'll not complain; for who 's displeas'd with
   love,
If it sincere, discreet, and constant prove?
But that I fear; not that I think you base,
Or doubt the blooming beauties of my
   face;   40
But all your sex is subject to deceive,
And ours, alas, too willing to believe.
Yet others yield, and love o'ercomes the
   best:
But why should I not shine above the rest?
Fair Leda's story seems at first to be
A fit example ready found for me.
But she was cozen'd by a borrow'd shape,
And under harmless feathers felt a rape.
If I should yield, what reason could I use?
By what mistake the loving crime excuse?
Her fault was in her pow'rful lover lost; 51
But of what Jupiter have I to boast?
Tho' you to heroes and to kings succeed,
Our famous race does no addition need;
And great alliances but useless prove
To one that's come herself from mighty
   Jove.
Go then, and boast in some less haughty
   place
Your Phrygian blood, and Priam's ancient
   race;

Which I would shew I valued, if I durst;
You are the fifth from Jove, but I the first.
The crown of Troy is pow'rful, I confess; 61
But I have reason to think ours no less.
Your letter, fill'd with promises of all
That men can good, or women pleasant
    call,
Gives expectation such an ample field,
As would move goddesses themselves to
    yield.
But if I e'er offend great Juno's laws,
Yourself shall be the dear, the only cause:
Either my honor I 'll to death maintain,
Or follow you, without mean thoughts of
    gain. 70
Not that so fair a present I despise;
We like the gift, when we the giver prize.
But 't is your love moves me, which made
    you take
Such pains, and run such hazards for my
    sake.
I have perceiv'd (tho' I dissembled too)
A thousand things that love has made you
    do.
Your eager eyes would almost dazzle mine,
In which, wild man, your wanton thoughts
    would shine.
Sometimes you 'd sigh, sometimes disorder'd
    stand,
And with unusual ardor press my hand; 80
Contrive just after me to take the glass,
Nor would you let the least occasion pass:
Which oft I fear'd, I did not mind alone,
And blushing sate for things which you
    have done:
Then murmur'd to myself: "He 'll for my
    sake
Do anything " — I hope 't was no mistake !
Oft have I read within this pleasing grove,
Under my name, those charming words, "I
    love."
I, frowning, seem'd not to believe your
    flame;
But now, alas, am come to write the same. 90
If I were capable to do amiss,
I could not but be sensible of this.
For O, your face has such peculiar charms,
That who can hold from flying to your
    arms !
But what I ne'er can have without offense,
May some blest maid possess with inno-
    cence.
Pleasure may tempt, but virtue more should
    move;
O learn of me to want the thing you love !

What you desire is sought by all mankind:
As you have eyes, so others are not blind. 100
Like you they see, like you my charms
    adore;
They wish not less, but you dare venture
    more.
O, had you then upon our coasts been
    brought,
My virgin love when thousand rivals sought,
You had I seen, you should have had my
    voice;
Nor could my husband justly blame my
    choice !
For both our hopes, alas, you come too
    late !
Another now is master of my fate.
More to my wish I could have liv'd with
    you,
And yet my present lot can undergo. 110
Cease to solicit a weak woman's will,
And urge not her you love to so much ill.
But let me live contented as I may,
And make not my unspotted fame your
    prey.
Some right you claim, since naked to your
    eyes
Three goddesses disputed beauty's prize:
One offer'd valor, t'other crowns; but she
Obtain'd her cause, who, smiling, promis'd
    me.
But first, I am not of belief so light,
To think such nymphs would shew you
    such a sight. 120
Yet, granting this, the other part is feign'd;
A bribe so mean your sentence had not
    gain'd.
With partial eyes I should myself regard,
To think that Venus made me her reward:
I humbly am content with human praise;
A goddess's applause would envy raise.
But be it as you say; for, 't is confess'd,
The men who flatter highest please us best.
That I suspect it, ought not to displease;
For miracles are not believ'd with ease. 130
One joy I have, that I had Venus' voice;
A greater yet, that you confirm'd her choice;
That proffer'd laurels, promis'd sov'reignty,
Juno and Pallas you contemn'd for me.
Am I your empire then, and your renown ?
What heart of rock, but must by this be
    won ?
And yet bear witness, O you pow'rs above,
How rude I am in all the arts of love !
My hand is yet untaught to write to men:
This is th' essay of my unpractic'd pen. 140

Happy those nymphs, whom use has perfect
    made !
I think all crime, and tremble at a shade.
Ev'n while I write, my fearful conscious
    eyes
Look often back, misdoubting a surprise.
For now the rumor spreads among the
    crowd,
At court in whispers, but in town aloud.
Dissemble you, whate'er you hear 'em say:
To leave off loving were your better way;
Yet if you will dissemble it, you may.
Love secretly; the absence of my lord   150
More freedom gives, but does not all afford:
Long is his journey, long will be his stay;
Call'd by affairs of consequence away.
To go, or not, when unresolv'd he stood,
I bid him make what swift return he could:
Then kissing me, he said: " I recommend
All to thy care, but most my Trojan friend."
I smil'd at what he innocently said,
And only answer'd: " You shall be obey'd."
Propitious winds have borne him far from
    hence,   160
But let not this secure your confidence.
Absent he is, yet absent he commands:
You know the proverb: " Princes have long
    hands."
My fame 's my burden: for the more I 'm
    prais'd,
A juster ground of jealousy is rais'd.
Were I less fair, I might have been more
    blest:
Great beauty thro' great danger is possess'd.
To leave me here his venture was not hard,
Because he thought my virtue was my
    guard.
He fear'd my face, but trusted to my life; 170
The beauty doubted, but believ'd the wife.
You bid me use th' occasion while I can,
Put in our hands by the good easy man.
I would, and yet I doubt, 'twixt love and
    fear;
One draws me from you, and one brings me
    near.
Our flames are mutual, and my husband 's
    gone:
The nights are long; I fear to lie alone.
One house contains us, and weak walls
    divide,
And you 're too pressing to be long denied.
Let me not live, but everything conspires 180
To join our loves, and yet my fear retires.
You court with words, when you should
    force employ:

A rape is requisite to shame-fac'd joy.
Indulgent to the wrongs which we receive,
Our sex can suffer what we dare not give.
What have I said ? for both of us 't were
    best,
Our kindling fires if each of us suppress'd.
The faith of strangers is too prone to
    change,
And, like themselves, their wand'ring pas-
    sions range.
Hypsipyle, and the fond Minoian maid, 190
Were both by trusting of their guests be-
    tray'd.
How can I doubt that other men deceive,
When you yourself did fair Œnone leave ?
But lest I should upbraid your treachery,
You make a merit of that crime to me.
Yet grant you were to faithful love in-
    clin'd,
Your weary Trojans wait but for a wind.
Should you prevail; while I assign the
    night,
Your sails are hoisted, and you take your
    flight :
Some bawling mariner our love destroys, 200
And breaks asunder our unfinish'd joys.
But I with you may leave the Spartan port,
To view the Trojan wealth and Priam's
    court:
Shown while I see, I shall expose my fame,
And fill a foreign country with my shame.
In Asia what reception shall I find ?
And what dishonor leave in Greece behind ?
What will your brothers, Priam, Hecuba,
And what will all your modest matrons
    say ?
Ev'n you, when on this action you reflect, 210
My future conduct justly may suspect;
And whate'er stranger lands upon your
    coast,
Conclude me, by your own example, lost.
I from your rage a strumpet's name shall
    hear,
While you forget what part in it you bear.
You, my crime's author, will my crime
    upbraid:
Deep under ground, O let me first be
    laid !
You boast the pomp and plenty of your
    land,
And promise all shall be at my command:
Your Trojan wealth, believe me, I de-
    spise; 220
My own poor native land has dearer ties.
Should I be injur'd on your Phrygian shore,

What help of kindred could I there im-
   plore ?
Medea was by Jason's flatt'ry won:
I may, like her, believe, and be undone.
Plain honest hearts, like mine, suspect no
   cheat,
And love contributes to its own deceit.
The ships, about whose sides loud tempests
   roar,
With gentle winds were wafted from the
   shore.
Your teeming mother dreamt a flaming
   brand,   230
Sprung from her womb, consum'd the Tro-
   jan land.
To second this, old prophecies conspire,
That Ilium shall be burnt with Grecian fire.
Both give me fear ; nor is it much allay'd,
That Venus is oblig'd our loves to aid:
For they, who lost their cause, revenge will
   take;
And for one friend two enemies you make.
Nor can I doubt, but, should I follow you,
The sword would soon our fatal crime pur-
   sue:
A wrong so great my husband's rage would
   rouse,   240
And my relations would his cause espouse.
You boast your strength and courage; but,
   alas !
Your words receive small credit from your
   face.
Let heroes in the dusty field delight:
Those limbs were fashion'd for another
   fight.
Bid Hector sally from the walls of Troy;
A sweeter quarrel should your arms em-
   ploy.
Yet fears like these should not my mind
   perplex,
Were I as wise as many of my sex.
But time and you may bolder thoughts in-
   spire;   250
And I perhaps may yield to your desire.
You last demand a private conference:
These are your words, but I can guess your
   sense.
Your unripe hopes their harvest must at-
   tend:
Be rul'd by me, and time may be your
   friend.
This is enough to let you understand,
For now my pen has tir'd my tender hand:
My woman knows the secret of my heart,
And may hereafter better news impart.

DIDO TO ÆNEAS

THE ARGUMENT

Æneas, the son of Venus and Anchises, having,
at the destruction of Troy, sav'd his gods,
his father, and son Ascanius, from the fire,
put to sea with twenty sail of ships ; and,
having bin long toss'd with tempests, was at
last cast upon the shore of Libya, where
Queen Dido, flying from the cruelty of Pygmalion, her brother, who had kill'd her husband Sichæus, had lately built Carthage.
She entertain'd Æneas and his fleet with
great civility, fell passionately in love with
him, and in the end denied him not the last
favors. But Mercury admonishing Æneas to
go in search of Italy, (a kingdom promis'd to
him by the gods,) he readily prepar'd to obey
him. Dido soon perceiv'd it, and having
in vain tried all other means to engage him to
stay, at last in despair writes to him as follows.

So, on Mæander's banks, when death is nigh,
The mournful swan sings her own elegy.
Not that I hope (for, O, that hope were
   vain !)
By words your lost affection to regain:
But, having lost whate'er was worth my
   care,
Why should I fear to lose a dying pray'r ?
'T is then resolv'd poor Dido must be left,
Of life, of honor, and of love bereft !
While you, with loosen'd sails, and vows,
   prepare
To seek a land that flies the searcher's
   care.   10
Nor can my rising tow'rs your flight re-
   strain,
Nor my new empire, offer'd you in vain.
Built walls you shun, unbuilt you seek;
   that land
Is yet to conquer, but you this command.
Suppose you landed where your wish de-
   sign'd,
Think what reception foreigners would find.
What people is so void of common sense,
To vote succession from a native prince ?
Yet there new scepters and new loves you
   seek,
New vows to plight, and plighted vows to
   break.   20
When will your tow'rs the height of Car-
   thage know ?
Or when your eyes discern such crowds
   below ?

If such a town and subjects you could see,
Still would you want a wife who lov'd like
    me.
For, O, I burn, like fires with incense
    bright:
Not holy tapers flame with purer light.
Æneas is my thoughts' perpetual theme;
Their daily longing, and their nightly
    dream.
Yet he ungrateful and obdurate still:
Fool that I am, to place my heart so ill ! 30
Myself I cannot to myself restore;
Still I complain, and still I love him more.
Have pity, Cupid, on my bleeding heart,
And pierce thy brother's with an equal
    dart.
I rave: nor canst thou Venus' offspring be,
Love's mother could not bear a son like
    thee.
From harden'd oak, or from a rock's cold
    womb,
At least thou art from some fierce tigress
    come;
Or on rough seas, from their foundation
    torn,
Got by the winds, and in a tempest born, 40
Like that which now thy trembling sailors
    fear;
Like that whose rage should still detain
    thee here.
Behold how high the foamy billows ride !
The winds and waves are on the juster
    side.
To winter weather and a stormy sea
I 'll owe, what rather I would owe to thee.
Death thou deserv'st from heav'n's aveng-
    ing laws.
But I 'm unwilling to become the cause.
To shun my love, if thou wilt seek thy fate,
'T is a dear purchase, and a costly hate. 50
Stay but a little, till the tempest cease,
And the loud winds are lull'd into a peace.
May all thy rage, like theirs, unconstant
    prove !
And so it will, if there be pow'r in love.
Know'st thou not yet what dangers ships
    sustain ?
So often wrack'd, how dar'st thou tempt
    the main ?
Which were it smooth, were every wave
    asleep,
Ten thousand forms of death are in the
    deep.
In that abyss the gods their vengeance
    store,

For broken vows of those who falsely
    swore.   60
There winged storms on sea-born Venus
    wait,
To vindicate the justice of her state.
Thus I to thee the means of safety show;
And, lost myself, would still preserve my
    foe.
False as thou art, I not thy death design:
O rather live, to be the cause of mine !
Should some avenging storm thy vessel
    tear,
(But Heav'n forbid my words should omen
    bear !)
Then in thy face thy perjur'd vows would
    fly,
And my wrong'd ghost be present to thy
    eye.   70
With threat'ning looks think thou behold'st
    me stare,
Gasping my mouth, and clotted all my hair.
Then, should fork'd lightning and red thun-
    der fall,
What couldst thou say, but: " I deserv'd
    'em all " ?
Lest this should happen, make not haste
    away;
To shun the danger will be worth thy stay.
Have pity on thy son, if not on me:
My death alone is guilt enough for thee.
What has his youth, what have thy gods
    deserv'd,
To sink in seas, who were from fires pre-
    serv'd ?   80
But neither gods nor parent didst thou bear;
(Smooth stories all, to please a woman's
    ear.)
False was the tale of thy romantic life,
Nor yet am I thy first deluded wife:
Left to pursuing foes Creüsa stay'd,
By thee, base man, forsaken and betray'd.
This, when thou told'st me, struck my
    tender heart,
That such requital follow'd such desert.
Nor doubt I but the gods, for crimes like
    these,
Sev'n winters kept thee wand'ring on the
    seas.   90
Thy starv'd companions, cast ashore, I fed,
Thyself admitted to my crown and bed.
To harbor strangers, succor the distress'd,
Was kind enough; but, O, too kind the
    rest !
Curst be the cave which first my ruin
    brought,

Where, from the storm, we common shel-
    ter sought!
A dreadful howling echoed round the place:
    "The mountain nymphs," thought I, "my
    nuptials grace."
I thought so then, but now too late I know
The Furies yell'd my funerals from below.
O chastity and violated fame,   101
Exact your dues to my dead husband's
    name!
By death redeem my reputation lost,
And to his arms restore my guilty ghost!
Close by my palace, in a gloomy grove,
Is rais'd a chapel to my murder'd love;
There, wreath'd with boughs and wool, his
    statue stands,
The pious monument of artful hands.
Last night, methought, he call'd me from
    the dome,
And thrice, with hollow voice, cried: "Dido,
    come!"   110
She comes; thy wife thy lawful summons
    hears,
But comes more slowly, clogg'd with con-
    scious fears.
Forgive the wrong I offer'd to thy bed;
Strong were his charms, who my weak
    faith misled.
His goddess mother, and his aged sire,
Borne on his back, did to my fall conspire.
O, such he was, and is, that, were he true,
Without a blush I might his love pursue!
But cruel stars my birthday did attend;
And, as my fortune open'd, it must end. 120
My plighted lord was at the altar slain,
Whose wealth was made my bloody bro-
    ther's gain.
Friendless, and follow'd by the murd'rer's
    hate,
To foreign countries I remov'd my fate;
And here, a suppliant, from the natives'
    hands
I bought the ground on which my city
    stands,
With all the coast that stretches to the
    sea;
Ev'n to the friendly port that shelter'd
    thee:
Then rais'd these walls, which mount into
    the air,
At once my neighbors' wonder, and their
    fear.   130
For now they arm; and round me leagues
    are made,
My scarce establish'd empire to invade.

To man my new-built walls I must pre-
    pare,
An helpless woman, and unskill'd in war.
Yet thousand rivals to my love pretend,
And for my person would my crown de-
    fend;
Whose jarring votes in one complaint
    agree,
That each unjustly is disdain'd for thee.
To proud Hyarbas give me up a prey;
(For that must follow, if thou go'st away):
Or to my husband's murd'rer leave my
    life,   141
That to the husband he may add the wife.
Go then, since no complaints can move thy
    mind;
Go, perjur'd man, but leave thy gods be-
    hind.
Touch not those gods, by whom thou art
    forsworn,
Who will in impious hands no more be
    borne:
Thy sacrilegious worship they disdain,
And rather would the Grecian fires sustain.
Perhaps my greatest shame is still to come,
And part of thee lies hid within my womb.
The babe unborn must perish by thy hate,
And perish guiltless in his mother's fate. 152
Some god, thou say'st, thy voyage does com-
    mand;
Would the same god had barr'd thee from
    my land!
The same, I doubt not, thy departure steers,
Who kept thee out at sea so many years;
Where thy long labors were a price so great,
As thou to purchase Troy wouldst not re-
    peat.
But Tiber now thou seek'st, to be at best,
When there arriv'd, a poor, precarious
    guest.   160
Yet it deludes thy search: perhaps it will
To thy old age lie undiscover'd still.
A ready crown and wealth in dow'r I bring,
And, without conqu'ring, here thou art a
    king.
Here thou to Carthage may'st transfer thy
    Troy:
Here young Ascanius may his arms employ;
And, while we live secure in soft repose,
Bring many laurels home from conquer'd
    foes.
By Cupid's arrows, I adjure thee, stay;
By all the gods, companions of thy way. 170
So may thy Trojans, who are yet alive,
Live still, and with no future fortune strive;

So may thy youthful son old age attain,
And thy dead father's bones in peace re-
    main;
As thou hast pity on unhappy me,
Who know no crime, but too much love of
    thee.
I am not born from fierce Achilles' line,
Nor did my parents against Troy combine.
To be thy wife if I unworthy prove,
By some inferior name admit my love. 180
To be secur'd of still possessing thee,
What would I do, and what would I not be !
Our Libyan coasts their certain seasons
    know,
When free from tempests passengers may
    go:
But now with northern blasts the billows
    roar,
And drive the floating seaweed to the
    shore.
Leave to my care the time to sail away;
When safe, I will not suffer thee to stay.
Thy weary men would be with ease con-
    tent;
Their sails are tatter'd, and their masts are
    spent.   190
If by no merit I thy mind can move,

What thou deny'st my merit, give my love.
Stay, till I learn my loss to undergo;
And give me time to struggle with my woe.
If not, know this, I will not suffer long;
My life's too loathsome, and my love too
    strong.
Death holds my pen, and dictates what I
    say,
While cross my lap thy Trojan sword I lay.
My tears flow down; the sharp edge cuts
    their flood,
And drinks my sorrows, that must drink my
    blood.   200
How well thy gift does with my fate agree !
My funeral pomp is cheaply made by thee.
To no new wounds my bosom I display;
The sword but enters where love made the
    way.
But thou, dear sister, and yet dearer friend,
Shalt my cold ashes to their urn attend.
Sichæus' wife let not the marble boast;
I lost that title, when my fame I lost.
This short inscription only let it bear:
" Unhappy Dido lies in quiet here.   210
The cause of death, and sword by which she
    died,
Æneas gave: the rest her arm supplied."

FOUR EPITAPHS

[The exact dates of the following epitaphs are unknown. The poems are grouped at this point for convenience in printing.]

UPON YOUNG MR. ROGERS OF GLOUCESTERSHIRE

[These verses were first printed, with title as above, in *Poetical Miscellanies, the Fifth Part*, published by Tonson in 1704, after Dryden's death. The miserable conceit in the last couplet suggests an early date of composition, perhaps before 1666, when Dryden wrote *Annus Mirabilis*. Nothing definite is known of the subject of the epitaph.]

OF gentle blood, his parents' only treasure,
Their lasting sorrow, and their vanish'd
    pleasure,
Adorn'd with features, virtues, wit, and
    grace,
A large provision for so short a race;
More mod'rate gifts might have prolong'd
    his date,
Too early fitted for a better state;

But, knowing heav'n his home, to shun de-
    lay,
He leap'd o'er age, and took the shortest
    way.

EPITAPH ON THE MONUMENT OF THE MARQUIS OF WIN-CHESTER

[John Paulet, fifth Marquis of Winchester, was among the most noted adherents of Charles I. After the siege of his mansion, Basing House, in Hampshire, by the Parliamentarians, from August, 1643, to October, 1645, and its final capture by Cromwell, he was called " the great loyalist." He died on March 5, 1675, and was buried at Englefield in Berkshire, where he had lived since the Restoration. Dryden's lines are engraved on his monument, followed by the inscription : " The Lady Mar-chioness Dowager (in testimony of her love and sorrow) gave this Monument to the memory of a most affectionate tender husband."

This epitaph was first printed, with title as above. in *Miscellaneous Poems and Translations*, published by Lintot in 1712. This volume, which contained the first form of *The Rape of the Lock*, and some minor poems by Pope, is commonly known as *Pope's Miscellany*. The present text is from a copy of the inscription on the monument.]

He who in impious times untainted stood,
And midst rebellion durst be just and good;
Whose arms asserted, and whose sufferings
  more
Confirm'd the cause for which he fought before,
Rests here, rewarded by an heav'nly prince,
For what his earthly could not recompense.
Pray, reader, that such times no more appear;
Or, if they happen, learn true honor here.

Ark of thy age's faith and loyalty,
Which, to preserve them, Heav'n confin'd in
  thee,   10
Few subjects could a king like thine deserve;
And fewer, such a king so well could serve.
Blest king, blest subject, whose exalted state
By suff'rings rose, and gave the law to fate.
Such souls are rare, but mighty patterns
  given
To earth, were meant for ornaments to
  heaven.

EPITAPH ON MRS. MARGARET PASTON

OF BARNINGHAM IN NORFOLK

[This epitaph was first printed, with title as above, in the same volume as the preceding. Nothing definite is known of the subject of the verses.]

So fair, so young, so innocent, so sweet, ⎫
So ripe a judgment, and so rare a wit, ⎬
Require at least an age in one to meet. ⎭
In her they met; but long they could not
  stay,
'T was gold too fine to fix without allay.
Heav'n's image was in her so well express'd,
Her very sight upbraided all the rest;
Too justly ravish'd from an age like this,
Now *she* is gone, the world is of a piece.

AN EPITAPH ON SIR PALMES FAIRBORNE'S TOMB IN WEST-MINSTER ABBEY

[This epitaph was first printed. with title as above, in *Examen Poeticum*, 1693. It is here reprinted from a copy of the inscription on the tomb, which varies very slightly from the text in *Examen Poeticum*. Dryden presumably did not write the prose introduction.]

Sacred to the immortal memory of Sir Palmes Fairborne, Knight, Governor of Tangier; in execution of which command he was mortally wounded by a shot from the Moors, then besieging the town, in the forty-sixth year of his age, October 24th, 1680.

Ye sacred relics, which your marble keep,
Here, undisturb'd by wars, in quiet sleep:
Discharge the trust, which, when it was ⎫
  below,   ⎪
Fairborne's undaunted soul did undergo, ⎬
And be the town's Palladium from the ⎪
  foe.   ⎭
Alive and dead these walls he will defend;
Great actions great examples must attend.
The Candian siege his early valor knew,
Where Turkish blood did his young hands
  imbrue.
From thence returning with deserv'd ap- ⎫
  plause,   10 ⎪
Against the Moors his well-flesh'd sword ⎬
  he draws;   ⎪
The same the courage, and the same the ⎪
  cause.   ⎭
His youth and age, his life and death ⎫
  combine,   ⎪
As in some great and regular design, ⎬
All of a piece throughout, and all divine. ⎭
Still nearer heaven his virtue shone more ⎫
  bright,   ⎪
Like rising flames expanding in their ⎬
  height;   ⎪
The martyr's glory crown'd the soldier's ⎪
  fight.   ⎭
More bravely British general never fell,
Nor general's death was e'er reveng'd so
  well;   20
Which his pleas'd eyes beheld before their
  close
Follow'd by thousand victims of his foes.

To his lamented loss for times to come
His pious widow consecrates this tomb.

PROLOGUE AND SONG FROM THE SPANISH FRIAR

OR, THE DOUBLE DISCOVERY

[This play, one of Dryden's best comedies, was probably acted late in 1680 or early in 1681; it was first printed in the latter year, being entered in the *Term Catalogue* for Trinity Term (June). The epilogue was "by a friend of the author's." The song is sung by Teresa, woman to Queen Leonora, the heroine of the play, in response to a request from her mistress:

> To soothe my sadness,
> Sing me the song which poor Olympia made,
> When false Bireno left her.]

PROLOGUE

Now, luck for us, and a kind hearty pit;
For he, who pleases, never fails of wit:
Honor is yours;
And you, like kings, at city-treats bestow it;
The writer kneels, and is bid rise a poet;
But you are fickle sovereigns, to our sorrow;
You dub to-day, and hang a man to-morrow:
You cry the same sense up, and down again,
Just like brass money once a year in Spain:
Take you i' th' mood, whate'er base metal
    come,   10
You coin as fast as groats at Bromingam:
Tho' 't is no more like sense, in ancient plays,
Than Rome's religion like St. Peter's days.
In short, so swift your judgments turn and
    wind,
You cast our fleetest wits a mile behind.
'T were well your judgments but in plays
    did range,
But ev'n your follies and debauches change
With such a whirl, the poets of your age
Are tir'd, and cannot score 'em on the stage;
Unless each vice in shorthand they indict,
Ev'n as notch'd prentices whole sermons
    write.   21
The heavy Hollanders no vices know, ⎫
But what they us'd a hundred years ago; ⎪
Like honest plants, where they were ⎬
    stuck, they grow. ⎭
They cheat, but still from cheating sires
    they come;
They drink, but they were christen'd first
    in mum.
Their patrimonial sloth the Spaniards keep,
And Philip first taught Philip how to sleep.
The French and we still change; but here's
    the curse,

They change for better, and we change for
    worse;   30
They take up our old trade of conquering,
And we are taking theirs, to dance and sing:
Our fathers did for change to France re-
    pair,
And they, for change, will try our English
    air;
As children, when they throw one toy away,
Straight a more foolish gewgaw comes in
    play:
So we, grown penitent, on serious thinking,
Leave whoring, and devoutly fall to drink-
    ing.
Scouring the watch grows out-of-fashion
    wit:
Now we set up for tilting in the pit,   40
Where 't is agreed by bullies, chicken-
    hearted,
To fright the ladies first, and then be parted.
A fair attempt has twice or thrice been
    made,
To hire night-murth'rers, and make death
    a trade.
When murther 's out, what vice can we ad-
    vance,
Unless the new-found pois'ning trick of
    France ?
And, when their art of ratsbane we have
    got,
By way of thanks, we 'll send 'em o'er **our**
    Plot.

SONG

I

FAREWELL, ungrateful traitor !
    Farewell, my perjur'd swain !
Let never injur'd creature
    Believe a man again.
The pleasure of possessing
Surpasses all expressing,
But 't is too short a blessing,
    And love too long a pain.

II

'T is easy to deceive us,
    In pity of your pain;   10
But when we love, you leave us
    To rail at you in vain.
Before we have descried it,
There is no bliss beside it;
But she that once has tried **it,**
    Will never love again.

III

The passion you pretended,
  Was only to obtain;
But when the charm is ended,
  The charmer you disdain.   20
Your love by ours we measure,
  Till we have lost our treasure;
But dying is a pleasure,
  When living is a pain.

EPILOGUE TO TAMERLANE THE GREAT

[This tragedy, by Charles Saunders, was probably acted late in 1680 or early in 1681; it was printed in 1681, being entered in the *Term Catalogue* for Easter Term (May) of that year. Dryden's epilogue was reprinted in the third edition (1702) of *Miscellany Poems, the First Part*, where it is called simply *An Epilogue by Mr. Dryden*. Langbaine says that Saunders was "a young gentleman whose wit began to bud as early as that of the incomparable Cowley, and was like him a King's Scholar [at Westminster School] when he writ a play called *Tamerlane the Great*." The young man seems not to have followed this first performance by any further work.]

LADIES, the beardless author of this day
Commends to you the fortune of his
    play.
A woman wit has often grac'd the stage,
But he's the first boy poet of our age.

Early as is the year his fancies blow,
Like young Narcissus peeping thro' the
    snow:
Thus Cowley blossom'd soon, yet flourish'd
    long;
This is as forward, and may prove as
    strong.
Youth with the fair should always favor
    find,
Or we are damn'd dissemblers of our
    kind.   10
What's all this love they put into our
    parts?
'T is but the pit-a-pat of two young hearts.
Should hag and graybeard make such ten- ⎫
    der moan,   ⎪
Faith, you'd e'en trust 'em to themselves ⎬
    alone,   ⎪
And cry: "Let's go, here's nothing to ⎭
    be done."
Since love's our business, as 't is your de-
    light,
The young, who best can practice, best can
    write.
What tho' he be not come to his full
    pow'r?
He's mending and improving every hour.
You sly she-jockeys of the box and pit   20
Are pleas'd to find a hot unbroken wit.
By management he may in time be made,
But there's no hopes of an old batter'd jade:
Faint and unnerv'd he runs into a sweat,
And always fails you at the second heat.

POEMS WRITTEN IN 1681

PROLOGUE

[The date and occasion of this prologue are unknown. It was not printed until 1693, when it appeared in *Examen Poeticum* with the heading, *Prologue by Mr. Dryden*. Christie places it in 1681 on account of its resemblance in style to the *Epilogue to Tamerlane the Great*, and this guess is as likely to be right as any other.]

GALLANTS, a bashful poet bids me say
He's come to lose his maidenhead to-day.
Be not too fierce, for he's but green of age,
And ne'er, till now, debauch'd upon the
    stage.
He wants the suff'ring part of resolution,
And comes with blushes to his execution.

E'er you deflow'r his Muse, he hopes the
    pit
Will make some settlement upon his wit.
Promise him well, before the play begin,
For he would fain be cozen'd into sin.   10
'T is not but that he knows you mean to ⎫
    fail;   ⎪
But, if you leave him after being frail,   ⎬
He'll have, at least, a fair pretense to ⎪
    rail;   ⎭
To call you base, and swear you us'd him
    ill,
And put you in the new Deserters' Bill.
Lord, what a troop of perjur'd men we see,
Enow to fill another *Mercury*!
But this the ladies may with patience brook:
Theirs are not the first colors you forsook!

He would be loth the beauties to offend; 20
But, if he should, he 's not too old to mend.
He 's a young plant, in his first year of
  bearing;
But his friend swears he will be worth the
  rearing.
His gloss is still upon him; tho' 't is true
He 's yet unripe, yet take him for the blue.
You think an apricot half green is best:
There 's sweet and sour, and one side good
  at least.
Mangoes and limes, whose nourishment is
  little,
Tho' not for food, are yet preserv'd for
  pickle.
So this green writer may pretend, at least,
To whet your stomachs for a better feast. 31
He makes this difference in the sexes too:
He sells to men, he gives himself to you.
To both he would contribute some delight,
A mere poetical hermaphrodite.
Thus he 's equipp'd, both to be woo'd and ⎫
  woo,   ⎪
With arms offensive and defensive too: ⎬
'T is hard, he thinks, if neither part will do. ⎭

PROLOGUE TO THE UNIVERSITY
  OF OXFORD

[This prologue was first printed in *Miscellany
Poems*, 1684. Scott's note upon it is of peculiar interest :
" This prologue must have been spoken at
Oxford during the residence of the Duke of
York in Scotland, in 1681–82. [More exactly,
from October, 1680, to March, 1682.] The
humor turns upon a part of the company having attended the duke to Scotland, where,
among other luxuries little known to my countrymen, he introduced, during his residence at
Holyrood House, the amusements of the theater. I can say little about the actors commemorated in the following verses, excepting that
their stage was erected in the tennis court of
the palace, which was afterwards converted
into some sort of manufactory, and finally
burned down many years ago. Besides these
deserters, whom Dryden has described very
ludicrously, he mentions a sort of strolling
company, composed, it would seem, of Irishmen, who had lately acted at Oxford."]

DISCORD and plots, which have undone our
  age,
With the same ruin have o'erwhelm'd the
  stage.

Our house has suffer'd in the common
  woe,
We have been troubled with Scotch rebels
  too.
Our brethren are from Thames to ⎫
  Tweed departed,   ⎪
And of our sisters all the kinder-hearted ⎬
To Edenborough gone, or coach'd, or   ⎪
  carted.   ⎭
With bonny bluecap there they act all
  night
For Scotch half-crown, in English three-
  pence hight.
One nymph, to whom fat Sir John Fal-
  staff 's lean,   10
There with her single person fills the
  scene.
Another, with long use and age decay'd,
Div'd here old woman, and rose there a
  maid.
Our trusty doorkeepers of former time
There strut and swagger in heroic rhyme.
Tack but a copper lace to drugget suit,
And there 's a hero made without dis-
  pute;
And that which was a capon's tail before,
Becomes a plume for Indian Emperor.
But all his subjects, to express the care 20
Of imitation, go, like Indians, bare:
Lac'd linen there would be a dangerous ⎫
  thing;   ⎪
It might perhaps a new rebellion bring; ⎬
The Scot who wore it would be chosen ⎪
  king.   ⎭
But why should I these renegades de-
  scribe,
When you yourselves have seen a lewder
  tribe ?
Teg has been here, and, to this learned
  pit,
With Irish action slander'd English wit:
You have beheld such barb'rous Macs ap-
  pear,
As merited a second massacre: 30
Such as, like Cain, were branded with dis-
  grace,
And had their country stamp'd upon their
  face.
When strollers durst presume to pick your
  purse,
We humbly thought our broken troop not
  worse.
How ill soe'er our action may deserve,
Oxford 's a place where wit can never
  sterve.

PROLOGUE TO THE UNIVERSITY OF OXFORD

[This prologue is of 1676 and should have been printed earlier: see *Notes*, p. 1054. It was first published in *Miscellany Poems*, 1684, where it immediately succeeds the prologue just printed.]

Tho' actors cannot much of learning boast,
Of all who want it, we admire it most:
We love the praises of a learned pit,
As we remotely are allied to wit.
We speak our poet's wit, and trade in ore,
Like those who touch upon the golden
      shore:
Betwixt our judges can distinction make,
Discern how much, and why, our poems
      take:
Mark if the fools, or men of sense, rejoice;
Whether th' applause be only sound or
      voice.   10
When our fop gallants, or our city folly
Clap over-loud, it makes us melancholy;
We doubt that scene which does their won-
      der raise,
And, for their ignorance, contemn their
      praise.
Judge then, if we who act, and they who
      write,
Should not be proud of giving you delight.
London likes grossly; but this nicer pit
Examines, fathoms all the depths of wit;
The ready finger lays on every blot;
Knows what should justly please, and what
      should not.   20
Nature herself lies open to your view;
You judge by her, what draught of her is
      true,
Where outlines false, and colors seem too
      faint,
Where bunglers daub, and where true
      poets paint.
But, by the sacred genius of this place,
By every Muse, by each domestic grace,
Be kind to wit, which but endeavors well,
And, where you judge, presumes not to
      excel.
Our poets hither for adoption come,
As nations sued to be made free of Rome: 30
Not in the suffragating tribes to stand,
But in your utmost, last, provincial band.
If his ambition may those hopes pursue,
Who with religion loves your arts and
      you,
Oxford to him a dearer name shall be,
Than his own mother-university.
Thebes did his green, unknowing youth in-
      gage;
He chooses Athens in his riper age.

PROLOGUE TO THE UNIVERSITY OF OXFORD, 1681

[This prologue was first printed, with the above heading, in *Examen Poeticum*, 1693. From the reference in lines 19, 20, it seems to have been delivered shortly after the dissolution of the Oxford Parliament on March 28, 1681.]

The fam'd Italian Muse, whose rhymes
      advance
Orlando and the Paladins of France,
Records that, when our wit and sense is
      flown,
'T is lodg'd within the circle of the moon
In earthen jars, which one, who thither
      soar'd,
Set to his nose, snuff'd up, and was restor'd.
Whate'er the story be, the moral 's true;
The wit we lost in town we find in you.
Our poets their fled parts may draw from
      hence,
And fill their windy heads with sober
      sense.   10
When London votes with Southwark's dis-
      agree,
Here may they find their long-lost loyalty.
Here busy senates, to th' old cause inclin'd,
May snuff the votes their fellows left be-
      hind:
Your country neighbors, when their grain
      grows dear,
May come, and find their last provision
      here:
Whereas we cannot much lament our loss,
Who neither carried back, nor brought one
      cross.
We look'd what representatives would
      bring;
But they help'd us, just as they did the
      king.   20
Yet we despair not, for we now lay forth
The Sibyl's books to those who know their
      worth;
And tho' the first was sacrific'd before,
These volumes doubly will the price re-
      store.
Our poet bade us hope this grace to find,

To whom by long prescription you are kind.
He whose undaunted Muse, with loyal rage,
Has never spar'd the vices of the age,
Here finding nothing that his spleen can
    raise,
Is forc'd to turn his satire into praise.   30

PROLOGUE AND EPILOGUE TO THE UNHAPPY FAVORITE

OR, THE EARL OF ESSEX

[This tragedy, by John Banks, was probably
acted in the spring or summer of 1681, since it
was published late in that year, being entered
in the *Term Catalogue* for Michaelmas Term
(November). This edition was dated 1682. As
it has been inaccessible, the text of the prologue is taken from the second edition of the
play, 1685. The epilogue is also printed, with
some variations of text, and with the heading,
An Epilogue for the King's House, in *Miscellany
Poems*, 1684, from which the present text is
taken.

The date of the royal visit referred to in the
prologue is unknown. It seems to have been
at the fifth performance of the play, since in
the printed copy Dryden's prologue is preceded by a *Prologue spoken by Major Mohun,
the first four days*. Perhaps it was upon the
return of the king to London after the Oxford
Parliament.]

PROLOGUE

SPOKEN TO THE KING AND QUEEN AT THEIR
COMING TO THE HOUSE, AND WRITTEN ON
PURPOSE BY MR. DRYDEN

When first the ark was landed on the
    shore,
And Heaven had vow'd to curse the ground
    no more;
When tops of hills the longing patriarch
    saw,
And the new scene of earth began to draw;
The dove was sent to view the waves de-
    crease,
And first brought back to man the pledge
    of peace.
'T is needless to apply, when those appear
Who bring the olive, and who plant it here.
We have before our eyes the royal dove;
Still Innocence is harbinger to Love: 10
The ark is open'd to dismiss the train,
And people with a better race the plain.

Tell me, you powers, why should vain
    man pursue,
With endless toil, each object that is
    new,
And for the seeming substance leave the
    true ?
Why should he quit for hopes his certain
    good,
And loathe the manna of his daily food ?
Must England still the scene of changes
    be,
Toss'd and tempestuous, like our ambient
    sea ?
Must still our weather and our wills
    agree ?   20
Without our blood our liberties we have:
Who that is free would fight to be a slave ?
Or, what can wars to aftertimes assure,
Of which our present age is not secure ?
All that our monarch would for us ordain,
Is but t' injoy the blessings of his reign.
Our land's an Eden, and the main's our
    fence,
While we preserve our state of innocence:
That lost, then beasts their brutal force
    employ,
And first their lord, and then themselves
    destroy.   30
What civil broils have cost we knew too
    well;
O let it be enough that once we fell,
And every heart conspire with every
    tongue,
Still to have such a king, and this king
    long !

EPILOGUE

We act by fits and starts, like drowning
    men,
But just peep up, and then dop down again.
Let those who call us wicked change their
    sense,
For never men liv'd more on Providence.
Not lott'ry cavaliers are half so poor,
Nor broken cits, nor a vacation whore;
Not courts, nor courtiers living on the
    rents
Of the three last ungiving parliaments:
So wretched, that, if Pharaoh could di-
    vine,
He might have spar'd his dream of seven
    lean kine,   10
And chang'd his vision for the Muses
    nine.

The comet, which, they say, portends a
    dearth,
Was but a vapor drawn from playhouse
    earth:
Pent there since our last fire, and, Lilly
    says,
Foreshews our change of state, and thin
    third-days.
'T is not our want of wit that keeps us poor;
For then the printer's press would suffer
    more.
Their pamphleteers each day their venom
    spit;
They thrive by treason, and we starve by
    wit.
Confess the truth, which of you *Looking* has not laid   20 *above.*
Four farthings out to buy *The Hatfield
    Maid?*
Or, which is duller yet, and more would
    spite us,
Democritus his wars with *Heraclitus?*

Such are the authors who have run us down,
And exercis'd you critics of the town.
Yet these are pearls to your lampooning
    rhymes,
Y' abuse yourselves more dully than the
    times.
Scandal, the glory of the English nation,
Is worn to rags, and scribbled out of fashion;
Such harmless thrusts, as if, like fencers
    wise,   30
They had agreed their play before their
    prize.
Faith, they may hang their harps upon the
    willows;
'T is just like children when they box with
    pillows.
Then put an end to civil wars for shame;
Let each knight-errant, who has wrong'd a
    dame,
Throw down his pen, and give her, as he
    can,
The satisfaction of a gentleman.

ABSALOM AND ACHITOPHEL

A POEM

*Si propius stes
Te capiet magis.*

[According to a note by Jacob Tonson, " in the year 1680 Mr. Dryden undertook the poem of *Absalom and Achitophel*, upon the desire of King Charles the Second : " see p. 137, below. The poem was printed as a folio pamphlet in 1681. A note on the copy of the satire owned by Narcissus Luttrell, " 17th November, *ex dono amici Jacobi Tonson.*" fixes the time of publication as on or shortly before that date : see note by Scott in Scott-Saintsbury edition, ix, 204. The poem was evidently meant to appear at the psychological moment for exciting public sentiment against Shaftesbury, who was brought before the grand jury, on a charge of high treason, on November 24. This first edition was anonymous ; and, though the authorship of the satire at once became known, and was acknowledged by Dryden in his *Discourse concerning Satire*, 1692 (see pp. 303, 313, below), Dryden's name was never directly joined to it during his lifetime. The second edition, in quarto, which appeared before the close of 1681, besides making some minor changes in the text, adds two important passages, lines 180-191 and 957-960. Seven other editions seem to have appeared before Dryden's death ; the sixth is included in *Miscellany Poems*, 1684 ; the tenth in the collected *Poems and Translations*, 1701. These editions are apparently mere printers' reprints, containing no variations for which Dryden can be held responsible. The present text follows the second edition.

Dryden seems to have taken the general idea of applying to contemporary politics the scriptural story of the revolt of Absalom (2 Samuel xiii-xviii), from an anonymous tract, published in 1680, *Absalom's Conspiracy, or The Tragedy of Treason*. This is reprinted by Scott: see Scott-Saintsbury edition, ix, 206-208.]

TO THE READER

'T is not my intention to make an apology for my poem : some will think it needs no excuse, and others will receive none. The design, I am sure, is honest ; but he who draws his pen for one party must expect to make enemies of the other. For wit and fool are consequents of Whig and Tory ; and every man is a knave or an ass to the contrary side. There 's a treasury of merits in the Fanatic Church, as well as in the Papist; and a pennyworth to be had of saintship, honesty, and poetry, for the lewd, the factious, and the blockheads; but the longest chapter in Deuteronomy has not curses enough for an anti-Bromingham. My comfort is, their manifest prejudice to my cause will render their judgment of less authority against me. Yet if a poem have a genius, it will force its own reception in the world; for there's a sweetness in good verse, which tickles even while it hurts, and no man can be heartily angry with him who pleases him against his will. The commendation of adversaries is the greatest triumph of a writer, because it never comes unless extorted. But I can be satisfied on more easy terms: if I happen to please the more moderate sort, I shall be sure of an honest party, and, in all probability, of the best judges; for the least concern'd are commonly the least corrupt. And, I confess, I have laid in for those, by rebating the satire (where justice would allow it) from carrying too sharp an edge. They who can criticise so weakly, as to imagine I have done my worst, may be convinc'd, at their own cost, that I can write severely with more ease than I can gently. I have but laugh'd at some men's follies, when I could have declaim'd against their vices; and other men's virtues I have commended, as freely as I have tax'd their crimes. And now, if you are a malicious reader, I expect you should return upon me that I affect to be thought more impartial than I am. But if men are not to be judg'd by their professions, God forgive you Commonwealth's-men for professing so plausibly for the government. You cannot be so unconscionable as to charge me for not subscribing of my name; for that would reflect too grossly upon your own party, who never dare, tho' they have the advantage of a jury to secure them. If you like not my poem, the fault may, possibly, be in my writing (tho' 't is hard for an author to judge against himself); but, more probably, 't is in your morals, which cannot bear the truth of it. The violent, on both sides, will condemn the character of Absalom, as either too favorably or too hardly drawn. But they are not the violent whom I desire to please. The fault on the right hand is to extenuate, palliate, and indulge; and, to confess freely, I have endeavor'd to commit it. Besides the respect which I owe his birth, I have a greater for his heroic virtues; and David himself could not be more tender of the young man's life than I would be of his reputation. But since the most excellent natures are always the most easy, and, as being such, are the soonest perverted by ill counsels, especially when baited with fame and glory; 't is no more a wonder that he withstood

not the temptations of Achitophel, than it was for Adam not to have resisted the two devils, the serpent and the woman. The conclusion of the story I purposely forbore to prosecute, because I could not obtain from myself to shew Absalom unfortunate. The frame of it was cut out but for a picture to the waist, and if the draught be so far true, 't is as much as I design'd.

Were I the inventor, who am only the historian, I should certainly conclude the piece with the reconcilement of Absalom to David. And who knows but this may come to pass? Things were not brought to an extremity where I left the story; there seems yet to be room left for a composure; hereafter there may only be for pity. I have not so much as an uncharitable wish against Achitophel, but am content to be accus'd of a good-natur'd error, and to hope with Origen, that the Devil himself may at last be sav'd. For which reason, in this poem, he is neither brought to set his house in order, nor to dispose of his person afterwards as he in wisdom shall think fit. God is infinitely merciful; and his vicegerent is only not so, because he is not infinite.

The true end of satire is the amendment of vices by correction. And he who writes honestly is no more an enemy to the offender, than the physician to the patient, when he prescribes harsh remedies to an inveterate disease; for those are only in order to prevent the chirurgeon's work of an *ense rescindendum*, which I wish not to my very enemies. To conclude all; if the body politic have any analogy to the natural, in my weak judgment, an act of oblivion were as necessary in a hot, distemper'd state, as an opiate would be in a raging fever.

ABSALOM AND ACHITOPHEL

In pious times, ere priestcraft did begin,
Before polygamy was made a sin;
When man on many multiplied his kind,
Ere one to one was cursedly confin'd;
When nature prompted, and no law denied
Promiscuous use of concubine and bride;
Then Israel's monarch after Heaven's own
    heart,
His vigorous warmth did variously impart
To wives and slaves; and, wide as his command, 9
Scatter'd his Maker's image thro' the land.
Michal, of royal blood, the crown did wear;
A soil ungrateful to the tiller's care:
Not so the rest; for several mothers bore
To godlike David several sons before.
But since like slaves his bed they did ascend,

No true succession could their seed attend.
Of all this numerous progeny was none
So beautiful, so brave, as Absalon:
Whether, inspir'd by some diviner lust,
His father got him with a greater gust;   20
Or that his conscious destiny made way,
By manly beauty, to imperial sway.
Early in foreign fields he won renown,
With kings and states allied to Israel's
    crown:
In peace the thoughts of war he could re-
    move,
And seem'd as he were only born for love.
Whate'er he did, was done with so much
    ease,
In him alone 't was natural to please:
His motions all accompanied with grace;
And paradise was open'd in his face.   30
With secret joy indulgent David view'd
His youthful image in his son renew'd:
To all his wishes nothing he denied;
And made the charming Annabel his bride.
What faults he had, (for who from faults is
    free ?)
His father could not, or he would not see.
Some warm excesses which the law forbore,
Were construed youth that purg'd by boil-
    ing o'er,
And Amnon's murther, by a specious name,
Was call'd a just revenge for injur'd fame.
Thus prais'd and lov'd the noble youth re-
    main'd,   41
While David, undisturb'd, in Sion reign'd.
But life can never be sincerely blest;
Heav'n punishes the bad, and proves the
    best.
The Jews, a headstrong, moody, murm'ring
    race,
As ever tried th' extent and stretch of
    grace;
God's pamper'd people, whom, debauch'd
    with ease,
No king could govern, nor no God could
    please;
(Gods they had tried of every shape and
    size,
That god-smiths could produce, or priests
    devise:)   50
These Adam-wits, too fortunately free,
Began to dream they wanted liberty;
And when no rule, no precedent was found,
Of men by laws less circumscrib'd and
    bound,
They led their wild desires to woods and
    caves,

And thought that all but savages were
    slaves.
They who, when Saul was dead, without a
    blow,
Made foolish Ishbosheth the crown forego;
Who banish'd David did from Hebron
    bring,
And with a general shout proclaim'd him
    king: 60
Those very Jews, who, at their very best,
Their humor more than loyalty express'd,
Now wonder'd why so long they had obey'd
An idol monarch, which their hands had
    made;
Thought they might ruin him they could
    create,
Or melt him to that golden calf, a State.
But these were random bolts; no form'd
    design,
Nor interest made the factious crowd to
    join:
The sober part of Israel, free from stain,
Well knew the value of a peaceful reign;   70
And, looking backward with a wise af-
    fright,
Saw seams of wounds, dishonest to the
    sight:
In contemplation of whose ugly scars
They curs'd the memory of civil wars.
The moderate sort of men, thus qualified,
Inclin'd the balance to the better side;
And David's mildness manag'd it so well,
The bad found no occasion to rebel.
But when to sin our bias'd nature leans,
The careful Devil is still at hand with
    means;   80
And providently pimps for ill desires.
The Good Old Cause reviv'd, a plot re-
    quires:
Plots, true or false, are necessary things,
To raise up commonwealths, and ruin kings.
    Th' inhabitants of old Jerusalem
Were Jebusites; the town so call'd from
    them;
And theirs the native right ——
But when the chosen people grew more
    strong,
The rightful cause at length became the
    wrong;
And every loss the men of Jebus bore,   90
They still were thought God's enemies the
    more.
Thus worn and weaken'd, well or ill content,
Submit they must to David's government:
Impoverish'd and depriv'd of all command,

Their taxes doubled as they lost their land;
And, what was harder yet to flesh and
    blood,
Their gods disgrac'd, and burnt like com-
    mon wood.
This set the heathen priesthood in a flame;
For priests of all religions are the same:
Of whatsoe'er descent their godhead be, 100
Stock, stone, or other homely pedigree,
In his defense his servants are as bold,
As if he had been born of beaten gold.
The Jewish rabbins, tho' their enemies,
In this conclude them honest men and
    wise:
For 't was their duty, all the learned think,
T' espouse his cause, by whom they eat
    and drink.
From hence began that Plot, the nation's
    curse,
Bad in itself, but represented worse;
Rais'd in extremes, and in extremes de-
    cried; 110
With oaths affirm'd, with dying vows de-
    nied;
Not weigh'd or winnow'd by the multitude;
But swallow'd in the mass, unchew'd and
    crude.
Some truth there was, but dash'd and
    brew'd with lies,
To please the fools, and puzzle all the
    wise.
Succeeding times did equal folly call,
Believing nothing, or believing all.
Th' Egyptian rites the Jebusites embrac'd;
Where gods were recommended by their
    taste.
Such sav'ry deities must needs be good, 120
As serv'd at once for worship and for food.
By force they could not introduce these
    gods,
For ten to one in former days was odds;
So fraud was us'd (the sacrificer's trade):
Fools are more hard to conquer than per-
    suade.
Their busy teachers mingled with the Jews,
And rak'd for converts even the court and
    stews:
Which Hebrew priests the more unkindly
    took,
Because the fleece accompanies the flock.
Some thought they God's anointed meant
    to slay 130
By guns, invented since full many a day:
Our author swears it not; but who can
    know

How far the Devil and Jebusites may go?
This Plot, which fail'd for want of common
    sense,
Had yet a deep and dangerous consequence:
For, as when raging fevers boil the blood,
The standing lake soon floats into a flood,
And ev'ry hostile humor, which before
Slept quiet in its channels, bubbles o'er;
So several factions from this first fer-
    ment 140
Work up to foam, and threat the govern-
    ment.
Some by their friends, more by themselves
    thought wise,
Oppos'd the pow'r to which they could not
    rise.
Some had in courts been great, and thrown
    from thence,
Like fiends were harden'd in impenitence.
Some, by their monarch's fatal mercy,
    grown
From pardon'd rebels kinsmen to the
    throne,
Were rais'd in pow'r and public office high;
Strong bands, if bands ungrateful men
    could tie.
Of these the false Achitophel was first; 150
A name to all succeeding ages curst:
For close designs and crooked counsels fit;
Sagacious, bold, and turbulent of wit;
Restless, unfix'd in principles and place;
In pow'r unpleas'd, impatient of disgrace:
A fiery soul, which, working out its way, ⎫
Fretted the pigmy body to decay,   ⎬
And o'er-inform'd the tenement of clay. ⎭
A daring pilot in extremity;
Pleas'd with the danger, when the waves
    went high, 160
He sought the storms; but, for a calm un-
    fit,
Would steer too nigh the sands, to boast
    his wit.
Great wits are sure to madness near allied,
And thin partitions do their bounds divide;
Else why should he, with wealth and honor
    blest,
Refuse his age the needful hours of rest?
Punish a body which he could not please;
Bankrupt of life, yet prodigal of ease?
And all to leave what with his toil he
    won,
To that unfeather'd two-legg'd thing, a
    son; 170
Got, while his soul did huddled notions try;
And born a shapeless lump, like anarchy.

In friendship false, implacable in hate;
Resolv'd to ruin or to rule the State.
To compass this the triple bond he broke;
The pillars of the public safety shook;
And fitted Israel for a foreign yoke:
Then seiz'd with fear, yet still affecting
 fame,
Usurp'd a patriot's all-atoning name.
So easy still it proves in factious times, 180
With public zeal to cancel private crimes.
How safe is treason, and how sacred ill,
Where none can sin against the people's
 will !
Where crowds can wink, and no offense be
 known,
Since in another's guilt they find their own !
Yet fame deserv'd no enemy can grudge;
The statesman we abhor, but praise the
 judge.
In Israel's courts ne'er sat an Abbethdin
With more discerning eyes, or hands more
 clean;
Unbrib'd, unsought, the wretched to re-
 dress;   190
Swift of dispatch, and easy of access.
O, had he been content to serve the crown,
With virtues only proper to the gown;
Or had the rankness of the soil been freed
From cockle, that oppress'd the noble
 seed;
David for him his tuneful harp had strung,
And Heav'n had wanted one immortal song.
But wild Ambition loves to slide, not stand,
And Fortune's ice prefers to Virtue's land.
Achitophel, grown weary to possess 200
A lawful fame, and lazy happiness,
Disdain'd the golden fruit to gather free,
And lent the crowd his arm to shake the
 tree.
Now, manifest of crimes contriv'd long
 since,
He stood at bold defiance with his prince;
Held up the buckler of the people's cause
Against the crown, and skulk'd behind the
 laws.
The wish'd occasion of the Plot he takes;
Some circumstances finds, but more he
 makes.
By buzzing emissaries fills the ears 210
Of list'ning crowds with jealousies and
 fears
Of arbitrary counsels brought to light,
And proves the king himself a Jebusite.
Weak arguments ! which yet he knew full
 well

Were strong with people easy to rebel.
For, govern'd by the moon, the giddy Jews
Tread the same track when she the prime
 renews;
And once in twenty years, their scribes re-
 cord,
By natural instinct they change their lord.
Achitophel still wants a chief, and none 220
Was found so fit as warlike Absalon:
Not that he wish'd his greatness to create,
(For politicians neither love nor hate,)
But, for he knew his title not allow'd,
Would keep him still depending on the
 crowd:
That kingly pow'r, thus ebbing out, might
 be
Drawn to the dregs of a democracy.
Him he attempts with studied arts to please,
And sheds his venom in such words as
 these:
 " Auspicious prince, at whose nativity 230
Some royal planet rul'd the southern sky;
Thy longing country's darling and desire;
Their cloudy pillar and their guardian fire:
Their second Moses, whose extended wand
Divides the seas, and shews the promis'd
 land;
Whose dawning day in every distant age
Has exercis'd the sacred prophets' rage:
The people's pray'r, the glad diviners'
 theme,
The young men's vision, and the old men's
 dream !
Thee, Savior, thee, the nation's vows con-
 fess,   240
And, never satisfied with seeing, bless:
Swift unbespoken pomps thy steps proclaim,
And stammering babes are taught to lisp
 thy name.
How long wilt thou the general joy detain,
Starve and defraud the people of thy
 reign ?
Content ingloriously to pass thy days
Like one of Virtue's fools that feeds on
 praise;
Till thy fresh glories, which now shine so
 bright,
Grow stale and tarnish with our daily sight.
Believe me, royal youth, thy fruit must
 be 250
Or gather'd ripe, or rot upon the tree.
Heav'n has to all allotted, soon or late,
Some lucky revolution of their fate;
Whose motions if we watch and guide with
 skill,

(For human good depends on human
   will,)
Our Fortune rolls as from a smooth descent,
And from the first impression takes the
   bent:
But, if unseiz'd, she glides away like wind,
And leaves repenting Folly far behind.
Now, now she meets you with a glorious
   prize,   260
And spreads her locks before her as she
   flies.
Had thus old David, from whose loins you
   spring,
Not dar'd, when Fortune call'd him, to be
   king,
At Gath an exile he might still remain,
And Heaven's anointing oil had been in
   vain.
Let his successful youth your hopes engage;
But shun th' example of declining age:
Behold him setting in his western skies,
The shadows lengthening as the vapors
   rise.   269
He is not now, as when on Jordan's sand ⎫
The joyful people throng'd to see him land, ⎪
Cov'ring the beach, and black'ning all the ⎬
   strand;   ⎭
But, like the Prince of Angels, from his
   height
Comes tumbling downward with diminish'd
   light;
Betray'd by one poor plot to public
   scorn,
(Our only blessing since his curst return;)
Those heaps of people which one sheaf did
   bind,
Blown off and scatter'd by a puff of wind.
What strength can he to your designs op-
   pose,   279
Naked of friends, and round beset with foes?
If Pharaoh's doubtful succor he should use,
A foreign aid would more incense the Jews:
Proud Egypt would dissembled friendship
   bring;
Foment the war, but not support the king:
Nor would the royal party e'er unite
With Pharaoh's arms t' assist the Jebusite;
Or if they should, their interest soon would
   break,
And with such odious aid make David weak.
All sorts of men by my successful arts,
Abhorring kings, estrange their alter'd
   hearts   290
From David's rule: and 't is the general cry,
' Religion, commonwealth, and liberty.'

If you, as champion of the public good,
Add to their arms a chief of royal blood,
What may not Israel hope, and what ap-
   plause
Might such a general gain by such a cause?
Not barren praise alone, that gaudy flow'r
Fair only to the sight, but solid pow'r;
And nobler is a limited command,
Giv'n by the love of all your native land,   300
Than a successive title, long and dark,
Drawn from the moldy rolls of Noah's ark."
   What cannot praise effect in mighty
   minds,
When flattery soothes, and when ambition
   blinds!
Desire of pow'r, on earth a vicious weed,
Yet, sprung from high, is of celestial seed:
In God 't is glory; and when men aspire,
'T is but a spark too much of heavenly fire.
Th' ambitious youth, too covetous of fame,
Too full of angels' metal in his frame,   310
Unwarily was led from virtue's ways,
Made drunk with honor, and debauch'd
   with praise.
Half loth, and half consenting to the ill,
(For loyal blood within him struggled still,)
He thus replied: " And what pretense
   have I
To take up arms for public liberty?
My father governs with unquestion'd right;
The faith's defender, and mankind's delight;
Good, gracious, just, observant of the laws:
And Heav'n by wonders has espous'd his
   cause.   320
Whom has he wrong'd in all his peaceful
   reign?
Who sues for justice to his throne in vain?
What millions has he pardon'd of his foes,
Whom just revenge did to his wrath ex-
   pose?
Mild, easy, humble, studious of our good;
Enclin'd to mercy, and averse from blood;
If mildness ill with stubborn Israel suit,
His crime is God's beloved attribute.
What could he gain, his people to betray,
Or change his right for arbitrary sway?   330
Let haughty Pharaoh curse with such a
   reign
His fruitful Nile, and yoke a servile train.
If David's rule Jerusalem displease,
The Dog-star heats their brains to this dis-
   ease.
Why then should I, encouraging the bad,
Turn rebel and run popularly mad?
Were he a tyrant, who, by lawless might

Oppress'd the Jews, and rais'd the Jebu-
site,
Well might I mourn; but nature's holy
bands
Would curb my spirits and restrain my
hands: 340
The people might assert their liberty;
But what was right in them were crime in
me.
His favor leaves me nothing to require,
Prevents my wishes, and outruns desire.
What more can I expect while David lives?
All but his kingly diadem he gives:
And that" — But there he paus'd; then
sighing, said —
"Is justly destin'd for a worthier head.
For when my father from his toils shall rest,
And late augment the number of the blest,
His lawful issue shall the throne ascend, 351
Or the collat'ral line, where that shall end.
His brother, tho' oppress'd with vulgar spite,
Yet dauntless, and secure of native right,
Of every royal virtue stands possess'd;
Still dear to all the bravest and the best.
His courage foes, his friends his truth pro-
claim;
His loyalty the king, the world his fame.
His mercy ev'n th' offending crowd will
find;
For sure he comes of a forgiving kind. 360
Why should I then repine at Heaven's de-
cree,
Which gives me no pretense to royalty?
Yet O that fate, propitiously inclin'd,
Had rais'd my birth, or had debas'd my
mind;
To my large soul not all her treasure lent,
And then betray'd it to a mean descent!
I find, I find my mounting spirits bold,
And David's part disdains my mother's
mold.
Why am I scanted by a niggard birth? 369
My soul disclaims the kindred of her earth;
And, made for empire, whispers me within,
'Desire of greatness is a godlike sin.'"
  Him staggering so when hell's dire agent
found,
While fainting Virtue scarce maintain'd her
ground,
He pours fresh forces in, and thus replies:
"Th' eternal God, supremely good and
wise,
Imparts not these prodigious gifts in vain:
What wonders are reserv'd to bless your
reign!

Against your will, your arguments have
shown, 379
Such virtue 's only giv'n to guide a throne.
Not that your father's mildness I contemn;
But manly force becomes the diadem.
'T is true he grants the people all they
crave;
And more, perhaps, than subjects ought to
have:
For lavish grants suppose a monarch tame,
And more his goodness than his wit pro-
claim.
But when should people strive their bonds
to break,
If not when kings are negligent or weak?
Let him give on till he can give no more,
The thrifty Sanhedrin shall keep him poor;
And every shekel which he can receive, 391
Shall cost a limb of his prerogative.
To ply him with new plots shall be my care;
Or plunge him deep in some expensive war;
Which when his treasure can no more sup-
ply,
He must, with the remains of kingship, buy.
His faithful friends, our jealousies and fears
Call Jebusites, and Pharaoh's pensioners;
Whom when our fury from his aid has
torn,
He shall be naked left to public scorn. 400
The next successor, whom I fear and hate,
My arts have made obnoxious to the State;
Turn'd all his virtues to his overthrow,
And gain'd our elders to pronounce a foe.
His right, for sums of necessary gold,
Shall first be pawn'd, and afterwards be
sold;
Till time shall ever-wanting David draw,
To pass your doubtful title into law:
If not, the people have a right supreme
To make their kings; for kings are made
for them. 410
All empire is no more than pow'r in trust,
Which, when resum'd, can be no longer
just.
Succession, for the general good design'd,
In its own wrong a nation cannot bind;
If altering that the people can relieve,
Better one suffer than a nation grieve.
The Jews well know their pow'r: ere Saul
they chose,
God was their king, and God they durst
depose.
Urge now your piety, your filial name,
A father's right, and fear of future fame;
The public good, that universal call, 421

To which even Heav'n submitted, answers
    all.
Nor let his love enchant your generous
    mind;
'T is Nature's trick to propagate her kind.
Our fond begett·rs, who would never die,
Love but themselves in their posterity.
Or let his kindness by th' effects be tried,
Or let him lay his vain pretense aside.
God said he lov'd your father; could he
    bring
A better proof, than to anoint him king ?
It surely shew'd he lov'd the shepherd
    well,   431
Who gave so fair a flock as Israel.
Would David have you thought his dar-
    ling son ?
What means he then, to alienate the
    crown ?
The name of godly he may blush to bear:
'T is after God's own heart to cheat his
    heir.
He to his brother gives supreme command,
To you a legacy of barren land:
Perhaps th' old harp, on which he thrums
    his lays,
Or some dull Hebrew ballad in your praise.
Then the next heir, a prince severe and
    wise,   441
Already looks on you with jealous eyes;
Sees thro' the thin disguises of your arts,
And marks your progress in the people's
    hearts.
Tho' now his mighty soul its grief contains,
He meditates revenge who least complains;
And, like a lion, slumb'ring in the way,
Or sleep dissembling, while he waits his
    prey,
His fearless foes within his distance draws,
Constrains his roaring, and contracts his
    paws;   450
Till at the last, his time for fury found,
He shoots with sudden vengeance from the
    ground;
The prostrate vulgar passes o'er and spares,
But with a lordly rage his hunters tears.
Your case no tame expedients will afford:
Resolve on death, or conquest by the sword,
Which for no less a stake than life you
    draw;
And self-defense is nature's eldest law.
Leave the warm people no considering
    time;
For then rebellion may be thought a
    crime.   460

Prevail yourself of what occasion gives,
But try your title while your father lives;
And that your arms may have a fair pre-
    tense,
Proclaim you take them in the king's de-
    fense;
Whose sacred life each minute would ex-
    pose
To plots, from seeming friends, and secret
    foes.
And who can sound the depth of David's
    soul ?
Perhaps his fear his kindness may con-
    trol.
He fears his brother, tho' he loves his son,
For plighted vows too late to be undone. 470
If so, by force he wishes to be gain'd;
Like women's lechery, to seem constrain'd.
Doubt not: but, when he most affects the
    frown,
Commit a pleasing rape upon the crown.
Secure his person to secure your cause:
They who possess the prince, possess the
    laws."
    He said, and this advice above the rest,
With Absalom's mild nature suited best:
Unblam'd of life, (ambition set aside,)
Not stain'd with cruelty, nor puff'd with
    pride;   480
How happy had he been, if destiny
Had higher plac'd his birth, or not so high !
His kingly virtues might have claim'd a
    throne,
And blest all other countries but his own.
But charming greatness since so few re-
    fuse,
'T is juster to lament him than accuse.
Strong were his hopes a rival to remove,
With blandishments to gain the public
    love;
To head the faction while their zeal was
    hot,
And popularly prosecute the Plot. 490
To farther this, Achitophel unites
The malcontents of all the Israelites;
Whose differing parties he could wisely
    join,
For several ends, to serve the same design:
The best, (and of the princes some were
    such,)
Who thought the pow'r of monarchy too
    much;
Mistaken men, and patriots in their hearts;
Not wicked, but seduc'd by impious arts.
By these the springs of property were bent,

And wound so high, they crack'd the government.   500
The next for interest sought t' embroil the State,
To sell their duty at a dearer rate;
And make their Jewish markets of the throne,
Pretending public good, to serve their own.
Others thought kings an useless heavy load,
Who cost too much, and did too little good.
These were for laying honest David by,
On principles of pure good husbandry.
With them join'd all th' haranguers of the throng,
That thought to get preferment by the tongue.   510
Who follow next, a double danger bring,
Not only hating David, but the king:
The Solymæan rout, well-vers'd of old
In godly faction, and in treason bold;
Cow'ring and quaking at a conqu'ror's sword;
But lofty to a lawful prince restor'd;
Saw with disdain an Ethnic plot begun,
And scorn'd by Jebusites to be outdone.
Hot Levites headed these; who, pull'd before
From th' ark, which in the Judges' days they bore,   520
Resum'd their cant, and with a zealous cry
Pursued their old belov'd Theocracy:
Where Sanhedrin and priest enslav'd the nation,
And justified their spoils by inspiration:
For who so fit for reign as Aaron's race,
If once dominion they could found in grace ?
These led the pack; tho' not of surest scent,
Yet deepest mouth'd against the government.
A numerous host of dreaming saints succeed,
Of the true old enthusiastic breed: 530
'Gainst form and order they their pow'r imploy,
Nothing to build, and all things to destroy.
But far more numerous was the herd of such,
Who think too little, and who talk too much.
These, out of mere instinct, they knew not why,

Ador'd their fathers' God and property;
And, by the same blind benefit of fate,
The Devil and the Jebusite did hate:
Born to be sav'd, even in their own despite,
Because they could not help believing right.   540
Such were the tools; but a whole Hydra more
Remains, of sprouting heads too long to score.
Some of their chiefs were princes of the land:
In the first rank of these did Zimri stand;
A man so various, that he seem'd to be
Not one, but all mankind's epitome:
Stiff in opinions, always in the wrong;
Was everything by starts, and nothing long;
But, in the course of one revolving moon,
Was chymist, fiddler, statesman, and buffoon: 550
Then all for women, painting, rhyming, drinking,
Besides ten thousand freaks that died in thinking.
Blest madman, who could every hour employ,
With something new to wish, or to enjoy !
Railing and praising were his usual themes;
And both (to shew his judgment) in extremes:
So over-violent, or over-civil,
That every man, with him, was God or Devil.
In squand'ring wealth was his peculiar art:
Nothing went unrewarded but desert.   560
Beggar'd by fools, whom still he found too late,
He had his jest, and they had his estate.
He laugh'd himself from court; then sought relief
By forming parties, but could ne'er be chief;
For, spite of him, the weight of business fell
On Absalom and wise Achitophel:
Thus, wicked but in will, of means bereft,
He left not faction, but of that was left.
Titles and names 't were tedious to rehearse
Of lords, below the dignity of verse.   570
Wits, warriors, Commonwealth's-men, were the best;
Kind husbands, and mere nobles, all the rest.

And therefore, in the name of dulness, be
The well-hung Balaam and cold Caleb,
    free;
And canting Nadab let oblivion damn,
Who made new porridge for the paschal
    lamb.
Let friendship's holy band some names as-
    sure;
Some their own worth, and some let scorn
    secure.
Nor shall the rascal rabble here have place,
Whom kings no titles gave, and God no
    grace: 580
Not bull-fac'd Jonas, who could statutes
    draw
To mean rebellion, and make treason law.
But he, tho' bad, is follow'd by a worse,
The wretch who Heav'n's anointed dar'd to
    curse:
Shimei, whose youth did early promise
Of zeal to God and hatred to his king,
Did wisely from expensive sins refrain,
And never broke the Sabbath, but for gain;
Nor ever was he known an oath to vent,
Or curse, unless against the government.
Thus heaping wealth, by the most ready
    way   591
Among the Jews, which was to cheat and
    pray,
The city, to reward his pious hate
Against his master, chose him magistrate.
His hand a vare of justice did uphold;
His neck was loaded with a chain of gold.
During his office, treason was no crime;
The sons of Belial had a glorious time;
For Shimei, tho' not prodigal of pelf,
Yet lov'd his wicked neighbor as him-
    self.   600
When two or three were gather'd to de-
    claim
Against the monarch of Jerusalem,
Shimei was always in the midst of them;
And if they curs'd the king when he was
    by,
Would rather curse than break good com-
    pany.
If any durst his factious friends accuse,
He pack'd a jury of dissenting Jews;
Whose fellow-feeling in the godly cause
Would free the suff'ring saint from human
    laws.
For laws are only made to punish those 610
Who serve the king, and to protect his
    foes.

If any leisure time he had from pow'r,
(Because 't is sin to misimploy an hour,)
His bus'ness was, by writing, to persuade
That kings were useless, and a clog to
    trade;
And, that his noble style he might refine,
No Rechabite more shunn'd the fumes of
    wine.
Chaste were his cellars, and his shrieval
    board
The grossness of a city feast abhorr'd:
His cooks, with long disuse, their trade
    forgot;   620
Cool was his kitchen, tho' his brains were
    hot.
Such frugal virtue malice may accuse,
But sure 't was necessary to the Jews;
For towns once burnt such magistrates re-
    quire
As dare not tempt God's providence by
    fire.
With spiritual food he fed his servants
    well,
But free from flesh that made the Jews
    rebel;
And Moses' laws he held in more account,
For forty days of fasting in the mount.
    To speak the rest, who better are for-
    got,   630
Would tire a well-breath'd witness of the
    Plot.
Yet, Corah, thou shalt from oblivion pass:
Erect thyself, thou monumental brass,
High as the serpent of thy metal made,
While nations stand secure beneath thy
    shade.
What tho' his birth were base, yet comets
    rise
From earthy vapors, ere they shine in
    skies.
Prodigious actions may as well be done
By weaver's issue, as by prince's son.
This arch-attestor for the public good   640
By that one deed ennobles all his blood.
Who ever ask'd the witnesses' high race,
Whose oath with martyrdom did Stephen
    grace?
Ours was a Levite, and as times went then,
His tribe were God Almighty's gentlemen.
Sunk were his eyes, his voice was harsh
    and loud,
Sure signs he neither choleric was nor
    proud:
His long chin prov'd his wit; his saintlike
    grace

A church vermilion, and a Moses' face.
His memory, miraculously great,   650
Could plots, exceeding man's belief, re-
     peat;
Which therefore cannot be accounted lies,
For human wit could never such devise.
Some future truths are mingled in his
     book;
But where the witness fail'd, the prophet
     spoke:
Some things like visionary flights appear;
The spirit caught him up, the Lord knows
     where;
And gave him his rabbinical degree,
Unknown to foreign university.
His judgment yet his mem'ry did excel; 660
Which piec'd his wondrous evidence so
     well,
And suited to the temper of the times,
Then groaning under Jebusitic crimes.
Let Israel's foes suspect his heav'nly call,
And rashly judge his writ apocryphal;
Our laws for such affronts have forfeits
     made:
He takes his life, who takes away his
     trade.
Were I myself in witness Corah's place,
The wretch who did me such a dire dis-
     grace,
Should whet my memory, tho' once for-
     got,   670
To make him an appendix of my plot.
His zeal to Heav'n made him his prince
     despise,
And load his person with indignities;
But zeal peculiar privilege affords,
Indulging latitude to deeds and words;
And Corah might for Agag's murther call,
In terms as coarse as Samuel us'd to Saul.
What others in his evidence did join,
(The best that could be had for love or
     coin,)
In Corah's own predicament will fall;   680
For *witness* is a common name to all.
     Surrounded thus with friends of every
     sort,
Deluded Absalom forsakes the court;
Impatient of high hopes, urg'd with re-
     nown,
And fir'd with near possession of a crown.
Th' admiring crowd are dazzled with sur-
     prise,
And on his goodly person feed their eyes.
His joy conceal'd, he sets himself to show,
On each side bowing popularly low;

His looks, his gestures, and his words he
     frames,   690
And with familiar ease repeats their names.
Thus form'd by nature, furnish'd out with
     arts,
He glides unfelt into their secret hearts.
Then, with a kind compassionating look,
And sighs, bespeaking pity ere he spoke,
Few words he said; but easy those and fit,
More slow than Hybla-drops, and far more
     sweet.
" I mourn, my countrymen, your lost es-
     tate;
Tho' far unable to prevent your fate:
Behold a banish'd man, for your dear cause
Expos'd a prey to arbitrary laws !   701
Yet O ! that I alone could be undone,
Cut off from empire, and no more a son !
Now all your liberties a spoil are made;
Egypt and Tyrus intercept your trade,
And Jebusites your sacred rites invade.
My father, whom with reverence yet I
     name,
Charm'd into ease, is careless of his fame;
And, brib'd with petty sums of foreign
     gold,
Is grown in Bathsheba's embraces old; 710
Exalts his enemies, his friends destroys;
And all his pow'r against himself imploys.
He gives, and let him give, my right away;
But why should he his own and yours be-
     tray?
He, only he, can make the nation bleed,
And he alone from my revenge is freed.
Take then my tears, (with that he wip'd
     his eyes,)
'T is all the aid my present pow'r supplies:
No court-informer can these arms accuse;
These arms may sons against their fathers
     use: 720
And 't is my wish, the next successor's reign
May make no other Israelite complain."
     Youth, beauty, graceful action seldom
     fail;
But common interest always will prevail;
And pity never ceases to be shown
To him who makes the people's wrongs
     his own.
The crowd, that still believe their kings
     oppress,
With lifted hands their young Messiah
     bless;
Who now begins his progress to ordain
With chariots, horsemen, and a num'rous
     train;   730

From east to west his glories he displays,
And, like the sun, the promis'd land sur-
veys.
Fame runs before him as the morning star,
And shouts of joy salute him from afar:
Each house receives him as a guardian god,
And consecrates the place of his abode.
But hospitable treats did most commend
Wise Issachar, his wealthy western friend.
This moving court, that caught the people's
eyes,
And seem'd but pomp, did other ends dis-
guise: 740
Achitophel had form'd it, with intent
To sound the depths, and fathom, where it
went,
The people's hearts; distinguish friends
from foes,
And try their strength, before they came
to blows.
Yet all was color'd with a smooth pretense
Of specious love, and duty to their prince.
Religion, and redress of grievances,
Two names that always cheat and always
please,
Are often urg'd; and good King David's
life
Endanger'd by a brother and a wife.   750
Thus in a pageant shew a plot is made,
And peace itself is war in masquerade.
O foolish Israel! never warn'd by ill!
Still the same bait, and circumvented still!
Did ever men forsake their present ease,
In midst of health imagine a disease;
Take pains contingent mischiefs to foresee,
Make heirs for monarchs, and for God de-
cree?
What shall we think! Can people give
away,
Both for themselves and sons, their native
sway?   760
Then they are left defenseless to the sword
Of each unbounded, arbitrary lord:
And laws are vain, by which we right en-
joy,
If kings unquestion'd can those laws de-
stroy.
Yet if the crowd be judge of fit and just,
And kings are only officers in trust,
Then this resuming cov'nant was declar'd
When kings were made, or is for ever
barr'd.
If those who gave the scepter could not tie
By their own deed their own posterity,   770
How then could Adam bind his future race?

How could his forfeit on mankind take
place?
Or how could heavenly justice damn us all,
Who ne'er consented to our father's fall?
Then kings are slaves to those whom they
command,
And tenants to their people's pleasure stand.
Add, that the pow'r for property allow'd
Is mischievously seated in the crowd;
For who can be secure of private right,
If sovereign sway may be dissolv'd by
might?   780
Nor is the people's judgment always true:
The most may err as grossly as the few;
And faultless kings run down, by common
cry,
For vice, oppression, and for tyranny.
What standard is there in a fickle rout,
Which, flowing to the mark, runs faster
out?
Nor only crowds, but Sanhedrins may be
Infected with this public lunacy,
And share the madness of rebellious times,
To murther monarchs for imagin'd
crimes.   790
If they may give and take whene'er they
please,
Not kings alone, (the Godhead's images,)
But government itself at length must fall
To nature's state, where all have right to
all.
Yet, grant our lords the people kings
can make,
What prudent men a settled throne would
shake?
For whatsoe'er their sufferings were be-
fore,
That change they covet makes them suf-
fer more.
All other errors but disturb a state,
But innovation is the blow of fate.   800
If ancient fabrics nod, and threat to fall,
To patch the flaws, and buttress up the
wall,
Thus far 't is duty: but here fix the mark;
For all beyond it is to touch our ark.
To change foundations, cast the frame
anew,
Is work for rebels, who base ends pursue,
At once divine and human laws control,
And mend the parts by ruin of the whole.
The tamp'ring world is subject to this curse,
To physic their disease into a worse.   810
Now what relief can righteous David
bring?

How fatal 't is to be too good a king!
Friends he has few, so high the madness
     grows:
Who dare be such, must be the people's
     foes.
Yet some there were, ev'n in the worst of
     days;
Some let me name, and naming is to praise.
  In this short file Barzillai first appears;
Barzillai, crown'd with honor and with
     years.
Long since, the rising rebels he withstood
In regions waste, beyond the Jordan's
     flood: 820
Unfortunately brave to buoy the State;
But sinking underneath his master's fate:
In exile with his godlike prince he mourn'd;
For him he suffer'd, and with him return'd.
The court he practic'd, not the courtier's
     art:
Large was his wealth, but larger was his
     heart,
Which well the noblest objects knew to
     choose,
The fighting warrior, and recording Muse.
His bed could once a fruitful issue boast;
Now more than half a father's name is
     lost.   830
His eldest hope, with every grace adorn'd,
By me (so Heav'n will have it) always
     mourn'd,
And always honor'd, snatch'd in manhood's
     prime
B' unequal fates, and Providence's crime;
Yet not before the goal of honor won, ⎤
All parts fulfill'd of subject and of son: ⎬
Swift was the race, but short the time ⎰
     to run.
O narrow circle, but of pow'r divine,
Scanted in space, but perfect in thy line!
By sea, by land, thy matchless worth was
     known,   840
Arms thy delight, and war was all thy own:
Thy force, infus'd, the fainting Tyrians
     propp'd;
And haughty Pharaoh found his fortune
     stopp'd.
O ancient honor! O unconquer'd hand,
Whom foes unpunish'd never could with-
     stand!
But Israel was unworthy of thy name;
Short is the date of all immoderate fame.
It looks as Heav'n our ruin had design'd,
And durst not trust thy fortune and thy
     mind.

Now, free from earth, thy disencumber'd
     soul   850
Mounts up, and leaves behind the clouds
     and starry pole:
From thence thy kindred legions mayst
     thou bring,
To aid the guardian angel of thy king.
Here stop, my Muse, here cease thy painful
     flight;
No pinions can pursue immortal height:
Tell good Barzillai thou canst sing no more,
And tell thy soul she should have fled be-
     fore.
Or fled she with his life, and left this verse
To hang on her departed patron's hearse?
Now take thy steepy flight from heav'n,
     and see   860
If thou canst find on earth another *he*:
Another *he* would be too hard to find;
See then whom thou canst see not far be-
     hind.
Zadoc the priest, whom, shunning pow'r
     and place,
His lowly mind advanc'd to David's grace.
With him the Sagan of Jerusalem,
Of hospitable soul, and noble stem;
Him of the western dome, whose weighty
     sense
Flows in fit words and heavenly eloquence.
The prophets' sons, by such example led, 870
To learning and to loyalty were bred:
For colleges on bounteous kings depend,
And never rebel was to arts a friend.
To these succeed the pillars of the laws;
Who best could plead, and best can judge
     a cause.
Next them a train of loyal peers ascend;
Sharp-judging Adriel, the Muses' friend;
Himself a Muse — in Sanhedrin's debate
True to his prince, but not a slave of state:
Whom David's love with honors did adorn,
That from his disobedient son were torn. 881
Jotham of piercing wit, and pregnant
     thought;
Endued by nature, and by learning taught
To move assemblies, who but only tried
The worse a while, then chose the better
     side:
Nor chose alone, but turn'd the balance
     too;
So much the weight of one brave man can
     do.
Hushai, the friend of David in distress;
In public storms, of manly steadfastness:
By foreign treaties he inform'd his youth,

And join'd experience to his native truth. 891
His frugal care supplied the wanting
    throne;
Frugal for that, but bounteous of his own:
'T is easy conduct when exchequers flow,
But hard the task to manage well the low;
For sovereign power is too depress'd or
    high,
When kings are forc'd to sell, or crowds to
    buy.
Indulge one labor more, my weary Muse,
For Amiel: who can Amiel's praise refuse?
Of ancient race by birth, but nobler yet 900
In his own worth, and without title great:
The Sanhedrin long time as chief he rul'd,
Their reason guided, and their passion
    cool'd:
So dext'rous was he in the crown's defense,
So form'd to speak a loyal nation's sense,
That, as their band was Israel's tribes in
    small,
So fit was he to represent them all.
Now rasher charioteers the seat ascend,
Whose loose careers his steady skill com-
    mend:
They, like th' unequal ruler of the day, 910
Misguide the seasons, and mistake the way;
While he withdrawn at their mad labor
    smiles,
And safe enjoys the sabbath of his toils.
These were the chief, a small but faith-⎤
    ful band   ⎥
Of worthies, in the breach who dar'd to ⎬
    stand,   ⎥
And tempt th' united fury of the land. ⎦
With grief they view'd such powerful en-
    gines bent,
To batter down the lawful government:
A numerous faction, with pretended frights,
In Sanhedrins to plume the regal rights; 920
The true successor from the court remov'd;
The Plot, by hireling witnesses, improv'd.
These ills they saw, and, as their duty
    bound,
They shew'd the king the danger of the
    wound;
That no concessions from the throne would
    please,
But lenitives fomented the disease;
That Absalom, ambitious of the crown,
Was made the lure to draw the people
    down;
That false Achitophel's pernicious hate
Had turn'd the Plot to ruin Church and
    State;   930

The council violent, the rabble worse;
That Shimei taught Jerusalem to curse.
With all these loads of injuries oppress'd,
And long revolving in his careful breast
Th' event of things, at last, his patience
    tir'd,
Thus from his royal throne, by Heav'n in-
    spir'd,
The godlike David spoke: with awful fear
His train their Maker in their master hear.
"Thus long have I, by native mercy
    sway'd,
My wrongs dissembled, my revenge de-
    lay'd: 940
So willing to forgive th' offending age;
So much the father did the king assuage.
But now so far my clemency they slight,
Th' offenders question my forgiving right.
That one was made for many, they con-
    tend;
But 't is to rule; for that 's a monarch's
    end.
They call my tenderness of blood, my fear;
Tho' manly tempers can the longest bear.
Yet, since they will divert my native course,
'T is time to shew I am not good by force.
Those heap'd affronts that haughty subjects
    bring,   951
Are burthens for a camel, not a king.
Kings are the public pillars of the State,
Born to sustain and prop the nation's
    weight;
If my young Samson will pretend a call
To shake the column, let him share the fall:
But O that yet he would repent and live!
How easy 't is for parents to forgive!
With how few tears a pardon might be won
From nature, pleading for a darling son! 960
Poor pitied youth, by my paternal care
Rais'd up to all the height his frame could
    bear!
Had God ordain'd his fate for empire born,
He would have giv'n his soul another turn:
Gull'd with a patriot's name, whose modern
    sense
Is one that would by law supplant his
    prince;
The people's brave, the politician's tool;
Never was patriot yet, but was a fool.
Whence comes it that religion and the laws
Should more be Absalom's than David's
    cause?   970
His old instructor, ere he lost his place,
Was never thought indued with so much
    grace.

Good heav'ns, how faction can a patriot
   paint !
My rebel ever proves my people's saint.
Would *they* impose an heir upon the throne ?
Let Sanhedrins be taught to give their own.
A king's at least a part of government,
And mine as requisite as their consent;
Without my leave a future king to choose,
Infers a right the present to depose.   980
True, they petition me t' approve their
   choice;
But Esau's hands suit ill with Jacob's voice.
My pious subjects for my safety pray;
Which to secure, they take my pow'r away.
From plots and treasons Heav'n preserve
   my years,
But save me most from my petitioners !
Unsatiate as the barren womb or grave;
God cannot grant so much as they can
   crave.
What then is left, but with a jealous eye
To guard the small remains of royalty ? 990
The law shall still direct my peaceful sway,
And the same law teach rebels to obey:
Votes shall no more establish'd pow'r con-
   trol —
Such votes as make a part exceed the
   whole:
No groundless clamors shall my friends
   remove,
Nor crowds have pow'r to punish ere they
   prove;
For gods and godlike kings their care ex-
   press,
Still to defend their servants in distress.
O that my pow'r to saving were confin'd !
Why am I forc'd, like Heav'n, against my
   mind,   1000
To make examples of another kind ?

Must I at length the sword of justice draw ?
O curst effects of necessary law !
How ill my fear they by my mercy scan !
Beware the fury of a patient man.
Law they require, let Law then shew her
   face;
They could not be content to look on Grace,
Her hinder parts, but with a daring eye
To tempt the terror of her front and die.
By their own arts, 't is righteously decreed,
Those dire artificers of death shall bleed.
Against themselves their witnesses will
   swear,   1012
Till viper-like their mother Plot they tear;
And suck for nutriment that bloody gore,
Which was their principle of life before.
Their Belial with their Belzebub will fight;
Thus on my foes, my foes shall do me
   right.
Nor doubt th' event; for factious crowds
   engage,
In their first onset, all their brutal rage.
Then let 'em take an unresisted course;
Retire, and traverse, and delude their
   force;   1021
But, when they stand all breathless, urge
   the fight,
And rise upon 'em with redoubled might;
For lawful pow'r is still superior found;
When long driv'n back, at length it stands
   the ground."
   He said. Th' Almighty, nodding, gave
   consent;
And peals of thunder shook the firmament.
Henceforth a series of new time began,
The mighty years in long procession ran:
Once more the godlike David was re-
   stor'd,   1030
And willing nations knew their lawful lord.

PROLOGUE AND EPILOGUE TO THE LOYAL BROTHER

OR, THE PERSIAN PRINCE

[This tragedy, the first play of Thomas Southerne (1660–1746), was printed in 1682, being entered in the *Term Catalogue* for Easter Term
(May). If we may judge from the description
of the annual pope-burning on "Queen Bess's
night," November 17 (see Prologue, line 18),
it was probably acted late in the preceding
year. The play had a political object : Tach-
mas, "the loyal brother," suggesting the Duke
of York ; and Ismael, "a villainous favorite,"
the Earl of Shaftesbury.

Pope, in his lines *To Mr. Thomas Southerne, on
his Birthday, 1742*, alludes to him as :

   Tom, whom Heav'n sent down to raise
   The price of prologues and of plays.

On this Warburton remarks :

"This alludes to a story Mr. Southerne told
about the same time to Mr. P[ope] and Mr.
W[arburton] of Dryden; who, when Southerne first wrote for the stage, was so famous
for his prologues that the players would act

nothing without that decoration. His usual price till then had been four guineas; but when Southerne came to him for the prologue he had bespoke, Dryden told him he must have six guineas for it; 'which,' said he, 'young man, is out of no disrespect to you, but the players have had my goods too cheap.'"

Dr. Johnson tells the same anecdote in his *Life of Dryden*; but, probably by a mere slip of memory, alters the figures to *two* guineas and *three*.]

PROLOGUE

POETS, like lawful monarchs, rul'd the stage,
Till critics, like damn'd Whigs, debauch'd our age.
Mark how they jump: critics would regulate
Our theaters, and Whigs reform our state:
Both pretend love, and both (plague rot 'em!) hate.
The critic humbly seems advice to bring;
The fawning Whig petitions to the king:
But one's advice into a satire slides;
T'other's petition a remonstrance hides.
These will no taxes give, and those no pence;   10
Critics would starve the poet, Whigs the prince.
The critic all our troops of friends discards;
Just so the Whig would fain pull down the guards.
Guards are illegal, that drive foes away,
As watchful shepherds, that fright beasts of prey.
Kings, who disband such needless aids as these,
Are safe — as long as e'er their subjects please:
And that would be till next Queen Bess's night,
Which thus grave penny chroniclers indite.
Sir Edmond-berry first, in woful wise,   20
Leads up the show, and milks their maudlin eyes.
There 's not a butcher's wife but dribs her part,
And pities the poor pageant from her heart;
Who, to provoke revenge, rides round the fire,
And, with a civil congee, does retire.
But guiltless blood to ground must never fall;
There 's Antichrist behind, to pay for all.
The punk of Babylon in pomp appears,

A lewd old gentleman of seventy years;
Whose age in vain our mercy would implore,   30
For few take pity on an old cast whore.
The Devil, who brought him to the shame, takes part;
Sits cheek by jowl, in black, to cheer his heart;
Like thief and parson in a Tyburn cart.
The word is giv'n, and with a loud huzza
The miter'd moppet from his chair they draw:
On the slain corpse contending nations fall:
Alas! what 's one poor pope among 'em all!
He burns; now all true hearts your triumphs ring:
And next (for fashion) cry: "God save the king!"   40
A needful cry in midst of such alarms,
When forty thousand men are up in arms.
But after he 's once sav'd, to make amends,
In each succeeding health they damn his friends:
So God begins, but still the Devil ends.
What if some one, inspir'd with zeal, should call:
"Come, let 's go cry: 'God save him at Whitehall'"?
His best friends would not like this overcare,
Or think him e'er the safer for that pray'r.
Five praying saints are by an act allow'd;
But not the whole Church-militant, in crowd.   51
Yet, should Heav'n all the true petitions drain
Of Presbyterians who would kings maintain,
Of forty thousand, five would scarce remain.

EPILOGUE

A VIRGIN poet was serv'd up to-day,
Who till this hour ne'er cackled for a play.
He 's neither yet a Whig nor Tory boy;
But, like a girl whom several would enjoy,
Begs leave to make the best of his own natural toy.
Were I to play my callow author's game,
The King's House would instruct me, by the name.
There 's loyalty to one: I wish no more;
A commonwealth sounds like a common whore.

Let husband or gallant be what they will,
One part of woman is true Tory still.   11
If any factious spirit should rebel,
Our sex, with ease, can every rising quell.
Then, as you hope we should your failings
    hide,
An honest jury for our play provide.
Whigs at their poets never take offense;
They save dull culprits who have murther'd
    sense:
Tho' nonsense is a nauseous heavy mass;
The vehicle call'd faction makes it pass.
Faction in play's the Commonwealth's-
    man's bribe,   20
The leaden farthing of the canting tribe;
Tho' void in payment laws and statutes
    make it,
The neighborhood, that knows the man,
    will take it.
'T is faction buys the votes of half the pit;
Theirs is the pension-parliament of wit.
In city clubs their venom let 'em vent,
For there 't is safe, in its own element:
Here, where their madness can have no pre-
    tense,
Let 'em forget themselves an hour in sense.
In one poor isle why should two fac-
    tions be ?   30
Small diff'rence in your vices I can see:
In drink and drabs both sides too well
    agree.
Would there were more preferments in the
    land;
If places fell, the party could not stand.
Of this damn'd grievance ev'ry Whig com-
    plains:
They grunt like hogs, till they have got
    their grains.
Meantime you see what trade our plots ad-
    vance:
We send each year good money into France;
And they, that know what merchandise we
    need,
Send o'er true Protestants to mend our
    breed.   40

PROLOGUE AND EPILOGUE TO THE PRINCESS OF CLEVES

[This tragi-comedy, by Lee, would seem, from
the reference to *Absalom and Achitophel*
(Prologue, line 25), which would have most
point when that poem was in its first heyday
of success, probably to have been acted late
in 1681 or early in 1682. Dryden's prologue
and epilogue were first printed in *Miscellany
Poems*, 1684. The early editions of the play,
of which the first appeared in 1689, do not contain either piece, but instead of them a prologue and epilogue apparently written by Lee
himself. The play is called *The Princess of
Cleve* in the early editions ; the spelling *Cleves*
is found, however, in *Miscellany Poems*, 1684.]

PROLOGUE

LADIES ! (I hope there's none behind to
    hear)
I long to whisper something in your ear:
A secret, which does much my mind per-
    plex —
There's treason in the play against our sex.
A man that's false to love, that vows and
    cheats,
And kisses every living thing he meets !
A rogue in mode — I dare not speak too
    broad —
One that does something to the very bawd.
Out on him, traitor, for a filthy beast !   9
Nay, and he's like the pack of all the rest:
None of 'em stick at mark; they all de- ⎤
    ceive. |
Some Jew has chang'd the text, I half   ⎬
    believe; |
Their Adam cozen'd our poor grandame |
    Eve.   ⎦
To hide their faults they rap out oaths and
    tear:
Now tho' we lie, we're too well bred to
    swear.
So we compound for half the sin we owe,
But men are dipp'd for soul and body too,
And when found out excuse themselves, pox
    cant 'em !
With Latin stuff, *perjuria ridet amantum.*
I'm not book-learn'd, to know that word in
    vogue,   20
But I suspect 't is Latin for a rogue.
I'm sure I never heard that scritch-owl
    hollow'd
In my poor ears, but separation follow'd.
How can such perjur'd villains e'er be saved !
Achitophel's not half so false to David.
With vows and soft expressions to allure,
They stand like foremen of a shop, de-
    mure;
No sooner out of sight, but they are gad-
    ding,
And for the next new face ride out a-pad-
    ding.

Yet, by their favor when they have bin kissing,   30
We can perceive the ready money missing.
Well! we may rail, but 't is as good e'en
wink;
Something we find, and something they
will sink.
But since they 're at renouncing, 't is our
parts
To trump their diamonds, as they trump our
hearts.

EPILOGUE

A QUALM of conscience brings me back
again
To make amends to you bespatter'd men !
We women love like cats, that hide their
joys
By growling, squalling, and a hideous noise.
I rail'd at wild young sparks, but, without
lying,
Never was man worse thought on for high-
flying:
The prodigal of love gives each her part,
And squand'ring shows, at least, a noble
heart.
I 've heard of men, who, in some lewd
lampoon,
Have hir'd a friend to make their valor
known.   10

That accusation straight this question
brings:
What is the man that does such naughty
things ?
The spaniel lover, like a sneaking fop,
Lies at our feet; he 's scarce worth tak-
ing up.
'T is true, such heroes in a play go far;
But chamber practice is not like the bar.
When men such vile, such faint petitions
make,
We fear to give, because they fear to take;
Since modesty 's the virtue of our kind,
Pray let it be to our own sex confin'd.   20
When men usurp it from the female nation,
'T is but a work of supererogation. —
We show'd a princess in the play, 't is true,
Who gave her Cæsar more than all his due;
Told her own faults; but I should much
abhor
To choose a husband for my confessor.
You see what fate follow'd the saintlike
fool,
For telling tales from out the nuptial
school.
Our play a merry comedy had prov'd,
Had she confess'd as much to him she
lov'd.   30
True Presbyterian wives the means
would try,
But damn'd confessing is flat Popery.

THE MEDAL

A SATIRE AGAINST SEDITION

BY THE AUTHOR OF ABSALOM AND ACHITOPHEL

*Per Graium populos, mediœque per Elidis urbem
Ibat ovans, divumque sibi poscebat honores.*

[On November 24, 1681, the government sought to indict the Earl of Shaftesbury of high
treason, but the London grand jury rejected the bill. What followed is well described by Sir
Walter Scott:

"The triumph of the Whigs was unbounded ; and, among other symptoms of exultation, it
displayed itself in that which gave rise to this poem of Dryden. This was a medal of Lord
Shaftesbury, struck by William [*sic*, really George] Bower, an artist who had executed some
popular pieces allusive to the Roman Catholic Plot. The obverse presented the bust of the Earl,
with the legend, *Antonio Comiti de Shaftesbury ;* the reverse, a view of London, the Bridge, and
the Tower ; the sun is rising above the Tower, and just in the act of dispersing a cloud ; the
legend around the exergue is *Lœtamur*, and beneath is the date of his acquittal, *24th November,
1681.* The partisans of the acquitted patriot wore these medals at their breasts, and care was
taken that this emblem should be made as general as possible.

"The success of *Absalom and Achitophel* made the Tories look to our author as the only poet
whose satire might check, or ridicule, the popular triumph of Shaftesbury. If the following

anecdote, which Spence has given on the authority of a Catholic priest, a friend of Pope, be absolutely correct, Charles himself engaged Dryden to write on this theme: 'One day as the king was walking in the Mall, and talking with Dryden, he said: "If I was a poet, and I think I am poor enough to be one, I would write a poem on such a subject, in the following manner." He then gave him the plan of *The Medal*. Dryden took the hint, carried the poem, as soon as it was written, to the king, and had a present of a hundred broad pieces for it.'" [Scott's quotation from Spence is not quite literal.]

The Medal was first published, as is evident from a manuscript note by Luttrell (Malone, I, 1, 163), about March 16, 1682. Of this first edition two issues are known, one of which lacks the quotation from Ovid at the end of the poem. The second edition appeared with *Miscellany Poems*, 1684, but has a separate title-page, dated 1683. A third edition was printed in 1692. The present text follows that of the issue lacking the quotation from Ovid, which, however, is added from the other issue of the first edition.]

EPISTLE TO THE WHIGS

For to whom can I dedicate this poem, with so much justice as to you? 'T is the representation of your own hero: 't is the picture drawn at length, which you admire and prize so much in little. None of your ornaments are wanting; neither the landscap of the Tower, nor the rising sun; nor the Anno Domini of your new sovereign's coronation. This must needs be a grateful undertaking to your whole party; especially to those who have not been so happy as to purchase the original. I hear the graver has made a good market of it: all his kings are bought up already; or the value of the remainder so inhanc'd, that many a poor Polander who would be glad to worship the image, is not able to go to the cost of him, but must be content to see him here. I must confess I am no great artist; but signpost painting will serve the turn to remember a friend by, especially when better is not to be had. Yet for your comfort the lineaments are true; and tho' he sate not five times to me, as he did to B., yet I have consulted history, as the Italian painters do, when they would draw a Nero or a Caligula; tho' they have not seen the man, they can help their imagination by a statue of him, and find out the coloring from Suetonius and Tacitus. Truth is, you might have spar'd one side of your Medal: the head would be seen to more advantage if it were plac'd on a spike of the Tower, a little nearer to the sun, which would then break out to better purpose.

You tell us in your preface to the *No-Protestant Plot*, that you shall be forc'd hereafter to leave off your modesty: I suppose you mean that little which is left you; for it was worn to rags when you put out this Medal. Never was there practic'd such a piece of notorious impudence in the face of an establish'd government. I believe when he is dead you will wear him in thumb-rings, as the Turks did Scanderbeg, as if there were virtue in his bones to preserve you against monarchy. Yet all this while you

pretend not only zeal for the public good, but a due veneration for the person of the king. But all men who can see an inch before them may easily detect those gross fallacies. That it is necessary for men in your circumstances to pretend both, is granted you; for without them there could be no ground to raise a faction. But I would ask you one civil question, what right has any man among you, or any association of men, (to come nearer to you,) who, out of Parliament, cannot be consider'd in a public capacity, to meet as you daily do in factious clubs, to vilify the government in your discourses, and to libel it in all your writings? Who made you judges in Israel? Or how is it consistent with your zeal of the public welfare to promote sedition? Does your definition of loyal, which is to serve the king according to the laws, allow you the license of traducing the executive power with which you own he is invested? You complain that his Majesty has lost the love and confidence of his people; and by your very urging it you endeavor, what in you lies, to make him lose them. All good subjects abhor the thought of arbitrary power, whether it be in one or many: if you were the patriots you would seem, you would not at this rate incense the multitude to assume it; for no sober man can fear it, either from the king's disposition, or his practice, or even, where you would odiously lay it, from his ministers. Give us leave to enjoy the government and the benefit of laws under which we were born, and which we desire to transmit to our posterity. You are not the trustees of the public liberty; and if you have not right to petition in a crowd, much less have you to intermeddle in the management of affairs, or to arraign what you do not like, which in effect is everything that is done by the king and council. Can you imagine that any reasonable man will believe you respect the person of his Majesty, when 't is apparent that your seditious pamphlets are stuff'd with particular reflections on him? If you have the confidence to deny this, 't is easy to be evinc'd from a thousand passages, which I only forbear to quote, because I desire they should die, and be forgotten. I have perus'd many of your papers, and to show you that I have, the third part of your *No-Protestant Plot* is much of it stolen from your dead author's pamphlet, call'd *The Growth of Popery;* as manifestly as Milton's *Defense of the English People* is from Buchanan, *De Jure Regni apud Scotos;* or your first Covenant and new Association from the Holy League of the French Guisards. Anyone who reads Davila may trace your practices all along. There were the same pretenses for reformation and loyalty, the same aspersions of the king, and the same grounds of a rebellion. I know not whether you will take the historian's word, who says it was reported that Poltrot, a Huguenot, murther'd Francis, Duke of Guise, by the instigations of Theodore Beza, or that it was a Huguenot minister, otherwise call'd a Presbyterian, (for our Church abhors so devilish a tenet,) who first writ a treatise of the lawfulness of deposing and murthering kings of a different persuasion in religion; but I am able to prove, from the doctrine of Calvin, and principles of Buchanan, that they set the people above the magistrate; which, if I mistake not, is your own fundamental, and which carries your loyalty no farther than your liking. When a vote of the House of Commons goes on your side, you are as ready to observe it as if it were pass'd into a law; but when you are pinch'd with any former, and yet unrepeal'd act of parliament, you declare that in some cases you will not be oblig'd by it. The passage is in the same third part of the *No-Protestant Plot,* and is too plain to be denied. The late copy of your intended Association, you neither wholly justify nor condemn; but as the Papists, when they are unoppos'd, fly out into all the pageantries of worship; but in times of war, when they are hard press'd by arguments, lie close intrench'd behind the Council of Trent: so now, when your affairs are in a low condition, you dare not pretend that to be a legal combination, but whensoever you are afloat, I doubt not but it will be maintain'd and justified to purpose. For indeed there is nothing to defend it but the sword; 't is the proper time to say anything, when men have all things in their power.

In the mean time, you would fain be nibbling at a parallel betwixt this Association and that in the time of Queen Elizabeth. But there is this small difference betwixt them, that the ends of the one are directly opposite to the other: one with the queen's approbation and conjunction, as head of it; the other without either the consent or knowledge of the king, against whose authority it is manifestly design'd. Therefore you do well to have recourse

to your last evasion, that it was contriv'd by your enemies, and shuffled into the papers that were seiz'd; which yet you see the nation is not so easy to believe as your own jury; but the matter is not difficult, to find twelve men in Newgate who would acquit a malefactor.

I have one only favor to desire of you at parting, that when you think of answering this poem, you would employ the same pens against it, who have combated with so much success against *Absalom and Achitophel;* for then you may assure yourselves of a clear victory, without the least reply. Rail at me abundantly; and, not to break a custom, do it without wit: by this method you will gain a considerable point, which is, wholly to waive the answer of my arguments. Never own the bottom of your principles, for fear they should be treason. Fall severely on the miscarriages of government; for if scandal be not allow'd, you are no freeborn subjects. If God has not blest you with the talent of rhyming, make use of my poor stock and welcome: let your verses run upon my feet; and, for the utmost refuge of notorious blockheads, reduc'd to the last extremity of sense, turn my own lines upon me, and, in utter despair of your own satire, make me satirize myself. Some of you have been driven to this bay already; but, above all the rest, commend me to the Nonconformist parson, who writ the *Whip and Key.* I am afraid it is not read so much as the piece deserves, because the bookseller is every week crying help at the end of his gazette, to get it off. You see I am charitable enough to do him a kindness, that it may be publish'd as well as printed; and that so much skill in Hebrew derivations may not lie for waste paper in the shop. Yet I half suspect he went no farther for his learning, than the index of Hebrew names and etymologies, which is printed at the end of some English Bibles. If Achitophel signify the brother of a fool, the author of that poem will pass with his readers for the next of kin. And perhaps 't is the relation that makes the kindness. Whatever the verses are, buy 'em up, I beseech you, out of pity; for I hear the conventicle is shut up, and the brother of Achitophel out of service.

Now footmen, you know, have the generosity to make a purse for a member of their society, who has had his livery pull'd over his ears; and even Protestant socks are bought up among you, out of veneration to the name. A dissenter in poetry from sense and English will make as good a Protestant rhymer, as a dissenter from the Church of England a Protestant parson. Besides, if you encourage a young beginner, who knows but he may elevate his style a little above the vulgar epithets of profane, and saucy Jack, and atheistic scribbler, with which he treats me, when the fit of enthusiasm is strong upon him ; by which well-manner'd and charitable expressions I was certain of his sect before I knew his name. What would you have more of a man ? He has damn'd me in your cause from Genesis to the Revelations ; and has half the texts of both the Testaments against me, if you will be so civil to yourselves as to take him for your interpreter, and not to take them for Irish witnesses. After all, perhaps you will tell me that you retain'd him only for the opening of your cause, and that your main lawyer is yet behind. Now if it so happen he meet with no more reply than his predecessors, you may either conclude that I trust to the goodness of my cause, or fear my adversary, or disdain him, or what you please, for the short on 't is, 't is indifferent to your humble servant, whatever your party says or thinks of him.

THE MEDAL

Of all our antic sights and pageantry,
Which English idiots run in crowds to see,
The Polish Medal bears the prize alone : ⎫
A monster, more the favorite of the town ⎬
Than either fairs or theaters have shown. ⎭
Never did art so well with nature strive,
Nor ever idol seem'd so much alive:
So like the man ; so golden to the sight,
So base within, so counterfeit and light.
One side is fill'd with title and with face; 10
And, lest the king should want a regal place,
On the reverse, a tow'r the town surveys;
O'er which our mounting sun his beams
    displays.
The word, pronounc'd aloud by shrieval
    voice,
Lœtamur, which, in Polish, is *rejoice*.
The day, month, year, to the great act are
    join'd ;
And a new canting holiday design'd.
Five days he sate for every cast and look;
Four more than God to finish Adam took.
But who can tell what essence angels are, 20
Or how long Heav'n was making Lucifer ?
O could the style that copied every grace,
And plow'd such furrows for an eunuch
    face,
Could it have form'd his ever-changing
    will,
The various piece had tir'd the graver's
    skill !
A martial hero first, with early care,

Blown, like a pigmy by the winds, to war.
A beardless chief, a rebel, ere a man:
(So young his hatred to his prince began.)
Next this, (how wildly will ambition steer !)
A vermin wriggling in th' usurper's ear. 31
Bart'ring his venal wit for sums of gold,
He cast himself into the saintlike mold;
Groan'd, sigh'd, and pray'd, while godliness
    was gain,
The loudest bagpipe of the squeaking train.
But, as 't is hard to cheat a juggler's eyes,
His open lewdness he could ne'er disguise.
There split the saint; for hypocritic zeal
Allows no sins but those it can conceal.
Whoring to scandal gives too large a scope;
Saints must not trade, but they may interlope. 41
Th' ungodly principle was all the same;
But a gross cheat betrays his partner's
    game.
Besides, their pace was formal, grave, and
    slack;
His nimble wit outran the heavy pack.
Yet still he found his fortune at a stay;
Whole droves of blockheads choking up his
    way:
They took, but not rewarded, his advice;
Villain and wit exact a double price.
Pow'r was his aim ; but, thrown from ⎫
    that pretense, 50 ⎪
The wretch turn'd loyal in his own de- ⎬
    fense, ⎪
And malice reconcil'd him to his prince. ⎭
Him in the anguish of his soul he serv'd,
Rewarded faster still than he deserv'd.
Behold him now exalted into trust;
His counsel 's oft convenient, seldom just.
Ev'n in the most sincere advice he gave,
He had a grudging still to be a knave.
The frauds he learnt in his fanatic years
Made him uneasy in his lawful gears: 60
At best as little honest as he could,
And, like white witches, mischievously
    good;
To his first bias longingly he leans,
And *rather* would be great by wicked
    means.
Thus, fram'd for ill, he loos'd our triple
    hold;
(Advice unsafe, precipitous, and bold.)
From hence those tears ! that Ilium of our
    woe !
Who helps a pow'rful friend, forearms a
    foe.
What wonder if the waves prevail so far,

When he cut down the banks that made
   the bar ?   70
Seas follow but their nature to invade,
But he by art our native strength betray'd.
So Samson to his foe his force confess'd;
And, to be shorn, lay slumb'ring on her
   breast.
But when this fatal counsel, found too
   late,
Expos'd its author to the public hate;
When his just sovereign, by no impious
   way,
Could be seduc'd to arbitrary sway;
Forsaken of that hope, he shifts the sail, ⌉
Drives down the current with a pop'lar |
   gale;   80 ⎬
And shews the fiend confess'd without a |
   veil.   ⌋
He preaches to the crowd that pow'r is
   lent,
But not convey'd to kingly government;
That claims successive bear no binding
   force,
That coronation oaths are things of course;
Maintains the multitude can never err,
And sets the people in the papal chair.
The reason's obvious: *int'rest never lies ;* ⌉
The most have still their int'rest in their |
   eyes;   ⎬
The pow'r is always theirs, and pow'r is |
   ever wise.   90 ⌋
Almighty crowd, thou shorten'st all dis-
   pute;
Pow'r is thy essence, wit thy attribute !
Nor faith nor reason make thee at a stay,
Thou leap'st o'er all eternal truths in thy
   Pindaric way!
Athens no doubt did righteously decide,
When Phocion and when Socrates were
   tried;
As righteously they did those dooms re-
   pent;
Still they were wise, whatever way they
   went.
Crowds err not, tho' to both extremes they
   run;
To kill the father and recall the son.   100
Some think the fools were most, as times
   went then;
But now the world's o'erstock'd with pru-
   dent men.
The common cry is ev'n religion's test:
The Turk's is at Constantinople best;
Idols in India; Popery at Rome;
And our own worship only true at home.

And true, but for the time; 't is hard to
   know
How long we please it shall continue so.
This side to-day, and that to-morrow burns;
So all are God-a'mighties in their turns. 110
A tempting doctrine, plausible and new:
What fools our fathers were, if this be
   true !
Who, to destroy the seeds of civil war,
Inherent right in monarchs did declare;
And, that a lawful pow'r might never cease,
Secur'd succession, to secure our peace.
Thus property and sovereign sway, at last,
In equal balances were justly cast:
But this new Jehu spurs the hot-mouth'd
   horse;   119
Instructs the beast to know his native force,
To take the bit between his teeth, and fly
To the next headlong steep of anarchy.
Too happy England, if our good we knew,
Would we possess the freedom we pursue !
The lavish government can give no more;
Yet we repine, and plenty makes us poor.
God tried us once: our rebel fathers fought;
He glutted 'em with all the pow'r they
   sought:
Till, master'd by their own usurping brave,
The freeborn subject sunk into a slave. 130
We loathe our manna, and we long for
   quails;
Ah, what is man, when his own wish pre-
   vails !
How rash, how swift to plunge himself in
   ill;
Proud of his pow'r, and boundless in his
   will !
That kings can do no wrong we must be-
   lieve;
None can they do, and must they all re-
   ceive ?
Help, Heaven ! or sadly we shall see an
   hour,
When neither wrong nor right are in their
   pow'r !
Already they have lost their best defense,
The benefit of laws which they dispense: 140
No justice to their righteous cause allow'd;
But baffled by an arbitrary crowd;
And medals grav'd, their conquest to record,
The stamp and coin of their adopted lord.
   The man who laugh'd but once, to see an
   ass
Mumbling to make the crossgrain'd thistles
   pass,
Might laugh again, to see a jury chaw

The prickles of unpalatable law.
The witnesses that, leech-like, liv'd on
    blood,
Sucking for them were med'cinally good;
But when they fasten'd on *their* fester'd ⎫
    sore,   151 ⎬
Then justice and religion they forswore; ⎬
Their maiden oaths debauch'd into a ⎬
    whore.   ⎭
Thus men are rais'd by factions, and de-
    cried;
And rogue and saint distinguish'd by their
    side.
They rack ev'n scripture to confess their
    cause,
And plead a call to preach in spite of laws.
But that's no news to the poor injur'd page:
It has been us'd as ill in every age;
And is constrain'd, with patience, all to
    take;   160
For what defense can Greek and Hebrew
    make?
Happy who can this talking trumpet seize;
They make it speak whatever sense they
    please!
'T was fram'd at first our oracle t' en- ⎫
    quire;   ⎬
But since our sects in prophecy grow ⎬
    higher,   ⎬
The text inspires not them, but they the ⎬
    text inspire.   ⎭
   London, thou great *emporium* of our isle,
O thou too bounteous, thou too fruitful Nile!
How shall I praise or curse to thy desert;
Or separate thy sound from thy corrupted
    part!   170
I call'd thee Nile; the parallel will stand:
Thy tides of wealth o'erflow the fatten'd
    land;
Yet monsters from thy large increase we
    find,
Engender'd on the slime thou leav'st be-
    hind.
Sedition has not wholly seiz'd on thee,
Thy nobler parts are from infection free.
Of Israel's tribes thou hast a numerous
    band,
But still the Canaanite is in the land.
Thy military chiefs are brave and true,
Nor are thy disinchanted burghers few. 180
The head is loyal which thy heart com-
    mands,
But what's a head with two such gouty
    hands?
The wise and wealthy love the surest way,

And are content to thrive and to obey.
But wisdom is to sloth too great a slave;
None are so busy as the fool and knave.
Those let me curse; what vengeance will
    they urge,
Whose ordures neither plague nor fire can
    purge;
Nor sharp experience can to duty bring,
Nor angry Heaven, nor a forgiving king! 190
In gospel-phrase their chapmen they be-
    tray;
Their shops are dens, the buyer is their prey.
The knack of trades is living on the spoil;
They boast, ev'n when each other they be-
    guile.
Customs to steal is such a trivial thing,
That 't is their charter to defraud their king.
All hands unite of every jarring sect;
They cheat the country first, and then in-
    fect.
They for God's cause their monarchs dare
    dethrone,
And they'll be sure to make his cause their
    own.   200
Whether the plotting Jesuit laid the plan
Of murth'ring kings, or the French Puritan,
Our sacrilegious sects their guides outgo,
And kings and kingly pow'r would murther
    too.
   What means their trait'rous combination
    less,
Too plain t' evade, too shameful to confess!
But treason is not own'd when 't is descried:
Successful crimes alone are justified.
The men, who no conspiracy would find,
Who doubts, but had it taken, they had
    join'd —   210
Join'd in a mutual cov'nant of defense,
At first without, at last against their
    prince?
If sovereign right by sovereign pow'r they
    scan,
The same bold maxim holds in God and
    man:
God were not safe, his thunder could they
    shun,
He should be forc'd to crown another son.
Thus, when the heir was from the vine-
    yard thrown,
The rich possession was the murth'rers' own.
In vain to sophistry they have recourse: ⎫
By proving theirs no plot, they prove 't is ⎬
    worse;   220 ⎬
Unmask'd rebellion, and audacious force; ⎭
Which tho' not actual, yet all eyes may see

'T is working in th' immediate pow'r to be;
For from pretended grievances they rise,
First to dislike, and after to despise;
Then, Cyclop-like, in human flesh to deal,
Chop up a minister at every meal;
Perhaps not wholly to melt down the king,
But clip his regal rights within the ring;
From thence t' assume the pow'r of peace
 and war;   230
And ease him by degrees of public care.
Yet, to consult his dignity and fame,
He should have leave to exercise the
 name,
And hold the cards, while commons play'd
 the game.
For what can pow'r give more than food
 and drink,
To live at ease, and not be bound to think?
These are the cooler methods of their crime,
But their hot zealots think 't is loss of time;
On utmost bounds of loyalty they stand,
And grin and whet like a Croatian band,
That waits impatient for the last com-
 mand.   241
Thus outlaws open villainy maintain,
They steal not, but in squadrons scour the
 plain;
And, if their pow'r the passengers subdue,
The most have right, the wrong is in the
 few.
Such impious axioms foolishly they show,
For in some soils republics will not grow:
Our temp'rate isle will no extremes sustain
Of pop'lar sway or arbitrary reign,
But slides between them both into the best,
Secure in freedom, in a monarch blest;   251
And tho' the climate, vex'd with various
 winds,
Works thro' our yielding bodies on our
 minds,
The wholesome tempest purges what it
 breeds,
To recommend the calmness that succeeds.
 But thou, the pander of the people's
 hearts,
(O crooked soul, and serpentine in arts!)
Whose blandishments a loyal land have
 whor'd,
And broke the bonds she plighted to her
 lord;
What curses on thy blasted name will
 fall!   260
Which age to age their legacy shall call;
For all must curse the woes that must
 descend on all.

Religion thou hast none; thy *mercury*
Has pass'd thro' every sect, or theirs thro'
 thee.
But what thou giv'st, that venom still re-
 mains;
And the pox'd nation feels thee in their
 brains.
What else inspires the tongues and swells
 the breasts
Of all thy bellowing renegado priests,
That preach up thee for God, dispense thy
 laws,
And with thy stum ferment their fainting
 cause,   270
Fresh fumes of madness raise, and toil and
 sweat
To make the formidable cripple great?
Yet should thy crimes succeed, should law-
 less pow'r
Compass those ends thy greedy hopes de-
 vour,
Thy canting friends thy mortal foes would
 be,
Thy God and theirs will never long agree;
For thine (if thou hast any) must be one
That lets the world and humankind alone;
A jolly god, that passes hours too well
To promise heav'n, or threaten us with
 hell;   280
That unconcern'd can at rebellion sit,
And wink at crimes he did himself commit.
A tyrant theirs; the heav'n their priest-
 hood paints
A conventicle of gloomy sullen saints;
A heav'n like Bedlam, slovenly and sad,
Foredoom'd for souls with false religion
 mad.
 Without a vision poets can foreshow
What all but fools by common sense may
 know;
If true succession from our isle should fail,
And crowds profane with impious arms
 prevail,   290
Not thou, nor those thy factious arts in-
 gage,
Shall reap that harvest of rebellious rage,
With which thou flatter'st thy decrepit
 age.
The swelling poison of the sev'ral sects,
Which, wanting vent, the nation's health
 infects,
Shall burst its bag; and, fighting out their
 way,
The various venoms on each other prey.
The presbyter, puff'd up with spiritual pride,

Shall on the necks of the lewd nobles ride,
His brethren damn, the civil pow'r defy, 300
And parcel out republic prelacy.
But short shall be his reign: his rigid yoke
And tyrant pow'r will puny sects provoke;
And frogs and toads, and all the tadpole
    train,
Will croak to Heav'n for help from this de-
    vouring crane.
The cutthroat sword and clamorous gown
    shall jar,
In sharing their ill-gotten spoils of war;
Chiefs shall be grudg'd the part which ⎫
    they pretend; ⎪
Lords envy lords, and friends with every ⎬
    friend   309
About their impious merit shall contend. ⎭

The surly commons shall respect deny,
And justle peerage out with property.
Their gen'ral either shall his trust betray,
And force the crowd to arbitrary sway;
Or they, suspecting his ambitious aim, ⎫
In hate of kings shall cast anew the frame; ⎪
And thrust out Collatine that bore their ⎬
    name. ⎭
Thus inborn broils the factions would ⎫
    ingage, ⎪
Or wars of exil'd heirs, or foreign rage, ⎬
Till halting vengeance overtook our age; ⎭
And our wild labors wearied into rest, 321
Reclin'd us on a rightful monarch's breast.

—— *Pudet hæc opprobria, vobis*
Et dici potuisse, et non potuisse refelli.

PROLOGUE TO HIS ROYAL HIGH-
NESS, UPON HIS FIRST AP-
PEARANCE AT THE DUKE'S
THEATER SINCE HIS RETURN
FROM SCOTLAND

SPOKEN BY MR. SMITH

[This prologue was first published as a broadside, in 1682; it was reprinted in the third
edition, 1702, of *Sylvæ*, with the addition of
1682 at the close of the title.
In March, 1682, the Duke of York was recalled from Scotland, where he had been living in honorable exile, as high commissioner,
since October, 1680. His first visit to the theater called by his name was on April 21.
Otway's *Venice Preserv'd, or A Plot Discover'd*,
a play of political tendency (first performed in
the preceding February), in which Antonio,
the villain, "a fine speaker in the senate," is
meant to suggest Anthony, Earl of Shaftesbury, was represented on this occasion. Date
and play are known to us from the heading
of the special epilogue, published as a broadside, which Otway wrote for this performance.
The play was first published in 1682; the
special prologue and epilogue were not printed
with it.]

IN those cold regions which no summers
    cheer,
When brooding darkness covers half the
    year,
To hollow caves the shivering natives go;
Bears range abroad, and hunt in tracks of
    snow·

But when the tedious twilight wears away,
And stars grow paler at th' approach of
    day,
The longing crowds to frozen mountains
    run;
Happy who first can see the glimmering
    sun!
The surly salvage offspring disappear,
And curse the bright successor of the
    year.   10
Yet, tho' rough bears in covert seek de- ⎫
    fense, ⎪
White foxes stay, with seeming innocence: ⎬
That crafty kind with daylight can dis- ⎪
    pense. ⎭
Still we are throng'd so full with Reynard's
    race,
That loyal subjects scarce can find a place:
Thus modest truth is cast behind the crowd;
Truth speaks too low, Hypocrisy too loud.
Let 'em be first to flatter in success;
Duty can stay, but guilt has need to press.
Once, when true zeal the sons of God did
    call,   20
To make their solemn show at heaven's
    Whitehall,
The fawning Devil appear'd among the rest,
And made as good a courtier as the best.
The friends of Job, who rail'd at him be-
    fore,
Came cap in hand when he had three times
    more.
Yet late repentance may, perhaps, be true;
Kings can forgive, if rebels can but sue:
A tyrant's pow'r in rigor is express'd;

The father yearns in the true prince's
    breast.
We grant, an o'ergrown Whig no grace
    can mend;   30
But most are babes, that know not they
    offend.
The crowd, to restless motion still enclin'd,
Are clouds, that rack according to the wind.
Driv'n by their chiefs, they storms of hail-
    stones pour;
Then mourn, and soften to a silent show'r.
O welcome to this much-offending land,
The prince that brings forgiveness in his
    hand !
Thus angels on glad messages appear;
Their first salute commands us not to fear:
Thus Heav'n, that could constrain us to ⎫
    obey,   40 ⎪
(With rev'rence if we might presume to ⎬
    say,)   ⎪
Seems to relax the rights of sov'reign ⎪
    sway;   ⎭
Permits to man the choice of good and ill,
And makes us happy by our own free will.

TO THE DUCHESS ON HER RE-
TURN FROM SCOTLAND IN
THE YEAR 1682

[This poem was first published as a broadside in 1682, with the heading, *Prologue to
the Duchess on her Return from Scotland*. It
was reprinted, with title as above, in *Examen
Poeticum*, 1693. The texts of the two editions
are identical.

This prologue is addressed to Mary of Este,
Princess of Modena, the second wife of the
Duke of York, whom he had married in 1673.
His first duchess, Anne Hyde, in whose honor
Dryden wrote some earlier verses (see p. 26,
above), died on March 31, 1671. On May 3,
1682, the duke sailed for Scotland to bring
back his wife, and suffered shipwreck on the
Lemmon Ore, off the Yorkshire coast, nearly
losing his life. (See the *Second Part of Absalom and Achitophel*, lines 1081–1084, and *Britannia Rediviva*, line 97.) The duke and duchess
returned in safety to England, reaching London on May 27 (Luttrell). The exact date of
the duchess's visit to the theater is unknown.]

WHEN factious rage to cruel exile drove
The Queen of Beauty, and the Court of
    Love,
The Muses droop'd, with their forsaken
    arts,

And the sad Cupids broke their useless
    darts;
Our fruitful plains to wilds and desarts
    turn'd,
Like Eden's face when banish'd man it
    mourn'd;
Love was no more, when Loyalty was gone,
The great supporter of his awful throne;
Love could no longer after Beauty stay, ⎫
But wandered northward to the verge ⎪
    of day,   10 ⎬
As if the sun and he had lost their way. ⎭
But now th' illustrious nymph, return'd
    again,
Brings every Grace triumphant in her
    train.
The wond'ring Nereids, tho' they rais'd no
    storm,
Foreslow'd her passage, to behold her form:
Some cried, a Venus; some, a Thetis
    pass'd;
But this was not so fair, nor that so chaste.
Far from her sight flew Faction, Strife, and
    Pride;
And Envy did but look on her, and died.
Whate'er we suffer'd from our sullen fate,
Her sight is purchas'd at an easy rate.   21
Three gloomy years against this day were
    set,
But this one mighty sum has clear'd the
    debt;
Like Joseph's dream, but with a better
    doom,
The famine past, the plenty still to come.
For her the weeping heav'ns become se-
    rene;
For her the ground is clad in cheerful
    green;
For her the nightingales are taught to
    sing,
And Nature has for her delay'd the spring.
The Muse resumes her long-forgotten ⎫
    lays,   30 ⎪
And Love, restor'd, his ancient realm ⎬
    surveys,   ⎪
Recalls our beauties, and revives our ⎪
    plays;   ⎭
His waste dominions peoples once again,
And from her presence dates his second
    reign.
But awful charms on her fair forehead sit,
Dispensing what she never will admit;
Pleasing, yet cold, like Cynthia's silver
    beam,
The people's wonder and the poet's theme.

Distemper'd Zeal, Sedition, canker'd Hate,
No more shall vex the Church, and tear the
    State: 40
No more shall Faction civil discords move,
Or only discords of too tender love:

Discord, like that of music's various parts;
Discord, that makes the harmony of hearts;
Discord, that only this dispute shall bring,
Who best shall love the duke, and serve the
    king.

MAC FLECKNOE

OR, A SATIRE UPON THE TRUE-BLUE-PROTESTANT POET

T. S.

BY THE AUTHOR OF ABSALOM AND ACHITOPHEL

[Thomas Shadwell, once Dryden's friend (see note, p. 83, above), now his enemy, and an ardent Whig, had published an answer to *The Medal*, entitled, *The Medal of John Bayes, a Satire against Folly and Knavery*, in which he assailed Dryden with foul and scurrilous abuse. Dryden's reply was the following poem, published, according to Malone (I, 1, 169), who probably had some authority for his statement, on October 4, 1682. It was "printed for D. Green," instead of for Tonson; part of the title-page is reproduced above. A second edition, with numerous changes in the text, appeared as the first piece in *Miscellany Poems*, 1684, from which the present text is taken.

In the preface to his translation of the *Tenth Satire of Juvenal*, 1687, Shadwell says that Dryden, when charged by him with writing *Mac Flecknoe*, denied the fact, "with all the execrations he could think of." This story deserves no attention; if true, it merely shows that Dryden was jesting at Shadwell's expense. Dryden admits the authorship in his *Discourse concerning Satire*, 1692: see p. 303, below. After the Revolution Shadwell was created poet laureate; Dr. Johnson wrongly states that Dryden wrote *Mac Flecknoe* to celebrate that occasion.]

ALL human things are subject to decay,
And when fate summons, monarchs must
    obey.
This Flecknoe found, who, like Augustus,
    young
Was call'd to empire, and had govern'd
    long;
In prose and verse, was own'd, without dis-
    pute,
Thro' all the realms of *Nonsense*, absolute.
This aged prince, now flourishing in peace,
And blest with issue of a large increase;
Worn out with business, did at length de-
    bate
To settle the succession of the State;   10
And, pond'ring which of all his sons was
    fit
To reign, and wage immortal war with wit,
Cried: "'T is resolv'd; for nature pleads,
    that he
Should only rule, who most resembles me.
Sh—— alone my perfect image bears,
Mature in dulness from his tender years:
Sh—— alone, of all my sons, is he
Who stands confirm'd in full stupidity.

The rest to some faint meaning make pre-
    tense,
But Sh—— never deviates into sense.   20
Some beams of wit on other souls may fall,
Strike thro', and make a lucid interval;
But Sh——'s genuine night admits no ray,
His rising fogs prevail upon the day,
Besides, his goodly fabric fills the eye,
And seems design'd for thoughtless majesty;
Thoughtless as monarch oaks that shade
    the plain,
And, spread in solemn state, supinely reign.
Heywood and Shirley were but types of
    thee,
Thou last great prophet of tautology.   30
Even I, a dunce of more renown than they,
Was sent before but to prepare thy way:
And, coarsely clad in Norwich drugget,
    came
To teach the nations in thy greater name.
My warbling lute, the lute I whilom strung,
When to King John of Portugal I sung,
Was but the prelude to that glorious day,
When thou on silver Thames didst cut thy
    way,

With well-tim'd oars before the royal barge,
Swell'd with the pride of thy celestial charge; 40
And big with hymn, commander of a host,
The like was ne'er in Epsom blankets toss'd.
Methinks I see the new Arion sail,
The lute still trembling underneath thy nail.
At thy well-sharpen'd thumb from shore to shore
The treble squeaks for fear, the basses roar;
Echoes from Pissing Alley Sh—— call,
And Sh —— they resound from Aston Hall.
About thy boat the little fishes throng,
As at the morning toast that floats along. 50
Sometimes, as prince of thy harmonious band,
Thou wield'st thy papers in thy threshing hand.
St. André's feet ne'er kept more equal time,
Not ev'n the feet of thy own *Psyche's* rhyme;
Tho' they in number as in sense excel:
So just, so like tautology, they fell,
That, pale with envy, Singleton forswore ⎤
The lute and sword, which he in triumph bore, ⎬
And vow'd he ne'er would act Villerius more." ⎦
Here stopp'd the good old sire, and wept for joy 60
In silent raptures of the hopeful boy.
All arguments, but most his plays, persuade,
That for anointed dulness he was made.
  Close to the walls which fair Augusta bind,
(The fair Augusta much to fears inclin'd,)
An ancient fabric rais'd t' inform the sight,
There stood of yore, and Barbican it hight:
A watchtower once; but now, so fate ordains,
Of all the pile an empty name remains.
From its old ruins brothel-houses rise, 70
Scenes of lewd loves, and of polluted joys,
Where their vast courts the mother-strumpets keep,
And, undisturb'd by watch, in silence sleep.
Near these a Nursery erects its head,
Where queens are form'd, and future heroes bred;

Where unfledg'd actors learn to laugh and cry, ⎤
Where infant punks their tender voices try, ⎬
And little Maximins the gods defy. ⎦
Great Fletcher never treads in buskins here,
Nor greater Jonson dares in socks appear; 80
But gentle Simkin just reception finds
Amidst this monument of vanish'd minds:
Pure clinches the suburbian Muse affords,
And Panton waging harmless war with words.
Here Flecknoe, as a place to fame well known,
Ambitiously design'd his Sh——'s throne;
For ancient Dekker prophesied long since, ⎤
That in this pile should reign a mighty prince, ⎬
Born for a scourge of wit, and flail of sense; ⎦
To whom true dulness should some *Psyches* owe, 90
But worlds of *Misers* from his pen should flow;
Humorists and *Hypocrites* it should produce,
Whole Raymond families, and tribes of Bruce.
  Now Empress Fame had publish'd the renown
Of Sh——'s coronation thro' the town.
Rous'd by report of Fame, the nations meet,
From near Bunhill, and distant Watling Street.
No Persian carpets spread th' imperial way,
But scatter'd limbs of mangled poets lay;
From dusty shops neglected authors come,
Martyrs of pies, and relics of the bum. 101
Much Heywood, Shirley, Ogleby there lay,
But loads of Sh—— almost chok'd the way.
Bilk'd stationers for yeomen stood prepar'd,
And Herringman was captain of the guard.
The hoary prince in majesty appear'd,
High on a throne of his own labors rear'd.
At his right hand our young Ascanius sate,
Rome's other hope, and pillar of the State.
His brows thick fogs, instead of glories, grace, 110
And lambent dulness play'd around his face.
As Hannibal did to the altars come,
Sworn by his sire a mortal foe to Rome;
So Sh—— swore, nor should his vow be vain,
That he till death true dulness would maintain;
And, in his father's right, and realm's defense,

Ne'er to have peace with wit, nor truce
with sense.
The king himself the sacred unction made,
As king by office, and as priest by trade.
In his sinister hand, instead of ball,   120
He plac'd a mighty mug of potent ale;
Love's Kingdom to his right he did convey,
At once his scepter, and his rule of sway;
Whose righteous lore the prince had prac-
tic'd young,
And from whose loins recorded *Psyche*
sprung.
His temples, last, with poppies were o'er-
spread,
That nodding seem'd to consecrate his head.
Just at that point of time, if fame not lie,
On his left hand twelve reverend owls did
fly.
So Romulus, 't is sung, by Tiber's brook, 130
Presage of sway from twice six vultures
took.
Th' admiring throng loud acclamations make,
And omens of his future empire take.
The sire then shook the honors of his head,
And from his brows damps of oblivion shed
Full on the filial dulness: long he stood,
Repelling from his breast the raging god;
At length burst out in this prophetic
mood:
  " Heavens bless my son, from Ireland let
him reign
To far Barbadoes on the western main; 140
Of his dominion may no end be known,
And greater than his father's be his throne;
Beyond *Love's Kingdom* let him stretch his
pen ! "
He paus'd, and all the people cried,
" Amen."
Then thus continued he: " My son, advance
Still in new impudence, new ignorance.
Success let others teach, learn thou from me
Pangs without birth, and fruitless industry.
Let *Virtuosos* in five years be writ;
Yet not one thought accuse thy toil of wit.
Let gentle George in triumph tread the
stage,   151
Make Dorimant betray, and Loveit rage;
Let Cully, Cockwood, Fopling, charm the
pit,
And in their folly shew the writer's wit.
Yet still thy fools shall stand in thy defense,
And justify their author's want of sense.
Let 'em be all by thy own model made
Of dulness, and desire no foreign aid;
That they to future ages may be known,

Not copies drawn, but issue of thy own. 160
Nay, let thy men of wit too be the same,
All full of thee, and differing but in name.
But let no alien S—dl—y interpose,
To lard with wit thy hungry *Epsom* prose.
And when false flowers of rhetoric thou
wouldst cull,
Trust nature, do not labor to be dull;
But write thy best, and top; and, in each
line,
Sir Formal's oratory will be thine:
Sir Formal, tho' unsought, attends thy quill,
And does thy northern dedications fill. 170
Nor let false friends seduce thy mind to
fame,
By arrogating Jonson's hostile name.
Let father Flecknoe fire thy mind with
praise,
And uncle Ogleby thy envy raise.
Thou art my blood, where Jonson has no
part:
What share have we in nature, or in art ?
Where did his wit on learning fix a brand,
And rail at arts he did not understand ?
Where made he love in Prince Nicander's
vein,
Or swept the dust in *Psyche's* humble strain ?
Where sold he bargains, ' whip-stitch, kiss
my arse,'   181
Promis'd a play and dwindled to a farce ?
When did his Muse from Fletcher scenes
purloin,
As thou whole Eth'rege dost transfuse to
thine ?
But so transfus'd, as oil on water's flow,
His always floats above, thine sinks below.
This is thy province, this thy wondrous way,
New humors to invent for each new play:
This is that boasted bias of thy mind,
By which one way, to dulness, 't is inclin'd;
Which makes thy writings lean on one side
still,   191
And, in all changes, that way bends thy will.
Nor let thy mountain-belly make pretense
Of likeness; thine 's a tympany of sense.
A tun of man in thy large bulk is writ,
But sure thou 'rt but a kilderkin of wit.
Like mine, thy gentle numbers feebly creep;
Thy tragic Muse gives smiles, thy comic
sleep.
With whate'er gall thou sett'st thyself to
write,
Thy inoffensive satires never bite. 200
In thy felonious heart tho' venom lies,
It does but touch thy Irish pen, and dies.

Thy genius calls thee not to purchase fame
In keen iambics, but mild anagram.
Leave writing plays, and choose for thy
  command
Some peaceful province in acrostic land.
There thou may'st wings display and altars
  raise,
And torture one poor word ten thousand
  ways.
Or, if thou wouldst thy diff'rent talents suit,

Set thy own songs, and sing them to thy lute."
  He said: but his last words were scarcely ⎫
    heard;   211 ⎪
For Bruce and Longvil had a trap prepar'd, ⎬
And down they sent the yet declaiming   ⎪
  bard.   ⎭
Sinking he left his drugget robe behind,
Borne upwards by a subterranean wind.
The mantle fell to the young prophet's part,
With double portion of his father's art.

THE SECOND PART OF

ABSALOM AND ACHITOPHEL

A POEM

Si quis tamen hæc quoque, si quis
Captus amore leget.

[According to an advertisement in the *Observator* (see Scott-Saintsbury edition, xviii, 295; and compare Malone, I, 1, 173) this poem was published about November 11, 1682; a second edition, with a few changes of text, appeared before the close of the year. No author's name was printed with either edition. To the third edition, which did not appear until 1716, in the fourth edition of the *Second Part of Miscellany Poems*, Tonson prefixed the following note, *To the Reader*, which is probably authentic, being confirmed by internal evidence:
"In the year 1680 Mr. Dryden undertook the poem of *Absalom and Achitophel*, upon the desire of King Charles the Second. The performance was applauded by everyone; and several persons pressing him to write a second part, he, upon declining it himself, spoke to Mr. Tate to write one, and gave him his advice in the direction of it; and that part beginning:
'Next these, a troop of busy spirits press,'
and ending:
'To talk like Doeg, and to write like thee,'
containing near two hundred verses, were intirely Mr. Dryden's compositions, besides some touches in other places."
Lines 310-509 may then be accepted as written by Dryden; in the rest of the poem his work cannot be distinguished with any certainty. Sir Walter Scott's opinion on the matter is however of much interest:
"To prevent Tate from suffering too much by comparison, Dryden has obviously contributed much to the poem at large. . . . Much of the character of Corah [lines 69-102], for example, is unquestionably Dryden's; so probably is that of Arod [lines 534-555] and the verses generally descriptive of the Green-ribbon Club [lines 522-533] which precede it. Such pungent satire is easily distinguished from the smooth insipid flow of other parts, in which Dryden's corrections probably left nothing for censure, and which Tate was unable to qualify with anything entitled to praise. The character of Michal [lines 51-68], of Dryden as Asaph [lines 1037-1064], and some of the encomiastic passages, seem to show the extent of Tate's powers, when unsupported by the vivifying assistance of his powerful auxiliary. They are just decently versified, but flat, commonplace, and uninteresting." (Scott-Saintsbury edition, ix, 321.)
The present text is that of the second edition.]

SINCE men, like beasts, each other's prey
  were made,
Since trade began, and priesthood grew a
  trade,
Since realms were form'd, none sure so
  curst as those

That madly their own happiness oppose;
There Heaven itself and godlike kings, in
  vain
Show'r down the *manna* of a gentle reign;
While pamper'd crowds to mad sedition
  run,

And monarchs by indulgence are undone.
Thus David's clemency was fatal grown,
While wealthy faction aw'd the wanting
   throne.   10
For now their sov'reign's orders to contemn
Was held the charter of Jerusalem,
His rights t' invade, his tributes to refuse,
A privilege peculiar to the Jews;
As if from heav'nly call this license fell,
And Jacob's seed were chosen to rebel!
  Achitophel with triumph sees his crimes
Thus suited to the madness of the times;
And Absalom, to make his hopes succeed,
Of flattering charms no longer stands in
   need;   20
While fond of change, tho' ne'er so dearly
   bought,
Our tribes outstrip the youth's ambitious
   thought;
His swiftest hopes with swifter homage
   meet,
And crowd their servile necks beneath his
   feet.
Thus to his aid while pressing tides repair,
He mounts and spreads his streamers in
   the air.
The charms of empire might his youth
   mislead,
But what can our besotted Israel plead?
Sway'd by a monarch, whose serene com-
   mand
Seems half the blessing of our promis'd
   land;   30
Whose only grievance is excess of ease;
Freedom our pain, and plenty our disease!
Yet, as all folly would lay claim to sense,
And wickedness ne'er wanted a pretense,
With arguments they'd make their treason
   good,
And righteous David's self with slanders
   load:
That arts of foreign sway he did affect,
And guilty Jebusites from law protect,
Whose very chiefs, convict, were never
   freed,
Nay, we have seen their sacrificers bleed! 40
Accusers' infamy is urg'd in vain,
While in the bounds of sense they did con-
   tain;
But soon they launch'd into th' unfathom'd
   tide,
And in the depths they knew disdain'd to
   ride.
For probable discoveries to dispense,
Was thought below a pension'd evidence;

Mere truth was dull, nor suited with the
   port
Of pamper'd Corah, when advanc'd to court.
No less than wonders now they will impose,
And projects void of grace or sense dis-
   close.   50
Such was the charge on pious Michal
   brought,
Michal that ne'er was cruel ev'n in thought,
The best of queens and most obedient wife,
Impeach'd of curst designs on David's life!
His life, the theme of her eternal pray'r,
'T is scarce so much his guardian angel's
   care.
Not summer morns such mildness can dis-
   close,
The Hermon lily, nor the Sharon rose.
Neglecting each vain pomp of majesty,
Transported Michal feeds her thoughts on
   high.   60
She lives with angels, and, as angels do,
Quits heav'n sometimes to bless the world
   below;
Where, cherish'd by her bounties' plenteous
   spring,
Reviving widows smile, and orphans sing.
O, when rebellious Israel's crimes at height
Are threaten'd with her lord's approaching
   fate,
The piety of Michal then remain
In Heaven's remembrance, and prolong his
   reign!
  Less desolation did the pest pursue,
That from Dan's limits to Beersheba slew, 70
Less fatal the repeated wars of Tyre,
And less Jerusalem's avenging fire.
With gentler terror these our state o'erran,
Than since our evidencing days began!
On every cheek a pale confusion sat,
Continued fear beyond the worst of fate!
Trust was no more, art, science, useless
   made,
All occupations lost but Corah's trade.
Meanwhile a guard on modest Corah wait,
If not for safety, needful yet for state. 80
Well might he deem each peer and prince
   his slave,
And lord it o'er the tribes which he could
   save:
Ev'n vice in him was virtue — what sad fate
But for his honesty had seiz'd our state?
And with what tyranny had we been curst,
Had Corah never prov'd a villain first?
T' have told his knowledge of th' intrigue
   in gross,

Had been, alas, to our deponent's loss:
The travel'd Levite had th' experience got,
To husband well, and make the best of 's
    plot;   90
And therefore, like an evidence of skill,
With wise reserves secur'd his pension still;
Nor quite of future pow'r himself bereft,
But limbos large for unbelievers left.
And now his writ such reverence had got,
'T was worse than plotting to suspect his plot.
Some were so well convinc'd, they made no
    doubt
Themselves to help the founder'd swearers
    out.
Some had their sense impos'd on by their
    fear,
But more for int'rest sake believe and
    swear: 100
Ev'n to that height with some the frenzy
    grew,
They rag'd to find their danger not prove
    true.
Yet, than all these a viler crew remain,
Who with Achitophel the cry maintain;
Not urg'd by fear, nor thro' misguided sense,
(Blind zeal and starving need had some
    pretense,)
But for the *Good Old Cause*, that did excite
Th' original rebels' wiles, revenge, and
    spite.
These raise the Plot, to have the scandal
    thrown
Upon the bright successor of the crown, 110
Whose virtue with such wrongs they had
    pursued,
As seem'd all hope of pardon to exclude.
Thus, while on private ends their zeal is
    built,
The cheated crowd applaud and share their
    guilt.
Such practices as these, too gross to lie
Long unobserv'd by each discerning eye,
The more judicious Israelites unspell'd,
Tho' still the charm the giddy rabble held.
Ev'n Absalom, amidst the dazzling beams
Of empire, and ambition's flattering
    dreams,   120
Perceives the Plot, (too foul to be excus'd,)
To aid designs, no less pernicious, us'd.
And, filial sense yet striving in his breast,
Thus to Achitophel his doubts express'd:
"Why are my thoughts upon a crown
    employ'd,
Which once obtain'd, can be but half en-
    joy'd?

Not so, when virtue did my arms require,
And to my father's wars I flew intire.
My regal pow'r how will my foes resent,
When I myself have scarce my own con-
    sent?   130
Give me a son's unblemish'd truth again,
Or quench the sparks of duty that remain.
How slight to force a throne that legions
    guard
The task to me; to prove unjust, how hard!
And if th' imagin'd guilt thus wound my
    thought,
What will it when the tragic scene is
    wrought?
Dire war must first be conjur'd from be-
    low,
The realm we 'd rule we first must over-
    throw;
And, when the civil furies are on wing   ⎤
That blind and undistinguish'd slaughters |
    fling,   140 ⎬
Who knows what impious chance may |
    reach the king?   ⎦
O rather let me perish in the strife,
Than have my crown the price of David's
    life!
Or if the tempest of the war he stand,
In peace, some vile officious villain's hand
His soul's anointed temple may invade,
Or, press'd by clamorous crowds, myself
    be made
His murtherer; rebellious crowds, whose
    guilt
Shall dread his vengeance till his blood be
    spilt.
Which if my filial tenderness oppose,   150
Since to the empire by their arms I rose,
Those very arms on me shall be employ'd,
A new usurper crown'd, and I destroy'd:
The same pretense of public good will ⎤
    hold, |
And new Achitophels be found as bold ⎬
To urge the needful change, perhaps the |
    old."   ⎦
  He said. The statesman with a smile
    replies
(A smile that did his rising spleen disguise):
"My thoughts presum'd our labors at an
    end,
And are we still with conscience to con-
    tend,   160
Whose want in kings as needful is allow'd,
As 't is for them to find it in the crowd?
Far in the doubtful passage you are gone,
And only can be safe by pressing on.

The crown's true heir, a prince severe and
    wise,
Has view'd your motions long with jealous
    eyes :
Your person's charms, your more prevail-
    ing arts,
And mark'd your progress in the people's
    hearts,
Whose patience is th' effect of stinted
    pow'r,
But treasures vengeance for the fatal
    hour;   170
And if remote the peril he can bring,
Your present danger's greater from the
    king.
Let not a parent's name deceive your sense,
Nor trust the father in a jealous prince !
Your trivial faults if he could so resent,
To doom you little less than banishment,
What rage must your presumption since
    inspire :
Against his orders your return from Tyre ?
Nor only so, but with a pomp more high,
And open court of popularity,   180
The factious tribes — " " And this reproof
    from thee ? "
The prince replies : " O statesman's winding
    skill,
They first condemn that first advis'd the
    ill ! "
" Illustrious youth," return'd Achitophel,
" Misconstrue not the words that mean you
    well.
The course you steer I worthy blame con-
    clude,
But 't is because you leave it unpursued.
A monarch's crown with fate surrounded
    lies,
Who reach, lay hold on death that miss the
    prize.
Did you for this expose yourself to show, 190
And to the crowd bow popularly low ?
For this your glorious progress next or-
    dain,
With chariots, horsemen, and a numerous
    train ;
With fame before you like the morning
    star,
And shouts of joy saluting from afar ?
O from the heights you've reach'd but take
    a view,
Scarce leading Lucifer could fall like you !
And must I here my shipwrack'd arts be-
    moan ?
Have I for this so oft made Israel groan ?

Your single interest with the nation
    weigh'd,   200
And turn'd the scale where your desires
    were laid ?
Ev'n when at helm a course so dang'rous
    mov'd
To land your hopes, as my removal
    prov'd ? "
  " I not dispute," the royal youth replies,
" The known perfection of your policies,
Nor in Achitophel yet grudge or blame
The privilege that statesmen ever claim ;
Who private interest never yet pursued,
But still pretended 't was for others' good :
What politician yet e'er scap'd his fate, 210
Who saving his own neck not sav'd the
    State ?
From hence on ev'ry hum'rous wind that
    veer'd,
With shifted sails a sev'ral course you
    steer'd.
What form of sway did David e'er pursue,
That seem'd like absolute, but sprung
    from you ?
Who at your instance quash'd each penal
    law,
That kept dissenting factious Jews in awe ;
And who suspends fix'd laws, may abro-
    gate,
That done, form new, and so enslave the
    State.
Ev'n property, whose champion now you
    stand,   220
And seem for this the idol of the land,
Did ne'er sustain such violence before,
As when your counsel shut the royal store ;
Advice, that ruin to whole tribes procur'd,
But secret kept till your own banks secur'd.
Recount with this the triple cov'nant broke,
And Israel fitted for a foreign yoke ;
Nor here your counsel's fatal progress
    stay'd,
But sent our levied powers to Pharaoh's aid.
Hence Tyre and Israel, low in ruins laid, 230
And Egypt, once their scorn, their common
    terror made.
Ev'n yet of such a season we can dream,
When royal rights you made your darling
    theme ;
For pow'r unlimited could reasons draw,
And place prerogative above the law ;
Which, on your fall from office, grew un-
    just,
The laws made king, the king a slave in
    trust :

Whom with statecraft, (to int'rest only
   true,)
You now accuse of ills contriv'd by you."
  To this Hell's agent: " Royal youth, fix
   here,   240
Let int'rest be the star by which I steer.
Hence to repose your trust in me was wise,
Whose int'rest most in your advancement
   lies,
A tie so firm as always will avail,
When friendship, nature, and religion fail:
On ours the safety of the crowd depends;
Secure the crowd, and we obtain our ends,
Whom I will cause so far our guilt to
   share,
Till they are made our champions by their
   fear.
What opposition can your rival bring,   250
While Sanhedrims are jealous of the king ?
His strength as yet in David's friendship
   lies,
And what can David's self without sup-
   plies ?
Who with exclusive bills must now dis-
   pense,
Debar the heir, or starve in his defense;
Conditions which our elders ne'er will quit,
And David's justice never can admit.
Or, forc'd by wants his brother to betray,
To your ambition next he clears the way;
For if succession once to naught they
   bring,   260
Their next advance removes the present
   king:
Persisting else his senates to dissolve,
In equal hazard shall his reign involve.
Our tribes, whom Pharaoh's pow'r so much
   alarms,
Shall rise without their prince t' oppose his
   arms;
Nor boots it on what cause at first they
   join,
Their troops, once up, are tools for our de-
   sign.
At least such subtile covenants shall be
   made,
Till peace itself is war in masquerade.
Associations of mysterious sense,   270
Against, but seeming for, the king's de-
   fense,
Ev'n on their courts of justice fetters draw,
And from our agents muzzle up their law.
By which a conquest if we fail to make,
'T is a drawn game at worst, and we secure
   our stake."

He said, and for the dire success depends
On various sects, by common guilt made
   friends,
Whose heads, tho' ne'er so diff'ring in their
   creed,
I' th' point of treason yet were well agreed.
'Mongst these, extorting Ishban first ap-
   pears,   280
Pursued b' a meager troop of bankrupt
   heirs.
Blest times, when Ishban, he whose occu-
   pation
So long has been to cheat, reforms the na-
   tion !
Ishban of conscience suited to his trade,
As good a saint as usurer e'er made.
Yet Mammon has not so engross'd him
   quite,
But Belial lays as large a claim of spite;
Who, for those pardons from his prince he
   draws,
Returns reproaches, and cries up the cause.
That year in which the city he did sway,   290
He left rebellion in a hopeful way.
Yet his ambition once was found so bold,
To offer talents of extorted gold;
Could David's wants have so been brib'd to
   shame
And scandalize our peerage with his name;
For which, his dear sedition he 'd forswear,
And e'en turn loyal to be made a peer.
Next him, let railing Rabsheka have place,
So full of zeal he has no need of grace;
A saint that can both flesh and spirit use,   300
Alike haunt conventicles and the stews:
Of whom the question difficult appears,
If most i' th' preachers' or the bawds' ar-
   rears.
What caution could appear too much in
   him
That keeps the treasure of Jerusalem !
Let David's brother but approach the town,
" *Double our guards*," he cries, " *we are un-*
   done."
Protesting that he dares not sleep in 's bed,
Lest he should rise next morn without his head.
Next these, a troop of busy spirits press,
Of little fortunes, and of conscience less; 311
With them the tribe, whose luxury had
   drain'd
Their banks, in former sequestrations gain'd;
Who rich and great by past rebellions grew,
And long to fish the troubled streams anew.
Some future hopes, some present payment
   draws,

To sell their conscience and espouse the
    cause.
Such stipends those vile hirelings best befit,
Priests without grace, and poets without
    wit.   319
Shall that false Hebronite escape our curse,
Judas, that keeps the rebels' pension-purse;
Judas, that pays the treason-writer's fee,
Judas, that well deserves his namesake's
    tree;
Who at Jerusalem's own gates erects
His college for a nursery of sects;
Young prophets with an early care secures,
And with the dung of his own arts manures !
What have the men of Hebron here to do ?
What part in Israel's promis'd land have
    you ?
Here Phaleg, the lay Hebronite, is come, 330
'Cause like the rest he could not live at
    home;
Who from his own possessions could not
    drain
An omer even of Hebronitish grain,
Here struts it like a patriot, and talks high
Of injur'd subjects, alter'd property;
An emblem of that buzzing insect just,
That mounts the wheel, and thinks she
    raises dust.
Can dry bones live ? or skeletons produce
The vital warmth of cuckoldizing juice ?
Slim Phaleg could, and at the table fed, 340
Return'd the grateful product to the bed.
A waiting-man to trav'ling nobles chose,
He his own laws would saucily impose,
Till bastinado'd back again he went,
To learn those manners he to teach was sent.
Chastis'd, he ought to have retreated home,
But he reads politics to Absalom;
For never Hebronite, tho' kick'd and
    scorn'd,
To his own country willingly return'd.
— But leaving famish'd Phaleg to be fed,
And to talk treason for his daily bread, 351
Let Hebron, nay, let hell produce a man
So made for mischief as Ben-Jochanan.
A Jew of humble parentage was he,
By trade a Levite, tho' of low degree:
His pride no higher than the desk aspir'd,
But for the drudgery of priests was hir'd
To read and pray in linen ephod brave,
And pick up single shekels from the grave.
Married at last, and finding charge come
    faster,   360
He could not live by God, but chang'd his
    master;

Inspir'd by want, was made a factious tool,
They got a villain, and we lost a fool:
Still violent, whatever cause he took,
But most against the party he forsook;
For renegadoes, who ne'er turn by halves,
Are bound in conscience to be double
    knaves.
So this prose-prophet took most monstrous
    pains
To let his masters see he earn'd his gains.
But as the Dev'l owes all his imps a
    shame,   370
He chose th' Apostate for his proper
    theme;
With little pains he made the picture true,
And from reflection took the rogue he
    drew:
A wondrous work, to prove the Jewish
    nation
In every age a murmuring generation;
To trace 'em from their infancy of sinning,
And shew 'em factious from their first be-
    ginning;
To prove they could rebel, and rail, and
    mock,
Much to the credit of the chosen flock;
A strong authority, which must convince,
That saints own no allegiance to their
    prince;   381
As 't is a leading card to make a whore,
To prove her mother had turn'd up before.
But, tell me, did the drunken patriarch
    bless
The son that shew'd his father's naked-
    ness ?
Such thanks the present Church thy pen
    will give,
Which proves rebellion was so primitive.
Must ancient failings be examples made ?
Then murtherers from Cain may learn
    their trade.
As thou the heathen and the saint hast
    drawn,   390
Methinks th' Apostate was the better man;
And thy hot father, (waiving my respect,)
Not of a mother church, but of a sect.
And such he needs must be of thy inditing;
This comes of drinking asses' milk and
    writing.
If Balak should be call'd to leave his
    place,
(As profit is the loudest call of grace,)
His temple dispossess'd of one, would be
Replenish'd with seven devils more by
    thee.

Levi, thou art a load, I 'll lay thee
  down,   400
And shew rebellion bare, without a gown;
Poor slaves in meter, dull and addle-pated,
Who rhyme below ev'n David's psalms
  translated;
Some in my speedy pace I must outrun,
As lame Mephibosheth the wizard's son;
To make quick way I 'll leap o'er heavy
  blocks,
Shun rotten Uzza, as I would the pox
And hasten Og and Doeg to rehearse,
Two fools that crutch their feeble sense on
  verse;
Who, by my Muse, to all succeeding
  times   410
Shall live, in spite of their own dogg'rel
  rhymes.
  Doeg, tho' without knowing how or why,
Made still a blund'ring kind of melody;
Spurr'd boldly on, and dash'd thro' thick
  and thin,
Thro' sense and nonsense, never out nor in;
Free from all meaning, whether good or
  bad,
And, in one word, heroically mad:
He was too warm on picking-work to ⎤
  dwell,   ⎟
But fagoted his notions as they fell,   ⎬
And if they rhym'd and rattled, all was   ⎟
  well.   420 ⎦
Spiteful he is not, tho' he wrote a satire,
For still there goes some *thinking* to ill-
  nature:
He needs no more than birds and beasts to
  think;
All his occasions are to eat and drink.
If he call rogue and rascal from a garret,
He means you no more mischief than a par-
  rot;
The words for friend and foe alike were
  made,
To fetter 'em in verse is all his trade.
For almonds he 'll cry whore to his own
  mother;
And call young Absalom King David's
  brother.   430
Let him be gallows-free by my consent,
And nothing suffer, since he nothing meant;
Hanging supposes human soul and reason,
This animal 's below committing treason.
Shall he be hang'd who never could rebel ?
That 's a preferment for Achitophel.
The woman that committed buggary,
Was rightly sentenc'd by the law to die;

But 't was hard fate that to the gallows led
The dog that never heard the statute
  read.   440
Railing in other men may be a crime,
But ought to pass for mere instinct in him:
Instinct he follows, and no farther knows,
For to write verse with him is to *trans-
  prose.*
'T were pity treason at his door to lay,
Who *makes heaven's gate a lock to its own
  key :*
Let him rail on, let his invective Muse
Have four and twenty letters to abuse,
Which if he jumbles to one line of sense,
Indict him of a capital offense.   450
In fireworks give him leave to vent his
  spite,
Those are the only serpents he can write;
The height of his ambition is, we know,
But to be master of a puppet show:
On that one stage his works may yet ap-
  pear,
And a month's harvest keeps him all the
  year.
  Now stop your noses, readers, all and ⎤
  some,   ⎟
For here 's a tun of midnight work to   ⎬
  come,   ⎟
Og, from a treason-tavern rolling home. ⎦
Round as a globe, and liquor'd ev'ry
  chink,   460
Goodly and great he sails behind his link.
With all this bulk there 's nothing lost in Og,
For ev'ry inch that is not fool is rogue:
A monstrous mass of foul corrupted matter,
As all the devils had spew'd to make the
  batter.
When wine has given him courage to blas-
  pheme,
He curses God, but God before curs'd him;
And if man could have reason, none has
  more,
That made his paunch so rich, and him so
  poor.
With wealth he was not trusted, for Heav'n
  knew   470
What 't was of old to pamper up a Jew;
To what would he on quail and pheasant
  swell,
That ev'n on tripe and carrion could rebel ?
But tho' Heav'n made him poor, (with
  rev'rence speaking,)
He never was a poet of God's making.
The midwife laid her hand on his thick
  skull,

With this prophetic blessing: *Be thou dull;*
Drink, swear, and roar, forbear no lewd
 delight
Fit for thy bulk, do anything but write:
Thou art of lasting make, like thoughtless
 men,   480
A strong nativity — but for the pen;
Eat opium, mingle arsenic in thy drink,
Still thou mayst live, avoiding pen and ink.
I see, I see, 't is counsel given in vain,
For treason botch'd in rhyme will be thy
 bane;
Rhyme is the rock on which thou art to
 wreck,
'T is fatal to thy fame and to thy neck:
Why should thy meter good King David
 blast ?
A psalm of his will surely be thy last.
Dar'st thou presume in verse to meet thy
 foes,   490
Thou whom the penny pamphlet foil'd in
 prose ?
Doeg, whom God for mankind's mirth has
 made,
O'ertops thy talent in thy very trade;
Doeg to thee, thy paintings are so coarse,
A poet is, tho' he 's the poets' horse.
A double noose thou on thy neck dost pull,
For writing treason, and for writing dull;
To die for faction is a common evil,
But to be hang'd for nonsense is the devil:
Hadst thou the glories of thy king ex-
 press'd,   500
Thy praises had been satire at the best;
But thou in clumsy verse, unlick'd, un-
 pointed,
Hast shamefully defied the Lord's
 anointed:
I will not rake the dunghill of thy crimes,
For who would read thy life that reads
 thy rhymes ?
But of King David's foes, be this the doom,
May all be like the young man Absalom;
And for my foes may this their blessing be,
To talk like Doeg, and to write like thee.
 Achitophel each rank, degree, and age, 510
For various ends, neglects not to engage;
The wise and rich for purse and counsel
 brought,
The fools and beggars for their number
 sought:
Who yet not only on the town depends,
For ev'n in court the faction had its friends;
These thought the places they possess'd
 too small,

And in their hearts wish'd court and king
 to fall:
Whose names the Muse disdaining, holds i'
 th' dark,
Thrust in the villain herd without a mark;
With parasites and libel-spawning imps, 520
Intriguing fops, dull jesters, and worse
 pimps.
Disdain the rascal rabble to pursue,
Their set cabals are yet a viler crew;
See where involv'd in common smoke they
 sit,
Some for our mirth, some for our satire fit:
These gloomy, thoughtful, and on mischief
 bent,
While those for mere good-fellowship fre-
 quent
Th' appointed club, can let sedition pass,
Sense, nonsense, anything t' employ the
 glass;   529
And who believe, in their dull honest hearts,
The rest talk treason but to shew their parts;
Who ne'er had wit or will for mischief
 yet,
But pleas'd to be reputed of a set.
But in the sacred annals of our Plot,
Industrious Arod never be forgot:
The labors of this midnight-magistrate
May vie with Corah's to preserve the State.
In search of arms he fail'd not to lay hold
On war's most powerful dang'rous weapon,
 GOLD.   539
And last, to take from Jebusites all odds,
Their altars pillag'd, stole their very gods.
Oft would he cry, when treasure he sur-
 pris'd:
" 'T is Baalish gold in David's coin dis-
 guis'd."
Which to his house with richer relicts came,
While lumber idols only fed the flame;
For our wise rabble ne'er took pains t' en-
 quire,
What 't was he burnt, so 't made a rousing
 fire.
With which our elder was enrich'd no more
Than false Gehazi with the Syrian's store;
So poor, that when our choosing-tribes were
 met,   550
Ev'n for his stinking votes he ran in debt;
For meat the wicked, and as authors think,
The saints he chous'd for his electing drink;
Thus ev'ry shift and subtle method pass'd,
And all to be no Zaken at the last.
 Now, rais'd on Tyre's sad ruins, Pha-
 raoh's pride

Soar'd high, his legions threat'ning far and
    wide;
As when a batt'ring storm ingender'd high,
By winds upheld, hangs hov'ring in the sky,
Is gaz'd upon by ev'ry trembling swain,   560
This for his vineyard fears, and that his
    grain;
For blooming plants, and flow'rs new open-
    ing; these
For lambs ean'd lately, and far-lab'ring
    bees:
To guard his stock each to the gods does call,
Uncertain where the fire-charg'd clouds will
    fall:
Ev'n so the doubtful nations watch his arms,
With terror each expecting his alarms.
Where, Judah, where was now thy lion's
    roar ?
Thou only couldst the captive lands restore;
But thou, with inbred broils and faction
    press'd,   570
From Egypt need'st a guardian with the
    rest:
Thy prince from Sanhedrims no trust
    allow'd,
Too much the representers of the crowd,
Who for their own defense give no supply,
But what the crown's prerogatives must
    buy;
As if their monarch's rights to violate
More needful were than to preserve the
    State !
From present dangers they divert their
    care,
And all their fears are of the royal heir;
Whom now the reigning malice of his foes
Unjudg'd would sentence, and ere crown'd
    depose.   581
Religion the pretense, but their decree
To bar his reign, whate'er his faith shall be !
By Sanhedrims and clam'rous crowds thus
    press'd,
What passions rent the righteous David's
    breast !
Who knows not how t' oppose, or to comply;
Unjust to grant, and dangerous to deny !
How near in this dark juncture Israel's fate,
Whose peace one sole expedient could cre-
    ate,   589
Which yet th' extremest virtue did require,
Ev'n in that prince whose downfall they
    conspire !
His absence David does with tears advise,
T' appease their rage; undaunted he com-
    plies.

Thus he, who, prodigal of blood and ease,
A royal life expos'd to winds and seas,
At once contending with the waves and fire,
And heading danger in the wars of Tyre,
Inglorious now forsakes his native sand,
And like an exile quits the promis'd land !
Our monarch scarce from pressing tears re-
    frains,   600
And painfully his royal state maintains,
Who now embracing on th' extremest shore
Almost revokes what he injoin'd before:
Concludes at last more trust to be allow'd
To storms and seas than to the raging
    crowd !
Forbear, rash Muse, the parting scene to
    draw,
With silence charm'd as deep as theirs that
    saw !
Not only our attending nobles weep,
But hardy sailors swell with tears the deep !
The tide restrain'd her course, and, more
    amaz'd,   610
The twin-stars on the royal brothers gaz'd:
While this sole fear ——
Does trouble to our suff'ring hero bring,
Lest next the popular rage oppress the king !
Thus parting, each for th' other's danger
    griev'd,
The shore the king, and seas the prince re-
    ceiv'd.
Go, injur'd hero, while propitious gales,
Soft as thy consort's breath, inspire thy
    sails;
Well may she trust her beauties on a flood
Where thy triumphant fleets so oft have
    rode !   620
Safe on thy breast reclin'd, her rest be deep,
Rock'd like a Nereid by the waves asleep;
While happiest dreams her fancy entertain,
And to Elysian fields convert the main !
Go, injur'd hero, while the shores of Tyre
At thy approach so silent shall admire,
Who on thy thunder still their thoughts
    imploy,
And greet thy landing with a trembling joy.
  On heroes thus the prophet's fate is
    thrown,
Admir'd by ev'ry nation but their own;   630
Yet while our factious Jews his worth deny,
Their aching conscience gives their tongue
    the lie.
Ev'n in the worst of men the noblest parts
Confess him, and he triumphs in their hearts,
Whom to his king the best respects com-
    mend

Of subject, soldier, kinsman, prince, and
    friend;
All sacred names of most divine esteem,
And to perfection all sustain'd by him,
Wise, just, and constant, courtly without
    art,
Swift to discern and to reward desert;   640
No hour of his in fruitless ease destroy'd,
But on the noblest subjects still employ'd;
Whose steady soul ne'er learnt to separate
Between his monarch's int'rest and the State,
But heaps those blessings on the royal
    head,
Which he well knows must be on subjects
    shed.
    On what pretense could then the vulgar
    rage
Against his worth, and native rights en-
    gage?
Religious fears their argument are made,
Religious fears his sacred rights invade! 650
Of future superstition they complain,
And Jebusitic worship in his reign:
With such alarms his foes the crowd de-
    ceive,
With dangers fright, which not themselves
    believe.
    Since nothing can our sacred rites re-
    move,
Whate'er the faith of the successor prove;
Our Jews their ark shall undisturb'd re-
    tain,
At least while their religion is their gain,
Who know by old experience Baal's com-
    mands
Not only claim'd their conscience, but their
    lands: 660
They grutch God's tythes, how therefore
    shall they yield
An idol full possession of the field?
Grant such a prince enthron'd, we must
    confess
The people's suff'rings than that monarch's
    less,
Who must to hard conditions still be bound,
And for his quiet with the crowd com-
    pound;
Or should his thoughts to tyranny incline,
Where are the means to compass the de-
    sign?
Our crown's revenues are too short a store,
And jealous Sanhedrims would give no
    more. 670
    As vain our fears of Egypt's potent aid;
Not so has Pharaoh learnt ambition's trade,

Nor ever with such measures can comply,
As shock the common rules of policy.
None dread like him the growth of Israel's
    king,
And he alone sufficient aids can bring;
Who knows that prince to Egypt can give
    law,
That on our stubborn tribes his yoke could
    draw.
At such profound expense he has not stood,
Nor dyed for this his hands so deep in
    blood; 680
Would ne'er thro' wrong and right his pro-
    gress take,
Grudge his own rest, and keep the world
    awake,
To fix a lawless prince on Judah's throne,
First to invade our rights and then his
    own;
His dear-gain'd conquests cheaply to de-
    spoil,
And reap the harvest of his crimes and toil.
We grant his wealth vast as our ocean's
    sand,
And curse its fatal influence on our land,
Which our brib'd Jews so num'rously per-
    take,
That ev'n an host his pensioners would
    make. 690
From these deceivers our divisions spring,
Our weakness, and the growth of Egypt's
    king;
These with pretended friendship to the
    State,
Our crowd's suspicion of their prince create,
Both pleas'd and frighten'd with the spe-
    cious cry
To guard their sacred rights and property.
To ruin, thus, the chosen flock are sold,
While wolves are ta'en for guardians of
    the fold;
Seduc'd by these, we groundlessly com-
    plain,
And loathe the manna of a gentle reign: 700
Thus our forefathers' crooked paths are
    trod,
We trust our prince no more then they
    their God.
But all in vain our reasoning prophets
    preach
To those whom sad experience ne'er could
    teach,
Who can commence new broils in bleeding
    scars,
And fresh remembrance of intestine wars;

When the same household mortal foes did
    yield,
And brothers stain'd with brothers' blood
    the field;
When sons' curst steel the fathers' gore did
    stain,
And mothers mourn'd for sons by fathers
    slain !   710
When thick as Egypt's locusts on the sand,
Our tribes lay slaughter'd thro' the promis'd
    land,
Whose few survivors with worse fate re-
    main,
To drag the bondage of a tyrant's reign:
Which scene of woes, unknowing, we re-
    new,
And madly ev'n those ills we fear pursue;
While Pharaoh laughs at our domestic
    broils,
And safely crowds his tents with nations'
    spoils.
Yet our fierce Sanhedrim, in restless rage,
Against our absent hero still engage,   720
And chiefly urge (such did their frenzy
    prove)
The only suit their prince forbids to move,
Which till obtain'd, they cease affairs of
    state,
And real dangers waive for groundless
    hate.
Long David's patience waits relief to bring,
With all th' indulgence of a lawful king,
Expecting till the troubled waves would
    cease,
But found the raging billows still increase.
The crowd, whose insolence forbearance
    swells,
While he forgives too far, almost rebels. 730
At last his deep resentments silence broke,
Th' imperial palace shook, while thus he
    spoke:
" Then Justice wake, and Rigor take her
    time,
For lo ! our mercy is become our crime.
While halting Punishment her stroke de-
    lays,
Our sov'reign right, Heav'n's sacred trust,
    decays;
For whose support ev'n subjects' interest
    calls —
Woe to that kingdom where the monarch
    falls !
That prince who yields the least of regal
    sway,
So far his people's freedom does betray. 740

Right lives by law, and law subsists by
    pow'r;
Disarm the shepherd, wolves the flock de-
    vour.
Hard lot of empire o'er a stubborn race,
Which Heav'n itself in vain has tried with
    grace !
When will our reason's long-charm'd eyes
    unclose,
And Israel judge between her friends and
    foes ?
When shall we see expir'd deceivers' sway,
And credit what our God and monarchs say ?
Dissembled patriots, brib'd with Egypt's
    gold,
Ev'n Sanhedrims in blind obedience hold; 750
Those patriots' falsehood in their actions
    see,
And judge by the pernicious fruit the tree:
If aught for which so loudly they declaim,
Religion, laws, and freedom, were their aim;
Our senates in due methods they had led,
T' avoid those mischiefs which they seem'd
    to dread;
But first ere yet they propp'd the sinking
    State,
T' impeach and charge, as urg'd by private
    hate,
Proves that they ne'er believ'd the fears
    they press'd,   760
But barb'rously destroy'd the nation's rest !
O ! whither will ungovern'd senates drive,
And to what bounds licentious votes arrive ?
When their injustice we are press'd to share,
The monarch urg'd t' exclude the lawful
    heir;
Are princes thus distinguish'd from the
    crowd,
And this the privilege of royal blood ?
But grant we should confirm the wrongs
    they press,
His sufferings yet were than the people's
    less;
Condemn'd for life the murd'ring sword to
    wield,
And on their heirs entail a bloody field: 770
Thus madly their own freedom they betray,
And for th' oppression which they fear
    make way;
Succession fix'd by Heav'n, the kingdom's
    bar,
Which once dissolv'd, admits the flood of
    war;
Waste, rapine, spoil, without th' assault
    begin,

And our mad tribes supplant the fence
    within.
Since then their good they will not under-
    stand,
'T is time to take the monarch's pow'r in
    hand;
Authority and force to join with skill,
And save the lunatics against their will. 780
The same rough means that swage the
    crowd, appease
Our senates raging with the crowd's disease.
Henceforth unbias'd measures let 'em draw
From no false gloss, but genuine text of
    law;
Nor urge those crimes upon religion's score,
Themselves so much in Jebusites abhor.
Whom laws convict, (and only they,) shall
    bleed,
Nor Pharisees by Pharisees be freed.
Impartial justice from our throne shall
    show'r,
All shall have right, and we our sov'reign
    pow'r."   790
    He said, th' attendants heard with awful
    joy,
And glad presages their fix'd thoughts im-
    ploy;
From Hebron now the suffering heir re-
    turn'd,
A realm that long with civil discord
    mourn'd,
Till his approach, like some arriving god,
Compos'd and heal'd the place of his abode;
The deluge check'd that to Judea spread,
And stopp'd sedition at the fountain's head.
Thus in forgiving David's paths he drives,
And chas'd from Israel, Israel's peace con-
    trives.   800
The field confess'd his pow'r in arms be-
    fore,
And seas proclaim'd his triumphs to the
    shore;
As nobly has his sway in Hebron shown,
How fit t' inherit godlike David's throne.
Thro' Sion's streets his glad arrival 's spread,
And conscious Faction shrinks her snaky
    head;
His train their sufferings think o'erpaid, to
    see
The crowd's applause with virtue once agree.
Success charms all, but zeal for worth dis-
    tress'd,
A virtue proper to the brave and best; 810
'Mongst whom was Jothran, Jothran always
    bent

To serve the crown, and loyal by descent,
Whose constancy so firm, and conduct just,
Deserv'd at once two royal masters' trust;
Who Tyre's proud arms had manfully with-
    stood
On seas, and gather'd laurels from the flood;
Of learning yet no portion was denied,
Friend to the Muses, and the Muses' pride.
Nor can Benaiah's worth forgotten lie,
Of steady soul when public storms were
    high;   820
Whose conduct, while the Moor fierce on-
    sets made,
Secur'd at once our honor and our trade.
Such were the chiefs who most his suff'rings
    mourn'd,
And view'd with silent joy the prince re-
    turn'd;
While those that sought his absence to be-
    tray,
Press first their nauseous false respects to
    pay;
Him still th' officious hypocrites molest,
And with malicious duty break his rest.
    While real transports thus his friends
    employ,
And foes are loud in their dissembled joy, 830
His triumphs, so resounded far and near,
Miss'd not his young ambitious rival's ear;
And as when joyful hunters' clam'rous train
Some slumb'ring lion wakes in Moab's plain,
Who oft had forc'd the bold assailants
    yield,
And scatter'd his pursuers thro' the field,
Disdaining, furls his mane and tears the
    ground,
His eyes enflaming all the desert round,
With roar of seas directs his chasers' way,
Provokes from far, and dares them to the
    fray;   840
Such rage storm'd now in Absalom's fierce
    breast,
Such indignation his fir'd eyes confess'd.
Where now was the instructor of his pride?
Slept the old pilot in so rough a tide,
Whose wiles had from the happy shore be-
    tray'd,
And thus on shelves the cred'lous youth
    convey'd?
In deep revolving thoughts he weighs his
    state,
Secure of craft, nor doubts to baffle fate;
At least, if his storm'd bark must go adrift,
To balk his charge, and for himself to
    shift,   850

In which his dext'rous wit had oft been shown,
And in the wreck of kingdoms sav'd his own;
But now with more than common danger press'd,
Of various resolutions stands possess'd,
Perceives the crowd's unstable zeal decay,
Lest their recanting chief the cause betray,
Who on a father's grace his hopes may ground,
And for his pardon with their heads compound.
Him therefore, ere his Fortune slip her time,
The statesman plots t' engage in some bold crime   860
Past pardon, whether to attempt his bed,
Or threat with open arms the royal head,
Or other daring method, and unjust,
That may confirm him in the people's trust.
But failing thus t' ensnare him, nor secure
How long his foil'd ambition may endure,
Plots next to lay him by, as past his date,
And try some new pretender's luckier fate;
Whose hopes with equal toil he would pursue,
Nor cares what claimer 's crown'd, except the true.   870
Wake, Absalom, approaching ruin shun,
And see, O see, for whom thou art undone !
How are thy honors and thy fame betray'd,
The property of desp'rate villains made !
Lost pow'r and conscious fears their crimes create,
And guilt in them was little less than fate;
But why shouldst thou, from ev'ry grievance free,
Forsake thy vineyards for their stormy sea ?
For thee did Canaan's milk and honey flow;
Love dress'd thy bow'rs, and laurels sought thy brow;   880
Preferment, wealth, and pow'r thy vassals were,
And of a monarch all things but the care.
O should our crimes, again, that curse draw down,
And rebel arms once more attempt the crown,
Sure ruin waits unhappy Absalon,
Alike by conquest or defeat undone !
Who could relentless see such youth and charms
Expire with wretched fate in impious arms:
A prince so form'd, with earth's and heav'n's applause,

To triumph o'er crown'd heads in David's cause ?   890
Or grant him victor, still his hopes must fail,
Who, conquering, would not for himself prevail;
The faction, whom he trusts for future sway,
Him and the public would alike betray;
Amongst themselves divide the captive State,
And found their hydra-empire in his fate !
Thus having beat the clouds with painful flight,
The pitied youth, with scepters in his sight,
(So have their cruel politics decreed,)
Must by that crew that made him guilty bleed !   900
For, could their pride brook any prince's sway,
Whom but mild David would they choose t' obey ?
Who once at such a gentle reign repine,
The fall of monarchy itself design;
From hate to that their reformations spring,
And David not their grievance, but the king.
Seiz'd now with panic fear the faction lies,
Lest this clear truth strike Absalom's charm'd eyes;
Lest he perceive, from long enchantment free,
What all beside the flatter'd youth must see.   910
But whate'er doubts his troubled bosom swell,
Fair carriage still became Achitophel;
Who now an envious festival enstalls,
And to survey their strength the faction calls,
Which fraud, religious worship too must gild —
But O how weakly does sedition build !
For lo ! the royal mandate issues forth,
Dashing at once their treason, zeal, and mirth !
So have I seen disastrous chance invade,
Where careful emmets had their forage laid,   920
Whether fierce Vulcan's rage the furzy plain
Had seiz'd, engender'd by some careless swain;
Or swelling Neptune lawless inroads made.

And to their cell of store his flood con-
vey'd;
The commonwealth broke up, distracted go,
And in wild haste their loaded mates o'er-
throw:
Ev'n so our scatter'd guests confus'dly
meet
With boil'd, bak'd, roast, all justling in the
street;
Dejected all, and ruefully dismay'd,
For *shekel*, without treat, or treason paid. 930
Sedition's dark eclipse now fainter shows,
More bright each hour the royal planet
grows,
Of force the clouds of envy to disperse,
In kind conjunction of assisting stars.
Here, lab'ring Muse, those glorious chiefs
relate
That turn'd the doubtful scale of David's
fate;
The rest of that illustrious band rehearse,
Immortaliz'd in laurel'd Asaph's verse:
Hard task! yet will not I thy flight recall,
View heav'n, and then enjoy thy glorious
fall.   940
First write Bezaliel, whose illustrious
name
Forestalls our praise, and gives his poet
fame.
The Kenites' rocky province his command,
A barren limb of fertile Canaan's land;
Which for its gen'rous natives yet could be
Held worthy such a president as he!
Bezaliel with each grace and virtue fraught;
Serene his looks, serene his life and thought;
On whom so largely Nature heap'd her
store,
There scarce remain'd for arts to give him
more!   950
To aid the Crown and State his greatest
zeal,
His second care that service to conceal;
Of dues observant, firm in ev'ry trust,
And to the needy always more than just;
Who truth from specious falsehood can di-
vide,
Has all the gownmen's skill without their
pride;
Thus crown'd with worth from heights of
honor won,
Sees all his glories copied in his son,
Whose forward fame should every Muse
engage;
Whose youth boasts skill denied to others'
age.   960

Men, manners, language, books of noblest
kind,
Already are the conquest of his mind.
Whose loyalty before its date was prime;
Nor waited the dull course of rolling time:
The monster *faction* early he dismay'd,
And David's cause long since confess'd his
aid.
Brave Abdael o'er the prophets' school
was plac'd;
Abdael with all his father's virtue grac'd;
A hero, who, while stars look'd wond'ring
down,
Without one Hebrew's blood restor'd the
crown.   970
That praise was his; what therefore did re-
main
For following chiefs, but boldly to main-
tain
That crown restor'd; and in this rank of
fame,
Brave Abdael with the first a place must
claim.
Proceed, illustrious, happy chief, proceed,
Foreseize the garlands for thy brow decreed,
While th' inspir'd tribe attend with noblest
strain
To register the glories thou shalt gain:
For sure the dew shall Gilboah's hills for-
sake,
And Jordan mix his stream with Sodom's
lake;   980
Or seas retir'd their secret stores disclose,
And to the sun their scaly brood expose,
Or swell'd above the clifts their billows
raise,
Before the Muses leave their patron's
praise.
Eliab our next labor does invite,
And hard the task to do Eliab right:
Long with the royal wanderer he rov'd,
And firm in all the turns of fortune prov'd!
Such ancient service and desert so large,
Well claim'd the royal household for his
charge.   990
His age with only one mild heiress blest,
In all the bloom of smiling nature dress'd,
And blest again to see his flow'r allied
To David's stock, and made young Othniel's
bride!
The bright restorer of his father's youth,
Devoted to a son's and subject's truth:
Resolv'd to bear that prize of duty home,
So bravely sought (while sought) by Absa-
lom.

Ah prince! th' illustrious planet of thy
 birth,
And thy more powerful virtue guard thy
 worth;   1000
That no Achitophel thy ruin boast:
Israel too much in one such wreck has
 lost.
Ev'n envy must consent to Helon's worth,
Whose soul (tho' Egypt glories in his birth)
Could for our captive ark its zeal retain,
And Pharaoh's altars in their pomp disdain:
To slight his gods was small; with nobler
 pride,
He all th' allurements of his court defied:
Whom profit nor example could betray,
But Israel's friend, and true to David's
 sway.   1010
What acts of favor in his province fall,
On merit he confers, and freely all.
Our list of nobles next let Amri grace,
Whose merits claim'd the Abbethdin's high
 place:
Who, with a loyalty that did excel,
Brought all th' endowments of Achitophel.
Sincere was Amri, and not only knew,
But Israel's sanctions into practice drew;
Our laws, that did a boundless ocean
 seem,
Were coasted all, and fathom'd all by him.
No rabbin speaks like him their mystic
 sense,   1021
So just, and with such charms of eloquence:
To whom the double blessing does belong,
With Moses' inspiration, Aaron's tongue.
 Than Sheva none more loyal zeal have
 shown,
Wakeful as Judah's lion for the crown,
Who for that cause still combats in his age,
For which his youth with danger did en-
 gage.
In vain our factious priests the cant re-
 vive;
In vain seditious scribes with libel strive
T' enflame the crowd, while he with watch-
 ful eye   1031
Observes, and shoots their treasons as they
 fly;
Their weekly frauds his keen replies de-
 tect;
He undeceives more fast than they infect.
So Moses, when the pest on *legions* prey'd,
Advanc'd his signal, and the plague was
 stay'd.
 Once more, my fainting Muse, thy pinions
 try,

And strength's exhausted store let *love* sup-
 ply.
What tribute, Asaph, shall we render thee?
We'll crown thee with a wreath from thy
 own tree!   1040
Thy laurel grove no envy's flash can blast;
The song of Asaph shall for ever last!
With wonder late posterity shall dwell
On Absalom and false Achitophel:
Thy strains shall be our slumb'ring pro-
 phets' dream;
And, when our Sion virgins sing, their
 theme.
Our *jubilees* shall with thy verse be grac'd;
The song of Asaph shall for ever last!
How fierce his satire loos'd; restrain'd, how
 tame;
How tender of th' offending *young man's*
 fame!   1050
How well his worth, and brave adventures
 styl'd;
Just to his virtues, to his error mild.
No page of thine that fears the strictest
 view,
But teems with just reproof, or praise as
 due;
Not Eden could a fairer prospect yield,
All paradise without one barren field:
Whose wit the censure of his foes has
 pass'd;
The song of Asaph shall for ever last!
What praise for such rich strains shall we
 allow?
What just rewards the grateful crown be-
 stow?   1060
While bees in flow'rs rejoice, and flow'rs in
 dew,
While stars and fountains to their course
 are true;
While Judah's throne and Sion's rock stand
 fast,
The song of Asaph and the fame shall
 last.
 Still Hebron's honor'd happy soil re-
 tains
Our royal hero's beauteous dear remains;
Who now sails off, with winds nor wishes
 slack,
To bring his suff'rings' bright companion
 back.
But ere such transport can our sense em-
 ploy,
A bitter grief must poison half our joy; 1070
Nor can our coasts restor'd those blessings
 see

Without a bribe to envious destiny !
Curs'd Sodom's doom for ever fix the tide
Where by inglorious chance the valiant
  died !
Give not insulting Askalon to know,
Nor let Gath's daughters triumph in our
  woe !
No sailor with the news swell Egypt's pride,
By what inglorious fate our valiant died !
Weep, Arnon ! Jordan, weep thy fountains
  dry,
While Sion's rock dissolves for a supply !
Calm were the elements, night's silence
  deep,   1081
The waves scarce murm'ring, and the
  winds asleep;
Yet fate for ruin takes so still an hour,
And treacherous sands the princely bark de-
  vour;
Then death unworthy seiz'd a gen'rous
  race,
To virtue's scandal, and the stars' dis-
  grace !
O ! had th' indulgent pow'rs vouchsaf'd to
  yield,
Instead of faithless shelves, a listed field;
A listed field of Heav'n's and David's
  foes,
Fierce as the troops that did his youth op-
  pose,   1090
Each life had on his slaughter'd heap re-
  tir'd,
Not tamely, and unconqu'ring thus expir'd:
But destiny is now their only foe,
And dying ev'n o'er that they triumph
  too;
With loud last breaths their master's scape
  applaud,
Of whom kind force could scarce the fates
  defraud,
Who for such followers lost (O matchless
  mind !)
At his own safety now almost repin'd !
Say, royal sir, by all your fame in arms,
Your praise in peace, and by Urania's
  charms;   1100
If all your suff'rings past so nearly press'd,
Or pierc'd with half so painful grief your
  breast.
  Thus some diviner Muse her hero forms,
Not sooth'd with soft delights, but toss'd in
  storms,
Not stretch'd on roses in the myrtle grove,
Nor crowns his days with mirth, his nights
  with love;

But far remov'd, in thund'ring camps is
  found,
His slumbers short, his bed the herbless
  ground;
In tasks of danger always seen the first,
Feeds from the hedge, and slakes with ice
  his thirst.   1110
Long must his patience strive with Fortune's
  rage,
And long opposing gods themselves en-
  gage,
Must see his country flame, his friends de-
  stroy'd,
Before the promis'd empire be enjoy'd:
Such toil of fate must build a man of
  fame,
And such, to Israel's crown, the godlike
  David came.
  What sudden beams dispel the clouds so
  fast,
Whose drenching rains laid all our vine-
  yards waste ?
The spring, so far behind her course de-
  lay'd,   1119
On th' instant is in all her bloom array'd;
The winds breathe low, the element se-
  rene;
Yet mark what motion in the waves is
  seen;
Thronging and busy as Hyblæan swarms,
Or straggled soldiers summon'd to their
  arms !
See where the princely bark, in loosest
  pride,
With all her guardian fleet, adorns the
  tide !
High on her deck the royal lovers stand,
Our crimes to pardon ere they touch'd our
  land.
Welcome to Israel and to David's breast !
Here all your toils, here all your suff'rings
  rest.   1130
  This year did Ziloah rule Jerusalem,
And boldly all sedition's surges stem,
Howe'er incumber'd with a viler pair
Than Ziph or Shimei to assist the chair;
Yet Ziloah's loyal labors so prevail'd
That faction at the next election fail'd,
When ev'n the common cry did justice
  sound,
And merit by the multitude was crown'd:
With David then was Israel's peace re-
  stor'd,
Crowds mourn'd their error, and obey'd
  their lord.   1140

PROLOGUE AND EPILOGUE TO THE KING AND QUEEN AT THE OPENING OF THEIR THEATER

[These two pieces, with heading on which the above is modeled, were published as a broadside in 1683. They were reprinted in the third edition, 1702, of *Miscellany Poems, the First Part*, the first of them having the title, *A Prologue to the King and Queen, upon the Union of the two Companies in the year 1689* [sic].

In 1682 the King's Company and the Duke's Company, which had been rivals for over twenty years, joined their forces. The articles of union (reprinted in FitzGerald : *A New History of the English Stage*, 1882 ; vol. i, pp. 154–158) are dated May 14, 1682 ; but the united companies did not give their first representation until November 16 (Malone, I, 1, 120, on the authority of a note by Luttrell).]

PROLOGUE

SPOKEN BY MR. BETTERTON

SINCE faction ebbs, and rogues grow out of
    fashion,
Their penny scribes take care t' inform the
    nation,
How well men thrive in this or that planta-
    tion:

How Pennsylvania's air agrees with Quak-
    ers,
And Carolina's with Associators:
Both e'en too good for madmen and for
    traitors.

Truth is, our land with saints is so run
    o'er,
And every age produces such a store,
That now there's need of two New Eng-
    lands more.

"What's this," you'll say, "to us and our
    vocation ? "   10
Only thus much, that we have left our sta-
    tion,
And made this theater our new plantation.

The factious natives never could agree;
But aiming, as they call'd it, to be free,
Those playhouse Whigs set up for property.

Some say they no obedience paid of late,
But would new fears and jealousies create,
Till topsy-turvy they had turn'd the State.

Plain sense, without the talent of foretell-
    ing,
Might guess 't would end in downright
    knocks and quelling;   20
For seldom comes there better of rebelling.

When men will, needlessly, their freedom
    barter
For lawless pow'r, sometimes they catch a
    Tartar;
(There's a damn'd word that rhymes to
    this, call'd Charter.)

But, since the victory with us remains,
You shall be call'd to twelve in all our gains;
(If you'll not think us saucy for our pains.)

Old men shall have good old plays to de-
    light 'em;
And you, fair ladies and gallants, that slight
    'em,
We'll treat with good new plays; if our
    new wits can write 'em.   30

We'll take no blund'ring verse, no fustian
    tumor,
No dribbling love, from this or that pre-
    sumer;
No dull fat fool shamm'd on the stage for
    humor.

For, faith, some of 'em such vile stuff have
    made,
As none but fools or fairies ever play'd;
But 't was, as shopmen say, to force a trade.

We've giv'n you tragedies, all sense defy-
    ing,
And singing men, in woful meter dying:
This 't is when heavy lubbers will be flying.

All these disasters we well hope to
    weather;   40
We bring you none of our old lumber
    hether:
Whig poets and Whig sheriffs may hang
    together.

EPILOGUE

SPOKEN BY MR. SMITH

NEW ministers, when first they get in place,
Must have a care to please; and that's our
    case:

Some laws for public welfare we de-
sign,
If you, the power supreme, will please to
join.
There are a sort of prattlers in the pit,
Who either have, or who pretend to wit:
These noisy sirs so loud their parts re-
hearse,
That oft the play is silenc'd by the farce.
Let such be dumb, this penalty to shun,
Each to be thought my lady's eldest son. 10
But stay; methinks some vizard-mask I
see
Cast out her lure from the mid gallery:
About her all the flutt'ring sparks are
rang'd;
The noise continues, tho' the scene is
chang'd:
Now growling, sputt'ring, wauling, such a
clutter;
'T is just like puss defendant in a gutter.
Fine love no doubt, but e'er two days are
o'er ye,
The surgeon will be told a woful story.
Let vizard-mask her naked face expose,
On pain of being thought to want a nose.
Then for your lackeys, and your train be-
side, 21
(By whate'er name or title dignified,)
They roar so loud, you'd think behind the
stairs
Tom Dove, and all the brotherhood of
bears:
They're grown a nuisance, beyond all dis-
asters;
We've none so great but their unpaying
masters.
We beg you, sirs, to beg your men, that
they
Would please to give you leave to hear the
play.
Next, in the playhouse spare your pre-
cious lives;
Think, like good Christians, on your bearns
and wives; 30
Think on your souls; but by your lugging
forth,
It seems you know how little they are
worth.
If none of these will move the warlike
mind,
Think on the helpless whore you leave behind !
We beg you last, our scene-room to forbear,

And leave our goods and chattels to our
care.
Alas, our women are but washy toys,
And wholly taken up in stage employs:
Poor willing tits they are ; but yet I
doubt
This double duty soon will wear 'em out.
Then you are watch'd besides, with jealous
care: 41
What if my lady's page should find you
there ?
My lady knows t' a tittle what there's in
ye;
No passing your gilt shilling for a guinea.
Thus, gentlemen, we have summ'd up in
short
Our grievances, from country, town, and
court:
Which humbly we submit to your good
pleasure;
But first vote money, then redress at lei-
sure.

PROLOGUE, EPILOGUES, AND SONG FROM THE DUKE OF GUISE

["In the year of his Majesty's happy Restoration," Dryden writes in his *Vindication of
The Duke of Guise,* "the first play I undertook
was *The Duke of Guise,* as the fairest way
which the Act of Indemnity had then left us
of setting forth the rise of the late rebellion.
. . . As this was my first essay, so it met
with the fortune of an unfinish'd piece ; that
is to say, it was damn'd in private, by the advice of some friends to whom I shew'd it ; who
freely told me that it was an excellent subject,
but not so artificially wrought as they could
have wish'd."
In 1682, at the request of Lee, Dryden accepted his aid in completing this play, which was
ready for acting before midsummer, though,
owing to objections from the government, the
first performance did not take place until November 30 (Malone, I, 1, 120, probably on
manuscript authority). As is obvious from the
following pieces, *The Duke of Guise* was a political play, directed against the Whig party.
The prologue and the first of the two epilogues are assigned to Dryden in the first edition of the play, 1683. They were also printed
in a broadside of the same date, which contains, in addition, the second epilogue. The
song occurs early in the second scene of the
fifth act, a portion of the play which Dryden
claims as his own.]

PROLOGUE

SPOKEN BY MR. SMITH

OUR play's a parallel: the Holy League
Begot our Cov'nant; Guisards got the
    Whig:
Whate'er our hot-brain'd sheriffs did ad-
    vance,
Was, like our fashions, first produc'd in
    France;
And when worn out, well-scourg'd, and
    banish'd there,
Sent over, like their godly beggars here.
Could the same trick, twice play'd, our na-
    tion gull?
It looks as if the Devil were grown dull;
Or serv'd us up, in scorn, his broken meat,
And thought we were not worth a better
    cheat.   10
The fulsome Cov'nant, one would think in
    reason,
Had giv'n us all our bellies-full of trea-
    son;
And yet, the name but chang'd, our nasty
    nation
Chaws its own excrement, th' Association.
'T is true we have not learn'd their pois'n-
    ing way,
For that's a mode but newly come in
    play;
Besides, your drug's uncertain to prevail, ⎫
But your true Protestant can never fail, ⎬
With that compendious instrument, a flail. ⎭
Go on, and bite, ev'n tho' the hook lies
    bare: 20
Twice in one age expel the lawful heir;
Once more decide religion by the sword,
And purchase for us a new tyrant lord.
Pray for your king, but yet your purses
    spare;
Make him not twopence richer by your
    prayer.
To show you love him much, chastise him
    more,
And make him very great, and very poor.
Push him to wars, but still no pence ad-
    vance;
Let him lose England, to recover France.
Cry freedom up with popular noisy votes,
And get enough to cut each other's throats.
Lop all the rights that fence your mon-
    arch's throne: 32
For fear of too much pow'r, pray leave him
    none.

A noise was made of arbitrary sway; ⎫
But, in revenge, you Whigs have found a ⎬
    way ⎭
An arbitrary duty now to pay.
Let his own servants turn, to save their stake;
Glean from his plenty, and his wants for-
    sake;
But let some Judas near his person stay,
To swallow the last sop, and then betray.
Make London independent of the Crown,
A realm apart, the kingdom of the town.
Let *ignoramus* juries find no traitors,   43
And *ignoramus* poets scribble satires.
And, that your meaning none may fail to ⎫
    scan, ⎪
Do what in coffee-houses you began: ⎬
Pull down the master, and set up the ⎪
    man. ⎭

EPILOGUE

SPOKEN BY MRS. COOKE

MUCH time and trouble this poor play has
    cost;
And, faith, I doubted once the cause was
    lost.
Yet no one man was meant, nor great nor
    small;
Our poets, like frank gamesters, threw at all.
They took no single aim ——
But, like bold boys, true to their prince and
    hearty,
Huzza'd, and fir'd broadsides at the whole
    party.
Duels are crimes; but, when the cause is
    right,
In battle every man is bound to fight.
For what should hinder me to sell my ⎫
    skin   10 ⎪
Dear as I could, if once my hand were in? ⎬
Se defendendo never was a sin. ⎭
'T is a fine world, my masters; right or
    wrong,
The Whigs must talk, and Tories hold their
    tongue.
They must do all they can ——
But we, forsooth, must bear a Christian
    mind,
And fight, like boys, with one hand tied
    behind;
Nay, and when one boy's down, 't were
    wondrous wise
To cry: "Box fair, and give him time to
    rise."

When fortune favors, none but fools will
    dally: 20
Would any of you sparks, if Nan or Mally
Tipp'd you th' inviting wink, stand, shall
    I, shall I?
A Trimmer cried, that heard me tell this
    story:
" Fie, Mistress Cooke! faith you 're too
    rank a Tory!
Wish not Whigs hang'd, but pity their
    hard cases;
You women love to see men make wry
    faces."
" Pray, sir," said I, " don't think me such a
    Jew;
I say no more, but give the Dev'l his due."
" Lenitives," says he, " suit best with our
    condition."
" Jack Ketch," says I, " 's an excellent
    physician."   30
" I love no blood. " — " Nor I, sir, as I
    breathe;
But hanging is a fine dry kind of death."
" We Trimmers are for holding all things
    even."
" Yes — just like him that hung 'twixt hell
    and heaven."
" Have we not had men's lives enow al-
    ready ? "
" Yes, sure, — but you 're for holding all
    things steady.
Now since the weight hangs all on one side,
    brother,
You Trimmers should, to poise it, hang on
    t'other."
Damn'd neuters, in their middle way of
    steering,
Are neither fish, nor flesh, nor good red
    herring;   40
Not Whigs, nor Tories they; nor this, nor
    that;
Not birds, nor beasts; but just a kind of bat:
A twilight animal, true to neither cause,
With Tory wings, but Whiggish teeth and
    claws.

ANOTHER EPILOGUE

INTENDED TO HAVE BEEN SPOKEN TO THE
PLAY BEFORE IT WAS FORBIDDEN LAST
SUMMER

Two houses join'd, two poets to a play ?
You noisy Whigs will sure be pleas'd to-
    day;

It looks so like two shrieves the city way.
But since our discords and divisions cease,
You, bilbo-gallants, learn to keep the peace;
Make here no tilts; let our poor stage
    alone;
Or if a decent murther must be done,
Pray take a civil turn to Marybone.
If not, I swear we 'll pull up all our benches;
Not for your sakes, but for our orange-
    wenches: 10
For you thrust wide sometimes; and many
    a spark,
That misses one, can hit the other mark.
This makes our boxes full; for men of
    sense
Pay their four shillings in their own de-
    fense,
That safe behind the ladies they may stay,
Peep o'er the fan, and judge the bloody
    fray.
But other foes give beauty worse alarms;
The *posse poetarum* 's up in arms:
No woman's fame their libels has escap'd;
Their ink runs venom, and their pens are
    clapp'd.   20
When sighs and pray'rs their ladies cannot
    move,
They rail, write treason, and turn Whigs
    to love.
Nay, and I fear they worse designs ad-
    vance;
There 's a damn'd love-trick new brought
    o'er from France.
We charm in vain, and dress, and keep a
    pother,
While those false rogues are ogling one
    another.
All sins beside admit some expiation,
But this against our sex is plain damna-
    tion.
They join for libels too, these women-
    haters;
And as they club for love, they club for
    satires.   30
The best on 't is they hurt not: for they
    wear
Stings in their tails; their only venom 's
    there.
'T is true, some shot at first the ladies hit,
Which able marksmen made and men of
    wit:
But now the fools give fire, whose bounce
    is louder;
And yet, like mere trainbands, they shoot
    but powder.

Libels, like plots, sweep all in their first fury;
Then dwindle like an *ignoramus* jury:
Thus age begins with towsing and with
    tumbling;
But grunts, and groans, and ends at last in
    fumbling.   40

SONG

SHEPHERDESS

TELL me, Thyrsis, tell your anguish;
Why you sigh, and why you languish:
    When the nymph whom you adore
    Grants the blessing of possessing,
What can love and I do more ?
What can love, what can love and I do
    more ?

SHEPHERD

Think it 's love beyond all measure
Makes me faint away with pleasure:
    Strength of cordial may destroy,
    And the blessing of possessing   10
Kills me with excess of joy.

SHEPHERDESS

Thyrsis, how can I believe you ?
But confess, and I 'll forgive you.
    Men are false and so are you:
    Never nature fram'd a creature
    To enjoy, and yet be true:
Never nature fram'd a creature
    To enjoy and yet be true;
    To enjoy and yet be true;
    And yet be true.   20

SHEPHERD

Mine 's a flame beyond expiring,
Still possessing, still desiring,
    Fit for love's imperial crown;
    Ever shining, and refining,
Still the more 't is melted down.

CHORUS TOGETHER

Mine 's a flame beyond expiring,
Still possessing, still desiring,
    Fit for love's imperial crown;
    Ever shining, and refining,
Still the more 't is melted down.   30

RELIGIO LAICI

OR, A LAYMAN'S FAITH

A POEM

Ornari res ipsa negat, contenta doceri.

[An advertisement in the *Observator* (see Scott-Saintsbury edition, xviii, 295) shows that this poem was first published about November 30, 1682. Two different issues of it appeared in that year, and a third in 1683; the variations in text are very minute and are probably not due to Dryden. The present edition follows what is apparently the earlier of the two copies of 1682. The early editions contain frequent italics, which are here generally disregarded; and several words printed in capital letters, which are here represented by small capitals.]

THE PREFACE

A POEM with so bold a title, and a name prefix'd from which the handling of so serious a subject would not be expected, may reasonably oblige the author to say somewhat in defense both of himself and of his undertaking. In the first place, if it be objected to me that, being a layman, I ought not to have concern'd myself with speculations which belong to the profession of divinity, I could answer that perhaps laymen, with equal advantages of parts and knowledge, are not the most incompetent judges of sacred things ; but, in the due sense of my own weakness and want of learning, I plead not this ; I pretend not to make myself a judge of faith in others, but only to make a confession of my own ; I lay no unhallowed hand upon the ark, but wait on it, with the reverence that becomes me, at a distance. In the next place I will ingenuously confess that the helps I have us'd in this small treatise were many of them taken from the works of our own reverend divines of the Church of England ; so that the weapons with which I combat irreligion are already consecrated ; tho' I suppose they may be taken down as lawfully as the sword of Goliah was by David, when they are to be employ'd for the common cause, against the enemies of piety. I intend not by this to

intitle them to any of my errors, which yet, I
hope, are only those of charity to mankind;
and such as my *own* charity has caus'd me to
commit, that of *others* may more easily excuse.
Being naturally inclin'd to scepticism in philosophy, I have no reason to impose my opinions in a subject which is above it; but whatever they are, I submit them with all reverence
to my Mother Church, accounting them no
further mine, than as they are authoriz'd, or at
least uncondemn'd by her. And, indeed, to secure myself on this side, I have us'd the necessary precaution of showing this paper before
it was publish'd to a judicious and learned
friend, a man indefatigably zealous in the service of the Church and State; and whose writings have highly deserv'd of both. He was
pleas'd to approve the body of the discourse,
and I hope he is more my friend than to do it
out of complaisance. 'T is true, he had too good
a taste to like it all; and amongst some other
faults recommended to my second view what I
have written, perhaps too boldly, on St. Athanasius, which he advis'd me wholly to omit. I
am sensible enough that I had done more *prudently* to have follow'd his opinion; but then
I could not have satisfied myself that I had
done honestly not to have written what was
my own. It has always been my *thought* that
heathens who never did, nor without miracle
could, hear of the name of Christ, were yet in
a possibility of salvation. Neither will it enter
easily into my belief that, before the coming
of our Savior, the whole world, excepting only
the Jewish nation, should lie under the inevitable necessity of everlasting punishment, for
want of that revelation which was confin'd to
so small a spot of ground as that of Pales-
tine. Among the sons of Noah we read of one
only who was accurst; and if a blessing in the
ripeness of time was reserv'd for Japhet, (of
whose progeny we are,) it seems unaccountable
to me why so many generations of the same
offspring, as preceded our Savior in the flesh,
should be all involv'd in one common condemnation, and yet that their posterity should be intitled to the hopes of salvation: as if a bill of
exclusion had pass'd only on the fathers, which
debarr'd not the sons from their succession.
Or that so many ages had been *deliver'd over*
to hell, and so many *reserv'd* for heaven, and
that the Devil had the first choice, and God the
next. Truly I am apt to think that the reveal'd religion which was taught by Noah to
all his sons might continue for some ages in
the whole posterity. That afterwards it was
included wholly in the family of Sem is manifest; but when the progenies of Cham and
Japhet swarm'd into colonies, and those colonies were subdivided into many others, in
process of time their descendants lost by little

and little the primitive and purer rites of divine worship, retaining only the notion of one
deity; to which succeeding generations added
others; for men took their degrees in those
ages from conquerors to gods. Revelation
being thus eclips'd to almost all mankind, the
light of nature, as the next in dignity, was
substituted; and that is it which St. Paul
concludes to be the rule of the heathens, and
by which they are hereafter to be judg'd. If
my supposition be true, then the consequence
which I have assum'd in my poem may be also
true; namely, that Deism, or the principles of
natural worship, are only the faint remnants
or dying flames of reveal'd religion in the posterity of Noah: and that our modern philosophers, nay, and some of our philosophizing divines, have too much exalted the faculties of our
souls, when they have maintain'd that by their
force mankind has been able to find out that
there is one supreme agent or intellectual being which we call God; that praise and prayer
are his due worship; and the rest of those de-
ducements, which I am confident are the remote effects of revelation, and unattainable by
our discourse; I mean as simply consider'd,
and without the benefit of divine illumination.
So that we have not lifted up ourselves to God
by the weak pinions of our reason, but he has
been pleas'd to descend to us; and what Socrates said of him, what Plato writ, and the rest
of the heathen philosophers of several nations,
is all no more than the twilight of revelation,
after the sun of it was set in the race of Noah.
That there is something above us, some principle of *motion*, our reason can apprehend, tho'
it cannot discover what it is, by its own virtue.
And indeed 't is very improbable that we, who
by the strength of our faculties cannot enter
into the knowledge of any *being*, not so much
as of our *own*, should be able to find out by
them that supreme nature, which we cannot
otherwise define than by saying it is infinite;
as if infinite were definable, or infinity a subject for our narrow understanding. They who
would prove religion by reason do but weaken
the cause which they endeavor to support: 't is
to take away the pillars from our faith, and to
prop it only with a twig; 't is to design a tower
like that of Babel, which, if it were possible
(as it is not) to reach heaven, would come to
nothing by the confusion of the workmen. For
every man is building a several way; impo-
tently conceited of his own model and his own
materials: reason is always striving, and always at a loss; and of necessity it must so come
to pass, while 't is exercis'd about that which is
not its proper object. Let us be content at
last to know God by his own methods; at least,
so much of him as he is pleas'd to reveal to us
in the sacred Scriptures; to apprehend them

to be the word of God is all our reason has to do; for all beyond it is the work of faith, which is the seal of heaven impress'd upon our human understanding.

And now for what concerns the holy bishop Athanasius, the preface of whose creed seems inconsistent with my opinion; which is, that heathens may possibly be sav'd: in the first place I desire it may be consider'd that it is the preface only, not the creed itself, which (till I am better inform'd) is of too hard a digestion for my charity. 'T is not that I am ignorant how many several texts of Scripture seemingly support that cause; but neither am I ignorant how all those texts may receive a kinder and more mollified interpretation. Every man who is read in Church history knows *that* belief was drawn up after a long contestation with Arius concerning the divinity of our blessed Savior, and his being one substance with the Father; and that, thus compil'd, it was sent abroad among the Christian churches, as a kind of test, which whosoever took was look'd on as an orthodox believer. 'T is manifest from hence that the heathen part of the empire was not concern'd in it; for its business was not to distinguish betwixt pagans and Christians, but betwixt heretics and true believers. This, well consider'd, takes off the heavy weight of censure, which I would willingly avoid from so venerable a man; for if this proportion, ' whosoever will be sav'd,' be restrain'd only to those to whom it was intended, and for whom it was compos'd, I mean the Christians; then the anathema reaches not the heathens, who had never heard of Christ, and were nothing interess'd in that dispute. After all, I am far from blaming even that prefatory addition to the creed, and as far from caviling at the continuation of it in the liturgy of the Church, where, on the days appointed, 't is publicly read: for I suppose there is the same reason for it now, in opposition to the Socinians, as there was then against the Arians; the one being a heresy which seems to have been refin'd out of the other; and with how much more plausibility of reason it combats our religion, with so much more caution to be avoided; and therefore the prudence of our Church is to be commended, which has interpos'd her authority for the recommendation of this creed. Yet, to such as are grounded in the true belief, those explanatory creeds, the Nicene and this of Athanasius, might perhaps be spar'd; for what is supernatural will always be a mystery in spite of exposition, and, for my own part, the plain Apostles' Creed is most suitable to my weak understanding, as the simplest diet is the most easy of digestion.

I have dwelt longer on this subject than I intended, and longer than, perhaps, I ought;

for having laid down, as my foundation, that the Scripture is a rule; that in all things needful to salvation it is clear, sufficient, and ordain'd by God Almighty for that purpose, I have left myself no right to interpret obscure places, such as concern the possibility of eternal happiness to heathens; because whatsoever is obscure is concluded not necessary to be known.

But, by asserting the Scripture to be the canon of our faith, I have unavoidably created to myself two sorts of enemies: the Papists indeed, more directly, because they have kept the Scripture from us, what they could; and have reserv'd to themselves a right of interpreting what they have deliver'd under the pretense of infallibility: and the Fanatics more collaterally, because they have assum'd what amounts to an infallibility in the private spirit; and have detorted those texts of Scripture which are not necessary to salvation, to the damnable uses of sedition, disturbance, and destruction of the civil government. To begin with the Papists, and to speak freely, I think them the less dangerous, at least in appearance, to our present State, for not only the penal laws are in force against them, and their number is contemptible; but also their peerage and commons are excluded from parliaments, and consequently those laws in no probability of being repeal'd. A general and uninterrupted plot of their clergy, ever since the Reformation, I suppose all Protestants believe. For 't is not reasonable to think but that so many of their orders, as were outed from their fat possessions, would endeavor a reëntrance against those whom they account heretics. As for the late design, Mr. Coleman's letters, for aught I know, are the best evidence; and what they discover, without wiredrawing their sense, or malicious glosses, all men of reason conclude credible. If there be anything more than this requir'd of me, I must believe it as well as I am able, in spite of the witnesses, and out of a decent conformity to the votes of parliament; for I suppose the Fanatics will not allow the private spirit in this case. Here the infallibility is at least in one part of the government; and our understandings as well as our wills are represented. But to return to the Roman Catholics, how can we be secure from the practice of Jesuited Papists in that religion? For not two or three of that order, as some of them would impose upon us, but almost the whole body of them, are of opinion that their infallible master has a right over kings, not only in spirituals but temporals. Not to name Mariana, Bellarmine, Emanuel Sa, Molina, Santarel, Simancha, and at least twenty others of foreign countries; we can produce, of our own nation, Campian, and Doleman or Parsons, besides many are nam'd whom I have not read, who all of them attest this doctrine, that the Pope can depose and give away the right of any sovereign prince, *si vel paulum deflexerit*, if he shall never so little warp ; but if he once comes to be excommunicated, then the bond of obedience is taken off from subjects; and they may and ought to drive him, like another Nebuchadnezzar, *ex hominum Christianorum dominatu*, from exercising dominion over Christians ; and to this they are bound by virtue of divine precept, and by all the ties of conscience under no less penalty than damnation. If they answer me (as a learned priest has lately written) that this doctrine of the Jesuits is not *de fide ;* and that consequently they are not oblig'd by it, they must pardon me if I think they have said nothing to the purpose ; for 'tis a maxim in their Church, where points of faith are not decided, and that doctors are of contrary opinions, they may follow which part they please ; but more safely the most receiv'd and most authoriz'd. And their champion Bellarmine has told the world, in his *Apology*, that the king of England is a vassal to the Pope, *ratione directi dominii*, and that he holds in villanage of his Roman landlord. Which is no new claim put in for England. Our chronicles are his authentic witnesses that King John was depos'd by the same plea, and Philip Augustus admitted tenant. And which makes the more for Bellarmine, the French king was again ejected when our king submitted to the Church, and the crown receiv'd under the sordid condition of a vassalage.

'T is not sufficient for the more moderate and well-meaning Papists (of which I doubt not there are many) to produce the evidences of their loyalty to the late king, and to declare their innocency in this Plot : I will grant their behavior in the first to have been as loyal and as brave as they desire ; and will be willing to hold them excus'd as to the second, (I mean when it comes to my turn, and after my betters ; for 't is a madness to be sober alone, while the nation continues drunk ;) but that saying of their Father Cres. is still running in my head, that they may be dispens'd with in their obedience to an heretic prince, while the necessity of the times shall oblige them to it : for that (as another of them tells us) is only the effect of Christian prudence ; but when once they shall get power to shake him off, an heretic is no lawful king, and consequently to rise against him is no rebellion. I should be glad, therefore, that they would follow the advice which was charitably given them by a reverend prelate of our Church ; namely, that they would join in a public act of disowning and detesting those Jesuitic principles ; and subscribe to all doctrines which deny the Pope's authority of deposing kings, and releasing subjects from

their oath of allegiance : to which I should think they might easily be induc'd, if it be true that this present Pope has condemn'd the doctrine of king-killing, (a thesis of the Jesuits,) amongst others, *ex cathedra*, (as they call it,) or in open consistory.

Leaving them, therefore, in so fair a way (if they please themselves) of satisfying all reasonable men of their sincerity and good meaning to the government, I shall make bold to consider that other extreme of our religion, I mean the Fanatics, or Schismatics, of the English Church. Since the Bible has been translated into our tongue, they have us'd it so, as if their business was not to be sav'd but to be damn'd by its contents. If we consider only them, better had it been for the English nation that it had still remain'd in the original Greek and Hebrew, or at least in the honest Latin of St. Jerome, than that several texts in it should have been prevaricated to the destruction of that government which put it into so ungrateful hands.

How many heresies the first translation of Tyndal produc'd in few years, let my Lord Herbert's history of Henry the Eighth inform you ; insomuch that for the gross errors in it, and the great mischiefs it occasion'd. a sentence pass'd on the first. edition of the Bible, too shameful almost to be repeated. After the short reign of Edward the Sixth, (who had continued to carry on the Reformation on other principles than it was begun,) everyone knows that not only the chief promoters of that work, but many others whose consciences would not dispense with Popery, were forc'd, for fear of persecution, to change climates : from whence returning at the beginning of Queen Elizabeth's reign, many of them who had been in France, and at Geneva, brought back the rigid opinions and imperious discipline of Calvin, to graff upon our Reformation. Which, tho' they cunningly conceal'd at first, (as well knowing how nauseously that drug would go down in a lawful monarchy, which was prescrib'd for a rebellious commonwealth,) yet they always kept it in reserve ; and were never wanting to themselves either in court or parliament, when either they had any prospect of a numerous party of Fanatic members in the one, or the encouragement of any favorite in the other, whose covetousness was gaping at the patrimony of the Church. They who will consult the works of our venerable Hooker, or the account of his life, or more particularly the letter written to him on this subject by George Cranmer, may see by what gradations they proceeded : from the dislike of cap and surplice, the very next step was admonitions to the parliament against the whole government ecclesiastical ; then came out volumes in English and Latin in de fense of their tenets; and immediately practices were set on foot to erect their discipline without authority. Those not succeeding, satire and railing was the next; and Martin Mar-prelate (the Marvell of those times) was the first Presbyterian scribbler who sanctified libels and scurrility to the use of the Good Old Cause. Which was done (says my author) upon this account; that (their serious treatises having been fully answer'd and refuted) they might compass by railing what they had lost by reasoning; and, when their cause was sunk in court and parliament, they might at least hedge in a stake amongst the rabble: for to their ignorance all things are wit which are abusive. But if Church and State were made the theme, then the doctoral degree of wit was to be taken at Billingsgate: even the most saintlike of the party, tho' they durst not excuse this contempt and vilifying of the government, yet were pleas'd, and grinn'd at it with a pious smile, and call'd it a judgment of God against the hierarchy. Thus Sectaries, we may see, were born with teeth, foul-mouth'd and scurrilous from their infancy; and if spiritual pride, venom, violence, contempt of superiors, and slander, had been the marks of orthodox belief, the Presbytery and the rest of our Schismatics, which are their spawn, were always the most visible Church in the Christian world. 'T is true, the government was too strong at that time for a rebellion; but to shew what proficiency they had made in Calvin's school, even then their mouths water'd at it; for two of their gifted brotherhood, (Hacket and Coppinger,) as the story tells us, got up into a pease-cart and harangued the people, to dispose them to an insurrection, and to establish their discipline by force: so that, however it comes about that now they celebrate Queen Elizabeth's birthnight as that of their saint and patroness, yet then they were for doing the work of the Lord by arms against her; and, in all probability, they wanted but a Fanatic lord mayor and two sheriffs of their party, to have compass'd it. Our venerable Hooker, after many admonitions which he had given them, toward the end of his preface breaks out into this prophetic speech: "There is in every one of these considerations most just cause to fear, lest our hastiness to embrace a thing of so perilous consequence" (meaning the Presbyterian discipline) "should cause posterity to feel those evils, which as yet are more easy for us to prevent, than they would be for them to remedy." How fatally this Cassandra has foretold, we know too well by sad experience: the seeds were sown in the time of Queen Elizabeth, the bloody harvest ripen'd in the reign of King Charles the Martyr; and, because all the

sheaves could not be carried off without shedding some of the loose grains, another crop is too like to follow; nay, I fear 't is unavoidable if the conventiclers be permitted still to scatter. A man may be suffer'd to quote an adversary to our religion, when he speaks truth; and 't is the observation of Maimbourg, in his *History of Calvinism*, that wherever that discipline was planted and embrac'd, rebellion, civil war, and misery attended it. And how indeed should it happen otherwise? Reformation of Church and State has always been the ground of our divisions in England. While we were Papists, our Holy Father rid us, by pretending authority out of the Scriptures to depose princes; when we shook off his authority, the Sectaries furnish'd themselves with the same weapons; and out of the same magazine, the Bible: so that the Scriptures, which are in themselves the greatest security of governors, as commanding express obedience to them, are now turn'd to their destruction; and never since the Reformation has there wanted a text of their interpreting to authorize a rebel. And 't is to be noted by the way that the doctrines of king-killing and deposing, which have been taken up only by the worst party of the Papists, the most frontless flatterers of the Pope's authority, have been espous'd, defended, and are still maintain'd by the whole body of Nonconformists and Republicans. 'T is but dubbing themselves the people of God, which 't is the interest of their preachers to tell them they are, and their own interest to believe; and after that, they cannot dip into the Bible, but one text or another will turn up for their purpose; if they are under persecution, (as they call it,) then that is a mark of their election; if they flourish, then God works miracles for their deliverance, and the saints are to possess the earth. They may think themselves to be too roughly handled in this paper; but I, who know best how far I could have gone on this subject, must be bold to tell them they are spar'd: tho' at the same time I am not ignorant that they interpret the mildness of a writer to them, as they do the mercy of the government; in the one they think it fear, and conclude it weakness in the other. The best way for them to confute me is, as I before advis'd the Papists, to disclaim their principles and renounce their practices. We shall all be glad to think them true Englishmen when they obey the king, and true Protestants when they conform to the Church discipline. It remains that I acquaint the reader that the verses were written for an ingenious young gentleman, my friend, upon his translation of the *Critical History of the Old Testament*, compos'd by the learned Father Simon: the verses therefore are address'd to the translator of that work, and the style of them is, what it ought to be, epistolary.

If anyone be so lamentable a critic as to require the smoothness, the numbers, and the turn of heroic poetry in this poem, I must tell him that, if he has not read Horace, I have studied him, and hope the style of his *Epistles* is not ill imitated here. The expressions of a poem design'd purely for instruction ought to be plain and natural, and yet majestic ; for here the poet is presum'd to be a kind of lawgiver, and those three qualities which I have nam'd are proper to the legislative style. The florid, elevated, and figurative way is for the passions ; for love and hatred, fear and anger, are begotten in the soul by shewing their objects out of their true proportion, either greater than the life, or less ; but instruction is to be given by shewing them what they naturally are. A man is to be cheated into passion, but to be reason'd into truth.

RELIGIO LAICI

DIM as the borrow'd beams of moon and stars
To lonely, weary, wand'ring travelers,
Is Reason to the soul ; and, as on high
Those rolling fires discover but the sky,
Not light us here, so Reason's glimmering ray
Was lent, not to assure our doubtful way,
But guide us upward to a better day.
And as those nightly tapers disappear,
When day's bright lord ascends our hemisphere ;
So pale grows Reason at Religion's sight ; 10
So dies, and so dissolves in supernatural light.
Some few, whose lamp shone brighter, have been led
From cause to cause, to nature's secret head ;
And found that one first principle must be :
But what, or who, that UNIVERSAL HE ;
Whether some soul incompassing this ball,
Unmade, unmov'd ; yet making, moving all ;
Or various atoms' interfering dance
Leapt into form, (the noble work of chance ;)
Or this great all was from eternity ; 20
Not ev'n the Stagirite himself could see,
And Epicurus guess'd as well as he :
As blindly grop'd they for a future state ;

As rashly judg'd of providence and fate :
But least of all could their endeavors find
What most concern'd the good of humankind ;
For happiness was never to be found,
But vanish'd from 'em like enchanted ground.
One thought content the good to be enjoy'd ;
This every little accident destroy'd : 30
The wiser madmen did for virtue toil,
A thorny, or at best a barren soil ;
In pleasure some their glutton souls would steep,
But found their line too short, the well too deep,
And leaky vessels which no bliss could keep.
Thus anxious thoughts in endless circles roll,
Without a center where to fix the soul ;
In this wild maze their vain endeavors end :
How can the less the greater comprehend ?
Or finite reason reach Infinity ? 40
For what could fathom GOD were more than He.
The Deist thinks he stands on firmer ground ;
Cries : " Εὕρεκα, the mighty secret 's found :
God is that spring of good ; supreme and best ;
We, made to serve, and in that service blest."
If so, some rules of worship must be given,
Distributed alike to all by Heaven :
Else God were partial, and to some denied
The means his justice should for all provide.
This general worship is to PRAISE and PRAY, 50
One part to borrow blessings, one to pay ;
And when frail nature slides into offense,
The sacrifice for crimes is penitence.
Yet, since th' effects of providence, we find,
Are variously dispens'd to humankind ;
That vice triumphs, and virtue suffers here,
(A brand that sovereign justice cannot bear ;)
Our reason prompts us to a future state,
The last appeal from fortune and from fate :
Where God's all-righteous ways will be declar'd, 60
The bad meet punishment, the good reward.

Side notes (right column):
Opinions of the several sects of philosophers concerning the *Summum Bonum.*

System of Deism.

Thus man by his own strength to heaven
would soar,   Of reveal'd
And would not be oblig'd to Religion.
God for more.
Vain, wretched creature, how art thou mis-
led
To think thy wit these godlike notions bred !
These truths are not the product of thy mind,
But dropp'd from heaven, and of a nobler
kind.
Reveal'd Religion first inform'd thy sight,
And Reason saw not, till Faith sprung the
light.
Hence all thy natural worship takes the
source: 70
'T is revelation what thou think'st discourse.
Else, how com'st thou to see these truths
so clear,
Which so obscure to heathens did appear ?
Not Plato these, nor Aristotle found;
Nor he whose wisdom oracles Socrates.
renown'd.
Hast thou a wit so deep, or so sublime,
Or canst thou lower dive, or higher climb ?
Canst thou, by Reason, more of Godhead
know
Than Plutarch, Seneca, or Cicero ?
Those giant wits, in happier ages born,   80
(When arms and arts did Greece and
Rome adorn,)
Knew no such system; no such piles could
raise
Of natural worship, built on pray'r and
praise,
To One Sole GOD:
Nor did remorse to expiate sin prescribe,
But slew their fellow creatures for a bribe:
The guiltless victim groan'd for their
offense,
And cruelty and blood was penitence.
If sheep and oxen could atone for men,
Ah ! at how cheap a rate the rich might
sin !   90
And great oppressors might Heaven's wrath
beguile,
By offering his own creatures for a spoil !
Dar'st thou, poor worm, offend Infinity ?
And must the terms of peace be given by
thee ?
Then thou art Justice in the last appeal:
Thy easy God instructs thee to rebel;
And, like a king remote, and weak, must
take
What satisfaction thou art pleas'd to make.
But if there be a pow'r too just and strong

To wink at crimes, and bear unpunish'd
wrong;   100
Look humbly upward, see his will disclose
The forfeit first, and then the fine impose:
A mulct thy poverty could never pay,
Had not eternal wisdom found the way,
And with celestial wealth supplied thy
store:
His justice makes the fine, his mercy quits
the score.
See God descending in thy human frame;
Th' offended suff'ring in th' offender's
name;
All thy misdeeds to him imputed see,
And all his righteousness devolv'd on thee.
For granting we have sinn'd, and that   111
th' offense
Of man is made against Omnipotence,
Some price that bears proportion must be
paid,
And infinite with infinite be weigh'd.
See then the Deist lost: remorse for vice,
Not paid; or paid, inadequate in price:
What farther means can Reason now direct,
Or what relief from human wit expect ?
That shews us sick; and sadly are we sure
Still to be sick, till Heav'n reveal the cure:
If then Heav'n's will must needs be under-
stood,   121
(Which must, if we want cure, and Heaven
be good,)
Let all records of will reveal'd be
shown;
With Scripture all in equal balance
thrown,
And our one sacred book will be that
one.
Proof needs not here, for whether we
compare
That impious, idle, superstitious ware
Of rites, lustrations, offerings, (which be-
fore,
In various ages, various countries bore,)
With Christian faith and virtues, we shall
find   130
None answ'ring the great ends of human-
kind,
But this one rule of life, that shews us
best
How God may be appeas'd, and mortals
blest.
Whether from length of time its worth we
draw,
The world is scarce more ancient than the
law:

Heav'n's early care prescrib'd for every
age;
First, in the soul, and after, in the page.
Or, whether more abstractedly we look,
Or on the writers, or the written book,
Whence, but from heav'n, could men un-
skill'd in arts,   140
In several ages born, in several parts,
Weave such agreeing truths? or how, or
why,
Should all conspire to cheat us with a lie?
Unask'd their pains, ungrateful their ad-
vice,
Starving their gain, and martyrdom their
price.
If on the book itself we cast our view,
Concurrent heathens prove the story true;
The doctrine, miracles; which must con-
vince,
For Heav'n in them appeals to human
sense:
And tho' they prove not, they confirm the
cause,   150
When what is taught agrees with nature's
laws.
Then for the style; majestic and divine,
It speaks no less than God in every line:
Commanding words; whose force is still
the same
As the first fiat that produc'd our frame.
All faiths beside or did by arms ascend,
Or sense indulg'd has made mankind their
friend:
This only doctrine does our lusts oppose,
Unfed by nature's soil, in which it grows;
Cross to our interests, curbing sense and
sin;   160
Oppress'd without, and undermin'd within,
It thrives thro' pain; its own tormentors
tires;
And with a stubborn patience still aspires.
To what can Reason such effects assign,
Transcending nature, but to laws divine?
Which in that sacred volume are contain'd;
Sufficient, clear, and for that use ordain'd.
But stay: the Deist here will Objection of
urge anew,   the Deist.
No supernatural worship can be true;
Because a general law is that alone   170
Which must to all, and everywhere, be
known;
A style so large as not this book can claim,
Nor aught that bears reveal'd Religion's
name.
'T is said the sound of a Messiah's birth

Is gone thro' all the habitable earth;
But still that text must be confin'd alone
To what was then inhabited, and known:
And what provision could from thence ac-
crue
To Indian souls, and worlds discover'd
new?
In other parts it helps, that, ages past, 180
The Scriptures there were known, and were
imbrac'd,
Till Sin spread once again the shades of
night:
What's that to these who never saw the
light?
Of all objections this indeed The objection
is chief   answer'd.
To startle Reason, stagger frail Belief:
We grant, 't is true, that Heav'n from hu-
man sense
Has hid the secret paths of Providence;
But boundless wisdom, boundless mercy,
may
Find ev'n for those bewilder'd souls a way:
If from his nature foes may pity claim, 190
Much more may strangers who ne'er heard
his name.
And tho' no name be for salvation known,
But that of his eternal Son's alone;
Who knows how far transcending goodness
can
Extend the merits of that Son to man?
Who knows what reasons may his mercy
lead,
Or ignorance invincible may plead?
Not only charity bids hope the best,
But more the great apostle has express'd:
That if the Gentiles (whom no law in-
spir'd)   200
By nature did what was by law requir'd;
They, who the written rule had never
known,
Were to themselves both rule and law
alone:
To nature's plain indictment they shall
plead,
And by their conscience be condemn'd or
freed.
Most righteous doom! because a rule re-
veal'd
Is none to those from whom it was con-
ceal'd.
Then those who follow'd Reason's dictates
right,
Liv'd up, and lifted high their natural
light;

With Socrates may see their Maker's
   face,   210
While thousand rubric-martyrs want a
   place.
Nor does it balk my charity, to find
Th' Egyptian bishop of another mind:
For tho' his creed eternal truth contains,
'T is hard for man to doom to endless
   pains
All who believ'd not all his zeal requir'd,
Unless he first could prove he was inspir'd.
Then let us either think he meant to say
This faith, where publish'd, was the only
   way;
Or else conclude that, Arius to confute, 220
The good old man, too eager in dispute,
Flew high; and, as his Christian fury rose,
Damn'd all for heretics who durst oppose.
   Thus far my charity this   Digression
     path has tried;   to the trans-
(A much unskilful, but well-   lator of
   meaning guide:)   Father
Yet what they are, ev'n these   Simon's *Crit-
   crude thoughts were   *ical History
   bred   *of the Old
By reading that which better thou hast   *Testament.*
   read:
Thy matchless author's work; which thou,
   my friend,
By well translating better dost commend:
Those youthful hours which of thy equals
   most   230
In toys have squander'd, or in vice have
   lost,
Those hours hast thou to nobler use em-
   ploy'd;
And the severe delights of truth enjoy'd.
Witness this weighty book, in which ap-
   pears
The crabbed toil of many thoughtful
   years,
Spent by thy author in the sifting care
Of Rabbins' old sophisticated ware
From gold divine; which he who well can
   sort
May afterwards make algebra a sport:
A treasure, which if country curates
   buy,   240
They Junius and Tremellius may defy;
Save pains in various readings and transla-
   tions,
And without Hebrew make most learn'd
   quotations:
A work so full with various learning
   fraught,

So nicely ponder'd, yet so strongly
   wrought,
As nature's height and art's last hand re-
   quir'd;
As much as man could compass, uninspir'd.
Where we may see what errors have been
   made
Both in the copier's and translator's trade;
How Jewish, Popish interests have pre-
   vail'd,   250
And where infallibility has fail'd.
   For some, who have his secret meaning
     guess'd,
Have found our author not too much a
   priest:
For fashion sake he seems to have recourse
To Pope, and councils, and tradition's force;
But he that old traditions could subdue,
Could not but find the weakness of the new:
If Scripture, tho' deriv'd from heav'nly
   birth,
Has been but carelessly preserv'd on earth;
If God's own people, who of God before 260
Knew what we know, and had been pro-
   mis'd more,
In fuller terms, of Heaven's assisting care,
And who did neither time nor study spare
To keep this book untainted, unperplex'd,
Let in gross errors to corrupt the text,
Omitted paragraphs, embroil'd the sense,
With vain traditions stopp'd the gaping
   fence,
Which every common hand pull'd up with
   ease;
What safety from such brushwood-helps as
   these ?
If written words from time are not secur'd,
How can we think have oral sounds en-
   dur'd ?   271
Which thus transmitted, if one mouth has
   fail'd,
Immortal lies on ages are intail'd;
And that some such have been, is prov'd
   too plain;
If we consider interest, Church, and gain.
   " O, but," says one, " tradi-   Of the infalli-
     tion set aside,   bility of tradi-
Where can we hope for an un-   tion in general.
   erring guide ?
For since th' original Scripture has been
   lost,
All copies disagreeing, maim'd the most,
Or Christian faith can have no certain
   ground,   280
Or truth in Church tradition must be found."

Such an omniscient Church we wish in-
    deed;
'T were worth both Testaments; and cast
    in the Creed:
But if this mother be a guide so sure,
As can all doubts resolve, all truth secure,
Then her infallibility as well
Where copies are corrupt or lame can tell;
Restore lost canon with as little pains,
As truly explicate what still remains;
Which yet no council dare pretend to do, ⎤
Unless like Esdras they could write it   ⎬
    new: 291
Strange confidence, still to interpret true, ⎦
Yet not be sure that all they have explain'd,
Is in the blest original contain'd.
More safe, and much more modest 't is, to
    say
God would not leave mankind without a
    way;
And that the Scriptures, tho' not every-
    where
Free from corruption, or intire, or clear,
Are uncorrupt, sufficient, clear, intire,
In all things which our needful faith re-
    quire.   300
If others in the same glass better see,
'T is for themselves they look, but not for
    me:
For MY salvation must its doom receive,
Not from what OTHERS but what *I* believe.
  Must all tradition then be   Objection in
    set aside ?   behalf of tra-
  This to affirm were ignorance dition, urg'd
    or pride.   Simon.
Are there not many points, some needful
    sure
To saving faith, that Scripture leaves ob-
    scure ?
Which every sect will wrest a several way
(For what one sect interprets, all sects may):
We hold, and say we prove from Scrip- ⎤
    ture plain,   311 ⎬
That Christ is GOD; the bold Socinian ⎬
From the same Scripture urges he 's but ⎦
    MAN.
Now what appeal can end th' important
    suit;
Both parts talk loudly, but the rule is mute ?
  Shall I speak plain, and in a nation free
Assume an honest layman's liberty ?
I think (according to my little skill,
To my own Mother Church submitting still)
That many have been sav'd, and many
    may,   320

Who never heard this question brought in
    play.
Th' unletter'd Christian, who believes in
    gross,
Plods on to heaven, and ne'er is at a loss;
For the strait gate would be made straiter
    yet,
Were none admitted there but men of wit.
The few by nature form'd, with learning
    fraught,
Born to instruct, as others to be taught,
Must study well the sacred page, and see
Which doctrine, this, or that, does best
    agree
With the whole tenor of the work divine, 330
And plainliest points to Heaven's reveal'd
    design;
Which exposition flows from genuine sense,
And which is forc'd by wit and eloquence.
Not that tradition's parts are useless here,
When general, old, disinteress'd and clear:
That ancient Fathers thus expound the page
Gives truth the reverend majesty of age;
Confirms its force, by biding every test;
For best authority's next rules are best.
And still the nearer to the spring we go, 340
More limpid, more unsoil'd the waters flow.
Thus, first traditions were a proof alone,
Could we be certain such they were, so
    known;
But since some flaws in long descent may
    be,
They make not truth, but probability.
Even Arius and Pelagius durst provoke
To what the centuries preceding spoke.
Such difference is there in an oft-told tale;
But truth by its own sinews will prevail. 349
Tradition written therefore more commends
Authority, than what from voice descends;
And this, as perfect as its kind can be,
Rolls down to us the sacred history,
Which, from the Universal Church receiv'd,
Is tried, and after for itself believ'd.
  The partial Papists would   The second
    infer from hence   objection.
Their Church, in last resort, should judge
    the sense;
But first they would assume, Answer to the
    with wondrous art,   objection.
Themselves to be the whole, who are but
    part
Of that vast frame, the Church; yet grant
    they were   360
The handers down, can they from thence
    infer

A right t' interpret? or would they alone
Who brought the present, claim it for their
      own?
The book's a common largess to mankind,
Not more for them than every man de-
      sign'd;
The welcome news is in the letter found;
The carrier's not commission'd to expound.
It speaks itself, and what it does contain,
In all things needful to be known, is plain.
  In times o'ergrown with rust and igno-
      rance,   370
A gainful trade their clergy did advance;
When want of learning kept the laymen
      low,
And none but priests were authoriz'd to
      know;
When what small knowledge was, in them
      did dwell,
And he a god who could but read or spell:
Then Mother Church did mightily prevail;
She parcell'd out the Bible by retail;
But still expounded what she sold or gave,
To keep it in her power to damn and save:
Scripture was scarce, and, as the market
      went,   380
Poor laymen took salvation on content;
As needy men take money, good or bad:
God's word they had not, but the priest's
      they had.
Yet, whate'er false conveyances they made,
The lawyer still was certain to be paid.
In those dark times they learn'd their
      knack so well,
That by long use they grew infallible:
At last, a knowing age began t' enquire
If they the book, or that did them inspire;
And, making narrower search, they found,
      tho' late,   390
That what they thought the priest's was
      their estate,
Taught by the will produc'd, (the written
      word,)
How long they had been cheated on re-
      cord.
Then every man who saw the title fair
Claim'd a child's part, and put in for a
      share;
Consulted soberly his private good,
And sav'd himself as cheap as e'er he
      could.
  'T is true, my friend, (and far be flattery
      hence,)
This good had full as bad a consequence:
The book thus put in every vulgar hand, 400

Which each presum'd he best could under-
      stand,
The common rule was made the common
      prey,
And at the mercy of the rabble lay.
The tender page with horny fists was
      gall'd,
And he was gifted most that loudest
      bawl'd:
The spirit gave the doctoral degree; ⎫
And every member of a company   ⎬
Was of his trade and of the Bible free. ⎭
Plain truths enough for needful use they
      found,
But men would still be itching to ex-
      pound: 410
Each was ambitious of th' obscurest place,
No measure ta'en from knowledge, all
      from GRACE.
Study and pains were now no more their
      care;
Texts were explain'd by fasting and by
      prayer:
This was the fruit the private spirit
      brought,
Occasion'd by great zeal and little thought.
While crowds unlearn'd, with rude devo-
      tion warm,
About the sacred viands buzz and swarm,
The fly-blown text creates a crawling
      brood,
And turns to maggots what was meant for
      food.   420
A thousand daily sects rise up and die;
A thousand more the perish'd race supply:
So all we make of Heaven's discover'd will
Is, not to have it, or to use it ill.
The danger's much the same; on several
      shelves
If others wreck us, or we wreck ourselves.
  What then remains, but, waiving each
      extreme,
The tides of ignorance and pride to stem?
Neither so rich a treasure to forego;
Nor proudly seek beyond our pow'r to
      know: 430
Faith is not built on disquisitions vain;
The things we must believe are few and
      plain:
But since men will believe more than they
      need,
And every man will make himself a creed,
In doubtful questions 't is the safest way
To learn what unsuspected ancients say;
For 't is not likely we should higher soar

In search of heav'n, than all the Church
  before;
Nor can we be deceiv'd, unless we see
The Scripture and the Fathers disagree. 440
If, after all, they stand suspected still,
(For no man's faith depends upon his will;)
'T is some relief that points not clearly
  known
Without much hazard may be let alone:
And after hearing what our Church can say,
If still our Reason runs another way,
That private Reason 't is more just to curb,

Than by disputes the public peace disturb.
For points obscure are of small use to
  learn;
But common quiet is mankind's concern. 450
  Thus have I made my own opinions clear;
Yet neither praise expect, nor censure fear:
And this unpolish'd, rugged verse, I chose,
As fittest for discourse, and nearest prose:
For while from sacred truth I do not
  swerve,
Tom Sternhold's, or Tom Sha—ll's rhymes
  will serve.

POEMS INCLUDED IN MISCELLANY POEMS (THE FIRST MISCELLANY), 1684

[In 1684 there was " printed for Jacob Tonson " a volume with title-page reading, *Miscellany Poems, containing a New Translation of Virgills Eclogues, Ovid's Love Elegies. Odes of Horace, and other Authors, with several Original Poems, by the most Eminent Hands;* and with the motto:

Et vos, O lauri, carpam, et te, proxima myrte;
Sic positæ quoniam suaveis miscetis odores.

This book is generally referred to as the *First Miscellany.* A second edition appeared in 1692, a third in 1702, and a fourth in 1716. (The title-page of the third edition reads, *Miscellany Poems, the First Part. . . . Publish'd by Mr. Dryden;* that of the fourth edition reads, *The First Part of Miscellany Poems. . . . Publish'd by Mr. Dryden.*) The collection has no preface and opens with new editions of *Mac Flecknoe, Absalom and Achitophel,* and *The Medal:* next come various translations from Greek and Latin authors, mixed with a few original poems; then follows a collection of prologues and epilogues; finally, after a few scattering poems, a translation of Virgil's *Eclogues* concludes the book. Among the "eminent hands" were Sir Charles Sedley, the Earl of Mulgrave, the Earl of Roscommon, the Earl of Rochester, Otway, Rymer, Tate, Duke, and Creech. Dryden was, however, by far the largest contributor to the volume. In the contents of the third and fourth editions, published after Dryden's death, Tonson, or an editor, made important changes.

The prologues and epilogues by Dryden have already been printed in their chronological order, so far as it could be ascertained. Of Virgil's *Eclogues* Dryden translated the fourth and ninth. These versions he reprinted, with some revision, in his complete translation of Virgil, published in 1697. They are therefore omitted at this point: the variant readings of the earlier texts are given in the notes to the *Virgil.* Of Dryden's work only the three following poems remain to be printed as first published in *Miscellany Poems,* 1684. The text follows the first edition.]

OVID'S ELEGIES

BOOK II, ELEGY XIX

[This translation is from the *Amores* of Ovid. Dryden later translated two more elegies from the same book: these are given below (pp. 729, 730), under the title of *Ovid's Amours.*]

IF for thyself thou wilt not watch thy whore,
Watch her for me, that I may love her more.
What comes with ease, we nauseously receive:

Who but a sot would scorn to love with
  leave?
With hopes and fears my flames are blown
  up higher:
Make me despair, and then I can desire.
Give me a jilt to tease my jealous mind;
Deceits are virtues in the female kind.
Corinna my fantastic humor knew,
Play'd trick for trick, and kept herself still
  new: 10
She, that next night I might the sharper
  come,
Fell out with me, and sent me fasting home;

Or some pretence to lie alone would take;
Whene'er she pleas'd, her head and teeth
  would ache:
Till, having won me to the highest strain,
She took occasion to be sweet again.
With what a gust, ye gods, we then im-
  brac'd!
How every kiss was dearer than the last!
  Thou whom I now adore, be edified;
Take care that I may often be denied.   20
Forget the promis'd hour, or feign some
  fright,
Make me lie rough on bulks each other
  night.
These are the arts that best secure thy
  reign,
And this the food that must my fires main-
  tain.
Gross easy love does, like gross diet, pall,
In squeasy stomachs honey turns to gall.
Had Danae not been kept in brazen tow'rs,
Jove had not thought her worth his golden
  show'rs.
When Juno to a cow turn'd Io's shape,   29
The watchman help'd her to a second leap.
Let him who loves an easy Whetstone whore,
Pluck leaves from trees, and drink the com-
  mon shore.
The jilting harlot strikes the surest blow,
A truth which I by sad experience know.
The kind poor constant creature we despise;
Man but pursues the quarry while it flies.
  But thou, dull husband of a wife too fair,
Stand on thy guard, and watch the precious
  ware;
If creaking doors, or barking dogs thou hear,
Or windows scratch'd, suspect a rival there.
An orange-wench would tempt thy wife
  abroad;   41
Kick her, for she 's a letter-bearing bawd;
In short, be jealous as the Devil in hell!
And set my wit on work to cheat thee well.
The sneaking city-cuckold is my foe;
I scorn to strike, but when he wards the
  blow.
Look to thy hits, and leave off thy conniv-
  ing;
I 'll be no drudge to any wittol living;
I have been patient, and forborne thee long,
In hope thou wouldst not pocket up thy
  wrong: 50
If no affront can rouse thee, understand
I 'll take no more indulgence at thy hand.
What. ne'er to be forbid thy house, and
  wife!

Damn him who loves to lead so dull a life.
Now I can neither sigh, nor whine, nor pray;
All those occasions thou hast ta'en away.
Why art thou so incorrigibly civil?
Do somewhat I may wish thee at the Devil.
For shame be no accomplice in my treason,
A pimping husband is too much in reason. 60
  Once more wear horns, before I quite for-
  sake her,
In hopes whereof, I rest thy cuckold-maker.

AMARYLLIS

OR, THE THIRD IDYLLIUM OF THEOCRI-
TUS, PARAPHRAS'D

To Amaryllis love compels my way;
My browzing goats upon the mountains
  stray:
O Tityrus, tend them well, and see them ⎫
  fed
In pastures fresh, and to their wat'ring ⎬
  led;
And 'ware the ridgeling with his butting ⎭
  head.
Ah, beauteous nymph, can you forget your
  love,
The conscious grottos, and the shady grove;
Where stretch'd at ease your tender limbs
  were laid,
Your nameless beauties nakedly display'd?
Then I was call'd your darling, your de-
  sire,   10
With kisses such as set my soul on fire;
But you are chang'd, yet I am still the
  same;
My heart maintains for both a double flame;
Griev'd, but unmov'd, and patient of your
  scorn:
So faithful I, and you so much forsworn!
I die, and death will finish all my pain;
Yet, ere I die, behold me once again:
Am I so much deform'd, so chang'd of late?
What partial judges are our love and hate!
Ten wildings have I gather'd for my dear; 20
How ruddy like your lips their streaks ap-
  pear!
Far off you view'd them with a longing eye
Upon the topmost branch (the tree was
  high):
Yet nimbly up, from bough to bough I
  swerv'd,
And for to-morrow have ten more re-
  serv'd.

Look on me kindly, and some pity shew,
Or give me leave at least to look on you.
Some god transform me by his heavenly
    pow'r
Ev'n to a bee to buzz within your bow'r,
The winding ivy-chaplet to invade,   30
And folded fern, that your fair forehead
    shade.
Now to my cost the force of Love I find;
The heavy hand he bears on humankind.
The milk of tigers was his infant food, ⎫
Taught from his tender years the taste   ⎪
    of blood;   ⎬
His brother whelps and he ran wild   ⎪
    about the wood.   ⎭
Ah nymph, train'd up in his tyrannic court,
To make the suff'rings of your slaves your
    sport!
Unheeded ruin! treacherous delight!
O polish'd hardness, soften'd to the sight! 40
Whose radiant eyes your ebon brows adorn,
Like midnight those, and these like break
    of morn!
Smile once again, revive me with your
    charms;
And let me die contented in your arms.
I would not ask to live another day,
Might I but sweetly kiss my soul away.
Ah, why am I from empty joys debarr'd?
For kisses are but empty when compar'd.
I rave, and in my raging fit shall tear
The garland which I wove for you to
    wear,   50
Of parsley, with a wreath of ivy bound,
And border'd with a rosy edging round.
What pangs I feel, unpitied and unheard!
Since I must die, why is my fate deferr'd!
I strip my body of my shepherd's frock:
Behold that dreadful downfall of a rock,
Where yon old fisher views the waves from
    high!
'T is that convenient leap I mean to try.
You would be pleas'd to see me plunge to
    shore,
But better pleas'd, if I should rise no
    more.   60
I might have read my fortune long ago,
When, seeking my success in love to know,
I tried th' infallible prophetic way,
A poppy-leaf upon my palm to lay:
I struck, and yet no lucky crack did follow;
Yet I struck hard, and yet the leaf lay
    hollow:
And, which was worse, if any worse could
    prove,

The with'ring leaf foreshew'd your with'r-
    ing love.
Yet farther (ah, how far a lover dares!)
My last recourse I had to sieve and
    shears;   70
And told the witch Agreo my disease:
(Agreo, that in harvest us'd to lease:
But harvest done, to charwork did aspire;
Meat, drink, and twopence was her daily
    hire.)
To work she went, her charms she mut- ⎫
    ter'd o'er,   ⎪
And yet the resty sieve wagg'd ne'er the ⎬
    more;   ⎪
I wept for woe, the testy beldame   ⎭
    swore;
And, foaming with her god, foretold my
    fate;
That I was doom'd to love, and you to hate.
A milk-white goat for you I did provide; 80
Two milk-white kids run frisking by her
    side,
For which the nut-brown lass, Erithacis,
Full often offer'd many a savory kiss.
Hers they shall be, since you refuse the
    price:
What madman would o'erstand his market
    twice?
My right eye itches, some good luck is ⎫
    near,   ⎬
Perhaps my Amaryllis may appear;   ⎪
I 'll set up such a note as she shall hear. ⎭
What nymph but my melodious voice
    would move?
She must be flint, if she refuse my love. 90
Hippomenes, who ran with noble strife ⎫
To win his lady, or to lose his life,   ⎪
(What shift some men will make to get   ⎬
    a wife!)   ⎭
Threw down a golden apple in her way;
For all her haste she could not choose but
    stay.
Renown said: "Run;" the glitt'ring bribe
    cried: "Hold;"
The man might have been hang'd, but for
    his gold.
Yet some suppose 't was love (some few
    indeed)
That stopp'd the fatal fury of her speed:
She saw, she sigh'd; her nimble feet re-
    fuse   100
Their wonted speed, and she took pains to
    lose.
A prophet some, and some a poet cry,
(No matter which, so neither of them lie,)

From steepy Othrys' top to Pylus drove
His herd; and for his pains enjoy'd his
    love:
If such another wager should be laid,
I 'll find the man, if you can find the maid.
Why name I men, when Love extended
    finds
His pow'r on high, and in celestial minds ?
Venus the shepherd's homely habit took, 110
And manag'd something else besides the
    crook;
Nay, when Adonis died, was heard to roar,
And never from her heart forgave the
    boar.
How blest is fair Endymion with his Moon,
Who sleeps on Latmos' top from night to
    noon!
What Jason from Medea's love possess'd,
You shall not hear, but know 't is like the
    rest.
My aching head can scarce support the
    pain;
This cursed love will surely turn my brain:
Feel how it shoots, and yet you take no
    pity; 120
Nay, then 't is time to end my doleful ditty.
A clammy sweat does o'er my temples
    creep;
My heavy eyes are urg'd with iron sleep:
I lay me down to gasp my latest breath,
The wolves will get a breakfast by my
    death;
Yet scarce enough their hunger to supply,
For love has made me carrion ere I die.

THE TEARS OF AMYNTA, FOR THE DEATH OF DAMON

SONG

On a bank, beside a willow,
Heav'n her cov'ring, earth her pillow,
    Sad Amynta sigh'd alone;
From the cheerless dawn of morning
Till the dews of night returning,
    Singing thus, she made her moan:
      " Hope is banish'd,
      Joys are vanish'd,
    Damon, my belov'd, is gone !

" Time, I dare thee to discover   10
Such a youth, and such a lover;
    O, so true, so kind was he !
Damon was the pride of nature,
Charming in his every feature;
    Damon liv'd alone for me:
      Melting kisses,
      Murmuring blisses ;
    Who so liv'd and lov'd as we !

" Never shall we curse the morning,
Never bless the night returning,   20
    Sweet embraces to restore;
Never shall we both lie dying,
Nature failing, love supplying
    All the joys he drain'd before.
      Death, come end me,
      To befriend me;
    Love and Damon are no more."

PROLOGUE TO THE DISAPPOINTMENT

OR, THE MOTHER IN FASHION

SPOKEN BY MR. BETTERTON

[This play, by Southerne, was acted and printed in 1684; it is noted in the *Term Catalogue* for Trinity Term (June) of that year. The prologue was reprinted in the third edition, 1702, of *Miscellany Poems, the First Part*, with the heading, *A Prologue, spoken by Mr. Betterton, written by Mr. Dryden.* The present text follows that printed with the play in 1684. On the epilogue to the same play, see *Appendix I*, p. 920, below.]

How comes it, gentlemen, that nowadays,
When all of you so shrewdly judge of plays,
Our poets tax you still with want of sense ?
All prologues treat you at your own expense.
Sharp citizens a wiser way can go;
They make you fools, but never call you so.
They in good manners seldom make a slip,
But treat a common whore with ladyship;
But here each saucy wit at random writes,
And uses ladies as he uses knights.   10
Our author, young, and grateful in his nature,
Vows that from him no nymph deserves a
    satyr;
Nor will he ever draw — I mean his rhyme,
Against the sweet partaker of his crime.
Nor is he yet so bold an undertaker,
To call *men* fools: 't is railing at their *Maker.*
Besides, he fears to split upon that shelf;

He 's young enough to be a *fop* himself:
And, if his praise can bring you all abed,
He swears such hopeful youth no nation
    ever bred.   20

Your nurses, we presume, in such a ⎤
    case,   ⎟
Your father chose, because he lik'd the ⎟
    face;   ⎬
And, often, they supplied your mother's ⎟
    place.   ⎦
The dry nurse was your mother's ancient
    maid,
Who knew some former slip she ne'er be-
    tray'd.
Betwixt 'em both, for milk and sugar candy,
Your sucking bottles were well stor'd with
    brandy.
Your father, to initiate your discourse, ⎤
Meant to have taught you first to swear ⎬
    and curse,   ⎟
But was prevented by each careful nurse. ⎦
For, leaving dad and mam, as names too
    common,   31
They taught you certain parts of man and
    woman.
I pass your schools; for there, when first
    you came,
You would be sure to learn the Latin name.
In colleges you scorn'd their art of think-
    ing,
But learn'd all moods and figures of good
    drinking:
Thence come to town, you practice play, to
    know
The virtues of the high dice, and the low.
Each thinks himself a *sharper* most pro-
    found:
He cheats by pence, is cheated by the
    pound.   40
With these perfections, and what else he ⎤
    gleans,   ⎟
The *spark* sets up for love behind our ⎬
    scenes;   ⎟
Hot in pursuit of princesses and queens. ⎦
There, if they know their man, with cun-
    ning carriage,
Twenty to one but it concludes in marriage.
He hires some homely room, love's fruits
    to gather,
And garret-high rebels against his father.
But he once dead —
Brings her in triumph, with her portion,
    down,
A twillet, dressing box, and half a crown.

Some marry first, and then they fall to
    scouring,   51
Which is, refining marriage into whoring.
Our women batten well on their good na-
    ture;
All they can rap and rend for the dear
    creature.
But while abroad so liberal the *dolt* is,
Poor *spouse* at home as ragged as a colt is.
Last, some there are, who take their first
    degrees
Of lewdness in our middle galleries;
The doughty *bullies* enter bloody drunk,
Invade and grabble one another's *punk:* 60
They caterwaul, and make a dismal rout;
Call *sons* of *whores*, and strike, but ne'er
    lug out:
Thus, while for paltry punk they roar and
    stickle,
They make it bawdier than a conventicle.

EPILOGUE TO CONSTANTINE
THE GREAT

SPOKEN BY MRS. COOKE

[This tragedy, by Lee, was first printed in
1684. The epilogue is not assigned to Dryden
in this edition or in the early collected editions
of Lee's works. It appears, however, in the
third edition, 1702, of *Miscellany Poems, the
First Part*, with the words, " written by Mr.
Dryden," after the title. The present text follows that printed with the play in 1684.]

Our hero 's happy in the play's conclu-
    sion;
The holy rogue at last has met confusion:
Tho' Arius all along appear'd a saint,
The last act shew'd him a True Protes-
    tant.
Eusebius (for you know I read Greek au-
    thors)
Reports that, after all these plots and
    slaughters,
The court of Constantine was full of glory,
And every Trimmer turn'd Addressing
    Tory.
They follow'd him in herds as they were
    mad;
When Clause was king, then all the world
    was glad: 10
Whigs kept the places they possess'd be-
    fore,
And most were in a way of getting more;

Which was as much as saying: "Gentle-
men,
Here's power and money to be rogues
again."
Indeed there were a sort of peaking tools,
(Some call them modest, but I call 'em
fools,)
Men much more loyal, tho' not half so
loud;
But these poor devils were cast behind the
crowd;
For bold knaves thrive without one grain
of sense,
But good men starve for want of impu-
dence.   20
Besides all these, there were a sort of
wights,
(I think my author calls them Teckelites,)
Such hearty rogues against the king and
laws,
They favor'd even a foreign rebel's cause.
When their own damn'd design was quash'd
and aw'd,
At least they gave it their good word
abroad.
As many a man, who, for a quiet life,
Breeds out his bastard, not to nose his
wife;
Thus o'er their darling plot these Trim- ⎫
mers cry, |
And tho' they cannot keep it in their ⎬
eye,   30 |
They bind it prentice to Count Teckely. ⎭
They believe not the last plot: may I be
curst,
If I believe they e'er believ'd the first !
No wonder their own plot no plot they
think;
The man that makes it, never smells the
stink.
And, now it comes into my head, I'll tell
Why these damn'd Trimmers lov'd the
Turks so well.
The original Trimmer, tho' a friend to no
man,
Yet in his heart ador'd a pretty woman;
He knew that Mahomet laid up for ever
Kind black-ey'd rogues for every true be-
liever;   41
And, which was more than mortal man e'er
tasted,
One pleasure that for threescore twelve-
months lasted.
To turn for this may surely be forgiven:
Who'd not be circumcis'd for such a heav'n !

TO THE EARL OF ROSCOMMON, ON HIS EXCELLENT ESSAY ON TRANSLATED VERSE

[*An Essay on Translated Verse*, by Wentworth Dillon, Earl of Roscommon, was first
published in 1684; a second edition, "corrected
and enlarged," appeared the next year. Dryden's poem is prefixed to both editions; in the
second it is slightly revised. Dryden several
times refers to Roscommon with warm admiration: see his *Preface to Ovid's Epistles* (p. 90,
above), his *Preface to Sylvæ* (pp. 176, 178, 179,
below), and his *Dedication of the Æneis* (p. 514,
below). In 1683 Roscommon prefixed a complimentary poem to the third issue of *Religio
Laici*.
The present text follows the second edition.]

WHETHER the fruitful Nile, or Tyrian shore,
The seeds of arts and infant science bore,
'T is sure the noble plant, translated first,
Advanc'd its head in Grecian gardens nurs'd.
The Grecians added verse; their tuneful
tongue
Made nature first and nature's God their
song.
Nor stopp'd translation here; for conquer-
ing Rome
With Grecian spoils brought Grecian num-
bers home,
Enrich'd by those Athenian Muses more
Than all the vanquish'd world could yield
before;   10
Till barb'rous nations, and more barb'rous
times,
Debas'd the majesty of verse to rhymes;
Those rude at first: a kind of hobbling
prose,
That limp'd along, and tinkled in the close.
But Italy, reviving from the trance
Of Vandal, Goth, and monkish ignorance,
With pauses, cadence, and well-vowel'd
words,
And all the graces a good ear affords,
Made rhyme an art, and Dante's polish'd
page
Restor'd a silver, not a golden age.   20
Then Petrarch follow'd, and in him we see ⎫
What rhyme improv'd in all its height |
can be: ⎬
At best a pleasing sound, and fair bar- |
barity.   ⎭
The French pursued their steps; and Britain,
last,
In manly sweetness all the rest surpass'd.

The wit of Greece, the gravity of Rome,
Appear exalted in the British loom;
The Muses' empire is restor'd again,
In Charles his reign, and by Roscommon's
    pen.
Yet modestly he does his work survey,   30
And calls a finish'd poem an *Essay ;*
For all the needful rules are scatter'd
    here;
Truth smoothly told, and pleasantly se-
    vere;
So well is art disguis'd, for nature to ap-
    pear.
Nor need those rules, to give translation
    light:
His own example is a flame so bright,
That he who but arrives to copy well,
Unguided will advance, unknowing will
    excel.
Scarce his own Horace could such rules
    ordain,
Or his own Virgil sing a nobler strain.   40
How much in him may rising Ireland boast,
How much in gaining him has Britain
    lost !
Their island in revenge has ours reclaim'd;
The more instructed we, the more we still
    are sham'd.
'T is well for us his generous blood did
    flow,
Deriv'd from British channels long ago;
That here his conquering ancestors were
    nurs'd,
And Ireland but translated England first:
By this reprisal we regain our right,
Else must the two contending nations fight;
A nobler quarrel for his native earth,   51
Than what divided Greece for Homer's
    birth.
To what perfection will our tongue ar-
    rive,
How will invention and translation thrive,
When authors nobly born will bear their
    part,
And not disdain th' inglorious praise of
    art !
Great generals thus, descending from com-
    mand,
With their own toil provoke the soldier's
    hand.
How will sweet Ovid's ghost be pleas'd to
    hear
His fame augmented by an The Earl of
    English peer;   60 Mulgrave.
How he embellishes his Helen's loves,

Outdoes his softness, and his sense im-
    proves ?
When these translate, and teach translators
    too,
Nor firstling kid, nor any vulgar vow
Should at Apollo's grateful altar stand:
Roscommon writes; to that auspicious
    hand,
Muse, feed the bull that spurns the yel-
    low sand:
Roscommon, whom both court and camps
    commend,
True to his prince, and faithful to his
    friend;
Roscommon, first in fields of honor known,
First in the peaceful triumphs of the
    gown,   71
Who both Minervas justly makes his
    own.
Now let the few belov'd by Jove, and
    they
Whom infus'd Titan form'd of better
    clay,
On equal terms with ancient wit ingage,
Nor mighty Homer fear, nor sacred Virgil's
    page:
Our English palace opens wide in state,
And without stooping they may pass the
    gate.

TO THE MEMORY OF MR. OLDHAM

[John Oldham, after Dryden and Butler the
ablest satirist of the Restoration period, died
on December 9, 1683, at the age of thirty. To
an edition of his *Remains in Verse and Prose,*
published late in the next year, Dryden prefixed the following noble tribute.]

FAREWELL, too little, and too lately known,
Whom I began to think and call my own:
For sure our souls were near allied, and
    thine
Cast in the same poetic mold with mine.
One common note on either lyre did strike,
And knaves and fools we both abhorr'd
    alike.
To the same goal did both our studies
    drive;
The last set out the soonest did arrive.
Thus Nisus fell upon the slippery place,
While his young friend perform'd and won
    the race.   10

O early ripe ! to thy abundant store
What could advancing age have added
    more ?
It might (what nature never gives the
    young)
Have taught the numbers of thy native
    tongue.
But satire needs not those, and wit will
    shine
Thro' the harsh cadence of a rugged line:
A noble error, and but seldom made,
When poets are by too much force be-
    tray'd.

Thy generous fruits, tho' gather'd ere
    their prime,
Still shew'd a quickness; and maturing
    time   20
But mellows what we write to the dull
    sweets of rhyme.
Once more, hail and farewell; farewell,
    thou young,
But ah too short, Marcellus of our tongue;
Thy brows with ivy, and with laurels
    bound;
But fate and gloomy night encompass thee
    around.

POEMS INCLUDED IN SYLVÆ (THE SECOND MISCELLANY), 1685

[Encouraged by the success of *Miscellany Poems*, 1684, Tonson and Dryden undertook a second volume of similar character, which was published in 1685 with a title reading, *Sylvæ, or The Second Part of Poetical Miscellanies;* and with the motto:

—— *Non deficit alter*
Aureus, et simili frondescit virga metallo. — VIRG.

This book is generally referred to as the *Second Miscellany*. Second, third, and fourth editions followed in the same years as those of its predecessor: 1692, 1702, and 1716. The third edition adds to the title the words, *Publish'd by Mr. Dryden;* the title of the fourth edition reads, *The Second Part of Miscellany Poems. . . . Publish'd by Mr. Dryden.* On the *Sylvæ* a passage in a letter from Dryden to Tonson, dated by Malone (I, 2, 21) in August or September, 1684, is of much interest: "Your opinion of the Miscellanyes is likewise mine: I will for once lay by the *Religio Laici* till another time. But I must also add, that since we are to have nothing but new, I am resolv'd we will have nothing but good, whomever we disoblige. You will have of mine, four Odes of Horace, which I have already translated; another small translation of forty lines from Lucretius; the whole story of Nisus and Eurialus, both in the fifth and the ninth of Virgil's Eneids: and I care not who translates them beside me, for let him be friend or foe, I will please myself, and not give off in consideration of any man. There will be forty lines more of Virgil in another place, to answer those of Lucretius: I meane those very lines which Montagne has compar'd in those two poets; and Homer shall sleep on for me, — I will not now meddle with him." Evidently Tonson proposed that no reprinted work be included in the new volume, and Dryden followed his suggestion.

After Dryden's preface, the *Sylvæ* opens with his translations from Virgil, Lucretius, Theocritus, and Horace. Other translations, mainly anonymous, with a few original poems, make up the rest of the volume. Among the contributions is a Latin poem, *Horti Arlingtoniani, ad Clarissimum Dominum, Henricum, Comitem Arlingtoniæ, &c.*, by Charles Dryden, eldest son of the poet. In the contents of the third and fourth editions of the *Sylvæ*, as of its predecessor, Tonson, or an editor, made important changes.

When Dryden made his complete translation of Virgil, he rewrote thoroughly the episodes from the *Æneid* included in the *Sylvæ*. His earlier texts are omitted at the present point, but are given in *Appendix II*, pp. 921–928, below.]

PREFACE

FOR this last half-year I have been troubled with the disease (as I may call it) of translation. The cold prose fits of it, which are always the most tedious with me, were spent in the *History of the League;* the hot, which succeeded them, in this volume of verse miscellanies. The truth is, I fancied to myself a kind of ease in the change of the paroxysm; never suspecting but the humor would have wasted itself in two or three pastorals of Theocritus, and as many odes of Horace. But finding, or at least thinking I found, something that was more pleasing in them than my ordinary productions, I encourag'd myself to renew my old acquaintance with Lucretius and Virgil; and immediately fix'd upon some parts of them, which had most affected me in the reading. These were my natural impulses for the undertaking; but there was an accidental motive which was full as forcible, and God forgive him who was the occasion of it. It was my Lord Roscommon's *Essay on Translated Verse;* which made me uneasy till I tried whether or no I was capable of following his rules, and of reducing the speculation into practice. For many a fair precept in poetry is like a seeming demonstration in the mathematics, very specious in the diagram, but failing in the mechanic operation. I think I have generally observ'd his instructions; I am sure my reason is sufficiently convinc'd both of their truth and usefulness; which, in other words, is to confess no less a vanity, than to pretend that I have at least in some places made examples to his rules. Yet, withal, I must acknowledge that I have many times exceeded my commission; for I have both added and omitted, and even sometimes very boldly made such expositions of my authors, as no Dutch commentator will forgive me. Perhaps, in such particular passages, I have thought that I discover'd some beauty yet undiscover'd by those pedants, which none but a poet could have found. Where I have taken away some of their expressions, and cut them shorter, it may possibly be on this consideration, that what was beautiful in the Greek or Latin, would not appear so shining in the English; and where I have enlarg'd them, I desire the false critics would not always think that those thoughts are wholly mine, but that either they are secretly in the poet, or may be fairly deduc'd from him; or at least, if both those considerations should fail, that my own is of a piece with his, and that if he were living, and an Englishman, they are such as he would probably have written.

For, after all, a translator is to make his author appear as charming as possibly he can, provided he maintains his character, and makes him not unlike himself. Translation is a kind of drawing after the life, where everyone will acknowledge there is a double sort of likeness, a good one and a bad. 'T is one thing to draw the outlines true, the features like, the proportions exact, the coloring itself perhaps tolerable; and another thing to make all these graceful, by the posture, the shadowings, and chiefly by the spirit which animates the whole. I cannot, without some indignation, look on an ill copy of an excellent original. Much less can I behold with patience Virgil, Homer, and some others, whose beauties I have been en-

deavoring all my life to imitate, so abus'd, as I may say, to their faces, by a botching interpreter. What English readers, unacquainted with Greek or Latin, will believe me, or any other man, when we commend those authors, and confess we derive all that is pardonable in us from their fountains, if they take those to be the same poets, whom our Oglebys have translated? But I dare assure them that a good poet is no more like himself, in a dull translation, than his carcass would be to his living body. There are many who understand Greek and Latin, and yet are ignorant of their mother tongue. The proprieties and delicacies of the English are known to few: 't is impossible even for a good wit to understand and practice them, without the help of a liberal education, long reading, and digesting of those few good authors we have amongst us, the knowledge of men and manners, the freedom of habitudes and conversation with the best company of both sexes; and, in short, without wearing off the rust which he contracted, while he was laying in a stock of learning. Thus difficult it is to understand the purity of English, and critically to discern not only good writers from bad, and a proper style from a corrupt, but also to distinguish that which is pure in a good author, from that which is vicious and corrupt in him. And for want of all these requisites, or the greatest part of them, most of our ingenious young men take up some cried-up English poet for their model, adore him, and imitate him, as they think, without knowing wherein he is defective, where he is boyish and trifling, wherein either his thoughts are improper to his subject, or his expressions unworthy of his thoughts, or the turn of both is unharmonious.

Thus it appears necessary that a man should be a nice critic in his mother tongue, before he attempts to translate a foreign language. Neither is it sufficient that he be able to judge of words and style, but he must be a master of them too; he must perfectly understand his author's tongue, and absolutely command his own. So that, to be a thorough translator, he must be a thorough poet. Neither is it enough to give his author's sense in good English, in poetical expressions, and in musical numbers; for, tho' all these are exceeding difficult to perform, there yet remains a harder task; and 't is a secret of which few translators have sufficiently thought. I have already hinted a word or two concerning it; that is, the maintaining the character of an author, which distinguishes him from all others, and makes him appear that individual poet whom you would interpret. For example, not only the thoughts, but the style and versification of Virgil and Ovid, are very different: yet I see, even in our best poets who have translated some parts of them, that they have confounded their several talents; and, by endeavoring only at the sweetness and harmony of numbers, have made them both so much alike, that if I did not know the originals, I should never be able to judge by the copies, which was Virgil, and which was Ovid. It was objected against a late noble painter, that he drew many graceful pictures, but few of them were like. And this happen'd to him, because he always studied himself, more than those who sate to him. In such translators I can easily distinguish the hand which perform'd the work, but I cannot distinguish their poet from another. Suppose two authors are equally sweet, yet there is a great distinction to be made in sweetness, as in that of sugar, and that of honey. I can make the difference more plain, by giving you (if it be worth knowing) my own method of proceeding, in my translations out of four several poets in this volume: Virgil, Theocritus, Lucretius, and Horace. In each of these, before I undertook them, I consider'd the genius and distinguishing character of my author. I look'd on Virgil as a succinct, and grave majestic writer; one who weigh'd not only every thought. but every word and syllable: who was still aiming to crowd his sense into as narrow a compass as possibly he could; for which reason he is so very figurative, that he requires (I may almost say) a grammar apart to construe him. His verse is everywhere sounding the very thing in your ears, whose sense it bears; yet the numbers are perpetually varied, to increase the delight of the reader; so that the same sounds are never repeated twice together. On the contrary, Ovid and Claudian, tho' they write in styles differing from each other, yet have each of them but one sort of music in their verses. All the versification and little variety of Claudian is included within the compass of four or five lines, and then he begins again in the same tenor; perpetually closing his sense at the end of a verse, and that verse commonly which they call golden, or two substantives and two adjectives, with a verb betwixt them to keep the peace. Ovid, with all his sweetness, has as little variety of numbers and sound as he; he is always, as it were, upon the handgallop, and his verse runs upon carpet-ground. He avoids, like the other, all synalephas, or cutting off one vowel when it comes before another in the following word; so that, minding only smoothness, he wants both variety and majesty. But to return to Virgil: tho' he is smooth where smoothness is requir'd, yet he is so far from affecting it, that he seems rather to disdain it; frequently makes use of synalephas, and concludes his sense in the middle of his verse. He is everywhere above conceits of epi-

grammatic wit, and gross hyperboles; he maintains majesty in the midst of plainness; he shines, but glares not; and is stately without ambition, which is the vice of Lucan. I drew my definition of poetical wit from my particular consideration of him: for propriety of thoughts and words are only to be found in him; and, where they are proper, they will be delightful. Pleasure follows of necessity, as the effect does the cause; and therefore is not to be put into the definition. This exact propriety of Virgil I particularly regarded, as a great part of his character; but must confess, to my shame, that I have not been able to translate any part of him so well, as to make him appear wholly like himself. For where the original is close, no version can reach it in the same compass. Hannibal Caro's, in the Italian, is the nearest, the most poetical, and the most sonorous of any translation of the Æneids: yet, tho' he takes the advantage of blank verse, he commonly allows two lines for one of Virgil, and does not always hit his sense. Tasso tells us, in his letters, that Sperone Speroni, a great Italian wit, who was his contemporary, observ'd of Virgil and Tully, that the Latin orator endeavor'd to imitate the copiousness of Homer, the Greek poet; and that the Latin poet made it his business to reach the conciseness of Demosthenes, the Greek orator. Virgil, therefore, being so very sparing of his words, and leaving so much to be imagin'd by the reader, can never be translated as he ought in any modern tongue. To make him copious, is to alter his character; and to translate him line for line is impossible, because the Latin is naturally a more succinct language than either the Italian, Spanish, French, or even than the English, which, by reason of its monosyllables, is far the most compendious of them. Virgil is much the closest of any Roman poet, and the Latin hexameter has more feet than the English heroic.

Besides all this, an author has the choice of his own thoughts and words, which a translator has not; he is confin'd by the sense of the inventor to those expressions which are the nearest to it: so that Virgil, studying brevity, and having the command of his own language, could bring those words into a narrow compass, which a translator cannot render without circumlocutions. In short, they who have call'd him the torture of grammarians, might also have call'd him the plague of translators; for he seems to have studied not to be translated. I own that, endeavoring to turn his *Nisus and Euryalus* as close as I was able, I have perform'd that episode too literally; that, giving more scope to *Mezentius and Lausus*, that version, which has more of the majesty of Virgil, has less of his conciseness; and all that I can promise for myself is only that I have done both better than Ogleby, and perhaps as well as Caro. So that, methinks, I come like a malefactor, to make a speech upon the gallows, and to warn all other poets, by my sad example, from the sacrilege of translating Virgil. Yet, by considering him so carefully as I did before my attempt, I have made some faint resemblance of him; and, had I taken more time, might possibly have succeeded better; but never so well, as to have satisfied myself.

He who excels all other poets in his own language, were it possible to do him right, must appear above them in our tongue; which, as my Lord Roscommon justly observes, approaches nearest to the Roman in its majesty: nearest indeed, but with a vast interval betwixt them. There is an inimitable grace in Virgil's words, and in them principally consists that beauty which gives so unexpressible a pleasure to him who best understands their force. This diction of his, I must once again say, is never to be copied; and, since it cannot, he will appear but lame in the best translation. The turns of his verse, his breakings, his propriety, his numbers, and his gravity, I have as far imitated as the poverty of our language and the hastiness of my performance would allow. I may seem sometimes to have varied from his sense; but I think the greatest variations may be fairly deduc'd from him; and where I leave his commentators, it may be I understand him better: at least I writ without consulting them in many places. But two particular lines in *Mezentius and Lausus* I cannot so easily excuse. They are indeed remotely allied to Virgil's sense; but they are too like the trifling tenderness of Ovid, and were printed before I had consider'd them enough to alter them. The first of them I have forgotten, and cannot easily retrieve, because the copy is at the press; the second is this:

When Lausus died, 1 was already slain.

This appears pretty enough at first sight; but I am convinc'd for many reasons that the expression is too bold; that Virgil would not have said it, tho' Ovid would. The reader may pardon it, if he please, for the freeness of the confession; and instead of that, and the former, admit these two lines, which are more according to the author:

Nor ask I life, nor fought with that design;
As I had us'd my fortune, use thou thine.

Having with much ado got clear of Virgil, I have, in the next place, to consider the genius of Lucretius, whom I have translated more happily in those parts of him which I undertook. If he was not of the best age of Roman poetry, he was at least of that which preceded it; and he himself refin'd it to that degree of perfection, both in the language and the thoughts, that he left an easy task to Virgil; who, as he succeeded him in time, so he copied his excellencies: for the method of the *Georgics* is plainly deriv'd from him. Lucretius had chosen a subject naturally crabbed; he therefore adorn'd it with poetical descriptions, and precepts of morality, in the beginning and ending of his books, which you see Virgil has imitated with great success, in those four books, which in my opinion are more perfect in their kind than even his divine *Æneids*. The turn of his verse he has likewise follow'd, in those places which Lucretius has most labor'd, and some of his very lines he has transplanted into his own works, without much variation. If I am not mistaken, the distinguishing character of Lucretius (I mean of his soul and genius) is a certain kind of noble pride, and positive assertion of his opinions. He is everywhere confident of his own reason, and assuming an absolute command, not only over his vulgar reader, but even his patron Memmius. For he is always bidding him attend, as if he had the rod over him, and using a magisterial authority, while he instructs him. From his time to ours, I know none so like him as our poet and philosopher of Malmesbury. This is that perpetual dictatorship which is exercis'd by Lucretius; who, tho' often in the wrong, yet seems to deal *bona fide* with his reader, and tells him nothing but what he thinks: in which plain sincerity, I believe, he differs from our Hobbes, who could not but be convinc'd, or at least doubt of some eternal truths, which he has oppos'd. But for Lucretius, he seems to disdain all manner of replies, and is so confident of his cause, that he is beforehand with his antagonists; urging for them whatever he imagin'd they could say, and leaving them, as he supposes, without an objection for the future; all this too, with so much scorn and indignation, as if he were assur'd of the triumph, before he enter'd into the lists. From this sublime and daring genius of his, it must of necessity come to pass, that his thoughts must be masculine, full of argumentation, and that sufficiently warm. From the same fiery temper proceeds the loftiness of his expressions, and the perpetual torrent of his verse, where the barrenness of his subject does not too much constrain the quickness of his fancy. For there is no doubt to be made, but that he could have been everywhere as poetical as he is in his descriptions, and in the moral part of his philosophy, if he had not aim'd more to instruct, in his *System of Nature*, than to delight. But he was bent upon making Memmius a materialist, and teaching him to defy an invisible power. In short, he was so much an atheist, that he forgot sometimes to be a poet. These are the considerations which I had of that author, before I attempted to translate some parts of him. And accordingly I laid by my natural diffidence and scepticism for a while, to take up that dogmatical way of his, which, as I said, is so much his character, as to make him that individual poet. As for his opinions concerning the mortality of the soul, they are so absurd, that I cannot, if I would, believe them. I think a future state demonstrable even by natural arguments; at least, to take away rewards and punishments, is only a pleasing prospect to a man, who resolves beforehand not to live morally. But on the other side, the thought of being nothing after death is a burden unsupportable to a virtuous man, even tho' a heathen. We naturally aim at happiness, and cannot bear to have it confin'd to the shortness of our present being, especially when we consider that virtue is generally unhappy in this world, and vice fortunate: so that 'tis hope of futurity alone that makes this life tolerable, in expectation of a better. Who would not commit all the excesses to which he is prompted by his natural inclinations, if he may do them with security while he is alive, and be uncapable of punishment after he is dead! If he be cunning and secret enough to avoid the laws, there is no band of morality to restrain him: for fame and reputation are weak ties; many men have not the least sense of them; powerful men are only aw'd by them, as they conduce to their interest, and that not always, when a passion is predominant; and no man will be contain'd within the bounds of duty, when he may safely transgress them. These are my thoughts abstractedly, and without ent'ring into the notions of our Christian faith, which is the proper business of divines.

But there are other arguments in this poem (which I have turn'd into English) not belonging to the mortality of the soul, which are strong enough to a reasonable man, to make him less in love with life, and consequently in less apprehensions of death: such as are the natural satiety proceeding from a perpetual enjoyment of the same things; the inconveniences of old age, which make him uncapable of corporeal pleasures; the decay of understanding and memory, which render him contemptible and useless to others. These, and many other reasons, so pathetically urg'd, so beautifully express'd, so adorn'd with examples, and so admirably rais'd by the prosopopeia of Nature, who is brought in speaking to her children, with so much authority and vigor, deserve the pains I have taken with them, which I hope have not been unsuccessful,

or unworthy of my author. At least I must take the liberty to own that I was pleas'd with my own endeavors, which but rarely happens to me, and that I am not dissatisfied upon the review of anything I have done in this author.

'T is true, there is something, and that of some moment, to be objected against my Englishing the *Nature of Love*, from the fourth book of Lucretius; and I can less easily answer why I translated it, than why I thus translated it. The objection arises from the obscenity of the subject, which is aggravated by the too lively and alluring delicacy of the verses. In the first place, without the least formality of an excuse, I own it pleas'd me: and let my enemies make the worst they can of this confession; I am not yet so secure from that passion, but that I want my author's antidotes against it. He has given the truest and most philosophical account both of the disease and remedy, which I ever found in any author: for which reasons I translated him. But it will be ask'd why I turn'd him into this luscious English — for I will not give it a worse word. Instead of an answer, I would ask again of my supercilious adversaries, whether I am not bound, when I translate an author, to do him all the right I can, and to translate him to the best advantage? If, to mince his meaning, which I am satisfied was honest and instructive, I had either omitted some part of what he said, or taken from the strength of his expression, I certainly had wrong'd him; and that freeness of thought and words being thus cashier'd in my hands, he had no longer been Lucretius. If nothing of this kind be to be read, physicians must not study nature, anatomies must not be seen, and somewhat I could say of particular passages in books, which, to avoid profaneness, I do not name. But the intention qualifies the act; and both mine and my author's were to instruct as well as please. 'T is most certain that barefac'd bawdry is the poorest pretense to wit imaginable. If I should say otherwise, I should have two great authorities against me. The one is the *Essay on Poetry*, which I publicly valued before I knew the author of it, and with the commendation of which my Lord Roscommon so happily begins his *Essay on Translated Verse*; the other is no less than our admir'd Cowley, who says the same thing in other words: for in his *Ode concerning Wit*, he writes thus of it:

Much less can that have any place,
At which a virgin hides her face:
Such dross the fire must purge away; 'tis just
The author blush, there where the reader must.

Here indeed Mr. Cowley goes farther than the *Essay*; for he asserts plainly that obscenity has no place in wit; the other only says, 'tis a poor pretense to it, or an ill sort of wit, which has nothing more to support it than barefac'd ribaldry; which is both unmannerly in itself, and fulsome to the reader. But neither of these will reach my case: for in the first place, I am only the translator, not the inventor; so that the heaviest part of the censure falls upon Lucretius, before it reaches me; in the next place, neither he nor I have us'd the grossest words, but the cleanliest metaphors we could find, to palliate the broadness of the meaning; and, to conclude, have carried the poetical part no farther than the philosophical exacted.

There is one mistake of mine which I will not lay to the printer's charge, who has enough to answer for in false pointings. 'T is in the word *viper;* I would have the verse run thus:

The scorpion, love, must on the wound be bruis'd.

There are a sort of blundering half-witted people, who make a great deal of noise about a verbal slip; tho' Horace would instruct them better in true criticism:

—— Non ego paucis
Offendor maculis quas aut incuria fudit,
Aut humana parum cavit natura.

True judgment in poetry, like that in painting, takes a view of the whole together, whether it be good or not; and where the beauties are more than the faults, concludes for the poet against the little judge. 'T is a sign that malice is hard driven, when 't is forc'd to lay hold on a word or syllable: to arraign a man is one thing, and to cavil at him is another. In the midst of an ill-natur'd generation of scribblers, there is always justice enough left in mankind to protect good writers; and they too are oblig'd, both by humanity and interest, to espouse each other's cause against false critics, who are the common enemies.

This last consideration puts me in mind of what I owe to the ingenious and learned translator of Lucretius. I have not here design'd to rob him of any part of that commendation which he has so justly acquir'd by the whole author, whose fragments only fall to my portion. What I have now perform'd, is no more than I intended above twenty years ago. The ways of our translation are very different; he follows him more closely than I have done, which became an interpreter of the whole poem: I take more liberty, because it best suited with my design, which was to make him as pleasing as I could. He had been too voluminous, had he us'd my method in so long a work; and I had certainly taken his, had I made it my business to translate the whole. The preference then is justly his; and I join with Mr. Evelyn in the confession of it, with this additional advantage to him, that his reputation is already establish'd in this poet, mine is to make its fortune in the world. If I have been anywhere obscure, in following our common author, or if Lucretius himself is to be condemn'd, I refer myself to his excellent annotations, which I have often read, and always with some new pleasure.

My preface begins already to swell upon me, and looks as if I were afraid of my reader, by so tedious a bespeaking of him: and yet I have Horace and Theocritus upon my hands; but the Greek gentleman shall quickly be dispatch'd, because I have more business with the Roman.

That which distinguishes Theocritus from all other poets, both Greek and Latin, and which raises him even above Virgil in his *Eclogues,* is the inimitable tenderness of his passions, and the natural expression of them in words so becoming of a pastoral. A simplicity shines thro' all he writes; he shows his art and learning by disguising both. His shepherds never rise above their country education in their complaints of love. There is the same difference betwixt him and Virgil, as there is betwixt Tasso's *Aminta* and the *Pastor Fido* of Guarini. Virgil's shepherds are too well-read in the philosophy of Epicurus and of Plato, and Guarini's seem to have been bred in courts; but Theocritus and Tasso have taken theirs from cottages and plains. It was said of Tasso, in relation to his similitudes, *mai esce del bosco;* that he never departed from the woods, that is, all his comparisons were taken from the country. The same may be said of our Theocritus. He is softer than Ovid; he touches the passions more delicately and performs all this out of his own *fond,* without diving into the arts and sciences for a supply. Even his Doric dialect has an incomparable sweetness in its clownishness, like a fair shepherdess in her country russet, talking in a Yorkshire tone. This was impossible for Virgil to imitate, because the severity of the Roman language denied him that advantage. Spenser has endeavor'd it in his *Shepherds' Calendar;* but neither will it succeed in English; for which reason I forbore to attempt it. For Theocritus writ to Sicilians, who spoke that dialect; and I direct this part of my translations to our ladies, who neither understand nor will take pleasure in such homely expressions. I proceed to Horace.

Take him in parts, and he is chiefly to be consider'd in his three different talents, as he was a critic, a satirist, and a writer of odes. His morals are uniform, and run thro' all of them; for, let his Dutch commentators say what they will, his philosophy was Epicurean; and he made use of gods and providence only to serve a turn in poetry. But since neither his criticisms, which are the most instructive of any that are written in this art, nor his satires, which are incomparably beyond Juvenal's, if to laugh and rally is to be preferr'd to railing and declaiming, are any part of my present undertaking, I confine myself wholly to his odes. These are also of several sorts: some of them are panegyrical, others moral, the rest jovial, or (if I may so call them) Bacchanalian. As difficult as he makes it, and as indeed it is, to imitate Pindar, yet, in his most elevated flights, and in the sudden changes of his subject with almost imperceptible connections, that Theban poet is his master. But Horace is of the more bounded fancy, and confines himself strictly to one sort of verse, or stanza, in every ode. That which will distinguish his style from all other poets is the elegance of his words, and the numerousness of his verse: there is nothing so delicately turn'd in all the Roman language. There appears in every part of his diction, or (to speak English) in all his expressions, a kind of noble and bold purity. His words are chosen with as much exactness as Virgil's; but there seems to be a greater spirit in them. There is a secret happiness attends his choice, which in Petronius is called *curiosa felicitas*, and which I suppose he had from the *feliciter audere* of Horace himself. But the most distinguishing part of all his character seems to me to be his briskness, his jollity, and his good humor; and those I have chiefly endeavor'd to copy. His other excellencies, I confess, are above my imitation. One ode, which infinitely pleas'd me in the reading, I have attempted to translate in Pindaric verse: 't is that which is inscrib'd to the present Earl of Rochester, to whom I have particular obligations, which this small testimony of my gratitude can never pay. 'T is his darling in the Latin, and I have taken some pains to make it my masterpiece in English; for which reason I took this kind of verse, which allows more latitude than any other. Everyone knows it was introduc'd into our language, in this age, by the happy genius of Mr. Cowley. The seeming easiness of it has made it spread; but it has not been consider'd enough, to be so well cultivated. It languishes in almost every hand but his, and some very few, whom, to keep the rest in countenance, I do not name. He, indeed, has brought it as near perfection as was possible in so short a time. But if I may be allow'd to speak my mind modestly, and without injury to his sacred ashes, somewhat of the purity of English, somewhat of more equal thoughts, somewhat of sweetness in the numbers, in one word, somewhat of a finer turn, and more lyrical verse, is yet wanting. As for the soul of it, which consists in the warmth and vigor of fancy, the masterly figures, and the copiousness of imagination, he has excell'd all others in this kind.

Yet, if the kind itself be capable of more perfection, tho' rather in the ornamental parts of it, than the essential, what rules of morality or respect have I broken, in naming the defects, that they may hereafter be amended? Imitation is a nice point, and there are few poets who deserve to be models in all they write. Milton's *Paradise Lost* is admirable; but am I therefore bound to maintain that there are no flats amongst his elevations, when 't is evident he creeps along sometimes, for above an hundred lines together? Cannot I admire the height of his invention, and the strength of his expression, without defending his antiquated words, and the perpetual harshness of their sound? 'T is as much commendation as a man can bear, to own him excellent; all beyond it is idolatry.

Since Pindar was the prince of lyric poets, let me have leave to say that, in imitating him, our numbers should, for the most part, be lyrical. For variety, or rather where the majesty of the thought requires it, they may be stretch'd to the English heroic of five feet, and to the French Alexandrine of six. But the ear must preside, and direct the judgment to the choice of numbers. Without the nicety of this, the harmony of Pindaric verse can never be complete: the cadency of one line must be a rule to that of the next; and the sound of the former must slide gently into that which follows, without leaping from one extreme into another. It must be done like the shadowings of a picture, which fall by degrees into a darker color. I shall be glad, if I have so explain'd myself as to be understood; but if I have not, *quod nequeo dicere, et sentio tantum*, must be my excuse.

There remains much more to be said on this subject; but, to avoid envy, I will be silent. What I have said is the general opinion of the best judges, and in a manner has been forc'd from me, by seeing a noble sort of poetry so happily restor'd by one man, and so grossly copied by almost all the rest. A musical ear, and a great genius, if another Mr. Cowley could arise, in another age may bring it to perfection. In the mean time:

—— Fungar vice cotis, acutum
Reddere quæ ferrum valet, expers ipsa secandi.

I hope it will not be expected from me that I should say anything of my fellow-undertakers in this *Miscellany*. Some of them are too nearly related to me to be commended without suspicion of partiality: others, I am sure, need it not; and the rest I have not perus'd.

To conclude, I am sensible that I have written this too hastily and too loosely: I fear I have been tedious, and, which is worse, it comes out from the first draught, and uncorrected.

This, I grant, is no excuse; for it may be reasonably urg'd, why did he not write with more leisure, or, if he had it not, (which was certainly my case,) why did he attempt to write on so nice a subject? The objection is unanswerable; but in part of recompense, let me assure the reader, that, in hasty productions, he is sure to meet with an author's present sense, which cooler thoughts would possibly have disguis'd. There is undoubtedly more of spirit, tho' not of judgment, in these uncorrect essays, and consequently, tho' my hazard be the greater, yet the reader's pleasure is not the less.

JOHN DRYDEN.

LUCRETIUS

THE BEGINNING OF THE FIRST BOOK

DELIGHT of humankind, and gods above,
Parent of Rome, propitious Queen of Love,
Whose vital pow'r, air, earth, and sea supplies,
And breeds whate'er is born beneath the rolling skies:
For every kind, by thy prolific might,
Springs, and beholds the regions of the light.
Thee, goddess, thee the clouds and tempests fear,
And at thy pleasing presence disappear:
For thee the land in fragrant flow'rs is dress'd;
For thee the ocean smiles, and smooths her wavy breast; 10
And heav'n itself with more serene and purer light is blest.
For when the rising spring adorns the mead,
And a new scene of nature stands display'd,
When teeming buds and cheerful greens appear,
And western gales unlock the lazy year;
The joyous birds thy welcome first express,
Whose native songs thy genial fire confess;
Then salvage beasts bound o'er their slighted food,
Strook with thy darts, and tempt the raging flood.
All nature is thy gift; earth, air, and sea: 20
Of all that breathes, the various progeny,
Stung with delight, is goaded on by thee.

O'er barren mountains, o'er the flow'ry plain,
The leavy forest, and the liquid main,
Extends thy uncontroll'd and boundless reign.
Thro' all the living regions dost thou move,
And scatter'st, where thou goest, the kindly seeds of love.
Since then the race of every living thing
Obeys thy pow'r; since nothing new can spring
Without thy warmth, without thy influence bear, 30
Or beautiful, or lovesome can appear;
Be thou my aid, my tuneful song inspire,
And kindle with thy own productive fire;
While all thy province, Nature, I survey,
And sing to Memmius an immortal lay
Of heav'n and earth, and everywhere thy wondrous pow'r display:
To Memmius, under thy sweet influence born,
Whom thou with all thy gifts and graces dost adorn.
The rather, then, assist my Muse and me,
Infusing verses worthy him and thee. 40
Meantime on land and sea let barb'rous discord cease,
And lull the list'ning world in universal peace.
To thee mankind their soft repose must owe,
For thou alone that blessing canst bestow;
Because the brutal business of the war
Is manag'd by thy dreadful servant's care;
Who oft retires from fighting fields, to prove
The pleasing pains of thy eternal love;
And, panting on thy breast, supinely lies,
While with thy heavenly form he feeds his famish'd eyes; 50
Sucks in with open lips thy balmy breath,
By turns restor'd to life, and plung'd in pleasing death.
There while thy curling limbs about him move,
Involv'd and fetter'd in the links of love,
When, wishing all, he nothing can deny,
Thy charms in that auspicious moment try;
With winning eloquence our peace implore,
And quiet to the weary world restore.

LUCRETIUS

THE BEGINNING OF THE SECOND BOOK

Suave mari magno, &c.

'T is pleasant, safely to behold from shore
The rolling ship, and hear the tempest
    roar:
Not that another's pain is our delight;
But pains unfelt produce the pleasing sight.
'T is pleasant also to behold from far
The moving legions mingled in the war;
But much more sweet thy lab'ring steps ⎫
    to guide   ⎪
To virtue's heights, with wisdom well ⎬
    supplied,   ⎪
And all the magazines of learning forti-⎭
    fied: 9
From thence to look below on humankind,
Bewilder'd in the maze of life, and blind:
To see vain fools ambitiously contend
For wit and pow'r; their lost endeavors bend
T' outshine each other, waste their time
    and health
In search of honor, and pursuit of wealth.
    O wretched man! in what a mist of life,
Inclos'd with dangers and with noisy strife,
He spends his little span, and overfeeds
His cramm'd desires with more than nature
    needs!
For nature wisely stints our appetite,   20
And craves no more than undisturb'd de-
    light:
Which minds, unmix'd with cares and fears,
    obtain;
A soul serene, a body void of pain.
So little this corporeal frame requires;
So bounded are our natural desires,
That wanting all, and setting pain aside,
With bare privation sense is satisfied.
If golden sconces hang not on the walls,
To light the costly suppers and the balls;
If the proud palace shines not with the
    state   30
Of burnish'd bowls, and of reflected plate;
If well-tun'd harps, nor the more pleasing
    sound
Of voices, from the vaulted roofs rebound;
Yet on the grass, beneath a poplar shade,
By the cool stream our careless limbs are
    laid;
With cheaper pleasures innocently blest,
When the warm spring with gaudy flow'rs
    is dress'd.

Nor will the raging fever's fire abate
With golden canopies and beds of state;
But the poor patient will as soon be sound
On the hard mattress, or the mother
    ground.   41
    Then since our bodies are not eas'd the
        more
By birth, or pow'r, or fortune's wealthy
    store,
'T is plain, these useless toys of every kind
As little can relieve the lab'ring mind:
Unless we could suppose the dreadful sight
Of marshal'd legions moving to the fight,
Could, with their sound and terrible array,
Expel our fears, and drive the thoughts of
    death away.
But, since the supposition vain appears, 50
Since clinging cares, and trains of inbred
    fears,
Are not with sounds to be affrighted thence,
But in the midst of pomp pursue the prince,
Not aw'd by arms, but in the presence bold,
Without respect to purple or to gold;
Why should not we these pageantries de-
    spise,
Whose worth but in our want of reason
    lies?
For life is all in wand'ring errors led;
And just as children are surpris'd with
    dread,
And tremble in the dark, so riper years 60
Ev'n in broad daylight are possess'd with
    fears,
And shake at shadows fanciful and vain
As those which in the breasts of children
    reign.
These bugbears of the mind, this inward
    hell,
No rays of outward sunshine can dispel;
But nature and right reason must display
Their beams abroad, and bring the dark-
    some soul to day.

LUCRETIUS

THE LATTER PART OF THE THIRD BOOK

AGAINST THE FEAR OF DEATH

WHAT has this bugbear death to frighten
    man,
If souls can die, as well as bodies can?
For, as before our birth we felt no pain,
When Punic arms infested land and main,

When heav'n and earth were in confusion
        hurl'd,
For the debated empire of the world,
Which aw'd with dreadful expectation lay,
Sure to be slaves, uncertain who should
        sway:
So, when our mortal frame shall be dis-
        join'd,
The lifeless lump uncoupled from the
        mind,   10
From sense of grief and pain we shall be
        free;
We shall not feel, because we shall not be.
Tho' earth in seas, and seas in heav'n were
        lost,
We should not move, we only should be
        toss'd.
Nay, ev'n suppose when we have suffer'd
        fate,
The soul could feel in her divided state,
What 's that to us ? for we are only we
While souls and bodies in one frame agree.
Nay, tho' our atoms should revolve by
        chance,
And matter leap into the former dance; 20
Tho' time our life and motion could re-
        store,
And make our bodies what they were be-
        fore,
What gain to us would all this bustle
        bring ?
The new-made man would be another
        thing.
When once an interrupting pause is made,
That individual being is decay'd.
We, who are dead and gone, shall bear no
        part
In all the pleasures, nor shall feel the
        smart
Which to that other mortal shall accrue,
Whom of our matter time shall mold
        anew.   30
For backward if you look on that long
        space
Of ages past, and view the changing face
Of matter, toss'd and variously combin'd
In sundry shapes, 't is easy for the mind
From thence t' infer, that seeds of things
        have been
In the same order as they now are seen:
Which yet our dark remembrance cannot
        trace,
Because a pause of life, a gaping space,
Has come betwixt, where memory lies
        dead,

And all the wand'ring motions from the
        sense are fled.   40
For whosoe'er shall in misfortunes live,
Must be, when those misfortunes shall ar-
        rive;
And since the man who is not, feels not
        woe,
(For death exempts him, and wards off the
        blow,
Which we, the living, only feel and bear,)
What is there left for us in death to fear ?
When once that pause of life has come be-
        tween,
'T is just the same as we had never been.
        And therefore if a man bemoan his lot,
That after death his mold'ring limbs shall
        rot,   50
Or flames, or jaws of beasts devour his
        mass,
Know, he 's an unsincere, unthinking ass.
A secret sting remains within his mind;
The fool is to his own cast offals kind.
He boasts no sense can after death re-
        main,
Yet makes himself a part of life again,
As if some other He could feel the pain.
If, while he live, this thought molest his
        head,
What wolf or vulture shall devour me
        dead ?
He wastes his days in idle grief, nor can 60
Distinguish 'twixt the body and the man;
But thinks himself can still himself survive;
And, what when dead he feels not, feels
        alive.
Then he repines that he was born to die,
Nor knows in death there is no other He,
No living He remains his grief to vent,
And o'er his senseless carcass to lament.
If after death 't is painful to be torn
By birds, and beasts, then why not so to
        burn;
Or, drench'd in floods of honey, to be
        soak'd;   70
Imbalm'd, to be at once preserv'd and
        chok'd;
Or on an airy mountain's top to lie,
Expos'd to cold and heav'n's inclemency;
Or crowded in a tomb to be oppress'd
With monumental marble on thy breast ?
        But to be snatch'd from all thy house-
        hold joys,
From thy chaste wife, and thy dear prat-
        tling boys,
Whose little arms about thy legs are cast,

And climbing for a kiss prevent their
    mother's haste,
Inspiring secret pleasure thro' thy breast —
All these shall be no more: thy friends op-
    press'd   81
Thy care and courage now no more shall
    free;
" Ah ! wretch ! " thou cry'st, " ah ! miser-
    able me !
One woful day sweeps children, friends, and
    wife,
And all the brittle blessings of my life ! "
Add one thing more, and all thou say'st is
    true;
Thy want and wish of them is vanish'd too:
Which, well consider'd, were a quick relief
To all thy vain imaginary grief.
For thou shalt sleep, and never wake
    again,   90
And, quitting life, shalt quit thy living pain.
But we, thy friends, shall all those sor-⎤
    rows find, |
Which in forgetful death thou leav'st ⎬
    behind; |
No time shall dry our tears, nor drive |
    thee from our mind.   ⎦
The worst that can befall thee, measur'd
    right,
Is a sound slumber, and a long good-night.
Yet thus the fools, that would be thought
    the wits,
Disturb their mirth with melancholy fits:
When healths go round, and kindly brim-
    mers flow,
Till the fresh garlands on their foreheads
    glow,   100
They whine, and cry: " Let us make haste
    to live.
Short are the joys that human life can give."
Eternal preachers, that corrupt the draught,
And pall the god, that never thinks, with
    thought;
Idiots with all that thought, to whom the
    worst
Of death is want of drink, and endless
    thirst,
Or any fond desire as vain as these.
For ev'n in sleep, the body, wrapp'd in ease,
Supinely lies, as in the peaceful grave;
And, wanting nothing, nothing can it
    crave.   110
Were that sound sleep eternal, it were
    death;
Yet the first atoms then, the seeds of
    breath,

Are moving near to sense; we do but shake
And rouse that sense, and straight we are
    awake.
Then death to us, and death's anxiety,
Is less than nothing, if a less could be.
For then our atoms, which in order lay,
Are scatter'd from their heap, and puff'd
    away,
And never can return into their place,
When once the pause of life has left an
    empty space.   120
    And last, suppose great Nature's voice
    should call
To thee, or me, or any of us all:
" What dost thou mean, ungrateful wretch,
    thou vain,
Thou mortal thing, thus idly to complain,
And sigh and sob that thou shalt be no
    more ?
For if thy life were pleasant heretofore,
If all the bounteous blessings, I could⎤
    give, |
Thou hast enjoy'd; if thou hast known ⎬
    to live, |
And pleasure not leak'd thro' thee like |
    a sieve;   ⎦
Why dost thou not give thanks as at a
    plenteous feast,   130
Cramm'd to the throat with life, and rise
    and take thy rest ?
But if my blessings thou hast thrown away,
If indigested joys pass'd thro', and would
    not stay,
Why dost thou wish for more to squander
    still ?
If life be grown a load, a real ill,
And I would all thy cares and labors end,
Lay down thy burden, fool, and know thy
    friend.
To please thee, I have emptied all my⎤
    store; |
I can invent and can supply no more,   ⎬
But run the round again, the round I ran |
    before.   140 ⎦
Suppose thou art not broken yet with
    years,
Yet still the selfsame scene of things ap-
    pears,
And would be ever, couldst thou ever live;
For life is still but life, there 's nothing new
    to give."
What can we plead against so just a bill ?
We stand convicted, and our cause goes ill.
    But if a wretch, a man oppress'd by fate,
Should beg of Nature to prolong his date,

She speaks aloud to him with more disdain:
" Be still, thou martyr fool, thou covetous
   of pain."   150
But if an old decrepit sot lament;
" What, thou," she cries, " who hast outliv'd
   content !
Dost thou complain, who hast enjoy'd my
   store ?
But this is still th' effect of wishing more.
Unsatisfied with all that Nature brings;
Loathing the present, liking absent things;
From hence it comes, thy vain desires, at
   strife
Within themselves, have tantaliz'd thy
   life;
And ghastly death appear'd before thy
   sight,
Ere thou hadst gorg'd thy soul and senses
   with delight.   160
Now leave those joys, unsuiting to thy age,
To a fresh comer, and resign the stage."
  Is Nature to be blam'd if thus she chide ?
No, sure; for 't is her business to provide,
Against this ever-changing frame's decay,
New things to come, and old to pass away.
One being, worn, another being makes;
Chang'd, but not lost; for Nature gives and
   takes:
New matter must be found for things to
   come,
And these must waste like those, and fol-
   low Nature's doom.   170
All things, like thee, have time to rise and
   rot;
And from each other's ruin are begot:
For life is not confin'd to him or thee;
'T is given to all for use, to none for pro-
   perty.
  Consider former ages past and gone,
Whose circles ended long ere thine begun,
Then tell me, fool, what part in them thou
   hast.
Thus may'st thou judge the future by the
   past.
What horror see'st thou in that quiet state ?
What bugbear dreams to fright thee after
   fate ?   180
No ghost, no goblins, that still passage keep;
But all is there serene, in that eternal
   sleep.
For all the dismal tales that poets tell
Are verified on earth, and not in hell.
No Tantalus looks up with fearful eye,
Or dreads th' impending rock to crush him
   from on high;

But fear of chance on earth disturbs our
   easy hours,
Or vain imagin'd wrath of vain imagin'd
   pow'rs.
No Tityus torn by vultures lies in hell;
Nor could the lobes of his rank liver
   swell   190
To that prodigious mass for their eternal
   meal:
Not tho' his monstrous bulk had cover'd
   o'er
Nine spreading acres, or nine thousand
   more;
Not tho' the globe of earth had been the
   giant's floor:
Nor in eternal torments could he lie,
Nor could his corpse sufficient food supply.
But he 's the Tityus, who by love op-
   press'd,
Or tyrant passion preying on his breast,
And ever-anxious thoughts, is robb'd of
   rest.
The Sisyphus is he, whom noise and strife
Seduce from all the soft retreats of life, 201
To vex the government, disturb the laws:
Drunk with the fumes of popular applause,
He courts the giddy crowd to make him
   great,
And sweats and toils in vain, to mount the
   sovereign seat.
For still to aim at pow'r, and still to fail,
Ever to strive, and never to prevail,
What is it, but, in reason's true account,
To heave the stone against the rising
   mount ?
Which urg'd, and labor'd, and forc'd up
   with pain,   210
Recoils, and rolls impetuous down, and
   smokes along the plain.
Then still to treat thy ever-craving mind
With ev'ry blessing, and of ev'ry kind,
Yet never fill thy rav'ning appetite;
Tho' years and seasons vary thy delight,
Yet nothing to be seen of all the store,
But still the wolf within thee barks for
   more;
This is the fable's moral, which they tell
Of fifty foolish virgins damn'd in hell
To leaky vessels, which the liquor spill; 220
To vessels of their sex, which none could
   ever fill.
As for the Dog, the Furies, and their
   snakes,
The gloomy caverns, and the burning lakes,
And all the vain infernal trumpery,

They neither are, nor were, nor e'er can be.
But here on earth the guilty have in view
The mighty pains to mighty mischiefs due;
Racks, prisons, poisons, the Tarpeian rock,
Stripes, hangmen, pitch, and suffocating
    smoke;
And last, and most, if these were cast be-
    hind,   230
Th' avenging horror of a conscious mind,
Whose deadly fear anticipates the blow,
And sees no end of punishment and woe;
But looks for more, at the last gasp of
    breath:
This makes a hell on earth, and life a
    death.
    Meantime, when thoughts of death dis-
      turb thy head;
Consider, Ancus, great and good, is dead;
Ancus, thy better far, was born to die;
And thou, dost thou bewail mortality?
So many monarchs with their mighty state,
Who rul'd the world, were overrul'd by
    fate.   241
That haughty king, who lorded o'er the
    main,
And whose stupendous bridge did the wild
    waves restrain,
(In vain they foam'd, in vain they threat-
    en'd wreck,
While his proud legions march'd upon their
    back,)
Him death, a greater monarch, overcame;
Nor spar'd his guards the more, for their
    immortal name.
The Roman chief, the Carthaginian dread,
Scipio, the thunderbolt of war, is dead,
And, like a common slave, by fate in tri-
    umph led.   250
The founders of invented arts are lost;
And wits, who made eternity their boast.
Where now is Homer, who possess'd the
    throne?
Th' immortal work remains, the mortal
    author's gone.
Democritus, perceiving age invade,
His body weaken'd, and his mind decay'd,
Obey'd the summons with a cheerful face;
Made haste to welcome death, and met
    him half the race.
That stroke ev'n Epicurus could not bar,
Tho' he in wit surpass'd mankind, as far
As does the midday sun the midnight
    star.   261
And thou, dost thou disdain to yield thy
    breath,

Whose very life is little more than death?
More than one half by lazy sleep pos-
    sess'd;
And when awake, thy soul but nods at
    best,
Day-dreams and sickly thoughts revolv-
    ing in thy breast.
Eternal troubles haunt thy anxious mind,
Whose cause and cure thou never hop'st to
    find;
But still uncertain, with thyself at strife,
Thou wander'st in the labyrinth of life. 270
    O, if the foolish race of man, who find
A weight of cares still pressing on their
    mind,
Could find as well the cause of this unrest,
And all this burden lodg'd within the breast;
Sure they would change their course, nor
    live as now,
Uncertain what to wish or what to vow.
Uneasy both in country and in town,
They search a place to lay their burden
    down.
One, restless in his palace, walks abroad,
And vainly thinks to leave behind the
    load;   280
But straight returns, for he's as restless
    there,
And finds there's no relief in open air.
Another to his villa would retire,
And spurs as hard as if it were on fire;
No sooner enter'd at his country door,
But he begins to stretch, and yawn, and
    snore;
Or seeks the city which he left before.
Thus every man o'erworks his weary
    will,
To shun himself, and to shake off his ill;
The shaking fit returns, and hangs upon
    him still.   290
No prospect of repose, nor hope of ease;
The wretch is ignorant of his disease;
Which known would all his fruitless
    trouble spare,
For he would know the world not worth
    his care;
Then would he search more deeply for the
    cause;
And study nature well, and nature's laws:
For in this moment lies not the debate,
But on our future, fix'd, eternal state;
That never-changing state, which all must
    keep,
Whom death has doom'd to everlasting
    sleep.   300

Why are we then so fond of mortal life,
Beset with dangers, and maintain'd with
    strife ?
A life which all our care can never save;
One fate attends us, and one common grave.
Besides, we tread but a perpetual round;
We ne'er strike out, but beat the former
    ground,
And the same mawkish joys in the same
    track are found.
For still we think an absent blessing
    best,
Which cloys, and is no blessing when
    possess'd;
A new arising wish expels it from the
    breast.   310
The fev'rish thirst of life increases still;
We call for more and more, and never
    have our fill,
Yet know not what to-morrow we shall try,
What dregs of life in the last draught may
    lie:
Nor, by the longest life we can attain,
One moment from the length of death
    we gain;
For all behind belongs to his eternal
    reign.
When once the Fates have cut the mortal
    thread,
The man as much to all intents is dead,
Who dies to-day, and will as long be so, 320
As he who died a thousand years ago.

LUCRETIUS

THE FOURTH BOOK

CONCERNING THE NATURE OF LOVE

BEGINNING AT THIS LINE

Sic igitur Veneris qui telis accipit ictum, &c.

THUS, therefore, he who feels the fiery
    dart
Of strong desire transfix his amorous
    heart,
Whether some beauteous boy's alluring
    face,
Or lovelier maid, with unresisted grace,
From her each part the winged arrow
    sends,
From whence he first was struck he thither
    tends;
Restless he roams, impatient to be freed,
And eager to inject the sprightly seed;   8

For fierce desire does all his mind employ,
And ardent love assures approaching joy.
Such is the nature of that pleasing smart,
Whose burning drops distil upon the heart,
The fever of the soul shot from the fair,
And the cold ague of succeeding care.
If absent, her idea still appears,
And. her sweet name is chiming in your
    ears.
But strive those pleasing phantoms to re-
    move,
And shun th' aërial images of love,
That feed the flame: when one molests thy
    mind,
Discharge thy loins on all the leaky kind;
For that's a wiser way than to restrain   21
Within thy swelling nerves that hoard of
    pain.
For every hour some deadlier symptom
    shows,
And by delay the gath'ring venom grows,
When kindly applications are not us'd;
The viper, love, must on the wound be
    bruis'd.
On that one object 't is not safe to stay,
But force the tide of thought some other
    way;
The squander'd spirits prodigally throw,
And in the common glebe of nature sow. 30
Nor wants he all the bliss that lovers feign,
Who takes the pleasure, and avoids the
    pain;
For purer joys in purer health abound,
And less affect the sickly than the sound.
  When love its utmost vigor does imploy,
Ev'n then 't is but a restless wand'ring joy;
Nor knows the lover in that wild excess,
With hands or eyes, what first he would
    possess;
But strains at all, and, fast'ning where he
    strains,   39
Too closely presses with his frantic pains;
With biting kisses hurts the twining fair,
Which shews his joys imperfect, unsincere:
For, stung with inward rage, he flings
    around,
And strives t' avenge the smart on that
    which gave the wound.
But love those eager bitings does restrain,
And mingling pleasure mollifies the pain.
For ardent hope still flatters anxious grief,
And sends him to his foe to seek relief:
Which yet the nature of the thing denies;
For love, and love alone of all our joys,   50
By full possession does but fan the fire;

The more we still enjoy, the more we still
   desire.
Nature for meat and drink provides a space,
And, when receiv'd, they fill their certain
   place;
Hence thirst and hunger may be satisfied,
But this repletion is to love denied:
Form, feature, color, whatsoe'er delight
Provokes the lover's endless appetite,
These fill no space, nor can we thence re-
   move
With lips, or hands, or all our instruments
   of love: 60
In our deluded grasp we nothing find,
But thin aërial shapes, that fleet before the
   mind.
As he, who in a dream with drought is curst,
And finds no real drink to quench his thirst,
Runs to imagin'd lakes his heat to steep,
And vainly swills and labors in his sleep;
So love with phantoms cheats our longing
   eyes,
Which hourly seeing never satisfies:
Our hands pull nothing from the parts
   they strain,
But wander o'er the lovely limbs in vain.
Nor when the youthful pair more closely
   join,   71
When hands in hands they lock, and thighs
   in thighs they twine,
Just in the raging foam of full desire,
When both press on, both murmur, both
   expire,
They gripe, they squeeze, their humid
   tongues they dart,
As each would force their way to t'other's
   heart:
In vain; they only cruise about the coast;
For bodies cannot pierce, nor be in bodies
   lost,
As sure they strive to be, when both en-
   gage
In that tumultuous momentary rage;   80
So 'tangled in the nets of love they lie,
Till man dissolves in that excess of joy.
Then, when the gather'd bag has burst its
   way,
And ebbing tides the slacken'd nerves be-
   tray,
A pause ensues; and nature nods a while,
Till with recruited rage new spirits boil;
And then the same vain violence returns,
With flames renew'd th' erected furnace
   burns;
Again they in each other would be lost,

But still by adamantine bars are cross'd.   90
All ways they try, successless all they
   prove,
To cure the secret sore of ling'ring love.
   Besides ——
They waste their strength in the venereal
   strife,
And to a woman's will enslave their life;
Th' estate runs out, and mortgages are ⎤
   made,
All offices of friendship are decay'd,   ⎬
Their fortune ruin'd, and their fame be- ⎟
   tray'd.   ⎦
Assyrian ointment from their temples flows,
And diamond buckles sparkle at their
   shoes;   100
The cheerful emerald twinkles on their
   hands,
With all the luxury of foreign lands;
And the blue coat, that with imbroid'ry
   shines,
Is drunk with sweat of their o'er-labor'd
   loins.
Their frugal fathers' gains they misemploy,
And turn to point, and pearl, and ev'ry
   female toy.
French fashions, costly treats are their de-
   light;
The park by day, and plays and balls by
   night.
In vain ——
For in the fountain, where their sweets are
   sought,   110
Some bitter bubbles up, and poisons all the
   draught.
First, guilty Conscience does the mirror
   bring,
Then sharp Remorse shoots out her angry
   sting;
And anxious thoughts, within themselves
   at strife,
Upbraid the long misspent, luxurious life.
Perhaps, the fickle fair one proves unkind, ⎤
Or drops a doubtful word, that pains his ⎬
   mind,   ⎟
And leaves a rankling jealousy behind. ⎦
Perhaps, he watches close her amorous
   eyes,
And in the act of ogling does surprise,   120
And thinks he sees upon her cheeks the ⎤
   while
The dimpled tracks of some foregoing ⎬
   smile;   ⎟
His raging pulse beats thick, and his ⎦
   pent spirits boil.

This is the product ev'n of prosp'rous love;
Think then what pangs disastrous passions
   prove !
Innumerable ills; disdain, despair,
With all the meager family of care.
   Thus, as I said, 't is better to prevent,
Than flatter the disease, and late repent;
Because to shun th' allurement is not hard
To minds resolv'd, forewarn'd, and well
   prepar'd;   131
But wondrous difficult, when once beset,
To struggle thro' the straits, and break th'
   involving net.
Yet, thus insnar'd, thy freedom thou may'st
   gain,
If, like a fool, thou dost not hug thy chain;
If not to ruin obstinately blind,   ⎫
And wilfully endeavoring not to find   ⎬
Her plain defects of body and of mind. ⎭
For thus the *Bedlam* train of lovers use
T' inhance the value, and the faults ex-
   cuse;   140
And therefore 't is no wonder if we see
They dote on dowdies and deformity.
Ev'n what they cannot praise, they will not
   blame,
But veil with some extenuating name.
The sallow skin is for the swarthy put,
And love can make a slattern of a slut;
If cat-ey'd, then a Pallas is their love;
If freckled, she 's a party-color'd dove;
If little, then she 's life and soul all o'er;
An Amazon, the large two-handed whore.
She stammers: O, what grace in lisping
   lies !   151
If she says nothing, to be sure she 's wise.
If shrill, and with a voice to drown a
   choir,
Sharp-witted she must be, and full of fire.
The lean, consumptive wench, with coughs
   decay'd,
Is call'd a pretty, tight, and slender maid;
Th' o'er-grown, a goodly Ceres is express'd,
A bedfellow for Bacchus at the least.
Flat-nose the name of Satyr never misses,
And hanging blobber lips but pout for
   kisses.   160
The task were endless all the rest to trace;
Yet grant she were a Venus for her face
And shape, yet others equal beauty share,
And time was you could live without the
   fair;
She does no more, in that for which you
   woo,
Then homelier women full as well can do.

Besides, she daubs, and stinks so much of
   paint,
Her own attendants cannot bear the scent,
But laugh behind, and bite their lips to
   hold.   169
Meantime, excluded, and expos'd to cold,
The whining lover stands before the gates,
And there with humble adoration waits;
Crowning with flow'rs the threshold and
   the floor,
And printing kisses on th' obdurate door;
Who, if admitted in that nick of time,
If some unsav'ry whiff betray the crime,
Invents a quarrel straight, if there be none,
Or makes some faint excuses to be gone;
And calls himself a doting fool to serve,
Ascribing more than woman can deserve.
Which well they understand, like cunning
   queans,   181
And hide their nastiness behind the scenes,
From him they have allur'd, and would re-
   tain;
But to a piercing eye 't is all in vain:
For common sense brings all their cheats
   to view,
And the false light discovers by the true;
Which a wise harlot owns, and hopes to
   find
A pardon for defects that run thro' all the
   kind.
   Nor always do they feign the sweets of
   love,
When round the panting youth their pliant
   limbs they move,   190
And cling, and heave, and moisten ev'ry
   kiss;
They often share, and more than share the
   bliss:
From every part, ev'n to their inmost soul,
They feel the trickling joys, and run with
   vigor to the goal.
Stirr'd with the same impetuous desire,
Birds, beasts, and herds, and mares, their
   males require;
Because the throbbing nature in their
   veins
Provokes them to assuage their kindly
   pains.
The lusty leap th' expecting female stands,
By mutual heat compell'd to mutual bands.
Thus dogs with lolling tongues by love are
   tied,   201
Nor shouting boys nor blows their union
   can divide;
At either end they strive the link to loose,

In vain, for stronger Venus holds the noose.
Which never would those wretched lovers ⎫
   do, ⎪
But that the common heats of love they ⎬
   know; ⎪
The pleasure therefore must be shar'd in ⎪
   common too. ⎭
And when the woman's more prevailing
   juice
Sucks in the man's, the mixture will pro-
   duce
The mother's likeness; when the man pre-
   vails,   210
His own resemblance in the seed he seals.
But when we see the new-begotten race
Reflect the features of each parent's face,
Then of the father's and the mother's blood
The justly temper'd seed is understood;
When both conspire, with equal ardor bent,
From every limb the due proportion sent,
When neither party foils, when neither
   foil'd,
This gives the blended features of the
   child.
Sometimes the boy the grandsire's image
   bears;   220
Sometimes the more remote progenitor he
   shares;
Because the genial atoms of the seed
Lie long conceal'd ere they exert the breed;
And, after sundry ages past, produce
The tardy likeness of the latent juice.
Hence, families such different figures take,
And represent their ancestors in face, and
   hair, and make;
Because of the same seed, the voice, and ⎫
   hair, ⎪
And shape, and face, and other members ⎬
   are, ⎪
And the same antique mold the likeness ⎪
   does prepare.   230 ⎭
Thus oft the father's likeness does prevail
In females, and the mother's in the male;
For, since the seed is of a double kind,
From that where we the most resemblance
   find,
We may conclude the strongest tincture sent,
And that was in conception prevalent.
   Nor can the vain decrees of pow'rs above
Deny production to the act of love,
Or hinder fathers of that happy name,
Or with a barren womb the matron shame;
As many think, who stain with victims'
   blood   241
The mournful altars, and with incense load,

To bless the show'ry seed with future life,
And to impregnate the well-labor'd wife.
In vain they weary Heav'n with prayer, or
   fly
To oracles, or magic numbers try;
For barrenness of sexes will proceed
Either from too condens'd, or wat'ry seed:
The wat'ry juice too soon dissolves away,
And in the parts projected will not stay; 250
The too condens'd, unsoul'd, unwieldy mass,
Drops short, nor carries to the destin'd
   place;
Nor pierces to the parts, nor, tho' injected
   home,
Will mingle with the kindly moisture of
   the womb.
For nuptials are unlike in their success;
Some men with fruitful seed some women
   bless,
And from some men some women fruitful
   are,
Just as their constitutions join or jar:
And many seeming barren wives have been,
Who after, match'd with more prolific men,
Have fill'd a family with prattling boys; 261
And many, not supplied at home with joys,
Have found a friend abroad to ease their
   smart,
And to perform the sapless husband's part.
So much it does import that seed with seed
Should of the kindly mixture make the
   breed;
And thick with thin, and thin with thick
   should join,
So to produce and propagate the line.
Of such concernment too is drink and food,
T' incrassate, or attenuate the blood.   270
Of like importance is the posture too,
In which the genial feat of love we do;
For, as the females of the four-foot kind
Receive the leapings of their males behind,
So the good wives, with loins uplifted high,
And leaning on their hands, the fruitful
   stroke may try:
For in that posture will they best conceive;
Not when, supinely laid, they frisk and
   heave;
For active motions only break the blow, ⎫
And more of strumpets than of wives ⎪
   they show,   280 ⎬
When, answering stroke with stroke, the ⎪
   mingled liquors flow. ⎭
Endearments eager, and too brisk a bound,
Throws off the plowshare from the furrow'd
   ground.

But common harlots in conjunction heave,
Because 't is less their business to conceive
Than to delight, and to provoke the deed;
A trick which honest wives but little need.
Nor is it from the gods, or Cupid's dart,
That many a homely woman takes the
    heart.
But wives well-humor'd, dutiful, and
    chaste,   290
And clean, will hold their wand'ring hus-
    bands fast;
Such are the links of love, and such a
    love will last.
For what remains, long habitude, and use,
Will kindness in domestic bands produce;
For custom will a strong impression leave.
Hard bodies, which the lightest stroke re-
    ceive,
In length of time will molder and decay,
And stones with drops of rain are wash'd
    away.

LUCRETIUS

FROM BOOK THE FIFTH

Tum porro puer, &c.

THUS, like a sailor by the tempest hurl'd
Ashore, the babe is shipwrack'd on the
    world:
Naked he lies, and ready to expire;
Helpless of all that human wants require;
Expos'd upon unhospitable earth,
From the first moment of his hapless birth.
Straight with foreboding cries he fills the
    room;
Too true presages of his future doom.
But flocks and herds, and every savage
    beast,
By more indulgent nature are increas'd. 10
They want no rattles for their froward
    mood,
Nor nurse to reconcile them to their food,
With broken words; nor winter blasts they
    fear,
Nor change their habits with the changing
    year;
Nor, for their safety, citadels prepare;
Nor forge the wicked instruments of war:
Unlabor'd Earth her bounteous treasure
    grants,
And Nature's lavish hand supplies their
    common wants.

THEOCRITUS: IDYLLIUM THE EIGHTEENTH

THE

EPITHALAMIUM OF HELEN AND MENELAUS

TWELVE Spartan virgins, noble, young, and
    fair,
With violet wreaths adorn'd their flowing
    hair,
And to the pompous palace did resort,
Where Menelaus kept his royal court.
There hand in hand a comely choir they
    led;
To sing a blessing to his nuptial bed,
With curious needles wrought, and painted
    flowers bespread.
Jove's beauteous daughter now his bride
    must be,
And Jove himself was less a god than he:
For this their artful hands instruct the lute
    to sound,   10
Their feet assist their hands, and justly
    beat the ground.
This was their song:
    "Why, happy bridegroom, why,
Ere yet the stars are kindled in the sky,
Ere twilight shades, or evening dews are
    shed,
Why dost thou steal so soon away to
    bed?
Has Somnus brush'd thy eyelids with his
    rod,
Or do thy legs refuse to bear their load
With flowing bowls of a more generous
    god?
If gentle slumber on thy temples creep,
(But, naughty man, thou dost not mean to
    sleep,)   20
Betake thee to thy bed, thou drowsy drone,
Sleep by thyself, and leave thy bride alone:
Go, leave her with her maiden mates to play
At sports more harmless, till the break of
    day:
Give us this evening; thou hast morn and
    night,
And all the year before thee, for delight.
O happy youth! to thee, among the crowd
Of rival princes, Cupid sneez'd aloud;
And every lucky *omen* sent before,
To meet thee landing on the Spartan shore.
Of all our heroes thou canst boast alone 31
That Jove, whene'er he thunders, calls thee
    son.

Betwixt two sheets thou shalt enjoy her
    bare,
With whom no Grecian virgin can com-
    pare;
So soft, so sweet, so balmy, and so fair.
A boy, like thee, would make a kingly line;
But O, a girl like her must be divine.
Her equals we, in years, but not in face,
Twelvescore *viragoes* of the Spartan race,
While naked to Eurotas' banks we bend, 40
And there in manly exercise contend,
When she appears, are all eclips'd and lost,
And hide the beauties that we made our
    boast.
So, when the night and winter disappear,
The purple Morning, rising with the year,
Salutes the Spring, as her celestial eyes
Adorn the world, and brighten all the
    skies:
So beauteous Helen shines among the rest,
Tall, slender, straight, with all the graces
    blest.
As pines the mountains, or as fields the
    corn, 50
Or as Thessalian steeds the race adorn;
So rosy-color'd Helen is the pride
Of Lacedæmon, and of Greece beside.
Like her no nymph can willing osiers
    bend
In basket-works, which painted streaks
    commend;
With Pallas in the loom she may con-
    tend.
But none, ah none can animate the lyre,
And the mute strings with vocal souls in-
    spire!
Whether the learn'd Minerva be her theme,
Or chaste Diana bathing in the stream; 60
None can record their heavenly praise so
    well
As Helen, in whose eyes ten thousand
    Cupids dwell.
O fair, O graceful! yet with maids inroll'd,
But whom to-morrow's sun a matron shall
    behold;
Yet ere to-morrow's sun shall show his
    head,
The dewy paths of meadows we will
    tread,
For crowns and chaplets to adorn thy
    head;
Where all shall weep, and wish for thy
    return,
As bleating lambs their absent mother
    mourn.

Our noblest maids shall to thy name be-
    queath 70
The boughs of *lotos*, form'd into a wreath.
This monument, thy maiden beauties' due,
High on a plane tree shall be hung to view;
On the smooth rind the passenger shall see
Thy name ingrav'd, and worship Helen's
    tree;
Balm, from a silver box distill'd around,
Shall all bedew the roots, and scent the
    sacred ground.
The balm, 'tis true, can aged plants pro-
    long,
But Helen's name will keep it ever young.
  "Hail bride, hail bridegroom, son-in-law
    to Jove! 80
With fruitful joys Latona bless your love!
Let Venus furnish you with full desires,
Add vigor to your wills, and fuel to your
    fires!
Almighty Jove augment your wealthy
    store,
Give much to you, and to his grandsons
    more!
From generous loins a generous race will
    spring;
Each girl, like her, a queen; each boy, like
    you, a king.
Now sleep, if sleep you can; but while you
    rest,
Sleep close, with folded arms, and breast to
    breast.
Rise in the morn; but O! before you
    rise, 90
Forget not to perform your morning sacri-
    fice.
We will be with you ere the crowing cock
Salutes the light, and struts before his
    feather'd flock.
Hymen, O Hymen, to thy triumphs run,
And view the mighty spoils thou hast in
    battle won."

THEOCRITUS: IDYLLIUM THE TWENTY-THIRD

THE DESPAIRING LOVER

WITH inauspicious love, a wretched swain
Pursued the fairest nymph of all the
    plain.
Fairest indeed, but prouder far than fair,
She plung'd him hopeless in a deep despair:
Her heavenly form too haughtily she priz'd,

His person hated, and his gifts despis'd;
Nor knew the force of Cupid's cruel darts,
Nor fear'd his awful pow'r on human hearts;
But either from her hopeless lover fled,
Or with disdainful glances shot him dead. 10
No kiss, no look, to cheer the drooping boy;
No word she spoke, she scorn'd ev'n to deny.
But, as a hunted panther casts about
Her glaring eyes, and pricks her list'ning
    ears to scout,
So she, to shun his toils, her cares im-
    ploy'd,
And fiercely in her savage freedom joy'd.
Her mouth she writh'd, her forehead taught
    to frown,
Her eyes to sparkle fires to love unknown:
Her sallow cheeks her envious mind did
    show,
And every feature spoke aloud the curst-
    ness of a shrew. 20
Yet could not he his obvious fate escape;
His love still dress'd her in a pleasing
    shape;
And every sullen frown, and bitter scorn,
But fann'd the fuel that too fast did burn.
Long time, unequal to his mighty pain,
He strove to curb it, but he strove in vain:
At last his woes broke out, and begg'd re-
    lief
With tears, the dumb petitioners of grief;
With tears so tender, as adorn'd his love,
And any heart, but only hers, would
    move. 30
Trembling before her bolted doors he stood,
And there pour'd out th' unprofitable flood:
Staring his eyes, and haggard was his look;
Then, kissing first the threshold, thus he
    spoke:
" Ah, nymph, more cruel than of human
    race !
Thy tigress heart belies thy angel face:
Too well thou show'st thy pedigree from
    stone;
Thy grandame's was the first by Pyrrha
    thrown:
Unworthy thou to be so long desir'd;
But so my love, and so my fate requir'd.
I beg not now (for 't is in vain) to live; 41
But take this gift, the last that I can give.
This friendly cord shall soon decide the
    strife
Betwixt my ling'ring love and loathsome
    life:
This moment puts an end to all my pain;
I shall no more despair, nor thou disdain.

Farewell, ungrateful and unkind ! I go
Condemn'd by thee to those sad shades be-
    low.
I go th' extremest remedy to prove, 49
To drink oblivion, and to drench my love;
There happily to lose my long desires —
But ah ! what draught so deep to quench my
    fires ?
Farewell, ye never-opening gates, ye stones,
And threshold guilty of my midnight
    moans !
What I have suffer'd here ye know too
    well;
What I shall do the gods and I can tell.
The rose is fragrant, but it fades in time;
The violet sweet, but quickly past the prime;
White lilies hang their heads, and soon de-
    cay,
And whiter snow in minutes melts away: 60
Such is your blooming youth, and withering
    so;
The time will come, it will, when you shall
    know
The rage of love; your haughty heart shall
    burn
In flames like mine, and meet a like re-
    turn.
    " Obdurate as you are, O hear at least
My dying prayers, and grant my last re-
    quest !
When first you ope your doors, and, pass-
    ing by,
The sad ill-omen'd object meets your eye,
Think it not lost, a moment if you stay;
The breathless wretch, so made by you,
    survey: 70
Some cruel pleasure will from thence arise,
To view the mighty ravage of your eyes.
I wish (but O ! my wish is vain, I fear)
The kind oblation of a falling tear:
Then loose the knot, and take me from the
    place,
And spread your mantle o'er my grisly face;
Upon my livid lips bestow a kiss:
O envy not the dead, they feel not bliss !
Nor fear your kisses can restore my breath;
Even you are not more pitiless than
    death. 80
Then for my corpse a homely grave pro-
    vide,
Which love and me from public scorn may
    hide;
Thrice call upon my name, thrice beat your
    breast,
And hail me thrice to everlasting rest;

Last let my tomb this sad inscription ⎫
    bear: .   ⎪
'A wretch whom love has kill'd lies ⎬
    buried here;   ⎪
O passengers, Amynta's eyes beware.' " ⎭
    Thus having said, and furious with his love,
He heav'd with more than human force to
    move
A weighty stone, (the labor of a team,) 90
And rais'd from thence he reach'd the
    neighboring beam;
Around its bulk a sliding knot he throws,
And fitted to his neck the fatal noose;
Then, spurning backward, took a swing,
    till death
Crept up, and stopp'd the passage of his
    breath.
    The bounce burst ope the door; the scorn-
      ful fair
Relentless look'd, and saw him beat his
    quivering feet in air;
Nor wept his fate, nor cast a pitying eye,
Nor took him down, but brush'd regardless
    by;
And, as she pass'd, her chance or fate was
    such,   100
Her garments touch'd the dead, polluted by
    the touch:
Next to the dance, thence to the bath did
    move —
The bath was sacred to the God of Love;
Whose injur'd image, with a wrathful eye,
Stood threat'ning from a pedestal on high:
Nodding a while, and watchful of his blow,
He fell; and falling crush'd th' ungrateful
    nymph below.
Her gushing blood the pavement all be-
    smear'd;
And this her last expiring voice was heard:
    " Lovers, farewell, revenge has reach'd
      my scorn: 110
    Thus warn'd, be wise, and love for love
      return."

DAPHNIS

FROM THEOCRITUS: IDYLLIUM THE
TWENTY-SEVENTH

DAPHNIS

The shepherd Paris bore the Spartan bride
By force away, and then by force enjoy'd;
But I by free consent can boast a bliss,
A fairer Helen, and a sweeter kiss.

CHLORIS

Kisses are empty joys, and soon are o'er.

DAPHNIS

A kiss betwixt the lips is something more.

CHLORIS

I wipe my mouth, and where's your kissing
    then ?

DAPHNIS

I swear you wipe it to be kiss'd again.

CHLORIS

Go, tend your herd, and kiss your cows at
    home;
I am a maid, and in my beauty's bloom. 10

DAPHNIS

'T is well remember'd; do not waste your
    time,
But wisely use it ere you pass your prime.

CHLORIS

Blown roses hold their sweetness to the last,
And raisins keep their luscious native taste.

DAPHNIS

The sun's too hot; those olive shades are
    near;
I fain would whisper something in your ear.

CHLORIS

'T is honest talking where we may be ⎫
    seen;   ⎪
God knows what secret mischief you may ⎬
    mean;   ⎪
I doubt you'll play the wag, and kiss ⎭
    again.

DAPHNIS

At least beneath yon elm you need not fear;
My pipe's in tune, if you're dispos'd to
    hear.   21

CHLORIS

Play by yourself, I dare not venture thither;
You, and your naughty pipe, go hang to-
    gether.

DAPHNIS

Coy nymph, beware, lest Venus you offend.

CHLORIS

I shall have chaste Diana still to friend.

DAPHNIS

You have a soul, and Cupid has a dart.

CHLORIS

Diana will defend, or heal my heart.
Nay, fie, what mean you in this open place?
Unhand me, or, I swear, I 'll scratch your
    face.
Let go for shame; you make me mad for
    spite;   30
My mouth 's my own; and, if you kiss, I 'll
    bite.

DAPHNIS

Away with your dissembling female tricks;
What, would you 'scape the fate of all your
    sex?

CHLORIS

I swear, I 'll keep my maidenhead till death,
And die as pure as Queen Elizabeth.

DAPHNIS

Nay, mum for that; but let me lay thee
    down;
Better with me than with some nauseous
    clown.

CHLORIS

I 'd have you know, if I were so inclin'd,
I have bin woo'd by many a wealthy
    hind;   39
But never found a husband to my mind.

DAPHNIS

But they are absent all, and I am here.

CHLORIS

The matrimonial yoke is hard to bear,
And marriage is a woful word to hear.

DAPHNIS

A scarecrow, set to frighten fools away;
Marriage has joys, and you shall have assay.

CHLORIS

Sour sauce is often mix'd with our de-
    light;
You kick by day more than you kiss by
    night.

DAPHNIS

Sham stories all; but say the worst you
    can,
A very wife fears neither God nor man.

CHLORIS

But childbirth is, they say, a deadly pain;
It costs at least a month to knit again.   51

DAPHNIS

Diana cures the wounds Lucina made;
Your goddess is a midwife by her trade.

CHLORIS

But I shall spoil my beauty, if I bear.

DAPHNIS

But Mam and Dad are pretty names to
    hear.

CHLORIS

But there 's a civil question us'd of late;
Where lies my jointure, where your own
    estate?

DAPHNIS

My flocks, my fields, my wood, my pastures
    take,
With settlement as good as law can make.

CHLORIS

Swear then you will not leave me on the
    common,   60
But marry me, and make an honest woman.

DAPHNIS

I swear by Pan, (tho' he wears horns you 'll
    say,)
Cudgell'd and kick'd, I 'll not be forc'd away.

CHLORIS

I bargain for a wedding bed at least,
A house, and handsome lodging for a guest.

DAPHNIS

A house well furnish'd shall be thine to
    keep;
And, for a flock bed, I can shear my sheep.

CHLORIS

What tale shall I to my old father tell?

DAPHNIS

'T will make him chuckle thou 'rt bestow'd
    so well.

CHLORIS

But, after all, in troth I am to blame   70
To be so loving, ere I know your name;
A pleasant-sounding name 's a pretty thing.

DAPHNIS

Faith, mine 's a very pretty name to sing.
They call me Daphnis; Lycidas my sire:
Both sound as well as woman can desire.
Nomæa bore me; farmers in degree;
He a good husband, a good housewife she.

CHLORIS

Your kindred is not much amiss, 't is true;
Yet I am somewhat better born than you.

DAPHNIS

I know your father, and his family;   80
And, without boasting, am as good as he:
Menalcas; and no master goes before.

CHLORIS

Hang both our pedigrees! not one word
    more;
But if you love me, let me see your living,
Your house, and home; for seeing is be-
    lieving.

DAPHNIS

See first yon cypress grove, a shade from
    noon.

CHLORIS

Browse on, my goats; for I 'll be with you
    soon.

DAPHNIS

Feed well, my bulls, to whet your appetite,
That each may take a lusty leap at night.

CHLORIS

What do you mean, uncivil as you are,   90
To touch my breasts, and leave my bosom
    bare?

DAPHNIS

These pretty bubbies, first, I make my own.

CHLORIS

Pull out your hand, I swear, or I shall
    swoon.

DAPHNIS

Why does thy ebbing blood forsake thy face?

CHLORIS

Throw me at least upon a cleaner place;
My linen ruffled, and my waistcoat soiling —
What, do you think new clothes were made
    for spoiling?

DAPHNIS

I 'll lay my lambskins underneath thy back.

CHLORIS

My headgear 's off; what filthy work you
    make.

DAPHNIS

To Venus, first, I lay these off'rings by.   100

CHLORIS

Nay, first look round, that nobody be nigh:
Methinks I hear a whisp'ring in the grove.

DAPHNIS

The cypress trees are telling tales of love.

CHLORIS

You tear off all behind me, and before me;
And I 'm as naked as my mother bore me.

DAPHNIS

I 'll buy thee better clothes than these I
    tear,
And lie so close I 'll cover thee from air.

CHLORIS

Y' are liberal now; but when your turn is
    sped,
You 'll wish me chok'd with every crust of
    bread.

DAPHNIS

I 'll give thee more, much more than I have
    told;   110
Would I could coin my very heart to gold!

CHLORIS

Forgive thy handmaid, huntress of the
    wood!
I see there 's no resisting flesh and blood!

DAPHNIS

The noble deed is done! My herds I 'll cull;
Cupid, be thine a calf; and, Venus, thine a
    bull.

CHLORIS

A maid I came, in an unlucky hour,
But hence return without my virgin flow'r.

DAPHNIS

A maid is but a barren name at best;
If thou canst hold, I bid for twins at least.

Thus did this happy pair their love dis-
  pense   120
With mutual joys, and gratified their
  sense:
The God of Love was there, a bidden
  guest,
And present at his own mysterious feast.
His azure mantle underneath he spread,
And scatter'd roses on the nuptial bed;
While folded in each other's arms they ⎤
  lay,   ⎥
He blew the flames, and furnish'd out the ⎬
  play,   ⎥
And from their foreheads wip'd the   ⎦
  balmy sweat away.
First rose the maid, and with a glowing
  face,
Her downcast eyes beheld her print upon
  the grass;   130
Thence to her herd she sped herself in ⎤
  haste: ⎥
The bridegroom started from his trance ⎬
  at last,   ⎥
And piping homeward jocundly he pass'd. ⎦

HORACE

THE THIRD ODE OF THE FIRST BOOK

INSCRIB'D TO THE EARL OF ROSCOMMON, ON
  HIS INTENDED VOYAGE TO IRELAND

So may th' auspicious Queen of Love,
And the Twin Stars, (the seed of Jove,)
And he who rules the raging wind,
To thee, O sacred ship, be kind;
And gentle breezes fill thy sails,
Supplying soft Etesian gales:
As thou, to whom the Muse commends
The best of poets and of friends,
Dost thy committed pledge restore,
And land him safely on the shore;   10
And save the better part of me
From perishing with him at sea;
Sure he, who first the passage tried, ⎤
In harden'd oak his heart did hide,   ⎬
And ribs of iron arm'd his side !   ⎦
Or his at least, in hollow wood
Who tempted first the briny flood;
Nor fear'd the winds' contending roar,
Nor billows beating on the shore;
Nor Hyades portending rain;   20
Nor all the tyrants of the main.
What form of death could him affright,

Who unconcern'd, with steadfast sight,
Could view the surges mounting steep,
And monsters rolling in the deep !
Could thro' the ranks of ruin go,
With storms above, and rocks below !
In vain did Nature's wise command
Divide the waters from the land,
If daring ships and men profane   3'
Invade th' inviolable main;
Th' eternal fences overleap,
And pass at will the boundless deep.
No toil, no hardship can restrain
Ambitious man, inur'd to pain;
The more confin'd, the more he tries,
And at forbidden quarry flies.
Thus bold Prometheus did aspire,
And stole from heaven the seed of fire:
A train of ills, a ghastly crew,   40
The robber's blazing track pursue;
Fierce Famine with her meager face,
And Fevers of the fiery race,
In swarms th' offending wretch surround,
All brooding on the blasted ground:
And limping Death, lash'd on by Fate,
Comes up to shorten half our date.
This made not Dedalus beware
With borrow'd wings to sail in air;
To hell Alcides forc'd his way,   50
Plung'd thro' the lake, and snatch'd the
  prey.
Nay, scarce the gods, or heav'nly climes,
Are safe from our audacious crimes;
We reach at Jove's imperial crown,
And pull the unwilling thunder down.

HORACE

THE NINTH ODE OF THE FIRST BOOK

I

BEHOLD yon mountain's hoary height,
  Made higher with new mounts of snow;
Again behold the winter's weight
  Oppress the lab'ring woods below;
And streams, with icy fetters bound,
Benumb'd and cramp'd to solid ground.

II

With well-heap'd logs dissolve the cold,
  And feed the genial hearth with fires;
Produce the wine, that makes us bold,
  And sprightly wit and love inspires: 10
For what hereafter shall betide,
God, if 't is worth his care, provide.

III

Let him alone, with what he made,
   To toss and turn the world below;
At his command the storms invade;
   The winds by his commission blow;
Till with a nod he bids 'em cease,
And then the calm returns, and all is
     peace.

IV

To-morrow and her works defy,
   Lay hold upon the present hour,   20
And snatch the pleasures passing by,
   To put them out of Fortune's pow'r:
Nor love, nor love's delights disdain;
Whate'er thou gett'st to-day is gain.

V

Secure those golden early joys
   That youth unsour'd with sorrow bears,
Ere with'ring time the taste destroys,
   With sickness and unwieldy years.
For active sports, for pleasing rest,
This is the time to be possess'd;   30
The best is but in season best.

VI

The pointed hour of promis'd bliss,
   The pleasing whisper in the dark,
The half-unwilling willing kiss,
   The laugh that guides thee to the mark,
When the kind nymph would coyness
     feign,
And hides but to be found again;
These, these are joys the gods for youth
     ordain.

HORACE

THE TWENTY-NINTH ODE OF THE THIRD
BOOK

PARAPHRAS'D IN PINDARIC VERSE, AND IN-
SCRIB'D TO THE RIGHT HONORABLE LAU-
RENCE, EARL OF ROCHESTER

I

DESCENDED of an ancient line,
   That long the Tuscan scepter sway'd,
Make haste to meet the generous wine,
   Whose piercing is for thee delay'd:
The rosy wreath is ready made;
   And artful hands prepare
The fragrant Syrian oil, that shall perfume
    thy hair.

II

When the wine sparkles from afar,
   And the well-natur'd friend cries,
    "Come away!"
Make haste, and leave thy business and thy
    care;   10
   No mortal int'rest can be worth thy
    stay.

III

Leave for a while thy costly country seat;
   And, to be great indeed, forget
The nauseous pleasures of the great:
   Make haste and come;
Come, and forsake thy cloying store;
   Thy turret that surveys, from high,
The smoke, and wealth, and noise of
    Rome;
   And all the busy pageantry
That wise men scorn, and fools adore: 20
Come, give thy soul a loose, and taste the
    pleasures of the poor.

IV

Sometimes 't is grateful to the rich to try
A short vicissitude, and fit of poverty:
   A savory dish, a homely treat,
   Where all is plain, where all is neat,
Without the stately spacious room,
The Persian carpet, or the Tyrian loom,
Clear up the cloudy foreheads of the great.

V

The sun is in the Lion mounted high;
    The Syrian star   30
    Barks from afar,
And with his sultry breath infects the
    sky;
The ground below is parch'd, the heav'ns
    above us fry.
The shepherd drives his fainting flock
Beneath the covert of a rock,
And seeks refreshing rivulets nigh:
The *sylvans* to their shades retire,
Those very shades and streams new shades
    and streams require,
And want a cooling breeze of wind to fan
    the raging fire.

VI

Thou, what befits the new Lord May'r, 40
And what the city faction dare,
And what the Gallic arms will do,
And what the quiver-bearing foe,
Art anxiously inquisitive to know;

But God has, wisely, hid from human sight
    The dark decrees of future fate,
And sown their seeds in depth of night:
He laughs at all the giddy turns of state,
When mortals search too soon, and fear too
    late.

VII

Enjoy the present smiling hour,   50
    And put it out of Fortune's pow'r;
The tide of bus'ness, like the running stream,
    Is sometimes high, and sometimes low,
    A quiet ebb, or a tempestuous flow,
    And always in extreme.
Now with a noiseless gentle course
    It keeps within the middle bed;
    Anon it lifts aloft the head,
And bears down all before it with impetu-
    ous force;   59
And trunks of trees come rolling down,
Sheep and their folds together drown:
Both house and homestead into seas are
    borne;
And rocks are from their old foundations
    torn,
And woods, made thin with winds, their
    scatter'd honors mourn.

VIII

Happy the man, and happy he alone,
    He, who can call to-day his own;
    He who, secure within, can say:
"To-morrow do thy worst, for I have
    liv'd to-day.
Be fair, or foul, or rain, or shine,
The joys I have possess'd, in spite of
    fate, are mine.   70
Not Heav'n itself upon the past has
    pow'r;
But what has been, has been, and I have
    had my hour."

IX

Fortune, that with malicious joy
    Does man her slave oppress,
    Proud of her office to destroy,
    Is seldom pleas'd to bless:
Still various, and unconstant still,
But with an inclination to be ill,
Promotes, degrades, delights in strife,
And makes a lottery of life.   80
I can enjoy her while she 's kind;
But when she dances in the wind,
And shakes her wings, and will not stay,
I puff the prostitute away:

The little or the much she gave is quietly
    resign'd;
Content with poverty, my soul I arm;
And virtue, tho' in rags, will keep me
    warm.

X

What is 't to me,
Who never sail in her unfaithful sea,   89
    If storms arise, and clouds grow black;
    If the mast split, and threaten wreck?
Then let the greedy merchant fear
    For his ill-gotten gain;
And pray to gods that will not hear,
While the debating winds and billows bear
    His wealth into the main.
For me, secure from Fortune's blows,
    (Secure of what I cannot lose,)
In my small pinnace I can sail,
Contemning all the blust'ring roar;   100
    And running with a merry gale,
    With friendly stars my safety seek,
    Within some little winding creek;
    And see the storm ashore.

HORACE

THE SECOND EPODE

"How happy in his low degree,
How rich in humble poverty, is he,
Who leads a quiet country life;
Discharg'd of business, void of strife,
And from the griping scrivener free!
(Thus, ere the seeds of vice were sown,
    Liv'd men in better ages born,
Who plow'd with oxen of their own
Their small paternal field of corn.)
Nor trumpets summon him to war,   10
    Nor drums disturb his morning sleep,
Nor knows he merchants' gainful care,
    Nor fears the dangers of the deep.
The clamors of contentious law,
    And court and state, he wisely shuns,
Nor brib'd with hopes, nor dar'd with
    awe,
    To servile salutations runs;
But either to the clasping vine
    Does the supporting poplar wed,
Or with his pruning-hook disjoin   20
    Unbearing branches from their head,
    And grafts more happy in their stead;
Or, climbing to a hilly steep,
    He views his herds in vales afar,

Or shears his overburden'd sheep,
  Or mead for cooling drink prepares,
  Of virgin honey in the jars.
Or, in the now declining year,
  When bounteous Autumn rears his
    head,
He joys to pull the ripen'd pear,   30
  And clust'ring grapes with purple spread.
The fairest of his fruit he serves,
  Priapus, thy rewards:
Sylvanus too his part deserves,
  Whose care the fences guards.
Sometimes beneath an ancient oak
  Or on the matted grass he lies,
No god of sleep he need invoke;
  The stream, that o'er the pebbles flies,
  With gentle slumber crowns his eyes.   40
The wind, that whistles thro' the sprays,
  Maintains the consort of the song;
And hidden birds, with native lays,
  The golden sleep prolong.
But when the blast of winter blows,
  And hoary frost inverts the year,
Into the naked woods he goes,
  And seeks the tusky boar to rear,
  With well-mouth'd hounds and pointed
    spear;
Or spreads his subtile nets from sight,   50
  With twinkling glasses, to betray
The larks that in the meshes light,
  Or makes the fearful hare his prey.
Amidst his harmless easy joys
  No anxious care invades his health,
Nor love his peace of mind destroys,
  Nor wicked avarice of wealth.
But if a chaste and pleasing wife,
  To ease the business of his life,
Divides with him his household care,   60
Such as the Sabine matrons were,
Such as the swift Apulian's bride,
  Sunburnt and swarthy tho' she be,
Will fire for winter nights provide,
  And without noise will oversee
His children and his family;
  And order all things till he come,
Sweaty and overlabor'd, home;
  If she in pens his flocks will fold,
  And then produce her dairy store,   70
With wine to drive away the cold,
  And unbought dainties of the poor;
Not oysters of the Lucrine lake
  My sober appetite would wish,
  Nor turbet, or the foreign fish
That rolling tempests overtake,
  And hither waft the costly dish.

Not heathpout, or the rarer bird
  Which Phasis or Ionia yields,
More pleasing morsels would afford   80
  Than the fat olives of my fields;
Than shards or mallows for the pot,
  That keep the loosen'd body sound,
Or than the lamb, that falls by lot
  To the just guardian of my ground.
Amidst these feasts of happy swains,
  The jolly shepherd smiles to see
His flock returning from the plains;
  The farmer is as pleas'd as he
To view his oxen, sweating smoke,   90
  Bear on their necks the loosen'd yoke:
To look upon his menial crew,
  That sit around his cheerful hearth,
And bodies spent in toil renew
  With wholesome food and country mirth."
This Morecraft said within himself,
  Resolv'd to leave the wicked town,
  And live retir'd upon his own.
He call'd his money in;
  But the prevailing love of pelf   100
Soon split him on the former shelf,
  And put it out again.

A NEW SONG

[This song was printed anonymously in the
first edition of *Sylvæ*; it is attributed to Dryden in the second edition of the book.]

I

SYLVIA, the fair, in the bloom of fifteen,
Felt an innocent warmth as she lay on the
    green;
She had heard of a pleasure, and something
    she guess'd
By the towzing, and tumbling, and touch-
    ing her breast.
She saw the men eager, but was at a loss,
What they meant by their sighing, and kiss-
    ing so close;
  By their praying and whining,
  And clasping and twining,
  And panting and wishing,
  And sighing and kissing,   10
And sighing and kissing so close.

II

" Ah ! " she cried, " ah ! for a languishing
    maid,
In a country of Christians, to die without
    aid !
Not a Whig, or a Tory, or Trimmer at least,

Or a Protestant parson, or Catholic priest,
To instruct a young virgin, that is at a loss,
What they meant by their sighing, and kiss-
   ing so close !
  By their praying and whining,
  And clasping and twining,
  And panting and wishing,   20
  And sighing and kissing,
And sighing and kissing so close."

III

Cupid, in shape of a swain, did appear,
He saw the sad wound, and in pity drew near;

Then show'd her his arrow, and bid her
  not fear,
For the pain was no more than a maiden
  may bear.
When the balm was infus'd, she was not at
  a loss,
What they meant by their sighing, and kiss-
  ing so close;
  By their praying and whining,
  And clasping and twining,   30
  And panting and wishing,
  And sighing and kissing,
And sighing and kissing so close.

FOUR SONGS

[Of these songs the first, third, and fourth were not published as Dryden's during his lifetime, so that their authenticity is not above suspicion. The four were mistakenly grouped
together in the first printing of the present book and cannot now be rearranged.]

THE FAIR STRANGER

[The following song was first printed in *A New Miscellany of Original Poems*. London, printed for Peter Buck . . . and George Strahan . . . *1701*, where it is ascribed to Dryden. Derrick stated, in his edition of Dryden (1760), that these verses celebrated the arrival in England in 1670, in the suite of the Duchess of Orleans, of Louise de Kéroualle, afterwards mistress of Charles II and Duchess of Portsmouth. This assertion has been often repeated by editors of Dryden. Christie notes that the poem would apply equally well to the Duchess of Mazarin, who arrived in England in January, 1676; but he adds pertinently : " There is no proof that the song was composed in honor of any great lady."]

I

HAPPY and free, securely blest,
No beauty could disturb my rest;
My amorous heart was in despair
To find a new victorious fair:

II

Till you descending on our plains,
With foreign force renew my chains;
Where now you rule without control
The mighty sovereign of my soul.

III

Your smiles have more of conquering charms
Than all your native country's arms: 10

Their troops we can expel with ease,
Who vanquish only when we please.

IV

But in your eyes, O there 's the spell !
Who can see them, and not rebel ?
You make us captives by your stay,
Yet kill us if you go away.

SONG

[This song was first printed, anonymously, in the first edition of *Sylvæ*, 1685; it is ascribed to Dryden in the second edition of that book, 1692, and is included in his *Poems on Various Occasions and Translations from Several Authors*, 1701.]

I

Go tell Amynta, gentle swain,
I would not die, nor dare complain:
Thy tuneful voice with numbers join,
Thy words will more prevail than mine.
To souls oppress'd, and dumb with grief,
The gods ordain this kind relief;
That music should in sounds convey
What dying lovers dare not say.

II

A sigh or tear, perhaps, she 'll give,
But love on pity cannot live.   10
Tell her that hearts for hearts were made,
And love with love is only paid.

Tell her my pains so fast encrease,
That soon they will be past redress;
But ah ! the wretch that speechless lies
Attends but death to close his eyes.

A SONG

[This song was first printed in *Poetical Miscellanies, the Fifth Part*, 1704.]

I

FAIR, sweet, and young, receive a prize
Reserv'd for your victorious eyes:
From crowds, whom at your feet you see,
O pity, and distinguish me !
As I from thousand beauties more
Distinguish you, and only you adore.

II

Your face for conquest was design'd,
Your ev'ry motion charms my mind;
Angels, when you your silence break,
Forget their hymns, to hear you speak;   10
But when at once they hear and view,
Are loth to mount, and long to stay with
     you.

III

No graces can your form improve,
But all are lost, unless you love;
While that sweet passion you disdain,
Your veil and beauty are in vain.

In pity then prevent my fate,
For after dying all reprieve 's too late.

SONG

[This song occurs anonymously, under the
title *An Ayre on a Ground*, in *Choice Ayres and
Songs*, 1683, whence it was reprinted in *The
Second Part of Miscellany Poems*, 1716. Another text occurs in *Poetical Miscellanies, the
Fifth Part*, 1704, where it is ascribed to Dryden. That text has been followed in the
present edition.]

HIGH state and honors to others impart,
     But give me your heart:
That treasure, that treasure alone,
     I beg for my own.
So gentle a love, so fervent a fire,
     My soul does inspire;
That treasure, that treasure alone,
     I beg for my own.

Your love let me crave;
Give me in possessing   10
     So matchless a blessing;
That empire is all I would have.

     Love 's my petition,
     All my ambition;
     If e'er you discover
     So faithful a lover,
     So real a flame,
     I 'll die, I 'll die,
     So give up my game.

THRENODIA AUGUSTALIS

A

FUNERAL-PINDARIC
POEM

SACRED TO THE HAPPY MEMORY
OF
KING CHARLES II

BY JOHN DRYDEN
SERVANT TO HIS LATE MAJESTY, AND TO THE PRESENT KING

Fortunati ambo, si quid mea carmina possunt,
Nulla dies unquam memori vos eximet œvo ! — VIRG.

[Charles II died on February 6, 1685, and this poem was published about a month later.
A second edition, with some changes of text, followed almost immediately. Advertisements in

the *Observator* (see Scott-Saintsbury edition, xviii, 295) show that the first edition appeared about March 14 and the second about March 25. Of the first edition two issues are known. The poem was also published in Dublin in 1685. It was not again reprinted until it was included in *Poems and Translations*, 1701. The present text follows the second edition.]

I

THUS long my grief has kept me dumb:
  Sure there 's a lethargy in mighty woe,
  Tears stand congeal'd and cannot flow;
And the sad soul retires into her inmost
    room;
Tears, for a stroke foreseen, afford relief;
  But, unprovided for a sudden blow,
  Like Niobe we marble grow,
    And petrify with grief.
Our British heav'n was all serene,
  No threat'ning cloud was nigh,   10
  Not the least wrinkle to deform the sky;
  We liv'd as unconcern'd and happily
As the first age in nature's golden scene;
  Supine amidst our flowing store,
We slept securely, and we dreamt of more:
  When suddenly the thunderclap was
    heard,
  It took us unprepar'd and out of guard,
  Already lost before we fear'd.
Th' amazing news of Charles at once were
    spread,
  At once the general voice declar'd,   20
  Our gracious prince was dead.
No sickness known before, no slow dis-
    ease,
  To soften grief by just degrees;
But like an hurricane on Indian seas
    The tempest rose;
  An unexpected burst of woes,
With scarce a breathing space betwixt,
This *now* becalm'd, and perishing the next.
As if great Atlas from his height
Should sink beneath his heavenly weight, 30
And with a mighty flaw, the flaming wall
    (As once it shall)
Should gape immense, and rushing down,
  o'erwhelm this nether ball;
So swift and so surprising was our fear:
Our Atlas fell indeed, but Hercules was
    near.

II

His pious brother, sure the best
  Who ever bore that name,
Was newly risen from his rest,
  And, with a fervent flame,
His usual morning vows had just address'd
  For his dear sovereign's health;   4?

And hop'd to have 'em heard,
  In long increase of years,
In honor, fame, and wealth:
Guiltless of greatness thus he always
    pray'd,
  Nor knew nor wish'd those vows he
    made
  On his own head should be repaid.
Soon as th' ill-omen'd rumor reach'd his
    ear,
  (Ill news is wing'd with fate, and flies
    apace,)
  Who can describe th' amazement in his
    face !   50
Horror in all his pomp was there,
Mute and magnificent without a tear:
And then the hero first was seen to fear.
Half unarray'd he ran to his relief,
So hasty and so artless was his grief:
Approaching greatness met him with her
    charms
  Of pow'r and future state;
But look'd so ghastly in a brother's fate,
  He shook her from his arms.
Arriv'd within the mournful room, he saw
  A wild distraction, void of awe,   61
And arbitrary grief unbounded by a law.
  God's image, God's anointed lay
    Without motion, pulse, or breath,
  A senseless lump of sacred clay,
    An image, now, of death:
Amidst his sad attendants' groans and
    cries,
  The lines of that ador'd, forgiving face,
  Distorted from their native grace;   69
An iron slumber sate on his majestic eyes.
The pious duke — forbear, audacious Muse,
No terms thy feeble art can use
Are able to adorn so vast a woe:
The grief of all the rest like subject-grief
    did show,
  His like a sovereign did transcend;
No wife, no brother, such a grief could
    know,
    Nor any name, but friend.

III

O wondrous changes of a fatal scene,
  Still varying to the last !
Heav'n, tho' its hard decree was past,   80

Seem'd pointing to a gracious turn again:
  And death's uplifted arm arrested in its
    haste.
Heav'n half repented of the doom,
And almost griev'd it had foreseen,
  What by foresight it will'd eternally to
    come.
Mercy above did hourly plead
  For her resemblance here below,
And mild forgiveness intercede
  To stop the coming blow.
New miracles approach'd th' ethereal throne,
Such as his wondrous life had oft and lately
    known,   91
And urg'd that still they might be shown.
  On earth his pious brother pray'd and
    vow'd,
    Renouncing greatness at so dear a
      rate,
  Himself defending, what he could,
    From all the glories of his future
      fate.
With him th' innumerable crowd
  Of armed prayers
Knock'd at the gates of heav'n, and knock'd
    aloud;
  The first, well-meaning, rude peti-
    tioners.   100
All for his life assail'd the throne,
All would have brib'd the skies by off'ring
    up their own.
So great a throng not heav'n itself could
    bar;
'T was almost borne by force, as in the
    giants' war.
The pray'rs, at least, for his reprieve were
    heard;
His death, like Hezekiah's, was deferr'd:
  Against the sun the shadow went;
  Five days, those five degrees, were
    lent
  To form our patience and prepare th'
    event.
The second causes took the swift com-
    mand,   110
The med'cinal head, the ready hand,
All eager to perform their part;
All but eternal doom was conquer'd by
    their art:
Once more the fleeting soul came back
  T' inspire the mortal frame;
And in the body took a doubtful stand,
  Doubtful and hov'ring like expiring flame,
That mounts and falls by turns, and trem-
    bles o'er the brand.

IV

The joyful short-liv'd news soon spread
    around,
Took the same train, the same impetuous
    bound: 120
The drooping town in smiles again was
    dress'd,
Gladness in every face express'd,
Their eyes before their tongues confess'd.
Men met each other with erected look,
The steps were higher that they took,
Friends to congratulate their friends made
    haste,
And long-inveterate foes saluted as they
    pass'd:
Above the rest heroic James appear'd
Exalted more, because he more had fear'd;
His manly heart, whose noble pride   130
    Was still above
Dissembled hate or varnish'd love,
Its more then common transport could not
    hide;
But like an *eagre* [1] rode in triumph o'er the
    tide.
Thus, in alternate course,
  The tyrant passions, hope and fear,
  Did in extremes appear,
And flash'd upon the soul with equal force.
Thus, at half ebb, a rolling sea
    Returns and wins upon the shore;   140
    The wat'ry herd, affrighted at the roar,
Rest on their fins a while, and stay,
Then backward take their wond'ring way:
The prophet wonders more than they,
  At prodigies but rarely seen before,
And cries, a *king* must fall, or kingdoms
    change their sway.
Such were our counter-tides at land, and so
Presaging of the fatal blow,
In their prodigious ebb and flow.
The royal soul, that like the laboring
    moon,   150
By charms of art was hurried down,
Forc'd with regret to leave her native
    sphere,
Came but a while on liking here:
Soon weary of the painful strife,
And made but faint essays of life:
    An evening light
    Soon shut in night;
A strong distemper, and a weak relief,
Short intervals of joy, and long returns of
    grief.

[1] An eagre is a tide swelling above another tide,
which I have myself observ'd on the river Trent.

V

The sons of art all med'cines tried,   160
And every noble remedy applied;
With emulation each essay'd
His utmost skill, nay more, they pray'd:
Never was losing game with better conduct
    play'd.
Death never won a stake with greater toil,
Nor e'er was fate so near a foil;
But, like a fortress on a rock,
Th' impregnable disease their vain at-
    tempts did mock.
They min'd it near, they batter'd from afar
With all the cannon of the med'cinal war;
No gentle means could be essay'd,   171
'T was beyond parley when the siege was
    laid.
Th' extremest ways they first ordain,
Prescribing such intolerable pain,
As none but Cæsar could sustain:
Undaunted Cæsar underwent
The malice of their art, nor bent
Beneath whate'er their pious rigor could
    invent.
In five such days he suffer'd more
Then any suffer'd in his reign before;   180
More, infinitely more, than he
Against the worst of rebels could decree,
A traitor, or twice pardon'd enemy.
Now art was tir'd without success,
No racks could make the stubborn malady
    confess.
    The vain *insurancers* of life,
And he who most perform'd and promis'd
    less,
    Even Short himself forsook th' unequal
      strife.
Death and despair was in their looks,
No longer they consult their memories or
    books;   190
Like helpless friends, who view from shore
The laboring ship, and hear the tempest
    roar;
    So stood they with their arms across;
Not to assist, but to deplore
    Th' inevitable loss.

VI

Death was denounc'd; that frightful sound
    Which ev'n the best can hardly bear,
    He took the summons void of fear;
And, unconcern'dly, cast his eyes around,
    As if to find and dare the grisly chal-
      lenger.   200
What death could do he lately tried,

When in four days he more then died.
The same assurance all his words did grace;
The same majestic mildness held its place;
Nor lost the monarch in his dying face.
Intrepid, pious, merciful, and brave,
He look'd as when he conquer'd and for-
    gave.

VII

As if some angel had been sent
To lengthen out his government,
And to foretell as many years again,   210
As he had number'd in his happy reign;
    So cheerfully he took the doom
Of his departing breath;
    Nor shrunk nor stepp'd aside for death;
      But with unalter'd pace kept on;
    Providing for events to come,
      When he resign'd the throne.
Still he maintain'd his kingly state;
And grew familiar with his fate.
Kind, good, and gracious, to the last,   220
On all he lov'd before his dying beams he
    cast:
O truly good, and truly great,
For glorious as he rose, benignly so he
    set !
All that on earth he held most dear,
He recommended to his care,
      To whom both Heav'n,
      The right had giv'n,
And his own love bequeath'd supreme com-
    mand:
He took and press'd that ever-loyal hand,
Which could in peace secure his reign,   230
Which could in wars his pow'r maintain,
That hand on which no plighted vows were
    ever vain.
Well for so great a trust, he chose
    A prince who never disobey'd;
    Not when the most severe commands
      were laid;
      Nor want, nor exile with his duty
      weigh'd:
A prince on whom, if Heav'n its eyes could
    close,
The welfare of the world it safely might
    repose.

VIII

That king who liv'd to God's own heart,
    Yet less serenely died than he: 240
    Charles left behind no harsh decree
For schoolmen with laborious art
    To salve from cruelty:

Those, for whom love could no excuses
  frame,
He graciously forgot to name.
Thus far my Muse, tho' rudely, has design'd
Some faint resemblance of his godlike mind;
But neither pen nor pencil can express
The parting brothers' *tenderness;*
Tho' that's a term too mean and low;　250
(The blest above a kinder word may know:)
  But what they did, and what they said,
The monarch who triumphant went,
  The militant who stay'd,
Like painters, when their height'ning arts
  are spent,
  I cast into a shade.
That all-forgiving king,
  The type of him above,
That inexhausted spring
  Of clemency and love;　260
Himself to his next self accus'd,
And ask'd that pardon which he ne'er re-
  fus'd:
For faults not his, for guilt and crimes
Of godless men, and of rebellious times;
For an hard exile, kindly meant,
When his ungrateful country sent
Their best Camillus into banishment,
And forc'd their sov'reign's act, they could
  not his consent.
O how much rather had that injur'd chief
  Repeated all his sufferings past,　270
  Then hear a pardon begg'd at last,
Which giv'n could give the dying no re-
  lief!
He bent, he sunk beneath his grief;
His dauntless heart would fain have held
From weeping, but his eyes rebell'd.
Perhaps the godlike hero in his breast
  Disdain'd, or was asham'd, to show
  So weak, so womanish a woe
Which yet the brother and the friend so
  plenteously confess'd.

IX

Amidst that silent show'r, the royal mind
  An easy passage found,　281
And left its sacred earth behind;
  Nor murm'ring groan express'd, nor
  laboring sound,
Nor any least tumultuous breath:
Calm was his life, and quiet was his death.
Soft as those gentle whispers were,
In which th' Almighty did appear;
By the still voice the prophet knew him
  there.

That peace which made thy prosperous
  reign to shine,
That peace thou leav'st to thy imperial
  line,　290
That peace, O happy shade, be ever thine!

X

For all those joys thy restoration brought,
For all the miracles it wrought,
  For all the healing balm thy mercy
  pour'd
Into the nation's bleeding wound,
And care that after kept it sound,
  For numerous blessings yearly show'r'd,
And property with plenty crown'd;
For freedom, still maintain'd alive,
Freedom, which in no other land will
  thrive,　300
Freedom, an English subject's sole pre-
  rogative,
Without whose charms ev'n peace would be
But a dull quiet slavery:
  For these, and more, accept our pious
  praise;
  'T is all the subsidy
  The present age can raise,
The rest is charg'd on late posterity.
  Posterity is charg'd the more,
  Because the large abounding store
To them and to their heirs is still entail'd
  by thee.　310
  Succession of a long descent
Which chastely in the channels ran,
And from our demigods began,
  Equal almost to time in its extent —
Thro' hazards numberless and great,
  Thou hast deriv'd this mighty blessing
  down,
  And fix'd the fairest gem that decks
  th' imperial crown:
Not faction, when it shook thy regal seat,
Not senates, insolently loud,
(Those echoes of a thoughtless crowd,)　320
Not foreign or domestic treachery,
Could warp thy soul to their unjust decree.
So much thy foes thy manly mind mistook,
Who judg'd it by the mildness of thy look;
Like a well-temper'd sword, it bent at will,
But kept the native toughness of the steel.

XI

Be true, O Clio, to thy hero's name!
  But draw him strictly so,
  That all who view, the piece may
  know;

He needs no trappings of fictitious fame: 330
The load's too weighty; thou may'st choose
Some parts of praise, and some refuse:
Write, that his annals may be thought more
    lavish than the Muse.
In scanty truth thou hast confin'd
The virtues of a royal mind,
Forgiving, bounteous, humble, just, and
    kind:
His conversation, wit, and parts,
His knowledge in the noblest, useful arts,
Were such, dead authors could not give;
But habitudes of those who live; 340
Who, lighting him, did greater lights re-
    ceive:
He drain'd from all, and all they knew;
His apprehension quick, his judgment true;
That the most learn'd, with shame, confess
His knowledge more, his reading only less.

XII

Amidst the peaceful triumphs of his reign,
    What wonder if the kindly beams he
        shed
Reviv'd the drooping arts again;
    If Science rais'd her head,
    And soft Humanity that from rebel-
        lion fled ! 350
Our isle, indeed, too fruitful was before;
    But all uncultivated lay
Out of the *solar* walk and heav'n's high
        way;
With rank Geneva weeds run o'er,
And cockle, at the best, amidst the corn it
    bore.
The royal husbandman appear'd,
    And plow'd, and sow'd, and till'd;
The thorns he rooted out, the rubbish
    clear'd,
    And bless'd th' obedient field:
When, straight, a double harvest rose; 360
Such as the swarthy Indian mows;
    Or happier climates near the line,
Or Paradise manur'd and dress'd by hands
    divine.

XIII

As when the newborn Phœnix takes his
        way,
His rich paternal regions to survey,
Of airy choristers a numerous train
Attend his wondrous progress o'er the plain;
So, rising from his father's urn,
So glorious did our Charles return:
Th' officious Muses came along, 370

A gay harmonious choir, like angels ever
        young;
(The Muse that mourns him now, his happy
        triumph sung.)
Even *they* could thrive in his auspicious
        reign;
    And such a plenteous crop they bore
Of purest and well-winnow'd grain,
    As Britain never knew before.
Tho' little was their hire, and light their
        gain,
Yet somewhat to their share he threw;
Fed from his hand, they sung and flew,
Like birds of Paradise, that liv'd on morn-
    ing dew. 380
O never let their lays his name forget !
The pension of a prince's praise is great.
Live then, thou great encourager of arts,
Live ever in our thankful hearts,
Live blest above, almost invok'd below;
Live and receive this pious vow,
Our patron once, our guardian angel now.
Thou Fabius of a sinking state,
Who didst by wise delays divert our fate,
When faction like a tempest rose, 390
    In death's most hideous form,
Then art to rage thou didst oppose,
    To weather out the storm:
Not quitting thy supreme command,
Thou held'st the rudder with a steady hand,
Till safely on the shore the bark did land;
The bark that all our blessings brought,
Charg'd with thyself and James, a doubly
        royal fraught.

XIV

O frail estate of human things,
    And slippery hopes below ! 400
Now to our cost your emptiness we
        know,
    (For 't is a lesson dearly bought,)
    Assurance here is never to be sought.
The best, and best belov'd of kings,
    And best deserving to be so,
When scarce he had escap'd the fatal blow
    Of faction and conspiracy,
Death did his promis'd hopes destroy:
He toil'd, he gain'd, but liv'd not to enjoy.
What mists of Providence are these 410
    Thro' which we cannot see !
    So saints, by supernatural pow'r set
        free,
    Are left at last in martyrdom to die;
Such is the end of oft-repeated miracles.
Forgive me, Heav'n, that impious thought,

'T was grief for Charles, to madness
   wrought,
  That question'd thy supreme decree!
Thou didst his gracious reign prolong,
Even in thy saints' and angels' wrong,
   His fellow-citizens of immortality: 420
For twelve long years of exile borne,
Twice twelve we number'd since his blest
   return:
So strictly wert thou just to pay,
Even to the driblet of a day.
Yet still we murmur, and complain,
The quails and manna should no longer rain:
Those miracles 't was needless to renew;
The chosen flock has now the promis'd land
  in view.

XV

A warlike prince ascends the regal state,
A prince long exercis'd by fate: 430
Long may he keep, tho' he obtains it late.
Heroes in Heaven's peculiar mold are cast,
They and their poets are not form'd in
  haste;
Man was the first in God's design, and man
  was made the last.
False heroes, made by flattery so,
Heav'n can strike out, like sparkles, at a
  blow;
But ere a prince is to perfection brought,
He costs Omnipotence a second thought.
   With toil and sweat,   439
  With hard'ning cold, and forming heat,
  The Cyclops did their strokes repeat,
Before th' impenetrable shield was wrought.
It looks as if the Maker would not own
The noble work for his,
Before 't was tried and found a master-
  piece.

XVI

View then a monarch ripen'd for a throne.
Alcides thus his race began;
O'er infancy he swiftly ran;
The future god at first was more than man:
Dangers and toils, and Juno's hate   450
Even o'er his cradle lay in wait;
And there he grappled first with fate:
In his young hands the hissing snakes he
  press'd,
So early was the deity confess'd;
Thus, by degrees, he rose to Jove's impe-
  rial seat;
Thus difficulties prove a soul *legitimately*
  great.

Like his, our hero's infancy was tried:
Betimes the Furies did their snakes pro-
  vide,
And to his infant arms oppose
His father's rebels, and his brother's foes;
The more oppress'd, the higher still he
  rose.   461
Those were the preludes of his fate,
That form'd his manhood, to subdue
The *Hydra* of the many-headed hissing
  crew.

XVII

As after Numa's peaceful reign,
  The martial Ancus did the scepter
   wield,
Furbish d the rusty sword again,
  Resum'd the long-forgotten shield,
  And led the Latins to the dusty field;
So James the drowsy *genius* wakes   470
Of Britain long entranc'd in charms,
Restiff and slumb'ring on its arms:
'T is rous'd, and with a new-strung nerve,
  the spear already shakes.
No neighing of the warrior steeds,
No drum, or louder trumpet, needs
T' inspire the coward, warm the cold;
His voice, his sole appearance makes 'em
  bold.
Gaul and Batavia dread th' impending blow;
Too well the vigor of that arm they know;
They lick the dust, and crouch beneath their
  fatal foe.   480
Long may they fear this awful prince,
And not provoke his ling'ring sword;
Peace is their only sure defense,
Their best security his word:
In all the changes of his doubtful state,
His truth, like Heav'n's, was kept inviolate,
For him to promise is to make it fate.
His *valor* can triumph o'er land and main;
With broken oaths his fame he will not
  stain;
With conquest basely bought, and with in-
  glorious gain.   490

XVIII

For once, O Heav'n, unfold thy adamantine
  book;
  And let his wond'ring *senate* see,
  If not thy firm, immutable decree,
  At least the second page of strong con-
   tingency;
  Such as consists with wills originally
  free:

Let them with glad amazement look
 On what their happiness may be;
Let them not still be obstinately blind,
Still to divert the good thou hast design'd,
 Or with malignant penury, 500
To sterve the royal virtues of his mind.
Faith is a Christian's and a subject's test;
O give them to believe, and they are surely
 blest.
They do; and with a distant view I see
Th' amended vows of English loyalty;
And all beyond that object, there appears
 The long retinue of a prosperous reign,

A series of successful years,
 In orderly array, a martial, manly
  train.
 Behold ev'n to remoter shores, 510
 A conquering navy proudly spread;
The British cannon formidably roars,
 While starting from his oozy bed,
 Th' asserted ocean rears his rever-
  end head,
To view and recognise his ancient lord
 again;
 And, with a willing hand, restores
The *fasces* of the main.

PROLOGUE AND EPILOGUE TO ALBION AND ALBANIUS

[Of this, his first opera, Dryden says in his preface: "It was all compos'd, and was just ready to have been perform'd, when he, in honor of whom it was principally made, was taken from us." After a slight alteration, made necessary by changed circumstances, the opera was presented early in June, 1685. It was published at about the same time; the prologue and epilogue were also printed as a broadside. The texts below follow those printed with the first edition of the opera.]

PROLOGUE

Full twenty years and more, our lab'ring
 stage
Has lost, on this incorrigible age;
Our poets, the John Ketches of the nation,
Have seem'd to lash ye, ev'n to excoria-
 tion:
But still no sign remains; which plainly
 notes,
You bore like heroes, or you brib'd like
 Oates.
What can we do, when mimicking a fop,
Like beating nut trees, makes a larger
 crop?
Faith, we'll e'en spare our pains; and, to
 content you,
Will fairly leave you what your Maker
 meant you. 10
Satire was once your physic, wit your food;
One nourish'd not, and t' other drew no
 blood:
We now prescribe, like doctors in despair,
The diet your weak appetites can bear.
Since hearty beef and mutton will not do,

Here's julep dance, ptisan of song and
 show:
Give you strong sense, the liquor is too
 heady;
You're come to farce, that's asses' milk,
 already.
Some hopeful youths there are, of callow
 wit,
Who one day may be men, if Heav'n think
 fit; 20
Sound may serve such, ere they to sense
 are grown,
Like leading strings, till they can walk
 alone.
But yet, to keep our friends in count'nance,
 know,
The wise Italians first invented show;
Thence into France the noble pageant
 pass'd:
'T is England's credit to be cozen'd last.
Freedom and zeal have chous'd you ⎫
 o'er and o'er;   ⎪
Pray give us leave to bubble you once ⎬
 more;   ⎪
You never were so cheaply fool'd before. ⎭
We bring you change, to humor your
 disease; 30
Change for the worse has ever us'd to
 please:
Then, 't is the mode of France; without
 whose rules
None must presume to set up here for
 fools.
In France, the oldest man is always ⎫
 young,   ⎪
Sees *operas* daily, learns the tunes so ⎬
 long,   ⎪
Till foot, hand, head, keep time with ⎪
 ev'ry song: ⎭

Each sings his part, echoing from pit and
box,
With his hoarse voice, half harmony, half
pox.
Le plus grand roi du monde is always ring-
ing,
They show themselves good subjects by
their singing.   40
On that condition, set up every throat:
You Whigs may sing, for you have chang'd
your note.
Cits and citesses, raise a joyful strain,
'T is a good omen to begin a reign;
Voices may help your charter to restoring,
And get by singing what you lost by roar-
ing.

EPILOGUE

AFTER our Æsop's fable shown to-day,
I come to give the moral of the play.
Feign'd Zeal, you saw, set out the speedier
pace;
But, the last heat, Plain Dealing won the
race:
Plain Dealing for a jewel has been known,
But ne'er till now the jewel of a crown.
When Heav'n made man, to show the work
divine,
Truth was his image, stamp'd upon the
coin:
And, when a king is to a god refin'd,
On all he says and does he stamps his
mind: 10
This proves a soul without allay, and pure;
Kings, like their gold, should every touch
endure.
To dare in fields is valor; but how few
Dare be so throughly valiant, to be true !
The name of great let other kings affect:
He 's great indeed, the prince that is direct.
His subjects know him now, and trust him
more
Than all their kings, and all their laws be-
fore.
What safety could their public acts afford ?
Those he can break; but cannot break his
word.   20
So great a trust to him alone was due;
Well have they trusted whom so well they
knew.
The saint, who walk'd on waves, securely
trod,
While he believ'd the beck'ning of his God;
But, when his faith no longer bore him out,

Began to sink, as he began to doubt.
Let us our native character maintain;
'T is of our growth, to be sincerely plain.
T' excel in truth we loyally may strive,
Set privilege against prerogative: 30
He plights his faith, and we believe him
just;
His honor is to promise, ours to trust.
Thus Britain's basis on a word is laid,
As by a word the world itself was made.

TO MY FRIEND, MR. J. NORTH-LEIGH

AUTHOR OF THE PARALLEL, ON HIS TRI-UMPH OF THE BRITISH MONARCHY

[John Northleigh (1657–1705) published, in
1682, *The Parallel, or the new specious Association an old rebellious Covenant;* and, in 1685, *The
Triumph of our Monarchy over the Plots and
Principles of our Rebels and Republicans.* To
the latter work Dryden prefixed the following
verses.]

So Joseph, yet a youth, expounded well
The boding dream, and did th' event fore-
tell;
Judged by the past, and drew the parallel.
Thus early Solomon the truth explor'd,
The right awarded, and the babe restor'd.
Thus Daniel, ere to prophecy he grew,
The perjur'd presbyters did first subdue,
And freed Susanna from the canting crew.
Well may our monarchy triumphant stand,
While warlike James protects both sea and
land;   10
And, under covert of his sev'nfold shield,
Thou send'st thy shafts to scour the dis-
tant field.
By law thy powerful pen has set us free;
Thou studi'st that, and that may study
thee.

TO THE PIOUS MEMORY OF THE ACCOMPLISH'D YOUNG LADY, MRS. ANNE KILLIGREW

EXCELLENT IN THE TWO SISTER-ARTS OF POESY AND PAINTING, AN ODE

[Anne Killigrew, daughter of Henry Killigrew, divine, and niece of the dramatists
Thomas and William Killigrew, was born

in 1660, and died in June, 1685. An edition of her *Poems* was licensed for the press on September 30 of that year; and, as is shown by an advertisement in the *Observator* (see Scott-Saintsbury edition, xviii, 295), was published about November 2, although it is dated 1686. The frontispiece of the volume is a mezzotint made from a painting of the poetess by herself. The title-page bears the motto *Immodicis brevis est œtas, et rara senectus* (Martial, vi. 29), to which Dryden refers in lines 147, 148 below. Dryden's *Ode* was first published in this volume; it was reprinted, with some changes of text, in *Examen Poeticum*, 1693. The later text is here followed.]

I

THOU youngest virgin-daughter of the skies,
Made in the last promotion of the blest;
Whose palms, new pluck'd from paradise,
In spreading branches more sublimely rise,
Rich with immortal green above the rest:
Whether, adopted to some neighboring star,
Thou roll'st above us, in thy wand'ring race,
  Or, in procession fix'd and regular,
  Mov'd with the heavens' majestic pace;
  Or, call'd to more superior bliss,   10
Thou tread'st, with seraphims, the vast abyss:
Whatever happy region is thy place,
Cease thy celestial song a little space;
(Thou wilt have time enough for hymns divine,
Since heav'n's eternal year is thine.)
Hear then a mortal Muse thy praise rehearse,
      In no ignoble verse;
But such as thy own voice did practice here,
When thy first fruits of poesy were giv'n,
To make thyself a welcome inmate there; 20
  While yet a young probationer,
  And candidate of heav'n.

II

If by traduction came thy mind,
  Our wonder is the less to find
A soul so charming from a stock so good;
Thy father was transfus'd into thy blood:
So wert thou born into the tuneful strain,
(An early, rich, and inexhausted vein.)
  But if thy preëxisting soul
  Was form'd, at first, with myriads more,

It did thro' all the mighty poets roll,   31
  Who Greek or Latin laurels wore,
And was that Sappho last, which once it was before.
If so, then cease thy flight, *O heav'n-born mind!*
Thou hast no dross to purge from thy rich ore;
Nor can thy soul a fairer mansion find,
Than was the beauteous frame she left behind:
Return, to fill or mend the choir of thy celestial kind.

III

May we presume to say, that at thy birth
New joy was sprung in heav'n, as well as here on earth?   40
For sure the milder planets did combine
On thy auspicious horoscope to shine,
And ev'n the most malicious were in trine.
Thy brother-angels at thy birth
Strung each his lyre, and tun'd it high,
That all the people of the sky
Might know a poetess was born on earth.
And then, if ever, mortal ears
Had heard the music of the spheres!
And if no clust'ring swarm of bees   50
On thy sweet mouth distill'd their golden dew,
  'T was that such vulgar miracles
  Heav'n had not leisure to renew:
For all the blest fraternity of love
Solemniz'd there thy birth, and kept thy holiday above.

IV

O gracious God! how far have we
Profan'd thy heav'nly gift of poesy!
Made prostitute and profligate the Muse,
Debas'd to each obscene and impious use,
Whose harmony was first ordain'd above 60
For tongues of angels, and for hymns of love!
O wretched we! why were we hurried down
  This lubric and adult'rate age,
(Nay, added fat pollutions of our own,)
  T' increase the steaming ordures of the stage?
What can we say t' excuse our *second fall*?
Let this thy *vestal*, Heav'n, atone for all:
Her Arethusian stream remains unsoil'd,

Unmix'd with foreign filth, and undefil'd;
Her wit was more than man, her innocence
    a child !   70

V

Art she had none, yet wanted none;
For nature did that want supply:
So rich in treasures of her own,
She might our boasted stores defy:
Such noble vigor did her verse adorn
That it seem'd borrow'd, where 't was only
    born.
Her morals too were in her bosom bred,
    By great examples daily fed,
What in the best of books, her father's
    life, she read.
And to be read herself she need not fear;
Each test, and ev'ry light, her Muse will
    bear,   81
Tho' Epictetus with his lamp were there.
Ev'n love (for love sometimes her Muse
    express'd)
Was but a *lambent flame* which play'd about
    her breast,
Light as the vapors of a morning dream:
So cold herself, whilst she such warmth
    express'd,
'T was Cupid bathing in Diana's stream.

VI

Born to the spacious empire of the Nine,
One would have thought she should have
    been content
To manage well that mighty government;
But what can young ambitious souls con-
    fine ?   91
To the next realm she stretch'd her ⎫
    sway,   ⎪
For *painture* near adjoining lay,   ⎬
A plenteous province, and alluring prey. ⎭
A chamber of dependences was fram'd,
(As conquerors will never want pretense,
    When arm'd, to justify th' offense,)
And the whole fief in right of poetry she
    claim'd.
The country open lay without defense;
For poets frequent inroads there had made,
    And perfectly could represent   101
    The shape, the face, with ev'ry linea-
      ment;
And all the large demains which the *Dumb
    Sister* sway'd,
    All bow'd beneath her government;
    Receiv'd in triumph wheresoe'er she
      went.

Her pencil drew whate'er her soul design'd,
And oft the happy draught surpass'd the
    image in her mind.
The *sylvan* scenes of herds and flocks,
And fruitful plains and barren rocks,
Of shallow brooks that flow'd so clear 110
The bottom did the top appear;
Of deeper too and ampler floods,
Which, as in mirrors, shew'd the woods;
Of lofty trees, with sacred shades,
And perspectives of pleasant glades,
Where nymphs of brightest form ap- ⎫
    pear,   ⎪
And shaggy satyrs standing near,   ⎬
Which them at once admire and fear: ⎭
The ruins too of some majestic piece,
Boasting the pow'r of ancient Rome, or
    Greece,   120
Whose statues, friezes, columns broken
    lie,
And, tho' defac'd, the wonder of the eye:
What nature, art, bold fiction, e'er durst
    frame,
Her forming hand gave feature to the
    name.
So strange a concourse ne'er was seen
    before,
But when the peopled ark the whole crea-
    tion bore.

VII

The scene then chang'd: with bold
    erected look
Our martial king the sight with reverence
    strook;
For, not content t' express his outward part,
Her hand call'd out the image of his
    heart: 130
His warlike mind, his soul devoid of ⎫
    fear,   ⎪
His high-designing thoughts were fig- ⎬
    ur'd there,   ⎪
As when, by magic, ghosts are made ap- ⎭
    pear.
Our Phœnix queen was portray'd too so
    bright,
Beauty alone could beauty take so right:
Her dress, her shape, her matchless grace,
Were all observ'd, as well as heav'nly
    face.
With such a peerless majesty she stands,
As in that day she took the crown from
    sacred hands;
Before a train of heroines was seen,   140
In beauty foremost, as in rank the queen.

Thus nothing to her *genius* was denied,
But like a ball of fire the further thrown,
Still with a greater blaze she shone,
And her bright soul broke out on ev'ry side.
What next she had design'd, Heaven only knows;
To such immod'rate growth her conquest rose
That fate alone its progress could oppose.

VIII

Now all those charms, that blooming grace,
The well-proportion'd shape, and beauteous face, 150
Shall never more be seen by mortal eyes:
In earth the much-lamented virgin lies !
Not wit, nor piety could fate prevent;
Nor was the cruel Destiny content
To finish all the murder at a blow,
To sweep at once her life and beauty too;
But, like a harden'd felon, took a pride
To work more mischievously slow,
And plunder'd first, and then destroy'd.
O double sacrilege on things divine, 160
To rob the relic, and deface the shrine !
But thus Orinda died:
Heav'n, by the same disease, did both translate;
As equal were their souls, so equal was their fate.

IX

Meantime her warlike brother on the seas
His waving streamers to the winds displays,
And vows for his return, with vain devotion, pays.
Ah, generous youth, that wish forbear,
The winds too soon will waft thee here !
Slack all thy sails, and fear to come, 170
Alas, thou know'st not, thou art wreck'd at home !
No more shalt thou behold thy sister's face,
Thou hast already had her last embrace.
But look aloft, and if thou kenn'st from far
Among the Pleiads a new kindled star;
If any sparkles than the rest more bright,
'T is she that shines in that propitious light.

X

When in mid-air the golden trump shall sound,
To raise the nations under ground;

When in the Valley of Jehosaphat 180
The judging God shall close the book of fate,
And there the last assizes keep
For those who wake and those who sleep;
When rattling bones together fly
From the four corners of the sky;
When sinews o'er the skeletons are spread,
Those cloth'd with flesh, and life inspires the dead;
The sacred poets first shall hear the sound, ⎫
And foremost from the tomb shall bound, ⎪
For they are cover'd with the lightest ⎬
   ground; 190 ⎭
And straight, with inborn vigor, on the wing,
Like mounting larks, to the new morning sing.
There thou, sweet saint, before the choir shalt go,
As harbinger of heav'n, the way to show,
The way which thou so well hast learn'd below.

A LETTER TO SIR GEORGE ETHEREGE

[Sir George Etherege, to whose comedy, *The Man of Mode,* Dryden had contributed an epilogue (see p. 78, above), was appointed in 1685 English minister to Ratisbon. On January 9, 1686, he sent a poetical epistle to the Secretary of State, the Earl of Middleton, who seems to have requested Dryden to write a reply in the same vein. Etherege's letter and Dryden's answer were published together in the third edition, 1702, of *Sylvæ, or The Second Part of Poetical Miscellanies.*]

To you who live in chill degree,
As map informs, of fifty-three,
And do not much for cold atone,
By bringing thither fifty-one,
Methinks all climes should be alike,
From tropic ev'n to pole artique;
Since you have such a constitution
As nowhere suffers diminution.
You can be old in grave debate,
And young in love-affairs of state; 10
And both to wives and husbands show
The vigor of a plenipo.
Like mighty missioner you come
Ad Partes Infidelium.
A work of wondrous merit sure,

So far to go, so much t' indure;
And all to preach to German dame,
Where sound of Cupid never came.
Less had you done, had you been sent,
As far as Drake or Pinto went,   20
For cloves and nutmegs to the line-a,
Or even for oranges to China.
That had indeed been charity;
Where lovesick ladies helpless lie,
Chapp'd, and for want of liquor dry.
But you have made your zeal appear
Within the circle of the Bear.
What region of the earth 's so dull,
That is not of your labors full ?
Triptolemus (so sung the Nine)   30
Strew'd plenty from his cart divine.
But spite of all these fable-makers,
He never sow'd on Almain acres:
No, that was left by fate's decree,
To be perform'd and sung by thee.
Thou break'st thro' forms with as much ease
As the French king thro' articles.
In grand affairs thy days are spent,
In waging weighty compliment,
With such as monarchs represent.   40
They who such vast fatigues attend,
Want some soft minutes to unbend,
To show the world that now and then
Great ministers are mortal men.
Then Rhenish rummers walk the round;
In bumpers ev'ry king is crown'd;
Besides three holy miter'd Hectors,
And the whole college of Electors.
No health of potentate is sunk,
That pays to make his envoy drunk.   50
These Dutch delights, I mention'd last,
Suit not, I know, your English taste:
For wine to leave a whore or play
Was ne'er your Excellency's way.
Nor need this title give offense,
For here you were your Excellence,
For gaming, writing, speaking, keeping,
His Excellence for all but sleeping.
Now if you tope in form, and treat,
'T is the sour sauce to the sweet meat,   60
The fine you pay for being great.
Nay, here 's a harder imposition,
Which is indeed the court's petition,
That setting worldly pomp aside,
Which poet has at font denied,
You would be pleas'd in humble way
To write a trifle call'd a play.
This truly is a degradation,
But would oblige the crown and nation
Next to your wise negotiation.   70

If you pretend, as well you may,
Your high degree, your friends will say,
The Duke St. Aignan made a play.
If Gallic wit convince you scarce,
His Grace of Bucks has made a farce,
And you, whose comic wit is terse all,
Can hardly fall below *Rehearsal.*
Then finish what you have began,
But scribble faster if you can;
For yet no George, to our discerning,   80
Has writ without a ten years' warning.

TO MY INGENIOUS FRIEND, MR. HENRY HIGDEN, ESQ.

ON HIS TRANSLATION OF THE TENTH SATIRE OF JUVENAL

[The following verses were prefixed to *A Modern Essay on the Tenth Satyr of Juvenal*, by Henry Higden, a lawyer. The book was licensed for the press June 2, 1686 ; it is dated 1687. The title-page bears the motto *ridendo monet.*]

THE Grecian wits, who *satire* first began,
Were pleasant *pasquins* on the life of
    man:
At mighty villains, who the State op-
    press'd,
They durst not rail; perhaps, they laugh'd
    at least,
And turn'd 'em out of office with a jest.
No fool could peep abroad, but ready stand
The drolls, to clap a bauble in his hand.
Wise legislators never yet could draw
A fop within the reach of common law;
For posture, dress, grimace, and affecta-
    tion,   10
Tho' foes to sense, are harmless to the na-
    tion.
Our last redress is dint of verse to try,
And *satire* is our Court of Chancery.
This way took Horace to reform an age
Not bad enough to need an author's rage.
But yours,* who liv'd in more   * Juvenal.
    degen'rate times,
Was forc'd to fasten deep, and worry
    crimes.
Yet you, my friend, have temper'd him so
    well,
You make him smile in spite of all his
    zeal:
An art peculiar to yourself alone,   20

To join the virtues of two styles in one.
    O ! were your author's principle re-⎫
        ceiv'd,   ⎪
Half of the lab'ring world would be re- ⎬
    liev'd;   ⎪
For not to wish, is not to be deceiv'd. ⎭
Revenge would into charity be chang'd,
Because it costs too dear to be reveng'd:
It costs our quiet and content of mind,
And when 't is compass'd, leaves a sting
    behind.
Suppose I had the better end o' th' staff,
Why should I help th' ill-natur'd world to
    laugh ?   30
'T is all alike to them, who gets the day;

They love the spite and mischief of the
    fray.
No: I have cur'd myself of that disease;
Nor will I be provok'd, but when I please:
But let me half that cure to you restore;
You gave the salve, I laid it to the sore.
    Our kind relief against a rainy day, ⎫
Beyond a tavern, or a tedious play,   ⎪
We take your book, and laugh our   ⎬
    spleen away.   ⎭
If all your tribe (too studious of debate) 40
Would cease false hopes and titles to
    create,
Led by the rare example you begun,
Clients would fail, and lawyers be undone.

THE HIND AND THE PANTHER

A POEM IN THREE PARTS

— Antiquam exquirite matrem. ⎫
Et vera, incessu, patuit dea. — ⎬ VIRG.

[*The Hind and the Panther* was published in the spring of 1687, being licensed for the press on April 11. Two more editions appeared in the same year ; a fourth (miscalled the third) was included in the folio *Poems and Translations*, 1701. An edition was also published at Edinburgh in 1687. Though Dryden's name did not appear on the original title-pages, his authorship of the poem was no secret. He apparently made a few corrections in the second edition, which is taken as the basis of the following text.]

TO THE READER

THE nation is in too high a ferment for me to expect either fair war, or even so much as fair quarter, from a reader of the opposite party. All men are engag'd either on this side or that ; and tho' conscience is the common word which is given by both, yet if a writer fall among enemies, and cannot give the marks of their conscience, he is knock'd down before the reasons of his own are heard. A preface, therefore, which is but a bespeaking of favor, is altogether useless. What I desire the reader should know concerning me, he will find in the body of the poem, if he have but the patience to peruse it. Only this advertisement let him take beforehand, which relates to the merits of the cause. No general characters of parties (call 'em either sects or churches) can be so fully and exactly drawn, as to comprehend all the several members of 'em ; at least all such as are receiv'd under that denomination. For example, there are some of the Church by law establish'd who envy not liberty of conscience to Dissenters ; as being well satisfied that, according to their own principles, they ought not

to persecute them. Yet these, by reason of their fewness, I could not distinguish from the numbers of the rest, with whom they are embodied in one common name. On the other side, there are many of our sects, and more indeed then I could reasonably have hop'd, who have withdrawn themselves from the communion of the Panther, and embrac'd this gracious indulgence of his Majesty in point of toleration. But neither to the one nor the other of these is this satire any way intended : 't is aim'd only at the refractory and disobedient on either side ; for those who are come over to the royal party are consequently suppos'd to be out of gunshot. Our physicians have observ'd that, in process of time, some diseases have abated of their virulence, and have in a manner worn out their malignity, so as to be no longer mortal ; and why may not I suppose the same concerning some of those who have formerly been enemies to kingly government, as well as Catholic religion ? I hope they have now another notion of both, as having found, by comfortable experience, that the doctrine of persecution is far from being an article of our faith.

'T is not for any private man to censure the proceedings of a foreign prince; but, without suspicion of flattery, I may praise our own, who has taken contrary measures, and those more suitable to the spirit of Christianity. Some of the Dissenters, in their addresses to his Majesty, have said, *that he has restor'd God to his empire over conscience.* I confess I dare not stretch the figure to so great a boldness; but I may safely say that conscience is the royalty and prerogative of every private man. He is absolute in his own breast, and accountable to no earthly power for that which passes only betwixt God and him. Those who are driven into the fold are, generally speaking, rather made hypocrites then converts.

This indulgence being granted to all the sects, it ought in reason to be expected that they should both receive it, and receive it thankfully. For at this time of day to refuse the benefit, and adhere to those whom they have esteem'd their persecutors, what is it else, but publicly to own, that they suffer'd not before for conscience sake, but only out of pride and obstinacy, to separate from a Church for those impositions, which they now judge may be lawfully obey'd? After they have so long contended for their classical ordination, (not to speak of rites and ceremonies,) will they at length submit to an episcopal? If they can go so far out of complaisance to their old enemies, methinks a little reason should persuade 'em to take another step, and see whether that would lead 'em.

Of the receiving this toleration thankfully I shall say no more, than that they ought, and I doubt not they will consider from what hands they receiv'd it. 'T is not from a Cyrus, a heathen prince, and a foreigner, but from a Christian king, their native sovereign; who expects a return *in specie* from them, that the kindness which he has graciously shown them may be retaliated on those of his own persuasion.

As for the poem in general, I will only thus far satisfy the reader, that it was neither impos'd on me, nor so much as the subject given me by any man. It was written during the last winter and the beginning of this spring, tho' with long interruptions of ill health and other hindrances. About a fortnight before I had finish'd it, his Majesty's Declaration for Liberty of Conscience came abroad: which if I had so soon expected, I might have spar'd myself the labor of writing many things which are contain'd in the third part of it. But I was always in some hope that the Church of England might have been persuaded to have taken off the penal laws and the Test, which was one design of the poem when I propos'd to myself the writing of it.

'T is evident that some part of it was only occasional, and not first intended. I mean that defense of myself to which every honest man is bound, when he is injuriously attack'd in print; and I refer myself to the judgment of those who have read the *Answer to the Defense of the late King's Papers,* and that of the *Duchess,* (in which last I was concern'd,) how charitably I have been represented there. I am now inform'd both of the author and supervisors of his pamphlet, and will reply when I think he can affront me; for I am of Socrates's opinion, that all creatures cannot. In the mean time let him consider, whether he deserv'd not a more severe reprehension then I gave him formerly, for using so little respect to the memory of those whom he pretended to answer; and, at his leisure, look out for some original *Treatise of Humility,* written by any Protestant in English, (I believe I may say in any other tongue:) for the magnified piece of Duncomb on that subject, which either he must mean, or none, and with which another of his fellows has upbraided me, was translated from the Spanish of Rodriguez; tho' with the omission of the seventeenth, the twenty-fourth, the twenty-fifth, and the last chapter, which will be found in comparing of the books.

He would have insinuated to the world that her late Highness died not a Roman Catholic. He declares himself to be now satisfied to the contrary, in which he has giv'n up the cause: for matter of fact was the principal debate betwixt us. In the mean time, he would dispute the motives of her change; how preposterously, let all men judge, when he seem'd to deny the subject of the controversy, the change itself. And because I would not take up this ridiculous challenge, he tells the world I cannot argue; but he may as well infer, that a Catholic cannot fast, because he will not take up the cudgels against Mrs. James, to confute the Protestant religion.

I have but one word more to say concerning the poem as such, and abstracting from the matters, either religious or civil, which are handled in it. The *first part,* consisting most in general characters and narration, I have endeavor'd to raise, and give it the majestic turn of heroic poesy. The *second,* being matter of dispute, and chiefly concerning Church authority, I was oblig'd to make as plain and perspicuous as possibly I could; yet not wholly neglecting the numbers, tho' I had not frequent occasions for the magnificence of verse. The *third,* which has more of the nature of domestic conversation, is, or ought to be, more free and familiar than the two former.

There are in it two *episodes,* or *fables,* which are interwoven with the main design; so that they are properly parts of it, tho' they are also distinct stories of themselves. In both of these I have made use of the commonplaces of *satire*, whether true or false, which are urg'd by the members of the one Church against the other : at which I hope no reader of either party will be scandaliz'd, because they are not of my invention, but as old, to my knowledge, as the times of Boccace and Chaucer on the one side, and as those of the Reformation on the other.

THE HIND AND THE PANTHER

THE FIRST PART

A MILK-WHITE Hind, immortal and un-chang'd,
Fed on the lawns, and in the forest rang'd;
Without unspotted, innocent within,
She fear'd no danger, for she knew no sin.
Yet had she oft been chas'd with horns and hounds
And Scythian shafts; and many winged wounds
Aim'd at her heart; was often forc'd to fly,
And doom'd to death, tho' fated not to die.
Not so her young; for their unequal line
Was hero's make, half human, half divine. 10
Their earthly mold obnoxious was to fate,
Th' immortal part assum'd immortal state.
Of these a slaughter'd army lay in blood,
Extended o'er the Caledonian wood,
Their native walk; whose vocal blood arose,
And cried for pardon on their perjur'd foes.
Their fate was fruitful, and the sanguine seed,
Endued with souls, encreas'd the sacred breed.
So captive Israel multiplied in chains,
A numerous exile, and enjoy'd her pains. 20
With grief and gladness mix'd, their mother view'd
Her martyr'd offspring, and their race re-new'd;
Their corps to perish, but their kind to last,
So much the deathless plant the dying fruit surpass'd.
Panting and pensive now she rang'd alone,
And wander'd in the kingdoms, once her own.
The common hunt, tho' from their rage restrain'd
By sov'reign pow'r, her company disdain'd;

Grinn'd as they pass'd, and with a glaring eye
Gave gloomy signs of secret enmity. 30
'Tis true, she bounded by, and tripp'd so light,
They had not time to take a steady sight;
For Truth has such a face and such a mien,
As to be lov'd needs only to be seen.
The bloody Bear, an *Independent* beast,
Unlick'd to form, in groans her hate ex-press'd.
Among the timorous kind the *Quaking Hare*
Profess'd neutrality, but would not swear.
Next her the *buffoon* Ape, as atheists use,
Mimick'd all sects, and had his own to choose: 40
Still when the Lion look'd, his knees he bent,
And paid at church a courtier's compli-ment.
The bristled *Baptist* Boar, impure as he,
(But whiten'd with the foam of sanctity,)
With fat pollutions fill'd the sacred place,
And mountains level'd in his furious race:
So first rebellion founded was in grace.
But since the mighty ravage which he made
In German forests had his guilt betray'd,
With broken tusks, and with a borrow'd name, 50
He shunn'd the vengeance, and conceal'd the shame;
So lurk'd in sects unseen. With greater guile
False Reynard fed on consecrated spoil:
The graceless beast by Athanasius first
Was chas'd from Nice; then, by Socinus nurs'd,
His impious race their blasphemy renew'd,
And nature's King thro' nature's optics view'd.
Revers'd, they view'd him lessen'd to their eye,
Nor in an infant could a God descry:
New swarming sects to this obliquely tend,
Hence they began, and here they all will end. 61
What weight of ancient witness can pre-vail,
If private reason hold the public scale ?
But, gracious God, how well dost thou pro-vide

For erring judgments an unerring guide !
Thy throne is darkness in th' abyss of
    light,
A blaze of glory that forbids the sight.
O teach me to believe thee thus conceal'd,
And search no farther than thyself re-
    veal'd;
But her alone for my director take,   70
Whom thou hast promis'd never to for-
    sake !
My thoughtless youth was wing'd with
    vain desires,
My manhood, long misled by wand'ring
    fires,
Follow'd false lights; and, when their
    glimpse was gone,
My pride struck out new sparkles of her
    own.
Such was I, such by nature still I am;
Be thine the glory, and be mine the shame.
Good life be now my task: my doubts are
    done:
(What more could fright my faith, than
    three in one ?)
Can I believe eternal God could lie   80 ⎤
Disguis'd in mortal mold and infancy ?   ⎥
That the great Maker of the world could   ⎬
    die ?   ⎦
And after that trust my imperfect sense,
Which calls in question his omnipotence ?
Can I my reason to my faith compel,
And shall my sight, and touch, and taste
    rebel ?
Superior faculties are set aside;
Shall their subservient organs be my guide ?
Then let the moon usurp the rule of day,
And winking tapers shew the sun his
    way;   90
For what my senses can themselves per-
    ceive,
I need no revelation to believe.
Can they who say the host should be de-
    scried
By sense, define a body glorified ?
Impassible, and penetrating parts ?
Let them declare by what mysterious arts
He shot that body thro' th' opposing might ⎤
Of bolts and bars impervious to the light, ⎬
And stood before his train confess'd in   ⎦
    open sight.
    For since thus wondrously he pass'd, 't is
    plain,   100
One single place two bodies did contain.
And sure the same Omnipotence as well
Can make one body in more places dwell.

Let Reason then at her own quarry fly,
But how can finite grasp infinity ?
    'T is urg'd again that faith did first com-
    mence
By miracles, which are appeals to sense,
And thence concluded, that our sense must
    be
The motive still of credibility.
For latter ages must on former wait,   110
And what began belief, must propagate.
    But winnow well this thought, and you *
    shall find
'T is light as chaff that flies before the
    wind.
Were all those wonders wrought by pow'r
    divine,
As means or ends of some more deep de-
    sign ?
Most sure as means, whose end was this
    alone,
To prove the Godhead of th' eternal Son.
God thus asserted: man is to believe
Beyond what sense and reason can con-
    ceive,
And for mysterious things of faith rely   120
On the proponent, Heav'n's authority.
If then our faith we for our guide admit,
Vain is the farther search of human wit;
As, when the building gains a surer stay,
We take th' unuseful scaffolding away.
Reason by sense no more can understand;
The game is play'd into another hand.
Why choose we then like bilanders to ⎤
    creep   ⎥
Along the coast, and land in view to keep, ⎬
When safely we may launch into the   ⎥
    deep ?   130   ⎦
In the same vessel which our Savior bore, ⎤
Himself the pilot, let us leave the shore, ⎬
And with a better guide a better world   ⎦
    explore.
Could he his Godhead veil with flesh and
    blood,
And not veil these again to be our food ?
His grace in both is equal in extent,
The first affords us life, the second nourish-
    ment.
And if he can, why all this frantic pain ⎤
To construe what his clearest words con- ⎥
    tain,   ⎬
And make a riddle what he made so   ⎥
    plain ?   140   ⎦
To take up half on trust, and half to
    try,
Name it not faith, but bungling bigotry.

Both knave and fool the merchant we
  may call,
To pay great sums, and to compound the
  small:
For who would break with Heav'n, and
  would not break for all ?
Rest then, my soul, from endless anguish
  freed:
Nor sciences thy guide, nor sense thy creed.
Faith is the best ensurer of thy bliss;
The bank above must fail before the ven-
  ture miss.
But heav'n and heav'n-born faith are far
  from thee,   150
Thou first apostate to divinity.
Unkennel'd range in thy Polonian plains;
A fiercer foe th' insatiate Wolf remains.
  Too boastful Britain, please thyself no
    more,
That beasts of prey are banish'd from thy
  shore;
The Bear, the Boar, and every salvage
  name,
Wild in effect, tho' in appearance tame,
Lay waste thy woods, destroy thy blissful
  bow'r,
And, muzzled tho' they seem, the mutes
  devour.
More haughty than the rest, the *wolfish*
  race   160
Appear with belly gaunt, and famish'd
  face:
Never was so deform'd a beast of grace.
His ragged tail betwixt his legs he wears,
Close clapp'd for shame; but his rough
  crest he rears,
And pricks up his predestinating ears.
His wild disorder'd walk, his haggard eyes,
Did all the bestial citizens surprise.
Tho' fear'd and hated, yet he rul'd a while,
As captain or companion of the spoil.
Full many a year his hateful head had
  been   170
For tribute paid, nor since in Cambria seen:
The last of all the litter scap'd by chance,
And from Geneva first infested France.
Some authors thus his pedigree will trace;
But others write him of an upstart race;
Because of Wycliffe's brood no mark he
  brings,
But his innate antipathy to kings.
These last deduce him from th' Helvetian
  kind,
Who near the Leman lake his consort lin'd:
That fi'ry Zuinglius first th' affection bred,
And meager Calvin bless'd the nuptial bed.
In Israel some believe him whelp'd long
  since,   182
When the proud Sanhedrim op-   *Vid.* pref. to
  press'd the prince,   Heyl. *Hist.*
Or, since he will be Jew, derive *of Presb.*
  him high'r,
When Corah with his brethren did conspire
From Moses' hand the sov'reign sway to
  wrest,
And Aaron of his ephod to devest:
Till opening earth made way for all to pass,
And could not bear the burden of a *class*.
The Fox and he came shuffled in the
  dark,   190
If ever they were stow'd in Noah's ark:
Perhaps not made; for all their barking
  train
The Dog (a common species) will contain.
And some wild curs, who from their mas-
  ters ran,
Abhorring the supremacy of man,
In woods and caves the rebel-race began.
  O happy pair, how well have you en-
    creas'd !
What ills in Church and State have you
  redress'd !
With teeth untried, and rudiments of claws,
Your first essay was on your native laws: 200
Those having torn with ease, and tram-
  pled down,
Your fangs you fasten'd on the miter'd
  crown,
And freed from God and monarchy your
  town.
What tho' your native kennel still be small,
Bounded betwixt a puddle and a wall;
Yet your victorious colonies are sent
Where the north ocean girds the continent.
Quicken'd with fire below, your monsters
  breed
In fenny Holland, and in fruitful Tweed:
And, like the first, the last effects to be 210
Drawn to the dregs of a democracy.
As, where in fields the fairy rounds are seen,
A rank sour herbage rises on the green;
So, springing where these midnight elves
  advance,
Rebellion prints the footsteps of the dance.
Such are their doctrines, such contempt
  they show
To Heav'n above, and to their prince be-
  low,
As none but traitors and blasphemers
  know.

God, like the tyrant of the skies, is plac'd,
And kings, like slaves, beneath the crowd
   debas'd.   220
So fulsome is their food that flocks re-
   fuse
To bite, and only dogs for physic use.
As, where the lightning runs along the
   ground,
No husbandry can heal the blasting wound;
Nor bladed grass, nor bearded corn suc-
   ceeds,
But scales of scurf and putrefaction breeds:
Such wars, such waste, such fiery tracks of
   dearth
Their zeal has left, and such a teemless
   earth.
But, as the poisons of the deadliest kind
Are to their own unhappy coasts confin'd; 230
As only Indian shades of sight deprive,
And magic plants will but in Colchos thrive;
So Presbyt'ry and pestilential zeal
Can only flourish in a commonweal.
   From Celtic woods is chas'd the *wolfish*
   crew;
But ah! some pity e'en to brutes is due:
Their native walks, methinks, they might
   enjoy,
Curb'd of their native malice to destroy.
Of all the tyrannies on humankind,
The worst is that which persecutes the
   mind.   240
Let us but weigh at what offense we strike;
'T is but because we cannot think alike.
In punishing of this, we overthrow
The laws of nations and of nature too.
Beasts are the subjects of tyrannic sway,
Where still the stronger on the weaker
   prey;
Man only of a softer mold is made,
Not for his fellows' ruin, but their aid:
Created kind, beneficent, and free,
The noble image of the Deity.   250
   One portion of informing fire was giv'n
To brutes, th' inferior family of heav'n:
The smith divine, as with a careless beat,
Struck out the mute creation at a heat;
But, when arriv'd at last to human race,
The Godhead took a deep consid'ring space;
And, to distinguish man from all the
   rest,
Unlock'd the sacred treasures of his breast;
And mercy mix'd with reason did impart,
One to his head, the other to his heart: 260
Reason to rule, but mercy to forgive;
The first is law, the last prerogative.

And like his mind his outward form ap-
   pear'd,
When, issuing naked to the wond'ring
   herd,
He charm'd their eyes; and, for they
   lov'd, they fear'd:
Not arm'd with horns of arbitrary might,
Or claws to seize their furry spoils in
   fight,
Or with increase of feet t' o'ertake 'em
   in their flight;
Of easy shape, and pliant ev'ry way;
Confessing still the softness of his clay, 270
And kind as kings upon their coronation
   day;
With open hands, and with extended space
Of arms, to satisfy a large embrace.
Thus kneaded up with milk, the new-made
   man
His kingdom o'er his kindred world began;
Till knowledge misapplied, misunderstood,
And pride of empire sour'd his balmy blood.
Then, first rebelling, his own stamp he
   coins;
The murth'rer Cain was latent in his loins:
And blood began its first and loudest cry 280
For diff'ring worship of the Deity.
Thus persecution rose, and farther space
Produc'd the mighty hunter of his race.
Not so the blessed Pan his flock encreas'd,
Content to fold 'em from the famish'd
   beast:
Mild were his laws; the Sheep and harm-
   less Hind
Were never of the persecuting kind.
Such pity now the pious Pastor shows,
Such mercy from the British Lion flows,
That both provide protection for their
   foes.   290
   O happy regions, Italy and Spain,
Which never did those monsters entertain!
The Wolf, the Bear, the Boar, can there
   advance
No native claim of just inheritance.
And self-preserving laws, severe in show,
May guard their fences from th' invading
   foe.
Where birth has plac'd 'em, let 'em safely
   share
The common benefit of vital air.
Themselves unharmful, let them live un-
   harm'd;
Their jaws disabled, and their claws dis-
   arm'd: 300
Here, only in nocturnal howlings bold,

They dare not seize the Hind, nor leap the
    fold.
More pow'rful, and as vigilant as they,
The Lion awfully forbids the prey.
Their rage repress'd, tho' pinch'd with ⎫
    famine sore,   ⎪
They stand aloof, and tremble at his ⎬
    roar: ⎪
Much is their hunger, but their fear is ⎪
    more.   ⎭
    These are the chief; to number o'er the
      rest,
And stand, like Adam, naming ev'ry beast,
Were weary work: nor will the Muse de-
    scribe   310
A slimy-born and sun-begotten tribe;
Who, far from steeples and their sacred
    sound,
In fields their sullen conventicles found.
These gross, half-animated lumps I leave;
Nor can I think what thoughts they can
    conceive.
But if they think at all, 't is sure no high'r
Than matter, put in motion, may aspire:
Souls that can scarce ferment their mass ⎫
    of clay: ⎪
So drossy, so divisible are they,   ⎬
As would but serve pure bodies for al- ⎪
    lay: 320 ⎭
Such souls as *shards* produce, such beetle
    things
As only buzz to heav'n with ev'ning wings;
Strike in the dark, offending but by chance,
Such are the blindfold blows of ignorance.
They know not beings, and but hate a
    name;
To them the Hind and Panther are the
    same.
    The Panther, sure the noblest, next the
      Hind,
And fairest creature of the spotted kind;
O, could her inborn stains be wash'd away,
She were too good to be a beast of prey!
How can I praise, or blame, and not of-
    fend,   331
Or how divide the frailty from the friend!
Her faults and virtues lie so mix'd that she
Nor wholly stands condemn'd, nor wholly
    free.
Then, like her injur'd Lion, let me speak;
He cannot bend her, and he would not
    break.
Unkind already, and estrang'd in part,
The Wolf begins to share her wand'ring
    heart.

Tho' unpolluted yet with actual ill,
She half commits, who sins but in her will.
If, as our dreaming Platonists report,   341
There could be spirits of a middle sort,
Too black for heav'n, and yet too white for
    hell,
Who just dropp'd halfway down, nor lower
    fell;
So pois'd, so gently she descends from
    high,
It seems a soft dismission from the sky.
Her house not ancient, whatsoe'er pretense
Her clergy heralds make in her defense;
A second century not halfway run,
Since the new honors of her blood begun.
A Lion, old, obscene, and furious made   351
By lust, compress'd her mother in a shade;
Then, by a left-hand marriage, weds the
    dame,
Cov'ring adult'ry with a specious name:
So Schism begot; and Sacrilege and she,
A well-match'd pair, got graceless Heresy.
God's and kings' rebels have the same
    good cause,
To trample down divine and human laws;
Both would be call'd reformers, and their
    hate
Alike destructive both to Church and
    State: 360
The fruit proclaims the plant; a lawless ⎫
    prince   ⎬
By luxury reform'd incontinence;   ⎪
By ruins, charity; by riots, abstinence. ⎭
Confessions, fasts, and penance set aside; ⎫
O, with what ease we follow such a   ⎪
    guide,   ⎬
Where souls are starv'd, and senses   ⎪
    gratified;   ⎭
Where marriage pleasures midnight ⎫
    pray'r supply,   ⎪
And matin bells (a melancholy cry)   ⎬
Are tun'd to merrier notes, *encrease* and ⎪
    multiply!   ⎭
Religion shows a rosy-color'd face;   370 ⎫
Not hatter'd out with drudging works of   ⎬
    grace: ⎪
A downhill reformation rolls apace.   ⎭
What flesh and blood would crowd the ⎫
    narrow gate,   ⎪
Or, till they waste their pamper'd   ⎬
    paunches, wait?   ⎪
All would be happy at the cheapest rate. ⎭
    Tho' our lean faith these rigid laws has
      giv'n,
The full-fed Mussulman goes fat to heav'n;

For his Arabian prophet with delights
Of sense allur'd his Eastern proselytes.
The jolly Luther, reading him, began   380
T' interpret Scriptures by his Alcoran;
To grub the thorns beneath our tender
    feet,
And make the paths of paradise more
    sweet:
Bethought him of a wife ere halfway gone,
(For 't was uneasy travailing alone;)
And, in this masquerade of mirth and
    love,
Mistook the bliss of heav'n for Bacchanals
    above.
Sure he presum'd of praise, who came to
    stock
Th' ethereal pastures with so fair a flock,
Burnish'd, and batt'ning on their food, to
    show   390
The diligence of careful herds below.
  Our Panther, tho' like these she chang'd
    her head,
Yet, as the mistress of a monarch's bed,
Her front erect with majesty she bore,
The crosier wielded, and the miter wore.
Her upper part of decent discipline
Shew'd affectation of an ancient line;
And Fathers, councils, Church and Church's
    head,
Were on her reverend phylacteries read.
But what disgrac'd and disavow'd the rest,
Was Calvin's brand, that stigmatiz'd the
    beast.   401
Thus, like a creature of a double kind,
In her own labyrinth she lives confin'd;
To foreign lands no sound of her is come,
Humbly content to be despis'd at home.
Such is her faith; where good cannot be
    had,
At least she leaves the refuse of the bad:
Nice in her choice of ill, tho' not of best,
And least deform'd, because reform'd the
    least.
In doubtful points betwixt her diff'ring
    friends,   410
Where one for substance, one for sign con-
    tends,
Their contradicting terms she strives to
    join;
Sign shall be substance, substance shall be
    sign.
A real presence all her sons allow, ⎫
And yet 't is flat idolatry to bow, ⎬
Because the Godhead 's there they know ⎭
    not how.

Her novices are taught that bread and ⎫
    wine ⎪
Are but the visible and outward sign, ⎬
Receiv'd by those who in communion ⎪
    join; ⎭
But th' inward grace, or the thing sig-
    nified,   420
His blood and body, who to save us died:
The faithful this thing signified receive.
What is 't those faithful then partake or
    leave ?
For what is signified and understood,
Is, by her own confession, flesh and blood.
Then, by the same acknowledgment, we
    know
They take the sign, and take the substance
    too.
The lit'ral sense is hard to flesh and blood,
But nonsense never can be understood.
  Her wild belief on ev'ry wave is
    toss'd;   430
But sure no Church can better morals
    boast:
True to her king her principles are found;
O that her practice were but half so sound !
Steadfast in various turns of state she
    stood,
And seal'd her vow'd affection with her
    blood:
Nor will I meanly tax her constancy, ⎫
That int'rest or obligement made the tie ⎬
(Bound to the fate of murder'd mon- ⎪
    archy.) ⎭
Before the sounding ax so falls the vine,
Whose tender branches round the poplar
    twine.   440
She chose her ruin, and resign'd her life,
In death undaunted as an Indian wife:
A rare example! but some souls we see
Grow hard, and stiffen with adversity:
Yet these by fortune's favors are undone; ⎫
Resolv'd, into a baser form they run, ⎬
And bore the wind, but cannot bear the ⎪
    sun. ⎭
Let this be Nature's frailty, or her fate,
Or * Isgrim's counsel, her new-   * The Wolf.
    chosen mate;
Still she 's the fairest of the fallen crew, 450
No mother more indulgent, but the true.
  Fierce to her foes, yet fears her force to
    try,
Because she wants innate auctority;
For how can she constrain them to obey,
Who has herself cast off the lawful sway ?
Rebellion equals all, and those who toil

In common theft will share the common
   spoil.
Let her produce the title and the right
Against her old superiors first to fight;
If she reform by text, ev'n that's as
   plain   460
For her own rebels to reform again.
As long as words a diff'rent sense will bear,
And each may be his own interpreter,
Our airy faith will no foundation find;
The word 's a weathercock for ev'ry wind:
The Bear, the Fox, the Wolf, by turns pre-
   vail;
The most in pow'r supplies the present
   gale.
The wretched Panther cries aloud for aid
To Church and councils, whom she first be-
   tray'd;
No help from Fathers or tradition's
   train: 470
Those ancient guides she taught us to dis-
   dain,
And by that Scripture which she once
   abus'd
To reformation stands herself accus'd.
What bills for breach of laws can she pre-
   fer,
Expounding which she owns herself may
   err ?
And, after all her winding ways are ⎤
   tried,
If doubts arise, she slips herself aside, ⎬
And leaves the private conscience for │
   the guide. ⎦
If then that conscience set th' offender
   free,
It bars her claim to Church auctority. 480
How can she censure, or what crime pre-
   tend,
But Scripture may be construed to defend ?
Ev'n those whom for rebellion she trans-
   mits
To civil pow'r, her doctrine first acquits;
Because no disobedience can ensue,
Where no submission to a judge is due;
Each judging for himself, by her consent,
Whom thus absolv'd she sends to punish-
   ment.
Suppose the magistrate revenge her cause,
'T is only for transgressing human laws. 490
How answ'ring to its end a Church is made,
Whose pow'r is but to counsel and per-
   suade ?
O solid rock, on which secure she stands !
Eternal house, not built with mortal hands !

O sure defense against th' infernal gate,
A patent during pleasure of the State !
  Thus is the Panther neither lov'd nor
   fear'd,
A mere mock queen of a divided herd,
Whom soon by lawful pow'r she might
   control,
Herself a part submitted to the whole. 500
Then, as the moon who first receives the
   light
By which she makes our nether regions
   bright,
So might she shine, reflecting from afar
The rays she borrow'd from a better star;
Big with the beams which from her mother
   flow,
And reigning o'er the rising tides below:
Now, mixing with a salvage crowd, she
   goes,
And meanly flatters her invet'rate foes;
Rul'd while she rules, and losing ev'ry
   hour
Her wretched remnants of precarious
   pow'r.   510
  One evening, while the cooler shade she
   sought,
Revolving many a melancholy thought,
Alone she walk'd, and look'd around in
   vain,
With rueful visage, for her vanish'd train :
None of her sylvan subjects made their
   court;
Levées and couchées pass'd without resort.
So hardly can usurpers manage well
Those whom they first instructed to rebel:
More liberty begets desire of more;
The hunger still encreases with the store. 520
Without respect they brush'd along the ⎤
   wood,
Each in his clan, and, fill'd with loath- ⎬
   some food,
Ask'd no permission to the neighb'ring │
   flood. ⎦
The Panther, full of inward discontent,
Since they would go, before 'em wisely
   went;
Supplying want of pow'r by drinking first,
As if she gave 'em leave to quench their
   thirst.
Among the rest, the Hind, with fearful
   face,
Beheld from far the common wat'ring
   place,
Nor durst approach; till with an awful
   roar   530

The sovereign Lion bade her fear no more.
Encourag'd thus she brought her young-
    lings nigh,
Watching the motions of her patron's eye,
And drank a sober draught; the rest amaz'd
Stood mutely still, and on the stranger
    gaz'd;
Survey'd her part by part, and sought to
    find
The ten-horn'd monster in the harmless
    Hind,
Such as the Wolf and Panther had de-
    sign'd.
They thought at first they dream'd; for
    't was offense
With them to question certitude of sense, 540
Their guide in faith; but nearer when
    they drew,
And had the faultless object full in view,
Lord, how they all admir'd her heav'nly
    hue !
Some, who before her fellowship dis-
    dain'd,
Scarce, and but scarce, from inborn rage
    restrain'd,
Now frisk'd about her, and old kindred
    feign'd.
Whether for love or int'rest, ev'ry sect
Of all the salvage nation shew'd respect:
The viceroy Panther could not awe the
    herd;
The more the company, the less they
    fear'd. 550
The surly Wolf with secret envy burst,
Yet could not howl; the Hind had seen
    him first:
But what he durst not speak, the Panther
    durst.
    For when the herd, suffis'd, did late re-
    pair
To ferny heaths, and to their forest lair,
She made a mannerly excuse to stay,
Proff'ring the Hind to wait her half the
    way;
That, since the sky was clear, an hour of
    talk
Might help her to beguile the tedious walk.
With much good will the motion was em-
    brac'd, 560
To chat a while on their adventures pass'd;
Nor had the grateful Hind so soon for-
    got
Her friend and fellow-suff'rer in the Plot.
Yet wond'ring how of late she grew es-
    trang'd,

Her forehead cloudy, and her count'nance
    chang'd,
She thought this hour th' occasion would
    present
To learn her secret cause of discontent,
Which well she hop'd might be with ease
    redress'd,
Consid'ring her a well-bred civil beast,
And more a gentlewoman than the
    rest. 570
After some common talk what rumors ran,
The lady of the spotted muff began.

THE SECOND PART

" Dame," said the Panther, " times are
    mended well,
Since late among the Philistines you fell.
The toils were pitch'd, a spacious tract of
    ground
With expert huntsmen was encompass'd
    round;
Th' enclosure narrow'd; the sagacious
    pow'r
Of hounds and death drew nearer ev'ry
    hour.
'T is true, the younger Lion scap'd the
    snare,
But all your priestly calves lay struggling
    there, 580
As sacrifices on their altars laid;
While you, their careful mother, wisely
    fled,
Not trusting destiny to save your head.
For, whate'er promises you have applied
To your unfailing Church, the surer
    side
Is four fair legs in danger to provide.
And whate'er tales of Peter's chair you
    tell,
Yet, saving reverence of the miracle,
The better luck was yours to scape so
    well."
    " As I remember," said the sober Hind,
" Those toils were for your own dear self
    design'd, 591
As well as me; and with the selfsame
    throw,
To catch the quarry and the vermin too:
(Forgive the sland'rous tongues that
    call'd you so.)
Howe'er you take it now, the common
    cry
Then ran you down for your rank loyalty.
Besides, in Popery they thought you nurs'd,

(As evil tongues will ever speak the worst,)
Because some forms, and ceremonies some
You kept, and stood in the main question
  dumb.   600
Dumb you were born indeed; but, thinking
  long,
The Test it seems at last has loos'd your
  tongue.
And, to explain what your forefathers
  meant,
By real presence in the sacrament,
(After long fencing, push'd against a
  wall,)
Your *salvo* comes, that he 's not there at
  all:
There chang'd your faith, and what may
  change may fall.
Who can believe what varies every day,
Nor ever was, nor will be at a stay ? "
  " Tortures may force the tongue un-
    truths to tell,   610
And I ne'er own'd myself infallible,"
Replied the Panther: " grant such presence
  were,
Yet in your sense I never own'd it there.
A real *virtue* we by faith receive,
And that we in the sacrament believe."
  " Then," said the Hind, " as you the mat-
    ter state,
Not only Jesuits can equivocate;
For *real* as you now the word expound,
From solid substance dwindles to a sound.
Methinks an Æsop's fable you repeat; 620
You know who took the shadow for the
  meat:
Your Church's substance thus you change
  at will,
And yet retain your former figure still.
I freely grant you spoke to save your life,
For then you lay beneath the butcher's
  knife.
Long time you fought, redoubled batt'ry
  bore,
But, after all, against yourself you swore:
Your former self; for ev'ry hour your form
Is chopp'd and chang'd, like winds before a
  storm.
Thus fear and int'rest will prevail with
  some;   630
For all have not the gift of martyrdom."
  The Panther grinn'd at this, and thus
    replied:
" That men may err was never yet denied.
But, if that common principle be true,
The cannon, dame, is level'd full at you.

But, shunning long disputes, I fain would
  see
That wondrous wight Infallibility.
Is he from heav'n, this mighty champion,
  come,
Or lodg d below in subterranean Rome ?
First, seat him somewhere, and derive his
  race,   640
Or else conclude that nothing has no place."
  " Suppose, (tho' I disown it,) " said the
    Hind,
" The certain mansion were not yet as-
    sign'd;
The doubtful residence no proof can bring
Against the plain existence of the thing.
Because philosophers may disagree,
If sight b' emission or reception be,
Shall it be thence inferr'd, I do not see ?
But you require an answer positive,
Which yet, when I demand, you dare not
  give;   650
For fallacies in universals live.
I then affirm that this unfailing guide
In Pope and gen'ral councils must reside;
Both lawful, both combin'd: what one
    decrees
By numerous votes, the other ratifies:
On this undoubted sense the Church re-
    lies.
'T is true, some doctors in a scantier space,
I mean, in each apart, contract the place.
Some, who to greater length extend the
  line,
The Church's after-acceptation join.   660
This last circumference appears too wide;
The Church diffus'd is by the council tied;
As members by their representatives
Oblig'd to laws which prince and senate
    gives.
Thus some contract, and some enlarge the
    space;
In Pope and council who denies the place,
Assisted from above with God's unfail-
    ing grace ?
Those canons all the needful points contain;
Their sense so obvious, and their words so
    plain,
That no disputes about the doubtful text 670
Have, hitherto, the lab'ring world per-
    plex'd.
If any should in aftertimes appear,
New councils must be call'd, to make the
    meaning clear;
Because in them the pow'r supreme resides,
And all the promises are to the guides.

This may be taught with sound and safe
   defense;
But mark how sandy is your own pretense,
Who, setting councils, Pope, and Church
   aside,
Are ev'ry man his own presuming guide.
The sacred books, you say, are full and
   plain, 680
And ev'ry needful point of truth contain:
All, who can read, interpreters may be.
Thus, tho' your sev'ral Churches disagree,
Yet ev'ry saint has to himself alone
The secret of this philosophic stone.
These principles your jarring sects unite,
When diff'ring doctors and disciples fight.
Tho' Luther, Zuinglius, Calvin, holy chiefs,
Have made a battle-royal of beliefs;
Or, like wild horses, sev'ral ways have
   whirl'd 690
The tortur'd text about the Christian world;
Each Jehu lashing on with furious force,
That Turk or Jew could not have us'd it
   worse;
No matter what dissension leaders make,
Where ev'ry private man may save a
   stake:
Rul'd by the Scripture and his own ad-
   vice,
Each has a blind by-path to Paradise;
Where, driving in a circle, slow or fast,
Opposing sects are sure to meet at last.
A wondrous charity you have in store 700
For all reform'd to pass the narrow door;
So much, that Mahomet had scarcely
   more:
For he, kind prophet, was for damning none;
But Christ and Moses were to save their
   own:
Himself was to secure his chosen race,
Tho' reason good for Turks to take the
   place,
And he allow'd to be the better man,
In virtue of his holier Alcoran."
   " True," said the Panther, " I shall ne'er
   deny
My brethren may be sav'd as well as I: 710
Tho' Huguenots contemn our ordination,
Succession, ministerial vocation;
And Luther, more mistaking what he read,
Misjoins the sacred body with the bread:
Yet, _lady_, still remember I maintain,
The word in needful points is only plain."
   " Needless, or needful, I not now con-
   tend,
For still you have a loophole for a friend;"

Rejoin'd the matron: " but the rule you
   lay
Has led whole flocks, and leads them still
   astray 720
In weighty points, and full damnation's
   way.
For did not Arius first, Socinus now,
The Son's eternal Godhead disavow ?
And did not these by gospel texts alone
Condemn our doctrine, and maintain their
   own ?
Have not all heretics the same pretense
To plead the Scriptures in their own de-
   fense ?
How did the Nicene Council then decide
That strong debate ? was it by Scripture
   tried ?
No, sure to those the rebel would not
   yield; 730
Squadrons of texts he marshal'd in the
   field;
That was but civil war, an equal set,
Where piles with piles, and eagles eagles
   met.
With texts point-blank and plain he fac'd
   the foe:
And did not Sathan tempt our Savior so ?
The good old bishops took a simpler way;
Each ask'd but what he heard his father
   say,
Or how he was instructed in his youth,
And by tradition's force upheld the truth."
   The Panther smil'd at this: " And
   when," said she, 740
" Were those first councils disallow'd by
   me ?
Or where did I at sure tradition strike,
Provided still it were apostolic ? "
   " Friend," said the Hind, " you quit
   your former ground,
Where all your faith you did on Scripture
   found:
Now 't is tradition join'd with Holy Writ;
But thus your memory betrays your wit."
   " No," said the Panther, " for in that I
   view
When your tradition 's forg'd, and when 't is
   true.
I set 'em by the rule, and, as they
   square,
Or deviate from undoubted doctrine 750
   there,
This oral fiction, that old faith declare."
   (_Hind._) " The Council steer'd, it seems,
   a diff'rent course;

They tried the Scripture by tradition's
    force:
But you tradition by the Scripture try;⎫
Pursued by sects, from this to that you⎬
    fly,
Nor dare on one foundation to rely.⎭
The word is then depos'd, and in this view
You rule the Scripture, not the Scripture
    you."
Thus said the *dame*, and, smiling, thus pur-
    sued: 760
" I see, tradition then is disallow'd,
When not evinc'd by Scripture to be true,
And Scripture, as interpreted by you.
But here you tread upon unfaithful
    ground;
Unless you could infallibly expound:
Which you reject as odious Popery,
And throw that doctrine back with scorn
    on me.
Suppose we on things traditive divide,
And both appeal to Scripture to decide;
By various texts we both uphold our
    claim,   770
Nay, often ground our titles on the same:
After long labor lost, and time's expense,
Both grant the words, and quarrel for the
    sense.
Thus all disputes for ever must depend,
For no dumb rule can controversies end.
Thus, when you said tradition must be
    tried
By Sacred Writ, whose sense yourselves
    decide,
You said no more, but that yourselves
    must be
The judges of the Scripture sense, not we.
Against our Church-tradition you de-
    clare,   780
And yet your clerks would sit in Moses'
    chair:
At least 't is prov'd against your argument,
The rule is far from plain, where all dis-
    sent."
" If not by Scriptures, how can we be
    sure,"
Replied the Panther, " what tradition's
    pure ?
For you may palm upon us new for old:
All, as they say, that glitters is not gold."
" How but by following her," replied the
    dame,
" To whom deriv'd from sire to son they
    came;
Where ev'ry age does on another move, 790

And trusts no farther than the next above;
Where all the rounds like Jacob's ladder
    rise,
The lowest hid in earth, the topmost in the
    skies."
Sternly the salvage did her answer mark,
Her glowing eyeballs glitt'ring in the dark,
And said but this: " Since lucre was your
    trade,
Succeeding times such dreadful gaps have
    made,
'T is dangerous climbing: to your sons and
    you
I leave the ladder, and its omen too."
    (*Hind.*) " The Panther's breath was ever
        fam'd for sweet;   800
But from the Wolf such wishes oft I meet:
You learn'd this language from the Blatant
    Beast,
Or rather did not speak, but were possess'd.
As for your answer, 't is but barely urg'd:
You must evince tradition to be forg'd;
Produce plain proofs; unblemish'd authors
    use,
As ancient as those ages they accuse;
Till when, 't is not sufficient to defame:
An old possession stands, till elder quits
    the claim.
Then for our int'rest, which is nam'd
    alone   810
To load with envy, we retort your own.
For when traditions in your faces fly,
Resolving not to yield, you must decry.
As, when the cause goes hard, the guilty
    man
Excepts, and thins his jury all he can;
So, when you stand of other aid bereft,
You to the twelve apostles would be left.
Your friend the Wolf did with more craft
    provide
To set those toys, traditions, quite aside;
And Fathers too, unless when, reason
    spent,   820
He cites 'em but sometimes for ornament.
But, madam Panther, you, tho' more sin-
    cere,
Are not so wise as your adulterer:
The private spirit is a better blind
Than all the dodging tricks your authors
    find.
For they, who left the Scripture to the⎫
    crowd,   ⎪
Each for his own peculiar judge allow'd; ⎬
The way to please 'em was to make 'em ⎪
    proud.   ⎭

Thus, with full sails, they ran upon the
  shelf:
Who could suspect a cozenage from him-
  self ?   830
On his own reason safer 't is to stand,
Than be deceiv'd and damn'd at second
  hand.
But you, who Fathers and traditions take,
And garble some, and some you quite for-
  sake,
Pretending Church auctority to fix,
And yet some grains of private spirit mix,
Are like a mule made up of diff'ring seed,
And that's the reason why you never breed;
At least not propagate your kind abroad,
For home dissenters are by statutes aw'd.
And yet they grow upon you ev'ry day, ⎫
While you (to speak the best) are at a ⎪
  stay,   842 ⎬
For sects that are extremes abhor a ⎪
  middle way. ⎭
Like tricks of state, to stop a raging ⎫
  flood, ⎪
Or mollify a mad-brain'd senate's mood, ⎬
Of all expedients never one was good. ⎭
Well may they argue, (nor can you deny,)
If we must fix on Church auctority,
Best on the best, the fountain, not the flood;
That must be better still, if this be good.
Shall she command, who has herself re-
  bell'd ?   851
Is Antichrist by Antichrist expell'd ?
Did we a lawful tyranny displace,
To set aloft a bastard of the race ?
Why all these wars to win the Book, if ⎫
  we ⎪
Must not interpret for ourselves, but she ? ⎬
Either be wholly slaves, or wholly free. ⎭
For *purging* fires traditions must not fight,
But they must prove episcopacy's right.
Thus those led horses are from service
  freed;   860
You never mount 'em but in time of need.
Like mercenaries, hir'd for home defense,
They will not serve against their native
  prince.
Against domestic foes of *hierarchy*
These are drawn forth, to make Fanatics
  fly;
But, when they see their countrymen at ⎫
  hand, ⎪
Marching against 'em under Church com- ⎬
  mand, ⎪
Straight they forsake their colors, and ⎪
  disband." ⎭

Thus she, nor could the Panther well
  enlarge
With weak defense against so strong a
  charge;   870
But said: "For what did Christ his word
  provide,
If still his Church must want a living
  guide ?
And if all saving doctrines are not there,
Or sacred penmen could not make 'em
  clear,
From after ages we should hope in vain
For truths which men inspir'd could not
  explain."
  "Before the word was written," said the
  Hind,
"Our Savior preach'd his faith to human-
  kind:
From his apostles the first age receiv'd
Eternal truth, and what they taught be-
  liev'd.   880
Thus by tradition faith was planted first;
Succeeding flocks succeeding pastors nurs'd.
This was the way our wise Redeemer ⎫
  chose, ⎪
(Who sure could all things for the best ⎬
  dispose,) ⎪
To fence his fold from their encroaching ⎪
  foes. ⎭
He could have writ himself, but well fore-
  saw
Th' event would be like that of Moses'
  law;
Some difference would arise, some doubts
  remain,
Like those which yet the jarring Jews
  maintain.
No written laws can be so plain, so pure,
But wit may gloss, and malice may ob-
  scure;   891
Not those indited by his first command —
A prophet grav'd the text, an angel held
  his hand.
Thus faith was ere the written word ap-
  pear'd,
And men believ'd, not what they read, but
  heard.
But since th' apostles could not be confin'd
To these, or those, but severally design'd
Their large commission round the world to
  blow,
To spread their faith, they spread their
  labors too.
Yet still their absent flock their pains did
  share;   900

They hearken'd still, for love produces care.
And, as mistakes arose, or discords fell,
Or bold seducers taught 'em to rebel;
As charity grew cold, or faction hot,
Or long neglect their lessons had forgot;
For all their wants they wisely did provide,
And preaching by epistles was supplied:
So great physicians cannot all attend,
But some they visit, and to some they send.
Yet all those letters were not writ to all;
Nor first intended, but occasional,   911
Their absent sermons; nor if they contain
All needful doctrines, are those doctrines
      plain.
Clearness by frequent preaching must be
      wrought,
They writ but seldom, but they daily taught.
And what one saint has said of holy Paul,
He darkly writ, is true applied to all.
For this obscurity could Heav'n provide ⎫
More prudently than by a living guide,   ⎬
As doubts arose, the difference to decide ? ⎭
A guide was therefore needful, therefore
      made;   921
And, if appointed, sure to be obey'd.
Thus, with due rev'rence to th' apostles' writ,
By which my sons are taught, to which sub-
      mit;
I think, those truths their sacred works con-
      tain,
The Church alone can certainly explain;
That following ages, leaning on the past,
May rest upon the primitive at last.
Nor would I thence the word no rule infer,
But none without the Church interpreter;
Because, as I have urg'd before, 't is mute,
And is itself the subject of dispute.   932
But what th' apostles their successors ⎫
      taught,   ⎪
They to the next, from them to us is ⎬
      brought,   ⎪
Th' undoubted sense which is in Scrip- ⎪
      ture sought.   ⎭
From hence the Church is arm'd, when ⎫
      errors rise,   ⎪
To stop their entrance, and prevent sur- ⎬
      prise;   ⎪
And, safe entrench'd within, her foes ⎪
      without defies.   ⎭
By these all fest'ring sores her coun- ⎫
      sels heal,   ⎪
Which time or has disclos'd, or shall re- ⎬
      veal;   940   ⎪
For discord cannot end without a last ⎪
      appeal.   ⎭

Nor can a council national decide,   ⎫
But with subordination to her guide: ⎪
(I wish the cause were on that issue   ⎬
      tried.)   ⎭
Much less the Scripture; for suppose debate
Betwixt pretenders to a fair estate,
Bequeath'd by some legator's last intent;
(Such is our dying Savior's testament:)
The will is prov'd, is open'd, and is read;
The doubtful heirs their diff'ring titles
      plead: 950
All vouch the words their int'rest to main-
      tain,
And each pretends by those his cause is
      plain.
Shall then the testament award the right ?
No, that's the Hungary for which they
      fight;
The field of battle, subject of debate;
The thing contended for, the fair estate.
The sense is intricate, 't is only clear
What vowels and what consonants are there.
Therefore 't is plain, its meaning must be
      tried
Before some judge appointed to decide." 960
"Suppose," the fair apostate said, "I grant
The faithful flock some living guide should
      want,
Your arguments an endless chase pursue: ⎫
Produce this vaunted leader to our view, ⎬
This mighty Moses of the chosen crew." ⎭
   The dame, who saw her fainting foe re-
      tir'd,
With force renew'd, to victory aspir'd;
And, looking upward to her kindred sky, ⎫
As once our Savior own'd his deity,   ⎬
Pronounc'd his words — *She whom ye seek* ⎪
      am I.   970   ⎭
Nor less amaz'd this voice the Panther
      heard,
Than were those Jews to hear a god de-
      clar'd.
Then thus the matron modestly renew'd:
"Let all your prophets and their sects be
      view'd,
And see to which of 'em yourselves think fit
The conduct of your conscience to submit:
Each proselyte would vote his doctor best,
With absolute exclusion to the rest;
Thus would your Polish diet disagree,
And end, as it began, in anarchy.   980
Yourself the fairest for election stand,
Because you seem crown-gen'ral of the land;
But soon against your superstitious lawn
Some Presbyterian saber would be drawn:

In your establish'd laws of sov'reignty
The rest some fundamental flaw would
    see,
And call rebellion gospel-liberty.
To Church decrees your articles require
Submission modified, if not entire;
Homage denied, to censures you proceed: 990
But when *Curtana* will not do the deed,
You lay that pointless clergy-weapon by,
And to the laws, your sword of justice,
    fly.
Now this your sects the more unkindly take,
(Those prying varlets hit the blots you
    make,)
Because some ancient friends of yours de-
    clare,
Your only rule of faith the Scriptures are,
Interpreted by men of judgment sound,
Which ev'ry sect will for themselves ex-
    pound;
Nor think less rev'rence to their doctors
    due   1000
For sound interpretation, than to you.
If then by able heads are understood
Your brother prophets, who reform'd abroad,
Those able heads expound a wiser way,
That their own sheep their shepherd should
    obey.
But if you mean yourselves are only
    sound,
That doctrine turns the Reformation
    round,
And all the rest are false reformers
    found;
Because in sundry points you stand alone,
Not in communion join'd with any
    one;   1010
And therefore must be all the Church,
    or none.
Then, till you have agreed whose judge is
    best,
Against this forc'd submission they protest:
While *sound* and *sound* a diff'rent sense ex-
    plains,
Both play at hardhead till they break their
    brains;
And from their chairs each other's force
    defy,
While unregarded thunders vainly fly.
I pass the rest, because your Church alone
Of all usurpers best could fill the throne.
But neither you, nor any sect beside,   1020
For this high office can be qualified
With necessary gifts requir'd in such a
    guide.

For that which must direct the whole
    must be
Bound in one bond of faith and unity,
But all your sev'ral Churches disagree.
The *consubstantiating* Church and priest
Refuse communion to the Calvinist:
The French reform'd from preaching you
    restrain,
Because you judge their ordination vain;
And so they judge of yours, but donors
    must ordain.   1030
In short, in doctrine, or in discipline,
Not one reform'd can with another join:
But all from each as from damnation fly;
No union they pretend, but in *non-Popery.*
Nor, should their members in a synod meet,
Could any Church presume to mount the
    seat
Above the rest, their discords to decide;
None would obey, but each would be the
    guide;
And face to face dissensions would en-
    crease,
For only distance now preserves the peace.
All in their turns accusers, and accus'd, 1041
Babel was never half so much confus'd.
What one can plead, the rest can plead
    as well;
For amongst equals lies no last appeal,
And all confess themselves are fallible.
Now since you grant some necessary guide,
All who can err are justly laid aside:
Because a trust so sacred to confer
Shows want of such a sure interpreter;
And how can he be needful who can
    err?   1050
Then, granting that unerring guide we want,
That such there is you stand oblig'd to
    grant:
Our Savior else were wanting to supply
Our needs, and obviate that necessity.
It then remains, that Church can only be
The guide, which owns unfailing certainty;
Or else you slip your hold, and change your
    side,
Relapsing from a necessary guide.
But this annex'd condition of the crown,
Immunity from errors, you disown;   1060
Here then you shrink, and lay your weak
    pretensions down.
For petty royalties you raise debate,
But this unfailing universal State
You shun, nor dare succeed to such a
    glorious weight;
And for that cause those promises detest,

With which our Savior did his Church invest;
But strive t' evade, and fear to find 'em true,
As conscious they were never meant to you:
All which the Mother Church asserts her own,
And with unrival'd claim ascends the throne.   1070
So when of old th' Almighty Father sate
In council, to redeem our ruin'd state,
Millions of millions, at a distance round,⎤
Silent the sacred consistory crown'd,   ⎬
To hear what mercy mix'd with justice   ⎪
    could propound;   ⎦
All prompt, with eager pity, to fulfil
The full extent of their Creator's will:
But when the stern conditions were declar'd,
A mournful whisper thro' the host was heard,
And the whole hierarchy, with heads hung down,   1080
Submissively declin'd the pond'rous proffer'd crown.
Then, not till then, th' eternal Son from high
Rose in the strength of all the Deity;
Stood forth t' accept the terms, and   ⎤
    underwent   ⎪
A weight which all the frame of heav'n   ⎬
    had bent,   ⎪
Nor he himself could bear, but as omni-   ⎪
    potent.   ⎦
Now, to remove the least remaining doubt,
That ev'n the blear-ey'd sects may find her out,
Behold what heav'nly rays adorn her   ⎤
    brows,   ⎪
What from his wardrobe her belov'd   ⎬
    allows   1090   ⎪
To deck the wedding day of his unspotted   ⎪
    spouse.   ⎦
Behold what marks of majesty she brings;
Richer than ancient heirs of Eastern kings:
Her right hand holds the scepter and the keys,
To shew whom she commands, and who obeys;
With these to bind, or set the sinner free,
With that t' assert spiritual royalty.
"One in herself, not rent by schism, but sound,

Entire, one solid shining diamond;
Not sparkles shatter'd into   Marks of
    sects like you: 1100 the Catholic
One is the Church, and must   Church from
    be to be true;   the Nicene
                                   Creed.
One central principle of unity.
" As undivided, so from errors free,   ⎫
As one in faith, so one in sanctity.   ⎬
Thus she, and none but she, th' insulting rage
Of heretics oppos'd from age to age:
Still when the giant-brood invades her ⎤
    throne,   ⎪
She stoops from heav'n, and meets 'em   ⎬
    halfway down,   ⎪
And with paternal thunder vindicates her⎪
    crown.   1109 ⎦
But like Egyptian sorcerers you stand, ⎤
And vainly lift aloft your magic wand, ⎪
To sweep away the swarms of vermin   ⎬
    from the land: ⎦
You could, like them, with like infernal force,
Produce the plague, but not arrest the course.
But when the boils and botches, with disgrace
And public scandal, sat upon the face,
Themselves attack'd, the *Magi* strove no⎤
    more,   ⎪
They saw God's finger, and their fate   ⎬
    deplore;   ⎪
Themselves they could not cure of the   ⎪
    dishonest sore.   ⎦
" Thus one, thus pure, behold her largely
    spread,   1120
Like the fair ocean from her mother-bed;
From east to west triumphantly she rides,
All shores are water'd by her wealthy tides:
The gospel-sound diffus'd from pole to pole,
Where winds can carry, and where waves can roll;
The selfsame doctrine of the sacred page
Convey'd to ev'ry clime, in ev'ry age.
" Here let my sorrow give my satire place,
To raise new blushes on my British race;
Our sailing ships like common shores we ⎤
    use,   1130 ⎬
And thro' our distant colonies diffuse   ⎪
The draughts of dungeons, and the stench ⎪
    of stews;   ⎦
Whom, when their home-bred honesty is lost,
We disembogue on some far Indian coast:

Thieves, panders, palliards, sins of ev'ry
    sort;
Those are the manufactures we export;
And these the *missioners* our zeal has
    made:
For, with my country's pardon be it said,
Religion is the least of all our trade.
    " Yet some improve their traffic more
        than we;   1140
For they on gain, their only god, rely;
And set a public price on piety.
Industrious of the needle and the chart,
They run full sail to their Japonian mart;
Prevention fear, and, prodigal of fame,
Sell all of Christian to the very name;
Nor leave enough of that to hide their
    naked shame.
    " Thus, of three marks, which in the
    Creed we view,
Not one of all can be applied to you:
Much less the fourth; in vain, alas, you
    seek   1150
Th' ambitious title of apostolic:
Godlike descent ! 't is well your blood can
    be
Prov'd noble in the third or fourth degree:
For all of ancient that you had before
(I mean what is not borrow'd from our
    store)
Was error fulminated o'er and o'er;
Old heresies condemn'd in ages past,
By care and time recover'd from the blast.
    " 'T is said with ease, but never can be
    prov'd,
The Church her old foundations has re-
    mov'd,   1160
And built new doctrines on unstable sands:
Judge that, ye winds and rains; you prov'd
    her, yet she stands.
Those ancient doctrines, charg'd on her for
    new,
Shew when, and how, and from what hands
    they grew.
We claim no pow'r, when heresies grow
    bold,
To coin new faith, but still declare the
    old.
How else could that obscene disease be
    purg'd,
When controverted texts are vainly urg'd ?
To prove tradition new, there 's somewhat
    more
Requir'd, than saying: ' 'T was not us'd be-
    fore.'   1170
Those monumental arms are never stirr'd,

Till schism or heresy call down Goliah's
    sword.
    " Thus, what you call corruptions are, in
    truth,
The first plantations of the gospel's youth;
Old standard faith; but cast your eyes
    again,
And view those errors which new sects
    maintain,
Or which of old disturb'd the Church's
    peaceful reign;
And we can point each period of the time,
When they began, and who begot the
    crime;   1179
Can calculate how long th' eclipse endur'd,
Who interpos'd, what digits were obscur'd:
Of all which are already pass'd away,
We know the rise, the progress, and de-
    cay.
    " Despair at our foundations then to
    strike,
Till you can prove your faith apostolic;
A limpid stream drawn from the native
    source;
Succession lawful in a lineal course.
Prove any Church, oppos'd to this our head,
So one, so pure, so unconfin'dly spread,
Under one chief of the spiritual State,   1190
The members all combin'd, and all subor-
    dinate.
Shew such a seamless coat, from schism
    so free,
In no communion join'd with heresy.
If such a one you find, let truth prevail;
Till when, your weights will in the bal-
    ance fail:
A Church unprincipled kicks up the scale.
    " But if you cannot think (nor sure
    you can
Suppose in God what were unjust in man)
That he, the fountain of eternal grace,
Should suffer Falsehood, for so long a
    space,   1200
To banish Truth, and to usurp her place ;
That sev'n successive ages should be lost,
And preach damnation at their proper cost;
That all your erring ancestors should die,
Drown'd in th' abyss of deep idolatry;
If piety forbid such thoughts to rise,
Awake, and open your unwilling eyes:
God has left nothing for each age undone,
From this to that wherein he sent his
    Son:
Then think but well of him, and half
    your work is done.   1210

"See how his Church, adorn'd with
    ev'ry grace,
With open arms, a kind forgiving face,
Stands ready to prevent her long-lost
    sons' embrace.
Not more did Joseph o'er his brethren weep,
Nor less himself could from discovery
    keep,
When in the crowd of suppliants they were
    seen,
And in their crew his best-beloved Ben-
    jamin.
That pious Joseph in the
    Church behold,
To feed your famine, and re-
    fuse your gold;
The Joseph you exil'd, the
    Joseph whom you
    sold."   1220

*The renun-
ciation of the
Benedictines
to the Abbey
Lands.*

    Thus, while with heav'nly charity she
        spoke,
A streaming blaze the silent shadows
    broke;
Shot from the skies a cheerful azure
    light;
The birds obscene to forests wing'd their
    flight,
And gaping graves receiv'd the wand'ring
    guilty sprite.
    Such were the pleasing triumphs of the
        sky
For James his late nocturnal victory;
The pledge of his Almighty Patron's love,
The fireworks which his angel made above.
I saw myself the lambent easy
    light   1230
Gild the brown horror, and dispel the
    night.
The messenger with speed the tidings
    bore;
News which three lab'ring nations did
    restore;
But heav'n's own *nuntius* was arriv'd
    before.
    By this, the Hind had reach'd her lonely
        cell,
And vapors rose, and dews unwholesome
    fell.
When she, by frequent observation wise,
As one who long on heav'n had fix'd her
    eyes,
Discern'd a change of weather in the
    skies.
The western borders were with crimson
    spread,   1240

*Poeta
loquitur.*

The moon descending look'd all flaming
    red;
She thought good manners bound her to
    invite
The stranger dame to be her guest that
    night.
'T is true, coarse diet, and a short repast,
(She said,) were weak inducements to
    the taste
Of one so nicely bred, and so unus'd to
    fast;
But what plain fare her cottage could
    afford,
A hearty welcome at a homely board,
Was freely hers; and, to supply the rest,
An honest meaning, and an open breast:
Last, with content of mind, the poor man's
    wealth,   1251
A grace cup to their common patron's
    health.
This she desir'd her to accept, and stay,
For fear she might be wilder'd in her way,
Because she wanted an unerring guide;
And then the dewdrops on her silken hide
Her tender constitution did declare,
Too lady-like a long fatigue to bear,
And rough inclemencies of raw nocturnal
    air.
But most she fear'd that, traveling so
    late,   1260
Some evil-minded beasts might lie in
    wait,
And without witness wreak their hidden
    hate.
    The Panther, tho' she lent a list'ning ear,
Had more of Lion in her than to fear:
Yet wisely weighing, since she had to deal
With many foes, their numbers might pre-
    vail,
Return'd her all the thanks she could
    afford,
And took her friendly hostess at her word;
Who, ent'ring first her lowly roof, (a
    shed
With hoary moss and winding ivy
    spread,   1270
Honest enough to hide an humble her-
    mit's head,)
Thus graciously bespoke her welcome
    guest:
"So might these walls, with your fair
    presence blest,
Become your dwelling place of everlast-
    ing rest,
Not for a night, or quick revolving year;

Welcome an owner, not a sojourner.
This peaceful seat my poverty secures;
War seldom enters but where wealth allures:
Nor yet despise it; for this poor abode
Has oft receiv'd, and yet receives a god;
A god victorious of the Stygian race   1281
Here laid his sacred limbs, and sanctified
 the place.
This mean retreat did mighty Pan contain:
Be emulous of him, and pomp disdain,
And dare not to debase your soul to gain."
 The silent stranger stood amaz'd to see
Contempt of wealth, and wilful poverty;
And, tho' ill habits are not soon controll'd,
Awhile suspended her desire of gold;
But civilly drew in her sharpen'd paws,
Not violating hospitable laws,   1291
And pacified her tail, and lick'd her
 frothy jaws.
 The Hind did first her country cates
 provide;
Then couch'd herself securely by her side.

THE THIRD PART

Much malice mingled with a little wit,
Perhaps, may censure this mysterious writ;
Because the Muse has peopled Caledon
With Panthers, Bears, and Wolves, and
 beasts unknown,
As if we were not stock'd with monsters
 of our own.
Let Æsop answer, who has set to view 1300
Such kinds as Greece and Phrygia never
 knew;
And Mother Hubbard, in her homely dress,
Has sharply blam'd a British Lioness,
That queen, whose feast the factious rabble keep,
Expos'd obscenely naked and asleep.
Led by those great examples, may not I
The wanted organs of their words supply?
If men transact like brutes, 't is equal then
For brutes to claim the privilege of men.
 Others our Hind of folly will endite, 1310
To entertain a dang'rous guest by night.
Let those remember that she cannot die
Till rolling time is lost in round eternity;
Nor need she fear the Panther, tho' untam'd,
Because the Lion's peace was now proclaim'd:
The wary salvage would not give offense,

To forfeit the protection of her prince;
But watch'd the time her vengeance to complete,
When all her furry sons in frequent senate
 met;
Meanwhile she quench'd her fury at the
 flood,   1320
And with a lenten salad cool'd her blood.
Their commons, tho' but coarse, were nothing scant,
Nor did their minds an equal banquet
 want.
 For now the Hind, whose noble nature
 strove
T' express her plain simplicity of love,
Did all the honors of her house so well,
No sharp debates disturb'd the friendly
 meal.
She turn'd the talk, avoiding that extreme,
To common dangers past, a sadly pleasing
 theme;
Rememb'ring ev'ry storm which toss'd
 the State,   1330
When both were objects of the public
 hate,
And dropp'd a tear betwixt for her own
 children's fate.
 Nor fail'd she then a full review to make
Of what the Panther suffer'd for her sake:
Her lost esteem, her truth, her loyal care,
Her faith unshaken to an exil'd heir,
Her strength t' endure, her courage to defy;
Her choice of honorable infamy.
On these, prolixly thankful, she enlarg'd;
Then with acknowledgments herself she
 charg'd;   1340
For friendship, of itself an holy tie,
Is made more sacred by adversity.
Now should they part, malicious tongues
 would say,
They met like chance companions on the
 way,
Whom mutual fear of robbers had possess'd:
While danger lasted, kindness was profess'd;
But that once o'er, the short-liv'd union
 ends;
The road divides, and there divide the
 friends.
 The Panther nodded when her speech
 was done,
And thank'd her coldly in a hollow tone, 1350
But said her gratitude had gone too far
For common offices of Christian care:
If to the lawful heir she had been true,
She paid but Cæsar what was Cæsar's due.

"I might," she added, "with like praise
 describe
Your suff'ring sons, and so return your
 bribe;
But incense from my hands is poorly priz'd,
For gifts are scorn'd where givers are de-
 spis'd.
I serv'd a turn, and then was cast away;
You, like the gaudy fly, your wings dis-
 play,   1360
And sip the sweets, and bask in your
 great *patron's* day."
 This heard, the matron was not slow to
 find
What sort of malady had seiz'd her mind:
Disdain, with gnawing envy, fell despite,
And canker'd malice stood in open sight;
Ambition, int'rest, pride without control,
And jealousy, the jaundice of the soul;
Revenge, the bloody minister of ill,
With all the lean tormentors of the will.
'T was easy now to guess from whence
 arose   1370
Her new-made union with her ancient foes,
Her forc'd civilities, her faint embrace,
Affected kindness with an alter'd face:
Yet durst she not too deeply probe the
 wound,
As hoping still the nobler parts were sound;
But strove with anodynes t' assuage the
 smart,
And mildly thus her med'cine did impart.
 "Complaints of lovers help to ease their
 pain;
It shows a rest of kindness to complain,
A friendship loth to quit its former hold,
And conscious merit may be justly bold.
But much more just your jealousy would
 show,   1382
If others' good were injury to you:
Witness, ye heav'ns, how I rejoice to see
Rewarded worth and rising loyalty.
Your warrior offspring that upheld the
 crown,
The scarlet honors of your peaceful gown,
Are the most pleasing objects I can find,
Charms to my sight, and cordials to my
 mind:
When virtue spooms before a prosp'rous
 gale,   1390
My heaving wishes help to fill the sail;
And if my pray'rs for all the brave were
 heard,
Cæsar should still have such, and such
 should still reward.

"The labor'd earth your pains have sow'd
 and till'd;
'T is just you reap the product of the field:
Yours be the harvest; 't is the beggar's
 gain
To glean the fallings of the loaded wain.
Such scatter'd ears as are not worth your
 care
Your charity for alms may safely spare,
And alms are but the vehicles of pray'r.
My daily bread is lit'rally implor'd;   1401
I have no barns nor granaries to hoard;
If Cæsar to his own his hand extends,
Say which of yours his charity offends:
You know he largely gives to more than
 are his friends.
Are you defrauded when he feeds the poor ?
Our mite decreases nothing of your store.
I am but few, and by your fare you see
My crying sins are not of luxury.
Some juster motive sure your mind with-
 draws,   1410
And makes you break our friendship's
 holy laws;
For barefac'd envy is too base a cause.
 "Show more occasion for your discon-
 tent;
Your love, the Wolf, would help you to in-
 vent:
Some German quarrel, or, as times go now,
Some French, where force is uppermost,
 will do.
When at the fountain's head, as merit ought
To claim the place, you take a swilling
 draught,
How easy 't is an envious eye to throw,
And tax the sheep for troubling streams
 below;   1420
Or call her (when no farther cause you
 find)
An enemy profess'd of all your kind.
But then, perhaps, the wicked world would
 think
The Wolf design'd to eat as well as drink."
 This last allusion gall'd the Panther more,
Because indeed it rubb'd upon the sore.
Yet seem'd she not to winch, tho' shrewdly
 pain'd,
But then her passive character maintain'd.
 "I never grudg'd, whate'er my foes re-
 port,
Your flaunting fortune in the Lion's
 court.   1430
You have your day, or you are much be-
 lied,

But I am always on the suff'ring side:
You know my doctrine, and I need not say
I will not, but I cannot disobey.
On this firm principle I ever stood;
He of my sons who fails to make it good,
By one rebellious act renounces to my
blood."
  "Ah," said the Hind, "how many sons
have you
Who call you mother, whom you never
knew !
But most of them who that relation plead,
Are such ungracious youths as wish you
dead.   1441
They gape at rich revenues which you hold,
And fain would nibble at your grandame
gold;
Enquire into your years, and laugh to find
Your crazy temper shews you much de-
clin'd.
Were you not dim, and doted, you might
see
A pack of cheats that claim a pedigree,
No more of kin to you, than you to me.
Do you not know, that for a little coin
Heralds can foist a name into the line; 1450
They ask you blessing but for what you
have,
But once possess'd of what with care you
save,
The wanton boys would piss upon your
grave.
  "Your sons of latitude that court your
grace,
Tho' most resembling you in form and
face,
Are far the worst of your pretended race.
And, but I blush your honesty to blot,
Pray God you prove 'em lawfully begot:
For in some Popish libels I have read,
The Wolf has been too busy in your bed; 1460
At least their hinder parts, the belly-piece,
The paunch, and all that Scorpio claims,
are his.
Their malice too a sore suspicion brings;
For, tho' they dare not bark, they snarl at
kings:
Nor blame 'em for intruding in your line;
Fat bishoprics are still of right divine.
  "Think you your new French proselytes
are come
To starve abroad, because they starv'd at
home ?
Your benefices twinkled from afar;
They found the new Messiah by the star: 1470

Those Swisses fight on any side for pay,
And 't is the living that conforms, not they.
Mark with what management their tribes
divide;
Some stick to you, and some to t'other
side,
That many Churches may for many
mouths provide.
More vacant pulpits would more converts
make;
All would have latitude enough to take:
The rest unbenefic'd your sects main-
tain;
For ordinations without cures are vain,
And chamber practice is a silent gain. 1480
Your sons of breadth at home are much
like these;
Their soft and yielding metals run with
ease:
They melt, and take the figure of the mold,
But harden and preserve it best in gold."
  "Your Delphic sword," the Panther then
replied,
"Is double-edg'd, and cuts on either side.
Some sons of mine, who bear upon their
shield
Three steeples argent in a sable field,
Have sharply tax'd your converts, who, un-
fed,
Have follow'd you for miracles of bread; 1490
Such who themselves of no religion are,
Allur'd with gain, for any will declare.
Bare lies with bold assertions they can face,
But dint of argument is out of place.
The grim logician puts 'em in a fright;
'T is easier far to flourish than to fight.
Thus our eighth Henry's marriage they
defame;
They say the schism of beds began the
game,
Divorcing from the Church to wed the
dame:
Tho' largely prov'd, and by himself pro-
fess'd,   1500
That conscience, conscience would not let
him rest;
I mean, not till possess'd of her he lov'd,
And old, uncharming Catherine was remov'd.
For sundry years before did he complain,
And told his ghostly confessor his pain.
With the same impudence, without a
ground,
They say, that look the Reformation
round,
No *Treatise of Humility* is found.

But if none were, the gospel does not
    want;
Our Savior preach'd it, and I hope you
    grant,   1510
The Sermon in the Mount was Protest-
    ant."
    "No doubt," replied the Hind, "as sure
        as all
The writings of Saint Peter and Saint
    Paul:
On that decision let it stand or fall.
Now for my converts, who, you say, un-
    fed,
Have follow'd me for miracles of bread;
Judge not by hearsay, but observe at least,
If since their change their loaves have been
    increas'd.
The Lion buys no converts; if he did,
Beasts would be sold as fast as he could
    bid.   1520
Tax those of int'rest who conform for gain,
Or stay the market of another reign:
Your broad-way sons would never be too
    nice
To close with Calvin, if he paid their price;
But rais'd three steeples high'r, would
    change their note,
And quit the cassock for the canting-coat.
Now, if you damn this censure as too bold,
Judge by yourselves, and think not others
    sold.
"Meantime my sons accus'd, by fame's
    report,
Pay small attendance at the Lion's court,
Nor rise with early crowds, nor flatter
    late;   1531
(For silently they beg who daily wait.)
Preferment is bestow'd that comes un-
    sought;
Attendance is a bribe, and then 't is bought.
How they should speed, their fortune is
    untried;
For not to ask is not to be denied.
For what they have, their God and king
    they bless,
And hope they should not murmur, had
    they less.
But, if reduc'd subsistence to implore,
In common prudence they would pass your
    door.   1540
Unpitied Hudibras, your champion friend,
Has shown how far your charities extend.
This lasting verse shall on his tomb be
    read,
He sham'd you living, and upbraids you dead.

"With odious atheist names you load
    your foes;
Your lib'ral clergy why did I expose?
It never fails in charities like those.
In climes where true religion is profess'd,
That imputation were no laughing jest.
But *imprimatur*, with a chaplain's name,
Is here sufficient license to defame.   1551
What wonder is 't that black detraction
    thrives?
The homicide of names is less than
    lives,
And yet the perjur'd murtherer sur-
    vives."
    This said, she paus'd a little, and sup-
        press'd
The boiling indignation of her breast;
She knew the virtue of her blade, nor
    would
Pollute her satire with ignoble blood:
Her panting foes she saw before her lie,
And back she drew the shining weapon
    dry.   1560
So, when the gen'rous Lion has in sight
His equal match, he rouses for the fight;
But when his foe lies prostrate on the
    plain,
He sheathes his paws, uncurls his angry
    mane,
And, pleas'd with bloodless honors of the
    day,
Walks over and disdains th' inglorious
    prey.
So JAMES, if great with less we may com-
    pare,
Arrests his rolling thunderbolts in air;
And grants ungrateful friends a lengthen'd
    space,
T' implore the remnants of long-suff'ring
    grace.   1570
    This breathing-time the matron took;
        and then
Resum'd the thrid of her discourse again.
"Be vengeance wholly left to pow'rs divine,
And let Heav'n judge betwixt your sons
    and mine:
If joys hereafter must be purchas'd here
With loss of all that mortals hold so dear,
Then welcome infamy and public shame,
And, last, a long farewell to worldly fame.
'T is said with ease, but, O, how hardly
    tried
By haughty souls to human honor tied!
O sharp convulsive pangs of agonizing
    pride!   1581

Down then, thou rebel, never more to
   rise,
And what thou didst, and dost, so dearly
   prize,
That fame, that darling fame, make that
   thy sacrifice.
'T is nothing thou hast giv'n, then add thy
   tears
For a long race of unrepenting years:
'T is nothing yet, yet all thou hast to
   give;
Then add those *may-be* years thou hast to
   live:
Yet nothing still; then poor and naked
   come,
Thy father will receive his unthrift
   home,   1590
And thy blest Savior's blood discharge
   the mighty sum.
  "Thus," she pursued, "I discipline a
   son,
Whose uncheck'd fury to revenge would
   run;
He champs the bit, impatient of his loss,
And starts aside, and flounders at the
   cross.
Instruct him better, gracious God, to know,
As thine is vengeance, so forgiveness too:
That, suff'ring from ill tongues, he bears no
   more
Than what his sovereign bears, and what
   his Savior bore.
  "It now remains for you to school your
   child,   1600
And ask why God's anointed he revil'd;
A king and princess dead! Did Shimei
   worse?
The curser's punishment should fright the
   curse: *Stillingfleet*
Your son was warn'd, and wisely gave it
   o'er, *Burnet*
But he who counsel'd him has paid the
   score:
The heavy malice could no higher tend,
But woe to him on whom the weights de-
   scend.
So to permitted ills the *dæmon* flies;
His rage is aim'd at him who rules the
   skies:
Constrain'd to quit his cause, no succor
   found,   1610
The foe discharges ev'ry tire around,
In clouds of smoke abandoning the fight;
But his own thund'ring peals proclaim his
   flight.

  "In Henry's change his charge as ill
   succeeds;
To that long story little answer needs;
Confront but Henry's words with Henry's
   deeds.
Were space allow'd, with ease it might be
   prov'd
What springs his blessed Reformation
   mov'd.
The dire effects appear'd in open sight,
Which from the cause he calls a distant
   flight,   1620
And yet no larger leap than from the
   sun to light.
  "Now last your sons a double pæan
   sound,
A *Treatise of Humility* is found.
'T is found, but better it had ne'er been
   sought,
Than thus in Protestant procession brought.
The fam'd original thro' Spain is known,
Rodriguez' work, my celebrated son,
Which yours by ill translating made his
   own;
Conceal'd its author, and usurp'd the name,
The basest and ignoblest theft of fame. 1630
My altars kindled first that living coal;
Restore, or practice better what you stole:
That virtue could this humble verse in-
   spire,
'T is all the restitution I require."
  Glad was the Panther that the charge
   was clos'd,
And none of all her fav'rite sons expos'd.
For laws of arms permit each injur'd man
To make himself a saver where he can.
Perhaps the plunder'd merchant cannot tell
The names of pirates in whose hands he
   fell;   1640
But at the den of thieves he justly flies,
And ev'ry Algerine is lawful prize.
No private person in the foe's estate
Can plead exemption from the public fate.
Yet Christian laws allow not such redress;
Then let the greater supersede the less.
But let th' abettors of the Panther's crime
Learn to make fairer wars another time.
Some characters may sure be found to
   write
Among her sons; for 't is no common
   sight,   1650
A spotted dam, and all her offspring
   white.
  The salvage, tho' she saw her plea con-
   troll'd,

Yet would not wholly seem to quit her hold,
But offer'd fairly to compound the strife,
And judge conversion by the convert's life.
" 'T is true," she said, " I think it somewhat
    strange,
So few should follow profitable change;
For present joys are more to flesh and
    blood,
Than a dull prospect of a distant good.
'T was well alluded by a son of mine,   1660
(I hope to quote him is not to purloin,)
Two magnets, heav'n and earth, allure to
    bliss;
The larger loadstone that, the nearer this:
The weak attraction of the greater fails;
We nod a while, but neighborhood prevails;
But when the greater proves the nearer too,
I wonder more your converts come so slow.
Methinks in those who firm with me re-
    main,
It shows a nobler principle than gain."
  "Your inf'rence would be strong," the
    Hind replied,   1670
" If yours were in effect the suff'ring side:
Your clergy sons their own in peace pos-
    sess,
Nor are their prospects in reversion less.
My proselytes are struck with awful dread;
Your bloody comet-laws hang blazing o'er
    their head:
The respite they enjoy but only lent,
The best they have to hope, protracted
    punishment.
Be judge yourself, if int'rest may prevail,
Which motives, yours or mine, will turn
    the scale.
While pride and pomp allure, and plen-⎤
    teous ease,   1680 |
That is, till man's predominant passions ⎬
    cease, |
Admire no longer at my slow encrease. ⎦
  " By education most have been misled;
So they believe, because they so were bred.
The *priest* continues what the nurse began,
And thus the child imposes on the man.
The rest I nam'd before, nor need repeat;
But int'rest is the most prevailing cheat,
The sly seducer both of age and youth:
They study that, and think they study
    truth.   1690
When int'rest fortifies an argument,   ⎤
Weak reason serves to gain the will's as- |
    sent;   ⎬
For souls already warp'd receive an easy |
    bent.   ⎦

" Add long prescription of establish'd
    laws,
And pique of honor to maintain a cause,
And shame of change, and fear of future
    ill,
And zeal, the blind conductor of the will;
And chief, among the still-mistaking⎤
    crowd, |
The fame of teachers obstinate and |
    proud,   ⎬
And, more than all, the private judge al- |
    low'd;   1700 ⎦
Disdain of Fathers, which the daunce be-⎤
    gan, |
And last, uncertain whose the narrower ⎬
    span, |
The clown unread, and half-read gentle- |
    man."   ⎦
  To this the Panther, with a scornful smile:
" Yet still you travail with unwearied toil,
And range around the realm without con-⎤
    trol, |
Among my sons for proselytes to prole, ⎬
And here and there you snap some silly |
    soul.   ⎦
You hinted fears of future change in state;
Pray Heav'n you did not prophesy your
    fate !   1710
Perhaps you think your time of triumph⎤
    near, |
But may mistake the season of the year; ⎬
The Swallows' fortune gives you cause to |
    fear."   ⎦
  " For charity," replied the matron, " tell
What sad mischance those pretty birds be-
    fell."
  " Nay, no mischance," the salvage⎤
    dame replied, |
" But want of wit in their unerring guide, ⎬
And eager haste, and gaudy hopes, and |
    giddy pride.   ⎦
Yet, wishing timely warning may prevail,
Make you the moral, and I 'll tell the
    tale.   1720
  " The Swallow, privileg'd above the rest
Of all the birds, as man's familiar guest,
Pursues the sun in summer brisk and bold,
But wisely shuns the persecuting cold:
Is well to chancels and to chimneys known,
Tho' 't is not thought she feeds on smoke
    alone.
From hence she has been held of heav'nly
    line,
Endued with particles of soul divine.
This merry chorister had long possess'd

Her summer seat, and feather'd well her
    nest: 1730
Till frowning skies began to change their
    cheer,
And time turn'd up the wrong side of the
    year;
The shedding trees began the ground to
    strow
With yellow leaves, and bitter blasts to
    blow.
Sad auguries of winter thence she drew,
Which by instinct, or prophecy, she knew:
When prudence warn'd her to remove be-
    times,
And seek a better heav'n and warmer climes.
  " Her sons were summon'd on a steeple's
    height,
And, call'd in common council, vote a flight;
The day was nam'd, the next that should ⌉
    be fair;   1741
All to the gen'ral rendezvous repair;   ⎬
They try their flutt'ring wings, and trust |
    themselves in air,   ⌋
But whether upward to the moon they go, ⌉
Or dream the winter out in caves below,   ⎬
Or hawk at flies elsewhere, concerns not   ⌋
    us to know.
  " Southwards, you may be sure, they bent
    their flight,
And harbor'd in a hollow rock at night:
Next morn they rose, and set up ev'ry sail;
The wind was fair, but blew a mack'rel gale:
The sickly young sat shiv'ring on the shore,
Abhorr'd salt water never seen before,   1752
And pray'd their tender mothers to delay
The passage, and expect a fairer day.
  " With these the Martin readily con-
    curr'd,
A church-begot, and church-believing bird;
Of little body, but of lofty mind,   ⌉
Round-bellied, for a dignity design'd,   ⎬
And much a dunce, as Martins are by |
    kind: ⌋
Yet often quoted canon-laws, and code, ⌉
And Fathers which he never under-   ⎬
    stood;   1761   ⌋
But little learning needs in noble blood.
For, sooth to say, the Swallow brought him
    in,
Her household chaplain, and her next of
    kin;
In superstition silly to excess,
And casting schemes by planetary guess:
In fine, short-wing'd, unfit himself to fly,
His fear foretold foul weather in the sky.

  " Besides, a Raven from a wither'd oak,
Left of their lodging, was observ'd to
    croak.   1770
That omen lik'd him not; so his advice ⌉
Was present safety, bought at any price;   ⎬
(A seeming pious care that cover'd cow- |
    ardice.)   ⌋
To strengthen this, he told a boding dream
Of rising waters and a troubled stream,
Sure signs of anguish, dangers, and distress;
With something more, not lawful to ex-
    press,
By which he slily seem'd to intimate
Some secret revelation of their fate.
For, he concluded, once upon a time,   1780
He found a leaf inscrib'd with sacred
    rhyme,
Whose antique characters did well denote
The Sibyl's hand of the Cumæan grot:
The mad divineress had plainly writ,
A time should come (but many ages yet) ⌉
In which, sinister destinies ordain,   ⎬
A dame should drown with all her fea- |
    ther'd train,   ⎬
And seas from thence be call'd the Cheli- |
    donian main.   ⌋
At this, some shook for fear; the more de-
    vout
Arose, and bless'd themselves from head
    to foot.   1790
  " 'T is true, some stagers of the wiser
    sort
Made all these idle wonderments their
    sport:
They said, their only danger was delay, ⌉
And he who heard what ev'ry fool could   ⎬
    say, |
Would never fix his thoughts, but trim |
    his time away.   ⌋
The passage yet was good; the wind, 't is ⌉
    true,   ⎬
Was somewhat high, but that was no- |
    thing new,   ⎬
Nor more than usual equinoxes blew.   ⌋
The sun (already from the Scales declin'd) ⌉
Gave little hopes of better days behind,   ⎬
But change from bad to worse of weather |
    and of wind.   1801   ⌋
Nor need they fear the dampness of the ⌉
    sky   ⎬
Should flag their wings, and hinder them |
    to fly,   ⎬
'T was only water thrown on sails too dry. ⌋
But, least of all, philosophy presumes
Of truth in dreams, from melancholy fumes:

Perhaps the Martin, hous'd in holy ground,
Might think of ghosts that walk their mid-
      night round,
Till grosser atoms, tumbling in the stream
Of fancy, madly met, and clubb'd into a
      dream: 1810
As little weight his vain presages bear
Of ill effect to such alone who fear.
Most prophecies are of a piece with these;
Each Nostradamus can foretell with ease:
Not naming persons, and confounding
      times,
One casual truth supports a thousand lying
      rhymes.
" Th' advice was true; but fear had seiz'd
      the most,
And all good counsel is on cowards lost.
The question crudely put, to shun delay,
'T was carried by the *major* part to stay. 1820
      " His point thus gain'd, Sir Martin dated
      thence
His pow'r, and from a priest became a
   * prince.
He order'd all things with a busy care,   ⎫
And cells and refectories did prepare,   ⎬
And large provisions laid of winter fare: ⎭
But now and then let fall a word or two   ⎫
Of hope that Heav'n some miracle might |
      show,   ⎬
And, for their sakes, the sun should back- |
      ward go;   ⎭
Against the laws of nature upward climb,
And, mounted on the Ram, renew the
      prime: 1830
For which two proofs in sacred story lay,
Of Ahaz' dial, and of Joshua's day.
In expectation of such times as these,
A chapel hous'd 'em, truly call'd of ease:
For Martin much devotion did not ask;
They pray'd sometimes, and that was all
      their task.
      " It happen'd (as beyond the reach of wit
Blind prophecies may have a lucky hit)
That this accomplish'd, or at least in part,
Gave great repute to their new Merlin's
      art.   1840
Some * Swifts, the giants of ⎫ * Otherwise
      the swallow kind, | call'd Mart-
Large-limb'd, stout-hearted, ⎬   lets.
      but of stupid mind, |
(For Swisses, or for Gibe- |
      onites design'd,)   ⎭
These lubbers, peeping thro' a broken pane,
To suck fresh air, survey'd the neighbor-
      ing plain,

And saw (but scarcely could believe their
      eyes)
New blossoms flourish, and new flow'rs
      arise;
As God had been abroad, and, walking
      there,
Had left his footsteps, and reform'd the
      year;
The sunny hills from far were seen to ⎫
      glow | 1850
With glittering beams, and in the meads ⎬
      below |
The burnish'd brooks appear'd with liquid |
      gold to flow.   ⎭
At last they heard the foolish Cuckow sing,
Whose note proclaim'd the holiday of
      spring.
      " No longer doubting, all prepare to fly,
And repossess their patrimonial sky.
The priest before 'em did his wings dis- ⎫
      play; |
And that good omens might attend their ⎬
      way, |
As luck would have it, 't was St. Martin's |
      day.   ⎭
      " Who but the Swallow now triumphs
      alone ?   186⦁
The canopy of heaven is all her own;
Her youthful offspring to their haunts re-
      pair,
And glide along in glades, and skim in air,
And dip for insects in the purling springs,
And stoop on rivers to refresh their wings.
Their mothers think a fair provision made,
That ev'ry son can live upon his trade:
And, now the careful charge is off their
      hands,
Look out for husbands, and new nuptial
      bands:
The youthful widow longs to be sup- ⎫
      plied; | 1870
But first the lover is by lawyers tied ⎬
To settle jointure-chimneys on the bride. ⎭
So thick they couple, in so short a space,
That Martin's marriage-off'rings rise apace;
Their ancient houses, running to decay,
Are furbish'd up, and cemented with clay:
They teem already; store of eggs are laid,
And brooding mothers call Lucina's aid.
Fame spreads the news, and foreign ⎫
      fowls appear |
In flocks to greet the new returning ⎬
      year, | 1880
To bless the founder, and partake the ⎭
      cheer.

" And now 't was time (so fast their
    numbers rise)
To plant abroad, and people colonies.
The youth drawn forth, as Martin had de-
    sir'd,
(For so their cruel destiny requir'd,)
Were sent far off on an ill-fated day; ⎫
The rest would need conduct 'em on ⎪
    their way, ⎬
And Martin went, because he fear'd ⎪
    alone to stay. ⎭
    " So long they flew with inconsiderate
    haste   1889
That now their afternoon began to waste;
And, what was ominous, that very morn
The sun was enter'd into Capricorn;
Which, by their bad astronomer's account,
That week the Virgin Balance should re-
    mount;
An infant moon eclips'd him in his way,
And hid the small remainders of his day.
The crowd, amaz'd, pursued no certain
    mark;
But birds met birds, and justled in the dark:
Few mind the public in a panic fright; 1899
And fear increas'd the horror of the night.
Night came, but unattended with repose; ⎫
Alone she came, no sleep their eyes to ⎪
    close; ⎬
Alone, and black she came; no friendly ⎪
    stars arose. ⎭
    " What should they do, beset with ⎫
    dangers round, ⎪
No neighb'ring dorp, no lodging to be ⎪
    found, ⎬
But bleaky plains, and bare unhospitable ⎪
    ground. ⎭
The latter brood, who just began to fly,
Sick-feather'd, and unpractic'd in the sky,
For succor to their helpless mother call; ⎫
She spread her wings; some few beneath ⎪
    'em crawl;   1910 ⎬
She spread 'em wider yet, but could not ⎪
    cover all. ⎭
T' augment their woes, the winds began to
    move
Debate in air, for empty fields above,
Till Boreas got the skies, and pour'd amain
His rattling hailstones mix'd with snow
    and rain.
    " The joyless morning late arose, and ⎫
    found ⎪
A dreadful desolation reign around, ⎬
Some buried in the snow, some frozen to ⎪
    the ground. ⎭

The rest were struggling still with death,
    and lay,
The Crows' and Ravens' rights, an un-
    defended prey: 1920
Excepting Martin's race; for they and he
Had gain'd the shelter of a hollow tree:
But, soon discover'd by a sturdy clown, ⎫
He headed all the rabble of a town, ⎪
And finish'd 'em with bats, or poll'd 'em ⎬
    down. ⎭
Martin himself was caught alive, and ⎫
    tried ⎪
For treas'nous crimes, because the laws ⎬
    provide ⎪
No Martin there in winter shall abide. ⎭
High on an oak, which never leaf shall
    bear,   1929
He breath'd his last, expos'd to open air;
And there his corps, unblest, are hanging
    still,
To show the change of winds with his pro-
    phetic bill "
    The patience of the Hind did almost fail,
For well she mark'd the malice of the
    tale:
Which ribald art their Church to Luther ⎫
    owes; ⎪
In malice it began, by malice grows; ⎬
He sow'd the serpent's teeth, an iron ⎪
    harvest rose. ⎭
But most in Martin's character and fate ⎫
She saw her slander'd sons, the Panther's ⎬
    hate, ⎪
The people's rage, the persecuting State: ⎭
Then said: " I take th' advice in friendly
    part;   1941
You clear your conscience, or at least your
    heart:
Perhaps you fail'd in your foreseeing skill,
For Swallows are unlucky birds to kill.
As for my sons, the family is blest,
Whose ev'ry child is equal to the rest;
No Church reform'd can boast a blameless
    line;
Such Martins build in yours, and more than
    mine:
Or else an old Fanatic author lies,
Who summ'd their scandals up by centu-
    ries.   1950
But thro' your parable I plainly see
The bloody laws, the crowd's barbarity;
The sunshine that offends the purblind
    sight —
Had some their wishes, it would soon be
    night.

Mistake me not: the charge concerns not
  you;
Your sons are malecontents, but yet are
  true,
As far as nonresistance makes 'em so;
But that's a word of neutral sense, you
  know,
A passive term, which no relief will bring,
But trims betwixt a rebel and a king." 1960
  "Rest well assur'd," the Pardelis re-
    plied,
"My sons would all support the regal
    side,
Tho' Heav'n forbid the cause by battle
    should be tried."
    The matron answer'd with a loud
      Amen,
And thus pursued her argument again:
"If, as you say, and as I hope no less,
Your sons will practice what yourself
    profess,
What angry pow'r prevents our present
    peace?
The Lion, studious of our common good,
Desires (and kings' desires are ill with-
    stood)   1970
To join our nations in a lasting love;
The bars betwixt are easy to remove,
For sanguinary laws were never made
    above.
If you condemn that prince of tyranny,
Whose mandate forc'd your Gallic friends
    to fly,
Make not a worse example of your own;
Or cease to rail at causeless rigor shown,
And let the guiltless person throw the
    stone.
His blunted sword your suff'ring brother-
    hood
Have seldom felt; he stops it short of
    blood: 1980
But you have ground the persecuting knife,
And set it to a razor-edge on life.
Curst be the wit which cruelty refines,
Or to his father's rod the scorpion joins;
Your finger is more gross than the great
    monarch's loins.
But you, perhaps, remove that bloody
    note,
And stick it on the first Reformers' coat.
O let their crime in long oblivion sleep:
'T was theirs indeed to make, 't is yours to
    keep.
Unjust, or just, is all the question now; 1990
'T is plain that, not repealing, you allow.

"To name the Test would put you in a
  rage;
You charge not that on any former age,
But smile to think how innocent you stand,
Arm'd by a weapon put into your hand.
Yet still remember that you wield a sword
Forg'd by your foes against your Sovereign
  Lord;
Design'd to hew th' imperial cedar down,
Defraud succession, and disheir the crown.
T' abhor the makers, and their laws ap-
  prove,   2000
Is to hate traitors, and the treason love.
What means it else, which now your chil-
  dren say,
'We made it not, nor will we take away'?
  "Suppose some great oppressor had by
    slight
Of law disseiz'd your brother of his
    right,
Your common sire surrend'ring in a
    fright;
Would you to that unrighteous title stand,
Left by the villain's will to heir the land?
More just was Judas, who his Savior sold;
The sacrilegious bribe he could not hold,
Nor hang in peace before he render'd
    back the gold.   2011
What more could you have done than now
  you do,
Had Oates and Bedloe, and their Plot been
  true?
Some specious reasons for those wrongs
  were found;
The dire magicians threw their mists
  around,
And wise men walk'd as on inchanted
  ground.
But now, when Time has made th' im-
  posture plain,
(Late tho' he follow'd Truth, and limp-
  ing held her train,)
What new delusion charms your cheated
  eyes again?
The painted harlot might a while bewitch,
But why the hag uncas'd, and all obscene
  with itch?   2021
  "The first Reformers were a modest race;
Our peers possess'd in peace their native
  place;
And when rebellious arms o'erturn'd the
  State,
They suffer'd only in the common fate:
But now the sov'reign mounts the regal
  chair,

And miter'd seats are full, yet David's
    bench is bare.
Your answer is, they were not dispossess'd;
They need but rub their metal on the Test
To prove their ore: 't were well if gold
    alone   2030
Were touch'd and tried on your discerning
    stone;
But that unfaithful Test unfound will pass
The dross of atheists, and sectarian brass:
As if th' experiment were made to hold
For base productions, and reject the gold.
Thus men ungodded may to places rise,
And sects may be preferr'd without disguise:
No danger to the Church or State from
    these;
The Papist only has his writ of ease.
No gainful office gives him the pretense 2040
To grind the subject, or defraud the prince.
Wrong conscience, or no conscience, may
    deserve
To thrive, but ours alone is privileg'd to
    sterve.
    " ' Still thank yourselves,' you cry; ' your
      noble race
We banish not, but they forsake the place:
Our doors are open.' True, but ere they
    come,
You toss your censing Test, and fume the
    room;
As if 't were Toby's rival to expel,
And fright the fiend who could not bear the
    smell."
    To this the Panther sharply had re-
      plied;   2050
But, having gain'd a verdict on her side,
She wisely gave the loser leave to chide;
Well satisfied to have the ' butt and
    peace,'
And for the plaintiff's cause she car'd the
    less,
Because she sued *in forma pauperis ;*
Yet thought it decent something should be
    said;
For secret guilt by silence is betray'd:
So neither granted all, nor much denied,
But answer'd with a yawning kind of pride.
" Methinks such terms of proffer'd peace
    you bring,   2060
As once Æneas to th' Italian king:
By long possession all the land is mine;
You strangers come with your intruding
    line,
To share my scepter, which you call to
    join.

You plead like him an ancient pedigree,
And claim a peaceful seat by fate's de-
    cree.
In ready pomp your sacrificer stands,
T' unite the Trojan and the Latin bands,
And, that the league more firmly may be
    tied,
Demand the fair Lavinia for your bride. 2070
Thus plausibly you veil th' intended wrong,
But still you bring your exil'd gods along;
And will endeavor, in succeeding space,
Those household poppits on our hearths to
    place.
Perhaps some barb'rous laws have been
    preferr'd;
I spake against the Test, but was not heard;
These to rescind, and peerage to restore,
My gracious sov'reign would my vote
    implore:
I owe him much, but owe my conscience
    more."
    " Conscience is then your plea," replied
      the dame,   2080
" Which, well inform'd, will ever be the
    same.
But yours is much of the *chameleon* hue,
To change the dye with ev'ry diff'rent view.
When first the Lion sat with awful sway,
Your conscience taught you duty to obey:
He might have had your statutes and your
    Test;
No conscience but of subjects was profess'd.
He found your temper, and no farther tried,
But on that broken reed, your Church, re-
    lied.
In vain the sects assay'd their utmost
    art,   2090
With offer'd treasure to espouse their
    part;
Their treasures were a bribe too mean to
    move his heart.
But when by long experience you had
    prov'd,
How far he could forgive, how well he lov'd;
A goodness that excell'd his godlike race,
And only short of Heav'n's unbounded
    grace;
A flood of mercy that o'erflow'd our isle,
Calm in the rise, and fruitful as the Nile;
Forgetting whence your Egypt was sup-
    plied,
You thought your sov'reign bound to send
    the tide;   2100
Nor upward look'd on that immortal spring,
But vainly deem'd, he durst not be a king.

Then Conscience, unrestrain'd by fear, be-
    gan
To stretch her limits, and extend the span;
Did his indulgence as her gift dispose,
And made a wise alliance with her foes.
Can Conscience own th' associating name, ⎫
And raise no blushes to conceal her   ⎪
    shame ?   ⎬
For sure she has been thought a bashful ⎪
    dame.   ⎭
But if the cause by battle should be ⎫
    tried,   2110   ⎪
You grant she must espouse the regal ⎬
    side: ⎪
O Proteus Conscience, never to be tied ! ⎭
What Phœbus from the tripod shall dis-
    close
Which are, in last resort, your friends or
    foes ?
Homer, who learn'd the language of the
    sky,
The seeming Gordian knot would soon un-
    tie;
Immortal pow'rs the term of Conscience
    know,
But Int'rest is her name with men below."
    " Conscience or Int'rest be 't, or both in
    one,"
The Panther answer'd in a surly tone,   2120
" The first commands me to maintain the
    crown,
The last forbids to throw my barriers down.
Our penal laws no sons of yours admit,
Our Test excludes your tribe from benefit.
These are my banks your ocean to with-
    stand,
Which proudly rising overlooks the land;
And, once let in, with unresisted sway,
Would sweep the pastors and their flocks
    away.
Think not my judgment leads me to com-
    ply
With laws unjust, but hard necessity: 2130
Imperious need, which cannot be withstood,
Makes ill authentic, for a greater good.
Possess your soul with patience, and attend:
A more auspicious planet may ascend;
Good fortune may present some happier
    time,
With means to cancel my unwilling crime
(Unwilling, witness all ye pow'rs above);
To mend my errors, and redeem your love:
That little space you safely may allow;
Your all-dispensing pow'r protects you
    now."   2140

" Hold," said the Hind, " 't is needless
    to explain;
You would *postpone* me to another reign;
Till when you are content to be unjust:
Your part is to possess, and mine to trust.
A fair exchange propos'd of future chance,
For present profit and inheritance.
Few words will serve to finish our dispute;
Who will not now repeal, would persecute:
To ripen green revenge your hopes attend,
Wishing that happier planet would as-
    cend.   2150
For shame, let Conscience be your plea ⎫
    no more;   ⎪
To will hereafter, proves she might be- ⎬
    fore;   ⎪
But she's a bawd to Gain, and holds the ⎭
    door.
    " Your care about your banks infers a
    fear
Of threat'ning floods and inundations near;
If so, a just reprise would only be
Of what the land usurp'd upon the sea;
And all your jealousies but serve to show
Your ground is, like your neighbor nation,
    low.
T' intrench in what you grant unrighteous
    laws,   2160
Is to distrust the justice of your cause,
And argues that the true religion lies
In those weak adversaries you despise.
    " Tyrannic force is that which least you
    fear;
The sound is frightful in a Christian's
    ear:
Avert it, Heav'n ! nor let that plague be
    sent
To us from the dispeopled continent.
    " But piety commands me to refrain;
Those pray'rs are needless in this mon-
    arch's reign.
Behold, how he protects your friends ⎫
    oppress'd,   2170   ⎪
Receives the banish'd, succors the dis- ⎬
    tress'd !   ⎪
Behold, for you may read an honest ⎭
    open breast.
He stands in daylight, and disdains to ⎫
    hide   ⎪
An act to which by honor he is tied,   ⎬
A generous, laudable, and kingly pride. ⎭
Your Test he would repeal, his peers re-
    store;
This when he says he means, he means no
    more."

"Well," said the Panther, "I believe him just,
And yet —— "
   "And yet, 't is but because you must;
You would be trusted, but you would not
   trust." 2180
The Hind thus briefly; and disdain'd t'
   inlarge
On pow'r of kings, and their superior
   charge,
As Heav'n's trustees before the people's ⎫
   choice: ⎪
Tho' sure the Panther did not much re- ⎬
   joice   ⎪
To hear those echoes giv'n of her once ⎪
   loyal voice. ⎭
  The matron woo'd her kindness to the
   last,
But could not win; her hour of grace was
   past.
Whom, thus persisting, when she could not
   bring
To leave the Wolf, and to believe her
   king,
She gave her up, and fairly wish'd her
   joy 2190
Of her late treaty with her new ally:
Which well she hop'd would more success-
   ful prove
Than was the Pigeons' and the Buzzard's
   love.
The Panther ask'd what concord there
   could be
Betwixt two kinds whose natures disagree.
The dame replied: "'T is sung in ev'ry
   street,
The common chat of gossips when they
   meet;
But, since unheard by you, 't is worth your
   while
To take a wholesome tale, tho' told in
   homely style.
  "A plain good man, whose name is
   understood, 2200
(So few deserve the name of plain and good,)
Of three fair lineal lordships stood possess'd,
And liv'd, as reason was, upon the best.
Inur'd to hardships from his early youth,
Much had he done and suffer'd for his
   truth:
At land and sea, in many a doubtful fight, ⎫
Was never known a more advent'rous ⎪
   knight,   ⎬
Who oft'ner drew his sword, and always ⎪
   for the right. ⎭

"As fortune would, (his fortune came,
   tho' late,)
He took possession of his just estate; 2210
Nor rack'd his tenants with increase of
   rent,
Nor liv'd too sparing, nor too largely
   spent;
But overlook'd his hinds; their pay was
   just,
And ready, for he scorn'd to go on trust:
Slow to resolve, but in performance quick;
So true, that he was awkward at a trick,
For little souls on little shifts rely, ⎫
And coward arts of mean expedients try; ⎪
The noble mind will dare do anything ⎬
   but lie. ⎭
False friends, (his deadliest foes,) could
   find no way 2220
But shows of honest bluntness, to betray:
That unsuspected plainness he believ'd;
He look'd into himself, and was deceiv'd.
Some lucky planet sure attends his birth,
Or Heav'n would make a miracle on earth;
For prosp'rous honesty is seldom seen
To bear so dead a weight, and yet to win.
It looks as fate with nature's law would
   strive,
To shew plain-dealing once an age may
   thrive;
And, when so tough a frame she could not
   bend, 2230
Exceeded her commission to befriend.
  "This grateful man, as Heav'n encreas'd
   his store,
Gave God again, and daily fed his poor.
His house with all convenience was pur-
   vey'd;
The rest he found, but rais'd the fabric
   where he pray'd;
And in that sacred place his beauteous wife
Employ'd her happiest hours of holy life.
  "Nor did their alms extend to those
   alone
Whom common faith more strictly made
   their own;
A sort of Doves were hous'd too near their
   hall, 2240
Who cross the proverb, and abound with
   gall.
Tho' some, 't is true, are passively inclin'd,
The greater part degenerate from their
   kind;
Voracious birds, that hotly bill and breed,
And largely drink, because on salt they
   feed.

Small gain from them their bounteous
    owner draws;
Yet, bound by promise, he supports their
    cause,
As corporations privileg'd by laws.
  "That house which harbor to their kind
    affords
Was built, long since, God knows, for better
    birds;   2250
But flutt'ring there, they nestle near the
    throne,
And lodge in habitations not their own,
By their high crops and corny gizzards
    known.
Like Harpies, they could scent a plenteous
    board,
Then to be sure they never fail'd their lord:
The rest was form, and bare attendance
    paid;
They drunk, and eat, and grudgingly obey'd.
The more they fed, they raven'd still for
    more;
They drain'd from Dan, and left Beersheba
    poor.   2259
All this they had by law, and none repin'd;
The pref'rence was but due to Levi's kind;
But when some lay-preferment fell by
    chance,
The gourmands made it their inheritance.
When once possess'd, they never quit their
    claim;
For then 't is sanctified to Heav'n's high
    name;
And, hallow'd thus, they cannot give con-
    sent
The gift should be profan'd by worldly
    management.
  "Their flesh was never to the table serv'd;
Tho' 't is not thence inferr'd the birds were
    starv'd;   2269
But that their master did not like the food,
As rank, and breeding melancholy blood.
Nor did it with his gracious nature suit,
Ev'n tho' they were not Doves, to persecute;
Yet he refus'd (nor could they take of-
    fense)
Their glutton kind should teach him absti-
    nence.
Nor consecrated grain their wheat he
    thought,
Which, new from treading, in their bills
    they brought;
But left his hinds each in his private pow'r,
That those who like the bran might leave
    the flour.

He for himself, and not for others, chose, 2280
Nor would he be impos'd on, nor impose;
But in their faces his devotion paid,
And sacrifice with solemn rites was made,
And sacred incense on his altars laid.
  "Besides these jolly birds, whose crops
    impure
Repaid their commons with their salt
    manure,
Another farm he had behind his house,
Not overstock'd, but barely for his use;
Wherein his poor domestic poultry fed,
And from his pious hands receiv'd their
    bread.   2290
Our pamper'd Pigeons, with malignant
    eyes,
Beheld these inmates, and their nurseries:
Tho' hard their fare, at ev'ning and at
    morn,
A cruse of water and an ear of corn;
Yet still they grudg'd that modicum, and
    thought
A sheaf in ev'ry single grain was brought:
Fain would they filch that little food away,
While unrestrain'd those happy gluttons
    prey.
And much they griev'd to see so nigh their
    hall
The bird that warn'd St. Peter of his fall;
That he should raise his miter'd crest on
    high,   2301
And clap his wings, and call his family
To sacred rites; and vex th' ethereal pow'rs
With midnight matins at uncivil hours:
Nay more, his quiet neighbors should mo-
    lest,
Just in the sweetness of their morning rest.
  "Beast of a bird, supinely when he might
Lie snug and sleep, to rise before the light!
What if his dull forefathers us'd that cry,
Could he not let a bad example die?   2310
The world was fall'n into an easier way;
This age knew better than to fast and pray.
Good sense in sacred worship would appear
So to begin, as they might end the year.
Such feats in former times had wrought
    the falls
Of crowing Chanticleers in cloister'd walls.
Expell'd for this, and for their lands,
    they fled;
And sister Partlet, with her hooded head,
Was hooted hence, because she would not
    pray abed.
The way to win the restiff world to God,
Was to lay by the disciplining rod,   2321

Unnatural fasts, and foreign forms of
    pray'r:
Religion frights us with a mien severe.
'T is prudence to reform her into ease,
And put her in undress to make her pleas:
A lively faith will bear aloft the mind,
And leave the luggage of good works be-
    hind.
    " Such doctrines in the Pigeon-house
        were taught:
You need not ask how wondrously they
    wrought;   2329
But sure the common cry was all for these,
Whose life and precept both encourag'd
    ease.
Yet fearing those alluring baits might fail,
And holy deeds o'er all their arts prevail;
(For vice, tho' frontless, and of harden'd
    face,
Is daunted at the sight of awful grace,)
An hideous figure of their foes they drew,⎤
Nor lines, nor looks, nor shades, nor   ⎟
    colors true;   ⎬
And this grotesque design expos'd to   ⎟
    public view.   ⎦
One would have thought it some Egyp-⎤
    tian piece,   ⎟
With garden-gods, and barking deities, ⎬
More thick than Ptolemy has stuck the   ⎟
    skies.   2341⎦
All so perverse a draught, so far unlike,
It was no libel where it meant to strike:
Yet still the daubing pleas'd, and great and
    small,
To view the monster, crowded Pigeon-hall.
There Chanticleer was drawn upon his knees
Adoring shrines, and stocks of sainted trees;
And by him, a misshapen, ugly race;
The curse of God was seen on ev'ry face:
No Holland emblem could that malice
    mend,   2350
But still the worse the look, the fitter for a
    fiend.
    " The master of the farm, displeas'd to
        find
So much of rancor in so mild a kind,
Enquir'd into the cause, and came to know
The Passive Church had struck the fore-
    most blow;
With groundless fears, and jealousies⎤
    possess'd,   ⎟
As if this troublesome intruding guest ⎬
Would drive the birds of Venus from   ⎟
    their nest: ⎦
A deed his inborn equity abhorr'd;

But Int'rest will not trust, tho' God should
    plight his word.   2360
    " A law, the source of many future harms,
Had banish'd all the poultry from the farms;
With loss of life, if any should be found
To crow or peck on this forbidden ground.
That bloody statute chiefly was design'd
For Chanticleer the white, of clergy kind;
But after-malice did not long forget
The lay that wore the robe and coronet.
For them, for their inferiors and allies,
Their foes a deadly shibboleth devise: 2370
By which unrighteously it was decreed ⎤
That none to trust, or profit, should suc-⎟
    ceed,   ⎬
Who would not swallow first a poisonous⎟
    wicked weed;   ⎦
Or that, to which old Socrates was curst,
Or henbane juice to swell 'em till they
    burst.
The patron (as in reason) thought it hard⎤
To see this inquisition in his yard,   ⎬
By which the sovereign was of subjects' ⎟
    use debarr'd.   ⎦
    " All gentle means he tried, which might
        withdraw
Th' effects of so unnatural a law;   2380
But still the Dove-house obstinately stood
Deaf to their own, and to their neighbors'
    good;
And which was worse (if any worse could be),
Repented of their boasted loyalty:
Now made the champions of a cruel cause,
And drunk with fumes of popular ap-
    plause;
For those whom God to ruin has design'd,
He fits for fate, and first destroys their
    mind.
    " New doubts indeed they daily strove to
        raise,
Suggested dangers, interpos'd delays;   2390
And emissary Pigeons had in store,
Such as the Meccan prophet us'd of yore,
To whisper counsels in their patron's ear;
And veil'd their false advice with zealous
    fear.
The master smil'd to see 'em work in vain
To wear him out, and make an idle reign:
He saw, but suffer'd their protractive arts,
And strove by mildness to reduce their
    hearts;
But they abus'd that grace to make allies,⎤
And fondly clos'd with former enemies; ⎬
For fools are double fools, endeav'ring to⎟
    be wise.   2401⎦

" After a grave consult what course were
    best,
One, more mature in folly than the rest,
Stood up, and told 'em, with his head aside,
That desp'rate cures must be to desp'rate
    ills applied;
And therefore, since their main impending
    fear
Was from th' encreasing race of Chanticleer,
Some potent bird of prey they ought to find
A foe profess'd to him and all his kind:
Some haggard Hawk, who had her eyry
    nigh,   2410
Well pounc'd to fasten, and well wing'd to
    fly;
One they might trust their common wrongs
    to wreak:
The Musket, and the Coystrel were too
    weak,
Too fierce the Falcon. — ' But, above the
    rest,
The noble Buzzard ever pleas'd me best;
Of small renown, 't is true; for, not to lie,
We call him but a Hawk by courtesy.
I know he haunts the Pigeon-house and
    farm,
And more, in time of war, has done us
    harm;
But all his hate on trivial points depends:
Give up our forms, and we shall soon be
    friends.   2421
For Pigeons' flesh he seems not much to
    care;
Cramm'd Chickens are a more delicious
    fare.
On this high potentate, without delay,
I wish you would confer the sovereign
    sway:
Petition him t' accept the government,
And let a splendid embassy be sent.'
    " This pithy speech prevail'd, and all
    agreed,
Old enmities forgot, the Buzzard should
    succeed.
    " Their welcome suit was granted soon
    as heard,   2430
His lodgings furnish'd, and a train pre-
    par'd,
With B's upon their breast, appointed for
    his guard.
He came, and, crown'd with great solem-
    nity,
'God save King Buzzard!' was the gen'ral
    cry.
    " A portly prince, and goodly to the sight,

He seem'd a son of Anak for his height:
Like those whom stature did to crowns
    prefer;
Black-brow'd, and bluff, like Homer's
    Jupiter;
Broad-back'd, and brawny-built for love's
    delight,
A prophet form'd to make a female prose-
    lyte.   2440
A theologue more by need than genial bent;
By breeding sharp, by nature confident.
Int'rest in all his actions was discern'd;
More learn'd than honest, more a wit than
    learn'd;
Or forc'd by fear, or by his profit led,
Or both conjoin'd, his native clime he fled;
But brought the virtues of his heav'n along,
A fair behavior, and a fluent tongue.
And yet with all his arts he could not
    thrive;
The most unlucky parasite alive.   2450
Loud praises to prepare his paths he sent,
And then himself pursued his compliment;
But, by reverse of fortune chas'd away,
His gifts no longer than their author stay:
He shakes the dust against th' ungrateful
    race,
And leaves the stench of ordures in the
    place.
Oft has he flatter'd and blasphem'd the
    same,
For in his rage he spares no sov'reign's
    name;
The hero and the tyrant change their style
By the same measure that they frown or
    smile.   2460
When well receiv'd by hospitable foes,
The kindness he returns, is to expose:
For courtesies, tho' undeserv'd and great, ⎫
No gratitude in felon-minds beget;   ⎪
As tribute to his wit, the churl receives ⎬
    the treat.   ⎪
                                          ⎭
His praise of foes is venomously nice;   ⎫
So touch'd, it turns a virtue to a vice: ⎬
A Greek, and bountiful, forewarns us twice.⎭
Sev'n sacraments he wisely does disown,
Because he knows confession stands for
    one;   2470
Where sins to sacred silence are convey'd,
And not for fear, or love, to be betray'd:
But he, uncall'd, his patron to control,
Divulg'd the secret whispers of his soul;
Stood forth th' accusing Sathan of his
    crimes,
And offer'd to the Moloch of the times.

Prompt to assail, and careless of defense,
Invulnerable in his impudence,
He dares the world; and, eager of a name,
He thrusts about, and justles into fame.
Frontless and satire-proof he scours the
    streets,   2481
And runs an Indian muck at all he meets.
So fond of loud report, that not to miss ⎫
Of being known (his last and utmost bliss) ⎬
He rather would be known for what he is. ⎭
    "Such was, and is the Captain of the ⎫
    Test,   ⎪
Tho' half his virtues are not here ex- ⎬
    press'd;   ⎪
The modesty of fame conceals the rest. ⎭
The spleenful Pigeons never could create
A prince more proper to revenge their
    hate: 2490
Indeed, more proper to revenge, than save;
A king whom in his wrath th' Almighty
    gave:
For all the grace the landlord had allow'd, ⎫
But made the Buzzard and the Pigeons ⎪
    proud;   ⎬
Gave time to fix their friends, and to se- ⎪
    duce the crowd.   ⎭
They long their fellow-subjects to in- ⎫
    thral,   ⎪
Their patron's promise into question call, ⎬
And vainly think he meant to make 'em ⎪
    lords of all.   ⎭
    "False fears their leaders fail'd not to
    suggest,
As if the Doves were to be dispossess'd;
Nor sighs, nor groans, nor goggling eyes
    did want,   2501
For now the Pigeons too had learn'd to cant.
The house of pray'r is stock'd with large
    encrease;
Nor doors, nor windows can contain the
    press:
For birds of ev'ry feather fill th' abode;
Ev'n atheists out of envy own a God:
And, reeking from the stews, adult'rers
    come,
Like Goths and Vandals to demolish Rome.
That Conscience which to all their crimes
    was mute
Now calls aloud, and cries to persecute;
No rigor of the laws to be releas'd,   2511
And much the less, because it was their
    lord's request:
They thought it great their sov'reign to
    control,
And nam'd their pride, nobility of soul.

    " 'T is true, the Pigeons, and their prince
    elect,
Were short of pow'r their purpose to effect;
But with their quills did all the hurt they
    could,
And cuff'd the tender Chickens from their
    food:
And much the Buzzard in their cause did ⎫
    stir,   ⎪
Tho' naming not the patron, to infer, 2520 ⎬
With all respect, he was a gross idolater. ⎭
    " But when th' imperial owner did espy
That thus they turn'd his grace to villainy,
Not suff'ring wrath to discompose his ⎫
    mind,   ⎪
He strove a temper for th' extremes to ⎬
    find,   ⎪
So to be just, as he might still be kind; ⎭
Then, all maturely weigh'd, pronounc'd a
    doom
Of sacred strength for ev'ry age to come.
By this the Doves their wealth and state
    possess,
No rights infring'd, but license to op-
    press: 2530
Such pow'r have they as factious lawyers
    long
To crowns ascrib'd, that kings can do no
    wrong.
But, since his own domestic birds have tried
The dire effects of their destructive pride,
He deems that proof a measure to the ⎫
    rest,   ⎪
Concluding well within his kingly breast, ⎬
His fowl of nature too unjustly were op- ⎪
    press'd.   ⎭
He therefore makes all birds of ev'ry ⎫
    sect   ⎪
Free of his farm, with promise to respect ⎬
Their sev'ral kinds alike, and equally pro- ⎪
    tect.   2540 ⎭
His gracious edict the same franchise ⎫
    yields   ⎪
To all the wild encrease of woods and ⎬
    fields,   ⎪
And who in rocks aloof, and who in ⎪
    steeples builds;   ⎭
To Crows the like impartial grace affords,
And Choughs and Daws, and such republic
    birds;
Secur'd with ample privilege to feed,
Each has his district, and his bounds de-
    creed:
Combin'd in common int'rest with his own,
But not to pass the Pigeons' Rubicon.

"Here ends the reign of this pre-
tended Dove;   2550
All prophecies accomplish'd from above,
For Shiloh comes the scepter to remove.
Reduc'd from her imperial high abode,
Like Dionysius to a private rod,
The Passive Church, that with pretended
grace
Did her distinctive mark in duty place,
Now touch'd, reviles her Maker to his
face.
"What after happen'd is not hard to
guess:
The small beginnings had a large en-
crease,
And arts and wealth succeed (the secret
spoils of peace).   2560
'T is said, the Doves repented, tho' too late,
Become the smiths of their own foolish fate:
Nor did their owner hasten their ill hour;
But, sunk in credit, they decreas'd in pow'r;
Like snows in warmth that mildly pass
away,
Dissolving in the silence of decay.
"The Buzzard, not content with equal
place,
Invites the feather'd Nimrods of his race,
To hide the thinness of their flock from sight,
And all together make a seeming goodly
flight: 2570

But each have sep'rate int'rests of their own,
Two *Czars* are one too many for a throne.
Nor can th' usurper long abstain from food;
Already he has tasted Pigeons' blood,
And may be tempted to his former fare,
When this indulgent lord shall late to
heav'n repair.
Bare benting times, and molting months
may come,
When, lagging late, they cannot reach their
home;
Or rent in schism (for so their fate decrees)
Like the tumultuous college of the bees, 2580
They fight their quarrel, by themselves op-
press'd:
The tyrant smiles below, and waits the
falling feast."
Thus did the gentle Hind her fable end,
Nor would the Panther blame it, nor com-
mend;
But, with affected yawnings at the close,
Seem'd to require her natural repose:
For now the streaky light began to peep,
And setting stars admonish'd both to sleep.
The dame withdrew, and, wishing to her
guest
The peace of heav'n, betook herself to
rest.   2590
Ten thousand angels on her slumbers wait,
With glorious visions of her future state.

A SONG FOR ST. CECILIA'S DAY, 1687

[About 1683 a musical society in London
began the custom of celebrating November
22, the Feast of St. Cecilia, the patroness of
music, by a public concert. Dryden wrote
the following ode, which was set to music by
an Italian composer, Giovanni Battista
Draghi, for the performance of 1687. The
ode was published as a broadside, "printed
for T. Dring, in Fleetstreet, 1687" (Macdonald); the only known copy is in the British
Museum. It was reprinted in *Examen
Poeticum*, 1693, from which the present text
is taken.]

I

FROM harmony, from heav'nly harmony
This universal frame began:
When Nature underneath a heap
Of jarring atoms lay,
And could not heave her head,
The tuneful voice was heard from high:
"Arise, ye more than dead."

Then cold, and hot, and moist, and dry,
In order to their stations leap,
And Music's pow'r obey.   10
From harmony, from heav'nly harmony
This universal frame began:
From harmony to harmony
Thro' all the compass of the notes it ran,
The diapason closing full in Man.

II

What passion cannot Music raise and
quell!
When Jubal struck the corded shell,
His list'ning brethren stood around,
And, wond'ring, on their faces fell
To worship that celestial sound. 20
Less than a god they thought there could
not dwell
Within the hollow of that shell
That spoke so sweetly and so well.
What passion cannot Music raise and
quell!

III

The Trumpet's loud clangor
  Excites us to arms,
  With shrill notes of anger,
  And mortal alarms.
The double double double beat
  Of the thund'ring Drum   30
Cries: "Hark! the foes come;
Charge, charge, 't is too late to retreat."

IV

The soft complaining Flute
  In dying notes discovers
  The woes of hopeless lovers,
Whose dirge is whisper'd by the warbling
      Lute.

V

Sharp Violins proclaim
Their jealous pangs, and desperation,
Fury, frantic indignation,
Depth of pains, and height of passion,   40
  For the fair, disdainful dame.

VI

But O! what art can teach,
  What human voice can reach,
The sacred Organ's praise?
  Notes inspiring holy love,
Notes that wing their heav'nly ways
  To mend the choirs above.

VII

Orpheus could lead the savage race;
And trees unrooted left their place,

Sequacious of the lyre;   50
But bright Cecilia rais'd the wonder high'r:
When to her Organ vocal breath was
      giv'n,
An angel heard, and straight appear'd,
  Mistaking earth for heav'n.

GRAND CHORUS

As from the pow'r of sacred lays
    The spheres began to move,
And sung the great Creator's praise
    To all the blest above;
So, when the last and dreadful hour
This crumbling pageant shall devour,   60
The Trumpet shall be heard on high,
The dead shall live, the living die,
And Music shall untune the sky.

EPIGRAM ON MILTON

[This epigram is engraved, without the
name of the author, beneath the portrait of
Milton which forms the frontispiece to Tonson's
folio edition of *Paradise Lost*, 1688. Dryden's
name is first joined to it in the second edition,
1716, of the *Sixth Part of Miscellany Poems*.]

THREE poets, in three distant ages born,
Greece, Italy, and England did adorn.
The first in loftiness of thought surpass'd,
The next in majesty, in both the last:
The force of Nature could no farther go;
To make a third, she join'd the former
      two.

BRITANNIA REDIVIVA

A POEM ON THE PRINCE, BORN ON THE TENTH OF JUNE, 1688

Dii Patrii Indigetes. et Romule, Vestaque Mater,
Quæ Tuscum Tiberim, et Romana Palatia servas,
Hunc saltem everso Puerum *succurrere sæclo*
Ne prohibete : satis jampridem sanguine nostro
Laomedonteæ luimus Perjuria *Trojæ.* — VIRG. *Georg.* I.

[This poem celebrates the birth of a son to James II on Trinity Sunday, June 10, 1688. It
was prepared in haste and licensed for the press on June 19. A folio edition was published by
Tonson; a quarto edition appeared at Edinburgh in the same year. About 1691 Tonson published a quarto edition, dated 1688, to be included in sets of Dryden's poems. After this
Britannia Rediviva was not reprinted during Dryden's lifetime.]

OUR vows are heard betimes! and Heaven
      takes care
To grant, before we can conclude the pray'r:

Preventing angels met it half way,
And sent us back to praise, who came to
      pray.

Just on the day, when the high-mounted
    sun
Did farthest in his northern progress run,
He bended forward, and ev'n stretch'd the
    sphere
Beyond the limits of the lengthen'd year,
To view a brighter sun in Britain born;
That was the bus'ness of his longest
    morn;   10
The glorious object seen, 't was time to
    turn.

Departing Spring could only stay to
    shed
Her bloomy beauties on the genial bed,
But left the manly Summer in her stead,
With timely fruit the longing land to cheer,
And to fulfil the promise of the year.
Betwixt two seasons comes th' auspicious
    heir,
This age to blossom, and the next to bear.
    (a) Last solemn Sabbath saw the Church
        attend;
The Paraclete in fiery pomp descend;   20
But when his wondrous (b) octave roll'd
    again,
He brought a royal infant in his train.
So great a blessing to so good a king,
None but th' Eternal Comforter could
    bring.
Or did the mighty Trinity conspire,
As once, in council to create our sire ?
It seems as if they sent the newborn guest
To wait on the procession of their feast;
And on their sacred anniverse decreed   29
To stamp their image on the promis'd seed.
Three realms united, and on one bestow'd,
An emblem of their mystic union show'd:
The Mighty Trine the triple empire shar'd,
As every person would have one to guard.

Hail, son of pray'rs, by holy violence
Drawn down from heav'n; but long be ban-
    ish'd thence,
And late to thy paternal skies retire !
To mend our crimes whole ages would re-
    quire;
To change th' inveterate habit of our sins,
And finish what thy godlike sire begins.   40
Kind Heav'n, to make us Englishmen again,
No less can give us than a patriarch's reign.

The sacred cradle to your charge receive,
Ye seraphs, and by turns the guard relieve;
Thy father's angel, and thy father join,
To keep possession, and secure the line;

(a) Whit Sunday.
(b) Trinity Sunday.

But long defer the honors of thy fate:
Great may they be like his, like his be late;
That James this running century may view,
And give his son an auspice to the new.   50
    Our wants exact at least that moderate
        stay:
For see the (c) Dragon winged on his
        way,
To watch the (d) travail, and devour the
        prey.
Or, if allusions may not rise so high,
Thus, when Alcides rais'd his infant cry,
The snakes besieg'd his young divinity;
But vainly with their forked tongues they
    threat,
For opposition makes a hero great.
To needful succor all the good will run,
And Jove assert the godhead of his son.   60
    O still repining at your present state,
Grudging yourselves the benefits of fate,
Look up, and read in characters of light
A blessing sent you in your own despite.
The manna falls, yet that celestial bread
Like Jews you munch, and murmur while
        you feed.
May not your fortune be like theirs, exil'd,
Yet forty years to wander in the wild;
Or if it be, may Moses live at least,
To lead you to the verge of promis'd rest. 70
    Tho' poets are not prophets, to fore-
        know
What plants will take the blight, and what
        will grow,
By tracing Heav'n his footsteps may be
    found:
Behold ! how awfully he walks the round !
God is abroad, and, wondrous in his ways,
The rise of empires and their fall surveys;
More (might I say) than with an usual
        eye,
He sees his bleeding Church in ruin lie,
And hears the souls of saints beneath his
        altar cry.
Already has he lifted high the (e) sign,   80
Which crown'd the conquering arms of
        Constantine:
The (f) moon grows pale at that presaging
        sight,
And half her train of stars have lost their
        light.

(c) Alluding only to the Commonwealth party, here
and in other places of the poem.
(d) Rev. xii, 4.
(e) The cross.
(f) The crescent, which the Turks bear for their
arms.

Behold another (g) Sylvester, to bless
The sacred standard, and secure success;
Large of his treasures, of a soul so great,
As fills and crowds his universal seat.
Now view at home a (h) second Con-
    stantine;
(The former, too, was of the British line;)
Has not his healing balm your breaches
    clos'd,   90
Whose exile many sought, and few oppos'd?
Or did not Heav'n by its eternal doom
Permit those evils, that this good might
    come?
So manifest, that ev'n the moon-ey'd sects
See *whom* and *what* this Providence pro-
    tects.
Methinks, had we within our minds no
    more
Than that one shipwrack on the fatal
    (i) ore,
That only thought may make us think
    again,
What wonders God reserves for such a
    reign.
To dream that chance his preservation
    wrought,   100
Were to think Noah was preserv'd for
    naught;
Or the surviving eight were not design'd
To people earth, and to restore their kind.
    When humbly on the royal babe we gaze,
The manly lines of a majestic face
Give awful joy: 't is paradise to look
On the fair frontispiece of Nature's book;
If the first opening page so charms the sight,
Think how th' unfolded volume will de-
    light!
    See how the venerable infant lies   110
In early pomp; how thro' the mother's
    eyes
The father's soul, with an undaunted view,
Looks out, and takes our homage as his
    due.
See on his future subjects how he smiles,
Nor meanly flatters, nor with craft be-
    guiles;
But with an open face, as on his throne,
Assures our birthrights and assumes his
    own.
Born in broad daylight, that th' ungrate-
    ful rout
May find no room for a remaining doubt;

(g) The Pope in the time of Constantine the Great,
alluding to the present Pope.
(h) King James the Second.
(i) The Lemmon Ore.

Truth, which itself is light, does darkness
    shun,   120
And the true eaglet safely dares the sun.
    (j) Fain would the fiends have made a
    dubious birth,
Loth to confess the godhead cloth'd in
    earth;
But sicken'd, after all their baffled lies,
To find an heir apparent of the skies,
Abandon'd to despair, still may they
    grudge,
And, owning not the Savior, prove the
    judge.
    Not great (k) Æneas stood in plainer
    day,
When, the dark mantling mist dissolv'd
    away,   129
He to the Tyrians shew'd his sudden face,
Shining with all his goddess mother's grace:
For she herself had made his count'nance
    bright,
Breath'd honor on his eyes, and her own
    purple light.
    If our victorious (l) Edward, as they say,
Gave Wales a prince on that propitious day,
Why may not years revolving with his fate
Produce his like, but with a longer date?
One who may carry to a distant shore
The terror that his fam'd forefather bore?
But why should James or his young hero
    stay   140
For slight presages of a name or day?
We need no Edward's fortune to adorn
That happy moment when our prince was
    born:
Our prince adorns his day, and ages hence
Shall wish his birthday for some future
    prince.
    (m) Great Michael, prince of all th' ethe-
    real hosts,
And whate'er inborn saints our Britain
    boasts;
And thou, (n) th' adopted patron of our
    isle,
With cheerful aspects on this infant smile:
The pledge of Heav'n, which, dropping
    from above,   150
Secures our bliss, and reconciles his love.
    Enough of ills our dire rebellion wrought,
When, to the dregs, we drank the bitter
    draught;

(j) Alluding to the temptations in the wilderness.
(k) Virgil, *Æneid* 1.
(l) Edward the Black Prince, born on Trinity Sunday.
(m) The motto of the poem explain'd.
(n) St. George.

Then airy atoms did in plagues conspire, ⎫
Nor did th' avenging angel yet retire, ⎬
But purg'd our still encreasing crimes ⎪
   with fire. ⎭
Then perjur'd Plots, the still impending
   Test,
And worse — but charity conceals the rest:
Here stop the current of the sanguine flood;
Require not, gracious God, thy martyrs'
   blood;   160
But let their dying pangs, their living toil,
Spread a rich harvest thro' their native soil:
A harvest ripening for another reign,
Of which this royal babe may reap the
   grain.
   Enough of early saints one womb has
     giv'n;
Enough encreas'd the family of heav'n:
Let them for his and our atonement go;
And reigning blest above, leave him to rule
   below.
   Enough already has the year foreslow'd
His wonted course, the seas have over-
   flow'd,   170
The meads were floated with a weeping
   spring,
And frighten'd birds in woods forgot to
   sing;
The strong-limb'd steed beneath his harness
   faints,
And the same shiv'ring sweat his lord at-
   taints.
When will the minister of wrath give o'er ?
Behold him, at (o) Araunah's threshing-
   floor:
He stops, and seems to sheathe his flaming
   brand,
Pleas'd with burnt incense from our David's
   hand.
David has bought the Jebusite's abode,
And rais'd an altar to the living God.   180
   Heav'n, to reward him, make his joys ⎫
     sincere; ⎪
No future ills nor accidents appear, ⎬
To sully and pollute the sacred infant's ⎪
   year ! ⎭
Five months to discord and debate were
   giv'n:
He sanctifies the yet remaining sev'n.
Sabbath of months ! henceforth in him be
   blest,
And prelude to the realm's perpetual rest !
   Let his baptismal drops for us atone;

(o) Alluding to the passage in the First Book of Kings
xxiv, 20.

Lustrations for (p) offenses not his own.
Let Conscience, which is Int'rest ill dis-
   guis'd,   190
In the same font be cleans'd, and all the
   land baptiz'd.
   (q) Unnam'd as yet; at least unknown to
     fame:
Is there a strife in heav'n about his name ?
Where every famous predecessor vies,
And makes a faction for it in the skies ?
Or must it be reserv'd to thought alone ?
Such was the sacred (r) *Tetragrammaton.*
Things worthy silence must not be reveal'd:
Thus the true name of (s) Rome was kept
   conceal'd,
To shun the spells and sorceries of those
Who durst her infant Majesty oppose.   201
But when his tender strength in time shall
   rise
To dare ill tongues, and fascinating eyes;
This isle, which hides the little thund'rer's
   fame,
Shall be too narrow to contain his name:
Th' artillery of heav'n shall make him
   known;
(t) Crete could not hold the god, when Jove
   was grown.
   As Jove's (u) increase, who from his
     brain was born,
Whom arms and arts did equally adorn,
Free of the breast was bred, whose milky
   taste   210
Minerva's name to Venus had debas'd;
So this imperial babe rejects the food
That mixes monarchs' with plebeian blood:
Food that his inborn courage might control,
Extinguish all the father in his soul,
And, for his Estian race, and Saxon strain,
Might reproduce some second Richard's
   reign.
Mildness he shares from both his parents'
   blood,
But kings too tame are despicably good:
Be this the mixture of this regal child,   220
By nature manly, but by virtue mild.
   Thus far the furious transport of the
     news
Had to prophetic madness fir'd the Muse;

(p) Original sin.
(q) The prince christen'd, but not nam'd.
(r) Jehovah, or the name of God, unlawful to be pronounc'd by the Jews.
(s) Some authors say that the true name of Rome was
kept a secret : *Ne hostes incantamentis deos elicerent.*
(t) Candie, or Jupiter was born and bred secretly.
(u) Pallas, or Minerva, said by the poets to have been
bred up by hand.

Madness ungovernable, uninspir'd,
Swift to foretell whatever she desir'd.
Was it for me the dark abyss to tread,
And read the book which angels cannot
  read ?
How was I punish'd, when the (v) sudden
  blast
The face of heav'n and our young sun o'er-
  cast !
Fame, the swift ill, encreasing as she roll'd,
Disease, despair, and death, at three re-
  prises told: 231
At three insulting strides she stalk'd the
  town,
And, like contagion, struck the loyal down.
Down fell the winnow'd wheat; but,
  mounted high,
The whirlwind bore the chaff, and hid the
  sky.
Here black rebellion shooting from be-⎫
  low,   ⎪
(As earth's (w) gigantic brood by mo- ⎬
  ments grow,)   ⎪
And here the sons of God are petrified ⎪
  with woe: ⎭
An apoplex of grief ! so low were driv'n
The saints, as hardly to defend their heav'n.
  As, when pent vapors run their hollow
    round,   241
Earthquakes, which are convulsions of the
  ground,
Break bellowing forth, and no confinement
  brook,
Till the third settles what the former shook;
Such heavings had our souls; till, slow and
  late,
Our life with his return'd, and faith pre-
  vail'd on fate:
By prayers the mighty blessing was im-
  plor'd,
To pray'rs was granted, and by pray'rs re-
  stor'd.
  So, ere the (x) Shunammite a son con-
    ceiv'd,
The prophet promis'd, and the wife be-
  liev'd.   250
A son was sent, the son so much desir'd;
But soon upon the mother's knees expir'd.
The troubled Seer approach'd the mourn-
  ful door,
Ran, pray'd, and sent his past'ral staff be-
  fore,

(v) The sudden false report of the prince's death.
(w) Those giants are feign'd to have grown fifteen ells
every day.
(x) In the Second Book of Kings iv.

Then stretch'd his limbs upon the child, and
  mourn'd,
Till warmth, and breath, and a new soul
  return'd.
  Thus Mercy stretches out her hand, and
    saves
Desponding Peter sinking in the waves.
  As when a sudden storm of hail and rain
Beats to the ground the yet unbearded
  grain,   260
Think not the hopes of harvest are destroy'd
On the flat field, and on the naked void;
The light, unloaded stem, from tempest
  freed,
Will raise the youthful honors of his head;
And, soon restor'd by native vigor, bear
The timely product of the bounteous year.
  Nor yet conclude all fiery trials past:
For Heav'n will exercise us to the last;
Sometimes will check us in our full career,
With doubtful blessings, and with mingled
  fear;   270
That, still depending on his daily grace,
His every mercy for an alms may pass;
With sparing hands will diet us to good,
Preventing surfeits of our pamper'd blood.
So feeds the mother bird her craving young
With little morsels, and delays 'em long.
  True, this last blessing was a royal feast;
But where 's the wedding garment on the
  guest ?
Our manners, as religion were a dream,
Are such as teach the nations to *blaspheme.*
In lusts we wallow, and with pride we swell,
And injuries with injuries repel;   282
Prompt to revenge, not daring to forgive,
Our lives unteach the doctrine we believe.
Thus Israel sinn'd, impenitently hard,
And vainly thought the (y) present ark
  their guard;
But when the haughty Philistines appear,⎫
They fled, abandon'd to their foes and fear; ⎪
Their God was absent, tho' his ark was ⎬
  there.   ⎭
Ah ! lest our crimes should snatch this
  pledge away   290
And make our joys the blessing of a day !
For we have sinn'd him hence, and that he
  lives,
God to his promise, not our practice gives.
Our crimes would soon weigh down the
  guilty scale,
But James, and Mary, and the Church pre-
  vail.

(y) 1 Samuel iv, 10.

Nor (z) Amalek can rout the chosen bands,
While Hur and Aaron hold up Moses' hands.
  By living well, let us secure his days,
Mod'rate in hopes, and humble in our ways.
No force the freeborn spirit can constrain,
But charity and great examples gain.   301
Forgiveness is our thanks for such a day,
'T is godlike God in his own coin to pay.
  But you, propitious queen, translated ⎤
    here, |
From your mild heav'n, to rule our ⎬
    rugged sphere, |
Beyond the sunny walks, and circling ⎦
    year:
You, who your native climate have bereft
Of all the virtues, and the vices left;
Whom piety and beauty make their boast,
Tho' beautiful is well in pious lost;   310
So lost, as starlight is dissolv'd away,
And melts into the brightness of the day;
Or gold about the regal diadem,
Lost to improve the luster of the gem:
What can we add to your triumphant
    day ?
Let the great gift the beauteous giver pay.
For, should our thanks awake the rising ⎤
    sun,
And lengthen, as his latest shadows run, ⎬
That, tho' the longest day, would soon, |
    too soon be done. ⎦
Let angels' voices with their harps con-
    spire,   320
But keep th' auspicious infant from the
    choir;
Late let him sing above, and let us know
No sweeter music than his cries below.
  Nor can I wish to you, great monarch,
    more
Than such an annual income to your store;
The day which gave this *unit* did not shine
For a less omen, than to fill the *trine.*
After a *prince*, an *admiral* beget;
The Royal Sov'reign wants an anchor yet.

        (z) Exod. xvii, 8.

Our isle has younger titles still in store, ⎤
And when th' exhausted land can yield |
    no more,   331 ⎬
Your line can force them from a foreign |
    shore. ⎦
  The name of Great your martial mind
    will suit,
But justice is your darling attribute:
Of all the Greeks, 't was but (a) one hero's
    due,
And in him Plutarch prophesied of you.
A prince's favors but on few can fall,
But justice is a virtue shar'd by all.
  Some kings the name of conqu'rors have
    assum'd,   339
Some to be great, some to be gods presum'd;
But boundless pow'r, and arbitrary lust,
Made tyrants still abhor the name of just;
They shunn'd the praise this godlike virtue
    gives,
And fear'd a title that reproach'd their lives.
  The pow'r, from which all kings derive
    their state,
Whom they pretend, at least, to imitate,
Is equal both to punish and reward;
For few would love their God, unless they
    fear'd.
  Resistless force and immortality
Make but a lame, imperfect deity;   350
Tempests have force unbounded to destroy,
And deathless being ev'n the damn'd enjoy;
And yet Heav'n's attributes, both last and
    first,
One without life, and one with life accurst;
But justice is Heav'n's self, so strictly he,
That, could it fail, the Godhead could not be.
This virtue is your own; but life and state
Are one to fortune subject, one to fate:
Equal to all, you justly frown or smile; ⎤
Nor hopes nor fears your steady hand |
    beguile;   360 ⎬
Yourself our balance hold, the world's, |
    our isle. ⎦

    (a) Aristides. See his life in Plutarch.

POEMS WRITTEN BETWEEN 1689 AND 1691

PROLOGUE AND EPILOGUE TO DON SEBASTIAN, KING OF PORTUGAL

[Dryden bestowed much labor upon this tragedy, the first play that he wrote on his return to dramatic work after the Revolution. Though of great literary merit, it seems from the author's preface to have had at first only moderate success on the stage. It was first acted on December 4, 1689; it was published in January, 1690. (See reference to the *London Gazette* in Scott-Saintsbury edition, xviii, 296.) The book was printed "for Jo. Hindmarsh," instead of for Tonson. The title-page bears the apt motto :

> — Nec tarda senectus
> Debilitat vires animi mutatque vigorem.
> VIRGIL, *Æneid*, ix, 610, 611.

The epilogue is closely connected with the play. The amour of Antonio, " a young, noble, amorous Portuguese," and the Mufti's daughter Morayma, who steals her father's jewel casket for her lover's sake, furnishes the secondary, comic intrigue of the drama, of which the love of Sebastian and Almeyda, "a captive queen of Barbary," later discovered to be Sebastian's sister, is the main plot. The true relation of Sebastian and Almeyda is disclosed by "an old counselor," Alvarez. The rest may be understood from hints in the epilogue itself.]

PROLOGUE

SPOKEN BY A WOMAN

THE judge remov'd, tho' he 's no more my lord,
May plead at bar, or at the council board:
So may cast poets write; there 's no pretension
To argue loss of wit, from loss of pension.
Your looks are cheerful; and in all this place
I see not one that wears a damning face.
The British nation is too brave, to show
Ignoble vengeance on a vanquish'd foe.
At least be civil to the wretch imploring,
And lay your paws upon him without roaring.   10
Suppose our poet was your foe before,
Yet now, the bus'ness of the field is o'er;
'T is time to let your civil wars alone,
When troops are into winter quarters gone.
Jove was alike to Latian and to Phrygian;
And you well know, a play 's of no religion.
Take good advice, and please yourselves this day
No matter from what hands you have the play
Among good fellows ev'ry health will pass,
That serves to carry round another glass:
When with full bowls of Burgundy you ⎫
   dine,   21 ⎬
Tho' at the mighty monarch you repine, ⎪
You grant him still Most Christian in his ⎪
   wine.   ⎭
  Thus far the poet; but his brains grow addle,
And all the rest is purely from this noddle.

You 've seen young ladies at the senate door
Prefer petitions, and your grace implore:
However grave the legislators were,
Their cause went ne'er the worse for being fair.
Reasons as weak as theirs, perhaps, I bring;   30
But I could bribe you with as good a thing.
I heard him make advances of good nature;
That he, for once, would sheathe his cutting satire.
Sign but his peace, he vows he 'll ne'er again
The sacred names of fops and beaus profane.
Strike up the bargain quickly; for I swear,
As times go now, he offers very fair.
Be not too hard on him with statutes ⎫
   neither; ⎪
Be kind; and do not set your teeth to- ⎬
   gether, ⎪
To stretch the laws, as cobblers do their ⎪
   leather.   40 ⎭
Horses by Papists are not to be ridden,
But sure the Muses' horse was ne'er forbidden;
For in no rate-book it was ever found
That Pegasus was valued at five pound;
Fine him to daily drudging and inditing,
And let him pay his taxes out in writing.

EPILOGUE

SPOKEN BETWIXT ANTONIO AND MORAYMA

Mor. I quak'd at heart, for fear the royal fashion
Should have seduc'd us two to separation:
To be drawn in, against our own desire,
Poor I to be a nun, poor you a friar.
Ant. I trembled, when the old man's hand was in,
He would have prov'd we were too near of kin,
Discovering old intrigues of love, like ⎫
   t'other, ⎪
Betwixt my father and thy sinful mother, ⎬
To make us sister Turk and Christian ⎪
   brother.   ⎭
Mor. Excuse me there; that league should have been rather   10
Betwixt your mother and my Mufti father

'T is for my own and my relations' credit,
Your friends should bear the bastard, mine
   should get it.
  Ant. Suppose us two Almeyda and
   Sebastian
With incest prov'd upon us —
  Mor.   Without question
Their conscience was too queasy of diges-
   tion.
  Ant. Thou wouldst have kept the coun-
   sel of thy brother,
And sinn'd till we repented of each other.
  Mor. Beast as you are, on nature's laws
   to trample !
'T were fitter that we follow'd their exam-
   ple;   20
And, since all marriage in repentance ends,
'T is good for us to part while we are
   friends.
To save a maid's remorses and confusions,
E'en leave me now before we try con-
   clusions.
  Ant. To copy their example, first make
   certain
Of one good hour, like theirs, before our
   parting;
Make a debauch o'er night of love and
   madness;
And marry, when we wake, in sober sad-
   ness.
  Mor. I 'll follow no new sects of your
   inventing;
One night might cost me nine long months'
   repenting.   30
First wed; and, if you find that life a fetter,
Die when you please; the sooner, sir, the
   better.
My wealth would get me love ere I could
   ask it:
O ! there's a strange temptation in the
   casket.
All these young sharpers would my grace
   importune,
And make me thund'ring votes of lives
   and fortune.

PROLOGUE TO THE PRO-
PHETESS

SPOKEN BY MR. BETTERTON

[Dryden wrote the following prologue for a
revival of Fletcher's *Prophetess*, "with alterations and additions after the manner of an
opera " (as the title-page has it) by Betterton,
and with music by Purcell (see Downes). The
date is fixed with some accuracy by the references to King William's campaign in Ireland,
from June 4 to September 6, 1690, during
which time Queen Mary acted as regent. The
prologue gave offense by its political references ; and, as Cibber tells us in his *Apology*,
" was forbid by the Lord Dorset after the first
day of its being spoken." " It must be confessed," Cibber adds, " that this prologue had
some familiar, metaphorical sneers at the Revolution itself ; and as the poetry of it was
good, the offense of it was less pardonable."
  This prologue was not printed with *The Prophetess* on its publication in 1690 ; it first appeared in the second edition, 1708, of *The Annual Miscellany for the Year 1694* (the *Fourth
Miscellany*).]

WHAT *Nostradame*, with all his art, can
   guess
The fate of our approaching *Prophetess ?*
A play, which, like a prospective set right,
Presents our vast expenses close to sight;
But turn the tube, and there we sadly view
Our distant gains; and those uncertain too:
A sweeping tax, which on ourselves we
   raise,
And all, like you, in hopes of better days.
When will our losses warn us to be wise!
Our wealth decreases, and our charges rise.
Money, the sweet allurer of our hopes,   11
Ebbs out in oceans and comes in by drops.
We raise new objects to provoke delight,
But you grow sated ere the second sight.
False men, even so you serve your mis-
   tresses:
They rise three stories in their tow'ring
   dress;
And, after all, you love not long enough
To pay the rigging, ere you leave 'em off:
Never content with what you had before,
But true to change, and Englishmen all
   o'er.   20
New honor calls you hence, and all your
   care
Is to provide the horrid pomp of war.
In plume and scarf, jack boots, and Bilbo
   blade,
Your silver goes, that should support our
   trade.
Go, unkind heroes, leave our stage to
   mourn,
Till rich from vanquish'd rebels you re-
   turn;
And the fat spoils of Teague in triumph
   draw,

His firkin butter, and his usquebaugh.
Go, conquerors of your male and female
   foes;
Men without hearts, and women without
   hose. 30
Each bring his love a Bogland captive
   home;
Such proper pages will long trains become;
With copper collars, and with brawny
   backs,
Quite to put down the fashion of our
   blacks.
Then shall the pious Muses pay their vows,
And furnish all their laurels for your
   brows;
Their tuneful voice shall rise for your de-
   lights;
We want not poets fit to sing your fights.
But you, bright beauties, for whose only
   sake
These doughty knights such dangers under-
   take, 40
When they with happy gales are gone ⎤
   away, |
With your propitious presence grace our ⎬
   play, |
And with a sigh their empty seats sur- |
   vey: ⎦
Then think: "On that bare bench my ser-
   vant sate;
I see him ogle still, and hear him chat,
Selling facetious bargains, and propounding
That witty recreation, call'd dumfounding."
Their loss with patience we will try to
   bear;
And would do more, to see you often here !
That our dead stage, reviv'd by your fair
   eyes, 50
Under a female regency may rise.

PROLOGUE, EPILOGUE, AND SONGS FROM AMPHITRYON

OR, THE TWO SOSIAS

[Dryden based his *Amphitryon* on the comedy of the same name by Molière, but borrowed some traits from Plautus and added
important features of his own invention. (See
Philipp Ott: *Ueber das Verhältnis des Lustspiel-
Dichters Dryden zu ... Molière.* Landshut,
1888.) The play was probably first acted in
October, 1690, and was published in the same
month. (See reference to the *London Gazette*
in Scott-Saintsbury edition, xviii, 296.)]

PROLOGUE

SPOKEN BY MRS. BRACEGIRDLE

THE lab'ring bee, when his sharp sting is
   gone,
Forgets his golden work, and turns a
   drone:
Such is a satire, when you take away
That rage in which his noble vigor lay.
What gain you by not suffering him to
   tease ye ?
He neither can offend you, now, nor please
   ye.
The honey-bag and venom lay so near, ⎤
That both together you resolv'd to tear; |
And lost your pleasure, to secure your ⎬
   fear. ⎦
How can he show his manhood, if you bind
   him 10
To box, like boys, with one hand tied be-
   hind him ?
This is plain leveling of wit, in which
The poor has all th' advantage, not the
   rich.
The blockhead stands excus'd for wanting
   sense,
And wits turn blockheads in their own de-
   fense.
Yet, tho' the stage's traffic is undone,
Still Julian's interloping trade goes on:
Tho' satire on the theater you smother,
Yet, in lampoons, you libel one another.
The first produces still a second jig; 20
You whip 'em out, like schoolboys, till
   they gig,
And with the same success, we readers
   guess,
For ev'ry one still dwindles to a less;
And much good malice is so meanly dress'd,
That we would laugh, but cannot find the
   jest.
If no advice your rhyming rage can stay,
Let not the ladies suffer in the fray:
Their tender sex is privileg'd from war;
'T is not like knights, to draw upon the fair.
What fame expect you from so mean a
   prize ? 30
We wear no murd'ring weapons but our
   eyes.
Our sex, you know, was after yours de- ⎤
   sign'd; |
The last perfection of the Maker's mind: ⎬
Heav'n drew out all the gold for us, and |
   left your dross behind. ⎦

Beauty for valor's best reward he chose;
Peace, after war; and after toil, repose.
Hence, ye profane, excluded from our ⎤
     sights; |
And, charm'd by day with honor's vain   }
     delights, |
Go, make your best of solitary nights.   ⎦
Recant betimes, 't is prudence to submit; 40
Our sex is still your overmatch in wit:
We never fail with new, successful arts,
To make fine fools of you, and all your
     parts.

EPILOGUE

SPOKEN BY PHÆDRA, MRS. MOUNTFORT

I 'M thinking (and it almost makes me mad)
How sweet a time those heathen ladies had.
Idolatry was ev'n their gods' own trade;
They worship'd the fine creatures they had
     made.
Cupid was chief of all the deities,
And love was all the fashion in the skies.
When the sweet nymph held up the lily
     hand,
Jove was her humble servant at command.
The treasury of heav'n was ne'er so bare,
But still there was a pension for the fair. 10
In all his reign adult'ry was no sin,
For Jove the good example did begin.
Mark, too, when he usurp'd the husband's
     name,
How civilly he sav'd the lady's fame.
The secret joys of love he wisely hid;
But you, sirs, boast of more than e'er you
     did.
You tease your cuckolds; to their face tor-
     ment 'em:
But Jove gave his new honors to content 'em;
And, in the kind remembrance of the fair,
On each exalted son bestow'd a star.   20
For those good deeds, as by the date ap-
     pears,
His godship flourish'd full two thousand
     years.
At last, when he and all his priests grew ⎤
     old, |
The ladies grew in their devotion cold, }
And that false worship would no longer |
     hold.   ⎦

Severity of life did next begin,
(And always does, when we no more can sin.)
That doctrine, too, so hard in practice lies,

That the next age may see another rise. 29
Then pagan gods may once again succeed, ⎤
And Jove or Mars be ready, at our need, |
To get young godlings, and so mend our   }
     breed.   ⎦

SONGS

I

SONG

I

CELIA, that I once was blest,
Is now the torment of my breast,
     Since, to curse me, you bereave me
Of the pleasures I possess'd:
     Cruel creature, to deceive me!
     First to love, and then to leave me!

II

Had you the bliss refus'd to grant,
Then I had never known the want;
     But possessing once the blessing
Is the cause of my complaint: 10
     Once possessing is but tasting;
     'T is no bliss that is not lasting.

III

Celia now is mine no more;
But I am hers, and must adore,
     Nor to leave her will endeavor:
Charms that captiv'd me before
     No unkindness can dissever;
     Love that 's true, is love forever.

II

MERCURY'S SONG TO PHÆDRA

I

FAIR Iris I love, and hourly I die,
But not for a lip, nor a languishing eye:
She 's fickle and false, and there we agree,
For I am as false and as fickle as she.
We neither believe what either can say;
And, neither believing, we neither betray.

II

'T is civil to swear, and say things of course;
We mean not the taking for better for worse.
When present, we love; when absent, agree:
I think not of Iris, nor Iris of me.   10
The legend of love no couple can find,
So easy to part, or so equally join'd.

III

A PASTORAL DIALOGUE BETWIXT THYRSIS
AND IRIS

I

Thyrsis. FAIR Iris and her swain
    Were in a shady bow'r;
    Where Thyrsis long in vain
    Had sought the shepherd's hour:
At length his hand advancing upon
    her snowy breast,
    He said: " O kiss me longer,
    And longer yet and longer,
    If you will make me blest."

II

Iris. An easy yielding maid
    By trusting is undone;   10
    Our sex is oft betray'd
    By granting love too soon.
If you desire to gain me, your
    suff'rings to redress,
    Prepare to love me longer,
    And longer yet, and longer,
    Before you shall possess.

III

Thyrsis. The little care you show
    Of all my sorrows past
    Makes death appear too slow
    And life too long to last.   20
Fair Iris, kiss me kindly, in pity
    of my fate;
    And kindly still, and kindly,
    Before it be too late.

IV

Iris. You fondly court your bliss,
    And no advances make;
    'T is not for maids to kiss,
    But 't is for men to take.
So you may kiss me kindly, and I
    will not rebel;
    And kindly still, and kindly,
    But kiss me not and tell.   30

V

A RONDEAU

Chorus. Thus at the height we love and
    live,
    And fear not to be poor:
We give, and give, and give, and
    give,
    Till we can give no more;

But what to-day will take away,
    To-morrow will restore.
Thus at the heighth we love and live,
    And fear not to be poor.

PROLOGUE TO THE MISTAKES

OR, THE FALSE REPORT

[This play, a tragi-comedy by Joseph Harris,
a comic actor of no great note, was probably
acted in 1690 ; it was published early in 1691,
being entered in the *Term Catalogue* for Hilary
Term (February). According to Giles Jacob,
in *The Poetical Register, or The Lives and
Characters of all the English Poets,* 1723, this
play was " originally composed by another person ; but being put into his [Harris's] hands,
he, by altering, spoiled it."]

Enter MR. BRIGHT

GENTLEMEN, we must beg your pardon;
here 's no prologue to be had to-day; our
new play is like to come on without a
frontispiece, as bald as one of you young
beaux without your periwig. I left our
young poet sniveling and sobbing behind
the scenes, and cursing somebody that has
deceiv'd him.

Enter MR. BOWEN

Hold your prating to the audience:
here 's honest Mr. Williams, just come in,
half mellow, from the Rose Tavern. He
swears he is inspir'd with claret, and will
come on, and that *extempore* too, either
with a prologue of his own or something
like one. O here he comes to his trial, at
all adventures; for my part I wish him a
good deliverance.

    [*Exeunt Mr. Bright and Mr. Bowen.*

Enter MR. WILLIAMS

Save ye, sirs, save ye ! I am in a
    hopeful way,
I should speak something, in rhyme,
    now, for the play:
But the deuce take me, if I know what
    to say.
I 'll stick to my friend the author, that I
    can tell ye,
To the last drop of claret in my belly.
So far I 'm sure 't is rhyme — that needs
    no granting:

And, if my verses' feet stumble — you see
  my own are wanting.
Our young poet has brought a piece of ⎤
  work, |
In which, tho' much of art there does ⎬
  not lurk, |
It may hold out three days — and that's |
  as long as Cork.   10 ⎦
But, for this play — (which till I have
  done, we show not)
What may be its fortune — by the Lord —
  I know not.
This I dare swear, no malice here is writ:
'T is innocent of all things; ev'n of wit.
He 's no high-flyer; he makes no sky-
  rockets,
His squibs are only level'd at your pock-
  ets.
And if his crackers light among your
  pelf,
You are blown up; if not, then he 's blown
  up himself.
By this time, I 'm something recover'd of
  my fluster'd madness:
And now a word or two in sober sad-
  ness.   20
Ours is a common play; and you pay
  down
A common harlot's price — just half a
  crown.
You 'll say, I play the pimp on my ⎤
  friend's score; |
But since 't is for a friend, your gibes ⎬
  give o'er: |
For many a mother has done that be- |
  fore.   ⎦
How 's this, you cry? an actor write? —
  we know it;
But Shakespeare was an actor and a poet.
Has not great Jonson's learning often
  fail'd?
But Shakespeare's greater genius still pre-
  vail'd.
Have not some writing actors, in this
  age,   30
Deserv'd and found success upon the stage?
To tell the truth, when our old wits are
  tir'd,
Not one of us but means to be inspir'd.
Let your kind presence grace our homely ⎤
  cheer; |
'Peace and the butt' is all our bus'ness ⎬
  here: |
So much for that — and the Devil take |
  small beer.   ⎦

PROLOGUE, EPILOGUE, AND SONGS FROM KING ARTHUR

OR, THE BRITISH WORTHY

[This opera Dryden originally designed as a sequel to *Albion and Albanius*. He had nearly completed it before the death of Charles II in February, 1685. The opera was finally acted, with many alterations from the original plan, in the spring of 1691, and published in the same year. Some copies of the first edition lack the prologue and the epilogue.]

PROLOGUE

SPOKEN BY MR. BETTERTON

SURE there 's a dearth of wit in this dull
  town,
When silly plays so savorly go down;
As, when clipp'd money passes, 't is a sign
A nation is not over-stock'd with coin.
Happy is he who, in his own defense,
Can write just level to your humble sense;
Who higher than your pitch can never
  go;
And, doubtless, he must creep, who writes
  below.
So have I seen, in hall of knight, or lord,
A weak arm throw on a long shovel-board;
He barely lays his piece, bar rubs and
  knocks,   11
Secur'd by weakness not to reach the box.
A feeble poet will his bus'ness do, ⎤
Who, straining all he can, comes up to |
  you;   ⎬
For, if you like yourselves, you like him |
  too.   ⎦
An ape his own dear image will embrace;
An ugly beau adores a hatchet face:
So, some of you, on pure instinct of na-
  ture,
Are led, by kind, t' admire your fellow
  creature.
In fear of which, our house has sent this
  day,   20
T' insure our new-built vessel, call'd a play;
No sooner nam'd, than one cries out:
  "These stagers
Come in good time, to make more work for
  wagers."
The town divides, if it will take or no; ⎤
The courtiers bet, the cits, the merchants ⎬
  too; |
A sign they have but little else to do. ⎦

Bets, at the first, were fool-traps; where
    the wise,
Like spiders, lay in ambush for the flies:
But now they 're grown a common trade
    for all,
And actions by the news-book rise and
    fall;   30
Wits, cheats, and fops, are free of wager-
    hall.
One policy as far as Lyons carries;
Another, nearer home, sets up for Paris.
Our bets, at last, would ev'n to Rome ex-
    tend,
But that the Pope has prov'd our trusty
    friend.
Indeed, it were a bargain worth our money,
Could we insure another Ottobuoni.
Among the rest there are a sharping set,
That pray for us, and yet against us bet.
Sure Heav'n itself is at a loss to know   40
If these would have their pray'rs be heard,
    or no:
For in great stakes, we piously suppose,
Men pray but very faintly they may lose.
Leave off these wagers; for, in conscience
    speaking,
The city needs not your new tricks for
    breaking:
And if you gallants lose, to all appearing,
You 'll want an equipage for volunteering;
While thus, no spark of honor left within
    ye,
When you should draw the sword, you
    draw the guinea.

EPILOGUE

SPOKEN BY MRS. BRACEGIRDLE

I 'VE had to-day a dozen *billets-doux*
From fops, and wits, and cits, and Bow
    Street *beaux ;*
Some from Whitehall, but from the Tem-
    ple more:
A Covent Garden porter brought me four.
I have not yet read all; but, without feigning,
We maids can make shrewd guesses at
    your meaning.
What if, to shew your styles, I read 'em
    here ?
Methinks I hear one cry: "O Lord, for-
    bear !
No, madam, no; by Heav'n, that 's too
    severe."
Well then, be safe —   10

But swear henceforwards to renounce all
    writing,
And take this solemn oath of my in-
    diting,
As you love ease, and hate campaigns and
    fighting.
Yet, faith, 't is just to make some few ex-
    amples:
What if I shew'd you one or two for
    samples ?
(*Pulls one out.*) Here 's one desires my
    ladyship to meet
At the kind couch above in Bridges Street.
O sharping knave ! that would have you
    know what,
For a poor sneaking treat of chocolate.
(*Pulls out another.*) Now, in the name of
    luck, I 'll break this open,   20
Because I dreamt last night I had a token:
The superscription is exceeding pretty:
To the desire of all the town and city.
Now, gallants, you must know, this pre-
    cious fop
Is foreman of a haberdasher's shop:
One who devoutly cheats, demure in carriage,
And courts me to the holy bands of mar-
    riage;
But with a civil innuendo too,
My overplus of love shall be for you.
(*Reads.*) "Madam, I swear your looks are
    so divine,   30
When I set up, your face shall be my sign:
Tho' times are hard, to shew how I adore you,
Here 's my whole heart, and half a guinea
    for you.
But have a care of *beaux ;* they 're false,
    my honey;
And, which is worse, have not one rag of
    money."
    See how maliciously the rogue would
    wrong ye !
But I know better things of some among ye.
My wisest way will be to keep the stage,
And trust to the good nature of the age;
And he that likes the music and the play 40
Shall be my favorite gallant to-day.

SONGS

I

SONG OF TRIUMPH OF THE BRITONS

"COME if you dare," our trumpets sound;
"Come if you dare," the foes rebound:

"We come, we come, we come, we come,"
Says the double, double, double beat of the
    thund'ring drum.

    Now they charge on amain,
    Now they rally again:
The gods from above the mad labor be-
    hold,
And pity mankind that will perish for
    gold.

The fainting Saxons quit their ground;
Their trumpets languish in the sound;   10
They fly, they fly, they fly, they fly:
"*Victoria, Victoria!*" the bold Britons cry.

    Now the victory's won,
    To the plunder we run:
We return to our lasses like fortunate
    traders,
Triumphant with spoils of the vanquish'd
    invaders.

II
SONG

Man sings. O SIGHT, the mother of de-
    sires,
What charming objects dost thou yield!
    'T is sweet, when tedious night ex-
    pires,
To see the rosy morning gild
The mountain-tops, and paint the field!
But when Clorinda comes in sight,
She makes the summer's day more bright;
And when she goes away, 't is night.
Chorus. When fair Clorinda comes in
    sight, &c.

Woman sings. 'T is sweet the blushing
    morn to view;   10
And plains adorn'd with pearly dew;
But such cheap delights to see,
    Heaven and nature
    Give each creature;
They have eyes, as well as we;
    This is the joy, all joys above,
      To see, to see,
      That only she,
    That only she we love!   19
Chorus. This is the joy, all joys above, &c.

Man sings. And, if we may discover,
What charms both nymph and lover,
    'T is when the fair at mercy lies,

With kind and amorous anguish,
To sigh, to look, to languish,
    On each other's eyes.
Chorus of all ⎫
men and wo- ⎬ And, if we may discover, &c.
men. ⎭

III
SONG

I

How happy the lover,
How easy his chain,
How pleasing his pain,
How sweet to discover,
    He sighs not in vain!
For love every creature
Is form'd by his nature;
    No joys are above
    The pleasures of love.

II

In vain are our graces,   10
In vain are your eyes,
    If love you despise;
When age furrows faces,
    'T is time to be wise.
Then use the short blessing
That flies in possessing:
    No joys are above
    The pleasures of love.

IV
HARVEST SONG

Comus. YOUR hay it is mow'd, and your
    corn is reap'd;
Your barns will be full, and your hovels
    heap'd:
    Come, my boys, come;
    Come, my boys, come;
And merrily roar out harvest-home;
    Harvest-home,
    Harvest-home;
And merrily roar out harvest-home.
Chorus. Come, my boys, come, &c.

First Man. We ha' cheated the parson,
    we 'll cheat him again,   10
For why should a blockhead ha' one in ten?
    One in ten,
    One in ten;
For why should a blockhead ha' one in ten?
Chorus. One in ten,
    One in ten;
For why should a blockhead ha' one in ten?

Second Man. For prating so long like a
  book-learn'd sot,
Till pudding and dumplin burn to pot;
          Burn to pot,   20
          Burn to pot;
Till pudding and dumplin burn to pot.
Chorus. Burn to pot, &c.

Third Man. We'll toss off our ale till we
  canno' stand,
And hoigh for the honor of old England;
          Old England,
          Old England;
And hoigh for the honor of old Eng-
  land.
Chorus. Old England, &c.

V

SONG SUNG BY VENUS IN HONOR OF
BRITANNIA

I

FAIREST isle, all isles excelling,
  Seat of pleasures and of loves;
Venus here will choose her dwelling,
  And forsake her Cyprian groves.

II

Cupid from his fav'rite nation
  Care and envy will remove;
Jealousy, that poisons passion,
  And despair, that dies for love.

III

Gentle murmurs, sweet complaining,
  Sighs that blow the fire of love;   10
Soft repulses, kind disdaining,
  Shall be all the pains you prove.

IV

Every swain shall pay his duty,
  Grateful every nymph shall prove;
And as these excel in beauty,
  Those shall be renown'd for love.

VI

SONG

I

She. YOU say 'tis love creates the pain
Of which so sadly you complain,
And yet would fain engage my heart
In that uneasy cruel part:

But how, alas, think you that I
Can bear the wound of which you die?

II

He. 'T is not my passion makes my care,
But your indiff'rence gives despair;
The lusty sun begets no spring,
Till gentle show'rs assistance bring: 10
So love that scorches and destroys,
Till kindness aids, can cause no joys.

III

She. Love has a thousand ways to please,
But more to rob us of our ease:
For wakeful nights and careful days
Some hours of pleasure he repays;
But absence soon, or jealous fears,
O'erflow the joys with floods of tears.

IV

He. By vain and senseless forms betray'd,
Harmless love's th' offender made,   20
While we no other pains endure,
Than those that we ourselves procure:
But one soft moment makes amends
For all the torment that attends.

V

Chorus of Both. Let us love, let us love,
      and to happiness haste;
Age and wisdom come too fast:
Youth for loving was design'd.
He alone. I'll be constant, you be kind.
She alone. You be constant, I'll be kind.
Both. Heav'n can give no greater blessing
Than faithful love, and kind possessing. 31

AN EPITAPH ON THE LADY
WHITMORE

[These lines were written in honor of Frances,
fourth daughter of Sir William Brooke (*alias*
Cobham) and sister of the second wife of Sir
John Denham, the poet. The lady married,
first (before May, 1665), Sir Thomas Whitmore
of Bridgenorth and Buddwas, who died in
1682; and, second, Matthew Harvey, Esq., of
Twickenham, who died in 1693: she herself
died in 1690. (See G. E. C.: *Complete Peerage
of England, etc.*, ii, 320, 321.) The Reverend
Henry P. Prosser, vicar of Twickenham, writes
to the present editor as follows:
  "There is in the lobby of our church a massive monument, a pedestal with an urn upon it.
On one side of the base it is thus inscribed,

*Here lyeth ye Body of Matthew Harvie Esqr., he
dyed ye 14th of Janu^y, 1693.* On the opposite
side to this inscription are Dryden's lines to
Lady Whitmore, whose name does not occur
on the monument at all."
  Dryden's verses were first printed in *Examen
Poeticum,* 1693. The text is essentially the
same as that on the monument.]

FAIR, kind, and true, a treasure each alone;
A wife, a mistress, and a friend in one;
Rest in this tomb, rais'd at thy husband's
    cost,
Here sadly summing what he had, and lost.
  Come, virgins, ere in equal bands you
    join,
Come first, and offer at her sacred shrine;
Pray but for half the virtues of this wife,
Compound for all the rest with longer life;
And wish your vows like hers may be re-
    turn'd,
So lov'd when living, and when dead so
    mourn'd.

EPITAPH ON THE POET'S NEPHEW, ERASMUS LAWTON

[On a mural tablet in the church of Great
Catworth, Huntingdonshire, there is the following inscription. The date of the verses
contained in it cannot be determined : they
are placed here for convenience.]

                        Near this Place
        Was interred Dr John Lawton and
          Mrs Rose Driden, his 2nd wife.
He was a Pious man and learned, both in Divinity : and
In Musick and diligently improved Both Studies to ͻ
          [Glory of God
        And to the good of His Neighbour.
She was daughter of Erasmus Driden : Son of Sr Erasmus
Driden of Canons Ashby in Northampton^shir and M^rs
          [Mary Pickering
His wife by whom He had 14 children, the Eldest was
John Dryden Es^qr the Laureat of his time who
Married the Lady Elizabeth Howard Daughter to Henry
          [Earl of Berkshire
By whom she [*sic*] had 3 sons, Charles, John & Erasmus
          [who all died fine young Gentle^men
The 2nd Brother to Mrs Lawton is the present Sr Eras-
          [mus Driden of Canons Ashby
By lineal descent an ancient Baronet.
She was very beautifull and Pleasant in Her Youth
          [allways Good &
Charitable allmost beyond her power, in which she
          [followed the rare Example
of her Exelent Mother.   Mrs Lawton lived in this
          [Town near 40 years
And died Lamented Decem 26. 1710. in the 77 Yeare
          [of her age
Having first buried her only child Erasmus Lawton
on whom her Brother wrote these lines

      Stay Stranger Stay and drop one Tear
      She allways weeps that layd him Here

And will do, till her race is Run
His Father's fifth, her only Son.

This was placed here by a Relation of Hers
Whos friendship reaches beyond the grave.

THE LADY'S SONG

[This song is printed, with title, *The Lady s
Song, by Mr. Dryden,* in *Poetical Miscellanies,
the Fifth Part,* 1704, from which the present
text is taken. It also appears, with the heading,
*The Beautiful Lady of the May, written by Mr.
Dryden in the year 1691,* in a volume of *Miscellaneous Works, written by his Grace, George, late
Duke of Buckingham . . . the second edition . . .
printed for S. Briscoe, 1704,* to which is added
a collection of *State Poems . . . by several
Hands.* The song obviously refers to the banishment of James II and his queen.]

I

A CHOIR of bright beauties in spring did
    appear,
To choose a May-lady to govern the year;
All the nymphs were in white, and the
    shepherds in green;
The garland was giv'n, and Phyllis was queen:
But Phyllis refus'd it, and sighing did say:
" I 'll not wear a garland while Pan is
    away."

II

While Pan and fair Syrinx are fled from
    our shore,
The Graces are banish'd, and Love is no
    more:
The soft god of pleasure, that warm'd our
    desires,
Has broken his bow, and extinguish'd his
    fires;   10
And vows that himself and his mother will
    mourn,
Till Pan and fair Syrinx in triumph return.

III

Forbear your addresses, and court us no
    more,
For we will perform what the deity swore;
But if you dare think of deserving our
    charms,
Away with your sheephooks, and take to
    your arms:
Then laurels and myrtles your brows shall
    adorn,
When Pan, and his son, and fair Syrinx
    return.

EPITAPH ON JOHN GRAHAM OF CLAVERHOUSE, VISCOUNT DUNDEE

[John Graham of Claverhouse, created Viscount Dundee in 1688, perhaps the most famous of the Scotch Jacobite leaders, was killed at the battle of Killiecrankie, July 17, 1689. In his honor Dr. Archibald Pitcairne, a noted physician and Latin poet, composed the following epitaph, which is printed, together with the free translation by Dryden given below, in *Poems on Affairs of State*, vol. iii, 1704.]

> Ultime Scotorum, potuit quo sospite solo
> Libertas patriæ salva fuisse tuæ :
> Te moriente novos accepit Scotia cives,
> Acceptitque novos te moriente deos.
> Illa nequit superesse tibi, tu non potes illi,
> Ergo Calidoniæ nomen inane vale ;
> Tuque vale nostræ gentis fortissime ductor,
> Optime Scotorum atque ultime Grahme vale.

Dryden's lines are also printed, in an inferior text, under the title, *Upon the Death of the Earl of Dundee*, in *Poetical Miscellanies, the Fifth Part*, 1704. The date of composition is unknown. It seems appropriate to print this Jacobite epitaph immediately after *The Lady's Song*.]

O LAST and best of Scots ! who didst maintain
Thy country's freedom from a foreign reign;
New people fill the land now thou art gone,
New gods the temples, and new kings the throne.
Scotland and thou did each in other live;
Thou wouldst not her, nor could she thee survive.
Farewell, who living didst support the State,
And couldst not fall but with thy country's fate.

ELEONORA

A PANEGYRICAL POEM DEDICATED TO THE MEMORY OF THE LATE COUNTESS OF ABINGDON

> — *Superas evadere ad auras,*
> *Hoc opus, hic labor est. Pauci, quos æquus amavit*
> *Juppiter, aut ardens evexit ad æthera virtus,*
> *Dis geniti potuere.*
> VIRGIL, *Æneid*, vi, 128-131.

[The following poem was written in memory of Eleonora, Countess of Abingdon, who died on May 31, 1691. Dryden, as he tells us in his dedication, was requested by the Earl of Abingdon, with whom he was not personally acquainted, to write an elegy upon his deceased wife, whom the poet had never seen. *Eleonora* was first published in March, 1692 (see reference to the *London Gazette* in Scott-Saintsbury edition, xviii, 296), and was not reprinted until it was included in the folio *Poems and Translations*, 1701.]

TO THE
RIGHT HONORABLE
THE
EARL OF ABINGDON, &c.

MY LORD,
THE commands with which you honor'd me some months ago are now perform'd : they had been sooner ; but betwixt ill health, some business, and many troubles, I was forc'd to defer them till this time. Ovid, going to his banishment, and writing from on shipboard to his friends, excus'd the faults of his poetry by his misfortunes ; and told them that good verses never flow but from a serene and compos'd spirit. Wit, which is a kind of Mercury, with wings fasten'd to his head and heels, can fly but slowly in a damp air. I therefore chose rather to obey you late than ill : if at least I am capable of writing anything, at any time, which is worthy your perusal and your patronage. I cannot say that I have escap'd from a shipwreck ; but have only gain'd a rock by hard swimming, where I may pant a while and gather breath ; for the doctors give me a sad assurance, that my disease never took its leave of any man, but with a purpose to return. However, my Lord, I have laid hold on the interval, and menag'd the small stock which age has left me, to the best advantage, in performing this inconsiderable service to my Lady's memory. We, who are priests of Apollo, have not the inspiration when we please ; but must

wait till the god comes rushing on us, and invades us with a fury which we are not able to resist: which gives us double strength while the fit continues, and leaves us languishing and spent, at its departure. Let me not seem to boast, my Lord, for I have really felt it on this occasion, and prophesied beyond my natural power. Let me add, and hope to be believ'd, that the excellency of the subject contributed much to the happiness of the execution ; and that the weight of thirty years was taken off me, while I was writing. I swam with the tide, and the water under me was buoyant. The reader will easily observe, that I was transported by the multitude and variety of my similitudes ; which are generally the product of a luxuriant fancy, and the wantonness of wit. Had I call'd in my judgment to my assistance, I had certainly retrench'd many of them. But I defend them not ; let them pass for beautiful faults amongst the better sort of critics : for the whole poem, tho' written in that which they call heroic verse, is of the Pindaric nature, as well in the thought as the expression ; and, as such, requires the same grains of allowance for it. It was intended, as your Lordship sees in the title, not for an elegy, but a panegyric : a kind of apotheosis, indeed, if a heathen word may be applied to a Christian use. And on all occasions of praise, if we take the ancients for our patterns, we are bound by prescription to employ the magnificence of words, and the force of figures, to adorn the sublimity of thoughts. Isocrates amongst the Grecian orators, and Cicero, and the younger Pliny, amongst the Romans, have left us their precedents for our security : for I think I need not mention the inimitable Pindar, who stretches on these pinions out of sight, and is carried upward, as it were, into another world.

This, at least, my Lord, I may justly plead, that, if I have not perform'd so well as I think I have, yet I have us'd my best endeavors to excel myself. One disadvantage I have had ; which is, never to have known or seen my Lady ; and to draw the lineaments of her mind, from the description which I have receiv'd from others, is for a painter to set himself at work without the living original before him : which, the more beautiful it is, will be so much the more difficult for him to conceive, when he has only a relation given him of such and such features by an acquaintance or a friend, without the nice touches which give the best resemblance and make the graces of the picture. Every artist is apt enough to flatter himself (and I amongst the rest) that their own ocular observations would have discover'd more perfections, at least others, than have been deliver'd to them : tho' I have receiv'd mine from

the best hands, that is, from persons who neither want a just understanding of my Lady's worth nor a due veneration for her memory.

Doctor Donne, the greatest wit, tho' not the greatest poet of our nation, acknowledges, that he had never seen Mrs. Drury, whom he has made immortal in his admirable *Anniversaries.* I have had the same fortune, tho' I have not succeeded to the same genius. However, I have follow'd his footsteps in the design of his panegyric ; which was to raise an emulation in the living, to copy out the example of the dead. And therefore it was, that I once intended to have call'd this poem *The Pattern :* and tho', on a second consideration, I chang'd the title into the name of that illustrious person, yet the design continues, and *Eleonora* is still the pattern of charity, devotion, and humility ; of the best wife, the best mother, and the best of friends.

And now, my Lord, tho' I have endeavor'd to answer your commands, yet I could not answer it to the world, nor to my conscience, if I gave not your Lordship my testimony of being the best husband now living : I say my testimony only ; for the praise of it is given you by yourself. They who despise the rules of virtue both in their practice and their morals, will think this a very trivial commendation. But I think it the peculiar happiness of the Countess of Abingdon, to have been so truly lov'd by you, while she was living, and so gratefully honor'd after she was dead. Few there are who have either had, or could have, such a loss ; and yet fewer who carried their love and constancy beyond the grave. The exteriors of mourning, a decent funeral, and black habits, are the usual stints of common husbands ; and perhaps their wives deserve no better than to be mourn'd with hypocrisy, and forgot with ease. But you have distinguish'd yourself from ordinary lovers, by a real and lasting grief for the deceas'd ; and by endeavoring to raise for her the most durable monument, which is that of verse. And so it would have prov'd, if the workman had been equal to the work, and your choice of the artificer as happy as your design. Yet as Phidias, when he had made the statue of Minerva, could not forbear to ingrave his own name, as author of the piece : so give me leave to hope that, by subscribing mine to this poem, I may live by the goddess, and transmit my name to posterity by the memory of hers. 'Tis no flattery to assure your Lordship that she is remember'd, in the present age, by all who have had the honor of her conversation and acquaintance ; and that I have never been in any company since the news of her death was first brought me, where they have not extoll'd her virtues, and even spoken the same things of her in prose, which I have done in verse.

I therefore think myself oblig'd to thank your Lordship for the commission which you have given me: how I have acquitted myself of it, must be left to the opinion of the world, in spite of any protestation which I can enter against the present age, as incompetent or corrupt judges. For my comfort, they are but Englishmen, and, as such, if they think ill of me to-day, they are inconstant enough to think well of me to-morrow. And, after all, I have not much to thank my fortune that I was born amongst them. The good of both sexes are so few, in England, that they stand like exceptions against general rules: and tho' one of them has deserv'd a greater commendation than I could give her, they have taken care that I should not tire my pen with frequent exercise on the like subjects; that praises, like taxes, should be appropriated, and left almost as individual as the person. They say, my talent is satire: if it be so, 't is a fruitful age, and there is an extraordinary crop to gather. But a single hand is insufficient for such a harvest: they have sown the dragon's teeth themselves, and 't is but just they should reap each other in lampoons. You, my Lord, who have the character of honor, tho' 't is not my happiness to know you, may stand aside, with the small remainders of the English nobility, truly such, and, unhurt yourselves, behold the mad combat. If I have pleas'd you, and some few others, I have obtain'd my end. You see I have disabled myself, like an elected Speaker of the House; yet like him I have undertaken the charge, and find the burden sufficiently recompens'd by the honor. Be pleas'd to accept of these my unworthy labors, this paper monument; and let her pious memory, which I am sure is sacred to you, not only plead the pardon of my many faults, but gain me your protection, which is ambitiously sought by,

> My Lord,
> Your Lordship's
> Most Obedient Servant,
> JOHN DRYDEN.

ELEONORA

As, when some great and gracious monarch
    dies,
Soft whispers, first, and mourn- *The introduc-*
    ful murmurs rise   *tion.*
Among the sad attendants; then the sound
Soon gathers voice, and spreads the news
    around
Thro' town and country, till the dreadful
    blast
Is blown to distant colonies at last;

Who, then, perhaps, were offering vows in
    vain,
For his long life, and for his happy reign:
So slowly, by degrees, unwilling fame
Did matchless Eleonora's fate proclaim, 10
Till public as the loss the news became.
  The nation felt it in th' extremest parts,
With eyes o'erflowing, and with bleeding
    hearts;
But most the poor, whom daily *Of her charity.*
    she supplied,
Beginning to be such, but when she died,
For, while she liv'd, they slept in peace by
    night,
Secure of bread, as of returning light;
And with such firm dependence on the day,
That need grew pamper'd, and forgot to
    pray:
So sure the dole, so ready at their call, 20
They stood prepar'd to see the manna fall.
  Such multitudes she fed, she cloth'd, she
    nurs'd,
That she herself might fear her wanting
    first.
Of her five talents, other five she made;
Heav'n, that had largely giv'n, was largely
    paid:
And in few lives, in wondrous few, we find
A fortune better fitted to the mind.
Nor did her alms from ostentation fall,
Or proud desire of praise; the soul gave
    all:
Unbrib'd it gave; or, if a bribe appear, 30
No less than heav'n, to heap huge treasures there.
Want pass'd for merit at her open door:
Heav'n saw, he safely might increase his
    poor,
And trust their sustenance with her so
    well,
As not to be at charge of miracle.
None could be needy, whom she saw, or
    knew;
All in the compass of her sphere she drew:
He, who could touch her garment, was as
    sure,
As the first Christians of th' apostles' cure.
The distant heard, by fame, her pious
    deeds, 40
And laid her up for their extremest needs;
A future cordial for a fainting mind;
For, what was ne'er refus'd, all hop'd to
    find,
Each in his turn: the rich might freely
    come,

As to a friend; but to the poor, 't was home.
As to some holy house th' afflicted came, ⎫
The hunger-starv'd, the naked and the ⎬
    lame; ⎪
Want and diseases fled before her name. ⎭
For zeal like hers her servants were too ⎫
    slow; ⎪
She was the first, where need requir'd, ⎬
    to go;   50 ⎪
Herself the foundress and attendant too. ⎭
  Sure she had guests sometimes to enter-
    tain,
Guests in disguise, of her great Master's
    train.
Her Lord himself might come, for aught
    we know,
Since in a servant's form he liv'd below:
Beneath her roof he might be pleas'd to
    stay;
Or some benighted angel, in his way,
Might ease his wings, and, seeing heav'n
    appear
In its best work of mercy, think it there,
Where all the deeds of charity and love 60
Were in as constant method, as above,
All carried on; all of a piece with theirs; ⎫
As free her alms, as diligent her cares; ⎬
As loud her praises, and as warm her ⎪
    pray'rs. ⎭
  Yet was she not profuse; but fear'd to
    waste,   Of her prudent
And wisely manag'd, that the management.
    stock might last;
That all might be supplied, and she not
    grieve,
When crowds appear'd, she had not to re-
    lieve:
Which to prevent, she still increas'd her
    store;
Laid up, and spar'd, that she might give
    the more.   70
So Pharaoh, or some greater king than he,
Provided for the sev'nth necessity;
Taught from above his magazines to frame,
That famine was prevented ere it came.
Thus Heav'n, tho' all-sufficient, shows a
    thrift
In his economy, and bounds his gift:
Creating, for our day, one single light;
And his reflection too supplies the night.
Perhaps a thousand other worlds, that lie
Remote from us, and latent in the sky, 80
Are lighten'd by his beams, and kindly
    nurs'd;
Of which our earthly dunghill is the worst.

  Now, as all virtues keep the middle line,
Yet somewhat more to one extreme incline,
Such was her soul; abhorring avarice,
Bounteous, but almost bounteous to a vice:
Had she giv'n more, it had profusion been,
And turn'd th' excess of goodness into sin.
  These virtues rais'd her fabric to the
    sky;   Of her
For that, which is next heav'n, humility.
    is charity.
But, as high turrets, for their airy steep, 91
Require foundations, in proportion deep;
And lofty cedars as far upward shoot,
As to the nether heav'ns they drive the
    root:
So low did her secure foundation lie,
She was not humble, but Humility.
Scarcely she knew that she was great, or ⎫
    fair, ⎪
Or wise, beyond what other women are, ⎬
Or, which is better, knew, but never durst ⎪
    compare. ⎭
For to be conscious of what all admire, 100
And not be vain, advances virtue high'r.
But still she found, or rather thought she
    found,
Her own worth wanting, others' to abound;
Ascrib'd above their due to ev'ry one,
Unjust and scanty to herself alone.
  Such her devotion was, as might give
    rules
Of speculation to disputing Of her piety.
    schools,
And teach us equally the scales to hold
Betwixt the two extremes of hot and cold;
That pious heat may mod'rately prevail, 110
And we be warm'd, but not be scorch'd
    with zeal.
Business might shorten, not disturb her
    pray'r;
Heav'n had the best, if not the greater
    share.
An active life long oraisons forbids;
Yet still she pray'd, for still she pray'd by
    deeds.
  Her ev'ry day was Sabbath; only free
From hours of pray'r, for hours of charity:
Such as the Jews from servile toil releas'd,
Where works of mercy were a part of rest;
Such as blest angels exercise above,   120
Varied with sacred hymns and acts of love:
Such Sabbaths as that one she now enjoys,
Ev'n that perpetual one, which she employs
(For such vicissitudes in heav'n there are)
In praise alternate, and alternate pray'r.

All this she practic'd here; that when she
    sprung
Amidst the choirs, at the first sight she
    sung:
Sung, and was sung herself in angels' lays;
For, praising her, they did her Maker
    praise.
All offices of heav'n so well she knew, 130
Before she came, that nothing there was
    new;
And she was so familiarly receiv'd,
As one returning, not as one arriv'd.

    Muse, down again precipitate thy flight:
For how can mortal eyes sus- Of her various
    tain immortal light!   virtues.
But as the sun in water we can bear,
Yet not the sun, but his reflection there,
So let us view her, here, in what she
    was,
And take her image in this wat'ry glass:
Yet look not ev'ry lineament to see; 140
Some will be cast in shades, and some
    will be
So lamely drawn, you'll scarcely know
    't is she.
For where such various virtues we recite,
'T is like the Milky Way, all over bright,
But sown so thick with stars, 't is undis-
    tinguish'd light.
Her virtue, not her virtues, let us call;
For one heroic comprehends 'em all:
One, as a constellation is but one,
Tho' 't is a train of stars, that, rolling on,
Rise in their turn, and in the zodiac
    run: 150
Ever in motion; now 't is Faith ascends,
Now Hope, now Charity, that upward
    tends,
And downwards with diffusive good de-
    scends.
    As in perfumes compos'd with art and
    cost,
'T is hard to say what scent is uppermost;
Nor this part musk or civet can we call,
Or amber, but a rich result of all;
So she was all a sweet, whose ev'ry part,
In due proportion mix'd, proclaim'd the
    Maker's art.
No single virtue we could most commend,
Whether the wife, the mother, or the
    friend; 161
For she was all, in that supreme degree,
That, as no one prevail'd, so all was she.
The sev'ral parts lay hidden in the piece;
Th' occasion but exerted that, or this.

    A wife as tender, and as true withal,
As the first woman was before Of her conju-
    her fall;   gal virtues.
Made for the man, of whom she was a
    part;
Made to attract his eyes, and keep his
    heart.
A second Eve, but by no crime accurs'd; 170
As beauteous, not as brittle as the first.
Had she been first, still Paradise had bin,
And death had found no entrance by her
    sin:
So she not only had preserv'd from ill
Her sex and ours, but liv'd their pattern
    still.
    Love and obedience to her lord she bore;
She much obey'd him, but she lov'd him
    more:
Not aw'd to duty by superior sway,
But taught by his indulgence to obey.
Thus we love God, as author of our good;
So subjects love just kings, or so they
    should. 181
Nor was it with ingratitude return'd;
In equal fires the blissful couple burn'd;
One joy possess'd 'em both, and in one
    grief they mourn'd.
His passion still improv'd; he lov'd so
    fast,
As if he fear'd each day would be her last:
Too true a prophet to foresee the fate
That should so soon divide their happy
    state;
When he to heav'n entirely must restore
That love, that heart, where he went
    halves before. 190
Yet as the soul is all in ev'ry part,
So God and he might each have all her
    heart.
    So had her children too; for Charity
Was not more fruitful, or more
    kind than she: Of her love
                              to her chil-
Each under other by degrees dren.
    they grew;
A goodly perspective of distant view.
Anchises look'd not with so pleas'd a face,
In numb'ring o'er his future Roman race,
And marshaling the heroes of his name,
As, in their order, next to light they came:
Nor Cybele with half so kind an eye 201
Survey'd her sons and daughters of the
    sky —
Proud, shall I say, of her immortal fruit?
As far as pride with heav'nly minds may
    suit.

Her pious love excell'd to all she bore;
New objects only multiplied it
more.   Her care of
                                         their educa-
And as the chosen found the tion.
pearly grain
As much as ev'ry vessel could contain;
As in the blissful vision each shall share ⎫
As much of glory as his soul can bear; ⎪
So did she love, and so dispense her ⎬
care.   211 ⎭
Her eldest thus, by consequence, was best,
As longer cultivated than the rest.
The babe had all that infant care beguiles,
And early knew his mother in her smiles:
But when dilated organs let in day
To the young soul, and gave it room to
play,
At his first aptness, the maternal love
Those rudiments of reason did improve.
The tender age was pliant to command;
Like wax it yielded to the forming hand:
True to th' artificer, the labor'd mind   222
With ease was pious, generous, just, and
kind;
Soft for impression from the first, prepar'd,
Till virtue with long exercise grew hard:
With ev'ry act confirm'd, and made at last
So durable as not to be effac'd,
It turn'd to habit; and, from vices free,
Goodness resolv'd into necessity.
Thus fix'd she Virtue's image, that 's her
own,   230
Till the whole mother in the children shone;
For that was their perfection: she was such,
They never could express her mind too
much.
So unexhausted her perfections were,
That, for more children, she had more to
spare;
For souls unborn, whom her untimely death
Depriv'd of bodies, and of mortal breath;
And (could they take th' impressions of her
mind)
Enough still left to sanctify her kind.   239
Then wonder not to see this soul extend
The bounds, and seek some Of her
other self, a friend.   friendship.
As swelling seas to gentle rivers glide,
To seek repose, and empty out the tide;
So this full soul, in narrow limits pent,
Unable to contain her, sought a vent,
To issue out, and in some friendly breast
Discharge her treasures, and securely rest:
T' unbosom all the secrets of her heart,
Take good advice, but better to impart.

For 't is the bliss of friendship's holy ⎫
state,   250 ⎪
To mix their minds, and to communicate; ⎬
Tho' bodies cannot, souls can penetrate. ⎭
Fix'd to her choice, inviolably true,
And wisely choosing, for she chose but few:
Some she must have; but in no one could
find
A tally fitted for so large a mind.
The souls of friends like kings in pro-
gress are;
Still in their own, tho' from the palace
far:
Thus her friend's heart her country dwell-
ing was,
A sweet retirement to a coarser place; 260
Where pomp and ceremonies enter'd not,
Where greatness was shut out, and bus'ness
well forgot.
This is th' imperfect draught; but ⎫
short as far ⎪
As the true height and bigness of a star ⎬
Exceeds the measures of th' astronomer. ⎭
She shines above, we know; but in what
place,
How near the throne, and Heav'n's imperial
face,
By our weak optics is but vainly guess'd;
Distance and altitude conceal the rest. 269
Tho' all these rare endowments of the
mind
Were in a narrow space of life Reflections
confin'd,   on the short-
                                 ness of her
The figure was with full per-   life.
fection crown'd;
Tho' not so large an orb, as truly round.
As when in glory, thro' the public place,
The spoils of conquer'd nations were to
pass,
And but one day for triumph was allow'd,
The consul was constrain'd his pomp to
crowd;
And so the swift procession hurried on,
That all, tho' not distinctly, might be
shown:
So, in the straiten'd bounds of life con-
fin'd,   280
She gave but glimpses of her glorious mind;
And multitudes of virtues pass'd along,
Each pressing foremost in the mighty
throng,
Ambitious to be seen, and then make room
For greater multitudes that were to come.
Yet unemploy'd no minute slipp'd away;
Moments were precious in so short a stay.

The haste of heav'n to have her was so
   great,
That some were single acts, tho' each
   complete;
But ev'ry act stood ready to repeat.   290
   Her fellow saints with busy care will look
For her blest name in fate's eternal book;
And, pleas'd to be outdone, with joy will
   see
Numberless virtues, endless charity:
But more will wonder at so short an age,
To find a blank beyond the thirtieth page;
And with a pious fear begin to
   doubt   *She died in*
The piece imperfect, and the *her thirty-*
   rest torn out.   *third year.*
But 't was her Savior's time; and, could
   there be
A copy near th' original, 't was she.   300
   As precious gums are not for lasting
   fire —
They but perfume the temple, and expire:
So was she soon exhal'd, and vanish'd hence;
A short sweet odor, of a vast expense.
She vanish'd, we can scarcely say she died;
For but a now did heav'n and earth divide:
She pass'd serenely with a single breath;
This moment perfect health, the next was
   death.
One sigh did her eternal bliss *The manner of*
   assure;   *her death.*
So little penance needs, when souls are
   almost pure.   310
As gentle dreams our waking thoughts
   pursue;
Or, one dream pass'd, we slide into a new;
So close they follow, such wild order keep,
We think ourselves awake, and are asleep:
So softly death succeeded life in her;
She did but dream of heav'n, and she was
   there.
   No pains she suffer'd, nor expir'd with
   noise;
Her soul was whisper'd out with God's still
   voice;
As an old friend is beckon'd to a feast,
And treated like a long familiar guest.   320
He took her as he found, but found her so,
As one in hourly readiness to *Her prepared-*
   go: *ness to die.*
Ev'n on that day, in all her trim prepar'd;
As early notice she from heav'n had heard,
And some descending courtier from above
Had giv'n her timely warning to remove;
Or counsel'd her to dress the nuptial room,

For on that night the bridegroom was to
   come.
He kept his hour, and found her where she
   lay   329
Cloth'd all in white, the liv'ry of the
   day: *She died on*
Scarce had she sinn'd in thought, *Whitsunday*
   or word, or act;   *night.*
Unless omissions were to pass for fact;
That hardly Death a consequence could draw,
To make her liable to nature's law.
And, that she died, we only have to show
The mortal part of her she left below;
The rest (so smooth, so suddenly she
   went)
Look'd like translation thro' the firma-
   ment,
Or like the fiery car on the third errand
   sent.   339
   O happy soul! if thou canst view from
   high,
Where thou art all intelligence, *Apostrophe*
   all eye,   *to her soul.*
If looking up to God, or down to us,
Thou find'st that any way be pervious,
Survey the ruins of thy house, and see
Thy widow'd, and thy orphan family:
Look on thy tender pledges left behind;
And, if thou canst a vacant minute find
From heav'nly joys, that interval afford
To thy sad children, and thy mourning lord.
See how they grieve, mistaken in their
   love,   350
And shed a beam of comfort from above;
Give 'em, as much as mortal eyes can bear,
A transient view of thy full glories there;
That they with mod'rate sorrow may sus-
   tain
And mollify their losses in thy gain.
Or else divide the grief; for such thou
   wert,
That should not all relations bear a part,
It were enough to break a single heart.
   Let this suffice: nor thou, great saint,
   refuse   *Epiphonema,*
This humble tribute of no vul- *or close of*
   gar Muse;   *the poem.*
Who, not by cares, or wants, or age de-
   press'd,   361
Stems a wild deluge with a dauntless
   breast;
And dares to sing thy praises in a clime
Where vice triumphs, and virtue is a crime;
Where ev'n to draw the picture of thy
   mind

Is satire on the most of humankind:
Take it, while yet 't is praise; before my
   rage,
Unsafely just, break loose on this bad age;
So bad, that thou thyself hadst no defense
From vice, but barely by departing hence.
  Be what, and where thou art: to wish
    thy place   371

Were, in the best, presumption more than
   grace.
Thy relics (such thy works of mercy are)
Have, in this poem, been my holy care.
As earth thy body keeps, thy soul the sky, ⎫
So shall this verse preserve thy memory: ⎪
For thou shalt make it live, because it ⎬
   sings of thee.   ⎭

ON THE DEATH OF A VERY YOUNG GENTLEMAN

[This elegy was first printed in *Poetical Miscellanies, the Fifth Part*, 1704. Christie infers, because of the resemblance of certain lines in this poem to passages in *Eleonora* (see notes), that the two pieces were written at about the same time.]

He who could view the book of destiny,
And read whatever there was writ of thee,
O *charming youth*, in the first op'ning page,
So many graces in so green an age,
Such wit, such modesty, such strength of
   mind,
A soul at once so manly, and so kind;
Would wonder, when he turn'd the volume
   o'er,
And after some few leaves should find no
   more,
Naught but a blank remain, a dead void
   space,
A step of life that promis'd such a race. 10
We must not, dare not think, that Heav'n
   began
A child, and could not finish him a man;
Reflecting what a mighty store was laid
Of rich materials, and a model made;
The cost already furnish'd; so bestow'd,
As more was never to one soul allow'd:
Yet after this profusion spent in vain,
Nothing but mold'ring ashes to remain.
I guess not, lest I split upon the shelf,
Yet durst I guess, Heav'n kept it for him-
   self;   20
And giving us the use, did soon recall,
Ere we could spare, the mighty principal.
  Thus then he disappear'd, was rarified;
For 't is improper speech to say he died:
He was exhal'd; his great Creator drew
His spirit, as the sun the morning dew.
'T is sin produces death; and he had none,
But the taint Adam left on ev'ry son.
He added not, he was so pure, so good,

'T was but th' original forfeit of his blood; 30
And that so little, that the river ran
More clear than the corrupted fount began.
Nothing remain'd of the first muddy clay;
The length of course had wash'd it in the
   way:
So deep, and yet so clear, we might behold
The gravel bottom, and that bottom gold.
  As such we lov'd, admir'd, almost ador'd,
Gave all the tribute mortals could afford.
Perhaps we gave so much, the pow'rs above
Grew angry at our superstitious love;   40
For when we more than human homage pay,
The charming cause is justly snatch'd away.
  Thus was the crime not his, but ours ⎫
    alone; ⎪
And yet we murmur that he went so soon, ⎬
Tho' miracles are short and rarely shown. ⎭
  Hear then, ye mournful parents, and
   divide
That love in many, which in one was tied.
That individual blessing is no more,
But multiplied in your remaining store.
The flame 's dispers'd, but does not all ex-
   pire;   50
The sparkles blaze, tho' not the globe of
   fire.
Love him by parts, in all your num'rous race,
And from those parts form one collected
   grace;
Then, when you have refin'd to that degree,
Imagine all in one, and think that one is he.

ON THE DEATH OF AMYNTAS

A PASTORAL ELEGY

[Nothing is known of the date or occasion of the following poem, which was first published in *Poetical Miscellanies, the Fifth Part*, 1704. It seems convenient to place it here, after another elegy, first printed in the same collection.]

'T was on a joyless and a gloomy morn,
Wet was the grass, and hung with pearls
   the thorn;
When Damon, who design'd to pass the day
With hounds and horns, and chase the fly-
   ing prey,
Rose early from his bed; but soon he ⎫
   found   ⎪
The welkin pitch'd with sullen clouds ⎬
   around,   ⎪
An eastern wind, and dew upon the ground. ⎭
Thus while he stood, and sighing did sur-
   vey
The fields, and curs'd th' ill omens of the
   day,
He saw Menalcas come with heavy pace; 10
Wet were his eyes, and cheerless was his
   face:
He wrung his hands, distracted with his
   care,
And sent his voice before him from afar.
   " Return," he cried, " return, unhappy
   swain,
The spongy clouds are fill'd with gath'ring
   rain;
The promise of the day not only cross'd,
But ev'n the spring, the spring itself is
   lost.
Amyntas — O ! " — he could not speak the
   rest,
Nor needed, for presaging Damon guess'd.
Equal with Heav'n young Damon lov'd the
   boy,   20
The boast of nature, both his parents'
   joy.
His graceful form revolving in his mind;
So great a genius, and a soul so kind,
Gave sad assurance that his fears were true;
Too well the envy of the gods he knew:
For when their gifts too lavishly are plac'd,
Soon they repent, and will not make them
   last.
For, sure, it was too bountiful a dole,
The mother's features, and the father's
   soul.
   Then thus he cried: " The Morn bespoke
   the news;   30
The Morning did her cheerful light dif-
   fuse;
But see how suddenly she chang'd her ⎫
   face,   ⎪
And brought on clouds and rain, the day's ⎬
   disgrace: ⎪
Just such, Amyntas, was thy promis'd ⎪
   race !   ⎭

What charms adorn'd thy youth, where
   nature smil'd,
And more than man was giv'n us in a child !
His infancy was ripe; a soul sublime
In years so tender that prevented time:
Heav'n gave him all at once; then ⎫
   snatch'd away,   ⎪
Ere mortals all his beauties could sur- ⎬
   vey,   40   ⎪
Just like the flow'r that buds and withers ⎪
   in a day."   ⎭

MENALCAS

The mother, lovely, tho' with grief op-
   press'd,
Reclin'd his dying head upon her breast.
The mournful family stood all around; ⎫
One groan was heard, one universal ⎪
   sound: ⎬
All were in floods of tears and endless ⎪
   sorrow drown'd.   ⎭
So dire a sadness sate on ev'ry look,
Ev'n Death repented he had giv'n the stroke.
He griev'd his fatal work had been or-
   dain'd,
But promis'd length of life to those who
   yet remain'd.   50
The mother's and her eldest daughter's
   grace,
It seems, had brib'd him to prolong their
   space.
The father bore it with undaunted soul,
Like one who durst his destiny control;
Yet with becoming grief he bore his part,
Resign'd his son, but not resign'd his heart:
Patient as Job; and may he live to see, ⎫
Like him, a new increasing family ! ⎪
                                      ⎪
DAMON   ⎬
                                      ⎪
Such is my wish, and such my pro- ⎪
   phecy,   ⎭
For yet, my friend, the beauteous mold re-
   mains;   60
Long may she exercise her fruitful pains !
But, ah ! with better hap, and bring a race
More lasting, and endued with equal grace !
Equal she may, but farther none can go;
For he was all that was exact below.

MENALCAS

Damon, behold yon breaking purple cloud;
Hear'st thou not hymns and songs divinely
   loud ?
There mounts Amyntas; the young cherubs
   play

About their godlike mate, and sing him on
  his way.
He cleaves the liquid air, behold, he flies, 70
And every moment gains upon the skies.
The new-come guest admires th' ethereal
  state,
The sapphire portal, and the golden gate;
And now admitted in the shining throng,
He shows the passport which he brought
  along.
His passport is his innocence and grace,
Well known to all the natives of the place.
Now sing, ye joyful angels, and admire
Your brother's voice that comes to mend
  your choir:
Sing you, while endless tears our eyes be-
  stow;   80
For like Amyntas none is left below.

TO MR. SOUTHERNE, ON HIS COMEDY CALL'D THE WIVES' EXCUSE

[After *The Loyal Brother* and *The Disappointment* (see pp. 122, 171, above), Southerne brought out *Sir Anthony Love, or The Rambling Lady* (1691) and *The Wives' Excuse, or Cuckolds Make Themselves* (1692). This last play had poor success on the stage. When it was published, early in 1692 — it is entered in the *Term Catalogue* for Hilary Term (February) — Dryden prefixed to it the following poem ; and in his *Epistle Dedicatory* Southerne boasts as follows:

" If Mr. Dryden's judgment goes for anything, I have it on my side: for, speaking of this play, he has publicly said, the town was kind to *Sir Anthony Love*, I needed 'em only to be just to this ; and to prove there was more than friendship in his opinion, upon the credit of this play with him, falling sick last summer, he bequeathed to my care the writing of half the last act of his tragedy of *Cleomenes*, which, when it comes into the world, you will find to be so considerable a trust, that all the town will pardon me for defending this play, that preferred me to it. If modesty be sometimes a weakness, what I say can hardly be a crime. In a fair English trial both parties are allowed to be heard ; and, without this vanity of mentioning Mr. Dryden, I had lost the best evidence of my cause."]

Sure there 's a fate in plays, and 't is in
  vain
To write, while these malignant planets
  reign:

Some very foolish influence rules the pit,
Not always kind to sense, or just to wit;
And whilst it lasts, let buffoonry succeed,
To make us laugh; for never was more
  need.
Farce, in itself, is of a nasty scent;
But the gain smells not of the excrement.
The Spanish nymph, a wit and beauty too,
With all her charms, bore but a single
  show;   10
But let a monster Muscovite appear,
He draws a crowded audience round the
  year.
Maybe thou hast not pleas'd the box⎫
  and pit,   ⎪
Yet those who blame thy tale commend ⎬
  thy wit;   ⎪
So Terence plotted, but so Terence writ.⎭
Like his thy thoughts are true, thy language clean;
Ev'n lewdness is made moral in thy scene.
The hearers may for want of Nokes repine;
But rest secure, the readers will be thine.
Nor was thy labor'd drama damn'd or
  hiss'd,   20
But with a kind civility dismiss'd;
With such good manners, as * The Wife in
  the * Wife did use,   the play, Mrs.
Who, not accepting, did but Friendall.
  just refuse.
There was a glance at parting; such a look,
As bids thee not give o'er, for one rebuke.
But if thou wouldst be seen, as well as
  read,
Copy one living author, and one dead:
The standard of thy style let Etherege be;
For wit, th' immortal spring of Wycherley.
Learn, after both, to draw some just design,   30
And the next age will learn to copy thine.

PROLOGUE, EPILOGUE, AND SONG FROM CLEOMENES, THE SPARTAN HERO

[This tragedy, written by Dryden with some aid from Southerne (see headnote to the preceding piece), was performed, after some opposition from the government, in May, 1692. (Malone, I, 1, 213, on the authority of Motteux's *Gentleman's Journal.*) The plot, of an exiled king seeking help in a foreign country, seemed capable of a political application. The play was first published in 1692.]

PROLOGUE

SPOKE BY MR. MOUNTFORT

I THINK, or hope at least, the coast is clear;
That none but men of wit and sense are
 here;
That our Bear Garden friends are all away,
Who bounce with hands and feet, and cry:
 " Play, play,"
Who, to save coach hire, trudge along the
 street,
Then print our matted seats with dirty feet;
Who, while we speak, make love to orange-
 wenches,
And, between acts, stand strutting on the
 benches;
Where got a-cock-horse, making vile gri-
 maces,   9
They to the boxes show their booby faces.
A merry-andrew such a mob will serve,
And treat 'em with such wit as they deserve.
Let 'em go people Ireland, where there 's
 need
Of such new planters to repair the breed;
Or to Virginia or Jamaica steer,
But have a care of some French privateer;
For, if they should become the prize of
 battle,
They 'll take 'em, black and white, for Irish
 cattle.
Arise, true judges, in your own defense,
Control those foplings, and declare for sense:
For, should the fools prevail, they stop not
 there,   21
But make their next descent upon the fair.
Then rise, ye fair; for it concerns you most,
That fools no longer should your favors
 boast;
'T is time you should renounce 'em, for we
 find
They plead a senseless claim to womankind:
Such squires are only fit for country towns,
To stink of ale, and dust a stand with
 clowns;
Who, to be chosen for the land's protectors,
Tope and get drunk before their wise
 electors.   30
Let not farce-lovers your weak choice up-
 braid,
But turn 'em over to the chambermaid;
Or, if they come to see our tragic scenes,
Instruct them what a Spartan hero means:
Teach 'em how manly passions ought to
 move,

For such as cannot think, can never love;
And, since they needs will judge the poet's
 art,
Point 'em with fescues to each shining part.
Our author hopes in you, but still in pain;
He fears your charms will be employ'd in
 vain.   40
You can make fools of wits, we find each
 hour;
But to make wits of fools, is past your
 power.

EPILOGUE

SPOKE BY MRS. BRACEGIRDLE

THIS day the poet, bloodily inclin'd,
Has made me die, full sore against my
 mind !
Some of you naughty men, I fear, will cry:
" Poor rogue ! would I might teach thee
 how to die ! "
Thanks for your love; but I sincerely say,
I never mean to die, your wicked way.
Well, since it is decreed all flesh must go,
(And I am flesh — at least for aught you
 know)
I first declare, I die with pious mind,
In perfect charity with all mankind.   10
Next for my will: I have in my dispose,
Some certain movables would please you
 beaux;
As, first, my youth; for, as I have been told,
Some of you modish sparks are dev'lish
 old.
My chastity I need not leave among ye;
For, to suspect old fops, were much to
 wrong ye.
You swear y' are sinners; but, for all your
 haste,
Your misses shake their heads, and find
 you chaste.
I give my courage to those bold com-
 manders
That stay with us, and dare not go to
 Flanders.   20
I leave my truth (to make his plot more
 clear)
To Mr. Fuller, when he next shall swear.
I give my judgment, craving all your
 mercies,
To those that leave good plays for damn'd
 dull farces.
My small devotion let the gallants share,
That come to ogle us at evening pray'r.

I give my person — let me well consider —
Faith, e'en to him that is the fairest bidder;
To some rich hunks, if any be so bold
To say those dreadful words, *To have and*
    hold.   30
But stay — to give, and be bequeathing still,
When I'm so poor, is just like Wickham's
    will:
Like that notorious cheat, vast sums I
    give,
Only that you may keep me while I live.
Buy a good bargain, gallants, while you may;
I'll cost you but your half a crown a day.

SONG

I

No, no, poor suff'ring heart, no change en-
    deavor,
Choose to sustain the smart, rather than
    leave her;
My ravish'd eyes behold such charms about
    her,
I can die with her, but not live without her;
One tender sigh of hers to see me languish,
Will more than pay the price of my past
    anguish:
Beware, O cruel fair, how you smile on me,
'Twas a kind look of yours that has undone
    me.

II

Love has in store for me one happy minute,
And she will end my pain, who did begin it;
Then no day void of bliss, or pleasure,
    leaving,   11
Ages shall slide away without perceiving:
Cupid shall guard the door, the more to
    please us,
And keep out Time and Death, when they
    would seize us;
Time and Death shall depart, and say, in
    flying,
Love has found out a way to live by dying.

EPILOGUE TO HENRY THE SECOND, KING OF ENGLAND, WITH THE DEATH OF ROSAMOND

SPOKE BY MRS. BRACEGIRDLE

[This tragedy was published in 1693, with
no author's name attached, but with an *epistle*
dedicatory* signed *Will. Mountfort*. Mountfort,
who was a noted actor and a minor dramatist,
does not, however, claim the play as his own.
Gildon, in his continuation of Langbaine's
English Dramatic Poets, 1699, assigns the play
to John Bancroft, a surgeon, who may have presented his work to Mountfort for revision. In
*Six Plays written by Mr. Mountfort: Printed
for J. Tonson, G. Strahan, and W. Mears, 1720*,
there occurs a preface, *The Booksellers to the
Reader*, which concludes as follows:
  " To the four pieces under his name . . . we
have annexed *King Edward the Third*, and
Henry the Second, which though not wholly
composed by him, it is presumed he had, at
least, a share in fitting them for the stage,
otherwise it cannot be supposed he would have
taken the liberty of writing dedications to
them, which we hope is sufficient authority
for this freedom, notwithstanding one of them *
was afterwards owned by another author.
        Henry the Second, by Mr. Bancroft."
  The play was probably acted in 1692;
Mountfort was killed on December 9 of that
year.]

THUS you the sad catastrophe have seen,
Occasion'd by a mistress and a queen.
Queen Eleanor the proud was French, they
    say;
But English manufacture got the day.
Jane Clifford was her name, as books aver;
Fair Rosamond was but her *nom de guerre*.
Now tell me, gallants, would you lead your
    life
With such a mistress, or with such a wife ?
If one must be your choice, which d'ye
    approve,
The curtain lecture, or the curtain love ? 10
Would ye be godly with perpetual strife,
Still drudging on with homely Joan your
    wife,
Or take your pleasure in a wicked way,
Like honest whoring Harry in the play ?
I guess your minds: the mistress would be
    taking,
And nauseous matrimony sent a packing.
The devil's in ye all; mankind's a rogue;
You love the bride, but you detest the clog.
After a year, poor spouse is left i' th'
    lurch,
And you, like Haynes, return to Mother
    Church.   20
Or, if the name of Church comes cross your
    mind,
Chapels of ease behind our scenes you find.
The playhouse is a kind of market place;

One chaffers for a voice, another for a face:
Nay, some of you, I dare not say how many,
Would buy of me a pen'worth for your
  penny.
Ev'n this poor face, which with my fan ⎱
  I hide,
Would make a shift my portion to provide,
With some small perquisites I have beside. ⎰

Tho' for your love, perhaps, I should not
  care,   30
I could not hate a man that bids me fair.
What might ensue, 't is hard for me to ⎱
  tell;
But I was drench'd to-day for loving well, ⎰
And fear the poison that would make me
  swell.

TRANSLATIONS FROM JUVENAL AND PERSIUS

[In October, 1692 (see advertisement in the *London Gazette*, referred to in the Scott-Saintsbury edition, xviii, 296), there appeared a folio volume with title-page reading as follows:

THE

SATIRES

of

Decimus Junius Juvenalis.

Translated into

ENGLISH VERSE

BY

Mr. *DRYDEN*,

AND

Several other Eminent Hands.

Together with the

SATIRES

OF

Aulus Persius Flaccus.

Made English by Mr. *Dryden*.

With Explanatory Notes at the end of each SATIRE.

To which is Prefix'd a Discourse concerning the Original and Progress of SATIRE. Dedicated to the Right Honourable *Charles* Earl of *Dorset*, &c. By Mr. *DRYDEN*.

Quicquid agunt homines, votum, timor, Ira, voluptas,
Gaudia, discursus, nostri est farrago libelli.

LONDON,

Printed for *Jacob Tonson* at the *Judge's-Head* in *Chancery-Lane*, near *Fleetstreet* MDCXCIII.

The translation of Persius has a separate title-page with the motto:

Sæpius in libro memoratur Persius uno
Quam levis in tota Marsus Amazonide. — MART.

To it there is prefixed a complimentary poem by Congreve.

Dryden's assistants on the *Juvenal* were Tate (*Satires* ii and xv), Bowles (*Satire* v), Stepney (*Satire* viii), Hervey (*Satire* ix), Congreve (*Satire* xi), Power (*Satire* xii), Creech (*Satire* xiii), an

unnamed writer (*Satire* iv), and his own sons, Charles and John (*Satires* vii and xiv respectively).
A second edition of the whole work, in octavo, appeared near the close of 1696 : it is entered in
the *Term Catalogue* for Michaelmas Term (November) of that year.]

TO THE

RIGHT HONORABLE CHARLES

EARL OF DORSET AND MIDDLESEX

LORD CHAMBERLAIN OF THEIR MAJES-
TIES' HOUSEHOLD, KNIGHT OF THE
MOST NOBLE ORDER OF THE GAR-
TER, &C.

MY LORD,

THE wishes and desires of all good men,
which have attended your Lordship from
your first appearance in the world, are at
length accomplish'd, in your obtaining those
honors and dignities which you have so long
deserv'd. There are no factions, tho' irreconcilable to one another, that are not united in
their affection to you, and the respect they
pay you. They are equally pleas'd in your
prosperity, and would be equally concern'd
in your afflictions. Titus Vespasian was not
more the delight of humankind. The universal empire made him only more known,
and more powerful, but could not make
him more belov'd. He had greater ability
of doing good, but your inclination to it
is not less; and tho' you could not extend
your beneficence to so many persons, yet
you have lost as few days as that excellent
emperor; and never had his complaint to
make when you went to bed, that the sun
had shone upon you in vain, when you had
the opportunity of relieving some unhappy
man. This, my Lord, has justly acquir'd
you as many friends as there are persons
who have the honor to be known to you.
Mere acquaintance you have none; you
have drawn them all into a nearer line;
and they who have convers'd with you are
for ever after inviolably yours. This is
a truth so generally acknowledg'd, that it
needs no proof: 't is of the nature of a
first principle, which is receiv'd as soon as
it is propos'd; and needs not the reformation which Descartes us'd to his; for we
doubt not, neither can we properly say we
think we admire and love you above all
other men; there is a certainty in the
proposition, and we know it. With the
same assurance I can say, you neither have
enemies, nor can scarce have any; for they
who have never heard of you, can neither
love or hate you; and they who have, can
have no other notion of you, than that
which they receive from the public, that
you are the best of men. After this, my
testimony can be of no farther use, than
to declare it to be daylight at high noon;
and all who have the benefit of sight, can
look up as well, and see the sun.

'T is true, I have one privilege which is
almost particular to myself, that I saw you
in the east at your first arising above the
hemisphere: I was as soon sensible as any
man of that light, when it was but just
shooting out, and beginning to travel upwards to the meridian. I made my early
addresses to your Lordship, in my *Essay of
Dramatic Poetry ;* and therein bespoke you
to the world, wherein I have the right of a
first discoverer. When I was myself in the
rudiments of my poetry, without name or
reputation in the world, having rather the
ambition of a writer, than the skill; when
I was drawing the outlines of an art, without any living master to instruct me in it;
an art which had been better prais'd than
studied here in England, wherein Shakespeare, who created the stage among us,
had rather written happily, than knowingly
and justly, and Jonson, who, by studying
Horace, had been acquainted with the rules,
yet seem'd to envy to posterity that knowledge, and, like an inventor of some useful
art, to make a monopoly of his learning;
when thus, as I may say, before the use of
the loadstone, or knowledge of the compass,
I was sailing in a vast ocean, without other
help than the polestar of the ancients, and
the rules of the French stage amongst the
moderns, which are extremely different
from ours, by reason of their opposite taste;
yet even then, I had the presumption to
dedicate to your Lordship — a very unfinish'd piece, I must confess, and which only
can be excus'd by the little experience of
the author, and the modesty of the title,
An Essay. Yet I was stronger in prophecy
than I was in criticism; I was inspir'd to
foretell you to mankind, as the restorer

of poetry, the greatest genius, the truest judge, and the best patron.

Good sense and good nature are never separated, tho' the ignorant world has thought otherwise. Good nature, by which I mean beneficence and candor, is the product of right reason; which of necessity will give allowance to the failings of others, by considering that there is nothing perfect in mankind; and by distinguishing that which comes nearest to excellency, tho' not absolutely free from faults, will certainly produce a candor in the judge. 'T is incident to an elevated understanding, like your Lordship's, to find out the errors of other men; but 't is your prerogative to pardon them; to look with pleasure on those things, which are somewhat congenial, and of a remote kindred to your own conceptions; and to forgive the many failings of those, who, with their wretched art, cannot arrive to those heights that you possess, from a happy, abundant, and native genius: which are as inborn to you, as they were to Shakespeare; and, for aught I know, to Homer; in either of whom we find all arts and sciences, all moral and natural philosophy, without knowing that they ever studied them.

There is not an English writer this day living, who is not perfectly convinc'd that your Lordship excels all others in all the several parts of poetry which you have undertaken to adorn. The most vain, and the most ambitious of our age, have not dar'd to assume so much as the competitors of Themistocles: they have yielded the first place without dispute; and have been arrogantly content to be esteem'd as second to your Lordship; and even that also, with a *longo, sed proximi intervallo*. If there have been, or are any, who go farther in their self-conceit, they must be very singular in their opinion; they must be like the officer in a play, who was call'd Captain, Lieutenant, and Company. The world will easily conclude whether such unattended generals can ever be capable of making a revolution in Parnassus.

I will not attempt, in this place, to say anything particular of your lyric poems, tho' they are the delight and wonder of this age, and will be the envy of the next. The subject of this book confines me to satire; and in that, an author of your own

quality (whose ashes I will not disturb) has given you all the commendation which his self-sufficiency could afford to any man:

The best good man, with the worst-natur'd Muse.

In that character, methinks, I am reading Jonson's verses to the memory of Shakespeare; an insolent, sparing, and invidious panegyric: where good nature, the most godlike commendation of a man, is only attributed to your person, and denied to your writings; for they are everywhere so full of candor, that, like Horace, you only expose the follies of men, without arraigning their vices; and in this excel him, that you add that pointedness of thought, which is visibly wanting in our great Roman. There is more of salt in all your verses than I have seen in any of the moderns, or even of the ancients; but you have been sparing of the gall, by which means you have pleas'd all readers, and offended none. Donne alone, of all our countrymen, had your talent; but was not happy enough to arrive at your versification; and were he translated into numbers, and English, he would yet be wanting in the dignity of expression. That which is the prime virtue, and chief ornament, of Virgil, which distinguishes him from the rest of writers, is so conspicuous in your verses, that it casts a shadow on all your contemporaries; we cannot be seen, or but obscurely, while you are present. You equal Donne in the variety, multiplicity, and choice of thoughts; you excel him in the manner and the words. I read you both with the same admiration, but not with the same delight. He affects the metaphysics, not only in his satires, but in his amorous verses, where nature only should reign; and perplexes the minds of the fair sex with nice speculations of philosophy, when he should ingage their hearts, and entertain them with the softnesses of love. In this (if I may be pardon'd for so bold a truth) Mr. Cowley has copied him to a fault; so great a one, in my opinion, that it throws his *Mistress* infinitely below his *Pindarics* and his latter compositions, which are undoubtedly the best of his poems, and the most correct. For my own part, I must avow it freely to the world, that I never attempted anything in satire, wherein I have not studied your writings as the most perfect model. I have continually laid them before me; and the greatest commendation which my own partiality can give to my productions, is, that they are copies, and no farther to be allow'd, than as they have something more or less of the original. Some few touches of your Lordship, some secret graces which I have endeavor'd to express after your manner, have made whole poems of mine to pass with approbation; but take your verses altogether, and they are inimitable. If therefore I have not written better, 't is because you have not written more. You have not set me sufficient copy to transcribe; and I cannot add one letter of my own invention, of which I have not the example there.

'T is a general complaint against your Lordship, and I must have leave to upbraid you with it, that, because you need not write, you will not. Mankind, that wishes you so well in all things that relate to your prosperity, have their intervals of wishing for themselves, and are within a little of grudging you the fulness of your fortune: they would be more malicious if you us'd it not so well, and with so much generosity.

Fame is in itself a real good, if we may believe Cicero, who was perhaps too fond of it; but even fame, as Virgil tells us, acquires strength by going forward. Let Epicurus give indolency as an attribute to his gods, and place in it the happiness of the blest; the divinity which we worship has given us not only a precept against it, but his own example to the contrary. The world, my Lord, would be content to allow you a seventh day for rest; or if you thought that hard upon you, we would not refuse you half your time : if you came out, like some great monarch, to take a town but once a year, as it were for your diversion, tho' you had no need to extend your territories. In short, if you were a bad, or, which is worse, an indifferent poet, we would thank you for our own quiet, and not expose you to the want of yours. But when you are so great and so successful, and when we have that necessity of your writing, that we cannot subsist in poetry without it, any more (I may almost say) than the world without the daily course of ordinary providence, methinks this argument might prevail with you, my Lord, to forego a little of your repose for the public benefit. 'T is not that you are under any force of working daily miracles, to prove your being; but now and then somewhat of extraordinary, that is, anything of your production, is requisite to refresh your character.

This, I think, my Lord, is a sufficient reproach to you; and should I carry it as far as mankind would authorise me, would be little less than satire. And, indeed, a provocation is almost necessary, in behalf of the world, that you might be induc'd sometimes to write; and in relation to a multitude of scribblers, who daily pester the world with their insufferable stuff, that they might be discourag'd from writing any more. I complain not of their lampoons and libels, tho' I have been the public mark for many years. I am vindictive enough to have repell'd force by force, if I could imagine that any of them had ever reach'd me; but they either shot at rovers, and therefore miss'd, or their powder was so weak, that I might safely stand them, at the nearest distance. I answer'd not *The Rehearsal*, because I knew the author sate to himself when he drew the picture, and was the very Bayes of his own farce; because also I knew that my betters were more concern'd than I was in that satire; and, lastly, because Mr. Smith and Mr. Johnson, the main pillars of it, were two such languishing gentlemen in their conversation, that I could liken them to nothing but to their own relations, those noble characters of men of wit and pleasure about the town. The like considerations have hinder'd me from dealing with the lamentable companions of their prose and doggrel. I am so far from defending my poetry against them, that I will not so much as expose theirs. And for my morals, if they are not proof against their attacks, let me be thought by posterity, what those authors would be thought, if any memory of them, or of their writings, could endure so long as to another age. But these dull makers of lampoons, as harmless as they have been to me, are yet of dangerous example to the public. Some witty men may perhaps succeed to their designs, and, mixing sense with malice, blast the reputation of the most innocent amongst men, and the most virtuous amongst women.

Heaven be prais'd, our common libelers are as free from the imputation of wit as of morality; and therefore whatever mischief they have design'd, they have perform'd but little of it. Yet these ill-writers, in all justice, ought themselves to be expos'd; as Persius has given us a fair example in his *First Satire*, which is level'd particularly at them; and none is so fit to correct their faults, as he who is not only clear from any in his own writings, but is also so just, that he will never defame the good; and is arm'd with the power of verse, to punish and make examples of the bad. But of this I shall have occasion to speak further, when I come to give the definition and character of true satires.

In the mean time, as a counselor bred up in the knowledge of the municipal and statute laws, may honestly inform a just prince how far his prerogative extends; so I may be allow'd to tell your Lordship, who, by an undisputed title, are the king of poets, what an extent of power you have, and how lawfully you may exercise it, over the petulant scribblers of this age. As Lord Chamberlain, I know, you are absolute by your office, in all that belongs to the decency and good manners of the stage. You can banish from thence scurrility and profaneness, and restrain the licentious insolence of poets, and their actors, in all things that shock the public quiet, or the reputation of private persons, under the notion of humor. But I mean not the authority which is annex'd to your office; I speak of that only which is inborn and inherent to your person; what is produc'd in you by an excellent wit, a masterly and commanding genius over all writers: whereby you are impower'd, when you please, to give the final decision of wit; to put your stamp on all that ought to pass for current; and set a brand of reprobation on clipp'd poetry, and false coin. A shilling dipp'd in the bath may go for gold amongst the ignorant, but the scepters on the guineas shew the difference. That your Lordship is form'd by nature for this supremacy, I could easily prove (were it not already granted by the world) from the distinguishing character of your writing: which is so visible to me, that I never

could be impos'd on to receive for yours, what was written by any others; or to mistake your genuine poetry for their spurious productions. I can farther add, with truth, (tho' not without some vanity in saying it,) that in the same paper, written by divers hands, whereof your Lordship's was only part, I could separate your gold from their copper; and tho' I could not give back to every author his own brass, (for there is not the same rule for distinguishing betwixt bad and bad, as betwixt ill and excellently good,) yet I never fail'd of knowing what was yours, and what was not; and was absolutely certain, that this, or the other part, was positively yours, and could not possibly be written by any other.

True it is, that some bad poems, tho' not all, carry their owners' marks about 'em. There is some peculiar awkwardness, false grammar, imperfect sense, or, at the least, obscurity; some brand or other on this buttock, or that ear, that 't is notorious who are the owners of the cattle, tho' they should not sign it with their names. But your Lordship, on the contrary, is distinguish'd, not only by the excellency of your thoughts, but by your style and manner of expressing them. A painter, judging of some admirable piece, may affirm, with certainty, that it was of Holbein, or Vandyck; but vulgar designs, and common draughts, are easily mistaken, and misapplied. Thus, by my long study of your Lordship, I am arriv'd at the knowledge of your particular manner. In the good poems of other men, like those artists, I can only say, this is like the draught of such a one, or like the coloring of another. In short, I can only be sure, that 't is the hand of a good master; but in your performances 't is scarcely possible for me to be deceiv'd. If you write in your strength, you stand reveal'd at the first view; and should you write under it, you cannot avoid some peculiar graces, which only cost me a second consideration to discover you: for I may say it, with all the severity of truth, that every line of yours is precious. Your Lordship's only fault is, that you have not written more; unless I could add another, and that yet greater, but I fear for the public the accusation would not be true — that you have written, and out of a vicious modesty will not publish.

Virgil has confin'd his works within the compass of eighteen thousand lines, and has not treated many subjects; yet he ever had, and ever will have, the reputation of the best poet. Martial says of him, that he could have excell'd Varius in tragedy, and Horace in lyric poetry, but out of deference to his friends, he attempted neither.

The same prevalence of genius is in your Lordship, but the world cannot pardon your concealing it on the same consideration; because we have neither a living Varius, nor a Horace, in whose excellencies, both of poems, odes, and satires, you had equall'd them, if our language had not yielded to the Roman majesty, and length of time had not added a reverence to the works of Horace. For good sense is the same in all or most ages, and course of time rather improves Nature than impairs her. What has been, may be again: another Homer, and another Virgil, may possibly arise from those very causes which produc'd the first; tho' it would be impudence to affirm, that any such have yet appear'd.

'T is manifest that some particular ages have been more happy than others in the production of great men, in all sorts of arts and sciences; as that of Euripides, Sophocles, Aristophanes, and the rest, for stage poetry amongst the Greeks; that of Augustus, for heroic, lyric, dramatic, elegiac, and indeed all sorts of poetry, in the persons of Virgil, Horace, Varius, Ovid, and many others; especially if we take into that century the latter end of the commonwealth, wherein we find Varro, Lucretius, and Catullus; and at the same time liv'd Cicero, and Sallust, and Cæsar. A famous age in modern times, for learning in every kind, was that of Lorenzo de Medici, and his son Leo the Tenth; wherein painting was reviv'd, and poetry flourish'd, and the Greek language was restor'd.

Examples in all these are obvious: but what I would infer is this; that in such an age, 't is possible some great genius may arise, to equal any of the ancients; abating only for the language. For great contemporaries whet and cultivate each other; and mutual borrowing, and commerce, makes the common riches of learning, as it does of the civil government.

But suppose that Homer and Virgil were the only of their species, and that Nature was so much worn out in producing them, that she is never able to bear the like again, yet the example only holds in heroic poetry: in tragedy and satire, I offer myself to maintain against some of our modern critics, that this age and the last, particularly in England, have excell'd the ancients in both those kinds; and I would instance in Shakespeare of the former, of your Lordship in the latter sort.

Thus I might safely confine myself to my native country; but if I would only cross the seas, I might find in France a living Horace and a Juvenal, in the person of the admirable Boileau; whose numbers are excellent, whose expressions are noble, whose thoughts are just, whose language is pure, whose satire is pointed, and whose sense is close; what he borrows from the ancients, he repays with usury of his own, in coin as good, and almost as universally valuable: for, setting prejudice and partiality apart, tho' he is our enemy, the stamp of a Louis, the patron of all arts, is not much inferior to the medal of an Augustus Cæsar. Let this be said without ent'ring into the interests of factions and parties, and relating only to the bounty of that king to men of learning and merit; a praise so just, that even we, who are his enemies, cannot refuse it to him.

Now if it may be permitted me to go back again to the consideration of epic poetry, I have confess'd that no man hitherto has reach'd, or so much as approach'd, to the excellencies of Homer, or of Virgil; I must farther add, that Statius, the best versificator next to Virgil, knew not how to design after him, tho' he had the model in his eye; that Lucan is wanting both in design and subject, and is besides too full of heat and affectation; that amongst the moderns, Ariosto neither design'd justly, nor observ'd any unity of action, or compass of time, or moderation in the vastness of his draught: his style is luxurious, without majesty or decency, and his adventures without the compass of nature and possibility. Tasso, whose design was regular, and who observ'd the rules of unity in time and place more closely than Virgil, yet was not so happy in his action; he confesses himself to have been too lyrical, that is, to have written beneath the dignity of heroic verse, in his episodes of Sophronia, Erminia, and Armida. His story is not so pleasing as Ariosto's; he is too flatulent sometimes, and sometimes too dry; many times unequal, and almost always forc'd; and, besides, is full of conceits, points of epigram, and witticisms; all which are not only below the dignity of heroic verse, but contrary to its nature: Virgil and Homer have not one of them. And those who are guilty of so boyish an ambition in so grave a subject, are so far from being consider'd as heroic poets, that they ought to be turn'd down from Homer to the *Anthologia*, from Virgil to Martial and Owen's *Epigrams*, and from Spenser to Flecknoe; that is, from the top to the bottom of all poetry. But to return to Tasso: he borrows from the invention of Boiardo, and in his alteration of his poem, which is infinitely for the worse, imitates Homer so very servilely, that (for example) he gives the King of Jerusalem fifty sons, only because Homer had bestow'd the like number on King Priam; he kills the youngest in the same manner, and has provided his hero with a Patroclus, under another name, only to bring him back to the wars, when his friend was kill'd. The French have perform'd nothing in this kind which is not far below those two Italians, and subject to a thousand more reflections, without examining their *St. Lewis*, their *Pucelle*, or their *Alaric*. The English have only to boast of Spenser and Milton, who neither of them wanted either genius or learning to have been perfect poets, and yet both of them are liable to many censures. For there is no uniformity in the design of Spenser: he aims at the accomplishment of no one action; he raises up a hero for every one of his adventures; and endows each of them with some particular moral virtue, which renders them all equal, without subordination or preference. Every one is most valiant in his own legend: only we must do him that justice to observe, that magnanimity, which is the character of Prince Arthur, shines throughout the whole poem; and succors the rest, when they are in distress. The original of every knight was then living in the court of Queen Elizabeth; and he attributed to each of them that virtue, which he thought was most conspicuous in them; an ingenious piece of flattery, tho' it turn'd not much to his account. Had he liv'd to finish his poem, in the six remaining legends, it had certainly been more of a piece; but could not have been perfect, because the model was not true. But Prince Arthur, or his chief patron Sir Philip Sidney, whom he intended to make happy by the marriage of his Gloriana, dying before him, depriv'd the poet both of means and spirit to accomplish his design. For the rest, his obsolete language, and the ill choice of his stanza, are faults but of the second magnitude; for, notwithstanding the first, he is still intelligible, at least after a little practice; and for the last, he is the more to be admir'd, that, laboring under such a difficulty, his verses are so numerous, so various, and so harmonious, that only Virgil, whom he profess'dly imitated, has surpass'd him among the Romans; and only Mr. Waller among the English.

As for Mr. Milton, whom we all admire with so much justice, his subject is not that of an heroic poem, properly so call'd. His design is the losing of our happiness; his event is not prosperous, like that of all other epic works; his heavenly machines are many, and his human persons are but two. But I will not take Mr. Rymer's work out of his hands: he has promis'd the world a critique on that author; wherein, tho' he will not allow his poem for heroic, I hope he will grant us, that his thoughts are elevated, his words sounding, and that no man has so happily copied the manner of Homer, or so copiously translated his Grecisms, and the Latin elegancies of Virgil. 'T is true, he runs into a flat of thought, sometimes for a hundred lines together, but 't is when he is got into a track of Scripture. His antiquated words were his choice, not his necessity; for therein he imitated Spenser, as Spenser did Chaucer. And tho', perhaps, the love of their masters may have transported both too far, in the frequent use of them, yet, in my opinion, obsolete words may then be laudably reviv'd, when either they are more sounding, or more significant, than those in practice; and when their obscurity is taken away, by joining other words to them which clear the sense; according to the rule of Horace, for the admission of new words. But in both cases a moderation is to be observ'd in the use of them: for unnecessary coinage, as well as unnecessary revival, runs into affectation; a fault to be avoided on either hand. Neither will I justify Milton for his blank verse, tho' I may excuse him, by the example of Hannibal Caro, and other Italians, who have us'd it; for whatever causes he alleges for the abolishing of rhyme, (which I have not now the leisure to examine,) his own particular reason is plainly this, that rhyme was not his talent; he had neither the ease of doing it, nor the graces of it; which is manifest in his *Juvenilia*, or verses written in his youth, where his rhyme is always constrain'd and forc'd, and comes hardly from him, at an age when the soul is most pliant, and the passion of love makes almost every man a rhymer, tho' not a poet.

By this time, my Lord, I doubt not but that you wonder, why I have run off from my bias so long together, and made so tedious a digression from satire to heroic poetry. But if you will not excuse it by the tattling quality of age, which, as Sir William Davenant says, is always narrative, yet I hope the usefulness of what I have to say on this subject will qualify the remoteness of it; and this is the last time I will commit the crime of prefaces, or trouble the world with my notions of anything that relates to verse. I have then, as you see, observ'd the failings of many great wits amongst the moderns, who have attempted to write an epic poem. Besides these, or the like animadversions of them by other men, there is yet a farther reason given, why they cannot possibly succeed so well as the ancients, even tho' we could allow them not to be inferior, either in genius or learning, or the tongue in which they write, or all those other wonderful qualifications which are necessary to the forming of a true accomplish'd heroic poet. The fault is laid on our religion; they say, that Christianity is not capable of those embellishments which are afforded in the belief of those ancient heathens.

And 't is true, that, in the severe notions of our faith, the fortitude of a Christian consists in patience, and suffering, for the love of God, whatever hardships can befall him in the world; not in any great attempt, or in performance of those enterprises which the poets call heroic, and which are commonly the effects of interest, ostentation, pride, and worldly honor: that humility and resignation are our prime virtues ; and that these include no action but that of the soul; when as, on the contrary, an heroic poem requires to its necessary design, and as its last perfection, some great action of war, the accomplishment of some extraordinary undertaking; which requires the strength and vigor of the body, the duty of a soldier, the capacity and prudence of a general, and, in short, as much, or more, of the active virtue, than the suffering. But to this the answer is very obvious. God has plac'd us in our several stations; the virtues of a private Christian are patience, obedience, submission, and the like; but those of a magistrate, or general, or a king, are prudence, counsel, active fortitude, coercive power, awful command, and the exercise of magnanimity, as well as justice. So that this objection hinders not but that an epic poem, or the heroic action of some great commander, enterpris'd for the common good, and honor of the Christian cause, and executed happily, may be as well written now, as it was of old by the heathens; provided the poet be endued with the same talents; and the language, tho' not of equal dignity, yet as near approaching to it, as our modern barbarism will allow; which is all that can be expected from our own, or any other now extant, tho' more refin'd; and therefore we are to rest contented with that only inferiority, which is not possibly to be remedied.

I wish I could as easily remove that other difficulty which yet remains. 'T is objected by a great French critic, as well as an admirable poet, yet living, and whom I have mention'd with that honor which his merit exacts from me, I mean Boileau, that the machines of our Christian religion, in heroic poetry, are much more feeble to support that weight than those of heathenism. Their doctrine, grounded as it was on ridiculous fables, was yet the belief of the two victorious monarchies, the Grecian and Roman. Their gods did not only interest themselves in the event of wars, (which is the effect of a superior providence,) but also espous'd the several parties in a visible corporeal descent, manag'd their intrigues, and fought their battles sometimes in opposition to each other: tho' Virgil (more discreet than Homer in that last particular) has contented himself with the partiality of his deities, their favors, their counsels or commands, to those whose cause they had espous'd, without bringing them to the outrageousness of blows. Now, our religion (says he) is depriv'd of the greatest part of those machines; at least the most shining in epic poetry. Tho' St. Michael, in Ariosto, seeks out Discord, to send her amongst the Pagans, and finds her in a convent of friars, where peace should reign, which indeed is fine satire; and Satan, in Tasso, excites Solyman to an attempt by night on the Christian camp, and brings an host of devils to his assistance; yet the archangel, in the former example, when Discord was restive, and would not be drawn from her belov'd monastery with fair words, has the whiphand of her, drags her out with many stripes, sets her, on God's name, about her business, and makes her know the difference of strength betwixt a nuncio of heaven, and a minister of hell. The same angel, in the latter instance from Tasso, (as if God had never another messenger belonging to the court, but was confin'd like Jupiter to Mercury, and Juno to Iris,) when he sees his time, that is, when half of the Christians are already kill'd, and all the rest are in a fair way to be routed, stickles betwixt the remainders of God's host, and the race of fiends; pulls the devils backward by their tails, and drives them from their quarry; or otherwise the whole business had miscarried, and Jerusalem remain'd untaken. This, says Boileau, is a very unequal match for the poor devils, who are sure to come by the worst of it in the combat; for nothing is more easy, than for an Almighty Power to bring his old rebels to reason when he pleases. Consequently, what pleasure, what entertainment, can be rais'd from so pitiful a machine, where we see the success of the battle from the very beginning of it; unless that, as we are Christians, we are glad that we have gotten God on our side, to maul our enemies, when we cannot do the work ourselves? For if the poet had given the faithful more courage, which had cost him nothing, or at least have made them exceed the Turks in number, he might have gain'd the victory for us Christians, without interesting Heaven in the quarrel; and that with as much ease,

and as little credit to the conqueror, as when a party of a hundred soldiers defeats another which consists only of fifty.

This, my Lord, I confess, is such an argument against our modern poetry, as cannot be answer'd by those mediums which have been us'd. We cannot hitherto boast, that our religion has furnish'd us with any such machines as have made the strength and beauty of the ancient buildings.

But what if I venture to advance an invention of my own, to supply the manifest defect of our new writers? I am sufficiently sensible of my weakness; and 't is not very probable that I should succeed in such a project, whereof I have not had the least hint from any of my predecessors, the poets, or any of their seconds and coadjutors, the critics. Yet we see the art of war is improv'd in sieges, and new instruments of death are invented daily; something new in philosophy and the mechanics is discover'd almost every year; and the science of former ages is improv'd by the succeeding. I will not detain you with a long preamble to that which better judges will, perhaps, conclude to be little worth.

'T is this, in short — that Christian poets have not hitherto been acquainted with their own strength. If they had search'd the Old Testament as they ought, they might there have found the machines which are proper for their work; and those more certain in their effect, than it may be the New Testament is, in the rules sufficient for salvation. The perusing of one chapter in the prophecy of Daniel, and accommodating what there they find with the principles of Platonic philosophy, as it is now Christianis'd, would have made the ministry of angels as strong an engine for the working up heroic poetry, in our religion, as that of the ancients has been to raise theirs by all the fables of their gods, which were only receiv'd for truths by the most ignorant and weakest of the people.

'T is a doctrine almost universally receiv'd by Christians, as well Protestants as Catholics, that there are guardian angels, appointed by God Almighty, as his vicegerents, for the protection and government of cities, provinces, kingdoms, and monarchies; and those as well of heathens, as of true believers. All this is so plainly prov'd from those texts of Daniel, that it admits of no farther controversy. The Prince of the Persians, and that other of the Grecians, are granted to be the guardians and protecting ministers of those empires. It cannot be denied that they were opposite, and resisted one another. St. Michael is mention'd by his name as the patron of the Jews, and is now taken by the Christians, as the protector-general of our religion. These tutelar genii, who presided over the several people and regions committed to their charge, were watchful over them for good, as far as their commissions could possibly extend. The general purpose and design of all was certainly the service of their Great Creator. But 't is an undoubted truth, that, for ends best known to the Almighty Majesty of Heaven, his providential designs for the benefit of his creatures, for the debasing and punishing of some nations, and the exaltation and temporal reward of others, were not wholly known to these his ministers; else why those factious quarrels, controversies, and battles amongst themselves, when they were all united in the same design, the service and honor of their common master? But being instructed only in the general, and zealous of the main design; and, as finite beings, not admitted into the secrets of government, the last resorts of providence, or capable of discovering the final purposes of God, who can work good out of evil as he pleases, and irresistibly sways all manner of events on earth, directing them finally for the best, to his creation in general, and to the ultimate end of his own glory in particular; they must, of necessity, be sometimes ignorant of the means conducing to those ends, in which alone they can jar and oppose each other. One angel, as we may suppose, the Prince of Persia, as he is call'd, judging that it would be more for God's honor, and the benefit of his people, that the Median and Persian monarchy, which deliver'd them from the Babylonish captivity, should still be uppermost; and the patron of the Grecians, to whom the will of God might be more particularly reveal'd, contending, on the other side, for the rise of Alexander and his successors, who were appointed to punish the backsliding Jews, and thereby to put them in mind of their offences, that they might repent, and become more virtuous, and more observant of the law reveal'd. But how far these controversies and appearing enmities of those glorious creatures may be carried; how these oppositions may best be manag'd, and by what means conducted, is not my business to shew or determine; these things must be left to the invention and judgment of the poet; if any of so happy a genius be now living, or any future age can produce a man, who, being conversant in the philosophy of Plato, as it is now accommodated to Christian use, for (as Virgil gives us to understand by his example) that is the only proper, of all others, for an epic poem; who, to his natural endowments, of a large invention, a ripe judgment, and a strong memory, has join'd the knowledge of the liberal arts and sciences, and particularly moral philosophy, the mathematics, geography, and history, and with all these qualifications is born a poet; knows, and can practice the variety of numbers, and is master of the language in which he writes — if such a man, I say, be now arisen, or shall arise, I am vain enough to think that I have propos'd a model to him by which he may build a nobler, a more beautiful, and more perfect poem, than any yet extant since the ancients.

There is another part of these machines yet wanting; but, by what I have said, it would have been easily supplied by a judicious writer. He could not have fail'd to add the opposition of ill spirits to the good; they have also their design, ever opposite to that of Heaven; and this alone has hitherto been the practice of the moderns: but this imperfect system, if I may call it such, which I have given, will infinitely advance and carry farther that hypothesis of the evil spirits contending with the good. For, being so much weaker, since their fall, than those blessed beings, they are yet suppos'd to have a permitted power from God of acting ill, as, from their own deprav'd nature, they have always the will of designing it. A great testimony of which we find in Holy Writ, when God Almighty suffer'd Satan to appear in the holy synod of the angels, (a thing not hitherto drawn into example by any of the poets,) and also gave him power over all things belonging to his servant Job, excepting only life.

Now, what these wicked spirits cannot compass, by the vast disproportion of their forces to those of the superior beings, they may by their fraud and cunning carry farther, in a seeming league, confederacy, or subserviency to the designs of some good angel, as far as consists with his purity to suffer such an aid, the end of which may possibly be disguis'd, and conceal'd from his finite knowledge. This is, indeed, to suppose a great error in such a being; yet since a devil can appear like an angel of light; since craft and malice may sometimes blind for a while a more perfect understanding; and, lastly, since Milton has given us an example of the like nature, when Satan, appearing like a cherub to Uriel, the Intelligence of the Sun, circumvented him even in his own province, and pass'd only for a curious traveler thro' those new-created regions, that he might observe therein the workmanship of God, and praise him in his works; I know not why, upon the same supposition, or some other, a fiend may not deceive a creature of more excellency than himself, but yet a creature; at least, by the connivance, or tacit permission, of the Omniscient Being.

Thus, my Lord, I have, as briefly as I could, given your Lordship, and by you the world, a rude draught of what I have been long laboring in my imagination, and what I had intended to have put in practice, (tho' far unable for the attempt of such a poem,) and to have left the stage (to which my genius never much inclin'd me) for a work which would have taken up my life in the performance of it. This, too, I had intended chiefly for the honor of my native country, to which a poet is particularly oblig'd. Of two subjects, both relating to it, I was doubtful whether I should choose that of King Arthur conquering the Saxons, which, being farther distant in time, gives the greater scope to my invention; or that of Edward, the Black Prince, in subduing Spain, and restoring it to the lawful prince, tho' a great tyrant, Don Pedro the Cruel: which, for the compass of time, including only the expedition of one year; for the greatness of the action, and its answerable event; for the magnanimity of the English hero, oppos'd to the ingrat-

itude of the person whom he restor'd; and for the many beautiful episodes, which I had interwoven with the principal design, together with the characters of the chiefest English persons; wherein, after Virgil and Spenser, I would have taken occasion to represent my living friends and patrons of the noblest families, and also shadow'd the events of future ages, in the succession of our imperial line. With these helps, and those of the machines, which I have mention'd, I might perhaps have done as well as some of my predecessors, or at least chalk'd out a way for others to amend my errors in a like design; but being encourag'd only with fair words by King Charles II, my little salary ill paid, and no prospect of a future subsistence, I was then discourag'd in the beginning of my attempt; and now age has overtaken me, and want, a more insufferable evil, thro' the change of the times, has wholly disenabled me. Tho' I must ever acknowledge, to the honor of your Lordship, and the eternal memory of your charity, that, since this revolution, wherein I have patiently suffer'd the ruin of my small fortune, and the loss of that poor subsistence which I had from two kings, whom I had serv'd more faithfully than profitably to myself — then your Lordship was pleas'd, out of no other motive but your own nobleness, without any desert of mine, or the least solicitation from me, to make me a most bountiful present, which at that time, when I was most in want of it, came most seasonably and unexpectedly to my relief. That favor, my Lord, is of itself sufficient to bind any grateful man to a perpetual acknowledgment, and to all the future service which one of my mean condition can be ever able to perform. May the Almighty God return it for me, both in blessing you here, and rewarding you hereafter! I must not presume to defend the cause for which I now suffer, because your Lordship is engag'd against it; but the more you are so, the greater is my obligation to you, for your laying aside all the considerations of factions and parties, to do an action of pure disinteress'd charity. This is one amongst many of your shining qualities, which distinguish you from others of your rank. But let me add a farther truth, that, without these ties of gratitude, and abstracting from them all, I have a most particular inclination to honor you; and, if it were not too bold an expression, to say, I love you. 'T is no shame to be a poet, tho' 't is to be a bad one. Augustus Cæsar of old, and Cardinal Richelieu of late, would willingly have been such; and David and Solomon were such. You, who, without flattery, are the best of the present age in England, and would have been so, had you been born in any other country, will receive more honor in future ages by that one excellency, than by all those honors to which your birth has intitled you, or your merits have acquir'd you.

Ne, forte, pudori
Sit tibi Musa lyræ solers, et cantor Apollo.

I have formerly said in this epistle, that I could distinguish your writings from those of any others; 't is now time to clear myself from any imputation of self-conceit on that subject. I assume not to myself any particular lights in this discovery; they are such only as are obvious to every man of sense and judgment who loves poetry, and understands it. Your thoughts are always so remote from the common way of thinking, that they are, as I may say, of another species than the conceptions of other poets; yet you go not out of nature for any of them. Gold is never bred upon the surface of the ground, but lies so hidden, and so deep, that the mines of it are seldom found; but the force of waters casts it out from the bowels of mountains, and exposes it amongst the sands of rivers; giving us of her bounty what we could not hope for by our search. This success attends your Lordship's thoughts, which would look like chance, if it were not perpetual. and always of the same tenor. If I grant that there is care in it, 't is such a care as would be ineffectual and fruitless in other men. 'T is the *curiosa felicitas* which Petronius ascribes to Horace in his *Odes*. We have not wherewithal to imagine so strongly, so justly, and so pleasantly; in short, if we have the same knowledge, we cannot draw out of it the same quintessence; we cannot give it such a turn, such a propriety, and such a beauty; something is deficient in the manner, or the words, but more in the nobleness of our conception. Yet when you have finish'd all, and it appears in its full luster, when the diamond is not only

found, but the roughness smooth'd, when it is cut into a form, and set in gold, then we cannot but acknowledge, that it is the perfect work of art and nature; and every one will be so vain, to think he himself could have perform'd the like, till he attempts it. 'T is just the description that Horace makes of such a finish'd piece: it appears so easy,

— ut sibi quivis
Speret idem, sudet multum, frustraque laboret,
Ausus idem.

And, besides all this, 't is your Lordship's particular talent to lay your thoughts so close together, that, were they closer, they would be crowded, and even a due connection would be wanting. We are not kept in expectation of two good lines, which are to come after a long parenthesis of twenty bad; which is the April poetry of other writers, a mixture of rain and sunshine by fits: you are always bright, even almost to a fault, by reason of the excess. There is continual abundance, a magazine of thought, and yet a perpetual variety of entertainment; which creates such an appetite in your reader, that he is not cloy'd with anything, but satisfied with all. 'T is that which the Romans call *cœna dubia;* where there is such plenty, yet withal so much diversity, and so good order, that the choice is difficult betwixt one excellency and another; and yet the conclusion, by a due climax, is evermore the best; that is, as a conclusion ought to be, ever the most proper for its place. See, my Lord, whether I have not studied your Lordship with some application; and, since you are so modest that you will not be judge and party, I appeal to the whole world, if I have not drawn your picture to a great degree of likeness, tho' 't is but in miniature, and that some of the best features are yet wanting. Yet what I have done is enough to distinguish you from any other, which is the proposition that I took upon me to demonstrate.

And now, my Lord, to apply what I have said to my present business. The *Satires* of Juvenal and Persius, appearing in this new English dress, cannot so properly be inscrib'd to any man as to your Lordship, who are the first of the age in that way of writing. Your Lordship, amongst many other favors, has given me your permission for this address; and you have particularly encourag'd me by your perusal and approbation of the *Sixth* and *Tenth Satires* of Juvenal, as I have translated them. My fellow-laborers have likewise commission'd me to perform, in their behalf, this office of a dedication to you; and will acknowledge, with all possible respect and gratitude, your acceptance of their work. Some of them have the honor to be known to your Lordship already, and they who have not yet that happiness desire it now. Be pleas'd to receive our common endeavors with your wonted candor, without intitling you to the protection of our common failings in so difficult an undertaking. And allow me your patience, if it be not already tir'd with this long epistle, to give you, from the best authors, the origin, the antiquity, the growth, the change, and the completement of satire among the Romans; to describe, if not define, the nature of that poem, with its several qualifications and virtues, together with the several sorts of it; to compare the excellencies of Horace, Persius, and Juvenal, and shew the particular manners of their satires; and, lastly, to give an account of this new way of version, which is attempted in our performance: all which, according to the weakness of my ability, and the best lights which I can get from others, shall be the subject of my following discourse.

The most perfect work of poetry, says our master Aristotle, is tragedy. His reason is, because it is the most united; being more severely confin'd within the rules of action, time, and place. The action is entire, of a piece, and one, without episodes; the time limited to a natural day; and the place circumscrib'd at least within the compass of one town, or city. Being exactly proportion'd thus, and uniform in all its parts, the mind is more capable of comprehending the whole beauty of it without distraction.

But, after all these advantages, an heroic poem is certainly the greatest work of human nature. The beauties and perfections of the other are but mechanical; those of the epic are more noble: tho' Homer has limited his place to Troy, and the fields about it; his actions to forty-eight natural days, whereof twelve are holidays, or cessation from business, during the funerals of

Patroclus. To proceed; the action of the epic is greater; the extension of time enlarges the pleasure of the reader, and the episodes give it more ornament, and more variety. The instruction is equal; but the first is only instructive, the latter forms a hero, and a prince.

If it signifies anything which of them is of the more ancient family, the best and most absolute heroic poem was written by Homer long before tragedy was invented. But, if we consider the natural endowments and acquir'd parts which are necessary to make an accomplish'd writer in either kind, tragedy requires a less and more confin'd knowledge; moderate learning, and observation of the rules, is sufficient, if a genius be not wanting. But in an epic poet, one who is worthy of that name, besides an universal genius, is requir'd universal learning, together with all those qualities and acquisitions which I have nam'd above, and as many more as I have, thro' haste or negligence, omitted. And, after all, he must have exactly studied Homer and Virgil as his patterns; Aristotle and Horace as his guides; and Vida and Bossu as their commentators; with many others, both Italian and French critics, which I want leisure here to recommend.

In a word, what I have to say in relation to this subject, which does not particularly concern satire, is, that the greatness of an heroic poem, beyond that of a tragedy, may easily be discover'd, by observing how few have attempted that work in comparison of those who have written dramas; and, of those few, how small a number have succeeded. But leaving the critics, on either side, to contend about the preference due to this or that sort of poetry, I will hasten to my present business, which is the antiquity and origin of satire, according to those informations which I have receiv'd from the learned Casaubon, Heinsius, Rigaltius, Dacier, and the Dauphin's *Juvenal;* to which I shall add some observations of my own.

There has been a long dispute amongst the modern critics, whether the Romans deriv'd their satire from the Grecians, or first invented it themselves. Julius Scaliger and Heinsius are of the first opinion; Casaubon, Rigaltius, Dacier, and the publisher of the Dauphin's *Juvenal* maintain the latter. If we take satire in the general signification of the word, as it is us'd in all modern languages, for an invective, 't is certain that it is almost as old as verse; and tho' hymns, which are praises of God, may be allow'd to have been before it, yet the defamation of others was not long after it. After God had curs'd Adam and Eve in Paradise, the husband and wife excus'd themselves by laying the blame on one another, and gave a beginning to those conjugal dialogues in prose which the poets have perfected in verse. The third chapter of Job is one of the first instances of this poem in holy Scripture; unless we will take it higher, from the latter end of the second, where his wife advises him to curse his Maker.

This original, I confess, is not much to the honor of satire; but here it was nature, and that deprav'd: when it became an art, it bore better fruit. Only we have learnt thus much already, that scoffs and revilings are of the growth of all nations; and, consequently, that neither the Greek poets borrow'd from other people their art of railing, neither needed the Romans to take it from them. But, considering satire as a species of poetry, here the war begins amongst the critics. Scaliger, the father, will have it descend from Greece to Rome; and derives the word satire from *Satyrus*, that mix'd kind of animal, or, as the ancients thought him, rural god, made up betwixt a man and a goat; with a human head, hook'd·nose, pouting lips, a bunch, or struma, under the chin, prick'd ears, and upright horns; the body shagg'd with hair, especially from the waist, and ending in a goat, with the legs and feet of that creature. But Casaubon, and his followers, with reason, condemn this derivation; and prove, that from *Satyrus*, the word *satira*, as ir signifies a poem, cannot possibly descend. For *satira* is not properly a substantive, but an adjective; to which the word *lanx* (in English, a charger, or large platter) is understood; so that the Greek poem, made according to the manners of a Satyr, and expressing his qualities, must properly be call'd satyrical, and not satire. And thus far 't is allow'd that the Grecians had such poems; but that they were wholly different *in specie* from that to which the Romans gave the name of satire.

Aristotle divides all poetry, in relation to the progress of it, into nature without art, art begun, and art completed. Mankind, even the most barbarous, have the seeds of poetry implanted in them. The first specimen of it was certainly shewn in the praises of the Deity, and prayers to him; and as they are of natural obligation, so they are likewise of divine institution: which Milton observing, introduces Adam and Eve every morning adoring God in hymns and prayers. The first poetry was thus begun, in the wild notes of nature, before the invention of feet and measures. The Grecians and Romans had no other original of·their poetry. Festivals and holidays soon succeeded to private worship, and we need not doubt but they were enjoin'd by the true God to his own people, as they were afterwards imitated by the heathens; who, by the light of reason, knew they were to invoke some superior being in their necessities, and to thank him for his benefits. Thus the Grecian holidays were celebrated with offerings to Bacchus, and Ceres, and other deities, to whose bounty they suppos'd they were owing for their corn and wine, and other helps of life; and the ancient Romans, as Horace tells us, paid their thanks to Mother Earth, or Vesta, to Silvanus, and their Genius, in the same manner. But as all festivals have a double reason of their institution, the first of religion, the other of recreation, for the unbending of our minds, so both the Grecians and Romans agreed, after their sacrifices were perform'd, to spend the remainder of the day in sports and merriments; amongst which, songs and dances, and that which they call'd wit, (for want of knowing better,) were the chiefest entertainments. The Grecians had a notion of Satyrs, whom I have already describ'd; and taking them, and the Sileni, that is, the young Satyrs and the old, for the tutors, attendants, and humble companions of their Bacchus, habited themselves like those rural deities, and imitated them in their rustic dances, to which they join'd songs, with some sort of rude harmony, but without certain numbers; and to these they added a kind of chorus.

The Romans, also, (as nature is the same in all places,) tho' they knew nothing of those Grecian demigods, nor had any communication with Greece, yet had certain young men, who, at their festivals, danc'd and sung, after their uncouth manner, to a certain kind of verse, which they call'd Saturnian. What it was, we have no very certain light from antiquity to discover; but we may conclude, that, like the Grecian, it was void of art, or at least with very feeble beginnings of it. Those ancient Romans, at these holidays, which were a mixture of devotion and debauchery, had a custom of reproaching each other with their faults, in a sort of *ex tempore* poetry, or rather of tunable hobbling verse; and they answer'd in the same kind of gross raillery; their wit and their music being of a piece. The Grecians, says Casaubon, had formerly done the same, in the persons of their petulant Satyrs. But I am afraid he mistakes the matter, and confounds the singing and dancing of the Satyrs with the rustical entertainments of the first Romans. The reason of my opinion is this: that Casaubon, finding little light from antiquity of these beginnings of poetry amongst the Grecians, but only these representations of Satyrs, who carried canisters and cornucopias full of several fruits in their hands, and danc'd with them at their public feasts; and afterwards reading Horace, who makes mention of his homely Romans jesting at one another in the same kind of solemnities, might suppose those wanton Satyrs did the same; and especially because Horace possibly might seem to him to have shewn the original of all poetry in general, including the Grecians as well as Romans; tho' 't is plainly otherwise, that he only describ'd the beginning and first rudiments of poetry in his own country. The verses are these, which he cites from the First Epistle of the Second Book, which was written to Augustus:

Agricolæ prisci, fortes, parvoque beati,
Condita post frumenta, levantes tempore festo
Corpus, et ipsum animum spe finis dura ferentem,
Cum sociis operum, et pueris, et conjuge fida,
Tellurem porco, Silvanum lacte piabant;
Floribus et vino Genium memorem brevis ævi.
Fescennina per hunc inventa licentia morem
Versibus alternis opprobria rustica fudit.

Our brawny clowns, of old, who turn'd the soil,
Content with little, and inur'd to toil,

At harvest-home, with mirth and country cheer,
Restor'd their bodies for another year;
Refresh'd their spirits, and renew'd their hope
Of such a future feast, and future crop.
Then, with their fellow-joggers of the plows,
Their little children, and their faithful spouse.
A sow they slew to Vesta's deity,
And kindly milk, Silvanus, pour'd to thee;
With flow'rs, and wine, their Genius they ador'd;
A short life, and a merry, was the word.
From flowing cups, defaming rhymes ensue,
And at each other homely taunts they threw.

Yet since it is a hard conjecture, that so great a man as Casaubon should misapply what Horace writ concerning ancient Rome, to the ceremonies and manners of ancient Greece, I will not insist on this opinion, but rather judge in general, that since all poetry had its original from religion, that of the Grecians and Rome had the same beginning. Both were invented at festivals of thanksgiving, and both were prosecuted with mirth and raillery, and rudiments of verses: amongst the Greeks, by those who represented Satyrs; and amongst the Romans, by real clowns.

For, indeed, when I am reading Casaubon on these two subjects, methinks I hear the same story told twice over with very little alteration. Of which Dacier taking notice, in his interpretation of the Latin verses which I have translated, says plainly, that the beginning of poetry was the same, with a small variety, in both countries; and that the mother of it, in all nations, was devotion. But, what is yet more wonderful, that most learned critic takes notice also, in his illustrations on the First Epistle of the Second Book, that as the poetry of the Romans, and that of the Grecians, had the same beginning, at feasts of thanksgiving, as it has been observ'd, and the Old Comedy of the Greeks, which was invective, and the satire of the Romans, which was of the same nature, were begun on the very same occasion, so the fortune of both, in process of time, was just the same; the Old Comedy of the Grecians was forbidden, for its too much licence in exposing of particular persons; and the rude satire of the Romans was also punish'd by a law of the Decemviri, as Horace tells us, in these words:

Libertasque recurrentes accepta per annos
Lusu amabiliter ; donec jam sævus apertam
In rabiem verti cœpit jocus, et per honestas
Ire domos impune minax : doluere cruento
Dente lacessiti ; fuit intactis quoque cura
Conditione super communi : quinetiam lex,
Pœnaque lata, malo quæ nollet carmine quem-
  quam
Describi : vertere modum, formidine fustis
Ad benedicendum delectandumque redacti.

The law of the Decemviri was this: *Siquis occentassit malum carmen, sire condidisit, quod infamiam faxit, flagitiumve alteri, capital esto.* A strange likeness, and barely possible; but the critics being all of the same opinion, it becomes me to be silent, and submit to better judgments than my own.

But, to return to the Grecians, from whose satyric dramas the elder Scaliger and Heinsius will have the Roman satire to proceed, I am to take a view of them first, and see if there be any such descent from them as those authors have pretended.

Thespis, or whosoever he were that invented tragedy, (for authors differ,) mingled with them a chorus and dances of Satyrs, which had before been us'd in the celebration of their festivals; and there they were ever afterwards retain'd. The character of them was also kept, which was mirth and wantonness; and this was given, I suppose, to the folly of the common audience, who soon grow weary of good sense, and, as we daily see in our own age and country, are apt to forsake poetry, and still ready to return to buffoonery and farce. From hence it came, that, in the Olympic games, where the poets contended for four prizes, the satyric tragedy was the last of them; for, in the rest, the Satyrs were excluded from the chorus. Amongst the plays of Euripides which are yet remaining, there is one of these satyrics, which is call'd the *Cyclops ;* in which we may see the nature of those poems, and from thence conclude what likeness they have to the Roman satire.

The story of this Cyclops, whose name was Polyphemus, so famous in the Grecian fables, was, that Ulysses, who, with his company, was driven on that coast of Sicily, where those Cyclops inhabited, coming to ask relief from Silenus, and the Satyrs, who were herdsmen to that one-ey'd giant,

was kindly receiv'd by them, and entertain'd; till, being perceiv'd by Polyphemus, they were made prisoners, against the rites of hospitality, for which Ulysses eloquently pleaded, were afterwards put down into the den, and some of them devour'd; after which Ulysses, having made him drunk, when he was asleep, thrust a great firebrand into his eye, and so, revenging his dead followers, escap'd with the remaining party of the living; and Silenus and the Satyrs were freed from their servitude under Polyphemus, and remitted to their first liberty of attending and accompanying their patron, Bacchus.

This was the subject of the tragedy; which, being one of those that end with a happy event, is therefore, by Aristotle, judg'd below the other sort, whose success is unfortunate. Notwithstanding which, the Satyrs, who were part of the *dramatis personæ*, as well as the whole chorus, were properly introduc'd into the nature of the poem, which is mix'd of farce and tragedy. The adventure of Ulysses was to entertain the judging part of the audience; and the uncouth persons of Silenus, and the Satyrs, to divert the common people with their gross railleries.

Your Lordship has perceiv'd by this time that this satyric tragedy, and the Roman satire, have little resemblance in any of their features. The very kinds are different; for what has a pastoral tragedy to do with a paper of verses satirically written? The character and raillery of the Satyrs is the only thing that could pretend to a likeness, were Scaliger and Heinsius alive to maintain their opinion. And the first farces of the Romans, which were the rudiments of their poetry, were written before they had any communication with the Greeks, or indeed any knowledge of that people.

And here it will be proper to give the definition of the Greek satyric poem from Casaubon, before I leave this subject. " The Satyric," says he, " is a dramatic poem, annex'd to a tragedy, having a chorus, which consists of Satyrs. The persons represented in it are illustrious men; the action of it is great; the style is partly serious, and partly jocular; and the event of the action most commonly is happy."

The Grecians, besides these satyric tragedies, had another kind of poem, which they call'd *silli*, which were more of kin to the Roman satire. Those *silli* were indeed invective poems, but of a different species from the Roman poems of Ennius, Pacuvius, Lucilius, Horace, and the rest of their successors. They were so call'd, says Casaubon in one place, from Silenus, the foster-father of Bacchus; but, in another place, bethinking himself better, he derives their name ἀπὸ τοῦ σιλλαίνειν, from their scoffing and petulancy. From some fragments of the *silli*, written by Timon, we may find, that they were satiric poems, full of parodies; that is, of verses patch'd up from great poets, and turn'd into another sense than their author intended them. Such, amongst the Romans, is the famous *Cento* of Ausonius; where the words are Virgil's, but, by applying them to another sense, they are made a relation of a wedding night; and the act of consummation fulsomely describ'd in the very words of the most modest amongst all poets. Of the same manner are our songs which are turn'd into burlesque, and the serious words of the author perverted into a ridiculous meaning. Thus in Timon's *silli* the words are generally those of Homer and the tragic poets; but he applies them, satirically, to some customs and kinds of philosophy, which he arraigns. But the Romans, not using any of these parodies in their satires — sometimes, indeed, repeating verses of other men, as Persius cites some of Nero's, but not turning them into another meaning — the *silli* cannot be suppos'd to be the original of Roman satire. To these *silli*, consisting of parodies, we may properly add the satires which were written against particular persons; such as were the iambics of Archilochus against Lycambes, which Horace undoubtedly imitated in some of his *Odes* and *Epodes*, whose titles bear sufficient witness of it. I might also name the invective of Ovid against Ibis, and many others; but these are the underwood of satire, rather than the timber trees: they are not of general extension, as reaching only to some individual person. And Horace seems to have purg'd himself from those splenetic reflections in those *Odes* and *Epodes*, before he undertook the noble work of *Satires*, which were properly so call'd.

Thus, my Lord, I have at length disengag'd myself from those antiquities of Greece; and have prov'd, I hope, from the best critics, that the Roman satire was not borrow'd from thence, but of their own manufacture. I am now almost gotten into my depth; at least, by the help of Dacier, I am swimming towards it. Not that I will promise always to follow him, any more than he follows Casaubon; but to keep him in my eye, as my best and truest guide; and where I think he may possibly mislead me, there to have recourse to my own lights, as I expect that others should do by me.

Quintilian says, in plain words, *Satira quidem tota nostra est ;* and Horace had said the same thing before him, speaking of his predecessor in that sort of poetry: *Et Græcis intacti carminis auctor.* Nothing can be clearer than the opinion of the poet, and the orator, both the best critics of the two best ages of the Roman Empire, than that satire was wholly of Latin growth, and not transplanted to Rome from Athens. Yet, as I have said, Scaliger, the father, according to his custom, that is, insolently enough, contradicts them both; and gives no better reason than the derivation of *satyrus* from σάθυ, *salacitas ;* and so, from the lechery of those fauns, thinks he has sufficiently prov'd that satire is deriv'd from them: as if wantonness and lubricity were essential to that sort of poem, which ought to be avoided in it. His other allegation, which I have already mention'd, is as pitiful; that the Satyrs carried platters and canisters full of fruit in their hands. If they had enter'd empty-handed, had they been ever the less Satyrs ? Or were the fruits and flowers which they offer'd anything of kin to satire ? Or any argument that this poem was originally Grecian? Casaubon judg'd better, and his opinion is grounded on sure authority, that satire was deriv'd from *satura*, a Roman word, which signifies full and abundant, and full also of variety, in which nothing is wanting to its due perfection. 'T is thus, says Dacier, that we say *a full color,* when the wool has taken the whole tincture, and drunk in as much of the dye as it can receive. According to this derivation, from *satur* comes *satura*, or *satira*, according to the new spelling, as *optumus* and *maxumus* are now spell'd *optimus* and *maximus*. *Satura,* as I have formerly noted, is an adjective, and relates to the word *lanx*, which is understood; and this *lanx*, in English a charger,

or large platter, was yearly fill'd with all
sorts of fruits, which were offer'd to the
gods at their festivals, as the *prémices*, or
first gatherings. These offerings of several
sorts, thus mingled, 't is true, were not unknown to the Grecians, who call'd them
πανκαρπὸν θυσίαν, a sacrifice of all sorts of
fruits; and πανσπερμίαν, when they offer'd
all kinds of grain. Virgil has mention'd
these sacrifices in his *Georgics :*

Lancibus et pandis fumantia reddimus exta,

and in another place, *lancesque et liba fe-
remus :* that is, *we offer the smoking entrails
in great platters,* and *we will offer the chargers and the cakes.*

This word *satura* has been afterward applied to many other sorts of mixtures; as
Festus calls it a kind of *olla,* or hotchpotch,
made of several sorts of meats. Laws were
also call'd *leges saturæ,* when they were of
several heads and titles, like our tack'd bills
of Parliament: and *per saturam legem ferre,*
in the Roman senate, was to carry a law
without telling the senators, or counting
voices, when they were in haste. Sallust
uses the word, *per saturam sententias ex-
quirere,* when the majority was visibly on
one side. From hence it might probably be
conjectur'd, that the *Discourses,* or *Satires,*
of Ennius, Lucilius, and Horace, as we now
call them, took their name; because they
are full of various matters, and are also written on various subjects, as Porphyrius says.
But Dacier affirms that it is not immediately from thence that these satires are so
call'd; for that name had been us'd formerly
for other things, which bore a nearer resemblance to those discourses of Horace.
In explaining of which, continues Dacier,
a method is to be pursued, of which Casaubon himself has never thought, and which
will put all things into so clear a light, that
no farther room will be left for the least
dispute.

During the space of almost four hundred
years, since the building of their city, the
Romans had never known any entertainments of the stage. Chance and jollity first
found out those verses which they call'd
Saturnian and *Fescennine ;* or rather human
nature, which is inclin'd to poetry, first produc'd them, rude and barbarous, and unpolish'd, as all other operations of the soul
are in their beginnings, before they are cul-

tivated with art and study. However, in
occasions of merriment they were first
practic'd; and this roughcast unhewn poetry was instead of stageplays for the space
of an hundred and twenty years together.
They were made *ex tempore,* and were, as the
French call them, *impromptus ;* for which
the Tarsians of old were much renown'd;
and we see the daily examples of them in
the Italian farces of Harlequin and Scaramucha. Such was the poetry of that salvage
people, before it was tun'd into numbers,
and the harmony of verse. Little of the
Saturnian verses is now remaining; we
only know from authors that they were
nearer prose than poetry, without feet, or
measure. They were ἔνρυθμοι, but not ἔμμε-
τροι. Perhaps they might be us'd in the solemn part of their ceremonies; and the Fescennine, which were invented after them,
in their afternoon's debauchery, because
they were scoffing and obscene.

The Fescennine and Saturnian were the
same; for as they were call'd Saturnian
from their ancientness, when Saturn reign'd
in Italy, they were also call'd Fescennine,
from Fescennia, a town in the same country,
where they were first practic'd. The actors,
with a gross and rustic kind of raillery, reproach'd each other with their failings; and
at the same time were nothing sparing of it
to their audience. Somewhat of this custom
was afterwards retain'd in their Saturnalia,
or feasts of Saturn, celebrated in December; at least all kind of freedom in speech
was then allow'd to slaves even against
their masters; and we are not without some
imitation of it in our Christmas gambols.
Soldiers also us'd those Fescennine verses,
after measure and numbers had been added
to them, at the triumph of their generals:
of which we have an example, in the triumph of Julius Cæsar over Gaul, in these
expressions:

Cæsar Gallias subegit, Nicomedes Cæsarem.
*Ecce Cæsar nunc triumphat, qui subegit Gal-
lias :*
Nicomedes non triumphat, qui subegit Cæsarem.

The vapors of wine made those first satirical poets amongst the Romans; which, says
Dacier, we cannot better represent, than by
imagining a company of clowns on a holiday, dancing lubberly, and upbraiding one
another, in *ex tempore* doggrel, with their

defects and vices, and the stories that were told of them in bakehouses and barbers' shops.

When they began to be somewhat better bred, and were ent'ring, as I may say, into the first rudiments of civil conversation, they left these hedge-notes for another sort of poem, somewhat polish'd, which was also full of pleasant raillery, but without any mixture of obscenity. This sort of poetry appear'd under the name of satire, because of its variety; and this satire was adorn'd with compositions of music, and with dances; but lascivious postures were banish'd from it. In the Tuscan language, says Livy, the word *hister* signifies a player; and therefore those actors, which were first brought from Etruria to Rome, on occasion of a pestilence, when the Romans were admonish'd to avert the anger of the gods by plays, in the year *ab urbe condita* CCCXC, those actors, I say, were therefore call'd *histriones ;* and that name has since remain'd, not only to actors Roman born, but to all others of every nation. They play'd not the former *ex tempore* stuff of Fescennine verses, or clownish jests; but what they acted was a kind of civil, cleanly farce, with music and dances, and motions that were proper to the subject.

In this condition Livius Andronicus found the stage, when he attempted first, instead of farces, to supply it with a nobler entertainment of tragedies and comedies. This man was a Grecian born, and being made a slave by Livius Salinator, and brought to Rome, had the education of his patron's children committed to him; which trust he discharg'd so much to the satisfaction of his master, that he gave him his liberty.

Andronicus, thus become a freeman of Rome, added to his own name that of Livius his master; and, as I observ'd, was the first author of a regular play in that commonwealth. Being already instructed, in his native country, in the manners and decencies of the Athenian theater, and conversant in the *Archæa Comœdia,* or Old Comedy of Aristophanes, and the rest of the Grecian poets, he took from that model his own designing of plays for the Roman stage; the first of which was represented in the year 514 since the building of Rome, as Tully, from the commentaries of Atticus,

has assur'd us: it was after the end of the first Punic war, the year before Ennius was born. Dacier has not carried the matter altogether thus far; he only says, that one Livius Andronicus was the first stage-poet at Rome. But I will adventure on this hint, to advance another proposition, which I hope the learned will approve. And tho' we have not anything of Andronicus remaining to justify my conjecture, yet 't is exceeding probable, that, having read the works of those Grecian wits, his countrymen, he imitated not only the groundwork, but also the manner of their writing; and how grave soever his tragedies might be, yet, in his comedies, he express'd the way of Aristophanes, Eupolis, and the rest, which was to call some persons by their own names, and to expose their defects to the laughter of the people: the examples of which we have in the foremention'd Aristophanes, who turn'd the wise Socrates into ridicule, and is also very free with the management of Cleon, Alcibiades, and other ministers of the Athenian government. Now if this be granted, we may easily suppose that the first hint of satirical plays on the Roman stage was given by the Greeks: not from their *Satyrica,* for that has been reasonably exploded in the former part of this discourse; but from their Old Comedy, which was imitated first by Livius Andronicus. And then Quintilian and Horace must be cautiously interpreted, where they affirm that satire is wholly Roman, and a sort of verse, which was not touch'd on by the Grecians. The reconcilement of my opinion to the standard of their judgment is not, however, very difficult, since they spoke of satire, not as in its first elements, but as it was form'd into a separate work; begun by Ennius, pursued by Lucilius, and completed afterwards by Horace. The proof depends only on this *postulatum,* that the comedies of Andronicus, which were imitations of the Greek, were also imitations of their railleries, and reflections on particular persons. For, if this be granted me, which is a most probable supposition, 't is easy to infer that the first light which was given to the Roman theatrical satire, was from the plays of Livius Andronicus; which will be more manifestly discover'd when I come to speak of Ennius. In the mean time I will return to Dacier.

The people, says he, ran in crowds to
these new entertainments of Andronicus, as
to pieces which were more noble in their
kind, and more perfect than their former
satires, which for some time they neglected
and abandon'd. But not long after, they
took them up again, and then they join'd
them to their comedies; playing them at
the end of every drama, as the French continue at this day to act their farces, in the
nature of a separate entertainment from
their tragedies. But more particularly they
were join'd to the *Atellane* fables, says
Casaubon; which were plays invented by
the Osci. Those fables, says Valerius Maximus, out of Livy, were temper'd with the
Italian severity, and free from any note
of infamy, or obsceneness; and, as an old
commentator on Juvenal affirms, the *Exo-
diarii*, which were singers and dancers, enter'd to entertain the people with light
songs, and mimical gestures, that they
might not go away oppress'd with melancholy, from those serious pieces of the
theater. So that the ancient satire of the
Romans was in extemporary reproaches;
the next was farce, which was brought from
Tuscany; to that succeeded the plays of
Andronicus, from the Old Comedy of the
Grecians; and out of all these sprung two
several branches of new Roman satire, like
different scions from the same root, which
I shall prove with as much brevity as the
subject will allow.

A year after Andronicus had open'd the
Roman stage with his new dramas, Ennius
was born; who, when he was grown to
man's estate, having seriously consider'd
the genius of the people, and how eagerly
they follow'd the first satires, thought it
would be worth his pains to refine upon
the project, and to write satires, not to be
acted on the theater, but read. He preserv'd
the groundwork of their pleasantry, their
venom, and their raillery on particular persons, and general vices; and by this means,
avoiding the danger of any ill success in a
public representation, he hop'd to be as well
receiv'd in the cabinet, as Andronicus had
been upon the stage. The event was answerable to his expectation. He made discourses in several sorts of verse, varied often in the same paper; retaining still in the
title their original name of satire. Both in
relation to the subjects, and the variety of

matters contain'd in them, the satires of
Horace are entirely like them; only Ennius,
as I said, confines not himself to one sort of
verse, as Horace does; but taking example
from the Greeks, and even from Homer
himself in his *Margites*, which is a kind of
satire, as Scaliger observes, gives himself
the license, when one sort of numbers
comes not easily, to run into another, as his
fancy dictates. For he makes no difficulty
to mingle hexameters with iambic trime-
ters, or with trochaic tetrameters; as appears by those fragments which are yet
remaining of him. Horace has thought
him worthy to be copied; inserting many
things of his into his own *Satires*, as Virgil
has done into his *Æneids*.

Here we have Dacier making out that
Ennius was the first satirist in that way of
writing, which was of his invention; that is,
satire abstracted from the stage, and new-
model'd into papers of verses on several
subjects. But he will have Ennius take
the groundwork of satire from the first
farces of the Romans, rather than from the
form'd plays of Livius Andronicus, which
were copied from the Grecian comedies. It
may possibly be so; but Dacier knows no
more of it than I do. And it seems to me
the more probable opinion, that he rather
imitated the fine railleries of the Greeks,
which he saw in the pieces of Andronicus,
than the coarseness of his old countrymen,
in their clownish extemporary way of jeer-
ing.

But besides this, 't is universally granted
that Ennius, tho' an Italian, was excellently
learn'd in the Greek language. His verses
were stuff'd with fragments of it, even to a
fault; and he himself believ'd, according to
the Pythagorean opinion, that the soul of
Homer was transfus'd into him; which Persius observes, in his *Sixth Satire: postquam
destertuit esse Mæonides*. But this being only
the private opinion of so inconsiderable a
man as I am, I leave it to the farther dis-
quisition of the critics, if they think it
worth their notice. Most evident it is, that
whether he imitated the Roman farce, or
the Greek comedies, he is to be acknowledg'd for the first author of Roman satire,
as it is properly so call'd, and distinguish'd
from any sort of stageplay.

Of Pacuvius, who succeeded him, there
is little to be said, because there is so little

remaining of him; only that he is taken to be the nephew of Ennius, his sister's son; that in probability he was instructed by his uncle, in his way of satire, which we are told he has copied: but what advances he made we know not.

Lucilius ·came into the world when Pacuvius flourish'd most. He also made satires after the manner of Ennius, but he gave them a more graceful turn, and endeavor'd to imitate more closely the *Vetus Comœdia* of the Greeks, of the which the old original Roman satire had no idea, till the time of Livius Andronicus. And tho' Horace seems to have made Lucilius the first author of satire in verse amongst the Romans, in these words:

—— *Quid ? cum est Lucilius ausus*
Primus in hunc operis componere carmina mo-
rem,

he is only thus to be understood; that Lucilius had given a more graceful turn to the satire of Ennius and Pacuvius, not that he invented a new satire of his own: and Quintilian seems to explain this passage of Horace in these words: *Satira quidem tota nostra est ; in qua primus insignem laudem adeptus est Lucilius.*

Thus, both Horace and Quintilian give a kind of primacy of honor to Lucilius, amongst the Latin satirists. For, as the Roman language grew more refin'd, so much more capable it was of receiving the Grecian beauties, in his time. Horace and Quintilian could mean no more, than that Lucilius writ better than Ennius and Pacuvius; and on the same account we prefer Horace to Lucilius. Both of them imitated the old Greek comedy; and so did Ennius and Pacuvius before them. The polishing of the Latin tongue, in the succession of times, made the only difference; and Horace himself, in two of his satires, written purposely on this subject, thinks the Romans of his age were too partial in their commendations of Lucilius; who writ not only loosely, and muddily, with little art, and much less care, but also in a time when the Latin tongue was not yet sufficiently purg'd from the dregs of barbarism; and many significant and sounding words, which the Romans wanted, were not admitted even in the times of Lucretius and Cicero, of which both complain.

But to proceed: Dacier justly taxes Casaubon for saying that the satires of Lucilius were wholly different *in specie* from those of Ennius and Pacuvius. Casaubon was led into that mistake by Diomedes the grammarian, who in effect says this: satire amongst the Romans, but not amongst the Greeks, was a biting invective poem, made after the model of the ancient comedy, for the reprehension of vices; such as were the poems of Lucilius, of Horace, and of Persius. But in former times the name of satire was given to poems which were compos'd of several sorts of verses, such as were made by Ennius and Pacuvius; more fully expressing the etymology of the word satire, from *satura*, which we have observ'd. Here 't is manifest, that Diomedes makes a specifical distinction betwixt the satires of Ennius, and those of Lucilius. But this, as we say in English, is only a distinction without a difference; for the reason of it is ridiculous, and absolutely false. This was that which cozen'd honest Casaubon, who, relying on Diomedes, had not sufficiently examin'd the origin and nature of those two satires; which were entirely the same, both in the matter and the form: for all that Lucilius perform'd beyond his predecessors, Ennius and Pacuvius, was only the adding of more politeness, and more salt, without any change in the substance of the poem. And tho' Lucilius put not together in the same satire several sorts of verses, as Ennius did, yet he compos'd several satires, of several sorts of verses, and mingled them with Greek verses: one poem consisted only of hexameters, and another was entirely of iambics; a third of trochaics; as is visible by the fragments yet remaining of his works. In short, if the satires of Lucilius are therefore said to be wholly different from those of Ennius, because he added much more of beauty and polishing to his own poems than are to be found in those before him, it will follow from hence that the satires of Horace are wholly different from those of Lucilius, because Horace has not less surpass'd Lucilius in the elegancy of his writing, than Lucilius surpass'd Ennius in the turn and ornament of his. This passage of Diomedes has also drawn Dousa, the son, into the same error of Casaubon, which I say, not to expose the little failings of those judicious men, but only to make it appear, with how much diffidence and caution we are to read their works, when they treat a subject of so much obscurity, and so very ancient, as is this of satire.

Having thus brought down the history of satire from its original to the times of Horace, and shewn the several changes of it, I should here discover some of those graces which Horace added to it, but that I think it will be more proper to defer that undertaking, till I make the comparison betwixt him and Juvenal. In the mean while, following the order of time, it will be necessary to say somewhat of another kind of satire, which also was descended from the ancient; 't is that which we call the Varronian satire, (but which Varro himself calls the Menippean,) because Varro, the most learn'd of the Romans, was the first author of it, who imitated, in his works, the manners of Menippus the Gadarenian, who profess'd the philosophy of the Cynics.

This sort of satire was not only compos'd of several sorts of verse, like those of Ennius, but was also mix'd with prose; and Greek was sprinkled amongst the Latin. Quintilian, after he had spoken of the satire of Lucilius, adds what follows: *There is another and former kind of satire, compos'd by Terentius Varro, the most learn'd of the Romans; in which he was not satisfied alone with mingling in it several sorts of verse.* The only difficulty of this passage is, that Quintilian tells us that this satire of Varro was of a former kind. For how can we possibly imagine this to be, since Varro, who was contemporary to Cicero, must consequently be after Lucilius? But Quintilian meant not, that the satire of Varro was in order of time before Lucilius; he would only give us to understand, that the Varronian satire, with mixture of several sorts of verses, was more after the manner of Ennius and Pacuvius, than that of Lucilius, who was more severe, and more correct, and gave himself less liberty in the mixture of his verses in the same poem.

We have nothing remaining of those Varronian satires, excepting some inconsiderable fragments, and those for the most part much corrupted. The titles of many of them are indeed preserv'd, and they are generally double; from whence, at least, we may understand, how many various subjects were treated by that author. Tully, in his *Academics*, introduces Varro himself giving us some light concerning the scope and design of these works. Wherein, after he had shewn his reasons why he did not *ex professo* write of philosophy, he adds what follows: *Notwithstanding, says he, that those pieces of mine, wherein I have imitated Menippus, tho' I have not translated him, are sprinkled with a kind of mirth and gaiety, yet many things are there inserted, which are drawn from the very intrails of philosophy, and many things severely argued; which I have mingled with pleasantries on purpose, that they may more easily go down with the common sort of unlearn'd readers.* The rest of the sentence is so lame, that we can only make thus much out of it, that in the composition of his satires he so temper'd philology with philosophy, that his work was a mixture of them both. And Tully himself confirms us in this opinion, when a little after he addresses himself to Varro in these words: *And you yourself have compos'd a most elegant and complete poem; you have begun philosophy in many places; sufficient to incite us, tho' too little to instruct us.* Thus it appears that Varro was one of those writers whom they call'd σπουδογέλοιοι, studious of laughter; and that, as learned as he was, his business was more to divert his reader, than to teach him. And he entitled his own satires Menippean; not that Menippus had written any satires, (for his were either dialogues or epistles,) but that Varro imitated his style, his manner, and his facetiousness. All that we know farther of Menippus and his writings, which are wholly lost, is that by some he is esteem'd, as, amongst the rest, by Varro; by others he is noted of cynical impudence and obscenity; that he was much given to those parodies which I have already mention'd; that is, he often quoted the verses of Homer and the tragic poets, and turn'd their serious meaning into something that was ridiculous; whereas Varro's satires are by Tully call'd absolute, and most elegant and various poems. Lucian, who was emulous of this Menippus, seems to have imitated both his manners and his style in many of his *Dialogues;* where Menippus himself is often introduc'd as a speaker in them, and as a perpetual buffoon;

particularly his character is express'd in the beginning of that dialogue which is call'd Νεκυομαντεία. But Varro, in imitating him, avoids his impudence and filthiness, and only expresses his witty pleasantry.

This we may believe for certain, that as his subjects were various, so most of them were tales or stories of his own invention. Which is also manifest from antiquity, by those authors who are acknowledg'd to have written Varronian satires, in imitation of his; of whom the chief is Petronius Arbiter, whose satire, they say, is now printing in Holland, wholly recover'd and made complete: when 't is made public, it will easily be seen by any one sentence, whether it be supposititious, or genuine. Many of Lucian's *Dialogues* may also properly be call'd Varronian satires, particularly his *True History ;* and consequently the *Golden Ass* of Apuleius, which is taken from him. Of the same stamp is the mock deification of Claudius, by Seneca; and the *Symposium* or *Cæsars* of Julian the Emperor. Amongst the moderns, we may reckon the *Encomium Moriæ* of Erasmus, Barclay's *Euphormio*, and a volume of German authors, which my ingenious friend, Mr. Charles Killegrew, once lent me. In the English, I remember none which are mix'd with prose, as Varro's were; but of the same kind is *Mother Hubbard's Tale*, in Spenser; and (if it be not too vain to mention anything of my own) the poems of *Absalom* and *Mac Flecknoe.*

This is what I have to say in general of satire; only, as Dacier has observ'd before me, we may take notice that the word *satire* is of a more general signification in Latin, than in French, or English. For amongst the Romans it was not only us'd for those discourses which decried vice, or expos'd folly, but for others also, where virtue was recommended. But in our modern languages we apply it only to invective poems, where the very name of satire is formidable to those persons who would appear to the world what they are not in themselves; for in English, to say satire, is to mean reflection, as we use that word in the worst sense; or as the French call it, more properly, *médisance*. In the criticism of spelling, it ought to be with *i*, and not with *y*, to distinguish its true derivation from *satura*, not from *satyrus*. And if this be so,

then 't is false spell'd thoughout this book; for here 't is written *satyr:* which having not consider'd at the first, I thought it not worth correcting afterwards. But the French are more nice, and never spell it any other ways than *satire.*

I am now arriv'd at the most difficult part of my undertaking, which is, to compare Horace with Juvenal and Persius. 'T is observ'd by Rigaltius, in his preface before Juvenal, written to Thuanus, that these three poets have all their particular partisans and favorers. Every commentator, as he has taken pains with any of them, thinks himself oblig'd to prefer his author to the other two; to find out their failings, and decry them, that he may make room for his own darling. Such is the partiality of mankind, to set up that interest which they have once espous'd, tho' it be to the prejudice of truth, morality, and common justice; and especially in the productions of the brain. As authors generally think themselves the best poets, because they cannot go out of themselves to judge sincerely of their betters; so it is with critics, who, having first taken a liking to one of these poets, proceed to comment on him, and to illustrate him; after which, they fall in love with their own labors, to that degree of blind fondness, that at length they defend and exalt their author, not so much for his sake as for their own. 'T is a folly of the same nature with that of the Romans themselves, in their games of the Circus. The spectators were divided in their factions, betwixt the Veneti and the Prasini; some were for the charioteer in blue, and some for him in green. The colors themselves were but a fancy; but when once a man had taken pains to set out those of his party, and had been at the trouble of procuring voices for them, the case was alter'd; he was concern'd for his own labor, and that so earnestly, that disputes and quarrels, animosities, commotions, and bloodshed, often happen'd; and in the declension of the Grecian Empire, the very sovereigns themselves ingag'd in it, even when the barbarians were at their doors, and stickled for the preference of colors, when the safety of their people was in question. I am now myself on the brink of the same precipice; I have spent some time on the translation of Juvenal and Persius; and it behoves me to be wary, lest, for that reason, I should be partial to them, or take a prejudice against Horace. Yet, on the other side, I would not be like some of our judges, who would give the cause for a poor man, right or wrong; for, tho' that be an error on the better hand, yet it is still a partiality; and a rich man, unheard, cannot be concluded an oppressor. I remember a saying of K. Charles the Second, on Sir Matthew Hale, (who was doubtless an uncorrupt and upright man,) that his servants were sure to be cast on any trial which was heard before him; not that he thought the judge was possibly to be brib'd, but that his integrity might be too scrupulous; and that the causes of the crown were always suspicious, when the privileges of subjects were concern'd.

It had been much fairer, if the modern critics, who have imbark'd in the quarrels of their favorite authors, had rather given to each his proper due; without taking from another's heap, to raise their own. There is praise enough for each of them in particular, without encroaching on his fellows, and detracting from them, or enriching themselves with the spoils of others. But to come to particulars. Heinsius and Dacier are the most principal of those who raise Horace above Juvenal and Persius. Scaliger the father, Rigaltius, and many others, debase Horace, that they may set up Juvenal; and Casaubon, who is almost single, throws dirt on Juvenal and Horace, that he may exalt Persius, whom he understood particularly well, and better than any of his former commentators; even Stelluti, who succeeded him. I will begin with him, who, in my opinion, defends the weakest cause, which is that of Persius; and laboring, as Tacitus professes of his own writing, to divest myself of partiality, or prejudice, consider Persius, not as a poet whom I have wholly translated, and who has cost me more labor and time than Juvenal, but according to what I judge to be his own merit; which I think not equal, in the main, to that of Juvenal or Horace, and yet in some things to be preferr'd to both of them.

First, then, for the verse; neither Casaubon himself, nor any for him, can defend either his numbers, or the purity of his Latin. Casaubon gives this point for lost, and pretends not to justify either the measures or the words of Persius; he is

evidently beneath Horace and Juvenal in both.

Then, as his verse is scabrous and hobbling, and his words not everywhere well chosen, the purity of Latin being more corrupted than in the time of Juvenal, and consequently of Horace, who writ when the language was in the heighth of its perfection, so his diction is hard, his figures are generally too bold and daring, and his tropes, particularly his metaphors, insufferably strain'd.

In the third place, notwithstanding all the diligence of Casaubon, Stelluti, and a Scotch gentleman, (whom I have heard extremely commended for his illustrations of him,) yet he is still obscure: whether he affected not to be understood, but with difficulty; or whether the fear of his safety under Nero compell'd him to this darkness in some places; or that it was occasion'd by his close way of thinking, and the brevity of his style, and crowding of his figures; or lastly, whether, after so long a time, many of his words have been corrupted, and many customs, and stories relating to them, lost to us: whether some of these reasons, or all, concurr'd to render him so cloudy, we may be bold to affirm, that the best of commentators can but guess at his meaning, in many passages; and none can be certain that he has divin'd rightly.

After all, he was a young man, like his friend and contemporary Lucan; both of them men of extraordinary parts, and great acquir'd knowledge, considering their youth: but neither of them had arriv'd to that maturity of judgment which is necessary to the accomplishing of a form'd poet. And this consideration, as, on the one hand, it lays some imperfections to their charge, so, on the other side, 't is a candid excuse for those failings which are incident to youth and inexperience; and we have more reason to wonder how they, who died before the thirtieth year of their age, could write so well, and think so strongly, than to accuse them of those faults from which human nature, and more especially in youth, can never possibly be exempted.

To consider Persius yet more closely: he rather insulted over vice and folly, than expos'd them, like Juvenal and Horace; and as chaste and modest as he is esteem'd, it cannot be denied but that in some places he is broad and fulsome, as the latter verses of the *Fourth Satire*, and of the *Sixth*, sufficiently witness. And 't is to be believ'd that he who commits the same crime often, and without necessity, cannot but do it with some kind of pleasure.

To come to a conclusion: he is manifestly below Horace, because he borrows most of his greatest beauties from him; and Casaubon is so far from denying this, that he has written a treatise purposely concerning it, wherein he shews a multitude of his translations from Horace, and his imitations of him, for the credit of his author; which he calls *Imitatio Horatiana*.

To these defects, which I casually observ'd while I was translating this author, Scaliger has added others; he calls him, in plain terms, a silly writer and a trifler, full of ostentation of his learning, and, after all, unworthy to come into competition with Juvenal and Horace.

After such terrible accusations, 't is time to hear what his patron Casaubon can allege in his defense. Instead of answering, he excuses for the most part; and, when he cannot, accuses others of the same crimes. He deals with Scaliger, as a modest scholar with a master. He compliments him with so much reverence, that one would swear he fear'd him as much at least as he respected him. Scaliger will not allow Persius to have any wit; Casaubon interprets this in the mildest sense, and confesses his author was not good at turning things into a pleasant ridicule; or, in other words, that he was not a laughable writer. That he was *ineptus*, indeed, but that was *non aptissimus ad jocandum;* but that he was ostentatious of his learning, that, by Scaliger's good favor, he denies. Persius shew'd his learning, but was no boaster of it; he did *ostendere*, but not *ostentare ;* and so, he says, did Scaliger: where, methinks, Casaubon turns it handsomely upon that supercilious critic, and silently insinuates that he himself was sufficiently vainglorious, and a boaster of his own knowledge. All the writings of this venerable censor, continues Casaubon, which are χρυσοῦ χρυσότερα, more golden than gold itself, are everywhere smelling of that thyme which, like a bee, he has gather'd from ancient authors; but

far be ostentation and vainglory from a gentleman so well born, and so nobly educated as Scaliger. But, says Scaliger, he is so obscure, that he has got himself the name of Scotinus, a dark writer. Now, says Casaubon, 't is a wonder to me that anything could be obscure to the divine wit of Scaliger, from which nothing could be hidden. This is indeed a strong compliment, but no defense; and Casaubon, who could not but be sensible of his author's blind side, thinks it time to abandon a post that was untenable. He acknowledges that Persius is obscure in some places; but so is Plato, so is Thucydides; so are Pindar, Theocritus, and Aristophanes, amongst the Greek poets; and even Horace and Juvenal, he might have added, amongst the Romans. The truth is, Persius is not sometimes, but generally, obscure; and therefore Casaubon, at last, is forc'd to excuse him, by alleging that it was *se defendendo*, for fear of Nero; and that he was commanded to write so cloudily by Cornutus, in virtue of holy obedience to his master. I cannot help my own opinion; I think Cornutus needed not to have read many lectures to him on that subject. Persius was an apt scholar; and when he was bidden to be obscure in some places, where his life and safety were in question, took the same counsel for all his book; and never afterwards wrote ten lines together clearly. Casaubon, being upon this chapter, has not fail'd, we may be sure, of making a compliment to his own dear comment. If Persius, says he, be in himself obscure, yet my interpretation has made him intelligible. There is no question but he deserves that praise which he has given to himself; but the nature of the thing, as Lucretius says, will not admit of a perfect explanation. Besides many examples which I could urge, the very last verse of his last satire, upon which he particularly values himself in his preface, is not yet sufficiently explicated. 'T is true, Holyday has endeavor'd to justify his construction; but Stelluti is against it; and, for my part, I can have but a very dark notion of it. As for the chastity of his thoughts, Casaubon denies not but that one particular passage, in the *Fourth Satire: At si unctus cesses*, &c., is not only the most obscure, but the most obscene of all his works. I understood it, but for that reason turn'd it over. In defense of his boist'rous metaphors, he quotes Longinus, who accounts them as instruments of the sublime; fit to move and stir up the affections, particularly in narration. To which it may be replied, that where the trope is farfetch'd and hard 't is fit for nothing but to puzzle the understanding; and may be reckon'd amongst those things of Demosthenes which Æschines call'd θαύματα, not ῥήματα, that is, prodigies, not words. It must be granted to Casaubon, that the knowledge of many things is lost in our modern ages, which were of familiar notice to the ancients; and that satire is a poem of a difficult nature in itself, and is not written to vulgar readers: and thro' the relation which it has to comedy, the frequent change of persons makes the sense perplex'd, when we can but divine who it is that speaks; whether Persius himself, or his friend and monitor; or, in some places, a third person. But Casaubon comes back always to himself, and concludes, that if Persius had not been obscure, there had been no need of him for an interpreter. Yet when he had once enjoin'd himself so hard a task, he then consider'd the Greek proverb, that he must χελώνης φαγεῖν ἢ μὴ φαγεῖν, either eat the whole snail, or let it quite alone; and so he went thro' with his laborious task, as I have done with my difficult translation.

Thus far, my Lord, you see it has gone very hard with Persius: I think he cannot be allow'd to stand in competition either with Juvenal or Horace. Yet for once I will venture to be so vain as to affirm, that none of his hard metaphors, or forc'd expressions, are in my translation. But more of this in its proper place, where I shall say somewhat in particular of our general performance, in making these two authors English. In the mean time, I think myself oblig'd to give Persius his undoubted due, and to acquaint the world, with Casaubon, in what he has equal'd, and in what excell'd, his two competitors.

A man who is resolv'd to praise an author, with any appearance of justice, must be sure to take him on the strongest side, and where he is least liable to exceptions. He is therefore oblig'd to choose his mediums accordingly. Casaubon, who saw that Persius could not laugh with a becoming grace, that he was not made for jesting, and that a merry conceit was not his talent, turn'd his feather, like an Indian, to another light, that he might give it the better gloss. Moral doctrine, says he, and urbanity, or well-manner'd wit, are the two things which constitute the Roman satire; but of the two, that which is most essential to this poem, and is, as it were, the very soul which animates it, is the scourging of vice and exhortation to virtue. Thus wit, for a good reason, is already almost out of doors; and allow'd only for an instrument, a kind of tool, or a weapon, as he calls it, of which the satirist makes use in the compassing of his design. The end and aim of our three rivals is consequently the same. But by what methods they have prosecuted their intention is farther to be consider'd. Satire is of the nature of moral philosophy, as being instructive: he, therefore, who instructs most usefully, will carry the palm from his two antagonists. The philosophy in which Persius was educated, and which he professes thro' his whole book, is the Stoic; the most noble, most generous, most beneficial to humankind, amongst all the sects, who have given us the rules of ethics, thereby to form a severe virtue in the soul; to raise in us an undaunted courage against the assaults of fortune; to esteem as nothing the things that are without us, because they are not in our power; not to value riches, beauty, honors, fame, or health, any farther than as conveniences, and so many helps to living as we ought, and doing good in our generation: in short, to be always happy, while we possess our minds with a good conscience, are free from the slavery of vices, and conform our actions and conversation to the rules of right reason. See here, my Lord, an epitome of Epictetus; the doctrine of Zeno, and the education of our Persius: and this he express'd, not only in all his satires, but in the manner of his life. I will not lessen this commendation of the Stoic philosophy by giving you an account of some absurdities in their doctrine, and some perhaps impieties, if we consider them by the standard of Christian faith. Persius has fall'n into none of them; and therefore is free from those imputations. What he teaches might be taught from pulpits, with more profit to the audience than all the nice speculations of divinity, and controversies concerning faith;

which are more for the profit of the shepherd than for the edification of the flock. Passion, interest, ambition, and all their bloody consequences of discord and of war, are banish'd from this doctrine. Here is nothing propos'd but the quiet and tranquillity of mind; Virtue lodg'd at home, and afterwards diffus'd in her general effects, to the improvement and good of humankind. And therefore I wonder not that the present Bishop of Salisbury has recommended this our author, and the *Tenth Satire* of Juvenal, in his Pastoral Letter, to the serious perusal and practice of the divines in his diocese, as the best commonplaces for their sermons, as the storehouses and magazines of moral virtues, from whence they may draw out, as they have occasion, all manner of assistance for the accomplishment of a virtuous life, which the Stoics have assign'd for the great end and perfection of mankind. Herein then it is, that Persius has excell'd both Juvenal and Horace. He sticks to his one philosophy; he shifts not sides, like Horace, who is sometimes an Epicurean, sometimes a Stoic, sometimes an Eclectic, as his present humor leads him; nor declaims like Juvenal against vices, more like an orator than a philosopher. Persius is everywhere the same; true to the dogmas of his master. What he has learnt, he teaches vehemently; and what he teaches, that he practices himself. There is a spirit of sincerity in all he says; you may easily discern that he is in earnest, and is persuaded of that truth which he inculcates. In this I am of opinion that he excels Horace, who is commonly in jest, and laughs while he instructs; and is equal to Juvenal, who was as honest and serious as Persius, and more he could not be.

Hitherto I have follow'd Casaubon, and enlarg'd upon him, because I am satisfied that he says no more than truth; the rest is almost all frivolous. For he says that Horace, being the son of a taxgatherer, or a collector, as we call it, smells everywhere of the meanness of his birth and education: his conceits are vulgar, like the subjects of his satire; that he does *plebeium sapere*, and writes not with that elevation which becomes a satirist: that Persius, being nobly born, and of an opulent family, had likewise the advantage of a better master; Cornutus being the most learned of his time, a man

of a most holy life, the chief of the Stoic sect at Rome, and not only a great philosopher, but a poet himself, and in probability a coadjutor of Persius: that, as for Juvenal, he was long a declaimer, came late to poetry, and had not been much conversant in philosophy.

'T is granted that the father of Horace was *libertinus*, that is, one degree remov'd from his grandfather, who had been once a slave. But Horace, speaking of him, gives him the best character of a father which I ever read in history; and I wish a witty friend of mine, now living, had such another. He bred him in the best school, and with the best company of young noblemen; and Horace, by his gratitude to his memory, gives a certain testimony that his education was ingenuous. After this, he form'd himself abroad, by the conversation of great men. Brutus found him at Athens, and was so pleas'd with him that he took him thence into the army, and made him *tribunus militum*, a colonel in a legion, which was the preferment of an old soldier. All this was before his acquaintance with Mæcenas, and his introduction into the court of Augustus, and the familiarity of that great emperor; which, had he not been well-bred before, had been enough to civilize his conversation, and render him accomplish'd and knowing in all the arts of complacency and good behavior; and, in short, an agreeable companion for the retir'd hours and privacies of a favorite, who was first minister. So that, upon the whole matter, Persius may be acknowledg'd to be equal with him in those respects, tho' better born, and Juvenal inferior to both. If the advantage be anywhere, 't is on the side of Horace; as much as the court of Augustus Cæsar was superior to that of Nero. As for the subjects which they treated, it will appear hereafter that Horace writ not vulgarly on vulgar subjects, nor always chose them. His style is constantly accommodated to his subject, either high or low. If his fault be too much lowness, that of Persius is the fault of the hardness of his metaphors, and obscurity: and so they are equal in the failings of their style; where Juvenal manifestly triumphs over both of them.

The comparison betwixt Horace and Juvenal is more difficult, because their forces were more equal. A dispute has always been, and ever will continue, betwixt the favorers of the two poets. *Non nostrum est tantas componere lites.* I shall only venture to give my own opinion, and leave it for better judges to determine. If it be only argued in general, which of them was the better poet, the victory is already gain'd on the side of Horace; Virgil himself must yield to him in the delicacy of his turns, his choice of words, and perhaps the purity of his Latin. He who says that Pindar is inimitable, is himself inimitable in his *Odes.* But the contention betwixt these two great masters is for the prize of satire; in which controversy all the *Odes* and *Epodes* of Horace are to stand excluded. I say this, because Horace has written many of them satirically, against his private enemies; yet these, if justly consider'd, are somewhat of the nature of the Greek *silli,* which were invectives against particular sects and persons. But Horace had purg'd himself of this choler before he enter'd on those discourses which are more properly call'd the Roman satire. He has not now to do with a Lyce, a Canidia, a Cassius Severus, or a Menas; but is to correct the vices and the follies of his time, and to give the rules of a happy and virtuous life. In a word, that former sort of satire, which is known in England by the name of lampoon, is a dangerous sort of weapon, and for the most part unlawful. We have no moral right on the reputation of other men. 'T is taking from them what we cannot restore to them. There are only two reasons for which we may be permitted to write lampoons; and I will not promise that they can always justify us. The first is revenge, when we have been affronted in the same nature, or have been any ways notoriously abus'd, and can make ourselves no other reparation. And yet we know, that, in Christian charity, all offenses are to be forgiven, as we expect the like pardon for those which we daily commit against Almighty God. And this consideration has often made me tremble when I was saying our Savior's prayer; for the plain condition of the forgiveness which we beg is the pardoning of others the offenses which they have done to us; for which reason I have many times avoided the commission of that fault, ev'n when I have been notoriously provok'd. Let not this, my Lord, pass for vanity in me; for 't is truth. More libels

have been written against me, than almost any man now living; and I had reason on my side, to have defended my own innocence. I speak not of my poetry, which I have wholly given up to the critics: let them use it as they please; posterity, perhaps, may be more favorable to me; for interest and passion will lie buried in another age, and partiality and prejudice be forgotten. I speak of my morals, which have been sufficiently aspers'd: that only sort of reputation ought to be dear to every honest man, and is to me. But let the world witness for me, that I have been often wanting to myself in that particular; I have seldom answer'd any scurrilous lampoon, when it was in my power to have expos'd my enemies; and, being naturally vindicative, have suffer'd in silence, and possess'd my soul in quiet.

Anything, tho' never so little, which a man speaks of himself, in my opinion, is still too much; and therefore I will waive this subject, and proceed to give the second reason which may justify a poet when he writes against a particular person; and that is, when he is become a public nuisance. All those whom Horace in his *Satires,* and Persius and Juvenal have mention'd in theirs, with a brand of infamy, are wholly such. 'T is an action of virtue to make examples of vicious men. They may and ought to be upbraided with their crimes and follies; both for their own amendment, if they are not yet incorrigible, and for the terror of others, to hinder them from falling into those enormities which they see are so severely punish'd in the persons of others. The first reason was only an excuse for revenge; but this second is absolutely of a poet's office to perform: but how few lampooners are there now living, who are capable of this duty! When they come in my way, 't is impossible sometimes to avoid reading them. But, good God! how remote they are, in common justice, from the choice of such persons as are the proper subject of satire! And how little wit they bring for the support of their injustice! The weaker sex is their most ordinary theme, and the best and fairest are sure to be the most severely handled. Amongst men, those who are prosperously unjust are intitled to a panegyric, but afflicted virtue is insolently stabb'd with all manner of reproaches; no decency is consider'd, no fulsomeness omitted; no venom is wanting, as far as dulness can supply it: for there is a perpetual dearth of wit, a barrenness of good sense and entertainment. The neglect of the readers will soon put an end to this sort of scribbling. There can be no pleasantry where there is no wit; no impression can be made where there is no truth for the foundation. To conclude: they are like the fruits of the earth in this unnatural season; the corn which held up its head is spoil'd with rankness; but the greater part of the harvest is laid along, and little of good income and wholesome nourishment is receiv'd into the barns. This is almost a digression, I confess to your Lordship; but a just indignation forc'd it from me. Now I have remov'd this rubbish, I will return to the comparison of Juvenal and Horace.

I would willingly divide the palm betwixt them, upon the two heads of profit and delight, which are the two ends of poetry in general. It must be granted by the favorers of Juvenal, that Horace is the more copious and profitable in his instructions of human life; but, in my particular opinion, which I set not up for a standard to better judgments, Juvenal is the more delightful author. I am profited by both, I am pleas'd with both; but I owe more to Horace for my instruction, and more to Juvenal for my pleasure. This, as I said, is my particular taste of these two authors: they who will have either of them to excel the other in both qualities, can scarce give better reasons for their opinion than I for mine. But all unbias'd readers will conclude that my moderation is not to be condemn'd: to such impartial men I must appeal; for they who have already form'd their judgment may justly stand suspected of prejudice; and tho' all who are my readers will set up to be my judges, I enter my *caveat* against them, that they ought not so much as to be of my jury; or, if they be admitted, 't is but reason that they should first hear what I have to urge in the defense of my opinion.

That Horace is somewhat the better instructor of the two, is prov'd from hence, that his instructions are more general, Juvenal's more limited. So that, granting that the counsels which they give are equally good for moral use, Horace, who gives the most various advice, and most applicable to all occasions which can occur to us in the course of our lives — as including in his discourses not only all the rules of morality, but also of civil conversation — is undoubtedly to be preferr'd to him who is more circumscrib'd in his instructions, makes them to fewer people, and on fewer occasions, than the other. I may be pardon'd for using an old saying, since 't is true, and to the purpose: *Bonum quo communius, eo melius.* Juvenal, excepting only his *First Satire*, is in all the rest confin'd to the exposing of some particular vice; that he lashes, and there he sticks. His sentences are truly shining and instructive; but they are sprinkled here and there. Horace is teaching us in every line, and is perpetually moral: he had found out the skill of Virgil, to hide his sentences; to give you the virtue of them, without shewing them in their full extent; which is the ostentation of a poet, and not his art: and this Petronius charges on the authors of his time, as a vice of writing which was then growing on the age: *ne sententiæ extra corpus orationis emineant:* he would have them weav'd into the body of the work, and not appear emboss'd upon it, and striking directly on the reader's view. Folly was the proper quarry of Horace, and not vice; and as there are but few notoriously wicked men, in comparison with a shoal of fools and fops, so 't is a harder thing to make a man wise than to make him honest; for the will is only to be reclaim'd in the one, but the understanding is to be inform'd in the other. There are blind sides and follies, even in the professors of moral philosophy; and there is not any one sect of them that Horace has not expos'd: which, as it was not the design of Juvenal, who was wholly employ'd in lashing vices, some of them the most enormous that can be imagin'd, so, perhaps, it was not so much his talent.

Omne vafer vitium ridenti Flaccus amico
Tangit, et admissus circum præcordia ludit.

This was the commendation which Persius gave him: where, by *vitium*, he means those little vices which we call follies, the defects of human understanding, or, at most, the peccadillos of life, rather than the tragical vices, to which men are hurried by their unruly passions and exorbitant desires. But in the word *omne*, which is universal, he concludes with me, that the divine wit of Horace left nothing un-touch'd; that he enter'd into the inmost recesses of nature; found out the imper-fections even of the most wise and grave, as well as of the common people; discover-ing, even in the great Trebatius, to whom he addresses the *First Satire*, his hunting after business, and following the court, as well as in the persecutor Crispinus, his impertinence and importunity. 'T is true, he exposes Crispinus openly, as a common nuisance; but he rallies the other, as a friend, more finely. The exhortations of Persius are confin'd to noblemen; and the Stoic philosophy is that alone which he recommends to them; Juvenal exhorts to particular virtues, as they are oppos'd to those vices against which he declaims; but Horace laughs to shame all follies, and in-sinuates virtue rather by familiar examples than by the severity of precepts.

This last consideration seems to incline the balance on the side of Horace, and to give him the preference to Juvenal, not only in profit, but in pleasure. But, after all, I must confess that the delight which Horace gives me is but languishing. Be pleas'd still to understand, that I speak of my own taste only: he may ravish other men; but I am too stupid and insensible to be tickled. Where he barely grins him-self, and, as Scaliger says, only shews his white teeth, he cannot provoke me to any laughter. His urbanity, that is, his good manners, are to be commended, but his wit is faint; and his salt, if I may dare to say so, almost insipid. Juvenal is of a more vigorous and masculine wit; he gives me as much pleasure as I can bear; he fully satisfies my expectation; he treats his sub-ject home: his spleen is rais'd, and he raises mine: I have the pleasure of con-cernment in all he says; he drives his reader along with him; and when he is at the end of his way, I willingly stop with him. If he went another stage, it would be too far; it would make a journey of a progress, and turn delight into fatigue. When he gives over, 't is a sign the sub-ject is exhausted, and the wit of man can carry it no farther. If a fault can be justly found in him, 't is that he is sometimes too luxuriant, too redundant; says more than he needs, like my friend the *Plain Dealer*, but never more than pleases. Add to this,

that his thoughts are as just as those of Horace, and much more elevated. His expressions are sonorous and more noble; his verse more numerous, and his words are suitable to his thoughts, sublime and lofty. All these contribute to the pleasure of the reader; and the greater the soul of him who reads, his transports are the greater. Horace is always on the amble, Juvenal on the gallop; but his way is per-petually on carpet-ground. He goes with more impetuosity than Horace, but as se-curely; and the swiftness adds a more lively agitation to the spirits. The low style of Horace is according to his subject, that is, generally groveling. I question not but he could have rais'd it; for the First Epistle of the Second Book, which he writes to Augustus, (a most instructive satire concerning poetry,) is of so much dignity in the words, and of so much elegancy in the numbers, that the author plainly shews the *sermo pedestris*, in his other satires, was rather his choice than his necessity. He was a rival to Lucilius, his predecessor, and was resolv'd to sur-pass him in his own manner. Lucilius, as we see by his remaining fragments, minded neither his style, nor his numbers, nor his purity of words, nor his run of verse. Hor-ace therefore copes with him in that humble way of satire, writes under his own force, and carries a dead weight, that he may match his competitor in the race. This, I imagine, was the chief reason why he minded only the clearness of his satire, and the cleanness of expression, without ascending to those heights to which his own vigor might have carried him. But, limit-ing his desires only to the conquest of Lucilius, he had his ends of his rival, who liv'd before him; but made way for a new conquest over himself, by Juvenal, his suc-cessor. He could not give an equal pleasure to his reader, because he us'd not equal in-struments. The fault was in the tools, and not in the workman. But versification and numbers are the greatest pleasures of po-etry: Virgil knew it, and practic'd both so happily, that, for aught I know, his greatest excellency is in his diction. In all other parts of poetry, he is faultless; but in this he plac'd his chief perfection. And give me leave, my Lord, since I have here an apt occasion, to say that Virgil could have written sharper satires than either Horace or Juvenal, if he would have employ'd his talent that way. I will produce a verse and half of his, in one of his *Eclogues*, to justify my opinion; and with commas after every word, to shew that he has given almost as many lashes as he has written syllables. 'T is against a bad poet, whose ill verses he describes:

—— *non tu, in triviis, indocte, solebas*
Stridenti, miserum, stipula, disperdere carmen?

But to return to my purpose. When there is anything deficient in numbers and sound, the reader is uneasy and unsatisfied; he wants something of his complement, desires somewhat which he finds not: and this being the manifest defect of Horace, 't is no wonder that, finding it supplied in Juvenal, we are more delighted with him. And, besides this, the sauce of Juvenal is more poignant, to create in us an appetite of reading him. The meat of Horace is more nourishing; but the cookery of Juvenal more exquisite: so that, granting Horace to be the more general philosopher, we cannot deny that Juvenal is the greater poet, I mean in satire. His thoughts are sharper; his indignation against vice is more vehement; his spirit has more of the commonwealth genius; he treats tyranny, and all the vices attending it, as they deserve, with the utmost rigor: and consequently, a noble soul is better pleas'd with a zealous vindicator of Roman liberty, than with a temporizing poet, a well-manner'd court slave, and a man who is often afraid of laughing in the right place; who is ever decent, because he is naturally servile. After all, Horace had the disadvantage of the times in which he liv'd; they were better for the man, but worse for the satirist. 'T is generally said, that those enormous vices which were practic'd under the reign of Domitian, were unknown in the time of Augustus Cæsar; that therefore Juvenal had a larger field than Horace. Little follies were out of doors, when oppression was to be scourg'd instead of avarice: it was no longer time to turn into ridicule the false opinions of philosophers, when the Roman liberty was to be asserted. There was more need of a Brutus in Domitian's days, to redeem or mend, than of a Horace, if he had then been living, to laugh at a fly-catcher. This

reflection at the same time excuses Horace, but exalts Juvenal. I have ended, before I was aware, the comparison of Horace and Juvenal, upon the topics of instruction and delight; and, indeed, I may safely here conclude that commonplace; for, if we make Horace our minister of state in satire, and Juvenal of our private pleasures, I think the latter has no ill bargain of it. Let profit have the preëminence of honor, in the end of poetry. Pleasure, tho' but the second in degree, is the first in favor. And who would not choose to be lov'd better, rather than to be more esteem'd? But I am enter'd already upon another topic, which concerns the particular merits of these two satirists. However, I will pursue my business where I left it, and carry it farther than that common observation of the several ages in which these authors flourish'd. When Horace writ his *Satires*, the monarchy of his Cæsar was in its newness, and the government but just made easy to the conquer'd people. They could not possibly have forgotten the usurpation of that prince upon their freedom, nor the violent methods which he had us'd in the compassing of that vast design: they yet remember'd his proscriptions, and the slaughter of so many noble Romans, their defenders: amongst the rest, that horrible action of his, when he forc'd Livia from the arms of her husband, who was constrain'd to see her married, as Dion relates the story, and, big with child as she was, convey'd to the bed of his insulting rival. The same Dion Cassius gives us another instance of the crime before mention'd; that Cornelius Sisenna being reproach'd, in full senate, with the licentious conduct of his wife, return'd this answer, that he had married her by the counsel of Augustus; intimating, says my author, that Augustus had oblig'd him to that marriage, that he might, under that covert, have the more free access to her. His adulteries were still before their eyes, but they must be patient where they had not power. In other things that emperor was moderate enough: propriety was generally secur'd; and the people entertain'd with public shows and donatives, to make them more easily digest their lost liberty. But Augustus, who was conscious to himself of so many crimes which he had committed, thought, in the first place, to provide for his own reputation, by making an edict against lampoons and satires, and the authors of those defamatory writings which my author Tacitus, from the law-term, calls *famosos libellos*.

In the first book of his *Annals*, he gives the following account of it, in these words: *Primus Augustus cognitionem de famosis libellis, specie legis ejus, tractavit; commotus Cassii Severi libidine, qua viros fœminasque illustres, procacibus scriptis diffamaverat.* Thus in English: "Augustus was the first who under the color of that law took cognizance of lampoons, being provok'd to it by the petulancy of Cassius Severus, who had defam'd many illustrious persons of both sexes in his writings." The law to which Tacitus refers was *Lex lœsœ Majestatis;* commonly call'd, for the sake of brevity, *Majestas;* or, as we say, high treason. He means not that this law had not been enacted formerly: for it had been made by the Decemviri, and was inscrib'd amongst the rest in the Twelve Tables; to prevent the aspersion of the Roman majesty, either of the people themselves, or their religion, or their magistrates: and the infringement of it was capital; that is, the offender was whipp'd to death with the *fasces*, which were borne before their chief officers of Rome. But Augustus was the first who restor'd that intermitted law. By the words, *under color of that law,* he insinuates that Augustus caus'd it to be executed, on pretense of those libels which were written by Cassius Severus against the nobility; but, in truth, to save himself from such defamatory verses. Suetonius likewise makes mention of it thus: *Sparsos de se in curia famosos libellos, nec expavit, et magna cura redarguit. Ac ne requisitis quidem auctoribus, id modo censuit, cognoscendum posthac de iis qui libellos aut carmina ad infamiam cujuspiam sub alieno nomine edant.* "Augustus was not afraid of libels," says that author; "yet he took all care imaginable to have them answer'd; and then decreed, that for the time to come the authors of them should be punish'd." But Aurelius makes it yet more clear, according to my sense, that this emperor for his own sake durst not permit them: *Fecit id Augustus in speciem, et quasi gratificaretur populo Romano, et primoribus urbis; sed revera ut sibi consuleret: nam habuit in animo, comprimere nimiam quorundam procacitatem in loquendo, a qua nec ipse exemptus fuit. Nam suo nomine compescere erat invidiosum, sub alieno facile et utile. Ergo specie legis tractavit, quasi populi Romani majestas infamaretur.* This, I think, is a sufficient comment on that passage of Tacitus. I will add only by the way, that the whole family of the Cæsars, and all their relations, were included in the law; because the majesty of the Romans, in the time of the empire, was wholly in that house; *omnia Cæsar erat:* they were all accounted sacred who belong'd to him. As for Cassius Severus, he was contemporary with Horace; and was the same poet against whom he writes in his *Epodes*, under this title, *In Cassium Severum maledicum poetam;* perhaps intending to kill two crows, according to our proverb, with one stone, and revenge both himself and his emperor together.

From hence I may reasonably conclude, that Augustus, who was not altogether so good as he was wise, had some by-respect in the enacting of this law; for to do anything for nothing was not his maxim. Horace, as he was a courtier, complied with the interest of his master; and, avoiding the lashing of greater crimes, confin'd himself to the ridiculing of petty vices and common follies; excepting only some reserv'd cases, in his *Odes* and *Epodes*, of his own particular quarrels, which either with permission of the magistrate, or without it, every man will revenge, tho' I say not that he should; for *prior lœsit* is a good excuse in the civil law, if Christianity had not taught us to forgive. However, he was not the proper man to arraign great vices, at least if the stories which we hear of him are true, that he practic'd some, which I will not here mention, out of honor to him. It was not for a Clodius to accuse adulterers, especially when Augustus was of that number; so that tho' his age was not exempted from the worst of villainies, there was no freedom left to reprehend them, by reason of the edict; and our poet was not fit to represent them in an odious character, because himself was dipp'd in the same actions. Upon this account, without farther insisting on the different tempers of Juvenal and Horace, I conclude, that the subjects which Horace chose for satire are of a lower nature than those of which Juvenal has written.

Thus I have treated, in a new method, the

comparison betwixt Horace, Juvenal, and Persius; somewhat of their particular manner belonging to all of them is yet remaining to be consider'd. Persius was grave, and particularly oppos'd his gravity to lewdness, which was the predominant vice in Nero's court at the time when he publish'd his *Satires*, which was before that emperor fell into the excess of cruelty. Horace was a mild admonisher, a court satirist, fit for the gentle times of Augustus, and more fit, for the reasons which I have already given. Juvenal was as proper for his times, as they for theirs; his was an age that deserv'd a more severe chastisement; vices were more gross and open, more flagitious, more encourag'd by the example of a tyrant, and more protected by his authority. Therefore, wheresoever Juvenal mentions Nero, he means Domitian, whom he dares not attack in his own person, but scourges him by proxy. Heinsius urges in praise of Horace, that, according to the ancient art and law of satire, it should be nearer to comedy than to tragedy; not declaiming against vice, but only laughing at it. Neither Persius nor Juvenal were ignorant of this, for they had both studied Horace. And the thing itself is plainly true. But as they had read Horace, they had likewise read Lucilius, of whom Persius says, *secuit urbem; et genuinum fregit in illis;* meaning Mutius and Lupus; and Juvenal also mentions him in these words: *Ense velut stricto, quoties Lucilius ardens Infremuit,* &c. So that they thought the imitation of Lucilius was more proper to their purpose than that of Horace. "They chang'd satire," says Holyday, "but they chang'd it for the better; for the business being to reform great vices, chastisement goes farther than admonition; whereas a perpetual grin, like that of Horace, does rather anger than amend a man."

Thus far that learned critic, Barten Holyday, whose interpretation and illustrations of Juvenal are as excellent, as the verse of his translation and his English are lame and pitiful. For 't is not enough to give us the meaning of a poet, which I acknowledge him to have perform'd most faithfully, but he must also imitate his genius and his numbers, as far as the English will come up to the elegance of the original. In few words, 't is only for a poet to translate a poet. Holyday and Stapylton had not enough consider'd this, when they attempted Juvenal: but I forbear reflections; only I beg leave to take notice of this sentence, where Holyday says: "A perpetual grin, like that of Horace, rather angers than amends a man." I cannot give him up the manner of Horace in low satire so easily. Let the chastisements of Juvenal be never so necessary for his new kind of satire; let him declaim as wittily and sharply as he pleases; yet still the nicest and most delicate touches of satire consist in fine raillery. This, my Lord, is your particular talent, to which even Juvenal could not arrive. 'T is not reading, 't is not imitation of an author, which can produce this fineness; it must be inborn; it must proceed from a genius, and particular way of thinking, which is not to be taught; and therefore not to be imitated by him who has it not from nature. How easy it is to call rogue and villain, and that wittily! But how hard to make a man appear a fool, a blockhead, or a knave, without using any of those opprobrious terms! To spare the grossness of the names, and to do the thing yet more severely, is to draw a full face, and to make the nose and cheeks stand out, and yet not to employ any depth of shadowing. This is the mystery of that noble trade, which yet no master can teach to his apprentice; he may give the rules, but the scholar is never the nearer in his practice. Neither is it true, that this fineness of raillery is offensive. A witty man is tickled while he is hurt in this manner, and a fool feels it not. The occasion of an offense may possibly be given, but he cannot take it. If it be granted, that in effect this way does more mischief; that a man is secretly wounded, and tho' he be not sensible himself, yet the malicious world will find it for him; yet there is still a vast difference betwixt the slovenly butchering of a man, and the fineness of a stroke that separates the head from the body, and leaves it standing in its place. A man may be capable, as Jack Ketch's wife said of his servant, of a plain piece of work, a bare hanging; but to make a malefactor die sweetly, was only belonging to her husband. I wish I could apply it to myself, if the reader would be kind enough to think it belongs to me. The character of Zimri in my *Absalom* is, in my opinion, worth the whole poem: 't is not bloody, but 't is ridiculous enough; and he for whom it was intended was too witty to resent it as an injury. If I had rail'd, I might have suffer'd for it justly; but I manag'd my own work more happily, perhaps more dext'rously. I avoided the mention of great crimes, and applied myself to the representing of blind sides, and little extravagancies; to which, the wittier a man is, he is generally the more obnoxious. It succeeded as I wish'd; the jest went round, and he was laugh'd at in his turn who began the frolic.

And thus, my Lord, you see I have preferr'd the manner of Horace, and of your Lordship, in this kind of satire, to that of Juvenal, and, I think, reasonably. Holyday ought not to have arraign'd so great an author for that which was his excellency and his merit; or if he did, on such a palpable mistake, he might expect that some one might possibly arise, either in his own time, or after him, to rectify his error, and restore to Horace that commendation of which he has so unjustly robb'd him. And let the *manes* of Juvenal forgive me, if I say that this way of Horace was the best for amending manners, as it is the most difficult. His was an *ense rescindendum ;* but that of Horace was a pleasant cure, with all the limbs preserv'd entire; and, as our mountebanks tell us in their bills, without keeping the patient within-doors for a day. What they promise only, Horace has effectually perform'd: yet I contradict not the proposition which I formerly advanc'd. Juvenal's times requir'd a more painful kind of operation; but if he had liv'd in the age of Horace, I must needs affirm that he had it not about him. He took the method which was prescrib'd him by his own genius, which was sharp and eager; he could not rally, but he could declaim; and as his provocations were great, he has reveng'd them tragically. This notwithstanding, I am to say another word, which, as true as it is, will yet displease the partial admirers of our Horace. I have hinted it before, but 't is time for me now to speak more plainly.

This manner of Horace is indeed the best; but Horace has not executed it altogether so happily, at least not often. The manner of Juvenal is confess'd to be inferior to the former, but Juvenal has excell'd him in his performance. Juvenal has rail'd more wittily than Horace has rallied. Horace means to make his reader laugh, but he is not sure

of his experiment. Juvenal always intends to move your indignation, and he always brings about his purpose. Horace, for aught I know, might have tickled the people of his age; but amongst the moderns he is not so successful. They who say he entertains so pleasantly may perhaps value themselves on the quickness of their own understandings, that they can see a jest farther off than other men. They may find occasion of laughter in the wit-battle of the two buffoons, Sarmentus and Cicerrus; and hold their sides for fear of bursting, when Rupilius and Persius are scolding. For my own part, I can only like the characters of all four, which are judiciously given; but for my heart I cannot so much as smile at their insipid raillery. I see not why Persius should call upon Brutus to revenge him on his adversary; and that because he had kill'd Julius Cæsar, for endeavoring to be a king, therefore he should be desir'd to murther Rupilius, only because his name was Mr. King. A miserable clench, in my opinion, for Horace to record: I have heard honest Mr. Swan make many a better, and yet have had the grace to hold my countenance. But it may be puns were then in fashion, as they were wit in the sermons of the last age, and in the court of King Charles the Second. I am sorry to say it, for the sake of Horace; but certain it is, he has no fine palate who can feed so heartily on garbidge.

But I have already wearied myself, and doubt not but I have tir'd your Lordship's patience, with this long, rambling, and, I fear, trivial discourse. Upon the one half of the merits, that is, pleasure, I cannot but conclude that Juvenal was the better satirist. They who will descend into his particular praises may find them at large in the *Dissertation* of the learned Rigaltius to Thuanus. As for Persius, I have given the reasons why I think him inferior to both of them; yet I have one thing to add on that subject.

Barten Holyday, who translated both Juvenal and Persius, has made this distinction betwixt them, which is no less true than witty; that in Persius the difficulty is to find a meaning, in Juvenal to choose a meaning: so crabbed is Persius, and so copious is Juvenal; so much the understanding is employ'd in one, and so much the judgment in the other; so difficult it is to find any sense in the former, and the best sense of the latter.

If, on the other side, any one suppose I have commended Horace below his merit, when I have allow'd him but the second place, I desire him to consider, if Juvenal, a man of excellent natural endowments, besides the advantages of diligence and study, and coming after him, and building upon his foundations, might not probably, with all these helps, surpass him; and whether it be any dishonor to Horace to be thus surpass'd, since no art or science is at once begun and perfected, but that it must pass first thro' many hands, and even thro' several ages. If Lucilius could add to Ennius, and Horace to Lucilius, why, without any diminution to the fame of Horace, might not Juvenal give the last perfection to that work? Or rather, what disreputation is it to Horace, that Juvenal excels in the tragical satire, as Horace does in the comical? I have read over attentively both Heinsius and Dacier, in their commendations of Horace; but I can find no more in either of them, for the preference of him to Juvenal, than the instructive part; the part of wisdom, and not that of pleasure; which, therefore, is here allow'd him, notwithstanding what Scaliger and Rigaltius have pleaded to the contrary for Juvenal. And, to shew I am impartial, I will here translate what Dacier has said on that subject:

"I cannot give a more just idea of the two books of *Satires* made by Horace, than by comparing them to the statues of the Sileni, to which Alcibiades compares Socrates in the *Symposium*. They were figures which had nothing of agreeable, nothing of beauty, on their outside; but when any one took the pains to open them, and search into them, he there found the figures of all the deities. So, in the shape that Horace presents himself to us in his *Satires*, we see nothing, at the first view, which deserves our attention: it seems that he is rather an amusement for children, than for the serious consideration of men. But, when we take away his crust, and that which hides him from our sight, when we discover him to the bottom, then we find all the divinities in a full assembly; that is to say, all the virtues which ought to be the continual exercise of those who seriously endeavor to correct their vices."

'Tis easy to observe, that Dacier, in this noble similitude, has confin'd the praise of his author wholly to the instructive part; the commendation turns on this, and so does that which follows:

"In these two books of satire, 'tis the business of Horace to instruct us how to combat our vices, to regulate our passions, to follow nature, to give bounds to our desires, to distinguish betwixt truth and falsehood, and betwixt our conceptions of things, and things themselves; to come back from our prejudicate opinions, to understand exactly the principles and motives of all our actions; and to avoid the ridicule into which all men necessarily fall, who are intoxicated with those notions which they have receiv'd from their masters, and which they obstinately retain, without examining whether or no they are founded on right reason.

"In a word, he labors to render us happy in relation to ourselves; agreeable and faithful to our friends; and discreet, serviceable, and well-bred, in relation to those with whom we are oblig'd to live, and to converse. To make his figures intelligible, to conduct his readers thro' the labyrinth of some perplex'd sentence, or obscure parenthesis, is no great matter; and, as Epictetus says, there is nothing of beauty in all this, or what is worthy of a prudent man. The principal business, and which is of most importance to us, is to shew the use, the reason, and the proof of his precepts.

"They who endeavor not to correct themselves according to so exact a model, are just like the patients who have open before them a book of admirable receipts for their diseases, and please themselves with reading it, without comprehending the nature of the remedies, or how to apply them to their cure."

Let Horace go off with these encomiums, which he has so well deserv'd.

To conclude the contention betwixt our three poets, I will use the words of Virgil, in his fifth *Æneid*, where Æneas proposes the rewards of the foot race to the three first who should reach the goal:

—— *tres præmia primi*
Accipient, flavaque caput nectentur oliva.

Let these three ancients be preferr'd to all the moderns, as first arriving at the goal; let them all be crown'd, as victors, with the wreath that properly belongs to satire; but, after that, with this distinction amongst themselves:

Primus equum phaleris insignem victor habeto : —

let Juvenal ride first in triumph:

*Alter Amazoniam pharetram, plenamque sagittis
Threiciis, lato quam circumplectitur auro
Balteus, et tereti subnectit fibula gemma : —*

let Horace, who is the second, and but just the second, carry off the quivers and the arrows, as the badges of his satire, and the golden belt, and the diamond button:

Tertius Argolico hoc clypeo contentus abito : —

and let Persius, the last of the first three worthies, be contented with this Grecian shield, and with victory, not only over all the Grecians, who were ignorant of the Roman satire, but over all the moderns in succeeding ages, excepting Boileau and your Lordship.

And thus I have given the history of satire, and deriv'd it as far as from Ennius to your Lordship; that is, from its first rudiments of barbarity to its last polishing and perfection; which is, with Virgil, in his address to Augustus:

*—— nomen fama tot ferre per annos,
Tithoni prima quot abest ab origine Cæsar.*

I said only from Ennius; but I may safely carry it higher, as far as Livius Andronicus; who, as I have said formerly, taught the first play at Rome, in the year *ab urbe condita* 514. I have since desir'd my learn'd friend, Mr. Maidwell, to compute the difference of times betwixt Aristophanes and Livius Andronicus; and he assures me, from the best chronologers, that *Plutus*, the last of Aristophanes his plays, was represented at Athens, in the year of the 97th Olympiad, which agrees with the year *urbis conditæ* 364. So that the difference of years betwixt Aristophanes and Andronicus is 150; from whence I have probably deduc'd, that Livius Andronicus, who was a Grecian, had read the plays of the Old Comedy, which were satirical, and also of the New; for Menander was fifty years before him, which must needs be a great light to him in his

own plays, that were of the satirical nature. That the Romans had farces before this, 't is true; but then they had no communication with Greece; so that Andronicus was the first who wrote after the manner of the Old Comedy in his plays: he was imitated by Ennius, about thirty years afterwards. Tho' the former writ fables, the latter, speaking properly, began the Roman satire; according to that description which Juvenal gives of it in his *First*:

*Quicquid agunt homines, votum, timor, ira, vo-
    luptas.
Gaudia, discursus, nostri est farrago libelli.*

This is that in which I have made bold to differ from Casaubon, Rigaltius, Dacier, and indeed from all the modern critics, that not Ennius, but Andronicus was the first; who, by the *Archæa Comœdia* of the Greeks, added many beauties to the first rude and barbarous Roman satire: which sort of poem, tho' we had not deriv'd from Rome, yet nature teaches it mankind in all ages, and in every country.

'T is but necessary, that after so much has been said of satire, some definition of it should be given. Heinsius, in his *Dissertations on Horace*, makes it for me, in these words: " Satire is a kind of poetry, without a series of action, invented for the purging of our minds; in which human vices, ignorance, and errors, and all things besides, which are produc'd from them in every man, are severely reprehended; partly dramatically, partly simply, and sometimes in both kinds of speaking; but, for the most part, figuratively, and occultly; consisting in a low familiar way, chiefly in a sharp and pungent manner of speech; but partly, also, in a facetious and civil way of jesting; by which either hatred, or laughter, or indignation is mov'd." — Where I cannot but observe, that this obscure and perplex'd definition, or rather description, of satire, is wholly accommodated to the Horatian way; and excluding the works of Juvenal and Persius, as foreign from that kind of poem. The clause in the beginning of it, *without a series of action*, distinguishes satire properly from stageplays, which are all of one action, and one continued series of action. The end or scope of satire is to purge the passions; so far it is common to the satires of Juvenal and Persius. The rest which follows is also generally belonging to all three; till he comes upon us, with the excluding clause, *consisting in a low familiar way of speech*, which is the proper character of Horace; and from which the other two, for their honor be it spoken, are far distant. But how come lowness of style, and the familiarity of words, to be so much the propriety of satire, that without them a poet can be no more a satirist, than without risibility he can be a man? Is the fault of Horace to be made the virtue and standing rule of this poem? Is the *grande sophos* of Persius, and the sublimity of Juvenal, to be circumscrib'd with the meanness of words and vulgarity of expression? If Horace refus'd the pains of numbers, and the loftiness of figures, are they bound to follow so ill a precedent? Let him walk afoot, with his pad in his hand, for his own pleasure; but let not them be accounted no poets, who choose to mount, and shew their horsemanship. Holyday is not afraid to say, that there was never such a fall, as from his *Odes* to his *Satires*, and that he, injuriously to himself, untun'd his harp. The majestic way of Persius and Juvenal was new when they began it, but 't is old to us; and what poems have not, with time, receiv'd an alteration in their fashion? "Which alteration," says Holyday, "is to aftertimes as good a warrant as the first." Has not Virgil chang'd the manners of Homer's heroes in his *Æneis*? Certainly he has, and for the better: for Virgil's age was more civiliz'd, and better bred; and he writ according to the politeness of Rome, under the reign of Augustus Cæsar, not to the rudeness of Agamemnon's age, or the times of Homer. Why should we offer to confine free spirits to one form, when we cannot so much as confine our bodies to one fashion of apparel? Would not Donne's *Satires*, which abound with so much wit, appear more charming, if he had taken care of his words, and of his numbers? But he follow'd Horace so very close, that of necessity he must fall with him; and I may safely say it of this present age, that if we are not so great wits as Donne, yet certainly we are better poets.

But I have said enough, and it may be too much, on this subject. Will your Lordship be pleas'd to prolong my audience, only so far, till I tell you my own trivial thoughts, how a modern satire should be made. I will not deviate in the least from the precepts and examples of the ancients, who were always our best masters. I will only illustrate them, and discover some of the hidden beauties in their designs, that we thereby may form our own in imitation of them. Will you please but to observe, that Persius, the least in dignity of all the three, has notwithstanding been the first who has discover'd to us this important secret in the designing of a perfect satire — that it ought only to treat of one subject; to be confin'd to one particular theme; or at least, to one principally. If other vices occur in the management of the chief, they should only be transiently lash'd, and not be insisted on, so as to make the design double. As in a play of the English fashion, which we call a tragi-comedy, there is to be but one main design; and tho' there be an underplot, or second walk of comical characters and adventures, yet they are subservient to the chief fable, carried along under it, and helping to it; so that the drama may not seem a monster with two heads. Thus, the Copernican system of the planets makes the moon to be mov'd by the motion of the earth, and carried about her orb, as a dependent of hers. Mascardi, in his discourse of the *Doppia favola*, or double tale in plays, gives an instance of it in the famous pastoral of Guarini, call'd *Il Pastor Fido;* where Corisca and the Satyr are the under parts; yet we may observe that Corisca is brought into the body of the plot, and made subservient to it. 'T is certain that the divine wit of Horace was not ignorant of this rule — that a play, tho' it consists of many parts, must yet be one in the action, and must drive on the accomplishment of one design; for he gives this very precept, *sit quodvis simplex duntaxat et unum;* yet he seems not much to mind it in his *Satires*, many of them consisting of more arguments than one; and the second without dependence on the first. Casaubon has observ'd this before me, in his preference of Persius to Horace; and will have his own belov'd author to be the first who found out and introduc'd this method of confining himself to one subject. I know it may be urg'd in defense of Horace, that this unity is not necessary; because the very word *satura* signifies a dish plentifully stor'd with all variety of fruits and grains. Yet

Juvenal, who calls his poems a *farrago*, which is a word of the same signification with *satura*, has chosen to follow the same method of Persius, and not of Horace; and Boileau, whose example alone is a sufficient authority, has wholly confin'd himself, in all his *Satires*, to this unity of design. That variety, which is not to be found in any one satire, is at least in many, written on several occasions. And if variety be of absolute necessity in every one of them, according to the etymology of the word, yet it may arise naturally from one subject, as it is diversely treated, in the several subordinate branches of it, all relating to the chief. It may be illustrated accordingly with variety of examples in the subdivisions of it, and with as many precepts as there are members of it; which, altogether, may complete that *olla*, or hotchpotch, which is properly a satire.

Under this unity of theme, or subject, is comprehended another rule for perfecting the design of true satire. The poet is bound, and that *ex officio*, to give his reader some one precept of moral virtue, and to caution him against some one particular vice or folly. Other virtues, subordinate to the first, may be recommended under that chief head; and other vices or follies may be scourg'd, besides that which he principally intends. But he is chiefly to inculcate one virtue, and insist on that. Thus Juvenal, in every satire excepting the *First*, ties himself to one principal instructive point, or to the shunning of moral evil. Even in the *Sixth*, which seems only an arraignment of the whole sex of womankind, there is a latent admonition to avoid ill women, by shewing how very few who are virtuous and good are to be found amongst them. But this, tho' the wittiest of all his satires, has yet the least of truth or instruction in it. He has run himself into his old declamatory way, and almost forgotten that he was now setting in for a moral poet.

Persius is never wanting to us in some profitable doctrine, and in exposing the opposite vices to it. His kind of philosophy is one, which is the Stoic; and every satire is a comment on one particular dogma of that sect, unless we will except the *First*, which is against bad writers; and yet ev'n there he forgets not the precepts of the Porch. In general, all virtues are every-

where to be prais'd and recommended to practice; and all vices to be reprehended, and made either odious or ridiculous; or else there is a fundamental error in the whole design.

I have already declar'd who are the only persons that are the adequate object of private satire, and who they are that may properly be expos'd by name for public examples of vices and follies; and therefore I will trouble your Lordship no farther with them. Of the best and finest manner of satire, I have said enough in the comparison betwixt Juvenal and Horace: 't is that sharp, well-manner'd way of laughing a folly out of countenance, of which your Lordship is the best master in this age. I will proceed to the versification which is most proper for it, and add somewhat to what I have said already on that subject. The sort of verse which is call'd *burlesque*, consisting of eight syllables, or four feet, is that which our excellent Hudibras has chosen. I ought to have mention'd him before, when I spoke of Donne; but by a slip of an old man's memory he was forgotten. The worth of his poem is too well known to need my commendation, and he is above my censure. His satire is of the Varronian kind, tho' unmix'd with prose. The choice of his numbers is suitable enough to his design, as he has manag'd it; but in any other hand, the shortness of his verse, and the quick returns of rhyme, had debas'd the dignity of style. And besides, the double rhyme (a necessary companion of burlesque writing) is not so proper for manly satire; for it turns earnest too much to jest, and gives us a boyish kind of pleasure. It tickles awkwardly with a kind of pain, to the best sort of readers: we are pleas'd ungratefully, and, if I may say so, against our liking. We thank him not for giving us that unseasonable delight, when we know he could have given us a better, and more solid. He might have left that task to others, who, not being able to put in thought, can only make us grin with the excrescence of a word of two or three syllables in the close. 'T is, indeed, below so great a master to make use of such a little instrument. But his good sense is perpetually shining thro' all he writes; it affords us not the time of finding faults. We pass thro' the levity of his rhyme, and are immediately carried into some admirable useful thought. After all, he has chosen this kind of verse, and has written the best in it; and had he taken another, he would always have excell'd: as we say of a court favorite, that whatsoever his office be, he still makes it uppermost, and most beneficial to himself.

The quickness of your imagination, my Lord, has already prevented me; and you know beforehand, that I would prefer the verse of ten syllables, which we call the English heroic, to that of eight. This is truly my opinion; for this sort of number is more roomy: the thought can turn itself with greater ease in a larger compass. When the rhyme comes too thick upon us, it straitens the expression; we are thinking of the close, when we should be employ'd in adorning the thought. It makes a poet giddy with turning in a space too narrow for his imagination; he loses many beauties, without gaining one advantage. For a burlesque rhyme I have already concluded to be none; or, if it were, 't is more easily purchas'd in ten syllables than in eight. In both occasions 't is as in a tennis court, when the strokes of greater force are given, when we strike out and play at length. Tassoni and Boileau have left us the best examples of this way, in the *Secchia Rapita*, and the *Lutrin*; and next them Merlin Coccaius in his *Baldus*. I will speak only of the two former, because the last is written in Latin verse. The *Secchia Rapita* is an Italian poem, a satire of the Varronian kind. 'T is written in the stanza of eight, which is their measure for heroic verse. The words are stately, the numbers smooth, the turn both of thoughts and words is happy. The first six lines of the stanza seem majestical and severe; but the two last turn them all into a pleasant ridicule. Boileau, if I am not much deceiv'd, has model'd from hence his famous *Lutrin*. He had read the burlesque poetry of Scarron with some kind of indignation, as witty as it was, and found nothing in France that was worthy of his imitation; but he copied the Italian so well, that his own may pass for an original. He writes it in the French heroic verse, and calls it an heroic poem; his subject is trivial, but his verse is noble. I doubt not but he had Virgil in his eye, for we find many admirable imitations of him, and some parodies; as particularly this passage in the fourth of the *Æneids*:

Nec tibi diva parens, generis nec Dardanus auctor,
Perfide; sed duris genuit te cautibus horrens
Caucasus; Hyrcanæque admorunt ubera tigres:

which he thus translates, keeping to the words, but altering the sense:

Non, ton père à Paris ne fut point boulanger;
Et tu n'es point du sang de Gervais, horloger:
Ta mère ne fut point la maitresse d'un coche;
Caucase dans ses flancs te forma d'une roche:
Une tigresse affreuse, en quelque antre écarté,
Te fit, avec son lait, sucer sa cruauté.

And, as Virgil in his *Fourth Georgic*, of the Bees, perpetually raises the lowness of his subject by the loftiness of his words, and ennobles it by comparisons drawn from empires, and from monarchs:

Admiranda tibi levium spectacula rerum,
Magnanimosque duces, totiusque ordine gentis
Mores et studia, et populos, et prælia dicam;

and again:

Sed genus immortale manet; multosque per annos
Stat fortuna domus, et avi numerantur avorum;

we see Boileau pursuing him in the same flights, and scarcely yielding to his master. This, I think, my Lord, to be the most beautiful and most noble kind of satire. Here is the majesty of the heroic, finely mix'd with the venom of the other; and raising the delight which otherwise would be flat and vulgar, by the sublimity of the expression. I could say somewhat more of the delicacy of this and some other of his satires; but it might turn to his prejudice, if 't were carried back to France.

I have given your Lordship but this bare hint, in what verse and in what manner this sort of satire may best be manag'd. Had I time, I could enlarge on the beautiful turns of words and thoughts, which are as requisite in this, as in heroic poetry itself, of which this satire is undoubtedly a species. With these beautiful turns, I confess myself to have been unacquainted, till about twenty years ago, in a conversation which I had with that noble wit of Scotland, Sir George Mackenzie, he ask'd me why I did not imitate in my verses the turns of Mr. Waller and Sir John Denham, of which he repeated many to me. I had often read with pleasure, and with some profit, those two fathers of our English poetry, but had not seriously enough consider'd those beauties which give the last perfection to their works. Some sprinklings of this kind I had also formerly in my plays; but they were casual, and not design'd. But this hint, thus seasonably given me, first made me sensible of my own wants, and brought me afterwards to seek for the supply of them in other English authors. I look'd over the darling of my youth, the famous Cowley; there I found, instead of them, the points of wit, and quirks of epigram, even in the *Davideis*, a heroic poem, which is of an opposite nature to those puerilities; but no elegant turns either on the word or on the thought. Then I consulted a greater genius, (without offense to the *manes* of that noble author,) I mean Milton; but as he endeavors everywhere to express Homer, whose age had not arriv'd to that fineness, I found in him a true sublimity, lofty thoughts, which were cloth'd with admirable Grecisms, and ancient words, which he had been digging from the mines of Chaucer and of Spenser, and which, with all their rusticity, had somewhat of venerable in them. But I found not there neither that for which I look'd. At last I had recourse to his master, Spenser, the author of that immortal poem call'd *The Fairy Queen*, and there I met with that which I had been looking for so long in vain. Spenser had studied Virgil to as much advantage as Milton had done Homer, and amongst the rest of his excellencies had copied that. Looking farther into the Italian, I found Tasso had done the same; nay more, that all the sonnets in that language are on the turn of the first thought; which Mr. Walsh, in his late ingenious preface to his poems, has observ'd. In short, Virgil and Ovid are the two principal fountains of them in Latin poetry. And the French at this day are so fond of them, that they judge them to be the first beauties: *délicat et bien tourné* are the highest commendations which they bestow on somewhat which they think a masterpiece.

An example of the turn on words, amongst a thousand others, is that in the last book of Ovid's *Metamorphoses*:

Heu! quantum scelus est, in viscera, viscera condi!
Congestoque avidum pinguescere corpore corpus;
Alteriusque animantem animantis vivere leto.

An example on the turn both of thoughts and words is to be found in Catullus, in the complaint of Ariadne, when she was left by Theseus:

Tum jam nulla viro juranti fœmina credat;
Nulla viri speret sermones esse fideles;
Qui, dum aliquid cupiens animus prægestit
*   apisci,*
Nil metuunt jurare, nihil promittere parcunt:
Sed simul ac cupidæ mentis satiata libido est,
Dicta nihil metuere, nihil perjuria curant.

An extraordinary turn upon the words is that in Ovid's *Epistolæ Heroidum*, of Sappho to Phaon:

Si, nisi quæ forma poterit te digna videri,
Nulla futura tua est, nulla futura tua est.

Lastly, a turn, which I cannot say is absolutely on words, for the thought turns with them, is in the *Fourth Georgic* of Virgil; where Orpheus is to receive his wife from hell, on express condition not to look on her till she was come on earth:

Cum subita incautum dementia cepit amantem;
Ignoscenda quidem, scirent si ignoscere manes.

I will not burthen your Lordship with more of them, for I write to a master who understands them better than myself. But I may safely conclude them to be great beauties. I might descend also to the mechanic beauties of heroic verse; but we have yet no English *prosodia*, not so much as a tolerable dictionary, or a grammar; so that our language is in a manner barbarous; and what government will encourage any one, or more, who are capable of refining it, I know not: but nothing under a public expense can go thro' with it. And I rather fear a declination of the language, than hope an advancement of it in the present age.

I am still speaking to you, my Lord, tho', in all probability, you are already out of hearing. Nothing which my meanness can produce is worthy of this long attention. But I am come to the last petition of Abraham; if there be ten righteous lines in this vast preface, spare it for their sake; and also spare the next city, because it is but a little one.

I would excuse the performance of this translation, if it were all my own; but the better, tho' not the greater part, being the work of some gentlemen who have succeeded very happily in their undertaking, let their excellencies atone for my imperfections, and those of my sons. I have perus'd some of the satires which are done by other hands, and they seem to me as perfect in their kind as anything I have seen in English verse. The common way which we have taken is not a literal translation, but a kind of paraphrase; or somewhat which is yet more loose, betwixt a paraphrase and imitation. It was not possible for us, or any men, to have made it pleasant any other way. If rend'ring the exact sense of these authors, almost line for line, had been our business, Barten Holyday had done it already to our hands; and, by the help of his learned notes and illustrations, not only Juvenal and Persius, but, what yet is more obscure, his own verses, might be understood.

But he wrote for fame, and wrote to scholars; we write only for the pleasure and entertainment of those gentlemen and ladies, who, tho' they are not scholars, are not ignorant: persons of understanding and good sense, who, not having been conversant in the original, or at least not having made Latin verse so much their business as to be critics in it, would be glad to find if the wit of our two great authors be answerable to their fame and reputation in the world. We have, therefore, endeavor'd to give the public all the satisfaction we are able in this kind.

And if we are not altogether so faithful to our author, as our predecessors Holyday and Stapylton, yet we may challenge to ourselves this praise, that we shall be far more pleasing to our readers. We have follow'd our authors at greater distance, tho' not step by step, as they have done: for oftentimes they have gone so close, that they have trod on the heels of Juvenal and Persius, and hurt them by their too near approach. A noble author would not be pursued too close by a translator. We lose his spirit, when we think to take his body. The grosser part remains with us, but the soul is flown away in some noble expression, or some delicate turn of words or thought. Thus Holyday, who made this way his choice, seiz'd the meaning of Juvenal; but the poetry has always scap'd him.

They who will not grant me that pleasure is one of the ends of poetry, but that it is only a means of compassing the only end, which is instruction, must yet allow, that, without the means of pleasure, the instruction is but a bare and dry philosophy: a crude preparation of morals, which we may have from Aristotle and Epictetus, with more profit than from any poet. Neither Holyday nor Stapylton have imitated Juvenal in the poetical part of him, his diction and his elocution. Nor had they been poets, as neither of them were, yet, in the way they took, it was impossible for them to have succeeded in the poetic part.

The English verse which we call heroic consists of no more than ten syllables; the Latin hexameter sometimes rises to seventeen; as, for example, this verse in Virgil:

Pulverulenta putrem sonitu quatit ungula campum.

Here is the difference of no less than seven syllables in a line, betwixt the English and the Latin. Now the medium of these is about fourteen syllables; because the dactyl is a more frequent foot in hexameters than the spondee. But Holyday, without considering that he writ with the disadvantage of four syllables less in every verse, endeavors to make one of his lines to comprehend the sense of one of Juvenal's. According to the falsity of the proposition was the success. He was forc'd to crowd his verse with ill-sounding monosyllables, of which our barbarous language affords him a wild plenty; and by that means he arriv'd at his pedantic end, which was to make a literal translation. His verses have nothing of verse in them, but only the worst part of it, the rhyme; and that, into the bargain, is far from good. But, which is more intolerable, by cramming his ill-chosen and worse-sounding monosyllables so close together, the very sense which he endeavors to explain is become more obscure than that of his author; so that Holyday himself cannot be understood, without as large a commentary as that which he makes on his two authors. For my own part, I can make a shift to find the meaning of Juvenal without his notes; but his translation is more difficult than his author. And I find beauties in the Latin to recompense my pains; but, in Holyday and Stapylton, my ears, in the first place, are mortally offended; and then their sense is so perplex'd, that I return to the original, as the more pleasing task, as well as the more easy. This must be said for our translation,

that, if we give not the whole sense of Juvenal, yet we give the most considerable
part of it : we give it, in general, so clearly,
that few notes are sufficient to make us
intelligible. We make our author at least
appear in a poetic dress. We have actually
made him more sounding, and more elegant,
than he was before in English; and have endeavor'd to make him speak that kind of
English which he would have spoken had
he liv'd in England, and had written to this
age. If sometimes any of us (and 't is but
seldom) make him express the customs and
manners of our native country rather than
of Rome, 't is either when there was some
kind of analogy betwixt their customs and
ours, or when, to make him more easy to
vulgar understandings, we gave him those
manners which are familiar to us. But I
defend not this innovation; 't is enough if I
can excuse it. For, to speak sincerely, the
manners of nations and ages are not to be
confounded; we should either make them
English, or leave them Roman. If this can
neither be defended nor excus'd, let it be
pardon'd at least, because it is acknowledg'd;
and so much the more easily, as being a
fault which is never committed without some
pleasure to the reader.

Thus, my Lord, having troubled you with
a tedious visit, the best manners will be
shewn in the least ceremony. I will slip
away while your back is turn'd, and while
you are otherwise employ'd; with great confusion for having entertain'd you so long
with this discourse, and for having no other
recompense to make you, than the worthy
labors of my fellow-undertakers in this
work, and the thankful acknowledgments,
prayers, and perpetual good wishes, of,

MY LORD,
            Your Lordship's
        Most oblig'd, most humble,
    And most obedient Servant,
                    JOHN DRYDEN.
Aug. 18, 1692.

THE FIRST SATIRE OF
JUVENAL

THE ARGUMENT

The poet gives us first a kind of humorous
reason for his writing : that being provok'd
by hearing so many ill poets rehearse their

works, he does himself justice on them, by
giving them as bad as they bring. But since
no man will rank himself with ill writers,
't is easy to conclude, that if such wretches
could draw an audience, he thought it no
hard matter to excel them, and gain a greater
esteem with the public. Next he informs us
more openly, why he rather addicts himself
to satire, than any other kind of poetry. And
here he discovers that it is not so much his
indignation to ill poets, as to ill men, which
has prompted him to write. He therefore
gives us a summary and general view of the
vices and follies reigning in his time. So that
this first satire is the natural groundwork of
all the rest. Herein he confines himself to no
one subject, but strikes indifferently at all
men in his way : in every following satire he
has chosen some particular moral which he
would inculcate ; and lashes some particular vice or folly (an art with which our lampooners are not much acquainted). But our
poet being desirous to reform his own age,
and not daring to attempt it by an overt
act of naming living persons, inveighs only
against those who were infamous in the
times immediately preceding his, whereby
he not only gives a fair warning to great
men, that their memory lies at the mercy of
future poets and historians, but also, with
a finer stroke of his pen, brands ev'n the
living, and personates them under dead men's
names.

I have avoided as much as I could possibly
the borrow'd learning of marginal notes and
illustrations, and for that reason have translated this satire somewhat largely ; and freely
own (if it be a fault) that I have likewise
omitted most of the proper names, because I
thought they would not much edify the reader.
To conclude, if in two or three places I have
deserted all the commentators, 't is because I
thought they first deserted my author, or at
least have left him in so much obscurity, that
too much room is left for guessing.

STILL shall I hear, and never quit the
            score,
Stunn'd with hoarse Codrus'[1] *Theseid*, o'er
            and o'er ?
Shall this man's elegies and t'other's play
Unpunish'd murther a long summer's day ?
Huge *Telephus*,[2] a formidable page,
Cries vengeance; and *Orestes'*[3] bulky rage,
Unsatisfied with margins closely writ,
Foams o'er the covers, and not finish'd yet.
No man can take a more familiar note
Of his own home, than I of Vulcan's grot,

Or Mars his grove,[4] or hollow winds that
   blow   11
From Ætna's top, or tortur'd ghosts below.
I know by rote the fam'd exploits of
   Greece;
The Centaurs' fury, and the Golden Fleece;
Thro' the thick shades th' eternal scribbler
   bawls,
And shakes the statues on their pedestals.
The best and worst[5] on the same theme
   employs
His Muse, and plagues us with an equal
   noise.
   Provok'd by these incorrigible fools,
I left declaiming in pedantic schools;   20
Where, with men-boys, I strove to get re-
   nown,
Advising Sylla[6] to a private gown.
But, since the world with writing is pos-
   sess'd,
I'll versify in spite; and do my best,
To make as much waste paper as the
   rest.
   But why I lift aloft the Satire's rod,
And tread the path which fam'd Lucilius[7]
   trod,
Attend the causes which my Muse have led:
When sapless eunuchs mount the marriage-
   bed;
When mannish Mævia,[8] that two-handed
   whore,   30
Astride on horseback hunts the Tuscan boar;
When all our lords are by his wealth out-
   vied,
Whose razor[9] on my callow beard was
   tried;
When I behold the spawn of conquer'd
   Nile,
Crispinus,[10] both in birth and manners vile,
Pacing in pomp, with cloak of Tyrian dye,
Chang'd oft a day for needless luxury;
And finding oft occasion to be fann'd,
Ambitious to produce his lady-hand;
Charg'd with light summer-rings[11] his fin-
   gers sweat,   40
Unable to support a gem of weight —
Such fulsome objects meeting everywhere,
'T is hard to write, but harder to forbear.
   To view so lewd a town, and to refrain,
What hoops of iron could my spleen con-
   tain !
When pleading Matho,[12] borne abroad for
   air,
With his fat paunch fills his new-fashion'd
   chair,

And after him the wretch in pomp convey'd,
Whose evidence his lord and friend betray'd,
And but the wish'd occasion does attend
From the poor nobles the last spoils to
   rend,   51
Whom ev'n spies dread as their superior
   fiend,
And bribe with presents; or, when presents
   fail,
They send their prostituted wives for bail:
When night-performance holds the place of
   merit,
And brawn and back the next of kin dis-
   herit;
For such good parts are in preferment's
   way,
The rich old madam never fails to pay
Her legacies, by nature's standard giv'n,
One gains an ounce, another gains eleven:
A dear-bought bargain, all things duly
   weigh'd,   61
For which their thrice concocted blood is
   paid:
With looks as wan, as he who in the brake
At unawares has trod upon a snake;
Or play'd at Lyons[13] a declaiming prize,
For which the vanquish'd rhetorician dies.
   What indignation boils within my veins,
When perjur'd guardians, proud with im-
   pious gains,
Choke up the streets, too narrow for their
   trains !
Whose wards, by want betray'd, to crimes
   are led   70
Too foul to name, too fulsome to be read !
When he who pill'd his province scapes the
   laws,
And keeps his money, tho' he lost his cause:
His fine begg'd off, contemns his infamy,
Can rise at twelve, and get him drunk ere
   three;
Enjoys his exile, and, condemn'd in vain,
Leaves thee, prevailing province,[14] to com-
   plain !
   Such villainies rous'd Horace[15] into
   wrath;
And 't is more noble to pursue his path,
Than an old tale of Diomede to repeat,
Or lab'ring after Hercules to sweat,   81
Or wand'ring in the winding maze of
   Crete;
Or with the winged smith aloft to fly,
Or flutt'ring perish with his foolish boy.
   With what impatience must the Muse
   behold

The wife by her procuring husband sold ?
For tho' the law makes null th' adulterer's
   deed
Of lands to her, the cuckold may succeed;
Who his taught eyes up to the ceiling
   throws,   89
And sleeps all over but his wakeful nose.
When he dares hope a colonel's command,
Whose coursers kept, ran out his father's
   land;
Who, yet a stripling, Nero's chariot ⎤
   drove,   ⎥
Whirl'd o'er the streets, while his vain ⎬
   master strove   ⎥
With boasted art to please his eunuch-   ⎦
   love.[16]
Would it not make a modest author dare
To draw his table-book within the square,
And fill with notes, when lolling at his ease,
Mæcenas-like,[17] the happy rogue he sees 99
Borne by six wearied slaves in open view,
Who cancel'd an old will and forg'd a new;
Made wealthy at the small expense of sign-
   ing
With a wet seal, and a fresh interlining ?
   The lady, next, requires a lashing line,
Who squeez'd a toad into her husband's
   wine:
So well the fashionable med'cine thrives,
That now 't is practic'd ev'n by country
   wives;
Pois'ning, without regard of fame or fear:
And spotted corps are frequent on the bier.
Wouldst thou to honors and preferments
   climb,   110
Be bold in mischief, dare some mighty
   crime,
Which dungeons, death, or banishment de-
   serves:
For virtue is but dryly prais'd, and sterves.
Great men, to great crimes, owe their ⎤
   plate emboss'd,   ⎥
Fair palaces, and furniture of cost;   ⎬
And high commands: a sneaking sin is ⎥
   lost.   ⎦
Who can behold that rank old lecher keep
His son's corrupted wife, and hope to
   sleep ? [18]
Or that male-harlot, or that unfledg'd boy,
Eager to sin, before he can enjoy ?   120
If nature could not, anger would indite
Such woful stuff as I or S——ll write.
   Count from the time, since old Deuca-
   lion's [19] boat,
Rais'd by the flood, did on Parnassus float;

And scarcely mooring on the cliff, implor'd
An oracle how man might be restor'd;
When soften'd stones and vital breath en-
   sued,
And virgins naked were by lovers view'd;
Whatever since that Golden Age was done,
What humankind desires, and what they
   shun,   130
Rage, passions, pleasures, impotence of will,
Shall this satirical collection fill.
   What age so large a crop of vices bore,
Or when was avarice extended more ?
When were the dice with more profusion
   thrown ?
The well-fill'd fob not emptied now alone,
But gamesters for whole patrimonies play;
The steward brings the deeds which must
   convey
The lost estate: what more than madness
   reigns,
When one short sitting many hundreds
   drains,   140
And not enough is left him to supply ⎤
Board-wages, or a footman's livery ?   ⎬
   What age so many summer seats did ⎥
     see ?   ⎦
Or which of our forefathers far'd so well,
As on seven dishes, at a private meal?
Clients of old were feasted; now a poor
Divided dole is dealt at th' outward door,
Which by the hungry rout is soon dis-
   patch'd:
The paltry largess, too, severely watch'd
Ere given; and every face observ'd with
   care,   150
That no intruding guest usurp a share.
Known, you receive: the crier calls aloud ⎤
Our old nobility of Trojan blood,   ⎬
Who gape among the crowd for their   ⎥
   precarious food.   ⎦
The prætors' and the tribunes' voice is
   heard;
The freedman justles, and will be preferr'd;
"First come, first serv'd," he cries; "and I,
   in spite
Of your great lordships, will maintain my
   right.
Tho' born a slave, tho' my torn ears are
   bor'd,[20]
'T is not the birth, 't is money makes the
   lord.   160
The rents of five fair houses I receive;
What greater honors can the purple give ?
The poor patrician [21] is reduc'd to keep
In melancholy walks a grazier's sheep:

Not Pallas nor Licinius [22] had my treasure;
Then let the sacred tribunes wait my lei-
    sure.
Once a poor rogue, 't is true, I trod the
    street,
And trudg'd to Rome upon my naked
    feet:
Gold is the greatest god; tho' yet we see
No temples rais'd to Money's majesty, 170
No altars fuming to her pow'r divine,
Such as to Valor, Peace, and Virtue shine,
And Faith, and Concord: where the stork ⎤
    on high [23]   ⎟
Seems to salute her infant progeny,   ⎬
Presaging pious love with her auspicious ⎟
    cry."   ⎦
But since our knights and senators account
To what their sordid begging vails amount,
Judge what a wretched share the poor at-
    tends,
Whose whole subsistence on those alms de-
    pends !
Their household fire, their raiment, and
    their food,   180
Prevented by those harpies; [24] when a wood
Of litters thick besiege the donor's gate,
And begging lords and teeming ladies wait
The promis'd dole: nay, some have learn'd
    the trick
To beg for absent persons; feign them sick,
Close mew'd in their sedans, for fear of ⎤
    air;   ⎟
And for their wives produce an empty ⎬
    chair.   ⎟
"This is my spouse: dispatch her with her ⎟
    share." [25]   ⎦
'T is Galla." [25] "Let her ladyship but
    peep."
"No, sir, 't is pity to disturb her sleep." 190
Such fine employments our whole days
    divide:
The salutations of the morning tide
Call up the sun; those ended, to the hall
We wait the patron, hear the lawyers bawl;
Then to the statues; [26] where, amidst the ⎤
    race   ⎟
Of conqu'ring Rome, some Arab shews ⎬
    his face,   ⎟
Inscrib'd with titles, and profanes the ⎟
    place;   ⎦
Fit to be piss'd against, and somewhat more.
The great man, home conducted, shuts his
    door: 199
Old clients, wearied out with fruitless care,
Dismiss their hopes of eating, and despair;

Tho' much against the grain, forc'd to re-
    tire,
Buy roots for supper, and provide a fire.
Meantime his lordship lolls within at ease,
Pamp'ring his paunch with foreign rarities;
Both sea and land are ransack'd for the
    feast,
And his own gut the sole invited guest.
Such plate, such tables, dishes dress'd so
    well,
That whole estates are swallow'd at a meal.
Ev'n parasites are banish'd from his board:
(At once a sordid and luxurious lord:) 211
Prodigious throat, for which whole boars
    are dress'd;
(A creature form'd to furnish out a feast.)
But present punishment pursues his maw,
When, surfeited and swell'd, the peacock
    raw
He bears into the bath; whence want of
    breath,
Repletions, apoplex, intestate death.
His fate makes table talk, divulg'd with
    scorn,
And he, a jest, into his grave is borne.
No age can go beyond us; future times 220
Can add no farther to the present crimes.
Our sons but the same things can wish ⎤
    and do;   ⎟
Vice is at stand, and at the highest flow. ⎬
Then, Satire, spread thy sails; take all ⎟
    the winds can blow.   ⎦
Some may, perhaps, demand what Muse can
    yield
Sufficient strength for such a spacious field;
From whence can be deriv'd so large a
    vein,
Bold truths to speak, and spoken to main-
    tain,
When godlike freedom is so far bereft
The noble mind, that scarce the name is
    left.   230
Ere *scandalum magnatum* was begot,
No matter if the great forgave or not:
But if that honest license now you take, ⎤
If into rogues omnipotent you rake, ⎬
Death is your doom, impal'd upon a stake, ⎦
Smear'd o'er with wax, and set on fire, to
    light
The streets, and make a dreadful blaze by
    night.
Shall they, who drench'd three uncles in
    a draught
Of pois'nous juice, be then in triumph
    brought,

Make lanes among the people where they ⎫
    go,   240 ⎪
And, mounted high on downy chariots, ⎬
    throw ⎪
Disdainful glances on the crowd below ? ⎭
Be silent, and beware, if such you see;
'T is defamation but to say: " That 's he ! "
Against bold Turnus [27] the great Trojan
    arm,
Amidst their strokes the poet gets no
    harm:
Achilles may in epic verse be slain,
And none of all his Myrmidons complain:
Hylas may drop his pitcher, none will cry;
Not if he drown himself for company: 250
But when Lucilius brandishes his pen,
And flashes in the face of guilty men,
A cold sweat stands in drops on ev'ry part;
And rage succeeds to tears, revenge to
    smart.
Muse, be advis'd; 't is past consid'ring time,
When enter'd once the dangerous lists of
    rhyme:
Since none the living villains dare implead,
Arraign them in the persons of the dead.

EXPLANATORY NOTES ON THE FIRST SATIRE

1 *Codrus*, or it may be Cordus, a bad poet who wrote the life and actions of Theseus.

2 *Telephus*, the name of a tragedy.

3 *Orestes*, another tragedy.

4 *Mars his grove*. Some commentators take this grove to be a place where poets were us'd to repeat their works to the people ; but more probably, both this and Vulcan's grot, or cave, and the rest of the places and names here mention'd, are only meant for the commonplaces of Homer in his *Iliads* and *Odysses*.

5 *The best and worst ;* that is, the best and the worst poets.

6 *Advising Sylla*, &c. This was one of the themes given in the schools of rhetoricians, in the deliberative kind ; whether Sylla should lay down the supreme power of dictatorship, or still keep it.

7 *Lucilius*, the first satirist of the Romans, who wrote long before Horace.

8 *Mœvia*, a name put for any impudent or mannish woman.

9 *Whose razor*, &c. Juvenal's barber now grown wealthy.

10 *Crispinus*, an Egyptian slave ; now by his riches transform'd into a nobleman.

11 *Charg'd with light summer-rings*, &c. The Romans were grown so effeminate in Juvenal's time, that they wore light rings in the summer and heavier in the winter.

12 *Matho*, a famous lawyer, mention'd in other places by Juvenal and Martial.

13 *At Lyons*. A city in France, where annual sacrifices and games were made in honor of Augustus Cæsar.

14 *Prevailing province*, &c. Here the poet complains that the governors of provinces, being accus'd for their unjust exactions, tho' they were condemn'd at their trials, yet got off by bribery.

15 *Horace*, who wrote satires: 't is more noble, says our author, to imitate him in that way, than to write the labors of Hercules, the sufferings of Diomedes and his followers, or the flight of Dædalus, who made the Labyrinth, and the death of his son Icarus.

16 *His eunuch-love*. Nero married Sporus, an eunuch ; tho' it may be, the poet meant Nero's mistress in man's apparel.

17 *Mœcenas-like*. Mæcenas is often tax'd by Seneca and others for his effeminacy.

18 *And hope to sleep*. The meaning is, that the very consideration of such a crime will hinder a virtuous man from taking his repose.

19 *Deucalion* and Pyrrha, when the world was drown'd, escap'd to the top of Mount Parnassus, and were commanded to restore mankind, by throwing stones over their heads: the stones he threw became men, and those she threw became women.

20 *Tho' my torn ears are bor'd*. The ears of all slaves were bor'd, as a mark of their servitude ; which custom is still usual in the East Indies, and in other parts, even for whole nations, who bore prodigious holes in their ears, and wear vast weights at them.

21 *The poor patrician*. The poor nobleman.

22 *Pallas, or Licinius*. Pallas, a slave freed by Claudius Cæsar, and rais'd by his favor to great riches. Licinius was another wealthy freedman, belonging to Augustus.

23 *Where the stork on high*, &c. Perhaps the storks were us'd to build on the top of the temple dedicated to Concord.

24 *Prevented by those harpies*. He calls the Roman knights, &c., harpies, or devourers. In those days the rich made doles intended for the poor ; but the great were either so coveteous, or so needy, that they came in their litters to demand their shares of the largess, and thereby prevented, and consequently starv'd, the poor.

25 *'T is Galla*, &c. The meaning is, that noblemen would cause empty litters to be carried to the giver's door, pretending their wives were within them. " 'T is Galla," that is, " my wife ; " the next words, " Let her ladyship but peep," are of the servant who distributes the dole ; " Let me see her, that I may be sure she is within the litter." The husband answers : " She is asleep, and to open the litter would disturb her rest."

26 *Next to the statues*, &c. The poet here tells you how the idle pass'd their time ; in going first to the levees of the great, then to the hall, that is, to the temple of Apollo, to hear the lawyers plead, then to the marketplace of Augustus, where the statues of the famous Romans were set in ranks on pedestals, amongst which statues were seen those of foreigners, such as Arabs, &c., who, for no desert, but only on the account of

their wealth or favor, were plac'd amongst the noblest

27 *Against bold Turnus, &c.* A poet may safely write an heroic poem, such as that of Virgil who describes the duel of Turnus and Æneas; or of Homer, who writes of Achilles and Hector; or the death of Hylas, the catamite of Hercules, who, stooping for water, dropp'd his pitcher, and fell into the well after it. But 't is dangerous to write satire, like Lucilius.

THE THIRD SATIRE OF JUVENAL

THE ARGUMENT

The story of this satire speaks itself. Umbritius, the suppos'd friend of Juvenal, and himself a poet, is leaving Rome, and retiring to Cumæ. Our author accompanies him out of town. Before they take leave of each other, Umbritius tells his friend the reasons which oblige him to lead a private life, in an obscure place. He complains that an honest man cannot get his bread at Rome; that none but flatterers make their fortunes there; that Grecians and other foreigners raise themselves by those sordid arts which he describes, and against which he bitterly inveighs. He reckons up the several inconveniencies which arise from a city life, and the many dangers which attend it; upbraids the noblemen with covetousness, for not rewarding good poets; and arraigns the government for starving them. The great art of this satire is particularly shown in commonplaces, and drawing in as many vices as could naturally fall into the compass of it.

GRIEV'D tho' I am an ancient friend to lose, }
I like the solitary seat he chose, }
In quiet Cumæ [1] fixing his repose: }
Where, far from noisy Rome, secure he lives,
And one more citizen to Sibyl gives;
The road to Bajæ,[2] and that soft recess,
Which all the gods with all their bounty bless.
Tho' I in Prochyta [3] with greater ease
Could live, than in a street of palaces.   9
What scene so desart, or so full of fright, }
As tow'ring houses tumbling in the night, }
And Rome on fire beheld by its own blazing light ? }
But worse than all, the clatt'ring tiles; and worse
Than thousand padders, is the poet's curse;

Rogues that in dog days [4] cannot rhyme forbear:
But without mercy read, and make you hear.
Now while my friend, just ready to depart,
Was packing all his goods in one poor cart;
He stopp'd a little at the Conduit-gate,
Where Numa [5] model'd once the Roman State,   20
In mighty councils with his nymph [6] retir'd:
Tho' now the sacred shades and founts are hir'd
By banish'd Jews, who their whole wealth can lay
In a small basket, on a wisp of hay;
Yet such our avarice is, that every tree
Pays for his head; not sleep itself is free:
Nor place, nor persons, now are sacred held;
From their own grove the Muses are expell'd.
Into this lonely vale our steps we bend,
I and my sullen discontented friend: 30
The marble caves, and aqueducts we view;
But how adult'rate now, and different from the true !
How much more beauteous had the fountain been,
Embellish'd with her first created green,
Where crystal streams thro' living turf had run,
Contented with an urn of native stone !
   Then thus Umbritius (with an angry frown,
And looking back on this degen'rate town):
" Since noble arts in Rome have no support,
And ragged virtue not a friend at court,   40
No profit rises from th' ungrateful stage,
My poverty encreasing with my age,
'T is time to give my just disdain a vent,
And, cursing, leave so base a government.
Where Dædalus[7] his borrow'd wings laid by,
To that obscure retreat I choose to fly:
While yet few furrows on my face are seen, }
While I walk upright, and old age is green, }
And Lachesis [8] has somewhat left to spin. }
Now, now 't is time to quit this cursed place,   50
And hide from villains my too honest face:
Here let Arturius [9] live, and such as he;
Such manners will with such a town agree.
Knaves who in full assemblies have the knack

Of turning truth to lies, and white to black;
Can hire large houses, and oppress the poor
By farm'd excise; can cleanse the common
    shore,
And rent the fishery; can bear the dead;⎫
And teach their eyes dissembled tears to⎪
    shed: ⎪
All this for gain; for gain they sell their ⎬
    very head.   60⎭
These fellows (see what Fortune's pow'r can
    do)
Were once the minstrels of a country show:
Follow'd the prizes thro' each paltry town,
By trumpet-cheeks and bloated faces known.
But now, grown rich, on drunken holi-
    days,
At their own costs exhibit public plays;
Where, influenc'd by the rabble's bloody
    will,
With thumbs bent back,[10] they popularly
    kill.
From thence return'd, their sordid avarice
    rakes
In excrements again, and hires the jakes. 70
Why hire they not the town, not ev'ry-
    thing,
Since such as they have Fortune in a string,
Who, for her pleasure, can her fools ad-
    vance,
And toss 'em topmost on the wheel of
    chance ?
What's Rome to me, what bus'ness have I
    there,
I who can neither lie, nor falsely swear ?
Nor praise my patron's undeserving rhymes,
Nor yet comply with him, nor with his
    times;
Unskill'd in schemes by planets to foreshow,
Like canting rascals, how the wars will go:
I neither will, nor can prognosticate   81
To the young gaping heir, his father's fate;
Nor in the entrails of a toad have pried,
Nor carried bawdy presents to a bride:
For want of these town virtues, thus, alone,
I go conducted on my way by none:
Like a dead member from the body rent;
Maim'd, and unuseful to the government.
    " Who now is lov'd, but he who loves the
    times,
Conscious of close intrigues, and dipp'd in
    crimes;   90
Lab'ring with secrets which his bosom burn,
Yet never must to public light return ?
They get reward alone who can betray:
For keeping honest counsels none will pay.

He who can Verres,[11] when he will, accuse,
The purse of Verres may at pleasure use:
But let not all the gold which Tagus [12] hides,
And pays the sea in tributary tides,
Be bribe sufficient to corrupt thy breast,
Or violate with dreams thy peaceful rest. 100
Great men with jealous eyes the friend be-
    hold,
Whose secrecy they purchase with their
    gold.
    " I haste to tell thee, nor shall shame
    oppose,
What confidents our wealthy Romans chose;
And whom I most abhor: to speak my mind,
I hate, in Rome, a Grecian town to find:
To see the scum of Greece transplanted
    here,
Receiv'd like gods, is what I cannot bear.
Nor Greeks alone, but Syrians here abound;
Obscene Orontes,[13] diving under ground, 110
Conveys his wealth to Tiber's [14] hungry
    shores,
And fattens Italy with foreign whores:
Hether their crooked harps and customs
    come;
All find receipt in hospitable Rome.
The barbarous harlots crowd the public⎫
    place: ⎪
Go, fools, and purchase an unclean em- ⎬
    brace;   ⎪
The painted miter court, and the more ⎪
    painted face.   ⎭
Old Romulus,[15] and Father Mars, look⎫
    down !   ⎪
Your herdsman primitive, your homely ⎬
    clown   ⎪
Is turn'd a beau in a loose tawdry gown. ⎭
His once unkemb'd and horrid locks, be-
    hold   121
Stilling sweet oil: his neck inchain'd with
    gold;
Aping the foreigners, in ev'ry dress,
Which, bought at greater cost, becomes
    him less.
Meantime they wisely leave their native
    land;
From Sicyon, Samos, and from Alaband,
And Amydon, to Rome they swarm in
    shoals:
So sweet and easy is the gain from fools.
Poor refugees at first, they purchase here;
And, soon as denizen'd, they domineer; 130
Grow to the great flatt'ring servile rout:
Work themselves inward, and their patrons
    out:

Quick - witted, brazen - fac'd, with fluent
    tongues,
Patient of labors, and dissembling wrongs.
Riddle me this, and guess him if you can,
Who bears a nation in a single man ?
A cook, a conjurer, a rhetorician, ⎫
A painter, pedant, a geometrician, ⎬
A dancer on the ropes, and a physician. ⎭
All things the hungry Greek exactly knows:
And bid him go to heav'n, to heav'n he
    goes: 141
In short, no Scythian, Moor, or Thracian
    born,
But in that town [16] which arms and arts
    adorn.
Shall he be plac'd above me at the board,
In purple cloth'd, and lolling like a lord ?
Shall he before me sign, whom t'other ⎫
    day ⎪
A small-craft vessel hither did convey; ⎬
Where, stow'd with prunes, and rotten ⎪
    figs, he lay ? ⎭
How little is the privilege become
Of being born a citizen of Rome !   150
The Greeks get all by fulsome flatteries;
A most peculiar stroke they have at lies.
They make a wit of their insipid friend;
His blobber lips, and beetle brows commend;
His long crane neck, and narrow shoulders
    praise —
You 'd think they were describing Hercules.
A creaking voice for a clear treble goes;
Tho' harsher than a cock that treads and
    crows.
We can as grossly praise; but, to our grief,
No flatt'ry but from Grecians gains belief.
Besides these qualities, we must agree 161
They mimic better on the stage than we:
The wife, the whore, the shepherdess they
    play,
In such a free, and such a graceful way,
That we believe a very woman shown,
And fancy something underneath the gown.
But not Antiochus, nor Stratocles,[17] ⎫
Our ears and ravish'd eyes can only ⎬
    please: ⎪
The nation is compos'd of such as these. ⎭
All Greece is one comedian: laugh, and
    they   170
Return it louder than an ass can bray:
Grieve, and they grieve; if you weep ⎫
    silently, ⎪
There seems a silent echo in their eye: ⎬
They cannot mourn like you; but they ⎪
    can cry. ⎭

Call for a fire, their winter clothes they
    take:
Begin but you to shiver, and they shake:
In frost and snow, if you complain of heat,
They rub th' unsweating brow, and swear
    they sweat.
We live not on the square with such as
    these;   179
Such are our betters who can better please;
Who day and night are like a looking-glass,
Still ready to reflect their patron's face;
The panegyric hand, and lifted eye,
Prepar'd for some new piece of flattery.
Ev'n nastiness occasions will afford;
They praise a belching, or well-pissing lord.
Besides, there 's nothing sacred, nothing free
From bold attempts of their rank lechery.
Thro' the whole family their labors run; ⎫
The daughter is debauch'd, the wife is ⎪
    won: 190 ⎬
Nor scapes the bridegroom, or the bloom- ⎪
    ing son. ⎭
If none they find for their lewd purpose fit,
They with the walls and very floors commit.
They search the secrets of the house, and
    so
Are worship'd there, and fear'd for what
    they know.
" And, now we talk of Grecians, cast a ⎫
    view ⎪
On what, in schools, their men of morals ⎬
    do; ⎪
A rigid Stoic [18] his own pupil slew: ⎭
A friend, against a friend, of his own cloth,
Turn'd evidence, and murther'd on his oath.
What room is left for Romans in a town 201
Where Grecians rule, and cloaks control
    the gown ?
Some Diphilus, or some Protogenes,[19]
Look sharply out, our senators to seize:
Engross 'em wholly, by their native art,
And fear no rivals in their bubble's heart:
One drop of poison in my patron's ear,
One slight suggestion of a senseless fear,
Infus'd with cunning, serves to ruin me;
Disgrac'd and banish'd from the family. 210
In vain forgotten services I boast;
My long dependence in an hour is lost:
Look round the world, what country will
    appear,
Where friends are left with greater ease
    than here ?
At Rome (nor think me partial to the poor)
All offices of ours are out of door:
In vain we rise, and to their levees run:

My lord himself is up, before, and gone;
The prætor bids his lictors mend their pace,
Lest his colleague outstrip him in the
　　race;　　　　　　　　　　　　　　220
The childless matrons are, long since,
　　awake,
And for affronts the tardy visits take.
　" 'T is frequent, here, to see a freeborn
　　son
On the left hand of a rich hireling run;
Because the wealthy rogue can throw away,
For half a brace of bouts, a tribune's pay:
But you, poor sinner, tho' you love the vice
And like the whore, demur upon the price;
And, frighted with the wicked sum, forbear
To lend a hand, and help her from the
　　chair.　　　　　　　　　　　　　230
　" Produce a witness of unblemish'd life,
Holy as Numa, or as Numa's wife,
Or him who bid [20] th' unhallow'd flames
　　retire,
And snatch'd the trembling goddess from
　　the fire;
The question is not put, how far extends
His piety, but what he yearly spends:
Quick, to the bus'ness; how he lives and
　　eats;
How largely gives; how splendidly he
　　treats;
How many thousand acres feed his sheep;
What are his rents; what servants does he
　　keep?　　　　　　　　　　　　　240
Th' account is soon cast up; the judges
　　rate
Our credit in the court by our estate.
Swear by our gods, or those the Greeks
　　adore,
Thou art as sure forsworn, as thou art poor;
The poor must gain their bread by per-⎫
　　jury;　　　　　　　　　　　　　　｜
And even the gods, that other means ⎬
　　deny,　　　　　　　　　　　　　　｜
In conscience must absolve 'em, when ｜
　　they lie.　　　　　　　　　　　　⎭
　" Add, that the rich have still a gibe in
　　store;
And will be monstrous witty on the poor:
For the torn surtout and the tatter'd vest,
The wretch and all his wardrobe are a jest;
The greasy gown, sullied with often turn-
　　ing,　　　　　　　　　　　　　　252
Gives a good hint, to say: ' The man 's in
　　mourning: '
Or if the shoe be ripp'd, or patches put:
' He 's wounded! see the plaster on his foot.'

Want is the scorn of ev'ry wealthy fool;
And wit in rags is turn'd to ridicule.
　" ' Pack hence, and from the cover'd
　　　benches rise,'
The master of the ceremonies cries,
' This is no place for you, whose small estate
Is not the value of the settled rate;　　261
The sons of happy punks, the pander's ⎫
　　heir,　　　　　　　　　　　　　　｜
Are privileg'd to sit in triumph there, ⎬
To clap the first, and rule the theater. ⎭
Up to the galleries, for shame, retreat;
For, by the Roscian law,[21] the poor can
　　claim no seat.'
Who ever brought to his rich daughter's bed
The man that poll'd but twelvepence for
　　his head?
Who ever nam'd a poor man for his heir,
Or call'd him to assist the judging chair?
The poor were wise, who, by the rich op-
　　press'd,　　　　　　　　　　　　271
Withdrew, and sought a sacred place of
　　rest.
Once they did well, to free themselves from
　　scorn;
But had done better never to return.
Rarely they rise by virtue's aid, who lie
Plung'd in the depth of helpless poverty.
　" At Rome 't is worse; where house-⎫
　　rent by the year　　　　　　　　　｜
And servants' bellies cost so dev'lish dear; ⎬
And tavern bills run high for hungry ｜
　　cheer.　　　　　　　　　　　　　｜
To drink or eat in earthenware we ⎨
　　scorn,　　　　　　　　　　　　280 ｜
Which cheaply country cupboards does ⎬
　　adorn;　　　　　　　　　　　　　｜
And coarse blue hoods on holidays are ｜
　　worn.　　　　　　　　　　　　　⎭
Some distant parts of Italy are known,
Where none, but only dead men,[22] wear a
　　gown;
On theaters of turf, in homely state,
Old plays they act, old feasts they cele-
　　brate;
The same rude song returns upon the crowd,
And, by tradition, is for wit allow'd.
The mimic yearly gives the same delights;
And in the mother's arms the clownish in-
　　fant frights.　　　　　　　　　　290
Their habits (undistinguish'd by degree) ⎫
Are plain, alike; the same simplicity, ⎬
Both on the stage, and in the pit, you see. ⎭
In his white cloak the magistrate appears;
The country bumpkin the same liv'ry wears.

But here, attir'd beyond our purse we go,
For useless ornament and flaunting show:
We take on trust, in purple robes to shine;
And poor, are yet ambitious to be fine.
This is a common vice, tho' all things here
Are sold, and sold unconscionably dear. 301
What will you give that Cossus [23] may but
    view
Your face, and in the crowd distinguish
    you;
May take your incense like a gracious god,
And answer only with a civil nod ?
To please our patrons, in this vicious age,
We make our entrance by the fav'rite page;
Shave his first down, and when he polls his
    hair,
The consecrated locks to temples bear;
Pay tributary cracknels, which he sells, 310
And, with our offerings, help to raise his
    vails.
    " Who fears, in country towns, a house's
    fall,
Or to be caught betwixt a riven wall ?
But we inhabit a weak city, here;
Which buttresses and props but scarcely
    bear:
And 't is the village mason's daily calling,
To keep the world's metropolis from fall-
    ing,
To cleanse the gutters, and the chinks to
    close,
And, for one night, secure his lord's repose.
At Cumæ we can sleep, quite round the
    year, 320
Nor falls, nor fires, nor nightly dangers fear;
While rolling flames from Roman turrets
    fly,
And the pale citizens for buckets cry.
Thy neighbor has remov'd his wretched
    store,
(Few hands will rid the lumber of the
    poor;)
Thy own third story smokes, while thou,
    supine,
Art drench'd in fumes of undigested wine.
For if the lowest floors already burn,
Cocklofts and garrets soon will take the
    turn,
Where thy tame pigeons [24] next the tiles
    were bred, 330
Which, in their nests unsafe, are timely fled.
    " Codrus [25] had but one bed, so short to
    boot,
That his short wife's short legs hung dan-
    gling out;

His cupboard's head six earthen pitchers
    grac'd,
Beneath 'em was his trusty tankard plac'd;
And, to support this noble plate, there lay
A bending Chiron cast from honest clay;
His few Greek books a rotten chest con-
    tain'd,
Whose covers much of moldiness com-
    plain'd: 339
Where mice and rats devour'd poetic bread,
And with heroic verse luxuriously were fed.
'T is true, poor Codrus nothing had to boast,
And yet poor Codrus all that nothing lost;
Begg'd naked thro' the streets of wealthy
    Rome;
And found not one to feed, or take him
    home.
    " But if the palace of Arturius burn,
The nobles change their clothes, the ma-
    trons mourn;
The city prætor will no pleadings hear; ⎫
The very name of fire we hate and fear,   ⎬
And look aghast, as if the Gauls were   ⎪
    here. 350 ⎭
While yet it burns, th' officious nation flies,
Some to condole, and some to bring supplies:
One sends him marble to rebuild; and one
White naked statues of the Parian stone,
The work of Polyclete, that seem to live;
While others images for altars give;
One books and screens, and Pallas to the
    breast;
Another bags of gold; and he gives best.
Childless Arturius, vastly rich before,
Thus by his losses multiplies his store; 360
Suspected for accomplice to the fire,
That burnt his palace but to build it higher.
    " But, could you be content to bid adieu
To the dear playhouse, and the players too;
Sweet country seats are purchas'd ev'ry- ⎫
    where,   ⎪
With lands and gardens, at less price ⎬
    than here   ⎪
You hire a darksome doghole by the year: ⎭
A small convenience, decently prepar'd,
A shallow well, that rises in your yard,
That spreads his easy crystal streams
    around, 370
And waters all the pretty spot of ground.
There, love the fork, thy garden cultivate,
And give thy frugal friends a Pythago-
    rean treat. [26]
'T is somewhat to be lord of some small
    ground,
In which a lizard may, at least, turn round.

" 'T is frequent, here, for want of sleep
  to die;
Which fumes of undigested feasts deny;
And, with imperfect heat, in languid
  stomachs fry.
What house secure from noise the poor can
  keep,
When ev'n the rich can scarce afford to
  sleep ?   380
So dear it costs to purchase rest in Rome;
And hence the sources of diseases come.
The drover who his fellow-drover meets
In narrow passages of winding streets;
The wagoners, that curse their standing
  teams,
Would wake ev'n drowsy Drusus from his
  dreams.
And yet the wealthy will not brook de-
  lay,
But sweep above our heads; and make
  their way,
In lofty litters borne, and read and write,
Or sleep at ease: the shutters make it
  night.   390
Yet still he reaches, first, the public place:
The prease before him stops the client's
  pace.
The crowd that follows crush his panting
  sides,
And trip his heels; he walks not, but he
  rides.
One elbows him, one justles in the shole,
A rafter breaks his head, or chairman's
  pole:
Stocking'd with loads of fat town-dirt
  he goes;
And some rogue-soldier, with his hob-
  nail'd shoes,
Indents his legs behind in bloody rows.
" See with what smoke our doles we
  celebrate: 400
A hundred guests, invited, walk in state;
A hundred hungry slaves, with their
  Dutch kitchens, wait.
Huge pans the wretches on their heads
  must bear,
Which scarce gigantic Corbulo [27] could
  rear:
Yet they must walk upright beneath the
  load;
Nay, run, and, running, blow the sparkling
  flames abroad.
Their coats, from botching newly brought,
  are torn;
Unwieldy timber-trees in wagons borne,

Stretch'd at their length, beyond their car-
  riage lie,
That nod, and threaten ruin from on high;
For, should their axle break, its over-
  throw   411
Would crush, and pound to dust, the
  crowd below;
Nor friends their friends, nor sires their
  sons could know:
Nor limbs, nor bones, nor carcass would
  remain:
But a mash'd heap, a hotchpotch of the
  slain;
One vast destruction; not the soul alone,
But bodies, like the soul, invisible are
  flown.
Meantime, unknowing of their fellows'
  fate,
The servants wash the platter, scour the
  plate,
Then blow the fire, with puffing cheeks,
  and lay   420
The rubbers, and the bathing-sheets dis-
  play;
And oil them first; and each is handy in
  his way.
But he, for whom this busy care they take,
Poor ghost, is wand'ring by the Stygian
  lake;
Affrighted with the ferryman's [28] grim face,
New to the horrors of that uncouth place,
His passage begs with unregarded pray'r,
And wants two farthings to discharge his
  fare.
" Return we to the dangers of the night:
And, first, behold our houses' dreadful
  height;   430
From whence come broken potsherds
  tumbling down;
And leaky ware, from garret windows
  thrown:
Well may they break our heads, that
  mark the flinty stone.
'T is want of sense to sup abroad too late,
Unless thou first hast settled thy estate.
As many fates attend, thy steps to meet,
As there are waking windows in the street.
Bless the good gods, and think thy chance
  is rare,
To have a pisspot only for thy share.
" The scouring drunkard, if he does not
  fight   440
Before his bedtime, takes no rest that
  night;
Passing the tedious hours in greater pain

Than stern Achilles,[29] when his friend was
   slain:
'T is so ridiculous, but so true withal,
A bully cannot sleep without a brawl:
Yet tho' his youthful blood be fir'd with
   wine,
He wants not wit, the danger to decline;
Is cautious to avoid the coach and six,
And on the lackeys will no quarrel fix.
His train of flambeaux, and embroider'd
   coat,   450
May privilege my lord to walk secure on
   foot.
But me, who must by moonlight home-
   ward bend,
Or lighted only with a candle's end,
Poor me he fights, if that be fighting, where
He only cudgels, and I only bear.
He stands, and bids me stand; I must
   abide;
For he 's the stronger, and is drunk beside.
" ' Where did you whet your knife to-
   night ? ' he cries,
' And shred the leeks that in your stomach
   rise ?
Whose windy beans have stuff'd your guts,
   and where   460
Have your black thumbs been dipp'd in
   vinegar ?
With what companion cobbler have you fed,
On old ox-cheeks, or he-goat's tougher
   head ?
What, are you dumb ? Quick, with your
   answer, quick,
Before my foot salutes you with a kick.
Say, in what nasty cellar, under ground,
Or what church porch, your rogueship may
   be found ? '
Answer, or answer not, 't is all the same:
He lays me on, and makes me bear the
   blame.
Before the bar, for beating him, you come;
This is a poor man's liberty in Rome.   471
You beg his pardon; happy to retreat
With some remaining teeth, to chew your
   meat.
" Nor is this all; for, when retir'd, you
   think
To sleep securely; when the candles wink,
When every door with iron chains is barr'd,
And roaring taverns are no longer heard;
The ruffian robbers, by no justice aw'd,
And unpaid cutthroat soldiers, are abroad,
Those venal souls, who, harden'd in each
   ill,   480

To save complaints and prosecution, kill.
Chas'd from their woods and bogs, the
   padders come
To this vast city, as their native home;
To live at ease, and safely skulk in
   Rome.
" The forge in fetters only is employ'd;
Our iron mines exhausted and destroy'd
In shackles; for these villains scarce allow
Goads for the teams, and plowshares for
   the plow.
O happy ages of our ancestors,   489
Beneath the kings [30] and tribunitial pow'rs !
One jail did all their criminals restrain,
Which, now, the walls of Rome can scarce
   contain.
" More I could say, more causes I could
   show
For my departure; but the sun is low;
The wagoner grows weary of my stay,
And whips his horses forwards on their
   way.
" Farewell; and when, like me, o'er-
   whelm'd with care,
You to your own Aquinum [31] shall repair,
To take a mouthful of sweet country air,
Be mindful of your friend; and send me
   word,   500
What joys your fountains and cool shades
   afford:
Then, to assist your satires, I will come;
And add new venom, when you write of
   Rome."

EXPLANATORY NOTES ON THE THIRD SATIRE

1 *Cumæ*, a small city in Campania, near Pu-
teoli, or Puzzolo, as it is call'd. The habitation
of the Cumæan Sibyl.
2 *Bajæ*, another little town in Campania, near
the sea ; a pleasant place.
3 *Prochyta*, a small barren island belonging to
the kingdom of Naples.
4 *In dog days.* The poets in Juvenal's time
us'd to rehearse their poetry in August.
5 *Numa*, the second king of Rome, who made
their laws, and instituted their religion.
6 *Nymph.* Egeria, a nymph, or goddess, with
whom Numa feign'd to converse by night, and
to be instructed by her in modeling his superstitions.
7 *Where Dædalus*, &c., meaning at Cumæ.
8 *Lachesis*, one of the three Destinies, whose
office was to spin the life of every man ; as it
was of Clotho to hold the distaff, and Atropos
to cut the thread.
9 *Arturius*, any debauch'd, wicked fellow,
who gains by the times.

10 *With thumbs bent backward.* In a prize of sword-players, when one of the fencers had the other at his mercy, the vanquish'd party implor'd the clemency of the spectators. If they thought he deserv'd it not, they held up their thumbs and bent them backwards in sign of death.

11 *Verres*, prætor in Sicily, contemporary with Cicero, by whom, accus'd of oppressing the province, he was condemn'd: his name is us'd here for any rich vicious man.

12 *Tagus*, a famous river in Spain, which discharges itself into the ocean near Lisbon, in Portugal. It was held of old to be full of golden sands.

13 *Orontes*, the greatest river of Syria. The poet here puts the river for the inhabitants of Syria.

14 *Tiber*, the river which runs by Rome.

15 *Romulus*, first king of Rome; son of Mars, as the poets feign. The first Romans were originally herdsmen.

16 *But in that town*, &c. He means Athens, of which Pallas, the Goddess of Arms and Arts, was patroness.

17 *Antiochus* and *Stratocles*, two famous Grecian mimics, or actors, in the poet's time.

18 *A rigid Stoic*, &c. Publius Egnatius, a Stoic, falsely accus'd Bareas Soranus, as Tacitus tells us.

19 *Diphilus* and *Protogenes*, &c., were Grecians living in Rome.

20 *Or him who bade*, &c. Lucius Metellus, the high priest, who, when the temple of Vesta was on fire, sav'd the Palladium.

21 *For, by the Roscian law*, &c. Roscius, a tribune, who order'd the distinction of places in public shows betwixt the noblemen of Rome and the plebeians.

22 *Where none, but only dead men*, &c. The meaning is, that men in some parts of Italy never wore a gown (the usual habit of the Romans) till they were buried in one.

23 *Cossus* is here taken for any great man.

24 *Where the tame pigeons*, &c. The Romans us'd to breed their tame pigeons in their garrets.

25 *Codrus*, a learned man, very poor: by his books, suppos'd to be a poet; for, in all probability, the heroic verses here mention'd, which rats and mice devour'd, were Homer's works.

26 *A Pythagorean treat.* He means herbs, roots, fruits, and salads.

27 *Gigantic Corbulo.* Corbulo was a famous general, in Nero's time, who conquer'd Armenia, and was afterwards put to death by that tyrant, when he was in Greece, in reward of his great services. His stature was not only tall, above the ordinary size, but he was also proportionably strong.

28 *The ferryman's*, &c. Charon, the ferryman of hell, whose fare was a halfpenny for every soul.

29 *Stern Achilles.* The friend of Achilles was Patroclus, who was slain by Hector.

30 *Beneath the kings*, &c. Rome was originally rul'd by kings, till, for the rape of Lucretia, Tarquin the Proud was expell'd; after which it was govern'd by two consuls, yearly chosen; but they oppressing the people, the commoners mutinied and procur'd tribunes to be created, who defended their privileges and often oppos'd the consular authority and the senate.

31 *Aquinum* was the birthplace of Juvenal.

THE SIXTH SATIRE OF JUVENAL

THE ARGUMENT

This satire, of almost double length to any of the rest, is a bitter invective against the fair sex. 'T is, indeed, a commonplace, from whence all the moderns have notoriously stolen their sharpest railleries. In his other satires, the poet has only glanc'd on some particular women and generally scourg'd the men. But this he reserv'd wholly for the ladies. How they had offended him I know not; but upon the whole matter he is not to be excus'd for imputing to all the vices of some few amongst them. Neither was it generously done of him, to attack the weakest as well as the fairest part of the creation; neither do I know what moral he could reasonably draw from it. It could not be to avoid the whole sex, if all had been true which he alleges against them; for that had been to put an end to humankind. And to bid us beware of their artifices, is a kind of silent acknowledgment, that they have more wit than men: which turns the satire upon us, and particularly upon the poet; who thereby makes a compliment, where he meant a libel. If he intended only to exercise his wit, he has forfeited his judgment, by making the one half of his readers his mortal enemies; and amongst the men, all the happy lovers, by their own experience, will disprove his accusations. The whole world must allow this to be the wittiest of his satires; and truly he had need of all his parts, to maintain, with so much violence, so unjust a charge. I am satisfied he will bring but few over to his opinion; and on that consideration chiefly I ventur'd to translate him. Tho' there wanted not another reason, which was, that no one else would undertake it: at least, Sir C. S., who could have done more right to the author, after a long delay, at length absolutely refus'd so ungrateful an employment; and everyone will grant that the work must have been imperfect and lame, if it had appear'd without one of the principal members belonging to it. Let the poet there

fore bear the blame of his own invention ;
and let me satisfy the world that I am not of
his opinion. Whatever his Roman ladies were,
the English are free from all his imputations. They will read with wonder and abhorrence the vices of an age which was the
most infamous of any on record. They will
bless themselves when they behold those
examples related of Domitian's time; they
will give back to antiquity those monsters
it produc'd; and believe with reason that the
species of those women is extinguish'd, or at
least that they were never here propagated.
I may safely therefore proceed to the argument of a satire, which is no way relating
to them ; and first observe that my author
makes their lust the most heroic of their
vices : the rest are in a manner but digression. He skims them over ; but he dwells
on this : when he seems to have taken his
last leave of it, on the sudden he returns to
it : 't is one branch of it in Hippia, another
in Messalina, but lust is the main body of
the tree. He begins with this text in the
first line, and takes it up with intermissions
to the end of the chapter. Every vice is a
loader, but that 's a ten. The fillers, or intermediate parts, are their revenge; their contriv-
ances of secret crimes; their arts to hide them ;
their wit to excuse them ; and their impudence to own them, when they can no longer
be kept secret. Then, the persons to whom
they are most addicted, and on whom they
commonly bestow the last favors : as stage-
players, fiddlers, singing-boys, and fencers.
Those who pass for chaste amongst them,
are not really so ; but only, for their vast dow-
ries, are rather suffer'd, than lov'd, by their
own husbands. That they are imperious, domi-
neering, scolding wives ; set up for learning
and criticism in poetry, but are false judges.
Love to speak Greek (which was then the
fashionable tongue, as French is now with
us). That they plead causes at the bar, and
play prizes at the bear garden. That they
are gossips and newsmongers ; wrangle with
their neighbors abroad, and beat their servants at home. That they lie in for new faces
once a month ; are sluttish with their husbands in private ; and paint and dress in public for their lovers. That they deal with Jews,
diviners, and fortune tellers ; learn the arts of
miscarrying, and barrenness. Buy children,
and produce them for their own. Murther
their husband's sons, if they stand in their way
to his estate, and make their adulterers his
heirs. From hence the poet proceeds to
shew the occasions of all these vices, their
original, and how they were introduc'd in
Rome, by peace, wealth, and luxury. In conclusion, if we will take the word of our malicious author, bad women are the general
standing rule ; and the good, but some few
exceptions to it.

IN Saturn's reign,[1] at Nature's early birth,
There was that thing call'd chastity on earth;
When in a narrow cave, their common shade,
The sheep, the shepherds, and their gods
    were laid:
When reeds, and leaves, and hides of ⎫
    beasts were spread   ⎪
By mountain huswifes for their homely ⎬
    bed,   ⎪
And mossy pillows rais'd, for the rude ⎭
    husband's head.
Unlike the niceness of our modern dames,
(Affected nymphs with new affected
    names,)   9
The Cynthias and the Lesbias of our years,
Who for a sparrow's death dissolve in
    tears;
Those first unpolish'd matrons, big and
    bold,
Gave suck to infants of gigantic mold;
Rough as their savage lords who rang'd
    the wood,
And fat with acorns[2] belch'd their windy
    food.
For when the world was buxom, fresh, and
    young,
Her sons were undebauch'd and therefore
    strong;
And whether born in kindly beds of earth,
Or struggling from the teeming oaks to
    birth,
Or from what other atoms they begun,   20
No sires they had, or, if a sire, the sun.
Some thin remains of chastity appear'd,
Ev'n under Jove,[3] but Jove without a
    beard;
Before the servile Greeks had learnt to
    swear
By heads of kings; while yet the bounteous
    year
Her common fruits in open plains expos'd,
Ere thieves were fear'd, or gardens were
    enclos'd.
At length uneasy Justice[4] upwards flew,
And both the sisters to the stars withdrew;
From that old era whoring did begin,   30
So venerably ancient is the sin.
Adult'rers next invade the nuptial state,
And marriage beds creak'd with a foreign
    weight;
All other ills did iron times adorn,
But whores and silver in one age were born.

Yet thou, they say, for marriage dost
provide:
Is this an age to buckle with a bride?
They say thy hair the curling art is taught,
The wedding ring perhaps already bought:
A sober man like thee to change his life!
What fury would possess thee with a wife?
Art thou of ev'ry other death bereft,   42
No knife, no ratsbane, no kind halter left?
(For every noose compar'd to hers is cheap)
Is there no city bridge from whence to
leap?
Wouldst thou become her drudge, who dost
enjoy
A better sort of bedfellow, thy boy?
He keeps thee not awake with nightly
brawls,
Nor with a begg'd reward thy pleasure
palls;
Nor with insatiate heavings calls for more,
When all thy spirits were drain'd out be-
fore.   51
But still Ursidius courts the marriage bait,
Longs for a son to settle his estate,
And takes no gifts, tho' ev'ry gaping heir
Would gladly grease the rich old bachelor.
What revolution can appear so strange,
As such a lecher, such a life to change?
A rank, notorious whoremaster, to choose
To thrust his neck into the marriage noose!
He who so often in a dreadful fright   60
Had in a coffer scap'd the jealous cuckold's
sight,
That he, to wedlock dotingly betray'd,
Should hope in this lewd town to find a
maid!
The man's grown mad: to ease his frantic
pain,
Run for the surgeon; breathe the middle
vein:
But let a heifer with gilt horns be led
To Juno, regent of the marriage bed,
And let him every deity adore,   ⎫
If his new bride prove not an arrant whore ⎬
In head and tail, and every other pore. ⎭
On Ceres' feast,[5] restrain'd from their de-
light,   71
Few matrons, there, but curse the tedious
night;
Few whom their fathers dare salute, such
lust
Their kisses have, and come with such a
gust.
With ivy now adorn thy doors, and wed;
Such is thy bride, and such thy genial bed.

Think'st thou one man is for one woman
meant?
She, sooner, with one eye would be con-
tent.
   And yet, 't is nois'd, a maid did once ap-
pear
In some small village, tho' fame says not
where: 80
'T is possible; but sure no man she found;
'T was desart, all, about her father's ground:
And yet some lustful god might there
make bold;
Are Jove and Mars[6] grown impotent and
old?
Many a fair nymph has in a cave been
spread,
And much good love without a feather bed.
Whither wouldst thou to choose a wife re-
sort,
The Park, the Mall, the Playhouse, or the
Court?
Which way soever thy adventures fall,
Secure alike of chastity in all.   90
   One sees a dancing master cap'ring high,
And raves, and pisses, with pure ecstasy;
Another does with all his motions move,
And gapes, and grins, as in the feat of love;
A third is charm'd with the new opera
notes,
Admires the song, but on the singer dotes:
The country lady in the box appears,   ⎫
Softly she warbles over all she hears; ⎬
And sucks in passion, both at eyes and ears. ⎭
   The rest, (when now the long vacation's
come,   100
The noisy hall and theaters grown dumb,)
Their memories to refresh, and cheer their
hearts,
In borrow'd breeches act the players' parts.
The poor, that scarce have wherewithal to
eat,
Will pinch, to make the singing-boy a treat:
The rich, to buy him, will refuse no price;
And stretch his quail-pipe, till they crack
his voice.
Tragedians, acting love, for lust are sought:
(Tho' but the parrots of a poet's thought.)
The pleading lawyer, tho' for counsel us'd,
In chamber practice often is refus'd.   111
Still thou wilt have a wife, and father heirs;
(The product of concurring theaters.)
Perhaps a fencer did thy brows adorn,
And a young swordman to thy lands is born.
   Thus Hippia loath'd her old patrician
lord,

And left him for a brother of the sword:
To wond'ring Pharos [7] with her love she
   fled,
To shew one monster more than Afric bred:
Forgetting house and husband, left be- ⎤
   hind,   120 ⎟
Ev'n children too; she sails before the ⎬
   wind;   ⎟
False to 'em all, but constant to her kind. ⎦
But, stranger yet, and harder to conceive,
She could the playhouse and the players
   leave.
Born of rich parentage, and nicely bred,
She lodg'd on down, and in a damask bed;
Yet daring now the dangers of the deep,
On a hard mattress is content to sleep.
Ere this, 't is true, she did her fame expose:
But that, great ladies with great ease can
   lose.   130
The tender nymph could the rude ocean
   bear:
So much her lust was stronger than her fear.
But, had some honest cause her passage
   press'd,
The smallest hardship had disturb'd her
   breast:
Each inconvenience makes their virtue cold;
But womankind, in ills, is ever bold.
Were she to follow her own lord to sea,
What doubts and scruples would she raise
   to stay ?
Her stomach sick, and her head giddy
   grows;   139
The tar and pitch are nauseous to her nose.
But in love's voyage nothing can offend;
Women are never seasick with a friend.
Amidst the crew, she walks upon the ⎤
   board;   ⎟
She eats, she drinks, she handles every ⎬
   cord;   ⎟
And if she spews, 't is thinking of her ⎟
   lord.   ⎦
Now ask, for whom her friends and fame she
   lost ?
What youth, what beauty could th' adul-
   t'rer boast ?
What was the face, for which she could
   sustain
To be call'd mistress to so base a man ?
The gallant of his days had known the ⎤
   best: 150 ⎟
Deep scars were seen indented on his ⎬
   breast;   ⎟
And all his batter'd limbs requir'd their ⎟
   needful rest.   ⎦

A promontory wen, with grisly grace,
Stood high, upon the handle of his face:
His blear eyes ran in gutters to his chin:
His beard was stubble, and his cheeks were
   thin.
But 't was his fencing did her fancy move:
'T is arms and blood and cruelty they love.
But should he quit his trade, and sheathe
   his sword,
Her lover would begin to be her lord.   160
   This was a private crime; but you shall
   hear
What fruits the sacred brows of monarchs
   bear:
The good old sluggard but began to snore,
When from his side up rose th' imperial
   whore: [8]
She who preferr'd the pleasures of the
   night
To pomps, that are but impotent delight;
Strode from the palace, with an eager
   pace,
To cope with a more masculine embrace;
Muffled she march'd, like Juno in a cloud,
Of all her train but one poor wench allow'd;
One whom in secret service she could trust,
The rival and companion of her lust.   172
To the known brothel-house she takes her ⎤
   way;   ⎟
And for a nasty room gives double pay; ⎬
That room in which the rankest harlot ⎟
   lay.   ⎦
Prepar'd for fight, expectingly she lies,
With heaving breasts, and with desiring
   eyes:
Still as one drops, another takes his place,
And baffled still succeeds to like disgrace.
At length, when friendly darkness is ex-
   pir'd,   180
And every strumpet from her cell retir'd,
She lags behind, and, ling'ring at the gate,
With a repining sigh submits to fate:
All filth without, and all a fire within,
Tir'd with the toil, unsated with the sin.
Old Cæsar's bed the modest matron seeks;
The steam of lamps still hanging on her
   cheeks
In ropy smut: thus foul, and thus bedight,
She brings him back the product of the
   night.
   Now should I sing what poisons they
   provide,   190
With all their trumpery of charms beside,
And all their arts of death, it would be
   known

Lust is the smallest sin the sex can own;
Cæsinia still, they say, is guiltless found
Of every vice, by her own lord renown'd:
And well she may, she brought ten thou-
    sand pound.
She brought him wherewithal to be call'd
    chaste;
His tongue is tied in golden fetters fast:
He sighs, adores, and courts her every hour;
Who would not do as much for such a
    dower ?   200
She writes love letters to the youth in grace;
Nay, tips the wink before the cuckold's face;
And might do more; her portion makes it
    good;
Wealth has the privilege [9] of widowhood.
  These truths with his example you dis-
    prove,
Who with his wife is monstrously in love:
But know him better; for I heard him
    swear,
'T is not that she 's his wife, but that she 's
    fair.
Let her but have three wrinkles in her face,
Let her eyes lessen, and her skin unbrace, 210
Soon you will hear the saucy steward say:
" Pack up with all your trinkets, and away;
You grow offensive both at bed and board:
Your betters must be had to please my
    lord."
  Meantime she 's absolute upon the throne;
And, knowing time is precious, loses none:
She must have flocks of sheep, with wool
    more fine
Than silk, and vineyards of the noblest wine;
Whole droves of pages for her train she
    craves,
And sweeps the prisons for attending
    slaves.   220
In short, whatever in her eyes can come,
Or others have abroad, she wants at home.
When winter shuts the seas, and fleecy
    snows
Make houses white, she to the merchant
    goes;
Rich crystals of the rock she takes up
    there,
Huge agate vases, and old China ware:
Then Berenice's ring [10] her finger proves,
More precious made by her incestuous loves,
And infamously dear; a brother's bribe,
Ev'n God's anointed, and of Judah's tribe;
Where barefoot they approach the sacred
    shrine,   231
And think it only sin to feed on swine.

  But is none worthy to be made a wife
In all this town ? Suppose her free from
    strife,
Rich, fair, and fruitful, of unblemish'd
    life;
Chaste as the Sabines, whose prevailing
    charms
Dismiss'd their husbands', and their bro-
    thers' arms:
Grant her, besides, of noble blood, that
    ran
In ancient veins ere heraldry began:
Suppose all these, and take a poet's word, 240
A black swan is not half so rare a bird.
A wife, so hung with virtues, such a freight,
What mortal shoulders could support the
    weight !
Some country girl, scarce to a curtsy bred,
Would I much rather than Cornelia [11] wed:
If supercilious, haughty, proud, and vain,
She brought her father's triumphs in her
    train.
Away with all your Carthaginian state;
Let vanquish'd Hannibal without doors
    wait,
Too burly and too big to pass my narrow
    gate.   250
" O Pæan," [12] cries Amphion, " bend thy
    bow
Against my wife, and let my children
    go ! "
But sullen Pæan shoots at sons and
    mothers too.
His Niobe and all his boys he lost:
Ev'n her who did her num'rous offspring
    boast,
As fair and fruitful as the sow that carried
The thirty pigs [13] at one large litter far-
    row'd.
  What beauty or what chastity can bear
So great a price, if, stately and severe
She still insults, and you must still adore ?
Grant that the honey 's much, the gall is
    more.   261
Upbraided with the virtues she displays,
Sev'n hours in twelve you loathe the wife
    you praise.
Some faults, tho' small, intolerable grow;
For what so nauseous and affected too,
As those that think they due perfection
    want,
Who have not learnt to lisp the Grecian
    cant ? [14]
In Greece, their whole accomplishments
    they seek;

Their fashion, breeding, language, must be
  Greek: 269
But, raw in all that does to Rome belong,
They scorn to cultivate their mother tongue.
In Greek they flatter, all their fears they
  speak,
Tell all their secrets; nay, they scold in
  Greek:
Ev'n in the feat of love, they use that
  tongue.
Such affectations may become the young;
But thou, old hag, of threescore years and
  three,
Is shewing of thy parts in Greek for thee?
Ζωὴ καὶ ψυχή ! All those tender words
The momentary trembling bliss affords,
The kind soft murmurs of the private
  sheets,   280
Are bawdy, while thou speak'st in public
  streets.
Those words have fingers; and their force
  is such,
They raise the dead, and mount him with
  a touch:
But all provocatives from thee are vain;
No blandishment the slacken'd nerve can
  strain.
  If then thy lawful spouse thou canst not
  love,
What reason should thy mind to marriage
  move ?
Why all the charges of the nuptial feast,
Wine and desserts, and sweetmeats to digest;
Th' indowing gold that buys the dear de-
  light,   290
Giv'n for thy first and only happy night ?
If thou art thus uxoriously inclin'd,
To bear thy bondage with a willing mind,
Prepare thy neck, and put it in the yoke;
But for no mercy from thy woman look.
For tho', perhaps, she loves with equal fires,
To absolute dominion she aspires;
Joys in the spoils, and triumphs o'er thy
  purse;
The better husband makes the wife the
  worse.
Nothing is thine to give, or sell, or buy, 300 ⎫
All offices of ancient friendship die;   ⎬
Nor hast thou leave to make a legacy.   ⎭
By thy imperious wife thou art bereft
A privilege,[15] to pimps and panders left.
Thy testament 's her will; where she pre- ⎫
  fers   ⎬
Her ruffians, drudges, and adulterers,   ⎬
Adopting all thy rivals for thy heirs.   ⎭

" Go drag that slave to death ! " [16] " Your
  reason, why [17]
Should the poor innocent be doom'd to die ?
What proofs ? For, when man's life is in
  debate,   310
The judge can ne'er too long deliberate."
" Call'st thou that slave a man ? " [18] the wife
  replies;
" Prov'd, or unprov'd the crime, the villain
  dies.
I have the sovereign pow'r to save or kill,
And give no other reason but my will."
  Thus the she-tyrant reigns, till, pleas'd
  with change,
Her wild affections to new empires range:
Another subject-husband she desires;
Divorc'd from him, she to the first retires,
While the last wedding feast is scarcely
  o'er,   320
And garlands hang yet green upon the
  door.
So still the reck'ning rises; and appears,
In total sum, eight husbands in five years.
The title for a tombstone might be fit,
But that it would too commonly be writ.
  Her mother living, hope no quiet day; ⎫
She sharpens her, instructs her how to flay ⎬
Her husband bare, and then divides the ⎪
  prey.   ⎭
She takes love letters, with a crafty smile,
And in her daughter's answer mends the
  style.   330
In vain the husband sets his watchful spies;
She cheats their cunning, or she bribes
  their eyes.
The doctor 's call'd; the daughter, taught
  the trick,
Pretends to faint; and in full health is sick.
The panting stallion, at the closet door,
Hears the consult, and wishes it were o'er.
Canst thou, in reason, hope, a bawd so
  known
Should teach her other manners than her
  own ?
Her int'rest is in all th' advice she gives:
'T is on the daughter's rents the mother
  lives.   340
  No cause is tried at the litigious bar,
But women plaintiffs or defendants are;
They form the process, all the briefs they ⎫
  write;   ⎬
The topics furnish, and the pleas indite;   ⎬
And teach the toothless lawyer how to ⎪
  bite.   ⎭
  They turn viragoes too; the wrastler's toil

They try, and smear their naked limbs with
     oil:
Against the post their wicker shields they
     crush,
Flourish the sword, and at the plastron
     push.
Of every exercise the mannish crew   350
Fulfils the parts, and oft excels us too;
Prepar'd not only in feign'd fights t' engage,
But rout the gladiators on the stage.
What sense of shame in such a breast can
     lie,
Inur'd to arms, and her own sex to fly?
Yet to be wholly man she would disclaim; ⎫
To quit her tenfold pleasure at the game, ⎬
For frothy praises and an empty name. ⎭
O what a decent sight 't is to behold
All thy wife's magazine by auction sold ! 360
The belt, the crested plume, the several
     suits
Of armor, and the Spanish-leather boots !
Yet these are they, that cannot bear the
     heat
Of figur'd silks, and under sarcenet sweat.
Behold the strutting Amazonian whore:
She stands in guard with her right foot be-
     fore;
Her coats tuck'd up, and all her motions
     just;
She stamps, and then cries Hah ! at every
     thrust:
But laugh to see her, tir'd with many a
     bout,
Call for the pot, and like a man piss out. 370
The ghosts of ancient Romans, should they
     rise,
Would grin to see their daughters play a
     prize.
Besides, what endless brawls by wives are
     bred !
The curtain lecture makes a mournful bed.
Then, when she has thee sure within the
     sheets,
Her cry begins, and the whole day repeats.
Conscious of crimes herself, she teases
     first;
Thy servants are accus'd; thy whore is
     curst;
She acts the jealous, and at will she cries;
For women's tears are but the sweat of
     eyes.   380
Poor cuckold-fool, thou think'st that love
     sincere,
And suck'st between her lips the falling
     tear;

But search her cabinet, and thou shalt find
Each tiller there with love epistles lin'd.
Suppose her taken in a close embrace,   ⎫
This you would think so manifest a case, ⎪
No rhetoric could defend, no impudence ⎬
     outface: ⎭
And yet even then she cries: "The marriage
     vow
A mental reservation must allow;
And there 's a silent bargain still implied, ⎫
The parties should be pleas'd on either   ⎪
     side;   391 ⎬
And both may for their private needs pro- ⎪
     vide.   ⎭
Tho' men yourselves, and women us you
     call,
Yet _homo_ is a common name for all."
There 's nothing bolder than a woman
     caught;
Guilt gives 'em courage to maintain their
     fault.
  You ask from whence proceed these mon-
     strous crimes.
Once poor, and therefore chaste, in former
     times,
Our matrons were: no luxury found room
In low-roof'd houses, and bare walls of
     loam;   400
Their hands with labor harden'd while 't was
     light,
And frugal sleep supplied the quiet night;
While pinch'd with want, their hunger held
     'em straight,
When Hannibal [19] was hov'ring at the gate:
But wanton now, and lolling at our ease,
We suffer all th' invet'rate ills of peace,
And wasteful riot; whose destructive
     charms
Revenge the vanquish'd world of our vic-
     torious arms.
No crime, no lustful postures are unknown;
Since Poverty, our guardian god, is gone:
Pride, laziness, and all luxurious arts,   411
Pour like a deluge in, from foreign parts;
Since gold obscene and silver found the ⎫
     way,   ⎪
Strange fashions, with strange bullion, to ⎬
     convey,   ⎪
And our plain simple manners to betray. ⎭
  What care our drunken dames to whom
     they spread ?
Wine no distinction makes of tail or head:
Who, lewdly dancing at a midnight ball,
For hot eringoes and fat oysters call;
Full brimmers to their fuddled noses thrust,

Brimmers, the last provocatives of lust; 421
When vapors to their swimming brains ad-
    vance,
And double tapers on the tables dance.
  Now think what bawdy dialogues they
    have,
What Tullia talks to her confiding slave,
At Modesty's old statue; when by night
They make a stand, and from their litters
    light:
The good man early to the levee goes,
And treads the nasty paddle of his spouse.
  The secrets of the goddess nam'd the
    Good,[20]   430
Are even by boys and barbers understood:
Where the rank matrons, dancing to the
    pipe,
Gig with their bums, and are for action
    ripe;
With music rais'd, they spread abroad their
    hair,
And toss their heads like an enamor'd
    mare:
Laufella lays her garland by, and proves
The mimic lechery of manly loves.
Rank'd with the lady the cheap sinner lies;
For here not blood, but virtue, gives the
    prize.
Nothing is feign'd in this venereal strife; 440
'T is downright lust, and acted to the life.
So full, so fierce, so vigorous, and so strong,
That looking on would make old Nestor [21]
    young.
Impatient of delay, a general sound,   ⎫
An universal groan of lust goes round;   ⎪
For then, and only then, the sex sincere   ⎬
    is found.   ⎪
" Now is the time of action; now begin,"   ⎭
They cry, " and let the lusty lovers in."
" The whoresons are asleep." " Then bring
    the slaves,
And watermen, a race of strong-back'd
    knaves."   450
  I wish, at least, our sacred rites were
    free
From those pollutions of obscenity:
But 't is well known what singer,[22] how dis-
    guis'd,
A lewd audacious action enterpriz'd:
Into the fair, with women mix'd, he went,
Arm'd with a huge two-handed instrument;
A grateful present to those holy choirs,
Where the mouse, guilty of his sex, retires,
And even male pictures modestly are veil'd:
Yet no profaneness on that age prevail'd; 460

No scoffers at religious rites were found;
Tho' now, at every altar they abound.
  I hear your cautious counsel, you would
    say:
" Keep close your women under lock and
    key."
But, who shall keep those keepers ? Wo-
    men, nurs'd
In craft, begin with those, and bribe 'em
    first.
The sex is turn'd all whore; they love the
    game:
And mistresses and maids are both the
    same.
  The poor Ogulnia, on the poet's day,
Will borrow clothes, and chair, to see the
    play;   470
She, who before had mortgag'd her estate,
And pawn'd the last remaining piece of
    plate.
Some are reduc'd their utmost shifts to try,
But women have no shame of poverty.
They live beyond their stint; as if their
    store,
The more exhausted, would increase the
    more:
Some men, instructed by the lab'ring ant,
Provide against th' extremities of want;
But womankind, that never knows a mean,
Down to the dregs their sinking fortune
    drain: 480
Hourly they give, and spend, and waste,
    and wear,
And think no pleasure can be bought too
    dear.
  There are, who in soft eunuchs place their
    bliss,[23]
To shun the scrubbing of a bearded kiss,
And scape abortion; but their solid joy
Is when the page, already past a boy,
Is capon'd late, and to the gelder shown,
With his two pounders to perfection grown;
When all the navel-string could give, ap-
    pears;
All but the beard, and that 's the barber's
    loss, not theirs.   490
Seen from afar, and famous for his ware,
He struts into the bath, among the fair:
Th' admiring crew to their devotions fall;
And, kneeling, on their new Priapus [24] call.
Kerv'd for his lady's use, with her he lies;
And let him drudge for her, if thou art
    wise,
Rather than trust him with thy fav'rite boy;
He proffers death, in proffering to enjoy.

If songs they love, the singer's voice they
    force
Beyond his compass, till his quail-pipe 's
    hoarse;   500
His lute and lyre with their embrace is
    worn;
With knots they trim it, and with gems
    adorn:
Run over all the strings, and kiss the case;
And make love to it in the master's place.
   A certain lady once, of high degree,
To Janus vow'd, and Vesta's deity,
That Pollio [25] might, in singing, win the
    prize;
Pollio the dear, the darling of her eyes:
She pray'd, and brib'd; what could she
    more have done
For a sick husband, or an only son ?   510
With her face veil'd, and heaving up her
    hands,
The shameless suppliant at the altar stands;
The forms of prayer she solemnly pursues;
And, pale with fear, the offer'd entrails
    views.
Answer, ye pow'rs: for, if you heard her
    vow,
Your godships, sure, had little else to do.
   This is not all; for actors [26] they implore:
An impudence unknown to Heav'n before.
Th' Aruspex,[27] tir'd with this religious rout,
Is forc'd to stand so long, he gets the
    gout.   520
But suffer not thy wife abroad to roam:
If she love singing, let her sing at home;
Not strut in streets, with Amazonian pace,
For that 's to cuckold thee before thy face.
   Their endless itch of news comes next in
    play;
They vent their own, and hear what others
    say :
Know what in Thrace, or what in France is
    done;
Th' intrigues betwixt the stepdam and the
    son :
Tell who loves who, what favors some par-
    take;
And who is jilted for another's sake: 530
What pregnant widow in what month was
    made;
How oft she did, and, doing, what she said.
   She, first, beholds the raging comet rise;
Knows whom it threatens, and what lands
    destroys.
Still for the newest news she lies in wait,
And takes reports just ent'ring at the gate.

Wrecks, floods, and fires, whatever she can
    meet,
She spreads; and is the Fame of every
    street.
   This is a grievance; but the next is worse,
A very judgment, and her neighbors'
    curse: 540
For if their barking dog disturb her ease,
No pray'r can bend her, no excuse appease.
Th' unmanner'd malefactor is arraign'd;
But first the master, who the cur maintain'd,
Must feel the scourge; by night she leaves
    her bed,
By night her bathing equipage is led,
That marching armies a less noise create;
She moves in tumult, and she sweats in
    state.
Meanwhile, her guests their appetites must
    keep;
Some gape for hunger, and some gasp for
    sleep.   550
At length she comes, all flush'd; but ere
    she sup,
Swallows a swingeing preparation cup;
And then, to clear her stomach, spews it
    up.
The deluge-vomit all the floor o'erflows,
And the sour savor nauseates every nose.
She drinks again; again she spews a lake;
Her wretched husband sees, and dares not
    speak;
But mutters many a curse against his wife,
And damns himself for choosing such a life.
   But of all plagues, the greatest is untold;
The book-learn'd wife, in Greek and Latin
    bold: 561
The critic-dame, who at her table sits,
Homer and Virgil quotes, and weighs
    their wits;
And pities Dido's agonizing fits.
She has so far th' ascendant of the board,
The prating pedant puts not in one word:
The man of law is non-plus'd in his suit,
Nay, every other female tongue is mute.
Hammers and beating anvils, you would
    swear,   569
And Vulcan [28] with his whole militia there.
Tabors and trumpets [29] cease; for she alone
Is able to redeem the lab'ring Moon.
Ev'n wit 's a burthen, when it talks too
    long;
But she, who has no continence of tongue,
Should walk in breeches, and should wear
    a beard,
And mix among the philosophic herd.

O what a midnight curse has he, whose side
Is pester'd with a mood and figure bride ! [30]
Let mine, ye gods, (if such must be my
    fate,)
No logic learn, nor history translate;   580
But rather be a quiet, humble fool:
I hate a wife to whom I go to school,
Who climbs the grammar tree, distinctly
    knows
Where noun, and verb, and participle grows;
Corrects her country neighbor; and, abed,
For breaking Priscian's,[31] breaks her hus-
    band's head.
    The gaudy gossip, when she 's set agog,
In jewels dress'd, and at each ear a bob,
Goes flaunting out, and, in her trim of pride,
Thinks all she says or does is justified. 590
When poor, she 's scarce a tolerable evil;
But rich, and fine, a wife 's a very devil.
    She duly, once a month, renews her face;
Meantime, it lies in daub, and hid in grease:
Those are the husband's nights; she craves
    her due,
He takes fat kisses, and is stuck in glue.
But, to the lov'd adult'rer when she steers,
Fresh from the bath, in brightness she
    appears:
For him the rich Arabia sweats her gum, ⎫
And precious oils from distant Indies ⎪
    come,   600 ⎬
How haggardly soe'er she looks at home. ⎭
Th' eclipse then vanishes; and all her face
Is open'd, and restor'd to ev'ry grace;
The crust remov'd, her cheeks, as smooth
    as silk,
Are polish'd with a wash of asses' milk;
And should she to the farthest North be
    sent,
A train of these [32] attend her banishment.
But, hadst thou seen her plaister'd up before,
'T was so unlike a face, it seem'd a sore.
    'T is worth our while to know what all
    the day   610
They do, and how they pass their time
    away;
For, if o'ernight the husband has been ⎫
    siack,   ⎪
Or counterfeited sleep, and turn'd his ⎬
    back,   ⎪
Next day, be sure, the servants go to ⎪
    wrack.   ⎭
The chambermaid and dresser are call'd
    whores,
The page is stripp'd, and beaten out of
    doors;

The whole house suffers for the master's
    crime,
And he himself is warn'd to wake another
    time.
    She hires tormentors by the year; she
    treats
Her visitors, and talks, but still she beats; 620
Beats while she paints her face, surveys
    her gown,
Casts up the day's account, and still beats
    on:
Tir'd out, at length, with an outrageous
    tone,
She bids 'em in the Devil's name be gone.
Compar'd with such a proud, insulting
    dame,
Sicilian tyrants [33] may renounce their name.
    For, if she hastes abroad to take the air,
Or goes to Isis' church, (the bawdyhouse
    of pray'r,)
She hurries all her handmaids to the task;
Her head, alone, will twenty dressers ask.
Psecas, the chief, with breast and shoulders
    bare,   631
Trembling, considers every sacred hair;
If any straggler from his rank be found,
A pinch must for the mortal sin compound.
Psecas is not in fault; but, in the glass,
The dame 's offended at her own ill face.
That maid is banish'd; and another girl,
More dextrous, manages the comb and curl;
The rest are summon'd on a point so nice;
And first, the grave old woman gives ad-
    vice.   640
The next is call'd, and so the turn goes
    round,
As each for age, or wisdom, is renown'd:
Such counsel, such delib'rate care they take,
As if her life and honor lay at stake:
With curls on curls, they build her head
    before,
And mount it with a formidable tow'r.[34]
A giantess she seems; but, look behind,
And then she dwindles to the pigmy kind.
Duck-legg'd, short-waisted, such a dwarf
    she is,
That she must rise on tiptoes for a kiss. 650
Meanwhile her husband's whole estate is
    spent;
He may go bare, while she receives his
    rent.
She minds him not; she lives not as a wife,
But like a bawling neighbor, full of strife:
Near him in this alone, that she extends
Her hate to all his servants and his friends.

Bellona's priests,[35] an eunuch at their
    head,
About the streets a mad procession lead;
The venerable gelding, large and high,
O'erlooks the herd of his inferior fry.   660
His awkward clergymen about him prance,
And beat the timbrels to their mystic
    dance;
Guiltless of testicles, they tear their throats,
And squeak, in treble, their unmanly notes.
Meanwhile, his cheeks the miter'd prophet
    swells,
And dire presages of the year foretells;
Unless with eggs (his priestly hire) they
    haste
To expiate, and avert th' autumnal blast;
And add beside [36] a murrey-color'd vest,
Which, in their places, may receive the
    pest;   670
And, thrown into the flood, their crimes
    may bear
To purge th' unlucky omens of the year.
Th' astonish'd matrons pay, before the rest;
That sex is still obnoxious to the priest.
    Thro' ice they beat, and plunge into the
    stream,
If so the god has warn'd 'em in a dream.
Weak in their limbs, but in devotion
    strong,
On their bare hands and feet they crawl
    along
A whole field's length, the laughter of the
    throng.
Should Io (Io's priest I mean) command
A pilgrimage to Meroe's burning sand,   681
Thro' desarts they would seek the secret
    spring;
And holy water, for lustration, bring.
How can they pay their priests too much
    respect,
Who trade with heav'n, and earthly gains
    neglect?
With him, domestic gods discourse by
    night;
By day, attended by his choir in white,
The baldpate tribe runs madding thro'
    the street,
And smile to see with how much ease they
    cheat.   689
The ghostly sire forgives the wife's delights,
Who sins, thro' frailty, on forbidden nights,
And tempts her husband in the holy time,
When carnal pleasure is a mortal crime.
The sweating image shakes its head, but he
With mumbled prayers atones the deity.

The pious priesthood the fat goose receive,
And they once brib'd, the godhead must
    forgive.
    No sooner these remove, but, full of fear,
A gypsy Jewess whispers in your ear,
And begs an alms; an high priest's daugh-
    ter she,   700
Vers'd in their Talmud, and divinity,
And prophesies beneath a shady tree.
Her goods a basket, and old hay her bed,
She strolls, and, telling fortunes, gains her
    bread:
Farthings, and some small moneys, are her
    fees;
Yet she interprets all your dreams for
    these;
Foretells th' estate, when the rich uncle
    dies,
And sees a sweetheart in the sacrifice.
Such toys a pigeon's entrails can disclose,
Which yet th' Armenian augur far outgoes;
In dogs, a victim more obscene, he rakes,   711
And murder'd infants for inspection takes:
For gain his impious practice he pursues;
For gain, will his accomplices accuse.
    More credit, yet, is to Chaldeans [37] giv'n;
What they foretell, is deem'd the voice of
    Heav'n.
Their answers, as from Hammon's altar,
    come;
Since now the Delphian oracles are dumb.
And mankind, ignorant of future fate,
Believes what fond astrologers relate.   720
    Of these the most in vogue is he, who
    sent
Beyond seas, is return'd from banishment;
His art who to aspiring Otho [38] sold,
And sure succession to the crown foretold:
For his esteem is in his exile plac'd;
The more believ'd, the more he was dis-
    grac'd.
No astrologic wizard honor gains,
Who has not oft been banish'd, or in chains.
He gets renown, who, to the halter near,
But narrowly escapes, and buys it dear.
    From him your wife enquires the planets'
    will,   731
When the black jaundice shall her mother
    kill;
Her sister's and her uncle's end, would
    know;
But, first, consults his art, when you shall
    go;
And, what's the greatest gift that Heav'n
    can give.

If, after her, th' adulterer shall live.
She neither knows nor cares to know the
     rest;
If Mars and Saturn [39] shall the world infest;
Or Jove and Venus, with their friendly
     rays,
Will interpose, and bring us better days. 740
  Beware the woman, too, and shun her
     sight,
Who in these studies does herself delight;
By whom a greasy almanac is borne,
With often handling, like chaf'd amber,
     worn:
Not now consulting, but consulted, she
Of the twelve houses, and their lords, is free.
She, if the scheme a fatal journey show,
Stays safe at home, but lets her husband
     go.
If but a mile she travel out of town,
The planetary hour must first be known, 750
And lucky moment; if her eye but aches
Or itches, its decumbiture she takes;
No nourishment receives in her disease,
But what the stars and Ptolemy [40] shall
     please.
  The middle sort, who have not much to ⎤
     spare,   ⎪
To chiromancers' cheaper art repair,   ⎬
Who clap the pretty palm, to make the   ⎪
     lines more fair.   ⎦
But the rich matron, who has more to
     give,
Her answers from the Brachman [41] will re-
     ceive:
Skill'd in the globe and sphere, he gravely
     stands,   760
And, with his compass, measures seas and
     lands.
  The poorest of the sex have still an itch
To know their fortunes, equal to the rich.
The dairymaid enquires, if she shall take
The trusty tailor, and the cook forsake.
  Yet these, tho' poor, the pain of childbed
     bear;
And, without nurses, their own infants rear:
You seldom hear of the rich mantle, spread
For the babe, born in the great lady's bed.
Such is the pow'r of herbs; such arts they
     use   770
To make them barren, or their fruit to lose.
But thou, whatever slops she will have
     brought,
Be thankful, and supply the deadly draught;
Help her to make manslaughter; let her
     bleed,

And never want for savin at her need.
For, if she holds till her nine months be
     run,
Thou mayst be father to an Ethiop's son; [42]
A boy, who ready gotten to thy hands,
By law is to inherit all thy lands;
One of that hue, that should he cross the
     way,   780
His omen [43] would discolor all the day.
  I pass the foundling by, a race unknown,
At doors expos'd, whom matrons make their
     own;
And into noble families advance
A nameless issue, the blind work of chance.
Indulgent Fortune does her care employ,
And, smiling, broods upon the naked boy:
Her garment spreads, and laps him in the
     fold,
And covers with her wings from nightly
     cold:
Gives him her blessing; puts him in a way;
Sets up the farce, and laughs at her own
     play.   791
Him she promotes; she favors him alone,
And makes provision for him as her own.
  The craving wife the force of magic
     tries,
And philters for th' unable husband buys:
The potion works not on the part design'd;
But turns his brain, and stupefies his mind.
The sotted mooncalf gapes, and, staring on,
Sees his own business by another done:
A long oblivion, a benumbing frost,   800
Constrains his head; and yesterday is lost:
Some nimbler juice would make him foam
     and rave,
Like that Cæsonia [44] to her Caius gave;
Who, plucking from the forehead of the
     foal
His mother's love, infus'd it in the bowl:
The boiling blood ran hissing in his veins,
Till the mad vapor mounted to his brains.
The Thund'rer [45] was not half so much on
     fire,
When Juno's girdle kindled his desire.
What woman will not use the pois'ning
     trade,   810
When Cæsar's wife the precedent has made?
Let Agrippina's [46] mushroom be forgot,
Giv'n to a slav'ring, old, unuseful sot,
That only clos'd the driveling dotard's eyes,
And sent his godhead downward to the
     skies:
But this fierce potion calls for fire and
     sword,

Nor spares the commons, when it strikes the
   lord;
So many mischiefs were in one combin'd;
So much one single pois'ner cost mankind.
If stepdames seek their sons-in-law to
   kill,   820
'T is venial trespass; let them have their
   will:
But let the child, entrusted to the care
Of his own mother, of her bread beware:
Beware the food she reaches with her hand;
The morsel is intended for thy land.
Thy tutor be thy taster, ere thou eat;
There's poison in thy drink and in thy meat.
   You think this feign'd; the satire in a
   rage
Struts in the buskins of the tragic stage,
Forgets his bus'ness is to laugh and bite; 830
And will of deaths and dire revenges
   write.
Would it were all a fable that you read;
But Drymon's wife [47] pleads guilty to the
   deed.
" I," she confesses, " in the fact was caught,
Two sons dispatching at one deadly
   draught."
" What two ! two sons, thou viper, in one
   day ! "
" Yes, sev'n," she cries, " if sev'n were in
   my way."
Medea's [48] legend is no more a lie;
Our age adds credit to antiquity.
Great ills, we grant, in former times did
   reign,   840
And murthers then were done: but not for
   gain.
Less admiration to great crimes is due,
Which they thro' wrath, or thro' revenge
   pursue.
For, weak of reason, impotent of will,
The sex is hurried headlong into ill;
And, like a cliff from its foundations torn
By raging earthquakes, into seas is borne.
But those are fiends, who crimes from
   thought begin;
And, cool in mischief, meditate the sin.
They read th' example of a pious wife, 850
Redeeming, with her own, her husband's
   life;
Yet, if the laws did that exchange afford,
Would save their lapdog sooner than their
   lord.
   Where'er you walk, the Belides [49] you
   meet;
And Clytemnestras [50] grow in every street.

But here's the difference; Agamemnon's
   wife
Was a gross butcher with a bloody knife;
But murther, now, is to perfection grown,
And subtle poisons are employ'd alone;
Unless some antidote prevents their arts, 860
And lines with balsam all the noble parts:
In such a case, reserv'd for such a need,
Rather than fail, the dagger does the deed.

EXPLANATORY NOTES ON THE SIXTH
SATIRE

1 In the Golden Age, when Saturn reign'd.
2 *Fat with acorns.* Acorns were the bread of
mankind, before corn was found.
3 *Under Jove.* When Jove had driven his
father into banishment, the Silver Age began,
according to the poets.
4 *Uneasy Justice,* &c. The poet makes Justice and Chastity sisters; and says that they fled
to heaven together, and left earth for ever.
5 *Ceres' feast.* When the Roman women were
forbidden to bed with their husbands.
6 *Jove and Mars,* of whom more fornicating
stories are told than any of the other gods.
7 *Wond'ring Pharos.* She fled to Egypt,
which wonder'd at the enormity of her crime.
8 He tells the famous story of Messalina, wife
to the Emperor Claudius.
9 *Wealth has the privilege,* &c. His meaning
is, that a wife who brings a large dowry may do
what she pleases, and has all the privileges of a
widow.
10 *Berenice's ring.* A ring of great price,
which Herod Agrippa gave to his sister Berenice. He was King of the Jews, but tributary
to the Romans.
11 *Cornelia,* mother to the Gracchi, of the
family of the Cornelii, from whence Scipio the
African was descended, who triumph'd over
Hannibal.
12 *O Pæan,* &c. He alludes to the known
fable of Niobe, in Ovid. Amphion was her
husband. Pæan is Apollo, who with his arrows
kill'd her children, because she boasted that
she was more fruitful than Latona, Apollo's
mother.
13 *The thirty pigs,* &c. He alludes to the
white sow in Virgil, who farrow'd thirty pigs.
14 *The Grecian cant.* Women then learnt
Greek, as ours speak French.
15 All the Romans, even the most inferior
and most infamous sort of them, had the power
of making their wills.
16 " *Go drag that slave,* &c. These are the
words of the wife.
17 "*Your reason, why,* &c. The answer of
the husband.
18 " *Call'st thou that slave a man?*" The
wife again.
19 *Hannibal,* a famous Carthaginian captain,
who was upon the point of conquering the Romans.

20 *The Good Goddess*, at whose feasts no men were to be present.

21 *Nestor*, who liv'd three hundred years.

22 *What singer*, &c. He alludes to the story of P. Clodius, who, disguis'd in the habit of a singing woman, went into the house of Cæsar, where the feast of the Good Goddess was celebrated, to find an opportunity with Cæsar's wife, Pompeia.

23 He taxes women with their loving eunuchs, who can get no children ; but adds that they only love such eunuchs as are gelded when they are already at the age of manhood.

24 *Priapus*, the God of Lust.

25 *Pollio*, a famous singing-boy.

26 That such an actor whom they love might obtain the prize.

27 *Th' Aruspex*. He who inspects the entrails of the sacrifice, and from thence foretells the successor.

28. *Vulcan*, the god of smiths.

29 *Tabors and trumpets*, &c. The ancients thought that with such sounds they could bring the Moon out of her eclipse.

30 *A mood and figure bride.* A woman who has learn'd logic.

31 A woman-grammarian, who corrects her husband for speaking false Latin, which is call'd breaking Priscian's head.

32 *A train of these.* That is, of she-asses.

33 *Sicilian tyrants* are grown to a proverb, in Latin, for their cruelty.

34 This dressing up the head so high, which we call a tow'r, was an ancient way amongst the Romans.

35 *Bellona's priests* were a sort of fortune tellers, and the high priest an eunuch.

36 *And add beside*, &c. A garment was given to the priest, which he threw into the river ; and that, they thought, bore all the sins of the people, which were drown'd with it.

37 *Chaldeans* are thought to have been the first astrologers.

38 *Otho* succeeded Galba in the empire, which was foretold him by an astrologer.

39 *Mars and Saturn* are the two unfortunate planets ; Jupiter and Venus the two fortunate.

40 *Ptolemy*, a famous astrologer ; an Egyptian.

41 *The Brachmans* are Indian philosophers, who remain to this day, and hold, after Pythagoras, the translation of souls from one body to another.

42 *To an Ethiop's son.* His meaning is, help her to any kind of slops which may cause her to miscarry, for fear she may be brought to bed of a blackmoor, which thou, being her husband, art bound to father ; and that bastard may, by law, inherit thy estate.

43 *His omen*, &c. The Romans thought it ominous to see a blackmoor in the morning, if he were the first man they met.

44 *Cæsonia*, wife to Caius Caligula, the great tyrant. 'T is said she gave him a love potion, which, flying up into his head, distracted him, and was the occasion of his committing so many acts of cruelty.

45 *The Thunderer*, &c. The story is in Homer, where Juno borrow'd the girdle of Venus, call'd *cestos*, to make Jupiter in love with her, while the Grecians and Trojans were fighting, that he might not help the latter.

46 *Agrippina* was the mother of the tyrant Nero, who poison'd her husband Claudius, that Nero might succeed, who was her son, and not Britannicus, who was the son of Claudius by a former wife.

47 *The widow* of Drymon poison'd her sons, that she might succeed to their estate. This was done either in the poet's time, or just before it.

48 *Medea*, out of revenge to Jason, who had forsaken her, kill'd the children which she had by him.

49 The Belides, who were fifty sisters, married to fifty young men, their cousin-germans, and kill'd them all on their wedding night, excepting Hypermnestra, who sav'd her husband Linus.

50 *Clytemnestra*, the wife of Agamemnon, who, in favor to her adulterer, Ægisthus, was consenting to his murther.

THE TENTH SATIRE OF JUVENAL

THE ARGUMENT

The poet's design, in this divine satire, is to represent the various wishes and desires of mankind, and to set out the folly of 'em. He runs thro' all the several heads of riches, honors, eloquence, fame for martial achievements, long life, and beauty ; and gives instances, in each, how frequently they have prov'd the ruin of those that own'd them. He concludes, therefore, that since we generally choose so ill for ourselves, we should do better to leave it to the gods to make the choice for us. All we can safely ask of Heaven lies within a very small compass. 'T is but health of body and mind. And if we have these, 't is not much matter what we want besides, for we have already enough to make us happy.

Look round the habitable world: how few
Know their own good; or knowing it, pursue.
How void of reason are our hopes and fears !
What in the conduct of our life appears
So well design'd, so luckily begun,
But, when we have our wish, we wish
    undone ?
  Whole houses, of their whole desires
    possess'd,
Are often ruin'd, at their own request.

In wars, and peace, things hurtful we require,
When made obnoxious to our own desire. 10
  With laurels some have fatally been ⎫
    crown'd;   ⎬
Some, who the depths of eloquence have
  found,
In that unnavigable stream were drown'd. ⎭
  The brawny fool,[1] who did his vigor
    boast,
In that presuming confidence was lost;
But more have been by avarice oppress'd,
And heaps of money crowded in the chest:
Unwieldy sums of wealth, which higher
  mount
Than files of marshal'd figures can account;
To which the stores of Crœsus, in the ⎫
  scale,   20 ⎬
Would look like little dolphins, when they
  sail   ⎭
In the vast shadow of the British whale.
  For this, in Nero's arbitrary time,
When virtue was a guilt, and wealth a
  crime,
A troop of cutthroat guards were sent to
  seize
The rich men's goods, and gut their palaces:
The mob, commission'd by the government,
Are seldom to an empty garret sent.
The fearful passenger, who travels late,
Charg'd with the carriage of a paltry plate,
Shakes at the moonshine shadow of a
  rush,   31
And sees a redcoat rise from every bush:
The beggar sings, ev'n when he sees the
  place
Beset with thieves, and never mends his
  pace.
  Of all the vows, the first and chief re-
    quest
Of each is, to be richer than the rest;
And yet no doubts the poor man's draught
  control,
He dreads no poison in his homely bowl.
Then fear the deadly drug, when gems di-
  vine
Enchase the cup, and sparkle in the wine. 40
  Will you not now the pair of sages praise,
Who the same end pursued, by several
  ways ?
One pitied, one contemn'd the woful times;
One laugh'd at follies, one lamented crimes:
Laughter is easy; but the wonder lies,
What stores of brine supplied the weeper's
  eyes.
Democritus could feed his spleen, and shake

His sides and shoulders till he felt 'em ache;
Tho' in his country town no lictors were,
Nor rods, nor ax, nor tribune did appear; 59
Nor all the foppish gravity of show
Which cunning magistrates on crowds be-
  stow.
  What had he done, had he beheld, on
  high,
Our prætor seated, in mock majesty ?
His chariot rolling o'er the dusty place,
While, with dumb pride, and a set formal
  face,
He moves in the dull ceremonial track,
With Jove's embroider'd coat upon his
  back:
A suit of hangings had not more oppress'd
His shoulders, than that long, laborious vest:
A heavy gewgaw, (call'd a crown,) that
  spread   61
About his temples, drown'd his narrow
  head;
And would have crush'd it with the massy
  freight,
But that a sweating slave sustain'd the
  weight:
A slave in the same chariot seen to ride,
To mortify the mighty madman's pride.
Add now th' imperial eagle, rais'd on high,
With golden beak (the mark of majesty),
Trumpets before, and on the left and right,
A cavalcade of nobles, all in white: 70
In their own natures false and flatt'ring
  tribes,
But made his friends by places and by
  bribes.
  In his own age, Democritus could find
Sufficient cause to laugh at humankind:
Learn from so great a wit: a land of bogs
With ditches fenc'd, a heaven fat with fogs,
May form a spirit fit to sway the State;
And make the neighb'ring monarchs fear
  their fate.
  He laughs at all the vulgar cares and
  fears;
At their vain triumphs, and their vainer
  tears: 80
An equal temper in his mind he found,
When Fortune flatter'd him, and when she
  frown'd.
'T is plain, from hence, that what our vows
  request
Are hurtful things, or useless at the best.
  Some ask for envied pow'r; which public
  hate
Pursues, and hurries headlong to their fate:

Down go the titles; and the statue crown'd
Is by base hands in the next river drown'd.
The guiltless horses, and the chariot wheel,
The same effects of vulgar fury feel: 90
The smith prepares his hammer for the
      stroke,
While the lung'd bellows hissing fire pro-
      voke;
Sejanus,[2] almost first of Roman names,
The great Sejanus crackles in the flames:
Form'd in the forge, the pliant brass is ⎤
      laid |
On anvils; and of head and limbs are ⎬
      made |
Pans, cans, and pisspots, a whole kitchen ⎦
      trade.

  Adorn your doors with laurels; and a bull,
Milk-white, and large, lead to the Capitol;
Sejanus with a rope is dragg'd along,   100
The sport and laughter of the giddy throng !
" Good Lord," they cry, " what Ethiop lips
      he has,
How foul a snout, and what a hanging face !
By Heav'n, I never could endure his sight;
But say, how came his monstrous crimes to
      light ?
What is the charge, and who the evidence
(The savior of the nation and the prince) ? "
" Nothing of this; but our old Cæsar sent
A noisy letter to his parliament."
" Nay, sirs, if Cæsar writ, I ask no more —
He 's guilty; and the question 's out of
      door."   111
How goes the mob ? (for that 's a mighty
      thing.)
When the king 's trump, the mob are for
      the king:
They follow Fortune, and the common cry
Is still against the rogue condemn'd to die.
  But the same very mob, that rascal crowd,
Had cried Sejanus, with a shout as loud,
Had his designs (by Fortune's favor blest)
Succeeded, and the prince's age oppress'd,
But long, long since, the times have chang'd
      their face,   120
The people grown degenerate and base;
Not suffer'd now the freedom of their choice,
To make their magistrates, and sell their
      voice.
  Our wise forefathers, great by sea and
      land,
Had once the pow'r and absolute command;
All offices of trust, themselves dispos'd;
Rais'd whom they pleas'd, and whom they
      pleas'd depos'd.

But we, who give our native rights away,
And our inslav'd posterity betray,
Are now reduc'd to beg an alms, and go   130
On holidays to see a puppet show.
  " There was a damn'd design," cries one,
      " no doubt;
For warrants are already issued out:
I met Brutidius in a mortal fright;
He 's dipp'd for certain, and plays least in
      sight:
I fear the rage of our offended prince,
Who thinks the senate slack in his defense !
Come, let us haste, our loyal zeal to show,
And spurn the wretched corpse of Cæsar's
      foe: 139
But let our slaves be present there, lest they
Accuse their masters, and for gain betray."
  Such were the whispers of those jealous
      times
About Sejanus' punishment and crimes.
  Now, tell me truly, wouldst thou change
      thy fate
To be, like him, first minister of state ?
To have thy levees crowded with resort,
Of a depending, gaping, servile court;
Dispose all honors of the sword and gown,
Grace with a nod, and ruin with a frown;
To hold thy prince in pupilage, and sway
That monarch whom the master'd world
      obey ?   151
While he, intent on secret lusts alone,
Lives to himself, abandoning the throne;
Coop'd in a narrow isle,[3] observing dreams
With flatt'ring wizards, and erecting
      schemes !
  I well believe, thou wouldst be great as
      he;
For every man 's a fool to that degree;
All wish the dire prerogative to kill;
Ev'n they would have the pow'r, who want
      the will:
But wouldst thou have thy wishes under-
      stood,   160
To take the bad together with the good ?
Wouldst thou not rather choose a small re-
      nown,
To be the may'r of some poor paltry town,
Bigly to look, and barb'rously to speak;
To pound false weights, and scanty mea-
      sures break ?
Then, grant we that Sejanus went astray
In ev'ry wish, and knew not how to pray:
For he who grasp'd the world's exhausted
      store,
Yet never had enough, but wish'd for more,

Rais'd a top-heavy tow'r, of monstrous
    height,   170
Which mold'ring, crush'd him underneath
    the weight.
What did the mighty Pompey's fall be-
    get;
And ruin'd him,[4] who, greater than the
    Great,
The stubborn pride of Roman nobles broke,
And bent their haughty necks beneath his
    yoke?
What else but his immoderate lust of
    pow'r,
Pray'rs made and granted in a luckless
    hour?
For few usurpers to the shades descend
By a dry death, or with a quiet end.
The boy, who scarce has paid his entrance
    down   180
To his proud pedant, or declin'd a noun,
(So small an elf, that, when the days are
    foul,
He and his satchel must be borne to school,)
Yet prays, and hopes, and aims at nothing
    less,
To prove a Tully, or Demosthenes:[5]
But both those orators, so much renown'd,
In their own depths of eloquence were
    drown'd:
The hand and head were never lost of those
Who dealt in dogg'rel, or who punn'd in
    prose.
  " Fortune foretun'd the dying notes of
    Rome: 190
Till I, thy consul sole, consol'd thy doom." [6]
His fate had crept below the lifted swords,
Had all his malice been to murther words.
I rather would be Mævius, thrash for
    rhymes
Like his, the scorn and scandal of the times,
Than that *Philippic*,[7] fatally divine,
Which is inscrib'd the *Second*, should be
    mine.
Nor he, the wonder of the Grecian throng,
Who drove them with the torrent of his
    tongue,
Who shook the theaters, and sway'd the
    state   200
Of Athens, found a more propitious fate:
Whom, born beneath a boding horoscope,
His sire, the blear-ey'd Vulcan of a shop,
From Mars his forge, sent to Minerva's
    schools,
To learn th' unlucky art of wheedling fools.
  With itch of honor and opinion vain,

All things beyond their native worth we
    strain:
The spoils [8] of war, brought to Feretrian
    Jove,
An empty coat of armor hung above
The conqueror's chariot, and in triumph
    borne,   210
A streamer from a boarded galley torn,
A chap-fall'n beaver loosely hanging by
The cloven helm, an arch of victory,
On whose high convex sits a captive foe,
And sighing casts a mournful look below;
Of ev'ry nation each illustrious name,
Such toys as these have cheated into fame:
Exchanging solid quiet, to obtain
The windy satisfaction of the brain.
  So much the thirst of honor fires the
    blood;   220
So many would be great, so few be good.
For who would Virtue for herself regard,
Or wed, without the portion of reward?
Yet this mad chase of fame, by few pur-
    sued,
Has drawn destruction on the multitude:
This avarice of praise in times to come,
Those long inscriptions, crowded on the
    tomb,
Should some wild fig tree take her native
    bent,
And heave below the gaudy monument,
Would crack the marble titles, and dis-
    perse   230
The characters of all the lying verse.
For sepulchers themselves must crumbling
    fall
In time's abyss, the common grave of all.
  Great Hannibal within the balance lay,
And tell how many pounds his ashes weigh;
Whom Afric was not able to contain,
Whose length runs level with th' Atlantic
    main,
And wearies fruitful Nilus, to convey
His sun-beat waters by so long a way;
Which Ethiopia's double clime divides, 240
And elephants in other mountains hides.
Spain first he won, the Pyrenæans pass'd,
And steepy Alps, the mounds that Nature
    cast;
And with corroding juices, as he went,
A passage thro' the living rocks he rent.
Then, like a torrent, rolling from on high,
He pours his headlong rage on Italy;
In three victorious battles overrun;
Yet, still uneasy, cries: "There's nothing
    done,

Till level with the ground their gates are laid, 250
And Punic flags on Roman tow'rs display'd."
  Ask what a face belong'd to this high fame:
His picture scarcely would deserve a frame;
A signpost dauber would disdain to paint
The one-ey'd hero on his elephant.
Now what's his end, O charming Glory! say,
What rare fifth act to crown this huffing play?
In one deciding battle overcome,
He flies, is banish'd from his native home;
Begs refuge in a foreign court, and there
Attends, his mean petition to prefer; 261
Repuls'd by surly grooms, who wait before
The sleeping tyrant's interdicted door.
  What wondrous sort of death has ⎫
Heav'n design'd,   ⎬
Distinguish'd from the herd of human- ⎪
kind,   ⎭
For so untam'd, so turbulent a mind!
Nor swords at hand, nor hissing darts afar,
Are doom'd t' avenge the tedious bloody war;
But poison, drawn thro' a ring's hollow plate,
Must finish him; a sucking infant's fate. 270
Go, climb the rugged Alps, ambitious fool,
To please the boys, and be a theme at school.
  One world suffic'd not Alexander's mind:
Coop'd up, he seem'd in earth and seas confin'd;
And, struggling, stretch'd his restless limbs about
The narrow globe, to find a passage out.
Yet, enter'd in the brick-built town,[9] he tried
The tomb, and found the strait dimensions wide:
" Death only this mysterious truth unfolds,
The mighty soul, how small a body holds."
  Old Greece a tale of Athos [10] would make out, 281
Cut from the continent, and sail'd about;
Seas hid with navies, chariots passing o'er
The channel, on a bridge from shore to shore:
Rivers, whose depth no sharp beholder sees,
Drunk at an army's dinner, to the lees;
With a long legend of romantic things,
Which in his cups the bowsy poet sings.
But how did he return, this haughty brave,

Who whipp'd the winds, and made the sea his slave? 290
(Tho' Neptune took unkindly to be ⎫
bound;   ⎪
And Eurus never such hard usage found ⎬
In his Æolian prisons under ground;) ⎪
What god so mean, ev'n he who points the way,[11]
So merciless a tyrant to obey!
But how return'd he? let us ask again: ⎫
In a poor skiff he pass'd the bloody main, ⎪
Chok'd with the slaughter'd bodies of ⎬
his train.   ⎭
For fame he pray'd, but let th' event declare
He had no mighty penn'worth of his pray'r.
" Jove, grant me length of life, and years' good store 301
Heap on my bending back; I ask no more."
Both sick and healthful, old and young, conspire
In this one silly mischievous desire.
Mistaken blessing, which old age they call!
'T is a long, nasty, darksome hospital,
A ropy chain of rheums; a visage rough,
Deform'd, unfeatur'd, and a skin of buff;
A stitch-fall'n cheek, that hangs below the jaw;
Such wrinkles, as a skilful hand would draw 310
For an old grandam ape, when, with a grace,
She sits at squat, and scrubs her leathern face.
  In youth, distinctions infinite abound;
No shape or feature just alike are found;
The fair, the black, the feeble, and the ⎫
strong;   ⎪
But the same foulness does to age belong, ⎬
The selfsame palsy, both in limbs and ⎪
tongue;   ⎭
The skull and forehead one bald barren plain,
And gums unarm'd to mumble meat in vain:
Besides th' eternal drivel, that supplies 320
The dropping beard, from nostrils, mouth, and eyes.
His wife and children loathe him, and, what's worse,
Himself does his offensive carrion curse!
Flatt'rers forsake him too; for who would kill
Himself, to be remember'd in a will?
His taste not only pall'd to wine and meat,
But to the relish of a nobler treat.

The limber nerve, in vain provok'd to rise,
Inglorious from the field of battle flies:
Poor feeble dotard, how could he advance
With his blue headpiece, and his broken
    lance ?   331
Add, that endeavoring still without effect,
A lust more sordid justly we suspect.
    Those senses lost, behold a new defeat,
The soul dislodging from another seat.
What music, or enchanting voice, can cheer
A stupid, old, impenetrable ear ?
No matter in what place, or what degree
Of the full theater, he sits to see;
Cornets and trumpets cannot reach his ear:
Under an actor's nose he 's never near.   341
    His boy must bawl, to make him under-
        stand
The hour o' th' day, or such a lord 's at hand:
The little blood that creeps within his veins,
Is but just warm'd in a hot fever's pains.
In fine, he wears no limb about him sound;
With sores and sicknesses beleaguer'd round:
Ask me their names, I sooner could relate
How many drudges on salt Hippia wait;
What crowds of patients the town doctor
    kills,   350
Or how, last fall, he rais'd the weekly bills;
What provinces by Basilus were spoil'd;
What herds of heirs by guardians are be-
    guil'd;
How many bouts a day that bitch has tried;
How many boys that pedagogue can ride;
What lands and lordships for their owners
    know
My quondam barber, but his worship now.
This dotard of his broken back com-
    plains,
One his legs fail, and one his shoulder
    pains;
Another is of both his eyes bereft,   360
And envies who has one for aiming left.
A fifth with trembling lips expecting stands,
As in his childhood, cramm'd by others'
    hands;
One, who at sight of supper open'd wide ⎤
His jaws before, and whetted grinders │
    tried;   ⎬
Now only yawns, and waits to be sup- │
    plied: ⎦
Like a young swallow, when with weary
    wings
Expected food her fasting mother brings.
    His loss of members is a heavy curse,
But all his faculties decay'd, a worse !   370
His servants' names he has forgotten quite;

Knows not his friend who supp'd with him
    last night:
Not ev'n the children he begot and bred;
Or his will knows 'em not; for, in their
    stead,
In form of law, a common hackney jade,
Sole heir, for secret services, is made:
So lewd, and such a batter'd brothel whore,
That she defies all comers at her door.
Well, yet suppose his senses are his own,
He lives to be chief mourner for his son: 380
Before his face his wife and brother burns;
He numbers all his kindred in their urns.
These are the fines he pays for living long,
And dragging tedious age in his own wrong:
Griefs always green, a household still in ⎤
    tears,   │
Sad pomps, a threshold throng'd with   ⎬
    daily biers,   │
And liveries of black for length of years. ⎦
    Next to the raven's age, the Pylian king [12]
Was longest liv'd of any two-legg'd thing;
Blest, to defraud the grave so long, to
    mount   390
His number'd years, and on his right hand
    count [13]
Three hundred seasons, guzzling must of
    wine !
But, hold a while, and hear himself repine
At fate's unequal laws; and at the clue
Which, merciless in length, the midmost
    sister [14] drew.
When his brave son upon the fun'ral pyre
He saw extended, and his beard on fire,
He turn'd, and weeping, ask'd his friends
    what crime
Had curs'd his age to this unhappy time.
    Thus mourn'd old Peleus for Achilles
        slain,   400
And thus Ulysses' father did complain.
    How fortunate an end had Priam made,
Among his ancestors a mighty shade,
While Troy yet stood; when Hector, with
    the race
Of royal bastards, might his funeral grace:
Amidst the tears of Trojan dames inurn'd,
And by his loyal daughters truly mourn'd !
Had Heav'n so blest him, he had died before
The fatal fleet to Sparta Paris bore.
But mark what age produc'd; he liv'd to
    see   410
His town in flames, his falling monarchy:
In fine, the feeble sire, reduc'd by fate,
To change his scepter for a sword, too late,
His last effort before Jove's altar tries; [15]

A soldier half, and half a sacrifice:
Falls like an ox, that waits the coming
    blow;
Old and unprofitable to the plow.
    At least, he died a man; his queen [16] sur-
        viv'd,
To howl, and in a barking body liv'd.
    I hasten to our own; nor will relate   420
Great Mithridates' [17] and rich Crœsus' [18] fate;
Whom Solon wisely counsel'd to attend
The name of happy, till he knew his end.
    That Marius was an exile, that he fled,
Was ta'en, in ruin'd Carthage begg'd his
    bread,
All these were owing to a life too long:
For whom had Rome beheld so happy,
    young!
High in his chariot, and with laurel crown'd,
When he had led the Cimbrian captives
    round
The Roman streets; descending from his
    state,   430
In that blest hour he should have begg'd
    his fate:
Then, then, he might have died of all ad-
    mir'd,
And his triumphant soul with shouts ex-
    pir'd.
    Campania, Fortune's malice to prevent,
To Pompey [19] an indulgent fever sent;
But public pray'rs impos'd on Heav'n, to
    give
Their much-lov'd leader an unkind reprieve.
The city's fate and his conspir'd to save
The head reserv'd for an Egyptian slave.
    Cethegus,[20] tho' a traitor to the State,   440
And tortur'd, scap'd this ignominous fate:
And Sergius,[21] who a bad cause bravely
    tried,
All of a piece, and undiminish'd, died.
    To Venus the fond mother makes a
        pray'r,
That all her sons and daughters may be
        fair:
True, for the boys a mumbling vow she
        sends;
But, for the girls, the vaulted temple rends:
They must be finish'd pieces; 't is allow'd
Diana's beauty made Latona proud,
And pleas'd, to see the wond'ring people
        pray   450
To the new-rising sister of the day.
    And yet Lucretia's fate would bar that
        vow;
And fair Virginia [22] would her fate bestow

On Rutila, and change her faultless make
For the foul rumple of her camel back.
    But, for his mother's boy, the beau, what
        frights
His parents have by day, what anxious
        nights!
Form join'd with virtue is a sight too rare:
Chaste is no epithet to suit with fair.
Suppose the same traditionary strain   460
Of rigid manners in the house remain;
Inveterate truth, an old plain Sabine's heart;
Suppose that Nature, too, has done her part;
Infus'd into his soul a sober grace,
And blush'd a modest blood into his face,
(For Nature is a better guardian far
Than saucy pedants, or dull tutors are:)
Yet still the youth must ne'er arrive at
        man;
(So much almighty bribes and presents
        can;)
Ev'n with a parent, where persuasions fail,
Money is impudent, and will prevail.   471
    We never read of such a tyrant king,
Who gelt a boy deform'd, to hear him sing.
Nor Nero, in his more luxurious rage,
E'er made a mistress of an ugly page:
Sporus, his spouse, nor crooked was, nor ⎫
        lame,   ⎪
With mountain back, and belly, from the ⎬
        game   ⎪
Cross-barr'd; but both his sexes well ⎪
        became.   ⎭
Go, boast your springal, by his beauty curst
To ills, nor think I have declar'd the
        worst: 480
His form procures him journeywork; a strife
Betwixt town-madams, and the merchant's
        wife:
Guess, when he undertakes this public war,
What furious beasts offended cuckolds are.
    Adult'rers are with dangers round beset;
Born under Mars, they cannot scape the
        net;
And from revengeful husbands oft have
        tried
Worse handling than severest laws provide:
One stabs; one slashes; one, with cruel art,
Makes colon suffer for the peccant part.   490
    But your Endymion, your smooth, smock-
        fac'd boy,
Unrival'd, shall a beauteous dame enjoy.
Not so: one more salacious, rich, and old,
Outbids, and buys her pleasure for her gold:
Now he must moil and drudge for one he
        loathes;

She keeps him high in equipage and clothes;
She pawns her jewels and her rich attire,
And thinks the workman worthy of his hire:
In all things else immoral, stingy, mean;
But, in her lusts, a conscionable quean. 500
  " She may be handsome, yet be chaste,"
    you say —
Good observator, not so fast away:
Did it not cost the modest youth [23] his life,
Who shunn'd th' embraces of his father's
    wife ?
And was not t'other stripling [24] forc'd to ⎫
    fly,   ⎪
Who coldly did his patron's queen deny,   ⎬
And pleaded laws of hospitality ?   ⎭
The ladies charg'd 'em home, and turn'd
    the tale;
With shame they redden'd, and with spite
    grew pale.
'T is dang'rous to deny the longing dame;
She loses pity, who has lost her shame. 511
  Now Silius wants thy counsel, give ad-
    vice;
Wed Cæsar's wife,[25] or die; the choice is
    nice.
Her comet-eyes she darts on ev'ry grace,
And takes a fatal liking to his face.
Adorn'd with bridal pomp she sits in state;
The public notaries and auspex wait:
The genial bed is in the garden dress'd, 518 ⎫
The portion paid, and ev'ry rite express'd ⎬
Which in a Roman marriage is profess'd. ⎭
'T is no stol'n wedding this; rejecting awe,
She scorns to marry, but in form of law.
In this moot case, your judgment: to re-
    fuse
Is present death, besides the night you
    lose:
If you consent, 't is hardly worth your pain;
A day or two of anxious life you gain,
Till loud reports thro' all the town have
    pass'd,
And reach the prince; for cuckolds hear
    the last.
Indulge thy pleasure, youth, and take thy
    swing;
For not to take is but the selfsame thing:
Inevitable death before thee lies, 531
But looks more kindly thro' a lady's eyes.
  What then remains ? Are we depriv'd
    of will;
Must we not wish, for fear of wishing
    ill ?
Receive my counsel, and securely move;
Intrust thy fortune to the pow'rs above.

Leave them to manage for thee, and to
    grant
What their unerring wisdom sees thee want:
In goodness as in greatness they excel;
Ah, that we lov'd ourselves but half so
    well ! 540
We, blindly by our headstrong passions led,
Are hot for action, and desire to wed;
Then wish for heirs: but to the gods alone ⎫
Our future offspring, and our wives are   ⎪
    known;   ⎬
Th' audacious strumpet, and ungracious   ⎪
    son.   ⎭
  Yet, not to rob the priests of pious gain,
That altars be not wholly built in vain;
Forgive the gods the rest, and stand con-
    fin'd
To health of body, and content of mind:
A soul, that can securely death defy, 550
And count it nature's privilege to die;
Serene and manly, harden'd to sustain
The load of life, and exercis'd in pain;
Guiltless of hate, and proof against desire;
That all things weighs, and nothing can ad-
    mire;
That dares prefer the toils of Hercules
To dalliance, banquets, and ignoble ease.
The path to peace is virtue: what I show,
Thyself may freely on thyself bestow;
Fortune was never worship'd by the wise;
But, set aloft by fools, usurps the skies. 561

EXPLANATORY NOTES ON THE TENTH
SATIRE

1 Milo, of Crotona ; who, for a trial of his
strength, going to rend an oak, perish'd in the
attempt, for his arms were caught in the trunk
of it, and he was devour'd by wild beasts.
  2 *Sejanus* was Tiberius's first favorite ; and,
while he continued so, had the highest marks of
honor bestow'd on him : statues and triumphal
chariots were everywhere erected to him. But,
as soon as he fell into disgrace with the emperor,
these were all immediately dismounted, and the
senate and common people insulted over him as
meanly as they had fawn'd on him before.
  3 The island of Capreæ, which lies about a
league out at sea from the Campanian shore,
was the scene of Tiberius's pleasures in the latter part of his reign. There he liv'd, for some
years, with diviners, soothsayers, and worse
company ; and from thence dispatch'd all his
orders to the senate.
  4 Julius Cæsar, who got the better of Pompey, that was styl'd " the Great."
  5 *Demosthenes* and *Tully* both died for their
oratory: Demosthenes gave himself poison, to
avoid being carried to Antipater, one of Alexander's captains, who had then made himself

master of Athens. Tully was murther'd by M. Antony's order, in return for those invectives he had made against him.

6 The Latin of this couplet is a famous verse of Tully's, in which he sets out the happiness of his own consulship, famous for the vanity and the ill poetry of it; for Tully, as he had a good deal of the one, so he had no great share of the other.

7 The orations of Tully against M. Antony were styl'd by him *Philippics*, in imitation of Demosthenes, who had given that name before to those he made against Philip of Macedon.

8 This is a mock account of a Roman triumph.

9 Babylon, where Alexander died.

10 Xerxes is represented in history after a very romantic manner: affecting fame beyond measure, and doing the most extravagant things to compass it. Mount Athos made a prodigious promontory in the Ægean Sea; he is said to have cut a channel thro' it, and to have sail'd round it. He made a bridge of boats over the Hellespont, where it was three miles broad; and order'd a whipping for the winds and seas, because they had once cross'd his designs; as we have a very solemn account of it in Herodotus. But, after all these vain boasts, he was shamefully beaten by Themistocles at Salamis; and return'd home, leaving most of his fleet behind him.

11 Mercury, who was a god of the lowest size, and employ'd always in errands between heaven and hell; and mortals us'd him accordingly: for his statues were anciently plac'd where roads met, with directions on the fingers of 'em, pointing out the several ways to travelers.

12 Nestor, King of Pylus; who was three hundred years old, according to Homer's account; at least as he is understood by his expositors.

13 The ancients counted by their fingers. Their left hands serv'd 'em till they came up to an hundred. After that they us'd their right, to express all greater numbers.

14 The Fates were three sisters, which had all some peculiar business assign'd 'em by the poets, in relation to the lives of men. The first held the distaff, the second spun the thread, and the third cut it.

15 Whilst Troy was sacking by the Greeks, old King Priam is said to have buckled on his armor to oppose 'em; which he had no sooner done, but he was met by Pyrrhus, and slain before the altar of Jupiter, in his own palace; as we have the story finely told in Virgil's second *Æneid*.

16 Hecuba, his queen, escap'd the swords of the Grecians, and outliv'd him. It seems she behav'd herself so fiercely and uneasily to her husband's murtherers while she liv'd, that the poets thought fit to turn her into a bitch when she died.

17 *Mithridates*, after he had disputed the empire of the world for forty years together, with the Romans, was at last depriv'd of life and empire by Pompey the Great.

18 *Crœsus*, in the midst of his prosperity, making his boast to Solon how happy he was, receiv'd this answer from the wise man: that no one could pronounce himself happy, till he saw what his end should be. The truth of this Crœsus found, when he was put in chains by Cyrus, and condemn'd to die.

19 *Pompey*, in the midst of his glory, fell into a dangerous fit of sickness at Naples. A great many cities then made public supplications for him. He recover'd; was beaten at Pharsalia; fled to Ptolemy, King of Egypt; and, instead of receiving protection at his court, had his head struck off by his order, to please Cæsar.

20 *Cethegus* was one that conspir'd with Catiline, and was put to death by the Senate.

21 Catiline died fighting.

22 *Virginia* was kill'd by her own father, to prevent her being expos'd to the lust of Appius Claudius, who had ill designs upon her. The story at large is in Livy's third book; and 't is a remarkable one, as it gave occasion to the putting down the power of the Decemviri, of whom Appius was one.

23 Hippolytus, the son of Theseus, was lov'd by his mother-in-law, Phædria; but he not complying with her, she procur'd his death.

24 Bellerophon, the son of King Glaucus, residing some time at the court of Pœtus, King of the Argives, the queen, Sthenobæa, fell in love with him; but he refusing her, she turn'd the accusation upon him, and he narrowly scap'd Pœtus's vengeance.

25 Messalina, wife to the Emperor Claudius, infamous for her lewdness. She set her eyes upon C. Silius, a fine youth; forc'd him to quit his own wife, and marry her, with all the formalities of a wedding, whilst Claudius Cæsar was sacrificing at Hostia. Upon his return, he put both Silius and her to death.

THE SIXTEENTH SATIRE OF JUVENAL

THE ARGUMENT

The poet in this satire proves that the condition of a soldier is much better than that of a countryman: first, because a countryman, however affronted, provok'd, and struck himself, dares not strike a soldier who is only to be judg'd by a court-martial; and, by the law of Camillus, which obliges him not to quarrel without the trenches, he is also assur'd to have a speedy hearing and quick dispatch: whereas, the townsman or peasant is delay'd in his suit by frivolous pretenses, and not sure of justice when he is heard in the court. The soldier is also privileg'd to make a will, and to give away his estate, which he got in war, to whom he pleases, without consideration of parentage or relations, which is denied to all other Romans. This satire was written by Juvenal when he

was a commander in Egypt: 't is certainly
his, tho' I think it not finish'd. And, if it be
well observ'd, you will find he intended an
invective against a standing army.

WHAT vast prerogatives, my Gallus, are
Accruing to the mighty man of war !
For, if into a lucky camp I light,
Tho' raw in arms, and yet afraid to fight,
Befriend me, my good stars, and all goes
    right:
One happy hour is to a soldier better,
Than Mother Juno's [1] recommending let-
    ter,
Or Venus, when to Mars she would prefer
My suit, and own the kindness done to her.
  See what our common privileges are: 10
As, first, no saucy citizen shall dare
To strike a soldier, nor, when struck, re-
    sent
The wrong, for fear of farther punish-
    ment:
Not tho' his teeth are beaten out, his eyes
Hang by a string, in bumps his forehead
    rise,
Shall he presume to mention his disgrace,
Or beg amends for his demolish'd face.
A booted judge shall sit to try his cause,
Not by the statute, but by martial laws,
Which old Camillus [2] order'd, to confine   20
The brawls of soldiers to the trench and
    line:
A wise provision; and from thence 't is
    clear,
That officers a soldier's cause should hear;
And, taking cognizance of wrongs receiv'd,
An honest man may hope to be reliev'd.
So far 't is well: but with a general cry,
The regiment will rise in mutiny,
The freedom of their fellow-rogue demand,
And, if refus'd, will threaten to disband.
Withdraw thy action, and depart in peace;
The remedy is worse than the disease;   31
This cause is worthy him,[3] who in the hall
Would for his fee, and for his client, bawl:
But wouldst thou, friend, who hast two legs
    alone,
(Which, Heav'n be prais'd, thou yet mayst
    call thy own,)
Wouldst thou to run the gauntlet these
    expose
To a whole company of hobnail'd shoes ? [4]
Sure the good breeding of wise citizens
Should teach 'em more good nature to their
    shins.

Besides, whom canst thou think so much
    thy friend ?
Who dares appear thy business to defend ?   40
Dry up thy tears, and pocket up th'
    abuse,
Nor put thy friend to make a bad ex-
    cuse:
The judge cries out: "Your evidence pro-
    duce."
Will he, who saw the soldier's mutton fist,
And saw thee maul'd, appear within the
    list,
To witness truth ? When I see one so brave,
The dead, think I, are risen from the
    grave;
And with their long spade beards and mat-
    ted hair,
Our honest ancestors are come to take the
    air.   50
Against a clown, with more security,
A witness may be brought to swear a lie,
Than, tho' his evidence be full and fair,
To vouch a truth against a man of war.
  More benefits remain, and claim'd as
    rights,
Which are a standing army's perquisites.
If any rogue vexatious suits advance
Against me for my known inheritance,
Enter by violence my fruitful grounds,
Or take the sacred landmark from my
    bounds,   60
Those bounds which, with procession and
    with pray'r,
And offer'd cakes, have been my annual
    care; [5]
Or if my debtors do not keep their day,
Deny their hands, and then refuse to pay;
I must with patience all the terms attend,
Among the common causes that depend,
Till mine is call'd; and that long-look'd-for
    day
Is still encumber'd with some new delay.
Perhaps the cloth of state is only spread,[6]
Some of the quorum may be sick abed;   70
That judge is hot, and doffs his gown, while
    this
O'ernight was bowsy, and goes out to piss:
So many rubs appear, the time is gone
For hearing, and the tedious suit goes on;
But buff and beltmen never know these
    cares,
No time, nor trick of law, their action bars:
Their cause they to an easier issue put;
They will be heard, or they lug out, and
    cut.

Another branch of their revenue still
Remains, beyond their boundless right
    to kill,   80
Their father yet alive, impow'r'd to
    make a will.[7]
For, what their prowess gain'd, the law de-
    clares,
Is to themselves alone, and to their heirs:
No share of that goes back to the be-
    getter,
But if the son fights well, and plunders
    better,
Like stout Coranus, his old shaking sire
Does a remembrance in his will desire;
Inquisitive of fights, and longs in vain
To find him in the number of the slain:
But still he lives, and, rising by the war,
Enjoys his gains, and has enough to
    spare;   91
For 't is a noble general's prudent part
To cherish valor, and reward desert:
Let him be daub'd with lace, live high, and
    whore;
Sometimes be lousy, but be never poor.

EXPLANATORY NOTES ON THE SIX-TEENTH SATIRE

1 *Juno* was mother to Mars, the God of War ; Venus was his mistress.

2 *Camillus,* who, being first banish'd by his ungrateful countrymen the Romans, afterwards return'd, and freed them from the Gauls, made a law which prohibited the soldiers from quarreling without the camp, lest upon that pretense they might happen to be absent when they ought to be on duty.

3 *This cause is worthy him,* &c. The poet names a Modenese lawyer, whom he calls Vagellius, who was so impudent that he would plead any cause, right or wrong, without shame or fear.

4 *Hobnail'd shoes.* The Roman soldiers wore plates of iron under their shoes, or stuck them with nails, as countrymen do now.

5 *Landmarks* were us'd by the Romans almost in the same manner as now ; and as we go once a year in procession about the bounds of parishes, and renew them, so they offer'd cakes upon the stone, or landmark.

6 The courts of judicature were hung, and spread, as with us ; but spread only before the hundred judges were to sit and judge public causes, which were call'd by lot.

7 The Roman soldiers had the privilege of making a will, in their father's lifetime, of what they had purchas'd in the wars, as being no part of their patrimony. By this will they had power of excluding their own parents, and giving the estate so gotten to whom they pleas'd. Therefore, says the poet, Coranus (a soldier

contemporary with Juvenal, who had rais'd his fortune by the wars) was courted by his own father to make him his heir.

THE FIRST SATIRE OF PERSIUS

ARGUMENT OF THE PROLOGUE TO THE FIRST SATIRE

The design of the author was to conceal his name and quality. He liv'd in the dangerous times of the tyrant Nero, and aims particularly at him in most of his satires. For which reason, tho' he was a Roman knight, and of a plentiful fortune, he would appear in this *Prologue* but a beggarly poet, who writes for bread. After this, he breaks into the business of the *First Satire;* which is chiefly to decry the poetry then in fashion, and the impudence of those who were endeavoring to pass their stuff upon the world.

PROLOGUE TO THE FIRST SATIRE

I NEVER did on cleft Parnassus [1] dream,
Nor taste the sacred Heliconian stream;
Nor can remember when my brain, in-
    spir'd,
Was by the Muses into madness fir'd.
My share in pale Pyrene [2] I resign,
And claim no part in all the mighty
    Nine.
Statues,[3] with winding ivy crown'd, be-
    long
To nobler poets, for a nobler song:
Heedless of verse, and hopeless of the
    crown,
Scarce half a wit, and more than half a
    clown,   10
Before the shrine [4] I lay my rugged num-
    bers down.
Who taught the parrot human notes to
    try,
Or with a voice endued the chatt'ring pie ?
'T was witty want, fierce hunger to ap-
    pease;
Want taught their masters, and their masters these.
Let gain, that gilded bait, be hung on
    high;
The hungry witlings have it in their eye:
Pies, crows, and daws, poetic presents
    bring;
You say they squeak, but they will swear
    they sing.

THE FIRST SATIRE

IN DIALOGUE

BETWIXT THE POET AND HIS FRIEND OR MONITOR

THE ARGUMENT

I need not repeat that the chief aim of the author is against bad poets in this satire. But I must add that he includes also bad orators, who began at that time (as Petronius in the beginning of his book tells us) to enervate manly eloquence by tropes and figures, ill plac'd, and worse applied. Amongst the poets, Persius covertly strikes at Nero, some of whose verses he recites with scorn and indignation. He also takes notice of the noblemen and their abominable poetry, who, in the luxury of their fortune, set up for wits and judges. The satire is in dialogue, betwixt the author and his friend or monitor; who dissuades him from this dangerous attempt of exposing great men. But Persius, who is of a free spirit, and has not forgotten that Rome was once a commonwealth, breaks thro' all those difficulties, and boldly arraigns the false judgment of the age in which he lives, The reader may observe that our poet was a Stoic philosopher; and that all his moral sentences, both here and in all the rest of his satires, are drawn from the dogmas of that sect.

PERSIUS. How anxious are our cares, and
    yet how vain
The bent of our desires !
  FRIEND.   Thy spleen contain;
For none will read thy satires.
  PER.   This to me ?
  FRIEND. None; or what 's next to none,
    but two or three.
'T is hard, I grant.
  PER.   'T is nothing; I can bear
That paltry scribblers have the public ear:
That this vast universal fool, the Town,
Should cry up Labeo's stuff,[1] and cry me
    down.
They damn themselves; nor will my Muse
    descend
To clap with such, who fools and knaves
    commend: 10
Their smiles and censures are to me the
    same;
I care not what they praise, or what they
    blame.
In full assemblies let the crowd prevail:
I weigh no merit by the common scale.

The conscience is the test of ev'ry mind;
" Seek not thyself, without thyself, to find."
But where 's that Roman ? — Somewhat I
    would say,
But fear — let Fear, for once, to Truth
    give way.
Truth lends the Stoic courage: when I look
On human acts, and read in Nature's book,
From the first pastimes of our infant age,
To elder cares, and man's severer page; 22
When stern as tutors, and as uncles hard,
We lash the pupil, and defraud the ward:
Then, then I say — or would say, if I
    durst —
But thus provok'd, I must speak out, or
    burst.
  FRIEND. Once more forbear.
  PER.   I cannot rule my spleen;
My scorn rebels, and tickles me within.
  First, to begin at home: our authors write
In lonely rooms, secur'd from public sight;
Whether in prose, or verse, 't is all the
    same;   31
The prose is fustian, and the numbers
    lame:
All noise, and empty pomp, a storm of
    words,
Lab'ring with sound, that little sense affords.
They comb,[2] and then they order ev'ry
    hair:
A gown, or white, or scour'd to whiteness,
    wear;
A birthday jewel bobbing at their ear:
Next, gargle well their throats, and thus
    prepar'd,
They mount, a-God's name, to be seen and
    heard,
From their high scaffold, with a trumpet
    cheek,   40
And ogling all their audience ere they
    speak.
The nauseous nobles, ev'n the chief of
    Rome,
With gaping mouths to these rehearsals
    come,
And pant with pleasure, when some lusty
    line
The marrow pierces, and invades the chine;
At open fulsome bawdry they rejoice,
And slimy jests applaud with broken voice.
Base prostitute, thus dost thou gain thy
    bread ?
Thus dost thou feed their ears, and thus
    art fed ?

At his own filthy stuff he grins and brays,
And gives the sign where he expects their
       praise.   51
   Why have I learn'd, say'st thou, if, thus
       confin'd,
I choke the noble vigor of my mind ?
Know, my wild fig tree,[3] which in rocks is
       bred,
Will split the quarry, and shoot out the
       head.
Fine fruits of learning ! old ambitious fool,
Dar'st thou apply that adage of the school;
As if 't is nothing worth that lies conceal'd,
And " science is not science till reveal'd " ?
O, but 't is brave to be admir'd, to see   60
The crowd, with pointing fingers, cry:
       " That 's he:
That 's he whose wondrous poem is become
A lecture for the noble youth of Rome !
Who, by their fathers, is at feasts renown'd;
And often quoted when the bowls go round."
Full gorg'd and flush'd, they wantonly re-
       hearse,
And add to wine the luxury of verse.
One, clad in purple, not to lose his time,
Eats, and recites some lamentable rhyme:
Some senseless Phyllis, in a broken note, 70
Snuffling at nose, or croaking in his throat.
Then graciously the mellow audience nod;
Is not th' immortal author made a god ?
Are not his manes blest, such praise to have ?
Lies not the turf more lightly on his grave ?
And roses (while his loud applause they
       sing)
Stand ready from his sepulcher to spring ?
   All these, you cry, but light objections
       are;
Mere malice, and you drive the jest too far.
For does there breathe a man who can re-
       ject   80
A general fame, and his own lines neglect ?
In cedar tablets [4] worthy to appear,   ⎤
That need not fish, or frankincense to |
       fear ?   ⎬
   Thou, whom I make the adverse part |
       to bear,   ⎦
Be answer'd thus. — If I by chance succeed
In what I write, (and that 's a chance in-
       deed,)
Know, I am not so stupid, or so hard,
Not to feel praise, or fame's deserv'd re-
       ward:
But this I cannot grant, that thy applause
Is my work's ultimate, or only cause.   90
Prudence can ne'er propose so mean a prize;

For mark what vanity within it lies.
Like Labeo's *Iliads*, in whose verse is found
Nothing but trifling care, and empty sound:
Such little elegies as nobles write,
Who would be poets, in Apollo's spite.
Them and their woful works the Muse de-
       fies:
Products of citron beds,[5] and golden cano-
       pies.
To give thee all thy due, thou hast the   ⎤
       heart |
To make a supper, with a fine dessert; 100 ⎬
And to thy threadbare friend, a cast old |
       suit impart.   ⎦
   Thus brib'd, thou thus bespeak'st him:
       " Tell me, friend,
(For I love truth, nor can plain speech
       offend,)
What says the world of me and of my
       Muse ? "
   The poor dare nothing tell but flatt'ring
       news:
But shall I speak ? Thy verse is wretched
       rhyme,
And all thy labors are but loss of time.
Thy strutting belly swells, thy paunch is
       high;
Thou writ'st not, but thou pissest poetry.
   All authors to their own defects are
       blind;   110
Hadst thou but, Janus-like,[6] a face behind,
To see the people, what splaymouths they
       make;
To mark their fingers, pointed at thy back;
Their tongues loll'd out, a foot beyond
       the pitch,
When most athirst, of an Apulian bitch:
But noble scribblers are with flatt'ry fed;
For none dare find their faults, who eat
       their bread.
   To pass the poets of patrician blood,
What is 't the common reader takes for
       good ?
The verse in fashion is, when numbers
       flow,   120
Soft without sense, and without spirit slow:
So smooth and equal, that no sight can find
The rivet, where the polish'd piece was
       join'd:
So even all, with such a steady view,
As if he shut one eye to level true.
Whether the vulgar vice his satire stings,
The people's riots, or the rage of kings,
The gentle poet is alike in all;
His reader hopes no rise, and fears no fall.

FRIEND. Hourly we see some raw pin-
feather'd thing   130
Attempt to mount, and fights and heroes
sing;
Who for false quantities was whipp'd at
school
But t'other day, and breaking grammar
rule;
Whose trivial art was never tried above
The bare description of a native grove;
Who knows not how to praise the coun- ⌉
try store, |
The feasts, the baskets, nor the fatted |
boar;   ⎬
Nor paint the flow'ry fields, that paint |
themselves before;   ⌋
Where Romulus [7] was bred, and Quintius
born,
Whose shining plowshare was in furrows
worn,   140
Met by his trembling wife, returning home,
And rustically joy'd, as chief of Rome:
She wip'd the sweat from the dictator's ⌉
brow, |
And o'er his back his robe did rudely ⎬
throw; |
The lictors bore in state their lord's tri- |
umphant plow.   ⌋
  Some love to hear the fustian poet roar,
And some on antiquated authors pore;
Rummage for sense, and think those only
good
Who labor most, and least are understood.
When thou shalt see the blear-ey'd fathers
teach   150
Their sons this harsh and moldy sort of
speech;
Or others new affected ways to try,
Of wanton smoothness, female poetry;
One would enquire from whence this mot-
ley style
Did first our Roman purity defile:
For our old dotards cannot keep their seat,
But leap and catch at all that's obsolete.
  Others, by foolish ostentation led,
When call'd before the bar, to save their
head,
Bring trifling tropes, instead of solid sense,
And mind their figures more than their de-
fense;   161
Are pleas'd to hear their thick-skull'd
judges cry:
"Well mov'd, O finely said, and decently!"
"Theft," says th' accuser, "to thy charge
I lay,

O Pedius!" What does gentle Pedius say?
Studious to please the genius of the times,
With periods,[8] points, and tropes, he slurs
his crimes:
"He robb'd not, but he borrow'd from the
poor;
And took but with intention to restore."
He lards with flourishes his long harangue;
"'T is fine," say'st thou;— what, to be
prais'd and hang?   171
Effeminate Roman, shall such stuff prevail
To tickle thee, and make thee wag thy
tail?
Say, should a shipwrack'd sailor sing his
woe,
Wouldst thou be mov'd to pity, or bestow
An alms? What's more prepost'rous than
to see
A merry beggar? Mirth in misery?
  PER. He seems a trap for charity to lay,
And cons, by night, his lesson for the day.
  FRIEND. But to raw numbers, and un-
finish'd verse,   180
Sweet sound is added now, to make it terse:
"'T is tagg'd with rhyme, like Berecyn-
thian Atys,[9]
The mid-part chimes with art, which never
flat is.
The dolphin brave, that cut the liquid wave,
Or he who in his line can chine the long-
ribb'd Apennine."
  PER. All this is dogg'rel stuff.
  FRIEND.   What if I bring
A nobler verse? "Arms and the man I
sing." [10]
  PER. Why name you Virgil with such
fops as these?
He's truly great, and must for ever please;
Not fierce, but awful is his manly page; 190
Bold is his strength, but sober is his rage.
  FRIEND. What poems think you soft?
and to be read
With languishing regards, and bending
head?
  PER. "Their crooked horns [11] the Mi-
mallonian crew
With blasts inspir'd; and Bassaris who slew
The scornful calf, with sword advanc'd on
high,
Made from his neck his haughty head to fly.
And Mænas, when with ivy bridles bound, ⌉
She led the spotted lynx, then Evion |
rung around;   ⎬
Evion from woods and floods repairing |
echoes sound."   200 ⌋

Could such rude lines a Roman mouth
become,
Were any manly greatness left in Rome ?
Mænas and Atys [12] in the mouth were bred,
And never hatch'd within the lab'ring head:
No blood from bitten nails those poems
drew;
But churn'd, like spettle, from the lips they
flew.
FRIEND. 'T is fustian all; 't is execra-
bly bad:
But if they will be fools, must you be mad ?
Your satires, let me tell you, are too fierce;
The great will never bear so blunt a verse.
Their doors are barr'd against a bitter flout:
Snarl, if you please, but you shall snarl
without. 212
Expect such pay as railing rhymes deserve,
Y' are in a very hopeful way to starve.
PER. Rather than so, uncensur'd let 'em
be ;
All, all is admirably well, for me.
My harmless rhyme shall scape the dire
disgrace
Of common shores, and ev'ry pissing-place.
Two painted serpents [13] shall on high appear:
" 'T is holy ground; you must not urine
here." 220
This shall be writ to fright the fry away,
Who draw their little baubles, when they
play.
Yet old Lucilius [14] never fear'd the times,
But lash'd the city, and dissected crimes.
Mutius and Lupus both by name he brought;
He mouth'd 'em, and betwixt his grinders
caught.
Unlike in method, with conceal'd design,
Did crafty Horace his low numbers join;
And, with a sly insinuating grace,
Laugh'd at his friend, and look'd him in the
face; 230
Would raise a blush, where secret vice he
found,
And tickle, while he gently prob'd the
wound;
With seeming innocence the crowd be-
guil'd,
But made the desperate passes, when he
smil'd.
Could he do this, and is my Muse con-
troll'd
By servile awe? Born free, and not be
bold ?
At least, I 'll dig a hole within the ground,
And to the trusty earth commit the sound:

The reeds shall tell you what the poet
fears: 239
" King Midas [15] has a snout, and ass's ears."
This mean conceit, this darling mystery,
Which thou think'st nothing, friend, thou
shalt not buy;
Nor will I change for all the flashy wit
That flatt'ring Labeo in his *Iliads* writ.
Thou, if there be a thou in this base town,
Who dares, with angry Eupolis,[16] to frown;
He who, with bold Cratinus, is inspir'd
With zeal, and equal indignation fir'd;
Who at enormous villainy turns pale, 249
And steers against it with a full-blown sail,
Like Aristophanes; let him but smile
On this my honest work, tho' writ in homely
style:
And if two lines or three in all the vein
Appear less drossy, read those lines again.
May they perform their author's just intent,
Glow in thy ears, and in thy breast ferment.
But from the reading of my book and me,
Be far, ye foes of virtuous poverty:
Who Fortune's fault [17] upon the poor can
throw, 259
Point at the tatter'd coat and ragged shoe;
Lay Nature's failings to their charge, and
jeer
The dim weak eyesight, when the mind is
clear:
When thou thyself, thus insolent in state,
Art but, perhaps, some country magistrate;
Whose pow'r extends no farther than to
speak
Big on the bench, and scanty weights to
break.
Him, also, for my censor I disdain,
Who thinks all science, as all virtue, vain;
Who counts geometry and numbers toys,
And with his foot [18] the sacred dust de-
stroys; 270
Whose pleasure is to see a strumpet tear
A Cynic's beard, and lug him by the hair.
Such, all the morning, to the pleadings ⎤
run; ⎟
But, when the bus'ness of the day is done, ⎬
On dice, and drink, and drabs, they ⎟
spend their afternoon. ⎦

EXPLANATORY NOTES ON THE
PROLOGUE

1 *Parnassus* and Helicon were hills consecrated to the Muses, and the suppos'd place of
their abode. Parnassus was fork'd on the top;

and from Helicon ran a stream, the spring of which was call'd the Muses' Well.

2 *Pyrene*, a fountain in Corinth, consecrated also to the Muses.

3 *Statues*, &c. The statues of the poets were crown'd with ivy about their brows.

4 *Before the shrine ;* that is, before the shrine of Apollo, in his temple at Rome, call'd the Palatine.

EXPLANATORY NOTES ON THE FIRST SATIRE

1 *Labeo's stuff.* Nothing is remaining of Atticus Labeo (so he is call'd by the learned Casaubon); nor is he mention'd by any other poet besides Persius. Casaubon, from an old commentator on Persius, says that he made a very foolish translation of Homer's *Iliads*.

2 *They comb*, &c. He describes a poet preparing himself to rehearse his works in public, which was commonly perform'd in August. A room was hir'd, or lent by some friend ; a scaffold was rais'd, and a pulpit plac'd for him who was to hold forth ; who borrow'd a new gown, or scour'd his old one, and adorn'd his ears with jewels, &c.

3 *My wild fig tree.* Trees of that kind grow wild in many parts of Italy, and make their way thro' rocks, sometimes splitting the tombstones.

4 The Romans wrote on cedar and cypress tables, in regard of the duration of the wood. Ill verses might justly be afraid of frankincense, for the papers in which they were written were fit for nothing but to wrap it up.

5 *Products of citron beds*, &c. Writings of noblemen, whose bedsteads were of the wood of citron.

6 *Janus-like*, &c. Janus was the first king of Italy, who refug'd Saturn when he was expell'd, by his son Jupiter, from Crete (or, as we now call it, Candia). From his name the first month of the year is call'd January. He was pictur'd with two faces, one before and one behind, as regarding the past time and the future. Some of the mythologists think he was Noah, for the reason given above.

7 *Where Romulus*, &c. He speaks of the country in the foregoing verses ; the praises of which are the most easy theme for poets, but which a bad poet cannot naturally describe : then he makes a digression to Romulus, the first king of Rome, who had a rustical education ; and enlarges upon Quintius Cincinnatus, a Roman senator, who was call'd from the plow to be dictator of Rome.

8 *In periods*, &c. Persius here names antitheses, or seeming contradictions ; which, in this place, are meant for rhetorical flourishes, as I think, with Casaubon.

9 *Berecynthian Atys* (or *Attin*), &c. Foolish verses of Nero, which the poet repeats ; and which cannot be translated properly into English.

10 " *Arms and the man*, &c. The first line of Virgil's *Æneids*.

11 " *Their crooked horns*, &c. Other verses of Nero, that were mere bombast. I only note that the repetition of these and the former verses of Nero might justly give the poet a caution to conceal his name.

12 *Mœnas and Atys.* Poems on the Mænades, who were priestesses of Bacchus ; and of Atys, who made himself an eunuch to attend on the sacrifices of Cybele, call'd Berecynthia by the poets. She was mother of the gods.

13 *Two painted serpents*, &c. Two snakes, twin'd with each other, were painted on the walls, by the ancients, to shew the place was holy.

14 *Yet old Lucilius*, &c. Lucilius wrote long before Horace, who imitates his manner of satire, but far excels him in the design.

15 " *King Midas*, &c. The story is vulgar, that Midas, King of Phrygia, was made judge betwixt Apollo and Pan, who was the best musician : he gave the prize to Pan ; and Apollo, in revenge, gave him ass's ears. He wore his hair long to hide them ; but his barber discovering them, and not daring to divulge the secret, dug a hole in the ground, and whisper'd into it : the place was marshy ; and, when the reeds grew up, they repeated the words which were spoken by the barber. By Midas, the poet meant Nero.

16 *Eupolis* and *Cratinus*, as also *Aristophanes*, mention'd afterwards, were all Athenian poets ; who wrote that sort of comedy which was call'd the Old Comedy, where the people were nam'd who were satiriz'd by those authors.

17 *Who Fortune's fault*, &c. The people of Rome, in the time of Persius, were apt to scorn the Grecian philosophers, particularly the Cynics and Stoics, who were the poorest of them.

18 *And with his foot*, &c. Arithmetic and geometry were taught on floors which were strew'd with dust, or sand ; in which the numbers and diagrams were made and drawn, which they might strike out again at pleasure.

THE SECOND SATIRE OF PERSIUS

DEDICATED TO HIS FRIEND PLOTIUS MACRINUS, ON HIS BIRTHDAY

THE ARGUMENT

This satire contains a most grave and philosophical argument, concerning prayers and wishes. Undoubtedly it gave occasion to Juvenal's *Tenth Satire ;* and both of them had their original from one of Plato's dialogues, call'd the *Second Alcibiades.* Our author has induc'd it with great mastery of art, by taking his rise from the birthday of his friend ; on which occasions prayers were made, and sacrifices offer'd by the native. Persius, commending first the purity of his friend's vows, descends to the impious and immoral requests of others. The satire is divided into three parts. The first is the exordium to Macrinus, which the poet confines within the compass of four verses; the second relates to the matter of the prayers and vows, and an enumeration of those things, wherein men commonly sinn'd against right reason, and offended in their requests; the third part consists in shewing the repugnancies of those prayers and wishes to those of other men, and inconsistencies with themselves. He shews the original of these vows, and sharply inveighs against them; and, lastly, not only corrects the false opinion of mankind concerning them, but gives the true doctrine of all addresses made to Heaven, and how they may be made acceptable to the pow'rs above, in excellent precepts, and more worthy of a Christian than a heathen.

LET this auspicious morning be express'd
With a white stone,[1] distinguish'd from the rest,
White as thy fame, and as thy honor clear;
And let new joys attend on thy new-added year.
Indulge thy genius, and o'erflow thy soul,
Till thy wit sparkle, like the cheerful bowl.
Pray; for thy pray'rs the test of Heav'n will bear;
Nor need'st thou take the gods aside, to hear;
While others, ev'n the mighty men of Rome,
Big swell'd with mischief, to the temples come;   10
And in low murmurs, and with costly smoke,
Heaven's help, to prosper their black vows, invoke.
So boldly to the gods mankind reveal
What from each other they, for shame, conceal.
"Give me good fame, ye pow'rs, and make me just; "
Thus much the rogue to public ears will trust:
In private then: — "When wilt thou, mighty Jove,
My wealthy uncle from this world remove ? "
Or — " O thou Thund'rer's son, great Hercules,[2]   19
That once thy bounteous deity would please
To guide my rake upon the chinking sound
Of some vast treasure, hidden under ground !

" O were my pupil fairly knock'd o' th' head;
I should possess th' estate, if he were dead !
He 's so far gone with rickets, and with th' evil,
That one small dose would send him to the devil.
" This is my neighbor Nerius his third spouse,
Of whom in happy time he rids his house;
But my eternal wife ! — Grant Heav'n I may
Survive to see the fellow of his day ! "   30
Thus, that thou mayst the better bring about
Thy wishes, thou art wickedly devout:
In Tiber ducking thrice, by break of day,
To wash th' obscenities of night [3] away.
But pr'ythee tell me, ('t is a small request,)
With what ill thoughts of Jove art thou possess'd ?
Wouldst thou prefer him to some man ? Suppose
I dipp'd among the worst, and Staius chose ?
Which of the two would thy wise head declare
The trustier tutor to an orphan heir ?   40
Or, put it thus: — Unfold to Staius, straight,
What to Jove's ear thou didst impart of late:
He 'll stare, and, "O good Jupiter ! " will cry;
" Canst thou indulge him in this villainy ? "
And think'st thou, Jove himself, with patience, then,
Can hear a pray'r condemn'd by wicked men ?
That, void of care, he lolls supine in state,
And leaves his bus'ness to be done by fate ?
Because his thunder splits some burly tree,
And is not darted at thy house and thee ?   50
Or that his vengeance falls not at the time,
Just at the perpetration of thy crime:
And makes thee a sad object of our eyes,
Fit for Ergenna's pray'r [4] and sacrifice ?
What well-fed off'ring to appease the god,
What pow'rful present to procure a nod,
Hast thou in store ? What bribe hast thou prepar'd,
To pull him, thus unpunish'd, by the beard ?
Our superstitions with our life begin:
Th' obscene old grandam, or the next of kin,   60
The newborn infant from the cradle takes,
And first of spettle a lustration [5] makes;

Then in the spawl her middle finger dips,
Anoints the temples, forehead, and the
    lips,
Pretending force of witchcraft to prevent,
By virtue of her nasty excrement;
Then dandles him with many a mutter'd
    pray'r
That Heav'n would make him some rich
    miser's heir,
Lucky to ladies, and in time a king;
Which to insure, she adds a length of na-
    vel-string.   70
But no fond nurse is fit to make a pray'r:
And Jove, if Jove be wise, will never
    hear;
Not tho' she prays in white, with lifted
    hands.
A body made of brass the crone demands
For her lov'd nursling, strung with nerves
    of wire,
Tough to the last, and with no toil to tire:
Unconscionable vows ! which when we use,
We teach the gods, in reason, to refuse.
Suppose they were indulgent to thy wish:
Yet the fat entrails, in the spacious dish, 80
Would stop the grant; the very over-care,
And nauseous pomp, would hinder half the
    pray'r.
Thou hop'st with sacrifice of oxen slain
To compass wealth, and bribe the God of
    Gain,
To give thee flocks and herds, with large
    increase;
Fool ! to expect 'em from a bullock's
    grease !
And think'st that when the fatten'd flames
    aspire,
Thou seest th' accomplishment of thy de-
    sire !
Now, now, my bearded harvest gilds the ⎤
    plain,   ⎥
The scanty folds can scarce my sheep ⎰
    contain,   90 ⎟
And show'rs of gold come pouring in ⎟
    amain !   ⎦
Thus dreams the wretch, and vainly thus
    dreams on,
Till his lank purse declares his money gone.
   Should I present thee with rare figur'd
    plate,
Or gold as rich in workmanship as weight;
O how thy rising heart would throb and
    beat,
And thy left side, with trembling pleasure,
    sweat !

Thou measur'st by thyself the pow'rs di-
    vine;
Thy gods are burnish'd gold, and silver is
    their shrine.
Thy puny godlings of inferior race,   100
Whose humble statues are content with
    brass,
Should some of these, in visions purg'd
    from phlegm,[6]
Foretell events, or in a morning dream;
Ev'n those thou wouldst in veneration hold;
And, if not faces, give 'em beards of gold.
The priests in temples now no longer care
For Saturn's brass,[7] or Numa's earthen-
    ware,[8]
Or vestal urns, in each religious rite:
This wicked gold has put 'em all to flight.
O souls, in whom no heav'nly fire is found,
Fat minds, and ever groveling on the
    ground !   111
We bring our manners to the blest abodes,
And think what pleases us must please the
    gods.
Of oil and cassia one th' ingredients takes,
And, of the mixture, a rich ointment makes;
Another finds the way to dye in grain,
And make Calabrian wool [9] receive the Tyr-
    ian stain;
Or from the shells their orient treasure
    takes,
Or, for their golden ore, in rivers rakes;
Then melts the mass. All these are vani-
    ties !   120
Yet still some profit from their pains may
    rise:
But tell me, priest, if I may be so bold,
What are the gods the better for this gold ?
The wretch that offers from his wealthy
    store
These presents, bribes the pow'rs to give
    him more;
As maids to Venus [10] offer baby-toys,
To bless the marriage bed with girls and
    boys.
But let us for the gods a gift prepare,
Which the great man's great chargers can-
    not bear:
A soul, where laws, both human and di-
    vine,   130
In practice more than speculation shine;
A genuine virtue, of a vigorous kind,
Pure in the last recesses of the mind;
When with such off'rings to the gods I
    come,
A cake thus giv'n [11] is worth a hecatomb.

EXPLANATORY NOTES ON THE SECOND SATIRE

1 *White stone.* The Romans were us'd to mark their fortunate days, or anything that luckily befell 'em, with a white stone, which they had from the island Creta, and their unfortunate with a coal.

2 *Hercules* was thought to have the key and power of bestowing all hidden treasure.

3 The ancients thought themselves tainted and polluted by night itself, as well as bad dreams in the night; and therefore purified themselves by washing their heads and hands every morning, which custom the Turks observe to this day.

4 When anyone was thunderstruck, the soothsayer (who is here call'd Ergenna) immediately repair'd to the place, to expiate the displeasure of the gods by sacrificing two sheep.

5 The poet laughs at the superstitious ceremonies which the old women made use of in their lustration, or purification days, when they nam'd their children, which was done on the eighth day to females, and on the ninth to males.

6 *In visions purg'd from phlegm,* &c. It was the opinion both of Grecians and Romans, that the gods, in visions or dreams, often reveal'd to their favorites a cure for their diseases, and sometimes those of others. Thus Alexander dreamt of an herb which cur'd Ptolemy. These gods were principally Apollo and Æsculapius, but in aftertimes the same virtue and good will was attributed to Isis and Osiris. Which brings to my remembrance an odd passage in Sir Tho. Browne's *Religio Medici,* or in his *Vulgar Errors;* the sense whereof is, that we are beholding, for many of our discoveries in physic, to the courteous revelation of spirits. By the expression of *visions purg'd from phlegm,* our author means such dreams or visions as proceed not from natural causes, or humors of the body, but such as are sent from heaven; and are, therefore, certain remedies.

7 *For Saturn's brass,* &c. Brazen vessels, in which the public treasures of the Romans was kept: it may be the poet means only old vessels, which were all call'd Κρόνια, from the Greek name of Saturn. Note also that the Roman treasury was in the temple of Saturn.

8 *Numa's earthenware.* Under Numa, the second king of Rome and for a long time after him, the holy vessels for sacrifice were of earthenware; according to the superstitious rites which were introduc'd by the same Numa: tho' afterwards, when Memmius had taken Corinth, and Paulus Æmilius had conquer'd Macedonia, luxury began amongst the Romans, and then their utensils of devotion were of gold and silver, &c.

9 *And make Calabrian wool,* &c. The wool of Calabria was of the finest sort in Italy, as Juvenal also tells us. The Tyrian stain is the purple color dyed at Tyrus; and I suppose, but dare not positively affirm, that the richest of that dye was nearest our crimson, and not scar-let, or that other color more approaching to the blue. I have not room to justify my conjecture.

10 *As maids to Venus,* &c. Those baby-toys were little babies, or poppets, as we call them; in Latin, *pupæ:* which the girls, when they came to the age of puberty, or childbearing, offer'd to Venus; as the boys, at fourteen or fifteen years of age, offer'd their *bullæ,* or bosses.

11 *A cake thus giv'n,* &c. A cake of barley, or coarse wheat meal, with the bran in it: the meaning is that God is pleas'd with the pure and spotless heart of the offerer, and not with the riches of the offering. Laberius, in the fragments of his *Mimes,* has a verse like this: *Puras Deus non plenas aspicit manus.* — What I had forgotten before, in its due place, I must here tell the reader, that the first half of this satire was translated by one of my sons, now in Italy; but I thought so well of it that I let it pass without any alteration.

THE THIRD SATIRE OF PERSIUS

THE ARGUMENT

Our author has made two satires concerning study; the *First* and the *Third:* the *First* related to men; this to young students, whom he desir'd to be educated in the Stoic philosophy: he himself sustains the person of the master, or preceptor, in this admirable satire, where he upbraids the youth of sloth and negligence in learning. Yet he begins with one scholar reproaching his fellow students with late rising to their books. After which he takes upon him the other part, of the teacher; and, addressing himself particularly to young noblemen, tells them that, by reason of their high birth, and the great possessions of their fathers, they are careless of adorning their minds with precepts of moral philosophy: and, withal, inculcates to them the miseries which will attend them in the whole course of their life, if they do not apply themselves betimes to the knowledge of virtue, and the end of their creation, which he pathetically insinuates to them. The title of this satire, in some ancient manuscripts, was *The Reproach of Idleness;* tho' in others of the scholiasts 't is inscrib'd, *Against the Luxury and Vices of the Rich.* In both of which the intention of the poet is pursued, but principally in the former.

I remember I translated this satire, when I was a King's Scholar at Westminster School, for a Thursday-night's exercise; and believe that it, and many other of my exercises of this nature, in English verse, are still in the hands of my learned master, the Reverend Doctor Busby.

" Is this thy daily course ? The glaring
   sun
Breaks in at ev'ry chink; the cattle run
To shades, and noontide rays of summer
   shun;
Yet plung'd in sloth we lie; and snore su-
   pine,
As fill'd with fumes of undigested wine."
   This grave advice some sober student
     bears,
And loudly rings it in his fellow's ears.
The yawning youth, scarce half awake, es-
   says
His lazy limbs and dozy head to raise;
Then rubs his gummy eyes, and scrubs his
   pate,   10
And cries: " I thought it had not been so
   late:
My clothes; make haste: why when ! " If
   none be near,
He mutters first, and then begins to swear;
And brays aloud, with a more clam'rous
   note,
Than an Arcadian ass can stretch his
   throat.
   With much ado, his book before him
     laid,
And parchment [1] with the smoother side
   display'd,
He takes the papers; lays 'em down again,
And with unwilling fingers tries the pen:
Some peevish quarrel straight he strives to
   pick;   20
His quill writes double, or his ink's too
   thick:
Infuse more water; now 't is grown so thin,
It sinks, nor can the character be seen.
O wretch, and still more wretched ev'ry
   day !
Are mortals born to sleep their lives away ?
Go back to what thy infancy began,
Thou who wert never meant to be a man:
Eat pap and spoon-meat; for thy gewgaws
   cry:
Be sullen, and refuse the lullaby.
No more accuse thy pen; but charge the
   crime   30
On native sloth, and negligence of time.
Think'st thou thy master, or thy friends,
   to cheat ?
Fool, 't is thyself, and that 's a worse deceit.
Beware the public laughter of the town;
Thou spring'st a leak already in thy crown.
A flaw is in thy ill-bak'd vessel found;
'T is hollow, and returns a jarring sound.

Yet, thy moist clay is pliant to command;
Unwrought, and easy to the potter's hand:
Now take the mold; now bend thy mind
   to feel   40
The first sharp motions of the forming
   wheel.
But thou hast land; a country seat, se-
   cure
By a just title; costly furniture;
A fuming-pan [2] thy Lares to appease:
What need of learning when a man 's at
   ease ?
If this be not enough to swell thy soul,
Then please thy pride, and search the her-
   ald's roll,
Where thou shalt find thy famous pedi-
   gree
Drawn from the root [3] of some old Tuscan
   tree;
And thou, a thousand off, a fool of long
   degree;   50
Who, clad in purple, [4] canst thy censor
   greet,
And loudly call him cousin in the street.
   Such pageantry be to the people shown;
There boast thy horse's trappings, and thy
   own:
I know thee to thy bottom; from within
Thy shallow center, to thy outmost skin:
Dost thou not blush to live so like a beast,
So trim, so dissolute, so loosely dress'd ?
   But 't is in vain: the wretch is drench'd
     too deep,
His soul is stupid, and his heart asleep; 60
Fatten'd in vice, so callous, and so gross,
He sins, and sees not, senseless of his loss.
Down goes the wretch at once, unskill'd to
   swim,
Hopeless to bubble up and reach the water's
   brim.
   Great Father of the Gods, when, for our
     crimes,
Thou send'st some heavy judgment on the
   times;
Some tyrant king, the terror of his age,
The type, and true vicegerent of thy rage;
Thus punish him: set Virtue in his sight,
With all her charms adorn'd, with all her
   graces bright;   70
But set her distant, make him pale to see
His gains outweigh'd by lost felicity !
   Sicilian tortures, [5] and the brazen bull,
Are emblems, rather than express the full
Of what he feels; yet what he fears is
   more:

The wretch, who sitting [6] at his plenteous
  board,
Look'd up, and view'd on high the pointed
  sword
Hang o'er his head, and hanging by a twine,
Did with less dread, and more securely dine.
Ev'n in his sleep he starts, and fears the
  knife,   80
And, trembling, in his arms takes his ac-
  complice wife:
Down, down he goes; and from his darling
  friend
Conceals the woes his guilty dreams por-
  tend.
  When I was young, I, like a lazy fool,
Would blear my eyes with oil to stay from
  school,
Averse from pains, and loth to learn the
  part
Of Cato, dying with a dauntless heart;
Tho' much my master that stern virtue
  prais'd,
Which o'er the vanquisher the vanquish'd
  rais'd;
And my pleas'd father came with pride to
  see   90
His boy defend the Roman liberty.
But then my study was to cog the dice,
And dext'rously to throw the lucky sice;
To shun ames-ace, that swept my stakes ⎤
  away; |
And watch the box, for fear they should ⎬
  convey |
False bones, and put upon me in the play; ⎦
Careful, besides, the whirling top to whip,
And drive her giddy, till she fell asleep.
  Thy years are ripe, nor art thou yet to
  learn
What's good or ill, and both their ends
  discern: 100
Thou, in the Stoic Porch,[7] severely bred,
Hast heard the dogmas of great Zeno read;
Where on the walls, by Polygnotus'[8] hand,
The conquer'd Medians in trunk-breeches
  stand;
Where the shorn youth to midnight lec-
  tures rise,
Rous'd from their slumbers to be early
  wise;
Where the coarse cake, and homely husks
  of beans,
From pamp'ring riot the young stomach
  weans;
And where the Samian Y [9] directs thy steps
  to run

To Virtue's narrow steep, and broad-way
  Vice to shun.   110
And yet thou snor'st; thou draw'st thy
  drunken breath,
Sour with debauch; and sleep'st the sleep
  of death:
Thy chaps are fallen, and thy frame dis-
  join'd;
Thy body as dissolv'd as is thy mind.
  Hast thou not yet propos'd some certain
  end,
To which thy life, thy ev'ry act may tend?
Hast thou no mark at which to bend thy
  bow?
Or like a boy pursu'st the carrion crow
With pellets, and with stones, from tree to
  tree:
A fruitless toil, and liv'st extempore?   120
  Watch the disease in time; for, when
  within
The dropsy rages and extends the skin,
In vain for hellebore the patient cries,
And fees the doctor; but too late is wise:
Too late for cure, he proffers half his
  wealth;
Conquest and Gibbons cannot give him
  health.
  Learn, wretches, learn the motions of ⎤
  the mind, |
Why you were made, for what you ⎬
  were design'd; |
And the great moral end of humankind. ⎦
Study thyself, what rank or what degree 130
The wise Creator has ordain'd for thee;
And all the offices of that estate
Perform, and with thy prudence guide thy
  fate.
  Pray justly, to be heard; nor more de-
  sire
Than what the decencies of life require.
Learn what thou ow'st thy country, and thy
  friend;
What's requisite to spare, and what to
  spend:
Learn this; and after, envy not the store
Of the greas'd advocate, that grinds the
  poor,
Fat fees [10] from the defended Umbrian
  draws,   140
And only gains the wealthy client's cause;
To whom the Marsians [11] more provision
  send,
Than he and all his family can spend.
Gammons, that give a relish to the taste,
And potted fowl, and fish come in so fast,

That, ere the first is out, the second stinks,
And moldy mother gathers on the brinks.
  But here some captain of the land or
    fleet,
Stout of his hands, but of a soldier's wit,
Cries: "I have sense to serve my turn, in
    store;   150
And he's a rascal who pretends to more.
Damme, whate'er those book-learn'd block-
    heads say,
Solon's the veriest fool in all the play.
Top-heavy drones, and always looking down,
(As overballasted within the crown!)
Mutt'ring betwixt their lips some mystic
    thing,
Which, well examin'd, is flat conjuring,
Mere madmen's dreams: for what the ⎫
    schools have taught,   ⎪
Is only this, that nothing can be brought ⎬
From nothing; and, what is, can ne'er   ⎪
    be turn'd to naught.   160   ⎭
Is it for this they study? to grow pale,
And miss the pleasures of a glorious meal?
For this, in rags accouter'd, they are seen,
And made the May-game of the public
    spleen?"
  Proceed, my friend, and rail; but hear
    me tell
A story, which is just thy parallel.
  A spark, like thee, of the man-killing
    trade,
Fell sick, and thus to his physician said:
"Methinks I am not right in ev'ry part;
I feel a kind of trembling at my heart: 170
My pulse unequal, and my breath is strong;
Besides, a filthy fur upon my tongue."
The doctor heard him, exercis'd his skill;
And, after, bade him for four days be still.
Three days he took good counsel, and be-
    gan
To mend, and look like a recov'ring man;
The fourth, he could not hold from drink,
    but sends
His boy to one of his old trusty friends,
Adjuring him, by all the pow'rs divine, ⎫
To pity his distress, who could not dine 180 ⎬
Without a flagon of his healing wine. ⎭
He drinks a swilling draught; and, lin'd
    within,
Will supple in the bath his outward skin:
Whom should he find but his physician
    there,
Who, wisely, bade him once again beware:
"Sir, you look wan, you hardly draw your
    breath;

Drinking is dangerous, and the bath is
    death."
"'T is nothing," says the fool. "But," says
    the friend,
"This nothing, sir, will bring you to your
    end.
Do I not see your dropsy-belly swell? 190
Your yellow skin?" — "No more of that;
    I'm well.
I have already buried two or three   ⎫
That stood betwixt a fair estate and me, ⎬
And, doctor, I may live to bury thee. ⎭
Thou tell'st me, I look ill, and thou look'st
    worse."
"I've done," says the physician; "take your
    course."
The laughing sot, like all unthinking men,
Bathes and gets drunk; then bathes and
    drinks again.
His throat half throttled with corrupted
    phlegm,
And breathing thro' his jaws a belching
    stream,   200
Amidst his cups with fainting shiv'ring
    seiz'd,
His limbs disjointed, and all o'er diseas'd,
His hand refuses to sustain the bowl, ⎫
And his teeth chatter, and his eyeballs ⎬
    roll,   ⎭
Till, with his meat, he vomits out his soul:
Then trumpets, torches, and a tedious crew
Of hireling mourners, for his funeral due.
Our dear departed brother lies in state, ⎫
His heels stretch'd out, [12] and pointing ⎪
    to the gate;   ⎬
And slaves, now manumiz'd, on their ⎪
    dead master wait.   210   ⎭
They hoist him on the bier, and deal the
    dole;
And there's an end of a luxurious fool.
  "But what's thy fulsome parable to me?
My body is from all diseases free:
My temperate pulse does regularly beat; ⎫
Feel, and be satisfied, my hands and feet: ⎬
These are not cold, nor those oppress'd ⎪
    with heat.   ⎭
Or lay thy hand upon my naked heart,
And thou shalt find me hale in ev'ry part."
  I grant this true: but, still, the deadly
    wound   220
Is in thy soul; 't is there thou art not
    sound.
Say, when thou seest a heap of tempting
    gold,
Or a more tempting harlot dost behold;

Then, when she casts on thee a sidelong
    glance,
Then try thy heart, and tell me if it dance.
Some coarse cold salad is before thee ⎱
    set; ⎰
Bread, with the bran perhaps, and broken ⎬
    meat:
Fall on, and try thy appetite to eat. ⎰
These are not dishes for thy dainty tooth:
What, hast thou got an ulcer in thy mouth ?
Why stand'st thou picking ? Is thy palate
    sore,   231
That beet and radishes will make thee
    roar ?
Such is th' unequal temper of thy mind;
Thy passions in extremes, and unconfin'd:
Thy hair so bristles with unmanly fears,
As fields of corn that rise in bearded ears;
And, when thy cheeks with flushing fury ⎱
    glow, ⎰
The rage of boiling caldrons is more slow; ⎬
When fed with fuel and with flames be- ⎰
    low.
With foam upon thy lips, and sparkling
    eyes,   240
Thou say'st and dost in such outrageous
    wise,
That mad Orestes, [13] if he saw the show,
Would swear thou wert the madder of the
    two.

EXPLANATORY NOTES ON THE THIRD SATIRE

1 *And parchment*, &c. The students us'd to
write their notes on parchments ; the inside, on
which they wrote, was white ; the other side
was hairy, and commonly yellow. Quintilian
reproves this custom, and advises rather tablebooks, lin'd with wax, and a style, like that we
use in our vellum tablebooks, as more easy.

2 *A fuming-pan*, &c. Before eating, it was
customary to cut off some part of the meat,
which was first put into a pan, or little dish,
then into the fire, as an offering to the household gods: this they called a libation.

3 *Drawn from the root*, &c. The Tuscans
were accounted of most ancient nobility. Horace observes this in most of his compliments to
Mæcenas, who was deriv'd from the old kings of
Tuscany, now the dominion of the Great Duke.

4 *Who, clad in purple*, &c. The Roman
knights, attir'd in the robe call'd *trabea*, were
summon'd by the censor to appear before him,
and to salute him in passing by, as their names
were call'd over. They led their horses in their
hand. See more of this in Pompey's life, written by Plutarch.

5 *Sicilian tortures*, &c. Some of the Sicilian
kings were so great tyrants, that the name is

become proverbial. The brazen bull is a known
story of Phalaris, one of those tyrants, who,
when Perillus, a famous artist, had presented
him with a bull of that metal hollow'd within,
which, when the condemn'd person was inclos'd
in it, would render the sound of a bull's roaring,
caus'd the workman to make the first experiment — *docuitque suum mugire juvencum.*

6 *The wretch, who sitting*, &c. He alludes
to the story of Damocles, a flatterer of one
of those Sicilian tyrants, namely Dionysius.
Damocles had infinitely extoll'd the happiness
of kings. Dionysius, to convince him of the contrary, invited him to a feast, and cloth'd him
in purple ; but caus'd a sword, with the point
downward, to be hung over his head by a silken
twine ; which when he perceiv'd, he could eat
nothing of the delicates that were set before
him.

7 *Thou, in the Stoic Porch*, &c. The Stoics
taught their philosophy under a *porticus*, to
secure their scholars from the weather. Zeno
was the chief of that sect.

8 *Polygnotus*, a famous painter, who drew the
pictures of the Medes and Persians conquer'd
by Miltiades, Themistocles, and other Athenian
captains, on the walls of the portico, in their
natural habits.

9 *And where the Samian Y*, &c. Pythagoras,
of Samos, made the allusion of the Y, or Greek
upsilon, to Vice and Virtue. One side of the
letter, being broad, characters Vice, to which
the ascent is wide and easy ; the other side represents Virtue, to which the passage is strait
and difficult ; and perhaps our Savior might
also allude to this, in those noted words of the
evangelist, " The way to heaven," &c.

10 *Fat fees*, &c. Casaubon here notes that
among all the Romans who were brought up to
learning, few besides the orators, or lawyers,
grew rich.

11 *The Marsians* and *Umbrians* were the most
plentiful of all the provinces in Italy.

12 *His heels stretch'd out*, &c. The Romans
were buried without the city ; for which reason
the poet says that the dead man's heels were
stretch'd out towards the gate.

13 *That mad Orestes*. Orestes was son to Agamemnon and Clytemnestra. Agamemnon, at
his return from the Trojan wars, was slain
by Ægisthus, the adulterer of Clytemnestra.
Orestes, to revenge his father's death, slew both
Ægisthus and his mother ; for which he was
punish'd with madness by the Eumenides, or
Furies, who continually haunted him.

THE FOURTH SATIRE OF PERSIUS

THE ARGUMENT

Our author, living in the time of Nero, was
contemporary and friend to the noble poet
Lucan ; both of them were sufficiently sensible, with all good men, how unskilfully

he manag'd the commonwealth; and perhaps might guess at his future tyranny by some passages during the latter part of his first five years; tho' he broke not out into his greater excesses, while he was restrain'd by the counsels and authority of Seneca. Lucan has not spar'd him in the poem of his *Pharsalia;* for his very compliment look'd asquint, as well as Nero. Persius has been bolder, but with caution likewise. For here, in the person of young Alcibiades, he arraigns his ambition of meddling with state affairs, without judgment or experience. 'T is probable that he makes Seneca, in this satire, sustain the part of Socrates, under a borrow'd name; and, withal, discovers some secret vices of Nero, concerning his lust, his drunkenness, and his effeminacy, which had not yet arriv'd to public notice. He also reprehends the flattery of his courtiers, who endeavor'd to make all his vices pass for virtues. Covetousness was undoubtedly none of his faults; but it is here describ'd as a veil cast over the true meaning of the poet, which was to satirize his prodigality and voluptuousness; to which he makes a transition. I find no instance in history of that emperor's being a pathic, tho' Persius seems to brand him with it. From the two dialogues of Plato, both call'd *Alcibiades,* the poet took the arguments of the *Second* and *Third Satire,* but he inverted the order of them; for the *Third Satire* is taken from the first of those dialogues.

The commentators before Casaubon were ignorant of our author's secret meaning, and thought he had only written against young noblemen in general, who were too forward in aspiring to public magistracy; but this excellent scholiast has unravel'd the whole mystery, and made it apparent that the sting of the satire was particularly aim'd at Nero.

WHOE'ER thou art, whose forward years are bent
On state affairs, to guide the government;
Hear, first, what Socrates [1] of old has said
To the lov'd youth, whom he at Athens bred:
"Tell me, thou pupil to great Pericles,[2]
Our second hope, my Alcibiades,
What are the grounds, from whence thou dost prepare
To undertake, so young, so vast a care?
Perhaps thy wit: (a chance not often heard,
That parts and prudence should prevent the beard:)   10
'T is seldom seen, that senators so young

Know when to speak, and when to hold their tongue.
Sure thou art born to some peculiar fate;
When the mad people rise against the State,
To look them into duty; and command
An awful silence with thy lifted hand.
Then to bespeak 'em thus: 'Athenians, know
Against right reason all your counsels go;
This is not fair; nor profitable that;
Nor t'other question proper for debate.'   20
But thou, no doubt, canst set the business right,
And give each argument its proper weight;
Know'st, with an equal hand, to hold the scale;
Seest where the reasons pinch, and where they fail,
And where exceptions o'er the general rule prevail;
And, taught by inspiration, in a trice,
Canst punish crimes,[3] and brand offending vice.
"Leave, leave to fathom such high points as these,
Nor be ambitious, ere thy time, to please;
Unseasonably wise, till age and cares   30
Have form'd thy soul to manage great affairs.
Thy face, thy shape, thy outside, are but vain;
Thou hast not strength such labors to sustain:
Drink hellebore,[4] my boy, drink deep, and purge thy brain.
"What aim'st thou at, and whither tends thy care?
In what thy utmost good? Delicious fare;
And then, to sun thyself in open air.
"Hold, hold; are all thy empty wishes such?
A good old woman would have said as much.   39
But thou art nobly born: 't is true; go boast
Thy pedigree, the thing thou valu'st most.
Besides, thou art a beau: what's that, my child?
A fop, well-dress'd, extravagant, and wild:
She that cries herbs has less impertinence;
And, in her calling, more of common sense."
None, none descends into himself, to find
The secret imperfections of his mind:
But ev'ryone is eagle-ey'd, to see
Another's faults and his deformity.   49

"Say, dost thou know Vectidius ? " [5] " Who,
   the wretch
Whose lands beyond the Sabines largely
   stretch;
Cover the country, that a sailing kite
Can scarce o'erfly 'em in a day and night ?
Him dost thou mean, who, spite of all his
   store,
Is ever craving, and will still be poor ?
Who cheats for halfpence, and who doffs
   his coat,
To save a farthing in a ferryboat ?
Ever a glutton, at another's cost,
But in whose kitchen dwells perpetual
   frost ?
Who eats and drinks with his domestic
   slaves;   60
A verier hind than any of his knaves ?
Born with the curse and anger of the gods,
And that indulgent genius he defrauds ?
At harvest-home, and on the shearing day,
When he should thanks [6] to Pan and Pales
   pay,
And better Ceres, trembling to approach
The little barrel, which he fears to broach:
He 'says the wimble, often draws it back,
And deals to thirsty servants but a smack.
To a short meal he makes a tedious grace, 70
Before the barley pudding comes in place:
Then, bids fall on; himself, for saving
   charges,
A peel'd slic'd onion eats, and tipples ver-
   juice."
" Thus fares the drudge: but thou, whose
   life 's a dream
Of lazy pleasures, tak'st a worse extreme.
'T is all thy bus'ness, bus'ness how to shun;
To bask thy naked body in the sun,
Suppling thy stiffen'd joints with fragrant
   oil;
Then, in thy spacious garden, walk a while,
To suck the moisture up, and soak it in: 80
And this, thou think'st, but vainly think'st,
   unseen.
But know, thou art observ'd; and there
   are those
Who, if they durst, would all thy secret
   sins expose:
The depilation of thy modest part; [7] ⎫
Thy catamite, the darling of thy heart, ⎬
His engine-hand, and ev'ry lewder art; ⎭
When, prone to bear, and patient to re-
   ceive,
Thou tak'st the pleasure which thou canst
   not give.

With odorous oil thy head and hair are
   sleek;
And then thou kemb'st the tuzzes on thy
   cheek: 90
Of these thy barbers take a costly care,
While thy salt tail is overgrown with hair.
Not all thy pincers, nor unmanly arts,
Can smooth the roughness of thy shameful
   parts:
Not five, the strongest [8] that the Circus
   breeds,
From the rank soil can root those wicked
   weeds,
Tho' suppled first with soap, to ease thy
   pain;
The stubborn fern springs up, and sprouts
   again.
" Thus others we with defamations wound,
While they stab us ; and so the jest goes
   round.   100
Vain are thy hopes, to scape censorious eyes;
Truth will appear thro' all the thin disguise:
Thou hast an ulcer which no leech can heal,
Tho' thy broad shoulder belt the wound
   conceal.
Say thou art sound and hale in ev'ry part,
We know, we know thee rotten at thy heart.
We know thee sullen, impotent, and proud:
Nor canst thou cheat thy nerve,[9] who cheat'st
   the crowd."
" But when they praise me, in the neigh-
   borhood,
When the pleas'd people take me for a
   god,   110
Shall I refuse their incense ? Not receive
The loud applauses which the vulgar give ? "
" If thou dost wealth with longing eyes
   behold,
And greedily art gaping after gold;
If some alluring girl, in gliding by, ⎫
Shall tip the wink, with a lascivious eye, ⎬
And thou with a consenting glance reply; ⎭
If thou thy own solicitor become,
And bidd'st arise the lumpish pendulum;
If thy lewd lust provokes an empty
   storm,   120
And prompts to more than nature can per-
   form;
If with thy guards [10] thou scour'st the streets
   by night,
And dost in murthers, rapes, and spoils de-
   light;
Please not thyself, the flatt'ring crowd to
   hear;
'T is fulsome stuff to feed thy itching ear·

Reject the nauseous praises of the times;
Give thy base poets back their cobbled
    rhymes:
Survey thy soul,[11] not what thou dost appear,
But what thou art, and find the beggar
    there."

EXPLANATORY NOTES ON THE FOURTH SATIRE

1 *Socrates*, whom the oracle of Delphos prais'd as the wisest man of his age, liv'd in the time of the Peloponnesian War. He, finding the uncertainty of natural philosophy, applied himself wholly to the moral. He was master to Xenophon and Plato, and to many of the Athenian young noblemen; amongst the rest, to Alcibiades, the most lovely youth then living; afterwards a famous captain, whose life is written by Plutarch.

2 *Pericles* was tutor, or rather overseer, of the will of Clinias, father to Alcibiades. While Pericles liv'd, who was a wise man, and an excellent orator, as well as a great general, the Athenians had the better of the war.

3 *Canst punish crimes*, &c. That is, by death. When the judges would condemn a malefactor, they cast their votes into an urn; as, according to the modern custom, a balloting-box. If the suffrages were mark'd with Θ, they signified the sentence of death to the offender; as being the first letter of Θάνατος, which, in English, is death.

4 *Drink hellebore*, &c. The poet would say, that such an ignorant young man as he here describes is fitter to be govern'd himself than to govern others. He therefore advises him to drink hellebore, which purges the brain.

5 "*Say, dost thou know Vectidius?*" &c. The name of Vectidius is here us'd appellatively, to signify any rich covetous man, tho' perhaps there might be a man of that name then living. I have translated this passage paraphrastically and loosely; and leave it for those to look on, who are not unlike the picture.

6 *When he should thanks*, &c. Pan, the god of shepherds, and Pales, the goddess presiding over rural affairs; whom Virgil invocates in the beginning of his *Second Georgic*. I give the epithet of *better* to Ceres, because she first taught the use of corn for bread, as the poets tell us; men, in the first rude ages, feeding only on acorns, or mast, instead of bread.

7 . . .

8 *Not five, the strongest*, &c. The learned Holyday (who has made us amends for his bad poetry in this and the rest of these satires, with his excellent illustrations) here tells us, from good authority, that the number five does not allude to the five fingers of one man, . . . but to five strong men, such as were skilful in the five robust exercises then in practice at Rome, and were perform'd in the Circus, or public place ordain'd for them. These five he reckons up in this manner: 1. The *cæstus*,

or whirlbats, describ'd by Virgil in his fifth *Æneid*; and this was the most dangerous of all the rest. The second was the *foot race*; the third the *discus*, like the throwing a weighty ball, a sport now us'd in Cornwall and other parts of England; we may see it daily practic'd in Red Lion Fields. The fourth was the *saltus*, or leaping; and the fifth, *wrestling* naked and besmear'd with oil. They who were practic'd in these five manly exercises were call'd Πέντα-θλοι.

9 *Thy nerve*, &c. That is, thou canst not deceive thy obscene part, which is weak or impotent, tho' thou mak'st ostentation of thy performances with women.

10 *If with thy guards*, &c. Persius durst not have been so bold with Nero as I dare now; and therefore there is only an intimation of that in him which I publicly speak: I mean, of Nero's walking the streets by night in disguise, and committing all sorts of outrages, for which he was sometimes well beaten.

11 *Survey thy soul*, &c. That is, look into thyself, and examine thy own conscience; there thou shalt find that how wealthy soever thou appear'st to the world, yet thou art but a beggar; because thou art destitute of all virtues, which are the riches of the soul. This also was a parodox of the Stoic school.

THE FIFTH SATIRE OF PERSIUS

INSCRIB'D TO THE REVEREND DR. BUSBY

THE ARGUMENT

The judicious Casaubon, in his proem to this satire, tells us that Aristophanes the grammarian, being ask'd what poem of Archilochus his *Iambics* he preferr'd before the rest, answer'd, the longest. His answer may justly be applied to this *Fifth Satire;* which, being of a greater length than any of the rest, is also by far the most instructive. For this reason I have selected it from all the others, and inscrib'd it to my learned master, Doctor Busby; to whom I am not only oblig'd myself for the best part of my own education, and that of my two sons, but have also receiv'd from him the first and truest taste of Persius. May he be pleas'd to find in this translation the gratitude, or at least some small acknowledgment, of his unworthy scholar, at the distance of forty-two years from the time when I departed from under his tuition.

This satire consists of two distinct parts: the first contains the praises of the Stoic philosopher Cornutus, master and tutor to our Persius. It also declares the love and piety of Persius to his well-deserving master, and the mutual friendship which continued betwixt them, after Persius was now grown a man; as also his exhortation to young noblemen, that they would enter themselves into his institution. From hence he makes an artful transition into the second part of his subject: wherein he first complains of the sloth of scholars, and afterwards persuades them to the pursuit of their true liberty. Here our author excellently treats that paradox of the Stoics which affirms, that the wise or virtuous man is only free, and that all vicious men are naturally slaves; and, in the illustration of this dogma, he takes up the remaining part of this inimitable satire.

THE SPEAKERS PERSIUS AND CORNUTUS

PER. Of ancient use to poets it belongs,
To wish themselves an hundred mouths and
    tongues:
Whether to the well-lung'd tragedian's rage
They recommend their labors of the stage,
Or sing the Parthian, when transfix'd he
    lies,
Wrenching the Roman javelin from his
    thighs.
    CORN. And why wouldst thou these
        mighty morsels choose,
Of words unchaw'd, and fit to choke the
    Muse?
Let fustian poets with their stuff be gone,
And suck the mists that hang o'er Helicon;
When Progne's[1] or Thyestes'[2] feast they
    write;   11
And, for the mouthing actor, verse indite.
Thou neither, like a bellows, swell'st thy
    face,
As if thou wert to blow the burning mass
Of melting ore; nor canst thou strain thy
    throat,
Or murmur in an undistinguish'd note,
Like rolling thunder, till it breaks the
    cloud,
And rattling nonsense is discharg'd aloud.
Soft elocution does thy style renown,
And the sweet accents of the peaceful
    gown: 20
Gentle or sharp, according to thy choice,
To laugh at follies, or to lash at vice.
Hence draw thy theme, and to the stage
    permit
Raw-head and bloody-bones, and hands
    and feet,
Ragousts for Tereus or Thyestes dress'd;
'T is task enough for thee t' expose a Roman
    feast.

PER. 'T is not, indeed, my talent to en-
    gage
In lofty trifles, or to swell my page
With wind and noise; but freely to impart,
As to a friend, the secrets of my heart; 30
And, in familiar speech, to let thee know
How much I love thee, and how much I
    owe.
Knock on my heart: for thou hast skill to ⌉
    find
If it sound solid, or be fill'd with wind; ⎬
And, thro' the vale of words, thou view'st
    the naked mind.   ⌋
    For this a hundred voices I desire,
To tell thee what an hundred tongues would
    tire;
Yet never could be worthily express'd,
How deeply thou art seated in my breast.
    When first my childish robe[3] resign'd the
        charge,   40
And left me, unconfin'd, to live at large;
When now my golden bulla (hung on ⌉
    high |
To household gods) declar'd me past a ⎬
    boy, |
And my white shield[4] proclaim'd my lib-
    erty;   ⌋
When, with my wild companions, I could
    roll
From street to street, and sin without con-
    trol;
Just at that age, when manhood set me free,
I then depos'd myself, and left the reins to
    thee.
On thy wise bosom I repos'd my head,
And by my better Socrates[5] was bred.   50
Then thy straight rule set virtue in my
    sight,
The crooked line reforming by the right.
My reason took the bent of thy command,
Was form'd and polish'd by thy skilful
    hand:
Long summer days thy precepts I rehearse,
And winter nights were short in our con-
    verse;
One was our labor, one was our repose,
One frugal supper did our studies close.
    Sure on our birth some friendly planet
        shone;
And, as our souls, our horoscope was one:[6]
Whether the mounting Twins[7] did heav'n
    adorn,   61
Or with the rising Balance[8] we were born;
Both have the same impressions from
    above.

And both have Saturn's rage, repell'd by
    Jove.[9]
What star I know not, but some star, I find,
Has giv'n thee an ascendant o'er my mind.
    CORN. Nature is ever various in her
        frame;
Each has a different will, and few the same:
The greedy merchants, led by lucre, run
To the parch'd Indies, and the rising sun; [70]
From thence hot pepper and rich drugs
        they bear,
Bart'ring for spices their Italian ware;
The lazy glutton safe at home will keep,
Indulge his sloth, and batten with his sleep:
One bribes for high preferments in the
        State;
A second shakes the box, and sits up late;
Another shakes the bed, dissolving there,
Till knots upon his gouty joints appear,
And chalk is in his crippled fingers found;
Rots like a dodder'd oak, and piecemeal
        falls to ground; [80]
Then his lewd follies he would late repent;
And his past years, that in a mist were
        spent.
    PER. But thou art pale in nightly stud-
        ies grown,
To make the Stoic institutes thy own; [10]
Thou long with studious care hast till'd our
        youth,
And sown our well-purg'd ears with whole-
        some truth.
From thee both old and young with profit ⎫
        learn   ⎪
The bounds of good and evil to discern.   ⎬
    CORN. Unhappy he who does this   ⎪
        work adjourn   ⎭
And to to-morrow would the search delay: [90]
His lazy morrow will be like to-day.
    PER. But is one day of ease too much
        to borrow ?
    CORN. Yes, sure: for yesterday was once
        to-morrow.
That yesterday is gone, and nothing gain'd;
And all thy fruitless days will thus be
        drain'd;
For thou hast more to-morrows yet to ask,
And wilt be ever to begin thy task;
Who, like the hindmost chariot wheels, art
        curst,
Still to be near, but ne'er to reach the first.
    O freedom ! first delight of human-
        kind ! [100]
Not that which bondmen from their mas-
        ters find,

The privilege of doles; [11] nor yet t' inscribe
Their names in this or t'other Roman
        tribe: [12]
That false enfranchisement with ease is
        found;
Slaves are made citizens by turning round.[13]
    "How," replies one, "can any be more
        free ?
Here 's Dama, once a groom of low degree
Not worth a farthing, and a sot beside;
So true a rogue, for lying's sake he lied:
But, with a turn, a freeman he became; [110]
Now Marcus Dama is his worship's name.[14]
Good gods ! who would refuse to lend a
        sum,
If wealthy Marcus surety will become !
Marcus is made a judge, and for a proof
Of certain truth, 'He said it,' is enough.
A will is to be prov'd; put in your claim;
'T is clear, if Marcus has subscrib'd his
        name.[15]
This is true liberty, as I believe;   ⎫
What farther can we from our caps re-   ⎪
        ceive,[16]   ⎬
Than as we please without control to   ⎪
        live ?   [120]⎭
Not more to noble Brutus[17] could belong."
    "Hold," says the Stoic, "your assump-
        'tion 's wrong:
I grant true freedom you have well de-   ⎫
        fin'd;   ⎪
But, living as you list, and to your mind,   ⎬
Are loosely tack'd, and must be left be-   ⎪
        hind."   ⎭
    "What ! since the prætor did my fetters
        loose,
And left me freely at my own dispose,
May I not live without control or awe,
Excepting still the letter of the law ? " [18]
    "Hear me with patience, while thy mind
        I free   [130]
From those fond notions of false liberty:
'T is not the prætor's province to bestow ⎫
True freedom; nor to teach mankind to   ⎪
        know   ⎬
What to ourselves, or to our friends, we ⎪
        owe.   ⎭
He could not set thee free from cares and
        strife,
Nor give the reins to a lewd vicious life:
As well he for an ass a harp might string,
Which is against the reason of the thing;
For reason still is whisp'ring in your ear:
'Where you are sure to fail, th' attempt
        forbear.' [140]

No need of public sanctions this to bind,
Which Nature has implanted in the mind:
Not to pursue the work, to which we 're not design'd.
" Unskill'd in hellebore, if thou shouldst try
To mix it, and mistake the quantity,
The rules of physic would against thee cry.
The high-shoed plowman, should he quit the land,
To take the pilot's rudder in his hand,
Artless of stars, and of the moving sand,
The gods would leave him to the waves and wind, 150
And think all shame was lost in human-kind.
" Tell me, my friend, from whence hadst thou the skill,
So nicely to distinguish good from ill ?
Or by the sound to judge of gold and brass,
What piece is tinker's metal, what will pass ?
And what thou art to follow, what to fly,
This to condemn, and that to ratify ?
When to be bountiful, and when to spare,
But never craving, or oppress'd with care ?
The baits of gifts and money to despise, 160
And look on wealth with undesiring eyes ?
When thou canst truly call these virtues thine,
Be wise and free, by Heav'n's consent, and mine.
" But thou, who lately of the common strain,
Wert one of us, if still thou dost retain
The same ill habits, the same follies too,
Gloss'd over only with a saintlike show,
Then I resume the freedom which I gave;
Still thou art bound to vice, and still a slave.
Thou canst not wag thy finger, or begin 170
The least light motion, but it tends to sin."
" How 's this ? Not wag my finger ? " he replies.
" No, friend; nor fuming gums, nor sacrifice,
Can ever make a madman free, or wise.
*Virtue and Vice are never in one soul :
A man is wholly wise, or wholly is a fool.*[19]
A heavy bumpkin, taught with daily care,
Can never dance three steps with a becoming air."
PER. In spite of this, my freedom still remains.

CORN. Free ! what, and fetter'd with so many chains ? 180
Canst thou no other master understand
Than him that freed thee by the prætor's wand ?[20]
Should he, who was thy lord, command thee now,
With a harsh voice, and supercilious brow,
To servile duties, thou wouldst fear no more;
The gallows and the whip are out of door.
But if thy passions lord it in thy breast,
Art thou not still a slave, and still oppress'd ?
Whether alone, or in thy harlot's lap,
When thou wouldst take a lazy morning's nap, 190
" Up, up," says Avarice; thou snor'st again,
Stretchest thy limbs, and yawn'st, but all in vain:
The tyrant Lucre no denial takes;
At his command th' unwilling sluggard wakes.
" What must I do ? " he cries: " What ? " says his lord:
" Why rise, make ready, and go straight aboard:
With fish, from Euxine seas, thy vessel freight;
Flax, castor, Coan wines, the precious weight
Of pepper, and Sabæan incense, take
With thy own hands, from the tir'd camel's back: 200
And with posthaste thy running markets make.
Be sure to turn the penny: lie and swear;
'T is wholesome sin." " But Jove," thou say'st, " will hear."
" Swear, fool, or starve; for the dilemma 's even:
A tradesman thou ! and hope to go to heav'n ? "
Resolv'd for sea, the slaves thy baggage pack,
Each saddled with his burden on his back;
Nothing retards thy voyage, now, unless
Thy other lord forbids, Voluptuousness:
And he may ask this civil question: " Friend, 210
What dost thou make a-shipboard ? to what end ?
Art thou of Bethlem's noble college free ?
Stark, staring mad, that thou wouldst tempt the sea ?

Cubb'd in a cabin, on a mattress laid,
On a brown george, with lousy swabbers
   fed,
Dead wine, that stinks of the borachio,
   sup
From a foul jack, or greasy maple cup ?
Say, wouldst thou bear all this, to raise thy
   store
From six i' th' hundred, to six hundred
   more ?
Indulge, and to thy Genius freely give; 220
For, not to live at ease, is not to live;
Death stalks behind thee, and each flying
   hour
Does some loose remnant of thy life de-
   vour.
Live, while thou liv'st; for death will make
   us all
A name, a nothing but an old wife's tale."
   Speak; wilt thou Avarice, or Pleasure
   choose
To be thy lord ? Take one, and one re-
   fuse.
But both, by turns, the rule of thee will
   have,
And thou, bewixt 'em both, wilt be a slave.
   Nor think, when once thou hast resisted
   one,   230
That all thy marks of servitude are gone:
The struggling greyhound gnaws his leash
   in vain,
If, when 't is broken, still he drags the
   chain.
   Says Phædria [21] to his man: " Believe me,
   friend,
To this uneasy love I 'll put an end.
Shall I run out of all ? my friends dis-
   grace,
And be the first lewd unthrift of my race ?
Shall I the neighbors' nightly rest invade
At her deaf doors, with some vile sere-
   nade ? "
" Well hast thou freed thyself," his man
   replies,   240
" Go, thank the gods, and offer sacrifice."
" Ah," says the youth, " if we unkindly
   part,
Will not the poor fond creature break her
   heart ? "
" Weak soul ! and blindly to destruction
   led !
She break her heart ! she 'll sooner break
   your head.
She knows her man, and when you rant and
   swear,

Can draw you to her *with a single hair*."
" But shall I not return ? Now, when she
   sues,
Shall I my own, and her desires refuse ? "
" Sir, take your course; but my advice is
   plain: 250
Once freed, 't is madness to resume your
   chain."
   Ay; there 's the man, who, loos'd from
   lust and pelf,
Less to the prætor owes, than to himself.
But write him down a slave, who, humbly
   proud,
With presents begs preferments from the
   crowd;
That early suppliant,[22] who salutes the
   tribes,
And sets the mob to scramble for his bribes,
That some old dotard, sitting in the sun,
On holidays may tell that such a feat was
   done:
In future times this will be counted rare. 260
   Thy superstition too may claim a share:
When flow'rs are strew'd, and lamps in or-
   der plac'd,
And windows with illuminations grac'd,
On Herod's day; [23] when sparkling bowls go
   round,
And tunny's tails in savory sauce are
   drown'd,
Thou mutter'st prayers obscene; nor dost
   refuse
The fasts and Sabbaths of the curtail'd
   Jews.
Then a crack'd eggshell thy sick fancy
   frights,[24]
Besides the childish fear of walking sprites.
Of o'ergrown gelding priests thou art
   afraid;   270
The timbrel, and the squintifego maid
Of Isis, awe thee; lest the gods, for sin,
Should with a swelling dropsy stuff thy
   skin:
Unless three garlic heads the curse avert,
Eaten each morn, devoutly, next thy heart.
   " Preach this among the brawny guards,"
   say'st thou,
" And see if they thy doctrine will al-
   low:"
The dull fat captain, with a hound's deep
   throat,
Would bellow out a laugh, in a bass
   note;
And prize a hundred Zenos just as much 280
As a clipp'd sixpence, or a schilling Dutch.

EXPLANATORY NOTES ON THE FIFTH SATIRE

1 *Progne* was wife to Tereus, King of Thracia. Tereus fell in love with Philomela, sister to Progne, ravish'd her, and cut out her tongue ; in revenge of which, Progne kill'd Itys, her own son by Tereus, and serv'd him up at a feast, to be eaten by his father.

2 *Thyestes* and Atreus were brothers, both kings. Atreus, to revenge himself of his unnatural brother, kill'd the sons of Thyestes, and invited him to eat them.

3 By the childish robe is meant the *prætexta*, or first gowns which the Roman children of quality wore. These were welted with purple, and on those welts were fasten'd the *bullæ*, or little bells ; which, when they came to the age of puberty, were hung up, and consecrated to the *Lares*, or household gods.

4 The first shields which the Roman youths wore were white, and without any impress or device on them, to shew they had yet achiev'd nothing in the wars.

5 *Socrates*, by the oracle, was declar'd to be the wisest of mankind : he instructed many of the Athenian young noblemen in morality, and amongst the rest Alcibiades.

6 Astrologers divide the heaven into twelve parts, according to the number of the twelve signs of the zodiac. The sign, or constellation, which rises in the east at the birth of any man, is call'd the Ascendant : Persius therefore judges that Cornutus and he had the same or a like nativity.

7 The sign of Gemini.

8 The sign of Libra.

9 Astrologers have an axiom that whatsoever Saturn ties is loos'd by Jupiter. They account Saturn to be a planet of a malevolent nature, and Jupiter of a propitious influence.

10 Zeno was the great master of the Stoic philosophy, and Cleanthes was second to him in reputation. Cornutus, who was master or tutor to Persius, was of the same school.

11 When a slave was made free, he had the privilege of a Roman born ; which was to have a share in the donatives, or doles of bread, &c., which were distributed by the magistrates amongst the people.

12 The Roman people was distributed into several tribes. He who was made free was inroll'd into some one of them, and thereupon enjoy'd the common privileges of a Roman citizen.

13 The master who intended to infranchise a slave carried him before the city prætor, and turn'd him round, using these words : " I will that this man be free."

14 Slaves had only one name before their freedom ; after it they were admitted to a *prænomen*, like our christen'd names : so Dama is now call'd Marcus Dama.

15 At the proof of a testament, the magistrates were to subscribe their names, as allowing the legality of the will.

16 Slaves, when they were set free, had a cap given them, in sign of their liberty.

17 *Brutus* freed the Roman people from the tyranny of the Tarquins, and chang'd the form of the government into a glorious commonwealth.

18 The text of the Roman laws was written in red letters, which was call'd the Rubric ; translated here, in more general words, " The letter of the law."

19 The Stoics held this paradox, that any one vice, or notorious folly, which they call'd madness, hinder'd a man from being virtuous ; that a man was of a piece, without a mixture, either wholly vicious, or good ; one virtue or vice, according to them, including all the rest.

20 The prætor held a wand in his hand, with which he softly struck the slave on the head, when he declar'd him free.

21 This alludes to the play of Terence, call'd *The Eunuch ;* which was excellently imitated of late in English, by Sir Charles Sedley. In the first scene of that comedy Phædria was introduc'd with his man, Pamphilus, discoursing whether he should leave his mistress Thais, or return to her, now that she had invited him.

22 He who sued for any office amongst the Romans was call'd a candidate, because he wore a white gown ; and sometimes chalk'd it, to make it appear whiter. He rose early, and went to the levees of those who headed the people ; saluted also the tribes severally, when they were gather'd together to choose their magistrates ; and distributed a largess amongst them, to bribe them for their voices ; much resembling our elections of Parliament-men.

23 The commentators are divided what Herod this was, whom our author mentions ; whether Herod the Great, whose birthday might possibly be celebrated, after his death, by the Herodians, a sect amongst the Jews, who thought him their Messiah ; or Herod Agrippa, living in the author's time and after it. The latter seems the more probable opinion.

24 The ancients had a superstition, contrary to ours, concerning eggshells : they thought that if an eggshell were crack'd, or a hole bor'd in the bottom of it, they were subject to the power of sorcery. We as vainly break the bottom of an eggshell, and cross it, when we have eaten the egg, lest some hag should make use of it in bewitching us, or sailing over the sea in it, if it were whole.

The rest, of the priests of Isis, and her one-ey'd or squinting priestess, is more largely treated in the *Sixth Satire* of Juvenal, where the superstitions of women are related.

THE SIXTH SATIRE OF PERSIUS

TO CÆSIUS BASSUS, A LYRIC POET

THE ARGUMENT

This *Sixth Satire* treats an admirable commonplace of moral philosophy ; of the true use

of riches. They are certainly intended, by
the power who bestows them, as instruments
and helps of living commodiously ourselves,
and of administ'ring to the wants of others
who are oppress'd by fortune. There are two
extremes in the opinions of men concerning
them. One error, tho' on the right hand, yet
a great one, is that they are no helps to a
virtuous life; the other places all our happiness in the acquisition and possession of
them; and this is, undoubtedly, the worse
extreme. The mean betwixt these is the
opinion of the Stoics; which is that riches
may be useful to the leading a virtuous life,
in case we rightly understand how to give
according to right reason; and how to receive what is given us by others. The virtue
of giving well is call'd liberality; and 't is of
this virtue that Persius writes in this satire,
wherein he not only shews the lawful use of
riches, but also sharply inveighs against the
vices which are oppos'd to it; and especially
of those which consist in the defects of giving or spending, or in the abuse of riches.
He writes to Cæsius Bassus, his friend, and
a poet also; enquires first of his health and
studies, and afterwards informs him of his
own, and where he is now resident. He gives
an account of himself, that he is endeavoring by little and little to wear off his vices;
and particularly, that he is combating ambition and the desire of wealth. He dwells
upon the latter vice; and being sensible that
few men either desire or use riches as they
ought, he endeavors to convince them of
their folly; which is the main design of the
whole satire.

HAS winter caus'd thee, friend, to change
    thy seat,
And seek, in Sabine air,[1] a warm retreat?
Say, dost thou yet the Roman harp com-
    mand?
Do the strings answer to thy noble hand?
Great master of the Muse, inspir'd to sing
The beauties of the first created spring;
The pedigree of nature to rehearse,
And sound the Maker's work, in equal
    verse;
Now sporting on thy lyre[2] the loves of
    youth,
Now virtuous age, and venerable truth;   10
Expressing justly Sappho's wanton art
Of odes, and Pindar's more majestic part.
    For me, my warmer constitution wants
More cold, than our Ligurian winter grants;
And therefore, to my native shores re-
    tir'd,
I view the coast old Ennius once admir'd;

Where clifts on either side their points }
    display; }
And, after, opening in an ampler way, }
Afford the pleasing prospect of the bay. }
" 'T is worth your while, O Romans, to re-
    gard   20
The Port of Luna," says our learned
    bard;
Who, in a drunken dream,[3] beheld his
    soul
The fifth within the transmigrating roll;
Which first a peacock, then Euphorbus }
    was, }
Then Homer next, and next Pythagoras; }
And last of all the line did into Ennius }
    pass. }
    Secure and free from business of the
    State,
And more secure of what the vulgar prate,
Here I enjoy my private thoughts, nor
    care
What rots for sheep the southern winds
    prepare;   30
Survey the neighb'ring fields, and not re-
    pine,
When I behold a larger crop than mine.
To see a beggar's brat in riches flow,
Adds not a wrinkle to my even brow;
Nor, envious at the sight, will I forbear
My plenteous bowl, nor bate my bounteous
    cheer;
Nor yet unseal the dregs of wine that
    stink
Of cask, nor in a nasty flagon drink: }
Let others stuff their guts with homely }
    fare; }
For men of diff'rent inclinations are,   40 }
Tho' born, perhaps, beneath one common }
    star. }
In minds and manners twins oppos'd we
    see
In the same sign, almost the same de-
    gree:
One, frugal, on his birthday fears to }
    dine, }
Does at a penny's cost in herbs repine, }
And hardly dares to dip his fingers in the }
    brine; }
Prepar'd as priest of his own rites to stand,
He sprinkles pepper with a sparing hand.
His jolly brother, opposite in sense, }
Laughs at his thrift; and, lavish of ex- }
    pense,   50 }
Quaffs, crams, and guttles in his own de- }
    fense. }

For me, I 'll use my own, and take my
    share,
Yet will not turbots for my slaves pre-
    pare;
Nor be so nice in taste myself, to know
If what I swallow be a thrush, or no.
Live on thy annual income ! Spend thy ⎫
    store,   ⎬
And freely grind from thy full threshing
    floor: ⎭
Next harvest promises as much, or more.
Thus I would live; but friendship's ⎫
    holy band,   ⎪
And offices of kindness, hold my hand: 60 ⎬
My friend is shipwreck'd on [4] the Bruttian ⎪
    strand,   ⎭
His riches in th' Ionian main are lost;
And he himself stands shiv'ring on the
    coast;
Where, destitute of help, forlorn, and bare,
He wearies the deaf gods with fruitless
    pray'r.
Their images, the relics of the wrack,
Torn from the naked poop, are tided back
By the wild waves; and, rudely thrown
    ashore,
Lie impotent, nor can themselves restore.
The vessel sticks, and shews her open'd
    side,   70
And on her shatter'd mast the mews in
    triumph ride.
From thy new hope,[5] and from thy growing
    store,
Now lend assistance, and relieve the poor.
Come, do a noble act of charity;
A pittance of thy land will set him free.
Let him not bear the badges of a wrack,
Nor beg with a blue table [6] on his back;
Nor tell me that thy frowning heir will
    say:
" 'T is mine, that wealth thou squander'st
    thus away."
What is 't to thee, if he neglects thy urn, 80
Or without spices [7] lets thy body burn ?
If odors to thy ashes he refuse,
Or buys corrupted cassia from the Jews ?
" All these," the wiser Bestius will reply,
" Are empty pomp, and dead men's lux-
    ury."
We never knew this vain expense, before
Th' effeminated Grecians brought it o'er:
Now toys and trifles from their Athens
    come,
And dates and pepper have unsinew'd
    Rome.

Our sweating hinds their salads, now,
    defile,   90
Infecting homely herbs with fragrant oil.
But to thy fortune be not thou a slave,
For what hast thou to fear beyond the
    grave ?
And thou who gap'st for my estate, draw
    near;
For I would whisper somewhat in thy
    ear.
Hear'st thou the news, my friend ? Th' ex-
    press is come
With laurel'd letters from the camp to
    Rome:
Cæsar salutes [8] the queen and senate thus:
" My arms are on the Rhine victorious.
From mourning altars sweep the dust
    away: 100
Cease fasting, and proclaim a fat thanks-
    giving day."
The goodly empress,[9] jollily inclin'd,
Is to the welcome bearer wondrous kind;
And, setting her good housewif'ry aside,
Prepares for all the pageantry of pride.
The captive Germans,[10] of gigantic size,
Are rank'd in order, and are clad in frize.
The spoils of kings and conquer'd camps we
    boast,
Their arms in trophies hang on the trium-
    phal post.
Now, for so many glorious actions done 110
In foreign parts, and mighty battles won;
For peace at home, and for the public
    wealth,
I mean to crown a bowl to Cæsar's health:
Besides, in gratitude for such high mat-
    ters,
Know, I have vow'd two hundred gladia-
    tors.[11]
Say, wouldst thou hinder me from this
    expense ?
I disinherit thee, if thou dar'st take of-
    fense.
Yet more, a public largess I design
Of oil and pies, to make the people dine:
Control me not, for fear I change my
    will.   120
And yet methinks I hear thee grumbling
    still:
" You give as if you were the Persian
    king;
Your land does no such large revenues
    bring."
Well, on my terms thou wilt not be **my**
    heir;

If thou car'st little, less shall be my
    care:
Were none of all my father's sisters left;
Nay, were I of my mother's kin bereft;
None by an uncle's or a grandam's side,
Yet I could some adopted heir provide.   129
I need but take my journey half a day ⎫
From haughty Rome, and at Aricia stay, ⎪
Where fortune throws poor Manius in ⎬
    my way. ⎭
Him will I choose. "What; him, of hum-
    ble birth,
Obscure, a foundling, and a son of earth ?"
Obscure! Why pr'ythee what am I? I
    know
My father, grandsire, and great grandsire
    too:
If farther I derive my pedigree,
I can but guess beyond the fourth degree.
The rest of my forgotten ancestors
Were sons of earth, like him, or sons of
    whores.   140
    Yet why shouldst thou, old covetous
        wretch, aspire
To be my heir, who mightst have been my
    sire ?
In nature's race, shouldst thou demand of
    me
My torch,[12] when I in course run after
    thee ?
Think I approach thee like the God of
    Gain,
With wings on head and heels, as poets
    feign:
Thy mod'rate fortune from my gift receive;
Now fairly take it, or as fairly leave;
But take it as it is, and ask no more.
"What, when thou hast embezzled all thy
    store ?   150
Where's all thy father left ?" 'T is true,
    I grant,
Some I have mortgag'd, to supply my want:
The legacies of Tadius too are flown;
All spent, and on the selfsame errand
    gone.
"How little then to my poor share will
    fall ! "
Little indeed; but yet that little 's all.
    Nor tell me, in a dying father's tone:
"Be careful still of the main chance, my
    son;
Put out the principal in trusty hands:
Live of the use; and never dip thy lands." 160
"But yet what 's left for me ? " What 's
    left, my friend !

Ask that again, and all the rest I spend.
Is not my fortune at my own command ?
Pour oil, and pour it with a plenteous
    hand,
Upon my salads, boy: shall I be fed
With sodden nettles, and a sing'd sow's
    head ?
'T is holiday; provide me better cheer;
'T is holiday, and shall be round the year.
Shall I my household gods and genius
    cheat,
To make him rich, who grudges me my
    meat,   170
That he may loll at ease; and, pamper'd
    high,
When I am laid, may feed on giblet pie ?
And, when his throbbing lust extends the
    vein,
Have wherewithal his whores to enter-
    tain ?
Shall I in homespun cloth be clad, that he
His paunch in triumph may before him
    see ?
    Go, miser, go; for lucre sell thy soul;
Truck wares for wares, and trudge from
    pole to pole,
That men may say, when thou art dead and
    gone:
" See what a vast estate he left his son ! 180
How large a family of brawny knaves,
Well fed, and fat as Cappadocian slaves ! " [13]
Encrease thy wealth, and double all thy ⎫
    store. ⎪
'T is done: now double that and swell the ⎬
    score; ⎪
To ev'ry thousand add ten thousand ⎭
    more.
Then say, Chrysippus,[14] thou who wouldst
    confine
Thy heap, where I shall put an end to mine.

EXPLANATORY NOTES ON THE SIXTH
SATIRE

1 *And seek, in Sabine air*, &c. All the studious, and particularly the poets, about the end
of August, began to set themselves on work,
refraining from writing during the heats of the
summer. They wrote by night, and sate up
the greatest part of it; for which reason the
product of their studies was call'd their elucu-
brations, or nightly labors. They who had country seats retir'd to them while they studied, as
Persius did to his, which was near the Port of
the Moon in Etruria; and Bassus to his, which
was in the country of the Sabines, nearer
Rome.
2 *Now sporting on thy lyre*, &c. This proves

Cæsius Bassus to have been a lyric poet. 'T is said of him that by an eruption of the flaming mountain Vesuvius, near which the greatest part of his fortune lay, he was burnt himself, together with all his writings.

3 *Who, in a drunken dream*, &c. I call it a drunken dream of Ennius ; not that my author in this place gives me any encouragement for the epithet, but because Horace and all who mention Ennius say he was an excessive drinker of wine. In a dream, or vision, call you it which you please, he thought it was reveal'd to him that the soul of Pythagoras was transmigrated into him ; as Pythagoras before him believ'd that himself had been Euphorbus in the wars of Troy. Commentators differ in placing the order of this soul, and who had it first. I have here given it to the peacock, because it looks more according to the order of nature that it should lodge in a creature of an inferior species, and so by gradation rise to the informing of a man. And Persius favors me, by saying that Ennius was the fifth from the Pythagorean peacock.

4 *My friend is shipwreck'd on*, &c. Perhaps this is only a fine transition of the poet, to introduce the business of the satire ; and not that any such accident had happen'd to one of the friends of Persius. But, however, this is the most poetical description of any in our author ; and since he and Lucan were so great friends, I know not but Lucan might help him in two or three of these verses, which seem to be written in his style : certain it is, that besides this description of a shipwreck, and two lines more, which are at the end of the *Second Satire*, our poet has written nothing elegantly. I will therefore transcribe both the passages, to justify my opinion. The following are the last verses, saving one, of the *Second Satire* :

Compositum jus, fasque animi ; sanctosque recessus Mentis, et incoctum generoso pectus honesto.

The others are those in this present satire, which are subjoin'd :

—— trabe rupta, Bruttia saxa Prendit amicus inops : remque omnem, surdaque vota Condidit Ionio, jacet ipse in littore, et una Ingentes de puppe Dei, jamque obvia mergis Costa ratis laceræ.

5 *From thy new hope*, &c. The Latin is, *Nunc et de cespite vivo frange aliquid*. Casaubon only opposes the *cespes vivus*, which, word for word, is the living turf, to the harvest, or annual income ; I suppose the poet rather means, sell a piece of land already sown, and give the money of it to my friend, who has lost all by shipwreck ; that is, do not stay till thou hast reap'd, but help him immediately, as his wants require.

6 *Not beg with a blue table*, &c. Holyday translates it a green table. The sense is the same, for the table was painted of the sea-color, which the shipwreck'd person carried on his back, expressing his losses thereby, to excite the charity of the spectators.

7 *Or without spices*, &c. The bodies of the rich, before they were burnt, were imbalm'd with spices ; or rather spices were put into the urn with the relics of the ashes. Our author here names cinnamum and cassia, which cassia was sophisticated with cherry gum, and probably enough by the Jews, who adulterate all things which they sell. But whether the ancients were acquainted with the spices of the Molucca Islands, Ceylon, and other parts of the Indies, or whether their pepper and cinnamon, &c., were the same with ours, is another question. As for nutmegs and mace, 't is plain that the Latin names of them are modern.

8 *Cæsar salutes*, &c. The Cæsar here mention'd is Caius Caligula, who affected to triumph over the Germans, whom he never conquer'd, as he did over the Britains ; and accordingly sent letters, wrapp'd about with laurels, to the senate and the Empress Cæsonia, whom I here call *queen*, tho' I know that name was not us'd amongst the Romans ; but the word *empress* would not stand in that verse, for which reason I adjourn'd it to another. The dust which was to be swept away from the altars, was either the ashes which were left there after the last sacrifice for victory, or might perhaps mean the dust or ashes which were left on the altars since some former defeat of the Romans by the Germans ; after which overthrow the altars had been neglected.

9 *Cæsonia*, wife to Caius Caligula, who afterwards, in the reign of Claudius, was propos'd, but ineffectually, to be married to him, after he had executed Messalina for adultery.

10 *The captive Germans*, &c. He means only such as were to pass for Germans in the triumph, large-bodied men, as they are still, whom the empress cloth'd new, with coarse garments, for the greater ostentation of the victory.

11 *Know, I have vow'd two hundred gladiators.* A hundred pair of gladiators were beyond the purse of a private man to give ; therefore this is only a threat'ning to his heir, that he could do what he pleas'd with his estate.

12 *Shouldst thou demand of me my torch*, &c. Why shouldst thou, who art an old fellow, hope to outlive me, and be my heir, who am much younger ? He who was first in the course, or race, deliver'd the torch which he carried to him who was second.

13 *Well fed, and fat as Cappadocian slaves !* " Who were famous for their lustiness, and being, as we call it, in good liking. They were set on a stall when they were expos'd to sale, to shew the good habit of their body ; and made to play tricks before the buyers, to shew their activity and strength.

14 *Then say, Chrysippus*, &c. Chrysippus, the Stoic, invented a kind of argument, consisting of more than three propositions, which is call'd *sorites*, or a heap. But as Chrysippus could never bring his propositions to a certain stint, so neither can a covetous man bring his craving desires to any certain measure of riches, beyond which he could not wish for any more.

POEMS INCLUDED IN EXAMEN POETICUM (THE THIRD MISCELLANY), 1693

[In 1693 Tonson published a miscellany with title-page reading, *Examen Poeticum: being The Third Part of Miscellany Poems. Containing Variety of New Translations of the Ancient Poets. Together with many Original Copies, by the Most Eminent Hands.*

> *Hæc potior soboles : hinc cœli tempore certo,*
> *Dulcia mella premes.* — VIRGIL, *Geor.* IV.
>
> *In medium quæsita reponunt.* — Ibid.

Dryden's translations from the *Metamorphoses* occupy the place of honor in the volume. Besides the material printed below, the collection contains the first edition of some minor pieces by Dryden, which have been printed above in their probable chronological order (see pp. 20, 102, 104, 106, 252, 267, above); and reprints of some of his earlier work, notably his *Ode to Mrs. Anne Killigrew* (see p. 211, above). Among the other contributors to the volume were the Earl of Mulgrave, Prior, Congreve, Granville, Henry Cromwell, and Yalden.

Two slightly different issues of this first edition are known ; the variations apparently do not affect Dryden's work. A second edition, with title unchanged, appeared in 1706; and a third, with title-page reading, *The Third Part of Miscellany Poems . . . Publish'd by Mr. Dryden,* in 1716. The second edition omits nearly all Dryden's poetical contributions ; the third has a still different table of contents.]

TO THE

RIGHT HONORABLE MY LORD RADCLIFFE

MY LORD,

THESE *Miscellany Poems* are by many titles yours. The first they claim from your acceptance of my promise to present them to you, before some of them were yet in being. The rest are deriv'd from your own merit, the exactness of your judgment in poetry, and the candor of your nature ; easy to forgive some trivial faults, when they come accompanied with countervailing beauties. But, after all, tho' these are your equitable claims to a dedication from other poets, yet I must acknowledge a bribe in the case, which is your particular liking of my verses. 'T is a vanity common to all writers, to overvalue their own productions ; and 't is better for me to own this failing in myself, than the world to do it for me. For what other reason have I spent my life in so unprofitable a study ? Why am I grown old in seeking so barren a reward as fame ? The same parts and application which have made me a poet might have rais'd me to any honors of the gown, which are often given to men of as little learning and less honesty than myself. No government has ever been, or ever can be, wherein timeservers and blockheads will not be uppermost. The persons are only chang'd, but the same jugglings in state, the same hypocrisy in religion, the same self-interest and mismanagement, will remain for ever. Blood and money will be lavish'd in all ages, only for the preferment of new faces, with old consciences. There is too

often a jaundice in the eyes of great men ; they see not those whom they raise in the same colors with other men. All whom they affect look golden to them, when the gilding is only in their own distemper'd sight. These considerations have given me a kind of contempt for those who have risen by unworthy ways. I am not asham'd to be little, when I see them so infamously great ; neither do I know why the name of poet should be dishonorable to me, if I am truly one, as I hope I am ; for I will never do anything that shall dishonor it. The notions of morality are known to all men ; none can pretend ignorance of those ideas which are inborn in mankind : and if I see one thing and practice the contrary, I must be disingenuous, not to acknowledge a clear truth ; and base, to act against the light of my own conscience. For the reputation of my honesty, no man can question it, who has any of his own ; for that of my poetry, it shall either stand by its own merit, or fall for want of it. Ill writers are usually the sharpest censors ; for they, as the best poet and the best patron said :

> When in the full perfection of decay,
> Turn vinegar, and come again in play.

Thus the corruption of a poet is the generation of a critic : I mean of a critic in the general acceptation of this age, for formerly they were quite another species of men. They were defenders of poets and commentators on their works : to illustrate obscure beauties ; to place some passages in a better light ; to redeem others from malicious interpretations ; to help out an author's modesty, who is not ostentatious of his wit, and, in short, to shield him from the ill nature of those fellows, who were then call'd Zoili and Momi, and now take upon themselves the venerable name of censors. But neither Zoilus, nor he who endeavor'd to defame Virgil, were ever adopted into the name of critics by the ancients: what their reputation was then, we know; and their successors in this age deserve no better. Are our auxiliary forces turn'd our enemies? Are they, who at best are but wits of the second order, and whose only credit amongst readers is what they obtain'd by being subservient to the fame of writers; are these become rebels of slaves, and usurpers of subjects? or, to speak in the most honorable terms of them, are they from our seconds become principals against us? Does the ivy undermine the oak, which supports its weakness? What labor would it cost them to put in a better line than the worst of those which they expunge in a true poet! Petronius, the greatest wit perhaps of all the Romans, yet when his envy prevail'd upon his judgment to fall on Lucan, he fell himself in his attempt: he perform'd worse in his *Essay of the Civil War*, than the author of the *Pharsalia;* and, avoiding his errors, has made greater of his own. Julius Scaliger would needs turn down Homer, and abdicate him after the possession of three thousand years. Has he succeeded in his attempt? He has indeed shown us some of those imperfections in him, which are incident to humankind; but who had not rather be that Homer than this Scaliger? You see the same hypercritic, when he endeavors to mend the beginning of Claudian (a faulty poet, and living in a barbarous age), yet how short he comes of him, and substitutes such verses of his own as deserve the *ferula*. What a censure has he made of Lucan, that he rather seems to bark than sing! Would any but a dog have made so snarling a comparison? One would have thought he had learn'd Latin, as late as they tell us he did Greek. Yet he came off with a *pace tua*, by your good leave, Lucan; he call'd him not by those outrageous names, of fool, booby, and blockhead: he had somewhat more of good manners than his successors, as he had much more knowledge. We have two sorts of those gentlemen in our nation: some of them, proceeding with a seeming moderation and pretense of respect to the dramatic writers of the last age, only scorn and vilify the present poets, to set up their predecessors. But this is only in appearance; for their real design is nothing less than to do honor to any man besides themselves. Horace took notice of such men in his age:

—— Non ingeniis favet ille sepultis;
Nostra sed impugnat; nos nostraque lividus odit.

'T is not with an ultimate intention to pay reverence to the manes of Shakespeare, Fletcher, and Ben Jonson, that they commend their writings, but to throw dirt on the writers of this age: their declaration is one thing, and their practice is another. By a seeming veneration to our fathers, they would thrust out us, their lawful issue, and govern us themselves, under a specious pretense of reformation If they could compass their intent, what would wit and learning get by such a change? If we are bad poets, they are worse; and when any of their woful pieces come abroad, the difference is so great betwixt them and good writers, that there need no criticisms on our part to decide it. When they describe the writers of this age, they draw such monstrous figures of them, as resemble none of us; our pretended pictures are so unlike, that 't is evident we never sate to them: they are all grotesque; the products of their wild imaginations, things out of nature, so far from being copied from us, that they resemble nothing that ever was, or ever can be. But there is another sort of insects, more venomous than the former: those who manifestly aim at the destruction of our poetical Church and State; who allow nothing to their countrymen, either of this or of the former age. These attack the living by raking up the ashes of the dead; well knowing that if they can subvert their original title to the stage, we who claim under them must fall of course. Peace be to the venerable shades of Shakespeare and Ben Jonson! None of the living will presume to have any competition with them: as they were our predecessors, so they were our masters. We trail our plays under them, but (as at the funerals of a Turkish emperor) our ensigns are furl'd or dragg'd upon the ground, in honor to the dead; so we may lawfully advance our own, afterwards, to show that we succeed: if less in dignity, yet on the same foot and title, which we think too we can maintain against the insolence of our own janizaries. If I am the man, as I have reason to believe, who am seemingly courted, and secretly undermin'd, I think I shall be able to defend myself, when I am openly attack'd; and to shew besides that the Greek writers only gave us the rudiments of a stage, which they never finish'd; that many of the tragedies in the former age amongst us were without comparison beyond those of Sophocles and Euripides. But at present, I have neither the leisure nor the means for such an undertaking. 'T is ill going to law for an estate with him who is in possession of it and enjoys the present profits to feed his cause. But the *quantum mutatus* may be remember'd in due time. In the mean while, I leave the world to judge who gave the provocation.

This, my Lord, is, I confess, a long digression, from Miscellany Poems to Modern Tragedies; but I have the ordinary excuse of an injur'd man, who will be telling his tale unseasonably to his betters: tho', at the same time, I am certain you are so good a friend, as to take a concern in all things which belong to one who so truly honors you. And besides, being yourself a critic of the genuine sort, who have read the best authors in their own languages, who perfectly distinguish of their several merits, and in general prefer them to the moderns, yet, I know, you judge for the English tragedies against the Greek and Latin, as well as against the French, Italian, and Spanish, of these latter ages. Indeed there is a vast difference betwixt arguing like Perrault in behalf of the French poets, against Homer and Virgil, and betwixt giving the English poets their undoubted due of excelling Æschylus, Euripides, and Sophocles. For if we, or our greater fathers, have not yet brought the drama to an absolute perfection, yet at least we have carried it much farther than those ancient Greeks: who, beginning from a chorus, could never totally exclude it, as we have done, who find it an unprofitable incumbrance, without any necessity of entertaining it amongst us; and without the possibility of establishing it here, unless it were supported by a public charge. Neither can we accept of those lay bishops, as some call them, who, under pretense of reforming the stage, would intrude themselves upon us as our superiors, being indeed incompetent judges of what is manners, what religion, and, least of all, what is poetry and good sense. I can tell them, in behalf of all my fellows, that when they come to exercise a jurisdiction over us, they shall have the stage to themselves, as they have the laurel. As little can I grant that the French dramatic writers excel the English: our authors as far surpass them in genius, as our soldiers excel theirs in courage. 'T is true, in conduct they surpass us either way; yet that proceeds not so much from their greater knowledge, as from the difference of tastes in the two nations. They content themselves with a thin design, without episodes, and manag'd by few persons. Our audience will not be pleas'd but with variety of accidents, an underplot, and many actors. They follow the ancients too servilely in the mechanic rules, and we assume too much license to ourselves, in keeping them only in view at too great a distance. But if our audience had their tastes, our poets could more easily comply with them than the French writers could come up to the sublimity of our thoughts, or to the difficult variety of our designs. However it be, I dare establish it for a rule of practice on the stage, that we are bound to please those whom we pretend to entertain; and that at any price, religion and good manners only excepted; and I care not much if I give this handle to our

bad illiterate poetasters, for the defense of their *scriptions*, as they call them. There is a sort of merit in delighting the spectators; which is a name more proper for them than that of auditors; or else Horace is in the wrong, when he commends Lucilius for it. But these commonplaces I mean to treat at greater leisure: in the mean time, submitting that little I have said to your Lordship's approbation, or your censure, and choosing rather to entertain you this way, as you are a judge of writing, than to oppress your modesty with other commendations; which, tho' they are your due, yet would not be equally receiv'd in this satirical and censorious age. That which cannot without injury be denied to you is the easiness of your conversation, far from affectation or pride, not denying even to enemies their just praises. And this, if I would dwell on any theme of this nature, is no vulgar commendation to your Lordship. Without flattery, my Lord, you have it in your nature to be a patron and encourager of good poets, but your fortune has not yet put into your hands the opportunity of expressing it. What you will be hereafter, may be more than guess'd by what you are at present. You maintain the character of a nobleman, without that haughtiness which generally attends too many of the nobility; and when you converse with gentlemen, you forget not that you have been of their order. You are married to the daughter of a king, who, amongst her other high perfections, has deriv'd from him a charming behavior, a winning goodness, and a majestic person. The Muses and the Graces are the ornaments of your family. While the Muse sings, the Grace accompanies her voice: even the servants of the Muse have sometimes had the happiness to hear her, and to receive their inspirations from her.

I will not give myself the liberty of going farther; for 't is so sweet to wander in a pleasing way, that I should never arrive at my journey's end. To keep myself from being belated in my letter, and tiring your attention, I must return to the place where I was setting out. I humbly dedicate to your Lordship my own labors in this *Miscellany;* at the same time, not arrogating to myself the privilege of inscribing to you the works of others who are join'd with me in this undertaking, over which I can pretend no right. Your Lady and you have done me the favor to hear me read my translations of Ovid, and you both seem'd not to be displeas'd with them. Whether it be the partiality of an old man to his youngest child, I know not; but they appear to me the best of all my endeavors in this kind. Perhaps this poet is more easy to be translated than some others whom I have lately attempted; perhaps, too, he was more according to my genius. He is certainly more palatable to the reader than any of the Roman wits, tho' some of them are more lofty, some more instructive, and others more correct. He had learning enough to make him equal in the best. But, as his verse came easily, he wanted the toil of application to amend it. He is often luxuriant both in his fancy and expressions, and, as it has lately been observ'd, not always natural. If wit be pleasantry, he has it to excess; but if it be propriety, Lucretius, Horace, and, above all, Virgil are his superiors. I have said so much of him already, in my preface to his *Heroical Epistles*, that there remains little to be added in this place. For my own part, I have endeavor'd to copy his character what I could in this translation, even, perhaps, farther than I should have done; to his very faults. Mr. Chapman, in his translation of Homer, professes to have done it somewhat paraphrastically, and that on set purpose; his opinion being that a good poet is to be translated in that manner. I remember not the reason which he gives for it; but I suppose it is, for fear of omitting any of his excellencies: sure I am, that if it be a fault, 't is much more pardonable than that of those who run into the other extreme of a literal and close translation, where the poet is confin'd to his author's words that he wants elbowroom to express his elegancies. He leaves him obscure; he leaves him prose, where he found him verse: and no better than thus has Ovid been serv'd by the so much admir'd Sandys. This is at least the idea which I have remaining of his translation; for I never read him since I was a boy. They who take him upon content, from the praises which their fathers gave him, may inform their judgment by reading him again, and see (if they understand the original) what is become of Ovid's poetry, in his version; whether it be not all, or the greatest part of it, evaporated. But this proceeded from the wrong judgment of the age in which he liv'd. They neither knew good verse nor lov'd it; they were scholars, 't is true, but they were pedants. And for a just reward of their pedantic pains, all their translations want to be translated into English. If I flatter not myself, or if my friends have not flatter'd me, I have given my author's sense for the most part truly: for to mistake sometimes is incident to all men, and not to follow the Dutch commentators always may be forgiven to a man who thinks them, in the general, heavy gross-witted fellows, fit only to gloss on their own dull poets. But I leave a farther satire on their wit, till I have a better opportunity to shew how much I love and honor them. I have likewise attempted to restore Ovid to his native sweetness, easiness, and smoothness; and to give my poetry a kind of cadence, and,

as we call it, a run of verse, as like the original, as the English can come up to the Latin. As he seldom uses any *synalephas*, so I have endeavor'd to avoid them, as often as I could: I have likewise given him his own turns, both on the words and on the thought, which I cannot say are inimitable, because I have copied them; and so may others, if they use the same diligence: but certainly they are wonderfully graceful in this poet. Since I have nam'd the *synalepha*, which is the cutting off one vowel immediately before another, I will give an example of it from Chapman's *Homer*, which lies before me; for the benefit of those who understand not the Latin *prosodia*. 'T is in the first line of the argument to the first *Iliad* :

Apollo's priest to th' Argive fleet doth bring, &c.

There we see he makes it not *the Argive*, but *th' Argive*, to shun the shock of the two vowels immediately following each other. But in his second argument, in the same page, he gives a bad example of the quite contrary kind:

Alpha the pray'r of Chryses sings;
The army's plague, the strife of kings.

In these words *the army's*, *the* ending with a vowel, and *army's* beginning with another vowel, without cutting off the first, which by it had been *th' army's*, there remains a most horrible ill-sounding gap betwixt those words. I cannot say that I have everywhere observ'd the rule of this *synalepha* in my translation; but wheresoever I have not, 't is a fault in sound. The French and Italians have made it an inviolable precept in their versification, therein following the severe example of the Latin poets. Our countrymen have not yet reform'd their poetry so far, but content themselves with following the licentious practice of the Greeks; who, tho' they sometimes use *synalephas*, yet make no difficulty very often, to sound one vowel upon another; as Homer does in the very first line of *Alpha* :

Μῆνιν ἄειδε, Θεὰ, Πηληιάδεω 'Αχιλῆος.

'T is true, indeed, that in the second line, in these words μυρί' 'Αχαιοῖς, and ἄλγε' ἔθηκεν, the *synalepha* in revenge is twice observ'd. But it becomes us, for the sake of euphony, rather *Musas colere severiores*, with the Romans, than to give into the looseness of the Grecians.

I have tir'd myself, and have been summon'd by the press to send away this dedication; otherwise I had expos'd some other faults which are daily committed by our English poets; which, with care and observation, might be amended. For, after all, our language is both copious, significant, and majestical, and might be reduc'd into a more harmonious sound. But, for want of public encouragement, in this *iron age*, we are so far from making any progress in the improvement of our tongue, that in few years we shall speak and write as barbarously as our neighbors.

Notwithstanding my haste, I cannot forbear to tell your Lordship that there are two fragments of Homer translated in this *Miscellany*; one by Mr. Congreve (whom I cannot mention without the honor which is due to his excellent parts, and that entire affection which I bear him), and the other by myself. Both the subjects are pathetical, and I am sure my friend has added to the tenderness which he found in the original, and, without flattery, surpass'd his author. Yet I must needs say this in reference to Homer, that he is much more capable of exciting the manly passions than those of grief and pity. To cause admiration is indeed the proper and adequate design of an epic poem, and in that he has excell'd even Virgil; yet, without presuming to arraign our master, I may venture to affirm that he is somewhat too talkative, and more than somewhat too digressive. This is so manifest that it cannot be denied, in that little parcel which I have translated, perhaps too literally: there Andromache, in the midst of her concernment and fright for Hector, runs off her bias, to tell him a story of her pedigree, and of the lamentable death of her father, her mother, and her seven brothers. The devil was in Hector if he knew not all this matter, as well as she who told it him, for she had been his bedfellow for many years together; and if he knew it, then it must be confess'd that Homer, in this long digression, has rather given us his own character than that of the fair lady whom he paints. His dear friends the commentators, who never fail him at a pinch, will needs excuse him, by making the present sorrow of Andromache to occasion the remembrance of all the past; but others think that she had enough to do with that grief which now oppress'd her, without running for assistance to her family. Virgil, I am confident, would have omitted such a work of supererogation. But Virgil had the gift of expressing much in little, and sometimes in silence; for tho' he yielded much to Homer in invention, he more excell'd him in his admirable judgment. He drew the passion of Dido for Æneas in the most lively and most natural colors that are imaginable. Homer was ambitious enough of moving pity, for he has attempted twice on the same subject of Hector's death: first, when Priam and Hecuba beheld his corpse, which was dragg'd after the chariot of Achilles; and then in the lamentation which was made over him, when his body was redeem'd by Priam; and the same persons again bewail his death, with a chorus of others to help the cry. But if this last excite compassion in you, as I doubt not but it will, you are more oblig'd to the translator than the poet. For Homer, as I observ'd before, can move rage better than he can pity: he stirs up the irascible appetite, as our philosophers call it; he provokes to murther, and the destruction of God's images; he forms and equips those ungodly man-killers, whom we poets, when we flatter them, call heroes; a race of men who can never enjoy quiet in themselves, till they have taken it from all the world. This is Homer's commendation, and such as it is, the lovers of peace, or at least of more moderate heroism, will never envy him. But let Homer and Virgil contend for the prize of honor betwixt themselves, I am satisfied they will never have a third concurrent. I wish Mr. Congreve had the leisure to translate him, and the world the good nature and justice to encourage him in that noble design, of which he is more capable than any man I know. The Earl of Mulgrave and Mr. Waller, two the best judges of our age, have assur'd me that they could never read over the translation of Chapman without incredible pleasure and extreme transport. This admiration of theirs must needs proceed from the author himself; for the translator has thrown him down as low as harsh numbers, improper English, and a monstrous length of verse could carry him. What then would he appear in the harmonious version of one of the best writers, living in a much better age than was the last? I mean for versification, and the art of numbers; for in the drama we have not arriv'd to the pitch of Shakespeare and Ben Jonson. But here, my Lord, I am forc'd to break off abruptly, without endeavoring at a compliment in the close. This *Miscellany* is, without dispute, one of the best of the kind which has hitherto been extant in our tongue. At least, as Sir Samuel Tuke has said before me, a modest man may praise what's not his own. My fellows have no need of any protection, but I humbly recommend my part of it, as much as it deserves, to your patronage and acceptance, and all the rest to your forgiveness.

I am,
My Lord,
Your Lordship's most
Obedient Servant,
JOHN DRYDEN.

THE FIRST BOOK
OF

OVID'S METAMORPHOSES

OF bodies chang'd to various forms I sing:
Ye gods, from whom these miracles did
      spring,

Inspire my numbers with celestial heat;
Till I my long laborious work complete,
And add perpetual tenor to my rhymes,
Deduc'd from nature's birth to Cæsar's
   times.
Before the seas, and this terrestrial ball,
And heav'n's high canopy, that covers all,
One was the face of nature, if a face;
Rather a rude and indigested mass;   10
A lifeless lump, unfashion'd, and unfram'd,
Of jarring seeds, and justly Chaos nam'd.
No sun was lighted up, the world to view;
No moon did yet her blunted horns renew:
Nor yet was earth suspended in the sky;
Nor, pois'd, did on her own foundations lie:
Nor seas about the shores their arms had
   thrown,
But earth and air and water were in one.
Thus air was void of light, and earth un-
   stable,
And water's dark abyss unnavigable.   20
No certain form on any was impress'd;
All were confus'd, and each disturb'd the
   rest:
For hot and cold were in one body fix'd,
And soft with hard, and light with heavy
   mix'd.
  But God, or Nature, while they thus
   contend,
To these intestine discords put an end.
Then earth from air, and seas from earth
   were driv'n,
And grosser air sunk from ethereal heav'n.
Thus disembroil'd, they take their pro- ⎫
   per place;   ⎬
The next of kin contiguously embrace, 30 |
And foes are sunder'd by a larger space. ⎭
The force of fire ascended first on high,
And took its dwelling in the vaulted sky.
Then air succeeds, in lightness next to fire;
Whose atoms from unactive earth retire.
Earth sinks beneath, and draws a numer-
   ous throng
Of ponderous, thick, unwieldy seeds along.
About her coasts unruly waters roar,
And, rising on a ridge, insult the shore.
Thus when the God, whatever God was
   he,   40
Had form'd the whole, and made the parts
   agree,
That no unequal portions might be found,
He molded earth into a spacious round;
Then, with a breath, he gave the winds to
   blow,
And bade the congregated waters flow.

He adds the running springs and standing
   lakes,
And bounding banks for winding rivers
   makes.
Some part in earth are swallow'd up, the
   most
In ample oceans, disimbogued, are lost.
He shades the woods, the valleys he re-
   strains   50
With rocky mountains, and extends the
   plains.
  And as five zones th' ethereal regions
   bind,
Five, correspondent, are to earth assign'd:
The sun, with rays directly darting down,
Fires all beneath, and fries the middle
   zone:
The two beneath the distant poles com-
   plain
Of endless winter, and perpetual rain.
Betwixt th' extremes, two happier climates
   hold
The temper that partakes of hot and cold.
The fields of liquid air, inclosing all,   60
Surround the compass of this earthly ball;
The lighter parts lie next the fires above,
The grosser near the wat'ry surface move:
Thick clouds are spread, and storms en- ⎫
   gender there, |
And thunder's voice, which wretched ⎬
   mortals fear, |
And winds that on their wings cold win- ⎭
   ter bear.
Nor were those blust'ring brethren left at
   large,
On seas and shores their fury to discharge:
Bound as they are, and circumscrib'd in
   place,
They rend the world, resistless, where they
   pass,   70
And mighty marks of mischief leave be-
   hind;
Such is the rage of their tempestuous kind.
First Eurus to the rising morn is sent,
(The regions of the balmy continent,)
And eastern realms, where early Persians
   run
To greet the blest appearance of the sun.
Westward the wanton Zephyr wings his
   flight,
Pleas'd with the remnants of departing
   light:
Fierce Boreas with his offspring issues
   forth,
T' invade the frozen Wagon of the North; 80

While frowning Auster seeks the southern
    sphere,
And rots, with endless rain, th' unwhole-
    some year.
High o'er the clouds, and empty realms
    of wind,
The God a clearer space for heav'n design'd;
Where fields of light, and liquid ether flow,
Purg'd from the pond'rous dregs of earth
    below.
Scarce had the pow'r distinguish'd these,
    when straight
The stars, no longer overlaid with weight,
Exert their heads from underneath the ⎤
    mass,   ⎟
And upward shoot, and kindle as they ⎬
    pass,   90 ⎟
And with diffusive light adorn their ⎟
    heav'nly place.   ⎦
Then, every void of nature to supply,
With forms of gods he fills the vacant sky:
New herds of beasts he sends, the plains ⎤
    to share;   ⎟
New colonies of birds, to people air; ⎬
And to their oozy beds the finny fish re- ⎟
    pair.   ⎦
A creature of a more exalted kind
Was wanting yet, and then was Man de-
    sign'd;
Conscious of thought, of more capacious
    breast,   99
For empire form'd, and fit to rule the rest:
Whether with particles of heav'nly fire
The God of Nature did his soul inspire;
Or earth, but new divided from the sky,
And pliant still, retain'd the ethereal energy;
Which wise Prometheus temper'd into
    paste,
And, mix'd with living streams, the god-
    like image cast.
Thus, while the mute creation downward
    bend
Their sight, and to their earthy mother
    tend,
Man looks aloft, and with erected eyes
Beholds his own hereditary skies.   110
From such rude principles our form began,
And earth was metamorphos'd into man.

THE GOLDEN AGE

The Golden Age was first; when man, ⎤
    yet new,   ⎟
No rule but uncorrupted reason knew; ⎬
And, with a native bent, did good pursue. ⎦

Unforc'd by punishment, unaw'd by fear,
His words were simple, and his soul sincere:
Needless was written law, where none op-
    press'd;
The law of man was written in his breast;
No suppliant crowds before the judge ap-
    pear'd;   120 ⎤
No court erected yet, nor cause was ⎟
    hear'd;   ⎬
But all was safe, for conscience was their ⎟
    guard.   ⎦
The mountain trees in distant prospect
    please,
Ere yet the pine descended to the seas;
Ere sails were spread, new oceans to ⎤
    explore;   ⎟
And happy mortals, unconcern'd for more, ⎬
Confin'd their wishes to their native ⎟
    shore.   ⎦
No walls were yet, nor fence, nor moat, nor
    mound;
Nor drum was heard, nor trumpet's angry
    sound:
Nor swords were forg'd; but, void of care
    and crime,   130
The soft creation slept away their time.
The teeming earth, yet guiltless of the
    plow,
And unprovok'd, did fruitful stores allow:
Content with food, which nature freely
    bred,
On wildings and on strawberries they fed;
Cornels and bramble berries gave the rest,
And falling acorns furnish'd out a feast.
The flow'rs, unsown, in fields and meadows
    reign'd,
And western winds immortal spring main-
    tain'd.
In following years the bearded corn ensued
From earth unask'd, nor was that earth
    renew'd;   141
From veins of valleys milk and nectar
    broke,
And honey sweating thro' the pores of oak.

THE SILVER AGE

But when good Saturn, banish'd from
    above,
Was driv'n to hell, the world was under
    Jove.
Succeeding times a Silver Age behold,
Excelling brass, but more excell'd by gold.
Then Summer, Autumn, Winter did ap-
    pear;

And Spring was but a season of the year.
The sun his annual course obliquely made,
Good days contracted, and enlarg'd the
    bad.   151
Then air with sultry heats began to glow;
The wings of winds were clogg'd with ice
    and snow;
And shivering mortals, into houses driv'n,
Sought shelter from th' inclemency of
    heav'n.
Those houses, then, were caves, or homely
    sheds,
With twining osiers fenc'd, and moss their
    beds.
Then plows, for seed, the fruitful furrows
    broke,
And oxen labor'd first beneath the yoke.

THE BRAZEN AGE

To this next came in course the Brazen
    Age: 160
A warlike offspring, prompt to bloody rage,
Not impious yet ——

THE IRON AGE

                —— Hard Steel succeeded then;
And stubborn as the metal were the men.
Truth, Modesty, and Shame, the world
    forsook;
Fraud, Avarice, and Force, their places
    took.
Then sails were spread to every wind that
    blew;
Raw were the sailors, and the depths were
    new:
Trees, rudely hollow'd, did the waves sus-
    tain,
Ere ships in triumph plow'd the wat'ry
    plain.
    Then landmarks limited to each his
    right: 170
For all before was common as the light.
Nor was the ground alone requir'd to bear
Her annual income to the crooked share;
But greedy mortals, rummaging her store,
Digg'd from her entrails first the precious
    ore,
Which next to hell the prudent gods had
    laid,
And that alluring ill to sight display'd.
Thus cursed steel, and more accursed gold,
Gave mischief birth, and made that mis-
    chief bold;

And double death did wretched man in-
    vade,   180
By steel assaulted, and by gold betray'd.
Now (brandish'd weapons glittering in their
    hands)
Mankind is broken loose from moral bands;
No rights of hospitality remain:
The guest, by him who harbor'd him, is
    slain;
The son-in-law pursues the father's life;
The wife her husband murders, he the wife;
The stepdame poison for the son prepares;
The son inquires into his father's years.
Faith flies, and Piety in exile mourns;   190
And Justice, here oppress'd, to heav'n re-
    turns.

THE GIANTS' WAR

Nor were the gods themselves more safe
    above:
Against beleaguer'd heav'n the giants move.
Hills pil'd on hills, on mountains mountains
    lie,
To make their mad approaches to the sky.
Till Jove, no longer patient, took his time
T' avenge with thunder their audacious
    crime:
Red lightning play'd along the firmament,
And their demolish'd works to pieces rent.
Sing'd with the flames, and with the bolts
    transfix'd,   200
With native earth their blood the monsters
    mix'd;
The blood, indued with animating heat,
Did in th' impregnant earth new sons be-
    get:
They, like the seed from which they sprung,
    accurst,
Against the gods immortal hatred nurs'd:
An impious, arrogant, and cruel brood;
Expressing their original from blood.
    Which when the King of Gods beheld
    from high,
(Withal revolving in his memory
What he himself had found on earth of
    late,   210
Lycaon's guilt, and his inhuman treat,)
He sigh'd, nor longer with his pity strove,
But kindled to a wrath becoming Jove:
    Then call'd a general council of the gods;
Who, summon'd, issue from their blest
    abodes,
And fill th' assembly with a shining train.
A way there is in heaven's expanded plain,

Which, when the skies are clear, is seen be-
    low,
And mortals by the name of Milky know.
The groundwork is of stars; thro' which
    the road   220
Lies open to the Thunderer's abode.
The gods of greater nations dwell around,
And on the right and left the palace bound;
The commons where they can; the nobler
    sort,
With winding doors wide open, front the
    court.
This place, as far as earth with heav'n may
    vie,
I dare to call the Louvre of the sky.
When all were plac'd, in seats distinctly
    known,
And he, their father, had assum'd the throne,
Upon his iv'ry scepter first he leant,   230
Then shook his head, that shook the firma-
    ment:
Air, earth, and seas, obey'd th' almighty
    nod;
And with a gen'ral fear confess'd the god.
At length, with indignation, thus he broke
His awful silence, and the pow'rs bespoke:
    "I was not more concern'd in that debate
Of empire, when our universal state
Was put to hazard, and the giant race
Our captive skies were ready to imbrace:
For tho' the foe was fierce, the seeds of all
Rebellion sprung from one original;   241
Now, wheresoever ambient waters glide,
All are corrupt, and all must be destroy'd.
Let me this holy protestation make:
By hell, and hell's inviolable lake,
I tried whatever in the godhead lay; ⎫
But gangren'd members must be lopp'd ⎬
    away,   ⎬
Before the nobler parts are tainted to ⎬
    decay.   ⎭
There dwells below a race of demigods,   249
Of nymphs in waters, and of fawns in woods;
Who, tho' not worthy yet in heav'n to live,
Let 'em at least enjoy that earth we give.
Can these be thought securely lodg'd below,
When I myself, who no superior know,
I, who have heav'n and earth at my com-
    mand,
Have been attempted by Lycaon's hand?"
    At this a murmur thro' the synod went,
And with one voice they vote his punish-
    ment.
Thus, when conspiring traitors dar'd to
    doom

The fall of Cæsar, and in him of Rome, 260
The nations trembled with a pious fear;
All anxious for their earthly Thunderer:
Nor was their care, O Cæsar, less esteem'd
By thee, than that of heav'n for Jove was
    deem'd;
Who, with his hand, and voice, did first re-
    strain
Their murmurs, then resum'd his speech
    again.
The gods to silence were compos'd, and
    sate
With reverence due to his superior state.
    "Cancel your pious cares; already he
Has paid his debt to justice, and to me. 270
Yet what his crimes, and what my judg-
    ments were,
Remains for me thus briefly to declare.
The clamors of this vile degenerate age,
The cries of orphans, and th' oppressor's
    rage,
Had reach'd the stars: 'I will descend,'
    said I,
' In hope to prove this loud complaint a lie.'
Disguis'd in human shape, I travel'd round
The world, and more than what I heard
    I found.
O'er Mænalus I took my steepy way,
By caverns infamous for beasts of prey; 280
Then cross'd Cyllene, and the piny shade,
More infamous by curst Lycaon made.
Dark night had cover'd heav'n and earth,
    before
I enter'd his unhospitable door.
Just at my entrance, I displayed the sign
That somewhat was approaching of divine.
The prostrate people pray: the tyrant grins;
And, adding profanation to his sins,
' I 'll try,' said he, 'and if a god appear,
To prove his deity shall cost him dear.' 290
'T was late; the graceless wretch my death
    prepares,
When I should soundly sleep, oppress'd with
    cares:
This dire experiment he chose, to prove
If I were mortal, or undoubted Jove;
But first he had resolv'd to taste my pow'r.
Not long before, but in a luckless hour,
Some legates, sent from the Molossian state,
Were on a peaceful errant come to treat.
Of these he murders one; he boils the flesh,
And lays the mangled morsels in a dish: 300
Some part he roasts; then serves it up,
    so dress'd,
And bids me welcome to this human feast.

Mov'd with disdain, the table I o'erturn'd,
And with avenging flames the palace burn'd.
The tyrant, in a fright, for shelter gains
The neighb'ring fields, and scours along the
   plains.
Howling he fled, and fain he would have
   spoke,
But human voice his brutal tongue forsook.
About his lips the gather'd foam he ⎤
   churns,   ⎥
And, breathing slaughters, still with rage ⎬
   he burns,   310 ⎥
But on the bleating flock his fury turns. ⎦
His mantle, now his hide, with rugged
   hairs
Cleaves to his back; a famish'd face he
   bears;
His arms descend, his shoulders sink away,
To multiply his legs for chase of prey.
He grows a wolf, his hoariness remains,
And the same rage in other members reigns.
His eyes still sparkle in a narr'wer space,
His jaws retain the grin, and violence of
   face.
  " This was a single ruin, but not one   320
Deserves so just a punishment alone.
Mankind's a monster, and th' ungodly times,
Confed'rate into guilt, are sworn to crimes.
All are alike involv'd in ill, and all
Must by the same relentless fury fall."
  Thus ended he; the greater gods as-⎤
   sent,   ⎥
By clamors urging his severe intent;   ⎬
The less fill up the cry for punishment. ⎦
Yet still with pity they remember man,
And mourn as much as heav'nly spirits
   can.   330
They ask, when those were lost of human
   birth,
What he would do with all this waste of
   earth;
If his dispeopled world he would resign
To beasts, a mute, and more ignoble line:
Neglected altars must no longer smoke,
If none were left to worship and invoke.
To whom the Father of the Gods replied:⎤
  " Lay that unnecessary fear aside: ⎬
  Mine be the care new people to provide. ⎦
I will from wondrous principles ordain 340
A race unlike the first, and try my skill
   again."
  Already had he toss'd the flaming brand ⎤
And roll'd the thunder in his spacious ⎬
   hand,   ⎥
Preparing to discharge on seas and land; ⎦

But stopp'd, for fear, thus violently driven,
The sparks should catch his axletree of
   heav'n:
Rememb'ring, in the Fates, a time when
   fire
Should to the battlements of heav'n aspire,
And all his blazing worlds above should
   burn,   349
And all th' inferior globe to cinders turn.
His dire artill'ry thus dismiss'd, he bent
His thoughts to some securer punishment;
Concludes to pour a wat'ry deluge down,
And, what he durst not burn, resolves to
   drown.
The northern breath, that freezes floods, he
   binds,
With all the race of cloud-dispelling winds:
The South he loos'd, who night and horror
   brings;
And fogs are shaken from his flaggy wings.
From his divided beard two streams he
   pours;
His head and rheumy eyes distil in show-
   ers;   360
With rain his robe and heavy mantle flow,
And lazy mists are low'ring on his brow.
Still as he swept along, with his clench'd
   fist
He squeez'd the clouds; th' imprison'd
   clouds resist:
The skies, from pole to pole, with peals re-
   sound;
And show'rs inlarg'd come pouring on the
   ground.
Then, clad in colors of a various dye,
Junonian Iris breeds a new supply,
To feed the clouds: impetuous rain descends;
The bearded corn beneath the burthen
   bends;   370
Defrauded clowns deplore their perish'd
   grain,
And the long labors of the year are vain.
  Nor from his patrimonial heav'n alone
Is Jove content to pour his vengeance
   down:
Aid from his brother of the seas he craves,
To help him with auxiliary waves.
The wat'ry tyrant calls his brooks and
   floods;
Who roll from mossy caves, their moist
   abodes,
And with perpetual urns his palace fill: 379
To whom, in brief, he thus imparts his will:
  " Small exhortation needs : your pow'rs
   employ,

And this bad world (so Jove requires) de-
stroy.
Let loose the reins to all your wat'ry store;
Bear down the dams, and open every door."
The floods, by nature enemies to land,
And proudly swelling with their new com-
mand,
Remove the living stones that stopp'd
their way,
And, gushing from their source, augment
the sea.
Then, with his mace, their monarch ⎫
struck the ground: ⎪
With inward trembling earth receiv'd the ⎬
wound,   390 ⎪
And rising streams a ready passage found. ⎭
Th' expanded waters gather on the plain,
They float the fields, and overtop the grain;
Then rushing onwards, with a sweepy sway,
Bear flocks, and folds, and lab'ring hinds
away.
Nor safe their dwellings were; for, sapp'd
by floods,
Their houses fell upon their household gods.
The solid piles, too strongly built to fall,
High o'er their heads behold a wat'ry
wall: 399
Now seas and earth were in confusion lost;
A world of waters, and without a coast.
    One climbs a cliff; one in his boat is
borne,
And plows above, where late he sow'd his
corn.
Others o'er chimney tops and turrets row,
And drop their anchors on the meads below;
Or downward driv'n, they bruise the tender
vine,
Or toss'd aloft, are knock'd against a pine;
And where of late the kids had cropp'd the
grass,
The monsters of the deep now take their
place.
Insulting Nereids on the cities ride,   410
And wond'ring dolphins o'er the palace
glide;
On leaves and masts of mighty oaks they
browse,
And their broad fins entangle in the boughs.
The frighted wolf now swims amongst the
sheep;
The yellow lion wanders in the deep:
His rapid force no longer helps the boar;
The stag swims faster than he ran before:
The fowls, long beating on their wings in
vain,

Despair of land, and drop into the main.
Now hills and vales no more distinction
know,   420
And level'd nature lies oppress'd below.
The most of mortals perish in the flood,
The small remainder dies for want of food.
    A mountain of stupendous height there
stands
Betwixt th' Athenian and Bœotian lands,
The bound of fruitful fields, while fields
they were,
But then a field of waters did appear:
Parnassus is its name; whose forky rise
Mounts thro' the clouds, and mates the
lofty skies.   429
High on the summit of this dubious cliff,
Deucalion, wafting, moor'd his little skiff.
He with his wife were only left behind
Of perish'd man; they two were human-
kind.
The mountain nymphs and Themis they
adore,
And from her oracles relief implore.
The most upright of mortal men was he;
The most sincere and holy woman, she.
    When Jupiter, surveying earth from
high,
Beheld it in a lake of water lie,   439
That, where so many millions lately liv'd,
But two, the best of either sex, surviv'd,
He loos'd the northern wind; fierce Boreas
flies
To puff away the clouds, and purge the
skies:
Serenely, while he blows, the vapors, driven,
Discover heav'n to earth, and earth to
heav'n.
The billows fall, while Neptune lays his
mace
On the rough sea, and smooths its furrow'd
face.
Already Triton, at his call, appears   448 ⎫
Above the waves; a Tyrian robe he wears, ⎬
And in his hand a crooked trumpet bears. ⎭
The sovereign bids him peaceful sounds
inspire,
And give the waves the signal to retire.
His writhen shell he takes, whose narrow
vent
Grows by degrees into a large extent;
Then gives it breath: the blast, with dou-
bling sound,
Runs the wide circuit of the world around.
The sun first heard it, in his early east,
And met the rattling echoes in the west. 458

The waters, list'ning to the trumpet's roar,
Obey the summons, and forsake the shore.
    A thin circumference of land appears;
And Earth, but not at once, her visage rears,
And peeps upon the seas from upper grounds:
The streams, but just contain'd within their
        bounds,
By slow degrees into their channels crawl;
And earth increases as the waters fall.
In longer time the tops of trees appear,
Which mud on their dishonor'd branches
        bear.
    At length the world was all restor'd to
        view,
But desolate, and of a sickly hue: 470
Nature beheld herself, and stood aghast;
A dismal desart, and a silent waste.
    Which when Deucalion, with a piteous
        look,
Beheld, he wept, and thus to Pyrrha
        spoke:
"O wife, O sister, O of all thy kind ⎫
The best and only creature left behind, ⎬
By kindred, love, and now by dangers ⎟
        join'd; ⎭
Of multitudes who breath'd the common
        air
We two remain; a species in a pair:
The rest the seas have swallow'd; nor have
        we   480
Ev'n of this wretched life a certainty.
The clouds are still above; and, while I
        speak,
A second deluge o'er our heads may break.
Should I be snatch'd from hence, and ⎫
        thou remain, ⎟
Without relief, or partner of thy pain, ⎬
How couldst thou such a wretched life ⎟
        sustain? ⎭
Should I be left, and thou be lost, the sea,
That buried her I lov'd, should bury me.
O could our father his old arts inspire,   489
And make me heir of his informing fire,
That so I might abolish'd man retrieve,
And perish'd people in new souls might
        live!
But Heav'n is pleas'd, nor ought we to com-
        plain,
That we, th' examples of mankind, remain."
He said: the careful couple join their tears,
And then invoke the gods, with pious
        prayers.
    Thus in devotion having eas'd their grief,
From sacred oracles they seek relief;
And to Cephisus' brook their way pursue:

The stream was troubled, but the ford they
        knew.   500
With living waters, in the fountain bred, ⎫
They sprinkle first their garments and ⎟
        their head; ⎬
Then took the way which to the temple ⎟
        led. ⎭
The roofs were all defil'd with moss and
        mire,
The desart altars void of solemn fire.
Before the gradual, prostrate they ador'd;
The pavement kiss'd, and thus the saint im-
        plor'd:
    "O righteous Themis, if the pow'rs above
By pray'rs are bent to pity, and to love;
If human miseries can move their mind; 510
If yet they can forgive, and yet be kind;
Tell how we may restore, by second birth,
Mankind, and people desolated earth."
    Then thus the gracious goddess, nodding,
        said:
"Depart, and with your vestments veil your
        head;
And stooping lowly down, with loosen'd
        zones,
Throw each behind your backs your mighty
        mother's bones."
    Amaz'd the pair, and mute with wonder
        stand,
Till Pyrrha first refus'd the dire command.
"Forbid it Heav'n," said she, "that I should
        tear   520
Those holy relics from the sepulcher."
They ponder'd the mysterious words again,
For some new sense; and long they sought
        in vain:
At length Deucalion clear'd his cloudy
        brow,
And said: "The dark enigma will allow
A meaning, which, if well I understand,
From sacrilege will free the god's command:
This earth our mighty mother is, the stones
In her capacious body are her bones:
These we must cast behind." With hope and
        fear   530
The woman did the new solution hear:
The man diffides in his own augury,
And doubts the gods; yet both resolve to
        try.
Descending from the mount, they first un-
        bind
Their vests; and, veil'd, they cast the stones
        behind:
The stones (a miracle to mortal view,
But long tradition makes it pass for true)

Did first the rigor of their kind expel,
And suppled into softness as they fell;
Then swell'd, and, swelling, by degrees grew
  warm;   540
And took the rudiments of human form:
Imperfect shapes — in marble such are seen,
When the rude chisel does the man begin;
While yet the roughness of the stone re-
  mains,
Without the rising muscles and the veins.
The sappy parts, and next resembling juice,
Were turn'd to moisture, for the body's use,
Supplying humors, blood, and nourishment:
The rest, too solid to receive a bent,
Converts to bones; and what was once a
  vein,   550
Its former name and nature did retain.
By help of pow'r divine, in little space, ⎫
What the man threw assum'd a manly   ⎪
  face;   ⎬
And what the wife, renew'd the female   ⎪
  race.   ⎭
Hence we derive our nature, born to bear
Laborious life, and harden'd into care.
  The rest of animals, from teeming earth
Produc'd, in various forms receiv'd their
  birth.
The native moisture, in its close retreat,
Digested by the sun's ethereal heat,   560
As in a kindly womb, began to breed;
Then swell'd and quicken'd by the vital seed.
And some in less, and some in longer space,
Were ripen'd into form, and took a several
  face.
Thus when the Nile from Pharian fields is
  fled,
And seeks, with ebbing tides, his ancient bed,
The fat manure with heav'nly fire is
  warm'd;
And crusted creatures, as in wombs, are
  form'd:
These, when they turn the glebe, the pea-
  sants find;   569
Some rude, and yet unfinish'd in their kind;
Short of their limbs, a lame imperfect birth;
One half alive, and one of lifeless earth.
  For heat and moisture, when in bodies
  join'd,
The temper that results from either kind
Conception makes; and, fighting till they
  mix,
Their mingled atoms in each other fix.
Thus Nature's hand the genial bed prepares
With friendly discord, and with fruitful
  wars.

  From hence the surface of the ground,
    with mud
And slime besmear'd (the fæces of the
    flood),   580
Receiv'd the rays of heav'n; and, sucking
    in
The seeds of heat, new creatures did begin:
Some were of sev'ral sorts produc'd before,
But of new monsters Earth created more.
  Unwillingly, but yet she brought to ⎫
    light   ⎪
Thee, Python, too, the wond'ring world ⎬
    to fright;   ⎪
And the new nations, with so dire a sight: ⎭
So monstrous was his bulk, so large a space
Did his vast body and long train embrace.
Whom Phœbus basking on a bank espied:
Ere now the god his arrows had not tried,
But on the trembling deer, or mountain goat:
At this new quarry he prepares to shoot. 593
Tho' every shaft took place, he spent the ⎫
    store   ⎪
Of his full quiver; and 't was long before ⎬
Th' expiring serpent wallow'd in his gore. ⎭
Then, to preserve the fame of such a deed,
For Python slain he Pythian games decreed,
Where noble youths for mastership should
    strive,
To quoit, to run, and steeds and chariots
    drive: 600
The prize was fame; in witness of renown
An oaken garland did the victor crown.
The laurel was not yet for triumphs born, ⎫
But every green alike by Phœbus worn   ⎪
Did, with promiscuous grace, his flowing ⎬
    locks adorn.   ⎭

THE TRANSFORMATION OF DAPHNE INTO
A LAUREL

  The first and fairest of his loves was she
Whom not blind Fortune, but the dire de-
    cree
Of angry Cupid forc'd him to desire:
Daphne her name, and Peneus was her
    sire.
Swell'd with the pride that new success at-
    tends,   610
He sees the stripling, while his bow he bends,
And thus insults him: "Thou lascivious boy,
Are arms like these for children to employ?
Know, such achievements are my proper
    claim,
Due to my vigor and unerring aim:
Resistless are my shafts, and Python late

In such a feather'd death has found his
   fate.
Take up thy torch, and lay my weapons by;
With that the feeble souls of lovers fry." 619
To whom the son of Venus thus replied:
" Phœbus, thy shafts are sure on all beside;
But mine on Phœbus: mine the fame shall
   be
Of all thy conquests, when I conquer thee."
   He said, and soaring, swiftly wing'd his
   flight;
Nor stopp'd but on Parnassus' airy height.
Two diff'rent shafts he from his quiver
   draws;
One to repel desire, and one to cause.
One shaft is pointed with refulgent gold,
To bribe the love, and make the lover
   bold:
One blunt, and tipp'd with lead, whose base
   allay 630
Provokes disdain, and drives desire away.
The blunted bolt against the nymph he
   dress'd,
But with the sharp transfix'd Apollo's
   breast.
   Th' enamor'd deity pursues the chase;
The scornful damsel shuns his loath'd em-
   brace;
In hunting beasts of prey her youth em-
   ploys,
And Phœbe rivals in her rural joys.
With naked neck she goes, and shoulders
   bare,
And with a fillet binds her flowing hair.
By many suitors sought, she mocks their
   pains, 640
And still her vow'd virginity maintains.
Impatient of a yoke, the name of bride
She shuns, and hates the joys she never
   tried.
On wilds and woods she fixes her desire,
Nor knows what youth and kindly love
   inspire.
Her father chides her oft: " Thou ow'st,"
   says he,
" A husband to thyself, a son to me."
She, like a crime, abhors the nuptial bed;
She glows with blushes, and she hangs her
   head.
Then, casting round his neck her tender
   arms, 650
Soothes him with blandishments, and filial
   charms.
"Give me, my lord," she said, " to live,
   and die,

A spotless maid, without the marriage tie.
'T is but a small request; I beg no more
Than what Diana's father gave before."
The good old sire was soften'd to consent,
But said her wish would prove her punish-
   ment;
For so much youth, and so much beauty
   join'd,
Oppos'd the state which her desires de-
   sign'd. 659
   The God of Light, aspiring to her bed,
Hopes what he seeks, with flattering fan-
   cies fed;
And is by his own oracles misled.
And as in empty fields the stubble burns,
Or nightly travelers, when day returns,
Their useless torches on dry hedges throw,
That catch the flames, and kindle all the
   row;
So burns the god, consuming in desire,
And feeding in his breast a fruitless fire:
Her well-turn'd neck he view'd (her neck
   was bare) 669
And on her shoulders her dishevel'd hair:
" O were it comb'd," said he, " with what
   a grace
Would every waving curl become her
   face ! "
He view'd her eyes, like heavenly lamps
   that shone;
He view'd her lips, too sweet to view
   alone,
Her taper fingers, and her panting breast;
He praises all he sees, and for the rest,
Believes the beauties yet unseen are best.
Swift as the wind, the damsel fled away,
Nor did for these alluring speeches stay:
" Stay, nymph," he cried, " I follow, not a
   foe: 680
Thus from the lion trips the trembling
   doe;
Thus from the wolf the frighten'd lamb
   removes,
And from pursuing falcons fearful doves;
Thou shunn'st a god, and shunn'st a god
   that loves.
Ah, lest some thorn should pierce thy ten-
   der foot,
Or thou shouldst fall in flying my pursuit !
To sharp uneven ways thy steps decline;
Abate thy speed, and I will bate of mine.
Yet think from whom thou dost so rashly
   fly; 689
Nor basely born, nor shepherd's swain am I.
Perhaps thou know'st not my superior state,

And from that ignorance proceeds thy hate.
Me Claros, Delphos, Tenedos obey;
These hands the Patareian scepter sway.
The King of Gods begot me: what shall be,
Or is, or ever was, in fate, I see.
Mine is th' invention of the charming lyre;
Sweet notes, and heav'nly numbers I inspire.
Sure is my bow, unerring is my dart;
But ah! more deadly his, who pierc'd my
   heart.   700
Med'cine is mine: what herbs and simples ⎤
   grow |
In fields and forests, all their pow'rs I ⎬
   know, |
And am the great physician call'd below.   ⎦
Alas, that fields and forests can afford
No remedies to heal their love-sick lord!
To cure the pains of love no plant avails,
And his own physic the physician fails."
   She heard not half, so furiously she flies,
And on her ear th' imperfect accent dies.
Fear gave her wings; and as she fled, the
   wind,   710
Increasing, spread her flowing hair behind,
And left her legs and thighs expos'd to
   view;
Which made the god more eager to pursue.
The god was young, and was too hotly
   bent
To lose his time in empty compliment;
But led by love, and fir'd with such a sight,
Impetuously pursued his near delight.
   As when th' impatient greyhound, slipp'd
   from far,
Bounds o'er the glebe, to course the fearful hare,   719
She in her speed does all her safety lay,
And he with double speed pursues the prey;
O'erruns her at the sitting turn, and licks
His chaps in vain, and blows upon the flix;
She scapes, and for the neighb'ring covert
   strives,
And gaining shelter, doubts if yet she lives:
If little things with great we may compare,
Such was the god, and such the flying fair:
She, urg'd by fear, her feet did swiftly
   move,
But he more swiftly, who was urg'd by
   love.   729
He gathers ground upon her in the chase; ⎤
Now breathes upon her hair, with nearer |
   pace,   ⎬
And just is fast'ning on the wish'd embrace ⎦

The nymph grew pale, and in a mortal
   fright,
Spent with the labor of so long a flight;
And now despairing, cast a mournful look
Upon the streams of her paternal brook:
"O help," she cried, " in this extremest need,
If water gods are deities indeed:
Gape, earth, and this unhappy wretch intomb;
Or change my form whence all my sorrows
   come."   740
Scarce had she finish'd, when her feet she
   found
Benumb'd with cold, and fasten'd to the
   ground:
A filmy rind about her body grows;
Her hair to leaves, her arms extend to
   boughs:
The nymph is all into a laurel gone,
The smoothness of her skin remains alone.
Yet Phœbus loves her still, and, casting
   round
Her bole his arms, some little warmth he
   found.   748
The tree still panted in th' unfinish'd part,
Not wholly vegetive, and heav'd her heart.
He fix'd his lips upon the trembling rind;
It swerv'd aside, and his embrace declin'd.
To whom the god: " Because thou canst
   not be
My mistress, I espouse thee for my tree:
Be thou the prize of honor and renown;
The deathless poet, and the poem, crown.
Thou shalt the Roman festivals adorn,
And, after poets, be by victors worn.
Thou shalt returning Cæsar's triumph grace,
When pomps shall in a long procession pass;
Wreath'd on the posts before his palace wait,
And be the sacred guardian of the gate; 762
Secure from thunder, and unharm'd by Jove,
Unfading as th' immortal pow'rs above:
And, as the locks of Phœbus are unshorn,
So shall perpetual green thy boughs adorn."
The grateful tree was pleas'd with what he
   said,
And shook the shady honors of her head.

THE TRANSFORMATION OF IO INTO A HEIFER.

An ancient forest in Thessalia grows,
Which Tempe's pleasing valley does inclose: 770
Thro' this the rapid Peneus takes his course,
From Pindus rolling with impetuous force;

Mists from the river's mighty fall arise,
And deadly damps inclose the cloudy skies;
Perpetual fogs are hanging o'er the wood,
And sounds of waters deaf the neighborhood.
Deep in a rocky cave he makes abode,
A mansion proper for a mourning god.
Here he gives audience, issuing out decrees
To rivers, his dependent deities.   780
On this occasion hither they resort,
To pay their homage, and to make their
    court;
All doubtful, whether to congratulate
His daughter's honor, or lament her fate.
Sperchæus, crown'd with poplar, first ap-
    pears;
Then old Apidanus came, crown'd with
    years:
Enipeus turbulent, Amphrysos tame;
And Æas last, with lagging waters, came.
Then of his kindred brooks a numerous
    throng   789
Condole his loss, and bring their urns along.
Not one was wanting of the wat'ry train
That fill'd his flood, or mingled with the
    main,
But Inachus, who in his cave, alone,
Wept not another's losses, but his own;
For his dear Io, whether stray'd, or dead,
To him uncertain, doubtful tears he shed.
He sought her thro' the world, but sought
    in vain;
And, nowhere finding, rather fear'd her
    slain.
    Her, just returning from her father's
    brook,
Jove had beheld, with a desiring look;   800
And: "O fair daughter of the flood," he
    said,
"Worthy alone of Jove's imperial bed,
Happy, whoever shall those charms possess!
The King of Gods (nor is thy lover less)
Invites thee to yon cooler shades, to shun
The scorching rays of the meridian sun.
Nor shalt thou tempt the dangers of the
    grove
Alone, without a guide; thy guide is Jove:
No puny pow'r, but he whose high com-
    mand
Is unconfin'd, who rules the seas and
    land,   810
And tempers thunder in his awful hand.
O fly not — " for she fled from his embrace:
O'er Lerna's pastures he pursued the chase,
Along the shades of the Lyrcæan plain.
At length the god, who never asks in vain,

Involv'd with vapors, imitating night,
Both air and earth; and then suppress'd
    her flight,
And, mingling force with love, enjoy'd
    the full delight.
    Meantime the jealous Juno, from on
    high,
Survey'd the fruitful fields of Arcady;   820
And wonder'd that the mist should overrun
The face of daylight, and obscure the sun.
No nat'ral cause she found, from brooks or
    bogs,
Or marshy lowlands, to produce the fogs:
Then round the skies she sought for Jupiter,
Her faithless husband; but no Jove was
    there.
Suspecting now the worst: "Or I," she said,
"Am much mistaken, or am much be-
    tray'd."
With fury she precipitates her flight,   829
Dispels the shadows of dissembled night,
And to the day restores his native light.
Th' almighty lecher, careful to prevent
The consequence, foreseeing her descent,
Transforms his mistress in a trice; and
    now
In Io's place appears a lovely cow.
So slick her skin, so faultless was her make,
Ev'n Juno did unwilling pleasure take
To see so fair a rival of her love;
And what she was, and whence, enquir'd of
    Jove;   839
Of what fair herd, and from what pedigree.
The god, half-caught, was forc'd upon a
    lie;
And said she sprung from earth. She took
    the word,
And begg'd the beauteous heifer of her
    lord.
What should he do? 'Twas equal shame
    to Jove
Or to relinquish, or betray his love;
Yet to refuse so slight a gift would be
But more t' increase his consort's jealousy:
Thus fear and love by turns his heart
    assail'd,
And stronger love had sure at length pre-
    vail'd;
But some faint hope remain'd, his jealous
    queen   850
Had not the mistress thro' the heifer seen.
The cautious goddess, of her gift possess'd,
Yet harbor'd anxious thoughts within her
    breast;
As she who knew the falsehood of her Jove,

And justly fear'd some new relapse of love.
Which to prevent, and to secure her care,
To trusty Argus she commits the fair.
　　The head of Argus (as with stars the skies)
Was compass'd round, and wore an hundred
　　　eyes.
But two by turns their lids in slumber ⎫
　　steep;　　　　　　　　　　860 ⎬
The rest on duty still their station keep; ⎭
Nor could the total constellation sleep.
Thus, ever present to his eyes and mind,
His charge was still before him, tho' behind.
In fields he suffer'd her to feed by day;
But, when the setting sun to night gave way,
The captive cow he summon'd with a call,
And drove her back, and tied her to the stall.
On leaves of trees and bitter herbs she fed,
Heav'n was her canopy, bare earth her bed;
So hardly lodg'd: and, to digest her food, 871
She drank from troubled streams, defil'd
　　with mud.
Her woful story fain she would have told,
With hands upheld, but had no hands to
　　hold.
Her head to her ungentle keeper bow'd,
She strove to speak; she spoke not, but she
　　low'd:
Affrighted with the noise, she look'd around,
And seem'd t' inquire the author of the
　　sound.
　　Once on the banks where often she had
　　　play'd,
(Her father's banks) she came, and there
　　survey'd　　　　　　　　　　880
Her alter'd visage, and her branching head;
And, starting, from herself she would have
　　fled.
Her fellow-nymphs, familiar to her eyes,
Beheld, but knew her not in this disguise.
Ev'n Inachus himself was ignorant,
And in his daughter did his daughter want.
She follow'd where her fellows went, as she
Were still a partner of the company:
They stroke her neck; the gentle heifer
　　stands,　　　　　　　　　　889
And her neck offers to their stroking hands.
Her father gave her grass; the grass she ⎫
　　took,　　　　　　　　　　　　⎬
And lick'd his palms, and cast a piteous ⎬
　　look,　　　　　　　　　　　　⎬
And in the language of her eyes she spoke. ⎭
She would have told her name, and ask'd
　　relief;
But, wanting words, in tears she tells her
　　grief,

Which with her foot she makes him under-
　　stand;
And prints the name of Io in the sand.
" Ah wretched me ! " her mournful father
　　cried;
She, with a sigh, to " wretched me " re-
　　plied:
About her milk-white neck his arms he
　　threw;　　　　　　　　　　　900
And wept, and then these tender words
　　ensue:
" And art thou she, whom I have sought
　　around
The world, and have at length so sadly found ?
So found, is worse than lost: with mutual
　　words
Thou answer'st not, no voice thy tongue
　　affords;
But sighs are deeply drawn from out thy
　　breast,
And speech denied by lowing is express'd.
Unknowing, I prepar'd thy bridal bed,
With empty hopes of happy issue fed;
But now the husband of a herd must be 910
Thy mate, and bell'wing sons thy progeny.
O, were I mortal, death might bring relief !
But now my godhead but extends my grief;
Prolongs my woes, of which no end I see,
And makes me curse my immortality ! "
More had he said, but, fearful of her stay,
The starry guardian drove his charge away
To some fresh pasture; on a hilly height
He sate himself, and kept her still in sight.

THE EYES OF ARGUS TRANSFORM'D INTO
A PEACOCK'S TRAIN

　　Now Jove no longer could her suff'rings
　　　bear;　　　　　　　　　　920
But call'd in haste his airy messenger,
The son of Maia, with severe decree
To kill the keeper, and to set her free.
With all his harness soon the god was sped;
His flying hat was fasten'd on his head;
Wings on his heels were hung, and in his
　　hand
He holds the virtue of the snaky wand.
The liquid air his moving pinions wound,
And, in the moment, shoot him on the ground.
Before he came in sight, the crafty god 930
His wings dismiss'd, but still retain'd his rod:
That sleep-procuring wand wise Hermes
　　took,
But made it seem to sight a shepherd's hook.
With this he did a herd of goats control;

Which by the way he met, and slyly stole.
Clad like a country swain, he pip'd, and sung;
And, playing, drove his jolly troop along.

 With pleasure Argus the musician heeds,
But wonders much at those new vocal reeds;
And: " Whosoe'er thou art, my friend,"
    said he,   940
" Up hither drive thy goats, and play by
    me:
This hill has browse for them, and shade
    for thee."
The god, who was with ease induc'd to climb,
Began discourse to pass away the time;
And still, betwixt, his tuneful pipe he plies;
And watch'd his hour to close the keeper's
    eyes.
With much ado, he partly kept awake,
Not suff'ring all his eyes repose to take;
And ask'd the stranger, who did reeds in-
    vent,   949
And whence began so rare an instrument.

THE TRANSFORMATION OF SYRINX
INTO REEDS

 Then Hermes thus: " A nymph of late
    there was,
Whose heav'nly form her fellows did sur-
    pass:
The pride and joy of fair Arcadia's plains;
Belov'd by deities, ador'd by swains:
Syrinx her name; by Sylvans oft pursued,
As oft she did the lustful gods delude;
The rural and the woodland pow'rs dis-
    dain'd;
With Cynthia hunted, and her rites main-
    tain'd.
Like Phœbe clad, even Phœbe's self she
    seems,
So tall, so straight, such well-proportion'd
    limbs: 960
The nicest eye did no distinction know,
But that the goddess bore a golden bow:
Distinguish'd thus, the sight she cheated
    too.
Descending from Lycæus, Pan admires
The matchless nymph, and burns with new
    desires.
A crown of pine upon his head he wore,
And thus began her pity to implore.
But ere he thus began, she took her flight
So swift, she was already out of sight;
Nor stay'd to hear the courtship of the god,
But bent her course to Ladon's gentle
    flood: 971

There by the river stopp'd, and, tir'd be-
    fore,
Relief from water nymphs her pray'rs
    implore.
 " Now while the lustful god, with
    speedy pace,
Just thought to strain her in a strict em-
    brace,
He fills his arms with reeds, new rising
    on the place.
And while he sighs, his ill success to find,
The tender canes were shaken by the wind;
And breath'd a mournful air, unheard be-
    fore,
That, much surprising Pan, yet pleas'd
    him more.   980
Admiring this new music: ' Thou,' he said,
' Who canst not be the partner of my bed,
At least shalt be the consort of my mind;
And often, often, to my lips be join'd.'
He form'd the reeds, proportion'd as they
    are:
Unequal in their length, and wax'd with
    care,
They still retain the name of his ungrate-
    ful fair."

 While Hermes pip'd, and sung, and told
    his tale,
The keeper's winking eyes began to fail, 989
And drowsy slumber on the lids to creep;
Till all the watchman was, at length,
    asleep.
Then soon the god his voice and song sup-
    press'd,
And with his pow'rful rod confirm'd his
    rest;
Without delay his crooked faulchion drew,
And at one fatal stroke the keeper slew.
Down from the rock fell the dissever'd
    head,
Opening its eyes in death, and falling bled;
And mark'd the passage with a crimson
    trail:
Thus Argus lies in pieces, cold and pale;
And all his hundred eyes, with all their
    light,   1000
Are clos'd at once in one perpetual night.
These Juno takes, that they no more may
    fail,
And spreads them in her peacock's gaudy
    tail.
 Impatient to revenge her injur'd bed,
She wreaks her anger on her rival's head;
With furies frights her from her native
    home,

And drives her gadding round the world
 to roam:
Nor ceas'd her madness and her flight,
 before
She touch'd the limits of the Pharian
 shore.   1009
At length, arriving on the banks of Nile,
Wearied with length of ways, and worn
 with toil,
She laid her down; and, leaning on her
 knees,
Invok'd the cause of all her miseries;
And cast her languishing regards above,
For help from heav'n, and her ungrateful
 Jove.
She sigh'd, she wept, she low'd; 't was all
 she could,
And with unkindness seem'd to tax the god.
Last, with an humble pray'r, she begg'd
 repose,
Or death at least, to finish all her woes. 1019
Jove heard her vows, and with a flatt'ring
 look,
In her behalf to jealous Juno spoke.
He cast his arms about her neck, and said:
" Dame, rest secure; no more thy nuptial bed
This nymph shall violate; by Styx I swear,
And every oath that binds the Thunderer."
The goddess was appeas'd; and at the word
Was Io to her former shape restor'd.
The rugged hair began to fall away;
The sweetness of her eyes did only stay,
Tho' not so large; her crooked horns de-
 crease;   1030
The wideness of her jaws and nostrils cease:
Her hoofs to hands return, in little space;
The five long taper fingers take their place;
And nothing of the heifer now is seen,
Beside the native whiteness of the skin.
Erected on her feet she walks again,
And two the duty of the four sustain.
She tries her tongue, her silence softly breaks,
And fears her former lowings when she
 speaks:
A goddess now, thro' all th' Egyptian state,
And serv'd by priests, who in white linen
 wait.   1041
 Her son was Epaphus, at length believ'd
The son of Jove, and as a god receiv'd.
With sacrifice ador'd and public pray'rs,
He common temples with his mother shares.
Equal in years, and rival in renown ⎫
With Epaphus, the youthful Phaeton, ⎬
 Like honor claims, and boasts his sire the ⎭
 Sun.

His haughty looks, and his assuming air,
The son of Isis could no longer bear: 1050
" Thou tak'st thy mother's word too far,"
 said he,
" And hast usurp'd thy boasted pedigree.
Go, base pretender to a borrow'd name ! "
Thus tax'd, he blush'd with anger, and with
 shame;
But shame repress'd his rage: the daunted
 youth
Soon seeks his mother, and enquires the truth.
"Mother," said he, "this infamy was thrown
By Epaphus on you, and me your son.
He spoke in public, told it to my face;
Nor durst I vindicate the dire disgrace: 1060
Ev'n I, the bold, the sensible of wrong,
Restrain'd by shame, was forc'd to hold my
 tongue.
To bear an open slander is a curse;
But not to find an answer, is a worse.
If I am heav'n-begot, assert your son ⎫
By some sure sign; and make my father ⎪
 known,   ⎬
To right my honor, and redeem your ⎪
 own."   ⎭
He said, and saying cast his arms about
Her neck, and begg'd her to resolve the
 doubt.   1069
 'T is hard to judge if Clymene were mov'd
More by his pray'r, whom she so dearly lov'd,
Or more with fury fir'd, to find her name
Traduc'd, and made the sport of common
 fame.
She stretch'd her arms to heav'n, and fix'd
 her eyes
On that fair planet that adorns the skies:
" Now by those beams," said she, " whose
 holy fires
Consume my breast, and kindle my desires;
By him who sees us both, and cheers our
 sight,
By him the public minister of light,
I swear that Sun begot thee: if I lie, 1080
Let him his cheerful influence deny;
Let him no more this perjur'd creature
 see,
And shine on all the world but only me.
If still you doubt your mother's innocence,
His eastern mansion is not far from hence;
With little pains you to his _levé_ go,
And from himself your parentage may
 know."
With joy th' ambitious youth his mother
 heard,
And eager, for the journey soon prepar'd. 1089

He longs the world beneath him to survey;
To guide the chariot, and to give the day:
From Meroe's burning sands he bends his
    course,
Nor less in India feels his father's force;
His travel urging, till he came in sight,
And saw the palace by the purple light.

THE FABLE OF IPHIS AND
IANTHE

FROM THE NINTH BOOK OF THE
METAMORPHOSES

THE fame of this, perhaps, thro' Crete had
    flown;
But Crete had newer wonders of her own,
In Iphis chang'd; for near the Gnossian
    bounds,
(As loud report the miracle resounds,)
At Phæstus dwelt a man of honest blood, ⎤
But meanly born, and not so rich as good; ⎟
Esteem'd and lov'd by all the neighbor- ⎬
    hood: ⎟
Who to his wife, before the time assign'd ⎦
For childbirth came, thus bluntly spoke his
    mind:
" If Heav'n," said Lygdus, " will vouch- ⎤
    safe to hear,   10 ⎟
I have but two petitions to prefer; ⎬
Short pains for thee, for me a son and ⎟
    heir. ⎦
Girls cost as many throes in bringing forth;
Beside, when born, the tits are little worth;
Weak puling things, unable to sustain
Their share of labor, and their bread to
    gain.
If, therefore, thou a creature shalt pro-
    duce,
Of so great charges, and so little use,
(Bear witness, Heav'n, with what reluc-
    tancy,)
Her hapless innocence I doom to die."   20
He said, and tears the common grief dis-
    play
Of him who bade, and her who must obey.
  Yet Telethusa still persists, to find
Fit arguments to move a father's mind;
T' extend his wishes to a larger scope,
And in one vessel not confine his hope.
Lygdus continues hard: her time drew
    near,
And she her heavy load could scarcely
    bear;

When slumb'ring, in the latter shades of
    night,
Before th' approaches of returning light, 30
She saw, or thought she saw, before her bed,
A glorious train, and Isis at their head:
Her moony horns were on her forehead
    plac'd,
And yellow sheaves her shining temples
    grac'd:
A miter, for a crown, she wore on high;
The dog and dappled bull were waiting by;
Osiris, sought along the banks of Nile;
The silent god; the sacred crocodile;
And, last, a long procession moving on,
With timbrels, that assist the lab'ring
    moon.   40
Her slumbers seem'd dispell'd, and, broad
    awake,
She heard a voice that thus distinctly
    spake:
" My votary, thy babe from death defend,
Nor fear to save whate'er the gods will send.
Delude with art thy husband's dire de- ⎤
    cree: ⎟
When danger calls, repose thy trust on ⎬
    me;   ⎟
And know thou hast not serv'd a thank- ⎟
    less deity."   ⎦
This promise made, with night the goddess
    fled:
With joy the woman wakes, and leaves her
    bed;
Devoutly lifts her spotless hands on high, 50
And prays the pow'rs their gift to ratify.
  Now grinding pains proceed to bearing
    throes,
Till its own weight the burden did disclose.
'T was of the beauteous kind, and brought
    to light
With secrecy, to shun the father's sight.
Th' indulgent mother did her care employ,
And pass'd it on her husband for a boy.
The nurse was conscious of the fact alone;
The father paid his vows as for a son;
And call'd him Iphis, by a common name 60
Which either sex with equal right may
    claim.
Iphis his grandsire was; the wife was
    pleas'd,
Of half the fraud by fortune's favor eas'd:
The doubtful name was us'd without deceit,
And truth was cover'd with a pious cheat.
The habit shew'd a boy, the beauteous face
With manly fierceness mingled female
    grace.

Now thirteen years of age were swiftly ⎤
   run,   ⎥
When the fond father thought the time ⎬
   drew on   ⎥
Of settling in the world his only son. 70 ⎦
Ianthe was his choice; so wondrous fair,
Her form alone with Iphis could compare:
A neighbor's daughter of his own degree,
And not more blest with fortune's goods
   than he.
They soon espous'd; for they with ease
   were join'd,
Who were before contracted in the mind:
Their age the same, their inclinations too;
And, bred together, in one school they grew.
Thus, fatally dispos'd to mutual fires,
They felt, before they knew, the same de-
   sires.   80
Equal their flame, unequal was their care;
One lov'd with hope, one languish'd in despair.
The maid accus'd the ling'ring days alone;
For whom she thought a man, she thought
   her own.
But Iphis bends beneath a greater grief;
As fiercely burns, but hopes for no relief.
Ev'n her despair adds fuel to her fire:
A maid with madness does a maid desire.
   And, scarce refraining tears: "Alas!"
     said she,
"What issue of my love remains for me! 90
How wild a passion works within my breast!
With what prodigious flames am I possess'd!
Could I the care of Providence deserve,
Heav'n must destroy me, if it would preserve.
And that's my fate, or sure it would have sent
Some usual evil for my punishment;
Not this unkindly curse, to rage and burn,
Where nature shews no prospect of return.
Nor cows for cows consume with fruitless fire;
Nor mares, when hot, their fellow-mares
   desire: 100
The father of the fold supplies his ewes; ⎤
The stag through secret woods his hind ⎥
   pursues;   ⎬
And birds for mates the males of their own ⎥
   species choose.   ⎦
Her females Nature guards from female ⎤
   flame,   ⎥
And joins two sexes to preserve the game: ⎬
Would I were nothing, or not what I am! ⎦
Crete, fam'd for monsters, wanted of her
   store,
Till my new love produc'd one monster more.
The daughter of the Sun a bull desir'd,
And yet, ev'n then, a male a female fir'd: 110

Her passion was extravagantly new,
But mine is much the madder of the two.
To things impossible she was not bent,
But found the means to compass her intent.
To cheat his eyes she took a different shape;
Yet still she gain'd a lover, and a leap.
Should all the wit of all the world conspire,
Should Dædalus assist my wild desire,
What art can make me able to enjoy,
Or what can change Ianthe to a boy?   120
Extinguish then thy passion, hopeless maid,
And recollect thy reason for thy aid.
Know what thou art, and love as maidens
   ought,
And drive these golden wishes from thy
   thought.
Thou canst not hope thy fond desires to
   gain;
Where hope is wanting, wishes are in vain.
"And yet no guards against our joys con-
   spire;
No jealous husband hinders our desire:
My parents are propitious to my wish,
And she herself consenting to the bliss. 130
All things concur to prosper our design;
All things to prosper any love but mine.
And yet I never can enjoy the fair;
'T is past the pow'r of Heav'n to grant my
   pray'r.
Heav'n has been kind, as far as Heav'n can be;
Our parents with our own desires agree;
But Nature, stronger than the gods above,
Refuses her assistance to my love;
She sets the bar that causes all my pain:
One gift refus'd makes all their bounty vain.
And now the happy day is just at hand, 141
To bind our hearts in Hymen's holy band —
Our hearts, but not our bodies: thus, accurst,
In midst of water I complain of thirst.
Why com'st thou, Juno, to these barren rites,
To bless a bed defrauded of delights?
Or why should Hymen lift his torch on high,
To see two brides in cold embraces lie?"
   Thus love-sick Iphis her vain passion
   mourns:
With equal ardor fair Ianthe burns,   150
Invoking Hymen's name, and Juno's pow'r,
To speed the work, and haste the happy
   hour.
   She hopes, while Telethusa fears the day,
And strives to interpose some new delay:
Now feigns a sickness, now is in a fright
For this bad omen, or that boding sight.
But having done whate'er she could devise,
And emptied all her magazine of lies,

The time approach'd; the next ensuing day
The fatal secret must to light betray.   160
Then Telethusa had recourse to pray'r,
She and her daughter with dishevel'd hair;
Trembling with fear, great Isis they ador'd,
Embrac'd her altar, and her aid implor'd:
" Fair queen, who dost on fruitful Egypt
    smile,
Who sway'st the scepter of the Pharian
    isle,
And sev'nfold falls of disemboguing Nile;
Relieve, in this our last distress," she said,
" A suppliant mother, and a mournful maid.
Thou, goddess, thou wert present to my
    sight;   170
Reveal'd I saw thee, by thy own fair light:
I saw thee in my dream, as now I see,
With all thy marks of awful majesty,
The glorious train that compass'd thee
    around;
And heard the hollow timbrel's holy sound.
Thy words I noted, which I still retain;
Let not thy sacred oracles be vain.
That Iphis lives, that I myself am free
From shame and punishment, I owe to thee.
On thy protection all our hopes depend: 180
Thy counsel sav'd us, let thy pow'r defend."
    Her tears pursued her words, and, while
    she spoke,
The goddess nodded, and her altar shook:
The temple doors, as with a blast of wind,
Were heard to clap; the lunar horns that
    bind
The brows of Isis cast a blaze around;
The trembling timbrel made a murm'ring
    sound.
    Some hopes these happy omens did impart;
Forth went the mother with a beating
    heart,
Not much in fear, nor fully satisfied;   190
But Iphis follow'd with a larger stride:
The whiteness of her skin forsook her face,
Her looks embolden'd with an awful grace;
Her features and her strength together
    grew,
And her long hair to curling locks with-
    drew.
Her sparkling eyes with manly vigor
    shone;
Big was her voice, audacious was her tone.
The latent parts, at length reveal'd, began
To shoot, and spread, and burnish into
    man.   199
The maid becomes a youth; no more delay
Your vows, but look, and confidently pay.

Their gifts the parents to the temple bear;
The votive tables this inscription wear:
" Iphis, the man, has to the goddess paid
The vows that Iphis offer'd when a maid."
    Now when the star of day had shewn
    his face,
Venus and Juno with their presence grace
The nuptial rites; and, Hymen from above
Descending to complete their happy love,
The gods of marriage lend their mutual
    aid,   210
And the warm youth enjoys the lovely
    maid.

THE FABLE OF ACIS, POLYPHE-
MUS, AND GALATEA

FROM THE THIRTEENTH BOOK OF THE
METAMORPHOSES

GALATEA RELATES THE STORY

Acis, the lovely youth, whose loss I
    mourn,
From Faunus and the nymph Symethis
    born,
Was both his parents' pleasure; but to me
Was all that love could make a lover be.
The gods our minds in mutual bands did
    join;
I was his only joy, as he was mine.
Now sixteen summers the sweet youth had
    seen,
And doubtful down began to shade his
    chin;
When Polyphemus first disturb'd our joy,
And lov'd me fiercely, as I lov'd the boy. 10
Ask not which passion in my soul was
    high'r,
My last aversion, or my first desire:
Nor this the greater was, nor that the less;
Both were alike, for both were in excess.
Thee, Venus, thee, both heav'n and earth
    obey;
Immense thy pow'r, and boundless is thy
    sway.
The Cyclops, who defied th' ethereal throne,
And thought no thunder louder than his
    own;
The terror of the woods, and wilder far
Than wolves in plains, or bears in forests
    are;   20
Th' inhuman host, who made his bloody
    feasts

On mangled members of his butcher'd
    guests,
Yet felt the force of love and fierce desire,
And burnt for me with unrelenting fire:
Forgot his caverns, and his woolly care; ⎫
Assum'd the softness of a lover's air;   ⎪
And comb'd, with teeth of rakes, his ⎬
    rugged hair.   ⎭
Now with a crooked scythe his beard he
    sleeks,
And mows the stubborn stubble of his
    cheeks;
Now in the crystal stream he looks, to try
His simagres, and rolls his glaring eye. 31
His cruelty and thirst of blood are lost,
And ships securely sail along the coast.
    The prophet Telemus (arriv'd by chance
Where Etna's summits to the sea's ad-
    vance,
Who mark'd the tracts of every bird that
    flew,
And sure presages from their flying drew)
Foretold the Cyclops that Ulysses' hand
In his broad eye should thrust a flaming
    brand.
The giant, with a scornful grin, replied: 40
"Vain augur, thou hast falsely prophesied;
Already Love his flaming brand has toss'd;
Looking on two fair eyes, my sight I lost."
Thus, warn'd in vain, with stalking pace
    he strode,
And stamp'd the margin of the briny flood
With heavy steps; and, weary, sought again
The cool retirement of his gloomy den.
    A promontory, sharp'ning by degrees,
Ends in a wedge, and overlooks the seas;
On either side, below, the water flows: 50
This airy walk the giant lover chose.
Here on the midst he sate; his flocks, unled,
Their shepherd follow'd, and securely fed.
A pine so burly, and of length so vast,
That sailing ships requir'd it for a mast,
He wielded for a staff, his steps to guide;
But laid it by, his whistle while he tried.
A hundred reeds, of a prodigious growth,
Scarce made a pipe proportion'd to his
    mouth;
Which when he gave it wind, the rocks
    around,   60
And wat'ry plains, the dreadful hiss re-
    sound.
I heard the ruffian shepherd rudely blow,
Where, in a hollow cave, I sat below;
On Acis' bosom I my head reclin'd;
And still preserve the poem in my mind.

"O lovely Galatea, whiter far
Than falling snows and rising lilies are;
More flow'ry than the meads, as crystal
    bright;
Erect as alders, and of equal height;   69
More wanton than a kid; more sleek thy skin
Than orient shells that on the shores are seen;
Than apples fairer, when the boughs they
    lade;
Pleasing as winter suns or summer shade;
More grateful to the sight than goodly planes;
And softer to the touch than down of swans,
Or curds new turn'd; and sweeter to the
    taste
Than swelling grapes that to the vintage
    haste;
More clear than ice, or running streams, that
    stray
Thro' garden plots, but ah ! more swift than
    they.
    "Yet, Galatea, harder to be broke 80 ⎫
Than bullocks, unreclaim'd to bear the ⎪
    yoke;   ⎬
And far more stubborn than the knotted ⎪
    oak: ⎭
Like sliding streams, impossible to hold;
Like them fallacious; like their fountains,
    cold;
More warping than the willow, to decline
My warm embrace; more brittle than the
    vine;
Immovable, and fix'd in thy disdain;
Rough as these rocks, and of a harder grain;
More violent than is the rising flood;   89
And the prais'd peacock is not half so proud;
Fierce as the fire, and sharp as thistles are;
And more outrageous than a mother bear;
Deaf as the billows to the vows I make;
And more revengeful than a trodden snake;
In swiftness fleeter than the flying hind,
Or driven tempests, or the driving wind:
All other faults with patience I can bear;
But swiftness is the vice I only fear.
    "Yet, if you knew me well, you would
    not shun
My love, but to my wish'd embraces run;
Would languish in your turn, and court my
    stay   101
And much repent of your unwise delay.
    "My palace, in the living rock, is made ⎫
By Nature's hand; a spacious pleasing ⎪
    shade,   ⎬
Which neither heat can pierce, nor cold ⎪
    invade.   ⎭
My garden fill'd with fruits you may behold,

And grapes in clusters, imitating gold;
Some blushing bunches of a purple hue:
And these, and those, are all reserv'd for you.
Red strawberries, in shades, expecting stand,
Proud to be gather'd by so white a hand.   111
Autumnal cornels latter fruit provide,
And plums, to tempt you, turn their glossy
        side;
Not those of common kinds, but such alone
As in Phæacian orchards might have grown;
Nor chestnuts shall be wanting to your food,
Nor garden fruits, nor wildings of the wood;
The laden boughs for you alone shall bear;
And yours shall be the product of the year.
  "The flocks you see, are all my own, ⎫
        beside   120 ⎪
The rest that woods and winding valleys ⎬
        hide,   ⎪
And those that folded in the caves abide. ⎭
Ask not the numbers of my growing store;
Who knows how many, knows he has no
        more.
Nor will I praise my cattle; trust not me,
But judge yourself, and pass your own
        decree:
Behold their swelling dugs; the sweepy
        weight
Of ewes that sink beneath the milky freight;
In the warm folds their tender lambkins lie,
Apart from kids that call with human cry.
New milk in nut-brown bowls is duly serv'd
For daily drink; the rest for cheese reserv'd.
Nor are these household dainties all my ⎫
        store: 133 ⎪
The fields and forests will afford us more; ⎬
The deer, the hare, the goat, the salvage ⎪
        boar,   ⎭
All sorts of ven'son; and of birds the best,
A pair of turtles taken from the nest.
I walk'd the mountains, and two cubs I found,
Whose dam had left 'em on the naked ground,
So like, that no distinction could be seen; 140
So pretty, they were presents for a queen:
And so they shall: I took 'em both away;
And keep, to be companions of your play.
  "O raise, fair nymph, your beauteous
        face above
The waves; nor scorn my presents, and my
        love:
Come, Galatea, come, and view my face; ⎫
I late beheld it in the wat'ry glass,   ⎬
And found it lovelier than I fear'd it was. ⎭
Survey my tow'ring stature, and my size:
Not Jove, the Jove you dream that rules
        the skies,   150

Bears such a bulk, or is so largely spread.
My locks, the plenteous harvest of my head,
Hang o'er my manly face; and, dangling
        down,
As with a shady grove my shoulders crown.
Nor think, because my limbs and body bear
A thickset underwood of bristling hair,
My shape deform'd: what fouler sight can
        be
Than the bald branches of a leafless tree ?
Foul is the steed, without a flowing mane;
And birds, without their feathers, and their
        train.   160
Wool decks the sheep; and man receives a
        grace
From bushy limbs, and from a bearded face.
My forehead with a single eye is fill'd,
Round as a ball, and ample as a shield.
The glorious lamp of heav'n, the radiant sun,
Is Nature's eye; and she's content with one.
Add, that my father sways your seas, and I,
Like you, am of the wat'ry family.
I make you his, in making you my own;
You I adore, and kneel to you alone: 170
Jove, with his fabled thunder, I despise,
And only fear the lightning of your eyes.
Frown not, fair nymph; yet I could bear to
        be
Disdain'd, if others were disdain'd with me.
But to repulse the Cyclops, and prefer
The love of Acis, heav'ns ! I cannot bear.
But let the stripling please himself; nay
        more,
Please you, tho' that's the thing I most
        abhor;
The boy shall find, if e'er we cope in fight,
These giant limbs endued with giant might.
His living bowels, from his belly torn,   181
And scatter'd limbs, shall on the flood be
        borne:
Thy flood, ungrateful nymph; and fate
        shall find
That way for thee and Acis to be join'd.
For O ! I burn with love, and thy disdain
Augments at once my passion and my pain.
Translated Etna flames within my heart,
And thou, inhuman, wilt not ease my
        smart."
  Lamenting thus in vain, he rose, and
        strode
With furious paces to the neighb'ring
        wood.   190
Restless his feet, distracted was his walk;
Mad were his motions, and confus'd his
        talk:

Mad as the vanquish'd bull, when forc'd to
    yield
His lovely mistress, and forsake the field.
   Thus far unseen I saw: when, fatal
    chance
His looks directing, with a sudden glance,
Acis and I were to his sight betray'd;
Where, naught suspecting, we securely
   play'd.
From his wide mouth a bellowing cry he
   cast:
" I see, I see; but this shall be your last."
A roar so loud made Etna to rebound; 201
And all the Cyclops labor'd in the sound.
Affrighted with his monstrous voice, I fled,
And in the neighb'ring ocean plung'd my
   head.
Poor Acis turn'd his back, and: " Help,"
   he cried,
" Help, Galatea ! help, my parent gods,
And take me dying to your deep abodes ! "
The Cyclops follow'd; but he sent before
A rib, which from the living rock he tore:
Tho' but an angle reach'd him of the
   stone, 210
The mighty fragment was enough alone
To crush all Acis; 't was too late to save,
But what the fates allow'd to give, I gave:
That Acis to his lineage should return;
And roll, among the river gods, his urn.
Straight issued from the stone a stream of
   blood,
Which lost the purple, mingling with the
   flood.
Then like a troubled torrent it appear'd:
The torrent, too, in little space was clear'd.
The stone was cleft, and thro' the yawning
   chink 220
New reeds arose, on the new river's brink.
The rock, from out its hollow womb, dis-
   clos'd
A sound like water in its course oppos'd:
When (wondrous to behold) full in the
   flood
Up starts a youth, and navel high he stood.
Horns from his temples rise; and either
   horn
Thick wreaths of reeds (his native growth)
   adorn.
Were not his stature taller than before,
His bulk augmented, and his beauty more,
His color blue, for Acis he might pass: 230
And Acis chang'd into a stream he was.
But mine no more; he rolls along the plains
With rapid motion, and his name retains.

SONG TO A FAIR YOUNG LADY

GOING OUT OF THE TOWN IN THE SPRING

I

Ask not the cause, why sullen Spring
  So long delays her flow'rs to bear;
Why warbling birds forget to sing,
  And winter storms invert the year.
Chloris is gone, and fate provides
To make it spring where she resides.

II

Chloris is gone, the cruel fair:
  She cast not back a pitying eye;
But left her lover in despair,
  To sigh, to languish, and to die. 10
Ah, how can those fair eyes endure
To give the wounds they will not cure !

III

Great God of Love, why hast thou made
  A face that can all hearts command,
That all religions can invade,
  And change the laws of ev'ry land ?
Where thou hadst plac'd such pow'r before,
Thou shouldst have made her mercy more.

IV

When Chloris to the temple comes,
  Adoring crowds before her fall: 20
She can restore the dead from tombs,
  And ev'ry life but mine recall.
I only am by Love design'd
To be the victim for mankind.

VENI CREATOR SPIRITUS

TRANSLATED IN PARAPHRASE

Creator Spirit, by whose aid
The world's foundations first were laid,
Come visit ev'ry pious mind;
Come pour thy joys on humankind;
From sin and sorrow set us free,
And make thy temples worthy thee.
  O source of uncreated light,
The Father's promis'd Paraclite !
Thrice holy fount, thrice holy fire,
Our hearts with heav'nly love inspire; 10
Come, and thy sacred unction bring
To sanctify us, while we sing !
  Plenteous of grace, descend from high,
Rich in thy sev'nfold energy,

Thou strength of his almighty hand,
Whose pow'r does heav'n and earth com-
    mand !
Proceeding Spirit, our defense, ⎫
Who dost the gift of tongues dis- ⎬
    pense, ⎭
And crown'st thy gift with eloquence !
    Refine and purge our earthy parts;   20
But, O, inflame and fire our hearts !
Our frailties help, our vice control,
Submit the senses to the soul;
And when rebellious they are grown,
Then lay thy hand, and hold 'em down.
    Chase from our minds th' infernal foe,
And peace, the fruit of love, bestow;
And lest our feet should step astray,
Protect and guide us in the way.
    Make us eternal truths receive,   30
And practice all that we believe:
Give us thyself, that we may see
The Father and the Son, by thee.
    Immortal honor, endless fame,
Attend th' Almighty Father's name:
The Savior Son be glorified,
Who for lost man's redemption died;
And equal adoration be,
Eternal Paraclete, to thee.

RONDELAY

I

CHLOE found Amyntas lying,
    All in tears, upon the plain;
Sighing to himself, and crying:
    " Wretched I, to love in vain !
Kiss me, dear, before my dying;
    Kiss me once, and ease my pain ! "

II

Sighing to himself, and crying:
    " Wretched I, to love in vain !
Ever scorning, and denying
    To reward your faithful swain;   10
Kiss me, dear, before my dying;
    Kiss me once, and ease my pain.

III

" Ever scorning, and denying
    To reward your faithful swain." —
Chloe, laughing at his crying,
    Told him that he lov'd in vain. —
" Kiss me, dear, before my dying:
    Kiss me once, and ease my pain."

IV

Chloe, laughing at his crying,
    Told him that he lov'd in vain;   20
But repenting, and complying,
    When he kiss'd, she kiss'd again:
Kiss'd him up before his dying;
    Kiss'd him up, and eas'd his pain.

THE LAST PARTING OF HECTOR
AND ANDROMACHE

FROM THE SIXTH BOOK OF HOMER'S
ILIADS

ARGUMENT

Hector, returning from the field of battle, to
visit Helen his sister-in-law, and his brother
Paris, who had fought unsuccessfully hand
to hand with Menelaus, from thence goes to
his own palace to see his wife Andromache,
and his infant son Astyanax. The description of that interview is the subject of this
translation.

THUS having said, brave Hector went to
    see
His virtuous wife, the fair Andromache.
He found her not at home; for she was ⎫
    gone, ⎬
Attended by her maid and infant son, ⎭
To climb the steepy tow'r of Ilion:
From whence, with heavy heart, she might
    survey
The bloody business of the dreadful day.
Her mournful eyes she cast around the plain,
And sought the lord of her desires in vain.
    But he, who thought his peopled palace
    bare,   10
When she, his only comfort, was not there,
Stood in the gate, and ask'd of ev'ry one,
Which way she took, and whither she was
    gone;
If to the court, or, with his mother's train,
In long procession to Minerva's fane.
The servants answer'd, neither to the court,
Where Priam's sons and daughters did re-
    sort,
Nor to the temple was she gone, to move
With prayers the blue-ey'd progeny of
    Jove;
But, more solicitous for him alone.   20
Than all their saf ty, to the tow'r was
    gone,
There to survey the labors of the field,

Where the Greeks conquer, and the Tro-
jans yield;
Swiftly she pass'd, with fear and fury
wild;
The nurse went lagging after with the child.
　This heard, the noble Hector made no
stay;
Th' admiring throng divide to give him
way;
He pass'd thro' every street by which he
came,
And at the gate he met the mournful
dame.
　His wife beheld him, and with eager
pace　　　　　　　　　　　　　　30
Flew to his arms, to meet a dear embrace:
His wife, who brought in dow'r Cilicia's
crown,
And in herself a greater dow'r alone;
Aetion's heir, who on the woody plain
Of Hippoplacus did in Thebe reign.
Breathless she flew, with joy and passion
wild;
The nurse came lagging after with her
child.
　The royal babe upon her breast was laid,
Who, like the morning star, his beams dis-
play'd.
Scamandrius was his name, which Hector
gave,　　　　　　　　　　　　　40
From that fair flood which Ilion's wall did
lave;
But him Astyanax the Trojans call,
From his great father, who defends the wall.
Hector beheld him with a silent smile;
His tender wife stood weeping by, the while:
Press'd in her own, his warlike hand she
took,
Then sigh'd, and thus prophetically spoke:
　" Thy dauntless heart, (which I foresee
too late,)
Too daring man, will urge thee to thy fate:
Nor dost thou pity, with a parent's mind,　50
This helpless orphan, whom thou leav'st
behind;
Nor me, th' unhappy partner of thy bed,
Who must in triumph by the Greeks be
led:
They seek thy life, and, in unequal fight,
With many will oppress thy single might:
Better it were for miserable me
To die, before the fate which I foresee.
For ah ! what comfort can the world be-
queath
To Hector's widow, after Hector's death ?

" Eternal sorrow and perpetual tears　60
Began my youth, and will conclude my
years:
I have no parents, friends, nor brothers
left;
By stern Achilles all of life bereft.
Then when the walls of Thebes he o'er-
threw,
His fatal hand my royal father slew;
He slew Aetion, but despoil'd him not,
Nor in his hate the funeral rites forgot;
Arm'd as he was he sent him whole below,
And reverenc'd thus the manes of his foe:
A tomb he rais'd; the mountain nymphs
around　　　　　　　　　　　　70
Enclos'd with planted elms the holy ground.
　" My sev'n brave brothers in one fatal
day
To Death's dark mansions took the mourn-
ful way,
Slain by the same Achilles, while they keep
The bellowing oxen and the bleating sheep.
My mother, who the royal scepter sway'd,
Was captive to the cruel victor made,
And hither led; but, hence redeem'd with
gold,
Her native country did again behold,
And but beheld; for soon Diana's dart　80
In an unhappy chase transfix'd her heart.
　" But thou, my Hector, art thyself alone
My parents, brothers, and my lord in one.
O kill not all my kindred o'er again,
Nor tempt the dangers of the dusty
plain;
But in this tow'r, for our defense, re-
main.
Thy wife and son are in thy ruin lost:
This is a husband's and a father's post.
The Scæan gate commands the plains
below;
Here marshal all thy soldiers as they
go,　　　　　　　　　　　　　90
And hence with other hands repel the
foe.
By yon wild fig tree lies their chief ascent,
And thither all their pow'rs are daily bent:
The two Ajaces have I often seen,
And the wrong'd husband of the Spartan
queen;
With him his greater brother; and with
these
Fierce Diomede and bold Meriones.
Uncertain if by augury, or chance,
But by this easy rise they all advance:
Guard well that pass, secure of all beside."

To whom the noble Hector thus replied: 101
" That and the rest are in my daily care;
But, should I shun the dangers of the war,
With scorn the Trojans would reward my
    pains,
And their proud ladies with their sweep-
    ing trains.
The Grecian swords and lances I can bear;
But loss of honor is my only fear.
Shall Hector, born to war, his birthright
    yield;
Belie his courage, and forsake the field ?
Early in rugged arms I took delight, 110
And still have been the foremost in the
    fight:
With dangers dearly have I bought re-
    nown,
And am the champion of my father's
    crown.
    " And yet my mind forebodes, with sure
    presage,
That Troy shall perish by the Grecian rage.
The fatal day draws on, when I must fall,
And universal ruin cover all.
Not Troy itself, tho' built by hands divine,
Nor Priam, nor his people, nor his line,
My mother, nor my brothers of renown, 120
Whose valor yet defends th' unhappy town;
Not these, nor all their fates which I fore-
    see,
Are half of that concern I have for thee.
I see, I see thee in that fatal hour,
Subjected to the victor's cruel pow'r;
Led hence a slave to some insulting sword,
Forlorn, and trembling at a foreign lord;
A spectacle in Argos, at the loom,
Gracing with Trojan fights a Grecian room;
Or from deep wells the living stream to
    take, 130
And on thy weary shoulders bring it back:
While, groaning under this laborious life,
They insolently call thee Hector's wife;
Upbraid thy bondage with thy husband's
    name,
And from my glory propagate thy shame.
This when they say, thy sorrows will ⎫
    encrease   ⎪
With anxious thoughts of former happi- ⎬
    ness;   ⎪
That he is dead who could thy wrongs ⎭
    redress.
But I, oppress'd with iron sleep before,
Shall hear thy unavailing cries no more." 140
He said —
Then, holding forth his arms, he took his boy

(The pledge of love and other hope of Troy).
The fearful infant turn'd his head away,
And on his nurse's neck reclining lay,
His unknown father shunning with affright,
And looking back on so uncouth a sight;
Daunted to see a face with steel o'erspread,
And his high plume that nodded o'er his
    head.
His sire and mother smil'd with silent joy,
And Hector hasten'd to relieve his boy; 151
Dismiss'd his burnish'd helm, that shone afar
(The pride of warriors, and the pomp of
    war):
Th' illustrious babe, thus reconcil'd, he took;
Hugg'd in his arms, and kiss'd, and thus he
    spoke:
" Parent of gods and men, propitious Jove,
And you bright synod of the pow'rs above;
On this my son your gracious gifts bestow;
Grant him to live, and great in arms to grow;
To reign in Troy, to govern with renown,
To shield the people, and assert the crown:
That, when hereafter he from war shall come,
And bring his Trojans peace and triumph
    home, 163
Some aged man, who lives this act to see,
And who in former times remember'd me,
May say the son in fortitude and fame
Outgoes the mark, and drowns his father's
    name:
That at these words his mother may re-
    joice,
And add her suffrage to the public voice."
    Thus having said, 170
He first with suppliant hands the gods ador'd,
Then to the mother's arms the child restor'd:
With tears and smiles she took her son, and
    press'd
Th' illustrious infant to her fragrant breast.
He, wiping her fair eyes, indulg'd her grief,
And eas'd her sorrows with this last relief:
    " My wife and mistress, drive thy fears
    away,
Nor give so bad an omen to the day:
Think not it lies in any Grecian's pow'r,
To take my life before the fatal hour. 180
When that arrives, nor good nor bad can
    fly
Th' irrevocable doom of destiny.
Return, and to divert thy thoughts at ⎫
    home,   ⎪
There task thy maids, and exercise the ⎬
    loom,   ⎪
Employ'd in works that womankind be- ⎭
    come:

The toils of war and feats of chivalry
Belong to men, and most of all to me."
    At this, for new replies he did not stay,
But lac'd his crested helm, and strode away.
His lovely consort to her house return'd,
And looking often back in silence mourn'd.

Home when she came, her secret woe she
    vents, 192
And fills the palace with her loud laments:
Those loud laments her echoing maids re-
    store,
And Hector, yet alive, as dead deplore.

POEMS WRITTEN BETWEEN 1693 AND 1696

PROLOGUE, EPILOGUE, AND SONGS FROM LOVE TRIUMPHANT

OR, NATURE WILL PREVAIL

[This tragi-comedy, Dryden's last play, was produced near the close of 1693, or early in 1694 (Malone, I, 1, 213–217, on the authority of Motteux's *Gentleman's Journal*; and *Letter from Dryden to Walsh*, in Scott-Saintsbury edition, xviii, 189), and was published in 1694. It was a failure on the stage.]

PROLOGUE

SPOKEN BY MR. BETTERTON

As when some treasurer lays down the stick,
Warrants are sign'd for ready money thick,
And many desperate debentures paid,
Which never had been, had his lordship
    stay'd;
So now, this poet, who forsakes the stage,
Intends to gratify the present age.
One warrant shall be sign'd for every man;
All shall be wits that will, and beaux that can:
Provided still, this warrant be not shown,
And you be wits but to yourselves alone;
Provided, too, you rail at one another, 11
For there 's no one wit will allow a brother;
Provided, also, that you spare this story,
Damn all the plays that e'er shall come be-
    fore ye.
If one by chance prove good in half a score,
Let that one pay for all, and damn it more.
For if a good one scape among the crew, ⎫
And you continue judging as you do, ⎬
Every bad play will hope for damning too. ⎭
You might damn this, if it were worth ⎫
    your pains; 20
Here 's nothing you will like; no fustian ⎬
    scenes,
And nothing, too, of — you know what he ⎭
    means.

No *double-entendres*, which you sparks allow,
To make the ladies look they know not how;
Simply as 't were, and knowing both to-
    gether,
Seeming to fan their faces in cold weather.
But here 's a story, which no books relate,
Coin'd from our own old poet's addle-pate.
The fable has a moral, too, if sought; ⎫
But let that go; for, upon second thought, ⎬
He fears but few come hither to be taught. ⎭
Yet if you will be profited, you may; 32
And he would bribe you too, to like his play.
He dies, at least to us, and to the stage,
And what he has he leaves this noble age.
He leaves you, first, all plays of his inditing,
The whole estate which he has got by writ-
    ing.
The beaux may think this nothing but ⎫
    vain praise; ⎪
They 'll find it something, the testator ⎬
    says; ⎪
For half their love is made from scraps ⎭
    of plays. 40
To his worst foes he leaves his honesty,
That they may thrive upon 't as much as he.
He leaves his manners to the roaring boys,
Who come in drunk, and fill the house with
    noise.
He leaves to the dire critics of his wit,
His silence and contempt of all they writ.
To Shakespeare's critic, he bequeaths the
    curse,
To find his faults, and yet himself make
    worse;
A precious reader in poetic schools, 49
Who by his own examples damns his rules.
Last, for the fair, he wishes you may be,
From your dull critics, the lampooners, free.
Tho' he pretends no legacy to leave you,
An old man may at least good wishes give
    you.
Your beauty names the play; and may it
    prove,
To each, an omen of Triumphant Love!

EPILOGUE

Now, in good manners, nothing should be said
Against this play, because the poet 's dead.
The prologue told us of a moral here:
Would I could find it ! but the Devil knows where.
If in my part it lies, I fear he means
To warn us of the sparks behind our scenes.
For, if you 'll take it on Dalinda's word,
'T is a hard chapter to refuse a lord.
The poet might pretend this moral too,
That, when a wit and fool together woo,   10
The damsel (not to break an ancient rule)
Should leave the wit, and take the wealthy fool.
This he might mean: but there 's a truth ⎤
  behind, ⎟
And, since it touches none of all our kind ⎬
But masks and misses, faith, I 'll speak ⎟
  my mind. ⎦
What if he taught our sex more cautious carriage,
And not to be too coming before marriage;
For fear of my misfortune in the play,
A kid brought home upon the wedding day ?
I fear there are few Sanchos in the pit,   20
So good as to forgive, and to forget;
That will, like him, restore us into favor,
And take us after on our good behavior.
Few, when they find the money-bag is rent,
Will take it for good payment on content.
But in the telling, there the difference is,
Sometimes they find it more than they could wish.
Therefore be warn'd, you misses and you masks,
Look to your hits, nor give the first that asks.
Tears, sighs, and oaths, no truth of passion prove;   30
True settlement, alone, declares true love.
For him that weds a puss, who kept her first,
I say but little, but I doubt the worst.
The wife that was a cat may mind her ⎤
  house, ⎟
And prove an honest, and a careful spouse; ⎬
But, faith, I would not trust her with a ⎟
  mouse. ⎦

SONGS

I

SONG OF JEALOUSY

I

What state of life can be so blest
As love, that warms a lover's breast ?
Two souls in one, the same desire
To grant the bliss, and to require !
But if in heav'n a hell we find,
  'T is all from thee,
    O Jealousy !
  'T is all from thee,
    O Jealousy !
Thou tyrant, tyrant Jealousy,   10
Thou tyrant of the mind !

II

All other ills, tho' sharp they prove,
Serve to refine, and perfect love:
In absence, or unkind disdain,
Sweet Hope relieves the lover's pain.
But, ah ! no cure but death we find,
  To set us free
  From Jealousy:
  O Jealousy !
Thou tyrant, tyrant Jealousy,   20
Thou tyrant of the mind !

III

False in thy glass all objects are,
Some set too near, and some too far;
Thou art the fire of endless night,
The fire that burns and gives no light.
All torments of the damn'd we find
  In only thee,
  O Jealousy !
Thou tyrant, tyrant Jealousy,
Thou tyrant of the mind !   30

II

SONG FOR A GIRL

I

Young I am, and yet unskill'd
How to make a lover yield;
How to keep, or how to gain,
When to love, and when to feign.

II

Take me, take me, some of you,
While I yet am young and true;

Ere I can my soul disguise,
Heave my breasts, and roll my eyes.

III

Stay not till I learn the way,
How to lie, and to betray: 10
He that has me first, is blest,
For I may deceive the rest.

IV

Could I find a blooming youth,
Full of love, and full of truth,
Brisk, and of a jaunty mien,
I should long to be fifteen.

TO MY DEAR FRIEND MR. CONGREVE, ON HIS COMEDY CALL'D THE DOUBLE-DEALER

[This play by Congreve was first acted in November, 1693 (Malone, I, 1, 229; on the authority of Motteux's *Gentleman's Journal*). Of it Dryden writes as follows in a letter to Walsh: "His [Congreve's] Double Dealer is much censurd by the greater part of the Town: and is defended onely by the best judges, who, you know, are commonly the fewest yet it gets ground daily, and has already been acted Eight times." (Scott-Saintsbury edition, xviii, 189, 190.) To the first edition of the play, published in 1694, he prefixed the following fine poem, which shows his critical appreciation of the comedy and his personal affection for its author. Congreve fulfilled the charge laid upon him in the last lines, by editing an edition of Dryden's dramatic works, published in 1717.]

WELL then, the promis'd hour is come at last;
The present age of wit obscures the past:
Strong were our sires, and as they fought they writ,
Conqu'ring with force of arms, and dint of wit;
Theirs was the giant race, before the flood;
And thus, when Charles return'd, our empire stood.
Like Janus he the stubborn soil manur'd,
With rules of husbandry the rankness cur'd;
Tam'd us to manners, when the stage was rude;
And boist'rous English wit with art indued.   10
Our age was cultivated thus at length,
But what we gain'd in skill we lost in strength.
Our builders were with want of genius curst;
The second temple was not like the first:
Till you, the best Vitruvius, come at length;
Our beauties equal, but excel our strength.
Firm Doric pillars found your solid base; ⎫
The fair Corinthian crowns the higher space: ⎬
Thus all below is strength, and all above is grace. ⎭
In easy dialogue is Fletcher's praise;   20
He mov'd the mind, but had not power to raise.
Great Jonson did by strength of judgment please;
Yet, doubling Fletcher's force, he wants his ease.
In differing talents both adorn'd their age;
One for the study, t'other for the stage:
But both to Congreve justly shall submit,
One match'd in judgment, both o'ermatch'd in wit.
In him all beauties of this age we see, ⎫
Etherege his courtship, Southerne's purity, ⎬
The satire, wit, and strength of Manly Wycherley.   30 ⎭
All this in blooming youth you have achiev'd,
Nor are your foil'd contemporaries griev'd,
So much the sweetness of your manners move,
We cannot envy you, because we love.
Fabius might joy in Scipio, when he saw
A beardless consul made against the law;
And join his suffrage to the votes of Rome,
Tho' he with Hannibal was overcome.
Thus old Romano bow'd to Raphael's fame,
And scholar to the youth he taught became.   40
O that your brows my laurel had sustain'd;
Well had I been depos'd, if you had reign'd!
The father had descended for the son;
For only you are lineal to the throne.
Thus, when the state one Edward did depose,
A greater Edward in his room arose.
But now, not I, but poetry is curst;
For Tom the Second reigns like Tom the First.

But let 'em not mistake my patron's part,
Nor call his charity their own desert.   50
Yet this I prophesy: thou shalt be seen
(Tho' with some short parenthesis be-
     tween)
High on the throne of wit; and, seated
     there,
Not mine — that's little — but thy laurel
     wear.
Thy first attempt an early promise made;
That early promise this has more than
     paid.
So bold, yet so judiciously you dare,
That your least praise is to be regular.
Time, place, and action, may with pains be
     wrought;
But genius must be born, and never can be
     taught.   60
This is your portion; this your native ⎤
     store;   ⎟
Heav'n, that but once was prodigal be-   ⎬
     fore,   ⎟
To Shakespeare gave as much; she could ⎦
     not give him more.
   Maintain your post: that's all the fame
     you need;
For 't is impossible you should proceed.
Already I am worn with cares and age,
And just abandoning th' ungrateful stage;
Unprofitably kept at Heav'n's expense,
I live a rent-charge on his providence:
But you, whom ev'ry Muse and Grace
     adorn,   70
Whom I foresee to better fortune born,
Be kind to my remains; and O defend,
Against your judgment, your departed
     friend !
Let not the insulting foe my fame pursue,
But shade those laurels which descend to
     you;
And take for tribute what these lines ex-
     press:
You merit more; nor could my love do less.

TO SIR GODFREY KNELLER

[Early in 1694 (see letter from Dryden to
Walsh, Scott-Saintsbury edition, xviii, 191)
Tonson published a volume entitled, *The An-
nual Miscellany for the Year 1694, being the Fourth
Part of Miscellany Poems*, which is commonly
referred to as the *Fourth Miscellany*. To this
Dryden contributed only a translation of *The
Third Book of Virgil's Georgics* and the follow-
ing epistle *To Sir Godfrey Kneller*. Among the

other writers for the volume were Addison,
Congreve, Prior, Dennis, Yalden, and Charles
Dryden, the poet's son. A second edition of
the volume, with the same title, but with many
changes in the contents, appeared in 1708 ; and
a third, with title-page reading, *The Fourth
Part of Miscellany Poems . . . Publish'd by Mr.
Dryden*, and with further changes in the contents, in 1716. Tonson did not carry out his
plan of an *Annual Miscellany*, perhaps because
Dryden, now busy with his *Virgil*, was unable
to give him further help. A fifth part of the
series appeared, however, in 1704, after Dryden's
death ; and a sixth in 1709 : second editions of
these last two volumes were printed in 1716.
   Dryden reprinted his version of *The Third
Book of Virgil's Georgics*, with very slight
changes, in his complete *Virgil*. It is therefore
omitted at this point.
   The epistle *To Sir Godfrey Kneller* was probably written as an acknowledgment of a painting of Shakespeare, copied from the well-known
Chandos portrait, which Kneller had presented
to Dryden : see line 73 below. It was reprinted
in the folio *Poems and Translations*, 1701, with
the omission of lines 91-94, 115-123, 164, 165
of the *Miscellany* text, and with some minor
changes of reading. It is at least doubtful
whether these alterations were due to Dryden
himself. The present text follows that of the
Miscellany.]

ONCE I beheld the fairest of her kind:
(And still the sweet idea charms my mind:)
True, she was dumb ; for Nature gaz'd so
     long,
Pleas'd with her work, that she forgot her
     tongue,
But, smiling, said : " She still shall gain the
     prize ;
I only have transferr'd it to her eyes."
Such are thy pictures, Kneller: such thy
     skill,
That Nature seems obedient to thy will;
Comes out, and meets thy pencil in the
     draught;
Lives there, and wants but words to speak
     her thought.   10
At least thy pictures look a voice; and we ⎤
Imagine sounds, deceiv'd to that degree, ⎬
We think 't is somewhat more than just to ⎦
     see.
   Shadows are but privations of the light;
Yet, when we walk, they shoot before the
     sight;
With us approach, retire, arise, and fall;
Nothing themselves, and yet expressing all.
Such are thy pieces, imitating life

So near, they almost conquer'd in the strife;
And from their animated canvas came,   20
Demanding souls, and loosen'd from the
    frame.
  Prometheus, were he here, would cast
    away
His Adam, and refuse a soul to clay;
And either would thy noble work inspire,
Or think it warm enough without his fire.
  But vulgar hands may vulgar likeness
    raise;
This is the least attendant on thy praise:
From hence the rudiments of art began;
A coal, or chalk, first imitated man:
Perhaps the shadow, taken on a wall,   30
Gave outlines to the rude original;
Ere canvas yet was strain'd, before the ⎫
    grace   ⎪
Of blended colors found their use and   ⎬
    place,   ⎪
Or cypress tablets first receiv'd a face. ⎭
  By slow degrees, the godlike art advanc'd;
As man grew polish'd, picture was inhanc'd:
Greece added posture, shade, and perspec-
    tive;
And then the mimic piece began to live.
Yet perspective was lame, no distance true,
But all came forward in one common view: 40
No point of light was known, no bounds of art;
When light was there, it knew not to depart,
But glaring on remoter objects play'd;
Not languish'd and insensibly decay'd.
  Rome rais'd not art, but barely kept alive,
And with old Greece unequally did strive;
Till Goths and Vandals, a rude northern race,
Did all the matchless monuments deface.
Then all the Muses in one ruin lie,
And rhyme began t' enervate poetry.   50
Thus, in a stupid military state,
The pen and pencil find an equal fate.
Flat faces, such as would disgrace a screen,
Such as in Bantam's embassy were seen,
Unrais'd, unrounded, were the rude delight
Of brutal nations, only born to fight.
  Long time the sister arts, in iron sleep,
A heavy sabbath did supinely keep:
At length, in Raphael's age, at once they
    rise,
Stretch all their limbs, and open all their
    eyes.   60
  Thence rose the Roman and the Lombard
    line;
One color'd best, and one did best design.
Raphael's, like Homer's, was the nobler part,
But Titian's painting look'd like Virgil's art.

Thy genius gives thee both; where true
    design,
Postures unforc'd, and lively colors join.
Likeness is ever there; but still the best,
Like proper thoughts in lofty language
    dress'd:
Where light, to shades descending, plays, not
    strives,
Dies by degrees, and by degrees revives.   70
Of various parts a perfect whole is wrought:
Thy pictures think, and we divine their
    thought.
  Shakespeare,* thy gift, I   * Shakespeare's
    place before my sight;   picture, drawn
With awe, I ask his bless-   by Sir Godfrey
    ing ere I write;   Kneller and
With reverence look on his   given to the
    majestic face.   author.
Proud to be less, but of his godlike race.
His soul inspires me, while thy praise I write,
And I, like Teucer, under Ajax fight:
Bids thee, thro' me, be bold; with dauntless
    breast
Contemn the bad, and emulate the best.   80
Like his, thy critics in th' attempt are lost:
When most they rail, know then, they envy
    most.
In vain they snarl aloof; a noisy crowd,
Like women's anger, impotent and loud.
While they their barren industry deplore,
Pass on secure, and mind the goal before.
Old as she is, my Muse shall march behind,
Bear off the blast, and intercept the wind.
Our arts are sisters, tho' not twins in birth;
For hymns were sung in Eden's happy earth
By the first pair, while Eve was yet a saint,
Before she fell with pride, and learn'd to
    paint.   92
Forgive th' allusion; 't was not meant to bite,
But satire will have room, where'er I write.
For O the painter Muse, tho' last in place,
Has seiz'd the blessing first, like Jacob's race.
Apelles' art an Alexander found,   ⎫
And Raphael did with Leo's gold abound;   ⎪
But Homer was with barren laurel   ⎬
    crown'd.   ⎭
Thou hadst thy Charles a while, and so
    had I;   100
But pass we that unpleasing image by.
Rich in thyself, and of thyself divine,
All pilgrims come and offer at thy shrine.
A graceful truth thy pencil can command:
The fair themselves go mended from thy
    hand.
Likeness appears in every lineament;

But likeness in thy work is eloquent.
Tho' Nature there her true resemblance
    bears,
A nobler beauty in thy piece appears.
So warm thy work, so glows the gen'rous
    frame, 110
Flesh looks less living in the lovely dame.
Thou paint'st as we describe, improving ⎤
    still, |
When on wild nature we ingraft our ⎬
    skill; |
But not creating beauties at our will. ⎦
   Some other hand perhaps may reach a
    face,
But none like thee a finish'd figure place:
None of this age; for that 's enough for ⎤
    thee,   ⎬
The first of these inferior times to be, |
Not to contend with heroes' memory. ⎦
Due honors to those mighty names we
    grant, 120
But shrubs may live beneath the lofty
    plant;
Sons may succeed their greater parents
    gone:
Such is thy lot, and such I wish my own.
   But poets are confin'd in narr'wer space,
To speak the language of their native
    place:
The painter widely stretches his command;
Thy pencil speaks the tongue of ev'ry land.
From hence, my friend, all climates are
    your own,
Nor can you forfeit, for you hold of none.
All nations all immunities will give 130
To make you theirs, where'er you please ⎤
    to live;   ⎬
And not seven cities, but the world |
    would strive. ⎦
   Sure some propitious planet then did
    smile,
When first you were conducted to this
    isle:
Our genius brought you here, t' inlarge
    our fame,
For your good stars are ev'rywhere the
    same.
Thy matchless hand, of ev'ry region free,
Adopts our climate, not our climate thee.
   Great Rome and Venice *   * He travel'd
    early did impart   very young
To thee th' examples of their   into Italy.
    wondrous art. 140
Those masters then, but seen, not under-
    stood,

With generous emulation fir'd thy blood;
For what in nature's dawn the child ad-
    mir'd,
The youth endeavor'd, and the man ac-
    quir'd.
   That yet thou hast not reach'd their high
    degree,
Seems only wanting to this age, not thee.
Thy genius, bounded by the times, like ⎤
    mine, |
Drudges on petty draughts, nor dare ⎬
    design |
A more exalted work, and more divine. ⎦
For what a song, or senseless opera 150
Is to the living labor of a play;
Or what a play to Virgil's work would be,
Such is a single piece to history.
   But we, who life bestow, ourselves must
    live;
Kings cannot reign unless their subjects
    give;
And they who pay the taxes bear the rule:
Thus thou, sometimes, art forc'd to draw
    a fool;
But so his follies in thy posture sink,
The senseless idiot seems at least to think.
   Good Heav'n ! that sots and knaves should
    be so vain, 160
To wish their vile resemblance may re-
    main !
And stand recorded, at their own request,
To future days, a libel or a jest !
Meantime, while just incouragement you
    want,
You only paint to live, not live to paint.
   Else should we see your noble pencil
    trace
Our unities of action, time, and place;
A whole compos'd of parts, and those the
    best,
With ev'ry various character express'd;
Heroes at large, and at a nearer view; 170
Less, and at distance, an ignobler crew;
While all the figures in one action join,
As tending to complete the main design.
   More cannot be by mortal art express'd,
But venerable age shall add the rest:
For Time shall with his ready pencil stand;
Retouch your figures with his ripening
    hand;
Mellow your colors, and imbrown the teint;
Add every grace, which Time alone can
    grant;
To future ages shall your fame convey, 180
And give more beauties than he takes away.

AN ODE ON THE DEATH OF MR. HENRY PURCELL

LATE SERVANT TO HIS MAJESTY, AND ORGANIST OF THE CHAPEL ROYAL, AND OF ST. PETER'S, WESTMINSTER

[Henry Purcell, the greatest musician of his time, died on November 21, 1695, at the age of thirty-seven. Dryden's ode was published in the next year, in a broadside, where it is twice printed, first by itself, and then with music written for it by Dr. John Blow. It also appeared as one of several poems prefixed to *Orpheus Britannicus*, a collection of Purcell's music published in 1698.]

I

MARK how the lark and linnet sing;
　　With rival notes
　They strain their warbling throats,
　　To welcome in the spring.
　But in the close of night,
When Philomel begins her heav'nly lay,
　They cease their mutual spite,
　Drink in her music with delight,
And list'ning and silent, and silent and list'ning, and list'ning and silent obey.

II

So ceas'd the rival crew, when Purcell
　　came;　　　　　　　　　　　　　10
They sung no more, or only sung his fame;
Struck dumb, they all admir'd the godlike
　man:
　　The godlike man,
　　Alas! too soon retir'd,
　　As he too late began.
We beg not hell our Orpheus to restore:
　　Had he been there,
　　Their sovereigns' fear
　Had sent him back before.
The pow'r of harmony too well they know:
He long ere this had tun'd their jarring
　sphere,　　　　　　　　　　　　21
　And left no hell below.

III

The heav'nly choir, who heard his notes
　from high,
Let down the scale of music from the sky:
　They handed him along,
And all the way he taught, and all the way
　they sung.
Ye brethren of the lyre, and tuneful voice,
Lament his lot; but at your own rejoice:

　Now live secure, and linger out your
　　days;
The gods are pleas'd alone with Pur-
　cell's lays,　　　　　　　　　　　30
Nor know to mend their choice.

PREFACE AND EPILOGUE TO THE HUSBAND HIS OWN CUCKOLD

[This comedy, by John Dryden, Jr., the poet's second son, was published in July, 1696 (Malone, I, 1, 425, on the authority of an advertisement in the *London Gazette*), with a prologue by Congreve, and a dedication to Sir Robert Howard, the author's uncle. The play bore the appropriate Virgilian motto:

Et pater Æneas et avunculus excitet Hector. — (*Æneid*, III, 343.)

Dryden's preface furnishes a delightful proof of his fatherly kindliness. So also, in a different fashion, does the following excerpt from a letter to Tonson (Malone, I, 2, 48):
"Send word, if you please, Sir, what is the most you will give for my sonn's play, that I may take the fairest chapman, as I am bound to do for his benefit."]

PREFACE

I HAVE thought convenient to acquaint the reader with somewhat concerning this comedy, tho' perhaps not worth his knowledge. It was sent me from Italy some years since, by my second son, to try its fortune on the stage; and being the essay of a young unexperienc'd author, to confess the truth, I thought it not worthy of that honor. 'T is true, I was not willing to discourage him so far as to tell him plainly my opinion, but it seems he guess'd somewhat of my mind, by my long delays of his expectation; and therefore, in my absence from the town last summer, took the boldness to dedicate his play to that person of honor whose name you will find before his epistle. It was receiv'd by that noble gentleman with so much candor and generosity, as neither my son nor I could deserve from him. Then the play was no longer in my power; the patron demanding it in his own right, it was deliver'd to him. And he was farther pleas'd, during my sickness, to put it into that method in which you find it; the loose scenes digested into order, and knit into a tale.

As it is, I think it may pass amongst the rest of our new plays: I know but two authors, and they are both my friends, who have done better since the Revolution. This I dare venture to maintain, that the taste of the age is wretchedly deprav'd in all sorts of poetry; nothing almost but what is abominably bad can please. The young hounds, who ought to come behind, now lead the pack; but they miserably mistake the scent. Their poets, worthy of such an audience, know not how to distinguish their characters; the manners are all alike, inconsistent and interfering with each other. There is scarce a man or woman of God's making in all their farces: yet they raise an unnatural sort of laughter, the common effect of buffoon'ry; and the rabble, which takes this for wit, will endure no better, because 't is above their understanding. This account I take from the best judges; for I thank God, I have had the grace hitherto to avoid the seeing or reading of their gallimaufries. But 't is the latter end of a century, and I hope the next will begin better.

This play, I dare assure the reader, is none of those; it may want beauties, but the faults are neither gross nor many. Perfection in any art is not suddenly obtain'd: the author of this, to his misfortune, left his country at a time when he was to have learn'd the language. The story he has treated was an accident which happen'd at Rome, tho' he has transferr'd the scene to England. If it shall please God to restore him to me, I may perhaps inform him better of the rules of writing; and if I am not partial, he has already shewn that a genius is not wanting to him. All that I can reasonably fear is, that the perpetual good success of ill plays may make him endeavor to please by writing worse, and by accommodating himself to the wretched capacity and liking of the present audience, from which, Heaven defend any of my progeny! A poet, indeed, must live by the many; but a good poet will make it his business to please the few. I will not proceed farther on a subject which arraigns so many of the readers.

For what remains, both my son and I are extremely oblig'd to my dear friend, Mr. Congreve, whose excellent prologue was one of the greatest ornaments of the play. Neither is my epilogue the worst which I have written; tho' it seems, at the first sight, to expose our young clergy with too much freedom. It was on that consideration that I had once begun it otherwise, and deliver'd the copy of it to be spoken, in case the first part of it had given offense. This I will give you, partly in my own justification, and partly too because I think it not unworthy of your sight; only rememb'ring you that the last line connects the sense to the ensuing part of it. — Farewell, reader: if you are a father, you will forgive me; if not, you will when you are a father.

Time was, when none could preach without degrees,
And seven years' toil at universities;
But when the canting saints came once in play,
The spirit did their bus'ness in a day:
A zealous cobbler, with the gift of tongue,
If he could pray six hours, might preach as long.
Thus, in the primitive times of poetry,
The stage to none but men of sense was free.
But thanks to your judicious taste, my masters,
It lies in common, now, to poetasters.
You set them up, and till you dare condemn,
The satire lies on you, and not on them.
When mountebanks their drugs at market cry,
Is it their fault to sell, or yours to buy?
'T is true, they write with ease, and well they may; ⎫
Flyblows are gotten every summer's day;   ⎬
The poet does but buzz, and there 's a play.   ⎭
Wit 's not his business, &c.

EPILOGUE

SPOKEN BY MRS. BRACEGIRDLE

LIKE some raw sophister that mounts the pulpit,
So trembles a young poet at a full pit.
Unus'd to crowds, the parson quakes for fear,
And wonders how the devil he durst come there;
Wanting three talents needful for the place,
Some beard, some learning, and some little grace:
Nor is the puny poet void of care;   ⎫
For authors, such as our new authors are,   ⎬
Have not much learning, nor much wit to spare; ⎭
And as for grace, to tell the truth, there 's scarce one   10
But has as little as the very parson.
Both say, they preach and write for your instruction;
But 't is for a third day, and for induction.
The difference is, that tho' you like the play,
The poet's gain is ne'er beyond his day;
But with the parson 't is another case;
He, without holiness, may rise to grace.
The poet has one disadvantage more,   ⎫
That if his play be dull, he 's damn'd all o'er,   ⎬
Not only a damn'd blockhead, but damn'd poor.   20 ⎭
But dulness well becomes the sable garment;
I warrant that ne'er spoil'd a priest's preferment:

Wit's not his business, and, as wit now
  goes,
Sirs, 't is not so much yours as you suppose,
For you like nothing now but nauseous
  beaux.
You laugh not, gallants, as by proof appears,
At what his beauship says, but what he
  wears;
So 't is your eyes are tickled, not your
  ears:
The tailor and the furrier find the stuff,
The wit lies in the dress, and monstrous
  muff.   30

The truth on 't is, the payment of the
  pit
Is like for like, clipp'd money for clipp'd
  wit.
You cannot from our absent author hope, ·
He should equip the stage with such a
  fop:
Fools change in England, and new fools
  arise;
For tho' th' immortal species never dies,
Yet ev'ry year new maggots make new
  flies.
But where he lives abroad, he scarce can
  find
One fool, for million that he left behind.

TRANSLATION OF VIRGIL

[From the close of 1693 (see letter to Walsh, December 12, 1693, in Scott-Saintsbury edition, xviii, 191) until the summer of 1697, Dryden devoted nearly all his energies to his translation of Virgil. On June 28, 1697, an advertisement in the *London Gazette* states: "Virgil . . .
will be finished this week, and be ready next week to be delivered, as subscribed for, in Quires,
upon bringing the Receipt for the first Payment, and paying the second." This first edition is a
stately folio, with title-page reading as follows:

THE

WORKS

OF

VIRGIL:

Containing His
PASTORALS,
GEORGICS,
AND
ÆNEIS.

Translated into English Verse; By
Mr. *DRYDEN.*

Adorn'd with a Hundred Sculptures.

Sequiturque Patrem non passibus Æquis. Virg. Æn. 2.

LONDON,
Printed for *Jacob Tonson,* at the *Judges-Head* in *Fleetstreet,*
near the *Inner-Temple-Gate,* MDCXCVII.

The volume contained, besides the work of Dryden here reprinted, a *Life of Virgil* and a
Preface to the Pastorals by Knightly Chetwood, an *Essay on the Georgics* by Addison, who also
wrote "all the arguments in prose to the whole translation" (see p. 519, below, and *Notes,*

p. 1009, below), and, finally, several complimentary poems, and lists of subscribers to the work. The *sculptures* were from the plates, somewhat retouched, that had formerly been used for Ogleby's *Virgil*.

Soon after the volume was published, Dryden undertook a revision of it, which occupied him for only nine days. (See letter from Dryden to Tonson: Malone, I, 2, 61.) The second edition, which is the basis of the present text, was also in folio, and appeared in 1698. The third edition, in three volumes, octavo, was not printed until 1709.]

PASTORALS

TO THE

RIGHT HONORABLE
HUGH, LORD CLIFFORD

BARON OF CHUDLEIGH

My Lord,

I HAVE found it not more difficult to translate Virgil, than to find such patrons as I desire for my translation. For, tho' England is not wanting in a learned nobility, yet such are my unhappy circumstances, that they have confin'd me to a narrow choice. To the greater part I have not the honor to be known; and to some of them I cannot shew at present, by any public act, that grateful respect which I shall ever bear them in my heart. Yet I have no reason to complain of fortune, since in the midst of that abundance I could not possibly have chosen better than the worthy son of so illustrious a father. He was the patron of my manhood, when I flourish'd in the opinion of the world; tho' with small advantage to my fortune, till he awaken'd the remembrance of my royal master. He was that Pollio, or that Varus, who introduc'd me to Augustus; and, tho' he soon dismiss'd himself from state affairs, yet in the short time of his administration he shone so powerfully upon me, that, like the heat of a Russian summer, he ripen'd the fruits of poetry in a cold climate, and gave me wherewithal to subsist, at least, in the long winter which succeeded. What I now offer to your Lordship is the wretched remainder of a sickly age, worn out with study, and oppress'd by fortune; without other support than the constancy and patience of a Christian. You, my Lord, are yet in the flower of your youth, and may live to enjoy the benefits of the peace which is promis'd Europe: I can only hear of that blessing; for years, and, above all things, want of health, have shut me out from sharing in the happiness. The poets, who condemn their Tantalus to hell, had added to his torments if they had plac'd him in Elysium, which is the proper emblem of my condition. The fruit and the water may reach my lips, but cannot enter; and, if they could, yet I want a palate as well as a digestion. But it is some kind of pleasure to me, to please those whom I respect. And I am not altogether out of hope that these *Pastorals* of Virgil may give your Lordship some delight, tho' made English by one who scarce remembers that passion which inspir'd my author when he wrote them. These were his first essay in poetry, (if the *Ceiris* was not his,) and it was more excusable in him to describe love when he was young, than for me to translate him when I am old. He died at the age of fifty-two; and I began this work in my great climacteric. But having perhaps a better constitution than my author, I have wrong'd him less, considering my circumstances, than those who have attempted him before, either in our own, or any modern language. And, tho' this version is not void of errors, yet it comforts me that the faults of others are not worth finding. Mine are neither gross nor frequent in those eclogues wherein my master has rais'd himself above that humble style in which pastoral delights, and which I must confess is proper to the education and converse of shepherds; for he found the strength of his genius betimes, and was even in his youth preluding to his *Georgics* and his *Æneis*. He could not forbear to try his wings, tho' his pinions were not harden'd to maintain a long laborious flight. Yet sometimes they bore him to a pitch as lofty as ever he was able to reach afterwards. But, when he was admonish'd by his subject to descend, he came down gently circling in the air, and singing, to the ground; like a lark, melodious in her mounting, and continuing her song till she alights, still preparing for a higher flight at her next sally, and tuning her voice to better music. The *Fourth*, the *Sixth*, and the *Eighth Pastorals* are clear evidences of this truth. In the three first he contains himself within his bounds; but, addressing to Pollio, his great patron, and himself no vulgar poet, he no longer could restrain the freedom of his spirit, but began to assert his native character, which is sublimity — putting himself under the conduct of the same Cumæan Sibyl whom afterwards he gave for a guide to Æneas. 'T is true he was sensible of his own boldness; and we know it by the *paulo majora* which begins his *Fourth Eclogue*. He remember'd, like young Manlius, that he was forbidden to engage; but what avails an express command to a youthful courage which presages victory in the attempt? Encourag'd with success, he proceeds farther in the *Sixth*, and invades the province of philosophy. And notwithstanding that Phœbus had forewarn'd him of singing wars, as he there confesses, yet he presum'd that the search of nature was as free to him as to Lucretius, who at his age explain'd it according to the principles of Epicurus. In his *Eighth Eclogue* he has innovated nothing; the former part of it being the complaint and despair of a forsaken lover; the latter, a charm of an enchantress, to renew a lost affection. But the complaint perhaps contains some topics which are above the condition of his persons; and our author seems to have made his herdsmen somewhat too learn'd for their profession: the charms are also of the same nature; but both were copied from Theocritus, and had receiv'd the applause of former ages in their original. There is a kind of rusticity in all those pompous verses; somewhat of a holiday shepherd strutting in his country buskins. The like may be observ'd both in the *Pollio* and the *Silenus*, where the similitudes are drawn from the woods and meadows. They seem to me to represent our poet betwixt a farmer and a courtier, when he left Mantua for Rome, and dress'd himself in his best habit to appear before his patron, somewhat too fine for the place from whence he came, and yet retaining part of its simplicity. In the *Ninth Pastoral* he collects some beautiful passages which were scatter'd in Theocritus, which he could not insert into any of his former eclogues, and yet was unwilling they should be lost. In all the rest he is equal to his Sicilian master, and observes, like him, a just decorum both of the subject and the persons; as particularly in the *Third Pastoral*, where one of his shepherds describes a bowl, or mazer, curiously carv'd:

In medio duo signa: Conon, et quis fuit alter,
Descripsit radio totum qui gentibus orbem?

He remembers only the name of Conon, and forgets the other on set purpose; (whether he means Anaximander, or Eudoxus, I dispute not;) but he was certainly forgotten, to shew his country swain was no great scholar.

After all, I must confess that the boorish dialect of Theocritus has a secret charm in it which the Roman language cannot imitate, tho' Virgil has drawn it down as low as possibly he could; as in the *cujum pecus*, and some other words, for which he was so unjustly blam'd by the bad critics of his age, who could not see the beauties of that *merum rus* which the poet describ'd in those expressions. But Theocritus may justly be preferr'd as the original, without injury to Virgil, who modestly contents himself with the second place, and glories only in being the first who transplanted pastoral

into his own country, and brought it there to bear as happily as the cherry trees which Lucullus brought from Pontus.

Our own nation has produc'd a third poet in this kind, not inferior to the two former. For the *Shepherds' Kalendar* of Spenser is not to be match'd in any modern language, not even by Tasso's *Aminta*, which infinitely transcends Guarini's *Pastor Fido*, as having more of nature in it, and being almost wholly clear from the wretched affectation of learning. I will say nothing of the *Piscatory Eclogues*, because no modern Latin can bear criticism. 'T is no wonder that rolling down, thro' so many barbarous ages, from the spring of Virgil, it bears along with it the filth and ordures of the Goths and Vandals. Neither will I mention Monsieur Fontenelle, the living glory of the French. 'T is enough for him to have excell'd his master Lucian, without attempting to compare our miserable age with that of Virgil or Theocritus. Let me only add, for his reputation:

—— Si Pergama dextra
Defendi possint, etiam hac defensa fuissent.

But Spenser, being master of our northern dialect, and skill'd in Chaucer's English, has so exactly imitated the Doric of Theocritus that his love is a perfect image of that passion which God infus'd into both sexes, before it was corrupted with the knowledge of arts, and the ceremonies of what we call good manners.

My Lord, I know to whom I dedicate; and could not have been induc'd by any motive to put this part of Virgil, or any other, into unlearned hands. You have read him with pleasure, and, I dare say, with admiration, in the Latin, of which you are a master. You have added to your natural endowments, which, without flattery, are eminent, the superstructures of study, and the knowledge of good authors. Courage, probity, and humanity are inherent in you. These virtues have ever been habitual to the ancient house of Cumberland, from whence you are descended, and of which our chronicles make so honorable mention in the long wars betwixt the rival families of York and Lancaster. Your forefathers have asserted the party which they chose till death, and died for its defense in the fields of battle. You have, besides, the fresh remembrance of your noble father, from whom you never can degenerate.

—— Nec imbellem feroces
Progenerant aquilæ columbam.

It being almost morally impossible for you to be other than you are by kind, I need neither praise nor invite your virtue. You are acquainted with the Roman history, and know without my information that patronage and clientship always descended from the fathers to the sons, and that the same plebeian houses had recourse to the same patrician line which had formerly protected them, and follow'd their principles and fortunes to the last. So that I am your Lordship's by descent, and part of your inheritance. And the natural inclination which I have to serve you adds to your paternal right ; for I was wholly yours from the first moment when I had the happiness and honor of being known to you. Be pleas'd therefore to accept the rudiments of Virgil's poetry, coarsely translated, I confess, but which yet retains some beauties of the author, which neither the barbarity of our language, nor my unskilfulness, could so much sully, but that they appear sometimes in the dim mirror which I hold before you. The subject is not unsuitable to your youth, which allows you yet to love, and is proper to your present scene of life. Rural recreations abroad, and books at home, are the innocent pleasures of a man who is early wise, and gives Fortune no more hold of him than of necessity he must. 'T is good, on some occasions, to think beforehand as little as we can ; to enjoy as much of the present as will not endanger our futurity ; and to provide ourselves of the virtuoso's saddle, which will be sure to amble, when the world is upon the hardest trot. What I humbly offer to your Lordship is of this nature. I wish it pleasant, and am sure 't is innocent. May you ever continue your esteem for Virgil, and not lessen it for the faults of his translator ; who is, with all manner of respect and sense of gratitude,

My Lord,

Your Lordship's most humble,
and most obedient servant,
JOHN DRYDEN.

THE FIRST PASTORAL

OR, TITYRUS AND MELIBŒUS

THE ARGUMENT

The occasion of the *First Pastoral* was this. When Augustus had settled himself in the Roman Empire, that he might reward his veteran troops for their past service, he distributed among 'em all the lands that lay about Cremona and Mantua, turning out the right owners for having sided with his enemies. Virgil was a sufferer among the rest, who afterwards recover'd his estate by Mæcenas's intercession ; and, as an instance of his gratitude, compos'd the following pastoral, where he sets out his own good fortune in the person of Tityrus, and the calamities of his Mantuan neighbors in the character of Melibœus.

MELIBŒUS

BENEATH the shade which beechen boughs diffuse,
You, Tit'rus, entertain your sylvan Muse:
Round the wide world in banishment we roam,
Forc'd from our pleasing fields and native home;
While, stretch'd at ease, you sing your happy loves,
And Amaryllis fills the shady groves.

TITYRUS

These blessings, friend, a deity bestow'd;
For never can I deem him less than god.
The tender firstlings of my woolly breed
Shall on his holy altar often bleed.   10
He gave my kine to graze the flow'ry plain,
And to my pipe renew'd the rural strain.

MELIBŒUS

I envy not your fortune, but admire,
That, while the raging sword and wasteful fire
Destroy the wretched neighborhood around,
No hostile arms approach your happy ground.
Far diff'rent is my fate; my feeble goats
With pains I drive from their forsaken cotes:
And this, you see, I scarcely drag along,
Who, yeaning, on the rocks has left her young,   20
The hope and promise of my failing fold.
My loss, by dire portents, the gods foretold;
For, had I not been blind, I might have seen
Yon riven oak, the fairest of the green;
And the hoarse raven, on the blasted bough,
By croaking from the left, presag'd the coming blow.
But tell me, Tityrus, what heav'nly power
Preserv'd your fortunes in that fatal hour ?

TITYRUS

Fool that I was, I thought imperial Rome
Like Mantua, where on market days we come,   30
And thether drive our tender lambs from home.
So kids and whelps their sires and dams express,
And so the great I measur'd by the less.

But country towns, compar'd with her,
    appear
Like shrubs when lofty cypresses are near.

MELIBŒUS

What great occasion call'd you hence to
    Rome ?

TITYRUS

Freedom, which came at length, tho' slow
    to come.
Nor did my search of liberty begin,
Till my black hairs were chang'd upon my
    chin;
Nor Amaryllis would vouchsafe a look,   40
Till Galatea's meaner bonds I broke.
Till then a helpless, hopeless, homely
    swain,
I sought not freedom, nor aspir'd to gain:
Tho' many a victim from my folds was
    bought,
And many a cheese to country markets
    brought,
Yet all the little that I got, I spent,
And still return'd as empty as I went.

MELIBŒUS

We stood amaz'd to see your mistress
    mourn,
Unknowing that she pin'd for your re-
    turn;
We wonder'd why she kept her fruit so
    long,   50
For whom so late th' ungather'd apples
    hung.
But now the wonder ceases, since I see
She kept them only, Tityrus, for thee:
For thee the bubbling springs appear'd to
    mourn,
And whisp'ring pines made vows for thy
    return.

TITYRUS

What should I do ! While here I was en-
    chain'd,
No glimpse of godlike liberty remain'd;
Nor could I hope, in any place but there,
To find a god so present to my pray'r.
There first the youth of heav'nly birth I
    view'd,   60
For whom our monthly victims are re-
    new'd.
He heard my vows, and graciously decreed
My grounds to be restor'd, my former
    flocks to feed.

MELIBŒUS

O fortunate old man ! whose farm re-
    mains
For you sufficient, and requites your
    pains;
Tho' rushes overspread the neighb'ring
    plains,
Tho' here the marshy grounds approach
    your fields,
And there the soil a stony harvest yields.
Your teeming ewes shall no strange mead-
    ows try,
Nor fear a rot from tainted company.   70
Behold ! yon bord'ring fence of sallow trees
Is fraught with flow'rs, the flow'rs are
    fraught with bees:
The busy bees, with a soft murm'ring strain,
Invite to gentle sleep the lab'ring swain;
While, from the neighb'ring rock, with
    rural songs,
The pruner's voice the pleasing dream pro-
    longs;
Stockdoves and turtles tell their am'rous
    pain,
And, from the lofty elms, of love complain.

TITYRUS

Th' inhabitants of seas and skies shall
    change,
And fish on shore and stags in air shall
    range,   80
The banish'd Parthian dwell on Arar's
    brink,
And the blue German shall the Tigris
    drink,
Ere I, forsaking gratitude and truth,
Forget the figure of that godlike youth.

MELIBŒUS

But we must beg our bread in climes un-
    known,
Beneath the scorching or the freezing zone;
And some to far Oaxis shall be sold,
Or try the Libyan heat, or Scythian cold;
The rest among the Britons be confin'd,   89
A race of men from all the world dis-
    join'd.
O ! must the wretched exiles ever mourn,
Nor after length of rolling years return ?
Are we condemn'd by fate's unjust decree
No more our houses and our homes to
    see ?
Or shall we mount again the rural throne,
And rule the country kingdoms, once our
    own ?

Did we for these barbarians plant and
  sow ?
On these, on these, our happy fields be-
  stow ?
Good Heav'n ! what dire effects from
  civil discord flow !
Now let me graff my pears, and prune the
  vine ;   100
The fruit is theirs, the labor only mine.
Farewell, my pastures, my paternal stock,
My fruitful fields, and my more fruitful
  flock !
No more, my goats, shall I behold you
  climb
The steepy cliffs, or crop the flow'ry thyme !
No more, extended in the grot below,
Shall see you browsing on the mountain's
  brow
The prickly shrubs ; and after, on the bare,
Lean down the deep abyss, and hang in
  air.
No more my sheep shall sip the morn-
  ing dew ;   110
No more my song shall please the rural
  crew :
Adieu, my tuneful pipe ! and all the
  world, adieu !

TITYRUS

This night, at least, with me forget your
  care ;
Chestnuts and curds and cream shall be
  your fare :
The carpet-ground shall be with leaves o'er-
  spread,
And boughs shall weave a cov'ring for your
  head.
For see yon sunny hill the shade extends,
And curling smoke from cottages ascends.

THE SECOND PASTORAL

OR, ALEXIS

THE ARGUMENT

The commentators can by no means agree on
the person of Alexis, but are all of opinion
that some beautiful youth is meant by him, to
whom Virgil here makes love, in Corydon's
language and simplicity. His way of courtship is wholly pastoral : he complains of the
boy's coyness ; recommends himself for his
beauty and skill in piping ; invites the youth
into the country, where he promises him
the diversions of the place, with a suitable

present of nuts and apples ; but when he
finds nothing will prevail, he resolves to
quit his troublesome amour, and betake himself again to his former business.

YOUNG Corydon, th' unhappy shepherd
  swain,
The fair Alexis lov'd, but lov'd in vain ;
And underneath the beechen shade, alone,
Thus to the woods and mountains made
  his moan :
Is this, unkind Alexis, my reward ?
And must I die unpitied, and unheard ?
Now the green lizard in the grove is laid,
The sheep enjoy the coolness of the shade,
And Thestylis wild thyme and garlic beats
For harvest hinds, o'erspent with toil and
  heats ;   10
While in the scorching sun I trace in vain
Thy flying footsteps o'er the burning plain.
The creaking locusts with my voice con-
  spire,
They fried with heat, and I with fierce
  desire.
How much more easy was it to sustain
Proud Amaryllis and her haughty reign,
The scorns of young Menalcas, once my
  care,
Tho' he was black, and thou art heav'nly
  fair !
Trust not too much to that enchanting face ;
Beauty 's a charm, but soon the charm will
  pass.   20
White lilies lie neglected on the plain,
While dusky hyacinths for use remain.
My passion is thy scorn ; nor wilt thou
  know
What wealth I have, what gifts I can
  bestow ;
What stores my dairies and my folds con-
  tain —
A thousand lambs, that wander on the
  plain ;
New milk, that all the winter never fails,
And all the summer overflows the pails.
Amphion sung not sweeter to his herd,
When summon'd stones the Theban turrets
  rear'd.   30
Nor am I so deform'd ; for late I stood
Upon the margin of the briny flood :
The winds were still ; and, if the glass be
  true,
With Daphnis I may vie, tho' judg'd by
  you.
O leave the noisy town ! O come and see
Our country cots, and live content with me !

To wound the flying deer, and from their
　　cotes
With me to drive afield the browsing goats;
To pipe and sing, and, in our country strain,
To copy, or perhaps contend with Pan.　40
Pan taught to join with wax unequal reeds;
Pan loves the shepherds, and their flocks
　　he feeds.
Nor scorn the pipe: Amyntas, to be taught,
With all his kisses would my skill have
　　bought.
Of seven smooth joints a mellow pipe I
　　have,
Which with his dying breath Damœtas
　　gave,
And said: " This, Corydon, I leave to thee;
For only thou deserv'st it after me."
His eyes Amyntas durst not upward lift;
For much he grudg'd the praise, but more
　　the gift.　50
Besides, two kids, that in the valley stray'd,
I found by chance, and to my fold convey'd:
They drain two bagging udders every day;
And these shall be companions of thy play;
Both fleck'd with white, the true Arcadian
　　strain,
Which Thestylis had often begg'd in vain:
And she shall have them, if again she sues,
Since you the giver and the gift refuse.
Come to my longing arms, my lovely care,
And take the presents which the nymphs
　　prepare.　60
White lilies in full canisters they bring,
With all the glories of the purple spring.
The daughters of the flood have search'd
　　the mead
For violets pale, and cropp'd the poppy's
　　head,
The short narcissus and fair daffodil,
Pansies to please the sight, and cassia
　　sweet to smell;
And set soft hyacinths with iron blue,
To shade marsh marigolds of shining hue;
Some bound in order, others loosely strow'd,
To dress thy bow'r, and trim thy new
　　abode.　70
Myself will search our planted grounds at
　　home
For downy peaches and the glossy plum;
And thrash the chestnuts in the neighb'ring
　　grove,
Such as my Amaryllis us'd to love.
The laurel and the myrtle sweets agree,
And both in nosegays shall be bound for thee.
　　Ah, Corydon! ah, poor unhappy swain!

Alexis will thy homely gifts disdain:
Nor, shouldst thou offer all thy little store,
Will rich Iolas yield, but offer more.　80
What have I done, to name that wealthy
　　swain,
So powerful are his presents, mine so mean !
The boar amidst my crystal streams I bring;
And southern winds to blast my flow'ry
　　spring.
Ah, cruel creature, whom dost thou despise ?
The gods, to live in woods, have left the
　　skies;
And godlike Paris, in th' Idæan grove,
To Priam's wealth preferr'd Œnone's love.
In cities which she built let Pallas reign;
Tow'rs are for gods, but forests for the swain.
The greedy lioness the wolf pursues,　91
The wolf the kid, the wanton kid the browse;
Alexis, thou art chas'd by Corydon:
All follow sev'ral games, and each his own.
See, from afar, the fields no longer smoke;
The sweating steers, unharness'd from the
　　yoke,
Bring, as in triumph, back the crooked plow;
The shadows lengthen as the sun goes low.
Cool breezes now the raging heats remove:
Ah, cruel Heaven, that made no cure for
　　love !　100
I wish for balmy sleep, but wish in vain;
Love has no bounds in pleasure, or in pain.
What frenzy, shepherd, has thy soul pos-
　　sess'd ?
Thy vineyard lies half prun'd, and half un-
　　dress'd.
Quench, Corydon, thy long unanswer'd fire;
Mind what the common wants of life require:
On willow twigs employ thy weaving care,
And find an easier love, tho' not so fair.

THE THIRD PASTORAL

OR, PALÆMON

MENALCAS, DAMŒTAS, PALÆMON

THE ARGUMENT

Damœtas and Menalcas, after some smart
strokes of country raillery, resolve to try who
has the most skill at a song; and accordingly make their neighbor Palæmon judge
of their performances; who, after a full
hearing of both parties, declares himself
unfit for the decision of so weighty a controversy, and leaves the victory undetermin'd.

MENALCAS

Ho, swain, what shepherd owns those ragged
sheep ?

DAMŒTAS

Ægon's they are: he gave 'em me to keep.

MENALCAS

Unhappy sheep, of an unhappy swain !   ⎫
While he Neæra courts, but courts in vain,   ⎬
And fears that I the damsel shall obtain;   ⎭
Thou, varlet, dost thy master's gains de-
   vour;
Thou milk'st his ewes, and often twice an
   hour;
Of grass and fodder thou defraud'st the
   dams,
And of their mothers' dugs the starving
   lambs.

DAMŒTAS

Good words, young catamite, at least to
   men.   10
We know who did your business, how, and
   when;
And in what chapel too you play'd your ⎫
   prize,   ⎪
And what the goats observ'd with leer- ⎬
   ing eyes: ⎪
The nymphs were kind, and laugh'd; and   ⎭
   there your safety lies.

MENALCAS

Yes, when I cropp'd the hedges of the leys,
Cut Micon's tender vines, and stole the
   stays !

DAMŒTAS

Or rather, when, beneath yon ancient oak,
The bow of Daphnis and the shafts you
   broke,
When the fair boy receiv'd the gift of
   right;
And, but for mischief, you had died for
   spite.   20

MENALCAS

What nonsense would the fool thy master
   prate,
When thou, his knave, canst talk at such a
   rate !
Did I not see you, rascal, did I not,
When you lay snug to snap young Damon's
   goat ?
His mungril bark'd; I ran to his relief,

And cried: " There, there he goes ! stop,
   stop the thief ! "
Discover'd, and defeated of your prey,
You skulk'd behind the fence, and sneak'd
   away.

DAMŒTAS

An honest man may freely take his own;
The goat was mine, by singing fairly won.
A solemn match was made; he lost the ⎫
   prize.   31 ⎬
Ask Damon, ask if he the debt denies.   ⎪
I think he dares not; if he does, he lies. ⎭

MENALCAS

Thou sing with him, thou booby ! Never
   pipe
Was so profan'd to touch that blubber'd
   lip.
Dunce at the best ! in streets but scarce
   allow'd
To tickle, on thy straw, the stupid crowd.

DAMŒTAS

To bring it to the trial, will you dare
Our pipes, our skill, our voices, to com-
   pare ?
My brinded heifer to the stake I lay;   40
Two thriving calves she suckles twice a
   day,
And twice besides her beestings never fail
To store the dairy with a brimming pail.
Now back your singing with an equal stake.

MENALCAS

That should be seen, if I had one to make.
You know too well, I feed my father's
   flock;
What can I wager from the common stock ?
A stepdame too I have, a cursed she,
Who rules my henpeck'd sire, and orders
   me.
Both number twice a day the milky dams;
And once she takes the tale of all the
   lambs.   51
But, since you will be mad, and since you
   may
Suspect my courage, if I should not lay,
The pawn I proffer shall be full as good:
Two bowls I have, well turn'd, of beechen
   wood;
Both by divine Alcimedon were made;
To neither of them yet the lip is laid.
The lids are ivy; grapes in clusters lurk
Beneath the carving of the curious work.

Two figures on the sides emboss'd ap-
　　pear —　　　　　　　　　　　60
Conon, and what 's his name who made
　　the sphere,
And shew'd the seasons of the sliding
　　year,
Instructed in his trade the lab'ring swain,
And when to reap, and when to sow the
　　grain ?

DAMŒTAS

And I have two, to match your pair, at
　　home:
The wood the same; from the same hand
　　they come
(The kimbo handles seem with bear's-foot
　　carv'd),
And never yet to table have been serv'd;
Where Orpheus on his lyre laments his love,
With beasts encompass'd, and a dancing
　　grove.　　　　　　　　　　　70
But these, nor all the proffers you can
　　make,
Are worth the heifer which I set to
　　stake.

MENALCAS

No more delays, vain boaster, but begin !
I prophesy beforehand I shall win.
Palæmon shall be judge how ill you rhyme;
I 'll teach you how to brag another time.

DAMŒTAS

Rhymer, come on, and do the worst you
　　can !
I fear not you, nor yet a better man.
With silence, neighbor, and attention, wait;
For 't is a business of a high debate.　　80

PALÆMON

Sing then; the shade affords a proper
　　place:
The trees are cloth'd with leaves, the fields
　　with grass;
The blossoms blow, the birds on bushes sing,
And Nature has accomplish'd all the spring.
The challenge to Damœtas shall belong;
Menalcas shall sustain his undersong.
Each in his turn your tuneful numbers
　　bring;
By turns the tuneful Muses love to sing.

DAMŒTAS

From the great Father of the Gods above
My Muse begins; for all is full of Jove: 90

To Jove the care of heav'n and earth be-
　　longs;
My flocks he blesses, and he loves my songs.

MENALCAS

Me Phœbus loves; for he my Muse inspires,
And in her songs the warmth he gave re-
　　quires.
For him, the god of shepherds and their
　　sheep,
My blushing hyacinths and my bays I keep.

DAMŒTAS

My Phyllis me with pelted apples plies;
Then tripping to the woods the wanton
　　hies,
And wishes to be seen before she flies.

MENALCAS

But fair Amyntas comes unask'd to
　　me,　　　　　　　　　　　　100
And offers love, and sits upon my knee:
Not Delia to my dogs is known so well
　　as he.

DAMŒTAS

To the dear mistress of my lovesick mind,
Her swain a pretty present has design'd:
I saw two stockdoves billing, and ere long
Will take the nest, and hers shall be the
　　young.

MENALCAS

Ten ruddy wildings in the wood I found,
And stood on tiptoes, reaching from the
　　ground:
I sent Amyntas all my present store; 109
And will, to-morrow, send as many more.

DAMŒTAS

The lovely maid lay panting in my arms,
And all she said and did was full of charms.
Winds, on your wings to heav'n her accents
　　bear;
Such words as heav'n alone is fit to hear.

MENALCAS

Ah ! what avails it me, my love's delight,
To call you mine, when absent from my sight !
I hold the nets, while you pursue the prey,
And must not share the dangers of the day.

DAMŒTAS

I keep my birthday: send my Phyllis home;
At shearing time, Iolas, you may come. 120

MENALCAS

With Phyllis I am more in grace than you; ⎫
Her sorrow did my parting steps pursue: ⎪
"Adieu, my dear," she said, "a long ⎬
    adieu!" ⎭

DAMŒTAS

The nightly wolf is baneful to the fold,
Storms to the wheat, to buds the bitter
    cold;
But, from my frowning fair, more ills I
    find,
Than from the wolves, and storms, and
    winter wind.

MENALCAS

The kids with pleasure browse the bushy
    plain;
The show'rs are grateful to the swelling
    grain;
To teeming ewes the sallow's tender tree; 130
But, more than all the world, my love to me.

DAMŒTAS

Pollio my rural verse vouchsafes to read:
A heifer, Muses, for your patron breed.

MENALCAS

My Pollio writes himself: a bull be bred,
With spurning heels, and with a butting head.

DAMŒTAS

Who Pollio loves, and who his Muse ad-
    mires,
Let Pollio's fortune crown his full desires.
Let myrrh instead of thorn his fences fill,
And show'rs of honey from his oaks distil.

MENALCAS

Who hates not living Bavius, let him be, 140
Dead Mævius, damn'd to love thy works and
    thee!
The same ill taste of sense would serve to
    join
Dog-foxes in the yoke, and shear the swine.

DAMŒTAS

Ye boys, who pluck the flow'rs, and spoil
    the spring,
Beware the secret snake that shoots a sting.

MENALCAS

Graze not too near the banks, my jolly sheep;
The ground is false, the running streams are
    deep:

See, they have caught the father of the
    flock,
Who dries his fleece upon the neighb'ring
    rock.

DAMŒTAS

From rivers drive the kids, and sling your
    hook; 150
Anon I'll wash 'em in the shallow brook.

MENALCAS

To fold, my flock! When milk is dried with
    heat,
In vain the milkmaid tugs an empty teat.

DAMŒTAS

How lank my bulls from plenteous pasture
    come!
But love, that drains the herd, destroys the
    groom.

MENALCAS

My flocks are free from love, yet look so
    thin,
Their bones are barely cover'd with their
    skin.
What magic has bewitch'd the woolly dams,
And what ill eyes beheld the tender lambs?

DAMŒTAS

Say, where the round of heav'n, which ⎫
    all contains, 160 ⎪
To three short ells on earth our sight re- ⎬
    strains: ⎪
Tell that, and rise a Phœbus for thy pains. ⎭

MENALCAS

Nay, tell me first, in what new region
    springs
A flow'r that bears inscrib'd the names of
    kings;
And thou shalt gain a present as divine
As Phœbus' self; for Phyllis shall be thine.

PALÆMON

So nice a diff'rence in your singing lies,
That both have won, or both deserv'd the
    prize.
Rest equal happy both; and all who prove
The bitter sweets, and pleasing pains, of
    love. 170
Now dam the ditches, and the floods re-
    strain;
Their moisture has already drench'd the
    plain.

THE FOURTH PASTORAL

OR, POLLIO

THE ARGUMENT

The poet celebrates the birthday of Saloninus, the son of Pollio, born in the consulship of his father, after the taking of Salonæ, a city in Dalmatia. Many of the verses are translated from one of the Sibyls, who prophesy of our Savior's birth.

SICILIAN Muse, begin a loftier strain!
Tho' lowly shrubs, and trees that shade the plain,
Delight not all; Sicilian Muse, prepare
To make the vocal woods deserve a consul's care.
The last great age, foretold by sacred rhymes,
Renews its finish'd course: Saturnian times
Roll round again; and mighty years, begun
From their first orb, in radiant circles run.
The base degenerate iron offspring ends;
A golden progeny from heav'n descends. 10
O chaste Lucina, speed the mother's pains,
And haste the glorious birth! thy own Apollo reigns!
The lovely boy, with his auspicious face, ⎫
Shall Pollio's consulship and triumph grace; ⎬
Majestic months set out with him to their appointed race. ⎭
The father banish'd virtue shall restore,
And crimes shall threat the guilty world no more.
The son shall lead the life of gods, and be
By gods and heroes seen, and gods and heroes see.
The jarring nations he in peace shall bind, 20
And with paternal virtues rule mankind.
Unbidden Earth shall wreathing ivy bring, ⎫
And fragrant herbs (the promises of spring), ⎬
As her first off'rings to her infant king. ⎭
The goats with strutting dugs shall homeward speed,
And lowing herds secure from lions feed.
His cradle shall with rising flow'rs be crown'd:
The serpent's brood shall die; the sacred ground
Shall weeds and pois'nous plants refuse to bear;
Each common bush shall Syrian roses wear. 30

But when heroic verse his youth shall raise,
And form it to hereditary praise,
Unlabor'd harvests shall the fields adorn,
And cluster'd grapes shall blush on every thorn;
The knotted oaks shall show'rs of honey weep,
And thro' the matted grass the liquid gold shall creep.
Yet of old fraud some footsteps shall remain:
The merchant still shall plow the deep for gain;
Great cities shall with walls be compass'd round,
And sharpen'd shares shall vex the fruitful ground; 40
Another Tiphys shall new seas explore;
Another Argo land the chiefs upon th' Iberian shore;
Another Helen other wars create,
And great Achilles urge the Trojan fate.
But when to ripen'd manhood he shall grow,
The greedy sailer shall the seas forego;
No keel shall cut the waves for foreign ware,
For every soil shall every product bear.
The laboring hind his oxen shall disjoin; ⎫
No plow shall hurt the glebe, no pruning hook the vine; ⎬ 50
Nor wool shall in dissembled colors shine. ⎭
But the luxurious father of the fold,
With native purple, or unborrow'd gold,
Beneath his pompous fleece shall proudly sweat;
And under Tyrian robes the lamb shall bleat.
The Fates, when they this happy web have spun,
Shall bless the sacred clew, and bid it smoothly run.
Mature in years, to ready honors move,
O of celestial seed! O foster son of Jove!
See, lab'ring Nature calls thee to sustain 60
The nodding frame of heav'n, and earth, and main!
See to their base restor'd, earth, seas, and air;
And joyful ages, from behind, in crowding ranks appear.
To sing thy praise, would Heav'n my breath prolong,
Infusing spirits worthy such a song,

Not Thracian Orpheus should transcend
    my lays,
Nor Linus crown'd with never - fading
    bays;
Tho' each his heav'nly parent should in-
    spire;
The Muse instruct the voice, and Phœbus
    tune the lyre.
Should Pan contend in verse, and thou my
    theme,   70
Arcadian judges should their god con-
    demn.
Begin, auspicious boy, to cast about
Thy infant eyes, and, with a smile, thy
    mother single out:
Thy mother well deserves that short de-
    light,
The nauseous qualms of ten long months
    and travel to requite.
Then smile: the frowning infant's doom is
    read;
No god shall crown the board, nor goddess
    bless the bed.

THE FIFTH PASTORAL

OR, DAPHNIS

THE ARGUMENT

Mopsus and Menalcas, two very expert shepherds at a song, begin one by consent to the
memory of Daphnis, who is suppos'd by the
best critics to represent Julius Cæsar. Mopsus laments his death; Menalcas proclaims
his divinity; the whole eclogue consisting of
an elegy and an apotheosis.

MENALCAS

SINCE on the downs our flocks together
    feed,
And since my voice can match your tune-
    ful reed,
Why sit we not beneath the grateful
    shade
Which hazels, intermix'd with elms, have
    made ?

MOPSUS

Whether you please that sylvan scene to
    take,
Where whistling winds uncertain shadows
    make;
Or will you to the cooler cave succeed,
Whose mouth the curling vines have over-
    spread ?

MENALCAS

Your merit and your years command the
    choice;
Amyntas only rivals you in voice.   10

MOPSUS

What will not that presuming shepherd
    dare,
Who thinks his voice with Phœbus may
    compare ?

MENALCAS

Begin you first: if either Alcon's praise,
Or dying Phyllis, have inspir'd your lays;
If her you mourn, or Codrus you commend,
Begin, and Tityrus your flock shall tend.

MOPSUS

Or shall I rather the sad verse repeat,
Which on the beech's bark I lately writ ?
I writ, and sung betwixt. Now bring the
    swain
Whose voice you boast, and let him try the
    strain.   20

MENALCAS

Such as the shrub to the tall olive shows,
Or the pale sallow to the blushing rose;
Such is his voice, if I can judge aright,
Compar'd to thine, in sweetness and in
    height.

MOPSUS

No more, but sit and hear the promis'd
    lay;
The gloomy grotto makes a doubtful day.
The nymphs about the breathless body wait
Of Daphnis, and lament his cruel fate.
The trees and floods were witness to their
    tears;
At length the rumor reach'd his mother's
    ears.   30
The wretched parent, with a pious haste,
Came running, and his lifeless limbs em-
    brac'd.
She sigh'd, she sobb'd; and, furious with
    despair,
She rent her garments, and she tore her
    hair,
Accusing all the gods, and every star.
The swains forgot their sheep, nor near the
    brink
Of running waters brought their herds to
    drink.
The thirsty cattle, of themselves, abstain'd

From water, and their grassy fare dis-
  dain'd.
The death of Daphnis woods and hills
  deplore;   40
They cast the sound to Libya's desart
  shore;
The Libyan lions hear, and hearing roar.
Fierce tigers Daphnis taught the yoke to
  bear,
And first with curling ivy dress'd the spear:
Daphnis did rites to Bacchus first ordain,
And holy revels for his reeling train.
As vines the trees, as grapes the vines
  adorn,
As bulls the herds, and fields the yellow
  corn;
So bright a splendor, so divine a grace,
The glorious Daphnis cast on his illustrious
  race.   50
When envious Fate the godlike Daphnis
  took,
Our guardian gods the fields and plains
  forsook;
Pales no longer swell'd the teeming grain,
Nor Phœbus fed his oxen on the plain;
No fruitful crop the sickly fields return,
But oats and darnel choke the rising corn;
And where the vales with violets once were
  crown'd,
Now knotty burs and thorns disgrace the
  ground.
Come, shepherds, come, and strow with
  leaves the plain;
Such funeral rites your Daphnis did or-
  dain.   60
With cypress boughs the crystal fountains
  hide,
And softly let the running waters glide.
A lasting monument to Daphnis raise,
With this inscription to record his praise:
" Daphnis, the fields' delight, the shepherd's
  love,
Renown'd on earth, and deified above;
Whose flock excell'd the fairest on the plains,
But less than he himself surpass'd the
  swains."

Menalcas

O heavenly poet ! such thy verse appears,
So sweet, so charming to my ravish'd ears,
As to the weary swain, with cares oppress'd,
Beneath the sylvan shade, refreshing rest;
As to the feverish traveler, when first   73
He finds a crystal stream to quench his thirst.
In singing, as in piping, you excel;

And scarce your master could perform so
  well.
O fortunate young man, at least your lays
Are next to his, and claim the second praise.
Such as they are, my rural songs I join,
To raise our Daphnis to the pow'rs di-
  vine;   80
For Daphnis was so good, to love what-
  e'er was mine.

Mopsus

How is my soul with such a promise rais'd !
For both the boy was worthy to be prais'd,
And Stimichon has often made me long
To hear, like him, so soft, so sweet a song.

Menalcas

Daphnis, the guest of heav'n, with wond'ring
  eyes,
Views, in the Milky Way, the starry skies,
And far beneath him, from the shining sphere,
Beholds the moving clouds, and rolling year.
For this, with cheerful cries the woods
  resound,   90
The purple spring arrays the various
  ground,
The nymphs and shepherds dance, and Pan
  himself is crown'd.
The wolf no longer prowls for nightly spoils,
Nor birds the springes fear, nor stags the
  toils;
For Daphnis reigns above, and deals from
  thence
His mother's milder beams, and peaceful in-
  fluence.
The mountain tops unshorn, the rocks re-
  joice;
The lowly shrubs partake of human voice.
Assenting Nature, with a gracious nod,
Proclaims him, and salutes the new-admit-
  ted god.   100
Be still propitious, ever good to thine !
Behold, four hallow'd altars we design;
And two to thee, and two to Phœbus rise;
On both are offer'd annual sacrifice.
The holy priests, at each returning year,
Two bowls of milk, and two of oil shall
  bear;
And I myself the guests with friendly
  bowls will cheer.
Two goblets will I crown with sparkling
  wine,
The gen'rous vintage of the Chian vine;
These will I pour to thee, and make the
  nectar thine.   110

In winter shall the genial feast be made
Before the fire; by summer, in the shade.
Damœtas shall perform the rites divine,
And Lyctian Ægon in the song shall join.
Alphesibœus, tripping, shall advance,
And mimic Satyrs in his antic dance.
When to the nymphs our annual rites we
    pay,
And when our fields with victims we survey;
While savage boars delight in shady woods,
And finny fish inhabit in the floods;   120
While bees on thyme, and locusts feed on
    dew,
Thy grateful swains these honors shall
    renew.
Such honors as we pay to pow'rs divine,
To Bacchus and to Ceres, shall be thine.
Such annual honors shall be giv'n; and
    thou
Shalt hear, and shalt condemn thy suppli-
    ants to their vow.

MOPSUS

What present worth thy verse can Mop-
    sus find!
Not the soft whispers of the southern
    wind,
That play thro' trembling trees, delight
    me more;
Nor murm'ring billows on the sounding
    shore;   130
Nor winding streams, that thro' the valley
    glide,
And the scarce-cover'd pebbles gently
    chide.

MENALCAS

Receive you first this tuneful pipe, the
    same
That play'd my Corydon's unhappy flame;
The same that sung Neæra's conqu'ring
    eyes,
And, had the judge been just, had won the
    prize.

MOPSUS

Accept from me this sheephook in ex-
    change;
The handle brass, the knobs in equal range.
Antigenes, with kisses, often tried
To beg this present, in his beauty's pride,
When youth and love are hard to be de-
    nied.   141
But what I could refuse to his request,
Is yours unask'd, for you deserve it best.

THE SIXTH PASTORAL

OR, SILENUS

THE ARGUMENT

Two young shepherds, Chromis and Mnasylus, having been often promis'd a song by Silenus, chance to catch him asleep in this pastoral; where they bind him hand and foot, and then claim his promise. Silenus, finding they would be put off no longer, begins his song, in which he describes the formation of the universe, and the original of animals, according to the Epicurean philosophy; and then runs thro' the most surprising transformations which have happen'd in Nature since her birth. This pastoral was design'd as a compliment to Syro the Epicurean, who instructed Virgil and Varus in the principles of that philosophy. Silenus acts as tutor, Chromis and Mnasylus as the two pupils.

I FIRST transferr'd to Rome Sicilian strains;
Nor blush'd the Doric Muse to dwell on
    Mantuan plains.
But when I tried her tender voice, too
    young,
And fighting kings and bloody battles sung,
Apollo check'd my pride, and bade me feed
My fatt'ning flocks, nor dare beyond the
    reed.
Admonish'd thus, while every pen prepares
To write thy praises, Varus, and thy wars,
My past'ral Muse her humble tribute brings,
And yet not wholly uninspir'd she sings. 10
For all who read, and, reading, not disdain
These rural poems, and their lowly strain,
The name of Varus oft inscrib'd shall see ⎤
In every grove, and every vocal tree, ⎬
And all the sylvan reign shall sing of ⎦
    thee:
Thy name, to Phœbus and the Muses ⎤
    known, ⎪
Shall in the front of every page be shown; ⎬
For he who sings thy praise secures his ⎦
    own.
    Proceed, my Muse!—Two Satyrs, on
    the ground,
Stretch'd at his ease, their sire Silenus
    found.   20
Doz'd with his fumes, and heavy with his ⎤
    load, ⎪
They found him snoring in his dark abode, ⎬
And seiz'd with youthful arms the drunken ⎦
    god.
His rosy wreath was dropp'd not long before,

Borne by the tide of wine, and floating on
the floor.
His empty can, with ears half worn away,
Was hung on high, to boast the triumph of
the day.
Invaded thus, for want of better bands,
His garland they unstring, and bind his
hands;
For, by the fraudful god deluded long,   30
They now resolve to have their promis'd
song.
Ægle came in, to make their party good —
The fairest Nais of the neighboring flood —
And, while he stares around with stupid
eyes,
His brows with berries, and his temples,
dyes.
He finds the fraud, and, with a smile, de-
mands
On what design the boys had bound his
hands.
"Loose me," he cried, " 't was impudence to
find
A sleeping god; 't is sacrilege to bind.
To you the promis'd poem I will pay;   40
The nymph shall be rewarded in her way."
He rais'd his voice; and soon a num'rous
throng
Of tripping Satyrs crowded to the song;
And sylvan Fauns and savage beasts ad-
vanc'd,
And nodding forests to the numbers danc'd.
Not by Hæmonian hills the Thracian bard, ⎫
Nor awful Phœbus was on Pindus heard ⎬
With deeper silence, or with more regard. ⎭
He sung the secret seeds of nature's frame;
How seas, and earth, and air, and active
flame,   50
Fell thro' the mighty void, and, in their fall,
Were blindly gather'd in this goodly ball.
The tender soil then, stiff'ning by degrees,
Shut from the bounded earth the bounding
seas.
Then earth and ocean various forms disclose,
And a new sun to the new world arose;
And mists, condens'd to clouds, obscure the
sky;
And clouds, dissolv'd, the thirsty ground
supply;
The rising trees the lofty mountains ⎫
grace; ⎬
The lofty mountains feed the savage ⎬
race,   60 ⎬
Yet few, and strangers, in th' unpeopled ⎬
place. ⎭

From thence the birth of man the song pur-
sued,
And how the world was lost, and how re-
new'd;
The reign of Saturn, and the Golden Age;
Prometheus' theft, and Jove's avenging rage;
The cries of Argonauts for Hylas drown'd,
With whose repeated name the shores re-
sound;
Then mourns the madness of the Cretan
queen —
Happy for her if herds had never been.
What fury, wretched woman, seiz'd thy
breast !   70
The maids of Argos (tho', with rage pos-
sess'd,
Their imitated lowings fill'd the grove)
Yet shunn'd the guilt of thy prepost'rous
love,
Nor sought the youthful husband of the ⎫
herd; ⎬
Tho' lab'ring yokes on their own necks ⎬
they fear'd, ⎬
And felt for budding horns on their smooth ⎬
foreheads rear'd. ⎭
Ah, wretched queen, you range the path-
less wood,
While on a flow'ry bank he chaws the cud,
Or sleeps in shades, or thro' the forest
roves,
And roars with anguish for his absent
loves. —   80
"Ye nymphs, with toils his forest walk
surround,
And trace his wand'ring footsteps on the
ground.
But, ah ! perhaps my passion he disdains,
And courts the milky mothers of the
plains.
We search th' ungrateful fugitive abroad,
While they at home sustain his happy
load." —
He sung the lover's fraud; the longing
maid,
With golden fruit, like all the sex, be-
tray'd;
The sisters mourning for their brother's loss;
Their bodies hid in barks, and furr'd with
moss;   90
How each a rising alder now appears,
And o'er the Po distils her gummy tears:
Then sung, how Gallus, by a Muse's hand,
Was led and welcom'd to the sacred strand;
The senate rising to salute their guest;
And Linus thus their gratitude express'd:

" Receive this present, by the Muses made,
The pipe on which th' Ascræan pastor
    play'd;
With which of old he charm'd the savage
    train,
And call'd the mountain ashes to the plain.
Sing thou on this thy Phœbus, and the
    wood   101
Where once his fane of Parian marble stood;
On this his ancient oracles rehearse,
And with new numbers grace the God of
    Verse."
Why should I sing the double Scylla's fate ?
(The first by love transform'd, the last by
    hate —
A beauteous maid above; but magic arts
With barking dogs deform'd her nether
    parts:)
What vengeance on the passing fleet she
    pour'd,
The master frighted, and the mates de-
    vour'd.   110
Then ravish'd Philomel the song express'd;
The crime reveal'd; the sister's cruel feast;
And how in fields the lapwing Tereus reigns,
The warbling nightingale in woods com-
    plains;
While Progne makes on chimney tops her
    moan,
And hovers o'er the palace once her own.
Whatever songs besides the Delphian god
Had taught the laurels, and the Spartan
    flood,
Silenus sung: the vales his voice rebound,
And carry to the skies the sacred sound.   120
And now the setting sun had warn'd the
    swain
To call his counted cattle from the plain:
Yet still th' unwearied sire pursues the
    tuneful strain,
Till, unperceiv'd, the heav'ns with stars
    were hung,
And sudden night surpris'd the yet un-
    finish'd song.

THE SEVENTH PASTORAL

OR, MELIBŒUS

THE ARGUMENT

Melibœus here gives us the relation of a sharp
poetical contest between Thyrsis and Corydon, at which he himself and Daphnis were
present; who both declar'd for Corydon.

BENEATH a holm repair'd two jolly swains
(Their sheep and goats together graz'd the
    plains),
Both young Arcadians, both alike inspir'd
To sing, and answer as the song requir'd.
Daphnis, as umpire, took the middle seat,
And fortune thether led my weary feet;
For, while I fenc'd my myrtles from the cold,
The father of my flock had wander'd from
    the fold.
Of Daphnis I enquir'd: he, smiling, said:
" Dismiss your fear;" and pointed where
    he fed;   10
" And, if no greater cares disturb your mind,
Sit here with us, in covert of the wind.
Your lowing heifers, of their own accord,
At wat'ring time will seek the neighb'ring
    ford.
Here wanton Mincius winds along the meads,
And shades his happy banks with bending
    reeds.
And see, from yon old oak that mates the
    skies,
How black the clouds of swarming bees
    arise."
What should I do ! Nor was Alcippe nigh,
Nor absent Phyllis could my care supply,   20
To house, and feed by hand my weaning
    lambs,
And drain the strutting udders of their
    dams.
Great was the strife betwixt the singing
    swains;
And I preferr'd my pleasure to my gains.
Alternate rhyme the ready champions chose:
These Corydon rehears'd, and Thyrsis those.

CORYDON

Ye Muses, ever fair, and ever young,
Assist my numbers, and inspire my song.
With all my Codrus, O inspire my breast !
For Codrus, after Phœbus, sings the best.   30
Or, if my wishes have presum'd too high,
And stretch'd their bounds beyond mortal-
    ity,
The praise of artful numbers I resign,
And hang my pipe upon the sacred pine.

THYRSIS

Arcadian swains, your youthful poet crown
With ivy wreaths; tho' surly Codrus frown:
Or, if he blast my Muse with envious praise,
Then fence my brows with amulets of bays,
Lest his ill arts, or his malicious tongue,   39
Should poison, or bewitch my growing song.

CORYDON

These branches of a stag, this tusky boar
(The first essay of arms untried before)
Young Micon offers, Delia, to thy shrine:
But speed his hunting with thy pow'r di-
    vine;
Thy statue then of Parian stone shall stand;
Thy legs in buskins with a purple band.

THYRSIS

This bowl of milk, these cakes (our ⎤
    country fare),   ⎬
For thee, Priapus, yearly we prepare, ⎪
Because a little garden is thy care; ⎦
But, if the falling lambs increase my fold,
Thy marble statue shall be turn'd to gold. 51

CORYDON

Fair Galatea, with thy silver feet,
O, whiter than the swan, and more than
    Hybla sweet,
Tall as a poplar, taper as the bole,
Come, charm thy shepherd, and restore my
    soul !
Come, when my lated sheep at night return,
And crown the silent hours, and stop the
    rosy morn !

THYRSIS

May I become as abject in thy sight
As seaweed on the shore, and black as night;
Rough as a bur; deform'd like him who
    chaws   60
Sardinian herbage to contract his jaws;
Such and so monstrous let thy swain ap-
    pear,
If one day's absence looks not like a year.
Hence from the field, for shame: the flock
    deserves
No better feeding while the shepherd
    starves.

CORYDON

Ye mossy springs, inviting easy sleep,
Ye trees, whose leafy shades those mossy
    fountains keep,
Defend my flock ! The summer heats are
    near,
And blossoms on the swelling vines ap-
    pear.

THYRSIS

With heapy fires our cheerful hearth is
    crown'd;   70
And firs for torches in the woods abound:

We fear not more the winds and wintry
    cold,
Than streams the banks, or wolves the
    bleating fold.

CORYDON

Our woods, with juniper and chestnuts ⎤
    crown'd,   ⎪
With falling fruits and berries paint the ⎪
    ground;   ⎬
And lavish Nature laughs, and strows ⎪
    her stores around: ⎦
But, if Alexis from our mountains fly,
Ev'n running rivers leave their channels
    dry.

THYRSIS

Parch'd are the plains, and frying is the
    field,
Nor with'ring vines their juicy vintage
    yield;   80
But, if returning Phyllis bless the plain, ⎤
The grass revives, the woods are green ⎪
    again,   ⎬
And Jove descends in show'rs of kindly ⎪
    rain.   ⎦

CORYDON

The poplar is by great Alcides worn;
The brows of Phœbus his own bays adorn;
The branching vine the jolly Bacchus loves;
The Cyprian queen delights in myrtle
    groves;
With hazel Phyllis crowns her flowing ⎤
    hair;   ⎪
And, while she loves that common wreath ⎬
    to wear,   ⎪
Nor bays, nor myrtle boughs, with hazel ⎪
    shall compare.   90 ⎦

THYRSIS

The tow'ring ash is fairest in the woods;
In gardens pines, and poplars by the floods:
But, if my Lycidas will ease my pains,
And often visit our forsaken plains,
To him the tow'ring ash shall yield in
    woods,
In gardens pines, and poplars by the floods.

MELIBŒUS

These rhymes I did to memory commend,
When vanquish'd Thyrsis did in vain con-
    tend;
Since when 't is Corydon among the swains,
Young Corydon without a rival reigns. 100

THE EIGHTH PASTORAL

OR, PHARMACEUTRIA

THE ARGUMENT

This pastoral contains the songs of Damon and Alphesibœus. The first of 'em bewails the loss of his mistress, and repines at the success of his rival Mopsus. The other repeats the charms of some enchantress, who endeavor'd by her spells and magic to make Daphnis in love with her.

THE mournful Muse of two despairing swains,
The love rejected, and the lovers' pains;
To which the salvage lynxes list'ning stood,
The rivers stood on heaps, and stopp'd the running flood;
The hungry herd their needful food refuse —
Of two despairing swains, I sing the mournful Muse.
　Great Pollio! thou, for whom thy Rome prepares
The ready triumph of thy finish'd wars,
Whether Timavus or th' Illyrian coast,
Whatever land or sea thy presence boast; 10
Is there an hour in fate reserv'd for me,
To sing thy deeds in numbers worthy thee ?
In numbers like to thine could I rehearse
Thy lofty tragic scenes, thy labor'd verse,
The world another Sophocles in thee,
Another Homer should behold in me.
Amidst thy laurels let this ivy twine:
Thine was my earliest Muse; my latest shall be thine.
　Scarce from the world the shades of night withdrew,
Scarce were the flocks refresh'd with morning dew, 20
When Damon, stretch'd beneath an olive shade,
And wildly staring upwards, thus inveigh'd
Against the conscious gods, and curs'd the cruel maid:
　" Star of the morning, why dost thou delay ?
Come, Lucifer, drive on the lagging day,
While I my Nisa's perjur'd faith deplore —
Witness, ye pow'rs, by whom she falsely swore !

The gods, alas ! are witnesses in vain;
Yet shall my dying breath to Heav'n complain.
Begin with me, my flute, the sweet Mænalian strain. 30
　" The pines of Mænalus, the vocal grove,
Are ever full of verse, and full of love:
They hear the hinds, they hear their god complain,
Who suffer'd not the reeds to rise in vain.
Begin with me, my flute, the sweet Mænalian strain.
　" Mopsus triumphs; he weds the willing fair :
When such is Nisa's choice, what lover can despair !
Now griffons join with mares; another age
Shall see the hound and hind their thirst assuage,
Promiscuous at the spring. Prepare the lights, 40
O Mopsus, and perform the bridal rites.
Scatter thy nuts among the scrambling boys:
Thine is the night, and thine the nuptial joys.
For thee the sun declines: O happy swain !
Begin with me, my flute, the sweet Mænalian strain.
　" O, Nisa, justly to thy choice condemn'd !
Whom hast thou taken, whom hast thou contemn'd !
For him, thou hast refus'd my browsing herd,
Scorn'd my thick eyebrows, and my shaggy beard.
Unhappy Damon sighs and sings in vain, 50
While Nisa thinks no god regards a lover's pain.
Begin with me, my flute, the sweet Mænalian strain.
　" I view'd thee first, (how fatal was the view !)
And led thee where the ruddy wildings grew,
High on the planted hedge, and wet with morning dew.
Then scarce the bending branches I could win;
The callow down began to clothe my chin.
I saw; I perish'd; yet indulg'd my pain.
Begin with me, my flute, the sweet Mænalian strain.
　" I know thee, Love ! in desarts thou wert bred, 60
And at the dugs of salvage tigers fed;

Alien of birth, usurper of the plains !
Begin with me, my flute, the sweet Mæna-
    lian strains.
" Relentless Love the cruel mother led
The blood of her unhappy babes to shed.
Love lent the sword; the mother struck
    the blow;
Inhuman she; but more inhuman thou:
Alien of birth, usurper of the plains !
Begin with me, my flute, the sweet Mæna-
    lian strains.
" Old doting Nature, change thy course
    anew,   70
And let the trembling lamb the wolf pur-
    sue;
Let oaks now glitter with Hesperian fruit,
And purple daffodils from alder shoot;
Fat amber let the tamarisk distil,
And hooting owls contend with swans in
    skill;
Hoarse Tit'rus strive with Orpheus in the
    woods,
And challenge fam'd Arion on the floods.
Or, O ! let Nature cease, and Chaos reign !
Begin with me, my flute, the sweet Mæna-
    lian strain.
" Let earth be sea; and let the whelm-
    ing tide   80
The lifeless limbs of luckless Damon
    hide:
Farewell, ye secret woods, and shady
    groves,
Haunts of my youth, and conscious of my
    loves !
From yon high cliff I plunge into the ⎫
    main: ⎪
Take the last present of thy dying swain; ⎬
And cease, my silent flute, the sweet   ⎪
    Mænalian strain."   ⎭
  Now take your turns, ye Muses, to re-
    hearse
His friend's complaints, and mighty magic
    verse:
" Bring running water; bind those altars
    round
With fillets, and with vervain strow the
    ground: 90
Make fat with frankincense the sacred
    fires,
To re-inflame my Daphnis with desires.
'T is done: we want but verse. — Restore,
    my charms,
My ling'ring Daphnis to my longing arms.
" Pale Phœbe, drawn by verse, from
    heav'n descends;

And Circe chang'd with charms Ulysses'
    friends.
Verse breaks the ground, and penetrates
    the brake,
And in the winding cavern splits the snake:
Verse fires the frozen veins. — Restore, my
    charms,
My ling'ring Daphnis to my longing arms.
" Around his waxen image first I wind 101
Three woolen fillets, of three colors join'd;
Thrice bind about his thrice-devoted head,
Which round the sacred altar thrice is
    led.
Unequal numbers please the gods. — My
    charms,
Restore my Daphnis to my longing arms.
" Knit with three knots the fillets; knit
    'em straight;
And say: ' These knots to love I conse-
    crate.'
Haste, Amaryllis, haste. — Restore, my
    charms,
My lovely Daphnis to my longing arms. 110
" As fire this figure hardens, made of
    clay,
And this of wax with fire consumes away;
Such let the soul of cruel Daphnis be,
Hard to the rest of women, soft to me.
Crumble the sacred mole of salt and
    corn:
Next in the fire the bays with brimstone
    burn;
And, while it crackles in the sulphur,
    say,
' This I for Daphnis burn; thus Daphnis
    burn away !
This laurel is his fate.' — Restore, my
    charms,
My lovely Daphnis to my longing arms. 120
" As when the raging heifer, thro' the
    grove,
Stung with desire, pursues her wand'ring
    love;
Faint at the last, she seeks the weedy
    pools,
To quench her thirst, and on the rushes
    rolls,
Careless of night, unmindful to return;
Such fruitless fires perfidious Daphnis
    burn,
While I so scorn his love ! — Restore, my
    charms,
My ling'ring Daphnis to my longing arms.
" These garments once were his, and left
    to me,

The pledges of his promis'd loyalty,   130
Which underneath · my threshold I be-
        stow:
These pawns, O sacred earth, to me my
        Daphnis owe.
As these were his, so mine is he. — My
        charms,
Restore their ling'ring lord to my deluded
        arms.
    " These pois'nous plants, for magic use
        design'd,
(The noblest and the best of all the baneful
        kind,)
Old Mœris brought me from the Pontic
        strand,
And cull'd the mischief of a bounteous
        land.
Smear'd with these pow'rful juices, on the
        plain,
He howls a wolf among the hungry train;
And oft the mighty negromancer boasts, 141
With these, to call from tombs the stalking
        ghosts,
And from the roots to tear the standing
        corn,
Which, whirl'd aloft, to distant fields is
        borne.
Such is the strength of spells. — Restore, my
        charms,
My ling'ring Daphnis to my longing arms.
    " Bear out these ashes; cast 'em in the
        brook;
Cast backwards o'er your head; nor turn
        your look:
Since neither gods nor godlike verse can
        move,
Break out, ye smother'd fires, and kindle
        smother'd love.   150
Exert your utmost pow'r, my ling'ring
        charms;
And force my Daphnis to my longing
        arms.
    " See, while my last endeavors I delay,
The waking ashes rise, and round our al-
        tars play !
Run to the threshold, Amaryllis, hark !
Our Hylas opens, and begins to bark.
Good Heav'n, may lovers what they wish
        believe !
Or dream their wishes, and those dreams
        deceive !
No more — my Daphnis comes: no more,
        my charms !
He comes, he runs, he leaps to my desiring
        arms."   160

THE NINTH PASTORAL

OR, LYCIDAS AND MŒRIS

THE ARGUMENT

When Virgil, by the favor of Augustus, had
recover'd his patrimony near Mantua, and
went in hope to take possession, he was in
danger to be slain by Arius the centurion, to
whom those lands were assign'd by the Emperor, in reward of his service against Brutus and Cassius. This pastoral, therefore,
is fill'd with complaints of his hard usage ;
and the persons introduc'd are the bailiff
of Virgil, Mœris, and his friend Lycidas.

LYCIDAS

Ho, Mœris ! whether on thy way so fast ?
This leads to town.

MŒRIS

                        O Lycidas, at last
The time is come I never thought to see,
(Strange revolution for my farm and me !)
When the grim captain in a surly tone
Cries out: " Pack up, ye rascals, and be
        gone."
Kick'd out, we set the best face on 't we ⎫
        could;   ⎪
And these two kids, t' appease his angry ⎬
        mood,   ⎪
I bear — of which the Furies give him   ⎭
        good !

LYCIDAS

Your country friends were told another
        tale;   10
That, from the sloping mountain to the
        vale,
And dodder'd oak, and all the banks
        along,
Menalcas sav'd his fortune with a song.

MŒRIS

Such was the news, indeed; but songs and
        rhymes
Prevail as much in these hard iron times,
As would a plump of trembling fowl, that
        rise
Against an eagle sousing from the skies.
And, had not Phœbus warn'd me, by the
        croak
Of an old raven from a hollow oak,
To shun debate, Menalcas had been slain, 20
And Mœris not surviv'd him, to complain.

LYCIDAS

Now Heav'n defend ! Could barb'rous rage
    induce
The brutal son of Mars t' insult the sacred
    Muse !
Who then should sing the nymphs, or who
    rehearse
The waters gliding in a smoother verse !
Or Amaryllis praise — that heav'nly lay,
That shorten'd, as we went, our tedious
    way:
" O Tit'rus, tend my herd, and see them
    fed;
To morning pastures, evening waters, led;
And 'ware the Libyan ridgil's butting
    head."   30

MŒRIS

Or what unfinish'd he to Varus read:
" Thy name, O Varus, (if the kinder pow'rs
Preserve our plains, and shield the Mantuan
    tow'rs,
Obnoxious by Cremona's neighb'ring crime,)
The wings of swans, and stronger-pinion'd
    rhyme,
Shall raise aloft, and soaring bear above,
Th' immortal gift of gratitude to Jove."

LYCIDAS

Sing on, sing on; for I can ne'er be cloy'd:
So may thy swarms the baleful yew avoid;
So may thy cows their burden'd bags dis-
    tend,   40
And trees to goats their willing branches
    bend.
Mean as I am, yet have the Muses made
Me free, a member of the tuneful trade:
At least the shepherds seem to like my
    lays;
But I discern their flatt'ry from their
    praise:
I nor to Cinna's ears, nor Varus', dare as-
    pire,
But gabble, like a goose, amidst the swan-
    like choir.

MŒRIS

'T is what I have been conning in my mind;
Nor are they verses of a vulgar kind.
" Come, Galatea, come, the seas forsake: 50
What pleasures can the tides with their
    hoarse murmurs make ?
See, on the shore inhabits purple spring,
Where nightingales their love-sick ditty
    sing:

See, meads with purling streams, with ⎫
    flow'rs the ground,   ⎪
The grottoes cool, with shady poplars ⎬
    crown'd;   ⎪
And creeping vines on arbors weav'd ⎪
    around.   ⎭
Come then, and leave the waves' tumultu-
    ous roar;
Let the wild surges vainly beat the shore."

LYCIDAS

Or that sweet song I heard with such de-
    light;
The same you sung alone one starry night. 60
The tune I still retain, but not the words.

MŒRIS

" Why, Daphnis, dost thou search in old re-
    cords,
To know the seasons when the stars arise ?
See, Cæsar's lamp is lighted in the skies:
The star whose rays the blushing grapes
    adorn,
And swell the kindly ripening ears of corn.
Under this influence, graft the tender shoot:
Thy children's children shall enjoy the fruit."
The rest I have forgot; for cares and time
Change all things, and untune my soul to
    rhyme.   70
I could have once sung down a summer's
    sun;
But now the chime of poetry is done:
My voice grows hoarse; I feel the notes
    decay,
As if the wolves had seen me first to-day.
But these, and more than I to mind can bring,
Menalcas has not yet forgot to sing.

LYCIDAS

Thy faint excuses but inflame me more:
And now the waves roll silent to the shore;
Hush'd winds the topmost branches scarcely
    bend,
As if thy tuneful song they did attend: 80
Already we have half our way o'ercome;
Far off I can discern Bianor's tomb.
Here, where the laborer's hands have form'd
    a bow'r
Of wreathing trees, in singing waste an hour.
Rest here thy weary limbs; thy kids lay
    down:
We 've day before us yet to reach the town;
Or if, ere night, the gath'ring clouds we
    fear.
A song will help the beating storm to bear.

And, that thou may'st not be too late
    abroad,
Sing, and I 'll ease thy shoulders of thy
    load.   90

MŒRIS

Cease to request me; let us mind our way:
Another song requires another day.
When good Menalcas comes, if he rejoice,
And find a friend at court, I 'll find a voice.

THE TENTH PASTORAL

OR, GALLUS

THE ARGUMENT

Gallus, a great patron of Virgil, and an excellent poet, was very deeply in love with
one Cytheris, whom he calls Lycoris, and
who had forsaken him for the company
of a soldier. The poet therefore supposes
his friend Gallus retir'd, in his heighth of
melancholy, into the solitudes of Arcadia
(the celebrated scene of pastorals), where
he represents him in a very languishing condition, with all the rural deities about him,
pitying his hard usage, and condoling his
misfortune.

THY sacred succor, Arethusa, bring,
To crown my labor ('t is the last I sing),
Which proud Lycoris may with pity view:
The Muse is mournful, tho' the numbers
    few.
Refuse me not a verse, to grief and
    Gallus due:
So may thy silver streams beneath the
    tide,
Unmix'd with briny seas, securely glide.
Sing then my Gallus, and his hopeless
    vows;
Sing, while my cattle crop the tender
    browse.
The vocal grove shall answer to the sound,
And echo, from the vales, the tuneful voice
    rebound.   11
What lawns or woods withheld you from
    his aid,
Ye nymphs, when Gallus was to love be-
    tray'd;
To love, unpitied by the cruel maid ?
Not steepy Pindus could retard your course,
Nor cleft Parnassus, nor th' Aonian source:
Nothing that owns the Muses could suspend
Your aid to Gallus — Gallus is their friend.

For him the lofty laurel stands in tears,
And hung with humid pearls the lowly
    shrub appears.   20
Mænalian pines the godlike swain be-
    moan,
When, spread beneath a rock, he sigh'd
    alone;
And cold Lycæus wept from every drop-
    ping stone.
The sheep surround their shepherd, as he
    lies:
Blush not, sweet poet, nor the name de-
    spise —
Along the streams, his flock Adonis fed;
And yet the Queen of Beauty bless'd his
    bed.
The swains and tardy neatherds came, and
    last,
Menalcas, wet with beating winter mast.
Wond'ring, they ask'd from whence arose
    thy flame;   30
Yet more amaz'd, thy own Apollo came.
Flush'd were his cheeks, and glowing were
    his eyes:
" Is she thy care ? is she thy care ? " he
    cries.
"Thy false Lycoris flies thy love and
    thee,
And, for thy rival, tempts the raging sea,
The forms of horrid war, and heav'n's in-
    clemency."
Silvanus came: his brows a country crown
Of fennel, and of nodding lilies, drown.
Great Pan arriv'd; and we beheld him
    too,
His cheeks and temples of vermilion hue.
" Why, Gallus, this immod'rate grief ? " he
    cried.   41
" Think'st thou that love with tears is sat-
    isfied ?
The meads are sooner drunk with morning
    dews,
The bees with flow'ry shrubs, the goats
    with browse."
    Unmov'd, and with dejected eyes, he
    mourn'd:
He paus'd, and then these broken words
    return'd:
" 'T is past; and pity gives me no relief;
But you, Arcadian swains, shall sing my
    grief,
And on your hills my last complaints renew:
So sad a song is only worthy you.   50
How light would lie the turf upon my
    breast,

If you my suff'rings in your songs ex-
    press'd !
Ah ! that your birth and bus'ness had been
    mine;
To pen the sheep, and press the swelling
    vine !
Had Phyllis or Amyntas caus'd my pain,
Or any nymph, or shepherd on the plain,
(Tho' Phyllis brown, tho' black Amyntas
    were,
Are violets not sweet, because not fair ?)
Beneath the sallows, and the shady vine,
My loves had mix'd their pliant limbs with
    mine: 60
Phyllis with myrtle wreaths had crown'd
    my hair,
And soft Amyntas sung away my care.
Come, see what pleasures in our plains
    abound;
The woods, the fountains, and the flow'ry
    ground.
As you are beauteous, were you half so
    true,
Here could I live, and love, and die with
    only you.
Now I to fighting fields am sent afar,
And strive in winter camps with toils of
    war;
While you, (alas, that I should find it
    so !)
To shun my sight, your native soil forego,
And climb the frozen Alps, and tread th'
    eternal snow.   71
Ye frosts and snows, her tender body
    spare !
Those are not limbs for icicles to tear.
For me, the wilds and desarts are my choice;
The Muses, once my care; my once harmo-
    nious voice.
There will I sing, forsaken and alone:
The rocks and hollow caves shall echo to my
    moan.
The rind of ev'ry plant her name shall know;
And, as the rind extends, the love shall grow.
Then on Arcadian mountains will I chase 80
(Mix'd with the woodland nymphs) the sav-
    age race;
Nor cold shall hinder me, with horns and
    hounds
To thrid the thickets, or to leap the mounds.
And now methinks o'er steepy rocks I go,
And rush thro' sounding woods, and bend the
    Parthian bow;
As if with sports my sufferings I could ease,
Or by my pains the God of Love appease.

My frenzy changes; I delight no more
On mountain tops to chase the tusky boar:
No game but hopeless love my thoughts
    pursue —   90
Once more, ye nymphs, and songs, and sound-
    ing woods, adieu !
Love alters not for us his hard decrees,
Not tho' beneath the Thracian clime we
    freeze,
Or Italy's indulgent heav'n forego,
And in midwinter tread Sithonian snow;
Or, when the barks of elms are scorch'd, we
    keep
On Meroe's burning plains the Libyan sheep.
In hell, and earth, and seas, and heav'n above,
Love conquers all; and we must yield to
    Love."
    My Muses, here your sacred raptures
    end: 100
The verse was what I ow'd my suff'ring
    friend.
This while I sung, my sorrows I deceiv'd,
And bending osiers into baskets weav'd.
The song, because inspir'd by you, shall shine;
And Gallus will approve, because 't is mine —
Gallus, for whom my holy flames renew
Each hour, and ev'ry moment rise in view;
As alders, in the spring, their boles extend,
And heave so fiercely that the bark they rend.
Now let us rise; for hoarseness oft invades
The singer's voice, who sings beneath the
    shades.   111
From juniper unwholesome dews distil,
That blast the sooty corn, the with'ring
    herbage kill.
Away, my goats, away ! for you have
    brows'd your fill.

GEORGICS

TO THE

RIGHT HONORABLE PHILIP, EARL OF CHESTERFIELD, &c.

MY LORD,
I CANNOT begin my address to your Lordship
better than in the words of Virgil:

    —— *Quod optanti divum promittere nemo*
    Auderet, volvenda dies, en, attulit ultro.

Seven years together I have conceal'd the
longing which I had to appear before you : a
time as tedious as Æneas pass'd in his wan-
d'ring voyage, before he reach'd the promis'd
Italy. But I consider'd that nothing which my

meanness could produce was worthy of your patronage. At last this happy occasion offer'd, of presenting to you the best poem of the best poet. If I balk'd this opportunity, I was in despair of finding such another; and, if I took it, I was still uncertain whether you would vouchsafe to accept it from my hands. 'T was a bold venture which I made, in desiring your permission to lay my unworthy labors at your feet. But my rashness has succeeded beyond my hopes; and you have been pleas'd not to suffer an old man to go discontented out of the world, for want of that protection of which he had been so long ambitious. I have known a gentleman in disgrace, and not daring to appear before King Charles the Second, tho' he much desir'd it: at length he took the confidence to attend a fair lady to the court, and told his Majesty that, under her protection, he had presum'd to wait on him. With the same humble confidence I present myself before your Lordship, and, attending on Virgil, hope a gracious reception. The gentleman succeeded, because the powerful lady was his friend; but I have too much injur'd my great author, to expect he should intercede for me. I would have translated him; but, according to the literal French and Italian phrases, I fear I have traduc'd him. 'T is the fault of many a well-meaning man, to be officious in a wrong place, and do a prejudice where he had endeavor'd to do a service. Virgil wrote his *Georgics* in the full strength and vigor of his age, when his judgment was at the height, and before his fancy was declining. He had (according to our homely saying) his full swing at this poem, beginning it about the age of thirty-five, and scarce concluding it before he arriv'd at forty. 'T is observ'd both of him and Horace, (and I believe it will hold in all great poets,) that, tho' they wrote before with a certain heat of genius which inspir'd them, yet that heat was not perfectly digested. There is requir'd a continuance of warmth to ripen the best and noblest fruits. Thus Horace, in his First and Second Book of *Odes*, was still rising, but came not to his meridian till the Third; after which his judgment was an overpoise to his imagination: he grew too cautious to be bold enough; for he descended in his Fourth by slow degrees, and, in his *Satires* and *Epistles*, was more a philosopher and a critic than a poet. In the beginning of summer the days are almost at a stand, with little variation of length or shortness, because at that time the diurnal motion of the sun partakes more of a right line than of a spiral. The same is the method of nature in the frame of man. He seems at forty to be fully in his summer tropic; somewhat before, and somewhat after, he finds in his soul but small increases or decays. From fifty to three-score, the balance generally holds even,

in our colder climates: for he loses not much in fancy; and judgment, which is the effect of observation, still increases. His succeeding years afford him little more than the stubble of his own harvest: yet, if his constitution be healthful, his mind may still retain a decent vigor; and the gleanings of that Ephraim, in comparison with others, will surpass the vintage of Abiezer. I have call'd this somewhere, by a bold metaphor, a green old age; but Virgil has given me his authority for the figure:

Jam senior; sed cruda Deo, viridisque senectus.

Amongst those few who enjoy the advantage of a latter spring your Lordship is a rare example; who, being now arriv'd at your great climacteric, yet give no proof of the least decay in your excellent judgment and comprehension of all things which are within the compass of human understanding. Your conversation is as easy as it is instructive; and I could never observe the least vanity, or the least assuming, in anything you said, but a natural unaffected modesty, full of good sense, and well digested; a clearness of notion, express'd in ready and unstudied words. No man has complain'd, or ever can, that you have discours'd too long on any subject: for you leave us in an eagerness of learning more; pleas'd with what we hear, but not satisfied, because you will not speak so much as we could wish. I dare not excuse your Lordship from this fault; for, tho' 't is none in you, 't is one to all who have the happiness of being known to you. I must confess, the critics make it one of Virgil's beauties, that, having said what he thought convenient, he always left somewhat for the imagination of his readers to supply; that they might gratify their fancies by finding more in what he had written than at first they could; and think they had added to his thought, when it was all there beforehand, and he only sav'd himself the expense of words. However it was, I never went from your Lordship but with a longing to return, or without a hearty curse to him who invented ceremonies in the world, and put me on the necessity of withdrawing, when it was my interest, as well as my desire, to have given you a much longer trouble. I cannot imagine (if your Lordship will give me leave to speak my thoughts) but you have had a more than ordinary vigor in your youth; for too much of heat is requir'd at first, that there may not too little be left at last. A prodigal fire is only capable of large remains; and yours, my Lord, still burns the clearer in declining. The blaze is not so fierce as at the first; but the smoke is wholly vanish'd; and your friends who stand about you are not only sensible of a cheerful warmth, but are kept at an awful distance by its force. In my small observations of mankind,

I have ever found that such as are not rather too full of spirit when they are young, degenerate to dulness in their age. Sobriety in our riper years is the effect of a well-concocted warmth; but, where the principles are only phlegm, what can be expected from the waterish matter but an insipid manhood and a stupid old infancy; discretion in leading strings, and a confirm'd ignorance on crutches? Virgil, in his *Third Georgic*, when he describes a colt who promises a courser for the race, or for the field of battle, shews him the first to pass the bridge which trembles under him, and to stem the torrent of the flood. His beginnings must be in rashness — a noble fault; but time and experience will correct that error, and tame it into a deliberate and well-weigh'd courage, which knows both to be cautious and to dare, as occasion offers. Your Lordship is a man of honor, not only so unstain'd, but so unquestion'd, that you are the living standard of that heroic virtue; so truly such, that if I would flatter you, I could not. It takes not from you, that you were born with principles of generosity and probity; but it adds to you, that you have cultivated nature, and made those principles the rule and measure of all your actions. The world knows this, without my telling; yet poets have a right of recording it to all posterity:

Dignum laude virum Musa vetat mori.

Epaminondas, Lucullus, and the two first Cæsars were not esteem'd the worse commanders for having made philosophy and the liberal arts their study. Cicero might have been their equal, but that he wanted courage. To have both these virtues, and to have improv'd them both with a softness of manners and a sweetness of conversation — few of our nobility can fill that character. One there is, and so conspicuous by his own light, that he needs not

Digito monstrari, et dicier, " Hic est."

To be nobly born, and of an ancient family, is in the extremes of fortune, either good or bad; for virtue and descent are no inheritance. A long series of ancestors shews the native with great advantage at the first; but if he any way degenerate from his line, the least spot is visible on ermine. But, to preserve this whiteness in its original purity, you, my Lord, have, like that ermine, forsaken the common track of business, which is not always clean: you have chosen for yourself a private greatness, and will not be polluted with ambition. It has been observ'd in former times that none have taken been so greedy of employments, and of managing the public, as they who have least deserv'd their stations. But such only merit to be call'd patriots, under

whom we see their country flourish. I have laugh'd sometimes (for who would always be a Heraclitus?) when I have reflected on those men who from time to time have shot themselves into the world. I have seen many successions of them; some bolting out upon the stage with vast applause, and others hiss'd off, and quitting it with disgrace. But, while they were in action, I have constantly observ'd that they seem'd desirous to retreat from business: greatness, they said, was nauseous, and a crowd was troublesome; a quiet privacy was their ambition. Some few of them, I believe, said this in earnest, and were making a provision against future want, that they might enjoy their age with ease: they saw the happiness of a private life, and promis'd to themselves a blessing which every day it was in their power to possess. But they deferr'd it, and linger'd still at court, because they thought they had not yet enough to make them happy: they would have more, and laid in, to make their solitude luxurious — a wretched philosophy, which Epicurus never taught them in his garden. They lov'd the prospect of this quiet in reversion, but were not willing to have it in possession: they would first be old, and made as sure of health and life as if both of them were at their dispose. But put them to the necessity of a present choice, and they preferr'd continuance in power; like the wretch who call'd Death to his assistance, but refus'd it when he came. The great Scipio was not of their opinion, who indeed sought honors in his youth, and indur'd the fatigues with which he purchas'd them. He serv'd his country when it was in need of his courage and his conduct, till he thought it was time to serve himself; but dismounted from the saddle when he found the beast which bore him began to grow restiff and ungovernable. But your Lordship has given us a better example of moderation. You saw betimes that ingratitude is not confin'd to commonwealths; and therefore, tho' you were form'd alike for the greatest of civil employments and military commands, yet you push'd not your fortune to rise in either, but contented yourself with being capable, as much as any whosoever, of defending your country with your sword, or assisting it with your counsel, when you were call'd. For the rest, the respect and love which was paid you, not only in the province where you live, but generally by all who had the happiness to know you, was a wise exchange for the honors of the court — a place of forgetfulness, at the best. for well-deservers. 'T is necessary, for the polishing of manners, to have breath'd that air; but 't is infectious, even to the best morals, to live always in it. 'T is a dangerous commerce, where an honest man is sure at the first of being cheated, and he recovers not his losses but by learning to cheat others. The undermining smile becomes at length habitual; and the drift of his plausible conversation is only to flatter one, that he may betray another. Yet 't is good to have been a looker-on, without venturing to play; that a man may know false dice another time, tho' he never means to use them. I commend not him who never knew a court, but him who forsakes it because he knows it. A young man deserves no praise, who, out of melancholy zeal, leaves the world before he has well tried it, and runs headlong into religion. He who carries a maidenhead into a cloister is sometimes apt to lose it there, and to repent of his repentance. He only is like to endure austerities who has already found the inconvenience of pleasures. For almost every man will be making experiments in one part or another of his life, and the danger is the less when we are young; for, having tried it early, we shall not be apt to repeat it afterwards. Your Lordship therefore may properly be said to have chosen a retreat, and not to have chosen it till you had maturely weigh'd the advantages of rising higher, with the hazards of the fall. *Res, non parta labore, sed relicta*, was thought by a poet to be one of the requisites to a happy life. Why should a reasonable man put it into the power of Fortune to make him miserable, when his ancestors have taken care to release him from her? Let him venture, says Horace, *qui zonam perdidit*. He who has nothing plays securely; for he may win, and cannot be poorer if he loses. But he who is born to a plentiful estate, and is ambitious of offices at court, sets a stake to Fortune which she can seldom answer: if he gains nothing, he loses all, or part of what was once his own; and if he gets, he cannot be certain but he may refund. In short, however he succeeds, 't is covetousness that induc'd him first to play; and covetousness is the undoubted sign of ill sense at bottom. The odds are against him that he loses; and one loss may be of more consequence to him than all his former winnings. 'T is like the present war of the Christians against the Turk: every year they gain a victory, and by that a town; but, if they are once defeated, they lose a province at a blow, and endanger the safety of the whole empire. You, my Lord, enjoy your quiet in a garden, where you have not only the leisure of thinking, but the pleasure to think of nothing which can discompose your mind. A good conscience is a port which is landlock'd on every side, and where no winds can possibly invade, no tempests can arise. There a man may stand upon the shore, and not only see his own image, but that of his Maker, clearly reflected from the undisturb'd

and silent waters. Reason was intended for a blessing; and such it is to men of honor and integrity, who desire no more than what they are able to give themselves; like the happy old Corycian whom my author describes in his *Fourth Georgic*, whose fruits and salads, on which he liv'd contented, were all of his own growth, and his own plantation. Virgil seems to think that the blessings of a country life are not complete without an improvement of knowledge by contemplation and reading:

> *O fortunatos nimium, bona si sua norint,*
> *Agricolas!*

'T is but half possession not to understand that happiness which we possess. A foundation of good sense and a cultivation of learning are requir'd to give a seasoning to retirement, and make us taste the blessing. God has bestow'd on your Lordship the first of these; and you have bestow'd on yourself the second. Eden was not made for beasts, tho' they were suffer'd to live in it, but for their master, who studied God in the works of his creation. Neither could the Devil have been happy there with all his knowledge; for he wanted innocence to make him so. He brought envy, malice, and ambition into Paradise, which sour'd to him the sweetness of the place. Wherever inordinate affections are, 't is hell. Such only can enjoy the country, who are capable of thinking when they are there, and have left their passions behind them in the town. Then they are prepar'd for solitude; and in that solitude is prepar'd for them:

> *Et secura quies, et nescia fallere vita.*

As I began this dedication with a verse of Virgil, so I conclude it with another. The continuance of your health, to enjoy that happiness which you so well deserve, and which you have provided for yourself, is the sincere and earnest wish of

> Your Lordship's most devoted
> And most obedient Servant,
> JOHN DRYDEN.

THE FIRST BOOK OF THE GEORGICS

THE ARGUMENT

The poet, in the beginning of this book, propounds the general design of each *Georgic;* and, after a solemn invocation of all the gods who are any way related to his subject, he addresses himself in particular to Augustus, whom he compliments with divinity: and after strikes into his business. He shews the different kinds of tillage proper to different soils; traces out the original of agriculture; gives a catalogue of the husbandman's tools; specifies the employments peculiar to each season; describes the changes of the weather, with the signs in heaven and earth that forebode them; instances many of the prodigies that happen'd near the time of Julius Cæsar's death; and shuts up all with a supplication to the gods for the safety of Augustus, and the preservation of Rome.

WHAT makes a plenteous harvest, when to turn
The fruitful soil, and when to sow the corn;
The care of sheep, of oxen, and of kine,
And how to raise on elms the teeming vine;
The birth and genius of the frugal bee,
I sing, Mæcenas, and I sing to thee.
Ye deities, who fields and plains protect,
Who rule the seasons, and the year direct,
Bacchus and fost'ring Ceres, pow'rs divine,
Who gave us corn for mast, for water, wine;   10
Ye Fauns, propitious to the rural swains,
Ye nymphs, that haunt the mountains and the plains,
Join in my work, and to my numbers bring
Your needful succor; for your gifts I sing.
And thou, whose trident struck the teeming earth,
And made a passage for the courser's birth;
And thou, for whom the Cæan shore sustains
Thy milky herds, that graze the flow'ry plains;
And thou, the shepherds' tutelary god,
Leave, for a while, O Pan, thy lov'd abode;   20
And, if Arcadian fleeces be thy care,
From fields and mountains to my song repair.
Inventor, Pallas, of the fatt'ning oil,
Thou founder of the plow, and plowman's toil;
And thou, whose hands the shroud-like ⎫
   cypress rear,   ⎬
Come, all ye gods and goddesses, that ⎪
   wear   ⎭
The rural honors, and increase the year: ⎭
You, who supply the ground with seeds of grain;
And you, who swell those seeds with kindly rain;
And chiefly thou, whose undetermin'd state

Is yet the business of the gods' debate,   31
Whether in after times to be declar'd
The patron of the world, and Rome's peculiar guard,
Or o'er the fruits and seasons to preside,
And the round circuit of the year to guide —
Pow'rful of blessings, which thou strew'st around,
And with thy goddess-mother's myrtle crown'd.
Or wilt thou, Cæsar, choose the wat'ry reign,
To smooth the surges, and correct the main?
Then mariners, in storms, to thee shall ⎫
   pray;   40 ⎪
Ev'n utmost Thule shall thy pow'r obey, ⎬
And Neptune shall resign the fasces of ⎪
   the sea;   ⎭
The wat'ry virgins for thy bed shall strive,
And Tethys all her waves in dowry give.
Or wilt thou bless our summers with thy rays,
And, seated near the Balance, poise the days,
Where, in the void of heav'n, a space is free,
Betwixt the Scorpion and the Maid, for thee?
The Scorpion, ready to receive thy laws,
Yields half his region, and contracts his claws.   50
Whatever part of heav'n thou shalt obtain —
For let not hell presume of such a reign;
Nor let so dire a thirst of empire move
Thy mind, to leave thy kindred gods above —
Tho' Greece admires Elysium's blest retreat,
Tho' Proserpine affects her silent seat,
And, importun'd by Ceres to remove,
Prefers the fields below to those above, —
But thou, propitious Cæsar, guide my course,
And to my bold endeavors add thy force: 60
Pity the poet's and the plowman's cares; ⎫
Int'rest thy greatness in our mean affairs, ⎬
And use thyself betimes to hear and grant ⎪
   our pray'rs.   ⎭
   While yet the spring is young, while Earth unbinds
Her frozen bosom to the western winds;
While mountain snows dissolve against the sun,

And streams, yet new, from precipices run;
Ev'n in this early dawning of the year,
Produce the plow, and yoke the sturdy
    steer,
And goad him till he groans beneath his
    toil,   70
Till the bright share is buried in the soil.
That crop rewards the greedy peasant's ⎤
    pains,   │
Which twice the sun, and twice the cold ⎪
    sustains,   ⎬
And bursts the crowded barns with more │
    than promis'd gains.   ⎦
But, ere we stir the yet unbroken ground,
The various course of seasons must be
    found;
The weather, and the setting of the winds,
The culture suiting to the sev'ral kinds
Of seeds and plants, and what will thrive
    and rise,
And what the genius of the soil denies. 80
This ground with Bacchus, that with Ceres
    suits;
That other loads the trees with happy fruits;
A fourth with grass, unbidden, decks the
    ground.
Thus Tmolus is with yellow saffron crown'd:
India black ebon and white ivory bears;
And soft Idume weeps her od'rous tears.
Thus Pontus sends her beaver stones from
    far;
And naked Spaniards temper steel for war:
Epirus for th' Elean chariot breeds,
In hopes of palms, a race of running steeds.
This is the orig'nal contract; these the
    laws   91
Impos'd by Nature, and by Nature's
    cause,
On sundry places, when Deucalion hurl'd
His mother's entrails on the desart world;
Whence men, a hard laborious kind, ⎤
    were born.   │
Then borrow part of winter for thy corn, ⎬
And early with thy team the glebe in │
    furrows turn;   ⎦
That, while the turf lies open and un-
    bound,
Succeeding suns may bake the mellow
    ground.
But, if the soil be barren, only scar   100
The surface, and but lightly print the
    share,
When cold Arcturus rises with the sun;
Lest wicked weeds the corn should overrun
In wat'ry soils, or lest the barren sand

Should suck the moisture from the thirsty
    land.
Both these unhappy soils the swain for-
    bears,
And keeps a sabbath of alternate years,
That the spent earth may gather heart
    again,
And, better'd by cessation, bear the grain.
At least where vetches, pulse, and tares
    have stood,   110
And stalks of lupines grew (a stubborn
    wood),
Th' ensuing season, in return, may bear
The bearded product of the golden year.
For flax and oats will burn the tender
    field,
And sleepy poppies harmful harvests yield;
But sweet vicissitudes of rest and toil
Make easy labor, and renew the soil.
Yet sprinkle sordid ashes all around,
And load with fatt'ning dung thy fallow
    ground.
Thus change of seeds for meager soils is
    best;   120
And earth manur'd, not idle, tho' at rest.
  Long practice has a sure improvement
    found,
With kindled fires to burn the barren
    ground,
When the light stubble, to the flames re-
    sign'd,
Is driv'n along, and crackles in the wind:
Whether from hence the hollow womb of
    Earth
Is warm'd with secret strength for better
    birth;
Or, when the latent vice is cur'd by fire,
Redundant humors thro' the pores expire;
Or that the warmth distends the chinks,
    and makes   130
New breathings, whence new nourishment
    she takes;
Or that the heat the gaping grounds con-
    strains.
New knits the surface, and new strings the
    veins;
Lest soaking show'rs should pierce her ⎤
    secret seat,   │
Or freezing Boreas chill her genial heat, ⎬
Or scorching suns too violently beat.   ⎦
  Nor is the profit small the peasant makes,
Who smooths with harrows, or who pounds
    with rakes
The crumbling clods; nor Ceres from on
    high

Regards his labors with a grudging eye; 140
Nor his, who plows across the furrow'd
grounds,
And on the back of earth inflicts new
wounds;
For he with frequent exercise commands
Th' unwilling soil, and tames the stubborn
lands.
  Ye swains, invoke the pow'rs who rule
the sky,
For a moist summer, and a winter dry;
For winter drought rewards the peasant's
pain,
And broods indulgent on the buried grain.
Hence Mysia boasts her harvests, and the
tops
Of Gargarus admire their happy crops. 150
When first the soil receives the fruitful
seed,
Make no delay, but cover it with speed:
So fenc'd from cold, the pliant furrows
break
Before the surly clod resists the rake.
And call the floods from high, to rush
amain
With pregnant streams, to swell the teem-
ing grain.
Then, when the fiery suns too fiercely play,
And shrivel'd herbs on with'ring stems de-
cay,
The wary plowman, on the mountain's
brow,
Undams his wat'ry stores — huge torrents
flow, 160
And, rattling down the rocks, large mois-
ture yield,
Temp'ring the thirsty fever of the field —
And lest the stem, too feeble for the
freight,
Should scarce sustain the head's unwieldy
weight,
Sends in his feeding flocks betimes, t' in-
vade
The rising bulk of the luxuriant blade,
Ere yet th' aspiring offspring of the grain
O'ertops the ridges of the furrow'd plain;
And drains the standing waters, when they
yield
Too large a bev'rage to the drunken field:
But most in autumn, and the show'ry
spring, 171
When dubious months uncertain weather
bring;
When fountains open, when impetuous
rain

Swells hasty brooks, and pours upon the
plain;
When earth with slime and mud is cover'd
o'er,
Or hollow places spew their wat'ry store.
Nor yet the plowman, nor the lab'ring
steer,
Sustain alone the hazards of the year:
But glutton geese, and the Strymonian
crane,
With foreign troops invade the tender
grain; 180
And tow'ring weeds malignant shadows
yield;
And spreading succ'ry chokes the rising
field.
The sire of gods and men, with hard de-
crees,
Forbids our plenty to be bought with ease,
And wills that mortal men, inur'd to toil,
Should exercise, with pains, the grudging
soil.
Himself invented first the shining share,
And whetted human industry by care;
Himself did handicrafts and arts ordain,
Nor suffer'd sloth to rust his active reign.
Ere this, no peasant vex'd the peaceful
ground, 191
Which only turfs and greens for altars
found:
No fences parted fields, nor marks nor
bounds
Distinguish'd acres of litigious grounds;
But all was common, and the fruitful Earth
Was free to give her unexacted birth.
Jove added venom to the viper's brood,
And swell'd with raging storms the peace-
ful flood;
Commission'd hungry wolves t' infest the
fold,
And shook from oaken leaves the liquid
gold; 200
Remov'd from human reach the cheerful
fire,
And from the rivers bade the wine retire;
That studious need might useful arts ex-
plore,
From furrow'd fields to reap the foodful
store,
And force the veins of clashing flints t'
expire
The lurking seeds of their celestial fire.
Then first on seas the hollow'd alder swam;
Then sailors quarter'd heav'n, and found a
name

For ev'ry fix'd and ev'ry wand'ring star:
The Pleiads, Hyads, and the Northern
    Car.   210
Then toils for beasts, and lime for birds
    were found,
And deep-mouth dogs did forest walks sur-
    round;
And casting nets were spread in shallow
    brooks,
Drags in the deep, and baits were hung on
    hooks.
Then saws were tooth'd, and sounding axes
    made,
(For wedges first did yielding wood in-
    vade;)
And various arts in order did succeed:
What cannot endless labor, urg'd by
    need?
    First Ceres taught the ground with grain
    to sow,
And arm'd with iron shares the crooked
    plow;   220
When now Dodonian oaks no more sup-
    plied
Their mast, and trees their forest fruit de-
    nied.
Soon was his labor doubled to the swain,
And blasting mildews blacken'd all his
    grain;
Tough thistles chok'd the fields, and kill'd
    the corn,
And an unthrifty crop of weeds was born:
Then burs and brambles, an unbidden crew
Of graceless guests, th' unhappy field sub-
    due;
And oats unblest, and darnel domineers,
And shoots its head above the shining ears;
So that, unless the land with daily care   231
Is exercis'd, and with an iron war
Of rakes and harrows the proud foes ex-
    pell'd,
And birds with clamors frighted from the
    field;
Unless the boughs are lopp'd that shade
    the plain,
And Heav'n invok'd with vows for fruitful
    rain,
On other crops you may with envy look,
And shake for food the long-abandon'd oak.
Nor must we pass untold what arms they
    wield,
Who labor tillage and the furrow'd field;   240
Without whose aid the ground her corn
    denies,
And nothing can be sown, and nothing rise:

The crooked plow, the share, the tow'ring
    height
Of wagons, and the cart's unwieldy weight;
The sled, the tumbril, hurdles, and the
    flail,
The fan of Bacchus, with the flying sail —
These all must be prepar'd, if plowmen
    hope
The promis'd blessing of a bounteous crop.
Young elms, with early force, in copses
    bow,
Fit for the figure of the crooked plow.   250
Of eight foot long a fasten'd beam pre-
    pare;
On either side the head produce an ear,
And sink a socket for the shining share:
Of beech the plow-tail and the bending
    yoke,
Or softer linden harden'd in the smoke.
    I could be long in precepts; but I fear
So mean a subject might offend your ear.
Delve of convenient depth your thrashing
    floor:
With temper'd clay then fill and face it
    o'er;
And let the weighty roller run the round,
To smooth the surface of th' unequal
    ground;   261
Lest, crack'd with summer heats, the floor-
    ing flies,
Or sinks, and thro' the crannies weeds
    arise.
For sundry foes the rural realm surround;
The field mouse builds her garner under
    ground
For gather'd grain; the blind laborious
    mole
In winding mazes works her hidden hole;
In hollow caverns vermin make abode —
The hissing serpent, and the swelling toad;
The corn-devouring weasel here abides,   270
And the wise ant her wintry store provides.
    Mark well the flow'ring almonds in the
    wood:
If od'rous blooms the bearing branches
    load,
The glebe will answer to the sylvan reign;
Great heats will follow, and large crops of
    grain.
But if a wood of leaves o'ershade the tree,
Such and so barren will thy harvest be:
In vain the hind shall vex the thrashing
    floor;
For empty chaff and straw will be thy
    store.

Some steep their seed, and some in caldrons
   boil,   280
With vigorous niter and with lees of oil,
O'er gentle fires, th' exuberant juice to
   drain,
And swell the flatt'ring husks with fruitful
   grain.
Yet is not the success for years assur'd,
Tho' chosen is the seed, and fully cur'd,
Unless the peasant, with his annual pain,
Renews his choice, and culls the largest
   grain.
Thus all below, whether by Nature's curse,
Or Fate's decree, degen'rate still to worse.
So the boat's brawny crew the current
   stem,   290
And, slow advancing, struggle with the
   stream;
But if they slack their hands, or cease to
   strive,
Then down the flood with headlong haste
   they drive.
Nor must the plowman less observe the
   skies,
When the Kids, Dragon, and Arcturus rise,
Than sailors homeward bent, who cut their
   way
Thro' Helle's stormy straits, and oyster-
   breeding sea.
But, when Astræa's Balance, hung on high,
Betwixt the nights and days divides the sky,
Then yoke your oxen, sow your winter
   grain,   300
Till cold December comes with driving
   rain.
Linseed and fruitful poppy bury warm,
In a dry season, and prevent the storm.
Sow beans and clover in a rotten soil,
And millet rising from your annual toil:
When with his golden horns, in full ca- ⎫
   reer,   ⎪
The Bull beats down the barriers of the ⎬
   year,   ⎪
And Argos and the Dog forsake the   ⎭
   northern sphere.
But if your care to wheat alone extend, ⎫
Let Maia with her sisters first descend, ⎪
And the bright Gnossian diadem down- ⎬
   ward bend,   311 ⎭
Before you trust in earth your future hope;
Or else expect a listless lazy crop.
Some swains have sown before; but most
   have found
A husky harvest from the grudging ground.
Vile vetches would you sow, or lentils lean,

The growth of Egypt, or the kidney bean?
Begin when the slow wagoner descends,
Nor cease your sowing till midwinter ends:
For this, thro' twelve bright signs Apollo
   guides   320
The year, and earth in sev'ral climes di-
   vides.
Five girdles bind the skies: the torrid zone
Glows with the passing and repassing sun;
Far on the right and left, th' extremes of
   heav'n
To frosts and snows and bitter blasts are
   giv'n;
Betwixt the midst and these, the gods as-
   sign'd
Two habitable seats for humankind,
And cross their limits cut a sloping way,
Which the twelve signs in beauteous order
   sway.
Two poles turn round the globe; one seen
   to rise   330
O'er Scythian hills, and one in Libyan
   skies;
The first sublime in heav'n, the last is
   whirl'd
Below the regions of the nether world.
Around our pole the spiry Dragon glides,
And, like a winding stream, the Bears di-
   vides —
The less and greater, who, by Fate's decree,
Abhor to dive beneath the southern sea.
There, as they say, perpetual night is found
In silence brooding on th' unhappy ground:
Or, when Aurora leaves our northern sphere,
She lights the downward heav'n, and rises
   there;   341
And, when on us she breathes the living
   light,
Red Vesper kindles there the tapers of the
   night.
From hence uncertain seasons we may know,
And when to reap the grain, and when to
   sow;
Or when to fell the furzes; when 't is meet
To spread the flying canvas for the fleet.
Observe what stars arise, or disappear;
And the four quarters of the rolling year.
But, when cold weather and continued rain
The lab'ring husband in his house restrain,
Let him forecast his work with timely ⎫
   care,   352 ⎪
Which else is huddled when the skies   ⎬
   are fair: ⎪
Then let him mark the sheep, or whet   ⎭
   the shining share,

Or hollow trees for boats, or number o'er
His sacks, or measure his increasing store,
Or sharpen stakes, or head the forks, or
   twine
The sallow twigs to tie the straggling vine;
Or wicker baskets weave, or air the corn,
Or grinded grain betwixt two marbles
   turn.   360
No laws, divine or human, can restrain
From necessary works the lab'ring swain.
Ev'n holidays and feasts permission yield
To float the meadows, or to fence the field,
To fire the brambles, snare the birds, and
   steep
In wholesome waterfalls the woolly sheep.
And oft the drudging ass is driv'n, with
   toil,
To neighb'ring towns with apples and with
   oil;
Returning late, and loaden, home with gain
Of barter'd pitch, and handmills for the
   grain.   370
The lucky days, in each revolving moon,
For labor choose: the fifth be sure to shun;
That gave the Furies and pale Pluto birth,
And arm'd, against the skies, the sons of
   earth.
With mountains pil'd on mountains, thrice
   they strove
To scale the steepy battlements of Jove;
And thrice his lightning and red thunder
   play'd,
And their demolish'd works in ruin laid.
The sev'nth is, next the tenth, the best to
   join
Young oxen to the yoke, and plant the
   vine;   380
Then, weavers, stretch your stays upon the
   weft.
The ninth is good for travel, bad for theft.
Some works in dead of night are better
   done,
Or when the morning dew prevents the sun.
Parch'd meads and stubble mow by Phœbe's
   light,
Which both require the coolness of the
   night;
For moisture then abounds, and pearly
   rains
Descend in silence to refresh the plains.
The wife and husband equally conspire
To work by night, and rake the winter
   fire: 390
He sharpens torches in the glimm'ring
   room;

She shoots the flying shuttle thro' the loom,
Or boils in kettles must of wine, and skims
With leaves the dregs that overflow the
   brims;
And, till the watchful cock awakes the
   day,
She sings, to drive the tedious hours away.
But in warm weather, when the skies are
   clear,
By daylight reap the product of the year;
And in the sun your golden grain display,
And thrash it out, and winnow it by day.
Plow naked, swain, and naked sow the
   land;   401
For lazy winter numbs the lab'ring hand.
In genial winter, swains enjoy their store,
Forget their hardships, and recruit for
   more;
The farmer to full bowls invites his friends,
And, what he got with pains, with pleasure
   spends.
So sailors, when escap'd from stormy seas,
First crown their vessels, then indulge
   their ease.
Yet that's the proper time to thrash the
   wood
For mast of oak, your fathers' homely
   food;   410
To gather laurel berries, and the spoil
Of bloody myrtles, and to press your oil;
For stalking cranes to set the guileful
   snare;
T' inclose the stags in toils, and hunt the
   hare;
With Balearic slings, or Gnossian bow,
To persecute from far the flying doe —
Then, when the fleecy skies new clothe the
   wood,
And cakes of rustling ice come rolling
   down the flood.
  Now sing we stormy stars, when ⎫
The year, and adds to nights, and shortens ⎬
   days,   420 ⎭
And suns declining shine with feeble rays:
What cares must then attend the toiling ⎫
   swain; |
Or when the low'ring spring, with lavish ⎬
   rain, |
Beats down the slender stem and bearded ⎭
   grain,
While yet the head is green, or, lightly
   swell'd
With milky moisture, overlooks the field.
Ev'n when the farmer, now secure of fear,

Sends in the swains to spoil the finish'd year;
Ev'n while the reaper fills his greedy hands,
And binds the golden sheafs in brittle bands;   430
Oft have I seen a sudden storm arise
From all the warring winds that sweep the skies:
The heavy harvest from the root is torn,
And whirl'd aloft the lighter stubble borne;
With such a force the flying rack is driv'n,
And such a winter wears the face of heav'n:
And oft whole sheets descend of sluicy rain,
Suck'd by the spongy clouds from off the main;
The lofty skies at once come pouring down,
The promis'd crop and golden labors drown.   440
The dykes are fill'd, and with a roaring sound
The rising rivers float the nether ground;
And rocks the bellowing voice of boiling seas rebound.
The Father of the Gods his glory shrouds,
Involv'd in tempests, and a night of clouds;
And, from the middle darkness flashing out,
By fits he deals his fiery bolts about.
Earth feels the motions of her angry god;
Her entrails tremble, and her mountains nod,
And flying beasts in forests seek abode:
Deep horror seizes ev'ry human breast; 451
Their pride is humbled and their fear confess'd,
While he from high his rolling thunder throws,
And fires the mountains with repeated blows.
The rocks are from their old foundations rent;
The winds redouble, and the rains augment:
The waves on heaps are dash'd against the shore;
And now the woods, and now the billows roar.
In fear of this, observe the starry signs,
Where Saturn houses, and where Hermes joins.   460
But first to Heav'n thy due devotions pay,
And annual gifts on Ceres' altars lay.

When winter's rage abates, when cheerful hours
Awake the spring, and spring awakes the flow'rs,
On the green turf thy careless limbs display,
And celebrate the Mighty Mother's day:
For then the hills with pleasing shades are crown'd,
And sleeps are sweeter on the silken ground;
With milder beams the sun securely shines;
Fat are the lambs, and luscious are the wines.   470
Let ev'ry swain adore her pow'r divine,
And milk and honey mix with sparkling wine:
Let all the choir of clowns attend the show
In long procession, shouting as they go;
Invoking her to bless their yearly stores,
Inviting plenty to their crowded floors.
Thus in the spring, and thus in summer's heat,
Before the sickles touch the ripening wheat,
On Ceres call; and let the lab'ring hind
With oaken wreaths his hollow temples bind: 480
On Ceres let him call, and Ceres praise,
With uncouth dances, and with country lays.
And that by certain signs we may presage
Of heats and rains, and wind's impetuous rage,
The sov'reign of the heav'ns has set on high
The moon, to mark the changes of the sky;
When southern blasts should cease, and when the swain
Should near their folds his feeding flocks restrain.
For, ere the rising winds begin to roar,
The working seas advance to wash the shore;   490
Soft whispers run along the leavy woods,
And mountains whistle to the murm'ring floods.
Ev'n then the doubtful billows scarce abstain
From the toss'd vessel on the troubled main;
When crying cormorants forsake the sea,
And stretching to the covert wing their way;
When sportful coots run skimming o'er the strand;
When watchful herons leave their wat'ry stand,

And mounting upward, with erected flight,
Gain on the skies, and soar above the
   sight.   500
And oft, before tempest'ous winds arise,
The seeming stars fall headlong from the
   skies,
And, shooting thro' the darkness, gild the
   night
With sweeping glories, and long trails of
   light;
And chaff with eddy-winds is whirl'd
   around,
And dancing leaves are lifted from the
   ground;
And floating feathers on the waters play.
But when the winged thunder takes his
   way
From the cold North, and East and West
   ingage,
And at their frontiers meet with equal
   rage,   510
The clouds are crush'd; a glut of gather'd ⌉
   rain |
The hollow ditches fills, and floats the |
   plain;   }
And sailors furl their dropping sheets |
   amain.   ⌋
Wet weather seldom hurts the most un-
   wise;
So plain the signs, such prophets are the
   skies.
The wary crane foresees it first, and sails
Above the storm, and leaves the lowly
   vales;
The cow looks up, and from afar can find
The change of heav'n, and snuffs it in the
   wind;
The swallow skims the river's wat'ry face;
The frogs renew the croaks of their lo-
   quacious race;   521
The careful ant her secret cell forsakes,
And drags her eggs along the narrow
   tracks:
At either horn the rainbow drinks the ⌉
   flood; |
Huge flocks of rising rooks forsake their   }
   food, |
And, crying, seek the shelter of the |
   wood.   ⌋
Besides, the sev'ral sorts of wat'ry fowls
That swim the seas, or haunt the standing
   pools,
The swans that sail along the silver flood,
And dive with stretching necks to search
   their food,   530

Then lave their backs with sprinkling dews
   in vain,
And stem the stream to meet the pro-
   mis'd rain.
The crow with clam'rous cries the show'r
   demands,
And single stalks along the desart sands.
The nightly virgin, while her wheel she
   plies,
Foresees the storm impending in the skies,
When sparkling lamps their sputt'ring light
   advance,
And in the sockets oily bubbles dance.
   Then, after show'rs, 't is easy to descry
Returning suns, and a serener sky: 540
The stars shine smarter; and the moon
   adorns,
As with unborrow'd beams, her sharpen'd
   horns.
The filmy gossamer now flits no more,
Nor halcyons bask on the short sunny
   shore;
Their litter is not toss'd by sows unclean:
But a blue droughty mist descends upon
   the plain;
And owls, that mark the setting sun, de-
   clare
A starlight evening, and a morning fair.
Tow'ring aloft, avenging Nisus flies,
While, dar'd below, the guilty Scylla lies.
Wherever frighted Scylla flies away,   551
Swift Nisus follows, and pursues his prey;
Where injur'd Nisus takes his airy course,
Thence trembling Scylla flies, and shuns
   his force:
This punishment pursues th' unhappy maid,
And thus the purple hair is dearly paid.
Then, thrice the ravens rend the liquid air,
And croaking notes proclaim the settled
   fair;
Then, round their airy palaces they fly,
To greet the sun; and, seiz'd with secret
   joy,   560
When storms are overblown, with food
   repair
To their forsaken nests and callow care.
Not that I think their breasts with heav'nly
   souls
Inspir'd, as man, who destiny controls;
But with the changeful temper of the
   skies,
As rains condense, and sunshine rarefies,
So turn the species in their alter'd minds,
Compos'd by calms, and discompos'd by
   winds:

From hence proceeds the birds' harmonious
    voice;
From hence the crows exult, and frisking
    lambs rejoice.   570
Observe the daily circle of the sun,
And the short year of each revolving
    moon:
By them thou shalt foresee the following
    day,
Nor shall a starry night thy hopes betray.
When first the moon appears, if then she
    shrouds
Her silver crescent, tipp'd with sable clouds,
Conclude she bodes a tempest on the main,
And brews for fields impetuous floods of
    rain;
Or, if her face with fiery flushing glow,
Expect the rattling winds aloft to blow. 580
But, four nights old, (for that 's the surest
    sign,)
With sharpen'd horns if glorious then she
    shine,
Next day, nor only that, but all the moon,
Till her revolving race be wholly run,
Are void of tempests, both by land and sea,
And sailors in the port their promis'd vow
    shall pay.
    Above the rest, the sun, who never lies,
Foretells the change of weather in the
    skies:
For if he rise unwilling to his race,
Clouds on his brows, and spots upon his
    face,   590
Or if thro' mists he shoots his sullen beams,
Frugal of light, in loose and straggling
    streams;
Suspect a drizzling day, with southern rain,
Fatal to fruits, and flocks, and promis'd
    grain.
Or if Aurora, with half-open'd eyes,
And a pale sickly cheek, salute the skies;
How shall the vine, with tender leaves, de-
    fend
Her teeming clusters, when the storms de-
    scend,
When ridgy roofs and tiles can scarce avail
To bar the ruin of the rattling hail ?   600
But, more than all, the setting sun survey,
When down the steep of heav'n he drives
    the day,
For oft we find him finishing his race
With various colors erring on his face.
If fiery red his glowing globe descends,
High winds and furious tempests he por-
    tends:

But if his cheeks are swoln with livid blue,
He bodes wet weather by his wat'ry hue.
If dusky spots are varied on his brow,
And, streak d with red, a troubled color
    show;   610
That sullen mixture shall at once declare
Winds, rain, and storms, and elemental
    war:
What desp'rate madman then would ven-
    ture o'er
The *frith*, or haul his cables from the shore ?
But if with purple rays he brings the light,
And a pure heav'n resigns to quiet night,
No rising winds or falling storms are ⎫
    nigh;   ⎪
But northern breezes thro' the forest fly, ⎬
And drive the rack, and purge the ruffled ⎪
    sky.   619 ⎭
Th' unerring sun by certain signs declares
What the late ev'n or early morn prepares,
And when the south projects a stormy day,
And when the clearing north will puff the
    clouds away.
The sun reveals the secrets of the sky;
And who dares give the source of light the
    lie ?
The change of empires often he declares,
Fierce tumults, hidden treasons, open wars.
He first the fate of Cæsar did foretell,
And pitied Rome, when Rome in Cæsar
    fell;
In iron clouds conceal'd the public light, 630
And impious mortals fear'd eternal night.
Nor was the fact foretold by him alone:
Nature herself stood forth, and seconded
    the sun.
Earth, air, and seas with prodigies were
    sign'd;
And birds obscene, and howling dogs divin'd.
What rocks did Ætna's bellowing mouth
    expire
From her torn entrails ! and what floods of
    fire !
What clanks were heard, in German skies
    afar,
Of arms and armies, rushing to the war !
Dire earthquakes rent the solid Alps be-
    low,   640
And from their summets shook th' eternal
    snow;
Pale specters in the close of night were
    seen,
And voices heard of more than mortal men;
In silent groves dumb sheep and oxen
    spoke;

And streams ran backward, and their beds
    forsook;
The yawning earth disclos'd th' abyss of
    hell;
The weeping statues did the wars foretell,
And holy sweat from brazen idols fell.
Then, rising in his might, the king of floods
Rush'd thro' the forests, tore the lofty
    woods;   650
And, rolling onward, with a sweepy sway,
Bore houses, herds, and lab'ring hinds away.
Blood sprang from wells, wolfs howl'd in
    towns by night,
And boding victims did the priests affright;
Such peals of thunder never pour'd from
    high,
Nor forky lightnings flash'd from such a
    sullen sky.
Red meteors ran across th' ethereal space;
Stars disappear'd, and comets took their
    place.
For this, th' Emathian plains once more
    were strow'd
With Roman bodies, and just Heav'n
    thought good   660
To fatten twice those fields with Roman
    blood.
Then, after length of time, the lab'ring swains
Who turn the turfs of those unhappy plains
Shall rusty piles from the plow'd furrows
    take,
And over empty helmets pass the rake;
Amaz'd at antic titles on the stones,
And mighty relics of gigantic bones.
Ye home-born deities, of mortal birth!
Thou Father Romulus, and Mother Earth,
Goddess unmov'd! whose guardian arms
    extend   670
O'er Tuscan Tiber's course, and Roman
    tow'rs defend;
With youthful Cæsar your joint pow'rs
    ingage,
Nor hinder him to save the sinking age.
O let the blood already spilt atone
For the past crimes of curst Laomedon!
Heav'n wants thee there; and long the
    gods, we know,
Have grudg'd thee, Cæsar, to the world
    below,
Where fraud and rapine right and wrong
    confound,
Where impious arms from ev'ry part re-
    sound,
And monstrous crimes in ev'ry shape are
    crown'd.   680

The peaceful peasant to the wars is press'd;
The fields lie fallow in inglorious rest;
The plain no pasture to the flock affords;
The crooked scythes are straighten'd into
    swords:
And there Euphrates her soft offspring
    arms,
And here the Rhine rebellows with alarms;
The neighb'ring cities range on sev'ral
    sides,
Perfidious Mars long-plighted leagues
    divides,
And o'er the wasted world in triumph
    rides.
So four fierce coursers, starting to the
    race,   690
Scour thro' the plain, and lengthen ev'ry
    pace;
Nor reins, nor curbs, nor threat'ning cries
    they fear,
But force along the trembling charioteer.

THE SECOND BOOK OF THE GEORGICS

THE ARGUMENT

The subject of the following book is planting:
in handling of which argument the poet
shews all the different methods of raising
trees, describes their variety, and gives rules
for the management of each in particular.
He then points out the soils in which the several plants thrive best, and thence takes occasion to run out into the praises of Italy: after
which he gives some directions for discovering the nature of every soil, prescribes rules
for the dressing of vines, olives, &c., and concludes the *Georgic* with a panegyric on a
country life.

THUS far of tillage, and of heav'nly signs:
Now sing, my Muse, the growth of gen'rous
    vines,
The shady groves, the woodland progeny,
And the slow product of Minerva's tree.
    Great Father Bacchus! to my song re-
    pair;
For clust'ring grapes are thy peculiar care:
For thee, large bunches load the bending
    vine,
And the last blessings of the year are thine.
To thee his joys the jolly Autumn owes,
When the fermenting juice the vat o'er-
    flows.   10

Come, strip with me, my god ! come, drench
　　all o'er
Thy limbs in must of wine, and drink at
　　ev'ry pore.
　　Some trees their birth to bounteous Na-
　　　ture owe;
For some without the pains of planting
　　grow.
With osiers thus the banks of brooks
　　abound,
Sprung from the wat'ry genius of the
　　ground.
From the same principles gray willows
　　come,
Herculean poplar, and the tender broom.
But some from seeds inclos'd in earth
　　arise;
For thus the mastful chestnut mates the
　　skies.   20
Hence rise the branching beech and vocal
　　oak,
Where Jove of old oraculously spoke.
Some from the root a rising wood disclose:
Thus elms, and thus the salvage cherry
　　grows;
Thus the green bay, that binds the poet's
　　brows,
Shoots, and is shelter'd by the mother's
　　boughs.
　　These ways of planting Nature did or-
　　　dain
For trees and shrubs, and all the sylvan
　　reign.
Others there are, by late experience found:
Some cut the shoots, and plant in furrow'd
　　ground;   30
Some cover rooted stalks in deeper mold;
Some, cloven stakes; and (wondrous to be-
　　hold !)
Their sharpen'd ends in earth their footing
　　place,
And the dry poles produce a living race.
Some bow their vines, which buried in the
　　plain,
Their tops in distant arches rise again.
Others no root require; the lab'rer cuts
Young slips, and in the soil securely puts.
Ev'n stumps of olives, bar'd of leaves, and
　　dead,
Revive, and oft redeem their wither'd head.
'T is usual now an inmate graff to see   41
With insolence invade a foreign tree:
Thus pears and quinces from the crab tree
　　come,
And thus the ruddy cornel bears the plum.

Then let the learned gard'ner mark with
　　care
The kinds of stocks, and what those kinds
　　will bear;
Explore the nature of each sev'ral tree,
And, known, improve with artful industry:
And let no spot of idle earth be found,
But cultivate the genius of the ground; 50
For open Ismarus will Bacchus please;
Taburnus loves the shade of olive trees.
　　The virtues of the sev'ral soils I sing —
Mæcenas, now thy needful succor bring !
O thou ! the better part of my renown,
Inspire thy poet, and thy poem crown,
Embark with me, while I new tracts ex-
　　plore,
With flying sails, and breezes from the
　　shore:
Not that my song, in such a scanty space,
So large a subject fully can embrace —   60
Not tho' I were supplied with iron lungs,
A hundred mouths, fill'd with as many
　　tongues —
But steer my vessel with a steady hand,
And coast along the shore in sight of land.
Nor will I tire thy patience with a train
Of preface, or what ancient poets feign.
The trees which of themselves advance in
　　air
Are barren kinds, but strongly built and
　　fair;
Because the vigor of the native earth
Maintains the plant, and makes a manly
　　birth.   70
Yet these, receiving graffs of other kind,
Or thence transplanted, change their sal-
　　vage mind,
Their wildness lose, and, quitting nature's
　　part,
Obey the rules and discipline of art.
The same do trees that, sprung from bar-
　　ren roots,
In open fields transplanted bear their fruits;
For, where they grow, the native energy
Turns all into the substance of the tree,
Starves and destroys the fruit, is only made
For brawny bulk, and for a barren shade.
The plant that shoots from seed, a sullen
　　tree,   81
At leisure grows, for late posterity;
The gen'rous flavor lost, the fruits decay,
And salvage grapes are made the birds'
　　ignoble prey.
Much labor is requir'd in trees, to tame
Their wild disorder, and in ranks reclaim.

Well must the ground be digg'd, and better
    dress'd,
New soil to make, and meliorate the rest.
Old stakes of olive trees in plants revive; ⎤
By the same methods Paphian myrtles ⎬
    live;   90
But nobler vines by propagation thrive. ⎦
From roots hard hazels; and from cions rise
Tall ash, and taller oak that mates the
    skies;
Palm, poplar, fir, descending from the
    steep
Of hills, to try the dangers of the deep.
The thin-leav'd arbute hazel graffs re-
    ceives;
And planes huge apples bear, that bore but
    leaves.
Thus mastful beech the bristly chestnut
    bears,
And the wild ash is white with blooming
    pears,
And greedy swine from grafted elms are
    fed   100
With falling acorns, that on oaks are bred.
  But various are the ways to change the
    state
Of plants, to bud, to graff, t' inoculate.
For, where the tender rinds of trees dis-
    close
Their shooting gems, a swelling knot there
    grows;
Just in that space a narrow slit we make,
Then other buds from bearing trees we take;
Inserted thus, the wounded rind we close,
In whose moist womb th' admitted infant
    grows.
But, when the smoother bole from knots is
    free,   110
We make a deep incision in the tree,
And in the solid wood the slip inclose:
The batt'ning bastard shoots again and
    grows;
And in short space the laden boughs arise,
With happy fruit advancing to the skies.
The mother plant admires the leaves un-
    known
Of alien trees, and apples not her own.
  Of vegetable woods are various kinds,
And the same species are of sev'ral minds.
Lotes, willows, elms, have diff'rent forms
    allow'd;   120
So fun'ral cypress, rising like a shroud:
Fat olive trees of sundry sorts appear,
Of sundry shapes their unctuous berries
    bear.

Radii long olives, Orchits round produce,
And bitter Pausia, pounded for the juice.
Alcinoüs' orchard various apples bears;
Unlike are bergamotes and pounder pears.
Nor our Italian vines produce the shape,
Or taste, or flavor, of the Lesbian grape.
The Thasian vines in richer soils abound; 130
The Mareotic grow in barren ground.
The Psythian grape we dry; Lagæan juice
Will stamm'ring tongues and stagg'ring
    feet produce.
Rathe ripe are some, and some of later
    kind;
Of golden some, and some of purple rind.
How shall I praise the Ræthean grape di-
    vine,
Which yet contends not with Falernian
    wine?
Th' Aminean many a consulship survives,
And longer than the Lydian vintage lives,
Or high Phanæus, king of Chian growth; 140
But for large quantities and lasting, both,
The less Argitis bears the prize away.
The Rhodian, sacred to the solemn day,
In second services is pour'd to Jove,
And best accepted by the gods above.
Nor must Bumastus his old honors lose,
In length and largeness like the dugs of
    cows.
I pass the rest, whose ev'ry race, and name,
And kinds, are less material to my theme;
Which who would learn, as soon may tell
    the sands,   150
Driv'n by the western wind on Libyan
    lands;
Or number, when the blust'ring Eurus
    roars,
The billows beating on Ionian shores.
  Nor ev'ry plant on ev'ry soil will grow:
The sallow loves the wat'ry ground, and low;
The marshes, alders; nature seems t' ordain
The rocky cliff for the wild ash's reign;
The baleful yew to northern blasts assigns,
To shores the myrtles, and to mounts the
    vines.
  Regard th' extremest cultivated coast, 160
From hot Arabia to the Scythian frost:
All sort of trees their sev'ral countries ⎤
    know;   ⎬
Black ebon only will in India grow,   ⎪
And od'rous frankincense on the Sabæan ⎦
    bough.
Balm slowly trickles thro' the bleeding
    veins
Of happy shrubs in Idumæan plains.

The green Egyptian thorn, for med'cine
    good,
With Ethiops' hoary trees and woolly wood,
Let others tell; and how the Seres spin
Their fleecy forests in a slender twine; 170
With mighty trunks of trees on Indian
    shores,
Whose height above the feather'd arrow
    soars,
Shot from the toughest bow, and by the
    brawn
Of expert archers with vast vigor drawn.
Sharp-tasted citrons Median climes pro-
    duce,
(Bitter the rind, but gen'rous is the juice,)
A cordial fruit, a present antidote
Against the direful stepdam's deadly
    draught,
Who, mixing wicked weeds with words im-
    pure,   179
The fate of envied orphans would procure.
Large is the plant, and like a laurel grows,
And, did it not a diff'rent scent disclose,
A laurel were: the fragrant flow'rs contemn
The stormy winds, tenacious of their stem.
With this the Medes to lab'ring age be-
    queath
New lungs, and cure the sourness of the
    breath.
    But neither Median woods (a plenteous
    land),
Fair Ganges, Hermus rolling golden sand,
Nor Bactria, nor the richer Indian fields,
Nor all the gummy stores Arabia yields, 190
Nor any foreign earth of greater name, ⎫
Can with sweet Italy contend in fame.   ⎬
No bulls whose nostrils breathe a living ⎭
    flame
Have turn'd our turf; no teeth of serpents
    here
Were sown, an armed host and iron crop to
    bear.
But fruitful vines, and the fat olive's freight,
And harvests heavy with their fruitful
    weight,
Adorn our fields; and on the cheerful green
The grazing flocks and lowing herds are
    seen.
The warrior horse, here bred, is taught to
    train;   200
There flows Clitumnus thro' the flow'ry
    plain,
Whose waves, for triumphs after pros-
    p'rous war,
The victim ox and snowy sheep prepare.

Perpetual spring our happy climate sees: ⎫
Twice breed the cattle, and twice bear   ⎬
    the trees;   ⎪
And summer suns recede by slow degrees. ⎭
    Our land is from the rage of tigers freed,
Nor nourishes the lion's angry seed;
Nor pois'nous aconite is here produc'd,
Or grows unknown, or is, when known, re-
    fus d;   210
Nor in so vast a length our serpents glide,
Or rais'd on such a spiry volume ride.
    Next add our cities of illustrious name,
Their costly labor, and stupendous frame;
Our forts on steepy hills, that far below
See wanton streams in winding valleys
    flow;
Our twofold seas, that, washing either side,
A rich recruit of foreign stores provide;
Our spacious lakes; thee, Larius, first; and
    next
Benacus, with tempest'ous billows vex'd. 220
Or shall I praise thy ports, or mention
    make
Of the vast mound that binds the Lucrine
    lake ?
Or the disdainful sea, that, shut from
    thence,
Roars round the structure, and invades the
    fence,
There, where secure the Julian waters glide,
Or where Avernus' jaws admit the Tyrrhene
    tide ?
Our quarries, deep in earth, were fam'd of
    old
For veins of silver, and for ore of gold.
Th' inhabitants themselves their country
    grace:
Hence rose the Marsian and Sabellian race,
Strong-limb'd and stout, and to the wars
    inclin'd,   231
And hard Ligurians, a laborious kind,
And Volscians arm'd with iron - headed
    darts.
Besides, an offspring of undaunted hearts,
The Decii, Marii, great Camillus, came
From hence, and greater Scipio's double
    name;
And mighty Cæsar, whose victorious arms
To farthest Asia carry fierce alarms,
Avert unwarlike Indians from his Rome;
Triumph abroad, secure our peace at home.
    Hail, sweet Saturnian soil ! of fruitful
    grain   241
Great parent, greater of illustrious men !
For thee my tuneful accents will I raise,

And treat of arts disclos'd in ancient days;
Once more unlock for thee the sacred
   spring,
And old Ascræan verse in Roman cities
   sing.
The nature of their sev'ral soils now
   see,
Their strength, their color, their fertility:
And first for heath, and barren hilly
   ground,
Where meager clay and flinty stones
   abound;   250
Where the poor soil all succor seems to
   want —
Yet this suffices the Palladian plant.
Undoubted signs of such a soil are found;
For here wild olive shoots o'erspread
   the ground,
And heaps of berries strew the fields
   around.
But where the soil, with fatt'ning moisture
   fill'd,
Is cloth'd with grass, and fruitful to be
   till'd,
Such as in cheerful vales we view from
   high,
Which dripping rocks with rolling streams
   supply,
And feed with ooze; where rising hillocks
   run   260
In length, and open to the southern sun;
Where fern succeeds, ungrateful to the
   plow —
That gentle ground to gen'rous grapes al-
   low.
Strong stocks of vines it will in time pro-
   duce,
And overflow the vats with friendly juice,
Such as our priests in golden goblets pour
To gods, the givers of the cheerful hour,
Then when the bloated Tuscan blows his
   horn,
And reeking entrails are in chargers
   borne.
If herds or fleecy flocks be more thy
   care,   270
Or goats that graze the field, and burn it
   bare,
Then seek Tarentum's lawns, and farthest
   coast,
Or such a field as hapless Mantua lost,
Where silver swans sail down the wat'ry
   road,
And graze the floating herbage of the flood.
There crystal streams perpetual tenor keep,

Nor food nor springs are wanting to thy
   sheep;
For, what the day devours, the nightly dew
Shall to the morn in pearly drops renew.
Fat crumbling earth is fitter for the plow,
Putrid and loose above, and black below;
For plowing is an imitative toil,   282
Resembling nature in an easy soil.
No land for seed like this; no fields afford
So large an income to the village lord:
No toiling teams from harvest labor come
So late at night, so heavy-laden home.
The like of forest land is understood,
From whence the surly plowman grubs
   the wood,
Which had for length of ages idle stood:
Then birds forsake the ruins of their seat,
And, flying from their nests, their callow
   young forget.   292
The coarse lean gravel, on the mountain
   sides,
Scarce dewy bev'rage for the bees provides;
Nor chalk nor crumbling stones, the food
   of snakes,
That work in hollow earth their winding
   tracks.
The soil exhaling clouds of subtile dews,
Imbibing moisture which with ease she
   spews,
Which rusts not iron, and whose mold is
   clean,
Well cloth d with cheerful grass, and ever
   green,   300
Is good for olives, and aspiring vines,
Embracing husband elms in am'rous twines;
Is fit for feeding cattle, fit to sow,
And equal to the pasture and the plow.
Such is the soil of fat Campanian fields;
Such large increase the land that joins
   Vesuvius yields;
And such a country could Acerra boast,
Till Clanius overflow'd th' unhappy coast.
   I teach thee next the diff'ring soils to
   know,
The light for vines, the heavier for the
   plow.   310
Choose first a place for such a purpose fit:
There dig the solid earth, and sink a pit;
Next fill the hole with its own earth again.
And trample with thy feet, and tread it in:
Then, if it rise not to the former height
Of superfice, conclude that soil is light,
A proper ground for pasturage and vines.
But if the sullen earth, so press'd, repines
Within its native mansion to retire,

And stays without, a heap of heavy mire,
'T is good for arable, a glebe that asks   321
Tough teams of oxen, and laborious tasks.
  Salt earth and bitter are not fit to sow,
Nor will be tam'd or mended with the plow.
Sweet grapes degen'rate there; and fruits, declin'd
From their first flav'rous taste, renounce their kind.
This truth by sure experiment is tried;
For first an osier colander provide
Of twigs thick wrought (such toiling peasants twine,
When thro' strait passages they strain their wine):   330
In this close vessel place that earth accurst,
But fill'd brimful with wholesome water first;
Then run it thro': the drops will rope around,
And by the bitter taste disclose the ground.
The fatter earth by handling we may find,
With ease distinguish'd from the meager kind:
Poor soil will crumble into dust; the rich
Will to the fingers cleave like clammy pitch:
Moist earth produces corn and grass, but both
Too rank and too luxuriant in their growth.   340
Let not my land so large a promise boast,
Lest the lank ears in length of stem be lost.
The heavier earth is by her weight betray'd;
The lighter in the poising hand is weigh'd.
'T is easy to distinguish by the sight
The color of the soil, and black from white;
But the cold ground is difficult to know; ⎫
Yet this the plants that prosper there   ⎬
  will show: ⎪
Black ivy, pitch trees, and the baleful ⎭
  yew.
These rules consider'd well, with early care   350
The vineyard destin'd for thy vines prepare;
But, long before the planting, dig the ground
With furrows deep that cast a rising mound:
The clods, expos'd to winter winds, will bake;
For putrid earth will best in vineyards take,

And hoary frosts, after the painful toil
Of delving hinds, will rot the mellow soil.
  Some peasants, not t' omit the nicest care,
Of the same soil their nursery prepare   359
With that of their plantation; lest the tree,
Translated, should not with the soil agree.
Beside, to plant it as it was, they mark
The heav'n's four quarters on the tender bark,
And to the north or south restore the side
Which at their birth did heat or cold abide.
So strong is custom; such effects can use
In tender souls of pliant plants produce.
  Choose next a province for thy vineyard's reign,
On hills above, or in the lowly plain.
If fertile fields or valleys be thy choice,   370
Plant thick; for bounteous Bacchus will rejoice
In close plantations there; but if the vine
On rising ground be plac'd, or hills supine,
Extend thy loose battalions largely wide,
Opening thy ranks and files on either side,
But marshal'd all in order as they stand;
And let no soldier straggle from his band.
As legions in the field their front display,
To try the fortune of some doubtful day,
And move to meet their foes with sober pace,   380
Strict to their figure, tho' in wider space,
Before the battle joins, while from afar
The field yet glitters with the pomp of war,
And equal Mars, like an impartial lord,
Leaves all to fortune, and the dint of sword;
So let thy vines in intervals be set,
But not their rural discipline forget:
Indulge their width, and add a roomy space,
That their extremest lines may scarce embrace:
Nor this alone t' indulge a vain delight, 390
And make a pleasing prospect for the sight;
But, for the ground itself, this only way ⎫
Can equal vigor to the plants convey,   ⎬
Which, crowded, want the room their ⎪
  branches to display.   ⎭
  How deep they must be planted, wouldst thou know?
In shallow furrows vines securely grow.
Not so the rest of plants; for Jove's own tree,
That holds the woods in awful sov'reignty,

Requires a depth of lodging in the ground,
And, next the lower skies, a bed profound:
High as his topmost boughs to heav'n as-
    cend,   401
So low his roots to hell's dominion tend.
Therefore, nor winds, nor winter's rage o'er-
    throws
His bulky body, but unmov'd he grows;
For length of ages lasts his happy reign,
And lives of mortal man contend in vain:
Full in the midst of his own strength he
    stands,
Stretching his brawny arms, and leafy
    hands;
His shade protects the plains, his head
    the hills commands.
   The hurtful hazel in thy vineyard shun;
Nor plant it to receive the setting sun;   411
Nor break the topmost branches from the
    tree;
Nor prune, with blunted knife, the pro-
    geny.
Root up wild olives from thy labor'd lands;
For sparkling fire, from hinds' unwary
    hands,
Is often scatter'd o'er their unctuous rinds,
And after spread abroad by raging winds:
For first the smould'ring flame the trunk
    receives;
Ascending thence, it crackles in the leaves;
At length victorious to the top aspires,   420
Involving all the wood in smoky fires;
But most, when, driv'n by winds, the flam-
    ing storm
Of the long files destroys the beauteous
    form.
In ashes then th' unhappy vineyard lies;
Nor will the blasted plants from ruin rise;
Nor will the wither'd stock be green again;
But the wild olive shoots, and shades th'
    ungrateful plain.
Be not seduc'd with wisdom's empty shows,
To stir the peaceful ground when Boreas
    blows.
When winter frosts constrain the field with
    cold,   430
The fainty root can take no steady hold;
But when the golden spring reveals the
    year,
And the white bird returns, whom serpents
    fear,
That season deem the best to plant thy
    vines:
Next that, is when autumnal warmth de-
    clines,

Ere heat is quite decay'd, or cold begun,
Or Capricorn admits the winter sun.
   The spring adorns the woods, renews the
    leaves;
The womb of Earth the genial seed receives:
For then almighty Jove descends, and
    pours   440
Into his buxom bride his fruitful show'rs;
And, mixing his large limbs with hers, he
    feeds
Her births with kindly juice, and fosters
    teeming seeds.
Then joyous birds frequent the lonely grove,
And beasts, by nature stung, renew their
    love.
Then fields the blades of buried corn dis-
    close;
And, while the balmy western spirit
    blows,
Earth to the breath her bosom dares ex-
    pose.
With kindly moisture then the plants
    abound;
The grass securely springs above the ground;
The tender twig shoots upward to the
    skies,   451
And on the faith of the new sun relies.
The swerving vines on the tall elms pre-
    vail,
Unhurt by southern show'rs, or northern
    hail;
They spread their gems, the genial warmth
    to share,
And boldly trust their buds in open air.
In this soft season (let me dare to sing)
The world was hatch'd by heav'n's im-
    perial king:
In prime of all the year, and holidays of
    spring.
Then did the new creation first appear;
Nor other was the tenor of the year,   461
When laughing heav'n did the great birth
    attend,
And eastern winds their wintry breath
    suspend:
Then sheep first saw the sun in open fields,
And salvage beasts were sent to stock the
    wilds,
And golden stars flew up to light the skies,
And man's relentless race from stony quar-
    ries rise.
Nor could the tender, new creation bear
Th' excessive heats or coldness of the year;
But, chill'd by winter, or by summer fir'd,
The middle temper of the spring requir'd,

When warmth and moisture did at once
    abound,   472
And heav'n's indulgence brooded on the
    ground.
  For what remains, in depth of earth se-
    cure
Thy cover'd plants, and dung with hot ma-
    nure,
And shells and gravel in the ground inclose;
For thro' their hollow chinks the water
    flows,
Which, thus imbib'd, returns in misty dews,
And, steaming up, the rising plant renews.
Some husbandmen, of late, have found ⎫
    the way,   480 ⎪
A hilly heap of stones above to lay,   ⎬
And press the plants with sherds of pot-   ⎪
    ters' clay.   ⎭
This fence against immod'rate rain they
    found,
Or when the Dog-star cleaves the thirsty
    ground.
Be mindful, when thou hast intomb'd the
    shoot,
With store of earth around to feed the
    root;
With iron teeth of rakes and prongs to
    move
The crusted earth, and loosen it above.
Then exercise thy sturdy steers to plow
Betwixt thy vines, and teach thy feeble
    row   490
To mount on reeds and wands, and, up-
    ward led,
On ashen poles to raise their forky head.
On these new crutches let them learn to
    walk,
Till, swerving upwards, with a stronger
    stalk,
They brave the winds, and, clinging to
    their guide,
On tops of elms at length triumphant ride.
But, in their tender nonage, while they
    spread
Their springing leafs, and lift their infant
    head,
And upward while they shoot in open air,
Indulge their childhood, and the nursling
    spare.   500
Nor exercise thy rage on newborn life;
But let thy hand supply the pruning knife,
And crop luxuriant stragglers, nor be loth
To strip the branches of their leafy growth:
But when the rooted vines, with steady
    hold,

Can clasp their elms, then, husbandman, be
    bold
To lop the disobedient boughs, that stray'd
Beyond their ranks; let crooked steel in-
    vade
The lawless troops, which discipline dis-
    claim,
And their superfluous growth with rigor
    tame.   510
Next, fenc'd with hedges and deep ditches
    round,
Exclude th' incroaching cattle from thy
    ground,
While yet the tender gems but just ap-
    pear,
Unable to sustain th' uncertain year;
Whose leaves are not alone foul winter's
    prey,
But oft by summer suns are scorch'd away,
And, worse than both, become th' un- ⎫
    worthy browse   ⎪
Of buffaloes, salt goats, and hungry cows. ⎬
For not December's frost, that burns the   ⎪
    boughs,   ⎭
Nor dog days' parching heat, that splits ⎫
    the rocks,   520 ⎪
Are half so harmful as the greedy flocks, ⎬
Their venom'd bite, and scars indented on ⎪
    the stocks.   ⎭
For this, the malefactor goat was laid
On Bacchus' altar, and his forfeit paid.
At Athens thus Old Comedy began,
When round the streets the reeling actors
    ran,
In country villages, and crossing ways,
Contending for the prizes of their plays;
And, glad with Bacchus, on the grassy
    soil,
Leapt o'er the skins of goats besmear'd
    with oil.   530
Thus Roman youth, deriv'd from ruin'd
    Troy,
In rude Saturnian rhymes express their joy;
With taunts, and laughter loud, their audi-
    ence please,
Deform'd with vizards, cut from barks of
    trees.
In jolly hymns they praise the God of ⎫
    Wine,   ⎪
Whose earthen images adorn the pine,   ⎬
And there are hung on high, in honor of   ⎪
    the vine: ⎭
A madness so devout the vineyard fills.
In hollow valleys and on rising hills,   539
On whate'er side he turns his honest face,

And dances in the wind, those fields are in
  his grace.
To Bacchus therefore let us tune our lays,
And in our mother tongue resound his
  praise.
Thin cakes in chargers, and a guilty goat,
Dragg'd by the horns, be to his altars
  brought;
Whose offer'd entrails shall his crime re-
  proach,
And drip their fatness from the hazel
  broach.
To dress thy vines, new labor is requir'd;
Nor must the painful husbandman be tir'd:
For thrice, at least, in compass of the
  year,   550
Thy vineyard must employ the sturdy steer
To turn the glebe, besides thy daily pain
To break the clods, and make the surface
  plain,
T' unload the branches, or the leaves to
  thin,
That suck the vital moisture of the vine.
Thus in a circle runs the peasant's pain,
And the year rolls within itself again.
Ev'n in the lowest months, when storms
  have shed
From vines the hairy honors of their head,
Not then the drudging hind his labor ends,
But to the coming year his care extends: 561
Ev'n then the naked vine he persecutes;
His pruning knife at once reforms and
  cuts.
Be first to dig the ground; be first to burn
The branches lopp'd; and first the props
  return
Into thy house, that bore the burden'd
  vines;
But last to reap the vintage of thy wines.
Twice in the year luxuriant leaves o'er-
  shade
The incumber'd vine; rough brambles twice
  invade:
Hard labor both! Commend the large ex-
  cess   570
Of spacious vineyards; cultivate the less.
Besides, in woods the shrubs of prickly
  thorn,
Sallows and reeds, on banks of rivers born,
Remain to cut; for vineyards useful
  found,
To stay thy vines, and fence thy fruitful
  ground.
Nor, when thy tender trees at length are
  bound,

When peaceful vines from pruning hooks
  are free,
When husbands have survey'd the last
  degree,
And utmost files of plants, and order'd
  ev'ry tree;
Ev'n when they sing at ease in full con-
  tent,   580
Insulting o'er the toils they underwent,
Yet still they find a future task remain,
To turn the soil, and break the clods again:
And, after all, their joys are unsincere,
While falling rains on ripening grapes they
  fear.
Quite opposite to these are olives found:
No dressing they require, and dread no
  wound,
Nor rakes nor harrows need; but, fix'd be-
  low,
Rejoice in open air, and unconcern'dly grow.
The soil itself due nourishment supplies: 590
Plow but the furrows, and the fruits arise;
Content with small endeavors, till they
  spring.
Soft peace they figure, and sweet plenty
  bring:
Then olives plant, and hymns to Pallas
  sing.
    Thus apple trees, whose trunks are strong
      to bear
Their spreading boughs, exert themselves
  in air,
Want no supply, but stand secure alone,
Not trusting foreign forces, but their
  own,
Till with the ruddy freight the bending
  branches groan.
Thus trees of nature, and each common
  bush,   600
Uncultivated thrive, and with red berries
  blush.
Vile shrubs are shorn for browse; the
  tow'ring height
Of unctuous trees are torches for the night.
And shall we doubt (indulging easy sloth),
To sow, to set, and to reform their growth?
To leave the lofty plants — the lowly kind
Are for the shepherd or the sheep design'd.
Ev'n humble broom and osiers have their
  use,
And shade for sleep, and food for flocks
  produce;
Hedges for corn, and honey for the bees, 610
Besides the pleasing prospect of the trees.
How goodly looks Cytorus, ever green

With boxen groves ! with what delight are
    seen
Narycian woods of pitch, whose gloomy
    shade
Seems for retreat of heav'nly Muses made !
But much more pleasing are those fields to
    see,
That need not plows, nor human industry.
Ev'n cold Caucasian rocks with trees are
    spread,
And wear green forests on their hilly head.
Tho' bending from the blast of eastern
    storms,   620
Tho' shent their leaves, and shatter'd are
    their arms,
Yet Heav'n their various plants for use de-
    signs;
For houses, cedars; and, for shipping, pines;
Cypress provides for spokes and wheels of
    wains,
And all for keels of ships, that scour the
    wat'ry plains.
Willows in twigs are fruitful, elms in leaves;
The war from stubborn myrtle shafts re-
    ceives;
From cornels, jav'lins; and the tougher
    yew
Receives the bending figure of a bow.
Nor box, nor limes, without their use ⎫
    are made;   630 ⎪
Smooth-grain'd, and proper for the ⎬
    turner's trade;   ⎪
Which curious hands may kerve, and ⎪
    steel with ease invade.   ⎭
Light alder stems the Po's impetuous tide,
And bees in hollow oaks their honey hide.
Now balance with these gifts the fumy joys
Of wine, attended with eternal noise.
Wine urg'd to lawless lust the Centaurs'
    train;
Thro' wine they quarrel'd, and thro' wine
    were slain.
O happy, if he knew his happy state,
The swain, who, free from business and
    debate,   640
Receives his easy food from Nature's hand,
And just returns of cultivated land !
No palace, with a lofty gate, he wants,
T' admit the tides of early visitants,
With eager eyes devouring, as they pass,
The breathing figures of Corinthian brass.
No statues threaten from high pedestals;
No Persian arras hides his homely walls
With antic vests, which thro' their shady
    fold

Betray the streaks of ill-dissembled gold.
He boasts no wool whose native white is
    dyed   651
With purple poison of Assyrian pride;
No costly drugs of Araby defile,
With foreign scents, the sweetness of his
    oil;
But easy quiet, a secure retreat,
A harmless life that knows not how to
    cheat,
With home-bred plenty the rich owner
    bless,
And rural pleasures crown his happiness.
Unvex'd with quarrels, undisturb'd with
    noise,
The country king his peaceful realm enjoys:
Cool grots, and living lakes, the flow'ry
    pride   661
Of meads, and streams that thro' the valley
    glide,
And shady groves that easy sleep invite,
And, after toilsome days, a soft repose at
    night.
Wild beasts of nature in his woods abound;
And youth, of labor patient, plow the
    ground,
Inur'd to hardship, and to homely fare.
Nor venerable age is wanting there
In great examples to the youthful train;
Nor are the gods ador'd with rites profane.
From hence Astræa took her flight; and
    here   671
The prints of her departing steps appear.
    Ye sacred Muses ! with whose beauty
        fir'd
My soul is ravish'd, and my brain inspir'd;
Whose priest I am, whose holy fillets wear;
Would you your poet's first petition hear;
Give me the ways of wand'ring stars to
    know,
The depths of heav'n above, and earth be-
    low:
Teach me the various labors of the moon,
And whence proceed th' eclipses of the
    sun;   680
Why flowing tides prevail upon the main,
And in what dark recess they shrink again;
What shakes the solid earth; what cause
    delays
The summer nights, and shortens winter
    days.
But, if my heavy blood restrain the flight ⎫
Of my free soul, aspiring to the height   ⎬
Of nature, and unclouded fields of light, ⎭
My next desire is, void of care and strife,

To lead a soft, secure, inglorious life —
A country cottage near a crystal flood,   690
A winding valley, and a lofty wood.
Some god conduct me to the sacred shades
Where Bacchanals are sung by Spartan
    maids,
Or lift me high to Hæmus' hilly crown,
Or in the plains of Tempe lay me down,
Or lead me to some solitary place,
And cover my retreat from human race !
  Happy the man, who, studying nature's
    laws,
Thro' known effects can trace the secret
    cause;
His mind possessing in a quiet state,   700
Fearless of fortune, and resign'd to fate !
And happy too is he who decks the bow'rs
Of Sylvans, and adores the rural pow'rs;
Whose mind, unmov'd, the bribes of courts
    can see,
Their glitt'ring baits, and purple slavery;
Nor hopes the people's praise, nor fears ⎫
    their frown,   ⎪
Nor, when contending kindred tear the ⎬
    crown,   ⎪
Will set up one, or pull another down. ⎭
  Without concern he hears, but hears from
    far,
Of tumults, and descents, and distant war;
Nor with a superstitious fear is aw'd   711
For what befalls at home, or what abroad.
Nor envies he the rich their heapy store,
Nor his own peace disturbs with pity for the
    poor.
He feeds on fruits, which, of their own
    accord,
The willing ground and laden trees afford.
From his lov'd home no lucre him can ⎫
    draw;   ⎪
The senate's mad decrees he never saw; ⎬
Nor heard, at bawling bars, corrupted ⎪
    law.   ⎭
Some to the seas, and some to camps re-
    sort,   720
And some with impudence invade the court:
In foreign countries others seek renown;
With wars and taxes others waste their
    own,
And houses burn, and household gods de-
    face,
To drink in bowls which glitt'ring gems
    enchase,
To loll on couches, rich with citron steads,
And lay their guilty limbs in Tyrian beds.
This wretch in earth intombs his golden ore,

Hov'ring and brooding on his buried store.
Some patriot fools to pop'lar praise aspire, 730
Or public speeches, which worse fools ad-
    mire,
While from both benches, with redoubled
    sounds,
Th' applause of lords and commoners
    abounds.
Some thro' ambition, or thro' thirst of gold,
Have slain their brothers, or their country
    sold;
And, leaving their sweet homes, in exile run
To lands that lie beneath another sun.
  The peasant, innocent of all these ills, ⎫
With crooked plows the fertile fallows ⎬
    tills,   ⎪
And the round year with daily labor fills. ⎭
From hence the country markets are sup-
    plied;   741
Enough remains for household charge be-
    side,
His wife and tender children to sustain,
And gratefully to feed his dumb deserving
    train.
Nor cease his labors till the yellow field
A full return of bearded harvest yield:
A crop so plenteous, as the land to load,
O'ercome the crowded barns, and lodge on
    ricks abroad.
Thus ev'ry sev'ral season is employ'd,
Some spent in toil, and some in ease en-
    joy'd.   750
The yeaning ewes prevent the springing
    year;
The laded boughs their fruits in autumn
    bear:
'T is then the vine her liquid harvest yields,
Bak'd in the sunshine of ascending fields.
The winter comes; and then the falling
    mast
For greedy swine provides a full repast;
Then olives, ground in mills, their fatness
    boast,
And winter fruits are mellow'd by the frost.
His cares are eas'd with intervals of bliss:
His little children, climbing for a kiss,   760
Welcome their father's late return at night;
His faithful bed is crown'd with chaste de-
    light.
His kine with swelling udders ready stand,
And, lowing for the pail, invite the milker's
    hand.
His wanton kids, with budding horns pre-
    par'd,
Fight harmless battles in his homely yard:

Himself, in rustic pomp, on holidays,
To rural pow'rs a just oblation pays,
And on the green his careless limbs dis-
    plays.
The hearth is in the midst; the herdsmen,
    round   770
The cheerful fire, provoke his health in
    goblets crown'd.
He calls on Bacchus, and propounds the
    prize:
The groom his fellow-groom at butts de-
    fies,
And bends his bow, and levels with his
    eyes;
Or, stripp'd for wrestling, smears his limbs
    with oil,
And watches with a trip his foe to foil.
Such was the life the frugal Sabines led;
So Remus and his brother god were bred,
From whom th' austere Etrurian virtue rose;
And this rude life our homely fathers chose.
Old Rome from such a race deriv'd her
    birth   781
(The seat of empire, and the conquer'd
    earth),
Which now on sev'n high hills triumphant
    reigns,
And in that compass all the world contains.
Ere Saturn's rebel son usurp'd the skies,
When beasts were only slain for sacrifice,
While peaceful Crete enjoy'd her ancient
    lord,
Ere sounding hammers forg'd th' inhuman
    sword,
Ere hollow drums were beat, before the
    breath   789
Of brazen trumpets rung the peals of death,
The good old god his hunger did assuage
With roots and herbs, and gave the Golden
    Age.
But, overlabor'd with so long a course,
'T is time to set at ease the smoking horse.

THE THIRD BOOK OF THE GEORGICS

THE ARGUMENT

This book begins with an invocation of some
rural deities, and a compliment to Augustus;
after which Virgil directs himself to Mæcenas, and enters on his subject. He lays down
rules for the breeding and management of
horses, oxen, sheep, goats, and dogs; and in-
terweaves several pleasant descriptions of a
chariot race, of the battle of the bulls, of the
force of love, and of the Scythian winter. In
the latter part of the book he relates the diseases incident to cattle; and ends with the
description of a fatal murrain that formerly
rag'd among the Alps.

THY fields, propitious Pales, I rehearse;
And sing thy pastures in no vulgar verse,
Amphrysian shepherd; the Lycæan woods,
Arcadia's flow'ry plains, and pleasing floods.
    All other themes that careless minds in-
    vite
Are worn with use, unworthy me to write.
Busiris' altars, and the dire decrees
Of hard Eurystheus, ev'ry reader sees;
Hylas the boy, Latona's erring isle,
And Pelops' iv'ry shoulder, and his toil   10
For fair Hippodame, with all the rest
Of Grecian tales, by poets are express'd:
New ways I must attempt, my groveling
    name
To raise aloft, and wing my flight to fame.
    I, first of Romans, shall in triumph come
From conquer'd Greece and bring her tro-
    phies home,
With foreign spoils adorn my native place,
And with Idume's palms my Mantua grace.
Of Parian stone a temple will I raise,
Where the slow Mincius thro' the valley
    strays,   20
Where cooling streams invite the flocks to
    drink,
And reeds defend the winding water's
    brink.
Full in the midst shall mighty Cæsar stand,
Hold the chief honors, and the dome com-
    mand.
Then I, conspicuous in my Tyrian gown,
(Submitting to his godhead my renown,)
A hundred coursers from the goal will
    drive:
The rival chariots in the race shall strive.
All Greece shall flock from far, my
    games to see;
The whorlbat and the rapid race shall
    be   30
Reserv'd for Cæsar, and ordain'd by me.
Myself, with olive crown'd, the gifts will
    bear:
Ev'n now methinks the public shouts I
    hear;
The passing pageants and the pomps ap-
    pear.
I to the temple will conduct the crew,

The sacrifice and sacrificers view,
From thence return, attended with my train,
Where the proud theaters disclose the scene,
Which interwoven Britons seem to raise,
And shew the triumph which their shame displays. 40
High o'er the gate in elephant and gold,
The crowd shall Cæsar's Indian war behold:
The Nile shall flow beneath; and, on the side,
His shatter'd ships on brazen pillars ride.
Next him Niphates, with inverted urn,
And dropping sedge, shall his Armenia mourn;
And Asian cities in our triumph borne.
With backward bows the Parthians shall be there,
And, spurring from the fight, confess their fear.
A double wreath shall crown our Cæsar's brows: 50
Two differing trophies, from two different foes.
Europe with Afric in his fame shall join;
But neither shore his conquest shall confine.
The Parian marble there shall seem to move
In breathing statues, not unworthy Jove,
Resembling heroes, whose ethereal root
Is Jove himself, and Cæsar is the fruit.
Tros and his race the sculptor shall employ;
And he, the god, who built the walls of Troy.
Envy herself at last, grown pale and dumb,
(By Cæsar combated and overcome,) 61
Shall give her hands, and fear the curling snakes
Of lashing Furies, and the burning lakes;
The pains of famish'd Tantalus shall feel,
And Sisyphus, that labors up the hill
The rolling rock in vain; and curst Ixion's wheel.
Meantime we must pursue the sylvan lands,
(Th' abode of nymphs,) untouch'd by former hands;
For such, Mæcenas, are thy hard commands.
Without thee, nothing lofty can I sing: 70
Come then, and with thyself thy genius bring,

With which inspir'd, I brook no dull delay:
Cithæron loudly calls me to my way;
Thy hounds, Taygetus, open, and pursue their prey.
High Epidaurus urges on my speed,
Fam'd for his hills, and for his horses' breed:
From hills and dales the cheerful cries rebound;
For Echo hunts along, and propagates the sound.
A time will come, when my maturer Muse
In Cæsar's wars a nobler theme shall choose,
And thro' more ages bear my sovereign's praise, 81
Than have from Tithon pass'd to Cæsar's days.
The generous youth, who, studious of the prize,
The race of running coursers multiplies,
Or to the plow the sturdy bullock breeds,
May know that from the dam the worth of each proceeds.
The mother cow must wear a low'ring look,
Sour-headed, strongly neck'd, to bear the yoke.
Her double dewlap from her chin descends,
And at her thighs the pond'rous burthen ends. 90
Long are her sides and large; her limbs are great;
Rough are her ears, and broad her horny feet;
Her color shining black, but fleck'd with white.
She tosses from the yoke; provokes the fight:
She rises in her gait, is free from fears,
And in her face a bull's resemblance bears.
Her ample forehead with a star is crown'd,
And with her length of tail she sweeps the ground.
The bull's insult at four she may sustain;
But, after ten, from nuptial rites refrain. 100
Six seasons use; but then release the cow,
Unfit for love, and for the lab'ring plow.
Now, while their youth is fill'd with kindly fire,
Submit thy females to the lusty sire:
Watch the quick motions of the frisking tail;
Then serve their fury with the rushing male,
Indulging pleasure, lest the breed should fail.

In youth alone, unhappy mortals live;
But, ah! the mighty bliss is fugitive: 109
Discolor'd sickness, anxious labors, come,
And age, and death's inexorable doom.
Yearly thy herds in vigor will impair.
Recruit and mend 'em with thy yearly care:
Still propagate, for still they fall away;
'T is prudence to prevent th' entire decay.
  Like diligence requires the courser's race,
In early choice, and for a longer space.
The colt that for a stallion is design'd ⎫
By sure presages shows his generous   ⎬
   kind;   ⎪
Of able body, sound of limb and wind. 120 ⎭
Upright he walks, on pasterns firm and
   straight;
His motions easy; prancing in his gait;
The first to lead the way, to tempt the
   flood,
To pass the bridge unknown, nor fear the
   trembling wood;
Dauntless at empty noises; lofty neck'd,
Sharp - headed, barrel - bellied, broadly
   back'd;
Brawny his chest, and deep; his color ⎫
   gray;   ⎪
For beauty, dappled, or the brightest ⎬
   bay: ⎪
Faint white and dun will scarce the rear- ⎭
   ing pay.
  The fiery courser, when he hears from far
The sprightly trumpets and the shouts of
   war,   131
Pricks up his ears; and, trembling with
   delight,
Shifts place, and paws, and hopes the
   promis'd fight.
On his right shoulder his thick mane, re-
   clin'd,
Ruffles at speed, and dances in the wind.
His horny hoofs are jetty black and ⎫
   round;   ⎪
His chine is double; starting, with a ⎬
   bound   ⎪
He turns the turf, and shakes the solid ⎭
   ground.
Fire from his eyes, clouds from his nostrils
   flow:
He bears his rider headlong on the foe. 140
  Such was the steed in Grecian poets
   fam'd,
Proud Cyllarus, by Spartan Pollux tam'd:
Such coursers bore to fight the god of
   Thrace;
And such, Achilles, was thy warlike race.

In such a shape, grim Saturn did restrain
His heav'nly limbs, and flow'd with such a
   mane,
When, half-surpris'd, and fearing to be
   seen,
The lecher gallop'd from his jealous queen,
Ran up the ridges of the rocks amain,
And with shrill neighings fill'd the neigh-
   b'ring plain.   150
  But, worn with years, when dire diseases
   come,
Then hide his not ignoble age at home,
In peace t' enjoy his former palms and
   pains;
And gratefully be kind to his remains.
For, when his blood no youthful spirits
   move,
He languishes and labors in his love;
And, when the sprightly seed should swiftly
   come,
Dribbling he drudges, and defrauds the
   womb:
In vain he burns, like hasty stubble fires,
And in himself his former self requires. 160
  His age and courage weigh; nor those
   alone,
But note his father's virtues and his own:
Observe if he disdains to yield the prize,
Of loss impatient, proud of victories.
  Hast thou beheld, when from the goal
   they start,
The youthful charioteers with heaving
   heart
Rush to the race; and, panting, scarcely
   bear
Th' extremes of feverish hope and chilling
   fear;
Stoop to the reins, and lash with all their
   force ?
The flying chariot kindles in the course; 170
And now alow, and now aloft they fly,
As borne thro' air, and seem to touch the
   sky.
No stop, no stay; but clouds of sand arise,
Spurn'd, and cast backward on the follower's
   eyes.
The hindmost blows the foam upon the
   first:
Such is the love of praise, an honorable
   thirst.
  Bold Erichthonius was the first who
   join'd
Four horses for the rapid race design'd,
And o'er the dusty wheels presiding sate:
The Lapithæ to chariots add the state 180

Of bits and bridles; taught the steed to
    bound,
To run the ring, and trace the mazy round;
To stop, to fly, the rules of war to know;
T' obey the rider, and to dare the foe.
    To choose a youthful steed with courage
    fir'd,
To breed him, break him, back him, are
    requir'd
Experienc'd masters, and in sundry ways;
Their labors equal, and alike their praise.
But, once again, the batter'd horse beware:
The weak old stallion will deceive thy
    care,   190
Tho' famous in his youth for force and
    speed,
Or was of Argos or Epirian breed,
Or did from Neptune's race, or from
    himself proceed.
    These things premis'd, when now the
    nuptial time
Approaches for the stately steed to climb,
With food inable him to make his court;
Distend his chine, and pamper him for
    sport.
Feed him with herbs, whatever thou canst
    find,
Of generous warmth, and of salacious kind;
Then water him, and (drinking what he
    can)   200
Encourage him to thirst again, with bran.
Instructed thus, produce him to the fair,
And join in wedlock to the longing mare.
For, if the sire be faint, or out of case,
He will be copied in his famish'd race,
And sink beneath the pleasing task assign'd
(For all 's too little for the craving kind).
    As for the females, with industrious care
Take down their mettle; keep 'em lean and
    bare:
When conscious of their past delight, and
    keen   210
To take the leap, and prove the sport again,
With scanty measure then supply their
    food;
And, when athirst, restrain 'em from the
    flood:
Their bodies harass; sink 'em when they
    run;
And fry their melting marrow in the sun.
Starve 'em, when barns beneath their bur-
    then groan,
And winnow'd chaff by western winds is
    blown;
For fear the rankness of the swelling womb

Should scant the passage, and confine the
    room;
Lest the fat furrows should the sense de-
    stroy   220
Of genial lust, and dull the seat of joy.
But let 'em suck the seed with greedy
    force,
And close involve the vigor of the horse.
    The male has done: thy care must now
    proceed
To teeming females, and the promis'd breed.
First let 'em run at large, and never know
The taming yoke, or draw the crooked
    plow.
Let 'em not leap the ditch, or swim the
    flood,
Or lumber o'er the meads, or cross the
    wood;
But range the forest, by the silver side   230
Of some cool stream, where nature shall
    provide
Green grass and fatt'ning clover for their
    fare,
And mossy caverns for their noontide lair,
With rocks above, to shield the sharp
    nocturnal air.
    About th' Alburnian groves, with holly
    green,
Of winged insects mighty swarms are seen.
This flying plague (to mark its quality)
Œstros the Grecians call; Asylus, we;
A fierce loud-buzzing breeze: their stings
    draw blood,   239
And drive the cattle gadding thro' the wood.
Seiz'd with unusual pains, they loudly cry:
Tanagrus hastens thence, and leaves his
    channel dry.
This curse the jealous Juno did invent,
And first imploy'd for Io's punishment.
To shun this ill, the cunning leech ordains,
In summer's sultry heats (for then it
    reigns)
To feed the females ere the sun arise,
Or late at night, when stars adorn the
    skies.
When she has calv'd, then set the dam
    aside,
And for the tender progeny provide.   250
Distinguish all betimes with branding fire,
To note the tribe, the lineage, and the sire;
Whom to reserve for husband of the herd,
Or who shall be to sacrifice preferr'd;
Or whom thou shalt to turn thy glebe allow,
To smooth the furrows, and sustain the
    plow:

The rest, for whom no lot is yet decreed,
May run in pastures, and at pleasure feed.
The calf, by nature and by genius made
To turn the glebe, breed to the rural trade.
Set him betimes to school; and let him be
Instructed there in rules of husbandry, 262
While yet his youth is flexible and green,
Nor bad examples of the world has seen.
Early begin the stubborn child to break:
For his soft neck a supple collar make
Of bending osiers; and (with time and care
Enur'd that easy servitude to bear)
Thy flattering method on the youth pursue.
Join'd with his schoolfellows by two and
        two,   270
Persuade 'em first to lead an empty wheel,
That scarce the dust can raise, or they can
        feel:
In length of time produce the lab'ring yoke,
And shining shares, that make the furrow
        smoke.
Ere the licentious youth be thus restrain'd,
Or moral precepts on their minds have
        gain'd,
Their wanton appetites not only feed
With delicates of leaves, and marshy weed,
But with thy sickle reap the rankest land,
And minister the blade with bounteous
        hand;   280
Nor be with harmful parsimony won
To follow what our homely sires have done,
Who fill'd the pail with beestings of the
        cow,
But all her udder to the calf allow.
If to the warlike steed thy studies bend,
Or for the prize in chariots to contend,
Near Pisa's flood the rapid wheels to guide,
Or in Olympian groves aloft to ride,
The generous labors of the courser, first,
Must be with sight of arms and sounds of
        trumpets nurs'd;   290
Inur'd the groaning axletree to bear —
And let him clashing whips in stables hear.
Soothe him with praise, and make him un-
        derstand
The loud applauses of his master's hand:
This, from his weaning, let him well be
        taught;
And then betimes in a soft snaffle wrought,
Before his tender joints with nerves are knit,
Untried in arms, and trembling at the bit.
But when to four full springs his years ad-
        vance,
Teach him to run the round, with pride to
        prance,   300

And (rightly manag'd) equal time to beat,
To turn, to bound in measure, and curvet.
Let him to this, with easy pains, be brought,
And seem to labor, when he labors not.
Thus, form'd for speed, he challenges the
        wind,
And leaves the Scythian arrow far behind;
He scours along the field, with loosen'd
        reins,
And treads so light, he scarcely prints the
        plains.
Like Boreas in his race, when, rushing
        forth,
He sweeps the skies, and clears the cloudy
        north —   310
The waving harvest bends beneath his blast,
The forest shakes, the groves their honors
        cast;
He flies aloft, and with impetuous roar
Pursues the foaming surges to the shore —
Thus, o'er th' Elean plains, thy well-breath'd
        horse
Impels the flying car, and wins the course;
Or, bred to Belgian wagons, leads the way,
Untir'd at night, and cheerful all the day.
When once he 's broken, feed him full and
        high;
Indulge his growth, and his gaunt sides
        supply.   320
Before his training, keep him poor and low;
For his stout stomach with his food will
        grow:
The pamper'd colt will discipline disdain,
Impatient of the lash, and restiff to the
        rein.
Wouldst thou their courage and their
        strength improve?
Too soon they must not feel the stings of
        love.
Whether the bull or courser be thy care,
Let him not leap the cow, nor mount the
        mare.
The youthful bull must wander in the wood
Behind the mountain, or beyond the flood,
Or in the stall at home his fodder find,   331
Far from the charms of that alluring kind.
With two fair eyes his mistress burns his
        breast:
He looks, and languishes, and leaves his
        rest,
Forsakes his food, and, pining for the lass,
Is joyless of the grove, and spurns the grow-
        ing grass.
The soft seducer, with enticing looks,
The bellowing rivals to the fight provokes.

A beauteous heifer in the woods is bred:
The stooping warriors, aiming head to head,
Engage their clashing horns; with dread-
ful sound   341
The forest rattles, and the rocks rebound.
They fence, they push, and, pushing, loudly
roar:
Their dewlaps and their sides are bath'd in
gore.
Nor, when the war is over, is it peace;
Nor will the vanquish'd bull his claim re-
lease;
But, feeding in his breast his ancient fires,
And cursing fate, from his proud foe re-
tires.
Driv'n from his native land to foreign
grounds,   349
He with a gen'rous rage resents his wounds,
His ignominious flight, the victor's boast,
And, more than both, the loves, which un-
reveng'd he lost.
Often he turns his eyes, and, with a groan,
Surveys the pleasing kingdoms, once his
own;
And therefore to repair his strength he ⎫
tries,   ⎪
Hard'ning his limbs with painful exer- ⎬
cise,   ⎪
And rough upon the flinty rock he lies. ⎭
On prickly leaves and on sharp herbs he
feeds,
Then to the prelude of a war proceeds.
His horns, yet sore, he tries against a tree,
And meditates his absent enemy.   361
He snuffs the wind; his heels the sand ⎫
excite;   ⎪
But when he stands collected in his ⎬
might,   ⎪
He roars, and promises a more successful ⎪
fight.   ⎭
Then, to redeem his honor at a blow,
He moves his camp, to meet his careless
foe.
Not with more madness, rolling from afar,
The spumy waves proclaim the wat'ry war;
And mounting upwards, with a mighty roar,
March onwards, and insult the rocky shore.
They mate the middle region with their
height,   371
And fall no less than with a mountain's
weight;
The waters boil, and, belching, from below
Black sands as from a forceful engine
throw.
Thus every creature, and of every kind,

The secret joys of sweet coition find:
Not only man's imperial race, but they
That wing the liquid air, or swim the sea,
Or haunt the desart, rush into the flame;
For Love is lord of all, and is in all the
same.   380
'T is with this rage the mother lion stung
Scours o'er the plain, regardless of her
young:
Demanding rites of love, she sternly stalks,
And hunts her lover in his lonely walks.
'T is then the shapeless bear his den forsakes;
In woods and fields a wild destruction
makes:
Boars whet their tusks; to battle tigers
move,
Enrag'd with hunger, more enrag'd with
love:
Then woe to him that in the desart land
Of Libya travels, o'er the burning sand !
The stallion snuffs the well-known scent
afar,   391
And snorts and trembles for the distant
mare;
Nor bits nor bridles can his rage restrain,
And rugged rocks are interpos'd in vain:
He makes his way o'er mountains, and
contemns
Unruly torrents, and unforded streams.
The bristled boar, who feels the pleasing
wound,
New grinds his arming tusks, and digs the
ground.
The sleepy lecher shuts his little eyes;
About his churning chaps the frothy bubbles
rise: 400
He rubs his sides against a tree; prepares
And hardens both his shoulders for the
wars.
What did the youth, when Love's unerring
dart
Transfix'd his liver, and inflam'd his heart ?
Alone, by night, his wat'ry way he took:
About him, and above, the billows broke;
The sluices of the sky were open spread,
And rolling thunder rattled o'er his head.
The raging tempest call'd him back in vain,
And every boding omen of the main;   410
Nor could his kindred, nor the kindly force
Of weeping parents, change his fatal course:
No, not the dying maid, who must deplore
His floating carcass on the Sestian shore.
  I pass the wars that spotted lynxes make
With their fierce rivals, for the females'
sake;

The howling wolves', the mastiffs' amorous
    rage;
When ev'n the fearful stag dares for his
    hind engage.
But, far above the rest, the furious mare,
Barr'd from the male, is frantic with
    despair: 420
For, when her pouting vent declares her
    pain,
She tears the harness, and she rends the
    rein.
For this (when Venus gave them rage ⎤
    and pow'r)   ⎟
Their masters' mangled members they ⎬
    devour,   ⎟
Of love defrauded in their longing hour. ⎦
For love, they force thro' thickets of the
    wood;
They climb the steepy hills, and stem the
    flood.
    When, at the spring's approach, their
    marrow burns,
(For with the spring their genial warmth
    returns,)
The mares to cliffs of rugged rocks repair,
And with wide nostrils snuff the western
    air: 431
When (wondrous to relate!) the parent
    wind,
Without the stallion, propagates the kind.
Then, fir'd with amorous rage, they take
    their flight
Thro' plains, and mount the hills' unequal
    height;
Nor to the north, nor to the rising sun,
Nor southward to the rainy regions run,
But boring to the west, and hov'ring there,
With gaping mouths they draw prolific air;
With which impregnate, from their groins
    they shed   440
A slimy juice, by false conception bred.
The shepherd knows it well, and calls by
    name
Hippomanes, to note the mother's flame.
This, gather'd in the planetary hour,
With noxious weeds, and spell'd with words
    of pow'r,
Dire stepdames in the magic bowl infuse,
And mix, for deadly draughts, the pois'nous
    juice.
But time is lost, which never will ⎤
    renew,   ⎟
While we too far the pleasing path ⎬
    pursue,   ⎟
Surveying nature with too nice a view. ⎦

Let this suffice for herds: our following
    care   451
Shall woolly flocks and shaggy goats
    declare.
Nor can I doubt what oil I must bestow,
To raise my subject from a ground so low;
And the mean matter which my theme
    affords
T' embellish with magnificence of words.
But the commanding Muse my chariot
    guides,
Which o'er the dubious cliff securely rides;
And pleas'd I am, no beaten road to take,
But first the way to new discov'ries make.
    Now, sacred Pales, in a lofty strain   461
I sing the rural honors of thy reign.
First, with assiduous care from winter keep,
Well fodder'd in the stalls, thy tender
    sheep:
Then spread with straw the bedding of thy
    fold,
With fern beneath, to fend the bitter cold;
That free from gouts thou mayst preserve
    thy care,
And clear from scabs, produc'd by freezing
    air.
Next, let thy goats officiously be nurs'd,
And led to living streams, to quench their
    thirst.   470
Feed 'em with winter browse; and, for their
    lair,
A cote that opens to the south prepare;
Where basking in the sunshine they may lie,
And the short remnants of his heat enjoy.
This during winter's drizzly reign be done,
Till the new Ram receives th' exalted sun;
For hairy goats of equal profit are
With woolly sheep, and ask an equal care.
'T is true, the fleece, when drunk with Tyr-
    ian juice,
Is dearly sold; but not for needful use: 480
For the salacious goat encreases more,
And twice as largely yields her milky store.
The still distended udders never fail,
But, when they seem exhausted, swell the
    pail.
Meantime the pastor shears their hoary
    beards,
And eases of their hair the loaden herds.
Their camelots, warm in tents, the soldier
    hold,
And shield the shiv'ring mariner from cold.
    On shrubs they browse, and on the bleaky
    top
Of rugged hills the thorny bramble crop.

Attended with their bleating kids they
   come   491
At night, unask'd, and mindful of their
   home;
And scarce their swelling bags the
   threshold overcome.
So much the more thy diligence bestow
In depth of winter, to defend the snow,
By how much less the tender helpless kind
For their own ills can fit provision find.
Then minister the browse with bounteous
   hand,
And open let thy stacks all winter stand.
But, when the western winds with vital
   pow'r   500
Call forth the tender grass and budding
   flow'r;
Then, at the last, produce in open air
Both flocks, and send 'em to their sum-
   mer fare.
Before the sun, while Hesperus appears,
First let 'em sip from herbs the pearly tears
Of morning dews, and after break their
   fast
On greensward ground — a cool and grate-
   ful taste.
But, when the day's fourth hour has drawn
   the dews,
And the sun's sultry heat their thirst re-
   news;
When creaking grasshoppers on shrubs com-
   plain,   510
Then lead 'em to their wat'ring troughs
   again.
In summer's heat, some bending valley
   find,
Clos'd from the sun, but open to the wind;
Or seek some ancient oak, whose arms
   extend
In ample breadth, thy cattle to defend,
Or solitary grove, or gloomy glade,
To shield 'em with its venerable shade.
Once more to wat'ring lead; and feed
   again
When the low sun is sinking to the main,
When rising Cynthia sheds her silver dews,
And the cool evening breeze the meads re-
   news,   521
When linnets fill the woods with tuneful
   sound,
And hollow shores the halcyon's voice re-
   bound.
   Why should my Muse enlarge on Libyan
   swains,
Their scatter'd cottages, and ample plains,

Where oft the flocks without a leader
   stray,
Or thro' continued desarts take their way,
And, feeding, add the length of night to
   day?
Whole months they wander, grazing as they
   go;
Nor folds nor hospitable harbor know: 530
Such an extent of plains, so vast a space
Of wilds unknown, and of untasted grass,
Allures their eyes: the shepherd last ap-
   pears,
And with him all his patrimony bears;
His house and household gods, his trade of
   war,
His bow and quiver, and his trusty cur.
Thus, under heavy arms, the youth of
   Rome
Their long laborious marches overcome;
Cheerly their tedious travels undergo,
And pitch their sudden camp before the
   foe.   540
   Not so the Scythian shepherd tends his
   fold,
Nor he who bears in Thrace the bitter
   cold,
Nor he who treads the bleak Mæotian
   strand,
Or where proud Ister rolls his yellow sand.
Early they stall their flocks and herds; for
   there
No grass the fields, no leaves the forests
   wear:
The frozen earth lies buried there, below
A hilly heap, sev'n cubits deep in snow;
And all the west allies of stormy Boreas
   blow.
   The sun from far peeps with a sickly
   face,   550
Too weak the clouds and mighty fogs to
   chase,
When up the skies he shoots his rosy head,
Or in the ruddy ocean seeks his bed.
Swift rivers are with sudden ice constrain'd;
And studded wheels are on its back sus-
   tain'd,
An hostry now for wagons, which before
Tall ships of burthen on its bosom bore.
The brazen caldrons with the frost are
   flaw'd;
The garment, stiff with ice, at hearths is
   thaw'd;
With axes first they cleave the wine; and
   thence,   560
By weight, the solid portions they dispense.

From locks uncomb'd, and from the frozen
    beard,
Long icicles depend, and crackling sounds
    are heard.
Meantime perpetual sleet, and driving snow,
Obscure the skies, and hang on herds below.
The starving cattle perish in their stalls;
Huge oxen stand enclos'd in wintry walls
Of snow congeal'd; whole herds are buried
    there
Of mighty stags, and scarce their horns ap-
    pear.
The dext'rous huntsman wounds not these
    afar   570
With shafts or darts, or makes a distant
    war
With dogs, or pitches toils to stop their
    flight,
But close engages in unequal fight;
And, while they strive in vain to make their
    way
Thro' hills of snow, and pitifully bray,
Assaults with dint of sword, or pointed
    spears,
And homeward, on his back, the joyful bur-
    then bears.
The men to subterranean caves retire,
Secure from cold, and crowd the cheerful
    fire:
With trunks of elms and oaks the hearth
    they load,   580
Nor tempt th' inclemency of heav'n abroad.
Their jovial nights in frolics and in play
They pass, to drive the tedious hours away,
And their cold stomachs with crown'd gob-
    lets cheer
Of windy cider, and of barmy beer.
Such are the cold Riphæan race, and such
The savage Scythian, and unwarlike Dutch,
Where skins of beasts the rude barbarians
    wear,
The spoils of foxes, and the furry bear.
    Is wool thy care? Let not thy cattle go
Where bushes are, where burs and thistles
    grow;   591
Nor in too rank a pasture let 'em feed;
Then of the purest white select thy breed.
Ev'n tho' a snowy ram thou shalt behold,
Prefer him not in haste for husband to thy
    fold:
But search his mouth; and, if a swarthy
    tongue
Is underneath his humid palate hung,
Reject him, lest he darken all the flock,
And substitute another from thy stock.

'T was thus, with fleeces milky white, (if we
May trust report,) Pan, god of Arcady,   601
Did bribe thee, Cynthia; nor didst thou
    disdain,
When call'd in woody shades, to cure a
    lover's pain.
    If milk be thy design, with plenteous
    hand
Bring clover grass; and from the marshy
    land
Salt herbage for the fodd'ring rack provide,
To fill their bags, and swell the milky tide.
These raise their thirst, and to the taste
    restore
The savor of the salt on which they fed be-
    fore.
    Some, when the kids their dams too
    deeply drain,   610
With gags and muzzles their soft mouths
    restrain.
Their morning milk the peasants press at
    night;
Their evening meal, before the rising light,
To market bear; or sparingly they steep
With seas'ning salt, and stor'd for winter
    keep.
    Nor, last, forget thy faithful dogs; but
    feed
With fatt'ning whey the mastiffs' gen'rous
    breed,
And Spartan race, who, for the fold's relief,
Will prosecute with cries the nightly thief,
Repulse the prowling wolf, and hold at bay
The mountain robbers rushing to the prey.
With cries of hounds, thou mayst pursue
    the fear   622
Of flying hares, and chase the fallow deer;
Rouse from their desart dens the bristled
    rage
Of boars, and beamy stags in toils engage.
    With smoke of burning cedar scent thy
    walls,
And fume with stinking galbanum thy stalls,
With that rank odor from thy dwelling
    place
To drive the viper's brood, and all the
    venom'd race;
For often under stalls unmov'd they lie,
Obscure in shades, and shunning heav'n's
    broad eye;   631
And snakes, familiar, to the hearth succeed,
Disclose their eggs, and near the chimney
    breed:
Whether to roofy houses they repair,
Or sun themselves abroad in open air,

In all abodes, of pestilential kind
To sheep and oxen and the painful hind.
Take, shepherd, take a plant of stubborn
oak,
And labor him with many a sturdy stroke, 640
Or with hard stones demolish from afar
His haughty crest, the seat of all the war;
Invade his hissing throat and winding
spires;
Till, stretch'd in length, th' unfolded foe
retires.
He drags his tail, and for his head pro-
vides,
And in some secret cranny slowly glides;
But leaves expos'd to blows his back and
batter'd sides.
    In fair Calabria's woods a snake is bred,
With curling crest, and with advancing
head:
Waving he rolls, and makes a winding
track;
His belly spotted, burnish'd is his back. 650
While springs are broken, while the south-
ern air
And dropping heav'ns the moisten'd earth
repair,
He lives on standing lakes and trembling
bogs,
And fills his maw with fish, or with loqua-
cious frogs:
But when in muddy pools the water sinks,
And the chapp'd earth is furrow'd o'er with
chinks,
He leaves the fens, and leaps upon the
ground,
And, hissing, rolls his glaring eyes around.
With thirst inflam'd, impatient of the heats,
He rages in the fields, and wide destruction
threats. 660
O let not sleep my closing eyes invade
In open plains, or in the secret shade,
When he, renew'd in all the speckled pride
Of pompous youth, has cast his slough aside,
And in his summer liv'ry rolls along,
Erect, and brandishing his forky tongue,
Leaving his nest and his imperfect young;
And, thoughtless of his eggs, forgets to
rear
The hopes of poison for the foll'wing year.
    The causes and the signs shall next be
told 670
Of ev'ry sickness that infects the fold.
A scabby tetter on their pelts will stick,
When the raw rain has pierc'd them to the
quick,

Or searching frosts have eaten thro' the
skin,
Or burning icicles are lodg'd within;
Or, when the fleece is shorn, if sweat re-
mains
Unwash'd, and soaks into their empty veins;
When their defenseless limbs the brambles
tear,
Short of their wool, and naked from the
shear.
    Good shepherds, after shearing, drench
their sheep; 680
And their flock's father (forc'd from high
to leap)
Swims down the stream, and plunges in
the deep.
They oint their naked limbs with mother'd
oil;
Or, from the founts where living sulphurs
boil,
They mix a med'cine to foment their limbs,
With scum that on the molten silver swims.
Fat pitch and black bitumen add to these;
Besides, the waxen labor of the bees,
And hellebore, and squills deep-rooted in
the seas.
Receipts abound; but, searching all thy
store, 690
The best is still at hand, to launch the sore,
And cut the head; for, till the core be found,
The secret vice is fed, and gathers ground;
While, making fruitless moan, the shep-
herd stands,
And, when the launching-knife requires
his hands,
Vain help, with idle pray'rs, from heav'n
demands.
Deep in their bones when fevers fix their
seat,
And rack their limbs, and lick the vital
heat,
The ready cure to cool the raging pain
Is underneath the foot to breathe a vein. 700
This remedy the Scythian shepherds found:
Th' inhabitants of Thracia's hilly ground
And Gelons use it, when for drink and food
They mix their cruddled milk with horses'
blood.
    But where thou seest a single sheep re-
main
In shades aloof, or couch'd upon the plain,
Or listlessly to crop the tender grass,
Or late to lag behind, with truant pace;
Revenge the crime, and take the traitor's
head,

Ere in the faultless flock the dire contagion
   spread. 710
On winter seas we fewer storms behold,
Than foul diseases that infect the fold.
Nor do those ills on single bodies prey,
But oft'ner bring the nation to decay,
And sweep the present stock and future
   hope away.
   A dire example of this truth appears,
When, after such a length of rolling years,
We see the naked Alps, and thin remains
Of scatter'd cots, and yet unpeopled
   plains,
Once fill'd with grazing flocks, the shep-
   herds' happy reigns. 720
   Here, from the vicious air and sickly skies,
A plague did on the dumb creation rise:
During th' autumnal heats ·th' infection
   grew,
Tame cattle and the beasts of nature slew,
Pois'ning the standing lakes, and pools im-
   pure;
Nor was the foodful grass in fields secure.
Strange death ! for, when the thirsty fire had
   drunk
Their vital blood, and the dry nerves were
   shrunk,
When the contracted limbs were cramp'd,
   ev'n then
A wat'rish humor swell'd and ooz'd again,
Converting into bane the kindly juice 731
Ordain'd by nature for a better use.
The victim ox, that was for altars press'd,
Trimm'd with white ribbons, and with gar-
   lands dress'd,
Sunk of himself, without the god's com-
   mand,
Preventing the slow sacrificer's hand.
Or, by the holy butcher if he fell,
Th' inspected entrails could no fates fore-
   tell;
Nor, laid on altars, did pure flames arise;
But clouds of smold'ring smoke forbade
   the sacrifice: 740
Scarcely the knife was redden'd with his
   gore.
Or the black poison stain'd the sandy floor.
The thriven calves in meads their food for-
   sake,
And render their sweet souls before the
   plenteous rack.
The fawning dog runs mad; the wheezing
   swine
With coughs is chok'd, and labors from the
   chine.

The victor horse, forgetful of his food,
The palm renounces, and abhors the flood;
He paws the ground; and on his hanging
   ears
A doubtful sweat in clammy drops ap-
   pears: 750
Parch'd is his hide, and rugged are his
   hairs.
Such are the symptoms of the young dis-
   ease;
But, in time's process, when his pains en-
   crease,
He rolls his mournful eyes; he deeply
   groans
With patient sobbing, and with manly
   moans.
He heaves for breath; which, from his
   lungs supplied,
And fetch'd from far, distends his lab'ring
   side.
To his rough palate his dry tongue suc-
   ceeds;
And ropy gore he from his nostrils bleeds.
A drench of wine has with success been
   us'd, 760
And thro' a horn the gen'rous juice infus'd;
Which, timely taken, op'd his closing jaws,
But, if too late, the patient's death did
   cause:
For the too vig'rous dose too fiercely
   wrought,
And added fury to the strength it brought.
Recruited into rage, he grinds his teeth
In his own flesh, and feeds approaching
   death.
Ye gods, to better fate good men dispose,
And turn that impious error on our foes !
   The steer, who to the yoke was bred to
   bow, 770
(Studious of tillage, and the crooked plow,)
Falls down and dies; and, dying, spews a
   flood
Of foamy madness, mix'd with clotted
   blood.
The clown, who, cursing Providence, re-
   pines,
His mournful fellow from the team dis-
   joins;
With many a groan forsakes his fruitless
   care,
And in th' unfinish'd furrow leaves the
   share.
The pining steer no shades of lofty woods
Nor flow'ry meads can ease, nor crystal
   floods

Roll'd from the rock: his flabby flanks de-
crease;   780
His eyes are settled in a stupid peace;
His bulk too weighty for his thighs is grown,
And his unwieldy neck hangs drooping
down.
Now what avails his well-deserving toil
To turn the glebe, or smooth the rugged
soil !
And yet he never supp'd in solemn state,
Nor undigested feasts did urge his fate,
Nor day to night luxuriously did join,
Nor surfeited on rich Campanian wine.
Simple his bev'rage, homely was his food,
The wholesome herbage, and the running
flood: 791
No dreadful dreams awak'd him with af-
fright;
His pains by day secur'd his rest by night.
  'Twas then that buffaloes, ill pair'd,
were seen
To draw the car of Jove's imperial queen,
For want of oxen; and the lab'ring swain ⎤
Scratch'd, with a rake, a furrow for his   ⎪
grain,   ⎬
And cover'd with his hand the shallow   ⎪
seed again.   ⎦
He yokes himself, and up the hilly height
With his own shoulders draws the wagon's
weight.   800
  The nightly wolf, that round th' enclosure
prowl'd
To leap the fence, now plots not on the
fold,
Tam'd with a sharper pain. The fearful ⎤
doe   ⎪
And flying stag amidst the greyhounds   ⎬
go,   ⎪
And round the dwellings roam of man,   ⎪
their fiercer foe.   ⎦
The scaly nations of the sea profound,
Like shipwreck'd carcasses, are driv'n
aground,
And mighty *phocæ*, never seen before
In shallow streams, are stranded on the
shore.   809
The viper dead within her hole is found:
Defenseless was the shelter of the ground.
The water snake, whom fish and paddocks
fed,
With staring scales lies poison'd in his bed:
To birds their native heav'ns contagious
prove;
From clouds they fall, and leave their souls
above.

  Besides, to change their pasture 't is in
vain,
Or trust to physic; physic is their bane.
The learned leeches in despair depart,
And shake their heads, desponding of their
art.   819
  Tisiphone, let loose from under ground,
Majestically pale, now treads the round,
Before her drives diseases and affright, ⎤
And every moment rises to the sight,   ⎪
Aspiring to the skies, encroaching on the ⎬
light.   ⎦
The rivers, and their banks, and hills around,
With lowings and with dying bleats resound.
At length, she strikes an universal blow;
To death at once whole herds of cattle go;
Sheep, oxen, horses, fall; and, heap'd on
high,
The diff'ring species in confusion lie,   830
Till, warn'd by frequent ills, the way they
found
To lodge their loathsome carrion under-
ground:
For useless to the currier were their hides;
Nor could their tainted flesh with ocean
tides
Be freed from filth; nor could Vulcanian
flame
The stench abolish, or the savor tame.
Nor safely could they shear their fleecy
store,
(Made drunk with pois'nous juice, and stiff
with gore,)
Or touch the web: but, if the vest they
wear,
Red blisters rising on their paps appear, 840
And flaming carbuncles, and noisome sweat,
And clammy dews, that loathsome lice be-
get;
Till the slow-creeping evil eats his way,
Consumes the parching limbs, and makes
the life his prey.

THE FOURTH BOOK OF THE GEORGICS

THE ARGUMENT

Virgil has taken care to raise the subject of
each *Georgic*. In the first, he has only dead
matter on which to work. In the second, he
just steps on the world of life, and describes
that degree of it which is to be found in
vegetables. In the third, he advances to ani

mals; and, in the last, singles out the bee,
which may be reckon'd the most sagacious
of 'em, for his subject.

In this *Georgic* he shews us what station is most
proper for the bees, and when they begin to
gather honey; how to call 'em home when
they swarm; and how to part 'em when they
are engag'd in battle. From hence he takes
occasion to discover their different kinds;
and, after an excursion, relates their prudent
and politic administration of affairs, and the
several diseases that often rage in their hives,
with the proper symptoms and remedies of
each disease. In the last place, he lays down
a method of repairing their kind, supposing
their whole breed lost; and gives at large
the history of its invention.

THE gifts of heav'n my foll'wing song
    pursues,
Aërial honey, and ambrosial dews.
Mæcenas, read this other part, that sings ⎫
Embattled squadrons, and advent'rous   ⎬
    kings: ⎭
A mighty pomp, tho' made of little things.
Their arms, their arts, their manners, I
    disclose,
And how they war, and whence the people
    rose:
Slight is the subject, but the praise not
    small,
If Heav'n assist, and Phœbus hear my
    call.

First, for thy bees a quiet station find, 10
And lodge 'em under covert of the wind,
(For winds, when homeward they return,
    will drive
The loaded carriers from their ev'ning hive,)
Far from the cows' and goats' insulting
    crew,
That trample down the flow'rs, and brush
    the dew.
The painted lizard, and the birds of prey,
Foes of the frugal kind, be far away;
The titmouse, and the peckers' hungry
    brood,
And Progne, with her bosom stain'd in
    blood:
These rob the trading citizens, and bear 20 ⎫
The trembling captives thro' the liquid ⎪
    air,   ⎬
And for their callow young a cruel feast ⎪
    prepare.   ⎭
But near a living stream their mansion
    place,
Edg'd round with moss and tufts of mat-
    ted grass;

And plant (the winds' impetuous rage to
    stop)
Wild olive trees, or palms, before the busy
    shop;
That, when the youthful prince, with proud
    alarm,
Calls out the vent'rous colony to swarm;
When first their way thro' yielding air they
    wing,
New to the pleasures of their native spring;
The banks of brooks may make a cool re-
    treat   31
For the raw soldiers from the scalding
    heat,
And neighb'ring trees with friendly shade
    invite
The troops, unus'd to long laborious flight.
Then o'er the running stream, or standing
    lake,
A passage for thy weary people make;
With osier floats the standing water strow;
Of massy stones make bridges, if it flow;
That basking in the sun thy bees may lie,
And, resting there, their flaggy pinions
    dry,   40
When, late returning home, the laden host
By raging winds is wreck'd upon the coast.
Wild thyme and sav'ry set around their
    cell,
Sweet to the taste, and fragrant to the
    smell;
Set rows of rosemary with flow'ring stem,
And let the purple vi'lets drink the stream.

Whether thou build the palace of thy
    bees
With twisted osiers, or with barks of trees,
Make but a narrow mouth; for, as the cold
Congeals into a lump the liquid gold, 50
So 't is again dissolv'd by summer's heat,
And the sweet labors both extremes de-
    feat.
And therefore, not in vain, th' industrious
    kind
With dauby wax and flow'rs the chinks
    have lin'd,
And, with their stores of gather'd glue, con-
    trive
To stop the vents and crannies of their
    hive.
Not birdlime, or Idæan pitch, produce
A more tenacious mass of clammy juice.
  Nor bees are lodg'd in hives alone, but
    found
In chambers of their own, beneath the
    ground;   60

Their vaulted roofs are hung in pumices,
And in the rotten trunks of hollow trees.
  But plaister thou the chinky hives with
    clay,
And leafy branches o'er their lodgings lay:
Nor place them where too deep a water
    flows,
Or where the yew, their pois'nous neigh-
    bor, grows;
Nor roast red crabs, t' offend the nice-
    ness of their nose;
Nor near the steaming stench of muddy
    ground;
Nor hollow rocks that render back the
    sound,
And doubled images of voice rebound. 70
  For what remains, when golden suns ap-
    pear,
And under earth have driv'n the winter
    year,
The winged nation wanders thro' the skies,
And o'er the plains and shady forest flies;
Then, stooping on the meads and leafy
    bow'rs,
They skim the floods, and sip the purple
    flow'rs.
Exalted hence, and drunk with secret joy,
Their young succession all their cares em-
    ploy:
They breed, they brood, instruct, and edu-
    cate,
And make provision for the future state; 80
They work their waxen lodgings in their
    hives,
And labor honey to sustain their lives.
But when thou seest a swarming cloud arise,
That sweeps aloft, and darkens all the
    skies,
The motions of their hasty flight attend;
And know, to floods or woods their airy
    march they bend.
Then melfoil beat, and honeysuckles
    pound;
With these alluring savors strew the
    ground,
And mix with tinkling brass the cymbals'
    droning sound.
Straight to their ancient cells, recall'd from
    air, 90
The reconcil'd deserters will repair.
But if intestine broils alarm the hive,
(For two pretenders oft for empire strive,)
The vulgar in divided factions jar;
And murm'ring sounds proclaim the civil
    war.

Inflam'd with ire, and trembling with dis-
    dain,
Scarce can their limbs their mighty souls
    contain.
With shouts the cowards' courage they ex-
    cite,
And martial clangors call 'em out to fight;
With hoarse alarms the hollow camp re-
    bounds, 100
That imitates the trumpets' angry sounds;
Then to their common standard they re-
    pair;
The nimble horsemen scour the fields of
    air,
In form of battle drawn, they issue forth,
And ev'ry knight is proud to prove his
    worth.
Press'd for their country's honor, and
    their king's,
On their sharp beaks they whet their
    pointed stings,
And exercise their arms, and tremble
    with their wings.
Full in the midst the haughty monarchs
    ride;
The trusty guards come up, and close the
    side; 110
With shouts the daring foe to battle is
    defied.
Thus, in the season of unclouded spring,
To war they follow their undaunted king,
Crowd thro' their gates, and in the fields of
    light
The shocking squadrons meet in mortal
    fight.
Headlong they fall from high, and,
    wounded, wound,
And heaps of slaughter'd soldiers bite the
    ground.
Hard hailstones lie not thicker on the plain,
Nor shaken oaks such show'rs of acorns rain.
With gorgeous wings, the marks of sov'reign
    sway, 120
The two contending princes make their
    way;
Intrepid thro' the midst of danger go,
Their friends encourage, and amaze the foe.
With mighty souls in narrow bodies press'd,
They challenge, and encounter breast to
    breast;
So fix'd on fame, unknowing how to fly,
And obstinately bent to win or die,
That long the doubtful combat they main-
    tain,
Till one prevails — for one can only reign.

Yet all those dreadful deeds, this deadly
    fray,   130
A cast of scatter'd dust will soon allay,
And undecided leave the fortune of the
    day.
When both the chiefs are sunder'd from
    the fight,
Then to the lawful king restore his right;
And let the wasteful prodigal be slain,
That he who best deserves alone may reign.
With ease distinguish'd is the regal race:
One monarch wears an honest open face;
Shap'd to his size, and godlike to behold,
His royal body shines with specks of gold,
And ruddy scales; for empire he design'd,
Is better born, and of a nobler kind.   142
That other looks like nature in disgrace:
Gaunt are his sides, and sullen is his face;
And like their grisly prince appears his
    gloomy race,
Grim, ghastly, rugged, like a thirsty train
That long have travel'd thro' a desart
    plain,
And spet from their dry chaps the gather'd
    dust again.
The better brood, unlike the bastard crew,
Are mark'd with royal streaks of shining
    hue;   150
Glitt'ring and ardent, tho' in body less:
From these, at pointed seasons, hope to
    press
Huge heavy honeycombs, of golden juice,
Not only sweet, but pure, and fit for use,
T' allay the strength and hardness of the
    wine,
And with old Bacchus new metheglin join.
    But when the swarms are eager of their
    play,
And loathe their empty hives, and idly
    stray,
Restrain the wanton fugitives, and take
A timely care to bring the truants back. 160
The task is easy — but to clip the wings
Of their high-flying arbitrary kings.
At their command, the people swarm away:
Confine the tyrant, and the slaves will stay.
    Sweet gardens, full of saffron flow'rs,
    invite
The wand'ring gluttons, and retard their
    flight;
Besides, the god obscene, who frights away,
With his lath sword, the thiefs and birds of
    prey.
With his own hand, the guardian of the
    bees

For slips of pines may search the mountain
    trees,   170
And with wild thyme and sav'ry plant the
    plain,
Till his hard horny fingers ache with
    pain;
And deck with fruitful trees the fields
    around,
And with refreshing waters drench the
    ground
    Now, did I not so near my labors end,
Strike sail, and hast'ning to the harbor
    tend,
My song to flow'ry gardens might extend:
To teach the vegetable arts, to sing
The Pæstan roses, and their double spring;
How succ'ry drinks the running streams,
    and how   180
Green beds of parsley near the river grow;
How cucumers along the surface creep
With crooked bodies, and with bellies deep;
The late narcissus, and the winding trail
Of bear's-foot, myrtles green, and ivy pale.
For, where with stately tow'rs Tarentum
    stands,
And deep Galæsus soaks the yellow sands,
I chanc'd an old Corycian swain to know,
Lord of few acres, and those barren too,
Unfit for sheep or vines, and more unfit
    to sow: 190
Yet, lab'ring well his little spot of ground,
Some scatt'ring pot-herbs here and there he
    found,
Which, cultivated with his daily care,
And bruis'd with vervain, were his frugal
    fare.
Sometimes white lilies did their leaves
    afford,
With wholesome poppy flow'rs, to mend his
    homely board;
For, late returning home, he supp'd at
    ease,
And wisely deem'd the wealth of mon-
    archs less:
The little of his own, because his own,
    did please.
To quit his care, he gather'd, first of a'l, 200
In spring the roses, apples in the fall;
And, when cold winter split the rocks in
    twain,
And ice the running rivers did restrain,
He stripp'd the bear's-foot of its leafy
    growth,
And, calling western winds, accus'd the
    spring of sloth.

He therefore first among the swains was }
   found
To reap the product of his labor'd ground, }
And squeeze the combs with golden }
   liquor crown'd.
His limes were first in flow'rs; his lofty
   pines,
With friendly shade, secur'd his tender
   vines.   210
For ev'ry bloom his trees in spring afford,
An autumn apple was by tale restor'd.
He knew to rank his elms in even rows, }
For fruit the grafted pear tree to dispose, }
And tame to plums the sourness of the }
   sloes.
With spreading planes he made a cool re-
   treat,
To shade good fellows from the summer's
   heat.
But, straiten'd in my space, I must forsake
This task, for others afterwards to take.
   Describe we next the nature of the bees,
Bestow'd by Jove for secret services,   221
When, by the tinkling sound of timbrels
   led,
The King of Heav'n in Cretan caves they
   fed.
Of all the race of animals, alone,
The bees have common cities of their own;
And, common sons, beneath one law they
   live,
And with one common stock their traffic
   drive.
Each has a certain home, a sev'ral stall;
All is the State's, the State provides for all.
Mindful of coming cold, they share the
   pain,   230
And hoard, for winter's use, the summer's
   gain.
Some o'er the public magazines preside,
And some are sent new forage to provide;
These drudge in fields abroad, and those }
   at home
Lay deep foundations for the labor'd }
   comb, }
With dew, narcissus leaves, and clammy }
   gum.
To pitch the waxen flooring some contrive;
Some nurse the future nation of the hive;
Sweet honey some condense; some purge
   the grout;
The rest, in cells apart, the liquid nectar
   shut: 240
All, with united force, combine to drive
The lazy drones from the laborious hive;

With envy stung, they view each other's
   deeds;
With diligence the fragrant work proceeds.
As when the Cyclops, at th' almighty nod,
New thunder hasten for their angry god,
Subdued in fire the stubborn metal lies;
One brawny smith the puffing bellows plies,
And draws and blows reciprocating air:
Others to quench the hissing mass prepare;
With lifted arms they order ev'ry blow, }
And chime their sounding hammers in a }
   row;   252
With labor'd anvils Ætna groans be- }
   low:
Strongly they strike; huge flakes of flames
   expire;
With tongs they turn the steel, and vex it
   in the fire.
If little things with great we may com-
   pare,
Such are the bees, and such their busy care;
Studious of honey, each in his degree,
The youthful swain, the grave experienc'd
   bee:
That in the field; this, in affairs of state 260
Employ'd at home, abides within the gate,
To fortify the combs, to build the wall,
To prop the ruins, lest the fabric fall:
But, late at night, with weary pinions come
The lab'ring youth, and heavy laden, home.
Plains, meads, and orchards, all the day
   he plies;
The gleans of yellow thyme distend his
   thighs:
He spoils the saffron flow'rs; he sips the
   blues
Of vi'lets, wilding blooms, and willow dews.
Their toil is common, common is their
   sleep;   270
They shake their wings when morn begins
   to peep,
Rush thro' the city gates without delay,
Nor ends their work, but with declining
   day.
Then, having spent the last remains of
   light,
They give their bodies due repose at night,
When hollow murmurs of their ev'ning
   bells
Dismiss the sleepy swains, and toll 'em to
   their cells.
When once in beds their weary limbs they
   steep,
No buzzing sounds disturb their golden
   sleep.

'T is sacred silence all. Nor dare they
   stray, 280
When rain is promis'd, or a stormy day;
But near the city walls their wat'ring take,
Nor forage far, but short excursions make.
   And as, when empty barks on billows
   float,
With sandy ballast sailors trim the boat;
So bees bear gravel stones, whose poising
   weight
Steers thro' the whistling winds their
   steady flight.
   But, what 's more strange, their modest
   appetites,
Averse from Venus, fly the nuptial rites.
No lust enervates their heroic mind, 290
Nor wastes their strength on wanton
   womankind;
But in their mouths reside their genial
   pow'rs:
They gather children from the leaves
   and flow'rs.
Thus make they kings to fill the regal ⎫
   seat,   ⎪
And thus their little citizens create,   ⎬
And waxen cities build and palaces of ⎪
   state.   ⎭
And oft on rocks their tender wings they
   tear,
And sink beneath the burthens which they
   bear:
Such rage of honey in their bosom beats,
And such a zeal they have for flow'ry
   sweets. 300
   Thus tho' the race of life they quickly
   run,
Which in the space of sev'n short years is
   done,
Th' immortal line in sure succession ⎫
   reigns;   ⎪
The fortune of the family remains,   ⎬
And grandsires' grandsons the long list ⎪
   contains.   ⎭
Besides, not Egypt, India, Media, more,
With servile awe their idol king adore:
While he survives, in concord and con- ⎫
   tent   ⎪
The commons live, by no divisions rent; ⎬
But the great monarch's death dissolves ⎪
   the government. 310 ⎭
All goes to ruin; they themselves contrive
To rob the honey, and subvert the hive.
The king presides, his subjects' toil surveys;
The servile rout their careful Cæsar praise:
Him they extol; they worship him alone;

They crowd his levees, and support his
   throne;
They raise him on their shoulders with a
   shout;
And, when their sov'reign's quarrel calls
   'em out,
His foes to mortal combat they defy,
And think it honor at his feet to die. 320
   Induc'd by such examples, some have
   taught
That bees have portions of ethereal
   thought;
Endued with particles of heavenly fires:
For God the whole created mass inspires;
Thro' heav'n, and earth, and ocean's depth
   he throws
His influence round, and kindles as he
   goes.
Hence flocks, and herds, and men, and
   beasts, and fowls
With breath are quicken'd and attract
   their souls;
Hence take the forms his prescience did
   ordain,
And into him at length resolve again. 330
No room is left for death: they mount the
   sky,
And to their own congenial planets fly.
   Now, when thou hast decreed to seize
   their stores,
And by prerogative to break their doors,
With sprinkled water first the city choke,
And then pursue the citizens with smoke.
Two honey harvests fall in ev'ry year:
First, when the pleasing Pleiades appear,
And, springing upward, spurn the briny
   seas; 339
Again, when their affrighted choir surveys
The wat'ry Scorpion mend his pace be- ⎫
   hind,   ⎪
With a black train of storms, and winter ⎬
   wind,   ⎪
They plunge into the deep, and safe pro- ⎪
   tection find.   ⎭
Prone to revenge, the bees, a wrathful race,
When once provok'd, assault th' aggressor's
   face,
And thro' the purple veins a passage find;
There fix their stings, and leave their souls
   behind.
   But if a pinching winter thou foresee,
And wouldst preserve thy famish'd family;
With fragrant thyme the city fumigate, 350
And break the waxen walls to save the state.
For lurking lizards often lodge, by stealth,

Within the suburbs, and purloin their
  wealth;
And worms, that shun the light, a dark
  retreat
Have found in combs, and undermin'd the
  seat;
Or lazy drones, without their share of pain,
In winter quarters free, devour the gain;
Or wasps infest the camp with loud alarms,
And mix in battle with unequal arms;
Or secret moths are there in silence fed; 360
Or spiders in the vault their snary webs
  have spread.
The more oppress'd by foes, or famine-pin'd,
The more increase thy care to save the sink-
  ing kind:
With greens and flow'rs recruit their empty
  hives,
And seek fresh forage to sustain their lives.
  But, since they share with man one com-
    mon fate,
In health and sickness, and in turns of state;
Observe the symptoms when they fall away,
And languish with insensible decay.
They change their hue; with haggard eyes
  they stare;   370
Lean are their looks, and shagged is their
  hair;
And crowds of dead, that never must ⎤
  return |
To their lov'd hives, in decent pomp are ⎬
  borne: |
Their friends attend the hearse; the next |
  relations mourn.   ⎦
The sick for air before the portal gasp,
Their feeble legs within each other clasp,
Or idle in their empty hives remain,
Benumb'd with cold, and listless of their
  gain.
Soft whispers then, and broken sounds are
  heard,
As when the woods by gentle winds are
  stirr'd;   380
Such stifled noise as the close furnace hides,
Or dying murmurs of departing tides.
This when thou seest, galbanean odors use,
And honey in the sickly hive infuse.
Thro' reeden pipes convey the golden flood,
T' invite the people to their wonted food.
Mix it with thicken'd juice of sodden wines,
And raisins from the grapes of Psythian
  vines:
To these add pounded galls, and roses dry,
And, with Cecropian thyme, strong-scented
  centaury.   390

A flow'r there is, that grows in meadow
  ground,
Amellus call'd, and easy to be found;
For, from one root, the rising stem bestows
A wood of leaves, and vi'let-purple boughs:
The flow'r itself is glorious to behold,
And shines on altars like refulgent gold;
Sharp to the taste; by shepherds near the
  stream
Of Mella found; and thence they gave the
  name.
Boil this restoring root in gen'rous wine,
And set beside the door, the sickly stock to
  dine.   400
But, if the lab'ring kind be wholly lost,
And not to be retriev'd with care or cost;
'T is time to touch the precepts of an art
Th' Arcadian master did of old impart;
And how he stock'd his empty hives again,
Renew'd with putrid gore of oxen slain.
An ancient legend I prepare to sing,
And upward follow Fame's immortal
  spring: —
  For, where with sev'nfold horns myste-
    rious Nile
Surrounds the skirts of Egypt's fruitful
  isle,   410
And where in pomp the sunburnt people
  ride
On painted barges o'er the teeming tide,
Which, pouring down from Ethiopian lands,
Makes green the soil with slime, and black
  prolific sands;
That length of region, and large tract of
  ground,
In this one art a sure relief have found.
First, in a place by nature close, they build
A narrow flooring, gutter'd, wall'd, and
  til'd.
In this, four windows are contriv'd, that
  strike
To the four winds oppos'd their beams
  oblique.   420
A steer of two years old they take, whose
  head
Now first with burnish'd horns begins to
  spread;
They stop his nostrils, while he strives in
  vain
To breathe free air, and struggles with his
  pain.
Knock'd down, he dies: his bowels, bruis'd
  within,
Betray no wound on his unbroken skin.
Extended thus, in this obscene abode

They leave the beast; but first sweet flow'rs
are strow'd
Beneath his body, broken boughs and
thyme,
And pleasing cassia just renew'd in prime.
This must be done, ere spring makes equal
day,   431
When western winds on curling waters play;
Ere painted meads produce their flow'ry
crops,
Or swallows twitter on the chimney tops.
The tainted blood, in this close prison pent,
Begins to boil, and thro' the bones ferment.
Then, wondrous to behold, new creatures
rise,
A moving mass at first, and short of thighs;
Till, shooting out with legs, and imp'd with
wings,
The grubs proceed to bees with pointed
stings;   440
And, more and more affecting air, they try
Their tender pinions, and begin to fly:
At length, like summer storms from spread-
ing clouds,
That burst at once, and pour impetuous
floods;
Or flights of arrows from the Parthian
bows,
When from afar they gall embattled foes;
With such a tempest thro' the skies they
steer,
And such a form the winged squadrons
bear.
　　What god, O Muse! this useful science
taught?
Or by what man's experience was it
brought?   450
　　Sad Aristæus from fair Tempe fled,   ⎤
His bees with famine or diseases dead: ⎟
On Peneus' banks he stood, and near his   ⎬
holy head;   ⎟
And, while his falling tears the stream   ⎦
supplied,
Thus, mourning, to his mother goddess cried:
"Mother Cyrene! mother, whose abode
Is in the depth of this immortal flood!
What boots it, that from Phœbus' loins I
spring,
The third, by him and thee, from heav'n's
high king?
O where is all thy boasted pity gone,   460
And promise of the skies to thy deluded
son?
Why didst thou me, unhappy me, create,
Odious to gods, and born to bitter fate?

Whom scarce my sheep, and scarce my   ⎤
painful plow,   ⎟
The needful aids of human life allow: ⎬
So wretched is thy son, so hard a mother ⎟
thou!   ⎦
Proceed, inhuman parent, in thy scorn;   ⎤
Root up my trees; with blights destroy   ⎟
my corn;   ⎬
My vineyards ruin, and my sheepfolds   ⎟
burn.   ⎦
Let loose thy rage; let all thy spite be
shown,   470
Since thus thy hate pursues the praises of
thy son."
　　But, from her mossy bow'r below the   ⎤
ground,   ⎟
His careful mother heard the plaintive   ⎬
sound,   ⎟
Encompass'd with her sea-green sisters   ⎦
round.
One common work they plied; their distaffs
full
With carded locks of blue Milesian wool:
Spio, with Drymo brown, and Xanthe fair,
And sweet Phyllodoce with long dishevel'd
hair;
Cydippe with Lycorias, one a maid,
And one that once had call'd Lucina's aid;
Clio and Beroe, from one father both;   481
Both girt with gold, and clad in party-col-
or'd cloth;
Opis the meek, and Deiopeia proud;
Nisæa softly, with Ligea loud;
Thalia joyous, Ephyre the sad,   ⎤
And Arethusa, once Diana's maid,   ⎬
But now (her quiver left) to love betray'd. ⎦
To these Clymene the sweet theft declares
Of Mars, and Vulcan's unavailing cares;
And all the rapes of gods, and ev'ry love, 490
From ancient Chaos down to youthful Jove.
　　Thus while she sings, the sisters turn
the wheel,
Empty the woolly rock, and fill the reel.
A mournful sound again the mother hears;
Again the mournful sound invades the sis-
ters' ears.
Starting at once from their green seats,
they rise;
Fear in their heart, amazement in their
eyes.
But Arethusa, leaping from her bed,   ⎤
First lifts above the waves her beauteous ⎟
head,   ⎬
And, crying from afar, thus to Cyrene   ⎟
said: 500 ⎦

"O sister, not with causeless fear pos-
sess'd !
No stranger voice disturbs thy tender breast.
'T is Aristæus, 't is thy darling son,
Who to his careless mother makes his moan.
Near his paternal stream he sadly stands,
With downcast eyes, wet cheeks, and folded
hands,
Upbraiding heav'n, from whence his lineage
came;
And cruel calls the gods, and cruel thee, by
name."
    Cyrene, mov'd with love, and seiz'd with
fear,
Cries out: "Conduct my son, conduct him
here: 510
'T is lawful for the youth, deriv'd from
gods,
To view the secrets of our deep abodes."
At once she wav'd her hand on either side;
At once the ranks of swelling streams di-
vide.
Two rising heaps of liquid crystal stand,
And leave a space betwixt of empty sand.
Thus safe receiv'd, the downward track he
treads,
Which to his mother's wat'ry palace leads.
With wond'ring eyes he views the secret
store
Of lakes, that pent in hollow caverns roar:
He hears the crackling sound of coral
woods,   521
And sees the secret source of subterranean
floods;
And where, distinguish'd in their sev'ral
cells,
The fount of Phasis, and of Lycus, dwells;
Where swift Enipeus in his bed appears,
And Tiber his majestic forehead rears;
Whence Anio flows, and Hypanis, profound,
Breaks thro' th' opposing rocks with rag-
ing sound;
Where Po first issues from his dark abodes,
And, awful in his cradle, rules the floods:
Two golden horns on his large front he
wears,   531
And his grim face a bull's resemblance
bears;
With rapid course he seeks the sacred
main,
And fattens, as he runs, the fruitful plain.
    Now, to the court arriv'd, th' admiring
son
Beholds the vaulted roofs of pory stone;
Now to his mother goddess tells his grief,

Which she with pity hears, and promises re-
lief.
Th' officious nymphs, attending in a ring,
With waters drawn from their perpetual
spring,   540
From earthly dregs his body purify,
And rub his temples with fine towels dry;
Then load tne tables with a lib'ral feast,
And honor with full bowls their friendly
guest.
The sacred altars are involv'd in smoke,
And the bright choir their kindred gods
invoke.
Two bowls the mother fills with Lydian ⎤
wine;   ⎪
Then thus: "Let these be pour'd, with ⎬
rites divine,   ⎪
To the great authors of our wat'ry line: ⎦
To Father Ocean, this; and this," she ⎤
said,   550 ⎪
"Be to the nymphs his sacred sisters paid, ⎬
Who rule the wat'ry plains, and hold the ⎪
woodland shade."   ⎦
She sprinkled thrice, with wine, the Vestal
fire;
Thrice to the vaulted roof the flames as-
pire.
Rais'd with so blest an omen, she begun,
With words like these, to cheer her droop-
ing son:
"In the Carpathian bottom makes abode
The shepherd of the seas, a prophet and a
god.
High o'er the main in wat'ry pomp he rides;
His azure car and finny coursers guides: 560
Proteus his name — to his Pallenian port
I see from far the weary god resort.
Him not alone we river gods adore,
But aged Nereus hearkens to his lore.
With sure foresight, and with unerring
doom,
He sees what is, and was, and is to come.
This Neptune gave him, when he gave to
keep
His scaly flocks, that graze the wat'ry deep.
Implore his aid; for Proteus only knows
The secret cause, and cure, of all thy woes.
But first the wily wizard must be caught; ⎤
For, unconstrain'd, he nothing tells for ⎪
naught;   572 ⎬
Nor is with pray'rs, or bribes, or flatt'ry ⎪
bought.   ⎦
Surprise him first, and with hard fetters
bind;
Then all his frauds will vanish into wind.

I will myself conduct thee on thy way;
When next the southing sun inflames the
day,
When the dry herbage thirsts for dews in
vain,
And sheep, in shades, avoid the parching
plain:
Then will I lead thee to his secret seat, ⎤
When, weary with his toil, and scorch'd |
with heat, 581 ⎬
The wayward sire frequents his cool re- |
treat. ⎦
His eyes with heavy slumber overcast;
With force invade his limbs, and bind him
fast.
Thus surely bound, yet be not over bold:
The slipp'ry god will try to loose his hold,
And various forms assume, to cheat thy
sight,
And with vain images of beasts affright:
With foamy tusks will seem a bristly boar,
Or imitate the lion's angry roar; 590
Break out in crackling flames to shun thy
snares,
Or hiss a dragon, or a tiger stares;
Or, with a wile thy caution to betray,
In fleeting streams attempt to slide away.
But thou, the more he varies forms, beware
To strain his fetters with a stricter care;
Till, tiring all his arts, he turns again
To his true shape, in which he first was
seen."
This said, with nectar she her son anoints,
Infusing vigor thro' his mortal joints: 600
Down from his head the liquid odors ran;
He breath'd of heav'n, and look'd above a
man.
Within a mountain's hollow womb there
lies
A large recess, conceal'd from human eyes,
Where heaps of billows, driv'n by wind ⎤
and tide, |
In form of war their wat'ry ranks divide, ⎬
And there, like sentries set, without the |
mouth abide: ⎦
A station safe for ships, when tempests roar,
A silent harbor, and a cover'd shore.
Secure within resides the various god, 610
And draws a rock upon his dark abode.
Hether with silent steps, secure from ⎤
sight, |
The goddess guides her son, and turns ⎬
him from the light: |
Herself, involv'd in clouds, precipitates |
her flight. ⎦

'T was noon; the sultry Dog-star from
the sky
Scorch'd Indian swains; the rivel'd grass
was dry;
The sun with flaming arrows pierc'd the
flood,
And, darting to the bottom, bak'd the mud;
When weary Proteus, from the briny waves,
Retir'd for shelter to his wonted caves. 620
His finny flocks about their shepherd play,
And, rolling round him, spirt the bitter sea;
Unwieldily they wallow first in ooze,
Then in the shady covert seek repose.
Himself, their herdsman, on the middle
mount,
Takes of his muster'd flocks a just account.
So, seated on a rock, a shepherd's groom
Surveys his ev'ning flocks returning home,
When lowing calves and bleating lambs,
from far, 629
Provoke the prowling wolf to nightly war.
Th' occasion offers, and the youth complies:
For scarce the weary god had clos'd his
eyes,
When, rushing on, with shouts, he binds in
chains
The drowsy prophet, and his limbs con-
strains.
He, not unmindful of his usual art,
First in dissembled fire attempts to part:
Then roaring beasts and running streams
he tries,
And wearies all his miracles of lies;
But, having shifted ev'ry form to scape,
Convinc'd of conquest, he resum'd his
shape, 640
And thus, at length, in human accent spoke:
"Audacious youth! what madness could
provoke
A mortal man t' invade a sleeping god?
What bus'ness brought thee to my dark
abode?"
To this th' audacious youth: "Thou
know'st full well
My name and bus'ness, god; nor need I tell.
No man can Proteus cheat; but, Proteus,
leave
Thy fraudful arts, and do not thou deceive.
Foll'wing the gods' command, I come t'
implore
Thy help, my perish'd people to restore."
The seer, who could not yet his wrath
assuage, 651
Roll'd his green eyes, that sparkled with
his rage,

And gnash'd his teeth, and cried: "No
  vulgar god
Pursues thy crimes, nor with a common
  rod.
Thy great misdeeds have met a due re-
  ward;
And Orpheus' dying pray'rs at length are
  heard.
For crimes not his the lover lost his life,
And at thy hands requires his murther'd
  wife;
Nor (if the Fates assist not) canst thou
  scape
The just revenge of that intended rape. 660
To shun thy lawless lust, the dying bride,
Unwary, took along the river's side,
Nor at her heels perceiv'd the deadly snake
That kept the bank, in covert of the brake.
But all her fellow-nymphs the mountains
  tear
With loud laments, and break the yielding
  air:
The realms of Mars remurmur'd all around,
And echoes to th' Athenian shores rebound.
Th' unhappy husband, husband now no ⎫
  more, ⎪
Did on his tuneful harp his loss deplore, ⎬
And sought his mournful mind with ⎪
  music to restore.   671 ⎭
On thee, dear wife, in desarts all alone, ⎫
He call'd, sigh'd, sung: his griefs with ⎪
  day begun, ⎬
Nor were they finish'd with the setting ⎪
  sun. ⎭
Ev'n to the dark dominions of the night
He took his way, thro' forests void of light,
And dar'd amidst the trembling ghosts to
  sing,
And stood before th' inexorable king.
Th' infernal troops like passing shadows
  glide,
And, list'ning, crowd the sweet musician's
  side.   680
Not flocks of birds, when driv'n by storms
  or night,
Stretch to the forest with so thick a flight:
Men, matrons, children, and th' un- ⎫
  married maid, ⎪
The mighty hero's more majestic shade,* ⎬
And youths on fun'ral piles before their ⎪
  parents laid. ⎭
All these Cocytus bounds with squalid
  reeds,

* This whole line is taken from the Marquess of Normanby's translation.

With muddy ditches, and with deadly
  weeds;
And baleful Styx encompasses around,
With nine slow circling streams, th' un-
  happy ground.
Ev'n from the depths of hell the damn'd
  advance;   690
Th' infernal mansions, nodding, seem to
  dance;
The gaping three-mouth'd dog forgets to
  snarl;
The Furies hearken, and their snakes
  uncurl;
Ixion seems no more his pains to feel,
But leans attentive on his standing wheel.
  " All dangers pass'd, at length the lovely
  bride
In safety goes, with her melodious guide,
Longing the common light again to share,
And draw the vital breath of upper air: 699
He first; and close behind him follow'd she;
For such was Proserpine's severe decree —
When strong desires th' impatient youth
  invade,
By little caution and much love betray'd:
A fault which easy pardon might receive,
Were lovers judges, or could Hell forgive.
For, near the confines of ethereal light,
And longing for the glimm'ring of a sight,
Th' unwary lover cast his eyes behind,
Forgetful of the law, nor master of his
  mind.
Straight all his hopes exhal'd in empty
  smoke,   710
And his long toils were forfeit for a look.
Three flashes of blue lightning gave the sign
Of cov'nants broke; three peals of thunder
  join.
Then thus the bride: 'What fury seiz'd on
  thee,
Unhappy man ! to lose thyself and me ?
Dragg'd back again by cruel destinies,
An iron slumber shuts my swimming eyes.
And now, farewell ! Involv'd in shades of
  night,
Forever I am ravish'd from thy sight.
In vain I reach my feeble hands, to join 720
In sweet embraces — ah ! no longer thine !'
She said; and from his eyes the fleeting ⎫
  fair ⎬
Retir'd like subtile smoke dissolv'd in air, ⎪
And left her hopeless lover in despair. ⎭
In vain, with folding arms, the youth assay'd
To stop her flight, and strain the flying
  shade:

He prays, he raves, all means in vain he }
   tries,
With rage inflam'd, astonish'd with sur- }
   prise;
But she return'd no more, to bless his }
   longing eyes,
Nor would th' infernal ferryman once
   more   730
Be brib'd to waft him to the farther shore.
What should he do, who twice had lost his
   love?
What notes invent? what new petitions
   move?
Her soul already was consign'd to fate,
And shiv'ring in the leaky sculler sate.
For sev'n continued months, if fame say
   true,
The wretched swain his sorrows did renew.
By Strymon's freezing streams he sate
   alone:
The rocks were mov'd to pity with his
   moan;
Trees bent their heads to hear him sing his
   wrongs;   740
Fierce tigers couch'd around, and loll'd
   their fawning tongues.
  "So, close in poplar shades, her children
   gone,
The mother nightingale laments alone,
Whose nest some prying churl had found,
   and thence
By stealth convey'd th' unfeather'd inno-
   cence.
But she supplies the night with mournful
   strains;
And melancholy music fills the plains.
Sad Orpheus thus his tedious hours em-
   ploys,
Averse from Venus, and from nuptial joys.
Alone he tempts the frozen floods, alone 750
Th' unhappy climes, where spring was never
   known:
He mourn'd his wretched wife, in vain re-
   stor'd,
And Pluto's unavailing boon deplor'd.
  "The Thracian matrons, who the youth
   accus'd
Of love disdain'd and marriage rites re-
   fus'd,
With furies and nocturnal orgies fir'd,
At length against his sacred life conspir'd,
Whom ev'n the savage beasts had spar'd,
   they kill'd,
And strew'd his mangled limbs about the
   field.

Then, when his head, from his fair shoulders
   torn,   760
Wash'd by the waters, was on Hebrus borne,
Ev'n then his trembling tongue invok'd his }
   bride;
With his last voice, 'Eurydice,' he cried. }
'Eurydice,' the rocks and river banks re- }
   plied."
This answer Proteus gave; nor more he }
   said,
But in the billows plung'd his hoary head; }
And, where he leap'd, the waves in circles }
   widely spread.
  The nymph return'd, her drooping son to
   cheer,
And bade him banish his superfluous fear:
"For now," said she, "the cause is known,
   from whence   770
Thy woe succeeded, and for what offense.
The nymphs, companions of th' unhappy
   maid,
This punishment upon thy crimes have laid;
And sent a plague among thy thriving bees.
With vows and suppliant pray'rs their
   pow'rs appease:
The soft Napæan race will soon repent
Their anger, and remit the punishment.
The secret in an easy method lies:
Select four brawny bulls for sacrifice,
Which on Lycæus graze without a guide; 780
Add four fair heifers yet in yoke untried.
For these, four altars in their temple rear,
And then adore the woodland pow rs with
   pray'r.
From the slain victims pour the streaming
   blood,
And leave their bodies in the shady wood:
Nine mornings thence, Lethæan poppy
   bring,
T' appease the manes of the poets' king;
And, to propitiate his offended bride,
A fatted calf and a black ewe provide.
This finish'd, to the former woods repair." }
  His mother's precepts he performs with }
   care,   791
The temple visits, and adores with pray'r; }
Four altars raises; from his herd he culls,
For slaughter, four the fairest of his bulls:
Four heifers from his female store he took,
All fair, and all unknowing of the yoke.
Nine mornings thence, with sacrifice and
   pray'rs,
The pow'rs aton'd, he to the grove repairs.
Behold a prodigy! for, from within
The broken bowels and the bloated skin, 800

A buzzing noise of bees his ears alarms:
Straight issue thro' the sides assembling
   swarms.
Dark as a cloud, they make a wheeling
   flight,
Then on a neighb'ring tree, descending,
   light:
Like a large cluster of black grapes they
   show,
And make a large dependence from the
   bough.
   Thus have I sung of fields, and flocks, and
   trees,
And of the waxen work of lab'ring bees;
While mighty Cæsar, thund'ring from afar,
Seeks on Euphrates' banks the spoils of war;
With conqu'ring arms asserts his country's
   cause,   811
With arts of peace the willing people draws;
On the glad earth the Golden Age renews,
And his great father's path to heav'n pur-
   sues;
While I at Naples pass my peaceful days,
Affecting studies of less noisy praise;
And, bold thro' youth, beneath the beechen
   shade,
The lays of shepherds, and their loves, have
   play'd.

ÆNEIS

TO THE

MOST HONORABLE
JOHN, LORD MARQUIS OF
NORMANBY

EARL OF MULGRAVE, &C.

AND KNIGHT OF THE MOST NOBLE ORDER
OF THE GARTER

A HEROIC poem, truly such, is undoubtedly
the greatest work which the soul of man is
capable to perform. The design of it is to
form the mind to heroic virtue by example.
'T is convey'd in verse, that it may delight,
while it instructs: the action of it is always
one, entire, and great. The least and most
trivial episodes, or underactions, which are
interwoven in it, are parts either necessary
or convenient to carry on the main design;
either so necessary, that, without them, the
poem must be imperfect, or so convenient,
that no others can be imagin'd more suitable

to the place in which they are. There is
nothing to be left void in a firm building;
even the cavities ought not to be fill'd with
rubbish, (which is of a perishable kind, destructive to the strength,) but with brick
or stone, tho' of less pieces, yet of the same
nature, and fitted to the crannies. Even the
least portions of them must be of the epic
kind: all things must be grave, majestical,
and sublime; nothing of a foreign nature,
like the trifling *novels* which Ariosto and
others have inserted in their poems; by
which the reader is misled into another
sort of pleasure, opposite to that which is
design'd in an epic poem. One raises the
soul, and hardens it to virtue; the other
softens it again, and unbends it into vice.
One conduces to the poet's aim, the completing of his work, which he is driving on,
laboring and hast'ning in every line; the
other slackens his pace, diverts him from
his way, and locks him up, like a knight-
errant, in an enchanted castle, when he
should be pursuing his first adventure.
Statius, as Bossu has well observ'd, was
ambitious of trying his strength with his
master Virgil, as Virgil had before tried
his with Homer. The Grecian gave the two
Romans an example, in the games which
were celebrated at the funerals of Patroclus. Virgil imitated the invention of
Homer, but chang'd the sports. But both
the Greek and Latin poet took their occasions from the subject; tho', to confess the
truth, they were both ornamental, or at best
convenient parts of it, rather than of necessity arising from it. Statius, who, thro'
his whole poem, is noted for want of conduct and judgment, instead of staying, as he
might have done, for the death of Capaneus,
Hippomedon, Tydeus, or some other of his
seven champions, (who are heroes all alike,)
or more properly for the tragical end of
the two brothers, whose exequies the next
successor had leisure to perform when the
siege was rais'd, and in the interval betwixt
the poet's first action and his second, went
out of his way, as it were on prepense
malice, to commit a fault. For he took his
opportunity to kill a royal infant by the
means of a serpent (that author of all evil),
to make way for those funeral honors which
he intended for him. Now if this innocent
had been of any relation to his *Thebais ;*
if he had either farther'd or hinder'd the

taking of the town; the poet might have found some sorry excuse at least for detaining the reader from the promis'd siege. On these terms, this Capaneus of a poet ingag'd his two immortal predecessors; and his success was answerable to his enterprise.

If this economy must be observ'd in the minutest parts of an epic poem, which, to a common reader, seem to be detach'd from the body, and almost independent of it; what soul, tho' sent into the world with great advantages of nature, cultivated with the liberal arts and sciences, conversant with histories of the dead, and enrich'd with observations on the living, can be sufficient to inform the whole body of so great a work? I touch here but transiently, without any strict method, on some few of those many rules of imitating nature which Aristotle drew from Homer's *Iliads* and *Odysses*, and which he fitted to the drama; furnishing himself also with observations from the practice of the theater when it flourish'd under Æschylus, Euripides, and Sophocles: for the original of the stage was from the epic poem. Narration, doubtless, preceded acting, and gave laws to it; what at first was told artfully, was, in process of time, represented gracefully to the sight and hearing. Those episodes of Homer which were proper for the stage, the poets amplified each into an action; out of his limbs they form'd their bodies; what he had contracted, they enlarg'd; out of one Hercules were made infinite of pigmies, yet all endued with human souls; for from him, their great creator, they have each of them the *divinæ particulam auræ*. They flow'd from him at first, and are at last resolv'd into him. Nor were they only animated by him, but their measure and symmetry was owing to him. His one, entire, and great action was copied by them according to the proportions of the drama. If he finish'd his orb within the year, it suffic'd to teach them, that their action being less, and being also less diversified with incidents, their orb, of consequence, must be circumscrib'd in a less compass, which they reduc'd within the limits either of a natural or an artificial day; so that, as he taught them to amplify what he had shorten'd, by the same rule, applied the contrary way, he taught them to shorten what he had amplified. Tragedy is the miniature of human life; an epic poem

is the draught at length. Here, my Lord, I must contract also; for, before I was aware, I was almost running into a long digression, to prove that there is no such absolute necessity that the time of a stage action should so strictly be confin'd to twenty-four hours as never to exceed them, for which Aristotle contends, and the Grecian stage has practic'd. Some longer space, on some occasions, I think, may be allow'd, especially for the English theater, which requires more variety of incidents than the French. Corneille himself, after long practice, was inclin'd to think that the time allotted by the ancients was too short to raise and finish a great action: and better a mechanic rule were stretch'd or broken, than a great beauty were omitted. To raise, and afterwards to calm the passions; to purge the soul from pride, by the examples of human miseries, which befall the greatest; in few words, to expel arrogance, and introduce compassion, are the great effects of tragedy; great, I must confess, if they were altogether as true as they are pompous. But are habits to be introduc'd at three hours' warning? Are radical diseases so suddenly remov'd? A mountebank may promise such a cure, but a skilful physician will not undertake it. An epic poem is not in so much haste: it works leisurely; the changes which it makes are slow; but the cure is likely to be more perfect. The effects of tragedy, as I said, are too violent to be lasting. If it be answer'd that, for this reason, tragedies are often to be seen, and the dose to be repeated, this is tacitly to confess that there is more virtue in one heroic poem than in many tragedies. A man is humbled one day, and his pride returns the next. Chymical medicines are observ'd to relieve oft'ner than to cure; for 't is the nature of spirits to make swift impressions, but not deep. Galenical decoctions, to which I may properly compare an epic poem, have more of body in them; they work by their substance and their weight. It is one reason of Aristotle's to prove that tragedy is the more noble, because it turns in a shorter compass; the whole action being circumscrib'd within the space of four-and-twenty hours. He might prove as well that a mushroom is to be preferr'd before a peach, because it shoots up in the compass of a night. A chariot may be driven round the pillar in less space than a large machine, because the bulk is not so great. Is the Moon a more noble planet than Saturn, because she makes her revolution in less than thirty days, and he in little less than thirty years? Both their orbs are in proportion to their several magnitudes; and consequently the quickness or slowness of their motion, and the time of their circumvolutions, is no argument of the greater or less perfection. And, besides, what virtue is there in a tragedy which is not contain'd in an epic poem, where pride is humbled, virtue rewarded, and vice punish'd; and those more amply treated than the narrowness of the drama can admit? The shining quality of an epic hero, his magnanimity, his constancy, his patience, his piety, or whatever characteristical virtue his poet gives him, raises first our admiration. We are naturally prone to imitate what we admire; and frequent acts produce a habit. If the hero's chief quality be vicious, as, for example, the choler and obstinate desire of vengeance in Achilles, yet the moral is instructive: and, besides, we are inform'd in the very proposition of the *Iliads* that this anger was pernicious; that it brought a thousand ills on the Grecian camp. The courage of Achilles is propos'd to imitation, not his pride and disobedience to his general, nor his brutal cruelty to his dead enemy, nor the selling his body to his father. We abhor these actions while we read them; and what we abhor we never imitate. The poet only shews them, like rocks or quicksands, to be shunn'd.

By this example the critics have concluded that it is not necessary the manners of the hero should be virtuous. They are poetically good, if they are of a piece: tho', where a character of perfect virtue is set before us, 't is more lovely; for there the whole hero is to be imitated. This is the Æneas of our author; this is that idea of perfection in an epic poem which painters and statuaries have only in their minds, and which no hands are able to express. These are the beauties of a god in a human body. When the picture of Achilles is drawn in tragedy, he is taken with those warts, and moles, and hard features, by those who represent him on the stage, or he is no more Achilles; for his creator, Homer, has so describ'd him. Yet even thus he

appears a perfect hero, tho' an imperfect character of virtue. Horace paints him after Homer, and delivers him to be copied on the stage with all those imperfections. Therefore they are either not faults in a heroic poem, or faults common to the drama. After all, on the whole merits of the cause, it must be acknowledg'd that the epic poem is more for the manners, and tragedy for the passions. The passions, as I have said, are violent; and acute distempers require medicines of a strong and speedy operation. Ill habits of the mind are like chronical diseases, to be corrected by degrees, and cur'd by alteratives; wherein, tho' purges are sometimes necessary, yet diet, good air, and moderate exercise have the greatest part. The matter being thus stated, it will appear that both sorts of poetry are of use for their proper ends. The stage is more active; the epic poem works at greater leisure, yet is active too, when need requires; for dialogue is imitated by the drama from the more active parts of it. One puts off a fit, like the *quinquina*, and relieves us only for a time; the other roots out the distemper, and gives a healthful habit. The sun enlightens and cheers us, dispels fogs, and warms the ground with his daily beams; but the corn is sow'd, increases, is ripen'd, and is reap'd for use in process of time, and in its proper season. I proceed from the greatness of the action to the dignity of the actors; I mean to the persons employ'd in both poems. There likewise tragedy will be seen to borrow from the epopee; and that which borrows is always of less dignity, because it has not of its own. A subject, 't is true, may lend to his sovereign; but the act of borrowing makes the king inferior, because he wants, and the subject supplies. And suppose the persons of the drama wholly fabulous, or of the poet's invention, yet heroic poetry gave him the examples of that invention, because it was first, and Homer the common father of the stage. I know not of any one advantage which tragedy can boast above heroic poetry, but that it is represented to the view, as well as read, and instructs in the closet, as well as on the theater. This is an uncontended excellence, and a chief branch of its prerogative; yet I may be allow'd to say, without partiality, that herein the actors share the poet's praise. Your Lordship knows some modern tragedies which are beautiful on the stage, and yet I am confident you would not read them. Tryphon the stationer complains they are seldom ask'd for in his shop. The poet who flourish'd in the scene is damn'd in the *ruelle ;* nay more, he is not esteem'd a good poet by those who see and hear his extravagances with delight. They are a sort of stately fustian, and lofty childishness. Nothing but nature can give a sincere pleasure; where that is not imitated, 't is grotesque painting; the fine woman ends in a fish's tail.

I might also add that many things which not only please, but are real beauties in the reading, would appear absurd upon the stage; and those not only the *speciosa miracula*, as Horace calls them, of transformations, of Scylla, Antiphates, and the Læstrygons, which cannot be represented even in operas; but the prowess of Achilles or Æneas would appear ridiculous in our dwarf heroes of the theater. We can believe they routed armies, in Homer or in Virgil; but *ne Hercules contra duos* in the drama. I forbear to instance in many things which the stage cannot, or ought not to represent; for I have said already more than I intended on this subject, and should fear it might be turn'd against me, that I plead for the preëminence of epic poetry because I have taken some pains in translating Virgil, if this were the first time that I had deliver'd my opinion in this dispute. But I have more than once already maintain'd the rights of my two masters against their rivals of the scene, even while I wrote tragedies myself, and had no thoughts of this present undertaking. I submit my opinion to your judgment, who are better qualified than any man I know to decide this controversy. You come, my Lord, instructed in the cause, and needed not that I should open it. Your *Essay of Poetry,* which was publish'd without a name, and of which I was not honor'd with the confidence. I read over and over with much delight, and as much instruction, and, without flattering you, or making myself more moral than I am, not without some envy. I was loth to be inform'd how an epic poem should be written, or how a tragedy should be contriv'd and manag'd, in better verse, and with more judgment, than I could teach others. A native of Parnassus, and bred up in the studies of its fundamental laws, may receive new lights from his contemporaries; but 't is a grudging kind of praise which he gives his benefactors. He is more oblig'd than he is willing to acknowledge; there is a tincture of malice in his commendations; for where I own I am taught, I confess my want of knowledge. A judge upon the bench may, out of good nature, or at least interest, encourage the pleadings of a puny counselor; but he does not willingly commend his brother sergeant at the bar, especially when he controls his law, and exposes that ignorance which is made sacred by his place. I gave the unknown author his due commendation, I must confess; but who can answer for me and for the rest of the poets who heard me read the poem, whether we should not have been better pleas'd to have seen our own names at the bottom of the title-page ? Perhaps we commended it the more, that we might seem to be above the censure. We are naturally displeas'd with an unknown critic, as the ladies are with the lampooner, because we are bitten in the dark, and know not where to fasten our revenge. But great excellencies will work their way thro' all sorts of opposition. I applauded rather out of decency than affection; and was ambitious, as some yet can witness, to be acquainted with a man with whom I had the honor to converse, and that almost daily, for so many years together. Heaven knows if I have heartily forgiven you this deceit. You extorted a praise which I should willingly have given, had I known you. Nothing had been more easy than to commend a patron of a long standing. The world would join with me, if the *encomiums* were just; and, if unjust, would excuse a grateful flatterer. But to come anonymous upon me, and force me to commend you against my interest, was not altogether so fair, give me leave to say, as it was politic; for by concealing your quality, you might clearly understand how your work succeeded, and that the general approbation was given to your merit, not your titles. Thus, like Apelles, you stood unseen behind your own Venus, and receiv'd the praises of the passing multitude; the work was commended, not the author; and I doubt not this was one of the most pleasing adventures of your life.

I have detain'd your Lordship longer than I intended in this dispute of preference betwixt the epic poem and the drama, and yet have not formally answer'd any of the arguments which are brought by Aristotle on the other side, and set in the fairest light by Dacier. But I suppose, without looking on the book, I may have touch'd on some of the objections; for, in this address to your Lordship, I design not a treatise of heroic poetry, but write in a loose epistolary way, somewhat tending to that subject, after the example of Horace, in his First Epistle of the Second Book, to Augustus Cæsar, and of that to the Pisos, which we call his *Art of Poetry;* in both of which he observes no method that I can trace, whatever Scaliger the Father or Heinsius may have seen, or rather think they had seen. I have taken up, laid down, and resum'd as often as I pleas'd, the same subject; and this loose proceeding I shall use thro' all this prefatory dedication. Yet all this while I have been sailing with some side wind or other toward the point I propos'd in the beginning, the greatness and excellency of an heroic poem, with some of the difficulties which attend that work. The comparison, therefore, which I made betwixt the epopee and the tragedy was not altogether a digression; for 't is concluded on all hands that they are both the masterpieces of human wit.

In the mean time, I may be bold to draw this corollary from what has been already said, that the file of heroic poets is very short; all are not such who have assum'd that lofty title in ancient or modern ages, or have been so esteem'd by their partial and ignorant admirers.

There have been but one great *Ilias,* and one *Æneis,* in so many ages. The next, but the next with a long interval betwixt, was the *Jerusalem:* I mean not so much in distance of time, as in excellency. After these three are enter'd, some Lord Chamberlain should be appointed, some critic of authority should be set before the door, to keep out a crowd of little poets, who press for admission, and are not of quality. Mævius would be deaf'ning your Lordship's ears with his

Fortunam Priami cantabo, et nobile bellum —

mere fustian, as Horace would tell you from behind, without pressing forward, and

more smoke than fire. Pulci, Boiardo, and Ariosto would cry out: " Make room for the Italian poets, the descendants of Virgil in a right line." Father Le Moyne, with his *Saint Louis;* and Scudéry with his *Alaric:* " for a godly king and a Gothic conqueror;" and Chapelain would take it ill that his *Maid* should be refus'd a place with Helen and Lavinia. Spenser has a better plea for his *Fairy Queen,* had his action been finish'd, or had been one; and Milton, if the Devil had not been his hero, instead of Adam; if the giant had not foil'd the knight, and driven him out of his stronghold, to wander thro' the world with his lady errant; and if there had not been more machining persons than human in his poem. After these, the rest of our English poets shall not be mention'd. I have that honor for them which I ought to have; but, if they are worthies, they are not to be rank'd amongst the three whom I have nam'd, and who are establish'd in their reputation.

Before I quitted the comparison betwixt epic poetry and tragedy, I should have acquainted my judge with one advantage of the former over the latter, which I now casually remember out of the preface of Segrais before his translation of the *Æneis,* or out of Bossu, no matter which. The style of the heroic poem is, and ought to be, more lofty than that of the drama. The critic is certainly in the right, for the reason already urg'd; the work of tragedy is on the passions, and in dialogue; both of them abhor strong metaphors, in which the epopee delights. A poet cannot speak too plainly on the stage: for *volat irrevocabile verbum;* the sense is lost, if it be not taken flying; but what we read alone, we have leisure to digest. There an author may beautify his sense by the boldness of his expression, which if we understand not fully at the first, we may dwell upon it till we find the secret force and excellence. That which cures the manners by alterative physic, as I said before, must proceed by insensible degrees; but that which purges the passions must do its business all at once, or wholly fail of its effect, at least in the present operation, and without repeated doses. We must beat the iron while 't is hot, but we may polish it at leisure. Thus, my Lord, you pay the fine of my forgetfulness; and yet the merits of both causes are where they were, and undecided, till you declare whether it be more for the benefit of mankind to have their manners in general corrected, or their pride and hard-heartedness remov'd.

I must now come closer to my present business, and not think of making more invasive wars abroad, when, like Hannibal, I am call'd back to the defense of my own country. Virgil is attack'd by many enemies; he has a whole confederacy against him; and I must endeavor to defend him as well as I am able. But their principal objections being against his moral, the duration or length of time taken up in the action of the poem, and what they have to urge against the manners of his hero, I shall omit the rest as mere cavils of grammarians; at the worst, but casual slips of a great man's pen, or inconsiderable faults of an admirable poem, which the author had not leisure to review before his death. Macrobius has answer'd what the ancients could urge against him; and some things I have lately read in Tanneguy le Fèvre, Valois, and another whom I name not, which are scarce worth answering. They begin with the moral of his poem, which I have elsewhere confess'd, and still must own, not to be so noble as that of Homer. But let both be fairly stated; and, without contradicting my first opinion. I can shew that Virgil's was as useful to the Romans of his age, as Homer's was to the Grecians of his, in what time soever he may be suppos'd to have liv'd and flourish'd. Homer's moral was to urge the necessity of union, and of a good understanding betwixt confederate states and princes engag'd in a war with a mighty monarch; as also of discipline in an army, and obedience in the several chiefs to the supreme commander of the joint forces. To inculcate this, he sets forth the ruinous effects of discord in the camp of those allies, occasion'd by the quarrel betwixt the general and one of the next in office under him. Agamemnon gives the provocation, and Achilles resents the injury. Both parties are faulty in the quarrel, and accordingly they are both punish'd: the aggressor is forc'd to sue for peace to his inferior on dishonorable conditions; the deserter refuses the satisfaction offer'd, and his obstinacy costs him his best friend. This works the natural effect of choler, and turns his rage against him by

whom he was last affronted, and most sensibly. The greater anger expels the less; but his character is still preserv'd. In the mean time, the Grecian army receives loss on loss, and is half destroy'd by a pestilence into the bargain:

Quicquid delirant reges, plectuntur Achivi.

As the poet, in the first part of the example, had shewn the bad effects of discord, so, after the reconcilement, he gives the good effects of unity; for Hector is slain, and then Troy must fall. By this 't is probable that Homer liv'd when the Median monarchy was grown formidable to the Grecians, and that the joint endeavors of his countrymen were little enough to preserve their common freedom from an encroaching enemy. Such was his moral, which all critics have allow'd to be more noble than that of Virgil, tho' not adapted to the times in which the Roman poet liv'd. Had Virgil flourish'd in the age of Ennius, and address'd to Scipio, he had probably taken the same moral, or some other not unlike it. For then the Romans were in as much danger from the Carthaginian commonwealth as the Grecians were from the Assyrian or Median monarchy. But we are to consider him as writing his poem in a time when the old form of government was subverted, and a new one just establish'd by Octavius Cæsar, in effect by force of arms, but seemingly by the consent of the Roman people. The commonwealth had receiv'd a deadly wound in the former civil wars betwixt Marius and Sylla. The commons, while the first prevail'd, had almost shaken off the yoke of the nobility; and Marius and Cinna, like the captains of the mob, under the specious pretense of the public good, and of doing justice on the oppressors of their liberty, reveng'd themselves, without form of law, on their private enemies. Sylla, in his turn, proscrib'd the heads of the adverse party: he too had nothing but liberty and reformation in his mouth; for the cause of religion is but a modern motive to rebellion, invented by the Christian priesthood, refining on the heathen. Sylla, to be sure, meant no more good to the Roman people than Marius before him, whatever he declar'd; but sacrific'd the lives and took the estates of all his enemies, to gratify those who brought him into power.

Such was the reformation of the government by both parties. The senate and the commons were the two bases on which it stood, and the two champions of either faction each destroy'd the foundations of the other side; so the fabric, of consequence, must fall betwixt them, and tyranny must be built upon their ruins. This comes of altering fundamental laws and constitutions; like him, who, being in good health, lodg'd himself in a physician's house, and was overpersuaded by his landlord to take physic, of which he died, for the benefit of his doctor. *Stavo ben;* (was written on his monument,) *ma, per star meglio, sto qui.*

After the death of those two usurpers, the commonwealth seem'd to recover, and held up its head for a little time. But it was all the while in a deep consumption, which is a flattering disease. Pompey, Crassus, and Cæsar had found the sweets of arbitrary power; and, each being a check to the other's growth, struck up a false friendship amongst themselves, and divided the government betwixt them, which none of them was able to assume alone. These were the public-spirited men of their age; that is, patriots for their own interest. The commonwealth look'd with a florid countenance in their management, spread in bulk, and all the while was wasting in the vitals. Not to trouble your Lordship with the repetition of what you know: after the death of Crassus, Pompey found himself outwitted by Cæsar, broke with him, overpower'd him in the senate, and caus'd many unjust decrees to pass against him. Cæsar, thus injur'd, and unable to resist the faction of the nobles, which was now uppermost, (for he was a Marian,) had recourse to arms; and his cause was just against Pompey, but not against his country, whose constitution ought to have been sacred to him, and never to have been violated on the account of any private wrong. But he prevail'd; and, Heav'n declaring for him, he became a providential monarch, under the title of perpetual dictator. He being murther'd by his own son, whom I neither dare commend, nor can justly blame, (tho' Dante, in his *Inferno,* has put him and Cassius, and Judas Iscariot betwixt them, into the great devil's mouth,) the commonwealth popp'd up its head for the third time, under Brutus and Cassius, and then sunk for ever.

Thus the Roman people were grossly gull'd, twice or thrice over, and as often enslav'd in one century, and under the same pretense of reformation. At last the two battles of Philippi gave the decisive stroke against liberty; and, not long after, the commonwealth was turn'd into a monarchy by the conduct and good fortune of Augustus. 'T is true that the despotic power could not have fallen into better hands than those of the first and second Cæsar. Your Lordship well knows what obligations Virgil had to the latter of them: he saw, beside, that the commonwealth was lost without resource; the heads of it destroy'd; the senate, new molded, grown degenerate, and either bought off, or thrusting their own necks into the yoke, out of fear of being forc'd. Yet I may safely affirm for our great author, (as men of good sense are generally honest,) that he was still of republican principles in heart.

Secretisque piis, his dantem jura Catonem.

I think I need use no other argument to justify my opinion, than that of this one line, taken from the Eighth Book of the *Æneis.* If he had not well studied his patron's temper, it might have ruin'd him with another prince. But Augustus was not discontented, at least that we can find, that Cato was plac'd, by his own poet, in Elysium, and there giving laws to the holy souls who deserv'd to be separated from the vulgar sort of good spirits. For his conscience could not but whisper to the arbitrary monarch, that the kings of Rome were at first elective, and govern'd not without a senate; that Romulus was no hereditary prince; and tho', after his death, he receiv'd divine honors for the good he did on earth, yet he was but a god of their own making; that the last Tarquin was expell'd justly, for overt acts of tyranny and maladministration; for such are the conditions of an elective kingdom: and I meddle not with others, being, for my own opinion, of Montaigne's principles, that an honest man ought to be contented with that form of government, and with those fundamental constitutions of it, which he receiv'd from his ancestors, and under which himself was born; tho' at the same time he confess'd freely, that if he could have chosen his place of birth, it should have been at

Venice; which, for many reasons, I dislike, and am better pleas'd to have been born an Englishman.

But, to return from my long rambling, I say that Virgil, having maturely weigh'd the condition of the times in which he liv'd; that an entire liberty was not to be retriev'd; that the present settlement had the prospect of a long continuance in the same family, or those adopted into it; that he held his paternal estate from the bounty of the conqueror, by whom he was likewise enrich'd, esteem'd, and cherish'd; that this conqueror, tho' of a bad kind, was the very best of it; that the arts of peace flourish'd under him; that all men might be happy, if they would be quiet; that, now he was in possession of the whole, yet he shar'd a great part of his authority with the senate; that he would be chosen into the ancient offices of the commonwealth, and rul'd by the power which he deriv'd from them, and prorogued his government from time to time, still, as it were, threat'ning to dismiss himself from public cares, which he exercis'd more for the common good than for any delight he took in greatness — these things, I say, being consider'd by the poet, he concluded it to be the interest of his country to be so govern'd; to infuse an awful respect into the people towards such a prince; by that respect to confirm their obedience to him, and by that obedience to make them happy. This was the moral of his divine poem; honest in the poet; honorable to the emperor, whom he derives from a divine extraction; and reflecting part of that honor on the Roman people, whom he derives also from the Trojans; and not only profitable, but necessary, to the present age, and likely to be such to their posterity. That it was the receiv'd opinion that the Romans were descended from the Trojans, and Julius Cæsar from Julus the son of Æneas, was enough for Virgil; tho' perhaps he thought not so himself, or that Æneas ever was in Italy; which Bochartus manifestly proves. And Homer, where he says that Jupiter hated the house of Priam, and was resolv'd to transfer the kingdom to the family of Æneas, yet mentions nothing of his leading a colony into a foreign country and settling there. But that the Romans valued themselves on their Trojan ancestry is so undoubted a truth that I need not

prove it. Even the seals which we have remaining of Julius Cæsar, which we know to be antique, have the star of Venus over them, tho' they were all graven after his death, as a note that he was deified. I doubt not but it was one reason why Augustus should be so passionately concern'd for the preservation of the _Æneis_, which its author had condemn'd to be burnt, as an imperfect poem, by his last will and testament; was because it did him a real service, as well as an honor; that a work should not be lost where his divine original was celebrated in verse which had the character of immortality stamp'd upon it.

Neither were the great Roman families which flourish'd in his time less oblig'd by him than the emperor. Your Lordship knows with what address he makes mention of them, as captains of ships, or leaders in the war; and even some of Italian extraction are not forgotten. These are the single stars which are sprinkled thro' the _Æneis_; but there are whole constellations of them in the Fifth Book. And I could not but take notice, when I translated it, of some favorite families to which he gives the victory and awards the prizes, in the person of his hero, at the funeral games which were celebrated in honor of Anchises. I insist not on their names; but am pleas'd to find the Memmii amongst them, deriv'd from Mnestheus, because Lucretius dedicates to one of that family, a branch of which destroy'd Corinth. I likewise either found or form'd an image to myself of the contrary kind; that those who lost the prizes were such as had disoblig'd the poet, or were in disgrace with Augustus, or enemies to Mæcenas; and this was the poetical revenge he took. For _genus irritabile vatum_, as Horace says. When a poet is throughly provok'd, he will do himself justice, however dear it cost him; _animamque in vulnere ponit_. I think these are not bare imaginations of my own, tho' I find no trace of them in the commentators; but one poet may judge of another by himself. The vengeance we defer is not forgotten. I hinted before that the whole Roman people were oblig'd by Virgil, in deriving them from Troy; an ancestry which they affected. We and the French are of the same humor: they would be thought to descend from a son, I think, of Hector; and we would have our Britain both nam'd and planted by a descendant of Æneas. Spenser favors this opinion what he can. His Prince Arthur, or whoever he intends by him, is a Trojan. Thus the hero of Homer was a Grecian, of Virgil a Roman, of Tasso an Italian.

I have transgress'd my bounds, and gone farther than the moral led me. But, if your Lordship is not tir'd, I am safe enough.

Thus far, I think, my author is defended. But, as Augustus is still shadow'd in the person of Æneas, (of which I shall say more when I come to the manners which the poet gives his hero,) I must prepare that subject by shewing how dext'rously he manag'd both the prince and people, so as to displease neither, and to do good to both; which is the part of a wise and an honest man, and proves that it is possible for a courtier not to be a knave. I shall continue still to speak my thoughts like a free-born subject, as I am; tho' such things, perhaps, as no Dutch commentator could, and I am sure no Frenchman durst. I have already told your Lordship my opinion of Virgil, that he was no arbitrary man. Oblig'd he was to his master for his bounty; and he repays him with good counsel, how to behave himself in his new monarchy, so as to gain the affections of his subjects, and deserve to be call'd the father of his country. From this consideration it is that he chose, for the groundwork of his poem, one empire destroy'd, and another rais'd from the ruins of it. This was just the parallel. Æneas could not pretend to be Priam's heir in a lineal succession; for Anchises, the hero's father, was only of the second branch of the royal family; and Helenus, a son of Priam, was yet surviving, and might lawfully claim before him. It may be Virgil mentions him on that account. Neither has he forgotten Priamus, in the Fifth of his *Æneis*, the son of Polites, youngest son to Priam, who was slain by Pyrrhus, in the Second Book. Æneas had only married Creüsa, Priam's daughter, and by her could have no title while any of the male issue were remaining. In this case the poet gave him the next title, which is that of an elective king. The remaining Trojans chose him to lead them forth, and settle them in some foreign country. Ilioneus, in his speech to Dido, calls him expressly by the name of king. Our poet, who

all this while had Augustus in his eye, had no desire he should seem to succeed by any right of inheritance deriv'd from Julius Cæsar, (such a title being but one degree remov'd from conquest,) for what was introduc'd by force, by force may be remov'd. 'T was better for the people that they should give, than he should take; since that gift was indeed no more at bottom than a trust. Virgil gives us an example of this in the person of Mezentius: he govern'd arbitrarily; he was expell'd, and came to the deserv'd end of all tyrants. Our author shews us another sort of kingship, in the person of Latinus. He was descended from Saturn, and, as I remember, in the third degree. He is describ'd a just and a gracious prince, solicitous for the welfare of his people, always consulting with his senate to promote the common good. We find him at the head of them, when he enters into the council hall, speaking first, but still demanding their advice, and steering by it, as far as the iniquity of the times would suffer him. And this is the proper character of a king by inheritance, who is born a father of his country. Æneas, tho' he married the heiress of the crown, yet claim'd no title to it during the life of his father-in-law. *Pater arma Latinus habeto*, &c., are Virgil's words. As for himself, he was contented to take care of his country gods, who were not those of Latium; wherein our divine author seems to relate to the after-practice of the Romans, which was to adopt the gods of those they conquer'd, or receiv'd as members of their commonwealth. Yet, withal, he plainly touches at the office of the high-priesthood, with which Augustus was invested, and which made his person more sacred and inviolable than even the tribunitial power. It was not therefore for nothing that the most judicious of all poets made that office vacant by the death of Panthus in the Second Book of the *Æneis*, for his hero to succeed in it, and consequently for Augustus to enjoy. I know not that any of the commentators have taken notice of that passage. If they have not, I am sure they ought; and if they have, I am not indebted to them for the observation. The words of Virgil are very plain:

Sacra, suosque tibi commendat Troja penates.

As for Augustus, or his uncle Julius, claiming by descent from Æneas, that title is already out of doors. Æneas succeeded not, but was elected. Troy was foredoom'd to fall for ever:

Postquam res Asiæ Priamique evertere regnum Immeritum visum superis.
— Æneis, lib. iii, lin. 1.

Augustus, 't is true, had once resolv'd to rebuild that city, and there to make the seat of empire; but Horace writes an ode on purpose to deter him from that thought, declaring the place to be accurst, and that the gods would as often destroy it as it should be rais'd. Hereupon the emperor laid aside a project so ungrateful to the Roman people. But by this, my Lord, we may conclude that he had still his pedigree in his head, and had an itch of being thought a divine king, if his poets had not given him better counsel.

I will pass by many less material objections, for want of room to answer them: what follows next is of great importance, if the critics can make out their charge; for 't is level'd at the manners which our poet gives his hero, and which are the same which were eminently seen in his Augustus. Those manners were piety to the gods and a dutiful affection to his father, love to his relations, care of his people, courage and conduct in the wars, gratitude to those who had oblig'd him, and justice in general to mankind.

Piety, as your Lordship sees, takes place of all, as the chief part of his character; and the word in Latin is more full than it can possibly be express'd in any modern language; for there it comprehends not only devotion to the gods, but filial love and tender affection to relations of all sorts. As instances of this, the deities of Troy and his own Penates are made the companions of his flight: they appear to him in his voyage, and advise him; and at last he replaces them in Italy, their native country. For his father, he takes him on his back; he leads his little son; his wife follows him; but, losing his footsteps thro' fear or ignorance, he goes back into the midst of his enemies to find her, and leaves not his pursuit till her ghost appears, to forbid his farther search. I will say nothing of his duty to his father while he liv'd, his sorrow for his death, of the games

instituted in honor of his memory, or seeking him, by his command, even after death, in the Elysian fields. I will not mention his tenderness for his son, which everywhere is visible — of his raising a tomb for Polydorus, the obsequies for Misenus, his pious remembrance of Deiphobus, the funerals of his nurse, his grief for Pallas, and his revenge taken on his murtherer, whom otherwise, by his natural compassion, he had forgiven: and then the poem had been left imperfect; for we could have had no certain prospect of his happiness, while the last obstacle to it was unremov'd. Of the other parts which compose his character, as a king or as a general, I need say nothing; the whole *Æneis* is one continued instance of some one or other of them; and where I find anything of them tax'd, it shall suffice me, as briefly as I can, to vindicate my divine master to your Lordship, and by you to the reader. But herein Segrais, in his admirable preface to his translation of the *Æneis*, as the author of the Dauphin's *Virgil* justly calls it, has prevented me. Him I follow, and what I borrow from him, am ready to acknowledge to him. For, impartially speaking, the French are as much better critics than the English, as they are worse poets. Thus we generally allow that they better understand the management of a war than our islanders; but we know we are superior to them in the day of battle. They value themselves on their generals, we on our soldiers. But this is not the proper place to decide that question, if they make it one. I shall say perhaps as much of other nations and their poets, excepting only Tasso; and hope to make my assertion good, which is but doing justice to my country; part of which honor will reflect on your Lordship, whose thoughts are always just; your numbers harmonious, your words chosen, your expressions strong and manly, your verse flowing, and your turns as happy as they are easy. If you would set us more copies, your example would make all precepts needless. In the mean time, that little you have written is own'd, and that particularly by the poets, (who are a nation not over lavish of praise to their contemporaries,) as a principal ornament of our language; but the sweetest essences are always confin'd in the smallest glasses.

When I speak of your Lordship, 't is never

a digression, and therefore I need beg no pardon for it; but take up Segrais where I left him, and shall use him less often than I have occasion for him; for his preface is a perfect piece of criticism, full and clear, and digested into an exact method; mine is loose, and, as I intended it, epistolary. Yet I dwell on many things which he durst not touch; for 't is dangerous to offend an arbitrary master, and every patron who has the power of Augustus has not his clemency. In short, my Lord, I would not translate him, because I would bring you somewhat of my own. His notes and observations on every book are of the same excellency; and, for the same reason, I omit the greater part.

He takes notice that Virgil is arraign'd for placing piety before valor, and making that piety the chief character of his hero. I have said already from Bossu, that a poet is not oblig'd to make his hero a virtuous man; therefore, neither Homer nor Tasso are to be blam'd for giving what predominant quality they pleas'd to their first character. But Virgil, who design'd to form a perfect prince, and would insinuate that Augustus, whom he calls Æneas in his poem, was truly such, found himself oblig'd to make him without blemish, thoroughly virtuous; and a thorough virtue both begins and ends in piety. Tasso, without question, observ'd this before me, and therefore split his hero in two; he gave Godfrey piety, and Rinaldo fortitude, for their chief qualities or manners. Homer, who had chosen another moral, makes both Agamemnon and Achilles vicious; for his design was to instruct in virtue by shewing the deformity of vice. I avoid repetition of that I have said above. What follows is translated literally from Segrais:

"Virgil had consider'd that the greatest virtues of Augustus consisted in the perfect art of governing his people; which caus'd him to reign for more than forty years in great felicity. He consider'd that his emperor was valiant, civil, popular, eloquent, politic, and religious; he has given all these qualities to Æneas. But, knowing that piety alone comprehends the whole duty of man towards the gods, towards his country, and towards his relations, he judg'd that this ought to be his first character, whom he would set for a pattern of perfection. In reality, they who believe that the praises which arise from valor are superior to those which proceed from any other virtues, have not consider'd (as they ought) that valor, destitute of other virtues, cannot render a man worthy of any true esteem. That quality, which signifies no more than an intrepid courage, may be separated from many others which are good, and accompanied with many which are ill. A man may be very valiant, and yet impious and vicious. But the same cannot be said of piety, which excludes all ill qualities, and comprehends even valor itself, with all other qualities which are good. Can we, for example, give the praise of valor to a man who should see his gods profan'd, and should want the courage to defend them? To a man who should abandon his father, or desert his king in his last necessity?"

Thus far Segrais, in giving the preference to piety before valor. I will now follow him, where he considers this valor, or intrepid courage, singly in itself; and this also Virgil gives to his Æneas, and that in a heroical degree.

Having first concluded that our poet did for the best in taking the first character of his hero from that essential virtue on which the rest depend, he proceeds to tell us that in the ten years' war of Troy he was consider'd as the second champion of his country (allowing Hector the first place); and this, even by the confession of Homer, who took all occasions of setting up his own countrymen the Grecians, and of undervaluing the Trojan chiefs. But Virgil (whom Segrais forgot to cite) makes Diomede give him a higher character for strength and courage. His testimony is this, in the Eleventh Book:

—— *Stetimus tela aspera contra,*
Contulimusque manus: experto credite, quantus
In clypeum assurgat, quo turbine torqueat hastam.
Si duo præterea tales Idæa tulisset
Terra viros, ultro Inachias venisset ad urbes
Dardanus, et versis lugeret Græcia fatis.
Quicquid apud duræ cessatum est mœnia Trojæ,
Hectoris Æneæque manu victoria Graium
Hæsit, et in decumum vestigia retulit annum.
Ambo animis, ambo insignes præstantibus armis:
Hic pietate prior. ——

I give not here my translation of these verses, (tho' I think I have not ill succeeded in them,) because your Lordship is so great a master of the original that I have no reason to desire you should see Virgil and me so near together. But you may please, my Lord, to take notice that the Latin author refines upon the Greek, and insinuates that Homer had done his hero wrong in giving the advantage of the duel to his own countryman; tho' Diomedes was manifestly the second champion of the Grecians; and Ulysses preferr d him before Ajax, when he chose him for the companion of his nightly expedition; for he had a headpiece of his own, and wanted only the fortitude of another to bring him off with safety, and that he might compass his design with honor.

The French translator thus proceeds: "They who accuse Æneas for want of courage, either understand not Virgil, or have read him slightly; otherwise they would not raise an objection so easy to be answer'd." Hereupon he gives so many instances of the hero's valor, that to repeat them after him would tire your Lordship, and put me to the unnecessary trouble of transcribing the greatest part of the three last *Æneids*. In short, more could not be expected from an Amadis, a Sir Lancelot, or the whole Round Table, than he performs. *Proxima quœque metit gladio*, is the perfect account of a knight-errant. "If it be replied," continues Segrais, "that it was not difficult for him to undertake and achieve such hardy enterprises, because he wore enchanted arms; that accusation, in the first place, must fall on Homer, ere it can reach Virgil." Achilles was as well provided with them as Æneas, tho' he was invulnerable without them. And Ariosto, the two Tassos (Bernardo and Torquato), even our own Spenser, in a word, all modern poets, have copied Homer as well as Virgil: he is neither the first nor last, but in the midst of them; and therefore is safe, if they are so. "Who knows," says Segrais, "but that his fated armor was only an allegorical defense, and signified no more than that he was under the peculiar protection of the gods? — born, as the astrologers will tell us out of Virgil, (who was well vers'd in the Chaldæan mysteries,) under the favorable influence of Jupiter, Venus, and the Sun." But I insist not on this, because I know you believe not there is such an art; tho' not only Horace and Persius, but Augustus himself, thought otherwise. But, in defense of Virgil, I dare positively say that he has been more cautious in this particular

than either his predecessor or his descendants; for Æneas was actually wounded in the Twelfth of the *Æneis*, tho' he had the same godsmith to forge his arms as had Achilles. It seems he was no warluck, as the Scots commonly call such men, who, they say, are iron-free, or lead-free. Yet, after this experiment that his arms were not impenetrable, when he was cur'd indeed by his mother's help, because he was that day to conclude the war by the death of Turnus, the poet durst not carry the miracle too far, and restore him wholly to his former vigor: he was still too weak to overtake his enemy; yet we see with what courage he attacks Turnus, when he faces and renews the combat. I need say no more; for Virgil defends himself without needing my assistance, and proves his hero truly to deserve that name. He was not then a second-rate champion, as they would have him who think fortitude the first virtue in a hero. But, being beaten from this hold, they will not yet allow him to be valiant, because he wept more often, as they think, than well becomes a man of courage.

In the first place, if tears are arguments of cowardice, what shall I say of Homer's hero? Shall Achilles pass for timorous because he wept, and wept on less occasions than Æneas? Herein Virgil must be granted to have excell'd his master. For once both heroes are describ'd lamenting their lost loves: Briseis was taken away by force from the Grecian; Creüsa was lost for ever to her husband. But Achilles went roaring along the salt sea-shore, and, like a booby, was complaining to his mother, when he should have reveng'd his injury by arms. Æneas took a nobler course; for, having secur'd his father and his son, he repeated all his former dangers to have found his wife, if she had been above ground. And here your Lordship may observe the address of Virgil; it was not for nothing that this passage was related with all these tender circumstances. Æneas told it; Dido heard it. That he had been so affectionate a husband was no ill argument to the coming dowager that he might prove as kind to her. Virgil has a thousand secret beauties, tho' I have not leisure to remark them.

Segrais, on this subject of a hero's shedding tears, observes that historians commend Alexander for weeping when he read

the mighty actions of Achilles; and Julius
Cæsar is likewise prais'd, when, out of the
same noble envy, he wept at the victories of
Alexander. But, if we observe more closely,
we shall find that the tears of Æneas were
always on a laudable occasion. Thus he
weeps out of compassion and tenderness of
nature, when, in the temple of Carthage,
he beholds the pictures of his friends, who
sacrific'd their lives in defense of their
country. He deplores the lamentable end
of his pilot Palinurus, the untimely death of
young Pallas his confederate, and the rest,
which I omit. Yet, even for these tears,
his wretched critics dare condemn him.
They make Æneas little better than a kind
of St. Swithen hero, always raining. One of
these censors is bold enough to argue him
of cowardice, when, in the beginning of the
First Book, he not only weeps, but trembles
at an approaching storm:

Extemplo Æneæ solvuntur frigore membra :
Ingemit, et duplices tendens ad sidera palmas, &c.

But to this I have answer'd formerly,
that his fear was not for himself, but for
his people. And who can give a sovereign
a better commendation, or recommend a
hero more to the affection of the reader ?
They were threaten'd with a tempest, and
he wept; he was promis'd Italy, and therefore he pray'd for the accomplishment of
that promise. All this in the beginning
of a storm; therefore he shew'd the more
early piety, and the quicker sense of compassion. Thus much I have urg'd elsewhere
in the defense of Virgil; and, since, I have
been inform'd by Mr. Moyle, a young gentleman whom I can never sufficiently commend, that the ancients accounted drowning an accursed death; so that, if we grant
him to have been afraid, he had just occasion for that fear, both in relation to himself and to his subjects. I think our adversaries can carry this argument no farther,
unless they tell us that he ought to have
had more confidence in the promise of the
gods. But how was he assur'd that he had
understood their oracles aright ? Helenus
might be mistaken; Phœbus might speak
doubtfully; even his mother might flatter
him that he might prosecute his voyage,
which if it succeeded happily, he should be
the founder of an empire. For that she
herself was doubtful of his fortune is appar-

ent by the address she made to Jupiter on
his behalf; to which the god makes answer
in these words:

Parce metu. Cytherea : manent immota tuorum
Fata tibi, &c.

notwithstanding which, the goddess, tho'
comforted, was not assur'd; for even after
this, thro' the course of the whole *Æneis*,
she still apprehends the interest which Juno
might make with Jupiter against her son.
For it was a moot point in heaven, whether
he could alter fate, or not. And indeed
some passages in Virgil would make us suspect that he was of opinion Jupiter might
defer fate, tho' he could not alter it. For
in the latter end of the Tenth Book he introduces Juno begging for the life of Turnus, and flattering her husband with the
power of changing destiny — *Tua, qui potes,*
orsa reflectas ! To which he graciously
answers:

Si mora præsentis lethi, tempusque caduco
Oratur juveni, meque hoc ita ponere sentis,
Tolle fuga Turnum, atque instantibus eripe fatis.
Hactenus indulsisse vacat.   Sin altior istis
Sub precibus venia ulla latet, totumque moveri
Mutarive putas bellum, spes pascis inaneis.

But that he could not alter those decrees,
the King of Gods himself confesses, in the
book above cited, when he comforts Hercules for the death of Pallas, who had invok'd his aid before he threw his lance at
Turnus:

—— Trojæ sub mœnibus altis
Tot nati cecidere deum ; quin occidit una
Sarpedon, mea progenies. Etiam sua Turnum
Fata manent, metasque dati pervenit ad ævi ——

where he plainly acknowledges that he could
not save his own son, or prevent the death
which he foresaw. Of his power to defer
the blow I once occasionally discours'd with
that excellent person Sir Robert Howard,
who is better conversant than any man
that I know in the doctrine of the Stoics;
and he set me right, from the concurrent
testimony of philosophers and poets, that
Jupiter could not retard the effects of fate,
even for a moment. For, when I cited
Virgil as favoring the contrary opinion in
that verse,

Tolle fuga Turnum, atque instantibus eripe
fatis, &c.

he replied, and, I think, with exact judgment, that, when Jupiter gave Juno leave to withdraw Turnus from the present danger, it was because he certainly foreknew that his fatal hour was not come; that it was in destiny for Juno at that time to save him; and that himself obey'd destiny in giving her that leave.

I need say no more in justification of our hero's courage, and am much deceiv'd if he ever be attack'd on this side of his character again. But he is arraign'd with more shew of reason by the ladies, who will make a numerous party against him, for being false to love, in forsaking Dido. And I cannot much blame them; for, to say the truth, 't is an ill precedent for their gallants to follow. Yet, if I can bring him off with flying colors, they may learn experience at her cost, and, for her sake, avoid a cave, as the worst shelter they can choose from a shower of rain, especially when they have a lover in their company.

In the first place, Segrais observes with much acuteness that they who blame Æneas for his insensibility of love when he left Carthage, contradict their former accusation of him for being always crying, compassionate, and effeminately sensible of those misfortunes which befell others. They give him two contrary characters; but Virgil makes him of a piece, always grateful, always tender-hearted. But they are impudent enough to discharge themselves of this blunder, by laying the contradiction at Virgil's door. He, they say, has shewn his hero with these inconsistent characters, acknowledging and ungrateful, compassionate and hard-hearted, but, at the bottom, fickle and self-interested; for Dido had not only receiv'd his weather-beaten troops before she saw him, and given them her protection, but had also offer'd them an equal share in her dominion:

Vultis et his mecum pariter considere regnis ?
Urbem quam statuo, vestra est.

This was an obligement never to be forgotten; and the more to be consider'd, because antecedent to her love. That passion, 't is true, produc'd the usual effects, of generosity, gallantry, and care to please; and thither we refer them. But when she had made all these advances, it was still in his power to have refus'd them; after the in-

trigue of the cave (call it marriage, or enjoyment only) he was no longer free to take or leave; he had accepted the favor, and was oblig'd to be constant, if he would be grateful.

My Lord, I have set this argument in the best light I can, that the ladies may not think I write booty; and perhaps it may happen to me, as it did to Doctor Cudworth, who has rais'd such strong objections against the being of a God, and Providence, that many think he has not answer'd them. You may please at least to hear the adverse party. Segrais pleads for Virgil, that no less than an absolute command from Jupiter could excuse this insensibility of the hero, and this abrupt departure, which looks so like extreme ingratitude. But, at the same time, he does wisely to remember you, that Virgil had made piety the first character of Æneas; and, this being allow'd, (as I am afraid it must,) he was oblig'd, antecedent to all other considerations, to search an asylum for his gods in Italy — for those very gods, I say, who had promis'd to his race the universal empire. Could a pious man dispense with the commands of Jupiter, to satisfy his passion, or (take it in the strongest sense) to comply with the obligations of his gratitude ? Religion, 't is true, must have moral honesty for its groundwork, or we shall be apt to suspect its truth; but an immediate revelation dispenses with all duties of morality. All casuists agree that theft is a breach of the moral law; yet, if I might presume to mingle things sacred with profane, the Israelites only spoil'd the Egyptians, not robb'd them, because the propriety was transferr'd by a revelation to their lawgiver. I confess Dido was a very infidel in this point; for she would not believe, as Virgil makes her say, that ever Jupiter would send Mercury on such an immoral errand. But this needs no answer, at least no more than Virgil gives it:

Fata obstant ; placidasque viri deus obstruit aures.

This notwithstanding, as Segrais confesses, he might have shewn a little more sensibility when he left her; for that had been according to his character.

But let Virgil answer for himself. He still lov'd her, and struggled with his inclinations to obey the gods:

—— Curam sub corde premebat,
Multa gemens, magnoque animum labefactus
amore.

Upon the whole matter, and humanly speaking, I doubt there was a fault somewhere; and Jupiter is better able to bear the blame than either Virgil or Æneas. The poet, it seems, had found it out, and therefore brings the deserting hero and the forsaken lady to meet together in the lower regions, where he excuses himself when 't is too late; and accordingly she will take no satisfaction, nor so much as hear him. Now Segrais is forc'd to abandon his defense, and excuses his author by saying that the *Æneis* is an imperfect work, and that death prevented the divine poet from reviewing it; and for that reason he had condemn'd it to the fire; tho', at the same time, his two translators must acknowledge that the Sixth Book is the most correct of the whole *Æneis*. O, how convenient is a machine sometimes in a heroic poem! This of Mercury is plainly one; and Virgil was constrain'd to use it here, or the honesty of his hero would be ill defended. And the fair sex, however, if they had the deserter in their power, would certainly have shewn him no more mercy than the Bacchanals did Orpheus: for, if too much constancy may be a fault sometimes, then want of constancy, and ingratitude after the last favor, is a crime that never will be forgiven. But of machines, more in their proper place; where I shall shew with how much judgment they have been us'd by Virgil; and, in the mean time, pass to another article of his defense on the present subject; where, if I cannot clear the hero, I hope at least to bring off the poet; for here I must divide their causes. Let Æneas trust to his machine, which will only help to break his fall; but the address is incomparable. Plato, who borrow'd so much from Homer, and yet concluded for the banishment of all poets, would at least have rewarded Virgil before he sent him into exile. But I go farther, and say that he ought to be acquitted, and deserv'd, beside, the bounty of Augustus and the gratitude of the Roman people. If, after this, the ladies will stand out, let them remember that the jury is not all agreed; for Octavia was of his party, and was of the first quality in Rome; she was also present at the reading of the *Sixth Æneid*, and we know not

that she condemn'd Æneas; but we are sure she presented the poet for his admirable elegy on her son Marcellus.

But let us consider the secret reasons which Virgil had for thus framing this noble episode, wherein the whole passion of love is more exactly describ'd than in any other poet. Love was the theme of his Fourth Book: and, tho' it is the shortest of the whole *Æneis*, yet there he has given its beginning, its progress, its traverses, and its conclusion; and had exhausted so entirely this subject, that he could resume it but very slightly in the eight ensuing books.

She was warm'd with the graceful appearance of the hero; she smother'd those sparkles out of decency; but conversation blew them up into a flame. Then she was forc'd to make a confident of her whom she best might trust, her own sister, who approves the passion, and thereby augments it; then succeeds her public owning it; and, after that, the consummation. Of Venus and Juno, Jupiter and Mercury, I say nothing, for they were all machining work; but, possession having cool'd his love, as it increas'd hers, she soon perceiv'd the change, or at least grew suspicious of a change; this suspicion soon turn'd to jealousy, and jealousy to rage; then she disdains and threatens, and again is humble, and intreats, and, nothing availing, despairs, curses, and at last becomes her own executioner. See here the whole process of that passion, to which nothing can be added. I dare go no farther, lest I should lose the connection of my discourse.

To love our native country, and to study its benefit and its glory, to be interested in its concerns, is natural to all men, and is indeed our common duty. A poet makes a farther step; for, endeavoring to do honor to it, 't is allowable in him even to be partial in its cause; for he is not tied to truth, or fetter'd by the laws of history. Homer and Tasso are justly prais'd for choosing their heroes out of Greece and Italy; Virgil indeed made his a Trojan; but it was to derive the Romans and his own Augustus from him. But all the three poets are manifestly partial to their heroes, in favor of their country; for Dares Phrygius reports of Hector that he was slain cowardly: Æneas, according to the best account, slew not Mezentius, but was slain by him; and the chronicles of Italy tell us little of that Rinaldo d' Este who conquers Jerusalem in Tasso. He might be a champion of the Church; but we know not that he was so much as present at the siege. To apply this to Virgil, he thought himself engag'd in honor to espouse the cause and quarrel of his country against Carthage. He knew he could not please the Romans better, or oblige them more to patronize his poem, than by disgracing the foundress of that city. He shews her ungrateful to the memory of her first husband, doting on a stranger; enjoy'd, and afterwards forsaken by him. This was the original, says he, of the immortal hatred betwixt the two rival nations. 'T is true, he colors the falsehood of Æneas by an express command from Jupiter, to forsake the queen who had oblig'd him; but he knew the Romans were to be his readers, and them he brib'd, perhaps at the expense of his hero's honesty; but he gain'd his cause, however, as pleading before corrupt judges. They were content to see their founder false to love, for still he had the advantage of the amour: it was their enemy whom he forsook, and she might have forsaken him, if he had not got the start of her: she had already forgotten her vows to her Sichæus; and *varium et mutabile semper femina* is the sharpest satire, in the fewest words, that ever was made on womankind; for both the adjectives are neuter, and *animal* must be understood, to make them grammar. Virgil does well to put those words into the mouth of Mercury. *If a god had not spoken them, neither durst he have written them, nor I translated them.* Yet the deity was forc'd to come twice on the same errand; and the second time, as much a hero as Æneas was, he frighted him. It seems he fear'd not Jupiter so much as Dido; for your Lordship may observe that, as much intent as he was upon his voyage, yet he still delay'd it, till the messenger was oblig'd to tell him plainly, that, if he weigh'd not anchor in the night, the queen would be with him in the morning. *Notumque furens quid femina possit —* she was injur'd; she was revengeful; she was powerful. The poet had likewise before hinted that her people were naturally perfidious; for he gives their character in their queen, and makes a proverb of *Punica fides.* many ages before it was invented.

Thus I hope, my Lord, that I have made good my promise, and justified the poet, whatever becomes of the false knight. And sure a poet is as much privileg'd to lie as an ambassador, for the honor and interest of his country; at least as Sir Henry Wotton has defin'd.

This naturally leads me to the defense of the famous anachronism, in making Æneas and Dido contemporaries; for 't is certain that the hero liv'd almost two hundred years before the building of Carthage. One who imitates Bocaline says that Virgil was accus'd before Apollo for this error. The god soon found that he was not able to defend his favorite by reason, for the case was clear: he therefore gave this middle sentence, that anything might be allow'd to his son Virgil, on the account of his other merits; that, being a monarch, he had a dispensing power, and pardon'd him. But, that this special act of grace might never be drawn into example, or pleaded by his puny successors in justification of their ignorance, he decreed for the future, no poet should presume to make a lady die for love two hundred years before her birth. To moralize this story, Virgil is the Apollo who has this dispensing power. His great judgment made the laws of poetry; but he never made himself a slave to them: chronology, at best, is but a cobweb law, and he broke thro' it with his weight. They who will imitate him wisely must choose, as he did, an obscure and a remote *æra*, where they may invent at pleasure, and not be easily contradicted. Neither he, nor the Romans, had ever read the Bible, by which only his false computation of times can be made out against him. This Segrais says in his defense, and proves it from his learned friend Bochartus, whose letter on this subject he has printed at the end of the *Fourth Æneid*, to which I refer your Lordship and the reader. Yet the credit of Virgil was so great that he made this fable of his own invention pass for an authentic history, or at least as credible as anything in Homer. Ovid takes it up after him, even in the same age, and makes an ancient heroine of Virgil's new-created Dido; dictates a letter for her, just before her death, to the ingrateful fugitive; and, very unluckily for himself, is for measuring a sword with a man so much superior in force to him, on the same subject. I think I may be judge of this, because I have translated both. The famous author of the *Art of Love* has nothing of his own; he borrows all from a greater master in his own profession; and, which is worse, improves nothing which he finds. Nature fails him; and, being forc'd to his old shift, he has recourse to witticism. This passes indeed with his soft admirers, and gives him the preference to Virgil in their esteem. But let them like for themselves, and not prescribe to others; for our author needs not their admiration.

The motives that induc'd Virgil to coin this fable I have shew'd already; and have also begun to shew that he might make this anachronism by superseding the mechanic rules of poetry, for the same reason that a monarch may dispense with or suspend his own laws, when he finds it necessary so to do, especially if those laws are not altogether fundamental. Nothing is to be call'd a fault in poetry, says Aristotle, but what is against the art; therefore a man may be an admirable poet without being an exact chronologer. Shall we dare, continues Segrais, to condemn Virgil for having made a fiction against the order of time, when we commend Ovid and other poets who have made many of their fictions against the order of nature? For what else are the splendid miracles of the *Metamorphoses*? Yet these are beautiful as they are related, and have also deep learning and instructive mythologies couch'd under them; but to give, as Virgil does in this episode, the original cause of the long wars betwixt Rome and Carthage, to draw truth out of fiction after so probable a manner, with so much beauty, and so much for the honor of his country, was proper only to the divine wit of Maro; and Tasso, in one of his discourses, admires him for this particularly. 'T is not lawful, indeed, to contradict a point of history which is known to all the world, as, for example, to make Hannibal and Scipio contemporaries with Alexander; but, in the dark recesses of antiquity, a great poet may and ought to feign such things as he finds not there, if they can be brought to embellish that subject which he treats. On the other side, the pains and diligence of ill poets is but thrown away when they want the genius to invent and feign agreeably. But if the fictions be delightful; (which they always are, if they be natural;) if they be of a piece; if the beginning, the middle, and the end be in their due places, and artfully united to each other, such works can never fail of their deserv'd success. And such is Virgil's episode of Dido and Æneas; where the sourest critic must acknowledge that, if he had depriv'd his *Æneis* of so great an ornament because he found no traces of it in antiquity, he had avoided their unjust censure, but had wanted one of the greatest beauties of his poem. I shall say more of this in the next article of their charge against him, which is want of invention. In the mean time I may affirm, in honor of this episode, that it is not only now esteem'd the most pleasing entertainment of the *Æneis*, but was so accounted in his own age, and before it was mellow'd into that reputation which time has given it; for which I need produce no other testimony than that of Ovid, his contemporary:

> *Nec pars ulla magis legitur de corpore toto,*
> *Quam non legitimo fœdere junctus amor.*

Where, by the way, you may observe, my Lord, that Ovid, in those words, *non legitimo fœdere junctus amor*, will by no means allow it to be a lawful marriage betwixt Dido and Æneas. He was in banishment when he wrote those verses, which I cite from his letter to Augustus: "You, sir," saith he, "have sent me into exile for writing my *Art of Love*, and my wanton *Elegies;* yet your own poet was happy in your good graces, tho' he brought Dido and Æneas into a cave, and left them there not over honestly together. May I be so bold to ask your Majesty, is it a greater fault to teach the art of unlawful love, than to shew it in the action?" But was Ovid, the court poet, so bad a courtier as to find no other plea to excuse himself than by a plain accusation of his master? Virgil confess'd it was a lawful marriage betwixt the lovers, that Juno, the goddess of matrimony, had ratified it by her presence; for it was her business to bring matters to that issue. That the ceremonies were short, we may believe; for Dido was not only amorous, but a widow. Mercury himself, tho' employ'd on a quite contrary errand, yet owns it a marriage by an *innuendo: pulchramque uxorius urbem Exstruis.* He calls Æneas not only a husband, but upbraids him for being a fond husband, as the word *uxorius* implies. Now mark a little, if your Lordship pleases, why Virgil is so much concern'd to make this marriage (for he seems to be the father of the bride himself, and to give her to the bridegroom): it was to make way for the divorce which he intended afterwards; for he was a finer flatterer than Ovid, and I more than conjecture that he had in his eye the divorce which not long before had pass'd betwixt the emperor and Scribonia. He drew this dimple in the cheek of Æneas, to prove Augustus of the same family, by so remarkable a feature in the same place. Thus, as we say in our homespun English proverb, *he kill'd two birds with one stone;* pleas'd the emperor, by giving him the resemblance of his ancestor, and gave him such a resemblance as was not scandalous in that age. For to leave one wife, and take another, was but a matter of gallantry at that time of day among the Romans. *Neque hæc in fœdera veni* is the very excuse which Æneas makes, when he leaves his lady: " I made no such bargain with you at our marriage, to live always drudging on at Carthage: my business was Italy; and I never made a secret of it. If I took my pleasure, had not you your share of it? I leave you free, at my departure, to comfort yourself with the next stranger who happens to be shipwreck'd on your coast. Be as kind a hostess as you have been to me, and you can never fail of another husband. In the mean time, I call the gods to witness that I leave your shore unwillingly; for, tho' Juno made the marriage, yet Jupiter commands me to forsake you." This is the effect of what he saith, when it is dishonor'd out of Latin verse into English prose. If the poet argued not aright, we must pardon him for a poor blind heathen, who knew no better morals.

I have detain'd your Lordship longer than I intended on this objection, which would indeed weigh something in a spiritual court; but I am not to defend our poet there. The next, I think, is but a cavil, tho' the cry is great against him, and hath continued from the time of Macrobius to this present age. I hinted it before. They lay no less than want of invention to his charge — a capital crime, I must acknowledge; for a poet is a maker, as the word signifies; and who

cannot make, that is, invent, hath his name for nothing. That which makes this accusation look so strange at the first sight, is, that he has borrow'd so many things from Homer, Apollonius Rhodius, and others who preceded him. But in the first place, if invention is to be taken in so strict a sense, that the matter of a poem must be wholly new, and that in all its parts, then Scaliger hath made out, saith Segrais, that the history of Troy was no more the invention of Homer than of Virgil. There was not an old woman, or almost a child, but had it in their mouths, before the Greek poet or his friends digested it into this admirable order in which we read it. At this rate, as Solomon hath told us, there is nothing new beneath the sun. Who then can pass for an inventor, if Homer, as well as Virgil, must be depriv'd of that glory? Is Versailles the less a new building, because the architect of that palace hath imitated others which were built before it? Walls, doors and windows, apartments, offices, rooms of convenience and magnificence, are in all great houses. So descriptions, figures, fables, and the rest, must be in all heroic poems; they are the common materials of poetry, furnish'd from the magazine of nature; every poet hath as much right to them as every man hath to air or water. *Quid prohibetis aquas? Usus communis aquarum est.* But the argument of the work, that is to say, its principal action, the economy and disposition of it; these are the things which distinguish copies from originals. The poet who borrows nothing from others is yet to be born; he and the Jews' Messias will come together. There are parts of the *Æneis* which resemble some parts both of the *Ilias* and of the *Odysses;* as, for example, Æneas descended into hell, and Ulysses had been there before him; Æneas lov'd Dido, and Ulysses lov'd Calypso: in few words, Virgil hath imitated Homer's *Odysses* in his first six books, and in his six last the *Ilias.* But from hence can we infer that the two poets write the same history? Is there no invention in some other parts of Virgil's *Æneis?* The disposition of so many various matters, is not that his own? From what book of Homer had Virgil his episode of Nisus and Euryalus, of Mezentius and Lausus? From whence did he borrow his design of bringing Æneas into Italy? of establishing the Roman empire on the foundations of a Trojan colony? to say nothing of the honor he did his patron, not only in his descent from Venus, but in making him so like him in his best features, that the goddess might have mistaken Augustus for her son. He had indeed the story from common fame, as Homer had his from the Egyptian priestess. *Æneadum genetrix* was no more unknown to Lucretius than to him. But Lucretius taught him not to form his hero, to give him piety or valor for his manners, and both in so eminent a degree, that, having done what was possible for man, to save his king and country, his mother was forc'd to appear to him, and restrain his fury, which hurried him to death in their revenge. But the poet made his piety more successful; he brought off his father and his son; and his gods witness'd to his devotion, by putting themselves under his protection, to be replac'd by him in their promis'd Italy. Neither the invention nor the conduct of this great action were owing to Homer or any other poet. 'T is one thing to copy, and another thing to imitate from nature. The copier is that servile imitator, to whom Horace gives no better a name than that of animal; he will not so much as allow him to be a man. Raphael imitated nature; they who copy one of Raphael's pieces imitate but him, for his work is their original. They translate him, as I do Virgil; and fall as short of him, as I of Virgil. There is a kind of invention in the imitation of Raphael; for, tho' the thing was in nature, yet the idea of it was his own. Ulysses travel'd; so did Æneas: but neither of them were the first travelers; for Cain went into the land of Nod before they were born, and neither of the poets ever heard of such a man. If Ulysses had been kill'd at Troy, yet Æneas must have gone to sea, or he could never have arriv'd in Italy. But the designs of the two poets were as different as the courses of their heroes; one went home, and the other sought a home. To return to my first similitude: suppose Apelles and Raphael had each of them painted a burning Troy, might not the modern painter have succeeded as well as the ancient, tho' neither of them had seen the town on fire? for the draughts of both were taken from the ideas which they had of nature. Cities had been burnt before either of them were in being. But, to close the simile as I began it,

they would not have design'd it after the same manner: Apelles would have distinguish'd Pyrrhus from the rest of all the Grecians, and shew'd him forcing his entrance into Priam's palace; there he had set him in the fairest light, and given him the chief place of all his figures; because he was a Grecian, and he would do honor to his country. Raphael, who was an Italian, and descended from the Trojans, would have made Æneas the hero of his piece; and perhaps not with his father on his back, his son in one hand, his bundle of gods in the other, and his wife following; for an act of piety is not half so graceful in a picture as an act of courage: he would rather have drawn him killing Androgeos, or some other, hand to hand; and the blaze of the fires should have darted full upon his face, to make him conspicuous amongst his Trojans. This, I think, is a just comparison betwixt the two poets, in the conduct of their several designs. Virgil cannot be said to copy Homer; the Grecian had only the advantage of writing first. If it be urg'd that I have granted a resemblance in some parts, yet therein Virgil has excell'd him. For what are the tears of Calypso for being left, to the fury and death of Dido? Where is there the whole process of her passion and all its violent effects to be found, in the languishing *episode* of the *Odysses*? If this be to copy, let the critics shew us the same disposition, features, or coloring, in their original. The like may be said of the descent to hell, which was not of Homer's invention neither; he had it from the story of Orpheus and Eurydice. But to what end did Ulysses make that journey? Æneas undertook it by the express commandment of his father's ghost: there he was to shew him all the succeeding heroes of his race, and, next to Romulus (mark, if you please, the address of Virgil,) his own patron, Augustus Cæsar. Anchises was likewise to instruct him how to manage the Italian war, and how to conclude it with his honor; that is, in other words, to lay the foundations of that empire which Augustus was to govern. This is the noble invention of our author; but it hath been copied by so many sign-post daubers, that now 't is grown fulsome, rather by their want of skill than by the commonness.

In the last place, I may safely grant that,

by reading Homer, Virgil was taught to imitate his invention; that is, to imitate like him; which is no more than if a painter studied Raphael, that he might learn to design after his manner. And thus I might imitate Virgil, if I were capable of writing an heroic poem, and yet the invention be my own; but I should endeavor to avoid a servile copying. I would not give the same story under other names, with the same characters, in the same order, and with the same sequel; for every common reader to find me out at the first sight for a plagiary, and cry: "This I read before in Virgil, in a better language, and in better verse. This is like Merry Andrew on the low rope, copying lubberly the same tricks which his master is so dext'rously performing on the high."

I will trouble your Lordship but with one objection more, which I know not whether I found in Le Fèvre, or Valois; but I am sure I have read it in another French critic, whom I will not name, because I think it is not much for his reputation. Virgil, in the heat of action — suppose, for example, in describing the fury of his hero in a battle, when he is endeavoring to raise our concernments to the highest pitch — turns short on the sudden into some similitude, which diverts, say they, your attention from the main subject, and misspends it on some trivial image. He pours cold water into the caldron, when his business is to make it boil.

This accusation is general against all who would be thought heroic poets; but I think it touches Virgil less than any. He is too great a master of his art, to make a blot which may so easily be hit. Similitudes, as I have said, are not for tragedy, which is all violent, and where the passions are in a perpetual ferment; for there they deaden where they should animate; they are not of the nature of dialogue, unless in comedy: a metaphor is almost all the stage can suffer, which is a kind of similitude comprehended in a word. But this figure has a contrary effect in heroic poetry; there 't is employ'd to raise the admiration, which is its proper business; and admiration is not of so violent a nature as fear or hope, compassion or horror, or any concernment we can have for such or such a person on the stage. Not but I confess that similitudes

and descriptions, when drawn into an unreasonable length, must needs nauseate the reader. Once, I remember, and but once, Virgil makes a similitude of fourteen lines; and his description of Fame is about the same number. He is blam'd for both; and I doubt not but he would have contracted them, had he liv'd to have review'd his work; but faults are no precedents. This I have observ'd of his similitudes in general, that they are not plac'd, as our unobserving critics tell us, in the heat of any action, but commonly in its declining. When he has warm'd us in his description as much as possibly he can, then, lest that warmth should languish, he renews it by some apt similitude, which illustrates his subject, and yet palls not his audience. I need give your Lordship but one example of this kind, and leave the rest to your observation, when next you review the whole Æneis in the original, unblemish'd by my rude translation. 'T is in the First Book, where the poet describes Neptune composing the ocean, on which Æolus had rais'd a tempest without his permission. He had already chidden the rebellious winds for obeying the commands of their usurping master; he had warn'd them from the seas; he had beaten down the billows with his mace, dispell'd the clouds, restor'd the sunshine, while Triton and Cymothoe were heaving the ships from off the quicksands, before the poet would offer at a similitude for illustration:

Ac, veluti magno in populo cum sæpe coorta est
Seditio, sævitque animis ignobile vulgus,
Jamque faces et saxa volant; furor arma ministrat;
Tum, pietate gravem ac meritis si forte virum quem
Conspexere, silent, arrectisque auribus adstant;
Ille regit dictis animos, et pectora mulcet:
Sic cunctus pelagi cecidit fragor, æquora postquam
Prospiciens genitor cæloque invectus aperto
Flectit equos, curruque volans dat lora secundo.

This is the first similitude which Virgil makes in this poem, and one of the longest in the whole; for which reason I the rather cite it. While the storm was in its fury, any allusion had been improper; for the poet could have compar'd it to nothing more impetuous than itself; consequently he could have made no illustration. If he could have illustrated, it had been an ambitious ornament out of season, and would have diverted our concernment: *nunc non erat hisce locus;* and therefore he deferr'd it to its proper place.

These are the criticisms of most moment which have been made against the *Æneis* by the ancients or moderns. As for the particular exceptions against this or that passage, Macrobius and Pontanus have answer'd them already. If I desir'd to appear more learned than I am, it had been as easy for me to have taken their objections and solutions, as it is for a country parson to take the expositions of the fathers out of Junius and Tremellius, or not to have nam'd the authors from whence I had them; for so Ruæus, otherwise a most judicious commentator on Virgil's works, has us'd Pontanus, his greatest benefactor; of whom he is very silent; and I do not remember that he once cites him.

What follows next is no objection; for that implies a fault: and it had been none in Virgil, if he had extended the time of his action beyond a year. At least Aristotle has set no precise limits to it. Homer's, we know, was within two months: Tasso, I am sure, exceeds not a summer; and, if I examin'd him, perhaps he might be reduc'd into a much less compass. Bossu leaves it doubtful whether Virgil's action were within the year, or took up some months beyond it. Indeed, the whole dispute is of no more concernment to the common reader, than it is to a plowman, whether February this year had 28 or 29 days in it. But, for the satisfaction of the more curious, of which number I am sure your Lordship is one, I will translate what I think convenient out of Segrais, whom perhaps you have not read; for he has made it highly probable that the action of the *Æneis* began in the spring, and was not extended beyond the autumn. And we have known campaigns that have begun sooner and have ended later.

Ronsard, and the rest whom Segrais names, who are of opinion that the action of this poem takes up almost a year and half, ground their calculation thus. Anchises died in Sicily at the end of winter, or beginning of the spring. Æneas, immediately after the interment of his father, puts to sea for Italy. He is surpris'd by the tempest describ'd in the beginning of the First

Book; and there it is that the scene of the poem opens, and where the action must commence. He is driven by this storm on the coasts of Afric; he stays at Carthage all that summer, and almost all the winter following, sets sail again for Italy just before the beginning of the spring, meets with contrary winds, and makes Sicily the second time. This part of the action completes the year. Then he celebrates the anniversary of his father's funerals, and shortly after arrives at Cumes; and from thence his time is taken up in his first treaty with Latinus, the overture of the war, the siege of his camp by Turnus, his going for succors to relieve it, his return, the raising of the siege by the first battle, the twelve days' truce, the second battle, the assault of Laurentum, and the single fight with Turnus; all which, they say, cannot take up less than four or five months more; by which account we cannot suppose the entire action to be contain'd in a much less compass than a year and half.

Segrais reckons another way; and his computation is not condemn'd by the learned Ruæus, who compil'd and publish'd the commentaries on our poet which we call the Dauphin's *Virgil.*

He allows the time of year when Anchises died to be in the latter end of winter, or the beginning of the spring: he acknowledges that, when Æneas is first seen at sea afterwards, and is driven by the tempest on the coast of Afric, is the time when the action is naturally to begin: he confesses, farther, that Æneas left Carthage in the latter end of winter; for Dido tells him in express terms, as an argument for his longer stay:

Quinetiam hiberno moliris sidere classem.

But, whereas Ronsard's followers suppose that when Æneas had buried his father, he set sail immediately for Italy, (tho' the tempest drove him on the coast of Carthage,) Segrais will by no means allow that supposition, but thinks it much more probable that he remain'd in Sicily till the midst of July, or the beginning of August; at which time he places the first appearance of his hero on the sea, and there opens the action of the poem. From which beginning to the death of Turnus, which concludes the action, there need not be suppos'd above ten months of intermediate time: for, arriving at Carthage in the latter end of summer, staying there the winter following, departing thence in the very beginning of the spring, making a short abode in Sicily the second time, landing in Italy, and making the war, may be reasonably judg'd the business but of ten months. To this the Ronsardians reply, that, having been for seven years before in quest of Italy, and having no more to do in Sicily than to inter his father — after that office was perform'd, what remain'd for him, but, without delay, to pursue his first adventure? To which Segrais answers, that the obsequies of his father, according to the rites of the Greeks and Romans, would detain him for many days; that a longer time must be taken up in the refitting of his ships after so tedious a voyage, and in refreshing his weatherbeaten soldiers on a friendly coast. These indeed are but suppositions on both sides; yet those of Segrais seem better grounded. For the feast of Dido, when she entertain'd Æneas first, has the appearance of a summer's night, which seems already almost ended when he begins his story; therefore the love was made in autumn: the hunting follow'd properly, when the heats of that scorching country were declining; the winter was pass'd in jollity, as the season and their love requir'd; and he left her in the latter end of winter, as is already prov'd. This opinion is fortified by the arrival of Æneas at the mouth of Tiber, which marks the season of the spring; that season being perfectly describ'd by the singing of the birds, saluting the dawn, and by the beauty of the place, which the poet seems to have painted expressly in the *Seventh Æneid :*

Aurora in roseis fulgebat lutea bigis,
Cum venti posuere ; variæ circumque supraque
Assuetæ ripis volucres et fluminis alveo
Æthera mulcebant cantu. ──

The remainder of the action requir'd but three months more: for, when Æneas went for succor to the Tuscans, he found their army in a readiness to march, and wanting only a commander; so that, according to this calculation, the *Æneis* takes not up above a year complete, and may be comprehended in less compass.

This, amongst other circumstances treated more at large by Segrais, agrees with the rising of Orion. which caus'd the tempest describ'd in the beginning of the First Book. By some passages in the *Pastorals,* but more particularly in the *Georgics,* our poet is found to be an exact astronomer, according to the knowledge of that age. Now Ilioneus (whom Virgil twice employs in embassies, as the best speaker of the Trojans) attributes that tempest to Orion, in his speech to Dido:

Cum subito assurgens fluctu nimbosus Orion.

He must mean either the *heliacal* or *achronical* rising of that sign. The *heliacal* rising of a constellation is when it comes from under the rays of the sun and begins to appear before daylight. The *achronical* rising, on the contrary, is when it appears at the close of day, and in opposition of the sun's diurnal course.

The *heliacal* rising of Orion is at present computed to be about the sixth of July; and about that time it is that he either causes or presages tempests on the seas.

Segrais has observ'd farther, that, when Anna counsels Dido to stay Æneas during the winter, she speaks also of Orion:

Dum pelago desævit hiems, et aquosus Orion.

If therefore Ilioneus, according to our supposition, understand the *heliacal* rising of Orion, Anna must mean the *achronical,* which the different epithets given to that constellation seem to manifest. Ilioneus calls him *nimbosus ;* Anna, *aquosus.* He is tempestuous in the summer, when he rises *heliacally,* and rainy in the winter, when he rises *achronically.* Your Lordship will pardon me for the frequent repetition of these cant words, which I could not avoid in this abbreviation of Segrais, who, I think, deserves no little commendation in this new criticism.

I have yet a word or two to say of Virgil's machines, from my own observation of them. He has imitated those of Homer, but not copied them. It was establish'd long before this time, in the Roman religion as well as in the Greek, that there were gods; and both nations, for the most part, worship'd the same deities; as did also the Trojans, from whom the Romans, I suppose, would rather be thought to derive the rites of their religion than from the Grecians; because they thought themselves descended from them. Each of those gods had his proper office, and the chief of them their particular attendants. Thus Jupiter had in propriety Ganymede and Mercury, and Juno had Iris. It was not for Virgil then to create new ministers; he must take what he found in his religion. It cannot therefore be said that he borrow'd them from Homer, any more than Apollo, Diana, and the rest, whom he uses as he finds occasion for them, as the Grecian poet did; but he invents the occasions for which he uses them. Venus, after the destruction of Troy, had gain'd Neptune entirely to her party; therefore we find him busy in the beginning of the *Æneis*, to calm the tempest rais'd by Æolus, and afterwards conducting the Trojan fleet to Cumes in safety, with the loss only of their pilot, for whom he bargains. I name those two examples amongst a hundred which I omit, to prove that Virgil, generally speaking, employ'd his machines in performing those things which might possibly have been done without them. What more frequent than a storm at sea, upon the rising of Orion? What wonder, if, amongst so many ships, there should one be overset, which was commanded by Orontes, tho' half the winds had not been there which Æolus employ'd? Might not Palinurus, without a miracle, fall asleep, and drop into the sea, having been overwearied with watching, and secure of a quiet passage, by his observation of the skies? At least Æneas, who knew nothing of the machine of Somnus, takes it plainly in this sense:

O nimium cœlo et pelago confise sereno,
Nudus in ignota, Palinure, jacebis arena.

But machines sometimes are specious things, to amuse the reader and give a color of probability to things otherwise incredible. And, besides, it sooth'd the vanity of the Romans, to find the gods so visibly concern'd in all the actions of their predecessors. We, who are better taught by our religion, yet own every wonderful accident which befalls us for the best, to be brought to pass by some special providence of Almighty God, and by the care of guardian angels; and from hence I might infer that no heroic poem can be writ on the Epicurean principles; which I could easily demonstrate, if there were need to prove it, or I had leisure.

When Venus opens the eyes of her son

Æneas, to behold the gods who combated against Troy in that fatal night when it was surpris'd, we share the pleasure of that glorious vision (which Tasso has not ill copied in the sacking of Jerusalem). But the Greeks had done their business, tho' neither Neptune, Juno, or Pallas had given them their divine assistance. The most crude machine which Virgil uses is in the episode of Camilla, where Opis, by the command of her mistress, kills Aruns. The next is in the *Twelfth Æneid*, where Venus cures her son Æneas. But in the last of these the poet was driven to a necessity; for Turnus was to be slain that very day; and Æneas, wounded as he was, could not have engag'd him in single combat, unless his hurt had been miraculously heal'd. And the poet had consider'd that the *dittany* which she brought from Crete could not have wrought so speedy an effect, without the juice of *ambrosia*, which she mingled with it. After all, that his machine might not seem too violent, we see the hero limping after Turnus. The wound was skinn'd, but the strength of his thigh was not restor'd. But what reason had our author to wound Æneas at so critical a time? And how came the cuisses to be worse temper'd than the rest of his armor, which was all wrought by Vulcan and his journeymen? These difficulties are not easily to be solv'd, without confessing that Virgil had not life enough to correct his work; tho' he had review'd it, and found those errors which he resolv'd to mend: but, being prevented by death, and not willing to leave an imperfect work behind him, he ordain'd, by his last testament, that his *Æneis* should be burn'd. As for the death of Aruns, who was shot by a goddess, the machine was not altogether so outrageous as the wounding Mars and Venus by the sword of Diomede. Two divinities, one would have thought, might have pleaded their prerogative of impassibility, or at least not have been wounded by any mortal hand; beside that the ἐΐχωρ which they shed was so very like our common blood, that it was not to be distinguish'd from it, but only by the name and color. As for what Horace says in his *Art of Poetry*, that no machines are to be us'd, unless on some extraordinary occasion:

Nec deus intersit, nisi dignus vindice nodus —

that rule is to be applied to the theater, of which he is then speaking; and means no more than this, that, when the knot of the play is to be untied, and no other way is left for making the discovery; then, and not otherwise, let a god descend upon a rope, and clear the business to the audience. But this has no relation to the machines which are us'd in an epic poem.

In the last place, for the *Dira*, or flying pest, which, flapping on the shield of Turnus, and fluttering about his head, dishearten'd him in the duel, and presag'd to him his approaching death, I might have plac'd it more properly amongst the objections; for the critics who lay want of courage to the charge of Virgil's hero quote this passage as a main proof of their assertion. They say our author had not only secur'd him before the duel, but also, in the beginning of it, had given him the advantage in impenetrable arms, and in his sword; for that of Turnus was not his own, which was forg'd by Vulcan for his father, but a weapon which he had snatch'd in haste, and by mistake, belonging to his charioteer Metiscus; that, after all this, Jupiter, who was partial to the Trojan, and distrustful of the event, tho' he had hung the balance, and given it a jog of his hand to weigh down Turnus, thought convenient to give the Fates a collateral security, by sending the screech owl to discourage him: for which they quote these words of Virgil :

——— *Non me tua turbida virtus*
Terret, ait : dii me terrent, et Jupiter hostis.

In answer to which, I say that this machine is one of those which the poet uses only for ornament, and not out of necessity. Nothing can be more beautiful or more poetical than his description of the three *Diræ*, or the setting of the balance, which our Milton has borrow'd from him, but employ'd to a different end: for, first, he makes God Almighty set the scales for St. Gabriel and Satan, when he knew no combat was to follow; then he makes the good angel's scale descend, and the Devil's mount, quite contrary to Virgil, if I have translated the three verses according to my author's sense:

Jupiter ipse duas æquato examine lances
Sustinet ; et fata imponit diversa duorum ;
Quem damnet labor, et quo vergat pondere letum.

For I have taken these words, *quem damnet labor,* in the sense which Virgil gives them in another place — *damnabis tu quoque votis* — to signify a prosperous event. Yet I dare not condemn so great a genius as Milton: for I am much mistaken if he alludes not to the text in Daniel, where Belshazzar was put into the balance and found too light. This is digression; and I return to my subject. I said above that these two machines of the balance and the *Dira* were only ornamental, and that the success of the duel had been the same without them. For, when Æneas and Turnus stood fronting each other before the altar, Turnus look'd dejected, and his color faded in his face, as if he desponded of the victory before the fight; and not only he, but all his party, when the strength of the two champions was judg'd by the proportion of their limbs, concluded it was *impar pugna*, and that their chief was overmatch'd: whereupon Juturna (who was of the same opinion) took this opportunity to break the treaty and renew the war. Juno herself had plainly told the nymph beforehand that her brother was to fight

Imparibus fatis, nec diis nec viribus æquis ;

so that there was no need of an apparition to fright Turnus: he had the presage within himself of his impending destiny. The *Dira* only serv'd to confirm him in his first opinion, that it was his destiny to die in the ensuing combat; and in this sense are those words of Virgil to be taken:

——— *Non me tua turbida virtus*
Terret, ait : dii me terrent, et Jupiter hostis.

I doubt not but the adverb *solum* is to be understood: " 'T is not your valor *only* that gives me this concernment; but I find also, by this portent, that Jupiter is my enemy." For Turnus fled before, when his first sword was broken, till his sister supplied him with a better; which indeed he could not use, because Æneas kept him at a distance with his spear. I wonder Ruæus saw not this, where he charges his author so unjustly, for giving Turnus a second sword to no purpose. How could he fasten a blow, or make a thrust, when he was not suffer'd to approach ? Besides, the chief errand of the *Dira* was to warn Juturna from the field, for she could have brought the chariot again, when she saw her brother worsted in the duel. I might farther add, that Æneas was so eager of the fight that he left the city, now almost in his possession, to decide his quarrel with Turnus by the sword; whereas Turnus had manifestly declin'd the combat, and suffer'd his sister to convey him as far from the reach of his enemy as she could. I say, not only suffer'd her, but consented to it; for 't is plain he knew her, by these words:

O soror, et dudum agnovi. cum prima per artem
Fœdera turbasti, teque hœc in bella dedisti ;
Et nunc nequicquam fallis dea. ——

I have dwelt so long on this subject, that I must contract what I have to say in reference to my translation, unless I would swell my preface into a volume, and make it formidable to your Lordship, when you see so many pages yet behind. And indeed what I have already written, either in justification or praise of Virgil, is against myself, for presuming to copy, in my coarse English, the thoughts and beautiful expressions of this inimitable poet, who flourish'd in an age when his language was brought to its last perfection, for which it was particularly owing to him and Horace. I will give your Lordship my opinion, that those two friends had consulted each other's judgment, wherein they should endeavor to excel; and they seem to have pitch'd on propriety of thought, elegance of words, and harmony of numbers. According to this model, Horace writ his *Odes* and *Epodes :* for his *Satires* and *Epistles*, being intended wholly for instruction, requir'd another style:

Ornari res ipsa negat, contenta doceri —

and therefore, as he himself professes, are *sermoni propiora*, nearer prose than verse. But Virgil, who never attempted the lyric verse, is everywhere elegant, sweet, and flowing in his hexameters. His words are not only chosen, but the places in which he ranks them for the sound; he who removes them from the station wherein their master sets them, spoils the harmony. What he says of the Sibyl's prophecies may be as properly applied to every word of his: they must be read in order as they lie; the least breath discomposes them; and somewhat of their divinity is lost. I cannot boast that I have been thus exact in my verses; but

I have endeavor'd to follow the example of my master, and am the first Englishman, perhaps, who made it his design to copy him in his numbers, his choice of words, and his placing them for the sweetness of the sound. On this last consideration I have shunn'd the *cæsura* as much as possibly I could: for, wherever that is us'd, it gives a roughness to the verse; of which we can have little need in a language which is overstock'd with consonants. Such is not the Latin, where the vowels and consonants are mix'd in proportion to each other; yet Virgil judg'd the vowels to have somewhat of an overbalance, and therefore tempers their sweetness with *cæsuras*. Such difference there is in tongues, that the same figure which roughens one, gives majesty to another; and that was it which Virgil studied in his verses. Ovid uses it but rarely; and hence it is that his versification cannot so properly be call'd sweet, as luscious. The Italians are forc'd upon it once or twice in every line, because they have a redundancy of vowels in their language. Their metal is so soft that it will not coin without alloy to harden it. On the other side, for the reason already nam'd, 't is all we can do to give sufficient sweetness to our language: we must not only choose our words for elegance, but for sound; to perform which, a mastery in the language is requir'd; the poet must have a magazine of words, and have the art to manage his few vowels to the best advantage, that they may go the farther. He must also know the nature of the vowels — which are more sonorous, and which more soft and sweet — and so dispose them as his present occasions require: all which, and a thousand secrets of versification beside, he may learn from Virgil, if he will take him for his guide. If he be above Virgil, and is resolv'd to follow his own *verve*, (as the French call it,) the proverb will fall heavily upon him: "Who teaches himself, has a fool for his master."

Virgil employ'd eleven years upon his *Æneis ;* yet he left it, as he thought himself, imperfect. Which when I seriously consider, I wish that, instead of three years, which I have spent in the translation of his works, I had four years more allow'd me to correct my errors, that I might make my version somewhat more tolerable than it is: for a poet cannot have too great a reverence for his readers, if he expects his labors should survive him. Yet I will neither plead my age nor sickness, in excuse of the faults which I have made: that I wanted time, is all I have to say; for some of my subscribers grew so clamorous that I could no longer defer the publication. I hope, from the candor of your Lordship, and your often experienc'd goodness to me, that, if the faults are not too many, you will make allowances with Horace:

Si plura nitent in carmine, non ego paucis
Offendar maculis, quas aut incuria fudit,
Aut humana parum cavit natura.

You may please also to observe, that there is not, to the best of my remembrance, one vowel gaping on another for want of a *cæsura*, in this whole poem; but, where a vowel ends a word, the next begins either with a consonant, or what is its equivalent; for our *W* and *H* aspirate, and our diphthongs, are plainly such. The greatest latitude I take is in the letter *Y*, when it concludes a word and the first syllable of the next begins with a vowel. Neither need I have call'd this a latitude, which is only an explanation of this general rule, that no vowel can be cut off before another when we cannot sink the pronunciation of it; as *he, she, me, I,* &c. Virgil thinks it sometimes a beauty to imitate the license of the Greeks, and leave two vowels opening on each other, as in that verse of the *Third Pastoral:*

Et succus pecori, et lac subducitur agnis.

But, *nobis non licet esse tam disertis,* at least if we study to refine our numbers. I have long had by me the materials of an English *prosodia,* containing all the mechanical rules of versification, wherein I have treated with some exactness of the feet, the quantities, and the pauses. The French and Italians know nothing of the two first; at least their best poets have not practic'd them. As for the pauses, Malherbe first brought them into France, within this last century; and we see how they adorn their *Alexandrins.* But, as Virgil propounds a riddle, which he leaves unsolv'd:

Dic, quibus in terris, inscripti nomina regum
Nascantur flores; et Phyllida solus habeto;

so I will give your Lordship another, and leave the exposition of it to your acute judgment. I am sure there are few who make verses have observ'd the sweetness of these two lines in *Cooper's Hill:*

Tho' deep, yet clear; tho' gentle, yet not dull;
Strong without rage; without o'erflowing, full.

And there are yet fewer who can find the reason of that sweetness. I have given it to some of my friends in conversation, and they have allow'd the criticism to be just. But, since the evil of false quantities is difficult to be cur'd in any modern language; since the French and the Italians, as well as we, are yet ignorant what feet are to be us'd in heroic poetry; since I have not strictly observ'd those rules myself which I can teach others; since I pretend to no dictatorship among my fellow poets; since, if I should instruct some of them to make well-running verses, they want genius to give them strength as well as sweetness; and, above all, since your Lordship has advis'd me not to publish that little which I know, I look on your counsel as your command, which I shall observe inviolably, till you shall please to revoke it, and leave me at liberty to make my thoughts public. In the mean time, that I may arrogate nothing to myself, I must acknowledge that Virgil in Latin, and Spenser in English, have been my masters. Spenser has also given me the boldness to make use sometimes of his *Alexandrin* line, which we call, tho' improperly, the Pindaric, because Mr. Cowley has often employ'd it in his *Odes.* It adds a certain majesty to the verse, when 't is us'd with judgment, and stops the sense from overflowing into another line. Formerly the French, like us and the Italians, had but five feet, or ten syllables, in their heroic verse; but since Ronsard's time, as I suppose, they found their tongue too weak to support their epic poetry without the addition of another foot. That indeed has given it somewhat of the run and measure of a *trimeter;* but it runs with more activity than strength: their language is not strung with sinews, like our English. It has the nimbleness of a greyhound, but not the bulk and body of a mastiff. Our men and our verses overbear them by their weight; and *pondere, non numero,* is the

British motto. The French have set up purity for the standard of their language; and a masculine vigor is that of ours. Like their tongue is the genius of their poets, light and trifling in comparison of the English; more proper for sonnets, madrigals, and elegies, than heroic poetry. The turn on thoughts and words is their chief talent, but the epic poem is too stately to receive those little ornaments. The painters draw their nymphs in thin and airy habits; but the weight of gold and of embroideries is reserv'd for queens and goddesses. Virgil is never frequent in those turns, like Ovid, but much more sparing of them in his *Æneis* than in his *Pastorals* and *Georgics*.

Ignoscenda quidem, scirent si ignoscere manes.

That turn is beautiful indeed; but he employs it in the story of Orpheus and Eurydice, not in his great poem. I have us'd that license in his *Æneis* sometimes, but I own it as my fault. 'Twas given to those who understand no better. 'T is like Ovid's

Semivirumque bovem, semibovemque virum.

The poet found it before his critics, but it was a darling sin, which he would not be persuaded to reform. The want of genius, of which I have accus'd the French, is laid to their charge by one of their own great authors, tho' I have forgotten his name, and where I read it. If rewards could make good poets, their great master has not been wanting on his part in his bountiful encouragements; for he is wise enough to imitate Augustus, if he had a Maro. The triumvir and proscriber had descended to us in a more hideous form than they now appear, if the emperor had not taken care to make friends of him and Horace. I confess the banishment of Ovid was a blot in his escutcheon: yet he was only banish'd; and who knows but his crime was capital, and then his exile was a favor? Ariosto, who, with all his faults, must be acknowledg'd a great poet, has put these words into the mouth of an evangelist; but whether they will pass for gospel now, I cannot tell:

Non fu si santo ni benigno Augusto,
Come la tuba di Virgilio suona.
L' haver havuto in poesia buon gusto,
La proscrittione iniqua gli perdona.

But heroic poetry is not of the growth of France, as it might be of England, if it were cultivated. Spenser wanted only to have read the rules of Bossu; for no man was ever born with a greater genius, or had more knowledge to support it. But the performance of the French is not equal to their skill; and hitherto we have wanted skill to perform better. Segrais, whose preface is so wonderfully good, yet is wholly destitute of elevation, tho' his version is much better than that of the two brothers, or any of the rest who have attempted Virgil. Hannibal Caro is a great name amongst the Italians; yet his translation of the *Æneis* is most scandalously mean, tho' he has taken the advantage of writing in blank verse, and freed himself from the shackles of modern rhyme, (if it be modern; for Le Clerc has told us lately, and I believe has made it out, that David's Psalms were written in as errant rhyme as they are translated.) Now, if a Muse cannot run when she is unfetter'd, 't is a sign she has but little speed. I will not make a digression here, tho' I am strangely tempted to it; but will only say, that he who can write well in rhyme, may write better in blank verse. Rhyme is certainly a constraint even to the best poets, and those who make it with most ease; tho' perhaps I have as little reason to complain of that hardship as any man, excepting Quarles and Withers. What it adds to sweetness, it takes away from sense; and he who loses the least by it may be call'd a gainer. It often makes us swerve from an author's meaning; as, if a mark be set up for an archer at a great distance, let him aim as exactly as he can, the least wind will take his arrow, and divert it from the white. I return to our Italian translator of the *Æneis*. He is a foot-poet, he lackeys by the side of Virgil at the best, but never mounts behind him. Doctor Morelli, who is no mean critic in our poetry, and therefore may be presum'd to be a better in his own language, has confirm'd me in this opinion by his judgment, and thinks, withal, that he has often mistaken his master's sense. I would say so, if I durst, but am afraid I have committed the same fault more often, and more grossly; for I have forsaken Ruæus (whom generally I follow) in many places, and made expositions of my own in some, quite contrary to him. Of which I will give but two examples, because they are so near each other, in the *Tenth Æneid:*

—— *Sorti pater æquus utrique.*

Pallas says it to Turnus, just before they fight. Ruæus thinks that the word *pater* is to be referr'd to Evander, the father of Pallas. But how could he imagine that it was the same thing to Evander, if his son were slain, or if he overcame? The poet certainly intended Jupiter, the common father of mankind; who, as Pallas hop'd, would stand an impartial spectator of the combat, and not be more favorable to Turnus than to him. The second is not long after it, and both before the duel is begun. They are the words of Jupiter, who comforts Hercules for the death of Pallas, which was immediately to ensue, and which Hercules could not hinder, (tho' the young hero had address'd his prayers to him for his assistance,) because the gods cannot control destiny. — The verse follows:

Sic ait; atque oculos Rutulorum rejicit arvis,

which the same Ruæus thus construes: Jupiter, after he had said this, immediately turns his eyes to the Rutulian fields, and beholds the duel. I have given this place another exposition, that he turn'd his eyes from the field of combat, that he might not behold a sight so unpleasing to him. The word *rejicit,* I know, will admit of both senses; but Jupiter having confess'd that he could not alter fate, and being griev'd he could not, in consideration of Hercules, it seems to me that he should avert his eyes, rather than take pleasure in the spectacle. But of this I am not so confident as the other, tho' I think I have follow'd Virgil's sense.

What I have said, tho' it has the face of arrogance, yet is intended for the honor of my country; and therefore I will boldly own that this English translation has more of Virgil's spirit in it than either the French or the Italian. Some of our countrymen have translated episodes and other parts of Virgil with great success; as particularly your Lordship, whose version of *Orpheus and Eurydice* is eminently good. Amongst the dead authors, the *Silenus* of my Lord Roscommon cannot be too much commended. I say nothing of Sir John Denham, Mr. Waller, and Mr. Cowley; 't is the

utmost of my ambition to be thought their equal, or not to be much inferior to them, and some others of the living. But 't is one thing to take pains on a fragment, and translate it perfectly; and another thing to have the weight of a whole author on my shoulders. They who believe the burthen light, let them attempt the *Fourth, Sixth,* or *Eighth Pastoral;* the *First* or *Fourth Georgic;* and, amongst the *Æneids,* the *Fourth,* the *Fifth,* the *Seventh,* the *Ninth,* the *Tenth,* the *Eleventh,* or the *Twelfth;* for in these I think I have succeeded best.

Long before I undertook this work, I was no stranger to the original. I had also studied Virgil's design, his disposition of it, his manners, his judicious management of the figures, the sober retrenchments of his sense, which always leaves somewhat to gratify our imagination, on which it may enlarge at pleasure; but, above all, the elegance of his expressions, and the harmony of his numbers. For, as I have said in a former dissertation, the words are in poetry what the colors are in painting. If the design be good, and the draught be true, the coloring is the first beauty that strikes the eye. Spenser and Milton are the nearest, in English, to Virgil and Horace in the Latin; and I have endeavor'd to form my style by imitating their masters. I will farther own to you, my Lord, that my chief ambition is to please those readers who have discernment enough to prefer Virgil before any other poet in the Latin tongue. Such spirits as he desir'd to please, such would I choose for my judges, and would stand or fall by them alone. Segrais has distinguish'd the readers of poetry, according to their capacity of judging, into three classes; (he might have said the same of writers too, if he had pleas'd.) In the lowest form he places those whom he calls *les petits esprits;* such things as are our upper-gallery audience in a playhouse, who like nothing but the husk and rind of wit; prefer a quibble, a conceit, an epigram, before solid sense and elegant expression; these are mob readers. If Virgil and Martial stood for Parliament-men, we know already who would carry it. But, tho' they make the greatest appearance in the field, and cry the loudest, the best on 't is, they are but a sort of French Huguenots, or Dutch boors, brought over in herds, but not naturaliz'd; who have not land of two pounds *per annum* in Parnassus, and therefore are not privileg'd to poll. Their authors are of the same level, fit to represent them on a mountebank's stage, or to be masters of the ceremonies in a bear garden. Yet these are they who have the most admirers. But it often happens, to their mortification, that, as their readers improve their stock of sense, (as they may by reading better books, and by conversation with men of judgment,) they soon forsake them; and when the torrent from the mountains falls no more, the swelling writer is reduc'd into his shallow bed, like the Mançanares at Madrid, with scarce water to moisten his own pebbles. There are a middle sort of readers, (as we hold there is a middle state of souls,) such as have a farther insight than the former, yet have not the capacity of judging right; for I speak not of those who are brib'd by a party, and know better, if they were not corrupted; but I mean a company of warm young men, who are not yet arriv'd so far as to discern the difference betwixt fustian, or ostentatious sentences, and the true sublime. These are above liking Martial, or Owen's *Epigrams*, but they would certainly set Virgil below Statius or Lucan. I need not say their poets are of the same paste with their admirers. They affect greatness in all they write: but 't is a bladder'd greatness, like that of the vain man whom Seneca describes; an ill habit of body, full of humors, and swell'd with dropsy. Even these too desert their authors, as their judgment ripens. The young gentlemen themselves are commonly misled by their *pædagogue* at school, their tutor at the university, or their governor in their travels. And many of those three sorts are the most positive blockheads in the world. How many of those flatulent writers have I known who have sunk in their reputation after seven or eight editions of their works! for indeed they are poets only for young men. They had great success at their first appearance; but, not being of God, as a wit said formerly, they could not stand.

I have already nam'd two sorts of judges; but Virgil wrote for neither of them: and, by his example, I am not ambitious of pleasing the lowest or the middle form of readers.

He chose to please the most judicious, souls of the highest rank and truest understanding. These are few in number; but whoever is so happy as to gain their approbation can never lose it, because they never give it blindly. Then they have a certain *magnetism* in their judgment, which attracts others to their sense. Every day they gain some new proselyte, and in time become the Church. For this reason, a well-weigh'd judicious poem, which at its first appearance gains no more upon the world than to be just receiv'd, and rather not blam'd than much applauded, insinuates itself by insensible degrees into the liking of the reader: the more he studies it, the more it grows upon him; every time he takes it up, he discovers some new graces in it. And whereas poems which are produc'd by the vigor of imagination only, have a gloss upon them at the first which time wears off, the works of judgment are like the diamond; the more they are polish'd, the more luster they receive. Such is the difference betwixt Virgil's *Æneis* and Marini's *Adone*. And, if I may be allow'd to change the metaphor, I would say that Virgil is like the Fame which he describes:

Mobilitate viget, viresque acquirit eundo.

Such a sort of reputation is my aim, tho' in a far inferior degree, according to my motto in the title-page: *Sequiturque patrem non passibus æquis:* and therefore I appeal to the highest court of judicature, like that of the peers, of which your Lordship is so great an ornament.

Without this ambition which I own, of desiring to please the *judices natos*, I could never have been able to have done anything at this age, when the fire of poetry is commonly extinguish'd in other men. Yet Virgil has given me the example of Entellus for my encouragement: when he was well heated, the younger champion could not stand before him. And we find the elder contended not for the gift, but for the honor: *nec dona moror.* For Dampier has inform'd us, in his *Voyages*, that the air of the country which produces gold is never wholesome.

I had long since consider'd that the way to please the best judges is not to translate a poet literally, and Virgil least of any other. For, his peculiar beauty lying in his choice of words, I am excluded from it by the narrow compass of our heroic verse, unless I would make use of monosyllables only, and those clogg'd with consonants, which are the dead weight of our mother tongue. 'T is possible, I confess, tho' it rarely happens, that a verse of monosyllables may sound harmoniously; and some examples of it I have seen. My first line of the *Æneis* is not harsh:

Arms, and the man I sing, who, forc'd by fate, &c.

But a much better instance may be given from the last line of Manilius, made English by our learned and judicious Mr. Creech:

Nor could the world have borne so fierce a flame —

where the many liquid consonants are plac'd so artfully that they give a pleasing sound to the words, tho' they are all of one syllable. 'T is true, I have been sometimes forc'd upon it in other places of this work; but I never did it out of choice: I was either in haste, or Virgil gave me no occasion for the ornament of words; for it seldom happens but a monosyllable line turns verse to prose; and even that prose is rugged and unharmonious. Philarchus, I remember, taxes Balzac for placing twenty monosyllables in file, without one dissyllable betwixt them. The way I have taken is not so strait as metaphrase, nor so loose as paraphrase: some things too I have omitted, and sometimes have added of my own. Yet the omissions, I hope, are but of circumstances, and such as would have no grace in English; and the additions, I also hope, are easily deduc'd from Virgil's sense. They will seem (at least I have the vanity to think so) not stuck into him, but growing out of him. He studies brevity more than any other poet; but he had the advantage of a language wherein much may be comprehended in a little space. We, and all the modern tongues, have more articles and pronouns, besides signs of tenses and cases, and other barbarities on which our speech is built by the faults of our forefathers. The Romans founded theirs upon the Greek: and the Greeks, we know, were laboring many hundred years upon their language before they brought it to perfection. They rejected all those signs, and cut off as many articles as they could spare;

comprehending in one word what we are constrain'd to express in two; which is one reason why we cannot write so concisely as they have done. The word *pater*, for example, signifies not only *a* father, but *your* father, *my* father, *his* or *her* father, all included in a word.

This inconvenience is common to all modern tongues; and this alone constrains us to employ more words than the ancients needed. But having before observ'd that Virgil endeavors to be short, and at the same time elegant, I pursue the excellence and forsake the brevity. For there he is like ambergris, a rich perfume, but of so close and glutinous a body that it must be open'd with inferior scents of musk or civet, or the sweetness will not be drawn out into another language.

On the whole matter, I thought fit to steer betwixt the two extremes of paraphrase and literal translation; to keep as near my author as I could, without losing all his graces, the most eminent of which are in the beauty of his words; and those words, I must add, are always figurative. Such of these as would retain their elegance in our tongue, I have endeavor'd to graff on it; but most of them are of necessity to be lost, because they will not shine in any but their own. Virgil has sometimes two of them in a line; but the scantiness of our heroic verse is not capable of receiving more than one; and that too must expiate for many others which have none. Such is the difference of the languages, or such my want of skill in choosing words. Yet I may presume to say, and I hope with as much reason as the French translator, that, taking all the materials of this divine author, I have endeavor'd to make Virgil speak such English as he would himself have spoken, if he had been born in England, and in this present age. I acknowledge, with Segrais, that I have not succeeded in this attempt according to my desire; yet I shall not be wholly without praise, if in some sort I may be allow'd to have copied the clearness, the purity, the easiness, and the magnificence of his style. But I shall have occasion to speak farther on this subject before I end the preface.

When I mention'd the Pindaric line, I should have added that I take another license in my verses; for I frequently make use of triplet rhymes, and for the same reason, because they bound the sense. And therefore I generally join these two licenses together, and make the last verse of the triplet a Pindaric: for, besides the majesty which it gives, it confines the sense within the barriers of three lines, which would languish if it were lengthen'd into four. Spenser is my example for both these privileges of English verses; and Chapman has follow'd him in his translation of Homer. Mr. Cowley has given in to them after both; and all succeeding writers after him. I regard them now as the *Magna Charta* of heroic poetry, and am too much an Englishman to lose what my ancestors have gain'd for me. Let the French and Italians value themselves on their regularity; strength and elevation are our standard. I said before, and I repeat it, that the affected purity of the French has unsinew'd their heroic verse. The language of an epic poem is almost wholly figurative; yet they are so fearful of a metaphor, that no example of Virgil can encourage them to be bold with safety. Sure they might warm themselves by that sprightly blaze, without approaching it so close as to singe their wings; they may come as near it as their master. Not that I would discourage that purity of diction in which he excels all other poets. But he knows how far to extend his franchises, and advances to the verge, without venturing a foot beyond it. On the other side, without being injurious to the memory of our English Pindar, I will presume to say that his metaphors are sometimes too violent, and his language is not always pure. But at the same time I must excuse him; for, thro' the iniquity of the times, he was forc'd to travel, at an age when, instead of learning foreign languages, he should have studied the beauties of his mother tongue, which, like all other speeches, is to be cultivated early, or we shall never write it with any kind of elegance. Thus by gaining abroad he lost at home; like the painter in the *Arcadia*, who, going to see a skirmish, had his arms lopp'd off, and return'd, says Sir Philip Sidney, well instructed how to draw a battle, but without a hand to perform his work.

There is another thing in which I have presum'd to deviate from him and Spenser. They both make hemistichs (or half verses)

breaking off in the middle of a line. I confess there are not many such in the *Fairy Queen ;* and even those few might be occasion'd by his unhappy choice of so long a stanza. Mr. Cowley had found out that no kind of staff is proper for a heroic poem, as being all too lyrical; yet, tho' he wrote in couplets, where rhyme is freer from constraint, he frequently affects half verses; of which we find not one in Homer, and I think not in any of the Greek poets, or the Latin, excepting only Virgil; and there is no question but he thought he had Virgil's authority for that license. But I am confident our poet never meant to leave him, or any other, such a precedent; and I ground my opinion on these two reasons. First, we find no example of a hemistich in any of his *Pastorals* or *Georgics ;* for he had given the last finishing strokes to both these poems: but his *Æneis* he left so uncorrect, at least so short of that perfection at which he aim'd, that we know how hard a sentence he pass'd upon it. And, in the second place, I reasonably presume that he intended to have fill'd up all those hemistichs, because in one of them we find the sense imperfect:

Quem tibi jam Troja ——

which some foolish grammarian has ended for him with a half line of nonsense:

—— *peperit fumante Creusa :*

for Ascanius must have been born some years before the burning of that city; which I need not prove. On the other side, we find also that he himself fill'd up one line in the *Sixth Æneid*, the enthusiasm seizing him while he was reading to Augustus:

Misenum Æolidem, quo non præstantior alter
Ære ciere viros ——

to which he added, in that transport, *Martemque accendere cantu:* and never was any line more nobly finish'd; for the reasons which I have given in the *Book of Painting.* On these considerations I have shunn'd hemistichs; not being willing to imitate Virgil to a fault, like Alexander's courtiers, who affected to hold their necks awry, because he could not help it. I am confident your Lordship is by this time of my opinion, and that you will look on those half lines hereafter as the imperfect products of a hasty Muse; like the frogs and serpents in the Nile; part of them kindled into life, and part a lump of unform'd unanimated mud.

I am sensible that many of my whole verses are as imperfect as those halves, for want of time to digest them better; but give me leave to make the excuse of Boccace, who, when he was upbraided that some of his novels had not the spirit of the rest, return'd this answer, that Charlemagne, who made the paladins, was never able to raise an army of them. The leaders may be heroes, but the multitude must consist of common men.

I am also bound to tell your Lordship, in my own defense, that, from the beginning of the *First Georgic* to the end of the last *Æneid,* I found the difficulty of translation growing on me in every succeeding book: for Virgil, above all poets, had a stock, which I may call almost inexhaustible, of figurative, elegant, and sounding words. I, who inherit but a small portion of his genius, and write in a language so much inferior to the Latin, have found it very painful to vary phrases, when the same sense returns upon me. Even he himself, whether out of necessity or choice, has often express'd the same thing in the same words, and often repeated two or three whole verses which he had us'd before. Words are not so easily coin'd as money; and yet we see that the credit not only of banks, but of exchequers, cracks, when little comes in and much goes out. Virgil call'd upon me in every line for some new word, and I paid so long, that I was almost bankrupt; so that the latter end must needs be more burdensome than the beginning or the middle; and, consequently, the *Twelfth Æneid* cost me double the time of the *First* and *Second.* What had become of me, if Virgil had tax'd me with another book? I had certainly been reduc'd to pay the public in hammer'd money, for want of mill'd; that is, in the same old words which I had us'd before; and the receivers must have been forc'd to have taken anything, where there was so little to be had.

Besides this difficulty (with which I have struggled, and made a shift to pass it over) there is one remaining, which is insuperable to all translators. We are bound to our author's sense, tho' with the latitudes already mention'd; for I think it not so

sacred, as that one *iota* must not be added or diminish'd, on pain of an *anathema.* But slaves we are, and labor on another man's plantation; we dress the vineyard, but the wine is the owner's: if the soil be sometimes barren, then we are sure of being scourg'd; if it be fruitful, and our care succeeds, we are not thank'd; for the proud reader will only say the poor drudge has done his duty. But this is nothing to what follows; for, being oblig'd to make his sense intelligible, we are forc'd to untune our own verses, that we may give his meaning to the reader. He who invents is master of his thoughts and words: he can turn and vary them as he pleases, till he renders them harmonious. But the wretched translator has no such privilege: for, being tied to the thoughts, he must make what music he can in the expression; and for this reason it cannot always be so sweet as that of the original. There is a beauty of sound, as Segrais has observ'd, in some Latin words, which is wholly lost in any modern language. He instances in that *mollis amaracus,* on which Venus lays Cupid, in the *First Æneid.* If I should translate it *sweet marjoram,* as the word signifies, the reader would think I had mistaken Virgil: for those village words, as I may call them, give us a mean idea of the thing; but the sound of the Latin is so much more pleasing, by the just mixture of the vowels with the consonants, that it raises our fancies to conceive somewhat more noble than a common herb, and to spread roses under him, and strew lilies over him; a bed not unworthy the grandson of the goddess.

If I cannot copy his harmonious numbers, how shall I imitate his noble flights, where his thoughts and words are equally sublime?

> *Quem quisquis studet æmulari,*
> *...... cœratis ope Dœdalea*
> *Nititur pennis. vitreo daturus*
> *Nomina ponto.*

What modern language, or what poet, can express the majestic beauty of this one verse, amongst a thousand others!

> *Aude, hospes, contemnere opes, et te quoque dignum*
> *Finge deo. ——*

For my part, I am lost in the admiration of it: I contemn the world when I think on it, and myself when I translate it.

Lay by Virgil, I beseech your Lordship, and all my better sort of judges, when you take up my version; and it will appear a passable beauty when the original Muse is absent. But, like Spenser's false Florimel made of snow, it melts and vanishes when the true one comes in sight. I will not excuse, but justify myself for one pretended crime, with which I am liable to be charg'd by false critics, not only in this translation, but in many of my original poems — that I Latinize too much. 'T is true that, when I find an English word significant and sounding, I neither borrow from the Latin or any other language; but, when I want at home, I must seek abroad.

If sounding words are not of our growth and manufacture, who shall hinder me to import them from a foreign country? I carry not out the treasure of the nation, which is never to return; but what I bring from Italy, I spend in England: here it remains, and here it circulates; for, if the coin be good, it will pass from one hand to another. I trade both with the living and the dead, for the enrichment of our native language. We have enough in England to supply our necessity; but, if we will have things of magnificence and splendor, we must get them by commerce. Poetry requires ornament; and that is not to be had from our old Teuton monosyllables: therefore, if I find any elegant word in a classic author, I propose it to be naturaliz'd by using it myself; and, if the public approves of it, the bill passes. But every man cannot distinguish betwixt pedantry and poetry: every man, therefore, is not fit to innovate. Upon the whole matter, a poet must first be certain that the word he would introduce is beautiful in the Latin; and is to consider, in the next place, whether it will agree with the English idiom. After this, he ought to take the opinion of judicious friends, such as are learned in both languages; and, lastly, since no man is infallible, let him use this license very sparingly; for, if too many foreign words are pour'd in upon us, it looks as if they were design'd not to assist the natives, but to conquer them.

I am now drawing towards a conclusion, and suspect your Lordship is very glad of it. But permit me first to own what helps I have had in this undertaking. The late Earl of Lauderdale sent me over his new translation of the Æneis, which he had ended before I ingag'd in the same design. Neither did I then intend it; but, some proposals being afterwards made me by my bookseller, I desir'd his Lordship's leave that I might accept them, which he freely granted; and I have his letter yet to shew for that permission. He resolv'd to have printed his work; which he might have done two years before I could publish mine; and had perform'd it, if death had not prevented him. But having his manuscript in my hands, I consulted it as often as I doubted of my author's sense; for no man understood Virgil better than that learned nobleman. His friends, I hear, have yet another and more correct copy of that translation by them, which had they pleas'd to have given the public, the judges must have been convinc'd that I have not flatter'd him. Besides this help, which was not inconsiderable, Mr. Congreve has done me the favor to review the Æneis, and compare my version with the original. I shall never be asham'd to own that this excellent young man has shew'd me many faults, which I have endeavor'd to correct. 'T is true, he might have easily found more, and then my translation had been more perfect.

Two other worthy friends of mine, who desire to have their names conceal'd, seeing me straiten'd in my time, took pity on me, and gave me the *Life of Virgil*, the two *Prefaces* to the *Pastorals* and the *Georgics*, and all the arguments in prose to the whole translation; which, perhaps, has caus'd a report that the two first poems are not mine. If it had been true that I had taken their verses for my own, I might have gloried in their aid; and, like Terence, have farther'd the opinion that Scipio and Lælius join'd with me. But the same style being continued thro' the whole, and the same laws of versification observ'd, are proofs sufficient that this is one man's work; and your Lordship is too well acquainted with my manner to doubt that any part of it is another's.

That your Lordship may see I was in earnest when I promis'd to hasten to an end, I will not give the reasons why I writ not always in the proper terms of navigation, land service, or in the cant of any profession. I will only say that Virgil has avoided those proprieties, because he writ not to mariners, soldiers, astronomers, gard'ners, peasants, &c., but to all in general, and in particular to men and ladies of the first quality, who have been better bred than to be too nicely knowing in the terms. In such cases, 't is enough for a poet to write so plainly, that he may be understood by his readers; to avoid impropriety, and not affect to be thought learn'd in all things.

I have omitted the four preliminary lines of the *First Æneid*, because I think them inferior to any four others in the whole poem, and consequently believe they are not Virgil's. There is too great a gap betwixt the adjective *vicina* in the second line, and the substantive *arva* in the latter end of the third, which keeps his meaning in obscurity too long, and is contrary to the clearness of his style.

Ut quamvis avidis

is too ambitious an ornament to be his; and

Gratum opus agricolis

are all words unnecessary, and independent of what he had said before.

Horrentia Martis arma

is worse than any of the rest. *Horrentia* is such a flat epithet as Tully would have given us in his verses. 'T is a mere filler, to stop a vacancy in the hexameter, and connect the preface to the work of Virgil. Our author seems to sound a charge, and begins like the clangor of a trumpet:

Arma virumque cano, Trojæ qui primus ab oris —

scarce a word without an *r*, and the vowels for the greater part sonorous. The preface began with *Ille ego*, which he was constrain'd to patch up in the fourth line with *at nunc*, to make the sense cohere; and if both those words are not notorious botches, I am much deceiv'd, tho' the French translator thinks otherwise. For my own part, I am rather of the opinion that they were added by Tucca and Varius, than retrench'd.

I know it may be answer'd by such as think Virgil the author of the four lines, that he asserts his title to the *Æneis* in the beginning of this work, as he did to the two former in the last lines of the *Fourth Georgic*. I will not reply otherwise to this than by desiring them to compare these four lines with the four others, which we know are his, because no poet but he alone could

write them. If they cannot distinguish creeping from flying, let them lay down Virgil, and take up Ovid *de Ponto* in his stead. My master needed not the assistance of that preliminary poet to prove his claim. His own majestic mien discovers him to be the king, amidst a thousand courtiers. It was a superfluous office; and therefore I would not set those verses in the front of Virgil, but have rejected them to my own preface.

I, who before, with shepherds in the groves,
Sung to my oaten pipe their rural loves,
And, issuing thence, compell'd the neighb'ring
    field
A plenteous crop of rising corn to yield,
Manur'd the glebe, and stock'd the fruitful
    plain,
(A poem grateful to the greedy swain) &c.

If there be not a tolerable line in all these six, the prefacer gave me no occasion to write better. This is a just apology in this place, but I have done great wrong to Virgil in the whole translation. Want of time, the inferiority of our language, the inconvenience of rhyme, and all the other excuses I have made, may alleviate my fault, but cannot justify the boldness of my undertaking. What avails it me to acknowledge freely that I have not been able to do him right in any line? For even my own confession makes against me; and it will always be return'd upon me: "Why then did you attempt it?" To which no other answer can be made, than that I have done him less injury than any of his former libelers.

What they call'd his picture had been drawn at length, so many times, by the daubers of almost all nations, and still so unlike him, that I snatch'd up the pencil with disdain; being satisfied beforehand that I could make some small resemblance of him, tho' I must be content with a worse likeness. A *Sixth Pastoral*, a *Pharmaceutria*, a single *Orpheus*, and some other features, have been exactly taken; but those holiday authors writ for pleasure, and only shew'd us what they could have done, if they would have taken pains to perform the whole.

Be pleas'd, my Lord, to accept with your wonted goodness this unworthy present which I make you. I have taken off one trouble from you, of defending it, by acknowledging its imperfections; and, tho' some part of them are cover'd in the verse, (as Erichthonius rode always in a chariot, to hide his lameness,) such of them as cannot be conceal'd, you will please to connive at, tho', in the strictness of your judgment, you cannot pardon. If Homer was allow'd to nod sometimes in so long a work, it will be no wonder if I often fall asleep. You took my *Aureng-Zebe* into your protection, with all his faults; and I hope here cannot be so many, because I translate an author who gives me such examples of correctness. What my jury may be, I know not; but 't is good for a criminal to plead before a favorable judge. If I had said partial, would your Lordship have forgiven me? Or will you give me leave to acquaint the world that I have many times been oblig'd to your bounty since the Revolution? Tho' I never was reduc'd to beg a charity, nor ever had the impudence to ask one, either of your Lordship, or your noble kinsman the Earl of Dorset, much less of any other; yet, when I least expected it, you have both remember'd me. So inherent it is in your family not to forget an old servant. It looks rather like ingratitude on my part, that, where I have been so often oblig'd, I have appear'd so seldom to return my thanks, and where I was also so sure of being well receiv'd. Somewhat of laziness was in the case, and somewhat too of modesty, but nothing of disrespect or of unthankfulness. I will not say that your Lordship has encourag'd me to this presumption, lest, if my labors meet with no success in public, I may expose your judgment to be censur'd. As for my own enemies, I shall never think them worth an answer; and, if your Lordship has any, they will not dare to arraign you for want of knowledge in this art, till they can produce somewhat better of their own than your *Essay on Poetry.* 'T was on this consideration that I have drawn out my preface to so great a length. Had I not address'd to a poet, and a critic of the first magnitude, I had myself been tax'd for want of judgment, and sham'd my patron for want of understanding. But neither will you, my Lord, so soon be tir'd as any other, because the discourse is on your art; neither will the learned reader think it tedious, because it is *ad clerum.* At least, when he begins to be weary, the church doors are open. That I may pursue the allegory with a short prayer after a long sermon:

May you live happily and long, for the service of your country, the encouragement of good letters, and the ornament of poetry; which cannot be wish'd more earnestly by any man, than by

Your Lordship's most humble,
Most oblig'd, and most obedient Servant,
JOHN DRYDEN.

THE FIRST BOOK OF THE ÆNEIS

THE ARGUMENT

The Trojans, after a seven years' voyage, set sail for Italy, but are overtaken by a dreadful storm, which Æolus raises at Juno's request. The tempest sinks one, and scatters the rest. Neptune drives off the Winds, and calms the sea. Æneas, with his own ship, and six more, arrives safe at an African port. Venus complains to Jupiter of her son's misfortunes. Jupiter comforts her, and sends Mercury to procure him a kind reception among the Carthaginians. Æneas, going out to discover the country, meets his mother in the shape of an huntress, who conveys him in a cloud to Carthage, where he sees his friends whom he thought lost, and receives a kind entertainment from the queen. Dido, by a device of Venus, begins to have a passion for him, and, after some discourse with him, desires the history of his adventures since the siege of Troy, which is the subject of the two following books.

ARMS, and the man I sing, who, forc'd by fate,
And haughty Juno's unrelenting hate,
Expell'd and exil'd, left the Trojan shore.
Long labors, both by sea and land, he bore,
And in the doubtful war, before he won
The Latian realm, and built the destin'd town;
His banish'd gods restor'd to rites divine,
And settled sure succession in his line,
From whence the race of Alban fathers come,
And the long glories of majestic Rome.   10
  O Muse! the causes and the crimes relate;
What goddess was provok'd, and whence her hate;
For what offense the Queen of Heav'n began
To persecute so brave, so just a man;
Involv'd his anxious life in endless cares,

Expos'd to wants, and hurried into wars!
Can heav'nly minds such high resentment
    show,
Or exercise their spite in human woe?
  Against the Tiber's mouth, but far away,
An ancient town was seated on the sea; 20
A Tyrian colony; the people made
Stout for the war, and studious of their
    trade:
Carthage the name; belov'd by Juno more
Than her own Argos, or the Samian shore.
Here stood her chariot; here, if Heav'n
    were kind,
The seat of awful empire she design'd.
Yet she had heard an ancient rumor fly,
(Long cited by the people of the sky,)
That times to come should see the Trojan
    race
Her Carthage ruin, and her tow'rs deface;
Nor thus confin'd, the yoke of sov'reign
    sway   31
Should on the necks of all the nations lay.
She ponder'd this, and fear'd it was in ⎫
    fate;   ⎪
Nor could forget the war she wag'd of ⎬
    late   ⎪
For conqu'ring Greece against the Trojan ⎪
    state.   ⎭
Besides, long causes working in her mind,
And secret seeds of envy, lay behind:
Deep graven in her heart the doom re-
    main'd
Of partial Paris, and her form disdain'd;
The grace bestow'd on ravish'd Ganymed,
Electra's glories, and her injur'd bed. 41
Each was a cause alone; and all combin'd
To kindle vengeance in her haughty mind.
For this, far distant from the Latian coast
She drove the remnants of the Trojan host;
And sev'n long years th' unhappy wand'ring
    train
Were toss'd by storms, and scatter'd thro'
    the main.
Such time, such toil, requir'd the Roman
    name,
Such length of labor for so vast a frame.
  Now scarce the Trojan fleet, with sails
    and oars,   50
Had left behind the fair Sicilian shores,
Ent'ring with cheerful shouts the wat'ry
    reign,
And plowing frothy furrows in the main;
When, lab'ring still with endless discon-
    tent,
The Queen of Heav'n did thus her fury vent:

" Then am I vanquish'd? must I yield?"
    said she,
" And must the Trojans reign in Italy?
So Fate will have it, and Jove adds his
    force;
Nor can my pow'r divert their happy course.
Could angry Pallas, with revengeful
    spleen,   60
The Grecian navy burn, and drown the men?
She, for the fault of one offending foe,
The bolts of Jove himself presum'd to
    throw:
With whirlwinds from beneath she toss'd
    the ship,
And bare expos'd the bosom of the deep;
Then, as an eagle gripes the trembling game,
The wretch, yet hissing with her father's
    flame,
She strongly seiz'd, and with a burning
    wound
Transfix'd, and naked, on a rock she bound.
But I, who walk in awful state above, 70
The majesty of heav'n, the sister wife of
    Jove,
For length of years my fruitless force em-
    ploy
Against the thin remains of ruin'd Troy!
What nations now to Juno's pow'r will
    pray,
Or off'rings on my slighted altars lay?"
  Thus rag'd the goddess; and, with fury
    fraught,
The restless regions of the storms she
    sought,
Where, in a spacious cave of living stone,
The tyrant Æolus, from his airy throne,
With pow'r imperial curbs the struggling
    winds,   80
And sounding tempests in dark prisons
    binds.
This way and that th' impatient captives
    tend,
And, pressing for release, the mountains
    rend.
High in his hall th' undaunted monarch
    stands,
And shakes his scepter, and their rage com-
    mands;
Which did he not, their unresisted sway
Would sweep the world before them in
    their way;
Earth, air, and seas thro' empty space would
    roll,
And heav'n would fly before the driving
    soul.

In fear of this, the Father of the Gods 90
Confin'd their fury to those dark abodes,
And lock'd 'em safe within, oppress'd
   with mountain loads;
Impos'd a king, with arbitrary sway,
To loose their fetters, or their force allay.
To whom the suppliant queen her pray'rs
   address'd,
And thus the tenor of her suit express'd:
" O Æolus ! for to thee the King of Heav'n
The pow'r of tempests and of winds has
   giv'n;
Thy force alone their fury can restrain,
And smooth the waves, or swell the troubled
   main —   100
A race of wand'ring slaves, abhorr'd by me,
With prosp'rous passage cut the Tuscan sea;
To fruitful Italy their course they steer,
And for their vanquish'd gods design new
   temples there.
Raise all thy winds; with night involve the
   skies;
Sink or disperse my fatal enemies.
Twice sev'n, the charming daughters of the
   main,
Around my person wait, and bear my train:
Succeed my wish, and second my design;
The fairest, Deiopeia, shall be thine,   110
And make thee father of a happy line."

   To this the god: " 'T is yours, O queen,
   to will
The work which duty binds me to fulfil.
These airy kingdoms, and this wide com-
   mand,
Are all the presents of your bounteous
   hand:
Yours is my sov'reign's grace; and, as
   your guest,
I sit with gods at their celestial feast;
Raise tempests at your pleasure, or subdue;
Dispose of empire, which I hold from you."
He said, and hurl'd against the mountain
   side   120
His quiv'ring spear, and all the god ap-
   plied.
The raging winds rush thro' the hollow
   wound,
And dance aloft in air, and skim along the
   ground;
Then, settling on the sea, the surges sweep,
Raise liquid mountains, and disclose the
   deep.
South, East, and West with mix'd confu-
   sion roar,
And roll the foaming billows to the shore.

The cables crack; the sailors' fearful
   cries
Ascend; and sable night involves the
   skies;
And heav'n itself is ravish'd from their
   eyes.   130
Loud peals of thunder from the poles en-
   sue;
Then flashing fires the transient light re-
   new;
The face of things a frightful image bears,
And present death in various forms ap-
   pears.
Struck with unusual fright, the Trojan
   chief,
With lifted hands and eyes, invokes relief;
And, " Thrice and four times happy those,"
   he cried,
" That under Ilian walls before their parents
   died !
Tydides, bravest of the Grecian train !
Why could not I by that strong arm be
   slain,   140
And lie by noble Hector on the plain,
Or great Sarpedon, in those bloody fields
Where Simoïs rolls the bodies and the
   shields
Of heroes, whose dismember'd hands yet
   bear
The dart aloft, and clench the pointed
   spear ! "

   Thus while the pious prince his fate be-
   wails,
Fierce Boreas drove against his flying sails,
And rent the sheets; the raging billows
   rise,
And mount the tossing vessel to the skies:
Nor can the shiv'ring oars sustain the
   blow;   150
The galley gives her side, and turns her
   prow;
While those astern, descending down the
   steep,
Thro' gaping waves behold the boiling deep.
Three ships were hurried by the southern
   blast,
And on the secret shelves with fury cast.
Those hidden rocks th' Ausonian sailors
   knew:
They call'd them Altars, when they rose in
   view,
And show'd their spacious backs above the
   flood.
Three more fierce Eurus, in his angry
   mood,

Dash'd on the shallows of the moving
sand,   160
And in mid ocean left them moor'd aland.
Orontes' bark, that bore the Lycian crew,
(A horrid sight!) ev'n in the hero's view,
From stem to stern by waves was over-
borne:
The trembling pilot, from his rudder torn,
Was headlong hurl'd; thrice round the
ship was toss'd,
Then bulg'd at once, and in the deep was
lost;
And here and there above the waves were
seen
Arms, pictures, precious goods, and floating
men.
The stoutest vessel to the storm gave way,
And suck'd thro' loosen'd planks the rush-
ing sea.   171
Ilioneus was her chief: Alethes old,
Achates faithful, Abas young and bold,
Endur'd not less; their ships, with gaping
seams,
Admit the deluge of the briny streams.
    Meantime imperial Neptune heard the
sound
Of raging billows breaking on the ground.
Displeas'd, and fearing for his wat'ry reign,
He rear'd his awful head above the main,
Serene in majesty; then roll'd his eyes   180
Around the space of earth, and seas, and
skies.
He saw the Trojan fleet dispers'd, dis-
tress'd,
By stormy winds and wintry heav'n op-
press'd.
Full well the god his sister's envy knew,
And what her aims and what her arts pur-
sue.
He summon'd Eurus and the western blast,
And first an angry glance on both he cast;
Then thus rebuk'd: " Audacious winds!
from whence
This bold attempt, this rebel insolence ?
Is it for you to ravage seas and land,   190
Unauthoriz'd by my supreme command ?
To raise such mountains on the troubled ⎫
main ?   ⎪
Whom I — but first 't is fit the billows   ⎬
to restrain;   ⎪
And then you shall be taught obedience   ⎪
to my reign.   ⎭
Hence ! to your lord my royal mandate
bear —
The realms of ocean and the fields of air

Are mine, not his. By fatal lot to me
The liquid empire fell, and trident of the
sea.
His pow'r to hollow caverns is confin'd:
There let him reign, the jailer of the wind,
With hoarse commands his breathing sub-
jects call,   201
And boast and bluster in his empty hall."
He spoke; and, while he spoke, he smooth'd
the sea,
Dispell'd the darkness, and restor'd the day.
Cymothoe, Triton, and the sea-green train
Of beauteous nymphs, the daughters of the
main,
Clear from the rocks the vessels with
their hands :   ⎫
The god himself with ready trident   ⎪
stands,   ⎬
And opes the deep, and spreads the mov-   ⎪
ing sands;   ⎭
Then heaves them off the shoals. Wher-   ⎫
e'er he guides   210 ⎪
His finny coursers and in triumph rides,   ⎬
The waves unruffle and the sea subsides.   ⎭
As, when in tumults rise th' ignoble crowd,
Mad are their motions, and their tongues
are loud;
And stones and brands in rattling volleys
fly,
And all the rustic arms that fury can sup-
ply:
If then some grave and pious man appear,
They hush their noise, and lend a list'ning
ear;
He soothes with sober words their angry
mood,
And quenches their innate desire of blood:
So, when the Father of the Flood appears, 221
And o'er the seas his sov'reign trident
rears,
Their fury falls: he skims the liquid ⎫
plains,   ⎪
High on his chariot, and, with loosen'd ⎬
reins,   ⎪
Majestic moves along, and awful peace ⎪
maintains.   ⎭
The weary Trojans ply their shatter'd oars
To nearest land, and make the Libyan
shores.
    Within a long recess there lies a bay:
An island shades it from the rolling sea,
And forms a port secure for ships to ⎫
ride;   230 ⎬
Broke by the jutting land, on either side, ⎪
In double streams the briny waters glide. ⎭

Betwixt two rows of rocks a sylvan scene
Appears above, and groves for ever green:
A grot is form'd beneath, with mossy seats,
To rest the Nereids, and exclude the heats.
Down thro' the crannies of the living walls
The crystal streams descend in murm'ring
　　falls:
No haulsers need to bind the vessels here,
Nor bearded anchors; for no storms they
　　fear.　　　　　　　　　　　　240
Sev'n ships within this happy harbor meet,
The thin remainders of the scatter'd fleet.
The Trojans, worn with toils, and spent
　　with woes,
Leap on the welcome land, and seek their
　　wish'd repose.
　　First, good Achates, with repeated
　　strokes
Of clashing flints, their hidden fire provokes:
Short flame succeeds; a bed of wither'd
　　leaves
The dying sparkles in their fall receives:
Caught into life, in fiery fumes they rise,
And, fed with stronger food, invade the
　　skies.　　　　　　　　　　　250
The Trojans, dropping wet, or stand around
The cheerful blaze, or lie along the ground:
Some dry their corn, infected with the
　　brine,
Then grind with marbles, and prepare to
　　dine.
Æneas climbs the mountain's airy brow,
And takes a prospect of the seas below,
If Capys thence, or Antheus he could spy,
Or see the streamers of Caïcus fly.
No vessels were in view; but, on the plain,
Three beamy stags command a lordly train
Of branching heads: the more ignoble
　　throng　　　　　　　　　　261
Attend their stately steps, and slowly graze
　　along.
He stood; and, while secure they fed below,
He took the quiver and the trusty bow
Achates us'd to bear: the leaders first
He laid along, and then the vulgar pierc'd;
Nor ceas'd his arrows, till the shady plain
Sev'n mighty bodies with their blood
　　distain.
For the sev'n ships he made an equal share,
And to the port return'd, triumphant from
　　the war.　　　　　　　　　　270
The jars of gen'rous wine (Acestes' gift,
When his Trinacrian shores the navy left)
He set abroach, and for the feast prepar'd,
In equal portions with the ven'son shar'd.

Thus while he dealt it round, the pious
　　chief
With cheerful words allay'd the common
　　grief:
" Endure, and conquer! Jove will soon
　　dispose
To future good our past and present woes.
With me, the rocks of Scylla you have
　　tried;
Th' inhuman Cyclops and his den defied. 280
What greater ills hereafter can you bear ?
Resume your courage and dismiss your
　　care.
An hour will come, with pleasure to relate
Your sorrows past, as benefits of Fate.
Thro' various hazards and events, we
　　move
To Latium and the realms foredoom'd by
　　Jove.
Call'd to the seat (the promise of the skies)
Where Trojan kingdoms once again may
　　rise,
Endure the hardships of your present state;
Live, and reserve yourselves for better
　　fate."　　　　　　　　　　290
　　These words he spoke, but spoke not
　　from his heart;
His outward smiles conceal'd his inward
　　smart.
The jolly crew, unmindful of the past,
The quarry share, their plenteous dinner
　　haste.
Some strip the skin; some portion out
　　the spoil;
The limbs, yet trembling, in the cal-
　　drons boil;
Some on the fire the reeking entrails
　　broil.
Stretch'd on the grassy turf, at ease they
　　dine,
Restore their strength with meat, and cheer
　　their souls with wine.
Their hunger thus appeas'd, their care
　　attends　　　　　　　　　　300
The doubtful fortune of their absent
　　friends:
Alternate hopes and fears their minds pos-
　　sess,
Whether to deem 'em dead, or in distress.
Above the rest, Æneas mourns the fate
Of brave Orontes, and th' uncertain state
Of Gyas, Lycus, and of Amycus.
The day, but not their sorrows, ended thus.
　　When, from aloft, almighty Jove sur-
　　veys

Earth, air, and shores, and navigable seas,
At length on Libyan realms he fix'd his
   eyes —   310
Whom, pond'ring thus on human miseries,
When Venus saw, she with a lowly look,
Not free from tears, her heav'nly sire be-
   spoke:
  "O King of Gods and Men! whose ⎫
    awful hand   ⎪
Disperses thunder on the seas and land, ⎬
Disposing all with absolute command; ⎭
How could my pious son thy pow'r incense?
Or what, alas! is vanish'd Troy's offense?
Our hope of Italy not only lost,   ⎫
On various seas by various tempests   ⎪
   toss'd,   320 ⎬
But shut from ev'ry shore, and barr'd ⎪
   from ev'ry coast.   ⎭
You promis'd once, a progeny divine
Of Romans, rising from the Trojan line,
In after times should hold the world in awe,
And to the land and ocean give the law.
How is your doom revers'd, which eas'd
   my care
When Troy was ruin'd in that cruel war?
Then fates to fates I could oppose; but
   now,
When Fortune still pursues her former
   blow,
What can I hope? What worse can still
   succeed?   330
What end of labors has your will decreed?
Antenor, from the midst of Grecian hosts,
Could pass secure, and pierce th' Illyrian
   coasts,
Where, rolling down the steep, Timavus
   raves
And thro' nine channels disembogues his
   waves.
At length he founded Padua's happy seat,
And gave his Trojans a secure retreat;
There fix'd their arms, and there renew'd
   their name,
And there in quiet rules, and crown'd with
   fame.
But we, descended from your sacred line,
Entitled to your heav'n and rites divine, 341
Are banish'd earth; and, for the wrath of
   one,
Remov'd from Latium and the promis'd
   throne.
Are these our scepters? these our due
   rewards?
And is it thus that Jove his plighted faith
   regards?"

To whom the Father of th' immortal
   race,
Smiling with that serene indulgent face,
With which he drives the clouds and clears
   the skies,
First gave a holy kiss; then thus replies:
  "Daughter, dismiss thy fears: to thy
    desire   350
The fates of thine are fix'd, and stand
   entire.
Thou shalt behold thy wish'd Lavinian
   walls;
And, ripe for heav'n, when fate Æneas calls,
Then shalt thou bear him up, sublime, to
   me:
No councils have revers'd my firm decree.
And, lest new fears disturb thy happy
   state,
Know, I have search'd the mystic rolls of
   Fate:
Thy son (nor is th' appointed season far)
In Italy shall wage successful war,
Shall tame fierce nations in the bloody
   field,   360
And sov'reign laws impose, and cities build,
Till, after ev'ry foe subdued, the sun
Thrice thro' the signs his annual race shall
   run:
This is his time prefix'd. Ascanius then,
Now call'd Iülus, shall begin his reign.
He thirty rolling years the crown shall
   wear,
Then from Lavinium shall the seat transfer,
And, with hard labor, Alba Longa build.
The throne with his succession shall be
   fill'd
Three hundred circuits more: then shall be
   seen   370
Ilia the fair, a priestess and a queen,
Who, full of Mars, in time, with kindly
   throes,
Shall at a birth two goodly boys disclose.
The royal babes a tawny wolf shall drain:
Then Romulus his grandsire's throne shall
   gain,
Of martial tow'rs the founder shall become,
The people Romans call, the city Rome.
To them no bounds of empire I assign,
Nor term of years to their immortal line.
Ev'n haughty Juno, who, with endless
   broils,   380
Earth, seas, and heav'n, and Jove himself
   turmoils;
At length aton'd, her friendly pow'r shall
   join,

To cherish and advance the Trojan line.
The subject world shall Rome's dominion
    own,
And, prostrate, shall adore the nation of
    the gown.
An age is ripening in revolving fate
When Troy shall overturn the Grecian
    state,
And sweet revenge her conqu'ring sons
    shall call,
To crush the people that conspir'd her fall.
Then Cæsar from the Julian stock shall
    rise,   390
Whose empire ocean, and whose fame the
    skies
Alone shall bound; whom, fraught with
    eastern spoils,
Our heav'n, the just reward of human toils,
Securely shall repay with rites divine;
And incense shall ascend before his sacred
    shrine.
Then dire debate and impious war shall
    cease,
And the stern age be soften'd into peace:
Then banish'd Faith shall once again re-
    turn,
And Vestal fires in hallow'd temples burn;
And Remus with Quirinus shall sustain 400
The righteous laws, and fraud and force
    restrain.
Janus himself before his fane shall wait,
And keep the dreadful issues of his gate,
With bolts and iron bars: within remains
Imprison'd Fury, bound in brazen chains;
High on a trophy rais'd, of useless arms,
He sits, and threats the world with vain
    alarms."
    He said, and sent Cyllenius with command
To free the ports, and ope the Punic land
To Trojan guests; lest, ignorant of fate,
The queen might force them from her town
    and state.   411
Down from the steep of heav'n Cyllenius
    flies,
And cleaves with all his wings the yielding
    skies.
Soon on the Libyan shore descends the god,
Performs his message, and displays his rod:
The surly murmurs of the people cease;
And, as the fates requir'd, they give the
    peace:
The queen herself suspends the rigid laws,
The Trojans pities, and protects their cause.
    Meantime, in shades of night Æneas
    lies: 420

Care seiz'd his soul, and sleep forsook his
    eyes.
But, when the sun restor'd the cheerful
    day,
He rose, the coast and country to survey,
Anxious and eager to discover more.
It look'd a wild uncultivated shore;
But, whether humankind, or beasts alone
Possess'd the new-found region, was un-
    known.
Beneath a ledge of rocks his fleet he ⎫
    hides: ⎪
Tall trees surround the mountain's shady ⎬
    sides;   ⎪
The bending brow above a safe retreat ⎪
    provides.   430 ⎭
Arm'd with two pointed darts, he leaves
    his friends,
And true Achates on his steps attends.
Lo! in the deep recesses of the wood,
Before his eyes his goddess mother stood:
A huntress in her habit and her mien;
Her dress a maid, her air confess'd a queen.
Bare were her knees, and knots her gar- ⎫
    ments bind;   ⎪
Loose was her hair, and wanton'd in the ⎬
    wind;   ⎪
Her hand sustain'd a bow; her quiver ⎪
    hung behind.   ⎭
She seem'd a virgin of the Spartan ⎫
    blood: 440 ⎪
With such array Harpalyce bestrode ⎬
Her Thracian courser and outstripp'd the ⎪
    rapid flood.   ⎭
" Ho, strangers! have you lately seen," ⎫
    she said,   ⎪
" One of my sisters, like myself array'd, ⎬
Who cross'd the lawn, or in the forest ⎪
    stray'd?   ⎭
A painted quiver at her back she bore; ⎫
Varied with spots, a lynx's hide she wore; ⎬
And at full cry pursued the tusky boar." ⎭
    Thus Venus: thus her son replied again:
" None of your sisters have we heard or
    seen,   450
O virgin! or what other name you bear
Above that style — O more than mortal
    fair!
Your voice and mien celestial birth betray!
If, as you seem, the sister of the day,
Or one at least of chaste Diana's train,
Let not an humble suppliant sue in vain;
But tell a stranger, long in tempests toss'd,
What earth we tread, and who commands
    the coast?

Then on your name shall wretched mortals
    call,
And offer'd victims at your altars fall." 460
" I dare not," she replied, "assume the
    name
Of goddess, or celestial honors claim:
For Tyrian virgins bows and quivers bear,
And purple buskins o'er their ankles wear.
Know, gentle youth, in Libyan lands you
    are —
A people rude in peace, and rough in war.
The rising city, which from far you see,
Is Carthage, and a Tyrian colony.
Phœnician Dido rules the growing state,
Who fled from Tyre, to shun her brother's
    hate.   470
Great were her wrongs, her story full of
    fate;
Which I will sum in short. Sichæus,
    known
For wealth, and brother to the Punic throne,
Possess'd fair Dido's bed; and either heart
At once was wounded with an equal dart.
Her father gave her, yet a spotless maid;
Pygmalion then the Tyrian scepter sway'd:
One who contemn'd divine and human laws.
Then strife ensued, and cursed gold the
    cause.
The monarch, blinded with desire of wealth,
With steel invades his brother's life by
    stealth;   481
Before the sacred altar made him bleed,
And long from her conceal'd the cruel deed.
Some tale, some new pretense, he daily
    coin'd,
To soothe his sister, and delude her mind.
At length, in dead of night, the ghost
    appears
Of her unhappy lord: the specter stares,
And, with erected eyes, his bloody bosom
    bares.
The cruel altars and his fate he tells,
And the dire secret of his house reveals, 490
Then warns the widow, with her household
    gods,
To seek a refuge in remote abodes.
Last, to support her in so long a way,
He shows her where his hidden treasure lay.
Admonish'd thus, and seiz'd with mortal
    fright,
The queen provides companions of her
    flight:
They meet, and all combine to leave the
    state,
Who hate the tyrant, or who fear his hate.

They seize a fleet, which ready rigg'd they
    find;
Nor is Pygmalion's treasure left behind. 500
The vessels, heavy laden, put to sea
With prosp'rous winds; a woman leads the
    way.
I know not, if by stress of weather driv'n,
Or was their fatal course dispos'd by
    Heav'n;
At last they landed, where from far your
    eyes
May view the turrets of new Carthage rise;
There bought a space of ground, which
    (Byrsa call'd,
From the bull's hide) they first inclos'd,
    and wall'd.
But whence are you? what country claims
    your birth?
What seek you, strangers, on our Libyan
    earth?"   510
    To whom, with sorrow streaming from
        his eyes,
And deeply sighing, thus her son replies:
" Could you with patience hear, or I re-
    late,
O nymph, the tedious annals of our fate!
Thro' such a train of woes if I should run,
The day would sooner than the tale be done !
From ancient Troy, by force expell'd, we
    came —
If you by chance have heard the Trojan
    name.
On various seas by various tempests toss'd,
At length we landed on your Libyan coast.
The good Æneas am I call'd — a name, 521
While Fortune favor'd, not unknown to
    fame.
My household gods, companions of my
    woes,
With pious care I rescued from our foes.
To fruitful Italy my course was bent;
And from the King of Heav'n is my de-
    scent.
With twice ten sail I cross'd the Phrygian
    sea;
Fate and my mother goddess led my way.
Scarce sev'n, the thin remainders of my
    fleet,
From storms preserv'd, within your harbor
    meet.   530
Myself distress'd, an exile, and unknown,
Debarr'd from Europe, and from Asia
    thrown,
In Libyan desarts wander thus alone."
    His tender parent could no longer bear;

But, interposing, sought to soothe his care.
" Whoe'er you are — not unbelov'd by
      Heav'n,
Since on our friendly shore your ships are
      driv'n —
Have courage: to the gods permit the rest,
And to the queen expose your just request.
Now take this earnest of success, for more:
Your scatter'd fleet is join'd upon the shore;
The winds are chang'd, your friends from
      danger free;   542
Or I renounce my skill in augury.
Twelve swans behold in beauteous order
      move,
And stoop with closing pinions from above;
Whom late the bird of Jove had driv'n
      along,
And thro' the clouds pursued the scatt'ring
      throng:
Now, all united in a goodly team,
They skim the ground, and seek the quiet
      stream.
As they, with joy returning, clap their
      wings,   550
And ride the circuit of the skies in rings;
Not otherwise your ships, and ev'ry friend,
Already hold the port, or with swift sails
      descend.
No more advice is needful; but pursue
The path before you, and the town in view."
      Thus having said, she turn'd, and made
      appear
Her neck refulgent, and dishevel'd hair,
Which, flowing from her shoulders, reach'd
      the ground,
And widely spread ambrosial scents around:
In length of train descends her sweeping
      gown;   560
And, by her graceful walk, the Queen of
      Love is known.
The prince pursued the parting deity
With words like these: " Ah! whither do
      you fly?
Unkind and cruel! to deceive your son
In borrow'd shapes, and his embrace to
      shun;
Never to bless my sight, but thus unknown;
And still to speak in accents not your
      own."
Against the goddess these complaints he
      made,
But took the path, and her commands
      obey'd.
They march obscure; for Venus kindly
      shrouds   570

With mists their persons, and involves in
      clouds,
That, thus unseen, their passage none might
      stay,
Or force to tell the causes of their way.
This part perform'd, the goddess flies sub-
      lime
To visit Paphos and her native clime;
Where garlands, ever green and ever fair,
With vows are offer'd, and with solemn
      pray'r:
A hundred altars in her temple smoke;
A thousand bleeding hearts her pow'r in-
      voke.
      They climb the next ascent, and, looking
      down,   580
Now at a nearer distance view the town.
The prince with wonder sees the stately
      tow'rs,
Which late were huts and shepherds'
      homely bow'rs,
The gates and streets; and hears, from
      ev'ry part,
The noise and busy concourse of the mart.
The toiling Tyrians on each other call
To ply their labor: some extend the wall;
Some build the citadel; the brawny throng
Or dig, or push unwieldy stones along.
Some for their dwellings choose a spot of
      ground,   590
Which, first design'd, with ditches they
      surround.
Some laws ordain; and some attend the
      choice
Of holy senates, and elect by voice.
Here some design a mole, while others
      there
Lay deep foundations for a theater;
From marble quarries mighty columns
      hew,
For ornaments of scenes, and future view.
Such is their toil, and such their busy
      pains,
As exercise the bees in flow'ry plains,
When winter past, and summer scarce
      begun,   600
Invites them forth to labor in the sun;
Some lead their youth abroad, while some
      condense
Their liquid store, and some in cells dis-
      pense;
Some at the gate stand ready to receive
The golden burthen, and their friends
      relieve;
All, with united force, combine to drive

The lazy drones from the laborious hive:
With envy stung, they view each other's
    deeds;
The fragrant work with diligence proceeds.
"Thrice happy you, whose walls already
    rise!"   610
Æneas said, and view'd, with lifted eyes,
Their lofty tow'rs; then, ent'ring at the
    gate,
Conceal'd in clouds (prodigious to relate)
He mix'd, unmark'd, among the busy
    throng,
Borne by the tide, and pass'd unseen along.
 Full in the center of the town there
    stood,
Thick set with trees, a venerable wood.
The Tyrians, landing near this holy ground,
And digging here, a prosp'rous omen
    found:
From under earth a courser's head they
    drew,   620
Their growth and future fortune to fore-
    shew.
This fated sign their foundress Juno gave,
Of a soil fruitful, and a people brave.
Sidonian Dido here with solemn state
Did Juno's temple build, and consecrate,
Enrich'd with gifts, and with a golden
    shrine;
But more the goddess made the place
    divine.
On brazen steps the marble threshold rose,
And brazen plates the cedar beams inclose:
The rafters are with brazen cov'rings
    crown'd;   630
The lofty doors on brazen hinges sound.
What first Æneas in this place beheld,
Reviv'd his courage, and his fear expell'd.
For while, expecting there the queen, he
    rais'd
His wond'ring eyes, and round the temple
    gaz'd,
Admir'd the fortune of the rising town,
The striving artists, and their arts' renown;
He saw, in order painted on the wall,
Whatever did unhappy Troy befall:
The wars that fame around the world had
    blown,   640
All to the life, and ev'ry leader known.
There Agamemnon, Priam here, he spies,
And fierce Achilles, who both kings defies.
He stopp'd, and weeping said: "O friend!
    ev'n here
The monuments of Trojan woes appear!
Our known disasters fill ev'n foreign lands:

See there, where old unhappy Priam stands!
Ev'n the mute walls relate the warrior's
    fame,   648
And Trojan griefs the Tyrians' pity claim."
He said (his tears a ready passage find), ⎫
Devouring what he saw so well design'd,   ⎬
And with an empty picture fed his mind: ⎭
For there he saw the fainting Grecians
    yield,
And here the trembling Trojans quit the
    field,
Pursued by fierce Achilles thro' the plain,
On his high chariot driving o'er the slain.
The tents of Rhesus next his grief renew,
By their white sails betray'd to nightly
    view;
And wakeful Diomede, whose cruel sword
The sentries slew, nor spar'd their slum-
    b'ring lord,   660
Then took the fiery steeds, ere yet the food
Of Troy they taste, or drink the Xanthian
    flood.
Elsewhere he saw where Troilus defied
Achilles, and unequal combat tried;
Then, where the boy disarm'd, with loosen'd
    reins,
Was by his horses hurried o'er the plains,
Hung by the neck and hair, and dragg'd ⎫
    around: ⎪
The hostile spear, yet sticking in his   ⎬
    wound,   ⎪
With tracks of blood inscrib'd the dusty ⎪
    ground.   ⎭
Meantime the Trojan dames, oppress'd ⎫
    with woe,   670   ⎪
To Pallas' fane in long procession go,   ⎬
In hopes to reconcile their heav'nly foe. ⎭
They weep, they beat their breasts, they ⎫
    rend their hair,   ⎪
And rich embroider'd vests for presents   ⎬
    bear;   ⎪
But the stern goddess stands unmov'd   ⎪
    with pray'r.   ⎭
Thrice round the Trojan walls Achilles
    drew
The corpse of Hector, whom in fight he
    slew.
Here Priam sues; and there, for sums of
    gold,
The lifeless body of his son is sold.
So sad an object, and so well express'd, 680
Drew sighs and groans from the griev'd
    hero's breast,
To see the figure of his lifeless friend,
And his old sire his helpless hand extend.

Himself he saw amidst the Grecian train,
Mix'd in the bloody battle on the plain;
And swarthy Memnon in his arms he knew,
His pompous ensigns, and his Indian crew.
Penthisilea there, with haughty grace,
Leads to the wars an Amazonian race:
In their right hands a pointed dart they
 wield;   690
The left, for ward, sustains the lunar shield.
Athwart her breast a golden belt she
 throws,
Amidst the press alone provokes a thou-
 sand foes,
And dares her maiden arms to manly
 force oppose.
 Thus while the Trojan prince employs
 his eyes,
Fix'd on the walls with wonder and surprise,
The beauteous Dido, with a num'rous train
And pomp of guards, ascends the sacred
 fane.
Such on Eurotas' banks, or Cynthus' height,
Diana seems; and so she charms the sight,
When in the dance the graceful goddess
 leads   701
The choir of nymphs, and overtops their
 heads:
Known by her quiver, and her lofty mien,
She walks majestic, and she looks their
 queen;
Latona sees her shine above the rest,
And feeds with secret joy her silent breast.
Such Dido was; with such becoming state,
Amidst the crowd, she walks serenely
 great.
Their labor to her future sway she speeds,
And passing with a gracious glance pro-
 ceeds;   710
Then mounts the throne, high plac'd before
 the shrine:
In crowds around, the swarming people
 join.
She takes petitions, and dispenses laws,
Hears and determines ev'ry private cause;
Their tasks in equal portions she divides,
And, where unequal, there by lots decides.
Another way by chance Æneas bends
His eyes, and unexpected sees his friends,
Antheus, Sergestus grave, Cloanthus strong,
And at their backs a mighty Trojan throng,
Whom late the tempest on the billows
 toss'd,   721
And widely scatter'd on another coast.
The prince, unseen, surpris'd with wonder
 stands,

And longs, with joyful haste, to join their
 hands;
But, doubtful of the wish'd event, he stays,
And from the hollow cloud his friends sur-
 veys,
Impatient till they told their present state,
And where they left their ships, and what
 their fate,
And why they came, and what was their
 request;
For these were sent, commission'd by the
 rest,   730
To sue for leave to land their sickly men,
And gain admission to the gracious queen.
Ent'ring, with cries they fill'd the holy
 fane;
Then thus, with lowly voice, Ilioneus be-
 gan:
 "O queen! indulg'd by favor of the
 gods
To found an empire in these new abodes,
To build a town, with statutes to restrain
The wild inhabitants beneath thy reign,
We wretched Trojans, toss'd on ev'ry shore,
From sea to sea, thy clemency implore. 740
Forbid the fires our shipping to deface !
Receive th' unhappy fugitives to grace,
And spare the remnant of a pious race !
We come not with design of wasteful prey,
To drive the country, force the swains
 away:
Nor such our strength, nor such is our desire;
The vanquish'd dare not to such thoughts
 aspire.
A land there is, Hesperia nam'd of old,
(The soil is fruitful, and the men are bold —
Th' Œnotrians held it once,) by common
 fame   750
Now call'd Italia, from the leader's name.
To that sweet region was our voyage bent,
When winds and ev'ry warring element
Disturb'd our course, and, far from sight of
 land,
Cast our torn vessels on the moving sand:
The sea came on; the South, with mighty
 roar,
Dispers'd and dash'd the rest upon the
 rocky shore.
Those few you see escap'd the storm, and
 fear,
Unless you interpose, a shipwreck here.
What men, what monsters, what inhuman
 race,   760
What laws, what barb'rous customs of the
 place,

Shut up a desart shore to drowning men,
And drive us to the cruel seas again ?
If our hard fortune no compassion draws, ⎫
Nor hospitable rights, nor human laws, ⎪
The gods are just, and will revenge our ⎬
    cause. ⎭
Æneas was our prince: a juster lord, ⎫
Or nobler warrior, never drew a sword; ⎪
Observant of the right, religious of his ⎬
    word. ⎭
If yet he lives, and draws this vital air, 770
Nor we, his friends, of safety shall despair;
Nor you, great queen, these offices repent,
Which he will equal, and perhaps aug-
    ment.
We want not cities, nor Sicilian coasts,
Where King Acestes Trojan lineage boasts.
Permit our ships a shelter on your shores,
Refitted from your woods with planks and
    oars,
That, if our prince be safe, we may renew
Our destin'd course, and Italy pursue.
But if, O best of men, the Fates ordain 780
That thou art swallow'd in the Libyan
    main,
And if our young Iülus be no more,
Dismiss our navy from your friendly shore,
That we to good Acestes may return,
And with our friends our common losses
    mourn."
Thus spoke Ilioneus: the Trojan crew
With cries and clamors his request renew.
    The modest queen a while, with downcast
      eyes,
Ponder'd the speech; then briefly thus re-
    plies:
"Trojans, dismiss your fears; my cruel
    fate,   790
And doubts attending an unsettled state,
Force me to guard my coast from foreign
    foes.
Who has not heard the story of your woes,
The name and fortune of your native place,
The fame and valor of the Phrygian race ?
We Tyrians are not so devoid of sense,
Nor so remote from Phœbus' influence.
Whether to Latian shores your course ⎫
    is bent, ⎪
Or, driv'n by tempests from your first ⎬
    intent, ⎪
You seek the good Acestes' government, ⎭
Your men shall be receiv'd, your fleet re-
    pair'd,   801
And sail, with ships of convoy for your
    guard:

Or, would you stay, and join your ⎫
    friendly pow'rs ⎪
To raise and to defend the Tyrian ⎬
    tow'rs, ⎪
My wealth, my city, and myself are ⎪
    yours. ⎭
And would to Heav'n, the storm, you felt,
    would bring
On Carthaginian coasts your wand'ring
    king.
My people shall, by my command, explore
The ports and creeks of ev'ry winding
    shore,
And towns, and wilds, and shady woods, in
    quest   810
Of so renown'd and so desir'd a guest."
    Rais'd in his mind the Trojan hero
      stood,
And long'd to break from out his ambient
    cloud:
Achates found it, and thus urg'd his way:
"From whence, O goddess-born, this long
    delay ?
What more can you desire, your welcome
    sure,
Your fleet in safety, and your friends se-
    cure ?
One only wants; and him we saw in vain
Oppose the storm, and swallow'd in the
    main.
Orontes in his fate our forfeit paid;   820
The rest agrees with what your mother
    said."
Scarce had he spoken, when the cloud
    gave way,
The mists flew upward and dissolv'd in day.
The Trojan chief appear'd in open sight,
August in visage, and serenely bright.
His mother goddess, with her hands divine,
Had form'd his curling locks, and made
    his temples shine,
And giv'n his rolling eyes a sparkling
    grace,
And breath'd a youthful vigor on his face;
Like polish'd iv'ry, beauteous to behold, 830
Or Parian marble, when enchas'd in gold:
Thus radiant from the circling cloud he
    broke,
And thus with manly modesty he spoke:
    "He whom you seek am I; by tempests
      toss'd,
And sav'd from shipwreck on your Libyan
    coast;
Presenting, gracious queen, before your
    throne,

A prince that owes his life to you alone.
Fair majesty, the refuge and redress
Of those whom fate pursues, and wants
    oppress,
You, who your pious offices employ   840
To save the relics of abandon'd Troy;
Receive the shipwreck'd on your friendly
    shore,
With hospitable rites relieve the poor;
Associate in your town a wand'ring train,
And strangers in your palace entertain:
What thanks can wretched fugitives return,
Who, scatter'd thro' the world, in exile
    mourn?
The gods, if gods to goodness are inclin'd;
If acts of mercy touch their heav'nly mind,
And, more than all the gods, your gen'rous
    heart,   850
Conscious of worth, requite its own desert!
In you this age is happy, and this earth,
And parents more than mortal gave you
    birth.
While rolling rivers into seas shall run,
And round the space of heav'n the radiant
    sun;
While trees the mountain tops with shades
    supply,
Your honor, name, and praise shall never
    die.
Whate'er abode my fortune has assign'd,
Your image shall be present in my mind."
Thus having said, he turn'd with pious
    haste,   860
And joyful his expecting friends em-
    brac'd:
With his right hand Ilioneus was grac'd,
Serestus with his left; then to his breast
Cloanthus and the noble Gyas press'd;
And so by turns descended to the rest.
    The Tyrian queen stood fix'd upon his
    face,
Pleas'd with his motions, ravish'd with his
    grace;
Admir'd his fortunes, more admir'd the
    man;
Then recollected stood, and thus began:
"What fate, O goddess-born! what angry
    pow'rs   870
Have cast you shipwrack'd on our barren
    shores?
Are you the great Æneas, known to fame,
Who from celestial seed your lineage
    claim?
The same Æneas whom fair Venus bore
To fam'd Anchises on th' Idæan shore?

It calls into my mind, tho' then a child,
When Teucer came, from Salamis exil'd,
And sought my father's aid, to be restor'd:
My father Belus then with fire and sword
Invaded Cyprus, made the region bare,   880
And, conqu'ring, finish'd the successful
    war.
From him the Trojan siege I understood,
The Grecian chiefs, and your illustrious
    blood.
Your foe himself the Dardan valor prais'd,
And his own ancestry from Trojans rais'd.
Enter, my noble guest, and you shall find,
If not a costly welcome, yet a kind:
For I myself, like you, have been dis-
    tress'd,
Till Heav'n afforded me this place of rest;
Like you, an alien in a land unknown,   890
I learn to pity woes so like my own."
She said, and to the palace led her guest;
Then offer'd incense, and proclaim'd a feast.
Nor yet less careful for her absent friends,
Twice ten fat oxen to the ships she sends;
Besides a hundred boars, a hundred lambs,
With bleating cries, attend their milky
    dams;
And jars of gen'rous wine and spacious
    bowls
She gives, to cheer the sailors' drooping
    souls.
Now purple hangings clothe the palace
    walls,   900
And sumptuous feasts are made in splendid
    halls:
On Tyrian carpets, richly wrought, they
    dine;
With loads of massy plate the sideboards
    shine,
And antique vases, all of gold emboss'd
(The gold itself inferior to the cost),
Of curious work, where on the sides were
    seen
The fights and figures of illustrious men,
From their first founder to the present
    queen.
    The good Æneas, whose paternal care
Iülus' absence could no longer bear,   910
Dispatch'd Achates to the ships in haste,
To give a glad relation of the past,
And, fraught with precious gifts, to bring
    the boy,
Snatch'd from the ruins of unhappy Troy:
A robe of tissue, stiff with golden wire;
An upper vest, once Helen's rich attire,
From Argos by the fam'd adultress brought,

With golden flow'rs and winding foliage
    wrought,
Her mother Leda's present, when she came
To ruin Troy and set the world on flame;
The scepter Priam's eldest daughter bore,
Her orient necklace, and the crown she
    wore;   922
Of double texture, glorious to behold,
One order set with gems, and one with
    gold.
Instructed thus, the wise Achates goes,
And in his diligence his duty shows.
    But Venus, anxious for her son's affairs,
New counsels tries, and new designs pre-
    pares·
That Cupid should assume the shape and
    face
Of sweet Ascanius, and the sprightly grace;
Should bring the presents, in her nephew's
    stead,   931
And in Eliza's veins the gentle poison shed:
For much she fear'd the Tyrians, double-
    tongued,
And knew the town to Juno's care be-
    long'd.
These thoughts by night her golden slumbers
    broke,
And thus alarm'd, to winged Love she
    spoke:
" My son, my strength, whose mighty pow'r
    alone
Controls the Thund'rer on his awful
    throne,
To thee thy much-afflicted mother flies,
And on thy succor and thy faith relies. 940
Thou know'st, my son, how Jove's revenge-
    ful wife,
By force and fraud, attempts thy brother's
    life;
And often hast thou mourn'd with me his ⎫
    pains.   ⎪
Him Dido now with blandishment de- ⎬
    tains;   ⎪
But I suspect the town where Juno   ⎭
    reigns.
For this 't is needful to prevent her art,
And fire with love the proud Phœnician's
    heart:
A love so violent, so strong, so sure,
As neither age can change, nor art can cure.
How this may be perform'd, now take my
    mind: 950
Ascanius by his father is design'd
To come, with presents laden, from the
    port,

To gratify the queen, and gain the court.
I mean to plunge the boy in pleasing sleep,
And, ravish'd, in Idalian bow'rs to keep,
Or high Cythera, that the sweet deceit
May pass unseen, and none prevent the
    cheat.
Take thou his form and shape. I beg ⎫
    the grace   ⎪
But only for a night's revolving space: ⎬
Thyself a boy, assume a boy's dissembled ⎪
    face;   960   ⎭
That when, amidst the fervor of the feast,
The Tyrian hugs and fonds thee on her
    breast,
And with sweet kisses in her arms con-
    strains,
Thou may'st infuse thy venom in her
    veins."
The God of Love obeys, and sets aside
His bow and quiver, and his plumy pride;
He walks Iülus in his mother's sight,
And in the sweet resemblance takes delight.
    The goddess then to young Ascanius
    flies,
And in a pleasing slumber seals his eyes: 970
Lull'd in her lap, amidst a train of Loves,
She gently bears him to her blissful
    groves,
Then with a wreath of myrtle crowns his
    head,
And softly lays him on a flow'ry bed.
Cupid meantime assum'd his form and
    face,
Foll'wing Achates with a shorter pace,
And brought the gifts. The queen already
    sate
Amidst the Trojan lords, in shining state,
High on a golden bed: her princely guest
Was next her side; in order sate the
    rest.   980
Then canisters with bread are heap'd ⎫
    on high;   ⎪
Th' attendants water for their hands sup- ⎬
    ply,   ⎪
And, having wash'd, with silken towels ⎭
    dry.
Next fifty handmaids in long order bore
The censers, and with fumes the gods adore:
Then youths, and virgins twice as many,
    join
To place the dishes, and to serve the wine.
The Tyrian train, admitted to the feast,
Approach, and on the painted couches rest.
All on the Trojan gifts with wonder
    gaze,   990

But view the beauteous boy with more
amaze,
His rosy-color'd cheeks, his radiant eyes,
His motions, voice, and shape, and all the
god's disguise;
Nor pass unprais'd the vest and veil divine,
Which wand'ring foliage and rich flow'rs
entwine.
But, far above the rest, the royal dame,
(Already doom'd to love's disastrous flame,)
With eyes insatiate, and tumultuous joy,
Beholds the presents, and admires the boy.
The guileful god about the hero long, 1000
With children's play, and false embraces,
hung;
Then sought the queen: she took him to
her arms
With greedy pleasure, and devour'd his
charms.
Unhappy Dido little thought what guest,
How dire a god, she drew so near her
breast;
But he, not mindless of his mother's ⎫
pray'r, ⎪
Works in the pliant bosom of the fair, ⎬
And molds her heart anew, and blots ⎪
her former care. ⎭
The dead is to the living love resign'd;
And all Æneas enters in her mind. 1010
Now, when the rage of hunger was ap-
peas'd,
The meat remov'd, and ev'ry guest was
pleas'd,
The golden bowls with sparkling wine are
crown'd,
And thro' the palace cheerful cries resound.
From gilded roofs depending lamps display
Nocturnal beams, that emulate the day.
A golden bowl, that shone with gems ⎫
divine, ⎪
The queen commanded to be crown'd with ⎬
wine: ⎪
The bowl that Belus us'd, and all the ⎪
Tyrian line. ⎭
Then, silence thro' the hall proclaim'd, she
spoke: 1020
" O hospitable Jove ! we thus invoke,
With solemn rites, thy sacred name and
pow'r;
Bless to both nations this auspicious hour !
So may the Trojan and the Tyrian line
In lasting concord from this day combine.
Thou, Bacchus, god of joys and friendly
cheer,
And gracious Juno, both be present here !

And you, my lords of Tyre, your vows
address
To Heav'n with mine, to ratify the peace."
The goblet then she took, with nectar
crown'd, 1030
(Sprinkling the first libations on the ground,)
And rais'd it to her mouth with sober grace;
Then, sipping, offer'd to the next in place.
'T was Bitias whom she call'd, a thirsty
soul;
He took the challenge, and embrac'd the
bowl,
With pleasure swill'd the gold, nor ceas'd
to draw,
Till he the bottom of the brimmer saw.
The goblet goes around: Iopas brought
His golden lyre, and sung what ancient
Atlas taught: 1039
The various labors of the wand'ring moon,
And whence proceed th' eclipses of the sun;
Th' original of men and beasts; and ⎫
whence ⎪
The rains arise, and fires their warmth ⎬
dispense, ⎪
And fix'd and erring stars dispose their ⎪
influence; ⎭
What shakes the solid earth; what cause
delays
The summer nights and shortens winter
days.
With peals of shouts the Tyrians praise the
song;
Those peals are echo'd by the Trojan throng.
Th' unhappy queen with talk prolong'd the
night,
And drank large draughts of love with vast
delight; 1050
Of Priam much enquir'd, of Hector more; ⎫
Then ask'd what arms the swarthy Mem- ⎪
non wore, ⎬
What troops he landed on the Trojan ⎪
shore; ⎭
The steeds of Diomede varied the discourse,
And fierce Achilles, with his matchless
force;
At length, as fate and her ill stars requir'd,
To hear the series of the war desir'd.
" Relate at large, my godlike guest," she
said,
" The Grecian stratagems, the town be-
tray'd:
The fatal issue of so long a war, 1060
Your flight, your wand'rings, and your
woes, declare;
For, since on ev'ry sea, on ev'ry coast,

Your men have been distress'd, your navy
toss'd,
Sev'n times the sun has either tropic view'd,
The winter banish'd, and the spring renew'd."

THE SECOND BOOK OF THE ÆNEIS

THE ARGUMENT

Æneas relates how the city of Troy was
taken, after a ten years' siege, by the treachery of Sinon, and the stratagem of a wooden
horse. He declares the fix'd resolution he
had taken not to survive the ruins of his
country, and the various adventures he met
with in the defense of it. At last, having
been before advis'd by Hector's ghost, and
now by the appearance of his mother Venus,
he is prevail'd upon to leave the town, and
settle his household gods in another country.
In order to this, he carries off his father on
his shoulders, and leads his little son by the
hand, his wife following him behind. When
he comes to the place appointed for the general rendezvouze, he finds a great conflu-
ence of people, but misses his wife, whose
ghost afterwards appears to him, and tells
him the land which was design'd for him.

ALL were attentive to the godlike man,
When from his lofty couch he thus began:
" Great queen, what you command me to
relate
Renews the sad remembrance of our fate:
An empire from its old foundations rent,
And ev'ry woe the Trojans underwent;
A peopled city made a desart place;
All that I saw, and part of which I was:
Not ev'n the hardest of our foes could
hear,
Nor stern Ulysses tell without a tear.   10
And now the latter watch of wasting night,
And setting stars, to kindly rest invite;
But, since you take such int'rest in our
woe,
And Troy's disastrous end desire to know,
I will restrain my tears, and briefly tell
What in our last and fatal night befell.
" By destiny compell'd, and in despair,
The Greeks grew weary of the tedious
war,
And by Minerva's aid a fabric rear'd,
Which like a steed of monstrous height
appear'd: 20

The sides were plank'd with pine; they
feign'd it made
For their return, and this the vow they paid
Thus they pretend, but in the hollow side
Selected numbers of their soldiers hide:
With inward arms the dire machine they
load,
And iron bowels stuff the dark abode.
In sight of Troy lies Tenedos, an isle
(While Fortune did on Priam's empire
smile)
Renown'd for wealth; but, since, a faith-
less bay,
Where ships expos'd to wind and weather
lay.   30
There was their fleet conceal'd. We
thought, for Greece
Their sails were hoisted, and our fears re-
lease.
The Trojans, coop'd within their walls so
long,
Unbar their gates, and issue in a throng,
Like swarming bees, and with delight sur-
vey
The camp deserted, where the Grecians
lay:
The quarters of the sev'ral chiefs they
show'd;
Here Phœnix, here Achilles, made abode;
Here join'd the battles; there the navy
rode.
Part on the pile their wond'ring eyes em-
ploy: 40
The pile by Pallas rais'd to ruin Troy.
Thymœtes first ('t is doubtful whether
hir'd,
Or so the Trojan destiny requir'd)
Mov'd that the ramparts might be broken
down,
To lodge the monster fabric in the town.
But Capys, and the rest of sounder mind,
The fatal present to the flames design'd,
Or to the wat'ry deep; at least to bore
The hollow sides, and hidden frauds ex-
plore.
The giddy vulgar, as their fancies guide, 50
With noise say nothing, and in parts divide.
Laocoon, follow'd by a num'rous crowd,
Ran from the fort, and cried, from far,
aloud:
' O wretched countrymen! what fury reigns ?
What more than madness has possess'd
your brains ?
Think you the Grecians from your coasts
are gone ?

And are Ulysses' arts no better known ?
This hollow fabric either must inclose,
Within its blind recess, our secret foes;
Or 't is an engine rais'd above the town,   60
T' o'erlook the walls, and then to batter
    down.
Somewhat is sure design'd, by fraud or
    force:
Trust not their presents, nor admit the
    horse.'
Thus having said, against the steed he
    threw
His forceful spear, which, hissing as it flew,
Pierc'd thro' the yielding planks of jointed
    wood,
And trembling in the hollow belly stood.
The sides, transpierc'd, return a rattling
    sound,
And groans of Greeks inclos'd come issuing
    thro' the wound.
And, had not Heav'n the fall of Troy de-
    sign'd,   70
Or had not men been fated to be blind,
Enough was said and done t' inspire a
    better mind.
Then had our lances pierc'd the treach'rous
    wood,
And Ilian tow'rs and Priam's empire stood.
Meantime, with shouts, the Trojan shep-
    herds bring
A captive Greek, in bands, before the king;
Taken, to take; who made himself their
    prey,
T' impose on their belief, and Troy betray;
Fix'd on his aim, and obstinately bent
To die undaunted, or to circumvent.   80
About the captive, tides of Trojans flow;
All press to see, and some insult the foe.
Now hear how well the Greeks their wiles
    disguis'd;
Behold a nation in a man compris'd.
Trembling the miscreant stood, unarm'd
    and bound,
He star'd, and roll'd his haggard eyes
    around,
Then said: ' Alas ! what earth remains, what
    sea
Is open to receive unhappy me ?
What fate a wretched fugitive attends,
Scorn'd by my foes, abandon'd by my
    friends ? '   90
He said, and sigh'd, and cast a rueful eye:
Our pity kindles, and our passions die.
We cheer the youth to make his own de-
    fense,

And freely tell us what he was, and whence:
What news he could impart, we long to
    know,
And what to credit from a captive foe.
    " His fear at length dismiss'd, he said:
' Whate'er
My fate ordains, my words shall be sincere:
I neither can nor dare my birth disclaim;
Greece is my country, Sinon is my name.   100
Tho' plung'd by Fortune's pow'r in misery,
'T is not in Fortune's pow'r to make me lie.
If any chance has hither brought the name
Of Palamedes, not unknown to fame,
Who suffer'd from the malice of the times,
Accus'd and sentenc'd for pretended crimes,
Because these fatal wars he would prevent;
Whose death the wretched Greeks too late
    lament —
Me, then a boy, my father, poor and bare
Of other means, committed to his care,   110
His kinsman and companion in the war.
While Fortune favor'd, while his arms sup-
    port
The cause, and rul'd the counsels, of the
    court,
I made some figure there; nor was my
    name
Obscure, nor I without my share of fame.
But when Ulysses, with fallacious arts,
Had made impression in the people's hearts,
And forg'd a treason in my patron's name
(I speak of things too far divulg'd by fame),
My kinsman fell. Then I, without sup-
    port,   120
In private mourn'd his loss, and left the
    court.
Mad as I was, I could not bear his fate
With silent grief, but loudly blam'd the
    state,
And curs'd the direful author of my woes.
'T was told again; and hence my ruin rose.
I threaten'd, if indulgent Heav'n once
    more
Would land me safely on my native shore,
His death with double vengeance to re-
    store.
This mov'd the murderer's hate; and soon
    ensued
Th' effects of malice from a man so proud.   130
Ambiguous rumors thro' the camp he
    spread,
And sought, by treason, my devoted head;
New crimes invented; left unturn'd no
    stone,
To make my guilt appear, and hide his own;

Till Calchas was by force and threat'ning
    wrought —
But why — why dwell I on that anxious
    thought ?
If on my nation just revenge you seek,
And 't is t' appear a foe, t' appear a Greek;
Already you my name and country know;
Assuage your thirst of blood, and strike the
    blow: 140
My death will both the kingly brothers
    please,
And set insatiate Ithacus at ease.'
This fair unfinish'd tale, these broken ⎤
    starts,   ⎬
Rais'd expectations in our longing
    hearts;   ⎭
Unknowing as we were in Grecian arts.
His former trembling once again renew'd,
With acted fear, the villain thus pursued:
   " ' Long had the Grecians (tir'd with fruit-
    less care,
And wearied with an unsuccessful war)
Resolv'd to raise the siege, and leave the
    town;   150
And, had the gods permitted, they had
    gone;
But oft the wintry seas and southern winds
Withstood their passage home, and chang'd
    their minds.
Portents and prodigies their souls amaz'd;
But most, when this stupendous pile was
    rais'd:
Then flaming meteors, hung in air, were
    seen,
And thunders rattled thro' a sky serene.
Dismay'd, and fearful of some dire event,
Eurypylus t' enquire their fate was sent.
He from the gods this dreadful answer ⎤
    brought: 160 ⎮
"O Grecians, when the Trojan shores ⎬
    you sought,   ⎮
Your passage with a virgin's blood was ⎮
    bought: ⎦
So must your safe return be bought again,
And Grecian blood once more atone the
    main."
The spreading rumor round the people ran;
All fear'd, and each believ'd himself the
    man.
Ulysses took th' advantage of their fright;
Call'd Calchas, and produc'd in open sight:
Then bade him name the wretch, ordain'd
    by fate
The public victim, to redeem the state. 170
Already some presag'd the dire event,

And saw what sacrifice Ulysses meant.
For twice five days the good old seer with-
    stood
Th' intended treason, and was dumb to
    blood,
Till, tir'd with endless clamors and pursuit
Of Ithacus, he stood no longer mute;
But, as it was agreed, pronounc'd that I
Was destin'd by the wrathful gods to die.
All prais'd the sentence, pleas'd the storm
    should fall
On one alone, whose fury threaten'd all. 180
The dismal day was come; the priests
    prepare
Their leaven'd cakes, and fillets for my
    hair.
I follow'd nature's laws, and must avow
I broke my bonds and fled the fatal blow.
Hid in a weedy lake all night I lay,
Secure of safety when they sail'd away.
But now what further hopes for me re-
    main,
To see my friends, or native soil, again;
My tender infants, or my careful sire, 189
Whom they returning will to death require;
Will perpetrate on them their first design,
And take the forfeit of their heads for
    mine ?
Which, O ! if pity mortal minds can move,
If there be faith below, or gods above,
If innocence and truth can claim desert,
Ye Trojans, from an injur'd wretch avert.'
" False tears true pity move; the king
    commands
To loose his fetters, and unbind his hands:
Then adds these friendly words: ' Dismiss
    thy fears;
Forget the Greeks; be mine as thou wert
    theirs.   200
But truly tell, was it for force or guile,
Or some religious end, you rais'd the pile ? '
Thus said the king. He, full of fraudful
    arts,
This well-invented tale for truth imparts:
' Ye lamps of heav'n ! ' he said, and lifted
    high
His hands now free, ' thou venerable sky !
Inviolable pow'rs, ador'd with dread !   ⎤
Ye fatal fillets, that once bound this ⎮
    head !   ⎬
Ye sacred altars, from whose flames I ⎮
    fled !   ⎦
Be all of you adjur'd; and grant I may, 210
Without a crime, th' ungrateful Greeks
    betray,

Reveal the secrets of the guilty state,
And justly punish whom I justly hate!
But you, O king, preserve the faith you
gave,
If I, to save myself, your empire save.
The Grecian hopes, and all th' attempts they
made,
Were only founded on Minerva's aid.
But from the time when impious Diomede,
And false Ulysses, that inventive head,
Her fatal image from the temple drew, 220
The sleeping guardians of the castle slew,
Her virgin statue with their bloody hands
Polluted, and profan'd her holy bands;
From thence the tide of fortune left their
shore,
And ebb'd much faster than it flow'd be-
fore:
Their courage languish'd, as their hopes
decay'd;
And Pallas, now averse, refus'd her aid.
Nor did the goddess doubtfully declare
Her alter'd mind and alienated care.
When first her fatal image touch'd the
ground, 230
She sternly cast her glaring eyes around,
That sparkled as they roll'd, and seem'd to
threat:
Her heav'nly limbs distill'd a briny sweat.
Thrice from the ground she leap'd, was
seen to wield
Her brandish'd lance, and shake her horrid
shield.
Then Calchas bade our host for flight pre-
pare,
And hope no conquest from the tedious
war,
Till first they sail'd for Greece; with
pray'rs besought
Her injur'd pow'r, and better omens
brought.
And now their navy plows the wat'ry
main, 240
Yet soon expect it on your shores again,
With Pallas pleas'd; as Calchas did or-
dain.
But first, to reconcile the blue-ey'd maid
For her stol'n statue and her tow'r betray'd,
Warn'd by the seer, to her offended name
We rais'd and dedicate this wondrous frame,
So lofty, lest thro' your forbidden gates
It pass, and intercept our better fates:
For, once admitted there, our hopes are lost;
And Troy may then a new Palladium boast;
For so religion and the gods ordain, 251

That, if you violate with hands profane
Minerva's gift, your town in flames shall
burn,
(Which omen, O ye gods, on Græcia turn!)
But if it climb, with your assisting hands,
The Trojan walls, and in the city stands;
Then Troy shall Argos and Mycenæ burn,
And the reverse of fate on us return.'
  " With such deceits he gain'd their easy
hearts,
Too prone to credit his perfidious arts. 260
What Diomede, nor Thetis' greater son,
A thousand ships, nor ten years' siege,
had done —
False tears and fawning words the city
won.
  " A greater omen, and of worse por-
tent,
Did our unwary minds with fear torment,
Concurring to produce the dire event.
Laocoon, Neptune's priest by lot that year,
With solemn pomp then sacrific'd a steer;
When, dreadful to behold, from sea we
spied
Two serpents, rank'd abreast, the seas
divide, 270
And smoothly sweep along the swelling
tide.
Their flaming crests above the waves they
show;
Their bellies seem to burn the seas below;
Their speckled tails advance to steer their
course,
And on the sounding shore the flying billows
force.
And now the strand, and now the plain they
held;
Their ardent eyes with bloody streaks were
fill'd;
Their nimble tongues they brandish'd as
they came,
And lick'd their hissing jaws, that sputter'd
flame.
We fled amaz'd; their destin'd way they
take, 280
And to Laocoon and his children make;
And first around the tender boys they
wind,
Then with their sharpen'd fangs their limbs
and bodies grind.
The wretched father, running to their aid
With pious haste, but vain, they next in-
vade;
Twice round his waist their winding vol-
umes roll'd:

And twice about his gasping throat they
    fold.
The priest thus doubly chok'd, their crests
    divide,
And tow'ring o'er his head in triumph ride.
With both his hands he labors at the
    knots;   290
His holy fillets the blue venom blots;
His roaring fills the flitting air around.
Thus, when an ox receives a glancing
    wound,
He breaks his bands, the fatal altar flies,
And with loud bellowings breaks the yield-
    ing skies.
Their tasks perform'd, the serpents quit
    their prey,
And to the tow'r of Pallas make their way:
Couch'd at her feet, they lie protected there
By her large buckler and protended spear.
Amazement seizes all; the gen'ral cry 300
Proclaims Laocoon justly doom'd to die,
Whose hand the will of Pallas had with-
    stood,
And dar'd to violate the sacred wood.
All vote t' admit the steed, that vows be
    paid
And incense offer'd to th' offended maid.
A spacious breach is made; the town lies
    bare;
Some hoisting-levers, some the wheels pre-
    pare
And fasten to the horse's feet; the rest
With cables haul along th' unwieldy beast.
Each on his fellow for assistance calls; 310
At length the fatal fabric mounts the
    walls,
Big with destruction. Boys with chaplets
    crown'd,
And choirs of virgins, sing and dance
    around.
Thus rais'd aloft, and then descending
    down,
It enters o'er our heads. and threats the
    town.
O sacred city, built by hands divine !
O valiant heroes of the Trojan line !
Four times he struck: as oft the clashing
    sound
Of arms was heard, and inward groans re-
    bound.
Yet, mad with zeal, and blinded with our
    fate,   320
We haul along the horse in solemn state;
Then place the dire portent within the
    tow'r.

Cassandra cried, and curs'd th' unhappy
    hour;
Foretold our fate; but, by the god's decree,
All heard, and none believ'd the prophecy.
With branches we the fanes adorn, and
    waste,
In jollity, the day ordain'd to be the last.
Meantime the rapid heav'ns roll'd down
    the light,
And on the shaded ocean rush'd the night;
Our men, secure, nor guards nor sentries
    held,   330
But easy sleep their weary limbs compell'd.
The Grecians had embark'd their naval
    pow'rs
From Tenedos, and sought our well-known
    shores,
Safe under covert of the silent night,
And guided by th' imperial galley's light;
When Sinon, favor'd by the partial gods,
Unlock'd the horse, and op'd his dark
    abodes;
Restor'd to vital air our hidden foes,
Who joyful from their long confinement
    rose.
Tysander bold, and Sthenelus their guide,
And dire Ulysses down the cable slide: 341
Then Thoas, Athamas, and Pyrrhus haste;
Nor was the Podalirian hero last,
Nor injur'd Menelaüs, nor the fam'd
Epeüs, who the fatal engine fram'd.
A nameless crowd succeed; their forces
    join
T' invade the town, oppress'd with sleep and
    wine.
Those few they find awake first meet their
    fate;
Then to their fellows they unbar the gate.
" 'T was in the dead of night, when sleep
    repairs   350
Our bodies worn with toils, our minds with
    cares,
When Hector's ghost before my sight ap-
    pears:
A bloody shroud he seem'd, and bath'd in
    tears;
Such as he was, when, by Pelides slain,
Thessalian coursers dragg'd him o'er the
    plain.
Swoln were his feet, as when the thongs
    were thrust
Thro' the bor'd holes; his body black with
    dust;
Unlike that Hector who return'd from toils
Of war, triumphant, in Æacian spoils,

Or him who made the fainting Greeks re-
    tire,   360
And launch'd against their navy Phrygian
    fire.
His hair and beard stood stiffen'd with his
    gore;
And all the wounds he for his country bore
Now stream'd afresh, and with new pur-
    ple ran.
I wept to see the visionary man,
And, while my trance continued, thus
    began:
'O light of Trojans, and support of Troy,
Thy father's champion, and thy country's
    joy!
O, long expected by thy friends! from
    whence
Art thou so late return'd for our defense?
Do we behold thee, wearied as we are   371
With length of labors, and with toils of
    war?
After so many fun'rals of thy own
Art thou restor'd to thy declining town?
But say, what wounds are these? What
    new disgrace
Deforms the manly features of thy face?'
    "To this the specter no reply did frame,
But answer'd to the cause for which he
    came,
And, groaning from the bottom of his breast,
This warning in these mournful words ex-
    press'd: 380
'O goddess-born! escape, by timely flight,
The flames and horrors of this fatal night.
The foes already have possess'd the wall;
Troy nods from high, and totters to her fall.
Enough is paid to Priam's royal name,
More than enough to duty and to fame.
If by a mortal hand my father's throne
Could be defended, 't was by mine alone.
Now Troy to thee commends her future
    state,   389
And gives her gods companions of thy fate:
From their assistance happier walls expect,
Which, wand'ring long, at last thou shalt
    erect.'
He said, and brought me, from their blest
    abodes,
The venerable statues of the gods,
With ancient Vesta from the sacred choir,
The wreaths and relics of th' immortal fire.
    "Now peals of shouts come thund'ring
        from afar,
Cries, threats, and loud laments, and min-
        gled war:

The noise approaches, tho' our palace stood
Aloof from streets, encompass'd with a
    wood.   400
Louder, and yet more loud, I hear th' alarms
Of human cries distinct, and clashing arms.
Fear broke my slumbers; I no longer
    stay,
But mount the terrace, thence the town
    survey,
And hearken what the frightful sounds
    convey.
Thus, when a flood of fire by wind is borne,
Crackling it rolls, and mows the standing
    corn;
Or deluges, descending on the plains,
Sweep o er the yellow year, destroy the
    pains
Of lab'ring oxen and the peasant's
    gains;   410
Unroot the forest oaks, and bear away
Flocks, folds, and trees, an undistinguish'd
    prey:
The shepherd climbs the cliff, and sees from
    far
The wasteful ravage of the wat'ry war.
Then Hector's faith was manifestly
    clear'd,
And Grecian frauds in open light appear'd.
The palace of Deïphobus ascends
In smoky flames, and catches on his friends.
Ucalegon burns next: the seas are bright
With splendor not their own, and shine with
    Trojan light.   420
New clamors and new clangors now arise,
The sound of trumpets mix'd with fighting
    cries.
With frenzy seiz'd, I run to meet th' alarms,
Resolv'd on death, resolv'd to die in arms,
But first to gather friends, with them t' op-
    pose
(If fortune favor'd) and repel the foes;
Spurr'd by my courage, by my country
    fir'd,
With sense of honor and revenge inspir'd.
    "Pantheus, Apollo's priest, a sacred name,
Had scap'd the Grecian swords, and pass'd
    the flame: 430
With relics loaden, to my doors he fled,
And by the hand his tender grandson led.
'What hope, O Pantheus? whither can we
    run?
Where make a stand? and what may yet
    be done?'
Scarce had I said, when Pantheus, with a
    groan:

'Troy is no more, and Ilium was a town!
The fatal day, th' appointed hour, is come,
When wrathful Jove's irrevocable doom
Transfers the Trojan state to Grecian hands.
The fire consumes the town, the foe com-
 mands; 440
And armed hosts, an unexpected force,
Break from the bowels of the fatal horse.
Within the gates, proud Sinon throws about
The flames; and foes for entrance press
 without,
With thousand others, whom I fear to name,
More than from Argos or Mycenæ came.
To sev'ral posts their parties they divide;
Some block the narrow streets, some scour
 the wide:
The bold they kill, th' unwary they sur-
 prise;
Who fights finds death, and death finds him
 who flies. 450
The warders of the gate but scarce maintain
Th' unequal combat, and resist in vain.'
 " I heard; and Heav'n, that well-born
  souls inspires,
Prompts me thro' lifted swords and rising
 fires
To run where clashing arms and clamor
 calls,
And rush undaunted to defend the walls.
Ripheus and Iph'itus by my side engage,
For valor one renown'd, and one for age.
Dymas and Hypanis by moonlight knew
My motions and my mien, and to my party
 drew; 460
With young Corœbus, who by love was led
To win renown and fair Cassandra's bed,
And lately brought his troops to Priam's
 aid,
Forewarn'd in vain by the prophetic maid.
Whom when I saw resolv'd in arms to fall,
And that one spirit animated all:
'Brave souls!' said I, — 'but brave, alas!
 in vain —
Come, finish what our cruel fates ordain.
You see the desp'rate state of our affairs,
And heav'n's protecting pow'rs are deaf to
 pray'rs. 470
The passive gods behold the Greeks defile
Their temples, and abandon to the spoil
Their own abodes: we, feeble few, conspire
To save a sinking town, involv'd in fire.
Then let us fall, but fall amidst our foes:
Despair of life the means of living shows.'
So bold a speech incourag'd their desire
Of death, and added fuel to their fire.

" As hungry wolves, with raging appetite,
Scour thro' the fields, nor fear the stormy
 night — 480
Their whelps at home expect the promis'd
 food,
And long to temper their dry chaps in
 blood —
So rush'd we forth at once; resolv'd to die,
Resolv'd, in death, the last extremes to try.
We leave the narrow lanes behind, and ⎫
 dare   ⎪
Th' unequal combat in the public square: ⎬
Night was our friend; our leader was ⎪
 despair.   ⎭
What tongue can tell the slaughter of that
 night?
What eyes can weep the sorrows and
 affright?
An ancient and imperial city falls; 490
The streets are fill'd with frequent funerals;
Houses and holy temples float in blood,
And hostile nations make a common flood.
Not only Trojans fall; but, in their turn,
The vanquish'd triumph, and the victors
 mourn.
Ours take new courage from despair and
 night:
Confus'd the fortune is, confus'd the fight.
All parts resound with tumults, plaints, and
 fears;
And grisly Death in sundry shapes appears.
Androgeos fell among us, with his band, 500
Who thought us Grecians newly come to
 land.
'From whence,' said he, 'my friends, this
 long delay?
You loiter, while the spoils are borne away:
Our ships are laden with the Trojan store;
And you, like truants, come too late
 ashore.'
He said, but soon corrected his mistake,
Found, by the doubtful answers which we
 make:
Amaz'd, he would have shunn'd th' unequal
 fight;
But we, more num'rous, intercept his
 flight. 509
As when some peasant, in a bushy brake,
Has with unwary footing press'd a snake;
He starts aside, astonish'd, when he ⎫
 spies   ⎪
His rising crest, blue neck, and rolling ⎬
 eyes;   ⎪
So from our arms surpris'd Androgeos ⎭
 flies.

In vain; for him and his we compass'd
round,
Possess'd with fear, unknowing of the
ground,
And of their lives an easy conquest found.
Thus Fortune on our first endeavor smil'd.
Corœbus then, with youthful hopes beguil'd,
Swoln with success, and of a daring mind,
This new invention fatally design'd.   521
'My friends,' said he, 'since Fortune shows
the way,
'T is fit we should th' auspicious guide
obey.
For what has she these Grecian arms
bestow'd,
But their destruction, and the Trojans'
good ?
Then change we shields, and their devices
bear:
Let fraud supply the want of force in war.
They find us arms.' This said, himself he
dress'd
In dead Androgeos' spoils, his upper vest,
His painted buckler, and his plumy
crest.   530
Thus Ripheus, Dymas, all the Trojan train,
Lay down their own attire, and strip the
slain.
Mix'd with the Greeks, we go with ill
presage,
Flatter'd with hopes to glut our greedy
rage;
Unknown, assaulting whom we blindly
meet,
And strew with Grecian carcasses the
street.
Thus while their straggling parties we
defeat,
Some to the shore and safer ships retreat;
And some, oppress'd with more ignoble
fear,
Remount the hollow horse, and pant in
secret there.   540
"But, ah ! what use of valor can be
made,
When heav'n's propitious pow'rs refuse
their aid !
Behold the royal prophetess, the fair
Cassandra, dragg'd by her dishevel'd hair,
Whom not Minerva's shrine, nor sacred
bands,
In safety could protect from sacrilegious
hands:
On heav'n she cast her eyes, she sigh'd,
she cried —

'T was all she could — her tender arms
were tied.
So sad a sight Corœbus could not bear;
But, fir'd with rage, distracted with de-
spair,   550
Amid the barb'rous ravishers he flew:
Our leader's rash example we pursue.
But storms of stones, from the proud tem-
ple's height,
Pour down, and on our batter'd helms
alight:
We from our friends receiv'd this fatal
blow,
Who thought us Grecians, as we seem'd
in show.
They aim at the mistaken crests, from
high;
And ours beneath the pond'rous ruin lie.
Then, mov'd with anger and disdain, to
see
Their troops dispers'd, the royal virgin
free,   560
The Grecians rally, and their pow'rs unite,
With fury charge us, and renew the fight.
The brother kings with Ajax join their
force,
And the whole squadron of Thessalian
horse.
"Thus, when the rival winds their quar-
rel try,
Contending for the kingdom of the sky,
South, east, and west, on airy coursers
borne;
The whirlwind gathers, and the woods are
torn:
Then Nereus strikes the deep; the billows
rise,
And, mix'd with ooze and sand, pollute the
skies.   570
The troops we squander'd first again ap-
pear
From sev'ral quarters, and enclose the
rear.
They first observe, and to the rest betray,
Our diff'rent speech; our borrow'd arms
survey.
Oppress'd with odds, we fall; Corœbus
first,
At Pallas' altar, by Peneleus pierc'd.
Then Ripheus follow'd, in th' unequal
fight;
Just of his word, observant of the right:
Heav'n thought not so. Dymas their fate
attends,
With Hypanis, mistaken by their friends.

Nor, Pantheus, thee, thy miter, nor the
    bands   581
Of awful Phœbus, sav'd from impious
    hands.
Ye Trojan flames, your testimony bear,
What I perform'd, and what I suffer'd there;
No sword avoiding in the fatal strife,
Expos'd to death, and prodigal of life !
Witness, ye heav'ns ! I live not by my
    fault:
I strove to have deserv'd the death I
    sought.
But, when I could not fight, and would
    have died,
Borne off to distance by the growing tide,
Old Iphitus and I were hurried thence, 591
With Pelias wounded, and without de-
    fense.
New clamors from th' invested palace ring:
We run to die, or disengage the king.
So hot th' assault, so high the tumult rose,
While ours defend, and while the Greeks
    oppose,
As all the Dardan and Argolic race
Had been contracted in that narrow space;
Or as all Ilium else were void of fear,
And tumult, war, and slaughter, only
    there.   600
Their targets in a tortoise cast, the foes,
Secure advancing, to the turrets rose:
Some mount the scaling ladders; some,
    more bold,
Swerve upwards, and by posts and pillars
    hold;
Their left hand gripes their bucklers in th'
    ascent,
While with the right they seize the battle-
    ment.
From their demolish'd tow'rs the Trojans
    throw
Huge heaps of stones, that, falling, crush
    the foe;
And heavy beams and rafters from the
    sides   609
(Such arms their last necessity provides)
And gilded roofs, come tumbling from on
    high,
The marks of state and ancient royalty.
The guards below, fix'd in the pass, attend
The charge undaunted, and the gate defend.
Renew'd in courage with recover'd breath,
A second time we ran to tempt our death,
To clear the palace from the foe, succeed
The weary living, and revenge the dead.
    " A postern door, yet unobserv'd and free,

Join'd by the length of a blind gallery, 620
To the king's closet led: a way well known
To Hector's wife, while Priam held the
    throne,
Thro' which she brought Astyanax, unseen,
To cheer his grandsire and his grandsire's
    queen.
Thro' this we pass, and mount the tow'r,
    from whence
With unavailing arms the Trojans make
    defense.
From this the trembling king had oft de-
    scried
The Grecian camp, and saw their navy ride.
Beams from its lofty height with swords
    we hew,
Then, wrenching with our hands, th' assault
    renew;   630
And, where the rafters on the columns meet,
We push them headlong with our arms and
    feet.
The lightning flies not swifter than the fall,
Nor thunder louder than the ruin'd wall:
Down goes the top at once; the Greeks be-
    neath
Are piecemeal torn, or pounded into death.
Yet more succeed, and more to death are
    sent;
We cease not from above, nor they below
    relent.
Before the gate stood Pyrrhus, threat'ning
    loud,
With glitt'ring arms conspicuous in the
    crowd.   640
So shines, renew'd in youth, the crested
    snake,
Who slept the winter in a thorny brake,
And, casting off his slough when spring
    returns,
Now looks aloft, and with new glory burns;
Restor'd with pois'nous herbs, his ardent
    sides
Reflect the sun; and rais'd on spires he rides,
High o'er the grass, hissing he rolls along,
And brandishes by fits his forky tongue.
Proud Periphas, and fierce Automedon,
His father's charioteer, together run   650
To force the gate; the Scyrian infantry
Rush on in crowds, and the barr'd passage
    free.
Ent'ring the court, with shouts the skies
    they rend;
And flaming firebrands to the roofs ascend.
Himself, among the foremost, deals his
    blows.

And with his ax repeated strokes bestows
On the strong doors; then all their shoulders ply,
Till from the posts the brazen hinges fly.
He hews apace; the double bars at length
Yield to his ax and unresisted strength. 660
A mighty breach is made: the rooms con-
ceal'd
Appear, and all the palace is reveal'd;
The halls of audience, and of public state,
And where the lonely queen in secret sate.
Arm'd soldiers now by trembling maids
are seen,
With not a door, and scarce a space, be-
tween.
The house is fill'd with loud laments and
cries,
And shrieks of women rend the vaulted
skies;
The fearful matrons run from place to place,
And kiss the thresholds, and the posts em-
brace. 670
The fatal work inhuman Pyrrhus plies,
And all his father sparkles in his eyes;
Nor bars, nor fighting guards, his force sus-
tain:
The bars are broken, and the guards are
slain.
In rush the Greeks, and all the apartments
fill;
Those few defendants whom they find, they
kill.
Not with so fierce a rage the foaming flood
Roars, when he finds his rapid course with-
stood;
Bears down the dams with unresisted sway,
And sweeps the cattle and the cots away. 680
These eyes beheld him when he march'd
between
The brother kings: I saw th' unhappy queen,
The hundred wives, and where old Priam
stood,
To stain his hallow'd altar with his blood.
The fifty nuptial beds (such hopes had he,
So large a promise, of a progeny),
The posts, of plated gold, and hung with
spoils,
Fell the reward of the proud victor's toils.
Where'er the raging fire had left a space,
The Grecians enter and possess the place.
  "Perhaps you may of Priam's fate en-
quire. 691
He, when he saw his regal town on fire,
His ruin'd palace, and his ent'ring foes,
On ev'ry side inevitable woes,

In arms, disus'd, invests his limbs, decay'd,
Like them, with age; a late and useless
aid.
His feeble shoulders scarce the weight
sustain;
Loaded, not arm'd, he creeps along with
pain,
Despairing of success, ambitious to be
slain !
Uncover'd but by heav'n, there stood in
view 700
An altar; near the hearth a laurel grew,
Dodder'd with age, whose boughs encom-
pass round
The household gods, and shade the holy
ground.
Here Hecuba, with all her helpless train
Of dames, for shelter sought, but sought in
vain.
Driv'n like a flock of doves along the sky,
Their images they hug, and to their altar
fly.
The queen, when she beheld her trembling
lord,
And hanging by his side a heavy sword,
'What rage,' she cried, 'has seiz'd my hus-
band's mind ? 710
What arms are these, and to what use de-
sign'd ?
These times want other aids ! Were Hec-
tor here,
Ev'n Hector now in vain, like Priam, would
appear.
With us, one common shelter thou shalt
find,
Or in one common fate with us be join'd.'
She said, and with a last salute embrac'd
The poor old man, and by the laurel plac'd.
Behold ! Polites, one of Priam's sons,
Pursued by Pyrrhus, there for safety runs.
Thro' swords and foes, amaz'd and hurt, he
flies 720
Thro' empty courts and open galleries.
Him Pyrrhus, urging with his lance, pursues,
And often reaches, and his thrusts renews.
The youth, transfix'd, with lamentable
cries,
Expires before his wretched parent's eyes:
Whom gasping at his feet when Priam saw,
The fear of death gave place to nature's
law;
And, shaking more with anger than with
age,
'The gods,' said he, 'requite thy brutal
rage !

As sure they will, barbarian, sure they
   must,   730
If there be gods in heav'n, and gods be
   just —
Who tak'st in wrongs an insolent delight;
With a son's death t' infect a father's
   sight.
Not he, whom thou and lying fame con-
   spire
To call thee his — not he, thy vaunted sire,
Thus us'd my wretched age: the gods he
   fear'd,
The laws of nature and of nations heard.
He cheer'd my sorrows, and, for sums of
   gold,
The bloodless carcass of my Hector sold;
Pitied the woes a parent underwent,   740
And sent me back in safety from his tent.'
   " This said, his feeble hand a javelin
   threw,
Which, flutt'ring, seem'd to loiter as it
   flew:
Just, and but barely, to the mark it held,
And faintly tinkled on the brazen shield.
   " Then Pyrrhus thus: ' Go thou from me
   to fate,
And to my father my foul deeds relate.
Now die ! ' With that he dragg'd the
   trembling sire,
Slidd'ring thro' clotter'd blood and holy
   mire,
(The mingled paste his murder'd son had ⎫
   made,)   750
Haul'd from beneath the violated shade, ⎬
And on the sacred pile the royal victim
   laid.   ⎭
His right hand held his bloody fauchion
   bare,
His left he twisted in his hoary hair;
Then, with a speeding thrust, his heart he ⎫
   found:
The lukewarm blood came rushing thro' ⎬
   the wound,
And sanguine streams distain'd the sacred
   ground.   ⎭
Thus Priam fell, and shar'd one common
   fate
With Troy in ashes, and his ruin'd state:
He, who the scepter of all Asia sway'd, 760
Whom monarchs like domestic slaves
   obey'd.
On the bleak shore now lies th' abandon'd
   king,
A headless carcass, and a nameless thing.*

* This whole line is taken from Sir John Denham.

   " Then, not before, I felt my cruddled
   blood
Congeal with fear, my hair with horror
   stood:
My father's image fill'd my pious mind,
Lest equal years might equal fortune find.
Again I thought on my forsaken wife,
And trembled for my son's abandon'd life.
I look'd about, but found myself alone, 770
Deserted at my need ! My friends were
   gone.
Some spent with toil, some with despair
   oppress'd,
Leap'd headlong from the heights; the
   flames consum'd the rest.
Thus, wand'ring in my way, without a
   guide,
The graceless Helen in the porch I spied
Of Vesta's temple; there she lurk'd alone;
Muffled she sate, and, what she could,
   unknown:
But, by the flames that cast their blaze
   around,
That common bane of Greece and Troy I
   found.
For Ilium burnt, she dreads the Trojan ⎫
   sword;   780
More dreads the vengeance of her injur'd ⎬
   lord;
Ev'n by those gods who refug'd her
   abhorr'd.   ⎭
Trembling with rage, the strumpet I regard,
Resolv'd to give her guilt the due reward:
' Shall she triumphant sail before the wind,
And leave in flames unhappy Troy behind ?
Shall she her kingdom and her friends
   review,
In state attended with a captive crew,
While unreveng'd the good old Priam
   falls,
And Grecian fires consume the Trojan
   walls ?   790
For this the Phrygian fields and Xanthian
   flood
Were swell'd with bodies, and were drunk
   with blood ?
'T is true, a soldier can small honor gain,
And boast no conquest, from a woman
   slain:
Yet shall the fact not pass without applause,
Of vengeance taken in so just a cause;
The punish'd crime shall set my soul at
   ease,
And murm'ring manes of my friends
   appease.'

Thus while I rave, a gleam of pleasing
   light
Spread o'er the place; and, shining
   heav'nly bright,   800
My mother stood reveal'd before my
   sight.
Never so radiant did her eyes appear;
Not her own star confess'd a light so clear:
Great in her charms, as when on gods
   above
She looks, and breathes herself into their
   love.
She held my hand, the destin'd blow to
   break;
Then from her rosy lips began to speak:
'My son, from whence this madness, this
   neglect
Of my commands, and those whom I pro-
   tect?
Why this unmanly rage? Recall to mind
Whom you forsake, what pledges leave
   behind.   811
Look if your helpless father yet survive,
Or if Ascanius or Creüsa live.
Around your house the greedy Grecians
   err;
And these had perish'd in the nightly
   war,
But for my presence and protecting care.
Not Helen's face, nor Paris, was in fault;
But by the gods was this destruction
   brought.
Now cast your eyes around, while I dissolve
The mists and films that mortal eyes in-
   volve,   820
Purge from your sight the dross, and make
   you see
The shape of each avenging deity.
Enlighten'd thus, my just commands fulfil,
Nor fear obedience to your mother's will.
Where yon disorder'd heap of ruin lies,
Stones rent from stones; where clouds of
   dust arise —
Amid that smother Neptune holds his
   place,
Below the wall's foundation drives his
   mace,
And heaves the building from the solid
   base.
Look where, in arms, imperial Juno
   stands   830
Full in the Scæan gate, with loud com-
   mands,
Urging on shore the tardy Grecian
   bands.

See! Pallas, of her snaky buckler proud,
Bestrides the tow'r, refulgent thro' the
   cloud:
See! Jove new courage to the foe supplies,
And arms against the town the partial
   deities.
Haste hence, my son; this fruitless labor
   end:
Haste, where your trembling spouse and
   sire attend:
Haste; and a mother's care your passage
   shall befriend.'
She said, and swiftly vanish'd from my
   sight,   840
Obscure in clouds and gloomy shades of
   night.
I look'd, I listen'd; dreadful sounds I
   hear;
And the dire forms of hostile gods appear.
Troy sunk in flames I saw (nor could
   prevent),
And Ilium from its old foundations rent;
Rent like a mountain ash, which dar'd the
   winds,
And stood the sturdy strokes of lab'ring
   hinds.
About the roots the cruel ax resounds;
The stumps are pierc'd with oft-repeated
   wounds:
The war is felt on high; the nodding
   crown   850
Now threats a fall, and throws the leafy
   honors down.
To their united force it yields, tho' late,
And mourns with mortal groans th' ap-
   proaching fate:
The roots no more their upper load sus-
   tain;
But down she falls, and spreads a ruin thro'
   the plain.
  " Descending thence, I scape thro' foes
   and fire:
Before the goddess, foes and flames retire.
Arriv'd at home, he, for whose only sake,
Or most for his, such toils I undertake,
The good Anchises, whom, by timely flight,
I purpos'd to secure on Ida's height,   861
Refus'd the journey, resolute to die
And add his fun'rals to the fate of Troy,
Rather than exile and old age sustain.
'Go you, whose blood runs warm in ev'ry
   vein.
Had Heav'n decreed that I should life en-
   joy,
Heav'n had decreed to save unhappy Troy.

'T is, sure, enough, if not too much, for
  one,
Twice to have seen our Ilium overthrown.
Make haste to save the poor remaining
  crew,   870
And give this useless corpse a long adieu.
These weak old hands suffice to stop my
  breath;
At least the pitying foes will aid my
  death,
To take my spoils, and leave my body
  bare:
As for my sepulcher, let Heav'n take care.
'T is long since I, for my celestial wife
Loath'd by the gods, have dragg'd a
  ling'ring life;
Since ev'ry hour and moment I expire,
Blasted from heav'n by Jove's avenging
  fire.'
This oft repeated, he stood fix'd to ⎤
  die: 880 ⎟
Myself, my wife, my son, my family, ⎬
Intreat, pray, beg, and raise a doleful ⎟
  cry — ⎦
' What, will he still persist, on death re-
  solve,
And in his ruin all his house involve ! '
He still persists his reasons to maintain;
Our pray'rs, our tears, our loud laments,
  are vain.
  " Urg'd by despair, again I go to try
The fate of arms, resolv'd in fight to die:
' What hope remains, but what my death
  must give ?
Can I, without so dear a father, live ? 890
You term it prudence, what I baseness call:
Could such a word from such a parent
  fall ?
If Fortune please, and so the gods or- ⎤
  dain,   ⎟
That nothing should of ruin'd Troy re- ⎬
  main,   ⎟
And you conspire with Fortune to be ⎦
  slain,
The way to death is wide, th' approaches
  near:
For soon relentless Pyrrhus will appear,
Reeking with Priam's blood — the wretch ⎤
  who slew   ⎟
The son (inhuman) in the father's view, ⎬
And then the sire himself to the dire ⎦
  altar drew.   900
O goddess mother, give me back to Fate;
Your gift was undesir'd, and came too
  late !

Did you, for this, unhappy me convey
Thro' foes and fires, to see my house a
  prey ?
Shall I my father, wife, and son behold,
Welt'ring in blood, each other's arms in-
  fold ?
Haste ! gird my sword, tho' spent and
  overcome:
'T is the last summons to receive our doom.
I hear thee, Fate; and I obey thy call !
Not unreveng'd the foe shall see my fall.
Restore me to the yet unfinish'd fight: 911
My death is wanting to conclude the night.'
Arm'd once again, my glitt'ring sword I ⎤
  wield,   ⎟
While th' other hand sustains my weighty ⎬
  shield,   ⎟
And forth I rush to seek th' abandon'd ⎦
  field.
I went; but sad Creüsa stopp'd my way,
And cross the threshold in my passage lay,
Embrac'd my knees, and, when I would
  have gone,
Shew'd me my feeble sire and tender son:
' If death be your design, at least,' said
  she,   920
' Take us along to share your destiny.
If any farther hopes in arms remain,
This place, these pledges of your love,
  maintain.
To whom do you expose your father's life,
Your son's, and mine, your now forgotten
  wife ! '
While thus she fills the house with clam'r-
  ous cries,
Our hearing is diverted by our eyes:
For, while I held my son, in the short
  space
Betwixt our kisses and our last embrace;
Strange to relate, from young Iülus' ⎤
  head   930 ⎟
A lambent flame arose, which gently ⎬
  spread   ⎟
Around his brows, and on his temples ⎦
  fed.
Amaz'd, with running water we prepare
To quench the sacred fire, and slake his
  hair;
But old Anchises, vers'd in omens, rear'd
His hands to heav'n, and this request pre-
  ferr'd:
' If any vows, almighty Jove, can bend ⎤
Thy will; if piety can pray'rs commend, ⎬
Confirm the glad presage which thou art ⎦
  pleas'd to send.'

Scarce had he said, when, on our left, we
    hear   940
A peal of rattling thunder roll in air:
There shot a streaming lamp along the
    sky,
Which on the winged lightning seem'd to
    fly;
From o'er the roof the blaze began to
    move,
And, trailing, vanish'd in th' Idæan grove.
It swept a path in heav'n, and shone a
    guide,
Then in a steaming stench of sulphur died.
    "The good old man with suppliant
    hands implor'd
The gods' protection, and their star ador'd.
'Now, now,' said he, 'my son, no more de-
    lay!   950
I yield, I follow where Heav'n shews the
    way.
Keep, O my country gods, our dwelling
    place,
And guard this relic of the Trojan race,
This tender child! These omens are your
    own,
And you can yet restore the ruin'd town.
At least accomplish what your signs fore-
    show:
I stand resign'd, and am prepar'd to go.'
    "He said. The crackling flames appear
    on high,
And driving sparkles dance along the sky.
With Vulcan's rage the rising winds con-
    spire,   960
And near our palace roll the flood of fire.
'Haste, my dear father, ('t is no time to
    wait,)
And load my shoulders with a willing
    freight.
Whate'er befalls, your life shall be my
    care;
One death, or one deliv'rance, we will
    share.
My hand shall lead our little son; and
    you,
My faithful consort, shall our steps pur-
    sue.
Next, you, my servants, heed my strict
    commands:
Without the walls a ruin'd temple stands,
To Ceres hallow'd once; a cypress nigh   970
Shoots up her venerable head on high,
By long religion kept; there bend your
    feet,
And in divided parties let us meet.

Our country gods, the relics, and the
    bands,
Hold you, my father, in your guiltless
    hands:
In me 't is impious holy things to bear,
Red as I am with slaughter, new from
    war,
Till in some living stream I cleanse the
    guilt
Of dire debate, and blood in battle spilt.'
Thus, ord'ring all that prudence could pro-
    vide,   980
I clothe my shoulders with a lion's hide
And yellow spoils; then, on my bending
    back,
The welcome load of my dear father take;
While on my better hand Ascanius hung,
And with unequal paces tripp'd along.
Creüsa kept behind; by choice we stray
Thro' ev'ry dark and ev'ry devious way.
I, who so bold and dauntless, just before,
The Grecian darts and shock of lances
    bore,   989
At ev'ry shadow now am seiz'd with fear,
Not for myself, but for the charge I bear;
Till, near the ruin'd gate arriv'd at last,
Secure, and deeming all the danger past,
A frightful noise of trampling feet we
    hear.
My father, looking thro' the shades, with
    fear,
Cried out: 'Haste, haste, my son, the foes
    are nigh;
Their swords and shining armor I descry.'
Some hostile god, for some unknown of-
    fense,
Had sure bereft my mind of better sense,
For, while thro' winding ways I took my
    flight,   1000
And sought the shelter of the gloomy
    night,
Alas! I lost Creüsa: hard to tell
If by her fatal destiny she fell,
Or weary sate, or wander'd with affright;
But she was lost for ever to my sight.
I knew not, or reflected, till I meet
My friends, at Ceres' now deserted seat.
We met: not one was wanting; only she
Deceiv'd her friends, her son, and wretched
    me.
    "What mad expressions did my tongue
    refuse!   1010
Whom did I not, of gods or men, accuse!
This was the fatal blow, that pain'd me
    more

Than all I felt from ruin'd Troy before.
Stung with my loss, and raving with de-
    spair,
Abandoning my now forgotten care,
Of counsel, comfort, and of hope bereft,
My sire, my son, my country gods I left.
In shining armor once again I sheathe
My limbs, not feeling wounds, nor fearing
    death. 1019
Then headlong to the burning walls I run,
And seek the danger I was forc'd to shun.
I tread my former tracks; thro' night ex-
    plore
Each passage, ev'ry street I cross'd before.
All things were full of horror and affright,
And dreadful ev'n the silence of the night.
Then to my father's house I make repair,
With some small glimpse of hope to find
    her there.
Instead of her, the cruel Greeks I met;
The house was fill'd with foes, with flames
    beset.
Driv'n on the wings of winds, whole sheets
    of fire, 1030
Thro' air transported, to the roofs aspire.
From thence to Priam's palace I resort,
And search the citadel and desart court.
Then, unobserv'd, I pass by Juno's church:
A guard of Grecians had possess'd the porch;
There Phœnix and Ulysses watch the prey,
And thither all the wealth of Troy convey:
The spoils which they from ransack'd houses
    brought,
And golden bowls from burning altars
    caught,
The tables of the gods, the purple vests, 1040
The people's treasure, and the pomp of
    priests.
A rank of wretched youths, with pinion'd
    hands,
And captive matrons, in long order stands.
Then, with ungovern'd madness, I proclaim,
Thro' all the silent street, Creüsa's name:
Creüsa still I call; at length she hears,
And sudden thro' the shades of night ap-
    pears —
Appears, no more Creüsa, nor my wife,
But a pale specter, larger than the life.
Aghast, astonish'd, and struck dumb with
    fear, 1050
I stood; like bristles rose my stiffen'd hair.
Then thus the ghost began to soothe my
    grief:
'Nor tears, nor cries, can give the dead
    relief.

Desist, my much-lov'd lord, t' indulge your
    pain;
You bear no more than what the gods
    ordain.
My fates permit me not from hence to fly;
Nor he, the great controller of the sky.
Long wand'ring ways for you the pow'rs
    decree:
On land hard labors, and a length of sea.
Then, after many painful years are past, 1060
On Latium's happy shore you shall be cast,
Where gentle Tiber from his bed beholds
The flow'ry meadows, and the feeding folds.
There end your toils; and there your fates
    provide
A quiet kingdom, and a royal bride:
There fortune shall the Trojan line restore,
And you for lost Creüsa weep no more.
Fear not that I shall watch, with servile
    shame,
Th' imperious looks of some proud Grecian
    dame;
Or, stooping to the victor's lust, disgrace
My goddess mother, or my royal race. 1071
And now, farewell ! The parent of the gods
Restrains my fleeting soul in her abodes:
I trust our common issue to your care.'
She said, and gliding pass'd unseen in air.
I strove to speak: but horror tied my
    tongue;
And thrice about her neck my arms I
    flung,
And, thrice deceiv'd, on vain embraces
    hung.
Light as an empty dream at break of day,
Or as a blast of wind, she rush'd away. 1080
  " Thus having pass'd the night in fruitless
    pain,
I to my longing friends return again,
Amaz'd th' augmented number to behold,
Of men and matrons mix'd, of young and
    old;
A wretched exil'd crew together brought,
With arms appointed, and with treasure
    fraught,
Resolv'd, and willing, under my command,
To run all hazards both of sea and land.
The Morn began, from Ida, to display
Her rosy cheeks; and Phosphor led the
    day: 1090
Before the gates the Grecians took their
    post,
And all pretense of late relief was lost.
I yield to Fate, unwillingly retire,
And, loaded, up the hill convey my sire."

THE THIRD BOOK OF THE ÆNEIS

THE ARGUMENT

Æneas proceeds in his relation: he gives an account of the fleet with which he sail'd, and the success of his first voyage to Thrace. From thence he directs his course to Delos, and asks the oracle what place the gods had appointed for his habitation. By a mistake of the oracle's answer, he settles in Crete; his household gods give him the true sense of the oracle, in a dream. He follows their advice, and makes the best of his way for Italy. He is cast on several shores, and meets with very surprising adventures, till at length he lands on Sicily, where his father Anchises dies. This is the place which he was sailing from, when the tempest rose, and threw him upon the Carthaginian coast.

" WHEN Heav'n had overturn'd the Trojan
        state
And Priam's throne, by too severe a fate;
When ruin'd Troy became the Grecians'
        prey,
And Ilium's lofty tow'rs in ashes lay;
Warn'd by celestial omens, we retreat,
To seek in foreign lands a happier seat.
Near old Antandros, and at Ida's foot,
The timber of the sacred groves we cut,
And build our fleet; uncertain yet to find
What place the gods for our repose as-
        sign'd.   10
Friends daily flock; and scarce the kindly
        spring
Began to clothe the ground, and birds to
        sing,
When old Anchises summon'd all to sea:
The crew my father and the Fates obey.
With sighs and tears I leave my native
        shore,
And empty fields, where Ilium stood
        before.
My sire, my son, our less and greater gods,
All sail at once, and cleave the briny
        floods.
    " Against our coast appears a spacious
        land,
Which once the fierce Lycurgus did
        command,   20
(Thracia the name — the people bold in
        war;
Vast are their fields, and tillage is their
        care,)

A hospitable realm while Fate was kind,
With Troy in friendship and religion
        join'd.
I land; with luckless omens then adore
Their gods, and draw a line along the
        shore;
I lay the deep foundations of a wall,
And Ænos, nam'd from me, the city call.
To Dionæan Venus vows are paid,
And all the pow'rs that rising labors
        aid;   30
A bull on Jove's imperial altar laid.
Not far, a rising hillock stood in view;
Sharp myrtles on the sides, and cornels
        grew.
There, while I went to crop the sylvan
        scenes,
And shade our altar with their leafy
        greens,
I pull'd a plant — with horror I relate
A prodigy so strange and full of fate.
The rooted fibers rose, and from the wound
Black bloody drops distill'd upon the
        ground.
Mute and amaz'd, my hair with terror
        stood;   40
Fear shrunk my sinews, and congeal'd my
        blood.
Mann'd once again, another plant I try:
That other gush'd with the same sanguine
        dye.
Then, fearing guilt for some offense un-
        known,
With pray'rs and vows the Dryads I atone,
With all the sisters of the woods, and most
The God of Arms, who rules the Thracian
        coast,
That they, or he, these omens would avert,
Release our fears, and better signs impart.
Clear'd, as I thought, and fully fix'd at
        length   50
To learn the cause, I tugg'd with all my
        strength:
I bent my knees against the ground; once
        more
The violated myrtle ran with gore.
Scarce dare I tell the sequel: from the
        womb
Of wounded earth, and caverns of the
        tomb,
A groan, as of a troubled ghost, renew'd
My fright, and then these dreadful words
        ensued:
' Why dost thou thus my buried body
        rend ?

O spare the corpse of thy unhappy friend !
Spare to pollute thy pious hands with
  blood: 60
The tears distil not from the wounded
  wood;
But ev'ry drop this living tree contains
Is kindred blood, and ran in Trojan veins.
O fly from this unhospitable shore,
Warn'd by my fate; for I am Polydore !
Here loads of lances, in my blood embrued,
Again shoot upward, by my blood renew'd.'
  " My falt'ring tongue and shiv'ring limbs
    declare
My horror, and in bristles rose my hair.
When Troy with Grecian arms was ⎤
  closely pent,   70 ⎬
Old Priam, fearful of the war's event,   ⎟
This hapless Polydore to Thracia sent: ⎦
Loaded with gold, he sent his darling, ⎤
  far   ⎟
From noise and tumults, and destructive ⎬
  war,   ⎟
Committed to the faithless tyrant's care; ⎦
Who, when he saw the pow'r of Troy de-
  cline,
Forsook the weaker, with the strong to
  join;
Broke ev'ry bond of nature and of truth,
And murder'd, for his wealth, the royal
  youth.
O sacred hunger of pernicious gold !   80
What bands of faith can impious lucre
  hold ?
Now, when my soul had shaken off her
  fears,
I call my father and the Trojan peers;
Relate the prodigies of Heav'n, require
What he commands, and their advice de-
  sire.
All vote to leave that execrable shore,
Polluted with the blood of Polydore;
But, ere we sail, his fun'ral rites prepare,
Then, to his ghost, a tomb and altars rear.
In mournful pomp the matrons walk the ⎤
  round,   90 ⎟
With baleful cypress and blue fillets ⎬
  crown'd,   ⎟
With eyes dejected, and with hair un-   ⎦
  bound.
Then bowls of tepid milk and blood we
  pour,
And thrice invoke the soul of Polydore.
  " Now, when the raging storms no longer
    reign,
But southern gales invite us to the main,

We launch our vessels, with a prosp'rous
  wind,
And leave the cities and the shores behind.
  " An island in th' Ægæan main appears;
Neptune and wat'ry Doris claim it theirs.
It floated once, till Phœbus fix'd the
  sides   101
To rooted earth, and now it braves the
  tides.
Here, borne by friendly winds, we come ⎤
  ashore,   ⎟
With needful ease our weary limbs re- ⎬
  store,   ⎟
And the Sun's temple and his town ⎟
  adore.   ⎦
  " Anius, the priest and king, with laurel
    crown'd,
His hoary locks with purple fillets bound,
Who saw my sire the Delian shore ascend,
Came forth with eager haste to meet his
  friend;
Invites him to his palace; and, in sign 110
Of ancient love, their plighted hands they
  join.
Then to the temple of the god I went,
And thus, before the shrine, my vows pre-
  sent:
'Give, O Thymbræus, give a resting place
To the sad relics of the Trojan race;
A seat secure, a region of their own,
A lasting empire, and a happier town.
Where shall we fix ? where shall our labors
  end ?
Whom shall we follow, and what fate at-
  tend ?
Let not my pray'rs a doubtful answer
  find;   120
But in clear auguries unveil thy mind.'
Scarce had I said: he shook the holy ⎤
  ground,   ⎟
The laurels, and the lofty hills around; ⎬
And from the tripos rush'd a bellowing ⎟
  sound.   ⎦
Prostrate we fell; confess'd the present
  god,
Who gave this answer from his dark abode:
' Undaunted youths, go, seek that mother
  earth
From which your ancestors derive their
  birth.
The soil that sent you forth, her ancient
  race
In her old bosom shall again embrace.   130
Thro' the wide world th' Æneian house
  shall reign,

And children's children shall the crown
    sustain.'
Thus Phœbus did our future fates disclose:
A mighty tumult, mix'd with joy, arose.
    " All are concern'd to know what place
      the god
Assign'd, and where determin'd our abode.
My father, long revolving in his mind
The race and lineage of the Trojan kind,
Thus answer'd their demands: ' Ye princes,
    hear
Your pleasing fortune, and dispel your fear.
The fruitful isle of Crete, well known to
    fame,   141
Sacred of old to Jove's imperial name,
In the mid ocean lies, with large command,
And on its plains a hundred cities stand.
Another Ida rises there, and we
From thence derive our Trojan ancestry.
From thence, as 't is divulg'd by certain
    fame,
To the Rhœtean shores old Teucrus came;
There fix'd, and there the seat of empire
    chose,
Ere Ilium and the Trojan tow'rs arose.   150
In humble vales they built their soft ⎫
    abodes,   ⎬
Till Cybele, the mother of the gods,   ⎭
With tinkling cymbals charm'd th' Idæan
    woods.
She secret rites and ceremonies taught,
And to the yoke the salvage lions brought.
Let us the land which Heav'n appoints, ex-
    plore;
Appease the winds, and seek the Gnossian
    shore.
If Jove assists the passage of our fleet,
The third propitious dawn discovers Crete.'
Thus having said, the sacrifices, laid   160
On smoking altars, to the gods he paid:
A bull, to Neptune an oblation due,
Another bull to bright Apollo slew;
A milk-white ewe, the western winds to
    please,
And one coal-black, to calm the stormy seas.
Ere this, a flying rumor had been spread
That fierce Idomeneus from Crete was fled,
Expell'd and exil'd; that the coast was free
Erom foreign or domestic enemy.
    " We leave the Delian ports, and put to
      sea;   170
By Naxos, fam'd for vintage, make our
    way;
Then green Donysa pass; and sail in sight
Of Paros' isle, with marble quarries white.

We pass the scatter'd isles of Cyclades,
That, scarce distinguish'd, seem to stud the
    seas.
The shouts of sailors double near the shores;
They stretch their canvas, and they ply
    their oars.
' All hands aloft ! for Crete ! for Crete !'
    they cry,
And swiftly thro' the foamy billows fly.
Full on the promis'd land at length we bore,
With joy descending on the Cretan shore. 181
With eager haste a rising town I frame,
Which from the Trojan Pergamus I name:
The name itself was grateful; I exhort
To found their houses, and erect a fort.
Our ships are haul'd upon the yellow
    strand;
The youth begin to till the labor'd land;
And I myself new marriages promote,
Give laws, and dwellings I divide by lot;
When rising vapors choke the wholesome
    air,   190
And blasts of noisome winds corrupt the
    year;
The trees devouring caterpillars burn;
Parch'd was the grass, and blighted was the
    corn:
Nor scape the beasts; for Sirius, from on ⎫
    high,   ⎬
With pestilential heat infects the sky: ⎪
My men — some fall, the rest in fevers ⎭
    fry.
Again my father bids me seek the shore
Of sacred Delos, and the god implore,
To learn what end of woes we might ex-
    pect,   199
And to what clime our weary course direct.
    " 'T was night, when ev'ry creature, void
      of cares,
The common gift of balmy slumber shares:
The statues of my gods (for such they
    seem'd),
Those gods whom I from flaming Troy re-
    deem'd,
Before me stood, majestically bright,
Full in the beams of Phœbe's ent'ring light.
Then thus they spoke, and eas'd my
    troubled mind:
' What from the Delian god thou go'st to
    find,
He tells thee here, and sends us to relate.
Those pow'rs are we, companions of thy
    fate,   210
Who from the burning town by thee were
    brought,

Thy fortune follow'd, and thy safety
    wrought.
Thro' seas and lands as we thy steps attend,
So shall our care thy glorious race befriend.
An ample realm for thee thy fates ordain,
A town that o'er the conquer'd world shall
    reign.
Thou, mighty walls for mighty nations
    build;
Nor let thy weary mind to labors yield:
But change thy seat; for not the Delian
    god,
Nor we, have giv'n thee Crete for our
    abode.   220
A land there is, Hesperia call'd of old,
(The soil is fruitful, and the natives bold —
Th' Œnotrians held it once,) by later fame
Now call'd Italia, from the leader's name.
Iasius there and Dardanus were born;
From thence we came, and thither must
    return.
Rise, and thy sire with these glad tidings
    greet.
Search Italy; for Jove denies thee Crete.'
" Astonish'd at their voices and their
    sight,
(Nor were they dreams, but visions of the
    night;   230
I saw, I knew their faces, and descried,
In perfect view, their hair with fillets tied;)
I started from my couch; a clammy sweat
On all my limbs and shiv'ring body sate.
To heav'n I lift my hands with pious haste,
And sacred incense in the flames I cast.
Thus to the gods their perfect honors done,
More cheerful, to my good old sire I run,
And tell the pleasing news. In little space
He found his error of the double race; 240
Not, as before he deem'd, deriv'd from
    Crete;
No more deluded by the doubtful seat:
Then said: ' O son, turmoil'd in Trojan
    fate !
Such things as these Cassandra did relate.
This day revives within my mind what she
Foretold of Troy renew'd in Italy,
And Latian lands; but who could then ⎫
    have thought   ⎪
That Phrygian gods to Latium should be ⎬
    brought,   ⎪
Or who believ'd what mad Cassandra ⎭
    taught ?
Now let us go where Phœbus leads the
    way.'   250
" He said; and we with glad consent obey,

Forsake the seat, and, leaving few behind,
We spread our sails before the willing wind.
Now from the sight of land our galleys
    move,
With only seas around and skies above;
When o'er our heads descends a burst of
    rain,
And night with sable clouds involves the
    main;
The ruffling winds the foamy billows raise;
The scatter'd fleet is forc'd to sev'ral ways;
The face of heav'n is ravish'd from our
    eyes,   260
And in redoubled peals the roaring thunder
    flies.
Cast from our course, we wander in the
    dark;
No stars to guide, no point of land to mark.
Ev'n Palinurus no distinction found
Betwixt the night and day; such darkness
    reign'd around.
Three starless nights the doubtful navy
    strays,
Without distinction, and three sunless days;
The fourth renews the light, and, from our
    shrouds,
We view a rising land, like distant clouds;
The mountain-tops confirm the pleasing
    sight,   270
And curling smoke ascending from their
    height.
The canvas falls; their oars the sailors ply;
From the rude strokes the whirling waters
    fly.
At length I land upon the Strophades,
Safe from the danger of the stormy seas.
Those isles are compass'd by th' Ionian
    main,
The dire abode where the foul Harpies reign,
Forc'd by the winged warriors to repair
To their old homes, and leave their costly
    fare.
Monsters more fierce offended Heav'n ne'er
    sent   280
From hell's abyss, for human punishment:
With virgin faces, but with wombs ob- ⎫
    scene,   ⎪
Foul paunches, and with ordure still ⎬
    unclean;   ⎪
With claws for hands, and looks for ever ⎭
    lean.
" We landed at the port, and soon beheld
Fat herds of oxen graze the flow'ry field,
And wanton goats without a keeper stray'd.
With weapons we the welcome prey invade,

Then call the gods for partners of our feast,
And Jove himself, the chief invited guest.
We spread the tables on the greensward ground; 291
We feed with hunger, and the bowls go round;
When from the mountain-tops, with hideous cry,
And clatt'ring wings, the hungry Harpies fly:
They snatch the meat, defiling all they find,
And, parting, leave a loathsome stench behind.
Close by a hollow rock, again we sit,
New dress the dinner, and the beds refit,
Secure from sight, beneath a pleasing shade,
Where tufted trees a native arbor made.
Again the holy fires on altars burn; 301
And once again the rav'nous birds return,
Or from the dark recesses where they lie,
Or from another quarter of the sky;
With filthy claws their odious meal repeat,
And mix their loathsome ordures with their meat.
I bid my friends for vengeance then prepare,
And with the hellish nation wage the war.
They, as commanded, for the fight provide,
And in the grass their glitt'ring weapons hide; 310
Then, when along the crooked shore we hear
Their clatt'ring wings, and saw the foes appear,
Misenus sounds a charge: we take th' alarm,
And our strong hands with swords and bucklers arm.
In this new kind of combat all employ
Their utmost force, the monsters to destroy.
In vain — the fated skin is proof to wounds;
And from their plumes the shining sword rebounds.
At length rebuff'd, they leave their mangled prey,
And their stretch'd pinions to the skies display. 320
Yet one remain'd — the messenger of Fate:
High on a craggy cliff Celæno sate,
And thus her dismal errand did relate:

' What ! not contented with our oxen slain,
Dare you with Heav'n an impious war maintain,
And drive the Harpies from their native reign ?
Heed therefore what I say; and keep in mind
What Jove decrees, what Phœbus has design'd,
And I, the Furies' queen, from both relate —
You seek th' Italian shores, foredoom'd by fate: 330
Th' Italian shores are granted you to find,
And a safe passage to the port assign'd.
But know, that ere your promis'd walls you build,
My curses shall severely be fulfill'd.
Fierce famine is your lot for this misdeed,
Reduc'd to grind the plates on which you feed.'
She said, and to the neighb'ring forest flew.
Our courage fails us, and our fears renew.
Hopeless to win by war, to pray'rs we fall,
And on th' offended Harpies humbly call, 340
And whether gods or birds obscene they were,
Our vows for pardon and for peace prefer.
But old Anchises, off'ring sacrifice,
And lifting up to heav'n his hands and eyes,
Ador'd the greater gods : ' Avert,' said he,
' These omens; render vain this prophecy,
And from th' impending curse a pious people free ! '
" Thus having said, he bids us put to sea;
We loose from shore our haulsers, and obey,
And soon with swelling sails pursue the wat'ry way. 350
Amidst our course, Zacynthian woods appear;
And next by rocky Neritos we steer:
We fly from Ithaca's detested shore,
And curse the land which dire Ulysses bore.
At length Leucate's cloudy top appears,
And the Sun's temple, which the sailor fears.
Resolv'd to breathe a while from labor past,
Our crooked anchors from the prow we cast,
And joyful to the little city haste.

Here, safe beyond our hopes, our vows we
    pay   360
To Jove, the guide and patron of our way.
The customs of our country we pursue,
And Trojan games on Actian shores renew.
Our youth their naked limbs besmear with
    oil,
And exercise the wrastlers' noble toil;
Pleas'd to have sail'd so long before the
    wind,
And left so many Grecian towns behind.
The sun had now fulfill'd his annual course,
And Boreas on the seas display'd his
    force:
I fix'd upon the temple's lofty door   370
The brazen shield which vanquish'd Abas
    bore;
The verse beneath my name and action
    speaks:
'These arms Æneas took from conqu'ring
    Greeks.'
Then I command to weigh; the seamen ply
Their sweeping oars; the smoking billows
    fly.
The sight of high Phæacia soon we lost,
And skimm'd along Epirus' rocky coast.
  "Then to Chaonia's port our course we
    bend,
And, landed, to Buthrotus' heights ascend.
Here wondrous things were loudly blaz'd
    by fame: 380
How Helenus reviv'd the Trojan name,
And reign'd in Greece; that Priam's cap-
    tive son
Succeeded Pyrrhus in his bed and throne;
And fair Andromache, restor'd by fate,
Once more was happy in a Trojan mate.
I leave my galleys riding in the port,
And long to see the new Dardanian court.
By chance, the mournful queen, before the
    gate,
Then solemniz'd her former husband's fate.
Green altars, rais'd of turf, with gifts ⎤
    she crown'd,   390 |
And sacred priests in order stand around, ⎬
And thrice the name of hapless Hector |
    sound.   ⎦
The grove itself resembles Ida's wood;
And Simoïs seem'd the well-dissembled
    flood.
But when at nearer distance she beheld
My shining armor and my Trojan shield,
Astonish'd at the sight, the vital heat
Forsakes her limbs; her veins no longer
    beat:

She faints, she falls, and scarce recov'ring
    strength,
Thus, with a falt'ring tongue, she speaks at
    length: 400
  "'Are you alive, O goddess-born?' she
    said,
'Or if a ghost, then where is Hector's
    shade?'
At this, she cast a loud and frightful cry.
With broken words I made this brief reply:
'All of me that remains appears in sight;
I live, if living be to loathe the light.
No phantom; but I drag a wretched life,
My fate resembling that of Hector's wife.
What have you suffer'd since you lost your
    lord?
By what strange blessing are you now
    restor'd?   410
Still are you Hector's? or is Hector fled,
And his remembrance lost in Pyrrhus'
    bed?'
With eyes dejected, in a lowly tone,
After a modest pause she thus begun:
  "'O only happy maid of Priam's race,
Whom death deliver'd from the foes'
    embrace!
Commanded on Achilles' tomb to die,   ⎤
Not forc'd, like us, to hard captivity, ⎬
Or in a haughty master's arms to lie. ⎦
In Grecian ships unhappy we were borne,
Endur'd the victor's lust, sustain'd the
    scorn: 421
Thus I submitted to the lawless pride
Of Pyrrhus, more a handmaid than a bride
Cloy'd with possession, he forsook my bed,
And Helen's lovely daughter sought to
    wed;
Then me to Trojan Helenus resign'd,
And his two slaves in equal marriage join'd
Till young Orestes, pierc'd with deep ⎤
    despair, |
And longing to redeem the promis'd fair, ⎬
Before Apollo's altar slew the ravisher. ⎦
By Pyrrhus' death the kingdom we re-
    gain'd: 431
At least one half with Helenus remain'd.
Our part, from Chaon, he Chaonia calls,
And names from Pergamus his rising
    walls.
But you, what fates have landed on our
    coast?
What gods have sent you, or what storms
    have toss'd?
Does young Ascanius life and health enjoy,
Sav'd from the ruins of unhappy Troy?

O tell me how his mother's loss he bears,
What hopes are promis'd from his bloom-
  ing years,   440
How much of Hector in his face ap-
  pears ? '
She spoke; and mix'd her speech with
  mournful cries,
And fruitless tears came trickling from her
  eyes.
  "At length her lord descends upon the
  plain,
In pomp, attended with a num'rous train;
Receives his friends, and to the city leads,
And tears of joy amidst his welcome sheds.
Proceeding on, another Troy I see,
Or, in less compass, Troy's epitome.
A riv'let by the name of Xanthus ran,   450
And I embrace the Scæan gate again.
My friends in porticoes were entertain'd,
And feasts and pleasures thro' the city
  reign'd.
The tables fill'd the spacious hall around,
And golden bowls with sparkling wine were
  crown'd.
Two days we pass'd in mirth, till friendly
  gales,
Blown from the south, supplied our swell-
  ing sails.
Then to the royal seer I thus began:
' O thou, who know'st, beyond the reach of
  man,
The laws of heav'n, and what the stars
  decree;   460
Whom Phœbus taught unerring pro-
  phecy,
From his own tripod, and his holy tree;
Skill'd in the wing'd inhabitants of air,
What auspices their notes and flights de-
  clare:
O say — for all religious rites portend
A happy voyage, and a prosp'rous end;
And ev'ry pow'r and omen of the sky
Direct my course for destin'd Italy;
But only dire Celæno, from the gods,
A dismal famine fatally forebodes —   470
O say what dangers I am first to shun,
What toils to vanquish, and what course to
  run.'
  "The prophet first with sacrifice adores
The greater gods; their pardon then im-
  plores;
Unbinds the fillet from his holy head;
To Phœbus, next, my trembling steps he
  led,
Full of religious doubts and awful dread.

Then, with his god possess'd, before the
  shrine,
These words proceeded from his mouth
  divine:
' O goddess-born, (for Heav'n's appointed
  will,   480
With greater auspices of good than ill,
Foreshows thy voyage, and thy course di-
  rects;
Thy fates conspire, and Jove himself pro-
  tects,)
Of many things some few I shall explain,
Teach thee to shun the dangers of the
  main,
And how at length the promis'd shore to
  gain.
The rest the fates from Helenus conceal,
And Juno's angry pow'r forbids to tell.
First, then, that happy shore, that seems
  so nigh,
Will far from your deluded wishes fly;   490
Long tracts of seas divide your hopes
  from Italy:
For you must cruise along Sicilian shores,
And stem the currents with your struggling
  oars;
Then round th' Italian coast your navy
  steer;
And, after this, to Circe's island veer;
And, last, before your new foundations
  rise,
Must pass the Stygian lake, and view the
  nether skies.
Now mark the signs of future ease and
  rest,
And bear them safely treasur'd in thy
  breast.
When, in the shady shelter of a wood,   500
And near the margin of a gentle flood,
Thou shalt behold a sow upon the ground,
With thirty sucking young encompass'd
  round;
The dam and offspring white as falling
  snow —
These on thy city shall their name be-
  stow,
And there shall end thy labors and thy
  woe.
Nor let the threaten'd famine fright thy
  mind,
For Phœbus will assist, and Fate the way
  will find.
Let not thy course to that ill coast be bent,
Which fronts from far th' Epirian con-
  tinent: 510

Those parts are all by Grecian foes pos-
sess'd;
The salvage Locrians here the shores infest;
There fierce Idomeneus his city builds,
And guards with arms the Salentinian
fields;
And on the mountain's brow Petilia stands,
Which Philoctetes with his troops com-
mands.
Ev'n when thy fleet is landed on the shore,
And priests with holy vows the gods adore,
Then with a purple veil involve your eyes,
Lest hostile faces blast the sacrifice.   520
These rites and customs to the rest com-
mend,
That to your pious race they may descend.
  "'When, parted hence, the wind, that
ready waits
For Sicily, shall bear you to the straits
Where proud Pelorus opes a wider way,
Tack to the larboard, and stand off to sea:
Veer starboard sea and land. Th' Italian
shore
And fair Sicilia's coast were one, before
An earthquake caus'd the flaw: the roar-⎤
ing tides   ⎟
The passage broke that land from land   ⎬
divides;   530   ⎟
And where the lands retir'd, the rushing   ⎦
ocean rides.
Distinguish'd by the straits, on either hand,
Now rising cities in long order stand,
And fruitful fields: so much can time in-
vade
The mold'ring work that beauteous Nature
made.
Far on the right, her dogs foul Scylla ⎤
hides;   ⎟
Charybdis roaring on the left presides,⎬
And in her greedy whirlpool sucks the ⎟
tides;   ⎦
Then spouts them from below: with fury
driv'n,
The waves mount up and wash the face of
heav'n.   540
But Scylla from her den, with open jaws,
The sinking vessel in her eddy draws,
Then dashes on the rocks. A human face,
And virgin bosom, hides her tail's disgrace:
Her parts obscene below the waves descend,
With dogs inclos'd, and in a dolphin end.
'T is safer, then, to bear aloof to sea,
And coast Pachynus, tho' with more delay,
Than once to view misshapen Scylla near,
And the loud yell of wat'ry wolves to hear.

  "'Besides, if faith to Helenus be due,
And if prophetic Phœbus tell me true,   552
Do not this precept of your friend forget,
Which therefore more than once I must
repeat:
Above the rest, great Juno's name adore;
Pay vows to Juno; Juno's aid implore.
Let gifts be to the mighty queen design'd,
And mollify with pray'rs her haughty mind.
Thus, at the length, your passage shall be
free,
And you shall safe descend on Italy.   560
Arriv'd at Cumæ, when you view the flood
Of black Avernus, and the sounding wood,
The mad prophetic Sibyl you shall find,
Dark in a cave, and on a rock reclin'd.
She sings the fates, and, in her frantic fits,
The notes and names, inscrib'd, to leafs
commits.
What she commits to leafs, in order laid,
Before the cavern's entrance are display'd:
Unmov'd they lie; but, if a blast of wind
Without, or vapors issue from behind,   570
The leafs are borne aloft in liquid air,
And she resumes no more her museful care,
Nor gathers from the rocks her scatter'd
verse,
Nor sets in order what the winds disperse.
Thus, many not succeeding, most upbraid⎤
The madness of the visionary maid,   ⎬
And with loud curses leave the mystic ⎟
shade.   ⎦
  "'Think it not loss of time a while to
stay,
Tho' thy companions chide thy long delay;
Tho' summon'd to the seas, tho' pleasing
gales   580
Invite thy course, and stretch thy swelling
sails:
But beg the sacred priestess to relate
With willing words, and not to write thy
fate.
The fierce Italian people she will show, ⎤
And all thy wars, and all thy future   ⎟
woe,   ⎬
And what thou may'st avoid, and what   ⎟
must undergo.   ⎦
She shall direct thy course, instruct thy
mind,
And teach thee how the happy shores to find.
This is what Heav'n allows me to relate:⎤
Now part in peace; pursue thy better   ⎟
fate,   590   ⎬
And raise, by strength of arms, the   ⎟
Trojan state.'   ⎦

" This when the priest with friendly voice
 declar'd,
He gave me license, and rich gifts pre-
 par'd:
Bounteous of treasure, he supplied my
 want
With heavy gold, and polish'd elephant;
Then Dodonæan caldrons put on board,
And ev'ry ship with sums of silver stor'd.
A trusty coat of mail to me he sent,
Thrice chain'd with gold, for use and orna-
 ment;
The helm of Pyrrhus added to the rest, 600
That flourish'd with a plume and waving
 crest.
Nor was my sire forgotten, nor my
 friends;
And large recruits he to my navy sends:
Men, horses, captains, arms, and warlike
 stores;
Supplies new pilots, and new sweeping
 oars.
Meantime, my sire commands to hoist our
 sails,
Lest we should lose the first auspicious
 gales.
 " The prophet bless'd the parting crew,
 and last,
With words like these, his ancient friend
 embrac'd: 609
' Old happy man, the care of gods above,
Whom heav'nly Venus honor'd with her
 love,
And twice preserv'd thy life, when Troy
 was lost,
Behold from far the wish'd Ausonian
 coast:
There land; but take a larger compass
 round,
For that before is all forbidden ground.
The shore that Phœbus has design'd for
 you,
At farther distance lies, conceal'd from
 view.
Go happy hence, and seek your new
 abodes,
Blest in a son, and favor'd by the gods:
For I with useless words prolong your
 stay,   620
When southern gales have summon'd you
 away.'
 " Nor less the queen our parting thence
 deplor'd,
Nor was less bounteous than her Trojan
 lord.

A noble present to my son she brought,
A robe with flow'rs on golden tissue
 wrought,
A Phrygian vest; and loads with gifts
 beside
Of precious texture, and of Asian pride.
' Accept,' she said, ' these monuments of
 love,
Which in my youth with happier hands I
 wove:
Regard these trifles for the giver's sake; 630
'T is the last present Hector's wife can
 make.
Thou call'st my lost Astyanax to mind;
In thee his features and his form I find:
His eyes so sparkled with a lively flame;⎫
Such were his motions; such was all his ⎬
 frame;   ⎭
And ah ! had Heav'n so pleas'd, his years
 had been the same.'
 " With tears I took my last adieu, and
 said:
' Your fortune, happy pair, already made,
Leaves you no farther wish. My diff'rent
 state,
Avoiding one, incurs another fate.   640
To you a quiet seat the gods allow:
You have no shores to search, no seas to
 plow,
Nor fields of flying Italy to chase:
(Deluding visions, and a vain embrace !)
You see another Simoïs, and enjoy
The labor of your hands, another Troy,
With better auspice than her ancient
 tow'rs,
And less obnoxious to the Grecian pow'rs.
If e'er the gods, whom I with vows adore,
Conduct my steps to Tiber's happy shore;
If ever I ascend the Latian throne,   651
And build a city I may call my own;
As both of us our birth from Troy de-⎫
 rive,   ⎪
So let our kindred lines in concord live, ⎬
And both in acts of equal friendship ⎪
 strive.   ⎭
Our fortunes, good or bad, shall be the
 same:
The double Troy shall differ but in name;
That what we now begin may never end,
But long to late posterity descend.'
 " Near the Ceraunian rocks our course
 we bore;   660
The shortest passage to th' Italian shore.
Now had the sun withdrawn his radiant
 light,

And hills were hid in dusky shades of night:
We land, and, on the bosom of the ground,
A safe retreat and a bare lodging found.
Close by the shore we lay; the sailors keep
Their watches, and the rest securely sleep.
The night, proceeding on with silent pace,
Stood in her noon, and view'd with equal face
Her steepy rise and her declining race.
Then wakeful Palinurus rose, to spy 671
The face of heav'n, and the nocturnal sky;
And listen'd ev'ry breath of air to try;
Observes the stars, and notes their sliding course,
The Pleiads, Hyads, and their wat'ry force;
And both the Bears is careful to behold,
And bright Orion, arm'd with burnish'd gold.
Then, when he saw no threat'ning tempest nigh,
But a sure promise of a settled sky,
He gave the sign to weigh; we break our sleep, 680
Forsake the pleasing shore, and plow the deep.
" And now the rising morn with rosy light
Adorns the skies, and puts the stars to flight;
When we from far, like bluish mists, descry
The hills, and then the plains, of Italy.
Achates first pronounc'd the joyful sound;
Then, ' Italy ! ' the cheerful crew rebound.
My sire Anchises crown'd a cup with wine,
And, off'ring, thus implor'd the pow'rs divine:
' Ye gods, presiding over lands and seas,
And you who raging winds and waves appease, 691
Breathe on our swelling sails a prosp'rous wind,
And smooth our passage to the port assign'd ! '
The gentle gales their flagging force renew,
And now the happy harbor is in view.
Minerva's temple then salutes our sight,
Plac'd, as a landmark, on the mountain's height.
We furl our sails, and turn the prows to shore;

The curling waters round the galleys roar.
The land lies open to the raging east, 700
Then, bending like a bow, with rocks compress'd,
Shuts out the storms; the winds and waves complain,
And vent their malice on the cliffs in vain.
The port lies hid within; on either side
Two tow'ring rocks the narrow mouth divide.
The temple, which aloft we view'd before,
To distance flies, and seems to shun the shore.
Scarce landed, the first omens I beheld
Were four white steeds that cropp'd the flow'ry field.
' War, war is threaten'd from this foreign ground,' 710
My father cried, ' where warlike steeds are found.
Yet, since reclaim'd to chariots they submit,
And bend to stubborn yokes, and champ the bit,
Peace may succeed to war.' Our way we bend
To Pallas, and the sacred hill ascend;
There prostrate to the fierce *virago* pray,
Whose temple was the landmark of our way.
Each with a Phrygian mantle veil'd his head,
And all commands of Helenus obey'd,
And pious rites to Grecian Juno paid. 720
These dues perform'd, we stretch our sails, and stand
To sea, forsaking that suspected land.
" From hence Tarentum's bay appears in view,
For Hercules renown'd, if fame be true.
Just opposite, Lacinian Juno stands;
Caulonian tow'rs, and Scylacæan strands,
For shipwrecks fear'd. Mount Ætna thence we spy,
Known by the smoky flames which cloud the sky.
Far off we hear the waves with surly sound
Invade the rocks, the rocks their groans rebound. 730
The billows break upon the sounding strand,
And roll the rising tide, impure with sand.
Then thus Anchises, in experience old:
' 'T is that Charybdis which the seer foretold,

And those the promis'd rocks ! Bear off to
   sea ! '
With haste the frighted mariners obey.
First Palinurus to the larboard veer'd;
Then all the fleet by his example steer'd.
To heav'n aloft on ridgy waves we ride,
Then down to hell descend, when they
   divide;   740
And thrice our galleys knock'd the stony
   ground,
And thrice the hollow rocks return'd the
   sound,
And thrice we saw the stars, that stood
   with dews around.
The flagging winds forsook us, with the sun;
And, wearied, on Cyclopian shores we run.
The port capacious, and secure from wind,
Is to the foot of thund'ring Ætna join'd.
By turns a pitchy cloud she rolls on high;
By turns hot embers from her entrails
   fly,
And flakes of mounting flames, that lick
   the sky.   750
Oft from her bowels massy rocks are
   thrown,
And, shiver'd by the force, come piecemeal
   down.
Oft liquid lakes of burning sulphur flow,
Fed from the fiery springs that boil below.
Enceladus, they say, transfix'd by Jove,
With blasted limbs came tumbling from
   above;
And, where he fell, th' avenging father
   drew
This flaming hill, and on his body threw.
As often as he turns his weary sides,
He shakes the solid isle, and smoke the
   heavens hides.   760
In shady woods we pass the tedious
   night,
Where bellowing sounds and groans our
   souls affright,
Of which no cause is offer'd to the sight;
For not one star was kindled in the sky,
Nor could the moon her borrow'd light
   supply;
For misty clouds involv'd the firmament,
The stars were muffled, and the moon was
   pent.
  " Scarce had the rising sun the day re-
   veal'd,
Scarce had his heat the pearly dews dis-
   pell'd,
When from the woods there bolts, before
   our sight,   770

Somewhat betwixt a mortal and a sprite,
So thin, so ghastly meager, and so wan,
So bare of flesh, he scarce resembled man.
This thing, all tatter'd, seem'd from far
   t' implore
Our pious aid, and pointed to the shore.
We look behind, then view his shaggy
   beard;
His clothes were tagg'd with thorns, and
   filth his limbs besmear'd;
The rest, in mien, in habit, and in face,
Appear'd a Greek, and such indeed he was.
He cast on us, from far, a frightful view, 780
Whom soon for Trojans and for foes he
   knew;
Stood still, and paus'd; then all at once
   began
To stretch his limbs, and trembled as he
   ran.
Soon as approach'd, upon his knees he falls,
And thus with tears and sighs for pity
   calls:
' Now, by the pow'rs above, and what we
   share
From Nature's common gift, this vital air,
O Trojans, take me hence ! I beg no more;
But bear me far from this unhappy shore.
'Tis true, I am a Greek, and farther own, 790
Among your foes besieg'd th' imperial town.
For such demerits if my death be due,
No more for this abandon'd life I sue;
This only favor let my tears obtain,
To throw me headlong in the rapid main:
Since nothing more than death my crime
   demands,
I die content, to die by human hands.'
He said, and on his knees my knees em-
   brac'd:
I bade him boldly tell his fortune past,
His present state, his lineage, and his name,
Th' occasion of his fears, and whence he
   came.   801
The good Anchises rais'd him with his
   hand;
Who, thus encourag'd, answer'd our de-
   mand:
' From Ithaca, my native soil, I came
To Troy; and Achæmenides my name.
Me my poor father with Ulysses sent;
(O had I stay'd, with poverty content !)
But, fearful for themselves, my country-
   men
Left me forsaken in the Cyclops' den.
The cave, tho' large, was dark; the dismal
   floor   810

Was pav'd with mangled limbs and putrid
  gore.
Our monstrous host, of more than human
  size,
Erects his head, and stares within the skies;
Bellowing his voice, and horrid is his hue.
Ye gods, remove this plague from mortal
  view !
The joints of slaughter'd wretches are his
  food;
And for his wine he quaffs the streaming
  blood.
These eyes beheld, when with his spacious
  hand
He seiz'd two captives of our Grecian band;
Stretch'd on his back, he dash'd against the
  stones   820
Their broken bodies, and their crackling
  bones:
With spouting blood the purple pavement
  swims,
While the dire glutton grinds the trem-
  bling limbs.
" ' Not unreveng'd Ulysses bore their fate,
Nor thoughtless of his own unhappy state;
For, gorg'd with flesh, and drunk with human
  wine,
While fast asleep the giant lay supine,
Snoring aloud, and belching from his maw
His indigested foam, and morsels raw;
We pray; we cast the lots, and then sur-
  round   830
The monstrous body, stretch'd along the
  ground:
Each, as he could approach him, lends a
  hand
To bore his eyeball with a flaming brand.
Beneath his frowning forehead lay his eye;
For only one did the vast frame supply —
But that a globe so large, his front it fill'd,
Like the sun's disk or like a Grecian shield.
The stroke succeeds; and down the pupil
  bends:
This vengeance follow'd for our slaugh-
  ter'd friends.
But haste, unhappy wretches, haste to fly ! 840
Your cables cut, and on your oars rely !
Such, and so vast as Polypheme appears,
A hundred more this hated island bears:
Like him, in caves they shut their woolly
  sheep;
Like him, their herds on tops of moun-
  tains keep;
Like him, with mighty strides, they stalk
  from steep to steep.

And now three moons their sharpen'd horns
  renew,
Since thus, in woods and wilds, obscure
  from view,
I drag my loathsome days with mortal
  fright,
And in deserted caverns lodge by night; 850
Oft from the rocks a dreadful prospect
  see
Of the huge Cyclops, like a walking tree:
From far I hear his thund'ring voice re-
  sound,
And trampling feet that shake the solid
  ground.
Cornels and salvage berries of the wood,
And roots and herbs, have been my meager
  food.
While all around my longing eyes I cast,
I saw your happy ships appear at last.
On those I fix'd my hopes, to these I run;
'T is all I ask, this cruel race to shun; 860
What other death you please, yourselves
  bestow.'
  " Scarce had he said, when on the moun-
  tain's brow
We saw the giant shepherd stalk before
His following flock, and leading to the
  shore:
A monstrous bulk, deform'd, depriv'd of
  sight;
His staff a trunk of pine, to guide his steps
  aright.
His pond'rous whistle from his neck de-
  scends;
His woolly care their pensive lord attends:
This only solace his hard fortune sends.
Soon as he reach'd the shore and touch'd
  the waves,   870
From his bor'd eye the gutt'ring blood he
  laves:
He gnash'd his teeth, and groan'd; thro'
  seas he strides,
And scarce the topmost billows touch'd his
  sides.
  " Seiz'd with a sudden fear, we run to
  sea,
The cables cut, and silent haste away;
The well-deserving stranger entertain;
Then, buckling to the work, our oars divide
  the main.
The giant harken'd to the dashing sound:
But, when our vessels out of reach he found,
He strided onward, and in vain essay'd 880
Th' Ionian deep, and durst no farther
  wade.

With that he roar'd aloud: the dreadful ⎤
 cry   ⎬
Shakes earth, and air, and seas; the bil- ⎭
 lows fly
Before the bellowing noise to distant Italy.
The neighb'ring Ætna trembling all around,
The winding caverns echo to the sound.
His brother Cyclops hear the yelling roar,
And, rushing down the mountains, crowd
 the shore.
We saw their stern distorted looks, from
 far,
And one-eye'd glance, that vainly threaten'd
 war: 890
A dreadful council, with their heads on
 high;
(The misty clouds about their foreheads
 fly;)
Not yielding to the tow'ring tree of Jove,
Or tallest cypress of Diana's grove.
New pangs of mortal fear our minds ⎤
 assail;   ⎬
We tug at ev'ry oar, and hoist up ev'ry ⎮
 sail,   ⎬
And take th' advantage of the friendly ⎮
 gale.   ⎭
Forewarn'd by Helenus, we strive to shun
Charybdis' gulf, nor dare to Scylla run.
An equal fate on either side appears: 900
We, tacking to the left, are free from
 fears;
For, from Pelorus' point, the North arose,
And drove us back where swift Pantagias
 flows.
His rocky mouth we pass, and make our
 way
By Thapsus and Megara's winding bay.
This passage Achæmenides had shown,
Tracing the course which he before had
 run.
  "Right o'er against Plemmyrium's
 wat'ry strand,
There lies an isle, once call'd th' Ortygian
 land.
Alpheüs, as old fame reports, has found
From Greece a secret passage under
 ground,   911
By love to beauteous Arethusa led;
And, mingling here, they roll in the same
 sacred bed.
As Helenus enjoin'd, we next adore
Diana's name, protectress of the shore.
With prosp'rous gales we pass the quiet
 sounds
Of still Elorus, and his fruitful bounds.

Then, doubling Cape Pachynus, we survey
The rocky shore extended to the sea.
The town of Camarine from far we see,
And fenny lake, undrain'd by fate's de-
 cree.   921
In sight of the Geloan fields we pass,
And the large walls, where mighty Gela
 was;
Then Agragas with lofty summets crown'd,
Long for the race of warlike steeds re-
 nown'd.
We pass'd Selinus, and the palmy land, ⎤
And widely shun the Lilybæan strand, ⎬
Unsafe, for secret rocks and moving ⎮
 sand.   ⎭
At length on shore the weary fleet ar-
 riv'd,   929
Which Drepanum's unhappy port receiv'd.
Here, after endless labors, often toss'd ⎤
By raging storms, and driv'n on ev'ry ⎬
 coast,   ⎬
My dear, dear father, spent with age, I ⎮
 lost: ⎭
Ease of my cares, and solace of my pain,
Sav'd thro' a thousand toils, but sav'd in
 vain.
The prophet, who my future woes re-
 veal'd,
Yet this, the greatest and the worst, con-
 ceal'd;
And dire Celæno, whose foreboding skill
Denounc'd all else, was silent of this ill.
This my last labor was. Some friendly
 god   940
From thence convey'd us to your blest
 abode."
  Thus, to the list'ning queen, the royal
 guest
His wand'ring course and all his toils ex-
 press'd;
And here concluding, he retir'd to rest.

THE FOURTH BOOK OF THE ÆNEIS

THE ARGUMENT

Dido discovers to her sister her passion for
Æneas, and her thoughts of marrying him.
She prepares a hunting match for his entertainment. Juno, by Venus's consent, raises
a storm, which separates the hunters, and
drives Æneas and Dido into the same cave,
where their marriage is suppos'd to be
completed. Jupiter dispatches Mercury to

Æneas, to warn him from Carthage. Æneas secretly prepares for his voyage. Dido finds out his design, and, to put a stop to it, makes use of her own and her sister's entreaties, and discovers all the variety of passions that are incident to a neglected lover. When nothing would prevail upon him, she contrives her own death, with which this book concludes.

BUT anxious cares already seiz'd the queen:
She fed within her veins a flame unseen;
The hero's valor, acts, and birth inspire
Her soul with love, and fan the secret fire.
His words, his looks, imprinted in her heart,
Improve the passion, and increase the smart.
Now, when the purple morn had chas'd away
The dewy shadows, and restor'd the day,
Her sister first with early care she sought,
And thus in mournful accents eas'd her thought: 10
" My dearest Anna, what new dreams affright
My lab'ring soul ! what visions of the night
Disturb my quiet, and distract my breast
With strange ideas of our Trojan guest !
His worth, his actions, and majestic air,
A man descended from the gods declare.
Fear ever argues a degenerate kind;
His birth is well asserted by his mind.
Then, what he suffer'd, when by Fate betray'd !
What brave attempts for falling Troy he made!   20
Such were his looks, so gracefully he spoke,
That, were I not resolv'd against the yoke
Of hapless marriage, never to be curst
With second love, so fatal was my first,
To this one error I might yield again;
For, since Sichæus was untimely slain,
This only man is able to subvert
The fix'd foundations of my stubborn heart.
And, to confess my frailty, to my shame, ⎫
Somewhat I find within, if not the same, 30 ⎬
Too like the sparkles of my former flame. ⎭
But first let yawning earth a passage rend,
And let me thro' the dark abyss descend;
First let avenging Jove, with flames ⎫
from high, ⎪
Drive down this body to the nether sky, ⎬
Condemn'd with ghosts in endless night ⎪
to lie, ⎭

Before I break the plighted faith I gave ! ⎫
No ! he who had my vows shall ever ⎪
have; ⎬
For, whom I lov'd on earth, I worship in ⎪
the grave." ⎭
She said: the tears ran gushing from her eyes,   40
And stopp'd her speech. Her sister thus replies:
" O dearer than the vital air I breathe,
Will you to grief your blooming years bequeath,
Condemn'd to waste in woes your lonely life,
Without the joys of mother or of wife ?
Think you these tears, this pompous train of woe,
Are known or valued by the ghosts below ?
I grant that, while your sorrows yet were green,
It well became a woman, and a queen,
The vows of Tyrian princes to neglect,   50
To scorn Hyarbas, and his love reject,
With all the Libyan lords of mighty name;
But will you fight against a pleasing flame !
This little spot of land, which Heav'n bestows,
On ev'ry side is hemm'd with warlike foes;
Gætulian cities here are spread around,
And fierce Numidians there your frontiers bound;
Here lies a barren waste of thirsty land,
And there the Syrtes raise the moving sand;
Barcæan troops besiege the narrow shore, 60
And from the sea Pygmalion threatens more.
Propitious Heav'n, and gracious Juno, lead
This wand'ring navy to your needful aid:
How will your empire spread, your city rise,
From such a union, and with such allies !
Implore the favor of the pow'rs above,
And leave the conduct of the rest to love.
Continue still your hospitable way,
And still invent occasions of their stay,
Till storms and winter winds shall cease to threat,   70
And planks and oars repair their shatter'd fleet."
These words, which from a friend and ⎫
sister came, ⎪
With ease resolv'd the scruples of her ⎬
fame, ⎪
And added fury to the kindled flame. ⎭
Inspir'd with hope, the project they pursue;

On ev'ry altar sacrifice renew:
A chosen ewe of two years old they pay
To Ceres, Bacchus, and the God of Day;
Preferring Juno's pow'r, for Juno ties
The nuptial knot and makes the marriage
    joys.   80
The beauteous queen before her altar
    stands,
And holds the golden goblet in her hands.
A milk-white heifer she with flow'rs
    adorns,
And pours the ruddy wine betwixt her
    horns;
And, while the priests with pray'r the gods
    invoke,
She feeds their altars with Sabæan smoke,
With hourly care the sacrifice renews,
And anxiously the panting entrails views.
What priestly rites, alas! what pious art,
What vows avail to cure a bleeding
    heart!   90
A gentle fire she feeds within her veins,
Where the soft god secure in silence
    reigns.
    Sick with desire, and seeking him she
    loves,
From street to street the raving Dido
    roves.
So when the watchful shepherd, from the
    blind,
Wounds with a random shaft the careless
    hind,
Distracted with her pain she flies the woods,
Bounds o'er the lawn, and seeks the silent
    floods,
With fruitless care; for still the fatal dart
Sticks in her side, and rankles in her
    heart.   100
And now she leads the Trojan chief along
The lofty walls, amidst the busy throng;
Displays her Tyrian wealth, and rising
    town,
Which love, without his labor, makes his
    own.
This pomp she shows, to tempt her
    wand'ring guest;
Her falt'ring tongue forbids to speak the
    rest.
When day declines, and feasts renew the
    night,
Still on his face she feeds her famish'd
    sight;
She longs again to hear the prince relate
His own adventures and the Trojan
    fate.   110

He tells it o'er and o'er; but still in vain,
For still she begs to hear it once again.
The hearer on the speaker's mouth de-
    pends,
And thus the tragic story never ends.
    Then, when they part, when Phœbe's
    paler light
Withdraws, and falling stars to sleep in-
    vite,
She last remains, when ev'ry guest is gone,
Sits on the bed he press'd, and sighs alone;
Absent, her absent hero sees and hears;
Or in her bosom young Ascanius bears, 120
And seeks the father's image in the child,
If love by likeness might be so beguil'd.
    Meantime the rising tow'rs are at a
    stand;
No labors exercise the youthful band,
Nor use of arts, nor toils of arms they
    know;
The mole is left unfinish'd to the foe;
The mounds, the works, the walls, neg-
    lected lie,
Short of their promis'd heighth, that seem'd
    to threat the sky.
    But when imperial Juno, from above,
Saw Dido fetter'd in the chains of love, 130
Hot with the venom which her veins in-
    flam'd,
And by no sense of shame to be reclaim'd,
With soothing words to Venus she begun:
" High praises, endless honors, you have
    won,
And mighty trophies, with your worthy
    son!
Two gods a silly woman have undone!
Nor am I ignorant, you both suspect
This rising city, which my hands erect:
But shall celestial discord never cease?
'T is better ended in a lasting peace.   140
You stand possess'd of all your soul
    desir'd:
Poor Dido with consuming love is fir'd.
Your Trojan with my Tyrian let us join;⎫
So Dido shall be yours, Æneas mine: ⎬
One common kingdom, one united line. ⎭
Eliza shall a Dardan lord obey,
And lofty Carthage for a dow'r convey."
Then Venus, who her hidden fraud de- ⎫
    scried, ⎪
Which would the scepter of the world ⎬
    misguide ⎪
To Libyan shores, thus artfully replied: ⎭
" Who, but a fool, would wars with Juno
    choose,   151

And such alliance and such gifts refuse,
If Fortune with our joint desires comply?
The doubt is all from Jove and destiny;
Lest he forbid, with absolute command,
To mix the people in one common land —
Or will the Trojan and the Tyrian line
In lasting leagues and sure succession
join?
But you, the partner of his bed and throne,
May move his mind; my wishes are your
own."   160
"Mine," said imperial Juno, "be the
care;
Time urges, now, to perfect this affair:
Attend my counsel, and the secret share.
When next the Sun his rising light dis-
plays,
And gilds the world below with purple
rays,
The queen, Æneas, and the Tyrian court
Shall to the shady woods, for sylvan game,
resort.
There, while the huntsmen pitch their toils
around,
And cheerful horns from side to side re-
sound,
A pitchy cloud shall cover all the plain   170
With hail, and thunder, and tempestuous
rain;
The fearful train shall take their speedy
flight,
Dispers'd, and all involv'd in gloomy night;
One cave a grateful shelter shall afford
To the fair princess and the Trojan lord.
I will myself the bridal bed prepare,
If you, to bless the nuptials, will be there:
So shall their loves be crown'd with due
delights,
And Hymen shall be present at the rites."
The Queen of Love consents, and closely
smiles   180
At her vain project, and discover'd wiles.
The rosy morn was risen from the main,
And horns and hounds awake the princely
train:
They issue early thro' the city gate,
Where the more wakeful huntsmen ready
wait,
With nets, and toils, and darts, beside the
force
Of Spartan dogs, and swift Massylian
horse.
The Tyrian peers and officers of state
For the slow queen in antechambers wait;
Her lofty courser, in the court below,   190

Who his majestic rider seems to know,
Proud of his purple trappings, paws the
ground,
And champs the golden bit, and spreads
the foam around.
The queen at length appears; on either
hand
The brawny guards in martial order stand.
A flow'r'd simar with golden fringe she
wore,
And at her back a golden quiver bore;
Her flowing hair a golden caul restrains,
A golden clasp the Tyrian robe sustains.
Then young Ascanius, with a sprightly
grace,   200
Leads on the Trojan youth to view the chase.
But far above the rest in beauty shines
The great Æneas, when the troop he joins;
Like fair Apollo, when he leaves the frost
Of wint'ry Xanthus, and the Lycian coast,
When to his native Delos he resorts,
Ordains the dances, and renews the sports;
Where painted Scythians, mix'd with Cretan
bands,
Before the joyful altars join their hands:
Himself, on Cynthus walking, sees below   210
The merry madness of the sacred show.
Green wreaths of bays his length of hair
inclose;
A golden fillet binds his awful brows;
His quiver sounds: not less the prince is
seen
In manly presence, or in lofty mien.
Now had they reach'd the hills, and
storm'd the seat
Of salvage beasts, in dens, their last
retreat.
The cry pursues the mountain goats: they
bound
From rock to rock, and keep the craggy
ground;
Quite otherwise the stags, a trembling ⎫
train,   220 ⎬
In herds unsingled, scour the dusty plain, ⎪
And a long chase in open view maintain. ⎭
The glad Ascanius, as his courser guides,
Spurs thro' the vale, and these and those
outrides.
His horse's flanks and sides are forc'd to
feel
The clanking lash, and goring of the steel.
Impatiently he views the feeble prey,
Wishing some nobler beast to cross his way,
And rather would the tusky boar attend,
Or see the tawny lion downward bend.   230

Meantime, the gath'ring clouds obscure
    the skies:
From pole to pole the forky lightning flies;
The rattling thunders roll; and Juno pours
A wintry deluge down, and sounding
    show'rs.
The company, dispers'd, to coverts ride,
And seek the homely cots, or mountain's
    hollow side.
The rapid rains, descending from the hills,
To rolling torrents raise the creeping rills.
The queen and prince, as love or fortune
    guides,
One common cavern in her bosom hides. 240
Then first the trembling earth the signal
    gave,
And flashing fires enlighten all the cave;
Hell from below, and Juno from above,
And howling nymphs, were conscious to
    their love.
From this ill-omen'd hour in time arose
Debate and death, and all succeeding woes.
    The queen, whom sense of honor could
    not move,
No longer made a secret of her love,
But call'd it marriage, by that specious
    name
To veil the crime and sanctify the shame. 250
The loud report thro' Libyan cities goes.
Fame, the great ill, from small beginnings
    grows:
Swift from the first; and ev'ry moment
    brings
New vigor to her flights, new pinions to her
    wings.
Soon grows the pigmy to gigantic size;
Her feet on earth, her forehead in the
    skies.
Inrag'd against the gods, revengeful Earth
Produc'd her last of the Titanian birth.
Swift is her walk, more swift her winged
    haste:
A monstrous phantom, horrible and vast. 260
As many plumes as raise her lofty flight,
So many piercing eyes inlarge her sight;
Millions of opening mouths to Fame be-
    long,
And ev'ry mouth is furnish'd with a
    tongue,
And round with list'ning ears the flying
    plague is hung.
She fills the peaceful universe with cries;
No slumbers ever close her wakeful eyes;
By day, from lofty tow'rs her head she
    shews,

And spreads thro' trembling crowds disas-
    trous news;
With court informers haunts, and royal
    spies;   270
Things done relates, not done she feigns,
    and mingles truth with lies.
Talk is her business, and her chief delight
To tell of prodigies and cause affright.
She fills the people's ears with Dido's name,
Who, lost to honor and the sense of shame,
Admits into her throne and nuptial bed
A wand'ring guest, who from his country
    fled:
Whole days with him she passes in delights,
And wastes in luxury long winter nights,
Forgetful of her fame and royal trust,   280
Dissolv'd in ease, abandon'd to her lust.
    The goddess widely spreads the loud
    report,
And flies at length to King Hyarba's court.
When first possess'd with this unwelcome
    news,
Whom did he not of men and gods accuse?
This prince, from ravish'd Garamantis born,
A hundred temples did with spoils adorn,
In Ammon's honor, his celestial sire;
A hundred altars fed with wakeful fire;
And, thro' his vast dominions, priests or-
    dain'd,   290
Whose watchful care these holy rites main-
    tain'd.
The gates and columns were with garlands
    crown'd,
And blood of victim beasts enrich'd the
    ground.
    He, when he heard a fugitive could move
The Tyrian princess, who disdain'd his love,
His breast with fury burn'd, his eyes with
    fire,
Mad with despair, impatient with desire;
Then on the sacred altars pouring wine,
He thus adorn with pray'rs implor'd his sire
    divine:
"Great Jove! propitious to the Moorish
    race,   300
Who feast on painted beds, with off'rings
    grace
Thy temples, and adore thy pow'r divine
With blood of victims, and with sparkling
    wine,
Seest thou not this? or do we fear in vain
Thy boasted thunder, and thy thoughtless
    reign?
Do thy broad hands the forky lightnings
    lance?

Thine are the bolts, or the blind work of
  chance ?
A wand'ring woman builds, within our state,
A little town, bought at an easy rate;
She pays me homage, and my grants allow
A narrow space of Libyan lands to plow; 311
Yet, scorning me, by passion blindly led,
Admits a banish'd Trojan to her bed !
And now this other Paris, with his train
Of conquer'd cowards, must in Afric reign !
(Whom, what they are, their looks and
  garb confess,
Their locks with oil perfum'd, their Lydian
  dress.)
He takes the spoil, enjoys the princely
  dame;
And I, rejected I, adore an empty name."
  His vows, in haughty terms, he thus pre-
    ferr'd,   320
And held his altar's horns. The mighty
  Thund'rer heard;
Then cast his eyes on Carthage, where he
  found
The lustful pair in lawless pleasure
  drown'd,
Lost in their loves, insensible of shame,
And both forgetful of their better fame.
He calls Cyllenius, and the god attends,
By whom his menacing command he sends:
" Go, mount the western winds, and cleave
  the sky;
Then, with a swift descent, to Carthage
  fly:
There find the Trojan chief, who wastes his
  days   330
In slothful riot and inglorious ease,
Nor minds the future city, giv'n by fate.
To him this message from my mouth
  relate:
' Not so fair Venus hop'd, when twice she
  won
Thy life with pray'rs, nor promis'd such a
  son.
Hers was a hero, destin'd to command
A martial race, and rule the Latian land,
Who should his ancient line from Teucer
  draw,
And on the conquer'd world impose the
  law.'
If glory cannot move a mind so mean, 340
Nor future praise from fading pleasure
  wean,
Yet why should he defraud his son of fame,
And grudge the Romans their immortal
  name !

What are his vain designs ! what hopes h̲
  more
From his long ling'ring on a hostile shore,
Regardless to redeem his honor lost,
And for his race to gain th' Ausonian coast !
Bid him with speed the Tyrian court for-
  sake;
With this command the slumb'ring warrior
  wake."
  Hermes obeys; with golden pinions binds
His flying feet, and mounts the western
  winds: 351
And, whether o'er the seas or earth he
  flies,
With rapid force they bear him down the
  skies.
But first he grasps within his awful hand
The mark of sov'reign pow'r, his magic wand;
With this he draws the ghosts from hollow
  graves;
With this he drives them down the Stygian
  waves;
With this he seals in sleep the wakeful
  sight,
And eyes, tho' clos'd in death, restores to
  light.
Thus arm'd, the god begins his airy race, 360
And drives the racking clouds along the
  liquid space;
Now sees the tops of Atlas, as he flies,
Whose brawny back supports the starry
  skies;
Atlas, whose head, with piny forests crown'd,
Is beaten by the winds, with foggy vapors
  bound.
Snows hide his shoulders; from beneath his
  chin
The founts of rolling streams their race
  begin;
A beard of ice on his large breast depends.
Here, pois'd upon his wings, the god de-
  scends:
Then, rested thus, he from the tow'ring
  height   370
Plung'd downward, with precipitated flight,
Lights on the seas, and skims along the
  flood.
As waterfowl, who seek their fishy food,
Less, and yet less, to distant prospect show;
By turns they dance aloft, and dive below:
Like these, the steerage of his wings he
  plies,
And near the surface of the water flies,
Till, having pass'd the seas, and cross'd the
  sands,

He clos'd his wings, and stoop'd on Libyan
     lands:
Where shepherds once were hous'd in
     homely sheds,   380
Now tow'rs within the clouds advance their
     heads.
Arriving there, he found the Trojan prince
New ramparts raising for the town's de-
     fense.
A purple scarf, with gold embroider'd o'er,
(Queen Dido's gift,) about his waist he
     wore;
A sword, with glitt'ring gems diversified,
For ornament, not use, hung idly by his
     side.
     Then thus, with winged words, the god
          began,
Resuming his own shape: " Degenerate man,
Thou woman's property, what mak'st thou
     here,   390
These foreign walls and Tyrian tow'rs to
     rear,
Forgetful of thy own ? All-pow'rful Jove,
Who sways the world below and heav'n
     above,
Has sent me down with this severe command:
What means thy ling'ring in the Libyan
     land ?
If glory cannot move a mind so mean,
Nor future praise from flitting pleasure
     wean,
Regard the fortunes of thy rising heir:
The promis'd crown let young Ascanius
     wear,
To whom th' Ausonian scepter, and the
     state   400
Of Rome's imperial name is ow'd by fate.''
So spoke the god; and, speaking, took his
     flight,
Involv'd in clouds, and vanish'd out of sight.
     The pious prince was seiz'd with sudden
          fear;
Mute was his tongue, and upright stood his
     hair.
Revolving in his mind the stern command,
He longs to fly, and loathes the charming
     land.
What should he say ? or how should he ⎫
     begin ?   ⎪
What course, alas ! remains to steer be- ⎬
     tween   ⎪
Th' offended lover and the pow'rful ⎪
     queen ?   410 ⎭
This way and that he turns his anxious
     mind,

And all expedients tries, and none can find.
Fix'd on the deed, but doubtful of the
     means,
After long thought, to this advice he leans:
Three chiefs he calls, commands them to
     repair
The fleet, and ship their men with silent
     care;
Some plausible pretense he bids them find,
To color what in secret he design'd.
Himself, meantime, the softest hours would
     choose,
Before the love-sick lady heard the news;
And move her tender mind, by slow de-
     grees,   421
To suffer what the sov'reign pow'r decrees:
Jove will inspire him, when, and what to
     say.
They hear with pleasure, and with haste
     obey.
     But soon the queen perceives the thin
          disguise:
(What arts can blind a jealous woman's
     eyes !)
She was the first to find the secret fraud,
Before the fatal news was blaz'd abroad.
Love the first motions of the lover hears,
Quick to presage, and ev'n in safety fears.
Nor impious Fame was wanting to report ⎫
The ships repair'd, the Trojans' thick re- ⎪
     sort,   432 ⎬
And purpose to forsake the Tyrian court. ⎭
Frantic with fear, impatient of the wound,
And impotent of mind, she roves the city
     round.
Less wild the Bacchanalian dames ap- ⎫
     pear,   ⎪
When, from afar, their nightly god they ⎬
     hear,   ⎪
And howl about the hills, and shake the ⎪
     wreathy spear.   ⎭
At length she finds the dear perfidious man;
Prevents his form'd excuse, and thus began:
" Base and ungrateful ! could you hope to
     fly,   441
And undiscover'd scape a lover's eye ?
Nor could my kindness your compassion
     move,
Nor plighted vows, nor dearer bands of
     love ?
Or is the death of a despairing queen
Not worth preventing, tho' too well fore-
     seen ?
Ev'n when the wintry winds command your
     stay,

You dare the tempests, and defy the sea.
False as you are, suppose you were not
   bound
To lands unknown, and foreign coasts to
   sound;   450
Were Troy restor'd, and Priam's happy
   reign,
Now durst you tempt, for Troy, the raging
   main ?
See whom you fly ! am I the foe you shun ?
Now, by those holy vows, so late begun,
By this right hand, (since I have nothing
   more
To challenge, but the faith you gave be-
   fore;)
I beg you by these tears too truly shed,
By the new pleasures of our nuptial bed;
If ever Dido, when you most were kind,
Were pleasing in your eyes, or touch'd your
   mind;   460
By these my pray'rs, if pray'rs may yet
   have place,
Pity the fortunes of a falling race.
For you I have provok'd a tyrant's hate,
Incens'd the Libyan and the Tyrian state;
For you alone I suffer in my fame,
Bereft of honor, and expos'd to shame.
Whom have I now to trust, ungrateful
   guest ?
(That only name remains of all the rest !)
What have I left ? or whither can I fly ?
Must I attend Pygmalion's cruelty,   470
Or till Hyarba shall in triumph lead
A queen that proudly scorn'd his proffer'd
   bed ?
Had you deferr'd, at least, your hasty ⎤
   flight,   ⎮
And left behind some pledge of our de- ⎮
   light,   ⎬
Some babe to bless the mother's mourn- ⎮
   ful sight,   ⎦
Some young Æneas, to supply your place,
Whose features might express his father's
   face;
I should not then complain to live bereft
Of all my husband, or be wholly left."
   Here paus'd the queen. Unmov'd he ⎤
     holds his eyes,   480 ⎮
By Jove's command; nor suffer'd love to ⎬
   rise,   ⎮
Tho' heaving in his heart; and thus at ⎮
   length replies: ⎦
" Fair queen, you never can enough repeat
Your boundless favors, or I own my debt;
Nor can my mind forget Eliza's name,

While vital breath inspires this mortal
   frame.
This only let me speak in my defense:
I never hop'd a secret flight from hence,
Much less pretended to the lawful claim
Of sacred nuptials, or a husband's name. 490
For, if indulgent Heav'n would leave me
   free,
And not submit my life to fate's decree,
My choice would lead me to the Trojan ⎤
   shore,   ⎬
Those relics to review, their dust adore, ⎮
And Priam's ruin'd palace to restore. ⎦
But now the Delphian oracle commands,
And fate invites me to the Latian lands.
That is the promis'd place to which I steer,
And all my vows are terminated there.
If you, a Tyrian, and a stranger born,   500
With walls and tow'rs a Libyan town
   adorn,
Why may not we — like you, a foreign
   race —
Like you, seek shelter in a foreign place ?
As often as the night obscures the skies
With humid shades, or twinkling stars
   arise,
Anchises' angry ghost in dreams appears,
Chides my delay, and fills my soul with
   fears;
And young Ascanius justly may complain
Of his defrauded fate and destin'd reign.
Ev'n now the herald of the gods ap-
   pear'd: 510
Waking I saw him, and his message heard.
From Jove he came commission'd, heav'nly
   bright
With radiant beams, and manifest to sight
(The sender and the sent I both attest):
These walls he enter'd, and those words
   express'd.
Fair queen, oppose not what the gods
   command;
Forc'd by my fate, I leave your happy
   land."
   Thus while he spoke, already she began,
With sparkling eyes, to view the guilty
   man;
From head to foot survey'd his person
   o'er,   520
Nor longer these outrageous threats fore-
   bore:
" False as thou art, and, more than false,
   forsworn !
Not sprung from noble blood, nor goddess-
   born,

But hewn from harden'd entrails of a rock !
And rough Hyrcanian tigers gave thee
    suck !
Why should I fawn ? what have I worse ⎱
    to fear ?
Did he once look, or lent a list'ning ear, ⎬
Sigh'd when I sobb'd, or shed one kindly
    tear ? —
All symptoms of a base ungrateful mind,
So foul, that, which is worse, 't is hard to
    find.   530
Of man's injustice why should I complain ?
The gods, and Jove himself, behold in
    vain
Triumphant treason; yet no thunder ⎱
    flies,
Nor Juno views my wrongs with equal ⎬
    eyes;
Faithless is earth, and faithless are the
    skies !
Justice is fled, and Truth is now no more !
I sav'd the shipwrack'd exile on my shore;
With needful food his hungry Trojans
    fed;
I took the traitor to my throne and bed:
Fool that I was — 't is little to repeat   540
The rest — I stor'd and rigg'd his ruin'd
    fleet.
I rave, I rave ! A god's command he pleads,
And makes Heav'n accessary to his deeds.
Now Lycian lots, and now the Delian god,
Now Hermes is employ'd from Jove's abode,
To warn him hence; as if the peaceful
    state
Of heav'nly pow'rs were touch'd with human
    fate !
But go ! thy flight no longer I detain —
Go seek thy promis'd kingdom thro' the
    main !
Yet, if the heav'ns will hear my pious
    vow,   550
The faithless waves, not half so false as
    thou,
Or secret sands, shall sepulchers afford
To thy proud vessels, and their perjur'd
    lord.
Then shalt thou call on injur'd Dido's ⎱
    name:
Dido shall come in a black sulph'ry flame, ⎬
When death has once dissolv'd her mortal
    frame;
Shall smile to see the traitor vainly weep: ⎱
Her angry ghost, arising from the deep, ⎬
Shall haunt thee waking, and disturb thy
    sleep.

At least my shade thy punishment shall
    know,   560
And Fame shall spread the pleasing news
    below."
Abruptly here she stops; then turns away
Her loathing eyes, and shuns the sight of
    day.
Amaz'd he stood, revolving in his mind
What speech to frame, and what excuse to
    find.
Her fearful maids their fainting mistress
    led,
And softly laid her on her iv'ry bed.
But good Æneas, tho' he much desir'd
To give that pity which her grief requir'd;
Tho' much he mourn'd, and labor'd with his
    love,   570
Resolv'd at length, obeys the will of Jove;
Reviews his forces: they with early care
Unmoor their vessels, and for sea prepare.
The fleet is soon afloat, in all its pride,
And well-calk'd galleys in the harbor ride.
Then oaks for oars they fell'd; or, as they
    stood,
Of its green arms despoil'd the growing
    wood,
Studious of flight. The beach is cover'd
    o'er
With Trojan bands, that blacken all the
    shore:
On ev'ry side are seen, descending down, 580
Thick swarms of soldiers, loaden from the
    town.
Thus, in battalia, march embodied ants,
Fearful of winter, and of future wants,
T' invade the corn, and to their cells con-
    vey
The plunder'd forage of their yellow prey.
The sable troops, along the narrow tracks,
Scarce bear the weighty burthen on their
    backs:
Some set their shoulders to the pond'rous ⎱
    grain;
Some guard the spoil; some lash the ⎬
    lagging train;
All ply their sev'ral tasks, and equal toil
    sustain.   590
    What pangs the tender breast of Dido
    tore,
When, from the tow'r, she saw the cov-
    er'd shore,
And heard the shouts of sailors from afar,
Mix'd with the murmurs of the wat'ry war !
All-pow'rful Love ! what changes canst thou
    cause

In human hearts, subjected to thy laws!
Once more her haughty soul the tyrant
   bends:
To pray'rs and mean submissions she de-
   scends.
No female arts or aids she left untried,
Nor counsels unexplor'd, before she died. 600
"Look, Anna! look! the Trojans crowd to
   sea;
They spread their canvas, and their anchors
   weigh.
The shouting crew their ships with garlands
   bind,
Invoke the sea gods, and invite the wind.
Could I have thought this threat'ning blow
   so near,
My tender soul had been forewarn'd to
   bear.
But do not you my last request deny; ⎫
With you perfidious man your int'rest ⎪
   try,   ⎬
And bring me news, if I must live or ⎪
   die.   ⎭
You are his fav'rite; you alone can find 610
The dark recesses of his inmost mind:
In all his trusted secrets you have part,
And know the soft approaches to his heart.
Haste then, and humbly seek my haughty
   foe;
Tell him, I did not with the Grecians go,
Nor did my fleet against his friends em-
   ploy,
Nor swore the ruin of unhappy Troy,
Nor mov'd with hands profane his father's
   dust:
Why should he then reject a suit so just!
Whom does he shun, and whither would
   he fly!   620
Can he this last, this only pray'r deny!
Let him at least his dang'rous flight delay,
Wait better winds, and hope a calmer sea.
The nuptials he disclaims I urge no more:
Let him pursue the promis'd Latian shore.
A short delay is all I ask him now;
A pause of grief, an interval from woe,
Till my soft soul be temper'd to sustain
Accustom'd sorrows, and inur'd to pain.
If you in pity grant this one request,   630
My death shall glut the hatred of his
   breast."
This mournful message pious Anna bears,
And seconds with her own her sister's
   tears:
But all her arts are still employ'd in vain;
Again she comes, and is refus'd again.

His harden'd heart nor pray'rs nor threat'n-
   ings move;
Fate, and the god, had stopp'd his ears to
   love.
  As, when the winds their airy quarrel
   try,
Justling from ev'ry quarter of the sky,
This way and that the mountain oak they
   bend,   640
His boughs they shatter, and his branches
   rend;
With leaves and falling mast they spread
   the ground;
The hollow valleys echo to the sound:
Unmov'd, the royal plant their fury
   mocks,
Or, shaken, clings more closely to the
   rocks;
Far as he shoots his tow'ring head on high,
So deep in earth his fix'd foundations lie.
No less a storm the Trojan hero bears; ⎫
Thick messages and loud complaints he ⎪
   hears,   ⎬
And bandied words, still beating on his ⎪
   ears.   650 ⎭
Sighs, groans, and tears proclaim his in-
   ward pains;
But the firm purpose of his heart remains.
   The wretched queen, pursued by cruel
   fate,
Begins at length the light of heav'n to
   hate,
And loathes to live. Then dire portents
   she sees,
To hasten on the death her soul decrees:
Strange to relate! for when, before the
   shrine,
She pours in sacrifice the purple wine,
The purple wine is turn'd to putrid blood,
And the white offer'd milk converts to
   mud.   660
This dire presage. to her alone reveal'd,
From all, and ev'n her sister, she con-
   ceal'd.
A marble temple stood within the grove,
Sacred to death, and to her murther'd
   love;
That honor'd chapel she had hung around
With snowy fleeces, and with garlands
   crown'd:
Oft, when she visited this lonely dome,
Strange voices issued from her husband's
   tomb;
She thought she heard him summon her
   away,

Invite her to his grave, and chide her stay.
Hourly 't is heard, when with a boding
   note   671
The solitary screech owl strains her throat,
And, on a chimney's top, or turret's height,
With songs obscene disturbs the silence of
   the night.
Besides, old prophecies augment her fears;
And stern Æneas in her dreams appears,
Disdainful as by day: she seems, alone,
To wander in her sleep, thro' ways un-
   known,
Guideless and dark; or, in a desart plain,
To seek her subjects, and to seek in vain:
Like Pentheus, when, distracted with his
   fear,   681
He saw two suns, and double Thebes, ap-
   pear;
Or mad Orestes, when his mother's ghost
Full in his face infernal torches toss'd,
And shook her snaky locks: he shuns the ⎤
   sight, |
Flies o'er the stage, surpris'd with mor- |
   tal fright;   ⎬
The Furies guard the door and intercept |
   his flight.   ⎦
   Now, sinking underneath a load of grief,
From death alone she seeks her last relief;
The time and means resolv'd within her
   breast,   690
She to her mournful sister thus address'd
(Dissembling hope, her cloudy front she
   clears,
And a false vigor in her eyes appears):
"Rejoice!" she said.   "Instructed from
   above,
My lover I shall gain, or lose my love.
Nigh rising Atlas, next the falling sun,
Long tracts of Ethiopian climates run:
There a Massylian priestess I have found,
Honor'd for age, for magic arts renown'd:
Th' Hesperian temple was her trusted care;
'T was she supplied the wakeful dragon's
   fare.   701
She poppy seeds in honey taught to steep,
Reclaim'd his rage, and sooth'd him into
   sleep.
She watch'd the golden fruit; her charms
   unbind
The chains of love, or fix them on the
   mind:
She stops the torrents, leaves the channel
   dry,
Repels the stars, and backward bears the
   sky.

The yawning earth rebellows to her call,
Pale ghosts ascend, and mountain ashes
   fall.
Witness, ye gods, and thou my better part,
How loth I am to try this impious art! 711
Within the secret court, with silent care,
Erect a lofty pile, expos'd in air:
Hang on the topmost part the Trojan vest,
Spoils, arms, and presents, of my faithless
   guest.
Next, under these, the bridal bed be plac'd,
Where I my ruin in his arms embrac'd:
All relics of the wretch are doom'd to fire;
For so the priestess and her charms re-
   quire."
   Thus far she said, and farther speech for-
   bears;   720
A mortal paleness in her face appears:
Yet the mistrustless Anna could not find ⎤
The secret fun'ral in these rites de- |
   sign'd;   ⎬
Nor thought so dire a rage possess'd her |
   mind.   ⎦
Unknowing of a train conceal'd so well,
She fear'd no worse than when Sichæus fell;
Therefore obeys. The fatal pile they rear,
Within the secret court, expos'd in air.
The cloven holms and pines are heap'd on
   high,
And garlands on the hollow spaces lie. 730
Sad cypress, vervain, yew, compose the
   wreath,
And ev'ry baleful green denoting death.
The queen, determin'd to the fatal deed, ⎤
The spoils and sword he left, in order |
   spread,   ⎬
And the man's image on the nuptial bed. ⎦
   And now (the sacred altars plac'd ⎤
   aroun') |
The priestess enters, with her hair un- ⎬
   bound, |
And thrice invokes the pow'rs below the |
   ground.   ⎦
Night, Erebus, and Chaos she proclaims,
And threefold Hecate, with her hundred
   names,   740
And three Dianas: next, she sprinkles
   round
With feign'd Avernian drops the hallow'd
   ground;
Culls hoary simples, found by Phœbe's
   light,
With brazen sickles reap'd at noon of night;
Then mixes baleful juices in the bowl,
And cuts the forehead of a newborn foal,

Robbing the mother's love. The destin'd
    queen
Observes, assisting at the rites obscene;
A leaven'd cake in her devoted hands   749
She holds, and next the highest altar stands:
One tender foot was shod, her other bare;
Girt was her gather'd gown, and loose her
    hair.
Thus dress'd, she summon'd, with her dying
    breath,
The heav'ns and planets conscious of her
    death,
And ev'ry pow'r, if any rules above,
Who minds, or who revenges, injur'd love.
    'T was dead of night, when weary bodies
    close
Their eyes in balmy sleep and soft repose:
The winds no longer whisper thro' the
    woods,
Nor murm'ring tides disturb the gentle
    floods.   760
The stars in silent order mov'd around;
And Peace, with downy wings, was brood-
    ing on the ground.
The flocks and herds, and party-color'd
    fowl,
Which haunt the woods, or swim the weedy
    pool,
Stretch'd on the quiet earth, securely lay,
Forgetting the past labors of the day.
All else of nature's common gift partake:
Unhappy Dido was alone awake.
Nor sleep nor ease the furious queen can
    find;
Sleep fled her eyes, as quiet fled her mind.
Despair, and rage, and love divide her
    heart;   771
Despair and rage had some, but love the
    greater part.
    Then thus she said within her secret
    mind:
"What shall I do? what succor can I
    find?
Become a suppliant to Hyarba's pride,
And take my turn, to court and be denied?
Shall I with this ungrateful Trojan go,
Forsake an empire, and attend a foe?
Himself I refug'd, and his train reliev'd —
'T is true — but am I sure to be receiv'd?
Can gratitude in Trojan souls have place!
Laomedon still lives in all his race!   782
Then, shall I seek alone the churlish crew,
Or with my fleet their flying sails pursue?
What force have I but those whom scarce
    before

I drew reluctant from their native shore?
Will they again embark at my desire,
Once more sustain the seas, and quit their
    second Tyre?
Rather with steel thy guilty breast invade,
And take the fortune thou thyself hast
    made.   790
Your pity, sister, first seduc'd my mind,
Or seconded too well what I design'd.
These dear-bought pleasures had I never
    known,
Had I continued free, and still my own;
Avoiding love, I had not found despair,
But shar'd with salvage beasts the common
    air.
Like them, a lonely life I might have led,
Not mourn'd the living, nor disturb'd the
    dead."
These thoughts she brooded in her anxious
    breast.
On board, the Trojan found more easy
    rest.   800
Resolv'd to sail, in sleep he pass'd the
    night;
And order'd all things for his early flight.
    To whom once more the winged god ⎤
    appears;   ⎪
His former youthful mien and shape ⎬
    he wears,   ⎪
And with this new alarm invades his ears: ⎦
"Sleep'st thou, O goddess-born! and canst
    thou drown
Thy needful cares, so near a hostile town,
Beset with foes; nor hear'st the western
    gales
Invite thy passage, and inspire thy sails?
She harbors in her heart a furious hate,   810
And thou shalt find the dire effects too
    late;
Fix'd on revenge, and obstinate to die.
Haste swiftly hence, while thou hast pow'r
    to fly.
The sea with ships will soon be cover'd o'er,
And blazing firebrands kindle all the shore.
Prevent her rage, while night obscures the
    skies,
And sail before the purple morn arise.
Who knows what hazards thy delay may
    bring?
Woman's a various and a changeful thing."
Thus Hermes in the dream; then took his
    flight   820
Aloft in air unseen, and mix'd with night.
    Twice warn'd by the celestial messenger,
The pious prince arose with hasty fear;

Then rous'd his drowsy train without de-
    lay:
"Haste to your banks; your crooked
    anchors weigh,
And spread your flying sails, and stand to
    sea.
A god commands: he stood before my
    sight,
And urg'd us once again to speedy flight.
O sacred pow'r, what pow'r soe'er thou art,
To thy blest orders I resign my heart. 830
Lead thou the way; protect thy Trojan
    bands,
And prosper the design thy will commands."
He said; and, drawing forth his flaming
    sword,
His thund'ring arm divides the many-
    twisted cord.
An emulating zeal inspires his train:
They run; they snatch; they rush into the
    main.
With headlong haste they leave the desert
    shores,
And brush the liquid seas with lab'ring
    oars.
   Aurora now had left her saffron bed,
And beams of early light the heav'ns o'er-
    spread, 840
When, from a tow'r, the queen, with wake-
    ful eyes,
Saw day point upward from the rosy skies.
She look'd to seaward; but the sea was
    void,
And scarce in ken the sailing ships de-
    scried.
Stung with despite, and furious with de-
    spair,
She struck her trembling breast, and tore
    her hair.
"And shall th' ungrateful traitor go," she
    said,
"My land forsaken, and my love be-
    tray'd?
Shall we not arm? not rush from ev'ry
    street, 849
To follow, sink, and burn his perjur'd fleet?
Haste, haul my galleys out! pursue the
    foe!
Bring flaming brands! set sail, and swiftly
    row!
What have I said? where am I? Fury
    turns
My brain; and my distemper'd bosom burns.
Then, when I gave my person and my
    throne,

This hate, this rage, had been more timely
    shown.
See now the promis'd faith, the vaunted
    name,
The pious man, who, rushing thro' the
    flame,
Preserv'd his gods, and to the Phrygian
    shore
The burthen of his feeble father bore! 860
I should have torn him piecemeal; strow'd
    in floods
His scatter'd limbs, or left expos'd in woods;
Destroy'd his friends and son; and, from
    the fire,
Have set the reeking boy before the sire.
Events are doubtful, which on battles wait:
Yet where's the doubt, to souls secure of
    fate?
My Tyrians, at their injur'd queen's com-
    mand,
Had toss'd their fires amid the Trojan band;
At once extinguish'd all the faithless
    name;
And I myself, in vengeance of my shame,
Had fall'n upon the pile, to mend the
    fun'ral flame. 871
Thou Sun, who view'st at once the world
    below;
Thou Juno, guardian of the nuptial vow;
Thou Hecate, hearken from thy dark
    abodes!
Ye Furies, fiends, and violated gods,
All pow'rs invok'd with Dido's dying breath,
Attend her curses and avenge her death!
If so the Fates ordain, and Jove commands,
Th' ungrateful wretch should find the
    Latian lands,
Yet let a race untam'd, and haughty foes,
His peaceful entrance with dire arms
    oppose: 881
Oppress'd with numbers in th' unequal
    field,
His men discourag'd, and himself expell'd,
Let him for succor sue from place to place,
Torn from his subjects, and his son's
    embrace.
First, let him see his friends in battle slain,
And their untimely fate lament in vain;
And when, at length, the cruel war shall
    cease,
On hard conditions may he buy his peace:
Nor let him then enjoy supreme com-
    mand; 890
But fall, untimely, by some hostile hand,
And lie unburied on the barren sand!

These are my pray'rs, and this my dying
will;
And you, my Tyrians, ev'ry curse fulfil.
Perpetual hate and mortal wars proclaim,
Against the prince, the people, and the
name.
These grateful off'rings on my grave
bestow;
Nor league, nor love, the hostile nations
know !
Now, and from hence, in ev'ry future age,
When rage excites your arms, and strength
supplies the rage,   900
Rise some avenger of our Libyan blood,
With fire and sword pursue the perjur'd
brood;
Our arms, our seas, our shores, oppos'd to
theirs;
And the same hate descend on all our
heirs ! "
   This said, within her anxious mind she
weighs
The means of cutting short her odious days.
Then to Sichæus' nurse she briefly said
(For, when she left her country, hers was
dead):
" Go, Barce, call my sister. Let her care
The solemn rites of sacrifice prepare;   910
The sheep, and all th' atoning off'rings,
bring,
Sprinkling her body from the crystal spring
With living drops; then let her come, and
thou
With sacred fillets bind thy hoary brow.
Thus will I pay my vows to Stygian Jove,
And end the cares of my disastrous love;
Then cast the Trojan image on the fire,
And, as that burns, my passion shall expire."
   The nurse moves onward, with officious
care,   919
And all the speed her aged limbs can bear.
But furious Dido, with dark thoughts in-
volv'd,
Shook at the mighty mischief she resolv'd.
With livid spots distinguish'd was her face;
Red were her rolling eyes, and discompos'd
her pace;
Ghastly she gaz'd, with pain she drew her
breath,
And nature shiver'd at approaching death.
   Then swiftly to the fatal place she pass'd,
And mounts the fun'ral pile with furious
haste;
Unsheathes the sword the Trojan left be-
hind

(Not for so dire an enterprise design'd). 930
But when she view'd the garments loosely
spread,
Which once he wore, and saw the conscious
bed,
She paus'd, and with a sigh the robes ⎫
embrac'd;   ⎪
Then on the couch her trembling body ⎬
cast,   ⎪
Repress'd the ready tears, and spoke her ⎭
last:
" Dear pledges of my love, while Heav'n so
pleas'd,
Receive a soul, of mortal anguish eas'd:
My fatal course is finish'd; and I go,
A glorious name, among the ghosts below.
A lofty city by my hands is rais'd,   940
Pygmalion punish'd, and my lord appeas'd.
What could my fortune have afforded more,
Had the false Trojan never touch'd my
shore ! "
Then kiss'd the couch; and, " Must I die,"
she said,
" And unreveng'd ? 'T is doubly to be
dead !
Yet ev'n this death with pleasure I receive·
On any terms, 't is better than to live.
These flames, from far, may the false
Trojan view;
These boding omens his base flight
pursue ! "
   She said, and struck; deep enter'd in
her side   950
The piercing steel, with reeking purple
dyed:
Clogg'd in the wound the cruel weapon
stands;
The spouting blood came streaming on her
hands.
Her sad attendants saw the deadly stroke,
And with loud cries the sounding palace
shook.
Distracted, from the fatal sight they fled,
And thro' the town the dismal rumor
spread.
First from the frighted court the yell
began;
Redoubled, thence from house to house it
ran:
The groans of men, with shrieks, laments,
and cries   960
Of mixing women, mount the vaulted skies.
Not less the clamor, than if — ancient
Tyre,
Or the new Carthage, set by foes on fire —

The rolling ruin, with their lov'd abodes,
Involv'd the blazing temples of their gods.
  Her sister hears; and, furious with de-
    spair,
She beats her breast, and rends her yellow
    hair,
And, calling on Eliza's name aloud,
Runs breathless to the place, and breaks
    the crowd.
" Was all that pomp of woe for this
    prepar'd;   970
These fires, this fun'ral pile, these altars
    rear'd ?
Was all this train of plots contriv'd," said
    she,
" All only to deceive unhappy me ?
Which is the worst ? Didst thou in death
    pretend
To scorn thy sister, or delude thy friend ?
Thy summon'd sister, and thy friend, had
    come;
One sword had serv'd us both, one common
    tomb:
Was I to raise the pile, the pow'rs invoke,
Not to be present at the fatal stroke ?
At once thou hast destroy'd thyself and
    me,   980
Thy town, thy senate, and thy colony !
Bring water; bathe the wound; while I in
    death
Lay close my lips to hers, and catch the
    flying breath."
This said, she mounts the pile with eager
    haste,
And in her arms the gasping queen em-
    brac'd;
Her temples chaf'd; and her own garments
    tore,
To stanch the streaming blood, and cleanse
    the gore.
Thrice Dido tried to raise her drooping head,
And, fainting thrice, fell grov'ling on the
    bed;
Thrice op'd her heavy eyes, and sought ⎫
    the light,   990 ⎬
But, having found it, sicken'd at the sight, ⎭
And clos'd her lids at last in endless
    night.
  Then Juno, grieving that she should
    sustain
A death so ling'ring, and so full of pain,
Sent Iris down, to free her from the strife
Of lab'ring nature, and dissolve her life.
For since she died, not doom'd by Heav'n's
    decree,

Or her own crime, but human casualty,
And rage of love, that plung'd her in
    despair,
The Sisters had not cut the topmost
    hair,   1000
Which Proserpine and they can only know;
Nor made her sacred to the shades below.
Downward the various goddess took her
    flight,
And drew a thousand colors from the
    light;
Then stood above the dying lover's head,
And said: " I thus devote thee to the dead.
This off'ring to th' infernal gods I bear." ⎫
Thus while she spoke, she cut the fatal   ⎪
    hair: ⎬
The struggling soul was loos'd, and life ⎪
    dissolv'd in air.   ⎭

THE FIFTH BOOK OF THE ÆNEIS

THE ARGUMENT

Æneas, setting sail from Afric, is driven by a
storm on the coasts of Sicily, where he is hospitably receiv'd by his friend Acestes, king
of part of the island, and born of Trojan
parentage. He applies himself to celebrate
the memory of his father with divine honors,
and accordingly institutes funeral games,
and appoints prizes for those who should conquer in them. While the ceremonies were
performing, Juno sends Iris to persuade the
Trojan women to burn the ships, who, upon
her instigation, set fire to them ; which
burnt four, and would have consum'd the
rest, had not Jupiter, by a miraculous shower,
extinguish'd it. Upon this, Æneas, by the
advice of one of his generals, and a vision of
his father, builds a city for the women, old
men, and others, who were either unfit for
war, or weary of the voyage, and sails for
Italy. Venus procures of Neptune a safe voyage for him and all his men, excepting only
his pilot Palinurus, who is unfortunately lost.

MEANTIME the Trojan cuts his wat'ry way,
Fix'd on his voyage, thro' the curling sea;
Then, casting back his eyes, with dire
    amaze,
Sees on the Punic shore the mounting blaze
The cause unknown; yet his presaging ⎫
    mind   ⎬
The fate of Dido from the fire divin'd; ⎪
He knew the stormy souls of womankind, ⎭

What secret springs their eager passions
    move,
How capable of death for injur'd love.
Dire auguries from hence the Trojans
    draw;   10
Till neither fires nor shining shores they
    saw.
Now seas and skies their prospect only
    bound;
An empty space above, a floating field
    around.
But soon the heav'ns with shadows were
    o'erspread;
A swelling cloud hung hov'ring o'er their
    head:
Livid it look'd, the threat'ning of a storm;
Then night and horror ocean's face deform.
The pilot, Palinurus, cried aloud:
' What gusts of weather from that
    gath'ring cloud
My thoughts presage ! Ere yet the tempest
    roars,   20
Stand to your tackle, mates, and stretch
    your oars;
Contract your swelling sails, and luff to
    wind."
The frighted crew perform the task assign'd.
Then, to his fearless chief: " Not Heav'n," } said he,
" Tho' Jove himself should promise Italy, }
Can stem the torrent of this raging sea. }
Mark how the shifting winds from west
    arise,
And what collected night involves the skies !
Nor can our shaken vessels live at sea, }
Much less against the tempest force their }
    way.   30 }
'T is fate diverts our course, and fate we }
    must obey. }
Not far from hence, if I observ'd aright
The southing of the stars, and polar light,
Sicilia lies, whose hospitable shores
In safety we may reach with struggling
    oars."
Æneas then replied: " Too sure I find
We strive in vain against the seas and wind:
Now shift your sails; what place can please
    me more
Than what you promise, the Sicilian shore,
Whose hallow'd earth Anchises' bones con-
    tains,   40
And where a prince of Trojan lineage
    reigns ? "
The course resolv'd, before the western
    wind

They scud amain, and make the port as-
    sign'd.
Meantime Acestes, from a lofty stand,
Beheld the fleet descending on the land;
And, not unmindful of his ancient race, }
Down from the cliff he ran with eager }
    pace, }
And held the hero in a strict embrace. }
Of a rough Libyan bear the spoils he wore,
And either hand a pointed jav'lin bore.   50
His mother was a dame of Dardan blood;
His sire Crinisus, a Sicilian flood.
He welcomes his returning friends ashore
With plenteous country cates and homely
    store.
    Now, when the following morn had chas'd
    away
The flying stars, and light restor'd the day,
Æneas call'd the Trojan troops around,
And thus bespoke them from a rising
    ground:
"Offspring of heav'n, divine Dardanian race !
The sun, revolving thro' th' ethereal space,
The shining circle of the year has fill'd,   61
Since first this isle my father's ashes held:
And now the rising day renews the year;
A day for ever sad, for ever dear.
This would I celebrate with annual games,
With gifts on altars pil'd, and holy flames,
Tho' banish'd to Gætulia's barren sands,
Caught on the Grecian seas, or hostile lands:
But since this happy storm our fleet has
    driv'n
(Not, as I deem, without the will of Heav'n)
Upon these friendly shores and flow'ry
    plains,   71
Which hide Anchises and his blest remains,
Let us with joy perform his honors due,
And pray for prosp'rous winds, our voyage
    to renew;
Pray, that in towns and temples of our } own, }
The name of great Anchises may be } known, }
And yearly games may spread the gods' } renown. }
Our sports Acestes, of the Trojan race,
With royal gifts ordain'd, is pleas'd to grace:
Two steers on ev'ry ship the king bestows;
His gods and ours shall share your equal
    vows.   81
Besides, if, nine days hence, the rosy morn
Shall with unclouded light the skies adorn,
That day with solemn sports I mean to
    grace:

Light galleys on the seas shall run a wat'ry
    race;
Some shall in swiftness for the goal con-
    tend,
And others try the twanging bow to bend;
The strong, with iron gauntlets arm'd, shall
    stand
Oppos'd in combat on the yellow sand.
Let all be present at the games prepar'd, 90
And joyful victors wait the just reward.
But now assist the rites, with garlands
    crown'd."
He said, and first his brows with myrtle
    bound.
Then Helymus, by his example led,
And old Acestes, each adorn'd his head;
Thus young Ascanius, with a sprightly
    grace,
His temples tied, and all the Trojan race.
    Æneas then advanc'd amidst the train,
By thousands follow'd thro' the flow'ry
    plain,
To great Anchises' tomb; which when he
    found, 100
He pour'd to Bacchus, on the hallow'd
    ground,
Two bowls of sparkling wine, of milk two
    more,
And two (from offer'd bulls) of purple gore.
With roses then the sepulcher he strow'd,
And thus his father's ghost bespoke aloud:
"Hail, O ye holy manes! hail again,
Paternal ashes, now review'd in vain!
The gods permitted not, that you, with
    me,
Should reach the promis'd shores of
    Italy,
Or Tiber's flood, what flood soe'er it
    be." 110
Scarce had he finish'd, when, with speckled
    pride,
A serpent from the tomb began to glide;
His hugy bulk on sev'n high volumes roll'd;
Blue was his breadth of back, but streak'd
    with scaly gold:
Thus riding on his curls, he seem'd to pass
A rolling fire along, and singe the grass.
More various colors thro' his body run,
Than Iris when her bow imbibes the sun.
Betwixt the rising altars, and around,
The sacred monster shot along the ground;
With harmless play amidst the bowls he
    pass'd, 121
And with his lolling tongue assay'd the
    taste:

Thus fed with holy food, the wondrous
    guest
Within the hollow tomb retir'd to rest.
The pious prince, surpris'd at what he
    view'd,
The fun'ral honors with more zeal re-
    new'd,
Doubtful if this the place's genius were,
Or guardian of his father's sepulcher.
Five sheep, according to the rites, he
    slew;
As many swine, and steers of sable hue; 130
New gen'rous wine he from the goblets
    pour'd,
And call'd his father's ghost, from hell
    restor'd.
The glad attendants in long order come,
Off'ring their gifts at great Anchises'
    tomb:
Some add more oxen; some divide the
    spoil;
Some place the chargers on the grassy
    soil;
Some blow the fires, and offer'd entrails
    broil.
    Now came the day desir'd. The skies
    were bright
With rosy luster of the rising light:
The bord'ring people, rous'd by sounding
    fame 140
Of Trojan feasts and great Acestes' name,
The crowded shore with acclamations fill,
Part to behold, and part to prove their
    skill.
And first the gifts in public view they
    place,
Green laurel wreaths, and palm, the vic-
    tors' grace:
Within the circle, arms and tripods lie,
Ingots of gold and silver, heap'd on
    high,
And vests embroider'd, of the Tyrian
    dye.
The trumpet's clangor then the feast pro-
    claims,
And all prepare for their appointed games.
Four galleys first, which equal rowers
    bear, 151
Advancing, in the wat'ry lists appear.
The speedy Dolphin, that outstrips the
    wind,
Bore Mnestheus, author of the Memmian
    kind:
Gyas the vast Chimæra's bulk commands,
Which rising, like a tow'ring city stands;

Three Trojans tug at ev'ry lab'ring oar;
Three banks in three degrees the sailors bore;
Beneath their sturdy strokes the billows roar.
Sergesthus, who began the Sergian race,
In the great Centaur took the leading place;   161
Cloanthus on the sea-green Scylla stood,
From whom Cluentius draws his Trojan blood.
  Far in the sea, against the foaming shore,
There stands a rock: the raging billows roar
Above his head in storms; but, when 't is clear,
Uncurl their ridgy backs, and at his foot appear.
In peace below the gentle waters run;
The cormorants above lie basking in the sun.
On this the hero fix'd an oak in sight,   170
The mark to guide the mariners aright.
To bear with this, the seamen stretch their oars;
Then round the rock they steer, and seek the former shores.
The lots decide their place. Above the rest,
Each leader shining in his Tyrian vest;
The common crew with wreaths of poplar boughs
Their temples crown, and shade their sweaty brows:
Besmear'd with oil, their naked shoulders shine.
All take their seats, and wait the sounding sign:
They gripe their oars; and ev'ry panting breast   180
Is rais'd by turns with hope, by turns with fear depress'd.
The clangor of the trumpet gives the sign;
At once they start, advancing in a line:
With shouts the sailors rend the starry skies;
Lash'd with their oars, the smoky billows rise;
Sparkles the briny main, and the vex'd ocean fries.
Exact in time, with equal strokes they row:
At once the brushing oars and brazen prow
Dash up the sandy waves, and ope the depths below.

Not fiery coursers, in a chariot race,   190
Invade the field with half so swift a pace;
Not the fierce driver with more fury lends
The sounding lash, and, ere the stroke descends,
Low to the wheels his pliant body bends.
The partial crowd their hopes and fears divide,
And aid with eager shouts the favor'd side.
Cries, murmurs, clamors, with a mixing sound,
From woods to woods, from hills to hills rebound.
  Amidst the loud applauses of the shore,
Gyas outstripp'd the rest, and sprung before: 200
Cloanthus, better mann'd, pursued him fast,
But his o'er-masted galley check'd his haste.
The Centaur and the Dolphin brush the brine
With equal oars, advancing in a line;
And now the mighty Centaur seems to lead,
And now the speedy Dolphin gets ahead;
Now board to board the rival vessels row,
The billows lave the skies, and ocean groans below.
They reach'd the mark. Proud Gyas and his train
In triumph rode, the victors of the main;   210
But, steering round, he charg'd his pilot stand
More close to shore, and skim along the sand —
"Let others bear to sea!" Menœtes heard;
But secret shelves too cautiously he fear'd,
And, fearing, sought the deep; and still aloof he steer'd.
With louder cries the captain call'd again:
"Bear to the rocky shore, and shun the main."
He spoke, and, speaking, at his stern he saw
The bold Cloanthus near the shelvings draw.
Betwixt the mark and him the Scylla stood,   220
And in a closer compass plow'd the flood.
He pass'd the mark; and, wheeling, got before:

Gyas blasphem'd the gods, devoutly swore,
Cried out for anger, and his hair he tore.
Mindless of others' lives (so high was grown
His rising rage) and careless of his own,
The trembling dotard to the deck he drew;
Then hoisted up, and overboard he threw;
This done, he seiz'd the helm; his fellows
  cheer'd,
Turn'd short upon the shelfs, and madly
  steer'd. 230
Hardly his head the plunging pilot rears,
Clogg'd with his clothes, and cumber'd with
  his years:
Now dropping wet, he climbs the cliff with
  pain.
The crowd, that saw him fall and float again,
Shout from the distant shore; and loudly
  laugh'd,
To see his heaving breast disgorge the
  briny draught.
The following Centaur, and the Dolphin's
  crew,
Their vanish'd hopes of victory renew;
While Gyas lags, they kindle in the race,
To reach the mark. Sergesthus takes the
  place; 240
Mnestheus pursues; and, while around they
  wind,
Comes up, not half his galley's length be-
  hind;
Then, on the deck, amidst his mates ap-
  pear'd,
And thus their drooping courages he
  cheer'd:
" My friends, and Hector's followers here-
  tofore,
Exert your vigor; tug the lab'ring oar;
Stretch to your strokes, my still unconquer'd
  crew,
Whom from the flaming walls of Troy I
  drew.
In this, our common int'rest, let me find
That strength of hand, that courage of the
  mind, 250
As when you stemm'd the strong Malean
  flood,
And o'er the Syrtes' broken billows row'd.
I seek not now the foremost palm to gain;
Tho' yet — but, ah ! that haughty wish is
  vain !
Let those enjoy it whom the gods ordain.
But to be last, the lags of all the race ! —
Redeem yourselves and me from that dis-
  grace."
Now, one and all, they tug amain; they row

At the full stretch, and shake the brazen
  prow.
The sea beneath 'em sinks; their lab'ring
  sides 260
Are swell'd, and sweat runs gutt'ring down
  in tides.
Chance aids their daring with unhop'd suc-
  cess:
Sergesthus, eager with his beak to press
Betwixt the rival galley and the rock,
Shuts up th' unwieldy Centaur in the lock.
The vessel struck; and, with the dreadful
  shock,
Her oars she shiver'd; and her head she
  broke.
The trembling rowers from their banks
  arise,
And, anxious for themselves, renounce the
  prize.
With iron poles they heave her off the
  shores, 270
And gather from the sea their floating oars.
The crew of Mnestheus, with elated minds,
Urge their success, and call the willing
  winds;
Then ply their oars, and cut their liquid way
In larger compass on the roomy sea.
As, when the dove her rocky hold forsakes,
Rous'd in a fright, her sounding wings she
  shakes;
The cavern rings with clatt'ring; out she
  flies,
And leaves her callow care, and cleaves
  the skies:
At first she flutters; but at length she
  springs 280
To smoother flight, and shoots upon her
  wings:
So Mnestheus in the Dolphin cuts the sea;
And, flying with a force, that force assists
  his way.
Sergesthus in the Centaur soon he pass'd,
Wedg'd in the rocky shoals, and sticking
  fast.
In vain the victor he with cries implores,
And practices to row with shatter'd oars.
Then Mnestheus bears with Gyas, and out-
  flies: 288
The ship, without a pilot, yields the prize.
Unvanquish'd Scylla now alone remains;
Her he pursues, and all his vigor strains.
Shouts from the fav'ring multitude arise;
Applauding Echo to the shouts replies;
Shouts, wishes, and applause run rattling
  thro' the skies.

These clamors with disdain the Scylla heard,
Much grudg'd the praise, but more the robb'd reward:
Resolv'd to hold their own, they mend their pace,
All obstinate to die, or gain the race.
Rais'd with success, the Dolphin swiftly ran;
For they can conquer, who believe they can.   300
Both urge their oars, and fortune both supplies,
And both perhaps had shar'd an equal prize;
When to the seas Cloanthus holds his hands,
And succor from the wat'ry pow'rs demands:
" Gods of the liquid realms, on which I row !
If, giv'n by you, the laurel bind my brow,
Assist to make me guilty of my vow !
A snow-white bull shall on your shore be slain;
His offer'd entrails cast into the main,
And ruddy wine, from golden goblets thrown,   310
Your grateful gift and my return shall own."
The choir of nymphs, and Phorcus, from below,
With virgin Panopea, heard his vow;
And old Portunus, with his breadth of hand,
Push'd on, and sped the galley to the land.
Swift as a shaft, or winged wind, she flies,
And, darting to the port, obtains the prize.
The herald summons all, and then proclaims
Cloanthus conqu'ror of the naval games.
The prince with laurel crowns the victor's head,   320
And three fat steers are to his vessel led,
The ship's reward; with gen'rous wine beside,
And sums of silver, which the crew divide.
The leaders are distinguish'd from the rest;
The victor honor'd with a nobler vest,
Where gold and purple strive in equal rows,
And needlework its happy cost bestows.
There Ganymede is wrought with living art,

Chasing thro' Ida's groves the trembling hart: 329
Breathless he seems, yet eager to pursue;
When from aloft descends, in open view,
The bird of Jove, and, sousing on his prey,
With crooked talons bears the boy away.
In vain, with lifted hands and gazing eyes,
His guards behold him soaring thro' the skies,
And dogs pursue his flight with imitated cries.
    Mnestheus the second victor was declar'd;
And, summon'd there, the second prize he shar'd.
A coat of mail, which brave Demoleüs bore,
More brave Æneas from his shoulders tore,   340
In single combat on the Trojan shore:
This was ordain'd for Mnestheus to possess;
In war for his defense, for ornament in peace.
Rich was the gift, and glorious to behold,
But yet so pond'rous with its plates of gold,
That scarce two servants could the weight sustain;
Yet, loaded thus, Demoleüs o'er the plain
Pursued and lightly seiz'd the Trojan train.
The rest, succeeding to the last reward,
Two goodly bowls of massy silver shar'd,   350
With figures prominent, and richly wrought,
And two brass caldrons from Dodona brought.
Thus all, rewarded by the hero's hands,
Their conqu'ring temples bound with purple bands;
And now Sergesthus, clearing from the rock,
Brought back his galley shatter'd with the shock.
Forlorn she look'd, without an aiding oar,
And, houted by the vulgar, made to shore.
As when a snake, surpris'd upon the road,
Is crush'd athwart her body by the load   360
Of heavy wheels; or with a mortal wound
Her belly bruis'd, and trodden to the ground:
In vain, with loosen'd curls, she crawls along;
Yet, fierce above, she brandishes her tongue;

Glares with her eyes, and bristles with her
  scales;
But, groveling in the dust, her parts un-
  sound she trails:
So slowly to the port the Centaur tends,
But, what she wants in oars, with sails
  amends.
Yet, for his galley sav'd, the grateful prince
Is pleas'd th' unhappy chief to recom-
  pense.   370
Pholoe, the Cretan slave, rewards his care,
Beauteous herself, with lovely twins as fair.

From thence his way the Trojan hero bent
Into the neighb'ring plain, with mountains
  pent,
Whose sides were shaded with surrounding
  wood.
Full in the midst of this fair valley stood
A native theater, which, rising slow
By just degrees, o'erlook'd the ground be-
  low.   378
High on a sylvan throne the leader sate;
A num'rous train attend in solemn state.
Here those that in the rapid course delight,
Desire of honor and the prize invite.
The rival runners without order stand;
The Trojans mix'd with the Sicilian band.
First Nisus, with Euryalus, appears;
Euryalus a boy of blooming years,
With sprightly grace and equal beauty
  crown'd;
Nisus, for friendship to the youth renown'd.
Diores next, of Priam's royal race,
Then Salius, join'd with Patron, took their
  place;   390
(But Patron in Arcadia had his birth,
And Salius his from Acarnanian earth;)
Then two Sicilian youths — the names of
  these,
Swift Helymus, and lovely Panopes:
Both jolly huntsmen, both in forests bred,
And owning old Acestes for their head;
With sev'ral others of ignobler name,
Whom time has not deliver'd o'er to fame.
  To these the hero thus his thoughts ex-
  plain'd,
In words which gen'ral approbation gain'd:
"One common largess is for all design'd, 401
(The vanquish'd and the victor shall be
  join'd,)
Two darts of polish'd steel and Gnosian
  wood,
A silver-studded ax, alike bestow'd.
The foremost three have olive wreaths de-
  creed:

The first of these obtains a stately steed,
Adorn'd with trappings; and the next in
  fame,
The quiver of an Amazonian dame,
With feather'd Thracian arrows well sup-
  plied:
A golden belt shall gird his manly side, 410
Which with a sparkling diamond shall be
  tied.
The third this Grecian helmet shall con-
  tent."
He said. To their appointed base they went;
With beating hearts th' expected sign re-
  ceive,
And, starting all at once, the barrier leave.
Spread out, as on the winged winds, they
  flew,
And seiz'd the distant goal with greedy view.
Shot from the crowd, swift Nisus all o'er-
  pass'd;
Nor storms, nor thunder, equal half his
  haste.
The next, but, tho' the next, yet far dis-
  join'd,   420
Came Salius, and Euryalus behind;
Then Helymus, whom young Diores plied,
Step after step, and almost side by side,
His shoulders pressing; and, in longer space,
Had won, or left at least a dubious race.
  Now, spent, the goal they almost reach
  at last,
When eager Nisus, hapless in his haste,
Slipp'd first, and, slipping, fell upon the
  plain,
Soak'd with the blood of oxen newly slain.
The careless victor had not mark'd his
  way;   430
But, treading where the treach'rous puddle
  lay,
His heels flew up; and on the grassy floor
He fell, besmear'd with filth and holy gore.
Not mindless then, Euryalus, of thee,
Nor of the sacred bonds of amity,
He strove th' immediate rival's hope to
  cross,
And caught the foot of Salius as he rose.
So Salius lay extended on the plain;
Euryalus springs out, the prize to gain,
And leaves the crowd: applauding peals
  attend   440
The victor to the goal, who vanquish'd by
  his friend.
Next Helymus; and then Diores came,
By two misfortunes made the third in
  fame.

But Salius enters, and, exclaiming loud
For justice, deafens and disturbs the crowd;
Urges his cause may in the court be heard;
And pleads the prize is wrongfully con-
    ferr'd.
But favor for Euryalus appears;
His blooming beauty, with his tender tears,
Had brib'd the judges for the promis'd
    prize.   450
Besides, Diores fills the court with cries,
Who vainly reaches at the last reward,
If the first palm on Salius be conferr'd.
Then thus the prince: "Let no disputes
    arise:
Where fortune plac'd it, I award the prize.
But fortune's errors give me leave to mend,
At least to pity my deserving friend."
He said, and, from among the spoils, he
    draws
(Pond'rous with shaggy mane and golden
    paws)
A lion's hide: to Salius this he gives.   460
Nisus with envy sees the gift, and grieves.
"If such rewards to vanquish'd men are
    due,"
He said, "and falling is to rise by you,
What prize may Nisus from your bounty
    claim,
Who merited the first rewards and fame?
In falling, both an equal fortune tried;
Would fortune for my fall so well provide!"
With this he pointed to his face, and show'd
His hands and all his habit smear'd with
    blood.
Th' indulgent father of the people smil'd, 470
And caus'd to be produc'd an ample shield,
Of wondrous art, by Didymaon wrought,
Long since from Neptune's bars in triumph
    brought.
This giv'n to Nisus, he divides the rest,
And equal justice in his gifts express'd.
    The race thus ended, and rewards be-
    stow'd,
Once more the prince bespeaks th' attentive
    crowd:
"If there be here whose dauntless courage
    dare
In gauntlet-fight, with limbs and body
    bare,
His opposite sustain in open view,   480
Stand forth the champion, and the games
    renew.
Two prizes I propose, and thus divide:
A bull with gilded horns, and fillets tied,
Shall be the portion of the conqu'ring chief;

A sword and helm shall cheer the loser's
    grief."
Then haughty Dares in the lists appears;
Stalking he strides, his head erected bears:
His nervous arms the weighty gauntlet
    wield,
And loud applauses echo thro' the field.
Dares alone in combat us'd to stand   490
The match of mighty Paris, hand to hand;
The same, at Hector's fun'rals, undertook
Gigantic Butes, of th' Amycian stock,
And, by the stroke of his resistless hand,
Stretch'd the vast bulk upon the yellow
    sand.
Such Dares was; and such he strode along,
And drew the wonder of the gazing
    throng.
His brawny back and ample breast he shows;
His lifted arms around his head he throws,
And deals in whistling air his empty
    blows.   500
His match is sought; but, thro' the trem-
    bling band,
Not one dares answer to the proud demand.
Presuming of his force, with sparkling eyes
Already he devours the promis'd prize.
He claims the bull with awless insolence,
And having seiz'd his horns, accosts the
    prince:
"If none my matchless valor dares op-
    pose,
How long shall Dares wait his dastard
    foes?
Permit me, chief, permit without delay,
To lead this uncontended gift away."   510
The crowd assents, and with redoubled
    cries
For the proud challenger demands the prize.
    Acestes, fir'd with just disdain, to see
The palm usurp'd without a victory,
Reproach'd Entellus thus, who sate beside,
And heard and saw, unmov'd, the Trojan's
    pride:
"Once, but in vain, a champion of renown,
So tamely can you bear the ravish'd crown,
A prize in triumph borne before your sight,
And shun, for fear, the danger of the
    fight?   520
Where is our Eryx now, the boasted name,
The god who taught your thund'ring arm
    the game?
Where now your baffled honor? Where
    the spoil

That fill'd your house, and fame that fill'd
    our isle ? "
Entellus, thus: "My soul is still the same,
Unmov'd with fear, and mov'd with mar-
    tial fame;
But my chill blood is curdled in my veins,
And scarce the shadow of a man remains.
O could I turn to that fair prime again,
That prime of which this boaster is so
    vain,   530
The brave, who this decrepid age defies,
Should feel my force, without the promis'd
    prize."
    He said; and, rising at the word, he threw
Two pond'rous gauntlets down in open
    view;
Gauntlets which Eryx wont in fight to
    wield,
And sheathe his hands with in the listed
    field.
With fear and wonder seiz'd, the crowd
    beholds
The gloves of death, with sev'n distin-
    guish'd folds
Of tough bull hides; the space within is
    spread
With iron, or with loads of heavy lead: 540
Dares himself was daunted at the sight,
Renounc'd his challenge, and refus'd to
    fight.
Astonish'd at their weight, the hero stands,
And pois'd the pond'rous engines in his
    hands.
" What had your wonder," said Entel- ⎤
    lus, " been,   ⎟
Had you the gauntlets of Alcides seen,   ⎬
Or view'd the stern debate on this un-   ⎟
    happy green !   ⎦
These which I bear your brother Eryx
    bore,
Still mark'd with batter'd brains and
    mingled gore.
With these he long sustain'd th' Herculean
    arm;   550
And these I wielded while my blood was
    warm,
This languish'd frame while better spirits
    fed,
Ere age unstrung my nerves, or time o'er-
    snow'd my head.
But if the challenger these arms refuse,
And cannot wield their weight, or dare not
    use;
If great Æneas and Acestes join
In his request, these gauntlets I resign;

Let us with equal arms perform the fight,
And let him leave to fear, since I resign
    my right."
    This said, Entellus for the strife pre-
    pares;   560
Stripp'd of his quilted coat, his body
    bares;
Compos'd of mighty bones and brawn he
    stands,
A goodly tow'ring object on the sands.
Then just Æneas equal arms supplied,
Which round their shoulders to their wrists
    they tied.
Both on the tiptoe stand, at full extent,
Their arms aloft, their bodies inly bent;
Their heads from aiming blows they bear
    afar;
With clashing gauntlets then provoke the
    war.
One on his youth and pliant limbs re-
    lies;   570
One on his sinews and his giant size.
The last is stiff with age, his motion ⎤
    slow;   ⎟
He heaves for breath, he staggers to   ⎬
    and fro,   ⎟
And clouds of issuing smoke his nostrils ⎟
    loudly blow.   ⎦
Yet equal in success, they ward, they
    strike;
Their ways are diff'rent, but their art
    alike.
Before, behind, the blows are dealt;
    around
Their hollow sides the rattling thumps
    resound.
A storm of strokes, well meant, with fury
    flies,
And errs about their temples, ears, and
    eyes.   580
Nor always errs; for oft the gauntlet
    draws
A sweeping stroke along the crackling
    jaws.
Heavy with age, Entellus stands his
    ground,
But with his warping body wards the
    wound.
His hand and watchful eye keep even
    pace;
While Dares traverses and shifts his
    place,
And, like a captain who beleaguers round
Some strong-built castle on a rising
    ground,

Views all th' approaches with observing
eyes:
This and that other part in vain he
tries,   590
And more on industry than force relies.
With hands on high, Entellus threats
the foe;
But Dares watch'd the motion from be-
low,
And slipp'd aside, and shunn'd the long
descending blow.
Entellus wastes his forces on the wind,
And, thus deluded of the stroke design'd,
Headlong and heavy fell; his ample breast
And weighty limbs his ancient mother
press'd.
So falls a hollow pine, that long had stood
On Ida's height, or Erymanthus' wood, 600
Torn from the roots. The diff'ring nations
rise,
And shouts and mingled murmurs rend
the skies.
Acestes runs with eager haste, to raise
The fall'n companion of his youthful days.
Dauntless he rose, and to the fight re-
turn'd;
With shame his glowing cheeks, his eyes
with fury burn'd.
Disdain and conscious virtue fir'd his breast,
And with redoubled force his foe he
press'd.
He lays on load with either hand, amain,
And headlong drives the Trojan o'er the
plain;   610
Nor stops, nor stays; nor rest nor breath
allows;
But storms of strokes descend about his
brows,
A rattling tempest, and a hail of blows.
But now the prince, who saw the wild
increase
Of wounds, commands the combatants
to cease,
And bounds Entellus' wrath, and bids
the peace.
First to the Trojan, spent with toil, he
came,
And sooth'd his sorrow for the suffer'd
shame.
" What fury seiz'd my friend ? The gods,"
said he,
" To him propitious, and averse to thee, 620
Have giv'n his arm superior force to thine.
'T is madness to contend with strength
divine."

The gauntlet fight thus ended, from the
shore
His faithful friends unhappy Dares bore:
His mouth and nostrils pour'd a purple
flood,
And pounded teeth came rushing with his
blood.
Faintly he stagger'd thro' the hissing
throng,
And hung his head, and trail'd his legs
along.
The sword and casque are carried by his
train;   629
But with his foe the palm and ox remain.
    The champion, then, before Æneas came,
Proud of his prize, but prouder of his
fame:
" O goddess-born, and you, Dardanian
host,
Mark with attention, and forgive my
boast;
Learn what I was, by what remains; and
know
From what impending fate you sav'd my
foe."
Sternly he spoke, and then confronts the
bull;
And, on his ample forehead aiming full,
The deadly stroke, descending, pierc'd
the skull.
Down drops the beast, nor needs a second
wound,   640
But sprawls in pangs of death, and spurns
the ground.
Then, thus: " In Dares' stead I offer this.
Eryx, accept a nobler sacrifice;
Take the last gift my wither'd arms can
yield:
Thy gauntlets I resign, and here renounce
the field."
    This done, Æneas orders, for the close,
The strife of archers with contending bows.
The mast Sergesthus' shatter'd galley bore
With his own hands he raises on the shore.
A flutt'ring dove upon the top they tie, 650
The living mark at which their arrows fly.
The rival archers in a line advance,
Their turn of shooting to receive from
chance.
A helmet holds their names; the lots are
drawn:
On the first scroll was read Hippocoön.
The people shout. Upon the next was found
Young Mnestheus, late with naval honors
crown'd.

The third contain'd Eurytion's noble name,
Thy brother, Pandarus, and next in fame,
Whom Pallas urg'd the treaty to con-
found,   660
And send among the Greeks a feather'd
wound.
Acestes in the bottom last remain'd,
Whom not his age from youthful sports
restrain'd.
Soon all with vigor bend their trusty bows,
And from the quiver each his arrow chose.
Hippocoön's was the first: with forceful
sway
It flew, and, whizzing, cut the liquid way.
Fix'd in the mast the feather'd weapon
stands:
The fearful pigeon flutters in her bands,
And the tree trembled, and the shouting
cries   670
Of the pleas'd people rend the vaulted skies.
Then Mnestheus to the head his arrow ⎫
drove,   ⎪
With lifted eyes, and took his aim above, ⎬
But made a glancing shot, and miss'd the   ⎪
dove;   ⎭
Yet miss'd so narrow, that he cut the cord
Which fasten'd by the foot the flitting bird.
The captive thus releas'd, away she flies,
And beats with clapping wings the yielding
skies.
His bow already bent, Eurytion stood;   679
And, having first invok'd his brother god,
His winged shaft with eager haste he sped.
The fatal message reach'd her as she fled:
She leaves her life aloft; she strikes the
ground,
And renders back the weapon in the wound.
Acestes, grudging at his lot, remains,
Without a prize to gratify his pains.
Yet, shooting upward, sends his shaft, to
show
An archer's art, and boast his twanging bow.
The feather'd arrow gave a dire portent,
And latter augurs judge from this event. 690
Chaf'd by the speed, it fir'd; and, as it flew,
A trail of following flames ascending drew:
Kindling they mount, and mark the shiny ⎫
way;   ⎬
Across the skies as falling meteors play, ⎪
And vanish into wind, or in a blaze decay.⎭
The Trojans and Sicilians wildly stare,
And, trembling, turn their wonder into
pray'r.
The Dardan prince put on a smiling face,
And strain'd Acestes with a close embrace;

Then, hon'ring him with gifts above the
rest,   700
Turn'd the bad omen, nor his fears con-
fess'd.
" The gods," said he, " this miracle have
wrought,
And order'd you the prize without the lot.
Accept this goblet, rough with figur'd gold,
Which Thracian Cisseus gave my sire of
old:
This pledge of ancient amity receive,
Which to my second sire I justly give."
He said, and, with the trumpets' cheerful
sound,
Proclaim'd him victor, and with laurel
crown'd.
Nor good Eurytion envied him the prize, 710
Tho' he transfix'd the pigeon in the skies.
Who cut the line, with second gifts was
grac'd;
The third was his whose arrow pierc'd the
mast.
   The chief, before the games were wholly
done,
Call'd Periphantes, tutor to his son,
And whisper'd thus: " With speed Ascanius
find;
And, if his childish troop be ready join'd,
On horseback let him grace his grandsire's
day,
And lead his equals arm'd in just array."
He said; and, calling out, the cirque he
clears.   720
The crowd withdrawn, an open plain ap-
pears.
And now the noble youths, of form divine, ⎫
Advance before their fathers, in a line: ⎬
The riders grace the steeds; the steeds   ⎪
with glory shine.   ⎭
   Thus marching on in military pride,
Shouts of applause resound from side to
side.
Their casques adorn'd with laurel wreaths
they wear,
Each brandishing aloft a cornel spear.
Some at their backs their gilded quivers
bore;
Their chains of burnish'd gold hung down
before.   730
Three graceful troops they form'd upon ⎫
the green;   ⎪
Three graceful leaders at their head were ⎬
seen;   ⎪
Twelve follow'd ev'ry chief, and left a   ⎪
space between.   ⎭

The first young Priam led; a lovely boy,
Whose grandsire was th' unhappy king of
　　Troy;
His race in after times was known to ⎫
　　fame,　　　　　　　　　　　　　　⎬
New honors adding to the Latian name; ⎬
And well the royal boy his Thracian steed ⎭
　　became.
White were the fetlocks of his feet before,
And on his front a snowy star he bore.　740
Then beauteous Atys, with Iülus bred,
Of equal age, the second squadron led.
The last in order, but the first in place,
First in the lovely features of his face,
Rode fair Ascanius on a fiery steed,
Queen Dido's gift, and of the Tyrian breed.
Sure coursers for the rest the king ordains,
With golden bits adorn'd, and purple reins.
　The pleas'd spectators peals of shouts
　　renew,
And all the parents in the children view;　750
Their make, their motions, and their
　　sprightly grace,
And hopes and fears alternate in their face.
　Th' unfledg'd commanders and their mar-
　　tial train
First make the circuit of the sandy plain
Around their sires, and, at th' appointed
　　sign,
Drawn up in beauteous order, form a line.
The second signal sounds, the troop divides
In three distinguish'd parts, with three dis-
　　tinguish'd guides.
Again they close, and once again disjoin;
In troop to troop oppos'd, and line to line.
They meet; they wheel; they throw their
　　darts afar　　　　　　　　　　　761
With harmless rage and well-dissembled
　　war.
Then in a round the mingled bodies run:
Flying they follow, and pursuing shun;
Broken, they break; and, rallying, they
　　renew
In other forms the military shew.
At last, in order, undiscern'd they join,
And march together in a friendly line.
And, as the Cretan labyrinth of old,
With wand'ring ways and many a winding
　　fold,　　　　　　　　　　　　　770
Involv'd the weary feet, without redress,
In a round error, which denied recess;
So fought the Trojan boys in warlike play,
Turn'd and return'd, and still a diff'rent
　　way.
Thus dolphins in the deep each other chase

In circles, when they swim around the
　　wat'ry race.
This game, these carousels, Ascanius taught;
And, building Alba, to the Latins brought;
Shew'd what he learn'd: the Latin sires im-
　　part
To their succeeding sons the graceful art;
From these imperial Rome receiv'd the
　　game,　　　　　　　　　　　　781
Which Troy, the youths the Trojan troop,
　　they name.
　Thus far the sacred sports they cele-
　　brate:
But Fortune soon resum'd her ancient hate;
For, while they pay the dead his annual
　　dues,
Those envied rites Saturnian Juno views;
And sends the goddess of the various
　　bow,
To try new methods of revenge below;
Supplies the winds to wing her airy way,
Where in the port secure the navy lay.　790
Swiftly fair Iris down her arch descends,
And, undiscern'd, her fatal voyage ends.
She saw the gath'ring crowd; and, gliding
　　thence,
The desart shore, and fleet without de-
　　fense.
The Trojan matrons, on the sands alone,
With sighs and tears Anchises' death be-
　　moan:
Then, turning to the sea their weeping
　　eyes,
Their pity to themselves renews their cries.
"Alas!" said one, "what oceans yet re-
　　main
For us to sail! what labors to sustain!"
All take the word, and, with a gen'ral
　　groan,　　　　　　　　　　　801
Implore the gods for peace, and places of
　　their own.
　The goddess, great in mischief, views
　　their pains,
And in a woman's form her heav'nly limbs
　　restrains.
In face and shape old Beroe she became, ⎫
Doryclus' wife, a venerable dame,　　　⎬
Once blest with riches, and a mother's ⎬
　　name.　　　　　　　　　　　　　⎭
Thus chang'd, amidst the crying crowd she
　　ran,
Mix'd with the matrons, and these words
　　began:
"O wretched we, whom not the Grecian
　　pow'r,　　　　　　　　　　　810

Nor flames, destroy'd, in Troy's unhappy
    hour !
O wretched we, reserv'd by cruel fate,
Beyond the ruins of the sinking state !
Now sev'n revolving years are wholly run,
Since this improsp'rous voyage we begun;
Since, toss'd from shores to shores, from
    lands to lands,
Inhospitable rocks and barren sands,
Wand'ring in exile thro' the stormy sea,
We search in vain for flying Italy.
Now cast by fortune on this kindred ⎤
    land,   820 ⎥
What should our rest and rising walls ⎬
    withstand,   ⎥
Or hinder here to fix our banish'd band ? ⎦
O country lost, and gods redeem'd in vain,
If still in endless exile we remain !
Shall we no more the Trojan walls renew,
Or streams of some dissembled Simoïs
    view !
Haste, join with me, th' unhappy fleet con-
    sume !
Cassandra bids; and I declare her doom.
In sleep I saw her; she supplied my hands
(For this I more than dreamt) with flaming
    brands: 830
'With these,' said she, 'these wand'ring ⎤
    ships destroy: ⎥
These are your fatal seats, and this your ⎬
    Troy.'   ⎥
Time calls you now; the precious hour ⎥
    employ: ⎦
Slack not the good presage, while Heav'n
    inspires
Our minds to dare, and gives the ready
    fires.
See ! Neptune's altars minister their brands:
The god is pleas'd; the god supplies our
    hands."
Then from the pile a flaming fire she drew,
And, toss'd in air, amidst the galleys threw.
    Wrapp'd in amaze, the matrons wildly
    stare: 840
Then Pyrgo, reverenc'd for her hoary hair,
Pyrgo, the nurse of Priam's num'rous race:
"No Beroe this, tho' she belies her face !
What terrors from her frowning front arise !
Behold a goddess in her ardent eyes !
What rays around her heav'nly face are
    seen !
Mark her majestic voice, and more than
    mortal mien !
Beroe but now I left, whom, pin'd with
    pain,

Her age and anguish from these rites de-
    tain."
She said. The matrons, seiz'd with new
    amaze,   850
Roll their malignant eyes, and on the navy
    gaze.
They fear, and hope, and neither part
    obey:
They hope the fated land, but fear the
    fatal way.
The goddess, having done her task below,
Mounts up on equal wings, and bends her
    painted bow.
Struck with the sight, and seiz'd with rage
    divine,
The matrons prosecute their mad design:
They shriek aloud; they snatch, with im-
    pious hands,
The food of altars; fires and flaming brands.
Green boughs and saplings, mingled in their
    haste,   860
And smoking torches, on the ships they
    cast.
The flame, unstopp'd at first, more fury
    gains,
And Vulcan rides at large with loosen'd
    reins:
Triumphant to the painted sterns he soars,
And seizes, in his way, the banks and crack-
    ling oars.
Eumelus was the first the news to bear,
While yet they crowd the rural theater.
Then, what they hear, is witness'd by their
    eyes:
A storm of sparkles and of flames arise.
Ascanius took th' alarm, while yet he led 870
His early warriors on his prancing steed,
And, spurring on, his equals soon o'erpass'd;
Nor could his frighted friends reclaim his
    haste.
Soon as the royal youth appear'd in view,
He sent his voice before him as he flew:
"What madness moves you, matrons, to de-
    stroy
The last remainders of unhappy Troy !
Not hostile fleets, but your own hopes, you
    burn,
And on your friends your fatal fury turn.
Behold your own Ascanius ! " While he ⎤
    said,   880 ⎥
He drew his glitt'ring helmet from his ⎬
    head,   ⎥
In which the youths to sportful arms he ⎥
    led.   ⎦
By this, Æneas and his train appear;

And now the women, seiz'd with shame and
    fear,
Dispers'd, to woods and caverns take their
    flight,
Abhor their actions, and avoid the light;
Their friends acknowledge, and their error
    find,
And shake the goddess from their alter'd
    mind.
  Not so the raging fires their fury cease,
But, lurking in the seams, with seeming
    peace,   890
Work on their way amid the smold'ring tow,
Sure in destruction, but in motion slow.
The silent plague thro' the green timber
    eats,
And vomits out a tardy flame by fits.
Down to the keels, and upward to the sails,
The fire descends, or mounts, but still pre-
    vails;
Nor buckets pour'd, nor strength of human
    hand,
Can the victorious element withstand.
  The pious hero rends his robe, and throws
To heav'n his hands, and with his hands his
    vows.   900
" O Jove," he cried, " if pray'rs can yet
    have place;
If thou abhorr'st not all the Dardan race;
If any spark of pity still remain;   ⎫
If gods are gods, and not invok'd in vain; ⎬
Yet spare the relics of the Trojan train ! ⎭
Yet from the flames our burning vessels
    free,
Or let thy fury fall alone on me !
At this devoted head thy thunder throw,
And send the willing sacrifice below ! "
  Scarce had he said, when southern storms
    arise: 910
From pole to pole the forky lightning flies;
Loud rattling shakes the mountains and the
    plain;
Heav'n bellies downward, and descends in
    rain.
Whole sheets of water from the clouds are
    sent,
Which, hissing thro' the planks, the flames
    prevent,
And stop the fiery pest. Four ships alone
Burn to the waist, and for the fleet atone.
  But doubtful thoughts the hero's heart
    divide;
If he should still in Sicily reside,
Forgetful of his fates, or tempt the main,
In hope the promis'd Italy to gain.   921

Then Nautes, old and wise, to whom alone
The will of Heav'n by Pallas was fore-
    shown;
Vers'd in portents, experienc'd, and inspir'd
To tell events, and what the fates requir'd;
Thus while he stood, to neither part inclin'd,
With cheerful words reliev'd his lab'ring
    mind:
" O goddess-born, resign'd in ev'ry state,
With patience bear, with prudence push
    your fate.
By suff'ring well, our Fortune we subdue;
Fly when she frowns, and, when she calls,
    pursue.   931
Your friend Acestes is of Trojan kind;
To him disclose the secrets of your mind:
Trust in his hands your old and useless
    train:
Too num'rous for the ships which yet
    remain:
The feeble, old, indulgent of their ease,
The dames who dread the dangers of the
    seas,
With all the dastard crew, who dare not
    stand
The shock of battle with your foes by land.
Here you may build a common town for all,
And, from Acestes' name, Acesta call."
The reasons, with his friend's experience
    join'd,   942
Encourag'd much, but more disturb'd his
    mind.
  'T was dead of night; when to his slum-
    b'ring eyes
His father's shade descended from the
    skies,
And thus he spoke: " O more than vital
    breath,
Lov'd while I liv'd, and dear ev'n after
    death;
O son, in various toils and troubles toss'd,
The King of Heav'n employs my careful
    ghost
On his commands: the god, who sav'd from
    fire   950
Your flaming fleet, and heard your just
    desire.
The wholesome counsel of your friend
    receive,
And here the coward train and women
    leave:
The chosen youth, and those who nobly
    dare,
Transport, to tempt the dangers of the war.
The stern Italians will their courage try;

Rough are their manners, and their minds
    are high.
But first to Pluto's palace you shall go,
And seek my shade among the blest below:
For not with impious ghosts my soul
    remains,   960
Nor suffers with the damn'd perpetual
    pains,
But breathes the living air of soft Elysian
    plains.
The chaste Sibylla shall your steps convey,
And blood of offer'd victims free the way.
There shall you know what realms the
    gods assign,
And learn the fates and fortunes of your
    line.
But now, farewell! I vanish with the
    night,
And feel the blast of heav'n's approach-
    ing light."
He said, and mix'd with shades, and took
    his airy flight.
" Whither so fast ? " the filial duty cried;
" And why, ah why, the wish'd embrace de-
    nied ? "   971
He said, and rose: as holy zeal inspires,
He rakes hot embers, and renews the fires;
His country gods and Vesta then adores
With cakes and incense, and their aid im-
    plores.
Next, for his friends and royal host he sent,
Reveal'd his vision, and the gods' intent,
With his own purpose. All, without delay,
The will of Jove, and his desires obey.
They list with women each degenerate
    name,   980
Who dares not hazard life for future fame.
These they cashier: the brave remaining
    few,
Oars, banks, and cables, half consum'd,
    renew.
The prince designs a city with the plow;
The lots their sev'ral tenements allow.
This part is nam'd from Ilium, that from
    Troy,
And the new king ascends the throne with
    joy;
A chosen senate from the people draws;
Appoints the judges, and ordains the laws.
Then, on the top of Eryx, they begin   990
A rising temple to the Paphian queen.
Anchises, last, is honor'd as a god;
A priest is added, annual gifts bestow'd,
And groves are planted round his blest
    abode.

Nine days they pass in feasts, their temples
    crown'd;
And fumes of incense in the fanes abound.
Then from the south arose a gentle breeze
That curl'd the smoothness of the glassy
    seas;
The rising winds a ruffling gale afford,
And call the merry mariners aboard.   1000
    Now loud laments along the shores re-
    sound,
Of parting friends in close embraces bound.
The trembling women, the degenerate train,
Who shunn'd the frightful dangers of the
    main,
Ev'n those desire to sail, and take their
    share
Of the rough passage and the promis'd
    war:
Whom good Æneas cheers, and recom-
    mends
To their new master's care his fearful
    friends.
On Eryx' altars three fat calves he lays;
A lamb new-fallen to the stormy seas;   1010
Then slips his haulsers, and his anchors
    weighs.
High on the deck the godlike hero stands,
With olive crown'd, a charger in his hands;
Then cast the reeking entrails in the brine,
And pour'd the sacrifice of purple wine.
Fresh gales arise; with equal strokes they
    vie,
And brush the buxom seas, and o'er the
    billows fly.
    Meantime the mother goddess, full of
    fears,
To Neptune thus address'd, with tender
    tears:
" The pride of Jove's imperious queen, the
    rage,   1020
The malice which no suff'rings can as-
    suage,
Compel me to these pray'rs; since neither
    fate,
Nor time, nor pity, can remove her hate:
Ev'n Jove is thwarted by his haughty
    wife;
Still vanquish'd, yet she still renews the
    strife.
As if 't were little to consume the town
Which aw'd the world, and wore th' im-
    perial crown,
She prosecutes the ghost of Troy with pains,
And gnaws, ev'n to the bones, the last re-
    mains.

Let her the causes of her hatred tell;   1030
But you can witness its effects too well.
You saw the storm she rais'd on Libyan
    floods,
That mix'd the mounting billows with the
    clouds;
When, bribing Æolus, she shook the main,
And mov'd rebellion in your wat'ry reign.
With fury she possess'd the Dardan dames,
To burn their fleet with execrable flames,
And forc'd Æneas, when his ships were
    lost,
To leave his foll'wers on a foreign coast.
For what remains, your godhead I im-
    plore,   1040
And trust my son to your protecting pow'r.
If neither Jove's nor Fate's decree with-
    stand,
Secure his passage to the Latian land."
Then thus the mighty Ruler of the Main:
"What may not Venus hope from Nep-
    tune's reign?
My kingdom claims your birth; my late
    defense
Of your indanger'd fleet may claim your
    confidence.
Nor less by land than sea my deeds de-
    clare
How much your lov'd Æneas is my care.
Thee, Xanthus, and thee, Simoïs, I at-
    test: 1050
Your Trojan troops when proud Achilles
    press'd,
And drove before him headlong on the ⎫
    plain,   ⎪
And dash'd against the walls the trem-   ⎬
    bling train;   ⎪
When floods were fill'd with bodies of   ⎭
    the slain;
When crimson Xanthus, doubtful of his ⎫
    way,   ⎪
Stood up on ridges to behold the sea;   ⎬
(New heaps came tumbling in, and chok'd ⎪
    his way;)   ⎭
When your Æneas fought, but fought with
    odds
Of force unequal, and unequal gods;
I spread a cloud before the victor's sight,
Sustain'd the vanquish'd, and secur'd his
    flight;   1061
Ev'n then secur'd him, when I sought with
    joy
The vow'd destruction of ungrateful Troy.
My will's the same: fair goddess, fear no
    more,

Your fleet shall safely gain the Latian shore;
Their lives are giv'n; one destin'd head
    alone
Shall perish, and for multitudes atone."
Thus having arm'd with hopes her anxious
    mind,
His finny team Saturnian Neptune join'd,
Then adds the foamy bridle to their jaws, 1070
And to the loosen'd reins permits the laws.
High on the waves his azure car he guides; ⎫
Its axles thunder, and the sea subsides,   ⎪
And the smooth ocean rolls her silent   ⎬
    tides.   ⎭
The tempests fly before their father's face,
Trains of inferior gods his triumph grace,
And monster whales before their master
    play,
And choirs of Tritons crowd the wat'ry way
The marshal'd pow'rs in equal troops di- ⎫
    vide   ⎪
To right and left; the gods his better   ⎬
    side   1080   ⎪
Inclose, and on the worse the Nymphs   ⎪
    and Nereids ride.   ⎭
Now smiling hope, with sweet vicissitude,
Within the hero's mind his joys renew'd.
He calls to raise the masts, the sheets dis- ⎫
    play;   ⎪
The cheerful crew with diligence obey;   ⎬
They scud before the wind, and sail in   ⎪
    open sea.   ⎭
Ahead of all the master pilot steers;
And, as he leads, the following navy veers.
The steeds of Night had travel'd half the
    sky,
The drowsy rowers on their benches lie,
When the soft God of Sleep, with easy
    flight,   1091
Descends, and draws behind a trail of light.
Thou, Palinurus, art his destin'd prey;
To thee alone he takes his fatal way.
Dire dreams to thee, and iron sleep, he
    bears;
And, lighting on thy prow, the form of
    Phorbas wears.
Then thus the traitor god began his tale: ⎫
"The winds, my friend, inspire a pleasing ⎬
    gale;   ⎪
The ships, without thy care, securely sail. ⎭
Now steal an hour of sweet repose; and I
Will take the rudder and thy room sup-
    ply."   1101
To whom the yawning pilot, half asleep:
"Me dost thou bid to trust the treach'rous
    deep,

The harlot smiles of her dissembling face,
And to her faith commit the Trojan race?
Shall I believe the Siren South again,
And, oft betray'd, not know the monster
main?"
He said: his fasten'd hands the rudder
keep,
And, fix'd on heav'n, his eyes repel in-
vading sleep.
The god was wroth, and at his temples
threw   1110
A branch in Lethe dipp'd, and drunk with
Stygian dew:
The pilot, vanquish'd by the pow'r divine,
Soon clos'd his swimming eyes, and lay su-
pine.
Scarce were his limbs extended at their
length,
The god, insulting with superior strength,
Fell heavy on him, plung'd him in the sea,
And, with the stern, the rudder tore away.
Headlong he fell, and, struggling in the
main,
Cried out for helping hands, but cried in
vain.
The victor dæmon mounts obscure in air, 1120
While the ship sails without the pilot's
care.
On Neptune's faith the floating fleet re-
lies;
But what the man forsook, the god sup-
plies,
And o'er the dang'rous deep secure the
navy flies;
Glides by the Sirens' cliffs, a shelfy coast,
Long infamous for ships and sailors lost,
And white with bones. Th' impetuous ocean
roars,
And rocks rebellow from the sounding
shores.
The watchful hero felt the knocks, and
found
The tossing vessel sail'd on shoaly ground.
Sure of his pilot's loss, he takes him-
self   1131
The helm, and steers aloof, and shuns the
shelf.
Inly he griev'd, and, groaning from the
breast,
Deplor'd his death; and thus his pain ex-
press'd:
" For faith repos'd on seas, and on the flat-
t'ring sky,
Thy naked corpse is doom'd on shores un-
known to lie."

THE SIXTH BOOK OF THE ÆNEIS

THE ARGUMENT

The Sibyl foretells Æneas the adventures he
should meet with in Italy. She attends him
to hell; describing to him the various scenes
of that place, and conducting him to his
father Anchises, who instructs him in those
sublime mysteries of the soul of the world,
and the transmigration; and shews him that
glorious race of heroes which was to descend
from him, and his posterity.

HE said, and wept; then spread his sails
before
The winds, and reach'd at length the
Cuman shore:
Their anchors dropp'd, his crew the ves-
sels moor.
They turn their heads to sea, their sterns
to land,
And greet with greedy joy th' Italian
strand.
Some strike from clashing flints their fiery
seed;
Some gather sticks, the kindled flames to
feed,
Or search for hollow trees, and fell the
woods,
Or trace thro' valleys the discover'd floods.
Thus, while their sev'ral charges they ful-
fil,   10
The pious prince ascends the sacred hill
Where Phœbus is ador'd; and seeks the
shade
Which hides from sight his venerable maid.
Deep in a cave the Sibyl makes abode;
Thence full of fate returns, and of the god.
Thro' Trivia's grove they walk; and now
behold,
And enter now, the temple roof'd with gold.
When Dædalus, to fly the Cretan shore,
His heavy limbs on jointed pinions bore,
(The first who sail'd in air,) 't is sung by
Fame,   20
To the Cumæan coast at length he came,
And, here alighting, built this costly
frame.
Inscrib'd to Phœbus, here he hung on high
The steerage of his wings, that cut the sky:
Then o'er the lofty gate his art emboss'd
Androgeos' death, and off'rings to his ghost;
Sev'n youths from Athens yearly sent, to
meet

The fate appointed by revengeful Crete.
And next to those the dreadful urn was
　　plac'd,
In which the destin'd names by lots were
　　cast:　　　　　　　　　　　　　　30
The mournful parents stand around in tears,
And rising Crete against their shore ap-
　　pears.
There too, in living sculpture, might be seen
The mad affection of the Cretan queen;
Then how she cheats her bellowing lover's
　　eye;　　·
The rushing leap, the doubtful progeny,
The lower part a beast, a man above,
The monument of their polluted love.
Nor far from thence he grav'd the won-
　　drous maze,
A thousand doors, a thousand winding
　　ways:　　　　　　　　　　　　　　40
Here dwells the monster, hid from human
　　view,
Not to be found, but by the faithful clew;
Till the kind artist, mov'd with pious grief,
Lent to the loving maid this last relief,
And all those erring paths describ'd so well
That Theseus conquer'd and the monster
　　fell.
Here hapless Icarus had found his part,
Had not the father's grief restrain'd his
　　art.
He twice assay'd to cast his son in gold;
Twice from his hands he dropp'd the form-
　　ing mold.　　　　　　　　　　　　50
　　All this with wond'ring eyes Æneas
　　view'd;
Each varying object his delight renew'd:
Eager to read the rest — Achates came, ⎫
And by his side the mad divining dame, ⎪
The priestess of the god, Deïphobe her ⎬
　　name. ⎭
"Time suffers not," she said, "to feed your
　　eyes
With empty pleasures; haste the sacrifice.
Sev'n bullocks, yet unyok'd, for Phœbus
　　choose,
And for Diana sev'n unspotted ewes."
This said, the servants urge the sacred
　　rites,　　　　　　　　　　　　　　60
While to the temple she the prince invites.
A spacious cave, within its farmost part,
Was hew'd and fashion'd by laborious art
Thro' the hill's hollow sides: before the
　　place,
A hundred doors a hundred entries grace;
As many voices issue, and the sound

Of Sibyl's words as many times rebound.
Now to the mouth they come. Aloud she
　　cries:
"This is the time; enquire your destinies.
He comes; behold the god!" Thus while
　　she said,　　　　　　　　　　　　70
(And shiv'ring at the sacred entry stay'd,)
Her color chang'd; her face was not the
　　same,
And hollow groans from her deep spirit
　　came.
Her hair stood up; convulsive rage pos-
　　sess'd
Her trembling limbs, and heav'd her la-
　　b'ring breast.
Greater than humankind she seem'd to
　　look,
And with an accent more than mortal
　　spoke.
Her staring eyes with sparkling fury roll;
When all the god came rushing on her
　　soul.
Swiftly she turn'd, and, foaming as she
　　spoke:　　　　　　　　　　　　　80
"Why this delay?" she cried — "the
　　pow'rs invoke!
Thy pray'rs alone can open this abode;
Else vain are my demands, and dumb the
　　god."
　　She said no more. The trembling Tro-
　　jans hear,
O'erspread with a damp sweat and holy
　　fear.
The prince himself, with awful dread pos-
　　sess'd,
His vows to great Apollo thus address'd:
"Indulgent god, propitious pow'r to Troy,
Swift to relieve, unwilling to destroy,
Directed by whose hand the Dardan dart　90
Pierc'd the proud Grecian's only mortal
　　part:
Thus far, by fate's decrees and thy com-
　　mands,
Thro' ambient seas and thro' devouring
　　sands,
Our exil'd crew has sought th' Ausonian
　　ground;
And now, at length, the flying coast is
　　found.
Thus far the fate of Troy, from place to
　　place,
With fury has pursued her wand'ring race.
Here cease, ye pow'rs, and let your ven-
　　geance end:
Troy is no more, and can no more offend.

And thou, O sacred maid, inspir'd to see   100
Th' event of things in dark futurity;
Give me what Heav'n has promis'd to my
    fate,
To conquer and command the Latian state;
To fix my wand'ring gods, and find a place
For the long exiles of the Trojan race.
Then shall my grateful hands a temple
    rear
To the twin gods, with vows and solemn
    pray'r;
And annual rites, and festivals, and games,
Shall be perform'd to their auspicious
    names.
Nor shalt thou want thy honors in my
    land;   110
For there thy faithful oracles shall stand,
Preserv'd in shrines; and ev'ry sacred lay,
Which, by thy mouth, Apollo shall convey:
All shall be treasur'd by a chosen train
Of holy priests, and ever shall remain.
But O ! commit not thy prophetic mind
To flitting leaves, the sport of ev'ry wind,
Lest they disperse in air our empty fate;
Write not, but, what the pow'rs ordain,
    relate."
  Struggling in vain, impatient of her
    load,   120
And lab'ring underneath the pond'rous god,
The more she strove to shake him from her
    breast,
With more and far superior force he press'd;
Commands his entrance, and, without con-
    trol,
Usurps her organs and inspires her soul.
Now, with a furious blast, the hundred ⎫
    doors |
Ope of themselves; a rushing whirlwind ⎬
    roars |
Within the cave, and Sibyl's voice re- |
    stores: ⎭
" Escap'd the dangers of the wat'ry reign,
Yet more and greater ills by land re-
    main.   130
The coast, so long desir'd (nor doubt th'
    event),
Thy troops shall reach, but, having reach'd,
    repent.
Wars, horrid wars, I view — a field of blood,
And Tiber rolling with a purple flood.
Simoïs nor Xanthus shall be wanting there:
A new Achilles shall in arms appear,
And he, too, goddess-born. Fierce Juno's
    hate,
Added to hostile force, shall urge thy fate.

To what strange nations shalt not thou re-
    sort,
Driv'n to solicit aid at ev'ry court !   140
The cause the same which Ilium once op-
    press'd;
A foreign mistress, and a foreign guest.
But thou, secure of soul, unbent with woes,
The more thy fortune frowns, the more
    oppose.
The dawnings of thy safety shall be shown
From whence thou least shalt hope, a Gre-
    cian town."
  Thus, from the dark recess, the Sibyl ⎫
    spoke, |
And the resisting air the thunder broke; ⎬
The cave rebellow'd, and the temple |
    shook.   ⎭
Th' ambiguous god, who rul'd her lab'r- ⎫
    ing breast,   150 |
In these mysterious words his mind ex- ⎬
    press'd; |
Some truths reveal'd, in terms involv'd the |
    rest.   ⎭
At length her fury fell, her foaming ceas'd,
And, ebbing in her soul, the god decreas'd.
Then thus the chief: " No terror to my
    view,
No frightful face of danger can be new.
Inur'd to suffer, and resolv'd to dare,
The Fates, without my pow'r, shall be with-
    out my care.
This let me crave, since near your grove ⎫
    the road |
To hell lies open, and the dark abode   160 ⎬
Which Acheron surrounds, th' innavi- |
    gable flood;   ⎭
Conduct me thro' the regions void of light,
And lead me longing to my father's sight.
For him, a thousand dangers I have ⎫
    sought, |
And, rushing where the thickest Grecians ⎬
    fought, |
Safe on my back the sacred burthen |
    brought.   ⎭
He, for my sake, the raging ocean tried, ⎫
And wrath of Heav'n, my still auspicious |
    guide,   ⎬
And bore beyond the strength decrepid |
    age supplied.   ⎭
Oft, since he breath'd his last, in dead of
    night   170
His reverend image stood before my sight;
Enjoin'd to seek, below, his holy shade;
Conducted there by your unerring aid.
But you, if pious minds by pray'rs are won,

Oblige the father, and protect the son.
Yours is the pow'r; nor Proserpine in vain
Has made you priestess of her nightly reign.
If Orpheus, arm'd with his enchanting lyre,
The ruthless king with pity could inspire,
And from the shades below redeem his
  wife;   180
If Pollux, off'ring his alternate life,
Could free his brother, and can daily go
By turns aloft, by turns descend below —
Why name I Theseus, or his greater friend,
Who trod the downward path, and upward
  could ascend ?
Not less than theirs, from Jove my lineage
  came;
My mother greater, my descent the same."
So pray'd the Trojan prince, and, while he
  pray'd,
His hand upon the holy altar laid.   189
  Then thus replied the prophetess divine:
" O goddess-born, of great Anchises' line,
The gates of hell are open night and day;
Smooth the descent, and easy is the way:
But to return, and view the cheerful skies,
In this the task and mighty labor lies.
To few great Jupiter imparts this grace,
And those of shining worth and heav'nly
  race.
Betwixt those regions and our upper light,
Deep forests and impenetrable night
Possess the middle space: th' infernal
  bounds   200
Cocytus, with his sable waves, surrounds.
But if so dire a love your soul invades,
As twice below to view the trembling
  shades;
If you so hard a toil will undertake,
As twice to pass th' innavigable lake;
Receive my counsel. In the neighb'ring
  grove
There stands a tree; the queen of Stygian
  Jove
Claims it her own; thick woods and gloomy
  night
Conceal the happy plant from human sight.
One bough it bears; but (wondrous to be-
  hold !)   210
The ductile rind and leaves of radiant gold:
This from the vulgar branches must be torn,
And to fair Proserpine the present borne,
Ere leave be giv'n to tempt the nether⎫
  skies.   ⎪
The first thus rent, a second will arise, ⎬
And the same metal the same room   ⎪
  supplies.   ⎭

Look round the wood, with lifted eyes, to
  see
The lurking gold upon the fatal tree:
Then rend it off, as holy rites command;
The willing metal will obey thy hand,   220
Following with ease, if, favor'd by thy fate,
Thou art foredoom'd to view the Stygian
  state:
If not, no labor can the tree constrain;
And strength of stubborn arms and steel
  are vain.
Besides, you know not, while you here
  attend,
Th' unworthy fate of your unhappy friend:
Breathless he lies; and his unburied ghost,
Depriv'd of fun'ral rites, pollutes your host.
Pay first his pious dues; and, for the dead,
Two sable sheep around his hearse be
  led;   230
Then, living turfs upon his body lay: ⎫
This done, securely take the destin'd   ⎬
  way,   ⎪
To find the regions destitute of day."   ⎭
  She said, and held her peace. Æneas⎫
  went   ⎪
Sad from the cave, and full of discontent, ⎬
Unknowing whom the sacred Sibyl meant. ⎭
Achates, the companion of his breast,
Goes grieving by his side, with equal cares
  oppress'd.
Walking, they talk'd, and fruitlessly divin'd
What friend the priestess by those words
  design'd.   240
But soon they found an object to deplore:
Misenus lay extended on the shore;
Son of the God of Winds: none so renown'd
The warrior trumpet in the field to sound,
With breathing brass to kindle fierce
  alarms,
And rouse to dare their fate in honorable
  arms.
He serv'd great Hector, and was ever near,
Not with his trumpet only, but his spear.
But by Pelides' arms when Hector fell,
He chose Æneas; and he chose as well. 250
Swoln with applause, and aiming still at
  more,
He now provokes the sea gods from the
  shore;
With envy Triton heard the martial sound,
And the bold champion, for his challenge,
  drown'd;
Then cast his mangled carcass on the strand:
The gazing crowd around the body stand.
All weep; but most Æneas mourns his fate,

And hastens to perform the funeral state.
In altar-wise, a stately pile they rear;
The basis broad below, and top advanc'd
  in air.   260
An ancient wood, fit for the work design'd,
(The shady covert of the salvage kind,)
The Trojans found: the sounding ax is
  plied;
Firs, pines, and pitch trees, and the tow'ring
  pride
Of forest ashes, feel the fatal stroke,
And piercing wedges cleave the stubborn
  oak.
Huge trunks of trees, fell'd from the steepy
  crown
Of the bare mountains, roll with ruin down.
Arm'd like the rest the Trojan prince
  appears,
And by his pious labor urges theirs.   270
  Thus while he wrought, revolving in his
  mind
The ways to compass what his wish de-
  sign'd,
He cast his eyes upon the gloomy grove,
And then with vows implor'd the Queen
  of Love:
" O may thy pow'r, propitious still to me,
Conduct my steps to find the fatal tree,
In this deep forest; since the Sibyl's breath
Foretold, alas ! too true, Misenus' death."
Scarce had he said, when, full before ⎫
  his sight,   ⎪
Two doves, descending from their airy ⎬
  flight,   280   ⎪
Secure upon the grassy plain alight. ⎭
He knew his mother's birds; and thus he
  pray'd:
" Be you my guides, with your auspicious
  aid,
And lead my footsteps, till the branch be
  found,
Whose glitt'ring shadow gilds the sacred
  ground.
And thou, great parent, with celestial care,
In this distress be present to my pray'r ! "
Thus having said, he stopp'd, with watch-
  ful sight,
Observing still the motions of their flight,
What course they took, what happy signs ⎫
  they shew.   290   ⎪
They fed, and, flutt'ring, by degrees ⎬
  withdrew   ⎪
Still farther from the place, but still ⎪
  in view: ⎭
Hopping and flying, thus they led him on

To the slow lake, whose baleful stench to
  shun
They wing'd their flight aloft; then, stoop-
  ing low,
Perch'd on the double tree that bears the
  golden bough.
Thro' the green leafs the glitt'ring shadows
  glow;
As, on the sacred oak, the wintry mistletoe,
Where the proud mother views her pre-
  cious brood,
And happier branches, which she never
  sow'd.   300
Such was the glitt'ring; such the ruddy rind,
And dancing leaves, that wanton'd in the
  wind.
He seiz'd the shining bough with griping
  hold,
And rent away, with ease, the ling'ring
  gold;
Then to the Sibyl's palace bore the prize. ⎫
  Meantime the Trojan troops, with ⎪
    weeping eyes,   ⎬
To dead Misenus pay his obsequies. ⎭
First, from the ground a lofty pile they
  rear,
Of pitch trees, oaks, and pines, and unc-
  tuous fir:
The fabric's front with cypress twigs they
  strew,   310
And stick the sides with boughs of baleful
  yew.
The topmost part his glitt'ring arms adorn;
Warm waters, then, in brazen caldrons
  borne,
Are pour'd to wash his body, joint by joint,
And fragrant oils the stiffen'd limbs anoint.
With groans and cries Misenus they de-
  plore:
Then on a bier, with purple cover'd o'er,
The breathless body, thus bewail'd, they ⎫
  lay,   ⎪
And fire the pile, their faces turn'd away— ⎬
Such reverend rites their fathers us'd to ⎪
  pay.   320   ⎭
Pure oil and incense on the fire they throw,
And fat of victims, which his friends bestow.
These gifts the greedy flames to dust de-
  vour;
Then on the living coals red wine they
  pour;
And, last, the relics by themselves dispose,
Which in a brazen urn the priests inclose.
Old Corynæus compass'd thrice the crew,
And dipp'd an olive branch in holy dew;

Which thrice he sprinkled round, and thrice
  aloud
Invok'd the dead, and then dismiss'd the
  crowd.   330
But good Æneas order'd on the shore ⎤
A stately tomb, whose top a trumpet ⎬
  bore,
A soldier's fauchion, and a seaman's oar. ⎦
Thus was his friend interr'd; and deathless
  fame
Still to the lofty cape consigns his name.
  These rites perform'd, the prince, with-
  out delay,
Hastes to the nether world his destin'd way.
Deep was the cave; and, downward as it
  went
From the wide mouth, a rocky rough de-
  scent;
And here th' access a gloomy grove de-
  fends,   340
And there th' unnavigable lake extends,
O'er whose unhappy waters, void of light,
No bird presumes to steer his airy flight;
Such deadly stenches from the depth arise,
And steaming sulphur, that infects the
  skies.
From hence the Grecian bards their legends
  make,
And give the name Avernus to the lake.
Four sable bullocks, in the yoke untaught,
For sacrifice the pious hero brought.
The priestess pours the wine betwixt their
  horns;   350
Then cuts the curling hair; that first obla-
  tion burns,
Invoking Hecate hither to repair:
A pow'rful name in hell and upper air.
The sacred priests with ready knives be-
  reave
The beasts of life, and in full bowls re-
  ceive
The streaming blood: a lamb to Hell and
  Night
(The sable wool without a streak of white)
Æneas offers; and, by fate's decree,
A barren heifer, Proserpine, to thee.
With holocausts he Pluto's altar fills;   360
Sev'n brawny bulls with his own hand he
  kills;
Then on the broiling entrails oil he pours;
Which, ointed thus, the raging flame de-
  vours.
Late the nocturnal sacrifice begun,
Nor ended till the next returning sun.
Then earth began to bellow, trees to dance,

And howling dogs in glimm'ring light ad-
  vance,
Ere Hecate came. "Far hence be souls
  profane ! "
The Sibyl cried, "and from the grove ab-
  stain !
Now, Trojan, take the way thy fates
  afford;   370
Assume thy courage, and unsheathe thy
  sword."
She said, and pass'd along the gloomy space;
The prince pursued her steps with equal
  pace.
  Ye realms, yet unreveal'd to human
  sight,
Ye gods who rule the regions of the night,
Ye gliding ghosts, permit me to relate
The mystic wonders of your silent state !
  Obscure they went thro' dreary shades,
  that led
Along the waste dominions of the dead.
Thus wander travelers in woods by night,
By the moon's doubtful and malignant
  light,   381
When Jove in dusky clouds involves the
  skies,
And the faint crescent shoots by fits before
  their eyes.
Just in the gate and in the jaws of hell,
Revengeful Cares and sullen Sorrows dwell,
And pale Diseases, and repining Age,
Want, Fear, and Famine's unresisted rage;
Here Toils, and Death, and Death's half-
  brother, Sleep,
Forms terrible to view, their sentry keep;
With anxious Pleasures of a guilty mind,
Deep Frauds before, and open Force be-
  hind;   391
The Furies' iron beds; and Strife, that
  shakes
Her hissing tresses and unfolds her snakes.
Full in the midst of this infernal road,
An elm displays her dusky arms abroad:
The God of Sleep there hides his heavy
  head,
And empty dreams on ev'ry leaf are spread.
Of various forms unnumber'd specters more,
Centaurs, and double shapes, besiege the
  door.   399
Before the passage, horrid Hydra stands,
And Briareus with all his hundred hands;
Gorgons, Geryon with his triple frame;
And vain Chimæra vomits empty flame.
The chief unsheath'd his shining steel, pre-
  par'd,

Tho' seiz'd with sudden fear, to force the
    guard,
Off'ring his brandish'd weapon at their
    face;
Had not the Sibyl stopp'd his eager pace,
And told him what those empty phantoms
    were:
Forms without bodies, and impassive air.
Hence to deep Acheron they take their
    way,   410
Whose troubled eddies, thick with ooze and
    clay,
Are whirl'd aloft, and in Cocytus lost.
There Charon stands, who rules the dreary
    coast —
A sordid god: down from his hoary chin
A length of beard descends, uncomb'd,
    unclean;
His eyes, like hollow furnaces on fire;
A girdle, foul with grease, binds his ob-
    scene attire.
He spreads his canvas; with his pole he
    steers;
The freights of flitting ghosts in his thin
    bottom bears.
He look'd in years; yet in his years were
    seen   420
A youthful vigor and autumnal green.
An airy crowd came rushing where he
    stood,
Which fill'd the margin of the fatal flood:
Husbands and wives, boys and unmarried
    maids,
And mighty heroes' more majestic shades,
And youths, intomb'd before their fathers'
    eyes,
With hollow groans, and shrieks, and feeble
    cries.
Thick as the leaves in autumn strow the
    woods,
Or fowls, by winter forc'd, forsake the
    floods,
And wing their hasty flight to happier
    lands;   430
Such, and so thick, the shiv'ring army
    stands,
And press for passage with extended
    hands.
  Now these, now those, the surly boat-
    man bore:
The rest he drove to distance from the
    shore.
The hero, who beheld with wond'ring eyes
The tumult mix'd with shrieks, laments, and
    cries,

Ask'd of his guide, what the rude con-
    course meant;
Why to the shore the thronging people
    bent;
What forms of law among the ghosts were
    us'd;
Why some were ferried o'er, and some re-
    fus'd.   440
" Son of Anchises, offspring of the gods,"
The Sibyl said, " you see the Stygian floods,
The sacred stream which heav'n's imperial
    state
Attests in oaths, and fears to violate.
The ghosts rejected are th' unhappy crew
Depriv'd of sepulchers and fun'ral due:
The boatman, Charon; those, the buried
    host,
He ferries over to the farther coast;
Nor dares his transport vessel cross the
    waves
With such whose bones are not compos'd in
    graves.   450
A hundred years they wander on the shore;
At length, their penance done, are wafted
    o'er."
The Trojan chief his forward pace repress'd,
Revolving anxious thoughts within his
    breast.
He saw his friends, who, whelm'd beneath
    the waves,
Their fun'ral honors claim'd, and ask'd
    their quiet graves.
The lost Leucaspis in the crowd he knew,
And the brave leader of the Lycian crew,
Whom, on the Tyrrhene seas, the tempests
    met;   459
The sailors master'd, and the ship o'erset.
  Amidst the spirits, Palinurus press'd,
Yet fresh from life, a new-admitted guest,
Who, while he steering view'd the stars,
    and bore
His course from Afric to the Latian shore,
Fell headlong down. The Trojan fix'd his
    view,
And scarcely thro' the gloom the sullen
    shadow knew.
Then thus the prince: " What envious
    pow'r, O friend,
Brought your lov'd life to this disastrous
    end ?
For Phœbus, ever true in all he said,   469
Has in your fate alone my faith betray'd.
The god foretold you should not die, before
You reach'd, secure from seas, th' Italian
    shore.

Is this th' unerring pow'r?" The ghost re-
plied:
"Nor Phœbus flatter'd, nor his answers
lied;
Nor envious gods have sent me to the
deep:
But, while the stars and course of heav'n
I keep,
My wearied eyes were seiz'd with fatal
sleep.
I fell; and, with my weight, the helm con-
strain'd
Was drawn along, which yet my gripe re-
tain d.
Now by the winds and raging waves I
swear,   480
Your safety, more than mine, was then my
care;
Lest, of the guide bereft, the rudder lost,
Your ship should run against the rocky
coast.
Three blust'ring nights, borne by the south-
ern blast,
I floated, and discover'd land at last:
High on a mounting wave my head I bore,
Forcing my strength, and gath'ring to the
shore.
Panting, but past the danger, now I seiz'd
The craggy cliffs, and my tir'd members
eas'd.
While, cumber'd with my dropping clothes,
I lay,   490
The cruel nation, covetous of prey,
Stain'd with my blood th' unhospitable
coast;
And now, by winds and waves, my lifeless
limbs are toss'd:
Which O avert, by yon ethereal light,
Which I have lost for this eternal night!
Or, if by dearer ties you may be won,
By your dead sire, and by your living son,
Redeem from this reproach my wand'ring
ghost;
Or with your navy seek the Velin coast,
And in a peaceful grave my corpse compose;
Or, if a nearer way your mother shows, 501
Without whose aid you durst not under-
take
This frightful passage o'er the Stygian
lake,
Lend to this wretch your hand, and waft
him o'er
To the sweet banks of yon forbidden shore."
Scarce had he said, the prophetess began:
"What hopes delude thee, miserable man?

Think'st thou, thus unintomb'd, to cross ⎫
the floods,   ⎪
To view the Furies and infernal gods, 509 ⎬
And visit, without leave, the dark abodes? ⎭
Attend the term of long revolving years;
Fate, and the dooming gods, are deaf to
tears.
This comfort of thy dire misfortune take:
The wrath of Heav'n, inflicted for thy sake,
With vengeance shall pursue th' inhuman
coast,
Till they propitiate thy offended ghost,
And raise a tomb, with vows and solemn
pray'r;
And Palinurus' name the place shall bear."
This calm'd his cares; sooth'd with his fu-
ture fame,
And pleas'd to hear his propagated name.
    Now nearer to the Stygian lake they
draw: 521
Whom, from the shore, the surly boatman
saw;
Observ'd their passage thro' the shady wood,
And mark'd their near approaches to the
flood.
Then thus he call'd aloud, inflam'd with
wrath:
"Mortal, whate'er, who this forbidden path
In arms presum'st to tread, I charge thee,
stand,
And tell thy name, and bus'ness in the
land.
Know this, the realm of night — the Styg-
ian shore:
My boat conveys no living bodies o'er; 530
Nor was I pleas'd great Theseus once to
bear,
Who forc'd a passage with his pointed spear,
Nor strong Alcides — men of mighty fame,
And from th' immortal gods their lineage
came.
In fetters one the barking porter tied,   ⎫
And took him trembling from his   ⎪
sov'reign's side: ⎬
Two sought by force to seize his beau-   ⎪
teous bride."   ⎭
To whom the Sibyl thus: "Compose thy
mind;
Nor frauds are here contriv'd, nor force
design'd.
Still may the dog the wand'ring troops ⎫
constrain   540 ⎪
Of airy ghosts, and vex the guilty train, ⎬
And with her grisly lord his lovely queen ⎪
remain.   ⎭

The Trojan chief, whose lineage is from
   Jove,
Much fam'd for arms, and more for filial
   love,
Is sent to seek his sire in your Elysian
   grove.
If neither piety, nor Heav'n's command,
Can gain his passage to the Stygian strand,
This fatal present shall prevail, at least."
Then shew'd the shining bough, conceal'd
   within her vest.
No more was needful: for the gloomy
   god   550
Stood mute with awe, to see the golden rod;
Admir'd the destin'd off'ring to his queen —
A venerable gift, so rarely seen.
His fury thus appeas'd, he puts to land;
The ghosts forsake their seats at his com-
   mand:
He clears the deck, receives the mighty
   freight;
The leaky vessel groans beneath the weight.
Slowly she sails, and scarcely stems the
   tides;
The pressing water pours within her sides.
His passengers at length are wafted o'er, 560
Expos'd, in muddy weeds, upon the miry
   shore.
   No sooner landed, in his den they found
The triple porter of the Stygian sound,
Grim Cerberus, who soon began to rear
His crested snakes, and arm'd his bristling
   hair.
The prudent Sibyl had before prepar'd
A sop, in honey steep'd, to charm the guard;
Which, mix'd with pow'rful drugs, she cast
   before
His greedy grinning jaws, just op'd to roar.
With three enormous mouths he gapes;
   and straight,   570
With hunger press'd, devours the pleasing
   bait.
Long draughts of sleep his monstrous limbs
   enslave;
He reels, and, falling, fills the spacious
   cave.
The keeper charm'd, the chief without
   delay
Pass'd on, and took th' irremeable way.
Before the gates, the cries of babes new
   born,
Whom fate had from their tender mothers
   torn,
Assault his ears: then those, whom form
   of laws

Condemn'd to die, when traitors judg'd
   their cause.   579
Nor want they lots, nor judges to review
The wrongful sentence, and award a new.
Minos, the strict inquisitor, appears;
And lives and crimes, with his assessors,
   hears.
Round in his urn the blended balls he rolls,
Absolves the just, and dooms the guilty
   souls.
The next, in place and punishment, are
   they
Who prodigally throw their souls away;
Fools, who, repining at their wretched state,
And loathing anxious life, suborn'd their
   fate.
With late repentance now they would
   retrieve   590
The bodies they forsook, and wish to live;
Their pains and poverty desire to bear,
To view the light of heav'n, and breathe
   the vital air:
But fate forbids; the Stygian floods op-
   pose,
And with nine circling streams the captive
   souls inclose.
   Not far from thence, the Mournful Fields
   appear,
So call'd from lovers that inhabit there.
The souls whom that unhappy flame
   invades,
In secret solitude and myrtle shades
Make endless moans, and, pining with
   desire,   600
Lament too late their unextinguish'd fire.
Here Procris, Eriphyle here he found,
Baring her breast, yet bleeding with the
   wound
Made by her son. He saw Pasiphae there,
With Phædra's ghost, a foul incestuous
   pair.
There Laodamia, with Evadne, moves;
Unhappy both, but loyal in their loves:
Cæneus, a woman once, and once a man,
But ending in the sex she first began.
Not far from these Phœnician Dido stood,
Fresh from her wound, her bosom bath'd
   in blood;   611
Whom when the Trojan hero hardly knew,
Obscure in shades, and with a doubtful
   view,
(Doubtful as he who sees, thro' dusky
   night,
Or thinks he sees, the moon's uncertain
   light,)

With tears he first approach'd the sullen
  shade;
And, as his love inspir'd him, thus he said:
"Unhappy queen! then is the common
  breath
Of rumor true, in your reported death,
And I, alas! the cause? By Heav'n, I
  vow,   620
And all the pow'rs that rule the realms
  below,
Unwilling I forsook your friendly state,
Commanded by the gods, and forc'd by
  fate —
Those gods, that fate, whose unresisted ⎤
  might   ⎪
Have sent me to these regions void of light, ⎬
Thro' the vast empire of eternal night.   ⎦
Nor dar'd I to presume, that, press'd with
  grief,
My flight should urge you to this dire re-
  lief.
Stay, stay your steps, and listen to my vows:
'T is the last interview that fate allows!" 630
In vain he thus attempts her mind to move
With tears, and pray'rs, and late-repenting
  love.
Disdainfully she look'd; then turning round,
But fix'd her eyes unmov'd upon the ground,
And what he says and swears, regards no
  more
Than the deaf rocks, when the loud billows
  roar;
But whirl'd away, to shun his hateful sight,
Hid in the forest and the shades of night;
Then sought Sichæus thro' the shady grove,
Who answer'd all her cares, and equal'd all
  her love.   640
  Some pious tears the pitying hero paid,
And follow'd with his eyes the flitting
  shade.
Then took the forward way, by fate or- ⎤
  dain'd,   ⎪
And, with his guide, the farther fields at- ⎬
  tain'd,   ⎪
Where, sever'd from the rest, the warrior ⎪
  souls remain'd.   ⎦
Tydeus he met, with Meleager's race, ⎤
The pride of armies, and the soldiers' ⎬
  grace;   ⎦
And pale Adrastus with his ghastly face.
Of Trojan chiefs he view'd a num'rous train,
All much lamented, all in battle slain;   650
Glaucus and Medon, high above the rest,
Antenor's sons, and Ceres' sacred priest.
And proud Idæus, Priam's charioteer,

Who shakes his empty reins, and aims his
  airy spear.
The gladsome ghosts, in circling troops, at-
  tend,
And with unwearied eyes behold their
  friend;
Delight to hover near, and long to know
What bus'ness brought him to the realms
  below.
But Argive chiefs, and Agamemnon's train,
When his refulgent arms flash'd thro' the
  shady plain,   660
Fled from his well-known face, with ⎤
  wonted fear,   ⎪
As when his thund'ring sword and pointed ⎬
  spear   ⎪
Drove headlong to their ships, and glean'd ⎪
  the routed rear.   ⎦
They rais'd a feeble cry, with trembling
  notes;
But the weak voice deceiv'd their gasping
  throats.
  Here Priam's son, Deïphobus, he found,
Whose face and limbs were one continued
  wound:
Dishonest, with lopp'd arms, the youth ap-
  pears,
Spoil'd of his nose, and shorten'd of his ears.
He scarcely knew him, striving to disown 670
His blotted form, and blushing to be known;
And therefore first began: "O Teucer's ⎤
  race,   ⎪
Who durst thy faultless figure thus de- ⎬
  face?   ⎪
What heart could wish, what hand inflict, ⎪
  this dire disgrace?   ⎦
'T was fam'd, that in our last and fatal night
Your single prowess long sustain'd the fight,
Till tir'd, not forc'd, a glorious fate you
  chose,
And fell upon a heap of slaughter'd foes.
But, in remembrance of so brave a deed,
A tomb and fun'ral honors I decreed;   680
Thrice call'd your manes on the Trojan
  plains:
The place your armor and your name re-
  tains.
Your body too I sought, and, had I found,
Design'd for burial in your native ground."
  The ghost replied: "Your piety has paid
All needful rites, to rest my wand'ring
  shade;
But cruel fate, and my more cruel wife,
To Grecian swords betray'd my sleeping life.
These are the monuments of Helen's love:

The shame I bear below, the marks I bore
 above.   690
You know in what deluding joys we pass'd
The night that was by Heav'n decreed our
 last:
For, when the fatal horse, descending down,
Pregnant with arms, o'erwhelm'd th' un-
 happy town,
She feign'd nocturnal orgies; left my bed,
And, mix'd with Trojan dames, the dances
 led;
Then, waving high her torch, the signal
 made,
Which rous'd the Grecians from their am-
 buscade.
With watching overworn, with cares ⎫
 oppress'd,   ⎬
Unhappy I had laid me down to rest, 700 ⎪
And heavy sleep my weary limbs pos- ⎭
 sess'd.
Meantime my worthy wife our arms mis-
 laid,
And from beneath my head my sword con-
 vey'd;
The door unlatch'd, and, with repeated calls,
Invites her former lord within my walls.
Thus in her crime her confidence she plac'd,
And with new treasons would redeem the
 past.
What need I more? Into the room they ran,
And meanly murther'd a defenseless man.
Ulysses, basely born, first led the way. 710 ⎫
Avenging pow'rs! with justice if I pray, ⎬
That fortune be their own another day! ⎭
But answer you; and in your turn relate,
What brought you, living, to the Stygian
 state:
Driv'n by the winds and errors of the ⎫
 sea,   ⎬
Or did you Heav'n's superior doom obey? ⎪
Or tell what other chance conducts your ⎭
 way,
To view with mortal eyes our dark re-
 treats,
Tumults and torments of th' infernal seats."
 While thus in talk the flying hours they
 pass,   720
The sun had finish'd more than half his race:
And they, perhaps, in words and tears had
 spent
The little time of stay which Heav'n had
 lent;
But thus the Sibyl chides their long delay:
"Night rushes down, and headlong drives
 the day:

'T is here, in different paths, the way di-
 vides;
The right to Pluto's golden palace guides; ⎫
The left to that unhappy region tends, ⎪
Which to the depth of Tartarus descends; ⎬
The seat of night profound, and punish'd ⎪
 fiends."   730 ⎭
Then thus Deïphobus: "O sacred maid,
Forbear to chide, and be your will obey'd!
Lo! to the secret shadows I retire,
To pay my penance till my years expire.
Proceed, auspicious prince, with glory
 crown'd,
And born to better fates than I have found."
He said; and, while he said, his steps he
 turn'd
To secret shadows, and in silence mourn'd.
 The hero, looking on the left, espied
A lofty tow'r, and strong on ev'ry side 740
With treble walls, which Phlegethon sur- ⎫
 rounds,   ⎪
Whose fiery flood the burning empire ⎬
 bounds;   ⎪
And, press'd betwixt the rocks, the bel- ⎭
 lowing noise resounds.
Wide is the fronting gate, and, rais'd on
 high
With adamantine columns, threats the sky.
Vain is the force of man, and Heav'n's as
 vain,
To crush the pillars which the pile sustain.
Sublime on these a tow'r of steel is rear'd;
And dire Tisiphone there keeps the ward,
Girt in her sanguine gown, by night and
 day,   750
Observant of the souls that pass the down-
 ward way.
From hence are heard the groans of ghosts,
 the pains
Of sounding lashes and of dragging chains.
The Trojan stood astonish'd at their cries,
And ask'd his guide from whence those
 yells arise;
And what the crimes, and what the tortures
 were,
And loud laments that rent the liquid air.
 She thus replied: "The chaste and holy
 race
Are all forbidden this polluted place.
But Hecate, when she gave to rule the ⎫
 woods,   760 ⎪
Then led me trembling thro' these dire ⎬
 abodes,   ⎪
And taught the tortures of th' aveng- ⎭
 ing gods.

These are the realms of unrelenting fate;
And awful Rhadamanthus rules the state.
He hears and judges each committed crime;
Enquires into the manner, place, and time.
The conscious wretch must all his acts re-
    veal,
(Loth to confess, unable to conceal,)
From the first moment of his vital breath,
To his last hour of unrepenting death. 770
Straight, o'er the guilty ghost, the Fury ⎫
    shakes   ⎪
The sounding whip and brandishes her ⎬
    snakes,   ⎪
And the pale sinner, with her sisters, ⎪
    takes.   ⎭
Then, of itself, unfolds th' eternal door;
With dreadful sounds the brazen hinges
    roar.
You see, before the gate, what stalking ghost
Commands the guard, what sentries keep
    the post.
More formidable Hydra stands within,
Whose jaws with iron teeth severely grin.
The gaping gulf low to the center lies, 780
And twice as deep as earth is distant from
    the skies.
The rivals of the gods, the Titan race,
Here, sing'd with lightning, roll within th'
    unfathom'd space.
Here lie th' Alæan twins, (I saw them both,)
Enormous bodies, of gigantic growth,
Who dar'd in fight the Thund'rer to defy,
Affect his heav'n, and force him from the
    sky.
Salmoneus, suff'ring cruel pains, I found,
For emulating Jove; the rattling sound
Of mimic thunder, and the glitt'ring blaze 790
Of pointed lightnings, and their forky rays.
Thro' Elis and the Grecian towns he flew;
Th' audacious wretch four fiery coursers
    drew:
He wav'd a torch aloft, and, madly vain,
Sought godlike worship from a servile
    train.
Ambitious fool ! with horny hoofs to pass
O'er hollow arches of resounding brass,
To rival thunder in its rapid course,
And imitate inimitable force !
But he, the King of Heav'n, obscure on
    high,   800
Bar'd his red arm, and, launching from the
    sky
His writhen bolt, not shaking empty smoke,
Down to the deep abyss the flaming felon
    strook.

There Tityus was to see, who took his birth
From heav'n, his nursing from the foodful
    earth.
Here his gigantic limbs, with large em-
    brace,
Infold nine acres of infernal space.
A rav'nous vulture, in his open'd side,
Her crooked beak and cruel talons tried;
Still for the growing liver digg'd his breast;
The growing liver still supplied the feast;
Still are his entrails fruitful to their pains:
Th' immortal hunger lasts, th' immortal
    food remains.   813
Ixion and Perithoüs I could name,
And more Thessalian chiefs of mighty fame.
High o'er their heads a mold'ring rock is
    plac'd,
That promises a fall, and shakes at ev'ry
    blast.
They lie below, on golden beds display'd;
And genial feasts with regal pomp are
    made.
The Queen of Furies by their sides is set,
And snatches from their mouths th' un-
    tasted meat,   821
Which if they touch, her hissing snakes she
    rears,
Tossing her torch, and thund'ring in their
    ears.
Then they, who brothers' better claim dis-
    own,
Expel their parents, and usurp the throne;
Defraud their clients, and, to lucre sold,
Sit brooding on unprofitable gold;
Who dare not give, and ev'n refuse to
    lend
To their poor kindred, or a wanting friend.
Vast is the throng of these; nor less the
    train   830
Of lustful youths, for foul adult'ry slain;
Hosts of deserters, who their honor sold,
And basely broke their faith for bribes of
    gold.
All these within the dungeon's depth re-
    main,
Despairing pardon, and expecting pain.
Ask not what pains; nor farther seek to
    know
Their process, or the forms of law below.
Some roll a weighty stone; some, laid
    along,
And bound with burning wires, on spokes
    of wheels are hung.
Unhappy Theseus, doom'd for ever there,
Is fix'd by fate on his eternal chair;   841

And wretched Phlegyas warns the world
 with cries
(Could warning make the world more just
 or wise):
'Learn righteousness, and dread th'
 avenging deities.'
To tyrants others have their country sold,
Imposing foreign lords, for foreign gold;
Some have old laws repeal'd, new statutes
 made,
Not as the people pleas'd, but as they paid;
With incest some their daughters' bed pro-
 fan'd:
All dar'd the worst of ills, and, what they
 dar'd, attain'd. 850
Had I a hundred mouths, a hundred
 tongues,
And throats of brass, inspir'd with iron
 lungs,
I could not half those horrid crimes repeat,
Nor half the punishments those crimes have
 met.
But let us haste our voyage to pursue:
The walls of Pluto's palace are in view;
The gate, and iron arch above it, stands
On anvils labor'd by the Cyclops' hands.
Before our farther way the Fates allow,
Here must we fix on high the golden
 bough." 860
 She said: and thro' the gloomy shades
 they pass'd,
And chose the middle path. Arriv'd at last,
The prince with living water sprinkled o'er
His limbs and body; then approach'd the
 door,
Possess'd the porch, and on the front above
He fix'd the fatal bough requir'd by Pluto's
 love.
These holy rites perform'd, they took their
 way
Where long extended plains of pleasure lay:
The verdant fields with those of heav'n may
 vie,
With ether vested, and a purple sky; 870
The blissful seats of happy souls below.
Stars of their own, and their own suns, they
 know;
Their airy limbs in sports they exercise,
And on the green contend the wrestler's
 prize.
Some in heroic verse divinely sing;
Others in artful measures lead the ring.
The Thracian bard, surrounded by the rest,
There stands conspicuous in his flowing
 vest;

His flying fingers, and harmonious quill,
Strike sev'n distinguish'd notes, and sev'n
 at once they fill. 880
Here found they Teucer's old heroic race,
Born better times and happier years to
 grace.
Assaracus and Ilus here enjoy
Perpetual fame, with him who founded
 Troy.
The chief beheld their chariots from afar,
Their shining arms, and coursers train'd
 to war:
Their lances fix'd in earth, their steeds
 around,
Free from their harness, graze the flow'ry
 ground.
The love of horses which they had, alive,
And care of chariots, after death survive. 890
Some cheerful souls were feasting on the
 plain;
Some did the song, and some the choir
 maintain,
Beneath a laurel shade, where mighty Po
Mounts up to woods above, and hides his
 head below.
Here patriots live, who, for their country's
 good,
In fighting fields, were prodigal of blood:
Priests of unblemish'd lives here make
 abode,
And poets worthy their inspiring god;
And searching wits, of more mechanic parts,
Who grac'd their age with new-invented
 arts: 900
Those who to worth their bounty did ex-
 tend,
And those who knew that bounty to com-
 mend.
The heads of these with holy fillets bound,
And all their temples were with garlands
 crown'd.
 To these the Sibyl thus her speech
 address'd,
And first to him surrounded by the rest
(Tow'ring his height, and ample was his
 breast):
"Say, happy souls, divine Musæus, say,
Where lives Anchises, and where lies our
 way
To find the hero, for whose only sake 910
We sought the dark abodes, and cross'd the
 bitter lake?"
To this the sacred poet thus replied:
"In no fix'd place the happy souls reside.
In groves we live, and lie on mossy beds,

By crystal streams, that murmur thro' the
　　meads:
But pass yon easy hill, and thence descend;
The path conducts you to your journey's
　　end."
This said, he led them up the mountain's
　　brow,
And shews them all the shining fields
　　below.
They wind the hill, and thro' the blissful
　　meadows go.　　　　　　　　　　920
　　But old Anchises, in a flow'ry vale,
Review'd his muster'd race, and took the
　　tale:
Those happy spirits, which, ordain'd by
　　fate,
For future beings and new bodies wait —
With studious thought observ'd th' illustri-
　　ous throng,
In nature's order as they pass'd along:
Their names, their fates, their conduct, and
　　their care,
In peaceful senates and successful war.
He, when Æneas on the plain appears,
Meets him with open arms, and falling
　　tears.　　　　　　　　　　　　930
"Welcome," he said, "the gods' un-
　　doubted race !
O long expected to my dear embrace !
Once more 't is giv'n me to behold your
　　face !
The love and pious duty which you pay
Have pass'd the perils of so hard a way.
' Tis true, computing times, I now believ'd
The happy day approach'd; nor are my
　　hopes deceiv'd.
What length of lands, what oceans have
　　you pass'd;
What storms sustain'd, and on what shores
　　been cast ?
How have I fear'd your fate ! but fear'd it
　　most,　　　　　　　　　　　　940
When love assail'd you, on the Libyan
　　coast."
To this, the filial duty thus replies:
"Your sacred ghost before my sleeping
　　eyes
Appear'd, and often urg'd this painful
　　enterprise.
After long tossing on the Tyrrhene sea,
My navy rides at anchor in the bay.
But reach your hand, O parent shade, nor
　　shun
The dear embraces of your longing son !"
He said: and falling tears his face bedew:

Then thrice around his neck his arms he
　　threw;　　　　　　　　　　950
And thrice the flitting shadow slipp'd away,
Like winds, or empty dreams that fly the
　　day.
　　Now, in a secret vale, the Trojan sees
A sep'rate grove, thro' which a gentle
　　breeze
Plays with a passing breath, and whispers
　　thro' the trees;
And, just before the confines of the wood,
The gliding Lethe leads her silent flood.
About the boughs an airy nation flew,
Thick as the humming bees, that hunt the
　　golden dew;
In summer's heat on tops of lilies feed,　960
And creep within their bells, to suck the
　　balmy seed:
The winged army roams the fields around;
The rivers and the rocks remurmur to the
　　sound.
Æneas wond'ring stood, then ask'd the
　　cause
Which to the stream the crowding people
　　draws.
Then thus the sire: " The souls that throng
　　the flood
Are those to whom, by fate, are other
　　bodies ow'd:
In Lethe's lake they long oblivion taste,
Of future life secure, forgetful of the past.
Long has my soul desir'd this time and
　　place,　　　　　　　　　　　970
To set before your sight your glorious race,
That this presaging joy may fire your mind
To seek the shores by destiny design'd." —
" O father, can it be, that souls sublime
Return to visit our terrestrial clime,
And that the gen'rous mind, releas'd by
　　death,
Can covet lazy limbs and mortal breath ? "
Anchises then, in order, thus begun
To clear those wonders to his godlike son:
" Know, first, that heav'n, and earth's com-
　　pacted frame,　　　　　　　　980
And flowing waters, and the starry flame,
And both the radiant lights, one common
　　soul
Inspires and feeds, and animates the whole.
This active mind, infus'd thro' all the space,
Unites and mingles with the mighty mass.
Hence men and beasts the breath of life
　　obtain,
And birds of air, and monsters of the main.
Th' ethereal vigor is in all the same,

And every soul is fill'd with equal flame;
As much as earthy limbs, and gross allay
Of mortal members, subject to decay, 991
Blunt not the beams of heav'n and edge
    of day.
From this coarse mixture of terrestrial
    parts,
Desire and fear by turns possess their
    hearts,
And grief, and joy; nor can the groveling
    mind,
In the dark dungeon of the limbs confin'd,
Assert the native skies, or own its heav'nly
    kind:
Nor death itself can wholly wash their
    stains;
But long-contracted filth ev'n in the soul
    remains.
The relics of inveterate vice they wear, 1000
And spots of sin obscene in ev'ry face ap-
    pear.
For this are various penances enjoin'd;
And some are hung to bleach upon the wind,
Some plung'd in waters, others purg'd in
    fires,
Till all the dregs are drain'd, and all the
    rust expires.
All have their *manes*, and those *manes*
    bear:
The few, so cleans'd, to these abodes re-
    pair,
And breathe, in ample fields, the soft
    Elysian air.
Then are they happy, when by length of
    time
The scurf is worn away of each committed
    crime;   1010
No speck is left of their habitual stains,
But the pure ether of the soul remains.
But, when a thousand rolling years are past,
(So long their punishments and penance
    last,)
Whole droves of minds are, by the driving
    god,
Compell'd to drink the deep Lethæan flood,
In large forgetful draughts to steep the
    cares
Of their past labors, and their irksome years,
That, unrememb'ring of its former pain,
The soul may suffer mortal flesh again." 1020
    Thus having said, the father spirit leads
The priestess and his son thro' swarms of
    shades,
And takes a rising ground, from thence to
    see

The long procession of his progeny.
"Survey," pursued the sire, "this airy
    throng,
As, offer'd to thy view, they pass along.
These are th' Italian names, which fate will
    join
With ours, and graff upon the Trojan line.
Observe the youth who first appears in
    sight,
And holds the nearest station to the light,
Already seems to snuff the vital air,   1031
And leans just forward, on a shining spear:
Silvius is he, thy last-begotten race,
But first in order sent, to fill thy place;
An Alban name, but mix'd with Dardan
    blood,
Born in the covert of a shady wood:
Him fair Lavinia, thy surviving wife,
Shall breed in groves, to lead a solitary life.
In Alba he shall fix his royal seat,
And, born a king, a race of kings beget. 1040
Then Procas, honor of the Trojan name,
Capys, and Numitor, of endless fame.
A second Silvius after these appears;
Silvius Æneas, for thy name he bears;
For arms and justice equally renown'd,
Who, late restor'd, in Alba shall be crown'd.
How great they look! how vig'rously they
    wield
Their weighty lances, and sustain the shield !
But they, who crown'd with oaken wreaths
    appear,
Shall Gabian walls and strong Fidena rear;
Nomentum, Bola, with Pometia, found; 1051
And raise Collatian tow'rs on rocky ground.
All these shall then be towns of mighty
    fame,
Tho' now they lie obscure, and lands with-
    out a name.
See Romulus the great, born to restore
The crown that once his injur'd grandsire
    wore.
This prince a priestess of your blood shall
    bear,
And like his sire in arms he shall appear.
Two rising crests his royal head adorn;
Born from a god, himself to godhead born:
His sire already signs him for the skies, 1061
And marks the seat amidst the deities.
Auspicious chief ! thy race, in times to come,
Shall spread the conquests of imperial
    Rome —
Rome, whose ascending tow'rs shall heav'n
    invade.
Involving earth and ocean in her shade;

High as the Mother of the Gods in place,
And proud, like her, of an immortal race.
Then, when in pomp she makes the Phryg-
    ian round,
With golden turrets on her temples
    crown'd;   1070
A hundred gods her sweeping train supply;
Her offspring all, and all command the sky.
" Now fix your sight, and stand intent, to
    see
Your Roman race, and Julian progeny.
The mighty Cæsar waits his vital hour,
Impatient for the world, and grasps his
    promis'd pow'r.
But next behold the youth of form divine,
Cæsar himself, exalted in his line;
Augustus, promis'd oft, and long foretold, ⎤
Sent to the realm that Saturn rul'd of   ⎟
    old;   1080 ⎬
Born to restore a better age of gold.   ⎦
Afric and India shall his pow'r obey;   ⎤
He shall extend his propagated sway   ⎬
Beyond the solar year, without the starry ⎦
    way,
Where Atlas turns the rolling heav'ns
    around,
And his broad shoulders with their lights
    are crown'd.
At his foreseen approach, already quake
The Caspian kingdoms and Mæotian lake:
Their seers behold the tempest from afar,
And threat'ning oracles denounce the war.
Nile hears him knocking at his sev'nfold
    gates,   1091
And seeks his hidden spring, and fears his
    nephew's fates.
Nor Hercules more lands or labors knew,
Not tho' the brazen-footed hind he slew,
Freed Erymanthus from the foaming boar,
And dipp'd his arrows in Lernæan gore;
Nor Bacchus, turning from his Indian war,
By tigers drawn triumphant in his car,
From Nisus' top descending on the plains,
With curling vines around his purple reins.
And doubt we yet thro' dangers to pursue 1101
The paths of honor, and a crown in view ?
But what's the man, who from afar ap-
    pears ?
His head with olive crown'd, his hand a
    censer bears.
His hoary beard and holy vestments bring
His lost idea back: I know the Roman king.
He shall to peaceful Rome new laws ordain,
Call'd from his mean abode a scepter to sus-
    tain.

Him Tullus next in dignity succeeds,
An active prince, and prone to martial deeds.
He shall his troops for fighting fields pre-
    pare,   1111
Disus'd to toils, and triumphs of the war.
By dint of sword his crown he shall in-
    crease,
And scour his armor from the rust of peace.
Whom Ancus follows, with a fawning air,
But vain within, and proudly popular.
Next view the Tarquin kings, th' avenging
    sword
Of Brutus, justly drawn, and Rome restor'd.
He first renews the rods and ax severe, 1119
And gives the consuls royal robes to wear
His sons, who seek the tyrant to sustain,
And long for arbitrary lords again,
With ignominy scourg'd, in open sight,
He dooms to death deserv'd, asserting pub-
    lic right.
Unhappy man, to break the pious laws
Of nature, pleading in his children's cause !
Howe'er the doubtful fact is understood, ⎤
'T is love of honor, and his country's good: ⎬
The consul, not the father, sheds the   ⎦
    blood.
Behold Torquatus the same track pursue;
And, next, the two devoted Decii view: 1131
The Drusian line, Camillus loaded home
With standards well redeem'd, and foreign
    foes o'ercome.
The pair you see in equal armor shine,
Now, friends below, in close embraces join;
But, when they leave the shady realms of
    night,
And, cloth'd in bodies, breathe your upper
    light,
With mortal hate each other shall pursue:
What wars, what wounds, what slaughter
    shall ensue !
From Alpine heights the father first de- ⎤
    scends;   1140 ⎟
His daughter's husband in the plain at-   ⎬
    tends: ⎟
His daughter's husband arms his eastern   ⎦
    friends.
Embrace again, my sons, be foes no more;
Nor stain your country with her children's
    gore !
And thou, the first, lay down thy lawless
    claim,
Thou, of my blood, who bear'st the Julian
    name !
Another comes, who shall in triumph ride,
And to the Capitol his chariot guide,

From conquer'd Corinth, rich with Grecian
   spoils.
And yet another, fam'd for warlike toils,
On Argos shall impose the Roman laws, 1151
And on the Greeks revenge the Trojan cause;
Shall drag in chains their Achillean race; ⎫
Shall vindicate his ancestors' disgrace, ⎬
And Pallas, for her violated place. ⎭
Great Cato there, for gravity renown'd,
And conqu'ring Cossus goes with laurels
   crown'd.
Who can omit the Gracchi ? who declare
The Scipios' worth, those thunderbolts of
   war,
The double bane of Carthage ? Who can see
Without esteem for virtuous poverty, 1161
Severe Fabricius, or can cease t' admire
The plowman consul in his coarse attire ?
Tir'd as I am, my praise the Fabii claim;
And thou, great hero, greatest of thy name,
Ordain'd in war to save the sinking state,
And, by delays, to put a stop to fate !
Let others better mold the running mass ⎫
Of metals, and inform the breathing brass, ⎬
And soften into flesh a marble face; 1170 ⎭
Plead better at the bar; describe the skies,
And when the stars descend, and when they
   rise.
But, Rome, 't is thine alone, with awful ⎫
   sway, ⎪
To rule mankind, and make the world ⎬
   obey, ⎪
Disposing peace and war thy own majes- ⎪
   tic way; ⎭
To tame the proud, the fetter'd slave to
   free:
These are imperial arts, and worthy thee."
   He paus'd; and, while with wond'ring
   eyes they view'd
The passing spirits, thus his speech renew'd:
" See great Marcellus ! how, untir'd in toils,
He moves with manly grace, how rich with
   regal spoils !   1181
He, when his country, threaten'd with
   alarms,
Requires his courage and his conqu'ring
   arms,
Shall more than once the Punic bands af-
   fright;
Shall kill the Gaulish king in single fight;
Then to the Capitol in triumph move,
And the third spoils shall grace Feretrian
   Jove."
Æneas here beheld, of form divine,
A godlike youth in glitt'ring **armor shine,**

With great Marcellus keeping equal pace;
But gloomy were his eyes, dejected was his
   face.   1191
He saw, and, wond'ring, ask'd his airy guide,
What and of whence was he, who press'd
   the hero's side:
" His son, or one of his illustrious name ?
How like the former, and almost the same !
Observe the crowds that compass him
   around;
All gaze, and all admire, and raise a shout-
   ing sound:
But hov'ring mists around his brows are
   spread,
And night, with sable shades, involves his
   head."
" Seek not to know," the ghost replied with
   tears,   1200
" The sorrows of thy sons in future years.
This youth (the blissful vision of a day)
Shall just be shown on earth, and snatch'd
   away.
The gods too high had rais'd the Roman
   state,
Were but their gifts as permanent as great.
What groans of men shall fill the Martian
   field !
How fierce a blaze his flaming pile shall
   yield !
What fun'ral pomp shall floating Tiber see,
When, rising from his bed, he views the
   sad solemnity !   1209
No youth shall equal hopes of glory give,
No youth afford so great a cause to grieve;
The Trojan honor, and the Roman boast,
Admir'd when living, and ador'd when lost !
Mirror of ancient faith in early youth !
Undaunted worth, inviolable truth !
No foe, unpunish'd, in the fighting field
Shall dare thee, foot to foot, with sword
   and shield;
Much less in arms oppose thy matchless
   force,
When thy sharp spurs shall urge thy foam-
   ing horse.
Ah ! couldst thou break thro' fate's severe
   decree,   1220
A new Marcellus shall arise in thee !
Full canisters of fragrant lilies bring,
Mix'd with the purple roses of the spring;
Let me with fun'ral flow'rs his body strow; ⎫
This gift which parents to their children ⎪
   owe, ⎬
This unavailing gift, at least, I may be- ⎪
   stow !' "

Thus having said, he led the hero round
The confines of the blest Elysian ground;
Which when Anchises to his son had shown,
And fir'd his mind to mount the promis'd
     throne,   1230
He tells the future wars, ordain'd by fate;
The strength and customs of the Latian
     state;
The prince, and people; and forearms his
     care
With rules, to push his fortune, or to bear.
   Two gates the silent house of Sleep
     adorn;
Of polish'd iv'ry this, that of transparent
     horn:
True visions thro' transparent horn arise;
Thro' polish'd iv'ry pass deluding lies.
Of various things discoursing as he pass'd,
Anchises hither bends his steps at last. 1240
Then, thro' the gate of iv'ry, he dismiss'd
His valiant offspring and divining guest.
Straight to the ships Æneas took his way,⎫
Embark'd his men, and skimm'd along ⎬
   the sea, ⎭
Still coasting, till he gain'd Cajeta's bay.
At length on oozy ground his galleys moor;
   Their heads are turn'd to sea, their sterns
     to shore.

THE SEVENTH BOOK OF THE ÆNEIS

THE ARGUMENT

King Latinus entertains Æneas, and promises
   him his only daughter, Lavinia, the heiress
   of his crown. Turnus, being in love with
   her, favor'd by her mother, and stirr'd up
   by Juno and Alecto, breaks the treaty which
   was made, and engages in his quarrel Mezentius, Camilla, Messapus, and many others
   of the neighboring princes; whose forces, and
   the names of their commanders, are here
   particularly related.

AND thou, O matron of immortal fame,
Here dying, to the shore hast left thy name;
Cajeta still the place is call'd from thee,
The nurse of great Æneas' infancy.
Here rest thy bones in rich Hesperia's
     plains;
Thy name ('t is all a ghost can have) re-
     mains.
   Now, when the prince her fun'ral rites
     had paid,

He plow'd the Tyrrhene seas with sails dis-
     play'd.
From land a gentle breeze arose by night,⎫
Serenely shone the stars, the moon was ⎪
   bright,   10 ⎬
And the sea trembled with her silver ⎪
   light. ⎭
Now near the shelves of Circe's shores they
     run,
(Circe the rich, the daughter of the Sun,)
A dang'rous coast: the goddess wastes her
     days
In joyous songs; the rocks resound her lays:
In spinning, or the loom, she spends the
     night,
And cedar brands supply her father's light.
From hence were heard, rebellowing to the
     main,
The roars of lions that refuse the chain,
The grunts of bristled boars, and groans of
     bears,   20
And herds of howling wolves that stun the
     sailors' ears.
These from their caverns, at the close of
     night,
Fill the sad isle with horror and affright.
Darkling they mourn their fate, whom
   Circe's pow'r,
(That watch'd the moon and planetary hour,)
With words and wicked herbs from human-
     kind
Had alter'd, and in brutal shapes confin'd.
Which monsters lest the Trojans' pious host
Should bear, or touch upon th' inchanted
     coast,
Propitious Neptune steer'd their course by
   night   30
With rising gales that sped their happy
     flight.
Supplied with these, they skim the sound-
     ing shore,
And hear the swelling surges vainly roar.
Now, when the rosy morn began to rise,
And wav'd her saffron streamer thro' the
     skies;
When Thetis blush'd in purple not her own,
And from her face the breathing winds
     were blown,
A sudden silence sate upon the sea,
And sweeping oars, with struggling, urge
     their way.
   The Trojan, from the main, beheld a
     wood,   40
Which thick with shades and a brown hor-
     ror stood:

Betwixt the trees the Tiber took his course,
With whirlpools dimpled; and with down-
 ward force,
That drove the sand along, he took his way,
And roll'd his yellow billows to the sea.
About him, and above, and round the wood,
The birds that haunt the borders of his
 flood,
That bath'd within, or basked upon his side,
To tuneful songs their narrow throats ap-
 plied.
The captain gives command; the joyful
 train   50
Glide thro' the gloomy shade, and leave the
 main.
 Now, Erato, thy poet's mind inspire,
And fill his soul with thy celestial fire!
Relate what Latium was; her ancient kings;
Declare the past and present state of things,
When first the Trojan fleet Ausonia sought,
And how the rivals lov'd, and how they
 fought.
These are my theme, and how the war be-
 gan,
And how concluded by the godlike man:
For I shall sing of battles, blood, and rage,
Which princes and their people did engage;
And haughty souls, that, mov'd with mu-
 tual hate,   62
In fighting fields pursued and found their
 fate;
That rous'd the Tyrrhene realm with loud
 alarms,
And peaceful Italy involv'd in arms.
A larger scene of action is display'd;
And, rising hence. a greater work is weigh'd.
 Latinus, old and mild, had long possess'd
The Latian scepter, and his people blest:
His father Faunus; a Laurentian dame   70
His mother; fair Marica was her name.
But Faunus came from Picus: Picus drew
His birth from Saturn, if records be true.
Thus King Latinus, in the third degree,
Had Saturn author of his family.
But this old peaceful prince, as Heav'n de-
 creed,
Was blest with no male issue to succeed:
His sons in blooming youth were snatch'd
 by fate;
One only daughter heir'd the royal state.
Fir'd with her love, and with ambition
 led,   80
The neighb'ring princes court her nuptial
 bed.
Among the crowd, but far above the rest,

Young Turnus to the beauteous maid ad-
 dress'd.
Turnus, for high descent and graceful mien,
Was first, and favor'd by the Latian queen;
With him she strove to join Lavinia's hand,
But dire portents the purpos'd match with-
 stand.
Deep in the palace, of long growth, there
 stood
A laurel's trunk, a venerable wood;
Where rites divine were paid; whose holy
 hair   90
Was kept and cut with superstitious care.
This plant Latinus, when his town he
 wall'd,
Then found, and from the tree Laurentum
 call'd;
And last, in honor of his new abode,
He vow'd the laurel to the laurel's god.
It happen'd once (a boding prodigy!)
A swarm of bees, that cut the liquid sky,
(Unknown from whence they took their
 airy flight,)
Upon the topmost branch in clouds alight;
There with their clasping feet together
 clung,   100
And a long cluster from the laurel hung.
An ancient augur prophesied from hence:
"Behold on Latian shores a foreign prince!
From the same parts of heav'n his navy ⎫
 stands,   ⎪
To the same parts on earth; his army   ⎬
 lands;   ⎪
The town he conquers, and the tow'r   ⎭
 commands."
 Yet more, when fair Lavinia fed the fire
Before the gods, and stood beside her sire,
(Strange to relate!) the flames, involv'd in
 smoke
Of incense, from the sacred altar broke, 110
Caught her dishevel'd hair and rich attire;
Her crown and jewels crackled in the fire:
From thence the fuming trail began to
 spread,
And lambent glories danc'd about her head.
This new portent the seer with wonder
 views,
Then pausing, thus his prophecy renews:
"The nymph, who scatters flaming fires
 around,
Shall shine with honor, shall herself be
 crown'd;
But, caus'd by her irrevocable fate,
War shall the country waste, and change
 the state."   120

Latinus, frighted with this dire ostent,
For counsel to his father Faunus went,
And sought the shades renown'd for pro-
   phecy
Which near Albunea's sulph'rous fountain
   lie.
To these the Latian and the Sabine land
Fly, when distress'd, and thence relief de-
   mand.
The priest on skins of off'rings takes his
   ease,
And nightly visions in his slumber sees;
A swarm of thin aërial shapes appears,
And, flutt'ring round his temples, deafs his
   ears: 130
These he consults, the future fates to know,
From pow'rs above, and from the fiends
   below.
Here, for the gods' advice, Latinus flies,
Off'ring a hundred sheep for sacrifice:
Their woolly fleeces, as the rites requir'd,
He laid beneath him, and to rest retir'd.
No sooner were his eyes in slumber bound,
When, from above, a more than mortal
   sound
Invades his ears; and thus the vision ⎫
   spoke: ⎬
"Seek not, my seed, in Latian bands to ⎭
   yoke   140
Our fair Lavinia, nor the gods provoke.
A foreign son upon thy shore descends,
Whose martial fame from pole to pole ex-
   tends.
His race, in arms and arts of peace re- ⎫
   nown'd,   ⎪
Not Latium shall contain, nor Europe ⎬
   bound: ⎪
'T is theirs whate'er the sun surveys ⎭
   around."
These answers, in the silent night receiv'd,
The king himself divulg'd, the land be-
   liev'd:
The fame thro' all the neighb'ring nations
   flew,
When now the Trojan navy was in view. 150
  Beneath a shady tree, the hero spread ⎫
His table on the turf, with cakes of bread; ⎬
And, with his chiefs, on forest fruits he ⎭
   fed.
They sate; and, (not without the god's com-
   mand,)
Their homely fare dispatch'd, the hungry
   band
Invade their trenchers next, and soon de-
   vour,

To mend the scanty meal, their cakes of
   flour.
Ascanius this observ'd, and smiling said:
"See, we devour the plates on which we
   fed."
The speech had omen, that the Trojan race
Should find repose, and this the time and
   place.   161
Æneas took the word, and thus replies,
Confessing fate with wonder in his eyes:
"All hail, O earth! all hail, my household
   gods!
Behold the destin'd place of your abodes!
For thus Anchises prophesied of old,
And this our fatal place of rest foretold:
'When, on a foreign shore, instead of meat,
By famine forc'd, your trenchers you shall
   eat,
Then ease your weary Trojans will attend,
And the long labors of your voyage end. 171
Remember on that happy coast to build,
And with a trench inclose the fruitful field.'
This was that famine, this the fatal place
Which ends the wand'ring of our exil'd
   race.
Then, on to-morrow's dawn, your care em- ⎫
   ploy,   ⎪
To search the land, and where the cities ⎬
   lie,   ⎪
And what the men; but give this day to ⎭
   joy.
Now pour to Jove; and, after Jove is blest,
Call great Anchises to the genial feast: 180
Crown high the goblets with a cheerful
   draught;
Enjoy the present hour; adjourn the future
   thought."
  Thus having said, the hero bound his
   brows
With leafy branches, then perform'd his
   vows;
Adoring first the genius of the place,
Then Earth, the mother of the heav'nly
   race,
The nymphs, and native godheads yet un-
   known,
And Night, and all the stars that gild her
   sable throne,
And ancient Cybel, and Idæan Jove,
And last his sire below, and mother queen
   above.   190
Then heav'n's high monarch thunder'd
   thrice aloud,
And thrice he shook aloft a golden cloud.
Soon thro' the joyful camp a rumor flew,

The time was come their city to renew.
Then ev'ry brow with cheerful green is
crown'd,
The feasts are doubled, and the bowls go
round.
When next the rosy morn disclos'd the
day,
The scouts to sev'ral parts divide their way,
To learn the natives' names, their towns
explore,
The coasts and trendings of the crooked
shore: 200
Here Tiber flows, and here Numicus stands;
Here warlike Latins hold the happy lands.
The pious chief, who sought by peaceful
ways
To found his empire, and his town to raise,
A hundred youths from all his train selects,
And to the Latian court their course directs,
(The spacious palace where their prince
resides,)
And all their heads with wreaths of olive
hides.
They go commission'd to require a peace,
And carry presents to procure access.   210
Thus while they speed their pace, the prince
designs
His new-elected seat, and draws the lines.
The Trojans round the place a rampire cast,
And palisades about the trenches plac'd.
Meantime the train, proceeding on their
way,
From far the town and lofty tow'rs survey;
At length approach the walls. Without the
gate,
They see the boys and Latian youth debate
The martial prizes on the dusty plain:
Some drive the cars, and some the coursers
rein;   220
Some bend the stubborn bow for victory,
And some with darts their active sinews
try.
A posting messenger, dispatch'd from
hence,
Of this fair troop advis'd their aged prince,
That foreign men of mighty stature came;
Uncouth their habit, and unknown their
name.
The king ordains their entrance, and ascends
His regal seat, surrounded by his friends.
The palace built by Picus, vast and ⎤
    proud,   ⎥
Supported by a hundred pillars stood, 230 ⎬
And round incompass'd with a rising   ⎥
    wood.   ⎦

The pile o'erlook'd the town, and drew the
sight;
Surpris'd at once with reverence and de-
light.
There kings receiv'd the marks of ⎤
    sov'reign pow'r;   ⎥
In state the monarchs march'd; the lic- ⎬
    tors bore   ⎥
Their awful axes and the rods before. ⎦
Here the tribunal stood, the house of pray'r,
And here the sacred senators repair;
All at large tables, in long order set,
A ram their off'ring, and a ram their meat.
Above the portal, carv'd in cedar wood, 241
Plac'd in their ranks, their godlike grand-
sires stood;
Old Saturn, with his crooked scythe, on
high;
And Italus, that led the colony;
And ancient Janus, with his double face,
And bunch of keys, the porter of the place.
There good Sabinus, planter of the vines, ⎤
On a short pruning hook his head reclines, ⎥
And studiously surveys his gen'rous ⎬
    wines;   ⎦
Then warlike kings, who for their country
    fought,   250
And honorable wounds from battle brought.
Around the posts hung helmets, darts, ⎤
    and spears,   ⎥
And captive chariots, axes, shields, and ⎬
    bars,   ⎥
And broken beaks of ships, the trophies ⎥
    of their wars.   ⎦
Above the rest, as chief of all the band, ⎤
Was Picus plac'd, a buckler in his hand; ⎬
His other wav'd a long divining wand.   ⎦
Girt in his Gabin gown the hero sate,
Yet could not with his art avoid his fate:
For Circe long had lov'd the youth in
    vain,   260
Till love, refus'd, converted to disdain:
Then, mixing pow'rful herbs, with magic
art,
She chang'd his form, who could not change
his heart;
Constrain'd him in a bird, and made him fly,
With party-color'd plumes, a chatt'ring
pie.
In this high temple, on a chair of state,
The seat of audience, old Latinus sate;
Then gave admission to the Trojan train;
And thus with pleasing accents he began:
" Tell me, ye Trojans, for that name you
    own,   270

Nor is your course upon our coasts un-
  known —
Say what you seek, and whither were you
  bound:
Were you by stress of weather cast
  aground ?
(Such dangers as on seas are often seen,
And oft befall to miserable men,)
Or come, your shipping in our ports to lay,
Spent and disabled in so long a way ?
Say what you want: the Latians you shall
  find
Not forc'd to goodness, but by will inclin'd;
For, since the time of Saturn's holy reign,
His hospitable customs we retain.   281
I call to mind (but time the tale has worn)
Th' Arunci told, that Dardanus, tho' born
On Latian plains, yet sought the Phrygian
  shore,
And Samothracia, Samos call'd before.
From Tuscan Coritum he claim'd his birth;
But after, when exempt from mortal earth,
From thence ascended to his kindred skies,
A god, and, as a god, augments their sacri-
  fice."
  He said. Ilioneus made this reply: 290
" O king, of Faunus' royal family !
Nor wintry winds to Latium forc'd our
  way,
Nor did the stars our wand'ring course be-
  tray.
Willing we sought your shores; and, hither
  bound,
The port, so long desir'd, at length we
  found;
From our sweet homes and ancient realms
  expell'd;
Great as the greatest that the sun beheld.
The god began our line, who rules above;
And, as our race, our king descends from
  Jove:
And hither are we come, by his command,
To crave admission in your happy land.   301
How dire a tempest, from Mycenæ pour'd,
Our plains, our temples, and our town de-
  vour'd;
What was the waste of war, what fierce
  alarms
Shook Asia's crown with European arms;
Ev'n such have heard, if any such there be,
Whose earth is bounded by the frozen sea;
And such as, born beneath the burning sky
And sultry sun, betwixt the tropics lie.
From that dire deluge, thro' the wat'ry
  waste,   310

Such length of years, such various perils
  past,)
At last escap'd, to Latium we repair, ⎫
To beg what you without your want ⎬
  may spare: ⎭
The common water, and the common air;
Sheds which ourselves will build, and mean
  abodes,
Fit to receive and serve our banish'd gods.
Nor our admission shall your realm dis-
  grace,
Nor length of time our gratitude efface.
Besides, what endless honor you shall gain,
To save and shelter Troy's unhappy train !
Now, by my sov'reign, and his fate, I
  swear,   321
Renown'd for faith in peace, for force in
  war;
Oft our alliance other lands desir'd,
And, what we seek of you, of us requir'd.
Despise not then, that in our hands we bear
These holy boughs, and sue with words of
  pray'r.
Fate and the gods, by their supreme com-
  mand,
Have doom'd our ships to seek the Latian
  land.
To these abodes our fleet Apollo sends; 329
Here Dardanus was born, and hither tends;
Where Tuscan Tiber rolls with rapid force,
And where Numicus opes his holy source.
Besides, our prince presents, with his re-
  quest,
Some small remains of what his sire pos-
  sess'd.
This golden charger, snatch'd from burn-
  ing Troy,
Anchises did in sacrifice employ;
This royal robe and this tiara wore
Old Priam, and this golden scepter bore
In full assemblies, and in solemn games;
These purple vests were weav'd by Dardan
  dames."   340
  Thus while he spoke, Latinus roll'd
  around
His eyes, and fix'd a while upon the ground.
Intent he seem'd, and anxious in his breast;
Not by the scepter mov'd, or kingly vest,
But pond'ring future things of wondrous
  weight;
Succession, empire, and his daughter's fate.
On these he mus'd within his thoughtful
  mind,
And then revolv'd what Faunus had divin'd.
This was the foreign prince, by fate decreed

To share his scepter, and Lavinia's bed; 350
This was the race that sure portents fore-
  shew
To sway the world, and land and sea subdue.
At length he rais'd his cheerful head, and
  spoke:
" The pow'rs," said he, "the pow'rs we both
  invoke,
To you, and yours, and mine, propitious be,
And firm our purpose with their augury !
Have what you ask; your presents I receive;
Land, where and when you please, with
  ample leave;
Partake and use my kingdom as your own;
All shall be yours, while I command the
  crown: 360
And, if my wish'd alliance please your king,
Tell him he should not send the peace, but
  bring.
Then let him not a friend's embraces fear;
The peace is made when I behold him here.
Besides this answer, tell my royal guest,
I add to his commands my own request:
One only daughter heirs my crown and
  state,
Whom not our oracles, nor Heav'n, nor fate,
Nor frequent prodigies, permit to join
With any native of th' Ausonian line. 370
A foreign son-in-law shall come from far
(Such is our doom), a chief renown'd in war,
Whose race shall bear aloft the Latian name,
And thro' the conquer'd world diffuse our
  fame.
Himself to be the man the fates require,
I firmly judge, and, what I judge, desire."
  He said, and then on each bestow'd a steed.
Three hundred horses, in high stables fed,
Stood ready, shining all, and smoothly
  dress'd:
Of these he chose the fairest and the best, 380
To mount the Trojan troop. At his com-
  mand
The steeds caparison'd with purple stand,
With golden trappings, glorious to behold,
And champ betwixt their teeth the foaming
  gold.
Then to his absent guest the king decreed
A pair of coursers born of heav'nly breed,
Who from their nostrils breath'd ethereal
  fire;
Whom Circe stole from her celestial sire,
By substituting mares produc'd on earth,
Whose wombs conceiv'd a more than mortal
  birth. 390
These draw the chariot which Latinus sends,

And the rich present to the prince com-
  mends.
Sublime on stately steeds the Trojans borne,
To their expecting lord with peace return.
  But jealous Juno, from Pachynus' height,
As she from Argos took her airy flight,
Beheld with envious eyes this hateful sight.
She saw the Trojan and his joyful train
Descend upon the shore, desert the main,
Design a town, and, with unhop'd suc-
  cess, 400
Th' embassadors return with promis'd peace.
Then, pierc'd with pain, she shook her
  haughty head,
Sigh'd from her inward soul, and thus she
  said:
" O hated offspring of my Phrygian foes !
O fates of Troy, which Juno's fates oppose !
Could they not fall unpitied on the plain,
But slain revive, and, taken, scape again ?
When execrable Troy in ashes lay,
Thro' fires and swords and seas they forc'd
  their way. 490
Then vanquish'd Juno must in vain conte[cut off]
Her rage disarm'd, her empire at an end.
Breathless and tir'd, is all my fury spent ?
Or does my glutted spleen at length relent ?
As if 't were little from their town to chase,
I thro' the seas pursued their exil'd race;
Ingag'd the heav'ns, oppos'd the stormy
  main;
But billows roar'd, and tempests rag'd in
  vain.
What have my Scyllas and my Syrtes done,
When these they overpass, and those they
  shun ? 419
On Tiber's shores they land, secure of fate,
Triumphant o'er the storms and Juno's hate.
Mars could in mutual blood the Centaurs
  bathe,
And Jove himself gave way to Cynthia's
  wrath,
Who sent the tusky boar to Calydon;
(What great offense had either people
  done ?)
But I, the consort of the Thunderer,
Have wag'd a long and unsuccessful war,
With various arts and arms in vain have
  toil'd, 428
And by a mortal man at length am foil'd.
If native pow'r prevail not, shall I doubt
To seek for needful succor from without ?
If Jove and Heav'n my just desires deny,
Hell shall the pow'r of Heav'n and Jove
  supply.

Grant that the Fates have firm'd, by their
   decree,
The Trojan race to reign in Italy;
At least I can defer the nuptial day,
And with protracted wars the peace delay:
With blood the dear alliance shall be
   bought,
And both the people near destruction
   brought;
So shall the son-in-law and father join, 440
With ruin, war, and waste of either line.
O fatal maid, thy marriage is endow'd
With Phrygian, Latian, and Rutulian blood!
Bellona leads thee to thy lover's hand; ⎫
Another queen brings forth another brand, ⎬
To burn with foreign fires another land! ⎭
A second Paris, diff'ring but in name,
Shall fire his country with a second flame."
   Thus having said, she sinks beneath the
   ground,
With furious haste, and shoots the Stygian
   sound, 450
To rouse Alecto from th' infernal seat
[...] er dire sisters, and their dark retreat.
This Fury, fit for her intent, she chose;
One who delights in wars and human woes.
Ev'n Pluto hates his own misshapen race;
Her sister Furies fly her hideous face;
So frightful are the forms the monster
   takes,
So fierce the hissings of her speckled snakes.
Her Juno finds, and thus inflames her spite:
" O virgin daughter of eternal Night,   460
Give me this once thy labor, to sustain
My right, and execute my just disdain.
Let not the Trojans, with a feign'd pretense
Of proffer'd peace, delude the Latian prince.
Expel from Italy that odious name,
And let not Juno suffer in her fame.
'T is thine to ruin realms, o'erturn a state, ⎫
Betwixt the dearest friends to raise de- ⎬
   bate, ⎭
And kindle kindred blood to mutual hate.
Thy hand o'er towns the fun'ral torch dis-
   plays, 470
And forms a thousand ills ten thousand
   ways.
Now shake, from out thy fruitful breast, the
   seeds
Of envy, discord, and of cruel deeds:
Confound the peace establish'd, and prepare
Their souls to hatred, and their hands to
   war."
   Smear'd as she was with black Gorgonian
   blood,

The Fury sprang above the Stygian flood;
And on her wicker wings, sublime thro'
   night,
She to the Latian palace took her flight:
There sought the queen's apartment, stood
   before 480
The peaceful threshold, and besieg'd the
   door.
Restless Amata lay, her swelling breast ⎫
Fir'd with disdain for Turnus dispossess'd, ⎬
And the new nuptials of the Trojan guest. ⎭
From her black bloody locks the Fury
   shakes
Her darling plague, the fav'rite of her
   snakes;
With her full force she threw the pois'nous
   dart,
And fix'd it deep within Amata's heart,
That, thus envenom'd, she might kindle
   rage,
And sacrifice to strife her house and hus-
   band's age. 490
Unseen, unfelt, the fiery serpent skims
Betwixt her linen and her naked limbs;
His baleful breath inspiring, as he glides,
Now like a chain around her neck he rides,
Now like a fillet to her head repairs,
And with his circling volumes folds her
   hairs.
At first the silent venom slid with ease,
And seiz'd her cooler senses by degrees;
Then, ere th' infected mass was fir'd too
   far,
In plaintive accents she began the war, 500
And thus bespoke her husband: " Shall,"
   she said,
" A wand'ring prince enjoy Lavinia's bed?
If nature plead not in a parent's heart,
Pity my tears, and pity her desert.
I know, my dearest lord, the time will come,
You would, in vain, reverse your cruel
   doom;
The faithless pirate soon will set to sea,
And bear the royal virgin far away!
A guest like him, a Trojan guest before, ⎫
In shew of friendship sought the Spartan ⎬
   shore, 510 ⎥
And ravish'd Helen from her husband ⎭
   bore.
Think on a king's inviolable word;
And think on Turnus, her once plighted
   lord:
To this false foreigner you give your throne,
And wrong a friend, a kinsman, and a son.
Resume your ancient care; and, if the god

Your sire, and you, resolve on foreign blood,
Know all are foreign, in a larger sense,
Not born your subjects, or deriv'd from
   hence.   519
Then, if the line of Turnus you retrace,
He springs from Inachus of Argive race."
   But when she saw her reasons idly spent,
And could not move him from his fix'd in-
   tent,
She flew to rage; for now the snake possess'd
Her vital parts, and poison'd all her breast;
She raves, she runs with a distracted pace,
And fills with horrid howls the public place.
And, as young striplings whip the top for
   sport,
On the smooth pavement of an empty court;
The wooden engine flies and whirls about, 530
Admir'd, with clamors, of the beardless rout;
They lash aloud; each other they provoke,
And lend their little souls at ev'ry stroke:
Thus fares the queen; and thus her fury
   blows
Amidst the crowd, and kindles as she goes.
Nor yet content, she strains her malice
   more,
And adds new ills to those contriv'd before:
She flies the town, and, mixing with a throng
Of madding matrons, bears the bride along,
Wand'ring thro' woods and wilds, and devi-
   ous ways,   540
And with these arts the Trojan match de-
   lays.
She feign'd the rites of Bacchus; cried aloud,
And to the buxom god the virgin vow'd.
" Evoe ! O Bacchus ! " thus began the song;
And " Evoe ! " answer'd all the female
   throng.
" O virgin ! worthy thee alone ! " she cried;
" O worthy thee alone ! " the crew replied.
" For thee she feeds her hair, she leads thy
   dance,
And with thy winding ivy wreathes her
   lance."
Like fury seiz'd the rest; the progress
   known,   550
All seek the mountains, and forsake the
   town:
All, clad in skins of beasts, the jav'lin ⎫
   bear,   ⎪
Give to the wanton winds their flowing ⎬
   hair,   ⎪
And shrieks and shoutings rend the suf- ⎪
   f'ring air.   ⎭
The queen herself, inspir'd with rage divine,
Shook high above her head a flaming pine;

Then roll'd her haggard eyes around the
   throng,
And sung, in Turnus' name, the nuptial
   song:
" Io, ye Latian dames ! if any here
Hold your unhappy queen, Amata, dear; 560
If there be here," she said, " who dare main-
   tain
My right, nor think the name of mother
   vain;
Unbind your fillets, loose your flowing hair,
And orgies and nocturnal rites prepare."
   Amata's breast the Fury thus invades,
And fires with rage, amid the sylvan shades;
Then, when she found her venom spread so
   far,
The royal house embroil'd in civil war,
Rais'd on her dusky wings, she cleaves the
   skies,
And seeks the palace where young Turnus
   lies.   570
His town, as fame reports, was built of old
By Danae, pregnant with almighty gold,
Who fled her father's rage, and, with a ⎫
   train   ⎪
Of following Argives, thro' the stormy ⎬
   main,   ⎪
Driv'n by the southern blasts, was fated ⎪
   here to reign.   ⎭
'T was Ardua once; now Ardea's name it
   bears;
Once a fair city, now consum'd with years.
Here, in his lofty palace, Turnus lay,
Betwixt the confines of the night and day,
Secure in sleep. The Fury laid aside 580 ⎫
Her looks and limbs, and with new ⎬
   methods tried   ⎪
The foulness of th' infernal form to hide. ⎭
Propp'd on a staff, she takes a trembling
   mien:
Her face is furrow'd, and her front obscene;
Deep-dinted wrinkles on her cheek she
   draws;
Sunk are her eyes, and toothless are her
   jaws;
Her hoary hair with holy fillets bound,
Her temples with an olive wreath are crown'd.
Old Chalybe, who kept the sacred fane ⎫
Of Juno. now she seem'd, and thus ⎪
   began,   590 ⎬
Appearing in a dream, to rouse the care- ⎪
   less man: ⎭
" Shall Turnus then such endless toil sustain
In fighting fields, and conquer towns in
   vain ?

Win, for a Trojan head to wear the prize,
Usurp thy crown, enjoy thy victories ?
The bride and scepter which thy blood has
  bought,
The king transfers; and foreign heirs are
  sought.
Go now, deluded man, and seek again
New toils, new dangers, on the dusty plain.
Repel the Tuscan foes; their city seize; 600
Protect the Latians in luxurious ease.
This dream all-pow'rful Juno sends; I bear
Her mighty mandates, and her words you
  hear.
Haste; arm your Ardeans; issue to the
  plain;
With fate to friend, assault the Trojan
  train:
Their thoughtless chiefs, their painted ships,
  that lie
In Tiber's mouth, with fire and sword de-
  stroy.
The Latian king, unless he shall submit,
Own his old promise, and his new forget —
Let him, in arms, the pow'r of Turnus
  prove, 610
And learn to fear whom he disdains to love.
For such is Heav'n's command." The youth-
  ful prince
With scorn replied, and made this bold de-
  fense:
"You tell me, mother, what I knew before:
The Phrygian fleet is landed on the shore.
I neither fear nor will provoke the war;
My fate is Juno's most peculiar care.
But time has made you dote, and vainly tell
Of arms imagin'd in your lonely cell.
Go; be the temple and the gods your
  care; 620
Permit to men the thought of peace and
  war."
    These haughty words Alecto's rage pro-
  voke,
And frighted Turnus trembled as she spoke.
Her eyes grow stiffen'd, and with sulphur
  burn;
Her hideous looks and hellish form return;
Her curling snakes with hissings fill the
  place,
And open all the furies of her face:
Then, darting fire from her malignant
  eyes,
She cast him backward as he strove to
  rise,
And, ling'ring, sought to frame some new
  replies. 630

High on her head she rears two twisted
  snakes;
Her chains she rattles, and her whip she
  shakes;
And, churning bloody foam, thus loudly
  speaks:
"Behold whom time has made to dote, and
  tell
Of arms imagin'd in her lonely cell !
Behold the Fates' infernal minister !
War, death, destruction, in my hand I bear."
    Thus having said, her smold'ring torch,
  impress'd
With her full force, she plung'd into his
  breast.
Aghast he wak'd; and, starting from his
  bed, 640
Cold sweat, in clammy drops, his limbs o'er-
  spread.
"Arms ! arms ! " he cries: "my sword and
  shield prepare ! "
He breathes defiance, blood, and mortal war.
So, when with crackling flames a caldron
  fries,
The bubbling waters from the bottom rise:
Above the brims they force their fiery way;
Black vapors climb aloft, and cloud the day.
    The peace polluted thus, a chosen band
He first commissions to the Latian land,
In threat'ning embassy; then rais'd the
  rest, 650
To meet in arms th' intruding Trojan guest,
To force the foes from the Lavinian shore,
And Italy's indanger'd peace restore.
Himself alone an equal match he boasts,
To fight the Phrygian and Ausonian hosts.
The gods invok'd, the Rutuli prepare
Their arms, and warm each other to the
  war.
His beauty these, and those his blooming
  age,
The rest his house and his own fame ingage.
    While Turnus urges thus his enter-
  prise, 660
The Stygian Fury to the Trojans flies;
New frauds invents, and takes a steepy
  stand,
Which overlooks the vale with wide com-
  mand;
Where fair Ascanius and his youthful
  train,
With horns and hounds, a hunting match
  ordain,
And pitch their toils around the shady
  plain.

The Fury fires the pack; they snuff, they
    vent,
And feed their hungry nostrils with the scent.
'T was of a well-grown stag, whose antlers
    rise
High o'er his front; his beams invade the
    skies.   670
From this light cause th' infernal maid pre-
    pares
The country churls to mischief, hate, and
    wars.
    The stately beast the two Tyrrhidæ bred,
Snatch'd from his dam, and the tame young-
    ling fed.
Their father Tyrrheus did his fodder bring,
Tyrrheus, chief ranger to the Latian king:
Their sister Silvia cherish'd with her care
The little wanton, and did wreaths prepare
To hang his budding horns, with ribbons
    tied
His tender neck, and comb'd his silken
    hide,   680
And bath'd his body. Patient of command
In time he grew, and, growing us'd to hand,
He waited at his master's board for food;
Then sought his salvage kindred in the
    wood,
Where grazing all the day, at night he
    came
To his known lodgings, and his country
    dame.
    This household beast, that us'd the wood-
    land grounds,
Was view'd at first by the young hero's
    hounds,
As down the stream he swam, to seek re-
    treat
In the cool waters, and to quench his
    heat.   690
Ascanius, young, and eager of his game,
Soon bent his bow, uncertain in his aim;
But the dire fiend the fatal arrow guides,
Which pierc'd his bowels thro' his panting
    sides.
The bleeding creature issues from the
    floods,
Possess'd with fear, and seeks his known
    abodes,
His old familiar hearth and household
    gods.
He falls; he fills the house with heavy
    groans,
Implores their pity, and his pain bemoans.
Young Silvia beats her breast, and cries
    aloud   700

For succor from the clownish neighborhood:
The churls assemble; for the fiend, who
    lay
In the close woody covert, urg'd their way.
One with a brand yet burning from the
    flame,
Arm'd with a knotty club another came:
Whate'er they catch or find, without their
    care,
Their fury makes an instrument of war.
Tyrrheus, the foster father of the beast,
Then clench'd a hatchet in his horny fist,
But held his hand from the descending
    stroke,   710
And left his wedge within the cloven oak,
To whet their courage and their rage pro-
    voke.
And now the goddess, exercis'd in ill,
Who watch'd an hour to work her impious
    will,
Ascends the roof, and to her crooked horn,
Such as was then by Latian shepherds
    borne,
Adds all her breath: the rocks and woods
    around,
And mountains, tremble at th' infernal
    sound.
The sacred lake of Trivia from afar,
The Veline fountains, and sulphureous
    Nar,   720
Shake at the baleful blast, the signal of
    the war.
Young mothers wildly stare, with fear
    possess'd,
And strain their helpless infants to their
    breast.
    The clowns, a boist'rous, rude, ungovern'd
    crew,
With furious haste to the loud summons
    flew.
The pow'rs of Troy, then issuing on the
    plain,
With fresh recruits their youthful chief sus-
    tain:
Not theirs a raw and unexperienc'd train,
But a firm body of embattled men.
At first, while fortune favor'd neither
    side,   730
The fight with clubs and burning brands was
    tried;
But now, both parties reinforc'd, the fields
Are bright with flaming swords and brazen
    shields.
A shining harvest either host displays,
And shoots against the sun with equal rays.

Thus, when a black-brow'd gust begins to
   rise,
White foam at first on the curl'd ocean
   fries;
Then roars the main, the billows mount
   the skies;
Till, by the fury of the storm full blown,
The muddy bottom o'er the clouds is
   thrown.   740
First Almon falls, old Tyrrheus' eldest care,
Pierc'd with an arrow from the distant war:
Fix'd in his throat the flying weapon stood,
And stopp'd his breath, and drank his vital
   blood.
Huge heaps of slain around the body rise:
Among the rest, the rich Galesus lies;
A good old man, while peace he preach'd in
   vain,
Amidst the madness of th' unruly train:
Five herds, five bleating flocks, his pastures
   fill d;
His lands a hundred yoke of oxen till'd. 750
   Thus, while in equal scales their fortune
     stood,
The Fury bath'd them in each other's blood;
Then, having fix'd the fight, exulting flies,
And bears fulfill'd her promise to the skies.
To Juno thus she speaks: "Behold ! 't is
   done,
The blood already drawn, the war begun;
The discord is complete; nor can they cease
The dire debate, nor you command the peace.
Now, since the Latian and the Trojan brood
Have tasted vengeance and the sweets of
   blood;   760
Speak, and my pow'r shall add this office
   more:
The neighb'ring nations of th' Ausonian
   shore
Shall hear the dreadful rumor, from afar,
Of arm'd invasion, and embrace the war."
Then Juno thus: "The grateful work is
   done,
The seeds of discord sow'd, the war begun;
Frauds, fears, and fury have possess'd the
   state,
And fix'd the causes of a lasting hate.
A bloody Hymen shall th' alliance join
Betwixt the Trojan and Ausonian line: 770
But thou with speed to night and hell
   repair;
For not the gods, nor angry Jove, will
   bear
Thy lawless wand'ring walks in upper
   air.

Leave what remains to me." Saturnia
   said:
The sullen fiend her sounding wings dis-
   play'd,
Unwilling left the light, and sought the
   nether shade.
   In midst of Italy, well known to fame,
There lies a lake (Amsanctus is the name)
Below the lofty mounts: on either side
Thick forests the forbidden entrance
   hide.   780
Full in the center of the sacred wood
An arm arises of the Stygian flood,
Which, breaking from beneath with bellow-
   ing sound,
Whirls the black waves and rattling stones
   around.
Here Pluto pants for breath from out his
   cell,
And opens wide the grinning jaws of hell.
To this infernal lake the Fury flies;
Here hides her hated head, and frees the
   lab'ring skies.
Saturnian Juno now, with double care,
Attends the fatal process of the war.   790
The clowns, return'd, from battle bear the
   slain,
Implore the gods, and to their king com-
   plain.
The corps of Almon and the rest are
   shown;
Shrieks, clamors, murmurs, fill the frighted
   town.
Ambitious Turnus in the press appears,
And, aggravating crimes, augments their
   fears;
Proclaims his private injuries aloud,
A solemn promise made, and disavow'd;
A foreign son is sought, and a mix'd mun-
   gril brood.
Then they, whose mothers, frantic with
   their fear,   800
In woods and wilds the flags of Bacchus
   bear,
And lead his dances with dishevel'd hair,
Increase the clamor, and the war demand,
(Such was Amata's interest in the land,)
Against the public sanctions of the peace,
Against all omens of their ill success.
With fates averse, the rout in arms resort,
To force their monarch, and insult the court.
But, like a rock unmov'd, a rock that
   braves
The raging tempest and the rising
   waves —   810

Propp'd on himself he stands; his solid
    sides
Wash off the seaweeds, and the sounding
    tides —
So stood the pious prince, unmov'd, and long
Sustain'd the madness of the noisy throng.
But, when he found that Juno's pow'r pre-
    vail'd,
And all the methods of cool counsel fail'd,
He calls the gods to witness their offense,
Disclaims the war, asserts his innocence.
" Hurried by fate," he cries, " and borne
    before
A furious wind, we leave the faithful
    shore.   820
O more than madmen ! you yourselves shall
    bear
The guilt of blood and sacrilegious war:
Thou, Turnus, shalt atone it by thy fate,
And pray to Heav'n for peace, but pray too
    late.
For me, my stormy voyage at an end,
I to the port of death securely tend.
The fun'ral pomp which to your kings you
    pay,
Is all I want, and all you take away."
He said no more, but, in his walls confin'd,
Shut out the woes which he too well
    divin'd;   830
Nor with the rising storm would vainly
    strive,
But left the helm, and let the vessel drive.
    A solemn custom was observ'd of old,
Which Latium held, and now the Romans
    hold,
Their standard when in fighting fields they ⎤
    rear
Against the fierce Hyrcanians, or declare ⎬
The Scythian, Indian, or Arabian war; ⎦
Or from the boasting Parthians would re-
    gain
Their eagles, lost in Carrhæ's bloody plain.
Two gates of steel (the name of Mars they
    bear,   840
And still are worship'd with religious fear)
Before his temple stand: the dire abode,
And the fear'd issues of the furious god,
Are fenc'd with brazen bolts; without the
    gates,
The wary guardian Janus doubly waits.
Then, when the sacred senate votes the ⎤
    wars,
The Roman consul their decree declares, ⎬
And in his robes the sounding gates un- ⎦
    bars.

The youth in military shouts arise,
And the loud trumpets break the yielding
    skies.   850
These rites, of old by sov'reign princes
    us'd,
Were the king's office; but the king re-
    fus'd,
Deaf to their cries, nor would the gates
    unbar
Of sacred peace, or loose th' imprison'd
    war;
But hid his head, and, safe from loud
    alarms,
Abhorr'd the wicked ministry of arms.
Then heav'n's imperious queen shot down
    from high:
At her approach the brazen hinges fly;
The gates are forc'd, and ev'ry falling bar;
And, like a tempest, issues out the war.   860
    The peaceful cities of th' Ausonian shore,
Lull'd in their ease, and undisturb'd before,
Are all on fire; and some, with studious
    care,
Their restiff steeds in sandy plains pre-
    pare;
Some their soft limbs in painful marches
    try,
And war is all their wish, and arms the
    gen'ral cry.
Part scour the rusty shields with seam;
    and part
New grind the blunted ax, and point the
    dart:
With joy they view the waving ensigns fly,
And hear the trumpet's clangor pierce the
    sky.   870
Five cities forge their arms: th' Atinian
    pow'rs,
Antemnæ, Tibur with her lofty tow'rs,
Ardea the proud, the Crustumerian town:
All these of old were places of renown.
Some hammer helmets for the fighting field;
Some twine young sallows to support the
    shield;
The croslet some, and some the cuishes
    mold,
With silver plated, and with ductile gold.
The rustic honors of the scythe and share
Give place to swords and plumes, the pride
    of war.   880
Old fauchions are new temper'd in the
    fires;
The sounding trumpet ev'ry soul inspires.
The word is giv'n; with eager speed they
    lace

The shining headpiece, and the shield em-
  brace.
The neighing steeds are to the chariot
  tied;
The trusty weapon sits on ev'ry side.
  And now the mighty labor is begun —
Ye Muses, open all your Helicon.
Sing you the chiefs that sway'd th' Auso-
  nian land,
Their arms, and armies under their com-
  mand;   890
What warriors in our ancient clime were
  bred;
What soldiers follow'd, and what heroes
  led.
For well you know, and can record alone,
What fame to future times conveys but
  darkly down.
Mezentius first appear'd upon the plain:
Scorn sate upon his brows, and sour dis-
  dain,
Defying earth and heav'n. Etruria lost,
He brings to Turnus' aid his baffled host.
The charming Lausus, full of youthful fire,
Rode in the rank, and next his sullen
  sire;   900
To Turnus only second in the grace
Of manly mien, and features of the face.
A skilful horseman, and a huntsman bred,
With fates averse a thousand men he led:
His sire unworthy of so brave a son;
Himself well worthy of a happier throne.
Next Aventinus drives his chariot round
The Latian plains, with palms and laurels
  crown'd.
Proud of his steeds, he smokes along the
  field;
His father's hydra fills his ample shield: 910
A hundred serpents hiss about the brims;⎫
The son of Hercules he justly seems   ⎪
By his broad shoulders and gigantic   ⎬
  limbs;   ⎭
Of heav'nly part, and part of earthly
  blood,
A mortal woman mixing with a god.
For strong Alcides, after he had slain
The triple Geryon, drove from conquer'd
  Spain
His captive herds; and, thence in triumph
  led,
On Tuscan Tiber's flow'ry banks they fed.
Then on Mount Aventine the son of
  Jove   920
The priestess Rhea found, and forc'd to
  love.

For arms, his men long piles and jav'lins
  bore;
And poles with pointed steel their foes in
  battle gore.
Like Hercules himself his son appears,
In salvage pomp; a lion's hide he wears;
About his shoulders hangs the shaggy skin;
The teeth and gaping jaws severely grin.
Thus, like the god his father, homely dress'd,
He strides into the hall, a horrid guest.
  Then two twin brothers from fair Tibur
  came,   930
(Which from their brother Tiburs took the
  name,)
Fierce Coras and Catillus, void of fear:
Arm'd Argive horse they led, and in the
  front appear.
Like cloud-born Centaurs, from the moun-
  tain's height
With rapid course descending to the fight;
They rush along; the rattling woods give
  way;
The branches bend before their sweepy
  sway.
  Nor was Præneste's founder wanting
  there,
Whom fame reports the son of Mulciber:
Found in the fire, and foster'd in the ⎫
  plains,   940⎪
A shepherd and a king at once he reigns, ⎬
And leads to Turnus' aid his country   ⎪
  swains.   ⎭
His own Præneste sends a chosen band,
With those who plow Saturnia's Gabine
  land;
Besides the succor which cold Anien yields,
The rocks of Hernicus, and dewy fields,
Anagnia fat, and Father Amasene —
A num'rous rout, but all of naked men:
Nor arms they wear, nor swords and
  bucklers wield,
Nor drive the chariot thro' the dusty
  field,   950
But whirl from leathern slings huge balls
  of lead,
And spoils of yellow wolves adorn their
  head;
The left foot naked, when they march to
  fight,
But in a bull's raw hide they sheathe the
  right.
  Messapus next, (great Neptune was his
  sire,)
Secure of steel, and fated from the fire,
In pomp appears, and with his ardor warms

A heartless train, unexercis'd in arms:
The just Faliscans he to battle brings,
And those who live where Lake Ciminia
  springs;   960
And where Feronia's grove and temple
  stands,
Who till Fescennian or Flavinian lands.
All these in order march, and marching
  sing
The warlike actions of their sea-born king;
Like a long team of snowy swans on high,
Which clap their wings, and cleave the
  liquid sky,
When, homeward from their wat'ry pastures
  borne,
They sing, and Asia's lakes their notes re-
  turn.
Not one who heard their music from afar,
Would think these troops an army train'd
  to war,   970
But flocks of fowl, that, when the tempests
  roar,
With their hoarse gabbling seek the silent
  shore.
  Then Clausus came, who led a num'rous
    band
Of troops embodied from the Sabine land,
And, in himself alone, an army brought.
'T was he the noble Claudian race begot,
The Claudian race, ordain'd, in times to
  come,
To share the greatness of imperial Rome.
He led the Cures forth, of old renown,   979
Mutuscans from their olive-bearing town,
And all th' Eretian pow'rs; besides a band
That follow'd from Velinum's dewy land,
And Amiternian troops, of mighty fame,
And mountaineers, that from Severus came,
And from the craggy cliffs of Tetrica,   ⎫
And those where yellow Tiber takes his   ⎬
  way,   ⎪
And where Himella's wanton waters play.   ⎭
Casperia sends her arms, with those that
  lie
By Fabaris, and fruitful Foruli:
The warlike aids of Horta next appear,   990
And the cold Nursians come to close the
  rear,
Mix'd with the natives born of Latine blood,
Whom Allia washes with her fatal flood.
Not thicker billows beat the Libyan main,
When pale Orion sets in wintry rain;
Nor thicker harvests on rich Hermus rise,
Or Lycian fields, when Phœbus burns the
  skies,

Than stand these troops: their bucklers
  ring around;
Their trampling turns the turf, and shakes
  the solid ground.
  High in his chariot then Halesus came, 1000
A foe by birth to Troy's unhappy name:
From Agamemnon born — to Turnus' aid
A thousand men the youthful hero led,
Who till the Massic soil, for wine re-
  nown'd,
And fierce Auruncans from their hilly
  ground,
And those who live by Sidicinian shores,
And where with shoaly fords Vulturnus
  roars,
Cales' and Osca's old inhabitants,
And rough Saticulans, inur'd to wants:
Light demi-lances from afar they throw,
Fasten'd with leathern thongs, to gall the
  foe.   1011
Short crooked swords in closer fight they
  wear,
And on their warding arm light bucklers
  bear.
  Nor, Œbalus, shalt thou be left unsung,
From nymph Semethis and old Telon
  sprung,
Who then in Teleboan Capri reign'd;
But that short isle th' ambitious youth dis-
  dain'd,
And o'er Campania stretch'd his ample
  sway,
Where swelling Sarnus seeks the Tyrrhene
  sea;
O'er Batulum, and where Abella sees,   1020
From her high tow'rs, the harvest of her
  trees.
And these (as was the Teuton use of old)
Wield brazen swords, and brazen bucklers
  hold;
Sling weighty stones, when from afar they
  fight;
Their casques are cork, a covering thick
  and light.
  Next these in rank, the warlike Ufens
    went,
And led the mountain troops that Nursia
  sent.
The rude Equicolæ his rule obey'd;
Hunting their sport, and plund'ring was
  their trade.
In arms they plow'd, to battle still pre-
  par'd: 1030
Their soil was barren, and their hearts were
  hard.

Umbro the priest the proud Marrubians
led,
By King Archippus sent to Turnus' aid,
And peaceful olives crown'd his hoary
head.
His wand and holy words, the viper's rage,
And venom'd wounds of serpents could as-
suage.
He, when he pleas'd with powerful juice to
steep
Their temples, shut their eyes in pleasing
sleep.
But vain were Marsian herbs, and magic art,
To cure the wound giv'n by the Dardan
dart: 1040
Yet his untimely fate th' Angitian woods
In sighs remurmur'd to the Fucine floods.
  The son of fam'd Hippolytus was there,
Fam'd as his sire, and, as his mother, fair;
Whom in Egerian groves Aricia bore,
And nurs'd his youth along the marshy
shore,
Where great Diana's peaceful altars flame,
In fruitful fields; and Virbius was his name.
Hippolytus, as old records have said,
Was by his stepdam sought to share her
bed;   1050
But, when no female arts his mind could
move,
She turn'd to furious hate her impious love.
Torn by wild horses on the sandy shore,
Another's crimes th' unhappy hunter bore,
Glutting his father's eyes with guiltless
gore.
But chaste Diana, who his death deplor'd,
With Æsculapian herbs his life restor'd.
Then Jove, who saw from high, with just
disdain,
The dead inspir'd with vital breath again,
Struck to the center, with his flaming
dart,   1060
Th' unhappy founder of the godlike art.
But Trivia kept in secret shades alone
Her care, Hippolytus, to fate unknown;
And call'd him Virbius in th' Egerian grove,
Where then he liv'd obscure, but safe from
Jove.
For this, from Trivia's temple and her
wood
Are coursers driv'n, who shed their mas-
ter's blood,
Affrighted by the monsters of the flood.
His son, the second Virbius, yet retain'd
His father's art, and warrior steeds he
rein'd.   1070

Amid the troops, and like the leading
god,
High o'er the rest in arms the graceful
Turnus rode:
A triple pile of plumes his crest adorn'd,
On which with belching flames Chimæra
burn'd:
The more the kindled combat rises high'r,
The more with fury burns the blazing fire.
Fair Io grac'd his shield; but Io now
With horns exalted stands, and seems to
low —
A noble charge ! Her keeper by her side,
To watch her walks, his hundred eyes ap-
plied;   1080
And on the brims her sire, the wat'ry god,
Roll'd from a silver urn his crystal flood.
A cloud of foot succeeds, and fills the fields
With swords, and pointed spears, and
clatt'ring shields;
Of Argives, and of old Sicanian bands,
And those who plow the rich Rutulian lands;
Auruncan youth, and those Sacrana yields,
And the proud Labicans, with painted
shields,
And those who near Numician streams
reside,
And those whom Tiber's holy forests
hide,   1090
Or Circe's hills from the main land di-
vide;
Where Ufens glides along the lowly lands,
Or the black water of Pomptina stands.
  Last, from the Volscians fair Camilla
came,
And led her warlike troops, a warrior dame;
Unbred to spinning, in the loom unskill'd,
She chose the nobler Pallas of the field.
Mix'd with the first, the fierce virago
fought,
Sustain'd the toils of arms, the danger
sought,
Outstripp'd the winds in speed upon the
plain,   1100
Flew o'er the fields, nor hurt the bearded
grain:
She swept the seas, and, as she skimm'd
along,
Her flying feet unbath'd on billows hung.
Men, boys, and women, stupid with surprise,
Where'er she passes, fix their wond'ring
eyes:
Longing they look, and, gaping at the sight,
Devour her o'er and o'er with vast delight;
Her purple habit sits with such a grace

On her smooth shoulders, and so suits her
   face;
Her head with ringlets of her hair is
   crown'd, 1110
And in a golden caul the curls are bound.
She shakes her myrtle jav'lin; and, behind,
Her Lycian quiver dances in the wind.

THE EIGHTH BOOK OF THE ÆNEIS

THE ARGUMENT

The war being now begun, both the generals
   make all possible preparations. Turnus
   sends to Diomedes. Æneas goes in person to
   beg succors from Evander and the Tuscans.
   Evander receives him kindly, furnishes him
   with men, and sends his son Pallas with him.
   Vulcan, at the request of Venus, makes arms
   for her son Æneas, and draws on his shield
   the most memorable actions of his posterity.

WHEN Turnus had assembled all his pow'rs,
His standard planted on Laurentum's tow'rs;
When now the sprightly trumpet, from afar,
Had giv'n the signal of approaching war,
Had rous'd the neighing steeds to scour the
   fields,
While the fierce riders clatter'd on their
   shields;
Trembling with rage, the Latian youth pre-
   pare
To join th' allies, and headlong rush to war.
Fierce Ufens, and Messapus, led the crowd,
With bold Mezentius, who blasphem'd
   aloud. 10
These thro' the country took their waste-
   ful course,
The fields to forage, and to gather force.
Then Venulus to Diomede they send,
To beg his aid Ausonia to defend,
Declare the common danger, and inform
The Grecian leader of the growing storm:
Æneas, landed on the Latian coast,
With banish'd gods, and with a baffled host,
Yet now aspir'd to conquest of the state, 19
And claim'd a title from the gods and fate;
What num'rous nations in his quarrel came,
And how they spread his formidable name.
What he design'd, what mischief might
   arise,
If fortune favor'd his first enterprise,
Was left for him to weigh, whose equal fears,
And common interest, was involv'd in theirs.

While Turnus and th' allies thus urge
   the war,
The Trojan, floating in a flood of care,
Beholds the tempest which his foes prepare.
This way and that he turns his anxious
   mind; 30
Thinks, and rejects the counsels he design'd;
Explores himself in vain, in ev'ry part,
And gives no rest to his distracted heart.
So, when the sun by day, or moon by night,
Strike on the polish'd brass their trembling
   light,
The glitt'ring species here and there divide,
And cast their dubious beams from side to
   side;
Now on the walls, now on the pavement
   play,
And to the ceiling flash the glaring day.
'T was night; and weary nature lull'd
   asleep 40
The birds of air, and fishes of the deep,
And beasts, and mortal men. The Trojan
   chief
Was laid on Tiber's banks, oppress'd with
   grief,
And found in silent slumber late relief.
Then, thro' the shadows of the poplar wood,
Arose the father of the Roman flood;
An azure robe was o'er his body spread,
A wreath of shady reeds adorn'd his head:
Thus, manifest to sight, the god appear'd,
And with these pleasing words his sorrow
   cheer'd: 50
" Undoubted offspring of ethereal race,
O long expected in this promis'd place !
Who thro' the foes hast borne thy banish'd
   gods,
Restor'd them to their hearths, and old
   abodes;
This is thy happy home, the clime where
   fate
Ordains thee to restore the Trojan state.
Fear not ! The war shall end in lasting peace,
And all the rage of haughty Juno cease.
And that this nightly vision may not seem
Th' effect of fancy, or an idle dream, 60
A sow beneath an oak shall lie along,
All white herself, and white her thirty
   young.
When thirty rolling years have run their
   race,
Thy son Ascanius, on this empty space,
Shall build a royal town, of lasting fame,
Which from this omen shall receive the
   name.

Time shall approve the truth. For what
   remains,
And how with sure success to crown thy
   pains,
With patience next attend. A banish'd band,
Driv'n with Evander from th' Arcadian
   land,   70
Have planted here, and plac'd on high their
   walls;
Their town the founder Pallanteum calls,
Deriv'd from Pallas, his great-grandsire's
   name:
But the fierce Latians old possession claim,
With war infesting the new colony.
These make thy friends, and on their aid
   rely.
To thy free passage I submit my streams.
Wake, son of Venus, from thy pleasing
   dreams;
And, when the setting stars are lost in day,
To Juno's pow'r thy just devotion pay;   80
With sacrifice the wrathful queen appease:
Her pride at length shall fall, her fury cease.
When thou return'st victorious from the
   war,
Perform thy vows to me with grateful care.
The god am I, whose yellow water flows
Around these fields, and fattens as it goes:
Tiber my name; among the rolling floods
Renown'd on earth, esteem'd among the gods.
This is my certain seat. In times to come,
My waves shall wash the walls of mighty
   Rome."   90
   He said, and plung'd below. While yet
   he spoke,
His dream Æneas and his sleep forsook.
He rose, and looking up, beheld the skies
With purple blushing, and the day arise.
Then water in his hollow palm he took
From Tiber's flood, and thus the pow'rs be-
   spoke:
" Laurentian nymphs, by whom the streams
   are fed,
And Father Tiber, in thy sacred bed
Receive Æneas, and from danger keep.
Whatever fount, whatever holy deep,   100
Conceals thy wat'ry stores; where'er they
   rise,
And, bubbling from below, salute the skies;
Thou, king of horned floods, whose plen-
   teous urn
Suffices fatness to the fruitful corn,
For this thy kind compassion of our woes,
Shalt share my morning song and ev'ning
   vows.

But, O be present to thy people's aid,
And firm the gracious promise thou hast
   made ! "
Thus having said, two galleys, from his
   stores,
With care he chooses, mans, and fits with
   oars.   110
Now on the shore the fatal swine is found.
Wondrous to tell ! — She lay along the
   ground:
Her well-fed offspring at her udders hung;
She white herself, and white her thirty
   young.
Æneas takes the mother and her brood,
And all on Juno's altar are bestow'd.
   The foll'wing night, and the succeeding
   day,
Propitious Tiber smooth'd his wat'ry way:
He roll'd his river back, and pois'd he stood,
A gentle swelling, and a peaceful flood.   120
The Trojans mount their ships; they put
   from shore,
Borne on the waves, and scarcely dip an oar.
Shouts from the land give omen to their
   course,
And the pitch'd vessels glide with easy
   force.
The woods and waters wonder at the gleam
Of shields, and painted ships that stem the
   stream.
One summer's night and one whole day they
   pass
Betwixt the greenwood shades, and cut the
   liquid glass.
The fiery sun had finish'd half his race,
Look'd back, and doubted in the middle
   space,   130
When they from far beheld the rising
   tow'rs,
The tops of sheds, and shepherds' lowly
   bow'rs,
Thin as they stood, which, then of homely
   clay,
Now rise in marble, from the Roman sway.
These cots (Evander's kingdom, mean and
   poor)
The Trojan saw, and turn'd his ships to
   shore.
'T was on a solemn day: th' Arcadian states,
The king and prince, without the city gates,
Then paid their off'rings in a sacred grove
To Hercules, the warrior son of Jove.   140
Thick clouds of rolling smoke involve the
   skies,
And fat of entrails on his altar fries.

But, when they saw the ships that
  stemm'd the flood,
And glitter'd thro' the covert of the wood,
They rose with fear, and left th' unfinish'd
  feast,
Till dauntless Pallas reassur'd the rest
To pay the rites. Himself without delay
A jav'lin seiz'd, and singly took his way;
Then gain'd a rising ground, and call'd
  from far:
" Resolve me, strangers, whence, and what
  you are;   150
Your bus'ness here; and bring you peace
  or war ? "
High on the stern Æneas took his stand,
And held a branch of olive in his hand,
While thus he spoke: " The Phrygians'
  arms you see,
Expell'd from Troy, provok'd in Italy
By Latian foes, with war unjustly made;
At first affianc'd, and at last betray'd.
This message bear: ' The Trojans and their
  chief
Bring holy peace, and beg the king's relief.' "
Struck with so great a name, and all on
  fire,   160
The youth replies : " Whatever you require,
Your fame exacts. Upon our shores de-
  scend,
A welcome guest, and, what you wish, a
  friend."
He said, and, downward hasting to the
  strand,
Embrac'd the stranger prince, and join'd
  his hand.
Conducted to the grove, Æneas broke
The silence first, and thus the king bespoke:
" Best of the Greeks, to whom, by fate's
  command,
I bear these peaceful branches in my hand,
Undaunted I approach you, tho' I know 170
Your birth is Grecian, and your land my
  foe;
From Atreus tho' your ancient lineage came,
And both the brother kings your kindred
  claim;
Yet, my self-conscious worth, your high re-
  nown,
Your virtue, thro' the neighb'ring nations
  blown,
Our fathers' mingled blood, Apollo's voice,
Have led me hither, less by need than choice.
Our founder Dardanus, as fame has sung,
And Greeks acknowledge, from Electra
  sprung:

Electra from the loins of Atlas came; 180
Atlas, whose head sustains the starry frame.
Your sire is Mercury, whom long before
On cold Cyllene's top fair Maia bore.
Maia the fair, on fame if we rely,
Was Atlas' daughter, who sustains the sky.
Thus from one common source our streams
  divide;
Ours is the Trojan, yours th' Arcadian
  side.
Rais'd by these hopes, I sent no news be-
  fore,
Nor ask'd your leave, nor did your faith
  implore;
But come, without a pledge, my own am-
  bassador.   190
The same Rutulians, who with arms pursue
The Trojan race, are equal foes to you.
Our host expell'd, what farther force can
  stay
The victor troops from universal sway ?
Then will they stretch their pow'r athwart
  the land,
And either sea from side to side command.
Receive our offer'd faith, and give us thine;
Ours is a gen'rous and experienc'd line:
We want not hearts nor bodies for the war;
In council cautious, and in fields we dare."
  He said; and while he spoke, with pierc-
  ing eyes 201
Evander view'd the man with vast surprise,
Pleas'd with his action, ravish'd with his
  face:
Then answer'd briefly, with a royal grace:
" O valiant leader of the Trojan line,
In whom the features of thy father shine,
How I recall Anchises ! how I see
His motions, mien, and all my friend, in
  thee !
Long tho' it be, 't is fresh within my mind,
When Priam to his sister's court design'd
A welcome visit, with a friendly stay, 211
And thro' th' Arcadian kingdom took his
  way.
Then, past a boy, the callow down began
To shade my chin, and call me first a man.
I saw the shining train with vast delight,
And Priam's goodly person pleas'd my
  sight:
But great Anchises, far above the rest,
With awful wonder fir'd my youthful breast.
I long'd to join in friendship's holy bands
Our mutual hearts, and plight our mutual
  hands. 220
I first accosted him: I sued, I sought,

And, with a loving force, to Pheneus
  brought.
He gave me, when at length constrain'd to
  go,
A Lycian quiver and a Gnossian bow,
A vest embroider'd, glorious to behold,
And two rich bridles, with their bits of
  gold,
Which my son's coursers in obedience
  hold.
The league you ask, I offer, as your right;
And, when to-morrow's sun reveals the
  light,
With swift supplies you shall be sent
  away.   230
Now celebrate with us this solemn day,
Whose holy rites admit no long delay.
Honor our annual feast; and take your
  seat,
With friendly welcome, at a homely treat."
Thus having said, the bowls (remov'd for
  fear)
The youths replac'd, and soon restor'd the
  cheer.
On sods of turf he set the soldiers round:
A maple throne, rais'd higher from the
  ground,
Receiv'd the Trojan chief; and, o'er the
  bed,
A lion's shaggy hide for ornament they
  spread.   240
The loaves were serv'd in canisters; the
  wine
In bowls; the priest renew'd the rites di-
  vine:
Broil'd entrails are their food, and beef's
  continued chine.
  But when the rage of hunger was re-
  press'd,
Thus spoke Evander to his royal guest:
"These rites, these altars, and this feast,
  O king,
From no vain fears or superstition spring,
Or blind devotion, or from blinder chance,
Or heady zeal, or brutal ignorance;
But, sav'd from danger, with a grateful
  sense,   250
The labors of a god we recompense.
See, from afar, yon rock that mates the sky,
About whose feet such heaps of rubbish lie;
Such indigested ruin; bleak and bare,
How desart now it stands, expos'd in air!
'T was once a robber's den, inclos'd around
With living stone, and deep beneath the
  ground.

The monster Cacus, more than half a beast,
This hold, impervious to the sun, possess'd.
The pavement ever foul with human gore;
Heads, and their mangled members, hung
  the door.   261
Vulcan this plague begot; and, like his sire,
Black clouds he belch'd, and flakes of livid
  fire.
Time, long expected, eas'd us of our load,
And brought the needful presence of a god.
Th' avenging force of Hercules, from
  Spain,
Arriv'd in triumph, from Geryon slain:
Thrice liv'd the giant, and thrice liv'd
  in vain.
His prize, the lowing herds, Alcides drove
Near Tiber's bank, to graze the shady
  grove.   270
Allur'd with hope of plunder, and intent
By force to rob, by fraud to circumvent,
The brutal Cacus, as by chance they stray'd,
Four oxen thence, and four fair kine con-
  vey'd;
And, lest the printed footsteps might be
  seen,
He dragg'd 'em backwards to his rocky
  den.
The tracks averse a lying notice gave,
And led the searcher backward from the
  cave.
  "Meantime the herdsman hero shifts his
  place,
To find fresh pasture and untrodden grass.
The beasts, who miss'd their mates, fill'd
  all around   281
With bellowings, and the rocks restor'd the
  sound.
One heifer, who had heard her love com-
  plain,
Roar'd from the cave, and made the pro-
  ject vain.
Alcides found the fraud; with rage he shook,
And toss'd about his head his knotted oak.
Swift as the winds, or Scythian arrows'
  flight,
He clomb, with eager haste, th' aërial height.
Then first we saw the monster mend his
  pace;
Fear in his eyes, and paleness in his face, 290
Confess'd the god's approach. Trembling
  he springs,
As terror had increas'd his feet with wings;
Nor stay'd for stairs; but down the depth
  he threw
His body, on his back the door he drew

(The door, a rib of living rock; with pains
His father hew'd it out, and bound with
   iron chains):
He broke the heavy links, the mountain
   clos'd,
And bars and levers to his foe oppos'd.
The wretch had hardly made his dungeon
   fast;
The fierce avenger came with bounding
   haste;   300
Survey'd the mouth of the forbidden hold,
And here and there his raging eyes he roll'd.
He gnash'd his teeth; and thrice he com-
   pass'd round
With winged speed the circuit of the ground.
Thrice at the cavern's mouth he pull'd in
   vain,
And, panting, thrice desisted from his pain.
A pointed flinty rock, all bare and black,
Grew gibbous from behind the mountain's
   back;
Owls, ravens, all ill omens of the night,
Here built their nests, and hither wing'd
   their flight.   310
The leaning head hung threat'ning o'er the
   flood,
And nodded to the left. The hero stood
Adverse, with planted feet, and, from the
   right,
Tugg'd at the solid stone with all his might.
Thus heav'd, the fix'd foundations of the
   rock
Gave way; heav'n echo'd at the rattling
   shock.
Tumbling, it chok'd the flood: on either side
The banks leap backward, and the streams
   divide;
The sky shrunk upward with unusual dread,
And trembling Tiber div'd beneath his
   bed.   320
The court of Cacus stands reveal'd to sight;
The cavern glares with new-admitted light.
So the pent vapors, with a rumbling sound,
Heave from below, and rend the hollow
   ground;
A sounding flaw succeeds; and, from on
   high,
The gods with hate beheld the nether sky:
The ghosts repine at violated night,
And curse th' invading sun, and sicken at
   the sight.
The graceless monster, caught in open day,
Inclos'd, and in despair to fly away,   330
Howls horrible from underneath, and fills
His hollow palace with unmanly yells.

The hero stands above, and from afar
Plies him with darts, and stones, and dis-
   tant war.
He, from his nostrils and huge mouth, ex-
   pires
Black clouds of smoke, amidst his father's
   fires,
Gath'ring, with each repeated blast, the
   night,
To make uncertain aim, and erring sight.
The wrathful god then plunges from above,
And, where in thickest waves the sparkles
   drove,   340
There lights; and wades thro' fumes, and
   gropes his way,
Half sing'd, half stifled, till he grasps his
   prey.
The monster, spewing fruitless flames,
   he found;
He squeez'd his throat; he writh'd his
   neck around,
And in a knot his crippled members
   bound;
Then from their sockets tore his burning
   eyes:
Roll'd on a heap, the breathless robber lies.
The doors, unbarr'd, receive the rushing
   day,
And thoro' lights disclose the ravish'd prey.
The bulls, redeem'd, breathe open air again.
Next, by the feet, they drag him from his
   den.   351
The wond'ring neighborhood, with glad
   surprise,
Behold his shagged breast, his giant size,
His mouth that flames no more, and his
   extinguish'd eyes.
From that auspicious day, with rites divine,
We worship at the hero's holy shrine.
Potitius first ordain'd these annual vows:
As priests, were added the Pinarian house,
Who rais'd this altar in the sacred shade,
Where honors, ever due, for ever shall be
   paid.   360
For these deserts, and this high virtue
   shown,
Ye warlike youths, your heads with gar-
   lands crown:
Fill high the goblets with a sparkling flood,
And with deep draughts invoke our com-
   mon god."
   This said, a double wreath Evander
   twin'd,
And poplars black and white his temples
   bind.

Then brims his ample bowl. With like de-
sign
The rest invoke the gods, with sprinkled
wine.
Meantime the sun descended from the skies,
And the bright evening star began to rise.
And now the priests, Potitius at their head,
In skins of beasts involv'd, the long pro-
cession led;   372
Held high the flaming tapers in their hands,
As custom had prescrib'd their holy bands;
Then with a second course the tables load,
And with full chargers offer to the god.
The Salii sing, and cense his altars round
With Saban smoke, their heads with pop-
lar bound —
One choir of old, another of the young, 379
To dance, and bear the burthen of the song.
The lay records the labors, and the praise,
And all th' immortal acts of Hercules:
First, how the mighty babe, when swath'd
in bands,
The serpents strangled with his infant
hands;
Then, as in years and matchless force he
grew,
Th' Œchalian walls, and Trojan, overthrew.
Besides, a thousand hazards they relate,
Procur'd by Juno's and Eurystheus' hate:
"Thy hands, unconquer'd hero, could sub-
due
The cloud-born Centaurs, and the monster
crew: 390
Nor thy resistless arm the bull withstood,
Nor he, the roaring terror of the wood.
The triple porter of the Stygian seat, ⎤
With lolling tongue, lay fawning at thy │
feet,   ⎬
And, seiz'd with fear, forgot his mangled │
meat.   ⎦
Th' infernal waters trembled at thy sight;
Thee, god, no face of danger could affright;
Not huge Typhœus, nor th' unnumber'd
snake,
Increas'd with hissing heads, in Lerna's
lake.
Hail, Jove's undoubted son! an added
grace   400
To heav'n and the great author of thy race!
Receive the grateful off'rings which we pay,
And smile propitious on thy solemn day!"
In numbers thus they sung; above the rest,
The den and death of Cacus crown the feast.
The woods to hollow vales convey the
sound,

The vales to hills, and hills the notes re-
bound.
The rites perform'd, the cheerful train re-
tire.
Betwixt young Pallas and his aged sire,
The Trojan pass'd, the city to survey, 410
And pleasing talk beguil'd the tedious
way.
The stranger cast around his curious eyes,
New objects viewing still, with new sur-
prise;
With greedy joy enquires of various things,
And acts and monuments of ancient kings.
Then thus the founder of the Roman tow'rs:
"These woods were first the seat of sylvan
pow'rs,
Of Nymphs and Fauns, and salvage men,
who took
Their birth from trunks of trees and stub-
born oak.
Nor laws they knew, nor manners, nor ⎤
the care   420 │
Of lab'ring oxen, or the shining share, ⎬
Nor arts of gain, nor what they gain'd to │
spare.   ⎦
Their exercise the chase; the running flood
Supplied their thirst, the trees supplied
their food.
Then Saturn came, who fled the pow'r of
Jove,
Robb'd of his realms, and banish'd from
above.
The men, dispers'd on hills, to towns he
brought,
And laws ordain'd, and civil customs taught,
And Latium call'd the land where safe he
lay
From his unduteous son, and his usurping
sway.   430
With his mild empire, peace and plenty
came;
And hence the golden times deriv'd their
name.
A more degenerate and discolor'd age
Succeeded this, with avarice and rage.
Th' Ausonians then, and bold Sicanians
came;
And Saturn's empire often chang'd the
name.
Then kings, gigantic Tybris, and the rest,
With arbitrary sway the land oppress'd:
For Tiber's flood was Albula before,
Till, from the tyrant's fate, his name it
bore.   440
I last arriv'd, driv'n from my native home

By fortune's pow'r, and fate's resistless
　　doom.
Long toss'd on seas, I sought this happy
　　land,
Warn'd by my mother nymph, and call'd
　　by Heav'n's command."
　　Thus, walking on, he spoke, and shew'd
　　　　the gate,
Since call'd Carmental by the Roman state;
Where stood an altar, sacred to the name
Of old Carmenta, the prophetic dame,
Who to her son foretold th' Ænean race,
Sublime in fame, and Rome's imperial
　　place:　　　　　　　　　　　　450
Then shews the forest, which, in after
　　times,
Fierce Romulus for perpetrated crimes
A sacred refuge made; with this, the shrine
Where Pan below the rock had rites divine:
Then tells of Argus' death, his murder'd
　　guest,
Whose grave and tomb his innocence attest.
Thence, to the steep Tarpeian rock he
　　leads;
Now roof'd with gold, then thatch'd with
　　homely reeds.
A reverent fear (such superstition reigns
Among the rude) ev'n then possess'd the
　　swains.　　　　　　　　　　　460
Some god, they knew — what god, they
　　could not tell —
Did there amidst the sacred horror dwell.
Th' Arcadians thought him Jove; and said
　　they saw
The mighty Thund'rer with majestic awe,
Who took his shield, and dealt his bolts
　　around,
And scatter'd tempests on the teeming
　　ground.
Then saw two heaps of ruins, (once they
　　stood
Two stately towns, on either side the flood,)
Saturnia's and Janicula's remains;
And either place the founder's name re-
　　tains.　　　　　　　　　　　470
Discoursing thus together, they resort
Where poor Evander kept his country court.
They view'd the ground of Rome's litigious
　　hall;
(Once oxen low'd, where now the lawyers
　　bawl;)
Then, stooping, thro' the narrow gate they
　　press'd,
When thus the king bespoke his Trojan
　　guest:

" Mean as it is, this palace, and this door,
Receiv'd Alcides, then a conqueror.
Dare to be poor; accept our homely food,
Which feasted him, and emulate a god."
Then underneath a lowly roof he led　481 ⎫
The weary prince, and laid him on a bed; ⎬
The stuffing leaves, with hides of bears ⎪
　　o'erspread.　　　　　　　　　　⎭
　　Now Night had shed her silver dews
　　　　around,
And with her sable wings embrac'd the
　　ground,
When love's fair goddess, anxious for her
　　son,
(New tumults rising, and new wars begun,)
Couch'd with her husband in his golden bed,
With these alluring words invokes his aid;
And, that her pleasing speech his mind may
　　move,　　　　　　　　　　　490
Inspires each accent with the charms of
　　love:
" While cruel fate conspir'd with Grecian
　　pow'rs,
To level with the ground the Trojan tow'rs,
I ask'd not aid th' unhappy to restore,
Nor did the succor of thy skill implore;
Nor urg'd the labors of my lord in vain,
A sinking empire longer to sustain,
Tho' much I ow'd to Priam's house, and
　　more
The dangers of Æneas did deplore.
But now, by Jove's command, and fate's
　　decree,　　　　　　　　　　　500
His race is doom'd to reign in Italy:
With humble suit I beg thy needful art,
O still propitious pow'r, that rules my
　　heart !
A mother kneels a suppliant for her son.
By Thetis and Aurora thou wert won
To forge impenetrable shields, and grace
With fated arms a less illustrious race.
Behold, what haughty nations are combin'd
Against the relics of the Phrygian kind,
With fire and sword my people to de-
　　stroy,　　　　　　　　　　　510
And conquer Venus twice, in conqu'ring
　　Troy."
She said; and straight her arms, of snowy
　　hue,
About her unresolving husband threw.
Her soft embraces soon infuse desire; ⎫
His bones and marrow sudden warmth ⎪
　　inspire; ⎬
And all the godhead feels the wonted ⎪
　　fire. ⎭

Not half so swift the rattling thunder flies,
Or forky lightnings flash along the skies.
The goddess, proud of her successful wiles,
And conscious of her form, in secret
    smiles.   520
  Then thus the pow'r, obnoxious to her
    charms,
Panting, and half dissolving in her arms:
" Why seek you reasons for a cause so just,
Or your own beauties or my love distrust ?
Long since, had you requir'd my helpful
    hand,
Th' artificer and art you might command,
To labor arms for Troy: nor Jove, nor fate,
Confin'd their empire to so short a date.
And, if you now desire new wars to wage,
My skill I promise, and my pains engage.
Whatever melting metals can conspire,   531
Or breathing bellows, or the forming fire,
Is freely yours: your anxious fears remove,
And think no task is difficult to love."
Trembling he spoke; and, eager of her
    charms,
He snatch'd the willing goddess to his
    arms;
Till, in her lap infus'd, he lay possess'd
Of full desire, and sunk to pleasing rest.
Now when the Night her middle race had
    rode,
And his first slumber had refresh'd the
    god —   540
The time when early housewives leave the
    bed;
When living embers on the hearth they
    spread,
Supply the lamp, and call the maids to
    rise —
With yawning mouths, and with half-open'd
    eyes,
They ply the distaff by the winking light,
And to their daily labor add the night:
Thus frugally they earn their children's
    bread,
And uncorrupted keep the nuptial bed —
Not less concern'd, nor at a later hour,
Rose from his downy couch the forging
    pow'r.   550
  Sacred to Vulcan's name, an isle there
    lay,
Betwixt Sicilia's coasts and Lipare,
Rais'd high on smoking rocks; and, deep
    below,
In hollow caves the fires of Ætna glow.
The Cyclops here their heavy hammers
    deal;

Loud strokes, and hissings of tormented
    steel,
Are heard around; the boiling waters roar,
And smoky flames thro' fuming tunnels
    soar.
Hether the Father of the Fire, by night,
Thro' the brown air precipitates his flight.
On their eternal anvils here he found   561
The brethren beating, and the blows go
    round.
A load of pointless thunder now there lies
Before their hands, to ripen for the skies:
These darts, for angry Jove, they daily
    cast;
Consum'd on mortals with prodigious waste.
Three rays of writhen rain, of fire three
    more,
Of winged southern winds and cloudy store
As many parts, the dreadful mixture frame;
And fears are added, and avenging flame.
Inferior ministers, for Mars, repair   571
His broken axletrees and blunted war,
And send him forth again with furbish'd
    arms,
To wake the lazy war with trumpets' loud
    alarms.
The rest refresh the scaly snakes that fold
The shield of Pallas, and renew their gold.
Full on the crest the Gorgon's head they
    place,
With eyes that roll in death, and with dis-
    torted face.
  " My sons," said Vulcan, " set your tasks
    aside;
Your strength and master-skill must now
    be tried.   580
Arms for a hero forge; arms that require
Your force, your speed, and all your form-
    ing fire."
He said. They set their former work aside,
And their new toils with eager haste divide.
A flood of molten silver, brass, and gold,
And deadly steel, in the large furnace
    roll'd:
Of this, their artful hands a shield prepare,
Alone sufficient to sustain the war.
Sev'n orbs within a spacious round they
    close:
One stirs the fire, and one the bellows
    blows.   590
The hissing steel is in the smithy drown'd;
The grot with beaten anvils groans around.
By turns their arms advance, in equal time;
By turns their hands descend, and hammers
    chime.

They turn the glowing mass with crooked tongs;
The fiery work proceeds, with rustic songs.
 While, at the Lemnian god's command, they urge
Their labors thus, and ply th' Æolian forge,
The cheerful morn salutes Evander's eyes,
And songs of chirping birds invite to rise. 600
He leaves his lowly bed: his buskins meet
Above his ankles; sandals sheathe his feet:
He sets his trusty sword upon his side,
And o'er his shoulder throws a panther's hide.
Two menial dogs before their master press'd.
Thus clad, and guarded thus, he seeks his kingly guest.
Mindful of promis'd aid, he mends his pace,
But meets Æneas in the middle space.
Young Pallas did his father's steps attend,
And true Achates waited on his friend. 610
They join their hands; a secret seat they choose;
Th' Arcadian first their former talk renews:
" Undaunted prince, I never can believe
The Trojan empire lost, while you survive.
Command th' assistance of a faithful friend;
But feeble are the succors I can send.
Our narrow kingdom here the Tiber bounds;
That other side the Latian state surrounds,
Insults our walls, and wastes our fruitful grounds.
But mighty nations I prepare, to join 620
Their arms with yours, and aid your just design.
You come, as by your better genius sent,
And fortune seems to favor your intent.
Not far from hence there stands a hilly town,
Of ancient building, and of high renown,
Torn from the Tuscans by the Lydian race,
Who gave the name of Cære to the place,
Once Agyllina call'd. It flourish'd long,
In pride of wealth and warlike people strong,
Till curs'd Mezentius, in a fatal hour, 630
Assum'd the crown, with arbitrary pow'r.
What words can paint those execrable times,
The subjects' suff'rings, and the tyrant's crimes !
That blood, those murthers, O ye gods, replace

On his own head, and on his impious race !
The living and the dead at his command
Were coupled, face to face, and hand to hand,
Till, chok'd with stench, in loath'd embraces tied,
The ling'ring wretches pin'd away and died.
Thus plung'd in ills, and meditating more — 640
The people's patience, tir'd, no longer bore
The raging monster; but with arms beset
His house, and vengeance and destruction threat.
They fire his palace: while the flame ascends,
They force his guards, and execute his friends.
He cleaves the crowd, and, favor'd by the night,
To Turnus' friendly court directs his flight.
By just revenge the Tuscans set on fire,
With arms, their king to punishment require:
Their num'rous troops, now muster'd on the strand, 650
My counsel shall submit to your command.
Their navy swarms upon the coasts; they cry
To hoist their anchors, but the gods deny.
An ancient augur, skill'd in future fate,
With these foreboding words restrains their hate:
' Ye brave in arms, ye Lydian blood, the flow'r
Of Tuscan youth, and choice of all their pow'r,
Whom just revenge against Mezentius arms,
To seek your tyrant's death by lawful arms; 659
Know this: no native of our land may lead
This pow'rful people; seek a foreign head.'
Aw'd with these words, in camps they still abide,
And wait with longing looks their promis'd guide.
Tarchon, the Tuscan chief, to me has sent
Their crown, and ev'ry regal ornament:
The people join their own with his desire;
And all my conduct, as their king, require.
But the chill blood that creeps within my veins,
And age, and listless limbs unfit for pains,
And a soul conscious of its own decay, 670
Have forc'd me to refuse imperial sway.

My Pallas were more fit to mount the
    throne,
And should, but he 's a Sabine mother's
    son,
And half a native; but, in you, combine
A manly vigor, and a foreign line.
Where Fate and smiling Fortune shew the
    way,
Pursue the ready path to sov'reign sway.
The staff of my declining days, my son,
Shall make your good or ill success his
    own;
In fighting fields from you shall learn to
    dare,   680
And serve the hard apprentiship of war;
Your matchless courage and your conduct
    view,
And early shall begin t' admire and copy you.
Besides, two hundred horse he shall com-
    mand;
Tho' few, a warlike and well-chosen band.
These in my name are listed; and my son
As many more has added in his own."
    Scarce had he said; Achates and his
    guest,
With downcast eyes, their silent grief ex-
    press'd;
Who, short of succors, and in deep de-
    spair,   690
Shook at the dismal prospect of the war.
But his bright mother, from a breaking
    cloud,
To cheer her issue, thunder'd thrice aloud;
Thrice forky lightning flash'd along the
    sky,
And Tyrrhene trumpets thrice were heard
    on high.
Then, gazing up, repeated peals they hear;
And, in a heav'n serene, refulgent arms
    appear:
Redd'ning the skies, and glitt'ring all
    around,
The temper'd metals clash, and yield a
    silver sound.
The rest stood trembling, struck with awe
    divine;   700
Æneas only, conscious to the sign,
Presag'd th' event, and joyful view'd,
    above,
Th' accomplish'd promise of the Queen of
    Love.
Then, to th' Arcadian king: " This prodigy
(Dismiss your fear) belongs alone to me.
Heav'n calls me to the war: th' expected
    sign

Is giv'n of promis'd aid, and arms divine.
My goddess mother, whose indulgent care
Foresaw the dangers of the growing war,
This omen gave, when bright Vulcanian
    arms,   710
Fated from force of steel by Stygian
    charms,
Suspended, shone on high: she then fore-
    show'd
Approaching fights, and fields to float in
    blood.
Turnus shall dearly pay for faith for-
    sworn;
And corps, and swords, and shields, on
    Tiber borne,
Shall choke his flood: now sound the loud
    alarms;
And, Latian troops, prepare your perjur'd
    arms."
    He said, and, rising from his homely
    throne,
The solemn rites of Hercules begun,
And on his altars wak'd the sleeping
    fires;   720
Then cheerful to his household gods re-
    tires;
There offers chosen sheep. Th' Arcadian
    king
And Trojan youth the same oblations
    bring.
Next, of his men and ships he makes re-
    view;
Draws out the best and ablest of the crew.
Down with the falling stream the refuse
    run,
To raise with joyful news his drooping son.
Steeds are prepar'd to mount the Trojan
    band,
Who wait their leader to the Tyrrhene
    land.
A sprightly courser, fairer than the
    rest,   730
The king himself presents his royal guest:
A lion's hide his back and limbs infold,
Precious with studded work, and paws of
    gold.
Fame thro' the little city spreads aloud
Th' intended march, amid the fearful crowd:
The matrons beat their breasts, dissolve in
    tears,
And double their devotion in their fears.
The war at hand appears with more affright,
And rises ev'ry moment to the sight.
    Then old Evander, with a close em-
    brace,   740

Strain'd his departing friend; and tears
    o'erflow his face.
"Would Heav'n," said he, "my strength
    and youth recall,
Such as I was beneath Præneste's wall;
Then when I made the foremost foes retire,
And set whole heaps of conquer'd shields
    on fire;
When Herilus in single fight I slew,
Whom with three lives Feronia did endue;
And thrice I sent him to the Stygian shore,
Till the last ebbing soul return'd no more —
Such if I stood renew'd, not these alarms,
Nor death, should rend me from my Pallas'
    arms;   751
Nor proud Mezentius, thus unpunish'd,
    boast
His rapes and murthers on the Tuscan
    coast.
Ye gods, and mighty Jove, in pity bring
Relief, and hear a father and a king !
If fate and you reserve these eyes, to see
My son return with peace and victory;
If the lov'd boy shall bless his father's
    sight;
If we shall meet again with more delight;
Then draw my life in length; let me sus-
    tain,   760
In hopes of his embrace, the worst of pain.
But if your hard decrees — which, O ! I
    dread —
Have doom'd to death his undeserving
    head;
This, O this very moment, let me die !
While hopes and fears in equal balance lie;
While, yet possess'd of all his youthful
    charms,
I strain him close within these aged arms;
Before that fatal news my soul shall
    wound ! "
He said, and, swooning, sunk upon the
    ground.
His servants bore him off, and softly
    laid   770
His languish'd limbs upon his homely bed.
    The horsemen march; the gates are open'd
    wide;
Æneas at their head, Achates by his side.
Next these, the Trojan leaders rode along;
Last follows in the rear th' Arcadian
    throng.
Young Pallas shone conspicuous o'er the
    rest;
Gilded his arms, embroider'd was his vest.
So, from the seas, exerts his radiant head

The star by whom the lights of heav'n are
    led;
Shakes from his rosy locks the pearly dews,
Dispels the darkness, and the day re-
    news.   781
The trembling wives the walls and turrets
    crowd,
And follow, with their eyes, the dusty
    cloud,
Which winds disperse by fits, and shew
    from far
The blaze of arms, and shields, and shining
    war.
The troops, drawn up in beautiful array,
O'er heathy plains pursue the ready way.
Repeated peals of shouts are heard
    around;
The neighing coursers answer to the
    sound,
And shake with horny hoofs the solid
    ground.   790
    A greenwood shade, for long religion
    known,
Stands by the streams that wash the Tus-
    can town,
Incompass'd round with gloomy hills above,
Which add a holy horror to the grove.
The first inhabitants, of Grecian blood,
That sacred forest to Silvanus vow'd,
The guardian of their flocks and fields; and
    pay
Their due devotions on his annual day.
Not far from hence, along the river's side,
In tents secure, the Tuscan troops
    abide,   800
By Tarchon led. Now, from a rising ground,
Æneas cast his wond'ring eyes around,
And all the Tyrrhene army had in sight,
Stretch'd on the spacious plain from left to
    right.
Thether his warlike train the Trojan led,
Refresh'd his men, and wearied horses fed.
    Meantime the mother goddess, crown'd
    with charms,
Breaks thro' the clouds, and brings the
    fated arms.
Within a winding vale she finds her son,
On the cool river's banks, retir'd alone.   810
She shews her heav'nly form without dis-
    guise,
And gives herself to his desiring eyes.
"Behold," she said, "perform'd in ev'ry
    part,
My promise made, and Vulcan's labor'd art.
Now seek, secure, the Latian enemy,

And haughty Turnus to the field defy."
She said; and, having first her son embrac'd,
The radiant arms beneath an oak she plac'd.
Proud of the gift, he roll'd his greedy sight
Around the work, and gaz'd with vast de-
    light.   820
He lifts, he turns, he poises, and admires
The crested helm, that vomits radiant fires:
His hands the fatal sword and corslet hold,
One keen with temper'd steel, one stiff with
    gold:
Both ample, flaming both, and beamy
    bright;
So shines a cloud, when edg'd with adverse
    light.
He shakes the pointed spear, and longs to
    try
The plated cuishes on his manly thigh;
But most admires the shield's mysterious
    mold,
And Roman triumphs rising on the gold:
For these, emboss'd, the heav'nly smith had
    wrought   831
(Not in the rolls of future fate untaught)
The wars in order, and the race divine
Of warriors issuing from the Julian line.
The cave of Mars was dress'd with mossy
    greens:
There, by the wolf, were laid the martial
    twins.
Intrepid on her swelling dugs they hung;
The foster dam loll'd out her fawning
    tongue:
They suck'd secure, while, bending back
    her head,
She lick'd their tender limbs, and form'd
    them as they fed.   840
Not far from thence new Rome appears,
    with games
Projected for the rape of Sabine dames.
The pit resounds with shrieks; a war suc-
    ceeds,
For breach of public faith, and unexampled
    deeds.
Here for revenge the Sabine troops contend;
The Romans there with arms the prey de-
    fend.
Wearied with tedious war, at length they
    cease;
And both the kings and kingdoms plight the
    peace.
The friendly chiefs before Jove's altar
    stand,
Both arm'd, with each a charger in his
    hand: 850

A fatted sow for sacrifice is led,
With imprecations on the perjur'd head.
Near this, the traitor Metius, stretch'd be-
    tween
Four fiery steeds, is dragg'd along the
    green,
By Tullus' doom: the brambles drink his
    blood,
And his torn limbs are left the vulture's
    food.
There, Porsena to Rome proud Tarquin
    brings,
And would by force restore the banish'd
    kings.
One tyrant for his fellow-tyrant fights;
The Roman youth assert their native
    rights.   860
Before the town the Tuscan army lies,
To win by famine, or by fraud surprise.
Their king, half-threat'ning, half-disdaining
    stood,
While Cocles broke the bridge, and stemm'd
    the flood.
The captive maids there tempt the raging
    tide,
Scap'd from their chains, with Clœlia for
    their guide.
High on a rock heroic Manlius stood,
To guard the temple, and the temple's god.
Then Rome was poor; and there you might
    behold
The palace thatch'd with straw, now roof'd
    with gold.   870
The silver goose before the shining gate
There flew, and, by her cackle, sav'd the
    state.
She told the Gauls' approach; th' approach-
    ing Gauls,
Obscure in night, ascend, and seize the
    walls.
The gold dissembled well their yellow hair,
And golden chains on their white necks
    they wear.
Gold are their vests; long Alpine spears
    they wield,
And their left arm sustains a length of
    shield.
Hard by, the leaping Salian priests ad-
    vance;
And naked thro' the streets the mad Luperci
    dance,   880
In caps of wool; the targets dropp'd from
    heav'n.
Here modest matrons, in soft litters driv'n,
To pay their vows in solemn pomp appear,

And odorous gums in their chaste hands
  they bear.
Far hence remov'd, the Stygian seats are
  seen;
Pains of the damn'd, and punish'd Catiline
Hung on a rock — the traitor; and, around,
The Furies hissing from the nether ground.
Apart from these, the happy souls he draws,
And Cato's holy ghost dispensing laws. 890
  Betwixt the quarters flows a golden sea;
But foaming surges there in silver play.
The dancing dolphins with their tails di-
  vide
The glitt'ring waves, and cut the precious
  tide.
Amid the main, two mighty fleets engage
Their brazen beaks, oppos'd with equal rage.
Actium surveys the well-disputed prize;
Leucate's wat'ry plain with foamy billows
  fries.
Young Cæsar, on the stern, in armor
  bright,
Here leads the Romans and their gods to
  fight: 900
His beamy temples shoot their flames afar,
And o'er his head is hung the Julian star.
Agrippa seconds him, with prosp'rous gales,
And, with propitious gods, his foes assails:
A naval crown, that binds his manly
  brows,
The happy fortune of the fight foreshows.
Rang'd on the line oppos'd, Antonius brings
Barbarian aids, and troops of Eastern kings;
Th' Arabians near, and Bactrians from
  afar,
Of tongues discordant, and a mingled
  war: 910
And, rich in gaudy robes, amidst the strife,
His ill fate follows him — th' Egyptian wife.
Moving they fight; with oars and forky
  prows
The froth is gather'd, and the water glows.
It seems, as if the Cyclades again
Were rooted up, and justled in the main;
Or floating mountains floating mountains
  meet:
Such is the fierce encounter of the fleet.
Fireballs are thrown, and pointed jav'lins
  fly;
The fields of Neptune take a purple dye. 920
The queen herself, amidst the loud alarms,
With cymbals toss'd her fainting soldiers
  warms —
Fool as she was ! who had not yet divin'd
Her cruel fate, nor saw the snakes behind.

Her country gods, the monsters of the sky,
Great Neptune, Pallas, and Love's Queen
  defy:
The dog Anubis barks, but barks in vain,
Nor longer dares oppose th' ethereal train.
Mars in the middle of the shining shield
Is grav'd, and strides along the liquid
  field. 930
The Diræ souse from heav'n with swift
  descent;
And Discord, dyed in blood, with garments
  rent,
Divides the prease: her steps Bellona
  treads,
And shakes her iron rod above their heads.
This seen, Apollo, from his Actian height,
Pours down his arrows; at whose winged
  flight
The trembling Indians and Egyptians yield,
And soft Sabæans quit the wat'ry field.
The fatal mistress hoists her silken sails,
And, shrinking from the fight, invokes the
  gales. 940
Aghast she looks, and heaves her breast
  for breath,
Panting, and pale with fear of future death.
The god had figur'd her as driv'n along
By winds and waves, and scudding thro' the
  throng.
Just opposite, sad Nilus opens wide
His arms and ample bosom to the tide,
And spreads his mantle o'er the winding
  coast,
In which he wraps his queen, and hides the
  flying host.
The victor to the gods his thanks express'd,
And Rome, triumphant, with his presence
  bless'd. 950
Three hundred temples in the town he
  plac'd;
With spoils and altars ev'ry temple grac'd.
Three shining nights, and three succeed-⎫
  ing days,   ⎪
The fields resound with shouts, the streets ⎬
  with praise,   ⎪
The domes with songs, the theaters with ⎪
  plays.   ⎭
All altars flame: before each altar lies,
Drench'd in his gore, the destin'd sacrifice.
Great Cæsar sits sublime upon his throne,
Before Apollo's porch of Parian stone;
Accepts the presents vow'd for victory, 960
And hangs the monumental crowns on high.
Vast crowds of vanquish'd nations march
  along,

Various in arms, in habit, and in tongue.
Here, Mulciber assigns the proper place
For Carians, and th' ungirt Numidian race;
Then ranks the Thracians in the second row,
With Scythians, expert in the dart and bow.
And here the tam'd Euphrates humbly
　　glides,
And there the Rhine submits her swelling
　　tides,
And proud Araxes, whom no bridge ⎫
　　could bind;　　　　　　　　　970
The Danes' unconquer'd offspring march ⎬
　　behind,
And Morini, the last of humankind. ⎭
These figures, on the shield divinely ⎫
　　wrought,
By Vulcan labor'd, and by Venus brought, ⎬
With joy and wonder fill the hero's
　　thought. ⎭
Unknown the names, he yet admires the
　　grace,
And bears aloft the fame and fortune of his
　　race.

THE NINTH BOOK OF THE ÆNEIS

THE ARGUMENT

Turnus takes advantage of Æneas' absence,
fires some of his ships, (which are transform'd
into sea nymphs,) and assaults his camp.
The Trojans, reduc'd to the last extremities, send Nisus and Euryalus to recall
Æneas; which furnishes the poet with that
admirable episode of their friendship, generosity, and the conclusion of their adventures.

WHILE these affairs in distant places pass'd,
The various Iris Juno sends with haste,
To find bold Turnus, who, with anxious
　　thought,
The secret shade of his great grandsire
　　sought.
Retir'd alone she found the daring man,
And op'd her rosy lips, and thus began:
"What none of all the gods could grant thy
　　vows,
That, Turnus, this auspicious day bestows.
Æneas, gone to seek th' Arcadian prince,
Has left the Trojan camp without defense;
And, short of succors there, employs his
　　pains　　　　　　　　　　　　11
In parts remote to raise the Tuscan swains.

Now snatch an hour that favors thy designs;
Unite thy forces, and attack their lines."
This said, on equal wings she pois'd her
　　weight,
And form'd a radiant rainbow in her flight.
The Daunian hero lifts his hands and eyes,
And thus invokes the goddess as she flies:
"Iris, the grace of heav'n, what pow'r di-
　　vine
Has sent thee down, thro' dusky clouds to
　　shine?　　　　　　　　　　　　20
See, they divide; immortal day appears,
And glitt'ring planets dancing in their
　　spheres!
With joy, these happy omens I obey,
And follow to the war the god that leads
　　the way."
Thus having said, as by the brook he stood,
He scoop'd the water from the crystal flood;
Then with his hands the drops to heav'n he
　　throws,
And loads the pow'rs above with offer'd
　　vows.
　Now march the bold confed'rates thro'
　　the plain,
Well hors'd, well clad; a rich and shining
　　train.　　　　　　　　　　　　30
Messapus leads the van; and, in the rear,
The sons of Tyrrheus in bright arms appear.
In the main battle, with his flaming crest,
The mighty Turnus tow'rs above the rest.
Silent they move, majestically slow,
Like ebbing Nile, or Ganges in his flow.
The Trojans view the dusty cloud from far,
And the dark menace of the distant war.
Caïcus from the rampire saw it rise,
Black'ning the fields, and thick'ning thro'
　　the skies.　　　　　　　　　　40
Then to his fellows thus aloud he calls:
"What rolling clouds, my friends, approach
　　the walls?
Arm! arm! and man the works! prepare
　　your spears
And pointed darts! the Latian host ap-
　　pears."
Thus warn'd, they shut their gates; with
　　shouts ascend
The bulwarks, and, secure, their foes at-
　　tend:
For their wise gen'ral, with foreseeing care,
Had charg'd them not to tempt the doubt-
　　ful war,
Nor, tho' provok'd, in open fields advance,
But close within their lines attend their
　　chance.　　　　　　　　　　　50

Unwilling, yet they keep the strict com-
mand,
And sourly wait in arms the hostile band.
The fiery Turnus flew before the rest: ⎫
A piebald steed of Thracian strain he ⎪
press'd; ⎬
His helm of massy gold, and crimson ⎪
was his crest. ⎭
With twenty horse to second his designs,
An unexpected foe, he fac'd the lines.
"Is there," he said, "in arms, who bravely
dare
His leader's honor and his danger share?"
Then spurring on, his brandish'd dart he
threw, 60
In sign of war: applauding shouts ensue.
Amaz'd to find a dastard race, that run
Behind the rampires and the battle shun,
He rides around the camp, with rolling
eyes,
And stops at ev'ry post, and ev'ry passage
tries.
So roams the nightly wolf about the fold:
Wet with descending show'rs, and stiff with
cold,
He howls for hunger, and he grins for
pain,
(His gnashing teeth are exercis'd in vain,)
And, impotent of anger, finds no way 70
In his distended paws to grasp the prey.
The mothers listen; but the bleating lambs
Securely swig the dug, beneath the dams.
Thus ranges eager Turnus 'er the plain,
Sharp with desire, and furious with dis-
dain;
Surveys each passage with a piercing sight,
To force his foes in equal field to fight.
Thus while he gazes round, at length he
spies,
Where, fenc'd with strong redoubts, their
navy lies,
Close underneath the walls; the washing
tide 80
Secures from all approach this weaker side.
He takes the wish'd occasion, fills his hand
With ready fires, and shakes a flaming
brand.
Urg'd by his presence, ev'ry soul is warm'd,
And ev'ry hand with kindled firs is arm'd.
From the fir'd pines the scatt'ring sparkles
fly;
Fat vapors, mix'd with flames, involve the
sky.
What pow'r, O Muses, could avert the
flame

Which threaten'd, in the fleet, the Trojan
name?
Tell: for the fact, thro' length of time
obscure, 90
Is hard to faith; yet shall the fame endure.
'T is said that, when the chief prepar'd
his flight,
And fell'd his timber from Mount Ida's
height,
The grandam goddess then approach'd her
son,
And with a mother's majesty begun:
"Grant me," she said, "the sole request I
bring,
Since conquer'd heav'n has own'd you for
its king.
On Ida's brows, for ages past, there stood,
With firs and maples fill'd, a shady wood;
And on the summit rose a sacred grove, 100
Where I was worship'd with religious love.
Those woods, that holy grove, my long de-
light,
I gave the Trojan prince, to speed his flight.
Now, fill'd with fear, on their behalf I come;
Let neither winds o'erset, nor waves intomb
The floating forests of the sacred pine;
But let it be their safety to be mine."
Then thus replied her awful son, who rolls
The radiant stars, and heav'n and earth
controls:
"How dare you, mother, endless date de-
mand 110
For vessels molded by a mortal hand?
What then is fate? Shall bold Æneas ride,
Of safety certain, on th' uncertain tide?
Yet, what I can, I grant: when, wafted o'er,
The chief is landed on the Latian shore,
Whatever ships escape the raging storms,
At my command shall change their fading
forms
To nymphs divine, and plow the wat'ry
way,
Like Dotis and the daughters of the sea."
To seal his sacred vow, by Styx he swore,
The lake of liquid pitch, the dreary shore,
And Phlegethon's innavigable flood, 122 ⎫
And the black regions of his brother god. ⎪
He said; and shook the skies with his ⎬
imperial nod. ⎭
And now at length the number'd hours
were come,
Prefix'd by fate's irrevocable doom,
When the great Mother of the Gods was
free
To save her ships, and finish Jove's decree.

First, from the quarter of the morn, there
  sprung
A light that sign'd the heav'ns, and shot
  along;   130
Then from a cloud, fring'd round with
  golden fires,
Were timbrels heard, and Berecynthian
  choirs;
And, last, a voice, with more than mortal
  sounds,
Both hosts, in arms oppos'd, with equal
  horror wounds:
" O Trojan race, your needless aid forbear,
And know, my ships are my peculiar care.
With greater ease the bold Rutulian may,
With hissing brands, attempt to burn the
  sea,
Than singe my sacred pines. But you, my
  charge,
Loos'd from your crooked anchors, launch
  at large,   140
Exalted each a nymph: forsake the sand,
And swim the seas, at Cybele's command."
No sooner had the goddess ceas'd to speak,
When, lo! th' obedient ships their haulsers
  break;
And, strange to tell, like dolphins, in the
  main
They plunge their prows, and dive, and
  spring again:
As many beauteous maids the billows sweep,
As rode before tall vessels on the deep.
  The foes, surpris'd with wonder, stood
  aghast;   149
Messapus curb'd his fiery courser's haste;
Old Tiber roar'd, and, raising up his head,
Call'd back his waters to their oozy bed.
Turnus alone, undaunted, bore the shock,
And with these words his trembling troops
  bespoke:
" These monsters for the Trojans' fate are
  meant,
And are by Jove for black presages sent.
He takes the cowards' last relief away; ⎤
For fly they cannot, and, constrain'd to │
  stay,   ⎬
Must yield unfought, a base inglorious │
  prey.   ⎦
The liquid half of all the globe is lost; 160
Heav'n shuts the seas, and we secure the
  coast.
Theirs is no more than that small spot of
  ground
Which myriads of our martial men surround.
Their fates I fear not, or vain oracles.

'T was giv'n to Venus they should cross the
  seas,
And land secure upon the Latian plains:
Their promis'd hour is pass'd, and mine re-
  mains.
'T is in the fate of Turnus to destroy,
With sword and fire, the faithless race of
  Troy.   169
Shall such affronts as these alone inflame
The Grecian brothers, and the Grecian
  name ?
My cause and theirs is one; a fatal strife,
And final ruin, for a ravish'd wife.
Was 't not enough, that, punish'd for the
  crime,
They fell; but will they fall a second time ?
One would have thought they paid enough
  before,
To curse the costly sex, and durst offend no
  more.
Can they securely trust their feeble wall,
A slight partition, a thin interval,
Betwixt their fate and them; when Troy,
  tho' built   180
By hands divine, yet perish'd by their guilt ?
Lend me, for once, my friends, your valiant
  hands,
To force from out their lines these dastard
  bands.
Less than a thousand ships will end this war,
Nor Vulcan needs his fated arms prepare.
Let all the Tuscans, all th' Arcadians, join!
Nor these, nor those, shall frustrate my
  design.
Let them not fear the treasons of the ⎤
  night,   │
The robb'd Palladium, the pretended ⎬
  flight: 189 │
Our onset shall be made in open light. ⎦
No wooden engine shall their town betray;
Fires they shall have around, but fires by
  day.
No Grecian babes before their camp appear,
Whom Hector's arms detain'd to the tenth
  tardy year.
Now, since the sun is rolling to the west,
Give we the silent night to needful rest:
Refresh your bodies, and your arms prepare;
The morn shall end the small remains of
  war."
  The post of honor to Messapus falls,
To keep the nightly guard, to watch the
  walls,   200
To pitch the fires at distances around,
And close the Trojans in their scanty ground.

Twice seven Rutulian captains ready stand,
And twice seven hundred horse these chiefs
    command;
All clad in shining arms the works invest,
Each with a radiant helm and waving crest.
Stretch'd at their length, they press the
    grassy ground;
They laugh, they sing, (the jolly bowls go
    round,)
With lights and cheerful fires renew the
    day,
And pass the wakeful night in feasts and
    play.   210
    The Trojans, from above, their foes be-
    held,
And with arm'd legions all the rampires
    fill'd.
Seiz'd with affright, their gates they first
    explore;
Join works to works with bridges, tow'r to
    tow'r:
Thus all things needful for defense abound.
Mnestheus and brave Seresthus walk the
    round,
Commission'd by their absent prince to
    share
The common danger, and divide the care.
The soldiers draw their lots, and, as they
    fall,
By turns relieve each other on the wall.   220
    Nigh where the foes their utmost guards
    advance,
To watch the gate was warlike Nisus'
    chance.
His father Hyrtacus of noble blood;
His mother was a huntress of the wood,
And sent him to the wars. Well could he
    bear
His lance in fight, and dart the flying spear,
But better skill'd unerring shafts to send.
Beside him stood Euryalus, his friend:
Euryalus, than whom the Trojan host
No fairer face, or sweeter air, could boast —
Scarce had the down to shade his cheeks
    begun.   231
One was their care, and their delight was
    one:
One common hazard in the war they shar'd,
And now were both by choice upon the
    guard.
    Then Nisus thus: " Or do the gods in-
    spire
This warmth, or make we gods of our de-
    sire ?
A gen'rous ardor boils within my breast,

Eager of action, enemy to rest:
This urges me to fight, and fires my mind
To leave a memorable name behind.   240
Thou see'st the foe secure; how faintly
    shine
Their scatter'd fires ! the most, in sleep su-
    pine
Along the ground, an easy conquest lie:
The wakeful few the fuming flagon ply;
All hush'd around. Now hear what I re-
    volve —
A thought unripe — and scarcely yet re-
    solve.
Our absent prince both camp and council
    mourn;
By message both would hasten his return:
If they confer what I demand on thee,
(For fame is recompense enough for me,) 250
Methinks, beneath yon hill, I have espied
A way that safely will my passage guide."
    Euryalus stood list'ning while he spoke,
With love of praise and noble envy struck;
Then to his ardent friend expos'd his ⎫
    mind: ⎪
" All this, alone, and leaving me behind ! ⎬
Am I unworthy, Nisus, to be join'd ?   ⎭
Think'st thou I can my share of glory
    yield,
Or send thee unassisted to the field ?
Not so my father taught my childhood
    arms;   260
Born in a siege, and bred among alarms !
Nor is my youth unworthy of my friend,
Nor of the heav'n-born hero I attend.
The thing call'd life, with ease I can dis-
    claim,
And think it over-sold to purchase fame."
    Then Nisus thus: " Alas ! thy tender
    years
Would minister new matter to my fears.
So may the gods, who view this friendly
    strife,
Restore me to thy lov'd embrace with life,
Condemn'd to pay my vows, (as sure I
    trust,)   270
This thy request is cruel and unjust.
But if some chance — as many chances are,
And doubtful hazards, in the deeds of war —
If one should reach my head, there let it
    fall,
And spare thy life; I would not perish all.
Thy bloomy youth deserves a longer date:
Live thou to mourn thy love's unhappy fate;
To bear my mangled body from the foe,
Or buy it back, and fun'ral rites bestow.

Or, if hard fortune shall those dues deny, 280
Thou canst at least an empty tomb supply.
O let not me the widow's tears renew !
Nor let a mother's curse my name pursue:
Thy pious parent, who, for love of thee,
Forsook the coasts of friendly Sicily,
Her age committing to the seas and wind,
When ev'ry weary matron stay'd behind."
To this, Euryalus: " You plead in vain,
And but protract the cause you cannot gain.
No more delays, but haste !" With that, he
      wakes   290
The nodding watch: each to his office takes.
The guard reliev'd, the gen'rous couple
      went
To find the council at the royal tent.

All creatures else forgot their daily care,
And sleep, the common gift of nature,
      share;
Except the Trojan peers, who wakeful sate
In nightly council for th' indanger'd state.
They vote a message to their absent chief,
Shew their distress, and beg a swift relief.
Amid the camp a silent seat they chose,
Remote from clamor, and secure from
      foes.   301
On their left arms their ample shields they
      bear,
The right reclin'd upon the bending spear.
Now Nisus and his friend approach the ⎫
      guard,   ⎪
And beg admission, eager to be heard: ⎬
Th' affair important, not to be deferr'd. ⎭
Ascanius bids 'em be conducted in,
Ord'ring the more experienc'd to begin.
Then Nisus thus: " Ye fathers, lend your
      ears:
Nor judge our bold attempt beyond our
      years.   310
The foe, securely drench'd in sleep and
      wine,
Neglect their watch; the fires but thinly
      shine;
And, where the smoke in cloudy vapors
      flies,
Cov'ring the plain, and curling to the skies,
Betwixt two paths, which at the gate ⎫
      divide,   ⎪
Close by the sea, a passage we have spied, ⎬
Which will our way to great Æneas   ⎪
      guide.   ⎭
Expect each hour to see him safe again,
Loaded with spoils of foes in battle slain.
Snatch we the lucky minute while we may;
Nor can we be mistaken in the way;   321

For, hunting in the vale, we both have seen
The rising turrets, and the stream between,
And know the winding course, with ev'ry
      ford."
He ceas'd; and old Alethes took the word:
" Our country gods, in whom our trust we
      place,
Will yet from ruin save the Trojan race,
While we behold such dauntless worth ap-
      pear
In dawning youth, and souls so void of
      fear."
Then into tears of joy the father broke; ⎫
Each in his longing arms by turns he   ⎪
      took;   331   ⎬
Panted and paus'd; and thus again he   ⎪
      spoke: ⎭
" Ye brave young men, what equal gifts
      can we,
In recompense of such desert, decree ?
The greatest, sure, and best you can re-
      ceive,
The gods and your own conscious worth
      will give.
The rest our grateful gen'ral will bestow,
And young Ascanius till his manhood owe."
" And I, whose welfare in my father
      lies,"
Ascanius adds, " by the great deities,   340
By my dear country, by my household
      gods,
By hoary Vesta's rites and dark abodes,
Adjure you both, (on you my fortune
      stands;
That and my faith I plight into your
      hands,)
Make me but happy in his safe return,
Whose wanted presence I can only mourn;
Your common gift shall two large goblets
      be,
Of silver, wrought with curious imagery,
And high emboss'd, which, when old Priam
      reign'd,   349
My conqu'ring sire at sack'd Arisba gain'd;
And more, two tripods cast in antic mold,
With two great talents of the finest gold;
Beside a costly bowl, ingrav'd with art,
Which Dido gave, when first she gave her
      heart.
But, if in conquer'd Italy we reign,
When spoils by lot the victor shall obtain —
Thou saw'st the courser by proud Turnus
      press'd:
That, Nisus, and his arms, and nodding
      crest,

And shield, from chance exempt, shall ⎫
  be thy share: ⎪
Twelve lab'ring slaves, twelve handmaids ⎬
  young and fair,   360 ⎪
All clad in rich attire, and train'd with ⎪
  care;   ⎭
And, last, a Latian field with fruitful
  plains,
And a large portion of the king's domains.
But thou, whose years are more to mine
  allied —
No fate my vow'd affection shall divide
From thee, heroic youth ! Be wholly mine;
Take full possession; all my soul is thine.
One faith, one fame, one fate, shall both
  attend;
My life's companion, and my bosom friend:
My peace shall be committed to thy care, 370
And to thy conduct my concerns in war."
Then thus the young Euryalus replied:
" Whatever fortune, good or bad, betide,
The same shall be my age, as now my
  youth;
No time shall find me wanting to my truth.
This only from your goodness let me gain
(And, this ungranted, all rewards are vain):
Of Priam's royal race my mother came —
And sure the best that ever bore the name —
Whom neither Troy nor Sicily could hold 380
From me departing, but, o'erspent and old,
My fate she follow'd. Ignorant of this
(Whatever) danger, neither parting kiss,
Nor pious blessing taken, her I leave,
And in this only act of all my life deceive.
By this right hand and conscious Night I
  swear,
My soul so sad a farewell could not bear.
Be you her comfort; fill my vacant place
(Permit me to presume so great a grace);
Support her age, forsaken and distress'd. 390
That hope alone will fortify my breast
Against the worst of fortunes, and of fears."
He said. The mov'd assistants melt in
  tears.
Then thus Ascanius, wonderstruck to see
That image of his filial piety:
"So great beginnings, in so green an age,
Exact the faith which I again ingage.
Thy mother all the dues shall justly claim,
Creüsa had, and only want the name.
Whate'er event thy bold attempt shall
  have,   400
'T is merit to have borne a son so brave.
Now by my head. a sacred oath, I swear,
(My father us'd it,) what, returning here

Crown'd with success, I for thyself prepare,
That, if thou fail, shall thy lov'd mother
  share."
He said, and weeping, while he spoke the
  word,
From his broad belt he drew a shining
  sword,
Magnificent with gold. Lycaon made,
And in an iv'ry scabbard sheath'd the
  blade.
This was his gift. Great Mnestheus gave
  his friend   410
A lion's hide, his body to defend;
And good Alethes furnish'd him, beside,
With his own trusty helm, of temper tried.
  Thus arm'd they went. The noble Tro-
  jans wait
Their issuing forth, and follow to the gate
With prayers and vows. Above the rest
  appears
Ascanius, manly far beyond his years,
And messages committed to their care,
Which all in winds were lost, and flitting
  air.
  The trenches first they pass'd; then took
  their way   420
Where their proud foes in pitch'd pavilions
  lay;
To many fatal, ere themselves were slain.
They found the careless host dispers'd upon
  the plain,
Who, gorg'd, and drunk with wine, supinely
  snore.
Unharnass'd chariots stand along the shore:
Amidst the wheels and reins, the goblet by,
A medley of debauch and war, they lie.
Observing Nisus shew'd his friend the sight:
" Behold a conquest gain'd without a fight.
Occasion offers, and I stand prepar'd;   430
There lies our way: be thou upon the
  guard,
And look around, while I securely go,
And hew a passage thro' the sleeping foe."
Softly he spoke; then striding took his way,
With his drawn sword, where haughty
  Rhamnes lay:
His head rais'd high on tapestry beneath,
And heaving from his breast, he drew his
  breath;
A king and prophet, by King Turnus lov'd:
But fate by prescience cannot be remov'd.
Him and his sleeping slaves he slew; then
  spies   440
Where Remus, with his rich retinue, lies.
His armor-bearer first, and next he kills

His charioteer, intrench'd betwixt the
    wheels
And his lov'd horses; last invades their
    lord;
Full on his neck he drives the fatal sword:
The gasping head flies off; a purple flood
Flows from the trunk, that welters in the
    blood,
Which, by the spurning heels dispers'd
    around,
The bed besprinkles and bedews the ground.
Lamus the bold, and Lamyrus the strong, 450
He slew, and then Serranus fair and young.
From dice and wine the youth retir'd to
    rest,
And puff'd the fumy god from out his
    breast:
Ev'n then he dreamt of drink and lucky
    play —
More lucky, had it lasted till the day.
The famish'd lion thus, with hunger bold,
O'erleaps the fences of the nightly fold,
And tears the peaceful flocks: with silent
    awe
Trembling they lie, and pant beneath his
    paw.
    Nor with less rage Euryalus employs 460
The wrathful sword, or fewer foes de-
    stroys;
But on th' ignoble crowd his fury flew:
He Fadus, Hebesus, and Rhœtus slew.
Oppress'd with heavy sleep the former
    fall,
But Rhœtus wakeful, and observing all:
Behind a spacious jar he slink'd for fear;
The fatal iron found and reach'd him
    there;
For, as he rose, it pierc'd his naked side,
And, reeking, thence return'd in crimson
    dyed.
The wound pours out a stream of wine and
    blood;   470
The purple soul comes floating in the flood.
    Now, where Messapus quarter'd, they
    arrive.
The fires were fainting there, and just
    alive;
The warrior-horses, tied in order, fed.
Nisus observ'd the discipline, and said:
" Our eager thirst of blood may both be-
    tray;
And see the scatter'd streaks of dawning
    day,
Foe to nocturnal thefts. No more, my
    friend;

Here let our glutted execution end.
A lane thro' slaughter'd bodies we have
    made."   480
The bold Euryalus, tho' loth, obey'd.
Of arms, and arras, and of plate, they find
A precious load; but these they leave be-
    hind.
Yet, fond of gaudy spoils, the boy would
    stay
To make the rich caparison his prey,
Which on the steed of conquer'd Rham-
    nes lay.
Nor did his eyes less longingly behold
The girdle-belt, with nails of burnish'd
    gold.
This present Cædicus the rich bestow'd
On Remulus, when friendship first they
    vow'd,   490
And, absent, join'd in hospitable ties:
He, dying, to his heir bequeath'd the
    prize;
Till, by the conqu'ring Ardean troops op-
    press'd,
He fell; and they the glorious gift possess'd.
These glitt'ring spoils (now made the
    victor's gain)
He to his body suits, but suits in vain:
Messapus' helm he finds among the rest,
And laces on, and wears the waving crest.
Proud of their conquest, prouder of their
    prey,
They leave the camp, and take the ready
    way.   500
    But far they had not pass'd, before they
    spied
Three hundred horse, with Volscens for
    their guide.
The queen a legion to King Turnus sent;
But the swift horse the slower foot pre-
    vent,
And now, advancing, sought the leader's
    tent.
They saw the pair; for, thro' the doubt-
    ful shade,
His shining helm Euryalus betray'd,
On which the moon with full reflection
    play'd.
" 'T is not for naught," cried Volscens from
    the crowd,
" These men go there; " then rais'd his voice
    aloud: 510
" Stand ! stand ! why thus in arms ? And
    whither bent ?
From whence, to whom, and on what errand
    sent ? "

Silent they scud away, and haste their flight
To neighb'ring woods, and trust themselves
    to night.
The speedy horse all passages belay,
And spur their smoking steeds to cross their
    way,
And watch each entrance of the winding
    wood.
Black was the forest: thick with beech it
    stood,
Horrid with fern, and intricate with thorn;
Few paths of human feet, or tracks of beasts,
    were worn.   520
The darkness of the shades, his heavy prey,
And fear, misled the younger from his way.
But Nisus hit the turns with happier haste,
And, thoughtless of his friend, the forest
    pass'd,
And Alban plains, from Alba's name so
    call'd,
Where King Latinus then his oxen stall'd;
Till, turning at the length, he stood his
    ground,
And miss'd his friend, and cast his eyes
    around:
" Ah wretch ! " he cried, " where have I left
    behind
Th' unhappy youth ? where shall I hope to
    find ?   530
Or what way take ? " Again he ventures
    back,
And treads the mazes of his former track.
He winds the wood, and, list'ning, hears the
    noise
Of trampling coursers, and the riders' voice.
The sound approach'd; and suddenly he
    view'd
The foes inclosing, and his friend pursued,
Forelaid and taken, while he strove in vain
The shelter of the friendly shades to gain.
What should he next attempt ? what arms
    employ,
What fruitless force, to free the captive
    boy ?   540
Or desperate should he rush and lose his
    life,
With odds oppress'd, in such unequal strife ?
  Resolv'd at length, his pointed spear he
    shook;
And, casting on the moon a mournful look:
" Guardian of groves, and goddess of the
    night,
Fair queen," he said, " direct my dart
    aright.
If e'er my pious father, for my sake,

Did grateful off'rings on thy altars make,
Or I increas'd them with my sylvan toils,
And hung thy holy roofs with savage spoils,
Give me to scatter these." Then from his
    ear   551
He pois'd, and aim'd, and launch'd the
    trembling spear.
The deadly weapon, hissing from the grove,
Impetuous on the back of Sulmo drove;
Pierc'd his thin armor, drank his vital blood,
And in his body left the broken wood.
He staggers round; his eyeballs roll in
    death,
And with short sobs he gasps away his
    breath.
All stand amaz'd — a second jav'lin flies
With equal strength, and quivers thro' the
    skies.   560
This thro' thy temples, Tagus, forc'd the
    way,
And in the brainpan warmly buried lay.
Fierce Volscens foams with rage, and, gaz-
    ing round,
Descried not him who gave the fatal wound,
Nor knew to fix revenge: " But thou," he
    cries,
"Shalt pay for both," and at the pris'ner
    flies
With his drawn sword. Then, struck with
    deep despair,
That cruel sight the lover could not bear;
But from his covert rush'd in open view,
And sent his voice before him as he flew:
" Me ! me ! " he cried — " turn all your
    swords alone   571
On me — the fact confess'd, the fault my
    own.
He neither could nor durst, the guiltless
    youth:
Ye moon and stars, bear witness to the
    truth !
His only crime (if friendship can offend)
Is too much love to his unhappy friend."
Too late he speaks: the sword, which fury
    guides,
Driv'n with full force, had pierc'd his ten-
    der sides.
Down fell the beauteous youth: the yawning
    wound
Gush'd out a purple stream, and stain'd the
    ground.   580
His snowy neck reclines upon his breast,
Like a fair flow'r by the keen share op-
    press'd;
Like a white poppy sinking on the plain,

Whose heavy head is overcharg'd with
    rain.
Despair, and rage, and vengeance justly
    vow'd,
Drove Nisus headlong on the hostile crowd.
Volscens he seeks; on him alone he bends:
Borne back and bor'd by his surrounding
    friends,
Onward he press'd, and kept him still in
    sight;
Then whirl'd aloft his sword with all his
    might: 590
Th' unerring steel descended while he
    spoke,
Pierc'd his wide mouth, and thro' his weazon
    broke.
Dying, he slew; and, stagg'ring on the plain,
With swimming eyes he sought his lover
    slain;
Then quiet on his bleeding bosom fell,
Content, in death, to be reveng'd so well.
    O happy friends! for, if my verse can
    give
Immortal life, your fame shall ever live,
Fix'd as the Capitol's foundation lies,
And spread, where'er the Roman eagle
    flies!   600
    The conqu'ring party first divide the
    prey,
Then their slain leader to the camp convey.
With wonder, as they went, the troops were
    fill'd,
To see such numbers whom so few had
    kill'd.
Serranus, Rhamnes, and the rest, they ⎤
    found; |
Vast crowds the dying and the dead sur- ⎬
    round; |
And the yet reeking blood o'erflows the |
    ground.   ⎦
All knew the helmet which Messapus lost,
But mourn'd a purchase that so dear had
    cost.
Now rose the ruddy morn from Tithon's
    bed,   610
And with the dawns of day the skies o'er-
    spread;
Nor long the sun his daily course withheld,
But added colors to the world reveal'd:
When early Turnus, wak'ning with the
    light,
All clad in armor, calls his troops to fight.
His martial men with fierce harangue she
    fir'd,
And his own ardor in their souls inspir'd.

This done — to give new terror to his foes,
The heads of Nisus and his friend he shows,
Rais'd high on pointed spears — a ghastly
    sight: 620
Loud peals of shouts ensue, and barbarous
    delight.
    Meantime the Trojans run, where danger
    calls;
They line their trenches, and they man their
    walls.
In front extended to the left they stood;
Safe was the right, surrounded by the flood.
But, casting from their tow'rs a frightful
    view,
They saw the faces, which too well they
    knew,
Tho' then disguis'd in death, and smear'd
    all o'er
With filth obscene, and dropping putrid gore.
Soon hasty fame thro' the sad city bears 630
The mournful message to the mother's ears.
An icy cold benumbs her limbs; she shakes;
Her cheeks the blood, her hand the web
    forsakes.
She runs the rampires round amidst the ⎤
    war, |
Nor fears the flying darts; she rends her ⎬
    hair, |
And fills with loud laments the liquid air. ⎦
" Thus, then, my lov'd Euryalus appears!
Thus looks the prop of my declining years!
Was 't on this face my famish'd eyes I
    fed?
Ah! how unlike the living is the dead! 640
And could'st thou leave me, cruel, thus
    alone?
Not one kind kiss from a departing son!
No look, no last adieu before he went,
In an ill-boding hour to slaughter sent!
Cold on the ground, and pressing foreign
    clay,
To Latian dogs and fowls he lies a prey!
Nor was I near to close his dying eyes,
To wash his wounds, to weep his obsequies,
To call about his corpse his crying friends,
Or spread the mantle (made for other
    ends)   650
On his dear body, which I wove with care,
Nor did my daily pains or nightly labor
    spare.
Where shall I find his corpse? what earth
    sustains
His trunk dismember'd, and his cold re-
    mains?
For this, alas! I left my needful ease,

Expos'd my life to winds and winter seas!
If any pity touch Rutulian hearts,
Here empty all your quivers, all your
    darts;
Or, if they fail, thou, Jove, conclude my
    woe,
And send me thunderstruck to shades be-
    low!"   660
Her shrieks and clamors pierce the Tro-
    jans' ears,
Unman their courage, and augment their
    fears;
Nor young Ascanius could the sight sus-
    tain,
Nor old Ilioneus his tears restrain,
But Actor and Idæus jointly sent,
To bear the madding mother to her tent.
    And now the trumpets terribly, from far,
With rattling clangor, rouse the sleepy
    war.
The soldiers' shouts succeed the brazen
    sounds;
And heav'n, from pole to pole, the noise
    rebounds.   670
The Volscians bear their shields upon their
    head,
And, rushing forward, form a moving shed.
These fill the ditch; those pull the bul-
    warks down:
Some raise the ladders; others scale the
    town.
But, where void spaces on the walls ap-
    pear,
Or thin defense, they pour their forces
    there.
With poles and missive weapons, from
    afar,
The Trojans keep aloof the rising war.
Taught, by their ten years' siege, defensive
    fight,
They roll down ribs of rocks, an unresisted
    weight,   680
To break the penthouse with the pond'rous
    blow,
Which yet the patient Volscians undergo:
But could not bear th' unequal combat
    long;
For, where the Trojans find the thickest
    throng,
The ruin falls: their shatter'd shields give
    way,
And their crush'd heads become an easy
    prey.
They shrink for fear, abated of their rage,
Nor longer dare in a blind fight engage;

Contented now to gall them from below
With darts and slings, and with the distant
    bow.   690
    Elsewhere Mezentius, terrible to view,
A blazing pine within the trenches threw.
But brave Messapus, Neptune's warlike
    son,
Broke down the palisades, the trenches
    won,
And loud for ladders calls, to scale the
    town.
    Calliope, begin! Ye sacred Nine,
Inspire your poet in his high design,
To sing what slaughter manly Turnus
    made,
What souls he sent below the Stygian
    shade,
What fame the soldiers with their captain
    share,   700
And the vast circuit of the fatal war;
For you in singing martial facts excel;
You best remember, and alone can tell.
    There stood a tow'r, amazing to the
    sight,
Built up of beams, and of stupendous
    height:
Art, and the nature of the place, conspir'd
To furnish all the strength that war re-
    quir'd.
To level this, the bold Italians join;
The wary Trojans obviate their design;
With weighty stones o'erwhelm their troops
    below,   710
Shoot thro' the loopholes, and sharp jav'lins
    throw.
Turnus, the chief, toss'd from his thun-
    d'ring hand,
Against the wooden walls, a flaming brand:
It stuck, the fiery plague; the winds were
    high;
The planks were season'd, and the timber
    dry.
Contagion caught the posts; it spread
    along,
Scorch'd, and to distance drove the scatter'd
    throng.
The Trojans fled; the fire pursued amain,
Still gath'ring fast upon the trembling
    train;   719
Till, crowding to the corners of the wall,
Down the defense and the defenders fall.
The mighty flaw makes heav'n itself re-
    sound:
The dead and dying Trojans strew the
    ground.

The tow'r, that follow'd on the fallen crew,
Whelm'd o'er their heads, and buried whom
    it slew:
Some stuck upon the darts themselves had
    sent;
All the same equal ruin underwent.
   Young Lycus and Helenor only scape;
Sav'd — how, they know not — from the
    steepy leap.
Helenor, elder of the two: by birth,   730
On one side royal, one a son of earth,
Whom to the Lydian king Licymnia bare, ⎤
And sent her boasted bastard to the war ⎟
(A privilege which none but freemen   ⎬
    share). ⎦
Slight were his arms, a sword and silver
    shield:
No marks of honor charg'd its empty field.
Light as he fell, so light the youth arose,
And rising, found himself amidst his foes;
Nor flight was left, nor hopes to force his
    way.
Embolden'd by despair, he stood at bay; 740
And — like a stag, whom all the troop sur-
    rounds
Of eager huntsmen and invading hounds —
Resolv'd on death, he dissipates his fears,
And bounds aloft against the pointed
    spears:
So dares the youth, secure of death; and
    throws
His dying body on his thickest foes.
But Lycus, swifter of his feet by far,
Runs, doubles, winds, and turns, amidst the
    war;
Springs to the walls, and leaves his foes
    behind,   749
And snatches at the beam he first can find;
Looks up, and leaps aloft at all the stretch,
In hopes the helping hand of some kind
    friend to reach.
But Turnus follow'd hard his hunted prey
(His spear had almost reach'd him in the
    way,
Short of his reins, and scarce a span be-
    hind):
"Fool!" said the chief, "tho' fleeter than
    the wind,
Couldst thou presume to scape, when I
    pursue?"
He said, and downward by the feet he
    drew
The trembling dastard; at the tug he falls;
Vast ruins come along, rent from the smok-
    ing walls.   760

Thus on some silver swan, or tim'rous
    hare,
Jove's bird comes sousing down from up-
    per air;
Her crooked talons truss the fearful prey:
Then out of sight she soars, and wings her
    way.
So seizes the grim wolf the tender lamb,
In vain lamented by the bleating dam.
   Then rushing onward, with a barb'rous
    cry,
The troops of Turnus to the combat fly.
The ditch with fagots fill'd, the daring
    foe
Toss'd firebrands to the steepy turrets
    throw.   770
Ilioneus, as bold Lucetius came
To force the gate, and feed the kindling
    flame,
Roll'd down the fragment of a rock so
    right,
It crush'd him double underneath the
    weight.
Two more young Liger and Asylas slew: ⎤
To bend the bow young Liger better   ⎬
    knew; ⎟
Asylas best the pointed jav'lin threw. ⎦
Brave Cæneus laid Ortygius on the plain;
The victor Cæneus was by Turnus slain.
By the same hand, Clonius and Itys fall, 780
Sagar, and Ida, standing on the wall.
From Capys' arms his fate Privernus found:
Hurt by Themilla first — but slight the
    wound —
His shield thrown by, to mitigate the
    smart,
He clapp'd his hand upon the wounded
    part:
The second shaft came swift and unespied,
And pierc'd his hand, and nail'd it to his
    side,
Transfix'd his breathing lungs and beating
    heart:
The soul came issuing out, and hiss'd
    against the dart.
   The son of Arcens shone amid the rest,
In glitt'ring armor and a purple vest,   791
(Fair was his face, his eyes inspiring love,)
Bred by his father in the Martian grove,
Where the fat altars of Palicus flame,
And sent in arms to purchase early fame.
Him when he spied from far, the Tuscan
    king
Laid by the lance, and took him to the
    sling,

Thrice whirl'd the thong around his head,
    and threw:
The heated lead half melted as it flew;
It pierc'd his hollow temples and his brain;
The youth came tumbling down, and
    spurn'd the plain.   801
  Then young Ascanius, who, before this
    day,
Was wont in woods to shoot the savage
    prey,
First bent in martial strife the twanging
    bow,
And exercis'd against a human foe —
With this bereft Numanus of his life,
Who Turnus' younger sister took to wife.
Proud of his realm, and of his royal
    bride,
Vaunting before his troops, and length-
    en'd with a stride,
In these insulting terms the Trojans he
    defied: 810
"Twice-conquer'd cowards, now your shame
    is shown —
Coop'd up a second time within your town!
Who dare not issue forth in open field,
But hold your walls before you for a shield.
Thus threat you war? thus our alliance
    force?
What gods, what madness, hether steer'd
    your course?
You shall not find the sons of Atreus here,
Nor need the frauds of sly Ulysses fear.
Strong from the cradle, of a sturdy brood,
We bear our newborn infants to the flood;
There bath'd amid the stream, our boys we
    hold,   821
With winter harden'd, and inur'd to cold.
They wake before the day to range the
    wood,
Kill ere they eat, nor taste unconquer'd
    food.
No sports, but what belong to war, they
    know:
To break the stubborn colt, to bend the
    bow.
Our youth, of labor patient, earn their
    bread;
Hardly they work, with frugal diet fed.
From plows and harrows sent to seek re-
    nown,
They fight in fields, and storm the shaken
    town.   830
No part of life from toils of war is free,
No change in age, or diff'rence in degree.
We plow and till in arms; our oxen feel,

Instead of goads, the spur and pointed
    steel;
Th' inverted lance makes furrows in the
    plain.
Ev'n time, that changes all, yet changes us
    in vain:
The body, not the mind; nor can control
Th' immortal vigor, or abate the soul.
Our helms defend the young, disguise the
    gray:
We live by plunder, and delight in prey.
Your vests embroider'd with rich purple
    shine;   841
In sloth you glory, and in dances join.
Your vests have sweeping sleeves; with
    female pride
Your turbants underneath your chins are
    tied.
Go, Phrygians, to your Dindymus again!
Go, less than women, in the shapes of men!
Go, mix'd with eunuchs, in the Mother's
    rites,
Where with unequal sound the flute in-
    vites;
Sing, dance, and howl, by turns, in Ida's
    shade:
Resign the war to men, who know the mar-
    tial trade!"   850
  This foul reproach Ascanius could not
    hear
With patience, or a vow'd revenge forbear.
At the full stretch of both his hands he
    drew,
And almost join'd the horns of the tough
    yew.
But, first, before the throne of Jove he
    stood,
And thus with lifted hands invok'd the
    god:
"My first attempt, great Jupiter, suc-
    ceed!
An annual off'ring in thy grove shall bleed;
A snow-white steer, before thy altar led,
Who, like his mother, bears aloft his head,
Butts with his threat'ning brows, and bel-
    lowing stands,   861
And dares the fight, and spurns the yellow
    sands."
  Jove bow'd the heav'ns, and lent a gra-
    cious ear,
And thunder'd on the left, amidst the
    clear.
Sounded at once the bow; and swiftly flies
The feather'd death, and hisses thro' the
    skies.

The steel thro' both his temples forc'd the
    way:
Extended on the ground, Numanus lay.
" Go now, vain boaster, and true valor
    scorn !
The Phrygians, twice subdued, yet make
    this third return."   870
Ascanius said no more. The Trojans shake
The heav'ns with shouting, and new vigor
    take.
  Apollo then bestrode a golden cloud,
To view the feats of arms, and fighting
    crowd;
And thus the beardless victor he bespoke
    aloud:
" Advance, illustrious youth, increase in
    fame,
And wide from east to west extend thy
    name;
Offspring of gods thyself; and Rome shall
    owe
To thee a race of demigods below.
This is the way to heav'n: the pow'rs di-
    vine   880
From this beginning date the Julian line.
To thee, to them, and their victorious heirs,
The conquer'd war is due, and the vast
    world is theirs.
Troy is too narrow for thy name." He
    said,
And plunging downward shot his radiant
    head;
Dispell'd the breathing air, that broke his
    flight:
Shorn of his beams, a man to mortal sight.
Old Butes' form he took, Anchises' squire,
Now left, to rule Ascanius, by his sire:
His wrinkled visage, and his hoary hairs,
His mien, his habit, and his arms, he
    wears,   891
And thus salutes the boy, too forward for
    his years:
" Suffice it thee, thy father's worthy son,
The warlike prize thou hast already won.
The god of archers gives thy youth a part
Of his own praise, nor envies equal art.
Now tempt the war no more." He said,
    and flew
Obscure in air, and vanish'd from their
    view.
The Trojans, by his arms, their patron
    know,
And hear the twanging of his heav'nly bow.
Then duteous force they use, and Phœbus'
    name,   901

To keep from fight the youth too fond of
    fame.
Undaunted, they themselves no danger
    shun;
From wall to wall the shouts and clamors
    run.
They bend their bows; they whirl their
    slings around;
Heaps of spent arrows fall, and strew the
    ground;
And helms, and shields, and rattling
    arms resound.
The combat thickens, like the storm that
    flies
From westward, when the show'ry Kids
    arise;
Or patt'ring hail comes pouring on the
    main,   910
When Jupiter descends in harden'd rain,
Or bellowing clouds burst with a stormy
    sound,
And with an armed winter strew the
    ground.
  Pand'rus and Bitias, thunderbolts of war,
Whom Hiera to bold Alcanor bare
On Ida's top, two youths of height and
    size
Like firs that on their mother mountain
    rise,
Presuming on their force, the gates unbar,
And of their own accord invite the war.
With fates averse, against their king's
    command,   920
Arm'd, on the right and on the left they
    stand,
And flank the passage: shining steel they
    wear,
And waving crests above their heads ap-
    pear.
Thus two tall oaks, that Padus' banks
    adorn,
Lift up to heav'n their leafy heads unshorn,
And, overpress'd with nature's heavy load,
Dance to the whistling winds, and at each
    other nod.
In flows a tide of Latians, when they see
The gate set open, and the passage free;
Bold Quercens, with rash Tmarus, rushing
    on,   930
Equicolus, that in bright armor shone,
And Hæmon first; but soon repuls'd they
    fly,
Or in the well-defended pass they die.
These with success are fir'd, and those with
    rage,

And each on equal terms at length ingage.
Drawn from their lines, and issuing on the plain,
The Trojans hand to hand the fight maintain.
Fierce Turnus in another quarter fought,
When suddenly th' unhop'd-for news was brought,
The foes had left the fastness of their place, 940
Prevail'd in fight, and had his men in chase.
He quits th' attack, and, to prevent their fate,
Runs where the giant brothers guard the gate.
The first he met, Antiphates the brave,
But base-begotten on a Theban slave,
Sarpedon's son, he slew: tl deadly dart
Found passage thro' his breast, and pierc'd his heart.
Fix'd in the wound th' Italian cornel stood,
Warm'd in his lungs, and in his vital blood.
Aphidnus next, and Erymanthus dies, 950
And Meropes, and the gigantic size
Of Bitias, threat'ning with his ardent eyes.
Not by the feeble dart he fell oppress'd
(A dart were lost within that roomy breast),
But from a knotted lance, large, heavy, strong,
Which roar'd like thunder as it whirl'd along:
Not two bull hides th' impetuous force withhold,
Nor coat of double mail, with scales of gold.
Down sunk the monster bulk and press'd the ground;
His arms and clatt'ring shield on the vast body sound, 960
Not with less ruin than the Bajan mole,
Rais'd on the seas, the surges to control —
At once comes tumbling down the rocky wall;
Prone to the deep, the stones disjointed fall
Of the vast pile; the scatter'd ocean flies;
Black sands, discolor'd froth, and mingled mud arise:
The frighted billows roll, and seek the shores;
Then trembles Prochyta, then Ischia roars:
Typhœus, thrown beneath, by Jove's command,

Astonish'd at the flaw that shakes the land, 970
Soon shifts his weary side, and, scarce awake,
With wonder feels the weight press lighter on his back.
The warrior god the Latian troops inspir'd,
New strung their sinews, and their courage fir'd,
But chills the Trojan hearts with cold affright:
Then black despair precipitates their flight.
When Pandarus beheld his brother kill'd,
The town with fear and wild confusion fill'd,
He turns the hinges of the heavy gate
With both his hands, and adds his shoulders to the weight; 980
Some happier friends within the walls inclos'd;
The rest shut out, to certain death expos'd:
Fool as he was, and frantic in his care,
T' admit young Turnus, and include the war !
He thrust amid the crowd, securely bold,
Like a fierce tiger pent amid the fold.
Too late his blazing buckler they descry,
And sparkling fires that shot from either eye,
His mighty members, and his ample breast,
His rattling armor, and his crimson crest.
Far from that hated face the Trojans fly, 991
All but the fool who sought his destiny.
Mad Pandarus steps forth, with vengeance vow'd
For Bitias' death, and threatens thus aloud:
" These are not Ardea's walls, nor this the town
Amata proffers with Lavinia's crown:
'T is hostile earth you tread. Of hope bereft,
No means of safe return by flight are left."
To whom, with count'nance calm, and soul sedate,
Thus Turnus: " Then begin, and try thy fate: 1000
My message to the ghost of Priam bear;
Tell him a new Achilles sent thee there."
A lance of tough ground ash the Trojan threw,
Rough in the rind, and knotted as it grew:
With his full force he whirl'd it first around;

But the soft yielding air receiv'd the
wound:
Imperial Juno turn'd the course before,
And fix'd the wand'ring weapon in the door.
"But hope not thou," said Turnus, "when
I strike,
To shun thy fate: our force is not alike,
Nor thy steel temper'd by the Lemnian
god."   1011
Then rising, on his utmost stretch he stood,
And aim'd from high: the full descending
blow
Cleaves the broad front and beardless
cheeks in two.
Down sinks the giant with a thund'ring ⎫
sound: ⎪
His pond'rous limbs oppress the trem- ⎬
bling ground;   ⎪
Blood, brains, and foam gush from the ⎪
gaping wound: ⎭
Scalp, face, and shoulders the keen steel
divides,
And the shar'd visage hangs on equal sides.
The Trojans fly from their approaching
fate;   1020
And, had the victor then secur'd the gate,
And to his troops without unclos'd the bars,
One lucky day had ended all his wars.
But boiling youth, and blind desire of
blood,
Push'd on his fury, to pursue the crowd.
Hamstring'd behind, unhappy Gyges died;
Then Phalaris is added to his side.
The pointed jav'lins from the dead he drew,
And their friends' arms against their fellows
threw.
Strong Halys stands in vain; weak Phlegys
flies;   1030
Saturnia, still at hand, new force and fire
supplies.
Then Halius, Prytanis, Alcander fall —
Ingag'd against the foes who scal'd the
wall:
But, whom they fear'd without, they found
within.
At last, tho' late, by Lynceus he was seen.
He calls new succors, and assaults the
prince:
But weak his force, and vain is their de-
fense.
Turn'd to the right, his sword the hero
drew,
And at one blow the bold aggressor slew.
He joints the neck; and, with a stroke so
strong,   1040

The helm flies off, and bears the head
along.
Next him, the huntsman Amycus he kill'd,
In darts invenom'd and in poison skill'd.
Then Clytius fell beneath his fatal spear,
And Creteus, whom the Muses held so
dear:
He fought with courage, and he sung the
fight;
Arms were his bus'ness, verses his delight.
The Trojan chiefs behold, with rage and
grief,
Their slaughter'd friends, and hasten their
relief.
Bold Mnestheus rallies first the broken
train,   1050
Whom brave Seresthus and his troop sus-
tain.
To save the living, and revenge the dead,
Against one warrior's arms all Troy they
led.
"O, void of sense and courage!" Mnes-
theus cried,
"Where can you hope your coward heads
to hide?
Ah! where beyond these rampires can you
run?
One man, and in your camp inclos'd, you
shun!
Shall then a single sword such slaughter
boast,
And pass unpunish'd from a num'rous host?
Forsaking honor, and renouncing fame, 1060
Your gods, your country, and your king
you shame!"
This just reproach their virtue does excite:
They stand, they join, they thicken to the
fight.
Now Turnus doubts, and yet disdains to
yield,
But with slow paces measures back the
field,
And inches to the walls, where Tiber's
tide,
Washing the camp, defends the weaker
side.
The more he loses, they advance the more,
And tread in ev'ry step he trod before.
They shout: they bear him back; and, whom
by might   1070
They cannot conquer, they oppress with
weight.
As, compass'd with a wood of spears
around,
The lordly lion still maintains his ground;

Grins horrible, retires, and turns again;
Threats his distended paws, and shakes his
   mane;
He loses while in vain he presses on,
Nor will his courage let him dare to run:
So Turnus fares, and, unresolv'd of flight,
Moves tardy back, and just recedes from
   fight.
Yet twice, inrag'd, the combat he renews,
Twice breaks, and twice his broken foes
   pursues.   1081
But now they swarm, and, with fresh troops
   supplied,
Come rolling on, and rush from ev'ry side:
Nor Juno, who sustain'd his arms before,
Dares with new strength suffice th' ex-
   hausted store;
For Jove, with sour commands, sent Iris
   down,
To force th' invader from the frighted
   town.
With labor spent, no longer can he wield
The heavy fauchion, or sustain the shield,
O'erwhelm'd with darts, which from afar
   they fling: 1090
The weapons round his hollow temples
   ring;
His golden helm gives way, with stony
   blows
Batter'd, and flat, and beaten to his brows.
His crest is rash'd away; his ample shield
Is falsified, and round with jav'lins fill'd.
  The foe, now faint, the Trojans over-
   whelm;
And Mnestheus lays hard load upon his
   helm.
Sick sweat succeeds; he drops at ev'ry
   pore;
With driving dust his cheeks are pasted
   o'er;
Shorter and shorter ev'ry gasp he takes;
And vain efforts and hurtless blows he
   makes.   1101
Arm'd as he was, at length he leap'd from
   high,
Plung'd in the flood, and made the waters
   fly.
The yellow god the welcome burthen
   bore,
And wip'd the sweat, and wash'd away the
   gore;
Then gently wafts him to the farther
   coast,
And sends him safe to cheer his anxious
   host.

THE TENTH BOOK OF THE ÆNEIS

THE ARGUMENT

Jupiter, calling a council of the gods, forbids
them to engage in either party. At Æneas's
return there is a bloody battle: Turnus killing Pallas; Æneas, Lausus and Mezentius.
Mezentius is describ'd as an atheist; Lausus,
as a pious and virtuous youth. The different
actions and death of these two are the subject
of a noble episode.

THE gates of heav'n unfold: Jove summons
   all
The gods to council in the common hall.
Sublimely seated, he surveys from far
The fields, the camp, the fortune of the war,
And all th' inferior world. From first to
   last,
The sov'reign senate in degrees are plac'd.
  Then thus th' almighty sire began: " Ye
   gods,
Natives or denizens of blest abodes,
From whence these murmurs, and this
   change of mind,
This backward fate from what was first
   design'd?   10
Why this protracted war, when my com-
   mands
Pronounc'd a peace, and gave the Latian
   lands?
What fear or hope on either part divides
Our heav'ns, and arms our pow'rs on dif-
   f'rent sides?
A lawful time of war at length will come,
(Nor need your haste anticipate the
   doom,)
When Carthage shall contend the world
   with Rome,
Shall force the rigid rocks and Alpine chains,
And, like a flood, come pouring on the
   plains.
Then is your time for faction and debate,
For partial favor, and permitted hate.   21
Let now your immature dissension cease;
Sit quiet, and compose your souls to peace."
  Thus Jupiter in few unfolds the charge;
But lovely Venus thus replies at large:
" O pow'r immense, eternal energy,
(For to what else protection can we fly?)
Seest thou the proud Rutulians, how they
   dare
In fields, unpunish'd, and insult my care?
How lofty Turnus vaunts amidst his train,

In shining arms, triumphant on the plain ? 31
Ev'n in their lines and trenches they contend,
And scarce their walls the Trojan troops defend:
The town is fill'd with slaughter, and o'erfloats,
With a red deluge, their increasing moats.
Æneas, ignorant, and far from thence,
Has left a camp expos'd, without defense.
This endless outrage shall they still sustain ?
Shall Troy renew'd be forc'd and fir'd again ?
A second siege my banish'd issue fears, 40
And a new Diomede in arms appears.
One more audacious mortal will be found;
And I, thy daughter, wait another wound.
Yet, if with fates averse, without thy leave,
The Latian lands my progeny receive,
Bear they the pains of violated law,
And thy protection from their aid withdraw.
But, if the gods their sure success foretell;
If those of heav'n consent with those of hell,
To promise Italy; who dare debate 50
The pow'r of Jove, or fix another fate ?
What should I tell of tempests on the main,
Of Æolus usurping Neptune's reign ?
Of Iris sent, with Bacchanalian heat
T' inspire the matrons, and destroy the fleet ?
Now Juno to the Stygian sky descends,
Solicits hell for aid, and arms the fiends.
That new example wanted yet above:
An act that well became the wife of Jove !
Alecto, rais'd by her, with rage inflames 60
The peaceful bosoms of the Latian dames.
Imperial sway no more exalts my mind;
(Such hopes I had indeed, while Heav'n was kind;)
Now let my happier foes possess my place,
Whom Jove prefers before the Trojan race;
And conquer they, whom you with conquest grace.
Since you can spare, from all your wide command,
No spot of earth, no hospitable land,
Which may my wand'ring fugitives receive;
(Since haughty Juno will not give you leave;)
Then, father, (if I still may use that name,) 70
By ruin'd Troy, yet smoking from the flame,
I beg you, let Ascanius, by my care,

Be freed from danger, and dismiss'd the war:
Inglorious let him live, without a crown:
The father may be cast on coasts unknown,
Struggling with fate; but let me save the son.
Mine is Cythera, mine the Cyprian tow'rs:
In those recesses, and those sacred bow'rs,
Obscurely let him rest; his right resign 80
To promis'd empire, and his Julian line.
Then Carthage may th' Ausonian towns destroy,
Nor fear the race of a rejected boy.
What profits it my son to scape the fire,
Arm'd with his gods, and loaded with his sire;
To pass the perils of the seas and wind;
Evade the Greeks, and leave the war behind;
To reach th' Italian shores; if, after all,
Our second Pergamus is doom'd to fall ?
Much better had he curb'd his high desires, 90
And hover'd o'er his ill-extinguish'd fires.
To Simoïs' banks the fugitives restore,
And give them back to war, and all the woes before."
  Deep indignation swell'd Saturnia's heart:
" And must I own," she said, " my secret smart —
What with more decence were in silence kept,
And, but for this unjust reproach, had slept ?
Did god or man your fav'rite son advise,
With war unhop'd the Latians to surprise ?
By fate, you boast, and by the gods' decree,
He left his native land for Italy ! 101
Confess the truth; by mad Cassandra, more
Than Heav'n inspir'd, he sought a foreign shore !
Did I persuade to trust his second Troy
To the raw conduct of a beardless boy,
With walls unfinish'd, which himself forsakes,
And thro' the waves a wand'ring voyage takes ?
When have I urg'd him meanly to demand
The Tuscan aid, and arm a quiet land ?
Did I or Iris give this mad advice, 110
Or made the fool himself the fatal choice ?
You think it hard, the Latians should destroy
With swords your Trojans, and with fires your Troy !
Hard and unjust indeed, for men to draw

Their native air, nor take a foreign law!
That Turnus is permitted still to live,
To whom his birth a god and goddess give!
But yet 't is just and lawful for your line
To drive their fields, and force with fraud
    to join;
Realms, not your own, among your clans
    divide,   120
And from the bridegroom tear the promis'd
    bride;
Petition, while you public arms prepare;
Pretend a peace, and yet provoke a war!
'T was giv'n to you, your darling son to ⎫
    shroud,   ⎪
To draw the dastard from the fighting ⎬
    crowd,   ⎪
And, for a man, obtend an empty cloud. ⎭
From flaming fleets you turn'd the fire
    away,
And chang'd the ships to daughters of the
    sea.
But 't is my crime — the Queen of Heav'n
    offends,
If she presume to save her suff'ring
    friends!   130
Your son, not knowing what his foes decree,
You say, is absent: absent let him be.
Yours is Cythera, yours the Cyprian tow'rs,
The soft recesses, and the sacred bow'rs.
Why do you then these needless arms pre-
    pare,
And thus provoke a people prone to war?
Did I with fire the Trojan town deface,
Or hinder from return your exil'd race?
Was I the cause of mischief, or the man
Whose lawless lust the fatal war began?
Think on whose faith th' adult'rous youth
    relied;   141
Who promis'd, who procur'd, the Spartan
    bride?
When all th' united states of Greece com-
    bin'd,
To purge the world of the perfidious kind,
Then was your time to fear the Trojan
    fate:
Your quarrels and complaints are now too
    late."
    Thus Juno. Murmurs rise, with mix'd
    applause,
Just as they favor or dislike the cause.
So winds, when yet unfledg'd in woods they
    lie,
In whispers first their tender voices try, 150
Then issue on the main with bellowing rage,
And storms to trembling mariners presage.

    Then thus to both replied th' imperial
    god,
Who shakes heav'n's axles with his awful
    nod.
(When he begins, the silent senate stand
With rev'rence, list'ning to the dread com-
    mand:
The clouds dispel; the winds their breath
    restrain;
And the hush'd waves lie flatted on the
    main.)
"Celestials, your attentive ears incline! ⎫
Since," said the god, "the Trojans must ⎪
    not join   160   ⎬
In wish'd alliance with the Latian line; ⎭
Since endless jarrings and immortal hate ⎫
Tend but to discompose our happy state; ⎬
The war henceforward be resign'd to fate: ⎭
Each to his proper fortune stand or fall;
Equal and unconcern'd I look on all.
Rutulians, Trojans, are the same to me;
And both shall draw the lots their fates
    decree.
Let these assault, if Fortune be their
    friend;   169
And, if she favors those, let those defend:
The Fates will find their way." The Thun-
    d'rer said,
And shook the sacred honors of his head,
Attesting Styx, th' inviolable flood,   ⎫
And the black regions of his brother god. ⎪
Trembled the poles of heav'n, and earth ⎬
    confess'd the nod.   ⎭
This end the sessions had: the senate rise,
And to his palace wait their sov'reign thro'
    the skies.
    Meantime, intent upon their siege, the
    foes
Within their walls the Trojan host inclose:
They wound, they kill, they watch at ev'ry
    gate;   180
Renew the fires, and urge their happy fate.
Th' Æneans wish in vain their wanted
    chief,
Hopeless of flight, more hopeless of relief.
Thin on the tow'rs they stand; and ev'n
    those few
A feeble, fainting, and dejected crew.
Yet in the face of danger some there stood:
The two bold brothers of Sarpedon's blood,
Asius and Acmon; both th' Assaraci;
Young Hæmon, and tho' young, resolv'd to
    die.
With these were Clarus and Thymœtes
    join'd;   190

Tibris and Castor, both of Lycian kind.
From Acmon's hands a rolling stone there
　came,
So large, it half deserv'd a mountain's
　name:
Strong-sinew'd was the youth, and big of ⎫
　bone;　　　　　　　　　　　　　　　⎪
His brother Mnestheus could not more ⎬
　have done,　　　　　　　　　　　　　⎪
Or the great father of th' intrepid son. ⎭
Some firebrands throw, some flights of
　arrows send;
And some with darts, and some with stones
　defend.
　Amid the press appears the beauteous
　　boy,
The care of Venus, and the hope of Troy. 200
His lovely face unarm'd, his head was bare;
In ringlets o'er his shoulders hung his hair.
His forehead circled with a diadem;
Distinguish'd from the crowd, he shines a
　gem,
Enchas'd in gold, or polish'd iv'ry set,
Amidst the meaner foil of sable jet.
Nor Ismarus was wanting to the war,
Directing ointed arrows from afar,
And death with poison arm'd — in Lydia
　born,
Where plenteous harvests the fat fields
　adorn;　　　　　　　　　　　　　210
Where proud Pactolus floats the fruitful
　lands,
And leaves a rich manure of golden sands.
There Capys, author of the Capuan name, ⎤
And there was Mnestheus too, increas'd ⎪
　in fame,　　　　　　　　　　　　⎬
Since Turnus from the camp he cast with ⎪
　shame.　　　　　　　　　　　　⎦
　Thus mortal war was wag'd on either side.
Meantime the hero cuts the nightly tide:
For, anxious, from Evander when he went,
He sought the Tyrrhene camp, and Tar-
　chon's tent;
Expos'd the cause of coming to the chief; 220
His name and country told, and ask'd relief;
Propos'd the terms; his own small strength
　declar'd;
What vengeance proud Mezentius had pre-
　par'd;
What Turnus, bold and violent, design'd;
Then shew'd the slipp'ry state of human-
　kind,
And fickle fortune; warn'd him to beware,
And to his wholesome counsel added pray'r.
Tarchon, without delay, the treaty signs,

And to the Trojan troops the Tuscan joins.
　They soon set sail; nor now the fates
　　withstand;　　　　　　　　　　230
Their forces trusted with a foreign hand.
Æneas leads; upon his stern appear ⎫
Two lions carv'd, which rising Ida ⎬
　bear —　　　　　　　　　　　⎭
Ida, to wand'ring Trojans ever dear.
Under their grateful shade Æneas sate,
Revolving war's events, and various fate.
His left young Pallas kept, fix'd to his side,
And oft of winds enquir'd, and of the tide;
Oft of the stars, and of their wat'ry way;
And what he suffer'd both by land and
　sea.　　　　　　　　　　　　　240
　Now, sacred sisters, open all your spring !
The Tuscan leaders, and their army sing,
Which follow'd great Æneas to the war:
Their arms, their numbers, and their names,
　declare.
　A thousand youths brave Massicus obey,
Borne in the Tiger thro' the foaming sea;
From Asium brought, and Cosa, by his care:
For arms, light quivers, bows and shafts,
　they bear.
Fierce Abas next: his men bright armor
　wore;
His stern Apollo's golden statue bore.　250
Six hundred Populonia sent along,
All skill'd in martial exercise, and strong.
Three hundred more for battle Ilva joins,
An isle renown'd for steel, and unexhausted
　mines.
Asylas on his prow the third appears,
Who heav'n interprets, and the wand'ring
　stars;
From offer'd entrails prodigies expounds,
And peals of thunder, with presaging sounds.
A thousand spears in warlike order stand,
Sent by the Pisans under his command. 260
　Fair Astur follows in the wat'ry field,
Proud of his manag'd horse and painted
　shield.
Gravisca, noisome from the neighb'ring fen,
And his own Cære, sent three hundred men;
With those which Minio's fields and Pyrgi
　gave,
All bred in arms, unanimous, and brave.
　Thou, Muse, the name of Cinyras renew,
And brave Cupavo follow'd but by few;
Whose helm confess'd the lineage of the
　man,
And bore, with wings display'd, a silver
　swan.　　　　　　　　　　　　270
Love was the fault of his fam'd ancestry,

Whose forms and fortunes in his ensigns fly.
For Cycnus lov'd unhappy Phaeton,
And sung his loss in poplar groves, alone,
Beneath the sister shades, to soothe his grief.
Heav'n heard his song, and hasten'd his
   relief,
And chang'd to snowy plumes his hoary hair,
And wing'd his flight, to chant aloft in air.
His son Cupavo brush'd the briny flood:
Upon his stern a brawny Centaur stood, 280
Who heav'd a rock, and, threat'ning still to
   throw,
With lifted hands alarm'd the seas below:
They seem'd to fear the formidable sight,
And roll'd their billows on, to speed his
   flight.
Ocnus was next, who led his native train
Of hardy warriors thro' the wat'ry plain:
The son of Manto by the Tuscan stream,
From whence the Mantuan town derives the
   name —
An ancient city, but of mix'd descent:
Three sev'ral tribes compose the govern-
   ment; 290
Four towns are under each; but all obey
The Mantuan laws, and own the Tuscan
   sway.
Hate to Mezentius arm'd five hundred ⎫
   more,   ⎪
Whom Mincius from his sire Benacus ⎬
   bore: ⎪
Mincius, with wreaths of reeds his fore-⎪
   head cover'd o'er.   ⎭
These grave Auletes leads: a hundred
   sweep
With stretching oars at once the glassy
   deep.
Him and his martial train the Triton bears;
High on his poop the sea-green god appears:
Frowning he seems his crooked shell to
   sound, 300
And at the blast the billows dance around.
A hairy man above the waist he shows;
A porpoise tail beneath his belly grows;
And ends a fish: his breast the waves di-
   vides,
And froth and foam augment the murm'r-
   ing tides.
Full thirty ships transport the chosen
   train
For Troy's relief, and scour the briny main.
Now was the world forsaken by the sun,
And Phœbe half her nightly race had run.
The careful chief, who never clos'd his
   eyes, 310

Himself the rudder holds, the sails sup-
   plies.
A choir of Nereids meet him on the flood,
Once his own galleys, hewn from Ida's
   wood;
But now, as many nymphs, the sea they
   sweep,
As rode, before, tall vessels on the deep.
They know him from afar; and in a ring
Inclose the ship that bore the Trojan king.
Cymodoce, whose voice excell'd the rest,
Above the waves advanc'd her snowy
   breast;
Her right hand stops the stern; her left
   divides 320
The curling ocean, and corrects the tides.
She spoke for all the choir, and thus began
With pleasing words to warn th' unknow-
   ing man:
"Sleeps our lov'd lord ? O goddess-born,
   awake !
Spread ev'ry sail, pursue your wat'ry track,
And haste your course. Your navy once
   were we,
From Ida's height descending to the sea;
Till Turnus, as at anchor fix'd we stood,
Presum'd to violate our holy wood.
Then, loos'd from shore, we fled his fires ⎫
   profane 330   ⎪
(Unwillingly we broke our master's ⎬
   chain),   ⎪
And since have sought you thro' the Tus-⎪
   can main.   ⎭
The mighty Mother chang'd our forms to
   these,
And gave us life immortal in the seas.
But young Ascanius, in his camp distress'd,
By your insulting foes is hardly press'd.
Th' Arcadian horsemen, and Etrurian host,
Advance in order on the Latian coast:
To cut their way the Daunian chief designs,
Before their troops can reach the Trojan
   lines. 340
Thou, when the rosy morn restores the
   light,
First arm thy soldiers for th' ensuing fight:
Thyself the fated sword of Vulcan wield,
And bear aloft th' impenetrable shield.
To-morrow's sun, unless my skill be vain,
Shall see huge heaps of foes in battle slain."
Parting, she spoke; and with immortal
   force
Push'd on the vessel in her wat'ry course;
For well she knew the way. Impell'd be-
   hind,

The ship flew forward, and outstripp'd the
wind.   350
The rest make up. Unknowing of the
cause,
The chief admires their speed, and happy
omens draws.
Then thus he pray'd, and fix'd on heav'n
his eyes:
" Hear thou, great Mother of the deities.
With turrets crown'd ! (on Ida's holy hill
Fierce tigers, rein'd and curb'd, obey thy
will.)
Firm thy own omens; lead us on to fight;
And let thy Phrygians conquer in thy right."
He said no more. And now renewing
day   359
Had chas'd the shadows of the night away.
He charg'd the soldiers, with preventing ⎤
care,   │
Their flags to follow, and their arms pre- ⎬
pare;   │
Warn'd of th' ensuing fight, and bade 'em │
hope the war.   ⎦
Now, from his lofty poop, he view'd below
His camp incompass'd, and th' inclosing
foe.
His blazing shield, imbrac'd, he held on
high;
The camp receive the sign, and with loud
shouts reply.
Hope arms their courage: from their tow'rs
they throw
Their darts with double force, and drive
the foe.
Thus, at the signal giv'n, the cranes arise 370
Before the stormy south, and blacken all
the skies.
King Turnus wonder'd at the fight re-
new'd,
Till, looking back, the Trojan fleet he
view'd,
The seas with swelling canvas cover'd o'er,
And the swift ships descending on the shore.
The Latians saw from far, with dazzled
eyes,
The radiant crest that seem'd in flames to
rise,
And dart diffusive fires around the field,
And the keen glitt'ring of the golden
shield.
Thus threat'ning comets, when by night they
rise,   380
Shoot sanguine streams, and sadden all the
skies:
So Sirius, flashing forth sinister lights,

Pale humankind with plagues and with dry
famine frights.
Yet Turnus with undaunted mind is bent
To man the shores, and hinder their de-
scent,
And thus awakes the courage of his friends:
" What you so long have wish'd, kind For-
tune sends;
In ardent arms to meet th' invading foe:
You find, and find him at advantage now.
Yours is the day: you need but only dare;
Your swords will make you masters of the
war.   391
Your sires, your sons, your houses, and your
lands,
And dearest wifes, are all within your
hands.
Be mindful of the race from whence you
came,
And emulate in arms your fathers' fame.
Now take the time, while stagg'ring yet
they stand
With feet unfirm, and prepossess the strand:
Fortune befriends the bold." Nor more
he said,
But balanc'd whom to leave, and whom to
lead;
Then these elects, the landing to prevent;
And those he leaves, to keep the city
pent.   401
Meantime the Trojan sends his troops
ashore:
Some are by boats expos'd, by bridges more.
With lab'ring oars they bear along the
strand,
Where the tide languishes, and leap aland.
Tarchon observes the coast with careful
eyes,
And, where no ford he finds, no water
fries,
Nor billows with unequal murmurs roar,
But smoothly slide along, and swell the
shore,
That course he steer'd, and thus he gave
command: 410
" Here ply your oars, and at all hazard
land:
Force on the vessel, that her keel may
wound
This hated soil, and furrow hostile ground.
Let me securely land — I ask no more;
Then sink my ships, or shatter on the
shore."
This fiery speech inflames his fearful
friends:

They tug at ev'ry oar, and ev'ry stretcher
   bends;
They run their ships aground; the vessels
   knock,
(Thus forc'd ashore,) and tremble with the
   shock.
Tarchon's alone was lost, that stranded
   stood,   420
Stuck on a bank, and beaten by the flood:
She breaks her back; the loosen'd sides
   give way,
And plunge the Tuscan soldiers in the sea.
Their broken oars and floating planks ⎫
   withstand   ⎪
Their passage, while they labor to the   ⎬
   land,   ⎪
And ebbing tides bear back upon th' un- ⎪
   certain sand.   ⎭
   Now Turnus leads his troops without
   delay,
Advancing to the margin of the sea.
The trumpets sound: Æneas first assail'd
The clowns new-rais'd and raw, and soon
   prevail'd.   430
Great Theron fell, an omen of the fight;
Great Theron, large of limbs, of giant
   height.
He first in open field defied the prince:
But armor scal'd with gold was no defense
Against the fated sword, which open'd wide
His plated shield, and pierc'd his naked side.
Next, Lichas fell, who, not like others born,
Was from his wretched mother ripp'd and
   torn;
Sacred, O Phœbus, from his birth to thee;
For his beginning life from biting steel was
   free.   440
Not far from him was Gyas laid along,
Of monstrous bulk; with Cisseus fierce and
   strong:
Vain bulk and strength! for, when the
   chief assail'd,
Nor valor nor Herculean arms avail'd,
Nor their fam'd father, wont in war to go
With great Alcides, while he toil'd below.
The noisy Pharos next receiv'd his death:
Æneas writh'd his dart, and stopp'd his
   bawling breath.
Then wretched Cydon had receiv'd his
   doom,
Who courted Clytius in his beardless
   bloom,   450
And sought with lust obscene polluted joys:
The Trojan sword had cur'd his love of
   boys,

Had not his sev'n bold brethren stopp'd the
   course
Of the fierce champion, with united force.
Sev'n darts were thrown at once; and some
   rebound
From his bright shield, some on his helmet
   sound:
The rest had reach'd him; but his mother's
   care
Prevented those, and turn'd aside in air.
   The prince then call'd Achates, to supply
The spears that knew the way to vic-
   tory —   460
"Those fatal weapons, which, inur'd to
   blood,
In Grecian bodies under Ilium stood:
Not one of those my hand shall toss in vain
Against our foes, on this contended plain."
He said; then seiz'd a mighty spear, and
   threw;
Which, wing'd with fate, thro' Mæon's
   buckler flew,
Pierc'd all the brazen plates, and reach'd
   his heart:
He stagger'd with intolerable smart.
Alcanor saw; and reach'd, but reach'd in
   vain,
His helping hand, his brother to sustain. 470
A second spear, which kept the former
   course,
From the same hand, and sent with equal
   force,
His right arm pierc'd, and holding on, be-
   reft
His use of both, and pinion'd down his left.
Then Numitor from his dead brother
   drew
Th' ill-omen'd spear, and at the Trojan
   threw:
Preventing fate directs the lance awry,
Which, glancing, only mark'd Achates'
   thigh.
   In pride of youth the Sabine Clausus
   came,
And, from afar, at Dryops took his aim. 480
The spear flew hissing thro' the middle
   space,
And pierc'd his throat, directed at his
   face;
It stopp'd at once the passage of his wind,
And the free soul to flitting air resign'd:
His forehead was the first that struck the
   ground;
Lifeblood and life rush'd mingled thro' the
   wound.

He slew three brothers of the Borean
    race,
And three, whom Ismarus, their native
    place,
Had sent to war, but all the sons of
    Thrace.
Halesus, next, the bold Aurunci leads: 490
The son of Neptune to his aid succeeds,
Conspicuous on his horse. On either hand,
These fight to keep, and those to win, the
    land.
With mutual blood th' Ausonian soil is
    dyed,
While on its borders each their claim de-
    cide.
As wintry winds, contending in the sky,
With equal force of lungs their titles try:
They rage, they roar; the doubtful rack of
    heav'n
Stands without motion, and the tide un-
    driv'n: 499
Each bent to conquer, neither side to yield,
They long suspend the fortune of the field.
Both armies thus perform what courage
    can;
Foot set to foot, and mingled man to man.
   But, in another part, th' Arcadian horse
With ill success ingage the Latin force:
For, where th' impetuous torrent, rushing
    down,
Huge craggy stones and rooted trees had
    thrown,
They left their coursers, and, unus'd to
    fight
On foot, were scatter'd in a shameful flight.
Pallas, who with disdain and grief had
    view'd   510
His foes pursuing, and his friends pursued,
Us'd threat'nings mix'd with pray'rs, his
    last resource,
With these to move their minds, with
    those to fire their force.
" Which way, companions ? whether would
    you run ?
By you yourselves, and mighty battles
    won,
By my great sire, by his establish'd name,
And early promise of my future fame;
By my youth, emulous of equal right
To share his honors — shun ignoble flight !
Trust not your feet: your hands must hew
    your way   520
Thro' yon black body, and that thick array:
'T is thro' that forward path that we must
    come;

There lies our way, and that our passage
    home.
Nor pow'rs above, nor destinies below
Oppress our arms: with equal strength
    we go,
With mortal hands to meet a mortal foe.
See on what foot we stand: a scanty shore,
The sea behind, our enemies before;
No passage left, unless we swim the main;
Or, forcing these, the Trojan trenches
    gain."   530
This said, he strode with eager haste along,
And bore amidst the thickest of the throng.
Lagus, the first he met, with fate to foe,
Had heav'd a stone of mighty weight, to
    throw:
Stooping, the spear descended on his chine,
Just where the bone distinguish'd either
    loin:
It stuck so fast, so deeply buried lay,
That scarce the victor forc'd the steel
    away.
Hisbon came on: but, while he mov'd too
    slow
To wish'd revenge, the prince prevents his
    blow;   540
For, warding his at once, at once he press'd,
And plung'd the fatal weapon in his breast.
Then lewd Anchemolus he laid in dust,
Who stain'd his stepdam's bed with im-
    pious lust.
And, after him, the Daucian twins were
    slain,
Laris and Thymbrus, on the Latian plain;
So wondrous like in feature, shape, and size,
As caus'd an error in their parents' eyes —
Grateful mistake ! but soon the sword de-
    cides   549
The nice distinction, and their fate divides:
For Thymbrus' head was lopp'd; and Laris'
    hand,
Dismember'd, sought its owner on the
    strand:
The trembling fingers yet the fauchion
    strain,
And threaten still th' intended stroke in
    vain.
   Now, to renew the charge, th' Arca-
    dians came:
Sight of such acts, and sense of honest
    shame,
And grief, with anger mix'd, their minds
    inflame.
Then, with a casual blow was Rhœteus
    slain,

Who chanc'd, as Pallas threw, to cross the
    plain:
The flying spear was after Ilus sent;   560
But Rhœteus happen'd on a death unmeant:
From Teuthras and from Tyres while he
    fled,
The lance, athwart his body, laid him dead:
Roll'd from his chariot with a mortal wound,
And intercepted fate, he spurn'd the
    ground.
As when, in summer, welcome winds arise,
The watchful shepherd to the forest flies,
And fires the midmost plants; contagion
    spreads,
And catching flames infect the neighb'ring
    heads;
Around the forest flies the furious ⎫
    blast,   570 ⎬
And all the leafy nation sinks at last,   ⎪
And Vulcan rides in triumph o'er the   ⎬
    waste;   ⎪
                                        ⎭
The pastor, pleas'd with his dire victory,
Beholds the satiate flames in sheets ascend
    the sky:
So Pallas' troops their scatter'd strength
    unite,
And, pouring on their foes, their prince de-
    light.
Halesus came, fierce with desire of blood;
But first collected in his arms he stood:
Advancing then, he plied the spear so well,
Ladon, Demodocus, and Pheres fell.   580
Around his head he toss'd his glitt'ring
    brand,
And from Strymonius hew'd his better
    hand,
Held up to guard his throat; then hurl'd a
    stone
At Thoas' ample front, and pierc'd the
    bone:
It struck beneath the space of either eye;
And blood, and mingled brains, together
    fly.
Deep skill'd in future fates, Halesus' sire
Did with the youth to lonely groves retire:
But, when the father's mortal race was
    run,
Dire destiny laid hold upon the son,   590
And haul'd him to the war, to find, beneath
Th' Evandrian spear, a memorable death.
Pallas th' encounter seeks, but, ere he
    throws,
To Tuscan Tiber thus address'd his vows:
" O sacred stream, direct my flying dart,
And give to pass the proud Halesus' heart !

His arms and spoils thy holy oak shall
    bear."
Pleas'd with the bribe, the god receiv'd his
    pray'r:
For, while his shield protects a friend dis-
    tress'd,
The dart came driving on, and pierc'd his
    breast.   600
But Lausus, no small portion of the war,
Permits not panic fear to reign too far,
Caus'd by the death of so renown'd a
    knight;
But by his own example cheers the fight.
Fierce Abas first he slew; Abas, the stay
Of Trojan hopes, and hind'rance of the day.
The Phrygian troops escap'd the Greeks in
    vain:
They, and their mix'd allies, now load the
    plain.
To the rude shock of war both armies came;
Their leaders equal, and their strength the
    same.   610
The rear so press'd the front, they could
    not wield
Their angry weapons, to dispute the field.
Here Pallas urges on, and Lausus there: ⎫
Of equal youth and beauty both appear, ⎬
But both by fate forbid to breathe their ⎬
    native air.   ⎭
Their congress in the field great Jove with-
    stands:
Both doom'd to fall, but fall by greater
    hands.
    Meantime Juturna warns the Daunian
        chief
Of Lausus' danger, urging swift relief. 619
With his driv'n chariot he divides the crowd,
And, making to his friends, thus calls aloud:
" Let none presume his needless aid to join;
Retire, and clear the field; the fight is
    mine:
To this right hand is Pallas only due;
O were his father here, my just revenge to
    view ! "
From the forbidden space his men retir'd.
Pallas their awe, and his stern words, ad-
    mir'd;
Survey'd him o'er and o'er with wond'ring
    sight,
Struck with his haughty mien, and tow'ring
    height.
Then to the king: " Your empty vaunts
    forbear;   630
Success I hope, and fate I cannot fear;
Alive or dead, I shall deserve a name;

Jove is impartial, and to both the same."
He said, and to the void advanc'd his pace:
Pale horror sate on each Arcadian face.
Then Turnus, from his chariot leaping light,
Address'd himself on foot to single fight.
And, as a lion — when he spies from far
A bull that seems to meditate the war,
Bending his neck, and spurning back the
　sand —　640
Runs roaring downward from his hilly
　stand:
Imagine eager Turnus not more slow,
To rush from high on his unequal foe.
　Young Pallas, when he saw the chief ad-
　vance
Within due distance of his flying lance,
Prepares to charge him first, resolv'd to try
If fortune would his want of force supply;
And thus to Heav'n and Hercules address'd:
" Alcides, once on earth Evander's guest,
His son adjures you by those holy rites, 650
That hospitable board, those genial nights;
Assist my great attempt to gain this prize,
And let proud Turnus view, with dying
　eyes,
His ravish'd spoils." 'T was heard, the
　vain request;
Alcides mourn'd, and stifled sighs within
　his breast.
Then Jove, to soothe his sorrow, thus ⎤
　began: ⎟
" Short bounds of life are set to mortal ⎟
　man. ⎬
'T is virtue's work alone to stretch the ⎟
　narrow span. ⎦
So many sons of gods, in bloody fight,
Around the walls of Troy, have lost the
　light:　660
My own Sarpedon fell beneath his foe;
Nor I, his mighty sire, could ward the
　blow.
Ev'n Turnus shortly shall resign his
　breath,
And stands already on the verge of death."
This said, the god permits the fatal fight,
But from the Latian fields averts his sight.
　Now with full force his spear young Pal-
　las threw,
And, having thrown, his shining fauchion
　drew.
The steel just graz'd along the shoulder
　joint,
And mark'd it slightly with the glancing
　point.　670
Fierce Turnus first to nearer distance drew,

And pois'd his pointed spear, before he
　threw:
Then, as the winged weapon whizz'd along,
" See now," said he, " whose arm is better
　strung."
The spear kept on the fatal course, unstay'd
By plates of ir'n, which o'er the shield were
　laid:
Thro' folded brass and tough bull hides it
　pass'd,
His corslet pierc'd, and reach'd his heart
　at last.
In vain the youth tugs at the broken
　wood;
The soul comes issuing with the vital blood:
He falls; his arms upon his body sound; 681
And with his bloody teeth he bites the
　ground.
　Turnus bestrode the corpse: " Arcadians,
　hear,"
Said he; " my message to your master bear:
Such as the sire deserv'd, the son I send;
It costs him dear to be the Phrygians'
　friend.
The lifeless body, tell him, I bestow,
Unask'd, to rest his wand'ring ghost below."
He said, and trampled down with all the
　force
Of his left foot, and spurn'd the wretched
　corse;　690
Then snatch'd the shining belt, with gold
　inlaid;
The belt Eurytion's artful hands had made,
Where fifty fatal brides, express'd to ⎤
　sight, ⎟
All in the compass of one mournful night, ⎬
Depriv'd their bridegrooms of returning ⎟
　light. ⎦
　In an ill hour insulting Turnus tore
Those golden spoils, and in a worse he
　wore.
O mortals, blind in fate, who never know
To bear high fortune, or endure the low !
The time shall come, when Turnus, but in
　vain,　700
Shall wish untouch'd the trophies of the
　slain;
Shall wish the fatal belt were far away,
And curse the dire remembrance of the
　day.
　The sad Arcadians, from th' unhappy
　field,
Bear back the breathless body on a shield.
O grace and grief of war ! at once restor'd,
With praises, to thy sire, at once deplor'd !

One day first sent thee to the fighting
    field,
Beheld whole heaps of foes in battle
    kill'd;
One day beheld thee dead, and borne
    upon thy shield.   710
This dismal news, not from uncertain fame,
But sad spectators, to the hero came:
His friends upon the brink of ruin stand,
Unless reliev'd by his victorious hand.
He whirls his sword around, without delay,
And hews thro' adverse foes an ample way,
To find fierce Turnus, of his conquest proud:
Evander, Pallas, all that friendship ow'd
To large deserts, are present to his eyes;
His plighted hand, and hospitable ties.   720
    Four sons of Sulmo, four whom Ufens
    bred,
He took in fight, and living victims led,
To please the ghost of Pallas, and expire,
In sacrifice, before his fun'ral fire.
At Magus next he threw: he stoop'd below
The flying spear, and shunn'd the promis'd
    blow;
Then, creeping, clasp'd the hero's knees,
    and pray'd:
"By young Iülus, by thy father's shade,
O spare my life, and send me back to see
My longing sire, and tender progeny!   730
A lofty house I have, and wealth untold,
In silver ingots, and in bars of gold:
All these, and sums besides, which see no
    day,
The ransom of this one poor life shall pay.
If I survive, will Troy the less prevail?
A single soul's too light to turn the scale."
He said. The hero sternly thus replied:
"Thy bars and ingots, and the sums beside,
Leave for thy children's lot. Thy Turnus
    broke
All rules of war by one relentless stroke, 740
When Pallas fell: so deems, nor deems alone
My father's shadow, but my living son."
Thus having said, of kind remorse bereft,
He seiz'd his helm, and dragg'd him with
    his left;
Then with his right hand, while his neck he
    wreath'd,
Up to the hilts his shining fauchion sheath'd.
Apollo's priest, Emonides, was near;
His holy fillets on his front appear;
Glitt'ring in arms, he shone amidst the
    crowd;
Much of his god, more of his purple,
    proud.   750

Him the fierce Trojan follow'd thro' the
    field:
The holy coward fell; and, forc'd to yield,
The prince stood o'er the priest, and, at one
    blow,
Sent him an off'ring to the shades below.
His arms Seresthus on his shoulders bears,
Design'd a trophy to the God of Wars.
    Vulcanian Cæculus renews the fight,
And Umbro, born upon the mountains'
    height.
The champion cheers his troops t' encoun-
    ter those,
And seeks revenge himself on other foes. 760
At Anxur's shield he drove; and, at the
    blow,
Both shield and arm to ground together go.
Anxur had boasted much of magic charms,
And thought he wore impenetrable arms,
So made by mutter'd spells; and, from the
    spheres,
Had life secur'd, in vain, for length of years.
Then Tarquitus the field in triumph trod;
A nymph his mother, and his sire a god.
Exulting in bright arms, he braves the
    prince:
With his protended lance he makes de-
    fense;   770
Bears back his feeble foe; then, pressing on,
Arrests his better hand, and drags him
    down;
Stands o'er the prostrate wretch, and, as he
    lay,
Vain tales inventing, and prepar'd to pray,
Mows off his head: the trunk a moment
    stood,
Then sunk, and roll'd along the sand in
    blood.
The vengeful victor thus upbraids the slain:
"Lie there, proud man, unpitied, on the
    plain;
Lie there, inglorious, and without a tomb,
Far from thy mother and thy native
    home,   780
Expos'd to savage beasts, and birds of
    prey,
Or thrown for food to monsters of the sea."
    On Lycas and Antæus next he ran,
Two chiefs of Turnus, and who led his van.
They fled for fear; with these, he chas'd
    along
Camers the yellow-lock'd, and Numa
    strong;
Both great in arms, and both were fair
    and young.

Camers was son to Volscens lately slain,
In wealth surpassing all the Latian train,
And in Amycla fix'd his silent easy
   reign.   790
And, as Ægæon, when with heav'n he
   strove,
Stood opposite in arms to mighty Jove;
Mov'd all his hundred hands, provok'd the
   war,
Defied the forky lightning from afar;
At fifty mouths his flaming breath expires,
And flash for flash returns, and fires for
   fires;
In his right hand as many swords he
   wields,
And takes the thunder on as many shields:
With strength like his, the Trojan hero
   stood;
And soon the fields with falling corps
   were strow'd,   800
When once his fauchion found the taste
   of blood.
With fury scarce to be conceiv'd, he flew
Against Niphæus, who-n four coursers
   drew.
They, when they see the fiery chief ad-
   vance,
And pushing at their chests his pointed
   lance,
Wheel'd with so swift a motion, mad with
   fear,
They threw their master headlong from the
   chair.
They stare, they start, nor stop their course,
   before
They bear the bounding chariot to the
   shore.
   Now Lucagus and Liger scour the
     plains,   810
With two white steeds; but Liger holds
   the reins,
And Lucagus the lofty seat maintains:
Bold brethren both. The former wav'd
   in air
His flaming sword: Æneas couch'd his
   spear,
Unus'd to threats, and more unus'd to
   fear.
Then Liger thus: "Thy confidence is
   vain
To scape from hence, as from the Trojan
   plain:
Nor these the steeds which Diomede be-
   strode,
Nor this the chariot where Achilles rode;

Nor Venus' veil is here, nor Neptune's
   shield;   820
Thy fatal hour is come, and this the field."
Thus Liger vainly vaunts: the Trojan
   peer
Return'd his answer with his flying spear.
As Lucagus, to lash his horses, bends,
Prone to the wheels, and his left foot pro-
   tends,
Prepar'd for fight; the fatal dart arrives,
And thro' the borders of his buckler drives;
Pass'd thro', and pierc'd his groin: the
   deadly wound,
Cast from his chariot, roll'd him on the
   ground.
Whom thus the chief upbraids with scorn-
   ful spite: 830
"Blame not the slowness of your steeds in
   flight;
Vain shadows did not force their swift re-
   treat;
But you yourself forsake your empty seat."
He said, and seiz'd at once the loosen'd
   rein;
For Liger lay already on the plain,
By the same shock: then, stretching out
   his hands,
The recreant thus his wretched life de-
   mands:
"Now, by thyself, O more than mortal
   man!
By her and him from whom thy breath
   began,
Who form'd thee thus divine, I beg thee,
   spare   840
This forfeit life, and hear thy suppliant's
   pray'r."
Thus much he spoke, and more he would
   have said;
But the stern hero turn'd aside his head,
And cut him short: "I hear another man;
You talk'd not thus before the fight began.
Now take your turn; and, as a brother
   should,
Attend your brother to the Stygian flood."
Then thro' his breast his fatal sword he
   sent,
And the soul issued at the gaping vent.
   As storms the skies, and torrents tear
     the ground,   850
Thus rag'd the prince, and scatter'd deaths
   around.
At length Ascanius and the Trojan train
Broke from the camp, so long besieg'd in
   vain.

Meantime the King of Gods and Mortal Man
Held conference with his queen, and thus began:
" My sister goddess, and well-pleasing wife,
Still think you Venus' aid supports the strife —
Sustains her Trojans — or themselves, alone,
With inborn valor force their fortune on ?
How fierce in fight, with courage undecay'd !
Judge if such warriors want immortal aid."
To whom the goddess with the charming eyes,   862
Soft in her tone, submissively replies:
" Why, O my sov'reign lord, whose frown I fear,
And cannot, unconcern'd, your anger bear;
Why urge you thus my grief ? when, if I still
(As once I was) were mistress of your will,
From your almighty pow'r your pleasing wife
Might gain the grace of length'ning Turnus' life,
Securely snatch him from the fatal fight,
And give him to his aged father's sight. 871
Now let him perish, since you hold it good,
And glut the Trojans with his pious blood.
Yet from our lineage he derives his name,
And, in the fourth degree, from god Pilumnus came;
Yet he devoutly pays you rites divine,
And offers daily incense at your shrine."
Then shortly thus the sov'reign god replied:
" Since in my pow'r and goodness you confide,
If for a little space, a lengthen'd span, 880
You beg reprieve for this expiring man,
I grant you leave to take your Turnus hence
From instant fate, and can so far dispense.
But, if some secret meaning lies beneath,
To save the short-liv'd youth from destin'd death,
Or if a farther thought you entertain,
To change the fates; you feed your hopes in vain."
To whom the goddess thus, with weeping eyes:
" And what if that request, your tongue denies,
Your heart should grant; and not a short reprieve,   890
But length of certain life, to Turnus give ?

Now speedy death attends the guiltless youth,
If my presaging soul divines with truth;
Which, O ! I wish, might err thro' causeless fears,
And you (for you have pow'r) prolong his years ! "
Thus having said, involv'd in clouds, she flies,
And drives a storm before her thro' the skies.
Swift she descends, alighting on the plain,
Where the fierce foes a dubious fight maintain.   899
Of air condens'd a specter soon she made;
And, what Æneas was, such seem'd the shade.
Adorn'd with Dardan arms, the phantom bore
His head aloft; a plumy crest he wore:
This hand appear'd a shining sword to wield,
And that sustain'd an imitated shield.
With manly mien he stalk'd along the ground,
Nor wanted voice belied, nor vaunting sound.
(Thus haunting ghosts appear to waking sight,
Or dreadful visions in our dreams by night.)
The specter seems the Daunian chief to dare,   910
And flourishes his empty sword in air.
At this, advancing, Turnus hurl'd his spear:
The phantom wheel'd, and seem'd to fly for fear.
Deluded Turnus thought the Trojan fled,
And with vain hopes his haughty fancy fed.
" Whether, O coward ? " (thus he calls aloud,
Nor found he spoke to wind, and chas'd a cloud,)
" Why thus forsake your bride ! Receive from me   918
The fated land you sought so long by sea."
He said, and, brandishing at once his blade,
With eager pace pursued the flying shade.
By chance a ship was fasten'd to the shore,
Which from old Clusium King Osinius bore:
The plank was ready laid for safe ascent; ⎱
For shelter there the trembling shadow bent,   ⎰
And skipp't and skulk'd, and under hatches went.
Exulting Turnus, with regardless haste,
Ascends the plank, and to the galley pass'd.

Scarce had he reach'd the prow: Saturnia's
   hand
The haulsers cuts, and shoots the ship from
   land.   930
With wind in poop, the vessel plows the sea,
And measures back with speed her former
   way.
Meantime Æneas seeks his absent foe,
And sends his slaughter'd troops to shades
   below.
   The guileful phantom now forsook the
   shroud,
And flew sublime, and vanish'd in a cloud.
Too late young Turnus the delusion found,
Far on the sea, still making from the
   ground.
Then, thankless for a life redeem'd by
   shame,
With sense of honor stung, and forfeit
   fame,   940
Fearful besides of what in fight had pass'd,
His hands and haggard eyes to heav'n he
   cast:
" O Jove !" he cried, "for what offense
   have I
Deserv'd to bear this endless infamy ?
Whence am I forc'd, and whether am I
   borne ?
How, and with what reproach, shall I re-
   turn ?
Shall ever I behold the Latian plain,
Or see Laurentum's lofty tow'rs again ?
What will they say of their deserting
   chief ?
The war was mine: I fly from their re-
   lief;   950
I led to slaughter, and in slaughter leave;
And ev'n from hence their dying groans
   receive.
Here, overmatch'd in fight, in heaps they lie;
There, scatter'd o'er the fields, ignobly fly.
Gape wide, O earth, and draw me down ⎱
   alive !   ⎰
Or, O ye pitying winds, a wretch relieve ! ⎱
On sands or shelves the splitting vessel ⎰
   drive;
Or set me shipwrack'd on some desart
   shore,
Where no Rutulian eyes may see me more,
Unknown to friends, or foes, or conscious
   Fame,   960
Lest she should follow, and my flight pro-
   claim."
   Thus Turnus rav'd, and various fates re-
   volv'd:

The choice was doubtful, but the death re-
   solv'd.
And now the sword, and now the sea took
   place,
That to revenge, and this to purge disgrace.
Sometimes he thought to swim the stormy
   main,
By stretch of arms the distant shore to
   gain.
Thrice he the sword assay'd, and thrice the
   flood;
But Juno, mov'd with pity, both withstood,
And thrice repress'd his rage; strong gales
   supplied,   970
And push'd the vessel o'er the swelling tide.
At length she lands him on his native
   shores,
And to his father's longing arms restores.
   Meantime, by Jove's impulse, Mezentius
   arm'd,
Succeeding Turnus, with his ardor warm'd
His fainting friends, reproach'd their
   shameful flight,
Repell'd the victors, and renew'd the fight.
Against their king the Tuscan troops con-
   spire;
Such is their hate, and such their fierce de-
   sire
Of wish'd revenge: on him, and him
   alone,   980
All hands employ'd, and all their darts are
   thrown.
He, like a solid rock by seas inclos'd,
To raging winds and roaring waves oppos'd,
From his proud summit looking down, dis-
   dains
Their empty menace, and unmov'd remains.
   Beneath his feet fell haughty Hebrus
   dead,
Then Latagus, and Palmus as he fled.
At Latagus a weighty stone he flung:
His face was flatted, and his helmet rung.
But Palmus from behind receives his
   wound;   990
Hamstring'd he falls, and grovels on the
   ground:
His crest and armor, from his body torn,
Thy shoulders, Lausus, and thy head adorn.
Evas and Mimas, both of Troy, he slew.
Mimas his birth from fair Theano drew,
Born on that fatal night, when, big with
   fire,
The queen produc'd young Paris to his
   sire:
But Paris in the Phrygian fields was slain,

Unthinking Mimas on the Latian plain.
  And, as a savage boar, on mountains
    bred,   1000
With forest mast and fatt'ning marshes fed,
When once he sees himself in toils inclos'd,
By huntsmen and their eager hounds op-
    pos'd —
He whets his tusks, and turns, and dares
    the war;
Th' invaders dart their jav'lins from afar:
All keep aloof, and safely shout around;
But none presumes to give a nearer wound:
He frets and froths, erects his bristled hide,
And shakes a grove of lances from his
    side:
Not otherwise the troops, with hate in-
    spir'd,   1010
And just revenge against the tyrant fir'd,
Their darts with clamor at a distance
    drive,
And only keep the languish'd war alive.
  From Coritus came Acron to the fight,
Who left his spouse betroth'd, and uncon-
    summate night.
Mezentius sees him thro' the squadrons
    ride,
Proud of the purple favors of his bride.
Then, as a hungry lion, who beholds
A gamesome goat, who frisks about the
    folds,
Or beamy stag, that grazes on the plain —
He runs, he roars, he shakes his rising
    mane,   1021
He grins, and opens wide his greedy jaws;
The prey lies panting underneath his paws:
He fills his famish'd maw; his mouth runs
    o'er
With unchew'd morsels, while he churns
    the gore:
So proud Mezentius rushes on his foes,
And first unhappy Acron overthrows:
Stretch'd at his length, he spurns the
    swarthy ground;
The lance, besmear'd with blood, lies
    broken in the wound.
  Then with disdain the haughty victor
    view'd   1030
Orodes flying, nor the wretch pursued,
Nor thought the dastard's back deserv'd a
    wound,
But, running, gain'd th' advantage of
    the ground:
Then turning short, he met him face to
    face,
To give his victory the better grace.

Orodes falls, in equal fight oppress'd:
Mezentius fix'd his foot upon his breast,
And rested lance; and thus aloud he cries:
" Lo ! here the champion of my rebels
    lies ! "
The fields around with *Io Pæan !* ring;
And peals of shouts applaud the conqu'ring
    king.   1041
At this the vanquish'd, with his dying
    breath,
Thus faintly spoke, and prophesied in
    death:
" Nor thou, proud man, unpunish'd shalt
    remain:
Like death attends thee on this fatal
    plain."
Then, sourly smiling, thus the king replied:
" For what belongs to me, let Jove pro-
    vide;
But die thou first, whatever chance ensue."
He said, and from the wound the weapon
    drew.
A hov'ring mist came swimming o'er his
    sight,   1050
And seal'd his eyes in everlasting night.
  By Cædicus, Alcathoüs was slain;
Sacrator laid Hydaspes on the plain;
Orses the strong to greater strength must
    yield;
He, with Parthenius, were by Rapo kill'd.
Then brave Messapus Ericetes slew,
Who from Lycaon's blood his lineage drew.
But from his headstrong horse his fate ⎫
    he found,   ⎪
Who threw his master, as he made a ⎬
    bound: ⎪
The chief, alighting, stuck him to the ⎪
    ground;   1060 ⎭
Then Clonius, hand to hand, on foot assails:
The Trojan sinks, and Neptune's son pre-
    vails.
Agis the Lycian, stepping forth with pride,
To single fight the boldest foe defied;
Whom Tuscan Valerus by force o'ercame,
And not belied his mighty father's fame.
Salius to death the great Antronius sent:
But the same fate the victor underwent,
Slain by Nealces' hand, well-skill'd to throw
The flying dart, and draw the far-deceiving
    bow.   1070
  Thus equal deaths are dealt with equal
    chance;
By turns they quit their ground, by turns
    advance:
Victors and vanquish'd, in the various field,

Nor wholly overcome, nor wholly yield.
The gods from heav'n survey the fatal
    strife,
And mourn the miseries of human life.
Above the rest, two goddesses appear
Concern'd for each: here Venus, Juno there.
Amidst the crowd, infernal Ate shakes
Her scourge aloft, and crest of hissing
    snakes.   1080
  Once more the proud Mezentius, with
    disdain,
Brandish'd his spear, and rush'd into the
    plain,
Where tow'ring in the midmost ranks he
    stood,
Like tall Orion stalking o'er the flood
(When with his brawny breast he cuts the
    waves,
His shoulders scarce the topmost billow
    laves),
Or like a mountain ash, whose roots are
    spread,
Deep fix'd in earth; in clouds he hides his
    head.   1088
  The Trojan prince beheld him from afar,
And dauntless undertook the doubtful war.
Collected in his strength, and like a rock,
Pois'd on his base, Mezentius stood the
    shock.
He stood, and, measuring first with careful
    eyes
The space his spear could reach, aloud he
    cries:
" My strong right hand, and sword, assist
    my stroke !
(Those only gods Mezentius will invoke.)
His armor, from the Trojan pirate torn,
By my triumphant Lausus shall be worn."
He said; and with his utmost force he
    threw
The massy spear, which, hissing as it flew,
Reach'd the celestial shield, that stopp'd
    the course;   1101
But, glancing thence, the yet unbroken
    force
Took a new bent obliquely, and betwixt
The side and bowels fam'd Anthores fix'd.
Anthores had from Argos travel'd far,
Alcides' friend, and brother of the war;
Till, tir'd with toils, fair Italy he chose,
And in Evander's palace sought repose.
Now, falling by another's wound, his eyes
He cast to heav'n, on Argos thinks, and
    dies.   1110
  The pious Trojan then his jav'lin sent;

The shield gave way; thro' treble plates it
    went
Of solid brass, of linen trebly roll'd,
And three bull hides which round the buck-
    ler fold.
All these it pass'd, resistless in the course,
Transpierc'd his thigh, and spent its dying
    force.
The gaping wound gush'd out a crimson
    flood.
The Trojan, glad with sight of hostile blood,
His fauchion drew, to closer fight address'd,
And with new force his fainting foe op-
    press'd.   1120
  His father's peril Lausus view'd with
    grief;
He sigh'd, he wept, he ran to his relief.
And here, heroic youth, 't is here I must
To thy immortal memory be just,
And sing an act so noble and so new,
Posterity will scarce believe 't is true.
Pain'd with his wound, and useless for the
    fight,
The father sought to save himself by flight:
Incumber'd, slow he dragg'd the spear
    along,
Which pierc'd his thigh, and in his buckler
    hung.   1130
The pious youth, resolv'd on death, below ⎫
The lifted sword springs forth to face   ⎪
    the foe;   ⎬
Protects his parent, and prevents the   ⎪
    blow.   ⎭
Shouts of applause ran ringing thro' the
    field,
To see the son the vanquish'd father shield.
All, fir'd with gen'rous indignation, strive,
And with a storm of darts to distance drive
The Trojan chief, who, held at bay from
    far,
On his Vulcanian orb sustain'd the war.
  As, when thick hail comes rattling in the
    wind,   1140
The plowman, passenger, and lab'ring hind
For shelter to the neighb'ring covert fly,
Or hous'd, or safe in hollow caverns lie;
But, that o'erblown, when heav'n above 'em
    smiles,
Return to travel, and renew their toils:
Æneas thus, o'erwhelm'd on ev'ry side, ⎫
The storm of darts, undaunted, did abide; ⎪
And thus to Lausus loud with friendly ⎬
    threat'ning cried: ⎭
" Why wilt thou rush to certain death, and
    rage

In rash attempts, beyond thy tender age, 1150
Betray'd by pious love ? " Nor, thus for-
borne,
The youth desists, but with insulting scorn
Provokes the ling'ring prince, whose pa-
tience, tir'd,
Gave place; and all his breast with fury
fir'd.
For now the Fates prepar'd their sharpen'd
shears;
And lifted high the flaming sword appears,
Which, full descending with a frightful ⎫
sway, ⎪
Thro' shield and corslet forc'd th' impet- ⎬
uous way, ⎪
And buried deep in his fair bosom lay. ⎭
The purple streams thro' the thin armor
strove, 1160
And drench'd th' imbroider'd coat his mo-
ther wove;
And life at length forsook his heaving
heart,
Loth from so sweet a mansion to depart.
　But when, with blood and paleness all
o'erspread,
The pious prince beheld young Lausus
dead,
He griev'd; he wept; the sight an image
brought
Of his own filial love, a sadly pleasing
thought:
Then stretch'd his hand to hold him up,
and said:
" Poor hapless youth ! what praises can be
paid
To love so great, to such transcendent
store 1170
Of early worth, and sure presage of more ?
Accept whate'er Æneas can afford;
Untouch'd thy arms, untaken be thy sword;
And all that pleas'd thee living, still remain
Inviolate, and sacred to the slain.
Thy body on thy parents I bestow, ⎫
To rest thy soul, at least, if shadows ⎬
know, ⎪
Or have a sense of human things below. ⎭
There to thy fellow ghosts with glory tell:
' 'T was by the great Æneas' hand I fell.' "
With this, his distant friends he beckons
near, 1181
Provokes their duty, and prevents their
fear:
Himself assists to lift him from the ground,
With clotted locks, and blood that well'd
from out the wound.

　Meantime, his father, now no father,
stood,
And wash'd his wounds by Tiber's yellow
flood:
Oppress'd with anguish, panting, and o'er-
spent,
His fainting limbs against an oak he leant.
A bough his brazen helmet did sustain;
His heavier arms lay scatter'd on the
plain: 1190
A chosen train of youth around him stand;
His drooping head was rested on his hand:
His grisly beard his pensive bosom sought;
And all on Lausus ran his restless thought.
Careful, concern'd his danger to prevent,
He much enquir'd, and many a message
sent
To warn him from the field — alas ! in vain !
Behold, his mournful followers bear him
slain !
O'er his broad shield still gush'd the yawn-
ing wound,
And drew a bloody trail along the
ground. 1200
Far off he heard their cries, far off divin'd
The dire event, with a foreboding mind.
With dust he sprinkled first his hoary ⎫
head; ⎪
Then both his lifted hands to heav'n he ⎬
spread; ⎪
Last, the dear corpse embracing, thus he ⎭
said:
" What joys, alas ! could this frail being
give,
That I have been so covetous to live ?
To see my son, and such a son, resign
His life, a ransom for preserving mine !
And am I then preserv'd, and art thou
lost ? 1210
How much too dear has that redemption
cost !
'T is now my bitter banishment I feel:
This is a wound too deep for time to heal.
My guilt thy growing virtues did defame;
My blackness blotted thy unblemish'd
name.
Chas'd from a throne, abandon'd, and exil'd
For foul misdeeds, were punishments too
mild:
I ow'd my people these, and, from their
hate,
With less resentment could have borne my
fate.
And yet I live, and yet sustain the sight 1220
Of hated men, and of more hated light:

But will not long." With that he rais'd
    from ground
His fainting limbs, that stagger'd with his
    wound;
Yet, with a mind resolv'd, and unappall'd
With pains or perils, for his courser call'd;
Well-mouth'd, well-manag'd, whom him-⎤
    self did dress   ⎮
With daily care, and mounted with suc-   ⎬
    cess;   ⎮
His aid in arms, his ornament in peace.   ⎦
    Soothing his courage with a gentle stroke,
The steed seem'd sensible, while thus
    he spoke: 1230
"O Rhœbus, we have liv'd too long for
    me —
If life and long were terms that could
    agree !
This day thou either shalt bring back the
    head
And bloody trophies of the Trojan dead;
This day thou either shalt revenge my woe,
For murther'd Lausus, on his cruel foe;
Or, if inexorable fate deny
Our conquest, with thy conquer'd master
    die:
For, after such a lord, I rest secure,
Thou wilt no foreign reins, or Trojan load
    endure."   1240
He said; and straight th' officious courser
    kneels,
To take his wonted weight. His hands he
    fills
With pointed jav'lins; on his head he lac'd
His glitt'ring helm, which terribly was
    grac'd
With waving horsehair, nodding from afar;
Then spurr'd his thund'ring steed amidst
    the war.
Love, anguish, wrath, and grief, to madness
    wrought,
Despair, and secret shame, and conscious
    thought
Of inborn worth, his lab'ring soul oppress'd,
Roll'd in his eyes, and rag'd within his
    breast.   1250
Then loud he call'd Æneas thrice by name:
The loud repeated voice to glad Æneas
    came.
"Great Jove," he said, "and the far-
    shooting god,
Inspire thy mind to make thy challenge
    good ! "
He spoke no more; but hasten'd, void of
    fear,

And threaten'd with his long protended
    spear.
To whom Mezentius thus: " Thy vaunts
    are vain.
My Lausus lies extended on the plain:
He 's lost ! thy conquest is already won;
The wretched sire is murther'd in the
    son.   1260
Nor fate I fear, but all the gods defy.   ⎤
Forbear thy threats: my bus'ness is to   ⎮
    die;   ⎬
But first receive this parting legacy."   ⎦
He said; and straight a whirling dart he
    sent;
Another after, and another went.
Round in a spacious ring he rides the ⎤
    field,   ⎮
And vainly plies th' impenetrable shield. ⎬
Thrice rode he round; and thrice Æneas ⎮
    wheel'd,   ⎦
Turn'd as he turn'd: the golden orb with-
    stood
The strokes, and bore about an iron wood.
Impatient of delay, and weary grown,   1271
Still to defend, and to defend alone,
To wrench the darts which in his buckler
    light,
Urg'd and o'er-labor'd in unequal fight;
At length resolv'd, he throws with all his
    force
Full at the temples of the warrior horse.
Just where the stroke was aim'd, th' uner-
    ring spear
Made way, and stood transfix'd thro' either
    ear.
Seiz'd with unwonted pain, surpris'd with
    fright,
The wounded steed curvets, and, rais'd up-
    right.   1280
Lights on his feet before; his hoofs behind
Spring up in air aloft, and lash the wind.
Down comes the rider headlong from his
    height:
His horse came after with unwieldy weight,
And, flound'ring forward, pitching on his
    head,
His lord's incumber'd shoulder overlaid.
    From either host, the mingled shouts and
    cries
Of Trojans and Rutulians rend the skies.
Æneas, hast'ning, wav'd his fatal sword
High o'er his head, with this reproachful
    word: 1290
" Now; where are now thy vaunts, the
    fierce disdain

Of proud Mezentius, and the lofty strain ? "
Struggling, and wildly staring on the
    skies,
With scarce recover'd sight he thus replies:
" Why these insulting words, this waste of
    breath,
To souls undaunted, and secure of death ?
'T is no dishonor for the brave to die,
Nor came I here with hope of victory;
Nor ask I life, nor fought with that design:
As I had us'd my fortune, use thou thine.
My dying son contracted no such band; 1301
The gift is hateful from his murd'rer's
    hand.
For this, this only favor let me sue,
If pity can to conquer'd foes be due:
Refuse it not; but let my body have
The last retreat of humankind, a grave.
Too well I know th' insulting people's hate;
Protect me from their vengeance after fate:
This refuge for my poor remains provide, ⎤
And lay my much-lov'd Lausus by my ⎪
    side."   1310 ⎬
He said, and to the sword his throat ap- ⎪
    plied.   ⎦
The crimson stream distain'd his arms
    around,
And the disdainful soul came rushing thro'
    the wound.

THE ELEVENTH BOOK OF THE ÆNEIS

THE ARGUMENT

Æneas erects a trophy of the spoils of Mezentius, grants a truce for burying the dead,
and sends home the body of Pallas with
great solemnity. Latinus calls a council, to
propose offers of peace to Æneas ; which occasions great animosity betwixt Turnus and
Drances. In the mean time there is a sharp
engagement of the horse ; wherein Camilla
signalizes herself ; is kill'd ; and the Latine
troops are entirely defeated.

SCARCE had the rosy Morning rais'd her
    head
Above the waves, and left her wat'ry bed;
The pious chief, whom double cares attend
For his unburied soldiers and his friend,
Yet first to Heav'n perform'd a victor's
    vows:
He bar'd an ancient oak of all her boughs;
Then on a rising ground the trunk he plac'd,

Which with the spoils of his dead foe he
    grac'd.
The coat of arms by proud Mezentius worn,
Now on a naked snag in triumph borne, 10
Was hung on high, and glitter'd from afar,
A trophy sacred to the God of War.
Above his arms, fix'd on the leafless wood,
Appear'd his plumy crest, besmear'd with
    blood:
His brazen buckler on the left was seen;
Truncheons of shiver'd lances hung be-
    tween;
And on the right was plac'd his corslet,
    bor'd;
And to the neck was tied his unavailing
    sword.
    A crowd of chiefs inclose the godlike
    man,
Who thus, conspicuous in the midst, began:
"Our toils, my friends, are crown'd with
    sure success;   21
The greater part perform'd, achieve the
    less.
Now follow cheerful to the trembling town;
Press but an entrance, and presume it won.
Fear is no more, for fierce Mezentius lies,
As the first fruits of war, a sacrifice.
Turnus shall fall extended on the plain,
And, in this omen, is already slain.
Prepar'd in arms, pursue your happy chance;
That none unwarn'd may plead his igno-
    rance,   30
And I, at Heav'n's appointed hour, may find
Your warlike ensigns waving in the wind.
Meantime the rites and fun'ral pomps pre-
    pare,
Due to your dead companions of the war:
The last respect the living can bestow,
To shield their shadows from contempt be-
    low.
That conquer'd earth be theirs, for which
    they fought,
And which for us with their own blood they
    bought;
But first the corpse of our unhappy friend
To the sad city of Evander send,   40
Who, not inglorious, in his age's bloom,
Was hurried hence by too severe a doom."
    Thus, weeping while he spoke, he took
    his way,
Where, new in death, lamented Pallas lay.
Accetes watch'd the corpse; whose youth
    deserv'd
The father's trust; and now the son he
    serv'd

With equal faith, but less auspicious care.
Th' attendants of the slain his sorrow share.
A troop of Trojans mix'd with these appear,
And mourning matrons with dishevel'd
   hair.   50
Soon as the prince appears, they raise a
   cry;
All beat their breasts, and echoes rend the
   sky.
They rear his drooping forehead from the
   ground;
But, when Æneas view'd the grisly wound
Which Pallas in his manly bosom bore,
And the fair flesh distain'd with purple
   gore;
First, melting into tears, the pious man
Deplor'd so sad a sight, then thus began:
"Unhappy youth! when Fortune gave the
   rest
Of my full wishes, she refus'd the best! 60
She came; but brought not thee along, to
   bless
My longing eyes, and share in my success:
She grudg'd thy safe return, the triumphs
   due
To prosp'rous valor, in the public view.
Not thus I promis'd, when thy father lent
Thy needless succor with a sad consent;
Embrac'd me, parting for th' Etrurian land,
And sent me to possess a large command.
He warn'd, and from his own experience
   told,
Our foes were warlike, disciplin'd, and
   bold.   70
And now perhaps, in hopes of thy return,
Rich odors on his loaded altars burn,
While we, with vain officious pomp, pre-
   pare
To send him back his portion of the war,
A bloody breathless body, which can owe
No farther debt, but to the pow'rs below.
The wretched father, ere his race is run,
Shall view the fun'ral honors of his son.
These are my triumphs of the Latian war,
Fruits of my plighted faith and boasted
   care!   80
And yet, unhappy sire, thou shalt not see
A son whose death disgrac'd his ancestry;
Thou shalt not blush, old man, however
   griev'd:
Thy Pallas no dishonest wound receiv'd.
He died no death to make thee wish, too
   late,
Thou hadst not liv'd to see his shameful
   fate:

But what a champion has th' Ausonian
   coast,
And what a friend hast thou, Ascanius,
   lost!"
   Thus having mourn'd, he gave the word
   around,
To raise the breathless body from the
   ground;   90
And chose a thousand horse, the flow'r of
   all
His warlike troops, to wait the funeral,
To bear him back and share Evander's
   grief:
A well-becoming, but a weak relief.
Of oaken twigs they twist an easy bier,
Then on their shoulders the sad burden rear.
The body on this rural hearse is borne:
Strew'd leaves and funeral greens the bier
   adorn.
All pale he lies, and looks a lovely flow'r,
New cropp'd by virgin hands, to dress the
   bow'r: 100
Unfaded yet, but yet unfed below,
No more to mother earth or the green
   stem shall owe.
Then two fair vests, of wondrous work
   and cost,
Of purple woven, and with gold emboss'd,
For ornament the Trojan hero brought,
Which with her hands Sidonian Dido
   wrought.
One vest array'd the corpse; and one they
   spread
O'er his clos'd eyes, and wrapp'd around
   his head,
That, when the yellow hair in flame should
   fall,
The catching fire might burn the golden
   caul.   110
Besides, the spoils of foes in battle slain,
When he descended on the Latian plain;
Arms, trappings, horses, by the hearse are
   led
In long array — th' achievements of the
   dead.
Then, pinion'd with their hands behind, ap-
   pear
Th' unhappy captives, marching in the
   rear,
Appointed off'rings in the victor's name,
To sprinkle with their blood the fun'ral
   flame.
Inferior trophies by the chiefs are borne;
Gauntlets and helms their loaded hands
   adorn;   120

And fair inscriptions fix'd, and titles read
Of Latian leaders conquer'd by the dead.
Accœtes on his pupil's corpse attends,
With feeble steps, supported by his friends.
Pausing at ev'ry pace, in sorrow drown'd,
Betwixt their arms he sinks upon the
   ground;
Where grov'ling while he lies in deep de-
   spair,
He beats his breast, and rends his hoary
   hair.
The champion's chariot next is seen to
   roll,
Besmear'd with hostile blood, and honorably
   foul. 130
To close the pomp, Æthon, the steed of
   state,
Is led, the fun'rals of his lord to wait.
Stripp'd of his trappings, with a sullen
   pace
He walks; and the big tears run rolling
   down his face.
The lance of Pallas, and the crimson crest,
Are borne behind: the victor seiz'd the
   rest.
The march begins: the trumpets hoarsely
   sound;
The pikes and lances trail along the ground.
Thus while the Trojan and Arcadian horse
To Pallantean tow'rs direct their course, 140
In long procession rank'd, the pious chief
Stopp'd in the rear, and gave a vent to
   grief:
"The public care," he said, "which war
   attends,
Diverts our present woes, at least suspends.
Peace with the manes of great Pallas
   dwell!
Hail, holy relics! and a last farewell!"
He said no more, but, inly tho' he mourn'd,
Restrain'd his tears, and to the camp re-
   turn'd.
Now suppliants, from Laurentum sent,
   demand
A truce, with olive branches in their
   hand; 150
Obtest his clemency, and from the plain
Beg leave to draw the bodies of their
   slain.
They plead, that none those common rites
   deny
To conquer'd foes that in fair battle die.
All cause of hate was ended in their death;
Nor could he war with bodies void of
   breath.

A king, they hop'd, would hear a king's re-
   quest,
Whose son he once was call'd, and once his
   guest.
   Their suit, which was too just to be de-
   nied,
The hero grants, and farther thus replied:
"O Latian princes, how severe a fate 161
In causeless quarrels has involv'd your
   state,
And arm'd against an unoffending man,
Who sought your friendship ere the war
   began!
You beg a truce, which I would gladly
   give,
Not only for the slain, but those who live.
I came not hether but by Heav'n's com-
   mand,
And sent by fate to share the Latian land.
Nor wage I wars unjust: your king denied
My proffer'd friendship, and my promis'd
   bride; 170
Left me for Turnus. Turnus then should
   try
His cause in arms, to conquer or to die.
My right and his are in dispute: the slain
Fell without fault, our quarrel to maintain.
In equal arms let us alone contend;
And let him vanquish, whom his fates be-
   friend.
This is the way (so tell him) to possess
The royal virgin, and restore the peace.
Bear this my message back, with ample
   leave,
That your slain friends may fun'ral rites
   receive." 180
   Thus having said — th' embassadors,
   amaz'd,
Stood mute a while, and on each other
   gaz'd.
Drances, their chief, who harbor'd in his
   breast
Long hate to Turnus, as his foe profess'd,
Broke silence first, and to the godlike
   man,
With graceful action bowing, thus began:
"Auspicious prince, in arms a mighty
   name,
But yet whose actions far transcend your
   fame;
Would I your justice or your force express,
Thought can but equal; and all words are
   less. 190
Your answer we shall thankfully relate,
And favors granted to the Latian state.

If wish'd success our labor shall attend,
Think peace concluded, and the king your
    friend:
Let Turnus leave the realm to your com-
    mand,
And seek alliance in some other land:
Build you the city which your fates assign;
We shall be proud in the great work to
    join."
    Thus Drances; and his words so well
        persuade
The rest impower'd, that soon a truce is
    made.   200
Twelve days the term allow'd: and, during
    those,
Latians and Trojans, now no longer foes,
Mix'd in the woods, for fun'ral piles pre-
    pare
To fell the timber, and forget the war.
Loud axes thro' the groaning groves re-
    sound;
Oak, mountain ash, and poplar spread the
    ground;
Firs fall from high; and some the trunks
    receive
In loaden wains; with wedges some they
    cleave.
    And now the fatal news by Fame is blown
Thro' the short circuit of th' Arcadian
    town,   210
Of Pallas slain — by Fame, which just be-
    fore
His triumphs on distended pinions bore.
Rushing from out the gate, the people
    stand,
Each with a fun'ral flambeau in his hand.
Wildly they stare, distracted with amaze:
The fields are lighten'd with a fiery blaze,
That cast a sullen splendor on their friends,
The marching troop which their dead prince
    attends.
Both parties meet: they raise a doleful ⎤
    cry;   ⎟
The matrons from the walls with shrieks ⎜
    reply,   220 ⎟
And their mix'd mourning rends the ⎜
    vaulted sky.   ⎦
The town is fill'd with tumult and with
    tears,
Till the loud clamors reach Evander's ears:
Forgetful of his state, he runs along,
With a disorder'd pace, and cleaves the
    throng;
Falls on the corpse; and groaning there he
    lies,

With silent grief, that speaks but at his
    eyes.
Short sighs and sobs succeed; till sorrow
    breaks
A passage, and at once he weeps and speaks:
    " O Pallas ! thou hast fail'd thy plighted
        word,   230
To fight with caution, not to tempt the
    sword !
I warn'd thee, but in vain; for well I knew
What perils youthful ardor would pursue,
That boiling blood would carry thee too
    far,
Young as thou wert in dangers, raw to war !
O curst essay of arms, disastrous doom,
Prelude of bloody fields, and fights to come !
Hard elements of unauspicious war,
Vain vows to Heav'n, and unavailing care !
Thrice happy thou, dear partner of my
    bed,   240
Whose holy soul the stroke of Fortune fled,
Præscious of ills, and leaving me behind,
To drink the dregs of life by fate assign'd !
Beyond the goal of nature I have gone:
My Pallas late set out, but reach'd too soon.
If, for my league against th' Ausonian state,
Amidst their weapons I had found my fate,
(Deserv'd from them,) then I had been re-
    turn'd
A breathless victor, and my son had
    mourn'd.   249
Yet will I not my Trojan friend upbraid,
Nor grudge th' alliance I so gladly made.
'T was not his fault, my Pallas fell so young,
But my own crime, for having liv'd too
    long.
Yet, since the gods had destin'd him to die,
At least he led the way to victory:
First for his friends he won the fatal ⎤
    shore,   ⎟
And sent whole herds of slaughter'd foes ⎬
    before;   ⎟
A death too great, too glorious to deplore. ⎦
Nor will I add new honors to thy grave,
Content with those the Trojan hero gave: 260
That funeral pomp thy Phrygian friends
    design'd,
In which the Tuscan chiefs and army join'd.
Great spoils and trophies, gain'd by thee,
    they bear:
Then let thy own achievements be thy
    share.
Even thou, O Turnus, hadst a trophy stood,
Whose mighty trunk had better grac'd the
    wood,

If Pallas had arriv'd, with equal length
Of years, to match thy bulk with equal
   strength.
But why, unhappy man, dost thou detain
These troops, to view the tears thou shedd'st
   in vain?   270
Go, friends, this message to your lord re-
   late:
Tell him, that, if I bear my bitter fate,
And, after Pallas' death, live ling'ring on,
'T is to behold his vengeance for my son.
I stay for Turnus, whose devoted head
Is owing to the living and the dead.
My son and I expect it from his hand;
'T is all that he can give, or we demand.
Joy is no more; but I would gladly go,
To greet my Pallas with such news below."
   The morn had now dispell'd the shades
   of night,   281
Restoring toils, when she restor'd the light.
The Trojan king and Tuscan chief com-
   mand
To raise the piles along the winding strand.
Their friends convey the dead to fun'ral
   fires;
Black smold'ring smoke from the green
   wood expires;
The light of heav'n is chok'd, and the
   new day retires.
Then thrice around the kindled piles they
   go
(For ancient custom had ordain'd it so);
Thrice horse and foot about the fires are
   led;   290
And thrice, with loud laments, they hail
   the dead.
Tears, trickling down their breasts, bedew
   the ground,
And drums and trumpets mix their mourn-
   ful sound.
Amid the blaze, their pious brethren throw
The spoils, in battle taken from the foe:
Helms, bits emboss'd, and swords of shin-
   ing steel;
One casts a target, one a chariot wheel;
Some to their fellows their own arms re-
   store:
The fauchions which in luckless fight they
   bore,
Their bucklers pierc'd, their darts bestow'd
   in vain,   300
And shiver'd lances gather'd from the plain.
Whole herds of offer'd bulls, about the fire,
And bristled boars, and woolly sheep ex-
   pire.

Around the piles a careful troop attends,
To watch the wasting flames, and weep
   their burning friends;
Ling'ring along the shore, till dewy night
New decks the face of heav'n with starry
   light.
   The conquer'd Latians, with like pious
   care,
Piles without number for their dead pre-
   pare.
Part in the places where they fell are laid;
And part are to the neighb'ring fields con-
   vey'd.   311
The corps of kings, and captains of renown,
Borne off in state, are buried in the town;
The rest, unhonor'd, and without a name,
Are cast a common heap to feed the
   flame.
Trojans and Latians vie with like desires
To make the field of battle shine with
   fires,
And the promiscuous blaze to heav'n as-
   pires.
   Now had the morning thrice renew'd the
   light,
And thrice dispell'd the shadows of the
   night,   320
When those who round the wasted fires re-
   main,
Perform the last sad office to the slain.
They rake the yet warm ashes from below;
These, and the bones unburn'd, in earth be-
   stow;
These relics with their country rites they
   grace,
And raise a mount of turf to mark the
   place.
But, in the palace of the king, appears
A scene more solemn, and a pomp of tears.
Maids, matrons, widows, mix their common
   moans;
Orphans their sires, and sires lament their
   sons.   330
All in that universal sorrow share,
And curse the cause of this unhappy war:
A broken league, a bride unjustly sought,
A crown usurp'd, which with their blood is
   bought!
These are the crimes with which they load
   the name
Of Turnus, and on him alone exclaim:
"Let him who lords it o'er th' Ausonian
   land
Engage the Trojan hero hand to hand:
His is the gain; our lot is but to serve;

'T is just, the sway he seeks, he should de-
        serve."   340
This Drances aggravates; and adds, with
        spite:
" His foe expects, and dares him to the
        fight."
Nor Turnus wants a party, to support
His cause and credit in the Latian court.
His former acts secure his present fame,
And the queen shades him with her mighty
        name.
    While thus their factious minds with
        fury burn,
The legates from th' Ætolian prince re-
        turn:
Sad news they bring, that, after all the
        cost
And care employ'd, their embassy is lost;
That Diomede refus'd his aid in war,   351
Unmov'd with presents, and as deaf to
        pray'r.
Some new alliance must elsewhere be
        sought,
Or peace with Troy on hard conditions
        bought.
    Latinus, sunk in sorrow, finds too late,
A foreign son is pointed out by fate;
And, till Æneas shall Lavinia wed,
The wrath of Heav'n is hov'ring o'er his
        head.
The gods, he saw, espous'd the juster ⎤
        side, |
When late their titles in the field were }
        tried: 360 |
Witness the fresh laments, and fun'ral |
        tears undried.   ⎦
    Thus, full of anxious thought, he summons
        all
The Latian senate to the council hall.
The princes come, commanded by their
        head,
And crowd the paths that to the palace
        lead.
Supreme in pow'r, and reverenc'd for his
        years,
He takes the throne, and in the midst ap-
        pears.
Majestically sad, he sits in state,
And bids his envoys their success relate.
    When Venulus began, the murmuring
        sound   370
Was hush'd, and sacred silence reign'd
        around.
" We have," said he, " perform'd your high
        command,

And pass'd with peril a long tract of land:
We reach'd the place desir'd; with wonder
        fill'd,
The Grecian tents and rising tow'rs beheld.
Great Diomede has compass d round with
        walls
The city, which Argyripa he calls,
From his own Argos nam d. We touch'd,
        with joy,
The royal hand that raz'd unhappy Troy.
When introduc'd, our presents first we
        bring,   380
Then crave an instant audience from the
        king.
His leave obtain'd, our native soil we name,
And tell th' important cause for which we
        came.
Attentively he heard us, while we spoke;
Then, with soft accents, and a pleasing
        look,
Made this return: ' Ausonian race, of old
Renown'd for peace, and for an age of gold,
What madness has your alter'd minds pos-
        sess d,
To change for war hereditary rest,
Solicit arms unknown, and tempt the
        sword,   390
A needless ill your ancestors abhorr'd ?
We — for myself I speak, and all the name
Of Grecians, who to Troy's destruction
        came,
Omitting those who were in battle slain,
Or borne by rolling Simoïs to the main —
Not one but suffer'd, and too dearly bought
The prize of honor which in arms he
        sought;
Some doom'd to death, and some in exile
        driv'n,
Outcasts, abandon'd by the care of Heav'n;
So worn, so wretched, so despis d a crew, 400
As ev'n old Priam might with pity view.
Witness the vessels by Minerva toss'd
In storms; the vengeful Capharean coast;
Th' Eubœan rocks ! the prince, whose bro-
        ther led
Our armies to revenge his injur'd bed,
In Egypt lost ! Ulysses with his men
Have seen Charybdis and the Cyclops' den.
Why should I name Idomeneus, in vain ⎤
Restor'd to scepters, and expell'd again ? }
Or young Achilles, by his rival slain ? 410 ⎦
Ev'n he, the King of Men, the foremost
        name
Of all the Greeks, and most renown'd by
        fame,

The proud revenger of another's wife,
Yet by his own adult'ress lost his life;
Fell at his threshold; and the spoils of Troy
The foul polluters of his bed enjoy.
The gods have envied me the sweets of life,
My much lov'd country, and my more lov'd
    wife:
Banish'd from both, I mourn; while in the
    sky,
Transform'd to birds, my lost companions
    fly: 420
Hov'ring about the coasts, they make their
    moan,
And cuff the cliffs with pinions not their
    own.
What squalid specters, in the dead of night,
Break my short sleep, and skim before my
    sight !
I might have promis'd to myself those
    harms,
Mad as I was, when I, with mortal arms,
Presum'd against immortal pow'rs to move,
And violate with wounds the Queen of
    Love.
Such arms this hand shall never more em-
    ploy;
No hate remains with me to ruin'd Troy.   430
I war not with its dust; nor am I glad
To think of past events, or good or bad.
Your presents I return: whate'er you bring
To buy my friendship, send the Trojan king.
We met in fight; I know him, to my cost:
With what a whirling force his lance he
    toss'd !
Heav'ns ! what a spring was in his arm, to
    throw !
How high he held his shield, and rose at
    ev'ry blow !
Had Troy produc'd two more his match in
    might,
They would have chang'd the fortune of the
    fight: 440
Th' invasion of the Greeks had been re-
    turn'd,
Our empire wasted, and our cities burn'd.
The long defense the Trojan people made,
The war protracted, and the siege delay'd,
Were due to Hector's and this hero's hand:
Both brave alike, and equal in command;
Æneas, not inferior in the field,
In pious reverence to the gods excell'd.
Make peace, ye Latians, and avoid with care
Th' impending dangers of a fatal war.'   450
He said no more; but, with this cold excuse,
Refus'd th' alliance, and advis'd a truce."

Thus Venulus concluded his report.
A jarring murmur fill'd the factious court:
As, when a torrent rolls with rapid force,
And dashes o'er the stones that stop the
    course,
The flood, constrain'd within a scanty space,
Roars horrible along th' uneasy race;
White foam in gath'ring eddies floats
    around;
The rocky shores rebellow to the sound.   460
    The murmur ceas'd: then from his lofty
    throne
The king invok'd the gods, and thus begun:
" I wish, ye Latins, what we now debate
Had been resolv'd before it was too late.
Much better had it been for you and me,
Unforc'd by this our last necessity,
To have been earlier wise, than now to
    call
A council, when the foe surrounds the wall.
O citizens, we wage unequal war,
With men not only Heav'n's peculiar care,
But Heav'n's own race; unconquer'd in the
    field,   471
Or, conquer'd, yet unknowing how to yield.
What hopes you had in Diomede, lay down:
Our hopes must center on ourselves alone.
Yet those how feeble, and, indeed, how vain,
You see too well; nor need my words ex-
    plain.
Vanquish'd without resource; laid flat by
    fate;
Factions within, a foe without the gate !
Not but I grant that all perform'd their
    parts
With manly force, and with undaunted
    hearts: 480
With our united strength the war we wag'd;
With equal numbers, equal arms, engag'd.
You see th' event. — Now hear what I pro-
    pose,
To save our friends, and satisfy our foes.
A tract of land the Latins have possess'd
Along the Tiber, stretching to the west,
Which now Rutulians and Auruncans till,
And their mix'd cattle graze the fruitful
    hill.
Those mountains fill'd with firs, that lower
    land,   489
If you consent, the Trojan shall command,
Call'd into part of what is ours; and there,
On terms agreed, the common country
    share.
There let 'em build and settle, if they
    please;

Unless they choose once more to cross the seas,
In search of seats remote from Italy,
And from unwelcome inmates set us free.
Then twice ten galleys let us build with speed,
Or twice as many more, if more they need.
Materials are at hand; a well-grown wood
Runs equal with the margin of the flood:
Let them the number and the form assign;
The care and cost of all the stores be mine.
To treat the peace, a hundred senators　503
Shall be commission'd hence with ample pow'rs,
With olive crown'd: the presents they ⎫
　shall bear,　　　　　　　　　　　　　⎪
A purple robe, a royal iv'ry chair,　　　⎬
And all the marks of sway that Latian ⎪
　monarchs wear,　　　　　　　　　　⎭
And sums of gold. Among yourselves debate
This great affair, and save the sinking state."
　Then Drances took the word,who grudg'd, long since,　　　　　　　　　　510
The rising glories of the Daunian prince.
Factious and rich, bold at the council ⎫
　board,　　　　　　　　　　　　　　⎪
But cautious in the field, he shunn'd the ⎬
　sword;　　　　　　　　　　　　　⎪
A close caballer, and tongue-valiant lord. ⎭
Noble his mother was, and near the throne;
But, what his father's parentage, unknown.
He rose, and took th' advantage of the times,
To load young Turnus with invidious crimes.
" Such truths, O king," said he, "your words contain,　　　　　　　　519
As strike the sense, and all replies are vain;
Nor are your loyal subjects now to seek
What common needs require, but fear to speak.
Let him give leave of speech, that haughty man,
Whose pride this unauspicious war began;
For whose ambition (let me dare to say,
Fear set apart, tho' death is in my way)
The plains of Latium run with blood around;
So many valiant heroes bite the ground;
Dejected grief in ev'ry face appears;
A town in mourning, and a land in tears;
While he, th' undoubted author of our harms,　　　　　　　　　　531
The man who menaces the gods with arms,
Yet, after all his boasts, forsook the fight,

And sought his safety in ignoble flight.
Now, best of kings, since you propose to send
Such bounteous presents to your Trojan friend;
Add yet a greater at our joint request,
One which he values more than all the rest:
Give him the fair Lavinia for his bride; ⎫
With that alliance let the league be tied, ⎪
And for the bleeding land a lasting peace ⎬
　provide.　　　　　　　　　　541　⎪
Let insolence no longer awe the throne;　⎭
But, with a father's right, bestow your own.
For this maligner of the general good,
If still we fear his force, he must be woo'd;
His haughty godhead we with pray'rs implore,
Your scepter to release, and our just rights restore.
O cursed cause of all our ills, must we
Wage wars unjust, and fall in fight, for thee !
What right hast thou to rule the Latian state,　　　　　　　　　　550
And send us out to meet our certain fate ?
'T is a destructive war: from Turnus' hand
Our peace and public safety we demand.
Let the fair bride to the brave chief remain;
If not, the peace, without the pledge, is vain.
Turnus, I know you think me not your friend,
Nor will I much with your belief contend:
I beg your greatness not to give the law
In others' realms, but, beaten, to withdraw.
Pity your own, or pity our estate;　　560
Nor twist our fortunes with your sinking fate.
Your interest is, the war should never cease;
But we have felt enough to wish the peace:
A land exhausted to the last remains,
Depopulated towns, and driven plains.
Yet, if desire of fame, and thirst of pow'r,
A beauteous princess, with a crown in dow'r,
So fire your mind, in arms assert your right,
And meet your foe, who dares you to the fight.
Mankind, it seems, is made for you alone;
We, but the slaves who mount you to the throne:　　　　　　　　　　571

A base ignoble crowd, without a name,
Unwept, unworthy of the fun'ral flame,
By duty bound to forfeit each his life,
That Turnus may possess a royal wife.
Permit not, mighty man, so mean a crew ⎱
Should share such triumphs, and detain ⎰
    from you
The post of honor, your undoubted due. ⎰
Rather alone your matchless force employ,
To merit what alone you must enjoy."   580
    These words, so full of malice mix'd with
      art,
Inflam'd with rage the youthful hero's
    heart.
Then, groaning from the bottom of his
    breast,
He heav'd for wind, and thus his wrath ex-
    press'd:
" You, Drances, never want a stream of
    words,
Then, when the public need requires our
    swords.
First in the council hall to steer the state,
And ever foremost in a tongue-debate,
While our strong walls secure us from the
    foe,
Ere yet with blood our ditches overflow: 590
But let the potent orator declaim,
And with the brand of coward blot my
    name;
Free leave is giv'n him, when his fatal ⎱
    hand
Has cover'd with more corps the sanguine ⎰
    strand,
And high as mine his tow'ring trophies ⎰
    stand.
If any doubt remains, who dares the most,
Let us decide it at the Trojans' cost,
And issue both abreast, where honor calls —
Foes are not far to seek without the
    walls —
Unless his noisy tongue can only fight,   600
And feet were giv'n him but to speed his
    flight.
I beaten from the field ?   I forc'd away ?
Who, but so known a dastard, dares to
    say ?
Had he but ev'n beheld the fight, his eyes
Had witness'd for me what his tongue de-
    nies:
What heaps of Trojans by this hand were
    slain,
And how the bloody Tiber swell'd the
    main.
All saw, but he, th' Arcadian troops retire

In scatter'd squadrons, and their prince ex-
    pire.
The giant brothers, in their camp, have
    found,   610
I was not forc'd with ease to quit my
    ground.
Not such the Trojans tried me, when, in-
    clos'd,
I singly their united arms oppos'd:
First forc'd an entrance thro' their thick
    array;
Then, glutted with their slaughter, freed
    my way.
'T is a destructive war ?   So let it be,
But to the Phrygian pirate, and to thee !
Meantime proceed to fill the people's ears
With false reports, their minds with panic
    fears:
Extol the strength of a twice-conquer'd
    race;   620
Our foes encourage, and our friends debase.
Believe thy fables, and the Trojan town
Triumphant stands; the Grecians are o'er-
    thrown;
Suppliant at Hector's feet Achilles lies,
And Diomede from fierce Æneas flies.
Say rapid Aufidus with awful dread
Runs backward from the sea, and hides his
    head,
When the great Trojan on his bank appears;
For that 's as true as thy dissembled fears
Of my revenge. Dismiss that vanity: 630
Thou, Drances, art below a death from me.
Let that vile soul in that vile body rest;
The lodging is well worthy of the guest.
    " Now, royal father, to the present state
Of our affairs, and of this high debate:
If in your arms thus early you diffide,
And think your fortune is already tried;
If one defeat has brought us down so low,
As never more in fields to meet the foe;
Then I conclude for peace: 't is time to
    treat,   640
And lie like vassals at the victor's feet.
But, O ! if any ancient blood remains,
One drop of all our fathers', in our veins,
That man would I prefer before the rest,
Who dar'd his death with an undaunted
    breast;
Who comely fell, by no dishonest wound,
To shun that sight, and, dying, gnaw'd the
    ground.
But, if we still have fresh recruits in store,
If our confederates can afford us more;
If the contended field we bravely fought, 650

And not a bloodless victory was bought;
Their losses equal'd ours; and, for their slain,
With equal fires they fill'd the shining plain,
Why thus, unforc'd, should we so tamely yield,
And, ere the trumpet sounds, resign the field?
Good unexpected, evils unforeseen,
Appear by turns, as fortune shifts the scene:
Some, rais'd aloft, come tumbling down amain;
Then fall so hard, they bound and rise again.
If Diomede refuse his aid to lend,   660
The great Messapus yet remains our friend:
Tolumnius, who foretells events, is ours;
Th' Italian chiefs and princes join their pow'rs:
Nor least in number, nor in name the last,
Your own brave subjects have your cause embrac'd.
Above the rest, the Volscian Amazon
Contains an army in herself alone,
And heads a squadron, terrible to sight,
With glitt'ring shields, in brazen armor bright.
Yet, if the foe a single fight demand,   670
And I alone the public peace withstand;
If you consent, he shall not be refus'd,
Nor find a hand to victory unus'd
This new Achilles, let him take the field,
With fated armor, and Vulcanian shield!
For you, my royal father, and my fame,
I, Turnus, not the least of all my name,
Devote my soul. He calls me hand to hand,
And I alone will answer his demand.   679
Drances shall rest secure, and neither share
The danger, nor divide the prize of war."
   While they debate, nor these nor those will yield,
Æneas draws his forces to the field,
And moves his camp. The scouts with flying speed
Return, and thro' the frighted city spread
Th' unpleasing news, the Trojans are descried,
In battle marching by the river side,
And bending to the town. They take th' alarm:
Some tremble, some are bold; all in confusion arm.
Th' impetuous youth press forward to the field;   690

They clash the sword, and clatter on the shield:
The fearful matrons raise a screaming cry:
Old feeble men with fainter groans reply;
A jarring sound results, and mingles in the sky,
Like that of swans remurm'ring to the floods,
Or birds of diff'ring kinds in hollow woods.
Turnus th' occasion takes, and cries aloud:
"Talk on, ye quaint haranguers of the crowd:
Declaim in praise of peace, when danger calls,
And the fierce foes in arms approach the walls."   700
He said, and, turning short, with speedy pace,
Casts back a scornful glance, and quits the place:
"Thou, Volusus, the Volscian troops command
To mount; and lead thyself our Ardean band.
Messapus and Catillus, post your force
Along the fields, to charge the Trojan horse.
Some guard the passes, others man the wall;
Drawn up in arms. the rest attend my call."
   They swarm from ev'ry quarter of the town,
And with disorder'd haste the rampires crown.   710
Good old Latinus, when he saw, too late,
The gath'ring storm just breaking on the state,
Dismiss'd the council till a fitter time,
And own'd his easy temper as his crime,
Who, forc'd against his reason, had complied
To break the treaty for the promis'd bride.
   Some help to sink new trenches; others aid
To ram the stones, or raise the palisade.
Hoarse trumpets sound th' alarm; around the walls
Runs a distracted crew, whom their last labor calls.   720
A sad procession in the streets is seen,
Of matrons, that attend the mother queen:
High in her chair she sits, and, at her side,
With downcast eyes appears the fatal bride.
They mount the cliff, where Pallas' temple stands;

Pray'rs in their mouths, and presents in
their hands.
With censers first they fume the sacred
shrine,
Then in this common supplication join:
"O patroness of arms, unspotted maid,
Propitious hear, and lend thy Latins aid ! 730
Break short the pirate's lance; pronounce
his fate,
And lay the Phrygian low before the gate."
Now Turnus arms for fight. His back
and breast
Well-temper'd steel and scaly brass invest:
The cuishes which his brawny thighs in-
fold
Are mingled metal damask'd o'er with gold.
His faithful fauchion sits upon his side;
Nor casque, nor crest, his manly features
hide:
But, bare to view. amid surrounding friends,
With godlike grace, he from the tow'r
descends   740
Exulting in his strength, he seems to dare
His absent rival, and to promise war.
Freed from his keepers, thus, with broken
reins,
The wanton courser prances o'er the plains,
Or in the pride of youth o'erleaps the
mounds,
And snuffs the females in forbidden grounds,
Or seeks his wat'ring in the well-known
flood,
To quench his thirst, and cool his fiery blood:
He swims luxuriant in the liquid plain,
And o'er his shoulder flows his waving
mane: 750
He neighs, he snorts, he bears his head on
high;
Before his ample chest the frothy waters
fly.
Soon as the prince appears without the
gate,
The Volscians, with their virgin leader, wait
His last commands. Then, with a grace-
ful mien,
Lights from her lofty steed the warrior
queen:
Her squadron imitates, and each descends;
Whose common suit Camilla thus com-
mends:
"If sense of honor, if a soul secure
Of inborn worth, that can all tests endure,
Can promise aught, or on itself rely   761
Greatly to dare, to conquer or to die;
Then, I alone, sustain'd by these, will meet

The Tyrrhene troops, and promise their de-
feat.
Ours be the danger, ours the sole renown:
You, gen'ral, stay behind, and guard the
town."
Turnus a while stood mute, with glad
surprise,
And on the fierce virago fix'd his eyes;
Then thus return'd: "O grace of Italy, 769
With what becoming thanks can I reply ?
Not only words lie lab'ring in my breast,
But thought itself is by thy praise op-
press'd.
Yet rob me not of all; but let me join
My toils, my hazard, and my fame, with
thine.
The Trojan, not in stratagem unskill'd,
Sends his light horse before to scour the
field:
Himself, thro' steep ascents and thorny
brakes,
A larger compass to the city takes.
This news my scouts confirm, and I prepare
To foil his cunning, and his force to dare;
With chosen foot his passage to forelay, 781
And place an ambush in the winding way.
Thou, with thy Volscians, face the Tuscan
horse:
The brave Messapus shall thy troops in-
force
With those of Tibur, and the Latian band,
Subjected all to thy supreme command."
This said, he warns Messapus to the war,
Then ev'ry chief exhorts with equal care.
All thus encourag'd, his own troops he joins,
And hastes to prosecute his deep designs.
Inclos'd with hills, a winding valley lies,
By nature form'd for fraud, and fitted for
surprise.   792
A narrow track, by human steps untrode,
Leads, thro' perplexing thorns, to this ob-
scure abode.
High o'er the vale a steepy mountain stands,
Whence the surveying sight the nether
ground commands.
The top is level, an offensive seat
Of war; and from the war a safe retreat:
For, on the right and left, is room to press
The foes at hand, or from afar distress; 800
To drive 'em headlong downward, and to
pour
On their descending backs a stony show'r.
Thither young Turnus took the well-known
way,
Possess'd the pass, and in blind ambush lay.

Meantime, Latonian Phœbe, from the
skies,
Beheld th' approaching war with hateful
eyes,
And call'd the light-foot Opis to her aid,
Her most belov'd and ever-trusty maid;
Then with a sigh began: "Camilla goes
To meet her death amidst her fatal foes:
The nymph I lov'd of all my mortal train,
Invested with Diana's arms, in vain.   812
Nor is my kindness for the virgin new:
'T was born with her; and with her years
it grew.
Her father Metabus, when forc'd away
From old Privernum, for tyrannic sway,
Snatch'd up, and sav'd from his prevailing
foes,
This tender babe, companion of his woes.
Casmilla was her mother; but he drown'd
One hissing letter in a softer sound,   820
And call'd Camilla. Thro' the woods he
flies;
Wrapp'd in his robe the royal infant lies.
His foes in sight, he mends his weary
pace;
With shouts and clamors they pursue the
chase.
The banks of Amasene at length he gains: ⎤
The raging flood his farther flight re- ⎬
strains,   ⎭
Rais'd o'er the borders with unusual rains. ⎦
Prepar'd to plunge into the stream, he
fears,
Not for himself, but for the charge he
bears.
Anxious, he stops a while, and thinks in
haste;   830
Then, desp'rate in distress, resolves at last.
A knotty lance of well-boil'd oak he bore;
The middle part with cork he cover'd o'er:
He clos'd the child within the hollow space;
With twigs of bending osier bound the case;
Then pois'd the spear, heavy with human
weight,
And thus invok'd my favor for the freight:
' Accept, great goddess of the woods,' he
said,
' Sent by her sire, this dedicated maid !
Thro' air she flies a suppliant to thy
shrine;   840
And the first weapons that she knows, are
thine.'
He said; and with full force the spear he
threw:
Above the sounding waves Camilla flew.

Then, press'd by foes, he stemm'd the
stormy tide,
And gain'd, by stress of arms, the farther
side.
His fasten'd spear he pull'd from out the
ground,
And, victor of his vows, his infant nymph
unbound;
Nor, after that, in towns which walls in-
close,
Would trust his hunted life amidst his foes;
But, rough, in open air he chose to lie; 850
Earth was his couch, his cov'ring was the
sky.
On hills unshorn, or in a desart den,
He shunn'd the dire society of men.
A shepherd's solitary life he led;
His daughter with the milk of mares he
fed.
The dugs of bears, and ev'ry salvage beast,
He drew, and thro' her lips the liquor
press'd.
The little Amazon could scarcely go:
He loads her with a quiver and a bow;
And, that she might her stagg'ring steps
command,   860
He with a slender jav'lin fills her hand.
Her flowing hair no golden fillet bound;
Nor swept her trailing robe the dusty
ground.
Instead of these, a tiger's hide o'erspread
Her back and shoulders, fasten'd to her
head.
The flying dart she first attempts to fling,
And round her tender temples toss'd the
sling;
Then, as her strength with years in- ⎤
creas'd, began   ⎬
To pierce aloft in air the soaring swan, ⎬
And from the clouds to fetch the heron ⎭
and the crane.   870
The Tuscan matrons with each other vied,
To bless their rival sons with such a bride;
But she disdains their love, to share with
me
The sylvan shades and vow'd virginity.
And, O ! I wish, contented with my cares
Of salvage spoils, she had not sought the
wars:
Then had she been of my celestial train,
And shunn'd the fate that dooms her to be
slain.
But since, opposing Heav'n's decree, she
goes   879
To find her death among forbidden foes,

Haste with these arms, and take thy steepy
    flight,
Where, with the gods averse, the Latins
    fight.
This bow to thee, this quiver I bequeath,
This chosen arrow, to revenge her death:
By whate'er hand Camilla shall be slain,
Or of the Trojan or Italian train,
Let him not pass unpunish'd from the
    plain.
Then, in a hollow cloud, myself will aid
To bear the breathless body of my maid:
Unspoil'd shall be her arms, and unpro-
    fan'd   890
Her holy limbs with any human hand,
And in a marble tomb laid in her native
    land."
She said. The faithful nymph descends
    from high
With rapid flight, and cuts the sounding
    sky:
Black clouds and stormy winds around
    her body fly.
By this, the Trojan and the Tuscan horse,
Drawn up in squadrons, with united force,
Approach the walls: the sprightly coursers
    bound,
Press forward on their bits, and shift their
    ground.
Shields, arms, and spears flash horribly
    from far;   900
And the fields glitter with a waving war.
Oppos'd to these, come on with furious
    force
Messapus, Coras, and the Latian horse;
These in the body plac'd, on either hand
Sustain'd and clos'd by fair Camilla's band.
Advancing in a line, they couch their spears;
And less and less the middle space appears.
Thick smoke obscures the field; and scarce
    are seen
The neighing coursers, and the shouting
    men.
In distance of their darts they stop their
    course;   910
Then man to man they rush, and horse to
    horse.
The face of heav'n their flying jav'lins hide,
And deaths unseen are dealt on either side.
Tyrrhenus, and Aconteus, void of fear,
By mettled coursers borne in full career,
Meet first oppos'd; and, with a mighty
    shock,
Their horses' heads against each other
    knock.

Far from his steed is fierce Aconteus cast,
As with an engine's force, or lightning's
    blast:
He rolls along in blood, and breathes his
    last.   920
The Latin squadrons take a sudden fright,
And sling their shields behind, to save their
    backs in flight.
Spurring at speed, to their own walls they
    drew;
Close in the rear the Tuscan troops pursue,
And urge their flight: Asylas leads the
    chase;
Till, seiz'd with shame, they wheel about
    and face,
Receive their foes, and raise a threat'ning
    cry.
The Tuscans take their turn to fear and fly.
So swelling surges, with a thund'ring roar,
Driv'n on each other's backs, insult the
    shore,   930
Bound o'er the rocks, incroach upon the
    land,
And far upon the beach eject the sand;
Then backward, with a swing, they take
    their way,
Repuls'd from upper ground, and seek their
    mother sea;
With equal hurry quit th' invaded shore,
And swallow back the sand and stones they
    spew'd before.
  Twice were the Tuscans masters of the
    field,
Twice by the Latins, in their turn, repell'd.
Asham'd at length, to the third charge they
    ran;
Both hosts resolv'd, and mingled man to
    man.   940
Now dying groans are heard; the fields are
    strow'd
With falling bodies, and are drunk with
    blood.
Arms, horses, men, on heaps together lie:
Confus'd the fight, and more confus'd the
    cry.
Orsilochus, who durst not press too near
Strong Remulus, at distance drove his
    spear,
And stuck the steel beneath his horse's
    ear.
The fiery steed, impatient of the wound,
Curvets, and, springing upward with a
    bound,
His helpless lord cast backward on the
    ground.   950

Catillus pierc'd Iolas first; then drew
His reeking lance, and at Herminius
    threw,
The mighty champion of the Tuscan
    crew.
His neck and throat unarm'd, his head was
    bare,
But shaded with a length of yellow hair:
Secure, he fought, expos'd on ev'ry part,
A spacious mark for swords, and for the
    flying dart.
Across the shoulders came the feather'd
    wound;
Transfix'd, he fell, and doubled to the
    ground.
The sands with streaming blood are san-
    guine dyed,   960
And death with honor sought on either
    side.
Resistless thro' the war Camilla rode,
In danger unappall'd, and pleas'd with
    blood.
One side was bare for her exerted breast;
One shoulder with her painted quiver
    press'd.
Now from afar her fatal jav'lins play;
Now with her ax's edge she hews her way:
Diana's arms upon her shoulder sound;
And when, too closely press'd, she quits
    the ground,
From her bent bow she sends a backward
    wound.   970
Her maids, in martial pomp, on either side,
Larina, Tulla, fierce Tarpeia, ride:
Italians all; in peace, their queen's delight;
In war, the bold companions of the fight.
So march'd the Thracian Amazons of old,
When Thermodon with bloody billows
    roll'd:
Such troops as these in shining arms were
    seen,
When Theseus met in fight their maiden
    queen:
Such to the field Penthisilea led,
From the fierce virgin when the Grecians
    fled;   980
With such, return'd triumphant from the
    war,
Her maids with cries attend the lofty car;
They clash with manly force their moony
    shields;
With female shouts resound the Phrygian
    fields.
Who foremost, and who last, heroic
    maid,

On the cold earth were by thy courage
    laid ?
Thy spear, of mountain ash, Eumenius first,
With fury driv'n, from side to side trans-
    pierc'd:
A purple stream came spouting from the
    wound;
Bath'd in his blood he lies, and bites the
    ground.   990
Liris and Pagasus at once she slew:
The former, as the slacken'd reins he drew
Of his faint steed; the latter, as he
    stretch'd
His arm to prop his friend, the jav'lin
    reach'd.
By the same weapon, sent from the same
    hand,
Both fall together, and both spurn the sand.
Amastrus next is added to the slain:
The rest in rout she follows o'er the plain:
Tereus, Harpalycus, Demophoön,   999
And Chromis, at full speed her fury shun.
Of all her deadly darts, not one she lost;
Each was attended with a Trojan ghost.
Young Ornithus bestrode a hunter steed,
Swift for the chase, and of Apulian breed.
Him from afar she spied, in arms unknown:
O'er his broad back an ox's hide was
    thrown;
His helm a wolf, whose gaping jaws were
    spread
A cov'ring for his cheeks, and grinn'd
    around his head.
He clench'd within his hand an iron prong,
And tower'd above the rest, conspicuous in
    the throng.   1010
Him soon she singled from the flying train,
And slew with ease; then thus insults the
    slain:
"Vain hunter, didst thou think thro' woods
    to chase
The savage herd, a vile and trembling
    race ?
Here cease thy vaunts, and own my victory:
A woman warrior was too strong for thee.
Yet, if the ghosts demand the conqu'ror's
    name,
Confessing great Camilla, save thy shame."
Then Butes and Orsilochus she slew,
The bulkiest bodies of the Trojan crew; 1020
But Butes breast to breast: the spear
    descends
Above the gorget, where his helmet ends,
And o'er the shield which his left side
    defends.

Orsilochus and she their coursers ply:
He seems to follow, and she seems to fly;
But in a narrower ring she makes the race;
And then he flies, and she pursues the
    chase.
Gath'ring at length on her deluded foe,
She swings her ax, and rises to the blow;
Full on the helm behind, with such a sway
The weapon falls, the riven steel gives
    way: 1031
He groans, he roars, he sues in vain for
    grace;
Brains, mingled with his blood, besmear his
    face.
    Astonish'd Aunus just arrives by chance,
To see his fall, nor farther dares advance;
But, fixing on the horrid maid his eye,
He stares, and shakes, and finds it vain to
    fly;
Yet, like a true Ligurian, born to cheat,
(At least while fortune favor'd his deceit,)
Cries out aloud: " What courage have you
    shown,   1040
Who trust your courser's strength, and not
    your own ?
Forego the vantage of your horse, alight,
And then on equal terms begin the fight:
It shall be seen, weak woman, what you
    can,
When, foot to foot, you combat with a man."
He said. She glows with anger and dis-
    dain,
Dismounts with speed to dare him on the
    plain,
And leaves her horse at large among her
    train;
With her drawn sword defies him to the
    field,   1049
And, marching, lifts aloft her maiden shield.
The youth, who thought his cunning did suc-
    ceed,
Reins round his horse, and urges all his
    speed;
Adds the remembrance of the spur, and
    hides
The goring rowels in his bleeding sides.
" Vain fool, and coward ! " cries the lofty
    maid,
" Caught in the train which thou thyself
    hast laid !
On others practice thy Ligurian arts;
Thin stratagems and tricks of little hearts
Are lost on me: nor shalt thou safe retire,
With vaunting lies, to thy fallacious sire."
At this, so fast her flying feet she sped, 1061

That soon she strain'd beyond his horse's
    head:
Then turning short, at once she seiz'd the
    rein,
And laid the boaster grov'ling on the plain.
Not with more ease the falcon, from above,
Trusses in middle air the trembling dove,
Then plumes the prey, in her strong
    pounces bound:
The feathers, foul with blood, come tum-
    bling to the ground.
    Now mighty Jove, from his superior
    height,
With his broad eye surveys th' unequal
    fight.   1070
He fires the breast of Tarchon with disdain,
And sends him to redeem th' abandon'd
    plain.
Betwixt the broken ranks the Tuscan rides,
And these encourages, and those he chides;
Recalls each leader, by his name, from
    flight;
Renews their ardor, and restores the fight.
" What panic fear has seiz'd your souls ?
    O shame,
O brand perpetual of th' Etrurian name !
Cowards incurable, a woman's hand
Drives, breaks, and scatters your ignoble
    band !   1080
Now cast away the sword, and quit the
    shield !
What use of weapons which you dare not
    wield ?
Not thus you fly your female foes by night,
Nor shun the feast, when the full bowls
    invite;
When to fat off'rings the glad augur calls,
And the shrill hornpipe sounds to baccha-
    nals.
These are your studied cares, your lewd
    delight:
Swift to debauch, but slow to manly fight."
Thus having said, he spurs amid the foes,
Not managing the life he meant to lose.
The first he found he seiz'd, with headlong
    haste,   1091
In his strong gripe, and clasp'd around the
    waist:
'T was Venulus, whom from his horse he
    tore,
And, laid athwart his own, in triumph bore.
Loud shouts ensue; the Latins turn their
    eyes,
And view th' unusual sight with vast sur-
    prise.

The fiery Tarchon, flying o'er the plains,
Press'd in his arms the pond'rous prey sustains;
Then, with his shorten'd spear, explores around   1099
His jointed arms, to fix a deadly wound.
Nor less the captive struggles for his life:
He writhes his body to prolong the strife,
And, fencing for his naked throat, exerts
His utmost vigor, and the point averts.
So stoops the yellow eagle from on high,
And bears a speckled serpent thro' the sky,
Fast'ning his crooked talons on the prey:
The pris'ner hisses thro' the liquid way;
Resists the royal hawk; and, tho' oppress'd,
She fights in volumes, and erects her crest: 1110
Turn'd to her foe, she stiffens ev'ry scale,
And shoots her forky tongue, and whisks her threat'ning tail.
Against the victor, all defense is weak:
Th' imperial bird still plies her with his beak;
He tears her bowels, and her breast he gores;
Then claps his pinions, and securely soars.
Thus, thro' the midst of circling enemies,
Strong Tarchon snatch'd and bore away his prize.
The Tyrrhene troops, that shrunk before, now press
The Latins, and presume the like success. 1120
  Then Aruns, doom'd to death, his arts assay'd,
To murther, unespied, the Volscian maid:
This way and that his winding course he bends,
And, wheresoe'er she turns, her steps attends.
When she retires victorious from the chase,
He wheels about with care, and shifts his place;
When, rushing on, she seeks her foes in fight,
He keeps aloof, but keeps her still in sight:
He threats, and trembles, trying ev'ry way,
Unseen to kill, and safely to betray.   1130
  Chloreus, the priest of Cybele, from far,
Glitt'ring in Phrygian arms amidst the war,
Was by the virgin view'd. The steed he press'd
Was proud with trappings, and his brawny chest
With scales of gilded brass was cover'd o'er;
A robe of Tyrian dye the rider wore.

With deadly wounds he gall'd the distant foe;
Gnossian his shafts, and Lycian was his bow:
A golden helm his front and head surrounds;
A gilded quiver from his shoulder sounds.   1140
Gold, weav'd with linen, on his thighs he wore,
With flowers of needlework distinguish'd o'er,
With golden buckles bound, and gather'd up before.
Him the fierce maid beheld with ardent eyes,
Fond and ambitious of so rich a prize,
Or that the temple might his trophies hold,
Or else to shine herself in Trojan gold.
Blind in her haste, she chases him alone,
And seeks his life, regardless of her own.
  This lucky moment the sly traitor chose;   1150
Then, starting from his ambush, up he rose,
And threw, but first to Heav'n address'd his vows:
"O patron of Soracte's high abodes,
Phœbus, the ruling pow'r among the gods,
Whom first we serve, whole woods of unctuous pine
Are fell'd for thee, and to thy glory shine;
By thee protected, with our naked soles,
Thro' flames unsing'd we march, and tread the kindled coals:
Give me, propitious pow'r, to wash away
The stains of this dishonorable day: 1160
Nor spoils, nor triumph, from the fact I claim,
But with my future actions trust my fame.
Let me, by stealth, this female plague o'ercome,
And from the field return inglorious home."
Apollo heard, and, granting half his pray'r,
Shuffled in winds the rest, and toss'd in empty air.
He gives the death desir'd: his safe return
By southern tempests to the seas is borne.
  Now, when the jav'lin whizz'd along the skies,
Both armies on Camilla turn'd their eyes,   1170
Directed by the sound. Of either host,
Th' unhappy virgin, tho' concern'd the most,
Was only deaf; so greedy was she bent
On golden spoils, and on her prey intent:
Till in her pap the winged weapon stood

Infix'd, and deeply drunk the purple blood.
Her sad attendants hasten to sustain
Their dying lady, drooping on the plain.
Far from their sight the trembling Aruns
  flies,
With beating heart, and fear confus'd with
  joys;   1180
Nor dares he farther to pursue his blow,
Or ev'n to bear the sight of his expiring foe.
As, when the wolf has torn a bullock's hide
At unawares, or ranch'd a shepherd's side,
Conscious of his audacious deed, he flies,
And claps his quiv'ring tail between his
  thighs:
So, speeding once, the wretch no more
  attends,
But, spurring forward, herds among his
  friends.
  She wrench'd the jav'lin with her dying
  hands,
But wedg'd within her breast the weapon
  stands;   1190
The wood she draws, the steely point re-
  mains;
She staggers in her seat with agonizing
  pains:
(A gath'ring mist o'erclouds her cheerful
  eyes,
And from her cheeks the rosy color flies:)
Then turns to her, whom of her female train
She trusted most, and thus she speaks with
  pain:
" Acca, 't is past ! he swims before my sight,
Inexorable Death; and claims his right.
Bear my last words to Turnus; fly with
  speed,   1199
And bid him timely to my charge succeed,
Repel the Trojans, and the town relieve:
Farewell ! and in this kiss my parting breath
  receive."
She said, and, sliding, sunk upon the plain:
Dying, her open'd hand forsakes the rein;
Short, and more short, she pants: by slow
  degrees
Her mind the passage from her body frees.
She drops her sword; she nods her plumy
  crest,
Her drooping head declining on her breast:
In the last sigh her struggling soul expires,
And, murm'ring with disdain, to Stygian
  sounds retires.   1210
  A shout, that struck the golden stars, en-
  sued;
Despair and rage the languish'd fight re-
  new'd.

The Trojan troops and Tuscans, in a line,
Advance to charge; the mix'd Arcadians
  join.
But Cynthia's maid, high seated, from
  afar
Surveys the field, and fortune of the war,
Unmov'd a while, till, prostrate on the
  plain,
Welt'ring in blood, she sees Camilla slain,
And, round her corpse, of friends and
  foes a fighting train.
Then, from the bottom of her breast, she
  drew   1220
A mournful sigh, and these sad words ensue:
" Too dear a fine, ah much lamented maid,
For warring with the Trojans, thou hast
  paid !
Nor aught avail'd, in this unhappy strife,
Diana's sacred arms, to save thy life.
Yet unreveng'd thy goddess will not leave
Her vot'ry's death, nor with vain sorrow
  grieve.
Branded the wretch, and be his name ab-
  horr'd;
But after ages shall thy praise record.
Th' inglorious coward soon shall press the
  plain: 1230
Thus vows thy queen, and thus the Fates
  ordain."
  High o'er the field there stood a hilly
  mound,
Sacred the place, and spread with oaks
  around,
Where, in a marble tomb, Dercennus lay,
A king that once in Latium bore the sway.
The beauteous Opis thither bent her flight,
To mark the traitor Aruns from the height.
Him in refulgent arms she soon espied,
Swoln with success; and loudly thus she
  cried:
" Thy backward steps, vain boaster, are
  too late;   1240
Turn like a man, at length, and meet thy
  fate.
Charg'd with my message, to Camilla go,
And say I sent thee to the shades below,
An honor undeserv'd from Cynthia's
  bow."
  She said, and from her quiver chose with
  speed
The winged shaft, predestin'd for the deed;
Then to the stubborn yew her strength ap-
  plied,
Till the far distant horns approach'd on
  either side.

The bowstring touch'd her breast, so strong
  she drew;
Whizzing in air the fatal arrow flew.   1250
At once the twanging bow and sounding
  dart
The traitor heard, and felt the point within
  his heart.
Him, beating with his heels in pangs of
  death,
His flying friends to foreign fields bequeath.
The conqu'ring damsel, with expanded
  wings,
The welcome message to her mistress
  brings.
  Their leader lost, the Volscians quit the
  field;
And, unsustain'd, the chiefs of Turnus yield.
The frighted soldiers, when their captains
  fly,
More on their speed than on their strength
  rely.   1260
Confus'd in flight, they bear each other
  down,
And spur their horses headlong to the town.
Driv'n by their foes, and to their fears re-
  sign'd,
Not once they turn, but take their wounds
  behind.
These drop the shield, and those the lance
  forego,
Or on their shoulders bear the slacken'd
  bow.
The hoofs of horses, with a rattling sound,
Beat short and thick, and shake the rotten
  ground.
Black clouds of dust come rolling in the sky,
And o'er the darken'd walls and rampires
  fly.   1270
The trembling matrons, from their lofty
  stands,
Rend heav'n with female shrieks, and wring
  their hands.
All pressing on, pursuers and pursued,
Are crush'd in crowds, a mingled multitude.
Some happy few escape: the throng too late
Rush on for entrance, till they choke the
  gate.
Ev'n in the sight of home, the wretched sire
Looks on, and sees his helpless son expire.
Then, in a fright, the folding gates they
  close,
But leave their friends excluded with their
  foes.   1280
The vanquish'd cry; the victors loudly
  shout;

'T is terror all within, and slaughter all
  without.
Blind in their fear, they bounce against the
  wall,
Or, to the moats pursued, precipitate their
  fall.
  The Latian virgins, valiant with despair,
Arm'd on the tow'rs, the common danger
  share:
So much of zeal their country's cause in-
  spir'd;
So much Camilla's great example fir'd.
Poles, sharpen'd in the flames, from high
  they throw,
With imitated darts to gall the foe.   1290
Their lives for godlike freedom they be-
  queath,
And crowd each other to be first in death.
  Meantime to Turnus, ambush'd in the
  shade,
With heavy tidings came th' unhappy
  maid:
" The Volscians overthrown, Camilla kill'd;
The foes, entirely masters of the field,
Like a resistless flood, come rolling on:
The cry goes off the plain, and thickens to
  the town.''
Inflam'd with rage, (for so the Furies fire
The Daunian's breast, and so the Fates re-
  quire,)   1300
He leaves the hilly pass, the woods in vain
Possess'd, and downward issues on the
  plain.
Scarce was he gone, when to the straits,
  now freed
From secret foes, the Trojan troops suc-
  ceed.
Thro' the black forest and the ferny brake,
Unknowingly secure, their way they take;
From the rough mountains to the plain
  descend,
And there, in order drawn, their line ex-
  tend.
Both armies now in open fields are seen;
Nor far the distance of the space between.
Both to the city bend.   Æneas sees, 1311
Thro' smoking fields, his hast'ning enemies;
And Turnus views the Trojans in array,
And hears th' approaching horses proudly
  neigh.
Soon had their hosts in bloody battle join'd;
But westward to the sea the sun declin'd.
Intrench'd before the town both armies lie,
While Night with sable wings involves the
  sky.

THE TWELFTH BOOK OF THE ÆNEIS

THE ARGUMENT

Turnus challenges Æneas to a single combat:
articles are agreed on, but broken by the Rutili, who wound Æneas. He is miraculously
cur'd by Venus, forces Turnus to a duel, and
concludes the poem with his death.

WHEN Turnus saw the Latins leave the field,
Their armies broken, and their courage
quell'd,
Himself become the mark of public spite,
His honor question'd for the promis'd fight;
The more he was with vulgar hate oppress'd,
The more his fury boil'd within his breast:
He rous'd his vigor for the last debate,
And rais'd his haughty soul to meet his fate.
As, when the swains the Libyan lion chase,
He makes a sour retreat, nor mends his
pace;   10
But, if the pointed jav'lin pierce his side,
The lordly beast returns with double pride:
He wrenches out the steel, he roars for pain;
His sides he lashes, and erects his mane:
So Turnus fares; his eyeballs flash with fire,
Thro' his wide nostrils clouds of smoke ex-
pire.
Trembling with rage, around the court he
ran,
At length approach'd the king, and thus be-
gan:
"No more excuses or delays: I stand
In arms prepar'd to combat, hand to
hand,   20
This base deserter of his native land.
The Trojan, by his word, is bound to take
The same conditions which himself did
make.
Renew the truce; the solemn rites prepare,
And to my single virtue trust the war.
The Latians unconcern'd shall see the fight;
This arm unaided shall assert your right:
Then, if my prostrate body press the plain,
To him the crown and beauteous bride re-
main."   29
To whom the king sedately thus replied:
"Brave youth, the more your valor has
been tried,
The more becomes it us, with due respect,
To weigh the chance of war, which you neg-
lect.
You want not wealth, or a successive throne,
Or cities which your arms have made your
own:
My towns and treasures are at your com-
mand,
And stor'd with blooming beauties is my
land;
Laurentum more than one Lavinia sees,
Unmarried, fair, of noble families.
Now let me speak, and you with patience
hear,   40
Things which perhaps may grate a lover's
ear,
But sound advice, proceeding from a heart
Sincerely yours, and free from fraudful art.
The gods, by signs, have manifestly shown,
No prince Italian born should heir my
throne:
Oft have our augurs, in prediction skill'd,
And oft our priests, a foreign son reveal'd.
Yet, won by worth that cannot be with-
stood,
Brib'd by my kindness to my kindred blood,
Urg'd by my wife, who would not be de-
nied,   50
I promis'd my Lavinia for your bride:
Her from her plighted lord by force I took;
All ties of treaties, and of honor, broke:
On your account I wag'd an impious
war —
With what success, 'tis needless to de-
clare;
I and my subjects feel, and you have had
your share.
Twice vanquish'd, while in bloody fields we
strive,
Scarce in our walls we keep our hopes alive:
The rolling flood runs warm with human
gore;
The bones of Latians blanch the neighb'ring
shore.   60
Why put I not an end to this debate,
Still unresolv'd, and still a slave to fate?
If Turnus' death a lasting peace can give,
Why should I not procure it whilst you
live?
Should I to doubtful arms your youth be-
tray,
What would my kinsmen the Rutulians
say?
And, should you fall in fight, (which
Heav'n defend!)
How curse the cause which hasten'd to
his end
The daughter's lover and the father's
friend?

Weigh in your mind the various chance of
    war;   70
Pity your parent's age, and ease his care."
   Such balmy words he pour'd, but all in
    vain:
The proffer'd med'cine but provok'd the
    pain.
The wrathful youth, disdaining the relief,
With intermitting sobs thus vents his grief:
"The care, O best of fathers, which you
    take
For my concerns, at my desire forsake.
Permit me not to languish out my days,
But make the best exchange of life for
    praise.
This arm, this lance, can well dispute the
    prize;   80
And the blood follows, where the weapon
    flies.
His goddess mother is not near, to shroud
The flying coward with an empty cloud."
   But now the queen, who fear'd for
    Turnus' life,
And loath'd the hard conditions of the
    strife,
Held him by force; and, dying in his death,
In these sad accents gave her sorrow breath:
"O Turnus, I adjure thee by these tears,
And whate'er price Amata's honor bears
Within thy breast, since thou art all my
    hope,   90
My sickly mind's repose, my sinking age's
    prop;
Since on the safety of thy life alone
Depends Latinus, and the Latian throne:
Refuse me not this one, this only pray'r,
To waive the combat, and pursue the war.
Whatever chance attends this fatal strife,
Think it includes, in thine, Amata's life.
I cannot live a slave, or see my throne
Usurp'd by strangers, or a Trojan son."
   At this, a flood of tears Lavinia shed;
A crimson blush her beauteous face o'er-
    spread,   101
Varying her cheeks by turns with white
    and red.
The driving colors, never at a stay,
Run here and there, and flush, and fade
    away.
Delightful change! Thus Indian iv'ry
    shows,
Which with the bord'ring paint of pur-
    ple glows;
Or lilies damask'd by the neighb'ring
    rose.

   The lover gaz'd, and, burning with desire,
The more he look'd, the more he fed the
    fire:
Revenge, and jealous rage, and secret
    spite,   110
Roll in his breast, and rouse him to the
    fight.
Then fixing on the queen his ardent eyes,
Firm to his first intent, he thus replies:
"O mother, do not by your tears prepare
Such boding omens, and prejudge the war.
Resolv'd on fight, I am no longer free
To shun my death, if Heav'n my death de-
    cree."
Then turning to the herald, thus pursues:
"Go, greet the Trojan with ungrateful
    news;
Denounce from me, that, when to-morrow's
    light   120
Shall gild the heav'ns, he need not urge
    the fight;
The Trojan and Rutulian troops no more
Shall dye, with mutual blood, the Latian
    shore:
Our single swords the quarrel shall decide,
And to the victor be the beauteous bride."
   He said, and striding on, with speedy
    pace,
He sought his coursers of the Thracian
    race.
At his approach they toss their heads on
    high,
And, proudly neighing, promise victory.
The sires of these Orythia sent from far, 130
To grace Pilumnus, when he went to war.
The drifts of Thracian snows were scarce
    so white,
Nor northern winds in fleetness match'd
    their flight.
Officious grooms stand ready by his side;⎞
And some with combs their flowing manes |
    divide,   ⎬
And others stroke their chests and gently |
    soothe their pride.   ⎠
   He sheath'd his limbs in arms; a tem-
    per'd mass
Of golden metal those, and mountain brass.
Then to his head his glitt'ring helm he tied,
And girt his faithful fauchion to his side. 140
In his Ætnæan forge, the God of Fire
That fauchion labor'd for the hero's sire;
Immortal keenness on the blade bestow'd,
And plung'd it hissing in the Stygian flood.
Propp'd on a pillar, which the ceiling bore,
Was plac'd the lance Auruncan Actor wore;

Which with such force he brandish'd in his
hand,
The tough ash trembled like an osier wand:
Then cried: " O pond'rous spoil of Actor
slain,
And never yet by Turnus toss'd in vain, 150
Fail not this day thy wonted force; but go,
Sent by this hand, to pierce the Trojan foe !
Give me to tear his corslet from his breast,
And from that eunuch head to rend the
crest;
Dragg'd in the dust, his frizzled hair to soil,
Hot from the vexing ir'n, and smear'd with
fragrant oil ! "
 Thus while he raves, from his wide nos-
trils flies
A fiery steam, and sparkles from his eyes.
So fares the bull in his lov'd female's sight:
Proudly he bellows, and preludes the
fight; 160
He tries his goring horns against a tree,
And meditates his absent enemy;
He pushes at the winds; he digs the strand
With his black hoofs, and spurns the yellow
sand.
 Nor less the Trojan, in his Lemnian arms,
To future fight his manly courage warms:
He whets his fury, and with joy prepares
To terminate at once the ling'ring wars;
To cheer his chiefs and tender son, relates
What Heav'n had promis'd, and expounds
the fates. 170
Then to the Latian king he sends, to cease
The rage of arms, and ratify the peace.
 The morn ensuing, from the mountain's
height,
Had scarcely spread the skies with rosy
light;
Th' ethereal coursers, bounding from the sea,
From out their flaming nostrils breath'd the
day;
When now the Trojan and Rutulian guard,
In friendly labor join'd, the list prepar'd.
Beneath the walls they measure out the ⎫
space;   ⎟
Then sacred altars rear, on sods of ⎬
grass, 180 ⎟
Where, with religious rites, their com-⎟
mon gods they place.   ⎭
In purest white the priests their heads at-
tire,
And living waters bear, and holy fire;
And, o'er their linen hoods and shaded hair,
Long twisted wreaths of sacred vervain
wear.

In order issuing from the town appears
The Latin legion, arm'd with pointed spears;
And from the fields, advancing on a line,
The Trojan and the Tuscan forces join:
Their various arms afford a pleasing sight;
A peaceful train they seem, in peace pre-
par'd for fight. 191
Betwixt the ranks the proud commanders
ride,
Glitt'ring with gold, and vests in purple
dyed;
Here Mnestheus, author of the Memmian
line,
And there Messapus, born of seed divine.
The sign is giv'n; and, round the listed
space,
Each man in order fills his proper place.
Reclining on their ample shields, they stand,
And fix their pointed lances in the sand.
Now, studious of the sight, a num'rous
throng 200
Of either sex promiscuous, old and young,
Swarm from the town: by those who rest
behind,
The gates and walls and houses' tops are
lin'd.
 Meantime the Queen of Heav'n beheld
the sight,
With eyes unpleas'd, from Mount Albano's
height
(Since call'd Albano by succeeding fame,
But then an empty hill, without a name).
She thence survey'd the field, the Trojan
pow'rs,
The Latian squadrons, and Laurentine
tow'rs.
Then thus the goddess of the skies be-
spake, 210
With sighs and tears, the goddess of the
lake,
King Turnus' sister, once a lovely maid,
Ere to the lust of lawless Jove betray'd:
Compress'd by force, but, by the grateful
god,
Now made the Naïs of the neighb'ring flood.
" O nymph, the pride of living lakes," said
she,
" O most renown'd, and most belov'd by me,
Long hast thou known, nor need I to record,
The wanton sallies of my wand'ring lord.
Of ev'ry Latian fair whom Jove misled 220
To mount by stealth my violated bed,
To thee alone I grudg'd not his embrace,
But gave a part of heav'n, and an unenvied
place.

Now learn from me thy near approaching
        grief,
Nor think my wishes want to thy relief.
While fortune favor'd, nor Heav'n's King
        denied
To lend my succor to the Latian side,
I sav'd thy brother, and the sinking state:
But now he struggles with unequal fate,
And goes, with gods averse, o'ermatch'd ⎫
        in might,   230
To meet inevitable death in fight;   ⎬
Nor must I break the truce, nor can
        sustain the sight.   ⎭
Thou, if thou dar'st, thy present aid supply;
It well becomes a sister's care to try."
    At this the lovely nymph, with grief op-
        press'd,
Thrice tore her hair, and beat her comely
        breast.
To whom Saturnia thus: " Thy tears are
        late:
Haste, snatch him, if he can be snatch'd
        from fate:
New tumults kindle; violate the truce:
Who knows what changeful fortune may
        produce ?   240
'T is not a crime t' attempt what I decree;
Or, if it were, discharge the crime on me."
She said, and, sailing on the winged wind,
Left the sad nymph suspended in her mind.
    And now in pomp the peaceful kings
        appear:
Four steeds the chariot of Latinus bear;
Twelve golden beams around his temples
        play,
To mark his lineage from the God of Day.
Two snowy coursers Turnus' chariot yoke,
And in his hand two massy spears he shook:
Then issued from the camp, in arms divine,
Æneas, author of the Roman line;   252
And by his side Ascanius took his place,
The second hope of Rome's immortal race.
Adorn'd in white, a rev'rend priest ap- ⎫
        pears,   ⎪
And off'rings to the flaming altars bears; ⎬
A porket, and a lamb that never suffer'd   ⎪
        shears.   ⎭
Then to the rising sun he turns his eyes,
And strews the beasts, design'd for sacrifice,
With salt and meal: with like officious
        care   260
He marks their foreheads, and he clips their
        hair.
Betwixt their horns the purple wine he
        sheds;

With the same gen'rous juice the flame he
        feeds.
Æneas then unsheath'd his shining sword,
And thus with pious pray'rs the gods
        ador'd:
" All-seeing sun, and thou, Ausonian soil,
For which I have sustain'd so long a toil,
Thou, King of Heav'n, and thou, the Queen
        of Air,
Propitious now, and reconcil'd by pray'r;
Thou, God of War, whose unresisted sway
The labors and events of arms obey;   271
Ye living fountains, and ye running floods,
All pow'rs of ocean, all ethereal gods,
Hear, and bear record: if I fall in field,
Or, recreant in the fight, to Turnus yield,
My Trojans shall encrease Evander's town;
Ascanius shall renounce th' Ausonian crown:
All claims, all questions of debate, shall
        cease;
Nor he, nor they, with force infringe the
        peace.
But, if my juster arms prevail in fight, 280
(As sure they shall, if I divine aright,)
My Trojans shall not o'er th' Italians reign:
Both equal, both unconquer'd shall remain,
Join'd in their laws, their lands, and their
        abodes;
I ask but altars for my weary gods.
The care of those religious rites be mine;
The crown to King Latinus I resign:
His be the sov'reign sway.   Nor will I
        share
His pow'r in peace, or his command in war.
For me, my friends another town shall
        frame,   290
And bless the rising tow'rs with fair La-
        vinia's name."
    Thus he.   Then, with erected eyes and
        hands,
The Latian king before his altar stands.
" By the same heav'n," said he, " and earth,
        and main,
And all the pow'rs that all the three con-
        tain;
By hell below, and by that upper god
Whose thunder signs the peace, who seals
        it with his nod;
So let Latona's double offspring hear,
And double-fronted Janus, what I swear:
I touch the sacred altars, touch the flames,
And all those pow'rs attest, and all their
        names;   301
Whatever chance befall on either side,
No term of time this union shall divide:

No force, no fortune, shall my vows unbind,
Or shake the steadfast tenor of my mind;
Not tho' the circling seas should break their
  bound,
O'erflow the shores, or sap the solid ground;
Not tho' the lamps of heav'n their spheres
  forsake,
Hurl'd down, and hissing in the nether lake:
Ev'n as this royal scepter " (for he bore 310
A scepter in his hand) " shall never more
Shoot out in branches, or renew the birth:
An orphan now, cut from the mother earth
By the keen ax, dishonor'd of its hair,
And cas'd in brass, for Latian kings to
  bear."
  When thus in public view the peace was
    tied
With solemn vows, and sworn on either
  side,
All dues perform'd which holy rites re-
  quire;
The victim beasts are slain before the fire,
The trembling entrails from their bodies
  torn,   320
And to the fatten'd flames in chargers
  borne.
  Already the Rutulians deem their man
O'ermatch'd in arms, before the fight be-
  gan.
First rising fears are whisper'd thro' the
  crowd;
Then, gath'ring sound, they murmur more
  aloud.
Now, side to side, they measure with their
  eyes
The champions' bulk, their sinews, and
  their size:
The nearer they approach, the more is
  known
Th' apparent disadvantage of their own.
Turnus himself appears in public sight 330
Conscious of fate, desponding of the fight.
Slowly he moves, and at his altar stands
With eyes dejected, and with trembling
  hands;
And, while he mutters undistinguish'd
  pray'rs,
A livid deadness in his cheeks appears.
  With anxious pleasure when Juturna
    view'd
Th' increasing fright of the mad multitude,
When their short sighs and thick'ning sobs
  she heard,
And found their ready minds for change
  prepar'd;   339

Dissembling her immortal form, she took
Camertus' mien, his habit, and his look;
A chief of ancient blood: in arms well
  known
Was his great sire, and he his greater son.
His shape assum'd, amid the ranks she ran,
And humoring their first motions, thus
  began:
" For shame, Rutulians, can you bear the
    sight
Of one expos'd for all, in single fight ?
Can we, before the face of heav'n, confess
Our courage colder, or our numbers less ?
View all the Trojan host, th' Arcadian
  band,   350
And Tuscan army; count 'em as they stand:
Undaunted to the battle if we go,
Scarce ev'ry second man will share a foe.
Turnus, 't is true, in this unequal strife,
Shall lose, with honor, his devoted life,
Or change it rather for immortal fame,
Succeeding to the gods, from whence he
  came:
But you, a servile and inglorious band,
For foreign lords shall sow your native
  land,
Those fruitful fields your fighting fathers
  gain'd,   360
Which have so long their lazy sons sus-
  tain'd."
With words like these, she carried her
  design:
A rising murmur runs along the line.
Then ev'n the city troops, and Latians,
  tir'd
With tedious war, seem with new souls in-
  spir'd:
Their champion's fate with pity they lament,
And of the league, so lately sworn, repent.
  Nor fails the goddess to foment the rage
With lying wonders, and a false presage;
But adds a sign, which, present to their
  eyes,   370
Inspires new courage, and a glad surprise.
For, sudden, in the fiery tracts above,
Appears in pomp th' imperial bird of Jove:
A plump of fowl he spies, that swim the
  lakes,
And o'er their heads his sounding pinions
  shakes;
Then, stooping on the fairest of the train,
In his strong talons truss'd a silver swan.
Th' Italians wonder at th' unusual sight;
But, while he lags, and labors in his flight,
Behold, the dastard fowl return anew, 380

And with united force the foe pursue:
Clam'rous around the royal hawk they fly,
And, thick'ning in a cloud, o'ershade the
sky.
They cuff, they scratch, they cross his airy
course;
Nor can th' incumber'd bird sustain their
force;
But vex'd, not vanquish'd, drops the pon-
d'rous prey,
And, lighten'd of his burthen, wings his
way.
Th' Ausonian bands with shouts salute
the sight,
Eager of action, and demand the fight.
Then King Tolumnius, vers'd in augurs'
arts,   390
Cries out, and thus his boasted skill imparts:
"At length 't is granted, what I long de-
sir'd!
This, this is what my frequent vows requir'd.
Ye gods, I take your omen, and obey.
Advance, my friends, and charge! I lead
the way.
These are the foreign foes, whose impious
band,
Like that rapacious bird, infest our land:
But soon, like him, they shall be forc'd to
sea
By strength united, and forego the prey. 399
Your timely succor to your country bring;
Haste to the rescue, and redeem your king."
  He said; and, pressing onward thro' the
crew,
Pois'd in his lifted arm, his lance he threw.
The winged weapon, whistling in the wind,
Came driving on, nor miss'd the mark
design'd.
At once the cornel rattled in the skies;
At once tumultuous shouts and clamors
rise.
Nine brothers in a goodly band there stood,
Born of Arcadian mix'd with Tuscan blood,
Gylippus' sons: the fatal jav'lin flew,   410
Aim'd at the midmost of the friendly crew.
A passage thro' the jointed arms it found, ⎤
Just where the belt was to the body |
bound,   ⎬
And struck the gentle youth extended on |
the ground.   ⎦
Then, fir'd with pious rage, the gen'rous
train
Run madly forward to revenge the slain.
And some with eager haste their jav'lins
throw;

And some with sword in hand assault the
foe.
The wish'd insult the Latine troops em-
brace,   419
And meet their ardor in the middle space.
The Trojans, Tuscans, and Arcadian line,
With equal courage obviate their design.
Peace leaves the violated fields, and hate
Both armies urges to their mutual fate.
With impious haste their altars are o'er-
turn'd,
The sacrifice half-broil'd, and half-unburn'd.
Thick storms of steel from either army fly,
And clouds of clashing darts obscure the
sky;
Brands from the fire are missive weapons
made,
With chargers, bowls, and all the priestly
trade.   430
Latinus, frighted, hastens from the fray,
And bears his unregarded gods away.
These on their horses vault; those yoke the
car;
The rest, with swords on high, run headlong
to the war.
  Messapus, eager to confound the peace,
Spurr'd his hot courser thro' the fighting
prease,
At King Aulestes, by his purple known ⎤
A Tuscan prince, and by his regal crown; ⎬
And, with a shock encount'ring, bore him |
down.   ⎦
Backward he fell; and, as his fate design'd,
The ruins of an altar were behind: 441
There, pitching on his shoulders and his
head,
Amid the scatt'ring fires he lay supinely
spread.
The beamy spear, descending from above,
His cuirass pierc'd, and thro' his body
drove.
Then, with a scornful smile, the victor cries:
"The gods have found a fitter sacrifice."
Greedy of spoils, th' Italians strip the dead
Of his rich armor, and uncrown his head.
  Priest Corynæus arm'd his better hand,
From his own altar, with a blazing brand;
And, as Ebusus with a thund'ring pace 452
Advanc'd to battle, dash'd it on his face:
His bristly beard shines out with sudden
fires;
The crackling crop a noisome scent ex-
pires.
Following the blow, he seiz'd his curling
crown

With his left hand; his other cast him
down.
The prostrate body with his knees he
press'd,
And plung'd his holy poniard in his breast.
　While Podalirius, with his sword, pur-
sued   460
The shepherd Alsus thro' the flying crowd,
Swiftly he turns, and aims a deadly blow
Full on the front of his unwary foe.
The broad ax enters with a crashing ⎤
sound,   ⎟
And cleaves the chin with one continued ⎬
wound;   ⎟
Warm blood, and mingled brains, besmear ⎟
his arms around.   ⎦
An iron sleep his stupid eyes oppress'd,
And seal'd their heavy lids in endless rest.
　But good Æneas rush'd amid the bands;
Bare was his head, and naked were his
hands,   470
In sign of truce: then thus he cries aloud:
" What sudden rage, what new desire of
blood,
Inflames your alter'd minds ?   O Trojans,
cease
From impious arms, nor violate the peace !
By human sanctions, and by laws divine,
The terms are all agreed; the war is mine.
Dismiss your fears, and let the fight ensue;
This hand alone shall right the gods and
you:
Our injur'd altars, and their broken vow,
To this avenging sword the faithless Tur-
nus owe."   480
　Thus while he spoke, unmindful of de-
fense,
A winged arrow struck the pious prince.
But, whether from some human hand it
came,
Or hostile god, is left unknown by fame:
No human hand or hostile god was found,
To boast the triumph of so base a wound.
　When Turnus saw the Trojan quit the
plain,
His chiefs dismay'd, his troops a fainting
train,
Th' unhop'd event his heighten'd soul in-
spires: 489
At once his arms and coursers he requires;
Then, with a leap, his lofty chariot gains,
And with a ready hand assumes the reins.
He drives impetuous, and, where'er he
goes,
He leaves behind a lane of slaughter'd foes.

These his lance reaches; over those he
rolls
His rapid car, and crushes out their souls:
In vain the vanquish'd fly; the victor sends
The dead men's weapons at their living
friends.
Thus, on the banks of Hebrus' freezing
flood,
The God of Battles, in his angry mood, 500
Clashing his sword against his brazen shield,
Lets loose the reins, and scours along the
field:
Before the wind his fiery coursers fly;
Groans the sad earth, resounds the rattling
sky.
Wrath, Terror, Treason, Tumult, and ⎤
Despair   ⎟
(Dire faces, and deform'd) surround the ⎬
car;   ⎟
Friends of the god, and followers of the ⎟
war.   ⎦
　With fury not unlike, nor less disdain,
Exulting Turnus flies along the plain:
His smoking horses, at their utmost speed,
He lashes on, and urges o'er the dead.   511
Their fetlocks run with blood; and, when
they bound,
The gore and gath'ring dust are dash'd
around.
Thamyris and Pholus, masters of the war,
He kill'd at hand, but Sthenelus afar:
From far the sons of Imbracus he slew,
Glaucus and Lades, of the Lycian crew;
Both taught to fight on foot, in battle
join'd,
Or mount the courser that outstrips the
wind.
　Meantime Eumedes, vaunting in the
field,   520
New fir'd the Trojans, and their foes
repell'd.
This son of Dolon bore his grandsire's
name,
But emulated more his father's fame;
His guileful father, sent a nightly spy,
The Grecian camp and order to descry:
Hard enterprise ! and well he might require
Achilles' car and horses, for his hire:
But, met upon the scout, th' Ætolian prince
In death bestow'd a juster recompense.
Fierce Turnus view'd the Trojan from
afar,   530
And launch'd his jav'lin from his lofty car;
Then lightly leaping down, pursued the
blow,

And, pressing with his foot his prostrate
        foe,
Wrench'd from his feeble hold the shining
        sword,
And plung'd it in the bosom of its lord.
" Possess," said he, " the fruit of all thy
        pains,
And measure, at thy length, our Latian
        plains.
Thus are my foes rewarded by my hand;
Thus may they build their town, and thus
        enjoy the land ! "
Then Dares, Butes, Sybaris he slew,   540
Whom o'er his neck his flound'ring courser
        threw.
As when loud Boreas, with his blust'ring
        train,
Stoops from above, incumbent on the main;
Where'er he flies, he drives the rack before,
And rolls the billows on th' Ægæan shore:
So, where resistless Turnus takes his course,
The scatter'd squadrons bend before his
        force;
His crest of horses' hair is blown behind
By adverse air, and rustles in the wind.
This haughty Phegeus saw with high ⎤
        disdain,   550 ⎬
And, as the chariot roll'd along the plain, ⎪
Light from the ground he leapt, and   ⎦
        seiz'd the rein.
Thus hung in air, he still retain'd his hold,
The coursers frighted, and their course
        controll'd.
The lance of Turnus reach'd him as he hung,
And pierc'd his plated arms, but pass'd
        along,
And only raz'd the skin. He turn'd, and
        held
Against his threat'ning foe his ample shield;
Then call'd for aid: but, while he cried in
        vain,
The chariot bore him backward on the
        plain.   560
He lies revers'd; the victor king descends,
And strikes so justly where his helmet ends,
He lops the head. The Latian fields are
        drunk
With streams that issue from the bleeding
        trunk.
While he triumphs, and while the Trojans
        yield,
The wounded prince is forc'd to leave the
        field:
Strong Mnestheus, and Achates often tried,
And young Ascanius, weeping by his side,

Conduct him to his tent. Scarce can he
        rear
His limbs from earth, supported on his
        spear.   570
Resolv'd in mind, regardless of the smart,
He tugs with both his hands, and breaks
        the dart.
The steel remains. No readier way he
        found
To draw the weapon, than t' inlarge the
        wound.
Eager of fight, impatient of delay,
He begs; and his unwilling friends obey.
Iapis was at hand to prove his art,
Whose blooming youth so fir'd Apollo's
        heart,
That, for his love, he proffer'd to bestow
His tuneful harp and his unerring bow. 580
The pious youth, more studious how to save
His aged sire, now sinking to the grave,
Preferr'd the pow'r of plants, and silent
        praise
Of healing arts, before Phœbean bays.
    Propp'd on his lance the pensive hero
        stood,
And heard and saw, unmov'd, the mourning
        crowd.
The fam'd physician tucks his robes around
With ready hands, and hastens to the
        wound.
With gentle touches he performs his part, ⎤
This way and that, soliciting the dart, 590 ⎬
And exercises all his heav'nly art.   ⎦
All soft'ning simples, known of sov'reign
        use,
He presses out, and pours their noble juice.
These first infus'd, to lenify the pain,
He tugs with pincers, but he tugs in vain.
Then to the patron of his art he pray'd:
The patron of his art refus'd his aid.
    Meantime the war approaches to the
        tents;
Th' alarm grows hotter, and the noise
        augments:
The driving dust proclaims the danger ⎤
        near;   600 ⎬
And first their friends, and then their ⎪
        foes appear: ⎪
Their friends retreat; their foes pursue ⎦
        the rear.
The camp is fill'd with terror and affright:
The hissing shafts within the trench alight;
An undistinguish'd noise ascends the sky,
The shouts of those who kill, and groans of
        those who die.

But now the goddess mother, mov'd with grief,
And pierc'd with pity, hastens her relief.
A branch of healing dittany she brought,
Which in the Cretan fields with care she
sought: 610
Rough is the stem, which woolly leafs
surround;
The leafs with flow'rs, the flow'rs with
purple crown'd,
Well known to wounded goats; a sure
relief
To draw the pointed steel, and ease the
grief.
This Venus brings, in clouds involv'd, and
brews
Th' extracted liquor with ambrosian dews,
And od'rous *panacee.* Unseen she stands,
Temp'ring the mixture with her heav'nly
hands,
And pours it in a bowl, already crown'd
With juice of med'c'nal herbs prepar'd to
bathe the wound. 620
The leech, unknowing of superior art ⎫
Which aids the cure, with this foments │
the part; ⎬
And in a moment ceas'd the raging │
smart. ⎭
Stanch'd is the blood, and in the bottom
stands:
The steel, but scarcely touch'd with tender
hands.
Moves up, and follows of its own accord,
And health and vigor are at once restor'd.
Iapis first perceiv'd the closing wound,
And first the footsteps of a god he found.
" Arms ! arms ! " he cries: " the sword and
shield prepare, 630
And send the willing chief, renew'd, to war.
This is no mortal work, no cure of mine,
Nor art's effect, but done by hands divine.
Some god our general to the battle sends;
Some god preserves his life for greater
ends."
The hero arms in haste; his hands in-
fold
His thighs with cuishes of refulgent gold:
Inflam'd to fight, and rushing to the field,
That hand sustaining the celestial shield,
This gripes the lance, and with such vigor
shakes, 640
That to the rest the beamy weapon quakes.
Then with a close embrace he strain'd his
son,
And, kissing thro' his helmet, thus begun:

" My son, from my example learn the ⎫
war, │
In camps to suffer, and in fields to dare; ⎬
But happier chance than mine attend thy │
care ! ⎭
This day my hand thy tender age shall
shield,
And crown with honors of the conquer'd
field:
Thou, when thy riper years shall send thee
forth 649
To toils of war, be mindful of my worth;
Assert thy birthright, and in arms be
known,
For Hector's nephew, and Æneas' son."
He said; and, striding, issued on the plain.
Anteus and Mnestheus, and a num'rous
train,
Attend his steps; the rest their weapons
take,
And, crowding to the field, the camp for-
sake.
A cloud of blinding dust is rais'd around,
Labors beneath their feet the trembling
ground.
Now Turnus, posted on a hill, from far
Beheld the progress of the moving war: 660
With him the Latins view'd the cover'd
plains,
And the chill blood ran backward in their
veins.
Juturna saw th' advancing troops appear,
And heard the hostile sound, and fled for
fear.
Æneas leads; and draws a sweeping train,
Clos'd in their ranks, and pouring on the
plain.
As when a whirlwind, rushing to the shore
From the mid ocean, drives the waves be-
fore;
The painful hind with heavy heart foresees
The flatted fields, and slaughter of the
trees; 670
With like impetuous rage the prince ap-
pears
Before his doubled front, nor less destruc-
tion bears.
And now both armies shock in open field;
Osiris is by strong Thymbræus kill'd.
Archetius, Ufens, Epulon, are slain
(All fam'd in arms, and of the Latian train)
By Gyas', Mnestheus', and Achates' hand.
The fatal augur falls, by whose command
The truce was broken, and whose lance, em-
brued

With Trojan blood, th' unhappy fight re-
new'd.   680
Loud shouts and clamors rend the liquid
sky,
And o'er the field the frighted Latins fly.
The prince disdains the dastards to pursue,
Nor moves to meet in arms the fighting
few;
Turnus alone, amid the dusky plain,
He seeks, and to the combat calls in vain.
Juturna heard, and, seiz'd with mortal fear,
Forc'd from the beam her brother's char-
ioteer;
Assumes his shape, his armor, and his
mien,
And, like Metiscus, in his seat is seen. 690
  As the black swallow near the palace
plies;
O'er empty courts, and under arches, flies;
Now hawks aloft, now skims along the
flood,
To furnish her loquacious nest with food:
So drives the rapid goddess o'er the plains;
The smoking horses run with loosen'd reins.
She steers a various course among the foes;
Now here, now there, her conqu'ring brother
shows;
Now with a straight, now with a wheeling
flight,
She turns, and bends, but shuns the single
fight.   700
Æneas, fir'd with fury, breaks the crowd,
And seeks his foe, and calls by name aloud:
He runs within a narrower ring, and tries
To stop the chariot; but the chariot flies.
If he but gain a glimpse, Juturna fears,
And far away the Daunian hero bears.
  What should he do ! Nor arts nor arms
avail;
And various cares in vain his mind assail.
The great Messapus, thund'ring thro' the
field,
In his left hand two pointed jav'lins held: 710
Encount'ring on the prince, one dart he
drew,
And with unerring aim and utmost vigor
threw.
Æneas saw it come, and, stooping low
Beneath his buckler, shunn'd the threat'n-
ing blow.
The weapon hiss'd above his head, and tore
The waving plume which on his helm he
wore.
Forc'd by this hostile act, and fir'd with
spite,

That flying Turnus still declin'd the fight,
The prince, whose piety had long re-
pell'd
His inborn ardor, now invades the field; 720
Invokes the pow'rs of violated peace,
Their rites and injur'd altars to redress;
Then, to his rage abandoning the rein,
With blood and slaughter'd bodies fills the
plain.
  What god can tell, what numbers can
display,
The various labors of that fatal day;
What chiefs and champions fell on either
side,
In combat slain, or by what deaths they
died;
Whom Turnus, whom the Trojan hero
kill'd;
Who shar'd the fame and fortune of the
field !   730
Jove, could'st thou view, and not avert ⎤
thy sight, |
Two jarring nations join'd in cruel fight, ⎬
Whom leagues of lasting love so shortly |
shall unite !   ⎦
  Æneas first Rutulian Sucro found,
Whose valor made the Trojans quit their
ground;
Betwixt his ribs the jav'lin drove so just,
It reach'd his heart, nor needs a second
thrust.
Now Turnus, at two blows, two brethren
slew;
First from his horse fierce Amycus he
threw:
Then, leaping on the ground, on foot as-
sail'd   740
Diores, and in equal fight prevail'd.
Their lifeless trunks he leaves upon the
place;
Their heads, distilling gore, his chariot
grace.
  Three cold on earth the Trojan hero
threw,
Whom without respite at one charge he
slew:
Cethegus, Tanaïs, Tagus, fell oppress'd,
And sad Onythes, added to the rest,
Of Theban blood, whom Peridia bore.
  Turnus two brothers from the Lycian
shore,
And from Apollo's fane to battle sent, 750
O'erthrew; nor Phœbus could their fate
prevent.
Peaceful Menœtes after these he kill'd,

Who long had shunn'd the dangers of the
field:
On Lerna's lake a silent life he led,
And with his nets and angle earn'd his
bread;
Nor pompous cares, nor palaces, he knew,
But wisely from th' infectious world with-
drew:
Poor was his house; his father's painful
hand
Discharg'd his rent, and plow'd another's
land.
    As flames among the lofty woods are
        thrown   760
On diff'rent sides, and both by winds are
blown;
The laurels crackle in the sputt'ring fire;
The frighted sylvans from their shades
retire:
Or as two neighb'ring torrents fall from
high;
Rapid they run; the foamy waters fry;
They roll to sea with unresisted force,
And down the rocks precipitate their course:
Not with less rage the rival heroes take
Their diff'rent ways, nor less destruction
make.
With spears afar, with swords at hand, they
strike;   770
And zeal of slaughter fires their souls alike.
Like them, their dauntless men maintain
the field;
And hearts are pierc'd, unknowing how to
yield:
They blow for blow return, and wound for
wound;
And heaps of bodies raise the level ground.
    Murranus, boasting of his blood, that
springs
From a long royal race of Latian kings,
Is by the Trojan from his chariot thrown,
Crush'd with the weight of an unwieldy
stone:
Betwixt the wheels he fell; the wheels,
that bore   780
His living load, his dying body tore.
His starting steeds, to shun the glitt'ring
sword,
Paw down his trampled limbs, forgetful of
their lord.
    Fierce Hyllus threaten'd high, and, face
to face,
Affronted Turnus in the middle space:
The prince encounter'd him in full career,
And at his temples aim'd the deadly spear;

So fatally the flying weapon sped,
That thro' his brazen helm it pierc'd his
head.
Nor, Cisseus, couldst thou scape from Tur-
nus' hand,   790
In vain the strongest of th' Arcadian band:
Nor to Cupentus could his gods afford
Availing aid against th' Ænean sword,
Which to his naked heart pursued the
course;
Nor could his plated shield sustain the
force.
Iolas fell, whom not the Grecian pow'rs,
Nor great subverter of the Trojan tow'rs,
Were doom'd to kill, while Heav'n prolong'd
his date;
But who can pass the bounds prefix'd by
fate ?
In high Lyrnessus, and in Troy, he held 800
Two palaces, and was from each expell'd:
Of all the mighty man, the last remains
A little spot of foreign earth contains.
    And now both hosts their broken troops
unite
In equal ranks, and mix in mortal fight.
Seresthus and undaunted Mnestheus join
The Trojan, Tuscan, and Arcadian line:
Sea-born Messapus, with Atinas, heads
The Latin squadrons, and to battle leads.
They strike, they push, they throng the ⎱
scanty space,   810 ⎪
Resolv'd on death, impatient of disgrace; ⎬
And, where one falls, another fills his ⎪
place.   ⎰
    The Cyprian goddess now inspires her
son
To leave th' unfinish'd fight, and storm the
town:
For, while he rolls his eyes around the plain
In quest of Turnus, whom he seeks in vain,
He views th' unguarded city from afar,
In careless quiet, and secure of war.
Occasion offers, and excites his mind
To dare beyond the task he first design'd. 820
Resolv'd, he calls his chiefs; they leave the
fight:
Attended thus, he takes a neighb'ring
height;
The crowding troops about their gen'ral
stand,
All under arms, and wait his high command.
Then thus the lofty prince: " Hear and
obey,
Ye Trojan bands, without the least delay.
Jove is with us; and what I have decreed

Requires our utmost vigor, and our speed.
Your instant arms against the town prepare,
The source of mischief, and the seat of
war.   830
This day the Latian tow'rs, that mate the
sky,
Shall level with the plain in ashes lie:
The people shall be slaves, unless in time
They kneel for pardon, and repent their
crime.
Twice have our foes been vanquish'd on the
plain:
Then shall I wait till Turnus will be slain ?
Your force against the perjur'd city bend:
There it began, and there the war shall
end.
The peace profan'd our rightful arms re-
quires;
Cleanse the polluted place with purging
fires."   840
He finish'd; and, one soul inspiring all,
Form'd in a wedge, the foot approach the
wall.
Without the town, an unprovided train
Of gaping, gazing citizens are slain.
Some firebrands, others scaling ladders
bear,
And those they toss aloft, and these they
rear:
The flames now launch'd, the feather'd
arrows fly,
And clouds of missive arms obscure the
sky.
Advancing to the front, the hero stands,
And, stretching out to heav'n his pious
hands,   850
Attests the gods, asserts his innocence,
Upbraids with breach of faith th' Ausonian
prince;
Declares the royal honor doubly stain'd,
And twice the rites of holy peace profan'd.
Dissenting clamors in the town arise;
Each will be heard, and all at once advise.
One part for peace, and one for war con-
tends;
Some would exclude their foes, and some
admit their friends.
The helpless king is hurried in the throng,
And, whate'er tide prevails, is borne along.
Thus, when the swain, within a hollow
rock,   861
Invades the bees with suffocating smoke,
They run around, or labor on their wings,
Disus'd to flight, and shoot their sleepy
stings;

To shun the bitter fumes in vain they try;
Black vapors, issuing from the vent, in-
volve the sky.
But fate and envious fortune now prepare
To plunge the Latins in the last despair.
The queen, who saw the foes invade the
town,
And brands on tops of burning houses
thrown,   870
Cast round her eyes, distracted with her
fear —
No troops of Turnus in the field appear.
Once more she stares abroad, but still in
vain,
And then concludes the royal youth is slain.
Mad with her anguish, impotent to bear
The mighty grief, she loathes the vital air.
She calls herself the cause of all this ill,
And owns the dire effects of her ungovern'd
will;
She raves against the gods; she beats her
breast;
She tears with both her hands her purple
vest: 880
Then round a beam a running noose she
tied,
And, fasten'd by the neck, obscenely died.
Soon as the fatal news by Fame was
blown,
And to her dames and to her daughter
known,
The sad Lavinia rends her yellow hair
And rosy cheeks; the rest her sorrow
share:
With shrieks the palace rings, and mad-
ness of despair.
The spreading rumor fills the public
place:
Confusion, fear, distraction, and disgrace,
And silent shame, are seen in ev'ry face.
Latinus tears his garments as he goes, 891
Both for his public and his private woes;
With filth his venerable beard besmears,
And sordid dust deforms his silver hairs.
And much he blames the softness of his
mind,
Obnoxious to the charms of womankind,
And soon seduc'd to change what he so
well design'd;
To break the solemn league so long desir'd,
Nor finish what his fates, and those of Troy,
requir'd.
Now Turnus rolls aloof o'er empty plains,
And here and there some straggling foes he
gleans.   903

His flying coursers please him less and less,
Asham'd of easy fight and cheap success.
Thus half-contented, anxious in his mind,
The distant cries come driving in the wind,
Shouts from the walls, but shouts in murmurs drown'd;
A jarring mixture, and a boding sound.
"Alas!" said he, "what mean these dismal cries?
What doleful clamors from the town arise?"
Confus'd, he stops, and backward pulls the reins.   910
She who the driver's office now sustains,
Replies: "Neglect, my lord, these new alarms;
Here fight, and urge the fortune of your arms:
There want not others to defend the wall.
If by your rival's hand th' Italians fall,
So shall your fatal sword his friends oppress,
In honor equal, equal in success."
  To this, the prince: "O sister — for I knew
The peace infring'd proceeded first from you;
I knew you, when you mingled first in fight;
And now in vain you would deceive my sight —   921
Why, goddess, this unprofitable care?
Who sent you down from heav'n, involv'd in air,
Your share of mortal sorrows to sustain,
And see your brother bleeding on the plain?
For to what pow'r can Turnus have recourse,
Or how resist his fate's prevailing force?
These eyes beheld Murranus bite the ground:
Mighty the man, and mighty was the wound.
I heard my dearest friend, with dying breath,   930
My name invoking to revenge his death.
Brave Ufens fell with honor on the place,
To shun the shameful sight of my disgrace.
On earth supine, a manly corpse he lies;
His vest and armor are the victor's prize.
Then, shall I see Laurentum in a flame,
Which only wanted, to complete my shame?
How will the Latins hoot their champion's flight!
How Drances will insult and point them to the sight!

Is death so hard to bear? Ye gods below,   940
(Since those above so small compassion show,)
Receive a soul unsullied yet with shame,
Which not belies my great forefather's name!"
  He said; and while he spoke, with flying speed
Came Sages urging on his foamy steed:
Fix'd on his wounded face a shaft he bore,
And, seeking Turnus, sent his voice before:
"Turnus, on you, on you alone, depends
Our last relief: compassionate your friends!
Like lightning, fierce Æneas, rolling on,   950
With arms invests, with flames invades the town:
The brands are toss'd on high; the winds conspire
To drive along the deluge of the fire.
All eyes are fix'd on you: your foes rejoice;
Ev'n the king staggers, and suspends his choice;
Doubts to deliver or defend the town,
Whom to reject, or whom to call his son.
The queen, on whom your utmost hopes were plac'd,
Herself suborning death, has breath'd her last.
'T is true, Messapus, fearless of his fate,   960
With fierce Atinas' aid, defends the gate:
On ev'ry side surrounded by the foe,
The more they kill, the greater numbers grow;
An iron harvest mounts, and still remains to mow.
You, far aloof from your forsaken bands,
Your rolling chariot drive o'er empty sands."
  Stupid he sate, his eyes on earth declin'd,
And various cares revolving in his mind:
Rage, boiling from the bottom of his breast,
And sorrow mix'd with shame, his soul oppress'd;   970
And conscious worth lay lab'ring in his thought,
And love by jealousy to madness wrought.
By slow degrees his reason drove away
The mists of passion, and resum'd her sway.
Then, rising on his car, he turn'd his look,
And saw the town involv'd in fire and smoke.
A wooden tow'r with flames already blaz'd,

Which his own hands on beams and rafters
　rais'd;
And bridges laid above to join the space,
And wheels below to roll from place to
　place.　　　　　　　　　　　980
"Sister, the Fates have vanquish'd: let us
　go
The way which Heav'n and my hard for-
　tune show.
The fight is fix'd; nor shall the branded
　name
Of a base coward blot your brother's fame.
Death is my choice; but suffer me to try
My force, and vent my rage before I die."
He said; and, leaping down without delay,
Thro' crowds of scatter'd foes he freed his
　way.
Striding he pass'd, impetuous as the wind,
And left the grieving goddess far behind. 990
As when a fragment, from a mountain
　torn
By raging tempests, or by torrents borne,
Or sapp'd by time, or loosen'd from the
　roots —
Prone thro' the void the rocky ruin shoots,
Rolling from crag to crag, from steep to
　steep;
Down sink, at once, the shepherds and their
　sheep:
Involv'd alike, they rush to nether ground;
Stunn'd with the *shock* they fall, and
　stunn'd from *earth* rebound:
So Turnus, hasting headlong to the town,
Should'ring and shoving, bore the squadrons
　down.　　　　　　　　　　1000
Still pressing onward, to the walls he ⎱
　drew,　　　　　　　　　　⎰
Where shafts, and spears, and darts pro-
　miscuous flew,
And sanguine streams the slipp'ry ground
　embrue.
First stretching out his arm, in sign of
　peace,
He cries aloud, to make the combat cease:
"Rutulians, hold! and Latin troops, retire!
The fight is mine; and me the gods require.
'T is just that I should vindicate alone
The broken truce, or for the breach atone.
This day shall free from wars th' Ausonian
　state,　　　　　　　　　　1010
Or finish my misfortunes in my fate."
　Both armies from their bloody work
　desist,
And, bearing backward, form a spacious
　list.

The Trojan hero, who receiv'd from fame
The welcome sound, and heard the cham-
　pion's name,
Soon leaves the taken works and mounted
　walls,
Greedy of war where greater glory calls.
He springs to fight, exulting in his force;
His jointed armor rattles in the course.
Like Eryx, or like Athos, great he
　shows,　　　　　　　　　　1020
Or Father Apennine, when, white with
　snows,
His head divine obscure in clouds he hides,
And shakes the sounding forest on his sides.
The nations, overaw'd, surcease the fight;
Immovable their bodies, fix'd their sight.
Ev'n death stands still; nor from above
　they throw
Their darts, nor drive their batt'ring-rams
　below.
In silent order either army stands,
And drop their swords, unknowing, from
　their hands.
Th' Ausonian king beholds, with wond'ring
　sight,　　　　　　　　　　1030
Two mighty champions match'd in single
　fight,
Born under climes remote, and brought by
　fate,
With swords to try their titles to the state.
　Now, in clos'd field, each other from afar
They view; and, rushing on, begin the war.
They launch their spears; then hand to
　hand they meet;
The trembling soil resounds beneath their
　feet:
Their bucklers clash; thick blows descend
　from high,
And flakes of fire from their hard helmets
　fly.
Courage conspires with chance, and both
　ingage　　　　　　　　　　1040
With equal fortune yet, and mutual rage.
As when two bulls for their fair female
　fight
In Sila's shades, or on Taburnus' height;
With horns adverse they meet; the keeper
　flies;
Mute stands the herd; the heifers roll their
　eyes,
And wait th' event; which victor they shall
　bear,
And who shall be the lord, to rule the lusty
　year:
With rage of love the jealous rivals burn,

And push for push, and wound for wound
    return;
Their dewlaps gor'd, their sides are lav'd in
    blood;   1050
Loud cries and roaring sounds rebellow
    thro' the wood:
Such was the combat in the listed ground;
So clash their swords, and so their shields
    resound.
    Jove sets the beam: in either scale he
    lays
The champions' fate, and each exactly
    weighs.
On this side, life and lucky chance ascends;
Loaded with death, that other scale de-
    scends.
Rais'd on the stretch, young Turnus aims a
    blow
Full on the helm of his unguarded foe:
Shrill shouts and clamors ring on either
    side,   1060
As hopes and fears their panting hearts di-
    vide.
But all in pieces flies the traitor sword,
And, in the middle stroke, deserts his lord.
Now 't is but death, or flight; disarm'd he
    flies,
When in his hand an unknown hilt he spies.
Fame says that Turnus, when his steeds ⎤
    he join'd,   ⎟
Hurrying to war, disorder'd in his mind, ⎬
Snatch'd the first weapon which his haste ⎟
    could find.   ⎦
'T was not the fated sword his father bore,
But that his charioteer Metiscus wore. 1070
This, while the Trojans fled, the toughness
    held;
But, vain against the great Vulcanian shield,
The mortal-temper'd steel deceiv'd his
    hand:
The shiver'd fragments shone amid the sand.
    Surpris'd with fear, he fled along the
    field,
And now forthright, and now in orbits
    wheel'd:
For here the Trojan troops the list sur-
    round,
And there the pass is clos'd with pools and
    marshy ground.
Æneas hastens, tho' with heavier pace —
His wound, so newly knit, retards the
    chase,   1080
And oft his trembling knees their aid re-
    fuse —
Yet, pressing foot by foot, his foe pursues.

    Thus, when a fearful stag is clos'd around
With crimson toils, or in a river found,
High on the bank the deep-mouth'd hound
    appears,
Still opening, following still, where'er he
    steers;
The persecuted creature, to and fro,
Turns here and there, to scape his Umbrian
    foe:
Steep is th' ascent, and, if he gains the land,
The purple death is pitch'd along the
    strand.   1090
His eager foe, determin'd to the chase,
Stretch'd at his length, gains ground at
    ev'ry pace;
Now to his beamy head he makes his way,
And now he holds, or thinks he holds, his
    prey:
Just at the pinch, the stag springs out with
    fear;
He bites the wind, and fills his sounding
    jaws with air:
The rocks, the lakes, the meadows ring
    with cries;
The mortal tumult mounts, and thunders
    in the skies.
Thus flies the Daunian prince, and, flying,
    blames
His tardy troops, and, calling by their
    names,   1100
Demands his trusty sword. The Trojan
    threats
The realm with ruin, and their ancient
    seats
To lay in ashes, if they dare supply
With arms or aid his vanquish'd enemy:
Thus menacing, he still pursues the course,
With vigor, tho' diminish'd of his force.
Ten times already round the listed place
One chief had fled, and t'other giv'n the
    chase:
No trivial prize is play'd; for on the life
Or death of Turnus now depends the strife.
    Within the space, an olive tree had ⎤
    stood,   1111   ⎟
A sacred shade, a venerable wood,   ⎬
For vows to Faunus paid, the Latins' ⎟
    guardian god.   ⎦
Here hung the vests, and tablets were in-
    grav'd,
Of sinking mariners from shipwrack sav'd.
With heedless hands the Trojans fell'd the
    tree,
To make the ground inclos'd for combat
    free.

Deep in the root, whether by fate, or chance,
Or erring haste, the Trojan drove his lance;
Then stoop'd, and tugg'd with force im-
    mense, to free   1120
Th' incumber'd spear from the tenacious
    tree;
That, whom his fainting limbs pursued in
    vain,
His flying weapon might from far attain.
  Confus'd with fear, bereft of human aid,
Then Turnus to the gods, and first to Fau-
    nus pray'd:
" O Faunus, pity ! and thou Mother Earth,
Where I thy foster son receiv'd my birth,
Hold fast the steel ! If my religious hand
Your plant has honor'd, which your foes
    profan'd,
Propitious hear my pious pray'r ! " He
    said,   1130
Nor with successless vows invok'd their aid.
Th' incumbent hero wrench'd, and pull'd,
    and strain'd;
But still the stubborn earth the steel de-
    tain'd.
Juturna took her time; and, while in vain
He strove, assum'd Metiscus' form again,
And, in that imitated shape, restor'd
To the despairing prince his Daunian
    sword.
The Queen of Love, who, with disdain and
    grief,
Saw the bold nymph afford this prompt
    relief,
T' assert her offspring with a greater deed,
From the tough root the ling'ring weapon
    freed.   1141
  Once more erect, the rival chiefs ad-⎫
    vance: ⎪
One trusts the sword, and one the pointed ⎬
    lance;   ⎪
And both resolv'd alike to try their fatal ⎪
    chance.   ⎭
  Meantime imperial Jove to Juno spoke,
Who from a shining cloud beheld the
    shock:
" What new arrest, O Queen of Heav'n,
    is sent
To stop the Fates now lab'ring in th'
    event ?
What farther hopes are left thee to pur-⎫
    sue ?   ⎪
Divine Æneas, (and thou know'st it ⎬
    too,)   1150   ⎪
Foredoom'd, to these celestial seats is ⎪
    due.   ⎭

What more attempts for Turnus can be
    made,
That thus thou ling'rest in this lonely
    shade ?
Is it becoming of the due respect
And awful honor of a god elect,
A wound unworthy of our state to feel,
Patient of human hands and earthly steel ?
Or seems it just, the sister should re-⎫
    store   ⎪
A second sword, when one was lost be- ⎬
    fore,   ⎪
And arm a conquer'd wretch against his ⎪
    conqueror ?   1160   ⎭
For what, without thy knowledge and
    avow,
Nay more, thy dictate, durst Juturna do ?
At last, in deference to my love, forbear
To lodge within thy soul this anxious care;
Reclin'd upon my breast, thy grief unload:
Who should relieve the goddess, but the
    god ?
Now all things to their utmost issue tend,
Push'd by the Fates to their appointed end.
While leave was giv'n thee, and a lawful
    hour
For vengeance, wrath, and unresisted
    pow'r,   1170
Toss'd on the seas, thou couldst thy foes
    distress,
And, driv'n ashore, with hostile arms op-
    press;
Deform the royal house; and, from the
    side
Of the just bridegroom, tear the plighted
    bride:
Now cease at my command." The Thun-
    d'rer said;
And, with dejected eyes, this answer Juno
    made:
" Because your dread decree too well I
    knew,
From Turnus and from earth unwilling I
    withdrew.
Else should you not behold me here, alone,
Involv'd in empty clouds, my friends be-
    moan,   1180
But, girt with vengeful flames, in open
    sight
Engag'd against my foes in mortal fight.
'T is true, Juturna mingled in the strife
By my command, to save her brother's life—
At least to try; but, by the Stygian lake,
(The most religious oath the gods can
    take,)

With this restriction, not to bend the bow,
Or toss the spear, or trembling dart to
      throw.
And now, resign'd to your superior might,
And tir'd with fruitless toils, I loathe the
      fight.   1190
This let me beg (and this no fates with-
      stand)
Both for myself and for your father's land,
That, when the nuptial bed shall bind the
      peace,
(Which I, since you ordain, consent to
      bless.)
The laws of either nation be the same;
But let the Latins still retain their name,
Speak the same language which they spoke
      before,
Wear the same habits which their grand-
      sires wore.
Call them not Trojans: perish the renown
And name of Troy, with that detested
      town.   1200
Latium be Latium still; let Alba reign,
And Rome's immortal majesty remain."
   Then thus the founder of mankind re-
      plies
(Unruffled was his front, serene his eyes):
" Can Saturn's issue, and heav'n's other
      heir,
Such endless anger in her bosom bear ?
Be mistress, and your full desires obtain;
But quench the choler you foment in vain.
From ancient blood th' Ausonian people
      sprung,
Shall keep their name, their habit, and
      their tongue.   1210
The Trojans to their customs shall be ⎤
      tied: ⎟
I will, myself, their common rites pro-   ⎬
      vide;   ⎟
The natives shall command, the foreign-   ⎦
      ers subside.
All shall be Latium; Troy without a name;
And her lost sons forget from whence they
      came.
From blood so mix'd, a pious race shall
      flow,
Equal to gods, excelling all below.
No nation more respect to you shall pay,
Or greater off'rings on your altars lay."
Juno consents, well pleas'd that her desires
Had found success, and from the cloud re-
      tires.   1221
   The peace thus made, the Thund'rer next
      prepares

To force the wat'ry goddess from the wars.
Deep in the dismal regions void of light,
Three daughters at a birth were born to
      Night:
These their brown mother, brooding on ⎤
      her care,   ⎟
Indued with windy wings to flit in air,   ⎬
With serpents girt alike, and crown'd with ⎟
      hissing hair.   ⎦
In heav'n the Diræ call'd, and still at hand,
Before the throne of angry Jove they stand,
His ministers of wrath, and ready still 1231
The minds of mortal men with fears to fill,
Whene'er the moody sire, to wreak his hate
On realms or towns deserving of their fate,
Hurls down diseases, death, and deadly
      care,
And terrifies the guilty world with war.
One sister plague of these from heav'n he
      sent,
To fright Juturna with a dire portent.
The pest comes whirling down: by far
      more slow
Springs the swift arrow from the Parthian
      bow,   1240
Or Cydon yew, when, traversing the skies,
And drench'd in pois'nous juice, the sure
      destruction flies.
With such a sudden and unseen a flight
Shot thro' the clouds the daughter of the
      night.
Soon as the field inclos'd she had in view,
And from afar her destin'd quarry knew,
Contracted, to the boding bird she turns,
Which haunts the ruin'd piles and hallow'd
      urns,
And beats about the tombs with nightly
      wings,
Where songs obscene on sepulchers she
      sings.   1250
Thus lessen'd in her form, with frightful ⎤
      cries   ⎟
The Fury round unhappy Turnus flies,   ⎬
Flaps on his shield, and flutters o'er his ⎟
      eyes.   ⎦
   A lazy chillness crept along his blood;
Chok'd was his voice; his hair with horror
      stood.
Juturna from afar beheld her fly,
And knew th' ill omen, by her screaming
      cry
And stridor of her wings.   Amaz'd with
      fear,
Her beauteous breast she beat, and rent
      her flowing hair.

" Ah me ! " she cries, " in this unequal strife 1260
What can thy sister more to save thy life ?
Weak as I am, can I, alas ! contend
In arms with that inexorable fiend ?
Now, now, I quit the field ! forbear to fright
My tender soul, ye baleful birds of night !
The lashing of your wings I know too well,
The sounding flight, and fun'ral screams of hell !
These are the gifts you bring from haughty Jove,
The worthy recompense of ravish'd love !
Did he for this exempt my life from fate ?
O hard conditions of immortal state, 1271
'Tho' born to death, not privileg'd to die,
But forc'd to bear impos'd eternity !
Take back your envious bribes, and let me go
Companion to my brother's ghost below !
The joys are vanish'd: nothing now remains
Of life immortal, but immortal pains.
What earth will open her devouring womb,
To rest a weary goddess in the tomb ! "
She drew a length of sighs; nor more she said, 1280
But in her azure mantle wrapp'd her head,
Then plung'd into her stream, with deep despair,
And her last sobs came bubbling up in air.
  Now stern Æneas waves his weighty spear
Against his foe, and thus upbraids his fear:
" What farther subterfuge can Turnus find ?
What empty hopes are harbor'd in his mind ?
'T is not thy swiftness can secure thy flight;
Not with their feet, but hands, the valiant fight.
Vary thy shape in thousand forms, and dare 1290
What skill and courage can attempt in war;
Wish for the wings of winds, to mount the sky;
Or hid, within the hollow earth to lie ! "
The champion shook his head, and made this short reply:
" No threats of thine my manly mind can move;
'T is hostile heav'n I dread, and partial Jove."
He said no more, but, with a sigh, repress'd
The mighty sorrow in his swelling breast.

Then, as he roll'd his troubled eyes around,
An antique stone he saw, the common bound 1300
Of neighb'ring fields, and barrier of the ground;
So vast, that twelve strong men of modern days
Th' enormous weight from earth could hardly raise.
He heav'd it at a lift, and, pois'd on high,
Ran stagg'ring on against his enemy,
But so disorder'd, that he scarcely knew
His way, or what unwieldy weight he threw.
His knocking knees are bent beneath the load,
And shiv'ring cold congeals his vital blood.
The stone drops from his arms, and, falling short 1310
For want of vigor, mocks his vain effort.
And as, when heavy sleep has clos'd the sight,
The sickly fancy labors in the night;
We seem to run; and, destitute of force,
Our sinking limbs forsake us in the course:
In vain we heave for breath; in vain we cry;
The nerves, unbrac'd, their usual strength deny;
And on the tongue the falt'ring accents die:
So Turnus far'd; whatever means he tried,
All force of arms and points of art employ'd, 1320
The Fury flew athwart, and made th' endeavor void.
  A thousand various thoughts his soul confound;
He star'd about, nor aid nor issue found;
His own men stop the pass, and his own walls surround.
Once more he pauses, and looks out again,
And seeks the goddess charioteer in vain.
Trembling he views the thund'ring chief advance,
And brandishing aloft the deadly lance:
Amaz'd he cow'rs beneath his conqu'ring foe,
Forgets to ward, and waits the coming blow. 1330
Astonish'd while he stands, and fix'd with fear,
Aim'd at his shield he sees th' impending spear.

The hero measur'd first, with narrow
    view,
The destin'd mark; and, rising as he
    threw,
With its full swing the fatal weapon flew.
Not with less rage the rattling thunder
    falls,
Or stones from batt'ring-engines break the
    walls:
Swift as a whirlwind, from an arm so strong,
The lance drove on, and bore the death
    along.
Naught could his sev'nfold shield the
    prince avail,   1340
Nor aught, beneath his arms, the coat of
    mail:
It pierc'd thro' all, and with a grisly
    wound
Transfix'd his thigh, and doubled him to
    ground.
With groans the Latins rend the vaulted
    sky:
Woods, hills, and valleys, to the voice
    reply.
Now low on earth the lofty chief is laid,
With eyes cast upward, and with arms
    display'd,
And, recreant, thus to the proud victor
    pray'd:
"I know my death deserv'd, nor hope to
    live:
Use what the gods and thy good fortune
    give.   1350
Yet think, O think, if mercy may be
    shown —
Thou hadst a father once, and hast a son —
Pity my sire, now sinking to the grave;
And for Anchises' sake old Daunus save!
Or, if thy vow'd revenge pursue my death,
Give to my friends my body void of
    breath!
The Latian chiefs have seen me beg my
    life;
Thine is the conquest, thine the royal
    wife:
Against a yielded man, 't is mean ignoble
    strife."
In deep suspense the Trojan seem'd to
    stand,   1360
And, just prepar'd to strike, repress'd his
    hand.
He roll'd his eyes, and ev'ry moment felt
His manly soul with more compassion melt;
When, casting down a casual glance, he
    spied

The golden belt that glitter'd on his side,
The fatal spoils which haughty Turnus
    tore
From dying Pallas, and in triumph wore.
Then, rous'd anew to wrath, he loudly cries
(Flames, while he spoke, came flashing
    from his eyes):
"Traitor, dost thou, dost thou to grace
    pretend,   1370
Clad, as thou art, in trophies of my friend?
To his sad soul a grateful off'ring go!
'T is Pallas, Pallas gives this deadly blow."
He rais'd his arm aloft, and, at the word,
Deep in his bosom drove the shining sword.
The streaming blood distain'd his arms
    around,
And the disdainful soul came rushing thro'
    the wound.

FINIS

POSTSCRIPT TO THE READER

WHAT Virgil wrote in the vigor of his age, in plenty and at ease, I have undertaken to *translate* in my declining years; struggling with wants, oppress'd with sickness, curb'd in my genius, liable to be misconstrued in all I write; and my judges, if they are not very equitable, already prejudic'd against me, by the *lying character* which has been given them of my morals. Yet, steady to my principles, and not dispirited with my afflictions, I have, by the blessing of God on my endeavors, overcome all difficulties, and, in some measure, acquitted myself of the debt which I ow'd the public when I undertook this work. In the first place, therefore, I thankfully acknowledge to the Almighty Power the assistance he has given me in the beginning, the prosecution, and *conclusion* of my present studies, which are more happily perform'd than I could have promis'd to myself, when I labor'd under such discouragements. For what I have done, imperfect as it is for want of health and leisure to correct it, will be judg'd in after ages, and possibly in the present, to be no dishonor to my native country, whose language and poetry would be more esteem'd abroad, if they were better understood. Somewhat (give me leave to say) I have added to both of them in the choice of *words*, and harmony of numbers, which were wanting (especially the last) in all our poets, even in those who, being endued with genius, yet have not cultivated their mother tongue with sufficient care; or, relying on the beauty of their thoughts, have judg'd the ornament of words, and sweetness of sound, unnecessary. One is for raking in Chaucer (our English Ennius) for antiquated words, which are never to be reviv'd but when sound or significancy is wanting in the present language. But many of his deserve not this redemption, any more than the crowds of men who daily die, or are slain for sixpence in a battle, merit to be restor'd to life, if a wish could revive them. Others have no ear for verse, nor choice of words, nor distinction of thoughts; but mingle farthings with their gold, to make up the sum. Here is a field of satire open'd to me; but, since the Revolution, I have wholly renounc'd that talent: for who would give physic to the great, when he is uncall'd — to do his patient no good, and indanger himself for his prescription? Neither am I ignorant, but I may justly be condemn'd for many of those faults of which I have too liberally arraign'd others:

Cynthius aurem vellit, et admonuit.

'T is enough for me, if the Government will let me pass unquestion'd. In the mean time, I am oblig'd, in gratitude, to return my thanks to many of them, who have not only distinguish'd me from others of the same party, by a particular exception of grace, but, without considering the man, have been bountiful to the poet; have encourag'd Virgil to speak such English as I could teach him, and rewarded his interpreter for the pains he has taken in bringing him over into Britain, by defraying the charges of his voyage. Even Cerberus, when he had receiv'd the sop, permitted Æneas to pass freely to Elysium. Had it been offer'd me, and I had refus'd it, yet still some gratitude is due to such who were willing to oblige me; but how much more to those from whom I have receiv'd the favors which they have offer'd to one of a different persuasion! Amongst whom I cannot omit naming the Earls of Darby and of Peterborough. To the first of these I have not the honor to be known; and therefore his liberality [was] as much unexpected as it was undeserv'd. The present Earl of Peterborough has been pleas'd long since to accept the tenders of my service: his favors are so frequent to me that I receive them almost by prescription. No difference of interests or opinion have been able to withdraw his protection from me; and I might justly be condemn'd for the most unthankful of mankind, if I did not always preserve for him a most profound respect and inviolable gratitude. I must also add, that, if the last Æneid shine amongst its fellows, 't is owing to the commands of Sir William Trumball, one of the principal secretaries of state, who recommended it, as his favorite. to my care; and, for his sake particularly, I have made it mine: for who would confess weariness, when he enjoin'd a

fresh labor? I could not but invoke the assistance of a Muse, for this last office:

Extremum hunc, Arethusa —
—— Negat quis carmina Gallo ?

Neither am I to forget the noble present which was made me by Gilbert Dolben, Esq., the worthy son of the late Archbishop of York, who, when I began this work, enrich'd me with all the several editions of Virgil, and all the commentaries of those editions in Latine; amongst which I could not but prefer the Dolphin's, as the last, the shortest, and the most judicious Fabrini I had also sent me from Italy; but either he understands Virgil very imperfectly, or I have no knowledge of my author.

Being invited by that worthy gentleman, Sir William Bowyer, to Denham Court, I translated the *First Georgic* at his house, and the greatest part of the last Æneid. A more friendly entertainment no man ever found. No wonder, therefore, if both those versions surpass the rest, and own the satisfaction I receiv'd in his converse, with whom I had the honor to be bred in Cambridge, and in the same college. The *Seventh Æneid* was made English at Burleigh, the magnificent abode of the Earl of Exeter. In a village belonging to his family I was born; and under his roof I endeavor'd to make that Æneid appear in English with as much luster as I could; tho' my author has not given the finishing strokes either to it, or to the *Eleventh*, as I perhaps could prove in both, if I durst presume to criticise my master.

By a letter from Will. Walsh, of Abberley, Esq., (who has so long honor'd me with his friendship, and who, without flattery, is the best critic of our nation.) I have been inform'd that his Grace the Duke of Shrewsbury has procur'd a printed copy of the *Pastorals, Georgics,* and six first Æneids. from my bookseller, and has read them in the country, together with my friend. This noble person having been pleas'd to give them a commendation, which I presume not to insert, has made me vain enough to boast of so great a favor, and to think I have succeeded beyond my hopes; the character of his excellent judgment, the acuteness of his wit, and his general knowledge of good letters, being known as well to all the world, as the sweetness of his disposition, his humanity, his easiness of access, and desire of obliging those who stand in need of his protection, are known to all who have approach'd him, and to me in particular, who have formerly had the honor of his conversation. Whoever has given the world the translation of part of the *Third Georgic,* which he calls *The Power of Love,* has put me to sufficient pains to make my own not inferior to his; as my Lord Roscommon's *Silenus* had formerly given me the same trouble. The most ingenious Mr. Addison of Oxford has also been as troublesome to me as the other two, and on the same account. After his *Bees*, my latter swarm is scarcely worth the hiving. Mr. Cowley's *Praise of a Country Life* is excellent, but 't is rather an imitation of Virgil than a version. That I have recover'd, in some measure, the health which I had lost by too much application to this work, is owing, next to God's mercy, to the skill and care of Dr. Gibbons and Dr. Hobbs, the two ornaments of their profession, whom I can only pay by this acknowledgment. The whole faculty has always been ready to oblige me, and the only one of them who endeavor'd to defame me had it not in his power. I desire pardon from my readers for saying so much in relation to myself, which concerns not them; and, with my acknowledgments to all my subscribers, have only to add, that the few *Notes* which follow are *par manière d'acquit*, because I had oblig'd myself by articles to do somewhat of that kind. These scattering observations are rather guesses at my author's meaning in some passages than proofs that so he meant. The unlearn'd may have recourse to any poetical dictionary in English, for the names of persons, places, or fables, which the learned need not; but that little which I say is either new or necessary. And the first of these qualifications never fails to invite a reader, if not to please him.

NOTES AND OBSERVATIONS ON VIRGIL'S WORKS IN ENGLISH

PASTORAL I, line 60. *There first the youth of heavenly birth I view'd.* Virgil means Octavius Cæsar, heir to Julius, who perhaps had not arriv'd to his twentieth year when Virgil saw him first. *Vide* his *Life.* Of heavenly birth, or heavenly blood, because the Julian family was deriv'd from Julus, son to Æneas, and grandson to Venus.

PAST. II, line 65. *The short narcissus.* That is, of short continuance.

PAST. III, line 95. *For him, the god of shepherds and their sheep.* Phœbus, not Pan, is here call'd the god of shepherds. The poet alludes to the same story which he touches in the beginning of the *Second Georgic*, where he calls Phœbus the Amphrysian shepherd, because he fed the sheep and oxen of Admetus (with whom he was in love) on the hill Amphrysus.

PAST. IV, line 72. *Begin, auspicious boy, &c.* In Latin thus, *Incipe, parve puer, risu cognoscere matrem, &c.* I have translated the passage to this sense; that the infant, smiling on his mother, singles her out from the rest of the company about him. Erythræus, Bembus, and Joseph

Scaliger are of this opinion. Yet they and I may be mistaken; for, immediately after, we find these words, *cui non risere parentes*, which imply another sense, as if the parents smil'd on the newborn infant; and that the babe on whom they vouchsaf'd not to smile was born to ill fortune. For they tell a story, that when Vulcan, the only son of Jupiter and Juno, came into the world, he was so hard-favor'd that both his parents frown'd on him, and Jupiter threw him out of heaven: he fell on the island Lemnos, and was lame ever afterwards. The last line of the pastoral seems to justify this sense: *Nec deus hunc mensa, dea nec dignata cubili est.* For, tho' he married Venus, yet his mother Juno was not present at the nuptials to bless them; as appears by his wife's incontinence. They say also that he was banish'd from the banquets of the gods. If so, that punishment could be of no long continuance; for Homer makes him present at their feasts, and composing a quarrel betwixt his parents with a bowl of nectar. The matter is of no great consequence; and therefore I adhere to my translation, for these two reasons. First, Virgil had this following line, *Matri longa decem tulerunt fastidia menses*, as if the infant's smiling on his mother was a reward to her for bearing him ten months in her body, four weeks longer than the usual time. Secondly, Catullus is cited by Joseph Scaliger as favoring this opinion, in his *Epithalamium* of Manlius Torquatus:

> *Torquatus, volo, parvolus,*
> *Matris e gremio suæ*
> *Porrigens teneras manus,*
> *Dulce rideat ad patrem, &c.*

What if I should steer betwixt the two extremes, and conclude that the infant who was to be happy must not only smile on his parents, but also they on him? For Scaliger notes that the infants who smil'd not at their birth were observ'd to be ἀγέλαστοι, or sullen (as I have translated it) during all their life; and Servius and almost all the modern commentators affirm that no child was thought fortunate on whom his parents smil'd not at his birth. I observe farther, that the ancients thought the infant who came into the world at the end of the tenth month was born to some extraordinary fortune, good or bad. Such was the birth of the late Prince of Condé's father, of whom his mother was not brought to bed till almost eleven months were expir'd after his father's death; yet the College of Physicians at Paris concluded he was lawfully begotten. My ingenious friend, Anthony Henley, Esq., desir'd me to make a note on this passage of Virgil; adding (what I had not read) that the Jews have been so superstitious as to observe not only the first look or action of an infant, but also the first word which the parent or any of the assistants spoke after the birth; and from thence they gave a name to the child, alluding to it.

PAST. VI. My Lord Roscommon's notes on this pastoral are equal to his excellent translation of it; and thither I refer the reader.

PAST. VIII. The *Eighth* and *Tenth Pastorals* are already translated to all manner of advantage by my excellent friend Mr. Stafford. So is the episode of Camilla, in the *Eleventh Æneid.* This *Eighth Pastoral* is copied by our author from two *Bucolics* of Theocritus. Spenser has follow'd both Virgil and Theocritus in the charms which he employs for curing Britomartis of her love. But he had also our poet's *Ceiris* in his eye ; for there not only the inchantments are to be found, but also the very name of Britomartis.

PAST. IX. In the *Ninth Pastoral* Virgil has made a collection of many scattering passages which he had translated from Theocritus, and here he has bound them into a nosegay.

GEORGIC I. The poetry of this book is more sublime than any part of Virgil, if I have any taste. And if ever I have copied his majestic style, 't is here. The compliment he makes Augustus, almost in the beginning, is ill imitated by his successors, Lucan and Statius. They dedicated to tyrants, and their flatteries are gross and fulsome. Virgil's address is both more lofty and more just. In the three last lines of this *Georgic,* I think I have discover'd a secret compliment to the emperor which none of the commentators have observ'd. Virgil had just before describ'd the miseries which Rome had undergone betwixt the triumvirs and the commonwealth party ; in the close of all, he seems to excuse the crimes committed by his patron Cæsar, as if he were constrain'd against his own temper to those violent proceedings, by the necessity of the times in general, but more particularly by his two partners, Anthony and Lepidus :

Fertur equis auriga, nec audit currus habenas.

They were the headstrong horses who hurried Octavius, the trembling charioteer, along, and were deaf to his reclaiming them. I observe, farther, that the present wars, in which all Europe and a part of Asia are ingag'd at present, are wag'd in the same places here describ'd :

Atque hinc Euphrates, illinc Germania bellum, &c.

as if Virgil had prophesied of this age.

GEOR. II. The *Praises of Italy* (translated by the learned and every way excellent Mr. Chetwood), which are printed in one of my *Miscellany Poems,* are the greatest ornament of this book : wherein, for want of sufficient skill in gardening, agriculture, &c., I may possibly be mistaken in some terms. But concerning grafting, my honor'd friend Sir William Bowyer has assur'd me that Virgil has shewn more of poetry than skill, at least in relation to our more northern climates ; and that many of our stocks will not receive such grafts as our poet tells us would bear in Italy. Nature has conspir'd with art to make the garden at Denham Court, of Sir William's own plantation, one of the most delicious spots of ground in England : it contains not above five acres (just the compass of Alcinoüs his garden, describ'd in the *Odysses*) ; but Virgil says, in this very *Georgic :*

—— *Laudato ingentia rura ;*
Exiguum colito.

GEOR. III, line 45. *Next him Niphates, with inverted urn,* &c. It has been objected to me that I understood not this passage of Virgil, because I call Niphates a river, which is a mountain in Armenia. But the river arising from the same mountain is also call'd Niphates ; and, having spoken of Nile before, I might reasonably think that Virgil rather meant to couple two rivers than a river and a mountain.

Line 224. *The male has done,* &c. The transition is obscure in Virgil. He began with cows, then proceeds to treat of horses, now returns to cows.

Line 476. *Till the new Ram receives th' exalted sun.* Astrologers tell us that the sun receives his exaltation in the sign Aries : Virgil perfectly understood both astronomy and astrology.

GEOR. IV, line 27. *That, when the youthful prince.* My most ingenious friend, Sir Henry Shere, has observ'd, thro' a glass hive, that the young prince of the bees, or heir presumptive of the crown, approaches the king's apartment with great reverence, and for three successive mornings demands permission to lead forth a colony of that year's bees. If his petition be granted, which he seems to make by humble hummings, the swarm arises under his conduct ; if the answer be, *le roi s'avisera,* that is, if the old monarch think it not convenient for the public good to part with so many of his subjects, the next morning the prince is found dead before the threshold of the palace.

Line 477. The poet here records the names of fifty river nymphs, and for once I have translated them all. But in the *Æneis* I thought not myself oblig'd to be so exact ; for, in naming many men who were kill'd by heroes, I have omitted some which would not sound in English verse.

Line 656. The *episode* of Orpheus and Eurydice begins here, and contains the only machine which Virgil uses in the *Georgics.* I have observ'd, in the epistle before the *Æneis,* that our author seldom employs machines but to adorn his poem, and that the action which they seemingly perform is really produc'd without them. Of this nature is the legend of the bees restor'd by miracle, when the receipt which the poet gives would do the work without one. The only beautiful machine which I remember in the modern poets is in Ariosto, where God commands St. Michael to take care that Paris, then besieg'd by the Saracens, should be succor'd by Rinaldo. In order to this, he enjoins the archangel to find Silence and Discord ; the first to conduct the Christian army to relieve the town, with so much secrecy that their march should not be discover'd ; the latter to enter the camp of the infidels, and there to sow dissension among the principal commanders. The heavenly messenger takes his way to an ancient monastery, not doubting there to find Silence in her primitive abode ; but, instead of Silence, finds Discord : the monks, being divided into factions about the choice of some new officer, were at *snic* and *snee* with their drawn knives. The satire needs no explanation. And here it may be also observ'd that ambition, jealousy, and worldly interest, and point of honor, had made variance both in the *cloister* and the camp; and strict discipline had done the work of Silence, in conducting the Christian army to surprise the Turks.

ÆNEID I, line 111. *And make thee father of a happy line.* This was an obliging promise to Æolus, who had been so unhappy in his former children, Macareus and Canace.

Line 196.

The realms of ocean and the fields of air
Are mine, not his.

Poetically speaking, the *fields of air* are under the command of Juno and her vicegerent Æolus. Why then does Neptune call them his? I answer, because, being god of the seas, Æolus could raise no tempest in the *atmosphere* above them without his leave. But why does Juno address his own substitute? I answer, he had an immediate power over the winds, whom Juno desires to employ on her revenge. That power was absolute by land; which Virgil plainly insinuates: for, when Boreas and his brethren were let loose, he says at first, *terras turbine perflant;* then adds, *incubuere mari.* To raise a tempest on the sea was usurpation on the prerogative of Neptune, who had given him no leave, and therefore was inrag'd at his attempt. I may also add, that they who are in a passion, as Neptune then was, are apt to assume to themselves more than is properly their due.

Line 451.

O virgin! . . .
If, as you seem, the sister of the day,
Or one at least of chaste Diana's train.

Thus in the original —

O quam te memorem, virgo ——
Aut Phœbi soror, aut nympharum sanguinis una?

This is a family compliment, which Æneas here bestows on Venus. His father Anchises had us'd the very same to that goddess when he courted her. This appears by that very ancient Greek poem in which that amour is so beautifully describ'd, and which is thought Homer's, tho' it seems to be written before his age.

Line 980.

Her princely guest
Was next her side.

This, I confess, is improperly translated, and according to the modern fashion of sitting at table. But the ancient custom of lying on beds had not been understood by the unlearn'd reader.

ÆNEID II. The destruction of Veii is here shadow'd under that of Troy. Livy in his description of it seems to have emulated in his prose, and almost equal'd, the beauty of Virgil's verse.

ÆNEID III, line 132.

And children's children shall the crown sustain.

Et nati natorum, et qui nascentur ab illis.

Virgil translated this verse from Homer, Homer had it from Orpheus, and Orpheus from an ancient oracle of Apollo. On this account it is that Virgil immediately subjoins these words, *hœc Phœbus,* &c. Eustathius takes notice that the old poets were wont to take whole paragraphs from one another, which justifies our poet for what he borrows from Homer. Bochartus, in his letter to Segrais, mentions an oracle which he found in the fragments of an old Greek historian, the sense whereof is this in English, that, when the empire of the Priamidæ should be destroy'd, the line of Anchises should succeed. Venus therefore, says the *historian*, was desirous to have a son by Anchises, tho' he was then in his decrepid age; accordingly she had Æneas. After this she sought occasion to ruin the race of Priam, and set on foot the intrigue of Alexander (or Paris) with Helena. She being ravish'd, Venus pretended still to favor the Trojans, lest they should restore Helen, in case they should be reduc'd to the last necessity. Whence it appears that the controversy betwixt Juno and Venus was on no trivial account, but concern'd the succession to a great empire.

ÆNEID IV, line 944.

And, "Must I die," she said,
"And unreveng'd? 'T is doubly to be dead!
Yet even this death with pleasure I receive:
On any terms, 't is better than to live."

This is certainly the sense of Virgil, on which I have paraphras'd, to make it plain. His words are these:

—— *Moriemur inultœ?*
Sed moriamur, ait; sic, sic juvat ire sub umbras.

Servius makes an interrogation at the word *sic*; thus: *Sic? Sic juvat ire sub umbras;* which Mr. Cowley justly censures. But his own judgment may perhaps be question'd; for he would retrench the latter part of the verse, and leave it a hemistich — *Sed moriamur, ait.* That Virgil never intended to have left any hemistich, I have prov'd already in the preface. That this verse was fill'd up by him with these words, *sic, [sic] juvat ire sub umbras,* is very probable, if we consider the weight of them; for this procedure of Dido does not only contain that *dira execratio, quœ nullo expiatur carmine,* (as Horace observes in his *Canidia,*) but, besides that, Virgil, who is full of allusions to history, under another name describes the Decii devoting themselves to death this way, tho' in a better cause, in order to the destruction of the enemy. The reader who will take the pains to consult Livy in his accurate description of those Decii thus devoting themselves, will find a great resemblance betwixt these two passages. And 't is judiciously observ'd upon that verse:

—— *Nulla fides populis nec fœdera sunto,*

that Virgil uses, in the word *sunto,* a *verbum juris,* a form of speaking on solemn and religious occasions. Livy does the like. Note also, that Dido puts herself into the *habitus Gabinus,* which was the girding herself round with one sleeve of her vest, which is also according to the Roman *pontifical,* in this dreadful ceremony, as Livy has observ'd; which is a farther confirmation of this conjecture. So that, upon the whole matter, Dido only doubts whether she should die before she had taken her revenge, which she rather wish'd; but, considering that this devoting herself was the most certain and infallible way of compassing her vengeance, she thus exclaims:

Sic, sic juvat ire sub umbras!
Hauriat hunc oculis ignem crudelis ab alto
Dardanus, et nostræ secum ferat omina mortis ?

. Those flames from far may the false Trojan view;
Those boding omens his base flight pursue!

which translation I take to be according to the sense of Virgil. I should have added a note on that former verse,

Infelix Dido, nunc te fata impia tangunt —

which, in the edition of Heinsius, is thus printed. *nunc te facta impia tangunt ?* The word *facta,* instead of *fata,* is reasonably alter'd; for Virgil says afterwards, she died not by fate, nor by any deserv'd death, *nec fato, merita nec morte peribat,* &c. When I translated that passage, I doubted of the sense, and therefore omitted that hemistich, *nunc te fata impia tangunt.* But Heinsius is mistaken only in making an interrogation point instead of a period. The words *facta impia* I suppose are genuine; for she had perjur'd herself in her second marriage, having firmly resolv'd, as she told her sister in the beginning of this *Æneid,* never to love again, after the death of her first husband; and had confirm'd this resolution by a curse on herself, if she should alter it:

Sed mihi vel tellus, optem, prius ima dehiscat, &c.
Ante, pudor, quam te violem, aut tua jura resolvam.
Ille meos, primus qui me sibi junxit, amores
Abstulit: ille habeat secum, servetque sepulcro.

ÆNEID V. A great part of this book is borrow'd from Apollonius Rhodius; and the reader may observe the great judgment and distinction of our author, in what he borrows from the ancients, by comparing them. I conceive the reason why he omits the horse race in the funeral games, was, because he shews Ascanius afterwards on horseback. with his troops of boys, and would not wear that subject threadbare, which Statius, in the next age, describ'd so happily. Virgil seems to me to have excell'd Homer in all those sports, and to have labor'd them the more in honor of Octavius, his patron, who instituted the like games for perpetuating the memory of his uncle Julius; piety, as Virgil calls it, or dutifulness to parents, being a most popular virtue among the Romans.

ÆNEID VI, line 586.

The next, in place and punishment, are they
Who prodigally throw their lives away.

Proxima sorte tenent mœsti loca, qui sibi letum
Insontes peperere manu, lucemque perosi,
Projecere animas, &c.

This was taken, amongst many other things, from the tenth book of Plato *de Republica;* no commentator besides Fabrini has taken notice of it. Self-murther was accounted a great crime by that divine philosopher; but the instances which he brings are too many to be inserted in these short notes. Sir Robert Howard, in his translation of this *Æneid,* which was printed with his poems in the year 1660, has given us the most learned and the most judicious observations on this book which are extant in our language.
Line 733.

Lo ! to the secret shadows I retire,
To pay my penance till my years expire.

These two verses in English seem very different from the Latine:

Discedam, explebo numerum, reddarque tenebris.

Yet they are the sense of Virgil; at least, according to the common interpretation of this place: "I will withdraw from your company, retire to the shades, and perform my penance of a thousand years." But I must confess, the interpretation of those two words, *explebo numerum,* is somewhat violent, if it be thus understood, *minuam numerum;* that is: "I will lessen your company by my departure;" for Deïphobus, being a ghost, can hardly be said to be of their number. Perhaps the poet means by *explebo numerum, absolvam sententiam;* as if Deïphobus replied to the Sibyl, who was angry at his long visit: "I will only take my last leave of Æneas, my kinsman and my friend, with one hearty good wish for his health and welfare, and then leave you to prosecute your voyage." That wish is express'd in the words immediately following, *i decus, i nostrum,* &c., which contain a direct answer to what the Sibyl said before, when she upbraided their long discourse, *nos flendo ducimus horas.* This conjecture is new, and therefore left to the discretion of the reader.
Line 980.

Know, first, that heav'n, and earth's compacted frame,
And flowing waters, and the starry flame,
And both the radiant lights, &c.

Principio cœlum, et terras, camposque liquentes,
Lucentemque globum lunæ, Titaniaque astra, &c.

Here the sun is not express'd, but the moon only, tho' a less, and also a less radiant light. Perhaps the copies of Virgil are all false, and that, instead of *Titaniaque astra,* he writ, *Titanaque, et astra;* and according to those words I have made my *translation.* 'T is most certain that the sun ought not to be omitted, for he is frequently call'd the life and soul of all the world ; and nothing bids so fair for a visible divinity to those who know no better, than that glorious luminary. The Platonists call God the *archetypal* sun, and the sun the visible deity, the inward vital spirit in the center of the universe, or that body to which that spirit is united, and by which it exerts itself most powerfully. Now it was the receiv'd hypothesis amongst the Pythagoreans, that the sun was situate in the center of the world. Plato had it from them, and was himself of the same opinion, as appears by a passage in the *Timæus* : from which noble dialogue is this part of Virgil's poem taken. Line 1156.

Great Cato there, for gravity renown'd, &c.

Quis te, magne Cato, &c.

There is no question but Virgil here means Cato Major, or the Censor. But the name of Cato being also mention'd in the *Eighth Æneid*, I doubt whether he means the same man in both places. I have said in the preface that our poet was of republican principles ; and have given this for one reason of my opinion, that he prais'd Cato in that line,

Secretisque piis, his dantem jura Catonem,

and accordingly plac'd him in the Elysian fields. Montaigne thinks this was Cato the Utican, the great enemy of arbitrary power, and a profess'd foe to Julius Cæsar. Ruæus would persuade us that Virgil meant the Censor. But why should the poet name Cato twice, if he intended the same person ? Our author is too frugal of his words and sense to commit tautologies in either. His memory was not likely to betray him into such an error. Nevertheless I continue in the same opinion concerning the principles of our poet. He declares them sufficiently in this book, where he praises the first Brutus for expelling the Tarquins, giving liberty to Rome, and putting to death his own children, who conspir'd to restore tyranny. He calls him only an unhappy man, for being forc'd to that severe action :

Infelix, utcunque ferent ea facta minores,
Vincet amor patriæ, laudumque immensa cupido.

Let the reader weigh these two verses, and he must be convinc'd that I am in the right, and that I have not much injur'd my master in my translation of them. Line 1143.

Embrace again, my sons, be foes no more ;
Nor stain your country with her children's gore !
And thou, the first, lay down thy lawless claim,
Thou, of my blood, who bear'st the Julian name !

This note, which is out of its proper place, I deferr'd on purpose, to place it here, because it discovers the principles of our poet more plainly than any of the rest.

Tuque prior, tu parce, genus qui ducis Olympo :
Projice tela manu, sanguis meus !

Anchises here speaks to Julius Cæsar, and commands him first to lay down arms ; which is a plain condemnation of his cause. Yet observe our poet's incomparable address ; for, tho' he shews himself sufficiently to be a Commonwealth's-man, yet in respect to Augustus, who was his patron, he uses the authority of a parent, in the person of Anchises, who had more right to lay this injunction on Cæsar than on Pompey, because the latter was not of his blood. Thus our author cautiously veils his own opinion, and takes sanctuary under Anchises ; as if that ghost would have laid the same command on Pompey also, had he been lineally descended from him. What could be more judiciously contriv'd, when this was the *Æneid* which he chose to read before his master ? Line 1221. *A new Marcellus shall arise in thee !* In Virgil thus : *Tu Marcellus eris.*

How unpoetically and badly had this been translated : "Thou shalt Marcellus be ! " Yet some of my friends were of opinion that I mistook the sense of Virgil in my translation. The French interpreter observes nothing on this place, but that it appears by it the mourning of Octavia was yet fresh for the loss of her son Marcellus, whom she had by her first husband, and who died in the year *ab urbe condita* 731 ; and collects from thence that Virgil, reading this *Æneid* before her in the same year, had just finish'd it ; that from this time to that of the poet's death was little more than four years ; so that, supposing him to have written the whole *Æneis* in eleven years, the first six books must have taken up seven of those years ; on which account the six last must of necessity be less correct.

Now, for the false judgment of my friends, there is but this little to be said for them : the words of Virgil in the verse preceding are these :

—— *Si qua fata aspera rumpas* ——

as if the poet had meant : "If you break thro' your hard destiny, so as to be born, you shall be call'd Marcellus." But this cannot be the sense ; for, tho' Marcellus was born, yet he broke not thro' those hard decrees which doom'd him to so immature a death. Much less can Virgil mean: "You shall be the same Marcellus by the transmigration of his soul." For according to the system of our author a thousand years must be first elaps'd before the soul can return into a human body ; but the first Marcellus was slain in the second Punic war ; and how many hundred years were yet wanting to the accomplishing his penance, may with ease be gather'd by computing the time betwixt Scipio and Augustus. By which 't is plain that Virgil cannot mean the same Marcellus, but one of his descendants, whom I call a new Marcellus ; who so much resembled his ancestor, perhaps in his features and his person, but certainly in his military virtues, that Virgil cries out: *Quantum instar in ipso est !* which I have translated :

How like the former, and almost the same !

Line 1235.

Two gates the silent house of Sleep adorn ;
Of polish'd iv'ry this, that of transparent
horn.

Virgil borrow'd this imagination from Homer, *Odysses* the 19th, line 562. The translation gives the reason why true prophetic dreams are said to pass thro' the gate of horn, by adding the epithet *transparent*, which is not in Virgil, whose words are only these :

Sunt geminæ Somni portæ, quarum altera fertur
Cornea ——

What is pervious to the sight is clear ; and (alluding to this property) the poet infers such dreams are of divine revelation. Such as pass thro' the iv'ry gate are of the contrary nature, polish'd lies. But there is a better reason to be giv'n ; for the iv'ry alludes to the teeth, the horn to the eyes. What we see is more credible than what we only hear ; that is, words that pass thro' the portal of the mouth, or "hedge of the teeth ; " which is Homer's expression for *speaking.*
ÆNEID VII, line 109. (*Strange to relate!*) *the flames, involv'd in smoke*, &c. Virgil in this place takes notice of a great secret in the Roman divination : the lambent fires which rose above the head, or play'd about it, were signs of prosperity. Such were those which he observ'd in the *Second Æneid*, which were seen mounting from the crown of Ascanius :

Ecce, levis summo de vertice visus Iüli
Fundere lumen apex.

Smoky flames (or involv'd in smoke) were of a mix'd omen : such were those which are here describ'd ; for smoke signifies tears, because it produces them, and flames happiness. And therefore Virgil says that this ostent was not only *mirabile visu*, but *horrendum.*
Line 367. *One only daughter heirs my crown and state.* This has seem'd to some an odd passage ; that a king should offer his daughter and heir to a stranger prince, and a wanderer, before he had seen him, and when he had only heard of his arrival on his coasts. But these critics have not well consider'd the simplicity of former times, when the heroines almost courted the marriage of illustrious men. Yet Virgil here observes the rule of decency : Lavinia offers not herself ; 'tis Latinus who propounds the match ; and he had been foretold, both by an augur and an oracle, that he should have a foreign son-in-law, who was also a hero ; fathers, in those ancient ages, considering birth and virtue, more than fortune, in the placing of their daughters ; which I could prove by various examples. The contrary of which being now practic'd, I dare not say in our nation, but in France, has not a little darken'd the luster of their nobility. That Lavinia was averse to this marriage, and for what reason, I shall prove in its proper place.

Line 1020.

And where Abella sees,
From her high tow'rs, the harvest of her trees.

I observe that Virgil names not Nola, which was not far distant from Abella ; perhaps because that city (the same in which Augustus died afterwards) had once refus'd to give him entertainment, if we may believe the author of his life. Homer heartily curses another city which had us'd him on the same manner ; but our author thought his silence of the Nolans a sufficient correction. When a poet passes by a place or person, tho' a fair occasion offers of rememb'ring them, 't is a sign he is, or thinks himself, much disoblig'd.
ÆNEID VIII, line 34.

So, when the sun by day, or moon by night,
Strike on the polish'd brass their trembling
light, &c.

This similitude is literally taken from Apollonius Rhodius, and 't is hard to say whether the original or the translation excels. But in the shield which he describes afterwards in this *Æneid*, he as much transcends his master Homer, as the arms of Glaucus were richer than those of Diomedes — χρύσεα χαλκείων.
Line 115.

Æneas takes the mother and her brood,
And all on Juno's altar are bestow'd.

The translation is infinitely short of Virgil, whose words are these :

—— *Tibi*, enim, *tibi maxima Juno,*
Mactat, sacra ferens, et cum grege sistit ad aram—

for I could not turn the word *enim* into English with any grace, tho' it was of such necessity in the Roman rites that a sacrifice could not be perform'd without it. 'T is of the same nature (if I may presume to name that sacred mystery) in our words of consecration at the altar.
ÆNEID IX, line 853.

At the full stretch of both his hands he drew,
And almost join'd the horns of the tough yew.

The first of these lines is all of monosyllables, and both verses are very rough, but of choice ; for it had been easy for me to have smooth'd them. But either my ear deceives me, or they express the thing which I intended in their sound ; for the stress of a bow which is drawn to the full extent is express'd in the harshness of the first verse, clogg'd not only with monosyllables, but with consonants ; and these words, *the tough yew*, which conclude the second line, seem as forceful as they are unharmonious. Homer and Virgil are both frequent in their adapting sounds to the thing they signify. One example will serve for both ; because Virgil borrow'd the following verses from Homer's *Odysses :*

Una Eurusque Notusque ruunt, creberque procellis
Africus, et vastos volvunt ad litora fluctus.

Σὺν δ' Εὖροστε, Νότοστ' ἔπεσεν, Ζέφυροστε δυσαὴς,
Καὶ Βορέης αἰθρηγενετὴς, μέγα κῦμα κυλίνδων.

Our language is not often capable of these

beauties, tho' sometimes I have copied them, of which these verses are an instance.
Line 1094.

> *His ample shield*
> *Is falsified, and round with javelins fill'd.*

When I read this *Æneid* to many of my friends in company together, most of them quarrel'd at the word *falsified*, as an innovation in our language. The fact is confess'd; for I remember not to have read it in any English author, tho' perhaps it may be found in Spenser's *Fairy Queen*. But suppose it be not there, why am I forbidden to borrow from the Italian (a polish'd language) the word which is wanting in my native tongue? Terence has often Greciz'd; Lucretius has follow'd his example, and pleaded for it: *Sic quia me cogit patrii sermonis egestas.* Virgil has confirm'd it by his frequent practice; and even Cicero in prose, wanting terms of philosophy in the Latin tongue, has taken them from Aristotle's Greek. Horace has given us a rule for coining words, *si Græco fonte cadunt;* especially when other words are join'd with them, which explain the sense. I use the word *falsify* in this place to mean that the shield of Turnus was not of proof against the spears and jav'lins of the Trojans, which had pierc'd it thro' and thro' (as we say) in many places. The words which accompany this new one make my meaning plain, according to the precept which Horace gave. But I said I borrow'd the word from the Italian. *Vide* Ariosto, Cant. 26:

> *Ma sì l' usbergo d' ambi era perfetto,*
> *Che mai poter falsarlo in nessun canto.*

Falsar cannot otherwise be turn'd than by *falsified;* for *his shield was fals'd* is not English. I might indeed have contented myself with saying his shield was pierc'd, and bor'd, and stuck with javelins, *nec sufficit umbo ictibus.* They who will not admit a new word may take the old; the matter is not worth dispute.

ÆNEID X, line 241.

> *Now, sacred sisters, open all your spring!*
> *The Tuscan leaders, and their army sing.*

The poet here begins to tell the names of the Tuscan captains who follow'd Æneas to the war; and I observe him to be very particular in the description of their persons, and not forgetful of their manners; exact also in the relation of the numbers which each of them command. I doubt not but as, in the Fifth Book, he gave us the names of the champions who contended for the several prizes, that he might oblige many of the most ancient Roman families, their descendants; and as, in the Seventh Book, he muster'd the auxiliary forces of the Latins on the same account; so here he gratifies his Tuscan friends with the like remembrance of their ancestors, and, above the rest, Mæcenas, his great patron, who, being of a royal family in Etruria, was probably represented under one of the names here mention'd, then known among the Romans, tho', at so great a distance, unknown to us. And for his sake chiefly, as I guess, he makes Æneas (by whom he always means Augustus) to seek for aid in the country of Mæcenas, thereby to indear his protector to his emperor, as if there had been a former friendship betwixt their lines. And who knows but Mæcenas might pretend that the Cilnian family was deriv'd from Tarchon, the chief commander of the Tuscans?

Line 312. *A choir of Nereids, &c.* These were transform'd from ships to sea nymphs. This is almost as violent a machine as the death of Aruns by a goddess in the *episode* of Camilla. But the poet makes use of it with greater art; for here it carries on the main design. These new-made divinities not only tell Æneas what had pass'd in his camp during his absence, and what was the present distress of his besieg'd people, and that his horsemen, whom he had sent by land, were ready to join him at his descent; but warn him to provide for battle the next day, and foretell him good success: so that this *episodical* machine is properly a part of the great poem; for, besides what I have said, they push on his navy with celestial vigor, that it might reach the port more speedily, and take the enemy more unprovided to resist the landing. Whereas the machine relating to Camilla is only ornamental; for it has no effect which I can find, but to please the reader, who is concern'd that her death should be reveng'd.

Line 662. *Nor I, his mighty sire, could ward the blow.* I have mention'd this passage in my preface to the *Æneis*, to prove that fate was superior to the gods, and that Jove could neither defer nor alter its decrees. Sir Robert Howard has since been pleas'd to send me the concurrent testimony of Ovid: 't is in the last book of his *Metamorphoses*, where Venus complains that her descendant, Julius Cæsar, was in danger of being murther'd by Brutus and Cassius, at the head of the commonwealth faction, and desires them to prevent that barbarous assassination. They are mov'd to compassion; they are concern'd for Cæsar; but the poet plainly tells us that it was not in their power to change destiny. All they could do was to testify their sorrow for his approaching death by foreshewing it with signs and prodigies, as appears by the following lines:

> *Talia necquicquam toto Venus aurea cœlo*
> *Verba jacit; superosque movet: qui rumpere quan-*
> *quam*
> *Ferrea non possunt veterum decreta sororum,*
> *Signa tamen luctus dant haud incerta futuri.*

Then she addresses to her father, Jupiter, hoping aid from him, because he was thought omnipotent. But he, it seems, could do as little as the rest; for he answers thus:

> *—— sola insuperabile fatum,*
> *Nata, movere paras? Intres licet ipsa sororum*
> *Tecta trium; cernes illic, molimine vasto,*
> *Ex œre et solido rerum tabularia ferro,*
> *Quæ neque concursum cœli, neque fulminis iram,*
> *Nec metuunt ullas, tuta atque æterna, ruinas*
> *Invenies illic, incisa adamante perenni,*

Fata tui generis.   Legi ipse, animoque notavi ;
Et referam, ne sis etiamnum ignara futuri.
Hic sua complerit (pro quo, Cytherea, laboras)
Tempora, perfectis, quos terræ debuit, annis, &c.

Jupiter, you see, is only library keeper, or *custos rotulorum*, to the Fates ; for he offers his daughter a cast of his office, to give her a sight of their decrees, which the inferior gods were not permitted to read without his leave. This agrees with what I have said already in the preface ; that they, not having seen the records, might believe they were his own handwriting, and consequently at his disposing, either to blot out or alter, as he saw convenient. And of this opinion was Juno in those words, *tua, qui potes, orsa reflectas.* Now the abode of those Destinies being in hell, we cannot wonder why the swearing by Styx was an inviolable oath amongst the gods of heaven, and that Jupiter himself should fear to be accus'd of forgery by the Fates, if he alter'd anything in their decrees ; Chaos, Night, and Erebus being the most ancient of the deities, and instituting those fundamental laws by which he was afterwards to govern. Hesiod gives us the genealogy of the gods, and I think I may safely infer the rest. I will only add, that Homer was more a fatalist than Virgil ; for it has been observ'd that the word τυχη, or *fortune*, is not to be found in his two poems ; but, instead of it, always μοίρα.

ÆNEID XII, line 100.

At this, a flood of tears Lavinia shed ;
A crimson blush her beauteous face o'er-
   spread.
Varying her cheeks by turns with white and
   red.

Amata, ever partial to the cause of Turnus, had just before desir'd him, with all manner of earnestness, not to ingage his rival in single fight ; which was his present resolution. Virgil, tho', in favor of his hero, he never tells us directly that Lavinia preferr'd Turnus to Æneas, yet has insinuated this preference twice before. For mark, in the *Seventh Æneid* she left her father, who had promis'd her to Æneas without asking her consent, and follow'd her mother into the woods, with a troop of Bacchanals, where Amata sung the marriage song, in the name of Turnus ; which, if she had dislik'd, she might have oppos'd. Then, in the *Eleventh Æneid*, when her mother went to the temple of Pallas, to invoke her aid against Æneas, whom she calls by no better name than *Phrygius prædo*, Lavinia sits by her in the same chair or litter, *juxtaque comes Lavinia virgo — oculos dejecta decoros.* What greater sign of love than fear and concernment for the lover ? In the lines which I have quoted, she not only sheds tears, but changes color. She had been bred up with Turnus, and Æneas was wholly a stranger to her. Turnus, in probability, was her first love, and favor'd by her mother, who had the ascendant over her father. But I am much deceiv'd if (besides what I have said) there be not a secret satire against the sex, which is lurking under this description of Vir-

gil, who seldom speaks well of women ; better, indeed, of Camilla than any other, for he commends her beauty and valor, because he would concern the reader for her death. But valor is no very proper praise for womankind, and beauty is common to the sex. He says also somewhat of Andromache, but transiently ; and his Venus is a better mother than a wife ; for she owns to Vulcan she had a son by another man. The rest are Junos, Dianas, Didos, Amatas, two mad prophetesses, three Harpies on earth, and as many Furies under ground. This fable of Lavinia includes a secret moral : that women, in their choice of husbands, prefer the younger of their suitors to the elder ; are insensible of merit, fond of handsomeness, and, generally speaking, rather hurried away by their appetite than govern'd by their reason.

Line 808.

Sea-born Messapus, with Atinas, heads
The Latin squadrons, and to battle leads.

The poet had said, in the preceding lines, that Mnestheus, Seresthus, and Asylas led on the Trojans, the Tuscans, and the Arcadians ; but none of the printed copies which I have seen mention any leader of the Rutulians and Latins but Messapus the son of Neptune. Ruæus takes notice of this passage, and seems to wonder at it ; but gives no reason why Messapus is alone without a coadjutor. The four verses of Virgil run thus :

Totæ adeo conversæ acies, omnesque Latini,
Omnes Dardanidæ ; Mnestheus, acerque Seresthus,
Et Messapus equum domitor, et fortis Asylas,
Tuscorumque phalanx, Evandrique Arcadis alæ.

I doubt not but the third line was originally thus :

Et Messapus equum domitor, et fortis Atinas ;

for the two names of Asylas and Atinas are so like that one might easily be mistaken for the other by the transcribers. And to fortify this opinion, we find afterward, in the relation of Sages to Turnus, that Atinas is join'd with Messapus :

Soli, pro portis, Messapus et acer Atinas
Sustentant aciem. ——

In general I observe, not only in this *Æneid*, but in all the six last books, that Æneas is never seen on horseback, and but once before, as I remember, in the *Fourth*, when he hunts with Dido. The reason of this, if I guess aright, was a secret compliment which the poet made to his countrymen the Romans, the strength of whose armies consisted most in foot, which, I think, were all Romans and Italians. But their wings, or squadrons, were made up of their *allies*, who were foreigners.

Line 1191.

This let me beg (and this no fates withstand)
Both for myself and for your father's land, &c.

The words in the original are these : *Pro Latio obtestor, pro majestate tuorum.* Virgil very artfully uses here the word *majestas,* which the Romans lov'd so well that they appropriated it to themselves: *majestas populi Romani*. This title, applied to kings, is very modern; and that is all I will say of it at present, tho' the word requires a larger note. In the word *tuorum* is included the sense of my translation, *your father's land*, because Saturn, the father of Jove, had govern'd that part of Italy after his expulsion from Crete. But that on which I most insist is the address of the poet in this speech of Juno. Virgil was sufficiently sensible, as I have said in the preface, that whatever the common opinion was concerning the descent of the Romans from the Trojans, yet the ancient customs, rites, laws, and habits of those Trojans were wholly lost, and perhaps also that they had never been; and, for this reason, he introduces Juno in this place, requesting of Jupiter that no memory might remain of Troy (the town she hated), that the people hereafter should not be call'd Trojans, nor retain anything which belong'd to their predecessors. And why might not this also be concerted betwixt our author and his friend Horace, to hinder Augustus from rebuilding Troy, and removing thither the seat of empire, a design so unpleasing to the Romans? But of this I am not positive, because I have not consulted Dacier and the rest of the critics, to ascertain the time in which Horace writ the ode relating to that subject.

Line 1224.

Deep in the dismal regions void of light,
Three sisters at a birth were born to Night.

The father of these (not here mention'd) was Acheron; the names of the three were Alecto, Megæra, and Tisiphone. They were call'd Furies in hell, on earth Harpies, and in heaven Diræ. Two of these assisted at the throne of Jupiter, and were employ'd by him to punish the wickedness of mankind. These two must be Megæra and Tisiphone, not Alecto; for Juno expressly commands her to return to hell, from whence she came; and gives this reason:

Te super ætherias errare licentius auras
Haud pater ipse velit, summi regnator Olympi :
Cede locis.

Probably this Dira, unnam'd by the poet in this place, might be Tisiphone; for, tho' we find her in hell, in the *Sixth Æneid*, employ'd in the punishment of the damn'd:

Continuo sontes ultrix accincta flagello
Tisiphone quatit insultans, &c.,

yet afterwards she is on earth, in the *Tenth Æneid*, and amidst the battle: *Pallida Tisiphone media inter millia sævit*. Which I guess to be Tisiphone, the rather, by the etymology of her name, which is compounded of τίω, ulciscor, and φόνος, *cædes;* part of her errand being to affright Turnus with the stings of a guilty conscience, and denounce vengeance against him for breaking the first treaty, by refusing to yield Lavinia to Æneas, to whom she was promis'd by her father; and, consequently, for being the author of an unjust war; and also for violating the second treaty, by declining the single combat which he had stipulated with his rival and call'd the gods to witness before their altars. As for the names of the Harpies (so call'd on earth), Hesiod tells us they were Iris, Aello, and Ocypete. Virgil calls one of them Celæno: this, I doubt not, was Alecto, whom Virgil calls, in the *Third Æneid*, *Furiarum maxima*, and in the *Sixth* again by the same name: *Furiarum maxima juxta accubat*. That she was the chief of the Furies appears by her description in the *Seventh Æneid;* to which, for haste, I refer the reader.

TRANSLATIONS FROM OVID'S ART OF LOVE AND AMOURS

[The following translations were not published during Dryden's lifetime. On August 30, 1693, Dryden wrote to Tonson: "I have translated six hunderd lines of Ovid; but I believe I shall not compasse his 772 lines under nine hunderd or more of mine" (*Letters*, ed. Ward, p. 58). The words "his 772 lines" show that the reference is to the first book of *The Art of Love*. In December, 1697, Dryden again wrote to his publisher: "You told me not, but the Town says, you are printing Ovid de Arte Amandi; I know my Translation is very uncorrect; but at the same time I know no body else can do it better, with all their pains" (*Ibid.*, pp. 98, 99). The town was evidently mistaken. But in 1704 Tonson included in *Poetical Miscellanies, the Fifth Part,* two episodes from the first book of *The Art of Love* (lines 111–151 and 590–635 of Dryden's translation), under the titles of *The Rape of the Sabines* and *The Meeting of Bacchus with Ariadne;* and likewise two elegies from the *Amores (Amours)*, in versions that he ascribed to Dryden. Finally, in 1709, he published a volume entitled, *Ovid's Art of Love. In Three Books. Together with his Remedy of Love. Translated into English Verse by Several Eminent Hands. To which are added, The Court of Love, a Tale from Chaucer, and The History of Love.* The first book of *The Art of Love* is said to have been "translated, some years since, by Mr. Dryden." The translator of the second book is not named; the third book is ascribed to Congreve. — In the present volume the translation from *The Art of Love* should of course have been placed before that of *The Works of Virgil*. The dates of the versions of the two elegies are unknown.]

OVID'S ART OF LOVE

BOOK I

In Cupid's school whoe'er would take de-
gree,
Must learn his rudiments, by reading me.
Seamen with sailing arts their vessels
move;
Art guides the chariot; art instructs to
love.
Of ships and chariots others know the
rule;
But I am master in Love's mighty school.
Cupid indeed is obstinate and wild,
A stubborn god; but yet the god 's a child,
Easy to govern in his tender age,
Like fierce Achilles in his pupilage: 10
That hero, born for conquest, trembling
stood
Before the Centaur, and receiv'd the rod.
As Chiron mollified his cruel mind
With art, and taught his warlike hands to
wind
The silver strings of his melodious lyre;
So love's fair goddess does my soul inspire
To teach her softer arts, to soothe the
mind,
And smooth the rugged breasts of human-
kind.
Yet Cupid and Achilles each with scorn
And rage were fill'd; and both were god-
dess-born.   20
The bull, reclaim'd and yok'd, the burden
draws;
The horse receives the bit within his jaws;
And stubborn Love shall bend beneath my
sway,
Tho' struggling oft he strives to disobey.
He shakes his torch, he wounds me with
his darts;
But vain his force, and vainer are his arts.
The more he burns my soul, or wounds my
sight,
The more he teaches to revenge the spite.
I boast no aid the Delphian god affords,
Nor auspice from the flight of chattering
birds;   30
Nor Clio, nor her sisters have I seen,
As Hesiod saw them on the shady green:
Experience makes my work a truth so
tried,
You may believe; and Venus be my guide.
Far hence, you vestals be, who bind your
hair;

And wives, who gowns below your ankles
wear.
I sing the brothels loose and unconfin'd, ⎫
Th' unpunishable pleasures of the kind;   ⎬
Which all alike, for love, or money, find. ⎭
You, who in Cupid's rolls inscribe your
name,   40
First seek an object worthy of your flame;
Then strive, with art, your lady's mind to
gain;
And last, provide your love may long re-
main.
On these three precepts all my work shall
move:
These are the rules and principles of love.
Before your youth with marriage is op-
press'd,
Make choice of one who suits your humor
best:
And such a damsel drops not from the sky;
She must be sought for with a curious eye.
The wary angler, in the winding brook,
Knows what the fish, and where to bait his
hook.   51
The fowler and the huntsman know by
name
The certain haunts and harbor of their
game.
So must the lover beat the likeliest grounds,
Th' assemblies where his quarry most
abounds.
Nor shall my novice wander far astray;
These rules shall put him in the ready way.
Thou shalt not sail around the continent,
As far as Perseus, or as Paris went:
For Rome alone affords thee such a store,
As all the world can hardly shew thee
more.   61
The face of heav'n with fewer stars is
crown'd,
Than beauties in the Roman sphere are
found.
Whether thy love is bent on blooming
youth,
On dawning sweetness, in unartful truth;
Or courts the juicy joys of riper growth;
Here mayst thou find thy full desires in
both.
Or if autumnal beauties please thy sight,
(An age that knows to give and take
delight,)
Millions of matrons of the graver sort,   70
In common prudence, will not balk the
sport.
In summer heats thou need'st but only go

To Pompey's cool and shady portico,
Or Concord's fane, or that proud edifice
Whose turrets near the bawdy suburb rise;
Or to that other portico, where stands
The cruel father, urging his commands,
And fifty daughters wait the time of rest,
To plunge their poniards in the bridegroom's
breast;
Or Venus' temple, where, on annual nights,
They mourn Adonis with Assyrian rites. 81
Nor shun the Jewish walk, where the foul
drove,
On Sabbaths, rest from everything but
love;
Nor Isis' temple, for that sacred whore
Makes others what to Jove she was be-
fore.
And if the hall itself be not belied,
Even there the cause of love is often tried;
Near it at least, or in the palace yard,
From whence the noisy combatants are
heard.
The crafty counselors, in formal gown, 90
There gain another's cause, but lose their
own.
There eloquence is nonplus'd in the suit,
And lawyers, who had words at will, are
mute.
Venus, from her adjoining temple, smiles,
To see them caught in their litigious wiles.
Grave senators lead home the youthful
dame,
Returning clients, when they patrons came.
But above all, the playhouse is the place;
There 's choice of quarry in that narrow
chase.
There take thy stand, and sharply look-⎤
ing out, 100
Soon mayst thou find a mistress in the ⎬
rout,
For length of time, or for a single bout. ⎦
The theaters are berries for the fair:
Like ants on molehills, thither they repair;
Like bees to hives, so numerously they
throng,
It may be said, they to that place belong.
Thither they swarm, who have the public
voice:
There choose, if plenty not distracts thy
choice.
To see and to be seen, in heaps they run;
Some to undo, and some to be undone. 110
From Romulus the rise of plays began,
To his new subjects a commodious man;
Who, his unmarried soldiers to supply,

Took care the commonwealth should mul-
tiply;
Providing Sabine women for his braves,
Like a true king, to get a race of slaves:
His playhouse not of Parian marble made,
Nor was it spread with purple sails for
shade.
The stage with rushes or with leaves they
strow'd: 119
No scenes in prospect, no machining god.
On rows of homely turf they sate to see,
Crown'd with the wreaths of every common
tree.
There, while they sit in rustic majesty,
Each lover had his mistress in his eye;
And whom he saw most suiting to his mind,
For joys of matrimonial rape design'd.
Scarce could they wait the plaudit in their
haste;
But, ere the dances and the song were past,
The monarch gave the signal from his
throne;
And, rising, bade his merry men fall on.
The martial crew, like soldiers ready
press'd, 131
Just at the word (the word too was, The
Best)
With joyful cries each other animate;
Some choose, and some at hazard seize their
mate.
As doves from eagles, or from wolves the
lambs,
So from their lawless lovers fly the dames.
Their fear was one, but not one face of ⎤
fear;
Some rend the lovely tresses of their ⎬
hair;
Some shriek, and some are struck with
dumb despair. ⎦
Her absent mother one invokes in vain; ⎤
One stands amaz'd, not daring to com-
plain; 141 ⎬
The nimbler trust their feet, the slow re-
main. ⎦
But naught availing, all are captives led,
Trembling and blushing, to the genial bed.
She who too long resisted, or denied, ⎤
The lusty lover made by force a bride, ⎬
And, with superior strength, compell'd ⎦
her to his side:
Then sooth'd her thus: "My soul's far bet-
ter part,
Cease weeping, nor afflict thy tender heart;
For what thy father to thy mother was, 150
That faith to thee, that solemn vow I pass."

Thus Romulus became so popular;
This was the way to thrive in peace and
    war;
To pay his army, and fresh whores to bring:
Who would not fight for such a gracious
    king !
Thus love in theaters did first improve;
And theaters are still the scene of love:
Nor shun the chariots, and the courser's
    race;
The Circus is no inconvenient place.
No need is there of talking on the hand; 160
Nor nods, nor signs, which lovers under-
    stand.
But boldly next the fair your seat provide;
Close as you can to hers, and side by side.
Pleas'd or unpleas'd, no matter; crowding
    sit,
For so the laws of public shows permit.
Then find occasion to begin discourse;
Enquire whose chariot this, and whose that
    horse:
To whatsoever side she is inclin'd,
Suit all your inclinations to her mind;
Like what she likes: from thence your
    court begin;   170
And whom she favors, wish that he may
    win.
But when the statues of the deities,   ⎫
In chariots roll'd, appear before the   ⎬
    prize;   ⎪
When Venus comes, with deep devotion   ⎭
    rise.
If dust be on her lap, or grains of sand,
Brush both away with your officious hand.
If none be there, yet brush that nothing
    thence;
And still to touch her lap make some pre-
    tense.
Touch anything of hers; and if her ⎫
    train   ⎬
Sweep on the ground, let it not sweep in ⎪
    vain;   180   ⎭
But gently take it up, and wipe it clean;
And while you wipe it, with observing
    eyes,
Who knows but you may see her naked
    thighs !
Observe who sits behind her; and beware,
Lest his incroaching knee should press the
    fair.
Light service takes light minds; for some
    can tell
Of favors won by laying cushions well:
By fanning faces some their fortune meet;

And some by laying footstools for their
    feet.
These overtures of love the Circus gives;
Nor at the swordplay less the lover
    thrives: 191
For there the son of Venus fights his
    prize;
And deepest wounds are oft receiv'd from
    eyes.
One, while the crowd their acclamations
    make,
Or while he bets, and puts his ring to stake,
Is struck from far, and feels the flying
    dart,
And of the spectacle is made a part.
    Cæsar would represent a naval fight,
For his own honor, and for Rome's delight.
From either sea the youths and maidens
    come,   200
And all the world was then contain'd in
    Rome !
In this vast concourse, in this choice of
    game,
What Roman heart but felt a foreign
    flame ?
Once more our prince prepares to make us
    glad;
And the remaining East to Rome will add.
Rejoice, you Roman soldiers, in your ⎫
    urn;   ⎪
Your ensigns from the Parthians shall ⎬
    return,   ⎪
And the slain Crassi shall no longer ⎭
    mourn.
A youth is sent those trophies to demand;
And bears his father's thunder in his hand:
Doubt not th' imperial boy in wars un-
    seen;   211
In childhood all of Cæsar's race are men.
Celestial seeds shoot out before their day,
Prevent their years, and brook no dull
    delay.
Thus infant Hercules the snakes did press,
And in his cradle did his sire confess.
Bacchus, a boy, yet like a hero fought,
And early spoils from conquer'd India
    brought.
Thus you your father's troops shall lead to
    fight,
And thus shall vanquish in your father's
    right.   220
These rudiments you to your lineage owe;
Born to increase your titles, as you grow.
Brethren you had, revenge your brethren
    slain;

You have a father, and his rights maintain.
Arm'd by your country's parent, and your
own,
Redeem your country, and restore his
throne.
Your enemies assert an impious cause;
You fight both for divine and human laws.
Already in their cause they are o'ercome:
Subject them too, by force of arms, to
Rome.   230
Great Father Mars with greater Cæsar ⎫
join,   ⎬
To give a prosperous *omen* to your line: ⎪
One of you is, and one shall be divine.   ⎭
I prophesy you shall, you shall o'ercome:
My verse shall bring you back in triumph
home.
Speak in my verse, exhort to loud alarms:
O were my numbers equal to your arms !
Then will I sing the Parthians' overthrow;
Their shot averse sent from a flying bow:
The Parthians, who already flying fight, 240
Already give an *omen* of their flight.
O when will come the day, by Heaven de-
sign'd,
When thou, the best and fairest of man-
kind,
Drawn by white horses shalt in triumph
ride,
With conquer'd slaves attending on thy
side:
Slaves, that no longer can be safe in ⎫
flight —   ⎪
O glorious object, O surprising sight, ⎬
O day of public joy, too good to end in ⎪
night !   ⎭
On such a day, if thou, and, next to thee,
Some beauty sits, the spectacle to see: 250
If she enquire the names of conquer'd
kings,
Of mountains, rivers, and their hidden
springs,
Answer to all thou know'st; and, if need be,
Of things unknown seem to speak know-
ingly:
This is Euphrates, crown'd with reeds; and
there
Flows the swift Tigris, with his sea-green
hair.
Invent new names of things unknown be-
fore;
Call this Armenia, that the Caspian shore;
Call this a Mede, and that a Parthian
youth;
Talk probably: no matter for the truth. 260

In feasts, as at our shows, new means
abound;
More pleasure there than that of wine is
found.
The Paphian goddess there her ambush
lays;
And Love betwixt the horns of Bacchus
plays:
Desires encrease at ev'ry swilling draught;
Brisk vapors add new vigor to the thought.
There Cupid's purple wings no flight af-
ford;
But, wet with wine, he flutters on the
board.
He shakes his pinions, but he cannot
move;
Fix'd he remains, and turns a maudlin
Love.   270
Wine warms the blood, and makes the
spirits flow;
Care flies, and wrinkles from the forehead
go:
Exalts the poor, invigorates the weak;
Gives mirth and laughter, and a rosy
cheek.
Bold truths it speaks; and spoken, dares
maintain;
And brings our old simplicity again.
Love sparkles in the cup, and fills it
higher:
Wine feeds the flames, and fuel adds to
fire.
But choose no mistress in thy drunken fit;
Wine gilds too much their beauties and
their wit.   280
Nor trust thy judgment when the tapers
dance;
But sober, and by day, thy suit advance.
By daylight Paris judg'd the beauteous
three,
And for the fairest did the prize decree.
Night is a cheat, and all deformities
Are hid, or lessen'd in her dark disguise.
The sun's fair light each error will con-
fess,
In face, in shape, in jewels, and in dress.
 Why name I ev'ry place where youths
abound ?
'T is loss of time, and a too fruitful ground.
The Baian baths, where ships at anchor
ride,   291
And wholesome streams from sulphur foun-
tains glide;
Where wounded youths are by experience
taught,

The waters are less healthful than they
   thought:
Or Dian's fane, which near the suburb lies,
Where priests, for their promotion, fight a
   prize.
That maiden goddess is Love's mortal foe,
And much from her his subjects undergo.
   Thus far the sportful Muse, with myrtle
     bound,
Has sung where lovely lasses may be
    found.   300
Now let me sing, how she who wounds
   your mind,
With art, may be to cure your wounds in-
   clin'd.
Young nobles, to my laws attention lend;
And all you vulgar of my school, attend.
   First then believe, all women may be
    won;
Attempt with confidence, the work is done.
The grasshopper shall first forbear to sing
In summer season, or the birds in spring,
Than women can resist your flattering
   skill:
Ev'n she will yield, who swears she never
   will.   310
To secret pleasure both the sexes move;
But women most, who most dissemble
   love.
'T were best for us, if they would first
   declare,
Avow their passion, and submit to prayer.
The cow, by lowing, tells the bull her
   flame;
The neighing mare invites her stallion to
   the game.
Man is more temp'rate in his lust than they,
And, more than women, can his passion
   sway.
Biblis, we know, did first her love declare,
And had recourse to death in her despair.
Her brother she, her father Myrrha sought,
And lov'd, but lov'd not as a daughter
   ought.   322
Now from a tree she stills her odorous
   tears,
Which yet the name of her who shed 'em
   bears.
   In Ida's shady vale a bull appear'd,
White as the snow, the fairest of the herd;
A beauty spot of black there only rose,
Betwixt his equal horns and ample brows:
The love and wish of all the Cretan cows.
The queen beheld him as his head he
   rear'd;   330

And envied ev'ry leap he gave the herd.
A secret fire she nourish'd in her breast,
And hated ev'ry heifer he caress'd.
A story known, and known for true, I tell;
Nor Crete, tho' lying, can the truth con-
   ceal.
She cut him grass, (so much can Love
   command;)
She strok'd, she fed him with her royal
   hand:
Was pleas'd in pastures with the herd to
   roam;
And Minos by the bull was overcome.
   Cease, queen, with gems t' adorn thy
    beauteous brows;   340
The monarch of thy heart no jewel knows.
Nor in thy glass compose thy looks and
   eyes;
Secure from all thy charms thy lover lies:
Yet trust thy mirror, when it tells thee
   true;
Thou art no heifer to allure his view.
Soon wouldst thou quit thy royal diadem
To thy fair rivals, to be horn'd like them.
If Minos please, no lover seek to find;
If not, at least seek one of human kind.
   The wretched queen the Cretan court
    forsakes;   350
In woods and wilds her habitation makes:
She curses ev'ry beauteous cow she sees:
" Ah, why dost thou my lord and master
   please !
And think'st, ungrateful creature as thou
   art,
With frisking awkwardly, to gain his
   heart ! "
She said, and straight commands, with
   frowning look,
To put her, undeserving, to the yoke;
Or feigns some holy rites of sacrifice,
And sees her rival's death with joyful eyes:
Then, when the bloody priest has done his
   part,   360
Pleas'd, in her hand she holds the beating
   heart;
Nor from a scornful taunt can scarce re-
   frain:
"Go, fool, and strive to please my love
   again."
   Now she would be Europa, Io now:
(One bore a bull, and one was made a cow.)
Yet she at last her brutal bliss obtain'd,
And in a wooden cow the bull sustain'd;
Fill'd with his seed, accomplish'd her desire;
Till by his form the son betray'd the sire.

If Atreus' wife to incest had not run, 370
(But, ah, how hard it is to love but one !)
His coursers Phœbus had not driv'n away,
To shun that sight, and interrupt the day.
Thy daughter, Nisus, pull'd thy purple hair,
And barking sea-dogs yet her bowels tear.
At sea and land Atrides sav'd his life,
Yet fell a prey to his adult'rous wife.
Who knows not what revenge Medea sought,
When the slain offspring bore the father's fault ?
Thus Phœnix did a woman's love bewail;
And thus Hippolytus by Phædra fell. 381
These crimes revengeful matrons did commit:
Hotter their lust, and sharper is their wit.
Doubt not from them an easy victory:
Scarce of a thousand dames will one deny.
All women are content that men should woo;
She who complains, and she who will not do.
Rest then secure, whate'er thy luck may prove,
Not to be hated for declaring love.
And yet how canst thou miss, since womankind 390
Is frail and vain, and still to change inclin'd ?
Old husbands and stale gallants they despise,
And more another's than their own they prize.
A larger crop adorns our neighbor's field;
More milk his kine from swelling udders yield.
First gain the maid; by her thou shalt be sure
A free access and easy to procure:
Who knows what to her office does belong,
Is in the secret, and can hold her tongue.
Bribe her with gifts, with promises, and pray'rs; 400
For her good word goes far in love affairs.
The time and fit occasion leave to her,
When she most aptly can thy suit prefer.
The time for maids to fire their lady's blood,
Is, when they find her in a merry mood;
When all things at her wish and pleasure move:
Her heart is open then, and free to love.

Then mirth and wantonness to lust betray,
And smooth the passage to the lover's way.
Troy stood the siege, when fill'd with anxious care: 410
One merry fit concluded all the war.
If some fair rival vex her jealous mind,
Offer thy service to revenge in kind.
Instruct the damsel, while she combs her hair,
To raise the choler of that injur'd fair;
And, sighing, make her mistress understand,
She has the means of vengeance in her hand:
Then, naming thee, thy humble suit prefer,
And swear thou languishest and di'st for her. 419
Then let her lose no time, but push at all;
For women soon are rais'd, and soon they fall.
Give their first fury leisure to relent,
They melt like ice, and suddenly repent.
T' enjoy the maid, will that thy suit advance ?
'T is a hard question and a doubtful chance.
One maid, corrupted, bawds the better for 't;
Another for herself would keep the sport.
Thy bus'ness may be farther'd or delay'd;
But by my counsel, let alone the maid:
Ev'n tho' she should consent to do the feat, 430
The profit 's little and the danger great.
I will not lead thee thro' a rugged road;
But where the way lies open, safe, and broad.
Yet if thou find'st her very much thy friend,
And her good face her diligence commend,
Let the fair mistress have thy first embrace,
And let the maid come after in her place.
But this I will advise, and mark my words;
For 't is the best advice my skill affords:
If needs thou with the damsel wilt begin,
Before th' attempt is made, make sure to win; 441
For then the secret better will be kept;
And she can tell no tales when once she 's dipp'd.
'T is for the fowler's interest to beware,
The bird intangled should not scape the snare.
The fish, once prick'd, avoids the bearded hook,

And spoils the sport of all the neighb'ring
    brook.
But if the wench be thine, she makes thy
    way,
And, for thy sake, her mistress will betray;
Tell all she knows, and all she hears her
    say.   450
Keep well the counsel of thy faithful spy:
So shalt thou learn whene'er she treads
    awry.
All things the stations of their seasons
    keep;
And certain times there are to sow and
    reap.
Plowmen and sailors for the season stay,
One to plow land, and one to plow the
    sea:
So should the lover wait the lucky day.
Then stop thy suit, it hurts not thy design;
But think, another hour she may be thine.
And when she celebrates her birth at
    home,   460
Or when she views the public shows of
    Rome,
Know, all thy visits then are troublesome.
Defer thy work, and put not then to sea,
For that's a boding and a stormy day.
Else take thy time, and when thou canst,
    begin:
To break a Jewish Sabbath, think no sin;
Nor ev'n on superstitious days abstain;
Not when the Romans were at Allia slain.
Ill omens in her frowns are understood;
When she's in humor, ev'ry day is good.
But than her birthday seldom comes a
    worse;   471
When bribes and presents must be sent
    of course;
And that's a bloody day, that costs thy
    purse.
Be stanch; yet parsimony will be vain:
The craving sex will still the lover drain.
No skill can shift 'em off, nor art remove;
They will be begging, when they know we
    love.
The merchant comes upon th' appointed
    day,
Who shall before thy face his wares dis-
    play.
To choose for her she craves thy kind ad-
    vice;   480
Then begs again, to bargain for the price:
But when she has her purchase in her eye,
She hugs thee close, and kisses thee to
    buy:

" 'T is what I want, and 't is a pen'orth too;
In many years I will not trouble you."
If you complain you have no ready coin;
No matter, 't is but writing of a line,
A little bill, not to be paid at sight;
(Now curse the time when thou wert taught
    to write.)
She keeps her birthday; you must send the
    cheer,   490
And she'll be born a hundred times a year.
With daily lies she dribs thee into cost;
That earring dropp'd a stone, that ring is
    lost.
They often borrow what they never pay;
Whate'er you lend her, think it thrown
    away.
Had I ten mouths and tongues to tell each
    art,
All would be wearied ere I told a part.
    By letters, not by words, thy love begin;
And ford the dangerous passage with thy
    pen.
If to her heart thou aim'st to find the way,
Extremely flatter, and extremely pray. 501
Priam by pray'rs did Hector's body gain;
Nor is an angry god invok'd in vain.
With promis'd gifts her easy mind be-
    witch;
For ev'n the poor in promise may be rich.
Vain hopes a while her appetite will stay;
'T is a deceitful but commodious way.
Who gives is mad, but make her still be-
    lieve
'T will come, and that's the cheapest way
    to give.
Ev'n barren lands fair promises afford, 510
But the lean harvest cheats the starving
    lord.
Buy not thy first enjoyment, lest it prove
Of bad example to thy future love:
But get it *gratis* ; and she'll give thee
    more,
For fear of losing what she gave before.
The losing gamester shakes the box in
    vain,
And bleeds, and loses on, in hopes to gain.
    Write then, and in thy letter, as I said,
Let her with mighty promises be fed.
Cydippe by a letter was betray'd,   520
Writ on an apple to th' unwary maid.
She read herself into a marriage vow;
(And ev'ry cheat in love the gods allow.)
Learn eloquence, ye noble youth of Rome;
It will not only at the bar o'ercome:
Sweet words the people and the senate move;

But the chief end of eloquence is love.
But in thy letter hide thy moving arts;
Affect not to be thought a man of parts.
None but vain fools to simple women
  preach: 530
A learned letter oft has made a breach.
In a familiar style your thoughts convey,
And write such things as present you would
  say;
Such words as from the heart may seem
  to move:
'T is wit enough to make her think you love.
If seal'd she sends it back, and will not
  read,
Yet hope, in time, the business may suc-
  ceed.
In time the steer will to the yoke submit;
In time the restiff horse will bear the bit.
Ev'n the hard plowshare use will wear
  away,   540
And stubborn steel in length of time decay.
Water is soft, and marble hard; and yet
We see soft water thro' hard marble eat.
Tho' late, yet Troy at length in flames
  expir'd;
And ten years more Penelope had tir'd.
Perhaps thy lines unanswer'd she retain'd;
No matter; there 's a point already gain'd:
For she who reads, in time will answer too;
Things must be left by just degrees to
  grow.
Perhaps she writes, but answers with dis-
  dain,   550
And sharply bids you not to write again:
What she requires, she fears you should
  accord;
The jilt would not be taken at her word.
Meantime, if she be carried in her chair,
Approach, but do not seem to know she 's
  there.
Speak softly, to delude the standers-by;
Or, if aloud, then speak ambiguously.
If saunt'ring in the portico she walk,
Move slowly too, for that 's a time for talk;
And sometimes follow, sometimes be her
  guide;   560
But, when the crowd permits, go side by
  side.
Nor in the *playhouse* let her sit alone;
For she 's the *playhouse* and the *play* in one.
There thou mayst ogle, or by signs advance
Thy suit, and seem to touch her hand by
  chance.
Admire the dancer who her liking gains,
And pity in the *play* the lover's pains;

For her sweet sake the loss of time de-
  spise;
Sit while she sits, and when she rises rise.
But dress not like a fop, nor curl your hair,
Nor with a pumice make your body bare.
Leave those effeminate and useless toys 572
To *eunuchs*, who can give no solid joys.
Neglect becomes a man : this Theseus
  found;
Uncurl'd, uncomb'd, the nymph his wishes
  crown'd.
The rough Hippolytus was Phædra's care;
And Venus thought the rude Adonis fair.
Be not too finical; but yet be clean;
And wear well-fashion'd clothes, like other
  men.
Let not your teeth be yellow, or be foul;
Nor in wide shoes your feet too loosely
  roll.   581
Of a black muzzle and long beard beware;
And let a skilful barber cut your hair:
Your nails be pick'd from filth, and even
  par'd;
Nor let your nasty nostrils bud with beard.
Cure your unsav'ry breath, gargle your
  throat,
And free your armpits from the ram and
  goat.
Dress not, in short, too little or too much;
And be not wholly French nor wholly Dutch.
 Now Bacchus calls me to his jolly rites:
Wno would not follow, when a god invites ?
He helps the poet, and his pen inspires, 592
Kind and indulgent to his former fires.
 Fair Ariadne wander'd on the shore,
Forsaken now; and Theseus loves no more:
Loose was her gown, dishevel'd was her
  hair;
Her bosom naked, and her feet were bare.
Exclaiming, in the water's brink she stood;
Her briny tears augment the briny flood.
She shriek'd, and wept, and both became
  her face: 600
No posture could that heav'nly form dis-
  grace.
She beat her breast: "The traitor 's gone,"
  said she,
" What shall become of poor forsaken me ?
What shall become — " she had not time
  for more;
The sounding cymbals rattled on the shore.
She swoons for fear, she falls upon the
  ground;
No vital heat was in her body found.
The Mimallonian dames about her stood;

And scudding Satyrs ran before their god.
Silenus on his ass did next appear,   610
And held upon the mane; (the god was
    clear:)
The drunken *sire* pursues, the dames re-
    tire;
Sometimes the drunken dames pursue the
    drunken *sire*.
At last he topples over on the plain;
The Satyrs laugh, and bid him rise again.
And now the God of Wine came driving on,
High on his chariot by swift tigers drawn.
Her color, voice, and sense forsook the ⎤
    fair;   ⎟
Thrice did her trembling feet for flight ⎟
    prepare,   ⎬
And thrice affrighted did her flight for- ⎟
    bear.   620 ⎦
She shook, like leaves of corn when tem-
    pests blow,
Or slender reeds that in the marshes grow.
To whom the god: "Compose thy fearful
    mind;
In me a truer husband thou shalt find.
With heav'n I will endow thee, and thy ⎤
    star   ⎬
Shall with propitious light be seen afar, ⎟
And guide on seas the doubtful mariner." ⎦
He said, and from his chariot leaping light,
Lest the grim tigers should the nymph
    affright,
His brawny arms around her waist he
    threw;   630
(For gods, whate'er they will, with ease
    can do;)
And swiftly bore her thence: th' attending
    throng
Shout at the sight, and sing the nuptial
    song.
Now in full bowls her sorrow she may
    steep:
The bridegroom's liquor lays the bride
    asleep.
    But thou, when flowing cups in triumph
    ride,
And the lov'd nymph is seated by thy side;
Invoke the god, and all the mighty powers,
That wine may not defraud thy genial
    hours.
Then in ambiguous words thy suit prefer,
Which she may know were all address'd to
    her.   641
In liquid purple letters write her name,
Which she may read, and reading find thy
    flame.

Then may your eyes confess your mutual
    fires;
(For eyes have tongues, and glances tell
    desires.)
Whene'er she drinks, be first to take the
    cup;
And, where she laid her lips, the blessing
    sup.
When she to carving does her hand ad-
    vance,
Put out thy own, and touch it as by
    chance.   649
Thy service ev'n her husband must attend:
(A husband is a most convenient friend.)
Seat the fool cuckold in the highest place,
And with thy garland his dull temples
    grace.
Whether below, or equal in degree,   ⎤
Let him be lord of all the company,   ⎬
And what he says be seconded by thee. ⎦
'T is common to deceive thro' friendship's
    name;
But, common tho' it be, 't is still to blame:
Thus factors frequently their trust betray,
And to themselves their masters' gains
    convey.   660
Drink to a certain pitch, and then give
    o'er;
Thy tongue and feet may stumble, drink-
    ing more.
Of drunken quarrels in her sight beware;
Pot-valor only serves to fright the fair.
Eurytion justly fell, by wine oppress'd,
For his rude riot at a wedding feast.
Sing, if you have a voice; and shew your
    parts
In dancing, if endued with dancing arts.
Do anything within your power to please;
Nay, ev'n affect a seeming drunkenness:
Clip every word; and if by chance you
    speak   671
Too home, or if too broad a jest you break,
In your excuse the company will join,
And lay the fault upon the force of wine.
True drunkenness is subject to offend;
But when 't is feign'd, 't is oft a lover's
    friend.
Then safely you may praise her beauteous
    face,
And call him happy, who is in her grace.
Her husband thinks himself the man de-
    sign'd;
But curse the cuckold in your secret mind.
When all are risen and prepare to go,   681
Mix with the crowd, and tread upon her toe.

This is the proper time to make thy court,
For now she 's in the vein, and fit for sport.
Lay bashfulness, that rustic virtue, by;
To manly confidence thy thoughts apply.
On Fortune's foretop timely fix thy hold;
Now speak and speed, for Venus loves the
   bold.
No rules of rhetoric here I need afford;
Only begin, and trust the following word;
It will be witty of its own accord.   691
  Act well the lover; let thy speech abound
In dying words, that represent thy wound.
Distrust not her belief; she will be mov'd;
All women think they merit to be lov'd.
  Sometimes a man begins to love in jest,
And, after, feels the torments he profess'd.
For your own sakes be pitiful, ye fair;
For a feign'd passion may a true prepare.
By flatteries we prevail on womankind,   700
As hollow banks by streams are under-
  min'd.
Tell her, her face is fair, her eyes are
  sweet;
Her taper fingers praise, and little feet.
Such praises ev'n the chaste are pleas'd to
  hear;
Both maids and matrons hold their beauty
  dear.
  Once naked Pallas with Jove's queen ap-
  pear'd;
And still they grieve that Venus was pre-
  ferr'd.
Praise the proud peacock, and he spreads
  his train;
Be silent, and he pulls it in again.
Pleas'd is the courser in his rapid race;   710
Applaud his running, and he mends his pace.
But largely promise, and devoutly swear;
And, if need be, call ev'ry god to hear.
Jove sits above, forgiving with a smile
The perjuries that easy maids beguile.
He swore to Juno by the Stygian lake;
Forsworn, he dares not an example make,
Or punish falsehood, for his own dear sake.
'T is for our int'rest that the gods should
  be;
Let us believe 'em: I believe they see,   720
And both reward and punish equally —
Not that they live above, like lazy drones,
Or kings below, supine upon their thrones.
Lead then your lives as present in their ⎱
  sight;   ⎰
Be just in dealings, and defend the right; ⎰
By fraud betray not, nor oppress by might. ⎰
But 't is a venial sin to cheat the fair;

All men have liberty of conscience there.
On cheating nymphs a cheat is well de-
  sign'd;
'T is a profane and a deceitful kind.   730
  'T is said, that Egypt for nine years was
  dry,
Nor Nile did floods, nor heav'n did rain
  supply.
A foreigner at length inform'd the king
That slaughter'd guests would kindly mois-
  ture bring.
The king replied: " On thee the lot shall
  fall;
Be thou, my guest, the sacrifice for all."
Thus Phalaris Perillus taught to low,
And made him season first the brazen cow.
A rightful doom, the laws of nature cry;
'T is the artificers of death should die.   740
Thus justly women suffer by deceit;
Their practice authorizes us to cheat.
  Beg her, with tears, thy warm desires to
  grant;
For tears will pierce a heart of adamant.
If tears will not be squeez'd, then rub your
  eye,
Or noint the lids, and seem at least to cry.
Kiss, if you can: resistance if she make,
And will not give you kisses, let her take.
Fie, fie, you naughty man, are words of
  course;   749
She struggles, but to be subdued by force.
Kiss only soft, I charge you, and beware,
With your hard bristles not to brush the
  fair.
He who has gain'd a kiss, and gains no
  more,
Deserves to lose the bliss he got before.
If once she kiss, her meaning is express'd;
There wants but little pushing for the rest:
Which if thou dost not gain, by strength ⎱
  or art,   ⎰
The name of clown then suits with thy ⎰
  desert;   ⎰
'T is downright dulness, and a shameful ⎰
  part.   ⎰
Perhaps, she calls it force; but, if she
  scape,   760
She will not thank you for th' omitted rape.
The sex is cunning to conceal their fires;
They would be forc'd ev'n to their own
  desires.
They seem t' accuse you, with a downcast
  sight,
But in their souls confess you did them
  right.

Who might be forc'd, and yet untouch'd
depart,
Thank with their tongues, but curse you
with their heart.
Fair Phœbe and her sister did prefer
To their dull mates the noble ravisher.
What Deidamia did, in days of yore, 770
The tale is old, but worth the reading o'er.
When Venus had the golden apple
gain'd,
And the just judge fair Helen had obtain'd;
When she with triumph was at Troy re-
ceiv'd,
The Trojans joyful while the Grecians
griev'd;
They vow'd revenge of violated laws,
And Greece was arming in the cuckold's
cause:
Achilles, by his mother warn'd from war,
Disguis'd his sex, and lurk'd among the
fair.
What means Æacides to spin and sew ? ⎫
With spear and sword, in field thy valor ⎪
show; 781 ⎬
And, leaving this, the nobler Pallas ⎪
know. ⎭
Why dost thou in that hand the distaff
wield,
Which is more worthy to sustain a shield ?
Or with that other draw the woolly twine,
The same the Fates for Hector's thread
assign ?
Brandish thy fauchion in thy pow'rful
hand,
Which can alone the pond'rous lance
command.
In the same room by chance the royal ⎫
maid ⎪
Was lodg'd, and, by his seeming sex be- ⎬
tray'd, 790 ⎪
Close to her side the youthful hero laid. ⎭
I know not how his courtship he began,
But, to her cost, she found it was a man.
'T is thought she struggled; but withal
't is thought,
Her wish was to be conquer'd, when she
fought.
For when disclos'd, and hast'ning to the
field,
He laid his distaff down, and took the
shield,
With tears her humble suit she did prefer,
And thought to stay the grateful ravisher.
She sighs, she sobs, she begs him not to
part; 800

And now 't is nature, what before was art.
She strives by force her lover to detain,
And wishes to be ravish'd once again.
This is the sex: they will not first begin,
But, when compell'd, are pleas'd to suffer
sin.
Is there, who thinks that women first
should woo ?
Lay by thy self-conceit, thou foolish beau.
Begin, and save their modesty the shame;
'T is well for thee, if they receive thy
flame.
'T is decent for a man to speak his mind;
They but expect th' occasion to be kind. 811
Ask, that thou mayst enjoy; she waits for
this;
And on thy first advance depends thy bliss.
Ev'n Jove himself was forc'd to sue for
love;
None of the nymphs did first solicit Jove.
But if you find your pray'rs encrease her
pride,
Strike sail awhile, and wait another tide.
They fly when we pursue; but make delay,
And, when they see you slacken, they will
stay.
Sometimes it profits to conceal your end;
Name not yourself her lover, but her
friend. 821
How many skittish girls have thus been
caught ?
He prov'd a lover, who a friend was
thought.
Sailors by sun and wind are swarthy
made;
A tann'd complexion best becomes their
trade.
'T is a disgrace to plowmen to be fair ;
Bluff cheeks they have, and weather-beaten
hair.
Th' ambitious youth who seeks an olive
crown
Is sunburnt with his daily toil, and brown.
But if the lover hopes to be in grace, 830
Wan be his looks, and meager be his face.
That color from the fair compassion draws:
She thinks you sick, and thinks herself the
cause.
Orion wander'd in the woods for love: ⎫
His paleness did the nymphs to pity ⎬
move; ⎪
His ghastly visage argued hidden love. ⎭
Nor fail a nightcap, in full health, to wear;
Neglect thy dress, and discompose thy hair:
All things are decent that in love avail.

Read long by night, and study to be
    pale: 840
Forsake your food, refuse your needful
    rest;
Be miserable, that you may be blest.
    Shall I complain, or shall I warn you ⎫
      most ? ⎪
Faith, truth, and friendship in the world ⎬
    are lost; ⎪
A little and an empty name they boast. ⎭
Trust not thy friend, much less thy mis-
    tress praise:
If he believe, thou mayst a rival raise.
'T is true, Patroclus, by no lust misled,
Sought not to stain his dear companion's
    bed.
Nor Pylades Hermione embrac'd; 850
Ev'n Phædra to Perithous still was chaste.
But hope not thou, in this vile age, to find
Those rare examples of a faithful mind:
The sea shall sooner with sweet honey flow,
Or from the furzes pears and apples grow.
We sin with gust, we love by fraud to
    gain;
And find a pleasure in our fellows' pain.
From rival foes you may the fair defend;
But, would you ward the blow, beware your
    friend:
Beware your brother, and your next of
    kin; 860
But from your bosom friend your care
    begin.
Here I had ended, but experience finds
That sundry women are of sundry minds;
With various crotchets fill'd, and hard to
    please:
They therefore must be caught by various
    ways.
All things are not produc'd in any soil;
This ground for wine is proper, that for
    oil.
So 't is in men, but more in women-kind; ⎫
Diff'rent in face, in manners, and in ⎪
    mind: ⎬
But wise men shift their sails with ev'ry ⎪
    wind; 870 ⎭
As changeful Proteus varied oft his shape,
And did in sundry forms and figures
    scape;
A running stream, a standing tree became,
A roaring lion, or a bleating lamb.
Some fish with harpons, some with darts
    are struck,
Some drawn with nets, some hang upon the
    hook:

So turn thyself; and, imitating them,
Try sev'ral tricks, and change thy strata-
    gem.
One rule will not for diff'rent ages hold;
The jades grow cunning, as they grow more
    old. 880
Then talk not bawdy to the bashful maid;
Bug words will make her innocence afraid.
Nor to an ign'rant girl of learning speak;
She thinks you conjure, when you talk in
    Greek.
And hence 't is often seen, the simple shun
The learn'd, and into vile embraces run.
    Part of my task is done, and part to do:
But here 't is time to rest myself and you.

OVID'S AMOURS

BOOK I, ELEGY I

For mighty wars I thought to tune my
    lute,
And make my measures to my subject
    suit.
Six feet for ev'ry verse the Muse de- ⎫
    sign'd; ⎪
But Cupid, laughing, when he saw my ⎬
    mind, ⎪
From ev'ry second verse a foot purloin'd. ⎭
    " Who gave thee, boy, this arbitrary ⎫
      sway, ⎪
On subjects, not thy own, commands to ⎬
    lay, ⎪
Who Phœbus only and his laws obey ? ⎭
'T is more absurd, than if the Queen of
    Love
Should in Minerva's arms to battle move;
Or manly Pallas from that queen should
    take 11
Her torch, and o'er the dying lover shake.
In fields as well may Cynthia sow the corn,
Or Ceres wind in woods the bugle horn.
As well may Phœbus quit the trembling
    string
For sword and shield; and Mars may learn
    to sing.
Already thy dominions are too large;
Be not ambitious of a foreign charge.
If thou wilt reign o'er all, and ev'rywhere,
The God of Music for his harp may fear.
Thus when with soaring wings I seek re-
    nown, 21
Thou pluck'st my pinions, and I flutter
    down.

Could I on such mean thoughts my Muse
    employ,
I want a mistress or a blooming boy."
  Thus I complain'd: his bow the stripling
    bent,
And chose an arrow fit for his intent.
The shaft his purpose fatally pursues:
" Now, poet, there 's a subject for thy
    Muse."
He said : too well, alas, he knows his trade;
For in my breast a mortal wound he made.
Far hence, ye proud hexameters, remove;
My verse is pac'd and travel'd into love. 32
With myrtle wreaths my thoughtful brows
    inclose,
While in unequal verse I sing my woes.

BOOK I, ELEGY IV

To his mistress, whose husband is invited to a
    feast with them. The poet instructs her
    how to behave herself in his company.

YOUR husband will be with us at the treat;
May that be the last supper he shall eat.
And am poor I, a guest invited there,
Only to see, while he may touch the fair ?
To see you kiss and hug your nauseous
    lord,
While his lewd hand descends below the
    board ?
Now wonder not that Hippodamia's charms,
At such a sight, the Centaurs urg'd to
    arms;
That in a rage they threw their cups aside,
Assail'd the bridegroom, and would force
    the bride.   10
I am not half a horse, (I would I were,)
Yet hardly can from you my hands for-
    bear.
Take, then, my counsel; which, observ'd,
    may be
Of some importance both to you and me.
Be sure to come before your man be there:
There 's nothing can be done; but come
    howe'er.
Sit next him, (that belongs to decency,)
But tread upon my foot in passing by.
Read in my looks what silently they speak,
And slyly, with your eyes, your answer
    make.   20
My lifted eyebrow shall declare my pain;
My right hand to his fellow shall complain,
And on the back a letter shall design,

Besides a note that shall be writ in wine.
Whene'er you think upon our last embrace,
With your forefinger gently touch your face.
If any word of mine offend my dear,
Pull, with your hand, the velvet of your
    ear.
If you are pleas'd with what I do or say,
Handle your rings, or with your fingers
    play.   30
As suppliants use at altars, hold the board,
Whene'er you wish the devil may take
    your lord.
When he fills for you, never touch the cup,
But bid th' officious cuckold drink it up.
The waiter on those services employ:
Drink you, and I will snatch it from the
    boy;
Watching the part where your sweet mouth
    has been,
And thence, with eager lips, will suck it in.
If he, with clownish manners, thinks it fit
To taste, and offers you the nasty bit,   40
Reject his greasy kindness, and restore
Th' unsav'ry morsel he had chew'd before.
Nor let his arms embrace your neck, nor
    rest
Your tender cheek upon his hairy breast.
Let not his hand within your bosom stray,
And rudely with your pretty bubbies play.
But, above all, let him no kiss receive:
That 's an offense I never can forgive.
Do not, O do not that sweet mouth resign,
Lest I rise up in arms, and cry: " 'T is
    mine ! "   50
I shall thrust in betwixt, and void of fear
The manifest adult'rer will appear.
These things are plain to sight, but more I
    doubt
What you conceal beneath your petticoat.
Take not his leg between your tender
    thighs,
Nor, with your hand, provoke my foe to
    rise.
How many love-inventions I deplore,
Which I myself have practic'd all before ?
How oft have I been forc'd the robe to lift
In company; to make a homely shift   60
For a bare bout, ill huddled o'er in haste,
While o'er my side the fair her mantle
    cast.
You to your husband shall not be so kind;
But, lest you should, your mantle leave
    behind.
Encourage him to tope; but kiss him not,
Nor mix one drop of water in his pot.

If he be fuddled well, and snores apace,
Then we may take advice from time and
    place.
When all depart, when compliments are
    loud,   69
Be sure to mix among the thickest crowd;
There I will be, and there we cannot miss,
Perhaps to grubble, or at least to kiss.
Alas ! what length of labor I employ,
Just to secure a short and transient joy !
For night must part us; and, when night is
    come,
Tuck'd underneath his arms he leads you
    home.

He locks you in; I follow to the door,
His fortune envy, and my own deplore.
He kisses you, he more than kisses too;
Th' outrageous cuckold thinks it all his due.
But add not to his joy by your consent,   81
And let it not be giv'n, but only lent.
Return no kiss, nor move in any sort;
Make it a dull and a malignant sport.
Had I my wish, he should no pleasure take,
But slubber o'er your business for my
    sake.
And whate'er fortune shall this night be-
    fall,
Coax me to-morrow, by forswearing all.

ALEXANDER'S FEAST

OR, THE POWER OF MUSIC ; AN ODE IN HONOR OF ST. CECILIA'S DAY

[Dryden wrote this greatest of his lyric poems for the celebration of the Feast of St. Cecilia (November 22), 1697: compare note, p. 252, above. It was first set to music by Jeremiah Clarke ; next, in 1711, by Thomas Clayton: finally, in 1736, by Handel (Malone, I, 1, 296–307). It was published as a folio pamphlet in 1697, and was reprinted in the volume of *Fables*, 1700. In a letter to Tonson, written about the close of 1697, Dryden says: " I am glad to heare from all hands, that my Ode is esteem'd the best of all my poetry, by all the town : I thought so my self when I writ it ; but being old, I mistrusted my own judgment. I hope it has done you service, and will do more " (Malone, I, 2, 63).]

I

'T WAS at the royal feast, for Persia won
    By Philip's warlike son:
Aloft in awful state
The godlike hero sate
    On his imperial throne:
His valiant peers were plac'd around;
Their brows with roses and with myrtles
    bound:
(So should desert in arms be
    crown'd.)
The lovely Thais, by his side,
Sate like a blooming Eastern bride   10
In flow'r of youth and beauty's pride.
Happy, happy, happy pair !
    None but the brave,
    None but the brave,
    None but the brave deserves the
        fair.

CHORUS

Happy, happy, happy pair !
None but the brave,
None but the brave,
None but the brave deserves the fair.

II

Timotheus, plac'd on high   20
    Amid the tuneful choir,
    With flying fingers touch'd the lyre:
The trembling notes ascend the sky,
            And heav'nly joys inspire.
The song began from Jove,
Who left his blissful seats above,
(Such is the pow'r of mighty love.)
A dragon's fiery form belied the god:
Sublime on radiant spires he rode,
    When he to fair Olympia press'd;   30
    And while he sought her snowy breast:
Then, round her slender waist he curl'd,
And stamp'd an image of himself, a sov'-
    reign of the world.
The list'ning crowd admire the lofty sound;
" A present deity," they shout around;
" A present deity," the vaulted roofs re-
        bound:
        With ravish'd ears
        The monarch hears,
        Assumes the god,
        Affects to nod,   40
And seems to shake the spheres.

CHORUS

With ravish'd ears
The monarch hears,
Assumes the god,
Affects to nod,
And seems to shake the spheres.

III

The praise of Bacchus then the sweet mu-
    sician sung,
  Of Bacchus ever fair and ever young:
    The jolly god in triumph comes;   49
    Sound the trumpets; beat the drums;
      Flush'd with a purple grace
      He shews his honest face:
Now give the hautboys breath; he comes,
    he comes.
  Bacchus, ever fair and young,
    Drinking joys did first ordain;
  Bacchus' blessings are a treasure,
  Drinking is the soldier's pleasure:
      Rich the treasure,
      Sweet the pleasure,
    Sweet is pleasure after pain.   60

CHORUS

Bacchus' blessings are a treasure,
Drinking is the soldier's pleasure:
   Rich the treasure,
   Sweet the pleasure,
Sweet is pleasure after pain.

IV

Sooth'd with the sound, the king grew vain;
  Fought all his battles o'er again;
And thrice he routed all his foes; and
    thrice he slew the slain.
The master saw the madness rise;
  His glowing cheeks, his ardent eyes;   70
And, while he heav'n and earth defied,
Chang'd his hand, and check'd his pride.
    He chose a mournful Muse,
      Soft pity to infuse:
He sung Darius great and good,
      By too severe a fate,
Fallen, fallen, fallen, fallen,
     Fallen from his high estate,
      And welt'ring in his blood;
Deserted, at his utmost need,   80
By those his former bounty fed;
On the bare earth expos'd he lies,
With not a friend to close his eyes.

With downcast looks the joyless victor sate,
  Revolving in his alter'd soul

  The various turns of chance below;
And, now and then, a sigh he stole;
And tears began to flow.

CHORUS

Revolving in his alter'd soul
  The various turns of chance below;   90
And, now and then, a sigh he stole;
  And tears began to flow.

V

The mighty master smil'd, to see
That love was in the next degree:
'T was but a kindred sound to move,
For pity melts the mind to love.
  Softly sweet, in Lydian measures,
  Soon he sooth'd his soul to pleasures.
  "War," he sung, "is toil and trouble;
  Honor, but an empty bubble;   100
    Never ending, still beginning,
  Fighting still, and still destroying:
    If the world be worth thy winning,
  Think, O think it worth enjoying;
  Lovely Thais sits beside thee,
  Take the good the gods provide thee."

The many rend the skies with loud applause;
So Love was crown'd, but Music won the
    cause.
The prince, unable to conceal his pain,
    Gaz'd on the fair   110
      Who caus'd his care,
    And sigh'd and look'd, sigh'd and
      look'd,
  Sigh'd and look'd, and sigh'd again:
At length, with love and wine at once op-
    press'd,
The vanquish'd victor sunk upon her breast.

CHORUS

The prince, unable to conceal his pain,
    Gaz'd on the fair
     Who caus'd his care,
   And sigh'd and look'd, sigh'd and look'd,
  Sigh'd and look'd, and sigh'd again: 120
At length, with love and wine at once op-
    press'd,
The vanquish'd victor sunk upon her breast.

VI

Now strike the golden lyre again:
A louder yet, and yet a louder strain.
Break his bands of sleep asunder,
And rouse him, like a rattling peal of thun-
    der.

Hark, hark, the horrid sound
Has rais'd up his head:
As awak'd from the dead,
And amaz'd, he stares around.   130
" Revenge, revenge ! " Timotheus cries,
" See the Furies arise !
See the snakes that they rear,
How they hiss in their hair,
And the sparkles that flash from their eyes !
Behold a ghastly band,
Each a torch in his hand !
Those are Grecian ghosts, that in battle
were slain,
And unburied remain
Inglorious on the plain: 140
Give the vengeance due
To the valiant crew.
Behold how they toss their torches on high,
How they point to the Persian abodes,
And glitt'ring temples of their hostile
gods ! "
The princes applaud, with a furious joy;
And the king seiz'd a flambeau with zeal to
destroy;
Thais led the way,
To light him to his prey,   149
And, like another Helen, fir'd another Troy.

CHORUS

And the king seiz'd a flambeau with zeal to
  destroy ;
      Thais led the way,
      To light him to his prey,
And, like another Helen, fir'd another Troy.

VII

Thus, long ago,
Ere heaving bellows learn'd to blow,
While organs yet were mute;
Timotheus, to his breathing flute,
And sounding lyre,
Could swell the soul to rage, or kindle soft
desire.   160
At last, divine Cecilia came,
Inventress of the vocal frame;
The sweet enthusiast, from her sacred
store,
Enlarg'd the former narrow bounds,
And added length to solemn sounds,
With nature's mother wit, and arts un-
known before.
Let old Timotheus yield the prize,
Or both divide the crown;
He rais'd a mortal to the skies;
She drew an angel down.   170

GRAND CHORUS

At last, divine Cecilia came,
Inventress of the vocal frame ;
The sweet enthusiast, from her sacred store,
Enlarg'd the former narrow bounds,
And added length to solemn sounds,
With nature's mother wit, and arts unknown
  before.
Let old Timotheus yield the prize,
Or both divide the crown ;
He rais'd a mortal to the skies ;
She drew an angel down.   180

TO MR. GRANVILLE, ON HIS EXCELLENT TRAGEDY CALL'D HEROIC LOVE

[*Heroic Love*, a tragedy by George Granville, based on the story of Briseis in the *Iliad*,
was probably first acted in 1697 ; it had great
success on the stage (Downes). Dryden's epistle, with heading as above, was printed with
the first edition of the play, which was published on February 19, 1698 (Malone, I, 1, 310,
on the authority of an advertisement in the
London Gazette). Granville, who was created
Lord Lansdowne in 1711, is known in literature
as the friend of Pope as well as of Dryden.]

AUSPICIOUS poet, wert thou not my friend,
How could I envy, what I must commend !
But since 't is nature's law, in love and wit,
That youth should reign, and with'ring age
  submit,
With less regret those laurels I resign,
Which, dying on my brows, revive on
  thine.
With better grace an ancient chief may
  yield
The long contended honors of the field,
Than venture all his fortune at a cast,
And fight, like Hannibal, to lose at last. 10
Young princes, obstinate to win the prize,
Tho' yearly beaten, yearly yet they rise;
Old monarchs, tho' successful, still in
  doubt,
Catch at a peace, and wisely turn devout.
Thine be the laurel then; thy blooming
  age
Can best, if any can, support the stage;

Which so declines, that shortly we may see
Players and plays reduc'd to second in-
　fancy.
Sharp to the world, but thoughtless of re-
　nown.
They plot not on the stage, but on the
　town,　　　　　　　　　　　　　　20
And, in despair their empty pit to fill,
Set up some foreign monster in a bill.
Thus they jog on, still tricking, never
　thriving,
And murd'ring plays, which they miscall
　reviving.
Our sense is nonsense, thro' their pipes
　convey'd;
Scarce can a poet know the play he made,
'T is so disguis'd in death; nor thinks 't is
　he
That suffers in the mangled tragedy.
Thus Itys first was kill'd, and after dress'd
For his own sire, the chief invited guest. 30
I say not this of thy successful scenes,
Where thine was all the glory, theirs the
　gains.
With length of time, much judgment, and
　more toil,
Not ill they acted, what they could not
　spoil.
Their setting sun still shoots a glimm'ring
　ray,
Like ancient Rome, majestic in decay;
And better gleanings their worn soil can
　boast,
Than the crab vintage of the neighb'ring
　coast.
This difference yet the judging world will
　see;
Thou copiest Homer, and they copy thee. 40

TO MY FRIEND MR. MOTTEUX

[Peter Anthony Motteux was a French
Huguenot who settled in England in 1685, and
soon became noted as a man of letters; he is
best known in our day as a translator of Rabe-
lais and of *Don Quixote*. The following epistle
was prefixed to his tragedy, *Beauty in Distress*,
on its publication in 1698. The play is entered
in the *Term Catalogue* for Trinity Term (June)
of that year; it was probably acted late in
1697 or early in 1698.]

'T IS hard, my friend, to write in such an
　age,
As damns not only poets, but the stage.

That sacred art, by heav'n itself infus'd,
Which Moses, David, Solomon have us'd,
Is now to be no more: the Muses' foes
Would sink their Maker's praises into prose.
Were they content to prune the lavish vine
Of straggling branches, and improve the
　wine,
Who but a madman would his faults de-
　fend?
All would submit; for all but fools will
　mend.　　　　　　　　　　　　　　10
But when to common sense they give the
　lie,
And turn distorted words to blasphemy,
They give the scandal; and the wise dis-
　cern,
Their glosses teach an age too apt to learn.
What I have loosely or profanely writ,
Let them to fires, (their due desert,) com-
　mit;
Nor, when accus'd by me, let *them* com-
　plain:
Their faults and not their function I ar-
　raign.
Rebellion, worse than witchcraft, they
　pursued;
The pulpit preach'd the crime, the people
　rued.　　　　　　　　　　　　　　20
The stage was silenc'd; for the saints
　would see
In fields perform'd their plotted tragedy.
But let us first reform, and then so live,
That we may teach our teachers to forgive.
Our desk be plac'd below their lofty chairs;
Ours be the practice, as the precept theirs.
The moral part at least we may divide,
Humility reward, and punish pride;
Ambition, int'rest, avarice accuse:
These are the province of the Tragic Muse.
These hast thou chosen; and the public
　voice　　　　　　　　　　　　　　31
Has equal'd thy performance with thy
　choice.
Time, action, place, are so preserv'd by ⎫
　thee,　　　　　　　　　　　　　　　⎪
That ev'n Corneille might with envy see ⎬
Th' alliance of his tripled unity.　　　⎭
Thy incidents, perhaps, too thick are sown;
But too much plenty is thy fault alone:
At least but two can that good crime com-
　mit,
Thou in design, and Wycherley in wit.
Let thy own Gauls condemn thee, if they
　dare;　　　　　　　　　　　　　　40
Contented to be thinly regular.

Born there, but not for them, our fruitful
  soil
With more increase rewards thy happy toil.
Their tongue, infeebled, is refin d so much,
That, like pure gold, it bends at ev ry
  touch;
Our sturdy Teuton yet will art obey,
More fit for manly thought, and strengthen'd
  with allay.
But whence art thou inspir'd, and thou
  alone,
To flourish in an idiom not thine own ?
It moves our wonder, that a foreign guest
Should overmatch the most, and match the
  best.   51
In underpraising, thy deserts I wrong;
Here, find the first deficience of our
  tongue:
Words, once my stock, are wanting, to
  commend
So great a poet and so good a friend.

EPIGRAM ON TONSON

[In the third report of the *Royal Commission on Historical Manuscripts*. p. 193, there is
printed the following excerpt from a letter of
R. Powys to Matthew Prior, dated July 14,
1698 :]

Mr. Godfrey Kneller has drawn at length the
picture of your friend Jacob Tonson, which he
shewed Mr. Dryden, who desired to give a
touch of his pensill, and underneath it writ
these 3 verses : —

With leering look, bull faced and freckled fair,
With frowsy pores poisoning the ambient air,
With two left leggs and Judas coloured hair.

LINES TO MRS. CREED

[Mrs. Elizabeth Creed was the granddaughter of Sir John Pickering and of Susan, sister
of Erasmus Driden, the poet's father. She was
born in 1642. Malone (I, 1 ; 341, 342) prints the
following anecdote, from a manuscript note
which he conjectures to have been written by
a daughter of Mrs. Creed. Words in brackets
were supplied by Malone. The date of the
lines of course cannot be determined ; they
are printed in the present place for convenience.]

Conversation one day after dinner, at Mrs.
Creed's, running upon the or[igin of names],

Mr. Dryden bowed to the good old lady, and
spoke extempore the f[ollowing verses]:

So much religion in *your* name doth dwell,
Your soul must needs with piety excel.
Thus names, like [well-wrought] pictures drawn of old,
Their owners' nature and their story told. —
Your name but half expresses ; for in you
Belief and practice do together go.
My prayers shall be, while this short life endures,
These may go hand in hand with you and yours ;
Till faith hereafter is in vision drown'd,
And practice is with endless glory crown'd.

THE MONUMENT OF A FAIR MAIDEN LADY WHO DIED AT BATH AND IS THERE INTERR'D

[This epitaph was first printed, with title as
above, in the volume of *Fables*, 1700. It is
found on a mural tablet in Bath Abbey, where
it is preceded by the following words :
  " Here lyes the Body of Mary, third Daughter of Richard Frampton of Moreton in Dor-
setshire, Esq! and of Iane his Wife, sole Daughter of S! Francis Cottington of Founthill in
Wilts, who was born Ianuary yᵉ J^st 167⅔.
And Dyed after Seven Weeks sickness on the
6! of 7ber 1698. This Monument was Erected
by Cath. Frampton, her second Sister and Ex-
ecutress in testimony of her Grief, Affection,
and Gratitude."
  The tablet is surmounted by a bust of Mary
Frampton.
  The text above is from a copy of the tablet,
kindly furnished the present editor by the
Reverend S. A. Boyd, Rector of Bath. The
text of the poem follows that printed in the
Fables.]

BELOW this marble monument is laid
All that heav'n wants of this celestial maid.
Preserve, O sacred tomb, thy trust con-
  sign'd,
The mold was made on purpose for the
  mind;
And she would lose, if, at the latter day,
One atom could be mix'd of other clay.
Such were the features of her heav'nly
  face,
Her limbs were form'd with such harmo-
  nious grace;
So faultless was the frame, as if the whole
Had been an emanation of the soul,   10
Which her own inward symmetry reveal'd;
And like a picture shone, in glass anneal'd;
Or like the sun eclips'd, with shaded light;
Too piercing, else, to be sustain'd by sight.
Each thought was visible that roll'd within:

As thro' a crystal case the figur'd hours
    are seen.
And Heav'n did this transparent veil pro-
    vide,
Because she had no guilty thought to
    hide.
All white, a virgin saint, she sought the
    skies;
For marriage, tho' it sullies not, it dyes. 20
High tho' her wit, yet humble was her
    mind;
As if she could not, or she would not find
How much her worth transcended all her
    kind.
Yet she had learn'd so much of heav'n be-
    low,

That, when arriv'd, she scarce had more to
    know;
But only to refresh the former hint,
And read her Maker in a fairer print:
So pious, as she had no time to spare
For human thoughts, but was confin'd to
    pray'r.
Yet in such charities she pass'd the day, 30
'T was wondrous how she found an hour to
    pray.
A soul so calm, it knew not ebbs or flows;
Which passion could but curl, not discom-
    pose.
A female softness, with a manly mind;
A daughter duteous, and a sister kind;
In sickness patient, and in death resign'd.

FABLES, ANCIENT AND MODERN

[About March 5, 1700 (see Dryden's letter of March 12 to Mrs. Steward, cited on the next page), Tonson published a folio volume with title-page reading as follows:

FABLES

Ancient and *Modern ;*

Translated into VERSE,

FROM

Homer, Ovid,
Boccace, & Chaucer:

WITH

ORIGINAL POEMS.

By Mr *DRYDEN.*

Nunc ultrò ad Cineres ipsius & ossa parentis
(Haud equidem sine mente, reor, sine numine divum)
Adsumus.   Virg. Æn. lib. 5.

LONDON:
Printed for *Jacob Tonson,* within *Gray's Inn Gate* next
Gray's Inn Lane. MDCC.

This volume, the "last fruit off an old tree," contained, besides the material printed below, the epitaph on *The Monument of a Fair Maiden Lady* (p. 735, above) and a reprint of *Alexander's Feast.* The earliest of the new poems contained in it were probably written late in 1697 or early in 1698.

In Dryden's correspondence there are several charming references to this last great work of his pen. On February 2, 1699, he writes to his kinswoman Mrs. Steward:

"In the mean time, betwixt my intervalls of physique and other remedies which I am useing for my gravell, I am still drudgeing on: always a poet, and never a good one. I pass my time sometimes with Ovid, and sometimes with our old English poet, Chaucer; translateing such stories as best please my fancy; and intend besides them to add somewhat of my own : so that it is not impossible, but ere the summer be pass'd, I may come down to you with a volume in my hand, like a dog out of the water, with a duck in his mouth.'' (Malone, I, 2; 74, 75.)

In another letter, written March 4 of the same year, he tells the same correspondent:
"I am still drudging at a book of Miscellanyes, which I hope will be well enough; if otherwise, threescore and seven may be pardon'd.'' (Ibid. I, 2; 82, 83.)

On July 14, 1699, he writes to Samuel Pepys, the diarist:

"PADRON MIO,
"I REMEMBER, last year, when I had the honour of dineing with you, you were pleas'd to recommend to me the character of Chaucer's GOOD PARSON. Any desire of yours is a command to me; and accordingly I have put it into my English, with such additions and alterations as I thought fit. Having translated as many Fables from Ovid, and as many Novills from Boccace and Tales from Chaucer, as will make an indifferent large volume in folio, I intend them for the press in Michaelmass term next. In the mean time my PARSON desires the favour of being known to you, and promises, if you find any fault in his character, he will reform it. Whenever you please, he shall wait on you, and for the safer conveyance, I will carry him in my pocket; who am

My *Padrons* most obedient Servant,
JOHN DRYDEN." (Ibid. I, 2, 84-86.)

On November 7 the poet again writes to Mrs. Steward:
"If you desire to hear any thing more of my affairs, the Earl of Dorsett and your Cousin Montague [Charles Montague, later Earl of Halifax] have both seen the two poems, to the Duchess of Ormond, and my worthy Cousin Driden; and are of opinion that I never writt better. My other friends are divided in their judgments, which to preferr; but the greater part are for those to my dear kinsman; which I have corrected with so much care, that they will now be worthy of his sight, and do neither of us any dishonour after our death." (Ibid. I, 2; 93, 94.)

On March 12, 1700, Dryden writes once more to the same person, announcing the publication of his book:

"MADAM,
"'T is a week since I receiv'd the favour of a letter, which I have not yet acknowledg'd to you. About that time my new Poems were publish'd, which are not come till this day into my hands. They are a debt to you, I must confess; and I am glad, because they are so unworthy to be made a present. Your sisters, I hope, will be so kind to have them convey'd to you; that my writeings may have the honour of waiting on you, which is deny'd to me. The Town encourages them with more applause than any thing of mine deserves: and particularly my Cousin Driden accepted one from me so very indulgently, that it makes me more and more in love with him." (Ibid. I, 2; 127, 128.)

Finally, on April 11, 1700, only twenty days before his death, Dryden sends to Mrs. Steward a letter beginning:

"MADAM,
"THE ladies of the town have infected you at a distance : they are all of your opinion, and like my last book of Poems better than any thing they have formerly seen of mine. I always thought my Verses to my Cousin Driden were the best of the whole; and to my comfort, the Town thinks them so; and he, which pleases me most, is of the same judgment, as appears by a noble present he has sent me, which surpris'd me, because I did not in the least expect it." (Ibid. I, 2; 129, 130.)]

TO
HIS GRACE THE DUKE OF ORMOND

MY LORD,
SOME estates are held in England by paying a fine at the change of every lord. I have enjoy'd the patronage of your family, from the time of your excellent grandfather to this present day. I have dedicated the *Lives* of Plutarch to the first duke; and have celebrated the memory of your heroic father. Tho' I am very short of the age of Nestor, yet I have liv'd to a third generation of your house; and by your Grace's favor am admitted still to hold from you by the same tenure.

I am not vain enough to boast that I have deserv'd the value of so illustrious a line; but my fortune is the greater, that for three descents they have been pleas'd to distinguish my poems from those of other men; and have accordingly made me their peculiar care. May it be permitted me to say, that as your grandfather and father were cherish'd and adorn'd with honors by two successive monarchs, so I have been esteem'd and patroniz'd by the grandfather, the father, and the son, descended from one of the most ancient, most conspicuous, and most deserving families in Europe.

'T is true that by delaying the payment of my last fine, when it was due by your Grace's accession to the titles and patrimonies of your house, I may seem, in rigor of law, to have made a forfeiture of my claim; yet my heart has always been devoted to your service; and since you have been graciously pleas'd, by your permission of this address, to accept the tender of my duty, 't is not yet too late to lay these poems at your feet.

The world is sensible that you worthily succeed, not only to the honors of your ancestors, but also to their virtues. The long chain of magnanimity, courage, easiness of access, and desire of doing good, even to the prejudice of your fortune, is so far from being broken in your Grace, that the precious metal yet runs pure to the newest link of it; which I will not call the last, because I hope and pray it may descend to late posterity; and your flourishing youth, and that of your excellent duchess, are happy omens of my wish.

'T is observ'd by Livy and by others that some of the noblest Roman families retain'd a resemblance of their ancestry, not only in their shapes and features, but also in their manners, their qualities, and the distinguishing characters of their minds. Some lines were noted for a stern, rigid virtue, salvage, haughty, parsimonious, and unpopular: others were more sweet and affable, made of a more pliant paste, humble, courteous, and obliging; studious of doing charitable offices, and diffusive of the goods which they enjoy'd. The last of these is the proper and indelible character of your Grace's family. God Almighty has endued you with a softness, a beneficence, an attractive behavior winning on the hearts of others; and so sensible of their misery, that the wounds of fortune seem not inflicted on them, but on yourself. You are so ready to redress that you almost prevent their wishes, and always exceed their expectations; as if what was yours was not your own, and not given you to possess, but to bestow on wanting merit. But this is a topic which I must cast in shades, lest I offend your modesty, which is so far from being ostentatious of the good you do that it blushes even to have it known; and therefore I must leave you to the satisfaction and testimony of your own conscience, which, tho' it be a silent panegyric, is yet the best.

You are so easy of access, that Poplicola was not more, whose doors were open'd on the outside to save the people even the common civility of asking entrance; where all were equally admitted; where nothing that was reasonable was denied; where misfortune was a powerful recommendation, and where, I can scarce forbear saying, that want itself was a powerful mediator, and was next to merit.

The history of Peru assures us that their Incas, above all their titles, esteem'd that the highest, which call'd them Lovers of the Poor: a name more glorious than the *Felix*, *Pius*, and *Augustus* of the Roman emperors; which were epithets of flattery, deserv'd by few of them, and not running in a blood, like the perpetual gentleness and inherent goodness of the Ormond family.

Gold, as it is the purest, so it is the softest and most ductile of all metals. Iron, which is the hardest, gathers rust, corrodes itself, and is therefore subject to corruption; it was never intended for coins and medals, or to bear the faces and inscriptions of the great. Indeed 't is fit for armor, to bear off insults, and preserve the wearer in the day of battle; but the danger once repell'd, 't is laid aside by the brave, as a garment too rough for civil conversation: a necessary guard in war, but too harsh and cumbersome in peace, and which keeps off the embraces of a more human life.

For this reason, my Lord, tho' you have courage in a heroical degree, yet I ascribe it to you but as your second attribute: mercy, beneficence, and compassion claim precedence, as they are first in the divine nature. An intrepid courage, which is inherent in your Grace, is at best but a holiday kind of virtue, to be seldom exercis'd, and never but in cases of necessity; affability, mildness, tenderness, and a word which I would fain bring back to its original signification of virtue, I mean good-nature, are of daily use: they are the bread of mankind, and staff of life: neither sighs, nor tears, nor groans, nor curses of the vanquish'd, follow acts of compassion and charity; but a sincere pleasure and serenity of mind in him who performs an action of mercy, which cannot suffer the misfortunes of another without redress, lest they should bring a kind of contagion along with them, and pollute the happiness which he enjoys.

Yet since the perverse tempers of mankind, since oppression on one side, and ambition on the other, are sometimes the unavoidable occasions of war; that courage, that magnanimity and resolution, which is born with you, cannot be too much commended. And here it grieves me that I am scanted in the pleasure of dwelling on many of your actions; but αἰδέομαι Τρῶας is an expression which Tully often uses, when he would do what he dares not, and fears the censure of the Romans.

I have sometimes been forc'd to amplify on others; but here, where the subject is so fruitful that the harvest overcomes the reaper, I am shorten'd by my chain, and can only see what is forbidden me to reach; since it is not permitted me to commend you according to the extent of my wishes, and much less is it in my power to make my commendations equal to your merits.

Yet in this frugality of your praises, there are some things which I cannot omit, without detracting from your character. You have so form'd your own education, as enables you to pay the debt you owe your country, or, more properly speaking, both your countries; because you were born, I may almost say, in purple, at the Castle of Dublin, when your grandfather was Lord Lieutenant, and have since been bred in the Court of England.

If this address had been in verse, I might have call'd you, as Claudian calls Mercury, *Numen commune, gemino faciens commercia mundo.* The better to satisfy this double obligation, you have early cultivated the genius you have to arms, that when the service of Britain or Ireland shall require your courage and your conduct, you may exert them both to the benefit of either country. You began in the cabinet what you afterwards practic'd in the camp; and thus both Lucullus and Cæsar (to omit a crowd of shining Romans) form'd themselves to the war by the study of history, and by the examples of the greatest captains, both of Greece and Italy, before their time. I name those two commanders in particular, because they were better read in chronicle than any of the Roman leaders; and that Lucullus in particular, having only the theory of war from books, was thought fit, without practice, to be sent into the field against the most formidable enemy of Rome. Tully indeed was call'd the Learn'd Consul in derision; but then he was not born a soldier: his head was turn'd another way; when he read the tactics, he was thinking on the bar, which was his field of battle. The knowledge of warfare is thrown away on a general who dares not make use of what he knows. I commend it only in a man of courage and of resolution: in him it will direct his martial spirit, and teach him the way to the best victories, which are those that are least bloody, and which, tho' achiev'd by the hand, are manag'd by the head. Science distinguishes a man of honor from one of those athletic brutes whom undeservedly we call heroes. Curst be the poet who first honor'd with that name a mere Ajax, a man-killing idiot. The Ulysses of Ovid upbraids his ignorance, that he understood not the shield for which he pleaded: there was engraven on it plans of cities, and maps of countries, which Ajax could not comprehend, but look'd on them as stupidly as his fellow beast, the lion. But on the other side, your Grace has given yourself the education of his rival; you have studied every spot of ground in Flanders, which for these ten years past has been the scene of battles and of sieges. No wonder if you perform'd your part with such applause on a theater which you understood so well.

If I design'd this for a poetical encomium, it were easy to enlarge on so copious a subject; but confining myself to the severity of truth, and to what is becoming me to say, I must not only pass over many instances of your military skill, but also those of your assiduous diligence in the war; and of your personal bravery, attended with an ardent thirst of honor; a long train of generosity; profuseness of doing good; a soul unsatisfied with all it has done; and an unextinguish'd desire of doing more. But all this is matter for your own historians; I am, as Virgil says, *Spatiis exclusus iniquis.*

Yet not to be wholly silent of all your charities, I must stay a little on one action, which preferr'd the relief of others to the consideration of yourself. When, in the battle of Landen, your heat of courage (a fault only pardonable to your youth) had transported you so far before your friends that they were unable to follow, much less to succor you; when you were not only dangerously, but, in all appearance, mortally wounded; when in that desperate condition you were made prisoner, and carried to Namur, at that time in possession of the French; then it was, my Lord, that you took a considerable part of what was remitted to you of your own revenues, and, as a memorable instance of your heroic charity, put it into the hands of Count Guiscard, who was governor of the place, to be distributed among your fellow prisoners. The French commander, charm'd with the greatness of your soul, accordingly consign'd it to the use for which it was intended by the donor; by which means the lives of so many miserable men were sav'd, and a comfortable provision made for their subsistence, who had otherwise perish'd, had not you been the companion of their misfortune; or rather sent by Providence, like another Joseph, to keep out famine from invading those whom in humility you call'd your brethren. How happy was it for those poor creatures, that your Grace was made their fellow sufferer! And how glorious for you, that you chose to want, rather than not relieve the wants of others! The heathen poet, in commending the charity of Dido to the Trojans, spoke like a Christian:

Non ignara mali, miseris succurrere disco.

All men, even those of a different interest and contrary principles, must praise this action, as the most eminent for piety, not only in this degenerate age, but almost in any of the former; when men were made *de meliore luto*, when examples of charity were frequent, and when there were in being:

> *Teucri pulcherrima proles,*
> *Magnanimi heroes nati melioribus annis.*

No envy can detract from this: it will shine in history; and, like swans, grow whiter the longer it endures; and the name of ORMOND will be more celebrated in his captivity than in his greatest triumphs.

But all actions of your Grace are of a piece, as waters keep the tenor of their fountains; your compassion is general, and has the same effect as well on enemies as friends. 'T is so much in your nature to do good, that your life is but one continued act of placing benefits on many, as the sun is always carrying his light to some part or other of the world. And were it not that your reason guides you where to give, I might almost say that you could not help bestowing more than is consisting with the fortune of a private man, or with the will of any but an Alexander.

What wonder is it then, that, being born for a blessing to mankind, your suppos'd death in that engagement was so generally lamented thro' the nation? The concernment for it was as universal as the loss; and tho' the gratitude might be counterfeit in some, yet the tears of all were real: where every man deplor'd his private part in that calamity, and even those who had not tasted of your favors, yet built so much on the fame of your beneficence, that they bemoan'd the loss of their expectations.

This brought the untimely death of your great father into fresh remembrance; as if the same decree had pass'd on two short successive generations of the virtuous; and I repeated to myself the same verses which I had formerly applied to him:

> *Ostendunt terris hunc tantum fata, nec ultra*
> *Esse sinunt.*

But to the joy not only of all good men, but of mankind in general, the unhappy omen took not place. You are still living to enjoy the blessings and applause of all the good you have perform'd, the prayers of multitudes whom you have oblig'd, for your long prosperity, and that your power of doing generous and charitable actions may be as extended as your will; which is by none more zealously desir'd than by

Your Grace's most humble,
most obliged, and most
obedient Servant,
JOHN DRYDEN.

PREFACE

'T IS with a poet, as with a man who designs to build, and is very exact, as he supposes, in casting up the cost beforehand; but, generally speaking, he is mistaken in his account, and reckons short of the expense he first intended. He alters his mind as the work proceeds, and will have this or that convenience more, of which he had not thought when he began. So has it happen'd to me; I have built a house, where I intended but a lodge; yet with better success than a certain nobleman, who, beginning with a dog kennel, never liv'd to finish the palace he had contriv'd.

From translating the first of Homer's *Iliads* (which I intended as an essay to the whole work) I proceeded to the translation of the twelfth book of Ovid's *Metamorphoses*, because it contains, among other things, the causes of the Trojan war. Here I ought in reason to have stopp'd; but the speeches of Ajax and Ulysses lying next in my way, I could not balk 'em. When I had compass'd them, I was so taken with the former part of the fifteenth book, (which is the masterpiece of the whole *Metamorphoses*,) that I enjoin'd myself the pleasing task of rend'ring it into English. And now I found, by the number of my verses, that they began to swell into a little volume; which gave me an occasion of looking backward on some beauties of my author, in his former books. There occurr'd to me the *Hunting of the Boar, Cinyras and Myrrha*, the good-natur'd story of *Baucis and Philemon*, with the rest, which I hope I have translated closely enough, and given them the same turn of verse which they had in the original; and this, I may say without vanity, is not the talent of every poet. He who has arriv'd the nearest to it, is the ingenious and learned Sandys, the best versifier of the former age; if I may properly call it by that name, which was the former part of this concluding century. For Spenser and Fairfax both flourish'd in the reign of Queen Elizabeth; great masters in our language, and who saw much farther into the beauties of our numbers than those who immediately follow'd them. Milton was the poetical son of Spenser, and Mr. Waller of Fairfax, for we have our lineal descents and clans as well as other families. Spenser more than once insinuates that the soul of Chaucer was transfus'd into his body, and that he was begotten by him two hundred years after his decease. Milton has acknowledg'd to me that Spenser was his original, and many besides myself have heard our famous Waller own that he deriv'd the harmony of his numbers from the *Godfrey of Bulloign*, which was turn'd into English by Mr. Fairfax. But to return. Having done with Ovid for this time, it came into my mind that our old English poet, Chaucer, in many things resembled him, and that with no disadvantage on the side of the modern author, as I shall endeavor to prove when I compare them; and as I am, and always have been, studious to promote the honor of my native country, so I soon resolv'd to put their merits to the trial, by turning some of the *Canterbury Tales* into our language, as it is now refin'd; for by this means, both the poets being set in the same light, and dress'd in the same English habit, story to be compar'd with story, a certain judgment may be made betwixt them by the reader, without obtruding my opinion on him. Or, if I seem partial to my countryman and predecessor in the laurel, the friends of antiquity are not few; and besides many of the learn'd, Ovid has almost all the beaux, and the whole fair sex, his declar'd patrons. Perhaps I have assum'd somewhat more to myself than they allow me, because I have adventur'd to sum up the evidence; but the readers are the jury, and their privilege remains entire, to decide according to the merits of the cause, or, if they please, to bring it to another hearing before some other court. In the mean time, to follow the thrid of my discourse, (as thoughts, according to Mr. Hobbes, have always some connection,) so from Chaucer I was led to think on Boccace, who was not only his contemporary, but also pursued the same studies; wrote novels in prose, and many works in verse; particularly is said to have invented the octave rhyme, or stanza of eight lines, which ever since has been maintain'd by the practice of all Italian writers, who are, or at least assume the title of, heroic poets. He and Chaucer, among other things, had this in common, that they refin'd their mother tongues; but with this difference, that Dante had begun to file their language, at least in verse, before the time of Boccace, who likewise receiv'd no little help from his master Petrarch. But the reformation of their prose was wholly owing to Boccace himself, who is yet the standard of purity in the Italian tongue; tho' many of his phrases are become obsolete, as in process of time it must needs happen. Chaucer (as you have formerly been told by our learn'd Mr. Rymer) first adorn'd and amplified our barren tongue from the Provençal, which was then the most polish'd of all the modern languages; but this subject has been copiously treated by that great critic, who deserves no little commendation from us his countrymen. For these reasons of time, and resemblance of genius in Chaucer and Boccace, I resolv'd to join them in my present work; to which I have added some original papers of my own; which, whether they are equal or inferior to my other poems, an author is the most

improper judge, and therefore I leave them wholly to the mercy of the reader. I will hope the best, that they will not be condemn'd; but if they should, I have the excuse of an old gentleman, who mounting on horseback before some ladies, when I was present, got up somewhat heavily, but desir'd of the fair spectators that they would count fourscore and eight before they judg'd him. By the mercy of God, I am already come within twenty years of his number, a cripple in my limbs; but what decays are in my mind, the reader must determine. I think myself as vigorous as ever in the faculties of my soul, excepting only my memory, which is not impair'd to any great degree; and if I lose not more of it, I have no great reason to complain. What judgment I had, increases rather than diminishes; and thoughts, such as they are, come crowding in so fast upon me, that my only difficulty is to choose or to reject; to run them into verse, or to give them the other harmony of prose. I have so long studied and practic'd both, that they are grown into a habit, and become familiar to me. In short, tho' I may lawfully plead some part of the old gentleman's excuse, yet I will reserve it till I think I have greater need, and ask no grains of allowance for the faults of this my present work, but those which are given of course to human frailty. I will not trouble my reader with the shortness of time in which I writ it, or the several intervals of sickness. They who think too well of their own performances are apt to boast in their prefaces how little time their works have cost them, and what other business of more importance interfer'd; but the reader will be as apt to ask the question, why they allow'd not a longer time to make their works more perfect, and why they had so despicable an opinion of their judges as to thrust their indigested stuff upon them, as if they deserv'd no better.

With this account of my present undertaking, I conclude the first part of this discourse; in the second part, as at a second sitting, tho' I alter not the draught, I must touch the same features over again, and change the dead coloring of the whole. In general, I will only say that I have written nothing which savors of immorality or profaneness; at least, I am not conscious to myself of any such intention. If there happen to be found an irreverent expression, or a thought too wanton, they are crept into my verses thro' my inadvertency; if the searchers find any in the cargo, let them be stav'd or forfeited, like counterbanded goods; at least, let their authors be answerable for them, as being but imported merchandise, and not of my own manufacture. On the other side, I have endeavor'd to choose such fables, both ancient and modern, as contain in each of them some instructive moral; which I could prove by induction, but the way is tedious, and they leap foremost into sight, without the reader's trouble of looking after them. I wish I could affirm, with a safe conscience, that I had taken the same care in all my former writings; for it must be own'd, that supposing verses are never so beautiful or pleasing, yet if they contain anything which shocks religion, or good manners, they are at best what Horace says of good numbers without good sense, *Versus inopes rerum, nugæque canoræ.* Thus far, I hope, I am right in court, without renouncing to my other right of self-defense, where I have been wrongfully accus'd, and my sense wiredrawn into blasphemy or bawdry, as it has often been by a religious lawyer, in a late pleading against the stage; in which he mixes truth with falsehood, and has not forgotten the old rule of calumniating strongly, that something may remain.

I resume the thrid of my discourse with the first of my translations, which was the *First Iliad* of Homer. If it shall please God to give me longer life, and moderate health, my intentions are to translate the whole *Ilias;* provided still that I meet with those encouragements from the public which may enable me to proceed in my undertaking with some cheerfulness. And this I dare assure the world beforehand, that I have found by trial Homer a more pleasing task than Virgil, (tho' I say not the translation will be less laborious.) For the Grecian is more according to my genius than the Latin poet. In the works of the two authors we may read their manners and natural inclinations, which are wholly different. Virgil was of a quiet, sedate temper; Homer was violent, impetuous, and full of fire. The chief talent of Virgil was propriety of thoughts, and ornament of words; Homer was rapid in his thoughts, and took all the liberties, both of numbers and of expressions, which his language, and the age in which he liv'd, allow'd him. Homer's invention was more copious, Virgil's more confin'd; so that if Homer had not led the way, it was not in Virgil to have begun heroic poetry; for nothing can be more evident than that the Roman poem is but the second part of the *Ilias;* a continuation of the same story, and the persons already form'd; the manners of Æneas are those of Hector superadded to those which Homer gave him. The adventures of Ulysses in the *Odysseis* are imitated in the first six books of Virgil's *Æneis;* and tho' the accidents are not the same, (which would have argued him of a servile, copying, and total barrenness of invention,) yet the seas were the same, in which both the heroes wander'd; and Dido cannot be denied to be the

poetical daughter of Calypso. The six latter books of Virgil's poem are the four and twenty *Iliads* contracted: a quarrel occasion'd by a lady, a single combat, battles fought, and a town besieg'd. I say not this in derogation to Virgil, neither do I contradict anything which I have formerly said in his just praise: for his episodes are almost wholly of his own invention; and the form which he has given to the telling makes the tale his own, even tho' the original story had been the same. But this proves, however, that Homer taught Virgil to design; and if invention be the first virtue of an epic poet, then the Latin poem can only be allow'd the second place. Mr. Hobbes, in the preface to his own bald translation of the *Ilias* (studying poetry as he did mathematics, when it was too late) — Mr. Hobbes, I say, begins the praise of Homer where he should have ended it. He tells us that the first beauty of an epic poem consists in diction, that is, in the choice of words, and harmony of numbers; now the words are the coloring of the work, which in the order of nature is last to be consider'd. The design, the disposition, the manners, and the thoughts, are all before it: where any of those are wanting or imperfect, so much wants or is imperfect in the imitation of human life; which is in the very definition of a poem. Words, indeed, like glaring colors, are the first beauties that arise and strike the sight: but if the draught be false or lame, the figures ill dispos'd, the manners obscure or inconsistent, or the thoughts unnatural, then the finest colors are but daubing, and the piece is a beautiful monster at the best. Neither Virgil nor Homer were deficient in any of the former beauties; but in this last, which is expression, the Roman poet is at least equal to the Grecian, as I have said elsewhere; supplying the poverty of his language by his musical ear, and by his diligence. But to return: our two great poets, being so different in their tempers, one choleric and sanguine, the other phlegmatic and melancholic; that which makes them excel in their several ways is that each of them has follow'd his own natural inclination, as well in forming the design as in the execution of it. The very heroes shew their authors: Achilles is hot, impatient, revengeful, *Impiger, iracundus, inexorabilis, acer* &c.; Æneas patient, considerate, careful of his people, and merciful to his enemies; ever submissive to the will of Heaven — *Quo fata trahunt retrahuntque sequamur.* I could please myself with enlarging on this subject, but am forc'd to defer it to a fitter time. From all I have said I will only draw this inference, that the action of Homer being more full of vigor than that of Virgil, according to the temper of the writer, is of consequence more pleasing to the reader. One warms you by degrees; the other sets you on fire all at once, and never intermits his heat. 'T is the same difference which Longinus makes betwixt the effects of eloquence in Demosthenes and Tully. One persuades; the other commands. You never cool while you read Homer, even not in the second book (a graceful flattery to his countrymen); but he hastens from the ships, and concludes not that book till he has made you an amends by the violent playing of a new machine. From thence he hurries on his action with variety of events, and ends it in less compass than two months. This vehemence of his, I confess, is more suitable to my temper; and therefore I have translated his first book with greater pleasure than any part of Virgil; but it was not a pleasure without pains. The continual agitations of the spirits must needs be a weak'ning of any constitution, especially in age; and many pauses are requir'd for refreshment betwixt the heats; the *Iliad* of itself being a third part longer than all Virgil's works together.

This is what I thought needful in this place to say of Homer. I proceed to Ovid and Chaucer, considering the former only in relation to the latter. With Ovid ended the golden age of the Roman tongue; from Chaucer the purity of the English tongue began. The manners of the poets were not unlike: both of them were well bred, well natur'd, amorous, and libertine, at least in their writings, it may be also in their lives. Their studies were the same, philosophy and philology. Both of them were knowing in astronomy, of which Ovid's books of the Roman feasts, and Chaucer's treatise of the Astrolabe, are sufficient witnesses. But Chaucer was likewise an astrologer, as were Virgil, Horace, Persius, and Manilius. Both writ with wonderful facility and clearness: neither were great inventors; for Ovid only copied the Grecian fables; and most of Chaucer's stories were taken from his Italian contemporaries, or their predecessors. Boccace his *Decameron* was first publish'd; and from thence our Englishman has borrow'd many of his *Canterbury Tales;* yet that of *Palamon and Arcite* was written in all probability by some Italian wit in a former age, as I shall prove hereafter. The tale of Grizild was the invention of Petrarch; by him sent to Boccace; from whom it came to Chaucer. *Troilus and Cressida* was also written by a Lombard author; but much amplified by our English translator, as well as beautified; the genius of our countrymen, in general, being rather to improve an invention, than to invent themselves; as is evident not only in our poetry, but in many of our manufactures. I find I have anticipated already, and taken up from Boccace before I come to him; but there is

so much less behind; and I am of the temper of most kings, *who love to be in debt,* are all for present money, no matter how they pay it afterwards: besides, the nature of a preface is rambling; never wholly out of the way, nor in it. This I have learn'd from the practice of honest Montaigne, and return at my pleasure to Ovid and Chaucer, of whom I have little more to say. Both of them built on the inventions of other men; yet since Chaucer had something of his own, as *The Wife of Bath's Tale, The Cock and the Fox,* which I have translated, and some others, I may justly give our countryman the precedence in that part; since I can remember nothing of Ovid which was wholly his. Both of them understood the manners, under which name I comprehend the passions, and, in a larger sense, the descriptions of persons, and their very habits; for an example, I see Baucis and Philemon as perfectly before me, as if some ancient painter had drawn them; and all the pilgrims in the *Canterbury Tales,* their humors, their features, and the very dress, as distinctly as if I had supp'd with them at the Tabard in Southwark; yet even there too the figures of Chaucer are much more lively, and set in a better light: which tho' I have not time to prove, yet I appeal to the reader, and am sure he will clear me from partiality. The thoughts and words remain to be consider'd in the comparison of the two poets; and I have sav'd myself one half of that labor, by owning that Ovid liv'd when the Roman tongue was in its meridian, Chaucer in the dawning of our language; therefore that part of the comparison stands not on an equal foot, any more than the diction of Ennius and Ovid, or of Chaucer and our present English. The words are given up as a post not to be defended in our poet, because he wanted the modern art of fortifying. The thoughts remain to be consider'd, and they are to be measur'd only by their propriety; that is, as they flow more or less naturally from the persons describ'd, on such and such occasions. The vulgar judges, which are nine parts in ten of all nations, who call conceits and jingles wit, who see Ovid full of them, and Chaucer altogether without them, will think me little less than mad, for preferring the Englishman to the Roman: yet, with their leave, I must presume to say that the things they admire are only glittering trifles, and so far from being witty, that in a serious poem they are nauseous, because they are unnatural. Would any man who is ready to die for love describe his passion like Narcissus? Would he think of *inopem me copia fecit,* and a dozen more of such expressions, pour'd on the neck of one another, and signifying all the same thing? If this were wit, was this a time to be witty, when the poor wretch was in the agony of death? This is just John Littlewit in *Bartholomew Fair*, who had a conceit (as he tells you) left him in his misery; a miserable conceit. On these occasions the poet should endeavor to raise pity; but instead of this, Ovid is tickling you to laugh. Virgil never made use of such machines, when he was moving you to commiserate the death of Dido: he would not destroy what he was building. Chaucer makes Arcite violent in his love, and unjust in the pursuit of it; yet when he came to die, he made him think more reasonably: he repents not of his love, for that had alter'd his character; but acknowledges the injustice of his proceedings, and resigns Emilia to Palamon. What would Ovid have done on this occasion? He would certainly have made Arcite witty on his deathbed. He had complain'd he was farther off from possession by being so near, and a thousand such boyisms, which Chaucer rejected as below the dignity of the subject. They who think otherwise would by the same reason prefer Lucan and Ovid to Homer and Virgil, and Martial to all four of them. As for the turn of words, in which Ovid particularly excels all poets, they are sometimes a fault, and sometimes a beauty, as they are us'd properly or improperly; but in strong passions always to be shunn'd, because passions are serious, and will admit no playing. The French have a high value for them; and I confess, they are often what they call delicate, when they are introduc'd with judgment; but Chaucer writ with more simplicity, and follow'd nature more closely, than to use them. I have thus far, to the best of my knowledge, been an upright judge betwixt the parties in competition, not meddling with the design nor the disposition of it; because the design was not their own, and in the disposing of it they were equal. It remains that I say somewhat of Chaucer in particular.

In the first place, as he is the father of English poetry, so I hold him in the same degree of veneration as the Grecians held Homer or the Romans Virgil. He is a perpetual fountain of good sense, learn'd in all sciences, and therefore speaks properly on all subjects: as he knew what to say, so he knows also when to leave off, a continence which is practic'd by few writers, and scarcely by any of the ancients, excepting Virgil and Horace. One of our late great poets is sunk in his reputation, because he could never forgive any conceit which came in his way, but swept like a drag-net, great and small. There was plenty enough, but the dishes were ill sorted; whole pyramids of sweetmeats for boys and women, but little of solid meat for men. All this proceeded not from any want of knowledge, but of judg-ment; neither did he want that in discerning the beauties and faults of other poets; but only indulg'd himself in the luxury of writing; and perhaps knew it was a fault, but hop'd the reader would not find it. For this reason, tho' he must always be thought a great poet, he is no longer esteem'd a good writer; and for ten impressions, which his works have had in so many successive years, yet at present a hundred books are scarcely purchas'd once a twelvemonth: for, as my last Lord Rochester said, tho' somewhat profanely, "Not being of God, he could not stand."

Chaucer follow'd Nature everywhere, but was never so bold to go beyond her; and there is a great difference of being *poeta* and *nimis poeta*, if we may believe Catullus, as much as betwixt a modest behavior and affectation. The verse of Chaucer, I confess, is not harmonious to us; but 'tis like the eloquence of one whom Tacitus commends, it was *auribus istius temporis accommodata:* they who liv'd with him, and some time after him, thought it musical; and it continues so even in our judgment, if compar'd with the numbers of Lydgate and Gower, his contemporaries: there is the rude sweetness of a Scotch tune in it, which is natural and pleasing, tho' not perfect. 'Tis true, I cannot go so far as he who publish'd the last edition of him; for he would make us believe the fault is in our ears, and that there were really ten syllables in a verse where we find but nine: but this opinion is not worth confuting; 'tis so gross and obvious an error, that common sense (which is a rule in everything but matters of faith and revelation) must convince the reader that equality of numbers in every verse which we call heroic was either not known, or not always practic'd, in Chaucer's age. It were an easy matter to produce some thousands of his verses, which are lame for want of half a foot, and sometimes a whole one, and which no pronunciation can make otherwise. We can only say, that he liv'd in the infancy of our poetry, and that nothing is brought to perfection at the first. We must be children before we grow men. There was an Ennius, and in process of time a Lucilius and a Lucretius, before Virgil and Horace; even after Chaucer there was a Spenser, a Harrington, a Fairfax, before Waller and Denham were in being: and our numbers were in their nonage till these last appear'd. I need say little of his parentage, life, and fortunes; they are to be found at large in all the editions of his works. He was employ'd abroad and favor'd by Edward the Third, Richard the Second, and Henry the Fourth, and was poet, as I suppose, to all three of them. In Richard's time, I doubt, he was a little dipp'd in the rebellion of the commons, and being brother-in-law to John of Ghant, it was no wonder if he follow'd the fortunes of that family, and was well with Henry the Fourth, when he had depos'd his predecessor. Neither is it to be admir'd, that Henry, who was a wise as well as a valiant prince, who claim'd by succession, and was sensible that his title was not sound, but was rightfully in Mortimer, who had married the heir of York ; it was not to be admir'd, I say, if that great politician should be pleas'd to have the greatest wit of those times in his interests, and to be the trumpet of his praises. Augustus had given him the example, by the advice of Mæcenas, who recommended Virgil and Horace to him ; whose praises help'd to make him popular while he was alive, and after his death have made him precious to posterity. As for the religion of our poet, he seems to have some little bias towards the opinions of Wycliffe, after John of Ghant his patron ; somewhat of which appears in the tale of Piers Plowman. Yet I cannot blame him for inveighing so sharply against the vices of the clergy in his age; their pride, their ambition, their pomp, their avarice, their worldly interest, deserv'd the lashes which he gave them, both in that and in most of his *Canterbury Tales :* neither has his contemporary Boccace spar'd them. Yet both those poets liv'd in much esteem with good and holy men in orders ; for the scandal which is given by particular priests reflects not on the sacred function. Chaucer's Monk, his Canon, and his Friar, took not from the character of his Good Parson. A satirical poet is the check of the laymen on bad priests. We are only to take care that we involve not the innocent with the guilty in the same condemnation. The good cannot be too much honor'd, nor the bad too coarsely us'd : for the corruption of the best becomes the worst. When a clergyman is whipp'd, his gown is first taken off, by which the dignity of his order is secur'd : if he be wrongfully accus'd, he has his action of slander ; and 'tis at the poet's peril if he transgress the law. But they will tell us that all kind of satire, tho' never so well deserv'd by particular priests, yet brings the whole order into contempt. Is then the peerage of England anything dishonor'd, when a peer suffers for his treason ? If he be libel'd or any way defam'd, he has his *scandalum magnatum* to punish the offender. They who use this kind of argument seem to be conscious to themselves of somewhat which has deserv'd the poet's lash, and are less concern'd for their public capacity than for their private ; at least there is pride at the bottom of their reasoning. If the faults of men in orders are only to be judg'd among themselves, they are all in some sort parties : for, since they say

the honor of their order is concern'd in every member of it, how can we be sure that they will be impartial judges ? How far I may be allow'd to speak my opinion in this case, I know not ; but I am sure a dispute of this nature caus'd mischief in abundance betwixt a king of England and an archbishop of Canterbury ; one standing up for the laws of his land, and the other for the honor (as he call'd it) of God's Church ; which ended in the murther of the prelate, and in the whipping of his Majesty from post to pillar for his penance. The learn'd and ingenious Dr. Drake has sav'd me the labor of inquiring into the esteem and reverence which the priests have had of old ; and I would rather extend than diminish any part of it : yet I must needs say, that when a priest provokes me without any occasion given him, I have no reason, unless it be the charity of a Christian, to forgive him : *prior læsit* is justification sufficient in the civil law. If I answer him in his own language, self-defense, I am sure, must be allow'd me ; and if I carry it farther, even to a sharp recrimination, somewhat may be indulg'd to human frailty. Yet my resentment has not wrought so far, but that I have follow'd Chaucer in his character of a holy man, and have enlarg'd on that subject with some pleasure, reserving to myself the right, if I shall think fit hereafter, to describe another sort of priests, such as are more easily to be found than the Good Parson ; such as have given the last blow to Christianity in this age, by a practice so contrary to their doctrine. But this will keep cold till another time. In the mean while I take up Chaucer where I left him. He must have been a man of a most wonderful comprehensive nature, because, as it has been truly observ'd of him, he has taken into the compass of his *Canterbury Tales* the various manners and humors (as we now call them) of the whole English nation, in his age. Not a single character has escap'd him. All his pilgrims are severally distinguish'd from each other ; and not only in their inclinations, but in their very physiognomies and persons. Baptista Porta could not have describ'd their natures better, than by the marks which the poet gives them. The matter and manner of their tales, and of their telling, are so suited to their different educations, humors, and callings, that each of them would be improper in any other mouth. Even the grave and serious characters are distinguish'd by their several sorts of gravity : their discourses are such as belong to their age, their calling, and their breeding ; such as are becoming of them, and of them only. Some of his persons are vicious, and some virtuous ; some are unlearn'd, or (as Chaucer calls them) lewd, and some are learn'd. Even the ribaldry of the low characters is different : the Reeve, the Miller, and the Cook are several men, and distinguish'd from each other, as much as the mincing Lady Prioress and the broad-speaking gap-tooth'd Wife of Bath. But enough of this : there is such a variety of game springing up before me, that I am distracted in my choice, and know not which to follow. 'T is sufficient to say, according to the proverb, that here is God's plenty. We have our forefathers and great-grandames all before us, as they were in Chaucer's days; their general characters are still remaining in mankind, and even in England, tho' they are call'd by other names than those of Monks and Friars, and Canons, and Lady Abbesses, and Nuns : for mankind is ever the same, and nothing lost out of nature, tho' everything is alter'd. May I have leave to do myself the justice — since my enemies will do me none, and are so far from granting me to be a good poet, that they will not allow me so much as to be a Christian, or a moral man — may I have leave, I say, to inform my reader that I have confin'd my choice to such tales of Chaucer as savor nothing of immodesty. If I had desir'd more to please than to instruct, the Reeve, the Miller, the Shipman, the Merchant, the Sumner, and, above all, the Wife of Bath, in the prologue to her tale, would have procur'd me as many friends and readers, as there are beaux and ladies of pleasure in the town. But I will no more offend against good manners : I am sensible, as I ought to be, of the scandal I have given by my loose writings ; and make what reparation I am able, by this public acknowledgment. If anything of this nature, or of profaneness, be crept into these poems, I am so far from defending it, that I disown it. *Totum hoc indictum volo.* Chaucer makes another manner of apology for his broad speaking, and Boccace makes the like ; but I will follow neither of them. Our countryman, in the end of his characters, before the *Canterbury Tales*, thus excuses the ribaldry, which is very gross in many of his novels :

> But first, I pray you of your courtesy,
> That ye ne arrete it nought my villany,
> Though that I plainly speak in this mattere
> To tellen you her words, and eke her chere :
> Ne though I speak her words properly,
> For this ye knowen as well as I,
> Who shall tellen a tale after a man,
> He mote rehearse as nye as ever he can :
> Everich word of it been in his charge,
> *All speke he never so rudely ne large.*
> Or else he mote tellen his tale untrue,
> Or feine things, or find words new :
> He may not spare, altho he were his brother,
> He mote as well say o word as another.
> Christ spake himself full broad in holy writ,
> And well I wote no villany is it.
> Eke Plato saith, who so can him rede,
> The words mote been cousin to the dede.

Yet if a man should have enquir'd of Boccace or of Chaucer, what need they had of introducing such characters, where obscene words were proper in their mouths, but very undecent to be heard ; I know not what answer they could have made : for that reason, such tales shall be left untold by me. You have here a specimen of Chaucer's language, which is so obsolete that his sense is scarce to be understood ; and you have likewise more than one example of his unequal numbers, which were mention'd before. Yet many of his verses consist of ten syllables, and the words not much behind our present English : as for example, these two lines, in the description of the carpenter's young wife :

> Wincing she was, as is a jolly colt,
> Long as a mast, and upright as a bolt.

I have almost done with Chaucer, when I have answer'd some objections relating to my present work. I find some people are offended that I have turn'd these tales into modern English ; because they think them unworthy of my pains, and look on Chaucer as a dry, old-fashion'd wit, not worth reviving. I have often heard the late Earl of Leicester say that Mr. Cowley himself was of that opinion ; who having read him over at my lord's request, declar'd he had no taste of him. I dare not advance my opinion against the judgment of so great an author ; but I think it fair, however, to leave the decision to the public : Mr. Cowley was too modest to set up for a dictator ; and being shock'd perhaps with his old style, never examin'd into the depth of his good sense. Chaucer, I confess, is a rough diamond, and must first be polish'd, ere he shines. I deny not, likewise, that, living in our early days of poetry, he writes not always of a piece, but sometimes mingles trivial things with those of greater moment. Sometimes also, tho' not often, he runs riot, like Ovid, and knows not when he has said enough. But there are more great wits, beside Chaucer, whose fault is their excess of conceits, and those ill sorted. An author is not to write all he can, but only all he ought. Having observ'd this redundancy in Chaucer, (as it is an easy matter for a man of ordinary parts to find a fault in one of greater.) I have not tied myself to a literal translation ; but have often omitted what I judg'd unnecessary, or not of dignity enough to appear in the company of better thoughts, I have presum'd farther, in some places, and added somewhat of my own where I thought my author was deficient, and had not given his thoughts their true luster, for want of words in the beginning of our language. And to this I was the more embolden'd, because (if I may be permitted to say it of myself) I found I had a soul congenial to his, and that

I had been conversant in the same studies. Another poet, in another age, may take the same liberty with my writings; if at least they live long enough to deserve correction. It was also necessary sometimes to restore the sense of Chaucer, which was lost or mangled in the errors of the press. Let this example suffice at present; in the story of *Palamon and Arcite*, where the temple of Diana is describ'd, you find these verses, in all the editions of our author:

> There saw I Danè turned unto a tree,
> I mean not the goddess Diane,
> But Venus daughter, which that hight Danè;

which after a little consideration I knew was to be reform'd into this sense, that Daphne, the daughter of Peneus, was turn'd into a tree. I durst not make thus bold with Ovid, lest some future Milbourne should arise, and say I varied from my author, because I understood him not.

But there are other judges, who think I ought not to have translated Chaucer into English, out of a quite contrary notion: they suppose there is a certain veneration due to his old language; and that it is little less than profanation and sacrilege to alter it. They are farther of opinion that somewhat of his good sense will suffer in this transfusion, and much of the beauty of his thoughts will infallibly be lost, which appear with more grace in their old habit. Of this opinion was that excellent person whom I mention'd, the late Earl of Leicester, who valued Chaucer as much as Mr. Cowley despis'd him. My lord dissuaded me from this attempt, (for I was thinking of it some years before his death,) and his authority prevail'd so far with me as to defer my undertaking while he liv'd, in deference to him: yet my reason was not convinc'd with what he urg'd against it. If the first end of a writer be to be understood, then as his language grows obsolete, his thoughts must grow obscure:

> *Multa renascentur quæ nunc cecidere ; cadentque,*
> *Quæ nunc sunt in honore vocabula, si volet usus,*
> *Quem penes arbitrium est et jus et norma loquendi.*

When an ancient word for its sound and significancy deserves to be reviv'd, I have that reasonable veneration for antiquity, to restore it. All beyond this is superstition. Words are not like landmarks, so sacred as never to be remov'd; customs are chang'd, and even statutes are silently repeal'd, when the reason ceases for which they were enacted. As for the other part of the argument, that his thoughts will lose of their original beauty, by the innovation of words; in the first place, not only their beauty, but their being is lost, where they are no longer understood, which is the present case. I grant that something must be lost in all transfusion, that is, in all translations; but the sense will remain, which would otherwise be lost, or at least

be maim'd, when it is scarce intelligible; and that but to a few. How few are there who can read Chaucer so as to understand him perfectly! And if imperfectly, then with less profit and no pleasure. 'T is not for the use of some old Saxon friends that I have taken these pains with him: let them neglect my version, because they have no need of it. I made it for their sakes who understand sense and poetry as well as they, when that poetry and sense is put into words which they understand. I will go farther, and dare to add, that what beauties I lose in some places, I give to others which had them not originally; but in this I may be partial to myself; let the reader judge, and I submit to his decision. Yet I think I have just occasion to complain of them, who, because they understand Chaucer, would deprive the greater part of their countrymen of the same advantage, and hoard him up, as misers do their grandam gold, only to look on it themselves and hinder others from making use of it. In sum, I seriously protest that no man ever had, or can have, a greater veneration for Chaucer, than myself. I have translated some part of his works, only that I might perpetuate his memory, or at least refresh it, amongst my countrymen. If I have alter'd him anywhere for the better, I must at the same time acknowledge that I could have done nothing without him: *facile est inventis addere*, is no great commendation; and I am not so vain to think I have deserv'd a greater. I will conclude what I have to say of him singly, with this one remark: a lady of my acquaintance, who keeps a kind of correspondence with some authors of the fair sex in France, has been inform'd by them, that Mademoiselle de Scudéry, who is as old as Sibyl, and inspir'd like her by the same God of Poetry, is at this time translating Chaucer into modern French. From which I gather that he has been formerly translated into the old Provençal (for how she should come to understand old English I know not). But the matter of fact being true, it makes me think that there is something in it like fatality; that, after certain periods of time, the fame and memory of great wits should be renew'd, as Chaucer is both in France and England. If this be wholly chance, 't is extraordinary, and I dare not call it more, for fear of being tax'd with superstition.

Boccace comes last to be consider'd, who, living in the same age with Chaucer, had the same genius, and follow'd the same studies: both writ novels, and each of them cultivated his mother tongue. But the greatest resemblance of our two modern authors being in their familiar style, and pleasing way of relating comical adventures, I may pass it over, because I have translated nothing from Boccace of that nature. In the serious part of poetry, the advantage is wholly on Chaucer's side; for tho' the Englishman has borrow'd many tales from the Italian, yet it appears that those of Boccace were not generally of his own making, but taken from authors of former ages, and by him only model'd; so that what there was of invention in either of them may be judg'd equal. But Chaucer has refin'd on Boccace, and has mended the stories which he has borrow'd, in his way of telling; tho' prose allows more liberty of thought, and the expression is more easy when unconfin'd by numbers. Our countryman carries weight, and yet wins the race at disadvantage. I desire not the reader should take my word, and therefore I will set two of their discourses on the same subject, in the same light, for every man to judge betwixt them. I translated Chaucer first, and, amongst the rest, pitch'd on *The Wife of Bath's Tale;* not daring, as I have said, to adventure on her prologue, because 't is too licentious: there Chaucer introduces an old woman of mean parentage, whom a youthful knight of noble blood was forc'd to marry, and consequently loath'd her; the crone being in bed with him on the wedding night, and finding his aversion, endeavors to win his affection by reason, and speaks a good word for herself (as who could blame her?) in hope to mollify the sullen bridegroom. She takes her topics from the benefits of poverty, the advantages of old age and ugliness, the vanity of youth, and the silly pride of ancestry and titles without inherent virtue, which is the true nobility. When I had clos'd Chaucer, I return'd to Ovid, and translated some more of his fables; and by this time had so far forgotten *The Wife of Bath's Tale,* that, when I took up Boccace, unawares I fell on the same argument of preferring virtue to nobility of blood, and titles, in the story of Sigismonda; which I had certainly avoided for the resemblance of the two discourses, if my memory had not fail'd me. Let the reader weigh them both; and if he thinks me partial to Chaucer, 't is in him to right Boccace.

I prefer in our countryman, far above all his other stories, the noble poem of *Palamon and Arcite,* which is of the epic kind, and perhaps not much inferior to the *Ilias* or the *Æneis:* the story is more pleasing than either of them, the manners as perfect, the diction as poetical, the learning as deep and various, and the disposition full as artful; only it includes a greater length of time, as taking up seven years at least; but Aristotle has left undecided the duration of the action; which yet is easily reduc'd into the compass of a year, by a narration of what preceded the return of Palamon to Athens. I had thought for the honor of our

nation, and more particularly for his, whose laurel, tho' unworthy, I have worn after him, that this story was of English growth, and Chaucer's own; but I was undeceiv'd by Boccace; for, casually looking on the end of his seventh *Giornata,* I found Dioneo (under which name he shadows himself) and Fiametta (who represents his mistress, the natural daughter of Robert, King of Naples), of whom these words are spoken: *Dioneo e Fiametta gran pezza cantarono insieme d' Arcita, e di Palamone:* by which it appears that this story was written before the time of Boccace, but, the name of its author being wholly lost, Chaucer is now become an original; and I question not but the poem has receiv'd many beauties by passing thro' his noble hands. Besides this tale, there is another of his own invention, after the manner of the Provençals, call'd *The Flower and the Leaf;* with which I was so particularly pleas'd, both for the invention and the moral, that I cannot hinder myself from recommending it to the reader.

As a corollary to this preface, in which I have done justice to others, I owe somewhat to myself: not that I think it worth my time to enter the lists with one M——, or one B——, but barely to take notice, that such men there are who have written scurrilously against me, without any provocation. M——, who is in orders, pretends amongst the rest this quarrel to me, that I have fallen foul on priesthood: if I have, I am only to ask pardon of good priests, and am afraid his part of the reparation will come to little. Let him be satisfied that he shall not be able to force himself upon me for an adversary. I contemn him too much to enter into competition with him. His own translations of Virgil have answer'd his criticisms on mine. If (as they say he has declar'd in print) he prefers the version of Ogleby to mine, the world has made him the same compliment: for 't is agreed on all hands, that he writes even below Ogleby: that, you will say, is not easily to be done; but what cannot M—— bring about? I am satisfied, however, that while he and I live together, I shall not be thought the worst poet of the age. It looks as if I had desir'd him underhand to write so ill against me; but upon my honest word I have not brib'd him to do me this service, and am wholly guiltless of his pamphlet. 'T is true, I should be glad if I could persuade him to continue his good offices, and write such another critique on anything of mine: for I find by experience he has a great stroke with the reader, when he condemns any of my poems, to make the world have a better opinion of them. He has taken some pains with my poetry, but nobody will be persuaded to take the same with his. If I had taken to the

Church, (as he affirms, but which was never in my thoughts,) I should have had more sense, if not more grace, than to have turn'd myself out of my benefice by writing libels on my parishioners. But his account of my manners and my principles are of a piece with his cavils and his poetry ; and so I have done with him for ever.

As for the City Bard, or Knight Physician, I hear his quarrel to me is that I was the author of *Absalom and Achitophel*, which, he thinks, is a little hard on his fanatic patrons in London.

But I will deal the more civilly with his two poems, because nothing ill is to be spoken of the dead ; and therefore peace be to the *manes* of his *Arthurs*. I will only say that it was not for this noble knight that I drew the plan of an epic poem on King Arthur, in my preface to the translation of Juvenal. The guardian angels of kingdoms were machines too ponderous for him to manage ; and therefore he rejected them, as Dares did the whirlbats of Eryx. when they were thrown before him by Entellus. Yet from that preface he plainly took his hint : for he began immediately upon the story, tho' he had the baseness not to acknowledge his benefactor, but, instead of it, to traduce me in a libel.

I shall say the less of Mr. Collier, because in many things he has tax'd me justly ; and I have pleaded guilty to all thoughts and expressions of mine which can be truly argued of obscenity, profaneness, or immorality ; and retract them. If he be my enemy, let him triumph ; if he be my friend, as I have given him no personal occasion to be otherwise, he will be glad of my repentance. It becomes me not to draw my pen in the defense of a bad cause, when I have so often drawn it for a good one. Yet it were not difficult to prove that in many places he has perverted my meaning by his glosses, and interpreted my words into blasphemy and bawdry, of which they were not guilty. Besides that, he is too much given to horseplay in his raillery, and comes to battle like a dictator from the plow. I will not say : " The zeal of God's house has eaten him up ; " but I am sure it has devour'd some part of his good manners and civility. It might also be doubted whether it were altogether zeal which prompted him to this rough manner of proceeding : perhaps it became not one of his function to rake into the rubbish of ancient and modern plays ; a divine might have employ'd his pains to better purpose than in the nastiness of Plautus and Aristophanes ; whose examples, as they excuse not me, so it might be possibly suppos'd that he read them not without some pleasure. They who have written commentaries on those poets, or on Horace, Juvenal,

and Martial, have explain'd some vices which, without their interpretation, had been unknown to modern times. Neither has he judg'd impartially betwixt the former age and us.

There is more bawdry in one play of Fletcher's, call'd *The Custom of the Country*, than in all ours together. Yet this has been often acted on the stage in my remembrance. Are the times so much more reform'd now than they were five and twenty years ago ? If they are, I congratulate the amendment of our morals. But I am not to prejudice the cause of my fellow poets, tho' I abandon my own defense : they have some of them answer'd for themselves, and neither they nor I can think Mr. Collier so formidable an enemy that we should shun him. He has lost ground at the latter end of the day, by pursuing his point too far, like the Prince of Condé at the battle of Seneffe : from immoral plays to no plays, *ab abusu ad usum, non valet consequentia*. But being a party, I am not to erect myself into a judge. As for the rest of those who have written against me, they are such scoundrels that they deserve not the least notice to be taken of them. B—— and M—— are only distinguish'd from the crowd by being remember'd to their infamy :

> —— *Demetri, teque Tigelli*
> *Discipulorum inter jubeo plorare cathedras.*

TO HER GRACE

THE DUCHESS OF ORMOND

WITH THE FOLLOWING POEM OF

PALAMON AND ARCITE

FROM CHAUCER

MADAM,

THE bard who first adorn'd our native tongue,
Tun'd to his British lyre this ancient song;
Which Homer might without a blush rehearse,
And leaves a doubtful palm in Virgil's verse:
He match'd their beauties, where they most excel;
Of love sung better, and of arms as well.
   Vouchsafe, illustrious Ormond, to behold
What pow'r the charms of beauty had of old;
Nor wonder if such deeds of arms were done,
Inspir'd by two fair eyes, that sparkled like your own.   10
   If Chaucer by the best idea wrought,
And poets can divine each other's thought,

The fairest nymph before his eyes he set;
And then the fairest was Plantagenet;
Who three contending princes made her
   prize,
And rul'd the rival nations with her eyes;
Who left immortal trophies of her fame,
And to the noblest order gave the name.
   Like her, of equal kindred to the throne,
You keep her conquests, and extend your
   own: 20
As when the stars, in their ethereal race, ⎤
At length have roll'd around the liquid ⎟
   space,   ⎬
At certain periods they resume their ⎟
   place,   ⎦
From the same point of heav'n their course
   advance,
And move in measures of their former
   dance;
Thus, after length of ages, she returns,
Restor'd in you, and the same place adorns;
Or you perform her office in the sphere,
Born of her blood, and make a new Pla-
   tonic year.
   O true Plantagenet, O race divine,   30
(For beauty still is fatal to the line,)
Had Chaucer liv'd that angel face to view,
Sure he had drawn his Emily from you;
Or had you liv'd to judge the doubtful
   right,
Your noble Palamon had been the knight;
And conqu'ring Theseus from his side had
   sent
Your gen'rous lord, to guide the Theban
   government.
   Time shall accomplish that; and I shall
   see
A Palamon in him, in you an Emily.
   Already have the Fates your path pre-
   par'd,   40
And sure presage your future sway de-
   clar'd:
When westward, like the sun, you took
   your way,
And from benighted Britain bore the day,
Blue Triton gave the signal from the shore,
The ready Nereids heard, and swam before,
To smooth the seas; a soft Etesian gale
But just inspir'd, and gently swell'd the sail;
Portunus took his turn, whose ample ⎤
   hand   ⎟
Heav'd up the lighten'd keel, and sunk ⎬
   the sand,   ⎟
And steer'd the sacred vessel safe to ⎟
   land.   50 ⎦

The land, if not restrain'd, had met your
   way,
Projected out a neck, and jutted to the
   sea.
Hibernia, prostrate at your feet, ador'd,
In you, the pledge of her expected lord,
Due to her isle; a venerable name;
His father and his grandsire known to
   fame:
Aw'd by that house, accustom'd to com- ⎤
   mand,   ⎬
The sturdy kerns in due subjection stand, ⎟
Nor hear the reins in any foreign hand. ⎦
   At your approach, they crowded to the
   port;   60
And scarcely landed, you create a court:
As Ormond's harbinger, to you they run;
For Venus is the promise of the sun.
   The waste of civil wars, their towns de-
   stroy'd,
Pales unhonor'd, Ceres unemploy'd,
Were all forgot; and one triumphant day
Wip'd all the tears of three campaigns
   away.
Blood, rapines, massacres, were cheaply
   bought,
So mighty recompense your beauty
   brought.
   As when the dove returning bore the
   mark   70
Of earth restor'd to the long-lab'ring ark,
The relics of mankind, secure of rest, ⎤
Op'd ev'ry window to receive the guest, ⎟
And the fair bearer of the message ⎬
   bless'd;   ⎦
So, when you came, with loud repeated ⎤
   cries,   ⎟
The nation took an omen from your eyes, ⎬
And God advanc'd his rainbow in the ⎟
   skies,   ⎦
To sign inviolable peace restor'd;
The saints, with solemn shouts, proclaim'd
   the new accord.
   When at your second coming you ap-
   pear,   80
(For I foretell that millenary year,)
The sharpen'd share shall vex the soil no
   more,
But earth unbidden shall produce her store;
The land shall laugh, the circling ocean
   smile,
And Heav'n's indulgence bless the holy isle.
   Heav'n from all ages has reserv'd for
   you
That happy clime which venom never knew:

Or if it had been there, your eyes alone
Have pow'r to chase all poison but their
  own.
  Now in this interval, which fate has
    cast   90
Betwíxt your future glories and your past,
This pause of pow'r, 't is Ireland's hour to
  mourn,
While England celebrates your safe return,
By which you seem the seasons to com-
  mand,
And bring our summers back to their for-
  saken land.
  The vanquish'd isle our leisure must ⎤
    attend,   ⎟
Till the fair blessing we vouchsafe to ⎬
  send;   ⎟
Nor can we spare you long, tho' often we ⎦
  may lend.
The dove was twice employ'd abroad, be-
  fore
The world was dried and she return'd no
  more.   100
  Nor dare we trust so soft a messenger,
New from her sickness, to that northern
  air;
Rest here a while your luster to restore,
That they may see you as you shone be-
  fore,
For yet, th' eclipse not wholly past, you
  wade
Thro' some remains, and dimness of a
  shade.
  A subject in his prince may claim a
    right,
Nor suffer him with strength impair'd to
  fight;
Till force returns, his ardor we restrain,
And curb his warlike wish to cross the
  main.   110
  Now past the danger, let the learn'd be-
    gin
Th' enquiry where disease could enter in;
How those malignant atoms forc'd their
  way,
What in the faultless frame they found to
  make their prey;
Where ev'ry element was weigh'd so ⎤
  well,   ⎟
That Heav'n alone, who mix'd the mass, ⎬
  could tell   ⎟
Which of the four ingredients could re- ⎦
  bel;
And where, imprison'd in so sweet a cage,
A soul might well be pleas'd to pass an age.

And yet the fine materials made it
  weak;   120
Porcelain, by being pure, is apt to break:
Ev'n to your breast the sickness durst ⎤
  aspire;   ⎟
And, forc'd from that fair temple to re- ⎬
  tire,   ⎟
Profanely set the holy place on fire. ⎦
In vain your lord, like young Vespasian,
  mourn'd,
When the fierce flames the sanctuary
  burn'd;
And I prepar'd to pay in verses rude
A most detested act of gratitude:
Ev'n this had been your elegy, which now
Is offer'd for your health, the table of my
  vow.   130
  Your angel sure our Morley's mind in-
    spir'd,
To find the remedy your ill requir'd;
As once the Macedon, by Jove's decree,
Was taught to dream an herb for Ptolo-
  mee:
Or Heav'n, which had such over-cost be-
  stow'd,
As scarce it could afford to flesh and blood,
So lik'd the frame, he would not work
  anew,
To save the charges of another you.
Or by his middle science did he steer, ⎤
And saw some great contingent good ap- ⎬
  pear,   140 ⎟
Well worth a miracle to keep you here; ⎦
And, for that end, preserv'd the precious
  mold,
Which all the future Ormonds was to hold;
And meditated in his better mind
An heir from you, who may redeem the
  failing kind.
  Blest be the pow'r which has at once re-
    stor'd
The hopes of lost succession to your lord;
Joy to the first and last of each degree, ⎤
Virtue to courts, and, what I long'd to ⎬
  see,   ⎟
To you the Graces, and the Muse to me. ⎦
  O daughter of the rose, whose cheeks
    unite   151
The diff'ring titles of the red and white;
Who heav'n's alternate beauty well dis-
  play,
The blush of morning, and the milky way;
Whose face is paradise, but fenc'd from sin:
For God in either eye has plac'd a cheru-
  bin.

All is your lord's alone; ev'n absent, he
Employs the care of chaste Penelope.
For him you waste in tears your widow'd
    hours,
For him your curious needle paints the
    flow'rs;   160
Such works of old imperial dames were
    taught;
Such, for Ascanius, fair Elisa wrought.
    The soft recesses of your hours improve
The three fair pledges of your happy love:
All other parts of pious duty done,
You owe your Ormond nothing but a son;
To fill in future times his father's place,
And wear the garter of his mother's race.

PALAMON AND ARCITE

OR, THE KNIGHT'S TALE

IN THREE BOOKS

BOOK I

In days of old, there liv'd, of mighty fame,
A valiant prince, and Theseus was his
    name:
A chief, who more in feats of arms excell'd,
The rising nor the setting sun beheld.
Of Athens he was lord; much land he won,
And added foreign countries to his crown.
In Scythia with the warrior queen he
    strove,
Whom first by force he conquer'd, then by
    love;
He brought in triumph back the beauteous
    dame,
With whom her sister, fair Emilia, came. 10
With honor to his home let Theseus ride,
With Love to friend, and Fortune for his
    guide,
And his victorious army at his side.
I pass their warlike pomp, their proud
    array,
Their shouts, their songs, their welcome on
    the way:
But, were it not too long, I would recite
The feats of Amazons, the fatal fight
Betwixt the hardy queen and hero knight;
The town besieg'd, and how much blood it
    cost
The female army and th' Athenian host; 20
The spousals of Hippolyta the queen;
What tilts and turneys at the feast were
    seen;

The storm at their return, the ladies' fear:
But these, and other things, I must forbear.
The field is spacious I design to sow,
With oxen far unfit to draw the plow:
The remnant of my tale is of a length
To tire your patience, and to waste my
    strength;
And trivial accidents shall be forborne,
That others may have time to take their
    turn;   30
As was at first enjoin'd us by mine host —
That he whose tale is best, and pleases
    most,
Should win his supper at our common cost.
    And therefore where I left, I will
    pursue
This ancient story, whether false or true,
In hope it may be mended with a new.
The prince I mention'd, full of high renown,
In this array drew near th' Athenian town;
When in his pomp and utmost of his pride,
Marching, he chanc'd to cast his eye aside, 40
And saw a choir of mourning dames, who
    lay
By two and two across the common way:
At his approach they rais'd a rueful cry,
And beat their breasts, and held their hands
    on high,
Creeping and crying, till they seiz'd at last
His courser's bridle, and his feet embrac'd.
    "Tell me," said Theseus, "what and
    whence you are,
And why this funeral pageant you prepare.
Is this the welcome of my worthy deeds,
To meet my triumph in ill-omen'd weeds? 50
Or envy you my praise, and would destroy
With grief my pleasures, and pollute my
    joy?
Or are you injur'd, and demand relief?
Name your request, and I will ease your
    grief."
    The most in years of all the mourning
    train
Began; (but sounded first away for pain;)
Then, scarce recover'd, spoke: "Nor envy
    we
Thy great renown, nor grudge thy victory;
'T is thine, O king, th' afflicted to redress,
And fame has fill'd the world with thy
    success: 60
We wretched women sue for that alone,
Which of thy goodness is refus'd to none.
Let fall some drops of pity on our grief,
If what we beg be just, and we deserve
    relief:

For none of us, who now thy grace implore,
But held the rank of sovereign queen
    before;
Till, thanks to giddy Chance, which never
    bears
That mortal bliss should last for length of
    years,
She cast us headlong from our high estate,
And here in hope of thy return we wait; 70
And long have waited in the temple nigh,
Built to the gracious goddess Clemency.
But rev'rence thou the pow'r whose name
    it bears,
Relieve th' oppress'd, and wipe the widows'
    tears.
I, wretched I, have other fortune seen,
The wife of Capaneus, and once a queen:
At Thebes he fell; curst be the fatal day!
And all the rest thou seest in this array,
To make their moan, their lords in battle
    lost
Before that town besieg'd by our con-
    fed'rate host: 80
But Creon, old and impious, who commands
The Theban city, and usurps the lands,
Denies the rites of fun'ral fires to those
Whose breathless bodies yet he calls his
    foes.
Unburn'd, unburied, on a heap they lie;
Such is their fate, and such his tyranny;
No friend has leave to bear away the dead,
But with their lifeless limbs his hounds are
    fed.
At this she shriek'd aloud; the mournful
    train
Echo'd her grief, and grov'ling on the
    plain,   90
With groans, and hands upheld, to move
    his mind,
Besought his pity to their helpless kind !
  The prince was touch'd, his tears began
    to flow,
And, as his tender heart would break in
    two,
He sigh'd; and could not but their fate de-
    plore,
So wretched now, so fortunate before.
Then lightly from his lofty steed he flew,
And, raising one by one the suppliant crew,
To comfort each, full solemnly he swore,
That by the faith which knights to knight-
    hood bore,   100
And whate'er else to chivalry belongs,
He would not cease, till he reveng'd their
    wrongs;

That Greece should see perform'd what he
    declar'd,
And cruel Creon find his just reward.
He said no more, but, shunning all delay,
Rode on, nor enter'd Athens on his way;
But left his sister and his queen behind,
And wav'd his royal banner in the wind,
Where in an argent field the God of War
Was drawn triumphant on his iron car; 110
Red was his sword, and shield, and whole
    attire,
And all the godhead seem'd to glow with
    fire;
Ev'n the ground glitter'd where the stand-
    ard flew,
And the green grass was dyed to sanguine
    hue.
High on his pointed lance his pennon bore
His Cretan fight, the conquer'd Minotaur:
The soldiers shout around with generous
    rage,
And in that victory their own presage.
He prais'd their ardor, inly pleas'd to see
His host the flow'r of Grecian chivalry. 120
All day he march'd, and all th' ensuing
    night,
And saw the city with returning light.
The process of the war I need not tell,
How Theseus conquer'd, and how Creon
    fell;
Or after, how by storm the walls were won,
Or how the victor sack'd and burn'd the
    town;
How to the ladies he restor'd again
The bodies of their lords in battle slain;
And with what ancient rites they were in-
    terr'd —
All these to fitter time shall be deferr'd. 130
I spare the widows' tears, their woful cries,
And howling at their husbands' obsequies;
How Theseus at these fun'rals did assist,
And with what gifts the mourning dames
    dismiss'd.
  Thus when the victor chief had Creon
    slain,
And conquer'd Thebes, he pitch'd upon the
    plain
His mighty camp, and, when the day re-
    turn'd,
The country wasted, and the hamlets burn'd,
And left the pillagers, to rapine bred,   139
Without control to strip and spoil the dead.
  There, in a heap of slain, among the rest
Two youthful knights they found beneath
    a load oppress'd

Of slaughter'd foes, whom first to death
   they sent,
The trophies of their strength, a bloody
   monument.
Both fair, and both of royal blood they
   seem'd,
Whom kinsmen to the crown the heralds
   deem'd:
That day in equal arms they fought for
   fame;
Their swords, their shields, their surcoats
   were the same.
Close by each other laid, they press'd the
   ground,
Their manly bosoms pierc'd with many a
   griesly wound.   150
Nor well alive nor wholly dead they were,
But some faint signs of feeble life appear;
The wand'ring breath was on the wing to
   part,
Weak was the pulse, and hardly heav'd the
   heart.
These two were sisters' sons; and Arcite one,
Much fam'd in fields, with valiant Palamon.
From these their costly arms the spoilers
   rent,
And softly both convey'd to Theseus' tent:
Whom, known of Creon's line, and cur'd with
   care,   159
He to his city sent as pris'ners of the war,
Hopeless of ransom, and condemn'd to lie
In durance, doom'd a ling'ring death to die.
   This done, he march'd away with war- ⎫
     like sound,   ⎪
And to his Athens turn'd with laurels ⎬
     crown'd,   ⎪
Where happy long he liv'd, much lov'd, ⎪
     and more renown'd.   ⎭
But in a tow'r, and never to be loos'd,
The woful captive kinsmen are enclos'd.
   Thus year by year they pass, and day by
   day,
Till once ('t was on the morn of cheerful
   May)
The young Emilia, fairer to be seen   170
Than the fair lily on the flow'ry green,
More fresh than May herself in blossoms
   new,
For with the rosy color strove her hue,
Wak'd, as her custom was, before the day,
To do th' observance due to sprightly May:
For sprightly May commands our youth
   to keep
The vigils of her night, and breaks their
   sluggard sleep;

Each gentle breast with kindly warmth
   she moves,
Inspires new flames, revives extinguish'd
   loves.
In this remembrance Emily ere day   180
Arose, and dress'd herself in rich array;
Fresh as the month, and as the morning
   fair:
Adown her shoulders fell her length of
   hair;
A riband did the braided tresses bind,
The rest was loose, and wanton'd in the
   wind.
Aurora had but newly chas'd the night,
And purpled o'er the sky with blushing
   light,
When to the garden walk she took her ⎫
   way,   ⎪
To sport and trip along in cool of day, ⎬
And offer maiden vows in honor of the ⎪
   May.   190 ⎭
   At ev'ry turn she made a little stand,
And thrust among the thorns her lily hand
To draw the rose, and ev'ry rose she drew,
She shook the stalk, and brush'd away the
   dew;
Then party-color'd flow'rs of white and red
She wove, to make a garland for her head:
This done, she sung and carol'd out so
   clear
That men and angels might rejoice to hear;
Ev'n wond'ring Philomel forgot to sing,
And learn'd from her to welcome in the
   spring.   200
The tow'r, of which before was mention
   made,
Within whose keep the captive knights
   were laid,
Built of a large extent, and strong withal,
Was one partition of the palace wall;
The garden was enclos'd within the square
Where young Emilia took the morning air.
It happen'd Palamon, the pris'ner knight,
Restless for woe, arose before the light,
And with his jailer's leave desir'd to
   breathe
An air more wholesome than the damps
   beneath.   210
This granted, to the tow'r he took his way,
Cheer'd with the promise of a glorious day;
Then cast a languishing regard around, ⎫
And saw, with hateful eyes, the temples ⎪
   crown'd   ⎬
With golden spires, and all the hostile ⎪
   ground.   ⎭

He sigh'd, and turn'd his eyes, because he
   knew
'T was but a larger jail he had in view:
Then look'd below, and from the castle's
   height
Beheld a nearer and more pleasing sight;
The garden, which before he had not
   seen,   220
In spring's new livery clad of white and
   green,
Fresh flow'rs in wide parterres, and shady
   walks between.
This view'd, but not enjoy'd, with arms
   across
He stood, reflecting on his country's loss;
Himself an object of the public scorn,
And often wish'd he never had been born.
At last, (for so his destiny requir'd,)
With walking giddy, and with thinking
   tir'd,
He thro' a little window cast his sight,
Tho' thick of bars, that gave a scanty
   light;   230
But ev'n that glimmering serv'd him to
   descry
Th' inevitable charms of Emily.
   Scarce had he seen, but seiz'd with sud-
   den smart,
Stung to the quick, he felt it at his heart;
Struck blind with overpowering light he
   stood,
Then started back amaz'd, and cried aloud.
   Young Arcite heard, and up he ran with
   haste
To help his friend, and in his arms em-
   brac'd;
And ask'd him why he look'd so deadly
   wan,
And whence and how his change of cheer
   began,   240
Or who had done th' offense. " But if,"
   said he,
" Your grief alone is hard captivity,
For love of heav'n with patience undergo
A cureless ill, since fate will have it so:
So stood our horoscope in chains to lie,
And Saturn in the dungeon of the sky,
Or other baleful aspect, rul'd our birth,
When all the friendly stars were under
   earth:
Whate'er betides, by destiny 't is done;
And better bear like men than vainly seek
   to shun."   250
" Nor of my bonds," said Palamon again,
" Nor of unhappy planets I complain;

But when my mortal anguish caus'd my cry,
That moment I was hurt thro' either eye;
Pierc'd with a random shaft, I faint away,
And perish with insensible decay:
A glance of some new goddess gave the
   wound,
Whom, like Actæon, unaware I found.
Look how she walks along yon shady
   space:
Not Juno moves with more majestic
   grace;   260
And all the Cyprian queen is in her face.
If thou art Venus, (for thy charms confess
That face was form'd in heav'n, nor art
   thou less;
Disguis'd in habit, undisguis'd in shape,)
O help us captives from our chains to
   scape;
But if our doom be past in bonds to lie
For life, and in a loathsome dungeon die,
Then be thy wrath appeas'd with our dis-
   grace,
And shew compassion to the Theban race,
Oppress'd by tyrant pow'r ! " While yet he
   spoke,   270
Arcite on Emily had fix'd his look;
The fatal dart a ready passage found,
And deep within his heart infix'd the
   wound:
So that if Palamon were wounded sore,
Arcite was hurt as much as he, or more.
Then from his inmost soul he sigh'd, and
   said:
" The beauty I behold has struck me dead:
Unknowingly she strikes, and kills by
   chance;
Poison is in her eyes, and death in ev'ry
   glance.
O, I must ask; nor ask alone, but move   280
Her mind to mercy, or must die for love."
   Thus Arcite: and thus Palamon replies
(Eager his tone, and ardent were his eyes):
" Speak'st thou in earnest, or in jest-
   ing vein ? "
" Jesting," said Arcite, "suits but ill
   with pain."
" It suits far worse," said Palamon
   again,
And bent his brows, " with men who honor
   weigh,
Their faith to break, their friendship to
   betray;
But worst with thee, of noble lineage born,
My kinsman, and in arms my brother
   sworn.   290

Have we not plighted each our holy oath,
That one should be the common good of
both;
One soul should both inspire, and neither
prove
His fellow's hindrance in pursuit of love?
To this before the gods we gave our hands,
And nothing but our death can break the
bands.
This binds thee, then, to farther my design,
As I am bound by vow to farther thine.
Nor canst, nor dar'st thou, traitor, on the
plain
Appeach my honor, or thy own maintain, 300
Since thou art of my council, and the friend
Whose faith I trust, and on whose care
depend.
And wouldst thou court my lady's love,
which I
Much rather than release would choose to
die?
But thou, false Arcite, never shalt obtain
Thy bad pretense; I told thee first my pain,
For first my love began ere thine was born;
Thou, as my council, and my brother sworn,
Art bound t' assist my eldership of right,
Or justly to be deem'd a perjur'd knight."
    Thus Palamon; but Arcite with disdain
In haughty language thus replied again: 312
" Forsworn thyself: the traitor's odious
name
I first return, and then disprove thy claim.
If love be passion, and that passion nurs'd
With strong desires, I lov'd the lady first.
Canst thou pretend desire, whom zeal in-
flam'd
To worship, and a pow'r celestial nam'd?
Thine was devotion to the blest above;
I saw the woman, and desir'd her love; 320
First own'd my passion, and to thee com-
mend
Th' important secret, as my chosen friend.
Suppose (which yet I grant not) thy desire
A moment elder than my rival fire;
Can chance of seeing first thy title prove?
And know'st thou not, no law is made for
love?
Law is to things which to free choice re-
late;
Love is not in our choice, but in our fate:
Laws are but positive; love's pow'r, we see,
Is Nature's sanction, and her first decree. 330
Each day we break the bond of human laws
For love, and vindicate the common cause.
Laws for defense of civil rights are plac'd,

Love throws the fences down, and makes a
general waste:
Maids, widows, wives, without distinction
fall;
The sweeping deluge, love, comes on, and
covers all.
If then the laws of friendship I transgress, ⎫
I keep the greater, while I break the less; ⎬
And both are mad alike, since neither can ⎪
possess. ⎭
Both hopeless to be ransom'd, never more
To see the sun, but as he passes o'er. 341
    " Like Æsop's hounds contending for the
bone —
Each pleaded right, and would be lord
alone:
The fruitless fight continued all the day;
A cur came by and snatch'd the prize away.
As courtiers therefore justle for a grant,
And when they break their friendship,
plead their want,
So thou, if fortune will thy suit advance,
Love on, nor envy me my equal chance:
For I must love, and am resolv'd to try 350
My fate, or failing in th' adventure die."
    Great was their strife, which hourly was
renew'd,
Till each with mortal hate his rival view'd:
Now friends no more, nor walking hand in
hand;
But when they met, they made a surly stand;
And glar'd like angry lions as they pass'd,
And wish'd that ev'ry look might be their
last.
    It chanc'd at length, Perithous came t'
attend
This worthy Theseus, his familiar friend:
Their love in early infancy began, 360
And rose as childhood ripen'd into man,
Companions of the war; and lov'd so well, ⎫
That when one died, as ancient stories ⎬
tell, ⎪
His fellow to redeem him went to hell. ⎭
    But to pursue my tale; to welcome home
His warlike brother is Perithous come:
Arcite of Thebes was known in arms long
since,
And honor'd by this young Thessalian
prince.
Theseus, to gratify his friend and guest,
Who made our Arcite's freedom his re-
quest, 370
Restor'd to liberty the captive knight,
But on these hard conditions I recite:
That if hereafter Arcite should be found

Within the compass of Athenian ground,
By day or night, or on whate'er pretense,
His head should pay the forfeit of th'
    offense.
To this Perithous for his friend agreed,
And on his promise was the pris'ner freed.
    Unpleas'd and pensive hence he takes
    his way,
At his own peril; for his life must pay. 380
Who now but Arcite mourns his bitter fate,
Finds his dear purchase, and repents too
    late ?
"What have I gain'd," he said, " in prison
    pent,
If I but change my bonds for banishment ?
And, banish'd from her sight, I suffer more
In freedom than I felt in bonds before;
Forc'd from her presence, and condemn'd
    to live;
Unwelcome freedom, and unthank'd re-
    prieve:
Heav'n is not but where Emily abides,
And where she 's absent, all is hell be-
    sides. 390
Next to my day of birth, was that accurst
Which bound my friendship to Perithous
    first:
Had I not known that prince, I still had
    been
In bondage, and had still Emilia seen;
For tho' I never can her grace deserve,
'T is recompense enough to see and serve.
O Palamon, my kinsman and my friend,
How much more happy fates thy love
    attend !
Thine is th' adventure; thine the victory:
Well has thy fortune turn'd the dice for
    thee; 400
Thou on that angel's face may'st feed thy
    eyes —
In prison, no; but blissful paradise !
Thou daily see'st that sun of beauty shine,
And lov'st at least in love's extremest
    line.
I mourn in absence, love's eternal night;
And who can tell but since thou hast her
    sight,
And art a comely, young, and valiant
    knight,
Fortune (a various pow'r) may cease to
    frown,
And by some ways unknown thy wishes
    crown ?
But I, the most forlorn of humankind, 410
Nor help can hope, nor remedy can find;

But doom'd to drag my loathsome life in
    care,
For my reward, must end it in despair.
Fire, water, air, and earth, and force of
    fates,
That governs all, and Heav'n that all cre-
    ates,
Nor art, nor Nature's hand can ease my
    grief;
Nothing but death, the wretch's last relief:
Then farewell youth, and all the joys that
    dwell
With youth and life, and life itself, farewell !
    " But why, alas ! do mortal men in vain 420
Of Fortune, Fate, or Providence complain ?
God gives us what he knows our wants
    require,
And better things than those which we
    desire:
Some pray for riches; riches they obtain;
But, watched by robbers, for their wealth
    are slain:
Some pray from prison to be freed; and
    come,
When guilty of their vows, to fall at home;
Murder'd by those they trusted with their
    life,
A favor'd servant, or a bosom wife.
Such dear-bought blessings happen ev'ry
    day, 430
Because we know not for what things to
    pray.
Like drunken sots about the streets we
    roam:
Well knows the sot he has a certain home;
Yet knows not how to find th' uncertain
    place,
And blunders on, and staggers ev'ry pace.
Thus all seek happiness; but few can find,
For far the greater part of men are blind.
This is my case, who thought our utmost
    good
Was in one word of freedom understood:
The fatal blessing came; from prison free,
I starve abroad, and lose the sight of
    Emily." 441
    Thus Arcite; but if Arcite thus deplore
His suff'rings, Palamon yet suffers more.
For when he knew his rival freed and gone,
He swells with wrath; he makes outrageous
    moan:
He frets, he fumes, he stares, he stamps
    the ground;
The hollow tow'r with clamors rings
    around.

With briny tears he bath'd his fetter'd feet,
And dropp'd all o'er with agony of sweat.
"Alas!" he cried, "I, wretch, in prison
    pine,   450
Too happy rival, while the fruit is thine.
Thou liv'st at large, thou draw'st thy na-
    tive air,
Pleas'd with thy freedom, proud of my
    despair:
Thou may'st, since thou hast youth and
    courage join'd,
A sweet behavior and a solid mind,
Assemble ours, and all the Theban race,
To vindicate on Athens thy disgrace;
And after (by some treaty made) possess
Fair Emily, the pledge of lasting peace.
So thine shall be the beauteous prize,
    while I   460
Must languish in despair, in prison die.
Thus all th' advantage of the strife is
    thine;
Thy portion double joys, and double sor-
    rows mine."
    The rage of jealousy then fir'd his soul,
And his face kindled like a burning coal:
Now cold despair, succeeding in her stead,
To livid paleness turns the glowing red.
His blood, scarce liquid, creeps within his
    veins,
Like water which the freezing wind con-
    strains.
Then thus he said: "Eternal deities,   470
Who rule the world with absolute decrees,
And write whatever time shall bring to
    pass,
With pens of adamant, on plates of brass;
What is the race of humankind your care
Beyond what all his fellow creatures are?
He with the rest is liable to pain,
And like the sheep, his brother beast, is
    slain.
Cold, hunger, prisons, ills without a cure,
All these he must, and guiltless oft, endure:
Or does your justice, pow'r, or prescience
    fail;   480
When the good suffer, and the bad prevail?
What worse to wretched virtue could befall,
If Fate or giddy Fortune govern'd all?
Nay, worse than other beasts is our estate;
Them, to pursue their pleasures, you create;
We, bound by harder laws, must curb our
    will,
And your commands, not our desires, fulfil:
Then, when the creature is unjustly slain,
Yet after death at least he feels no pain;

But man in life surcharg'd with woe before,
Not freed when dead, is doomed to suffer
    more.   491
A serpent shoots his sting at unaware;
An ambush'd thief forelays a traveler:
The man lies murder'd, while the thief and
    snake,
One gains the thickets, and one thrids the
    brake.
This let divines decide; but well I know,
Just, or unjust, I have my share of woe,
Thro' Saturn seated in a luckless place,
And Juno's wrath, that persecutes my race;
Or Mars and Venus, in a quartil, move   500
My pangs of jealousy for Arcite's love."
    Let Palamon oppress'd in bondage mourn,
While to his exil'd rival we return.
By this, the sun, declining from his height,
The day had shorten'd to prolong the night;
The lengthen'd night gave length of misery
Both to the captive lover and the free;
For Palamon in endless prison mourns,
And Arcite forfeits life if he returns: 509
The banish'd never hopes his love to see,
Nor hopes the captive lord his liberty.
'T is hard to say who suffers greater pains:
One sees his love, but cannot break his
    chains;
One free, and all his motions uncontroll'd,
Beholds whate'er he would, but what he
    would behold.
Judge as you please, for I will haste to tell
What fortune to the banish'd knight befell.
    When Arcite was to Thebes return'd
    again,
The loss of her he lov'd renew'd his pain;
What could be worse, than never more to
    see   520
His life, his soul, his charming Emily?
He rav'd with all the madness of despair,
He roar'd, he beat his breast, he tore his hair;
Dry sorrow in his stupid eyes appears,
For, wanting nourishment, he wanted tears:
His eyeballs in their hollow sockets sink,
Bereft of sleep; he loathes his meat and
    drink.
He withers at his heart, and looks as wan
As the pale specter of a murder'd man:
That pale turns yellow, and his face re-
    ceives   530
The faded hue of sapless boxen leaves.
In solitary groves he makes his moan,
Walks early out, and ever is alone;
Nor, mix'd in mirth, in youthful pleasure
    shares,

But sighs when songs and instruments he
  hears.
His spirits are so low, his voice is drown'd, ⎫
He hears as from afar, or in a swound,   ⎬
Like the deaf murmurs of a distant sound: ⎭
Uncomb'd his locks, and squalid his attire,
Unlike the trim of love and gay desire; 540
But full of museful mopings, which presage
The loss of reason, and conclude in rage.
  This when he had endured a year and
    more,
Now wholly chang'd from what he was be-
    fore,
It happen'd once that slumb'ring as he lay,
He dreamt (his dream began at break of
    day)
That Hermes o'er his head in air appear'd,
And with soft words his drooping spirits
    cheer'd:
His hat, adorn'd with wings, disclos'd the
    god,
And in his hand he bore the sleep-compelling
    rod;   550
Such as he seem'd, when, at his sire's com-
    mand,
On Argus' head he laid the snaky wand.
" Arise," he said, " to conqu'ring Athens go,
There Fate appoints an end of all thy woe."
The fright awaken'd Arcite with a start;
Against his bosom bounc'd his heaving
    heart;
But soon he said, with scarce-recover'd
    breath:
" And thither will I go, to meet my death,
Sure to be slain; but death is my desire,
Since in Emilia's sight I shall expire." 560
By chance he spied a mirror while he spoke,
And gazing there beheld his alter'd look;
Wond'ring, he saw his features and his hue
So much were chang'd, that scarce himself
    he knew.
A sudden thought then starting in his mind:
" Since I in Arcite cannot Arcite find,
The world may search in vain with all their
    eyes,
But never penetrate thro' this disguise.
Thanks to the change which grief and sick-
    ness give,
In low estate I may securely live,   570
And see unknown my mistress day by day."
He said, and cloth'd himself in coarse array,
A lab'ring hind in shew; then forth he went,
And to th' Athenian tow'rs his journey
    bent.
One squire attended in the same disguise,

Made conscious of his master's enterprise.
Arriv'd at Athens, soon he came to court,
Unknown, unquestion'd, in that thick resort:
Proff'ring for hire his service at the gate,
To drudge, draw water, and to run or wait.
  So fair befell him, that for little gain 581
He serv'd at first Emilia's chamberlain;
And, watchful all advantages to spy,
Was still at hand, and in his master's eye;
And as his bones were big, and sinews strong,
Refus'd no toil that could to slaves belong;
But from deep wells with engines water
    drew,
And us'd his noble hands the wood to hew.
He pass'd a year at least attending thus
On Emily, and call'd Philostratus.   590
But never was there man of his degree
So much esteem'd, so well belov'd as he.
So gentle of condition was he known,
That thro' the court his courtesy was blown:
All think him worthy of a greater place,
And recommend him to the royal grace;
That, exercis'd within a higher sphere,
His virtues more conspicuous might appear.
Thus by the general voice was Arcite
    prais'd,   599
And by great Theseus to high favor rais'd;
Among his menial servants first enroll'd,
And largely entertain'd with sums of gold:
Besides what secretly from Thebes was sent,
Of his own income and his annual rent.
This well employ'd, he purchas'd friends
    and fame,
But cautiously conceal'd from whence it
    came.
Thus for three years he liv'd with large
    increase,
In arms of honor, and esteem in peace;
To Theseus' person he was ever near,   609
And Theseus for his virtues held him dear.

THE END OF THE FIRST BOOK

PALAMON AND ARCITE

OR, THE KNIGHT'S TALE

BOOK II

WHILE Arcite lives in bliss, the story turns
Where hopeless Palamon in prison mourns.
For six long years immur'd, the captive
    knight
Had dragg'd his chains and scarcely seen
    the light:

Lost liberty and love at once he bore;
His prison pain'd him much, his passion more;
Nor dares he hope his fetters to remove,
Nor ever wishes to be free from love.
　But when the sixth revolving year was run,
And May within the Twins receiv'd the sun —　　10
Were it by chance or forceful destiny,
Which forms in causes first whate'er shall be —
Assisted by a friend, one moonless night,
This Palamon from prison took his flight:
A pleasant beverage he prepar'd before
Of wine and honey mix'd, with added store
Of opium; to his keeper this he brought,
Who swallow'd unaware the sleepy draught,
And snor'd secure till morn, his senses bound　　19
In slumber, and in long oblivion drown'd.
Short was the night, and careful Palamon
Sought the next covert ere the rising sun.
A thick-spread forest near the city lay,
To this with lengthen'd strides he took his way
(For far he could not fly, and fear'd the day).
Safe from pursuit, he meant to shun the light,
Till the brown shadows of the friendly night
To Thebes might favor his intended flight.
When to his country come, his next design
Was all the Theban race in arms to join,　　30
And war on Theseus, till he lost his life,
Or won the beauteous Emily to wife.
Thus while his thoughts the ling'ring day beguile,
To gentle Arcite let us turn our style;
Who little dreamt how nigh he was to care,
Till treacherous Fortune caught him in the snare.
The morning lark, the messenger of day,
Saluted in her song the morning gray;
And soon the sun arose with beams so bright,
That all th' horizon laugh'd to see the joyous sight:　　40
He with his tepid rays the rose renews,
And licks the dropping leaves, and dries the dews;
When Arcite left his bed, resolv'd to pay
Observance to the month of merry May.
Forth on his fiery steed betimes he rode,

That scarcely prints the turf on which he trod:
At ease he seem'd, and, prancing o'er the plains,
Turn'd only to the grove his horse's reins,
The grove I nam'd before; and, lighting there,
A woodbind garland sought to crown his hair;　　50
Then turn'd his face against the rising day,
And rais'd his voice to welcome in the May:
"For thee, sweet month, the groves green liv'ries wear,
If not the first, the fairest of the year;
For thee the Graces lead the dancing hours,
And Nature's ready pencil paints the flow'rs:
When thy short reign is past, the fev'rish sun
The sultry tropic fears, and moves more slowly on.
So may thy tender blossoms fear no blight,
Nor goats with venom'd teeth thy tendrils bite,　　60
As thou shalt guide my wand'ring feet to find
The fragrant greens I seek, my brows to bind."
　His vows address'd, within the grove he stray'd,
Till Fate, or Fortune, near the place convey'd
His steps where secret Palamon was laid.
Full little thought of him the gentle knight,
Who, flying death, had there conceal'd his flight,
In brakes and brambles hid, and shunning mortal sight.
And less he knew him for his hated foe,
But fear'd him as a man he did not know.
But as it has been said of ancient years,　　71
That fields are full of eyes, and woods have ears;
For this the wise are ever on their guard,
For, unforeseen, they say, is unprepar'd.
Uncautious Arcite thought himself alone,
And less than all suspected Palamon,
Who list'ning heard him, while he search'd the grove,
And loudly sung his roundelay of love:
But on the sudden stopp'd, and silent stood,
As lovers often muse, and change their mood;　　80

Now high as heav'n, and then as low as hell;
Now up, now down, as buckets in a well;
For Venus, like her day, will change her
    cheer,
And seldom shall we see a Friday clear.
Thus Arcite having sung, with alter'd hue
Sunk on the ground, and from his bosom
    drew
A desp'rate sigh, accusing Heav'n and Fate,
And angry Juno's unrelenting hate.
"Curst be the day when first I did ap- ⎤
    pear;   ⎟
Let it be blotted from the calendar,   90 ⎬
Lest it pollute the month, and poison all ⎟
    the year.   ⎦
Still will the jealous queen pursue our race?
Cadmus is dead, the Theban city *was:*
Yet ceases not her hate; for all who come
From Cadmus are involv'd in Cadmus'
    doom.
I suffer for my blood: unjust decree!
That punishes another's crime on me.
In mean estate I serve my mortal foe,
The man who caus'd my country's over-
    throw.
This is not all; for Juno, to my shame, 100 ⎤
Has forc'd me to forsake my former   ⎬
    name;   ⎟
Arcite I was, Philostratus I am.   ⎦
That side of heav'n is all my enemy:
Mars ruin'd Thebes; his mother ruin'd me.
Of all the royal race remains but one
Beside myself, th' unhappy Palamon,
Whom Theseus holds in bonds, and will
    not free;
Without a crime, except his kin to me.
Yet these, and all the rest, I could endure;
But love's a malady without a cure: 110
Fierce Love has pierc'd me with his fiery
    dart;
He fries within, and hisses at my heart.
Your eyes, fair Emily, my fate pursue;
I suffer for the rest, I die for you.
Of such a goddess no time leaves record,
Who burn'd the temple where she was
    ador'd:
And let it burn, I never will complain,
Pleas'd with my suff'rings, if you knew my
    pain."   118
At this a sickly qualm his heart assail'd,
His ears ring inward, and his senses fail'd.
No word miss'd Palamon of all he spoke,
But soon to deadly pale he chang'd his look:
He trembled ev'ry limb, and felt a smart,
As if cold steel had glided thro' his heart;

Nor longer stay'd, but, starting from his
    place,
Discover'd stood, and shew'd his hostile
    face:
"False traitor Arcite, traitor to thy blood,
Bound by thy sacred oath to seek my good,
Now art thou found forsworn, for Emily;
And dar'st attempt her love, for whom I die.
So hast thou cheated Theseus with a wile,
Against thy vow, returning to beguile   132
Under a borrow'd name: as false to me,
So false thou art to him who set thee free.
But rest assur'd, that either thou shalt die,
Or else renounce thy claim in Emily:
For, tho' unarm'd I am, and (freed by
    chance)
Am here without my sword or pointed lance,
Hope not, base man, unquestion'd hence to
    go,
For I am Palamon, thy mortal foe."   140
Arcite, who heard his tale, and knew the
    man,
His sword unsheath'd, and fiercely thus
    began:
"Now by the gods who govern heav'n
    above,
Wert thou not weak with hunger, mad
    with love,
That word had been thy last, or in this grove
This hand should force thee to renounce
    thy love.
The surety which I gave thee, I defy: ⎤
Fool, not to know that love endures no tie, ⎬
And Jove but laughs at lovers' perjury. ⎦
Know, I will serve the fair in thy despite;
But, since thou art my kinsman, and a
    knight,   151
Here, have my faith, to-morrow in this
    grove
Our arms shall plead the titles of our love:
And Heav'n so help my right, as I alone
Will come, and keep the cause and quarrel
    both unknown,
With arms of proof both for myself and
    thee:
Choose thou the best, and leave the worst
    to me.
And, that at better ease thou may'st abide,
Bedding and clothes I will this night pro-
    vide,
And needful sustenance, that thou may'st
    be   160
A conquest better won, and worthy me."
His promise Palamon accepts; but pray'd,
To keep it better than the first he made.

Thus fair they parted till the morrow's
　　dawn,
For each had laid his plighted faith to
　　pawn.
O Love! thou sternly dost thy pow'r �
　　maintain, ⎫
And wilt not bear a rival in thy reign: ⎬
Tyrants and thou all fellowship disdain. ⎭
This was in Arcite prov'd, and Palamon:
Both in despair, yet each would love alone.
Arcite return'd, and, as in honor tied, 171
His foe with bedding and with food sup-
　　plied;
Then, ere the day, two suits of armor
　　sought,
Which borne before him on his steed he
　　brought:
Both were of shining steel, and wrought
　　so pure
As might the strokes of two such arms
　　endure.
Now, at the time, and in th' appointed
　　place,
The challenger and challeng'd, face to face,
Approach; each other from afar they knew,
And from afar their hatred chang'd their
　　hue. 180
So stands the Thracian herdsman with his
　　spear,
Full in the gap, and hopes the hunted bear,
And hears him rustling in the wood, and
　　sees
His course at distance by the bending trees,
And thinks: "Here comes my mortal
　　enemy,
And either he must fall in fight, or I."
This while he thinks, he lifts aloft his dart; ⎫
A gen'rous chillness seizes ev'ry part; ⎬
The veins pour back the blood, and fortify ⎪
　　the heart. ⎭
　　Thus pale they meet; their eyes with fury
　　　burn; 190
None greets, for none the greeting will
　　return;
But in dumb surliness, each arm'd with care
His foe profess'd, as brother of the war:
Then both, no moment lost, at once advance
Against each other, arm'd with sword and
　　lance:
They lash, they foin, they pass, they strive
　　to bore
Their corslets, and the thinnest parts ex-
　　plore.
Thus two long hours in equal arms they
　　stood,

And, wounded, wound; till both were bath'd
　　in blood;
And not a foot of ground had either got, 200
As if the world depended on the spot.
Fell Arcite like an angry tiger far'd,
And like a lion Palamon appear'd:
Or, as two boars, whom love to battle draws.
With rising bristles, and with frothy jaws —
Their adverse breasts with tusks oblique
　　they wound;
With grunts and groans the forest rings
　　around —
So fought the knights, and fighting must
　　abide,
Till Fate an umpire sends their diff'rence to
　　decide. 209
The pow'r that ministers to God's decrees,
And executes on earth what Heav'n foresees,
Call'd Providence, or Chance, or Fatal
　　Sway,
Comes with resistless force, and finds or
　　makes her way.
Nor kings, nor nations, nor united pow'r,
One moment can retard th' appointed hour,
And some one day, some wondrous chance
　　appears,
Which happen'd not in centuries of years:
For sure, whate'er we mortals hate, or love,
Or hope, or fear, depends on pow'rs above;
They move our appetites to good or ill, 220
And by foresight necessitate the will.
In Theseus this appears; whose youthful joy
Was beasts of chase in forests to destroy:
This gentle knight, inspir'd by jolly May, ⎫
Forsook his easy couch at early day, ⎬
And to the wood and wilds pursued his ⎪
　　way. ⎭
Beside him rode Hippolyta the queen,
And Emily attir'd in lively green,
With horns, and hounds, and all the tuneful
　　cry,
To hunt a royal hart within the covert
　　nigh; 230
And as he follow'd Mars before, so now
He serves the goddess of the silver bow.
The way that Theseus took was to the wood
Where the two knights in cruel battle stood:
The laund on which they fought, th' ap-
　　pointed place
In which th' uncoupled hounds began the
　　chase.
Thither forthright he rode to rouse the prey,
That shaded by the fern in harbor lay;
And thence dislodg'd, was wont to leave the
　　wood 239

For open fields, and cross the crystal flood.
Approach'd, and looking underneath the sun,
He saw proud Arcite and fierce Palamon
In mortal battle doubling blow on blow:
Like lightning flam'd their fauchions to and
    fro,
And shot a dreadful gleam; so strong they
    strook,
There seem'd less force requir'd to fell an
    oak.
He gaz'd with wonder on their equal might,
Look'd eager on, but knew not either
    knight:
Resolv'd to learn, he spurr'd his fiery steed
With goring rowels to provoke his speed.
The minute ended that began the race, 251
So soon he was betwixt 'em on the place;
And with his sword unsheath'd, on pain of
    life
Commands both combatants to cease their
    strife:
Then with imperious tone pursues his
    threat:
" What are you? why in arms together met?
How dares your pride presume against my
    laws,
As in a listed field to fight your cause?
Unask'd the royal grant; no marshal by,
As knightly rites require; nor judge to try?"
    Then Palamon, with scarce recover'd
    breath, 261
Thus hasty spoke: " We both deserve the
    death,
And both would die; for, look the world
    around,
A pair so wretched is not to be found.
Our life 's a load; encumber'd with the
    charge,
We long to set th' imprison'd soul at large.
Now, as thou art a sovereign judge, decree ⎤
The rightful doom of death to him and   ⎟
    me;   ⎬
Let neither find thy grace, for grace is   ⎟
    cruelty. 269 ⎦
Me first, O kill me first, and cure my woe;
Then sheathe the sword of justice on my foe:
Or kill him first; for when his name is
    heard,
He foremost will receive his due reward.
Arcite of Thebes is he; thy mortal foe,
On whom thy grace did liberty bestow,
But first contracted, that, if ever found
By day or night upon th' Athenian ground,
His head should pay the forfeit: see re-
    turn'd

The perjur'd knight, his oath and honor
    scorn'd. 279
For this is he, who, with a borrow'd name,
And proffer'd service, to thy palace came,
Now call'd Philostratus: retain'd by thee, ⎤
A traitor trusted, and in high degree,   ⎬
Aspiring to the bed of beauteous Emily. ⎦
My part remains; from Thebes my birth I
    own,
And call myself th' unhappy Palamon.
Think me not like that man; since no dis-
    grace
Can force me to renounce the honor of my
    race.
Know me for what I am: I broke thy chain,
Nor promis'd I thy pris'ner to remain: 290
The love of liberty with life is giv'n,
And life itself th' inferior gift of Heav'n.
Thus without crime I fled; but farther know,
I, with this Arcite, am thy mortal foe:
Then give me death, since I thy life pur-
    sue;
For safeguard of thyself, death is my due.
More wouldst thou know? I love bright
    Emily,
And, for her sake, and in her sight, will
    die.
But kill my rival too, for he no less   ⎤
Deserves; and I thy righteous doom will ⎟
    bless, 300   ⎬
Assur'd that what I lose he never shall   ⎟
    possess."   ⎦
    To this replied the stern Athenian prince,
And sourly smil'd: " In owning your offense
You judge yourself; and I but keep record
In place of law, while you pronounce the
    word.
Take your desert, the death you have de-
    creed;
I seal your doom and ratify the deed:
By Mars, the patron of my arms, you die."
    He said; dumb sorrow seiz'd the standers-
    by.
The queen, above the rest, by nature good,
(The pattern form'd of perfect woman-
    hood,) 311
For tender pity wept: when she began,
Thro' the bright choir th' infectious virtue
    ran.
All dropp'd their tears, ev'n the contended
    maid;
And thus among themselves they softly
    said:
" What eyes can suffer this unworthy
    sight!

Two youths of royal blood, renown'd in
    fight,
The mastership of heav'n in face and mind,
And lovers, far beyond their faithless kind:
See their wide streaming wounds; they
    neither came   320
From pride of empire, nor desire of fame.
Kings fight for kingdoms, madmen for ap-
    plause;
But love for love alone; that crowns the
    lover's cause."
This thought, which ever bribes the beau-
    teous kind,
Such pity wrought in ev'ry lady's mind,
They left their steeds, and, prostrate on the
    place,
From the fierce king implor'd th' offenders'
    grace.
    He paus'd a while, stood silent in his mood,
(For yet his rage was boiling in his blood;)
But soon his tender mind th' impression
    felt;   330
(As softest metals are not slow to melt,
And pity soonest runs in gentle minds:)
Then reasons with himself; and first he finds
His passion cast a mist before his sense,
And either made or magnified th' offense.
Offense ! of what ? to whom ? who judg'd
    the cause ?
The prison'r freed himself by nature's laws:
Born free, he sought his right: the man he
    freed
Was perjur'd, but his love excus'd the deed.
Thus pond'ring, he look'd under with his
    eyes   340
And saw the women's tears, and heard their
    cries;
Which mov'd compassion more: he shook
    his head,
And softly sighing to himself he said:
" Curse on th' unpard'ning prince, whom
    tears can draw
To no remorse; who rules by lions' law;
And deaf to pray'rs, by no submission
    bow'd,
Rends all alike; the penitent and proud ! "
At this, with look serene, he rais'd his
    head;
Reason resum'd her place, and passion fled:
Then thus aloud he spoke: " The pow'r of
    Love,   350
In earth, and seas, and air, and heav'n
    above,
Rules, unresisted, with an awful nod;
By daily miracles declar'd a god:

He blinds the wise, gives eyesight to the
    blind,
And molds and stamps anew the lover's
    mind.
Behold that Arcite, and this Palamon,
Freed from my fetters, and in safety gone —
What hinder'd either in their native soil
At ease to reap the harvest of their toil ?
But Love, their lord, did otherwise ordain,
And brought 'em in their own despite again,
To suffer death deserv'd; for well they
    know,   362
'T is in my pow'r, and I their deadly foe.
The proverb holds, that to be wise and love,
Is hardly granted to the gods above.
See how the madmen bleed ! behold the gains
With which their master, Love, rewards
    their pains.
For sev'n long years, on duty ev'ry day,
Lo their obedience, and their monarch's pay !
Yet, as in duty bound, they serve him on;
And, ask the fools, they think it wisely done;
Nor ease, nor wealth, nor life itself regard,
For 't is their maxim, love is love's reward.
This is not all; the fair, for whom they
    strove,   374
Nor knew before, nor could suspect their love,
Nor thought, when she beheld the fight
    from far,
Her beauty was th' occasion of the war.
But sure a gen'ral doom on man is pass'd,
And all are fools and lovers, first or last:
This, both by others and myself, I know, 380
For I have serv'd their sovereign, long ago;
Oft have been caught within the winding ⎫
    train   ⎪
Of female snares, and felt the lover's ⎬
    pain,   ⎪
And learn'd how far the god can human ⎪
    hearts constrain.   ⎭
To this remembrance, and the pray'rs of
    those
Who for th' offending warriors interpose,
I give their forfeit lives; on this accord,
To do me homage as their sov'reign lord;
And as my vassals, to their utmost might,
Assist my person, and assert my right." 390
    This freely sworn, the knights their grace
    obtain'd;
Then thus the king his secret thoughts ex-
    plain'd:
" If wealth, or honor, or a royal race,
Or each, or all, may win a lady's grace,
Then either of you knights may well de-
    serve

A princess born; and such is she you serve;
For Emily is sister to the crown,
And but too well to both her beauty known:
But should you combat till you both were
    dead,
Two lovers cannot share a single bed.   400
As therefore both are equal in degree,
The lot of both be left to destiny.
Now hear th' award, and happy may it prove
To her, and him who best deserves her love.
Depart from hence in peace, and, free as air,
Search the wide world, and where you
    please repair;
But on the day when this returning sun
To the same point thro' ev'ry sign has run,
Then each of you his hundred knights shall
    bring,
In royal lists, to fight before the king;   410
And then the knight, whom fate or happy
    chance
Shall with his friends to victory advance,
And grace his arms so far in equal fight,
From out the bars to force his opposite,
Or kill, or make him recreant on the plain,
The prize of valor and of love shall gain;
The vanquish'd party shall their claim
    release,
And the long jars conclude in lasting peace.
The charge be mine t' adorn the chosen
    ground,
The theater of war, for champions so re-
    nown'd;   420
And take the patron's place of either ⎤
    knight,   ⎥
With eyes impartial to behold the fight; ⎬
And Heav'n of me so judge as I shall   ⎥
    judge aright.   ⎦
If both are satisfied with this accord,
Swear by the laws of knighthood on my
    sword."
Who now but Palamon exults with joy?
And ravish'd Arcite seems to touch the sky:
The whole assembled troop was pleas'd as
    well,
Extoll'd th' award, and on their knees
    they fell
To bless the gracious king. The knights,
    with leave   430
Departing from the place, his last com-
    mands receive;
On Emily with equal ardor look,
And from her eyes their inspiration took;
From thence to Thebes' old walls pursue
    their way,
Each to provide his champions for the day.

It might be deem'd, on our historian's
    part,
Or too much negligence, or want of art,
If he forgot the vast magnificence
Of royal Theseus, and his large expense.
He first enclos'd for lists a level ground,
The whole circumference a mile around: 441
The form was circular; and all without
A trench was sunk, to moat the place about.
Within an amphitheater appear'd,
Rais'd in degrees; to sixty paces rear'd:
That when a man was plac'd in one de-
    gree,
Height was allow'd for him above to see.
Eastward was built a gate of marble
    white;
The like adorn'd the western opposite.
A nobler object than this fabric was,   450
Rome never saw; nor of so vast a space:
For, rich with spoils of many a conquer'd
    land,
All arts and artists Theseus could com-
    mand;
Who sold for hire, or wrought for better
    fame;
The master painters and the carvers came.
So rose within the compass of the year
An age's work, a glorious theater.
Then o'er its eastern gate was rais'd above
A temple, sacred to the Queen of Love:
An altar stood below; on either hand   460
A priest with roses crown'd, who held a
    myrtle wand.
The dome of Mars was on the gate op-
    pos'd,
And on the north a turret was enclos'd,
Within the wall, of alabaster white,   ⎤
And crimson coral, for the Queen of Night, ⎥
Who takes in sylvan sports her chaste   ⎬
    delight.   ⎦
Within these oratories might you see
Rich carvings, portraitures, and imagery,
Where ev'ry figure to the life express'd
The godhead's pow'r to whom it was ad-
    dress'd.   470
In Venus' temple, on the sides were seen
The broken slumbers of inamor'd men,
Pray'rs that ev'n spoke, and pity seem'd
    to call,
And issuing sighs that smok'd along the
    wall;
Complaints, and hot desires, the lover's
    hell,
And scalding tears that wore a channel
    where they fell:

And all around were nuptial bonds, the ties
Of love's assurance, and a train of lies,
That, made in lust, conclude in perjuries.
Beauty, and Youth, and Wealth, and Luxury, 480
And sprightly Hope, and short-enduring Joy;
And Sorceries to raise th' infernal pow'rs,
And Sigils fram'd in planetary hours;
Expense, and Afterthought, and idle Care,
And Doubts of motley hue, and dark Despair;
Suspicions, and fantastical Surmise,
And Jealousy suffus'd, with jaundice in her eyes,
Discoloring all she view'd, in tawny dress'd,
Down-look'd, and with a cuckow on her fist.
Oppos'd to her, on t'other side, advance 490
The costly feast, the carol, and the dance,
Minstrels, and music, poetry, and play,
And balls by night, and turnaments by day.
All these were painted on the wall, and more,
With acts and monuments of times before,
And others added by prophetic doom,
And lovers yet unborn, and loves to come:
For there th' Idalian mount, and Citheron,
The court of Venus, was in colors drawn.
Before the palace gate, in careless dress, 500
And loose array, sat portress Idleness;
There, by the fount, Narcissus pin'd alone;
There Samson was, with wiser Solomon,
And all the mighty names by love undone.
Medea's charms were there, Circean feasts,
With bowls that turn'd inamor'd youth to beasts.
Here might be seen that beauty, wealth, and wit,
And prowess, to the pow'r of love submit:
The spreading snare for all mankind is laid;
And lovers all betray, and are betray'd. 510
The goddess' self some noble hand had wrought;
Smiling she seem'd, and full of pleasing thought:
From ocean as she first began to rise,
And smooth'd the ruffled seas, and clear'd the skies;
She trode the brine all bare below the breast,
And the green waves but ill conceal'd the rest.

A lute she held, and on her head was seen
A wreath of roses red and myrtles green;
Her turtles fann'd the buxom air above;
And, by his mother, stood an infant Love,
With wings unfledg'd; his eyes were banded o'er; 521
His hands a bow, his back a quiver bore,
Supplied with arrows bright and keen, a deadly store.
But in the dome of mighty Mars the red
With diff'rent figures all the sides were spread;
This temple, less in form, with equal grace,
Was imitative of the first in Thrace:
For that cold region was the lov'd abode
And sov'reign mansion of the warrior god.
The landscape was a forest wide and bare,
Where neither beast nor humankind repair;
The fowl that scent afar the borders fly,
And shun the bitter blast, and wheel about the sky. 533
A cake of scurf lies baking on the ground,
And prickly stubs, instead of trees, are found;
Or woods with knots and knares deform'd and old;
Headless the most, and hideous to behold:
A rattling tempest thro' the branches went,
That stripp'd 'em bare, and one sole way they bent.
Heav'n froze above, severe; the clouds congeal, 540
And thro' the crystal vault appear'd the standing hail.
Such was the face without: a mountain stood
Threat'ning from high, and overlook'd the wood;
Beneath the low'ring brow, and on a bent,
The temple stood of Mars armipotent:
The frame of burnish'd steel, that cast a glare
From far, and seem'd to thaw the freezing air.
A strait, long entry to the temple led,
Blind with high walls, and horror over head:
Thence issued such a blast and hollow roar,
As threaten'd from the hinge to heave the door. 551
In thro' that door, a northern light there shone;
'T was all it had, for windows there were none.
The gate was adamant; eternal frame!

Which, hew'd by Mars himself, from Indian
    quarries came,
The labor of a god; and all along
Tough iron plates were clench'd to make it
    strong.
A tun about was ev'ry pillar there;
A polish'd mirror shone not half so clear.
There saw I how the secret felon wrought, ⎫
And treason lab'ring in the traitor's   ⎪
    thought,   561 ⎬
And midwife Time the ripen'd plot to   ⎪
    murder brought.   ⎭
There the red Anger dar'd the pallid Fear;
Next stood Hypocrisy, with holy leer;
Soft smiling, and demurely looking down,
But hid the dagger underneath the gown:
Th' assassinating wife, the household fiend;
And, far the blackest there, the traitor-
    friend.
On t'other side there stood Destruction bare;
Unpunish'd Rapine, and a waste of war;
Contest, with sharpen'd knives, in cloisters
    drawn,   571
And all with blood bespread the holy lawn.
Loud menaces were heard, and foul dis- ⎫
    grace,   ⎪
And bawling infamy, in language base; ⎬
Till sense was lost in sound, and silence ⎪
    fled the place.   ⎭
The slayer of himself yet saw I there;
The gore congeal'd was clotter'd in his hair:
With eyes half clos'd and gaping mouth he
    lay,
And grim, as when he breath'd his sullen
    soul away.   579
In midst of all the dome Misfortune sat,
And gloomy Discontent, and fell Debate,
And Madness laughing in his ireful mood,
And arm'd complaint on theft, and cries
    of blood.
There was the murder'd corpse, in covert laid,
And violent death in thousand shapes dis-
    play'd;
The city to the soldier's rage resign'd;
Successless wars, and poverty behind;
Ships burnt in fight, or forc'd on rocky shores,
And the rash hunter strangled by the boars;
The newborn babe by nurses overlaid;   590
And the cook caught within the raging fire
    he made.
All ills of Mars his nature, flame, and steel;
The gasping charioteer, beneath the wheel
Of his own car; the ruin'd house that falls
And intercepts her lord betwixt the walls;
The whole division that to Mars pertains,

All trades of death that deal in steel for
    gains,
Were there: the butcher, armorer, and
    smith,
Who forges sharpen'd fauchions, or the
    scythe.   599
The scarlet conquest on a tow'r was plac'd,
With shouts and soldiers' acclamations
    grac'd;
A pointed sword hung threat'ning o'er his
    head,
Sustain'd but by a slender twine of thread.
There saw I Mars his ides, the Capitol,
The seer in vain foretelling Cæsar's fall;
The last triumvirs, and the wars they move,
And Antony, who lost the world for love.
These, and a thousand more, the fane adorn;
Their fates were painted ere the men were
    born,
All copied from the heav'ns, and ruling
    force   610
Of the red star, in his revolving course.
The form of Mars high on a chariot stood,
All sheath'd in arms, and gruffly look'd the
    god;
Two geomantic figures were display'd ⎫
Above his head, a * warrior * Rubeus ⎪
    and a maid,   & Puella. ⎬
One when direct and one when retro-   ⎪
    grade.   ⎭
  Tir'd with deformities of death, I haste
To the third temple of Diana chaste.
A sylvan scene with various greens was
    drawn,
Shades on the sides, and on the midst a
    lawn: 620
The silver Cynthia, with her nymphs around,
Pursued the flying deer, the woods with
    horns resound;
Calisto there stood manifest of shame,
And, turn'd a bear, the northern star be-
    came;
Her son was next, and by peculiar grace
In the cold circle held the second place;
The stag Actæon in the stream had spied
The naked huntress, and, for seeing, died;
His hounds, unknowing of his change, pur-
    sue   629
The chase, and their mistaken master slew.
Peneian Daphne too was there to see,
Apollo's love before, and now his tree.
Th' adjoining fane th' assembled Greeks
    express'd,
And hunting of the Caledonian beast:
Œnides' valor, and his envied prize;

The fatal pow'r of Atalanta's eyes;
Diana's vengeance on the victor shown;
The murd'ress mother, and consuming son;
The Volscian queen extended on the plain;
The treason punish'd, and the traitor slain.
The rest were various huntings, well de-
sign'd,   641
And salvage beasts destroy'd, of ev'ry kind.
The graceful goddess was array'd in
green;
About her feet were little beagles seen,
That watch'd with upward eyes the mo-
tions of their queen.
Her legs were buskin'd, and the left
before
In act to shoot; a silver bow she bore,
And at her back a painted quiver wore.
She trod a wexing moon, that soon would
wane,   649
And, drinking borrow'd light, be fill'd again;
With downcast eyes, as seeming to survey
The dark dominions, her alternate sway.
Before her stood a woman in her throes,
And call'd Lucina's aid her burden to dis-
close.
All these the painter drew with such com-
mand,
That Nature snatch'd the pencil from his
hand,
Asham'd and angry that his art could feign
And mend the tortures of a mother's pain.
Theseus beheld the fanes of ev'ry god,
And thought his mighty cost was well be-
stow'd.   660
So princes now their poets should regard;
But few can write, and fewer can reward.
The theater thus rais'd, the lists enclos'd,
And all with vast magnificence dispos'd,
We leave the monarch pleas'd, and haste to
bring
The knights to combat, and their arms to
sing.

THE END OF THE SECOND BOOK

PALAMON AND ARCITE

OR, THE KNIGHT'S TALE

BOOK III

THE day approach'd when Fortune should
decide
Th' important enterprise, and give the bride;
For now the rivals round the world had
sought,

And each his number, well appointed,
brought.
The nations, far and near, contend in choice,
And send the flow'r of war by public voice;
That after, or before, were never known
Such chiefs, as each an army seem'd alone.
Beside the champions, all of high degree
Who knighthood lov'd, and deeds of chiv-
alry,   10
Throng'd to the lists, and envied to be-
hold
The names of others, not their own, in-
roll'd.
Nor seems it strange; for ev'ry noble
knight
Who loves the fair, and is endued with
might,
In such a quarrel would be proud to fight.
There breathes not scarce a man on British
ground
(An isle for love and arms of old renown'd)
But would have sold his life to purchase
fame,
To Palamon or Arcite sent his name;
And had the land selected of the best,   20
Half had come hence, and let the world
provide the rest.
A hundred knights with Palamon there
came,
Approv'd in fight, and men of mighty name;
Their arms were sev'ral, as their nations
were,
But furnish'd all alike with sword and spear.
Some wore coat armor, imitating scale;
And next their skins were stubborn shirts of
mail.
Some wore a breastplate and a light jup-
pon,
Their horses cloth'd with rich caparison:
Some for defense would leathern bucklers
use,   30
Of folded hides; and others shields of Pruce.
One hung a poleax at his saddlebow,
And one a heavy mace to stun the foe;
One for his legs and knees provided well,
With jambeux arm'd, and double plates of
steel;
This on his helmet wore a lady's glove,
And that a sleeve embroider'd by his love.
With Palamon, above the rest in place,
Lycurgus came, the surly king of Thrace;
Black was his beard, and manly was his
face;   40
The balls of his broad eyes roll'd in his
head.

And glar'd betwixt a yellow and a red:
He look'd a lion with a gloomy stare,
And o'er his eyebrows hung his matted
    hair;
Big-bon'd, and large of limbs, with sinews
    strong,
Broad-shoulder'd, and his arms were round
    and long.
Four milk-white bulls (the Thracian use of
    old)
Were yok'd to draw his car of burnish'd
    gold.
Upright he stood, and bore aloft his shield,
Conspicuous from afar, and overlook'd the
    field.   50
His surcoat was a bearskin on his back;
His hair hung long behind, and glossy
    raven-black.
His ample forehead bore a coronet
With sparkling diamonds and with rubies
    set.
Ten brace, and more, of greyhounds, ⎤
    snowy fair,   ⎮
And tall as stags, ran loose, and cours'd ⎮
    around his chair,   ⎬
A match for pards in flight, in grappling, ⎮
    for the bear;   ⎦
With golden muzzles all their mouths were
    bound,
And collars of the same their necks sur-
    round.
Thus thro' the fields Lycurgus took his way;
His hundred knights attend in pomp and
    proud array.   61
To match this monarch, with strong Arcite
    came
Emetrius, King of Inde, a mighty name,
On a bay courser, goodly to behold,
The trappings of his horse emboss'd with
    barb'rous gold.
Not Mars bestrode a steed with greater
    grace;
His surcoat o'er his arms was cloth of
    Thrace,
Adorn'd with pearls, all orient, round, and
    great;
His saddle was of gold, with emeralds set;
His shoulders large a mantle did attire,   70
With rubies thick, and sparkling as the
    fire;
His amber-color'd locks in ringlets run,
With graceful negligence, and shone against
    the sun.
His nose was aquiline, his eyes were blue,
Ruddy his lips, and fresh and fair his hue;

Some sprinkled freckles on his face were
    seen,
Whose dusk set off the whiteness of the
    skin.
His awful presence did the crowd surprise,
Nor durst the rash spectator meet his eyes;
Eyes that confess'd him born for kingly
    sway,   80
So fierce, they flash'd intolerable day.
His age in nature's youthful prime appear'd,
And just began to bloom his yellow beard.
Whene'er he spoke, his voice was heard
    around,
Loud as a trumpet, with a silver sound:
A laurel wreath'd his temples, fresh, and
    green;
And myrtle sprigs, the marks of love, were
    mix'd between.
Upon his fist he bore, for his delight,
An eagle well reclaim'd, and lily-white.
    His hundred knights attend him to the
        war,   90
All arm'd for battle; save their heads were
    bare.
Words and devices blaz'd on ev'ry shield,
And pleasing was the terror of the field.
For kings, and dukes, and barons you ⎤
    might see,   ⎮
Like sparkling stars, tho' diff'rent in   ⎬
    degree,   ⎮
All for th' increase of arms, and love of ⎮
    chivalry.   ⎦
Before the king tame leopards led the way,
And troops of lions innocently play.
So Bacchus thro' the conquer'd Indies rode,
And beasts in gambols frisk'd before their
    honest god.   100
    In this array the war of either side
Thro' Athens pass'd with military pride.
At prime, they enter'd on the Sunday morn;
Rich tap'stry spread the streets, and flow'rs
    the posts adorn.
The town was all a jubilee of feasts;
So Theseus will'd, in honor of his guests:
Himself with open arms the kings embrac'd,
Then all the rest in their degrees were
    grac'd.
No harbinger was needful for the night,
For ev'ry house was proud to lodge a
    knight.   110
I pass the royal treat, nor must relate
The gifts bestow'd, nor how the champions
    sate:
Who first, who last, or how the knights
    address'd

Their vows, or who was fairest at the
feast;
Whose voice, whose graceful dance did
most surprise;
Soft am'rous sighs, and silent love of eyes.
The rivals call my Muse another way,
To sing their vigils for th' ensuing day.
'T was ebbing darkness, past the noon of
night; 119
And Phosphor, on the confines of the light,
Promis'd the sun; ere day began to
spring,
The tuneful lark already stretch'd her
wing,
And, flick'ring on her nest, made short
essays to sing;
When wakeful Palamon, preventing day,
Took to the royal lists his early way,
To Venus at her fane, in her own house,
to pray.
There, falling on his knees before her
shrine,
He thus implor'd with pray'rs her pow'r
divine:
" Creator Venus, genial pow'r of love,
The bliss of men below and gods above !
Beneath the sliding sun thou runn'st thy
race, 131
Dost fairest shine, and best become thy
place;
For thee the winds their eastern blasts
forbear,
Thy month reveals the spring, and opens
all the year.
Thee, goddess, thee the storms of winter
fly,
Earth smiles with flow'rs renewing, laughs
the sky,
And birds to lays of love their tuneful
notes apply.
For thee the lion loathes the taste of blood,
And roaring hunts his female thro' the
wood;
For thee the bulls rebellow thro' the
groves, 140
And tempt the stream, and snuff their
absent loves.
'T is thine, whate'er is pleasant, good, or
fair;
All nature is thy province, life thy care:
Thou mad'st the world, and dost the
world repair.
Thou gladder of the mount of Cytheron,
Increase of Jove, companion of the sun;
If e'er Adonis touch'd thy tender heart,

Have pity, goddess, for thou know'st the
smart.
Alas ! I have not words to tell my grief;
To vent my sorrow would be some relief;
Light suff'rings give us leisure to complain;
We groan, but cannot speak, in greater
pain. 152
O goddess, tell thyself what I would say;
Thou know'st it, and I feel too much to
pray.
So grant my suit, as I enforce my might,
In love to be thy champion and thy knight;
A servant to thy sex, a slave to thee,
A foe profess'd to barren chastity.
Nor ask I fame or honor of the field,
Nor choose I more to vanquish than to
yield: 160
In my divine Emilia make me blest,
Let Fate, or partial Chance, dispose the rest:
Find thou the manner, and the means
prepare;
Possession, more than conquest, is my
care.
Mars is the warrior's god; in him it lies,
On whom he favors to confer the prize:
With smiling aspect you serenely move
In your fifth orb. and rule the realm of love.
The Fates but only spin the coarser clue,
The finest of the wool is left for you. 170
Spare me but one small portion of the
twine,
And let the sisters cut below your line:
The rest among the rubbish may they
sweep,
Or add it to the yarn of some old miser's
heap.
But, if you this ambitious pray'r deny,
(A wish, I grant, beyond mortality,)
Then let me sink beneath proud Arcite's
arms,
And I once dead, let him possess her
charms."
Thus ended he; then with observance
due
The sacred incense on her altar threw: 180
The curling smoke mounts heavy from the
fires;
At length it catches flame, and in a blaze
expires;
At once the gracious goddess gave the sign;
Her statue shook, and trembled all the
shrine.
Pleas'd Palamon the tardy omen took:
For, since the flames pursued the trailing
smoke,

He knew his boon was granted, but the day
To distance driv'n, and joy adjourn'd with long delay.
   Now morn with rosy light had streak'd the sky:
Up rose the sun, and up rose Emily;   190
Address'd her early steps to Cynthia's fane,
In state attended by her maiden train,
Who bore the vests that holy rites require,
Incense, and od'rous gums, and cover'd fire.
The plenteous horns with pleasant mead they crown,
Nor wanted aught besides in honor of the moon.
Now while the temple smok'd with hallow'd steam,
They wash the virgin in a living stream:
The secret ceremonies I conceal,
Uncouth, perhaps unlawful to reveal;   200
But such they were as pagan use requir'd,
Perform'd by women when the men retir'd,
Whose eyes profane their chaste mysterious rites
Might turn to scandal, or obscene delights.
Well-meaners think no harm; but for the rest,
Things sacred they pervert, and silence is the best.
Her shining hair, uncomb'd, was loosely spread;
A crown of mastless oak adorn'd her head.
When, to the shrine approach'd, the spotless maid
Had kindling fires on either altar laid,   210
(The rites were such as were observ'd of old,
By Statius in his Theban story told,)
Then, kneeling with her hands across her breast,
Thus lowly she preferr'd her chaste request:
   "O goddess, haunter of the woodland green,
To whom both heav'n and earth and seas are seen;
Queen of the nether skies, where half the year
Thy silver beams descend, and light the gloomy sphere;
Goddess of maids, and conscious of our hearts,
So keep me from the vengeance of thy darts,
(Which Niobe's devoted issue felt,   221

When hissing thro' the skies the feather'd deaths were dealt;)
As I desire to live a virgin life,
Nor know the name of mother or of wife.
Thy votress from my tender years I am,
And love, like thee, the woods and sylvan game.
Like death, thou know'st, I loathe the nuptial state,
And man, the tyrant of our sex, I hate —
A lowly servant, but a lofty mate;
Where love is duty on the female side;   230
On theirs mere sensual gust, and sought with surly pride.
Now by thy triple shape, as thou art seen
In heav'n, earth, hell, and ev'rywhere a queen,
Grant this my first desire: let discord cease,
And make betwixt the rivals lasting peace;
Quench their hot fire, or far from me remove
The flame, and turn it on some other love;
Or, if my frowning stars have so decreed,
That one must be rejected, one succeed,
Make him my lord, within whose faithful breast   240
Is fix'd my image, and who loves me best.
But, O, ev'n that avert; I choose it not,
But take it as the least unhappy lot.
A maid I am, and of thy virgin train;
O let me still that spotless name retain!
Frequent the forests, thy chaste will obey,
And only make the beasts of chase my prey!"
   The flames ascend on either altar clear,
While thus the blameless maid address'd her pray'r.
When lo! the burning fire that shone so bright   250
Flew off, all sudden, with extinguish'd light,
And left one altar dark, a little space;
Which turn'd self-kindled, and renew'd the blaze:
That other victor flame a moment stood,
Then fell, and lifeless left th' extinguish'd wood;
For ever lost, th' irrevocable light
Forsook the black'ning coals, and sunk to night:
At either end it whistled as it flew,
And as the brands were green, so dropp'd the dew,
Infected as it fell with sweat of sanguine hue.

The maid from that ill omen turn'd her
eyes,
And with loud shrieks and clamors rent
the skies,
Nor knew what signified the boding sign,
But found the pow'rs displeas'd, and fear'd
the wrath divine.
Then shook the sacred shrine, and sud-
den light
Sprung thro' the vaulted roof, and made
the temple bright.
The pow'r, behold ! the pow'r in glory shone,
By her bent bow and her keen arrows
known;
The rest, a huntress issuing from the wood,
Reclining on her cornel spear she stood: 270
Then gracious thus began: " Dismiss thy
fear,
And Heav'n's unchang'd decrees attentive
hear:
More pow'rful gods have torn thee from
my side,
Unwilling to resign, and doom'd a bride.
The two contending knights are weigh'd
above;
One Mars protects, and one the Queen of
Love:
But which the man, is in the Thund'rer's
breast —
This he pronounc'd, ' 'T is he who loves thee
best.'
The fire that, once extinct, reviv'd again,
Foreshews the love allotted to remain: 280
Farewell ! " she said, and vanish'd from
the place;
The sheaf of arrows shook, and rattled in
the case.
Aghast at this the royal virgin stood,
Disclaim'd, and now no more a sister of the
wood;
But to the parting goddess thus she ⎫
pray'd: ⎪
" Propitious still be present to my aid, ⎬
Nor quite abandon your once favor'd ⎪
maid." ⎭
Then sighing she return'd; but smil'd
betwixt,
With hopes, and fears, and joys with sor-
rows mix'd.
The next returning planetary hour 290
Of Mars, who shar'd the heptarchy of pow'r,
His steps bold Arcite to the temple bent,
T' adore with pagan rites the pow'r armi-
potent;
Then prostrate, low before his altar lay,

And rais'd his manly voice, and thus began
to pray:
" Strong God of Arms, whose iron scepter
sways
The freezing North, and Hyperborean seas,
And Scythian colds, and Thracia's wintry
coast,
Where stand thy steeds, and thou art
honor'd most —
There most; but ev'rywhere thy pow'r is
known,   300
The fortune of the fight is all thy own:
Terror is thine, and wild amazement, flung
From out thy chariot, withers ev'n the
strong;
And disarray and shameful rout ensue,
And force is added to the fainting crew.
Acknowledg'd as thou art, accept my
pray'r,
If aught I have achiev'd deserve thy care;
If to my utmost pow'r with sword and ⎫
shield ⎪
I dar'd the death, unknowing how to ⎬
yield, ⎪
And falling in my rank, still kept the ⎪
field: 310 ⎭
Then let my arms prevail, by thee sustain'd,
That Emily by conquest may be gain'd.
Have pity on my pains; nor those unknown
To Mars, which, when a lover, were his
own.
Venus, the public care of all above,
Thy stubborn heart has soften'd into love:
Now, by her blandishments and pow'rful
charms,
When yielded she lay curling in thy arms,
Ev'n by thy shame, if shame it may be
call'd,
When Vulcan had thee in his net inthrall'd;
(O envied ignominy, sweet disgrace,   321
When ev'ry god that saw thee wish'd thy
place !)
By those dear pleasures, aid my arms in
fight,
And make me conquer in my patron's
right:
For I am young, a novice in the trade,
The fool of love, unpractic'd to persuade;
And want the soothing arts that catch the
fair,
But, caught myself, lie struggling in the
snare:
And she I love, or laughs at all my pain,
Or knows her worth too well; and pays me
with disdain.   330

For sure I am, unless I win in arms,
To stand excluded from Emilia's charms;
Nor can my strength avail, unless, by thee
Endued with force, I gain the victory:
Then for the fire which warm'd thy gen'rous heart,
Pity thy subject's pains, and equal smart.
So be the morrow's sweat and labor mine,
The palm and honor of the conquest thine:
Then shall the war, and stern debate, and strife
Immortal, be the bus'ness of my life;   340
And in thy fane, the dusty spoils among,
High on the burnish'd roof, my banner shall be hung;
Rank'd with my champions' bucklers, and below,
With arms revers'd, th' achievements of my foe:
And while these limbs the vital spirit feeds,
While day to night, and night to day succeeds,
Thy smoking altar shall be fat with food
Of incense, and the grateful steam of blood;
Burnt off'rings morn and ev'ning shall be thine,
And fires eternal in thy temple shine.   350
This bush of yellow beard, this length of hair,
Which from my birth inviolate I bear,
Guiltless of steel, and from the razor free,
Shall fall a plenteous crop, reserv'd for thee.
So may my arms with victory be blest,
I ask no more; let fate dispose the rest."
    The champion ceas'd; there follow'd in the close
A hollow groan; a murm'ring wind arose;
The rings of ir'n that on the doors were hung   359
Sent out a jarring sound, and harshly rung:
The bolted gates flew open at the blast;
The storm rush'd in, and Arcite stood aghast:
The flames were blown aside, yet shone they bright,
Fann'd by the wind, and gave a ruffled light.
    Then from the ground a scent began to rise,
Sweet smelling, as accepted sacrifice.
This omen pleas'd, and, as the flames aspire,
With od'rous incense Arcite heaps the fire;
Nor wanted hymns to Mars, or heathen charms.

At length the nodding statue clash'd his arms,   370
And, with a sullen sound and feeble cry,
Half sunk, and half pronounc'd the word of victory.
For this, with soul devout, he thank'd the god;
And, of success secure, return'd to his abode.
    These vows, thus granted, rais'd a strife above.
Betwixt the God of War and Queen of Love.
She, granting first, had right of time to plead;
But he had granted too, nor would recede.
Jove was for Venus; but he fear'd his wife,
And seem'd unwilling to decide the strife; 380
Till Saturn from his leaden throne arose,
And found a way the diff'rence to compose:
Tho', sparing of his grace, to mischief bent,
He seldom does a good with good intent.
Wayward, but wise; by long experience taught,
To please both parties, for ill ends, he sought:
For this advantage age from youth has won,
As not to be outridden, tho' outrun.
By fortune he was now to Venus trin'd,
And with stern Mars in Capricorn was join'd: 390
Of him disposing in his own abode,
He sooth'd the goddess, while he gull'd the god:
"Cease, daughter, to complain, and stint the strife:
Thy Palamon shall have his promis'd wife;
And Mars, the lord of conquest, in the fight
With palm and laurel shall adorn his knight.
Wide is my course, nor turn I to my place
Till length of time, and move with tardy pace.
Man feels me, when I press th' ethereal plains;   399
My hand is heavy, and the wound remains.
Mine is the shipwreck in a wat'ry sign;
And in an earthy, the dark dungeon mine.
Cold shivering agues, melancholy care,   ⎫
And bitter blasting winds, and poison'd air, ⎟
Are mine, and wilful death, resulting from ⎬
    despair.   ⎭
The throttling quinsy 't is my star appoints,
And rheumatisms I send to rack the joints:
When churls rebel against their native prince,

I arm their hands, and furnish the pre-
tense;
And, housing in the Lion's hateful sign, 410
Bought senates, and deserting troops are
mine.
Mine is the privy pois'ning; I command
Unkindly seasons and ungrateful land.
By me kings' palaces are push'd to ground,
And miners crush'd beneath their mines
are found.
'T was I slew Samson, when the pillar'd
hall
Fell down and crush'd the many with the
fall.
My looking is the sire of pestilence,
That sweeps at once the people and the
prince.
Now weep no more, but trust thy grand-
sire's art; 420
Mars shall be pleas'd, and thou perform
thy part.
'T is ill, tho' diff'rent your complexions are,
The family of heav'n for men should war."
Th' expedient pleas'd, where neither lost
his right;
Mars had the day, and Venus had the night.
The management they left to Chronos' care;
Now turn we to th' effect, and sing the
war.
In Athens all was pleasure, mirth, and
play, 428
All proper to the spring and sprightly May;
Which ev'ry soul inspir'd with such delight,
'T was justing all the day, and love at night.
Heav'n smil'd, and gladded was the heart
of man,
And Venus had the world as when it first
began.
At length in sleep their bodies they com-
pose,
And dreamt the future fight, and early rose.
Now scarce the dawning day began to
spring,
As at a signal giv'n, the streets with cla-
mors ring:
At once the crowd arose; confus'd and
high,
Ev'n from the heav'n was heard a shout-
ing cry;
For Mars was early up, and rous'd the
sky. 440
The gods came downward to behold the
wars,
Sharp'ning their sights, and leaning from
their stars.

The neighing of the gen'rous horse was
heard,
For battle by the busy groom prepar'd;
Rustling of harness, rattling of the shield,
Clatt'ring of armor, furbish'd for the field.
Crowds to the castle mounted up the street,
Batt'ring the pavement with their coursers'
feet:
The greedy sight might there devour the
gold 449
Of glitt'ring arms, too dazzling to behold;
And polish'd steel, that cast the view aside,
And crested morions, with their plumy
pride.
Knights, with a long retinue of their squires,
In gaudy liv'ries march, and quaint attires.
One lac'd the helm, another held the lance;
A third the shining buckler did advance.
The courser paw'd the ground with rest-
less feet,
And snorting foam'd, and champ'd the
golden bit.
The smiths and armorers on palfreys ride,
Files in their hands, and hammers at
their side, 460
And nails for loosen'd spears, and thongs
for shields provide.
The yeomen guard the streets, in seemly
bands;
And clowns come crowding on with cudgels
in their hands.
The trumpets, next the gate, in order
plac'd,
Attend the sign to sound the martial blast;
The palace yard is fill'd with floating tides,
And the last comers bear the former to the
sides.
The throng is in the midst; the common
crew
Shut out, the hall admits the better few.
In knots they stand, or in a rank they walk,
Serious in aspect, earnest in their talk: 471
Factious, and fav'ring this or t'other side,
As their strong fancies and weak reason
guide.
Their wagers back their wishes; numbers
hold
With the fair freckled king, and beard of
gold:
So vig'rous are his eyes, such rays they cast,
So prominent his eagle's beak is plac'd.
But most their looks on the black monarch
bend,
His rising muscles and his brawn com-
mend;

His double-biting ax, and beamy spear, 480
Each asking a gigantic force to rear.
All spoke as partial favor mov'd the mind;
And, safe themselves, at others' cost divin'd.
  Wak'd by the cries, th' Athenian chief
    arose,
The knightly forms of combat to dispose;
And passing thro' th obsequious guards, he
    sate
Conspicuous on a throne, sublime in state;
There for the two contending knights he
    sent:
Arm'd *cap-a-pe*, with rev'rence low they
    bent;
He smil'd on both, and with superior look
Alike their offer'd adoration took.   491
The people press on ev'ry side to see
Their awful prince and hear his high de-
    cree.
Then, signing to the heralds with his hand,
They gave his orders from their lofty stand.
Silence is thrice enjoin'd; then thus aloud
The king at arms bespeaks the knights and
    list'ning crowd:
  "Our sovereign lord has ponder'd in his
    mind
The means to spare the blood of gentle kind;
And of his grace, and inborn clemency, 500
He modifies his first severe decree;
The keener edge of battle to rebate,
The troops for honor fighting, not for hate.
He wills, not death should terminate their
    strife;
And wounds, if wounds ensue, be short of
    life;
But issues, ere the fight, his dread com-
    mand,
That slings afar, and poniards hand to hand,
Be banish'd from the field; that none shall
    dare
With shorten'd sword to stab in closer war;
But in fair combat fight with manly
    strength,   510
Nor push with biting point, but strike at
    length.
The turney is allow'd but one career
Of the tough ash, with the sharp-grinded
    spear;
But knights unhors'd may rise from off the
    plain,
And fight on foot their honor to regain;
Nor, if at mischief taken, on the ground
Be slain, but pris'ners to the pillar bound,
At either barrier plac'd; nor, captives made,
Be freed, or arm'd anew the fight invade.

The chief of either side, bereft of life, 520
Or yielded to his foe, concludes the strife.
Thus dooms the lord: now valiant knights
    and young,
Fight each his fill with swords and maces
    long."
  The herald ends; the vaulted firmament
With loud acclaims and vast applause is
    rent:
" Heav'n guard a prince so gracious and so
    good,
So just, and yet so provident of blood ! "
This was the gen'ral cry. The trumpets
    sound,
And warlike symphony is heard around.
The marching troops thro' Athens take
    their way,   530
The great earl-marshal orders their array.
The fair from high the passing pomp be-
    hold;
A rain of flow'rs is from the windows roll'd.
The casements are with golden tissue
    spread,
And horses' hoofs, for earth, on silken
    tap'stry tread.
The king goes midmost, and the rivals ride
In equal rank, and close his either side.
Next after these, there rode the royal wife,
With Emily, the cause and the reward of
    strife.
The following cavalcade, by three and
    three,   540
Proceed by titles marshal'd in degree.
Thus thro' the southern gate they take their
    way,
And at the lists arriv'd ere prime of day.
There, parting from the king, the chiefs
    divide,
And wheeling east and west, before their
    many ride.
Th' Athenian monarch mounts his throne
    on high,
And after him the queen and Emily;
Next these, the kindred of the crown are
    grac'd
With nearer seats, and lords by ladies
    plac'd.
Scarce were they seated, when with clamors
    loud   550
In rush'd at once a rude promiscuous crowd;
The guards, and then each other overbare,
And in a moment throng the spacious
    theater.
Now chang'd the jarring noise to whispers
    low,

As winds forsaking seas more softly blow;
When, at the western gate, on which the car
Is plac'd aloft, that bears the God of War,
Proud Arcite, ent'ring arm'd before his train,
Stops at the barrier, and divides the plain.
Red was his banner, and display'd abroad
The bloody colors of his patron god.   561
    At that self moment enters Palamon
The gate of Venus and the rising Sun;
Wav'd by the wanton winds, his banner flies,
All maiden white, and shares the people's eyes.
From east to west, look all the world around,
Two troops so match'd were never to be found;
Such bodies built for strength, of equal age,
In stature siz'd; so proud an equipage:
The nicest eye could no distinction make,
Where lay th' advantage, or what side to take.   571
    Thus rang'd, the herald for the last proclaims
A silence, while they answer'd to their names:
For so the king decreed, to shun with care
The fraud of musters false, the common bane of war.
The tale was just, and then the gates were clos'd;
And chief to chief, and troop to troop oppos'd.
The heralds last retir'd, and loudly cried:
" The fortune of the field be fairly tried ! "
    At this, the challenger with fierce defy
His trumpet sounds; the challeng'd makes reply: 581
With clangor rings the field, resounds the vaulted sky.
Their vizors clos'd, their lances in the rest,
Or at the helmet pointed, or the crest,
They vanish from the barrier, speed the race,
And spurring see decrease the middle space.
A cloud of smoke envelops either host,
And all at once the combatants are lost:
Darkling they join adverse, and shock unseen,
Coursers with coursers justling, men with men;   590
As lab'ring in eclipse, a while they stay,
Till the next blast of wind restores the day.

They look anew; the beauteous form of fight
Is chang'd, and war appears a grisly sight.
Two troops in fair array one moment show'd,
The next, a field with fallen bodies strow'd:
Not half the number in their seats are found;
But men and steeds lie grov'ling on the ground.
The points of spears are stuck within the shield,
The steeds without their riders scour the field.   600
The knights, unhors'd, on foot renew the fight;
The glitt'ring fauchions cast a gleaming light:
Hauberks and helms are hew'd with many a wound;
Out spins the streaming blood and dyes the ground.
The mighty maces with such haste descend,
They break the bones, and make the solid armor bend.
This thrusts amid the throng with furious force;
Down goes, at once, the horseman and the horse:
That courser stumbles on the fallen steed,
And, flound'ring, throws the rider o'er his head.   610
One rolls along, a football to his foes;
One with a broken truncheon deals his blows.
This halting, this disabled with his wound,
In triumph led, is to the pillar bound,
Where by the king's award he must abide;
There goes a captive led on t'other side.
By fits they cease; and, leaning on the lance,
Take breath a while, and to new fight advance.
    Full oft the rivals met, and neither spar'd   619
His utmost force, and each forgot to ward.
The head of this was to the saddle bent,
That other backward to the crupper sent:
Both were by turns unhors'd; the jealous blows
Fall thick and heavy, when on foot they close.
So deep their fauchions bite, that ev'ry stroke

Pierc'd to the quick; and equal wounds
  they gave and took.
Borne far asunder by the tides of men,
Like adamant and steel they meet again.
  So when a tiger sucks the bullock's ⎫
    blood,   629
A famish'd lion issuing from the wood ⎬
Roars lordly fierce, and challenges the
    food.   ⎭
Each claims possession, neither will obey,
But both their paws are fasten'd on the
    prey;
They bite, they tear; and while in vain
    they strive,
The swains come arm'd between, and both
    to distance drive.
  At length, as Fate foredoom'd, and all
    things tend
By course of time to their appointed end;
So when the sun to west was far declin'd,
And both afresh in mortal battle join'd,
The strong Emetrius came in Arcite's aid,
And Palamon with odds was overlaid: 641
For, turning short, he struck with all his
    might
Full on the helmet of th' unwary knight.
Deep was the wound; he stagger'd with
    the blow
And turn'd him to his unexpected foe;
Whom with such force he struck, he fell'd
    him down,
And cleft the circle of his golden crown.
But Arcite's men, who now prevail'd in
    fight,
Twice ten at once surround the single
    knight:
O'erpower'd at length, they force him to
    the ground,   650
Unyielded as he was, and to the pillar
    bound;
And King Lycurgus, while he fought in
    vain
His friend to free, was tumbled on the
    plain.
  Who now laments but Palamon, com-
    pell'd
No more to try the fortune of the field !
And, worse than death, to view with hate-
    ful eyes
His rival's conquest, and renounce the
    prize !
  The royal judge on his tribunal plac'd,
Who had beheld the fight from first to last,
Bade cease the war; pronouncing from on
    high,   660

Arcite of Thebes had won the beauteous
    Emily.
  The sound of trumpets to the voice ⎫
    replied,   ⎪
And round the royal lists the heralds ⎬
    cried: ⎪
" Arcite of Thebes has won the beauteous ⎪
    bride."   ⎭
  The people rend the skies with vast
    applause:
All own the chief, when Fortune owns the
    cause.
Arcite is own'd ev'n by the gods above,
And conqu'ring Mars insults the Queen of
    Love:
So laugh'd he, when the rightful Titan
    fail'd,
And Jove's usurping arms in heav'n pre-
    vail'd.   670
Laugh'd all the pow'rs who favor tyranny;
And all the standing army of the sky.
But Venus with dejected eyes appears,
And weeping on the lists distill'd her tears;
Her will refus'd, which grieves a woman
    most,
And, in her champion foil'd, the cause of
    Love is lost:
Till Saturn said: " Fair daughter, now be
    still,
The blust'ring fool has satisfied his will;
His boon is giv'n; his knight has gain'd the
    day,
But lost the prize — th' arrears are yet to
    pay.   680
Thy hour is come, and mine the care shall
    be
To please thy knight, and set thy promise
    free."
  Now while the heralds run the lists
    around,
And " Arcite, Arcite," heav'n and earth
    resound;
A miracle (nor less it could be call'd)
Their joy with unexpected sorrow pall'd.
The victor knight had laid his helm aside,
Part for his ease, the greater part for pride.
Bareheaded, popularly low he bow'd,
And paid the salutations of the crowd; 690
Then, spurring at full speed, ran endlong on
Where Theseus sat on his imperial throne;
Furious he drove, and upward cast his eye,
Where next the queen was plac'd his
    Emily;
Then passing, to the saddlebow he bent —
A sweet regard the gracious virgin lent;

(For women, to the brave an easy prey,
Still follow Fortune, where she leads the
way.)
Just then, from earth sprung out a flash-
ing fire,
By Pluto sent, at Saturn's bad desire;   700
The startling steed was seiz'd with sudden
fright,
And, bounding, o'er the pommel cast the
knight:
Forward he flew, and pitching on his head,
He quiver'd with his feet, and lay for
dead.
Black was his count'nance in a little space,
For all the blood was gather'd in his face.
Help was at hand: they rear'd him from
the ground,
And from his cumbrous arms his limbs
unbound;
Then lanc'd a vein, and watch'd returning
breath;
It came, but clogg'd with symptoms of his
death.   710
The saddlebow the noble parts had press'd,
All bruis'd and mortified his manly breast.
Him still entranc'd, and in a litter laid,
They bore from field, and to his bed con-
vey'd.
At length he wak'd, and with a feeble cry,
The word he first pronounc'd was Emily.
Meantime the king, tho' inwardly he
mourn'd,
In pomp triumphant to the town return'd,
Attended by the chiefs, who fought the
field;
(Now friendly mix'd, and in one troop
compell'd;)   720
Compos'd his looks to counterfeited cheer,
And bade them not for Arcite's life to fear.
But that which gladded all the warrior
train,
Tho' most were sorely wounded, none were
slain.
The surgeons soon despoil'd 'em of their
arms,
And some with salves they cure, and some
with charms;
Foment the bruises, and the pains assuage,
And heal their inward hurts with sov'reign
draughts of sage.
The king in person visits all around,   729
Comforts the sick, congratulates the sound;
Honors the princely chiefs, rewards the rest,
And holds for thrice three days a royal
feast.

None was disgrac'd; for falling is no
shame,
And cowardice alone is loss of fame.
The vent'rous knight is from the saddle
thrown;
But 't is the fault of Fortune, not his own.
If crowds and palms the conqu'ring side
adorn,
The victor under better stars was born:
The brave man seeks not popular applause,
Nor, overpow'r'd with arms, deserts his
cause;   740
Unsham'd, tho' foil'd, he does the best he
can;
Force is of brutes, but honor is of man.
Thus Theseus smil'd on all with equal
grace;
And each was set according to his place.
With ease were reconcil'd the diff'ring
parts,
For envy never dwells in noble hearts.
At length they took their leave, the time
expir'd,
Well pleas'd, and to their sev'ral homes
retir'd.
Meanwhile the health of Arcite still im-
pairs;
From bad proceeds to worse, and mocks
the leeches' cares: 750
Swoln is his breast, his inward pains in-
crease;
All means are us'd, and all without suc-
cess.
The clotted blood lies heavy on his heart,
Corrupts, and there remains in spite of art:
Nor breathing veins, nor cupping will pre-
vail;
All outward remedies and inward fail.
The mold of Nature's fabric is destroy'd,
Her vessels discompos'd, her virtue void;
The bellows of his lungs begins to swell: ⎤
All out of frame is ev'ry secret cell,   760 ⎟
Nor can the good receive, nor bad expel. ⎦
Those breathing organs, thus within op-
press'd,
With venom soon distend the sinews of his
breast.
Naught profits him to save abandon'd life,
Nor vomit's upward aid, nor downward
laxatife.
The midmost region batter'd and destroy'd,
When nature cannot work, th' effect of
art is void:
For physic can but mend our crazy state,
Patch an old building, not a new create.

Arcite is doom'd to die in all his pride; ⎫
Must leave his youth, and yield his beau- ⎪
   teous bride,   771 ⎬
Gain'd hardly, against right, and unen- ⎪
   joy'd. ⎭
When 't was declar'd all hope of life was ⎫
   past, ⎪
Conscience, that of all physic works the ⎬
   last, ⎪
Caus'd him to send for Emily in haste. ⎭
With her, at his desire, came Palamon;
Then, on his pillow rais'd, he thus begun:
   " No language can express the smallest
     part
Of what I feel, and suffer in my heart,   779
For you, whom best I love and value most;
But to your service I bequeath my ghost;
Which from this mortal body when untied,
Unseen, unheard, shall hover at your side;
Nor fright you waking, nor your sleep of-
   fend,
But wait officious, and your steps attend.
How I have lov'd, excuse my falt'ring
   tongue,
My spirit 's feeble, and my pains are strong:
This I may say, I only grieve to die,
Because I lose my charming Emily:
To die, when Heav'n had put you in my
   pow'r,   790
Fate could not choose a more malicious
   hour !
What greater curse could envious Fortune
   give,
Than just to die, when I began to live !
Vain men, how vanishing a bliss we crave,
Now warm in love, now with'ring in the
   grave !
Never, O never more to see the sun !
Still dark, in a damp vault, and still alone !
This fate is common; but I lose my breath
Near bliss, and yet not blest before my
   death.   799
Farewell; but take me dying in your arms,
'T is all I can enjoy of all your charms:
This hand I cannot but in death resign;
Ah, could I live ! but while I live 't is mine.
I feel my end approach, and thus embrac'd,
Am pleas'd to die; but hear me speak my
   last.
Ah, my sweet foe, for you, and you alone,
I broke my faith with injur'd Palamon.
But love the sense of right and wrong
   confounds,
Strong love and proud ambition have no
   bounds.

And much I doubt, should Heav'n my life
   prolong,   810
I should return to justify my wrong:
For while my former flames remain within,
Repentance is but want of pow'r to sin.
With mortal hatred I pursued his life;
Nor he, nor you, were guilty of the strife;
Nor I, but as I lov'd: yet all combin'd,
Your beauty and my impotence of mind,
And his concurrent flame, that blew my
   fire;
For still our kindred souls had one desire.
He had a moment's right in point of time;
Had I seen first, then his had been the
   crime.   821
Fate made it mine, and justified his right;
Nor holds this earth a more deserving
   knight,
For virtue, valor, and for noble blood,
Truth, honor, all that is compris'd in good;
So help me Heav'n, in all the world is none
So worthy to be lov'd as Palamon.
He loves you too, with such a holy fire,
As will not, cannot, but with life expire:
Our vow'd affections both have often tried,
Nor any love but yours could ours divide.
Then, by my love's inviolable band,   832
By my long suff'ring, and my short com-
   mand,
If e'er you plight your vows when I am
   gone,
Have pity on the faithful Palamon."
   This was his last; for Death came on
   amain,
And exercis'd below his iron reign;
Then upward to the seat of life he goes:
Sense fled before him; what he touch'd he
   froze.
Yet could he not his closing eyes withdraw,
Tho' less and less of Emily he saw: 841
So, speechless, for a little space he lay;
Then grasp'd the hand he held, and sigh'd
   his soul away.
   But whither went his soul, let such re-
   late
Who search the secrets of the future state:
Divines can say but what themselves be-
   lieve;
Strong proofs they have, but not demon-
   strative:
For, were all plain, then all sides must
   agree,
And faith itself be lost in certainty.
To live uprightly then is sure the best,   850
To save ourselves, and not to damn the rest.

The soul of Arcite went where heathens go,
Who better live than we, tho' less they
  know.
  In Palamon a manly grief appears;
Silent, he wept, asham'd to shew his tears:
Emilia shriek'd but once, and then, op-
  press'd
With sorrow, sunk upon her lover's breast:
Till Theseus in his arms convey'd with
  care,   858
Far from so sad a sight, the swooning fair.
'T were, loss of time her sorrow to relate; ⎤
Ill bears the sex a youthful lover's fate,   ⎟
When just approaching to the nuptial   ⎬
  state.   ⎦
But like a low-hung cloud, it rains so fast,
That all at once it falls, and cannot last.
The face of things is chang'd, and Athens
  now,
That laugh'd so late, becomes the scene of
  woe:
Matrons and maids, both sexes, ev'ry state,
With tears lament the knight's untimely
  fate.
Not greater grief in falling Troy was seen
For Hector's death; but Hector was not
  then.   870
Old men with dust deform'd their hoary
  hair;
The women beat their breasts, their cheeks
  they tear.
" Why wouldst thou go," with one consent
  they cry,
" When thou hadst gold enough, and
  Emily ? "
  Theseus himself, who should have cheer'd
  the grief
Of others, wanted now the same relief;
Old Ægeus only could revive his son,
Who various changes of the world had
  known,
And strange vicissitudes of human fate,
Still alt'ring, never in a steady state;   880
Good after ill, and, after pain, delight;
Alternate like the scenes of day and night.
Since ev'ry man who lives is born to die,
And none can boast sincere felicity,
With equal mind, what happens, let us
  bear,
Nor joy nor grieve too much for things
  beyond our care.
Like pilgrims to th' appointed place we
  tend;
The world 's an inn, and death the journey's
  end.

Ev'n kings but play; and when their part
  is done,
Some other, worse or better, mount the
  throne.   890
With words like these the crowd was
  satisfied,
And so they would have been, had Theseus
  died.
  But he, their king, was lab'ring in his ⎤
  mind,   ⎟
A fitting place for fun'ral pomps to find, ⎬
Which were in honor of the dead de-   ⎟
  sign'd.   ⎦
And after long debate, at last he found
(As love itself had mark'd the spot of
  ground)
That grove for ever green, that conscious
  laund,
Where he with Palamon fought hand to
  hand:
That, where he fed his amorous desires 900
With soft complaints, and felt his hottest
  fires,
There other flames might waste his earthly
  part,
And burn his limbs, where love had burn'd
  his heart.
  This once resolv'd, the peasants were
  enjoin'd
Sear wood, and firs, and dodder'd oaks to
  find.
With sounding axes to the grove they go,
Fell, split, and lay the fuel on a row,
Vulcanian food: a bier is next prepar'd,
On which the lifeless body should be
  rear'd,
Cover'd with cloth of gold, on which was
  laid   910
The corpse of Arcite, in like robes array'd.
White gloves were on his hands, and on his
  head
A wreath of laurel, mix'd with myrtle,
  spread.
A sword keen-edg'd within his right he
  held,
The warlike emblem of the conquer'd field:
Bare was his manly visage on the bier;
Menac'd his count'nance, ev'n in death
  severe.
Then to the palace hall they bore the
  knight,
To lie in solemn state, a public sight.
Groans, cries, and howlings fill the crowded
  place,   920
And unaffected sorrow sat on ev'ry face.

Sad Palamon above the rest appears,
In sable garments, dew'd with gushing tears:
His auburn locks on either shoulder flow'd,
Which to the fun'ral of his friend he vow'd:
But Emily, as chief, was next his side,
A virgin widow, and a *Mourning Bride.*
And that the princely obsequies might be
Perform'd according to his high degree,
The steed that bore him living to the ⎤
   fight   930 ⎟
Was trapp'd with polish'd steel, all shin- ⎬
   ing bright, ⎟
And cover'd with th' achievements of the ⎦
   knight.
The riders rode abreast, and one his shield,
His lance of cornel wood another held;
The third his bow, and, glorious to behold,
The costly quiver, all of burnish'd gold.
The noblest of the Grecians next appear,
And, weeping, on their shoulders bore the
   bier;
With sober pace they march'd, and often
   stay'd,
And thro' the master-street the corpse
   convey'd.   940
The houses to their tops with black were
   spread,
And ev'n the pavements were with mourn-
   ing hid.
The right side of the pall old Ægeus kept,
And on the left the royal Theseus wept;
Each bore a golden bowl, of work di-
   vine,
With honey fill'd, and milk, and mix'd with
   ruddy wine.
Then Palamon, the kinsman of the slain,
And after him appear'd th' illustrious train:
To grace the pomp, came Emily the bright,
With cover'd fire, the fun'ral pile to light.
With high devotion was the service made,
And all the rites of pagan honor paid: 952
So lofty was the pile, a Parthian bow,
With vigor drawn, must send the shaft
   below.
The bottom was full twenty fathom broad,
With crackling straw beneath in due pro-
   portion strow'd.
The fabric seem'd a wood of rising green,
With sulphur and bitumen cast between,
To feed the flames: the trees were unc- ⎤
   tuous fir, ⎟
And mountain-ash, the mother of the ⎬
   spear;   960 ⎟
The mourner yew and builder oak were ⎦
   there;

The beech, the swimming alder, and the ⎤
   plane, ⎟
Hard box, and linden of a softer grain, ⎬
And laurels, which the gods for conqu'r- ⎟
   ing chiefs ordain. ⎦
How they were rank'd shall rest untold by
   me,
With nameless Nymphs that liv'd in ev'ry
   tree;
Nor how the Dryads and the woodland train,
Disherited, ran howling o'er the plain;
Nor how the birds to foreign seats repair'd,
Or beasts, that bolted out, and saw the
   forest bar'd;   970
Nor how the ground, now clear'd, with
   ghastly fright
Beheld the sudden sun, a stranger to the
   light.
   The straw, as first I said, was laid be-
   low:
Of chips and sear wood was the second row;
The third of greens and timber newly fell'd;
The fourth high stage the fragrant odors
   held,
And pearls, and precious stones, and rich
   array,
In midst of which, embalm'd, the body lay.
The service sung, the maid, with mourning
   eyes,
The stubble fir'd; the smold'ring flames
   arise: 980
This office done, she sunk upon the ground;
But what she spoke, recover'd from her
   swound,
I want the wit in moving words to dress;
But by themselves the tender sex may
   guess.
While the devouring fire was burning fast,
Rich jewels in the flame the wealthy cast;
And some their shields, and some their
   lances threw,
And gave the warrior's ghost a warrior's
   due.
Full bowls of wine, of honey, milk, and ⎤
   blood, ⎟
Were pour'd upon the pile of burning ⎬
   wood,   990 ⎟
And hissing flames receive, and hungry ⎦
   lick the food.
Then thrice the mounted squadrons ride
   around
The fire, and Arcite's name they thrice re-
   sound:
" Hail, and farewell! " they shouted thrice
   amain,

Thrice facing to the left, and thrice they
  turn'd again:
Still as they turn'd, they beat their clat-
  t'ring shields;
The women mix their cries; and clamor
  fills the fields.
The warlike wakes continued all the night,
And fun'ral games were play'd at new re-
  turning light:
Who naked wrestled best, besmear'd with
  oil,   1000
Or who with gauntlets gave or took the
  foil,
I will not tell you, nor would you attend;
But briefly haste to my long story's end.
  I pass the rest; the year was fully
  mourn'd,
And Palamon long since to Thebes return'd:
When, by the Grecians' general consent,
At Athens Theseus held his parliament.
Among the laws that pass'd it was decreed,
That conquer'd Thebes from bondage should
  be freed;   1009
Reserving homage to th' Athenian throne,
To which the sov'reign summon'd Palamon.
Unknowing of the cause, he took his way,
Mournful in mind, and still in black array.
  The monarch mounts the throne, and,
  plac'd on high,
Commands into the court the beauteous
  Emily:
So call'd, she came; the senate rose, and
  paid
Becoming rev'rence to the royal maid.
And first, soft whispers thro' th' assembly
  went;
With silent wonder then they watch'd th'
  event: 1019
All hush'd, the king arose with awful grace;
Deep thought was in his breast, and coun-
  sel in his face.
At length he sigh'd; and having first pre-
  par'd
Th' attentive audience, thus his will de-
  clar'd:
  "The Cause and Spring of motion, from
  above,
Hung down on earth the golden chain of
  love:
Great was th' effect, and high was his in-
  tent,
When peace among the jarring seeds he
  sent.
Fire, flood, and earth, and air by this were
  bound,

And love, the common link, the new cre-
  ation crown'd.
The chain still holds; for, tho' the forms
  decay,   1030
Eternal matter never wears away.
The same First Mover certain bounds has
  plac'd,
How long those perishable forms shall last;
Nor can they last beyond the time assign'd
By that all-seeing, and all-making mind:
Shorten their hours they may, for will is
  free,
But never pass th' appointed destiny.
So men oppress'd, when weary of their
  breath,
Throw off the burden, and suborn their
  death.
Then, since those forms begin, and have
  their end,   1040
On some unalter'd cause they sure depend:
Parts of the whole are we; but God the
  whole,
Who gives us life and animating soul.
For nature cannot from a part derive
That being which the whole can only give:
He perfect, stable; but imperfect we,
Subject to change, and diff'rent in degree;
Plants, beasts, and man; and as our organs
  are,
We more or less of his perfection share.
But by a long descent, th' ethereal fire
Corrupts; and forms, the mortal part, ex-
  pire: 1051
As he withdraws his virtue, so they pass,
And the same matter makes another mass.
This law th' Omniscient Pow'r was pleas'd
  to give,
That ev'ry kind should by succession live:
That individuals die, his will ordains;
The propagated species still remains.
The monarch oak, the patriarch of the trees,
Shoots rising up, and spreads by slow de-
  grees;
Three centuries he grows, and three he
  stays,   1060
Supreme in state, and in three more decays:
So wears the paving pebble in the street,
And towns and tow'rs their fatal periods
  meet;
So rivers, rapid once, now naked lie,
Forsaken of their springs, and leave their
  channels dry.
So man, at first a drop, dilates with heat;
Then, form'd, the little heart begins to
  beat;

Secret he feeds, unknowing, in the cell;
At length, for hatching ripe, he breaks the
   shell,   1069
And struggles into breath, and cries for aid;
Then, helpless, in his mother's lap is laid.
He creeps, he walks, and issuing into man,
Grudges their life, from whence his own
   began;
Rechless of laws, affects to rule alone,
Anxious to reign, and restless on the throne:
First vegetive, then feels, and reasons last;
Rich of three souls, and lives all three to
   waste.
Some thus; but thousands more in flow'r
   of age:
For few arrive to run the latter stage.
Sunk in the first, in battle some are slain,
And others whelm'd beneath the stormy
   main.   1081
What makes all this, but Jupiter the king,
At whose command we perish, and we
   spring ?
Then 't is our best, since thus ordain'd to die,
To make a virtue of necessity;
Take what he gives, since to rebel is vain;
The bad grows better, which we well sus-
   tain:
And could we choose the time, and choose
   aright,
'T is best to die, our honor at the height.
When we have done our ancestors no
   shame,   1090
But serv'd our friends, and well secur'd our
   fame;
Then should we wish our happy life to
   close,
And leave no more for fortune to dispose:
So should we make our death a glad relief
From future shame, from sickness, and
   from grief;
Enjoying while we live the present hour,
And dying in our excellence and flow'r.
Then round our deathbed ev'ry friend
   should run,
And joy us of our conquest, early won;
While the malicious world with envious
   tears   1100
Should grudge our happy end, and wish it
   theirs.
Since then our Arcite is with honor dead, ⎤
Why should we mourn, that he so soon is ⎟
   freed,   ⎬
Or call untimely what the gods decreed ? ⎦
With grief as just, a friend may be de-
   plor'd,

From a foul prison to free air restor'd.
Ought he to thank his kinsman or his wife,
Could tears recall him into wretched life !
Their sorrow hurts themselves; on him is
   lost;
And, worse than both, offends his happy
   ghost.   1110
What then remains, but, after past annoy,
To take the good vicissitude of joy ?
To thank the gracious gods for what they
   give,
Possess our souls, and while we live, to
   live ?
Ordain we then two sorrows to combine,
And in one point th' extremes of grief to
   join;
That thence resulting joy may be renew'd,
As jarring notes in harmony conclude.
Then I propose that Palamon shall be
In marriage join'd with beauteous Emily;
For which already I have gain'd th' assent
Of my free people in full parliament.   1122
Long love to her has borne the faithful
   knight,
And well deserv'd, had Fortune done him
   right:
'T is time to mend her fault, since Emily
By Arcite's death from former vows is free.
If you, fair sister, ratify th' accord,
And take him for your husband and your
   lord,
'T is no dishonor to confer your grace
On one descended from a royal race;   1130
And were he less, yet years of service past
From grateful souls exact reward at last:
Pity is Heav'n's and yours; nor can she find
A throne so soft as in a woman's mind."
  He said; she blush'd; and, as o eraw'd
   by might,
Seem'd to give Theseus what she gave the
   knight.
Then, turning to the Theban, thus he said
" Small arguments are needful to persuade
Your temper to comply with my com-
   mand; "   1139
And speaking thus, he gave Emilia's hand.
Smil'd Venus, to behold her own true ⎤
   knight   ⎟
Obtain the conquest, tho' he lost the fight; ⎬
And bless'd with nuptial bliss the sweet ⎟
   laborious night.   ⎦
Eros and Anteros, on either side,
One fir'd the bridegroom, and one warm'd
   the bride;
And long-attending Hymen from above

Shower'd on the bed the whole Idalian grove.
All of a tenor was their after life,
No day discolor'd with domestic strife;
No jealousy, but mutual truth believ'd,
Secure repose, and kindness undeceiv'd.
Thus Heav'n, beyond the compass of his
   thought,   1152
Sent him the blessing he so dearly bought.
  So may the Queen of Love long duty
   bless,
And all true lovers find the same success.

THE END OF THE THIRD BOOK

TO MY HONOR'D KINSMAN, JOHN DRIDEN, OF CHESTER-TON, IN THE COUNTY OF HUNTINGDON, ESQUIRE

How blest is he, who leads a country life,
Unvex'd with anxious cares, and void of
  strife !
Who, studying peace and shunning civil
  rage,
Enjoy'd his youth, and now enjoys his age:
All who deserve his love, he makes his own;
And, to be lov'd himself, needs only to be
  known.
  Just, good, and wise, contending neigh-
    bors come,
From your award to wait their final doom;
And, foes before, return in friendship
   home.
Without their cost, you terminate the
  cause,   10
And save th' expense of long litigious laws:
Where suits are travers'd, and so little won,
That he who conquers is but last undone.
Such are not your decrees; but so de-
   sign'd,
The sanction leaves a lasting peace be-
   hind:
Like your own soul, serene; a pattern of
   your mind.
  Promoting concord, and composing strife,
Lord of yourself, uncumber'd with a wife;
Where, for a year, a month, perhaps a
  night,
Long penitence succeeds a short delight: 20
Minds are so hardly match'd, that ev'n the
  first,
Tho' pair'd by Heav'n, in Paradise were
  curst.
For man and woman, tho' in one they grow,
Yet, first or last, retu n again to two. ..

He to God's image, she to his was made;
So, farther from the fount, the stream at
  random stray'd.
  How could he stand, when, put to double
   pain,
He must a weaker than himself sustain !
Each might have stood perhaps, but each
  alone;
Two wrestlers help to pull each other
  down.   30
  Not that my verse would blemish all
   the fair;
But yet if *some* be bad, 't is wisdom to be-
  ware;
And better shun the bait than struggle
  in the snare.
Thus have you shunn'd, and shun, the mar-
   ried state,
Trusting as little as you can to fate.
  No porter guards the passage of your
   door,
T' admit the wealthy, and exclude the poor;
For God, who gave the riches, gave the
  heart,
To sanctify the whole, by giving part.
Heav'n, who foresaw the will, the means
  has wrought,   40
And to the second son a blessing brought;
The first-begotten had his father's share,
But you, like Jacob, are Rebecca's heir.
  So may your stores and fruitful fields
  increase;
And ever be you blest, who live to bless.
As Ceres sow'd, where'er her chariot flew;
As Heav'n in desarts rain'd the bread of
  dew;
So free to many, to relations most,
You feed with manna your own Israel host.
  With crowds attended of your ancient
   race,   50
You seek the champian sports or sylvan
  chase;
With well-breath'd beagles you surround
  the wood,
Ev'n then industrious of the common good;
And often have you brought the wily fox
To suffer for the firstlings of the flocks;
Chas'd ev'n amid the folds, and made to
  bleed,
Like felons, where they did the murd'rous
  deed.
This fiery game your active youth main-
   tain'd,
Not yet by years extinguish'd, tho' re-
  strain'd:

You season still with sports your serious
   hours;   60
For age but tastes of pleasures, youth de-
   vours.
The hare in pastures or in plains is found,
Emblem of human life, who runs the round;
And after all his wand'ring ways are ⎫
   done,   ⎪
His circle fills and ends where he begun, ⎬
Just as the setting meets the rising sun. ⎭
   Thus princes ease their cares; but hap-
     pier he
Who seeks not pleasure thro' necessity,
Than such as once on slipp'ry thrones were
   plac'd;
And chasing, sigh to think themselves are
   chas'd.   70
   So liv'd our sires, ere doctors learn'd to
     kill,
And multiplied with theirs the weekly bill.
The first physicians by debauch were made;
Excess began, and sloth sustains the trade.
Pity the gen'rous kind their cares bestow
To search forbidden truths; (a sin to know:)
To which if human science could attain,
The doom of death, pronounc'd by God,
   were vain.
In vain the leech would interpose delay;
Fate fastens first, and vindicates the prey.
What help from art's endeavors can we ⎫
   have ?   81 ⎪
Gibbons but guesses, nor is sure to save; ⎬
But Maurus sweeps whole parishes, and ⎪
   peoples ev'ry grave; ⎭
And no more mercy to mankind will use,
Than when he robb'd and murder'd Maro's
   Muse.
Wouldst thou be soon dispatch'd, and per-
   ish whole ?
Trust Maurus with thy life, and M-lb-rne
   with thy soul.
   By chase our long-liv'd fathers earn'd
     their food;
Toil strung the nerves and purified the
   blood:
But we, their sons, a pamper'd race of men,
Are dwindled down to threescore years and
   ten.   91
Better to hunt in fields for health un-
   bought
Than fee the doctor for a nauseous draught.
The wise for cure on exercise depend;
God never made his work for man to mend.
   The tree of knowledge, once in Eden
     plac'd,

Was easy found, but was forbid the taste:
O had our grandsire walk'd without his
   wife,
He first had sought the better plant of life !
Now, both are lost; yet, wand'ring in the
   dark,   100
Physicians, for the tree, have found the
   bark.
They, lab'ring for relief of humankind, ⎫
With sharpen'd sight some remedies may ⎬
   find;   ⎪
Th' apothecary train is wholly blind. ⎭
From files a random recipe they take,
And many deaths of one prescription make.
Garth, gen'rous as his Muse, prescribes and
   gives;
The shopman sells, and by destruction lives:
Ungrateful tribe ! who, like the viper's
   brood,
From med'cine issuing, suck their mother's
   blood !   110
Let these obey, and let the learn'd pre-
   scribe,
That men may die without a double bribe:
Let them but under their superiors kill,
When doctors first have sign'd the bloody
   bill;
He scapes the best, who, nature to repair,
Draws physic from the fields, in draughts
   of vital air.
   You hoard not health for your own pri-
     vate use,
But on the public spend the rich produce;
When, often urg'd, unwilling to be great,
Your country calls you from your lov'd
   retreat,   120
And sends to senates, charg'd with com-
   mon care,
Which none more shuns, and none can bet-
   ter bear.
Where could they find another form'd so
   fit,
To poise with solid sense a sprightly wit ?
Were these both wanting, (as they both
   abound,)
Where could so firm integrity be found ?
   Well-born, and wealthy, wanting no sup-
     port,
You steer betwixt the country and the
   court;
Nor gratify whate'er the great desire,
Nor grudging give what public needs re-
   quire.   130
Part must be left, a fund when foes invade;
And part employ'd to roll the wat'ry trade:

Ev'n Canaan's happy land, when worn with
    toil,
Requir'd a sabbath year to mend the meager
    soil.
  Good senators (and such are you) so give,
That kings may be supplied, the people
    thrive.
And he, when want requires, is truly wise, ⎫
Who slights not foreign aids, nor over-   ⎬
    buys,   ⎬
But on our native strength, in time of ⎪
    need, relies. ⎭
Munster was bought, we boast not the
    success;   140
Who fights for gain, for greater makes his
    peace.
  Our foes, compell'd by need, have peace
    embrac'd;
The peace both parties want is like to last:
Which if secure, securely we may trade;
Or, not secure, should never have been
    made.
Safe in ourselves, while on ourselves we
    stand,
The sea is ours, and that defends the land.
Be, then, the naval stores the nation's care,
New ships to build, and batter'd to repair.
  Observe the war, in ev'ry annual course;
What has been done was done with British
    force;   151
Namur subdued is England's palm alone;
The rest besieg'd, but we constrain'd the
    town:
We saw th' event that follow'd our success;
France, tho' pretending arms, pursued the
    peace;
Oblig'd, by one sole treaty, to restore
What twenty years of war had won before.
Enough for Europe has our Albion fought:
Let us enjoy the peace our blood has
    bought.
When once the Persian king was put to
    flight.   160
The weary Macedons refus'd to fight,
Themselves their own mortality confess'd,
And left the son of Jove to quarrel for the
    rest.
  Ev'n victors are by victories undone; ⎫
Thus Hannibal, with foreign laurels won, ⎬
To Carthage was recall'd, too late to keep ⎪
    his own.   ⎭
While sore of battle, while our wounds are
    green,
Why should we tempt the doubtful die
    again?

In wars renew'd, uncertain of success;
Sure of a share, as umpires of the peace. 170
  A patriot both the king and country
    serves;
Prerogative and privilege preserves:
Of each our laws the certain limit show;
One must not ebb, nor t'other overflow.
Betwixt the prince and parliament we ⎫
    stand;   ⎬
The barriers of the state on either hand: ⎬
May neither overflow, for then they ⎪
    drown the land! ⎭
When both are full, they feed our blest
    abode;
Like those that water'd once the paradise
    of God.
  Some overpoise of sway by turns they
    share;   180
In peace the people, and the prince in
    war:
Consuls of mod'rate pow'r in calms were
    made;
When the Gauls came, one sole dictator
    sway'd.
  Patriots, in peace, assert the people's
    right;
With noble stubbornness resisting might:
No lawless mandates from the court re-
    ceive,
Nor lend by force, but in a body give.
Such was your gen'rous grandsire; free to
    grant
In parliaments that weigh'd their prince's
    want:
But so tenacious of the common cause, 190
As not to lend the king against his laws;
And, in a loathsome dungeon doom'd to ⎫
    lie,   ⎬
In bonds retain'd his birthright liberty, ⎬
And sham'd oppression, till it set him ⎪
    free. ⎭
  O true descendant of a patriot line,
Who, while thou shar'st their luster, lend'st
    'em thine,
Vouchsafe this picture of thy soul to see;
'T is so far good, as it resembles thee.
The beauties to th' original I owe;   199
Which when I miss, my own defects I show:
Nor think the kindred Muses thy disgrace;
A poet is not born in ev'ry race.
Two of a house few ages can afford;
One to perform, another to record.
Praiseworthy actions are by thee embrac'd;
And 't is my praise, to make thy praises
    last.

For ev'n when death dissolves our human
 frame,
The soul returns to heav'n, from whence
 it came;
Earth keeps the body, verse preserves the
 fame.

MELEAGER AND ATALANTA

OUT OF THE EIGHTH BOOK OF OVID'S METAMORPHOSES

CONNECTION TO THE FORMER STORY

Ovid, having told how Theseus had freed
Athens from the tribute of children which
was impos'd on them by Minos, King of Creta,
by killing the Minotaur, here makes a digression to the story of Meleager and Atalanta, which is one of the most inartificial
connections in all the *Metamorphoses*: for
he only says that Theseus obtain'd such
honor from that combat that all Greece
had recourse to him in their necessities;
and, amongst others, Calydon, tho' the hero
of that country, Prince Meleager, was then
living.

From him the Calydonians sought relief,
Tho' valiant Meleagrus was their chief.
The cause, a boar, who ravag'd far and
 near,
Of Cynthia's wrath th' avenging minister.
For Œneus with autumnal plenty blest,
By gifts to Heav'n his gratitude express'd:
Cull'd sheafs, to Ceres; to Lyæus, wine;
To Pan and Pales, offer'd sheep and kine;
And fat of olives, to Minerva's shrine.
Beginning from the rural gods, his hand 10
Was lib'ral to the pow'rs of high command:
Each deity in ev'ry kind was blest,
Till at Diana's fane th' invidious honor
 ceas'd.
 Wrath touches ev'n the gods; the Queen
 of Night,
Fir'd with disdain, and jealous of her right:
" Unhonor'd tho' I am, at least," said she,
" Not unreveng'd that impious act shall be."
Swift as the word, she sped the boar away,
With charge on those devoted fields to prey.
No larger bulls th' Egyptian pastures feed,
And none so large Sicilian meadows breed:
His eyeballs glare with fire, suffus'd with
 blood; 22
His neck shoots up a thickset thorny wood;
His bristled back a trench impal'd appears,

And stands erected, like a field of spears.
Froth fills his chaps, he sends a grunting
 sound,
And part he churns, and part befoams the
 ground.
For tusks with Indian elephants he strove,
And Jove's own thunder from his mouth
 he drove.
He burns the leaves; the scorching blast
 invades 30
The tender corn, and shrivels up the blades:
Or, suff'ring not their yellow beards to
 rear,
He tramples down the spikes, and intercepts
 the year.
In vain the barns expect their promis'd
 load;
Nor barns at home, nor reeks are heap'd
 abroad:
In vain the hinds the threshing-floor pre-
 pare,
And exercise their flails in empty air.
With olives ever green the ground is
 strow'd,
And grapes ungather'd shed their gen'rous
 blood.
Amid the fold he rages, nor the sheep 40
Their shepherds, nor the grooms their bulls
 can keep.
 From fields to walls the frighted rabble
 run,
Nor think themselves secure within the
 town;
Till Meleagros, and his chosen crew,
Contemn the danger, and the praise pursue.
Fair Leda's twins — in time to stars de-
 creed —
One fought on foot, one curb'd the fiery
 steed;
Then issued forth fam'd Jason after these,
Who mann'd the foremost ship that sail'd
 the seas;
Then Theseus, join'd with bold Perithous,
 came, 50
A single concord in a double name:
The Thestian sons, Idas who swiftly ran,
And Cæneus, once a woman, now a man.
Lynceus, with eagle's eyes, and lion's heart;
Leucippus, with his never-erring dart:
Acastus, Phileus, Phœnix, Telamon,
Echion, Lelex, and Eurytion,
Achilles' father, and great Phocus' son;
Dryas the fierce, and Hippasus the strong,
With twice old Iolas, and Nestor then but
 young; 60

Laertes active, and Ancæus bold;
Mopsus the sage, who future things fore-
   told,
And * t'other seer yet by his wife   * Amphi-
   unsold.   araus.
A thousand others of immortal fame;
Among the rest fair Atalanta came,
Grace of the woods: a diamond buckle
   bound
Her vest behind, that else had flow'd upon
   the ground,
And shew'd her buskin'd legs; her head was
   bare,
But for her native ornament of hair,
Which in a simple knot was tied above: 70
Sweet negligence ! unheeded bait of love !
Her sounding quiver on her shoulder tied,
One hand a dart, and one a bow supplied.
Such was her face, as in a nymph dis-
   play'd
A fair fierce boy, or in a boy betray'd
The blushing beauties of a modest maid.
The Calydonian chief at once the dame
Beheld, at once his heart receiv'd the flame,
With heav'ns averse.   "O happy youth," he
   cried,
"For whom thy fates reserve so fair a
   bride ! "   80
He sigh'd, and had no leisure more to say;
His honor call'd his eyes another way,
And forc'd him to pursue the now neg-
   lected prey.
    There stood a forest on a mountain's brow,
Which overlook'd the shaded plains below.
No sounding ax presum'd those trees to
   bite;
Coeval with the world, a venerable sight.
The heroes there arriv'd, some spread
   around
The toils, some search the footsteps on
   the ground,
Some from the chains the faithful dogs
   unbound.   90
Of action eager, and intent in thought,
The chiefs their honorable danger sought.
A valley stood below; the common drain
Of waters from above, and falling rain:
The bottom was a moist and marshy ground,
Whose edges were with bending osiers
   crown'd;
The knotty bulrush next in order stood,
And all within of reeds a trembling wood.
   From hence the boar was rous'd, and
      sprung amain,   99
Like lightning sudden, on the warrior train;

Beats down the trees before him, shakes
   the ground;
The forest echoes to the crackling sound;
Shout the fierce youth, and clamors ring
   around.
All stood with their protended spears pre-
   par'd;
With broad steel heads the brandish'd
   weapons glar'd.
The beast impetuous with his tusks aside
Deals glancing wounds; the fearful dogs
   divide:
All spend their mouth aloof, but none
   abide.
Echion threw the first, but miss'd his mark,
And stuck his boar-spear on a maple's bark.
Then Jason; and his javelin seem'd to take,
But fail'd with overforce, and whizz'd above
   his back.   112
Mopsus was next; but, ere he threw, ad-
   dress'd
To Phœbus thus: "O patron, help thy
   priest;
If I adore, and ever have ador'd
Thy pow'r divine, thy present aid afford;
That I may reach the beast." The god
   allow'd
His pray'r, and, smiling, gave him what he
   could:
He reach'd the savage, but no blood he
   drew;
Dian unarm'd the javelin as it flew.   120
   This chaf'd the boar, his nostrils flames
   expire,
And his red eyeballs roll with living fire.
Whirl'd from a sling, or from an engine
   thrown,
Amid the foes, so flies a mighty stone,
As flew the beast; the left wing put to
   flight,
The chiefs o'erborne, he rushes on the right.
Empalamos and Pelagon he laid
In dust, and next to death, but for their
   fellows' aid.
Onesimus far'd worse, prepar'd to fly;   129
The fatal fang drove deep within his thigh,
And cut the nerves; the nerves no more
   sustain
The bulk; the bulk unpropp'd falls head-
   long on the plain.
   Nestor had fail'd the fall of Troy to see;
But, leaning on his lance, he vaulted on a
   tree;
Then gath'ring up his feet, look'd down
   with fear.

And thought his monstrous foe was still too
  near.
Against a stump his tusk the monster
  grinds,
And in the sharpen'd edge new vigor finds;
Then, trusting to his arms, young Othrys
  found,
And ranch'd his hips with one continued
  wound.   140
Now Leda's twins, the future stars, appear;
White were their habits, white their horses
  were;
Conspicuous both, and both in act to throw,
Their trembling lances brandish'd at the foe:
Nor had they miss'd; but he to thickets fled,
Conceal'd from aiming spears, not pervious
  to the steed.
But Telamon rush'd in, and happ'd to meet
A rising root, that held his fasten'd feet;
So down he fell; whom, sprawling on the
  ground,
His brother from the wooden gyves un-
  bound.   150
  Meantime the virgin huntress was not
    slow
T' expel the shaft from her contracted bow:
Beneath his ear the fasten'd arrow stood,
And from the wound appear'd the trickling
  blood.
She blush'd for joy; but Meleagros rais'd
His voice with loud applause, and the fair
  archer prais'd.
He was the first to see, and first to show
His friends the marks of the successful
  blow.
"Nor shall thy valor want the praises due,"
He said; a virtuous envy seiz'd the crew.
They shout; the shouting animates their
  hearts,   161
And all at once employ their thronging
  darts;
But out of order thrown, in air they join;
And multitude makes frustrate the design.
With both his hands the proud Ancæus
  takes,
And flourishes his double-biting ax;
Then forward to his fate, he took a stride
Before the rest, and to his fellows cried:
"Give place, and mark the diff'rence, if
  you can,
Between a woman warrior and a man.   170
The boar is doom'd; nor, tho' Diana lend
Her aid, Diana can her beast defend."
Thus boasted he; then stretch'd, on tiptoe
  stood,

Secure to make his empty promise good.
But the more wary beast prevents the blow,
And upward rips the groin of his audacious
  foe.
Ancæus falls; his bowels from the wound
Rush out, and clotter'd blood distains the
  ground.
  Perithous, no small portion of the war,
Press'd on, and shook his lance; to whom
  from far   180
Thus Theseus cried: "O stay, my better
  part,
My more than mistress; of my heart, the
  heart:
The strong may fight aloof; Ancæus tried
His force too near, and by presuming died."
He said, and, while he spake, his javelin
  threw:
Hissing in air th' unerring weapon flew;
But on an arm of oak, that stood betwixt
The marksman and the mark, his lance he
  fix'd.
Once more bold Jason threw, but fail'd
  to wound
The boar, and slew an undeserving
  hound;   190
And thro' the dog the dart was nail'd to
  ground.
  Two spears from Meleager's hand were
    sent,
With equal force, but various in th' event:
The first was fix'd in earth, the second stood
On the boar's bristled back, and deeply
  drank his blood.
Now while the tortur'd salvage turns
  around,
And flings about his foam, impatient of the
  wound,
The wound's great author, close at hand,
  provokes
His rage, and plies him with redoubled
  strokes;
Wheels as he wheels, and with his pointed
  dart   200
Explores the nearest passage to his heart.
Quick and more quick he spins in giddy
  gires,
Then falls, and in much foam his soul ex-
  pires.
This act with shouts heav'n-high the friendly
  band
Applaud, and strain in theirs the victor
  hand.
Then all approach the slain with vast surprise,

Admire on what a breadth of earth he lies;
And, scarce secure, reach out their spears
    afar,
And blood their points, to prove their part-
    nership of war.
But he, the conqu'ring chief, his foot
    impress'd   210
On the strong neck of that destructive beast;
And, gazing on the nymph with ardent eyes,
"Accept," said he, "fair Nonacrine, my
    prize;
And, tho' inferior, suffer me to join
My labors, and my part of praise, with
    thine: "
At this presents her with the tusky head
And chine, with rising bristles roughly
    spread.
Glad, she receiv'd the gift; and seem'd to
    take
With double pleasure, for the giver's sake.
The rest were seiz'd with sullen discontent,
And a deaf murmur thro' the squadron went:
All envied; but the Thestyan brethren
    show'd   222
The least respect, and thus they vent their
    spleen aloud:
"Lay down those honor'd spoils, nor think
    to share,
Weak woman as thou art, the prize of war:
Ours is the title, thine a foreign claim,
Since Meleagros from our lineage came.
Trust not thy beauty; but restore the prize,
Which he, besotted on that face and eyes,
Would rend from us." At this, inflam'd
    with spite,   230
From her they snatch the gift, from him the
    giver's right.
    But soon th' impatient prince his fauchion
    drew,
And cried: "Ye robbers of another's due,
Now learn the diff'rence, at your proper
    cost,
Betwixt true valor and an empty boast."
At this advanc'd, and, sudden as the word,
In proud Plexippus' bosom plung'd the
    sword:
Toxeus amaz'd, and with amazement slow,
Or to revenge, or ward the coming blow,
Stood doubting; and, while doubting thus
    he stood,   240
Receiv'd the steel bath'd in his brother's
    blood.
    Pleas'd with the first, unknown the second
    news,
Althæa to the temples pays their dues

For her son's conquest; when at length
    appear
Her grisly brethren stretch'd upon the
    bier.
Pale at the sudden sight, she chang'd her
    cheer,
And with her cheer her robes; but hearing
    tell
The cause, the manner, and by whom they
    fell,
'T was grief no more, or grief and rage were
    one   249
Within her soul; at last 't was rage alone;
Which burning upwards in succession dries
The tears that stood consid'ring in her eyes.
    There lay a log unlighted on the hearth:
When she was lab'ring in the throes of birth
For th' unborn chief, the Fatal Sisters came,
And rais'd it up, and toss'd it on the flame:
Then on the rock a scanty measure place
Of vital flax, and turn'd the wheel apace;
And turning sung: "To this red brand and
    thee,
O newborn babe, we give an equal des-
    tiny: "   260
So vanish'd out of view. The frighted dame
Sprung hasty from her bed, and quench'd
    the flame:
The log, in secret lock'd, she kept with care;
And that, while thus preserv'd, preserv'd
    her heir.
This brand she now produc'd; and first she
    strows
The hearth with heaps of chips, and after
    blows;
Thrice heav'd her hand, and heav'd, she
    thrice repress'd:
The sister and the mother long contest,
Two doubtful titles in one tender breast;
And now her eyes and cheeks with fury
    glow,   270
Now pale her cheeks, her eyes with pity flow;
Now low'ring looks presage approaching
    storms,
And now prevailing love her face reforms.
Resolv'd, she doubts again; the tears she
    dried
With burning rage are by new tears sup-
    plied;
And as a ship, which winds and waves
    assail,
Now with the current drives, now with
    the gale,
Both opposite, and neither long prevail —
She feels a double force; by turns obeys

Th' imperious tempest, and th' impetuous
   seas: 280
So fares Althæa's mind; she first relents
With pity, of that pity then repents.
Sister and mother long the scales divide,
But the beam nodded on the sister's side.
Sometimes she softly sigh'd, then roar'd
   aloud;
But sighs were stifled in the cries of blood.
   The pious impious wretch at length de-
   creed,
To please her brother's ghost, her son should
   bleed;
And when the fun'ral flames began to rise,
" Receive," she said, " a sister's sacri-
   fice: 290
A mother's bowels burn." High in her hand,
Thus while she spoke, she held the fatal
   brand;
Then thrice before the kindled pile she
   bow'd,
And the three Furies thrice invok'd aloud:
" Come, come, revenging sisters, come and
   view
A sister paying her dead brothers' due:
A crime I punish, and a crime commit;
But blood for blood, and death for death is
   fit;
Great crimes must be with greater crimes
   repaid,
And second funerals on the former laid. 300
Let the whole household in one ruin fall,
And may Diana's curse o'ertake us all.
Shall fate to happy Œneus still allow ⎫
One son, while Thestius stands depriv'd ⎬
   of two ?   ⎪
Better three lost, than one unpunish'd go. ⎭
Take then, dear ghosts, (while yet, admitted
   new
In hell, you wait my duty,) take your due;
A costly off'ring on your tomb is laid,
When with my blood the price of yours is
   paid.
   " Ah ! whither am I hurried ? Ah ! for-
   give, 310
Ye shades, and let your sister's issue live;
A mother cannot give him death; tho' he
Deserves it, he deserves it not from me.
   " Then shall th' unpunish'd wretch insult
   the slain ?
Triumphant live ? nor only live, but reign ?
While you, thin shades, the sport of winds,
   are toss'd
O'er dreary plains, or tread the burning
   coast.

I cannot, cannot bear; 't is past, 't is done;
Perish this impious, this detested son;
Perish his sire, and perish I withal; 320
And let the house's heir and the hop'd king-
   dom fall.
   " Where is the mother fled, her pious love,
And where the pains with which ten months
   I strove !
Ah ! hadst thou died, my son, in infant years,
Thy little hearse had been bedew'd with
   tears.
   " Thou liv'st by me; to me thy breath
   resign;
Mine is the merit, the demerit thine.
Thy life by double title I require,
Once giv'n at birth, and once preserv'd from
   fire: 329
One murder pay, or add one murder more,
And me to them who fell by thee restore.
   " I would, but cannot: my son's image
   stands
Before my sight; and now their angry hands
My brothers hold, and vengeance these
   exact;
This pleads compassion, and repents the fact.
   " He pleads in vain, and I pronounce his
   doom:
My brothers, tho' unjustly, shall o'ercome.
But having paid their injur'd ghosts their
   due,
My son requires my death, and mine shall
   his pursue." 339
   At this, for the last time she lifts her hand,
Averts her eyes, and half unwilling drops
   the brand.
The brand, amid the flaming fuel thrown,
Or drew, or seem'd to draw, a dying groan;
The fires themselves but faintly lick'd their
   prey,
Then loath'd their impious food, and would
   have shrunk away.
   Just then the hero cast a doleful cry,
And in those absent flames began to fry:
The blind contagion rag'd within his veins,
But he with manly patience bore his pains;
He fear'd not fate, but only griev'd to die
Without an honest wound, and by a death
   so dry. 351
" Happy Ancæus," thrice aloud he cried,
" With what becoming fate in arms he
   died ! "
Then call'd his brothers, sisters, sire, around,
And her to whom his nuptial vows were
   bound;
Perhaps his mother; a long sigh he drew,

And his voice failing, took his last adieu:
For, as the flames augment, and as they stay
At their full height, then languish to decay;
They rise, and sink by fits; at last they soar
In one bright blaze, and then descend no
    more: 361
Just so his inward heats, at height, impair,
Till the last burning breath shoots out the
    soul in air.
    Now lofty Calydon in ruins lies;   ⎫
All ages, all degrees unsluice their eyes;   ⎬
And heav'n and earth resound with mur-   ⎪
    murs, groans, and cries.   ⎭
Matrons and maidens beat their breasts,
    and tear
Their habits, and root up their scatter'd
    hair.
The wretched father, father now no more,
With sorrow sunk, lies prostrate on the
    floor;   370
Deforms his hoary locks with dust obscene,
And curses age, and loathes a life prolong'd
    with pain.
By steel her stubborn soul his mother freed,
And punish'd on herself her impious deed.
    Had I a hundred tongues, a wit so large
As could their hundred offices discharge;
Had Phœbus all his Helicon bestow'd,
In all the streams inspiring all the god;
Those tongues, that wit, those streams, that
    god in vain
Would offer to describe his sisters' pain. 380
They beat their breasts with many a bruis-
    ing blow,
Till they turn'd livid, and corrupt the snow.
The corpse they cherish, while the corpse
    remains,
And exercise and rub with fruitless pains;
And when to fun'ral flames 't is borne away,
They kiss the bed on which the body lay:
And when those fun'ral flames no longer
    burn,
(The dust compos'd within a pious urn,)
Ev'n in that urn their brother they confess,
And hug it in their arms, and to their
    bosoms press.   390
    His tomb is rais'd; then, stretch'd along
    the ground,
Those living monuments his tomb surround:
Ev'n to his name, inscrib'd, their tears they
    pay,
Till tears and kisses wear his name away.
    But Cynthia now had all her fury spent,
Not with less ruin than a race content:
Excepting Gorge, perish'd all the seed,

And * her whom Heav'n for Hercules   * Deja-
    decreed.   nira.
Satiate at last, no longer she pursued   399
The weeping sisters; but with wings endued,
And horny beaks, and sent to flit in air;
Who yearly round the tomb in feather'd
    flocks repair.

SIGISMONDA AND GUISCARDO

FROM BOCCACE

WHILE   Norman   Tancred   in   Salerno
    reign'd,
The title of a gracious prince he gain'd;
Till, turn'd a tyrant in his latter days,
He lost the luster of his former praise;
And, from the bright meridian where he
    stood
Descending, dipp'd his hands in lovers'
    blood.
    This prince, of Fortune's favor long pos-
    sess'd,
Yet was with one fair daughter only blest;
And blest he might have been with her
    alone: 9
But O ! how much more happy had he none !
She was his care, his hope, and his de-
    light,
Most in his thought, and ever in his sight:
Next, nay beyond his life, he held her dear;
She liv'd by him, and now he liv'd in her.
For this, when ripe for marriage, he delay'd
Her nuptial bands, and kept her long a
    maid,
As envying any else should share a part
Of what was his, and claiming all her heart.
At length, as public decency requir'd,
And all his vassals eagerly desir'd,   20
With mind averse, he rather underwent
His people's will than gave his own consent.
So was she torn as from a lover's side,
And made almost in his despite a bride.
    Short were her marriage joys, for in the
    prime
Of youth her lord expir'd before his time;
And, to her father's court in little space ⎫
Restor'd anew, she held a higher place;   ⎬
More lov'd, and more exalted into grace.   ⎭
This princess, fresh and young, and fair and
    wise,   30
The worship'd idol of her father's eyes,
Did all her sex in ev'ry grace exceed,
And had more wit beside than women need.

Youth, health, and ease, and most an
 amorous mind,
To second nuptials had her thoughts in-
 clin'd;
And former joys had left a secret sting
 behind.
But, prodigal in ev'ry other grant,
Her sire left unsupplied her only want;
And she, betwixt her modesty and pride,
Her wishes, which she could not help, would
 hide.   40
Resolv'd at last to lose no longer time,
And yet to please herself without a crime,
She cast her eyes around the court, to find
A worthy subject suiting to her mind,
To him in holy nuptials to be tied,
A seeming widow, and a secret bride.
Among the train of courtiers, one she found
With all the gifts of bounteous nature
 crown'd,
Of gentle blood; but one whose niggard fate
Had set him far below her high estate. 50
Guiscard his name was call'd, of blooming
 age,
Now squire to Tancred, and before his
 page:
To him, the choice of all the shining crowd,
Her heart the noble Sigismonda vow'd.
Yet hitherto she kept her love conceal'd,
And with close glances ev'ry day beheld
The graceful youth; and ev'ry day increas'd
The raging fire that burn'd within her
 breast.
Some secret charm did all his acts attend,
And what his fortune wanted, hers could
 mend;   60
Till, as the fire will force its outward way,
Or, in the prison pent, consume the prey;
So long her earnest eyes on his were set,
At length their twisted rays together met;
And he, surpris'd with humble joy, survey'd
One sweet regard, shot by the royal maid:
Not well assur'd, while doubtful hopes he
 nurs'd,
A second glance came gliding like the first;
And he, who saw the sharpness of the dart,
Without defense receiv'd it in his heart. 70
In public tho' their passion wanted speech,
Yet mutual looks interpreted for each;
Time, ways, and means of meeting were
 denied;
But all those wants ingenious Love supplied.
Th' inventive god, who never fails his part,
Inspires the wit when once he warms the
 heart.

When Guiscard next was in the circle
 seen,
Where Sigismonda held the place of queen,
A hollow cane within her hand she brought,
But in the concave had enclos'd a note. 80
With this she seem'd to play, and, as in
 sport,
Toss'd to her love, in presence of the court:
"Take it," she said, "and when your needs
 require,
This little brand will serve to light your
 fire."
He took it with a bow, and soon divin'd
The seeming toy was not for naught de-
 sign'd;
But when retir'd, so long with curious eyes
He view'd the present, that he found the
 prize.
Much was in little writ; and all convey'd
With cautious care, for fear to be betray'd
By some false confident, or fav'rite maid.
The time, the place, the manner how to
 meet,   92
Were all in punctual order plainly writ;
But since a trust must be, she thought it
 best
To put it out of laymen's pow'r at least;
And for their solemn vows prepar'd a
 priest.
Guiscard (her secret purpose understood)
With joy prepar'd to meet the coming good;
Nor pains nor danger was resolv'd to spare,
But use the means appointed by the fair. 100
Near the proud palace of Salerno stood
A mount of rough ascent, and thick with
 wood.
Thro' this a cave was dug with vast expense;
The work it seem'd of some suspicious
 prince,
Who, when abusing pow'r with lawless
 might,
From public justice would secure his flight.
The passage made by many a winding way
Reach'd ev'n the room in which the tyrant
 lay,
Fit for his purpose; on a lower floor 109
He lodg'd, whose issue was an iron door;
From whence, by stairs descending to the
 ground,
In the blind grot a safe retreat he found.
Its outlet ended in a brake o'ergrown
With brambles, chok'd by time, and now
 unknown.
A rift there was, which from the mountain's
 height

Convey'd a glimm'ring and malignant light,
A breathing place to draw the damps away,
A twilight of an intercepted day.
The tyrant's den, whose use tho' lost to
    fame,   119
Was now th' apartment of the royal dame;
The cavern, only to her father known,
By him was to his darling daughter shown.
  Neglected long she let the secret rest,
Till love recall'd it to her lab'ring breast,
And hinted as the way by Heav'n design'd,
The teacher, by the means he taught, to
    blind.
What will not women do, when need inspires
Their wit, or love their inclination fires!
Tho' jealousy of state th' invention found,
Yet love refin'd upon the former ground.
That way the tyrant had reserv'd, to fly 131
Pursuing hate, now serv'd to bring two
    lovers nigh.
  The dame, who long in vain had kept
    the key,
Bold by desire, explor'd the secret way;
Now tried the stairs, and, wading thro' the
    night,
Search'd all the deep recess, and issued into
    light.
All this her letter had so well explain'd,
Th' instructed youth might compass what
    remain'd;
The cavern mouth alone was hard to find,
Because the path, disus'd, was out of mind:
But in what quarter of the copse it lay,   141
His eye by certain level could survey.
Yet (for the wood perplex'd with thorns he
    knew)
A frock of leather o'er his limbs he drew;
And thus provided, search'd the brake
    around,
Till the chok'd entry of the cave he found.
  Thus, all prepar'd, the promis'd hour
    arriv'd,
So long expected, and so well contriv'd:
With love to friend, th' impatient lover went,
Fenc'd from the thorns, and trod the deep
    descent.   150
The conscious priest, who was suborn'd be-
    fore,
Stood ready posted at the postern door;
The maids in distant rooms were sent to rest,
And nothing wanted but th' invited guest.
He came, and knocking thrice, with)ut
    delay,
The longing lady heard, and turn'd the key;
At once invaded him with all her charms,

And the first step he made was in her arms.
The leathern outside, boist'rous as it was,
Gave way, and bent beneath her strict em-
    brace;   160
On either side the kisses flew so thick,
That neither he nor she had breath to speak.
The holy man, amaz'd at what he saw,
Made haste to sanctify the bliss by law,
And mutter'd fast the matrimony o'er,
For fear committed sin should get before.
His work perform'd, he left the pair alone, ⎫
Because he knew he could not go too soon; ⎬
His presence odious, when his task was   ⎭
    done.
What thoughts he had beseems not me to ⎫
    say;   170⎪
Tho' some surmise he went to fast and   ⎬
    pray,   ⎪
And needed both to drive the tempting   ⎭
    thoughts away.
  The foe once gone, they took their full
    delight;
'T was restless rage and tempest all the
    night;
For greedy love each moment would em-
    ploy,
And grudg'd the shortest pauses of their joy.
  Thus were their loves auspiciously begun,
And thus with secret care were carried on;
The stealth itself did appetite restore,   179
And look'd so like a sin, it pleas'd the more.
  The cave was now become a common way;
The wicket, often open'd, knew the key:
Love rioted secure, and, long enjoy'd,
Was ever eager, and was never cloy'd.
  But as extremes are short, of ill and good,
And tides at highest mark regorge the flood;
So Fate, that could no more improve their
    joy,
Took a malicious pleasure to destroy.
  Tancred, who fondly lov'd, and whose de-
    light   189
Was plac'd in his fair daughter's daily sight,
Of custom, when his state affairs were done,
Would pass his pleasing hours with her
    alone;
And, as a father's privilege allow'd,
Without attendance of th' officious crowd.
  It happen'd once, that when in heat of day
He tried to sleep, as was his usual way,
The balmy slumber fled his wakeful eyes,
And forc'd him, in his own despite, to rise.
Of sleep forsaken, to relieve his care,
He sought the conversation of the fair;   200
But with her train of damsels she was gone.

In shady walks the scorching heat to shun.
He would not violate that sweet recess,
And found besides a welcome heaviness
That seiz'd his eyes; and slumber, which
    forgot,
When call'd before, to come, now came un-
    sought.
From light retir'd, behind his daughter's
    bed,
He for approaching sleep compos'd his head;
A chair was ready, for that use design'd,
So quilted, that he lay at ease reclin'd; 210
The curtains closely drawn, the light to
    screen,
As if he had contriv'd to lie unseen:
Thus cover'd with an artificial night,
Sleep did his office soon, and seal'd his sight.
    With Heav'n averse, in this ill-omen'd
    hour
Was Guiscard summon'd to the secret bow'r,
And the fair nymph, with expectation fir'd,
From her attending damsels was retir'd:
For, true to love, she measur'd time so right,
As not to miss one moment of delight.   220
The garden, seated on the level floor,
She left behind, and, locking ev'ry door,
Thought all secure; but little did she know,
Blind to her fate, she had inclos'd her foe.
Attending Guiscard, in his leathern frock,
Stood ready, with his thrice-repeated
    knock:
Thrice with a doleful sound the jarring
    grate
Rung deaf, and hollow, and presag'd their
    fate.
The door unlock'd, to known delight they
    haste,
And, panting, in each other's arms em-
    brac'd,   230
Rush to the conscious bed, a mutual freight,
And heedless press it with their wonted
    weight.
    The sudden bound awak'd the sleeping
    sire,
And shew'd a sight no parent can desire;
His opening eyes at once with odious view
The love discover'd, and the lover knew.
He would have cried; but, hoping that he
    dreamt,
Amazement tied his tongue, and stopp'd th'
    attempt.
Th' ensuing moment all the truth declar'd, ⎱
But now he stood collected and prepar'd; ⎰
For malice and revenge had put him on ⎰
    his guard.   241 ⎰

    So, like a lion that unheeded lay, ⎱
Dissembling sleep, and watchful to betray, ⎰
With inward rage he meditates his prey. ⎰
The thoughtless pair, indulging their de-
    sires,
Alternate kindled, and then quench'd their
    fires;
Nor thinking in the shades of death they ⎱
    play'd, ⎰
Full of themselves, themselves alone sur- ⎰
    vey'd, ⎰
And, too secure, were by themselves ⎰
    betray'd. ⎰
Long time dissolv'd in pleasure thus they
    lay,   250
Till nature could no more suffice their play;
Then rose the youth, and thro' the cave
    again
Return'd; the princess mingled with her
    train.
    Resolv'd his unripe vengeance to defer,
The royal spy, when now the coast was
    clear,
Sought not the garden, but retir'd unseen,
To brood in secret on his gather'd spleen,
And methodize revenge: to death he
    griev'd;
And, but he saw the crime, had scarce be-
    liev'd.
Th' appointment for th' ensuing night ⎱
    he heard,   260 ⎰
And therefore in the cavern had prepar'd ⎰
Two brawny yeoman of his trusty guard. ⎰
    Scarce had unwary Guiscard set his foot
Within the farmost entrance of the grot,
When these in secret ambush ready lay,
And rushing on the sudden seiz'd the prey.
Encumber'd with his frock, without de- ⎱
    fense, ⎰
An easy prize, they led the pris'ner ⎰
    thence, ⎰
And, as commanded, brought before the ⎰
    prince. ⎰
The gloomy sire, too sensible of wrong 270
To vent his rage in words, restrain'd his
    tongue,
And only said: "Thus servants are pre-
    ferr'd,
And, trusted, thus their sov'reigns they
    reward.
Had I not seen, had not these eyes receiv'd
Too clear a proof, I could not have be-
    liev'd."
    He paus'd and chok'd the rest. The
    youth, who saw

His forfeit life abandon'd to the law,
The judge th' accuser, and th' offense to him
Who had both pow'r and will t' avenge the
  crime,   279
No vain defense prepar'd, but thus replied:
" The faults of Love by Love are justified:
With unresisted might the monarch reigns,
He levels mountains, and he raises plains;
And, not regarding diff'rence of degree,
Abas'd your daughter, and exalted me."
    This bold return with seeming patience
      heard,
The pris'ner was remitted to the guard.
The sullen tyrant slept not all the night,
But, lonely walking by a winking light,
Sobb'd, wept, and groan'd, and beat his
  wither'd breast,   290
But would not violate his daughter's rest;
Who long expecting lay, for bliss prepar'd,
List'ning for noise, and griev'd that none
  she heard;
Oft rose, and oft in vain employ'd the key, ⎫
And oft accus'd her lover of delay;   ⎬
And pass'd the tedious hours in anxious   ⎭
  thoughts away.
    The morrow came, and at his usual hour
Old Tancred visited his daughter's bow'r;
Her cheek (for such his custom was) he
  kiss'd,
Then bless'd her kneeling, and her maids
  dismiss'd.   300
The royal dignity thus far maintain'd,
Now left in private, he no longer feign'd;
But all at once his grief and rage appear'd,
And floods of tears ran trickling down his
  beard.
" O Sigismonda," he began to say: ⎫
Thrice he began, and thrice was forc'd to ⎬
  stay,   ⎭
Till words with often trying found their
  way:
" I thought, O Sigismonda, (but how blind
Are parents' eyes, their children's faults to
  find !)   309
Thy virtue, birth, and breeding were above
A mean desire, and vulgar sense of love;
Nor less than sight and hearing could ⎫
  convince   ⎬
So fond a father, and so just a prince,   ⎭
Of such an unforeseen and unbeliev'd
  offense.
Then what indignant sorrow must I have,
To see thee lie subjected to my slave !
A man so smelling of the people's lee,
The court receiv'd him first for charity;

And since with no degree of honor grac'd,
But only suffer'd where he first was plac'd:
A grov'ling insect still, and so design'd   321
By Nature's hand, nor born of noble kind:
A thing, by neither man nor woman priz'd,
And scarcely known enough to be despis'd.
To what has Heav'n reserv'd my age ? Ah !
  why
Should man, when Nature calls, not choose
  to die,
Rather than stretch the span of life, to find
Such ills as Fate has wisely cast behind,
For those to feel, whom fond desire to live
Makes covetous of more than life can give !
Each has his share of good; and when 't is
  gone,   331
The guest, tho' hungry, cannot rise too soon.
But I, expecting more, in my own wrong
Protracting life, have liv'd a day too long.
If yesterday could be recall'd again,
Ev'n now would I conclude my happy reign;
But 't is too late, my glorious race is run,
And a dark cloud o'ertakes my setting sun.
Hadst thou not lov'd, or loving sav'd the
  shame,
If not the sin, by some illustrious name, 340
This little comfort had reliev'd my mind,
'T was frailty, not unusual to thy kind;
But thy low fall beneath thy royal blood
Shews downward appetite to mix with mud.
Thus not the least excuse is left for thee,
Nor the least refuge for unhappy me.
    " For him I have resolv'd: whom by sur-
      prise
I took, and scarce can call it in disguise;
For such was his attire, as, with intent
Of nature, suited to his mean descent.   350
The harder question yet remains behind, ⎫
What pains a parent and a prince can find ⎬
To punish an offense of this degenerate ⎭
  kind.
    " As I have lov'd, and yet I love thee,
      more
Than ever father lov'd a child before;
So that indulgence draws me to forgive:
Nature, that gave thee life, would have
  thee live.
But, as a public parent of the state,
My justice, and thy crime, requires thy
  fate.
Fain would I choose a middle course to
  steer;   360
Nature's too kind, and justice too severe:
Speak for us both, and to the balance bring,
On either side, the father and the king.

Heav'n knows, my heart is bent to favor
thee;
Make it but scanty weight, and leave the
rest to me."
Here stopping with a sigh, he pour'd a
flood
Of tears, to make his last expression good.
She, who had heard him speak, nor saw
alone   368
The secret conduct of her love was known,
But he was taken who her soul possess'd.
Felt all the pangs of sorrow in her breast:
And little wanted, but a woman's heart,
With cries and tears, had testified her
smart;
But inborn worth, that fortune can control,
New strung, and stiffer bent her softer soul;
The heroine assum'd the woman's place,
Confirm'd her mind, and fortified her face.
Why should she beg, or what could she pre-
tend,
When her stern father had condemn'd her
friend ?
Her life she might have had; but her de-
spair   380
Of saving his had put it past her care:
Resolv'd on fate, she would not lose her
breath,
But, rather than not die, solicit death.
Fix'd on this thought, she not, as women
use,
Her fault by common frailty would excuse;
But boldly justified her innocence,
And, while the fact was own'd, denied th'
offense:
Then with dry eyes, and with an open look,
She met his glance midway, and then un-
daunted spoke: 389
"Tancred, I neither am dispos'd to make
Request for life, nor offer'd life to take;
Much less deny the deed; but least of all
Beneath pretended justice weakly fall.
My words to sacred truth shall be confin'd,
My deeds shall shew the greatness of my
mind.
That I have lov'd, I own; that still I love,
I call to witness all the pow'rs above.
Yet more I own: to Guiscard's love I give
The small remaining time I have to live;
And if beyond this life desire can be,   400
Not fate itself shall set my passion free.
"This first avow'd; nor folly warp'd my
mind,
Nor the frail texture of the female kind
Betray'd my virtue; for too well I knew

What honor was, and honor had his due:
Before the holy priest my vows were tied;
So came I not a strumpet, but a bride.
This for my fame, and for the public voice:
Yet more, his merits justified my choice;
Which had they not, the first election thine,
That bond dissolv'd, the next is freely
mine.   411
Or, grant I err'd, (which yet I must deny,)
Had parents pow'r ev'n second vows to tie,
Thy little care to mend my widow'd nights ⎤
Has forced me to recourse of marriage   ⎮
rites,   ⎬
To fill an empty side, and follow known ⎮
delights.   ⎦
What have I done in this, deserving blame ?
State laws may alter; nature's are the same:
Those are usurp'd on helpless womankind,
Made without our consent, and wanting
pow'r to bind.   420
"Thou, Tancred, better shouldst have
understood,
That as thy father gave thee flesh and blood,
So gav'st thou me: not from the quarry
hew'd,
But of a softer mold, with sense endued:
Ev'n softer than thy own, of suppler kind,
More exquisite of taste, and more than man
refin'd.
Nor need'st thou by thy daughter to be told,
Tho' now thy sprightly blood with age be
cold,
Thou hast been young; and canst remember
still,
That when thou hadst the pow'r, thou hadst
the will;   430
And from the past experience of thy fires ⎤
Canst tell with what a tide our strong de- ⎮
sires   ⎬
Come rushing on in youth, and what their ⎮
rage requires.   ⎦
"And grant thy youth was exercis'd in
arms,
When love no leisure found for softer
charms;
My tender age in luxury was train'd,   ⎤
With idle ease and pageants entertain'd; ⎮
My hours my own, my pleasures unre-   ⎬
strain'd.   ⎦
So bred, no wonder if I took the bent
That seem'd ev'n warranted by thy con-
sent;   440
For, when the father is too fondly kind,
Such seed he sows, such harvest shall he
find.

Blame then thyself, as reason's law requires,
(Since nature gave, and thou foment'st my
　　fires.)
If still those appetites continue strong,
Thou may'st consider I am yet but young:
Consider too that, having been a wife,
I must have tasted of a better life,
And am not to be blam'd, if I renew,
By lawful means, the joys which then I
　　knew.　　　　　　　　　　450
Where was the crime, if pleasure I procur'd,
Young, and a woman, and to bliss inur'd?
That was my case, and this is my defense: ⎤
I pleas'd myself, I shunn'd incontinence,　⎟
And, urg'd by strong desires, indulg'd my　⎰
　　sense.

　"Left to myself, I must avow, I strove
From public shame to screen my secret
　　love,
And, well acquainted with thy native ⎤
　　pride,　　　　　　　　　　　　　⎟
Endeavor'd, what I could not help, to hide; ⎬
For which a woman's wit an easy way　　⎟
　　supplied.　　　　　　　460 ⎰
How this, so well contriv'd, so closely laid,
Was known to thee, or by what chance be-
　　tray'd,
Is not my care; to please thy pride alone,
I could have wish'd it had been still un-
　　known.

　"Nor took I Guiscard by blind fancy led,
Or hasty choice, as many women wed;
But with delib'rate care, and ripen'd
　　thought,
At leisure first design'd, before I wrought:
On him I rested, after long debate,　　469
And not without consid'ring, fix'd my fate.
His flame was equal, tho' by mine inspir'd;
(For so the diff'rence of our birth requir'd;)
Had he been born like me, like me his love
Had first begun what mine was forc'd to
　　move:
But thus beginning, thus we persevere; ⎤
Our passions yet continue what they were, ⎬
Nor length of trial makes our joys the　 ⎰
　　less sincere.

　"At this my choice, tho' not by thine al-
　　low'd,
(Thy judgment herding with the common
　　crowd,)　　　　　　　　　479
Thou tak'st unjust offense; and, led by them,
Dost less the merit than the man esteem.
Too sharply, Tancred, by thy pride betray'd,
Hast thou against the laws of kind inveigh'd;
For all th' offense is in opinion plac'd,

Which deems high birth by lowly choice
　　debas'd.
This thought alone with fury fires thy breast,
(For holy marriage justifies the rest,)
That I have sunk the glories of the state,
And mix'd my blood with a plebeian mate;
In which I wonder thou shouldst oversee ⎤
Superior causes, or impute to me　　491 ⎬
The fault of Fortune, or the Fates' decree. ⎰
Or call it Heav'n's imperial pow'r alone,
Which moves on springs of justice, tho' un-
　　known;
Yet this we see, tho' order'd for the best,
The bad exalted, and the good oppress'd;
Permitted laurels grace the lawless brow,
Th' unworthy rais'd, the worthy cast below.

　"But, leaving that, search we the secret
　　springs,　　　　　　　　499
And backward trace the principles of things:
There shall we find, that when the world
　　began,
One common mass compos'd the mold of
　　man;
One paste of flesh on all degrees bestow'd,
And kneaded up alike with moist'ning blood.
The same Almighty Pow'r inspir'd the
　　frame
With kindled life, and form'd the souls the
　　same:
The faculties of intellect and will　　 ⎤
Dispens'd with equal hand, dispos'd with ⎟
　　equal skill;　　　　　　　　　　 ⎬
Like liberty indulg'd, with choice of good ⎟
　　or ill.　　　　　　　　　　　 ⎰
Thus born alike, from virtue first began 510
The diff'rence that distinguish'd man from
　　man:
He claim'd no title from descent of blood,
But that which made him noble made him
　　good;
Warm'd with more particles of heav'nly ⎤
　　flame,　　　　　　　　　　　 ⎟
He wing'd his upward flight, and soar'd　⎬
　　to fame,　　　　　　　　　　 ⎟
The rest remain'd below, a tribe without ⎰
　　a name.

　"This law, tho' custom now diverts the
　　course,
As nature's institute, is yet in force;
Uncancel'd, tho' disus'd: and he, whose
　　mind
Is virtuous, is alone of noble kind;　　520
Tho' poor in fortune, of celestial race;
And he commits the crime, who calls him
　　base.

"Now lay the line, and measure all thy
court
By inward virtue, not external port;
And find whom justly to prefer above
The man on whom my judgment plac'd my
love:
So shalt thou see his parts and person shine;
And thus compar'd, the rest a base de-
gen'rate line.
Nor took I, when I first survey'd thy court,
His valor, or his virtues, on report;   530
But trusted what I ought to trust alone,
Relying on thy eyes, and not my own.
Thy praise (and thine was then the public
voice)
First recommended Guiscard to my choice:
Directed thus by thee, I look'd, and found
A man, I thought, deserving to be crown'd;
First by my father pointed to my sight,
Nor less conspicuous by his native light;
His mind, his mien, the features of his face
Excelling all the rest of human race.   540
These were thy thoughts, and thou couldst
judge aright,
Till int'rest made a jaundice in thy sight.
"Or should I grant thou didst not rightly
see;
Then thou wert first deceiv'd, and I deceiv'd
by thee.
But if thou shalt allege, thro' pride of
mind,
Thy blood with one of base condition join'd,
'T is false; for 't is not baseness to be poor;
His poverty augments thy crime the more;
Upbraids thy justice with the scant regard
Of worth: whom princes praise, they should
reward.   550
Are these the kings intrusted by the crowd
With wealth, to be dispens'd for common
good ?
The people sweat not for their king's delight,
T' enrich a pimp, or raise a parasite:
Theirs is the toil; and he who well has
serv'd
His country, has his country's wealth de-
serv'd.
"Ev'n mighty monarchs oft are meanly
born,
And kings by birth to lowest rank return;
All subject to the pow'r of giddy chance,
For fortune can depress, or can advance: 560
But true nobility is of the mind,
Not giv'n by chance, and not to chance re-
sign'd.
"For the remaining doubt of thy decree,

What to resolve, and how dispose of me,
Be warn'd to cast that useless care aside;
Myself alone will for myself provide.
If in thy doting and decrepit age,
Thy soul, a stranger in thy youth to rage,
Begins in cruel deeds to take delight,
Gorge with my blood thy barb'rous appe-
tite,   570
For I so little am dispos'd to pray
For life, I would not cast a wish away.
Such as it is, th' offense is all my own;
And what to Guiscard is already done,
Or to be done, is doom'd by thy decree; ⎱
That, if not executed first by thee, ⎰
Shall on my person be perform'd by me. ⎰
"Away ! with women weep, and leave me
here,
Fix'd like a man, to die without a tear; 579
Or save, or slay us both this present hour —
'T is all that fate has left within thy pow'r."
She said; nor did her father fail to find,
In all she spoke, the greatness of her mind;
Yet thought she was not obstinate to die,
Nor deem'd the death she promis'd was so
nigh.
Secure in this belief, he left the dame,
Resolv'd to spare her life and save her
shame;
But that detested object to remove,
To wreak his vengeance, and to cure her
love.
Intent on this, a secret order sign'd   590
The death of Guiscard to his guards en-
join'd;
Strangling was chosen, and the night the
time,
A mute revenge, and blind as was the crime.
His faithful heart, a bloody sacrifice,
Torn from his breast, to glut the tyrant's
eyes,
Clos'd the severe command: for (slaves to
pay)
What kings decree, the soldier must obey:
Wag'd against foes; and, when the wars are
o'er,
Fit only to maintain despotic pow'r;
Dang'rous to freedom, and desir'd alone 600
By kings who seek an arbitrary throne.
Such were these guards; as ready to have
slain
The prince himself, allur'd with greater
gain:
So was the charge perform'd with better
will,
By men inur'd to blood and exercis'd in ill.

Now, tho' the sullen sire had eas'd his
  mind,
The pomp of his revenge was yet behind,
A pomp prepar'd to grace the present he
  design'd.
A goblet rich with gems and rough with
  gold,
Of depth and breadth the precious pledge
  to hold,   610
With cruel care he chose: the hollow part
Inclos'd, the lid conceal'd the lover's heart.
Then of his trusted mischiefs one he sent,
And bade him with these words the gift
  present:
"Thy father sends thee this to cheer thy
  breast,
And glad thy sight with what thou lov'st the
  best;
As thou hast pleas'd his eyes and joy'd his
  mind
With what he lov'd the most of human-
  kind."
Ere this the royal dame, who well had
  weigh'd   619
The consequence of what her sire had said,
Fix'd on her fate, against th' expected hour,
Procur'd the means to have it in her pow'r.
For this she had distill'd, with early care,
The juice of simples friendly to despair,
A magazine of death, and thus prepar'd,
Secure to die, the fatal message heard:
Then smil'd severe, nor with a troubled
  look
Or trembling hand the fun'ral present took;
Ev'n kept her count'nance, when the lid
  remov'd
Disclos'd the heart, unfortunately lov'd.   630
She needed not be told within whose breast
It lodg'd; the message had explain'd the
  rest.
Or not amaz'd, or hiding her surprise,
She sternly on the bearer fix'd her eyes;
Then thus: "Tell Tancred, on his daughter's
  part,
The gold, tho' precious, equals not the
  heart:
But he did well to give his best; and I,
Who wish'd a worthier urn, forgive his
  poverty."
At this she curb'd a groan, that else had
  come,
And pausing, view'd the present in the
  tomb;   640
Then, to the heart ador'd devoutly glued
Her lips, and raising it, her speech renew'd:

"Ev'n from my day of birth, to this, the
  bound
Of my unhappy being, I have found
My father's care and tenderness express'd;
But this last act of love excels the rest:
For this so dear a present, bear him back
The best return that I can live to make."
  The messenger dispatch'd, again she
  view'd
The lov'd remains, and sighing thus pur-
  sued: 650
"Source of my life, and lord of my desires,
In whom I liv'd, with whom my soul ex-
  pires !
Poor heart, no more the spring of vital heat,
Curst be the hands that tore thee from thy
  seat !
The course is finish'd which thy fates de-
  creed,
And thou from thy corporeal prison freed:
Soon hast thou reach'd the goal with mended
  pace,
A world of woes dispatch'd in little space.
Forc'd by thy worth, thy foe, in death be-
  come   659
Thy friend, has lodg'd thee in a costly tomb.
There yet remain'd thy fun'ral exequies,
The weeping tribute of thy widow's eyes,
And those, indulgent Heav'n has found the
  way
That I, before my death, have leave to pay.
My father ev'n in cruelty is kind,
Or Heav'n has turn'd the malice of his
  mind
To better uses than his hate design'd;
And made th' insult, which in his gift ap-
  pears,
The means to mourn thee with my pious
  tears;   669
Which I will pay thee down, before I go,
And save myself the pains to weep below,
If souls can weep. Tho' once I meant to
  meet
My fate with face unmov'd, and eyes un-
  wet,
Yet since I have thee here in narrow room,
My tears shall set thee first afloat within
  thy tomb;
Then (as I know thy spirit hovers nigh)
Under thy friendly conduct will I fly
To regions unexplor'd, secure to share
Thy state; nor hell shall punishment ap-
  pear;
And heav'n is double heav'n, if thou art
  there."   680

She said: her brimful eyes, that ready
   stood,
And only wanted will to weep a flood,
Releas'd their wat'ry store, and pour'd
   amain,
Like clouds low hung, a sober show'r of
   rain;
Mute solemn sorrow, free from female
   noise,
Such as the majesty of grief destroys;
For, bending o'er the cup, the tears she
   shed
Seem'd by the posture to discharge her head,
O'erfill'd before; and oft (her mouth ap-
   plied
To the cold heart) she kiss'd at once and
   cried.   690
Her maids, who stood amaz'd, nor knew
   the cause
Of her complaining, nor whose heart it was;
Yet all due measures of her mourning kept,
Did office at the dirge, and by infection
   wept;
And oft enquir'd th' occasion of her grief,
(Unanswer'd but by sighs,) and offer'd vain
   relief.
At length, her stock of tears already shed,
She wip'd her eyes, she rais'd her drooping
   head,
And thus pursued: "O ever faithful heart,
I have perform'd the ceremonial part,   700
The decencies of grief; it rests behind,
That, as our bodies were, our souls be join'd;
To thy whate'er abode my shade convey,
And as an elder ghost, direct the way."
She said; and bade the vial to be brought,
Where she before had brew'd the deadly
   draught.
First pouring out the med'cinable bane,
The heart her tears had rins'd she bath'd
   again;
Then down her throat the death securely
   throws,
And quaffs a long oblivion of her woes.   710
  This done, she mounts the genial bed,
   and there
(Her body first compos'd with honest care)
Attends the welcome rest; her hands yet
   hold
Close to her heart the monumental gold;
Nor farther word she spoke, but clos'd her
   sight,
And quiet sought the covert of the night.
  The damsels, who the while in silence
   mourn'd,

Not knowing, nor suspecting death suborn'd,
Yet, as their duty was, to Tancred sent;
Who, conscious of th' occasion, fear'd th'
   event.   720
Alarm'd, and with presaging heart, he came,
And drew the curtains, and expos'd the
   dame
To loathsome light; then with a late relief
Made vain efforts to mitigate her grief.
She, what she could, excluding day, her
   eyes
Kept firmly seal'd, and sternly thus replies:
  "Tancred, restrain thy tears, unsought by
   me,
And sorrow, unavailing now to thee:
Did ever man before afflict his mind   729
To see th' effect of what himself design'd?
Yet, if thou hast remaining in thy heart
Some sense of love, some unextinguish'd
   part
Of former kindness, largely once pro- ⎫
   fess'd,   ⎪
Let me by that adjure thy harden'd   ⎬
   breast   ⎪
Not to deny thy daughter's last request. ⎭
The secret love which I so long enjoy'd,
And still conceal'd, to gratify thy pride,
Thou hast disjoin'd; but, with my dying
   breath,
Seek not, I beg thee, to disjoin our death:
Where'er his corpse by thy command is laid,
Thither let mine in public be convey'd;   741
Expos'd in open view, and side by side,
Acknowledg'd as a bridegroom and a bride."
  The prince's anguish hinder'd his reply;
And she, who felt her fate approaching
   nigh,
Seiz'd the cold heart, and heaving to her
   breast:
"Here, precious pledge," she said, "securely
   rest."
These accents were her last; the creeping
   death
Benumb'd her senses first, then stopp'd her
   breath.
  Thus she for disobedience justly died;   750
The sire was justly punish'd for his pride:
The youth, least guilty, suffer'd for th' of-
   fense,
Of duty violated to his prince;
Who, late repenting of his cruel deed,
One common sepulcher for both decreed;
Intomb'd the wretched pair in royal state,
And on their monument inscrib'd their
   fate.

BAUCIS AND PHILEMON

OUT OF THE EIGHTH BOOK OF OVID'S METAMORPHOSES

The author, pursuing the deeds of Theseus, relates how he with his friend Perithous were invited by Acheloüs, the river god, to stay with him till his waters were abated. Acheloüs entertains them with a relation of his own love to Perimele, who was chang'd into an island by Neptune at his request. Perithous, being an atheist, derides the legend, and denies the power of the gods to work that miracle. Lelex, another companion of Theseus, to confirm the story of Acheloüs, relates another metamorphosis of Baucis and Philemon into trees; of which he was partly an eye witness.

THUS Acheloüs ends: his audience hear
With admiration, and, admiring, fear
The pow'rs of heav'n; except Ixion's son,
Who laugh'd at all the gods, believ'd in
    none.
He shook his impious head, and thus replies:
" These legends are no more than pious lies:
You attribute too much to heavenly sway,
To think they give us forms, and take
    away."
    The rest, of better minds, their sense
        declar'd
Against this doctrine, and with horror
    heard.   10
Then Lelex rose, an old experienc'd man,
And thus with sober gravity began:
" Heav'n's pow'r is infinite; earth, air, and
    sea,
The manufactur'd mass, the making pow'r
    obey.
By proof to clear your doubt: in Phrygian
    ground
Two neighb'ring trees, with walls encom-
    pass'd round,
Stand on a mod'rate rise, with wonder
    shown,
One a hard oak, a softer linden one:
I saw the place and them, by Pittheus sent
To Phrygian realms, my grandsire's gov-
    ernment.   20
Not far from thence is seen a lake, the
    haunt
Of coots, and of the fishing cormorant:
Here Jove with Hermes came; but in dis-
    guise
Of mortal men conceal'd their deities:

One laid aside his thunder, one his rod;
And many toilsome steps together trod;
For harbor at a thousand doors they
    knock'd —
Not one of all the thousand but was lock'd.
At last an hospitable house they found,
A homely shed; the roof, not far from
    ground,   30
Was thatch'd with reeds and straw to-
    gether bound.
There Baucis and Philemon liv'd, and there
Had liv'd long married and a happy pair:
Now old in love; tho' little was their
    store,
Inur'd to want, their poverty they bore,
Nor aim'd at wealth, professing to be poor.
For master or for servant here to call,
Was all alike, where only two were all.
Command was none, where equal love was
    paid,
Or rather both commanded, both obey'd.   40
    " From lofty roofs the gods repuls'd be-
        fore,
Now, stooping, enter'd thro' the little door;
The man (their hearty welcome first ex-
    press'd)
A common settle drew for either guest,
Inviting each his weary limbs to rest.
But ere they sat, officious Baucis lays
Two cushions stuff'd with straw, the seat
    to raise;
Coarse, but the best she had; then rakes the
    load
Of ashes from the hearth, and spreads
    abroad
The living coals, and, lest they should ex-
    pire,   50
With leaves and barks she feeds her infant
    fire:
It smokes, and then with trembling breath
    she blows,
Till in a cheerful blaze the flames arose.
With brushwood and with chips she strength-
    ens these,
And adds at last the boughs of rotten
    trees.
The fire thus form'd, she sets the kettle on —
Like burnish'd gold the little seether
    shone —
Next took the coleworts which her husband
    got
From his own ground (a small well-water'd
    spot);
She stripp'd the stalks of all their leaves;
    the best

She cull'd, and then with handy care she
    dress'd.
High o'er the hearth a chine of bacon hung:
Good old Philemon seiz'd it with a prong,
And from the sooty rafter drew it down;
Then cut a slice, but scarce enough for one;
Yet a large portion of a little store,
Which for their sakes alone he wish'd were
    more.
This in the pot he plung'd without delay,
To tame the flesh and drain the salt away.
The time between, before the fire they sat, 70
And shorten'd the delay by pleasing chat.
    " A beam there was, on which a beechen
    pail
Hung by the handle, on a driven nail:
This fill'd with water, gently warm'd, ⎤
    they set |
Before their guests; in this they bath'd ⎬
    their feet, |
And after with clean towels dried their |
    sweat. ⎦
This done, the host produc'd the genial ⎤
    bed, |
Sallow the feet, the borders, and the ⎬
    stead, |
Which with no costly coverlet they |
    spread, ⎦
But coarse old garments; yet such robes as
    these   80
They laid alone, at feasts, on holidays.
The good old housewife, tucking up her
    gown,
The table sets; th' invited gods lie down.
The trivet table of a foot was lame —
A blot which prudent Baucis overcame,
Who thrusts beneath the limping leg a
    sherd;
So was the mended board exactly rear'd:
Then rubb'd it o'er with newly gather'd
    mint,
A wholesome herb, that breath'd a grateful
    scent.
Pallas began the feast, where first was
    seen   90
The party-color'd olive, black and green;
Autumnal cornels next in order serv'd,
In lees of wine well pickled and preserv'd;
A garden salad was the third supply,
Of endive, radishes, and succory;
Then curds and cream, the flow'r of ⎤
    country fare, |
And new-laid eggs, which Baucis' busy ⎬
    care |
Turn'd by a gentle fire, and roasted rear. ⎦

All these in earthenware were serv'd to ⎤
    board; |
And, next in place, an earthen pitcher, ⎬
    stor'd   100 |
With liquor of the best the cottage could |
    afford. ⎦
This was the table's ornament and pride,
With figures wrought: like pages at his side
Stood beechen bowls; and these were shin-
    ing clean,
Vernish'd with wax without, and lin'd
    within.
By this the boiling kettle had prepar'd
And to the table sent the smoking lard,
On which with eager appetite they dine,
A sav'ry bit, that serv'd to relish wine;
The wine itself was suiting to the rest, 110
Still working in the must, and lately
    press'd.
The second course succeeds like that before;
Plums, apples, nuts, and, of their wintry
    store,
Dry figs and grapes, and wrinkled dates
    were set
In canisters, t' enlarge the little treat.
All these a milk-white honeycomb sur-
    round,
Which in the midst the country banquet
    crown'd.
But the kind hosts their entertainment
    grace
With hearty welcome, and an open face:
In all they did you might discern with ease
A willing mind, and a desire to please. 121
    " Meantime the beechen bowls went
    round, and still,
Tho' often emptied, were observ'd to fill;
Fill'd without hands, and of their own ac-
    cord
Ran without feet, and danc'd about the
    board.
Devotion seiz'd the pair, to see the feast
With wine, and of no common grape, in-
    creas'd;
And up they held their hands, and fell to
    pray'r,
Excusing, as they could, their country fare.
    " One goose they had, ('t was all they ⎤
    could allow,)   130 ⎬
A wakeful sentry, and on duty now, |
Whom to the gods for sacrifice they vow: ⎦
Her, with malicious zeal, the couple view'd;
She ran for life, and, limping, they pursued.
Full well the fowl perceiv'd their bad in-
    tent,

And would not make her masters' compliment;
But, persecuted, to the pow'rs she flies,
And close between the legs of Jove she lies.
He, with a gracious ear, the suppliant heard,
And sav'd her life; then what he was declar'd,   140
And own'd the god. 'The neighborhood,'
        said he,
'Shall justly perish for impiety:
You stand alone exempted; but obey
With speed, and follow where we lead the
        way;
Leave these accurst, and to the mountain's
        height
Ascend, nor once look backward in your
        flight.'
"They haste, and what their tardy feet
        denied,
The trusty staff (their better leg) supplied.
An arrow's flight they wanted to the top,
And there secure, but spent with travel,
        stop;   150
Then turn their now no more forbidden
        eyes:
Lost in a lake the floated level lies;
A wat'ry desart covers all the plains;
Their cot alone, as in an isle, remains;
Wond'ring with weeping eyes, while they
        deplore
Their neighbors' fate, and country now no
        more,
Their little shed, scarce large enough for
        two,
Seems, from the ground increas'd, in
        height and bulk to grow.
A stately temple shoots within the skies;
The crotches of their cot in columns
        rise;   160
The pavement polish'd marble they behold,
The gates with sculpture grac'd, the spires
        and tiles of gold.
"Then thus the Sire of Gods, with look
        serene:
'Speak thy desire, thou only just of men;
And thou, O woman, only worthy found
To be with such a man in marriage bound.'
"A while they whisper; then, to Jove address'd,
Philemon thus prefers their joint request:
'We crave to serve before your sacred
        shrine,
And offer at your altars rites divine;   170
And since not any action of our life
Has been polluted with domestic strife,

We beg one hour of death; that neither
        she
With widow's tears may live to bury me,
Nor weeping I, with wither'd arms, may
        bear
My breathless Baucis to the sepulcher.'
"The godheads sign their suit. They run
        their race
In the same tenor all th' appointed space;
Then, when their hour was come, while
        they relate
These past adventures at the temple gate,
Old Baucis is by old Philemon seen   181
Sprouting with sudden leaves of sprightly
        green;
Old Baucis look'd where old Philemon
        stood,
And saw his lengthen'd arms a sprouting
        wood.
New roots their fasten'd feet begin to bind,
Their bodies stiffen in a rising rind:
Then, ere the bark above their shoulders
        grew,
They give and take at once their last adieu;
At once: 'Farewell, O faithful spouse,'
        they said;
At once th' incroaching rinds their closing
        lips invade.   190
Ev'n yet, an ancient Tyanæan shows
A spreading oak, that near a linden grows;
The neighborhood confirm the prodigy,
Grave men, not vain of tongue, or like to
        lie.
I saw myself the garlands on their boughs,
And tablets hung for gifts of granted vows;
And off'ring fresher up, with pious pray'r,
'The good,' said I, 'are God's peculiar
        care,
And such as honor Heav'n, shall heav'nly
        honor share.'"

PYGMALION AND THE STATUE

OUT OF THE TENTH BOOK OF OVID'S METAMORPHOSES

The Propœtides, for their impudent behavior, being turn'd into stone by Venus, Pygmalion, prince of Cyprus, detested all women for their sake, and resolv'd never to marry. He falls in love with a statue of his own making, which is chang'd into a maid, whom he marries. One of his descendants is Cinyras, the father of Myrrha: the daughter incestuously loves her own father; for which she is

chang'd into the tree which bears her name.
These two stories immediately follow each
other and are admirably well connected.

PYGMALION, loathing their lascivious life,
Abhorr'd all womankind, but most a wife:
So single chose to live, and shunn'd to wed,
Well pleas'd to want a consort of his bed;
Yet fearing idleness, the nurse of ill,
In sculpture exercis'd his happy skill;
And carv'd in iv'ry such a maid, so fair,
As Nature could not with his art compare,
Were she to work ; but, in her own defense,
Must take her pattern here, and copy hence.
Pleas'd with his idol, he commends, ad-
      mires,   11
Adores; and last, the thing ador'd desires.
A very virgin in her face was seen,
And, had she mov'd, a living maid had been.
One would have thought she could have
      stirr'd, but strove
With modesty, and was asham'd to move.
Art, hid with art, so well perform'd the
      cheat,
It caught the carver with his own deceit:
He knows 't is madness, yet he must adore,
And still the more he knows it, loves the
      more.   20
The flesh, or what so seems, he touches
      oft,
Which feels so smooth, that he believes it
      soft.
Fir'd with this thought, at once he strained
      the breast,
And on the lips a burning kiss impress'd.
'T is true, the harden'd breast resists the
      gripe,
And the cold lips return a kiss unripe:
But when, retiring back, he look'd again,
To think it iv'ry was a thought too mean;
So would believe she kiss'd, and courting
      more,
Again embrac'd her naked body o'er;   30
And straining hard the statue, was afraid
His hands had made a dint and hurt his
      maid;
Explor'd her, limb by limb, and fear'd to
      find
So rude a gripe had left a livid mark be-
      hind.
With flatt'ry now he seeks her mind to move,
And now with gifts (the pow'rful bribes of
      love).
He furnishes her closet first, and fills
The crowded shelves with rarities of shells;

Adds orient pearls, which from the conchs
      he drew,
And all the sparkling stones of various
      hue;   40
And parrots, imitating human tongue,
And singing-birds in silver cages hung;
And ev'ry fragrant flow'r, and od'rous
      green,
Were sorted well, with lumps of amber laid
      between.
Rich, fashionable robes her person deck,
Pendants her ears, and pearls adorn her
      neck;
Her taper'd fingers too with rings are
      grac'd,
And an embroider'd zone surrounds her
      slender waist.
Thus like a queen array'd, so richly dress'd,
Beauteous she shew'd, but naked shew'd
      the best.   50
Then from the floor he rais'd a royal bed,
With cov'rings of Sidonian purple spread;
The solemn rites perform'd, he calls her
      bride,
With blandishments invites her to his side;
And as she were with vital sense possess'd,
Her head did on a plumy pillow rest.
The feast of Venus came, a solemn day,
To which the Cypriots due devotion pay;
With gilded horns the milk-white heifers
      led,
Slaughter'd before the sacred altars, bled. 60
Pygmalion, off'ring, first approach'd the
      shrine,
And then with pray'rs implor'd the pow'rs
      divine:
" Almighty gods, if all we mortals want,
If all we can require, be yours to grant,
Make this fair statue mine," he would have
      said,
But chang'd his words for shame, and only
      pray'd:
" Give me the likeness of my iv'ry maid."
The golden goddess, present at the pray'r,
Well knew he meant th' inanimated fair,
And gave the sign of granting his desire; 70
For thrice in cheerful flames ascends the
      fire.
The youth, returning to his mistress, hies, ⎫
And, impudent in hope, with ardent eyes   ⎬
And beating breast, by the dear statue   ⎭
      lies.
He kisses her white lips, renews the bliss,
And looks and thinks they redden at th
      kiss —

He thought them warm before; nor longer
    stays,
But next his hand on her hard bosom lays:
Hard as it was, beginning to relent,
It seem'd the breast beneath his fingers
    bent.   80
He felt again, his fingers made a print;
'T was flesh, but flesh so firm, it rose against
    the dint.
The pleasing task he fails not to renew:
Soft, and more soft at ev'ry touch it grew;
Like pliant wax, when chafing hands re-
    duce
The former mass to form, and frame for
    use.
He would believe, but yet is still in pain, ⎫
And tries his argument of sense again; ⎬
Presses the pulse, and feels the leaping ⎭
    vein.
Convinc'd, o'erjoy'd, his studied thanks and
    praise   90
To her who made the miracle he pays:
Then lips to lips he join'd; now freed from
    fear,
He found the savor of the kiss sincere:
At this the waken'd image op'd her eyes,
And view'd at once the light and lover, with
    surprise.
The goddess, present at the match she made,
So bless'd the bed, such fruitfulness con-
    vey'd,
That ere ten moons had sharpen'd either
    horn,
To crown their bliss, a lovely boy was born;
Paphos his name, who, grown to manhood,
    wall'd   100
The city Paphos, from the founder call'd.

CINYRAS AND MYRRHA

OUT OF THE TENTH BOOK OF OVID'S
METAMORPHOSES

There needs no connection of this story with
the former : for the beginning of this immediately follows the end of the last. The reader
is only to take notice that Orpheus, who
relates both, was by birth a Thracian; and
his country far distant from Cyprus, where
Myrrha was born, and from Arabia, whither
she fled. You will see the reason of this
note, soon after the first lines of this fable.

Nor him alone produc'd the fruitful queen;
But Cinyras, who like his sire had been

A happy prince, had he not been a sire.
Daughters and fathers, from my song re-
    tire:
I sing of horror; and, could I prevail,
You should not hear, or not believe my tale.
Yet if the pleasure of my song be such,
That you will hear, and credit me too much,
Attentive listen to the last event,
And with the sin believe the punishment: 10
Since nature could behold so dire a crime,
I gratulate at least my native clime,
That such a land, which such a monster bore,
So far is distant from our Thracian shore.
Let Araby extol her happy coast,
Her cinnamon and sweet amomum boast,
Her fragrant flow'rs, her trees with pre- ⎫
    cious tears, ⎪
Her second harvests, and her double ⎬
    years — ⎪
How can the land be call'd so blest that ⎭
    Myrrha bears ?
Not all her od'rous tears can cleanse her
    crime;   20
Her plant alone deforms the happy clime.
Cupid denies to have inflam'd thy heart,
Disowns thy love, and vindicates his dart;
Some fury gave thee those infernal pains,
And shot her venom'd vipers in thy veins.
To hate thy sire, had merited a curse;
But such an impious love deserv'd a worse.
The neighb'ring monarchs, by thy beauty
    led,
Contend in crowds, ambitious of thy bed:
The world is at thy choice, except but one, 30
Except but him thou canst not choose alone.
She knew it too, the miserable maid, ⎫
Ere impious love her better thoughts be- ⎬
    tray'd, ⎪
And thus within her secret soul she said: ⎭
" Ah Myrrha! whither would thy wishes
    tend ?
Ye gods, ye sacred laws, my soul defend
From such a crime as all mankind detest,
And never lodg'd before in human breast !
But is it sin ?   Or makes my mind alone
Th' imagin'd sin ?   For nature makes it
    none.   40
What tyrant then these envious laws began,
Made not for any other beast but man !
The father bull his daughter may bestride,
The horse may make his mother mare a
    bride;
What piety forbids the lusty ram,
Or more salacious goat, to rut their dam ?
The hen is free to wed the chick she bore,

And make a husband, whom she hatch'd
   before.
All creatures else are of a happier kind, ⎤
Whom nor ill-natur'd laws from pleasure |
   bind,   50 ⎬
Nor thoughts of sin disturb their peace |
   of mind. ⎦
But man a slave of his own making lives;
The fool denies himself what nature gives:
Too busy senates, with an overcare
To make us better than our kind can bear,
Have dash'd a spice of envy in the laws,
And, straining up too high, have spoil'd the
   cause.
Yet some wise nations break their cruel
   chains,
And own no laws, but those which love or-
   dains;
Where happy daughters with their sires are
   join'd,   60
And piety is doubly paid in kind.
O that I had been born in such a clime,
Not here, where 't is the country makes the
   crime !
But whither would my impious fancy stray ?
Hence hopes, and ye forbidden thoughts,
   away !
His worth deserves to kindle my desires,
But with the love that daughters bear to
   sires.
Then had not Cinyras my father been,
What hinder'd Myrrha's hopes to be his
   queen ?
But the perverseness of my fate is such, 70
That he 's not mine, because he 's mine too
   much:
Our kindred blood debars a better tie;
He might be nearer, were he not so nigh.
Eyes and their objects never must unite;
Some distance is requir'd to help the sight:
Fain would I travel to some foreign shore, ⎤
Never to see my native country more,   ⎬
So might I to myself myself restore;   ⎦
So might my mind these impious thoughts
   remove,
And, ceasing to behold, might cease to
   love.   80
But stay I must, to feed my famish'd sight,
To talk, to kiss; and more, if more I might:
More, impious maid ! What more canst ⎤
   thou design ? |
To make a monstrous mixture in thy line, ⎬
And break all statutes human and divine ? ⎦
Canst thou be call'd (to save thy wretched
   life)

Thy mother's rival, and thy father's wife ?
Confound so many sacred names in one,
Thy brother's mother ! sister to thy son !
And fear'st thou not to see th' infernal
   bands,   90
Their heads with snakes, with torches arm'd
   their hands,
Full at thy face th' avenging brands to bear,
And shake the serpents from their hissing
   hair ?
But thou in time th' increasing ill control,
Nor first debauch the body by the soul;
Secure the sacred quiet of thy mind,
And keep the sanctions nature has design'd.
Suppose I should attempt, th' attempt were
   vain;
No thoughts like mine his sinless soul pro-
   fane:
Observant of the right; and O, that he 100
Could cure my madness, or be mad like
   me ! "
   Thus she; but Cinyras, who daily sees
A crowd of noble suitors at his knees,
Among so many, knew not whom to choose,
Irresolute to grant, or to refuse.
But, having told their names, enquir'd of
   her
Who pleas'd her best, and whom she would
   prefer.
The blushing maid stood silent with sur-
   prise,
And on her father fix'd her ardent eyes,
And looking sigh'd; and, as she sigh'd, be-
   gan   110
Round tears to shed, that scalded as they
   ran.
The tender sire, who saw her blush and
   cry,
Ascrib'd it all to maiden modesty;
And dried the falling drops, and, yet more
   kind,
He strok'd her cheeks, and holy kisses
   join'd.
She felt a secret venom fire her blood,
And found more pleasure than a daughter
   should;
And, ask'd again, what lover of the crew
She lik'd the best; she answer'd: "One like
   you."
Mistaking what she meant, her pious will 120
He prais'd, and bade her so continue still:
The word of "pious" heard, she blush'd
   with shame
Of secret guilt, and could not bear the
   name.

'T was now the mid of night, when slumbers close
Our eyes, and soothe our cares with soft repose;
But no repose could wretched Myrrha find,
Her body rolling, as she roll'd her mind.
Mad with desire, she ruminates her sin,
And wishes all her wishes o'er again: 129
Now she despairs, and now resolves to try;
Would not, and would again, she knows not why;
Stops and returns, makes and retracts the vow;
Fain would begin, but understands not how.
As when a pine is hew'd upon the plains,
And the last mortal stroke alone remains,
Lab'ring in pangs of death, and threat'ning all,
This way and that she nods, consid'ring where to fall;
So Myrrha's mind, impell'd on either side,
Takes ev'ry bent, but cannot long abide:
Irresolute on which she should rely, 140
At last unfix'd in all, is only fix'd to die.
On that sad thought she rests; resolv'd on death,
She rises, and prepares to choke her breath:
Then while about the beam her zone she ties,
" Dear Cinyras, farewell ! " she softly cries;
" For thee I die, and only wish to be
Not hated, when thou know'st I die for thee:
Pardon the crime, in pity to the cause."
This said, about her neck the noose she draws.
The nurse, who lay without, her faithful guard, 150
Tho' not the words, the murmurs overheard,
And sighs and hollow sounds: surpris'd with fright,
She starts, and leaves her bed, and springs a light;
Unlocks the door, and ent'ring out of breath,
The dying saw, and instruments of death.
She shrieks, she cuts the zone with trembling haste,
And in her arms her fainting charge embrac'd:
Next (for she now had leisure for her tears)
She weeping ask'd, in these her blooming years,
What unforeseen misfortune caus'd her care, 160

To loathe her life, and languish in despair !
The maid, with downcast eyes, and mute with grief,
For death unfinish'd, and ill-tim'd relief,
Stood sullen to her suit; the beldame press'd
The more to know, and bar'd her wither'd breast;
Adjur'd her, by the kindly food she drew
From those dry founts, her secret ill to shew.
Sad Myrrha sigh'd, and turn'd her eyes aside;
The nurse still urg'd, and would not be denied;
Nor only promis'd secrecy, but pray'd 170
She might have leave to give her offer'd aid.
" Good will," she said, " my want of strength supplies,
And diligence shall give what age denies.
If strong desires thy mind to fury move,
With charms and med'cines I can cure thy love;
If envious eyes their hurtful rays have cast,
More pow'rful verse shall free thee from the blast;
If Heav'n offended sends thee this disease,
Offended Heav'n with pray'rs we can appease.
What then remains that can these cares procure ? 180
Thy house is flourishing, thy fortune sure;
Thy careful mother yet in health survives,
And, to thy comfort, thy kind father lives."
The virgin started at her father's name,
And sigh'd profoundly, conscious of the shame;
Nor yet the nurse her impious love divin'd,
But yet surmis'd that love disturb'd her mind.
Thus thinking, she pursued her point, and laid
And lull'd within her lap the mourning maid;
Then softly sooth'd her thus: " I guess your grief; 190
You love, my child; your love shall find relief.
My long-experienc'd age shall be your guide;
Rely on that, and lay distrust aside:
No breath of air shall on the secret blow,
Nor shall (what most you fear) your father know."
Struck once again, as with a thunderclap,
The guilty virgin bounded from her lap,

And threw her body prostrate on the bed,
And, to conceal her blushes, hid her head:
There silent lay, and warn'd her with her
    hand   200
To go; but she receiv'd not the command,
Remaining still importunate to know.
Then Myrrha thus: " Or ask no more, or go:
I prethee go, or staying spare my shame;
What thou wouldst hear, is impious ev'n to
    name."
At this, on high the beldame holds her
    hands,
And trembling, both with age and terror,
    stands;
Adjures, and falling at her feet intreats,
Soothes her with blandishments, and frights
    with threats,
To tell the crime intended, or disclose   210
What part of it she knew, if she no farther
    knows;
And last, if conscious to her counsel made,
Confirms anew the promise of her aid.
    Now Myrrha rais'd her head; but soon,
        oppress'd
With shame, reclin'd it on her nurse's
        breast;
Bath'd it with tears, and strove to have
        confess'd;
Twice she began, and stopp'd; again she
    tried;
The falt'ring tongue its office still denied:
At last her veil before her face she spread,
And drew a long preluding sigh, and said,
" O happy mother, in thy marriage bed ! "
Then groan'd and ceas'd; the good old
    woman shook,   222
Stiff were her eyes, and ghastly was her look:
Her hoary hair upright with horror stood,
Made (to her grief) more knowing than she
    would.
Much she reproach'd, and many things she
    said,
To cure the madness of th' unhappy maid:
In vain; for Myrrha stood convict of ill;
Her reason vanquish'd, but unchang'd her
    will:
Perverse of mind, unable to reply,   230
She stood resolv'd or to possess, or die.
At length the fondness of a nurse prevail'd
Against her better sense, and virtue fail'd:
" Enjoy, my child, since such is thy desire,
Thy love," she said — she durst not say,
        " Thy sire; " —
" Live, tho' unhappy, live on any terms: "
Then with a second oath her faith confirms.

    The solemn feast of Ceres now was near,
When long white linen stoles the matrons
    wear;
Rank'd in procession walk the pious train, 240
Off'ring first fruits, and spikes of yellow
    grain:
For nine long nights the nuptial bed they
    shun,
And, sanctifying harvest, lie alone.
    Mix'd with the crowd, the queen forsook
    her lord,
And Ceres' pow'r with secret rites ador'd.
The royal couch now vacant for a time,
The crafty crone, officious in her crime,
The curst occasion took: the king she found
Easy with wine, and deep in pleasures
        drown'd,
Prepar'd for love: the beldame blew the
    flame,   250
Confess'd the passion, but conceal'd the
    name.
Her form she prais'd; the monarch ask'd
    her years,
And she replied: " The same thy Myrrha
    bears."
Wine and commended beauty fir'd his
    thought;
Impatient, he commands her to be brought.
Pleas'd with her charge perform'd, she hies
    her home,
And gratulates the nymph, the task was
    overcome.
Myrrha was joy'd the welcome news to
    hear;
But, clogg'd with guilt, the joy was un-
    sincere:
So various, so discordant is the mind,   260
That in our will a diff'rent will we find.
Ill she presag'd, and yet pursued her lust;
For guilty pleasures give a double gust.
'T was depth of night: Arctophylax had
    driv'n
His lazy wain half round the northern
    heav'n,
When Myrrha hasten'd to the crime de-
    sir'd;
The moon beheld her first, and first retir'd;
The stars amaz'd ran backward from the
    sight,
And, shrunk within their sockets, lost their
    light.
Icarius first withdraws his holy flame;   270
The Virgin sign, in heav'n the second name,
Slides down the belt, and from her station
    flies,

And night with sable clouds involves the
    skies.
Bold Myrrha still pursues her black in-
    tent:
She stumbled thrice (an omen of th'
    event);
Thrice shriek'd the fun'ral owl, yet on she
    went,
Secure of shame, because secure of sight —
Ev'n bashful sins are impudent by night.
Link'd hand in hand, th' accomplice and the
    dame,   279
Their way exploring, to the chamber came.
The door was ope, they blindly grope their
    way,
Where dark in bed th' expecting monarch
    lay:
Thus far her courage held, but here for-
    sakes;
Her faint knees knock at ev'ry step she
    makes.
The nearer to her crime, the more within
She feels remorse, and horror of her sin;
Repents too late her criminal desire,
And wishes that unknown she could retire.
Her ling'ring thus, the nurse (who fear'd
    delay
The fatal secret might at length betray)   290
Pull'd forward, to complete the work be-
    gun,
And said to Cinyras: " Receive thy own."
Thus saying, she deliver'd kind to kind,
Accurst, and their devoted bodies join'd.
The sire, unknowing of the crime, admits
His bowels, and profanes the hallow'd
    sheets:
He found she trembled, but believ'd she ⎫
    strove,   ⎪
With maiden modesty, against her love;   ⎬
And sought with flatt'ring words vain fan- ⎪
    cies to remove.   ⎭
Perhaps he said, " My daughter, cease thy
    fears,"   300
(Because the title suited with her years;)
And, " Father," she might whisper him
    again,
That names might not be wanting to the sin.
Full of her sire, she left th' incestuous bed,
And carried in her womb the crime she
    bred.
Another, and another night she came;
For frequent sin had left no sense of shame:
Till Cinyras desir'd to see her face,
Whose body he had held in close embrace,
And brought a taper; the revealer, light, 310

Expos'd both crime and criminal to sight.
Grief, rage, amazement, could no speech
    afford,
But from the sheath he drew th' avenging
    sword.
The guilty fled; the benefit of night,
That favor'd first the sin, secur'd the flight.
Long wand'ring thro' the spacious fields,
    she bent
Her voyage to th' Arabian continent;
Then pass'd the region which Panchæa
    join'd,
And, flying, left the palmy plains behind.
Nine times the moon had mew'd her horns;
    at length,   320
With travel weary, unsupplied with
    strength,
And with the burden of her womb op-
    press'd,
Sabæan fields afford her needful rest.
There, loathing life, and yet of death afraid,
In anguish of her spirit, thus she pray'd:
" Ye pow'rs, if any so propitious are
T' accept my penitence, and hear my pray'r,
Your judgments, I confess, are justly sent;
Great sins deserve as great a punishment:
Yet since my life the living will profane, 330
And since my death the happy dead will
    stain,
A middle state your mercy may bestow,
Betwixt the realms above and those be-
    low:
Some other form to wretched Myrrha give,
Nor let her wholly die, nor wholly live."
The pray'rs of penitents are never vain:
At least, she did her last request obtain;
For, while she spoke, the ground began to
    rise,
And gather'd round her feet, her legs and
    thighs:
Her toes in roots descend, and, spreading
    wide,   340
A firm foundation for the trunk provide;
Her solid bones convert to solid wood,
To pith her marrow, and to sap her blood;
Her arms are boughs, her fingers change
    their kind,
Her tender skin is harden'd into rind.
And now the rising tree her womb invests;
Now, shooting upwards still, invades her
    breasts,
And shades the neck; when, weary with de-
    lay,
She sunk her head within, and met it half
    the way.

And tho' with outward shape she lost her
 sense,   350
With bitter tears she wept her last offense;
And still she weeps, nor sheds her tears in
 vain;
For still the precious drops her name re-
 tain.
Meantime the misbegotten infant grows,
And, ripe for birth, distends with deadly
 throes
The swelling rind, with unavailing strife
To leave the wooden womb, and pushes
 into life.
The mother tree, as if oppress'd with pain,
Writhes here and there, to break the bark,
 in vain;
And, like a lab'ring woman, would have
 pray'd,   360
But wants a voice to call Lucina's aid:
The bending bole sends out a hollow sound,
And trickling tears fall thicker on the
 ground.
The mild Lucina came uncall'd, and stood
Beside the struggling boughs, and heard
 the groaning wood;
Then reach'd her midwife hand, to speed
 the throes,
And spoke the pow'rful spells that babes
 to birth disclose.
The bark divides, the living load to free,
And safe delivers the convulsive tree. 369
The ready nymphs receive the crying child,
And wash him in the tears the parent plant
 distill'd.
They swath'd him with their scarfs; beneath
 him spread
The ground with herbs; with roses rais'd
 his head.
The lovely babe was born with ev'ry grace;
Ev'n envy must have prais'd so fair a face.
Such was his form, as painters, when they
 show
Their utmost art, on naked Loves bestow;
And, that their arms no diff'rence might be-
 tray,
Give him a bow, or his from Cupid take
 away.   379
Time glides along, with undiscover'd haste,
The future but a length behind the past;
So swift are years: the babe, whom just be-
 fore
His grandsire got, and whom his sister
 bore;
The drop, the thing which late the tree in-
 clos'd,

And late the yawning bark to life expos'd;
A babe, a boy, a beauteous youth appears;
And lovelier than himself at riper years.
Now to the Queen of Love he gave desires,
And, with her pains, reveng'd his mother's
 fires.

THE FIRST BOOK OF HOMER'S ILIAS

THE ARGUMENT

Chryses, priest of Apollo, brings presents to
the Grecian princes, to ransom his daughter
Chryseis, who was prisoner in the fleet. Agamemnon, the general, whose captive and mistress the young lady was, refuses to deliver
her, threatens the venerable old man, and
dismisses him with contumely. The priest
craves vengeance of his god; who sends a
plague among the Greeks: which occasions
Achilles, their great champion, to summon a
council of the chief officers: he encourages
Calchas, the high priest and prophet, to tell
the reason why the gods were so much incens'd against them. Calchas is fearful of
provoking Agamemnon, till Achilles engages
to protect him; then, embolden'd by the
hero, he accuses the general as the cause of
all, by detaining the fair captive and refusing the presents offer'd for her ransom. By
this proceeding, Agamemnon is oblig'd,
against his will, to restore Chryseis, with
gifts, that he might appease the wrath of
Phœbus; but at the same time, to revenge
himself on Achilles, sends to seize his slave
Briseis. Achilles, thus affronted, complains
to his mother Thetis; and begs her to revenge his injury, not only on the general,
but on all the army, by giving victory to
the Trojans, till the ungrateful king became
sensible of his injustice. At the same time,
he retires from the camp into his ships,
and withdraws his aid from his countrymen.
Thetis prefers her son's petition to Jupiter,
who grants her suit. Juno suspects her errand, and quarrels with her husband for his
grant; till Vulcan reconciles his parents with
a bowl of nectar, and sends them peaceably
to bed.

THE wrath of Peleus' son, O Muse, resound;
Whose dire effects the Grecian army found,
And many a hero, king, and hardy knight,
Were sent, in early youth, to shades of
 night;
Their limbs a prey to dogs and vultures
 made:

So was the sov'reign will of Jove obey'd:
From that ill-omen'd hour when strife be-
     gun
Betwixt Atrides great and Thetis' godlike
     son.
  What pow'r provok'd, and for what cause,
     relate,
Sow'd in their breasts the seeds of stern
     debate: 10
Jove's and Latona's son his wrath express'd,
In vengeance of his violated priest,
Against the King of Men; who, swoln with
     pride,
Refus'd his presents, and his pray'rs denied.
For this the god a swift contagion spread
Amid the camp, where heaps on heaps lay
     dead.
  For venerable Chryses came to buy,
With gold and gifts of price, his daughter's
     liberty.
Suppliant before the Grecian chiefs he stood;
Awful, and arm'd with ensigns of his god: 20
Bare was his hoary head; one holy hand
Held forth his laurel crown, and one his
     scepter of command.
His suit was common; but, above the rest,
To both the brother princes thus address'd:
  "Ye sons of Atreus, and ye Grecian
     pow'rs,
So may the gods who dwell in heav'nly
     bow'rs
Succeed your siege, accord the vows you
     make,
And give you Troy's imperial town to take;
So, by their happy conduct, may you come
With conquest back to your sweet native
     home,   30
As you receive the ransom which I bring,
(Respecting Jove, and the far-shooting
     king,)
And break my daughter's bonds, at my de-
     sire,
And glad with her return her grieving sire."
  With shouts of loud acclaim the Greeks
     decree
To take the gifts, to set the damsel free.
The King of Men alone with fury burn'd;
And, haughty, these opprobrious words re-
     turn'd:
" Hence, holy dotard, and avoid my sight,
Ere evil intercept thy tardy flight;   40
Nor dare to tread this interdicted strand, ⎤
Lest not that idle scepter in thy hand,   ⎬
Nor thy god's crown, my vow'd revenge   ⎮
     withstand.   ⎦

Hence on thy life: the captive maid is
     mine;
Whom not for price or pray'rs I will re-
     sign.
Mine she shall be, till creeping age and
     time
Her bloom have wither'd, and consum'd her
     prime:
Till then my royal bed she shall attend;
And, having first adorn'd it, late ascend.
This, for the night; by day, the web and ⎤
     loom,   50 ⎮
And homely household task, shall be her ⎬
     doom,   ⎮
Far from thy lov'd embrace, and her   ⎮
     sweet native home."   ⎦
He said; the helpless priest replied no
     more,
But sped his steps along the hoarse-resound-
     ing shore:
Silent he fled; secure at length he stood,
Devoutly curs'd his foes, and thus invok'd
     his god:
" O source of sacred light, attend my
     pray'r,
God with the silver bow and golden hair,
Whom Chrysa, Cilla, Tenedos obeys,
And whose broad eye their happy soil sur-
     veys.   60
If, Smintheus, I have pour'd before thy
     shrine
The blood of oxen, goats, and ruddy wine,
And larded thighs on loaded altars laid,
Hear, and my just revenge propitious aid !
Pierce the proud Greeks, and with thy
     shafts attest
How much thy pow'r is injur'd in thy
     priest."
  He pray'd, and Phœbus, hearing, urg'd
     his flight,
With fury kindled, from Olympus' height;
His quiver o'er his ample shoulders threw;
His bow twang'd, and his arrows rattled as
     they flew.   70
Black as a stormy night, he rang'd around
The tents, and compass'd the devoted
     ground.
Then with full force his deadly bow he
     bent,
And feather'd fates among the mules and
     sumpters sent:
Th' essay of rage; on faithful dogs the next;
And last, in human hearts his arrows fix'd.
The god nine days the Greeks at rovers
     kill'd,

Nine days the camp with fun'ral fires was
    fill'd;
The tenth, Achilles, by the queen's com-
    mand,
Who bears heav'n's awful scepter in her
    hand,   80
A council summon'd; for the goddess griev'd
Her favor'd host should perish unreliev'd.
    The kings, assembled, soon their chief
    inclose;
Then from his seat the goddess-born arose,
And thus undaunted spoke: " What now re-
    mains,
But that once more we tempt the wat'ry
    plains,
And, wand'ring homeward, seek our safety
    hence,
In flight at least, if we can find defense ?
Such woes at once encompass us about,
The plague within the camp, the sword
    without.   90
Consult, O king, the prophets of th' event: ⎫
And whence these ills, and what the ⎪
    god's intent,   ⎬
Let them by dreams explore; for dreams ⎪
    from Jove are sent.   ⎭
What want of offer'd victims, what offense
In fact committed could the Sun incense,
To deal his deadly shafts ? What may re-
    move
His settled hate, and reconcile his love,
That he may look propitious on our toils,
And hungry graves no more be glutted with
    our spoils ? "   99
    Thus to the King of Men the hero spoke;
Then Calchas the desir'd occasion took:
Calchas the sacred seer, who had in view
Things present and the past, and things to
    come foreknew;
Supreme of augurs, who, by Phœbus taught,
The Grecian pow'rs to Troy's destruction
    brought.
Skill'd in the secret causes of their woes,
The reverend priest in graceful act arose,
And thus bespoke Pelides: " Care of Jove,
Favor'd of all th' immortal pow'rs above,
Wouldst thou the seeds deep sown of
    mischief know,   110
And why, provok'd, Apollo bends his bow ?
Plight first thy faith, inviolably true,
To save me from those ills that may ensue.
For I shall tell ungrateful truths to those
Whose boundless pow'r of life and death
    dispose;
And sov'reigns, ever jealous of their state,

Forgive not those whom once they mark for
    hate:
Ev'n tho' th' offense they seemingly digest.
Revenge, like embers, rak'd within their
    breast,
Bursts forth in flames; whose unresisted
    pow'r   120
Will seize th' unwary wretch, and soon
    devour.
Such and no less is he, on whom depends
The sum of things, and whom my tongue
    of force offends.
Secure me then from his foreseen intent,
That what his wrath may doom, thy valor
    may prevent."
    To this the stern Achilles made reply:
" Be bold, and on my plighted faith rely,
To speak what Phœbus has inspir'd thy soul
For common good; and speak without con-
    trol.
His godhead I invoke, by him I swear, 130
That while my nostrils draw this vital air,
None shall presume to violate those ⎫
    bands,   ⎪
Or touch thy person with unhallow'd ⎬
    hands;   ⎪
Ev'n not the King of Men, that all com- ⎪
    mands."   ⎭
    At this, resuming heart, the prophet said:
" Nor hecatombs unslain, nor vows unpaid,
On Greeks, accurst, this dire contagion
    bring,
Or call for vengeance from the bowyer king;
But he the tyrant, whom none dares resist,
Affronts the godhead in his injur'd priest: 140
He keeps the damsel captive in his chain,
And presents are refus'd, and pray'rs pre-
    ferr'd in vain.
For this th' avenging pow'r employs his
    darts,
And empties all his quiver in our hearts;
Thus will persist, relentless in his ire,
Till the fair slave be render'd to her sire,
And ransom-free restor'd to his abode,
With sacrifice to reconcile the god:
Then he, perhaps, aton'd by pray'r, may
    cease
His vengeance justly vow'd, and give the
    peace."   150
    Thus having said, he sate. Thus answer'd
    then,
Upstarting from his throne, the King of
    Men,
His breast with fury fill'd, his eyes with
    fire:

Which rolling round, he shot in sparkles on
the sire:
"Augur of ill, whose tongue was never
found
Without a priestly curse, or boding sound!
For not one blest event foretold to me
Pass'd thro' that mouth, or pass'd unwill-
ingly.
And now thou dost with lies the throne
invade,   159
By practice harden'd in thy sland'ring trade;
Obtending heav'n for whate'er ills befall,
And sputt'ring under specious names thy
gall.
Now Phœbus is provok'd, his rites and
laws
Are in his priest profan'd, and I the cause;
Since I detain a slave, my sov'reign prize,
And sacred gold, your idol god, despise.
I love her well, and well her merits claim
To stand preferr'd before my Grecian dame:
Not Clytemnestra's self in beauty's bloom
More charm'd, or better plied the various
loom: 170
Mine is the maid, and brought in happy
hour,
With every household grace adorn'd, to
bless my nuptial bow'r.
Yet shall she be restor'd, since public ⎫
good   ⎪
For private int'rest ought not be with-   ⎬
stood,   ⎪
To save th' effusion of my people's blood. ⎭
But right requires, if I resign my own,
I should not suffer for your sakes alone;
Alone excluded from the prize I gain'd,
And by your common suffrage have ob-
tain'd.
The slave without a ransom shall be sent: 180
It rests for you to make th' equivalent."
To this the fierce Thessalian prince re-
plied:
"O first in pow'r, but passing all in pride,
Griping, and still tenacious of thy hold,
Wouldst thou the Grecian chiefs, tho'
largely soul'd,
Should give the prizes they had gain'd be-
fore,
And with their loss thy sacrilege restore?
Whate'er by force of arms the soldier got,
Is each his own, by dividend of lot:
Which to resume, were both unjust and
base;   190
Not to be borne but by a servile race.
But this we can: if Saturn's son bestows

The sack of Troy, which he by promise
owes,
Then shall the conqu'ring Greeks thy loss
restore,
And with large int'rest make th' advantage
more."
To this Atrides answer'd: "Tho' thy
boast
Assumes the foremost name of all our host,
Pretend not, mighty man, that what is mine,
Controll'd by thee, I tamely should resign.
Shall I release the prize I gain'd by right, 200
In taken towns, and many a bloody fight,
While thou detain'st Briseis in thy bands,
By priestly glossing on the god's com-
mands?
Resolve on this, (a short alternative,)
Quit mine, or, in exchange, another give;
Else I, assure thy soul, by sov'reign right
Will seize thy captive in thy own despite;
Or from stout Ajax, or Ulysses, bear
What other prize my fancy shall prefer.
Then softly murmur, or aloud complain; 210
Rage as you please, you shall resist in vain.
But more of this, in proper time and place;
To things of greater moment let us pass.
A ship to sail the sacred seas prepare,   ⎫
Proud in her trim, and put on board the   ⎪
fair,   ⎬
With sacrifice and gifts, and all the pomp ⎪
of pray'r.   ⎭
The crew well chosen, the command   ⎫
shall be   ⎪
In Ajax; or, if other I decree,   ⎬
In Creta's king, or Ithacus, or, if I please, ⎪
in thee: ⎭
Most fit thyself to see perform'd th' in- ⎫
tent   220   ⎪
For which my pris'ner from my sight is   ⎬
sent,   ⎪
(Thanks to thy pious care,) that Phœbus   ⎭
may relent."
At this, Achilles roll'd his furious eyes,
Fix'd on the king askant, and thus replies:
"O impudent, regardful of thy own,
Whose thoughts are center'd on thyself
alone,
Advanc'd to sovereign sway for better ends
Than thus like abject slaves to treat thy
friends;
What Greek is he, that, urg'd by thy com-
mand,
Against the Trojan troops will lift his
hand?   230
Not I: nor such inforc'd respect I owe;

Nor Pergamus I hate, nor Priam is my foe.
What wrong from Troy remote could I
 sustain,
To leave my fruitful soil and happy reign,
And plow the surges of the stormy
 main ?
Thee, frontless man, we follow'd from afar;
Thy instruments of death, and tools of war.
Thine is the triumph; ours the toil alone:
We bear thee on our backs, and mount thee
 on the throne.
For thee we fall in fight; for thee re-
 dress   240
Thy baffled brother, not the wrongs of
 Greece.
And now thou threaten'st with unjust de-
 cree,
To punish thy affronting Heav'n, on me;
To seize the prize which I so dearly bought,
By common suffrage giv'n, confirm'd by
 lot;
Mean match to thine: for still, above the
 rest,
Thy hook'd rapacious hands usurp the best;
Tho' mine are first in fight, to force the
 prey,
And last sustain the labors of the day.
Nor grudge I thee the much the Grecians
 give,   250
Nor murm'ring take the little I receive.
Yet ev'n this little, thou, who wouldst in-
 gross
The whole, insatiate, envy'st as thy loss.
Know, then, for Phthia fix'd is my re-
 turn:
Better at home my ill-paid pains to
 mourn,
Than from an equal here sustain the pub-
 lic scorn."
 The king, whose brows with shining gold
 were bound,
Who saw his throne with scepter'd slaves
 incompass'd round,
Thus answer'd stern: " Go, at thy pleasure,
 go:
We need not such a friend, nor fear we
 such a foe.   260
There will not want to follow me in fight;
Jove will assist, and Jove assert my right.
But thou of all the kings (his care below)
Art least at my command, and most my
 foe.
Debates, dissensions, uproars are thy joy;
Provok'd without offense, and practic'd to
 destroy.

Strength is of brutes, and not thy boast
 alone;
At least 't is lent from heav'n, and not thy
 own.
Fly then, ill-manner'd, to thy native land,
And there thy ant-born Myrmidons com-
 mand.   270
But mark this menace; since I must resign
My black-ey'd maid, to please the pow'rs
 divine —
A well-rigg'd vessel in the port attends,
Mann'd at my charge, commanded by my
 friends !—
The ship shall waft her to her wish'd abode,
Full fraught with holy bribes to the far-
 shooting god.
This thus dispatch'd, I owe myself the care,
My fame and injur'd honor to repair:
From thy own tent, proud man, in thy de-
 spite,   279
This hand shall ravish thy pretended right.
Briseis shall be mine, and thou shalt see
What odds of awful pow'r I have on thee,
That others at thy cost may learn the
 diff'rence of degree."
 At this th' impatient hero sourly smil'd:
His heart, impetuous, in his bosom boil'd,
And, justled by two tides of equal sway,
Stood for a while suspended in his way,
Betwixt his reason and his rage untam'd;
One whisper'd soft, and one aloud re-
 claim'd:
That only counsel'd to the safer side;   290
This to the sword his ready hand applied.
Unpunish'd to support th' affront was hard,
Nor easy was th' attempt to force the
 guard.
But soon the thirst of vengeance fir'd his
 blood:
Half shone his falchion, and half sheath'd
 it stood.
 In that nice moment, Pallas, from above,
Commission'd by th' imperial wife of Jove,
Descended swift: (the white-arm'd queen
 was loth
The fight should follow, for she favor'd
 both:)
Just as in act he stood, in clouds inshrin'd, 300
Her hand she fasten'd on his hair behind;
Then backward by his yellow curls she drew;
To him, and him alone, confess'd in view.
Tam'd by superior force, he turn'd his eyes
Aghast at first, and stupid with surprise;
But by her sparkling eyes, and ardent look,
The virgin warrior known, he thus bespoke:

"Com'st thou, celestial, to behold my
    wrongs?
Then view the vengeance which to crimes
    belongs."
  Thus he. The blue-ey'd goddess thus
    rejoin'd: 310
"I come to calm thy turbulence of mind,
If Reason will resume her sovereign sway,
And, sent by Juno, her commands obey.
Equal she loves you both, and I protect:
Then give thy guardian gods their due
    respect;
And cease contention; be thy words severe,
Sharp as he merits, but the sword forbear.
An hour unhop'd already wings her way,
When he his dire affront shall dearly pay;
When the proud king shall sue, with treble
    gain,   320
To quit thy loss, and conquer thy disdain.
But thou, secure of my unfailing word,
Compose thy swelling soul, and sheathe the
    sword."
  The youth thus answer'd mild: " Auspi-
    cious maid,
Heav'n's will be mine, and your commands
    obey'd.
The gods are just, and when, subduing
    sense,
We serve their pow'rs, provide the recom-
    pense."
He said; with surly faith believ'd her word,
And in the sheath, reluctant, plung'd the
    sword.
Her message done, she mounts the blest
    abodes,   330
And mix'd among the senate of the gods.
  At her departure his disdain return d:
The fire she fann'd, with greater fury
    burn'd;
Rumbling within, till thus it found a vent:
"Dastard, and drunkard, mean and inso-
    lent;
Tongue-valiant hero, vaunter of thy might,
In threats the foremost, but the lag in flight;
When didst thou thrust amid the mingled
    prease,
Content to bide the war aloof in peace?
Arms are the trade of each plebeian soul; 340
'T is death to fight, but kingly to control;
Lord-like at ease, with arbitrary pow'r,
To peel the chiefs, the people to devour.
These, traitor, are thy talents; safer far
Than to contend in fields, and toils of war.
Nor couldst thou thus have dar'd the
    common hate,

Were not their souls as abject as their state.
But, by this scepter, solemnly I swear,
(Which never more green leaf or growing
    branch shall bear;
Torn from the tree, and giv'n by Jove to
    those   350
Who laws dispense, and mighty wrongs
    oppose,)
That when the Grecians want my wonted
    aid,
No gift shall bribe it, and no pray'r per-
    suade.
When Hector comes, the homicide, to wield
His conquering arms, with corps to strow
    the field;
Then shalt thou mourn thy pride, and late
    confess
My wrong repented, when 't is past redress."
He said; and with disdain, in open view,
Against the ground his golden scepter
    threw;
Then sate: with boiling rage Atrides burn'd,
And foam betwixt his gnashing grinders
    churn'd.   361
  But from his seat the Pylian prince arose,
With reas'ning mild, their madness to
    compose:
Words, sweet as honey, from his mouth
    distill'd:
Two centuries already he fulfill'd,
And now began the third; unbroken yet:
Once fam'd for courage; still in council
    great.
  "What worse," he said, " can Argos
    undergo;
What can more gratify the Phrygian foe,
Than these distemper'd heats? If both the
    lights   370
Of Greece their private int'rest disunites!
Believe a friend, with thrice your years in-
    creas'd,
And let these youthful passions be repress'd:
I flourish'd long before your birth; and ⎫
    then   ⎪
Liv'd equal with a race of braver men   ⎬
Than these dim eyes shall e'er behold   ⎪
    again.   ⎭
Cæneus and Dryas, and, excelling them,
Great Theseus, and the force of greater
    Polypheme.
With these I went, a brother of the war,
Their dangers to divide, their fame to share.
Nor idle stood with unassisting hands,   381
When salvage beasts, and men's more sal-
    vage bands,

Their virtuous toil subdued: yet those I
   sway'd
With pow'rful speech; I spoke, and they
   obey'd.
If such as those my counsels could reclaim,
Think not, young warriors, your diminish'd
   name
Shall lose of luster, by subjecting rage
To the cool dictates of experienc d age.
Thou, King of Men, stretch not thy sov-
   ereign sway
Beyond the bounds free subjects can obey;
But let Pelides in his prize rejoice,   391
Achiev'd in arms, allow'd by public voice.
Nor thou, brave champion, with his power
   contend,
Before whose throne ev'n kings their lower'd
   scepters bend:
The head of action he, and thou the hand;
Matchless thy force, but mightier his com-
   mand.
Thou first, O king, release the rights of
   sway;
Pow'r, self-restrain'd, the people best obey.
Sanctions of law from thee derive their
   source;
Command thyself, whom no commands can
   force.   400
The son of Thetis, rampire of our host,
Is worth our care to keep; nor shall my
   pray'rs be lost.''
   Thus Nestor said, and ceas'd: Atrides
   broke
His silence next; but ponder'd ere he spoke:
" Wise are thy words, and glad I would obey,
But this proud man affects imperial sway:
Controlling kings, and trampling on our
   state,
His will is law; and what he wills is fate.
The gods have giv'n him strength; but
   whence the style
Of lawless pow'r assum'd, or license to re-
   vile ? ''   410
   Achilles cut him short, and thus replied:
" My worth allow'd in words, is in effect de-
   nied.
For who but a poltron, possess'd with fear,
Such haughty insolence can tamely bear ?
Command thy slaves: my freeborn soul dis-
   dains
A tyrant's curb, and restiff breaks the
   reins.
Take this along, that no dispute shall rise
(Tho' mine the woman) for my ravish'd
   prize;

But, she excepted, as unworthy strife,
Dare not, I charge thee dare not, on thy
   life,   420
Touch aught of mine beside, by lot my due,
But stand aloof, and think profane to view:
This fauchion, else, not hitherto withstood,
These hostile fields shall fatten with thy
   blood.''
   He said, and rose the first; the council
   broke,
And all their grave consults dissolv'd in
   smoke.
The royal youth retir'd, on vengeance
   bent;
Patroclus follow'd silent to his tent.
   Meantime, the king with gifts a vessel
   stores;
Supplies the banks with twenty chosen oars;
And next, to reconcile the shooter god,   431
Within her hollow sides the sacrifice he
   stow'd.
Chryseis last was set on board; whose hand ⎫
Ulysses took, intrusted with command :   ⎬
They plow the liquid seas, and leave the   ⎭
   less'ning land.
   Atrides then, his outward zeal to boast,
Bade purify the sin-polluted host.
With perfect hecatombs the god they grac'd;
Whose offer'd entrails in the main were
   cast.   439
Black bulls and bearded goats on altars lie,
And clouds of sav'ry stench involve the
   sky.
These pomps the royal hypocrite design'd
For shew, but harbor'd vengeance in his
   mind;
Till holy malice, longing for a vent,
At length discover'd his conceal'd intent.
Talthybius, and Eurybates the just,
Heralds of arms, and ministers of trust,
He call'd, and thus bespoke: " Haste hence
   your way,
And from the goddess-born demand his prey.
If yielded, bring the captive; if denied, 450
The king (so tell him) shall chastise his
   pride,
And with arm'd multitudes in person come
To vindicate his pow'r, and justify his
   doom.''
   This hard command unwilling they ⎫
      obey,   ⎬
And o'er the barren shore pursue their ⎬
      way,   ⎭
Where quarter'd in their camp the fierce
   Thessalians lay.

Their sov'reign seated on his chair they
find,
His pensive cheek upon his hand reclin'd,
And anxious thoughts revolving in his
mind.
With gloomy looks he saw them ent'r-
ing in   460
Without salute; nor durst they first be-
gin,
Fearful of rash offense and death foreseen.
He soon, the cause divining, clear'd his brow,
And thus did liberty of speech allow:
" Interpreters of gods and men, be bold;
Awful your character, and uncontroll'd:
Howe'er unpleasing be the news you bring,
I blame not you, but your imperious king.
You come, I know, my captive to demand;
Patroclus, give her to the herald's hand. 470
But you authentic witnesses I bring,
Before the gods and your ungrateful king,
Of this my manifest: that never more
This hand shall combat on the crooked
shore:
No, let the Grecian pow'rs, oppress'd in
fight,
Unpitied perish in their tyrant's sight.
Blind of the future, and by rage misled,
He pulls his crimes upon his people's head;
Forc'd from the field in trenches to contend,
And his insulted camp from foes defend."
He said, and soon, obeying his intent, 481
Patroclus brought Briseis from her tent;
Then to th' intrusted messengers resign'd.
She wept, and often cast her eyes behind;
Forc'd from the man she lov'd: they led her
thence
Along the shore, a pris'ner to their prince.
Sole on the barren sands the suff'ring
chief
Roar'd out for anguish, and indulg'd his
grief;
Cast on his kindred seas a stormy look,
And his upbraided mother thus bespoke: 490
" Unhappy parent of a short-liv'd son,
Since Jove in pity by thy pray'rs was won
To grace my small remains of breath with
fame,
Why loads he this imbitter'd life with
shame,
Suff'ring his King of Men to force my slave,
Whom, well deserv'd in war, the Grecians
gave ? "
Set by old Ocean's side, the goddess heard;
Then from the sacred deep her head she
rear'd;

Rose like a morning mist, and thus begun
To soothe the sorrows of her plaintive son:
" Why cries my care, and why conceals his
smart ?   501
Let thy afflicted parent share her part."
Then, sighing from the bottom of his
breast,
To the sea goddess thus the goddess-born
address'd:
" Thou know'st my pain, which telling but
recalls:
By force of arms we raz'd the Theban
walls;
The ransack'd city, taken by our toils,
We left, and hither brought the golden
spoils:
Equal we shar'd them; but, before the rest,
The proud prerogative had seiz'd the best. 510
Chryseis was the greedy tyrant's prize,
Chryseis, rosy-cheek'd, with charming eyes.
Her sire, Apollo's priest, arriv'd to buy,
With proffer'd gifts of price, his daughter's
liberty.
Suppliant before the Grecians' chiefs he
stood,
Awful, and arm'd with ensigns of his god:
Bare was his hoary head, one holy hand
Held forth his laurel crown, and one, his
scepter of command.
His suit was common, but above the rest 519
To both the brother princes was address'd.
With shouts of loud acclaim the Greeks
agree
To take the gifts, to set the pris'ner free.
Not so the tyrant, who with scorn the priest
Receiv'd, and with opprobrious words dis-
miss'd.
The good old man, forlorn of human aid,
For vengeance to his heav'nly patron
pray'd:
The godhead gave a favorable ear,
And granted all to him he held so dear;
In an ill hour his piercing shafts he sped;
And heaps on heaps of slaughter'd Greeks
lay dead,   530
While round the camp he rang'd. At length
arose
A seer who well divin'd, and durst disclose
The source of all our ills: I took the word,
And urg'd the sacred slave to be restor'd,
The god appeas'd; the swelling monarch
storm'd,
And then the vengeance vow'd, he since
perform'd.
The Greeks, 't is true, their ruin to prevent

Have to the royal priest his daughter sent;
But from their haughty king his heralds
    came,
And seiz'd, by his command, my captive
    dame,   540
By common suffrage given; but, thou, be
    won,
If in thy pow'r, t' avenge thy injur'd son;
Ascend the skies, and supplicating move
Thy just complaint to cloud-compelling
    Jove.
If thou by either word or deed hast wrought
A kind remembrance in his grateful thought,
Urge him by that; for often hast thou said
Thy pow'r was once not useless in his aid.
When he, who high above the highest
    reigns,
Surpris'd by traitor gods, was bound in
    chains;   550
When Juno, Pallas, with ambition fir'd,
And his blue brother of the seas conspir'd,
Thou freed'st the sovereign from unworthy
    bands;
Thou brought'st Briareus with his hundred
    hands,
(So call'd in heav'n, but mortal men below
By his terrestrial name Ægeon know:
Twice stronger than his sire, who sate
    above,
Assessor to the throne of thund'ring Jove.)
The gods, dismay'd at his approach, with-
    drew,
Nor durst their unaccomplish'd crime pur-
    sue.   560
That action to his grateful mind recall:
Embrace his knees, and at his footstool fall;
That now, if ever, he will aid our foes;
Let Troy's triumphant troops the camp in-
    close:
Ours, beaten to the shore, the siege forsake,
And what their king deserves with him par-
    take;
That the proud tyrant, at his proper cost,
May learn the value of the man he lost."
    To whom the mother goddess thus re-
    plied,
Sigh'd ere she spoke, and while she spoke
    she cried: 570
" Ah wretched me ! by fates averse decreed
To bring thee forth with pain, with care to
    breed !
Did envious Heav'n not otherwise ordain, ⎫
Safe in thy hollow ships thou shouldst ⎬
    remain, ⎟
Nor ever tempt the fatal field again. ⎭

But now thy planet sheds his pois'nous rays,
And short and full of sorrow are thy days.
For what remains, to heav'n I will ascend,
And at the Thund'rer's throne thy suit com-
    mend.
Till then, secure in ships, abstain from fight;
Indulge thy grief in tears, and vent thy
    spite;   581
For yesterday the court of heav'n with
    Jove
Remov'd: 't is dead vacation now above.
Twelve days the gods their solemn revels
    keep,
And quaff with blameless Ethiops in the
    deep.
Return'd from thence, to heav'n my flight
    I take,
Knock at the brazen gates, and Providence
    awake;
Embrace his knees; and, suppliant to the
    sire,
Doubt not I will obtain the grant of thy
    desire."
    She said; and, parting, left him on the
    place,   590
Swoln with disdain, resenting his disgrace:
Revengeful thoughts revolving in his mind,
He wept for anger, and for love he pin'd.
    Meantime with prosperous gales Ulysses
    brought
The slave, and ship with sacrifices fraught,
To Chrysa's port: where, ent'ring with the
    tide,
He dropp'd his anchors, and his oars he
    plied;
Furl'd every sail, and, drawing down the
    mast,
His vessel moor'd, and made with haulsers
    fast.   599
Descending on the plain, ashore they bring
The hecatomb to please the shooter king.
The dame before an altar's holy fire
Ulysses led, and thus bespoke her sire:
    " Reverenc'd be thou, and be thy god
    ador'd:
The King of Men thy daughter has re-
    stor'd,
And sent by me with presents and with
    pray'r.
He recommends him to thy pious care;
That Phœbus at thy suit his wrath may
    cease,
And give the penitent offenders peace."
    He said, and gave her to her father's
    hands,   610

Who glad receiv'd her, free from servile
   bands.
This done, in order they, with sober grace,
Their gifts around the well-built altar place;
Then wash'd, and took the cakes; while
   Chryses stood
With hands upheld, and thus invok'd his
   god:
"God of the silver bow, whose eyes
   survey
The sacred Cilla; thou, whose awful sway
Chrysa the blest and Tenedos obey:
Now hear, as thou before my pray'r hast
   heard,
Against the Grecians and their prince pre-
   ferr'd.   620
Once thou hast honor'd, honor once again
Thy priest, nor let his second vows be vain;
But from th' afflicted host and humbled
   prince
Avert thy wrath, and cease thy pestilence."
Apollo heard, and, conquering his disdain,
Unbent his bow, and Greece respir'd again.
   Now when the solemn rites of pray'r were
   past,
Their salted cakes on crackling flames they
   cast;
Then, turning back, the sacrifice they sped;
The fatted oxen slew, and flay'd the dead;
Chopp'd off their nervous thighs, and next
   prepar'd   631
T' involve the lean in cauls, and mend with
   lard.
Sweetbreads and collops were with skewers
   prick'd
About the sides, inbibing what they deck'd.
The priest with holy hands was seen to tine
The cloven wood and pour the ruddy wine.
The youth approach'd the fire, and, as it
   burn'd,
On five sharp broachers rank'd, the roast
   they turn'd:
These morsels stay'd their stomachs; then
   the rest
They cut in legs and fillets for the feast; 640
Which drawn and serv'd, their hunger they
   appease
With sav'ry meat, and set their minds at
   ease.
Now when the rage of eating was repell'd,
The boys with generous wine the goblets
   fill'd.
The first libations to the gods they pour,
And then with songs indulge the genial hour.
Holy debauch! till day to night they bring,

With hymns and pæans to the bowyer king.
At sunset to their ship they make return,
And snore secure on decks till rosy morn.
   The skies with dawning day were purpled
   o'er;   651
Awak'd, with lab'ring oars they leave the
   shore:
The pow'r, appeas'd, with winds suffic'd the
   sail;
The bellying canvas strutted with the gale;
The waves indignant roar with surly pride,
And press against the sides, and beaten off
   divide.
They cut the foamy way, with force impell'd
Superior, till the Trojan port they held;
Then, hauling on the strand, their galley
   moor,
And pitch their tents along the crooked
   shore.   660
   Meantime the goddess-born in secret
   pin'd:
Nor visited the camp, nor in the council
   join'd;
But, keeping close, his gnawing heart he fed
With hopes of vengeance on the tyrant's
   head;
And wish'd for bloody wars and mortal
   wounds,
And of the Greeks oppress'd in fight to hear
   the dying sounds.
   Now, when twelve days complete had run
   their race,
The gods bethought them of the cares
   belonging to their place.
Jove at their head ascending from the sea,
A shoal of puny pow'rs attend his way. 670
Then Thetis, not unmindful of her son,
Emerging from the deep, to beg her boon,
Pursued their track; and, waken'd from his
   rest,
Before the sovereign stood a morning guest.
Him in the circle, but apart, she found;
The rest at awful distance stood around.
She bow'd, and ere she durst her suit begin,
One hand embrac'd his knees, one propp'd
   his chin.
Then thus: "If I, celestial sire, in aught
Have serv'd thy will, or gratified thy
   thought,   680
One glimpse of glory to my issue give,
Grac'd for the little time he has to live.
Dishonor'd by the King of Men he stands;
His rightful prize is ravish'd from his hands.
But thou, O father, in my son's defense,
Assume thy pow'r, assert thy providence.

Let Troy prevail, till Greece th' affront has
   paid
With doubled honors, and redeem'd his aid."
   She ceas'd, but the consid'ring god was
     mute: 689
Till she, resolv'd to win, renew'd her suit;
Nor loos'd her hold, but forc'd him to reply:
"Or grant me my petition, or deny.
Jove cannot fear: then tell me to my face
That I, of all the gods, am least in grace.
This I can bear." The Cloud-Compeller
   mourn'd,
And, sighing first, this answer he return'd:
"Know'st thou what clamors will disturb
   my reign,
What my stunn'd ears from Juno must sus-
   tain?
In council she gives license to her tongue,
Loquacious, brawling, ever in the wrong. 700
And now she will my partial pow'r upbraid,
If, alienate from Greece, I give the Trojans
   aid.
But thou depart, and shun her jealous sight;
The care be mine to do Pelides right.
Go then, and on the faith of Jove rely;
When, nodding to thy suit, he bows the sky.
This ratifies th' irrevocable doom:
The sign ordain'd, that what I will shall
   come;
The stamp of heav'n, and seal of fate." He
   said,
And shook the sacred honors of his head. 710
With terror trembled heav'n's subsiding
   hill,
And from his shaken curls ambrosial dews
   distil;
The goddess goes exulting from his sight,
And seeks the seas profound, and leaves the
   realms of light.
   He moves into his hall: the pow'rs resort,
Each from his house, to fill the sovereign's
   court.
Nor waiting summons, nor expecting stood;
But met with reverence, and receiv'd the
   god.
He mounts the throne; and Juno took her
   place;
But sullen discontent sate low'ring on her
   face.   720
With jealous eyes, at distance she had seen,
Whisp'ring with Jove, the silver-footed
   queen;
Then, impotent of tongue, (her silence
   broke,)
Thus turbulent in rattling tone she spoke:

"Author of ills, and close contriver Jove,
Which of thy dames, what prostitute of love,
Has held thy ear so long, and begg'd so hard,
For some old service done, some new
   reward?
Apart you talk'd, for that 's your special
   care;   729
The consort never must the council share.
One gracious word is for a wife too much:
Such is a marriage vow, and Jove's own
   faith is such."
   Then thus the sire of gods, and men
   below:
"What I have hidden, hope not thou to
   know.
Ev'n goddesses are women; and no wife
Has pow'r to regulate her husband's life:
Counsel she may; and I will give thy ear
The knowledge first, of what is fit to hear.
What I transact with others, or alone,
Beware to learn; nor press too near the
   throne."   740
   To whom the goddess with the charming
   eyes:
"What hast thou said, O tyrant of the
   skies?
When did I search the secrets of thy reign,
Tho' privileg'd to know, but privileg'd in
   vain?
But well thou dost, to hide from common
   sight
Thy close intrigues, too bad to bear the
   light.
Nor doubt I but the silver-footed dame,
Tripping from sea, on such an errand came,
To grace her issue, at the Grecians' cost,
And for one peevish man destroy an host."
   To whom the Thund'rer made this stern
   reply: 751
"My household curse, my lawful plague,
   the spy
Of Jove's designs, his other squinting
   eye;
Why this vain prying, and for what avail?
Jove will be master still, and Juno fail.
Should thy suspicious thoughts divine aright,
Thou but becom'st more odious to my sight
For this attempt: uneasy life to me,
Still watch'd and importun'd, but worse
   for thee.
Curb that impetuous tongue, before too
   late   760
The gods behold, and tremble at thy fate;
Pitying, but daring not, in thy defense,
To lift a hand against omnipotence."

This heard, the imperious queen sate
mute with fear,
Nor further durst incense the gloomy
Thunderer.
Silence was in the court at this rebuke,
Nor could the gods abash'd sustain their
sov'reign's look.
The limping smith observ'd the sadden'd
feast,
And hopping here and there (himself a
jest)   769
Put in his word, that neither might offend;
To Jove obsequious, yet his mother's friend:
" What end in heav'n will be of civil war,
If gods of pleasure will for mortals jar ?
Such discord but disturbs our jovial feast;
One grain of bad embitters all the best.
Mother, tho' wise yourself, my counsel
weigh;
'T is much unsafe my sire to disobey.
Not only you provoke him to your cost,
But mirth is marr'd, and the good cheer is
lost.
Tempt not his heavy hand, for he has
pow'r   780
To throw you headlong from his heav'nly
tow'r.
But one submissive word, which you let
fall,
Will make him in good humor with us
all."
   He said no more, but crown'd a bowl,
unbid;
The laughing nectar overlook'd the lid:
Then put it to her hand, and thus pursued:
" This cursed quarrel be no more renew'd.
Be, as becomes a wife, obedient still;
Tho' griev'd, yet subject to her husband's
will.
I would not see you beaten; yet afraid   790
Of Jove's superior force, I dare not aid.
Too well I know him, since that hapless
hour
When I and all the gods employ'd our
pow'r
To break your bonds: me by the heel he
drew,
And o'er heav'n's battlements with fury
threw:
All day I fell; my flight at morn begun,
And ended not but with the setting sun.
Pitch'd on my head, at length the Lemnian
ground
Receiv'd my batter'd skull, the Sinthians
heal'd my wound."

At Vulcan's homely mirth his mother
smil'd,   800
And smiling took the cup the clown had
fill'd.
The reconciler bowl went round the board,
Which, emptied, the rude skinker still re-
stor'd.
Loud fits of laughter seiz'd the guests, to
see
The limping god so deft at his new ministry.
The feast continued till declining light;
They drank, they laugh'd, they lov'd, and
then 't was night.
Nor wanted tuneful harp, nor vocal choir;
The Muses sung; Apollo touch'd the lyre.
Drunken at last, and drowsy they depart,
Each to his house, adorn'd with labor'd
art   811
Of the lame architect: the thund'ring god —
Ev'n he withdrew to rest, and had his load;
His swimming head to needful sleep ap-
plied,
And Juno lay unheeded by his side.

THE COCK AND THE FOX

OR, THE TALE OF THE NUN'S PRIEST

FROM CHAUCER

THERE liv'd, as authors tell, in days of yore,
A widow somewhat old, and very poor:
Deep in a dell her cottage lonely stood,
Well thatch'd, and under covert of a wood.
   This dowager, on whom my tale I found,
Since last she laid her husband in the
ground,
A simple sober life in patience led,
And had but just enough to buy her bread:
But huswifing the little Heav'n had lent,
She duly paid a groat for quarter rent;   10
And pinch'd her belly, with her daughters
two,
To bring the year about with much ado.
   The cattle in her homestead were three
sows,
An ewe call'd Mally, and three brinded
cows;
Her parlor window stuck with herbs
around,
Of sav'ry smell; and rushes strew'd the
ground.
A maple dresser in her hall she had,
On which full many a slender meal sne
made:

For no delicious morsel pass'd her throat;
According to her cloth she cut her coat. 20
No poynant sauce she knew, no costly treat;
Her hunger gave a relish to her meat:
A sparing diet did her health assure;
Or sick, a pepper posset was her cure.
Before the day was done, her work she
    sped,
And never went by candlelight to bed.
With exercise she sweat ill humors out;
Her dancing was not hinder'd by the gout.
Her poverty was glad, her heart content,
Nor knew she what the spleen or vapors
    meant. 30
    Of wine she never tasted thro' the year,
But white and black was all her homely
    cheer:
Brown bread, and milk, (but first she
    skimm'd her bowls,)
And rashers of sing'd bacon on the coals.
On holidays an egg, or two at most;
But her ambition never reach'd to roast.
    A yard she had, with pales enclos'd about,
Some high, some low, and a dry ditch with-
    out.
Within this homestead liv'd, without a peer
For crowing loud, the noble Chanticleer; 40
So hight her cock, whose singing did sur-
    pass
The merry notes of organs at the mass.
More certain was the crowing of the cock
To number hours, than is an abbey clock;
And sooner than the matin bell was rung,
He clapp'd his wings upon his roost, and
    sung:
For when degrees fifteen ascended right,
By sure instinct he knew 't was one at night.
High was his comb, and coral-red withal,
In dents embattled like a castle wall; 50
His bill was raven-black, and shone like
    jet;
Blue were his legs, and orient were his feet:
White were his nails, like silver to behold,
His body glitt'ring like the burnish'd gold.
    This gentle cock, for solace of his life,
Six misses had, beside his lawful wife;
Scandal, that spares no king, tho' ne'er so
    good,
Says they were all of his own flesh and
    blood,
His sisters both by sire and mother's side;
And sure their likeness show'd them near
    allied. 60
But make the worst, the monarch did no
    more,

Than all the Ptolemies had done before:
When incest is for int'rest of a nation,
'T is made no sin by holy dispensation.
Some lines have been maintain'd by this
    alone,
Which by their common ugliness are known.
    But passing this as from our tale apart,
Dame Partlet was the sovereign of his
    heart;
Ardent in love, outrageous in his play,
He feather'd her a hundred times a day: 70
And she, that was not only passing fair,
But was withal discreet and debonair,
Resolv'd the passive doctrine to fulfil,
Tho' loth; and let him work his wicked will:
At board and bed was affable and kind, ⎱
According as their marriage vow did bind, ⎬
And as the Church's precept had enjoin'd; ⎰
Ev'n since she was a sennight old, they ⎱
    say, ⎢
Was chaste and humble to her dying day, ⎬
Nor chick nor hen was known to disobey. ⎰
    By this her husband's heart she did ob-
        tain — 81
What cannot beauty, join'd with virtue,
    gain !
She was his only joy, and he her pride;
She, when he walk'd, went pecking by his
    side:
If, spurning up the ground, he sprung a
    corn,
The tribute in his bill to her was borne.
But O ! what joy it was to hear him sing
In summer, when the day began to spring,
Stretching his neck, and warbling in his
    throat;
Solus cum sola then was all his note. 90
For in the days of yore, the birds of parts
Were bred to speak, and sing, and learn
    the lib'ral arts.
    It happ'd that perching on the parlor
        beam,
Amidst his wives, he had a deadly dream,
Just at the dawn; and sigh'd, and groan'd
    so fast,
As ev'ry breath he drew would be his last.
Dame Partlet, ever nearest to his side,
Heard all his piteous moan, and how he
    cried
For help from gods and men; and, sore
    aghast,
She peck'd and pull'd, and waken'd him at
    last. 100
" Dear heart," said she, " for love of heav'n
    declare

Your pain, and make me partner of your
   care.
You groan, sir, ever since the morning light,
As something had disturb'd your noble
   sprite."
  " And, madam, well I might," said Chan-
   ticleer,
" Never was Shrovetide cock in such a fear.
Ev'n still I run all over in a sweat,
My princely senses not recover'd yet.
For such a dream I had of dire portent,
That much I fear my body will be shent: 110
It bodes I shall have wars and woful strife,
Or in a loathsome dungeon end my life.
Know, dame, I dreamt within my troubled ⎫
   breast,   ⎬
That in our yard I saw a murd'rous beast, ⎪
That on my body would have made arrest. ⎭
With waking eyes I ne'er beheld his fellow;
His color was betwixt a red and yellow:
Tipp'd was his tail, and both his pricking
   ears,
With black; and much unlike his other
   hairs;
The rest, in shape, a beagle's whelp through-
   out,   120
With broader forehead, and a sharper snout.
Deep in his front were sunk his glowing
   eyes,
That yet methinks I see him with surprise.
Reach out your hand, I drop with clammy
   sweat,
And lay it to my heart, and feel it beat."
  " Now fie for shame," quoth she, " by
   heav'n above,
Thou hast for ever lost thy lady's love;
No woman can endure a recreant knight;
He must be bold by day, and free by night.
Our sex desires a husband or a friend, 130
Who can our honor and his own defend;
Wise, hardy, secret, lib'ral of his purse;
A fool is nauseous, but a coward worse:
No bragging coxcomb, yet no baffled knight.
How dar'st thou talk of love, and dar'st not
   fight ?
How dar'st thou tell thy dame thou art
   afeard ?
Hast thou no manly heart, and hast a beard ?
  " If aught from fearful dreams may be
   divin'd,
They signify a cock of dunghill kind.
All dreams, as in old Galen I have read, 140
Are from repletion and complexion bred;
From rising fumes of indigested food,
And noxious humors that infect the blood:

And sure, my lord, if I can read aright,
These foolish fancies you have had to-night
Are certain symptoms (in the canting style)
Of boiling choler, and abounding bile;
This yellow gall that in your stomach floats
Ingenders all these visionary thoughts.
When choler overflows, then dreams are
   bred   150
Of flames, and all the family of red;
Red dragons and red beasts in sleep we
   view,
For humors are distinguish'd by their hue.
From hence we dream of wars and warlike
   things,
And wasps and hornets with their double
   wings.
  " Choler adust congeals our blood with
   fear;
Then black bulls toss us, and black devils
   tear.
In sanguine airy dreams aloft we bound,
With rheums oppress'd we sink in rivers
   drown'd.
  " More I could say, but thus conclude my
   theme,   160
The dominating humor makes the dream.
Cato was in his time accounted wise,
And he condemns them all for empty lies.
Take my advice, and when we fly to ⎫
   ground,   ⎬
With laxatives preserve your body sound, ⎪
And purge the peccant humors that ⎪
   abound.   ⎭
I should be loth to lay you on a bier;
And tho' there lives no 'pothecary near,
I dare for once prescribe for your disease,
And save long bills, and a damn'd doctor's
   fees.   170
  " Two sovereign herbs, which I by prac-
   tice know,
And both at hand, (for in our yard they
   grow,)
On peril of my soul shall rid you wholly
Of yellow choler, and of melancholy:
You must both purge and vomit; but obey,
And for the love of heav'n make no delay.
Since hot and dry in your complexion join,
Beware the sun when in a vernal sign;
For when he mounts exalted in the Ram,
If then he finds your body in a flame, 180
Replete with choler, I dare lay a groat,
A tertian ague is at least your lot.
Perhaps a fever (which the gods forefend !)
May bring your youth to some untimely end.
And therefore, sir, as you desire to live,

A day or two before your laxative,
Take just three worms, nor under nor above,
Because the gods unequal numbers love.
These digestives prepare you for your purge,
Of fumetery, centaury, and spurge;   190
And of ground-ivy add a leaf or two:
All which within our yard or garden grow.
Eat these, and be, my lord, of better cheer:
Your father's son was never born to fear."
    "Madam," quoth he, " gramercy for
        your care,
But Cato, whom you quoted, you may spare:
'T is true, a wise and worthy man he seems,
And (as you say) gave no belief to dreams;
But other men of more authority,
And, by th' immortal pow'rs, as wise as he,
Maintain, with sounder sense, that dreams
        forebode;   201
For Homer plainly says they come from
    God.
Nor Cato said it; but some modern fool,
Impos'd in Cato's name on boys at school.
    " Believe me, madam, morning dreams
        foreshow
Th' events of things, and future weal or
    woe:
Some truths are not by reason to be tried,
But we have sure experience for our guide.
An ancient author, equal with the best,
Relates this tale of dreams among the rest.
    " Two friends, or brothers, with devout
        intent,   211
On some far pilgrimage together went.
It happen'd so, that, when the sun was
    down,
They just arriv'd by twilight at a town.
That day had been the baiting of a bull;
'T was at a feast, and ev'ry inn so full,
That no void room in chamber, or on
    ground,
And but one sorry bed was to be found;
And that so little it would hold but one,
Tho' till this hour they never lay alone.   220
    " So were they forc'd to part; one stay'd
        behind,
His fellow sought what lodging he could
    find:
At last he found a stall where oxen stood,
And that he rather chose than lie abroad.
'T was in a farther yard without a door;
But, for his ease, well litter'd was the
    floor.
    " His fellow, who the narrow bed had
        kept,
Was weary, and without a rocker slept:

Supine he snor'd; but in the dead of night
He dreamt his friend appear'd before his
    sight,   230
Who, with a ghastly look and doleful cry,
Said: ' Help me, brother, or this night I
    die:
Arise, and help, before all help be vain,
Or in an ox's stall I shall be slain.'
    " Rous'd from his rest, he waken'd in a
        start,
Shiv'ring with horror, and with aching
    heart;
At length to cure himself by reason tries; ⎫
'T is but a dream, and what are dreams   ⎪
    but lies ?   ⎬
So thinking chang'd his side, and clos'd   ⎪
    his eyes.   ⎭
His dream returns; his friend appears ⎫
    again: 240   ⎪
' The murd'rers come; now help, or I am   ⎬
    slain: '   ⎪
'T was but a vision still, and visions are ⎪
    but vain.   ⎭
    " He dreamt the third; but now his friend
        appear'd
Pale, naked, pierc'd with wounds, with
    blood besmear'd:
' Thrice warn'd, awake,' said he; ' relief is
    late,
The deed is done; but thou revenge my
    fate:
Tardy of aid, unseal thy heavy eyes,
Awake, and with the dawning day arise;
Take to the western gate thy ready way,
For by that passage they my corpse con-
    vey.   250
My corpse is in a tumbril laid, among
The filth and ordure, and enclos'd with
    dung.
That cart arrest, and raise a common cry;
For sacred hunger of my gold I die:'
Then shew'd his grisly wounds; and last he
    drew
A piteous sigh, and took a long adieu.
    " The frighted friend arose by break of
        day,
And found the stall where late his fellow
    lay;
Then of his impious host enquiring more,
Was answer'd that his guest was gone be-
    fore: 260
' Mutt'ring he went,' said he, ' by morning
    light,
And much complain'd of his ill rest by
    night.'

This rais'd suspicion in the pilgrim's
    mind;
Because all hosts are of an evil kind,
And oft to share the spoil with robbers
    join'd.
  " His dream confirm'd his thought; with
    troubled look
Straight to the western gate his way he
    took;
There, as his dream foretold, a cart he
    found,
That carried compass forth to dung the
    ground.
This when the pilgrim saw, he stretch'd his
    throat,   270
And cried out murther, with a yelling note:
' My murther'd fellow in this cart lies dead;
Vengeance and justice on the villain's head!
You, magistrates, who sacred laws dis-
    pense,
On you I call to punish this offense.'
  " The word thus giv'n, within a little
    space,
The mob came roaring out, and throng'd
    the place.
All in a trice they cast the cart to ground,
And in the dung the murther'd body
    found;
Tho' breathless, warm, and reeking from
    the wound.   280
Good Heav'n, whose darling attribute we
    find
Is boundless grace, and mercy to mankind,
Abhors the cruel, and the deeds of night
By wondrous ways reveals in open light;
Murther may pass unpunish'd for a time,
But tardy justice will o'ertake the crime.
And oft a speedier pain the guilty feels;
The hue and cry of Heav'n pursues him at
    the heels,
Fresh from the fact; as, in the present
    case,   289
The criminals are seiz'd upon the place;
Carter and host confronted face to face.
Stiff in denial, as the law appoints,
On engines they distend their tortur'd
    joints:
So was confession forc'd, th' offense was
    known,
And public justice on th' offenders done.
  " Here may you see that visions are to
    dread;
And, in the page that follows this, I read
Of two young merchants, whom the hope
    of gain

Induc'd in partnership to cross the main:
Waiting till willing winds their sails sup-
    plied,   300
Within a trading town they long abide,
Full fairly situate on a haven's side.
  " One evening it befell, that, looking out,
The wind they long had wish'd was come
    about:
Well pleas'd they went to rest; and if the
    gale
Till morn continued, both resolv'd to sail.
But as together in a bed they lay,
The younger had a dream at break of day.
A man, he thought, stood frowning at
    his side,
Who warn'd him for his safety to pro-
    vide,   310
Nor put to sea, but safe on shore abide:
' I come, thy genius, to command thy
    stay;
Trust not the winds, for fatal is the day,
And death unhop'd attends the wat'ry
    way.'
  " The vision said; and vanish'd from his
    sight:
The dreamer waken'd in a mortal fright;
Then pull'd his drowsy neighbor, and de-
    clar'd
What in his slumber he had seen and heard.
His friend smil'd scornful, and with proud
    contempt
Rejects as idle what his fellow dreamt: 320
' Stay, who will stay; for me no fears re-
    strain,
Who follow Mercury the god of gain.
Let each man do as to his fancy seems;
I wait not, I, till you have better dreams.
Dreams are but interludes which fancy
    makes;
When monarch Reason sleeps, this mimic
    wakes;
Compounds a medley of disjointed things,
A mob of cobblers, and a court of kings.
Light fumes are merry, grosser fumes are
    sad;
Both are the reasonable soul run mad: 330
And many monstrous forms in sleep we see,
That neither were, nor are, nor e'er can be.
Sometimes forgotten things long cast be-
    hind
Rush forward in the brain, and come to
    mind.
The nurse's legends are for truths receiv'd,
And the man dreams but what the boy be-
    liev'd.

Sometimes we but rehearse a former
  play;
The night restores our actions done by
  day,
As hounds in sleep will open for their
  prey.
In short the farce of dreams is of a piece,
Chimeras all; and more absurd, or less: 341
You, who believe in tales, abide alone;
Whate'er I get this voyage is my own.'
  "Thus while he spoke, he heard the
    shouting crew
That call'd aboard, and took his last adieu.
The vessel went before a merry gale,
And for quick passage put on ev'ry sail;
But when least fear'd, and ev'n in open day,
The mischief overtook her in the way.
Whether she sprung a leak, I cannot find,
Or whether she was overset with wind, 351
Or that some rock below her bottom rent;
But down at once with all her crew she
  went:
Her fellow ships from far her loss descried;
But only she was sunk, and all were safe
  beside.
  " By this example you are taught again,
That dreams and visions are not always
  vain;
But if, dear Partlet, you are yet in doubt,
Another tale shall make the former out.
  "Kenelm, the son of Kenulph, Mercia's
    king,   360
Whose holy life the legends loudly sing,
Warn'd in a dream, his murther did fore-
  tell
From point to point as after it befell:
All circumstances to his nurse he told,
(A wonder from a child of sev'n years old.)
The dream with horror heard, the good old
  wife
From treason counsel'd him to guard his
  life,
But close to keep the secret in his mind,
For a boy's vision small belief would find.
The pious child, by promise bound, obey'd,
Nor was the fatal murther long delay'd: 371
By Quenda slain, he fell before his time,
Made a young martyr by his sister's crime.
The tale is told by Venerable Bede,
Which, at your better leisure, you may
  read.
  " Macrobius too relates the vision sent
To the great Scipio, with the fam'd event;
Objections makes, but after makes replies,
And adds that dreams are often prophecies.

  "Of Daniel you may read in holy
    writ,   380
Who, when the king his vision did forget,
Could word for word the wondrous dream
  repeat.
Nor less of patriarch Joseph understand,
Who by a dream inslav'd th' Egyptian land;
The years of plenty and of dearth foretold,
When, for their bread, their liberty they
  sold.
Nor must th' exalted butler be forgot,
Nor he whose dream presag'd his hanging
  lot.
  " And did not Croesus the same death
    foresee,
Rais'd in his vision on a lofty tree ? 390
The wife of Hector, in his utmost pride,
Dreamt of his death the night before he
  died;
Well was he warn'd from battle to re-
  frain,
But men to death decreed are warn'd in
  vain:
He dar'd the dream, and by his fatal foe
  was slain.
  " Much more I know, which I forbear to
    speak;
For, see, the ruddy day begins to break:
Let this suffice, that plainly I foresee
My dream was bad, and bodes adversity.
But neither pills nor laxatives I like; 400
They only serve to make a well man sick.
Of these his gain the sharp physician
  makes,
And often gives a purge, but seldom takes:
They not correct, but poison all the blood,
And ne'er did any but the doctors good.
Their tribe, trade, trinkets, I defy them
  all;
With ev'ry work of 'Pothecaries' Hall.
  " These melancholy matters I forbear;
But let me tell thee, Partlet mine, and
  swear,   409
That when I view the beauties of thy face,
I fear not death, nor dangers, nor disgrace:
So may my soul have bliss, as when I spy
The scarlet red about thy partridge eye,
While thou art constant to thy own true
  knight,
While thou art mine, and I am thy de-
  light,
All sorrows at thy presence take their
  flight.
For true it is, as *in principio*,
Mulier est hominis confusio.

Madam, the meaning of this Latin is,   419
That woman is to man his sovereign bliss.
For when by night I feel your tender side,
Tho' for the narrow perch I cannot ride,
Yet I have such a solace in my mind,
That all my boding cares are cast behind;
And ev'n already I forget my dream."
　He said, and downward flew from off the
　　beam,
For daylight now began apace to spring,
The thrush to whistle, and the lark to sing;
Then crowing clapp'd his wings, th' ap-
　　pointed call,
To chuck his wives together in the hall.   430
　By this the widow had unbarr'd the door,
And Chanticleer went strutting out before,
With royal courage, and with heart so light,
As shew'd he scorn'd the visions of the night.
Now, roaming in the yard, he spurn'd the
　　ground,
And gave to Partlet the first grain he found;
Then often feather'd her with wanton play,
And trod her twenty times ere prime of
　　day;
And took by turns and gave so much de-
　　light,
Her sisters pin'd with envy at the sight.   440
　He chuck'd again, when other corns he
　　found,
And scarcely deign'd to set a foot to ground,
But swagger'd like a lord about his hall,
And his sev'n wives came running at his
　　call.
　'T was now the month in which the world
　　began,
(If March beheld the first created man;)
And since the vernal equinox, the sun
In Aries twelve degrees, or more, had run;
When, casting up his eyes against the light,
Both month, and day, and hour he measur'd
　　right,   450
And told more truly than th' Ephemeris;
For art may err, but nature cannot miss.
　Thus numb'ring times and seasons in his
　　breast,
His second crowing the third hour confess'd.
Then turning, said to Partlet: "See, my
　　dear,
How lavish nature has adorn'd the year;
How the pale primrose and blue violet
　　spring,
And birds essay their throats disus'd to sing:
All these are ours; and I with pleasure
　　see   459
Man strutting on two legs, and aping me:

An unfledg'd creature, of a lumpish frame,
Indued with fewer particles of flame.
Our dame sits cow'ring o'er a kitchen fire;
I draw fresh air, and nature's works admire;
And ev'n this day in more delight abound,
Than, since I was an egg, I ever found."
　The time shall come when Chanticleer
　　shall wish
His words unsaid, and hate his boasted
　　bliss.
The crested bird shall by experience ⎫
　　know,   469 ⎪
Jove made not him his masterpiece below; ⎬
And learn the latter end of joy is woe.   ⎭
The vessel of his bliss to dregs is run,
And Heav'n will have him taste his other
　　tun.
　Ye wise, draw near, and hearken to my
　　tale,
Which proves that oft the proud by flatt'ry
　　fall:
The legend is as true, I undertake,
As *Tristram* is, and *Launcelot of the Lake*,
Which all our ladies in such rev'rence hold,
As if in *Book of Martyrs* it were told.   479
　A fox full-fraught with seeming sanctity,
That fear'd an oath, but, like the devil,
　　would lie;
Who look'd like Lent, and had the holy leer,
And durst not sin before he said his
　　pray'r —
This pious cheat, that never suck'd the ⎫
　　blood,   ⎪
Nor chaw'd the flesh of lambs, but when ⎬
　　he could,   ⎪
Had pass'd three summers in the neigh- ⎪
　　b'ring wood;   ⎭
And musing long, whom next to circum-
　　vent,
On Chanticleer his wicked fancy bent;
And in his high imagination cast,
By stratagem to gratify his taste.   490
　The plot contriv'd, before the break of
　　day,
Saint Reynard thro' the hedge had made
　　his way;
The pale was next, but proudly, with a
　　bound
He leapt the fence of the forbidden ground:
Yet fearing to be seen, within a bed
Of coleworts he conceal'd his wily head;
Then skulk'd till afternoon, and watch'd
　　his time,
(As murd'rers use,) to perpetrate his crime.
　O hypocrite, ingenious to destroy !

O traitor, worse than Sinon was to Troy! 500
O vile subverter of the Gallic reign,
More false than Gano was to Charlemagne !
O Chanticleer, in an unhappy hour
Didst thou forsake the safety of thy bow'r:
Better for thee thou hadst believ'd thy
    dream,
And not that day descended from the beam !
  But here the doctors eagerly dispute:
Some hold predestination absolute;
Some clerks maintain, that Heav'n at first
    foresees,
And in the virtue of foresight decrees.   510
If this be so, then prescience binds the
    will,
And mortals are not free to good or ill;
For what he first foresaw, he must ordain,
Or its eternal prescience may be vain:
As bad for us as prescience had not bin;
For first, or last, he 's author of the sin.
And who says that, let the blaspheming
    man
Say worse ev'n of the devil, if he can.
For how can that eternal pow'r be just, 519
To punish man, who sins because he must?
Or how can he reward a virtuous deed,
Which is not done by us, but first decreed ?
  I cannot bolt this matter to the bran,
As Bradwardin and holy Austin can;
If prescience can determine actions so
That we must do, because he did foreknow,
Or that foreknowing, yet our choice is free,
Not forc'd to sin by strict necessity.
This strict necessity they simple call;
Another sort there is, conditional.   530
The first so binds the will, that things fore-
    known
By spontaneity, not choice, are done.
Thus galley slaves tug willing at their ⎫
    oar,   ⎪
Consent to work, in prospect of the shore, ⎬
But would not work at all if not con-   ⎪
    strain'd before.   ⎭
That other does not liberty constrain,
But man may either act or may refrain.
Heav'n made us agents free to good or ill,
And forc'd it not, tho' he foresaw the will.
Freedom was first bestow'd on human
    race,   540
And prescience only held the second place.
  If he could make such agents wholly free,
I not dispute, the point 's too high for me;
For Heav'n's unfathom'd pow'r what man
    can sound,
Or put to his omnipotence a bound ?

He made us to his image all agree;   ⎫
That image is the soul, and that must be, ⎬
Or not the Maker's image, or be free.   ⎭
  But whether it were better man had been
By nature bound to good, not free to sin, 550
I waive, for fear of splitting on a rock.
The tale I tell is only of a cock,
Who had not run the hazard of his life,
Had he believ'd his dream, and not his wife:
For women, with a mischief to their kind,
Pervert with bad advice our better mind.
A woman's counsel brought us first to woe,
And made our man his Paradise forego,
Where at heart's ease he liv'd, and might
    have bin
As free from sorrow as he was from sin. 560
For what the devil had their sex to do,
That, born to folly, they presum'd to know,
And could not see the serpent in the grass ?
But I myself presume, and let it pass.
  Silence in times of suff'ring is the best;
'T is dang'rous to disturb a hornet's nest.
In other authors you may find enough,
But all they say of dames is idle stuff,
Legends of lying wits together bound —
The Wife of Bath would throw 'em to the
    ground.   570
These are the words of Chanticleer, not
    mine;
I honor dames, and think their sex divine.
  Now to continue what my tale begun.
Lay Madam Partlet basking in the sun,
Breast-high in sand; her sisters, in a row,
Enjoy'd the beams above, the warmth
    below.
The cock, that of his flesh was ever free,
Sung merrier than the mermaid in the sea.
And so befell, that as he cast his eye
Among the coleworts on a butterfly,   580
He saw false Reynard where he lay full low.
I need not swear he had no list to crow,
But cried: " Cock, cock," and gave a sud-
    den start,
As sore dismay'd and frighted at his heart.
For birds and beasts, inform'd by nature,
    know
Kinds opposite to theirs, and fly their foe.
So Chanticleer, who never saw a fox,
Yet shunn'd him as a sailor shuns the rocks.
  But the false loon, who could not work
    his will   589
By open force, employ'd his flatt'ring skill.
" I hope, my lord," said he, " I not offend;
Are you afraid of me, that am your friend ?
I were a beast indeed to do you wrong,

I, who have lov'd and honor'd you so long:
Stay, gentle sir, nor take a false alarm,
For on my soul I never meant you harm.
I come no spy, nor as a traitor press,
To learn the secrets of your soft recess —
Far be from Reynard so profane a thought —
But by the sweetness of your voice was
    brought: 600
For, as I bid my beads, by chance I heard
The song as of an angel in the yard;
A song that would have charm'd th' infernal
    gods,
And banish'd horror from the dark abodes:
Had Orpheus sung it in the nether sphere, ⎫
So much the hymn had pleas'd the   │
    tyrant's ear,   ⎬
The wife had been detain'd, to keep the │
    husband there.   ⎭
    "My lord, your sire familiarly I knew,
A peer deserving such a son as you:
He, with your lady mother, (whom Heav'n
    rest,)   610
Has often grac'd my house and been my
    guest.
To view his living features does me good,
For I am your poor neighbor in the wood;
And in my cottage should be proud to see
The worthy heir of my friend's family.
    "But since I speak of singing, let me say,
As with an upright heart I safely may,
That, save yourself, there breathes not on
    the ground
One like your father for a silver sound.
So sweetly would he wake the winter day,
That matrons to the church mistook their
    way,   621
And thought they heard the merry organ
    play.
And he to raise his voice with artful care,
(What will not beaux attempt to please the
    fair?)
On tiptoe stood to sing with greater strength,
And stretch'd his comely neck at all the
    length;
And while he pain'd his voice to pierce the
    skies,
As saints in raptures use, would shut his
    eyes,
That, the sound striving thro' the narrow
    throat,
His winking might avail to mend the note.
By this, in song, he never had his peer, 631
From sweet Cecilia down to Chanticleer;
Not Maro's Muse, who sung the mighty
    man,

Nor Pindar's heav'nly lyre, nor Horace
    when a swan.
Your ancestors proceed from race divine:
From Brennus and Belinus is your line;
Who gave to sov'reign Rome such loud
    alarms,
That ev'n the priests were not excus'd from
    arms.
    "Besides, a famous monk of modern times
Has left of cocks recorded in his rhymes, 640
That of a parish priest the son and heir,
(When sons of priests were from the prov-
    erb clear,)
Affronted once a cock of noble kind,
And either lam'd his legs or struck him
    blind;
For which the clerk his father was disgrac'd,
And in his benefice another plac'd.
Now sing, my lord, if not for love of me,
Yet for the sake of sweet Saint Charity;
Make hills, and dales, and earth, and heav'n
    rejoice,
And emulate your father's angel voice." 650
    The cock was pleas'd to hear him speak
    so fair,
And proud beside, as solar people are;
Nor could the treason from the truth descry,
So was he ravish'd with this flattery:
So much the more, as, from a little elf,
He had a high opinion of himself;
Tho' sickly, slender, and not large of limb,
Concluding all the world was made for him.
Ye princes, rais'd by poets to the gods,
And Alexander'd up in lying odes,   660
Believe not ev'ry flatt'ring knave's report,
There's many a Reynard lurking in the
    court;
And he shall be receiv'd with more regard,
And listen'd to, than modest truth is heard.
    This Chanticleer, of whom the story sings,
Stood high upon his toes, and clapp'd his
    wings;
Then stretch'd his neck, and wink'd with
    both his eyes,
Ambitious as he sought th' Olympic prize.
But while he pain'd himself to raise his
    note,
False Reynard rush'd, and caught him by
    the throat.   670
Then on his back he laid the precious load,
And sought his wonted shelter of the wood;
Swiftly he made his way, the mischief done,
Of all unheeded, and pursued by none.
    Alas, what stay is there in human state,
Or who can shun inevitable fate?

The doom was written, the decree was past,
Ere the foundations of the world were cast !
In Aries tho' the sun exalted stood,
His patron planet to procure his good;   680
Yet Saturn was his mortal foe, and he,
In Libra rais'd, oppos'd the same degree:
The rays both good and bad, of equal pow'r,
Each thwarting other, made a mingled hour.
　On Friday morn he dreamt this direful
　　dream,
Cross to the worthy native, in his scheme !
Ah blissful Venus, goddess of delight,
How couldst thou suffer thy devoted
　knight
On thy own day to fall by foe oppress'd,
The wight of all the world who serv'd thee
　best ?   690
Who, true to love, was all for recreation,
And minded not the work of propagation.
Gaufride, who couldst so well in rhyme
　complain
The death of Richard with an arrow slain,
Why had not I thy Muse, or thou my heart,
To sing this heavy dirge with equal art !
That I like thee on Friday might complain;
For on that day was Cœur de Lion slain.
　Not louder cries, when Ilium was in
　　flames,
Were sent to heav'n by woful Trojan
　dames,   700
When Pyrrhus toss'd on high his bur-⎤
　nish'd blade,   ⎪
And offer'd Priam to his father's shade, ⎬
Than for the cock the widow'd poultry   ⎪
　made.   ⎦
Fair Partlet first, when he was borne from
　sight,
With sovereign shrieks bewail'd her captive
　knight;
Far louder than the Carthaginian wife,
When Asdrubal her husband lost his life,
When she beheld the smold'ring flames as-
　cend,
And all the Punic glories at an end: 709
Willing into the fires she plung'd her head,
With greater ease than others seek their
　bed.
Not less aghast the matrons of renown,
When tyrant Nero burn'd th' imperial town,
Shriek'd for the downfall in a doleful cry,
For which their guiltless lords were doom'd
　to die.
　Now to my story I return again:
The trembling widow, and her daughters
　twain,

This woful cackling cry with horror heard,
Of those distracted damsels in the yard;
And starting up, beheld the heavy sight, 720
How Reynard to the forest took his flight,
And cross his back, as in triumphant scorn,
The hope and pillar of the house was borne.
　" The fox, the wicked fox," was all the
　　cry;
Out from his house ran ev'ry neighbor nigh.
The vicar first, and after him the crew,
With forks and staves the felon to pursue.
Ran Coll our dog, and Talbot with the
　band,
And Malkin, with her distaff in her hand;
Ran cow and calf, and family of hogs,   730
In panic horror of pursuing dogs;
With many a deadly grunt and doleful
　squeak,
Poor swine, as if their pretty hearts would
　break.
The shouts of men, the women in dismay,
With shrieks augment the terror of the day.
The ducks, that heard the proclamation
　cried,
And fear'd a persecution might betide,
Full twenty mile from town their voyage
　take,
Obscure in rushes of the liquid lake.
The geese fly o'er the barn; the bees in
　arms   740
Drive headlong from their waxen cells in
　swarms.
Jack Straw at London Stone, with all his
　rout,
Struck not the city with so loud a shout;
Not when with English hate they did pur-
　sue
A Frenchman or an unbelieving Jew;
Not when the welkin rung with "one and⎤
　all,"   ⎪
And echoes bounded back from Fox's hall: ⎬
Earth seem'd to sink beneath, and heav'n ⎪
　above to fall.   ⎦
With might and main they chas'd the mur-
　d'rous fox,
With brazen trumpets, and inflated box,   750
To kindle Mars with military sounds,
Nor wanted horns t' inspire sagacious
　hounds.
　But see how Fortune can confound the
　　wise,
And, when they least expect it, turn the dice.
The captive cock, who scarce could draw
　his breath,
And lay within the very jaws of death —

Yet in this agony his fancy wrought,
And fear supplied him with this happy
   thought:
" Yours is the prize, victorious prince," said
   he,
" The vicar my defeat, and all the village
   see.   760
Enjoy your friendly fortune while you may,
And bid the churls that envy you the prey
Call back their mungril curs, and cease ⎱
   their cry: ⎰
' See, fools, the shelter of the wood is nigh, ⎫
And Chanticleer in your despite shall die; ⎭
He shall be pluck'd and eaten to the bone.' "
  " 'T is well advis'd, in faith it shall be
   done; "
This Reynard said; but, as the word he
   spoke,
The pris'ner with a spring from prison
   broke;
Then stretch'd his feather'd fans with all
   his might,   770
And to the neighb'ring maple wing'd his
   flight.
   Whom when the traitor safe on tree be-
   held,
He curs'd the gods, with shame and sorrow
   fill'd;
Shame for his folly, sorrow out of time,
For plotting an unprofitable crime:
Yet mast'ring both, th' artificer of lies
Renews th' assault, and his last batt'ry tries.
  " Tho' I," said he, " did ne'er in thought
   offend,
How justly may my lord suspect his friend ?
Th' appearance is against me, I confess, 780
Who seemingly have put you in distress:
You, if your goodness does not plead my
   cause,
May think I broke all hospitable laws,
To bear you from your palace yard by
   might,
And put your noble person in a fright.
This, since you take it ill, I must repent,
Tho', Heav'n can witness, with no bad intent
I practic'd it, to make you taste your cheer
With double pleasure, first prepar'd by
   fear.   789
So loyal subjects often seize their prince, ⎫
Forc'd (for his good) to seeming violence, ⎬
Yet mean his sacred person not the least ⎭
   offense.
Descend; so help me Jove, as you shall find
That Reynard comes of no dissembling
   kind."

  " Nay," quoth the cock, " but I beshrew
   us both,
If I believe a saint upon his oath:
An honest man may take a knave's advice,
But idiots only will be cozen'd twice.
Once warn'd is well bewar'd; no flatt'ring ⎫
   lies   ⎪
Shall soothe me more to sing with wink- ⎬
   ing eyes,   800 ⎪
And open mouth, for fear of catching flies. ⎭
Who blindfold walks upon a river s brim,
When he should see, has he deserv'd to
   swim ? "
  " Better, sir cock, let all contention cease;
Come down," said Reynard, " let us treat
   of peace."
  " A peace with all my soul," said Chanti-
   cleer,
" But, with your favor, I will treat it here;
And, lest the truce with treason should be
   mix'd,
'T is my concern to have the tree betwixt."

THE MORAL

In this plain fable you th' effect may see 810
Of negligence and fond credulity:
And learn besides of flatt'rers to beware,
Then most pernicious when they speak too
   fair.
The cock and fox the fool and knave imply;
The truth is moral, tho' the tale a lie.
Who spoke in parables, I dare not say; ⎫
But sure he knew it was a pleasing way, ⎬
Sound sense, by plain example, to convey. ⎭
And in a heathen author we may find, ⎫
That pleasure with instruction should be ⎪
   join'd;   820 ⎬
So take the corn, and leave the chaff be- ⎪
   hind.   ⎭

THEODORE AND HONORIA

FROM BOCCACE

OF all the cities in Romanian lands,
The chief, and most renown'd, Ravenna
   stands,
Adorn'd in ancient times with arms and arts,
And rich inhabitants, with generous hearts.
But Theodore the brave, above the rest,
With gifts of fortune and of nature blest,
The foremost place for wealth and honor
   held,
And all in feats of chivalry excell'd.

This noble youth to madness lov'd a
  dame,
Of high degree; Honoria was her name; 10
Fair as the fairest, but of haughty mind,
And fiercer than became so soft a kind;
Proud of her birth, (for equal she had
  none,)
The rest she scorn'd, but hated him alone.
His gifts, his constant courtship, nothing
  gain'd;
For she, the more he lov'd, the more dis-
  dain'd.
He liv'd with all the pomp he could ⎫
  devise,   ⎪
At tilts and turnaments obtain'd the ⎬
  prize;   ⎪
But found no favor in his lady's eyes: ⎭
Relentless as a rock, the lofty maid   20
Turn'd all to poison that he did or said:
Nor pray'rs, nor tears, nor offer'd vows ⎫
  could move;   ⎪
The work went backward; and, the more ⎬
  he strove   ⎪
T' advance his suit, the farther from her ⎪
  love.   ⎭
  Wearied at length, and wanting remedy,
He doubted oft, and oft resolv'd to die;
But pride stood ready to prevent the blow,
For who would die to gratify a foe?
His generous mind disdain'd so mean a
  fate;
That pass'd, his next endeavor was to
  hate.   30
But vainer that relief than all the rest; ⎫
The less he hop'd, with more desire pos- ⎬
  sess'd;   ⎪
Love stood the siege, and would not ⎪
  yield his breast.   ⎭
  Change was the next, but change deceiv'd
  his care;
He sought a fairer, but found none so fair.
He would have worn her out by slow ⎫
  degrees,   ⎪
As men by fasting starve th' untam'd ⎬
  disease;   ⎪
But present love requir'd a present ease. ⎭
Looking he feeds alone his famish'd eyes,
Feeds ling'ring death, but, looking not, he
  dies.   40
Yet still he chose the longest way to fate,
Wasting at once his life and his estate.
  His friends beheld, and pitied him in
  vain,
For what advice can ease a lover's pain!
Absence, the best expedient they could find,

Might save the fortune, if not cure the
  mind:
This means they long propos'd, but little
  gain'd,
Yet after much pursuit at length obtain'd.
  Hard you may think it was to give con-
  sent,
But struggling with his own desires he
  went,   50
With large expense, and with a pompous ⎫
  train,   ⎪
Provided as to visit France or Spain, ⎬
Or for some distant voyage o'er the main. ⎭
But Love had clipp'd his wings, and cut him
  short,
Confin'd within the purlieus of his court.
Three miles he went, nor farther could
  retreat;
His travels ended at his country seat:
To Chassi's pleasing plains he took his way,
There pitch'd his tents, and there resolv'd
  to stay.
  The spring was in the prime; the neigh-
  b'ring grove   60
Supplied with birds, the choristers of love;
Music unbought, that minister'd delight
To morning walks, and lull'd his cares by
  night:
There he discharg'd his friends, but not th'
  expense
Of frequent treats, and proud magnifi-
  cence.
He liv'd as kings retire, tho' more at large
From public business, yet with equal
  charge;
With house and heart still open to receive;
As well content as love would give him
  leave:
He would have liv'd more free; but many
  a guest,   70
Who could forsake the friend, pursued the
  feast.
  It happ'd one morning, as his fancy led,
Before his usual hour he left his bed,
To walk within a lonely lawn, that stood
On ev'ry side surrounded by the wood.
Alone he walk'd, to please his pensive
  mind,
And sought the deepest solitude to find:
'T was in a grove of spreading pines he ⎫
  stray'd;   ⎪
The winds within the quiv'ring branches ⎬
  play'd,   ⎪
And dancing trees a mournful music ⎪
  made.   80   ⎭

The place itself was suiting to his care,
Uncouth and salvage as the cruel fair.
He wander'd on, unknowing where he went,
Lost in the wood, and all on love intent:
The day already half his race had run, ⎫
And summon'd him to due repast at noon, ⎪
But Love could feel no hunger but his ⎬
   own. ⎭
  Whilst list'ning to the murm'ring leaves
    he stood,
More than a mile immers'd within the
    wood,
At once the wind was laid; the whisp'ring
    sound   90
Was dumb; a rising earthquake rock'd the
    ground;
With deeper brown the grove was over- ⎫
    spread: ⎪
A sudden horror seiz'd his giddy head, ⎬
And his ears tinkled, and his color fled. ⎭
Nature was in alarm; some danger nigh
Seem'd threaten'd, tho' unseen to mortal
    eye.
Unus'd to fear, he summon'd all his soul,
And stood collected in himself, and whole;
Not long: for soon a whirlwind rose around,
And from afar he heard a screaming sound,
As of a dame distress'd, who cried for
    aid,   101
And fill'd with loud laments the secret
    shade.
  A thicket close beside the grove there
    stood,
With breers and brambles chok'd, and
    dwarfish wood;
From thence the noise, which now, approach-
    ing near,
With more distinguish'd notes invades his
    ear.
He rais'd his head, and saw a beauteous
    maid,
With hair dishevel'd, issuing thro' the
    shade;
Stripp'd of her clothes, and e'en those parts
    reveal'd,
Which modest Nature keeps from sight
    conceal'd.   110
Her face, her hands, her naked limbs were
    torn
With passing thro' the brakes and prickly
    thorn;
Two mastiffs gaunt and grim her flight
    pursued,
And oft their fasten'd fangs in blood
    embrued:

Oft they came up, and pinch'd her tender
    side,
"Mercy, O mercy, Heav'n," she ran, and
    cried;
When Heav'n was nam'd, they loos'd their
    hold again;
Then sprung she forth, they follow'd her
    amain.
  Not far behind, a knight of swarthy
    face,
High on a coal-black steed pursued the
    chase;   120
With flashing flames his ardent eyes were
    fill'd,
And in his hands a naked sword he held:
He cheer'd the dogs to follow her who fled,
And vow'd revenge on her devoted head.
  As Theodore was born of noble kind,
The brutal action rous'd his manly mind;
Mov'd with unworthy usage of the maid,
He, tho' unarm'd, resolv'd to give her aid.
A saplin pine he wrench'd from out the
    ground,
The readiest weapon that his fury found. 130
Thus furnish'd for offense, he cross'd the
    way
Betwixt the graceless villain and his prey.
  The knight came thund'ring on, but,
    from afar,
Thus in imperious tone forbade the war:
"Cease, Theodore, to proffer vain relief,
Nor stop the vengeance of so just a grief;
But give me leave to seize my destin'd
    prey,
And let eternal justice take the way:
I but revenge my fate, disdain'd, betray'd,
And suff'ring death for this ungrateful
    maid."   140
  He said, at once dismounting from the
    steed;
For now the hellhounds, with superior
    speed,
Had reach'd the dame, and, fast'ning on her
    side,
The ground with issuing streams of purple
    dyed.
Stood Theodore surpris'd in deadly fright,
With chatt'ring teeth, and bristling hair
    upright;
Yet arm'd with inborn worth: "Whate'er,"
    said he,
"Thou art, who know'st me better than I
    thee;
Or prove thy rightful cause, or be defied."
The specter, fiercely staring, thus replied:

"Know, Theodore, thy ancestry I claim,
And Guido Cavalcanti was my name.   152
One common sire our fathers did beget,
My name and story some remember yet:
Thee, then a boy. within my arms I laid,
When for my sins I lov'd this haughty
    maid;
Not less ador'd in life, nor serv'd by me,
Than proud Honoria now is lov'd by thee.
What did I not her stubborn heart to
    gain ?
But all my vows were answer'd with dis-
    dain: 160
She scorn'd my sorrows, and despis'd my
    pain.
Long time I dragg'd my days in fruitless
    care;
Then, loathing life, and plung'd in deep de-
    spair,
To finish my unhappy life, I fell
On this sharp sword, and now am damn'd
    in hell.
   "Short was her joy; for soon th' insult-
    ing maid
By Heav'n's decree in the cold grave was
    laid,
And, as in unrepenting sin she died,
Doom'd to the same bad place, is punish'd
    for her pride;   169
Because she deem'd I well deserv'd to die,
And made a merit of her cruelty.
There, then, we met; both tried and both
    were cast,
And this irrevocable sentence pass'd;
That she, whom I so long pursued in vain,
Should suffer from my hands a ling'ring
    pain:
Renew'd to life that she might daily die,
I daily doom'd to follow, she to fly.
No more a lover, but a mortal foe,
I seek her life (for love is none below):
As often as my dogs with better speed   180
Arrest her flight, is she to death decreed.
Then with this fatal sword, on which I died,
I pierce her open'd back, or tender side,
And tear that harden'd heart from out her
    breast,
Which, with her entrails, makes my hungry
    hounds a feast.
Nor lies she long, but, as her fates ordain,
Springs up to life, and fresh to second
    pain;
Is sav'd to-day, to-morrow to be slain."
   This, vers'd in death, th' infernal knight
    relates,

And then for proof fulfill'd their common
    fates;   190
Her heart and bowels thro' her back he
    drew,
And fed the hounds that help'd him to
    pursue.
Stern look'd the fiend, as frustrate of his
    will,
Not half suffic'd, and greedy yet to kill.
And now the soul, expiring thro' the
    wound,
Had left the body breathless on the
    ground,
When thus the grisly specter spoke again:
"Behold the fruit of ill-rewarded pain:
As many months as I sustain'd her hate,
So many years is she condemn'd by fate   200
To daily death; and ev'ry several place
Conscious of her disdain, and my disgrace,
Must witness her just punishment, and be
A scene of triumph and revenge to me.
As in this grove I took my last farewell,
As on this very spot of earth I fell,
As Friday saw me die, so she my prey
Becomes ev'n here, on this revolving day."
   Thus while he spoke, the virgin from the
    ground   209
Upstarted fresh, already clos'd the wound,
And, unconcern'd for all she felt before,
Precipitates her flight along the shore.
The hellhounds, as ungorg'd with flesh and
    blood,
Pursue their prey, and seek their wonted
    food;
The fiend remounts his courser, mends his
    pace,
And all the vision vanish'd from the place.
   Long stood the noble youth oppress'd
    with awe,
And stupid at the wondrous things he
    saw,
Surpassing common faith, transgressing
    nature's law.
He would have been asleep, and wish'd to
    wake,   220
But dreams, he knew, no long impression
    make,
Tho' strong at first; if vision, to what
    end,
But such as must his future state portend,
His love the damsel, and himself the
    fiend ?
But yet reflecting that it could not be
From Heav'n, which cannot impious acts
    decree,

Resolv'd within himself to shun the snare
Which Hell for his destruction did prepare;
And, as his better genius should direct,
From an ill cause to draw a good effect. 230
   Inspir'd from Heav'n, he homeward took
     his way,
Nor pall'd his new design with long delay;
But of his train a trusty servant sent,
To call his friends together at his tent.
They came, and, usual salutations paid,
With words premeditated thus he said:
" What you have often counsel'd, to remove
My vain pursuit of unregarded love,
By thrift my sinking fortune to repair,
Tho' late, yet is at last become my care: 240
My heart shall be my own; my vast
    expense
Reduc'd to bounds, by timely providence.
This only I require; invite for me
Honoria, with her father's family,
Her friends, and mine; the cause I shall
    display,
On Friday next, for that's th' appointed
    day."
   Well pleas'd were all his friends, the
    task was light;
The father, mother, daughter, they invite;
Hardly the dame was drawn to this repast;
But yet resolv'd, because it was the last. 250
The day was come, the guests invited
    came,
And, with the rest, th' inexorable dame;
A feast prepar'd with riotous expense,
Much cost, more care, and most magnifi-
    cence.
The place ordain'd was in that haunted
    grove
Where the revenging ghost pursued his
    love;
The tables in a proud pavilion spread,
With flow'rs below, and tissue overhead:
The rest in rank; Honoria, chief in place, ⎤
Was artfully contriv'd to set her face 260 ⎟
To front the thicket, and behold the ⎬
    chase. ⎦
The feast was serv'd, the time so well fore-
    cast,
That just when the dessert and fruits were
    plac'd,
The fiend's alarm began; the hollow ⎤
    sound ⎟
Sung in the leaves, the forest shook ⎬
    around, ⎟
Air blacken'd, roll'd the thunder, groan'd ⎦
    the ground.

   Nor long before the loud laments arise
Of one distress'd, and mastiffs' mingled cries;
And first the dame came rushing thro' ⎤
    the wood, ⎟
And next the famish'd hounds that sought ⎬
    their food, 270 ⎟
And grip'd her flanks, and oft essay'd ⎟
    their jaws in blood. ⎦
Last came the felon, on the sable steed,
Arm'd with his naked sword, and urg'd his
    dogs to speed.
She ran, and cried; her flight directly bent ⎤
 (A guest unbidden) to the fatal tent, ⎟
The scene of death, and place ordain'd ⎬
    for punishment. ⎦
Loud was the noise, aghast was every guest;
The women shriek'd, the men forsook the
    feast;
The hounds at nearer distance hoarsely ⎤
    bay'd; ⎟
The hunter close pursued the visionary ⎬
    maid; 280 ⎟
She rent the heav'n with loud laments, ⎦
    imploring aid.
   The gallants, to protect the lady's ⎤
    right, ⎟
Their fauchions brandish'd at the grisly ⎬
    sprite; ⎟
High on his stirrups he provok'd the ⎦
    fight.
Then on the crowd he cast a furious look,
And wither'd all their strength before he
    strook:
" Back, on your lives! let be," said he, " my
    prey,
And let my vengeance take the destin'd way.
Vain are your arms, and vainer your
    defense,
Against th' eternal doom of Providence: 290
Mine is th' ungrateful maid by Heav'n
    design'd;
Mercy she would not give, nor mercy shall
    she find."
At this the former tale again he told
With thund'ring tone, and dreadful to be-
    hold.
Sunk were their hearts with horror of the
    crime,
Nor needed to be warn'd a second time,
But bore each other back: some knew the ⎤
    face, ⎟
And all had heard the much lamented ⎬
    case ⎟
Of him who fell for love, and this the ⎦
    fatal place. 299

And now th' infernal minister advanc'd,
Seiz'd the due victim, and with fury launch'd
Her back, and, piercing thro' her inmost
    heart,
Drew backward as before th' offending
    part.
The reeking entrails next he tore away,
And to his meager mastiffs made a prey.
The pale assistants on each other star'd,
With gaping mouths for issuing words pre-
    par'd;
The stillborn sounds upon the palate hung,
And died imperfect on the falt'ring tongue.
The fright was general; but the female
    band   310
(A helpless train) in more confusion stand:
With horror shudd'ring, on a heap they ⎤
    run, |
Sick at the sight of hateful justice done; ⎬
For conscience rung th' alarm, and made |
    the case their own.   ⎦
So spread upon a lake, with upward eye,
A plump of fowl behold their foe on high;
They close their trembling troop, and all
    attend
On whom the sousing eagle will descend.
  But most the proud Honoria fear'd th'
    event,
And thought to her alone the vision sent. 320
Her guilt presents to her distracted mind ⎤
Heav'n's justice, Theodore's revengeful |
    kind,   ⎬
And the same fate to the same sin |
    assign'd —   ⎦
Already sees herself the monster's prey,
And feels her heart and entrails torn away.
'T was a mute scene of sorrow, mix'd with
    fear;
Still on the table lay th' unfinish'd cheer:
The knight and hungry mastiffs stood
    around,
The mangled dame lay breathless on the
    ground: 329
When on a sudden, reinspir'd with breath,
Again she rose, again to suffer death;
Nor stay'd the hellhounds, nor the hunter
    stay'd,
But follow'd, as before, the flying maid;
Th' avenger took from earth th' avenging
    sword,
And mounting light as air his sable steed
    he spurr'd:
The clouds dispell'd, the sky resum'd her
    light,
And Nature stood recover'd of her fright.

But fear, the last of ills, remain'd behind,
And horror heavy sat on ev'ry mind.
Nor Theodore incourag'd more his feast, 340
But sternly look'd, as hatching in his breast
Some deep design; which when Honoria
    view'd,
The fresh impulse her former fright re-
    new'd:
She thought herself the trembling dame
    who fled,
And him the grisly ghost that spurr'd th'
    infernal steed;
The more dismay'd, for when the guests ⎤
    withdrew, |
Their courteous host, saluting all the crew, ⎬
Regardless pass'd her o'er, nor grac'd |
    with kind adieu.   ⎦
That sting infix'd within her haughty ⎤
    mind, |
The downfall of her empire she divin'd; ⎬
And her proud heart with secret sorrow |
    pin'd.   351 ⎦
Home as they went, the sad discourse ⎤
    renew'd, |
Of the relentless dame to death pursued, ⎬
And of the sight obscene so lately view'd. ⎦
None durst arraign the righteous doom she
    bore;
Ev'n they who pitied most, yet blam'd her
    more:
The parallel they needed not to name,
But in the dead they damn'd the living
    dame.
  At ev'ry little noise she look'd behind,
For still the knight was present to her
    mind;   360
And anxious oft she started on the way,
And thought the horseman ghost came
    thund'ring for his prey.
Return'd, she took her bed, with little rest,
But in short slumbers dreamt the funeral
    feast:
Awak'd, she turn'd her side, and slept ⎤
    again; |
The same black vapors mounted in her ⎬
    brain, |
And the same dreams return'd with |
    double pain.   ⎦
  Now forc'd to wake, because afraid to
    sleep,
Her blood all fever'd, with a furious leap
She sprung from bed, distracted in her
    mind,   370
And fear'd, at ev'ry step, a twitching sprite
    behind.

Darkling and desp'rate, with a stagg'ring
 pace,
Of death afraid, and conscious of disgrace;
Fear, pride, remorse, at once her heart
 assail'd;
Pride put remorse to flight, but fear pre-
 vail'd.
Friday, the fatal day, when next it came,
Her soul forethought the fiend would
 change his game,
And her pursue, or Theodore be slain,
And two ghosts join their packs to hunt her
 o'er the plain.
 This dreadful image so possess'd her
 mind, 380
That desp'rate any succor else to find,
She ceas'd all farther hope; and now began
To make reflection on th' unhappy man.
Rich, brave, and young, who past expression
 lov'd,
Proof to disdain, and not to be remov'd:
Of all the men respected and admir'd;
Of all the dames, except herself, desir'd —
Why not of her, preferr'd above the rest
By him with knightly deeds, and open
 love profess'd ?
So had another been, where he his vows
 address'd. 390
This quell'd her pride, yet other doubts
 remain'd,
That, once disdaining, she might be dis-
 dain'd.
The fear was just, but greater fear pre-
 vail'd,
Fear of her life by hellish hounds assail'd:
He took a low'ring leave, but who can tell
What outward hate might inward love con-
 ceal ?
Her sex's arts she knew, and why not, then,
Might deep dissembling have a place in
 men ?
Here hope began to dawn; resolv'd to try,
She fix'd on this her utmost remedy: 400
Death was behind, but hard it was to die.
'T was time enough at last on death to call,
The precipice in sight: a shrub was all
That kindly stood betwixt to break the
 fatal fall.
 One maid she had, belov'd above the rest;
Secure of her, the secret she confess'd;
And now the cheerful light her fears dis-
 pell'd,
She with no winding turns the truth con-
 ceal'd,
But put the woman off, and stood reveal'd:

With faults confess'd commission'd her to
 go, 410
If pity yet had place, and reconcile her foe.
The welcome message made was soon re-
 ceiv'd;
'T was what he wish'd, and hop'd, but scarce
 believ'd:
Fate seem'd a fair occasion to present;
He knew the sex, and fear'd she might
 repent,
Should he delay the moment of consent.
There yet remain'd to gain her friends (a
 care
The modesty of maidens well might spare);
But she with such a zeal the cause embrac'd,
(As women, where they will, are all in
 haste,) 420
That father, mother, and the kin beside,
Were overborne by fury of the tide:
With full consent of all she chang'd her
 state,
Resistless in her love, as in her hate.
 By her example warn'd, the rest beware;
More easy, less imperious, were the fair;
And that one hunting, which the devil de-
 sign'd
For one fair female, lost him half the kind.

CEYX AND ALCYONE

[OUT OF THE ELEVENTH BOOK OF OVID'S
 METAMORPHOSES]

CONNECTION OF THIS FABLE WITH THE FORMER

Ceyx, the son of Lucifer (the morning star) and
 King of Trachin, in Thessaly, was married to
 Alcyone, daughter to Æolus, God of the
 Winds. Both the husband and the wife lov'd
 each other with an entire affection. Dædalion, the elder brother of Ceyx (whom he
 succeeded), having been turn'd into a falcon
 by Apollo, and Chione, Dædalion's daughter,
 slain by Diana, Ceyx prepares a ship to sail
 to Claros, there to consult the oracle of
 Apollo, and (as Ovid seems to intimate) to
 enquire how the anger of the gods might be
 aton'd.

THESE prodigies afflict the pious prince,
But, more perplex'd with those that hap-
 pen'd since,
He purposes to seek the Clarian god,
Avoiding Delphos, his more fam'd abode,
Since Phlegyan robbers made unsafe the
 road.

Yet could he not from her he lov'd so well,
The fatal voyage, he resolv'd, conceal:
But when she saw her lord prepar'd to
    part,
A deadly cold ran shiv'ring to her heart;
Her faded cheeks are chang'd to boxen
    hue,   10
And in her eyes the tears are ever new.
She thrice assay'd to speak; her accents
    hung,
And falt'ring died unfinish'd on her tongue,
Or vanish'd into sighs: with long delay
Her voice return'd, and found the wonted
    way.
  "Tell me, my lord," she said, " what ⎫
    fault unknown   ⎬
Thy once belov'd Alcyone has done.   ⎬
Whether, ah whether is thy kindness ⎭
    gone !
Can Ceyx then sustain to leave his wife,
And unconcern'd forsake the sweets of
    life ?   20
What can thy mind to this long journey
    move,
Or need'st thou absence to renew thy love ?
Yet, if thou go'st by land, tho' grief pos-
    sess
My soul ev'n then, my fears will be the
    less.
But ah ! be warn'd to shun the wat'ry way —
The face is frightful of the stormy sea;
For late I saw adrift disjointed planks,
And empty tombs erected on the banks.
Nor let false hopes to trust betray thy
    mind,
Because my sire in caves constrains the
    wind,   30
Can with a breath their clam'rous rage
    appease;
They fear his whistle, and forsake the seas.
Not so, for, once indulg'd, they sweep the
    main,
Deaf to the call, or, hearing, hear in vain;
But, bent on mischief, bear the waves be-
    fore,
And, not content with seas, insult the shore;
When ocean, air, and earth, at once ingage,
And rooted forests fly before their rage:
At once the clashing clouds to battle move,
And lightnings run across the fields above.
I know them well, and mark'd their rude
    comport,   41
While yet a child, within my father's court:
In times of tempest they command alone,
And he but sits precarious on the throne.

The more I know, the more my fears aug
    ment;
And fears are oft prophetic of th' event.
But if not fears or reasons will prevail,
If fate has fix'd thee obstinate to sail,
Go not without thy wife, but let me bear ⎫
My part of danger with an equal share, 50 ⎬
And present, what I suffer, only fear: ⎭
Then o'er the bounding billows shall we
    fly,
Secure to live together, or to die."
  These reasons mov'd her starlike hus-
    band's heart,
But still he held his purpose to depart:
For, as he lov'd her equal to his life,
He would not to the seas expose his wife;
Nor could be wrought his voyage to refrain,
But sought by arguments to soothe her
    pain.
Nor these avail'd; at length he lights on
    one,   60
With which so difficult a cause he won:
" My love, so short an absence cease to fear,
For, by my father's holy flame, I swear,
Before two moons their orb with light
    adorn,
If Heav'n allow me life, I will return."
This promise of so short a stay prevails:
He soon equips the ship, supplies the sails,
And gives the word to launch; she trem-
    bling views
This pomp of death, and parting tears re-
    news:
Last, with a kiss, she took a long farewell;
Sigh'd, with a sad presage, and swooning
    fell.   71
While Ceyx seeks delays, the lusty crew, ⎫
Rais'd on their banks, their oars in order ⎬
    drew   ⎬
To their broad breasts; the ship with fury ⎬
    flew.   ⎭
  The queen, recover'd, rears her humid
    eyes,
And first her husband on the poop espies,
Shaking his hand at distance on the main;
She took the sign, and shook her hand again.
Still as the ground recedes, contracts her
    view
With sharpen'd sight, till she no longer
    knew   80
The much-lov'd face; that comfort lost sup-
    plies
With less, and with the galley feeds her
    eyes;
The galley borne from view by rising gales,

She follow'd with her sight the flying sails:
When ev'n the flying sails were seen no
  more,
Forsaken of all sight, she left the shore.
  Then on her bridal bed her body throws,
And sought in sleep her wearied eyes to
  close;
Her husband's pillow, and the widow'd part
Which once he press'd, renew'd the former
  smart.   90
  And now a breeze from shore began to
  blow,
The sailors ship their oars, and cease to
  row;
Then hoist their yards atrip, and all their
  sails
Let fall, to court the wind, and catch the
  gales.
By this the vessel half her course had run,
And as much rested till the rising sun;
Both shores were lost to sight, when, at the
  close
Of day, a stiffer gale at east arose:
The sea grew white, the rolling waves from
  far,   99
Like heralds, first denounce the wat'ry war.
  This seen, the master soon began to cry:
"Strike, strike the topsail; let the main-
  sheet fly,
And furl your sails." The winds repel the
  sound,
And in the speaker's mouth the speech is
  drown'd;
Yet of their own accord, as danger taught,
Each in his way, officiously they wrought:
Some stow their oars, or stop the leaky
  sides;
Another bolder yet the yard bestrides,
And folds the sails; a fourth, with labor,
  laves
Th' intruding seas, and waves ejects on
  waves.   110
  In this confusion while their work they
  ply,
The winds augment the winter of the sky,
And wage intestine wars; the suff'ring seas
Are toss'd and mingled as their tyrants
  please.
The master would command, but, in despair
Of safety, stands amaz'd with stupid care;
Nor what to bid, or what forbid, he knows,
Th' ungovern'd tempest to such fury grows;
Vain is his force, and vainer is his skill,
With such a concourse comes the flood of
  ill.   120

The cries of men are mix'd with rattling
  shrouds;
Seas dash on seas, and clouds encounter
  clouds:
At once from east to west, from pole to
  pole,
The forky lightnings flash, the roaring thun-
  ders roll.
  Now waves on waves ascending scale the
  skies,
And, in the fires above, the water fries.
When yellow sands are sifted from below,
The glitt'ring billows give a golden show;
And when the fouler bottom spews the
  black,   129
The Stygian dye the tainted waters take:
Then frothy white appear the flatted seas,
And change their color, changing their dis-
  ease.
Like various fits the Trachin vessel finds,
And now sublime she rides upon the winds;
As from a lofty summit looks from high,
And from the clouds beholds the nether
  sky;
Now from the depth of hell they lift their
  sight,
And at a distance see superior light.
The lashing billows make a loud report,
And beat her sides, as batt'ring rams a
  fort: 140
Or as a lion, bounding in his way,
With force augmented bears against his
  prey,
Sidelong to seize; or, unappall'd with fear,
Springs on the toils and rushes on the
  spear:
So seas impell'd by winds with added pow'r
Assault the sides, and o'er the hatches
  tow'r.
  The planks (their pitchy cov'ring wash'd
  away)
Now yield, and now a yawning breach dis-
  play;
The roaring waters with a hostile tide
Rush thro' the ruins of her gaping side. 150
Meantime in sheets of rain the sky de-
  scends,
And ocean, swell'd with waters, upwards
  tends;
One rising, falling one, the heav'ns and sea
Meet at their confines, in the middle way:
The sails are drunk with show'rs, and drop
  with rain;
Sweet waters mingle with the briny main.
No star appears to lend his friendly light;

Darkness and tempest make a double night.
But flashing fires disclose the deep by turns;
And, while the lightnings blaze, the water
   burns.   160
  Now all the waves their scatter'd force
   unite,
And, as a soldier, foremost in the fight,
Makes way for others, and, an host alone,
Still presses on, and urging gains the town;
So, while th' invading billows come abreast,
The hero tenth, advanc'd before the rest,
Sweeps all before him with impetuous sway,
And from the walls descends upon the prey;
Part following enter, part remain without,
With envy hear their fellows' conqu'ring
   shout,   170
And mount on others' backs, in hope to
   share
The city, thus become the seat of war.
  An universal cry resounds aloud,
The sailors run in heaps, a helpless crowd;
Art fails, and courage falls, no succor near;
As many waves, as many deaths appear.
One weeps, and yet despairs of late relief;
One cannot weep, (his fears congeal his
   grief,)
But, stupid, with dry eyes expects his
   fate;
One with loud shrieks laments his lost
   estate,   180
And calls those happy whom their funer-
   als wait.
This wretch with pray'rs and vows the gods
   implores,
And ev'n the skies he cannot see, adores.
That other on his friends his thoughts be-
   stows,
His careful father, and his faithful spouse.
The covetous worldling in his anxious mind
Thinks only on the wealth he left behind.
  All Ceyx his Alcyone employs;
For her he grieves, yet in her absence joys:
His wife he wishes, and would still be
   near,   190
Not her with him, but wishes him with her.
Now with last looks he seeks his native
   shore,
Which fate has destin'd him to see no
   more:
He sought, but in the dark tempestuous
   night
He knew not whether to direct his sight.
So whirl the seas, such darkness blinds the
   sky,
That the black night receives a deeper dye.

  The giddy ship ran round; the tempest
   tore
Her mast, and overboard the rudder bore.
One billow mounts, and with a scornful
   brow,   200
Proud of her conquest gain'd, insults the
   waves below;
Nor lighter falls, than if some giant tore
Pindus and Athos, with the freight they
   bore,
And toss'd on seas: press'd with the pon-
   d'rous blow,
Down sinks the ship within th' abyss below;
Down with the vessel sink into the main
The many, never more to rise again.
Some few on scatter'd planks with fruitless
   care
Lay hold, and swim, but, while they swim,
   despair.
  Ev'n he, who late a scepter did com-
   mand,   210
Now grasps a floating fragment in his hand;
And, while he struggles on the stormy main,
Invokes his father, and his wife's, in vain.
But yet his consort is his greater care;
Alcyone he names amidst his pray'r,
Names as a charm against the waves and
   wind;
Most in his mouth, and ever in his mind:
Tir'd with his toil, all hopes of safety past,
From pray'rs to wishes he descends at last;
That his dead body, wafted to the sands, 220
Might have its burial from her friendly
   hands.
As oft as he can catch a gulp of air,
And peep above the seas, he names the fair;
And ev'n when plung'd beneath, on her he
   raves,
Murm'ring Alcyone below the waves:
At last a falling billow stops his breath,
Breaks o'er his head, and whelms him un-
   derneath.
Bright Lucifer unlike himself appears
That night, his heav'nly form obscur'd with
   tears;   229
And, since he was forbid to leave the skies,
He muffled with a cloud his mournful eyes.
  Meantime Alcyone (his fate unknown)
Computes how many nights he had been
   gone;
Observes the waning moon with hourly
   view,
Numbers her age, and wishes for a new;
Against the promis'd time provides with
   care,

And hastens in the woof the robes he was
    to wear;
And for herself employs another loom, ⎤
New-dress'd to meet her lord returning ⎥
    home,   ⎬
Flatt'ring her heart with joys that never ⎥
    were to come.   240 ⎦
She fum'd the temples with an od'rous ⎤
    flame,   ⎥
And oft before the sacred altars came, ⎬
To pray for him, who was an empty   ⎥
    name.   ⎦
All pow'rs implor'd, but, far above the
    rest,
To Juno she her pious vows address'd,
Her much-lov'd lord from perils to protect,
And safe o'er seas his voyage to direct;
Then pray'd that she might still possess
    his heart,
And no pretending rival share a part:
This last petition heard of all her pray'r, 250
The rest, dispers'd by winds, were lost in air.
    But she, the goddess of the nuptial bed,
Tir'd with her vain devotions for the dead,
Resolv'd the tainted hand should be re-
    pell'd,
Which incense offer'd, and her altar held:
Then Iris thus bespoke: "Thou faithful
    maid,
By whom thy queen's commands are well
    convey'd,
Haste to the house of Sleep, and bid the god,
Who rules the night by visions with a nod,
Prepare a dream, in figure and in form 260
Resembling him who perish'd in the storm:
This form before Alcyone present,
To make her certain of the sad event."
    Indued with robes of various hue she flies,
And flying draws an arch (a segment of the
    skies);
Then leaves her bending bow, and from the
    steep
Descends to search the silent house of Sleep.
    Near the Cimmerians, in his dark abode
Deep in a cavern, dwells the drowsy god;
Whose gloomy mansion nor the rising sun,
Nor setting, visits, nor the lightsome noon:
But lazy vapors round the region fly,   272
Perpetual twilight, and a doubtful sky.
No crowing cock does there his wings dis-
    play,
Nor with his horny bill provoke the day;
Nor watchful dogs, nor the more wakeful
    geese,
Disturb with nightly noise the sacred peace:

Nor beast of nature, nor the tame, are nigh,
Nor trees with tempests rock'd, nor human
    cry;
But safe repose, without an air of breath, 280
Dwells here, and a dumb quiet next to death.
    An arm of Lethe, with a gentle flow,
Arising upwards from the rock below,
The palace moats, and o'er the pebbles
    creeps,
And with soft murmurs calls the coming
    sleeps;
Around its entry nodding poppies grow,
And all cool simples that sweet rest bestow;
Night from the plants their sleepy virtue
    drains,
And passing, sheds it on the silent plains:
No door there was th' unguarded house to
    keep,   290
On creaking hinges turn'd, to break his sleep.
    But in the gloomy court was rais'd a bed,
Stuff'd with black plumes, and on an ebon
    stead:
Black was the cov'ring too, where lay the
    god,
And slept supine, his limbs display'd abroad.
About his head fantastic visions fly,
Which various images of things supply,
And mock their forms; the leaves on trees
    not more,
Nor bearded ears in fields, nor sands upon
    the shore.
    The virgin ent'ring bright indulg'd the
    day   300
To the brown cave, and brush'd the dreams
    away:
The god, disturb'd with this new glare of
    light
Cast sudden on his face, unseal'd his sight,
And rais'd his tardy head, which sunk again,
And sinking on his bosom knock'd his chin:
At length shook off himself; and ask'd the
    dame
(And asking yawn'd) for what intent she
    came.
    To whom the goddess thus: "O sacred
    Rest,
Sweet pleasing Sleep, of all the pow'rs the
    best!
O peace of mind, repairer of decay,   310 ⎤
Whose balms renew the limbs to labors ⎥
    of the day;   ⎬
Care shuns thy soft approach, and sullen ⎥
    flies away!   ⎦
Adorn a dream, expressing human form,
The shape of him who suffer'd in the storm,

And send it flitting to the Trachin court,
The wreck of wretched Ceyx to report:
Before his queen bid the pale specter stand,
Who begs a vain relief at Juno's hand."
She said, and scarce awake her eyes could
    keep,
Unable to support the fumes of sleep;   320
But fled, returning by the way she went,
And swerv'd along her bow with swift as-
    cent.
The god, uneasy till he slept again,
Resolv'd at once to rid himself of pain;
And, tho' against his custom, call'd aloud,
Exciting Morpheus from the sleepy crowd:
Morpheus of all his numerous train ex-
    press'd
The shape of man, and imitated best;
The walk, the words, the gesture could sup-
    ply,
The habit mimic, and the mien bely;   330
Plays well, but all his action is confin'd,
Extending not beyond our human kind.
Another birds, and beasts, and dragons apes,
And dreadful images, and monster shapes:
This demon Icelos in heav'n's high hall
The gods have nam'd, but men Phobetor
    call.
A third is Phantasus, whose actions roll
On meaner thoughts, and things devoid of
    soul;
Earth, fruits, and flow'rs he represents in
    dreams,
And solid rocks unmov'd, and running
    streams;   340
These three to kings and chiefs their scenes
    display,
The rest before th' ignoble commons play.
Of these the chosen Morpheus is dispatch'd:
Which done, the lazy monarch, over-
    watch'd,
Down from his propping elbow drops his
    head,
Dissolv'd in sleep, and shrinks within his bed.
Darkling the demon glides, for flight pre-
    par'd,
So soft that scarce his fanning wings are
    heard.
To Trachin, swift as thought, the flitting
    shade
Thro' air his momentary journey made: 350
Then lays aside the steerage of his wings,
Forsakes his proper form, assumes the king's;
And pale as death, despoil'd of his array,
Into the queen's apartment takes his way,
And stands before the bed at dawn of day.

Unmov'd his eyes, and wet his beard ap-
    pears;
And shedding vain, but seeming real tears;
The briny water dropping from his hairs:
Then staring on her, with a ghastly look
And hollow voice, he thus the queen be-
    spoke: 360
  " Know'st thou not me ? Not yet, un-
    happy wife ?
Or are my features perish'd with my life ?
Look once again, and, for thy husband lost,
Lo ! all that 's left of him, thy husband's
    ghost !
Thy vows for my return were all in vain;
The stor y south o'ertook us in the main;
And never shalt thou see thy living lord
    again.
Bear witness, Heav'n, I call'd on thee in
    death,
And while I call'd, a billow stopp'd my
    breath:
Think not that flying fame reports my
    fate;   370
I present, I appear, and my own wreck
    relate.
Rise, wretched widow, rise, nor unde-
    plor'd
Permit my ghost to pass the Stygian ford;
But rise, prepar'd in black, to mourn thy
    perish'd lord."
Thus said the player god; and, adding art
Of voice and gesture, so perform'd his part,
She thought (so like her love the shade
    appears)
That Ceyx spake the words, and Ceyx shed
    the tears.
She groan'd, her inward soul with grief
    oppress'd;
She sigh'd, she wept, and sleeping beat her
    breast: 380
Then stretch'd her arms t' embrace his
    body bare —
Her clasping arms inclose but empty air.
At this, not yet awake, she cried: "O stay,
One is our fate, and common is our way ! "
So dreadful was the dream, so loud she
    spoke,
That, starting sudden up, the slumber broke;
Then cast her eyes around, in hope to view
Her vanish'd lord, and find the vision true:
For now the maids, who waited her com-
    mands,
Ran in with lighted tapers in their hands.
Tir'd with the search, not finding what she
    seeks,   391

With cruel blows she pounds her blubber'd
    cheeks;
Then from her beaten breast the linen tare,
And cut the golden caul that bound her hair.
Her nurse demands the cause; with louder
    cries
She prosecutes her griefs, and thus replies:
  " No more Alcyone; she suffer'd death
With her lov'd lord, when Ceyx lost his
    breath:
No flatt'ry, no false comfort, give me none,
My shipwreck'd Ceyx is for ever gone; 400
I saw, I saw him manifest in view;
His voice, his figure, and his gestures knew.
His luster lost, and ev'ry living grace,
Yet I retain'd the features of his face;
Tho' with pale cheeks, wet beard, and
    dropping hair,
None but my Ceyx could appear so fair:
I would have strain'd him with a strict
    embrace,
But thro' my arms he slipp'd, and vanish'd
    from the place:
There, ev'n just there he stood; " and as
    she spoke,
Where last the specter was, she cast her
    look: 410
Fain would she hope, and gaz'd upon the
    ground,
If any printed footsteps might be found.
    Then sigh'd and said: " This I too well
    foreknew,
And my prophetic fear presag'd too true:
'T was what I begg'd, when with a bleeding
    heart
I took my leave, and suffer'd thee to part;
Or I to go along, or thou to stay,
Never, ah never to divide our way !
Happier for me, that all our hours assign'd
Together we had liv'd; e'en not in death
    disjoin'd ! 420
So had my Ceyx still been living here,
Or with my Ceyx I had perish'd there.
Now I die absent, in the vast profound,
And me without myself the seas have
    drown'd:
The storms were not so cruel, should I strive
To lengthen life, and such a grief survive;
But neither will I strive, nor wretched thee
In death forsake, but keep thee company.
If not one common sepulcher contains
Our bodies, or one urn our last remains, 430
Yet Ceyx and Alcyone shall join,
Their names remember'd in one common
    line."

No farther voice her mighty grief affords,
For sighs come rushing in betwixt her
    words,
And stopp'd her tongue; but what her
    tongue denied,
Soft tears, and groans, and dumb com-
    plaints supplied.
  'T was morning; to the port she takes
    her way,
And stands upon the margin of the sea:
That place, that very spot of ground she
    sought,
Or thither by her destiny was brought, 440
Where last he stood; and while she sadly ⎫
    said: ⎪
" 'T was here he left me, ling'ring here ⎬
    delay'd   ⎪
His parting kiss; and there his anchors ⎪
    weigh'd." —   ⎭
  Thus speaking, while her thoughts past
    actions trace,
And call to mind, admonish'd by the place,
Sharp at her utmost ken she cast her eyes,
And somewhat floating from afar descries;
It seem'd a corpse adrift, to distant sight,
But at a distance who could judge aright ?
It wafted nearer yet, and then she knew
That what before she but surmis'd, was
    true: 451
A corpse it was, but whose it was, unknown;
Yet mov'd, howe'er, she made the case
    her own;
Took the bad omen of a shipwreck'd man,
As for a stranger wept, and thus began:
  " Poor wretch, on stormy seas to lose
    thy life,
Unhappy thou, but more thy widow'd
    wife ! "
At this she paus'd; for now the flowing
    tide
Had brought the body nearer to the side:
The more she looks, the more her fears in-
    crease 460
At nearer sight, and she 's herself the less.
Now driv'n ashore, and at her feet it lies;
She knows too much, in knowing whom she
    sees —
Her husband's corpse: at this she loudly
    shrieks:
" 'T is he, 't is he," she cries, and tears her
    cheeks,
Her hair, her vest; and, stooping to the
    sands,
About his neck she cast her trembling
    hands.

" And is it thus, O dearer than my life,
Thus, thus return'st thou to thy longing
   wife ! "
She said, and to the neighb'ring mole she
   strode,   470
(Rais'd there to break th' incursions of the
   flood.)
Headlong from hence to plunge herself she
   springs,
But shoots along supported on her wings;
A bird new-made about the banks she
   plies,
Not far from shore, and short excursions
   tries;
Nor seeks in air her humble flight to raise,
Content to skim the surface of the seas:
Her bill, tho' slender, sends a creaking noise,
And imitates a lamentable voice.   479
Now lighting where the bloodless body lies,
She with a funeral note renews her cries.
At all her stretch her little wings she
   spread,
And with her feather'd arms embrac'd the
   dead;
Then flick'ring to his pallid lips, she strove
To print a kiss, the last essay of love.
Whether the vital touch reviv'd the dead,
Or that the moving waters rais'd his head
To meet the kiss, the vulgar doubt alone;
For sure a present miracle was shown.
The gods their shapes to winter birds trans-
   late,   490
But both obnoxious to their former fate.
Their conjugal affection still is tied,
And still the mournful race is multiplied.
They bill, they tread; Alcyone, compress'd,
Sev'n days sits brooding on her floating
   nest,
A wintry queen: her sire at length is kind,
Calms ev'ry storm, and hushes ev'ry wind;
Prepares his empire for his daughter's ease,
And for his hatching nephews smooths the
   seas.

THE FLOWER AND THE LEAF

OR, THE LADY IN THE ARBOR

A VISION [OUT OF CHAUCER]

Now turning from the wintry signs, the sun
His course exalted thro' the Ram had run,
And, whirling up the skies, his chariot drove
Thro' Taurus and the lightsome realms of
   love;

Where Venus from her orb descends in
   show'rs,
To glad the ground, and paint the fields
   with flow'rs:
When first the tender blades of grass ap-
   pear,
And buds, that yet the blast of Eurus fear,
Stand at the door of life, and doubt to
   clothe the year;
Till gentle heat and soft repeated rains   10
Make the green blood to dance within their
   veins:
Then, at their call, embolden'd out they
   come,
And swell the gems and burst the narrow
   room;
Broader and broader yet, their blooms dis-
   play,
Salute the welcome sun, and entertain the
   day.
Then from their breathing souls the sweet
   repair
To scent the skies, and purge th' unwhole-
   some air;
Joy spreads the heart, and, with a general
   song,
Spring issues out and leads the jolly months
   along.
In that sweet season, as in bed I lay   20
And sought in sleep to pass the night away,
I turn'd my weary side, but still in vain,
Tho' full of youthful health, and void of
   pain:
Cares I had none, to keep me from my rest,
For love had never enter'd in my breast;
I wanted nothing Fortune could supply,
Nor did she slumber till that hour deny.
I wonder'd then, but after found it true,
Much joy had dried away the balmy dew:
Seas would be pools, without the brush-
   ing air   30
To curl the waves; and sure some little
   care
Should weary Nature so, to make her
   want repair.
When Chanticleer the second watch had
   sung,
Scorning the scorner sleep, from bed I
   sprung;
And dressing, by the moon, in loose array,
Pass'd out in open air, preventing day,
And sought a goodly grove, as fancy led
   my way.
Straight as a line in beauteous order stood
Of oaks unshorn a venerable wood:

Fresh was the grass beneath; and ev'ry tree,
At distance planted in a due degree,   41
Their branching arms in air with equal space
Stretch'd to their neighbors with a long em-
    brace;
And the new leaves on ev'ry bough were
    seen,
Some ruddy-color'd, some of lighter green.
The painted birds, companions of the spring,
Hopping from spray to spray, were heard
    to sing;
Both eyes and ears receiv'd a like delight,
Enchanting music, and a charming sight.
On Philomel I fix'd my whole desire,   50
And listen'd for the queen of all the choir;
Fain would I hear her heav'nly voice to
    sing;
And wanted yet an omen to the spring.
  Attending long in vain, I took the way,
Which thro' a path but scarcely printed
    lay;
In narrow mazes oft it seem'd to meet,
And look'd as lightly press'd by fairy feet.
Wand'ring I walk'd alone, for still me-
    thought
To some strange end so strange a path was
    wrought;
At last it led me where an arbor stood,   60
The sacred receptacle of the wood.
This place unmark'd, tho' oft I walk'd the
    green,
In all my progress I had never seen;
And, seiz'd at once with wonder and delight,
Gaz'd all around me, new to the transport-
    ing sight.
'T was bench'd with turf, and goodly to be
    seen,
The thick young grass arose in fresher
    green:
The mound was newly made, no sight could
    pass
Betwixt the nice partitions of the grass;
The well-united sods so closely lay,   70
And all around the shades defended it from
    day,
For sycamores with eglantine were spread,
A hedge about the sides, a covering over
    head.
And so the fragrant brier was wove between,
The sycamore and flow'rs were mix'd with
    green,
That nature seem'd to vary the delight,
And satisfied at once the smell and sight.
The master workman of the bow'r was
    known

Thro' fairy lands, and built for Oberon;
Who twining leaves with such proportion
    drew,   80
They rose by measure, and by rule they
    grew:
No mortal tongue can half the beauty tell,
For none but hands divine could work so
    well.
Both roof and sides were like a parlor made,
A soft recess, and a cool summer shade:
The hedge was set so thick, no foreign eye
The persons plac'd within it could espy;
But all that pass'd without with ease was
    seen,
As if nor fence nor tree was plac'd between.
'T was border'd with a field; and some was
    plain   90
With grass, and some was sow'd with rising
    grain,
That (now the dew with spangles deck'd
    the ground)
A sweeter spot of earth was never found.
I look'd and look'd, and still with new de-
    light;
Such joy my soul, such pleasures fill'd my
    sight:
And the fresh eglantine exhal'd a breath,
Whose odors were of pow'r to raise from
    death.
Nor sullen discontent, nor anxious care,
Ev'n tho' brought thither, could inhabit
    there;
But thence they fled as from their mortal
    foe,   100
For this sweet place could only pleasure
    know.
  Thus, as I mus'd, I cast aside my eye,
And saw a medlar tree was planted nigh.
The spreading branches made a goodly show,
And full of opening blooms was ev'ry bough.
A goldfinch there I saw with gaudy pride
Of painted plumes, that hopp'd from side
    to side,
Still pecking as she pass'd; and still she
    drew
The sweets from ev'ry flow'r, and suck'd the
    dew:
Suffic'd at length, she warbled in her
    throat,   110
And tun'd her voice to many a merry note,
But indistinct, and neither sweet nor clear,
Yet such as sooth'd my soul and pleas'd
    my ear.
  Her short performance was no sooner
    tried,

When she I sought, the nightingale, re-
plied:
So sweet, so shrill, so variously she sung,
That the grove echo'd, and the valleys rung;
And I so ravish'd with her heav'nly note,
I stood intranc'd, and had no room for
thought,
But all o'erpow'r'd with ecstasy of bliss, 120
Was in a pleasing dream of Paradise.
At length I wak'd, and, looking round the
bow'r,
Search'd ev'ry tree, and pried on ev'ry
flow'r,
If anywhere by chance I might espy
The rural poet of the melody;
For still methought she sung not far away.
At last I found her on a laurel spray;
Close by my side she sate, and fair in sight,
Full in a line, against her opposite,
Where stood with eglantine the laurel
twin'd,   130
And both their native sweets were well
conjoin'd.
  On the green bank I sat, and listen'd
long;
(Sitting was more convenient for the song!)
Nor till her lay was ended could I move,
But wish'd to dwell forever in the grove.
Only methought the time too swiftly
pass'd,
And ev'ry note I fear'd would be the last.
My sight, and smell, and hearing were em-
ploy'd,
And all three senses in full gust enjoy'd.
And what alone did all the rest surpass, 140
The sweet possession of the fairy place;
Single, and conscious to myself alone
Of pleasures to th' excluded world un-
known:
Pleasures which nowhere else were to be
found,
And all Elysium in a spot of ground.
  Thus while I sat intent to see and hear,
And drew perfumes of more than vital air,
All suddenly I heard th' approaching sound
Of vocal music on th' enchanted ground:
An host of saints it seem'd, so full the ⎫
choir;   150 ⎬
As if the blest above did all conspire   ⎭
To join their voices and neglect the lyre.
At length there issued from the grove be-
hind
A fair assembly of the female kind:
A train less fair, as ancient fathers tell,
Seduc'd the sons of heaven to rebel.

I pass their forms, and ev'ry charming
grace;
Less than an angel would their worth de-
base;
But their attire, like liveries of a kind, 159
All rich and rare, is fresh within my mind.
In velvet, white as snow, the troop was
gown'd,
The seams with sparkling emeralds set
around;
Their hoods and sleeves the same, and pur-
fled o'er
With diamonds, pearls, and all the shining
store
Of Eastern pomp; their long descending
train,
With rubies edg'd, and sapphires, swept the
plain;
High on their heads, with jewels richly set,
Each lady wore a radiant coronet.
Beneath the circles, all the choir was grac'd
With chaplets green on their fair foreheads
plac'd.   170
Of laurel some, of woodbine many more,
And wreaths of *agnus castus* others bore:
These last, who with those virgin crowns
were dress'd,
Appear'd in higher honor than the rest.
They danc'd around; but in the midst ⎫
was seen   ⎪
A lady of a more majestic mien,   ⎬
By stature and by beauty mark'd their   ⎪
sovereign queen.   ⎭
  She in the midst began with sober grace;
Her servants' eyes were fix'd upon her
face,
And, as she mov'd or turn'd, her motions
view'd,   180
Her measures kept, and step by step pur-
sued.
Methought she trod the ground with greater
grace,
With more of godhead shining in her face;
And as in beauty she surpass'd the choir,
So, nobler than the rest, was her attire.
A crown of ruddy gold inclos'd her brow,
Plain without pomp, and rich without a
show:
A branch of *agnus castus* in her hand
She bore aloft (her scepter of command);
Admir'd, ador'd by all the circling crowd,
For wheresoe'er she turn'd her face, they
bow'd.   191
And as she danc'd, a roundelay she sung,
In honor of the laurel, ever young:

She rais'd her voice on high, and sung
    so clear,
The fawns came scudding from the
    groves to hear,
And all the bending forest lent an ear.
At ev'ry close she made, th' attending
    throng
Replied, and bore the burden of the song:
So just, so small, yet in so sweet a note,
It seem'd the music melted in the throat. 200
    Thus dancing on, and singing as they
    danc'd,
They to the middle of the mead advanc'd,
Till round my arbor a new ring they made,
And footed it about the secret shade.
O'erjoy'd to see the jolly troop so near,
But somewhat aw'd, I shook with holy fear;
Yet not so much, but that I noted well
Who did the most in song or dance excel.
    Not long I had observ'd, when from afar
I heard a sudden symphony of war;   210
The neighing coursers, and the soldiers' cry,
And sounding trumps that seem'd to tear
    the sky.
I saw soon after this, behind the grove
From whence the ladies did in order move,
Come issuing out in arms a warrior train,
That like a deluge pour'd upon the plain:
On barbed steeds they rode in proud array,
Thick as the college of the bees in May,
When swarming o'er the dusky fields they
    fly,
New to the flow'rs, and intercept the sky.
So fierce they drove, their coursers were so
    fleet,   221
That the turf trembled underneath their
    feet.
    To tell their costly furniture were long,
The summer's day would end before the
    song;
To purchase but the tenth of all their store
Would make the mighty Persian monarch
    poor.
Yet what I can, I will; before the rest
The trumpets issued in white mantles
    dress'd:
A numerous troop, and all their heads
    around
With chaplets green of cerrial oak were
    crown'd;   230
And at each trumpet was a banner bound,
Which, waving in the wind, display'd at
    large
Their master's coat of arms and knightly
    charge.

Broad were the banners, and of snowy hue,
A purer web the silkworm never drew.
The chief about their necks the scutcheons
    wore,
With orient pearls and jewels powder'd
    o'er;
Broad were their collars too, and ev'ry one
Was set about with many a costly stone.
Next these, of kings at arms a goodly
    train   240
In proud array came prancing o'er the plain;
Their cloaks were cloth of silver mix'd
    with gold,
And garlands green around their temples
    roll'd;
Rich crowns were on their royal scutcheons
    plac'd,
With sapphires, diamonds, and with rubies
    grac'd.
And as the trumpets their appearance
    made,
So these in habits were alike array'd;
But with a pace more sober and more slow,
And twenty, rank in rank, they rode arow.
The pursevants came next, in number
    more;   250
And like the heralds each his scutcheon
    bore:
Clad in white velvet all their troop they
    led,
With each an oaken chaplet on his head.
    Nine royal knights in equal rank suc-
    ceed,
Each warrior mounted on a fiery steed;
In golden armor glorious to behold;
The rivets of their arms were nail'd with
    gold.
Their surcoats of white ermine fur were
    made,
With cloth of gold between that cast a
    glitt'ring shade.
The trappings of their steeds were of the
    same;   260
The golden fringe ev'n set the ground on
    flame,
And drew a precious trail: a crown divine
Of laurel did about their temples twine.
    Three henchmen were for ev'ry knight
    assign'd,
All in rich livery clad, and of a kind;
White velvet, but unshorn, for cloaks they
    wore,
And each within his hand a truncheon bore:
The foremost held a helm of rare device;
A prince's ransom would not pay the price

The seeond bore the buckler of his
   knight,   270
The third of cornel wood a spear upright,
Headed with piercing steel, and polish'd
   bright.
Like to their lords their equipage was seen,
And all their foreheads crown'd with gar-
   lands green.
  And after these came arm'd with spear
   and shield
An host so great, as cover'd all the field;
And all their foreheads, like the knights
   before,
With laurels ever green were shaded o'er,
Or oak, or other leaves of lasting kind,
Tenacious of the stem, and firm against the
   wind.   280
Some in their hands, besides the lance and
   shield,
The boughs of woodbind or of hawthorn
   held,
Or branches for their mystic emblems took,
Of palm, of laurel, or of cerrial oak.
  Thus marching to the trumpets' lofty
   sound,
Drawn in two lines adverse they wheel'd
   around,
And in the middle meadow took their
   ground.
Among themselves the turney they divide,
In equal squadrons rang'd on either side;
Then turn'd their horses' heads, and man
   to man,   290
And steed to steed oppos'd, the justs began.
They lightly set their lances in the rest,
And, at the sign, against each other press'd:
They met; I sitting at my ease beheld
The mix'd events, and fortunes of the field.
Some broke their spears, some tumbled
   horse and man,
And round the field the lighten'd coursers
   ran.
An hour and more, like tides, in equal sway
They rush'd, and won by turns and lost the
   day:
At length the nine (who still together
   held)   300
Their fainting foes to shameful flight
   compell'd,
And with resistless force o'erran the field.
Thus, to their fame, when finish'd was the
   fight,
The victors from their lofty steeds alight:
Like them dismounted all the warlike train,
And two by two proceeded o'er the plain;

Till to the fair assembly they advanc'd,
Who near the secret arbor sung and danc'd.
  The ladies left their measures at the
   sight,
To meet the chiefs returning from the
   fight,   310
And each with open arms embrac'd her
   chosen knight.
Amid the plain a spreading laurel stood,
The grace and ornament of all the wood:
That pleasing shade they sought, a soft re-
   treat
From sudden April show'rs, a shelter from
   the heat.
Her leavy arms with such extent were
   spread,
So near the clouds was her aspiring head,
That hosts of birds, that wing the liquid
   air,
Perch'd in the boughs, had nightly lodging
   there;
And flocks of sheep beneath the shade from
   far   320
Might hear the rattling hail and wintry
   war;
From heav'n's inclemency here found re-
   treat,
Enjoy'd the cool, and shunn'd the scorching
   heat:
A hundred knights might there at ease
   abide,
And ev'ry knight a lady by his side;
The trunk itself such odors did bequeath,
That a Moluccan breeze to these was com-
   mon breath.
The lords and ladies here, approaching,
   paid
Their homage, with a low obeisance
   made,
And seem'd to venerate the sacred shade.
These rites perform'd, their pleasures they
   pursue,   331
With songs of love, and mix with measures
   new;
Around the holy tree their dance they
   frame,
And ev'ry champion leads his chosen dame.
  I cast my sight upon the farther field,
And a fresh object of delight beheld:
For from the region of the West I heard
New music sound, and a new troop ap-
   pear'd,
Of knights and ladies mix'd, a jolly band;
But all on foot they march'd, and hand in
   hand.   340

The ladies dress'd in rich simars were
    seen
Of Florence satin, flow'r'd with white and
    green,
And for a shade betwixt the bloomy
    gridelin.
The borders of their petticoats below
Were guarded thick with rubies on arow;
And ev'ry damsel wore upon her head
Of flow'rs a garland blended white and red.
Attir'd in mantles all the knights were seen,
That gratified the view with cheerful green:
Their chaplets of their ladies' colors were,
Compos'd of white and red, to shade their
    shining hair.   351
Before the merry troop the minstrels play'd:
All in their masters' liveries were array'd,
And clad in green, and on their temples wore
The chaplets white and red their ladies bore.
Their instruments were various in their kind,
Some for the bow, and some for breathing
    wind:
The sawtry, pipe, and hautboys' noisy band,
And the soft lute trembling beneath the
    touching hand.
A tuft of daisies on a flow'ry lay   360
They saw, and thitherward they bent their
    way;
To this both knights and dames their hom-
    age made,
And due obeisance to the daisy paid.
And then the band of flutes began to play,
To which a lady sung a virelay;
And still at ev'ry close she would repeat
The burden of the song, " The daisy is so
    sweet."
" The daisy is so sweet," when she begun,
The troop of knights and dames continued
    on.
The concert and the voice so charm'd my
    ear,   370
And sooth'd my soul, that it was heav'n to
    hear.
    But soon their pleasure pass'd; at noon
    of day,
The sun with sultry beams began to play:
Not Sirius shoots a fiercer flame from high,
When with his pois'nous breath he blasts
    the sky.
Then droop'd the fading flow'rs (their
    beauty fled)
And clos'd their sickly eyes, and hung
    the head;
And, rivel'd up with heat, lay dying in
    their bed.

The ladies gasp'd, and scarcely could re-
    spire;
The breath they drew, no longer air, but fire:
The fainty knights were scorch'd, and knew
    not where   381
To run for shelter, for no shade was near.
And after this the gath'ring clouds amain
Pour'd down a storm of rattling hail and
    rain,
And lightning flash'd betwixt; the field and
    flow'rs,
Burnt up before, were buried in the show'rs.
The ladies and the knights, no shelter nigh,
Bare to the weather and the wintry sky,
Were dropping wet, disconsolate and wan,
And thro' their thin array receiv'd the rain.
    While those in white, protected by the
    tree,   391
Saw pass the vain assault, and stood from
    danger free.
But as compassion mov'd their gentle minds,
When ceas'd the storm, and silent were the
    winds,
Displeas'd at what, not suff'ring, they had
    seen,
They went to cheer the faction of the green.
The queen in white array, before her band,
Saluting, took her rival by the hand;
So did the knights and dames, with courtly
    grace,
And with behavior sweet their foes embrace.
Then thus the queen with laurel on her
    brow: 401
" Fair sister, I have suffer'd in your woe;
Nor shall be wanting aught within my pow'r
For your relief in my refreshing bow'r."
That other answer'd with a lowly look,
And soon the gracious invitation took,
For ill at ease both she and all her train
The scorching sun had borne, and beating
    rain.
Like courtesy was us'd by all in white;
Each dame a dame receiv'd, and ev'ry
    knight a knight.   410
The laurel champions with their swords in-
    vade
The neighb'ring forests, where the justs
    were made,
And sear wood from the rotten hedges took,
And seeds of latent fire from flints provoke:
A cheerful blaze arose, and by the fire
They warm'd their frozen feet and dried
    their wet attire.
Refresh'd with heat, the ladies sought
    around

For virtuous herbs, which gather'd from
the ground,
They squeez'd the juice, and cooling oint-
ment made,
Which on their sunburnt cheeks and their
chapp'd skins they laid;   420
Then sought green salads, which they bade
'em eat,
A sovereign remedy for inward heat.
The Lady of the Leaf ordain'd a feast,
And made the Lady of the Flow'r her guest:
When lo! a bow'r ascended on the plain,
With sudden seats adorn'd, and large for
either train.
This bow'r was near my pleasant arbor
plac'd,
That I could hear and see whatever pass'd:
The ladies sat with each a knight between,
Distinguish'd by their colors, white and
green;   430
The vanquish'd party with the victors join'd,
Nor wanted sweet discourse, the banquet of
the mind.
Meantime the minstrels play'd on either
side,
Vain of their art, and for the mast'ry vied;
The sweet contention lasted for an hour,
And reach'd my secret arbor from the
bow'r.
The sun was set; and Vesper, to supply
His absent beams, had lighted up the sky:
When Philomel, officious all the day
To sing the service of th' ensuing May,   440
Fled from her laurel shade, and wing'd her
flight
Directly to the queen array'd in white;
And hopping sate familiar on her hand,
A new musician, and increas'd the band.
The goldfinch, who, to shun the scalding
heat,
Had chang'd the medlar for a safer seat,
And hid in bushes scap'd the bitter show'r,
Now perch'd upon the Lady of the Flow'r;
And either songster, holding out their
throats,
And folding up their wings, renew'd their
notes;   450
As if all day, preluding to the fight,
They only had rehears'd, to sing by night.
The banquet ended, and the battle done,
They danc'd by starlight and the friendly
moon;
And when they were to part, the laureat
queen
Supplied with steeds the Lady of the green,

Her and her train conducting on the way,
The moon to follow, and avoid the day.
This when I saw, inquisitive to know
The secret moral of the mystic show,   460
I started from my shade, in hopes to find
Some nymph to satisfy my longing mind;
And, as my fair adventure fell, I found
A lady all in white, with laurel crown'd,
Who clos'd the rear, and softly pac'd along,
Repeating to herself the former song.
With due respect my body I inclin'd,
As to some being of superior kind,
And made my court according to the day,
Wishing her queen and her a happy May.
"Great thanks, my daughter," with a gra-
cious bow   471
She said; and I, who much desir'd to know
Of whence she was, yet fearful how to
break
My mind, adventur'd humbly thus to speak:
"Madam, might I presume and not offend,
So may the stars and shining moon attend
Your nightly sports, as you vouchsafe to ⎫
tell   ⎪
What nymphs they were who mortal   ⎬
forms excel,   ⎪
And what the knights who fought in ⎭
listed fields so well."
To this the dame replied: "Fair daugh-
ter, know,   480
That what you saw was all a fairy show;
And all those airy shapes you now behold
Were human bodies once, and cloth'd with
earthly mold.
Our souls, not yet prepar'd for upper light,
Till doomsday wander in the shades of
night;
This only holiday of all the year,
We privileg'd in sunshine may appear:
With songs and dance we celebrate the
day,
And with due honors usher in the May.
At other times we reign by night alone,   490
And posting thro' the skies pursue the
moon;
But when the moon arises, none are found;
For cruel Demogorgon walks the round,
And if he finds a fairy lag in light,
He drives the wretch before, and lashes
into night.
"All courteous are by kind, and ever
proud
With friendly offices to help the good.
In every land we have a larger space
Than what is known to you of mortal race,

Where we with green adorn our fairy
   bow'rs,   500
And ev'n this grove, unseen before, is ours.
Know farther: ev'ry lady cloth'd in white,
And, crown'd with oak and laurel ev'ry
   knight,
Are servants to the Leaf, by liveries known
Of innocence; and I myself am one.
Saw you not her so graceful to behold
In white attire, and crown'd with radiant
   gold ?
The sovereign lady of our land is she,
Diana call'd, the queen of chastity;
And, for the spotless name of maid she
   bears,   510
That *agnus castus* in her hand appears;
And all her train, with leavy chaplets
   crown'd,
Were for unblam'd virginity renown'd;
But those the chief and highest in command
Who bear those holy branches in their hand:
The knights adorn'd with laurel crowns ⎤
   are they |
Whom death nor danger ever could dis- |
   may,   ⎬
Victorious names, who made the world |
   obey;   ⎦
Who, while they liv'd, in deeds of arms ex-
   cell'd,
And after death for deities were held.   520
But those who wear the woodbine on their
   brow
Were knights of love, who never broke
   their vow;
Firm to their plighted faith, and ever free
From fears, and fickle chance, and jealousy.
The lords and ladies who the woodbine
   bear
As true as Tristram and Isotta were."
  " But what are those," said I, " th' un-
   conquer'd nine,
Who crown'd with laurel wreaths in golden
   armor shine ?
And who the knights in green, and what
   the train   529
Of ladies dress'd with daisies on the plain ?
Why both the bands in worship disagree,
And some adore the Flow'r, and some the
   Tree ?"
  "Just is your suit, fair daughter," said
   the dame;
  " Those laurel'd chiefs were men of mighty
   seen;
Nine worthies were they call'd of diff'rent
   rites,

Three Jews, three Pagans, and three Chris-
   tian knights.
These, as you see, ride foremost in the ⎤
   field, |
As they the foremost rank of honor held, ⎬
And all in deeds of chivalry excell'd: ⎦
Their temples wreath'd with leafs, that
   still renew;   540
For deathless laurel is the victor's due.
Who bear the bows were knights in Ar-
   thur's reign,
Twelve they, and twelve the peers of Char-
   lemagne;
For bows the strength of brawny arms im-
   ply,
Emblems of valor and of victory.
Behold an order yet of newer date,
Doubling their number, equal in their state;
Our England's ornament, the crown's de-
   fense,
In battle brave, protectors of their prince;
Unchang'd by fortune, to their sovereign
   true,   550
For which their manly legs are bound with
   blue.
These, of the Garter call'd, of faith un- ⎤
   stain'd, |
In fighting fields the laurel have obtain'd, ⎬
And well repaid those honors which they |
   gain'd.   ⎦
The laurel wreaths were first by Cæsar
   worn,
And still they Cæsar's successors adorn;
One leaf of this is immortality,
And more of worth than all the world can
   buy."
  " One doubt remains," said I, " the dames
   in green,
What were their qualities, and who their
   queen ?"   560
" Flora commands," said she, "those nymphs
   and knights,
Who liv'd in slothful ease and loose de-
   lights;
Who never acts of honor durst pursue,
The men inglorious knights, the ladies all
   untrue:
Who, nurs'd in idleness and train'd in
   courts,
Pass'd all their precious hours in plays and
   sports,
Till Death behind came stalking on, unseen,
And wither'd (like the storm) the freshness
   of their green.

These, and their mates, enjoy the present
  hour,
And therefore pay their homage to the
  Flow'r.   570
But knights in knightly deeds should per-
  severe,
And still continue what at first they were;
Continue, and proceed in honor's fair
  career.
No room for cowardice or dull delay;
From good to better they should urge their
  way.
For this with golden spurs the chiefs are
  grac'd,
With pointed rowels arm'd to mend their
  haste;
For this with lasting leaves their brows
  are bound,
For laurel is the sign of labor crown'd,
Which bears the bitter blast, nor shaken
  falls to ground: 580
From winter winds it suffers no decay,
For ever fresh and fair, and ev'ry month is
  May.
Ev'n when the vital sap retreats below,
Ev'n when the hoary head is hid in snow,
The life is in she leaf, and still between
The fits of falling snows appears the streaky
  green.
Not so the flow'r, which lasts for little space,
A short-liv'd good, and an uncertain grace;
This way and that the feeble stem is driv'n,
Weak to sustain the storms and injuries of
  heav'n.   590
Propp'd by the spring, it lifts aloft the
  head,
But of a sickly beauty, soon to shed;
In summer living, and in winter dead.
For things of tender kind, for pleasure made,
Shoot up with swift increase, and sudden
  are decay'd."
  With humble words, the wisest I could
  frame,
And proffer'd service, I repaid the dame;
That, of her grace, she gave her maid to
  know
The secret meaning of this moral show.
And she, to prove what profit I had made
Of mystic truth, in fables first convey'd, 601
Demanded, till the next returning May,
Whether the Leaf or Flow'r I would obey ?
I chose the Leaf; she smil'd with sober
  cheer,
And wish'd me fair adventure for the year,
And gave me charms and sigils, for defense

Against ill tongues that scandal innocence.
" But I," said she, " my fellows must pursue,
Already past the plain and out of view."
  We parted thus; I homeward sped my
  way,   610
Bewilder'd in the wood till dawn of day,
And met the merry crew who danc'd about
  the May.
Then late, refresh'd with sleep, I rose to
  write
The visionary vigils of the night:
Blush, as thou may'st, my little book, for
  shame,
Nor hope with homely verse to purchase
  fame;
For such thy maker chose, and so design'd
Thy simple style to suit thy lowly kind.

THE TWELFTH BOOK OF OVID HIS METAMORPHOSES

WHOLLY TRANSLATED

CONNECTION TO THE END OF THE ELEVENTH BOOK

Æsacus, the son of Priam, loving a country
life, forsakes the court : living obscurely, he
falls in love with a nymph, who flying from
him was kill'd by a serpent; for grief of
this, he would have drown'd himself, but
by the pity of the gods is turn'd into a cormorant. Priam, not hearing of Æsacus, believes him to be dead, and raises a tomb to
preserve his memory. By this transition,
which is one of the finest in all Ovid, the poet
naturally falls into the story of the Trojan
war, which is summ'd up in the present book,
but so very briefly, in many places, that Ovid
seems more short than Virgil, contrary to
his usual style. Yet the House of Fame,
which is here describ'd, is one of the most
beautiful pieces in the whole *Metamorphoses*.
The fight of Achilles and Cygnus, and the
fray betwixt the Lapithæ and Centaurs,
yield to no other part of this poet; and particularly the loves and death of Cyllarus and
Hylonome, the male and female Centaur, are
wonderfully moving.

PRIAM, to whom the story was unknown,
As dead, deplor'd his metamorphos'd son;
A cenotaph his name and title kept,
And Hector round the tomb, with all his
  brothers, wept.
  This pious office Paris did not share;
Absent alone, and author of the war,

Which, for the Spartan queen, the Grecians
    drew
T' avenge the rape, and Asia to subdue.
  A thousand ships were mann'd, to sail
    the sea;
Nor had their just resentments found
    delay,   10
Had not the winds and waves oppos'd
    their way.
At Aulis, with united pow'rs, they meet;
But there, cross winds or calms detain'd
    the fleet.
  Now, while they raise an altar on the
    shore
And Jove with solemn sacrifice adore,
A boding sign the priests and people see:
A snake of size immense ascends a tree,
And in the leavy summit spied a nest,
Which, o'er her callow young, a sparrow
    press'd.
Eight were the birds unfledg'd; their
    mother flew   20
And hover'd round her care, but still in
    view;
Till the fierce reptile first devour'd the
    brood,
Then seiz'd the flutt'ring dam and drunk
    her blood.
This dire ostent the fearful people view;
Calchas alone, by Phœbus taught, foreknew
What Heav'n decreed; and, with a smiling
    glance,
Thus gratulates to Greece her happy
    chance:
"O Argives, we shall conquer; Troy is ours,
But long delays shall first afflict our pow'rs:
Nine years of labor the nine birds portend;
The tenth shall in the town's destruction
    end."   31
  The serpent, who his maw obscene had
    fill'd,
The branches in his curl'd embraces held;
But, as in spires he stood, he turn'd to stone:
The stony snake retain'd the figure still his
    own.
  Yet not for this the wind-bound navy
    weigh'd;
Slack were their sails, and Neptune dis-
    obey'd.
Some thought him loth the town should be
    destroy'd,
Whose building had his hands divine em-
    ploy'd:
Not so the seer; who knew, and known
    foreshow'd,   40

The virgin Phœbe with a virgin's blood
Must first be reconcil'd. The common cause
Prevail'd; and, pity yielding to the laws,
Fair Iphigenia, the devoted maid,
Was, by the weeping priests, in linen robes
    array'd.
All mourn her fate, but no relief appear'd;
The royal victim bound, the knife already
    rear'd:
When that offended pow'r, who caus'd their
    woe,
Relenting ceas'd her wrath, and stopp'd
    the coming blow.
A mist before the ministers she cast,   50
And in the virgin's room a hind she plac'd.
Th' oblation slain, and Phœbe reconcil'd,
The storm was hush'd, and dimpled ocean
    smil'd;
A favorable gale arose from shore,
Which to the port desir'd the Grecian gal-
    leys bore.
  Full in the midst of this created space,
Betwixt heav'n, earth, and skies, there
    stands a place
Confining on all three, with triple bound;
Whence all things, tho' remote, are view'd
    around,
And thither bring their undulating sound:
The palace of loud Fame, her seat of
    pow'r,   61
Plac'd on the summit of a lofty tow'r.
A thousand winding entries, long and wide,
Receive of fresh reports a flowing tide.
A thousand crannies in the walls are made;
Nor gate nor bars exclude the busy trade.
'T is built of brass, the better to diffuse
The spreading sounds, and multiply the
    news;
Where echoes in repeated echoes play: 69
A mart forever full, and open night and day.
Nor silence is within, nor voice express,
But a deaf noise of sounds that never cease;
Confus'd and chiding, like the hollow roar
Of tides receding from th' insulted shore;
Or like the broken thunder, heard from far,
When Jove to distance drives the rolling
    war.
The courts are fill'd with a tumultuous din
Of crowds, or issuing forth, or ent'ring in:
A thoroughfare of news, where some devise
Things never heard; some mingle truth
    with lies: 80
The troubled air with empty sounds they
    beat;
Intent to hear, and eager to repeat.

Error sits brooding there, with added train
Of vain Credulity, and Joys as vain:
Suspicion, with Sedition join'd, are near;
And Rumors rais'd, and Murmurs mix'd,
 and Panic Fear.
Fame sits aloft, and sees the subject ground,
And seas about, and skies above; enquiring
 all around.
 The goddess gives th' alarm, and soon is
 known   89
The Grecian fleet, descending on the town.
Fix'd on defense, the Trojans are not slow
To guard their shore from an expected foe.
They meet in fight; by Hector's fatal hand
Protesilaus falls, and bites the strand,
Which with expense of blood the Grecians
 won,
And prov'd the strength unknown of Priam's
 son;
And to their cost the Trojan leaders felt
The Grecian heroes, and what deaths they
 dealt.
 From these first onsets, the Sigæan shore
Was strew'd with carcasses and stain'd with
 gore: 100
Neptunian Cygnus troops of Greeks had
 slain;
Achilles in his car had scour'd the plain,
And clear'd the Trojan ranks: where'er he
 fought,
Cygnus, or Hector, thro' the fields he sought.
Cygnus he found; on him his force essay'd,
For Hector was to the tenth year delay'd.
His white-man'd steeds, that bow'd beneath
 the yoke,
He cheer'd to courage, with a gentle stroke;
Then urg'd his fiery chariot on the foe,
And rising shook his lance, in act to throw.
But first he cried: "O youth, be proud to
 bear   111
Thy death, ennobled by Pelides' spear."
The lance pursued the voice without delay;
Nor did the whizzing weapon miss the way,
But pierc'd his cuirass, with such fury sent,
And sign'd his bosom with a purple dint.
At this the seed of Neptune: "Goddess-
 born,
For ornament, not use, these arms are worn;
This helm and heavy buckler I can spare,
As only decorations of the war: 120
So Mars is arm'd for glory, not for need.
'T is somewhat more from Neptune to pro-
 ceed,
Than from a daughter of the sea to spring:
Thy sire is mortal; mine is ocean's king.

Secure of death, I should contemn thy dart,
Tho' naked, and impassible depart."
He said, and threw; the trembling
 weapon pass'd
Thro' nine bull hides, each under other
 plac'd
On his broad shield, and stuck within the
 last.   129
Achilles wrench'd it out, and sent again
The hostile gift: the hostile gift was vain.
He tried a third, a tough well-chosen spear;
Th' inviolable body stood sincere,
Tho' Cygnus then did no defense provide,
But scornful offer'd his unshielded side.
 Not otherwise th' impatient hero far'd,
Than as a bull, incompass'd with a guard,
Amid the circus roars, provok'd from far
By sight of scarlet and a sanguine war:
They quit their ground, his bended horns
 elude,   140
In vain pursuing and in vain pursued.
 Before to farther fight he would advance,
He stood considering and survey'd his lance;
Doubts if he wielded not a wooden spear
Without a point: he look'd, the point was
 there.
"This is my hand, and this my lance,"
 he said,
"By which so many thousand foes are
 dead.
O whither is their usual virtue fled!
I had it once; and the Lyrnessian wall
And Tenedos confess'd it in their fall.   150
Thy streams, Caïcus, roll'd a crimson flood;
And Thebes ran red with her own natives'
 blood.
Twice Telephus employ'd this piercing steel,
To wound him first, and afterward to heal.
The vigor of this arm was never vain;
And that my wonted prowess I retain,
Witness these heaps of slaughter on the
 plain."
He said, and, doubtful of his former deeds,
To some new trial of his force proceeds.
He chose Menœtes from among the rest;
At him he launch'd his spear, and pierc'd his
 breast: 161
On the hard earth the Lycian knock'd his
 head,
And lay supine; and forth the spirit fled.
 Then thus the hero: "Neither can I blame
The hand, or javelin; both are still the same.
The same I will employ against this foe;
And wish but with the same success to
 throw."

So spoke the chief; and while he spoke he
  threw.
The weapon with unerring fury flew,
At his left shoulder aim'd; nor entrance
  found;   170
But back, as from a rock, with swift re-
  bound
Harmless return'd: a bloody mark appear'd,
Which with false joy the flatter'd hero
  cheer'd.
Wound there was none; the blood that was
  in view,
The lance before from slain Menœtes drew.
  Headlong he leaps from off his lofty car,
And in close fight on foot renews the war;
Raging with high disdain, repeats his blows;
Nor shield nor armor can their force oppose.
Huge cantlets of his buckler strew the
  ground,   180
And no defense in his bor'd arms is found.
But on his flesh no wound or blood is seen;
The sword itself is blunted on the skin.
  This vain attempt the chief no longer
  bears,
But round his hollow temples and his ears
His buckler beats: the son of Neptune,
  stunn'd
With these repeated buffets, quits his
  ground;
A sickly sweat succeeds, and shades of
  night;
Inverted nature swims before his sight:
Th' insulting victor presses on the more, 190
And treads the steps the vanquish'd trod
  before,
Nor rest, nor respite gives. A stone there
  lay
Behind his trembling foe, and stopp'd his
  way:
Achilles took th' advantage which he found,
O'erturn'd, and push'd him backward on
  the ground.
His buckler held him under, while he
  press'd,
With both his knees above, his panting
  breast;
Unlac'd his helm: about his chin the twist
He tied, and soon the strangled soul dis-
  miss'd.
  With eager haste he went to strip the
  dead;   200
The vanish'd body from his arms was fled.
His sea god sire, t' immortalize his fame,
Had turn'd it to the bird that bears his
  name.

  A truce succeeds the labors of this day,
And arms suspended with a long delay.
While Trojan walls are kept with watch
  an.¹ ward,
The Greeks before their trenches mount
  the guard.
The feast approach'd; when to the blue-
  ey'd maid
His vows for Cygnus slain the victor paid,
And a white heifer on her altar laid. 210
The reeking entrails on the fire they threw,
And to the gods the grateful odor flew:
Heav'n had its part in sacrifice; the rest
Was broil'd and roasted for the future feast.
The chief invited guests were set around;
And, hunger first assuag'd, the bowls
  were crown'd,
Which in deep draughts their cares and
  labors drown'd.
The mellow harp did not their ears em-
  ploy,
And mute was all the warlike symphony.
Discourse, the food of souls, was their de-
  light,   220
And pleasing chat prolong'd the summer's
  night:
The subject, deeds of arms, and valor
  shown,
Or on the Trojan side, or on their own.
Of dangers undertaken, fame achiev'd,
They talk'd by turns; the talk by turns
  reliev'd.
What things but these could fierce Achilles
  tell,
Or what could fierce Achilles hear so well?
The last great act perform'd, of Cygnus
  slain,
Did most the martial audience entertain:
Wond'ring to find a body free by fate 230
From steel, and which could ev'n that steel
  rebate,
Amaz'd, their admiration they renew;
And scarce Pelides could believe it true.
  Then Nestor thus: "What once this age
  has known,
In fated Cygnus, and in him alone,
These eyes have seen in Cæneus long before,
Whose body not a thousand swords could
  bore.
Cæneus in courage and in strength ex-
  cell'd,
And still his Othrys with his fame is fill'd:
But what did most his martial deeds adorn,
(Tho' since he chang'd his sex,) a woman
  born."   241

A novelty so strange and full of fate,
His list'ning audience ask'd him to relate.
Achilles thus commends their common suit:
" O father, first for prudence in repute,
Tell, with that eloquence so much thy own,
What thou hast heard, or what of Cæneus
known:
What was he, whence his change of sex
begun,
What trophies, join'd in wars with thee, he
won ?
Who conquer'd him, and in what fatal
strife   250
The youth, without a wound, could lose his
life ? "
Neleides then: " Tho' tardy age and time
Have shrunk my sinews and decay'd my
prime;
Tho' much I have forgotten of my store,
Yet, not exhausted, I remember more.
Of all that arms achiev'd, or peace design'd,
That action still is fresher in my mind
Than aught beside. If reverend age can
give
To faith a sanction, in my third I live.   259
" 'T was in my second cent'ry I survey'd
Young Cænis, then a fair Thessalian maid:
Cænis the bright was born to high com-
mand;
A princess, and a native of thy land,
Divine Achilles: every tongue proclaim'd
Her beauty, and her eyes all hearts inflam'd.
Peleus, thy sire, perhaps had sought her
bed,
Among the rest; but he had either led
Thy mother then, or was by promise tied;
But she to him, and all alike, her love
denied.
" It was her fortune once to take her
way   270
Along the sandy margin of the sea:
The Pow'r of Ocean view'd her as she pass'd,
And, lov'd as soon as seen, by force em-
brac'd.
So fame reports. Her virgin treasure seiz'd,
And his new joys, the ravisher so pleas'd,
That thus, transported, to the nymph he
cried:
' Ask what thou wilt, no pray'r shall be
denied.'
This also fame relates: the haughty fair,
Who not the rape ev'n of a god could bear,
This answer, proud, return'd: ' To mighty
wrongs   280
A mighty recompense, of right, belongs.

Give me no more to suffer such a shame;
But change the woman for a better name;
One gift for all.' She said; and while she
spoke,
A stern, majestic, manly tone she took.
A man she was; and, as the godhead swore,
To Cæneus turn'd, who Cænis was before.
" To this the lover adds, without request,
No force of steel should violate his breast.
Glad of the gift, the new-made warrior
goes;   290
And arms among the Greeks, and longs for
equal foes.
" Now brave Perithous, bold Ixion's son,
The love of fair Hippodame had won.
The cloud-begotten race, half men, half
beast,
Invited, came to grace the nuptial feast:
In a cool cave's recess the treat was made,
Whose entrance trees with spreading boughs
o'ershade.
They sate; and summon'd by the bride-
groom came,
To mix with those, the Lapithæan name;
Nor wanted I: the roofs with joy resound,
And ' Hymen, Io Hymen,' rung around.   301
Rais'd altars shone with holy fires ; the
bride,
Lovely herself, (and lovely by her side
A bevy of bright nymphs,) with sober grace,
Came glitt'ring like a star, and took her
place.
Her heav'nly form beheld, all wish'd her
joy;
And little wanted but in vain their wishes
all employ.
" For one, most brutal of the brutal
brood,
Or whether wine or beauty fir'd his blood,
Or both at once, beheld with lustful eyes   310
The bride; at once resolv'd to make his
prize.
Down went the board; and, fast'ning on her
hair,
He seiz'd with sudden force the frighted
fair.
'T was Eurytus began: his bestial kind
His crime pursued; and each as pleas'd his
mind,
Or her whom chance presented, took: the
feast
An image of a taken town express'd.
" The cave resounds with female shrieks;
we rise,
Mad with revenge, to make a swift reprise:

And Theseus first: 'What frenzy has pos-
    sess'd,   320
O Eurytus,' he cried, ' thy brutal breast,
To wrong Perithous, and not him alone,
But, while I live, two friends conjoin'd in
    one ? '
" To justify his threat, he thrusts aside
The crowd of Centaurs, and redeems the
    bride.
The monster naught replied; for words were
    vain,
And deeds could only deeds unjust main-
    tain:
But answers with his hand, and forward
    press'd,
With blows redoubled, on his face and
    breast.
An ample goblet stood, of antic mold,   330
And rough with figures of the rising gold;
The hero snatch'd it up, and toss'd in air,
Full at the front of the foul ravisher.
He falls; and falling vomits forth a flood
Of wine, and foam, and brains, and mingled
    blood.
Half roaring, and half neighing thro' the
    hall,
' Arms, arms,' the double-form'd with fury
    call,
To wreak their brother's death: a medley
    flight
Of bowls and jars, at first, supply the fight,
Once instruments of feasts, but now of
    fate;   340
Wine animates their rage and arms their
    hate.
    " Bold Amycus from the robb'd vestry
    brings
The chalices of heav'n, and holy things
Of precious weight: a sconce, that hung on
    high,
With tapers fill'd, to light the sacristy,
Torn from the cord, with his unhallow'd
    hand
He threw amid the Lapithæan band.
On Celadon the ruin fell, and left
His face of feature and of form bereft;
So, when some brawny sacrificer knocks, 350
Before an altar led, an offer'd ox,
His eyeballs rooted out are thrown to ⎤
    ground: ⎟
His nose dismantled in his mouth is found, ⎬
His jaws, cheeks, front, one undistin-   ⎟
    guish'd wound.   ⎦
    " This, Belates, th' avenger, could not
    brook:

But by the foot a maple board he took,
And hurl'd at Amycus; his chin it bent
Against his chest, and down the Centaur
    sent;
Whom sputt'ring bloody teeth, the second
    blow
Of his drawn sword dispatch'd to shades
    below.   360
    " Grineus was near; and cast a furious
    look
On the side altar, cens'd with sacred smoke,
And bright with flaming fires. ' The gods,'
    he cried,
' Have with their holy trade our hands sup-
    plied:
Why use we not their gifts ? ' Then from
    the floor
An altar stone he heav'd, with all the load
    it bore:
Altar and altar's freight together flew ⎤
Where thickest throng'd the Lapithæan ⎬
    crew;   ⎦
And Broteas and, at once, Oryus slew:
Oryus' mother, Mycale, was known   370
Down from her sphere to draw the lab'ring
    moon.
    " Exadius cried: ' Unpunish'd shall not go
This fact, if arms are found against the foe.'
He look'd about, where on a pine were
    spread
The votive horns of a stag's branching head:
At Grineus these he throws; so just they
    fly
That the sharp antlers stuck in either eye.
Breathless and blind he fell; with blood
    besmear'd,
His eyeballs beaten out hung dangling on
    his beard.
Fierce Rhœtus from the hearth a burning
    brand   380
Selects, and whirling waves, till from his
    hand
The fire took flame; then dash'd it from the
    right,
On fair Charaxus' temples, near the sight:
The whistling pest came on and pierc'd the
    bone,
And caught the yellow hair, that shrivel'd
    while it shone;
Caught, like dry stubble fir'd, or like sear ⎤
    wood;   ⎟
Yet from the wound ensued no purple ⎬
    flood;   ⎟
But look'd a bubbling mass of frying ⎦
    blood.

His blazing locks sent forth a crackling
sound,
And hiss'd like red-hot iron within the
smithy drown'd.   390
The wounded warrior shook his flaming hair,
Then (what a team of horse could hardly
rear)
He heaves the threshold stone; but could
not throw:
The weight itself forbade the threaten'd
blow;
Which, dropping from his lifted arms, came
down
Full on Cometes' head, and crush'd his
crown.
Nor Rhœtus then retain'd his joy, but
said:
'So by their fellows may our foes be sped;'
Then with redoubled strokes he plies his
head:
The burning lever not deludes his pains, 400
But drives the batter'd skull within the
brains.
  "Thus flush'd, the conqueror, with force
renew'd,
Evagrus, Dryas, Corythus, pursued:
First Corythus, with downy cheeks, he slew;
Whose fall when fierce Evagrus had in
view,
He cried: 'What palm is from a beardless
prey?'
Rhœtus prevents what more he had to say;
And drove within his mouth the fiery death,
Which enter'd hissing in, and chok'd his
breath.   409
At Dryas next he flew, but weary chance
No longer would the same success advance;
For, while he whirl'd in fiery circles round
The brand, a sharpen'd stake strong
Dryas found,
And in the shoulder's joint inflicts the
wound.
The weapon stuck: which roaring out
with pain
He drew; nor longer durst the fight
maintain,
But turn'd his back, for fear; and fled
amain.
With him fled Orneus, with like dread
possess'd;
Thaumas, and Medon, wounded in the
breast;
And Mermeros, in the late race renown'd, 420
Now limping ran, and tardy with his
wound.

Pholus and Melaneus from fight withdrew,
And Abas maim'd, who boars encount'ring
slew;
And augur Astylos, whose art in vain
From fight dissuaded the four-footed
train,
Now beat the hoof with Nessus on the
plain;
But to his fellow cried: 'Be safely slow,
Thy death deferr'd is due to great Alcides'
bow.'
  "Meantime strong Dryas urg'd his
chance so well,
That Lycidas, Areos, Imbreus fell;   430
All one by one, and fighting face to face.
Crenæus fled, to fall with more disgrace:
For, fearful, while he look'd behind, he
bore,
Betwixt his nose and front, the blow be-
fore.
Amid the noise and tumult of the fray,
Snoring, and drunk with wine, Aphidas lay.
Ev'n then the bowl within his hand he kept,
And on a bear's rough hide securely slept.
Him Phorbas with his flying dart trans-
fix'd.
'Take thy next draught with Stygian waters
mix'd,   440
And sleep thy fill,' th' insulting victor
cried;
Surpris'd with death unfelt, the Centaur
died:
The ruddy vomit, as he breath'd his soul,
Repass'd his throat, and fill'd his empty
bowl.
  "I saw Petræus' arms employ'd around
A well-grown oak, to root it from the
ground.
This way and that he wrench'd the fibrous
bands;
The trunk was like a sapling in his hands,
And still obey'd the bent: while thus he
stood,
Perithous' dart drove on, and nail'd him to
the wood.   450
Lycus and Chromis fell, by him oppress'd;
Helops and Dictys added to the rest
A nobler palm: Helops, thro' either ear
Transfix'd, receiv'd the penetrating spear.
This Dictys saw; and, seiz'd with sudden
fright,
Leapt headlong from the hill of steepy
height;
And crush'd an ash beneath, that could
not bear his weight.

The shatter'd tree receives his fall, and
strikes,
Within his full-blown paunch, the sharpen'd
spikes.
Strong Aphareus had heav'd a mighty
stone,   460
The fragment of a rock, and would have
thrown;
But Theseus, with a club of harden'd oak, ⎫
The cubit-bone of the bold Centaur   ⎪
broke,   ⎬
And left him maim'd, nor seconded the ⎪
stroke;   ⎭
Then leapt on tall Bianor's back, (who bore
No mortal burden but his own before,)
Press'd with his knees his sides; the double
man,
His speed with spurs increas'd, unwilling
ran.
One hand the hero fasten'd on his locks;
His other plied him with repeated strokes:
The club rung round his ears and batter'd
brows;   471
He falls, and, lashing up his heels, his rider
throws.
  " The same Herculean arms Nedymnus
wound,
And lay by him Lycotas on the ground;
And Hippasus, whose beard his breast in-
vades;
And Ripheus, haunter of the woodland
shades:
And Tereus, us'd with mountain bears to
strive,
And from their dens to draw th' indignant
beasts alive.
  " Demoleon could not bear this hateful
sight,   479
Or the long fortune of th' Athenian knight;
But pull'd with all his force, to disengage
From earth a pine, the product of an age.
The root stuck fast; the broken trunk he
sent
At Theseus: Theseus frustrates his intent,
And leaps aside, by Pallas warn'd, the
blow
To shun: (for so he said; and we believ'd
it so.)
Yet not in vain th' enormous weight was
cast;
Which Crantor's body sunder'd at the waist:
Thy father's squire, Achilles, and his care;
Whom, conquer'd in the Dolopeian war,   490
Their king, his present ruin to prevent,
A pledge of peace implor'd, to Peleus sent.

  " Thy sire, with grieving eyes, beheld his
fate;
And cried: ' Not long, lov'd Crantor, shalt
thou wait
Thy vow'd revenge.' At once he said, and
threw
His ashen spear, which quiver'd as it flew,
With all his force and all his soul applied:
The sharp point enter'd in the Centaur's
side.
Both hands, to wrench it out, the monster
join'd;
And wrench'd it out, but left the steel
behind.   500
Stuck in his lungs it stood; inrag'd he rears
His hoofs, and down to ground thy father
bears.
Thus trampled under foot, his shield de-
fends
His head; his other hand the lance pro-
tends.
Ev'n while he lay extended on the dust,
He sped the Centaur with one single thrust.
Two more his lance before transfix'd from
far,
And two his sword had slain in closer war.
To these was added Dorylas, who spread
A bull's two goring horns around his head.
With these he push'd, in blood already
dyed: 511
Him, fearless, I approach'd, and thus defied:
' Now, monster, now, by proof it shall ap-
pear,
Whether thy horns are sharper, or my
spear.'
At this, I threw; for want of other ward,
He lifted up his hand, his front to guard.
His hand it pass'd, and fix'd it to his brow;
Loud shouts of ours attend the lucky blow.
Him Peleus finish'd, with a second wound, ⎫
Which thro' the navel pierc'd: he reel'd ⎪
around,   520 ⎬
And dragg'd his dangling bowels on the ⎪
ground;   ⎭
Trod what he dragg'd, and what he trod
he crush'd;
And to his mother earth with empty belly
rush'd.
  " Nor could thy form, O Cyllarus, fore-
slow
Thy fate (if form to monsters men allow):
Just bloom'd thy beard, thy beard of golden
hue;
**Thy locks, in golden waves, about thy
shoulders flew.**

Sprightly thy look; thy shapes in ev'ry part
So clean, as might instruct the sculptor's
    art,
As far as man extended: where began   530
The beast, the beast was equal to the man.
Add but a horse's head and neck, and he,
O Castor, was a courser worthy thee.
So was his back proportion'd for the seat;
So rose his brawny chest; so swiftly mov'd
    his feet.
Coal-black his color, but like jet it shone;
His legs and flowing tail were white alone.
Belov'd by many maidens of his kind,
But fair Hylonome possess'd his mind;
Hylonome, for features and for face   540
Excelling all the nymphs of double race:
Nor less her blandishments than beauty
    move,
At once both loving and confessing love.
For him she dress'd; for him with female
    care
She comb'd and set in curls her auburn
    hair.
Of roses, violets, and lilies mix'd,
And sprigs of flowing rosemary betwixt,
She form'd the chaplet that adorn'd her
    front.
In waters of the Pagasæan fount,
And in the streams that from the fountain
    play,   550
She wash'd her face, and bath'd her twice
    a day.
The scarf of furs that hung below her side
Was ermine, or the panther's spotted pride;
Spoils of no common beast: with equal flame
They lov'd; their sylvan pleasures were the
    same:
All day they hunted; and, when day expir'd,
Together to some shady cave retir'd.
Invited to the nuptials, both repair;
And, side by side, they both ingage in war.
  " Uncertain from what hand, a flying
    dart   560
At Cyllarus was sent, which pierc'd his
    heart.
The javelin drawn from out the mortal
    wound,
He faints with stagg'ring steps, and seeks
    the ground:
The fair within her arms receiv'd his fall,
And strove his wand'ring spirits to recall;
And, while her hand the streaming blood
    oppos'd,
Join'd face to face, his lips with hers she
    clos'd.

Stifled with kisses, a sweet death he dies;
She fills the fields with undistinguish'd cries:
At least her words were in her clamor
    drown'd,   570
For my stunn'd ears receiv'd no vocal sound.
In madness of her grief, she seiz'd the dart,
New-drawn, and reeking from her lover's
    heart;
To her bare bosom the sharp point ap-
    plied,
And wounded fell; and, falling by his side,
Embrac'd him in her arms, and thus em-
    bracing died.
  " Ev'n still, methinks, I see Phæocomes.
Strange was his habit, and as odd his dress.
Six lion's hides, with thongs together fast,
His upper part defended to his waist;   580
And where man ended, the continued vest,
Spread on his back, the houss and trappings
    of a beast.
A stump too heavy for a team to draw,
(It seems a fable, tho' the fact I saw,)
He threw at Pholon; the descending blow
Divides the skull, and cleaves his head in
    two.
The brains from nose and mouth and either
    ear
Came issuing out, as thro' a colander
The curdled milk, or from the press the
    whey,
Driv'n down by weights above, is drain'd
    away.   590
  " But him, while stooping down to spoil
    the slain,
Pierc'd thro' the paunch, I tumbled on the
    plain.
Then Chthonius and Teleboas I slew;
A fork the former arm'd, a dart his fellow
    threw.
The javelin wounded me; (behold the scar.)
Then was my time to seek the Trojan war;
Then I was Hector's match in open field;
But he was then unborn, at least a child;
Now, I am nothing.   I forbear to tell
By Periphantas how Pyretus fell,   600
The Centaur by the knight; nor will I
    stay
On Amphyx, or what deaths he dealt that
    day;
What honor with a pointless lance he won,
Stuck in the front of a four-footed man;
What fame young Macareus obtain'd in
    fight;
Or dwell on Nessus, now return'd from
    flight;

How prophet Mopsus not alone divin'd,
Whose valor equal'd his foreseeing mind.
" Already Cæneus, with his conquering
   hand,
Had slaughter'd five, the boldest of their
   band: 610
Pyrachmus, Helymus, Antimachus,
Bromus the brave, and stronger Styphelus.
Their names I number'd, and remember
   well,
No trace remaining, by what wounds they
   fell.
" Latreus, the bulkiest of the double race,
Whom the spoil'd arms of slain Halesus
   grace,
In years retaining still his youthful might,
Tho' his black hairs were interspers'd with
   white,   618
Betwixt th' imbattled ranks began to prance,
Proud of his helm and Macedonian lance,
And rode the ring around; that either host
Might hear him, while he made this empty
   boast:
' And from a strumpet shall we suffer
   shame ?
For Cænis still, not Cæneus is thy name;
And still the native softness of thy kind
Prevails, and leaves the woman in thy mind.
Remember what thou wert; what price was
   paid
To change thy sex, to make thee not a maid,
And but a man in shew: go, card and spin,
And leave the business of the war to men.'
" While thus the boaster exercis'd his
   pride,   631
The fatal spear of Cæneus reach'd his side;
Just in the mixture of the kinds it ran,
Betwixt the nether beast and upper man.
The monster, mad with rage, and stung with
   smart,
His lance directed at the hero's heart:
It strook, but bounded from his harden'd
   breast,
Like hail from tiles, which the safe house
   invest;
Nor seem'd the stroke with more effect to
   come,
Than a small pebble falling on a drum. 640
He next his fauchion tried, in closer fight;
But the keen fauchion had no pow'r to bite.
He thrust; the blunted point return'd again.
' Since downright blows,' he cried, ' and
   thrusts are vain,
I 'll prove his side.' In strong embraces
   held,

He prov'd his side; his side the sword re-
   pell'd:
His hollow belly echo'd to the stroke; ⎤
Untouch'd his body, as a solid rock; ⎟
Aim'd at his neck at last, the blade in ⎬
   shivers broke.   ⎦
" Th' impassive knight stood idle, to ⎤
   deride   650 ⎟
His rage, and offer'd oft his naked side: ⎬
At length: ' Now, monster, in thy turn,' ⎟
   he cried,   ⎦
' Try thou the strength of Cæneus.' At
   the word
He thrust, and in his shoulder plung'd the
   sword;
Then writh'd his hand; and, as he drove it
   down,
Deep in his breast, made many wounds in
   one.
" The Centaurs saw, inrag'd, th' unhop'd
   success;
And, rushing on, in crowds, together press;
At him, and him alone, their darts they
   threw:
Repuls'd they from his fated body flew. 660
Amaz'd they stood; till Monychus began:
' O shame, a nation conquer'd by a man !
A woman-man; yet more a man is he
Than all our race; and what he was, are we.
Now, what avail our nerves, the united
   force
Of two the strongest creatures, man and
   horse ?
Nor goddess-born, nor of Ixion's seed
We seem; (a lover built for Juno's bed;)
Master'd by this half man. Whole moun-
   tains throw   669
With woods at once, and bury him below.
This only way remains. Nor need we doubt
To choke the soul within, tho' not to force
   it out.
Heap weights, instead of wounds.' He
   chanc'd to see
Where southern storms had rooted up a
   tree;
This, rais'd from earth, against the foe he
   threw;
Th' example shewn, his fellow brutes pur-
   sue.
With forest loads the warrior they in- ⎤
   vade;   ⎟
Othrys and Pelion soon were void of ⎬
   shade,   ⎟
And spreading groves were naked moun- ⎟
   tains made.   ⎦

Press'd with the burden, Cæneus pants for
    breath,   680
And on his shoulders bears the wooden
    death.
To heave th' intolerable weight he tries;
At length it rose above his mouth and eyes.
Yet still he heaves; and, struggling with
    despair,
Shakes all aside, and gains a gulp of air;
A short relief, which but prolongs his pain;
He faints by fits, and then respires again:
At last, the burden only nods above,
As when an earthquake stirs th' Idæan
    grove.   689
Doubtful his death; he suffocated seem'd
To most; but otherwise our Mopsus deem'd,
Who said he saw a yellow bird arise
From out the pile, and cleave the liquid
    skies:
I saw it too, with golden feathers bright,
Nor e'er before beheld so strange a sight.
Whom Mopsus viewing, as it soar'd around
Our troop, and heard the pinions' rattling
    sound,
'All hail,' he cried, 'thy country's grace
    and love;
Once first of men below, now first of birds
    above.'
Its author to the story gave belief;   700
For us, our courage was increas'd by grief:
Asham'd to see a single man, pursued
With odds, to sink beneath a multitude,
We push'd the foe and forc'd to shameful
    flight;
Part fell, and part escap'd by favor of the
    night."
    This tale, by Nestor told, did much dis-
    please
Tlepolemus, the seed of Hercules,
For often he had heard his father say ⎞
That he himself was present at the fray, ⎟
And more than shar'd the glories of the ⎟
    day.   710⎠
  "Old Chronicle," he said, "among the
    rest,
You might have nam'd Alcides at the least:
Is he not worth your praise?" The Pylian
    prince
Sigh'd ere he spoke; then made this proud
    defense:
"My former woes, in long oblivion drown'd,
I would have lost; but you renew the
    wound:
Better to pass him o'er, than to relate
The cause I have your mighty sire to hate.

His fame has fill'd the world, and reach'd
    the sky
(Which, O, I wish with truth I could
    deny!)   720
We praise not Hector; tho' his name, we
    know,
Is great in arms: 'tis hard to praise a
    foe.
  "He, your great father, level'd to the
    ground
Messenia's tow'rs: nor better fortune found
Elis and Pylus; that, a neighb'ring state,
And this, my own, both guiltless of their
    fate.
  "To pass the rest, twelve, wanting one,
    he slew,
My brethren, who their birth from Neleus
    drew.
All youths of early promise, had they liv'd;
By him they perish'd: I alone surviv'd.   730
The rest were easy conquest, but the fate
Of Periclymenos is wondrous to relate.
To him our common grandsire of the main
Had giv'n to change his form, and chang'd,
    resume again.
Varied at pleasure, every shape he tried,
And in all beasts Alcides still defied;
Vanquish'd on earth, at length he soar'd
    above,
Chang'd to the bird that bears the bolt of
    Jove.
The new dissembled eagle, now endued   739
With beak and pounces, Hercules pursued,
And cuff'd his manly cheeks, and tore his
    face;
Then safe retir'd, and tow'r'd in empty
    space.
Alcides bore not long his flying foe;
But, bending his inevitable bow,
Reach'd him in air, suspended as he stood,
And in his pinion fix'd the feather'd wood.
Light was the wound; but in the sinew
    hung
The point, and his disabled wing unstrung.
He wheel'd in air, and stretch'd his vans in
    vain;   749
His vans no longer could his flight sustain:
For, while one gather'd wind, one unsup-
    plied
Hung drooping down, nor pois'd his other
    side.
He fell: the shaft that slightly was im-
    press'd,
Now from his heavy fall with weight in-
    creas'd.

Drove thro' his neck, aslant; he spurns the
  ground,
And the soul issues thro' the weazon's
  wound.
" Now, brave commander of the Rhodian
  seas,
What praise is due from me to Hercules ?
Silence is all the vengeance I decree
For my slain brothers; but 't is peace with
  thee."   760
Thus with a flowing tongue old Nestor
  spoke;
Then, to full bowls each other they provoke:
At length, with weariness and wine op-
  press'd,
The, rise from table, and withdraw to rest.
The sire of Cygnus, monarch of the ⎞
  main,   ⎪
Meantime laments his son in battle slain, ⎬
And vows the victor's death, nor vows in ⎪
  vain.   ⎠
For nine long years the smother'd pain he
  bore;
(Achilles was not ripe for fate before;)
Then, when he saw the promis'd hour was
  near,   770
He thus bespoke the god that guides the
  year:
" Immortal offspring of my brother Jove;
My brightest nephew, and whom best I love,
Whose hands were join'd with mine, to raise
  the wall
Of tott'ring Troy, now nodding to her fall;
Dost thou not mourn our pow'r employ'd in
  vain,
And the defenders of our city slain ?
To pass the rest, could noble Hector lie
Unpitied, dragg'd around his native Troy ?
And yet the murd'rer lives, himself by
  far   780
A greater plague than all the wasteful war:
He lives; the proud Pelides lives, to boast
Our town destroy'd, our common labor lost !
O, could I meet him ! But I wish too late;
To prove my trident is not in his fate.
But let him try (for that 's allow'd) thy
  dart,
And pierce his only penetrable part."
Apollo bows to the superior throne,
And to his uncle's anger adds his own.
Then, in a cloud involv'd, he takes his flight,
Where Greeks and Trojans mix'd in mortal
  fight,   791
And found out Paris, lurking where he
  stood,

And stain'd his arrows with plebeian blood.
Phœbus to him alone the god confess'd,
Then to the recreant knight he thus ad-
  dress'd:
" Dost thou not blush to spend thy shafts in
  vain
On a degenerate and ignoble train ?
If fame or better vengeance be thy care,
There aim, and with one arrow end the war."
He said; and shew'd from far the blaz- ⎞
  ing shield   800 ⎪
And sword, which but Achilles none could ⎬
  wield;   ⎪
And how he mov'd a god, and mow'd the ⎪
  standing field.   ⎠
The deity himself directs aright
Th' invenom'd shaft, and wings the fatal
  flight.
Thus fell the foremost of the Grecian
  name;
And he, the base adult'rer, boasts the fame:
A spectacle to glad the Trojan train,
And please old Priam, after Hector slain.
If by a female hand he had foreseen ⎞
He was to die, his wish had rather been 810 ⎬
The lance and double ax of the fair war- ⎪
  rior queen.   ⎠
And now, the terror of the Trojan field,
The Grecian honor, ornament, and shield,
High on a pile th' unconquer'd chief is plac'd;
The god that arm'd him first consum'd at
  last.
Of all the mighty man, the small remains
A little urn, and scarcely fill'd, contains.
Yet, great in Homer, still Achilles lives;
And, equal to himself, himself survives.
His buckler owns its former lord, and
  brings   820
New cause of strife betwixt contending
  kings;
Who worthiest, after him, his sword to wield,
Or wear his armor, or sustain his shield.
Ev'n Diomede sate mute, with downcast
  eyes,
Conscious of wanted worth to win the prize;
Nor Menelas presum'd these arms to claim,
Nor he, the King of Men, a greater name.
Two rivals only rose: Laertes' son,
And the vast bulk of Ajax Telamon.
The king, who cherish'd each with equal
  love,   830
And from himself all envy would remove,
Left both to be determin'd by the laws,
And to the Grecian chiefs transferr'd the
  cause.

THE SPEECHES OF AJAX AND ULYSSES

FROM OVID'S METAMORPHOSES, BOOK XIII

THE chiefs were set, the soldiers crown'd
    the field:
To these the master of the sevenfold shield
Upstarted fierce; and, kindled with disdain,
Eager to speak, unable to contain
His boiling rage, he roll'd his eyes around
The shore, and Grecian galleys haul'd
    aground;
Then, stretching out his hands: "O Jove,"
    he cried,
" Must then our cause before the fleet be
    tried ?
And dares Ulysses for the prize contend,
In sight of what he durst not once defend ?
But basely fled, that memorable day,   11
When I from Hector's hands redeem'd the
    flaming prey.
So much 't is safer at the noisy bar
With words to flourish, than ingage in war.
By different methods we maintain our right,
Nor am I made to talk, nor he to fight.
In bloody fields I labor to be great;
His arms are a smooth tongue, and soft
    deceit:
Nor need I speak my deeds, for those you
    see;
The sun and day are witnesses for me.   20
Let him who fights unseen relate his own,
And vouch the silent stars and conscious
    moon.
Great is the prize demanded, I confess,
But such an abject rival makes it less.
That gift, those honors, he but hop'd to gain,
Can leave no room for Ajax to be vain:
Losing he wins, because his name will be
Ennobled by defeat, who durst contend with
    me.
Were my known valor question'd, yet my
    blood
Without that plea would make my title
    good.   30
My sire was Telamon, whose arms, employ'd
With Hercules, these Trojan walls de-
    stroy'd;
And who before, with Jason, sent from
    Greece,
In the first ship brought home the Golden
    Fleece:
Great Telamon from Æacus derives
His birth (th' inquisitor of guilty lives

In shades below, where Sisyphus, whose son
This thief is thought, rolls up the restless
    heavy stone):
Just Æacus the King of Gods above
Begot: thus Ajax is the third from Jove.   40
Nor should I seek advantage from my line,
Unless, Achilles, it were mix'd with thine:
As next of kin Achilles' arms I claim;
This fellow would ingraft a foreign name
Upon our stock, and the Sisyphian seed
By fraud and theft asserts his father's
    breed.
Then must I lose these arms, because I
    came
To fight uncall'd, a voluntary name,
Nor shunn'd the cause, but offer'd you my
    aid,
While he long lurking was to war be-
    tray'd ?   50
Forc'd to the field he came, but in the rear,
And feign'd distraction to conceal his fear:
Till one more cunning caught him in the
    snare
(Ill for himself) and dragg'd him into war.
Now let a hero's arms a coward vest,
And he, who shunn'd all honors, gain the
    best;
And let me stand excluded from my right,
Robb'd of my kinsman's arms, who first
    appear'd in fight.
Better for us, at home had he remain'd,
Had it been true, the madness which he
    feign'd,   60
Or so believ'd; the less had been our shame,
The less his counsel'd crime which brands
    the Grecian name;
Nor Philoctetes had been left inclos'd
In a bare isle, to wants and pains expos'd,
Where to the rocks, with solitary groans,
His suff'rings and our baseness he bemoans;
And wishes (so may Heav'n his wish fulfil !)
The due reward to him who caus'd his ill.
Now he, with us to Troy's destruction
    sworn,
Our brother of the war, by whom are
    borne   70
Alcides' arrows, pent in narrow bounds,
With cold and hunger pinch'd, and pain'd
    with wounds,
To find him food and clothing, must employ
Against the birds the shafts due to the fate
    of Troy.
Yet still he lives, and lives from treason
    free,
Because he left Ulysses' company:

Poor Palamede might wish, so void of aid,
Rather to have been left, than so to death
    betray'd.
The coward bore the man immortal spite,
Who sham'd him out of madness into
    fight;   80
Nor daring otherwise to vent his hate,
Accus'd him first of treason to the state;
And then, for proof, produc'd the golden
    store
Himself had hidden in his tent before:
Thus of two champions he depriv'd our
    host,
By exile one, and one by treason lost.
Thus fights Ulysses, thus his fame extends,
A formidable man, but to his friends:
Great, for what greatness is in words and
    sound;
Ev'n faithful Nestor less in both is found. 90
But, that he might without a rival reign,
He left this faithful Nestor on the plain;
Forsook his friend ev'n at his utmost need,
Who, tir'd and tardy, with his wounded
    steed,
Cried out for aid, and call'd him by his
    name;
But cowardice has neither ears nor shame.
Thus fled the good old man, bereft of aid,
And, for as much as lay in him, betray'd.
That this is not a fable forg'd by me,
Like one of his, an Ulyssean lie,   100
I vouch ev'n Diomede, who, tho' his friend,
Cannot that act excuse, much less defend:
He call'd him back aloud, and tax'd his
    fear;
And sure enough he heard, but durst not
    hear.
" The gods with equal eyes on mortals
    look;
He justly was forsaken, who forsook;
Wanted that succor he refus'd to lend,
Found ev'ry fellow such another friend:
No wonder, if he roar'd that all might
    hear;
His elocution was increas'd by fear.   110
I heard, I ran, I found him out of breath,
Pale, trembling, and half dead with fear of
    death.
Tho' he had judg'd himself by his own laws,
And stood condemn'd, I help'd the com-
    mon cause;
With my broad buckler hid him from the
    foe —
Ev'n the shield trembled as he lay be-
    low —

And from impending fate the coward
    freed:
Good Heav'n forgive me for so bad a deed !
If still he will persist, and urge the strife,
First let him give me back his forfeit
    life: 120
Let him return to that opprobrious field;
Again creep under my protecting shield:
Let him lie wounded, let the foe be near,
And let his quiv'ring heart confess his
    fear;
There put him in the very jaws of fate,
And let him plead his cause in that estate.
And yet, when snatch'd from death, when
    from below
My lifted shield I loos'd and let him go,
Good heav'ns, how light he rose, with what
    a bound
He sprung from earth, forgetful of his
    wound !   130
How fresh, how eager then his feet to ply;
Who had not strength to stand, had speed
    to fly !
    " Hector came on, and brought the gods
    along;
Fear seiz'd alike the feeble and the strong:
Each Greek was an Ulysses; such a dread
Th' approach, and ev'n the sound of Hector
    bred;
Him, flesh'd with slaughter, and with con-
    quest crown'd,
I met, and overturn'd him to the ground.
When after, matchless as he deem'd in
    might,
He challeng'd all our host to single fight, 140
All eyes were fix'd on me; the lots were
    thrown,
But for your champion I was wish'd alone:
Your vows were heard, we fought, and
    neither yield;
Yet I return'd unvanquish'd from the field.
With Jove to friend th' insulting Trojan
    came,
And menac'd us with force, our fleet with
    flame:
Was it the strength of this tongue-valiant
    lord,
In that black hour, that sav'd you from the
    sword ?
Or was my breast expos'd alone, to brave
A thousand swords, a thousand ships to
    save —   150
The hopes of your return ? And can you
    yield,
For a sav'd fleet, less than a single shield ?

Think it no boast, O Grecians, if I deem
These arms want Ajax, more than Ajax
    them;
Or I with them an equal honor share,
They honor'd to be worn, and I to wear.
Will he compare my courage with his slight?
As well he may compare the day with night.
Night is indeed the province of his reign; ⎫
Yet all his dark exploits no more contain ⎬
Than a spy taken, and a sleeper slain; 161 ⎭
A priest made pris'ner, Pallas made a ⎫
    prey;   ⎪
But none of all these actions done by day; ⎬
Nor aught of these was done, and Dio-   ⎪
    med away.   ⎭
If on such petty merits you confer
So vast a prize, let each his portion share;
Make a just dividend: and, if not all,
The greater part to Diomed will fall.
But why for Ithacus such arms as those,
Who naked and by night invades his foes?
The glitt'ring helm by moonlight will pro-
    claim   171
The latent robber, and prevent his game;
Nor could he hold his tott'ring head up-
    right
Beneath that motion, or sustain the weight;
Nor that right arm could toss the beamy
    lance,
Much less the left that ampler shield ad-
    vance,
Pond'rous with precious weight, and rough
    with cost
Of the round world in rising gold emboss'd.
That orb would ill become his hand to wield,
And look as for the gold he stole the shield;
Which should your error on the wretch be-
    stow,   181
It would not frighten, but allure the foe.
Why asks he what avails him not in fight,
And would but cumber and retard his flight,
In which his only excellence is plac'd?
You give him death, that intercept his haste.
Add, that his own is yet a maiden shield,
Nor the least dint has suffer'd in the field,
Guiltless of fight; mine, batter'd, hew'd,
    and bor'd,
Worn out of service, must forsake his lord.
What farther need of words our right to
    scan?   191
My arguments are deeds, let action speak
    the man.
Since from a champion's arms the strife
    arose,
So cast the glorious prize amid the foes;

Then send us to redeem both arms and
    shield,
And let him wear who wins 'em in the field."
    He said; a murmur from the multitude,
Or somewhat like a stifled shout ensued!
Till from his seat arose Laertes' son,
Look'd down a while, and paus'd ere he
    begun;   200
Then to th' expecting audience rais'd his
    look,
And not without prepar'd attention spoke:
Soft was his tone, and sober was his face;
Action his words, and words his action grace:
" If Heav'n, my lords, had heard our com-
    mon pray'r,
These arms had caus'd no quarrel for an
    heir;
Still great Achilles had his own possess'd,
And we with great Achilles had been
    blest.
But since hard fate, and Heav'n's severe
    decree   209
Have ravish'd him away from you and me,
(At this he sigh'd, and wip'd his eyes, and
    drew,
Or seem'd to draw, some drops of kindly
    dew,)
Who better can succeed Achilles lost,
Than he who gave Achilles to your host?
This only I request, that neither he
May gain, by being what he seems to be,
A stupid thing, nor I may lose the prize,
By having sense, which Heav'n to him denies;
Since, great or small, the talent I enjoy'd
Was ever in the common cause employ'd.
Nor let my wit, and wonted eloquence, 221
Which often has been us'd in your defense
And in my own, this only time be brought
To bear against myself, and deem'd a fault.
Make not a crime, where nature made it
    none;
For ev'ry man may freely use his own.
The deeds of long descended ancestors
Are but by grace of imputation ours,
Theirs in effect; but, since he draws his line
From Jove, and seems to plead a right
    divine,   230
From Jove, like him, I claim my pedigree,
And am descended in the same degree:
My sire Laertes was Arcesius' heir,
Arcesius was the son of Jupiter;
No parricide, no banish'd man, is known
In all my line; let him excuse his own.
Hermes ennobles too my mother's side —
By both my parents to the gods allied;

But not because that on the female part
My blood is better, dare I claim desert, 240
Or that my sire from parricide is free;
But judge by merit betwixt him and me.
The prize be to the best; provided yet,
That Ajax for a while his kin forget,
And his great sire, and greater uncle's name,
To fortify by them his feeble claim:
Be kindred and relation laid aside,
And honor's cause by laws of honor tried;
For, if he plead proximity of blood,
That empty title is with ease withstood. 250
Peleus, the hero's sire, more nigh than he,
And Pyrrhus his undoubted progeny,
Inherit first these trophies of the field:
To Scyros, or to Phthia, send the shield:
And Teucer has an uncle's right; yet he
Waives his pretensions, nor contends with
  me.
  " Then, since the cause on pure desert is
  plac'd,
Whence shall I take my rise, what reckon
  last ?
I not presume on ev'ry act to dwell,
But take these few, in order as they fell.
  " Thetis, who knew the fates, applied her
  care   261
To keep Achilles in disguise from war;
And till the threat'ning influence were past,
A woman's habit on the hero cast:
All eyes were cozen'd by the borrow'd vest,
And Ajax (never wiser than the rest)
Found no Pelides there. At length I came
With proffer'd wares to this pretended
  dame;
She, not discover'd by her mien or voice, 269
Betray'd her manhood by her manly choice;
And, while on female toys her fellows ⎫
  look,   ⎪
Grasp'd in her warlike hand, a javelin ⎬
  shook;   ⎪
Whom, by this act reveal'd, I thus be- ⎪
  spoke: ⎭
' O goddess-born! resist not Heav'n's decree,
The fall of Ilium is reserv'd for thee;'
Then seiz'd him, and, produc'd in open light,
Sent blushing to the field the fatal knight.
Mine then are all his actions of the war;
Great Telephus was conquer'd by my spear,
And after cur'd: to me the Thebans owe
Lesbos and Tenedos their overthrow, 281
Scyros and Cilla: not on all to dwell,
By me Lyrnesus and strong Chrysa fell;
And, since I sent the man who Hector slew,
To me the noble Hector's death is due:

Those arms I put into his living hand,
Those arms, Pelides dead, I now demand.
  " When Greece was injur'd in the Spartan
  prince,
And met at Aulis to revenge th' offense,
'T was a dead calm, or adverse blasts, that
  reign'd,   290
And in the port the windbound fleet de-
  tain'd:
Bad signs were seen, and oracles severe
Were daily thunder'd in our general's ear,
That by his daughter's blood we must ap-
  pease
Diana's kindled wrath, and free the seas.
Affection, int'rest, fame, his heart assail'd;
But soon the father o'er the king prevail'd:
Bold, on himself he took the pious crime,
As angry with the gods as they with him.
No subject could sustain their sov'reign's
  look,   300
Till this hard enterprise I undertook:
I only durst th' imperial pow'r control,
And undermin'd the parent in his soul;
Forc'd him t' exert the king for common
  good,
And pay our ransom with his daughter's
  blood.
Never was cause more difficult to plead,
Than where the judge against himself de-
  creed:
Yet this I won by dint of argument; ⎫
The wrongs his injur'd brother underwent, ⎬
And his own office, sham'd him to consent. ⎭
  " 'T was harder yet to move the mother's
  mind,   311
And to this heavy task was I design'd.
Reasons against her love I knew were vain;
I circumvented whom I could not gain:
Had Ajax been employ'd, our slacken'd sails
Had still at Aulis waited happy gales.
  " Arriv'd at Troy, your choice was fix'd
  on me,
A fearless envoy, fit for a bold embassy.
Secure, I enter'd thro' the hostile court,
Glitt'ring with steel, and crowded with re-
  sort: 320
There, in the midst of arms, I plead our
  cause,
Urge the foul rape, and violated laws;
Accuse the foes, as authors of the strife,
Reproach the ravisher, demand the wife.
Priam, Antenor, and the wiser few,
I mov'd; but Paris and his lawless crew
Scarce held their hands, and lifted swords;
  but stood

In act to quench their impious thirst of blood.
This Menelaus knows, expos'd to share
With me the rough preludium of the war.
   " Endless it were to tell what I have
      done,   331
In arms, or council, since the siege begun:
The first encounters pass'd, the foe repell'd,
They skulk'd within the town, we kept the
    field.
War seem'd asleep for nine long years ; at
    length,
Both sides resolv'd to push, we tried our
    strength.
Now what did Ajax while our arms took
    breath,
Vers'd only in the gross mechanic trade of
    death ?
If you require my deeds, with ambush'd
    arms   339
I trapp'd the foe, or tir'd with false alarms;
Secur'd the ships, drew lines along the plain,
The fainting cheer'd, chastis'd the rebel
    train,
Provided forage, our spent arms renew'd;
Employ'd at home, or sent abroad, the com-
    mon cause pursued.
   " The king, deluded in a dream by Jove,
Despair'd to take the town, and order'd to
    remove.
What subject durst arraign the pow'r su-
    preme,
Producing Jove to justify his dream ?
Ajax might wish the soldiers to retain
From shameful flight, but wishes were in
    vain: 350
As wanting of effect had been his words,
Such as of course his thund'ring tongue
    affords.
But did this boaster threaten, did he pray, ⎫
Or by his own example urge their stay ? ⎪
None, none of these, but ran himself ⎬
    away.   ⎭
I saw him run, and was asham'd to see —
Who plied his feet so fast to get aboard as
    he ?
Then speeding thro' the place, I made a ⎫
    stand,   ⎪
And loudly cried : ' O base degenerate ⎬
    band,   ⎪
To leave a town already in your hand ! 360⎭
After so long expense of blood, for fame,
To bring home nothing but perpetual
    shame ! '
These words, or what I have forgotten since,
(For grief inspir'd me then with eloquence,)

Reduc'd their minds; they leave the crowded
    port,
And to their late forsaken camp resort:
Dismay'd the council met; this man was
    there,
But mute, and not recover'd of his fear:
Thersites tax'd the king, and loudly rail'd,
But his wide opening mouth with blows
    I seal'd.   370
Then, rising, I excite their souls to fame,
And kindle sleeping virtue into flame.
From thence, whatever he perform'd in fight
Is justly mine, who drew him back from
    flight.
   " Which of the Grecian chiefs consorts ⎫
    with thee ?   ⎪
But Diomede desires my company,   ⎬
And still communicates his praise with me.⎭
As guided by a god, secure he goes,
Arm'd with my fellowship, amid the foes;
And sure no little merit I may boast, 380
Whom such a man selects from such an
    host.
Unforc'd by lots, I went without affright,
To dare with him the dangers of the night;
On the same errand sent, we met the spy
Of Hector, double-tongued, and us'd to
    lie:
Him I dispatch'd, but not till, undermin'd,
I drew him first to tell what treacherous
    Troy design'd.
My task perform'd, with praise I had re-
    tir'd,
But not content with this, to greater praise
    aspir'd;
Invaded Rhœsus and his Thracian crew, 390
And him, and his, in their own strength, I
    slew;
Return'd a victor, all my vows complete,
With the king's chariot, in his royal seat.
Refuse me now his arms, whose fiery steeds
Were promis'd to the spy for his nocturnal
    deeds,
And let dull Ajax bear away my right,
When all his days outbalance this one night.
   " Nor fought I darkling still; the sun
    beheld
With slaughter'd Lycians when I strew'd
    the field.
You saw, and counted as I pass'd along, 400
Alastor, Chromius, Ceranos the strong,
Alcander, Prytanis, and Halius,
Noemon, Charopes, and Ennomus,
Choön, Chersidamas; and five beside,
Men of obscure descent, but courage tried:

All these this hand laid breathless on the
    ground;
Nor want I proofs of many a manly wound,
All honest, all before: believe not me;
Words may deceive, but credit what you
    see."
    At this he bar'd his breast and show'd
    his scars,   410
As of a furrow'd field, well plow'd with
    wars;
"Nor is this part unexercis'd," said he;
"That giant bulk of his from wounds is
    free:
Safe in his shield he fears no foe to try,
And better manages his blood than I.
But this avails me not; our boaster strove
Not with our foes alone, but partial Jove,
To save the fleet: this I confess is true,
(Nor will I take from any man his due,)
But thus assuming all, he robs from you. 420
Some part of honor to your share will fall;
He did the best indeed, but did not all.
Patroclus in Achilles' arms, and thought
The chief he seem'd, with equal ardor
    fought;
Preserv'd the fleet, repell'd the raging fire,
And forc'd the fearful Trojans to retire.
    "But Ajax boasts that he was only
    thought
A match for Hector, who the combat sought:
Sure he forgets the king, the chiefs, and me;
All were as eager for the fight as he;   430
He but the ninth, and, not by public voice
Or ours preferr'd, was only fortune's choice.
They fought, nor can our hero boast the
    event,
For Hector from the field unwounded went.
    "Why am I forc'd to name that fatal day
That snatch'd the prop and pride of Greece
    away?
I saw Pelides sink, with pious grief,
And ran in vain, alas! to his relief;
For the brave soul was fled: full of my
    friend,   439
I rush'd amid the war, his relics to defend;
Nor ceas'd my toil till I redeem'd the prey,
And, loaded with Achilles, march'd away:
Those arms, which on these shoulders then
    I bore,
'T is just you to these shoulders should re-
    store.
You see I want not nerves, who could sustain
The pond'rous ruins of so great a man;
Or, if in others equal force you find,
None is endued with a more grateful mind.

"Did Thetis then, ambitious in her care, ⎫
These arms thus labor'd for her son pre- ⎪
    pare,   450 ⎬
That Ajax after him the heav'nly gift ⎪
    should wear! ⎭
For that dull soul to stare, with stupid eyes,
On the learn'd unintelligible prize!
What are to him the sculptures of the shield,
Heav'n's planets, earth, and ocean's wat'ry
    field?
The Pleiads, Hyads; less and greater Bear,
Undipp'd in seas; Orion's angry star;
Two diff'ring cities, grav'd on either hand?
Would he wear arms he cannot understand?
    "Beside, what wise objections he pre-
    pares   460
Against my late accession to the wars?
Does not the fool perceive his argument
Is with more force against Achilles bent?
For, if dissembling be so great a crime,
The fault is common, and the same in him;
And if he taxes both of long delay,
My guilt is less, who sooner came away.
His pious mother, anxious for his life,
Detain'd her son; and me, my pious wife.
To them the blossoms of our youth were
    due,   470
Our riper manhood we reserv'd for you.
But grant me guilty, 't is not much my care,
When with so great a man my guilt I share:
My wit to war the matchless hero brought,
But by this fool I never had been caught.
    "Nor need I wonder that on me he threw
Such foul aspersions, when he spares not
    you.
If Palamede unjustly fell by me,
Your honor suffer'd in th' unjust decree: 479
I but accus'd, you doom'd; and yet he died,
Convinc'd of treason, and was fairly tried.
You heard not he was false; your eyes be-
    held
The traitor manifest, the bribe reveal'd.
    "That Philoctetes is on Lemnos left,
Wounded, forlorn, of human aid bereft,
Is not my crime, or not my crime alone;
Defend your justice, for the fact 's your
    own:
'T is true, th' advice was mine; that stay- ⎫
    ing there ⎪
He might his weary limbs with rest re- ⎬
    pair, ⎪
From a long voyage free, and from a ⎪
    longer war.   490 ⎭
He took the counsel, and he lives at least;
Th' event declares I counsel'd for the best:

Tho' faith is all, in ministers of state;
For who can promise to be fortunate ?
Now since his arrows are the fate of Troy,
Do not my wit, or weak address, employ;
Send Ajax there, with his persuasive sense,
To mollify the man and draw him thence:
But Xanthus shall run backward, Ida stand
A leafless mountain, and the Grecian band
Shall fight for Troy, if, when my counsels
          fail,   501
The wit of heavy Ajax can prevail.

" Hard Philoctetes, exercise thy spleen
Against thy fellows, and the King of Men;
Curse my devoted head, above the rest,
And wish in arms to meet me breast to
          breast:
Yet I the dang'rous task will undertake,
And either die myself, or bring thee back.
" Nor doubt the same success, as when
          before
The Phrygian prophet to these tents I bore,
Surpris'd by night, and forc'd him to de-
          clare   511
In what was plac'd the fortune of the war;
Heav'n's dark decrees and answers to dis-
          play,
And how to take the town, and where the
          secret lay:
Yet this I compass'd, and from Troy con-
          vey'd
The fatal image of their guardian maid —
That work was mine; for Pallas, tho' our
          friend,
Yet while she was in Troy, did Troy defend.
Now what has Ajax done, or what design'd,
A noisy nothing, and an empty wind ?   520
If he be what he promises in show,
Why was I sent, and why fear'd he to go ?
Our boasting champion thought the task
          not light
To pass the guards, commit himself to
          night;
Not only thro' a hostile town to pass,
But scale, with steep ascent, the sacred place;
With wand'ring steps to search the citadel,
And from the priests their patroness to
          steal:
Then thro' surrounding foes to force my
          way,   529
And bear in triumph home the heav'nly prey;
Which had I not, Ajax in vain had held,
Before that monstrous bulk, his sev'nfold
          shield.
That night to conquer Troy I might be said,
When Troy was liable to conquest made.

" Why point'st thou to my partner of the
          war ?
Tydides had indeed a worthy share
In all my toil and praise; but when thy
          might
Our ships protected, didst thou singly fight ?
All join'd, and thou of many wert but one;
I ask'd no friend, nor had, but him alone; 540
Who, had he not been well assur'd that art
And conduct were of war the better part,
And more avail'd than strength, my valiant
          friend
Had urg'd a better right than Ajax can
          pretend:
As good at least Eurypylus may claim,
And the more moderate Ajax of the name;
The Cretan king, and his brave charioteer,
And Menelaus bold with sword and spear —
All these had been my rivals in the shield,
And yet all these to my pretensions
          yield.   550
Thy boist'rous hands are then of use, when I
With this directing head those hands apply.
Brawn without brain is thine; my prudent
          care
Foresees, provides, administers the war.
Thy province is to fight; but when shall be
The time to fight, the king consults with
          me.
No dram of judgment with thy force is
          join'd;
Thy body is of profit, and my mind.
By how much more the ship her safety owes
To him who steers, than him that only
          rows;   560
By how much more the captain merits
          praise
Than he who fights, and fighting but obeys;
By so much greater is my worth than thine,
Who canst but execute what I design.
What gain'st thou, brutal man, if I confess
Thy strength superior, when thy wit is
          less ?
Mind is the man: I claim my whole desert
From the mind's vigor, and th' immortal
          part.
" But you, O Grecian chiefs, reward my
          care,
Be grateful to your watchman of the war.
For all my labors in so long a space,   571
Sure I may plead a title to your grace:
Enter the town; I then unbarr'd the gates,
When I remov'd their tutelary fates.
By all our common hopes, if hopes they be
Which I have now reduc'd to certainty;

By falling Troy, by yonder tott'ring tow'rs,
And by their taken gods, which now are
    ours;
Or if there yet a farther task remains, 579
To be perform'd by prudence or by pains;
If yet some desperate action rests behind,
That asks high conduct and a dauntless
    mind;
If aught be wanting to the Trojan doom,
Which none but I can manage and o'er-
    come;
Award those arms I ask, by your decree;
Or give to this what you refuse to me."
    He ceas'd; and, ceasing, with respect he
        bow'd,
And with his hand at once the fatal statue
    show'd.
Heav'n, air, and ocean rung with loud ap-
    plause,
And by the general vote he gain'd his
    cause.   590
Thus conduct won the prize, when courage
    fail'd,
And eloquence o'er brutal force prevail'd.

THE DEATH OF AJAX

He who could often, and alone, withstand
The foe, the fire, and Jove's own partial
    hand,
Now cannot his unmaster'd grief sustain,
But yields to rage, to madness, and dis-
    dain;
Then, snatching out his fauchion: "Thou,"
    said he,
"Art mine; Ulysses lays no claim to thee.
O often tried and ever trusty sword,
Now do thy last kind office to thy lord: 600
'T is Ajax who requests thy aid, to show
None but himself himself could overthrow."
He said, and with so good a will to die
Did to his breast the fatal point apply:
It found his heart, a way till then un-
    known,
Where never weapon enter'd but his own;
No hands could force it thence, so fix'd it
    stood,
Till out it rush'd, expell'd by streams of
    spouting blood.
The fruitful blood produc'd a flow'r, ⎫
    which grew   ⎪
On a green stem, and of a purple hue: 610 ⎬
Like his, whom unaware Apollo slew.   ⎭
Inscrib'd in both, the letters are the same,
But those express the grief, and these the
    name.

THE WIFE OF BATH, HER TALE

[FROM CHAUCER]

In days of old, when Arthur fill'd the
    throne,
Whose acts and fame to foreign lands were
    blown,
The king of elfs and little fairy queen
Gambol'd on heaths, and danc'd on ev'ry
    green;
And where the jolly troop had led the
    round,
The grass unbidden rose, and mark'd the
    ground:
Nor darkling did they dance; the silver ⎫
    light   ⎪
Of Phœbe serv'd to guide their steps   ⎬
    aright,   ⎪
And, with their tripping pleas'd, pro- ⎪
    long'd the night.   ⎭
Her beams they follow'd, where at full ⎫
    she play'd,   10 ⎪
Nor longer than she shed her horns they ⎬
    stay'd,   ⎪
From thence with airy flight to foreign ⎪
    lands convey'd.   ⎭
Above the rest our Britain held they dear; ⎫
More solemnly they kept their sabbaths ⎪
    here,   ⎬
And made more spacious rings, and   ⎪
    revel'd half the year.   ⎭
  I speak of ancient times, for now the ⎫
    swain   ⎪
Returning late may pass the woods in   ⎬
    vain,   ⎪
And never hope to see the nightly train; ⎭
In vain the dairy now with mints is   ⎫
    dress'd,   ⎪
The dairymaid expects no fairy guest, 20 ⎬
To skim the bowls, and after pay the feast. ⎭
She sighs, and shakes her empty shoes in
    vain,
No silver penny to reward her pain:
For priests with pray'rs, and other godly
    gear,
Have made the merry goblins disappear;
And where they play'd their merry pranks
    before,
Have sprinkled holy water on the floor;
And friars that thro' the wealthy regions
    run,
Thick as the motes that twinkle in the sun,
Resort to farmers rich, and bless their
    halls,   30

And exorcise the beds, and cross the walls:
This makes the fairy choirs forsake the
    place,
When once 't is hallow'd with the rites of
    grace.
But in the walks where wicked elves have
    been,
The learning of the parish now is seen,
The midnight parson, posting o'er the
    green,
With gown tuck'd up, to wakes, for Sun-
    day next
With humming ale encouraging his text;
Nor wants the holy leer to country girl
    betwixt.
From fiends and imps he sets the village
    free,   40
There haunts not any incubus but he.
The maids and women need no danger fear
To walk by night, and sanctity so near:
For by some haycock, or some shady thorn,
He bids his beads both evensong and morn.
  It so befell in this King Arthur's reign,
A lusty knight was pricking o'er the plain;
A bachelor he was, and of the courtly
    train.
It happen'd, as he rode, a damsel gay
In russet robes to market took her way; 50
Soon on the girl he cast an amorous eye,
So straight she walk'd, and on her pasterns
    high:
If seeing her behind he lik'd her pace,
Now turning short, he better lik'd her face.
He lights in haste, and, full of youthful
    fire,
By force accomplish'd his obscene desire:
This done, away he rode, not unespied,
For swarming at his back the country cried;
And once in view they never lost the sight,
But seiz'd, and pinion'd brought to court
    the knight.   60
  Then courts of kings were held in high
    renown,
Ere made the common brothels of the town:
There, virgins honorable vows receiv'd,
But chaste as maids in monasteries liv'd;
The king himself, to nuptial ties a slave,
No bad example to his poets gave;
And they, not bad, but in a vicious age,
Had not, to please the prince, debauch'd
    the stage.
  Now what should Arthur do? He lov'd
    the knight,
But sovereign monarchs are the source of
    right: 70

Mov'd by the damsel's tears and common
    cry,
He doom'd the brutal ravisher to die.
But fair Geneura rose in his defense,
And pray'd so hard for mercy from the
    prince,
That to his queen the king th' offender gave,
And left it in her pow'r to kill or save:
This gracious act the ladies all approve,
Who thought it much a man should die for
    love,
And with their mistress join'd in close
    debate,
(Covering their kindness with dissembled
    hate,)   80
If not to free him, to prolong his fate.
At last agreed, they call'd him by consent
Before the queen and female parliament;
And the fair speaker, rising from her chair,
Did thus the judgment of the house de-
    clare:
  "Sir knight, tho' I have ask'd thy life,
    yet still
Thy destiny depends upon my will;
Nor hast thou other surety than the grace
Not due to thee from our offended race.
But as our kind is of a softer mold,   90
And cannot blood without a sigh behold,
I grant thee life; reserving still the pow'r
To take the forfeit when I see my hour,
Unless thy answer to my next demand
Shall set thee free from our avenging hand.
The question, whose solution I require,
Is, *what the sex of women most desire.*
In this dispute thy judges are at strife;
Beware, for on thy wit depends thy life. 99
Yet (lest, surpris'd, unknowing what to say,
Thou damn thyself) we give thee farther
    day:
A year is thine to wander at thy will,
And learn from others, if thou want'st the
    skill.
But, not to hold our proffer['d boon] in scorn,
Good sureties will we have for thy return;
That at the time prefix'd thou shalt obey,
And at thy pledge's peril keep thy day."
  Woe was the knight at this severe com-
    mand;
But well he knew 't was bootless to with-
    stand:
The terms accepted, as the fair ordain, 110
He put in bail for his return again,
And promis'd answer at the day assign'd,
The best, with Heav'n's assistance, he could
    find.

His leave thus taken, on his way he went
With heavy heart, and full of discontent,
Misdoubting much, and fearful of th'
 event.
'T was hard the truth of such a point to find,
As was not yet agreed among the kind.
Thus on he went; still anxious more and
 more,
Ask'd all he met, and knock'd at ev'ry
 door;   120
Enquir'd of men, but made his chief re-
 quest
To learn from women what they lov'd the
 best.
They answer'd each according to her mind,
To please herself, not all the female kind.
One was for wealth, another was for place;
Crones, old and ugly, wish'd a better face.
The widow's wish was oftentimes to wed;
The wanton maids were all for sport abed.
Some said the sex were pleas'd with hand-
 some lies,
And some gross flatt'ry lov'd without dis-
 guise;   130
"Truth is," says one, "he seldom fails to
 win,
Who flatters well, for that 's our darling sin;
But long attendance, and a duteous mind,
Will work ev'n with the wisest of the kind."
One thought the sex's prime felicity
Was from the bonds of wedlock to be free;
Their pleasures, hours, and actions all their
 own,
And uncontroll'd to give account to none.
Some wish a husband-fool; but such are
 curst,
For fools perverse of husbands are the
 worst: 140
All women would be counted chaste and
 wise,
Nor should our spouses see, but with our
 eyes;
For fools will prate, and, tho' they want the
 wit
To find close faults, yet open blots will hit;
Tho' better for their ease to hold their
 tongue,
For womankind was never in the wrong.
So noise ensues, and quarrels last for life;
The wife abhors the fool, the fool the wife.
And some men say, that great delight have
 we,
To be for truth extoll'd, and secrecy; 150
And constant in one purpose still to dwell,
And not our husbands' counsels to reveal.

But that 's a fable, for our sex is frail,
Inventing rather than not tell a tale.
Like leaky sieves no secrets we can hold:
Witness the famous tale that Ovid told.
Midas the king, as in his book appears,
By Phœbus was endow'd with ass's ears,
Which under his long locks he well con-
 ceal'd,   159
(As monarchs' vices must not be reveal'd,)
For fear the people have 'em in the wind,
Who long ago were neither dumb nor blind,
Nor apt to think from heav'n their title
 springs,
Since Jove and Mars left off begetting
 kings.
This Midas knew; and durst communicate
To none but to his wife his ears of state:
One must be trusted, and he thought her fit,
As passing prudent, and a parlous wit.
To this sagacious confessor he went, 169
And told her what a gift the gods had sent;
But told it under matrimonial seal,
With strict injunction never to reveal.
The secret heard, she plighted him her troth,
(And sacred sure is every woman's oath,)
The royal malady should rest unknown,
Both for her husband's honor and her own;
But ne'ertheless she pin'd with discontent;
The counsel rumbled till it found a vent.
The thing she knew she was oblig'd to
 hide;
By int'rest and by oath the wife was
 tied;   180
But, if she told it not, the woman died.
Loth to betray a husband and a prince,
But she must burst, or blab, and no pre-
 tense
Of honor tied her tongue from self-de-
 fense.
A marshy ground commodiously was near;
Thither she ran, and held her breath for
 fear,
Lest if a word she spoke of anything,
That word might be the secret of the king.
Thus full of counsel to the fen she went,
Grip'd all the way, and longing for a vent;
Arriv'd, by pure necessity compell'd, 191
On her majestic mary-bones she kneel'd;
Then to the water's brink she laid her head,
And, as a bittor bumps within a reed,
"To thee alone, O lake," she said, "I tell,
(And, as thy queen, command thee to con-
 ceal,)
Beneath his locks the king my husband
 wears

A goodly royal pair of ass's ears:
Now I have eas'd my bosom of the pain,
Till the next longing fit return again!" 200
  Thus thro' a woman was the secret known;
Tell us, and in effect you tell the town.
But to my tale: the knight, with heavy
    cheer,
Wand'ring in vain, had now consum'd the
    year —
One day was only left to solve the doubt —
Yet knew no more than when he first set
    out.
But home he must, and, as th' award had
    been,
Yield up his body captive to the queen.
In this despairing state he happ'd to ride,
As fortune led him, by a forest side: 210
Lonely the vale, and full of horror stood,
Brown with the shade of a religious wood;
When full before him at the noon of
    night,
(The moon was up, and shot a gleamy
    light,)
He saw a choir of ladies in a round,
That featly footing seem'd to skim the
    ground:
Thus dancing hand in hand, so light they
    were,
He knew not where they trod, on earth or
    air.
At speed he drove, and came a sudden ⎫
    guest,   ⎪
In hope where many women were, at ⎬
    least,   220   ⎪
Some one by chance might answer his ⎪
    request.   ⎭
But faster than his horse the ladies flew,
And in a trice were vanish'd out of view
  One only hag remain'd; but fouler far
Than grandame apes in Indian forests are;
Against a wither'd oak she lean'd her ⎫
    weight,   ⎪
Propp'd on her trusty staff, not half up- ⎬
    right,   ⎪
And dropp'd an awkard court'sy to the ⎭
    knight.
Then said: "What make you, sir, so late
    abroad   229
Without a guide, and this no beaten road?
Or want you aught that here you hope to
    find,
Or travel for some trouble in your mind?
The last I guess; and, if I read aright,
Those of our sex are bound to serve a
    knight;

Perhaps good counsel may your grief as-
    suage:
Then tell your pain, for wisdom is in age."
  To this the knight: "Good mother, would
    you know
The secret cause and spring of all my woe?
My life must with to-morrow's light expire,
Unless I tell what women most desire. 240
Now could you help me at this hard essay,
Or for your inborn goodness, or for pay,
Yours is my life, redeem'd by your advice;
Ask what you please, and I will pay the
    price:
The proudest kerchief of the court shall
    rest
Well satisfied of what they love the best."
  "Plight me thy faith," quoth she, "that
    what I ask,
Thy danger over, and perform'd the task,
That shalt thou give for hire of thy de-
    mand;
Here take thy oath, and seal it on my
    hand;   250
I warrant thee, on peril of my life,
Thy words shall please both widow, maid,
    and wife."
  More words there needed not to move
    the knight
To take her offer, and his truth to plight.
With that she spread her mantle on the
    ground,
And, first enquiring whether he was bound,
Bade him not fear, tho' long and rough the
    way,
At court he should arrive ere break of day;
His horse should find the way without a ⎫
    guide,   259   ⎬
She said: with fury they began to ride, ⎭
He on the midst, the beldam at his side. ⎭
The horse, what devil drove, I cannot tell,
But only this, they sped their journey well;
And all the way the crone inform'd the
    knight,
How he should answer the demand aright.
  To court they came; the news was quickly
    spread
Of his returning to redeem his head.
The female senate was assembled soon,
With all the mob of women in the town;
The queen sate lord chief justice of the
    hall,   270
And bade the crier cite the criminal.
The knight appear'd, and silence they pro-
    claim:
Then first the culprit answer'd to his name:

And, after forms of laws, was last requir'd
To name the thing that women most desir'd.
    Th' offender, taught his lesson by the
        way,
And by his counsel order'd what to say,
Thus bold began : " My lady liege," said he,
" What all your sex desire is, Sovereignty.
The wife affects her husband to com-
    mand;   280
All must be hers, both money, house, and
    land.
The maids are mistresses ev'n in their
    name,
And of their servants full dominion claim.
This, at the peril of my head, I say,
A blunt plain truth, the sex aspires to
    sway,
You to rule all, while we, like slaves,
    obey."
    There was not one, or widow, maid, or
        wife,
But said the knight had well deserv'd his
    life.
Ev'n fair Geneura, with a blush, confess'd
The man had found what women love the
    best.   290
    Upstarts the beldam, who was there un-
        seen,
And, reverence made, accosted thus the
        queen:
" My liege," said she, " before the court
        arise,
May I, poor wretch, find favor in your eyes,
To grant my just request: 't was I who
        taught
The knight this answer, and inspir'd his
        thought;
None but a woman could a man direct
To tell us women what we most affect.
But first I swore him on his knightly troth,
(And here demand performance of his
    oath,)   300
To grant the boon that next I should desire;
He gave his faith, and I expect my hire:
My promise is fulfill'd; I sav'd his life,
And claim his debt, to take me for his
    wife."
The knight was ask'd, nor could his oath
        deny,
But hop'd they would not force him to
        comply.
The women, who would rather wrest the
        laws
Than let a sister plaintiff lose the cause,
(As judges on the bench more gracious are,

And more attent to brothers of the bar,) 310
Cried, one and all, the suppliant should
        have right,
And to the grandame hag adjudg'd the
        knight.
    In vain he sigh'd, and oft with tears
        desir'd,
Some reasonable suit might be requir'd.
But still the crone was constant to her note;
The more he spoke, the more she stretch'd
    her throat.
In vain he proffer'd all his goods, to save
His body destin'd to that living grave.
The liquorish hag rejects the pelf with
        scorn;
And nothing but the man would serve her
        turn.   320
" Not all the wealth of eastern kings," said
        she,
" Have pow'r to part my plighted love and
        me ;
And, old and ugly as I am, and poor,
Yet never will I break the faith I swore;
For mine thou art by promise, during life,
And I thy loving and obedient wife."
    " My love ! nay, rather my damnation
        thou,"
Said he, " nor am I bound to keep my vow;
The fiend thy sire has sent thee from
        below,
Else how couldst thou my secret sorrows
        know ?   330
Avaunt, old witch, for I renounce thy
        bed;
The queen may take the forfeit of my
        head,
Ere any of my race so foul a crone shall
        wed."
    Both heard, the judge pronounc'd against
        the knight:
So was he married in his own despite;
And all day after hid him as an owl,
Not able to sustain a sight so foul.
Perhaps the reader thinks I do him wrong,
To pass the marriage feast and nuptial
        song;
Mirth there was none, the man was à la
    mort,   340
And little courage had to make his court.
To bed they went, the bridegroom and the
        bride;
Was never such an ill-pair'd couple tied:
Restless he toss'd and tumbled to and fro,
And roll'd, and wriggled further off, for
        woe.

The good old wife lay smiling by his side,
And caught him in her quiv'ring arms, and
    cried:
"When you my ravish'd predecessor saw,⎫
You were not then become this man of
    straw;   ⎬
Had you been such, you might have scap'd⎪
    the law.   350⎭
Is this the custom of King Arthur's court?
Are all Round Table Knights of such a sort?
Remember I am she who sav'd your life,
Your loving, lawful, and complying wife;
Not thus you swore in your unhappy hour,
Nor I for this return employ'd my pow'r.
In time of need I was your faithful friend;
Nor did I since, nor ever will offend.
Believe me, my lov'd lord, 't is much un-
    kind;   359
What fury has possess'd your alter'd mind?
Thus on my wedding night — without pre-
    tense —
Come, turn this way, or tell me my offense.
If not your wife, let reason's rule persuade;
Name but my fault, amends shall soon be
    made."
    "Amends! nay, that 's impossible," said
    he,
"What change of age or ugliness can be!
Or, could Medea's magic mend thy face,⎫
Thou art descended from so mean a race,⎬
That never knight was match'd with such⎪
    disgrace.   369⎭
What wonder, madam, if I move my side,
When, if I turn, I turn to such a bride?"
    "And is this all that troubles you so
    sore!"
    "And what the devil couldst thou wish
    me more?"
    "Ah *benedicite*," replied the crone,
"Then cause of just complaining have you
    none.
The remedy to this were soon applied,
Would you be like the bridegroom to the
    bride.
But, for you say a long descended race,
And wealth, and dignity, and pow'r, and
    place,   379
Make gentlemen, and that your high degree
Is much disparag'd to be match'd with me;
Know this, my lord, nobility of blood
Is but a glitt'ring and fallacious good:
The nobleman is he whose noble mind
Is fill'd with inborn worth, unborrow'd from
    his kind.
The King of Heav'n was in a manger laid,

And took his earth but from an humble
    maid;
Then what can birth, or mortal men, bestow,
Since floods no higher than their fountains
    flow?   389
We, who for name and empty honor strive,
Our true nobility from him derive.
Your ancestors, who puff your mind with
    pride,
And vast estates to mighty titles tied,
Did not your honor, but their own advance;
For virtue comes not by inheritance.
If you tralineate from your father's mind,
What are you else but of a bastard kind?
Do as your great progenitors have done,
And, by their virtues, prove yourself their
    son.
No father can infuse or wit or grace;   400
A mother comes across, and mars the race.
A grandsire or a grandame taints the blood,
And seldom three descents continue good.
Were virtue by descent, a noble name
Could never villanize his father's fame;
But, as the first, the last of all the line
Would, like the sun, ev'n in descending
    shine.
Take fire, and bear it to the darkest house,
Betwixt King Arthur's court and Caucasus;
If you depart, the flame shall still remain, 410
And the bright blaze enlighten all the plain;
Nor, till the fuel perish, can decay,
By nature form'd on things combustible to
    prey.
Such is not man, who, mixing better seed
With worse, begets a base degenerate breed:
The bad corrupts the good, and leaves be-
    hind
No trace of all the great begetter's mind.
The father sinks within his son, we see,
And often rises in the third degree,
If better luck a better mother give: 420
Chance gave us being, and by chance we
    live.
Such as our atoms were, ev'n such are we,⎫
Or call it chance, or strong necessity: ⎬
Thus, loaded with dead weight, the will   ⎪
    is free.   ⎭
And thus it needs must be: for seed con-
    join'd
Lets into nature's work th' imperfect kind;
But fire, th' enliv'ner of the general frame,
Is one, its operation still the same.
Its principle is in itself, while ours
Works, as confederates war, with mingled
    pow'rs;   430

Or man or woman, whichsoever fails;
And, oft, the vigor of the worse prevails.
Ether with sulphur blended alters hue,
And casts a dusky gleam of Sodom blue.
Thus, in a brute, their ancient honor ends,
And the fair mermaid in a fish descends:
The line is gone; no longer duke or earl;
But, by himself degraded, turns a churl.
Nobility of blood is but renown
Of thy great fathers by their virtue
      known,   440
And a long trail of light, to thee descend-
      ing down.
If in thy smoke it ends, their glories shine;
But infamy and villanage are thine;
Then what I said before is plainly show'd,
That true nobility proceeds from God;
Nor left us by inheritance, but giv'n
By bounty of our stars, and grace of Heav'n.
Thus from a captive Servius Tullius rose,
Whom for his virtues the first Romans
      chose;   449
Fabricius from their walls repell'd the foe,
Whose noble hands had exercis'd the plow.
From hence, my lord, and love, I thus con-
      clude,
That, tho' my homely ancestors were rude,
Mean as I am, yet I may have the grace
To make you father of a generous race;
And noble then am I, when I begin,
In virtue cloth'd, to cast the rags of sin.
   If poverty be my upbraided crime,
And you believe in Heav'n, there was a time
When he, the great controller of our fate, 460
Deign'd to be man, and liv'd in low estate:
Which he who had the world at his dispose,
If poverty were vice, would never choose.
Philosophers have said, and poets sing,
That a glad poverty 's an honest thing.
Content is wealth, the riches of the mind;
And happy he who can that treasure find.
But the base miser starves amidst his
      store,
Broods on his gold, and, griping still at
      more,   469
Sits sadly pining, and believes he 's poor.
The ragged beggar, tho' he wants relief,
Has not to lose, and sings before the thief.
Want is a bitter and a hateful good,
Because its virtues are not understood;
Yet many things, impossible to thought,
Have been by need to full perfection
      brought:
The daring of the soul proceeds from thence,
Sharpness of wit, and active diligence;

Prudence at once, and fortitude, it gives,
And, if in patience taken, mends our
      lives;   480
For ev'n that indigence that brings me low,
Makes me myself, and him above, to know:
A good which none would challenge, few
      would choose,
A fair possession, which mankind refuse.
   " If we from wealth to poverty descend,
Want gives to know the flatt'rer from the
      friend.
If I am old and ugly, well for you,
No lewd adult'rer will my love pursue.
Nor jealousy, the bane of married life,
Shall haunt you for a wither'd homely wife;
For age and ugliness, as all agree,   491
Are the best guards of female chastity.
   " Yet since I see your mind is worldly
      bent,
I 'll do my best to further your content.
And therefore of two gifts in my dispose —
Think ere you speak — I grant you leave
      to choose:
Would you I should be still deform'd and
      old,
Nauseous to touch, and loathsome to be-
      hold;
On this condition to remain for life
A careful, tender, and obedient wife,   500
In all I can contribute to your ease,
And not in deed, or word, or thought dis-
      please ?
Or would you rather have me young and
      fair,
And take the chance that happens to your
      share ?
Temptations are in beauty, and in youth,
And how can you depend upon my truth ?
Now weigh the danger with the doubtful
      bliss,
And thank yourself, if aught should fall
      amiss."
   Sore sigh'd the knight, who this long
      sermon heard ;
At length, considering all, his heart he
      cheer'd,   510
And thus replied: " My lady, and my wife,
To your wise conduct I resign my life:
Choose you for me, for well you under-
      stand
The future good and ill, on either hand.
But if an humble husband may request,
Provide, and order all things for the best;
Yours be the care to profit, and to please;
And let your subject-servant take his ease."

"Then thus in peace," quoth she, "concludes the strife,
Since I am turn'd the husband, you the wife: 520
The matrimonial victory is mine,
Which, having fairly gain'd, I will resign;
Forgive, if I have said or done amiss,
And seal the bargain with a friendly kiss:
I promis'd you but one content to share,
But now I will become both good and fair.
No nuptial quarrel shall disturb your ease;
The business of my life shall be to please:
And for my beauty, that, as time shall try —
But draw the curtain first, and cast your eye."   530
He look'd, and saw a creature heav'nly fair,
In bloom of youth, and of a charming air.
With joy he turn'd and seiz'd her iv'ry arm;
And, like Pygmalion, found the statue warm.
Small arguments there needed to prevail,
A storm of kisses pour'd as thick as hail.
    Thus long in mutual bliss they lay embrac'd,
And their first love continued to the last:
One sunshine was their life, no cloud between;
Nor ever was a kinder couple seen.   540
    And so may all our lives like theirs be led:
Heav'n send the maids young husbands fresh in bed;
May widows wed as often as they can,
And ever for the better change their man,
And some devouring plague pursue their lives,
Who will not well be govern'd by their wives.

OF THE PYTHAGOREAN PHILOSOPHY

FROM OVID'S METAMORPHOSES, BOOK XV

The Fourteenth Book concludes with the death and deification of Romulus; the Fifteenth begins with the election of Numa to the crown of Rome. On this occasion, Ovid, following the opinion of some authors, makes Numa the scholar of Pythagoras, and to have begun his acquaintance with that philosopher at Crotona, a town in Italy; from thence he makes a digression to the moral and natural philosophy of Pythagoras: on both which our author enlarges; and which are the most learned and beautiful parts of the whole *Metamorphoses*.

A KING is sought to guide the growing state,
One able to support the public weight,
And fill the throne where Romulus had sate.
Renown, which oft bespeaks the public voice,
Had recommended Numa to their choice:
A peaceful, pious prince; who, not content
To know the Sabine rites, his study bent
To cultivate his mind; to learn the laws
Of nature, and explore their hidden cause.
Urg'd by this care, his country he forsook,
And to Crotona thence his journey took. 11
Arriv'd, he first enquir'd the founder's name
Of this new colony, and whence he came.
Then thus a senior of the place replies,
Well read, and curious of antiquities:
    " 'T is said, Alcides hither took his way
From Spain, and drove along his conquer'd prey;
Then, leaving in the fields his grazing cows,
He sought himself some hospitable house.
Good Croton entertain'd his godlike guest,
While he repair'd his weary limbs with rest.
The hero, thence departing, bless'd the place, 22
' And here,' he said, ' in time's revolving race,
A rising town shall take his name from thee.'
Revolving time fulfill'd the prophecy;
For Myscelos, the justest man on earth,
Alemon's son, at Argos had his birth.
Him Hercules, arm'd with his club of oak,
O'ershadow'd in a dream, and thus bespoke:
'Go, leave thy native soil, and make abode   30
Where Æsaris rolls down his rapid flood.'
He said; and sleep forsook him, and the god.
Trembling he wak'd, and rose with anxious heart:
His country laws forbade him to depart;
What should he do ? 'T was death to go away,
And the god menac'd if he dar'd to stay.
All day he doubted, and, when night came on,

Sleep, and the same forewarning dream,
  begun;
Once more the god stood threat'ning o'er
  his head,
With added curses if he disobey'd.   40
Twice warn'd, he studied flight; but would
  convey
At once his person and his wealth away.
Thus while he linger'd, his design was heard,
A speedy process form'd, and death declar'd.
Witness there needed none of his offense,
Against himself the wretch was evidence:
Condemn'd, and destitute of human aid,
To him for whom he suffer'd, thus he
  pray'd:
  "'O Pow'r, who hast deserv'd in heav'n
  a throne,
Not giv'n, but by thy labors made thy own, 50
Pity thy suppliant, and protect his cause,
Whom thou hast made obnoxious to the
  laws.'
  "A custom was of old, and still re-
  mains,
Which life or death by suffrages ordains;
White stones and black within an urn are
  cast,
The first absolve, but fate is in the last.
The judges to the common urn bequeath
Their votes, and drop the sable signs of
  death;
The box receives all black, but, pour'd from
  thence,
The stones came candid forth, the hue of
  innocence.   60
Thus Alemonides his safety won,
Preserv'd from death by Alcumena's son.
Then to his kinsman god his vows he pays,
And cuts with prosp'rous gales th' Ionian
  seas:
He leaves Tarentum, favor'd by the wind,
And Thurine bays, and Temises, behind;
Soft Sybaris, and all the capes that stand
Along the shore, he makes in sight of land;
Still doubling, and still coasting, till he
  found   69
The mouth of Æsaris, and promis'd ground:
Then saw where, on the margin of the flood,
The tomb that held the bones of Croton
  stood.
Here, by the god's command, he built and
  wall'd
The place predicted, and Crotona call'd:
Thus fame, from time to time, delivers
  down
The sure tradition of th' Italian town."

Here dwelt the man divine whom Samos
  bore,
But now self-banish'd from his native shore,
Because he hated tyrants, nor could bear
The chains which none but servile souls
  will wear: 80
He, tho' from heav'n remote, to heav'n
  could move,
With strength of mind, and tread th' abyss
  above;
And penetrate, with his interior light,
Those upper depths which Nature hid from
  sight;
And what he had observ'd, and learnt from
  thence,
Lov'd in familiar language to dispense.
  The crowd with silent admiration stand,
And heard him, as they heard their god's
  command;
While he discours'd of heav'n's mysterious
  laws,
The world's original, and nature's cause; 90
And what was God, and why the fleecy
  snows
In silence fell, and rattling winds arose;
What shook the steadfast earth, and whence
  begun
The dance of planets round the radiant sun;
If thunder was the voice of angry Jove,
Or clouds, with niter pregnant, burst above:
Of these, and things beyond the common
  reach,
He spoke, and charm'd his audience with
  his speech.
  He first the taste of flesh from tables
  drove,
And argued well, if arguments could move:
"O mortals! from your fellows' blood ab-
  stain,   101
Nor taint your bodies with a food profane:
While corn and pulse by nature are be-
  stow'd,
And planted orchards bend their willing
  load;
While labor'd gardens wholesome herbs
  produce,
And teeming vines afford their generous
  juice;
Nor tardier fruits of cruder kind are lost,
But tam'd with fire, or mellow'd by the
  frost;
While kine to pails distended udders bring,
And bees their honey redolent of spring; 110
While earth not only can your needs supply,
But, lavish of her store, provides for luxury;

A guiltless feast administers with ease,
And without blood is prodigal to please.
Wild beasts their maws with their slain
    brethren fill,
And yet not all, for some refuse to kill:
Sheep, goats, and oxen, and the nobler steed,
On browse and corn and flow'ry meadows
    feed.
Bears, tigers, wolves, the lion's angry brood,
Whom Heav'n endued with principles of
    blood,   120
He wisely sunder'd from the rest, to yell
In forests, and in lonely caves to dwell,
Where stronger beasts oppress the weak by
    might,
And all in prey and purple feasts delight.
    "O impious use! to Nature's laws oppos'd,
Where bowels are in other bowels clos'd;
Where, fatten'd by their fellows' fat, they
    thrive,
Maintain'd by murder, and by death they
    live.
'T is then for naught that Mother Earth pro-
    vides
The stores of all she shows, and all she
    hides,   130
If men with fleshy morsels must be fed,
And chaw with bloody teeth the breathing
    bread:
What else is this but to devour our guests,
And barb'rously renew Cyclopean feasts !
We, by destroying life, our life sustain,
And gorge th' ungodly maw with meats
    obscene.
    "Not so the Golden Age, who fed on fruit,
Nor durst with bloody meals their mouths
    pollute:
Then birds in airy space might safely move,
And timorous hares on heaths securely
    rove;   140
Nor needed fish the guileful hooks to fear,
For all was peaceful, and that peace sincere.
Whoever was the wretch (and curst be he)
That envied first our food's simplicity,
Th' essay of bloody feasts on brutes began,
And after forg'd the sword to murther man.
Had he the sharpen'd steel alone employ'd
On beasts of prey that other beasts de-
    stroy'd,
Or man invaded with their fangs and paws,
This had been justified by Nature's laws, 150
And self-defense; but who did feasts begin
Of flesh, he stretch'd necessity to sin.
To kill man-killers, man has lawful pow'r,
But not th' extended license to devour.

    "Ill habits gather by unseen degrees,
As brooks make rivers, rivers run to seas.
The sow, with her broad snout for rooting
    up
Th' intrusted seed, was judg'd to spoil the
    crop
And intercept the sweating farmer's hope;
The cov'tous churl, of unforgiving kind, 160
Th' offender to the bloody priest resign'd:
Her hunger was no plea; for that she died.
The goat came next in order to be tried;
The goat had cropp'd the tendrils of the
    vine:
In vengeance laity and clergy join,
Where one had lost his profit, one his
    wine.
Here was, at least, some shadow of of-
    fense;
The sheep was sacrific'd on no pretense,
But meek and unresisting innocence:
A patient, useful creature, born to bear 170
The warm and woolly fleece, that cloth'd
    her murderer,
And daily to give down the milk she bred,
A tribute for the grass on which she fed.
Living, both food and raiment she supplies,
And is of least advantage when she dies.
    "How did the toiling ox his death deserve,
A downright simple drudge, and born to
    serve ?
O tyrant ! with what justice canst thou hope
The promise of the year, a plenteous crop,
When thou destroy'st thy lab'ring steer,
    who till'd   180
And plow'd with pains thy else ungrateful
    field ?
From his yet reeking neck to draw the yoke,
(That neck with which the surly clods he
    broke,)
And to the hatchet yield thy husbandman,
Who finish'd autumn, and the spring began !
    "Nor this alone ! but, Heav'n itself to
    bribe,
We to the gods our impious acts ascribe;
First recompense with death their creatures'
    toil,
Then call the blest above to share the
    spoil.   189
The fairest victim must the pow'rs appease;
(So fatal 't is sometimes too much to please!)
A purple fillet his broad brows adorns,
With flow'ry garlands crown'd, and gilded
    horns.
He hears the murd'rous pray'r the priest
    prefers,

But understands not, 't is his doom he hears;
Beholds the meal betwixt his temples cast,
(The fruit and product of his labors past;)
And in the water views, perhaps, the knife
Uplifted, to deprive him of his life;
Then, broken up alive, his entrails sees, 200
Torn out for priests t' inspect the god's
    decrees.
  " From whence, O mortal men, this gust
    of blood
Have you deriv'd, and interdicted food ?
Be taught by me this dire delight to shun,
Warn'd by my precepts, by my practice
    won;
And when you eat the well-deserving beast,
Think, on the lab'rer of your field you feast !
  " Now since the god inspires me to pro-
    ceed.
Be that, whate'er inspiring pow'r, obey'd;
For I will sing of mighty mysteries, 210 ⎱
Of truths conceal'd before from human   ⎮
    eyes,   ⎬
Dark oracles unveil, and open all the   ⎮
    skies;   ⎰
Pleas'd as I am to walk along the sphere
Of shining stars, and travel with the year,
To leave the heavy earth, and scale the
    height
Of Atlas, who supports the heav'nly weight;
To look from upper light, and thence survey
Mistaken mortals wand'ring from the way,
And, wanting wisdom, fearful for the state
Of future things, and trembling at their
    fate ! 220
  " Those I would teach, and by right rea-
    son bring
To think of death, as but an idle thing.
Why thus affrighted at an empty name,
A dream of darkness, and fictitious flame ?
Vain themes of wit, which but in poems pass,
And fables of a world that never was !
What feels the body when the soul expires,
By time corrupted, or consum'd by fires ?
Nor dies the spirit, but new life repeats
In other forms, and only changes seats. 230
  " Ev'n I, who these mysterious truths
    declare,
Was once Euphorbus in the Trojan war;
My name and lineage I remember well,
And how in fight by Sparta's king I fell.
In Argive Juno's fane I late beheld
My buckler hung on high, and own'd my
    former shield.
  " Then death, so call'd, is but old matter
    dress'd

In some new figure, and a varied vest:
Thus all things are but alter'd, nothing dies;
And here and there th' unbodied spirit
    flies, 240
By time, or force, or sickness dispossess'd,
And lodges, where it lights, in man or beast;
Or hunts without, till ready limbs it find,
And actuates those according to their kind;
From tenement to tenement is toss'd;
The soul is still the same, the figure only
    lost.
And, as the soften'd wax new seals receives,
This face assumes, and that impression
    leaves;
Now call'd by one, now by another name;
The form is only chang'd, the wax is still
    the same: 250
So death, so call'd, can but the form de- ⎫
    face,   ⎮
Th' immortal soul flies out in empty space, ⎬
To seek her fortune in some other place. ⎭
  " Then let not piety be put to flight,
To please the taste of glutton appetite;
But suffer inmate souls secure to dwell,
Lest from their seats your parents you
    expel;
With rabid hunger feed upon your kind,
Or from a beast dislodge a brother's mind.
  " And since, like Tiphys, parting from the
    shore, 260
In ample seas I sail, and depths untried
    before,
This let me further add, that Nature knows
No steadfast station, but or ebbs or flows:
Ever in motion; she destroys her old,
And casts new figures in another mold.
Ev'n times are in perpetual flux, and run,
Like rivers from their fountain, rolling on;
For time, no more than streams, is at a stay:
The flying hour is ever on her way; 269
And, as the fountain still supplies her store,
(The wave behind impels the wave before,)
Thus in successive course the minutes run,
And urge their predecessor minutes on,
Still moving, ever new: for former things
Are set aside, like abdicated kings;
And every moment alters what is done,
And innovates some act till then unknown.
  " Darkness we see emerges into light,
And shining suns descend to sable night;
Ev'n heav'n itself receives another dye, 280
When wearied animals in slumbers lie
Of midnight ease; another, when the gray
Of morn preludes the splendor of the day
The disk of Phœbus, when he climbs on high,

Appears at first but as a bloodshot eye;
And, when his chariot downward drives to
    bed,
His ball is with the same suffusion red;
But, mounted high in his meridian race,
All bright he shines, and with a better face;
For there pure particles of ether flow,   290
Far from th' infection of the world below.
  "Nor equal light th' unequal moon
    adorns,
Or in her wexing, or her waning horns.
For ev'ry day she wanes, her face is less,
But gath'ring into globe, she fattens at in-
    crease.
  "Perceiv'st thou not the process of the
    year,
How the four seasons in four forms ap-
    pear,
Resembling human life in ev'ry shape
    they wear?
Spring first, like infancy, shoots out her
    head,   299
With milky juice requiring to be fed:
Helpless, tho' fresh, and wanting to be
    led.
The green stem grows in stature and in size,
But only feeds with hope the farmer's eyes;
Then laughs the childish year with flow'rets
    crown'd,
And lavishly perfumes the fields around,
But no substantial nourishment receives;
Infirm the stalks, unsolid are the leaves.
  "Proceeding onward whence the year
    began,
The Summer grows adult and ripens into
    man.
This season, as in men, is most replete   310
With kindly moisture and prolific heat.
  "Autumn succeeds, a sober tepid age,
Not froze with fear, nor boiling into rage;
More than mature, and tending to decay,
When our brown locks repine to mix with
    odious gray.
  "Last, Winter creeps along with tardy
    pace;
Sour is his front, and furrow'd is his face.
His scalp if not dishonor'd quite of hair,
The ragged fleece is thin, and thin is worse
    than bare.
  "Ev'n our own bodies daily change re-
    ceive;   320
Some part of what was theirs before, they
    leave;
Nor are to-day what yesterday they were,
Nor the whole same to-morrow will appear.

  "Time was, when we were sow'd, and just
    began,
From some few fruitful drops, the promise
    of a man.
Then Nature's hand (fermented as it was)
Molded to shape the soft, coagulated mass;
And when the little man was fully form'd,
The breathless embryo with a spirit warm'd;
But when the mother's throes begin to
    come,   330
The creature, pent within the narrow room,
Breaks his blind prison, pushing to repair
His stifled breath and draw the living air;
Cast on the margin of the world he lies,
A helpless babe, but by instinct he cries.
He next essays to walk, but, downward
    press'd,
On four feet imitates his brother beast:
By slow degrees he gathers from the ground
His legs, and to the rolling chair is bound;
Then walks alone; a horseman now be-
    come,   340
He rides a stick, and travels round the room.
In time he vaunts among his youthful peers,
Strong-bon'd, and strung with nerves, in
    pride of years.
He runs with mettle his first merry
    stage;
Maintains the next, abated of his rage,
But manages his strength, and spares his
    age.
Heavy the third and stiff, he sinks apace,
And, tho' 't is downhill all, but creeps along
    the race.
Now sapless on the verge of death he stands,
Contemplating his former feet and hands;
And, Milo-like, his slacken'd sinews
    sees,   351
And wither'd arms, once fit to cope with
    Hercules,
Unable now to shake, much less to tear,
    the trees.
  "So Helen wept, when her too faithful
    glass
Reflected to her eyes the ruins of her face,
Wond'ring what charms her ravishers could
    spy,
To force her twice, or ev'n but once enjoy!
  "Thy teeth, devouring Time, thine, envi-
    ous Age,
On things below still exercise your rage:
With venom'd grinders you corrupt your
    meat,   360
And then, at ling'ring meals, the morsels
    eat.

" Nor those, which elements we call,
 abide,
Nor to this figure, nor to that, are tied;
For this eternal world is said of old
But four prolific principles to hold,
Four different bodies; two to heaven as-
 cend,
And other two down to the center tend.
Fire, first, with wings expanded mounts on
 high,
Pure, void of weight, and dwells in upper
 sky;
Then Air, because unclogg'd in empty
 space, 370
Flies after Fire, and claims the second
 place;
But weighty Water, as her nature guides,
Lies on the lap of Earth, and Mother Earth
 subsides.
 " All things are mix'd of these, which all
 contain,
And into these are all resolv'd again:
Earth rarefies to Dew; expanded more,
The subtile Dew in Air begins to soar;
Spreads as she flies, and weary of her
 name
Extenuates still, and changes into Flame.
Thus having by degrees perfection won, 380
Restless they soon untwist the web they
 spun,
And Fire begins to lose her radiant hue,
Mix'd with gross Air, and Air descends to
 Dew;
And Dew, condensing, does her form forego,
And sinks, a heavy lump of Earth, below.
 " Thus are their figures never at a stand,
But chang'd by Nature's innovating hand;
All things are alter'd, nothing is destroy'd,
The shifted scene for some new show em-
 ploy'd.
 " Then, to be born, is to begin to be 390
Some other thing we were not formerly;
And what we call to die, is not t' appear
Or be the thing that formerly we were.
Those very elements which we partake,
Alive, when dead, some other bodies make;
Translated grow, have sense, or can dis-
 course;
But death on deathless substance has no
 force.
 "That forms are chang'd I grant, that
 nothing can
Continue in the figure it began;
The Golden Age to Silver was debas'd; 400
To Copper that; our metal came at last.

" The face of places, and their forms,
 decay;
And that is solid earth, that once was sea:
Seas, in their turn, retreating from the
 shore,
Make solid land what ocean was before;
And far from strands are shells of fishes
 found,
And rusty anchors fix'd on mountain
 ground;
And what were fields before, now wash'd
 and worn
By falling floods from high, to valleys turn,
And, crumbling still, descend to level lands,
And lakes and trembling bogs are barren
 sands; 411
And the parch'd desart floats in streams
 unknown,
Wond'ring to drink of waters not her own.
 " Here nature living fountains opes, and
 there
Seals up the wombs where living fountains
 were;
Or earthquakes stop their ancient course,
 and bring
Diverted streams to feed a distant spring.
So Lycus, swallow'd up, is seen no more,
But far from thence knocks out another
 door.
Thus Erasinus dives, and blind in earth 420
Runs on, and gropes his way to second birth;
Starts up in Argos' meads, and shakes his
 locks
Around the fields, and fattens all the flocks.
So Mysus by another way is led,
And, grown a river, now disdains his head;
Forgets his humble birth, his name for-
 sakes,
And the proud title of Caïcus takes.
Large Amenane, impure with yellow sands,
Runs rapid often, and as often stands;
And here he threats the drunken fields to
 drown, 430
And there his dugs deny to give their liquor
 down.
 " Anigros once did wholesome draughts
 afford,
But now his deadly waters are abhorr'd;
Since, hurt by Hercules, as fame resounds,
The Centaurs in his current wash'd their
 wounds.
The streams of Hypanis are sweet no more,
But, brackish, lose the taste they had before.
Antissa, Pharos, Tyre, in seas were pent,
Once isles, but now increase the continent;

While the Leucadian coast, mainland be-
    fore, 440
By rushing seas is sever'd from the shore.
So Zancle to th' Italian earth was tied,
And men once walk'd where ships at anchor
    ride;
Till Neptune overlook'd the narrow way,
And in disdain pour'd in the conqu'ring
    sea.
  "Two cities that adorn'd th' Achaian
    ground,
Buris and Helice, no more are found,
But, whelm'd beneath a lake, are sunk
    and drown'd;
And boatsmen thro' the crystal water show
To wond'ring passengers the walls below.
  "Near Trœzen stands a hill, expos'd in
    air 451
To winter winds, of leafy shadows bare:
This once was level ground; but (strange
    to tell)
Th' included vapors, that in caverns dwell,
Lab'ring with colic pangs, and close confin'd,
In vain sought issue for the rumbling wind:
Yet still they heav'd for vent, and heaving
    still
Inlarg'd the concave, and shot up the hill;
As breath extends a bladder, or the skins
Of goats are blown t' inclose the hoarded
    wines. 460
The mountain yet retains a mountain's face,
And gather'd rubbish heals the hollow
    space.
  "Of many wonders which I heard or
    knew,
Retrenching most, I will relate but few:
What, are not springs with qualities oppos'd
Endued at seasons, and at seasons lost?
Thrice in a day thine, Ammon, change their
    form,
Cold at high noon, at morn and evening
    warm;
Thine, Athaman, will kindle wood, if thrown
On the pil'd earth, and in the waning moon.
The Thracians have a stream, if any try 471
The taste, his harden'd bowels petrify;
Whate'er it touches it converts to stones,
And makes a marble pavement where it
    runs.
  "Crathis, and Sybaris her sister flood,
That slide thro' our Calabrian neighbor
    wood,
With gold and amber dye the shining hair,
And thither youth resort; (for who would
    not be fair?)

  "But stranger virtues yet in streams we
    find;
Some change not only bodies, but the mind:
Who has not heard of Salmacis obscene, 481
Whose waters into women soften men?
Of Ethiopian lakes, which turn the brain
To madness, or in heavy sleep constrain?
Clitorian streams the love of wine expel,
(Such is the virtue of th' abstemious well,)
Whether the colder nymph that rules the
    flood
Extinguishes and balks the drunken god;
Or that Melampus, (so have some assur'd,)
When the mad Prœtides with charms he
    cur'd, 490
And pow'rful herbs, both charms and sim-
    ples cast
Into the sober spring, where still their vir-
    tues last.
  "Unlike effects Lyncestis will produce;
Who drinks his waters, tho' with moderate
    use,
Reels as with wine, and sees with double
    sight;
His heels too heavy, and his head too light.
Ladon, once Pheneos, an Arcadian stream,
(Ambiguous in th' effects, as in the name,)
By day is wholesome bev'rage, but is thought
By night infected, and a deadly draught. 500
  "Thus running rivers, and the standing
    lake,
Now of these virtues, now of those partake:
Time was (and all things time and fate
    obey)
When fast Ortygia floated on the sea;
Such were Cyanean isles, when Tiphys
    steer'd
Betwixt their straits, and their collision
    fear'd;
They swam where now they sit; and, firmly
    join'd,
Secure of rooting up, resist the wind.
Nor Ætna vomiting sulphureous fire
Will ever belch, for sulphur will expire 510
(The veins exhausted of the liquid store):
Time was she cast no flames; in time will
    cast no more.
  "For whether earth's an animal, and air
Imbibes, her lungs with coolness to repair,
And what she sucks remits, she still requires
Inlets for air, and outlets for her fires;
When tortur'd with convulsive fits she
    shakes,
That motion chokes the vent, till other vent
    she makes;

Or when the winds in hollow caves are clos'd,
And subtile spirits find that way oppos'd, 520
They toss up flints in air; the flints that hide
The seeds of fire, thus toss'd in air, collide,
Kindling the sulphur, till, the fuel spent,
The cave is cool'd, and the fierce winds re-
        lent.
Or whether sulphur, catching fire, feeds on
Its unctuous parts, till, all the matter gone,
The flames no more ascend; for earth sup-
        plies
The fat that feeds them, and, when earth
        denies
That food, by length of time consum'd, the
        fire
Famish'd for want of fuel must expire. 530
    " A race of men there are, as fame has
        told,
Who shiv'ring suffer Hyperborean cold,
Till, nine times bathing in Minerva's lake,
Soft feathers to defend their naked sides
        they take.
'T is said, the Scythian wives (believe who
        will)
Transform themselves to birds by magic
        skill;
Smear'd over with an oil of wondrous
        might,
That adds new pinions to their airy flight.
    " But this by sure experiment we know,
That   living   creatures   from   corruption
        grow: 540
Hide in a hollow pit a slaughter'd steer,
Bees from his putrid bowels will appear;
Who like their parents haunt the fields, and
        bring
Their honey harvest home, and hope another
        spring.
The warlike steed is multiplied, we find,
To wasps and hornets of the warrior kind.
Cut from a crab his crooked claws, and hide
The rest in earth, a scorpion thence will
        glide,
And shoot his sting; his tail, in circles toss'd,
Refers the limbs his backward father lost.
And worms, that stretch on leaves their
        filmy loom,   551
Crawl from their bags, and butterflies be-
        come.
Ev'n slime begets the frog's loquacious race;
Short of their feet at first, in little space
With arms and legs endued, long leaps they
        take,
Rais'd on their hinder part, and swim the
        lake.

And waves repel: for Nature gives their
        kind,
To that intent, a length of legs behind.
    " The cubs of bears a living lump appear,
When whelp'd, and and no determin'd figure
        wear.   560
Their mother licks 'em into shape, and gives
As much of form as she herself receives.
    " The grubs from their sexangular abode
Crawl out unfinish'd, like the maggot's
        brood,
Trunks without limbs; till time at leisure
        brings
The thighs they wanted, and their tardy
        wings.
    " The bird who draws the car of Juno,
        vain
Of her crown'd head, and of her starry
        train;
And he that bears th' artillery of Jove,
The strong-pounc'd eagle and the billing
        dove;   570
And all the feather'd kind, who could sup-⎫
        pose   ⎪
(But   that from sight, the surest sense, ⎬
        he knows)   ⎪
They from th' included yolk, not ambient ⎪
        white, arose.   ⎭
    " There are who think the marrow of a
        man,
Which in the spine, while he was living, ran;
When dead, the pith corrupted, will become
A snake, and hiss within the hollow tomb.
    " All these receive their birth from other
        things,
But from himself the Phœnix only springs;
Self-born, begotten by the parent flame 580
In which he burn'd, another and the same:
Who not by corn or herbs his life sustains,
But the sweet essence of amomum drains,
And watches the rich gums Arabia bears,
While yet in tender dew they drop their
        tears.
He (his five centuries of life fulfill'd)
His nest on oaken boughs begins to build,
Or trembling tops of palm; and first he
        draws
The plan with his broad bill and crooked
        claws,
Nature's artificers; on this the pile   590
Is form'd, and rises round; then with the
        spoil
Of cassia, cinnamon, and stems of nard
(For softness strew'd beneath) his fun'ral
        bed is rear'd:

Fun'ral and bridal both; and all around
The borders with corruptless myrrh are
    crown'd,
On this incumbent; till ethereal flame
First catches, then consumes the costly
    frame;
Consumes him too, as on the pile he lies:
He liv'd on odors, and in odors dies.
    " An infant Phœnix from the former
        springs,   600
His father's heir, and from his tender wings
Shakes off his parent dust; his method he
    pursues,
And the same lease of life on the same terms
    renews.
When grown to manhood he begins his
    reign,
And with stiff pinions can his flight sus-
    tain,
He lightens of its load the tree that bore
His father's royal sepulcher before,
And his own cradle: this with pious care
Plac'd on his back, he cuts the buxom air,
Seeks the Sun's city, and his sacred church,
And decently lays down his burden in the
    porch.   611
" A wonder more amazing would we find ?
Th' hyæna shows it, of a double kind,
Varying the sexes in alternate years;
In one begets, and in another bears.
The thin chameleon, fed with air, receives
The color of the thing to which he cleaves.
    " India, when conquer'd, on the con-
        qu'ring god
For planted vines the sharp-ey'd lynx be-
    stow'd,
Whose urine shed, before it touches earth,
Congeals in air, and gives to gems their
    birth.   621
So coral, soft and white in ocean's bed,
Comes harden'd up in air, and glows with
    red.
    " All changing species should my song re-
        cite,
Before I ceas'd, would change the day to
    night.
Nations and empires flourish and decay,
By turns command, and in their turns
    obey;
Time softens hardy people, time again
Hardens to war a soft, unwarlike train.
Thus Troy, for ten long years, her foes
    withstood,   630
And, daily bleeding, bore th' expense of
    blood:

Now for thick streets it shows an empty
    space,
Or, only fill'd with tombs of her own per-
    ish'd race,
Herself becomes the sepulcher of what
    she was.
    " Mycenæ, Sparta, Thebes of mighty
        fame,
Are vanish'd out of substance into name,
And Dardan Rome, that just begins to
    rise,
On Tiber's banks, in time shall mate the
    skies;
Widening her bounds, and working on her
    way,
Ev'n now she meditates imperial sway: 640
Yet this is change, but she by changing
    thrives,
Like moons new-born, and in her cradle
    strives
To fill her infant horns; an hour shall come
When the round world shall be contain'd
    in Rome.
    " For thus old saws foretell, and Helenus
Anchises' drooping son enliven'd thus,
When Ilium now was in a sinking state,
And he was doubtful of his future fate:
' O goddess-born, with thy hard fortune
    strive;
Troy never can be lost, and thou alive. 650
Thy passage thou shalt free thro' fire and
    sword,
And Troy in foreign lands shall be restor'd.
In happier fields a rising town I see,
Greater than what e'er was, or is, or e'er
    shall be;
And Heav'n yet owes the world a race
    deriv'd from thee.
Sages and chiefs, of other lineage born,
The city shall extend, extended shall adorn;
But from Iülus he must draw his birth,
By whom thy Rome shall rule the conquer'd
    earth;
Whom Heav'n will lend mankind on earth
    to reign,   660
And late require the precious pledge again.'
This Helenus to great Æneas told,
Which I retain, e'er since in other mold
My soul was cloth'd; and now rejoice to
    view
My country walls rebuilt, and Troy reviv'd
    anew,
Rais'd by the fall; decreed by loss to gain;
Enslav'd but to be free, and conquer'd but
    to reign.

" 'Tis time my hard-mouth'd coursers to
control,
Apt to run riot and transgress the goal,
And therefore I conclude: whatever lies 670
In earth, or flits in air, or fills the skies,
All suffer change; and we, that are of soul
And body mix'd, are members of the whole.
Then, when our sires, or grandsires, shall
forsake
The forms of men, and brutal figures take,
Thus hous'd, securely let their spirits rest,
Nor violate thy father in the beast —
Thy friend, thy brother, any of thy kin;
If none of these, yet there's a man within:
O spare to make a Thyestean meal, 680
T' inclose his body, and his soul expel.
" Ill customs by degrees to habits rise,
Ill habits soon become exalted vice:
What more advance can mortals make in
sin,
So near perfection, who with blood begin?
Deaf to the calf that lies beneath the knife,
Looks up, and from her butcher begs her
life;
Deaf to the harmless kid, that, ere he dies, ⎫
All methods to procure thy mercy tries, ⎬
And imitates in vain thy children's cries. ⎭
Where will he stop, who feeds with house-
hold bread, 691
Then eats the poultry which before he fed?
Let plow thy steers; that, when they lose
their breath,
To nature, not to thee, they may impute
their death.
Let goats for food their loaded udders lend,
And sheep from winter cold thy sides de-
fend;
But neither springes, nets, nor snares em-
ploy,
And be no more ingenious to destroy.
Free, as in air, let birds on earth remain,
Nor let insidious glue their wings constrain;
Nor opening hounds the trembling stag
affright, 701
Nor purple feathers intercept his flight;
Nor hooks conceal'd in baits for fish prepare,
Nor lines to heave 'em twinkling up in air.
" Take not away the life you cannot give;
For all things have an equal right to live.
Kill noxious creatures, where 'tis sin to save;
This only just prerogative we have:
But nourish life with vegetable food,
And shun the sacrilegious taste of blood." 710
These precepts by the Samian sage were
taught,

Which godlike Numa to the Sabines
brought,
And thence transferr'd to Rome, by gift his
own,
A willing people, and an offer'd throne.
O happy monarch, sent by Heav'n to bless
A salvage nation with soft arts of peace;
To teach religion, rapine to restrain,
Give laws to lust, and sacrifice ordain:
Himself a saint, a goddess was his bride,
And all the Muses o'er his acts preside. 720

THE CHARACTER OF A GOOD PARSON

IMITATED FROM CHAUCER, AND INLARG'D

A PARISH priest was of the pilgrim train;
An awful, reverend, and religious man.
His eyes diffus'd a venerable grace,
And charity itself was in his face.
Rich was his soul, tho' his attire was poor, ⎫
(As God had cloth'd his own ambassador;) ⎬
For such, on earth, his blest Redeemer ⎭
bore.
Of sixty years he seem'd; and well might
last
To sixty more, but that he liv'd too fast; 9
Refin'd himself to soul, to curb the sense;
And made almost a sin of abstinence.
Yet had his aspect nothing of severe,
But such a face as promis'd him sincere.
Nothing reserv'd or sullen was to see, ⎫
But sweet regards and pleasing sanctity; ⎬
Mild was his accent, and his action free. ⎭
With eloquence innate his tongue was arm'd;
Tho' harsh the precept, yet the preacher
charm'd.
For, letting down the golden chain from
high,
He drew his audience upward to the sky; 20
And oft, with holy hymns, he charm'd their
ears
(A music more melodious than the spheres):
For David left him, when he went to rest,
His lyre, and after him he sung the best.
He bore his great commission in his look;
But sweetly temper'd awe, and soften'd all
he spoke.
He preach'd the joys of heav'n and pains ⎫
of hell, ⎬
And warn'd the sinner with becoming ⎬
zeal, ⎬
But on eternal mercy lov'd to dwell. 29 ⎭

He taught the gospel rather than the law,
And forc'd himself to drive, but lov'd to
    draw:
For fear but freezes minds; but love, like
    heat,
Exhales the soul sublime, to seek her na-
    tive seat.
    To threats the stubborn sinner oft is
      hard,
Wrapp'd in his crimes, against the storm
    prepar'd;
But, when the milder beams of mercy play,
He melts, and throws his cumbrous cloak
    away.
    Lightnings and thunder (heav'n's artil-
      lery)
As harbingers before th' Almighty fly: 39
Those but proclaim his style, and disappear;
The stiller sound succeeds, and God is there.
    The tithes his parish freely paid, he took;
But never sued, or curs'd with bell and book:
With patience bearing wrong, but off'ring
    none,
Since every man is free to lose his own.
The country churls, according to their kind,
(Who grudge their dues, and love to be
    behind,)
The less he sought his off'rings, pinch'd the
    more,
And prais'd a priest contented to be poor.
    Yet of his little he had some to spare, 50
To feed the famish'd, and to clothe the bare:
For mortified he was to that degree,
A poorer than himself he would not see.
True priests, he said, and preachers of the
    word,
Were only stewards of their sovereign
    Lord:
Nothing was theirs; but all the public store,
Intrusted riches, to relieve the poor;
Who, should they steal, for want of his
    relief,
He judg'd himself accomplice with the thief.
    Wide was his parish; not contracted
      close   60
In streets, but here and there a straggling
    house;
Yet still he was at hand, without request,
To serve the sick, to succor the distress'd;
Tempting, on foot, alone, without affright,
The dangers of a dark, tempestuous night.
    All this the good old man perform'd
      alone,
Nor spar'd his pains; for curate he had none.
Nor durst he trust another with his care;

Nor rode himself to Paul's, the public fair,
To chaffer for preferment with his gold, 70
Where bishoprics and sinecures are sold;
But duly watch'd his flock, by night and ⎫
    day,   ⎪
And from the prowling wolf redeem'd ⎬
    the prey,   ⎪
And hungry sent the wily fox away. ⎭
    The proud he tam'd, the penitent he
      cheer'd,
Nor to rebuke the rich offender fear'd.
His preaching much, but more his practice
    wrought;
(A living sermon of the truths he taught;)
For this by rules severe his life he squar'd,
That all might see the doctrine which they
    heard.   80
For priests, he said, are patterns for the rest;
(The gold of heav'n, who bear the God im-
    press'd;)
But when the precious coin is kept unclean,
The sovereign's image is no longer seen.
If they be foul on whom the people trust,
Well may the baser brass contract a rust.
    The prelate for his holy life he priz'd;
The worldly pomp of prelacy despis'd.
His Savior came not with a gaudy show,
Nor was his kingdom of the world below. 90
Patience in want, and poverty of mind, ⎫
These marks of Church and Churchmen ⎬
    he design'd,   ⎪
And living taught, and dying left behind.⎭
The crown he wore was of the pointed thorn;
In purple he was crucified, not born.
They who contend for place and high degree
Are not his sons, but those of Zebedee.
    Not but he knew the signs of earthly
      pow'r
Might well become Saint Peter's successor:
The holy father holds a double reign; 100
The prince may keep his pomp, the fisher
    must be plain.
    Such was the saint; who shone with every
      grace,
Reflecting, Moses-like, his Maker's face.
God saw his image lively was express'd,
And his own work, as in creation, bless'd.
    The tempter saw him too, with envious
      eye;
And, as on Job, demanded leave to try.
He took the time when Richard was depos'd,
And high and low with happy Harry clos'd.
This prince, tho' great in arms, the priest
    withstood;   110
Near tho' he was, yet not the next of blood.

Had Richard, unconstrain'd, resign'd the
    throne,
A king can give no more than is his own;
The title stood entail'd, had Richard had
    a son.
Conquest, an odious name, was laid aside,
Where all submitted, none the battle tried.
The senseless plea of right by providence
Was, by a flatt'ring priest, invented since;
And lasts no longer than the present sway,
But justifies the next who comes in play. 120
  The people's right remains; let those who
    dare
Dispute their pow'r, when they the judges
    are.
  He join'd not in their choice, because he
    knew
Worse might, and often did, from change
    ensue.
Much to himself he thought, but little spoke;
And, undepriv'd, his benefice forsook.
  Now, thro' the land, his cure of souls he
    stretch'd,
And like a primitive apostle preach'd:
Still cheerful, ever constant to his call;
By many follow'd, lov'd by most, admir'd
    by all.   130
With what he begg'd, his brethren he re-
    liev'd,
And gave the charities himself receiv'd;
Gave, while he taught; and edified the more,
Because he shew'd, by proof, 't was easy to
    be poor.
  He went not with the crowd to see a
    shrine,
But fed us, by the way, with food divine.
  In deference to his virtues, I forbear
To shew you what the rest in orders were:
This brilliant is so spotless and so bright,
He needs no foil, but shines by his own
    proper light.   140

CYMON AND IPHIGENIA

FROM BOCCACE

Poeta loquitur

OLD as I am, for ladies' love unfit,
The pow'r of beauty I remember yet,
Which once inflam'd my soul, and still
    inspires my wit.
If love be folly, the severe divine
Has felt that folly, tho' he censures mine;

Pollutes the pleasures of a chaste embrace,
Acts what I write, and propagates in
    grace,
With riotous excess, a priestly race.
Suppose him free, and that I forge th'
    offense,
He shew'd the way, perverting first my
    sense: 10
In malice witty, and with venom fraught,
He makes me speak the things I never
    thought.
Compute the gains of his ungovern'd zeal;
Ill suits his cloth the praise of railing well.
The world will think that what we loosely
    write,
Tho' now arraign'd, he read with some
    delight;
Because he seems to chew the cud again,
When his broad comment makes the text
    too plain;
And teaches more in one explaining page,
Than all the double meanings of the stage. 20
  What needs he paraphrase on what we
    mean?
We were at worst but wanton; he 's obscene.
I nor my fellows nor myself excuse;
But love 's the subject of the comic Muse:
Nor can we write without it, nor would you
A tale of only dry instruction view.
Nor love is always of a vicious kind,
But oft to virtuous acts inflames the mind,
Awakes the sleepy vigor of the soul,
And, brushing o'er, adds motion to the pool.
Love, studious how to please, improves our
    parts   31
With polish'd manners, and adorns with
    arts.
Love first invented verse, and form'd the
    rhyme,
The motion measur'd, harmoniz'd the chime ·
To lib'ral acts inlarg'd the narrow-soul'd,
Soften'd the fierce, and made the coward
    bold;
The world, when waste, he peopled with
    increase,
And warring nations reconcil'd in peace.
Ormond, the first, and all the fair may
    find,
In this one legend, to their fame design'd,
When beauty fires the blood, how love
    exalts the mind.   41

IN that sweet isle where Venus keeps her
    court,
And ev'ry grace, and all the loves, resort;

Where either sex is form'd of softer earth,
And takes the bent of pleasure from their
    birth;
There liv'd a Cyprian lord, above the rest
Wise, wealthy, with a num'rous issue blest.
    But, as no gift of fortune is sincere,
Was only wanting in a worthy heir:
His eldest born, a goodly youth to view, 50
Excell'd the rest in shape and outward
    shew;
Fair, tall, his limbs with due proportion
    join'd,
But of a heavy, dull, degenerate mind.
His soul belied the features of his face;
Beauty was there, but beauty in disgrace.
A clownish mien, a voice with rustic sound,
And stupid eyes that ever lov'd the ground.
He look'd like Nature's error, as the mind ⎤
And body were not of a piece design'd, ⎟
But made for two, and by mistake in one ⎬
    were join'd.   60 ⎦
    The ruling rod, the father's forming care,
Were exercis'd in vain on wit's despair;
The more inform'd, the less he understood,
And deeper sunk by flound'ring in the mud.
Now scorn'd of all, and grown the public
    shame,
The people from Galesus chang'd his name,
And Cymon call'd, which signifies a brute;
So well his name did with his nature suit.
    His father, when he found his labor lost,
And care employ'd that answer'd not the
    cost,   70
Chose an ungrateful object to remove,
And loath'd to see what Nature made him
    love;
So to his country farm the fool confin'd,
Rude work well suited with a rustic mind.
Thus to the wilds the sturdy Cymon went,
A squire among the swains, and pleas'd
    with banishment.
His corn and cattle were his only care,
And his supreme delight, a country fair.
    It happen'd on a summer's holiday,   ⎤
That to the greenwood shade he took his ⎟
    way;   80 ⎬
For Cymon shunn'd the church, and us'd ⎟
    not much to pray.   ⎦
His quarterstaff, which he could ne'er for-
    sake,
Hung half before, and half behind his back.
He trudg'd along, unknowing what he
    sought,
And whistled as he went, for want of
    thought.

By chance conducted, or by thirst con-
    strain'd,
The deep recesses of the grove he gain'd,
Where in a plain, defended by the wood, ⎤
Crept thro' the matted grass a crystal ⎟
    flood,   ⎬
By which an alabaster fountain stood; 90 ⎦
And on the margin of the fount was laid
(Attended by her slaves) a sleeping maid;
Like Dian and her nymphs, when, tir'd with
    sport,
To rest by cool Eurotas they resort.
The dame herself the goddess well ex-
    press'd,
Not more distinguish'd by her purple vest,
Than by the charming features of her face,
And, ev'n in slumber, a superior grace:
Her comely limbs compos'd with decent ⎤
    care,   ⎟
Her body shaded with a slight simar; 100 ⎬
Her bosom to the view was only bare, ⎦
Where two beginning paps were scarcely
    spied,
For yet their places were but signified.
The fanning wind upon her bosom blows, ⎤
To meet the fanning wind the bosom rose; ⎟
The fanning wind and purling streams ⎬
    continue her repose. ⎦
    The fool of nature stood with stupid eyes,
And gaping mouth, that testified surprise,
Fix'd on her face, nor could remove his sight,
New as he was to love, and novice in de-
    light: 110
Long mute he stood, and, leaning on his
    staff,
His wonder witness'd with an idiot laugh;
Then would have spoke, but by his glim-
    mering sense
First found his want of words, and fear'd
    offense;
Doubted for what he was he should be
    known,
By his clown accent and his country tone.
    Thro' the rude chaos thus the running
    light
Shot the first ray that pierc'd the native
    night;
Then day and darkness in the mass were
    mix'd,
Till, gather'd in a globe, the beams were
    fix'd;   120
Last shone the sun, who, radiant in his
    sphere,
Illumin'd heav'n and earth, and roll'd
    around the year.

So reason in this brutal soul began:
Love made him first suspect he was a man;
Love made him doubt his broad barbarian
    sound;
By love his want of words and wit he found;
That sense of want prepar'd the future way
To knowledge, and disclos'd the promise of
    a day.
    What not his father's care, nor tutor's art,
Could plant with pains in his unpolish'd
    heart,   130
The best instructor, Love, at once inspir'd,
As barren grounds to fruitfulness are fir'd:
Love taught him shame, and shame, with
    love at strife,
Soon taught the sweet civilities of life;
His gross material soul at once could find
Somewhat in her excelling all her kind,
Exciting a desire till then unknown,
Somewhat unfound, or found in her alone.
This made the first impression in his mind,
Above, but just above, the brutal kind: 140
For beasts can like, but not distinguish too,
Nor their own liking by reflection know;
Nor why they like or this or t'other face,
Or judge of this or that peculiar grace;
But love in gross, and stupidly admire;
As flies, allur'd by light, approach the fire.
Thus our man-beast, advancing by degrees,
First likes the whole, then sep'rates what he
    sees;
On sev'ral parts a sev'ral praise bestows,
The ruby lips, the well-proportion'd nose, 150
The snowy skin, the raven-glossy hair,
The dimpled cheek, the forehead rising
    fair,
And, ev'n in sleep itself, a smiling air.
From thence his eyes descending view'd the
    rest,
Her plump round arms, white hands, and
    heaving breast.
Long on the last he dwelt, tho' ev'ry part
A pointed arrow sped to pierce his heart.
    Thus in a trice a judge of beauty grown,
(A judge erected from a country clown,)
He long'd to see her eyes, in slumber hid,
And wish'd his own could pierce within the
    lid: 161
He would have wak'd her, but restrain'd
    his thought,
And love new-born the first good manners
    taught.
An awful fear his ardent wish withstood,
Nor durst disturb the goddess of the wood;
For such she seem'd by her celestial face,

Excelling all the rest of human race;
And things divine, by common sense he
    knew,
Must be devoutly seen, at distant view.
So, checking his desire, with trembling
    heart   170
Gazing he stood, nor would, nor could de-
    part;
Fix'd as a pilgrim wilder'd in his way,
Who dares not stir by night, for fear to
    stray,
But stands with awful eyes to watch the
    dawn of day.
    At length awaking, Iphigene the fair
(So was the beauty call'd, who caus'd his
    care)
Unclos'd her eyes, and double day reveal'd,
While those of all her slaves in sleep were
    seal'd.
    The slavering cudden, propp'd upon his
    staff,
Stood ready gaping with a grinning laugh,
To welcome her awake, nor durst begin 181
To speak, but wisely kept the fool within.
Then she: "What make you, Cymon, here
    alone?"
(For Cymon's name was round the country
    known,
Because descended of a noble race,
And for a soul ill sorted with his face.)
    But still the sot stood silent with surprise,
With fix'd regard on her new open'd eyes,
And in his breast receiv'd th' invenom'd
    dart,   189
A tickling pain that pleas'd amid the smart.
But conscious of her form, with quick dis-
    trust
She saw his sparkling eyes, and fear'd his
    brutal lust:
This to prevent, she wak'd her sleepy crew,
And rising hasty, took a short adieu.
    Then Cymon first his rustic voice essay'd,
With proffer'd service to the parting maid,
To see her safe; his hand she long denied,
But took at length, asham'd of such a guide.
So Cymon led her home, and, leaving there,
No more would to his country clowns re-
    pair,   200
But sought his father's house, with better
    mind;
Refusing in the farm to be confin'd.
    The father wonder'd at the son's return,
And knew not whether to rejoice or mourn;
But doubtfully receiv'd, expecting still
To learn the secret causes of his alter'd will.

Nor was he long delay'd; the first request 〕
He made, was like his brothers to be 〉
   dress'd, 〔
And, as his birth requir'd, above the rest. 〕
  With ease his suit was granted by his
   sire,   210
Distinguishing his heir by rich attire:
His body thus adorn'd, he next design'd
With lib'ral arts to cultivate his mind;
He sought a tutor of his own accord,
And studied lessons he before abhorr'd.
  Thus the man-child advanc'd, and learn'd
   so fast,
That in short time his equals he surpass'd:
His brutal manners from his breast exil'd,
His mien he fashion'd, and his tongue he
   fil'd;
In ev'ry exercise of all admir'd,   220
He seem'd, nor only seem'd, but was in-
   spir'd:
Inspir'd by love, whose business is to please;
He rode, he fenc'd, he mov'd with graceful
   ease,
More fam'd for sense, for courtly carriage
   more,
Than for his brutal folly known before.
  What then of alter'd Cymon shall we say,
But that the fire which chok'd in ashes lay,
A load too heavy for his soul to move,
Was upward blown below, and brush'd
   away by love?
Love made an active progress thro' his
   mind;   230
The dusky parts he clear'd, the gross re-
   fin'd,
The drowsy wak'd; and, as he went, im-
   press'd
The Maker's image on the human beast.
Thus was the man amended by desire,
And, tho' he lov'd perhaps with too much
   fire,
His father all his faults with reason scann'd,
And lik'd an error of the better hand;
Excus'd th' excess of passion in his mind,
By flames too fierce, perhaps too much re-
   fin'd.
So Cymon, since his sire indulg'd his will, 240
Impetuous lov'd, and would be Cymon still;
Galesus he disown'd, and chose to bear
The name of fool, confirm'd and bishop'd
   by the fair.
  To Cipseus by his friends his suit he
   mov'd,
Cipseus the father of the fair he lov'd.
But he was pre-ingag'd by former ties,

While Cymon was endeav'ring to be wise;
And Iphigene, oblig'd by former vows,
Had giv'n her faith to wed a foreign spouse:
Her sire and she to Rhodian Pasimond, 250
Tho' both repenting, were by promise bound,
Nor could retract; and thus, as fate decreed,
Tho' better lov'd, he spoke too late to speed.
  The doom was past, the ship already sent
Did all his tardy diligence prevent;
Sigh'd to herself the fair unhappy maid,
While stormy Cymon thus in secret said:
" The time is come for Iphigene to find
The miracle she wrought upon my mind:
Her charms have made me man, her ravish'd
   love   260
In rank shall place me with the blest above;
For, mine by love, by force she shall be
   mine,
Or death, if force should fail, shall finish my
   design."
  Resolv'd he said; and rigg'd with speedy
   care
A vessel strong, and well equipp'd for war.
The secret ship with chosen friends he
   stor'd;
And, bent to die or conquer, went aboard.
Ambush'd he lay behind the Cyprian shore,
Waiting the sail that all his wishes bore;
Nor long expected, for the following tide 270
Sent out the hostile ship and beauteous
   bride.
To Rhodes the rival bark directly steer'd,
When Cymon sudden at her back appear'd,
And stopp'd her flight; then, standing on
   his prow,
In haughty terms he thus defied the foe:
" Or strike your sails at summons, or pre-
   pare
To prove the last extremities of war."
Thus warn'd the Rhodians for the fight 〕
   provide; 〉
Already were the vessels side by side, 〔
These obstinate to save, and those to seize 〔
   the bride.   280 〕
But Cymon soon his crooked grapples 〕
   cast, 〔
Which with tenacious hold his foes em- 〉
   brac'd, 〔
And, arm'd with sword and shield, amid 〔
   the press he pass'd. 〕
Fierce was the fight, but, hast'ning to his
   prey,
By force the furious lover freed his way;
Himself alone dispers'd the Rhodian crew,
The weak disdain'd, the valiant overthrew;

Cheap conquest for his following friends
    remain'd,
He reap'd the field, and they but only
    glean'd.
  His victory confess'd, the foes retreat, 290
And cast their weapons at the victor's feet.
Whom thus he cheer'd: "O Rhodian youth,
    I fought
For love alone, nor other booty sought;
Your lives are safe; your vessel I resign;
Yours be your own, restoring what is mine:
In Iphigene I claim my rightful due,
Robb'd by my rival, and detain'd by you.
Your Pasimond a lawless bargain drove;
The parent could not sell the daughter's
    love;
Or if he could, my love disdains the laws, 300
And like a king by conquest gains his
    cause:
Where arms take place, all other pleas are
    vain;
Love taught me force, and force shall love
    maintain.
You, what by strength you could not keep,
    release,
And at an easy ransom buy your peace."
  Fear on the conquer'd side soon sign'd th'
    accord,
And Iphigene to Cymon was restor'd:
While to his arms the blushing bride he
    took,
To seeming sadness she compos'd her look;
As if by force subjected to his will,   310
Tho' pleas'd, dissembling, and a woman still.
And, for she wept, he wip'd her falling tears,
And pray'd her to dismiss her empty fears;
"For yours I am," he said, "and have de-
    serv'd
Your love much better, whom so long I
    serv'd,
Than he to whom your formal father tied
Your vows, and sold a slave, not sent a
    bride."
Thus while he spoke, he seiz'd the willing
    prey,
As Paris bore the Spartan spouse away;
Faintly she scream'd, and ev'n her eyes con-
    fess'd   320
She rather would be thought, than was dis-
    tress'd.
  Who now exults but Cymon in his ⎫
    mind?   ⎬
Vain hopes, and empty joys of human-   ⎪
    kind,   ⎭
Proud of the present, to the future blind! ⎭

Secure of fate while Cymon plows the sea,
And steers to Candy with his conquer'd
    prey,
Scarce the third glass of measur'd hours
    was run,
When like a fiery meteor sunk the sun;
The promise of a storm; the shifting gales
Forsake by fits, and fill, the flagging sails;
Hoarse murmurs of the main from far were
    heard,   331
And night came on, not by degrees prepar'd,
But all at once; at once the winds arise,
The thunders roll, the forky lightning flies.
In vain the master issues out commands,
In vain the trembling sailors ply their hands;
The tempest unforeseen prevents their care,
And from the first they labor in despair.
The giddy ship betwixt the winds and tides,
Forc'd back and forwards, in a circle rides,
Stunn'd with the diff'rent blows; then shoots
    amain,   341
Till counterbuff'd, she stops, and sleeps
    again.
Not more aghast the proud archangel fell,
Plung'd from the height of heav'n to deep-
    est hell,
Than stood the lover of his love possess'd,
Now curst the more, the more he had been
    blest;
More anxious for her danger than his own,
Death he defies, but would be lost alone.
  Sad Iphigene to womanish complaints
Adds pious pray'rs, and wearies all the
    saints;   350
Ev'n if she could, her love she would re-
    pent,
But since she cannot, dreads the punish-
    ment;
Her forfeit faith, and Pasimond betray'd,
Are ever present, and her crime upbraid.
She blames herself, nor blames her lover
    less;
Augments her anger, as her fears increase;
From her own back the burden would re-
    move,
And lays the load on his ungovern'd love,
Which interposing durst, in Heav'n's despite,
Invade and violate another's right: 360
The pow'rs incens'd a while deferr'd his
    pain,
And made him master of his vows in vain;
But soon they punish'd his presumptuous ⎫
    pride;   ⎬
That for his daring enterprise she died, ⎪
Who rather not resisted than complied.   ⎭

Then, impotent of mind, with alter'd
    sense,
She hugg'd th' offender, and forgave th'
    offense;
Sex to the last: meantime, with sails de-
    clin'd,
The wand'ring vessel drove before the
    wind;   369
Toss'd and retoss'd, aloft, and then alow,
Nor port they seek, nor certain course
    they know,
But ev'ry moment wait the coming blow.
Thus blindly driv'n, by breaking day they
    view'd
The land before 'em, and their fears re-
    new'd;
The land was welcome, but the tempest
    bore
The threaten'd ship against a rocky shore.
    A winding bay was near; to this they
    bent,
And just escap'd, their force already spent.
Secure from storms, and panting from the
    sea,   379
The land unknown at leisure they survey;
And saw (but soon their sickly sight with-
    drew)
The rising tow'rs of Rhodes at distant view;
And curs'd the hostile shore of Pasimond,
Sav'd from the seas, and shipwreck'd on the
    ground.
    The frighted sailors tried their strength
    in vain,
To turn the stern, and tempt the stormy
    main;
But the stiff wind withstood the lab'ring
    oar,
And forc'd them forward on the fatal shore!
The crooked keel now bites the Rhodian
    strand,
And the ship moor'd constrains the crew to
    land: 390
Yet still they might be safe, because un-
    known;
But, as ill fortune seldom comes alone,
The vessel they dismiss'd was driv'n before,
Already shelter'd on their native shore.
Known each, they know; but each with
    change of cheer;
The vanquish'd side exults; the victors fear
Not them but theirs, made pris'ners ere
    they fight,
Despairing conquest, and depriv'd of flight.
    The country rings around with loud
    alarms,

And raw in fields the rude militia swarms;
Mouths without hands; maintain'd at vast
    expense,   401
In peace a charge, in war a weak defense:
Stout once a month they march, a blust'ring
    band,
And ever, but in times of need, at hand.
This was the morn when, issuing on the
    guard,
Drawn up in rank and file they stood pre-
    par'd
Of seeming arms to make a short essay,
Then hasten to be drunk, the business of
    the day.
    The cowards would have fled, but that
    they knew   409
Themselves so many, and their foes so few;
But crowding on, the last the first impel,
Till overborne with weight the Cyprians
    fell.
Cymon inslav'd, who first the war begun,
And Iphigene once more is lost and won.
Deep in a dungeon was the captive cast,
Depriv'd of day, and held in fetters fast;
His life was only spar'd at their request,
Whom taken he so nobly had releas'd.
But Iphigenia was the ladies' care,
Each in their turn address'd to treat the
    fair;   420
While Pasimond and his the nuptial feast
    prepare.
    Her secret soul to Cymon was inclin'd,
But she must suffer what her fates as-
    sign'd;
So passive is the church of womankind.
What worse to Cymon could his Fortune
    deal,
Roll'd to the lowest spoke of all her wheel?
It rested to dismiss the downward weight,
Or raise him upward to his former height;
The latter pleas'd, and Love (concern'd
    the most)
Prepar'd th' amends for what by love he
    lost.   430
    The sire of Pasimond had left a son,
Tho' younger, yet for courage early known,
Ormisda call'd; to whom, by promise tied,
A Rhodian beauty was the destin'd bride:
Cassandra was her name, above the rest
Renown'd for birth, with fortune amply
    blest.
Lysimachus, who rul'd the Rhodian state,
Was then by choice their annual magis-
    trate:
He lov'd Cassandra too with equal fire,

But Fortune had not favor'd his desire; 440
Cross'd by her friends, by her not disap-
prov'd,
Nor yet preferr'd, or like Ormisda lov'd.
So stood th' affair; some little hope re-
main'd,
That, should his rival chance to lose, he
gain'd.
Meantime young Pasimond his marriage
press'd,
Ordain'd the nuptial day, prepar'd the feast;
And frugally resolv'd (the charge to shun, ⎤
Which would be double should he wed �
alone) ⎦
To join his brother's bridal with his own. ⎦
Lysimachus, oppress'd with mortal grief,
Receiv'd the news, and studied quick re-
lief. 451
The fatal day approach'd: if force were
us'd,
The magistrate his public trust abus'd;
To justice liable, as law requir'd,
For when his office ceas'd, his pow'r ex-
pir'd:
While pow'r remain'd, the means were in
his hand
By force to seize, and then forsake the land.
Betwixt extremes he knew not how to
move,
A slave to fame, but more a slave to love:
Restraining others, yet himself not free, 460
Made impotent by pow'r, debas'd by dig-
nity!
Both sides he weigh'd; but, after much de-
bate,
The man prevail'd above the magistrate.
Love never fails to master what he ⎤
finds, ⎮
But works a diff'rent way in diff'rent ⎮
minds, ⎬
The fool enlightens, and the wise he ⎮
blinds. ⎦
This youth, proposing to possess and scape,
Began in murder, to conclude in rape:
Unprais'd by me, tho' Heav'n sometime may
bless
An impious act with undeserv'd success; 470
The great, it seems, are privileg'd alone
To punish all injustice but their own.
But here I stop, not daring to proceed, ⎤
Yet blush to flatter an unrighteous deed; ⎬
For crimes are but permitted, not decreed. ⎦
Resolv'd on force, his wit the prætor bent,
To find the means that might secure th'
event;

Nor long he labor'd, for his lucky thought
In captive Cymon found the friend he
sought.
Th' example pleas'd: the cause and crime
the same; 480
An injur'd lover, and a ravish'd dame.
How much he durst he knew by what ⎤
he dar'd, ⎮
The less he had to lose, the less he car'd ⎬
To menage loathsome life when love was ⎮
the reward. ⎦
This ponder'd well, and fix'd on his in-
tent,
In depth of night he for the pris'ner sent;
In secret sent, the public view to shun;
Then with a sober smile he thus begun:
"The pow'rs above, who bounteously be-
stow 489
Their gifts and graces on mankind below,
Yet prove our merit first, nor blindly give
To such as are not worthy to receive;
For valor and for virtue they provide
Their due reward, but first they must be
tried.
These fruitful seeds within your mind they
sow'd;
'T was yours t' improve the talent they be-
stow'd:
They gave you to be born of noble kind;
They gave you love to lighten up your mind,
And purge the grosser parts; they gave
you care 499
To please, and courage to deserve the fair.
"Thus far they tried you, and by proof
they found
The grain intrusted in a grateful ground;
But still the great experiment remain'd —
They suffer'd you to lose the prize you
gain'd,
That you might learn the gift was theirs
alone,
And, when restor'd, to them the blessing
own.
Restor'd it soon will be; the means pre-
par'd,
The difficulty smooth'd, the danger shar'd:
Be but yourself, the care to me resign,
Then Iphigene is yours, Cassandra mine. 510
Your rival Pasimond pursues your life,
Impatient to revenge his ravish'd wife,
But yet not his; to-morrow is behind,
And Love our fortunes in one band has
join'd.
Two brothers are our foes, Ormisda mine,
As much declar'd as Pasimond is thine;

To-morrow must their common vows be ⎫
    tied: ⎪
With Love to friend, and Fortune for our ⎬
    guide,   ⎪
Let both resolve to die, or each redeem ⎪
    a bride.   ⎭
  " Right I have none, nor hast thou much
    to plead;   520
'T is force, when done, must justify the deed:
Our task perform'd, we next prepare for
    flight,
And let the losers talk in vain of right.
We with the fair will sail before the wind;
If they are griev'd, I leave the laws behind.
Speak thy resolves: if now thy courage
    droop,
Despair in prison, and abandon hope;
But if thou dar'st in arms thy love regain,
(For liberty without thy love were vain,)
Then second my design to seize the prey, 530
Or lead to second rape, for well thou know'st
    the way."
  Said Cymon, overjoy'd: " Do thou pro-
    pose
The means to fight, and only shew the foes:
For from the first, when love had fir'd my
    mind,
Resolv'd, I left the care of life behind."
  To this the bold Lysimachus replied:
" Let Heav'n be neuter, and the sword de-
    cide :
The spousals are prepar'd, already play
The minstrels, and provoke the tardy day;
By this the brides are wak'd, their grooms ⎫
    are dress'd;   540 ⎪
All Rhodes is summon'd to the nuptial ⎬
    feast,   ⎪
All but myself, the sole unbidden guest. ⎭
Unbidden tho' I am, I will be there,
And, join'd by thee, intend to joy the fair.
  " Now hear the rest: when day resigns
    the light,
And cheerful torches gild the jolly night,
Be ready at my call; my chosen few
With arms administer'd shall aid thy crew.
Then ent'ring unexpected will we seize
Our destin'd prey, from men dissolv'd in
    ease,   550
By wine disabled, unprepar'd for fight;
And, hast'ning to the seas, suborn our flight.
The seas are ours, for I command the fort;
A ship well mann'd expects us in the port:
If they, or if their friends, the prize contest,
Death shall attend the man who dares
    resist."

It pleas'd ! The pris'ner to his hold re- ⎫
    tir'd;   ⎪
His troop, with equal emulation fir'd, ⎬
All fix'd to fight, and all their wonted ⎪
    work requir'd.   ⎭
  The sun arose; the streets were throng'd
    around,   560
The palace open'd, and the posts were
    crown'd;
The double bridegroom at the door attends
Th' expected spouse, and entertains the
    friends.
They meet, they lead to church; the priests
    invoke
The pow'rs, and feed the flames with fra-
    grant smoke:
This done, they feast, and at the close of ⎫
    night   ⎪
By kindled torches vary their delight; ⎬
These lead the lively dance, and those the ⎪
    brimming bowls invite.   ⎭
  Now, at th' appointed place and hour as-
    sign'd,
With souls resolv'd the ravishers were
    join'd.   570
Three bands are form'd; the first is sent
    before
To favor the retreat and guard the shore,
The second at the palace gate is plac'd,
And up the lofty stairs ascend the last:
A peaceful troop they seem with shining
    vests,
But coats of mail beneath secure their
    breasts.
  Dauntless they enter, Cymon at their
    head,
And find the feast renew'd, the table spread:
Sweet voices, mix'd with instrumental
    sounds,
Ascend the vaulted roof, the vaulted roof
    rebounds.   580
When, like the harpies, rushing thro' the
    hall,
The sudden troop appears, the tables fall,
Their smoking load is on the pavement
    thrown;
Each ravisher prepares to seize his own:
The brides, invaded with a rude embrace,
Shriek out for aid, confusion fills the place.
Quick to redeem the prey, their plighted
    lords
Advance; the palace gleams with shining
    swords.
  But late is all defense, and succor vain;
The rape is made, the ravishers remain: 590

Two sturdy slaves were only sent before
To bear the purchas'd prize in safety to the
    shore.
The troop retires, the lovers close the
    rear,
With forward faces not confessing fear:
Backward they move, but scorn their pace
    to mend;
Then seek the stairs, and with slow haste
    descend.
 Fierce Pasimond, their passage to pre-⎤
    vent,   ⎟
Thrust full on Cymon's back in his de- ⎬
    scent;   ⎟
The blade return'd unbath'd, and to the ⎟
    handle bent.   ⎦
Stout Cymon soon remounts, and cleft in
    two   600
His rival's head with one descending
    blow;
And, as the next in rank Ormisda stood, ⎤
He turn'd the point; the sword, inur'd to ⎟
    blood,   ⎬
Bor'd his unguarded breast, which pour'd ⎟
    a purple flood.   ⎦
 With vow'd revenge the gath'ring crowd
    pursues,
The ravishers turn head, the fight re-
    news;
The hall is heap'd with corps; the sprinkled
    gore
Besmears the walls, and floats the marble
    floor.
Dispers'd at length the drunken squadron ⎤
    flies;   ⎟
The victors to their vessel bear the ⎬
    prize;   610 ⎟
And hear behind loud groans and lament-⎟
    able cries.   ⎦

The crew with merry shouts their an-⎤
    chors weigh,   ⎟
Then ply their oars, and brush the buxom ⎬
    sea,   ⎟
While troops of gather'd Rhodians crowd ⎟
    the key.   ⎦
What should the people do when left alone ?
The governor and government are gone;
The public wealth to foreign parts convey'd;
Some troops disbanded, and the rest unpaid.
Rhodes is the sovereign of the sea no more;
Their ships unrigg'd, and spent their naval
    store;   620
They neither could defend, nor can pursue,
But grind their teeth, and cast a helpless
    view:
In vain with darts a distant war they try;
Short, and more short, the missive weapons
    fly.
Meanwhile the ravishers their crimes enjoy,
And flying sails and sweeping oars employ:
The cliffs of Rhodes in little space are lost;
Jove's isle they seek, nor Jove denies his
    coast.
 In safety landed on the Candian shore,
With generous wines their spirits they re-
    store: 630
There Cymon with his Rhodian friend re-
    sides;
Both court, and wed at once the willing
    brides.
A war ensues, the Cretans own their cause,
Stiff to defend their hospitable laws:
Both parties lose by turns; and neither wins,
Till peace propounded by a truce begins.
The kindred of the slain forgive the deed,
But a short exile must for show precede:
The term expir'd, from Candia they remove,
And happy each at home enjoys his love. 640

PROLOGUE, EPILOGUE, SONG, AND SECULAR MASQUE FROM THE PILGRIM

[On April 11, 1700, Dryden writes to Mrs.
Steward : " Within this moneth there will be
play'd for my profit, an old play of Fletcher's,
call'd The Pilgrim, corrected by my good
friend, Mr. Vanbrook [i. e. Vanbrugh] ; to
which I have added a new Masque, and am to
write a new Prologue and Epilogue " (Malone,
I, 2 ; 131, 132). It is not known whether this
performance took place before May 1, the date
of Dryden's death. The play as printed, June
18, 1700 (Malone, I, 1 ; 330, 331, on the authority of an advertisement in the London Gazette),
closed with the following speech of the Governor : " I hope, before you go, sir, you 'll share
with us an entertainment the late great poet of
our age prepar'd to celebrate this day. Let the
masque begin." Late may or may not have
been inserted between the time of acting and
that of printing. It was probably the original
intention, as Malone suggests, to have the play
acted on March 25, on which day the year was
then considered to begin. The Secular Masque

would thus celebrate a day generally regarded as the opening of a new century.

The *Song* was probably written for the madhouse scene in the third act of the play. A scholar is there about to be discharged as sane, but immediately after shows his madness, fancying himself Neptune stilling a tempest; his *mistress* is Dryden's own invention.

The title of the play, as published in 1700, reads as follows: *The Pilgrim, a Comedy: As it is Acted at the Theatre-Royal, in Drury-Lane. Written Originally by Mr. Fletcher, and now very much Alter'd, with several Additions. Likewise a Prologue, Epilogue, Dialogue, and Masque, Written by the late Great Poet Mr. Dryden, just before his Death, being the last of his Works.]*

PROLOGUE

How wretched is the fate of those who write,
Brought muzzled to the stage, for fear they bite!
Where, like Tom Dove, they stand the common foe;
Lugg'd by the critic, baited by the beau.
Yet worse, their brother poets damn the play,
And roar the loudest, tho' they never pay.
The fops are proud of scandal, for they cry,
At every lewd, low character: "That 's I."
He who writes letters to himself would swear 9
The world forgot him, if he was not there.
What should a poet do? 'T is hard for one
To pleasure all the fools that would be shown,
And yet not two in ten will pass the town.
Most coxcombs are not of the laughing kind;
More goes to make a fop than fops can find.
Quack Maurus, tho' he never took degrees
In either of our universities,
Yet to be shown by some kind wit he looks,
Because he play'd the fool, and writ three books.
But, if he would be worth a poet's pen, 20
He must be more a fool, and write again;
For all the former fustian stuff he wrote
Was dead-born dogg'rel, or is quite forgot;

His man of Uz, stripp'd of his Hebrew robe,
Is just the proverb, and *as poor as Job.*
One would have thought he could no longer jog;
But *Arthur* was a level, *Job* 's a bog.
There, tho' he crept, yet still he kept in sight;
But here he founders in, and sinks downright.
Had he prepar'd us, and been dull by rule, 30
Tobit had first been turn'd to ridicule;
But our bold Briton, without fear or awe,
O'erleaps at once the whole Apocrypha;
Invades the Psalms with rhymes, and leaves no room
For any Vandal Hopkins yet to come.
But what if, after all, this godly gear
Is not so senseless as it would appear?
Our mountebank has laid a deeper train;
His cant, like Merry Andrew's noble vein,
Catcalls the sects, to draw 'em in again.
At leisure hours, in epic song he deals, 41
Writes to the rumbling of his coach's wheels,
Prescribes in haste, and seldom kills by rule,
But rides triumphant between stool and stool.
Well, let him go; 't is yet too early day,
To get himself a place in farce or play.
We know not by what name we should arraign him,
For no one category can contain him;
A pedant, canting preacher, and a quack,
Are load enough to break one ass's back: 50
At last grown wanton, he presum'd to write,
Traduc'd two kings, their kindness to requite;
One made the doctor, and one dubb'd the knight.

EPILOGUE

PERHAPS the parson stretch'd a point too far.
When with our theaters he wag'd a war.
He tells you that this very moral age
Receiv'd the first infection from the stage.
But sure, a banish'd court, with lewdness fraught,
The seeds of open vice, returning, brought.

Thus lodg'd, (as vice by great example
    thrives,)
It first debauch'd the daughters and the
    wives.
London, a fruitful soil, yet never bore
So plentiful a crop of horns before.   10
The poets, who must live by courts, or
    starve,
Were proud so good a government to serve;
And, mixing with buffoons and pimps pro-
    fane,
Tainted the stage, for some small snip of
    gain.
For they, like harlots, under bawds pro-
    fess'd,
Took all th' ungodly pains, and got the
    least.
Thus did the thriving malady prevail,
The court its head, the poets but the tail.
The sin was of our native growth, 't is
    true;
The scandal of the sin was wholly new.   20
Misses there were, but modestly conceal'd;
Whitehall the naked Venus first reveal'd,
Who standing, as at Cyprus, in her shrine,
The strumpet was ador'd with rites di-
    vine.
Ere this, if saints had any secret motion,
'T was chamber practice all, and close de-
    votion.
I pass the peccadillos of their time;
Nothing but open lewdness was a crime.
A monarch's blood was venial to the na-
    tion,
Compar'd with one foul act of fornication.
Now, they would silence us, and shut the
    door   31
That let in all the barefac'd vice before.
As for reforming us, which some pre-
    tend,   ⎫
That work in England is without an   ⎬
    end:
Well we may change, but we shall never   ⎭
    mend.
Yet, if you can but bear the present stage,
We hope much better of the coming
    age.
What would you say, if we should first ⎫
    begin   ⎪
To stop the trade of love behind the scene, ⎬
Where actresses make bold with married ⎪
    men ?   40   ⎭
For while abroad so prodigal the dolt is,
Poor spouse at home as ragged as a colt is.
In short, we 'll grow as moral as we can,

Save here and there a woman or a man;
But neither you, nor we, with all our ⎫
    pains,   ⎪
Can make clean work; there will be some ⎬
    remains,   ⎪
While you have still your Oates, and we ⎭
    our Haynes.

SONG OF A SCHOLAR AND HIS
MISTRESS, WHO, BEING CROSS'D
BY THEIR FRIENDS, FELL MAD
FOR ONE ANOTHER, AND NOW
FIRST MEET IN BEDLAM

Music within.

*The lovers enter at opposite doors, each held by a
keeper.*

Phyllis.   LOOK, look, I see — I see my love
                appear !
            'T is he —— 't is he alone;
            For like him there is none:
            'T is the dear, dear man; 't is thee,
                dear !

Amyntas.   Hark ! the winds war;
            The foamy waves roar;
            I see a ship afar,
            Tossing and tossing, and making
                to the shore:
              But what 's that I view,
              So radiant of hue —   10
            St. Hermo, St. Hermo, that sits
                upon the sails ?
              Ah ! No, no, no.
            St. Hermo never, never shone so
                bright;
            'T is Phyllis, only Phyllis, can
                shoot so fair a light;
            'T is Phyllis, 't is Phyllis, that
                saves the ship alone,
            For all the winds are hush'd, and
                the storm is overblown.

Phyllis.   Let me go, let me run, let me fly
                to his arms.

Amyntas.   If all the Fates combine,
            And all the Furies join,
            I 'll force my way to Phyllis, and
                break thro' the charms. 20

*Here they break from their keepers, run to each other,
and embrace.*

Phyllis.   Shall I marry the man I love ?
                And shall I conclude my
                pains ?
            Now blest be the powers above,
                I feel the blood bound in
                my veins;

With a lively leap it began to move,
    And the vapors leave my brains.

Amyntas. Body join'd to body, and heart join'd to heart,
    To make sure of the cure,
    Go call the man in black, to mumble o'er his part.

Phyllis. But suppose he should stay — 30

Amyntas. At worst if he delay,
    'T is a work must be done;
    We 'll borrow but a day,
    And the better the sooner begun.

Chorus of Both.
    At worst if he delay, &c.

They run out together hand in hand.

THE SECULAR MASQUE

Enter JANUS.

Janus. CHRONOS, Chronos, mend thy pace;
    An hundred times the rolling sun
    Around the radiant belt has run
    In his revolving race.
    Behold, behold, the goal in sight;
    Spread thy fans, and wing thy flight.

Enter CHRONOS, *with a scythe in his hand, and a great globe on his back, which he sets down at his entrance.*

Chronos. Weary, weary of my weight,
    Let me, let me drop my freight,
    And leave the world behind.
    I could not bear   10
    Another year
    The load of humankind.

Enter MOMUS, *laughing.*

Momus. Ha! ha! ha! ha! ha! ha! well hast thou done
    To lay down thy pack,
    And lighten thy back;
    The world was a fool, e'er since it begun,
    And since neither Janus, nor Chronos, nor I
    Can hinder the crimes,
    Or mend the bad times, 19
    'T is better to laugh than to cry.

Chorus of all Three.
    'T is better to laugh than to cry.

Janus. Since Momus comes to laugh below,
    Old Time, begin the show,
    That he may see, in every scene,
    What changes in this age have been.

Chronos. Then, goddess of the silver bow, begin.

Horns, or hunting music within.

Enter DIANA.

Diana. With horns and with hounds I waken the day,
    And hie to my woodland walks away;
    I tuck up my robe, and am buskin'd soon,
    And tie to my forehead a wexing moon.   30
    I course the fleet stag, unkennel the fox,
    And chase the wild goats o'er summits of rocks;
    With shouting and hooting we pierce thro' the sky,
    And Echo turns hunter, and doubles the cry.

Chorus of All.
    With shouting and hooting we pierce thro' the sky,
    And Echo turns hunter, and doubles the cry.

Janus. Then our age was in its prime:

Chronos. Free from rage:

Diana.   And free from crime:

Momus. A very merry, dancing, drinking,
    Laughing, quaffing, and unthinking time.   40

Chorus of All.
    Then our age was in its prime,
    Free from rage, and free from crime;
    A very merry, dancing, drinking,
    Laughing, quaffing, and unthinking time.

Dance of DIANA's *attendants.*

Enter MARS.

Mars. Inspire the vocal brass, inspire;
    The world is past its infant age:
    Arms and honor,
    Arms and honor,
    Set the martial mind on fire,
    And kindle manly rage.   50

Mars has look'd the sky to red;
And Peace, the lazy good, is fled.
Plenty, Peace, and Pleasure fly;
    The sprightly green
    In woodland walks no more is
        seen;
    The sprightly green has drunk
        the Tyrian dye.

Chorus of All.
    Plenty, Peace, &c.

Mars.   Sound the trumpet, beat the
        drum;
    Thro' all the world around,
    Sound a reveille, sound, sound,
    The warrior god is come.   61

Chorus of All.
    Sound the trumpet, &c.

Momus   Thy sword within the scabbard
        keep,
    And let mankind agree;
    Better the world were fast asleep,
    Than kept awake by thee.
    The fools are only thinner,
        With all our cost and care;
    But neither side a winner,   69
    For things are as they were.

Chorus of All.
    The fools are only, &c.
        Enter VENUS.

Venus.   Calms appear when storms are
        past,
    Love will have his hour at last:
    Nature is my kindly care;
    Mars destroys, and I repair;

Take me, take me, while you
    may;
Venus comes not ev'ry day.

Chorus of All.
    Take her, take her, &c.

Chronos.   The world was then so light,
    I scarcely felt the weight;   80
    Joy rul'd the day, and Love the
        night.
    But since the Queen of Pleasure
        left the ground,
    I faint, I lag,
    And feebly drag
    The pond'rous orb around.

Momus.   All, all of a piece through-
        out:
        Pointing to DIANA.
    Thy chase had a beast in
        view;
        To MARS.
    Thy wars brought nothing about;
        To VENUS.
    Thy lovers were all untrue.

Janus.   'T is well an old age is out: 90
Chronos.   And time to begin a new.

Chorus of All.
    All, all of a piece throughout:
    Thy chase had a beast in view;
    Thy wars brought nothing about;
    Thy lovers were all untrue.
    'T is well an old age is out,
    And time to begin a new.
        Dance of huntsmen, nymphs, warriors,
        and lovers.

ADDITIONAL POEMS

[Among the following poems, the *Translation of Epigram on Plutarch by Agathias* has been printed hitherto only in editions of Dryden containing his *Life of Plutarch*. Since 1916 it has been shown that the other poems, not previously included in the Cambridge edition, are certainly or probably by Dryden.]

EPILOGUE TO THE RIVAL LADIES

[Professor Roswell G. Ham, in an article on "Dryden's Epilogue to *The Rival Ladies*," in *The Review of English Studies*, xiii (1937), 76–80, states: "A manuscript purporting to be that of the missing epilogue is to be found in the Bodleian Library, in the same seventeenth-century hand, upon the same folio sheet as the authentic prologue, and immediately following it as though of one piece." He reprints the text, which in modernized form runs as given below. He argues in detail and convincingly that the epilogue is by Dryden, intended to be spoken with a change of costume by the same person who had recited the prologue (see page 20). In the manuscript, he finds, "prologue and epilogue have all the appearance of being the actor's scrip, conceived and written out as a unit for a single person to memorize." He remarks: "In his prologue to *The Wild Gallant* he [Dryden] presented two astrologers who prognosticated the brief span of the play. So, as a close parallel the next year, this epilogue in question produced a doctor to diagnose the ill-health of the poet and his muse, by way of an urinal." "How the epilogue came to be misplaced from Dryden's works," Professor Ham concludes, "is another question. The safest hazard would be that the playwright was not unduly proud of his handiwork; it was short and spiritless, particularly when sent up as a gift to Orrery [to whom Dryden dedicated *The Rival Ladies*], and the idea of it had already been utilized in an earlier comedy. Furthermore, the printer had brought the play to the bottom of a page. To print the ten-line epilogue would have required another gathering with some blank pages left over. Why not omit the thing altogether?"

The epilogue has been collated with a photostat of MS. Ashmole, foll. 267–8, kindly furnished by the Bodleian Library.]

EPILOGUE BY THE DOCTOR

'T is true, what as a jest our poet meant,
His little wit was in the prologue spent:

None left t' excuse my part, unless you would
Forbear to damn it till 't were understood.
'T would go ill with us, should you give our play
Half those hard words that I gave you to-day.

The DOCTOR'S *man comes and brings in an urinal with black water in it and whispers the* DOCTOR *in his ear.*

Whilst we in vain excuses waste our breath,
The poet and his muse are sick to death!
He 's past my cure; as his condition stands,
I leave him to these abler doctors' hands.

THE EPILOGUE SPOKEN TO THE KING AT THE OPENING OF THE PLAYHOUSE AT OXFORD ON SATURDAY LAST, BEING MARCH THE NINETEENTH, 1681

[In the early months of 1681 England was seething with excitement over the question of excluding from the throne the Catholic Duke of York. Charles II, fearing violence from Shaftesbury's followers, summoned parliament to meet at Oxford, a center of the Tory party, on March 21. The king and many of the members came there under arms. On March 28 Charles, finding that he could now count on popular support, dissolved this "Third Short Parliament" of his reign. See Biographical Sketch, page xli.

Dryden wrote this epilogue for a special performance of *Tamerlane the Great*, by Charles Saunders, given for the assembled members of parliament. (The name of the play is known from an item in *The True Protestant Mercury* for March 19–23, 1681: see W. G. Hiscock in *Times Literary Supplement* for October 13, 1932, and in *A Christ Church Miscellany*, 1946, pp. 113–115.) Slightly earlier he had written the epilogue for the first production of the same drama: see page 104 above. He now refers in dignified fashion to the troubled times and pleads for peace. His new epilogue is preserved in two extremely rare contemporary broadsides, one without indication of place or printer, the other "printed for Rich. Royston" in London. Of the first broadside, with heading as above, except that *of* is lacking after *opening*, a unique copy exists in the Christ Church Library at Oxford. Of it W. G. Hiscock edited a type facsimile, published in beautiful form by the Clarendon Press, 1932; he later included a photographic reproduction of it in *A Christ Church Miscellany*, 1946, p. 114. On that reproduction, with Mr. Hiscock's kind permission, the present text is based. Mr. Hiscock believes that the typography of this broadside shows it to have been printed by L. Lichfield Jun. at Oxford. Of the London broadside, according to Mr. Hiscock, "it is believed that five copies survive." The present editor has used for his notes a photostat of the copy owned by the William Andrews Clark Memorial Library in Los Angeles. To him this London broadside seems a mere catchpenny production, with no authority whatever. (But recently it caught several pennies, since, according to Mr. Hiscock, "as much as £340 was given for one at the Britwell Sale on March 30, 1927"!) R. G. Ham (*Times Literary Supplement*, December 27, 1928) drew attention to this London broadside and (*The London Mercury*, March, 1930) reprinted it.

It is peculiar that Dryden did not reprint this epilogue in *Miscellany Poems*, 1684, for it ranks among his very best work of its own sort. By failing to do so he gave Tom Brown a chance unconscionably to include it in the first collected edition of *The Works of Mr. Thomas Brown*. It occurs on page 96 of the third series of pagination in vol. iii, 1708. The half-title of this paging is: *A Walk Round London and Westminster, Exposing The Vices and Follies of the Town. By Mr. Tho. Brown.* Pages 91–121 are, *Poems upon several occasions. By Mr. T. Browne.* The piece was reprinted in later editions of Brown's *Works:* for instance it is in the seventh edition, 1730, vol. iv, p. 225. The last edition of Brown's *Works* was the ninth, in 1760. After that this epilogue disappeared from view until it was restored to Dryden in the present century.]

As from a darken'd room some optic glass
Transmits the distant species as they pass
(The world's large landscape is from far
  descried
And men contracted on the paper glide),
Thus crowded Oxford represents mankind
And in these walls Great Britain seems
  confin'd.
Oxford is now the public theater,
And you both audience are and actors here.
The gazing world on the new scene attend,

Admire the turns, and wish a prosp'rous
  end.   10
This place, the seat of peace, the quiet cell
Where arts remov'd from noisy business
  dwell,
Should calm your wills, unite the jarring
  parts,
And with a kind contagion seize your hearts:
O may its genius like soft music move
And tune you all to concord and to love!
Our ark that has in tempests long been
  toss'd
Could never land on so secure a coast.
From hence you may look back on civil rage
And view the ruins of the former age.   20
Here a new world its glories may unfold
And here be sav'd the remnants of the old.
  But while your days on public thoughts
  are bent,
Past ills to heal and future to prevent,
Some vacant hours allow to your delight: ⎫
Mirth is the pleasing business of the night, ⎬
The king's prerogative, the people's right. ⎭
Were all your hours to sullen cares confin'd,
The body would be jaded by the mind.
'T is wisdom's part betwixt extremes to
  steer: 30
Be gods in senates, but be mortals here.

PROLOGUE AND EPILOGUE SPOKEN AT MITHRIDATES, KING OF PONTUS, THE FIRST PLAY ACTED AT THE THEATER ROYAL THIS YEAR, 1681

[This prologue and epilogue are here reprinted from Luttrell's copy, now in the Henry E. Huntington Library. It is a single half-sheet of paper, printed on both sides, presumably designed to be sold at the theater. Luttrell marked his copy "13. Feb. 168$\frac{2}{1}$," thereby indicating both the date on which he acquired it and the approximate date of opening of the season at the Theater Royal in 1682. In the margin he made various changes of the text, which of course have no authority. At the close of the prologue he added, "John Dryden," and at the top of the epilogue, "by Mr Dryden." According to Mr. T. J. Wise (*A Dryden Library*, 1930, p. 33) another copy is signed at the close, "*J. Dryden*, in a contemporary hand." These signatures, joined to the internal evidence of the pieces themselves, make it almost certain that Dryden was the author. He had written another epilogue for *Mithridates* when it was first produced, in 1678: see page 81 above.

Aside from a photographic reproduction in

A Dryden Library, this prologue has apparently never been reprinted. The epilogue was reprinted by Scott (see Scott-Saintsbury edition, x. 351–353), who silently adopted some of Luttrell's marginal emendations.]

PROLOGUE

AFTER a four months' fast we hope at length
Your queasy stomachs have recover'd strength
That you can taste a play (your old coarse mess)
As honest and as plain as an address.
And therefore welcome from your several parts,
You that have gain'd kind country wenches' hearts;
Have watch'd returning milkmaids in the dark,
And sinn'd against the pales of every park!
Welcome, fair ladies of unblemish'd faith,
That left town bagnios for the fruitful Bath;   10
For when the season 's hot and lover 's there,
The waters never fail to get an heir!
Welcome, kind men that did your wives attend;
And welcome, he that was the husband's friend,
Who, holding chat, did silently encroach
With treacherous hand to grabble in the coach!
Hail, you Newmarket brothers of the switch, ⎤
That leap left strumpets, full of pox and itch, ⎬
A leap more dangerous than the devil's ditch! ⎦
Last, welcome, you who never did appear;   20
Gave out i'th' country, but lay fluxing here:
Now crawl abroad with stick, lean-chapp'd and thin,
And fair as lady that hath new lain in!
This winter let us reckon you our own,
For all wise men will let the state alone:
The Plot 's remov'd, a witness of renown
Has lodg'd it safe, at t'other end o'th' town;
And that it ne'er may fail, some pious ⎤
whore ⎬
Has cast her mite, and fairly at his door ⎥
Laid two small squalling evidences more; ⎦ 30
Which, well instructed, if we take their words,
In time may grow to hang two popish lords.

Heav'n grant the babes may live, for faith ⎤
there 's need! ⎥
Swearers fall off so fast; if none succeed ⎬
The land 's in danger quite to lose the ⎥
breed: ⎦
Unless you break an act, which were a sin,
And for recruit let Irish cattle in.
Well, after all, 't were better to compound
Then let the foolish frolic still go round:
Both sides have lost, and by my computation   40
None but Jack Ketch has gain'd in all the nation.

EPILOGUE

SPOKEN BY MR. GOODMAN

Pox on this playhouse; 't is an old tir'd jade!
'T will do no longer; we must force a trade.
What if we all turn witness of the Plot?
That 's overstock'd; there 's nothing to be got.
Shall we take orders? That will parts ⎤
require, ⎬
And colleges give no degrees for hire. ⎦
Would Salamanca was a little nigher!
Will nothing do? Oh, now 't is found, I hope!
Have not you seen the dancing of the rope?
When Andrew's wit was clean run off the score   10
And Jacob's cap'ring tricks could do no more,
A damsel does to the ladder's top advance
And with two heavy buckets drags a dance;
The yawning crowd perch'd up to see the sight
And slaver'd at the mouth for vast delight.
Oh, friends, there 's nothing to enchant the mind,
Nothing like that sweet sex to draw mankind:
The founder'd horse that switching will not stir,
Trots to the mare afore without a spur.
Faith, I 'll go scour the scene room and engage   20
Some toy within to save the falling stage.
                         [*Exit.*

Re-enters with Mrs. Cox

Who have we here again? what nymph 's i'th' stocks?
Your most obedient servant, sweet Madam Cox.
You 'd best be coy and blush for a pretense:
For shame, say something in your own defense!

Mrs. Cox. What shall I say? I have
    been hence so long
I 've e'en almost forgot my mother tongue.
If I can act I wish I were ten fathom
    Beneath —
Mr. Goodman. Oh, Lord! Pray you, no
    swearing, madam!
Mrs. Cox. Why, sir, if I had sworn to
    save the nation   30
I could find out some mental reservation.
Well, in plain terms, gallants, without a
    sham,
Will you be pleas'd to take me as I am:
Quite out of countenance, with a downcast
    look,
Just like a truant that returns to book.
Yet I 'm not old; but if I were, this place
Ne'er wanted art to piece a ruin'd face.
When graybeards govern'd I forsook the
    stage;
You know 't is piteous work to act with age.
Tho' there 's no sex amongst these beardless
    boys,   40
There 's what we women love: that 's mirth
    and noise.
These young beginners may grow up in time,
And the devil 's in 't if I am past my prime.

TRANSLATION OF EPIGRAM ON PLUTARCH BY AGATHIAS

[In 1683 Tonson published *Plutarchs Lives.
Translated from the Greek by Several Hands.
To which is prefixt the Life of Plutarch. The
First Volume.* The book was entered in the
Stationers' Register on April 25 and (according
to Macdonald) advertised in *The Observator*
for May 2. To this volume Dryden con-
tributed the *Epistle Dedicatory* to the Duke of
Ormond and the *Life of Plutarch.* Other
volumes followed, the fifth and last in 1686.
To these Dryden made no contributions.
His *Life of Plutarch* concludes as follows.]

The epigram of Agathias deserves also to
be remember'd. This author flourish'd about
the year five hundred, in the reign of the
Emperor Justinian. The verses are extant
in the *Anthologia*, and with the translation
of them I will conclude the praises of our
author, having first admonish'd you that
they are suppos'd to be written on a statue
erected by the Romans to his memory.

Σεῖο πολυκλήεντα τύπον στήσαντο, Χερωνεῦ
  Πλούταρχε, κρατερῶν υἷεες Αὐσονίων.
ὅττι παραλλήλοισι βίοις Ἕλληνας ἀρίστους
  Ῥώμης εὐπολέμοις ἥρμοσας ἐνναέταις.
ἀλλὰ τεοῦ βιότοιο παράλληλον βίον ἄλλον
  οὐδὲ σύ γ' ἂν γράψαις. οὐ γὰρ ὅμοιον ἔχεις.

CHÆRONEAN PLUTARCH, to thy deathless
    praise
Does martial Rome this grateful statue
    raise,
Because both Greece and she thy fame have
    shar'd
(Their heroes written and their lives com-
    par'd);
But thou thyself couldst never write thy
    own:
Their lives have parallels, but thine has
    none.

ON THE MARRIAGE OF THE FAIR AND VIRTUOUS LADY, MRS. ANASTASIA STAFFORD, WITH THAT TRULY WORTHY AND PIOUS GENT., GEORGE HOLMAN, ESQ.

A PINDARIC ODE, BY MR. DRYDEN

[This poem was first printed in *Tixall
Poetry, with Notes and Illustrations by Arthur
Clifford* (Edinburgh, 1813), pp. 207–212.

Tixall was an estate in Staffordshire, once
the seat of Walter Aston (1584–1639), who in
1627 became Lord Aston, Baron of Forfar in
Scotland. He was the patron of Drayton.
The Aston family were Catholics. The fifth
Lord Aston died in 1750, leaving only two
daughters, one of whom, Barbara, inherited
the estate of Tixall. She married in 1762 the
Hon. Henry Thomas Clifford. The Cliffords
in the first years of their marriage lived in
the old house, but by the nineteenth century
this had become a ruin. The estate passed
to their eldest son, Thomas Hugh Clifford.
His brother, Arthur Clifford, prepared, from
manuscripts that came from the old mansion,
a sumptuous quarto volume, *Tixall Poetry.*
In his Preface (p. xiii) Clifford explains: —
"The poems in the Fourth, and Last Division, consist of such pieces, as I found totally
unconnected with each other, and written
on backs of letters, or other scraps of paper.
These, for want of a better designation, I
have entitled 'Miscellaneous Poems.' I have
prefixed to them, a 'Pindaric Ode,' by Dryden; two small poems, by Sir Richard Fanshawe; one, by Sidney Godolphin; and one by
Waller: all of which I found in the old trunk,
and which, I believe, are now published for
the first time."
From *Tixall Poetry* this ode was reprinted
in the Aldine edition of Dryden, 1832, 1833
(vol. v, pp. 313–316), but with no indication
of its source. It reappeared in succeeding

Aldine editions. Finally B. H. Newdigate printed it in an article, "An Overlooked Ode by John Dryden," in *The London Mercury* for September, 1930 (vol. xxii, pp. 438–442), with references to *Tixall Poetry* and other editorial material.

Anastasia Stafford (1646–1719) was the fifth daughter of William Howard, Viscount Stafford (1614–80), a Catholic peer and the most noted victim of the Popish Plot. To quote from Ogg, *England in the Reign of Charles II* (Oxford, 1934, p. 604): —

"Having failed in their main object [the exclusion of the Duke of York from the succession], the Commons were eagerly looking about for a victim; this they found in the aged Lord Stafford, one of the five popish lords in the Tower.... At the trial ... Oates, Dugdale, and Turberville swore that he had procured a commission from the pope, and had tried to arrange the murder of the king. On this evidence the Commons secured a conviction, and their helpless victim was executed. This was the only successful impeachment by the Commons in the reign of Charles."

George Holman (1630–98) was the son of Philip Holman (1593–1669), a scrivener of London and apparently a dissenter, who purchased the manor of Warkworth in Northamptonshire. George Holman became a Catholic. Lines in the poem below indicate that he married Anastasia Stafford on or near Christmas Day, probably in 1685.

"I have no other authority to produce," Clifford states in his Notes (p. 379), "in proof of this Ode being the production of Dryden, but what is contained in the title, which is printed, just as it is in the original MS. The internal evidence is strongly in its favour. It has all the characters of Dryden's genius, and manner.

"When Dryden, on the accession of James II. became a Roman Catholic, it is very probable, that he would form an acquaintance with the principal families of that persuasion, in England, in his time. Among these, that of Stafford was one of the most conspicuous; and the more so, from the circumstance of Lord Stafford having most unjustly been put to death, in 1680, for his supposed participation in Oates's plot. The principal witness against him, was one Dugdale, who had been steward to Lord Aston, but was discharged from his service, for having defrauded his lordship of a large sum of money. This perjured wretch declared, that he had assisted at a great con-

sultation of Catholics, at Tixall, at which Lord Stafford was present; and swore, that his Lordship, on that occasion, had given his *full particular assent* to take away the life of the king. . . .

"As Tixall is only four miles from Stafford castle, which was the ancient seat of the Staffords; and, as there was always a close connexion between the two families, it can excite no surprise, that a copy of Dryden's poem should have been discovered there."

Newdigate comments pertinently: —

"No one can compare its [this poem's] opening lines with those of *Britannia Rediviva*, which Dryden wrote some two years later, without being sure of the common authorship of the two poems. In both there is the same play with the season of the year and the festivals of the Church's calendar — the winter solstice and the feasts of St. Lucy (December 13th), Christmas and Easter in the one; the summer solstice and Whitsuntide and Trinity in the other."

The present editor agrees that both external and internal evidence point to Dryden as the author of this ode. The poem is obviously unfinished, but whether its incomplete state be due to Dryden, to a copyist, or to the loss of part of the manuscript must remain uncertain.]

I

WHEN nature in our northern hemisphere
Had shorten'd daylight and deform'd the
    year;
        When the departing sun
        Was to our adverse tropic run;
And fair St. Lucy with the borrow'd light
Of moon and stars had lengthen'd night:
What more then summer's day slipp'd in
    by chance
        To beautify the calendar?
What made a spring in midst of winter to
    advance,
And the cold seasons leap into a youthful
    dance,   10
        To rouse the drooping year?
Was this by miracle, or did they rise
By the bright beams of Anastasia's eyes,
        To light our frozen clime;
And, happily for us, mistook their time?
'T was so, and 't was imported in her
    name;
From her their glorious resurrection came,
    And she renew'd their perish'd flame.
        The God of nature did the same:
His birth the depth of winter did adorn;   20

And she to marriage then, her second birth,
    was born.
Her pious family, in every state,
Their great Redeemer well can imitate.
They have a right in heaven, an early
    place;
The beauteous bride is of a martyr's race:
    And he above with joy looks down;
I see, I see him blaze with his immortal
    crown.
He on her nuptials does his beams dis-
    pense,
Blessing the day with better influence;
He looks from heaven with joy and gives
    her joy from thence.   30

II

Now let the reasonable beast, call'd man;
    Let those who never truly scan
    The effects of sacred Providence,
But measure all by the gross rules of
    sense;
Let those look up and steer their sight
    By the great Stafford's light!
The God that suffer'd him to suffer here
Rewards his race and blesses them below,
Their father's innocence and truth to
    show,
To show he holds the blood of martyrs dear.
He crown'd the father with a deathless
    diadem;   41
And all the days from him he took
He number'd out in his eternal book,
And said, Let these be safely kept for
    them,
The long descendants of that hallow'd
    stem.
To dry the mournful widow's tears,
Let all those days be turn'd to years,
And all those years be whiten'd too:
Still some new blessing let 'em bring
To those who from my martyr spring;
Still let them bloom, and still bestow 51
Some new content upon his race below.
    Let their first revolution
Bestow a bride upon his darling son
And crown those nuptials with a swift
    increase
Such as the emptied ark did bless;
Then, as the storms are more allay'd
    And waves decay'd,
Send out the beauteous blooming maid,
And let that virgin dove bring to her house
    again   60
An olive branch of peace, in triumph o'er
    the main.
For whom, ye Heavens! have ye reserv'd
    this joy?

Let us behold the man you chose;
    How well you can your cares employ,
    And to what arms your maid dispose,
Your maid whom you have chang'd, but
    cannot lose:
Chang'd as the morn into the day,
    As virgin snow that melts away
And by its kindly moisture makes new
    flowers to grow.
See then a bridegroom worthy such a
    bride!   70
Never was happy pair so fitly tied;
Never were virtues more allied:
United in a most auspicious hour —
A martyr's daughter weds a confessor!
When innocence and truth became a
    crime,
    By voluntary banishment
    He left our sacrilegious clime
And to a foreign country went,
Or rather there by Providence was sent:
For Providence design'd him to reside 80
    Where he from his abundant stock
    Might nourish God's afflicted flock
And, as his steward, for their wants pro-
    vide.
A troop of exiles on his bounty fed;
    They sought and found with him their
    daily bread:
As the large troop increas'd, the larger table
    spread.
The cruse ne'er emptied, nor the store
    Decreas'd the more;
For God supplied him still to give, who gave
    in God's own stead.
    Thus, when the raging dearth 90
    Afflicted all the Egyptian earth;
When scanty Nile no more his bounty
    dealt,
And Jacob even in Canaan famine felt,
    God sent a Joseph out before,
His father and his brethren to restore:
Their sacks were fill'd with corn, with
    generous wine
Their souls refresh'd; their ebbing store,
Still when they came, supplied with
    more;
    And doubled was their corn.
Joseph himself by giving greater grew,
And from his loins a double tribe increas'd
    the chosen crew.   101

PROLOGUE AND EPILOGUE TO THE WIDOW RANTER

OR, THE HISTORY OF BACON IN VIRGINIA

[This prologue and epilogue Dryden wrote
for a play by Mrs. Aphra Behn, who had

died April 16, 1689, before her drama was either acted or printed. Under the title *The Prologue and Epilogue to The History of Bacon in Virginia: written by Mr. Dryden,* Tonson published them as a folio sheet, presumably for sale at the theater, entering them on the *Stationers' Register,* November 20, 1689, a date that fixes the approximate time of production of the play. But when *The Widow Ranter* was printed by James Knapton in 1690 it was not accompanied by these pieces, but by a prologue that Dryden had written in 1678 for Shadwell's comedy, *A True Widow* (see page 83 above); and by an epilogue that, as far as is known, was first printed in *Covent Garden Drollery,* 1672, where it is termed a *prologue* to *The Double Marriage,* a drama of what Dryden called "the last age," probably by Fletcher and Massinger. Tonson's entry in the *Stationers' Register* attracted the attention of Malone (I, 1, 167) and puzzled him, but Tonson's broadside escaped the notice of students and editors of Dryden until the present century, when Professor R. G. Ham (*Times Literary Supplement,* Dec. 27, 1928) called attention to a copy of it preserved in the Bodleian Library and (*The London Mercury,* March, 1930) reprinted the two pieces. Before the work by Professor Ham had appeared, Mr. Percy J. Dobell in his *Bibliographical Memoranda,* 1922, had given a probable explanation of the problem. The present writer has not seen his book and cites him as quoted by Mr. J. M. Osborn (in *Modern Philology,* August, 1941, p. 96): —

"*The Widow Ranter* was published by James Knapton, and herein would seem to lie the key to the mystery, for, as the prologue and epilogue that were really written for *The Widow Ranter* were Tonson's property, he may have refused to give Knapton the right to print them, and so Knapton purloined the prologue to *The True Widow* and another prologue, and printed them as the prologue and epilogue to *The Widow Ranter.*"

Mr. Dobell's "purloined" is possibly too severe. *A True Widow* was first printed by Benjamin Tooke in 1679. Knapton seems to have acquired the unsold sheets of this edition, for in 1689 he reissued them (prologue and all), "with cancel title and epilogue leaves" (Macdonald, *Dryden Bibliography,* page 156).

Dryden's prologue and epilogue are here reprinted from the copy of Tonson's sheet in the William Andrews Clark Memorial Library in Los Angeles. Mr. Osborn (*Ibid.,* p. 94) states that there is a third copy in the library of William and Mary College.]

PROLOGUE

SPOKEN BY A WOMAN

PLAYS you will have, and to supply your
    store
Our poets trade to ev'ry foreign shore:
This is the product of Virginian ground
And to the port of Covent Garden bound.
Our cargo is, or should at least, be wit:
Bless us from you damn'd pirates of the pit;
And vizard-masks, those dreadful apparitions,
She-privateers, of venomous conditions,
That clap us oft aboard with French commissions!
You sparks, we hope, will wish us happy
    trading,   10
For you have ventures in our vessel's lading;
And tho' you touch at this or t'other nation,
Yet sure Virginia is your dear plantation.
Expect no polish'd scenes of love should rise
From the rude growth of Indian colonies:
Instead of courtship and a tedious pother
They only tip the wink at one another;
Nay, often the whole nation pig together.
You civil *beaus,* when you pursue the game,
With manners mince the meaning of —
    that same;   20
But ev'ry part has there its proper name.
Good Heav'ns defend me, who am yet unbroken,
From living there, where such bug words are
    spoken!
Yet surely, sirs, it does good stomachs show,
To talk so savor'ly of what they do.
But were I bound to that broad-speaking
    land,
Whate'er they said, I would not understand;
But innocently, with a lady's grace,
Would learn to whisk my fan about my face.
However, to secure you, let me swear   30
That no such base *mundungus* stuff is here.
We bring you of the best the soil affords:
Buy it for once, and take it on our words.
You would not think a country girl the
    worse,
If clean and wholesome, tho' her linen 's
    coarse.
Such are our scenes; and I dare boldly say,
You may laugh less at a far better play.
The story 's true, the fact not long ago;
The hero of our stage was English too;
And, bate him one small frailty of rebelling,   40
As brave as e'er was born at Iniskelling.

EPILOGUE

SPOKEN BY A WOMAN

By this time you have lik'd or damn'd our
    plot;
Which tho' I know, my epilogue knows not:
For if it could foretell, I should not fail,
In decent wise, to thank you or to rail.
But he who sent me here, is positive
This farce of government is sure to thrive.
Farce is a food as proper for your lips,
As for green sickness, crump'd tobacco pipes.
Besides, the author 's dead, and here you sit,
Like the infernal judges of the pit.   10
Be merciful, for 't is in you this day
To save or damn her soul — and that 's her
    play.
She who so well could love's kind passion
    paint,
We piously believe must be a saint.
Men are but bunglers when they would
    express

The sweets of love, the dying tenderness;
But women by their own abundance meas-
    ure,
And when they write, have deeper sense of
    pleasure.
Yet tho' her pen did to the mark arrive,
'T was common praise, to please you, when
    alive;   20
But of no other woman you have read,
Except this one, to please you, now she 's
    dead.
'T is like the fate of bees, whose golden pains,
Themselves extinguish'd, in their hive re-
    mains.
Or in plain terms to speak, before we go,
What you young gallants by experience
    know,
This is an orphan child, a bouncing boy;
'T is late to lay him out or to destroy.
Leave your dog tricks, to lie and to forswear;
Pay *you* for nursing, and we 'll keep him
    here.   30

APPENDIX I

POEMS ATTRIBUTED TO DRYDEN OR ONLY IN PART WRITTEN BY HIM

[The canon of Dryden's writings is not easy to determine. Dryden seems to have had no trace of petty vanity in regard to his own minor works. For one of Tonson's miscellany volumes he might gather together a dozen old prologues and songs that he had lying by him, but further than this he made no attempt to collect his occasional poems. Hence it is likely that among the anonymous pieces printed in miscellanies, between 1660 and 1700, by busy and conscienceless editors, there may be found some written by him. After his death many pieces, some certainly genuine, others as certainly spurious, were published under his name.

In the text of the present volume there are included several poems that are only in part by Dryden, or that may not be his work at all: see, for example, the headnotes on pages 76, 137. In the present *Appendix* there are included: (1) some pieces ascribed to Dryden in his own time, or shortly after it, but of doubtful authenticity; (2) some poems assigned to Dryden on internal evidence, in modern times; (3) a translation of Boileau's *Art of Poetry*, in which Dryden had some small share. Finally, there follows a series of titles of poems that have been printed in editions of Dryden's works, or have been otherwise attributed to him, but that are in all probability spurious. An explanatory note accompanies each title.]

PROLOGUE, EPILOGUE, AND SONG FROM THE INDIAN QUEEN

[This heroic play was first printed in *Four New Plays . . . written by . . . Sir Robert Howard*, 1665. It was first acted in January, 1664 (Pepys' *Diary*, January 27). Dryden's name was never joined to it in his lifetime; nor was the play included in the first collected edition of his dramatic works, published in 1701. But in his *Connection of The Indian Emperor to The Indian Queen* (Scott-Saintsbury edition, ii. 321) Dryden claims part of the latter drama as his own work. (Compare headnote, page 21.) It is therefore just possible that he is the author of one or more of the following pieces.]

PROLOGUE

As the music plays a soft air, the curtain rises softly, and discovers an Indian boy and girl sleeping under two plantain trees; and, when the curtain is almost up, the music turns into a tune expressing an alarm, at which the boy wakes, and speaks:

Boy. Wake, wake, Quevira! our soft rest
    must cease,
And fly together with our country's peace;
No more must we sleep under plantain shade,
Which neither heat could pierce, nor cold in-
    vade;
Where bounteous nature never feels decay,
And op'ning buds drive falling fruits away.
  Quevira. Why should men quarrel here,
    where all possess
As much as they can hope for by success?
None can have most, where nature is so kind
As to exceed man's use, tho' not his mind.   10
  Boy. By ancient prophecies we have been
    told,
Our world shall be subdued by one more old;
And, see, that world already's hither come.
  Que. If these be they, we welcome then our
    doom.
Their looks are such that mercy flows from
    thence,
More gentle than our native innocence.
  Boy. Why should we then fear these are
    enemies,
That rather seem to us like deities?

  Que. By their protection let us beg to live;
They came not here to conquer, but forgive. 20
If so, your goodness may your pow'r express,
And we shall judge both best by our success.

EPILOGUE

SPOKEN BY MONTEZUMA

You see what shifts we are inforc'd to try,
To help out wit with some variety;
Shows may be found that never yet were seen,
'Tis hard to find such wit as ne'er has been.
You have seen all that this old world could do,
We therefore try the fortune of the new,
And hope it is below your aim to hit
At untaught nature with your practic'd wit:
Our naked Indians, then, when wits appear,
Would as soon choose to have the Spaniards
    here.   10
'Tis true, y' have marks enough, the plot, the
    show,
The poet's scenes, nay, more, the painter's too;
If all this fail, considering the cost,
'Tis a true voyage to the Indies lost:
But if you smile on all, then these designs,
Like the imperfect treasure of our minds,
Will pass for current wheresoe'er they go,
When to your bounteous hands their stamps
    they owe.

SONG IS SUPPOS'D SUNG BY AERIAL SPIRITS

Poor mortals that are clogg'd with earth below
  Sink under love and care,
    While we that dwell in air
Such heavy passions never know.
  Why then should mortals be
  Unwilling to be free
  From blood, that sullen cloud
Which shining souls does shroud?
    Then they'll shew bright,
    And like us light,
When leaving bodies with their care,
  They slide to us and air.

A SONG

[This song is found in *Covent Garden Drollery*, 1672.
It is included here because of its resemblance to a song
in *An Evening's Love*: compare page 58. It may have
been a variation by Dryden on the same theme.]

I

FAIR was my mistress, and fine as a bride
   That is deck'd in her wedding attire;
Her eyes do protest I shall not be denied,
   And yet I dare hardly come nigh her.
I seem'd to be sad, and she smil'd,
Which I thought did a kindness betray;
   Then forward I go,
   But was dash'd with a no,
Yet came off with a ha ha ha ha ha ha ha ha;
Hey, ha ha ha ha ha.   10

II

Strange was she then as a politic nun,
   And I found my first courting was lost;
Her frowns put me farther then when I begun:
   O see how poor mortals are cross'd!
I then made another assault,
When her kindness began to display;
   And I brought her to this,
   That she gave me a kiss,
And came off with a ha ha ha ha ha ha ha ha;
Hey, ha ha ha ha ha.   20

III

High was my courage, but more my desire,
   Which fed my addresses with force,
That you could not distinguish whose eyes had
     most fire,
   Or who had the prettiest discourse.
Agreed we laid down and tumbled
Till both were aweary of play:
   Tho' I spent a full share,
   Yet by Cupid I swear,
I came off with a ha ha ha ha ha ha ha ha;
Hey, ha ha ha ha ha ha.   30

ENJOYMENT

A SONG AT THE KING'S HOUSE

[This song is found, with title as above, in *New Court
Songs and Poems, by R. V., Gent.*, 1672, from which
the following text is taken. It also occurs in *Covent
Garden Drollery*, 1672, where it is headed simply *Song*.
It is included here because of its resemblance to a song
in *Marriage à la Mode*: compare page 68. It may
have been a variation by Dryden on the same theme.]

I

So closely, closely press'd,
   In his Clymena's arms young Damon lay;
Panting in that transport so o'er-blest,
   He seem'd just ready, just to die away.
Clymena beheld him with amorous eyes,
And thus betwixt sighing and kissing she cries:
   "O make not such haste to be gone:
   'T is too much unkind,
   Whilst I stay behind,
For you to be dying alone."   10

II

This made the youth, now drawing to his end,
   The happy moment of his death suspend;
     But with so great a pain
     His soul he did retain,
That with himself he seem'd at strife
Whether to let out love or keep in life.
Then she, who already was hasting to death,
Said softly, and trembling, and all out of
     breath:
   "O now, my love, now let us go!
Die with me, Damon, now; for I die too."   20
Thus died they, but 't was of so sweet a death,
That so to die again they took new breath.

A SONG

[See headnote, page 68.]

I

FAREWELL, dear Revecchia, my joy and my
     grief,
Too long I have lov'd you and found no relief;
Undone by your jailer too strict and severe,
Your eyes gave me love and he gives me despair.
Now urg'd by your interest I seek to retire
Far off from the cause of so hopeless a fire;
To stay near you still were in vain to torment
Your ears with a passion you must not content.

II

To live in the country with fools is less pain
Then still to endure an unwilling disdain;   10
You 're the cause of my exile, and far off I 'll go,
That none of my suff'rings you ever may know.
But if some kind fate you should chance to con-
     vey,
And thro' woods where I 've been your journey
     should lay,
Your name when you find upon every tree,
You 'll say: "Poor Alexis! 't was written by
     thee."

PROLOGUE TO JULIUS CÆSAR

[This prologue was first printed in *Covent Garden
Drollery*, 1672, a miscellany which contains several of
Dryden's early poems: see headnotes on pages 51, 56,
64–66, 68. Mr. Bolton Corney, in *Notes and Queries*,
series I. ix. 95, 96, assigns this prologue to Dryden,
largely because the criticism of Shakespeare and Jonson
here expressed greatly resembles that embodied in Dryden's *Essay of Dramatic Poesy*. The present editor
finds much force in this argument and in that based
on the general style of the prologue. On the other
hand, it may be urged that Dryden never included the
piece in any of his miscellany volumes. In a man
of Dryden's careless habits, such reasoning has little
weight: compare headnotes on pages 65, 68.]

IN country beauties as we often see
Something that takes in their simplicity;
Yet while they charm, they know not they are
     fair,
And take without their spreading of the snare:
Such artless beauty lies in Shakespeare's wit,
'T was well in spite of him whate'er he writ.

His excellencies came and were not sought ;
His words like casual atoms made a thought,
Drew up themselves in rank and file and writ,
He wond'ring how the devil it were such wit.
Thus, like the drunken tinker in his play,   11
He grew a prince and never knew which way.
He did not know what trope or figure meant,
But to persuade is to be eloquent;
So in this *Cæsar* which this day you see,
Tully ne'er spoke as he makes Anthony.
Those then that tax his learning are to blame ;
He knew the thing, but did not know the name.
Great Jonson did that ignorance adore,
And, tho' he envied much, admir'd him more. 20
The faultless Jonson equally writ well ;
Shakespeare made faults, but then did more
    excel.
One close at guard like some old fencer lay ;
T'other more open, but he shew'd more play.
In imitation Jonson's wit was shown ;
Heaven made his men, but Shakespeare made
    his own.
Wise Jonson's talent in observing lay,
But others' follies still made up his play.
He drew the like in each elaborate line,
But Shakespeare like a master did design.   30
Jonson with skill dissected humankind,
And show'd their faults that they their faults
    might find ;
But then, as all anatomists must do,   ⎫
He to the meanest of mankind did go,   ⎬
And took from gibbets such as he would show. ⎭
Both are so great that he must boldly dare
Who both of 'em does judge and both com-
    pare.
If amongst poets one more bold there be,
The man that dare attempt in either way, is he.

LINES ON SETTLE'S EMPRESS OF MOROCCO

[In 1673 Elkanah Settle, a dramatist seventeen years younger than Dryden, won great success by his heroic play, *The Empress of Morocco*, and seemed in a fair way to eclipse the fame of the author of *The Conquest of Granada*. *The Empress of Morocco*, when published, was decorated with engravings, then first used in a drama, and was sold for two shillings, double the ordinary price. Dryden, bitterly mortified, joined Crowne and Shadwell in writing a scurrilous pamphlet, published in 1674, entitled *Notes and Observations on The Empress of Morocco ; or, Some few Erratas to be Printed instead of the Sculptures with the Second Edition of that Play*. Settle, in a reply published in the same year, treated Dryden as the principal author of this pamphlet ; but Crowne, in his epistle before *Caligula* (*Works*, 1874, iv. 353), claims three fourths of the piece as his own. From this least known of Dryden's works, which has never been reprinted in full, the following lines are taken. They parody a passage in *The Empress of Morocco* describing the approach of a fleet. Since they rise far above the general level of the pamphlet, they may be ascribed, though with some hesitation, to Dryden rather than to one of his collaborators.]

—— To jerk him a little the sharper, I will not trans-prose his verse, but by the help of his own words trans-nonsense sense, that by my **stuff** people may judge the better what his is :

GREAT boy, thy tragedy and sculptures done
From press and plates in fleets do homeward
    come,
And in ridiculous and humble pride
Their course in ballet-singers' baskets guide,
Whose greazy twigs do all new beauties take
From the gay shews thy dainty sculptures make.
Thy lines a mess of rhyming nonsense yield,
A senseless tale, with fluttering fustian fill'd.
No grain of sense does in one line appear ;
Thy words big bulks of boist'rous bombast
    bear ;   10
With noise they move, and from players' mouths
    rebound,
When their tongues dance to thy words' empty
    sound.
By thee inspir'd, thy rumbling verses roll,
As if that rhyme and bombast lent a soul ;
And with that soul they seem taught duty too.
To huffing words does humble nonsense bow,
As if it would thy worthless worth enhance,
To the lowest rank of fops thy praise advance,
To whom by instinct all thy stuff is dear ;
Their loud claps echo to the theater.   20
From breaths of fools thy commendation
    spreads ;
Fame sings thy praise with mouths of logger-
    heads ;
With noise and laughing each thy fustian
    greets ;
'T is clapp'd by choirs of empty-headed cits,
Who have their tribute sent and homage given,
As men in whispers send loud noise to heaven.

Thus I have daub'd him with his own puddle.

AN ESSAY UPON SATIRE

[This poem is here reprinted from *Poems on Affairs of State*, ed. 4, 1702. It was first printed early in 1680, being mentioned in the *Term Catalogue* for Hilary Term (February) of that year. According to the half-title preceding the poem, in *The Works of John Sheffield, Earl of Mulgrave, Marquis of Normanby, and Duke of Buckingham*, 1723, it was written in 1675. Dryden certainly had little share in writing this poem, perhaps no share at all. The evidence, which is inconsistent and perplexing, may be summarized as follows :

When the poem was circulated, apparently in manuscript, in 1679, Lord Rochester affected to believe Dryden the author, and in consequence of the attack on himself in lines 230-269 had him assaulted one evening in Rose Alley : see *Biographical Sketch*, pp. xxxviii-xl. The poem is assigned to Dryden in *Poems on Affairs of State*, ed. 4, 1702, and ed. 5, 1703. (The earlier editions have not been accessible to the present editor.) In *Spence's Anecdotes* there occurs the following passage, attributed to Dean Lockier, who knew Dryden well :

"Sheffield, Duke of Buckingham's famous essay, has certainly been cried up much more than it deserves, though corrected a good deal by Dryden. It was this which set him up for a poet ; and he was resolved to keep up that character, if he could, by any means, fair or foul. Could he be more impudent than his publishing that satire, for writing which Dryden was beat in Rose Alley (and which was so remarkably known by the name of the *Rose Alley Satire*), as his own ! He made, indeed, a few alterations in it first ; but these were only verbal, and generally for the worse."

On the other hand, the poem is attributed to Lord Mulgrave in *A New Collection of Poems relating to State Affairs*, 1705. More important, Mulgrave positively denied Dryden's authorship, in a passage of his own *Essay on Poetry*, first published in 1682. (For notice of publication, see the *Term Catalogue* for Michaelmas Term (November) of that year : this first edition of the *Essay* has not been accessible to the present editor.) In the second edition of the *Essay on Poetry*, 1691, he made the denial more emphatic by adding sidenotes : passage and notes are as follows :

The * *Laureat* here [in satire] may justly claim our Praise, Crown'd by ‖ *Mac-Fleckno* with immortal Bays ; Tho *prais'd* and *punish'd* for another's * Rhimes. His own deserve as great Applause sometimes ; But once his *Pegasus* has born *dead Weight*, Rid by some *lumpish* Minister of State.

* Mr. *D——n*. ‖ A famous Satyrical Poem of his. * A Libel, for which he was both applauded and wounded, tho intirely innocent of the whole matter.

In a later edition, 1713, of the *Essay on Poetry* (included by Tonson in one volume with *Poems by the Earl of Roscomon*, 1717), the last note becomes :

A Copy of Verses, call'd *An Essay on Satyr*, for which Mr. *Dryden* was both Applauded and Beaten, tho' not only Innocent but Ignorant, of the whole matter.

Finally, the *Essay upon Satire* appears in Mulgrave's *Works*, 1723.

Thus the evidence for Dryden's having a share in the authorship of the *Essay upon Satire* is extremely slender. The ascriptions of authorship in *Poems on Affairs of State* doubtless rested only on current gossip, and are of no authority. Lockier's testimony is emphatically at secondhand ; moreover, the first part of it seems inconsistent with the conclusion. Still, Mulgrave's vanity would lead him to minimize any aid he may have received from Dryden ; and even his footnote of 1713 does not state that Dryden was " ignorant " of the poem as a whole, but only of the attack on Rochester contained in it. The present editor, however, thinks it certain that Mulgrave was the real author of this poem, which is here reprinted because of its bearing on Dryden's biography, and because of the possibility that some parts of it may have been his work.]

How dull, and how insensible a beast
Is man, who yet would lord it o'er the rest!
Philosophers and poets vainly strove
In every age the lumpish mass to move:
But those were pedants, when compar'd with these,
Who know not only to instruct, but please.
Poets alone found the delightful way,
Mysterious morals gently to convey
In charming numbers ; so that as men grew
Pleas'd with their poems, they grew wiser too.
Satire has always shone among the rest, 11
And is the boldest way, if not the best,
To tell men freely of their foulest faults ;
To laugh at their vain deeds, and vainer thoughts.
In satire too the wise took different ways,
To each deserving its peculiar praise.
Some did all folly with just sharpness blame,
Whilst others laugh'd and scorn'd them into shame ;
But of these two, the last succeeded best,
As men aim rightest when they shoot in jest. 20
Yet, if we may presume to blame our guides,
And censure those who censure all besides,
In other things they justly are preferr'd ;
In this alone methinks the ancients err'd:

Against the grossest follies they declaim ;
Hard they pursue, but hunt ignoble game.
Nothing is easier than such blots to hit,
And 't is the talent of each vulgar wit :
Besides, 't is labor lost ; for who would preach
Morals to Armstrong, or dull Aston teach ? 30
'T is being devout at play, wise at a ball,
Or bringing wit and friendship to Whitehall.
But with sharp eyes those nicer faults to find,
Which lie obscurely in the wisest mind ;
That little speck which all the rest does spoil,
To wash off that would be a noble toil,
Beyond the loose-writ libels of this age,
Or the forc'd scenes of our declining stage :
Above all censure, too, each little wit
Will be so glad to see the greater hit ; 40
Who, judging better, tho' concern'd the most,
Of such correction will have cause to boast.
In such a satire all would seek a share,
And every fool will fancy he is there.
Old story-tellers too must pine and die,
To see their antiquated wit laid by ;
Like her who miss'd her name in a lampoon,
And griev'd to find herself decay'd so soon.
No common coxcomb must be mention'd here,
Nor the dull train of dancing sparks appear, 50
Nor fluttering officers who never fight :
Of such a wretched rabble who would write ?
Much less half wits : that 's more against our rules ;
For they are fops, the other are but fools.
Who would not be as silly as Dunbar ?
As dull as Monmouth, rather than Sir Carr ?
The cunning courtier should be slighted too,
Who with dull knavery makes so much ado ;
Till the shrewd fool, by thriving too too fast,
Like Æsop's fox becomes a prey at last. 60
Nor shall the royal mistresses be nam'd,
Too ugly, or too easy to be blam'd ;
With whom each rhyming fool keeps such a pother,
They are as common that way as the other :
Yet sauntering Charles between his beastly brace
Meets with dissembling still in either place,
Affected humor, or a painted face.
In loyal libels we have often told him,
How one has jilted him, the other sold him :
How that affects to laugh, how this to weep ; 70
But who can rail so long as he can sleep ?
Was ever prince by two at once misled,
False, foolish, old, ill-natur'd, and ill-bred ?
Earnely and Ayles—y, with all that race
Of busy blockheads, shall have here no place ;
At council set as foils on D—by's score,
To make that great false jewel shine the more ;
Who all that while was thought exceeding wise,
Only for taking pains and telling lies.
But there 's no meddling with such nauseous men ; 80
Their very names have tir'd my lazy pen ;
'T is time to quit their company, and choose
Some fitter subject for a sharper Muse.

First, let 's behold the merriest man alive
Against his careless genius vainly strive ;
Quit his dear ease, some deep design to lay,
'Gainst a set time, and then forget the day :

Yet he will laugh at his best friends, and be
Just as good company as Nokes and Lee.
But when he aims at reason or at rule,　90
He turns himself the best in ridicule.
Let him at business ne'er so earnest sit,
Shew him but mirth, and bait that mirth with
　　wit ;
That shadow of a jest shall be enjoy'd,
Tho' he left all mankind to be destroy'd.
So cat transform'd sat gravely and demure,
Till mouse appear'd, and thought himself secure;
But soon the lady had him in her eye,
And from her friend did just as oddly fly.
Reaching above our nature does no good ;　100
We must fall back to our old flesh and blood;
As by our little Machiavel we find, [E. of S—y.
That nimblest creature of the busy kind.
His limbs are crippled and his body shakes ; ⎫
Yet his hard mind, which all this bustle makes, ⎬
No pity of its poor companion takes.　　　⎭
What gravity can hold from laughing out,
To see him drag his feeble legs about ?
Like hounds ill-coupled, Jowler lugs him still
Thro' hedges, ditches, and thro' all that 's ill. 110
'T were crime in any man but him alone,
To use a body so, tho' 't is one's own :
Yet this false comfort never gives him o'er,
That whilst he creeps his vigorous thoughts can
　　soar.
Alas ! that soaring, to those few that know,
Is but a busy groveling here below.
So men in rapture think they mount the sky, ⎫
Whilst on the ground th' intranced wretches ⎬
　　lie :　　　　　　　　　　　　　　　⎭
So modern fops have fancied they could fly, ⎜
Whilst 't is their heads alone are in the air, 120
And for the most part building castles there ;
As the new earl, with parts deserving [E. of E—x.
　　praise,
And wit enough to laugh at his own ways ;
Yet loses all soft days and sensual nights,
Kind nature checks, and kinder fortune slights ;
Striving against his quiet all he can,
For the fine notion of a busy man.
And what is that at best, but one whose mind
Is made to tire himself and all mankind ?　129
For Ireland he would go ; faith, let him reign ;
For if some odd fantastic lord would fain
Carry in trunks, and all my drudgery do,
I 'll not only pay him but admire him too.
But is there any other beast that lives,
Who his own harm so wittily contrives ?
Will any dog that hath his teeth and stones
Refin'dly leave his bitches and his bones,
To turn a wheel ? and bark to be employ'd,
While Venus is by rival dogs enjoy'd ?　139
Yet this fond man, to get a statesman's name,
Forfeits his friends, his freedom, and his fame.
　Tho' satire nicely writ no humor stings
But those who merit praise in other things ;
Yet we must needs this one exception make,
And break our rules for folly Tropos' sake ;
Who was too much despis'd to be accus'd,
And therefore scarce deserves to be abus'd,
Rais'd only by his mercenary tongue,
From railing smoothly, and from reasoning
　　wrong.

As boys on holidays let loose to play,　150
Lay waggish traps for girls that pass that way ;
Then shout to see in dirt and deep distress
Some silly cit in flower'd foolish dress ;
So have I mighty satisfaction found,
To see his tinsel reason on the ground :
To see the florid fool despis'd (and know it)
By some who scarce have words enough to
　　show it ;
For sense sits silent, and condemns for weaker
The finer, nay sometimes the wittiest speaker.
But 't is prodigious so much eloquence　160
Should be acquir'd by such a little sense ;
For words and wit did anciently agree,
And Tully was no fool, tho' this man be :
At bar abusive, on the bench unable,
Knave on the woolsack, fop at council table.
These are the grievances of such fools as would
Be rather wise than honest, great than good.
　Some other kind of wits must be made known,
Whose harmless errors hurt themselves alone ;
Excess of luxury they think can please,　170
And laziness call loving of their ease :
To live dissolv'd in pleasures still they feign,
Tho' their whole life 's but intermitting pain :
So much of surfeits, headaches, claps are seen,
We scarce perceive the little time between :
Well-meaning men, who make this gross mis-
　　take,
And pleasure lose only for pleasure's sake.
Each pleasure has its price, and when we pay
Too much of pain, we squander life away.
Thus D—et, purring like a thoughtful cat,　180
Married, but wiser puss ne'er thought of that :
And first he worried her with railing rhyme,
Like Pembroke's mastives at his kindest time ;
Then for one night sold all his slavish life,
A teeming widow, but a barren wife.
Swell'd by contact of such a fulsome toad,
He lugg'd about the matrimonial load ;
Till Fortune, blindly kind as well as he,
Has ill restor'd him to his liberty ;
Which he would use in all his sneaking way, 190
Drinking all night and dozing all the day ;
Dull as Ned Howard, whom his brisker times
Had fam'd for dulness in malicious rhymes.
　Mul—ve had much ado to scape the snare,
Tho' learn'd in those ill arts that cheat the fair :
For after all his vulgar marriage mocks,
With beauty dazzled, Numps was in the stocks;
Deluded parents dried their weeping eyes,
To see him catch his Tartar for his prize :
Th' impatient town waited the wish'd-for
　　change,　　　　　　　　　　　　　200
And cuckolds smil'd in hopes of sweet revenge ;
Till Petworth plot made us with sorrow see,
As his estate, his person too was free.
Him no soft thoughts, no gratitude could move ;
To gold he fled from beauty and from love ;
Yet failing there, he keeps his freedom still,
Fore'd to live happily against his will :
'T is not his fault, if too much wealth and pow'r
Break not his boasted quiet every hour.
　And little Sid, for simile renown'd,　210
Pleasure has always sought but never found ;
Tho' all his thoughts on wine and women fall,
His are so bad, sure he ne'er thinks at all.

The flesh he lives upon is rank and strong,
His meat and mistresses are kept too long.
But sure we all mistake this pious man,
Who mortifies his person all he can :
What we uncharitably take for sin,
Are only rules of this old capuchin ;
For never hermit under grave pretense　　220
Has liv'd more contrary to common sense ;
And 't is a miracle, we may suppose,
No nastiness offends his skilful nose,
Which from all stink can with peculiar art
Extract perfume and essence from a f—t :
Expecting supper is his great delight ;
He toils all day but to be drunk at night ;
Then o'er his cups this night bird chirping sits,
Till he takes Hewet and Jack Hall for wits.
　Rochester I despise for 's want of wit,　　230
Tho' thought to have a tail and cloven feet ;
For while he mischief means to all mankind,
Himself alone the ill effects does find ;
And so like witches justly suffers shame,
Whose harmless malice is so much the same.
False are his words, affected is his wit ;
So often he does aim, so seldom hit ;
To every face he cringes while he speaks,
But when the back is turn'd, the head he
　　breaks :
Mean in each action, lewd in every limb,　　240
Manners themselves are mischievous in him;
A proof that chance alone makes every creature
A very Killigrew without good nature.
For what a Bessus has he always liv'd,
And his own kickings notably contriv'd ?
For (there 's the folly that 's still mix'd with
　　fear)
Cowards more blows than any hero bear ;
Of fighting sparks some may their pleasures say,
But 't is a bolder thing to run away.
The world may well forgive him all his ill,　　250
For every fault does prove his penance still ;
Falsely he falls into some dangerous noose,
And then as meanly labors to get loose.
A life so infamous is better quitting,
Spent in base injury and low submitting.
I 'd like to have left out his poetry,
Forgot by all almost as well as me.
Sometimes he has some humor, never wit ;
And if it rarely, very rarely, hit,
'T is under so much nasty rubbish laid,　　260
To find it out 's the cinder-woman's trade,
Who for the wretched remnants of a fire
Must toil all day in ashes and in mire.
So lewdly dull his idle works appear,
The wretched texts deserve no comments here ;
Where one poor thought 's sometimes left all
　　alone
For a whole page of dulness to atone :
'Mongst forty bad, one tolerable line,
Without expression, fancy, or design.　　269
　How vain a thing is man, and how unwise,
Ev'n he who would himself the most despise !
I, who so wise and humble seem to be,
Now my own vanity and pride can't see ;
While the world's nonsense is so sharply shown,
We pull down others but to raise our own ;
That we may angels seem, we paint them elves,
And are but Satyrs to set up ourselves.

I, who have all this while been finding fault,
Even with my masters who first satire taught,
And did by that describe the task so hard,　　280
It seems stupendous and above reward,
Now labor with unequal force to climb　·
That lofty hill, unreach'd by former time :
'T is just that I snould to the bottom fall,
Learn to write well, or not to write at all.

THE ART OF POETRY

WRITTEN IN FRENCH BY THE SIEUR DE BOILEAU, MADE ENGLISH

[This translation of Boileau's *Art Poétique* was first
published in 1683, with title as above, and with no indication of the translator's name. In 1708 Tonson
reprinted it in the second edition of *The Annual Miscellany for the Year 1694* (the *Fourth Miscellany*) with the
following advertisement :

" This translation of Monsieur Boileau's *Art of Poetry*
was made in the year 1680, by Sir William Soame of
Suffolk, Bart. ; who, being very intimately acquainted
with Mr. Dryden, desir'd his revisal of it. I saw the
manuscript lie in Mr. Dryden's hands for above six
months, who made very considerable alterations in it,
particularly the beginning of the fourth canto ; and
it being his opinion that it would be better to apply
the poem to English writers than keep to the French
names, as it was first translated, Sir William desir'd
he would take the pains to make that alteration ; and
accordingly that was entirely done by Mr. Dryden.
" The poem was first publish'd in the year 1683 ; Sir
William was after sent ambassador to Constantinople,
in the reign of King James, but died in the voyage.
　　　　　　　　　　　　　　　J. T."

The truth of Tonson's statement is confirmed by the
remarkable agreement in substance of lines 101, 102
and 555-557 in the present translation with passages in
Dryden's dedication to *The Spanish Friar* (Scott-Saintsbury edition, vi. 402-411). The general finish of the
verse probably owes much to Dryden's correcting hand.
　Collins : *Peerage of England*, ed. Brydges, vol. iv, p.
475, mentions a " William Soames, Esq., of Thurlowe,
in Suffolk, who was . . . created a baronet."
The present text follows that of 1683.]

CANTO I

RASH author, 't is a vain presumptuous crime
To undertake the sacred art of rhyme,
If at thy birth the stars that rul'd thy sense
Shone not with a poetic influence ;
In thy strait genius thou wilt still be bound,
Find Phœbus deaf, and Pegasus unsound.
　You then that burn with the desire to try
The dangerous course of charming poetry ;
Forbear in fruitless verse to lose your time,
Or take for genius the desire of rhyme ;　　10
Fear the allurements of a specious bait,
And well consider your own force and weight.
　Nature abounds in wits of every kind,
And for each author can a talent find :
One may in verse describe an amorous flame,
Another sharpen a short epigram ;
Waller a hero's mighty acts extol,
Spenser sing Rosalind in pastoral :
But authors that themselves too much esteem,
Lose their own genius, and mistake their theme.
Thus in times past Dubartas [1] vainly writ,　　21
　　　　　　　[1] Dubartas, translated by Sylvester.

Allaying sacred truth with trifling wit ;
Impertinently, and without delight,
Describ'd the Israelites' triumphant flight,
And following Moses o'er the sandy plain,
Perish'd with Pharaoh in th' Arabian main.
Whate'er you write of pleasant or sublime,
Always let Sense accompany your Rhyme :
Falsely they seem each other to oppose ;
Rhyme must be made with Reason's laws to
    close ; 30
And when to conquer her you bend your force,
The mind will triumph in the noble course ;
To Reason's yoke she quickly will incline,
Which, far from hurting, renders her divine :
But, if neglected, will as easily stray,
And master Reason, which she should obey.
Love Reason then ; and let whate'er you write
Borrow from her its beauty, force, and light.
Most writers, mounted on a resty Muse,
Extravagant and senseless objects choose ; 40
They think they err, if in their verse they fall
On any thought that 's plain or natural :
Fly this excess ; and let Italians be
Vain authors of false glitt'ring poetry.
All ought to aim at sense ; but most in vain
Strive the hard pass and slipp'ry path to gain :
You drown, if to the right or left you stray ;
Reason to go has often but one way.
Sometimes an author, fond of his own thought,
Pursues his object till it 's overwrought : 50
If he describes a house, he shews the face,
And after walks you round from place to place ;
Here is a *vista*, there the doors unfold,
Balconies here are baluster'd with gold ;
Then counts the rounds and ovals in the halls,
The festoons, friezes, and the astragals.[1]
Tir'd with his tedious pomp, away I run,
And skip o'er twenty pages to be gone.
Of such descriptions the vain folly see,
And shun their barren superfluity. 60
All that is needless carefully avoid ;
The mind once satisfied is quickly cloy'd :
He cannot write, who knows not to give o'er ;
To mend one fault, he makes a hundred more :
A verse was weak, you turn it much too strong,
And grow obscure, for fear you should be long.
Some are not gaudy, but are flat and dry ;
Not to be low, another soars too high.
Would you of every one deserve the praise ?
In writing, vary your discourse and phrase ; 70
A frozen style, that neither ebbs or flows,
Instead of pleasing, makes us gape and doze.
Those tedious authors are esteem'd by none,
Who tire us, humming the same heavy tone.
Happy, who in his verse can gently steer
From grave to light, from pleasant to severe ;
His works will be admir'd wherever found,
And oft with buyers will be compass'd round.
In all you write, be neither low nor vile ;
The meanest theme may have a proper style. 80
The dull burlesque appear'd with impudence,
And pleas'd by novelty, in spite of sense.
All, except trivial points, grew out of date ;
Parnassus spoke the cant of Belinsgate :
Boundless and mad, disorder'd Rhyme was
    seen ;

[1] Verse of Scudéry.

Disguis'd Apollo chang'd to Harlequin.
This plague, which first in country towns began,
Cities and kingdoms quickly overran ;
The dullest scribblers some admirers found,
And *The Mock-Tempest*[2] was a while renown'd :
But this low stuff the town at last despis'd, 91
And scorn'd the folly that they once had priz'd ;
Distinguish'd dull from natural and plain,
And left the villages to Flecknoe's reign.
Let not so mean a style your Muse debase,
But learn from Butler[3] the buffooning grace ;
And let burlesque in ballads be employ'd :
Yet noisy bumbast carefully avoid,
Nor think to raise, tho' on Pharsalia's plain,
Millions of mourning mountains of the slain :[4]
Nor, with Dubartas, bridle up the floods, 101
And periwig with wool the baldpate woods.[5]
Choose a just style ; be grave without constraint,
Great without pride, and lovely without paint :
Write what your reader may be pleas'd to hear ;
And for the measure have a careful ear.
On easy numbers fix your happy choice ;
Of jarring sounds avoid the odious noise :
The fullest verse and the most labor'd sense
Displease us, if the ear once take offense. 110
Our ancient verse (as homely as the times)
Was rude, unmeasur'd, only tagg'd with
    rhymes ;
Number and cadence, that have since been
    shown,
To those unpolish'd writers were unknown.
Fairfax[6] was he, who, in that darker age,
By his just rules restrain'd poetic rage.
Spenser did next in pastorals excel,
And taught the noble art of writing well ;
To stricter rules the stanza did restrain,
And found for poetry a richer vein. 120
Then Davenant came ; who, with a new-found
    art,
Chang'd all, spoil'd all, and had his way apart :
His haughty Muse all others did despise,
And thought in triumph to bear off the prize,
Till the sharp-sighted critics of the times,
In their mock *Gondibert*, expos'd his rhymes ;
The laurels he pretended did refuse,
And dash'd the hopes of his aspiring Muse.
This headstrong writer, falling from on high,
Made following authors take less liberty. 130
Waller came last, but was the first whose art
Just weight and measure did to verse impart ;
That of a well-plac'd word could teach the force,
And shew'd for poetry a nobler course.
His happy genius did our tongue refine,
And easy words with pleasing numbers join ;
His verses to good method did apply,
And chang'd harsh discord to soft harmony.
All own'd his laws ; which, long approv'd and
    tried,
To present authors now may be a *guide*. 140
Tread boldly in his steps, secure from fear,
And be, like him, in your expressions clear.
If in your verse you drag, and sense delay,
My patience tires, my fancy goes astray ;

[2] *The Mock-Tempest*, a play written by Mr. Duffet.
[3] *Hudibras*.
[4] Verse of Brébeuf.   [5] Verse of Dubartas.
[6] Fairfax in his translation of *Godfrey of Bullen*.

And from your vain discourse I turn my mind,
Nor search an author troublesome to find.
There is a kind of writer pleas'd with sound,
Whose fustian head with clouds is compass'd
round —
No reason can disperse 'em with its light:
Learn then to think ere you pretend to write.
As your idea 's clear, or else obscure,   151
Th' expression follows perfect or impure:
What we conceive, with ease we can express;
Words to the notions flow with readiness.
  Observe the language well in all you write,
And swerve not from it in your loftiest flight.
The smoothest verse and the exactest sense
Displease us, if ill English give offense:
A barb'rous phrase no reader can approve;
Nor bombast, noise, or affectation love.   160
In short, without pure language, what you write
Can never yield us profit or delight.
Take time for thinking; never work in haste;
And value not yourself for writing fast.
A rapid poem, with such fury writ,
Shews want of judgment, not abounding wit.
More pleas'd we are to see a river lead
His gentle streams along a flow'ry mead,
Than from high banks to hear loud torrents
roar,
With foamy waters on a muddy shore.   170
Gently make haste, of labor not afraid;
A hundred times consider what you 've said:
Polish, repolish, every color lay,
And sometimes add, but oft'ner take away.
'T is not enough, when swarming faults are
writ,
That here and there are scatter'd sparks of wit:
Each object must be fix'd in the due place,
And diff'ring parts have corresponding grace;
Till by a curious art dispos'd, we find
One perfect whole, of all the pieces join'd. 180
Keep to your subject close in all you say,
Nor for a sounding sentence ever stray.
The public censure for your writings fear,
And to yourself be critic most severe.
Fantastic wits their darling follies love:
But find you faithful friends that will reprove,
That on your works may look with careful eyes,
And of your faults be zealous enemies.
Lay by an author's pride and vanity,
And from a friend a flatterer descry,   190
Who seems to like, but means not what he says:
Embrace true counsel, but suspect false praise.
A sycophant will everything admire:
Each verse, each sentence sets his soul on fire;
All is divine! there 's not a word amiss!
He shakes with joy, and weeps with tenderness;
He overpow'rs you with his mighty praise.
Truth never moves in those impetuous ways:
A faithful friend is careful of your fame,
And freely will your heedless errors blame; 200
He cannot pardon a neglected line,
But verse to rule and order will confine;
Reproves of words the too affected sound:
Here the sense flags, and your expression 's
round;
Your fancy tires, and your discourse grows vain,
Your terms improper — make them just and
plain.

Thus 't is a faithful friend will freedom use;
But authors, partial to their darling Muse,
Think to protect it they have just pretense,
And at your friendly counsel take offense.   216
Said you of this, that the expression 's flat?
"Your servant, sir, you must excuse me that,"
He answers you. "This word has here no grace;
Pray leave it out." "That, sir, 's the proper'st
place."
"This turn I like not." "'T is approv'd by
all."
Thus, resolute not from a fault to fall,
If there 's a syllable of which you doubt,
'T is a sure reason not to blot it out.
Yet still he says you may his faults confute,
And over him your pow'r is absolute: 220
But of his feign'd humility take heed;
'T is a bait laid to make you hear him read.
And when he leaves you, happy in his Muse,
Restless he runs some other to abuse,
And often finds; for in our scribbling times
No fool can want a sot to praise his rhymes:
The flattest work has ever in the court
Met with some zealous *ass* for its support;
And in all times a forward, scribbling fop
Has found some greater fool to cry him up.   230

CANTO II

PASTORAL

As a fair nymph, when rising from her bed,
With sparkling diamonds dresses not her head,
But without gold, or pearl, or costly scents,
Gathers from neighb'ring fields her ornaments;
Such, lovely in its dress, but plain withal,
Ought to appear a perfect *Pastoral*.
Its humble method nothing has of fierce,
But hates the rattling of a lofty verse:
There native beauty pleases, and excites,
And never with harsh sounds the ear affrights.
But in this style a poet often spent,   241
In rage throws by his rural instrument,[1]
And vainly, when disorder'd thoughts abound,
Amidst the *Eclogue* makes the trumpet sound:
Pan flies, alarm'd, into the neighb'ring woods,
And frighted nymphs dive down into the floods.
Oppos'd to this, another, low in style,
Makes shepherds speak a language base and
vile:
His writings, flat and heavy, without sound,
Kissing the earth, and creeping on the ground;
You 'd swear that Randal, in his rustic strains,
Again was quav'ring to the country swains,   252
And changing, without care of sound or dress,
Strephon and Phyllis into Tom and Bess.
'Twixt these extremes 't is hard to keep the
right;
For guides take Virgil, and read Theocrite:
Be their just writings, by the gods inspir'd,
Your constant pattern, practic'd and admir'd.
By them alone you 'll easily comprehend
How poets, without shame, may condescend   260
To sing of gardens, fields, of flow'rs, and fruit,
To stir up shepherds, and to tune the flute;
Of love's rewards to tell the happy hour,

1 Flute pipe.

Daphne a tree, Narcissus made a flow'r,
And by what means the *Eclogue* yet has pow'r
To make the woods worthy a conqueror:[1]
This of their writings is the grace and flight;
Their risings lofty, yet not out of sight.

ELEGY

The *Elegy*, that loves a mournful style,
With unbound hair weeps at a funeral pile; 270
It paints the lover's torments and delights;
A mistress flatters, threatens, and invites:
But well these raptures if you'll make us see,
You must know love as well as poetry.
I hate those lukewarm authors, whose forc'd fire
In a cold style describes a hot desire;
That sigh by rule, and, raging in cold blood,
Their sluggish Muse whip to an amorous mood:
Their feign'd transports appear but flat and vain; 279
They always sigh, and always hug their chain,
Adore their prison, and their suff'rings bless,
Make sense and reason quarrel as they please.
'T was not of old in this affected tone
That smooth Tibullus made his amorous moan;
Nor Ovid, when, instructed from above,
By nature's rules he taught the *Art of Love*.
The heart in *Elegies* forms the discourse.

ODE

The *Ode* is bolder, and has greater force;
Mounting to heav'n in her ambitious flight,
Amongst the gods and heroes takes delight; 290
Of Pisa's wrestlers tells the sinewy force,
And sings the dusty conqueror's glorious course;
To Simois' streams does fierce Achilles bring,
And makes the Ganges bow to Britain's king.
Sometimes she flies, like an industrious bee,
And robs the flow'rs by nature's chymistry;
Describes the shepherds' dances, feasts, and bliss,
And boasts from Phyllis to surprise a kiss,
When gently she resists with feign'd remorse,
That what she grants may seem to be by force:
Her generous style at random oft will part, 301
And by a brave disorder shows her art:
Unlike those fearful poets, whose cold rhyme
In all their raptures keep exactest time,
That sing th' illustrious hero's mighty praise
(Lean writers!) by the terms of weeks and days,
And dare not from least circumstances part,
But take all towns by strictest rules of art.
Apollo drives those fops from his abode;
And some have said, that once the humorous god, 310
Resolving all such scribblers to confound,
For the short *Sonnet* order'd this strict bound:
Set rules for the just measure, and the time,
The easy running, and alternate rhyme;
But, above all, those licenses denied
Which in these writings the lame sense supplied;

[1] Virgil, *Eclogue IV*.

Forbade an useless line should find a place,
Or a repeated word appear with grace.
A faultless *Sonnet*, finish'd thus, would be
Worth tedious volumes of loose poetry. 320
A hundred scribbling authors, without ground,
Believe they have this only Phœnix found;
When yet th' exactest scarce have two or three,
Among whole tomes, from faults and censure free.
The rest, but little read, regarded less,
Are shovel'd to the pastry from the press.
Closing the sense within the measur'd time,
'T is hard to fit the reason to the rhyme.

EPIGRAM

The *Epigram*, with little art compos'd,
Is one good sentence in a distich clos'd. 330
These points, that by Italians first were priz'd,
Our ancient authors knew not, or despis'd:
The vulgar, dazzled with their glaring light,
To their false pleasures quickly they invite;
But public favor so increas'd their pride,
They overwhelm'd Parnassus with their tide.
The *Madrigal* at first was overcome,
And the proud *Sonnet* fell by the same doom;
With these grave *Tragedy* adorn'd her flights,
And mournful *Elegy* her funeral rites: 340
A hero never fail'd 'em on the stage,
Without his point a lover durst not rage;
The amorous shepherds took more care to prove
True to their point, than faithful to their love.
Each word, like Janus, had a double face;
And prose, as well as verse, allow'd it place:
The lawyer with conceits adorn'd his speech,
The parson without quibbling could not preach.
At last affronted reason look'd about,
And from all serious matters shut 'em out; 350
Declar'd that none should use 'em without shame,
Except a scattering in the *Epigram;*
Provided that by art, and in due time,
They turn'd upon the thought, and not the rhyme.
Thus in all parts disorders did abate;
Yet quibblers in the court had leave to prate:
Insipid jesters, and unpleasant fools,
A corporation of dull punning drolls.
'T is not, but that sometimes a dext'rous Muse
May with advantage a turn'd sense abuse, 360
And on a word may trifle with address;
But above all avoid the fond excess,
And think not, when your verse and sense are lame,
With a dull point to tag your *Epigram*.
Each poem his perfection has apart;
The *British Round* in plainness shows his art.
The *Ballad*, tho' the pride of ancient time,
Has often nothing but his humorous rhyme;
The *Madrigal*[2] may softer passions move,
And breathe the tender ecstasies of love: 370
Desire to show itself, and not to wrong,
Arm'd Virtue first with *Satire* in its tongue.

[2] An old way of writing, which began and ended with the same measure.

SATIRE

Lucilius was the man who, bravely bold,
To Roman vices did this mirror hold,
Protected humble goodness from reproach,
Show'd worth on foot, and rascals in the coach.
Horace his pleasing wit to this did add,
And none uncensur'd could be fool, or mad :
Unhappy was that wretch, whose name might be
Squar'd to the rules of their sharp poetry.   380
Persius, obscure, but full of sense and wit,
Affected brevity in all he writ :
And Juvenal, learn'd as those times could be,
Too far did stretch his sharp hyperbole ;
Tho' horrid truths thro' all his labors shine,
In what he writes there 's something of divine,
Whether he blames the Caprean debauch,
Or of Sejanus' fall tells the approach,
Or that he makes the trembling senate come
To the stern tyrant to receive their doom ;   390
Or Roman vice in coarsest habits shews,
And paints an empress reeking from the stews :
In all he writes appears a noble fire ;
To follow such a master then desire.
Chaucer alone, fix'd on this solid base,
In his old style conserves a modern grace :
Too happy, if the freedom of his rhymes
Offended not the method of our times.
The Latin writers decency neglect ;
But modern readers challenge our respect,   400
And at immodest writings take offense,
If clean expression cover not the sense.
I love sharp satire, from obsceneness free,
Not impudence that preaches modesty.
Our English, who in malice never fail,
Hence in lampoons and libels learnt to rail :
Pleasant detraction, that by singing goes
From mouth to mouth, and as it marches grows !
Our freedom in our poetry we see,
That child of joy, begot by liberty.   410
But, vain blasphemer, tremble when you choose
God for the subject of your impious Muse ;
At last, those jests which libertines invent,
Bring the lewd author to just punishment.
Ev'n in a song there must be art and sense ;
Yet sometimes we have seen that wine or
chance
Have warm'd cold brains, and given dull writers
mettle,
And furnish'd out a scene for Mr. S ——.
But for one lucky hit that made thee please,
Let not thy folly grow to a disease,   420
Nor think thyself a wit ; for in our age
If a warm fancy does some fop ingage,
He neither eats or sleeps till he has writ,
But plagues the world with his adulterate wit.
Nay, 'tis a wonder, if in his dire rage
He prints not his dull follies for the stage ;
And, in the front of all his senseless plays,
Makes David Logan [1] crown his head with bays.

CANTO III

TRAGEDY

THERE 's not a monster bred beneath the sky,
But, well-dispos'd by art, may please the eye ;   430

[1] D. Logan, a graver.

A curious workman, by his skill divine,
From an ill object makes a good design.
Thus, to delight us, *Tragedy*, in tears
For *Œdipus*,[2] provokes our hopes and fears ;
For parricide Orestes asks relief,
And, to encrease our pleasure, causes grief.
You then, that in this noble art would rise,
Come, and in lofty verse dispute the prize.
Would you upon the stage acquire renown,
And for your judges summon all the town ?   440
Would you your works for ever should remain,
And after ages past be sought again ?
In all you write observe with care and art
To move the passions and incline the heart.
If, in a labor'd act, the pleasing rage
Cannot our hopes and fears by turns ingage,
Nor in our mind a feeling pity raise,
In vain with learned scenes you fill your plays :
Your cold discourse can never move the mind
Of a stern critic, nat'rally unkind ;   450
Who, justly tir'd with your pedantic flight,
Or falls asleep, or censures all you write.
The secret is, attention first to gain ;
To move our minds, and then to entertain :
That, from the very op'ning of the scenes,
The first may show us what the author means.
I 'm tir'd to see an actor on the stage
That knows not whether he 's to laugh or rage ;
Who, an intrigue unraveling in vain,
Instead of pleasing, keeps my mind in pain.   460
I 'd rather much the nauseous dunce should say
Downright : " My name is Hector in the play ; "
Than with a mass of miracles, ill-join'd,
Confound my ears and not instruct my mind.
The subject 's never soon enough express'd ;
Your place of action must be fix'd, and rest.
A Spanish poet may, with good event,
In one day's space whole ages represent ;
There oft the hero of a wand'ring stage
Begins a child, and ends the play of age :   470
But we, that are by reason's rules confin'd,
Will that with art the poem be design'd,
That unity of action, time, and place,
Keep the stage full, and all our labors grace.
Write not what cannot be with ease conceiv'd ;
Some truths may be too strong to be believ'd.
A foolish wonder cannot entertain :
My mind 's not mov'd, if your discourse be vain.
You may relate what would offend the eye :
Seeing, indeed, would better satisfy ;   480
But there are objects that a curious art
Hides from the eyes, yet offers to the heart.
The mind is most agreeably surpris'd,
When a well-woven subject, long disguis'd,
You on a sudden artfully unfold,
And give the whole another face and mold.
    At first [3] the *Tragedy* was void of art ;
A song, where each man danc'd and sung his
part ;
And of god Bacchus roaring out the praise,
Sought a good vintage for their jolly days :   490
Then wine and joy were seen in each man's eyes,
And a fat goat was the best singer's prize.
Thespis was first, who, all besmear'd with lee,
Began this pleasure for posterity ;

[2] Writ by Mr. Dryden.
[3] The beginning and progress of tragedies.

And with his carted actors, and a song,
Amus'd the people as he pass'd along.
Next Æschylus the diff'rent persons plac'd,
And with a better mask his players grac'd ;
Upon a theater his verse express'd,
And show'd his hero with a buskin dress'd. 500
Then Sophocles, the genius of his age,
Increas'd the pomp and beauty of the stage,
Ingag'd the chorus song in every part,
And polish'd rugged verse by rules of art :
He in the Greek did those perfections gain,
Which the weak Latin never could attain.
Our pious fathers, in their priest-rid age,
As impious and profane abhorr'd the stage ;
A troop of silly pilgrims, as 't is said,
Foolishly zealous, scandalously play'd   510
(Instead of heroes, and of love's complaints)
The angels, God, the Virgin, and the saints.
At last, right Reason did his laws reveal,
And show'd the folly of their ill-plac'd zeal,
Silenc'd those nonconformists of the age,
And rais'd the lawful heroes of the stage :
Only th' Athenian mask was laid aside,
And chorus by the music was supplied.
Ingenious love, inventive in new arts,
Mingled in plays, and quickly touch'd our
        hearts :   520
This passion never could resistance find,
But knows the shortest passage to the mind.
Paint then, I 'm pleas'd my hero be in love ;
But let him not like a tame shepherd move ;
Let not Achilles be like Thyrsis seen,
Or for a Cyrus show an Artamène ;[1]
That, struggling oft, his passions we may find ;
The frailty, not the virtue of his mind.
Of romance heroes shun the low design ;
Yet to great hearts some human frailties join : 530
Achilles must with Homer's heat ingage ;
For an affront I 'm pleas'd to see him rage.
Those little failings in your hero's heart
Show that of man and nature he has part.
To leave known rules you cannot be allow'd :
Make Agamemnon covetous and proud,
Æneas in religious rites austere ;
Keep to each man his proper character.
Of countries and of times the humors know ;
From diff'rent climates diff'ring customs grow :
And strive to shun their fault, who vainly dress
An antique hero like some modern ass ;   542
Who make old Romans like our English move,
Show Cato sparkish, or make Brutus love.
In a romance those errors are excus'd ;
There 't is enough that, reading, we 're amus'd :
Rules too severe would then be useless found ;
But the strict scene must have a juster bound :
Exact decorum we must always find.
If then you form some hero in your mind,   550
Be sure your image with itself agree ;
For what he first appears, he still must be.
Affected wits will nat'rally incline
To paint their figures by their own design :
Your bully poets, bully heroes write ;   }
Chapman in *Bussy d'Ambois* took delight, }
And thought perfection was to huff and fight. }
Wise nature by variety does please :
Clothe diff'ring passions in a diff'ring dress ;

[1] Artamène, the name of Cyrus in Scudéry's romance.

Bold anger in rough haughty words appears ;
Sorrow is humble, and dissolves in tears.   561
Make not your Hecuba[2] with fury rage,
And show a ranting grief upon the stage ;
Or tell in vain how the rough Tanais bore
His sevenfold waters to the Euxine shore :
These swoln expressions, this affected noise,
Shows like some pedant that declaims to boys.
In sorrow, you must softer methods keep ;
And, to excite our tears, yourself must weep.
Those noisy words with which ill plays abound
Come not from hearts that are in sadness
        drown'd.   571
The theater for a young poet's rhymes
Is a bold venture in our knowing times ;
An author cannot eas'ly purchase fame ;
Critics are always apt to hiss and blame :
You may be judg'd by any ass in town :
The privilege is bought for half a crown.
To please, you must a hundred changes try ;
Sometimes be humble, then must soar on high :
In noble thoughts must everywhere abound,   580
Be easy, pleasant, solid, and profound :
To these you must surprising touches join,
And show us a new wonder in each line ;
That all, in a just method well-design'd,
May leave a strong impression in the mind.
These are the arts that *Tragedy* maintain.

THE EPIC

But the *Heroic* claims a loftier strain.
In the narration of some great design,
Invention, art, and fable, all must join :
Here fiction must employ its utmost grace ; 590
All must assume a body, mind, and face :
Each virtue a divinity is seen ;
Prudence is Pallas ; beauty, Paphos' Queen.
'T is not a cloud from whence swift lightnings
        fly,
But Jupiter, that thunders from the sky ;
Nor a rough storm that gives the sailor pain,
But angry Neptune, plowing up the main ;
Echo 's no more an empty airy sound,
But a fair nymph that weeps her lover drown'd.
Thus in the endless treasure of his mind   600
The poet does a thousand figures find ;
Around the work his ornaments he pours,
And strows with lavish hand his op'ning flow'rs.
'T is not a wonder if a tempest bore
The Trojan fleet against the Libyan shore ;
From faithless Fortune this is no surprise,
For every day 't is common to our eyes.
But angry Juno, that she might destroy
And overwhelm the rest of ruin'd Troy ;
That Æolus, with the fierce goddess join'd,   610
Open'd the hollow prisons of the wind,
Till angry Neptune, looking o'er the main,
Rebukes the tempest, calms the waves again,
Their vessels from the dang'rous quicksands
        steers —
These are the springs that move our hopes and
        fears :
Without these ornaments before our eyes
Th' unsinew'd poem languishes and dies ;
Your poet in his art will always fail,
And tell you but a dull insipid tale.

[2] Seneca Trag.

In vain have our mistaken authors tried   620
These ancient ornaments to lay aside,
Thinking our God, and prophets that he sent,
Might act like those the poets did invent,
To fright poor readers in each line with hell,
And talk of Satan, Ashtaroth, and Bel.
The mysteries which Christians must believe
Disdain such shifting pageants to receive :
The gospel offers nothing to our thoughts
But penitence, or punishment for faults ;   629
And mingling falsehoods with those mysteries
Would make our sacred truths appear like lies.
Besides, what pleasure can it be to hear
The howlings of repining Lucifer,
Whose rage at your imagin'd hero flies,
And oft with God himself disputes the prize?
Tasso, you 'll say, has done it with applause :
It is not here I mean to judge his cause ;
Yet, tho' our age has so extoll'd his name,
His works had never gain'd immortal fame,
If holy Godfrey in his ecstasies   640
Had only conquer'd Satan on his knees ;
If Tancred, and Armida's pleasing form,
Did not his melancholy theme adorn.
'T is not that Christian poems ought to be
Fill'd with the fictions of idolatry ;
But in a common subject to reject
The gods, and heathen ornaments neglect ;
To banish Tritons who the seas invade,
To take Pan's whistle, or the Fates degrade,
To hinder Charon in his leaky boat   650
To pass the shepherd with the man of note,
Is with vain scruples to disturb your mind,
And search perfection you can never find :
As well they may forbid us to present
Prudence or Justice for an ornament,
To paint old Janus with his front of brass ;
And take from Time his scythe, his wings, and
      glass ;
And everywhere, as 't were idolatry,
Banish descriptions from our poetry.
Leave 'em their pious follies to pursue,   660
But let our reason such vain fears subdue ;
And let us not, amongst our vanities,
Of the true God create a God of lies.
In fable we a thousand pleasures see,
And the smooth names seem made for poetry ;
As Hector, Alexander, Helen, Phyllis,
Ulysses, Agamemnon, and Achilles :
In such a crowd, the poet were to blame
To choose King Chilperic for his hero's name.
Sometimes, the name being well or ill applied,
Will the whole fortune of your work decide. 671
Would you your reader never should be tir'd ?
Choose some great hero, fit to be admir'd,
In courage signal, and in virtue bright ;
Let ev'n his very failings give delight ;
Let his great actions our attention bind ;
Like Cæsar, or like Scipio, frame his mind,
And not like Œdipus his perjur'd race ;
A common conqueror is a theme too base.
Choose not your tale of accidents too full ;   680
Too much variety may make it dull :
Achilles' rage alone, when wrought with skill,
Abundantly does a whole *Iliad* fll.
Be your narrations lively, short, and smart ;
In your descriptions show your noblest art :

There 't is your poetry may be employ'd ;
Yet you must trivial accidents avoid.
Nor imitate that fool,[1] who, to describe
The wondrous marches of the chosen tribe,
Plac'd on the sides, to see their armies pass,   690
The fishes staring thro' the liquid glass ;
Describ'd a child, who, with his little hand,
Pick'd up the shining pebbles from the sand.
Such objects are too mean to stay our sight ;
Allow your work a just and nobler flight.
Be your beginning plain, and take good heed
Too soon you mount not on the airy steed ;
Nor tell your reader, in a thund'ring verse,
" I sing the conqueror of the universe." [2]
What can an author after this produce ?   700
The lab'ring mountain must bring forth a mouse.
Much better are we pleas'd with his address,[3]
Who, without making such vast promises,
Says, in an easier style and plainer sense :
" I sing the combats of that pious prince,
Who from the Phrygian coast his armies bore,
And landed first on the Lavinian shore."
His op'ning Muse sets not the world on fire,
And yet performs more than we can require :
Quickly you 'll hear him celebrate the fame 71●
And future glory of the Roman name ;
Of Styx and Acheron describe the floods,
And Cæsars wand'ring in th' Elysian woods ;
With figures numberless his story grace,
And everything in beauteous colors trace.
At once you may be pleasing and sublime :
I hate a heavy melancholy rhyme ;
I 'd rather read Orlando's comic tale,
Than a dull author always stiff and stale,
Who thinks himself dishonor'd in his style,   720
If on his works the Graces do but smile.
'T is said that Homer, matchless in his art,
Stole Venus' girdle, to ingage the heart :
His works indeed vast treasures do unfold,
And whatsoe'er he touches turns to gold :
All in his hands new beauty does acquire ;
He always pleases, and can never tire.
A happy warmth he everywhere may boast,
Nor is he in too long digressions lost :
His verses without rule a method find,   730
And of themselves appear in order join'd :
All without trouble answers his intent ;
Each syllable is tending to th' event.
Let his example your indeavors raise ;
To love his writings is a kind of praise.
A poem where we all perfections find
Is not the work of a fantastic mind :
There must be care, and time, and skill, and
      pains ;
Not the first heat of unexperienc'd brains.
Yet sometimes artless poets, when the rage   740
Of a warm fancy does their minds ingage,
Puff'd with vain pride, presume they under-
      stand,
And boldly take the trumpet in their hand ;
Their fustian Muse each accident confounds ;
Nor can she fly, but rise by leaps and bounds,
Till, their small stock of learning quickly spent,
Their poem dies for want of nourishment.

1 St. Amant.
2 The first line of Scudéry's *Alaric.*
3 Virgil's *Æneids.*

In vain mankind the hot-brain'd fools decries,
No branding censures can unveil his eyes;
With impudence the laurel they invade,   750
Resolv'd to like the monsters they have made.
Virgil, compar'd to them, is flat and dry,
And Homer understood not poetry;
Against their merit if this age rebel,
To future times for justice they appeal.
But, waiting till mankind shall do 'em right,
And bring their works triumphantly to light,
Neglected heaps we in by-corners lay,
Where they become to worms and moths a prey;
Forgot, in dust and cobwebs let 'em rest,   760
Whilst we return from whence we first digress'd.
  The great success which tragic writers found,
In Athens first the *Comedy* renown'd.
Th' abusive Grecian there, by pleasing ways,
Dispers'd his nat'ral malice in his plays;
Wisdom and virtue, honor, wit, and sense,
Were subject to buffooning insolence:
Poets were publicly approv'd, and sought,
That vice extoll'd, and virtue set at naught;
And Socrates himself, in that loose age,   770
Was made the pastime of a scoffing stage.
At last the public took in hand the cause,
And cur'd this madness by the pow'r of laws;
Forbade at any time, or any place,
To name the person, or describe the face.
The stage its ancient fury thus let fall,
And comedy diverted without gall;
By mild reproofs recover'd minds diseas'd,
And, sparing persons, innocently pleas'd.
Each one was nicely shown in this new glass,   780
And smil'd to think he was not meant the ass:
A miser oft would laugh the first, to find
A faithful draught of his own sordid mind;
And fops were with such care and cunning writ,
They lik'd the piece for which themselves did sit.
You then that would the comic laurels wear,
To study nature be your only care:
Whoe'er knows man, and by a curious art
Discerns the hidden secrets of the heart;
He who observes and naturally can paint   790
The jealous fool, the fawning sycophant,
A sober wit, an enterprising ass,
A humorous Otter, or a Hudibras, —
May safely in these noble lists ingage,
And make 'em act and speak upon the stage.
Strive to be natural in all you write,
And paint with colors that may please the sight.
Nature in various figures does abound,
And in each mind are diff'rent humors found;
A glance, a touch, discovers to the wise,   800
But every man has not discerning eyes.
All-changing time does also change the mind,
And diff'rent ages diff'rent pleasures find:
Youth, hot and furious, cannot brook delay;
By flattering vice is eas'ly led away;
Vain in discourse, inconstant in desire;
In censure, rash; in pleasures, all on fire.
The manly age does steadier thoughts enjoy;
Pow'r and ambition do his soul employ:
Against the turns of fate he sets his mind,   810
And by the past the future hopes to find.
Decrepit age, still adding to his stores,

For others heaps the treasure he adores;
In all his actions keeps a frozen pace;
Past times extols, the present to debase:
Incapable of pleasures youth abuse,
In others blames what age does him refuse.
Your actors must by reason be controll'd;
Let young men speak like young, old men like
    old;
Observe the town, and study well the court,   820
For thither various characters resort:
Thus 't was great Jonson purchas'd his renown,
And in his art had borne away the crown;
If, less desirous of the people's praise,
He had not with low farce debas'd his plays;
Mixing dull buffoon'ry with wit refin'd,
And Harlequin with noble Terence join'd.
When in *The Fox* I see the tortoise hiss'd,
I lose the author of *The Alchymist.*
The comic wit, borne with the smiling air,   830
Must tragic grief and pompous verse forbear;
Yet may he not, as on a market place,
With bawdy jests amuse the populace.
With well-bred conversation you must please,
And your intrigue unravel'd be with ease;
Your action still should reason's rules obey,
Nor in an empty scene may lose its way.
Your humble style must sometimes gently rise,
And your discourse sententious be and wise;
The passions must to nature be confin'd,   840
And scenes to scenes with artful weaving join'd.
Your wit must not unseasonably play,
But follow bus'ness, never lead the way.
Observe how Terence does this error shun;
A careful father chides his am'rous son:
Then see that son, whom no advice can move,
Forget those orders, and pursue his love:
'T is not a well-drawn picture we discover;
'T is a true son, a father, and a lover.
I like an author that reforms the age,   850
And keeps the right decorum of the stage;
That always pleases by just reason's rule:
But for a tedious droll, a quibbling fool,
Who with low nauseous bawdry fills his plays,
Let him be gone, and on two trestles raise
Some Smithfield stage, where he may act his
    pranks,
And make Jack Puddings speak to mounte-
    banks.

Canto IV

In Florence dwelt a doctor of renown,
The scourge of God, and terror of the town,
Who all the cant of physic had by heart,   860
And never murder'd but by rules of art.
The public mischief was his private gain:
Children their slaughter'd parents sought in
    vain;
A brother here his poison'd brother wept;
Some bloodless died, and some by *opium* slept.
Colds, at his presence, would to frenzies turn,
And agues like malignant fevers burn.
Hated, at last, his practice gives him o'er;
One friend, unkill'd by drugs, of all his store,
In his new country house affords him place;   870
'T was a rich abbot, and a building ass.
Here first the doctor's talent came in play;

He seems inspir'd, and talks like Wren or
    May ; [1]
Of this new portico condemns the face,
And turns the entrance to a better place ;
Designs the staircase at the other end.
His friend approves, does for his mason send :
He comes ; the doctor's arguments prevail.
In short, to finish this our hum'rous tale,
He Galen's dang'rous science does reject,   880
And from ill doctor turn good architect.
  In this example we may have our part :
Rather be mason ('t is an useful art !)
Than a dull poet ; for that trade accurst
Admits no mean betwixt the best and worst.
In other sciences, without disgrace
A candidate may fill a second place ;
But poetry no medium can admit,
No reader suffers an indiff'rent wit ;
The ruin'd stationers against him bawl,   890
And Herringman degrades him from his stall.
Burlesque at least our laughter may excite,
But a cold writer never can delight.
The Counter Scuffle has more wit and art
Than the stiff formal style of *Gondibert*.
Be not affected with that empty praise
Which your vain flatterers will sometimes raise,
And when you read, with ecstasy will say,
" The finish'd piece ! the admirable play ! "
Which, when expos'd to censure and to light,   901
Cannot indure a critic's piercing sight.
A hundred authors' fates have been foretold,
And Sh——ll's works are printed, but not sold.
Hear all the world ; consider every thought ;
A fool by chance may stumble on a fault :
Yet, when Apollo does your Muse inspire,
Be not impatient to expose your fire ;
Nor imitate the Settles of our times,
Those tuneful readers of their own dull rhymes,
Who seize on all th' acquaintance they can
    meet,   910
And stop the passengers that walk the street :
There is no sanctuary you can choose
For a defense from their pursuing Muse.
I 've said before, be patient when they blame ;
To alter for the better is no shame.
Yet yield not to a fool's impertinence :
Sometimes conceited sceptics, void of sense,
By their false taste condemn some finish'd part,
And blame the noblest flights of wit and art.
In vain their fond opinions you deride ;   920
With their lov'd follies they are satisfied,
And their weak judgment, void of sense and
    light,
Thinks nothing can escape their feeble sight :
Their dang'rous counsels do not cure, but ⎫
    wound ; ⎪
To shun the storm they run your verse ⎬
    aground ; ⎪
And, thinking to escape a rock, are drown'd. ⎭
Choose a sure judge to censure what you write,
Whose reason leads, and knowledge gives you
    light,
Whose steady hand will prove your faithful
    guide,   929
And touch the darling follies you would hide :
He, in your doubts, will carefully advise,

[1] The king's architects.

And clear the mist before your feeble eyes.
'T is he will tell you to what noble height
A generous Muse may sometimes take her
    flight ;
When, too much fetter'd with the rules of art,
May from her stricter bounds and limits part :
But such a perfect judge is hard to see,
And every rhymer knows not poetry ;   938
Nay some there are, for writing verse extoll'd,
Who know not Lucan's dross from Virgil's gold.
  Would you in this great art acquire renown ?
Authors, observe the rules I here lay down.
In prudent lessons everywhere abound ;
With pleasant join the useful and the sound :
A sober reader a vain tale will slight ;
He seeks as well instruction as delight.
Let all your thoughts to virtue be confin'd,
Still off'ring noble figures to our mind :
I like not those loose writers, who employ   949
Their guilty Muse, good manners to destroy ;
Who with false colors still deceive our eyes,
And show us Vice dress'd in a fair disguise.
Yet do I not their sullen Muse approve,
Who from all modest writings banish love ;
That strip the playhouse of its chief intrigue,
And make a murderer of Roderigue : [2]
The lightest love, if decently express'd,
Will raise no vicious motions in our breast.
Dido in vain may weep, and ask relief ;
I blame her folly, whilst I share her grief.   960
A virtuous author, in his charming art,
To please the sense needs not corrupt the heart ;
His heat will never cause a guilty fire :
To follow virtue then be your desire.
In vain your art and vigor are express'd ;
Th' obscene expression shows th' infected
    breast.
But, above all, base jealousies avoid,
In which detracting poets are employ'd.
A noble wit dares lib'rally commend,   969
And scorns to grudge at his deserving friend.
Base rivals, who true wit and merit hate,
Caballing still against it with the great,
Maliciously aspire to gain renown
By standing up and pulling others down.
Never debase yourself by treacherous ways,
Nor by such abject methods seek for praise :
Let not your only bus'ness be to write ;
Be virtuous, just, and in your friends delight.
'T is not enough your poems be admir'd ;
But strive your conversation be desir'd :   980
Write for immortal fame, nor ever choose
Gold for the object of a gen'rous Muse.
I know a noble wit may, without crime,
Receive a lawful tribute for his time ;
Yet I abhor those writers who despise
Their honor, and alone their profit prize ;
Who their Apollo basely will degrade,
And of a noble science make a trade.
Before kind Reason did her light display,
And government taught mortals to obey,   996
Men, like wild beasts, did Nature's laws pursue ;
They fed on herbs, and drink from rivers drew ;
Their brutal force, on lust and rapine bent,
Committed murders without punishment.
Reason at last, by her all-conquering arts,

[2] *The Cid*, translated into English.

Reduc'd these savages and tun'd their hearts ;
Mankind from bogs, and woods, and caverns
    calls,
And towns and cities fortifies with walls :
Thus fear of justice made proud rapine cease,
And shelter'd innocence by laws and peace. 1000
    These benefits from poets we receiv'd,
From whence are rais'd those fictions since be-
    liev'd,
That Orpheus, by his soft harmonious strains,
Tam'd the fierce tigers of the Thracian plains ;
Amphion's notes, by their melodious pow'rs,
Drew rocks and woods, and rais'd the Theban
    tow'rs :
These miracles from numbers did arise ;
Since which, in verse Heav'n taught his mys-
    teries,
And by a priest, possess'd with rage divine,
Apollo spoke from his prophetic shrine. 1010
Soon after, Homer the great heroes prais'd,
And noble minds by great examples rais'd;
Then Hesiod did his Grecian swains incline
To till the fields, and prune the bounteous vine.
Thus useful rules were by the poets' aid,
In easy numbers, to rude men convey'd,
And pleasingly their precepts did impart ;
First charm'd the ear, and then ingag'd the
    heart :
The Muses thus their reputation rais'd, 1019
And with just gratitude in Greece were prais'd.
With pleasure mortals did their wonders see,
And sacrific'd to their divinity ;
But want, at last, base flatt'ry entertain'd,
And old Parnassus with this vice was stain'd :
Desire of gain dazzling the poets' eyes,
Their works were fill'd with fulsome flatteries.
Thus needy wits a vile revenue made,
And verse became a mercenary trade.
Debase not with so mean a vice thy art :
If gold must be the idol of thy heart, 1030
Fly, fly th' unfruitful Heliconian strand ;
Those streams are not inrich'd with golden
    sand :
Great wits, as well as warriors, only gain
Laurels and honors for their toil and pain.
But what ? an author cannot live on fame,
Or pay a reck'ning with a lofty name :
A poet to whom fortune is unkind,
Who when he goes to bed has hardly din'd,
Takes little pleasure in Parnassus' dreams,
Or relishes the Heliconian streams. 1040
Horace had ease and plenty when he writ, ⎫
And, free from cares for money or for meat, ⎬
Did not expect his dinner from his wit. ⎭
'Tis true ; but verse is cherish'd by the great,
And now none famish who deserve to eat :
What can we fear, when virtue, arts, and sense,
Receive the stars' propitious influence ;
When a sharp-sighted prince, by early grants,
Rewards your merits, and prevents your wants ?
Sing then his glory, celebrate his fame ; 1050
Your noblest theme is his immortal name.
Let mighty Spenser raise his reverend head,
Cowley and Denham start up from the dead ;
Waller his age renew, and off'rings bring ;
Our monarch's praise let bright-ey'd virgins
    sing ;

Let Dryden with new rules our stage refine,
And his great models form by this design :
But where 's a second Virgil, to rehearse
Our hero's glories in his epic verse ? 1059
What Orpheus sing his triumphs o'er the main,
And make the hills and forests move again ;
Show his bold fleet on the Batavian shore,
And Holland trembling as his cannons roar ;
Paint Europe's balance in his steady hand, ⎫
Whilst the two worlds in expectation stand ⎬
Of peace or war, that wait on his command ? ⎭
But, as I speak, new glories strike my eyes,
Glories which Heav'n itself does give, and prize,
Blessings of peace ; that with their milder rays
Adorn his reign, and bring Saturnian days. 1070
Now let rebellion, discord, vice, and rage,
That have in patriots' forms debauch'd our age,
Vanish, with all the ministers of hell :
His rays their pois'nous vapors shall dispel.
'Tis he alone our safety did create ; ⎫
His own firm soul secur'd the nation's fate, ⎬
Oppos'd to all the *boutefeus* of the state. ⎭
Authors, for him your great indeavors raise ;
The loftiest numbers will but reach his praise.
For me, whose verse in satire has been bred,
And never durst heroic measures tread ; 1081
Yet you shall see me, in that famous field,
With eyes and voice my best assistance yield ;
Offer you lessons that my infant Muse
Learnt, when she Horace for her guide did
    choose ;
Second your zeal with wishes, heart, and eyes,
And afar off hold up the glorious prize.
But pardon too, if, zealous for the right,
A strict observer of each noble flight,
From the fine gold I separate th' allay, 1090
And show how hasty writers sometimes stray :
Apter to blame, than knowing how to mend ;
A sharp, but yet a necessary friend.

ON THE YOUNG STATESMEN

[The following verses are reprinted from *Poems on Affairs of State, the fourth edition*, 1702, where they are headed *On the Young Statesman* [sic]. *By J. Dryden, 1680.* The style of this piece is entirely unlike Dryden's ; and the sneers at Danby and at Laurence Hyde, created Earl of Rochester in 1681, both of whom he compliments in dedications, are still more emphatically not in his manner. In *A New Collection of Poems relating to State Affairs*, 1705, this poem is ascribed to the Earl of Rochester [i. e. John Wilmot], who is much more likely to have been its author than is Dryden. Scott, on internal evidence, is "tempted to ascribe" the verses to the Earl of Dorset, whose poem *On the Countess of Dorchester* they resemble in "the turn of wit and structure of verse." H. C. Foxcroft (*Life and Letters of Sir George Savile, Bart., First Marquis of Halifax*, vol. i, p. 265) states that Burnet attributes them to the Duke of Buckingham.
    In *A Collection of Poems on Affairs of State*, 1689, there occurs a poem called *Young Statesman* on the title-page, but headed : *A Young Gentleman, desirous to be a Minister of State, thus pretends to qualife himself.* It has nothing in common with the present piece.]

I

CLARENDON had law and sense,
    Clifford was fierce and brave ;

Bennet's grave look was a pretense,
And D——y's matchless impudence
Help'd to support the knave.

II

But Sund——d, God——n, L—y,
These will appear such chits in story,
'T will turn all politics to jests,
To be repeated like John Dory,
When fiddlers sing at feasts.   10

III

Protect us, mighty Providence ;
What would these madmen have ?
First, they would bribe us without pence,
Deceive us without common sense,
And without pow'r enslave.

IV

Shall freeborn men in humble awe
Submit to servile shame ;
Who from consent and custom draw
The same right to be rul'd by law,
Which kings pretend, to reign ?   20

V

The duke shall wield his conqu'ring sword,
The chancellor make a speech ;
The king shall pass his honest word,
The pawn'd revenue sums afford —
And then, come kiss my breech.

VI

So have I seen a king on chess,
(His rooks and knights withdrawn,
His queen and bishops in distress,)
Shifting about, grow less and less,
With here and there a pawn.   30

ÆSACUS TRANSFORM'D INTO A COR-
MORANT

FROM OVID'S METAMORPHOSES, BOOK XI

[So far as the present editor can ascertain, the following piece was first printed in *Ovid's Metamorphoses, in
fifteen books, Translated by the most Eminent Hands*,
published by Tonson in 1717. It is assigned to Dryden
in the table of contents of this collection, which was
edited by Sir Samuel Garth. It was reprinted in the
edition of Dryden's *Original Poems and Translations*,
edited by Broughton, and published in 1743.]

THESE some old man sees wanton in the air,
And praises the unhappy constant pair ;
Then to his friend the long-neck'd corm'rant
    shows,
The former tale reviving others' woes.
" That sable bird," he cries, " which cuts the
    flood
With slender legs, was once of royal blood ;
His ancestors from mighty Tros proceed,
The brave Laomedon, and Ganymede,
(Whose beauty tempted Jove to steal the boy,)
And Priam, hapless prince ! who fell with
    Troy.   10
Himself was Hector's brother, and (had fate
But giv'n his hopeful youth a longer date)

Perhaps had rival'd warlike Hector's worth,
Tho' on the mother's side of meaner birth.
Fair Alyxothoe, a country maid,
Bare Æsacus by stealth in Ida's shade.
He fled the noisy town and pompous court,
Lov'd the lone hills and simple rural sport,
And seldom to the city would resort.
Yet he no rustic clownishness profess'd,   20
Nor was soft love a stranger to his breast.
The youth had long the nymph Hesperie woo'd ;
Oft thro' the thicket or the mead pursued :
Her haply on her father's bank he spied,
While fearless she her silver tresses dried.
Away she fled : not stags with half such speed
Before the prowling wolf scud o'er the mead ;
Not ducks, when they the safer flood forsake,
Pursued by hawks, so swift regain the lake.
As fast he follow'd in the hot career ;   30
Desire the lover wing'd, the virgin fear.
A snake unseen now pierc'd her heedless foot ;
Quick thro' the veins the venom'd juices shoot :
She fell, and 'scaped by death his fierce pur-
    suit.
Her lifeless body, frighted, he embrac'd,
And cried : ' Not this I dreaded, but thy haste :
O had my love been less, or less thy fear !
The victory, thus bought, is far too dear.
Accursed snake ! yet I more curst than he !   39
He gave the wound ; the cause was giv'n by me.
Yet none shall say that unreveng'd you died.'
He spoke ; then climb'd a cliff's o'erhanging
    side,
And, resolute, leap'd on the foaming tide.
Tethys receiv'd him gently on the wave ;
The death he sought denied, and feathers gave.
Debarr'd the surest remedy of grief,
And forc'd to live, he curs'd th' unask'd relief ;
Then on his airy pinions upward flies,
And at a second fall successless tries ;
The downy plume a quick descent denies.   50
Enrag'd, he often dives beneath the wave,
And there in vain expects to find a grave.
His ceaseless sorrow for th' unhappy maid
Meager'd his look, and on his spirits prey'd.
Still near the sounding deep he lives ; his name
From frequent diving and emerging came."

KING JAMES TO HIMSELF

[The following poem is taken from *Poems on Affairs
of State*, vol. ii, 1703, where it is ascribed to *Mr.
D——n*. Though the style has little of Dryden's vigor,
the piece is in itself not uninteresting.]

UNHAPPY I, who once ordain'd did bear
God's justice sword, and his vicegerent here,
Am now depos'd : 'gainst me my children rise ;
My life must be their only sacrifice.
Highly they me accuse, but nothing prove ;
But this is out of tenderness and love.
They seek to spill my blood ; 't is that alone
Must for the nation's crying sins atone.
But careful Heaven forewarn'd me in a dream,
And shew'd me that my dangers were extreme :
The heavenly vision spoke and bid me flee ;   11
Th' ungrateful wretches were not worthy me.
Alarm'd, I fled at the appointed time ;
Thus mere necessity was made my crime.

HYMNS ATTRIBUTED TO DRYDEN

[In 1693 Dryden published a translation of the hymn *Veni, Creator Spiritus:* see above, pages 406, 407.

In 1808 Scott printed as Dryden's work two more hymns, which he had received from manuscript sources: see the Scott-Saintsbury edition, vol. i, pp. xvi, 287–290. Later editors rashly accepted these hymns as authentic.

After the Reformation, certain devotional books, under the general title of *Primer*, were published for the use of English Catholic laymen. Among other things these books contain translations of the Latin church hymns. A *Primer* published in 1706 contains, among the 112 hymns included in it, both Dryden's acknowledged hymn and the two assigned to him by Scott. About 1883 Orby Shipley, a Catholic student of hymnology, discovered these facts; he also discovered that the same *Primer* contained various other hymns attributed to Dryden by Catholic tradition. He concluded that the majority of the hymns in the *Primer* of 1706, or even all of them, were translated by Dryden. His views found favor with the Rev. H. Leigh Bennett, who, in articles on "Dryden" and "Primers," contributed to Julian's *Dictionary of Hymnology* (1892), reinforced them by further arguments. In 1893 Saintsbury, in an appendix to his revision of Scott's edition of Dryden (vol. xviii, pp. 269–281), expressed general agreement with Shipley's position. He was followed by other writers.

So by the 1930's the idea had become prevalent that after his conversion to Catholicism Dryden had translated many Latin hymns; but, curiously enough, the hymns in the *Primer* of 1706 had never been reproduced as a whole except in reprints of that *Primer*, the last of which appeared in 1804. In 1937 they were reissued in *Hymns Attributed to John Dryden, edited with an Introduction and Notes by George Rapall Noyes and George Reuben Potter* (Berkeley, California). In their introduction the editors give a history of the controversy concerning the authorship of the translations and discuss the question independently. They argue: (1) that there is no valid external evidence that Dryden ever translated a single hymn other than the *Veni, Creator Spiritus;* (2) that the traits of style in the *Primer* hymns which have been thought to show Dryden's authorship really show that the translators simply used the poetic diction characteristic of the period or else were directly affected by specific passages in Dryden; and (3) that the hymns show certain traits of style at variance with Dryden's usage. They conclude that it is highly improbable that Dryden ever translated any other hymn than the *Veni*.

Below are given reprints of the two hymns published by Scott, preserving as a matter of curious interest Scott's text of them, which differs somewhat from that in the *Primer* of 1706.]

THE TE DEUM

THEE, Sovereign God, our grateful accents praise;
We own thee Lord, and bless thy wondrous ways;
To thee, Eternal Father, earth's whole frame,
With loudest trumpets, sounds immortal fame.
Lord God of Hosts! for thee the heavenly powers
With sounding anthems fill the vaulted towers.
Thy Cherubims thrice, Holy, Holy, Holy, cry; ⎫
Thrice, Holy, all the Seraphims reply, ⎬
And thrice returning echoes endless songs supply. ⎭

Both heaven and earth thy majesty display; 10
They owe their beauty to thy glorious ray.
Thy praises fill the loud apostles' choir;
The train of prophets in the song conspire.
Legions of martyrs in the chorus shine,
And vocal blood with vocal music join.
By these thy Church, inspir'd by heavenly art
Around the world maintains a second part;
And tunes her sweetest notes, O God, to thee,
The Father of unbounded majesty;
The Son, ador'd copartner of thy seat, 20
And equal everlasting Paraclete.
Thou King of Glory, Christ, of the most high,
Thou coeternal filial Deity;
Thou who, to save the world's impending doom,
Vouchsaf'dst to dwell within a Virgin's womb;
Old tyrant Death disarm'd, before thee flew
The bolts of heaven, and back the foldings drew,
To give access, and make thy faithful way;
From God's right hand thy filial beams display.
Thou art to judge the living and the dead; 30
Then spare those souls for whom thy veins have bled.
O take us up amongst thy blest above,
To share with them thy everlasting love.
Preserve, O Lord, thy people, and enhance
Thy blessing on thine own inheritance.
For ever raise their hearts, and rule their ways;
Each day we bless thee, and proclaim thy praise:
No age shall fail to celebrate thy name,
No hour neglect thy everlasting fame.
Preserve our souls, O Lord, this day from ill; 40
Have mercy on us, Lord, have mercy still:
As we have hop'd, do thou reward our pain;
We 've hop'd in thee — let not our hope be vain.

HYMN FOR ST. JOHN'S EVE

(29 June)

I

O SYLVAN prophet, whose eternal fame
Echoes from Judah's hills, and Jordan's stream,
The music of our numbers raise,
And tune our voices to thy praise.

II

A messenger from high Olympus came
To bear the tidings of thy life and name;
And told thy sire each prodigy
That Heaven design'd to work in thee.

III

Hearing the news, and doubting in surprise,
His falt'ring speech in fetter'd accent dies; 10
But Providence, with happy choice,
In thee restor'd thy father's voice.

IV

In the recess of nature's dark abode,
Tho' still inclos'd, yet knewest thou thy God!
Whilst each glad parent told and bless'd
The secrets of each other's breast.

THRENI CANTABRIGIENSES

[In 1661 there was published at Cambridge a volume entitled *Threni Cantabrigienses in Funere duorum Principum, Henrici Glocestrensis, et Mariæ Arausionensis, Serenissimi Regis Caroli II, Fratris et Sororis* (British Museum Catalogue). This contains, according to Malone (I, 1, 17), poems by Jonathan Dryden, a cousin of our author. The pieces are sometimes ascribed to John Dryden.]

SATIRE UPON THE DUTCH

WRITTEN BY MR. DRYDEN IN THE YEAR 1662

[A poem under this title is found in *Poems on Affairs of State*, vol. iii, 1704; and in *A New Collection of Poems relating to State Affairs*, 1705. See headnote, pages 70, 71.]

THE MALL

OR, THE MODISH LOVERS

[A comedy of this title, published in 1674, has a dedication, "To William Whitcomb, Junior, Esq.," signed "J. D." It has been conjectured that this piece is identical with *The Ladies à la Mode*, a play which Pepys saw on September 15, 1668, and which he terms "a translation out of French by Dryden." But, as an entry in the Lord Chamberlain's Department of the Public Record Office shows, the play that Pepys saw was *The Damoiselles a la Mode*, by Richard Flecknoe, a comedy based on Molière. See Allardyce Nicoll, *A History of Restoration Drama*, 1928, pp. 173, 306.
The Mall is printed in Dryden, *Works*, ed. Scott-Saintsbury, viii. 507–576.]

THE MISTAKEN HUSBAND

[A comedy of this title, "printed for J. Magnes and R. Bentley" in 1675, contains a short preface, *The Bookseller to the Reader*, signed "R. Bentley," which begins as follows:
"This play was left in Mr. Dryden's hands many years since. The author of it was unknown to him, and returned not to claim it; 't is therefore to be presum'd that he is dead. After twelve years' expectation, Mr. Dryden gave it to the players, having upon perusal of it found that it deserv'd a better fate than to be buried in obscurity. I have heard him say that finding a scene wanting he supplied it, and many have affirm'd that the style of it is proper to the subject, which is that the French call *basse comedy*."
A. C. Swinburne (in the *Gentleman's Magazine*, Oct., 1880; vol. ccxlix, pp. 416–423), while arguing that one scene of this play was mainly written by Dryden, condemns the prologue and epilogue as none of his work, but Saintsbury seems inclined to accept them. They are not intrinsically interesting, and have no claim to be reprinted in this edition. The play is included in Dryden, *Works*, ed. Scott-Saintsbury, viii. 577–643.]

TO BE WRITTEN UNDER THE DUCHESS OF PORTSMOUTH'S PICTURE

[In *Poems on Affairs of State . . . Part III . . . 1698*, there are found under this heading, with the additional words, "By Mr. Dryden," three epigrams, the first of which reads as below. This poem may possibly be by Dryden (the author of *All for Love*), though it occurs anonymously in *Examen Poeticum*, 1693, with the reading *the poet's* instead of *this poet's* in the fifth line. It is also found anonymously in *Poems on Affairs of State*, vol. iii, 1704; and in *A New Collection of Poems relating to State Affairs*, 1705. — In the volume of 1698 the three epigrams are printed like three stanzas of one poem, though their substance shows that they are not all by the same author. In the volume of 1704 the three epigrams likewise occur, but the second is termed *Answer* and the third (reprinted in Dryden, *Works*, ed. Scott-Saintsbury, xv. 266) is termed *Another;* the first two epigrams are left anonymous, but the third is ascribed in the index to "Mr. Dry—n." The first two epigrams are also found anonymously in the volume of 1705.]

HAD she but liv'd in Cleopatra's age,
When beauty did the earth's great lord engage,
Britain, not Egypt, had been glorious made;
Augustus then, like Julius, had obey'd:
A nobler theme had been this poet's boast,
That All the World for Love had Well been
    Lost.

SATIRE UPON ROMISH CONFESSORS

[A poem is printed under this title and attributed to Dryden in *Poems on Affairs of State*, 1704, and in *A New Collection of Poems relating to State Affairs*, 1705. It is really the epilogue to *The Spanish Friar*, lacking the first four lines. This epilogue was by one of Dryden's friends: see headnote, page 103.]

TO MR. CREECH, UPON HIS TRANSLATION OF LUCRETIUS INTO ENGLISH

[A poem under this heading, prefixed to the second edition of Creech's translation of Lucretius, 1683, was early attributed to Dryden; and on it was built a story that Dryden "incited Creech to translate Horace, that by his failure in that work he might lose the reputation which he had gained by his poetical version of Lucretius" (Malone). For this tale the only tangible evidence was that the verses were dated January 25, 1682, and contained the couplet:

Believe me, youth, for I am read in cares,
And bend beneath the weight of fifty years,

which tallies exactly with Dryden's age at the time. In 1800 Malone (I, 1, 505–511) refuted the calumny. Finally G. Thorn-Drury drew attention to a letter by Tonson, showing that Tonson was the real author of the verses: see *Review of English Studies*, i (1925), 195–197.]

ON THE DUKE OF BUCKS

[A lampoon on George Villiers, Duke of Buckingham, is printed under this title in *Poems on Affairs of State*, vol. ii, 1703, and ascribed to "Mr. D—n." It had been published anonymously at least as early as 1679, as a single folio sheet, undated, under the title *A Ballad;* it again appeared anonymously as *A New Ballad*, in *Poems on Affairs of State . . . Part III . . . 1698*. The style of the piece by no means suggests Dryden as the author.]

EPILOGUE TO DISAPPOINTMENT

OR, THE MOTHER IN FASHION

[The prologue to this play by Southerne has been printed on page 171. In the first edition of the play,

1684, and in the collected editions of Southerne's works, the epilogue is ascribed to the Hon. John Stafford. But it appears in the third edition, 1702, of *Miscellany Poems, the First Part,* under the heading *An Epilogue by Mr. Dryden.* The piece may be found in the Scott-Saintsbury edition, x. 421.]

AN EPITAPH UPON THE E. OF RO——S-TER'S BEING DISMISS'D FROM THE TREASURY IN 1687

[A lampoon on Laurence Hyde, Earl of Rochester, is found, ascribed to Dryden, in *Poems on Affairs of State* . . . *Part III* . . . 1698; and, under title as above, in *Poems on Affairs of State,* vol. ii, 1703. It cannot be by Dryden, who in 1692 dedicated *Cleomenes* to Rochester in terms of great respect. It is printed in Dryden, *Works,* ed. Scott-Saintsbury, xv. 265, 266.]

TARQUIN AND TULLIA

SUUM CUIQUE

[Under the title *Tarquin and Tullia* a poem violently attacking William and Mary is printed in *Poems on Affairs of State,* vol. iii, 1704, and in the index is ascribed to "Mr. D——n." It appears anonymously in *A New Collection of Poems relating to State Affairs,* 1705. In *The Life and Posthumous Works of Arthur Maynwaring, Esq.* [by John Oldmixon], 1715, pp. 9–13, Oldmixon gives quotations from this poem, which he says was one of Mainwaring's first productions. (On p. 14 he says that another poem by Mainwaring, *The King of Hearts,* was falsely attributed to Dryden.) Under the title *Tullius and Tarquin* the same poem was reprinted in *The St. James's Magazine* for November, 1762, where it is followed by a similar satire, *Suum Cuique.* A note to the editor from "B. T.," whom the contents page identifies as Bonnell Thornton, states: "These manuscripts were preserved in a family, that had been remarkably attached to the STUART line. You will therefore excuse my not being more particular, though your readers need not doubt of the authenticity of them. Indeed the argument, the style . . . are so many internal proofs that they must be the composition of DRYDEN, and DRYDEN only." Such is the value of tradition!

Scott had learned from Malone (I, 1, 546) that *Tarquin and Tullia* was by Mainwaring; and, presumably finding the two pieces together in *The St. James's Magazine,* concluded — perhaps correctly — that *Suum Cuique* was also by Mainwaring. Both poems may be found in Dryden, *Works,* ed. Scott-Saintsbury, xv. 258–265.]

SONGS FROM THE PROPHETESS

[Saintsbury conjectures, on what seems insufficient evidence, that certain songs in *The Prophetess* as revived in 1690 (see headnote, page 260) may have been written by Dryden. See Dryden, *Works,* ed. Scott-Saintsbury, viii. 10 and xviii. 302–308.]

A FAMILIAR EPISTLE TO MR. JULIAN SECRETARY OF THE MUSES

[A satire with this title, mainly directed against Sir Carr Scrope, is printed under Dryden's name in *The Sixth Part of Miscellany Poems,* 1716. It was first published independently, as a folio sheet, undated but as early as 1679, under the heading, *An Exclamation against Julian, Secretary to the Muses: with the Character of a Libeller. By a Person of Quality.* It was printed anonymously in *Poems on Affairs of State,* vol. iii, 1704. It was included in *Miscellaneous Works written by his Grace, George, late Duke of Buckingham,* 1705–07, vol. ii. It may be found in Dryden, *Works,* ed. Scott-Saintsbury, xv. 214–219. The style is unlike Dryden's, and the following couplet can scarcely have been written by him: —

Less art thou help'd by Dryden's bedrid age;
That drone has lost his sting upon the stage.]

OF A NOBLE RACE WAS SHENKIN

[A song by D'Urfey with this title has been attributed to Dryden: see *Notes and Queries,* series III. xi (1867), 316, 348. C. L. Day and E. B. Murray, in *English Song-Books, 1651–1702* (London, 1940), give the title (first line) as *Of noble race was Shinken;* and say that the song was first printed in *Thesaurus Musicus,* 1693, and reprinted in *Wit and Mirth; or, Pills to Purge Melancholy,* 1699.]

TO MATILDA

ON THE ANNIVERSARY OF OUR MARRIAGE

[In the Aldine edition of Dryden (London, 1832–33), vol. v, p. 317, there is found under this title a poem of eighteen lines, beginning, "When first in all thy youthful charms," which was reprinted in later Aldine editions. It was taken from *Tixall Poetry,* pp. 374, 375, and was really written by Arthur Clifford, the editor of that volume. On *Tixall Poetry* see headnote, pp. 906, 907.]

APPENDIX II

TRANSLATIONS FROM VIRGIL INCLUDED IN SYLVÆ (THE SECOND MISCELLANY), 1685

[The following episodes from the *Æneid,* first published in *Sylvæ,* 1685 (compare headnote, page 175), Dryden thoroughly recast when he made his complete translation of Virgil. In the texts printed below, lines which Dryden later retained unchanged are inclosed in brackets; those which he retained with minor changes are marked with a single bracket; those which he entirely rewrote are left unmarked. In *The Episode of Mezentius and Lausus,* which Dryden changed comparatively little in rewriting, passages which he left intact are indicated merely by the numbers of the lines in the later text.]

THE ENTIRE EPISODE OF NISUS AND EURYALUS, TRANSLATED FROM THE FIFTH AND NINTH BOOKS OF VIRGIL'S ÆNEIDS

[See pages 583, 584, lines 373–475, and pages 641–646, lines 221–600.]

Connection of the first part of the Episode in the Fifth Book with the rest of the foregoing poem.

Æneas having buried his father Anchises in Sicily, and setting sail from thence in search of Italy, is driven by a storm on the same coasts from whence he departed. After a year's wand'ring, he is hospitably received by his friend Acestes, king of that part of the island, who was born of Trojan parentage. He applies himself to celebrate the memory of his father with divine honors, and accordingly institutes funeral games, and appoints prizes for those who should conquer in them. One of these games was a foot race, in which Nisus and Euryalus were engag'd amongst other Trojans and Sicilians.

[FROM thence his way the Trojan hero bent]
[Into a grassy plain, with mountains pent,
[Whose brows were shaded with surrounding wood.
[Full in the midst of this fair valley stood]
[A native theater, which, rising slow]
[By just degrees, o'erlook'd the ground below.]
[A numerous train attend in solemn state;]
[High on the new-rais'd turf their leader sate.
[Here those who in the rapid race delight,
[Desire of honor and the prize invite.]   10
The Trojans and Sicilians mingled stand,
With Nisus and Euryalus, the foremost of the band:
Euryalus with youth and beauty crown'd,
[Nisus, for friendship to the boy renown'd.
[Diores next, of Priam's regal race,
[Then Salius, join'd with Patron, took his place;
But from Epirus one deriv'd his birth,
The other ow'd it to Arcadian earth:
[Then two Sicilian youths—the name of this   20
[Was Helymus, of that was Panopes;
[Two jolly huntsmen in the forest bred,
[And owning old Acestes for their head;]
[With many others of obscurer name,
[Whom time has not deliver'd o'er to fame.]
To these Æneas in the midst arose,
And pleasingly did thus his mind expose:
"Not one of you shall unrewarded go;
On each I will two Cretan spears bestow,
Pointed with polish'd steel; a battle-ax too,   30
With silver studded: these in common share;
[The foremost three shall olive garlands wear.
The victor, who shall first the race obtain,
Shall for his prize a well-breath'd courser gain,
[Adorn'd with trappings; to the next in fame,
[The quiver of an Amazonian dame,]
[With feather'd Thracian arrows well supplied,]
Hung on a golden belt, and with a jewel tied;
[The third this Grecian helmet must content."
[He said. To their appointed base they went;]
[With beating hearts th' expected sign receive,]
[And, starting all at once, the station leave.   41
[Spread out, as on the wings of winds they flew,

[And seiz'd the distant goal with eager view.
[Shot from the crowd, swift Nisus all o'er-pass'd;]
[Not storms, nor thunder, equal half his haste.
[The next, but, tho' the next, yet far disjoin'd,]
[Came Salius; then, a distant space behind,
Euryalus the third:
[Next Helymus, whom young Diores plied,
[Step after step, and almost side by side,] 50
[His shoulders pressing; and, in longer space,]
[Had won, or left at least a doubtful race.
    [Now, spent, the goal they almost reach at last,]
[When eager Nisus, hapless in his haste,]
[Slipp'd first, and, slipping, fell upon the plain,]
[Moist with the blood of oxen lately slain.
[The careless victor had not mark'd his way;]
[But, treading where the treacherous puddle lay,]
[His heels flew up, and on the grassy floor] 59
[He fell, besmear'd with filth and holy gore.]
[Nor mindless then, Euryalus, of thee,
[Nor of the sacred bonds of amity,]
[He strove th' immediate rival to oppose,
[And caught the foot of Salius as he rose.]
[So Salius lay extended on the plain;]
[Euryalus springs out, the prize to gain,]
[And cuts the crowd: applauding peals attend
[The conqu'ror to the goal, who conquer'd thro' his friend.
[Next Helymus; and then Diores came,]
[By two misfortunes now the third in fame. 70
    [But Salius enters, and, exclaiming loud]
[For justice, deafens and disturbs the crowd;]
[Urges his cause may in the court be heard;]
[And pleads the prize is wrongfully conferr'd.]
[But favor for Euryalus appears;]
[His blooming beauty and his graceful tears
[Had brib'd the judges to protect his claim;
[Besides, Diores does as loud exclaim,
[Who vainly reaches at the last reward,]
[If the first palm on Salius be conferr'd.]   80
[Then thus the prince: "Let no disputes arise;]
[Where Fortune plac'd it, I award the prize.]
[But give me leave her errors to amend,
[At least to pity a deserving friend."
Thus having said,
A lion's hide, amazing to behold,
[Pond'rous with bristles, and with paws of gold,
He gave the youth; which Nisus griev'd to view. —
[" If such rewards to vanquish'd men are due,"]
[Said he, "and falling is to rise by you,   90
[What prize may Nisus from your bounty claim,]
[Who merited the first rewards and fame?]
[In falling, both did equal fortune try;
[Would Fortune make me fall as happily!"
[With this he pointed to his face, and show'd]
[His hands and body all besmear'd with blood.
[Th' indulgent father of the people smil'd,]
[And caus'd to be produc'd a massy shield,
[Of wondrous art, by Didymaon wrought,]
[Long since from Neptune's bars in triumph brought:]   100

With this, the graceful youth he gratified;
Then the remaining presents did divide.

Connection of the remaining part of the Episode,
translated out of the Ninth Book of Virgil's *Æneids*,
with the foregoing part of the story.

The war being now broken out betwixt the Trojans and
Latins, and Æneas being overmatch'd in numbers by
his enemies, who were aided by King Turnus, he fortifies his camp, and leaves in it his young son Ascanius, under the direction of his chief counselors and
captains, while he goes in person to beg succors from
King Evander and the Tuscans. Turnus takes advantage of his absence, and assaults his camp. The Trojans in it are reduc'd to great extremities, which
gives the poet the occasion of continuing this admirable episode, wherein he describes the friendship, the generosity, the adventures, and the death of
Nisus and Euryalus.

The Trojan camp the common danger shar'd;
By turns they watch'd the walls, and kept the
          nightly guard.
To warlike Nisus fell the gate by lot,
Whom Hyrtacus on huntress Ida got,
And sent to sea Æneas to attend:
[Well could he dart the spear, and shafts
          unerring send.
[Beside him stood Euryalus, his ever faithful
          friend:
No youth in all the Trojan host was seen 110
More beautiful in arms, or of a nobler mien —
[Scarce was the down upon his chin begun.
[One was their friendship, their desire was one;
With minds united in the field they warr'd,
[And now were both by choice upon the guard.]
          [Then Nisus thus:
["Or do the gods this warlike warmth inspire,
[Or makes each man a god of his desire?
[A noble ardor boils within my breast,
[Eager of action, enemy of rest;   120
[That urges me to fight, or undertake
Some deed that may my fame immortal make.
[Thou see'st the foe secure; how faintly shine]
[Their scatter'd fires! the most, in sleep supine,]
Dissolv'd in ease, and drunk with victory;
[The few awake the fuming flagon ply:
[All hush'd around. Now hear what I revolve]
Within my mind, and what my laboring
          thoughts resolve.
[Our absent lord both camp and council mourn;
[By message both would hasten his return:] 130
[The gifts propos'd if they confer on thee,
[(For fame is recompense enough to me,)
[Methinks, beneath yon hill, I have espied]
[A way that safely will my passage guide."]
          [Euryalus stood list'ning while he spoke,
[With love of praise and noble envy strook;
[Then to his ardent friend expos'd his mind:]
[" All this, alone, and leaving me behind!]
[Am I unworthy, Nisus, to be join'd?] 139
[Think'st thou my share of honor I will yield,
[Or send thee unassisted to the field?]
[Not so my father taught my childhood arms;]
[Born in a siege, and bred amongst alarms!
[Nor is my youth unworthy of my friend,]
[Or of the heav'n-born hero I attend.
[The thing call'd life with ease I can disclaim,]
[And think it over-sold to purchase fame."]

To whom his friend:
["I could not think, alas, thy tender years
[Would minister new matter to my fears;] 150
Nor is it just thou shouldst thy wish obtain —
So Jove in triumph bring me back again
To those dear eyes; or if a god there be
To pious friends propitious more than he!
[But if some one — as many sure there are
Of adverse accidents in doubtful war —
[If one should reach my head, there let it fall,]
[And spare thy life; I would not perish all.]
[Thy youth is worthy of a longer date:
[Do thou remain to mourn thy lover's fate, 160
[To bear my mangled body from the foe,]
[Or buy it back, and fun'ral rites bestow;]
[Or, if hard fortune shall my corpse deny
Those dues, with empty marble to supply.
[O let not me the widow's tears renew!]
[Let not a mother's curse my name pursue;
[Thy pious mother, who, in love to thee,
[Left the fair coast of fruitful Sicily,
[Her age committing to the seas and wind,]
[When every weary matron stay'd behind."]
[To this, Euryalus: "Thou plead'st in vain, 171
[And but delay'st the cause thou canst not
          gain.
[No more! 'tis loss of time." With that he
          wakes
[The nodding watch: each to his office takes.]
[The guard reliev'd, in company they went
[To find the council at the royal tent.]
    Now every living thing lay void of care,
[And sleep, the common gift of nature, share:]
[Meantime the Trojan peers in council sate,
And call'd their chief commanders, to de-
          bate   180
[The weighty business of th' indanger'd
          state;
What next was to be done, who to be sent
T' inform Æneas of the foes' intent.
In midst of all the quiet camp they held
Nocturnal council; each sustains a shield
Which his o'er-labor'd arm can hardly rear,
And leans upon a long projected spear.
[Now Nisus and his friend approach the
          guard,]
[And beg admittance, eager to be heard:
[Th' affair important, not to be deferr'd.] 190
[Ascanius bids them be conducted in;
Then thus, commanded, Nisus does begin:
[" Ye Trojan fathers, lend attentive ears;
[Nor judge our undertaking by our years.
[The foes, securely drench'd in sleep and wine,
[Their watch neglect; their fires but thinly
          shine;
[And, where the smoke in thick'ning vapors
          flies,
[Cov'ring the plain, and clouding all the skies,
Betwixt the spaces we have mark'd a way,
Close by the gate, and coasting by the sea. 200
This passage undisturb'd, and unespied,
Our steps will safely to Æneas guide:
[Expect each hour to see him back again,]
[Loaded with spoils of foes in battle slain.]
[Snatch we the lucky minute while we may,]
[Nor can we be mistaken in the way;]
[For, hunting in the vale, we oft have seen

[The rising turrets with the stream between,
[And know its winding course, with every ford.''
  [He paus'd; and old Alethes took the word:
["Our country gods, in whom our trust we
    place,] 211
[Will yet from ruin save the Trojan race,]
[While we behold such springing worth appear
[In youth so brave, and breasts so void of fear.''
With this he took the hand of either boy,
Embrac'd them closely both, and wept for joy:
[" Ye brave young men, what equal gifts can
    we,]
[What recompense for such desert, decree!
[The greatest, sure, and best you can receive,]
[The gods, your virtue, and your fame will
    give. 220
[The rest our grateful general will bestow,]
[And young Ascanius till his manhood owe."]
  [" And I, whose welfare in my father lies,"]
[Ascanius adds, " by all the deities,
[By our great country, and our household gods,
[By hoary Vesta's rites and dark abodes,]
[Adjure you both (on you my fortune stands;]
[That and my faith I plight into your hands),]
[Make me but happy in his safe return,] 229
(For I no other loss but only his can mourn,)
[Nisus, your gift shall two large goblets be,
[Of silver, wrought with curious imagery,]
[And high emboss'd, which, when old Priam
    reign'd,]
[My conquering sire at sack'd Arisba gain'd;]
[And more, two tripods cast in antique mold,]
[With two great talents of the finest gold;]
[Besides a bowl which Tyrian art did grave,
The present that Sidonian Dido gave.
[But if in conquer'd Italy we reign,] 239
[When spoils by lot the victors shall obtain —
[Thou saw'st the courser by proud Turnus
    press'd;]
[That, and his golden arms, and sanguine crest,
[And shield, from lot exempted, thou shalt
    share:
[With these, twelve captive dam'sels young
    and fair;
Male slaves as many, well appointed all
With vests and arms, shall to thy portion fall;
And last, a fruitful field to thee shall rest,
The large demesnes the Latian king possess'd.
[But thou, whose years are more to mine al-
    lied —]
[No fate my vow'd affection shall divide] 250
[From thee, O wondrous youth! Be ever mine;
[Take full possession; all my soul is thine.]
[My life's companion, and my bosom friend,
[One faith, one fame, one fate, shall both at-
    tend.
[My peace shall be committed to thy care,]
[And to thy conduct my concerns in war."
  [Then thus the bold Euryalus replied:
[" Whatever fortune, good or bad, betide,]
[The same shall be my age, as now my youth;]
[No time shall find me wanting to my truth.]
[This only from your bounty let me gain 261
[(And this not granted, all rewards are vain):
[Of Priam's royal race my mother came —]
[And sure the best that ever bore the name —]
[Whom neither Troy nor Sicily could hold]

[From me departing, but, o'erspent and old,]
[My fate she follow'd. Ignorant of this]
[(Whatever) danger, neither parting kiss,]
[Nor pious blessing taken, her I leave,]
[And in this only act of all my life deceive.] 270
[By this your hand and conscious Night I
    swear,
[My youth so sad a farewell could not bear.
[Be you her patron; fill my vacant place
[(Permit me to presume so great a grace);]
[Support her age, forsaken and distress'd.]
[That hope alone will fortify my breast]
[Against the worst of fortunes, and of fears."]
[He said. Th' assistants shed presaging tears;
But, above all, Ascanius, mov'd to see
[That image of paternal piety. 280
  Then thus replied:
[" So great beginnings, in so green an age,]
[Exact that faith which firmly I engage.
[Thy mother all the privilege shall claim
[Creüsa had, and only want the name.]
[Whate'er event thy enterprise shall have,
['T is merit to have borne a son so brave.]
[By this my head, a sacred oath, I swear,]
[(My father us'd it,) what, returning here]
[Crown'd with success, I for thyself prepare,]
Thy parent and thy family shall share." 291
  [He said, and weeping, while he spoke the
    word,]
[From his broad belt he drew a shining sword,]
[Magnificent with gold. Lycaon made,]
[And in an iv'ry scabbard sheath'd the blade.]
[This was his gift; while Mnestheus did pro-
    vide,
For Nisus' arms, a grisly lion's hide,
[And true Alethes chang'd with him hi. helm
    of temper tried.
  [Thus arm'd they went. The noble Trojans
    wait]
[Their going forth, and follow to the gate 300
[With pray'rs and vows. Above the rest
    appears]
[Ascanius, manly far above his years,
[And messages committed to their care,]
[Which all in winds were lost, and empty air.
  [The trenches first they pass'd; then took
    their way]
[Where their proud foes in pitch'd pavilions
    lay;]
[To many fatal, e'er themselves were slain.]
[The careless host dispers'd upon the plain
[They found, who, drunk with wine, supinely
    snore. 309
[Unharness'd chariots stand upon the shore;
['Midst wheels and reins, and arms, the goblet
    by,
[A medley of debauch and war, they lie.]
[Observing Nisus shew'd his friend the sight;]
[Then thus: " Behold a conquest without fight!
[Occasion calls the sword to be prepar'd;
[Our way lies there: stand thou upon the
    guard,
[And look behind, while I securely go
[To cut an ample passage thro' the foe."
[Softly he spoke; then stalking took his way,
[With his drawn sword, where haughty Rham-
    nes lay:] 320

[His head rais'd high on tapestry beneath,]
[And heaving from his breast, he puff'd his
breath;
[A king and prophet, by King Turnus lov'd:]
[But fate by prescience cannot be remov'd.]
[Three sleeping slaves he soon subdues; then
spies
[Where Remus, with his proud retinue, lies.
[His armor-bearer first, and next he kills]
[His charioteer, entrench'd betwixt the wheels]
[And his lov'd horses; last invades their lord;]
[Full on his neck he aims the fatal sword: 330
[The gasping head flies off; a purple flood]
[Flows from the trunk, that wallows in the
blood,
[Which, by the spurning heels dispers'd
around,]
[The bed besprinkles and bedews the ground.]
Then Lamyrus with Lamus and the young
Serranus, who with gaming did prolong
The night: oppress'd with wine and slumber ⎫
lay
[The beauteous youth, and dreamt of lucky ⎬
play —
[More lucky, had it been protracted till the ⎭
day.
[The famish'd lion thus, with hunger bold,] 340
[O'erleaps the fences of the nightly fold,]
[The peaceful flock devours, and tears, and
draws:
[Wrapp'd up in silent fear, they lie and pant
beneath his paws.
[Nor with less rage Euryalus imploys]
[The vengeful sword, nor fewer foes destroys;
[But on th' ignoble crowd his fury flew,]
[Which Fadus, Hebesus, and Rhœtus slew,
With Abaris: in sleep the rest did fall,
[But Rhœtus waking, and observing all.
[Behind a mighty jar he slunk for fear; 350
[The sharp-edg'd iron found and reach'd him
there:
[Full as he rose he plung'd it in his side;
[The cruel sword return'd in crimson dyed.
[The wound a blended stream of wine and
blood
[Pours out; the purple soul comes floating in
the flood.
[Now, where Messapus quarter'd, they ar-
rive.]
[The fires were fainting there, and just alive;]
[The warlike horses, tied in order, fed.
[Nisus the discipline observ'd, and said:
["Our eagerness of blood may both betray; 360
[Behold the doubtful glimmering of the day,
[Foe to these nightly thefts. No more, my
friend;
[Here let our glutted execution end.]
[A lane thro' slaughter'd bodies we have
made."]
[The bold Euryalus, tho' loth, obey'd.]
Rich arms and arras, which they scatter'd find,
[And plate, a precious load, they leave behind.
[Yet, fond of gaudy spoils, the boy would stay]
[To make the proud caparisons his prey,
Which deck'd a neighb'ring steed. 370
[Nor did his eyes less longingly behold]
[The girdle, studded o'er with nails of gold,

Which Rhamnes wore. This present long ago
On Remulus did Cædicus bestow,
[And, absent, join'd in hospitable ties:]
[He, dying, to his heir bequeath'd the prize;]
[Till, by the conquering Rutuli oppress'd,
[He fell, and they the glorious gift possess'd.]
These gaudy spoils Euryalus now bears,
And vainly on his brawny shoulders wears: 380
[Messapus' helm he found amongst the dead,
Garnish'd with plumes, and fitted to his head.
[They leave the camp, and take the safest
road.
Meantime a squadron of their foes abroad,
Three hundred horse with bucklers arm'd,
they spied,
Whom Volscens by the king's command did
guide.
To Turnus these were from the city sent,
And to perform their message sought his
tent.
Approaching, near their utmost lines they
draw;
When, bending tow'rds the left, their captain
saw 390
[The faithful pair; for, thro' the doubtful ⎫
shade,
[His glitt'ring helm Euryalus betray'd, ⎬
[On which the moon with full reflection ⎭
play'd.]
["'T is not for naught," cried Volscens from
the crowd,]
["These men go there"; then rais'd his voice
aloud:]
["Stand! stand! why thus in arms? And
whether bent?]
[From whence, to whom, and on what errand
sent?"]
[Silent they make away, and haste their flight
[To neighb'ring woods, and trust themselves
to night.]
The speedy horsemen spur their steeds to
get 400
'Twixt them and home; and every path beset,
And all the windings of the well-known wood.
[Black was the brake, and thick with oak it
stood,
[With fern all horrid, and perplexing thorn,
Where tracks of bears had scarce a passage
worn.
[The darkness of the shades, his heavy prey,]
[And fear, misled the younger from his way.]
[But Nisus hit the turns with happier haste,]
Who now, unknowing, had the danger pass'd,
[And Alban lakes, from Alba's name so
call'd, 410
[Where King Latinus then his oxen stall'd;]
[Till, turning at the length, he stood his
ground,]
[And vainly cast his longing eyes around
For his lost friend!
["Ah wretch!" he cried, "where have I left
behind?]
[Where shall I hope th' unhappy youth to
find?
[Or what way take?" Again he ventures
back,]
[And treads the mazes of his former track]

Thro' the wild wood; at last he hears the noise
[Of trampling horses, and the riders' voice. 420
[The sound approach'd; and suddenly he view'd]
[His foes inclosing, and his friend pursued,
[Forelaid and taken, while he strove in vain]
[The covert of the neighb'ring wood to gain.
[What should he next attempt? what arms employ,]
[With fruitless force to free the captive boy?
Or tempt unequal numbers with the sword,
And die by him whom living he ador'd?
[Resolv'd on death, his dreadful spear he shook;
[And, casting to the moon a mournful look: 430 ⎫
"Fair queen," said he, "who dost in woods delight, ⎪
[Grace of the stars, and goddess of the ⎬
night, ⎪
[Be present, and direct my dart aright. ⎭
[If e'er my pious father, for my sake,]
[Did on thy altars grateful offerings make,
[Or I increas'd them with successful toils,
[And hung thy sacred roof with savage spoils,
Thro' the brown shadows guide my flying spear
To reach this troop." Then, poising from his ear, 439
The quiv'ring weapon with full force he threw.
Thro' the divided shades the deadly javelin flew;
On Sulmo's back it splits; the double dart
Drove deeper onward, and transfix'd his heart.
[He staggers round; his eyeballs roll in death,]
[And with short sobs he gasps away his breath.]
[All stand amaz'd — a second javelin flies]
From his stretch'd arm, and hisses thro' the skies.
[The lance thro' Tagus' temples forc'd its way,
[And in his brainpan warmly buried lay.
[Fierce Volscens foams with rage, and gazing round,] 450
[Descried no author of the fatal wound,
[Nor where to fix revenge: "But thou," he cries,
["Shalt pay for both," and at the pris'ner flies]
[With his drawn sword. Then, struck with deep despair,]
[That fatal sight the lover could not bear;
[But from his covert rush'd in open view,]
[And sent his voice before him as he flew:]
["Me, me, employ your sword on me alone:
[The crime confess'd; the fact was all my own.
[He neither could nor durst, the guiltless youth:] 460
[Ye moon and stars, bear witness to the truth!]
[His only fault (if that be to offend)
[Was too much loving his unhappy friend."
[Too late, alas, he speaks:
[The sword, which unrelenting fury guides,
[Driv'n with full force, had pierc'd his tender sides.]
[Down fell the beauteous youth: the gaping wound
[Gush'd out a crimson stream, and stain'd the ground.

[His nodding neck reclines on his white breast,
[Like a fair flow'r, in furrow'd fields oppress'd
By the keen share; or poppy on the plain, 471
[Whose heavy head is overcharg'd with rain.]
[Disdain, despair, and deadly vengeance vow'd,
[Drove Nisus headlong on the hostile crowd.]
[Volscens he seeks; at him alone he bends:
[Borne back, and push'd by his surrounding friends,
[He still press'd on, and kept him still in sight;
[Then whirl'd aloft his sword with all his might:]
Th' unerring weapon flew; and, wing'd with death,
Enter'd his gaping mouth and stopp'd his breath. 480
[Dying, he slew; and, stagg'ring on the plain,]
[Sought for the body of his lover slain;
[Then quietly on his dear breast he fell,
[Content, in death, to be reveng'd so well.]
[O happy pair! for, if my verse can give
[Eternity, your fame shall ever live,
[Fix'd as the Capitol's foundation lies,]
[And spread, where'er the Roman eagle flies.

THE ENTIRE EPISODE OF MEZENTIUS
AND LAUSUS, TRANSLATED OUT OF
THE TENTH BOOK OF VIRGIL'S
ÆNEIDS

[See pages 667–671, lines 1071–1313.]

Connection of the Episode with the foregoing story.

Mezentius was King of Etruria, or Tuscany, from whence he was expell'd by his subjects, for his tyrannical government and cruelty, and a new king elected. Being thus banish'd, he applies himself to King Turnus, in whose court he and his son Lausus take sanctuary. Turnus for the love of Lavinia making war with Æneas, Mezentius ingages in the cause of his benefactor, and performs many great actions, particularly in revenging himself on his late subjects, who now assisted Æneas, out of hatred to him. Mezentius is everywhere describ'd by Virgil as an atheist; his son Lausus is made the pattern of filial piety and virtue; and the death of those two is the subject of this noble episode.

[THUS equal deaths are dealt, and equal chance;
[1072–74]
[The gods from heav'n survey the doubtful strife,
[1077–79]
[Her scourge aloft, and hissing crest of snakes.
[Once more Mezentius, with a proud disdain,
[1082–83]
[Like vast Orion stalking o'er the flood.
[1085–88]
Thus arm'd, he took the field.
[The Trojan prince beheld him from afar,]
With joyful eyes, and undertook the war. 20
[Collected in himself, and like a rock,
[Pois'd on his base, Mezentius stood the shock]
Of his great foe. Then, measuring with his eyes

[The space his spear could reach, aloud he
    cries:]
["My own right hand, and sword, assist my
    stroke!
        [1096-97]
[Shall by my Lausus be in triumph worn."
[He said; and straight with all his force he
    threw   29
        [1100-14]
[All these it pass'd with unresisted course,
        [1116-20]
    [His father's danger Lausus view'd with
        grief;   51
[He sigh'd, he wept, he ran to his relief.]
[And here, O wondrous youth, 't is here I must
        [1124-25]
[Posterity shall scarce believe it true.
        [1127-30]
[The pious youth, resolv'd to undergo   61 ⎤
[The lifted sword, springs out to face his foe, ⎬
[Protects his father, and prevents the blow. ⎦
        [1134-35]
[All, fir'd with noble emulation, strive,
        [1137-54]
[For now the Fates prepar'd their cruel shears;
[And lifted high the conquering sword ap-
    pears,
[Which, full descending with a fearful sway, ⎤
[Thro' shield and cuirass forc'd th' impetu- ⎬
    ous way,   ⎭
[And buried deep in his fair bosom lay.] ⎦
[The springing streams thro' the thin armor
    strove,   90
[And drench'd the golden coat his careful
    mother wove;
        [1162-63]
    [But when, with blood and paleness all be-
        spread,
        [1165-67]
[Then stretch'd his hand to raise him up,   98
        [1169-76]
[To please thy ghost, at least, if shadows
    know,
[Or have a taste of human things below.
        [1179-80]
[With this, he bids his distant friends draw
    near,   111
[Provokes their duty, and prevents their fear:]
[Himself assists to raise him from the ground;
[His locks deform'd with blood, that well'd
    from out his wound.
[Meantime, the father, now no father, stood,
        [1186-87]
[His fainting limbs against a tree he leant.
        [1189-90]
[Of youth a chosen troop around him stand; 121
[His head hung down, and rested on his hand:
        [1193-95]
[Much he enquir'd, and many a message sent
        [1197-98]
[On their broad shields! Still gush'd the gap-
    ing wound,   129
        [1200-03]
[Then both his lifted arms to heav'n he spread;
        [1205-18]
[With less injustice could have borne my
    fate.

[And yet I live, and yet support the sight   150
[Of hateful men, and of more hated light!
        [1222-29]
[The horse seem'd sensible, while thus he
    spoke: 160
["O Rhœbus, we have liv'd too long for
    me —]
[If long and life were terms that could agree!
        [1233-44]
[With crested horsehair, nodding from afar;
        [1246-52]
["Great Jove," said he, "and the far-shoot-
    ing god,
[Inspire thy mind to make thy challenge
    good!"]
[He said no more; but hasten'd to appear,
        [1256-59]
This was my only way to be undone.   190
        [1261-72]
[To wrench the darts that in his buckler
    light,
[Urg'd and o'er-labor'd in unequal fight,]
[At last resolv'd, he throws with all his force
[Full at the temples of the warlike horse.
Betwixt the temples pass'd th' unerring spear,
[And, piercing, stood transfix'd from ear to
    ear.
[Seiz'd with the sudden pain, surpris'd with
    fright,   209
The courser bounds aloft and stands upright:
He beats his hoofs a while in air; then, press'd ⎤
With anguish, floundering falls the gen'rous ⎬
    beast,   ⎭
And his cast rider with his weight oppress'd.] ⎦
        [1287-93]
[With scarce recover'd breath, he thus re-
    plies:
["Why these insulting threats, this waste of
    breath,   222
        [1296-98]
But, with a glorious fate, to end my pain:
When Lausus fell, I was already slain.
[Nor ask I life:
[My dying son contracted no such band,]
[Nor would I take it from his murd'rer's hand.
[For this, this only favor let me sue,]   231
[If pity to a conquer'd foe be due:
[Refuse not that; but let my body have
[The last retreat of humankind, a grave.]
[Too well I know my injur'd people's hate;
        [1308-13]

THE SPEECH OF VENUS TO VULCAN

WHEREIN SHE PERSUADES HIM TO MAKE ARMS
FOR HER SON ÆNEAS, THEN ENGAG'D IN A
WAR AGAINST THE LATINS AND KING TUR-
NUS: TRANSLATED OUT OF THE EIGHTH
BOOK OF VIRGIL'S ÆNEIDS
    [See pages 631, 632, lines 484-538.]
Now Night with sable wings the world o'er-
    spread;
But Venus, not in vain, surpris'd with dread
Of Latian arms, before the tempest breaks,
Her husband's timely succor thus bespeaks,

[Couch'd in his golden bed;
[And, that her pleasing speech his mind may move,]
[Inspires it with diviner charms of love:
["While adverse fate conspir'd with Grecian pow'rs,
[To level with the ground the Trojan tow'rs,]
[I begg'd no aid th' unhappy to restore, 10
[Nor did thy succor, nor thy art implore;
[Nor sought, their sinking empire to sustain,
[To urge the labor of my lord in vain,
[Tho' much I ow'd to Priam's house, and more]
[The dangers of Æneas did deplore.]
[But now, by Jove's command, and fate's decree,]
[His race is doom'd to reign in Italy:]
[With humble suit I ask thy needful art,
[O still propitious pow'r, O sovereign of my heart!
[A mother stands a suppliant for a son. 20
[By silver-footed Thetis thou wert won
For fierce Achilles, and the rosy Morn
Mov'd thee with arms her Memnon to adorn.
Are these my tears less pow'rful on thy mind?
[Behold, what warlike nations are combin'd
[With fire and sword *my* people to destroy,]
And twice to triumph over *me* and Troy."
[She said; and straight her arms, of snowy hue,]
[About her unresolving husband threw.]

[Her soft embraces soon infuse desire;] 30
[His bones and marrow sudden warmth inspire;]
[And all the godhead feels the wonted fire.]
[Not half so swift the rolling thunder flies,
[Or streaks of lightning flash along the skies.
[The goddess, pleas'd with her successful wiles,
[And conscious of her conqu'ring beauty, smiles.
  [Then thus the good old god, sooth'd with her charms,
[Panting, and half dissolving in her arms:]
["Why seek you reasons for a cause so just,]
[Or your own beauty or my love distrust? 40
[Long since, had you requir'd my helpful hand,]
[You might the artist and his art command,
To arm your Trojans: nor did Jove or fate
[Confine their empire to so short a date.
[And, if you now desire new wars to wage,]
[My care, my skill, my labor I ingage.
[Whatever melting metals can conspire,]
[Or breathing bellows, or the forming fire,]
I freely promise: all your doubts remove,
[And think no task is difficult to love."] 50
[He said; and, eager to enjoy her charms,
[He snatch'd the lovely goddess to his arms;
[Till, all infus'd in joy, he lay possess'd
[Of full desire, and sunk to pleasing rest.]

NOTES

NOTES

The following Notes are to a considerable extent taken from Sir Walter Scott, whose edition of Dryden, first published in 1808, has become an English classic. The text printed in Professor Saintsbury's revision of Scott's edition (London and Edinburgh, 1882–93) has been used as a basis. When a note is taken from Scott with no change whatever, it is inclosed in quotation marks and his name is added. When Scott's note has been modified by the omission, alteration, or addition of even a single word, quotation marks are retained, but the name is inclosed in brackets [SCOTT]. When the note has been entirely rewritten, quotation marks are omitted, but the name, in brackets, is retained. The same notation is used for the comments, comparatively few in number, that have been taken from other critics.

Variant readings of Dryden's text are cited in the original spelling, punctuation, and capitals. Quotations from other authors of the seventeenth and eighteenth centuries, however, are usually given in modern spelling. Frequent references are made to the following works : —

The Critical and Miscellaneous Prose Works of John Dryden, edited by Edmond Malone, London, 1800. References to this work here, and in the headnotes throughout the volume, are in the form, "Malone, I, 1, 69; " i. e. vol. i. part i. page 69.

The Poetical Works of John Dryden, edited by W. D. Christie (Globe edition). (Unless otherwise specified, references to *Christie* are to this edition.)

Select Poems by Dryden, edited by W. D. Christie and C. H. Firth, ed. 5, Oxford, 1893.

The Satires of Dryden, edited by John Churton Collins, London, 1905.

Dryden : The Hind and the Panther, edited by W. H. Williams, London, 1900.

Essays of John Dryden, edited by W. P. Ker, Oxford, 1900.

In the headnotes throughout the volume there are many references to the *Term Catalogues*, as edited by Professor Arber, London, 1903–06. An expression such as "*Term Catalogue* for Easter Term (May), 1677" [p. 78], indicates that the *Catalogue* in question was itself published in May.

The system of reference in the following Notes and in the Glossary is as follows : the numbers go in pairs, in which the first (of heavier type) stands for the page, the second for the line on that page. When needed, an exponent indicates the column of the page. Thus **111**, 163 = page 111, line 163; **127¹**, 35 = page 127, column 1, line 35.

The following abbreviations are used : —

Arg. = argument.
B. S. = Biographical Sketch.
C. = Christie's Globe edition of Dryden.
C. D. = Century Dictionary.
CF. = Christie and Firth's *Select Poems by Dryden.*
cf. = compare.
D. N. B. = Dictionary of National Biography.
E. D. D. = English Dialect Dictionary.
Epil. = Epilogue.
f. = and the following.

l. = line.
ll. = lines.
N. E. D. = New English Dictionary.
p. = page.
pp. = pages.
Prol. = Prologue.
SS. = Scott-Saintsbury edition of Dryden.
v. = see.
v. n. = see note on.
v. n. **223**, 410 = see note on **223**, 410; *v.* **223**, 410, *n.* = see **223**, 410, and note.

GENERAL NOTES

DRYDEN'S RHYMES. For extended discussions of this topic, see A. J. ELLIS, *Early English Pronunciation*, pp. 1033–1039; DIERBERGER, *John Dryden's Reime*, Freiburg i. Br., 1895. The reader may find it useful to remember that, according to the pronunciation of the later seventeenth century, rhymes of the following types, among many others, that seem peculiar to a modern ear, were nearly or quite perfect : —

war : far ; **206**, 169.
hand : wand ; **765**, 460.
brought : fault ; **867**, 223.
draught : ought ; **236**, 1417.
desert : art ; **116**, 559.
garment : preferment ; **417**, 21.

wreck : back ; **187**, 244.
serv'd : starv'd ; **248**, 2268.
sea : way ; **27**, 42; cf. **850**, 360, **n.**
key : way ; **794**, 133.
foil'd : child ; **191**, 218.
coin : line ; **237**, 1449.

CHANGEABLE ACCENT OF ADJECTIVES. In Dryden there are numerous instances of "Schmidt's rule," according to which dissyllabic adjectives, normally accented on the second syllable, shift the accent to the first syllable when followed by a noun accented on the first syllable. Thus: *sub'lime soul,* **1**, 27; *di'vine progeny,* **2**, 104.

CORPSE. The usual spelling of this word in the early editions is *corps,* which is used both as a singular and as a plural: *v.* **780**, 911; **664**, 800. It may be construed as a plural (cf. *remains*) even when used of a single body: v. **243**, 1931. In the present volume *corpse* has been used as the singular and *corps* as the plural form.

NOTES ON TEXT.

1. Upon the Death of the Lord Hastings. v. B. S. xviii. Only the 1650 issue has been accessible to the present editor, who has depended on an account of the 1649 issue sent him from the British Museum.

27. *Orb.* Christie calls attention to parallel passages in *Stanzas on Cromwell*, *Absalom and Achitophel*, and *Eleonora:* v. **4**, 18; **120**, 838, 839; **274**, 272, 273.

43. *Tycho.* Tycho Brahe, the Danish astronomer (1546–1601), increased his reputation by the discovery of a *new star* in 1572.

14. *Others' beam.* Printed *others beam* in 1649 edition and *others Beam* in 1702 edition. C. and SS. insert no apostrophe and take *beam* as a verb.

2, 66. *Constellation.* Dryden occasionally employs, for the sake of rhyme, the archaic pronunciation of *-tion* as two syllables. Cf. **14**, 70; **54**[1], 2 (*Epil.*).

72. *Metempsuchosis.* So printed in the original edition. The word is here accented on the third syllable, as in Greek. Cf. **162**, 43, n.

81. *Three-legg'd graybeards.* The reference is of course to the riddle of the Sphinx. An old man's staff is his third leg.

82. *Achës.* Two syllables. In Dryden's time the noun *ache* was pronounced like the name of the letter " h."

84. *An antiquary's room.* The 1649 edition reads *an Antiquaries room ;* the 1702 edition omits *an ;* C. and SS. restore *an* but read *rooms.*

93. *O virgin-widow.* This refers to Hastings' betrothed, the daughter of Sir Theodore Turquet de Mayerne, a noted physician, who attended the young nobleman in his last illness. Mayerne's name is mentioned by other elegists in *Lachrymæ Musarum*, notably by Marvell.

97. *Platonic love.* This was a favorite subject of interest among the poets of the time: see an article by Professor J. B. Fletcher on " Précieuses at the Court of Charles I," in the *Journal of Comparative Literature*, i. 120–153. *Ideas* in l. 100 of course carries out the conceit; the *ideas* of Hastings' virtue, etc., would be, in the Platonic philosophy, their eternal archetypes. Cf. **6**, 103; **28**, 41.

3[1], 11. *Young eaglet.* Dryden alludes to the familiar story of the eagle, which mounts to heaven and renews its sight by gazing upon the sun. To it he gives a Puritanic flavor by his phrase *the Sun of Righteousness.*

20. *Helicon.* "Dryden confuses Helicon and Hippocrene. Helicon was a mount and not a fount." [Saintsbury.]

21. *Be.* On this use of *be* for *are*, cf. **11**, 22; **12**, 78. The form was already archaic in Dryden's time: in his *Defense of the Epilogue*

of The Conquest of Granada (published in 1672; v. SS. iv. 233) he condemns Ben Jonson for using it.

Letter to Madame Honor Dryden. On the date of this letter Malone makes the following comment: " Lest the date should too nearly discover her [Madame Honor's] age, the two latter figures have been almost obliterated, but the last numeral, when viewed through a microscope, is manifestly a 5; and that the other numeral, which, as being more material, was more carefully defaced, was not a 4, but a 5 also, may be collected not only from the lady's age, (for in 1645 she was probably not more than eight years old,) but from the time of our author's admission and residence at Cambridge." If this account be correct, it proves that Dryden continued at Cambridge after April, 1655, at which time Christie supposes that he had ceased to reside there: v. CF. pp. xv, xvi.

3[2], 11. *Persons.* That is, *parsons.* For the spelling, cf. *sterve*, *starve ; kerve*, *carve*, and the like. "An hour, measured by an hourglass fixed at the side of the pulpit, was the usual length of a sermon at this time." [Malone.]

4. Stanzas on Cromwell. The *Three Poems* text is the basis of the present edition, but its frequent italics are neglected, while the more sparing italics of the separate edition are usually preserved.

1. *And now 't is time.* Dryden apparently contrasts his own discretion in awaiting the time of Cromwell's funeral, with the haste of some other poets, who glorified him immediately after his death.

3. *Like eager Romans*, etc. An allusion to the Roman custom of letting fly from the funeral pyre of a deceased emperor an eagle, which was supposed to bear his soul to heaven. After that the emperor was worshiped among the other gods: v. Herodian, iv. 2. 11. [Scott.]

18. *A fame so truly circular.* The idea is a common one: v. **1**, 27, n. Christie quotes in illustration Horace's *fortis, et in se ipso totus, teres atque rotundus* (2 *Satires*, vii. 86), and Massinger's phrase, " Your wisdom is not circular" (*The Emperor of the East*, iii. 2. 9).

32. *Pompey.* "Pompey began to decline and Cromwell to rise at forty-five." Saintsbury.

5, 41. *Our former chiefs, like sticklers of the war*, etc. "Essex, Manchester, Sir William Waller, and the earlier generals of the Parliament, were all of the Presbyterian party, who, though they had drawn the sword against the king, had no will to throw away the scabbard. They were disposed so to carry on the war, that, neither party being too much weakened, a sound and honorable peace might have been accomplished on equal terms. Cromwell openly accused the Earl of Manchester of having refused to put an end to the war after the last battle at Newbury, when a single charge upon the King's rear might have dissipated his army for ever." [Scott.]

" Sticklers are seconds who first arrange a

fight, and then, if they can, part the combatants." [SAINTSBURY.]

48. *To stanch the blood by breathing of the vein.* The separate edition reads *stench*. On the meaning of *breathing*, cf. **336**, 65; **473**, 700. "This passage, which seems to imply nothing further than that Cromwell conducted the war so as to push it to a conclusion, was afterwards invidiously interpreted by Dryden's enemies as containing an explicit approbation of the execution of Charles I." [SCOTT.]

55. *Of conquests.* Christie construes this with *thick*, and compares *thick of bars* (**755**, 230). This seems a better interpretation than, following Saintsbury, to "take *of* with *maps*, and construe *thick* as an adverb with *strew'd.*"

56. *Is sown.* The separate edition reads *are sown*. This variant indicates that the separate edition is the older; Dryden later corrected his slip of grammar.

57. *His palms*, etc. Professor E. S. Parsons, in *Modern Language Notes*, xix. 47–49, gives for the first time a satisfactory explanation of this line. The idea that the palm, if loaded with heavy weights, does not give way, but grows with new vigor, is well known. In 1648–49 there had appeared a famous book, the *Eikon Basilike*, which was supposed to be by King Charles I, and to contain a "pourtraicture" of him "in his solitudes and sufferings." The frontispiece of this "represents Charles I in his royal robes, kneeling, . . . looking upward toward the heavenly crown, soon to be his. From a cloud in the background a beam of light shines out and rests on the king's head, . . . and two palms are disclosed, carrying heavy weights, with the motto: *Crescit sub Pondere Virtus.*" Cromwell's palms, though, unlike those of Charles, *under weights they did not stand, still thrived.* Cf. **17**, 151.

60. *And drew*, etc. Dryden's poems contain several references to the technique of painting: v. **6**, 94–96; **8**, 125–128; **414**, 41–44; **741²**, 44–49.

63. *Bologna's walls*, etc. During the siege of Bologna in 1512, according to a story told by Guicciardini, a mine was laid beneath a portion of the wall on which stood a chapel of the Virgin. When the mine was fired, the wall was blown into the air, so that through the breach the assailants could see the defenders, but a moment later it returned to its former place, as if it had never been moved.

66. *Treacherous Scotland.* The epithet probably refers rather to the general shifting course of the Scots during the Civil War than to any particular event.

71. *Influence . . . mien. Influence* is here used in its astrological sense, of the influence of the stars on human affairs. *Mien* is spelled *mine* in the *Three Poems* text, *mien* in the separate edition; perhaps the former spelling should be retained here, to mark the rhyme.

77, 78. *When past*, etc. These two lines are here punctuated as in the separate edition of 1659; the *Three Poems* text omits the comma

after *Jove*, and has commas after *depos'd* and *yield*. SS. and C. insert a comma after *when*, thereby making *depos'd* the verb of a subordinate clause. This certainly gives a better sense, but the change does not seem quite necessary.

Feretrian Jove. Pheretrian in the separate edition. To Jupiter Feretrius there were consecrated only the *spolia opima*, which were won but three times in Roman history. Dryden writes as if all spoils of war were offered to that divinity. As Christie points out, Dryden was apparently fond of the phrase, introducing it, without warrant from the Latin, into his translations of Juvenal and Virgil: v. **350**, 208; **609**, 1187.

84. *Her idol, gain.* Dryden loses no opportunity for expressing his hostility to the Dutch: see, for example, **233**, 1140–1147.

6, 90. *Mounsire.* The separate edition reads *Monsieur.*

91. *Where it was. Where e'er 't was* in the separate edition.

100. *Complexions.* The *complexion*, or temperament, was supposed to be determined by the mixture in the body of the four *humors*, blood, phlegm, choler, and melancholy.

103. *Ideas.* Cf. n. **2**, 97.

113. *He made us freemen*, etc. "The poet alludes to the exertions of the six thousand British auxiliaries whom Cromwell sent to join Marshal Turenne in Flanders. The English were made freemen of the continent by the cession of Dunkirk." [SCOTT.]

118. *Heard.* So the separate edition; the *Three Poems* text reads *har'd*, which perhaps should have been retained in the present edition.

120. *Alexander.* Alexander VII, pope from 1655 to 1667. "The thunder of his guns [those of Admiral Blake, cruising in the Mediterranean], every Puritan believed, would be heard in the castle of St. Angelo, and Rome itself would have to bow to the greatness of Cromwell." J. R. GREEN, *Short History of the English People*, ch. viii, § 10.

121. *By his command*, etc. "A powerful army and squadron were sent by Cromwell, 1654, under the command of Penn and Venables, to attack San Domingo. The main design misgave: they took, however, the island of Jamaica, whose importance long remained unknown; for, notwithstanding the manner in which Dryden has glossed over these operations in the West Indies, they were at the time universally considered as having been unfortunate." [SCOTT.]

136. *Under spoils decease* "Tarpeia, the virgin who betrayed a gate of Rome to the Sabines, demanded, in recompense, what they wore on their left arms, meaning their golden bracelets. But the Sabines, detesting her treachery, or not disposed to gratify her avarice, chose to understand that her request related to their bucklers, and flung them upon her in such numbers as to kill her." SCOTT.

137. *But first*, etc. Professor Firth (in *Notes*

and Queries, series VII. v. 404) well illustrates this stanza by a quotation from James Heath's *Flagellum*, 1663, p. 205:

"It pleased God to call him to an account of all that mischief he had perpetrated; ushering his end with a great whale, some three months before, on the second of June, that came up as far as Greenwich, and was there killed, and more immediately by a terrible storm of wind, the prognostic that the great Leviathan of men, that tempest and overthrow of government, was now going to his own place."

7, 144. *Halcyons.* Cf. **10,** 236; **845,** 495, n.

ASTRÆA REDUX. This title means *Justice Brought Back.* On the coming of the Iron Age, Astræa, the virgin Goddess of Justice, is fabled to have fled from earth to heaven: v. **335,** 28; **346**[2] (n. 4); **389,** 191; **462,** 671, 672; **630,** 425–432. Dryden's idea is that with the restoration of Charles, the Golden Age, when Saturn reigned, has been again established. His motto (VIRGIL, *Eclogues,* iv. 6; cf. **428,** 5–8) means: "Now too the Virgin returns, and the reign of Saturn returns."

On the title-pages of both the 1660 and the 1688 editions the poet's name is spelled *Driden.*

2. *A world divided from the rest.* Dryden borrows the thought from Virgil: v. **422,** 89, 90.

7. *An horrid stillness first invades the ear.* This line was much ridiculed by the wits of the time. Scott quotes a couplet parodying it:

A horrid silence does invade my eye,
While not one sound of voice from you I spy.

9. *Th' ambitious Swede,* etc. "The royal line of Sweden has produced more heroic and chivalrous monarchs than any dynasty of Europe. The gallant Charles X, who is here mentioned, did not degenerate from his warlike stem. He was a nephew of the great Gustavus Adolphus; and, like him, was continually engaged in war, particularly against Poland and Austria. He died at Gothenburg in 1660, and the peace of Sweden was soon afterwards restored by the treaty of Copenhagen." SCOTT.

13. *And Heaven,* etc. By the treaty of the Pyrenees in 1659 peace was concluded between France and Spain. The union was cemented by the marriage of Louis XIV to the Infanta Maria Theresa, on June 9, 1660, soon after this poem was written.

35. *The sacred purple,* etc. The *sacred purple* refers, as Christie indicates, to the Bishops, and the *scarlet gown* to the Peers. "The sight of them animated the people to such senseless fury as elephants, and many other animals, are said to show upon seeing any object of a red color." [SCOTT.]

37. *Typhoeus.* The giant who for a time expelled Jupiter from heaven, but was later overcome by him and imprisoned beneath Mount Ætna: v. **651,** 969–972. In the passage just cited the name appears, in accordance with the reading of the early editions, as *Typhæus.*

41. *The lesser gods,* etc. After the execution of Charles I, the House of Commons proceeded (1649) to abolish the House of Lords and to take the name of Parliament for itself.

45. *The Cyclops.* Polyphemus, who was blinded by Ulysses. Dryden has translated from Ovid one story in regard to him: v. **403–406.**

8, 57. *His wounds,* etc. "It is surely unnecessary to point out to the reader the confusion of metaphor, where virtue is said to dress the wounds of Charles with laurels; the impertinent antithesis of finding *light alone in dark afflictions* (l. 96); and the extravagance of representing the winds that wafted Charles as *out of breath with joy* (l. 244)." [SCOTT.]

67. *Soft Otho,* etc. The Roman emperor Galba, who reigned A. D. 68, 69, refused to make Otho his successor, on account of the latter's effeminate life, and adopted Piso as the heir to the throne. Otho then gained power by a revolt, but, after ruling only three months, was defeated by Vitellius at Brixellum, and slew himself.

74. *And all at Worc'ster but the honor lost.* "This is in imitation of the famous phrase which Francis I of France is said to have written to his mother after the battle of Pavia: 'Madam, all is lost except our honor.' That of Charles II certainly was not lost at Worcester. He gave many marks of personal courage, and was only hurried off the field by the torrent of fugitives." [SCOTT.]

94. *On Night,* etc. "That 'night brings counsel' is a well-nigh universal sentiment." [SAINTSBURY.]

98. *His famous grandsire.* "Henry IV of France, maternal grandfather of Charles II." SCOTT.

101. *A Covenanting League's vast pow'rs.* Cf. **154, 155.** There is a reference to the Solemn League and Covenant of 1643.

106. *Chronicles.* For the rhyme, cf. **208,** 414; **215,** 37.

108. *Epoches.* Three syllables, as is indicated by the spelling *epoche's* in the editions of 1660 and 1688.

117. *Rous'd by the lash,* etc. In illustration of this passage Professor W. A. Neilson of Harvard University kindly sends the following quotation: "By the tayle the boldnesse & heart of the Lyon is knowen, . . . for when the Lion is wroth, first he beateth the Earthe with his Tayle, and afterwarde, as the wrath increaseth, he smiteth and beateth his owne backe." *Batman uppon Bartholome,* London, 1582; lib. xviii, cap. 65.

121. *Portunus.* Portunus, the Roman god of harbors, was invoked to secure a safe return from a voyage: cf. **582,** 314, 315; **750,** 48–50.

125. *Yet as,* etc. Cf. n. **5,** 60.

9, 144. *As heav'n,* etc. v. Matthew xi. 12.

145. *Booth's forward valor.* After the death of Cromwell, Sir George Booth rose in Cheshire for Charles II, but was speedily defeated by General Lambert.

150. *Lay.* The grammatical subject of this verb is not clear.

151. *Monk.* General George Monk, the com-

mander of the English forces in Scotland. He took a prominent part in the restoration of Charles II.

154. *Did*, etc. Cf. **774**, 442.

162. *It shuns*, etc. "It is said, believe who list, that the ingenious Mr. Robert Boyle invented a metal which had all the properties of gold except malleability." SCOTT.

163. *How hard*, etc. The passage is far from clear: Dryden's style is not yet fully developed. Monk's task is explained in ll. 167, 168. In the natural body this is the charge of three distinct organs, muscles, nerves, and brain. The 1660 edition has no pause after *see* (l. 164); the 1688 edition has a semi-colon. Christie rightly restored the original punctuation.

182. *Whence Legion twice before was dispossess'd.* This alludes to Cromwell's dispersing the Rump Parliament, April, 1653, and Lambert's similar act, October, 1659.

195. *Th' incensed*, etc. v. **604**, 788–803.

201. *Sforza.* Lodovico Sforza (1451–1508) made himself Duke of Milan by the murder of his nephew. After a series of successful intrigues, he was finally captured by the French, and died in captivity.

205. *Suffer'd to live*, etc. Many prominent Puritans were deprived of the right to hold any public office. " Thus disqualified, the poet compares these republicans to the Spartan slaves, made drunk to excite the contempt of the youth for that degrading vice. By the bye, Dryden's kinsman, Sir Gilbert Pickering, was among the persons so incapacitated." [SCOTT.]

10, 211–214. *Like . . . renew.* This construction is supported by the authority of some good writers both before and after Dryden.

219. *Scheveline's.* "A small village near the Hague, at which Charles embarked on his joyful voyage." SCOTT. Now called Scheveningen.

230. *The Naseby.* "After dinner the king and duke altered the name of some of the ships, viz., the Naseby into Charles." *Pepys' Diary*, May 23, 1660.

235. *Gloc'ster's.* Henry, Duke of Gloucester (1639–60), fourth son of Charles I.

236. *Secure*, etc. Cf. **7**, 144; **845**, 495, n.

249. *Submitted fasces.* The *fasces*, a bundle of rods surrounding an ax, were the symbol of office of the highest Roman magistrates, showing their power both to flog and to put to death. Valerius Poplicola, consul in the first year of the city, when accused of ambition, defended himself before the people, Livy relates, with lowered fasces (*submissis fascibus*, whence Dryden's *submitted*), as a sign of submission to their superior power. Cf. **31**, 199, n; **312**[1], 27–30; **738**[2], 1 f.

251. *Th' approaching cliffs.* "The civility of such inanimate objects, according to the poets of this reign, was truly wonderful, considering their present insensibility." [SCOTT.]

262. *Thus, when*, etc. v. Exodus xxxiii. 20–23; xxxiv. 5–7.

267. *Your goodness only is above the laws.* Charles II pressed the Act of Indemnity upon the House of Lords in the most earnest terms.

284. *How shall I speak*, etc. "Charles II was born on May 29, 1630; and upon the same day of the same month, 1660, made his triumphal entry into London." [SCOTT.]

11, 288. *That star*, etc. "There was a star visible on Charles's birthday, May 29, 1630, a circumstance much dwelt on by his party during the civil wars. Lilly, the astrologer, assures us it was nothing more than the planet Venus, which is sometimes visible in the daytime." [SCOTT.] Cf. **29**, 69–72.

292. *Time's whiter series.* The use of *white* in the sense of *fortunate* is, as Christie indicates, a Latinism. On the line, cf. **29**, 71, n; **122**, 1028.

305. *Our merchants*, etc. The reference is to the commercial rivalry of England and Holland in the East: cf. **28**, 1–4; **71**, *Prol.* and *Epil.*

310. *France.* In June, 1654, owing to negotiations for an alliance between Louis XIV and Cromwell, Charles II left France. His presence there was dangerous only because it might be displeasing to Cromwell.

316. *Your edicts*, etc. This refers, as Professor Firth shows, to a proclamation by the king against vicious persons, including Cavaliers who by their riotous lives disgraced the cause they defended, issued on May 30, 1660, the day after his entrance into London. See *Somers Tracts*, vii. 423–425.

16. *Samson's riddle.* v. Judges xiv. 5–18.

26. *Rete mirabile.* "A network of blood vessels in the basis of the brain of quadrupeds." R. HOOPER, *Medical Dictionary.*

12, 31. *No atoms*, etc. A reference to the atomic theory, as set forth by Lucretius.

37. *Carry weight.* To be handicapped by carrying an extra burden.

68. *Achilles.* According to Statius, Thetis, the mother of Achilles, disguised her son as a maiden, hoping that in this way he might escape being sent to the Trojan War, where she knew he was fated to be slain. — Statius's bad poetry was a favorite object of attack for the critics of Dryden's time.

96. *Rufus'.* Verginius Rufus, who, in the reign of Nero, put down the rebellion of Vindex in Gaul, and later more than once resisted the attempts of his soldiers to make him emperor. He is said to have composed for himself the epitaph quoted in the margin: " Here lies Rufus, who once, defeating Vindex, upheld the empire, not for his own sake, but for his country's."

104. *Geniture.* "The author speaks the language of astrology, in which *geniture* signifies *nativity, horoscope.*" [SCOTT.] According to Malone (I, 1, 45) Howard's book was entered on the *Stationers' Register* April 16, 1660, so that it must have appeared at about the time of the king's return.

13, 18. *Some guilty months.* In Dryden's time the year was reckoned as beginning March 25.

Had Charles II been crowned before March 25, 1661, the two months (March 25–May 25, 1660) immediately preceding his return from exile would have been included in the year of his coronation.

14, 70. *Fruition.* For the rhyme, cf. **2,** 66, n.

79. *Sedition's.* The 1688 edition reads *seditious,* probably a mere misprint.

81. *The jealous sects,* etc. "The conferences held at Savoy House, in April, 1661, betwixt the Presbyterians and the bishops, excited hopes that these two powerful divisions of the Protestant Church might be reconciled to each other. The Quakers, Anabaptists, and other inferior sects, applied, by petitions and humble addresses, to the king, to be permitted to worship God according to their consciences. Thus the whole modeling of ecclesiastical matters seemed to be in the hands of the king." [SCOTT.] The Nonconformists relied on the king's promises in his Declaration from Breda, which he proved unable to fulfil.

104. *With Cæsar's heart.* Plutarch relates that Cæsar encouraged a timorous ship captain with the words: "Go on, my friend, and fear nothing; you carry Cæsar and his fortune in your boat."

107. *In stately frigates,* etc. Charles II had an amateur's interest and delight in shipbuilding and seamanship.

111. *Beyond your court,* etc. "By the improvements made by Charles II on St. James's Park there was a connection made with the river." [SCOTT.]

115. *The mistrustful fowl.* "The canal in St. James's Park formed a decoy for water-fowl, with which it was stocked." [SCOTT.]

127. *Two kingdoms,* etc. Portugal had revolted from Spain in 1640, but its independence was not secure. It received valuable aid from an alliance with England, confirmed by the marriage of Charles II to Catharine of Braganza, daughter to the King of Portugal. This marriage had been favored by France, but opposed by Spain. Spain and Portugal are then the two nations to which Dryden refers.

129. *Your Royal Oak.* "This is in allusion to a device exhibited over the triumphal arch through which the king passed on the day of his coronation. Behind a picture of the king appeared 'the Royal Oak, bearing crowns and scepters, instead of acorns, . . . as designing its reward for the shelter it afforded his Majesty after the fight at Worcester.'" [SCOTT.] The Royal Oak was that in which Charles once concealed himself, thereby escaping capture, after the battle of Worcester in 1651.

15, 5. *The Muses,* etc. In his youth Hyde was intimate with the most famous literary men of his time, but he was apparently never himself a writer of verse.

14. *As those that see,* etc. The Cardinals.

53. *Young David,* etc. v. 1 Samuel xvii. 38, 39.

16, 81. *Their subjects'.* Their *subjects* in 1688 edition; the 1662 text reads *the* instead of *their.*

106. *War's.* Wars in editions of 1662 and 1688.

119. *Envy,* etc. Clarendon's enemies finally triumphed, and secured his banishment in 1667. He died in exile at Rouen in 1674.

139. *Sometimes the hill,* etc. Christie calls attention to the following passage in Denham's *Cooper's Hill,* which was probably in Dryden's mind:

> Windsor the next . . . above the valley swells
> Into my eye, and doth itself present
> With such an easy and unforc'd ascent,
> That no stupend'ous precipice denies
> Access, no horror turns away our eyes;
> But such a rise as doth at once invite
> A pleasure and a rev'rence from the sight.

17, 151. *Without a weight.* Cf. **5,** 57, n.

TO MY HONOR'D FRIEND, DR CHARLETON. This poem is signed *John Driden* in both issues of 1663.

3. *The Stagirite.* Aristotle.

7. *Until 't was bought.* So both issues of 1663; the 1704 text reads *Till it was bought.*

18¹, 13. *Men, who.* So 1663 text, without *imprimatur,* and 1704 text; the 1663 text, with *imprimatur,* reads *men, that.*

22. *Th' English are not the least.* The 1663 text, with *imprimatur,* reads, *The English are not least;* the 1704 text reads, *Our nation 's not the least.*

25. *Gilbert.* William Gilbert (1540–1603), physician to Queen Elizabeth, wrote a treatise on the magnet, the first great physical book published in England.

27. *Boyle.* "The Hon. Robert Boyle (1627–91), who so laudably distinguished his name by his experimental researches, was a son of the great Earl of Cork. He was about this time actively engaged in the formation of the Royal Society. His *great brother* was Roger, Lord Broghill (1621–79), poet and politician, created upon the Restoration Earl of Orrery, to whom Dryden dedicated *The Rival Ladies.*" [SCOTT.] Cf. B. S. xxiv, n. 2.

31. *Harvey.* "William Harvey (1578–1657), the famous discoverer of the circulation of the blood. His last treatise was published in 1651, at the request of Dr. George Ent, a learned physician, mentioned by Dryden in the next line." [SCOTT.]

18², 50. *Joy'd with.* So the 1663 text, without *imprimatur,* and the 1704 text; the 1663 text, with *imprimatur,* reads *Chose by.*

52. *Rule.* So the 1663 text, without *imprimatur,* and the 1704 text; the 1663 text, with *imprimatur,* reads *sway.*

53. *These ruins,* etc. Charleton, in his dedication of *Chorea Gigantum* to Charles II, alludes to a visit which the king paid to Stonehenge immediately after the defeat of his army at Worcester in 1651.

54. *Then when from Wor'ster's fatal field he fled.* So both issues of 1663; the 1704 text reads, *When he from Wor'ster's fatal battle flea.*

55. *Royal.* So the 1663 text, without *imprimatur,* and the 1704 text; the 1663 text, with *imprimatur,* reads *kingly.*

13. *First Astrol.* Dryden by his frequent refer-

ences to astrology shows his interest in the science. A passage in one of his letters shows that he had faith in it: v. Malone, I, 2, 57; SS. xviii. 134: cf. **50,** 1165, n; **758,** 500, n.

19¹, 15. *Half an hour after three,* etc. This indicates the hour at which plays began at the time this comedy was first acted.

26. *The ascendant's.* The heavens were divided, by six great circles passing through the north and south poles of the horizon, into twelve *houses,* of which the *first,* or ascendant, lay just above the eastern horizon. As the houses were numbered downwards, the twelfth lay just above the first. In l. 36 Dryden puns on the double meaning of house.

28. *Denote.* The form of the verb is affected by the plural idea in the preceding clauses.

37. *Peregrine.* "Situated in a part of the zodiac where it has none of its essential dignities." N. E. D.

38. *One continued song.* This is probably, as Malone says, a reference to Davenant's *Siege of Rhodes,* a semi-operatic play, which had been acted with great success at the Duke's Theater in 1661. *The Wild Gallant* was presented at the rival house, the *Theater Royal.*

43. *A Spanish plot.* v. B. S. xxiii, xxiv.

19², 55. *Mistakes.* A reference, as Malone points out, to the mistakes of Teg, an Irish servant in *The Committee,* a comedy by Sir Robert Howard, Dryden's brother-in-law.

23. *Leander.* The lover of Hero, drowned in swimming the Hellespont.

20, 9. *Cato's virtue,* etc. The reference is to Lucan's famous line:

Victrix causa deis placuit sed victa Catoni.
(*Pharsalia,* i. 128.)

"The conquering cause pleased the gods; but the conquered cause, Cato." As Scott remarks, there is "little propriety in comparing the influence of the royal mistress to the virtue of Cato."

PROLOGUE TO THE RIVAL LADIES. The two editions of 1664 may be distinguished by the fact that one, "printed by W. W.," lacks the prose preface and has no author's name on the title-page. The other, "printed by T. N.," includes the prose preface, and is said to be *by John Driden, Esquire.*

21¹, 11. *Habits, dances,* etc. This is probably a reference to *The Siege of Rhodes:* cf. n. **19,** 38.

34. *All slighted maids.* There is a possible reference to *The Slighted Maid,* a comedy by Sir Robert Stapylton, acted and published in 1663.

PROLOGUE, . . . TO THE INDIAN EMPEROR. In *A Defense of an Essay of Dramatic Poesy,* printed with the second edition of *The Indian Emperor* in 1668, Dryden tells us that he has carefully corrected the text of the play since the first edition was published. The text of the second edition is therefore followed in the present volume.

21², 6. *Before the Spaniards came.* The Spaniards do not appear in *The Indian Queen.*

7-9. *Our prologue . . . beast.* These lines are found only in the first edition.

2 (Epil.). *Sends me.* So all editions from 1667 to 1686; editions from 1692 to 1701 read *sends you.*

22¹, 8. *Who write.* So all editions except the first, which reads, *That write.*

20. *To damn the Dutch.* Hostilities had broken out between England and Holland in 1664.

22², 5. *Which would too fast.* So all editions except the first, which reads, *that does too fast.*

22. ANNUS MIRABILIS. The first Latin motto is taken (with a change of order) from Pliny, *Epist.* x. 33, and means: "It matters much whether the occasion demands, or whether men wish to extend their power." The second is *Æneid,* ii. 363; cf. **542,** 490.

In the 1667 edition occurs a note *To the Readers :* "Notwithstanding the diligence which has been us'd in my absence, some faults have escap'd the press: and I have so many of my own to answer for, that I am not willing to be charg'd with those of the printer. I have only noted the grossest of them, not such as by false stops have confounded the sense, but such as by mistaken words have corrupted it." This is followed by a list of errata.

In the following notes the readings of the 1667 edition (in octavo) are marked O, due account being taken of the list of errata; those of the 1688 edition (in quarto) are marked Q. Insignificant variations are not recorded: in general O has the spellings *then, show, latter;* Q has *than, shew, later.*

23¹, 3. *It is.* O reads *is it.*

23². *Sir Robert Howard.* v. B. S. xx. This letter is dated from Charlton in Wiltshire, the residence of the Earl of Berkshire, Sir Robert Howard's father. The play to which Dryden refers (l. 9 of *Account*) is probably *Secret Love.*

24¹, 12. *Nobless.* That is, the nobility. O reads *noblesse,* which perhaps should have been retained in the text.

34. *Lucan.* Lucan (39?-65) wrote his *Pharsalia* on the war between Cæsar and Pompey · Silius Italicus, of about the same date, wrote his *Punica* on the second Punic war.

24², 9. *Female rhymes.* Rhymes in which an unaccented syllable follows the rhyming syllable, as *twenty : plenty.*

13. *Alarique . . . Pucelle.* By Georges de Scudéry (1601-67), on the conquest of Rome by Alaric; and by Chapelain (1595-1674), on Joan of Arc. Cf. **491²,** 5-9.

17. *Chapman.* Chapman's *Iliad* is really in verses of seven feet and his *Odyssey* in verses of five feet.

22. *Gondibert.* An epic poem by Sir William Davenant, in the same stanza as *Annus Mirabilis,* published in 1651. In the present essay Dryden draws some material from Davenant's preface to *Gondibert,* and from the *Answer* to it by Thomas Hobbes, the philosopher. What he borrows he improves, by expressing it in his own terse and elegant style.

30. *Art.* O reads *arts.*

36. *In general terms.* "Dryden changed his mind about *terms of art*, and in the *Dedication of the Æneis* has given the opposite view. The *Annus Mirabilis* is an Elizabethan poem, reckless in the use of minute particulars." [KER.] v. 519², 52, n.

40. *Descriptas,* etc. HORACE, *Ars Poet.* 86, 87. "Settled are the various forms and shades of style in poetry : if I lack the ability and knowledge to maintain these, how can I have the honored name of poet ? " (*Lonsdale and Lee's translation.*)

25¹, 5. *Omnia,* etc. "The earth, with perfect justice, gives back all things of its own free will." The line seems like one from a schoolboy's exercise, compounded of Virgil's *Georgics,* ii. 460 and *Eclogues,* iv. 39 and Ovid's *Metamorphoses,* i. 416, 417 and *Fasti,* iv. 370.

15. *It is.* O reads *is it.*

28. *Wit.* Dryden in the following passage is indebted to Davenant and Hobbes.

39. *Of imagination.* O reads, *of that imagination.*

47. *Paronomasia.* A pun: spelled *paranomasia* in O and Q.

57. *Deriving.* O reads *driving.*

25², 27. *Tho' he describes,* etc. Contrast Dryden's later comparison of Virgil and Ovid : v. 502, 503 ; 744¹, 4–10.

40. *Represents us with in.* So O and Q; Christie reads *within.* It seems better to retain the text as printed, and construe *represent* as *re-present.* Compare:

> Thy truth,
> Like a transparent mirror, represents
> My reason with my errors.
> FORD, *Love's Sacrifice,* Act v. sc. 3.

41. *So we.* O reads *we so.*

47. *Totamque,* etc. VIRGIL, *Æneid,* vi. 726, 727: cf. 606, 982, 983.

52. *Lumenque,* etc. *Ibid.* i. 590–93: cf. 532, 826–831.

26¹, 5. *Materiam,* etc. "The workmanship surpassed the material." *Metamorphoses,* ii. 5.

15. *Dixeris,* etc. "You will express yourself excellently, if a skilful combination makes a well-known word seem a new one." *Ars Poet.* 47, 48.

41. *Et nova,* etc. "And new and newly coined words will have credit, if they are only derived from a Greek source, a little altered in form." *Ars Poet.* 52, 53.

55. *Tediousness.* O reads *the tediousness.*

26², 7. *Antic.* Spelled *antique* in O and Q.

14. *Stantes,* etc. "Æmiliani standing in their chariots." JUVENAL, viii. 3.

17. *Spirantia,* etc. "Bronze statues that breathe more tenderly." *Æneid,* vi. 847, torn from its context.

24. *They said.* O reads, *they have said. Humi serpere.* "Crawl on the ground." Cf. Horace, *Ars Poet.* 28.

27. *Nunc non erat his locus.* "This was not the place for such things." HORACE, *Ars Poet.* 19. O and Q both read *hic* instead of *his.*

VERSES TO HER HIGHNESS THE DUCHESS. "The victory of June 3, 1665, was gained by

the British fleet, commanded by the Duke of York, over the Dutch, under the famous Opdam. — The duchess came down to Harwich to see her husband embark, and afterwards made the triumphant progress to the North which is here commemorated. — The poem itself is adapted to the capacity and taste of a lady." [SCOTT.]

27, 18. *As when,* etc. v. Exodus xiv. 21, 22.

28. *New vigor,* etc. v. Exodus xvii. 11–13.

30. *We heard the cannon play.* The battle was off the coast of Suffolk, near Lowestoft; the noise of the cannon could be heard even at London.

45. *The stubborn North.* After returning from this battle, the Duke of York was sent into Yorkshire, where a rising was apprehended, and whither the duchess accompanied him.

52. *The newborn Phœnix.* v. 886, 887, 578–611; cf. 208, 364–369.

10 (prose). *Nec sunt,* etc. "There are a good many people, who think they show critical ability by picking flaws in their friends." PLINY, *Epist.* vii. 28.

24 (prose). *The children.* So O; Q by an evident misprint omits *the.*

28, 1. *In thriving arts,* etc. Cf. n. 11, 305.

5. *Trade,* etc. There is an implied reference to Harvey's discovery: v. n. 18¹, 31.

11. *The Idumœan balm.* An imitation of Virgil: cf. 455, 165, 166.

13. *Their year.* So O; Q reads *the year,* probably by a mere misprint.

20. *Second Punic war.* The first English war against the Dutch (1652–54) had been carried on with great vigor by Cromwell. This second war, which Dryden trusted would result in a victory as complete as that of Rome over Hannibal, ended with the disgrace of England by the entrance of a Dutch fleet into the Thames in 1667. The comparison of Holland to Carthage later became famous by Shaftesbury's repetition of Cato's phrase, *Delenda est Carthago,* "Carthage must be destroyed:" cf. 71², 19, n.

32. *The babe of Spain.* Louis XIV was plotting to seize the Spanish Netherlands in the right of his wife, the elder half-sister of King Charles II of Spain, who was a sickly child. He sought, however, to conceal his designs, thus *rocking the cradle* of the Spanish king. He at first made a treaty to aid the Dutch against England; later, in 1667, when the English government agreed not to oppose his projects, he abandoned the cause of Holland.

41. *Ideas.* Cf. n. 2, 97.

29, 54. *He in himself did whole armadoes bring.* v. n. 14, 107.

59. *Cæruleus Proteus,* etc. Quoted incorrectly from *Georgics,* iv. 388, 394, 395: cf. 483, 557–568.

64. *Two glaring comets.* A comet had appeared in December, 1664, and another in the following April. By a poetical license (v. 50, 1162) Dryden continues the influence of these comets until the time of the Fire.

69. *Or one*, etc. **v. 11,** 288, n.

71. *A round,* etc. A Virgilian imitation: cf. **11,** 292, 293; **428,** 5–8.

73. *Victorious York.* v. **26, VERSES TO . . . THE DUCHESS,** and note.

81. *Lawson.* Sir John Lawson, vice admiral to the Duke of York, who died from a wound received in this battle. Lawson had won distinction under the Commonwealth, and had later helped to bring about the Restoration. His death is compared with that of Protesilaus, who was the first of the Greeks to leap on the Trojan shore, where he was killed by Hector: v. **855,** 94.

85. *Their chief,* etc. "Admiral Opdam blew up while alongside the Duke of York." [SCOTT.]

94. *The attempt at Berghen.* Two rich Dutch merchant fleets had taken refuge in the Norwegian harbor of Bergen. The King of Denmark, on a promise of a share in the profits connived at their capture by the English. The English, however, began the attack before his orders reached the governor of Bergen, and on August 3, 1665, were repulsed by the combined force of the Danes and the Dutch, and by a contrary wind. But when the Dutch fleet was proceeding on its way, it was shattered by a storm, and several vessels fell into the hands of the English (ll. 117–120).

95. *Southern climates,* etc. The war had opened with hostilities off the coast of Guinea.

30, 137. *Si bene,* etc. "If you reckon up things well, there is shipwreck everywhere." *Sat.* 115, with a change of *est* to *fit.* Christie points out that the three previous stanzas are suggested by the same chapter in Petronius.

145. *Munster's prelate.* The Bishop of Münster, on the payment of a subsidy by Charles, attacked Holland; later, when Louis XIV joined the Dutch, he retired.

146. *Nullos,* etc. "No men excel the Germans in fighting or in keeping their word." Tacitus (*Annals,* xiii. 54) reports these words (in a slightly different order) as the boast of two Frisian chiefs on an embassy to Nero. The Bishop of Münster had promised Sir William Temple, the English envoy, that he would keep his word *fide sincera et Germanica,* "with a sincere and German faith." (TEMPLE, *Works,* 1814, vol. i, p. 213.)

31, 165. *With France,* etc. Early in 1666 France and Denmark both joined Holland against England.

169. *Lewis,* etc. On the declaration of war, Louis XIV required all English subjects to leave France; Charles II, on the other hand, promised protection and religious toleration to any French or Dutch subjects who should come to England. [SCOTT.]

171. *Solomon.* v. 1 Kings iii. 16–28.

181. *The doubled charge,* etc. This refers to the enormous grants of money made to the king by parliament.

186. *Prince Rupert,* etc. Prince Rupert of Bavaria, the nephew of Charles I, had served with distinction in the civil wars. George Monk (v. **9.** 151, n) had on the Restoration been

created Duke of Albemarle. He had commanded the English fleet in a great victory over the Dutch in 1653: v. l. 198.

199. *Fasces.* v. n. **10,** 249. According to a story told by Herodotus (*History,* iv. 3, 4) the Scythians, being unable to suppress by arms a revolt of their slaves, laid aside their spears and bows, and went forth with only their horsewhips. "The slaves were so astounded that they forgot to fight, and immediately ran away."

32, 204. *Examina,* etc. "Swarms of children, and the future people." PLINY, *Panegyricus,* xxvi.

213. *Our fleet divides,* etc. "When Prince Rupert and Albemarle were about to sail from the Downs, they received advice from the king that the French had fitted out a strong squadron to join with the Dutch fleet, accompanied by a positive order that Prince Rupert, with seventy men-of-war, should sail in quest of the French, and fight them before the intended junction. This order occasioned the separation of the fleet, a circumstance which, as the intelligence concerning the supposed French squadron was totally false, occasioned a heavy, and, but for the bravery of Albemarle, an overwhelming disaster. On June 1 the duke descried the Dutch fleet, consisting of seventy-six sail, under the famous de Ruyter, whereas he himself had not above fifty. After a council of war, the duke began the battle, which was continued with incredible fury during that whole day." [SCOTT.]

228. *Lands unfix'd,* etc. *Æneid,* viii. 691, 692; cf. **637,** 915, 916.

231. *In its eye.* Against it.

33, 251. *With such respect.* "The Gauls, when they first entered the Roman senate, were so much struck with the solemn appearance of the venerable senators on their chairs of state, that for a time their fury was absorbed in veneration." SCOTT.

253. *Patroclus' body,* etc. v. *Iliad,* xvii.

267. *Berkeley alone, who nearest danger lay.* Christie states that the 1667 edition here reads, *not making equal way,* for the last half of this line: but the British Museum, Harvard, and Yale copies all read, *who neerest Danger lay.* If Christie is correct, there must have been two issues of the book. — Vice Admiral Sir William Berkeley was killed in this battle, after fighting bravely against heavy odds.

268. *Lost Creüsa.* v. **519,** 1002–1005.

287. *Of ships,* etc. "The Dutch, in the morning of June 2, were reinforced by a fresh squadron of sixteen men-of-war." [SCOTT.]

292. *Spem,* etc. *Æneid,* i. 209; *alto* should be *altum* : cf. **525,** 292.

34, 311. *Steer.* O reads *sheer.* Whether the change to *steer* was a misprint, or Dryden's substitution of a familiar word for an archaic one, must remain doubtful.

330. *Fiery Cacus.* v. **629,** 335–342.

35, 364. *From the noise.* O reads, *are from noise.*

366. *Foll'wing.* So O; Q reads *following.*

374. *As he*, etc. v. 1 Chronicles xiii. 7–10.
384. *Vestigia*, etc. *Æneid*, ix. 797, 798, quoted loosely: cf. **652, 653,** 1072–1081.
391. *Nec trucibus*, etc. Incorrectly quoted from *Sylvæ*, v. 4. 5, 6; *antennis* (*ac tenis* in O), should be *et terris:* "Fierce rivers have not their wonted sound; the uproar of the deep declines, and the seas, leaning on the lands, become calm."
396. *Two former victories.* "By the English fleet over the Dutch in 1653 and 1665. On the last occasion the fleets met on the third, though the Dutch avoided fighting till the fourth of the month." SCOTT.
36, 435. *Him, whom,* etc. Christie calls attention to the imitation of *Æneid*, ii. 726–728: cf. **549,** 988–991.
460. *Doth.* O reads *does.*
37, 472. *Joshua's.* v. Joshua x. 12, 13.
491. *Quum medii*, etc. *Georgics*, iii. 423, 424; cf. **473,** 644–646.
38, 514. *Dreadful*, etc. Christie remarks that there is here a fresh reminiscence of Virgil. Cf. **629,** 327, 328.
521. *So have*, etc. Cf. **396, 718**–725.
536. *Quos opimus*, etc. *Odes*, iv. 4. 51, 52.
545. *As when fiends.* v. Mark iii. 11.
553. *Unripe.* Cf. **28,** 10.
39, 573. *Fervet opus.* *Georgics*, iv. 169: cf. **479,** 230–273.
577. *Foundations.* O reads *foundation.*
586. *Friendly Sweden.* "Sweden was the only Continental power friendly to Britain during this war." [SCOTT.]
588. *Shakes.* So O and Q, whether by Dryden's error or the printer's.
601. *London.* "The former vessel, called the London, had been destroyed by fire. The city now built a new vessel, under the name of the Loyal London, and presented her as a free gift to Charles." SCOTT.
40, 629. *Saturn.* According to the Roman poets, Saturn, after his overthrow by his son Jupiter, came to Italy, introduced civilization, and established a reign of peace and happiness. v. **335,** 1; **388,** 113–145; **608,** 1080, 1081.
639. *Extra anni*, etc. *Æneid*, vi. 796: cf. **608,** 1084. For similar expressions, v. **208,** 353; **258,** 306.
649. *Measure of longitude.* O reads *knowledge of Longitudes.*
653. *Our globe's last verge.* This passage has been condemned as senseless. Lowell, however, in his *Essay on Dryden*, illustrates it by the American "jumping-off place," at the end of the world, which is thought of as a flat plate. There the sea meets the sky and *leans* upon it.
659. *The Royal Society.* Founded in 1660 for the promotion of science. Dryden himself was elected a member in November, 1662.
41, 669. *Already*, etc. "Notwithstanding the exertions of the English, the Dutch fleet, which needed fewer repairs, was first at sea, and their admirals braved the coast of England." [SCOTT.]
681. *Now come in.* O reads, *new come in.*

685. *Allen.* Sir Thomas Allen, an old Cavalier, had routed near Cadiz a large Dutch merchant fleet, on its way home from Smyrna, and had taken valuable prizes. [SCOTT.]
687. *Holmes.* Sir Robert Holmes had begun the war by aggressions on the coast of Guinea. He is compared here to Achates, the faithful follower of Æneas.
689. *Gen'rals'.* O and Q read *gen'rals*, which may mean either *gen'ral's* or *gen'rals'*.
691. *Cato.* Plutarch tells how Cato the Censor, as an argument for the destruction of Carthage, exhibited some fresh figs in the Roman senate, and reminded his hearers that they had been gathered in Africa, only three days' sail from Rome. Cf. **71**[2], 19, n.
693. *Sprag.* Sir Edward Sprag [Spragge], knighted and appointed rear admiral for bravery shown in the fight off Lowestoft.
695. *Harman.* Sir John Harman, who saved his vessel, the Henry, after it had twice been set on fire by the Dutch, in the battle of June 1–4.
697. *Hollis.* Sir Frescheville Hollis, who had lost an arm in the battle of June 3. His father had been distinguished in the civil wars; why his mother is here called a Muse is unknown. [SCOTT.]
701. *Thousands*, etc. A reminiscence of Virgil, as Christie indicates: cf. **583,** 397, 398.
42, 734. *Hosts.* O reads *host.*
736. *Levat*, etc. *Æneid*, i. 145, 146: cf. **524,** 208, 209.
741. *Second battle.* On July 25 and 26, 1666.
742. *Hast'ning.* O reads *hasting.*
760. *Possunt*, etc. *Æneid*, v. 231: cf. **582,** 300.
43, 773. *O famous leader*, etc. Michael Adrian de Ruyter, chosen lieutenant admiral of the States in 1666. Dryden compares him to Varro, who commanded the Romans at the battle of Cannæ, in which they were fatally defeated by Hannibal, and to whom the senate voted thanks, "because he had not despaired of the Republic." [SCOTT.]
778. *Close to fight.* O reads, *to the fight.*
801. *But whate'er*, etc. "The poet here follows up the doctrine he has laid down by a very bold averment, that Henry IV of France, and the first Prince of Orange, instructed in sound policy by their translation to the blessed, would, the one disown the war against Henry III, into which he was compelled to enter to vindicate his right of succession to the crown against the immediate possessor, and the other detest the Dutch naval power, although the only means which could secure his country's independence." SCOTT.
813. *Nor was this all*, etc. In August, 1666, the English under Sir Robert Holmes destroyed a large Dutch merchant fleet near the Vlie, the strait between the islands of Vlieland and Terschelling, and then burnt a town on the latter island.
824. *Turbants.* O reads *turbans.*
825. *English wool*, etc. Professor Firth explains that the Dutch undersold English cloth manufacturers in foreign markets. English

wool was exported to Holland, despite laws to the contrary.

827. *Doom into.* "Destine for." SAINTSBURY.

44, 836 (margin). *Transit.* O reads *Transitum.*

847. *Quum mare,* etc. Slightly altered from *Metamorphoses,* i. 257, 258; cf. **391,** 347–350.

863. *All was the Night's,* etc. The fire of London broke out on the night preceding September 2. The phrase, *All was the Night's* translates part of a line of Varro, *Omnia noctis erant, placida composta quiete,* quoted by the elder Seneca *(Controversiæ,* vii. 1 (16). 27).

881. *Hæc arte,* etc. "She artfully managed the greedy man, that privation might inflame his mind." Quoted freely from Terence, *Heautontimorumenos,* ii. 3. 125, 126.

45, 889. *The Bridge.* "London Bridge was a place allotted for affixing the heads of persons executed for treason. The skulls of the regicides, of the Fifth Monarchy insurgents, and of other fanatics, were placed on the Bridge and on other conspicuous places. The *sabbath notes,* imputed to this assembly of fanatic specters, are the infernal hymns chanted at the witches' sabbath — a meeting concerning which antiquity told and believed many strange things." [SCOTT.] Ghosts' voices were thought to be shrill and feeble.

922. *A blaze.* O reads *the blaze.*

922 (margin). *Sigœa,* etc. *Æneid,* ii. 312: cf. **541,** 419, 420.

926. *Simoeis.* The river Xanthus, which had endeavored to drown Achilles, was nearly dried up by Hephæstus. During the conflict it had called for aid on its tributary Simois. Dryden remembered in a general way Homer's account of the battle in *Iliad,* xxi.

46, 939. *Straggle.* So O; Q reads *struggle.*

949. *The king.* "It is not indeed imaginable how extraordinary the vigilance and activity of the king and the duke was, even laboring in person, and being present to command, order, reward, or encourage workmen; by which he showed his affection to his people, and gained theirs." *Evelyn's Diary,* Sept. 6, 1666.

47, 1004. *Tempests.* O reads *tempest.*

48, 1057. *Or, if,* etc. On the prayer of King Charles, cf. 1 Chronicles xxi. 12, 13, 17.

1066. *Spotted deaths.* "In 1665 the plague broke out in London with the most dreadful fury. In one year upwards of 90,000 inhabitants were cut off by this frightful visitation." [SCOTT.]

1077. *Threatings.* O reads *threatnings.*

1094. *In dust.* So O; Q reads, *in the Dust.*

49, 1099. *A poet's song.* Alluding to Waller's poem, addressed to Charles I, *Upon his Majesty's Repairing of St. Paul's.* The walls of Thebes were fabled to have been built by the music of Amphion's lyre: cf. **917,** 1005.

1113. *Th' empyrean heaven.* The highest heaven, the abode of God and the angels. The *Thrones* and the *Dominions* are the third and the fourth of the nine orders of angels.

1120. *Drive on.* O reads, *give on.*

1121. *An hollow.* etc. "The flames of London

are first a tallow candle; and secondly hawks, which, while pouncing on their quarry, are hooded with an extinguisher." [SCOTT.]

50, 1157. *The Jews,* etc. v. Ezra i–iii.

1165. *Trines.* Astrologers taught that a trine, that is, an aspect of two planets distant from each other 120 degrees (one third of the zodiac), had a benign influence. To this Dryden adds the happy omen of Jupiter in ascension. Cf. **18**[2], 13,'n; **758,** 500, n.

1168. *Works.* O reads *work.*

1177 (margin). *Augusta.* Cf. **135,** 64.

1185. *A maiden queen.* Compare the title of Dryden's play, **51.**

1195. *And Seine,* etc. This refers to the designs of Louis XIV on the Spanish Netherlands.

51, 1211. *Our trouble,* etc. "The disgraceful surprise of Chatham, in 1667, baffled this prophecy." SCOTT.

4. *The unities,* etc. v. B. S. xxiii.

52, 16 (Epil.). *[F]or.* CGD reads *or.*

PROLOGUE AND EPILOGUE TO THE WILD GALLANT, REVIV'D. Christie apparently makes a mistake in saying that these two pieces are printed in the *Covent Garden Drollery.*

53[1], 8 (Prol.). *Whetstone's Park.* This is a narrow street (now, and more usually in Dryden's time, called Whetstone Park) near Lincoln's Inn Fields. It was notorious for its brothels. Cf. **169**[1], 31.

15. *He thought,* etc. Pepys, who saw a court performance of *The Wild Gallant* on February 23, 1663, writes: "The play [was] so . . . little answering the name, that from beginning to end, I could not, nor can at this time, tell certainly which was the Wild Gallant."

53[2], 44. *Vests.* Charles II vainly attempted to introduce this garment into England. According to Pepys (October 15, 1666) the king's vest was "a long cassock close to the body, of black cloth, and pinked with white silk under it, and a coat over it, and the legs ruffled with black riband like a pigeon's leg." Pepys adds: "Upon the whole, I wish the king may keep it, for it is a very fine and handsome garment." But on November 22 Pepys has received the news, "how the King of France hath, in defiance to the King of England, caused all his footmen to be put into vests, and that the noblemen of France will do the like; which, if true, is the greatest indignity ever done by one prince to another, and would incite a stone to be revenged."

54[1], 10 (Prol.). *Woodcocks.* This word was a cant term for simpleton.

2 (Epil.). *Benediction.* For the rhyme, cf. **2,** 66, n.

54[2], 13 (Epil.). *Lilly.* William Lilly (1602–81), astrologer and almanac-maker. Cf. n. **11,** 288.

SONG I. In WD this song is headed, *A Song at the Duke's House.* The first line reads: "Make ready, fair Lady, to nights *Innocence.*"

SONG II. This song is imitated from one by Voiture, beginning, *L'amour sous sa loi:* see *Œuvres de Voiture,* 1856, p. 493.

55², 3. *Abroad.* So the editions of 1670 and 1690; that of 1676 reads *aboard.*

56¹, 5 (Epil.). *The rhyming Mounsieur,* etc. v. B. S. xxiii.

9. *King Richard's.* Referring, of course, to Shakespeare's *Richard III,* v. 3.

PROLOGUE TO ALBUMAZAR, REVIV'D. CGD contains the following variant readings: (4) *and fewer ;* (6) *And the best;* (8) *by this Astrologer ;* (9) *and I should suppose;* (10) *He likes my fashion well, that wears my Cloaths ;* (12) *became his Gold ;* (16) *a word ;* (21) *Who scarce ;* (28) *They stript the living, but they rob the dead ;* (29) *'T will with the mummey ;* (30) *to 'em ;* (33) *Yet such in Poetry ;* (35) *Such as in* Sparta *weight* [sic] *for Laurels stand ;* (37) *their benefit;* (39) *Where Broth to claim there's no one has the courage ;* (40) *after he has spit ;* (41) *y' are all ;* (43) *thefts will ;* (45, 46) omitted in CGD; (47) *Now should we Letters of reprizall seal.*

7 (Prol.). *Subtle.* The chief character in Jonson's *Alchemist.*

56², 25. *Toms.* "This seems to have been a cant name for highwaymen." [SCOTT.]

57², 33. *Thrice a year.* A reference to Dryden's recent contract to furnish three plays a year for the King's Company. v. B. S. xxxii.

4. *Like Jews,* etc. Cf. 1 Kings xxii. 17.

16. *The Feign'd Astrologue.* Dryden's play, as the second title indicates, is imitated from *Le Feint Astrologue* of Thomas Corneille, who again was indebted to *El Astrologo Fingido* of Calderon.

22. *This night or next.* Referring to the discussions over the unity of time. v. B. S. xxiii. The whole action of the play, as the title would indicate, takes place in one evening.

59¹. SONG IV. This song is a duet between Wildblood and Jacintha, the lively hero and heroine of the play.

59², 14. *And he, who servilely,* etc. Dryden writes as follows in his preface to the second edition of *Tyrannic Love:* "For the little critics, who pleas'd themselves with thinking they have found a flaw in that line of the prologue, 'And he . . . ,' as if I patroniz'd my own nonsense, I may reasonably suppose they have never read Horace. *Serpit humi tutus,* etc. [*Ars Poet.* 28] are his words: he who creeps after plain, dull, common sense, is safe from committing absurdities, but can never reach any height, or excellence of wit; and sure I could not mean that any excellence were to be found in nonsense."

18. *A tyrant.* Maximin, "tyrant of Rome," is the chief character in the play.

60¹, 30. *St. Cathar'n.* "In the *Wentworth Papers* Lady Wentworth and Lady Strafford, whose spelling of proper names is almost purely phonetic, write usually *Cathern.*" [SAINTSBURY.] St. Catharine was the heroine of the play, the *Royal Martyr.*

SONG. This is sung by a spirit, in order to tempt St. Catharine to love.

60², 1. *This jest,* etc. "The dress is said to have been begun by Nokes, a famous comic actor at the Duke's Theater, as a caricature of French attire when Henrietta of Orleans visited England in May, 1670." [SAINTSBURY.]

61¹, 27. *They bring,* etc. This may be a reference to *The Indian Emperor ;* v. **21.**

33. *To like.* As to like.

61², 38. *French farce,* etc. v. 65¹, 6; 73¹, 7; 74¹, 38.

19. *When forty comes,* etc. Dryden jests at his own expense; he was thirty-nine at the time.

25. *This year's delay.* Apparently alluding to the lapse of a year since the production of *Tyrannic Love,* despite Dryden's contract to write three plays a year.

26. *The women were away.* On Nell Gwyn, v. headnote: other actresses were apparently away for similar reasons.

62¹, 13. *Vizard-mask.* The mark of a courtesan.

62². EPILOGUE. To justify the arrogant tone of this epilogue Dryden published with the first three editions of his play a critical essay entitled *Defense of the Epilogue; or, An Essay on the Dramatic Poetry of the Last Age.*

6. *Cob's tankard,* etc. "The characters alluded to are Cob, the water-bearer, in *Every Man in his Humor ;* and Captain Otter, in *Epicœne; or, The Silent Woman,* whose humor it was to christen his drinking cups by the names of Horse, Bull, and Bear." SCOTT.

63. THE ZAMBRA DANCE. This heading merely indicates the occasion at which the song was sung in the play. The text of this song printed in WD under the title, *A Song at the King's House,* supplies the following variants: (2) *Which none but Love, for ;* (6) *Whilst ;* (7) *Flowers, that ;* (8) *bright Virgins;* (10) *temple . . . shady ;* (14) *that languish ;* (16) *can my bliss and you ;* (17) *lovely shade ;* (23) *For rather then ;* (27) *And yet, Thus, thus, she cry'd ;* (32) *I fancy I had done ;* (34) *Whilst ;* (35) *I must ease.* The text printed in the same collection under the title, *A Vision,* supplies the following variants: (2) *Which Jove for none ;* (10) *white shoulders ;* (11) *nor too ;* (13) *ev'ry part ;* (16) *will you ;* (17) *by Jove this lonesome shade ;* (24) *she spoke me-thought ;* (34) *your scorn.*

SONG II. In WD the last line in each stanza is repeated. That text also furnishes the following variants: (8) *heart burns ;* (11) *mine eyes;* (12) *sweet dream ;* (14) *Then I sigh ;* (15) *being rival ;* (19) *and ever.*

64. PROLOGUE . . . AFTER THE FIRE. CGD supplies the following variants: (2) *on bare ;* (4) *from a desert ;* (10) *of charity ;* (12) *Whilst . . . our guests ;* (13) *besides ;* (16) *cherish ;* (18) *the Fire ;* (23–30) omitted in CGD. — WD supplies the following variants: (2, 4, 10, 12, 13, 18) as in CGD ; (23) *doth ;* (24) *equald;* (25) *doth.*

20. *But as.* Cf. **44,** 847, 848.

65¹, 1. *With sickly actors,* etc. v. headnote, p. **64.**

7. *Broad bloody bills.* Apparently the *bills,* or advertisements of the French troupe, were red, or printed in red ink. v. Lowe's *Life of Betterton,* pp. 14, 15.

12. *Send lackeys.* Seats were not reserved at this time: *ibid.* pp. 16–18.

65², 6. *Wonted.* The 1684 text reads *wanted.*

13. *Burgundian.* A slang term for *bully, bragadoccio.* v. N. E. D. under *Burgullian.*

14. *Benches.* The pit seats were apparently without backs.

23. *Gaudy house.* v. headnote, p. **64.**

66², 26. *Too.* CGD reads *two.*

30. *Mamamouchi.* This refers to a play by Ravenscroft, *The Citizen turned Gentleman,* a free adaptation of Molière's *Le Bourgeois Gentilhomme,* which was acted at the Duke's Theater in 1671 or 1672. The *citizen* in the play is tricked into believing that he has been given the Turkish title of Mamamouchi, and is invested with the office amid much mock solemnity.

PROLOGUE AND EPILOGUE TO MARRIAGE À LA MODE. These pieces were spoken, as we learn from CGD, by Hart and Mohun, the two chief actors in the King's Company, who played the parts of Palamede and Rhodophil, the principal male characters in the play. The humor of the comedy consists in a double intrigue, between Palamede and Doralice, the wife of Rhodophil, and between Rhodophil and Melantha, the betrothed of Palamede. Neither couple can gain their end, and at the close of the play all resolve to respect one another's rights.

CGD furnishes the following variant readings: PROLOGUE, (4) *While Wig and Vizard Masks, no longer jar ;* (5) *hath swept ;* (7, 8) found only in CGD; (9) *went from home ;* (18) *the grinning ;* (23) *venter in ;* (24) *her half-Crown ;* (26) *heardly roame ;* (28) *with gaudy ;* (29) *For 't is presumed ;* (31) *cunning Morecraft, strut ;* (32) *Here's all . . . to do ;* (34, 37) *them* (for *'em*) ; (38) *falls. —* EPILOGUE, (7) *example ;* (8) *see and hear ;* (13) *Women faulty bare ;* (14) *them* (for *'em*) ; (15) *were less ;* (17) *Satyr lent ;* (18) *would fret ;* (19) *of Husband ;* (21) *which of them ;* (26) *are all ;* (31) *Town, nor Court.*

67¹, 5. *France,* etc. England was now in alliance with France against Holland.

18. *Grinning honor.* The phrase is borrowed from Shakespeare, *1 Henry IV,* v. 3. 62.

24. *Half-crown.* The price of admission to the pit.

25. *The Mall.* A walk in St. James Park: pronounced *Mell ;* cf. l. 20 of EPILOGUE.

31. *Cutting Morecraft.* In Beaumont and Fletcher's play, *The Scornful Lady,* Morecraft, a usurer, turns a gallant, and hence receives the title *cutting* (swaggering, ruffling) *Morecraft.* Malone, and Scott following him, see here a reference to the Mamamouchi episode in Ravenscroft's *Citizen turned Gentleman* (v. n. **66²**, 30), which is of a somewhat similar character, but this conjecture is far from convincing. There may have been a revival of *The Scornful Lady* at the Duke's Theater, of which record is lost.

67², 32. *The city.* The wives of the city merchants were conventionally regarded as the lawful prey of men of society.

68¹. SONG I. This song is sung by Doralice at the opening of the play, and is overheard by Palamede, who straightway begins his addresses to her. It thus forms the keynote of the action of the comedy.

NCS affords the following variants: (10) *further joys ;* (12) *can give ;* (15) *When all ;* (16) *And neither.*

SONG II. This is sung at a court masquerade. NCS reads *While* in l. 1. WD and CGD read *whilst* in l. 13, and *did* (for *died*) in ll. 19, 20.

68². A SONG. In CGD this song is addressed to *Arminda : The Rehearsal* gives the name as *Armida.* CGD furnishes the following variants: (2) *hope no ;* (6) *The fate ;* (11) *gave, though ;* (12) *My fall ;* (14) *would lay !*

69. THE ANSWER. CGD furnishes the following variants: (1) *Arminda ;* (8) *a fall ;* (9) *In Seas.*

70¹, 30. *Mamamouchi.* v. n. **66²**, 30. The gibberish quoted below is passed off for Turkish upon the *citizen* in Ravenscroft's play.

36, 37. *Touch you : Mamamouchi.* For the rhyme, cf. ll. 40, 41, *uneasy : please ye.*

45. *Haynes.* Joseph Haynes, a noted comic actor, who played the part of Benito, the fool in Dryden's comedy. Cf. **280²**, 20, n.

3. *Coleman Street.* "Coleman Street had an ancient notoriety. In Dekker's *Seven Deadly Sins of London* (1606), Lying 'musters together all the *Hackneymen* and *Horse-coursers* in and about *Coleman-streete.*'" (WARD: *History of English Dramatic Literature,* iii. 327.) Cowley wrote a play called, *Cutter of Coleman Street.* Cf. n. **67¹**, 31.

70². PROLOGUE . . . FROM AMBOYNA. The "cruelties of the Dutch" on which this play is founded occurred in 1622. Dryden dedicated *Amboyna* in terms of extravagant flattery to Lord Clifford, a colleague of the Earl of Shaftesbury in the Cabal ministry : cf. **419¹,** n. On the play, v. B. S. xxviii.

71¹, 12. *Love.* The 1673 text reads *loves,* by an evident misprint.

22. *States.* Republics: the Dutch Republic was frequently called simply the *States.*

33. *Least.* The 1673 text reads *lest ;* the text in the folio of 1701 reads *less.*

71², 1 (Epil.). *A poet,* etc. A reference to Tyrtæus, who inspired by his verses the Spartans, in their wars against the Messenians.

6. *Boor.* Spelled *bore* in the 1673 edition.

18. *Two kings' touch.* "The poet alludes to the king's evil [scrofula, which the king was supposed to heal by his touch], and to the joint war of France and England against Holland." SCOTT.

19. *Cato.* v. **41,** 691, n. After the incident of the figs, Cato is said to have concluded every speech by urging that Carthage should be destroyed. The comparison of Holland to Carthage was common at the time: cf. **28,** 17–20. Shaftesbury used of Holland the phrase *Delenda est Carthago* in a famous speech on the assembling of parliament in February, 1673, but this was after the date of Dryden's play.

73¹, 32. *The Lucretian way.* The reference is to the atomic theory, as set forth by Lucretius in his poem, *De Rerum Natura*.
40 *Prætorian bands.* The reference is to the violent election of Roman emperors by the Prætorian guards, in contrast to their legal choice by the senate.
7. *A French troop.* v. **61²**, 38; **65¹**, 6; **74¹**, 38.
73², 30. *Macbeth,* etc. This refers to the performance, at the Duke's Theater, of "the tragedy of Macbeth, altered by Sir William Davenant; being dressed in all its finery, as new clothes, new scenes; machines, as flyings for the witches; with all the singing and dancing in it." (DOWNES.) It was apparently first acted in 1664 and revived with greater magnificence in 1672, when it proved "a lasting play." It is notable that Dryden here seems to ridicule Davenant, whom, as we know, in general he valued highly at this time: cf. **24²**, 22, n. For the comparison with *Simon Magus* (Simon the Sorcerer), see Acts viii. 9.
74¹, 36. *Empty operas.* v. n. **73²**, 30.
38. *While troops.* v. **61²**, 38; **65¹**, 6; **73¹**, 7.
74², 53. *Machines and tempests.* This refers to the performance at the Duke's Theater of "*The Tempest . . .* made into an opera by Mr. Shadwell, having all new in it, as scenes, machines; particularly one scene painted with myriads of Ariel [*sic*] spirits; and another flying away, with a table furnished out with fruits, sweetmeats and all sorts of viands, just when Duke Trinculo and his companions were going to dinner." (DOWNES.) Cf. **917,** 90, n; and see supplementary information in *Additional Notes,* **1051, 1052.**
7. *Thro'. Tho'* in the 1684 text, probably by a mere misprint.
22. *But leave you,* etc. "This seems to be an allusion to the recent death of a Mr. Scroop, who, about this time, was stabbed in the theater at Dorset Gardens by Sir Thomas Armstrong. Langbaine says he witnessed this real tragedy, which happened during the representation of *Macbeth,* as altered and revised by Davenant." [SCOTT.]
75¹, 27. *Our house relieves,* etc. That is, Drury Lane was a more convenient situation for a theater than Dorset Gardens, where the rival house, the Duke's Theater, was situated.
32. *Three boys in buff.* This may possibly be a reference to a droll, *The Three Merry Boys,* founded on the comic scenes in Beaumont and Fletcher's *Rollo,* which was acted during the suppression of the theaters: see Ward, *English Dramatic Literature,* ii. 734; or perhaps, to the comic parts of *Rollo* itself. Scott, however, supposes that there is a reference to *The Bold Beauchamps,* an old play ascribed to Thomas Heywood, which must have been quite forgotten by Dryden's time.
33. *The poets' heads.* "Some part of the ornaments of Davenant's scenes probably presented the portraits of dramatic writers." SCOTT. Really, busts of the dramatic writers. That of Shakespeare was recovered in

1845: v. Sidney Lee, *Life of Shakespeare,* ch. xviii.
75², 13. *Man, the little world,* etc. Man was termed the *microcosm,* or little universe, in opposition to the exterior universe, or *macrocosm.* The *sphere of crystal* is described in Spenser's *Faerie Queene,* iii. 2. 18, 19.
24. *Muses so severe.* There is an implied reference to Martial, ix. 12 (11). 16, 17:

Nobis non licet esse tam disertis,
Qui Musas colimus severiores:

"We who serve severer Muses cannot be so eloquent." Cf. **385²**, 48; **512¹**, 36.
27. *Rather than,* etc. Cf. Exodus xxxiii. 20–23.
76¹, EPILOGUE TO OXFORD. The other text of this epilogue (see headnote) reads in l. 4, *He sought for quiet ;* and in l. 25, *Whose kindness.*
17. *Bathurst.* Ralph Bathurst (1620–1704) was vice chancellor of the University of Oxford from October 3, 1673, to October 9, 1676. (WOOD, *Fasti Oxonienses.*) He was celebrated as a writer of Latin prose and verse.
77¹, 21. *These peaceful triumphs,* etc. On the Continent France was now at war with a coalition led by the Prince of Orange. Charles II was seeking to remain on good terms with both sides in the struggle.
29. *One.* So the 1684 text; SS. and C. read *own,* which may be what the author intended.
PROLOGUE TO AURENG-ZEBE. On this play, v. B. S. xxx; and on the substance of the *Prologue,* cf. the passage quoted from the *Dedication,* in B. S. xl, xli. The play was probably acted in the spring or summer of 1675, since the entry in the *Stationers' Register* usually followed about half a year after the first production. It is entered in the *Term Catalogue* for Easter term, 1676.
12. *Correct.* Constructed according to the rules of dramatic criticism. Cf. the opening lines of the *Epilogue.*
15. *Romans.* Perhaps this should be printed *Roman's,* in reference to *Antony and Cleopatra.* Duke, in a poem addressed to Dryden (v. SS. vi. 288) has the line:

Envy not now the godlike Roman's rage.

77², 22. *The first,* etc. Dryden feels himself superior to the other authors of heroic plays, such as Settle and Crowne, but inferior to the great Elizabethan dramatists.
37. *We and our neighbors,* etc. This refers to the rivalry of the two theaters. For the comparison, v. **77¹**, 21, n.
78¹, 21. *Silk-weavers.* "Enemies, namely, like the English silk-weavers, to the manufactures of France." SCOTT.
22. *Bear Garden.* "Alluding to the prize fighting with broadswords at the Bear Garden." [SCOTT.]
EPILOGUE TO THE MAN OF MODE. "Sir Fopling Flutter was supposed to represent Sir George Hewet, one of the most choice coxcombs of the period. The satire being in fact personal, it followed as a matter of course that the *Epilogue* should disclaim all personality, that

being an attribute to be discovered by the audience, but not avowed by the poet." [SCOTT.] The identification of Sir Fopling with Hewet (cf. **916**, 229) is far from certain; it rests only on the authority of Oldys' sketch of Etherege in the *Biographia Britannica*.

78², 22. *The toss*, etc. "The *toss* was presumably a mode of shaking the voluminous wig-hair back, and the *wallow* either a deep courtesying bow or a rolling kind of strut in the walk. The *yard-long snake* must be the tail of the wig, and a *shog* is a shake like that of a wet dog." [SAINTSBURY.] In the present editor's opinion, the *snake* is simply the fop's cane; gentlemen at this time wore full flowing wigs, not those with cues.

79¹, 1. *Y' are.* The 1677 text reads *you' re.*

12. *Arbaces.* The chief character in Beaumont and Fletcher's *King and No King.* — *Volpone* is one of Jonson's best comedies.

15. *Slighted Maid.* Dryden elsewhere speaks contemptuously of this play: v. **21¹**, 34, n; SS. xvii. 325.

16. *Shakespeare's.* As Scott indicates, this statement, which is entirely incorrect, is doubtless founded only on the inferiority of Pericles as a play.

19. *All hawthorns.* "Alluding to the legend of the Glastonbury thorn, supposed to bloom on Christmas day." SCOTT.

24. *Stew'd.* Mr. W. A. Wright (v. C. xiii) suggested *sterv'd* (i. e. *starv'd*) as an emendation for this unintelligible word.

79², 1. *The blast*, etc. "Our author alludes to the verses addressed to him by Lee, on his drama called *The State of Innocence.* Dryden expresses some apprehension lest his friend and he should be considered as vouching for each other's genius, in the same manner that Bessus and the two swordsmen, in Beaumont and Fletcher's *King and No King* (act iv. sc. 3) grant certificates of cach other's courage, after having been all soundly beaten and kicked by Bacurius." [SCOTT.]

80¹, 31. *His heroic worth.* This probably refers to Sir Edward Spragge, who had in May, 1671, cut a boom defending the Bay of Bugia and attacked Algerine pirates there concealed. [SCOTT.] He had earlier distinguished himself against the Dutch: v. **41**, 693, n.

80². PROLOGUE . . . TO ALL FOR LOVE. On this play, v. B. S. xxx.

15. *Tonies. Tony*, the abbreviated form of *Antony*, was a cant term for simpleton.

81¹, 37. *And since*, etc. These lines indicate that the play was acted early in the winter season — say in October or November, 1677.

81², 17. *Mr. Bayes.* v. B. S. xxviii, xxxvi.

1. *You've.* The 1678 text reads, *Yo've.*

82¹. PROLOGUE . . . FROM THE KIND KEEPER. This play and its successors, *Œdipus, Troilus and Cressida*, and *The Spanish Friar*, Dryden gave to the Duke's Company. In 1678 his partners in the King's Company addressed a memorial to the Lord Chamberlain, in which, after setting forth their liberal treatment of Dryden, they complained of his

desertion of them. (Malone, I, 1, 72–75.) How the matter was settled is unknown. The memorial shows Dryden in a bad light, but we must not judge a suit at law merely from the brief for the plaintiff. If Dryden was really guilty of knavery, it is strange that none of his many literary foes made any mention of the affair. Cf. B. S. xxxii–xxxiv.

8. *Machining lumber.* Another fling at opera (cf. n. **73²**, 30; n. **74²**, 53), which had apparently lost its popularity at the Duke's Theater.

82², 16 (Prol.). *Sturbridge fair.* "The fair annually held at Cambridge between September 18 and October 10." SAINTSBURY.

23. *Nostradamus.* v. **242**, 1814, n.

EPILOGUE. Limberham, the *kind keeper* of the comedy, after being grossly betrayed by his mistress Mrs. Tricksy (nicknamed Pug), who intrigues with Woodal, finally marries her.

83¹, 22. *A Smithfield horse*, etc. "Alluding to an old proverb, that whoso goes to Westminster for a wife, to St. Paul's for a man, and to Smithfield for a horse, may meet with a whore, a knave, and a jade. Falstaff, on being informed that Bardolph is gone to Smithfield to buy him a horse, observes : 'I bought him in Paul's, and he'll buy me a horse in Smithfield. An I could get me but a wife in the stews, I were mann'd, hors'd, and wiv'd (*2 Henry IV*, i. 2. 58–61)." SCOTT.

9 (Prol.). *Cruse.* The text printed with *The Widow Ranter* reads *cause*, probably by a misprint.

83². PROLOGUE . . . TO ŒDIPUS. v. n. **82¹** (*Prol.*): This whole prologue shows the influence that Rymer's *Tragedies of the Last Age* had upon Dryden: cf. B. S. xxx, xxxi. For instance Rymer writes, early in his book: "And now it was that . . . Socrates set up for morality, and all the buzz in Athens was now about virtue and good life. Camerades with him, and confederates in his worthy design, were our Sophocles and Euripides; but these took a different method."

84¹, 25. *Mons.* On August 15, 1678, the Prince of Orange, aided by some English and Scotch regiments, attacked and defeated a French army blockading Mons. This date aids in determining the time of the play.

36. *The Woolen Act.* This provided that after August 1, 1678, all persons should be buried in woolen.

1. *What Sophocles*, etc. Sophocles, Seneca, and Corneille had all written tragedies on the subject of Œdipus: the last two writers proved unequal to their subject.

84², 34. *Burning of a pope.* "The burning a pope in effigy was a ceremony performed upon the anniversary of Queen Elizabeth's coronation." [SCOTT.] Cf. **87¹**, 11.

PROLOGUE . . . FROM TROILUS AND CRESSIDA. Of this play there seem to have been three issues in 1679, which differ in the imprint: one being *printed for Jacob Tonson*, the second *printed for Jacob Tonson . . . and Abel Swall*, and the third *printed for Abel Swall*

. . . *and Jacob Tonson.* The first two are in
the Harvard Library, the third is mentioned
in the *Catalogue of the Hoe Library,* vol. ii,
pp. 110, 111.

85. PROLOGUE SPOKEN BY MR. BETTERTON.
Betterton, the most famous actor of the
Duke's Company, took the part of Troilus in
the play.
  38. *How Trojan,* etc. "The conceit which our
  ancestors had adopted of their descent from
  Brutus, the great-grandson of Æneas, induced
  their poets to load the Grecian chiefs with
  every accusation of cowardice and treachery,
  and to extol the character of the Trojans in
  the same proportion." [SCOTT.] The *conceit*
  goes back to Geoffrey of Monmouth; on it cf.
  494², 52 f.
  40. *Homer's,* etc. Cf. 497², 34, n.

86¹, 26. *John Lilburne.* "John Lilburne (1614?–
57) the most turbulent, but the boldest and
most upright of men, had the merit of defying
and resisting the tyranny of the king, of the
parliament, and of the protector." [SCOTT.]
When on trial in 1649 and in 1653 he maintained a defiant attitude towards his judges,
but was on both occasions acquitted by the
jury.
  28. *The plot.* Dryden here avails himself of the
  anti-Catholic feeling roused by the Popish
  Plot.

86², 8. *Because,* etc. "An obvious reference to
the fate of *The Kind Keeper.*" [SAINTSBURY.]
  23. *Requests,* etc. "The Court of Requests was
  a general rendezvous for the newsmongers,
  politicians, and busybodies of the time.
  Swift, in his *Journal to Stella,* makes frequent
  mention of it as a scene of political bustle and
  intrigue." [SCOTT.]

87¹, 42. *The Pope,* etc. Dryden again avails
himself of the excitement caused by the
Popish Plot: cf. 86¹, 28, n. At the burning,
the Devil was prominent as the Pope's
counselor.
  7. *The Shrovetide crew.* Shrovetide is specifically
  the time between the evening before Quin-
  quagesima Sunday and the morning of Ash
  Wednesday; it is often used loosely for Shrove
  Tuesday. That was the traditional holiday
  of the London apprentices, when they were
  wont to "take the law in their own hands and
  do what they list." (DEKKER, *Seven Deadly
  Sins of London,* ed. Arber, p. 40.) Cf. **824,**
  106, n.
  11. *The Devil and the Pope.* Cf. 86¹, 28, n; 87¹,
  42, n.
  16. *The style of forty-one.* "The meaning is that
  the poets rebel against sense and criticism,
  as the parliament, in 1641, did against the
  king; and that the audience judge as ill as
  those who, in 1648, condemned Charles to the
  block." [SCOTT.]

87². PROLOGUE AT OXFORD. The text printed
with *Sophonisba,* 1681, furnishes the following
variant readings: (2) *in a cart ;* (5) *Eschilus*
[*Escalus* in *Miscellany*]; (6) *e're trod* [for
that trod]; (11) *some years . . . go on ;* (12)
will here ; (15) *you Heathen ;* (17, 18) not

found in this text; (19) *we want ;* (21–24)
not found in this text; (25) *Occam, Dun,
Scotus must, though learn'd, go down ;* (27)
Aristotle, for ; (30) *Shall thence be call'd a
Pipe of Inspiration.* After (30) this text adds
the following lines:

  Your wiser Judgments farther penetrate,
  Who late found out one Tare amongst the Wheat.
  This is our comfort, none e're cry'd us down,
  But who dislik'd both *Bishop* and a *Crown.*

  In Tory Oxford, Dryden ventures to ridicule the Popish Plot, instead of playing on the
passions raised by it, as he had done in earlier
prologues, and as he did later in *The Spanish
Friar.*
  4. *Dicitur,* etc. "Thespis is said to have carried
  his poems in wagons." HORACE, *Ars Poet.* 276.
  5. *In some page.* Really, in the following lines
  of the *Ars Poetica.*
  8. *A tennis court.* "Apparently a tennis court
  was the place where the temporary stage
  was erected at Oxford." SCOTT.
  18. *The Oxford Bells.* "Probably some pas-
  quinade against the Whigs, then current in
  the University." SCOTT.

88, 25 (verse). *Scot,* etc. Duns Scotus, Thomas
Aquinas, and William of Occam (mentioned
in the variant reading of this line) were
famous scholastic philosophers; Francisco
Suarez was a Spanish theologian: the triple
crown is of course that of the Pope.

TRANSLATIONS FROM OVID'S EPISTLES. The
text has been collated with that of the first
edition, 1680, which is the only one the present
editor has seen. The motto of the book is
from Ovid, *Ars Amat.* iii. 345, 346: "Or let
his *Epistles* be sung to thee with well-modu-
lated voice; that type of poetry, which others
knew not, he invented."

88¹, 4. *Mr. Sandys.* The translation of the
Metamorphoses by George Sandys was first
published in 1626, and was several times
reprinted.
  30. *A certain epigram.* MARTIAL, xi. 20.
  37. *That author's life.* Suetonius's life of
  Horace.

88², 36. *Cur,* etc. "Why did I behold anything?
Why did I make my eyes criminal?" OVID,
Tristia, ii. 103.

89¹, 19. *Nudam,* etc. "Diana naked and un-
clothed." Quoted inaccurately from *Tristia,*
ii. 105.
  40. *Cavalièrement.* With courtly grace.
  47. *He tells you himself,* etc. In *Tristia,* iv. 10.
  43–52. But there Ovid says that with Tibullus,
  as with Virgil, he was not personally acquainted.

89², 18. *Metamorphoses.* The 1680 text reads
Metamorphosis.
  30. *Nescivit,* etc. "He did not know how to
  leave alone what had gone well." From the
  elder Seneca, *Controversiæ,* ix. 5 (28). 17,
  with a change of tense.

90¹, 5. *Purpureus,* etc. "One or two purple
patches are sewn on, to glitter far and wide."
HORACE, *Ars Poet.* 15, 16.
  18. *Heinsius.* In his introductory note to the

Heroides, to which Dryden is also indebted at the close of this paragraph.

30. *Jupiter,* etc. "Jupiter used to go as suppliant to the heroines of olden times." OVID, *Ars Amat.* i. 713.

37. *Quam celer,* etc. "How swiftly did my Sabinus return from all parts of the world." OVID, *Amores,* ii. 18. 27.

40. *Arethusa to Lycotas.* PROPERTIUS, iv. 3.

90², 39. *To run division.* "The common old term for executing variations on a musical theme." KER.

45. *Nec verbum,* etc. *Ars Poet.* 133, 134.

48. *The Earl of Roscommon.* Roscommon translated the entire *Ars Poetica.*

55. *That servile,* etc. "Dryden has greatly improved his quotation by omitting four lines after the first couplet." KER.

91¹, 9. *Atque,* etc. "And the same winds will bear away your sails and your faith." OVID, *Heroides,* vii. 8: cf. **98**², 9.

33. *Brevis,* etc. "I try to be brief, and become obscure." *Ars Poet.* 25, 26.

39. *Dic mihi,* etc. Ibid. 141, 142.

48. *Denham and Cowley.* Dryden refers to Denham's preface to *The Destruction of Troy* (a translation from the second book of the *Æneid*), and Cowley's preface to his *Pindaric Odes.* Cf. **181**¹, 45, n; **319**², 50, n.

92², 3. *Et quæ,* etc. "You may drop that which you despair of making brilliant, if treated." Slightly altered from Horace, *Ars Poet.* 149, 150.

29. *The author.* Aphra Behn.

93, 39–42. *When . . . great.* These four lines are Dryden's own composition, without warrant in the Latin text. The inverted commas, which are here retained from the edition of 1680, were probably intended to call attention to this fact.

95. HELEN TO PARIS. The *foregoing epistle* mentioned in the argument, was that from Paris to Helen, translated by Duke.

97, 180. *Let me not live,* etc. A literal translation of the Latin would be: "May I perish, if all things do not invite us."

98, 17. *What people,* etc. Dryden has inserted into his poem a sly reference to the Exclusion Bill, by which the Whigs sought to deprive the Catholic Duke of York of the succession to the crown. The Latin says simply: "Who will yield the possession of their fields to men whom they know not?" Cf. **196**, 35, n.

100, 139. *Hyarbas.* Properly, *Iarbas.*

101. UPON YOUNG MR. ROGERS. "The family of Rogers seems to have been of considerable antiquity in Gloucestershire. They possessed the estate of Dowdeswell during the greater part of the sixteenth and seventeenth centuries. Many of their monuments are in the church of Dowdeswell, of which they were patrons. The subject of this epitaph was probably of this family." [SCOTT.]

EPITAPH ON THE MONUMENT OF THE MARQUIS OF WINCHESTER. The editor is indebted for a copy of this epitaph to the courtesy of the Reverend G. Gore Skipwith, rector of

Englefield. For the use of *Miscellany Poems,* 1712, he is indebted to Mrs. Edward Deshon Brandegee, of Faulkner Farm, Brookline, Massachusetts.

In line 1 the text of 1712 reads *undaunted* (for *untainted*).

102. EPITAPH ON MRS. MARGARET PASTON. "This is an ancient and distinguished family in Norfolk. The interest attaching to it from the *Paston Letters* is now considerable. Barningham is a charming Jacobean manor house between Aylsham and Cromer." [SCOTT and SAINTSBURY.]

EPITAPH ON SIR PALMES FAIRBORNE. The editor is indebted to the kindness of his friend Miss Elizabeth King, for a copy of the inscription in Westminster Abbey.

4. *Undaunted.* On the inscription *un-* seems to have been smoothed down and *dis-* substituted for it.

5. *Palladium.* The sacred image on which the safety of Troy was supposed to depend. *Balladium* on the inscription, by an evident mistake.

103¹. PROLOGUE . . . FROM THE SPANISH FRIAR. On this play, v. B. S. xxxv, xlii.

11. *Bromingam,* Birmingham acquired an evil repute for the coinage of counterfeit groats. Its name, under various forms, of which this is one (see N. E. D. under *Brummagem*), became a cant term for *spurious:* cf. **109**¹, 6, n.

21. *Notch'd.* N. E. D. explains as "having unevenly or closely cropped hair," and cites parallel passages. Scott comments: "It was anciently a part of the apprentice's duty . . . to take notes of the sermon for the edification of his master."

103², 43. *A fair attempt,* etc. The reference is to the assault on Dryden himself in Rose Alley on December 18, 1679, and probably also to the murder of Sir Edmund Berry Godfrey: v. n. **118,** 676.

46. *The new-found,* etc. The *Chambre Ardente* had been in session in 1679–80, investigating the Voisin and other notorious poisoning cases.

104¹, 3. *A woman wit,* etc. Aphra Behn.

7. *Cowley.* "Cowley published in his sixteenth year a book called *Poetical Blossoms.*" SCOTT.

104², 17 (Prol.). *Mercury.* This was a favorite title for newspapers at the time: a *Mercurius Domesticus,* published in 1679, may be intended here, though there need be no definite reference.

105¹, 25. *Take him for the blue. Blue* here seems equivalent to *bloom:* Dr. Johnson defines *bloom* as "the blue color upon plums and grapes newly gathered." The sense then is: "Accept the fruit, unripe as it is, since it is at least perfectly fresh."

1. *Discord and plots.* A reference to the disorders occasioned by the Popish Plot, and in particular (l. 4) to the suppression of the rebellion of the Scotch Covenanters by Monmouth in June, 1679.

105², 19. *Indian Emperor.* Dryden's own play: cf. **21.**

27. *Teg.* Cf. n. **19**², 55. But *Teg* seems to have

been the regular name for any stage Irishman, as Pat is to-day.

106¹, 31. *The suffragating tribes.* "The right of voting was only gradually extended to others than Romans proper." [SAINTSBURY.]

106², 35. *Oxford*, etc. This preference of Oxford to Cambridge must not be taken too seriously: cf. the quotation in headnote, p. **72**.

PROLOGUE TO OXFORD. The concluding lines of this prologue apparently refer to Dryden's political satires. If that is the case, too early a date has been assigned to the poem in the headnote.

1. *The fam'd Italian Muse*, etc. "Dryden seems, though perhaps unconsciously, to have borrowed the two first lines of this prologue from Drayton:

> The Tuscan poet doth advance
> The frantic Paladin of France.
> *Nymphidia.*" SCOTT.

The reference is to Ariosto, *Orlando Furioso*, xxxiv. 70, 82–86. (The editor is indebted for aid to Professor J. B. Fletcher, of Columbia University.)

11. *London votes.* London was the stronghold of the king's Whig opponents.

107¹. PROLOGUE . . . TO THE UNHAPPY FAVORITE. Christie suggests that this play was selected for the occasion because of a possible parallel between the story of Essex and that of Monmouth.

1. *When first*, etc. Cf. **750**, 70 f.

107². EPILOGUE. The text of this piece printed with the play furnishes the following variant readings: (11) *the Vision ;* (14) *Pent here ;* (18) *their venom daily spit ;* (20) *To the Upper Gallery* is inserted as a side-note; (22) *Or what is . . . does spite ;* (24) *These are the Authors that have ;* (25) *exercise ;* (31) *You had agreed your Play before the Prize ;* (32) *Faith you may hang your Harps ;* (36) *her if he.*

5. *Lott'ry cavaliers.* "The lottery cavaliers were the loyal indigent officers, to whom the right of keeping lotteries was granted by patent in the reign of Charles II." [SCOTT.]

8. *Three last ungiving parliaments.* "These were the parliaments of 1679, 1680, and the Oxford parliament of March, 1681. All three refused supplies to the crown, until they should obtain security, as they termed it, for the Protestant religion." [SCOTT.]

10. *Seven lean kine.* v. Genesis xli. 1–4.

108, 13. *Playhouse earth.* Cf. **117**, 636, 637.

14. *Our last fire.* v. headnote, p. **64**. On *Lilly*, v. n. **11**, 288; n. **54²**, 13 (*Epil.*).

15. *Third-days.* The third day of a play was the author's benefit performance : cf. **417**, 13 (*Epil.*).

21. *The Hatfield Maid.* This was a pamphlet telling of the apparition of a ghost of Whiggish inclinations to one Elizabeth Freeman, later called the Maid of Hatfield. [SCOTT.]

23. *Democritus*, etc. "*Heraclitus Ridens* was a paper published weekly on the part of the court, and answered by one called *Democritus on that* of the Whigs." [SCOTT.] Cf. **442²**, 3, n.

32. *Hang their harps*, etc. v. Psalm cxxxvii. 2. ABSALOM AND ACHITOPHEL. On the general occasion of this poem, see B. S. xliii, xliv. The motto: "If you stand nearer, it will attract you more," is from Horace, *Ars Poet.* 361, 362. In the following notes, F designates the first edition, Q the second; later editions are called ed. 3, ed. 4, etc. In 1716, in *The Second Part of Miscellany Poems*, Tonson published a *Key* to both parts of *Absalom and Achitophel*, to which all succeeding commentators are indebted.

108², 4. *Whig and Tory.* "These famous expressions of party distinction were just coming into fashion. Whig, a contraction of Whigamore, is derived from a word used by the peasantry in the west of Scotland in driving their horses, and gave a name to those fanatics who were the supporters of the Covenant in that part of Scotland. The Tories owe their name [Irish *toiridhe*, a pursuer] to the Irish banditti." [SCOTT.] Thus one side were *fanatic rebels*, the other *Popish thieves.*

109¹, 1. *A treasury of merits.* The saints, according to the Catholic doctrine, have merits more than sufficient for their own salvation; these merits may be applied to the saving of less holy persons.

6. *Enough.* F reads *enow.*

Anti-Bromingham. Anti-Whig. For the reputation of Birmingham, see **103¹**, 11, n. The Tories applied the term to the Whigs, perhaps in allusion to Monmouth's *spurious* pretensions to legitimacy. Or, according to another story, the Tories gave the name *Birmingham* Protestants to the Whigs, in sarcastic allusion to their claim of being the only *True Blue* Protestants: cf. the title of *Mac Flecknoe*, **134**. Cf. **124¹**, 40, n.

109², 20. *Origen.* Origen believed that salvation was possible for every rational creature. "The evil spirits which fell have not lost that spirit by which they are akin to God, which in its essence is inaccessible to evil, though it can be overgrown and overpowered." WESTCOTT, in *Dictionary of Christian Biography.*

33. *Ense rescindendum.* "Something that must be cut off with the sword." Ovid, *Met.* i. 191, has *ense recidendum ;* Virgil, *Æneid*, xii. 389, 390, has *ense . . . rescindant.* Cf. **314¹**, 27.

1 (verse). *In pious times*, etc. The profanity of these lines, which seek to excuse the profligacy of Charles II, aroused the wrath of a Nonconformist parson, who in 1682 published *A Whip for the Fools Back, who styles Honorable Marriage a Curs'd Confinement, in his Profane Poem of Absalom and Achitophel*, followed by, *A Key (with the Whip) to open the Mystery and Iniquity of the Poem call'd Absalom and Achitophel.* The two form one pamphlet, paged continuously: the first consists of just but crude raillery at the immorality of Dryden's opening lines. Dryden sneers at this writer in his *Epistle to the Whigs*, prefixed to *The Medal ;* v. **127²**, 30. Halkett and

Laing's *Dictionary of Anonymous and Pseudonymous Literature* identifies him with Christopher Nesse.

7. *Israel's monarch*, etc. David (v. 1 Samuel xiii. 14) and, in the parallel, King Charles II.

11. *Michal.* "Queen Catherine of Portugal, the wife of Charles II, resembled the daughter of Saul in the circumstance mentioned in the text." [SCOTT.] v. 1 Samuel xviii. 27; 2 Samuel vi. 23.

13. *Several mothers*, etc. This refers to Charles II's numerous family of illegitimate children.

110, 18. *Absalon.* F reads *Absolon.* The same variation occurs in line 221.

"James Scott, Duke of Monmouth and Buccleuch, was born at Rotterdam, April 9, 1649. He was the son of Charles II and of Lucy Walters, a beautiful young lady of a good Welsh family. After the Restoration, the king sent for this young gentleman to court, where the royal favor and his own personal and acquired accomplishments soon made him very remarkable. 'Nature,' says Count Hamilton, 'perhaps never formed anything so perfect as the external graces of his person.' Yet his mental qualities did not altogether support this prepossessing exterior. [Cf. **906,** 56.] — He was married, by the king's interference, to Anne Scott, Countess of Buccleuch, and heiress of the extensive estate which the powerful family she represented had acquired on the frontiers of Scotland. Thus favored at home, he was also fortunate enough to have an opportunity of acquiring military fame by serving two campaigns in Louis XIV's army against the Dutch, in 1672 and 1673. He also served with the Dutch against the French in 1678, and is on all hands allowed to have displayed great personal bravery. On his return to England, the duke met with a distinguished reception from Charles, by whom he was loaded with favors.

"Thus highly distinguished by rank, reputation, and royal favor, he appears for some time to have dedicated himself to the pleasures of the court. During the agitations over the Popish Plot, he was led to head the faction most inimical to the interests of the Duke of York, and speedily became distinguished by the name of the Protestant Duke. The prospect which now opened itself before Monmouth was such as might have turned the head of a man of deeper political capacity. The heir apparent, his personal enemy, had become the object of popular hatred to such a degree that the bill excluding him from the succession seemed to have every chance of being carried through the House of Lords, as it had already passed the Commons. It seems generally to have been believed that Charles was too fond of Monmouth, and too jealous of his brother, to hesitate at declaring this favorite youth his legitimate successor.

"Thus it is no wonder that Monmouth gave way to the dictates of ambition; and, while he probably conceived that he was only giving his father an opportunity to manifest

his secret partiality, he became more and more deeply involved in the plots of Shaftesbury, whose bustling and intriguing spirit saw at once the use to be made of Monmouth's favor with the king and popularity with the public. From that time their union became close and inseparable. Some of Monmouth's partisans had even the boldness to assert his legitimacy, which, however, was formally denied by the king. When the insurrection of the Covenanters broke out in Scotland, Monmouth was employed against them, a duty which he executed with fidelity and success. This was in the year 1679, and Monmouth's good fortune had then attained its summit. He was beloved by the people and general of all the forces; London was at the devotion of Shaftesbury; the Duke of York banished to Brussels, and universally detested on account of his religion. But either the king's attachment to the Catholic religion, or his sense of justice and hereditary right, occasioned an extraordinary alteration of measures at this momentous crisis. The Duke of York was summoned from abroad, and by his presence and activity at once assumed his ascendance over Charles. For although he was obliged to retire into Scotland to avoid the fury of the exclusionists, yet a sharper exile awaited his rival Monmouth, who, deprived of his commission as general, was sent into the foreign banishment from which his uncle had just been recalled. Accordingly he retired to Holland. Meanwhile the factions waxed still more furious, and Shaftesbury utterly embroiled the kingdom by persuading Monmouth to return to England (in November, 1679) without license from his father. This conduct deeply injured Monmouth in his father's favor, who refused to see him, had his chief offices taken from him, and caused him to be formally sent out of the kingdom by order in council. Monmouth, instead of leaving the country, in August, 1680, started on a quasi-royal progress through the west of England, with an affectation of popularity which gained the vulgar, but terrified the reflecting. Above all, by a close alliance with the Machiavel, Shaftesbury, he showed his avowed determination to maintain his pretensions against those of the lawful successor. This was the state of parties in 1681, when *Absalom and Achitophel* first appeared.

"The permission of so sharp a satire against the party of Monmouth, though much qualified as to his individual person, plainly showed the king's intention to proceed with energy against the leaders of the country party. Monmouth was arrested on September 20, 1682, and obliged to enter bail for his peaceable deportment and appearance when called on to answer any suit against him by the king. He was subsequently involved in the Rye House Plot, but was pardoned by the king. Being banished from court, he retreated to Holland, where he remained until after the

accession of James II. He then headed a
rebellion, which resulted in his entire defeat
and in his execution on the scaffold, July 15,
1685." [SCOTT.]

19. *Inspir'd by.* F reads *inspir'd with.*

34. *The charming Annabel.* See note on l. 18,
and B. S. xxi.

39. *Amnon's murther.* v. 2 Samuel xiii. 28, 29.
Scott and Christie think that this refers to an
assault in December, 1670, by some of Monmouth's troopers, upon Sir John Coventry,
a member of tne House of Commons who
had made a sarcastic allusion to the king's
amours. Coventry was not murdered, though
he was brutally disfigured, so that the parallel is not accurate.

42. *Sion.* London.

45. *The Jews.* The English.

51. *Adam-wits.* Probably only an allusion to
the state of Adam in Paradise, free except
that he was prohibited to eat of the tree of
knowledge. *Want* in the next line means *lack.*

57. *Saul.* Oliver Cromwell.

58. *Ishbosheth.* Richard Cromwell: v. 2 Samuel iii, iv.

59. *Hebron.* Scotland, where Charles had been
crowned on January 1, 1651; in England he
was not crowned until April 23, 1661. So
David reigned in Hebron before he reigned
in Jerusalem: v. 2 Samuel v. 4, 5.

66. *A State.* The word, as in l. 24, means *republic.*

82. *Good Old Cause.* That is, of the Commonwealth; Dryden's aim is to identify the Whigs
with the men who rebelled against Charles I.
There is, possibly, a more specific reference
to the intrigues between Charles I and the
Presbyterians and the parliament in 1647–48,
which led ultimately to the execution of the
king and the establishment of the Commonwealth.

85. *Jerusalem.* London.

86. *Jebusites.* Roman Catholics: for the name,
v. Judges i. 21; xix. 10.

87. *And theirs the native right.* As Professor
Collins points out, this and other unfinished
lines are probably in imitation of Virgil's
hemistichs: cf. 517[1], 55, n.

88. *The chosen people.* The Protestants.

90. *And every loss,* etc. The following lines do
not exaggerate the treatment of the Catholics
by the government and the people of England.

111, 104. *The Jewish rabbins.* "Doctors of the
Church of England." CHRISTIE.

108. *That Plot.* The Popish Plot, of which
Titus Oates gave the first information in
August, 1678. According to Oates' story,
Charles was to be murdered and James made
king as the agent of the Jesuits. A French
army was to support these schemes and aid
in suppressing Protestantism. Oates may
have had some slight foundation of truth for
his structure of lies.

114. *Some truth there was,* etc. A recent in-
vestigator of the Popish Plot, Mr. John Pollock, gives Dryden the following high (perhaps excessive) praise:

"Of all men whose reputation was made
or raised by the Popish Plot, none have since
maintained their fame at so even a height as
John Dryden. His person but not his name
suffered from the changes of fortune, and at
a distance of more than two centuries the sum
of continuous investigation has little to add
to the judgments passed on his times by the
greatest of satirists. The flashes of Dryden's
insight illumine more than the light shed by
many records. In politics, no less than in
society, his genius had ample room. The
Plot gave him a subject worthy of a master.
[Lines 114–117, 134–141 quoted.] The lines
are a witness against the two great parties
whose intrigues were woven to menace the
security of the English state. Oates' false
oaths ruined the hopes of the Roman Catholics: the designs of the English Whigs were
grounded on them." *The Popish Plot,* London,
1903, p. 222.

118. *Egyptian.* French: cf. **113,** 281–286. At
this time France was the leading Catholic
power. The following lines are a sneer at the
doctrine of transubstantiation, which Dryden
later defends in *The Hind and the Panther:*
v. **219, 220,** 85–153. Dryden is indebted to
the opening lines of Juvenal, xv, where, after
describing the Egyptian worship of animals,
the satirist exclaims: "It is impiety to violate and break with the teeth the leek and
the onion. O holy races, to whom such deities
as these are born in their gardens! Every
table abstains from woolly animals; it is impiety there to cut the throat of a young kid;
it is lawful to feed on human flesh." (*J. D.
Lewis's translation.*)

121. *As serv'd.* F reads *And serv'd.*

128. *Hebrew priests.* Anglican clergymen. The
fleece is of course the tithes paid by the parishioners; Dryden's sneers at priests are incessant.

150. *Of these,* etc. Professor Firth calls attention to the following passage in Coleridge's
Table Talk, August 6, 1832:

"You will find this a good gauge or crite-
rion of genius — whether it progresses and
evolves, or only spins upon itself. Take
Dryden's *Achitophel* and *Zimri:* . . . every
line adds to or modifies the character, which
is, as it were, a-building up to the very last
verse; whereas in Pope's *Timon,* &c., the first
two or three couplets contain all the pith of
the character, and the twenty or thirty lines
that follow are so much evidence or proof of
overt acts of jealousy, or pride, or whatever it
may be that is satirized."

Achitophel. Anthony Ashley Cooper (1621–
83), created Earl of Shaftesbury in 1672. He
inherited a large fortune, and became a member of parliament in 1640. On the outbreak
of the civil war he supported the king, and in
1643 raised troops in his aid. In 1644 he
changed sides, and performed military service under the parliamentary commanders.
He sat in the Barebone's Parliament in 1653,
where he was a leader of the moderate party,
and in later parliaments under Oliver Crom-

well and Richard Cromwell. He was also a
member of Cromwell's Council of State in
1653–54, but did not receive the usual salary
of £1000 for his services, and about the
close of 1654 became estranged from Cromwell, from whom he afterwards held aloof, and
whom he at times opposed. He actively promoted the Restoration, and after it became
prominent in the government. In 1661 he
was made Baron Ashley. In 1670–73 he was
a member of the Cabal ministry and in 1672–
73 Lord Chancellor. After the fall of the
Cabal he became the most conspicuous leader
of the Opposition. In 1678 and the following
years he took advantage of the belief in the
Popish Plot, and was the chief supporter of the
Exclusion Bill, which was brought forward
to deprive the Duke of York of the succession.
In 1679 he was for a short time in office as
Lord President of the Council. On July 2,
1681, he was arrested and confined to the
Tower on a charge of high treason, but was
released when the Middlesex grand jury refused to indict him. When set free, he remained in London, where he was safe so long
as Whig sheriffs remained in power. In 1682,
when the Tories had gained control of London,
Shaftesbury, with Monmouth and others,
formed fruitless plans for a rising against the
king. In November, 1682, he fled to Holland,
where he died on January 21 of the next year.
He was a constant supporter, though sometimes by unscrupulous means, of parliamentary government and, except as regards Catholics, whom he dreaded for political reasons, of
religious liberty. Dryden's wonderful satires
have done permanent injury, it may be
feared, to the reputation of a great man.

152. *Counsels.* F reads *Counsell.*

154. *Principles.* F reads *principle.*

156. *A fiery soul,* etc. A writer in *Notes and
Queries,* series I. ii. 468, cites the following
passages as possibly furnishing Dryden hints
for these lines:

"He was one of a lean body and visage, as
if his eager soul, biting for anger at the clog
of his body, desired to fret a passage through
it." FULLER, *The Holy State and the Profane
State* (in the life of Alva).

> The purest soul that e'er was sent
> Into a clayey tenement.
> CAREW, *Epitaph on the Lady Mary
> Villiers.*

The general idea of the contrast between
Shaftesbury's body and his mind is found in
Mulgrave's *Essay on Satire:* v. **915,** 100–116.

157. *Pigmy body.* In reference to Shaftesbury's
small stature.

163. *Great Wits,* etc. Seneca writes, quoting inaccurately from Aristotle (*Problems,* xxx. 1):
"There has been no great genius without a
mixture of madness." (*De Tranq. Animi,*
xvii.) But Dryden may have taken the idea
from Burton, *Anatomy of Melancholy,* i. 3. 3.

170. *To that unfeather'd,* etc. Shaftesbury's son
was a man of no capacity. Dryden contempt-

uously applies to him the definition of man
attributed to Plato: "A two-legged unfeather'd animal."

112, 175. *The triple bond he broke.* In 1668 a
triple alliance had been formed between England, Sweden, and the Dutch Republic,
against France. Shaftesbury played a prominent part in breaking up this alliance and
bringing on the Dutch war of 1672–74, in
which England was aided by France. He
was however not privy to any designs of
France against English freedom. In 1672
Dryden had been an ardent advocate of the
policy of the Cabal: v. B. S. xxviii; **70, 71.**
In 1673 dread of France, and of Catholic influence in England, replaced the previous
jealousy of Holland. There were fears, not
entirely groundless, of a French invasion in
the Catholic interest.

179. *Usurp'd a patriot's.* F reads *Assum'd a
Patron's.* The next twelve lines do not appear
at all in F. Their absence occasions an
abrupt and awkward transition. We may at
least conjecture — proof of course is impossible — that they were present in Dryden's
original draught of the poem, but omitted, in
order to deepen the satire on Shaftesbury,
when it was first published; and that line 179
was then altered in order partially to bridge
the gap caused by their omission. So far as
the editor can learn, Shaftesbury was not spe-
cially distinguished as a *patron,* nor can that
name be called *all-atoning.* If this conjecture be correct, Dryden in the second edition
simply reverted to his original text.

Patriot was the name affected by the faction
(the germ of the Whig party) that in 1680 sent
up petitions to Charles asking him to allow
Parliament to meet, that the Exclusion Bill
might be passed: cf. **121, 122,** 963–988.

188. *Abbethdin.* A rabbinical term for a certain
officer of the high court of justice of the Jews:
literally, *father of the house of judgment.* See
the *Jewish Encyclopedia* under *bet din.* It
is here applied to Shaftesbury as Lord Chancellor, the presiding judge in the Court of
Chancery.

196, 197. *David,* etc. Two interpretations are
possible for this couplet: David would have
made a song in honor of Achitophel, so that
(*a*) one of David's songs (perhaps Psalm iii,
or the lament of David for Absalom in 2
Samuel xviii. 33) would have been lacking; or
(*b*) that Dryden would have had no need
to write his immortal poem of *Absalom and
Achitophel.* The former meaning seems the
more likely to be true. The application to
Charles II is by no means clear.

198, 199. *But wild,* etc. "In Knolles' *History
of the Turks,* printed more than sixty years
before the appearance of *Absalom and Achitophel,* are the following verses, under a portrait of the Sultan Mustapha I:

> Greatnesse on Goodnesse loves to slide, not stand,
> And leaves for Fortune's ice Vertue's firme land.

The circumstance is the more remarkable,

because Dryden has really no couplet more
intensely Drydenian than this [lines 198, 199
of *A. and A.*], of which the whole thought,
and almost the whole expression, are stolen."
MACAULAY, *Essay on Temple*.

The poem from which this couplet is taken
is found on p. 1370 of the 1621 edition of
Knolles' work; it is in a continuation not included in the earlier editions. — The editor
is here indebted to Professor W. A. Neilson
of Harvard University.

204. *Manifest of crimes.* A Latinism, from Sallust's *manifestus sceleris* (*Jugurtha*, xxxv).
[CHRISTIE.] Cf. **767**, 623.

209. *More he makes.* Christie remarks that the
charge against Shaftesbury of fabricating
evidence for the Popish Plot is without foundation. Shaftesbury probably shared in the
belief in it by which he profited.

213. *Proves the king himself a Jebusite.* This
was, to quote Christie, "no calumnious invention of Shaftesbury." Charles II professed
himself a Catholic on his deathbed, and was
probably one in heart at the time of the
Restoration.

227. *Drawn*, etc. This line is repeated in *The
Hind and the Panther*, **220**, 211. The hint for
it he found in a couplet:

> It is decreed, we must be drain'd, I see,
> Down to the dregs of a democracy, —

which begins one of the poems in *Lachrymæ
Musarum*, 1649, the volume in which Dryden's poem *Upon the Death of the Lord Hastings* was first published. The poem is signed
M. N., which is expanded into M. Needham
in the copy of the book (in the issue of 1650)
once owned by the Countess of Huntingdon,
Hastings' mother, and now by Mr. Chew.

235. *Divides.* F reads *Shuts up.*

240. *Thee, Savior, thee*, etc. Dryden is indebted,
as Professor Collins shows, to Lucretius, i. 6:
Te, dea, te fugiunt venti (cf. **182**, 7); or to
Milton's imitation of that line in *Lycidas*, 39:

Thee, shepherd, thee the woods and desert caves, etc

113, 264. *Gath.* Explained in Tonson's *Key*,
published in *The Second Part of Miscellany
Poems*, 1716, as, "The Land of Exile, more
particularly Brussels, where King Charles II
long resided."

270–272. *He . . . strand.* Cf. **10**, 276–279.
Jordan's sand here means Dover, but in
120, 820 *Jordan's flood* is the Irish Channel.

281. *Pharaoh.* Louis XIV, with whom Charles
II was in alliance.

299. *And nobler*, etc. These lines probably express Shaftesbury's real motive. In desiring
a king who should hold power only by the
will of the people he anticipated the policy of
the Revolution.

310. *Metal. Metal* and *mettle* were at this time
not distinguished in spelling.

314. *Loyal.* So F and Q. Eds. 4, 5, and 6 read
Royal, probably by a misprint; the editor
has not seen ed. 3.

318. *Mankind's delight.* Copied from a phrase

used by Suetonius of the Emperor Titus:
amor ac deliciæ generis humani. Cf. **282**[1], 11 f.

114, 353. *His brother.* James, Duke of York. For
further tributes to him by Dryden, v. **204**,
36–77; **247**, 2200–2231.

381. *Contemn.* F reads *condemn.*

390. *Sanhedrin.* The high council of the Jews:
here, the *parliament.*

402. *My arts*, etc. "In 1679, when the antipathy to Popery had taken the deepest root
in men's minds, the House of Commons
passed a vote: 'That the Duke of York's being a Papist, and the hopes of his coming to
the crown, had given the highest countenance to the present conspiracies and designs
of the Papists against the king and the Protestant religion.' Charles endeavored to
parry the obvious consequences of this vote
by proposing to the Council a set of limi-
tations which deprived his successor, if a
Catholic, of the chief branches of royalty.
Shaftesbury, then President of the Council,
argued against this plan as totally ineffectual; urging that when the future king should
find a parliament to his mind the limita-
tions might be as effectually taken off as they
could be imposed. When the bill was brought
in, for the total exclusion of the Duke of York
from the succession, Shaftesbury favored it
with all his influence. It passed the Lower
House by a very large majority, but was rejected by the House of Lords, where Halifax
opposed it with very great ability. Shaftesbury, who had taken so decided a part against
the Duke of York in his dearest interests,
now could only look for safety in his ruin."
[SCOTT.]

416. *A nation.* F reads *a Million.*

418. *God was their king.* Alluding to the Commonwealth "without a king," established in
1649, which is compared to the condition of
Israel under the Judges. It was brought to
an end by the creation of the Protectorate
under Cromwell (*Saul*) in 1653.

115, 447. *A nation, and, like a lion*, etc. Cf. **795**, 242–244.

455. *Your case*, etc. Shaftesbury's party were
justly believed willing and anxious to raise
an armed rebellion against the king if they
could gain their ends in no other way.

116, 513. *Solymæan rout.* The London rabble:
Solyma is another name for Jerusalem. The
following lines refer to the submission of
the City to Cromwell, and its later turbu-
lency under Charles II.

517. *Ethnic plot.* The Popish Plot, made by the
Gentiles (τὰ ἔθνη): that is, here, the Jebusites,
or Catholics.

519. *Hot Levites.* The Presbyterian clergymen,
who in 1662 had been forced to leave the
Church of England by the Act of Uniformity,
which required unfeigned consent to everything contained in the Book of Common
Prayer as a condition of holding a benefice.
Their followers were mainly among the
tradesmen and merchants of the towns.

525. *Aaron's race.* The priesthood: v. 1 Chronicles vi. 49.

536. *Fathers'.* Q and eds. 5, 6 read *Father's;* F reads *fathers.*

539. *Born to be sav'd,* etc. A sneer at the Calvinistic doctrine of election.

544. *Zimri.* George Villiers, second Duke of Buckingham. On his relations with Dryden, v. B. S. xxviii, xliii. Dryden was fully aware of the genius shown in this portrait: v. **313, 314.** The portrait is not only brilliant but just. As Scott writes: "The Restoration put into the hands of the most lively, mercurial, ambitious, and licentious genius who ever lived, an estate of £20,000 a year, to be squandered in every wild scheme which the lust of power, of pleasure, of license, or of whim could dictate to an unrestrained imagination." Buckingham was a member of the Cabal ministry, but was dismissed from office in 1674. Changing sides, he strove to become a leader of the Opposition, and "made a most active figure in all proceedings which had relation to the Popish Plot." — "As Dryden owed the duke no favor, he has shown him none. Yet, even here, the ridiculous rather than the infamous part of his character is touched upon, and the unprincipled libertine, who slew the Earl of Shrewsbury while his adulterous countess held her lover's horse in the disguise of a page, is not exposed to hatred." Yet Dryden glances at this intrigue in the name *Zimri:* v. Numbers xxv. 6–15. A pamphlet, replying to Dryden, *Poetical Reflections on a late Poem entitled Absalom and Achitophel, by a Person of Honour,* is ascribed to Buckingham by Wood in *Athenæ Oxonienses.* Malone (I, 1; 36, 37) reprints the opening lines of it. It has none of the sparkle shown in *The Rehearsal.*

Professor Collins points out that Dryden drew hints for his portrait from Horace, *1 Satires,* iii. 1–20, and Juvenal, iii. 73–77: cf. **329,** 133–141.

Pope, in *Moral Essays,* iii. 297–314 (Cambridge edition, p. 169) gives a brilliant, though inaccurate, description of the death of Buckingham.

117, 574. *Balaam.* Theophilus Hastings, Earl of Huntingdon, younger brother of the Lord Hastings whom Dryden lamented in his first poem. At first an adherent of Monmouth, he later changed sides and joined the party of James II. — *Well-hung* may mean *fluent, voluble,* as in the following couplet, cited by Professor Firth:

> Flippant of talk and voluble of tongue,
> With words at will, no lawyer better hung.
> OLDHAM, Satire in Imitation of the Third of Juvenal.

It has also, however, a coarser meaning, which would make a truly Drydenian antithesis to *cold:* v. N. E. D. and E. D. D.

Caleb. Lord Grey, called cold because of the report that he consented to an intrigue between his wife and Monmouth.

575. *Nadab.* "William, Lord Howard of Escrick, although an abandoned debauchee, made occasional pretensions to piety. He

had served under Cromwell and been a preacher of the Anabaptists. Being accused of inspiring a treasonable libel on the court party, he was sent to the Tower, where he uttered and published a canting declaration, asserting his innocence, upon the truth of which he received the sacrament. He is said, however, to have taken the communion in *lamb's wool* — ale poured on roasted apples and sugar." [SCOTT.] There is a certain propriety in the name, since Nadab "offered strange fire before the Lord:" v. Leviticus x. 1.

581. *Jonas.* Sir William Jones, the attorney general who conducted the prosecution of those implicated in the Popish Plot. In November, 1679, he resigned his office, disgusted, it is said, with his work, and became an opponent of the court party. He drew up the Habeas Corpus Act, passed in 1679, which was a most important check on the arbitrary power of the government. Christie conjectures that he also draughted the Exclusion Bill.

585. *Shimei.* Slingsby Bethel, one of the two Whig sheriffs of London. He was a consistent republican, who had written both against royalty and against Cromwell. In lines 614, 615 Dryden probably refers to his recent tract, *The Interest of Princes and States.* Bethel's stinginess, in contrast to the hospitality expected of a sheriff, became proverbial. — By packing juries with Whigs, the sheriffs protected persons prosecuted by the court party, thus securing an *ignoramus* verdict on Shaftesbury himself shortly after this poem was published. — Dryden applies to him the name of the "man of the family of the house of Saul" who cursed David: v. 2 Samuel xvi. 5; 1 Kings ii. 36–46.

Youth did early. F reads, *early Youth did.*

598. *Sons of Belial.* For the phrase, cf. Deuteronomy xiii. 13 ; 1 Samuel x. 27.

617. *Rechabite.* v. Jeremiah xxxv. 14.

624. *Towns once burnt.* Referring to the great fire of London: cf. **44,** 833 f.

628. *Moses'.* Here and in l. 649 the early editions print *Moses's.*

632. *Corah.* Titus Oates (1649–1705), the contriver of the Popish Plot. Except that Korah was a rebellious Levite (v. Numbers xvi) there is no special appropriateness in the name. Oates was the son of an Anabaptist, of a family of ribbon-weavers, who later became a Church of England clergyman. He himself first took orders in the Church of England; then, being disgraced for misconduct, became ostensibly a Catholic. During his subsequent residence in Spain and France he professed to have received a degree from the University of Salamanca (l. 658), and to have gained a knowledge of Jesuit plots against the English government. In his testimony, he continually pieced out his original deposition by additional information, which he stated he had at first forgotten. During the reign of James II he was fined, whipped, and pilloried for his perjuries; under William III he received a pension.

633. *Erect thyself*, etc. Dryden sarcastically compares Oates to the brazen serpent made by Moses, which brought salvation to the children of Israel: v. Numbers xxi. 6–9.

118, 649. *A church vermilion*, etc. Jovial churchmen are proverbially of a ruddy complexion: Molière speaks of Tartuffe's *teint frais* and *bouche vermeille* in a line (v. *Tartuffe*, i. 4) that may have been in Dryden's mind. — And when Moses came down from Mount Sinai after his talk with the Lord, "the skin of his face shone:" v. Exodus xxxiv. 29–35 ; cf. **889,** 103.

665. *Writ.* F reads *Wit.*

676. *Agag's murther.* Sir Edmund Berry Godfrey, the magistrate before whom Oates had made his deposition, was soon after found dead in a field, with his sword run through his body. Oates hastened to assert that he had been murdered by Catholics, and by his complete success gained credence for his other stories. Dryden here represents Oates as instigating Godfrey's murder in order to profit by it, and, though the mystery will probably never be solved, his explanation has important arguments in its favor. (Of the most recent writers, John Pollock, in *The Popish Plot* (1903) maintains that Godfrey was killed by Jesuits, as Oates asserted ; Alfred Marks, in *Who killed Sir Edmund Berry Godfrey ?* (1905), argues that he committed suicide.) For the scriptural comparison, v. 1 Samuel xv: Samuel reproached Saul for not killing Agag, king of the Amalekites.

682. *Surrounded*, etc. v. n. **110,** 18.

688. *His joy conceal'd.* F reads *Dissembling Joy.*

697. *Hybla-drops.* The honey of Hybla in Sicily was famous: cf. **152,** 1123, n.

705. *Egypt and Tyrus.* France and Holland.

710. *Bathsheba.* Louise de Kéroualle, Duchess of Portsmouth, the reigning mistress of Charles II. The preceding line refers to the subsidies which Charles received from France.

727. *Believe.* F reads *believes.*

119, 738. *Wise Issachar.* Thomas Thynne, of Longleat in Wiltshire, who entertained Monmouth on his progress through the kingdom in 1680. *Wise* is sarcastic: compare the description (Genesis xlix. 14) of Issachar as "*a strong ass* couching down between two burdens."

742. *Depths.* F reads *depth.*

750. *A brother and a wife.* Oates attempted to involve both the Duke of York and Queen Catherine in the Popish Plot. The queen's failure to bear children, by opening the way for the Duke of York's succession, was in a sense the cause of the party strife in England.

759. *What shall we think ?* etc. In the remarkable passage that follows, Dryden sets forth his views on political philosophy. Unlike most Tories, he grounds the royal power not on *divine right*, but on a *covenant* made by the governed, to avoid the anarchy of a state of nature *where all have right to all* (l. 794). He thus shows his sceptical turn of mind by accepting a fundamental tenet of Hobbes. He will not, however, agree with Hobbes that this covenant once made is irrevocable, since such a conclusion leaves the people defenseless. Yet he sees, as well as Hobbes himself, that to admit that the governed can revoke their covenant, opens the door to anarchy. Unable to extricate himself from this logical dilemma, he subsides into a kind of opportunistic conservatism: innovation is justified in extreme cases, to preserve the falling State; otherwise, it is to be condemned. In *Religio Laici* (**165, 166,** 276–355) Dryden adopts a similarly shuffling attitude when discussing the relative authority of Scripture and tradition.

777. *Add, that the pow'r.* F reads, *That Pow'r, which is.*

The pow'r for property allow'd. The recognized possession of power.

785, 786. *What standard,* etc. The couplet is, for Dryden, singularly obscure. The fickle crowd is apparently compared to water, which, after rising to the *mark* or boundary it was intended to reach, overflows all the faster. (The editor is here somewhat indebted to a note by Professor Collins.)

804. *To touch our ark.* To commit sacrilege: for touching the ark of the covenant Uzzah was struck dead: v. 2 Samuel vi. 6, 7.

120, 817. *Barzillai.* James Butler, Duke of Ormond (1610–88). As Lord Lieutenant of Ireland (cf. l. 820) he had fought bravely on the side of Charles I. He was a companion in exile, and later a most loyal and honorable servant, of Charles II. To him Dryden dedicated in 1683 the translation of *Plutarch's Lives* for which he wrote the *Life of Plutarch.* Here he appropriately gives him the name of the aged benefactor of David, "a very great man:" v. 2 Samuel xix. 31–39.

829. *His bed,* etc. "The Duke of Ormond had eight sons and two daughters. Six of those sons were dead in 1681, when this poem was published." [SCOTT.]

831. *His eldest hope,* etc. Thomas, Earl of Ossory (1634–80). He had distinguished himself on sea in the Dutch wars of 1665–67 and 1672–74; and on land in 1677 and 1678, fighting with the Dutch under the Prince of Orange against the French. At the battle of Mons (v. n. **84¹,** 25) he had commanded the English auxiliaries. He died of a fever in 1680. — In ll. 832, 833 Dryden is indebted to Virgil, *Æneid,* v. 49, 50.

834. *Unequal fates.* Virgil's *fata iniqua* (unjust fates), *Æneid,* ii. 257; x. 380.

838. *O narrow circle,* etc. Cf. **4,** 18, n; **274,** 270–273.

844. *O ancient honor,* etc. Dryden is again indebted to Virgil; *Æneid,* vi. 878–880.

846. *Thy name.* F reads, *thy Birth ;* eds. 4, 5, 6 read, *his Name.*

847. *Fame.* F reads *Worth.*

858. *And left this verse,* etc. The hearse was, according to N. E. D.: "A temple-shaped structure of wood used in royal and noble funerals. . . . It was customary for friends to pin short poems or epitaphs upon it."

864. *Zadoc.* William Sancroft, Archbishop of Canterbury. v. 2 Samuel viii. 17.

866. *The Sagan of Jerusalem.* Henry Compton, Bishop of London, the youngest son of the second Earl of Northampton. Dryden takes the word *sagan* (more correctly *segen*), meaning *prefect, governor,* from the Hebrew. In post-biblical times the *segen* (abbreviated for *segen of the priests*) was the priest next in rank to the high priest. For this note, and for that on *abbethdin* (l. 188) the editor is indebted to Professor William Popper of the University of California.

868. *Him of the western dome.* John Dolben (1625–86), Dean of Westminster. By the *prophets' sons* (cf. 2 Kings ii. 3) Dryden means the boys of Westminster School. Dolben became Archbishop of York in 1683: cf. **708**[2], 5–7.

877. *Adriel.* John Sheffield (1648–1721), Earl of Mulgrave, and afterwards Marquis of Normanby (1694) and Duke of Buckingham and Normanby (1703). He was the patron to whom Dryden dedicated his *Aureng-Zebe* and his translation of the *Æneid.* He is probably called *sharp-judging* because of his *Essay on Satire* (v. **913–916**) and his *Essay on Poetry.* In 1679 Charles II bestowed on him the governorship of Hull, and the lord lieutenancy of Yorkshire, two of the offices that had been taken from Monmouth. For further details, v. B. S. xxxviii–xl.

882. *Jotham.* George Savile (1633–95), Viscount, Earl, and finally Marquis of Halifax, was the leader of the *Trimmers,* a small party that sought to mediate between the Whigs and the Tories, thus *trimming the boat.* From 1673 to 1679 he had been in opposition to the government, as a leader of the *Country* party, the predecessors of the Whigs; he was thus associated by political principles with Lord Shaftesbury, with whom he was also connected by marriage. From the first, however, he opposed the project of excluding the Duke of York from the succession; and by his eloquent speeches in the House of Lords, November 15, 1680, in opposition to Shaftesbury, he actually *turned the balance* against the Exclusion Bill (cf. n. **114**, 402). (So Jotham in a parable rebuked the conspirator Abimelech and his followers, and foretold their ruin: v. Judges ix.) His services to the king's party gained him a commanding influence in the government from May, 1681, to March, 1682. Dryden in 1691 dedicated to him his opera of *King Arthur.*

"Curiously enough, Halifax records, on the authority of Dryden himself, that the poet was at one time offered money to write verses against him (Devonshire House 'note book')." H. C. FOXCROFT: *Life and Letters of Sir George Savile, Bart., First Marquis of Halifax,* London, 1898, vol. i, p. 327.

Piercing. F reads *ready.*

888. *Hushai.* Laurence Hyde (1641–1711),

Viscount Hyde, later Earl of Rochester, son of the Earl of Clarendon, whom Dryden addressed in an early poem: v. **15**. Hyde, when young, held important diplomatic offices; in 1679 he was made First Lord of the Treasury, and became one of the most important ministers of the time. He was a patron of Dryden, to whom poems ridiculing him are falsely ascribed: v. **925, 929**. Hushai, the friend of David, was the chief agent in overthrowing the counsel of Achitophel: v. 2 Samuel xv–xvii.

121, 899. *Amiel.* "Edward Seymour was descended of the elder branch of the illustrious family of that name. [The then Duke of Somerset was descended from a younger branch of the same family.] He was Speaker of the House of Commons, 1673–79." [SCOTT.]

910. *Th' unequal ruler of the day.* Phaethon, the son of Apollo, god of the sun, who rashly attempted to drive his father's chariot.

944. *Th' offenders,* etc. The Whigs had questioned the king's power to pardon and commute punishment, notably in the cases of the Earl of Danby and Lord Stafford.

957–960. *But O . . . son!* These lines are not found in F; they were added to soften the satire on Monmouth.

965. *Patriot's.* v. n. **112**, 179.

966. *Supplant.* F reads *destroy;* the change is again in the direction of mildness.

971. *His old instructor,* etc. "Shaftesbury, who lost his place as Chancellor in November, 1673." CHRISTIE. But the line may possibly refer to Shaftesbury's dismissal in October, 1679, from the post of Lord President of the Council, to which he had been appointed in the preceding April: cf. **140**, 203.

122, 981. *They petition.* v. n. **112**, 179. The next line refers of course to Genesis xxvii. 22.

987. *Unsatiate,* etc. v. Proverbs xxx. 15, 16.

1006. *Law,* etc. Moses on Mount Sinai was not allowed to behold the face of the Lord, "For there shall no man see me, and live;" he was permitted, however, to see the "back parts" of the Lord (Exodus xxxiii. 20–23). Dryden here terms Grace the *hinder parts* of Law: the Whigs have clamored for Law against the Catholics and denied the king's power to grant pardon; hence they shall behold the face of Law and die themselves.

1010. *By their own arts,* etc. Dryden borrows from Ovid: cf. **727**, 739, 740.

1012. *Against themselves,* etc. "This is rather an imprudent avowal of what was actually the policy of the court faction at this time. They contrived to turn against Shaftesbury and his party many of those very witnesses by whom so many Catholics had been brought to execution." [SCOTT.]

1028. *Henceforth,* etc. Cf. **11**, 292, 293; **29**, 71, n.; **428**, 5–8.

PROLOGUE . . . TO THE LOYAL BROTHER. Neither of these pieces is directly assigned to Dryden in the 1682 edition of Southerne's play, from which the present texts are taken.

But in the dedicatory letter in which Southerne offers to the Duke of Richmond "the
first fruits of his Muse," there occurs the following sentence: " Nor durst I have attempted
thus far into the world, had not the Laureate's
own pen secur'd me, maintaining the out-
works, while I lay safe intrench'd within his
lines; and malice, ill nature, and censure
were forc'd to grin at a distance."

The two pieces were also published by Tonson as a broadside (undated), of which the
editor has used a copy made at the British
Museum. Here both pieces are ascribed to
Dryden, and the epilogue is said to have been
"spoken by Mrs. Sarah Cook:" cf. **155**²
(*Epil.*). The only variations of text of any
importance are *And* (for *But*) in l. 43 of the
Prologue, and *to* (for *till*) in l. 2 of the *Epilogue*. In ll. 36 and 46 of the *Prologue* the
text published with the play reads, *They
miter'd* and *inspire :* both obvious misprints.

123¹, 7. *Petitions.* v. n. **112**, 179.

13. *The Whig*, etc. This was part of the pro-
gram of Shaftesbury's party in 1681.

19. *Grave penny chroniclers*, etc. Scott printed
a copy (v. SS. vi. 237–240) of the identical
pamphlet to which Dryden refers, and of
which his verses might serve as a summary.
It describes the pope-burning of November 17,
1679.

20. *Sir Edmond-berry.* v. n. **118, 676.**

123², 50. *Five praying saints*, etc. The Conventicle Act of 1664 prohibited all religious meetings, not in accordance with the practice of
the Church of England, at which there should
be assembled " five persons or more . . . over
and above those of the same household."

7. *The King's House.* "Where the play was
acted." SCOTT.

124¹, 15. *An honest jury*, etc. Cf. n. **117**, 585.

21. *The leaden farthing.* "Alluding to the
tokens issued by tradesmen in place of copper
money, which, though not a legal tender of
payment, continued to be current by the
credit of the individual whose name they
bore." [SCOTT.]

25. *Pension-parliament.* "The parliament which
sat from the Restoration till 1678 bore this
ignominious epithet among the Whigs."
SCOTT.

40. *True Protestants.* A title that the Whigs
arrogated to themselves, insinuating that the
Tories were false ones, almost Papists: cf. n.
109¹, 6, and heading to *Mac Flecknoe*, **134.**
There is also an allusion to the emigration of
the French Huguenots into England, caused
by the persecuting spirit of the French government.

PROLOGUE . . . TO THE PRINCESS OF CLEVES.
Lee based his play on the celebrated romance
of the same title, by Mme. de La Fayette.
The virtuous Princess of Cleves confesses her
love for the Duke Nemours to her husband,
and claims his protection against herself.
The Prince of Cleves dies of grief at the
thought of her (assumed) infidelity. Thereupon her sense of honor and duty proves

stronger than her love for Nemours, whose
advances she rejects, afterwards retiring
entirely from life at court: v. *Epilogue*, ll.
23–32. This delicate central situation Lee
surrounds with an underplot unusually filthy
even for the Restoration stage. Nemours
is the person described in the opening lines
of the *Prologue*.

124², 19. *Perjuria*, etc. OVID, *Ars Amat.* i. 633:
cf. **727**, 714, 715.

125¹, 34. *Renouncing.* At this time, to *renounce*
was to fail to follow suit, though in possession
of a proper card. It now usually means to
fail to follow suit through the lack of a proper
card.

6. *High-flying.* An epithet applied to the extreme Tories, who supported lofty claims on
behalf of the authority of the king and the
Church.

THE MEDAL. On this poem, v. B. S. xliv–xlix.
The motto is from Virgil, *Æneid*, vi. 588,
589: cf. **604**, 792–795. As in the case of
Absalom and Achitophel, Dryden's name was
never directly joined to the poem during his
lifetime.

126¹, 14. *Polander.* "It was a standing joke
among the opponents of Shaftesbury, that he
hoped to be chosen King of Poland at the
vacancy in 1673–74 when John Sobieski was
elected." [SCOTT.] Hence his followers were
called Polanders.

23. *B.* George Bower, the artist of the Medal:
v. headnote.

34. *No-Protestant Plot.* A tract in three parts,
by Robert Ferguson (v. **142**, 321, n.) published in 1681–82. The full title of the first
part is: *No Protestant-Plot: or the pretended
conspiracy of Protestants against the King and
Government discovered to be a conspiracy of
the Papists against the King and his Protestant
Subjects.* Mr. T. F. Henderson writes in
D. N. B.: "The authorship of the first two
parts has usually been ascribed to Shaftesbury, but Ferguson claims the authorship of
the whole three." The object of it was to defend Shaftesbury and the Whigs from the
charge of having treasonable designs against
the king at Oxford.

42. *Scanderbeg.* An Albanian prince (1414?–
67), famous for his wars against the Turks.
When the Turks captured Alessio, where he
was buried, the janizaries disinterred his
bones, and used them as amulets.

126², 10. *Association.* Among Shaftesbury's papers there was found the draught of a project,
unsigned, and not in his handwriting, for an
Association to protect the Protestant religion,
the king's person, and the liberties of the subject, against the exercise of arbitrary power.
This was a main support of the charge of
high treason that had been rejected by the
grand jury.

Similar projects had also been mooted in
parliament. — "Another vote [in the House
of Commons of the second short parliament
1680] went much higher: it was for an Association, copied from that in Queen Elizabeth's

time, for the revenging the king's death upon all Papists, if he should happen to be killed. The precedent of that time was a specious color. But this difference was assigned between the two cases: Queen Elizabeth was in no danger but from Papists; so that Association struck a terror into that whole party, which did prove a real security to her, and therefore her ministers set it on. But now it was said there were many republicans still in the nation, and many of Cromwell's officers were yet alive, who seemed not to repent of what they had done; so some of these might by this means be encouraged to attempt on the king's life, presuming that both the suspicions and revenges of it would be cast upon the duke and the Papists. Great use was made of this to possess all people that this Association was intended to destroy the king instead of preserving him." BURNET.

"Lord Essex . . . moved [in the House of Lords of the same parliament] that an Association should be entered into to maintain those expedients [of limiting the royal power in case a Catholic should become king], and that some cautionary towns should be put into the hands of the Associators during the king's life to make them good after his death. The king looked on this as a deposing of himself . . . and as worse than the Exclusion." IBID.

37. *To petition in a crowd.* The Act of 13 Car. II. c. 5 (1661), provided that no persons, without previous legal permission, should procure more than twenty signatures to any petition, and that no petition should be presented to the king or the parliament by a body of more than ten persons.

127¹, 6. *Your dead author's pamphlet,* etc. The reference is to *An Account of the Growth of Popery and Arbitrary Government in England,* by Andrew Marvell (1621–78), published in 1677. "As it traced the intrigues of the court of England with that of France, it made a great impression on the nation." [SCOTT.]

9. *Buchanan.* George Buchanan (1506–82), famous as historian, political writer, and Latin poet. In the work mentioned in the text he defends *limited* monarchy. The book was a favorite with the men of the Long Parliament, but the editor can find no confirmation for the statement that Milton was particularly indebted to it.

12. *Guisards.* Cf. 154, 155 (Prol.); 8, 101, 102.
  Davila. An Italian historian (1576–1631). His *Storia delle Guerre Civili di Francia* is said to have gone through more than two hundred editions.

20. *Theodore Beza.* A French reformer (Théodore de Bèze, 1519–1605), the leader of the Calvinist party after the death of its founder.

35. *Some.* So in eds. 1 and 3; ed. 2 reads *same.*

53. *A parallel betwixt this Association,* etc. "In 1584 there was a general Association entered into by the subjects of Queen Elizabeth for the defense of her person, supposed to be

endangered by the plots of the Catholics and malcontents." [SCOTT.]

56. *Of the one.* Eds. 2 and 3 omit *the.*

127², 23. *Let your verses,* etc. Settle, for example, continually introduces parodies of Dryden's own verses into his *Absalom Senior,* which he wrote in reply to *Absalom and Achitophel;* cf. B. S. xlv.

30. *The Nonconformist parson,* etc. v. n. 109², 1 (verse).

41. *Is printed.* Eds. 2 and 3 read *are printed.*

61. *Saucy Jack. Jack* was a common epithet at this time for a low-bred or ill-mannered fellow.

128, 10 (prose). *Irish witnesses.* Certain Irishmen who, protected by Shaftesbury, had told of a Catholic plot in Ireland, later turned against him. The Whigs refused to credit them when they began to swear on the Tory side.

3 (verse). *Polish.* v. n. 126¹, 14.

26. *A martial hero,* etc. There is much misrepresentation in the following lines; v. n. 111, 150. Shaftesbury was twenty-three before he became a rebel; and, according to Christie, the charges in ll. 32–35, 38, lack authority, and that in l. 37 is exaggerated.

27. *Pigmy.* Cf. 111, 157, n.

41. *Interlope.* To traffic irregularly, without a proper license: cf. 261, 17.

62. *White witches.* Witches using their supernatural arts only for good purposes.

65. *He loos'd,* etc. v. 112, 175, n.

129, 73. *So Samson,* etc. v. Judges xvi. 15–20.

77. *When his just sovereign,* etc. In March, 1672, the king, supported by Ashley, who was shortly afterwards created Earl of Shaftesbury, issued a Declaration of Indulgence, granting toleration to Catholics and Dissenters. When parliament resisted this measure, as an abuse of the prerogative, Charles withdrew it, in March, 1673. Shaftesbury, who seems to have learned in the meantime of the intrigues of Charles with France for the establishment of the Catholic religion in England, then supported, in opposition to the king, the Test Act, by which all honest Catholics and most dissenters were excluded from office. Owing to this proceeding he lost his place as Chancellor in November, 1673, and ceased to be one of the king's advisers. He then entered on a course of violent opposition to the king.

94. *Thou leap'st,* etc. Dryden inserts this long line of fourteen syllables, for which he was unjustly ridiculed by contemporaries, to symbolize, by its departure from regular meter, the departures of the crowd from reason. (Cf. 429, 75, n; 785, 83, n; 820, 666; 891, 106, n; 897, 568.) At this time, also, Pindar was regarded as a peculiarly *wild and ungovernable* poet: v. 91², 26. Hence, in translating some of his odes, Cowley used an irregular versification, in which he frequently employed Alexandrine lines, of twelve syllables, hence called *Pindaric* lines; and occasionally still longer lines, of fourteen syllables: cf. 181. 512.

95. *Athens*, etc. The Athenians put to death Phocion on a charge of treason (B. C. 317) and Socrates on a charge of impiety (B. C. 399). In both cases they later repented of their acts, and raised statues to the memory of their victims.

119. *Jehu.* v. 2 Kings ix. 20.

131. *We loathe*, etc. v. Numbers xi.

135. *That kings*, etc. A Tory maxim, still maintained as an English legal fiction.

145. *The man*, etc. Dryden is probably indebted, as Saintsbury shows, to Sir Thomas Browne, *Pseudodoxia Epidemica*, vii. 16. 2. The story goes back ultimately to an anecdote concerning Marcus Licinius Crassus Agelastus (the *never-laughing*), the grandfather of the triumvir: v. *C. Lucilii Carminum Reliquiæ*, ed. F. Marx, Leipzig, 1904, vol. i, p. 89; vol. ii, pp. 412–414.

130, 149. *The witnesses*, etc. See note on *Irish witnesses*, **128**, 10 (prose). Other witnesses also had changed sides. The Whigs were loth to admit that they had been the dupes of men who lived by perjury, and yet could make no other tenable defense against the accusations brought against them.

156. *They rack*, etc. Referring to the dissenters' plea that each individual should interpret the Scriptures for himself; and to some extremists' claim of an immediate inspiration, which authorized them to preach in public, all laws to the contrary notwithstanding. Cf. **159**[2], 9–22; **167**, 398–426; **223, 224,** 452–496; **227, 676–708.**

173. *Yet monsters*, etc. A reminiscence of Ovid: cf. **394**, 565–572.

174. *Engender'd on.* So ed. 1 (without Latin motto) and eds. 2, 3; ed. 1 (with Latin motto) reads *Enlivend by.*

179–182. *Thy . . . hands.* So ed. 1 (without Latin motto), and eds. 2, 3; ed. 1 (with Latin motto) transposes the couplets 179, 180 and 181, 182, and in 182 reads, *But what's the Head.*

181. *The head*, etc. "As matters carried more and more the appearance of actual insurrection and civil war, the more wealthy of the citizens of London began to draw to the royal party. By means of this party Sir John Moore, a man favorable to the court, was elected Lord Mayor." [SCOTT.] He could, however, accomplish little while hampered by his *two gouty hands*, the Whig sheriffs, Shute and Pilkington. v. **152**, 1131–1140, and note on 1135.

201. *Whether*, etc. Cf. **127**[1], **159–161.**

205. *Their trait'rous combination.* The Association: v. n. **126**[2], 10.

217. *Thus*, etc. v. Matthew xxi. 33–39.

131, 226. *Cyclop-like.* A reference to the story of the Cyclops Polyphemus, who ate the flesh of men: v. *Odyssey*, ix.

229. *Clip . . . ring.* Until 1662, most of the money coined in England was hammered, not milled, and the hammered money continued in circulation after that date: cf. **518**[1], 45, n. Such coins were liable to be clipped on the edge: if the clipping extended within the ring inside which the sovereign's head was placed, the piece would not pass current. v. *Hamlet*, ii. 2. 447: "Pray God, your voice, like a piece of uncurrent gold, be not crack'd within the ring."

237. *Their crime.* Eds. 2 and 3 read *the Crime*

240. *Whet like a Croatian band.* Taken merely as a symbol of lawless ferocity, probably with an allusion to the wars between Austria and Turkey.

270. *Stum.* "New wine used to freshen up stale and cause a second fermentation." [SAINTSBURY.] Cf. n. **741**[1], 50.

272. *The formidable cripple.* For further satire on Shaftesbury's bodily infirmities, v. **915,** 100–114.

285. *Bedlam.* The popular term for a famous lunatic asylum, the Hospital of St. Mary of Bethlehem, in London: cf. **375**, 212.

287. *Without*, etc. Compare the conclusion to *The Hind and the Panther* (**252**, 2567 f) which similarly prophesies discord among the poet's opponents.

293. *Thy decrepit age.* "Shaftesbury was at this period little above sixty years old. But he was in a state of premature decrepitude; partly owing to natural feebleness of body, and partly to an injury which he received by an overturn in a Dutch carriage when he was in Holland, in 1660, as one of the Parliamentary Committee." [SCOTT.]

132, 317. *Collatine.* Lucius Tarquinius Collatinus took a prominent part in the dethronement of the last king of Rome, his kinsman Tarquinius Superbus, and was elected one of the first two consuls. He was later compelled to withdraw himself, owing to his bearing the name of Tarquin. Thus, Dryden predicts, Monmouth, if he ever became king, would be compelled to withdraw, owing to his kinship with the royal line.

323. *Pudet*, etc. OVID, *Metamorphoses*, i. 757, 758, with a change of *nobis* to *vobis* to suit the context. "Shameful is it that these insults could be spoken to you, and could not be refuted." Cf. **400**, 1063, 1064.

20. *Once, when*, etc. v. Job i. 6

21. *Whitehall.* Cf. **390**, 227, n.

133[1], 29. *The father*, etc. Cf. **121**, 957–960. To THE DUCHESS. Dryden had already (1677) dedicated *The State of Innocence* to this lady. Scott writes of her: "She was at this time in all the splendor of beauty; tall, and admirably formed in her person; dignified and graceful in her deportment, her complexion very fair, and her hair and eyebrows of the purest black. Her personal charms fully merited the encomiastic strains of the following epistle."

133[2], 22. *Three gloomy years.* The Duke of York's continuous residence in Scotland, as high commissioner, had begun only in October, 1680. But Dryden apparently counts the time since his withdrawal to the Low Countries, in March, 1679, during the excitement over the Popish Plot.

24. *Joseph's dream.* The dream of Pharaoh interpreted by Joseph: v. Genesis xli.

38. *The people's,* etc. Cf. **112,** 238, 239.

134. MAC FLECKNOE. For further details on the occasion of this poem, v. B. S. xxxvi–xxxviii. — Dr. Johnson was probably led into his misstatement in regard to it by a passage in Cibber's life of Dryden.

On *True-Blue-Protestant,* cf. **124**[1], 40, n.

3. *Flecknoe.* Flecknoe was, it is said, by birth an Irishman, and by profession a Catholic priest. Marvell saw him in Rome about 1645, and describes the meeting in a rough-hewn satire, *Flecknoe, an English Priest at Rome.* Dryden, who apparently had no personal quarrel with him, selected him for his purpose simply as a man who for a generation had been a notoriously bad poet. The verses in which Flecknoe complimented Dryden are as follows:

Dreyden the Muses darling and delight,
Than whom none ever flew so high a flight,
Some have their vains so drosie, as from *earth,*
Their Muses onely seem to have tane their birth.
Others but *water-Poets* are, have gon
No farther than to th' *Fount of Helicon:*
And they 'r but *aiery ones,* whose *Muse* soars up
No higher than to mount *Parnassus* top;
Whilst thou, with thine, dost seem to have mounted higher,
Then he who feteht [*sic*] from *Heaven* Celestial fire:
And dost as far surpass all others, as
Fire does all other elements surpass.
FLECKNOE, *Epigrams,* 1670, p. 70.

For a passage in which Dryden seems indebted to Flecknoe, v. **143,** 418–420, n.

11. *Was fit.* Ed. 1 reads *were fit.*

12. *War.* Ed. 1 reads *wars.*

15. *Sh——.* Ed. 1, here and elsewhere, reads *Shad——.*

"Thomas Shadwell (1642?–92) made several essays in verse, all of which are deplorably bad. But in comedy he was much more successful; and, in that capacity, Dryden does him great injustice in pronouncing him a dunce. On the contrary, I think most of Shadwell's comedies may be read with great pleasure. They do not, indeed, exhibit any brilliancy of wit, or ingenuity of intrigue; but the characters are truly dramatic, original, and well drawn, and the picture of manners which they exhibit gives us a lively idea of those of the author's age. As Shadwell proposed Jonson for his model, peculiarity of character, or what was then technically called *humor,* was what he chiefly wished to exhibit; and in this it cannot be denied that he has often succeeded admirably.

"In his *Epistle Dedicatory* to *Bury Fair* (1689) Shadwell complains of the hardships he suffered owing to his Whig principles: 'I never could recant in the worst of times, when my ruin was designed, and my life was sought, and for near ten years I was kept from the exercise of that profession which had afforded me a competent subsistence.' It is no wonder, therefore, he was among the first to hail the dawn of the Revolution, and that King William distinguished him by the laurel, of which Dryden was deprived. Shadwell did not long enjoy this triumph over his great enemy. His death is said to have been hastened by his taking an overdose of opium, to the use of which he was inordinately addicted. — In person, Shadwell was large, corpulent, and unwieldy, a circumstance which our author generally keeps in the eye of the reader." [SCOTT.] Cf. **153,** 33, n.

29. *Heywood and Shirley.* Thomas Heywood (d. 1650?) was probably the most prolific of the Elizabethan dramatists; he claims to have had a hand in the writing of two hundred and twenty plays, of which, however, only twenty-four are preserved. — James Shirley (1596–1666) the last of the Elizabethan dramatists, was also a prolific writer; thirty-six plays by him survive. These authors do not deserve the contempt here shown them by Dryden, who probably was ill acquainted with their writings. Heywood wrote a play called *The Late Lancashire Witches,* the title of which reappears in *The Lancashire Witches* of Shadwell; and in his *Love's Mistress* he treated the story of Psyche, which Shadwell took for the subject of an opera. But it may be doubted whether Dryden had these facts in mind when he made Heywood a *type* of Shadwell.

33. *And, coarsely,* etc. Ed. 1 reads:

I coursly Cloath'd in Drugget Russet, came.

Norwich drugget. "This stuff (a coarse woolen fabric) appears to have been sacred to the use of the poorer votaries of Parnassus; and it is somewhat odd that it seems to have been the dress of our poet himself in the earlier stage of his fortunes. An old gentleman who corresponded with the *Gentleman's Magazine* says he remembers our author in this dress." [SCOTT.]

"I remember plain John Dryden (before he paid his court with success to the great) in one uniform clothing of Norwich drugget. I have eat tarts with him and Madam Reeve at the Mulberry Garden, when our author advanced to a sword and chadreux wig." GENTLEMAN'S MAGAZINE, xv. 99 (February, 1745).

36. *King John of Portugal.* Flecknoe had visited Portugal, and boasts of being patronized by the king.

37. *The prelude.* Ed. 1 reads *a prelude.*

135, 41. *Commander.* Ed. 1 reads *commanders.*

42. *Epsom blankets,* etc. Tossing in a blanket is the punishment visited upon Sir Samuel Hearty (v. n. 136, 181) in *The Virtuoso:* see act ii of that play. There is also a reference to the title of Shadwell's play *Epsom Wells.*

43. *The new Arion.* Arion was an ancient Greek musician, who lived about B. C. 700. Once, when he was returning to Corinth from Sicily, where he had won the prize in a musical contest, his life was threatened by the rude sailors, who were greedy for his property. He gained permission once more to delight

himself with his music, placed himself in the
prow of the ship, sang and played upon his
lyre, and threw himself into the sea. The
song-loving dolphins that had crowded about
his ship carried him safe to land. — Dryden
in these lines apparently refers to some actual
festival, now lost to memory, in which Shadwell took part. Shadwell in his preface to
Psyche boasts of his skill in music.

44. *Trembling.* Ed. 1 reads *trembles.*

47. *Echoes.* Ed. 1 reads *Eccho.* *Pissing Alley* is
shown on a map in Stow's *Survey of London*,
1720 (book iv. between pp. 108 and 109), as a
passage between the Strand and Hollowell St.

48. *Aston Hall.* So ed. 1; ed. 2 reads *A —
Hall.* This allusion has never been explained.

50. *As at*, etc. Ed. 1 reads:

And gently waft the over all along.

52. *Papers*, etc. Ed. 1 reads, *Paper in thy
Thrashing-Hand.*

53. *St. André's.* Ed. 1 reads *St. Andrew's.*
"St. André was an eminent dancing master
of the period." [SCOTT.]

54. *Psyche.* "This unfortunate opera was
imitated from the French of Molière, and
finished, as Shadwell assures us, in the space
of five weeks. The author having no talents
for poetry and no ear for versification, *Psyche*
is one of the most contemptible of the frivolous dramatic class to which it belongs. It
was, however, *got up* with extreme magnificence, and received much applause on its
first appearance in 1674." [SCOTT.]
Some expressions in Shadwell's preface
might be interpreted as a sneer at the heroic
plays of Dryden, with whom, however, he
was apparently still on good terms: "Though
I expect more candor from the best writers
in rhyme, the more moderate of them . . .
are very much offended with me for leaving
my own province of comedy, to invade their
dominion of rhyme. But methinks they
might be satisfied, since I have made but a
small incursion, and am resolved to retire.
And were I never so powerful, they should
escape me, as the northern people did the
Romans, their craggy barren territories
being not worth the conquering."

57. *Singleton.* "Singleton was a musical performer of some eminence, and is mentioned
as such in Shadwell's *Bury Fair*, act iii, sc. 1.
Villerius, the Grand Master of Rhodes, is a
principal character in Davenant's *Siege of
Rhodes*, where a great part of the dialogue is in
a sort of lyrical recitative. — The combination of the lute and sword is taken from *The
Rehearsal* (act v), where Bayes informs his
critical friends that his whole battle is to be
represented by two persons: 'for I make 'em
both come out in armor, cap-a-pie, with
their swords drawn, and hung with a scarlet
ribbon at their wrists, (which, you know,
represents fighting enough,) each of 'em
holding a lute in his hand. . . . I make 'em,
sir, play the battle in *recitativo*.' The adverse generals enter accordingly, and perform

a sort of duet, in parody of passages in *The
Siege of Rhodes*." [SCOTT.]

58. *Bore.* Ed. 1 reads *wore.*

64. *Close to.* Ed. 1 reads *Close by.*
Augusta. v. **50, 1177,** n. The following
line alludes to the fears, especially rife in the
City, of Popish intrigues: cf. **141,** 306-309.
Professor Saintsbury points out that the
phrase, "Augusta is inclin'd to fears," is
found in [the prologue of] Crowne's *Calisto*
(1675). It is there also applied to London.

69. *Of all*, etc. Ed. 1 reads:

An Empty name of all the Pile Remains.

71. *Loves.* Ed. 1 reads *Love.*

72, 73. *Where . . . sleep.* A parody of a couplet in the first book of Cowley's *Davideis :*

Where their vast court the mother waters keep,
And, undisturb'd by moons, in silence sleep.

Another couplet in the same passage:

Beneath the dens where unfletcht tempests lie,
And infant winds their tender voices try, —

is parodied in lines 76, 77.

74. *Nursery.* This was a theater erected under a
patent issued by Charles II in 1664: "for
the makeing upp and supplying of a company
for acting of playes, and instructing boyes
and gyrles in the art of playing, to bee in the
nature of a Nursery, from time to time to be
removed to the said two severall theatres
abovementioned [that is, those of the King's
Company and of the Duke's Company], which
said company shall bee called by the name
of a Nursery" (*Shakespeare Society's Papers*,
vol. iii, 1847, p. 167). The patent adds: "We
doe expressly hereby prohibite that any obscene, scandalous, or offensive passages be
brought upon the stage, but such onely shalbe
there had and used, as may consist with
harmeless and inoffensive delights and recreations." The Nursery stood in Golding (later
Golden) Lane, which adjoins the Barbican,
a street which took its name in the manner
described by Dryden. It was much ridiculed
by the wits of the time. In Buckingham's
Rehearsal (act ii, sc. 2), Bayes, representing
Dryden, makes the following magnificent
threat: "I vow to gad, I have been so highly
disoblig'd by the peremptoriness of these
fellows, that I am resolv'd hereafter to bend
all my thoughts for the service of the Nursery,
and mump your proud players, i' gad."

78. *Maximins.* Dryden here ridicules the ranting hero of his own early play *Tyrannic Love.*

81. *Simkin.* Professor Collins states that a
piece entitled *The Humors of Simpkin* is
found in "a collection of drolls and farces,
compiled by Francis Kirkman in 1673."
Simpkin, he tells us, is "a stupid clown who
is represented as intriguing with an old man's
wife."

82. *Amidst*, etc. Ed. 1 reads:

Amidst these Monuments of Varnisht Minds.

Professor Collins points out that Dryden is
here indebted to Davenant:

This to a structure led, long known to fame,
And call'd the monument of vanish'd minds.
Gondibert, book ii, canto v, st. 36.

83. *Suburbian.* So ed. 2; ed. 1 reads *Suburbane.*

84. *Panton.* "A celebrated punster, according to Derrick." SCOTT.

87. *Dekker.* "Dekker, who did not altogether deserve the disgraceful classification which Dryden has here assigned to him, was a writer of the reign of James I, and the antagonist of Jonson. I suspect Dryden knew, or at least recollected, little more of him than that he was ridiculed by his more renowned adversary, under the character of Crispinus in *The Poetaster.*" [SCOTT.] v. *Additional Notes*, **1059.** Later critics are emphatic in their praise of Dekker. In *The Poetaster* Demetrius, not Crispinus, is his real representative.

88. *Pile.* Ed. 1 reads *Isle.*

91. *Misers*, etc. Shadwell wrote an adaptation of Molière's *L'Avare* under the title of *The Miser.* Raymond is "a gentleman of wit and honor" in his *Humorists*, and Bruce and Longvil (v. l. 212) are "gentlemen of wit and sense" in his *Virtuoso.* No special application of *hypocrites* is now known, unless Scott is right in his conjecture: "Perhaps Dryden means the characters of the Irish priest and Tory chaplain in *The Lancashire Witches.*"

92. *It should.* Ed. 1 reads, *his Pen should.*

94. *Empress Fame.* For the reference to Virgil, v. **567,** 251–281.

96. *Fame.* Ed. 1 reads *Pomp.*

97. *And distant.* Ed. 1 reads *to distant.*

98. *Carpets.* Ed. 1 reads *Carpet.*

102. *Ogleby.* John Ogleby (Ogilby), 1600–76. "This gentleman, whose name, thanks to our author and Pope, has become almost proverbial for a bad poet, was originally a Scottish dancing master. He translated the *Iliad*, the *Odyssey*, the *Æneid*, and *Æsop's Fables* into verse; and his versions were splendidly adorned with sculpture. He also wrote three epic poems, one of which was fortunately burned in the fire of London." [SCOTT.] For further comments on him by Dryden, v. **176**[2], 3–9; **748**[2], 40–46.

105. *Herringman.* So ed. 1; ed. 2 reads H— — —. On Herringman, see B. S. xix, xxxviii. He had published for Shadwell as well as for Dryden.

107. *Throne.* Ed. 1 reads *State.*

108. *Our young Ascanius*, etc. Dryden here adapts Virgil to his satiric purpose: cf. **548,** 926–932; **692,** 253, 254.

Sate. So ed. 1; ed. 2 reads *sat.*

111. *Around.* Ed. 1 reads *about.*

112. *As Hannibal*, etc. Hannibal, according to a story told by Livy, is said to have been forced by his father, when only nine years old, to swear eternal hatred to Rome.

115. *Till.* Ed. 1 reads *to.*

136, 117. *Ne'er to*, etc. Ed. 1 reads:

Wou'd bid defiance unto Wit and Sense.

121. *He plac'd.* Ed. 1 reads *Was plac'd.*

122. *Love's Kingdom.* A "pastoral tragi-

comedy" by Flecknoe, the only one of his plays ever acted.

124. *Lore.* Ed. 1 reads *Love.*

126. *Poppies.* Ed. 1 reads *Poppey.* "Perhaps in allusion to Shadwell's frequent use of opium, as well as to his dullness." SCOTT.

132. *Th' admiring.* Ed. 1 reads *Th' advancing.*

133. *His.* Ed. 1 reads *the.*

134. *Of his.* Ed. 1 reads *on his.*

135, 136. *Shed Full on the.* Ed. 1 reads, *Shed : Full of the.*

139. *Heavens.* Ed. 1 reads *Heaven.*

143. *Kingdom let him.* Ed. 1 reads *Kingdoms may he.*

148. *And fruitless.* Ed. 1 reads *a fruitless.*

149. *Let Virtuosos*, etc. "Shadwell's comedy *The Virtuoso* was first acted in 1676, with great applause. As the whole piece seems intended as a satire on the Royal Society, its scope could not be very pleasing to Dryden, even if he could have forgiven some hits leveled against him personally in the preface, prologue, and epilogue." [SCOTT.]

In the *Epistle Dedicatory* to *The Virtuoso* Shadwell complains of having scant time for writing, and in the preface to another comedy, *The Libertine*, he boasts of the speed with which he finished his work. Rochester, in his *Allusion to the Tenth Satire of the First Book of Horace*, terms him "hasty Shadwell." Dryden evidently knew the contrary to be the case: in his preface to *All for Love* (1678), written before his quarrel with Shadwell, he censures Rochester for calling "a slow man hasty." Cf. n. **135,** 54; **741**[2], 33–43.

150. *Toil.* Ed. 1 reads *Soul.*

151. *Gentle George.* v. headnote, p. **78.** In *The Man of Mode; or, Sir Fopling Flutter*, Dorimant is the betrayer of Mrs. Loveit. Cully is found in *The Comical Revenge; or, Love in a Tub*, and Cockwood in *She Would if She Could*, other comedies by the same writer.

In. Ed. 1 reads *with.*

157. *Let 'em be all by thy.* Ed. 1 reads: *Let them be all of thy.*

159. *Future.* Ed. 1 reads *after.*

160. *Issue of thy own.* Ed. 1 reads *issues of thine own.*

162. *Full of thee.* Ed. 1 reads *like to thee.*

163. *S—dl—y.* Ed. 1 reads *Sydney.*—Sir Charles Sedley was a noted wit and a minor poet and dramatist; a patron and friend of Dryden, who dedicated to him *The Assignation*, and introduced him, under the name of Lisideius, as one of the speakers in *An Essay of Dramatic Poesy.* He wrote a prologue for Shadwell's *Epsom Wells*, and was apparently suspected of aiding him in the comedy itself. Shadwell acknowledges receiving aid from him in another comedy, *A True Widow.*

167. *And top.* Ed. 1 reads *on th' top.*

168. *Sir Formal.* Sir Formal Trifle is a character in *The Virtuoso*, whom Shadwell justly terms "the orator, a florid coxcomb." In this line ed. 1 reads *Wit* instead of *will.*

170. *Does.* Ed. 1 reads *doth.*

Northern dedications. An allusion to Shadwell's frequent dedication of his plays to the Duke of Newcastle and his family. In his *Vindication of the Duke of Guise*, 1683, Dryden terms Shadwell "the northern dedicator."

172. *Jonson's hostile name.* Shadwell praises Jonson and professes himself his disciple with such fervor that he seems to claim kinship with him. In his *Epistle Dedicatory* to *The Virtuoso* he writes: "Nor do I hear of any professed enemies to the play, but some women, and some men of feminine understandings, who like slight plays only, that represent a little tattle-sort of conversation, like their own. But true humor is not liked or understood by them, and therefore even my attempt towards it is condemned by them. But the same people, to my great comfort, damn all Mr. Jonson's plays, who was incomparably the best dramatic poet that ever was, or, I believe, ever will be; and I had rather be author of one scene in his best comedies than of any play this age has produced."

175. *Has.* Ed. 1 reads *hath*.

177. *On.* Ed. 1 reads *or*. This line and the following probably refer to Shadwell's satire on the Royal Society in *The Virtuoso*.

178. *And.* Ed. 1 reads *Or*.

179. *Prince Nicander's vein.* Prince Nicander is a character in Shadwell's *Psyche*.

181. *Where sold he bargains. Selling bargains* consisted in answering innocent questions with coarse phrases like that quoted in the text: cf. **261**, 46.

Whip-stitch, etc. A similar phrase is a favorite with Sir Samuel Hearty in *The Virtuoso*, "one that by the help of humorous, nonsensical by-words, takes himself to be a great wit." In this line ed. 1 reads *mine* instead of *my*.

182. *Promis'd*, etc. This apparently refers to the *Epistle Dedicatory* of *The Virtuoso*. Here Shadwell writes, for example: "I say nothing of impossible, unnatural farce fools, which some intend for comical, who think it the easiest thing in the world to write a comedy, and yet will sooner grow rich upon their ill plays than write a good one."

183. *When . . .* Fletcher. Ed. 1 reads, *Where . . .* Fletchers.

184. *As thou,* etc. No commentator has investigated this charge of wholesale plagiarism, which is probably based mainly on Shadwell's *Epsom Wells*. Raines and Bevil, "men of wit and pleasure" in that play, and their ladyloves Lucia and Carolina, suggest the corresponding pairs Courtal and Freeman and Gatty and Ariana, in Etherege's *She Would if She Could;* and Shadwell's Mrs. Woodly has many traits of Etherege's Lady Cockwood. In each play the young men first meet the young women wearing vizards, and persuade them to unmask in somewhat the same fashion. Mrs. Woodly, who is carrying on an intrigue with Bevil, discovers his passion for Carolina, and entraps him by a forged letter,

just as Lady Cockwood endeavors to trick Courtal and Freeman by the same device. Mrs. Woodly again copies Lady Cockwood's behavior when she hides Bevil in her bedchamber; when she slanders Bevil and Raines to their sweethearts, saying that they have boasted of the favor accorded them ; and when, near the close of the play, she discards the faithless Bevil and tries to gain the affection of Raines. Lucia and Carolina behave towards their slandered lovers in much the same way as do Gatty and Ariana. — Furthermore, Kick and Cuff, two cheating bullies in *Epsom Wells*, resemble Wheedle and Palmer in Etherege's *Comical Revenge*, and trick Clodpate as their predecessors do Sir Nicholas Cully. At the end of the play Clodpate marries Mrs Jilt just as Sir Nicholas marries Mrs. Lucy.

Yet no fair-minded reader can deny the essential originality of *Epsom Wells*, inferior though its vulgar humor may be to the sprightly dialogue of the better scenes in Etherege. Other dramatists than these two have created pairs of rakish lovers, wanton damsels, and cowardly sharpers; and Etherege would have no good ground of complaint if Shadwell adopted the same familiar devices as himself. Shadwell probably took suggestions for some situations from Etherege, but he made these situations his own by his treatment of them. In another statement, however, Dryden is quite correct: certain scenes in *Epsom Wells* that Shadwell cannot even be accused of purloining, distinctly *sink below* those that remind one of Etherege.

Langbaine, who to be sure is always friendly to Shadwell, writes of *Epsom Wells*: "T is true that some endeavored to fix a calumny upon our author, alleging that this play was not ingenious; but this stain was quickly wiped off by the plea he makes for himself in the prologue spoken to the king and queen at Whitehall, where he says:

If this for him had been by others done,
After this honor sure they 'd claim their own."

185. *Oil*, etc. Ed. 1 reads, *Oyls on Water Flow;* ed. 2 reads *Oyl on Waters flow. Flow* is certainly a noun; it is not clear whether one should read *water's* or *waters'*.

187. *This is*, etc. "Four of the humors are entirely new; and (without vanity) I may say I ne'er produced a comedy that had not some natural humor in it not represented before, nor I hope ever shall." Shadwell, *Epistle Dedicatory* to *The Virtuoso. Province.* Ed. 1 reads *Promise*.

189. *This is that*, etc. The passage is a parody of four lines in the epilogue to Shadwell's *The Humorists:*

A humor is the bias of the mind,
By which with violence 't is one way inclin'd;
It makes our actions lean on one side still,
And in all changes that way bends the will.

Thy. Ed. 1 reads *the*.

191. *Lean.* Ed. 1 reads *lame.*
192. *Changes.* Ed. 1 reads *Charges.*
194. *Of likeness.* That is, to Ben Jonson.
196. *Thou 'rt but a.* Ed. 1 reads, *thou art a.*
199. *Sett'st.* Ed. 1 reads *sets.*
202. *Does.* Ed. 1 reads *doth.*

Thy Irish pen. In the *Epistle Dedicatory* to his translation of *The Tenth Satyr of Juvenal* (1687) Shadwell retorts indignantly: " — Sure he goes a little too far in calling me the *dullest*, and has no more reason for that than for giving me the Irish name of *Mack*, when he knows I never saw Ireland till I was three-and-twenty years old, and was there but four months."

137, 204. *Iambics.* Since the *iambic* was the appropriate meter for Greek satire, the name *iambics* has become equivalent to *satire*, even in languages like English, where it has no special fitness. In this line ed. 1 misprints *wild* instead of *mild.*

207. *There thou may'st wings display,* etc. "Among other efforts of gentle dulness may be noticed the singular fashion which prevailed during the earlier period of the seventeenth century, of writing in such changes of measure that by the different length and arrangement of the lines the poem was made to resemble an egg, an altar, a pair of wings, a cross, or some other fanciful figure." [Scott.] Dryden may possibly intend a specific reference to George Herbert's poems *An Altar* and *Easter Wings.*

209. *Diff'rent talents.* Ed. 1 reads *different Talent.*

212. *Bruce,* etc. v. n. **135**, 91. The two gentlemen are present at a scene in which their lady-loves, Clarinda and Miranda, entice Sir Formal to stand upon a secret trapdoor while he delivers a speech, and then dispose of him by releasing the trap. v. *The Virtuoso,* act. iii.

213. *Declaiming.* Ed. 1 reads *declaring.*

214. *His drugget robe.* Ed. 1 reads *the Drugget Robes.*

216. *The mantle,* etc. v. 2 Kings ii. 12–15, where "Elisha, dividing Jordan with Elijah's mantle, is acknowledged his successor."

217. *Double.* Ed. 1 reads *doubled.*

THE SECOND PART OF ABSALOM AND ACHITOPHEL. Nahum Tate (1652–1715) was a young Tory poet, for whose tragedy, *The Loyal General,* Dryden had written a prologue in 1679 (v. **87**). His best known works are an adaptation of *King Lear,* which held the stage until about 1840, and a version of the Psalms, which he made in conjunction with Nicholas Brady. He seems later to have changed his politics, for in 1692 he succeeded Shadwell as poet laureate.

The Grolier Club's *Catalogue of Original and Early Editions of English Writers from Wither to Prior,* New York, 1905, states that two issues of the first edition of this poem were printed in 1682. The editor has seen only that reading *Fleet-Street* (not *Fleetstreet*) on the title-page.

The notes on Tate's portion of the poem are made as brief as possible. Explanations of names that occur also in Dryden's poem are not repeated here.

138, 9. *Clemency was.* Ed. 1 reads, *Goodness was e'en.*

20. *Flattering.* Ed. 1 reads *Flatterie's.*

33. *As all.* Ed. 1 reads *since all.*

38. *Guilty Jebusites,* etc. Charles II was ambitious for power, and was well inclined to the Catholic religion. During the excitement caused by the Popish Plot, however, he did not deem it prudent to protect those Catholics as were accused, or to pardon those convicted. He refused, for example, to interfere, as he might well have done, in behalf of Lord Stafford.

40. *Nay,* etc. Christie glosses this line: "Some of those employed for sham plots whereby to sacrifice opponents have been executed." One Fitzharris, who swore that he had been bribed to concoct a sham plot and ascribe it to the Whigs, was later condemned and executed. But may not *sacrificers* here mean simply *priests ?*

48. *Pamper'd Corah,* etc. "The Salamanca doctor [Oates] . . . robed like a bishop and puffed with insolence . . . became the darling of the Whig party. . . . Each morning there waited at his lodgings to dress him two or three gentlemen who vied for the honor of holding his basin." JOHN POLLOCK, *The Popish Plot,* 1903, p. 227.

51. *Such was,* etc. On November 25, 1678, Oates accused Queen Catherine, before the king and council, of plotting against her husband's life.

58. *The Hermon,* etc. Cf. Song of Solomon ii. 1.

69. *The pest,* etc. The references are to the Great Plague of 1665, the Fire of London in 1666, and the wars with Holland (Tyre) in 1665–67 and 1672–74.

139, 95. *And now.* Ed. 1 reads *For now.*

96. *'T was worse,* etc. "The very breath of him was pestilential: and, if it brought not imprisonment or death over such on whom it fell, it surely poisoned reputation." NORTH, *Examen,* p. 205.

109. *These raise the Plot,* etc. The charge that Shaftesbury was the real author of the Popish Plot, and Oates merely his tool, is supported by no evidence, and is wholly incredible. Shaftesbury was, however, quick to take advantage of a situation that he did not create.

142. *O rather.* Ed. 2 reads *Oh ! rather ;* ed. 1, *Or rather.*

140, 165–170. *The crown's . . . hour.* Imitated from **115**, 441–446.

181. "*The factious tribes—*" "*And this reproof from thee ?*" As there are no quotation marks in the early editions, it is hard to tell where one speech ends and the other begins. The text follows C.; SS. makes Achitophel's speech extend through *from thee.*

189. *Who reach,* etc. Those who reach for the crown, but miss that prize, receive death.

190–195. *Did you . . . afar.* Imitated from **118, 119**, 688, 689, 729–734.

203. *My removal.* From the office of Lord President of the Council: v. n. **121,** 971.

216. *Who at your instance,* etc. This refers to *Shaftesbury's* support of the Declaration of Indulgence: v. n. **129,** 77.

220. *Ev'n property,* etc. At the opening of 1672, the king, being straitened for money, refused to repay £1,400,000 lent him by the goldsmiths, and arbitrarily reduced the interest from 12 to 6 per cent. This he seems to have done by the advice of Lord Clifford, and against the protest of Ashley, who, however, as a member of the Cabal ministry, received a large share of the blame. Nor is there any good evidence that Ashley turned the proceeding to his personal profit.

226. *Recount,* etc. Cf. **112,** 175, n.

141, 255. *Debar,* etc. The Commons had desired to make the passage of the Exclusion Bill the condition of their votes of supply: v. **107²,** 8, n.

268. *Subtile.* Ed. 1 reads *subtle.*

269. *Till peace,* etc. Cf. **119,** 752.

270. *Associations.* v. n. **126²,** 10.

280. *Ishban.* Sir Robert Clayton, alderman, and representative of the City in parliament. Other writers make the same charges against him as those in the text.

298. *Rabsheka.* "Sir Thomas Player, Chamberlain of the City of London, and one of the city members of parliament. When the Duke of York unexpectedly returned from Brussels, Player made his appearance before the Lord Mayor and Court of Aldermen, and gravely demanded that the city guards should be doubled. In the vehemence of his oratory a remarkable expression chanced to escape him, 'that he durst hardly go to sleep, for fear of awaking with his throat cut.'" [SCOTT.] For the name, v. 2 Kings xviii. 17–xix. 4.

310. *Next these,* etc. Cf. **599,** 461.

315. *Streams.* Ed. 1 reads *Waves.*

142, 321. *Judas.* Robert Ferguson (*d.* 1714), the "Plotter." He was a Nonconformist preacher, who, being ejected from his living by the Act of Uniformity in 1662, supported himself by teaching boys at Islington, near London. He aided Shaftesbury by his pamphlets (cf. n. **126¹,** 34), and fled with him to Holland. He became famous as a plotter against the governments of Charles, James, and William.

340. *Phaleg.* "James Forbes (1629?–1712), a Scotch dissenting clergyman of some distinction. He was placed by the Duke of Ormond as traveling tutor to the young Earl of Derby, who had married his granddaughter." [SCOTT.] The statements of the text seem to lack corroboration, especially as regards Forbes's relations with Ormond. Carte terms him "a gentleman of parts, virtue, and prudence, but of too mild a nature to manage his pupil," and tells how he was maltreated by the young earl and his riotous companions. (*Life of Ormond,* Oxford, 1851, vol. iv, pp. 488, 489.)

353. *Ben-Jochanan.* "The Reverend Samuel Johnson (1649–1703), a party writer of considerable merit. He was a native of Warwickshire, and took orders after a regular course of study at Cambridge. He obtained a small living of eighty pounds a year, the only church preferment he ever enjoyed. He later became chaplain to Lord Russell, the Whig leader in the House of Commons. During the dependence of the Bill of Exclusion, he endeavored at once to show the danger to a national religion from a sovereign who held opposite tenets, and to explode the doctrine of passive obedience, in a work entitled *Julian the Apostate : being a Short Account of his Life ; the Sense of the Primitive Christians about his Succession ; and their Behaviour towards him : together with a Comparison of Popery and Paganism* (London, 1682). There can be little doubt that, so far as the argument from the example of the primitive Christians is sound, Johnson has fairly made out his case. Indeed Dryden has little left to say, except that if they did resist Julian, which he seems to admit, they were very wrong in so doing, and the less that is said about it, the more will be the credit of the ancient Church.

" For this and subsequent writings, Johnson was fined, imprisoned, degraded from ecclesiastical orders, pilloried, and whipped. After the Revolution the proceedings against him were declared illegal, and he received a pension of £300 yearly, with £1000 in money, and a post for his son.

"The reader may contrast the character which Dryden has given of Johnson with that of John Hampden, who, in an account of him to the Duchess of Mazarin, says: 'Being two years with him in the same prison, I had the opportunity to know him perfectly well; and, to speak my thoughts of him in one word, I can assure your Grace that I never knew a man of better sense, of a more innocent life, nor of greater virtue, which was proof against all temptation, than Mr. Johnson.' See *Memorials* of his life prefixed to his *Works* in folio." [SCOTT.] The name Ben-Jochanan is taken as an equivalent of Johnson.

384. *But, tell me,* etc. v. Genesis ix. 18–27.

388, 389. *Made ? . . . trade.* Eds. 1 and 2 read *made, . . . Trade ?*

392. *And thy hot father,* etc. St. Gregory Nazianzenus. Johnson in his work relies for his argument largely on the invectives of St. Gregory Nazianzenus against Julian's memory. Gregory rebukes the dead Constantius for allowing Julian to succeed him; Julian he addresses as "Thou traitor next to Judas — only thou hast not testified thy repentance by hanging thyself, as he did." (*Op. cit.* p. 63.) Dryden rightly thinks that Gregory showed sectarian fury rather than Christian charity. He may have taken his cue from Johnson himself, who writes: "And yet how do the Christians treat this emperor ! One would take them to be the apostates; one while reproaching him, ruffling with him, and vexing every vein in his royal heart; another while . . . dancing and leaping for joy at his death, and insulting over his memory. But for the name of Christians, he had better have fallen amongst barbarians." (*Ibid.* p. 66.)

396. *Balak.* "The famous Gilbert Burnet was then preacher at the Rolls Chapel, under the patronage of Sir Harbottle Grimstone, Master of the Rolls. King Charles was so anxious that he should be dismissed, as to make it his particular request to Sir Harbottle, but the Master excused himself." [SCOTT.] Dryden later satirized him in *The Hind and the Panther* as the *Buzzard :* v. **250,** 2415, n.

143, 403. *David's psalms translated.* This refers to the old version by Sternhold and Hopkins, which later gave way to that by Tate and Brady: cf. **168,** 456.

405. *Mephibosheth.* Samuel Pordage, a minor writer of the time, the son of a Berkshire clergyman who had been ejected from his cure on a charge of intercourse with spirits. He is the reputed author of *Azaria and Hushai,* a reply to *Absalom and Achitophel,* and *The Medal Revers'd,* a reply to *The Medal.*

407. *Uzza.* In Tonson's *Key* (1716) this name is explained as J. H. The initials are thought to mean Jack Hall, a minor poet of the time, though no quarrel between him and Dryden is known. Cf. **916,** 229; n. **119, 804.**

412. *Doeg.* Elkanah Settle (1648–1724). On Dryden's quarrel with this writer, v. B. S. xxviii, xxix, xlv, xlvii. Settle had begun life as a Tory, then turned Whig; he later rejoined his original party. While on the Whig side, he was instrumental in arranging pope-burnings (cf. **122, 123**): to this Dryden refers in ll. 451, 452. He sank lower and lower in the literary scale, until, as Scott tells us, "finally he took the prophetic hint conveyed in Dryden's lines, and became, not indeed the master, but the assistant to a puppet show, kept by a Mrs. Mynn, in Bartholomew Fair." He lived to be ridiculed by Pope as well as by Dryden, and died in poverty, a pensioner of the Charterhouse. Cf. **920,** 418.

418. *He was too warm,* etc. Malone (I, 1, 170) cites the following from Flecknoe's *Enigmatical Characters.* 1658, p. 77, as giving Dryden the idea of this passage:

"For his [a schoolboy's] learning, 't is all capping verses, and fagoting poets' loose lines, which fall from him as disorderly as fagot-stick's, when the band is broke."

In *Notes and Observations on The Empress of Morocco,* 1674, p. 2 (v. B. S. xxix) Dryden (?) had already attacked Settle in a similar fashion:

"What stuff may not a silly unattending Audience swallow, wrapt up in Rhime: certainly our Poet writes by chance; is resolv'd upon the Rhime before hand, and for the rest of the Verse has a Lottery of words by him, and draws them that come next, let them make sense or nonsense when they come

together he matters not that; and his luck is so bad, that he seldom hits upon any that agree any more, than so many Men of several Languages would do."

444. *Transprose.* A reference to the title of Settle's poem, *Absalom Senior, or Achitophel Transpros'd.* This again refers to a jest in the first act of *The Rehearsal,* where Bayes boasts of his rule of *transversion,* or putting some one else's prose into his own verse. Johnson replies: "Methinks, Mr. Bayes, that putting verse into prose should be called transprosing; " and Bayes agrees: "By my troth, a very good notion, and hereafter it shall be so."

446. *Who makes,* etc. Settle's poem just mentioned begins:

In gloomy times, when priestcraft bore the sway, And made heav'n's gate a lock to their own key. —

448. *Four and twenty letters.* "I" and "j" were accounted one letter; so also were "u" and "v."

459. *Og.* Thomas Shadwell: v. n. **134,** 15.

144, 477. *Be thou dull.* Apparently the midwife's blessing is confined to these three words, which are printed in italics in the early editions.

524. *See where,* etc. The following verses describe the Green Ribbon Club, which met at the King's Head Tavern. It included among its members most of the prominent Whigs of the time, and many underlings of the party. v. POLLOCK, *The Popish Plot,* pp. 237–239.

535. *Arod.* "Sir William Waller, son of the parliamentary general of the same name, distinguished himself during the time of the Popish Plot by an uncommon degree of bustling activity." [SCOTT.] The charges here brought against him reflect contemporary report.

549. *Gehazi.* v. 2 Kings v. 20–27.

555. *Zaken.* An elder or magistrate (used, for example, in Exodus iii. 16). Commentators have stated that the word here means a member of parliament, but either this is incorrect, or Wood (*Athenæ Oxonienses,* 1721, ii. 419) is wrong in saying that Waller was elected to the Oxford parliament of 1681, the last that had met before the publication of this poem.

145, 574. *Who for.* v. **107²,** 8, n.

592. *His absence,* etc. In March, 1679, owing to the popular excitement over the Exclusion Bill, the Duke of York, at the king's request, left England, going first to Holland and then to Brussels.

627. *Thy thunder.* Referring to the Duke of York's earlier naval service against the Dutch: cf. **26.**

146, 642. *Subjects.* So ed. 1; ed. 2 reads *Subject's,* which may be correct, standing for *subject 's.*

661. *Grutch.* Cf. *grudge* (l. 682): the discrepancy is that of the early editions.

689. *Our brib'd Jews.* Some of the Whig leaders were as corrupt in receiving French bribes as was the king himself. Louis XIV aimed to weaken England by playing off one party against another.

148, 793. *From Hebron,* etc. In August, 1679, on the illness of the king, the Duke of York had come to England for a few days, but almost immediately returned to Brussels. In the following October he was permitted to change his place of exile for Scotland, whence he returned in February, 1680. In the next October he was again forced to retire to Scotland, and returned from there only in March, 1682: cf. headnote, p. **132.**

811. *Jothran.* George Legge (1648–91), created Baron of Dartmouth in 1682. He had won distinction in the wars with the Dutch, and later became admiral and commander-in-chief of the fleet. His father had been a noted royalist.

819. *Benaiah.* "General Edward Sackville, who had served at Tangier with great reputation, both for courage and judgment. He was expelled from the House of Commons for contemptuous words concerning those who believed in the Popish Plot." [Scott.]

825–828. *While . . . rest.* Cf. **132,** 14–25.

149, 864. *Confirm.* Ed. 1 reads *secure.*

891–906. *Or grant . . . king.* These lines are evidently inspired by a passage in *The Medal:* v. **131, 132,** 287–317.

913. *An envious festival,* etc. On April 20, 1682, the Duke of York was the guest of honor at a dinner given by the Artillery Company of London. The Whigs arranged for the following day a counter demonstration, consisting of a church service, followed by a dinner, in token of thanksgiving for the deliverance of England from Popish wiles. But the privy council meeting on April 19 unexpectedly forbade this gathering. (LUTTRELL, *Brief Relation,* i. 179.) Scott remarks: "This disappointment, trifling as it may seem, was of great disadvantage to the Whigs. It made them ridiculous, which is more fatal to a political party than any other misfortune."

150, 930. *For shekel,* etc. Tickets had been sold for the banquet at a guinea apiece.

938. *Asaph.* Dryden. Asaph was one of David's chief musicians: Psalms 1 and lxxiii–lxxxiii are ascribed to him.

941. *Bezaliel.* Henry Somerset, Marquis of Worcester, and later Duke of Beaufort; Lord President of the Council of Wales (*the Kenites' province*). Bezaleel was the artificer charged with making works of art required for the tabernacle in the wilderness: v. Exodus xxxi. 2–5.

958. *His son.* Charles Somerset, Marquis of Worcester.

967. *Abdael.* The Duke of Albemarle, son of General Monk, who had the chief share in restoring Charles II: v. **9,** 151, n. Though a man of small gifts, he became Chancellor of the University of Cambridge, here termed *the prophets' school.*

985. *Eliab.* Henry Bennet, Earl of Arlington, a member of the Cabal ministry, and Lord Chamberlain since 1674.

988. *Fortune.* Eds. 2 and 3 read *Fortunes,* probably by a misprint.

994. *Othniel's.* So ed. 3; eds. 1 and 2 read *Othriel's.* (For the name, v. Joshua xv. 17.) The Duke of Grafton, second son of Charles II by the Duchess of Cleveland, was married to the Lady Isabella Bennet, Arlington's only daughter. After the defection of Monmouth, the king attempted, as Scott says, "to set Grafton, in opposition to him, in the hearts of the people."

151, 1003. *Helon.* Louis Duras (1640?–1709) Earl of Feversham. He came of a noted French family, but had become an English subject in 1665.

1013. *Amri.* Heneage Finch, Earl of Nottingham, Lord Chancellor from 1674 to 1682: cf. **112,** 188, n. Tate's praise of his legal learning is just.

1025. *Sheva.* Sir Roger L'Estrange (1616–1704), a noted newspaper writer for the Tory party, and one of the founders of British journalism. He was licenser of the press under Charles II and James II. Sheva was a scribe of David: v. 2 Samuel xx. 25.

1035. *So Moses,* etc. v. Numbers xxi. 7–9, and cf. **117,** 632–635.

1041. *Thy laurel grove,* etc. "The thunder was anciently supposed to spare the laurel." SCOTT.

1065. *Still Hebron's,* etc. v. headnotes, **132, 133.**

1066. *Remains.* Referring to the Duchess of York, who remained behind in Scotland — a peculiar use of the word.

152, 1075. *Give not,* etc. v. 2 Samuel i. 20.

1095. *With loud last breaths,* etc. "The *Gazette* says that when the barge put off, the poor sailors, who remained to perish, manned the sides in the usual honorary form, and, indifferent to their own fate, hailed the duke's safety with three cheers." [SCOTT.]

1100. *Urania.* A title of Venus; here used of the Duchess of York.

1107. *Is.* "The grammar requires to read *he's.*" SCOTT.

1123. *Hyblæan swarms.* The honey from the hills about Hybla, in Sicily, is celebrated by the ancient poets: hence *Hyblæan swarms* means swarms of bees. Cf. **118,** 697.

1131. *Ziloah.* Sir John Moore: v. **130,** 181, n. The *viler pair* of l. 1133 were the Whig sheriffs, Shute and Pilkington, who are called worse than Cornish and Bethel (v. **117,** 585, n.), the sheriffs of the preceding year: their chief offense was in selecting the jury which refused to indict Shaftesbury.

1132. *Surges.* Eds. 1 and 2 read *Syrges,* by an evident misprint; ed. 3 reads *Syrtes,* by a mistaken correction of it.

1135. *Ziloah's loyal labors.* By unscrupulous political trickery, the court faction, aided by their tool Moore, brought about the election of two Tory sheriffs in September, 1682, as successors to Shute and Pilkington. This was followed by the choice of a Tory **lord** mayor, also secured by trickery.

153, 4. *Pennsylvania s air,* etc. In 1681 William Penn had received from the king the patent for his colony, and in September, 1682, he had sailed for America.

5. *Associators.* v. **126²,** 10, n. Shaftesbury was one of the nine individuals to whom the king made a grant of the province of Carolina in 1663, and he always took an active interest in the colony.

15. *Those playhouse Whigs,* etc Apparently a reference to some struggles of the actors against the patentees who controlled them.

24. *Charter.* The Charter of the City of London had kept it free in large measure from the encroachments of royal authority. In 1683 the king secured its forfeiture.

33. *No dull fat fool,* etc. A fresh attack on Shadwell: v n. **134,** 15. Apparently the Whig poet was set aside on the union of the companies.

42. *Whig sheriffs.* Cf. nn. **152,** 1131, 1135. The word *sheriffs* is to be pronounced as one syllable; cf. **56¹,** 13; **156²,** 3.

154, 12. *The mid gallery.* The eighteen-penny place, apparently the special haunt of women of the town; cf. **172²,** 58.

21. *Lackeys.* Mr. R. W. Lowe (*Life of Betterton,* p. 29) says that at this time servants were not admitted to the theater until the end of the fourth act. "While hanging about the entrances and lobbies their noise might be quite audible in the theater."

24. *Tom Dove.* A bear so called; cf. **899¹,** 3, n.

26. *Their unpaying masters.* For an interesting account of how theater-goers in Restoration times avoided payment of the entrance money, v. Lowe's *Life of Betterton,* pp. 22–25.

155¹, 1. *Holy League.* Cf. **8,** 97–102 and **127¹,** 10–12.

6. *Sent over,* etc. A reference to the French Huguenots who had sought shelter in England.

15. *Their pois'ning way.* Cf. **103²,** 46, n.

19. *A flail.* "A joiner named College made his fortune by inventing a pocket flail, tipped with lead, which was called the Protestant flail, and was to be used by sober citizens to brain 'Popish' assassins." (S. R. GARDINER, *Student's History of England,* p. 615.)

155², 2. *Once the cause was lost.* The government had for a long time refused to permit the play to be acted, fearing that the assassination of the Duke of Guise might be taken as suggesting that of Monmouth. In the next line Dryden denies, as he does more at length in his *Vindication* of the play, published in 1683, that any parallel between Monmouth and Guise was intended.

41. *London.* Cf. **153,** 24, n.

43. Ignoramus *juries.* A reference to the grand jury that refused to indict Shaftesbury, reporting *ignoramus.* Dryden of course puns on the legal and commonplace meanings of the word.

156¹, 23 *A Trimmer.* v. n. **120,** 882.

30. *Jack Ketch.* Cf. **210,** 3, n.

31. *Breathe.* Ed. 1 reads *breath.*

38. *You Trimmers,* etc. It is hard to say whether the quotation ends with this line or continues through the epilogue.

156², 8. *Marybone.* Marylebone Gardens, then a fashionable place of amusement.

14. *Pay their four shillings,* etc. The price of a box seat; the pit cost but half a crown.

157. RELIGIO LAICI. Of the two issues of this poem published in 1682, that described in the 1886 *Catalogue of the Rowfant Library,* is probably earlier than the other, number 315 in the Grolier Club's *Catalogue of Original and Early Editions of English Writers from Wither to Prior,* 1905. (This assertion contradicts one in *An Appendix to the Rowfant Library,* London, 1900.) In the latter (Grolier) copy the catch word at the end of the *Preface* is *To,* referring to the first complimentary poem *To Mr. Dryden,* which immediately follows in both issues; in the Rowfant copy it is *Religio,* referring to the title of the poem itself. This indicates that the complimentary poems were received after the *Rowfant* copy was already in type; hence it must be the first issue and *Grolier Club no. 315* the second. Mr. Beverly Chew, President of the Grolier Club, called the editor's attention to this circumstance.

Aside from frequent variations in spelling and punctuation, a collation shows only the following differences in reading between the two issues of 1682: **157²,** 6, (1) *ingenuously,* (2) *ingeniously;* **158²,** 58, (1) *its proper,* (2) *its own proper;* **160¹,** 36, (1) *Papists,* (2) *Papist;* **160²,** 17, (1) *had it been,* (2) *it had been.*

158¹, 1. *Intitle them to any of my errors.* "Father my errors on them." [SAINTSBURY.]

39. *Among the sons of Noah,* etc. v. Genesis ix. 24–27.

47. *Bill of exclusion.* A main argument against the Exclusion Bill (v. n **110,** 18) was the injustice done by it to the Duke of York's Protestant children.

159¹, 6. *The preface of whose creed,* etc. "Whosoever will be saved, before all things it is necessary that he hold the Catholic faith. Which faith except every one do keep whole and undefiled, without doubt he shall perish everlastingly."

159², 37. *Coleman's letters.* Edward Coleman, secretary to the Duchess of York, had carried on a correspondence with Père de La Chaise, a Jesuit, confessor to Louis XIV, relative to schemes for reëstablishing the Catholic religion in England. The discovery of his letters seemed to give at least partial confirmation to Oates's depositions. Coleman was one of the first men to be executed on account of the Popish Plot. Mr. Pollock (*The Popish Plot,* 1903) defends the truth of this sentence.

56. *Mariana,* etc. Catholic writers of the sixteenth and seventeenth centuries. All but the last (more correctly Simancas) were Jesuits.

59. *Campian.* Edmund Campian (Campion) and Robert Parsons were English Jesuits, who in 1580–81 tried to spread Catholicism in England. Campian was hanged; Parsons escaped from England. The latter published several works, one of them, *A Conference about the next Succession to the Crowne of England*, under the name of R. Doleman.

160[1], 7. *Nebuchadnezzar.* v Daniel iv. 28–33.

23. *Apology.* The full title is, *Apologia Roberti Bellarmini S. R. E. Cardinalis, pro responsione sua ad librum Jacobi Magnæ Britanniæ Regis, cujus titulus est, Triplici Nodo Triplex Cuneus.*

24. *Ratione directi dominii.* " After the manner of feudal tenure." The *dominium directum* is the right of the feudal lord in land, as distinguished from the *dominium utile*, or right of the vassal.

46. *Father Cres.* "Serenus Cressy, an English Benedictine monk, attendant on Queen Catherine. He was the principal conductor of controversy on the part of the Papists, and published many treatises against Stillingfleet and others." [SCOTT.]

160[2], 25. *Tyndal.* William Tyndal (Tyndale) (1490?–1536), one of the leaders of the English Reformation. He published translations of the New Testament, the Pentateuch, and the Book of Jonah, which, though condemned by Henry VIII, form the basis of the present Authorized Version.

Lord Herbert. Edward Herbert, Lord Herbert of Cherbury (1583–1648).

54. *Hooker.* Richard Hooker (1554?–1600), author of the *Ecclesiastical Polity.* To his life, by Izaak Walton, is appended a letter from his friend George Cranmer, grandnephew to the archbishop.

161[1], 4. *Martin Mar-prelate* Under this title there was issued from a secret press, in the years 1588–90, a series of bitter Puritan pamphlets. The man chiefly responsible for their publication was John Penry, a Welshman, who in 1593 was hanged as a traitor.

5. *Marvell.* Andrew Marvell, poet and controversialist; cf. **127**[1], 6, n.

23. *Thus Sectaries*, etc. "The court writers at this period were anxious to fix upon the Presbyterians and the Nonconformists in general the antimonarchical principles of the fanatics who brought Charles I to the scaffold." [SCOTT.]

35. *Hacket and Coppinger.* "In 1591, William Hacket, a former serving man, had his brain turned by enthusiasm, and seduced Coppinger and Arthington, two gentlemen, to sally forth with him into the streets of London, where he proclaimed himself to be the Messiah, and Coppinger and Arthington his prophet of mercy and his prophet of judgment. Hacket was executed; Arthington recanted; Coppinger starved himself to death in jail." [SCOTT.]

40. *Queen Elizabeth's birthnight.* v. headnote, p. **122**; n. **143**, 412; **235**, 1304, 1305.

44. *A Fanatic lord mayor*, etc. Cf. nn. **117**, 585 and **130**, 181.

50. " *There is*, etc. Preface to *Ecclesiastical Polity*, viii, 14.

161[2], 8. *Maimbourg.* The *Histoire du Calvinisme* of Louis Maimbourg had recently appeared,

in 1682. Dryden later (1684), at the command of King Charles, translated the *Histoire de la Ligue* of the same writer.

59. *Ingenious young gentleman.* This person, as is known from a complimentary poem by Duke, was named Henry Dickinson. His translation of *A Critical History of the Old Testament*, from the French of Richard Simon, appeared in 1682. Père Simon was one of the leading biblical scholars of his time.

162, 1, 2. *Stars : travelers.* Apparently *travelers* is pronounced with a strong secondary accent on the last syllable. Then the rhyme will be of the type *desert : art ;* cf. p. **939.**

21. *The Stagirite.* Aristotle.

28. *But vanish'd*, etc. Cf. **77**[1], 10.

43. Εὕρεκα. So 1683 ed. ; the issues of 1682 read εὑρεκα ; the correct form is εὕρηκα. The mistake and the meter indicate that Dryden was taught to accent Greek according to the Greek accents, instead of by the Latin rules, as is now usual in England. v. *Notes and Queries*, series VIII. vii. 451.

163, 76. *Hast thou*, etc. Cf. Job xi. 7, 8.

80. *Those giant wits*, etc. Christie thinks that the line was suggested by Virgil: cf. **605**, 881, 882.

164, 193. *Son's.* On the *pleonastic* genitive, v. Sweet, *New English Grammar*, § 2010.

165, 213. *Th' Egyptian bishop.* Athanasius, Bishop of Alexandria. Cf. **159**[1].

224 n. *Father Simon.* v n. **161**[2], 59.

241. *Junius and Tremellius.* " Calvinistic divines of the sixteenth century, who made translations of the Scripture, with commentaries, on which Père Simon makes learned criticisms." [SCOTT.] **167**, 16.

166, 283. *'T were worth*, etc. In this line *Testaments* is probably to be read *Test'ments ;* or the *Creed* may possibly be slurred to *th' Creed.*

291. *Esdras.* v. 2 Esdras xiv.

312. *Socinian.* The Socinians were a sect founded in the sixteenth century by the Italians Lælius and Faustus Socinus. They rejected the doctrine of the Trinity, maintaining that Christ was only man, but man by a miraculous conception.

322. *In gross.* In general, without inquiring into details.

339. *For best authority's next rules are best.* This is the reading of the first three issues, and seems intelligible in the sense: "The nearest (cf. l. 340) rules of the best authority are best." C. and SS. both read: "For best authorities, next rules, are best." This is somewhat easier to interpret, but is not necessarily an improvement.

346. *Arius and Pelagius.* Arius, the great heretic of the fourth century, denied the doctrine of the Trinity, asserting that Christ was a created being. His doctrine was condemned, largely through the efforts of Athanasius, at the Council of Nicæa (Nice) in 325. Pelagius, in the next century, is said to have denied original sin and the necessity for internal divine grace, and asserted the entire freedom

of the will, and man's perfectibility by his own unaided efforts.

167, 389. *If they,* etc. Cf. **130, 166.**

392. *The will produc'd.* Cf. **230,** 948, n.

419. *The fly-blown text,* etc. "Perhaps this idea is borrowed from Butler's *Hudibras,* iii. 2, ll. 1–12.

> The learned write, an insect breeze
> Is but a mongrel prince of bees,
> That falls before a storm on cows,
> And stings the founders of his house,
> From whose corrupted flesh that breed
> Of vermin did at first proceed.
> So, ere the storm of war broke out,
> Religion spawn'd a various rout
> Of petulant capricious sects,
> The maggots of corrupted texts,
> That first run all religion down,
> And after ev'ry swarm its own." [SCOTT.]

168, 456. *Tom Sternhold's,* etc. v. **143,** 402, 403, n; headnote, p. **134;** n. **134,** 15.

POEMS INCLUDED IN MISCELLANY POEMS, 1684. The editor has been unable to consult the second edition of this volume.

169¹, 31. *Whetstone.* v. **53¹,** 8, n; and for the introduction of contemporary references into a translation from an ancient writer, cf. **98,** 17, n; **196,** 35, n.

169². AMARYLLIS. Upon this piece, and upon those on pp. **192–198,** v. Pughe, *John Drydens Übersetzungen aus Theokrit,* Breslau, 1894.

171. PROLOGUE TO THE DISAPPOINTMENT. The 1684 edition of this play has not been accessible to the editor. The text has been collated with a copy made at the British Museum.

172¹, 38. *The high dice, and the low.* "Loaded dice, contrived some for high and others for low throws." SCOTT.

49. *Brings her,* etc. "Our author seems to copy himself in this passage. 'His old father in the country would have given him but little thanks for it, to see him bring down a fine-bred woman, with a lute, and a dressing box, and a handful of money to her portion.' *The Wild Gallant,* act iii, sc. 2." SCOTT.

172², 55, 56. *But while,* etc. Cf. **900,** 41, 42.

58. *Our middle galleries.* Cf. **154,** 12, n.

3. *Arius.* Lee made Arius the villain of his play: cf. **166,** 346, n.

4. *A True Protestant.* Cf. **124¹,** 40, n, and heading to *Mac Flecknoe,* p. **134.**

5. *Eusebius.* The historian of the Christian Church, who flourished about 300.

8. *Trimmer.* v. n. **120,** 882. In this epilogue Dryden apparently uses the word loosely, as equivalent to Whig.

Addressing Tory. Tories who presented to the king *addresses* in which they expressed their *abhorrence* of the acts of the *Petitioners.* v. n. **112,** 179.

10. *When Clause was king,* etc. This alludes to the rejoicing of the beggars when Clause is chosen their king: v. Fletcher's *Beggars' Bush,* act ii, sc. 1.

173¹, 22. *Teckelites.* "The severity of the Austrian government, in Hungary particularly, towards those who dissented from the Roman Catholic faith, occasioned several insurrections. The most memorable was headed by Count Teckely, who allied himself with the Sultan, assumed the crown of Transylvania as a vassal of the Porte, and joined with a considerable force the large army of Turks which besieged Vienna. A similarity of situation and of interest induced the Whig party in England to look with a favorable eye upon this Hungarian insurgent, and they hence gained the nickname of Teckelites." [SCOTT.]

28. *Nose.* The 1702 ed. reads *noise.*

32. *The last plot.* Possibly the Rye House Plot (1683), but more likely the Whig Combination of the same year, for participation in which Lord Russell was executed. The *first plot* (l. 33) is of course the Popish Plot.

173². TO THE EARL OF ROSCOMMON. Roscommon had prefixed a commendatory poem to the 1683 issue of *Religio Laici,* so that Dryden is now returning a compliment.

Pope praised Roscommon in the famous couplet:

> Unhappy Dryden! — In all Charles's days
> Roscommon only boasts unspotted bays.
> *First Epistle of the Second Book of Horace,*
> 213, 214.

Dryden's spelling here and elsewhere is *Roscomon.*

14. *Tinkled in the close.* Christie notes that Marvell had used the expression *tinkling rhyme* in his verses *On Paradise Lost.* By his dispraise of rhyme Dryden delicately flatters Roscommon, who in his *Essay* had advanced similar opinions; cf. n. **178¹,** 16.

174¹, 35. *Need.* In the sense of *are needed.*

36. *His own example,* etc. Roscommon translated from Virgil, *Eclogue* vi, and from Horace, *Odes* i. 22 and iii. 6, and the *Art of Poetry.*

41. *How much,* etc. "Roscommon, it must be remembered, was born in Ireland, where his property also was situated. But the Dillons were of English extraction." SCOTT.

47. *Were.* Ed. 1 reads *was,* a misprint of which Dryden complains in a letter to Tonson, where he also writes: "For my Lord Roscommon's *Essay,* I am of your opinion that you should reprint it, and that you may safely venture on a thousand more."

60. *An English peer.* Ed. 1 reads *a Brittish Peer.* For the reference, v. p. **95.** Roscommon had complimented Mulgrave at the opening of his *Essay;* cf. **179²,** 47, n.

174², 67. *Sand.* Both early editions place a full stop after this word.

72. *Who both.* Ed. 1 reads, *He both.*

74. *Infus'd Titan.* Prometheus: for the legend, v. **388,** 97–112; **414,** 22, n. Christie points out that Dryden is indebted to Juvenal, xiv. 34, 35:

> Forsitan hæc spernant juvenes, quibus arte benigna
> Et meliore luto finxit præcordia Titan.

9. *Thus Nisus,* etc. v. **583,** 373–441.

175, 23. *Marcellus.* A reference to Virgil's celebrated tribute to the nephew of Augustus,

the young Marcellus, who died in his twentieth year: v. **609**, 1188–1226.

POEMS INCLUDED IN SYLVÆ, 1685. The editor has been unable to consult the second
edition of this volume. The motto is *Æneid*,
vi. 143, 144: cf. **596**, 215, 216. In the letter
quoted Dryden refers to Montaigne, livre iii,
ch. 5, *Sur des Vers de Virgile*. (The editor is
here indebted to Professor C. H. C. Wright,
of Harvard University.)

175¹, 5 (prose). *History of the League*. v. n. **161**², 8.
176¹, 10. *Lord Roscommon's* Essay, etc. v. **173**², n.
27. *Dutch commentator*. Dryden's dilettante
patronizing of men like Franciscus Dousa
and Daniel and Nikolaes Heinsius reminds
one of certain literary critics of the present
day.

176², 8. *Our Oglebys*. v. **135**, 102, n; **748**², 40–46.
177¹, 8. *A late noble painter*. Sir Peter Lely
(1618–80), the court painter of Charles II.
50. *Hand-gallop*. An easy gallop, in which the
horse is kept well in hand.
51. *Carpet-ground*. Ground smooth as a carpet;
cf. **310**², 11.
52. *Synalephas*. v. **385**².

177², 5. *My definition of poetical wit*. "From
that which has been said, it may be collected
that the definition of wit . . . is only this:
that it is a propriety of thoughts and words;
or, in other terms, thoughts and words elegantly adapted to the subject." *The Author's
Apology for Heroic Poetry*, prefixed to *The
State of Innocence* (1677): v. SS. v. 124.

Dryden really took this idea from Rapin:
"La vertu la plus essentielle au discours,
après la clarté, c'est la pudeur et la modestie,
comme remarque Demetrius le Phaleréen.
Il faut, dit-il, *de la proportion entre les paroles et
les choses :* et rien n'est plus ridicule que de
traiter un petit sujet d'un grand style : parce
que ce qui est disproportionné, est ou tout-
à-fait faux, ou du moins badin et puerile."
Reflexions sur la Poëtique, part 1, § 30.

The source for Rapin is Demetrius Phale-
reus, *De Elocutione*, 120: "Fitness must be
observed, whatever the subject; or in other
words the style must be appropriate, —
subdued for humble topics, lofty for high
themes." (Roberts's translation.)

18. *Hannibal Caro* Lived 1507–66: on his
translation, cf. **513**², 14–19.
23. *Tasso*, etc. "Not in a letter, but at the end
of the first of his *Discorsi dell' Arte Poetica*."
KER.

178¹, 16. *Lord Roscommon*, etc.

O may I live to hail the glorious day,
And sing loud pæans through the crowded way,
When in triumphant state the British Muse,
True to herself, shall barb'rous aid [ι. e. rhyme] re-
    fuse,
And in the Roman majesty appear,
Which none know better, and none come so near.
        Essay on Translated Verse.

26. *Breakings*. Dryden may use *breaking* as
equivalent to *cæsura* (metrical pause), but
more likely as *hiatus* (the use of a word ending
in a vowel before one beginning with a vowel,

without elision): cf. **512**¹, 15–35, where
Dryden incorrectly uses *cæsura* in the sense
of *elision*.
44. *When Lausus died*, etc. The text reads
When Lausus fell; v. **935**, 226, and cf. **671**,
1299, 1300.
178², 29. *Our poet and philosopher of Malmesbury*. Thomas Hobbes (1588–1679).
179², 47. *Essay on Poetry*. By the Earl of Mulgrave; cf. **490**. Roscommon's *Essay* begins:

Happy that author, whose correct *Essay*
Repairs so well our old Horatian way.

Roscommon also, in the same *Essay*, condemns indecent verses.
180¹, 17. *Viper*. v. **188**, 26. The editor has naturally let the verse stand as the printer left it.
23. *Non ego*, etc. *Ars Poet*. 351–353.

But in a poem elegantly writ
I would not quarrel with a slight mistake,
Such as our nature's frailty may excuse.
        Roscommon's Translation.

41. *Translator of Lucretius*. Thomas Creech
(1659–1700), whose *Lucretius* appeared in
1682: cf. **928**². "In his translation he omitted
the indelicate part of the Fourth Book, a
deficiency which Dryden thought fit to supply,
for which he has above assigned some very
inadequate reasons." [SCOTT.]
181¹, 1. *His satires*, etc. Contrast Dryden's
later verdict, pp. **307–316**, which is in favor
of Juvenal.
4. *Any part*. Ed. 1 reads *no part*, but the mistake is corrected in the errata.
8. *As difficult*, etc. HORACE, *Odes*. iv. 2. 1–4.
26. *Curiosa felicitas*. "The felicity gained
through diligence." PETRONIUS, *Sat*. 118.
27. *Feliciter audere*. "To be happily bold:" v.
Horace, *2 Epistles*, i. 166.
33. *One ode*, etc. v. **199**. *The present Earl of
Rochester* was Laurence Hyde: v. **120**, 888, n.
Dryden distinguishes him from the nobleman mentioned in B. S. xxix, xxxviii, xxxix.
45. *Mr. Cowley*. For Dryden's varying estimate
of this author, v. **91**; **283**²; **320**¹; **514**¹, 53 f;
517¹; **744**¹, 53 f.
181², 36. *Quod nequeo*, etc. "What I cannot
express, but only feel;" adapted from Juvenal,
vii. 56, *Hunc qualem nequeo monstrare et sentio
tantum*.
48. *Fungar*, etc. HORACE, *Ars Poet*. 304, 305.

But I must rest contented as I am,
And only serve to whet that wit in you,
To which I willingly resign my claim.
        Roscommon's Translation.

185, 138. *Store*. Ed. 1 places a comma after this
word, and a semicolon after *more* in the next
line.
188, 26. *The viper*, etc. Cf. **180**¹, 17.
191, 218. *Neither*. Possibly a misprint for
neither's, as Saintsbury suggests.
253. *Nor pierces*, etc. "Notice here, what is
very unusual in Dryden, an Alexandrine
couplet." SAINTSBURY.
260. *Who after, match'd*, etc. Ed. 1 reads,
Who, after match'd, which may possibly be
correct. But cf. **180**¹, 14–16.

192[1], 18. *Hand supplies.* Ed. 1 reads, *Hands supplies.*

193, 72. *Beauties'.* Ed. 1 reads *beauties*, which may mean *beauty's*.

THEOCRITUS: IDYLLIUM THE TWENTY-THIRD. This piece and the following are probably not by Theocritus.

196, 35. *Queen Elizabeth.* For the introduction of the modern allusion, cf. **98**, 17, n; **169**[1], 31, n; **199**[2], 40; **324**, 122; **367**, 126.

44. *Scarecrow.* Ed. 1 reads *scar Crow.*

197, 82. *Menalcas.* Ed. 1 reads *Menelaus*, by a ludicrous misprint. The following words apparently mean: "He is a plain yeoman, not *Master* Menalcas." [SAINTSBURY.]

198. *The Earl of Roscommon.* v. **173.**

199[1], 32. *Pointed.* For the word, cf. **478**, 152.

HORACE, THE TWENTY-NINTH ODE, etc. v. **181**[1], 33, n.

199[2], 40. *The new Lord May'r*, etc. Cf. **152**, 1135, n. Dryden inserts political allusions even into his translations. Cf. **98**, 17, n; **196**, 35, n.

201, 14. *Trimmer.* v. n. **120**, 882.

202. THE FAIR STRANGER. The original edition does not separate or number the stanzas.

203[2]. SONG. In the text of this song in the *Second Part of Miscellany Poems*, 1716, lines 3, 4; 7, 8; 9, 10; 13, 14; 15, 16; 18, 19 form single lines. That text furnishes the following variant readings: l. 5, *so frequent a Fire*; l. 14, *and all my*; l. 16, *so faithful, so faithful a Lover*; l. 18, *I'll die, I'll die, I'll die.* The 1704 text is reprinted without change in the second edition, 1716, of *The Fifth Part of Miscellany Poems.*

203. THRENODIA AUGUSTALIS. Of the first edition of this poem there were two issues, both of which are owned by the Harvard Library. One of them (the later) is in larger type than the other. The second edition, as a careful comparison has shown, was apparently printed from the same type as the later issue of the first, without resetting, but with a few corrections of the text, apparently due to Dryden himself. The variations between the two issues of the first edition are very minute. The principal ones are as follows: l. 70 (small type) *sat*, (large type and ed. 2) *sate*; l. 125 (sm.) *then they*, (l. and ed. 2) *that they*; l. 232 (sm.) *in which*, (l. and ed. 2) *on which*; l. 259 (sm.) *inexhausting*, (l. and ed. 2) *inexhausted*; l. 484 (sm.) *The best*, (l.) *There best*, (ed. 2) *Their best.*

The text in *Poems and Translations*, 1701 (ed. 3), disregards Dryden's corrections and restores the readings of the later issue of ed. 1, from which it was evidently set up. But v. n. **206**, 188.

The motto of the poem is *Æneid*, ix. 446, 447; cf. **646**, 597, 598.

204, 7. *Niobe.* Niobe, stricken with grief for the loss of her children, who were slain by Apollo and Artemis, was turned into stone.

22. *No sickness*, etc. Charles, who had always been in the best of health, was taken seriously ill on the morning of February 2.

28. *This* now, etc. Cf. **275**, 306.

31. *The flaming wall.* Christie cites *flammantia moenia mundi*, "the flaming walls of the world" (Lucretius, i. 73).

36. *Our Atlas*, etc. "Alluding to the fable of Hercules supporting the heavenly sphere when Atlas was fatigued." SCOTT.

70. *An iron slumber.* Christie cites Virgil's *ferreus somnus* (*Æneid*, x. 745).

80. *Heav'n*, etc. On February 5, according to Macaulay, the *London Gazette* announced that the physicians thought Charles out of danger.

205, 100. *The first*, etc. "A very ill-timed sarcasm on those who petitioned Charles to call his parliament." SCOTT. v. n. **112**, 179.

Christie remarks: "The line must mean that these were the first *rude petitioners* who were *well-meaning*."

106. *His death*, etc. v. 2 Kings xx. 1–11; but the parallel is by no means exact.

126. *Friends*, etc. Eds. 1 and 3 read:

Each to congratulate his friend made haste.

150. *The laboring moon.* Cf. **342**, 571, 572.

"When the moon was eclipsed, it was supposed that magicians and witches were endeavoring to bring her down from heaven to aid them in their enchantments, and that she could be relieved from her sufferings by loud noises, beating of brass, sounding of trumpets, &c., to drown the voices of the enchanters." J. D. LEWIS, note on Juvenal, vi. 442.

153. *On liking.* "To engage *on liking* (an image rather too familiar for the occasion) is to take a temporary trial of a service, or business, with license to quit it at pleasure." [SCOTT.]

206, 164. *Never was losing.* Eds. 1 and 3 read *Was never losing.*

173. *Th' extremest ways*, etc. "The patient was bled largely. Hot iron was applied to his head. A loathsome volatile salt, extracted from human skulls, was forced into his mouth." MACAULAY.

188. *Even Short himself.* So eds. 1 and 2; ed. 3 reads *Even Short and Hobbs.* On this Christie well remarks: "Hobbes was a surgeon of eminence at the time of Dryden's death, and had attended Dryden in his last illness; but there is no other known mention of him among the medical men who attended the bedside of Charles II. This is a very suspicious change of the text in Tonson's volume of 1701." As a further proof that the change was not made by Dryden, it may be noted that in the preceding line (187) *he* remains in the text of ed. 3, but is altered to *They* in the errata.

"Dr. Thomas Short was a Catholic and a Tory. To this circumstance he probably owes the compliment paid him by our author." [SCOTT.]

236. *Exile.* Referring to the duke's enforced absence from England during the excitement over the Popish Plot: cf. **133**[2], 22, n.

239. *That king*, etc. v. 1 Kings ii. 1–9, where David charges his successor Solomon to take vengeance on certain of his enemies.

207, 244. *Those*, etc. A glance at Monmouth, of whom Charles made no mention when on his deathbed.

267. *Camillus.* Camillus, the Roman general who conquered Veii, went into exile rather than submit to an unjust fine.

288. *Still voice.* Eds. 1 and 3 read *still Sound.* For the reference, v. 1 Kings xix. 12.

311. *Succession*, etc. v. n. **110**, 18.

327. *Clio.* The Muse of History.

208, 353. *Out of*, etc. Cf. **40**, 639, n.

354. *Geneva weeds.* Referring of course to the influence of Calvinism in England. The Presbyterian clergy were driven from the Church of England by the Act of Uniformity of 1662.

364. *As when*, etc. Dryden had already used this comparison in his *Verses to the Duchess :* v. **27**, 52–57.

371. *Choir, like.* Ed. 2 reads *Quire like ;* eds. 1 and 3 read *Quire of.*

372. *The Muse*, etc. v. *Astræa Redux*, p. **7.**

377. *Tho' little*, etc. v. **238**, 1541, n.

388. *Thou Fabius*, etc. A reference to Q. Fabius Maximus, the Roman general who, continually avoiding a combat, thwarted Hannibal by his policy of delay. Dryden's praise of the king's statecraft is just. He overcame Shaftesbury and the Whigs by yielding at critical moments and awaiting a change of the public temper.

209, 421. *For twelve*, etc. Charles had been king *de jure* since the execution of his father, January 30, 1649; he returned to England king *de facto* on May 25, 1660, and was crowned on April 23 of the next year. Dryden's arithmetic is not quite exact.

430. *Long exercis'd by fate.* Christie cites Virgil's *Iliacis exercite fatis (Æneid,* iii. 182); cf. **554**, 243.

435. *False heroes*, etc. For a similar passage, v. **221**, 251–262.

441. *The Cyclops*, etc. v. **632**, **633**, 579–596.

447. *Alcides.* Hercules, the son of Jupiter and Alcmena. In his infancy he strangled two serpents sent against him by the jealous Juno; in maturity, one of his labors was to overcome the Lernean hydra; after his death he was numbered among the gods.

456. *Legitimately.* In reference to the defeat of the aspirations of the Duke of Monmouth, the illegitimate son of Charles II.

465. *As after*, etc. Numa was really followed by the *martial* Tullus Hostilius. Ancus *Martius* (hence, probably, Dryden's blunder), who succeeded Tullus, led the Romans *against* the Latins.

494. *Strong.* Eds. 1 and 3 read *great.*

210, 517. *The* fasces *of the main.* v. **10**, 249, n.

PROLOGUE AND EPILOGUE TO ALBION AND ALBANIUS. This opera celebrates the triumph of the royal brothers, Charles and James, over their Whig adversaries. — The editor has been unable to consult the broadside text of the prologue and epilogue.

3. *John Ketches.* The name of John Ketch (d. 1686), who seems to have been public

executioner from 1663 to his death, has become a nickname for his successors in office. Cf. **156**[1], 30; **313**[2], 46.

6. *Oates.* v. **117**, 632, n. In May, 1685, Oates was sentenced to so terrific a flogging that it is a wonder he survived. He was reported to have bribed the executioner to inflict the punishment lightly.

211[1], 4. *Plain Dealing.* "From this epilogue we learn, what is confirmed by many proofs elsewhere, that the attribute for which James desired to be distinguished and praised, was that of openness of purpose, and stern, undeviating inflexibility of conduct. He forgot that it was only the temporizing concessions of his brother which secured his way to the throne, when his exclusion, or a civil war, seemed the only alternatives." [SCOTT.] Contrast Dryden's praise of Charles, **208**, 388–398, n.

211[2]. TO MY FRIEND, MR. J. NORTHLEIGH. These verses have been collated with a copy of the first edition, made at the Bodleian Library. — For the scriptural references, v. Genesis xli. 25–36, 1 Kings iii. 16–28, and The History of Susanna (in the Apocrypha). In the last case there is of course a sarcastic reference to the Presbyterian party.

To MRS. ANNE KILLIGREW. The first edition of this poem has the following variant readings: (12) *be thy place ;* (124) *gave Shape unto the Name;* (128) *King the Eye;* (139–141):

> As in that Day she took from Sacred hands
> The Crown; 'mong num'rous Heroins was seen,
> More yet in Beauty, than in Rank, the Queen !

(148) *their Progress.*

Mrs. (Mistress) was in Dryden's time applied both to married and to unmarried women.

212, 26. *Thy father*, etc. Henry Killigrew had written a tragedy, *The Conspiracy*, published in 1638, and "reprinted in a revised form in 1653, under the title of *Pallantus and Eudora.*" (WARD.)

43. *In trine.* Cf. **50**, 1165, n.

50. *And if*, etc. An allusion to the fable that bees rested on the lips of the infant Plato.

68. *Arethusian.* Arethusa was the nymph of a famous well on the island of Ortygia, near Syracuse: cf. **439**, 1–7.

213, 79. *Her father's life.* Other writers do not concur in this praise of Henry Killigrew.

82. *Epictetus.* Dryden apparently confuses Epictetus with Diogenes, who is said to have 'it a lantern in the daytime, explaining: "I am looking for a *man.*"

128. *Our martial king.* James II.

134. *Our Phœnix queen.* "Mary of Este, as eminent for beauty as rank." [SCOTT.] She had been crowned Queen of England on April 23, 1685.

214, 147. *To such*, etc. Cf. the motto from Martial quoted in the headnote: "For extraordinary beings life is short and old age rare."

162. *Orinda.* "Mrs. Katherine Philips (1631–64), whom the affectation of her age called

Orinda." [SCOTT.] Her talents as a poetess were praised by Cowley and other eminent men, and, what is important in the present connection, by Anne Killigrew, who addressed some verses to her. Both Mrs. Philips and Anne Killigrew died of the smallpox.

165. *Her warlike brother.* Henry Killigrew (*d.* 1712), a captain in the navy, who later became admiral.

180. *The Valley of Jehosaphat.* v. Joel iii. 2.

A LETTER TO SIR GEORGE ETHEREGE. On Etherege's life, and the date of this *Letter*, v. Gosse, *Seventeenth Century Studies.*

2. *As map informs.* The latitude of Ratisbon is really about 49°: Dryden has followed a mistaken statement of Etherege in his letter to Middleton. The jests that follow are in reply to the same letter.

215, 28. *What region,* etc. A reference to Virgil's line:

> Quæ regio in terris nostri non plena laboris.
> *Æneid,* i. 460.

30. *Triptolemus.* Ceres gave a chariot drawn by dragons and laden with wheat to her favorite Triptolemus, who rode in it over the earth, spreading among men a knowledge of agriculture.

47. *Three holy miter'd Hectors.* The three ecclesiastical electors were the archbishops of Treves, Cologne, and Maintz. These, with five temporal lords (the Count Palatine and the rulers of Bohemia, Bavaria, Saxony, and Brandenburg), constituted at this time the college of Electors.

49. *Is sunk.* The 1702 ed. reads *is drunk ;* the correction is made in the following (fourth) edition of *Sylvæ* (1716).

73. *The Duke St. Aignan.* François de Beauvillers (1610?–87), a favorite of Louis XIV. A play called *Bradamante* was attributed to him. — The spelling of the edition of 1702 is *St. Agnon.*

75. *His Grace of Bucks.* v. B. S. xxviii. *The Rehearsal* is said to have been begun about 1663, though it was acted only in 1671.

7. *Bauble.* "A truncheon, with a fool's head and cap upon one end. It was carried by the ancient jester." [SCOTT.]

216, 22. *Your author's principle.* v. **354,** 533–561.

THE HIND AND THE PANTHER. Ed. 3 of this poem usually agrees with ed. 2; its readings, therefore, are ordinarily not recorded here.

The first line of the motto is from *Æneid,* iii. 96: "Seek thy ancient mother;" cf. **552,** 127. The second is from *Æneid,* i. 405: "The true goddess was made known by her stately movement;" cf. **529,** 561.

This poem produced a famous and truly humorous reply: *The Hind and the Panther transvers'd to the Story of the Country Mouse and the City Mouse,* by two young wits, Charles Montagu and Matthew Prior. In it Mr. Bayes and the two gentlemen of *The Rehearsal* were again brought to life.

Professor Williams's excellent commentary on this poem has assisted the editor in many cases not directly indicated in the following notes. Several of the references cited are due to it. A paper by B. Vildhaut, *Dryden's Fable of The Hind and The Panther* (Lüdinghausen, 1876), in general of very small value, has given hints for the notes on ll. 1550, 2190.

To the Reader. During the early part of his reign James II showed no tolerance for Protestant Dissenters, and tried to carry out his designs in behalf of the Catholic religion by the aid of his Tory Church of England subjects, who professed the doctrine of passive obedience. He disregarded in behalf of Catholics alone the Test Act of 1673, which excluded from office all men who refused to declare their disbelief in the doctrine of transubstantiation, and to receive the sacrament according to the rites of the Church of England. This had hitherto banished every honest Catholic, and most of the Dissenters, from any position under the government, but had not affected some of the less strenuous Dissenters. (The Test Act of 1678, which required of all members of parliament an oath professing disbelief in transubstantiation, but did not require the taking of the sacrament according to the Anglican rites, was aimed against Catholics alone.) Finding that he could not win the support of the Church of England for his dispensing power, James turned for help to the Dissenters, and on April 4, 1687, issued a Declaration of Indulgence, suspending the Test Act and all penal laws against both Catholics and Dissenters, and giving to both the freedom of public worship. By this he hoped to gain the Dissenters to his own side. But the more clear-headed among them saw that this temporary indulgence was only a political trick, and refused to be duped by it.

Dryden in this poem, planned and written while James was carrying out his earlier policy, breathes a spirit of hostility to the dissenting sects, such as the Wolf, the Bear, and the Fox. He hopes for a reconciliation of the Church of England with the Catholic Church (v. **222,** 327–330; **244, 245,** 1964–2049). The Declaration of Indulgence, issued only a week before *The Hind and the Panther,* was licensed for the press, probably startled Dryden as much as it did the rest of the nation not in the king's confidence. In this prose preface he adapts himself to changed circumstances, praises toleration, and censures those who refused to accept it from a Catholic king. Cf. n. **245,** 2090.

216², 22 (prose). *I hope,* etc. "Most readers will, I think, acknowledge with me the extreme awkwardness with which Dryden apologizes for hoping well of those sectaries against whom he had so often discharged the utmost severity of his pen." [SCOTT.]

217¹, 1. *'T is not,* etc. Referring to Louis XIV's revocation, in 1685, of the Edict of Nantes of 1598, which had secured religious freedom in France. A severe persecution of the Huguenots followed.

7. *That he has*, etc. Scott points out that a similar phrase is found in an actual address of the period.

28. *Classical ordination*. Ordination by a *classis* or presbytery; cf. n. **220**, 180.

38. *Cyrus*. v. Ezra i. 1–4.

41. *In specie*. In kind.

217², 1. *'T is evident*, etc. In 1685 and 1686 King James ordered published two papers in defense of the Catholic religion, said to have been written by King Charles II, and to have been found in his strong box, and a third paper, said to be by Anne, Duchess of York, the first wife of King James, telling how she came to adopt the same faith. An anonymous *Answer* to these papers soon appeared, of which Stillingfleet, a learned Church of England divine, was the principal author. This occasioned a *Defense of the Papers*, in the last division of which, concerning the paper of the Duchess of York, Dryden was concerned. Stillingfleet and his coadjutors then returned to the charge with *A Vindication of the Answer to some late Papers* (1687), to which Dryden here refers under the title *Answer to the Defense of the late King's Papers*. Cf. **237**, 1454, n.

12. *Socrates's*. So ed. 1; eds. 2 and 3 read *Socrate's*.

19. *Treatise of Humility*. At the end of his *Defense* Dryden had written: "In the mean time, the spirit of meekness and humble charity would become our author better than his boasts for this imaginary victory . . . but it is the less to be admired that he is such a stranger to that spirit, because, among all the volumes of divinity written by the Protestants, there is not one original treatise, at least that I have ever seen or heard of, which has handled distinctly, and by itself, that Christian virtue of humility." This Stillingfleet terms "a bare-faced assertion of a thing well known to be false, since within a few years such a book hath been published in London." Stillingfleet referred without doubt to *A Practical Discourse of Humility*, by W[illiam] A[llen], London, 1681. Dryden confuses this with a *magnified piece of Duncomb*, which turned out to be a translation from the Spanish Jesuit Alonso Rodriguez. Of Duncomb's work the editor can learn nothing: the British Museum Catalogue mentions "*A Treatise of Humilitie*, translated [by T. B.] into English" from Rodriguez, Rouen, 1631.

33. *Matter of fact*. Dryden echoes a phrase of Stillingfleet at the opening of the *Answer to the Defense of the Third Paper*, which concludes his *Vindication*: "I have now done as to matter of reason and argument: the third paper chiefly relates to matter of fact." But by *matter of fact* Stillingfleet does not refer to the mere question of the reality of the duchess's conversion. v. Stillingfleet, *Vindication*, page 102 (SS. xvii. 255). Cf. n. **239**, 1604.

42. *Mrs. James*. Eleanor James, a printer's wife who had published a pamphlet called *Mrs. James's Vindication of the Church of England*.

218, 1. *Hind*. The Catholic Church. Professor Williams points out that Dryden may have been influenced by scriptural passages such as Genesis xlix. 21; 2 Samuel xxii. 34; Proverbs v. 19.

6. *Scythian shafts*. "The Scythians tip their arrows with vipers' poison and human blood: for this frightful mixture there is no remedy; it brings death immediately at a slight touch." PLINY, *Natural History*, xi. 53 (115).

Professor Williams cites Ovid's *Scythica sagitta* (*Met*. x. 588).

13. *Of these*, etc. "The Roman Catholic priests executed in England at different times since the Reformation, and regarded as martyrs and saints by those of their communion." SCOTT.

14. *Caledonian wood*. "Not *Scottish*, but taken generally for Britain, as *Hercynian wood* might be for Germany." SAINTSBURY.

15. *Vocal blood*. Cf. Genesis iv. 10.

19. *So captive Israel*, etc. v. Exodus i. 7–14.

35. *Bear*. The Independents, (the predecessors of the modern Congregationalists,) who rejected all ecclesiastical authority above that of the individual congregation, and discarded most forms and ceremonies. Cf. **886**, 559–562.

37. *Hare*. The Quakers, who refused to take oaths of any sort, being guided by Matthew v. 34.

39. *Ape*. The Freethinkers. "The Earl of Sunderland, one of the principal ministers under Charles II and James II, was supposed to hold such opinions, for he made his change to Popery without even the form of previous instruction or conference. Dryden probably intended a sarcasm at him or some such time-serving courtier, for his occasional conformity with the royal faith, of which there were several instances at the time." [SCOTT.]

To this Christie replies: "Dryden would hardly wish to offend any Roman Catholic convert, and he was not at all likely at this time to run a risk of offending Sunderland, who was in power. He had flatteringly dedicated *Troilus and Cressida* to Sunderland in 1679." Finally, Sunderland apparently did not become a Catholic until many months after the date of this poem: v. H. C. Foxcroft, *Life of Halifax*, i. 508.

41. *Lion*. The King of England.

43. *Boar*. The Anabaptists. The sect originated in Germany, where their early history is connected with a revolt of the peasantry. In 1534 they seized the city of Münster, where their rule (ending in June, 1535) was marked by many excesses, which brought the sect into disrepute. The Baptists were severely persecuted in England: some of the Independent congregations seem to have held Baptist views.

44. *But whiten'd*, etc. "*The foam of sanctity* refers to the Anabaptist dogma that every true believer attains in this life perfect freedom from sin." WILLIAMS.

53. *Reynard.* Dryden chooses the Fox for his symbol of the Unitarians: v. nn. **166,** 312, 346. The Socinians had had much success in Poland, but had been driven out from the country by a law of 1658. Some of the refugees had been well received by Count Teckely. v. **220,** 150–152; **173**[1], 22, n.

61. *Hence,* etc. Cf. **700,** 838.

219, 71. *Whom thou,* etc. Cf. n. **226,** 675.

72. *My thoughtless youth,* etc. v. B. S. liii, liv.

80. *Can I believe,* etc. "The Protestant divines took a distinction; and, while they admitted they were obliged to surrender their human judgment in matters of divine revelation which were above their reason, they asserted the power of appealing to its guidance in those things of a finite nature which depend on the evidence of sense, and the consequent privilege of rejecting any doctrine which, being within the sphere of human comprehension, is nevertheless repugnant to the understanding: therefore, while they received the doctrine of the Trinity as an infinite mystery, far above their reason, they contended against that of transubstantiation as capable of being tried by human faculties, and as contradicted by an appeal to them." [SCOTT.]

95. *Penetrating parts.* This means, as Christie states, "penetrating the parts of matter, instead of separating them. Matter is impenetrable by matter." (Cf. **274,** 252.) Impenetrability, in physics, is defined by Webster as "that property in virtue of which two portions of matter cannot at the same time occupy the same portion of space." Dryden illustrates by a reference to John xx. 19. 24–29; and argues that as Christ's body penetrated the closed doors of the room where the disciples were gathered, so it could penetrate the elements of the consecrated host.

121. *Proponent.* Eds. 1 and 3 have a comma after this word; ed. 2 omits the comma, probably by a misprint, thereby converting *proponent* into an adjective. Christie, followed by C. D. (under *proponent*), adopts the reading of ed. 2.

134. *Could he,* etc. Contrast **111,** 118–121.

220, 153. *Wolf.* The Presbyterians.

163. *His ragged tail.* The Geneva gown of the Presbyterian clergy. — Their close-cropped hair and black skull cap made their ears prominent: to which fact, and to the Calvinistic doctrine of predestination, Dryden refers in l. 165.

168. *Tho' fear'd,* etc. A reference to the temporary power of the Presbyterian party in the days of the Long Parliament, as *captain,* and under Cromwell, as *companion of the spoil.*

170–173. *Full many . . . France.* Christie's explanation of this vague passage seems the most natural: Dryden, having styled the Presbyterians wolves, applies to them a story told by William of Malmesbury of King Edgar (about 973): "He designed to exterminate every beast of prey from his kingdom;

and commanded Judwall, King of the Welsh, to pay him yearly a tribute of three hundred wolves. This he performed for three years, but omitted in the fourth, declaring that he could find no more." Dryden next identifies them with *Wycliffe's brood,* who first resisted ecclesiastical authority in mediæval England, and supposes that the last Wycliffite, escaping persecution, started the Swiss reform movement. This is confused enough, but admissible for the purposes of satire. Scott, however, sees in the first two lines a reference to the story told by Bede, of the destruction (about 603) of twelve hundred Welsh monks of Bangor, as a punishment for their resistance to St. Augustine, and refusal to acknowledge him as their archbishop.

177. *Antipathy to kings.* Wycliffe, as Professor Williams notes, was accused of complicity in the rising of Wat Tyler.

180. *Zuinglius.* Ulric Zwingli (1484–1531) began to preach a reformed religion in Switzerland in 1516. John Calvin (1509–64) spent his life after 1536 for the most part in Geneva. The latter, in his *Institutes,* gave clear form to the presbyterian organization of church government, according to which ecclesiastical authority rests in a presbytery (otherwise called *classis* or *class,* l. 189), or assembly of presbyters (elders).

182. *In Israel,* etc. Dryden in the following lines draws on a work by Peter Heylyn, first published in 1670, *Aërius Redivivus; or, The History of the Presbyterians, containing . . . their Oppositions to Monarchical and Episcopal Government . . . and their Imbroilments in the Kingdoms and Estates of Christendom in the Pursuit of their Designs.* In his preface Heylyn writes: "I know that some out of pure zeal unto the cause would fain intitle them to a descent from the Jewish Sanhedrim, ordained by God himself in the time of Moses. And that it might comply the better with their ends and purposes, they have endeavored to make that famous consistory of the seventy elders not only a coördinate power with that of Moses, and after his decease with the kings and princes of that state in this public government, but a power paramount and supreme, from which lay no appeal to any but to God himself; a power by which they were enabled not only to control the actions of their kings and princes, but also to correct their persons." Heylyn denies that the Sanhedrim had any such authority, but adds: "And yet I shall not grutch them an antiquity as great as that which they desire, as great as that of Moses or the Jewish Sanhedrim." He then sarcastically attributes the origin of Presbyterianism to the rebellion of Korah, Dathan, and Abiram against Moses and Aaron (Numbers xvi. 1–35); a hint which Dryden follows in ll. 184–189.

189. *Class.* Cf. **217**[1], 28, n; n. **220,** 180.

197. *O happy pair,* etc. Cf. **160, 161,** nn.

204. *Your native kennel,* etc. The citizens of Geneva had been under the temporal as well

as the ecclesiastical authority of a bishop.
But, after they adopted the reformed religion
(1535), their city, famous as the home of Calvin, was regarded as the cradle of Presbytery.
As they made choice of a republican form of
government, our author infers that democracy is most congenial to their new form of
religion. — The territories of the little state
were bounded by its ramparts and the lake,
which Dryden contemptuously calls a puddle. [Scott.] Professor Williams, with more
probability, interprets the *wall* as the Alps

209. *Tweed.* Scotland. "If Dryden had looked
to his own times, he would have seen that the
Scottish Presbyterians made a very decided
stand for monarchy after the death of
Charles I; and even such as were engaged in
the conspiracy of Baillie of Jerviswood, which
was in some respects the counterpart of the
Rye House Plot, refused to take arms, because they suspected that the intentions of
Sidney, and others of the party in England,
were to establish a commonwealth." [Scott.]

210. *Effects.* Ed. 1 reads *affects.*

211. *Drawn,* etc. v. **112,** 227, n.

212. *As, where,* etc. Cf. **872, 873,** 1–45, and
241, 1806, n.

221, 222. *Dogs,* etc. Professor Williams aptly
quotes from Lyly's *Euphues* (ed. Arber, p. 61):
"The dog . . . eateth grasse and findeth
remedy."

235. *From Celtic woods,* etc. This probably
refers back to ll. 170, 171, though Scott,
Christie, and Williams think that there is an
allusion to the persecution of the Huguenots
in France: cf. n. **217¹,** 1. The whole passage,
through l. 307, refers undoubtedly, as Professor Williams suggests, to "the partial toleration granted in Scotland, February, 1687."

"A few days later James made his first
hesitating and ungracious advances towards
the Puritans. He had determined to begin
with Scotland, where his power to dispense
with acts of parliament had been admitted
by the obsequious Estates. On February 12,
accordingly, was published at Edinburgh a
proclamation granting relief to scrupulous
consciences. Even in the very act of making
concessions to the Presbyterians, James
could not conceal the loathing with which he
regarded them. The toleration given to the
Catholics was complete. But the indulgence
vouchsafed to the Presbyterians, who constituted the great body of the Scottish people,
was clogged by conditions which made it
almost worthless. For the old test, which
excluded Catholics and Presbyterians alike
from office, was substituted a new test, which
admitted the Catholics, but excluded most of
the Presbyterians. The Catholics were allowed to build chapels, and even to carry the
host in procession anywhere except in the
high streets of royal burghs; but the Presbyterians were interdicted from worshiping
God anywhere but in private dwellings; they
were not to presume to build meetinghouses;
they were not even to use a barn or an out-

house for religious exercises; and it was distinctly notified to them that, if they dared to
hold conventicles in the open air, the law
which denounced death against both preachers and hearers, should be enforced without
mercy. Any Catholic priest might say mass
but the privy council was directed to see that
no Presbyterian minister presumed to preach
without a special license from the government. Every line of this instrument, and of
the letters by which it was accompanied,
shows how much it cost the king to relax in
the smallest degree the rigor with which he
had ever treated the old enemies of his
house." Macaulay, ch. vii (abridged).

271. *Coronation day.* "Which is usually distinguished by an act of grace, or general pardon." Scott.

280. *And blood.* etc. v. Genesis iv. 1–10.

283. *The mighty hunter.* Nimrod. v. Genesis
x. 9.

284. *The blessed Pan.* Jesus Christ. In the
glosse on the *Shepheardes Calender* for May,
Spenser explains *great Pan* of his text as
follows: "Great Pan is Christ, the very God
of all shepheards, which calleth himselfe the
greate and good shepherd." The gloss further
explains that the idea originated in a connection that was made between the cruci-
fixion of Christ, and a story told by Plutarch
in his treatise, *Why the Oracles Cease to Give
Answers.*

289. *British Lion.* James II.

222. 321. *Shards.* Here undoubtedly in the
sense of *dung,* found in provincial English:
v. E. D. D. under *cowshard.*

326. *To them,* etc. "In Scotland, large conventicles were held in the mountains and
morasses by the fiercest of the Covenanters,
whom persecution had driven frantic. These
men, known now by the name of Cameronians,
considered popery and prelacy as synony-
mous terms." [Scott.]

327. *Panther.* The Church of England.

338. *The Wolf,* etc. v. n. **237,** 1454.

339. *Tho' unpolluted,* etc. Christie notes a resemblance to Juvenal, xiii. 209, 210: "He who
meditates any secret wickedness within himself incurs the guilt of the deed."

342. *Spirits of a middle sort.* Professor Williams
cites in illustration:

Those argent fields more likely habitants,
Translated Saints, or middle Spirits hold,
Betwixt the angelical and human kind.
                         Paradise Lost, iii. 460–462.

344. *Down.* So ed. 1; eds. 2 and 3 read *done.*

351. *A Lion, old.* etc. "Henry VIII's passion
for Anne Boleyn led the way to the Reformation." [Scott.]

Henry was born in 1491, met Anne Boleyn
in 1522, began open negotiations for a divorce
from Catherine of Aragon in 1527, was secretly married to Anne about January 25,
1533, and received a formal divorce from the
archiepiscopal court in May of that year.

354. *Cov'ring,* etc. Cf. **567,** 247–250.

361. *The fruit*, etc. "The following lines refer to the dissolution of the monasteries under Henry VIII." [WILLIAMS.]

367. *Where marriage*, etc. "The marriage of the clergy, licensed by the Reformation." SCOTT.

223, 385. *Travailing*. It is impossible to say whether the word here means *laboring* or *traveling*.

393. *Yet*, etc. "The king being owned the head of the Church of England, contrary to the doctrine of the other Reformed Churches." SCOTT.

402. *A creature*, etc. Referring to the Minotaur, half man and half bull, confined in the Cretan Labyrinth: cf. **594,** 33–46; **722,** 325–369.

410. *In doubtful points*, etc. The Catholics believe that in the Eucharist the bread and wine are transformed *into* the body and blood of Christ (transubstantiation); the Lutherans, that the body and blood of Christ are really present *in, with*, and *under* the elements (consubstantiation); the Calvinists deny entirely the real corporeal presence of the body and blood of Christ, teaching that they are present only spiritually, to be enjoyed by believers only. The doctrine of the Church of England, as expressed in Article 28, is practically Calvinistic; it admits a *real* (spiritual) *presence*, but does not exactly define the manner of that presence. The last part of the Article discountenances worship of the sacrament, which was regarded as idolatrous:

"The Supper of the Lord is not only a sign of the love that Christians ought to have among themselves one to another, but rather it is a sacrament of our redemption by Christ's death; insomuch that to such as rightly, worthily, and with faith receive the same, the bread which we break is a partaking of the body of Christ, and likewise the cup of blessing is a partaking of the blood of Christ. Transubstantiation, or the change of the substance of bread and wine, in the Supper of the Lord, cannot be proved by Holy Writ; but is repugnant to the plain words of Scripture, overthroweth the nature of a sacrament, and hath given occasion to many superstitions. The body of Christ is given, taken, and eaten in the Supper only after an heavenly and spiritual manner. And the mean whereby the body of Christ is received and eaten in the Supper is faith. The sacrament of the Lord's Supper was not by Christ's ordinance reserved, carried about, lifted up, or worshiped."

417. *Her novices*, etc. Referring to passages in *A Catechism* [of the Church of England], *that is to say, an instruction to be learned of every person, before he be brought to be confirmed by the bishop.*

"Q. What is the outward part or sign of the Lord's Supper?

"A. Bread and Wine, which the Lord hath commanded to be received.

"Q. What is the inward part, or thing signified?

"A. The Body and Blood of Christ, which are verily and indeed taken and received by the faithful in the Lord's Supper."

430. *Her wild*, etc. Cf. James i. 6.

431. *But sure*, etc. "The pretensions of the Church of England to loyalty were carried to a degree of extravagance which her divines were finally unable to support, unless they had meant to sign the destruction of their religion by a Catholic king." [SCOTT.]

In 1675 Danby, the head of the Tory and High Church party, had proposed a bill according to which, "no one was to be allowed to hold office or to sit in parliament unless he would swear that he believed resistance to the crown to be in all cases illegal, and that he would never endeavor to alter the government in Church or State." (GARDINER, *Student's History of England.*)

435. *And seal'd*, etc. "Alluding to the fate of the Church and monarchy of England, which fell together in the great rebellion." SCOTT.

442. *An Indian wife*. "Alluding to the voluntary self-immolation of Hindu widows (*suttee*)." [CHRISTIE.]

447. *And bore*, etc. Cf. **889,** 34, n.

449. *Isgrim*. The name of the wolf in the mediæval beast epic of which Reynard the Fox is the hero.

224, 460. *If she*, etc. Cf. **130,** 156–166.

497. *Thus*, etc. "That is, if the Church of England would be reconciled to Rome, she should be gratified with a delegated portion of innate authority over the rival sectaries, instead of being obliged to depend upon the civil power for protection." SCOTT.

225, 531. *The sovereign Lion*, etc. "Alluding to the exercise of the dispensing power." [SCOTT.]

Scott thinks that a reference to the Declaration of Indulgence is also intended, but this is impossible, unless the passage be a late addition to the poem. Cf. n. **216** (*To the Reader*).

537. *The ten-horn'd monster*. "The ten-horned monster (v. Revelation xvii) was usually explained by the reformers as typical of the Church of Rome." [SCOTT.]

540. *Certitude of sense*. v. n. **219,** 80.

552. *The Hind had seen him first*. "There was a classical superstition, that, if a wolf saw a man before he saw the wolf, the person lost his voice. (Cf. **438,** 73, 74.) Dryden has adopted, apparently without authority, the converse of this superstitious belief." [SCOTT.]

554. *Suffis'd*. So eds. 1 and 2; ed. 3 reads *suffic'd*.

563. *Her friend*, etc. "Although the Popish Plot was made the pretense of persecuting the Papists in the first instance, yet the high-flying party of the Church of England were also leveled at, and accused of being Tantivies, Papists in masquerade, etc." [SCOTT.] Cf. **124¹,** 40, n; **111,** 108, n.

579. *The younger Lion*. "James II, then Duke of York, whom Shaftesbury and his party involved in the odium of the Plot." SCOTT.

580. *Your priestly calves*. "Plunket, the titular primate of Ireland, Whitebread, provincial

of the Jesuits, and several other Catholic priests, suffered for the alleged plot." [SCOTT.]

226, 602. *The Test.* The Test Acts had removed any ambiguities in the Church of England's doctrine concerning the Eucharist. Cf. n. **216** (*To the Reader*).

635. *Cannon.* So in eds. 1, 2, 3; the pun with *canon* is obvious.

639. *Subterranean Rome.* The Catacombs; cf. *Evelyn's Diary,* April 11, 1645. [CHRISTIE.]

651. *For fallacies,* etc. "*Dolus versatur in generalibus* was an axiom of the Schools." SCOTT. Cf. **24**², 35–37.

652. *I then affirm,* etc. "Dryden does not plead the cause of infallibility so high as to declare it lodged in the Pope alone, but inclines to the milder and more moderate opinion which vests it in the Church and Pope jointly. This was the shape in which the doctrine was stated in the pamphlets generally dispersed from the king's printing press about this time." [SCOTT.]

675. *And all,* etc. "The Catholics interpret our Savior's promise: ' Lo, I am with you alway, even unto the end of the world' (Matthew xxviii. 20), as applicable to their own church exclusively." [SCOTT.]

227, 677. *But mark,* etc. "Dryden, like a good courtier, adopts here the arguments which converted his master, Charles II, and which are contained in the papers found in his strong box." [SCOTT.] Cf. n. **217**², 1.

692. *Jehu.* v. 2 Kings ix. 20.

713. *Luther.* Cf. n. **223,** 410.

722. *Arius, Socinus.* Cf. nn. **166,** 312, 346.

730. *To those.* The pronoun refers back not to *Scripture* in the preceding line, but to *Scriptures* in l. 727.

733. *Where piles,* etc.

Infestisque obvia signis
Signa, pares aquilas, et pila minantia pilis.
LUCAN, *Pharsalia,* i. 6, 7.

735. *Sathan.* v. Matthew iv. 6.

741. *Those first councils.* An act of 1559 (1 Eliz. c. 1, § 20) recognized the authority of the "first four general councils" in matters of faith.

742. *Sure tradition.* "We mean by traditions, ordinances made in the prime of Christian religion, established with that authority which Christ hath left to his Church for matters indifferent, and in that consideration requisite to be observed, till like authority see just and reasonable cause to alter them. So that traditions ecclesiastical are not rudely and in gross to be shaken off because the inventors of them were men." HOOKER, *Ecclesiastical Polity,* v. 65 (2). Cf. **166,** 316–355.

799. *Its omen.* "The gallows." SCOTT.

800. *The Panther's breath.* This was one of the current doctrines of the early natural history; v. Steele, *Mediæval Lore from Bartholomew Anglicus,* London, 1905, p. 166.

802. *The Blatant Beast.* "By the Blatant Beast (see Spenser's *Faerie Queene*) we are generally to understand slander. But it is here taken for the Wolf, or Presbyterian clergy, whose violent declamations against the Church of Rome filled up many sermons." [SCOTT.]

818. *The Wolf,* etc. "The Presbyterian Church appeals to the Scripture as the sole rule of faith." [SCOTT.]

229, 840. *Statutes.* James II had suspended these before the poem was published — cf. n. **216** (*To the Reader*) — but Dryden did not cancel this line. Cf. **240,** 1675, n; **243,** 1927, n.

858. *For purging fires.* The doctrine of purgatory, rejected by all the reformed churches, and defended by the Catholics more from tradition than from Scripture.

896. *Th' apostles.* So ed. 1; eds. 2 and 3 read *the Apostles.*

230, 917. *He darkly writ.* v. 2 Peter iii. 16.

939. *Counsels.* Ed. 1 reads *councils.*

948. *Testament.* "It is probable that from this passage Swift took the idea of comparing the Scripture to a testament in his *Tale of a Tub.*" SCOTT. Cf. **167,** 392.

954. *Hungary.* "Throughout the seventeenth century Austria and the Turks fought for Hungary." SAINTSBURY.

970. *Pronounc'd his words.* v. John xviii. 5, 6. Dryden repeats the latter part of the line in **532,** 834.

973. *Modestly.* Ed. 1 reads *modesty.*

979. *Polish diet.* In the Polish diets absolute unanimity was required for each decision. Hence they usually ended in anarchy, often in warfare. This was especially the case with those charged with the election of a new king. Armed rebellion (l. 987) was sanctioned by the laws of Poland. The term *crown-gen'ral* (l. 982), which is a translation of a Polish title (v. N. E. D.), *hetman koronny,* is particularly apt in this connection. Sobieski had been *hetman wielki koronny* (great crown-general) before his election to the Polish throne in 1674.

231, 988. *To Church decrees,* etc. "The Church hath power to decree rites or ceremonies, and authority in controversies of faith; and yet it is not lawful for the Church to ordain anything that is contrary to God's word written, neither may it so expound one place of Scripture that it be repugnant to another." Article xx.

991. *Curtana.* "This romantic name is given to the sword of mercy, which wants a point, and is said to have been that of Edward the Confessor. It is borne at the Coronation." [SCOTT.]

1026. *Consubstantiating* Church. The Lutherans: v. n. **223,** 410.

1028. *The French reform'd.* "The Huguenot preachers, being Calvinists, had received classical (v. n. **217**¹, 28) and not episcopal ordination; hence, unless reordained, they were not admitted to preach in the Church of England." [SCOTT.]

1030. *Donors,* etc. Those who give the right to preach must do the ordaining.

1061. *Here then,* etc. Scott points out that

much of Dryden's argument is identical with that of a passage in the second paper found in King Charles's strong box.

232, 1071. *So when of old,* etc. Cf. *Paradise Lost,* iii. 80–273.

1090. *What,* etc. Cf. Revelation xxi. 2.

1101 n. *Marks,* etc. Unity, Sanctity, Catholicity, and Apostolicity, in expansion of the clause of the Nicene Creed: "I believe one holy Catholic and Apostolic Church." (The word *holy* does not occur in the text of this creed in the *English Book of Common Prayer.*)

1110. *But like,* etc. "The magicians imitated Moses in producing the frogs which infested Egypt; but they could not relieve from that, or any of the other plagues. By that of boils and blains they were afflicted themselves, like the other Egyptians." [SCOTT.] v. Exodus viii, ix.

1130. *Our sailing ships,* etc. As Professor Firth explains, this is "a reference to the practice of transporting criminals to . . . the British colonies."

233, 1137. *Missioners.* Ed. 1 reads *Missionaires.*

1140. *Yet some,* etc. Catholic missionaries in the sixteenth century had some success in Japan, but were later driven out and their converts exterminated. Of the Europeans, only the Dutch retained the right to trade with Japan. For the sake of this privilege, according to a current report, they were required to abjure Christianity and to trample on the crucifix. [SCOTT.] Cf. **5,** 84, n.

1143. *Industrious of.* Cf. **784,** 53.

1154. *For all,* etc. "Alluding to the doctrines of Wycliffe and the Lollards, condemned as heresies in their own times, but revived by the reformers." SCOTT.

1159. *'T is said,* etc. v. Matthew vii. 24–27.

1171. *Monumental arms,* etc. Arms put up as a memento, or memorial.

1172. *Goliah's sword.* v. 1 Samuel xxi. 9.

1175. *Standard.* "Perhaps used with a reference to the sense given by Bailey for *standils* or *standards:* 'Trees reserved at the felling of wood for growth for timber.'" [WILLIAMS.]

1181. *What digits,* etc. "Astronomically. There are said to be twelve digits in the diameter of the sun or moon, and the extent of an eclipse is calculated by them." SAINTSBURY.

1202. *Sev'n.* Ed. 1 reads *nine.* St. Augustine, the missionary to the English, reached the country in 597. From that date Dryden apparently reckons, in ed. 1, to the time of Henry VIII; in ed. 2, to that of Wycliffe.

234, 1214. *Joseph.* v. Genesis xliii. 29, 30. "The English Benedictine monks executed a renunciation of the abbey lands, belonging to the order before the Reformation, in order to satisfy the minds of the possessors, and reconcile them to the reëstablishment of the ancient religion, by guaranteeing the stability of their property. There appeared, however, to the proprietors of these lands, little generosity in this renunciation, in case the monks were to remain in a condition of inability to support their pretended claim; and, on the other hand, some reason to suspect its validity, should they ever be strong enough to plead their title." [SCOTT.]

1223. *Skies a.* Ed. 1 makes no pause after skies; eds. 2 and 3 insert a colon.

1226. *Such were,* etc. Alluding to some extraordinary display of the aurora borealis at the time of the battle of Sedgemoor (July 6, 1685), in which King James's troops crushed Monmouth's rebellion. The battle was chiefly fought in the morning, before daybreak. [SCOTT.]

1234. *Nuntius.* v. GLOSSARY.

1251. *Content of mind.* Cf. **822, 823,** 1–30; n. **241,** 1806.

1252. *A grace cup.* N. E. D. defines *grace-drink* as "the drink taken by a company after the giving of thanks at the end of a meal." *Their common patron.* "King James." SCOTT.

1273. *So might,* etc. The following passage is reminiscent of Virgil: cf. **631,** 477–483.

235, 1283. *Mighty Pan.* v. **221,** 284, n.

1295. *Much malice,* etc. Montagu and Prior took this line for a motto of their satire on *The Hind and the Panther:* v. n. **216** (HIND AND PANTHER).

1302. *Mother Hubbard.* Spenser's *Mother Hubberd's Tale* is a political satire, in which the knavish Ape and Fox find the Lion (representing the allegory Queen Elizabeth) asleep, and usurp his functions as king of the beasts:

> The Lyon sleeping lay in secret shade,
> His crowne and scepter lying him beside,
> And having doft for heate his dreadfull hide.
> (Ll. 952–954.)

Mercury rebukes the Lion for his heedlessness:

> "Arise," said Mercurie, "thou sluggish beast,
> That here liest senseless, like the corpse deceast,
> The whilste thy kingdome from thy head is rent,
> And thy throne royall with dishonour blent."
> (Ll. 1327–1330.)

1304. *That queen,* etc. v. headnote, p. **122,** and **161¹,** 39–42.

1313. *Round eternity.* Cf. **4,** 18, n.

1315. *The Lion's peace.* "The Declaration of Indulgence." SCOTT. More probably, unless this line be a late addition to the poem, a reference to the king's earlier use of the dispensing power.

1319. *Furry sons.* "The clergy wearing the fur hoods of graduates." [WILLIAMS.] *Senate.* Convocation. [SCOTT.]

1336. *Her faith,* etc. "The adherence of the Church of England to the interests of James, while he was an exile at Brussels, and the Bill of Exclusion against him was in dependence, is here, as in other places, made the subject of panegyric. Had the Church joined with the Sectaries, the destruction of the Catholics at the time of the Plot would have been inevitable." SCOTT.

1354. *She paid,* etc. v. Matthew xxii. 21.

236, 1359. *I serv'd,* etc. "The Church of England complained, with great reason, of the coldness which they experienced from James, in whose behalf they had exerted themselves so successfully." SCOTT.

1415. *Some German quarrel. Une querelle d'Allemand* is a French phrase for a quarrel picked without cause. Louis XIV, conscious of superior force, could begin such when he chose.

237, 1436. *He of,* etc. Cf. **223,** 431, n.

1454. *Your sons of latitude.* On the phrase, cf. ll. 1481, 1523. "During the latter years of the reign of Charles II, the dissensions of the State began to creep into the Church. By far the greater part of the clergy were steady in their adherence to the court interest. But a party began to appear, who were distinguished by the name of Latitudinarians, which the High Churchmen conferred upon them. The chief amongst these were Tillotson, Stillingfleet, and Burnet. They distinguished themselves by a less violent ardor for the ceremonies and even the government of the Church; for all those particulars, in short, by which she is distinguished from other Protestant congregations. In 1668 a plan of this party for an accommodation with the Presbyterians was defeated by the uncompromising attitude of the House of Commons. As, on the one hand, the tenets of the moderate clergy approximated those of the Calvinists; so, on the other, their antipathy and opposition to the Church of Rome was more deeply rooted, in proportion to the slighter value which they attached to the particulars in which that of England resembled her. Hence some of the number looked with a favorable eye on the Exclusion Bill, directed against the Catholic Duke of York.

"The party was of course deeply hated by the Catholics, and hence the severity with which they are treated by Dryden, who objects to them as the illegitimate offspring of the Panther by the Wolf, and traces to their Presbyterian origin their indifference to the fasts and ascetic observances of the more rigid High Churchmen, and their covert disposition to resist regal domination. Their adherence to the English communion he ascribes only to the lucre of gain, and endeavors to draw an odious distinction between them and the rest of the Church." [SCOTT.]

Dryden had personal as well as public reasons for hostility to Stillingfleet; cf. n. **217²,** 1.

1462. *All that Scorpio claims.* "Alluding to the fact that the different parts of the body were assigned to different signs of the zodiac. The old almanacs have a naked figure in front, surrounded by the usual emblems of the signs, which dart their rays on the parts which they govern. What Scorpio claims, if not apparent from the context, may be found there." [SCOTT.]

1467. *Think you,* etc. "The Huguenot clergy who took refuge in England after the recall of the Edict of Nantes in 1685 did not all adhere to the same Protestant communion. Many conformed to the Church of England; and, having submitted to new ordination, some of them obtained benefices: others joined in communion with the Presbyterians and Dissenters of various kinds." [SCOTT.]

1482. *Yielding.* Ed. 1 reads *easie.*

1485. *Delphic.* i. e. ambiguous, and so doubleedged. [SAINTSBURY.] "The Δελφικὴ μάχαιρα of Aristotle, *Pol.* i. 2. 3." [WILLIAMS.]

1487. *Some,* etc. In the following paragraphs Dryden replies to the *Vindication* of Stillingfleet and his coadjutors; cf. **217²,** 1, n. "The *three steeples argent* obviously alludes to the pluralities enjoyed, perhaps by Stillingfleet, and certainly by some of the divines of the Established Church." [SCOTT.] Professor Williams, however, thinks that "it may refer to three Church dignitaries, such as Burnet, Stillingfleet, and Tillotson, whom Dryden supposed to be the authors of the three parts of the *Answer.* . . . *Argent* would then represent their professed purity, in strong contrast with the *sable field* of their real motives."

1489. *Have sharply tax'd,* etc. "I must not say the *poor* Bishop of Winchester is used unmercifully by him, for he calls him *that prelate of rich memory* [a phrase from Dryden's *Defense*]. . . . Had he a mind to tell us he was no poet ? or that he was out of the temptation of changing his religion for bread ?" STILLINGFLEET, *Vindication*, p. 105 (SS. xvii. 259, 260).

1491. *Such who,* etc. "If I thought there were no such thing in the world as true religion, and that the *priests of all religions are alike* [cf. **111,** 99], I might have been as nimble a convert, and as early a defender of the royal papers, as any one of these champions. For why should not one who believes no religion, declare for any ?" *Ibid.* p. 2 (SS. x. 208).

1493. *Bare lies,* etc. "But our grim logician proceeds from immediate and original to concomitant causes [of the English Reformation]; which, he saith, were revenge, ambition, and covetousness. But the skill of logicians used to lie in proving; but this is not our author's talent, for not a word is produced to that purpose. If bold sayings and confident declarations will do the business, he is never unprovided; but if you expect any reason from him, he begs your pardon ; he finds how ill the character of a grim logician suits with his inclination. However, he takes a leap from causes to effects; and here he tells us the immediate effects of this schism were sacrilege and a bloody persecution of such as denied the king's supremacy in matters wholly spiritual, which no layman, no King of Israel ever exercised." *Ibid.* p. 116 (SS. xvii. 277).

Stillingfleet writes these words at the close of an attempt to prove that Henry VIII's desire to divorce Catherine was caused by his tender conscience; and that the English casting off of the papal supremacy had "no relation at all" to the king's marriage to Anne Boleyn. Dryden in his *Defense* had applied the title *grim logician* to Stillingfleet (v. SS. xvii. 218), who here retorts it upon him.

1496. *'T is easier*, etc. "At the beginning of the *Vindication* Stillingfleet had said: 'But lest I be again thought to have a mind to flourish before I offer to pass.'" WILLIAMS.

1504. *For sundry*, etc. v. Stillingfleet, in SS. xvii. 267 f.

1508. *Treatise of Humility.* v. n. **217**², 19.

238, 1509. *But if*, etc. "Stillingfleet's argument: 'Suppose we had not such particular books, we think the Holy Scripture gives the best rules and examples of humility of any book in the world.'" WILLIAMS.

1541. *Hudibras.* Samuel Butler (1612–80). In 1683 Dryden had written, in a begging letter addressed to Laurence Hyde, Earl of Rochester, First Commissioner of the Treasury: "'T is enough for one age to have neglected Mr. Cowley, and sterv'd Mr. Butler." The guilt of neglect, as Scott remarks, belongs to "Charles II and his gay courtiers, who quoted *Hudibras* incessantly, and left the author to struggle with obscurity and indigence," not to the Church of England, which could have done nothing for the poet unless he had been in orders. Cf. **318**², 23, n.

1545. *With odious*, etc. v. **237**, 1491, 1493, nn. Stillingfleet (SS. xvii. 256) complains similarly of "civil and obliging epithets," such as *disingenuous*, *foul-mouthed*, and *shuffling*, which Dryden had bestowed upon him.

1550. *Imprimatur.* "Stillingfleet's *Vindication* bears this license: '*Imprimatur.* January 10, 1686. Henricus Maurice R^mo P. D. Wilhelmo Archiep. Cant. à Sacris.'" [SCOTT.] According to the law (14 Charles II, c. 33) the licensing power for all books except those on the common laws, history, affairs of state, and heraldry, was delegated to the Archbishop of Canterbury and the Bishop of London, and was thus beyond the immediate control of the king.

1573. *Be vengeance*, etc. "In the following beautiful lines, the poet, who had complained of Stillingfleet's having charged him with atheism, expresses his resolution [very imperfectly carried out] to submit to this reproach with Christian meekness, and without retaliation." [SCOTT.]

1575. *If joys*, etc. "In these lines Dryden versifies a sentence from the Duchess of York's paper: 'It will be plain enough to everybody, that I must lose all the friends and credit I have here by it; and have very well weighed which I could best part with, — my share in this world or the next: I thank God, I found no difficulty in the choice.'" WILLIAMS.

239, 1600. *It now*, etc. "The Hind having shown that her influence over Dryden was such as to induce him to submit patiently and without vengeance to injury and reproach, now calls upon the Panther to exert her authority in turn over Stillingfleet, for his irreverent attack upon the royal papers. Upon a careful perusal of the *Answer* and *Vindication* of that divine, it is impossible to find any grounds for the charge of his having *reviled*

Charles II or the Duchess of York. Dryden, however, like the other Catholics, was pleased to interpret the impugning and confuting the arguments used by the king and duchess into contempt and disrespect for their persons." [SCOTT.]

1602. *Shimei.* v. **117**, 585, n.

1604. *Your son*, etc. "In the beginning of the controversy, Stillingfleet had spoken dubiously of the authenticity of the paper ascribed to the duchess. In his *Vindication* he fully admitted that point, and insisted only upon the weakness of the reasons which she alleged for her conversion. This Dryden compares to a defeated vessel, bearing away under the smoke of her last broadside. (Cf. **217**², 29–43.)

"The person whom he states to have counseled Stillingfleet is probably Burnet; and the score which he paid is the severe description given of him under the character of the Buzzard (**250**, 2415 f). Dryden always seems to have viewed the *Answer* to the royal papers as the work of more than one hand. In his *Defense* (SS. xvii. 252) he affirms that the answerer's 'name is Legion, but tho' the body be possess'd with many evil spirits, it is but one of them who talks.'" [SCOTT.] Cf. **217**², 9.

1621. *Leap.* v. n. **237**, 1493.

1625. *Procession.* The word is especially applied to the ecclesiastical processions of the Catholic Church; hence Dryden's sarcastic *in Protestant procession.*

1627. *Rodriguez.* v. n. **217**², 19.

1631. *My altars*, etc. Cf. Isaiah vi. 6.

1638. *Make himself a saver.* "This apparently means 'to indemnify himself for damages.' A metaphor from bowls. Cf. Middleton, *No Wit, No Help like a Woman's*, ii. 3. 82: 'Yet if my bowl take bank, I shall go nigh to make myself a saver. Here's alley-room enough.'" WILLIAMS.

1649. *Some*, etc. Some among her sons may deserve to have their characters described in satire.

240, 1675. *Your bloody*, etc. The penal laws, though they were not strictly enforced, had never been abrogated. [SCOTT.] Cf. **225**, 531, n; **229**, 840, n; **243**, 1927, n.

1683. *By education*, etc. Cf. **116**, 535–538.

1713. *The Swallows' fortune*, etc. "The general application of the fable of the Swallows to the short gleam of Catholic prosperity during the reign of James II is sufficiently manifest. But it is probable that a more close and intimate allusion was intended to an event which took place in 1686, when the whole nation was in confusion at the measures of King James, so that the alarm had extended even to the Catholics, who were the objects of his favor. The following account is quoted from Ralph (*History*, 1744, p. 933), who cites as his authority *Secret Consults, etc. of the Roman Party*, p. 59:

"'While the nation was in a manner stunned with these outrageous proceeding, we are told there was a general meeting of the leading Roman Catholics at the Savoy, to consult how this favorable crisis might be most improved to the advantage of their cause. Father Petre had the chair, and at the very opening of the debates it appeared that the majority were more inclined to provide for their own security than to come to extremities with the Protestants. Notwithstanding the king's zeal, power, and success, they were afraid to push the experiment any farther. The people were already alarmed; the soldiery could not be depended upon; the very courtiers melted out of their grasp; all depended on a single life, which was already on the decline; and if that life should last yet a few years longer, and continue, as hitherto, devoted to their interest and service, they foresaw insurmountable difficulties in their way, and apprehended disappointments without end. Upon these considerations, therefore, some were for a petition to the king, that he would only so far interpose in their favor that their estates might be secured to them by Act of Parliament, with exemption from all employments, and liberty to worship God in their own way, in their own houses. Others were for obtaining the king's leave to sell their estates and transport themselves and their effects to France. All but Father Petre were for a compromise of some sort or another; but he disdained whatever had a tendency to moderation, and was for making the most of the voyage while the sea was smooth and the wind prosperous. All these several opinions, we are farther told, were laid before the king, who was pleased to answer that, before their desires were made known to him, he had provided a sure retreat and sanctuary for them in Ireland, in case all those endeavors which he was making for their security in England should be blasted, and which as yet gave him no reason to despair.'

"It will hardly, I think, be disputed that the fable of the Swallows about to cross the seas refers to this consultation of the Catholics; and it is a strong instance of Dryden's prejudice against priests of all persuasions, that, in the character of the Martin, who persuaded the Swallows to postpone the flight, he decidedly appears to have designed Petre, the king's confessor and prime adviser in state matters, both spiritual and temporal. The name of Martin may contain an allusion to the parish of St. Martin's in which Whitehall and the royal chapel are situated. But should this be thought fanciful, it is certain that the portrait of this vain, presumptuous, ambitious, bigoted Jesuit, as given by Burnet, is exactly that of the Martin. Burnet describes him as 'one Peter, descended from a noble family, a man of no learning, nor any way famed for his virtue, but who made all up in boldness and zeal.'

"The close correspondence of the fable with the real events may be further traced. The Raven (l. 1769) may be conjectured to mean Tenison, within whose parish Whitehall was situated, and who stood in the front of battle during all the Roman Catholic controversy. As Petre is the Martin who persuaded the Catholics not to leave the kingdom, his preparations for maintaining their ground there are also noticed. Lines 1823–1825 allude to the numerous schools and religious establishments which the Jesuits prepared to establish throughout England. The chapel which housed them (l. 1834) is obviously the royal chapel, where the priests were privileged to exercise their functions even during the subsistence of the penal laws. The transient gleam of sunshine (ll. 1844–1854) which invited the Swallows forth from their retirement, is the Declaration of Indulgence. The Irish Catholics, with the sanguine Talbot (Tyrconnel) at their head, may be the first who hailed the imaginary return of spring; they are painted as the Swifts (ll. 1841, 1842).

"I cannot help thinking that our author, still speaking in the character of the English Church, describes himself as the *foolish Cuckow* (l. 1853), whose premature annunciation of spring completed the Swallows' delusion. Perhaps he intended to mitigate the scornful description of Petre by talking of himself also as a Protestant would have talked of him. The foreign priests and Catholic officers whom hopes of promotion now brought into England are pointed out by the *foreign fowls* of l. 1879.

"The fable concludes in a prophetic strain by indicating the calamities which were likely to overwhelm the Catholics as soon as the death of James, or any similar event, should end their temporary prosperity. It is well known how exactly the event corresponded to the prophecy; even the circumstance of the rabble rising upon the Catholic priests was most literally verified. In most of the seaport towns they watched the coasts to prevent their escape; and, when King James was taken at Feversham, the fishermen by whom he was seized were employed in lying in wait for the fugitive priests." [SCOTT.]

The editor has been unable to verify all the details in the above note by Scott. Despite the fact that the Panther is supposed to be expressing the sentiments of the Church of England, it is probable that Dryden, himself a moderate Papist, had a personal antipathy for Petre and the Jesuit party in the Catholic Church; in ll. 1945–1948 the Hind admits the partial justice of the Panther's satire. — It is so surprising to find the court poet Dryden making a thinly disguised attack on the king's favorite counselor that Scott's identification of the Martin with Petre must be regarded as not absolutely beyond doubt. It is improbable, furthermore, that an allusion to the Declaration of Indulgence is intended in ll. 1844–1854; if so, that passage must be a late addition to the poem: cf. n. **216** (*To the Reader*) and **243**, 1953, n.

1728. *Endued*, etc. "Cf. *divinæ particulam auræ :* Horace, *2 Satires*, ii. 79." [WILLIAMS.]

241, 1732. *And time*, etc. Christie suggests that this phrase may be due to Horace's *simul inversum contristat Aquarius annum* (*1 Satires*, i. 36): cf. **406**[2], 4 (*Song*).

1750. *A* mack'rel *gale*. "A strong breeze such as mackerel are best caught in." N. E. D.

1759. *As Martins*, etc. "Perhaps another scoff at Martin Luther." WILLIAMS.

1769. *A Raven*, etc. Cf. **437**, 18, 19.

1776. *Signs*. Ed. 1 reads *sign*.

1783. *The Sibyl's hand*, etc. v. **558**, 561–577.

1788. *Chelidonian*. From χελιδών, a swallow. There is a reference to the fable of Icarus, who was drowned in the Ægean Sea, a part of which was called from him the Icarian.

1791. *The wiser sort*. Probably dramatic; the Church of England would naturally welcome a migration of the English Catholics to France.

1806. *Truth in dreams*, etc. Dryden had been reading Chaucer: v. **824**, 138–155; cf. **220**, 212, n.

242, 1814. *Nostradamus*. A famous French Jewish astrologer (1503–66), who published his prophecies in the form of rhymed quatrains. Cf. **260**[2], 1; **82**[2], 23.

1832. *Ahaz' dial*, etc. v. 2 Kings xx. 8–11; Joshua x. 12–14: cf. **205**, 106–109; **37**, 472.

1834. *A chapel*, etc. A chapel of ease is "a chapel built for the convenience of parishioners who live far from the parish church." N. E. D.

1843. *Gibeonites*. v. Joshua ix. 23.

1859. *St. Martin's day*. November 11.

1860. "*Who but*, etc. This turn of phrase may be another sign of Dryden's reading of Chaucer: cf. **757**, 381; **765**, 426; *Cant. Tales*, A 1870 (original of the latter passage).

1874. *Marriage-off'rings*. Ed. 1 reads *marr'age offsprings*.

1878. *Lucina*. The goddess in the Roman mythology who presides over childbirth.

243, 1887. *Need*. So eds. 1 and 2; ed. 3 reads *needs*, a proof that the adverbial *need* was already giving place to *needs*.

1898. *But birds*, etc. "A parody on Lee's famous rant in *Œdipus :*

May there not be a glimpse, one starry spark,
But gods meet gods, and jostle in the dark!"
SCOTT. Cf. 88. vi. 219.

1925. *Poll'd*. This word, found in eds. 1, 2, 3, seems to have caused needless trouble to commentators, and emendations to *pulled* or *poled* have been suggested. *Poll*, to clip or strip, a word used often in pruning trees, gives an excellent sense.

1927. *The laws*, etc. A law of Queen Elizabeth (27 Eliz. c. 2), confirmed under James I (1 Jac. I, c. 4), provided that any Jesuit or other Catholic priest found in England should be liable to the penalties of high treason; that is, to be hanged, drawn, and quartered. Any one harboring such a person the same law made guilty of felony, and liable to the death penalty.

1931. *And there*, etc. "It is a vulgar idea that a dead swallow, suspended in the air, intimates a change of wind by turning its bill to the point from which it is to blow." SCOTT. *Corps are.* v. general note, p. **939**.

1949. *An old fanatic author.* "John White, a Puritan member of the Long Parliament, had been very active in the ejectment of the clergy. In order to encourage and justify these violent measures, he published his famous treatise, *The First Century of Scandalous Malignant Priests, made and admitted into benefices by the Prelates* (1643), a tract which contains, as may be inferred from its name, a hundred instances of unworthiness, which had been either proved to have existed among the clergy of the Church of England, or had been invented to throw a slander upon them." [SCOTT.]

1953. *The sunshine*, etc. "The Hind intimates that, as the sunshine of Catholic prosperity, in the fable, depended upon the king's life, there existed those among her enemies who would fain have it shortened. But from this insinuation she exempts the Church of England, and only expresses her fears that her passive principles would incline her to neutrality." SCOTT. This passage is an additional proof that no allusion to the Declaration of Indulgence is intended in ll. 1844–1854: cf. n. **240**, 1713.

244, 1961. *Pardelis*. So eds. 1, 2, 3: *pardalis* is Latin (from the Greek) for a female panther.

1966. *If, as*, etc. The following passage is in support of the earlier policy of James II, cf. n. **216** (*To the Reader*). By making a declaration of his intention of maintaining the Church of England, the king hoped he could induce his Tory parliament to repeal the severe penal laws against the Catholics, and the Test Acts of 1673 and 1678. The conduct of the Church of England, in retaining the sanguinary penal laws of Elizabeth and James I, however laxly they might be enforced, is shown to be more cruel than that of Louis XIV, who in 1685 had revoked the Edict of Nantes, which, since 1598, had secured toleration for the Huguenots. Cf. n. **217**[1], 1.

1983. *Curst*, etc. v. 1 Kings xii. 6–11.

1992. *The Test*. The Test Act of 1678 — v. n. **216** (*To the Reader*) — had been brought forward at the height of the excitement over the Popish Plot. The Duke of York with difficulty secured the exemption of himself from its provisions. Shaftesbury, who had supported the Test Act of 1673, was particularly prominent in promoting this later measure, which Dryden, with much reason, represents as a prelude to the effort of the Whigs, in the Exclusion Bill of the next year, to set aside the succession of the Duke of York to the throne. "Though the Test Act was devised by a statesman whom they hated, and carried by a party whom they had opposed, the High Church clergy were not the less unwilling to part with it, when they found the advantages which it gave them against the Papists in King James's reign." [SCOTT.]

2009. *More just*, etc. v. Matthew xxvii. 3–5.

2013. *Oates.* v. n. **117**, 632. Bedloe was a scoundrel whose false testimony in the time of the Popish Plot excitement was second in importance only to that of Oates.

2020. *The painted*, etc. "The poet alludes to the enchantress Duessa (Falsehood), who, when disrobed by Prince Arthur, was changed from a beautiful woman into a loathsome hag (*Faerie Queene*, I. viii. 46–50)." [SCOTT.]

245, 2027. *Miter'd*, etc. The Anglican bishops retain their seats in the House of Lords; the Catholic peers, though spiritually kindred to the king, are excluded.

2029. *Metal.* Eds. 1, 2, 3 read *mettle ;* but the two words, etymologically the same, were not in Dryden's time separated in spelling.

2033. *Atheists*, etc. Who could freely deny transubstantiation, and therefore sit in parliament. Some of them might even feel justified in occasionally taking the sacrament according to the rites of the Church of England, as prescribed for office-holders by the Test Act of 1673. Cf. n. **216** (*To the Reader*).

2038. *To the Church.* Ed. 1 reads *from the church.*

2048. *Toby's rival*, etc. "The fiend in the Book of Tobit, who haunted Raguel's daughter, is frighted away by fumigation, by Tobias, her bridegroom." [SCOTT.] v. Tobit viii. 1–3.

2053. *Butt and peace.* The phrase is taken from Dryden's version of *The Tempest:* v. SS. iii. 166, 167, 191; it had evidently become proverbial. The sense is, "to have what one wants without fighting for it." Cf. **264**¹, 35.

2055. *In forma pauperis.* As a pauper, who was allowed writs and subpœnas gratis, and had counsel assigned him without fee.

2060. *Methinks*, etc. v. **611–615**, 68–352.

2084. *When first*, etc. During the first months of the reign of James II the readiness of the nation to trust and oblige him seemed unbounded.

2090. *In vain*, etc. It is impossible to say just what portions of Dryden's poem were written after the Declaration of Indulgence; v. n. **216** (*To the Reader*). Ll. 2090–92 would naturally, but not necessarily, have preceded it; l. 2105 contains a probable, but not a certain allusion to it; ll. 2186 f unquestionably followed it: v. nn. **247**, 2190, 2240; **251**, 2527. Perhaps ll. 2050–2185 are Dryden's attempt at a transition from one point of view to the other.

246, 2103. *Then Conscience*, etc. Lord Halifax (cf. n. **120**, 882), for example, published a pamphlet, *A Letter to a Dissenter*, urging the Dissenters to side with the Church of England, and not to be misled by the pretended toleration offered them by the other. But this may have been later than Dryden's poem.

2107. *Th' associating name.* A reminiscence of the times of Shaftesbury: cf. **126**², 10, n.

2112. *O Proteus*, etc. v. **483**, **484**, 557–598.

2117. *Immortal pow'rs*, etc. v. **819**, 554–556; **843**, 335, 336.

2119. *Conscience*, etc. Scott points out that the

arguments in this speech are versified almost literally from a contemporary tract.

2133. *Possess*, etc. Cf. **308**², 19: v. Luke xxi. 19.

2140. *Your*, etc. Cf. **225**, 531, n.

2150. *Wishing*, etc. "That is, wishing the accession of the Prince of Orange, then the presumptive heir of the crown." SCOTT.

2159. *Your neighbor nation.* Holland.

2170. *Your friends oppress'd.* The refugee Huguenots, whom James II had at first welcomed and protected, and the persecution of whom he had publicly denounced. In this he was not sincere: v. MACAULAY, ch. vi.

247, 2190. *She gave her up*, etc. A plain intimation of the king's abandonment of hope for a reconciliation between the Catholic Church and the Church of England.

2200. *A plain good man*, etc. James II, portrayed as he wished himself to be known.

2218. *Coward.* So eds. 1 and 2; ed. 3 reads *cowards.*

2235. *The fabric.* "The Catholic chapel at Whitehall." SCOTT.

2240. *Doves.* "The clergy of the Church of England, and those of London in particular. The virulent and abusive character which our author here draws of the clergy, and particularly those of the metropolis, differs so much from his description of the Church of England in the person of the Panther that we may conclude it was written after the publishing of the Declaration of Indulgence, when the king had decidedly turned his favor from the Established Church. Their quarrel was now irreconcilable, and at immediate issue; and Dryden therefore changes the tone of conciliation with which he had hitherto addressed the heretic Church into that of bitter and unrelenting satire. Dryden calls them Doves, in order to pave the way for terming them, as he does a little below (l. 2358), *birds of Venus*, as disowning the doctrine of celibacy. The popular opinion that a dove has no gall is well known." [SCOTT.]

2245. *Salt.* "Perhaps with reference to the state endowments of the Established Church (*salarium*, originally 'salt-money')." WILLIAMS.

248, 2247. *Bound by promise.* "His Majesty being dead, the duke, now King James II, went immediately to Council, and . . . told their Lordships that . . . he would endeavor . . . to maintain the government both in Church and State, as by law established, its principles being so firm for monarchy, and the members of it showing themselves so good and loyal subjects. . . . This being the substance of what he said, the Lords desired it might be published, as containing matter of great satisfaction to a jealous people upon this change, which his Majesty consented to." *Evelyn's Diary*, Feb. 4 (6), 1685.

2254. *Harpies.* v. **554**, **555**, 276–347.

2259. *Dan*, etc. Cf. 1 Samuel iii. 20.

2271. *Melancholy.* "Burton (*Anat. Mel.*, pt. i, sec. 2, mem. 2, subs. 1) includes pigeons among fowl whose flesh is 'hard, black, un-

wholesome, dangerous, melancholy meat.'"
WILLIAMS.

2289. *Domestic poultry.* "The Catholic clergy maintained by King James." [SCOTT.]

2300. *The bird,* etc. "The cock is made an emblem of the regular clergy of Rome, on account of their nocturnal devotions and matins." [SCOTT.]

2318. *Sister Partlet.* The nuns; v. **823,** 68.

2320. *Restiff.* Ed. 1 reads *restless.*

249, 2325. *Undress.* Ed. 1 reads *undrest.* At the end of the verse eds. 1, 2, and 3 read *pleas,* which modern editors have changed to *please. Please* may have been what Dryden intended, although N. E. D. cites no instance of the spelling *pleas* for *please* later than 1503, and the expression *make her pleas* in the sense of *plead her cause* seems intelligible.

2326. *A lively faith,* etc. A sarcasm upon Article XII: "Albeit that Good Works, which are the fruits of Faith, and follow after Justification, cannot put away our sins, and endure the severity of God's Judgment; yet are they pleasing and acceptable to God in Christ, and do spring out necessarily of a true and lively Faith; insomuch that by them a lively Faith may be as evidently known as a tree discerned by the fruit."

2336. *An hideous figure,* etc. "The Roman Catholic pamphlets of the time are filled with complaints that their principles were misrepresented by the Protestant divines." [SCOTT.]

2339. *Some Egyptian.* Ed. 1 reads, *an Ægyptian.*

2346. *There,* etc. "The worship of images, charged upon the Romish Church by Protestants as idolatrous." SCOTT.

2350. *No Holland emblem.* "The Dutch seem to have been remarkable for emblems, of which their old-fashioned prints and figured pantiles are existing evidence." [SCOTT.]

2361. *A law,* etc. v. n. **243,** 1927.

2370. *Shibboleth.* v. n. **244,** 1992 and n. **216** (*To the Reader*). On the word, v. Judges xii. 6.

2387. *For those,* etc. The idea of these lines goes back to Greek literature. Lycurgus, *In Leocratem,* 92, quotes a similar saying from "some of the old poets."

2392. *The Meccan prophet.* "The foolish fable of Mahomet accustoming a pigeon to pick peas from his ear, to found his pretensions to inspiration, is well known." [SCOTT.]

250, 2415. *Buzzard.* "Gilbert Burnet, well known as a historian, was born in Scotland in 1643. Being ordained, he obtained the living of Saltoun, in East Lothian. While in this living he drew up a memorial of the abuses of the Scotch bishops, and was instrumental in procuring the induction of some moderate Presbyterian divines into vacant churches. To measures so unfavorable for Episcopacy Dryden seems to allude in ll. 2418–2421. He was next created Professor of Divinity at Glasgow; but, as his active temper led him to mingle much in political life, he speedily distinguished himself rather as a politician than as a theologian. In 1672 he was made one of

the king's chaplains, and was in high favor both with Charles and his brother. He enjoyed much of the countenance of the Duke of Lauderdale; but a quarrel taking place between them, the duke represented Burnet's conduct in such terms that he was deprived of his chaplainry, and forced to resign his professor's chair and abandon Scotland. (He later had an opportunity of revenging himself upon Lauderdale; v. n. 2473.) During the time of the Popish Plot he again received a portion of the royal countenance. He was then preacher at the Rolls Chapel (v. n. **142,** 396), and enjoyed a high degree of public consideration. By a too frank letter to King Charles, in reproof of the faults of his character and government, he forfeited his favor, at least for a time. This freedom, with his Low Church tenets, gave also offense to the Duke of York, who was moreover offended with him for some interference in the affair of the Exclusion. At length his devotion to Lord Russell drew upon him the full resentment of both brothers. After a final breach with the court he went abroad, and settled in Holland at the court of the Prince of Orange. Here he did not fail, with that ready insinuation which seems to have distinguished him, to make himself of consequence to the prince, and especially to the princess, afterwards Queen Mary. From this place of refuge he sent forth several papers relating to the controversy in England; and the clergy, who had formerly looked upon him with some suspicion, began now to treat with great attention and respect a person so capable of serving their cause. He was consulted upon every emergency; which confidence was no doubt owing partly to his situation near the person of the Prince of Orange, the Protestant heir of the crown. He stood forward as the champion of the Church of England in the controversy with Parker, Bishop of Oxford, who advocated the repeal of the Test Act (v. l. 2486). In the *History of his own Time* he talks with complacency of the sway which circumstances had given him among the clergy, and of the important matters which fell under his management; for he was admitted into all the secrets of the English intrigues. These insinuations of Burnet's importance may, from the very satire of Dryden, be proved to have been well founded. This acquired importance of Burnet is the alliance between the Pigeon house and Buzzard which Dryden reprobates, believing, or wishing to make others believe, that Burnet held opinions unfavorable to Episcopacy. — This active politician had a very important share in the Revolution, and reaped his reward by being advanced to the see of Salisbury. He died in 1715." [SCOTT.]

In Dryden's time the word *buzzard* was often applied to a stupid, blundering, ignorant person.

2436. *Son of Anak.* v. Numbers xiii. 33.

2437. *Like those,* etc. Cf. **18,** 48–50.

2445. *His profit.* Ed. 1 reads *ambition*.

2466. *His praise*, etc. "This applies to the sketches of character introduced by Burnet in his controversial tracts." [SCOTT.]

2468. *A Greek*, etc. Imitated from Virgil's *timeo Danaos et dona ferentis* (*Æneid*, ii. 49).

2469. *Sev'n*, etc. The Anglican Church retains only two (baptism and the Lord's Supper) of the seven Catholic sacraments.

2473. *But he*, etc. In 1675 the House of Commons attacked the Duke of Lauderdale, the king's representative in Scotland, seeking his removal from office. Burnet, being summoned before a committee of that body, had testified that he had heard Lauderdale say "he wished the Presbyterians in Scotland would rebel, that he might bring over the Irish Papists to cut their throats." Burnet also gave other information of a private character unfavorable to Lauderdale. He defends himself against the charge of treachery, but admits that his conduct "had an ill appearance." Dryden's account is much exaggerated.

251, 2482. *An Indian muck.* "*To run amuck* is a phrase derived from a practice of the Malays. When one of them has sustained an insupportable calamity, he intoxicates himself and rushes into the streets, stabbing every one he meets, until he is cut down or shot, like a mad dog." [SCOTT.] *Amuck* was originally an adjective; it was falsely understood as *a muck*.

2497. *Their patron's promise.* v. n. **248**, 2247.

2521. *A gross idolater.* Burnet had merely reiterated the usual Protestant charge, that transubstantiation was an idolatrous doctrine. Cf. n. **223**, 410.

2527. *A doom.* The Declaration of Indulgence: v. n. **216** (*To the Reader*).

2530. *License.* Eds. 2 and 3 read *Licence ;* ed. 1 reads *licens'd*. This is doubtless a misprint, though it might be made into sense by placing a semicolon after *infring'd*, and commas after *but* and *oppress*.

2537. *Fowl of nature.* Wild birds, explained in ll. 2541–2549; cf. **842**, 278.

2549. *Rubicon.* A reference to Cæsar's famous passage (B. c. 49) of the Rubicon, the boundary of his province, by which he entered Italy and began war on the Senate.

252, 2552. *Shiloh.* v. Genesis xlix. 10.

2554. *Dionysius.* "The tyrant of Syracuse, who, after being dethroned, is said to have taught a school at Corinth." [SCOTT.]

2560. *And arts*, etc. "In the Declaration of Indulgence James expressed his conviction that persecution was unfavorable to population and trade." WILLIAMS.

2562. *The smiths*, etc. *In carminibus Appius ait fabrum esse quemque fortunæ.* (From the opening chapter of a piece attributed to Sallust, *Epistola* (*Secunda*) *ad Caesarem de Republica Ordinanda.*)

2572. *Two Czars*, etc. Peter the Great and his half-brother Ivan, at this time joint rulers of Russia. Dryden prophesies discord between the High and Low Church parties in the Anglican body. Compare the conclusion of *The Medal*, **131**, 287 f.

2577. *Benting times.* Times when pigeons are reduced to feed on *bents*, a sort of coarse grass.

2580. *College of the bees.* Probably nothing but a reference to Virgil: cf. **477, 478**, 92–156; **848**, 218.

SONG FOR ST. CECILIA'S DAY. Saintsbury notes: "In Dryden's copy of Spenser, preserved at Trinity College, Cambridge, the note, *Groundwork for a Song on St. Cecilia's Day*, is set against F. Q. VII. vii. 12."

17. *Jubal.* v. Genesis iv. 21.

253, 52. *Organ.* St. Cecilia is by tradition the patron saint of music, and an angel is said to have visited her while she was still on earth. But the editor cannot discover Dryden's authority for making her the inventress of the organ, or for representing that she drew an angel by her his notes. Cf. **733**, 161–170.

63. *Untune.* When this world and the heavenly bodies are destroyed, the music of the spheres will cease; thus *Music* (the blast of the divine *Trumpet*) will *untune* (make incapable of harmony) the *sky*. The antithesis of *music shall untune* continues that of *the dead shall live, the living die*, and is typically Drydenian in style. Thus the *universal frame* ends, as it began, *from harmony*. Cf. SS. xviii. 312.

EPIGRAM ON MILTON. "These lines were perhaps suggested by the distich written by Selvaggi in honor of the youthful poet, while he was at Rome, which Dryden has very happily amplified:

Græcia Mæonidem, jactet sibi Roma Maronem ;
Anglia Miltonum jactat utrique parem."
MALONE, I, 1, 205.

4. *Majesty.* "Impressive stateliness of character, expression, or action" (N. E. D.); hence not a repetition of *loftiness*.

BRITANNIA REDIVIVA. The heir of James II, the Princess Mary, was married to a Protestant, William, Prince of Orange. By the birth of a son to James her right to the throne after her father's death was set aside, and a Catholic succession seemed assured. Hence the exultation of the Catholic party, which Dryden expresses in this poem.

The motto is *Georgics*, i. 498–502; cf. **453**, 668–675. *Puerum*, which has been substituted for *juvenem* of the original, of course refers to the infant prince, and *perjuria* to the false testimony of Oates and others, in consequence of which many innocent Catholics lost their lives. Cf. **255, 256**, 146–164.

There are no significant variations of text in the two editions of 1688. The folio copy lacks the *imprimatur* that is found in the *quarto*, so that it is probably the later of the two.

254, 5. *The day.* June 10, 1688, of the *old style* corresponds to June 20 of the calendar now in use; Dryden here speaks of it as the longest day in the year.

9. *Sun.* The quibble on *sun*, *son* is unworthy of Dryden at this period. As far back as 1666 he had emphatically condemned *paronomasia:* cf. **25**[1], 47, n.

35. *Holy violence.* Referring to the claims of the Catholics that the prince was sent in answer to their prayers; cf. **9**, 139–144.

37. *And late,* etc. In imitation of Horace's, *Serus in cælum redeas* (*Odes,* i. 2. 45).

52. *For see,* etc. The opponents of James doubted the genuineness of the child; Dryden affects to believe that the doubts were confined to the Commonwealth party.

55. *Alcides.* v. **209**, 447, n.

65. *The manna,* etc. v. Numbers xi. 4–6.

80. *The sign.* A reference to the legend that Constantine the Great (272–337) beheld in the heavens, before his elevation to the throne, a luminous cross, with the inscription, τούτῳ νίκα (conquer by this). Adopting for his standard the symbol of Christianity, he triumphed over his enemies; as emperor, he favored and protected the Christians; shortly before his death he was himself baptized. So Dryden suggests that James's adoption of Catholicism was an omen of Christian success in the war going on between the German Empire and the Turks, in which the English king was much interested.

255, 84. *Sylvester. The present Pope* of Dryden's note, Innocent XI, was in reality opposed to the policy of James II, and disliked the Jesuits, whose influence was predominant with the English king.

86. *Large of his treasures.* Christie notes the imitation of Virgil's *largus opum* (*Æneid,* xi. 338). Innocent XI had given large sums to aid the German Empire in its war with the Turks.

89. *The former,* etc. Constantine spent part of his youth in Britain. A mistaken opinion was current that he was born there, and that his mother was a British princess.

91. *Whose exile,* etc. Cf. nn. **145**, 592; **148**, 793.

94. *Moon-ey'd.* Purblind. The king's brief attempt to conciliate the Dissenters having failed, Dryden resumes his natural antipathy to them.

97. *Shipwrack.* v. **151, 152**, 1065–1098, and headnote, p. **133.**

102. *The surviving eight.* v. Genesis vii. 13.

118. *Born,* etc. The birth took place at about ten o'clock in the morning, in the presence of numerous witnesses.

121. *Eaglet.* v. **3**[1], 11, n.

128. *Not,* etc. v. **532**, 822–833.

152. *Rebellion.* "The great Civil War." SCOTT.

256, 154. *Plagues.* v. **48**, 1066, n.

156. *Fire.* Cf. **44–51.**

157. *Plots.* v. **111**, 108, n.

Test. v. n. **216** (*To the Reader*); **244**, 1992, n.

158. *Worse.* The deaths of Catholics executed for supposed complicity in the Plot.

165. *Enough,* etc. "All the queen's former children died in infancy." SCOTT.

169. *Enough,* etc. "The year 1688, big with so many events of importance, commenced very unfavorably, with stormy weather, and an epidemical distemper among men and cattle." SCOTT.

176. *Araunah's,* etc. Dryden's reference should be to 2 Samuel xxiv. 18–25.

183. *Year!* The exclamation point is not found in the editions of 1688.

184. *Five months,* etc. "During the five months preceding the birth of the Chevalier de St. George, James was wholly engaged by those feuds and dissensions which tended to render irreparable the breach between him and his subjects. Dryden, like other men of sense, probably began to foresee the consequences of so violent and general irritation; and expresses himself in moderate and soothing language, both as to the past and future. Nothing is therefore dropped which can offend the Church of England." [SCOTT.]

190. *Conscience,* etc. Cf. **246**, 2117, 2118.

199. *Rome.* The Latin words in the footnote mean, "lest enemies should entice away the gods by incantations." When the gods had deserted a city, it was thought to be doomed; cf. **542**, 471–474; **15**, 19–22.

216. *Estian race.* Cf. headnote, p. **133.**

257, 237. *Gigantic brood.* Dryden's note exaggerates stories told, not of the giants, but of the Aloeidæ, Otus and Ephialtes, who, when only nine years old, threatened the Olympian gods with war, and would have succeeded in their rebellion had they been allowed to reach manhood. Cf. **604**, 784 f.

257. *Mercy,* etc. v. Matthew xiv. 31.

258, 296. *Amalek.* Cf. **27**[1], 28, n.

304. *But you,* etc. "The address to the queen has all the smoothness with which Dryden could vary the masculine character of his general poetry, when he addressed the female sex, and forms a marked contrast to the more majestic tone of the rest of the piece." [SCOTT.]

306. *Beyond,* etc. Cf. **40**, 639, n; **208**, 353.

259, 15. *Jove,* etc. Cf. **655**, 167.

21. *When,* etc. "An allusion to the gradual exclusion of French wine, owing to the war, which culminated, ten years later, in the Methuen treaty and the establishment of port as the staple drink." [SAINTSBURY.]

By the Methuen treaty (Dec. 27, 1703) England agreed to admit Portuguese wines on payment of two thirds of the duty imposed on French wines.

41. *Horses,* etc. "Alluding to the act for disarming the Catholics, which provided that no Papist should keep a horse or horses above the value of five pounds." [SCOTT.]

260, 36. *And make,* etc. "Alluding to the addresses upon the Revolution." SCOTT.

1. *Nostradame,* etc. Cf. **242**, 1814, n.

4. *Our vast expenses.* Owing to the elaborate scenery required for an opera.

261[1], 34. *Our blacks.* "It was the fashion, at this time, to have black boys in attendance, decorated with silver collars." [SCOTT.]

46. *Selling,* etc. v. **136**, 181, n.

47. *Dumfounding,* etc. "Explained by a stage direction in Shadwell's *Bury Fair* (act iii,

sc. 1), where 'Sir Humphrey dumfounds the count with a smart rap on the shoulders.' The humor seems to have consisted in doing this with such dexterity that the party dumfounded should be unable to discover to whom he was indebted for the favor." [SCOTT.]

261², 17. *Julian's.* "Julian, who styled himself Secretary to the Muses, made a dirty livelihood by copying and dispersing lampoons at Will's Coffee-House." [SCOTT.] Cf. **929²**. *Interloping.* Cf. **128**, 41, n.

20. *The first,* etc. "The poetasters of that age were so numerous and so active that the most deplorable attempt at wit or satire was usually answered in one which was yet worse. Parody and personal abuse were the implements of this warfare, which sometimes extended to answers, replies, rejoinders, rebutters, and surrebutters, all only distinguished by malignant scurrility." SCOTT. Cf. **308²**, 39–42.

262, MERCURY'S SONG TO PHÆDRA. The intrigue between these characters is of Dryden's own invention; Phædra is one of Alcmena's slaves.

263¹, 31. *Height.* This spelling, contrasting with *heighth* six lines later, is a fair sample of the inconsistencies of the early editions. Cf. *leafs, leaves* (**460**, 498, 515); *been, bin* (**829**, 515, 549); *elfs, elves* (**872**, 3; **873**, 34).

263², *Mr. Williams.* "This was quite in character. Cibber says of Williams (*Apology*, ch. vi), that his industry was not equal to his capacity, for he loved his bottle better than his business." SCOTT.

264¹, 10. *Cork.* "The taking of Cork was one of the first exploits of the renowned Marlborough. The assault began on September 25, 1690, and the city surrendered on September 28." [SCOTT.]

35. *Peace and the butt.* Cf. **245**, 2053, n.

264², 11. *He,* etc. Shovel-board was played by sliding coins or metal weights over a long smooth table. The highest score was gained by making the coin hang over the edge of the table; if it went the merest trifle further, it fell into the *box,* or trough placed to catch it. To score at all, the piece must cross a line drawn about four feet from the end of the table; this is apparently what is meant by *laying* the piece. v. Strutt, *Sports and Pastimes.*

265¹, 37. *Ottobuoni.* Cardinal Ottoboni became pope in 1689, as Alexander VIII, and died on February 1, 1691. He had been hostile to France, and friendly to the German Empire, hence to England as well. The policy of his successor was naturally a matter of much speculation. — This reference settles the date of presentation of King Arthur; Innocent XII, Alexander's successor, was elected on July 12.

Mrs. Bracegirdle. Anne Bracegirdle (1663?–1748), a beautiful and talented actress, and "a woman well reputed," spoke this indecent epilogue.

268¹, EPITAPH ON ERASMUS LAWTON. The text is from a copy of the inscription courteously furnished to the editor by the Reverend

William Woodward, Rector of Great Catworth.

268², THE LADY'S SONG. The text in *Buckingham's Works* reads *Ladies* (for *beauties*) in l. 1 and *the* (for *our*) in l. 7.

269, EPITAPH ON DUNDEE. The text in *Poetical Miscellanies* has the following variants: (5) Scotland *and Thee ;* (6) *Nor wou'dst thou her ;* (7) *dying did support.*

ELEONORA. For the motto, cf. **596**, 194–197: the original edition, after *Æneid,* reads only "l. 6;" in the last line it reads *Diis.*

269¹, 5 (prose). *Ovid.* v. *Tristia,* i. 1.

269², 10 (prose). *My disease.* The gout, according to Malone, who cites no authority for his statement.

270², 4. *Dr. Donne.* Cf. **283²**, 22–45; **317¹**, 43–51; n. **736**, 20. Donne states in a letter to George Gerrard (?): "Since I never saw the gentlewoman, I cannot be understood to have bound myself to have spoken just truth; but I would not be thought to have gone about to praise anybody in rhyme, except I took such a person as might be capable of all that I could say. If any of those ladies think that Mistress Drury was not so, let that lady make herself fit for all those praises in the book, and it shall be hers." GOSSE, *Life and Letters of John Donne,* i. 302.

271¹, 24. *The dragon's teeth.* Alluding to the legend of Cadmus, who, having slain a dragon, sowed its teeth, whereupon armed men sprang up, who immediately fell to fighting and slew one another, leaving only five survivors.

33. *An elected Speaker of the House.* The Speaker of the House of Commons has not the right to take part in debate.

272, 71. *Pharaoh,* etc. v. Genesis xli.

273, 181. *So subjects,* etc. A reproach to the English, who had driven into exile James II.

193. *Her children,* etc. "Lady Abingdon had six sons and three daughters." [SCOTT.] On *Charity,* cf. Spenser, *Faerie Queene,* I. x. 4, 16, 29–33.

197. *Anchises.* v. **606**, 921 f.

201. *Cybele.* The mother of Jupiter and other deities ; cf. **639**, 94, 127 ; **640**, 142.

274, 207. *And as,* etc. Apparently a loose reference to Exodus xvi. 11–31.

252. *Bodies.* Cf. **219**, 95, n.

273. *Orb.* Cf. **1**, 27, n.

275, 299. *Her Savior's time.* The age at which he is said to have been crucified.

325. *Courtier.* Christie well compares **132**, 20–23.

339. *The third errand.* "Enoch and Elijah were the two former instances, though the chariot is not especially mentioned in Enoch's case." [SAINTSBURY.] v. Genesis v. 24; 2 Kings ii. 11.

276, 7. *Would wonder,* etc. Cf. **275**, 295–298.

23. *Thus then,* etc. Cf. **275**, 303–305.

278, 9. *The Spanish nymph.* Apparently a reference to the "Spanish plot" of Southerne's play; cf. B. S. xxiii.

11. *But let,* etc. Cf. **734¹**, 21, 22.

18. *Nokes.* A celebrated actor of low comic parts; cf. **61¹**, 7; n. **60²**, 1.

27. *Copy*, etc. Etherege died early in 1691; Wycherley survived until 1716.

279², 22. *Mr. Fuller.* "William Fuller was an informer who pretended to make discovery of a formidable plot by the Jacobites against the government. The House of Commons, finding him unable to produce the witnesses to whom he referred, on February 24, 1692, declared him 'a notorious impostor, a cheat, and a false accuser.' He was prosecuted by the attorney general and punished by the pillory; notwithstanding which he did not profit by Mrs. Bracegirdle's legacy, for in 1702 he was sentenced to the same painful elevation for publishing more false statements." [SCOTT.]

280¹. *Mrs. Bracegirdle.* Cf. **265¹**, n. In *Henry the Second* she played the part of Rosamond, who dies of a draught of poison given her by Queen Eleanor.

280², 20. *Haynes.* "The facetious Joe Haynes became a Catholic in the latter part of James II's reign. But after the Revolution he read his recantation of the errors of Rome, in a penitentiary prologue." [SCOTT.] Cf. **70¹**, 45, n; **900²**, 47, n.

22. *Chapels of ease.* Cf. **242**, 1834, n.

281. TRANSLATIONS FROM JUVENAL AND PERSIUS. The editor has been unable to consult the second edition of this work. The first motto is Juvenal, i. 85, 86: cf. **324**, 130–132. The second is Martial, iv. 29. 7, 8: "Persius is more often noticed for his one book of *Satires* than the empty Marsus for his whole *Amazonid.*" — The following notes make almost no attempt to explain the substance of Juvenal and Persius, to comment on Dryden's deviations from the literal sense of the Latin, or to correct errors in his commentary. — The headings of Dryden's notes are taken literally from the original edition. In a few cases, as **334**, n. 10, they differ from the reading of the text. Cf. n. **418** (VIRGIL). This edition also follows the original in *omitting* the headings of certain notes.

282¹. *Dorset.* Charles Sackville (1638–1706), Earl of Dorset, to whom in 1668 Dryden had dedicated *An Essay of Dramatic Poesy.* He became Lord Chamberlain in 1689 and held the office until 1697. v. **412**, 48, n.

12. *The delight*, etc. Cf. **113**, 318, n.

283¹, 37. *Themistocles.* Every Greek general in the Persian wars voted for himself as the most deserving, but the majority assigned the *second* place to Themistocles. v. Herodotus, viii. 123.

41. *Longo*, etc. VIRGIL, *Æneid*, v. 320, with a change of *proximus* to *proximi:* cf. **583**, 420.

51. *Lyric poems.* "These lyrical pieces, after all, are only a few smooth songs, where wit is sufficiently overbalanced by indecency." SCOTT.

283², 4. *The best*, etc. Said of Dorset by Rochester, in *An Allusion to the Tenth Satire of the First Book of Horace.* On Rochester, v. B. S. xxix, xxxviii, xxxix: cf. **744²**, 11; **515¹**, 46–48.

"The satires of Lord Dorset seem to have consisted in short lampoons, if we may judge of those which have been probably lost from such as are known to us." [SCOTT.]

22. *Donne.* Pope probably took from this passage the hint for his *Satires of Dr. John Donne, Versified.* On Donne, cf. **270²**, 4, n.

38. *He affects*, etc. This passage probably suggested the title *metaphysical poets*, which Dr. Johnson gave to Donne, Cowley, and their school.

47. *Cowley.* v. **181¹**, 45, n.

284¹, 32. *Cicero. Tusc. Disp.* v. 16: Cicero, however, there passes over *fame*, as a matter of small consequence.

33. *Virgil.* Cf. **567**, 252–254.

35. *Epicurus.* v. Lucretius, vi. 58 f.

284², 25. *At rovers.* To *shoot at rovers* is, according to C. D.: "(a) To shoot an arrow for distance or at a mark, but with an elevation, not point-blank; or to shoot an arrow at a distant object, not the butt, which was nearer. (b) To shoot at random, or without any particular aim." Cf. **812**, 77.

28. *The Rehearsal.* v. B. S. xxviii. Davenant and the Howards were attacked in *The Rehearsal* as well as Dryden.

285¹, 47. *A shilling*, etc. "The four scepters were placed saltire-wise upon the reverse of guineas, till the gold coinage of his present majesty." SCOTT. "The *bath* is the chemist's bath, used for gilding." [KER.]

286¹, 2. *Eighteen thousand lines.* Really about fourteen thousand.

5. *Martial. Epigrams*, viii. 18.

286², 10. *Of your Lordship in the latter sort.* Ker emends to *In your . . . of the . . . ;* a reasonable but not a certain correction.

"Would it be imagined that, of this rival to antiquity, all the satires were little personal invectives, and that his longest composition was a song of eleven stanzas? The blame, however, of this exaggerated praise falls on the encomiast, not upon the author; whose performances are, what they pretend to be, the effusions of a man of wit; gay, vigorous, and airy." JOHNSON, *Life of Dorset.*

50. *Tasso.* Professor Ker points out that Dryden is indebted to Tasso's *Lettere Poetiche*, published with the first edition of his *Discorsi* in 1587, and probably also to Segrais' preface to his *Traduction de l'Eneïde* and to Rapin's *Reflexions sur la Poëtique*, ii. 13.

287¹, 15. *Owen's* Epigrams. The Latin epigrams of John Owen (1560?–1622) won popularity both in England and on the Continent; cf. **515¹**, 27.

32. *St. Lewis*, etc. Epic poems by Le Moyne, Chapelain, and Georges de Scudéry, all published in the years 1654–58: cf. **491²**, 4 f.

287², 5. *But Prince Arthur*, etc. Dryden's statement is without foundation in fact.

26. *His event is not prosperous*, etc. An idea reflected from René Le Bossu, *Traité du Poëme Epique*, ii. 17.

30. *Mr. Rymer's work.* "Mr. Rymer had promised to favor the public with 'some reflections

on that *Paradise Lost* of Milton's, which some are pleas'd to call a poem, and assert rhyme against the slender sophistry wherewith he attacks it.' But this promise, which is given at the end of his *Tragedies of the Last Age Considered and Examined*, he never filled up the measure of his presumption by attempting to fulfil." [SCOTT.]

On Dryden and Rymer, cf. B. S. xxx, xxxi; n. **382** (EX. POET.); **383**², 21, n; **410**, 47, n; **412**², 48, n; **741**¹, 50, n.

39. *A flat of thought.* Cf. **181**², 5–12.

53. *The rule of Horace. Ars Poet.* 47, 48.

288¹, 6. *Hannibal Caro.* Cf. **177**², 18, n; **513**², 14 f.

288², 42. *Boileau.* v. **922**, 620–663.

48. *Two victorious monarchies.* v. Daniel vii. The four beasts were interpreted as the Assyrian, Persian, Grecian, and Roman monarchies.

289¹, 9. *Ariosto*, etc. v. *Orlando Furioso*, xiv. 75–81; cf. **710**², 53 f.

13. *Tasso. Jerusalem Delivered*, ix.

37. *Boileau.* Boileau rather implies this than directly states it.

289², 23. *Philosophy.* Here used, as often, like the modern *science*, in the sense of "the study of natural objects and phenomena."

39. *Daniel.* v. Daniel x. Professor Ker notes that Cowley, with whom Dryden was of course familiar, had already used this passage in his *Discourse by way of Vision concerning the Government of Oliver Cromwell.*

41. *Platonic philosophy.* "Dryden was thinking of the Platonic opinion about dæmons as intermediary between heaven and earth. The idea of tutelar angels was familiar with the Platonists of Dryden's time." [KER.]

290¹, 9. *St. Michael.* v. Daniel x. 21; xii. 1.

290², 16. *Virgil.* "The most Platonic passages in Virgil, and those of which Dryden was probably thinking, are the *Fourth Eclogue* and the Sixth Book of the *Æneid.*" KER.

53. *Satan.* v. Job i. 6, 12; ii. 6.

291¹, 17. *Milton.* v. *Paradise Lost*, iii. 634 f. and *Arg.* "To every sphere of the heavens there is assigned an intelligence, or intelligences, which are angels." [KER.]

50. *Don Pedro*, etc. "Dryden refers to Don Pedro of Castile in his *Vindication of The Duke of Guise* (1683), with Mariana as authority. A *relation* quoted from Mariana shows that Dryden's projected poem might have been enlivened with modern applications to English politics, besides those which he indicates in this account of his design." [KER.] v. SS. vii. 182–184.

52. *One year.* Contemporary critics made this the limit of the action of an epic poem; v. Bossu, *op. cit.* iii. 13.

291², 16. *King Charles II.* Cf. B. S. xliv, xlv; **208**, 370–382; n. **238**, 1541.

292¹, 15. *Ne, forte*, etc. HORACE, *Ars Poet.* 406, 407: "Let not by any chance the Muse skilled in the lyre, and the singer Apollo, cause you shame."

43. *Curiosa felicitas.* v. **181**¹, 26, n.

292², 9. *Ut sibi*, etc. *Ars Poet.* 240–242: "That every one hopes to do the same, but sweats much and toils in vain, attempting the same."

28. *Cœna dubia.* TERENCE, *Phormio*, 342: "a hesitating banquet."

41. *Miniature.* F reads *meniature.*

293¹, 35. *Aristotle.* v. *Poetics*, 26. Dryden, in his *Apology for Heroic Poetry* (1677) [SS. v. 114], had praised heroic poetry as "the greatest work of human nature" and cited Aristotle as his authority. Now he cites Aristotle correctly, but opposes him. Cf. **490**¹, 35, n.

51. *Homer.* The time analysis of the *Iliad* here given may be due to Bossu, who, however (*op. cit.* ii. 18), gives the figures as *forty-seven* and *eleven.*

293², 5. *The instruction*, etc. The idea is common; Rapin entitles a chapter of his *Reflexions sur la Poëtique*, "La fin de ce poème [le poème épique] est d'instruire les grands," and writes in it: "La poésie héroïque . . . ne donne des leçons qu' aux grands pour gouverner les peuples." See also Sidney (*Apologie for Poetrie*, ed. Arber, pp. 46, 47) and Davenant (*Preface to Gondibert*). Davenant writes: "Nor is it needful that Heroick Poesie should be levell'd to the reach of common Men: for if the examples it presents prevail upon their Chiefs, the delight of Imitation . . . will rectifie by the rules which those Chiefs establish of their own lives, the lives of all that behold them; for the example of life doth as much surpass the force of Precept as Life doth exceed Death." Cf. **494**¹, 34, n.

27. *Vida.* The *De Arte Poetica* of the Italian Marco Girolamo Vida (1489?–1566) was counted an authority. On Bossu, v. B. S. xxxiv.

45. *Casaubon.* Isaac Casaubon (1559–1614), *De Satyrica Græcorum Poesi et Romanorum Satira*, Paris, 1605. (Page references in these notes are to that edition.) This is by far the most important in a scholarly sense of the sources of Dryden's *Discourse.*

Heinsius. Daniel Heinsius, *De Satyra Horatiana* (printed with his edition of Horace). Here cited from the Elzevir edition of 1629.

46. *Rigaltius.* Rigaltius (Nicolas Rigault, 1577–1654), *De Satyra Juvenalis*, published in his edition of Juvenal, 1616, and often reprinted. The editor has used the text included in the Leyden *Juvenal* of 1695.

Dacier. André Dacier, *Præfatio in Horatii Satiras*, printed with the edition of Horace *in usum Delphini.* (Professor Ker notes that Dacier's translation of Horace was published in the years 1681–89, and contained a *Preface sur les Satires d'Horace*, which was published in English in 1692, in Gildon's *Miscellany Poems.* Only the Latin form of this preface has been accessible to the present editor.) Notes and illustrations by Dacier are also found in the Delphin *Horace.*

The Dauphin's Juvenal. The *Delphin* editions (so called because they were prepared *in usum Delphini*, for the use of the Dauphin) of the Latin writers, with their copious notes, seem to have been those regularly used by Dryden.

52. *Julius Scaliger.* An Italian scholar (1484–1558), whose *Poetices Libri Septem*, i. 12, gives the etymology of satire referred to on the next page.

294¹, 36. *Hook'd nose.* Casaubon quotes from Isidorus: *Satyri homunciones sunt aduncis naribus* (l. i, c. 2, p. 85).

294², 1. *Aristotle*, etc. What follows, to **295²,** 26, is a free epitome of the first chapter of Casaubon, with some hints from Dacier.

296¹, 1. *Libertasque*, etc. HORACE, *2 Epistles*, i, 147–155.

10. *The law*, etc. Dryden found this *law* in a note by Dacier on this passage, in the Delphin *Horace*. It is not genuine, being made up on the basis of Cicero, *Rep*. iv. 10 (12).

24. *Thespis*, etc. In this paragraph Dryden follows Casaubon (l. i, c. 5), but in mentioning dramatic contests at the Olympic games he makes a blunder that is all his own !

48. *The story*, etc. Appended to the 1605 edition of Casaubon's work is *Cyclops Euripidæ Latinitate donata a Q. Septimo Florente Christiano.* One may doubt whether Dryden had read the original.

296², 44. *The definition*, etc. v. Casaubon, l. i, c. 3, pp. 130, 131.

297¹, 1. *Silli.* v. Casaubon, l. ii, c. 3, pp. 281–287. The editor cannot find that Casaubon anywhere derives σίλλοι from Σειληνός·

297², 5. *Dacier.* Whom Dryden now proceeds to follow, even in the quotations from Quintilian (*Inst. Orat.* x. 1. 93) and Horace (*1 Satires*, x. 66).

20. *Than that satire.* The careless repetition of *than* is probably due to Dryden rather than to the printer.

27. Σάθυ. Scaliger, *Poet*. i. 12; quoted, according to Ker, in the preface to the Delphin *Juvenal ; σάθν* should be *σάθη*.

40. *Casaubon.* l. ii, c. 4, pp. 317 f. The following discussion is mainly from the same writer, with some hints from Dacier.

298¹, 3. *Prémices.* A French word.

11. *Lancibus*, etc. *Georgics*, ii. 194, 394.

21. *Tack'd bills.* "When a measure was tacked to a money bill, so as to force its acceptance in the House of Lords." KER.

33. *Porphyrius.* Casaubon (l. ii, c. 4, pp. 319, 323) gives the name correctly, *Porphyrio ;* Dryden is misled by his frequent references to Porphyrius, as l. i, c. 2, pp. 82, 83.

298², 8. *Tarsians*, etc. From Casaubon, l. i, c. 5, pp. 201, 202.

10. *Scaramucha.* "The Italian comedy had been much in favor in Paris from the time of Charles IX; the most famous of all Scaramouches, Tiberio Fiorelli, was still alive when Dryden was writing this essay." [KER.] Scaramouche is a boaster and clown who is in mortal fear of the agile Harlequin. C. D. (*Names*.)

18. *Perhaps*, etc. This sentence seems not to be from Casaubon or Dacier, and is probably a

guess by Dryden. It is contradicted in the next sentence.

39. *Soldiers*, etc. Dryden here draws on Heinsius (p. 17), who quotes the Latin verses from Suetonius.

299¹, 15. *In the Tuscan language*, etc. From Dacier, who refers to Livy, vii. 2.

31. *Livius Andronicus.* v. Casaubon, l. i, c. 1, pp. 238 f.

300¹, 1. *The people*, etc. On what follows, v. Dacier, and Casaubon (l. ii, c. i, pp. 241 f).

300², 7. *As Scaliger observes.* The editor cannot find that Scaliger observes this, but Aristotle (*Poetics*, iv. 8) and Rigaltius do.

14. *Horace*, etc. Dacier says that Horace copied Ennius, but he says nothing about Virgil's doing so.

42. *Persius.* v. **378,** 20–26; **381,** n. 3. This story seems not to be quoted by Dacier or Casaubon in the essays that Dryden is following.

54. *Of Pacuvius*, etc. In the following paragraphs Dryden follows Dacier.

301¹, 18. *Quid*, etc. *2 Satires*, i, 62, 63.

24. *Quintilian.* Cf. **297²,** 13; n. **297²,** 5.

39. *Ennius and Pacuvius.* This is Dacier's view; Casaubon makes Lucilius the first follower, in Latin satire, of the spirit of the Greek Old Comedy: v. n. **301²,** 1.

301², 1. *Dacier*, etc. Dryden here follows Dacier in a total misinterpretation of Casaubon, who says distinctly: " Differentia præcipua Lucilianæ satiræ ab Enniana non fuit in genere carminis " (l. ii, c. 3, p. 273). The conclusion of Dryden's paragraph (l. 54 f.) is translated almost literally from Dacier: " Douzam quoque F.[ilium] fefellit iste Diomedis locus. Hoc non eo dixi quod errorem levem tantorum virorum notare gaudeam, sed solum ut demonstrem, quanta cum cura et cautela eorum opera legere oporteat, ubi de re agitur obscura adeo et antiqua." This is instructive as to Dryden's general methods of work. Casaubon's real doctrine is that Lucilius differed from Ennius in subject matter and manner of treatment: " Nam spectavit quidem ad doctrinam morum utraque hæc satira, sed Lucilius multo magis quam Ennius personis adhæsit. . . . Qua in re . . . visus dictusque fuit, mutato genere metri et facie poeseos, priscam Atheniensium comœdiam retulisse." From this to the view of Dacier is not a long step.

302¹, 19. *Varronian satire.* The account of this topic is taken from Casaubon (l. ii, c. 2, pp. 256–270) and Dacier.

30. *Quintilian. Inst. Orat.* x. 1. 95.

302², 4. *Academics. Acad.* i. 2.

31. Σπουδογέλοιοι. Rather, "blending jest with earnest."

303¹, 12. *Petronius.* The reference is to a supplement to Petronius published at about this time, which Bentley styles, in the introduction to his *Dissertation upon Phalaris*, "that scandal to all forgeries:" *Pet. Arb. Satyricon cum fragmentis Albæ Græcæ recuperatis anno 1688, Col. Agr. 1691.* Other editions were published at London, Paris, and Rotterdam in 1693 (Graesse, *Trésor de Livres Rares*).

22. *Mock deification.* The *Apocolocyntosis*, or *Pumpkinification*, a satire on Claudius.

27. *Barclay's* Euphormio. John Barclay (1582–1621), most famous as the author of the *Argenis*, adapted the style of Petronius to the needs of his own time. His first work, *Satyricon*, was published under the name of *Euphormio Lusininus.*

A volume. "Most probably the *Epistolæ Obscurorum Virorum*." KER. This was a collection of satirical letters in dog-Latin, published in 1515–17, of which Crotus Rubianus and Ulrich von Hutten were the chief authors.

303². *Satyr.* In the present volume the spelling *satire* is substituted, since the general practice of the edition is to employ modern spelling.

10. *Rigaltius.* Dryden greatly expands the hint taken from this critic.

304¹, 10. *Sir Matthew Hale.* This judge (1609–76) was universally celebrated for his justice and integrity. — F reads *Hales*, which perhaps should have been retained, as rather Dryden's error than the printer's.

33. *Casaubon.* His edition of Persius, with *Prolegomena*, to which Dryden constantly refers in the following pages, was published in 1605; Stelluti's in 1630.

304², 5. *More corrupted.* "This is a strange mistake in an author who translated Persius entirely and great part of Juvenal. The satires of Persius were written during the reign of Nero, and those of Juvenal in that of Domitian and later. This error is the more extraordinary, as Dryden mentions, a little lower, the very emperors under whom these poets flourished." [SCOTT.]

14. *A Scotch gentleman.* "David Wedderburn, of Aberdeen (1580–1646), whose edition of Persius, with a commentary, was published posthumously at Amsterdam, 1664." [SCOTT.]

34. *A young man.* Persius is said to have died in his twenty-eighth year (A. D. 62), and Lucan in his twenty-sixth (A. D. 65).

305¹, 16. *Imitatio.* "Casaubon's edition is accompanied *cum Persiana Horatii imitatione.*" SCOTT.

305², 17. *Even Horace.* Casaubon *does* add this of Horace, *Prolegomena*, p. 8 (in Duebner's edition, Leipzig, 1833). Most of the learning in this paragraph Dryden takes direct from these *Prolegomena.*

24. *Cornutus.* Cf. 372², *Arg.*

47. *Holyday.* Barten Holyday (1593–1661) was born at Oxford. His *Persius* appeared in 1616, his *Juvenal* not till 1673. v. 321.

306¹, 29. Χελώνης. Properly, *tortoise ;* Dryden adapts the proverb rather than mistranslates it.

307¹, 11. *Bishop of Salisbury.* Burnet; cf. 250, 2415, n. Dryden here mentions his *Discourse of the Pastoral Care* (1692) with apparent respect.

307², 11. *But Horace, etc.* "Dryden alludes to the beautiful description which Horace has given of his father's paternal and watchful affection, in *1 Satires*, vi. Wycherley, the friend for whom he wishes a father of equal tenderness, after having been gayest of the gay, applauded by theaters, and the object of a monarch's jealousy, was finally thrown into jail for debt, and lay there seven long years, his father refusing him any assistance." [SCOTT.]

308¹, 2. *Non nostrum,* etc. VIRGIL, *Ec.* iii. 108, slightly altered; cf. 427, 167, 168.

11. *He who says,* etc. v. *Odes,* iv. 2. 1–4.

308², 19. *Possess'd,* etc. Cf. 246, 2133, n.

40. *Lampooners.* Cf. 261², 20, n.

309¹, 28. *Juvenal is the more delightful.* Contrast 181¹, 1, 2, written only seven years before. Dryden in his earlier work quotes Horace more often than Juvenal.

309², 23. *Ne sententiæ,* etc. *Sat.* 118. Bossu, *Traité du Poëme Epique*, vi. 4, 5, dwells on this idea at length.

44. *Omne,* etc. PERSIUS, i. 116, 117; cf. 361, 227–230.

310¹, 54. *Plain Dealer.* Wycherley, author of the comedy of that name.

310², 11. *On carpet-ground.* Cf. 177¹, 51, n.

311¹, 10. *Non tu,* etc. *Ec.* iii. 26, 27: cf. 425, 36, 37.

311², 37. *Dion Cassius.* Dion, liv. 27, tells the anecdote of Sisenna, but makes no such express intimation as Dryden would have us believe. Dryden presumably is quoting, as usual, from some secondary authority.

312¹, 8. *Primus,* etc. TACITUS, *Annals,* i. 72. This paragraph is based on the notes to this passage in the Delphin *Tacitus*, where are found the quotations from Suetonius (*Augustus*, 55) and "Aurelius," used by Dryden.

49. *Aurelius.* Dryden evidently regards this person as a Roman historian. As the form of citation in the Delphin *Tacitus* indicates, he was really a commentator, Louis (Ludovicus) d'Orleans, who published at Paris, in 1622, *Novæ Cogitationes in Libr. Annalium C. Corneli Taciti, qui extant.* The editor of the Delphin *Tacitus* somewhat abbreviated the note by d'Orleans in transferring it to his own edition.

313¹, 22. *Heinsius,* etc. This is in accord with Heinsius's general theory of the connection between Roman satire and Greek dramatic poetry.

31. *Secuit,* etc. PERSIUS, i. 114, 115: cf. 361, 223–226.

34. *Ense,* etc. JUVENAL, i. 165, 166: cf. 326, 251–253.

38. " *They chang'd,* etc. Dryden has been making extensive use of Holyday's preface to his translation of Juvenal and Persius, Oxford, 1673. The passage here put in quotation marks is not taken literally from him, but represents his general sense.

55. *Stapylton.* Cf. 79¹, 15, n. Stapylton had published a translation of the first six satires of Juvenal in 1644, and a complete version in 1647.

313², 46. *Jack Ketch.* Cf. 156¹, 30; 210, 3, n.

55. *Too witty,* etc. "This is a strange averment.

considering the *Poetical Reflections on Absalom and Achitophel by a Person of Honour*, in composing and publishing which the Duke of Buckingham showed much resentment and very little wit." [SCOTT.] This tract is assigned to Buckingham only on the evidence of Wood's *Athenæ Oxonienses*. On Buckingham, cf. **116**, 544, n.

314¹, 27. *Ense rescindendum.* Cf. **109²**, 33, n.

314², 12. *Sarmentus*, etc. v. *1 Satires*, v, vii.

26. *Mr. Swan.* Professor Ker points out that the fame of this punster is preserved by Swift, Dennis, and others, as well as by Dryden.

315², 4. *Noble similitude.* Dacier took this similitude, along with most of his other material that is of any value, from Casaubon (l. i, c. 2, pp. 62–64), who, however, uses it in a different connection. It goes back ultimately to Plato, *Symposium*, 215 A.

49. *The words of Virgil.* Cf. **583**, 405–412.

316¹, 30. *Nomen*, etc. *Georgics*, iii. 47, 48; cf. **465**, 81, 82.

37. *Maidwell.* This may have been Lewis Maidwell, who published, in 1705, *An Essay upon the Necessity and Excellency of Education.*

316², 12. *Quicquid*, etc. Juvenal, i. 85, 86; cf. **324**, 130–132.

28. *Satire*, etc. Heinsius, p. 54.

317¹, 13. *Grande sophos.* "An oversight for the *grande aliquid* of Persius, i. 14. *Grande sophos*, 'the loud *bravo*,' occurs three times in Martial." [KER.] Dryden took the mistake, if it must be called such, from Rigaltius, who speaks (p. 2, col. 1) of the *grande Persii sophos.*

50. *Donne.* Cf. **270²**, 4, n.

317², 30. *Mascardi.* Professor Ker traces the reference to his *Discorso del' Unità della Favola Drammatica*, in his *Prose Volgari*, 1630.

32. *Guarini.* The *Pastor Fido* of Guarini (1537–1612), published in 1590, and the *Aminta* of Tasso are the most famous of the Italian pastoral dramas; cf. **420²**, 4–11.

318¹, 47. *Persius*, etc. Dryden is again indebted to Casaubon's *Prolegomena.*

318²,23. *Hudibras.* v. **238**,1541,n.Wood (*Ath.Ox.*,ed. 2, 1721, ii, 804) states that Butler joined Buckingham in his attack on Dryden in *The Rehearsal*. Butler's parody of the heroic manner in *Repartees between Cat and Puss* may have been the reason for Wood's assertion, which Dr. Johnson repeats.

51. *Such a little instrument.* "Dryden, in his *Letter to Sir George Etherege* (v. **214**, **215**), has shown, however, how completely he was master even of a measure he despised." [SCOTT.]

319¹, 30. *Tassoni.* (F reads *Tassone.*) Alessandro Tassoni (1565–1635) published his *Secchia Rapita* (*The Rape of the Bucket*) in 1622.

Boileau. The first four cantos of his *Lutrin* (*Lecturn*) were published in 1674, the remaining two in 1683.

32. *Merlin Coccaius.* The assumed name of Teofilo Folengo (1491–1544), an Italian poet who wrote in macaronic (burlesque Latin) verse. *Badus* is the hero of his comic epic *Macaroneæ.*

37. *Stanza of eight.* Cf. **741¹**, 34, n.

46. *Scarron.* Paul Scarron (1610–60), the first part of whose *Virgile Travesti* had appeared in 1648.

319², 3. *Nec*, etc. *Æneid.* iv. 365–367 (cf. **570**, 522–525), which Boileau imitated in his *Lutrin*, near the opening of the second canto. He later canceled the passage containing these verses, which do not appear in the editions subsequent to 1682. In the second line of the quotation *horloger* is a mistake of Dryden or the printer for *l'horloger.*

19. *Admiranda*, etc. *Georgics*, iv. 3–5, 208, 209; cf. **476**, 3–7; **480**, 303–305.

41. *Turns of words*, etc. Cf. **385²**,5 f; **513¹**, 7 f; **744¹**, 25 f. See Professor C. H. Herford's introduction (§ 24) to Spenser's *Shepheards Calender*, London, 1895; and Puttenham, *The Arte of English Poesie* (ed. Arber), p. 213.

48. *Mackenzie.* "Sir George Mackenzie (1636–91) of Rosehaugh was Lord Advocate for Scotland during the reigns of Charles II and his successor. His works are voluminous, and upon various subjects, but chiefly historical and juridical. He left, however, an heroic romance, *Aretina*, a poem called *Cœlia's Country House*, and some essays on moral subjects. His having been the zealous agent of the crown during the cruel persecution of the fanatical Cameronians renders him still execrated among the common people of Scotland. But he was an accomplished scholar, of lively talents and ready elocution, and very well deserved the appellation of a *noble wit of Scotland.*" [SCOTT.]

50. *Sir John Denham.* Cf. **91**; **512²**, 5; **514¹**, 52, n; **744²**, 52, n.

320¹, 12. *Cowley.* Cf. **181¹**, 45, n.

40. *Walsh.* William Walsh (1663–1708), critic and minor poet. Dryden had written a preface for his *Dialogue concerning Women*, published in 1691: v. SS. xviii. 1–7. He is known in literary history as the friend of Pope as well as of Dryden. The life of Walsh in Anderson's *British Poets* states that in 1692 he published *A Collection of Letters and Poems, Amorous and Gallant;* the present editor has been unable to find any other mention of this book. Walsh's *Preface*, as printed in the same collection, does not contain any such statement as is here referred to by Dryden. For another mention of Walsh, v. **708²**, 36.

53. *Hæu*, etc. *Met.* xv. 88–90; cf. **881**, 125–128.

320², 5. *Tum*, etc. CATULLUS, lxiv. 143–148.

14. *Si, nisi*, etc. *Heroïdes* [xv.] 39, 40, with a change of *facie* into *forma.* This epistle is of doubtful authenticity.

22. *Cum*, etc. *Georgics*, iv. 488, 489; cf. **485**, 702–705.

30. *Prosodia.* Cf. **512¹**, 36–42.

43. *Abraham.* v. Genesis xviii. 23–33.

321², 17. *Pulverulenta*, etc. *Æneid*, viii. 596, misquoted; the first word should be *quadrupedante.*

323, 14. *The Centaurs' fury.* v. **857–863**, 292–705.

62. *Thrice concocted blood.* Professor Saintsbury thinks that this is a reminiscence of the phrase *my thrice decocted blood*, in the last line of some verses headed *Ignoto*, attributed to Marlowe.

324, 122. *S——ll.* Shadwell: v. B. S. xxix, xxxvi–xxxviii, xlv–xlviii; **134,** 15, n: cf. **196,** 35, n.

327, 24. *Basket,* etc. Cf. **344,** 703.

334, 39 (Arg.). *Sir C. S.* v. **136,** 163, n.

335[1], 26. *Every vice,* etc. The metaphor is from dicing; a *loader* is a doublet.

335[2], 31. *Venerably.* F reads *ven'rably.*

336, 55. *Bachelor.* *Batchelour* in F; but the forms *bachiler, batcheler,* in use in Dryden's time, will account for the rhyme. Perhaps one of them should have been printed in the text.

90. *Secure . . . of.* Safe from finding.

337, 153. *Grisly.* F reads *griesly.*

184. *A fire.* So F: perhaps we should read *afire.*

339, 278. Ζωὴ καὶ ψυχή! Life and soul. Dryden of course copies these Greek words from his original Latin text.

341, 479, 480. *Knows . . . drain.* The discrepancy in number is a sign of Dryden's carelessness.

342, 538. *Fame.* Dryden introduces a Virgilian reference not found in his original: cf. **567,** 252–274.

571. *Tabors,* etc. v. n. **205,** 150

343, 578. *Mood and figure.* Terms of formal logic.

586. *Priscian.* A Roman grammarian of the fifth century: the mention of him here is of course an anachronism on Dryden's part.

344, 675. *Ice.* F reads *yee.*

688. *Runs.* Contrast *smile* in the next line; the careless grammar shows Dryden's haste in writing, or heedlessness in reading proof. Cf. **479,** 264–266; **400,** 1031, n.

703. *Basket,* etc. Cf. **327,** 24.

345, 736. *Adulterer.* F reads *Adult'rer.*

805. *His mother's love.* "*Hippomanes* is a lump of flesh on the forehead of a newborn foal which the dam was supposed to tear off with her teeth. It is also applied to a humor which runs from mares [v. **470,** 443]. In any case, it was supposed to stimulate the sexual passions, and also to drive people mad." J. D. LEWIS, note on Juvenal, vi. 133.

347, n. 33. *Sicilian tyrants.* Cf. **369,** nn. 5, 6.

n. 49. *Linus.* A mistake of Dryden or the printer for *Lynceus.*

348, 41. *The pair of sages.* Democritus and Heraclitus; cf. **442**[2], 3, n.

76. *Heaven.* F reads *Heav'n.*

349, 135. *Plays least in sight.* "An obscure phrase. If, as one would think, it equals *keeps out of the way,* this would not go very well with *met.*" [SAINTSBURY.]

351, 279. "*Death,* etc. The quotation marks, emphasizing the aphorism, are retained from F.

352, 359. *Shoulder pains.* F reads *Shoulders pain.*

353, 435. *Fever.* F reads *Favour.*

355, n. 23. *Phædria.* A blunder for *Phædra,* either by Dryden or by the printer.

n. 24. *Pætus.* A mistake for *Prœtus.*

n. 25. *Hostia.* i. e. Ostia.

THE SIXTEENTH SATIRE OF JUVENAL. The authenticity of this satire has been questioned.

356[1], 4 (Arg.). *Standing army.* Dryden loses no opportunity of expressing his dislike of a standing army, the establishment of which was an important part of King William's policy. Cf. **489**[2], 39, n; **743**[2], 2; **777,** 672; **799,** 596–601.

360, 194. *The Mimallonian crew.* Cf. **725,** 608.

199. *Evion.* The cry of the Bacchantes.

364, 102. *Phlegm.* F reads *fleam,* which might well have been retained, to mark the rhyme.

365, n. 6. *Æsculapius.* F reads *Esculapius.* On the story here told of Alexander, cf. **751,** 133, 134. The passage in Sir Thomas Browne to which Dryden refers is, as Professor Saintsbury shows: "I do think that many mysteries ascribed to our own inventions have been the courteous revelations of spirits." (*Religio Medici,* i. § 31.)

n. 7 (l. 2). *Treasures . . . was kept.* The peculiar grammar is probably nothing but a printer's error or a slip of the pen.

367, 126. *Conquest and Gibbons.* On William Gibbons (1649–1728), v. **709**[1], 13; **785,** 82; cf. **196,** 35, n.

370, 6 (Arg.). *Lucan,* etc. In *Pharsalia,* i. 33–38, Lucan explains that, if civil war were needed to secure the happy reign of Nero, he makes no complaint: "If such be the reward, even crimes and sin are pleasing." The compliment has sometimes been regarded as sarcastic.

35 (Arg.). *Casaubon.* Casaubon's theory has not been accepted by modern scholars.

371, 50. "*Say,* etc. F gives no indication of the changes of speakers in this line. In general, it is somewhat difficult to settle the position of quotation marks in this satire: they are not used in F.

372, n. 7. This note, and a few words from the following, are here omitted, — the only case of expurgation in the present edition.

Dr. Busby. Richard Busby (1606–95), headmaster of Westminster School from 1638. Though famous for his severity, he was beloved by his pupils.

374, 80. *Dodder'd.* F reads *Doddard.* v. GLOSSARY.

375, 212. *Bethlem's,* etc. v. **131,** 285, n.

376, 215. *Brown george.* "A loaf of a coarse kind of brown bread." N. E. D.

377, n. 21. *Sedley.* v. **136,** 163, n. Sedley founded his *Bellamira* on Terence's *Eunuchus.*

382, EXAMEN POETICUM. The mottoes are *Georgics,* iv. 100, 101, 157: cf. for the first, **478,** 152, 153; the second means: "They place in the center what they have sought for." The quotations are appropriate for a book of which the title is, *A Poetic Swarm of Bees.*

The dedication of this volume was not successful financially, and bade fair to involve Dryden in difficulties with the government.

In a letter to Tonson of August 30, 1693, he writes:

"I am sure you thought my Lord Radclyffe wou'd have done something: I ghess'd more truly, that he cou'd not; but I was too far ingag'd to desist; though I was tempted to it, by the melancholique prospect I had of it. . . .

"About a fortnight ago I had an intimation from a friend by letter, that one of the Secretaryes, I suppose Trenchard, had inform'd the Queen, that I had abus'd her Government, (those were the words) in my Epistle to my Lord Radcliffe; and that thereupon, she had commanded her Historiographer, Rymer, to fall upon my playes; which he assures me is now doeing. I doubt not his malice, from a former hint you gave me; and if he be employ'd, I am confident 't is of his own seeking, who, you know, has spoken slightly of me in his last critique: and that gave me occasion to snarl againe." v. n. **383²**, 21. After this, however, Rymer never *fell upon* Dryden's plays, at least in print.

Lord Radcliffe. "Lord Radcliffe was the eldest son of Francis, Earl of Derwentwater. He married Mary Tudor, a natural daughter of Charles II by Mary Davies." [Scott.]

382¹, 20. *The same parts*, etc. There was a story, mentioned for example by Settle in his *Absalom Senior*, that Dryden once wished to enter the priesthood. This Dryden elsewhere denies; cf. **748²**, 61 f.; v. B. S. lvi.

382², 23. *The best poet*, etc. The Earl of Dorset: v. n. **282.** The following quotation is from a satirical epistle by Dorset, *To Mr. Edward Howard, on his Incomparable, Incomprehensible Poem, called The British Princes:*

Wit, like tierce claret, when 't begins to pall,
Neglected lies, and 's of no use at all;
But, in its full perfection of decay,
Turns vinegar, and comes again in play.

(Howard, against whom Dorset's wit was directed, was Dryden's brother-in-law; cf. **915,** 192; B. S. xx.)

383¹, 2. *Zoili and Momi.* The name of Zoilus, a Greek grammarian famous for his attacks on Homer, became proverbial as that of a carping critic. Momus was a mythical personage, the personification of mockery and censure; cf. **901,** 13 f.

4. *He who*, etc. Dryden may refer to Carvilius Pictor, who, according to Donatus, wrote a book called *Æneidomastix*.

20. *Petronius*, etc. *Sat.* 118–124. Dryden may be indebted to Rapin, *Reflexions sur la Poétique*, ii. 15.

27. *Scaliger.* Scaliger attacks Homer in his *Poetices Libri Septem*, v. 3; in the following book (called *Hypercriticus*) he attempts to mend Claudian, and censures Lucan, as Dryden states: *Interdum mihi latrare, non canere videtur.*

57. *Non ingeniis.* 2 *Epistles*, i. 88, 89, quoted inaccurately, from memory: "He does not support buried genius, but attacks our writings; **us** and our writings he maliciously dislikes."

383², 21. *But there is*, etc. The following passage refers to Rymer — cf. B. S. xxx, xxxi; n. **382** (Ex. Poet.) — who in 1692 (v. Malone, I, 2, 30: title-page reads 1693) had published a new critical work, *A Short View of Tragedy, its Original, Excellency, and Corruption, with some Reflections on Shakespeare and other Practitioners for the Stage*, in which he continued his depreciation of the English school of tragedy. In his first chapter he gives an account of the *Persæ* of Æschylus, and sketches a plan for a similar English tragedy, to be called *The Invincible Armado.* He concludes his chapter: "If Mr. Dryden might try his pen on this subject, doubtless to an audience that heartily love their country, and glory in the virtue of their ancestors, his imitation of Æschylus would have better success, and would *pit, box, and gallery* far beyond anything now in possession of the stage, however wrought up by the unimitable Shakespeare." But, in this seemingly complimentary passage, *pit, box, and gallery* is a phrase that Buckingham had made famous by putting it into the mouth of Mr. Bayes in *The Rehearsal* (act i), and the covert condemnation of Dryden's praises of Shakespeare, and of his actual dramatic performance, is sufficiently pointed.

In a letter to Dennis, dated by Malone in March, 1694, Dryden writes: "You see what success this learned critick has found in the world, after his blaspheming Shakespeare. Almost all the faults which he has discover'd are truly there; yet who will read Mr. Rymer, or not read Shakspeare? For my own part I reverence Mr. Rymer's learning, but I detest his ill-nature and his arrogance. I indeed, and such as I, have reason to be afraid of him, but Shakspeare has not." (Malone, I, 2, 35.) Cf. **287²**, 30, n; **410**, 47, n; **412²**, 48, n. Dryden seems later to have become reconciled to Rymer: v. **741¹**, 50 f.

56. *Quantum mutatus.* "A reference to the *Epistle Dedicatory* of Rymer's *Short View* (to Lord Dorset): 'Three, indeed, of the epic (the two by Homer and Virgil's *Æneids*) are reckon'd in the degree of perfection, but amongst the tragedies, only the *Œdipus* of Sophocles. That by Corneille, and by others, of a modern cut, *quantum mutatus!*'" Ker. This is a direct attack on the *Œdipus* of Dryden and Lee, made more cutting by being addressed to Dryden's favorite patron; cf. **282**, n; **412**, 48, n; **413**, 49.

384¹, 14. *Perrault.* Charles Perrault (1628–1703) in his *Parallèle des Anciens et des Modernes* (1688–96) maintained the superiority of the modern writers of France to those of Greece and Rome. He was opposed by most of the great literary men of France, above all by Boileau.

22. *A chorus.* Rymer's *Short View* begins: "What reformation may not we expect now that in France they see the necessity of a *chorus* to their tragedies? . . . The chorus was the root and original, and is certainly always the most necessary part of tragedy."

33. *Poetry and good sense.* The close coupling of these two expressions is characteristic of Dryden and of his time.

384², 5. *Horace. 1 Satires,* x. 1–8.

385¹, 11. *Propriety.* v. **177²**, 5, n.

19. *Mr. Chapman.* See his poem *To the Reader,* prefaced to his *Iliad,* and his prose *Preface.*

34. *Sandys.* v. **88¹**, 4, n; **740²**, 40.

385², 5. *Turns,* etc. Cf. **319²**, 41, n; **513¹**, 7 f; **744¹**, 25 f.

48. *Musas,* etc. "To worship severer Muses;" cf. **75²**, 24, n; **512¹**, 36, n.

386¹, 8. *Congreve.* Congreve really translated two selections, *Priam's Lamentation and Petition to Achilles for the Body of his Son Hector,* and *The Lamentations of Hecuba, Andromache, and Helen, over the Dead Body of Hector.*

28. *Runs off her bias.* "Said of a bowl that does not run true." KER. Cf. **136**, 189, n.

386², 40. *Sir Samuel Tuke.* Dryden quotes *A modest . . . own,* from the prologue to Tuke's *Adventures of Five Hours.*

387, 5. *And add,* etc. "This odd phrase merely means, 'Let them go on unbroken.'" SAINTSBURY.

80. *Frozen Wagon.* "The constellation of the Great Bear (Charles's Wain)." SAINTSBURY.

390, 227. *Louvre.* Dryden here translates admirably the conceit of Ovid, whose word is *Palatia,* the palace of the Cæsars. Had he been well disposed to the English government, he would doubtless have used *Whitehall* instead of *Louvre;* cf. **132**, 21.

392, 417. *The stag,* etc. "Dryden, not Ovid, is answerable for the speed of the stag's exertions in the water." [SCOTT.]

393, 489. *Our father.* Dryden is somewhat inaccurate: Deucalion was the son of Prometheus, and Pyrrha the daughter of Epimetheus, the brother of Prometheus. Deucalion had addressed Pyrrha as *sister* only as a mark of tenderness.

395, 680. *Follow, not.* The comma is not found in the 1693 ed.; Ovid has *non insequor hostis.*

396, 718. *As when,* etc. Cf. **38**, 521–528.

400, 1031. *Cease.* The form of the verb is affected by the plural immediately preceding: cf. **439**, 38; **558**, 568; **589**, 869; **634**, 732; **813**, 115, n; **858**, 339. The construction is probably due rather to carelessness than to any settled principle of grammar. Cf. **344**, 688, n.

402, 109. *Daughter of the Sun.* Pasiphae: cf. **432**, 68–86; **594**, 33–46; **601**, 604; **722**, 325–369.

403, 208. *Rites,* etc. The 1693 ed. punctuates as follows: *Rites, . . . Love: . . . Marriage, . . . aid; . . .*

405, 112. *Latter.* Perhaps this should be emended to *later.*

166. *And she's.* So SS.; the 1693 ed. reads *and is,* which certainly cannot be correct.

406², 4 (Song). *Invert the year.* Cf. **241**, 1732, n. VENI CREATOR SPIRITUS. Cf. headnote, p. **927.**

7. *Uncreated light.* v. Genesis i. 3, in contrast to i. 1, 7.

8. *Paraclite.* So in 1693 ed.: cf. *Paraclete,* l. 39.

410, 1. *As.* A comma should be inserted after this word.

9. *Provided,* etc. "This seems to be an allusion to the pretended dukedom of Marine, in Beaumont and Fletcher's *Noble Gentleman,* which had been revived (in an altered form) in 1688, by Durfey, under the title of *A Fool's Preferment; or, The Three Dukes of Dunstable.*

> *Gent.* Hark you, sir: the king doth know you are a duke.
> *Mar.* No! does he?
> *Gent.* Yes, and is content you shall be; but with this caution,
> That none know it but yourself; for, if you do,
> He'll take it away by act of parliament.
> *Mar.* Here is my hand; and, whilst I live or breathe,
> No living wight shall know I am a duke.
> Act v (near close)." [SCOTT.]

47. *Shakespeare's critic.* Rymer: v. **287²**, 30, n. Rymer's own tragedy, *Edgar; or, The English Monarch* (published 1678, reprinted in 1691 and 1693) was a complete failure; it was never acted.

411¹, 2. *The poet's dead.* Cf. *Prologue,* l. 34.

7. *Dalinda.* The hoodwinking of the foolish Sancho by the crafty Dalinda (who of course speaks this epilogue) forms the underplot of the play.

411², 25. *The fire,* etc. There is a possible reminiscence of Milton's:

> — yet from those flames
> No light; but rather darkness visible. —
> *Paradise Lost,* i. 62, 63.

412¹, 7 (CONGREVE). *Janus.* The god Janus was fabled to have reigned as king in Italy, having his city near the hill Janiculum. Here he hospitably received Saturn, who was fleeing from his son Jupiter, and from whom he learned husbandry and other arts. Cf. **630**, 425–432; **631**, 467–470. Dryden here assigns to him a part that belongs rather to Saturn himself.

412², 14. *Second temple.* Referring to the rebuilding of the Jewish temple on the return from exile: v. Ezra v, vi. It was inferior to the temple of Solomon: v. Haggai ii. 1–3.

15. *Vitruvius.* The most famous Roman writer on architecture.

30. *Wycherley.* Called *Manly* in allusion to the name of the hero of his comedy, *The Plain Dealer.*

32. *Nor.* The 1694 ed., by an evident misprint, reads *Now; Nor* is found in the collected edition of Congreve's works, 1710.

35. *Fabius.* Scipio, on his return to Rome after successes in Spain, against the Carthaginians, was elected consul, though below the legal age. His policy of carrying the war into Africa was opposed by the old Fabius, who was in part moved by jealousy of the youthful conqueror. Dryden either made a blunder in his allusion, or he wishes to imply that, had Scipio been as charming as Congreve, Fabius might have rejoiced in his success, instead of envying it.

39. *Romano.* Dryden has made a serious mis-

take: Giulio Romano (1492–1546) was younger than Raphael (1483–1520), and was his pupil, not his master.

48. *Tom,* etc. "Thomas Shadwell [v. **134,** 15, n], who at the Revolution was promoted to Dryden's posts of Poet Laureate and Historiographer Royal, was succeeded in his office of Laureate by Nahum Tate, and in that of Historiographer by Thomas Rymer. Our author was at present on bad terms with Rymer; to whom, not to Tate, he applies the sarcastic title of Tom the Second. [Cf. **383²,** 21, n; **410,** 47, n.] The Earl of Dorset, although as Lord Chamberlain he was obliged to dispose of Dryden's offices to persons less politically obnoxious, bestowed at the same time such marks of generosity on the abdicated Laureate that Dryden here honors him with the title of *his patron.*" [SCOTT.] Cf. **282,** n; **291²,** 22–44.

413, 69. *His providence.* Christie notes that Dryden (*Defense of the Epilogue of The Conquest of Granada,* SS. iv. 233) condemns Jonson for his *ill syntax* in writing, "Tho' Heaven should speak with all *his* wrath at once;" and that he himself, in l. 63 of this poem, uses *she* referring to *Heav'n.*

To SIR GODFREY KNELLER. The title of this epistle in *Poems and Translations,* 1701, is, *To Sir Godfrey Kneller, Principal Painter to his Majesty.* That text furnishes the following variants, in addition to those mentioned in the headnote: (73, sidenote) *presented to;* (95) *But oh;* (114) *Yet not;* (145) *If yet;* (146) *'T is only.*

Kneller (1646–1723), born at Lübeck, settled in England in 1675, where he remained until his death.

414, 22. *Prometheus.* Prometheus stole fire from heaven and gave it to mortals; according to another legend, he created men out of earth and water: cf. **174²,** 74, n; **388,** 97–112. Dryden here mingles classical mythology and Scripture in an almost mediæval fashion.

54. *Bantam's embassy.* "Eight ambassadors from the King of Bantam were in England in 1682, and were treated with distinction by Charles II. Their faces were well known by portraits and engravings." [CHRISTIE.]

73. *Shakespeare.* "This portrait was copied from one in the possession of Mr. Betterton, and afterwards in that of the Chandos family. The copy presented by Kneller to Dryden is in the collection of Earl Fitzwilliam, at Wentworth House." [SCOTT.]

78. *Teucer.* Teucer, the best archer of the Greeks, sheltered himself behind the shield of Ajax; v. *Iliad,* viii. 266–272.

96. *Jacob's race.* v. Genesis xxvii.

100, 101. *Thou,* etc. This couplet is unpleasing, in view of Dryden's earlier adulation of Charles II.

415, 145. *That yet,* etc. "Mr. Walpole says that where Sir Godfrey 'offered one picture to fame, he sacrificed twenty to lucre; and he met with customers of so little judgment that they were fond of being painted by a man

who would gladly have disowned his works the moment they were paid for.' The same author gives us Sir Godfrey's apology for preferring the lucrative, though less honorable line, of portrait painting. 'Painters of history (said he) make the dead live, and do not begin to live themselves till they are dead. I paint the living, and they make me live.' *Anecdotes of Painting* (*Works,* 1798, vol iii, p. 359). Dryden seems to allude to this expression in ll. 150–154." [SCOTT.]

Walpole quotes Kneller's apology from "the author of the *Abregé.*"

416¹. ODE ON PURCELL. Perhaps the last three words of l. 12 should be made into a separate line, to point the rhyme of *admir'd* and *retir'd. Know* (l. 20) is printed *knew* in the separate text of 1696 and in *Orpheus Britannicus,* but appears as *know* in the text with music of 1696; cf. rhyme with *below.* The text with music of 1696 furnishes the following further variants: (6) *Heav'nly Lays;* (12) *the matchless man;* (21) *turn'd the jarring Spheres;* (24) *Musick from on high.*

PREFACE AND EPILOGUE TO THE HUSBAND HIS OWN CUCKOLD. According to Malone, John Dryden the younger was born in 1667 or 1668 and "probably went to Rome with his elder brother [Charles] about the end of the year 1692." He became an officer of the Pope's household, and seems never to have returned to England. He is said to have died in 1701. Cf. headnote, pp. **281, 282.**

416², 26 (prose). *Two authors.* "Probably Southerne and Congreve." SCOTT.

417, 13 (Epil.). *Third day,* etc. Cf. **108,** 15, n.

418, 36. *For tho',* etc. Cf. **480,** 303.

TRANSLATION OF VIRGIL. In the following notes, the first and second editions are called F1 and F2. When they agree, they are cited as FF. Dryden writes in a letter to Tonson: "You cannot take too great care of the printing this [second] edition exactly after my amendments; for a fault of that nature will disoblige me eternally" (Malone, I, 2, 63). From another letter we know that he "bestow'd nine entire days" on his work of revision (*Ibid.* 61). Accordingly F2 is made the basis of the present text: its readings are rejected only (*a*) when they seem evidently due to the printer's carelessness rather than to Dryden's correcting hand; or (*b*) in a few cases where the change, though probably due to Dryden himself, is obviously a perversion of the text rather than an improvement. Cf. notes on **481,** 354; **505¹,** 4; **601,** 614. Dryden was of course as capable of error in correcting his own work as in other things.

In the *errata* of F1 occurs the statement: "There are other errata, both in false pointing and omissions of words, both in the preface and the poem, which the reader will correct without my trouble. I omit them, because they only lame my English, not destroy my meaning."

The motto on the title-page is *Æneid,* ii. 724: "He follows his father with unequal steps."

The headings of some of Dryden's own notes do not correspond exactly with the text of his translation; these discrepancies are here preserved: see, for example, **601**, 586, 587, and Dryden's note (p. 712). Cf. n. **281**.

419[1]. *Hugh, Lord Clifford.* "The son of Lord Treasurer Clifford, a member of the Cabal administration." [SCOTT.] Cf **70**[2], n.

6. *A narrow choice.* "Dryden alludes to his religion and politics. I presume, Hugh, Lord Clifford, was a Catholic, like his father, and entertained the hereditary attachment to the line of Stuart, thus falling within the *narrow choice* to which Dryden was limited." SCOTT.

18, 19. *Pollio . . . Varus.* "The well-known patrons of Virgil." [SCOTT.] v. **428**, 14; **431**, 13. This passage indicates that Dryden was indebted to the elder Clifford for his appointment as Poet Laureate in 1668: v. B. S. xxvii.

419[2], 12. *Great climacteric.* "The sixty-third year of human life." [WEBSTER.] Cf. **441**[2], 15.

24. *He found,* etc. "In his prose you come upon passages that persuade you he is a poet, in spite of his verses so often turning state's evidence against him as to convince you he is none. He is a prose-writer, with a kind of Æolian attachment. For example, take this bit of prose from the dedication of his version of Virgil's *Pastorals :* 'He found . . . better music.' This is charming, and yet even this wants the ethereal tincture that pervades the style of Jeremy Taylor, making it, as Burke said of Sheridan's eloquence, ' neither prose nor poetry, but something better than either.'" LOWELL, *Essay on Dryden.*

51. *Manlius.* "Manlius, contrary to the general orders of his father, Manlius Torquatus, engaged and slew a Tuscan noble: his father caused his head to be struck off for disobedience." [SCOTT.]

420[1], 42. *In medio,* etc. Cf. **426**, 60, 61.

420[2], 6. *Shepherds'.* FF read *Shepherd's.*

9. *Guarini's* Pastor Fido. Cf. **317**[2], 32, n.

12. *Piscatory Eclogues.* Referring to the *Eclogæ Piscatoriæ* of the Italian poet Sannazaro (1458–1530). Malone states that they were published, "together with some pieces of Fracastorius and other Italians who have written Latin poetry, by Bishop Atterbury (then a student of Christ Church), in 1684."

18. *Fontenelle.* Petit de Julleville says of the *Pastorales* of Fontenelle (1657–1757): "Fontenelle, bel esprit, sec et prosaïque, était l'homme le moins fait pour célébrer la nature et faire parler les bergers." (*Leçons de Littérature Française,* ii. 141.) In the controversy as to the literary merits of the ancients and the moderns, Fontenelle took the side of the latter.

24. *Si Pergama,* etc. *Æneid,* ii. 291, 292; cf. **541**, 387, 388.

54. *Nec,* etc. HORACE, *Odes,* iv. 4. 31, 32. F1 reads *Aquilam Columbæ.*

421, 2. *Tit'rus.* FF read *Tity'rus.* So in **436**, 76; **438**, 28.

26. *By croaking from the left.* F1 reads, *With frequent Crokes.*

422, 56, 57. *What,* etc. F2 puts question marks after both these lines; F1 puts one after the second of them.

89. *Britons.* F1 reads *Britans;* F2, *Britains.*

425, 1. *Swain.* F1 reads *Groom.*

15. *Cropp'd.* SS. reads *cropt;* FF read *crept.*

426, 88. *By turns.* F1 reads *In turns.*

97. *My,* etc. F1 reads:

With pelted Fruit, me *Galatea* plyes.

427, 143. *Dog-foxes.* So SS.; FF read *Dog Foxes.*

428. THE FOURTH PASTORAL. This piece and *The Ninth Pastoral,* as is known from a letter of Dryden to Tonson (Malone, I, 2, 52), were printed from Dryden's wife's copy of *Miscellany Poems,* 1684, the text of which Dryden corrected for his complete *Virgil.*

3, 4. *Delight,* etc. The 1684 text reads :

Delight not all, if thither I repair,
My Song shall make 'em worth a Consul's care.

6. *Saturnian times.* Cf. **630**, 425–432.

28. *Serpent's.* FF read *Serpents.*

42–44. *Another,* etc. The 1684 text reads:

Another *Argos* on th' *Iberian* shore
Shall land the chosen Chiefs:
Another *Helen* other Wars create,
And great *Achilles* shall be sent to urge the *Trojan* Fate.

58. *Ready.* The 1684 text reads *awful.*

59. *Seed.* The 1684 text reads *Stem.*

63. *In crowding ranks.* The 1684 text reads *stand crowding to.*

429, 70. *In verse.* The 1684 text reads *with me.*

75. *The nauseous,* etc. The fourteen-syllable line is doubtless intended to symbolize the long *qualms and travel* of the mother; cf. **129**, 94, n.

5. *Whether,* etc. Dryden has not translated Virgil's line, *Tu maior; tibi me est æquum parere, Menalca.* Possibly a couplet translating it, on which the *whether . . . or* depended, disappeared in transcribing the manuscript or in printing; the use of *whether . . . or* in a direct question is hard to parallel in Dryden. Or the poet may have wished to give only four lines to Mopsus, to correspond with the four given to Menalcas.

430, 104. *On both are.* F1 reads, *On each is.*

432, 61. *Yet few,* etc. This line is not found in F1.

68. *The Cretan queen.* Pasiphae: cf. **402**, 109–120; **594**, 33–38; **601**, 604; **722**, 325–369.

75, 76. *Tho' lab'ring,* etc. In place of these two lines F1 reads:

Tho tender and untry'd the Yoke he fear'd.
Tho soft and white as flakes of falling Snow;
And scarce his budding Horns had arm'd his brow.

434, 97–100. *These rhymes,* etc. In place of these four lines F1 reads:

I 've heard: and, *Thyrsis,* you contend in vain:⎫
For *Corydon,* young *Corydon* shall reign,   ⎬
The Prince of Poets, on the *Mantuan* Plain. ⎭

435, 9. *Whether.* FF read *Whither.*

19. *Scarce,* etc. The text of F1 reads:

Scarce from our upper World the Shades with drew,—

which is changed in the errata to the form here printed.

436, 88. *Complaints.* F1 reads *Complaint.*

107. *Straight.* At once (translating the Latin *modo*).

437. THE NINTH PASTORAL. v. n. **428** (FOURTH PASTORAL). This piece is not ascribed to Dryden in *Miscellany Poems*, 1684, but is attributed to him in the third edition of that work, published in 1702.

7 (Arg.). *Pastoral.* The 1684 text reads *Eclogue.*

10 (Arg.). *Mœris . . . Lycidas.* The proper names are not found in the argument of the 1684 text.

9. *Furies.* The 1684 text reads *Devil.*

10. *Your,* etc. The 1684 text reads:

Good Gods, I heard a quite contrary Tale.

438, 22, 23. *Now,* etc. The 1684 text reads:

Now Heaven defend! could barbarous rage prevail
So far, the sacred Muses to assail ?

26. *Praise — that.* The 1684 text reads *praise that.*

43. *Free.* v. GLOSSARY, and cf. **375, 212.**

46. *Varus'.* FF read *Varus.*

56. *On.* The 1684 text reads *to.*

439, 91. *Request.* The 1684 text reads *entreat.*

38. *Drown.* Cf. **400,** 1031, n.

44. *Browze.* FF here read *Brouze,* possibly to point the rhyme; in l. 114 they have *browz'd.*

440², *Philip, Earl of Chesterfield.* "Philip Stanhope, second Earl of Chesterfield (1633–1713), was a man of considerable talent and political activity, and enjoyed at the court of Charles II several offices, but was now retired." [SCOTT.] Since he had refused to coöperate in the Revolution, had not taken office under William III, and had declined to join the Association in support of William's title, he was one of the small circle of patrons from whom Dryden could select: cf. **419¹,** 6, n; **487¹,** n. In his youth he had been notorious for dissipation; cf. **441²,** 48 f. A letter written to him in 1658 by the Lady Elizabeth Howard, later Dryden's wife, has been thought to imply a dishonorable intimacy between them: v. SS. i. 74, 75; cf. B. S. xx.

3 (prose). *Quod,* etc. *Æneid,* ix. 6, 7; cf. **638,** 7, 8. In the second line of the quotation F2 reads *auderit* (misprint).

441¹, 18. *Majesty.* F1 reads *M——.*

44. *Horace,* etc. Dryden apparently thought that the editions of Horace were arranged in chronological order. In reality, the *Satires* were, generally speaking, the earliest of the poet's works.

441², 7. *The gleanings,* etc. v. Judges viii. 2.

12. *Jam,* etc. *Æneid,* vi. 304; cf. **599,** 420, 421.

15. *Great climacteric.* v. **419²,** 12, n.

442¹, 5. *Principles.* Component parts of the body, elements.

30. *Dignum,* etc. "A man worthy of praise the Muse forbids to die." HORACE, *Odes,* iv. 8. 28.

42. *Digito,* etc. "To be pointed at with the finger, and to have people say of him, 'That is he.'" PERSIUS, i. 28; cf. **359,** 60, 61.

442², 3. *Heraclitus.* A Greek philosopher (about 535–475 B. c.), proverbial for his melancholy. He was called "the weeping philosopher" in contrast to Democritus, "the laughing philosopher." Cf. **108¹,** 23, n; **348,** 41 f.

33. *Scipio.* Scipio Africanus, the conqueror of Hannibal, in his later years was accused of corruption. He disdained to answer the charges brought against him, and avoided punishment by retiring to his villa at Liternum.

443¹, 27. *Res,* etc. "Wealth gained not by labor, but by inheritance." MARTIAL, x. 47. 3.

33. *Qui,* etc. "Who has lost his purse." *2 Epistles,* ii. 40. Horace tells the story of a soldier, who, after losing his purse, performed prodigies of valor, by which he gained wealth. Once rich, he refused to venture his life further.

52. *You,* etc. "The second Earl of Chesterfield, in the latter part of his life, passed much of his time at an elegant villa near Twickenham." MALONE.

443², 5. *Corycian.* v. **478, 479,** 186–217.

12. *O fortunatos,* etc. *Georgics,* ii. 458, 459; cf. **462,** 639–642.

36. *Et secura,* etc. *Georgics,* ii. 467, with a change of *at* to *et ;* cf. **462,** 655, 656.

6 (Arg.). *Compliments.* FF read *complements.*

444, 51. *Whatever,* etc. The following passage is somewhat incoherent, and the punctuation of it is difficult; FF punctuate as follows: (51) *obtain,* (52) *Reign ;* (54) *Mind, . . . above.* (55) *Retreat,* (56) *Seat,* (57) *remove,* (58) *above.*

63. *And grant.* F1 does not contain these words: for their insertion, cf. **517¹,** 2–5.

445, 93. *Deucalion.* v. **392–394,** 424–556.

447, 212. *Deep-mouth.* SS. emends to *deep-mouthed,* perhaps correctly.

448, 298. *Astræa's Balance.* The *Balance* is of course the symbol of justice; cf. n. 7 (ASTRÆA REDUX).

302. *Linseed.* FF read *Lineseed.*

310. *Maia.* FF read *Maja.*

337. *Southern.* "This must be a mistake of the pen or press." [SCOTT, following CAREY.]

449, 364. *To float,* etc. F1 reads:

The Meads to water, and to fence the Field.

452, 614. *Frith.* In italics in FF, as an unusual word.

453, 656. *Nor,* etc. F1 reads:

Nor Light'ning flash'd from so serene a Sky.

657. *Across.* F1 reads *along.*

454, 25. *Bay.* So SS.; FF read *Bays.*

455, 139. *And . . . lives, —* F1 prints *And . . . lives ?* The errata state: "The note of interrogation is false at the end of the line; it ought to be a period." F2, however, has a comma, which, as the Latin text shows, is undoubtedly correct.

456, 207. *Rage.* So F1; F2 reads *Land.*

214. *Stupendous.* FF read *stupend'ous,* which perhaps should have been retained, as marking a pronunciation *stupendyus,* the ancestor of the familiar *stupenjus.* Cf. n. **916,** 281.

457, 289. *Surly.* F1 reads *spleenful.*

306. The land that joins Vesuvius. F1 reads, *Vesuvian Nola.*

458, 330. Strait. FF read *streight.*

348, 349. *Show: yew.* For the rhyme, cf. **462,** 628, 629.

459, 421. *In smoky.* F1 reads *with smoky.*

457. *(Let me dare to sing).* F1 reads *(so sweet Poets sing).*

460–467. *Then . . . rise.* F1 reads:

> Earth knew no Season then, but Spring alone:
> On the moist Ground the Sun serenely shone:
> Then Winter Winds their blustring Rage forbear,
> And in a silent Pomp proceeds the mighty Year.
> Sheep soon were sent to people flow'ry Fields,
> And salvage Beasts were banish'd into Wilds.
> Then Heav'n was lighted up with Stars; and Man,
> A hard relentless Race, from Stones began.

460, 472. *When,* etc. F1 reads:

> When Infant Nature was with Quiet crown'd.

489. *Sturdy.* F1 reads *strugling.*

498, 515. *Leafs; leaves.* So FF; cf. **263¹,** 31, n.

525. *At Athens,* etc. Cf. **294, 295.**

540. *Honest face.* A translation of *caput honestum;* cf. **602,** 668; **732,** 52. This use of *honest* in the Latin sense of *comely, beautiful,* is apparently unusual in English of Dryden's time; N. E. D. cites no instance of it later than 1566.

461, 576. *Nor,* etc. "It is probable that Dryden meant to give the sentence a different construction from what it now presents, but, having changed his purpose, forgot to alter the beginning." [SCOTT.]

462, 615. *Heav'nly.* F1 reads *thoughtful.*

637. *Centaurs'.* v. **857–863,** 292–705.

671. *Astræa.* v. n. **7** (ASTRÆA REDUX).

676. *Poet's.* F1 reads *Virgil's.*

463, 714. *Nor,* etc. F1 reads:

> Nor with a helpless Hand condoles the Poor.

730. *Pop'lar.* So F1; F2 reads *popular.* The passage gives Dryden an opportunity to show his power as a satirist.

731. *Or.* F1 reads *By.*

464. THE THIRD BOOK OF THE GEORGICS. Variants found in *The Annual Miscellany for the Year 1694* (v. headnote, p. **413**) are here marked 4M. It is curious to see that, in ll. 131–233, Dryden, in revising his work, usually returned to the readings of 4M.

465, 39. *Britons.* Translating *Britanni;* 4M and FF read *Britains.*

74. *Taygetus.* This word, correctly *Ta-y'-ge-tus,* Dryden apparently pronounced as three syllables, *Tay-ge'-tus.*

93. *Fleck'd.* 4M reads *fleak'd.*

466, 131. *Trumpets.* So 4M and F2; F1 reads *Trumpet.*

142. *Pollux.* So 4M and F2; F1 reads *Castor.*

143. *God of Thrace.* Mars; cf. **766,** 524–529.

145. *Grim.* So 4M and F2; F1 reads *old.*

150. *Neighb'ring.* F1 reads *neighbo'ring;* 4M and F2, *neighbouring.* The present text, to be consistent, should read *neighboring.*

159. *Hasty.* So 4M and F2; F1 reads *fainty.*

162. *And his.* So 4M and F2; F1 reads *with his.*

166. *Heaving.* 4M and F1 read *beating.*

171, 172. *And now,* etc. So 4M and F2; F1 reads:

> And now aloft; and now alow they fly,
> Now seem to sink in Earth, and now to touch the Sky.

180. *Lapithæ.* For the story of their combat with the Centaurs, v. **857–863,** 292–705. *Add the.* So 4M and F2; F1 reads *added.*

467, 203. *The longing.* So FF; 4M reads *th' expecting.*

223. *Close involve.* 4M and F1 read, *there enclose.*

224, 225. *The male,* etc. So 4M and F2; F1 reads:

> No more of Coursers yet: We now proceed
> To teeming Kine; and their laborious breed.

4M has a side-note: *Here the Poet returns to Cows.*

233. *Noontide.* So 4M and F2; F1 reads *Evening.*

244. *Io's punishment.* v. **396–400,** 769–1041.

256. *Smooth the.* 4M and F1 read *harrow.*

468, 298. *Untried in.* 4M and F1 read *Guiltless of.*

316. *Impels the flying car.* 4M and F1 read *Sustains the goring spurs.*

469, 357. *And rough,* etc. In *Examen Poeticum* (v. headnote, p. **382**) is an anonymous piece headed, *Amor Omnibus Idem; or, The Force of Love in All Creatures, being a translation of some verses in Virgil's Third Georgick, from verse 209 to verse 285,* to which Dryden, in his *Postscript to the Reader,* refers in terms of high compliment: v. **708²,** 57 f. But he fails to state that from this piece he took three whole lines (**469,** 402; **470,** 431, 448), and suggestions for many others, for his own translation. The following excerpts will make the matter plain:

> Rough on the flinty Ground all Night he lies.
> [Cf. **469,** 357.]

> 'T is with this Rage the Lyoness is stung,
> When o're the Forrest (mindless of her Young)
> She sternly stalks: 'T is then the shapeless *Bear*
> With fierce desire does to the Woods repair,
> And wide Destruction makes.
> [Cf. **469,** 381–386.]

> See how the Winds the trembling Stallions fray,
> When first to their sagacious Nostrils they
> The distant Female's well-known scent convey!
> [Cf. **469,** 391, 392.]

> The *Sabine Boar* does then prepare to wound,
> And whets his foamy Tusks, and paws the Ground:
> His Sides against the rugged Trees does raise,
> And hardens both his Shoulders for the War.
> [Cf. **469,** 397–402.]

> What does the Youth in whose enraged Veins.
> [Cf. **469,** 408.]

> — whilst from the *Throne*
> Of Heav'n its loud *Artillery* rattles down
> On his devoted Head.
> [Cf. **469,** 408.]

> 'T were long to tell the spotted *Linx's* Wars,
> By Love excited: Or the furious Jars
> Of prowling Wolves, or Mastives head-strong Rage:
> Ev'n tim'rous Stags will for their Hinds engage.
> [Cf. **469, 470,** 415–418.]

With Rage incens'd they struck their Master dead,
And on his mangled Limbs by piecemeal fed.
[Cf. **470**, 424.]

When Spring's soft Fire their melting Marrow
burns
(For 't is in Spring the lusty warmth returns)
They to the tops of steepest hills repair,
And with wide nostrils snuff the *Western Air*,
Wherewith conceiving, (wonderful to tell)
Without the Stallions help their *Bellies* swell.
[Cf. **470**, 428–433.]

Till from their lustful Groins at last does fall
Their Off-spring, which the Shepherds rightly call
Hippomanes: A slimy, poisonous Juice,
Which muttering *Step-Dames* in *Inchantments*
use,
And in the *mystick Cup* their *powerful Herbs* in-
fuse.
But time is lost, which never will renew,
Whilst ravish'd, we the pleasing Theam pursue.
[Cf. **470**, 440–450.]

403. *The youth.* Leander, as a side-note in 4M
indicates: cf. **19**², 23, n.
470, 443. *Hippomanes.* v. n. **345**, 805.
453. *What oil.* 4M and FF read *what Oyl.* If
the text is right, it must refer to the student's
midnight oil, an idea without warrant in the
Latin. *What toil* would be an easy emendation.
472. *Cote.* 4M and F1 read *Cot.*
488. *Shiv'ring.* 4M and F1 read *wretched.*
490. *Rugged.* So FF; 4M reads *barren.*
471, 491. *Bleating kids.* 4M and F1 read *Family.*
501. *Flow'r.* FF read *Flower ;* here altered to
flow'r to conform to *pow'r* above.
510. *Creaking.* So FF; 4M reads *the shrill.*
519. *To the.* So FF; 4M reads *in the.*
549. *West allies.* So FF; 4M reads, — Western
Sons.
472, 587. *Dutch.* Dryden here departs slightly
from his original for the sake of gratifying his
animosity against the Dutch: cf. **5**, 84, n;
71, 72.
473, 637. *Painful.* So FF; 4M reads *sweating.*
673. *Them.* 4M and F1 read *'em.*
683. *Oint.* So FF; 4M reads *noint.*
474, 742. *Or.* In the sense of *before.*
475, 808. *Phocæ.* So FF; 4M reads *Sea-Calves.*
476, 27. *Proud.* F1 reads *loud.*
478, 137. *With ease,* etc. v. B. S. lx, lxi.
139. *Shap'd to his size.* F1 reads, *Large are his
Limbs.*
162. *High-flying.* Cf. **125**¹, 6, n.
479, 226. *And, common sons, beneath.* FF read,
And common Sons, beneath.
253. *Labor'd.* F1 reads *strokes of.*
257. *Busy.* F1 reads *native.*
266. *Plies.* Cf. **344**, 688, n.
480, 305. *Grandsires' grandsons.* This is probably an error for *grandsires' grandsires,* which
is adopted by SS.; Virgil has *avi numerantur
avorum.*
318. *Quarrel.* So F1; F2 reads *Quarrels.*
481, 354. *And worms, that shun the light.* So F1;
F2 reads *And Lizards shunning Light,* a
reading also found in the errata to F1. "As
lizards have been mentioned in the preceding
couplet, the correction itself seems erroneous."
[SCOTT.]

366. *Man.* F1 reads *us.*
482, 437. *Then,* etc. Cf. **886**, 539–544.
471. *Thy hate pursues.* F1 reads *thou hat'st.*
484. *Softly.* Dryden's construction is confused,
but the antithesis with *loud* shows that the
fault is his and not the printer's. SS. reads
lofty.
492. *Turn the wheel.* Dryden's mention of the
spinning wheel here is an anachronism, of
course without warrant in the original.
495. *Sisters'.* FF read *Sister's.*
483, 553. *The Vestal fire.* That is, the fire of
Vesta:
Ter liquido ardentem perfundit nectare Vestam.
484, 589. *Will seem.* F1 reads *he seems.*
590. *Imitate.* F1 reads *imitates.*
591. *Break.* F1 reads *Breaks.*
592. *Or hiss a dragon.* F1 reads, *A Dragon
hisses.* Dryden's alteration of this line introduces confusion, but has nevertheless been
followed, since the poet evidently attempted
to change the general construction of the
passage. It would be attractive to emend
stares to *stare* and to read *snare* in the line
above.
594. *Attempt.* F1 reads *attempts.*
486, 744. *Had.* So FF; perhaps a misprint for
has.
747. *And,* etc. In place of this line F1 reads:
With one continu'd Tenor still complains;
Which fills the Forrest and the neighb'ring Plains.
On revision Dryden evidently disliked the
jingle, *complains : plains.*
487¹, 801. *His.* F1 reads *their.*
811. *Arms.* So F1; F2 reads *Arts,* an evident
misprint caused by the *arts* of the following
line.
TO THE MOST, etc. The main sources for this
Dedication are the following two books:
Le Bossu, René, *Traité du Poëme Epique,*
Paris, 1675. (Here cited by book and chapter.)
Segrais, Jean Regnauld de, *Traduction de
l'Eneïde de Virgile,* Paris, 1668. (Cited by the
pages of vol. i of that edition.)
The first of these works, though now completely forgotten, was at the time a standard
authority in literary criticism. Dryden had
previously been much indebted to it: v. B. S.
xxxiv; **293**², 27; n. **287**², 26; n. **291**¹, 52.
Segrais (1624–1701) was a poet and prose
writer of some eminence, a member of the
circle of Mme. de La Fayette.
Besides these main sources, Dryden seems
to have been somewhat indebted to the following two books:
Dacier, André, *La Poëtique d'Aristote,
traduite en François, avec des remarques critiques sur tout l'ouvrage,* Paris, 1692. (Cited
by edition of Amsterdam, 1733. Dacier is the
same scholar whose work on Horace Dryden
used in his *Discourse concerning Satire:* v.
293², 46, n.)
Rapin, René, *Reflexions sur la Poëtique.*
(v. B. S. xxx, xxxiv. Dryden had not read this
book for a long time, and quotes from memory:

v. 513[1], 30, n. It is here cited by book and chapter of the edition of Amsterdam, 1709.) *John, Lord Marquis of Normanby.* v. n. **120,** 877. Mulgrave had been a stanch adherent of James II, and during most of the reign of William III was a member of the opposition. In 1696 he, like Chesterfield (v. **440[2],** n), refused to join the Association for the support of William as the "rightful and lawful king," against Jacobite attempts.

1. *A heroic poem,* etc. The idea is a commonplace; cf. Rapin, ii. 2, 4.

7. *The least,* etc. Cf. Bossu, ii. 6: "Les episodes sont les parties nécessaires de l'action, étendués avec des circonstances vrai-semblables." The idea of *convenient* might be deduced from Rapin, ii. 8, though it is not directly stated there.

487[2], 11. *Novels.* Used in the sense of *tale, short story* ; cf. **747[2],** 56.

Ariosto. "The early editions, by an absurd and continued blunder, read *Aristotle.* Ariosto, and indeed all the heroic Italian poets, Tasso excepted, have checkered their romantic fictions with lighter stories. But neither Ariosto nor his predecessors, Boiardo and Pulci, ever entertained the idea of writing a regular epic poem after the ancient rules. On the contrary, they often drop the mask in the middle of the romantic wonders which they relate, and plainly show how very far they are from considering the narrative as serious. It was, therefore, consistent with their plan to admit such light and frivolous narratives as might relieve the general gravity of their tale, which resembled an epic poem as little as a melodrama does a tragedy." [SCOTT.]

25. *Bossu. Op. cit.* ii. 8: in general, Bossu is never weary of berating Statius.

48. *Prepense.* So in SS.; FF read *propense.*

488[1], 3. *Siege.* After this word F1 has the following passage: *I can think of nothing to plead for him, but what I verily believe he thought himself ; which was, that as the Funerals of Anchises were solemniz'd in Sicily, so those of Archemorus should be celebrated in Candy. For the last was an Island ; and a better than the first, because Jove was born there.*

38. *Divinæ,* etc. "Particle of the divine air." HORACE, *2 Satires,* ii. 79. Cf. **240,** 1728.

45. *Within the year.* Bossu (iii. 12) assigns a year as the limit of duration of an epic poem.

488[2], 7. *For which.* "A real slip in grammar, it being impossible to adapt it to *practic'd.*" SAINTSBURY.

13. *Corneille,* etc. See his *Troisième Discours — Des Trois Unités.*

41. *Chymical medicines.* "Essences, strong medicines given in small doses; e. g. opium, arsenic, tartar emetic. *Galenical decoctions* are vegetable remedies, simples, given generally in a large drench. The terms belong to a controversy between the Spagirists or Paracelsians, who used chemical medicines, and the School of Paris, which imposed an

oath on its pupils never to use anything of the kind." [KER.]

"We, like subtile chymists, extract and refine our pleasure; while they, like fulsome Galenists, take it in gross." SHADWELL, *Epsom Wells,* act i.

47. *One reason of Aristotle's. Poetics,* xxvi.

489[1], 29. *The courage,* etc. "The cant of supposing that the *Iliad* contained an obvious and intentional moral was at this time established among the critics." [SCOTT.] Bossu insists that an epic poem is really a *fable,* teaching a moral just as do the fables of Æsop.

39. *The manners of the hero.* Dryden's discussion of this topic comes from Bossu, i. 12; iv. 4, 5, 9.

489[2], 13. *Ill habits,* etc. The idea is found in Dacier, pp. iv, 67.

25. *Quinquina.* Peruvian bark, producing quinine; its use was still a novelty in England, dating only from 1655.

39. *A subject . . . may lend,* etc. This is a bit of sarcasm at the expense of William III, and of the national debt, founded in 1693; cf. **356[1],** 4 (*Arg.*), n.

490[1], 4. *Tryphon the stationer.* "*Bibliopola Tryphon,* a character twice mentioned by Martial (iv. 72; xiii. 3); Dryden probably means Tonson." SCOTT.

7. *Ruelle.* "Properly the space or *lane* between the bed and the wall; later, the reception of visitors at the lady's toilette; then, generally, any party of ladies and gentlemen that pretended to wit." [KER.] The word is common in the French literature of Dryden's time.

13. *The fine woman,* etc.

— ut turpiter atrum
Desinat in piscem mulier formosa superne.
HORACE, *Ars Poet.* 3, 4.

18. *Speciosa miracula.* "Picturesque marvels." *Ibid.* 144: cf. **503[1],** 32.

20. *Antiphates.* So F1; F2 reads *Antiphanes.*

26. *Ne Hercules contra duos.* "Not even Hercules against two at once." The saying is first found, in literature, in Plato, *Phædo,* 89 C.

35. *But I have more than once,* etc. Cf. **293[1],** 47 f; SS. iv. 24, 25. But in *An Essay of Dramatic Poesy* Dryden seems to agree with Aristotle: v. SS. xv. 369.

490[2], 11. *Puny.* "i. e. *puisne,* junior." [KER.]

42. *Anonymous.* F1 prints this word in italics.

491[1], 18. *Scaliger the Father.* "On the contrary, Scaliger in the epistle before his *Poetices Libri Septem* says: *Nam et Horatius Artem quum inscripsit adeo sine ulla docet arte ut satyræ propius totum opus illud esse videatur.*" [KER.]

42. *The next,* etc. *Longo sed proxumus intervallo. Æneid,* v. 320. Tasso's *Jerusalem Delivered* was first published complete in 1581.

52. *Fortunam,* etc. "The fortune of Priam I will sing, and the noble war." HORACE, *Ars Poet.* 137. This bad opening line, attributed by Horace to a "cyclic writer," was by some commentators ascribed to Mævius, on whom **v. 427,** 141. [KER.]

491², 4. *Le Moyne,* etc. Cf. **287¹,** 32, n.
16. *Machining persons.* "Supernatural, who come *ex machina.*" [SAINTSBURY.]
30. *The style,* etc. Bossu (vi. 7) merely says that the expression of both epic poetry and tragedy should be on a high level, "belle, noble, et élevée."
38. *Volat,* etc. "The irrevocable word flies away." HORACE, *1 Epistles,* xviii. 71.
492¹, 22. *Macrobius.* A Roman grammarian of the early part of the fifth century. A large part of his *Saturnalia* is given up to the criticism of Virgil.
24. *Tanneguy le Fèvre.* (1615–72.) One of the most famous critics of his time, otherwise known as Tanaquillus Faber. An edition of Virgil with notes by him appeared at Saumur in 1675.
25. *Valois.* "Dryden perhaps means the *Valesiana, ou les Pensées critiques, historiques et morales, et les Poësies Latines de Monsieur de Valois Conseiller du Roi et Historiographe de France,* 1694. There are a few notes on Virgil in this collection." [KER.]
Another, etc. As Professor Ker indicates, this was probably St. Evremond (1613–1703), a distinguished French critic and satirist, who since 1661 had been living in exile in London. Dryden wrote a supplement to a *Character* of him, published with a collection of St. Évremond's *Miscellaneous Essays,* London, 1692. In it he refers to St. Evremond's strictures on Virgil, and attempts to refute some of them; v. SS. xviii. 14–16. His attitude there is more conciliatory than in the present essay: cf. **499¹,** 17 f; **506¹,** 23 f.
30. *But let,* etc. Taking a general notion from Bossu (i. 11), Dryden justifies it by historical reflections, apparently of his own composition. The blunder of making the Greeks of Homer's time in danger from the *Assyrian or Median* (or, as Dryden first wrote it, *Persian*) monarchy is all his own.
33. *Homer's* [*moral*], etc. Dryden's treatment of this topic is mainly from Bossu, i. 8.
492², 7. *Quicquid,* etc. "Whatever be the folly of the kings, the Achæans are the sufferers." HORACE, *1 Epistles,* ii. 14.
13. *Median.* F1 reads *Persian.*
27. *Assyrian or Median.* F1 reads *Persian.*
47. *The cause of religion,* etc. Another of Dryden's sneers at the Revolution. Cf. **493¹,** 8 f, 46.
493¹, 14. *Stavo,* etc. "I was well; but, endeavoring to be better, I am here." MALONE.
48. *His own son.* Plutarch states in his *Brutus* that Cæsar regarded Brutus as his son by his intrigue with Servilia.
50. *Dante.* v. *Inferno,* xxxiv. This is the only allusion to Dante in Dryden's works which even implies personal acquaintance with him. Elsewhere (**173²,** 19 ; **741¹,** 41 ; SS. vii. 233) he merely mentions him as a refiner of the Italian language.
493², 23. *Secretisque,* etc. *Æneid,* viii. 670 : the first words should be *secretosque pios :* cf. **637,** 889, 890; **713¹,** n. 1156.

47. *Montaigne's principles.* v. *Essais,* iii. **9.** But the editor cannot discover that Montaigne anywhere expresses the preference for Venice that Dryden attributes to him.
494¹, 34. *The moral,* etc. Dryden takes his general idea from Bossu, i. 11: "Il [Virgile] devoit leur faire perdre cette vieille aversion qu'ils avoient pour la monarchie, les persuader de la justice et du bon droit d'Auguste, leur ôter l'envie de s'opposer à ses desseins, et leur donner de l'amour et de la vénération pour ce prince." But Bossu regards the *Æneid* as written primarily for the instruction of Augustus and future Roman emperors; the people are only "le second objet de sa morale."
42. *The receiv'd opinion,* etc. Bossu (i. 11) and Segrais (pp. 31–35) agree that Virgil took from tradition the idea of Æneas's coming to Italy. Segrais cites reasons from Bochart for believing that Æneas was never actually in Italy. — Samuel Bochart (1599–1667) was a French Protestant theologian and philologian. His most famous work was a *Geographia Sacra.* He was called the most learned man of his time.
494², 5. *I doubt not but it was,* etc. This sentence is incoherent; the words *it was* are superfluous. They are here retained, as a mark of Dryden's general carelessness in correcting his work.
32. *Memmii.* A Mummius, not a Memmius, destroyed Corinth.
41. *Genus,* etc. "The irritable race of bards." *2 Epistles,* ii. 102. "I suspect our author spoke from recollection of some of his own satirical strokes." [SCOTT.] Cf. **714,** n. 1020.
44. *Animamque,* etc. "He lays down his life to inflict a wound." Imitated from Virgil, *Georgics,* iv. 238; cf. **480,** 344–347.
495¹, 1. *A descendant of Æneas.* Cf. **85,** 38, n.
11. *As Augustus,* etc. v. Bossu, i. 11; iv. 9; the first of these chapters is Dryden's general authority on this page.
43–46. *Neither . . . Book.* F1 reads: *Neither has he forgotten Atis, in the Fifth of his Æneis, the Son of* Polites, *youngest Son to* Priam ; *who was slain by* Pyrrhus, *in the Second Book.* Atis, *then, the Favourite Companion of* Ascanius, *had a better Right than he ; tho' I know he was introduc'd by* Virgil, *to do Honour to the Family, from which* Julius Cæsar *was descended by the Mothers side.* In the errata of F1, however, Dryden makes the following statement: "Where Atys is mention'd as having a claim by succession before Æneas, my memory betray'd me; for, had I consulted Virgil, he calls not the son of Polites by the name of Atys, but of Priamus. 'T is true he mentions Atys immediately afterwards, on the account of the Atian family, from which Julius Cæsar was descended by his grandmother, as I have there mention'd." Cf. **545,** 718; **588,** 734, 741.
51. *An elective king.* In writing this whole passage Dryden probably had in mind the circumstances of the Revolution of 1688. This is particularly marked in the sentence:

"Æneas, tho' he married the heiress of the crown, yet claim'd no title to it during the life of his father-in-law" (**495**², 27–30).

495², 30. *Pater*, etc. *Æneid*, xii. 192 (the first word is Dryden's slip for *socer*); cf. **692**, 287.

54. *Sacra*, etc. *Æneid*, ii. 293; cf. **541**, 389, 390.

496¹, 6. *Regnum immeritum*. Dryden's mistake for *gentem immeritam*.

10. *An ode. Odes*, iii. 3.

496², 24. *The author of the Dauphin's* Virgil. Ruæus (Charles de La Rue — 1643–1725); cf **507**¹, 18; **507**², 27. In his *argumentum* to the *Æneid*, Ruæus has the words: *Segresius, in egregia præfatione in Gallicam Æneidos interpretationem*. On the Delphin editions, cf. n. **293**², 46.

497¹, 18. *Takes notice*. So F1; F2, by an evident misprint, reads *takes no notice*.

21. *Bossu. Op. cit.* iv. 5.

43. *Virgil*, etc. From Segrais, pp. 37 f. Quotation marks are not used in FF.

497², 34. *Homer*, etc. According to the mediæval view, Homer wrote lies, favoring his countrymen the Greeks. The apocryphal accounts of the Trojan war attributed to Dares Phrygius, a priest of Hephæstus in Troy, and Dictys Cretensis, a follower of Idomeneus, were thought to be more historically accurate. v. Chaucer, *House of Fame*, 1464–1480 (Skeat), and cf. **501**², 52, n; **827**, 391, n.

41. *Stetimus*, etc. *Æneid*, xi. 282–292; cf. **677**, 435–448.

498¹, 16. *They who*, etc. v. Segrais, pp. 40–43. Dryden's translations merely give the general sense of his authority, in abridged form. He mingles some small material of his own with what he takes from Segrais.

27. *Proxima*, etc. *Æneid*, x. 513; cf. **663**, 715, 716.

36. *Invulnerable*. Achilles is not invulnerable in Homer; Dryden follows Segrais in this mistake.

498², 4. *Godsmith*. Used in a different sense in **110**, 50.

5. *Warlock*. "The Scots, about Dryden's time, had many superstitions concerning individuals whom they supposed to be shotproof, by virtue of a satanic charm. The famous Viscount Dundee [v. **269**] was supposed to be invulnerable to bullets of lead. But the word *warlock* [the more common spelling] means a male sorcerer in general, and has not, as Dryden seems to suppose, any reference to this particular charm." [SCOTT.]

35. *Grecian*. So F1; F2 reads *Grecians*, which is possibly an error for *Grecian's*.

499¹, 17. *Of St. Swithen*. F1 reads *of a St. Swithen*. Professor Ker shows that Dryden is probably thinking of a passage in Perrault (cf. **384**¹, 14, n). The day of St. Swithin (the usual spelling) is July 15. "The vulgar, to use Gay's account, believe:

How, if on Swithin's feast the welkin lowers,
And every pent house streams with hasty showers,
Twice twenty days shall clouds their fleeces drain,
And wash the pavements with incessant rain.
(*Trivia*, i. 183–186.)" SCOTT.

One of these censors. "Dryden was thinking (with grief) of St. Évremond, *Réflexions sur nos Traducteurs*, 1673." [KER.] Cf. **492**¹, 25, n : just below Dryden refers to his own *Character ;* v. SS. xviii. 15, 16.

22. *Extemplo*, etc. *Æneid*, i. 92, 93; cf. **523**, 135, 136.

37. *Moyle*. Walter Moyle (1672–1721), politician and student. He contributed to the translation of Lucian published in 1711. Dryden compliments him in his *Life of Lucian* prefixed to that work, and in his *Parallel of Poetry and Painting :* v. SS. xviii. 79 ; xvii. 315.

40. *Death*. FF place a period after this word.

499², 4. *Parce*, etc. *Æneid*, i. 257, 258; cf. **526**, 350, 351.

19. *Tua*, etc. *Æneid*, x. 632; cf. **665**, 894, 895.

22. *Si mora. Ibid.* 622–627; cf. **665**, 879–887. Dryden, by a queer mistake, inverts the order of his two quotations; Juno's flattery follows her husband's verdict instead of preceding it.

34. *Trojæ*, etc. *Ibid.* 469–472; cf. **662**, 659–662.

42. *Sir Robert Howard*. v. B. S. xx; **11**, **12**; cf. **715**², n. 662. Dryden follows Howard's idea in his translation; cf. **526**, 357.

44. *That I*. F1 omits *that*.

500¹, 1. *With exact*. F1 reads *with an exact*.

24. *Segrais*, etc. *Op. cit.* pp. 38–40.

45. *Vultis*, etc. *Æneid*, i. 572, 573; cf. **532**, 803–805.

500², 9. *Doctor Cudworth*. "Dr. Ralph Cudworth (1617–88), author of *The True Intellectual System of the Universe*, 1678." [MALONE.]

46. *Fata*, etc. *Æneid*, iv. 440; cf. **572**, 637.

501¹, 1. *Curam*, etc. *Ibid.* 332, 395; cf. **570**, 481, 482; **571**, 570.

3. *Humanly*. FF read *humanely*, which may mean either *humanly* or *humanely*.

18. *His two translators*. "Robert et Antoine le Chevalier d'Agneaux, frères, de Vire en Normandie. Their translation of Virgil was first published in 1582." [KER.]

28. *Orpheus*. v. **486**, 754–759.

52. *Was of*. F1 reads *was also of*.

53. *Was also*. F1 omits *also*.

501², 17. *Conversation*. Here used, of course, in the sense of *close acquaintance*.

37. *Discourse*. "I am afraid this passage, given as a just description of love, serves to prove that Dryden's ideas of the female sex and of the passion were very gross and malicious." [SCOTT.] Cf. **716**¹, n. 100; **1024**¹.

52. *Dares Phrygius*. Not Dares Phrygius, but Dictys Cretensis (*De Bello Trojano*, iii. 15) tells the story to which Dryden refers: cf. **497**², 34, n; **827**, 391, n.

502¹, 30. *Varium*, etc. *Æneid*, iv. 569, 570; cf. **574**, 819.

32. *Ever was*. F1 reads *was ever*.

49. *Notumque*, etc. *Æneid*, v. 6; cf. **577**, **578**, 7–9.

54. *Their queen*. So F1; F2 reads *the Queen*.

502², 6. *Sir Henry Wotton*. Walton, in his *Life of Sir Henry Wotton*, tells how Wotton wrote in a German's album "a pleasant definition of an ambassador, in these very words: *Legatus est vir bonus peregre missus ad mentiendum rei* *publicæ causa ;* which Sir Henry Wotton could have been content should have been thus Englished: 'An ambassador is an honest man, sent to lie [i. e. *sojourn*] abroad for the good of his country.'" But the jest would admit of an ill construction, and through the "malicious pen" of a Catholic writer became an occasion of scandal against the government of King James I.

13. *Bocaline.* "Trajano Boccalini (1556–1613) published his *Ragguagli di Parnaso* (*News of Parnassus*) in 1612–13, at Venice; the book was translated into English by Henry Cary, Earl of Monmouth, in 1656 (*Advertisements from Parnassus in two Centuries, with the Politick Touchstone . . .*). There were many imitators of Boccalini, but for this one it is perhaps unnecessary to make researches." [KER.]

40. *Segrais. Op. cit.* pp. 28-31.

48. *Ovid, etc.* Since 1666 Dryden has changed his opinion: cf. **25²**; also **744¹**, 4-10.

53. *Is for.* So F1; F2 reads *as for.*

503¹, 1. *I have translated both.* v. **98–101.**

22. *Nothing, etc.* Aristotle does not state this in so epigrammatic a form, but implies it in *Poetics,* xxv; Dryden follows Segrais: "On ne doit appeller faute, dit Aristote, que celles qui se font contre l'art qu'on professe. jusqueslà mesme qu'il y a des ignorances affectées qui ont bonne grace."

31. *Else are.* F1 reads *are else.*

32. *Splendid miracles. Speciosa miracula ;* cf. **490¹**, 18, n. Segrais does not name Ovid, but clearly has him in mind when he writes: "Pourquoi le [Virgile] condamnera-t-on d'avoir fait une fiction contre l'ordre du temps si on permet bien quelquefois aux autres poëtes de faire mesme contre l'ordre de la nature ?"

42. *Tasso.* The discourse referred to, as Professor Ker points out, is the second, *Dell' Arte Poetica.* Segrais mentions Tasso, but not his *Discorsi,* which Dryden had probably himself read. Cf. **286²**, 50, n.

503², 15. *In the mean time,* etc. What follows, to the end of the paragraph, seems to be original with Dryden.

24. *Nec pars,* etc. "Nor of the whole work is any part more read than the tale of a love not made lawful by marriage." *Tristia,* ii. 535, 536, somewhat incorrectly quoted.

53. *Pulchramque,* etc. "Devoted to thy wife, thou buildest a fair city." *Æneid,* iv. 266, 267.

504¹, 14. *Augustus.* "The Emperor Augustus divorced Scribonia, his second wife, in order to make room for his marriage with Livia. But the argument of our author from the *Æneid* seems far-fetched." SCOTT.

24. *Neque,* etc. *Æneid,* iv. 337, 339; cf. **570**, 489, 490.

40. *Saith.* F1 reads *says.*

45. *I have detain'd,* etc. In this paragraph Dryden follows very closely Segrais, pp. 24–27. His illustration from Raphael (**505¹**), however, seems to be original; in 1695 he had

published a translation of Du Fresnoy's *Art of Painting,* with a critical preface of his own.

50. *Hath.* F1 reads *has.*

504², 1, 9, 16, 22, 29, 30, 44. *Hath.* F1 reads *has.*

3. *Strange.* "Mr. Malone reads *strong,* but *strange* here seems to signify *alarming* or *startling.*" [SCOTT.] The present editor thinks Malone's emendation was very likely correct.

9. *Scaliger. Op. cit.* v. 2.

10. *Saith.* F1 reads *says.*

16. *Solomon.* v. Ecclesiastes i. 9.

31. *Quid,* etc. "Why do you deny me water ? The use of water is free to all." OVID, *Met.* vi. 349.

505¹, 4. *Him so like him.* So F1. That is, Æneas so like Augustus. F2 reads, *him so like her ;* evidently Dryden was confused in making this change, if it be due to him and not to the printer.

8. *Æneadum genetrix.* "Mother of Æneas's race," the opening words of Lucretius's poem *De Rerum Natura.*

26. *Horace. O imitatores, servum pecus :* "Imitators, ye servile herd." *1 Epistles,* xix. 19.

38. *Cain.* v. Genesis iv. 16.

53. *Cities had.* So F1; F2 reads *Cities have.*

505², 1. *It.* Not found in F1.

17. *Androgeos.* So F1; F2 reads *Androgeus.*

38. *Orpheus and Eurydice.* Cf. **485, 486,** 655-764.

51. *Hath.* F1 reads *has.*

506¹, 18. *Is so.* F1 omits *so.*

23. *Another French critic,* etc. "St. Évremond again, *Sur les Poëmes des Anciens,* 1685." [KER.] Cf. **492¹**, 25, n; **499¹**, 17, n.

40. *Similitudes,* etc. The frequent similes of Dryden's heroic plays were ridiculed in *The Rehearsal* (act ii, sc. 3):

"BAYES. Now, here she must make a *simile.*

"SMITH. Where's the necessity of that, Mr. Bayes ?

"BAYES. Because she's surpris'd. That's a general rule: you must ever make a simile when you are surpris'd; 't is the new way of writing."

[Chloris speaks a simile parodying one in *The Conquest of Granada.*]

Dryden acknowledges this fault in his preface to *Troilus and Cressida* (1679), where he has already adopted the view expressed here. — "No man is at leisure to make sentences and similes, when his soul is in an agony." v. SS. vi. 278. He probably drew from Bossu (vi. 3), who writes: "Il est rare qu'elles [comparaisons] soient naturelles et vraisemblables dans la bouche d'une personne passionée;" and quotes with disapprobation some verses from Seneca's *Medea.*

506², 35. *Ac,* etc. *Æneid,* i. 148-156; cf. **524,** 213-225.

507¹, 3. *Nunc,* etc. "Now was not the place for such things." HORACE, *Ars Poet.* 19, with a change of *his* to *hisce.*

10. *Macrobius.* Cf. **492¹**, 22, n.

Pontanus. His edition of Virgil was first published at Augsburg in 1599.

16. *Junius and Tremellius.* v. **165,** 241, n.
23. *What follows,* etc. From this point through
508², 40, Dryden draws most of his material
from Segrais, pp. 48 f.
31. *Bossu,* etc. Bossu himself (iii. 12) inclines
to reduce the action of the Æneid to a single
campaign, making it begin in summer and
close before the end of autumn of the same
year, but admits that his reasons are not conclusive.
42. *He has made,* etc. This is really Bossu's
view (cf. the previous note), which Dryden
remembered vaguely and mixed up with his
present subject. Really, Segrais gives the action nearly a year and includes winter in it:
v. **507²,** 41 f. The passage shows Dryden's
extreme carelessness.
47. *Ronsard.* In the preface to his *Franciade*
(1572).
507², 40. *Quinetiam,* etc. *Æneid,* iv. 309: cf.
569, 570, 447, 448.
508¹, 7. *Ten months.* F1 reads *three Months,* but
has the following statement in the errata:
" — towards the bottom of this page here [*sic*]
is a gross error, which is easily corrected by
reading *ten months* instead of *three ;* the sense
will direct you to the place." This gives an
interesting glimpse of Dryden's methods of
work. The sentence *From which . . . three
months* (**507²,** 51–**508¹,** 7), as it stood in F1,
was correct, though carelessly expressed.
Three months referred only to *landing in
Italy, and making the war,* and was taken from
Segrais' phrase: "Le reste [the action after
Æneas's arrival in Italy] *peut s'estre passé en
moins de trois mois.*" (Cf. **508¹,** 44.) Reading
over his own work, Dryden took as the subject of *may be judg'd* all the phrases from *arriving* through *making the war,* instead of only
the last two of them, and hence changed
three into *ten.*
20. *These,* etc. This sentence seems to be original with Dryden.
40. *Aurora,* etc. *Æneid,* vii. 26, 27, 32–34; cf.
610, 611, 34–49.
508², 10. *Cum subito,* etc. "When cloudy Orion,
suddenly rising from the waves." *Æneid,* i.
535.
26. *Dum pelago,* etc. "While winter and watery
Orion spend their rage on the sea." *Æneid,*
iv. 52.
509¹, 4. *For Virgil then.* F1 reads *then for
Virgil.*
8. *Than Apollo.* So F1; F2 reads *than from
Apollo.*
18. *I name,* etc. The view expressed in this sentence was the usual one in Dryden's time:
v. Bossu, v. 5, and cf. **921,** 587–619. Segrais
(p. 11) seems to differ: "Les anciens ont crû
que pour ce sujet il faloit encore se servir de
l'entremise des dieux, ne pouvant établir
autrement la vray-semblance de ces grands
évenemens qui touchent l'imagination, mais
contre qui le jugement se revolteroit d'abord
s'il n'estoit captivé par une foy aveugle."
This corresponds to the following paragraph
of Dryden.

36. *O nimium,* etc. *Æneid,* v. 870, 871; cf.
593, 1135, 1136.
38. *But machines,* etc. v. Segrais, in note on l.
18 above. Rapin (i. 23) writes: "Le changement de Niobé en rocher est une avanture
qui tient du merveilleux: mais elle devient
vray-semblable, dès qu'une divinité à qui ce
changement n'est pas impossible, s'en mêle."
48. *Guardian angels.* Cf. **288²–291¹**; **749¹,**
14–25.
50. *No heroic poem,* etc. Segrais (p. 12) was of
the same opinion: "Quelques modernes ont
voulu mettre les enchantemens en sa [*i. e.* des
dieux] place; et il faut du moins avoüer qu'ils
ont esté plus raisonnables que ceux qui n'ont
voulu ny dieux, ny anges, ny saints, ny en-
chantements. On le void par la ressemblance
qu'ont tous ces ouvrages qui pour entretenir
le merveilleux n'ont que des prodiges de valeur
et des avantures fortuites entassées les unes
sur les autres."
509², 4. *Tasso,* etc. *Gerusalemme Liberata,* xviii.
92–97.
10. *Camilla.* Cf. **715²,** n, 312.
46. *Not have.* F1 reads *not to have.*
47. Εἰχώρ. F1 reads ἔικωρ; the correct word is
ἰχώρ.
54. *Nec,* etc. "Let not a god intervene, unless
the difficulty be worthy a rescuer." *Ars Poet.*
191. Bossu (v. 5) emphasizes the contrast
between the drama and epic poetry in the use
of machines.
510¹, 35. *Non,* etc. Inaccurately quoted from
Æneid, xii. 894, 895: the first words should
be, *Non me tua fervida terrent Dicta, ferox.*
Cf. **706,** 1295, 1296.
42. *Milton,* etc. v. *Paradise Lost,* iv. 990–1015.
45. *St. Gabriel.* F1 reads *St. Michael.*
46. *Satan.* FF read *Sathan.*
52. *Jupiter,* etc. *Æneid,* xii. 725–727; cf. **703,**
1054–1057.
54. *Letum.* FF read *lethum,* which should have
been retained in the text, as in **499²,** 22.
510², 3. *Damnabis,* etc. *Eclogues,* v. 80; cf. **431,**
126.
7. *Daniel.* v. Daniel v. 27.
21. *Impar pugna.* "An unequal fight." *Æneid,*
xii. 216.
26. *Imparibus,* etc. "With the fates against
him, with unequal strength, with the gods
unfavorable." Apparently a line made up by
Dryden; cf. *Æneid,* xii. 149, 218.
511¹, 11. *O soror,* etc. *Æneid,* xii. 632–634; cf.
701, 918–921.
38. *Ornari,* etc. This line Dryden earlier took
for the motto of *Religio Laici ;* cf. **157,** n.
40. *Sermoni propiora.* HORACE, *1 Satires,* iv. 42.
41. *But Virgil,* etc. Cf. **286¹,** 5.
47. *What he says,* etc. v. **558,** 561–577.
511², 7. *Cæsura.* "Here used for elision of
vowels; called *synalepha* in **385¹,** 11." [KER.]
This is a blunder on Dryden's part; a *cæsura*
is really a metrical pause in the verse.
512¹, 12. *Si plura,* etc. "If there are many
beauties in a poem, I shall not be offended
by a few blots, which carelessness has let
drop, or against which human nature has

failed to guard." *Ars Poet.* 351–353, slightly
changed at the beginning.

35. *Et*, etc. *Eclogues*, iii. 6.

36. *Nobis*, etc. v. n. **75**², 24, n; cf. **385**², 46 f.
In the epigram referred to, Martial complains
that Roman poets cannot use the same metrical licenses as those of Greece.

46. *Malherbe.* Dryden makes too bold a deduction from Boileau's verses in *L'Art Poétique*, i :
Enfin Malherbe vint, et, le premier en France,
Fit sentir dans le vers une juste cadence.
Malherbe (1555–1628) was in some respects
the founder of the classic French literature;
the use of *pauses*, however, is known in the
earliest French poems.

51. *Dic*, etc. *Eclogues*, iii. 106, 107; cf. **427**,
163–166.

512,² 5. *Cooper's Hill.* By Sir John Denham;
cf. **514**¹, 52, n. Dryden's praise of the couplet
he quotes made it famous among eighteenth-
century critics.

42. *Ten syllables.* "Dryden probably judged
hastily, from the decasyllabic verse of
Ronsard's *Franciade* (1572), that the Alexandrine was not of long standing in French
poetry." [KER.] Dryden is of course wrong
in speaking of *feet* in French . or Italian
poetry. — Rapin writes (ii. 16) : "Le genre de
vers qu'il [Ronsard] a pris n'est pas assez
majestueux pour un poeme heroïque."

54. *Pondere, non numero.* "By weight, not by
number."

513¹, 1. *The French*, etc. Rapin (i. 31) develops
the thought: "La pureté du style qu'on
cherche en nôtre langue affoiblit la poësie."

7. *The turn*, etc. Cf. **319**², 41, n; **385**², 5 f;
744¹, 25 f.

18. *Ignoscenda*, etc. *Georgics*, iv. 489; cf. **485**,
704, 705.

25. *Semivirumque*, etc. "A bull half a man, and
a man half a bull." *Ars Amat.* ii. 24, with the
order of the hemistichs reversed. "The story,
as told by Seneca, is, that some of Ovid's
friends having requested him to leave out of
his works three verses which they should
name, he agreed, provided he might save
three, pointed out by himself. The lines,
being put by both parties into the hands of
arbitrators, proved the same. One of them
was that cited by our author. *Controversiæ*,
ii. 2 (10), 12." [MALONE.]

30. *One of their own great authors.* Rapin (ii. 20)
complains that French tragedy depends not
on terror and pity, but on *galanterie.* "Peut-
être que nôtre nation, qui est naturellement
galante, a été obligée par la necessité de son
caractere à se faire un systeme nouveau de
tragedie, pour s'accommoder à son humeur.
... C'est aussi peut-être par la galanterie que
nôtre siecle s'est avisé de sauver la foiblesse
de son genie, ne pouvant pas soûtenir toûjours
une même action par la grandeur des paroles
et des sentimens." Professor Ker thinks, however, that Dryden has St. Évremond in mind.

36. *Triumvir and proscriber.* The two nouns are
in italics in FF.

44. *His exile.* Cf. **88**, **89**¹.

49. *Non fu*, etc. "Augustus was not so holy or so
benign as the trumpet of Virgil proclaims; his
having had good taste in poetry wins him pardon for the unjust proscription." *Orlando
Furioso*, xxxv. 26, from the words of St. John
to Astolfo. (Dryden's spelling of the Italian
is here retained.) On the whole passage, cf.
745¹, 13–18.

513², 3. *Spenser.* By the allegorical scheme of
his poem, Spenser really is truer to the fundamental tenet of Bossu (cf. n. **489**¹, 29) than
is any other great epic poet.

12. *The two brothers.* v. **501**¹, 18, n.

14. *Hannibal Caro.* Cf. **177**², 18, n; **288**¹, 6.

20. *Le Clerc.* "Jean Le Clerc (1657–1736) in
Bibliothèque Universelle et Historique, t. ix.
p. 219 (*de l'Année* 1688) : *Essai de Critique,
où l'on tâche de montrer en quoi consiste la
Poësie des Hébreux.*" KER.

31. *Tho' perhaps*, etc. Dryden jestingly compares himself to these voluminous poets,
whom he somewhat unjustly despised. On
Wither (the correct form of the name), cf. SS.
xv. 288.

45. *Doctor Morelli.* "Dr. Henry Morelli, one of
the College of Physicians in our author's
time." [MALONE.]

514¹, 4. *Sorti*, etc. *Æneid*, x. 450; cf. **662**, 633.
Dryden is probably wrong here; Pallas's
words, "My father is able to bear either fate,"
are in reply to a taunt of Turnus, translated
in **661**, 625.

24. *Sic ait*, etc. *Ibid.* 473; cf. **662**, 665, 666.

48. *Your Lordship.* This refers to a translation
published anonymously in *Sylvæ* (1685) under
the title, *Part of Virgils 4th Georgick, Englished by an unknown hand.* It is reprinted in
Sheffield's *Works*, 1723.

50. *Lord Roscommon.* His translation of the
Sixth Eclogue was included in *Miscellany
Poems*, 1684; cf. **168.**

52. *Sir John Denham.* Denham translated *The
Destruction of Troy* (from *Æneid*, ii), and *The
Passion of Dido for Æneas* (from *Æneid*, iv):
cf. **91**; **319**², 50; **512**², 5; **744**², 52, n.

53. *Mr. Waller*, etc. Waller translated *Æneid*,
iv. 437–583; Cowley translated *Georgics*, ii.
458–540. On Cowley, cf. **181**¹, 45, n.

514², 23. *A former dissertation.* His *Parallel of
Poetry and Painting*, included in his preface to
his version of Du Fresnoy's *Art of Painting*
(cf. n. **504**¹, 45) : v SS. xvii. 328. Cf. **742**²,
20–24.

30. *And I have.* FF read *and have ;* the insertion
of *I* seems necessary.

38. *Segrais*, etc. Segrais (pp. 2–4) distinguishes
his three classes according to the predomi-
nance in them of *memory*, *wit* (esprit), or
judgment. The first class judges by *words*, the
second by *figures* or by *fine thoughts* (belles
pensées), the third by the *general structure* of a
work (discours). Dryden's three classes are
founded on *conceits*, *bombast*, and *true elevation of style*: compare his own literary development, as sketched in B. S. liii, liv. Taking
his general conception from Segrais, Dryden
develops it independently.

48. *Mob.* The word, as Professor Ker notes, was just coming into use at this time.

515¹, 14. *Mançanares.* Professor Ker thinks that for his illustration Dryden is indebted to Bouhours, *Entretiens d'Ariste et d'Eugène: II. La Langue Françoise.*

27. *Owen's Epigrams.* v. **287¹,** 15, n.

30. *Paste.* So FF; SS. and K. read *taste.* Cf. **738¹, 40; 798,** 503.

47. *A wit,* etc. Lord Rochester: cf. **744²,** 11; and, on Rochester's relations with Dryden, v. B. S. xxix, xxxviii, xxxix; **283²,** 4, n.

54. *He chose,* etc. Dryden now draws on a later section of **Segrais** (pp. 45–48), entitled: "Qu'il faut tascher de plaire seulement aux esprits relevez, et que ç'a esté la maxime de Virgile."

515², 18. *Imagination.* "Imagination has been degraded in meaning since Dryden explained its functions in the *Account of Annus Mirabilis;* what here is called *imagination* is there called *fancy,* or *invention and fancy.*" KER. Cf. **25.**

23. *Marini's Adone.* Published at Paris in 1623. The affectation of its style was proverbial. Marini (or *Marino*) (1569–1625) had some influence on English literature; Crashaw's *Sospetto d'Herode* is a free translation from him.

27. *Mobilitate,* etc. *Æneid,* iv. 175; cf. **567,** 253, 254.

40. *Entellus.* v. **586,** 605–613.

45. *Nec,* etc. "I care not for the gifts." *Æneid,* v. 400.

Dampier. "His *New Voyage round the World* came out in this year. Dampier is speaking of Quito, in the year 1684: 'I know no place where gold is found but what is very unhealthy' (ch. vi.)." [KER.]

516¹, 12. *Mr. Creech.* Cf. **180¹,** 41, n. Creech's version of Manilius was a new book, being printed in this same year, 1697.

25. *Phylarchus.* "Phyllarchus was Jean Goulu de St. François; his criticism of Balzac's style appeared in 1627, *Lettres de Phyllarque à Ariste où il est traicté de l'éloquence françoise.* Dryden refers, not quite accurately, to a passage in Letter xxi." [KER.] Balzac was regarded as the model of French prose style in the earlier seventeenth century.

42. *Articles.* Dryden expands a hint taken from Segrais (p. 64): "J'ay resolu d'enfermer le plus de sens que je pourrois en aussi peu de paroles que le desir de la netteté et la contrainte de notre langue, qui ne peut oublier les articles, me le pourroit permettre."

516², 15. *Ambergris.* FF read *Ambergreace.*

37. *Yet I may,* etc. Cf. Segrais (pp. 65, 66): "Enfin mettant en usage tous les materiaux de ce divin auteur, i'ay voulu donner l'Eneïde en françois, comme i'ay conceu qu'il l'eust donnée luy-mesme, s'il fust né sujet de nostre glorieux monarque; et en reconnoissant toûjours que j'estois bien éloigné de la sublimité de son genie."

517¹, 5. *A Pindaric.* "Now more commonly called an Alexandrine. Pope had perhaps this passage in his memory when he composed the famous triplet descriptive of Dryden's versification:

Waller was smooth; but Dryden taught to join }
The varying verse, the full resounding line, }
The long majestic march, and energy divine. }

(*First Epistle of the Second Book of Horace,* 267–269.)" SCOTT.

10. *Chapman.* "Triplets in Chapman's *Odyssey,* e. g. iv. 27, v. 361, vi. 351." [KER.]

12. *Mr. Cowley.* Professor Ker aptly quotes from Johnson's *Life of Cowley :* "Cowley was, I believe, the first poet that mingled Alexandrines at pleasure with the common heroic of ten syllables. . . . Of triplets in his *Davideis* he makes no use, and perhaps did not at first think them allowable; but he appears afterwards to have changed his mind, for, in the verses on the government of Cromwell, he inserts them liberally with great happiness." Cf. **181¹,** 45, n.

39. *But at,* etc. Cf. **417¹,** 24–34. "Cowley was forced abroad by the ill fate of the royal party in the civil wars." [SCOTT.]

55. *Hemistichs.* Cf. **110,** 87, n; **930,** 48, n. Dryden has changed his mind since writing *Absalom and Achitophel.*

517², 15. *Him,* or *any.* So F1, but with no comma; F2 reads *him any.*

29. *Quem,* etc. *Æneid,* iii. 340. "Whom to you, while Troy was already — smoking, Creüsa brought forth."

39. *Misenum,* etc. *Æneid,* vi. 164, 165. "Misenus the son of Æolus, than whom none was more excellent at rousing heroes with his trumpet — and kindling war by his song."

518¹, 2. *Nile.* v. **394,** 565–572; cf. **130,** 167–174; **886,** 553.

8. *Boccace,* etc. See his *Conclusione dell' Autore,* appended to the *Decamerone.* [KER.]

45. *Hammer'd money,* etc. v. **131,** 229, n. At this time there was great confusion and distress in England through the circulation of clipped hammered coins: v. Macaulay, ch. xxi. Dryden himself was a sufferer: see his letters to Tonson, SS. xviii. 126, 128. [KER.]

518², 24. *He instances,* etc. v. Segrais, p. 69.

26. *Cupid.* Dryden's slip for *Ascanius:* v. **534,** 969–974 (ll. 691–694 of the Latin).

30. *Give.* FF read *gives,* doubtless a misprint.

42. *Quem,* etc. Adapted from Horace, *Odes,* IV. 2: "Whoever is eager to emulate him, poises himself on wings waxened by the craft of Dædalus, and, [falling,] will give his name to the glassy sea."

49. *Aude,* etc. *Æneid,* viii. 364, 365; cf. **631,** 479, 480.

52. *I contemn.* "Nevertheless, our author, long before undertaking the translation of Virgil, had given a noble paraphrase of these lines in the Hind's address to the Panther." [SCOTT.] v. **235,** 1283–1285.

519¹, 5. *Florimel.* v. *Faerie Queene,* V. iii. 22–24.

54. *The late Earl of Lauderdale.* Richard Maitland (1653–95), fourth Earl of Lauderdale. Since the Revolution he had been living abroad, mainly in France, as an exile. His translation of Virgil was published posthumously in London.

519², 30. *Two other worthy friends.* These were Addison and Knightly Chetwood. That Addison wrote *An Essay on the Georgics* is known from Tickell's preface to Addison's collected works, 1721, and from Steele's preface to *The Drummer.* Dryden, in a letter to Tonson concerning the second edition of the *Virgil*, clearly indicates that Chetwood wrote the *Preface to the Pastorals:* "I have also written this day to Mr. Chetwood, and let him know, that the book is immediately goeing to the press again. My opinion is, that the printer shou'd begin with the first Pastoral, and print on to the end of the Georgiques, or farther, if occasion be, till Dr. Chetwood corrects his preface, which he writes me word is printed very false." (Malone, I, 2; 62, 63; SS. xviii. 139.) Malone (III, 547) states, without giving grounds for his opinion, that Chetwood also wrote the *Life of Virgil*, and Addison the *arguments in prose.*

36. *Caus'd.* F1 reads *occasion'd.*

52. *The proper terms.* Cf. **24²**, 36, n. Dryden has now adopted the view typical of the pseudo-classic period, which remained unchanged until the rise of the romantic school.

520¹, 10. *Four preliminary lines.*

Ille ego, qui quondam gracili modulatus avena
Carmen, et, egressus silvis, vicina coegi
Ut quamvis avido parerent arva colono,
Gratum opus agricolis; at nunc horrentia Martis.

These lines are rejected as spurious by most editors of Virgil.

42. *Of the opinion.* F1 omits *the.*

43. *Tucca and Varius.* Servius tells a story that, since Virgil had left his *Æneid* imperfect, Augustus bade the poet's friends Tucca and Varius edit the work, adding nothing, but destroying what was superfluous; and that they therefore retrenched the *four preliminary lines* of which Dryden speaks.

520², 21. *Place, but.* FF read, *place. But ;* and, in the next line, *Translation : Want.*

42. *Sixth Pastoral.* Cf. **514¹**, 50, n.

Pharmaceutria. Dryden refers to one of the two translations of *Eclogue* viii in *Miscellany Poems*, 1684; "by Mr. Stafford" and "by Mr. Chetwood;" probably to the former: v. **710¹**, n. Past. VIII.

43. *Orpheus.* v. n. **514¹**, 48.

521¹, 1. *Erichthonius.* Cf. **466, 467**, 177–184. The story to which Dryden alludes goes back to a note by Servius on that passage.

20. *Your noble kinsman.* "Their mothers were half-sisters." [SCOTT.]

39. *For want.* F1 reads *for your want.*

52. *Ad clerum.* "*i. e.* addressed to the learned." A Latin sermon preached before the Clergy assembled in Convocation, or in the Universities for degrees in divinity, is entitled *Concio ad Clerum.*" MALONE.

523, 102. *Thuscan.* FF here and often read *Thuscan*, but *Tuscan* is also found, as **640**, 186. FF have many similar variants, not recorded in these notes. It is difficult to decide

which of them are significant; perhaps *Alethes* (**524**, 172), for example, should be corrected to *Aletes.*

525, 249. *Fiery.* F1 reads *smoaking.*

526, 342, 343. *One: throne.* This rhyme was probably already somewhat archaic when Dryden wrote.

357. *Know*, etc. Cf. **499²**, 42, n.

365. *Iülus.* FF read *Julus.*

527, 394. *Repay.* F1 reads *reward.*

428. *Ledge of rocks.* F1 reads *hollow Rock.*

530, 622. *Fated.* F1 reads *fatal.*

671. *Procession.* F1 reads *Precession.*

531, 734. *Lowly.* F1 reads *humble.*

748. *A land*, etc. Cf. **554**, 221, n.

532, 763. *Drive.* F1 reads *drives.*

773. *Augment.* F1 reads *prevent.*

834. "*He*, etc. Cf. **230**, 970.

533, 842, 871. *Shipwreck'd ; shipwrack'd.* So FF.

873. *Claim ?* So SS.; FF read *claim!* Many similar cases occur later, as **574**, 774, 776; **575**, 866; **577**, 975; **596**, 185; **602**, 620; **609**, 1163; **639**, 89; **645**, 531, 539; **675**, 270; **681**, 770; **704**, 1153; **706**, 1261, 1263. Contrast **665**, 918, n.

905. *Cost).* So FF; SS. closes the parenthesis after *work* in the next line.

534, 949. *As.* F1 reads *That.*

535, 1000. *The hero.* F1 reads *his Father.*

536, 26. *And.* F1 reads *With.*

45. *Monster fabric.* F1 reads *fatal Engine.*

52. *Laocoon.* So printed in FF ; the word can be pronounced as three syllables wherever it occurs in Dryden: cf. **539**, 267, 281; **540**, 301.

538, 210. *Adjur'd.* So F1; F2 reads *abjur'd.*

540, 324. *God's.* FF read *Gods ;* but Virgil's *dei jussu* shows that a singular is intended.

354. *Pelides.* F1 reads *foul Treason.*

541, 416. *And.* F1 reads *The.*

542, 477. *Bold.* F1 reads *fierce.*

544, 646. *Rais'd on spires.* Cf. **731**, 29.

545, 660. *Yield.* So F1; F2 reads *yields*, an evident misprint.

546, 761. *Obey'd.* Followed by a comma in FF.

763. *A headless carcass*, etc. This is the last line of Denham's *Destruction of Troy ;* cf. **514¹**, 52, n. In the footnote FF read *Derhan*, by a misprint.

548, 934. *Slake.* So SS.; FF read *shake.*

549, 970. *Hallow'd.* F1 reads *hollow'd.*

551, 18. *Cleave.* F1 reads *tempt.*

40. *Terror.* F1 reads *Horror*, corrected to *Terrour* in the errata.

53. *With gore.* F1 reads *with purple Gore.*

553, 142. *Imperial.* F1 reads *Immortal.*

554, 221–224. *A land . . . name.* Cf. **531**, 748–751. The repetition occurs also in the Latin.

555, 356. *The Sun's.* F1 reads *Phœbus.*

558, 527. *Veer*, etc. This line is difficult to understand; Professor Saintsbury wishes to emend *veer* to *'ware.* But possibly *sea and land* may be taken as the subject of *veer :* "Let sea and land depart (shift their direction) to the starboard."

568. *Are display'd.* Cf. **400**, 1031, n.

559, 593. *He gave me license.* He let me go.

560, 728. *Cloud.* So F1; F2 reads *Clouds.*

561, 787. *From.* F1 reads *As.*

809. *Cyclops'.* FF read *Cyclop's*, but cf. **562**, 852.

563, 885. *Trembling.* F1 reads *trembled.*

564, 17, 18. *Fear*, etc. F1 reads:

Fear never harbours in a Noble Mind,
But Modesty, with just Assurance join'd.

51. *Hyarbas.* Cf. **570**, 471, n.

565, 105. *Wand'ring.* F1 reads *wond'ring.*

128. *Short of*, etc. F1 reads:

And, left unbuilt, are shorter of the Sky.

151–158. *Who*, etc. FF punctuate as follows: (151) *Fool, . . . chuse,* (152) *Alliance, . . . refuse?* (153) *comply:* (154) *Jove, . . . Destiny.* (155) *forbid, . . . Command,* (156) *Land.* (157) *Trojan, . . . Line,* (158) *Leagues, . . . join?* The rearrangement in the text follows SS., and is in accord with the Latin original. *Doubt* (154) is used half in its usual sense, half in that (common in Shakespeare) of *apprehension, dread;* hence it is followed first by *lest* and then by *or.*

566, 230. *Or see*, etc. F1 reads:

Or see the Lyon from the Hills descend.

567, 271. *Things done*, etc. The fourteen-syllable line may be meant to symbolize the tattling of the goddess. Cf. **129**, 94, n.

293. *Enrich'd.* So SS.; FF read *enrich*, which may possibly be what Dryden wrote: cf. **400**, 1031, n.

303. *Blood of.* F1 reads *offer'd.*

568, 360. *God begins.* So F1; F2 reads *Gods begins*, an evident misprint.

373. *Seek.* So F1; F2 reads *seeks.*

570, 471. *Hyarba.* Here and in **567**, 283; **564**, 51, the text follows FF. If FF are printed as Dryden intended, his usage varies between *Hyarba* and *Hyarbas.*

572, 603, 604. *Bind . . . wind.* F1 reads *binds . . . winds.*

631. *My death*, etc. F1 reads:

My Death shall leave you of my Crown possess'd.

574, 780. *'T is true.* F1 reads *Tis true;* — F2 reads *Tis true?* After this line F1 has the following, omitted in F2:

An Exile follows whom a Queen reliev'd!

791. *Sister.* Omitted in F2.

577, 22 (Arg.). *Who is.* F1 reads *who was.*

579, 99. *Flow'ry.* F1 reads *fruitful.*

115. *Thus riding*, etc. Cf. **731**, 29.

580, 160. *Sergesthus.* So F1, as ordinarily; F2 here reads *Sergestus*, but usually *Sergesthus.*

582, 307. *Guilty of my vow.* Translating *voti reus,* " bound by my vow (in case my request is granted)." Cf. **757**, 427.

339. *Demoleüs.* Here and in l. 347 FF read *Demoleus.*

583, 404. *Silver-studded.* So SS.; FF read *Silver'd studded.*

584, 450, 451. *Had brib'd*, etc. F1 reads (cf. **922**, 77, 78):

Had brib'd the Judges to protect his Claim;
Besides Diores does as loud exclaim.

479. *Gauntlet-fight.* FF read *Gauntlet fight*, suggesting, by the small letter, that *fight* be

taken as a verb; it is, however, far more natural to regard it as a noun.

587, 689. *Feather'd.* F1 reads *pointed.*

690. *Augurs.* FF read *Augures.*

707. *Give.* So F1; F2 reads *gave.*

588, 743. *Place.* "Dryden here uses *place* for eminence of rank. Ascanius was the last in order, but the first in dignity; this, by the way, is an Ovidian point superinduced upon the simplicity of *Virgil — Extremus, formaque ante omnes pulcher, Iulus.*" [SCOTT.] Cf. **513**[1], 7 f.

770. *Ways.* So F1; F2 reads *Wave.*

589, 838. *Fire.* F1, probably by a misprint, reads *Firr.*

840. *Wrapp'd in amaze.* FF read *Wrap'd in a maze;* SS. reads *Rapt in amaze.*

859. *Fires.* F1 reads *Firs.*

860. *Boughs.* F1 reads *Leaves.*

869. *Arise.* Cf. **400**, 1031, n.

591, 991. *A rising.* F1 reads *To raise a.*

592, 1090. *Lie.* So F1; F2 reads *lay.*

593, 1133. *The.* F1 reads *his.*

18. *Fly.* F1 reads *shun.*

594, 29. *Those.* F1 reads *these.*

34. *The Cretan queen.* Pasiphae; cf. **402**, 109, n.

49. *Assay'd.* F1 reads *essay'd.*

53. *Eager.* F1 reads *Prepar'd.*

596, 243. *Son of.* F1 reads *Son to.*

597, 285. *Glitt'ring.* FF read *glittering*, which should have been retained in the text; but in l. 312 FF have *glitt'ring.*

598, 381. *Malignant light.* Mistranslating *luce maligna,* " the scanty light." Cf. **794**, 116.

402. *Geryon.* The name is properly *Ge'ryon* or *Gery'ones;* Dryden here and in **628**, 267 mistakenly writes *Gery'on.*

599, 419. *Freights.* So F1; F2 reads *frights.*

435. *Wond'ring.* So F1; F2 reads *wand'ring.*

461. *Amidst*, etc. Cf. **141**, 310.

600, 519. *Calm'd.* So F1; F2 reads *claim'd.*

601, 558. *She sails.* So SS.; FF read *he sails.*

604. *Pasiphae.* Cf. **402**, 109, n.

605. *Phædra's ghost.* Cf. **723**, 381; **725**, 576; **729**, 851.

606. *There.* F1 reads *Chast.* Dryden accents incorrectly *Laoda'mia* instead of *Laodami'a :* cf. **730**, 7, n ; **854**, 44, n.

608. *Cæneus.* Cf. **856**, **857**, 234–287; **787**, 53.

614. *Sees.* So F1; F2 reads *runs.* The change, even if made by Dryden himself, is an evident deterioration of the text.

603, 733. *Lo.* So F1; F2 reads *Let.*

604, 784. *Th' Alcan twins.* Cf. **257**, 237, n.

605, 892. *The choir.* So F1; F2 reads *their Choir.*

606, 931. *Gods'.* F1 reads *Gods;* F2 reads *God's.*

948. *Embraces.* So F1; F2 reads *Embrace :* misprints are frequent in this part of F2.

962. *Fields.* So F1; F2 reads *Field.*

607, 1057. *Your.* F1 reads *our.*

1062. *The seat.* F1 reads *his Seat.*

608, 1092. *Nephew's.* So FF; perhaps *nephews'* should be substituted. *Nephew* is used in the sense of *descendant;* cf. **845**, 499.

1099. *Nisus'.* FF read *Nisus*, which may be a misprint for *Nisa's*, representing *Nysæ* of the Latin.

1111. *He shall,* etc. F1 reads:

For fighting Fields his Troops he shall prepare.

610, 1237, 1238. *True . . . lies.* These lines are not found in F1; but in the *Notes,* at the head of the note on l. 1235 (cf. **714**[1]) occurs the statement: *By the carelessness of the Amanuensis, the two next Lines are wanting, which I thus supply out of the Original Copy,* — (text as printed.) In F2 this statement is of course omitted.

7 (Arg.). *Others.* So F1; F2 reads *other.*
28. *Which.* So F1; F2 reads *With.*
38. *Sate.* So F1; F2 reads *sat.*
611, 84. *High.* F1 reads *great.*
612, 142. *Thy.* So F1; F2 reads *the.*
179. *Blest.* So F1; F2 reads *best.*
613, 205. *Selects.* F1 reads *elects.*
266. *In this.* F1 reads *On this,* by a misprint, corrected in the errata, but repeated in F2.
614, 302. *From.* So F1; omitted in F2, by a misprint.
328. *Seek.* So F1; F2 reads *see.*
615, 360. *All.* So F1; F2 reads *And.*
616, 439. *Near.* F1 reads *to.*
446. *Another.* F1 reads *her native,* changed in the errata.
617, 549. *Wreathes.* F1 reads *crowns,* corrected in the errata to *wreaths.*
554. *Suff'ring.* F1 reads *passive.*
619, 668. *Feed.* F1 reads *fill,* changed in the errata.
716. *Was.* So F1; omitted in F2 by a misprint.
620, 745. *Around.* F1 reads *above.*
621, 857. *Shot.* F1 reads *came.*
622, 910. *His ample.* So F1; F2 reads *the ample.*
925. *Pomp.* F2 has a colon after this word; F1 has no pause at all.
946. *Dewy.* F1 reads *rosie,* changed in the errata.
623, 1015. *Semethis.* So FF; perhaps merely a misprint for *Sebethis.*
1022. *And.* F1 reads *All.*
624, 1036. *Wounds.* So F1; F2 reads *wound.*
1047. *Altars.* So F1; F2 reads *Altar.*
1075. *The more,* etc. F1 reads:

The more the Winds his kindled Course inspire,
The more with fury burn'd the blazing Fire.

1097. *The nobler Pallas.* Cf. **728,** 782.
625, 20. *Fate.* FF place a period after this word, and a colon after *name* (l. 22).
23. *Mischief.* F1 reads *Mischiefs.*
626, 73. *Great-grandsire's.* This translates Virgil's *proavi ;* FF read *great Grandsire's.*
141, 142. *Skies . . . fries.* F1 reads *Sky : . . . fry.*
627, 183, 184. *Maia.* FF read *Maja.*
628, 267. *Geryon.* Cf. **598,** 402, n.
629, 313. *Adverse.* So F1; F2 reads *Averse.*
326. *Beheld.* So FF; SS. emends, perhaps correctly, into *behold.*
349. *Thoro'.* F1 reads *thorough ;* F2, *through.*
352. *Wond'ring.* So F1; F2 reads *wand'ring.*
353. *Behold.* So F1; F2 reads *Beheld.*
630, 398. *Typhœus.* So FF; Dryden has the name correctly, *Typhoeus,* in **7,** 37.

631, 446. *Carmental.* So F1; F2 reads *Carmetal.*
474. *Once,* etc. Dryden introduces a satirical touch not found in the original.
483. *With.* F1 reads *which.*
632, 524. *Or my.* So F1; F2 reads *of my.*
542. *When.* F1 reads *And.*
633, 641. *Tir'd.* So F1; F2 reads *try'd.*
669. *Listless.* F1 reads *lifeless,* changed in the errata.
634, 681. *Apprentiship.* So FF.
726. *Refuse.* Meaning, of course, nothing more than *the residue — pars cetera.* [SAINTSBURY.]
732. *Infold.* Cf. **400,** 1031, n.
636, 828. *Plated.* So F1; F2 reads *Plaited.*
637, 886. *Catiline.* FF place a colon after this word and make no pause after *rock* in the next line; the text follows SS.
928. *Th' ethereal.* F1 reads *th' Ætherial ;* F2, *the Ætherial.*
638, 1 (Arg.). *Æneas'.* FF read *Æneas's,* but forms occurring in verse show that Dryden did not make an extra syllable of the genitive ending after a final *s,* even though he wrote (or Tonson printed) an *—'s.*
640, 163. *Myriads . . . men.* F1 reads *Millions . . . Troops.*
643, 415. *Gate.* FF punctuate this and the succeeding lines as follows: *Gate. . . . vows, . . . Ascanius, . . . years,* — a punctuation which is retained from *Sylvæ* (1685), except that there no comma is found after *vows.* The present editor follows SS. in an almost certain emendation. The long inversion involved in the original punctuation seems entirely unlike Dryden's style.
644, 504. *Prevent.* F1 reads *outwent.*
645, 527. *At the length.* "At length." SAINTSBURY.
646, 588. *Bor'd.* v. GLOSSARY.
602. *Leader.* F1 reads *General.*
611. *Dawns.* So FF; perhaps a misprint for *dawn.* N. E. D. cites no similar passage.
647, 672. *Form.* F1 reads *from.*
650, 920. *With,* etc. SS. alters punctuation so as to take this line with the preceding rather than with the following clauses.
653, 17. *Contend.* F1 reads *Contest.*
654, 107. *Takes.* F1 reads *makes.*
655, 140. *Fatal.* F1 reads *bloody.*
656, 247. *Asium.* The word is here retained from FF, though it is probably a mere blunder for *Clusium,* caused by careless handwriting.
657, 284. *And roll'd,* etc. "This conceit is not Virgil's." [SCOTT.]
658, 368. *Courage.* F1 reads *Anger.*
388. *Ardent.* F1 reads *equal.*
660, 503. *Mingled.* F1 reads *crowded.*
520. *Trust,* etc. The antithesis of *feet* and *hands* is Dryden's, not Virgil's.
662, 639, 640. *War,* etc. FF punctuate *War ; . . . Neck, . . . Sand, . . .*
688. *Rest.* F1 reads *please.*
663, 735. *Will.* FF read *shall,* but the word is changed to *will* in the errata of F1.
664, 849. *Gaping.* F1 reads *bloody.*
665, 864. *Sov'reign.* F1 reads *loving,* changed in the errata to *Sov'raign.*

918. *Bride!* FF read *Bride ?* Similar cases are **669**, 1209; **698**, 730. Contrast **533**, 873, n.
924. *Plank was.* F1 reads *Planks were*, changed in the errata.
668, 1114. *Fold.* So the text in *Sylvæ;* FF read *rowl'd* (i. e. *roll'd*), which is evidently a misprint, by influence of the rhyme word just above.
669, 1155. *Sharpen'd.* F1 reads *cruel.*
670, 1270. *Wood.* Translating *silvam;* the play on words in *iron wood* is doubtless unintentional.
671, 1299. *Nor ask*, etc. Cf. **178**[1], 35–54.
1311. *To the sword his throat applied.* F1 reads, *to his Throat the Sword apply'd*, changed in the errata.
1312. *The crimson stream*, etc. Dryden repeats this couplet, with a slight change, in **707**, 1376, 1377. The jingle of *distain'd, disdainful* is sufficiently disagreeable.
14. *Besmear'd with.* F1 reads *distilling.*
672, 66. *Needless.* F1 reads *needful.*
90. *Breathless.* F1 reads *lifeless.*
120. *Loaded hands.* F1 reads *heads and hands*, changed in the errata.
673, 125. *Ev'ry.* So F1; F2 reads *every.*
674, 245. *My Pallas*, etc. This conceit is not found in Virgil.
678, 559. *Others'.* F1 reads *others ;* F2, *other.*
679, 578. *Undoubted.* F1 reads *unquestion'd.*
588. *In.* F1 reads *at.*
643. *Fathers'.* FF read *Father's.*
680, 659. *Then fall*, etc. This conceit is without warrant in the Latin, and is emphatically not in Virgil's manner.
681, 776. *Horse.* F1 reads *Foot.*
683, 900. *Horribly.* F1 reads *horrible.*
684, 957. *Flying.* This word is not found in F1.
958. *Feather'd.* F1 reads *flying.*
685, 1066. *Dove.* F1 reads *Drove.*
687, 1184. *A.* F1 reads *the.*
688, 1284. *The moats.* F1 reads *their Moats.*
1318. *Involves.* F1 reads *o'respreads.*
689, 2 (Arg.). *Rutili.* So FF.
16. *Thro'.* F1 reads *And.*
60. *Blanch.* So F1; F2 reads *glance.*
64. *Whilst.* F1 reads *while.*
691, 158. *Steam.* So F1; F2 reads *Stream.*
693, 322. *Deem.* F1 reads *deem'd.*
697, 671. *Like.* So F1; F2 reads *less.*
677. *Gyas', Mnestheus', Achates'.* The apostrophes are not found in FF.
698, 746. *Tagus.* So FF: an error, by Dryden or the printer, for *Talus ;* cf. l. 513 of the Latin text.
699, 787. *The.* F1 reads *his.*
798. *Heav'n.* So F1; F2 reads *Heaven.*
700, 836. *Will.* "Not a Scotticism, but *chooses to.*" SAINTSBURY.
838. *There*, etc. Cf. **218**, 61.
701, 939. *Insult.* F1 reads *be pleas'd.*
702, 1041. *Yet, and.* F1 reads *and with.*
705, 1192. *Father's.* In reference to Saturn; cf. **630**, 425–430. FF read *Fathers.*
1259. *Beauteous.* F1 reads *comely.*
707, 1376. *The streaming*, etc. Cf. **671**, 1312, n.
708[1], 20. *Cynthius*, etc. *Eclogues*, vi. 3, 4;

"Apollo plucks my ear, and warns me." Cf. **431**, 5.
32. *Cerberus*, etc. v. **601**, 562–575.
41. *Darby.* William George Richard Stanley (1655?–1702), ninth Earl of Derby.
Peterborough. Charles Mordaunt (1658–1735), third Earl of Peterborough, had been active in the Revolution as an adherent of William III. In 1705 and 1706 he became famous as the commander of the English forces in Spain. He was the friend of Pope, Swift, and Gay.
43. *Was.* Not in FF.
56. *Trumball.* So FF. Sir William Trumbull (1639–1716) was Secretary of State 1695–97. From 1705 to his death he was an intimate friend of Pope.
708[2], 3. *Extremum*, etc. *Eclogues*, x. 1, 3; *negat* is a mistake for *neget :* "Grant me this last favor, Arethusa. — Who denies songs to Gallus ?" Cf. **439**, 1–5.
6. *Gilbert Dolben.* On his father, cf. **120**, 868, n.
11. *The Dolphin's.* i. e. the Dauphin's; *dauphin* is the French form of the word *dolphin ;* cf. n. **293**[2], 46; **496**[2], 24, n.
13. *Fabrini.* First published at Venice in 1568, and often reprinted.
18. *Bowyer.* Cf. **710**[1], n. GEOR. II.
28. *Exeter.* John Cecil (1650?–1700), fifth Earl of Exeter. He was a non-juror, and lived in retirement at his noble seat of Burghley. [SCOTT.]
36. *Walsh.* v. **320**[1], 40, n.
40. *Shrewsbury.* Charles Talbot (1660–1718), twelfth Earl and only Duke of Shrewsbury. He took a prominent part in the Revolution, and later held important offices. "As to the personal attractions of Shrewsbury there is a general consensus of testimony." (A. W. Ward, in D. N. B.) He was the son of the Earl and Countess of Shrewsbury mentioned in n. **116**, 544.
57. *Whoever*, etc. v. n. **469**, 357. "From the high praise here given to these verses, which greatly exceeds their merit, I suspect that the concealed translator was our author's friend, George Granville, afterwards Lord Lansdowne [cf. **733**]. The poem which immediately preceded this in *Examen Poeticum* was written by him." [MALONE.]
709[1], 1. *Lord Roscommon's Silenus.* Cf. **514**[1], 50, n.
6. *Bees.* Alluding to *A Translation of all Virgil's 4th Georgick, except the Story of Aristeus. By Mr. Jo. Addison, of Magdalen Colledge, Oxon.*, included in *The Annual Miscellany for the Year 1694.*
7. *Mr. Cowley's*, etc. Cf. **181**[1], 45, n; **514**[1], 53 n.
13. *Dr. Gibbons.* Cf. **367**, 126; **785**, 82.
14. *Dr. Hobbs.* v. n. **206**, 188.
17. *The only one*, etc. Cf. **748**[2], 27, n; **785**, 83–87; **899**, 16–53.
24. *Par manière d'acquit.* "For form's sake" "A passage in a letter from our author to Jacob Tonson, dated by Malone, February, 1696, lets us know yet more plainly, that to the niggard disposition of this bookseller **we**

owe that the *Notes*, as here acknowledged, were rather slurred over than written with due care: 'I am not sorry that you will not allow any thing towards the Notes; for to make them good, wou'd have cost me half a yeare's time at least Those I write shall be only marginall, to help the unlearned, who understand not the poeticall fables. The Prefaces, as I intend them, will be somewhat more learned. It wou'd require seaven yeares to translate Virgil exactly. But I promise you once more to do my best in the four remaining books, as I have hitherto done in the foregoing. — Upon triall I find all of your trade are sharpers, and you not more than others; therefore I have not wholly left you. Mr. Aston does not blame you for getting as good a bargain as you cou'd, though I cou'd have gott an hundred pounds more: and you might have spared almost all your trouble, if you had thought fit to publish the proposals for the first subscriptions; for I have guinneas offer'd me every day, if there had been room; I believe, modestly speaking, I have refus'd already 25. I mislike nothing in your letter therefore, but onely your upbraiding me with the publique encouragement, and my own reputation concern'd in the notes; when I assure you I cou'd not make them to my mind in less than half a year's time.' "
[Scott.]

709², n. Past. IV. 72. *Dea nec*. So F1; F2 reads *dea non*.
　Virgil had. F1 reads *Virgil has*, which perhaps should have been retained in the text.
　Condé's father. F1 reads *Condé*, omitting *father*.

710¹, n. Geor. II. *The Praises of Italy*. Dryden refers to a piece printed in *Miscellany Poems*, 1684.
　My Miscellany. F1 reads *the* Miscellany. *Bowyer*. Cf. 708², 18.

710², n. Geor. II. *Laudato*. Georgics, ii. 412, 413: cf. 461, 570, 571.
　n. Geor. IV. 27. *Le roi*, etc. "The king will think it over;" the formula for refusing the royal assent to a bill passed by parliament.
　n. Geor. IV. 477. *Fifty*. Dryden's, or the printer's, mistake for *fifteen*.
　n. Geor. IV. 656. *Ariosto*. Cf. 289¹, 9, n.

711¹, n. Æn. I. 111. *Macareus and Canace*. Cf. 92-95.
　n. Æn. I. 196. *In a passion*. F1 reads *in Passion*.
　n. Æn. I. 451. *Ancient Greek poem*. The Homeric *Hymn to Aphrodite*.

711², n. Æn. III. 132. *Bochartus*. v. 494¹, 47, and n. 494¹, 42.
　n. Æn. IV. 944. *Dira*, etc. Garbled from, *Dira detestatio Nulla expiatur victima* (*Epode* v. 89, 90).

712¹, n. Æn. IV. 944. *Uses, in the*. F1 reads *uses in the*; F2 *uses the*.
　Omina. FF read *omnia*.

712², n. Æn. VI. 586. *Sir Robert Howard*. Cf. B. S. xx; 11.

713¹, n. Æn. VI. 1156. *Secretisque piis*. v. 493², 23, n.

714¹, n. Æn. VI. 1235. *Two gates*, etc. v. n. 610, 1237. Two lines below the first quotation F2 has *9th* (for *19th*, which is the reading of F1).
　n. Æn. VII. 367. *That Lavinia was averse*, etc. Cf. 716¹ (*n. Æn. XII. 100*).

714², n. Æn. VII. 1020. *On the same*. Perhaps a misprint for *in the same*.
　When a poet. Cf. 494², 41, n.
　n. Æn. VIII. 34. Χρύσεα χαλκείων "As gold [is richer] than brass." *Iliad*, vi. 236.
　n. Æn. IX. 853. Σὺν, etc. *Odyssey*, v. 295, 296.

715¹, n. Æn. IX. 1094. *Sic quia*, etc. "Because the poverty of my native language forces me to do so." Dryden writes from a hazy memory of Lucretius, i. 830-833; iii. 258-261.
　Si Græco, etc. Cf. 26¹, 41, n.
　Ma sì, etc. "Each man's cuirass was so perfect that it could not be pierced in any corner." *Orlando Furioso*, xxvi. 124.

715², n. Æn. X. 312. *Camilla*. Cf. 509², 10.
　n. Æn. X. 662. *Sir Robert Howard*. Cf. 499², 42, n.

716¹, n. Æn. X. 662. *Accus'd*. So F1; F2 reads *accurs'd*.

716², n. Æn. XII. 808. *Six last*. FF read *sixth last*.

717. Translations from Ovid's Art of Love, etc. It is not wholly impossible that Dryden withheld these pieces from the press because of their extreme indecency: cf. 741², 44 f; 746¹, 18 f. In the following notes the 1709 edition of the *Art of Love* is cited as ed. 1, and the 1704 texts as 5M.

719, 84. *Isis'*. v. 396-400, 769-1041.
　103. *Berries*. Probably *hillocks ;* less likely, *burrows :* v. N. E. D.
　127. *Plaudit*. In italics in ed. 1 and 5M.
　132. *The Best*. "Alluding to a well-known toast — a favorite with our straightforward fathers." Saintsbury. More definite information as to this toast may be gathered from the second stanza of Dorset's song to *Bonny Black Bess*. Cf. Byron, *Don Juan*, ix. 55-57.
　149. *Nor*. 5M reads *not*.

720, 206. *Urn*. Ed. 1 reads *Urns*, but cf. rhyme.

721, 253. *Know'st*. Ed. 1 reads *knowest*, which should have been retained in the text.
　291. *Baian*. Spelled *Bajan* in ed. 1.

722, 321. *Myrrha*. Cf. 806-811.
　325. *In Ida's*, etc. Cf. 402, 109-120; 432, 68-86; 594, 33-46; 601, 604.
　364. *Io*. v. 396-400, 769-1041.
　369. *The son*. "The Minotaur." Scott.

723, 374. *Thy daughter*. "Scylla." Scott.
　381. *Phædra*. Cf. 601, 605; 725, 576; 729, 851.

725, 577. *Adonis*. Cf. 811, 380-389.
　605. *On the shore*. So 5M; ed. 1 reads *in the shore*.
　608. *The Mimallonian dames*. Cf. 360, 194.

726, 610. *Silenus*. Cf. 297¹, 7; 431-433.
　611. *Clear*. Very drunk: v. N. E. D., under *Clear*, 24.

727, 737. *Phalaris*. "The famous brazen bull of Phalaris, tyrant of Agrigentum in Sicily (about B. C. 570), in which he burnt alive his victims, is here, for the sake of rhyme, converted into a cow. Perillus, the inventor of the engine of torture, was the first to suffer by it." [Scott.]

739. *A rightful doom*, etc. Cf. **122**, 1010, 1011.

728, 778. *Achilles*. Cf. **868**, 261–287.

782. *The nobler Pallas*. Cf. **624**, 1097.

799. *Grateful*. Here used for *pleasing*. [Scott.] Suggested by *gratum* in the Latin.

729, 851. *Perithous*. Cf. **787**, 50, n; **756**, 358.

871. *Proteus*. Cf. **483**, **484**, 557–598.

4. *But Cupid*, etc. Latin heroic poetry is written in hexameters; Latin elegiac poetry in couplets, the hexameter alternating with the pentameter: hence the term *unequal* (l. 34), which, however, is Dryden's, not Ovid's.

730, 7. *Hippodamia's*. Dryden accents incorrectly, *Hippoda'mia* instead of *Hippodami'a;* cf. **601**, 606, n. For the story, v. **857**, 292 f.

731. Alexander's Feast. On September 3, 1697, Dryden wrote in a letter to his sons at Rome: "I am writing a Song for St. Cecilia's Feast, who, you know, is the patroness of musick. This is troublesome, and no way beneficial; but I could not deny the Stewards of the Feast, who came in a body to me to desire that kindness, one of them being Mr. Bridgman, whose parents are your mother's friends." Notwithstanding this statement, which shows that Dryden had begun work on his poem nearly three months before St. Cecilia's Day, an apocryphal story has been often repeated, that he wrote *Alexander's Feast* at a single sitting. (The tale goes back to Warton, *Essay on the Genius and Writings of Pope*, § 8, where it is given on fifth-hand authority. Against it also is a statement in a lost letter by Dryden, referred to by Birch — see Malone, I, 1, 286 — that he spent almost a fortnight in composing and correcting the poem.) According to another story (first printed by Derrick), which may be true, Dryden ultimately received forty pounds for his work (*Ibid.* 287).

Malone relates that Lord Chief Justice Marlay, when a young man, frequented Will's Coffee-House, and, "*Alexander's Feast*, not long after its appearance, being the theme of every critic, young Marlay, among others, took an opportunity of paying his court to the author; and congratulated him on having produced the finest and noblest ode that had ever been written in any language. 'You are right, young gentleman,' replied Dryden, 'a nobler ode never *was* produced, nor ever *will*.'" (*Ibid.* 476, 477.)

It would be interesting to know Dryden's direct source for the incidents of this poem. Athenæus (576 D) writes: "Did not Alexander the Great keep with him Thais the Athenian courtesan, of whom Clitarchus relates that she was the cause of the burning of the palace in Persepolis?" The same writer (538 F) speaks of Timotheus as one of the flute-players at the marriage feast celebrated by Alexander after his capture of Darius. Suidas (under Τιμόθεος) relates that

Alexander was extremely fond of music, and that Timotheus so moved him by his strains, that, as he was listening to him, he jumped up to arms. (This Timotheus of Alexander's time must be distinguished from the great musician and poet Timotheus, who died in B. C. 357.) But Dryden is not likely to have read either Athenæus or Suidas.

Burton relates: "Timotheus the musician compelled Alexander to skip up and down and leave his dinner" (*Anatomy of Melancholy*, ii, § 2, mem. 6, subs. 3). This passage may be the germ of Dryden's ode. Burton's authority is Cardan, *De Subtilitate*, xiii: *Alterum Timothei, qui modo mutato Alexandrum coegit alacritate impulsum exilire e convivio*.

On St. Cecilia, v. n. **253**, 52.

9. *Thais*. Dryden originally wrote *Lais;* in a letter to Tonson he cautions him: "Remember in the copy of verses for St. Cecilia, to alter the name of *Lais*, which is twice there, for *Thais;* those two ladyes were contemporaryes, which caus'd that small mistake." (Malone, I, 2, 60.)

29. *Sublime*, etc. Cf. **544**, 646; **579**, 115.

30. *Olympia*. The name of Alexander's mother was *Olympias;* the change to *Olympia* may be either a blunder or a deliberate alteration to avoid accumulation of sibilants. [Saintsbury.]

40. *Affects to nod*. Cf. **655**, 153, 154.

732, 49. *The jolly god*, etc. Lines 49–60 might well be inclosed in quotation marks, which are not used at all in the original editions.

52. *Honest face*. Cf. **460**. 540, n; **769**, 100.

57 *Soldier's*. Ed. 1 and that in *Fables* read *Soldiers*, but *Soldier's* is found in l. 62, making it clear that a singular is intended.

67. *Battles*. The early texts read *Battails*.

107. *The many*, etc. Cf. **775**, 545, n; **777**, 665.

733. To Mr. Granville. In 1695 several of the leading actors, including Betterton and Mrs. Bracegirdle, seceded from the United Patentees (cf. headnote, p. **153**), whose theater was in Drury Lane, and established a house of their own in Lincoln's Inn Fields. Granville's play was acted by Betterton's company. Dryden's references, in this poem, to the rivalry between the two houses, brought forth a retort from George Powell, the principal actor at the theater in Drury Lane, in the preface to an anonymous tragedy, *The Fatal Discovery*, published in 1698. The following extracts are reprinted from Malone (I, 1; 311, 312):

"— Here I am afraid he makes but a coarse compliment, when this great wit, with his treacherous memory, forgets that he had given away his laurels upon record twice before, viz. once to Mr. Congreve [p. **412**] and another time to Mr. Southerne [p. **278**, but Powell exaggerates]. Pr'ythee, old Œdipus, expound this mystery! Dost thou set up thy transubstantiation miracle in the donation of thy idol bays, that thou hast them fresh, new, and whole, to give them three times over? . . .

" — For the most mortal stroke at us, he charges us with downright *murdering of plays, which we call reviving.* I will not derogate from the merit of those senior actors of both sexes, of the other house, that shine in their several perfections, in whose lavish praises he is so highly transported; but, at the same time, he makes himself but an arbitrary judge on our side, to condemn unheard, and that under no less a conviction than murder, when I cannot learn, for a fair judgment upon us, that his reverend crutches have ever brought him within our doors since the division of the companies. 'T is true, I think, we have revived some pieces of Dryden, as his *Sebastian, Maiden Queen, Marriage à la Mode, King Arthur,* etc. But here let us be tried by a Christian Jury, the Audience, and not receive the bowstring from his Mahometan Grand Signiorship. 'T is true, his more particular pique against us, as he has declared himself, is in relation to our reviving his *Almanzor* [*The Conquest of Granada*]. . . . I confess, he is a little severe, when he will allow our best performance to bear no better fruit than a crab vintage. Indeed, if we young actors spoke but half as sourly as his old gall scribbles, we should be all crab all over."

This is a peculiar diatribe, since it is obvious that all Dryden's strictures, with the exception of the *crab vintage* (l. '38), refer to the *senior actors* at Lincoln's Inn Fields. The text of the poem contained in *The Genuine Works in Verse and Prose of the Right Honourable George Granville, Lord Lansdowne,* 1736, contains the following notes: (on l. 35) "*Mr. Betterton's Company* in Lincolns-Inn Fields;" (on l. 38) "Drury Lane *Play-House.*" As these do not occur in the 1698 edition of *Heroic Love,* they can scarcely be due to Dryden himself.

The following passage in Downes's *Roscius Anglicanus* (ed. Knight, 1886, p. 46) will serve as a commentary on ll. 19–22: "In the space of Ten Years past, Mr. *Betterton* to gratify the desires and Fancies of the Nobility and Gentry; procur'd from Abroad the best Dances and Singers, as, Monsieur *L'Abbe,* Madam *Sublini,* Monsieur *Balon, Margarita Delpine, Maria Gallia* and divers others; who, being Exorbitantly Expensive,produc'd small Profit to him and his Company, but vast Gain to themselves." Apparently the Drury Lane Company adopted similar devices to win favor: v. Epilogue to Farquhar's *Love and a Bottle.*

734¹, 21. *And,* etc. Cf. **278,** 11.

29. *Itys.* Slain by his mother Procne, and offered by her as food to his father Tereus.

To my Friend Mr. Motteux. This epistle is in large part a feeble reply to Collier's *Short View:* v. B. S. lxi; n. **734²,** 18; and cf. **742¹,** 13–22; **745¹,** 29 f; **749¹,** 30 f; **873,** 61–68; **890,** 1–41; **899** (*Epil.*). Collier's book had a great and salutary influence on the morals of the English stage; Dryden seeks to confuse the issue by likening him to the Puritans, who in 1642 had suppressed the theater

entirely. Collier himself was a Tory, an High Churchman, and a fanatical adherent of James II.

734², 4. *Solomon.* Ed. 1698 reads *Salomon.*

18. *Their faults,* etc. "The poet here endeavors to vindicate himself from the charge of having often,and designedly, ridiculed the clerical function." Scott. This had been one of the charges pressed most vigorously by Collier against Dryden: cf. **745¹,** 23 f; and, for the grounds of the accusation, **111,** 99; **111,** 128, n; **492²,** 46–49.

19. *Rebellion,* etc. "Cf. 1 Samuel xv. 23: 'For rebellion is as the sin of witchcraft.'" [Christie.]

35. *His tripled unity.* v. B. S. xxiii.

735¹. Epigram on Tonson. *Faction Display'd,* a satirical poem first published in 1704, and attributed to William Shippen, contains the following passage:

> Now the Assembly to adjourn prepar'd, }
> When *Bibliopolo* from behind appear'd, }
> As well describ'd by th' old Satyrick Bard: }
> *With leering Looks, Bulfac'd, and Freckled fair,* }
> *With two left Legs, and Judas-colour'd Hair,* }
> *With Frowzy Pores, that taint the ambient Air.* }

In regard to this epigram, Malone (I, 1, 525) tells the following anecdote, the source of which the present editor has been unable to discover:

"On another occasion, Tonson having refused to advance him a sum of money for a work on which he was employed, he sent a second messenger to the bookseller, with a very satirical triplet; adding, 'Tell the dog that he who wrote these lines can write more.'"

Lines to Mrs. Creed. Mrs. Creed was the daughter of the Sir Gilbert Pickering mentioned in B. S. xviii. Of this Sir Gilbert Pickering both Dryden and his mother were own cousins (Malone, I, 1, 28).

Christie notes that "*skilful*" would do as well " as *well-wrought* to fill up the gap in the third line.

735². The Monument of a Fair Maiden Lady. The text on the monument in Bath Abbey reads *but seem'd* in l. 29. The other variations mentioned by Christie do not occur in the *Fables* or in the copy of the inscription sent to the editor by the Rector of Bath.

736, 20. *For marriage,* etc.

> But like a lampe of balsamum, desir'd
> Rather t' adorne then last, shee soone expird,
> Cloth'd in her virgin-white integritie;
> For marriage, though it doe not stain, doth dye.
>   Donne, *A Funerall Elegie* (ed. Grosart, i. 127; Riverside ed. p. 97).

Cf. **270²,** 4, n.

Fables. Dryden received from Tonson only £300 for this volume, of which £268, 15s. were paid to him at the time of contract, and the remainder to his heirs on the publication of a second edition in 1713.

The motto is from *Æneid,* v. 55–57: "Now are we near the ashes and the bones of our parent, surely, I think, not without the purpose and the guidance of the gods." The reference of course is to the translations from Chaucer in the volume.

The following excerpts from a letter of Wordsworth to Sir Walter Scott, November 7, 1805, are of special interest in connection with the *Fables :*

"I was much pleased to hear of your engagement with Dryden; not that he is, as a poet, any great favourite of mine. I admire his talents and genius highly, but his is not a poetical genius. The only qualities I can find in Dryden that are *essentially* poetical, are a certain ardour and impetuosity of mind, with an excellent ear. It may seem strange that I do not add to this great command of language; *that* he certainly has, and of such language too, as it is most desirable that a poet should possess, or rather, that he should not be without. But it is not language that is, in the highest sense of the word, poetical, being neither of the imagination nor of the passions — I mean of the amiable, the ennobling, or intense passions. I do not mean to say that there is nothing of this in Dryden, but as little, I think, as is possible, considering how much he has written. You will easily understand my meaning, when I refer to his versification of *Palamon and Arcite,* as contrasted with the language of Chaucer. Dryden has neither a tender heart, nor a lofty sense of moral dignity. Whenever his language is poetically impassioned, it is mostly upon unpleasing subjects, such as the follies, vices, and crimes of classes of men, or of individuals. That his cannot be the language of imagination, must have necessarily followed from this; that there is not a single image from nature in the whole body of his works; and in his translation from Virgil, whenever Virgil can be fairly said to have his *eye* upon his object, Dryden always soils [*spoils* ?] the passage.

" — I think his translations from Boccaccio are the best, at least the most poetical, of his poems. It is many years since I saw Boccaccio, but I remember that Sigismunda is not married by him to Guiscard (the names are different in Boccaccio in both tales, I believe, certainly in Theodore, &c.) [Really, only in the latter tale.] I think Dryden has much injured the story by the marriage, and degraded Sigismunda's character by it. He has also, to the best of my remembrance, degraded her still more, by making her love absolute sensuality and appetite; Dryden had no other notion of the passion. [Cf. n. **501**², 37.] With all these defects, and they are very gross ones, it is a noble poem. Guiscard's answer, when first reproached by Tancred, is noble in Boccaccio, nothing but this: *Amor può molto più che ne voi ne io possiamo.* This, Dryden has spoiled. He says first very well: 'The faults of love by love are justified,' and then come four lines of miserable rant, quite *à la Maximin*" [v. **135**, 78, n]. (KNIGHT, *Life of Wordsworth.* 1889. vol. ii, pp. 27–29.)

737¹. *The Duke of Ormond.* "James Butler (1665–1745), second Duke of Ormond, was second son of the gallant Earl of Ossory, and grandson to the great Duke of Ormond [v. n. **120**, 817], to whose honors he succeeded in 1688. After being favored by King William, and holding high office under Queen Anne, he entered into relations with the Pretender, and in 1715, soon after the accession of George I, he was impeached of high treason. He consulted his safety by flying abroad, and passed the remainder of his life in exile." [SCOTT.]

5. *The lives of Plutarch.* v. B. S. lii.

737², 2. *Your heroic father.* v. **120**, 831, n.

738¹, 43. *The last,* etc. "This character of the unfortunate nobleman was not exaggerated." [SCOTT.] He atoned by private virtues for lack of public capacity.

738², 1. *Poplicola.* Publius Valerius Publicola (or *Poplicola,* the name meaning "the people's friend"), the successor of Collatinus (v. n. **132**, 317) in the consulship. Cf. n. **10**, 249.

31. *Human.* So F; perhaps *humane* should be substituted, since the two words were not distinguished in spelling.

60. Αἰδέομαι Τρῶας. "I stand in awe of the Trojans." HOMER, *Iliad,* vi. 442; xxii. 105, quoted by Cicero *ad Atticum,* ii. 5 and elsewhere.

739¹, 24. *Numen commune,* etc. "A common divinity, having fellowship with two worlds." Adapted freely from *De Raptu Proserpinæ,* i. 89–91, where Claudian addresses Mercury as belonging both to the gods of heaven and to those of Hades.

39. *That.* "*That* often serves as a substitute for *because,* after *because* has been once used." [SAINTSBURY.]

60. *Ulysses,* etc. v. **870**, 449–459.

739², 24. *Spatiis,* etc. *Georgics,* iv. 147; cf. **479**, 218, 219.

28. *When,* etc. "At the battle of Landen, 29 July, 1693, after nearly losing his life amidst the terrible carnage of the day, he was taken prisoner by the French; but, after a brief captivity at Namur, where he found opportunities of munificence towards his fellow prisoners, he was exchanged for the Duke of Berwick." A. W. WARD, in D. N. B.

61. *Non ignara,* etc. *Æneid,* i. 630; cf. **533**, 890, 891.

740¹, 5. *De meliore luto.* "Of better clay." Juvenal, xiv. 35, with *de* added by Dryden. Cf. **174**², 74, n.

8. *Teucri,* etc. *Æneid,* vi. 648, 649; cf. **605**, 881, 882.

46. *Ostendunt.* *Æneid,* vi. 869, 870, with a change of tense from future to present; cf. **609**, 1202, 1203.

740², 5. *Of the expense.* So F; SS. reads *in the expense.* The original phrase is confused, but probably by Dryden's error rather than the printer's.

11. *A certain nobleman.* "This was, I suppose, our author's old foe, Villiers, Duke of Buckingham, the tardy progress of whose great

buildings at Cliefden was often the subject of satire." [Scott.] Cf. B. S. xxviii; **116**, 544, n.

40. *Sandys.* v. 88¹, 4, n; **385¹**, 34.

43. *Fairfax.* Cf. **917**, 115, n.

50. *Spenser*, etc.

> — Through infusion sweete
> Of thine [Chaucer's] owne spirit, which doth in
> me survive,
> I follow here the footing of thy feete.
>
> *Faerie Queene*, IV. ii. 34.

741¹, 29. *Mr. Hobbes.* v. *Leviathan*, i. 3: "Of the Consequence or *Train* of Imaginations."

34. *The octave rhyme.* "The stanza was used, in French, by Thibaut, King of Navarre, in the previous century, and before Boccaccio, in Italian, by the author of the *Cantare di Fiorio e Biancifiore.* But Boccaccio was the first author to give the octave its rank as the Italian *measure for heroic verse* [**319¹**, 38]." Ker.

50. *Mr. Rymer.* On this critic, v. B. S. xxx, xxxi; **287²**, 30, n. He is the source of Dryden's misinformation in this passage as to Chaucer, who was strongly affected by French and Italian literature, but not at all by Provençal.

"— And they, with us, that would write verse, as King *Richard, Savery de Mauleon*, and *Rob. Grostead*, finding the English stubborn and unweildy, fell readily to that of *Provence*, as more glib, and lighter on the Tongue. But they who attempted verse in English, down till *Chaucers* time, made an heavy pudder, and are always miserably put to 't for a word to clink: which commonly fall so awkard, and unexpectedly as dropping from the Clouds by some Machine or Miracle. "*Chaucer* found an Herculean labour on his Hands; And did perform to Admiration. He seizes all Provencal, French or Latin that came in his way, gives them a new garb and livery, and mingles them amongst our English: turns out English, gowty, or superannuated, to place in their room the foreigners, fit for service, train'd and accustomed to Poetical Discipline. "But tho' the Italian reformation was begun and finished well nigh at the same time by *Boccace, Dante*, and *Petrarch.* Our language retain'd something of the churl; something of the Stiff and Gothish did stick upon it, till long after *Chaucer.* "*Chaucer* threw in Latin, French, Provencial, and other Languages, like new Stum to raise a Fermentation: In Queen *Elizabeth's* time it grew fine, but came not to an Head and Spirit, did not shine and sparkle till Mr. *Waller* set it a running." *A Short View of Tragedy*, 1693, pp. 78, 79.

"Rymer knew something about Provençal poetry, and something about Chaucer, and through Dryden and Pope has made it a matter of traditional belief that Chaucer belongs, in some way or other, to 'the Provençal School.' Dryden seems not to have distinguished between Provençal and old French." [Ker.]

741², 22. *The other harmony of prose.* "A reminiscence of Aristotle, *Poetics*, iv., τῆς λεκτικῆς ἁρμονίας." Ker.

33. *They who*, etc. Cf. n. **135**, 54; n. **136**, 149. There may also be a reference to Blackmore; v. **748²**, 27, n; **899¹**, 16, n; **899²**, 41, n.

48. *Dead coloring.* Cf. **51**, 7: the *dead coloring* is the first coat of paint applied to the canvas, used as a foundation for the rest. Dryden seems to have had much interest in the technique of painting; cf. **5**, 60, n.

57. *Stav'd.* "Like contraband hogsheads." Ker.

742¹, 12. *Versus*, etc. *Ars Poet.* 322: "Verses empty of content, and tuneful trifles."

18. *A religious lawyer*, etc. Collier: v. B. S. lxi; **734** (Motteux), n.

23. *I resume.* etc. A letter of October, 1699, from Dryden to Charles Montagu, of which the earlier portion is given in n. **784** (To John Driden), concludes as follows:

"My thoughts at present are fix'd on Homer: and I find him a poet more according to my genius than Virgil, and consequently hope I may do him more justice, in his fiery way of writeing; which, as it is liable to more faults, so it is capable of more beauties than the exactness and sobriety of Virgil. Since 't is for my country's honour as well as for my own, that I am willing to undertake this task, I despair not of being encourag'd in it by your favour, who am,

Sir,
Your most obedient Servant,
John Dryden."

58. *Copying.* Possibly a word has dropped out at this point.

61. *Dido*, etc. Contrast **505²**, 27–35.

742², 15. *Mr. Hobbes*, etc. Hobbes completed his translation of Homer at eighty-six. His blunders in mathematics had brought ridicule upon him.

22. *Now the words are the coloring*, etc. Cf. **514²**, 23 f.

43. *Choleric*, etc. "Dryden had before him the *locus classicus* on humors: v. **824**, 138–161." [Ker.]

50. *Impiger*, etc. Horace, *Ars Poet.* 121.

53. *Quo fata*, etc. Virgil, *Æneid*, v. 709: "However much the fates may drag us to and fro, let us follow them."

743¹, 3. *Longinus*, etc. *On the Sublime*, ch. xii. Dryden knew the work in Boileau's translation; v. B. S. xxx.

10. *A new machine.* "Dryden's memory had misplaced the dream of Agamemnon, which in the second book comes *before* the Catalogue of the Ships." Ker.

43. *Chaucer's stories*, etc. Dryden's information on this topic is sadly at fault. There is no evidence that Chaucer was acquainted with the *Decameron.* He drew the plot, and much of the detail, of *Palamon and Arcite* from Boccaccio's epic the *Teseide.* The story of Griselda he took from Petrarch, whose source was Boccaccio. The main source of his

Troilus and Criseyde was Boccaccio's poem *Il Filostrato*. Though the direct originals of *The Wife of Bath's Tale* and *The Cock and the Fox* are unknown, Chaucer certainly did not invent the plot of either of them; the first story is probably of Celtic origin, the second is found in the mediæval beast epic of Reynard the Fox.

743², 2. *Who love*, etc. Cf. **356¹,** 4 (*Arg.*), n.

57. *Inopem*, etc. *Metamorphoses*, iii. 466: "Plenty has made me poor."

744¹, 2. *Bartholomew Fair.* By Ben Jonson. Dryden apparently remembers vaguely the general course of the action of the play, and the words of Littlewit at the opening of it: "A pretty conceit, and worth the finding! I have such luck to spin out these fine things still, and, like a silkworm, out of myself. . . . When a quirk or a quiblin does 'scape thee, and thou dost not watch and apprehend it, and bring it afore the constable of conceit, . . . let them carry thee out o' the archdeacon's court into his kitchen, and make a Jack of thee, instead of a John."

7. *Virgil*, etc. Cf. **25²; 502²,** 48, n.

22. *They who*, etc. Cf. **514², 515.**

25. *The turn of words*, etc. Cf. **319²,** 41, n; **385²,** 5 f; **513¹,** 7 f.

53. *One of our late great poets.* Cowley; cf. **181¹,** 45, n.

744², 11. *Lord Rochester.* Cf. **515¹,** 46–48; B. S. xxxviii, xxxix; **283²,** 4, n.

16. *Nimis poeta.* "Too much a poet." The source is not Catullus, but Martial, iii. 44.

21. *Auribus*, etc. "Fitted to the ears of that time." Tacitus (*Dialogus*, 21) describes an oration of Calvus as *auribus iudicum accommodata*.

29. *'T is true*, etc. This refers to a passage in Speght's preface to his edition of Chaucer, published in 1598 and 1602, reprinted in 1687, quoted by Scott: "And for his [Chaucer's] verses, although in divers places they seem to us to stand of unequal measures, yet a skilful reader, who can scan them in their nature, shall find it otherwise." Modern study of the pronunciation of English in Chaucer's time has shown the correctness of Speght's view, which is now universally accepted.

51. *Harrington.* "Sir John Harrington's translation of the *Orlando Furioso* of Ariosto appeared in 1591." [KER.]

52. *Our numbers*, etc. Rymer's summary of the contents of chapter vi of his *Short View of Tragedy*, from which an excerpt has already been given (n. **741¹,** 50) contains the passage: "*Chaucer* refin'd our English. Which in perfection by *Waller*. His Poem on the Navy Royal, beyond all modern Poetry in any Language. Before him our Poets better expressed their thoughts in Latin."

But, as Christie points out, Dryden had already written, in the dedication of *The Rival Ladies* (1664):

"— But the excellence and dignity of it [rhyme] were never fully known till Mr. Waller taught it: he first made writing easily an art; first show'd us to conclude the sense most commonly in distichs, which, in the verse of those before him, runs on for so many lines together that the reader is out of breath to overtake it. This sweetness of Mr. Waller's lyric poesy was afterwards follow'd in the epic by Sir John Denham, in his *Cooper's Hill*, a poem which, . . . for the majesty of the style, is, and ever will be, the exact standard of good writing." (SS. ii. 137.) Cf. **91; 319²,** 44 f; **512²,** 5; **514¹,** 52, n.

54. *I need*, etc. The little that Dryden says of Chaucer's life is of course inaccurate; see the Cambridge edition of Chaucer.

745¹, 13. *Augustus*, etc. Cf. **513¹,** 35–52.

22. *The tale of Piers Plowman.* Referring to *The Plowman's Tale*, a spurious poem included in all editions of Chaucer from 1542 to 1775, when Tyrwhitt rejected it from his *Canterbury Tales*.

31. *The scandal*, etc. Cf. **734²,** 18, n.

52. *Scandalum magnatum.* "Words spoken in derogation of a peer, a judge, or other great officer of the realm. This was distinct from mere slander in the earlier law, and was considered a more heinous offense." BOUVIER, *Law Dictionary.*

745², 7. *A king of England.* "It is almost unnecessary to mention their names — Henry II and Thomas à Becket." SCOTT.

13. *Dr. Drake.* Dr. James Drake wrote, in answer to Collier, a work called *The Antient and Modern Stages Survey'd; or, Mr. Collier's View of the Immorality and Profaneness of the English Stage set in a true light*, published anonymously in 1699.

21. *Prior læsit.* "He was the aggressor."

47. *Baptista Porta.* Giambattista della Porta (1543?–1615), Neapolitan physician. His *De Humana Physiognomia Libri IV* was published in 1586.

746¹, 19. *My enemies.* Collier and Blackmore, and possibly Milbourne also: cf. **734** (To MOTTEUX), n; **748²,** 27, nn.

40. *Totum*, etc. "I wish all this unsaid."

46. *Novels.* Cf. **487²,** 11, n.

746², 17. *Wincing*, etc. From *The Miller's Tale*, 77, 78.

25. *Reviving.* So SS. and K; F reads *receiving*.

26. *The late Earl of Leicester.* Philip Sidney (1619–98), third Earl of Leicester, to whom Dryden had dedicated *Don Sebastian* in 1690. He was the elder brother of Algernon Sidney.

747¹, 34. *My lord*, etc. For evidences of Dryden's earlier reading of Chaucer, v. **220,** 212, n; **241,** 1806, n; **242,** 1860, n. He may have been prompted to it by the appearance of a reprint of Speght's Chaucer in 1687; cf. n. **744²,** 29.

43. *Multa*, etc. HORACE, *Ars Poet.* 70–72: "Many words that now have declined shall be born again; and others, which are now in honor, shall fall, if usage wills it, on which depend the judgment and the law and the rules of our discourse." In the first line *nunc* is Dryden's error for *jam;* in the same line F reads *renascuntur*.

747², 6. *Some old Saxon friends.* The most distinguished Saxon student of Dryden's time was George Hickes (1642–1715), but the editor can find no evidence that he was a friend of Dryden. Professor Ker conjectures that "Dryden was probably thinking particularly of Rymer."

21. *Grandam gold.* Professor Ker points out that Dryden uses the phrase *old grandam-and-aunt gold* in *The Wild Gallant* (act iv, sc. 1; SS. ii. 93).

31. *Facile,* etc. "It is easy to add to what is already invented."

38. *Mademoiselle de Scudéry.* The famous French writer of chivalric romances (1607–1701): cf. B. S. xxiii. "Her huge romances, *Artamenes* and *Clelia,* were in my childhood still read in some old-fashioned Scottish families, though now absolutely forgotten, and in no chance of being revived." [SCOTT.]

43. *Provençal.* v. n. **741¹**, 50.

748¹, 49. *Palamon and Arcite.* On the real source of the poem, v. n. **743¹**, 43. On the duration of the action of an epic poem, v. **507¹**, 23 f.

748², 27. *M——.* Luke Milbourne (1649–1720), a clergyman of the Church of England, had himself planned a translation of Virgil. He attacked Dryden's version in *Notes on Dryden's Virgil* (1698), where he fortified his criticisms by specimens of his own verses. Scott states (SS. xi. 76) that he also attacked Dryden's "person, and principles political and religious." Cf. **785**, 87.

B——. Sir Richard Blackmore (1650?–1729), physician and poet, had written two epic poems, *Prince Arthur* (1695) and *King Arthur* (1697). In a passage of the preface to the former (quoted by Malone, III, 647–649) he attacked Dryden for the indecency of his writings, resulting from his "irreligion and folly." In *A Satyr against Wit,* dated 1700, but probably published in the previous year, he renewed the charge. (Among the books mentioned in the *Term Catalogue* for Hilary Term, 1700, is *A Satyr upon a late Pamphlet entituled A Satyr against Wit.*) Dr Johnson gives a specimen of Blackmore's raillery in this poem, and states that in a later edition of it, angered by Dryden's reply, he omitted a compliment to the poet which had mitigated the satire of the first edition. Cf. **785**, 83; **899¹**, 16, n.

41. *Ogleby.* v. **135**, 102, n; cf. **176²**, 3–9.

61. *If I,* etc. Cf. **382¹**, 20, n.

749¹, 20. *The guardian angels,* etc. Cf. **289²–291¹.**

23. *Dares,* etc. v. **585**, 533–559.

30. *Mr. Collier.* v. B. S. lxi; **734** (To MOTTEUX), n.

47. "*The zeal,*" etc. v. Psalm lxix. 9; John ii. 17.

749², 20. *Seneffe.* F reads *Senneph.* "The battle of Seneffe in Flanders, in which the Prince of Condé was opposed to the Prince of Orange, was fought on August 11, 1674. Condé, not content with having defeated the rear guard of the enemy, in attempting to destroy the remainder of the Prince of Orange's army,

who had left his flank exposed as he decamped, lost a great number of men." [MALONE.]

29. *Demetri,* etc. HORACE, *1 Satires,* x. 90, 91: "You, Demetrius and Tigellius, I bid lament among the chairs of your scholars." Blackmore had once been a schoolmaster.

To THE DUCHESS OF ORMOND. "Lady Mary Somerset, second wife of the duke. She was second daughter of Henry Somerset, first Duke of Beaufort." [SCOTT.] Cf. **150**, 941, n.

4 (verse). *A doubtful palm.* "Dryden here says of Chaucer in reference to Virgil what Juvenal said of Virgil in reference to Homer: 'The composer of the *Iliad* shall be sung, and the lays of high-sounding Maro, which make the palm of victory doubtful' (*Satires,* xi. 180, 181)." [CHRISTIE.]

750, 14. *Plantagenet.* Scott thought that the reference was to Blanche, first wife of John of Gaunt, Chaucer's patron, the fourth son of Edward III. Like her husband, this lady was a Plantagenet, being the daughter of Henry, Duke of Lancaster, the grandson of Edmund, brother of Edward I. But Professor Craik is doubtless right in rejecting this supposition. "The explanation" given by Scott, he writes, "leaves the principal part of the passage entirely unexplained. Chaucer's Plantagenet here is clearly not the Duchess Blanche, but Joan, daughter of Edmund of Woodstock, Earl of Kent, second son of Edward I by his second wife, Margaret of France, famous as the Fair Maid of Kent, married for the third and last time to Edward the Black Prince, by whom she was the mother of Richard II, having been previously the wife, first (it is understood) of Thomas Holland [later Earl of Kent], . . . secondly, of William Montague [Montacute], Earl of Salisbury (making the *three contending princes*), and commonly believed to be the Countess of Salisbury from whom the Order of the Garter, according to the well-known story, derived its name." (*History of English Literature,* 1871, vol. ii. pp. 116, 117.)

The fact that the *Fables* volume includes a version of *The Flower and the Leaf,* with its compliment to the Order of the Garter (v. **852**, 546–558), is an additional argument in favor of Professor Craik's explanation.

29. *Platonic year.* "A cycle imagined by some ancient astronomers, in which the heavenly bodies were supposed to go through all their possible movements and return to their original relative positions (after which, according to some, all events would recur in the same order as before)." N. E. D.

30. *O true Plantagenet,* etc. "John of Gaunt had by his mistress, Catharine Swynford, whom he afterwards married, three sons and a daughter, who were legitimated by act of parliament. John de Beaufort, the eldest of these, was created Earl of Somerset, and from him the ducal family of Beaufort are lineally descended. The patent of the first duke, the father of this Duchess of Ormond,

bears to be in consideration of his services, and of his most noble descent from Edward III." [Scott.]

46. *Etesian.* Properly, a name applied by Greek and Latin writers to certain annual winds, especially those that blow for forty days during the dog-days. Dryden uses it here of a gentle, steady breeze. N. E. D. quotes from *Phil. Trans.* xiv. 561 (1684): "These Eastern Winds (which I call our English Etesians)."

48. *Portunus.* Cf. **8**, 121, n; **582**, 314, 315.

51. *The land*, etc. Cf. **10**, 251, n.

59. *Nor hear the reins.* Christie aptly cites *Neque audit currus habenas.* (Virgil, *Georgics*, i. 514.)

62. *As Ormond's harbinger.* The Duchess of Ormond went to Ireland in April, 1697, and her husband followed in October. (Luttrell, *Brief Relation*, 1857, vol. iv, pp. 214, 288.)

64. *The waste*, etc. "Alluding to the wars of the Revolution in Ireland." Scott.

65. *Pales.* The god (goddess ?) of flocks and shepherds; Ceres, the goddess of agriculture: cf. **464**, 1; **787**, 7, 8.

70. *As when*, etc. Cf. **107**[1], 1 f.

751, 101. *Nor dare*, etc. "She seems to have been just recovered from a fever." Scott.

125. *Young Vespasian.* Titus Flavius Sabinus Vespasianus, better known, as a Roman emperor, by his first name. During the siege of Jerusalem, which he directed, he sought to spare the temple, and he mourned its destruction.

130. *The table of my vow.* The *tabula votiva* of Horace (*Odes*, i. 5. 13; *2 Satires*, i. 33). Persons saved from shipwreck used to hang up in the temple of Neptune or some other appropriate divinity a picture representing their escape; cf. **703**, 1114, 1115.

131. *Morley's.* "Dr. Christopher Love Morley, a physician of eminence." Scott.

133. *The Macedon*, etc. Alexander the Great; cf. **365**, note 6. The story is told by several writers, as Quintus Curtius, ix. 8.

752, 162. *Elisa.* Another name of Dido; cf. **12**, 65.

Palamon and Arcite. On this and Dryden's other translations and adaptations from early English, see Lounsbury, *Studies in Chaucer*, ch. vii; Schöpke, *Ueber Dryden's Bearbeitung Chaucer'scher Gedichte* (in *Anglia*, ii. 314–353, iii. 35–58); Tupper, *Dryden and Speght's Chaucer* (in *Modern Language Notes*, xii. 347–353).

12. *With Love*, etc. Repeated in **897**, 518.

753, 115. *His pennon.* "The poet here introduces a distinction well known in heraldry. The banner was a square flag, which only barons of a great lineage and power had a right to display. The pennon was a forked streamer borne by a knight: Theseus carried both to the field, each bearing a separate device. Chaucer says:

And by his baner born is his penoun."

Scott.

754, 175. *To do th' observance*, etc. Cf. **760**, 44, which translates Chaucer's:

And, for to doon his observaunce to May.

204. *Was one partition*, etc. "This may mean that the tower and the palace had a party wall in common, or that the tower was part of the outer wall of the palace." Saintsbury.

755, 222. *Shady walks between.* A reminiscence of Milton:

— a pillared shade
High overarched, and echoing walks between.
Paradise Lost, ix. 1106, 1107.

230. *Thick of bars.* Cf. **5**, 55, n. Chaucer's words are *thikke of many a barre.*

756, 301, 308. *Council.* So F; in Dryden's time *council* and *counsel* were not yet carefully distinguished: cf. **816**, 367.

358. *Perithous.* Dryden seems always to use this form in place of the correct *Pirithous;* cf. **787**, 50.

361. *Man.* F places a full stop after this word.

757, 404. *Extremest line.* Professor Saintsbury explains this as *outermost region.* Perhaps it is easier to suppose that Dryden was seeking to draw a metaphor from the two poles of the earth, where day and night are each six months long.

427. *Guilty of their vows.* "A Latinism, *voti reus;* cf. **582**, 307, n." [Christie.]

758, 500. *Or Mars*, etc. "Dryden has introduced Mars and the *quartil;* they are not in Chaucer." [Christie.] Cf. **18**[2], 13, n; **50**, 1165, n.

515. *Beholds*, etc. "This play of words, which is truly Ovidian, does not occur in Chaucer, nor is it in conformity with our author's general ideas of translating him: v. **743**[2], 45 f; **744**[1], 25 f." [Scott.]

759, 552. *Argus'.* v. **398**, **399**, 856–1003.

760, 12. *In causes.* "One of Dryden's frequent scholasticisms; *in their causes* would have been clearer." Saintsbury.

34. *Style.* Christie thinks that the word is used here in the sense of the Latin *stylus*, and refers for support to **151**, 1051. His argument is not convincing.

761, 88. *And angry*, etc. Cf. **521**, 2.

89. *Curst*, etc. Chaucer has simply, "Alas, that day that I was bore." Warton thinks that Dryden remembered Job iii. 3 f.

93. *Cadmus*, etc. Cf. **542**, 436.

115, 116. *Of such*, etc. This couplet (with the readings *times leave* and *That burnt*) concludes a short poem by Carew, *A Cruel Mistress.* Warton noted Dryden's appropriation of it.

149. *And Jove*, etc. Cf. **727**, 714, 715.

764, 364. *The proverb*, etc. *Amare et sapere vix deo conceditur.* "To love and to be wise is hardly granted to a god." From Publilius Syrus.

383. *Lover's.* F reads *Lovers.*

765, 414. *The bars.* "The palisades of the lists." [Scott.]

766, 483. *Sigils.* Cf. **853**, 606, n.

489. *Down-look'd.* With a downcast glance.

498. *Citheron.* Cf. **770**, 145, n.

515. *Below.* So F; but the sense requires *above.*

527. *Thrace.* Cf. **466**, 143.

548. *Strait.* F has *streight*, which, as often, obviously stands for *strait*, not *straight.*

767, 565. *Soft smiling.* So SS.; F reads *soft, smiling.*

580. *Sat.* So F; it might be better to substitute *sate*, to point the rhyme.

600. *Conquest.* This is personified, *Conquest*, in Chaucer; Dryden has confused the passage by prefixing the article.

614. *Two geomantic figures.* Chaucer wrote

> And over his heed ther shynen two figures
> Of sterres, that been cleped in scriptures,
> That oon Puella, that other Rubeus.

On this Speght comments, partially incorrectly: "The names of two figures in geomancy, representing two constellations in heaven. Puella signifieth Mars retrograde, and Rubeus Mars direct." This is sufficient to explain Dryden's rehandling of the passage; for an explanation of the subject matter, see Skeat's note on *Cant. Tales*, A 2045.

623. *Calisto.* A nymph of Diana, who was seduced by Jupiter. When her guilt had been discovered by Diana, as they were bathing, Juno turned her into a bear, in which form she was nearly slain by her son, Arcas. Jupiter, to avert this crime, gave mother and son places in the skies, as the constellations of the Great and the Little Bear. (F reads *Calistho;* the correct form is *Callisto.* Cf. p. **76**, where *Calisto* is retained from the early editions.) *Manifest of shame.* Cf. **112**, 204, n.

627. *Actæon.* A hunter who chanced to see Diana bathing. She changed him into a stag, and he was torn in pieces by his own dogs.

631. *Daphne.* v. **394**, 606 f.

634. *The Caledonian beast.* This is an error, by Dryden or the printer, for *Calydonian;* cf. **787**, 1, n. On the story, v. **787–792**.

768, 639. *The Volscian queen.* v. **624**, 1094 f; **681–688**, 753–1256.

661. *So princes*, etc. Dryden's complaint, not Chaucer's; cf. **414**, 100, n.

8. *Such chiefs*, etc. Cf. **623**, 975.

31. *Pruce.* Prussia. Scott.

769, 100. *Their honest god.* Cf. **460**, 540, n; **732**, 52.

104. *Posts.* The editions of 1700 and 1713 read *Pots.* The emendation to *posts*, adopted by all modern editors except Professor Saintsbury, seems practically certain; cf. **897**, 561.

770, 129. *Creator Venus*, etc. Dryden here mingles Lucretius with Chaucer; cf. **182**, 1–27. Spenser also imitates the same passage; v. *Faerie Queene*, IV. x. 44–47.

145. *Thou gladder*, etc. This line is directly from Chaucer; the island Cythera, not the mountain Cithæron, was really sacred to Venus. Cf. **766**, 498.

146. *Increase of Jove.* Cf. **256**, 208, and Dryden's footnote.

147. *Adonis.* Cf. **725**, 577; **811**, 382, n.

771, 201. *But such*, etc. Dryden here remembers Juvenal, vi. 314.

773, 381. *Leaden.* "His planetary metal." Saintsbury.

388. *Outridden.* Dryden has "most ridiculously mistaken" (Tyrwhitt) the sense of Chaucer's *outrede* (*at-rede* in Skeat's text), which really means *surpass in counsel.*

389. *Trin'd.* v. **50**, 1165, n.

774, 411. *Bought senates*, etc. "This line, containing a political allusion to the events of the Revolution, is Dryden's exclusively." [Scott.]

426. *Chronos'.* i. e. Saturn's.

442. *Leaning*, etc. Cf. **9**, 154.

775, 545. *Many.* In this substantive use of *many* there is probably confusion with the noun *meiny*, retinue; cf. **732**, 107.

777, 665. *The people*, etc. Cf. **732**, 107.

672. *The standing army.* Cf. **356**¹, 4 (*Arg.*), n.

689. *Popularly low.* Cf. **118**, 689.

778, 757, 758. *Destroy'd : void.* The repetition of this rhyme just below (ll. 766, 767) is a sign of Dryden's haste in writing.

779, 787. *Spirit 's.* F reads *Spirits.*

844–853. *But . . . know.* Dryden has modified Chaucer's lines into a passage that gives expression to his own sceptical temperament, which, however, did not preclude acceptance of the doctrines of the Catholic Church. On the concluding couplet, cf. **164**, **165**, 208–211.

780, 891. *With words*, etc. Here Dryden adds a touch of sarcasm not found in Chaucer.

781, 927. *Mourning Bride.* The italics (retained from F) point the compliment to Congreve's tragedy *The Mourning Bride*, acted and published in 1697.

960. *Mountain-ash.* So F.

982. *Swound.* F reads *Swoond.*

985. *While*, etc. In this description Dryden follows Chaucer closely, but compare also **675**, 281–303.

782, 1066. *A drop.* Cf. **811**, 384.

783, 1074. *Rechless.* F reads *Retchless.*

1144. *Eros and Anteros.* Here understood by Dryden as the gods of Love and Reciprocal Love.

784. To John Driden. This country gentleman was the second son of Sir John Driden, baronet, the elder brother of Erasmus Dryden (or Driden), the poet's father (Malone, I, 1, 321). He was born in 1635; he represented the county of Huntingdon in parliament in 1690, and from 1700 till his death in 1708.

Some interesting information as to this poem is contained in Dryden's letters. His former antagonist, Charles Montagu (v. n. **216**, Hind and Panther), was now First Lord of the Treasury, and a prominent member of the ministry to which John Driden of Chesterton, as is evident from ll. 127–134, 171–194, of the poem, was opposed. Desiring his patronage for his projected translation of Homer, the poet wrote to him in October, 1699, inclosing the epistle to his cousin:

"Sir,

"These verses had waited on you with the former [those *To the Duchess of Ormond*], but that they wanted that correction which I have given them, that they may the better endure the sight of so great a judge and poet. I am now in feare that I have purg'd them out of their spirit; as our Master Busby us'd to whip a boy so long, till he made him a confirm'd blockhead. My cousin Driden saw them in the country; and the greatest exception he made to them was, a satire against the Dutch valour in the last war. He desir'd me to omit it, (to use his own words) *out of the respect he had to his Sovereign.* I obey'd his commands, and left onely the praises, which I think are due to the gallantry of my own countrymen. In the description which I have made of a Parliament-man, I think I have not only drawn the features of my worthy kinsman, but have also given my own opinion of what an Englishman in Parliament ought to be; and deliver it as a memorial of my own principles to all posterity. I have consulted the judgment of my unbyass'd friends, who have some of them the honour to be known to you; and they think there is nothing which can justly give offence in that part of the poem. I say not this, to cast a blind on your judgment, (which I cou'd not do, if I indeavour'd it,) but to assure you, that nothing relateing to the publique shall stand without your permission; for it were to want common sence to desire your patronage, and resolve to disoblige you: And as I will not hazard my hopes of your protection, by refusing to obey you in any thing which I can perform with my conscience or my honour, so I am very confident you will never impose any other terms on me." (Malone, I, 2; 90, 91; the remainder of the letter is given in n. 742[1], 23.)

For other notices, see the excerpts on p. 737. Malone (I, 1, 325–327) mentions a tradition, of which he doubts the accuracy, that the *noble present* to which Dryden refers was the sum of five hundred pounds. Lines 7–13 of the poem, according to Scott, are added to John Driden's epitaph in the church at Chesterton.

43. *But you,* etc. "Sir Robert Driden inherited the paternal estate of Canons Ashby, while that of Chesterton descended to John, his second brother, to whom this poem is addressed, through his mother, daughter of Sir Robert Bevile." [SCOTT.]

53. *Industrious of.* Cf. **233,** 1143.

785, 75. *Pity,* etc. "It is a pity that the generous kind, etc." [CHRISTIE.]

82. *Gibbons.* Cf. **367,** 126, n; **709[1],** 13.

83. *Maurus.* Cf. **748[2],** 27, n; **899[1],** 16, n. The editor cannot find that Blackmore *robb'd and murder'd Maro's Muse,* and thinks that in l. 85 he may be confused with Milbourne. — "The fourteen-syllable line is of course used intentionally, and, as it were, pictorially. The sweep of the verse is as vast as that of Maurus." [SAINTSBURY.] Cf. **129,** 94, n.

87. *M-lb-rne.* Milbourne; cf. **748[2],** 27, n.

107. *Garth.* "Sir Samuel Garth (1661–1719), the ingenious author of *The Dispensary* (1699).

Although this celebrated wit and physician differed widely from Dryden in politics, being a violent Whig, they seem, nevertheless, to have lived in the most intimate terms. Sir Samuel had the honor to pronounce a Latin oration at the funeral of our poet. Garth's generosity consisted in maintaining a Dispensary for issuing advice and prescriptions gratis to the poor. This was highly disapproved of by the more selfish of his brethren, and by the apothecaries. The resulting disputes led to Sir Samuel's humorous poem." [SCOTT.]

109. *The viper's brood.*

Thou mak'st th' ingratefull *Viper* (at his birth) His dying Mother's belly to gnaw forth.
SYLVESTER, *Dubartas his First Weeke* (Sixth Day, ll. 250, 251).

118. *Produce.* F has periods after both this word and *bear* (l. 122); after *wit* (l. 124) it has an exclamation point, and after *found* (l. 126) a question mark. SS. and C. retain the period after *produce* and place a colon after *bear.*

786, 140. *Munster.* Cf. **30,** 145, n.

142. *Our foes,* etc. "A very bloody war had been recently concluded by the Peace of Ryswick in 1697. The House of Commons were averse to a renewal of the conflict, and, from fear of tyranny, were jealous of every attempt to maintain any military force. In 1698 the army was reduced to 7000 men, and in 1699 William saw himself compelled to dismiss his faithful and favorite Dutch guards. — The subsequent lines point obliquely at these measures, which were now matter of public discussion. Dryden's cousin was one of the Whig faction that opposed the king on the question of the army. As for the poet, his Jacobitical principles assented to everything that could embarrass King William. But, for the reasons which he has assigned in his letter to Montagu, he leaves his opinion concerning the disbanding of the army to be inferred from his panegyric on the navy, and his declamation against the renewal of the war." [SCOTT.] Cf. **356[1],** 4 (*Arg.*), n.

152. *Namur.* The capture of Namur in Belgium by William III in 1695 had led up to the Peace of Ryswick two years later.

188. *Your gen'rous grandsire.* Malone, and Scott following him, stated, apparently without other evidence than this poem, that this was Sir Robert Bevile, maternal grandfather of John Driden of Chesterton. Christie writes, on the other hand: "The laborious and accurate Mr. Holt White, in his MS. notes, ascertained that Sir Erasmus Dryden, the common grandfather of the two cousins, is referred to: and he refers to a list in Rushworth's *Historical Collections* (i. 473), where occurs the name of Sir Erasmus Draiton, as one of those sent to prison on account of the loan money, and liberated on the eve of the general election for Charles I's third parliament, 1628."

787, 1. *Calydonians.* F reads *Caledonians* (and

in l. 77 *Caledonian*), but prints *Calydon* in the *argument* just above, and *Calidon* in l. 364.

2, 44, 227. *Meleagrus . . . Meleagros.* So F.

7, 8. *Ceres . . . Pales.* Cf. **750**, 65, n.

50. *Perithous.* Cf. **756**, 358, n.

53. *Cæneus.* Cf. **856**, **857**, 234–287; **601**, 608.

790, 237. *Plexippus'.* F reads *Ploxippus*, probably by a misprint.

791, 288. *Brother's.* So F; in l. 296 F reads *Brothers.*

792. SIGISMONDA AND GUISCARDO. On this and on Dryden's other adaptations from Boccaccio, see Wieruszowski, *Untersuchungen über John Drydens Boccaccio-Paraphrasen*, Bonn, 1904.

Sigismonda and Guiscardo is from the first tale of the fourth day of the *Decameron.* The only essential change that Dryden has made in the plot is his introduction of a marriage between the hero and heroine. (v n. **736** (FABLES) for Wordsworth's opinion on this.) Wieruszowski thinks that the main aim of our argument-loving poet in this alteration was to provide Sigismonda with a new plea in her defense of her act; v. **797**, 402–420. Perhaps Dryden, despite the coarseness of ll. 147–172, really thought the change made the tale *savor less of immodesty*: cf. **746**¹, 25; and, for a similar change in *Cymon and Iphigenia*, v. n. **890** (CYMON).

Scott's criticism on the tale may be added to Wordsworth's: "— Dryden . . . made Boccaccio's story his own, and told it in his own way. One gross fault he has engrafted upon his original; I mean the coarseness of Sigismonda's character, whose love is that of temperament, not of affection. This error, grounded upon Dryden's false view of the passion and of the female character, and perhaps arising from the depravity of the age rather than of the poet, pervades and greatly injures the effect of the tale. Yet it is more than counterbalanced by preponderating beauties. Without repeating the praise, elsewhere given to the majesty of the poet's versification, and which this piece alone would be sufficient to justify, the reader's attention may be solicited to the colors with which Dryden has drawn a mind wrought up to the highest pitch of despair. Sigismonda is placed in that situation in which, above all others, the human disposition seems to acquire a sort of supernatural strength or obstinacy; for although guilty of a crime, she is punished in a degree far exceeding the measure of the offence. In such a situation, that acuteness of feeling, which would otherwise waste itself in fluctuations betwixt shame, fear, and remorse, is willingly and eagerly turned into the channel of resistance and recrimination; and perhaps no readier mode can be discovered of hardening the human heart, even to the consistence of the nether millstone. It is in this state that Sigismonda resolutely, and even joyfully, embraces death, in order to punish her father, and rejoin her lover. The previous arguments with Tancred sufficiently, and, in

the circumstances, naturally, intimate the tone of her mind, and are a striking instance of Dryden's power in painting passion wrought up to desperation." [SCOTT.]

793, 66. *The royal maid.* "Dryden constantly forces the rhyme for the sake of a word. But he very seldom, as here, forces a word for the sake of a rhyme. Sigismonda was not a maid." [SAINTSBURY.]

794, 116. *Malignant light.* Cf. **598**, 381, n.

154. *Nothing wanted.* "Nothing was wanting." [CHRISTIE.]

795, 242. *So, like*, etc. Cf. **115**, 445–454.

796, 306. *Thrice*, etc. Christie points out the imitation of *Paradise Lost*, i. 619–621:

> Thrice he assayed, and thrice, in spite of scorn,
> Tears, such as angels weep, burst forth : at last
> Words interwove with sighs found out their way.

332. *The guest*, etc. Saintsbury points out the influence of Lucretius; cf. **185**, 126–134.

798, 503. *One paste*, etc. Cf. **738**¹, 40.

799, 597. *The soldier.* Cf. **356**¹, 4 (*Arg.*), n.

802, 14. *Manufactur'd mass.* F reads *Manufacture Mass*, which, though retained by SS., seems to the present editor unintelligible.

803, 90. *Pallas.* "To whom the olive was sacred." SCOTT.

805, 41. *Parrots.* "These are of Dryden's introduction." [SCOTT.]

806. CINYRAS AND MYRRHA. Cf. **722**, 319–324.

809, 272. *The belt.* "The Zodiac." SAINTSBURY.

811, 382. *The babe.* Adonis: cf. **725**, 577; **770**, 147.

384. *The drop.* Cf. **782**, 1066.

812, 77. *At rovers.* Cf. **284**², 25, n.

813, 115. *Dispose.* The verb is apparently made plural by the influence of *those* in the preceding line; cf. **400**, 1031, n.

815, 295. *Falchion.* F reads *Faulchion.*

816, 328. *He said*, etc. "'What a difference,' he [Tennyson] would add, 'between Pope's little poisonous barbs, and Dryden's strong invective! And how much more real poetic force there is in Dryden! Look at Pope:

> He said, observant of the blue-eyed maid,
> Then in the sheath return'd the shining blade.

Then at Dryden:

> He said; with surly faith believ'd her word,
> And in the sheath, reluctant, plung'd the sword.'" HALLAM TENNYSON, *Alfred, Lord Tennyson*, 1898, vol. ii, p. 287.

367. *Council.* Cf. **756**, 301, n.

377. *Cæneus.* Cf. **856**, **857**, 234–287; **601**, 608; **787**, 53.

817, 385. *Counsels.* F reads *Councils;* cf. **756**, 301, n.

820, 634. *Inhibing.* "Not *drawing flavor from*, but *giving it to;* a sense now obsolete." SAINTSBURY. But apparently either sense will fit this passage; the original gives no aid in determining which to prefer.

666. *And of*, etc. Cf. **129**, 94, n.

822, 3. *Dell.* F reads *Cell;* the emendation was suggested, but not adopted, by Christie. Perhaps *Dale* (Chaucer's word) was what Dryden really wrote.

823, 21. *Poynant.* F reads *paynant,* probably by a misprint.

35. *Holidays.* F reads *Holy-Days;* the same spelling is often found elsewhere.

43. *The cock.* So Aldine and Riverside editions; F, followed by SS. and C., reads *a Cock,* which can hardly be correct.

65. *Some lines,* etc. "The exact object of this curious fling is not obvious. The cousinhood of William and Mary will not do, for many reasons. Perhaps the Hapsburgs and the 'Austrian lip' are glanced at." SAINTSBURY

824, 104. *Sprite.* F reads *Spright.*

106. *Shrovetide.* "The recognized and privileged time for cockfighting, and pelting cocks with sticks, especially in schools." SAINTSBURY. Cf. **87**¹, 7, n.

136. *Afeard.* F reads *affer'd;* Chaucer has *aferd.*

146. *The canting style.* "In technical terms;" used with a bit of sarcasm at doctors, not at Puritans.

161. *Humor.* Cf. **6,** 100, n.

162. *Cato.* The reference is to a work in easy Latin, used as a schoolbook in the middle ages, *Dionysii Catonis Disticha de Moribus ad Filium.* It has no connection with either of the two famous Catos of Roman history; hence ll. 203, 204, which are Dryden's addition to the story.

825, 187. *Under.* F reads *over,* an obvious mistake.

188. *Because,* etc. Cf. **436,** 105.

202. *For Homer,* etc. Dryden's addition; cf. **813,** 91–93.

254. *For sacred,* etc. Cf. **552,** 80.

826, 279. *Found.* F reads *bound.*

300. *Waiting,* etc. Cf. **10,** 223, 224.

328. *A mob,* etc. "There may be room to suspect that the line should run:

A court of cobblers, and a mob of kings, —

as better expressing the confusion of ideas incident to dreaming." SCOTT.

827, 391. *The wife,* etc. This vision Chaucer found, not in Homer, but in Dares Phrygius: cf. **497**², 34, n; **501**², 52, n.

417. *In principio.* "In the beginning," a reference to the opening words of the Gospel of John, which begin the "second Gospel," ordinarily read at the close of Mass.

418. *Mulier,* etc. "Woman is man's undoing," a mediæval saying that Chaucer is supposed to have taken from Vincent of Beauvais.

828, 460. *Man,* etc. Dryden's addition to the story; cf. **111,** 170, n.

473. *And Heav'n,* etc. "An allusion to Homer's allegory of the two tuns (*Iliad,* xxiv. 527 f), used by Achilles in consolation to the afflicted Priam." [WARTON.]

479. *Book of Martyrs.* The Catholic Dryden introduces a sarcastic reference to John Foxe's *Acts and Monuments,* commonly known as the *Book of Martyrs,* a favorite book with the English Protestants, and a work of which the accuracy is by no means equal to its anti-Catholic enthusiasm.

480. *A fox,* etc. "Indulging, as usual, his po-

litical antipathies, Dryden fails not to make the fox a Puritan." SCOTT.

499. *O hypocrite,* etc. "According to the romantic history of Charlemagne, Gano, or Ganelon, betrayed the Christian army at the battle of Roncesvalles, where Orlando and the peers of France were slain. The pun upon *Gallic* (Latin *gallus,* a cock), which is renewed in deriving the cock from Brennus and Belinus (l. 636), is entirely Dryden's." [SCOTT.]

829, 515, 549, 559. *Bin, been.* Cf. **263**¹, 31, n.

523. *I cannot,* etc. Dryden, true to his taste for argument in verse, expands the following passage; and, true to his Catholic faith, makes plain his preference for the free will solution: cf. **877,** 424. In ll. 517–522 there is a sneer at Calvinism; cf. **116,** 539, n.

524. *Bradwardin.* Thomas Bradwardine (1290?–1349), Archbishop of Canterbury. His work *On the Cause of God* earned him the title of Doctor Profundus, and remained a theological authority for ages. Austin is of course St. Augustine.

555. *With a mischief to their kind.* A mild curse — "deuce take 'em!"

565. *Silence,* etc. An expression of Dryden's own principles after the Revolution.

830, 599. *So profane.* So SS. and C.; F reads *to prophane.*

636. *Brennus and Belinus.* Brennus was the leader of the Gauls who overran Italy in B. C. 390. Belinus (or Belenus) was a divinity of the Gauls.

652. *Solar.* "That is, born under the influence of the sun; this addition to Chaucer well illustrates Dryden's interest in astrology." [SAINTSBURY.]

831, 686. *Native.* "In astrology, the person whose scheme of nativity is calculated." [SCOTT.]

693. *Gaufride,* etc. "Gaufride, or Geoffrey de Vinsauf, bewailed the death of Richard I in would-be plaintive hexameters, in which he particularly exclaims against Friday, the day on which that hero was shot by Bertrand de Gurdun." [SCOTT.] Chaucer's compliment is of course ironical.

728. *Talbot with the band.* "Probably Dryden took Talbot in its sense of *dog,* and then *band* will be as in *bandog,* 'the chained hound.'" [SAINTSBURY.]

742. *Jack Straw,* etc. "Dryden has given Jack Straw the national antipathies of the mob in his own time. The gathering cry *one and all* he also takes from modern London." [SCOTT.]

750. *And inflated box.* "Blew into musical instruments of boxwood;" or *inflated* may be taken as a participle.

832, 759. *Yours,* etc. "This excellent parody upon Virgil is introduced by Dryden, and marks his late labors." [SCOTT.] Cf. **707,** 1357, 1358.

790. *So loyal subjects,* etc. Another utterance of the Tory Dryden, capable of being applied to the events of the English Revolution.

806. "*A peace,* etc. This closing speech of the cock was added to the story by Dryden.

THEODORE AND HONORIA. This story is from the eighth tale of the fifth day of the *Decameron*. Dryden has altered the names of the characters, changing Nastagio degli Onesti into Theodore, the daughter of Paolo Traversaro into Honoria, and Guido degli Anastagi into Guido Cavalcanti. The last name is found in the tenth canto of Dante's *Inferno*, but Dryden is more likely to have taken it from the ninth tale of the sixth day of the *Decameron*. — In the plot the English poet makes but one essential change, greatly expanding (ll. 340–409) the description of the inward struggle of Honoria, which Boccaccio treats very summarily, in about ten lines.

Byron's praise of this tale is well known:

Sweet hour of twilight! — in the solitude
Of the pine forest, and the silent shore
Which bounds Ravenna's immemorial wood,
Rooted where once the Adrian wave flow'd o'er,
To where the last Cæsarean fortress stood,
Evergreen forest! which Boccaccio's lore
And Dryden's lay made haunted ground to me,
How have I loved the twilight hour and thee!

The shrill cicalas, people of the pine,
Making their summer lives one ceaseless song,
Were the sole echoes, save my steed's and mine,
And vesper bell's that rose the boughs along;
The specter huntsman of Onesti's line,
His hell-dogs, and their chase, and the fair throng
Which learn'd from this example not to fly
From a true lover, — shadow'd my mind's eye.
Don Juan, iii. 105, 106.

1. *Romanian lands.* Boccaccio's phrase is, *In Ravenna antichissima città di Romagna.*

835, 193. *Stern.* F reads *Stern'd.*

220. *Would.* "Used purposely here as expressing desire." [SAINTSBURY.]

836, 228. *Destruction.* F reads *Distruction.*

268. *Mastiffs'.* F reads *Mastiffs*, which may be either nominative or possessive, since the apostrophe is ordinarily not used in plural possessives.

280. *Close.* F reads *clos'd.*

838, 425. *Beware.* Since Dryden frequently shifts tenses in successive lines (as, for example, in **536,** 31, 32; **859,** 407, 408), this may be taken as a present tense: cf. **832,** 799.

CEYX AND ALCYONE. The words *out of . . . Metamorphoses* do not occur in the heading in F; they are supplied from the table of contents, which, however, has *Tenth* instead of *Eleventh*.

839, 51. *And present*, etc. "And, being present, fear nothing except what I actually suffer."

54. *Starlike.* Ovid's *sidereus;* Ceyx was the son of Lucifer, the morning star.

842, 278. *Beast of nature.* Wild beasts (*fera*); cf. **251,** 2537.

311. *Renew.* F reads *renews*, doubtless a misprint.

844, 395, 396. *Her nurse*, etc. The punctuation follows SS.; F has no stop after *cause*, and places commas after *Cries* and *Griefs.*

845, 495. *Sev'n days*, etc. These are the "halcyon days" (cf. **7,** 144; **10,** 236) of winter, when the sea is calm and the kingfisher sits brooding on her nest. Other authors give their number as fourteen.

THE FLOWER AND THE LEAF. The words *out of Chaucer* do not occur in the heading of this poem in F, but are found in the table of contents.

Modern students of Chaucer do not regard the original of this poem as one of his works. It probably dates from the middle of the fifteenth century, and seems to have been written by a woman (cf. **851,** 471). It is in a seven-line stanza, rhyming a b a b b c c (rhyme royal). Dryden is freer in handling this poem than in any other of his adaptations from early English, except of course *The Character of a Good Parson;* ll. 480–501, which identify the companies of knights and ladies with fairies, are his addition to the story.

29. *The balmy dew.* "That is, sleep." [SAINTSBURY.]

846, 46. *The painted birds.* Christie notes the borrowing from Virgil: *pictæ volucres, Georgics*, iii. 243.

53. *And wanted*, etc. "One prognostic was missing to add to the others that announced the spring." [SAINTSBURY.]

847, 129. *Her opposite.* "The goldfinch." SAINTSBURY.

155. *A train*, etc. "The mass of the Fathers (Justin, Athenagoras, Irenæus, Clement, Tertullian, Origen, Lactantius, Sulpicius, Ambrose, Nazianzen) hold that, though Satan fell from the beginning, the Angels fell before the deluge, falling in love with the daughters of men." NEWMAN, *Apologia*, ch. i (London, 1887, p. 29). Cf. Genesis vi. 2.

158. *Less.* "That is, a comparison less." [SAINTSBURY.]

159. *Of a kind.* "Of one kind; uniform." [SAINTSBURY.] After *kind* F has a comma, retained here and in SS.; C. deletes it.

848, 228. *Trumpets.* "In the sense of *trumpeters*. These and other warlike musicians long held some part of the character of heralds and of ancient minstrels. They were distinguished by collars and tabards, and often employed on messages, during which their persons were sacred." [SCOTT.]

233. *Charge.* "Bearings." SAINTSBURY.

257. *The rivets*, etc. "The joints of the armor were riveted with nails after the warrior had put it on." [SCOTT.]

264. *Henchmen.* "Personal attendants, who followed the knights in battle, and never quitted their side. Before a battle the henchmen carried, as in the text, the arms of the knight ready for use." [SCOTT.]

849, 297. *Coursers.* F reads *Courses.*

850, 345. *On arow.* F reads *on a-row.*

353. *Masters'.* F reads *Master's.*

360. *Lea.* F reads *Lay*, a spelling which helps to explain rhymes such as *sea : way*, **27,** 42.

851, 493. *Demogorgon.* "Demogorgon, one of the more apocryphal deities of mythology, has not much propriety here, except as supplying a name of excellent sound." [SAINTSBURY.]

852, 535. *Nine worthies.* "The common list of the nine worthies comprehends: Hector, Pompey, and Alexander, pagans; Joshua

David, and Judas Maccabeus, Jews: and Arthur, Charlemagne, and Godfrey of Boulogne, Christians; but it is sometimes varied." Scott.

542. *Who bear the bows*, etc. "This is a mistake of Dryden, who was misled by the spelling of his text of the old English; *bowes* here, but *boughes* in line corresponding to **849**, 282. The bow, though the youth trained to chivalry were taught to use it, made no part of a knight's proper weapons. But it is curious how Dryden, having fallen into an error, finds out a reason for his false reading, by alleging that the bows were borne as an emblem of strength of arm, valor, and victory." [Scott.]

853, 606. *Sigils*. "Planetary or other signs, used as talismans." [Saintsbury.] Dryden's addition; cf. **766**, 483.

854, 24. *Ostent*. "Dryden probably took this term (it is not in Ovid) from Chapman (*Iliad*, ii. 280), which, considering his previous condemnation of that translator (**386**², 21–29), was unkind." [Saintsbury.]

36. *Yet*, etc. Yet, despite this prodigy, the navy did not weigh anchor.

44. *Iphigenia*. Dryden accents incorrectly, *Iphige'nia* instead of *Iphigeni'a;* cf. **601**, 606, n; **730**, 7, n; **895**, 419.

855, 98. *Heroes*. Possibly this should be changed to *heroes'*.

856, 203. *The bird*. "The swan." Scott.

236. *These*. So SS.; F reads *Those*. On *Cæneus*, cf. **601**, 608; **787**, 53.

857, 294. *The cloud-begotten race*. "The Centaurs, a people of Thessaly, said to be begotten by Ixion, on the cloud which he took for Juno." Scott.

307. *And little wanted*, etc. "The translation is somewhat obscure; it means: 'All wished her joy, and it had nearly happened that all had wished it in vain.'" [Scott.]

858, 339. *Supply*. Cf. **400**, 1031, n.

861, 578. *Strange*, etc. *Habit* and *dress* are ordinarily synonyms. Scott thinks that here the former applies "to the furniture of the horse," but suggests as an alternative that it "means his mode of life." N. E. D. gives no instance of *habit* used in any such sense as *trappings of a horse*.

862, 607. *Divin'd*. F reads *devin'd*.

634. *Beast*. F reads *Breast;* the emendation was suggested, but not adopted, by Saintsbury.

863, 742. *Tow'r'd*. F reads *tour'd*.

864, 811. *Warrior*. So SS.; F reads *Warrious;* perhaps *warriors'* would be a better correction.

868, 254. *Phthia*. F reads *Pthya*.

869, 395. *The spy*. Dolon, whom Diomedes and Ulysses surprised setting out to explore the Greek camp: v. *Iliad*, x. 299–464; cf. **695**, 520–529.

871, 501. *Counsels*. So SS.; F reads *Counsel*, probably by a misprint.

872, 609. *A flow'r*. The hyacinth. This flower was fabled to have sprung from the blood of the beautiful youth Hyacinthus, a favorite of Apollo, and accidentally slain by him. It bore on its petals the Greek letters AI, an exclamation of woe, symbolizing the grief of Apollo for his loss. The same letters begin the name Αἴας, Ajax.

THE WIFE OF BATH, HER TALE. On this poem Professor Lounsbury writes:

"This is essentially a fairy story. In Chaucer the heroine is a young and beautiful woman who has by unmentioned, but evidently malignant agency been transformed into a foul, ill-favored crone. It is implied, though not asserted, that in this condition she must remain until some one can be prevailed upon to receive her as a bride with all her deformity, and ignorant of the transformation that is to restore her to her true shape. It is for this end, therefore, that she is laboring solely. But in Dryden's version she is no mere passive sufferer from a wrong inflicted by a malign and hostile influence possessed of preternatural power. She is herself a proficient in magic art. She has the infernal world at her command. When her offer is accepted by the knight, she spreads her mantle on the ground, and transfers him with furious rapidity to King Arthur's court, while his horse is also brought thither by some devil subject to her will [v. **875**, 253–265]. The alteration was objectionable because it was false to the original, false to the belief upon which the original was founded, and false to the central idea of the story. The beautiful woman of Chaucer, suffering from the influence of malignant hate, becomes in Dryden a practitioner of the black art, leagued with the powers of the lower world, and sharing in the privileges with which subservience to their will is rewarded." *Studies in Chaucer*, iii. 176, 177. Though this criticism is just, it merely shows Dryden's lack of knowledge and appreciation of mediæval literature. His contemporaries, if they noted his addition to the original, were probably pleased by it.

3. *Elfs*. On the discrepancy with *elves* (**873**, 34), cf. **263**¹, 31, n.

28. *Friars*. F reads *Fry'rs*.

873, 61–68. *Then courts*, etc. An oblique reply to Collier: v. B. S. lxi; n. **734** (Motteux); cf. **899** (*Epil.*).

73. *Geneura*. Guinevere.

80. *Covering*, etc. This line is Dryden's addition, and is very characteristic of him.

84. *Speaker*. The *speaker* of the House of Commons was so called because in the old days he was the *spokesman* of the Commons in their communications with the Crown. The older sense of the word survives here.

104. *But, not*, etc. The 1700 ed. reads *But not to hold our Proffer in Scorn;* that of 1713 inserts *turn'd* after *Proffer*. Some emendation is necessary, and that suggested in the text seems as likely as any.

874, 156. *Witness*, etc. "Ovid, indeed, tells the story in the *Metamorphoses*, lib. xi. But how will the fair reader excuse Chaucer for converting the talkative male domestic of Midas into that king's wife?" Scott.

194. *Bittor.* F reads *Bittour.*

Bumps. The name given to the cry of the bittern. "That a bittern maketh that mugient noise, or as we term it, *bumping,* by putting its bill into a reed, . . . is not so easily made out. For my own part, though after diligent enquiry, I could never behold them in this motion." Sir Thomas Browne, *Pseudodoxia Epidemica,* iii. 27, § 4.

875, 245. *Kerchief.* "I do not remember another example of this synecdoche, though the similar, but much less graceful, *petticoat,* is of course common." Saintsbury.

Chaucer has:
—the proudeste of hem alle,
That wereth on a coverchief or a calle.

876, 340. *À la mort.* F reads *a-la-mort.* This phrase was once completely naturalized in English, and felt as *all amort;* the italics of F show, however, that Dryden regarded it as still French.

877, 374. *Ah* benedicite, etc. The following passage, through l. 457, is greatly altered and expanded from Chaucer. Dryden owes much to Lucretius; cf. **191,** 208–236. Line 436, however, is from Horace; cf. **490**[1], 13, n.

387. *Earth.* "That is, his *earthly part, body.*" [Saintsbury.]

424. *The will is free.* Cf. **829,** 523, n.

878, 431. *Whichsoever.* One of the two.

434. *Sodom blue.* "That is, the blue flame of sulphur, wherewith Sodom perished." [Saintsbury.]

448. *Servius Tullius.* The sixth king of Rome, the son of a female captive, who was a slave in the family of Tarquinius Priscus, the fifth king. — F reads *Tullus,* probably by a misprint.

450. *Fabricius.* One of the poor and honest heroes of the Roman republic, famous for his exploits in the war against Pyrrhus. (Added to the story by Dryden.)

471. *The ragged beggar,* etc. From Juvenal, as Chaucer indicates; cf. **348,** 33, 34.

879, 534. *Pygmalion.* Added to the story by Dryden; v. **804–806.**

543. *Often as they.* So SS.; F reads *often they.*

3. *Sate.* F reads *sat,* but cf. rhyme.

16. *Alcides.* Hercules; cf. **628,** 266–270.

881, 160. *Cov'tous.* F reads *covet'ous.*

882, 260. *Tiphys.* The helmsman of the ship *Argo;* cf. **885,** 505.

883, 304. *Flow'rets.* F reads *Flourets.*

339. *The rolling chair.* "The *rolling chair,* or gocart, and the *stick* are not in Ovid." Saintsbury.

Dryden's addition here of concrete detail to Ovid's vague *aliquo conamine* is in contrast with his general tendency to abstraction.

343. *Years.* F places a comma after this word; SS., a colon.

884, 434. *Hurt by Hercules,* etc. Cf. **857,** 292 f, and **863,** 706–710.

885, 505. *Tiphys.* Cf. **882,** 260, n.

886, 539. *But this,* etc. Cf. **481–487,** 401–806.

541. *Hollow.* So SS.; F reads *hallow,* which may be a misprint for either *hollow* or *shallow.*

550. *Backward.* That is, walking backward, referring to the crab's gait.

583, 592. *Amomum . . . cassia, cinnamon . . . nard.* All these words are in italics in F.

586. *Centuries.* F reads *Cent'ries.*

887, 658. *Birth.* So SS.; F reads *Breath,* but cf. rhyme.

888, 702. *Nor purple feathers,* etc. "Alluding to the plan of fastening bright feathers to a string to frighten game." Saintsbury.

The Character of a Good Parson. "This piece may be considered as an *amende honorable* to the reverend order whom Dryden had often satirized, — cf. **734**(Motteux), n; **734**[2], 18, n; **111,** 99; **492**[2], 46–49, — and he himself seems to wish it to be viewed in that light (v. **745**[2], 26–35). With a freedom which he has frequently employed elsewhere, though to a less extent, Dryden has added the last thirty-five lines, in which, availing himself of the revolution which in Chaucer's time placed Henry IV on the throne, he represents the political principles of his priest as the same with those of the non-juring clergy of his own day. Indeed the whole piece is greatly enlarged upon Chaucer's sketch." [Scott.]

As we know from a letter (printed on p. **737**), Dryden wrote this poem at the suggestion of Samuel Pepys, the diarist. To the poet's letter Pepys replied as follows:

"*Friday, July* 14, 1699.

"Sir,

"You truly have obliged mee; and possibly in saying so, I am more in earnest then you can readily think; as verily hopeing from this your copy of one good parson, to fancy some amends made mee for the hourly offence I beare with from the sight of soe many lewd originalls.

"I shall with great pleasure attend you on this occasion, when ere you'l permit it; unless you would have the kindness to double it to mee, by suffering my coach to wayte on you (and who you can ga:'ne mee y[e] same favour from) hither, to a cold chicken and a sallade, any *noone* after Sunday, as being just stepping into the ayre for 2 days. I am most respectfully

Your hono[rd] and obed[nt] Servant,
S. P." (Malone I, 2, 86.)

The writer of the preface to the 1711 edition of *Expostulatoria,* a work attributed to Bishop Thomas Ken (1637–1711) applies to Ken Dryden's *Character of a Good Parson.* (The editor here follows the account of Ken by the Rev. William Hunt in D. N. B., which, however, gives the title of Ken's work as *Expostularia.*) The age of the parson, his writing of hymns (ll. 21–24), and his principles as a non-juror, all circumstances added to Chaucer by Dryden, favor this view, but external evidence is lacking.

19. *For, letting down,* etc. Dryden's addition; cf. **782,** 1024, 1025. The idea of the *chain of love* goes back to Boethius; v. Skeat's note on *Cant. Tales,* A 2991–93.

889, 34. *To threats*, etc. "A reference to the well-known fable of *The Sun, the Wind, and the Traveler*." SAINTSBURY. Cf. **223,** 447.

97. *Zebedee.* v. Mark x. 35–45.

98. *Not but*, etc. "This passage is obviously introduced by the author to apologize for the splendid establishment of the clergy of his own community. What follows applies, as has been noticed, to the non-juring clergy, who lost their benefices for refusing the oath of allegiance to King William." SCOTT.

103. *Reflecting*, etc. v. Exodus xxxiv. 29–35; cf. **118,** 649, n.

890, 115. *An odious name.* "How odious, Burnet found when his Pastoral Letter urging it was burnt by order of the Commons, January, 1693. The *flattering priest* below is, however, pretty certainly William Sherlock, Dean of St. Paul's, whose *Case of the Allegiance due to Sovereign Powers*, etc., appeared in 1690 or 1691. See Macaulay, ch. xvii, xix." [SAINTS-BURY.]

CYMON AND IPHIGENIA. This story is from the first tale of the fifth day of the *Decameron.* Dryden's principal alteration of the plot is that he makes Iphigenia respond to Cymon's love, so that she, as well as her father, regrets the previous contract to Pasimond (v. l. 251). The aim, as Wieruszowski conjectures, is probably to create some moral justification for the hero's acts. Cf. the similar change of *Sigismonda and Guiscardo ;* v. n. **792.**

This poem was reprinted in the third edition (1702) of *Sylvæ* (*The Second Miscellany*).

1–41. *Old*, etc. This passage is a reply to Collier's attack: v. B. S. lxi, and **734** (MOTTEUX), n, and references given there. Christie justly remarks: "Unable to make a good defense, Dryden resorts to abuse; and, a Roman Catholic convert, he denounces the marriage of Protestant clergymen."

39. *Ormond.* Cf. **749**[2] (ORMOND), n.

891, 67. *And Cymon*, etc. "Era chiamato Cimone, il che nella lor lingua sonava quanto nella nostra bestione."

106. *The fanning wind*, etc. The fourteen-syllable verse is used purposely to give a suggestion of prolonged repose; cf. **129,** 94, n.

892, 132. *As barren grounds*, etc. Dryden's addition; cf. **445,** 122–136.

894, 322. *Who now*, etc. Cf. **757,** 381; **765,** 426; **242,** 1860, n.

895, 400. *The rude militia.* "Dryden willingly seizes the opportunity of being witty at the expense of the militia of England." [SCOTT.]

419. *Iphigenia.* On the accent, cf. **854,** 44, n.

424. *So passive*, etc. A sarcastic allusion to the Church of England, which in time of stress had not adhered to its doctrine of passive obedience; cf. **236,** 1428; **237,** 1432–1437; **244,** 1956–1960.

427. *To dismiss*, etc. "That is, to shake him off altogether." [SAINTSBURY.]

897, 518. *With Love*, etc. Repeated from **752,** 12.

557. *Retir'd.* F, followed by SS. and C., places only a comma after this word, and has no pause after *troop* in the next line. Lines **558,** 559, mean clearly: "His soldiers . . . all determined to fight, and all begged for (demanded) their accustomed work (fighting)." (N. E. D., however, does not cite any instance of *fix* used in the sense of *determine* earlier than 1788.)

568. *These lead*, etc. Cf. **129,** 94, n.

898, 622. *Grind.* F reads *grin'd*, which may possibly mean *grinn'd*.

PROLOGUE . . . FROM THE PILGRIM. "Cibber informs us that Sir John Vanbrugh, who cast the parts, being pleased with the young actor's [Cibber's] moderation in contenting himself with those of the Stuttering Cook and Mad Englishman, assigned him also the creditable task of speaking the epilogue, which, as it was so much above the ordinary strain, highly gratified his vanity. Dryden himself, on hearing Cibber recite it, made him the further compliment of trusting him with the prologue also; an honorable distinction, which drew upon him the jealousy of the other actors (*Apology*, ch. viii)." [SCOTT.]

899[1], 3. *Tom Dove.* " The savage amusement of bear baiting was much in fashion in England during the seventeenth century. Tom Dove seems to have been a bear of great celebrity." [SCOTT.] Cf. **154,** 24.

16. *Maurus.* Blackmore. Cf. **748**[2], 27, n; **785,** 83. Blackmore took a B.A. from Oxford in 1674 and an M.A. in 1676, but had his medical degree from the University of Padua. He had just published — since Dryden wrote his preface to the *Fables* — *A Paraphrase on the Book of Job ; as likewise on the Songs of Moses, Deborah, David ; on four Select Psalms, some Chapters of Isaiah, and the Third Chapter of Habakkuk*, mentioned in the Term Catalogue for Trinity Term, 1700. In 1687 he was admitted fellow of the Royal College of Physicians, under the charter of James II; in 1697 he was knighted by William III. (The name is spelled *Marus* in the 1700 text, but cf. **785,** 83.)

899[2], 35. *Hopkins.* Cf. **143,** 403, n.

41. *At leisure hours*, etc. In his preface to *King Arthur* (1697) Blackmore states that *Prince Arthur* was written "by such catches and starts, and in such occasional, uncertain hours, as the business of my profession would afford me." He continues: "And therefore for the greatest part that poem was written in coffee-houses, and in passing up and down the streets, because I had little leisure elsewhere to apply to it." Cf. **741**[2], 33 f.

EPILOGUE. This is largely a reply to Collier; v. B. S. lxi, and **734** (MOTTEUX), n; cf. **873,** 61–68. (Collier in 1699 had published *A Defense of the Short View*, etc., in answer to attacks on his work by Congreve and Vanbrugh.)

900[1], 21. *Misses.* In italics in 1700 text.

41, 42. *For while*, etc. Repeated from **172, 55,** 56, with the alteration of two words.

900[2], 47. *Oates.* v. **117,** 632, n. Dryden here

alludes to his continual appendixes to his information concerning the Popish Plot.

Haynes. "The allusion seems to be partly to Bryan Haines, the Tory evidence against Shaftesbury and College, a fellow almost as infamous as Oates; but chiefly, by way of equivoque, to the wicked wag Joe Haynes [Haines], the comedian, who, amongst other pranks, chose, during the reign of James II, to become Roman Catholic. Whether he took this step from any serious prospect of advantage, or to throw ridicule on the new converts, is somewhat dubious; at least his apostasy was not founded upon conviction, for, after the Revolution, he abjured the errors of Popery, spoke a penitentiary prologue, and reconciled himself to the Church and theater of England." Scott. Cf. **70**, 45, n; **280²**, 20, n.

11. *St. Hermo.* "The electric appearances, sometimes seen on the masts or yards of a ship during stormy nights, called by sailors in the Mediterranean the Lights of St. Elmo. They are supposed to presage the safety of the vessel and the termination of the storm." [Scott.]

20. *Charms.* The 1700 text reads *Charm,* but cf. rhyme.

901. The Secular Masque. "The moral of this emblematical representation is sufficiently intelligible. By the introduction of the deities of the chase, of war, and of love, as governing the various changes of the seventeenth century, the poet alludes to the sylvan sports of James I, the bloody wars of his son, and the licentious gallantry which reigned in the courts of Charles II and James, his successor." [Scott.]

Janus is introduced here as the god of beginnings; Chronos, as the god of time; and Momus, as the personification of mockery and censure. Cf. **383¹**, 2, n.

Day writes (pp. 184, 185): "I have been unable to trace the music for the whole masque, but there is a manuscript in the British Museum . . . of the part composed by Daniel Purcell. His airs, moreover, were published in a volume entitled *A Collection of New Songs . . . Compos'd by Mr. Daniel Purcel. Perform'd in the Revis'd Comedy call'd the Pilgrim,* 1700, which contains the first, third, fourth, and fifth stanzas. . . . The passage sung by Venus beginning 'Calms appear when storms are past' was set to music by Gottfried Finger, a German, who is said to have left England in disgust when he was awarded the fourth prize in the competition to set Congreve's *Judgment of Paris* to music in 1701. There is a single-sheet edition in the British Museum . . . of the song of Venus as it was sung by Mrs. Campion. . . . The first stanza of the masque was

published with D. Purcell's music in *Mercurius Musicus,* May, 1700, . . . and as a single song."

902, 82. *But since,* etc. "There seems here to be a secret allusion to the exile of the beautiful queen of James II, so much admired by the Tory poets of the time." Scott. Cf. **268**, *The Lady's Song.*

903², 5. *Our.* This word is so carelessly written in the manuscript as to be illegible.

Epilogue Spoken to the King . . . 1681. The London broadside is headed simply *The Epilogue,* but in the margin, to the left of this heading, it has in small type the words, "Writ by Mr. Dreyden [sic], Spoke before His MAJESTY at *Oxford, March* 19, 1680 [*i. e.* 1680–1]." It has the following significant variants: (l. 3) *Landskip,* (l. 17) *hath in Tempest,* (l. 23) *Day-sun* (for *days on!*). Mr. Hiscock notes that in l. 8 the text given in Brown's *Works* reads:

And you both Audience and Actors are.

He thinks that this is what Dryden wrote. The present editor, however, regards that reading as clearly a degeneration "of the well-known type in which an obvious word [or phrase] is substituted for a more 'difficult' but more effective word [or phrase]" (Macdonald, p. 15 n). In this line, as in ll. 21, 22, 31 below, Dryden wished to throw emphasis on *here.*

904. Prologue . . . Mithridates. The original edition is headed, *A Prologue spoken,* etc. There is no separate heading, *Prologue,* but there is a heading, *Epilogue.* The date 1681 is for 1681–2.

905¹, 4. *Address.* A sarcastic reference to the addresses or petitions presented to the king by the Whigs in 1680: v. n. **112**, 179; **122**, 985–988; **123¹**, 1–17.

26. *Plot . . . witness.* v. **111**, 108, n; n. **117**, 632.

905², 36. *Break an act,* etc. The reference is to an act of 1666, "against importing Cattell from Ireland and other parts beyond the Seas," supplemented by "an additional act" in the following session of parliament.

41. *Jack Ketch.* v. **210**, 3, n. In this line *all* is lacking in the original edition; it is supplied by Luttrell.

Epilogue. The words, "Spoken by Mr. Goodman," have been added by the present editor: cf. **75¹, 76¹.** Goodman, one of the most noted actors in the Theater Royal company, played the part of Pharnaces in *Mithridates.* Mrs. Cox is not mentioned among the actors in the play either in the separate edition of 1693 or in that included in Lee's *Works,* 1712.

7. *Salamanca.* v. n. **117**, 632.

10. *Andrew's wit,* etc. "Alluding to St. André, the famous dancing-master, and

Jacob Hall, the performer on the slack rope." SCOTT. On St. André v. **135, 53**, n (on **1059**). Of Hall, Anthony Hamilton writes thus: "Jacob Hall (the famous rope-dancer) was at that time in vogue in London; his strength and agility charmed in public, even to a wish to know what he was in private. . . . The tumbler did not deceive Lady Castlemaine's expectations, if report may be believed; and as was intimated in many a song, much more to the honor of the rope-dancer than of the countess" (*Memoirs of Count Grammont*, London, 1896, p. 131).

23. *Servant.* Luttrell wished to substitute *slave*, a most unintelligent correction! Dryden intended that *Madam* should be pronounced as one syllable, *Mam.* In *An Evening's Love* (act iii, sc. i) Aurelia says to her servant Camilla: "Madam me no Madam, but learn to retrench your words; and say Mam."

906¹, 29. *Pray you.* The *you* has been inserted by the present editor. Some emendation was essential.

43. *I am.* The original edition reads *I'me.*

EPIGRAM ON PLUTARCH. Agathias died between 577 and 582; the Emperor Justinian reigned 527–565. The epigram is *Anthologia Planudea* 331. In the first line of it στήσαντο, Χερωνεῦ is an error found in all but one of the manuscripts and in the early editions. Later editions read correctly στῆσαν, Χαιρωνεῦ.

906². ON THE MARRIAGE OF . . . MRS. ANASTASIA STAFFORD. The material for the headnote has been taken from Clifford's editorial material in *Tixall Poetry*, Newdigate's article in *The London Mercury*, Burke's *Peerage* (ed. 93, 1935), *The Complete Peerage* (London, 1910), the *Dictionary of National Biography*, *Evelyn's Diary* (November 30, 1680, ff.), and Joseph Gillow, *A Literary and Biographical History or Bibliographical Dictionary of the English Catholics* (1885–1902). On *Tixall Poetry* see also nn. **22** (SONG), **52** (SONG) (on **1049**), **202** (THE FAIR STRANGER) (on **1063**). In Dryden's time the title *Mrs.* was not restricted to married women.

907, 17. *From her,* etc. "Anastasia, in Greek, means resurrection. The feast of St. Anastasia, martyr, is kept on Christmas Day." [CLIFFORD.]

908, 21. *And she,* etc. "From this line, I think, we may infer that the marriage was celebrated on Christmas day." CLIFFORD. Not a certain inference: the text implies no more than that the wedding was in "the depth of winter."

39. *Their father's,* etc. In *Tixall Poetry* there is a semicolon after this line and a colon after l. 40. Possibly the punctuation should be revised so as to connect l. 40 with what follows rather than with what precedes.

53. *Let their,* etc. These lines presumably refer to the marriage of Stafford's second son, John, to Mary Southcote on December 1, 1682, though that event did not come within the first revolution of the sun after December 29, 1680, the date of Stafford's execution.

59. *Send out,* etc. This and the following lines, through l. 89, seem to indicate that George Holman went abroad (ll. 75–78) "when innocence and truth became a crime": possibly in 1673, after the passage of the Test Act, though that act merely excluded Catholics from office, not making them criminals. In exile, he used his wealth to relieve the distress of his fellow English Catholic emigrants (ll. 79–89). Then, after the accession of James II in February, 1685 ("as the storms are more allay'd," l. 57) — or possibly earlier, during the Tory reaction that began about March, 1681, with the dissolution of the Oxford Parliament — Anastasia Stafford also went abroad, met Holman, and returned with him (ll. 60, 61) to be married about December, 1685. If Gillow is right in saying that Anastasia Stafford died in 1719 at the age of seventy-three, she would have been thirty-nine at the time of her marriage to Holman. Holman, according to the inscription on his grave (quoted at second-hand by Clifford, p. 380), was sixty-seven at his death in 1698, so that he was fifty-four at the time of his marriage. According to the same inscription the couple had nine children (Gillow says only four), of whom five survived their father.

74. *A confessor.* "One who avows his religion in the face of danger, and adheres to it under persecution and torture, but does not suffer martyrdom. (The earliest sense in English.) The pronunciation with the accent on the first syllable is found in all the poets, and is recognized by the dictionaries generally, down to Smart, 1836–49." [N. E. D.]

90. *Thus, when,* etc. See Genesis xlii ff., especially xlviii. 15–22.

909, 4. *Covent Garden.* The Drury Lane Theater, where the play was acted, was near Covent Garden.

19. *Beaus.* The italics, retained here from the original sheet, call attention to a foreign word. So likewise with *mundungus* below (l. 31), from the Spanish, meaning *trash, refuse.*

41. *Iniskelling.* That is, Enniskillen. The reference is to an episode in the Irish revolt of 1689. In Ireland James II had transferred both civil and military authority to Catholics, and the Protestant minority of the population feared a massacre. The Protestants of the south largely fled from the country; those of the north gathered at Londonderry and

Enniskillen. After losing his throne in England James II sought refuge in France, whence in March, 1689, he made an expedition to Ireland. There his general, Hamilton, besieged Londonderry. "The siege had lasted a hundred and five days, and only two days' food remained in Londonderry, when on the 28th of July an English ship broke the boom across the river, and the besiegers sullenly withdrew. Their defeat was turned into a rout by the men of Enniskillen, who struggled through a bog to charge an Irish force of double their number at Newtown Butler, and drove horse and foot before them in a panic which soon spread through Hamilton's whole army" (J. R. Green, *Short History of the English People*, ch. ix, sec. 8).

It is a bit surprising to find Dryden paying tribute to the enemies of James II, but after all Dryden was an Englishman and was writing for an English public.

910, 8. *Crump'd.* Crooked, bent.

911. POEMS ATTRIBUTED TO DRYDEN. The notes to pp. **911–927** have been made as brief as possible.

To the list of titles on pp. **928, 929** might be added, in order to avoid confusion, *The Happy Shepheard: or; The Young Gallants Courtship to his Coy Lady; To a pleasant New Tune, Sung in the last New Opera.* This is an undated broadside ballad, the first two stanzas of which the British Museum Catalogue (under *Shepherd*, p. 184) ascribes to Dryden. Those stanzas are indeed a song in *King Arthur* (v. **264**), act ii; they were omitted from the present edition because they seemed a part of the dramatic action rather than a detachable song: v. SS. viii. 158, 159; Day, p. 87. To them the broadside ballad adds five spurious stanzas.

On some other pieces that have been attributed to Dryden, see Macdonald, *John Dryden: a Bibliography*, pp. 180–184, and references there given.

PROLOGUE . . . FROM THE INDIAN QUEEN. On Howard, v. B. S. xx, xxi, xxiv. *The Indian Queen*, as might be inferred from the *Epilogue*, was presented with much magnificence. Pepys writes that it "for show, they say, exceeds *Henry the Eighth.*"

911², 17. *Will.* '*T will* in original edition.

SONG. Day comments (p. 142): "The passage in which this . . . song occur[s] resembles a similar incantation passage in *The Indian Emperour*, and therefore seems likely to be Dryden's."

912¹. A SONG and ENJOYMENT. G. Thorn-Drury in his excellent edition of *Covent Garden Drollery* (London, 1928), p. 135, comments crisply on these pieces: "Both strike me as obviously the work of some inferior imitator trying to take ad-

vantage of the popularity of . songs of Dryden, who is hardly likely to be thus feebly and, in the second case, almost without an interval repeating himself." The present editor now (1948) agrees with him.

3 (A Song). *Do.* CGD reads *do's.*

3 (Enjoyment). *So o'er-blest.* CGD reads *so over blest.*

9. *Whilst.* CGD reads *While.*

912², 14. *His soul.* CGD reads *His flying Soul.*

19, 20. "*O now,*" etc. CGD reads:

Oh! now my dear let us go.
Dye with me *Damon,* for now I dye too.

21. *Sweet.* CGD reads *secret.*

A SONG. Macdonald (p. 81, n. 1) terms these stanzas "something of a parody" on the song, *Farewell, fair Armeda* (v. **68²**), and comments, "There is, of course, not the slightest reason to suppose he [Dryden] wrote the piece."

The "A" of the heading is not found in CGD.

913¹. LINES ON SETTLE'S EMPRESS OF MOROCCO. If, as Settle himself asserts (Malone, II, 273), Shadwell had a hand in *Notes and Observations on The Empress of Morocco*, that pamphlet must have been written before the disagreement between Dryden and Shadwell referred to in nn. **74²**, 53 (on **1051, 1052²**).

913². AN ESSAY UPON SATIRE. v. B. S. xxxviii–xl. The headnote on pp. **913, 914** requires much revision. The poem discussed was written later than July 17, 1679, for "the new earl" of line 122 is the Earl of Halifax, whose creation was announced by the king on that date. (See H. C. Foxcroft, *Life and Letters of Sir George Savile, Bart., First Marquis of Halifax*, London, 1898: i, 176.) It was circulating among the London wits in November, 1679, for on November 22 Col. Edward Cooke wrote to the Duke of Ormond concerning this satire, which he terms "a most scurrilous, libellous copy of verse." He states that the Earl of Mulgrave is suspected to be "(if not guilty of the making, yet) guilty of being privy to the making of them." (See *Hist. MSS. Comm. Ormonde*, new ser. v, 242. For this reference and for varied information concerning this poem the present editor is indebted to an excellent article by Maurice Irvine, "Identification of Characters in Mulgrave's 'Essay upon Satyr,'" in *Studies in Philology*, xxxiv (1937), 533–551.) But Dryden was generally regarded as the author of it, as is plain from a letter written on November 27 by John Verney (*Hist. MSS. Comm., Seventh Report*, part i, p. 477). A month or so later Luttrell wrote in his *Brief Historical Relation of State Affairs* (Oxford, 1857; i. 30): "About the same time [the middle of

December] Mr. John Dryden was sett on in Covent Garden in the evening by three fellowes, who beat him very severely, and on peoples comeing in they run away; 'tis thought to be done by order of the dutchesse of Portsmouth; she being abused in a late libell called an Essay upon satyr, of which Mr. Dryden is suspected to be the author."

This shows that before the close of 1679 the piece had become notorious under the name, An Essay upon Satire. But it seems to have remained in manuscript until after the Revolution of 1688; ll. 61–73, on "sauntering Charles between his beastly brace" of mistresses, the Duchess of Portsmouth and Nell Gwyn, might have deterred even the most piratical publisher from issuing it during the reign of Charles II or James II. The first known printed text is in The Fourth (and Last) Collection of Poems, Satyrs, Songs, &c. . . . 1689, where the poem is said to be "by J. Dr—en Esquire." The piece is found also, attributed in similar fashion, in Poems on Affairs of State from the Time of Oliver Cromwell to the Abdication of K. James the Second . . . 1697, and in later editions of that volume, closing with the sixth, of 1710 and 1716. But it occurs, attributed to the Earl of Mulgrave, in A New Collection of Poems Relating to State Affairs . . . 1705. Finally, in a much revised text, it found its way into The Works of John Sheffield, Earl of Mulgrave, Marquis of Normanby, and Duke of Buckingham, 1723. The duke had died on February 24, 1721, and his works were edited for "Catharine his Duchesse" by Alexander Pope, so that the retouchings were probably from Pope's hand. Surely no mediocre squib ever had two more distinguished revisers than the piece called in this edition "An Essay on Satyre, written in the year 1675." That date, as has been already shown, is four years too early.

But in the Term Catalogues for Hilary Term (February), 1680, there occurs the entry:

"An Essay upon Satyr, or A Poem on the Times. To which is added, The Satyr against Separatists. Octavo. Price, stitcht, 6d. Printed for T. Dring in Fleet street."

This entry long remained a mystery, though it was universally regarded as referring to the Mulgrave-Dryden poem. In 1939 Hugh Macdonald stated in his Dryden Bibliography, "No copy of this edition, if it was ever published, seems to be known." But since that date two copies of the Essay upon Satyr issued in 1680 by Dring have come to light, one in the Henry E. Huntington Library in San Marino, California, the other in the library of Wellesley College, Welles-

ley, Massachusetts. It has nothing whatever in common with the Mulgrave-Dryden poem.

In 1648 there had appeared a pamphlet with a title-page reading in part, The Foure Ages of England: or, the Iron Age. With other select poems. Written by Mr. A. Cowley. The "other select poems" were only two in number: an address To my Lord Lieutenant of Ireland (Ormond), of 52 lines; and A Satyr against Separatists (Brownists, Independents), of 242 lines. The main item in the pamphlet, The Foure Ages of England: or, the Iron Age, is an ardent but dull royalist effusion of 1778 lines, which, as a passage in it makes plain, was composed late in 1646 or at some time in 1647. It traces the degeneration of English society, culminating in "the Iron Age" of the Civil War. In 1648 Abraham Cowley was living in France. Returning to England in 1654, in 1656 he published a folio edition of his Poems, in the preface to which he vigorously denied writing "a book entitled The Iron Age and published under my name during the time of my absence." "I wonder'd very much," he continued, "how one who could be so foolish to write so ill verses, should yet be so wise to set them forth as another man's rather than his own." Concerning the two minor poems in the pamphlet he was silent, and the problems connected with them need not be discussed here. This whole topic is discussed in greater detail in a paper, An Essay upon Satyr . . . London . . . Dring . . . 1680, by G. R. Noyes and H. R. Mead, Berkeley, California, 1948.

In 1675 two London booksellers thought that they could make a few pennies by reprinting this royalist pamphlet of 1648. Despite Cowley's disclaimer, they made no essential change in the title-page, which runs thus: The Four Ages of England: or, The Iron Age. With other select Poems: Written by Mr. A. Cowley, in the year 1648. . . . London: Printed by J. C. for Tho: Dring, and Joh. Leigh, at their Shops in Fleet-street. 1675. Apparently this reprint of material long since out of date had no particular success and plenty of copies remained on the booksellers' hands. Then, early in 1680, Tho. Dring seems to have had a bright idea. Taking advantage of the notoriety of the Dryden-Mulgrave Essay upon Satire, he reissued sets of The Four Ages of England with a fresh title-page, thus: An Essay upon Satyr, or A Poem on the Times; under the Names of the Golden Age, the Silver Age, the Brazen Age, and the Iron Age: to which is added, A Satyr against Separatists. [Four lines quoted from Brazen Age.] London, Printed for Tho. Dring at Chancery-Lane End in Fleet-

street, 1680. Tho. Dring obviously hoped that this cancel title-page would lead people to buy his left-over goods under the impression that they were getting something fresh and sparkling. He was doing nothing illegal: he made no pretense that his refurbished pamphlet had anything to do with Dryden or with Mulgrave or with any other living man; and nobody else had printed any *Essay upon Satyr,* so that he was infringing on no vested rights. But, if we may judge from the fact that only two copies of this reissue are now known to survive, Tho. Dring's scheme failed to work. All that he accomplished was to make trouble for bibliographers of a later epoch.

It has seemed needless to give full text variants for this poem.

914, 30. *Armstrong.* Cf. **74²,** 22, n.

Aston. Irvine (pp. 541, 542), following a suggestion by Scott, thinks that the reference is to Col. Edmund Aston, who was Mulgrave's second in a duel with Rochester: see V. D. Pinto, *Rochester* (London, 1935), pp. 112–114. Aston, according to Irvine, "fought a duel with Etherege and wrote scraps of verse."

55. *Dunbar.* "Robert Constable, third Viscount of Dunbar. He is elsewhere mentioned with the epithet of 'brawny Dunbar.'" SCOTT.

56. *Monmouth.* Cf. **110,** 18, n.

Sir Carr. Sir Carr Scrope (1649–80), courtier and minor poet. He contributed a version of *Sappho to Phaon* to the co-operative translation of *Ovid's Epistles* in which Dryden had a leading share (cf. **88–101**). See also headnote, **929²** (A FAMILIAR EPISTLE TO MR. JULIAN).

61. *The royal mistresses.* The reference has been interpreted as to the Duchess of Cleveland (1641–1709; v. headnote **20¹**) and the Duchess of Portsmouth (1649–1734; v. headnotes, **202¹, 928¹**). But Irvine comments (*Op. cit.,* p. 540): "The Duchess of Cleveland had by this time lost most of her influence as one of the royal mistresses and though she was still being coarsely reviled in contemporary satires, her name would not as readily as Nell Gwynn's have been coupled with that of the Duchess of Portsmouth." He finds support in a *Satyr* published in *Poems on Affairs of State,*' vol. iii, 1704, which (p. 125) brands Dryden as

He that could once call *Charles* a saun'tring Cully,
By *Portsmouth* sold, and jilted by Bitch *Nelly.*

The rivalry between the Duchess of Portsmouth and Nell Gwyn (1650–87) was notorious: see the article on Nell Gwyn in D. N. B. by Joseph Knight, who cites references. In 1679 a satirist could easily call each of these women "old" (l. 73).

72, 73. *Was ever prince,* etc. This couplet and that below, on Rochester (ll. 240, 241), whether or not they were written by Dryden, are worthy to rank with his best work.

74. *Earnely.* "Sir John Earnely was bred to the law, but became distinguished as a second-rate statesman. He was chancellor of the exchequer in 1686; and was made one of the commissioners of the treasury, in the room of the Earl of Rochester." SCOTT.

Ayles—y. "Robert Bruce, second Earl of Elgin, in Scotland; created after the Restoration an English peer, by the titles of Baron and Viscount Bruce, Earl of Ailesbury. In 1678 he was of the privy council and a gentleman of the bed chamber. In the reign of James II the Earl of Ailesbury succeeded to the office of lord chamberlain, upon the death of the Earl of Arlington, on July 30, 1685; an office which he held only two months, as he died on October 20 following." [SCOTT.]

76. *D—by's.* Thomas Osborne, Earl of Danby. Cf. **925** (ON THE YOUNG STATESMEN) and n. on **1043, 1044.**

84. *The merriest man alive.* The Duke of Buckingham, portrayed as Zimri in *Absalom and Achitophel:* v. **116,** 544, n.

915, 89. *Nokes and Lee.* James Nokes (or Noke, d. 1692?) and Anthony Leigh (or Lee, d. 1692) were both celebrated comic actors. Colley Cibber, in his *Apology,* ch. v, pays enthusiastic tribute to their talents.

102. *Machiavel.* The Earl of Shaftesbury; cf. **111,** 150, n. The 1702 text reads *Matchiavel,* which illustrates the pronunciation of the name in Dryden's time.

122. *The new earl.* The Earl of Halifax: v. n. **913²,** above. A sidenote in *Poems on Affairs of State* (reproduced in the present text) identifies *the new earl* with the Earl of Essex, that is, Arthur Capel (1631–83). But this is impossible, for Arthur Capel had been created Earl of Essex on April 20, 1661. The words "for Ireland he would go" caused the old commentator's blunder. The Earl of Essex had been Lord Lieutenant of Ireland from February, 1672, to April, 1677. A quotation from Gilbert Burnet, writing of English politics in the early autumn of 1679, will explain the rest: "Some gave it out that he [Halifax] pretended to be lord lieutenant of Ireland, and was uneasy when that was denied him; but he said to me that it was offered to him, and he had refused it. . . . He likewise saw that lord Essex had a mind to be again there, and he was confident he was better fitted for it than he himself was." *History of His Own Time* (London, 1850), p. 316.

145. *Tropos'*. As the reference in l. 165 to the *woolsack* (the seat of the lord chancellor in the House of Lords) makes perfectly clear, Tropos is Heneage Finch, who on December 19, 1674, became lord chancellor as successor to Shaftesbury. In *Absalom and Achitophel*, Part II, he is glorified as Amri: v. **151,** 1013–1024. Tate's praise is more trustworthy than Mulgrave's abuse. Osmond Airy writes in D. N. B.: "The fact that throughout an unceasing official career of more than twenty years, in a time of passion and intrigue, Finch was never once the subject of parliamentary attack, nor ever lost the royal confidence, is a remarkable testimony both to his probity and discretion."

180. *D—et.* Dorset; cf. **282**¹ (DORSET), n.

186. *Swell'd by contact.* So SS.; the texts of 1702 and 1703 read *Suckl'd by contract;* the line is not found in the 1723 edition.

192. *Ned Howard.* "Alluding to Dorset's verses *To Mr. Edward Howard, on his Incomparable, Incomprehensible Poem, called* The British Princes." [SCOTT.] Howard was Dryden's brother-in-law.

194. *Mul—ve.* The Earl of Mulgrave, author of the poem.

210. *Sid.* Sir Charles Sedley (Sidley); cf. **136,** 163, n. The texts of 1702 and 1703 read *Sid—y;* that of 1723 has *Sid.*

916, 229. *Hewet.* Cf. **78**¹ (EPIL. MAN OF MODE), n.

Jack Hall. Cf. **143,** 407, n. But V. D. Pinto, in *Sir Charles Sedley* (London, 1927), p. 146, comments thus on the present line: "The allusion to *Jack Hall* is more obscure. A Puritan poet of some merit called John Hall died in 1656, and a Dr. John Hall became Bishop of Bristol in 1691, but it is hardly likely that Mulgrave refers to either of these persons. It is more tempting to suppose that *Hall* is a printer's error for *Howe,* and that the person referred to is Jack Howe, the dissolute scribbler and politician [v. n. **267,** SONG VI, on **1067**], notorious for his violent speeches in the Parliaments of William III. Howe is said to have been 'an amorous spark of the Court' in his young days, and to have written some savage lampoons. His character would fit in very well with the sense of this context." So the present editor is doubtful whether any minor poet named *Jack Hall* was living in 1679.

230. *For's want.* So in the 1703 text; that of 1702 reads *for's meer want.*

243. *Killigrew.* Thomas Killigrew (1612–83), dramatist, theatrical manager, and wit. He was the uncle of the Mrs. Anne Killigrew whose talents are celebrated by Dryden; v. **211–214.**

244. *Bessus.* Cf. **80**¹, 8; n. **79**², 1.

266. *Thought's.* The texts of 1702 and 1703 read *Thought;* the line is not found in the 1723 edition.

281. *Stupendous.* So in 1703 text; the 1702 text reads *stupendious.* Cf. n. **456,** 214.

THE ART OF POETRY. The variant readings of this poem are omitted from these notes.

21. *Dubartas.* Joshua Sylvester (1563–1618) is chiefly known in literature by his translation of *Du Bartas his Divine Weekes and Workes.* The work was popular among the translator's contemporaries, but after 1660 it was comparatively little read; cf. n. **32,** 235, on **1048;** and **917,** 101, n.

917, 90. *The Mock-Tempest.* This play, by Thomas Duffet, was acted at the Theater Royal, in ridicule of the performance at the Duke's Theater of Shadwell's operatic version of Dryden and Davenant's adaptation of Shakespeare's *Tempest;* cf. n. **74**², 53. Duffet also wrote parodies of Settle's *Empress of Morocco* and Shadwell's *Psyche.*

98. *Bumbast.* On the discrepancy with *bombast* (**918,** 160), cf. **263**¹, 31, n.

101. *Nor,* etc. "Thus an injudicious poet, who aims at loftiness, runs easily into the swelling puffy style, because it looks like greatness. I remember, when I was a boy, I thought inimitable Spenser a mean poet in comparison of Sylvester's *Dubartas,* and was rapt into an ecstasy when I read these lines:

Now when the winter's keener breath began
To crystallize the Baltic ocean;
To glaze the lakes, to bridle up the floods,
And periwig with snow the baldpate woods.

I am much deceiv'd if this be not abominable fustian, that is, thoughts and words ill-sorted, and without the least relation to each other." DRYDEN, *Dedication of The Spanish Friar* (1681); SS. vi. 407, 408.

For the lines quoted (somewhat incorrectly) by Dryden, v. Sylvester, *Dubartas his Second Weeke:* Fourth Part of the First Day, ll. 184–187.

115. *Fairfax.* As a matter of fact, the translation of Tasso's *Jerusalem Delivered* by Edward Fairfax (d. 1635) was not published until 1600, after the death of Spenser (1552?–99). Dryden's views on literary history are generally not to be relied on.

126. *Their mock* Gondibert. Cf. **24**², 22, n. A group of wits, including, it is said, Denham and Donne, issued in 1653 two successive satires on *Gondibert,* entitled *Certain Verses written by severall of the Authors Friends, to be re-printed with the second edition of Gondibert* and *The Incomparable Poem Gondibert Vindicated,* etc. Professor F. N. Robinson writes to the editor that the first of these volumes (which alone is in the Harvard

Library) contains no poem called *The Mock Gondibert*, "though two of the pieces might be not inappropriately so characterized." The name *Mock Gondibert* was probably composed in imitation of *The Mock-Tempest* in l. 90. — Davenant in his *Preface* noted the errors of his predecessors in epic poetry, and praised his own originality. He constructed his poem, for example, on the model of a drama, "proportioning five books to five acts, and cantos to scenes."

918, 251. *Randal.* "It is difficult to guess who is meant. Certainly the description does not apply to Thomas Randolph, whose pastorals are rather ornate, and duly garnished with classical names. Probably Dryden, if he filled up this name, was contented to speak at large, from a general recollection, that Thomas Randolph, the 'adopted son' of Ben Jonson, had written pastorals." [SCOTT.]

920, 418. *S——.* Settle: v. B. S. xxviii, xxix, xlv–xlvii; **143,** 412, n; **913.** "These concluding lines are probably Dryden's, being marked with his usual inveteracy against Elkanah Settle, and his peculiar sense of that bard's presumption in prefixing an engraving of his portrait to *The Empress of Morocco* — a circumstance which Dryden took more to heart than was necessary, or becoming: David Logan was the engraver of this offensive plate." SCOTT.

This note is here retained as a sample of the less admirable side of Scott's editorial work. The real frontispiece of *The Empress of Morocco* is an exterior view of the Duke's Theater, engraved by Sherwin. Mrs. C. S. Whipple writes to the editor in regard to the private library of Mr. Robert Hoe of New York: "Mr. Hoe owns fifteen of Settle's works [including *The Empress of Morocco*], in none of which is a portrait."

921, 526. *Artamène.* Ed. 1683 reads *Artamen.* The reference is to *Artamène ou Le Grand Cyrus*, a romance written by Mlle. de Scudéry, but published under the name of her brother Georges de Scudéry.

555. *Your bully poets*, etc. "I have sometimes wonder'd, in the reading, what was become of those glaring colors which amaz'd me in *Bussy d'Ambois* upon the theater; but when I had taken up what I suppos'd a fallen star, I found I had been cozen'd with a jelly; nothing but a cold, dull mass, which glitter'd no longer than it was shooting; a dwarfish thought, dress'd up in gigantic words, repetition in abundance, looseness of expression, and gross hyperboles." DRYDEN, *Dedication of The Spanish Friar* (1681); SS. vi. 404.

Bussy d'Ambois and *The Revenge of Bussy d'Ambois* are the most famous tragedies of George Chapman (1559?–1634), the translator of Homer.

922, 620. *In vain*, etc. Cf. **288²,** 37 f.
923, 793. *Otter.* "A whimsical character in Jonson's *Epicœne.*" SCOTT.
828. *When*, etc. "In the *Volpone; or, The Fox* (act v, sc. 2) of Ben Jonson, Sir Politic Would-be, a foolish politician, disguises himself as a tortoise, and is detected on the stage: a machine much too farcical for the rest of the piece." [SCOTT.]
924, 891. *Herringman.* v. B. S. xix, xxxviii; **135,** 105.
894. *The Counter Scuffle.* "A burlesque poem on a quarrel and scuffle in the Counter Prison, printed in *The Third Part of Miscellany Poems*, 1716. It is written with considerable humor, though too long to be supported throughout." [SCOTT.]
925. ON THE YOUNG STATESMEN. Some details should be added to the headnote. The poem is found, without statement of authorship, in *A Third Collection of the Newest and Most Ingenious Poems, Satyrs, Songs, &c. against Popery and Tyranny . . .* 1689. It is found, attributed to Dryden, in *Poems on Affairs of State: from the Time of Oliver Cromwell, to the Abdication of K. James the Second*, 1697, a volume that went through various editions to a sixth in 1710 and 1716. — The poem was written before May 2, 1680, for in a letter to Halifax of that date Gilbert Burnet refers to it and attributes it to Buckingham, terming it "a new libel, that looks very like him, and I hear is own'd by him." (See *Some Unpublished Letters of Gilbert Burnet*, ed. Foxcroft, London, 1907, pp. 26, 27: *Camden Miscellany*, vol. xi.) It cannot have been written much before January, 1680, for not till then had the Whig and Trimmer leaders absolutely surrendered to the Tory *chits*. Despite Burnet, it cannot have been written by Buckingham, who had been a constant opponent of Clarendon and who (according to Harris: see below) had perpetrated a vituperative poem, still unpublished, *On the Late Lord Chancellor*. Nor can the verses have been by Rochester, who likewise had written against Clarendon in a poem *On the Lord Chancellor Hyde*: see *Collected Works of John Wilmot, Earl of Rochester*, ed. Hayward (London, 1926), p. 104. Besides this, if Rochester had been the author of the verses, Burnet would probably have known of the fact, for he was visiting that noble from October, 1679, to April, 1680. To the evidence against Dryden given in the headnote a few details may be added. In 1679 he had dedicated *Troilus and Cressida* to Sunderland. In 1681 he praised Laurence Hyde as Hushai in *Absalom and Achitophel*: v. **120, 121,** 888–897. His attitude to Danby varies disagreeably.

In 1678 he had dedicated *All for Love* to him in a tone of fulsome panegyric. But in 1680 or 1681 he had included in *The Spanish Friar*, IV, ii, 101–114, a passage obviously referring to circumstances attending the impeachment of Danby in December, 1678, and more than hinting that his conduct had been "infamously base." On the other hand, aside from the resemblances of style between *On the Young Statesmen* and Dorset's satirical poem *On the Countess of Dorchester*, the political attitude shown in *On the Young Statesmen* is exactly that of Dorset. Finally, *On the Young Statesmen* is attributed to Dorset in *Four Letters to a Friend in North Britain*, London, 1710, a pamphlet published four years after Dorset's death by Robert Walpole, first Earl of Orford, who had been Dorset's personal friend. The preceding account of things depends largely on an article by Brice Harris, entitled "Dorset's Poem, 'On the Young Statesmen,'" in the *Times Literary Supplement* for April 4, 1935.

926. ÆSACUS TRANSFORM'D INTO A CORMORANT. The 1717 text is followed in this edition.

KING JAMES TO HIMSELF. Case notes that in 1703 there were two editions of the book from which this poem is taken. One of them, he says, "may be a piracy." Another edition, called the second, followed in 1716.

927. THE TE DEUM. In *The Primer* this hymn is headed *The Hymn of S. Ambrose and S. Augustine. Te Deum Laudamus.* The *Primer* text has the following variant readings: (6) *thy vaulted;* (16) *with heav-'nly;* (18) *for Thee;* (24) *to stave;* (25) *Vouchsaf'st;* (28) *the Faithful;* (32) *the Blest;* (35) *thy own;* (39) *Nor hour.*

HYMN FOR ST. JOHN'S EVE. In *The Primer* this hymn is headed *On the Feast of the Nativity of S. John Baptist, June 24. The Hymn at Evensong. Ut queant laxis.* The *Primer* text has the following variant readings: (2) *Resounds from Jewry's;* (4) *tune our Voice to sing thy Praise;* (5) *Heav'ns Messenger;* (9) *He heard the News, and dubious with surprise;* (10) *Accents;* (13, 14):

From the Recess of Nature's inmost Room,
Thou knew'st thy Lord unborn from Womb to Womb.

It also adds a fifth stanza:

Glory to God the Father and the Son,
And Holy Ghost with both in Nature One;
Whose equal Pow'r unites the Three
In one eternal Trinity.

928¹. THE MALL. Flecknoe's play, *The Damoiselles à la Mode*, is based on

Molière's *École des femmes, École des maris*, and *Précieuses ridicules:* see J.-E. Gillet, *Molière en Angleterre, 1660–1670*, pp. 40–49 (*Académie Royale de Belgique, Classe des Lettres: Mémoires*, ser. 2, vol. 9, Brussels, 1912).

TO BE WRITTEN UNDER THE DUCHESS OF PORTSMOUTH'S PICTURE. On the Duchess of Portsmouth, the notorious French mistress of Charles II, see headnote, **202¹**, and **914**, 61, n.

928². ON THE DUKE OF BUCKS. Macdonald states (p. 213) that Luttrell's copy of the folio sheet, *A Ballad*, now in the British Museum, is dated 1679. Malone (I, 1, 95–97) gives a long excerpt from the lampoon.

929¹. AN EPITAPH, etc. On Dryden's relations with Rochester see B. S. xliv, xlv.

929². SONGS FROM THE PROPHETESS. These songs were included in *Philomela, or The vocal Musitian: being a Collection of the best and newest Songs; especially those in the two Operas, the 'Prophetess' and 'King* Arthur,' *written by Mr. Dryden: and set to Musick by Mr. Henry Purcell*, a book which is listed in the *Term Catalogues*, June, 1692, but of which no copy is known to have survived. Nevertheless it is highly improbable that Dryden was the author of them: see A. C. Sprague, *Beaumont and Fletcher on the Restoration Stage* (Cambridge, Massachusetts, 1926), pp. 69–71; and Day, who summarizes the evidence (pp. 168, 169).

A FAMILIAR EPISTLE TO MR. JULIAN. On Julian v. **261²**, 17, n. On Sir Carr Scrope (or Scroop) v. **914**, 56, n. Macdonald states (p. 215) that Luttrell's copy of the folio sheet "is inscribed '1679 1*d.*'" He adds, "In MS. Harl. 7319 it [the satire] is dated 1677 and signed 'John Dryden.'"

TO MATILDA. In *Tixall Poetry*, p. 374, Arthur Clifford prints the following note to *On his Mistresse Going a Voyage*, one of the "Poems collected by the Right Honourable Lady Aston":

"I am very much pleased with the structure, and metre, of this little poem, of which I have never met with an example any where else. As a further illustration of its structure, I submit the following composition to the reader, in which I have endeavoured to make the rhymes more exact than those in the text."

Then follows *To Matilda*, a sentimental poem in the taste of the early nineteenth century.

930, 48. *Euryalus the third.* On the hemistichs in these early translations from Virgil, cf. **110**, 87, n; **517¹**, 53 f.

932, 300. *Gate.* v. **643**, 415, n.

ADDITIONAL NOTES

THE NOTES below are for the most part based on books and articles published since 1909, the date of the first issue of the present edition. They supplement and often correct statements made on previous pages of this volume. Other notes, not found in the first edition of this book, have been incorporated in those to pages 900–932.

Among the most important recent books on Dryden and his period are the following: —

(1) Editions of Dryden.

The Poems of John Dryden, edited, with an introduction and textual notes, by John Sargeaunt, Oxford, 1910. (This volume does great service by preserving the spelling and other peculiarities of the original editions and giving photographic reproductions of many title-pages. The spelling and other features, however, are not necessarily those of Dryden's own manuscripts, which were usually copied by a clerk before being sent to press: see Dryden, *Letters*, ed. Ward, pp. 81, 83, 84.)

John Dryden, edited, with an introduction and notes, by George Saintsbury, London and New York, *c.* 1904. 2 vols. (These volumes in the Mermaid Series contain eight of the dramas. The editorial material is slight.)

Dryden: The Dramatic Works, edited by Montague Summers, London, 1931–32. 6 vols. (This is the only complete collection of the dramas that has appeared since the Scott-Saintsbury edition. The elaborate editorial material must be used with caution.)

The Songs of John Dryden, edited by Cyrus Lawrence Day, Cambridge, Massachusetts, 1932. (v. B. S. xxxv. Cited as *Day*. With the kind permission of Professor Day the present editor has here reprinted, without verification, the titles of various song-books cited by him, and has called attention to his reproductions of musical scores. But no attention is here paid to books printed later than 1700.)

The Letters of John Dryden, with Letters Addressed to Him, collected and edited by Charles E. Ward, Durham, North Carolina, 1942. (Cited as *Ward*. This volume supersedes previous collections of Dryden's correspondence.)

The Best of Dryden, edited, with an introduction and notes, by Louis I. Bredvold, New York, 1933. (This contains specimens of Dryden's prose as well as of his verse, together with excellent critical material. In his introduction Professor Bredvold summarizes his views on Dryden's intellectual outlook.)

(2) Bibliography.

John Dryden: a Bibliography of Early Editions and of Drydeniana, by Hugh Macdonald, Oxford, 1939. (This large book is probably the most important contribution to Dryden scholarship since Sir Walter Scott's great edition of 1808. It is not only a bibliography but a guide to all the literature on Dryden up to 1939. Cited as *Macdonald*. In this present reissue of the Cambridge edition of Dryden the editor is indebted to Macdonald at every turn. He has usually verified Macdonald's statements and then let his debt pass without specific acknowledgment. But frequently, as in quoting the advertisements of Dryden's works in contemporary newspapers, he has made no attempt to verify Macdonald's data, but has duly mentioned Macdonald as his authority.)

A Bibliography of English Poetical Miscellanies, 1521–1750, by Arthur Ellicott Case, Oxford, 1935. (This volume is a trustworthy guide to the large number of miscellanies that contain poems by Dryden or attributed to Dryden. Cited as *Case*.)

(3) Biography and criticism.

"Dryden and the Critical Canons of the Eighteenth Century," by Prosser Hall Frye. In *University Studies published by the University of Nebraska*, vol. vii (1907), no. 1. (An excellent account of the general traits of Dryden and his school, as contrasted with those of the Elizabethans and of the romantics.)

The Intellectual Milieu of John Dryden: Studies in Some Aspects of Seventeenth-Century Thought, by Louis I. Bredvold, Ann Arbor, 1934. (This book deals with Dryden's views on religion and politics, showing his relation to the intellectual currents of his time.)

John Dryden: Some Biographical Facts and Problems, by James M. Osborn, New York, 1940. (This volume treats of the progress of Dryden studies and makes important contributions to our knowledge of Dryden's life.)

John Dryden: a Study of His Poetry, by Mark Van Doren, New York, 1946. (This book deals exclusively with literary criticism. It is the best analysis of Dryden's genius as a poet that has been written.)

A History of Restoration Drama, 1660–1700, by Allardyce Nicoll: second edition, Cambridge, England, 1928. (This is the most adequate account of the Restoration drama. Cited as *Nicoll*. It is particularly valuable for its detailed factual information and for its account of the social environment of the Restoration theater.)

3. LETTER TO MADAME HONOR DRYDEN. For a photograph of this letter and for a description of the manuscript, the editor is deeply indebted to the administration of the Clark Library and above all to Mr. H. Richard Archer, Supervising Bibliographer, to whom he returns warm thanks.

The letter is on a folio sheet measuring about 11¼ by 8 inches. The text of the letter, opening with "Madame," begins on page 1 and continues into page 3, leaving page 4 blank. The sheet was then folded for sending, of course with the blank page outside, sealed, and addressed, "To the faire hands," etc. It was presumably sent by some friend of the household, just as a previous message had been dispatched by a clergyman ("the reverend Levite"), so that it required no further address. Dryden set off his verses by a double space and wrote them in a somewhat larger hand than his prose.

In line 7 of the verses only the first two letters of the fifth word are legible; a hole in the paper has been patched. Dryden may have written either *own* or *owne*.

The year at the close of the letter has now absolutely disappeared. Malone's reading of it as 1655 is probably wrong. At all events, among his manuscripts is found an entry from "one of the old books of Trinity College," "obligingly communicated" to him "by the Reverend Doctor Mansel, Master of that College," reading: "April 23, 1655. At the election of Scholars, Wilford is chosen into Sir *Dreyden's* place." (See Osborn, *John Dryden: Some Biographical Facts and Problems*, 1940, page 122.) If 1655 be thus ruled out, Ward's guess of 1653 as the date of the letter seems probable.

This letter was first printed in *The Gentleman's Magazine* for 1785, p. 337. The person who sent it in remarks: "The date of the year is almost obliterated," and wrongly interprets that date as "164 ."

4. STANZAS ON CROMWELL. The *Three Poems* edition gives the only text of this poem published in 1659. The separate edition with that date on the title-page was printed by Tonson about 1691, "to complete his made-up sets of Dryden's poems, &c.": see Macdonald, pp. 6, 7. Aside from the reprint of the *Three Poems* volume mentioned in the headnote, Dryden's poem was reprinted by itself for satiric purposes in 1681, 1682, and 1687. The title-page of the first of these reprints reads: *An Elegy on the Usurper O. C. by the Author of Absalom and Achitophel, published to shew the Loyalty and Integrity of the Poet.*

7. ASTRÆA REDUX. According to Macdonald this poem was advertised in *Mercurius Publicus*, June 21–28, 1660. Osborn writes: "Judging from the copy in the Thomason Tracts, this poem appeared on June 19, 1660 (*Catalogue*, II, 319). Professor Charles E. Ward, of Duke University, who called this date to my attention, points out that the poem was one among more than thirty written for the occasion" (*John Dryden: Some Biographical Facts and Problems*, p. 192, n. 4). Two states of the first edition are known, one of which reads in l. 208, *Like glass we clearness mixt.* — The volume of 1688 was "the first collected edition of Dryden's poems. When *Threnodia Augustalis* was published this 'Elegy' was added to the title, and copies . . . are sometimes found bound up with it" (Macdonald, pp. 15, 16). On the general title-page of the volume of 1688 the poet's name is spelled *Dryden*, but on the separate title-page of *Astræa Redux* in that volume the spelling is *Driden*.

11. TO . . . SIR ROBERT HOWARD. Since the volume of *Poems* by Howard was entered in the *Stationers' Register* on April 16, 1660, Dryden's address to the author is probably earlier than *Astræa Redux* and should have been printed before it in this edition. Like *Astræa Redux*, according to Macdonald Howard's book was advertised in *Mercurius Publicus*, June 21–28, 1660.

13. TO HIS SACRED MAJESTY. There are two states of the first edition, one of which reads in line 32, *Not only King of us but of the year* (Macdonald). The poem was reprinted (from this state) with a French translation in *Complementum Fortunatarum Insularum*, London, 1662.

15, 5. *The Muses*, etc. Clarendon says of himself in his youth: "He could not bring himself to an industrious pursuit of the law study, but rather loved polite learning and history" (*Life of Edward Earl of Clarendon*, Oxford, 1857, i. 8). He contributed a poem of ten lines to Davenant's *Tragedy of Albovine*, 1629. Davenant apparently lived for some time in Hyde's (Clarendon's) suite in the Middle Temple.

17. TO . . . DR. CHARLETON. Macdonald writes (p. 12): "Alterations were made in Dryden's verses as the book was going through the press. I give the differences between the first and the final state, but intermediate states are found." He then cites the variants noted by the present editor for ll. 13, 22, 50, 52, and 55, and adds a variant *in Ore* for l. 39 in the first state.

18. PROLOGUE . . . TO THE WILD GALLANT. Professor Allison Gaw, in his paper,

"Sir Samuel Tuke's *Adventures of Five Hours* in relation to the 'Spanish Plot' and to Dryden" (in *Studies in English Drama*, University of Pennsylvania, 1917), pp. 14–16, was the first to explain correctly the meaning of this prologue. "The first astrologer regrets that the play is straight comedy, since to succeed it should have been an 'opera' like *The Siege of Rhodes*. [v. n. **19**[1], 38.] The second astrologer believes that it is 'endangered by a Spanish plot,' *i. e.*, by the recent popularity of *The Adventures of Five Hours*." This play, by Sir Samuel Tuke, was an adaptation of *Los empeños de seis horas*, a comedy with a very complicated intrigue, attributed to Antonio Coello. Tuke's version "appears to have been the first of the group of Restoration translations from the Spanish drama" (Gaw, p. 23). It was presented at the Duke's Theater on January 8, 1663, and won an immediate triumph. Downes states: "It took successively 13 Days together, no other Play Intervening" (*Roscius Anglicanus*, ed. Knight, 1886, p. 23). "Turning upon this reference," Gaw continues, "and alluding to the opening of Tuke's prologue,

................I dare boldly say,
The English stage ne'r had so new a play,

the Prologue [to *The Wild Gallant*] declares that Dryden, on the contrary,

Bribes you not with anything that 's new.

Not all the wealth of Spain can make Tuke or his like the equals of Fletcher or Jonson. *The Wild Gallant* 'is English and the growth your own'; it will not admit inferiority to any Spanish plot. Moreover, the author is sure you will not censure his shortcomings, because 'in plays he finds you love mistakes'; a reference to the mistakes of Antonio, Henrique, and Carlos, in the complicated intrigue of *The Adventures*, probably also with a covert sneer at Tuke's literary shortcomings, especially in versification. [Gaw here controverts Malone: v. n. **19**[2], 55. He points out in a footnote that Dryden's phrase, "you love mistakes," "is enmeshed in a long passage the reference of which to *The Adventures* is unmistakable."] Finally, the audience is bound to defend the proposition that, in spite of the low opinion held of it by 'some' (*i. e.*, notably Tuke in his epilogue), English wit will continue to triumph."

Macdonald (pp. 99–101) and Osborn (in *Modern Philology*, xxxix, 1941, 83–85) show that two separate editions of *The Wild Gallant* appeared in 1669. No author's variants seem to be involved.

19[2], 13. *There is not*, etc. Gaw points out

(pp. 16, 17) that in the following passage Dryden, by his appeal to the judgment of well-dressed English gentlemen and ladies, resumes his attack on Tuke. In his own epilogue Tuke makes the servant Diego find fault with the play. Thereupon the gentleman Don Henrique, pointing to the humble auditors in the pit, replies:

Think'st thou, Impertinent,
That these, who know the Pangs of bringing forth
A Living Scene, should e'r destroy this Birth.
You ne'r can want such Writers, who aspire
To please the Judges of that Upper Tire.
The Knowing are his Peers, and for the rest
Of the Illiterate Croud (though finely drest)
The Author hopes, he never gave them cause
To think, he'd waste his Time for their Applause.

For other references to Tuke by Dryden see n. **67**[2], 4–6 (on **1050**); n. **386**[2], 40.

20. To THE LADY CASTLEMAINE, etc. This poem was first printed anonymously in *A New Collection of Poems and Songs. Written by several Persons. Never Printed before. Collected by John Bulteel.* London . . . Crook, . . . 1674. [Case, No. 157.] This book occurs in two other issues, the first of which (in the Harvard Library) is the source of the present note; it omits the editor's name from the title-page [Case, No. 157 (b).] A third issue [Case, No. 157 (c)] has a title-page beginning, *Melpomene: or, The Muses Delight*, and is dated 1678.

In this book the poem is headed *To the Dutchess of Cleaveland* and shows the following variants from the text in *Examen Poeticum*: l. 3, *labour'd for in vain;* l. 6, *Is cast;* l. 9, *Virtues;* l. 10, *When they;* l. 17, *Praise and Fame;* l. 18, *Smiles;* l. 29, *you use but for your own defence;* l. 34, *did wait;* l. 35, *With that assurance;* after l. 36 are the following lines, opening a new paragraph:

Well may I rest secure in your great Fate,
And dare my Stars to be unfortunate.

l. 38, *that castives* [sic]; l. 39, *would judge;* l. 43 begins a paragraph; l. 45, *her native;* l. 46, *drest her up;* l. 48, *of age;* l. 49, *But this vast growing Debt of Poesie;* l. 50, *You, Madam, justly.* After l. 52 are the following concluding lines:

Which, that the World as well as you may see,
Let these rude Verses your Acquittance be.
Receiv'd in full this present day and year,
One soveraign smile from Beauties general Heir.

42. *Some god descended*, etc. The Greek dramatists, particularly Euripides (as in his *Orestes* and *Hippolytus*), sometimes introduced a god at the close of a drama

in order to resolve the complications of its plot. Among the references to this practice are the lines of Horace, "Let not a god intervene unless a difficulty occurs worthy of such a deliverer" (*De arte poetica* 191, 192).

PROLOGUE TO THE RIVAL LADIES. Only one edition of this play (that "printed by W. W.") appeared in 1664. The supposition that there were two was caused by a copy of the 1675 edition in the Boston Public Library with a faked date. The edition of 1664 contains the prose preface (dedication to the Earl of Orrery). In stating otherwise the present editor was misled by an imperfect copy in the Boston Public Library. For correction of his error he is indebted to Mr. Haraszti and Miss Manning of the Rare Book Department of that library.

Pepys saw this "very innocent and most pretty witty play" on August 4, 1664. Macdonald dates the first performance "*c*. May, 1664," but there seems to be no positive evidence in the matter.

21. PROLOGUE . . . THE INDIAN EMPEROR. Macdonald (p. 92) points out that *last year* (Prologue, line 6) refers to *The Indian Queen*, acted in 1664, so that the first performance of *The Indian Emperor* must have been in 1665, and that the entry in the *Stationers' Register* shows it to have been in the spring.

22. SONG. Day reprints (pp. 7, 8) "an attractive musical setting by the gifted composer Pelham Humphrey" from *Choice Ayres, Songs, & Dialogues*, 1675 and 1676. He adds (p. 143) that texts of the words are included in *New Court-Songs, and Poems. By R. V. Gent.*, 1672; *Methinks the Poor Town has been troubled too long*, 1673 (two eds.); and *The Wits Academy*, 1677.

The same song, with many variant readings, is printed in *Tixall Poetry* (see headnote, pp. **906, 907**), p. 248 (misnumbered 348). The editor, Arthur Clifford, places it among his "Miscellaneous Poems." He comments (p. 393) that it is found in *New Court-Songs and Poems . . .* 1672; but he fails to recognize it as the work of Dryden. The variant readings of course have no authority, so that they are not cited here.

ANNUS MIRABILIS. See B. S. xxvii. Macdonald (pp. 13–15) distinguishes three issues of the first (1667) edition of this poem and notes also an edition of 1668, probably pirated. The Folger Shakespeare Library in Washington owns all four books and confirms all his statements. The original issue reads in l. 267:

Berkley alone, not making equal way,

and in ll. 417–420:

For now brave *Rupert's* Navy did appear,
  Whose waving streamers from afar he
    knows:
As in his fate something divine there were,
  Who dead and buried the third day arose.

Line 420 evidently gave offense as blasphemous, so that a cancel was inserted modifying the stanza to read as in the present volume. In a third issue (the commonest) a second cancel was inserted containing l. 267 as printed in this volume. "The line as first worded," Macdonald explains, "may have been considered a reflection on Sir William Berkeley, whose courage had been under suspicion in an engagement with the Dutch in the previous year."

In ll. 267 and 417–420 the edition of 1668 agrees with the first issue of 1667.

Macdonald doubts whether all the new readings in the edition of 1688 were due to Dryden. "It is of course possible that he was responsible for some of the small changes that were made, . . . but [others] . . . are clearly degenerations of the well-known type in which an obvious word is substituted for a more 'difficult' but more effective word, e. g. [l. 311] . . . *steer* for *sheer*."

28, 14. *Waxing*. O reads *wexing* in both text and sidenote.

32, 235. *The elephant*, etc.

But, his [the elephant's] huge strength, or subtile
    Wit, cannot
Defend him from the sly *Rhinocerot*:
Who (never with blind fury led) doth venter
Upon his Foe, but (yer the lists he enter)
Against a Rock he whetteth round about
The dangerous pike upon his armèd snout:
Then buckling close, doth not (at random)
    hack
On the hard Cuirass on his Enemie's back;
But under 's belly (cunning) findes a skin,
Where (and but there) his sharpned blade
    will in.
    SYLVESTER, *Dubartas his First Weeke*
    (Sixth Day, ll. 52–61).

39, 568. *Surgeons*. O reads *Chyrurg'ons*.
    581. *Sides*. So O and Q, possibly by an oversight on Dryden's part.
    600. *Into the road*. So O; Q reads *into Road*.

43, 801. *But whate'er*, etc. Mr. G. C. Macaulay (in *Modern Language Review*, v, 1910, 234) corrects the editor for accepting "without sufficient consideration" Scott's note on this passage. "Here there is certainly no reference to Henry III: the meaning is that the cause of the English was so just, that Henry IV, the first Bourbon, would in this instance refuse to side with his descendant, who was their enemy."

51, 7. *Dead colors*. Cf. **741**², 48, n.
52¹. EPILOGUE TO SECRET LOVE; OR, THE MAIDEN QUEEN. G. Thorn-Drury, in his edition of *Covent Garden Drollery, a*

Miscellany of 1672 (London, 1928, pp. 140–143), shows that this epilogue is not by Dryden. It was evidently written for a performance of *The Knight of the Burning Pestle* (a Beaumont and Fletcher play that is now generally regarded as the work of Beaumont alone), modernized so as to include ridicule of *Secret Love; or, The Maiden Queen.* In line 2 *swinge* means *beat, trounce;* and in line 4 *the fop who writ it* (*The Maiden Queen*) is Dryden. The epilogue was spoken by Nell Gwyn (l. 16). In *Covent Garden Drollery* the piece is headed simply *Epilogue* and it follows immediately a *Prologue to The Knight of the Burning Pestle.* Now Langbaine in his *Account of the English Dramatick Poets* (Oxford, 1691) states (p. 210) that *The Knight of the Burning Pestle* "was in vogue some years since, it being reviv'd by the King's House, and a new Prologue . . . being spoken by Mrs. Ellen Guin." It is therefore probable that the prologue and epilogue in *Covent Garden Drollery* were written for the revival of which Langbaine speaks. The date must have been between March 2, 1667, when Pepys described *The Maiden Queen* as "a new play of Dryden's" and 1671, when Nell Gwyn retired from the stage till 1677. It is not extraordinary for a performance at the Theater Royal to ridicule a play that had been staged at the same theater. Both *The Conquest of Granada* and *The Rehearsal* were presented by the Theater Royal company.

5. *The new peaching trick.* Thorn-Drury aptly cites lines from the epilogue to the second part of *The Conquest of Granada:* v. **62²**, 18–20.

16. *And Nell,* etc. "There is evidently something wrong with the text of the last line of it, which is not, I think, remedied by printing the word 'for' instead of 'or.'" [THORN-DRURY.]

Song. Day (p. 143) states: "This exquisite song never attained great popularity, and the music would appear to be irrevocably lost. It was printed in *The New Academy of Complements*, 1671."

The same song, with many variant readings, is printed in *Tixall Poetry* (see headnote, pp. **906, 907**), pp. 146–148, under the title, *Concealed Love.* The editor, Arthur Clifford, states that it came from a folio manuscript marked "Catherine Gage's Booke"; he explains (*Preface*, pp. xii, xiii): "She was the daughter of Sir Thomas Gage, Bart. . . . and the second wife of the third Lord Aston. I have therefore entitled this Third Division [pp. 107–205 of *Tixall Poetry*] 'Poems collected by the Right Honourable Lady Aston.'" Clifford did not notice that the song was by Dryden. The variant readings of course have no

authority, so that they are not cited here.

54. Song I. Day (p. 143) states that the words of this song are found in *The New Academy of Complements*, 1671, and *Windsor Drollery*, 1672, as well as in *Westminster Drollery*, 1671.

Song II. Day (p. 145) states that the words of this song are found in *The New Academy of Complements*, 1671.

57. Prologue . . . An Evening's Love. An entry in the Lord Chamberlain's Department of the Public Record Office shows that this play was acted as early as June 12, 1668: see Nicoll, p. 306. The play is noted in the *Term Catalogues* for February 13, 1671.

58. Song II. Day reprints (p. 25) a setting by Alphonso Marsh from *Choice Songs and Ayres for One Voyce*, 1673. He states (p. 149) that the same setting is found in *Choice Ayres, Songs, & Dialogues*, 1675 and 1676; and that the words are found in *Merry Drollery Complete. The First Part*, 1670 and 1691; *The New Academy of Complements*, 1671; and *Windsor Drollery*, 1672.

Song III. Day reprints (p. 27) a setting by Alphonso Marsh from *Choice Songs and Ayres for One Voyce*, 1673. He states (p. 149) that the same setting is found in *Choice Ayres, Songs, & Dialogues*, 1675 and 1676; and *Wit and Mirth: or Pills to Purge Melancholy*, 1699; and that the words alone are found in *The New Academy of Complements*, 1671; *Windsor Drollery*, 1672; *The Canting Academy*, 1673; *The Compleat Courtier*, 1683; and *Merry Drollery Compleat. The Second Part*, 1691.

59. Song IV. Day states (p. 150) that the words of this song are found in *The New Academy of Complements*, 1671; and *Windsor Drollery*, 1672; as well as in *Westminster Drollery*, 1671 and 1672.

The text in *Westminster Drollery* supplies the following variants: (3) *by your;* (9) *dam your;* (11) *as pale;* (16) *by anger;* (18) *Phisician;* (20) *Puts;* (21) *rowseth;* (22) *its onely;* (23) *guide to;* (26, 28) *do fall.*

Prologue . . . Tyrannic Love. This play was first acted in the last week of June, 1669. See Leslie Hotson, *The Commonwealth and Restoration Stage* (Cambridge, Massachusetts, 1928), pp. 250–253, 348–355, who quotes legal documents.

60. Song. Day states (p. 148) that the words of this song are found in *Windsor Drollery*, 1672. The song was set to music by Henry Purcell for a revival of the drama in 1695: see Purcell's *Works*, xxi (1917), 146, 147. The music with the first two of Dryden's stanzas is found in *Deliciæ Musicæ*, 1695 and 1696; and with the first stanza only in *Orpheus Britannicus*, 1698.

PROLOGUES ... THE CONQUEST OF GRA-
NADA. The First Part of this drama
was acted in December, 1670, and the
Second Part in January, 1671. On
January 2, 1671, Lady Mary Bertie
wrote from Westminster to her niece
Katherine Noel: "There is lately come
out a new play writ by Mr. Dreyden
who made the *Indian Emperor*. It is
caled the *Conquest of Granada*. My
brother Norreys tooke a box and carryed
my Lady Rochester and his mistresse
and all us to, and on Tuesday wee are
to goe see the second part of it which
is then the first tim acted" (*Historical Manuscripts Commission, Rutland,
Twelfth Report, Appendix, Part V,*
1889, p. 22). The play was entered on
the *Stationers' Register* not February
20, but February 25, 1671.

63. SONG I. Day reprints (p. 31) a setting
by John Banister from *Choice Songs and
Ayres for One Voyce*, 1673. He states
(p. 150) that the same setting is found in
Choice Ayres, Songs, & Dialogues, 1675
and 1676; and *Wit and Mirth: or Pills to
Purge Melancholy*, 1699; and that the
words alone are found in *Windsor Drollery*, as well as in *Westminster Drollery*,
1671 and 1672.

SONG II. Day reprints (p. 33) a setting
by Alphonso Marsh from *Choice Songs
and Ayres for One Voyce*, 1673. He
states (p. 151) that the same setting is
found in *Choice Ayres, Songs, & Dialogues*, 1675 and 1676; and *Wit and
Mirth: or Pills to Purge Melancholy*, 1699.
He mentions three other "early musical
settings," but none of them was certainly composed during Dryden's lifetime. He states that the words are in
The New Academy of Complements, 1671;
Windsor Drollery, 1672; and *The Wits
Academy*, 1677, as well as in *Westminster
Drollery*, 1671 and 1672.

64. SONG III. Day reprints (p. 37) a setting
by Nicholas Staggins from *Choice Songs
and Ayres for One Voyce*, 1673. He
states (p. 151) that the same setting is
found in *Choice Ayres, Songs, & Dialogues*, 1675 and 1676; and *Wit and
Mirth: or Pills to Purge Melancholy*, 1699.
He adds that the words alone are in *Westminster Drollery*, 1671 and 1672; *Windsor Drollery*, 1672; and *The New Academy of Complements*, 1671; and that an
imitation of the song under the title
"Concealed Love. A Song" is found in
Holborn Drollery, 1673.

PROLOGUE ... AFTER THE FIRE. G. Thorn-
Drury, in his edition of *Covent Garden
Drollery* (London, 1928), p. 124, quotes
from a manuscript of this prologue in
the British Museum: "The Curtaine
being drawne up all the Actors were discover'd on the stage in Melancholick
postures, & Moone [Mohun, who played

the part of Valentine in the drama] advancing before the rest speaks as follows, addressing himself chiefly to yᵉ
King then prsent."

65. PROLOGUE TO ARVIRAGUS, REVIV'D.
Macdonald (p. 69, n. 7) states that in
London Drollery, 1673, there are verses
referring to this revival and to Dryden's
prologue.

66. PROLOGUE ... MARRIAGE À LA MODE.
This play was written as early as the
summer of 1671 and may possibly have
been performed in that year. See Macdonald, p. 110, and references there
given, especially Charles E. Ward,
"The Dates of Two Dryden Plays," in
*Publications of the Modern Language
Association*, li. 786–788 (September,
1936). The play was entered on the
Stationers' Register March 18, 1673, advertised in *The London Gazette* for May
29–June 2 (according to Macdonald),
and is listed in the *Term Catalogues*
June 16, 1673.

67¹, 31. *And cutting Morecroft*, etc. G. Thorn-
Drury, in his edition of *Covent Garden
Drollery*, 1928, pp. 118–120, supplies a
probable explanation of this line. He
points out that the pronouns *they* and
'em in ll. 27, 29, 30, 34, 36, 37 all naturally refer to "our city friends." "It
seems to me reasonably clear," he continues, "that there had been in and
about 1672, either in the City itself or at
some place to which the citizens could
obtain access, entertainments in the
nature of masquerades which they
patronized and at which a prominent
feature had been a retiring-room provided with a couch, and it is to these that
this passage alludes." He supports this
conjecture by a quotation from *The
Prologue to the Widow*, in *London Drollery*, 1673.

67², 4–6. *Which men of easy phlegm*, etc.
This passage is a jibe at the opening lines
of *The Adventures of Five Hours*, by Sir
Samuel Tuke, in a third, much-revised
edition, 1671:

How happy are the Men of easie Phlegm,
Born on the Confines of Indifference.

Cf. n. **18** (PROLOGUE ... TO THE WILD
GALLANT), on **1046, 1047.**

68¹. SONG I. Day reprints (p. 41) a setting
by Robert Smith from *Choice Songs and
Ayres for One Voyce*, 1673. He states
(p. 155) that the same setting is found in
Choice Ayres, Songs, & Dialogues, 1675
and 1676.

SONG II. Day reprints (p. 43) a setting
by Nicholas Staggins from *Choice Songs
and Ayres for One Voyce*, 1673. He
states (p. 156) that the same setting is
found in *Choice Ayres, Songs, & Dialogues*, 1675 and 1676. To the list of
miscellanies mentioned in the headnote

as containing the words, he adds *The Canting Academy*, 1673, and *The Wits Academy*, 1677. See also headnote to *Enjoyment*, p. **912¹**, and n. **912¹** (on **1039**).

N. B. Allen writes in *The Sources of John Dryden's Comedies* (Ann Arbor, 1935), p. 115: "Professor L. I. Bredvold has called my attention to the fact that [this song] is imitated from a French madrigal which appeared in 1664 in *Recueil de quelques pieces nouvelles et galantes, tant en prose qu'en vers* (pp. 188–189)." He then cites the entire madrigal.

68². A SONG. This song and the following are also found in *Westminster Drollery*, 1672, pp. 125, 126, under the headings, *On Captain Digby's Death, to his Mistress*, and *Answer*. There are the following text variants for the first song: (2) *have I . . . hope no;* (6) *The Fate;* (8) *speedier;* (10) *My Danger;* (13) *would convey;* (14) *would lay;* (16) *You'd say*. Day reprints (p. 39) a setting by Robert Smith from *Choice Songs and Ayres for One Voyce*, 1673. He states (p. 155) that the same setting is found in *Choice Ayres, Songs, & Dialogues*, 1675 and 1676. In both collections the piece "is printed immediately after two indisputable songs of Dryden's." The composer, Robert Smith, wrote the settings for three songs certainly by Dryden: v. nn. **68¹** (*Song I*), **70, 71.** Day adds that there is a five-stanza burlesque of the song in *Mock Songs and Joking Poems*, 1675. Thorn-Drury says in his edition of *Covent Garden Drollery* (London, 1928), pp. 128, 129, that both this song and *The Answer* are found in *The Theatre of Complements*, 1688; and that the first piece alone is in *Windsor Drollery*, 1672, and *The Canting Academy*, ed. 2, 1674. Thorn-Drury argues against Dryden's authorship even of *Farewell, Fair Armeda;* Day effectively replies to him.

69. THE ANSWER. *Westminster Drollery* furnishes the following variants: (6) *your fate;* (8) *of a love;* (10) *the effect;* (14) *To my window*.

70. SONG. Day reprints (p. 45) a setting by Robert Smith from *Choice Songs and Ayres for One Voyce*, 1673. He states (p. 157) that the same setting is found in *Choice Ayres, Songs, & Dialogues*, 1675 and 1676; and that the words alone are in *London Drollery*, 1673, and *Methinks the Poor Town has been troubled too long*, 1673 (two editions).

PROLOGUE . . . AMBOYNA. The prologue cited from *Covent Garden Drollery* had appeared before in *Westminster Drollery*, which was entered on the *Stationers' Register* June 3, 1672, so that — unless the contents of that miscellany was altered after it was registered — Dryden's

play must have been performed before that date. See C. E. Ward, "The Dates of Two Dryden Plays," in *Publications of the Modern Language Association*, li (1936), 788–792.

71. SONG I. Day reprints (p. 47) a setting by Robert Smith from *Choice Songs and Ayres for One Voyce*, 1673. (The first stanza of the words is omitted.) He states (p. 157) that the same setting is found in *Choice Songs, & Dialogues*, 1675 and 1676; and that the words alone are found in *London Drollery*, 1673, and (lacking the first stanza) in *Methinks the Poor Town has been troubled too long*, ed. 2, 1673.

72. SONG II. Day states that this song appears in *Methinks the Poor Town has been troubled too long*, ed. 2, 1673.

PROLOGUE . . . OXFORD. Ward (*Letters of John Dryden*, 1942, p. 145) gives sound reasons for dating the letter from Dryden to Rochester referring to these pieces as not later than May 13, 1673. The Italian players to whom Dryden refers in ll. 11–20 of the *Epilogue* came to England in April, 1673: see *Calendar of Treasury Books*, 1672–75, p. 119. Thus the pieces themselves may be dated within narrow limits. In the letter Dryden speaks of sending them to Rochester. They had probably been published as a separate sheet, now lost.

73², 30. MACBETH. In the rough accounts of Sir Henry Herbert, Master of the Revels, for November 3, 1663, there is an item that probably refers to Davenant's revision of *Macbeth* (see J. Q. Adams, *Dramatic Records of Sir Henry Herbert*, New Haven, 1917, p. 138), but there is no evidence that the revised drama reached the stage in that year. On November 5, 1664, Pepys saw it and found it "a pretty good play, but admirably acted." The fact that Dryden in 1673 was in the employ of the King's Company explains sufficiently his slur on a production at the Duke's Theater, the house of the rival company.

74². 53. *Machines and tempests*. The alteration of *The Tempest* by Davenant and Dryden (v. p. **55**) was an exceptionally successful play, probably in part owing to the song and dance elements added to the text, Pepys saw it eight times from November 7, 1667, to January 21, 1669. Early in 1674 the Duke's Company decided that further songs and dances and more elaborate theatrical machinery would add fresh charm to the piece, and employed Shadwell to make operatic additions. (They could not turn to Dryden, since he was now under contract to write for the King's Company.) The results were as described by Downes: v. n. **74²**, 53, on p. **952**. The doubly refurbished drama (or "opera") seems to have been first acted in April, 1674; a document cited by Nicoll (p. 318) shows that it was still running in the middle of May. It was probably the most popular play of the Restoration period and continued in favor later; some of the additions to Shakespeare's text did not disappear from the stage till the nineteenth century. The closing line of Dryden's prologue "spoken at the opening of the New House [of the King's Company], March 26, 1674," obviously refers to this altered, magnificent, operatic version of *The Tempest*, with copious stage machinery, known to be in preparation by the Duke's Company, and expresses humorous apprehensions concerning its effect on the King's Company.

The Davenant-Dryden text of *The Tempest* was published early in 1670, being mentioned in the number of the *Term Catalogues* licensed on February 17. It was not reprinted until 1701, when it was included in the folio edition of Dryden's dramas. After that, according to Montague Summers, it was lost from sight (except for "a privately printed American edition") until 1922, when he included it in his *Shakespeare Adaptations*. Summers later printed it in his edition of *Dryden: The Dramatic Works*, 1931–32. The text as revised by Shadwell was printed late in 1674, being mentioned in the number of the *Term Catalogues* licensed on November 25. It was frequently reprinted, both by itself and in collections of Dryden's dramas; it is that found in SS. Summers included it in his edition of Shadwell's works, 1927. As published, it retained Dryden's prologue and epilogue of 1667 (those first printed in 1670), but a prologue and epilogue evidently written by Shadwell for his revision of 1674 have survived in a manuscript in the British Museum. The prologue replies to Dryden's prologue and epilogue of March 26, 1674. Shadwell's prologue and epilogue may be found in W. J. Lawrence, *The Elizabethan Playhouse and Other Studies*, 1912, pp. 200–202 (in an article reprinted from *Anglia*, xxvii. 205–217), and in Summers' edition of Shadwell.

Some of the statements above are controversial. For discussions of the questions involved see Macdonald, pp. 101–103, and references cited by him; also H. Spencer, *Shakespeare Improved* (Cambridge, Massachusetts, 1927), pp. 192–210, 238, 239.

76. EPILOGUE . . . CALISTO. Eleanore Boswell, in *The Restoration Court Stage* (Cambridge, Massachusetts, 1932), pp. 177–227, discusses at length this performance of *Calisto*, which she terms

(p. 208) "probably the most elaborate production staged at Whitehall during the entire Restoration period." She finds (p. 226) that the extant bills for it "come to no less than £3526. 19. 11¾." She thinks (p. 181) that the first performances (not rehearsals) of it were in February, 1675. See also Nicoll, pp. 319–322.

Professor W. B. Gardner, in an article on "Dryden and the Authorship of the Epilogue to Crowne's *Calisto*" (see *Studies in English*, Austin, Texas, June, 1948: xxvii. 234–238), finds that the epilogue printed by Crowne with *Calisto* when it was published in 1675 is essentially a modification of the present epilogue, and argues that both epilogues were written by Crowne. He states that the greatest difference between the two pieces is that lines 21–28 of the present text were toned down by "the deletion of certain specific references to the current war between the French and the Dutch," becoming:

And since Your Rule such joy to all procures,
All should contribute what they can to Yours.
Wit by Your Smiles a Lustre do's maintain,
And Beauty keeps a long and happy Raign.
Your Right in them is therefore so entire,
They, above all, Your Pleasure should conspire.

"The year 1675," Professor Gardner continues, "was a most critical one for King Charles, since he was attempting to steer his course between Scylla and Charybdis: on the one hand, Danby was pressing him to conclude an alliance with the Dutch; on the other hand, he had already begun negotiations for a secret treaty with King Louis. Therefore, it is evident that such undiplomatic lines as [those in the text of the present volume] were not acceptable in 1675, especially since they were to be spoken at Court. Hence Crowne was undoubtedly ordered to revise them, and [the passage quoted above] is the result. When the *Miscellany Poems* was published seven [*sic*, really nine] years later, the inclusion of the original epilogue could have no unfortunate repercussions."

Professor Gardner's explanation of the situation is plausible but by no means certain. He himself states an objection: "How [Crowne's first text] came to be included by Tonson — and apparently at the last moment almost like an afterthought — in the 1684 *Miscellany Poems*, which contains no other poem accredited to Crowne, cannot be determined." There seems to have been no bitterness between Dryden and Crowne at this time. In his address "To the Reader," published with *Calisto* in 1675, Crowne wrote: "Had it [*Calisto*] been written by him to whom by the double right of place and merit the honor of the employment belonged, the pleasure had been in all kinds complete." It is conceivable that Crowne asked Dryden to write an epilogue for his masque; and that later, when Dryden's version proved unacceptable for political reasons, Crowne rewrote it entirely, though out of courtesy he preserved some general features of Dryden's work, and published his own version with his play. Later Tonson, who was in close relations with Dryden but apparently not with Crowne, obtained Dryden's version for *Miscellany Poems*, 1684, though Dryden chose to withhold his name from the piece.

John Dennis, in a letter of 1719 (see *The Critical Works of John Dennis*, ed. Hooker, Baltimore, 1939–1943: ii. 405), says that Crowne was given the nomination for "writing the Mask of *Calypso*" [*sic*] through the malice of Rochester, "who design'd by that Preference to mortify Mr. *Dryden*." This statement, made forty-four years after the event, is partially confirmed by Crowne's own words, quoted above. And Dryden in his Dedication of *Aureng-Zebe* to Mulgrave (1676) has a passage that may refer to the matter: "In all courts there are too many who make it their business to ruin wit, and Montaigne . . . tells us what effects he found of their good natures. He describes them such, whose ambition, lust, or private interest seem to be the only end of their creation. If good accrue to any from them, it is only in order to their own designs: conferred most commonly on the base and infamous; and never given, but only happening sometimes on well-deservers." Finally Dennis, in his Epistle Dedicatory to Mulgrave of *The Advancement and Reformation of Modern Poetry* (1701), writes in reference to Dryden ("a Great Man deceas'd"): "'Tis known to all the observing World, that you generously began to espouse him, when he was more than half oppress'd, by a very formidable Party in the Court of King *Charles* II. a Faction that wanted neither Power nor Authority to crush him. . . . They, upon an unaccountable Pique which they had taken to his Person, would have oppress'd his growing Merit; Your Lordship, in Consideration of that rising Merit, cherish'd his Person, notwithstanding his pretended Frailties" (*Op. cit.*, i. 198). This passage harmonizes with the unswerving loyalty for Mulgrave that Dryden expressed throughout his life.

77. PROLOGUE . . . AURENG-ZEBE. A record in the Lord Chamberlain's Department of the Public Record Office indicates that this play was first acted November 17, 1675: see Nicoll, p. 307. According to Macdonald (p. 114) it was advertised in *The London Gazette* for February 17–

21, 1676, but it is not mentioned in the *Term Catalogues* until May 5 of that year.

78. EPILOGUE TO THE MAN OF MODE. An entry in the Lord Chamberlain's Department of the Public Record Office indicates that this play was first acted March 11, 1676: see Nicoll, p. 310. According to Macdonald the published play was advertised in *The London Gazette* for July 3–6, 1676, but it was not entered in the *Term Catalogues* until Michaelmas term (November) of that year.

PROLOGUE TO CIRCE. An entry in the Lord Chamberlain's Department of the Public Record Office shows that this play was acted as early as May 12, 1677: see Nicoll, p. 310. It was entered in the *Stationers' Register* for June 19, 1677.

80. PROLOGUE . . . ALL FOR LOVE. Nicoll states (p. 16 n.): "In *The Theatrical Inquisitor and Monthly Mirror* of July, 1816, a document is printed purporting to be a list of takings at the T[heater] R[oyal] for a performance of *All for Love* on Wed. Dec. 12, 1677." Macdonald says that the printed play was advertised in *The London Gazette* for March 21–25, 1678.

81. EPILOGUE TO MITHRIDATES. For the epilogue printed by Scott, see pp. **904–906**.

82. PROLOGUE . . . THE KIND KEEPER. An entry in the Lord Chamberlain's Department of the Public Record Office indicates that this play was acted as early as March 11, 1678: see Nicoll, p. 311.

83. PROLOGUE TO A TRUE WIDOW. See headnote, pp. **908, 909**.

86. SONG. Day reprints (p. 55) a setting by Thomas Farmer from *Choice Ayres and Songs*, 1681. He states (pp. 158, 159) that "there is a different setting of later date in *A Collection of Songs . . . Compos'd by Mr. John Eccles, ca. 1704*," and that the words were printed in *The Compleat Courtier*, 1683, and in a broadside.

102. AN EPITAPH ON SIR PALMES FAIRBORNE'S TOMB IN WESTMINSTER ABBEY. This poem appeared anonymously in *Poetical Recreations: . . . Part I. Occasionally written by Mrs. Jane Barker. Part II. By several Gentlemen of the Universities, and Others. . . . 1688*: pp. 6, 7 of Part II. It is there headed: *An Epitaph to the Memory (and fix't on the Tomb) of Sir Palme Fairborn, Governour of Tangier, who, in Execution of his Command, was Mortally Wounded by a Shot from the Moors, that then besieged the town, Octob. 24. 1680*. The last two lines are lacking and there are the following variant readings: (l. 1) *this Marble*, (l. 6) *he will these Walls*, (l. 16) *Vertues*, (l. 17) *the height*.

The text in *Examen Poeticum* has the following variant readings: (l. 16) *Vertues*, (l. 23) *time*.

103¹. PROLOGUE . . . THE SPANISH FRIAR. It would seem that Charles II saw this play, presumably at its first performance, on March 8, 1680: see entry in the Lord Chamberlain's Department of the Public Record Office, quoted by Nicoll, p. 311. On December 8, 1686, under James II, the drama was prohibited: see Nicoll, p. 10, n. 3. — The story of Olympia is told by Ariosto, *Orlando Furioso*, cantos ix–xi; Bireno deserts her in x. 19. The song that Dryden made for her is reprinted under the title, "The Farewel to Ingratitude," in *Female Poems on Several Occasions. Written by Ephelia;* ed. 2, 1682, p. 116: see Macdonald, p. 123, n. 4.

12, 13. *Tho'*, etc. These two lines are omitted in ed. 2 (1686); they are found in eds. 1, 3, and 4 (1681, 1690, 1695) and in the collected edition of Dryden's dramas (1701).

103². SONG. Day states (p. 160) that the original melody for this song was composed by "Captain Pack, an obscure musician of little skill." He reproduces it (p. 59) from a manuscript of about 1681. He adds that it was first printed in *Wit and Mirth; or Pills to Purge Melancholy*, 1707 and 1709; and that the words alone are found in *Wit and Drollery. Jovial Poems*, 1682, and *The Compleat Courtier*, 1683.

106¹. PROLOGUE TO THE UNIVERSITY OF OXFORD. W. J. Lawrence, in an article on "Oxford Restoration Prologues" in the *Times Literary Supplement* for January 16, 1930, states that this prologue is found in "a neatly penned quarto manuscript volume of miscellaneous late seventeenth-century verse" (Eng. Poet. E. 4) in the Bodleian Library, where it is described as "A Prologue to the University of Oxford at the Act 1676; by his Majesties Servants." R. G. Ham, in *The London Mercury*, xx. 421 (March, 1930), gives the same information. This establishes the date of the piece, which should have been printed earlier (page 78) in this edition of Dryden.

107. PROLOGUE . . . TO THE UNHAPPY FAVORITE. The text of the *Prologue* published with the play in 1682 shows no variants from that of 1685. The text of the *Epilogue* of 1682 agrees with that of 1685 in ll. 11, 14, 18, 20, 24, 25, 31, 32, 36. It adds the following variants: (15) *Fore-shows* [and so, with no hyphen, 1685 ed.]; (22) *Or what is . . . to spight us*.

108. ABSALOM AND ACHITOPHEL. Macdonald, confirmed by Osborn, lists seven London editions of this poem in 1681 and 1682, to say nothing of two different Latin translations printed at Oxford in 1682; two Dublin editions; and a cheap separate edition with a crude key, undated and without name of publisher. There were two folio editions in 1681, the first of which exists in "four issues or states": all these folio texts lack ll. 180–191 and 957–960. Two "second editions" in quarto, containing these lines, appeared in 1681. In 1684 the poem ("the sixth edition"!) was included in *Miscellany Poems* (v. p. **168**); thereafter it appeared repeatedly in various combinations. Apparently all forms of the poem after the earlier of the "second editions" of 1681 are mere printer's reprints, not reviewed by Dryden. So the text of the present volume is based on the earlier of the "second editions" of 1681.

References to "Oswald" in the notes on *Absalom and Achitophel*, *The Medal*, and *Mac Flecknoe* are to an unpublished University of California dissertation by Norman Hubert Oswald, *The Satires of John Dryden: a Critical Edition*, 1946.

109, 1. *In pious times*, etc. B. J. Pendlebury, in *Dryden's Heroic Plays* (London, 1923), p. 109, calls attention to the following soliloquy of Don John of Austria, the illegitimate son of the Emperor Charles V, at the opening of the second act of Otway's *Don Carlos* (1676):

Why should dull Law rule Nature, who first made
That Law by which herself is now betray'd?
E'er Man's Corruptions made him wretched, he
Was born most Noble that was born most Free:
Each of himself was Lord, and unconfin'd,
Obey'd the Dictates of his God-like Mind.
Law was an Innovation brought in since,
When Fools began to love Obedience,
And called their Slavery Safety and Defence.
My Glorious Father got me in his Heat,
When all he did was eminently Great;
When warlike Belgia felt his conqu'ring Pow'r,
And the proud Germans own'd him Emperor.
Why should it be a stain then on my Blood,
Because I came not in the common Road,
But born obscure, and so more like a God.

Pendlebury thinks that the "verbal echoes of this passage in the first twenty lines of *Absalom and Achitophel*" were "possibly intended as deliberate satire of Otway, with whom Dryden was not on good terms." The present editor regards them as more likely due to half-unconscious recollection of Otway's play, which was first produced about June, 1676.

110, 18. *So beautiful.* "But in all Israel there was none to be so much praised as Absalom for his beauty; from the sole of his foot even to the crown of his head there was no blemish in him." 2 Sam. xiv. 25.

111, 156. *A fiery soul*, etc. "In this description of Achitophel Dryden is thinking of the Aristotelian theory in which soul represents form and body represents matter. The word 'o'erinform'd' is used in the Aristotelian sense, and the 'fiery soul' recalls the theories of certain Greek philosophers. The classical associations of the passage are reinforced by the word 'pigmy' which is Greek in origin. What Dryden intends to convey is that in Shaftesbury there was too much 'form' for the 'matter.'" VERRALL, *Lectures on Dryden* (Cambridge, England, 1914), pp. 73, 74.

112, 179. *Patriot's.* According to Macdonald (p. 21) *Patron's* of two of the issues of the first folio edition of 1681 is a misprint; three other, more obvious, misprints occur on the same page. All four corrections are made in two of the issues of that edition. — In certain peculiarities of the first folio edition Macdonald finds "some confirmation" of the present editor's conjecture that lines 180–191 were in Dryden's original draft, but he adds: "It does not seem possible to explain the bibliographical eccentricity of this edition by the mere excision at the last moment of the twelve lines; and the fact that the only wrong catchword in the pamphlet . . . occurs here, may indicate that Dryden's text was not originally quite as it is in this edition or in its final form."

217. *When she the prime renews.* "Here the historical references are to the changes of government which took place within the memory of living men at intervals of about twenty years: the Long Parliament met in 1640, Charles II was restored in 1660, and the crisis of the Exclusion Bill was in 1680. Dryden's jest is that everything recurs, 'treads the same track,' as does even the inconstant moon when 'she the prime renews.' This last reference is not, I think, to the monthly change of the moon, but to the recurrence of similarity in the relative position of sun and moon which takes place about every twenty years. . . . When the discrepancy between sun and moon is reconciled by an adjustment of the Calendar, the moon may be said to recur to her original [starting] point, to 'renew the prime'; the cycle of the Jewish Calendar, at the end of which such a readjustment was made, was a period of 19 years." VERRALL, *Lectures on Dryden,* pp. 72, 73, n. Cf. **242,** 1830, n.

227. *Drawn,* etc. The copy of *Lachrymæ Musarum* mentioned in the note to this line on **960** is now (1948) in the Henry E. Huntington Library at San Marino, California.

239. *The young men's vision,* etc. "Your old men shall dream dreams, your young men shall see visions." Joel ii. 28.

113, 270. *He is not now,* etc. "What is the effect intended in the triplet? Is not the picture meant to be disagreeable? —

> *Cov'ring* the beach, and *black'ning* all the strand.

What does it call up to us? Beetles? Achitophel undoubtedly means to sneer at royalist sentiment and there is an involuntary recoil of feeling on the crowd, the populace, as such. This leads on consistently to his palpable sneer in the word 'tumbling': —

> Comes tumbling downward with diminish'd light, (274)

where the undignified words vaguely suggest the collapse of a sort of cockchafer-glow-worm. It is interesting to contrast this allusion by Achitophel with Dryden's own description of the same scene in his *Astræa Redux.*" VERRALL, *Lectures on Dryden,* p. 69. v. **10,** 276–283.

114, 373. *Him staggering,* etc. "Such inversion is not common in Dryden, nor is it in the manner proper to a narrative about contemporary politicians, or historical personages as such; it is obviously Miltonic, and a Latinism, and so carries with it a suggestion of Milton's Satan. And a comparison between the temptation of Monmouth and that of Adam is actually made by Dryden in the prefatory address, 'To the Reader.'" VERRALL, *Lectures on Dryden,* p. 55. v. **109**[1], 56–**109**[2], 3.

381. *Not that,* etc. "Here Dryden has to face one of the greatest difficulties inherent in his theme. Achitophel must criticise the king; but royal ears are rarely willing to hear criticism, and possibly the royal memory might retain the fact that the words had been written by Dryden, though they were put into the mouth of Achitophel. The peril is evaded with masterly skill. The criticism of Charles is made into an imputation of virtues. He is mild, he is lavishly generous to his subjects. It is true he is charged with real vices as well [**109,** 1–16]; but they are vices he was proud of, not vices he was ashamed of. He thought the better of himself for his amours, and his courtiers thought the better of him too. Thus lightly did Dryden skim over the dangerous ice; thus skilfully did he frame criticism so as to be more welcome to the subject of it than panegyric." HUGH WALKER, *English Satire and Satirists* (London, 1925), p. 153.

115, 458. *And self-defense,* etc. Oswald notes Dryden's reference to Hobbes, *Leviathan,* part I, ch. xiv: "And consequently it is a precept, or generall rule of Reason, *That every man, ought to en-*

deavour Peace, as farre as he has hope of obtaining it; and when he cannot obtain it, that he may seek, and use, all helps, and advantages of Warre. The first branch of which Rule, containeth the first, and Fundamentall Law of Nature; which is, *to seek Peace, and follow it.* The Second, the summe of the Right of Nature; which is, *By all means we can, to defend our selves.*"

476. *They who,* etc. The line, as Walker states (*Op. cit.*, p. 154), "is clearly suggested by the experience of the Civil War." Charles I was a prisoner in the hands of his opponents from May 5, 1646, to his execution on January 30, 1649.

116, 512. *Not only,* etc. "The line . . . indicates with unsurpassed neatness that the conflict had been, and still was with many, a conflict of political theories, and not merely a question of persons." WALKER, *Op. cit.*, p. 154.

544. *Zimri.* Lady Burghclere (*George Villiers, Second Duke of Buckingham,* New York, 1903, p. 195) shows that the charge that the "adulterous countess [of Shrewsbury] held her lover's horse in the disguise of a page," at the time of his duel with her husband, lacks foundation in fact.

J. Q. Wolf, in *Modern Language Notes,* xlvii (1932), 97–99, points out that Dryden probably had in mind not only the Zimri of Numbers xxv. 6–15, but the traitorous Zimri of 1 Kings xvi. 8–20.

117, 574. *Caleb.* The identification with Lord Grey depends on the *Key* of 1716 and is supported by the story (taken from Scott) cited on **961.** But in *A Key (with the Whip) to Open the Mystery and Iniquity of the Poem called Absalom and Achitophel,* 1682, Caleb is identified with Arthur Capel, Earl of Essex. E. S. de Beer, in the *Review of English Studies,* xvii (1941), 308, comments: "The resemblance of his family name, Capel, to Caleb, and his high moral character, both make the identification probable."

576. *Porridge.* E. S. de Beer, in the *Review of English Studies,* xvii (1941), 308 n. 1, remarks: "Dryden appears to be counter-attacking the nonconformists who described the Church services as 'porridge.'" Pepys, in his *Diary* for August 24, 1662, writes: "Among other things they tell me that there hath been a disturbance in a church in Friday street; a great many young people knotting together and crying out 'Porridge' often and seditiously in the church, and they took the Common Prayer Book, they say, away; and, some say, did tear it." On this Lord Braybrooke comments: "*Porridge* was the nickname given by the Dissenters to the Book of Common Prayer. . . . The meaning of

this word is fully explained in a rare contemporary tract, called *A Vindication of the Book of Common Prayer against the contumelious slanders of the Fanatic Party, terming it Porridge.*"

585. *Shimei.* Slingsby Bethel seems to have been stingy only in his official capacity. Narcissus Luttrell wrote about October 29, 1681; that is, less than three weeks before the publication of *Absalom and Achitophel:* "Slingsby Bethell esq., and lately one of the sheriffs of the citty of London, hath given to the two Compters and Ludgate prisons severall hundred pounds, for the relief of poor prisoners for debt" (*Brief Historical Relation of State Affairs,* Oxford, 1857: i. 140).

598. *The sons of Belial.* The phrase is biblical (Judges xix. 22; 1 Sam. ii. 12; 2 Sam. xxiii. 6) and Miltonic (*Paradise Lost,* i. 501, 502), but here it may have a special meaning. H. T. Cunningham, in the *Times Literary Supplement* for June 10, 1939, p. 342, notes that Balliol College "became the Whig headquarters for the short time the Oxford Parliament [v. B. S. xli] sat." Dryden's *Absalom, Achitophel,* Balaam (l. 574), and Caleb (l. 574, if the identification with Lord Grey be correct) were all lodged there. "It seems likely that the familiar old pun on 'Balliol' must have been applied to the Whigs by the Tories, and that the name stuck after their association with Balliol had ended."

118, 676. *Agag's murther.* E. S. de Beer, in the *Review of English Studies,* xvii (1941), 308, 309, writes pertinently: "Greatly as Godfrey's violent death helped Oates's rise, Oates certainly did not appeal to anyone in authority for his removal, much less for his murder; there is nothing to show that he had any direct part in Godfrey's death and it is extremely unlikely that he was an accessory of any kind to it. A far more likely identification is with Sir William Scroggs. As lord chief justice Scroggs had presided at the trial of Sir George Wakeman on 18 July 1679, and, in accordance with the evidence, had summed up in his favor; Wakeman was duly acquitted. The result was a shower of abuse on Scroggs, and in due course Oates and Bedloe presented to the Council, 'Articles of high misdemeanour' against him; Scroggs had no difficulty in answering them, and on 21 January 1680 the king and Council declared themselves satisfied with his reply. It is to Oates's articles against Scroggs that Dryden alludes; they are compared with Samuel's utterances in 1 Samuel xv."

119, 785, 786. *What standard,* etc. "I cannot accept Mr. Churton Collins's suggested explanation of [this] couplet, . . . which he calls 'very obscure.' . . . The lines are perhaps obscure — a rare fault in Dryden — but the metaphor is unmistakable: the 'mark' is the extreme high-water mark of a spring tide, and Dryden observes, quite accurately, that the higher the tide and consequently the greater the distance between high and low water-mark (the interval of time between tides remaining the same), the more rapid is the fall of the water at the ebb. The words 'flowing,' 'mark,' and 'runs out' would seem sufficient to indicate the metaphor, and all doubt is removed by the allusion in the next lines to another effect of the moon, mistress, in the opinion of the time, alike of madness and of the tides." VERRALL, *Lectures on Dryden*, p. 87.

120, 850, 851. *Now, free,* etc. Reminiscent of Virgil, *Ec.* v. 56, 57: cf. **430,** 86–89; **277, 278,** 66–75.

121, 939. *Thus long have I,* etc. v. B. S. xliii, xliv. Malone (I, 1, 154, 155) quotes portions of the Oxford speech (erroneously calling it "the King's Speech on *dissolving* the Parliament assembled at Oxford") and compares them with ll. 989–1011. The following excerpts are somewhat more ample, including sentences that resemble ll. 965–970:

"The unwarrantable Proceedings of the last House of Commons were the Occasion of My parting with the last Parliament; for I, who will never use arbitrary Government Myself, am resolved not to suffer it in others: I am unwilling to mention Particulars, because I am desirous to forget Faults; but whoever shall calmly consider what Offers I have formerly made, and what Assurances I renewed to the last Parliament, ... and shall then reflect upon the strange unsuitable Returns made to such Propositions by Men that were called together to consult, perhaps may wonder more that I had Patience so long, than that at last I grew weary of their Proceedings. I have thought it necessary to say thus much to you, that I may not have any new Occasion given Me to remember more of the late Miscarriages. It is as much My Interest, and shall be as much My Care, as yours, to preserve the Liberty of the Subject; because the Crown can never be safe when that is in Danger. And I would have you likewise be convinced, that neither your Liberties nor Properties can subsist long, when the just Rights and Prerogatives of the Crown are invaded, or the Honour of the Government brought low and into Disreputation. I let you see, by My calling this Parliament so soon, that no Irregularities in Parliament shall make Me out of Love with them; ... and at the same Time give One Evidence more, that I have not neglected My Part, to

give that general Satisfaction and Security, which, by the Blessing of God, may be attained, if you on your Parts bring suitable Dispositions towards it; and that the just Care you ought to have of Religion be not so managed and improved into unnecessary Fears, as to be made a Pretence for changing the Foundations of the Government. ... I conclude with this One Advice to you, That the Rules and Measures of all your Votes may be the known and established Laws of the Land, which neither can nor ought to be departed from nor changed, but by Act of Parliament; and I may the more reasonably require that you make the Laws of the Land your Rule, because I am resolved they shall be Mine."

122, 979, 980. *Without,* etc. Davies (p. 80 of article cited, B. S. xliv, n. 3) remarks that this couplet is "a reasonable paraphrase" of words in the *Declaration:* "We have reason to believe ... that if We could have been brought to give Our Consent to a Bill of Exclusion, the Intent was not to rest there, but to pass further, and to attempt some other Great and Important Changes even in Present."

987, 988. *Unsatiate,* etc. Davies (p. 81) regards this couplet as "a picturesque way of saying what the *Declaration* had complained of more prosaically — that the gracious concessions offered by the King had all been rejected as insufficient."

993, 994. *Votes,* etc. Davies (p. 80) thinks that this couplet "may well have been inspired by the complaint in the *Declaration:* 'By which Vote, without any regard to the Laws establish'd, they [Commons] assumed to themselves a Power of Suspending Acts of Parliament, ...'"

995, 996. *No groundless,* etc. Davies (p. 80) suspects that this couplet "may have been suggested by 'Strange illegal Votes, declaring divers eminent Persons to be enemies to the King and Kingdom, without any Order or Process of Law, ... or any Proof so much as offer'd against them.'"

1013. *Till viper-like,* etc. As Oswald indicates, the reference is to a familiar bit of the "unnatural natural history" still current in Dryden's time: see Sir Thomas Browne, *Pseudodoxia Epidemica,* book iii, ch. 16.

PROLOGUE ... THE LOYAL BROTHER. The approximate date of production of this play is established by Luttrell's note, "7 February 168⅔," on his copy of the broadside prologue and epilogue, now in the Huntington Library. This statement corrects the headnote.

124. PROLOGUE ... TO THE PRINCESS OF CLEVES. Macdonald aptly states (p. 69,

n. 10) that, since this prologue and epilogue were not printed with the early editions of the play, "they must have been written for a special performance." Presumably they were first printed on a separate sheet, now lost.

125. THE MEDAL. The two issues of the first edition of this poem mentioned in the headnote are both owned by the Harvard College Library. A copy of the first edition, *with* the Latin motto, owned by the University of California Library, agrees in lines 179–182 with the text of the Harvard copy *without* the Latin motto. Thus at least three issues of the first edition must be recognized. Macdonald mentions Edinburgh and Dublin editions of 1682. On the third edition (1692), mentioned in the headnote, see n. **134,** below.

The story told by Spence, related in the headnote, does not inspire confidence.

127¹, 12. *Davila.* Dryden had used this historian as a source when working on *The Duke of Guise.*

128, 41. *Interlope.* Mr. G. M. Trevelyan, in *England under the Stuarts* (New York, 1904, p. 48), describes how various chartered companies controlled English trade in different remote quarters of the globe, and protected Englishmen there, claiming in return "that no Interloper should drive an independent trade in those waters."

131, 287–322. *Without a vision,* etc. As Walker points out, in this passage Dryden refers to the history of England beginning with the Civil War and ending with the Restoration, and views with alarm a possible repetition of the same general course of events. "Dryden did not foresee the moderation of the new revolution towards which events were moving when he wrote. He believed there could be no half-way house between monarchy as he knew it and the rule of the multitude; and, like many of our greatest literary men from Shakespeare to Carlyle, he had a profound distrust of the multitude" (*English Satire and Satirists,* London, 1925, p. 155).

132, 304. *And frogs,* etc. Oswald remarks: "The reference, neatly combined with the reference to the plagues of Egypt, is to Æsop's fable concerning the frogs who asked Jupiter for a king." v. Exod. viii. 1–15. As Oswald says, Dryden probably had in mind La Fontaine's version of the fable.

PROLOGUE TO HIS ROYAL HIGHNESS, etc. There were two issues of the broadside edition of this piece.

133. TO THE DUCHESS, etc. On his copy of this prologue, now in the Huntington Library, Luttrell wrote, "At ye Dukes theater at Venice preserv'd &c Acted 31 May 1682." So the Duchess at-

tended the same play that her husband had witnessed on April 21 (see headnote, **132**). And Otway again wrote a special epilogue for the occasion (see Macdonald, p. 142, n. 2).

134. MAC FLECKNOE. Malone's authority for saying that the date of the first edition was October 4, 1682, was Luttrell's note on his copy of the book, now at Yale. This indicates only the time at which Luttrell acquired the piece, not the exact day of publication.

The information in the headnote is in part incorrect: v. B. S. xxxvi–xxxviii. The title of the poem on page **134** is from the 1682 edition and is probably not due to Dryden, for, to quote Macdonald (p. 30), it "has little relevance to the poem, which makes no reference to Shadwell's political or religious convictions." In general the 1682 edition must be regarded as unauthorized; Dryden's own text is that of 1684. In 1692 Tonson reprinted *Mac Flecknoe* together with *Absalom and Achitophel* ("the seventh edition") and *The Medal* ("the third edition"), in order "to make up collected sets of Dryden's poems" (Macdonald). In the present volume the poem should properly have been printed immediately after Dryden's *Prologue to A True Widow* (see **83**).

It has been alleged that in *Mac Flecknoe* Dryden was influenced by Boileau's serio-comic poem *Le Lutrin* (*The Lectern*), 1674. In his Author's Apology prefixed to *The State of Innocence* (1677) Dryden compliments Boileau as a critic and in his *Discourse concerning Satire* (1692) he praises *Le Lutrin* (v. **319¹**). He may well have read *Le Lutrin* before 1678, but one may doubt whether he was under any definite obligations to it. Serio-comic poetry was in the air at this time. No imitations of specific passages can be proved. When Dryden jeers at Shadwell's corpulence (ll. 25, 26) he is thinking of Shadwell's actual person, not of Boileau's words on a fat prelate. His words on Empress Fame (ll. 94, 95) reflect a commonplace that goes back to Virgil (v. **567,** 251–281), and need owe nothing to Boileau. The scanty evidence is summarized by Theodor Schenk, in *Sir Samuel Garth und seine Stellung zum komischen Epos* (Heidelberg, 1900), pp. 49–52.

It is noteworthy that John Dennis (1657–1734), a critic of real distinction, despite the fact that he had been on cordial personal terms with Dryden and that in general he admired him greatly, nevertheless found that in *Mac Flecknoe* Dryden was grossly unfair to Shadwell. In Letter III of *The Characters and Conduct of Sir John Edgar,* etc. (Part

II), published early in 1720, Dennis wrote thus:

"We have . had Libels which have pass'd for Satires, as *Absalom* and *Achitophel*, the *Medal, Mac Fleckno*. . . . They are indeed, if you please, beautiful Libels, but they are every where full of Flattery or Slander, and a just Satire admits of neither. In the two first, how many were abus'd only for being true to the Religion and Liberties of their Country? And on the other side, some were extoll'd only for being false to both. [Dennis, be it said, was of Whig sympathies.] The attempt to lessen *Shadwell* in *Mackflecno*, is every whit as unworthy of Satire. For *Shadwell* pretended to no Species of Poetry but the Comick, in which he was certainly very much superiour to *Dryden*." (*The Critical Works of John Dennis*, ed. Hooker, Baltimore, 1939–43: ii. 201.) Dennis was further of the opinion that, in the passage of his dedication to *Aureng-Zebe* (1676), quoted at the foot of B. S., p. xl, Dryden was thinking of Shadwell as one of the contemporaries who had "outdone" him in comedy. But it is much more probable that Dryden had in mind only Etherege and Wycherley.

21. *Some beams*, etc. Here Dryden is in debt to Cowley and possibly through him to Spenser.

There is a place deep, wondrous deep below,
Which genuine night and horror does o'er-
   flow; . . .
Here no dear glimpse of the sun's lovely face
Strikes through the solid darkness of the place;
No dawning morn does her kind reds display;
One slight weak beam would here be thought
   the day.
                    Davideis i. 81, 82, 85–88.
The wicked witch . . .
.by her hellish science raisd streight way
A foggy mist, that overcast the day,
And a dull blast, that, breathing on her face,
Dimmed her former beauties shining ray.
                    The Faerie Queene I. ii. 38.

Cf. **135**, 72, 73, n. The editor here follows Van Doren and Oswald.

134, 135, 35–50. *My warbling lute*, etc. In this passage, as Oswald indicates, there are some reminiscences of the first part of an early poem by Edmund Waller (1606–87), *Of the Danger His Majesty Escaped in the Road at Saint Andrews*, based on an incident in the return of Prince Charles (later Charles I) from Spain in September, 1623. See *The Poems of Edmund Waller*, ed. G. Thorn-Drury (London, 1893), pp. 1–7, 279–283. Details follow:

Healths to both kings, attended with the roar
Of cannons, echoed from the affrighted shore.
                    (Waller 7, 8; Dryden 45, 46.)
While to his harp divine Arion sings.
                    (Waller 11, Dryden 43.)

About the keel delighted dolphins play.
                    (Waller 34, Dryden 49.)
These mighty peers placed in the gilded barge,
Proud with the burden of so brave a charge.
                    (Waller 39, 40; Dryden 39, 40.)
On the smooth back of silver Thames to
   ride —
                    (Waller 62, Dryden 38.)

135, 53. *St. André's*. Shadwell, as Oswald indicates, states in the preface to his *Psyche*, mentioned in the next line: "The Dances were made by the most famous Master of France, Monsieur St. Andree." Cf. **905**[2], 10, n.

87. *Dekker*. In the preface to *Notes and Observations on The Empress of Morocco* (cf. B. S. xxii) the following passage occurs: "I knew indeed that to write against him [Settle], was to do him too great an honor; but I consider'd Ben Jonson had done it before to Dekker, our author's predecessor, whom he chastis'd in his *Poetaster* under the character of Crispinus, and brought him in vomiting up his fustian and nonsense."

92. *Hypocrites*. Shadwell seems to have written an unsuccessful play called *The Hypocrite*, which he never published. It is known only from this line and from a reference by Settle.

"Settle, in the course of his paper combat with Shadwell, . . . wrote in the preface to *Ibrahim* (published in 1677) some harsh . . . criticism of the works of his fellow-dramatist. There he classes *The Hypocrite* with *The Humourists* and *The Miser* as plays written in Shadwell's 'humbler and modester days' before he had become 'flusht with the Trophies of his *Epsom-Wells*.' He also brands Shadwell's remark concerning his own drudging for three years upon *The Conquest of China* as being 'as notoriously false, as that his *Hypocrite* was Acted six days.'" A. S. Borgman, *Thomas Shadwell* (New York, 1928), p. 23.

In ed. 1 the first three words of l. 92 are "Humorists and Hypocrite's," with no italics; in ed. 2 they are "*Humorists* and Hypocrites." This indicates that the clerk who prepared for press the text of *Miscellany Poems*, 1684, recognized the reference to Shadwell's *Humorists* and indicated it by italic type, but that the jibe at Shadwell's unprinted play, *The Hypocrite*, had already become obscure. In the 1909 and 1916 issues of the present edition "hypocrites" was printed in roman, without initial capital.

101. *Martyrs of pies*. Earlier Dryden had written, as Oswald indicates, near the opening of *An Essay of Dramatic Poesy* (SS. xv. 289): "They have bought more editions of his works than would serve to lay under all their pies at the Lord Mayor's Christmas."

136, 122. *Love's Kingdom*. This was *not* the

only play by Flecknoe ever acted: v. n. **928**[1] (THE MALL).

129. *Twelve reverend owls.* Oswald calls attention to a passage in Sir Thomas Browne, *Pseudodoxia Epidemica*, book v, ch. 23: "That owls and ravens are ominous appearers, and presignifying unlucky events, as Christians yet conceit, was also an augurial conception."

130. *So Romulus*, etc. The story is told by Plutarch in his life of Romulus.

134–138. *The sire*, etc. "Here Dryden combined the Homeric (and Virgilian) picture of Zeus with Virgil's description of the inspired Sibyl." R. A. Brower, in *Publications of the Modern Language Association*, lv (1940), 135. See *Æneid*, vi. 46–51, 77–82; cf. **594**, 72–79; **595**, 120–128. Two more parodies of Virgil follow immediately. See *Æneid*, ix. 641–644; xii. 435–440; cf. **650**, 876–884; **697**, 644–652.

145. *My son, advance*, etc. Oswald calls attention to lines 145, 146 of Denham's *Cooper's Hill*:

Can knowledge have no bound, but must advance
So far, to make us wish for ignorance.

148. *Pangs without birth.* The figure is common enough. Oswald points out parallels in Denham and Oldham, but he indicates that Dryden probably had in mind lines in Shadwell's epilogue to *The Virtuoso:*

But to the men of wit our poet flies,
And makes his fops to them a sacrifice:
You know the pangs and many laboring throes
By which your brains their perfect births
        disclose. . . .
And if this birth should want its perfect shape,
And cannot by your care its death escape,
Th' abortive issue came before its day
And th' poet has miscarried of a play.

149. *Let* Virtuosos, etc. Oswald writes aptly: "Dryden here assumes ironically that Shadwell had been working on *The Virtuoso* ever since he had produced *The Humorists*. In his Epistle Dedicatory to *The Virtuoso* Shadwell refers to his previous remarks on humors: 'As I have discoursed at large in the preface to *The Humorists*, written five years since.'"

160. *Not copies*, etc. Oswald points out that Shadwell had written in his epilogue to *The Humorists*, which is a panegyric on Ben Jonson:

Expect not then, since that most flourishing
        age,
Of BEN, to see true humor on the stage.
All that have since been writ, if they be
        scann'd,
Are but faint copies from that master's hand.

166. *Do not labor to be dull.* As Oswald indicates, Dryden probably had in mind

lines in Shadwell's prologue to *The History of Timon of Athens:*

Some scriblers will wit their whole bus'ness
        make,
For labor'd dulness grievous pains will take;
And when with many throes they've travail'd
        long,
They now and then bring forth a foolish song.

177, 178. *Where did*, etc. Oswald points out that these lines may refer not only to the Royal Society but to Sneake, a character in *The Humorists* whom Shadwell describes as "a young parson, fellow of a college, . . . one that speaks nothing but fustian with Greek and Latin."

180. *Psyche's humble strain*, etc. Oswald calls attention to a line in Shadwell's prologue to *Psyche:*

His subject 's humble, and his verse is so.

182. *Dwindled to a farce.* Oswald writes: "A reading of *The Virtuoso* will verify Dryden's charge. Several couples congregate in the same bedroom; some of the characters are attacked by crowds; one of the characters falls through a trapdoor. There are beatings, threatened duels, masks and mistaken identities, and a conclusion featuring wholesale marriages. Such devices are common in Restoration comedy, but the profusion of them in one play is remarkable, to say the least."

197. *Feebly creep.* Dryden, as Oswald indicates, probably once more has in mind a line in Shadwell's prologue to *Psyche:*

He would not soar too high, nor creep too low.

200. *Thy inoffensive satires never bite.* Oswald sees in this line a reference to the titles of the satires of Joseph Hall (1574–1656): *Virgidemiarum, Sixe Bookes. First three Bookes, of Toothlesse Satyrs* and *The three last Bookes. Of byting Satyres.* 1597–98.

137, 204. *Anagram.* As Oswald points out, even Cowley, in his ode, *Of Wit*, st. vi, had ridiculed anagram:

'T is not [wit is not] when two like words make
        up one noise,
Jests for Dutch men, and English boys:
In which who finds out wit, the same may see
In an'grams and acrostics poetry.

215. *A subterranean wind.* Shadwell had contributed to the "operatic" version (published in 1674) of the adaptation of Shakespeare's *Tempest* by Davenant and Dryden, act II, scene iv, a rhymed invocation beginning, "Arise, arise, ye subterranean winds!" (The present editor is indebted to A. S. Borgman, *Thomas Shadwell*, New York, 1928, p. 51.) v. n. **74**[2], 53, on **1051, 1052**.

The Second Part of Absalom and Achitophel. Luttrell's copy of the first edition, now in the Huntington Library, is marked "10 Nov." Macdonald (p. 32) distinguishes three issues of the first edition, with trifling variations of text, but "Dryden's portion seems to be the same in all the states." (Two issues are in the Huntington Library.) There was also a Dublin edition of 1682.

142, 384. *Patriarch.* Ed. 1 reads *Patriot!*

143, 405. *Mephibosheth.* Pordage, like Mephibosheth (v. 2 Sam. iv. 4), was lame.

407. *Uzza.* Explained in an earlier note (on **973**) as possibly Jack Hall, on whom v. n. **916**, 229.

429. *For almonds,* etc. A satirical poem called *A Trial of the Poets for the Bays* or *The Session of the Poets* had been circulated in manuscript as early as 1677: see Macdonald, p. 220, n. 4. Settle was one of the persons to whom it was attributed. In 1682 came a prose piece abusing Settle, *A Character of the True Blue Protestant Poet,* which represents Settle as giving to Otway, in order to avert a duel with him, a written statement running: "I confess *I* writ the *Session of the Poets,* and am very sorry for't, and am the Son of A Whore for doing it; Witness my hand *E. S.*" (Quoted by R. G. Ham in *Otway and Lee,* New Haven, 1931, pp. 110, 111; also in an article, "Dryden versus Settle," in *Modern Philology,* xxv. 409–416: May, 1928.) But in the next year, 1683, in another pamphlet, *A Supplement to the Narrative,* Settle included an indignant denial, writing (p. 17): ". . . amongst the Impudent Lyes and Detraction that fills that Paper, I was accused of being the Author of a Scandalous Copy of Verses call'd the *Sessions of the Poets,* an ill-natur'd scurrilous Lampoon, written some years since, and now laid as believed at the Fathers Door, being Printed amongst the Lord Rs. — [Rochester's] Poems." Later the poem was laid at the Duke of Buckingham's door, being included in his *Works,* 1704 (Macdonald, p. 220). There is no proof for any of the three attributions.

430. *And call,* etc. In Settle's *Absalom Senior* Absalom represents the Duke of York.

150, 967. *Prophets'.* *Prophet's* in eds. 1, 2, 3.

153. Prologue . . . Theater. Macdonald comments (p. 143): "The title of this prologue is a little misleading. The new Theatre Royal, built by Wren, had been opened on 26 March 1674 [see heading, **73**²]. This prologue and epilogue celebrate the union of the two companies in 1682, the united companies being henceforth known as the King's Company." Luttrell's copy of this folio sheet, with the manuscript date "16 Nov. 1682," is now in the Huntington Library. The sheet itself is dated ahead, 1683. For the same confusion of dates v. n. **154** (Prologue . . . The Duke of Guise). — There is another edition of these pieces, a broadside printed in two columns, without imprint. The Houghton Library at Harvard has a copy, possibly unique.

154. Prologue . . . The Duke of Guise. Malone's authority for the date of the first production of the play was a note by Luttrell on his copy of the broadside, now at the Huntington Library. Luttrell wrote "30 Nov." after "Duke of Guise" in the title and "4 Dec. 1682" after "Mr. Smith." R. G. Ham (in *Otway and Lee,* p. 237) thinks that the second date is that on which Luttrell acquired the piece. A note in the Lord Chamberlain's Department of the Public Record Office shows that places were engaged for the king and queen and maids of honor on December 1, 1682: see Nicoll, p. 311. The broadside is dated 1683: cf. n. **153** (Prologue . . . Theater). Macdonald states that the printed play was advertised in *The Observator* for February 13, 1683.

157. Song. Day reprints (pp. 62, 63) a setting by Captain Pack (cf. n. **103**) from *Choice Ayres and Songs,* 1683. It was also printed with the first edition of the play: see SS. vii. 112–115.

Religio Laici. The Latin motto on the title-page is Manilius iii. 39: "The topic refuses to be adorned, for it is content with being explained." — As Macdonald states (pp. 33–35), there were really two separate *editions* (mistakenly called *issues* by the present editor) of this poem in 1682. He cites from Percy J. Dobell, *John Dryden Bibliographical Memoranda,* 1922, arguments that support Mr. Chew's opinion that *Grolier Club No. 315* (Macdonald, No. 16 b) was the later edition. He adds of this later edition of 1682: "It is by no means an obviously pirated edition. . . . It is possible that there was a run on the poem and that Tonson had some copies printed in a hurry or by a rather careless printer."

Of the earlier edition of 1682, furthermore, there were three issues. Of the first issue only two copies are known: one, according to Macdonald, is in the Dyce Collection; the other, which formerly belonged to G. Thorn-Drury, is now in the William Andrews Clark Memorial Library in Los Angeles. Aside from some minor variations it reads *written* instead of *compos'd* as the last word on **161**: Dryden obviously made the change because he had used *written* only two lines earlier. More important, it contains an anti-Catholic thrust that was omitted from all later impressions. Immediately after the word *princes* in **161²**, 17, it has the following parenthesis: "(a Doctrine which, though some Papists may reject, no Pope has hitherto deny'd, nor ever will,)." Thorn-Drury, who knew of no other copy of this first issue than his own, made a note in it: "I have also Narcissus Luttrell's copy [of the second issue], dated Nov. 28. . . . Without going so far as to say that Luttrell *always* bought his tracts on the day of publication, one knows that he very often did so and it may well be doubted whether any other copy [of the first issue] escaped."

The second issue of the earlier edition of 1682 is fairly common. The third issue, according to Macdonald, differs from the second only in its title-page, which is undated and has *Mr. Dryden* "in italic lower-case instead of italic caps." Macdonald records only two copies of it, both in the Bodleian Library. — For several items in this note the editor is indebted to Mr. H. Richard Archer, Supervising Bibliographer of the Clark Library.

157², 12. *The sword of Goliah.* v. 1 Sam. xxi. 9.

161², 59. *Ingenious young gentleman.* Dickinson's translation of Simon's *Critical History* (v. B. S. xlix) was advertised (according to Ward) in *The Loyal Protestant and True Domestic Intelligence* for January 14, 1681–2. Dryden's acquaintance with the book apparently began with the English translation.

168. POEMS INCLUDED IN MISCELLANY POEMS, 1684. The volume *Miscellany Poems* was entered in the *Stationers' Register* February 4, 1684. Macdonald states (p. 68) that copies are found in slightly varying forms, and adds some details. Concerning the series of six volumes of *Miscellany Poems* printed by Tonson in 1716 he remarks (p. 78): "This edition has no very close relation to the former volumes of Miscellanies. The pieces reprinted frequently occur in the corresponding volumes of the original editions, but often they are in different volumes and many poems of earlier date such as Milton's *L'Allegro* are included."

171. PROLOGUE TO THE DISAPPOINTMENT. In the first edition of this play (1684), p. 69, the prologue is said to be "written by Mr. John Dryden" and the epilogue to be "by the Honourable John Stafford, Esquire." The prologue and epilogue were also published in 1684 as a single half-sheet, printed on both sides; the author of the prologue is not named, the epilogue is said to be "by another hand."

According to the Sotheby Sale Catalogue of June 12, 1939, "this copy [of the half-sheet] has been dated in MS. 67, Narcissus Luttrell, 5 April, 1684," establishing the approximate date of acting of the play. In the prologue there are no important variant readings between the two texts of 1684. The italics of the present edition represent words printed in capitals in the texts of 1684.

12. *Satyr.* So the texts of 1684. This spelling for *satire* predominates in the seventeenth century texts of Dryden. It is here retained because of the play on words involved. It might well have been retained throughout this volume. N. E. D. states under *satire:* "Formerly often confused or associated with *satyr.* . . . The words *satire* and *satyr* were probably at one time pronounced alike, as the derivatives *satiric* and *satyric* are still."

172, 60. *Grabble.* The single half-sheet reads *grubble.*

63, 64. *Paltry punk, bawdier.* These words are in italics in the half-sheet.

64. *Conventicle.* Capitals in the half-sheet, but roman with initial capital in the text printed with the play.

EPILOGUE TO CONSTANTINE THE GREAT. The prologue and epilogue to this play were "printed for C. Tebroc, 1683," as a single half-sheet, printed on both sides. No authors' names are given. Luttrell's copy is dated "12 Nov. 1683," indicating the approximate date of acting of the play: see photograph in Sotheby catalogue of sale of June 12, 1939, item 87. Tonson then issued a half-sheet with the epilogue only, printed on one side and headed thus: *A True Coppy of the Epilogue to Constantine the Great. That which was first Published being false printed and surreptitious. Written by Mr. Dryden.* This sheet is dated 1684, but Luttrell marked his copy of it "14 Nov. 1683": see photograph in the same catalogue, item 88.

Tonson's text shows no variants from that printed with the play, except that it omits, "Spoken by Mrs. Cooke," and that in l. 13 it omits the first *as.* The Tebroc text of the epilogue shows the following variants, mainly the obvious blunders of a piratical printer: (10) When *CAUSE;* (13) as to say — *Gentlemen;* (16) Some call 'em; (26) At last; (28) Sends out; (29, 30) Thus o're their Darling *Treason Trimmers* Cry, And though they dare not Her, it wants Supply; (36) my Mind; (37) Why those Damn'd *Trimmers* love the *TURK* so well; (38) Th' Original; (42) more then; (45) HEAVEN?

The prologue was by Otway, being printed in the 1712 edition of his *Works.* Both prologue and epilogue were printed as Lee's in the collected editions of his *Works*, 1713 and 1722. See J. G. Ghosh, "Prologue and Epilogue to Lee's *Constantine the Great*," in *Times Literary Supplement*, March 14, 1929.

173. TO THE EARL OF ROSCOMMON, etc. The letter by Dryden mentioned in n. **174¹**, 47 was probably written in August or September, 1684; and, as Malone (I, 2, 22) and Ward (p. 153) suggest, the second edition of Roscommon's *Essay* probably appeared before the close of that year, though the book is dated 1685.

175. POEMS INCLUDED IN SYLVÆ, 1685. This volume was entered in the *Stationers' Register* January 10, 1685; and, according to Macdonald, advertised in *The Observator* January 1, 1685. Macdonald notes some small variations between different copies of the first edition. A general title-page beginning *Miscellany Poems, In Two Parts*, was prepared for *Miscellany Poems*, 1684, and *Sylvæ*, 1685, when sold together. See also n. **202²**, below.

201. A NEW SONG. Day (p. 166) states that "an anonymous Latin translation of 'Mr. Dryden's pleasing and novel Song' was published by Motteux in *The Gentleman's Journal*, September, 1693"; and that the song, with a spurious fourth stanza, is found in *Wit's Cabinet*, c. 1699, pp. 150, 151. The song is included in Dryden's *Poems on Various Occasions and Translations from Several Authors*, 1701.

202¹. THE FAIR STRANGER. Case (No. 223) states that there are three issues of the book — "generally known as 'Gildon's Miscellany'" (Macdonald, p. 82) — from which this poem is taken. The original issue has a title-page beginning, *A New Collection of Poems*. The title-page of the issue cited on p. **202** is a cancel. A third issue has a cancel title-page beginning *A New Collection of Original Poems* and undated.

In *Tixall Poetry* (see headnote, pp. **906, 907**), p. 183, the editor, Arthur Clifford, prints from a manuscript a different text of this song, thus:

WITTY MR. HENNINGAM'S SONG

Happy and free, securely blest,
Noe beauty could disturb my rest:
My amorous hart no conquering faire
Had power to wound with new dispaire,
Till you descending on our plaines,
With forraigne force renew'd my chaines,
Where now you rule without controle,
The mighty sovraigne of my sole.

Your looks have more of conquering charmes,
Then all your native countryes armes;
Your troopes we can expell with ease,
They vanquish onely while we please;
But all the force that in us lies,
Yeilds no defence against your eyes.
They make us languish whilst in sight,
But absent, we must perish quite.

This text by no means settles the question of authorship. The heading probably means simply that "witty Mr. Henningam" used to sing the song, not that he wrote it. Clifford states in his Notes (p. 374): "There are also two very different copies of it [the song] in my MS. The Heveninghams, pronounced Henningham [*sic*], were a Roman Catholic family, and resided at Aston, near Stone, in Staffordshire."

202². SONG. This song should have been placed in the present edition among those included in *Sylvæ*, 1685. Day reprints (p. 74) a setting by Robert King from *The Theater of Music*, 1685, and states (p. 168) that the same setting is found in *Wit and Mirth: or, Pills to Purge Melancholy*, 1700 (and later); Day and Murrie add that the same setting is included in *A Collection of Twenty Four Songs*, 1685, and *The New Treasury of Musick*, 1695. Day states that a setting by Henry Purcell is found in a manuscript in the British Museum "dating from as early as 1686" and is included in *Orpheus Britannicus*, 1706: see Purcell's *Works*, xxii (1922), 133–136.

203². SONG. Day reprints (p. 134), under the title *An Ayre on a Ground*, a setting by John Abell from *Choice Ayres and Songs*, 1683. Day and Murrie add (p. 241, item 1375) that this setting is reprinted in *The New Treasury of Musick*, 1695, and that the words first appeared, anonymously, in *The Compleat Courtier*, 1683. In *Choice Ayres and Songs* there are the following variant readings (obviously for musical purposes): (l. 14) and all my Ambition; (l. 16) so faithful, so faithful a Lover; (l. 18) I'le dye, I'le dye, I'le dye.

203. THRENODIA AUGUSTALIS. Macdonald corrects the present editor concerning the early editions of this poem. "The first and second editions," he writes (p. 39) "were printed from the same setting of type and many states are found, slight changes and corrections having been made in the course of printing. At some point the words 'The Second Edition' were added to the title." The present editor in preparing his text consulted an edition also dated 1685, but set in smaller type, of which an apparently unique copy is owned by the Harvard Library. As Macdonald says, it is an entirely different edition, not a different issue.

210. PROLOGUE ... TO ALBION AND ALBANIUS. According to a manuscript note by Luttrell (see Malone I, 1, 188) the first performance of this opera was on June 6, 1685. Macdonald states that the first edition of the opera (words only) was advertised in *The Observator* for June 8, 1685.

214². A LETTER TO SIR GEORGE ETHEREGE.

poem, headed "*Mr. D.——— An-r*," was first printed in *The History of Auolphus, Prince of Russia*. . . . *By a Person of Quality. With a Collection of Songs and Love-Verses. By several hands. To which is added, Two Letters in Verse from Sir G. E. to the E. of M. with Mr. D. Answer to them. London,* . . . 1691. The "two letters in verse" from Etherege to Middleton (for which see *The Letterbook of Sir George Etherege,* ed. Sybil Rosenfeld, Oxford, 1928: pp. 62, 80) were of January 9/19 and April 19/29, 1686.

This text shows the following variants from that of *Sylvæ,* 1702: l. 6, *Pole Artick;* l. 8, *As cannot suffer;* l. 10, *Loves Affairs of State;* l. 11, *Husband;* l. 16, *so much endure;* l. 25, *Chop'd;* l. 28, *the World so dull;* l. 30, *Sing;* l. 32, *those;* l. 41, *whom* [*who* of the 1702 text may be a misprint]; l. 55, *the Title;* l. 56, *his Excellence;* l. 62, *there's;* l. 63, *the Court Petition;* l. 65, *defi'd;* l. 73, *St. Aignan;* l. 74, *If Gallick Peer affect you scarce;* l. 75, *Grace of B. —;* l. 78, *once began;* l. 81, *E'er Writ.*

1–4. *To you,* etc. Dryden seems rather stupidly to have misunderstood the opening lines of Etherege's second "letter in verse" to Middleton, which run:

> Since love and verse, as well as wine,
> Are brisker where the sun doth shine,
> 'T is something to lose two degrees,
> Now age itself begins to freeze.

London is about latitude 51° and Ratisbon about latitude 49°. Etherege meant that he lost two degrees from 51, giving 49, and thereby came into a "brisker," or *hotter,* climate. Dryden understood "brisker" as *chillier* and took "lose" as implying that Etherege had come into a more unfavorable, colder climate, two degrees farther north than London, and so, not looking at the map (despite his "map informs") wrote erroneously *fifty-three.* In line 4 *fifty-one* seems to refer to the age of Etherege at the time of his coming to Ratisbon. The exact date of his birth is unknown.

215, 13. *Our Court of Chancery.* Higden in 1686 had published *A Modern Essay on the Thirteenth Satyr of Juvenal,* Tonson being his printer. Higden suspected Tonson of dishonest conduct of the business and in April, 1686, brought a chancery suit against him. Tonson denied the charges; the outcome of the suit is unknown. Higden's later work, *A Modern Essay on the Tenth Satyr of Juvenal,* was "printed by T. Milbourn." See C. E. Ward, "Dryden, Higden and Tonson," in *Review of English Studies,* xiii (1937), 305, 306; and Macdonald, p. 43.

216. THE HIND AND THE PANTHER. Mac-

donald (pp. 45, 323) distinguishes various states of the first edition: cf. n. **250,** 2445, 2446, on **1065.** He also records a Dublin edition of 1687. The work was entered in the *Stationers' Register* on May 27, 1687.

As stated in 1909, the editor is indebted for various notes on this poem to Professor W. H. Williams of the University of Tasmania.

221, 298. *The common benefit of vital air.* Cf. *Æneid,* vii. 230; translated in **614,** 312–314.

222, 311. *A slimy-born,* etc. Cf. **394,** 565–572; **518**[1], 1–4; **886,** 553.

342. *Spirits of a middle sort.* "Also, besides the hosts of evil spirits, I considered there was a middle race, δαιμόνια, neither in heaven, nor in hell; partially fallen, capricious, wayward." NEWMAN, *Apologia,* ch. i (London, 1887, p. 28). Cf. n. **289**[2], 41.

354. *Cov'ring,* etc. A Virgilian echo: v. *Æneid,* iv. 172; cf. **567,** 249, 250.

223, 390. *Burnish'd.* Cf. Greene, *Frier Bacon,* x. 62: "And fortie kine with faire and burnisht heads." *Burnish,* of a stag, means to rub the dead skin, or "velvet," from its horns; it is also applied loosely to the annual renewal of the horns: v. N. E. D. Hence *burnished,* of cattle, apparently in the sense of "having bright, fresh horns."

233, 1172. *Goliah's sword.* v. 1 Sam. xxi. 9; cf. **157**[2], 5–15.

235, 1313. *Till rolling time,* etc. J. Bronowski (in *The Poet's Defence,* Cambridge, England, 1939, p. 7) is of the opinion that in writing this line Dryden was thinking of the opening verses of *The World,* by Henry Vaughan:

> I saw eternity the other night,
> Like a great ring of pure and endless light,
>   All calm, as it was bright;
> And round beneath it, time, in hours, days, years,
>   Driv'n by the spheres,
> Like a vast shadow mov'd, in which the world
>   And all her train were hurl'd.

238, 1515. *Now for my converts,* etc. Professor Bredvold, in *The Best of Dryden* (New York, 1933), p. 554, rightly stresses Dryden's defense of the English-Catholic converts. Dryden asserts that James II offers them no rewards; and that men who prefer to "conform [remain in the Church of England or join it] for gain" (l. 1521), or to "stay the market of another reign" (l. 1522) — that is, simply to remain in the Church of England and await the coming of William and Mary — may justly be accused of interested motives.

239, 1638. *Make himself a saver.* Cf. Jonson, *Epicœne,* iii. 1: "To make you good again, and, as it were, a saver in the main."

240, 1703. *Half-read gentleman.* Cf. Locke, *Conduct of the Understanding,* § 3: "A country gentleman, who, leaving Latin and learning in the university, removes thence to his mansion house, and associates with neighbors of the same strain, who relish nothing but hunting and a bottle; with those alone he spends his time, with those alone he converses, and can away with no company whose discourse goes beyond what claret and dissoluteness inspire."

1713. *The Swallows' fortune,* etc. Professor L. I. Bredvold, in *The Intellectual Milieu of John Dryden* (Ann Arbor, 1934), pp. 180–183, expresses partial dissent from Scott's interpretation of this passage, writing: "Anyone reading the *Secret Consults* [complete title, *A Full and Impartial Account of all the Secret Consults, Negotiations, Stratagems & Intrigues of the Romish Party in Ireland, From 1660, to this present Year 1689:* London, 1690] must be struck by the remarkable information of the author; but his information is hearsay and not trustworthy on details. This consultation at the Savoy, of which he speaks, must have been a very obscure event; no foreign ambassador mentioned it in his dispatches; no record of it remains except in this anti-Jacobite pamphlet. It seems more probable that the application of the fable was intended by Dryden to be more general, and that it refers, not to *one* consultation of the Catholics at the Savoy in 1686, but to almost every consultation by Catholics from the accession of James. It refers to that division of Catholic opinion which, as we have seen, existed as early as March, 1685, and became ever more marked as James unfolded his policy. . . . There is no doubt that Dryden in the poem betrays a personal dislike of Father Petres. But here, again, we may safely affirm that the application is broader, and that Dryden was putting into his poem some of the indignation against Petres [Edward Peters, Petre] and his influence felt by the moderate Catholics."

Professor Bredvold quotes from a letter that Dryden wrote to Etherege on February 16, 1687: "Oh, that our Monarch would encourage noble idleness by his own example as he of blessed memory did before him, for my mind misgives me that he will not much advance his affairs by stirring." He concludes: "After that letter I think there can be no doubt about Dryden's position among the moderate Catholics. In its light we may safely regard the fable of the swallows as the discreet expression of Catholic disapproval of James and his policies, and the tragic end of the swal-

lows as symbolizing what the Catholics were expecting with deep apprehension."

241, 1745. *Or dream,* etc. Cf. Fletcher, *The Night-Walker,* i. 1, 2, 3:

In what old hollow tree, or rotten wall,
Hast thou been, like a swallow, all this winter?

242, 1816. *One casual truth,* etc. "It is the peculiar and perpetual error of the human intellect to be more moved and excited by affirmatives than by negatives." BACON, *Novum Organum,* i. 46.

1830. *Renew the prime.* Here *prime* means *spring,* but with emphasis on spring as the first in the cycle of the four seasons: v. **112,** 217, n, and N. E. D.

249, 2392. *The Meccan prophet.* Cf. Massinger, *The Renegado,* iv. 3:

He taught a pigeon to feed in his ear,
Then made his credulous followers believe
It was an angel, that instructed him
In the framing of his Alcoran.

250, 2445, 2446. *Or forc'd by fear,* etc. The reading in the text is that of the second and third editions. Some copies of the first edition read:

Or forc'd by Fear, or by his Profit led,
Or both, his own unhappy clyme he fled; —

while others read:

Or forc'd by Fear, or by Ambition led,
Or both conjoyn'd, his Native clime he fled.

252. SONG FOR ST. CECILIA'S DAY. Verrall, in *Lectures on Dryden,* pp. 183–185, notes that Milton's poem, *At a Solemn Music,* "gave a most important hint" to Dryden for this ode. "The world, the cosmos, order, all is based on harmony, that is to say, on Music. The thought is platonic, but its application to poetry, as well as the use of intentional variation of rhythm, was suggested to Dryden by Milton's work." He notes further that Milton's phrases "jarred against Nature's chime" (l. 20) and "in perfect diapason" (l. 23) influenced Dryden's wording in lines 3, 4, 15.

Day (p. 167) states that manuscripts of Draghi's music are preserved in the library of the Sacred Harmonic Society and in the British Museum. Draghi's work has apparently never been printed, since it was eclipsed by Handel's later setting.

253, 54. *Mistaking,* etc. This line is identical with line 24 of Ben Jonson's poem *The Musical Strife:* see W. A. Eddy in *Modern Language Notes,* xlvi (1931), 40. The identity may be due to unconscious recollection — or even to mere accident.

63. *Untune.* Dryden was probably affected by lines in Cowley's Pindaric ode, *The Resurrection,* stanza 2:

Till all gentle notes be drown'd
In the last trumpet's dreadful sound,
That, to the spheres themselves, shall silence
  bring,
Untune the universal string.
Then all the wide extended sky,
And all th' harmonious worlds on high,
And Virgil's sacred work shall die.
And he himself shall see in one fire shine
Rich Nature's ancient Troy, though built by
  hands divine.

EPIGRAM ON MILTON. On a flyleaf bound up with a copy of the first edition of *Paradise Lost*, 1667, once owned by Mr. Beverly Chew of New York, now in the Henry E. Huntington Library at San Marino, California, there is a manuscript text of these lines, signed *John Dryden*, and written in a hand which, after comparison with undoubted autographs of the poet, Mr. Chew was inclined to regard as Dryden's own.

BRITANNIA REDIVIVA. The statement on **994** that the folio of 1688 lacks the *imprimatur* is incorrect; the *imprimatur* is found in the Huntington Library and the Harvard Library copies. Macdonald (pp. 16, 49, 50) is correct in regarding the folio edition as the first and in thinking that the quarto, dated 1688, was printed in 1691 or 1692 in order to enable Tonson to make up sets of Dryden's poems. Cf. n. **4** (on **1046**).

256, 199. *Rome.* J. G. Frazer, in *The Golden Bough* (ed. 2, 1900, vol. i, pp. 446, 447), discusses the superstition referred to by Dryden, and cites the classical authorities for it. None of the writers he mentions, however, seems to use the exact words of Dryden's footnote.

258. PROLOGUE . . . TO DON SEBASTIAN. The Latin motto of the play means: "Nor does slow old age weaken our strength of intellect or alter its vigor": cf. **649**, 836–838. — Boxes were reserved for the queen and the maids of honor at a performance of the play (probably the first) on December 4, 1689: see item from the Lord Chamberlain's Department of the Public Record Office, cited by Nicoll, p. 314.

260. PROLOGUE TO THE PROPHETESS. The headnote needs to be supplemented in various ways. The first performance of the play (about May, 1690) was of course shortly *before* King William's campaign in Ireland. Macdonald states (p. 162) that the printed drama was advertised in *The London Gazette* for June 12–16, 1690. Some copies of it contain the prologue on a separate leaf, which may have been inserted subsequently to the original printing. Macdonald writes: "I know of only two copies containing the prologue leaf, one in the library at Christ Church, the other belonging to Mr. Dobell." The prologue is also found in *Poems on Affairs of State*

from Oliver Cromwell to this present time. . . . *Part III.* . . . 1698, p. 223. Finally, it likewise occurs in *The Muses Mercury*, 1707, pp. 3–5, with a note that begins as follows:

This Prologue was forbidden to be spoken the second Night of the Representation of the *Prophetess.* Mr. *Shadwell* was the occasion of its being taken notice of by the Ministry in the last Reign. He happen'd to be at the House on the first Night, and taking the beginning of the Prologue to have a *double Meaning*, and that Meaning to reflect on the *Revolution*, he told a Gentleman, *He would immediately put a stop to it.* When that Gentleman ask'd, Why he wou'd do the Author such a Disservice? He said, *Because while Mr.* Dryden *was Poet Laureat, he wou'd never let any Play of his be Acted.* Mr. *Shadwell* informing the Secretary of State of it, and representing it in its worst Colours, the Prologue was never Spoken afterwards, and is not Printed in Mr. *Dryden*'s Works, or his Miscellanies.

This note is absolutely untrustworthy: see B. S. p. xlviii. One may doubt whether so ill-informed a person as this writer in *The Muses Mercury* of 1707 deserves credit for his assertion that Shadwell was responsible for the prohibition of Dryden's *Prologue to The Prophetess.*
The text on pp. **260, 261** has been revised from a photostat (kindly sent by the Christ Church Library, Oxford) of the prologue as printed with the play in 1690. Variants are given from the texts in ed. 2 (1708) of *The Annual Miscellany for the Year 1694* and in *Poems on Affairs of State, Part III*, 1698.

1. *Nostradame.* 1698 reads *Nosterdame.*
3. *Which.* 1698 reads *that.*
5. *There.* 1698 reads *then.*
6. *Gains.* 1698 reads *Gain.*
8. *Hopes.* 1698 reads *hope.*
9. *Wise!* 1698 and 1708 read *Wise?*
12. *In oceans and.* 1698 reads *by Oceans, but.*
14. *Grow.* 1698 reads *are.*
15. *Serve.* 1698 reads *use.*
18. *Leave.* 1698 reads *turn.*
21. *New.* 1698 and 1708 read *Now.*
22. *The horrid.* 1698 reads *for the fierce.*
24. *Your* . . . *that.* 1698 reads *The* . . . *which.* After this line 1698 has an additional line, making a triplet:

But we shall flourish, sure, when you are paid.

261[1], 33. *Collars.* 1698 reads *Culters* (an obvious misprint).
38. *Sing.* 1698 reads *Write.*
38. *Fights.* 1708 reads *Flights.*
39. *Bright.* 1698 reads *brisk.*
48. *Try.* 1698 reads *strive.*
50. *Fair.* 1698 reads *bright.*
PROLOGUE . . . AMPHITRYON. Boxes were reserved for the queen and the maids of honor at a performance of *Amphitryon* on April 30, 1690. These reservations

were canceled and then renewed for October 21. See items from the Lord Chamberlain's Department of the Public Record Office, cited by Nicoll, p. 314.

The songs were set to music by Henry Purcell: see his *Works*, vol. xvi (1906). The music was printed with the first edition of the play, of which there are two issues, one with date changed to 1691; it is reproduced in SS. viii. 113–122. Day states (p. 170) that words and music of the first two songs are also found in *Joyful Cuckoldom, c.* 1695, and *Wit and Mirth: or, Pills to Purge Melancholy*, 1700.

264. PROLOGUE ... KING ARTHUR. The copies of the first edition in which the prologue and epilogue were inserted vary in a perplexing fashion: see J. M. Osborn in *Modern Philology*, xxxix (1941), 92. — The music of this opera was by Henry Purcell: see his *Works*, vol. xxvi (1928). Day states (pp. 172, 176, 177) that *Song I* (with the music) is found in *Joyful Cuckoldom, c.* 1695, and in *Wit and Mirth: or, Pills to Purge Melancholy*, 1699; and that lines 6–9 of *Song III* and the first and third stanzas of *Song V* are found (with the music) in *Orpheus Britannicus*, 1698.

266¹, 4 (*Song I*). *Says the double*, etc. Dryden repeats from **253**, 29, 30.

267. SONG VI (*You say*, etc.) This song is not by Dryden; but, as the early editions indicate, "by Mr. Howe": that is, by John Grubham Howe (1657–1722), politician and very minor poet. Professor C. L. Day drew the editor's attention to this error.

268¹. EPITAPH ON ERASMUS LAWTON. This petty epitaph, not printed until 1860 (in *The Life of Edmond Malone*, by Sir James Prior, p. 265), and a passing reference in a letter of 1699 (see *Letters*, ed. Ward, p. 119) to a sister, probably Rose (Dryden) Lawton, seem to be the only proofs in Dryden's writings, including such of his letters as have survived, that he was aware of the existence of any of his three brothers and ten sisters. Rose Dryden was the third child and second daughter of Dryden's father and mother. See "The Brothers and Sisters of John Dryden the Poet," by P. D. Mundy, in *Notes and Queries*, cxciii (1948), 120–124.

277, 66–68. *Damon*, etc. Reminiscent of Virgil: cf. **120**, 850, 851, n (on **1057**).

278. TO MR. SOUTHERNE, etc. Southerne's *Epistle Dedicatory* to Thomas Wharton was not printed with the play in 1692; it appears in Southerne's *Works*, 1713 and 1721.

PROLOGUE ... CLEOMENES. Luttrell (*Brief Historical Relation of State Affairs*, 1857, ii. 413) writes on April 9, 1692: "By order of the queen, the lord chamberlain has sent an order to the playhouse pro-

hibiting the acting Mr. Drydens play called the tragedy of Cleomenes, reflecting much on the government." On April 16 he adds (*Ibid.*, p. 422): "Mr. Drydens play has been acted with applause, the reflecting passages upon this government being left out." Macdonald (p. 134) states that the printed play was advertised in *The London Gazette* for May 2–5, 1692.

280. SONG. The music for this song was by Henry Purcell: see his *Works*, vol. xvi (1906). Day states (p. 178) that words and music are found in *Comes Amoris*, 1693, and *Joyful Cuckoldom, c.* 1695.

EPILOGUE TO HENRY THE SECOND. An entry in the Lord Chamberlain's Department of the Public Record Office shows that boxes were engaged for the queen and the maids of honor at a performance of this play on November 14, 1692: see Nicoll, p. 314. Macdonald states (p. 163) that the printed play was advertised in *The London Gazette* for November 24–28, 1692.

281. TRANSLATIONS FROM JUVENAL AND PERSIUS. In the fourth edition (1711) the translator of *Satire IV* of Juvenal is stated to have been Richard Duke. — Stepney wrote to Leibnitz on March 8 (18), 1693: "Mr. Dryden, the first of our poets, who distributed the work among us and gave it to do, has reserved the sixth Satire for his own hand; and I can fully assure you, to his honour, that the original has lost none of its shamelessness through him, infamous as it is, but the excellence of his verses and the force of his expressions are admirable" (*State Papers and Correspondence ...* edited ... by John M. Kemble, London, 1857, p. 121).

327, 21. *Nymph.* F reads *Nymphs.* .

392, 447. *Sea.* The 1693 ed. reads *Seas.*

397, 814. *Lyrcæan.* The 1693 ed. reads *Lyrnæan*, by an error that is more probably due to the printer or the copying clerk than to Dryden.

406. SONG TO A FAIR YOUNG LADY. Day reprints (p. 103) from *Mercurius Musicus*, March, 1699, a musical setting attributed to John Blow.

407. RONDELAY. The modern spelling is *roundelay*. Day reprints (p. 106) from *Deliciæ Musicæ: ... the Second Book*, 1695, "the earliest musical setting," by John Gilbert. This was repeated in *Deliciæ Musicæ: ... the First Volume Compleat* (Day and Murrie, No. 148) and *Wit and Mirth: or, Pills to Purge Melancholy*, 1699. Day states (p. 182) that there is also a setting by John Blow in *Amphion Anglicus*, 1700.

408, 35. *Hippoplacus.* The form is a blunder. The literal translation of the passage is, "who dwelt beneath woody Placus, in Hypoplacian Thebe."

410. PROLOGUE ... LOVE TRIUMPHANT. John Evelyn wrote in his diary for January 11, 1694: "Supped at Mr. Edward Sheldon's, where was Mr. Dryden, the poet, who now intended to write no more plays, being intent on his translation of Virgil. He read to us his prologue and epilogue to his valedictory play now shortly to be acted." Macdonald states (p. 135) that the printed drama was advertised in *The London Gazette* for March 12–15, 1694.

411. SONG OF JEALOUSY. Day reprints (p. 109) from *Thesaurus Musicus*, 1694, a musical setting by John Eccles. He states (p. 180) that it is also found in *Joyful Cuckoldom, c.* 1695.

SONG FOR A GIRL. Day reprints (p. 111) from *The Gentleman's Journal*, January and February, 1694, a musical setting by John Eccles. He states (p. 181) that it is also found in *Thesaurus Musicus*, 1694, and in *Wit and Mirth: or, Pills to Purge Melancholy*, 1699; and that the words alone are found in *Wit's Cabinet, c.* 1699.

412. TO ... MR. CONGREVE. Though Congreve's play is dated 1694, Macdonald states (p. 55) that it was advertised in *The London Gazette* for December 4–7, 1693.

413. TO SIR GODFREY KNELLER. The letter cited in the headnote, date of December 12, 1693, refers to "Tonsons next Miscellanyes" (Ward, p. 64) as to be published in Hilary Term: that is, January, 1694. The book may have been delayed somewhat, since Macdonald (p. 75) quotes from *The Gentleman's Journal* for July, 1694: "We have had also the Fourth Part of Miscellany Poems."

R. G. Ham, in an article on "Dryden's Dedication for *The Music of The Prophetesse*, 1691," in *Publications of the Modern Language Association*, l (1935), 1065–1075, shows that in an unpublished bit of prose (which he prints in full) Dryden anticipated some of the ideas expressed in this poem, ll. 1–25, 124–127.

416. ODE ... PURCELL. Listed in the *Term Catalogues*, June, 1696.

PREFACE ... HUSBAND HIS OWN CUCKOLD. The motto, slightly altered from Virgil, means, "Let both his father Æneas and his uncle Hector spur him on!"

418. TRANSLATION OF VIRGIL. Publication of this book was somewhat delayed, for on July 29, 1697, Thomas Burnet of Kemney wrote thus to the Electress Sophia, casting a vivid light on the position that Dryden had gained among English men of letters:

"We are every hour impatiently expecting the coming out of Mr. Dreydens laborious versione of Virgil into English. Virgil was the most heroic poete that

ever sung in the most floorishing tymes of ingenious arts and witt in the Roman impyre; And Mr. Dreyden (for his vast learning, perfectione in our langwadge, noble fancie, richenesse of thought, rypenesse of age, and experience of more as 50 years in the practice, and the many triumphant pieces of his compositione, already extant) heth the fairest pretences to the immortal laurels of Virgil, as prince of all our english poets. He is so old that it is looked upon as his leaving the woreld of Poetry: And if he can bot make a good Exit, all that ere a Poete can wish for in his declyning dayes. If it fall out other wayes, they will say his Muse is at her dottage; and aught not to be heard. Whouever we all expect to feast ourselves upon this book when it comes forth; Then I shall shew your E. Hsse the relish the best criticks have of it. It is a disadvantage to be translating the best piece of Poetrie of the antients, wherof the versione being bot a coppie or imitatione, most come short of the origenal: And because the author heth bein so many yeirs about this work, as his last and cheifest work, our witts will criticise the same the more." (*State Papers and Correspondence.* Edited by John M. Kemble. London, 1857. P. 193.)

Dryden's revision of his translation for a second edition was probably made in December, 1697: see *The Letters of John Dryden*, ed. Ward, pp. 97, 179. Some copies of the work consist of the sheets of the second edition with the title-page of the first.

Dryden mentions some previous English translations of Virgil (v. 519[1], 54 ff; 708[2], 57 ff; 709[2], 64–66; 710[1], 1–4, 47–51); but, except as regards Lauderdale, Normanby (v. 485, 684) and Denham (v. 546, 763), he never alludes to the liberal use that he made of them — and of other translations that he does not mention.

In an excellent article on "Dryden's *Georgics* and English Predecessors," in *Huntington Library Quarterly*, ix (1946), 273–310, Helene Maxwell Hooker finds that Dryden took details for his version of the *Georgics* from nine (or possibly ten) other English translations. Most of the following data are (by permission) taken without verification from that paper. From Thomas May, whose translation of the *Georgics* appeared in 1628 and whom he never mentions, Dryden appropriated six lines without change and eight with slight changes; he also used at least 230 of May's rhyme words in identical places. From Lauderdale he took 241 rhyme words and five lines without change. From an anonymous translation of *Georgics* iii. 209–285, aside from sixteen rhyme words, he took three lines without change, his greatest debt to any other translation in proportion to its length: v. n. **469**, 357. It is particularly startling to find that from Ogleby (Ogilby), whom he mentions four times, and always with unadulterated contempt (v. **135**, 102; **136**, 174; **176**², 8; **748**², 40–46), Dryden took not only 105 rhyme words but a couplet that he modified only slightly. Ogleby's lines,

Then snares for beasts, and lime for birds was found,
And how dogs should the mighty woods surround —

become in Dryden,

Then toils for beasts, and lime for birds were found,
And deep-mouth dogs did forest walks surround. (**447**, 211, 212.)

Such practices seem to have been accepted as innocent in the seventeenth century; other translators besides Dryden acted in the same way. An examination of Dryden's versions of the *Pastorals* and the *Æneid* would probably show a similar state of things. Cf. **546**, 763, n, below. Apparently Lauderdale was heavily in debt to Dryden as well as Dryden to Lauderdale: see Van Doren, *John Dryden* (New York, 1946), p. 101, and Macdonald, pp. 323, 324.

447, 270. *The corn-devouring weasel*, etc. Ogleby's translation (ed. 1654) reads:

Thence Weesels plunder mighty hoords of Corn.

Here *Weesels* may be a misprint for *Weevels* (weevils), rendering Latin *curculio*. The 1684 edition of Ogleby has *Weesles*. Dryden, following Ogleby rather than looking up the Latin word, fell into a ludicrous blunder. Cf. J. M. Bottkol in *Philological Quarterly*, xxvi (1947), 119.

452, 570. *Crows exult.* FF, followed by subsequent editions (including earlier issues of the present volume), read absurdly, *cows exult*. Bottkol, in *Modern Philology*, xl (1942–43), 253, points out that Virgil's words *ovantes gutture corvi* indicate with certainty an error, whether due to the printer or to the copyist — or to a slip of Dryden's pen.

540, 318. *Four times he struck.* Here Dryden in general was following Denham: v. n. **546**, 763, below. He corrected Denham's "three times" into "four times" (*quater*); but through a blunder, whether by Dryden or by the copyist or by the printer, Denham's "it stuck" (*substitit*) became corrupted into "he struck," words entirely inappropriate in this passage. Cf. n. **452**, 570, above.

546, 763. *A headless carcass*, etc. This is the last line of *The Destruction of Troy*, by Sir John Denham (1615–69), a translation of *Æneid* ii. 1–558. Denham also published *The Passion of Dido for Æneas*, an abridged version of *Æneid* iv. 276–705. Dryden might profitably have expanded his footnote on page 546; for, as T. H. Banks, Jr., shows in the notes to his edition of *The Poetical Works of Sir John Denham* (New Haven, 1928), Dryden took suggestions from both pieces by Denham, sometimes copying his lines with only the smallest changes. The following are the closest resemblances, the line references being to Dryden, followed by the corresponding text of Denham:

Book II

48, 49. ......at least to search and bore
The sides, and what that space contains t' explore.
89, 90. What Land, what Sea, for me what Fate attends?
Caught by my Foes, condemned by my Friends.
154, 155. Chiefly when this stupendious Pile was rais'd
Strange noises fill'd the Air, we all amaz'd —
274, 275. Their winding tails advance and steer their course,
And 'gainst the shore the breaking Billow force.
318–327. Three times it stuck, as oft the clashing sound
Of Arms was heard, yet blinded by the Power
Of Fate, we place it in the sacred Tower.
Cassandra then foretels th' event, but she
Finds no belief (such was the Gods decree.)
The Altars with fresh flowers we crown, & wast
In Feasts that day, which was (alas) our last.
340, 341. *Ulysses, Stenelus, Tysander* slide
Down by a Rope, *Machaon* was their guide.
346–351. The Gates they seize, the Guards with sleep and wine
Opprest, surprize, and then their forces joyn.
'Twas then, when the first sweets of sleep repair
Our bodies spent with toil, our minds with care —
391–396. With them thy Fate, with them new Walls expect,
Which, tost on Seas, thou shalt at last erect;
Then brings old *Vesta* from her sacred Quire,
Her holy Wreaths, and her eternal Fire.
438–444. .... Our Glory and our Power

Incensed *Jove* transfers to Grecian hands,
The foe within, the burning Town commands;
And (like a smother'd fire) an unseen force
Breaks from the bowels of the fatal Horse:
Insulting *Synon* flings about the flame.

479, 480. Then re-inforc'd, as in a stormy night
Wolves urged by their raging appetite.

487. Darkness our Guide, Despair our Leader was.

498, 499. And now the Victors fall, on all sides, fears,
Groans and pale Death in all her shapes appears.

510–514.   . . . . . . As when an unseen Snake
A Travellers unwary foot hath prest,
Who trembling starts, when the Snakes azure Crest,
Swoln with his rising Anger, he espies,
So from our view surpriz'd *Androgeus* flies.

526. First change your Arms, and their distinctions bear.

567, 568.   And Eurus on his winged Coursers born
Triumphing in their speed, the woods are torn.

611, 612. The gilded Roofs, the marks of ancient state
They tumble down.

691, 692. Now *Priams* fate perhaps you may enquire,
Seeing his Empire lost, his *Troy* on fire —

714–721. Or here We shall a Sanctuary find,
Or as in life, we shall in death be joyn'd.
Then weeping, with kind force held & embrac'd
And on the sacred seat the King she plac'd;
Mean while *Polites* one of *Priams* sons
Flying the rage of bloudy *Pyrrhus*, runs
Through foes & swords, & ranges all the Court
And empty Galleries, amaz'd and hurt.

742. This said, his feeble Arm a Javelin flung.

760–763. He, whom such Titles swell'd, such Power made proud
To whom the Scepters of all *Asia* bow'd,
On the cold earth lies th' unregarded King,
A headless Carkass, and a nameless Thing.

Book IV

510, 511. And mighty *Joves* Ambassadour appear'd
With the same message, whom I saw and heard.

549. Go, go, pursue thy Kingdom through the Main.

636, 637. But him no Prayers, no Arguments can move,
The Fates resist, his Ears are stopt by *Jove*.

839, 840. *Aurora* now had left *Tithonus* bed,
And o're the world her blushing Raies did spread.

962, 963. As loud as if her *Carthage*, or old *Tyre*
The Foe had entred, and had set on Fire.

655, 149, 150. *So winds*, etc. Dryden is in debt to Cowley: v. n. **135,** 72, 73.

687, 1202. *And in this kiss*, etc. v. B. S. lix, lx.

719, 103. *Berries.* E. D. D. notes that *berry* is used in Berkshire and Hampshire in the sense of "a rabbit warren, a group of rabbit holes." Sargeaunt states (p. xviii) that the word "still has that sense in Dryden's own county [Northamptonshire]."

110. *Some to undo*, etc. As J. M. Bottkol notes in *Modern Philology*, xl (1942–43), 254, this line is taken literally from Denham, *Cooper's Hill*, l. 32.

731. ALEXANDER'S FEAST. Day remarks (pp. 182, 183) that Clarke's music for this ode was never published, but that "Händel's later musical setting has made the song known to many generations of music-lovers, and has often been reprinted, for example [in *Georg Friedrich Händels Werke*, vol. 12] by the German Händelsgesellschaft, Leipzig, 1862."

In an article on "Eine deutsche Anregung zu Drydens 'Alexander's Feast'?" in *Englische Studien*, lxi (1927), 177–182, Franz Harder raises the question whether Dryden was not under some obligations to a *Schlachtlied* by Jakob Vogel, printed in the *Unterricht von der teutschen Sprache und Poesie* of Daniel Georg Morhof (Kiel, 1682). The evidence is entertaining but (as the author indicates by his question mark) not conclusive. There is no reason to suppose that Dryden could read German.

Plutarch, in his life of Alexander, xxxviii, tells how at a drinking bout Thais, an Athenian courtesan, prompted Alexander to the burning of the Persian royal palace.

735¹. LINES TO MRS. CREED. In *John Dryden: Some Biographical Facts and Problems* Osborn publishes notes made by Malone in preparation for a second edition of his biography of Dryden. Malone found that he erred in stating (v. n. **735¹,** on **1023**) that Dryden's mother was a cousin of the Sir Gilbert Pickering (1612?–1668) who was the father of Mrs. Creed. The true state of affairs was as follows. Sir Gilbert Pickering (died 1613) had a son Sir John Pickering (died 1628), who married Susan Driden, sister of Erasmus Driden, the poet's father. This Sir John Pickering had a son Sir Gilbert Pickering (1612?–1668), who was the father of Mrs. Creed. — Sir Gilbert Pickering (died 1613) had a younger brother, Henry Pickering, who had a son, also named Henry Pickering, who became rector of Aldwincle All Saints (v. B. S. xvii). This second Henry Pickering had a daughter Mary, who married Erasmus Driden and became the mother of John Dryden, the poet. Thus Mary (Pickering) Driden, the poet's mother, was only second cousin (not first cousin) to Sir Gilbert Pickering (1612?–1668). See Osborn, *Op. cit.*, pp. 122, 143, and family tree facing p. 236.

744¹, 55. *Forgive.* So F and ed. 1713. Christie and some other modern editors read *forego*, which (or rather *forgoe*) may be what Dryden really wrote. N. E. D. gives no usage of *forgive* that is quite parallel to that in this passage. But the emendation may not be needed; E. D. D. defines *forgie* (Devonshire, a variant of *forgive*) as "forget, overlook, omit," and cites an example from Madox-Brown.

751, 155, 156. *Whose face*, etc. V. de S. Pinto, in *Notes and Queries*, cxcii (1947), 389, states that this couplet is "probably based on" lines in *The Virgin* (in *Carolina, or Loyal Poems*, 1683, p. 176), by Thomas Shipman (1632–80):

Her *Looks*, at *Sin* and *Lust* incens'd,
Like *Cherubim* her Eden fenc'd.

752. PALAMON AND ARCITE. On Dryden's translations and adaptations from early English see further W. H. Williams, "*Palamon and Arcite* and *The Knightes Tale*," in *Modern Language Review*, ix (1914), 161–172, 307–323; and W. Jünemann, *Drydens Fabeln und ihre Quellen* (*Britannica*, Heft 5), Hamburg, 1932. Jünemann rightly treats Dryden as a great master of what he terms the "barocco" style.

757, 404. *Extremest line.* Professor Williams, in *Modern Language Review*, vi (1911), 386, corrects the editor's note on this passage, pointing out that the phrase "is taken from Terence, *Eunuchus*, 640, where Phædria says:

si non tangendi copiast
eho ne uidendi quidem erit? si illud non licet,
saltem hoc licebit. *certe extrema linea*
amare haud nil est.

Lewis and Short well explain the meaning as 'to love at a distance, i.e. to see the beloved object only at a distance, not be able to speak to her!'"

783, 1126. *Free.* F places a colon after this word and a full stop after *lord*, two lines below.

799, 579. *Fix'd*, etc. F places commas after *fix'd* and *die* and has none after *man*.

803, 98. *Rear.* So F. The word *rare*, meaning *scantily cooked*, is of Anglo-Saxon origin, while *rare*, meaning *not dense, infrequent*, comes from Latin through French. In the seventeenth century the two words had not yet become fully identical in pronunciation; the first was usually spelled *rear, reare, reer, reere*, or *rere*, though the form *rare* already occurs. See N. E. D.

816, 339. *Bide.* F reads *bid*.

822, 11. *Daughters.* F by an evident misprint reads *Daughter*.

827, 418. *Mulier*, etc. F. N. Robinson in the Cambridge Chaucer points out that this is "a common sentiment in mediæval literature, for which no single source need be cited."

829, 534. *Consent.* So F. Some modern editions, including the earlier issues of the present volume, read *content*.

830, 605. *Orpheus.* F reads *Orphans!*

836, 266. *Groan'd the ground.* A Virgilian echo: v. *Æneid*, vi. 256; cf. **598,** 366.

849, 285–299. *Thus marching*, etc. Dryden has modified his source under the influence of Virgil: v. *Æneid*, v. 577–587; cf. **588,** 753–768.

301. *Flight.* F reads *Fight.*

850, 360. *Lay.* So F. The modern spelling is of course *lea;* cf. note on Dryden's rhymes, p. **939.**

873, 104. *But*, etc. Mr. Sargeaunt well conjectures that Dryden wrote:

But, not to hold our proffer as in scorn.

876, 322. *Have.* Cf. **400,** 1031, n.

887, 658. *Birth.* F reads *Breath.*

890, 139. *Brillant.* So F; a variant form of *brilliant.*

898. PROLOGUE . . . FROM THE PILGRIM. Macdonald indicates (p. 136) that certain copies of the edition of *The Pilgrim* in 1700 have the pages containing the *Song* and *The Secular Masque* renumbered and provided with a separate title-page, so that these pieces by Dryden could be sold by themselves; but that there is no evidence that they were so sold.

William Egerton, in his *Faithful Memoirs of . . . Mrs. Anne Oldfield*, 1731, p. 2, states, "*The Pilgrim* was indeed revived for the benefit of Mr. Dryden, *Ann.* 1700, but dying on the third night of its representation, his son attended the run of it, and the advantages accrued to his family." This would establish the first night of the production as April 29. Malone (I, 1, 331, 332) was unwilling to accept these words by Egerton, whom he terms "one of Curll's authors." Later writers have been less skeptical: see Macdonald, p. 135 and n. 4, and A. C. Sprague, *Beaumont and Fletcher on the Restoration Stage* (Cambridge, Massachusetts, 1926), p. 91.

GLOSSARY

This Glossary is for the most part compiled from the *New English Dictionary;* quotations from that work, however, are not indicated, except in a few special cases. It is designed merely to assist the reader, not to provide material for the study of Dryden's language. It includes (*a*) words the meaning of which might perplex persons unfamiliar with seventeenth-century English; (*b*) words which Dryden employs with a different accent from that now in common use; (*c*) a few words like *boatsman, fauchion, haulser,* which would probably cause no difficulty to the reader, but which by their unusual form might seem misprints when found in the text.

The following abbreviations are employed, in addition to those used in the Notes: —

adj. = adjective.	*p. p.* = past participle.
adv. = adverb.	*pl.* = plural.
fig. — figurative.	*prep.* = preposition.
Fr. = French.	*pret.* = preterit.
int. = interjection.	*sb.* = substantive.
intrans. = intransitive.	*trans.* = transitive.
Lat. = Latin.	*vb.* = verb.

Abate of, diminish, lessen in amount, **216**², 17.

Abbethdin. v. n. **112,** 188.

Ac'cessary.

Accident, incident, **384**¹, 47.

Achës. v. n. **2,** 82.

Achievement, an escutcheon or ensign armorial, granted in memory of some achievement or distinguished feat; sometimes used as " the arms . . . well marshaled with the supporters, helmet, wreath, and crests, etc.," **773,** 344. (Quotation is from *Gwillim,* cited in N. E. D.)

Acknowledging, grateful, **500**¹, 38.

Action (*Fr.*), share (of stock), **265**¹, 30.

Admiration, wonder, surprise, **95,** 19.

Admire, wonder, marvel.

Adown, down.

Adult'rate, of base origin, **3,** 25.

Adust, "*burnt up,*" dry; applied in medical sense to a certain condition of the body, **824,** 156.

Afeard, afraid, **824,** 136.

Affect, seek to obtain, **48,** 1091; like to frequent, **482,** 441; show ostentatiously a liking for, **494**², 52.

Affright (*sb.*), fright, **110,** 71.

Affright (*vb.*), frighten, **16,** 137.

Aland, on dry land, **524,** 161.

Alga, seaweed.

Allay, inferior metal mixed with one of greater value, alloy, **89**², 39.

Allow, approve of, sanction, **244,** 1991; admit, **496**², 30.

Allude, refer to, with symbolic meaning, **240,** 1660.

Almain, German.

Alow, low, downwards, **466,** 171; **895,** 370.

Amain, vehemently, violently; at full speed; immediately.

Amaze, amazement, bewilderment, **674,** 215.

Ambient, surrounding, **735,** 2 (*Tonson*).

Ambition, ostentation, **177**², 4.

Ames-ace, ambs-ace, double ace, the lowest throw at dice.

Amomum, an odoriferous plant.

Anneal'd, having colors burnt in, as glass, **735**², 12.

Anniverse, anniversary.

Annoy (*sb.*), trouble, discomfort.

Antic, Antique, grotesque, **26**², 7; ancient, **453,** 666. These two words, distinct in origin (one from Italian and one from French), were confused in Dryden's time. The spelling of the early editions varies between *antick* and *antique ;* the accent in each instance is on the first syllable.

Apoplex, apoplexy.

Apos'tolic.

Appeach, impeach, accuse, **756,** 300.

Ardent, flaming, fierce.

Arlequin, Harlequin, a merry-andrew; originally a droll rogue of the Italian comedy.

Armado, armada, fleet, **29,** 54.

Armipotent, mighty in arms, **766,** 545 (Chaucer).

Arow, in a row, **848,** 249.

Artificially, artistically, ingeniously, **154,** 12 (*prose*).

Artique', arctic, **214,** 6.

As, as if, **824,** 104.

Aspect, the relative positions of the heavenly bodies as they appear to an observer on the earth's surface; used with reference to the influence of such positions on the fortunes of men, **755,** 247.

Assay, essay, try, put to the proof.

Assist, be present.

Assistant, person present, bystander, **837,** 306.

Astragal, molding used on columns, **917,** 56 (Soame).

Atone, reconcile, bring into concord, make propitious.

Atrip, of yards: hoisted up and ready to be swayed across, **840,** 93.

Attend, wait, wait for; wait to see, **837,** 317.
Attent, attentive, **876,** 310.
At'tribute (*vb.*), **802,** 7.
Auctority, authority.
Auspex, one who took omens by the flight of birds; then, a director of marriage ceremonies, **354,** 517.
Auspice, propitious influence, patronage, **49,** 1150; a well-omened introduction, **254,** 50.
Authentic, authoritative, entitled to belief, **4,** 8; entitled to obedience or respect, **246,** 2132.
Awful, reverential, profoundly respectful, **255,** 106.

Bacchanals, Bacchanalia, drunken revels, **223,** 387; songs in honor of Bacchus, **463,** 693.
Baffled, disgraced, dishonored.
Balk, omit, pass over.
Band, bond, obligation, **671,** 1301.
Bank, bench for rowers, **575,** 825.
Banquier, banker, **58**[1], 34.
Bare, a space bare of grass, **423,** 108.
Barmy, frothy.
Bat, club, cudgel, **243,** 1925.
Bate of, **80**[2], 11. v. **Abate of.**
Battalia, battle array, **571,** 582.
Bauble. v. n. **215,** 7.
Bead, *bid beads,* offer prayers (with indirect reference to the use of the rosary).
Beam, the main trunk of a stag's horn, **619,** 670.
Beamy, antlered, **472,** 625; massive as a (weaver's) beam, **775,** 480.
Bear, push, press, **660,** 532.
Bearded, barbed, **525,** 240.
Bearn, child.
Becoming of, suitable to, **745**[2], 58.
Beestings, the first milk after calving, **425,** 42.
Beholding, indebted, **365,** n. 6.
Belinsgate, Billingsgate, abusive language (so called from a noted fish market in London), **917,** 84 (Soame?).
Bent, bare field, heath.
Benting times, times when pigeons are reduced to feeding on *bents* or coarse grass, **252,** 2577.
Bergamote, a fine kind of pear.
Berry. v. **719,** 103, nn (on **10**2**1, 1070**).
Bias, preponderating disposition (metaphor from game of bowls), **136,** 189; *to run off one's bias,* to depart from one's natural course, **288**[1], 22.
Bid, *bid beads.* v. **Bead.**
Big-corn'd, large-grained, **39,** 595.
Bilander (*Dutch*), coasting vessel, **219,** 128.
Bilbo-gallant, bully gallant, — from *bilbo,* a sword, originally one from Bilbao in Spain, **156,** 5.
Bishop'd, confirmed.
Bittor, bittern, **874,** 194.
Blatant, bellowing; cf. **228,** 802, n.
Bleaky, rather bleak, bleakish.
Bless, make the sign of the cross over, **241,** 1790.
Blind, a place of concealment, **565,** 95.
Bloomy, blooming.
Blubber'd, bewept, disfigured with weeping, **844,** 392.
Boatsman, boatman, **885,** 449.
Boist'rous, stiff, unyielding, **794,** 159.

Booty, to *play booty* is to play badly on purpose, in order to lose the game; hence *write booty,* **500**[2]**, 8.**
Boracho, a leathern wine bottle, **376,** 216.
Bore, push an opponent out of the course in racing, **646,** 588; thrust the head straight forward (of a horse), **470,** 438. (The Latin text points to this meaning rather than to that of " push forward by gradual persistent motion," which N. E. D. applies to this passage.)
Botch, boil, ulcer, pimple, **232,** 1115.
Bounce, knock, strike, **688,** 1283.
Boutefeu, incendiary, firebrand, **925,** 1077 (Soame).
Bowsy, boozy, drunken, **351,** 288.
Bowyer, archer, **813,** 138.
Boyism, puerility, **744**[1], 21.
Brave (*sb.*), bravo, bully.
Breathe, be redolent of, **484,** 602; *breathe a vein,* lance it so as to let blood, **5,** 48.
Breer, briar.
Breeze, gadfly, **467,** 239.
Brew, prepare by mixing several ingredients, **6,** 100, n.
Brim, fill to the brim.
Brimmer, goblet filled to the brim, **185,** 99.
Brinded, brindled, streaked, **822,** 14.
Brindice, brendice, bumper, cup in which a person's health is drunk, **72**[1], 6.
Broach (*sb.*), spit, **461,** 547.
Broacher, spit, **820,** 638.
Brown george. v. n. **376,** 215.
Browse, young shoots and twigs, used as food for cattle, **439,** 9.
Bubble (*sb.*), dupe, gull, **329,** 206.
Bug word, bugaboo (?) word, word meant to terrify, **729,** 882.
Built (*sb.*), build, **32,** 237.
Bumbast, bombast, **917,** 98 (Soame).
Bump. v. **874,** 194, n.
Burnish (*vb. intrans.*), grow plump or stout, **79**[1], 21; (*vb. trans.*), v. n. **223,** 390, on **1064.**
Buxom, pliant, yielding, favorable, kindly, **591,** 1017.
By-end, secret, selfish purpose.

Cadence'.
Cadency, cadence, rhythm.
Cæsura. v. **511**[2], 7, n.
Camelot, camlet, a stuff made of goats' hair; in **470,** 487, apparently used of the goats' hair itself, corresponding to *fleece* as used of sheep.
Candid, white, **880,** 60.
Cant (*sb.* and *adj.*), technical language, or pertaining to it; the peculiar phraseology of a religious sect (not necessarily hypocritical), **116,** 521.
Cant (*vb.*), use cant language, **824,** 146, n. The execration *pox cant 'em,* **124**[2]**, 18,** is probably only a euphemism for a vigorous oath. It may, however, as the context indicates, be more specific, *plague take their canting.*
Cantlet, piece cut off, fragment.
Captive (*vb.*), take captive.
Careful, attended with care or trouble, **242,** 1868.
Carousel, tournament, gorgeous equestrian display, **588,** 777.
Cashier, dismiss from service.

Cast (*vb.*), calculate astrologically, **241**, 1766.

Cast (*p. p.*), condemned, defeated in a law suit, **835**, 172.

Castor, beaver.

Cat, prostitute, **411**[1], 34.

Cates, provisions, food, or perhaps dainties, **235**, 1293.

Ce'ment (*vb.*), **242**, 1876.

Cense, burn incense before, perfume with burning incense.

Cerrial oak, evergreen oak, **848**, 230.

Cey'lon.

Cham, Ham, son of Noah.

Champian (*adj.*), of the champaign, or broad open country, **784**, 51.

Chapman, merchant, trader.

Charge, a device borne upon an escutcheon, a bearing, **848**, 233.

Charger, platter.

Chaw, chew; not necessarily with vulgar connotation; cf. **828**, 485.

Check, *fly at check*, to forsake the proper quarry and pursue base game, as crows, **34**, 344.

Cheer, face, expression, aspect.

Cherubin, cherub, **751**, 156; pl. *cherubims*, **927**[1], 7.

Chiromancer, one who tells fortunes by the hand, **345**, 756.

Chirurgeon, surgeon.

Chosen, well selected, **496**[2], 44.

Chymical, chemical; v. n. **488**[2], 41.

Cion, scion.

Circular. v. n. **4**, 18.

Cirque, natural amphitheater, **587**, 720; cf. **583**, 377.

Cit, citizen (used contemptuously), **65**[2], 23.

Class, classis, presbytery, **220**, 189.

Classical, pertaining to a *class* or presbytery, **217**[1], 28.

Clear. v. n. **726**, 611.

Clench, pun, quibble, **85**[1], 27.

Clift, cliff.

Clinch, same as **Clench**, **135**, 83.

Clip it, fly rapidly, **34**, 344.

Closely, secretly, covertly, **566**, 180.

Clotter'd, clotted.

Clue, clew, ball of thread, **16**, 71; thread, **9**, 155; thread of life, **770**, 169.

Cock, swagger, strut, brag, **78**, 9.

Cockle, a weed (*Lychnis Githago*) growing frequently in grain fields, especially among wheat.

Colewort, any plant of the cabbage kind.

Coming, forward, inclined to make advances, **498**[2], 49.

Commerce'.

Common shore. v. **Shore.**

Commonplace, collection of commonplaces, or striking, notable passages, valuable for quotation, **307**[1], 15.

Commonweal, commonwealth, republic, **221**, 234.

Complexion. v. n. **6**, 100.

Composs, compost, prepared manure, **826**, 269.

Composure, composing of differences, agreement, **109**[2], 16; literary or artistic composition, **11**, 6.

Conceit, strained or far-fetched turn of thought or figure.

Concernment, solicitude, anxiety.

Condition, character, nature, **759**, 593 (Chaucer).

Con'fessor.

Confident, trusty friend, person confided in.

Confining, bordering, **854**, 58.

Congee, bow, **123**, 25.

Con'globate, gathered into a ball, rounded, **1**, 35.

Connatural, agreeing in nature, allied, **26**[1], 7.

Conscious, privy to a secret, **576**, 932.

Consequent (*sb.*), consequence, **108**[2], 3.

Con'sistory, court, company surrounding a throne, **232**, 1074.

Consort, singing or playing in harmony, accompaniment (?), **201**, 42.

Consult, consultation (often with unfavorable connotation), **250**, 2402.

Contain, contain oneself, remain, **138**, 42 (Tate).

Contended, striven for, disputed.

Content, *on* (*upon*) *content*, without question or examination, **167**, 381.

Contra'ry. v. n. **437**, 10.

Con'venticle (or **Conventi'cle**), meeting of Nonconformists (illegal in Dryden's time), **131**, 284.

Conversation, familiar society, intimacy, **501**[2], 17.

Converse', talk, conversation, **19**[2], 20.

Convert (*vb. intrans.*), change, **810**, 342.

Convict' (*adj.*), proved guilty, **809**, 228.

Convince, convict, prove guilty, **870**, 481.

Cornel, fruit of cornel tree.

Corps. v. *General Notes*, **939.**

Couch, lay down (a person, or oneself).

Couchée, evening reception, **224**, 516.

Counter, city prison, **82**[2], 20 (*Epil.*).

Counterbanded, smuggled.

Counterbuff'd, rebuffed, struck in the opposite direction, **894**, 342.

Courtship, courtliness, **412**, 29.

Coystrel, kestrel, a species of small hawk.

Cozen, cheat, **8**, 128.

Cozenage, deception, fraud, **229**, 830.

Crack, crash, loud noise, **46**, 951.

Cracknel, cracker, crisp biscuit, **331**, 310.

Crazy, sickly, infirm, **237**, 1445.

Croslet, corslet, **621**, 877.

Cross (*prep.*), across.

Cross (*vb.*), contradict, contravene, **247**, 2241.

Crotch, pole with forked top, used as support, **804**, 160.

Cruddled, curdled, congealed.

Cruse, small earthen vessel for liquids, jug, **248**, 2294.

Cry, pack of hounds, **225**, 595, where, however, the meaning of *the public voice* may also be intended; cf. **249**, 2330.

Cuckow, cuckoo.

Cucumer, cucumber.

Cudden, born fool, dolt, **892**, 179.

Cuishes, Cuisses, armor for protecting the front part of the thighs.

Cully, dupe, gull, simpleton, **85**[2], 8.

Curious, skilfully or elaborately wrought.
Curtana. v. n. **231, 991.**
Cutting. v. n. **67¹, 31.**

Dare, *to dare larks,* to fascinate and daze them, in order to catch them, **43, 780.**
Darkling (*adv.*), in the dark.
Dash, bespatter, splash, **111, 114.**
Dauby, sticky.
Dead color (or coloring). v. n. **741², 48.**
Debenture, certificate of indebtedness issued by some government office, **410, 3.**
Decence, decency.
Decline (*vb. intrans.*), turn aside, deviate, **395, 687.**
Decrepid, decrepit.
Decumbiture, an astrological figure erected for the time of falling ill, affording prognostics of recovery or death, **345, 752.**
Deducement, deduction, inference.
Defend, prohibit, avert, **689, 67.**
Deficience, deficiency.
Defy, declaration of defiance, challenge to fight, **776, 580.**
Degree, row, tier, **580, 158.**
Delude, *delude their force,* **122, 1021,** apparently means *squander their energy ;* from the use of *delude* (*time*) in the sense of *spend, beguile.*
Demains, demesnes, domains, regions.
Denounce, announce, proclaim, **690, 120.**
Depend (*vb. intrans.*), hang down, **568, 368;** be in suspense, or undetermined, **228, 774.**
Dependence, something that hangs down, **487, 806.**
Designment, original draught or design.
Despite, spite, malice, hatred.
Destin'd, fated, doomed, **574, 747.**
Detort, twist, pervert, wrest, **159², 19.**
Devest, unclothe, strip, **220, 187.**
Diapason, grand burst of harmony, whole compass of an instrument, **252, 15.**
Diffide, distrust, lack faith.
Di'gestive (*sb.*), medicine or food promoting digestion, **825, 189** (Chaucer).
Diges'tive (*adj.*), having the function of digesting, tending to methodize and reduce to order, **8, 89.**
Dint, (assaulting) force, **237, 1494.**
Dip, immerse, involve, implicate; mortgage, **380, 160.**
Discourse, the faculty of reasoning; reasoning, ratiocination, **163, 71.**
Discover, make known, **476** (*Arg.*).
Disembogue, pour forth, empty out, **232, 1134.**
Disheir, deprive of an heir, **244, 1999.**
Disherited, disinherited, dispossessed.
Dishonest, shameful, ignominious, **232, 1119;** unseemly, hideous, **602, 668.**
Disinteress'd, disinterested, unbiased
Dismission, dismissal, leave to depart.
Dispel, become scattered, **655, 157.**
Dispose, disposal, control.
Disseize, dispossess wrongfully, **244, 2005.**
Distain, stain, discolor.
Dittany, a plant (*Dictamnus Creticus*) formerly famous for its supposed healing virtues, **697, 609.**

Divisible. In **222, 319,** equivalent to *material,* since matter is divisible and spirit indivisible.
Do (*sensu obscæno*).
Dodder'd. Used as an epithet of an oak, or other tree, that has lost its head and branches by decay, **780, 905; 545, 702.** This word was apparently first used in literature by Dryden.
Dolphin, Dauphin.
Done, exhausted, weary, **33, 277.**
Doom, statute, enactment, **164, 206; 251, 2527;** judgment, discernment, **483, 565;** fate, **466, 111.**
Doom into. v. n. **43, 827.**
Doom'd, sentenced (in contrast to *fated*), **218, 8;** fated, destined, **631, 501.**
Dop, descend suddenly into water, pop down, **107², 2.**
Dorp, village, **243, 1905.**
Doted, foolish, in second childhood.
Doubt, suspect, **744², 60;** mistrust, **97, 171;** *doubt of,* be undecided about, **178², 37.**
Draught, drawing, delineation, picture, **249, 2342.**
Dress, train, break in; or groom, curry (?), **670, 1226.**
Drib (*vb.*), let fall in drops or driblets, *i. e.* weep, **123, 22.**
Dropping, dripping, **760, 42.**
Dumfounding. v. n. **261, 47.**

Eagre, a tidal wave of unusual height, caused by the rushing of the tide up a narrowing estuary; used chiefly with reference to the Humber (and Trent) and the Severn, **205, 134.**
Ean, yean, bring forth lambs, **145, 563** (Tate).
Ease, Chapel of. v. n. **242, 1834.**
Ease, Writ of, certificate of discharge from employment, **81², 19.**
Economy, structure, arrangement, proportion of parts (of a poem or play), **504², 34.**
Effort'.
Elephant, ivory, **559, 595.**
Embodied, formed into a militant body, marshaled, **571, 582.**
Em'piric (Em'p'ric).
Emptiness, vacuum, **15, 42.**
Encrease. v. **Increase.**
Endlong, right along, straight on, **777, 691.**
Enquire, inquire of, seek information from, **130, 164.**
Enterpris'd, undertaken, **288², 24.**
Envy, malice, enmity; odium, unpopularity.
Epoche, epoch (v. n. **8, 108**).
Equal (*sb.*), person of same age as another, **587, 719.**
Equal (*adj.*), just, fair-minded, impartial, **655, 166.**
Eringo, the candied root of the sea holly, formerly used as a sweetmeat, and regarded as an aphrodisiac, **340, 419.**
Err, stray, wander, **547, 814.**
Errant (*sb.*), errand, **390, 298.**
Errant (*adj.*), downright, unquestionable, **513², 21.**
Error, action of wandering; devious course, **588, 772.**
Essay', first tentative effort, **38, 558; 740², 15;** result of an attempt, **434, 42.**

Etesian. v. n. **750,** 46.
Event, outcome, issue, **288²,** 50.
Evidence, witness, **138,** 46 (Tate).
Evince, prove, **228,** 762.
Exact, consummate, accomplished, **277, 65.**
Example, pattern, design to be copied, **393,** 494. (Ovid has *hominum exempla*.)
Excellency, excellence.
Excite, stir up (in physical sense), **469,** 362.
Exclusive, having the function of excluding, **141,** 254 (Tate).
Excursion, digression, **476** (*Arg*.).
Exequies, funeral rites.
Exercise, employ, train by practice or by ascetic discipline, or (possibly) harass, afflict, **209,** 430; till (the ground), **447,** 232.
Exert, bring to light, reveal, **273,** 165.
Exerted, thrust out, projecting, **684, 964.**
Exile'.
Expire (*vb. trans.*), breathe out, **789,** 203; give out under pressure, **446,** 205; (*vb. intrans.*), rush forth, **479,** 254.
Explicate, explain, **166,** 289.
Expose, put out, put ashore, **658,** 403; explain, set forth, **529,** 539.
Express (*adj.*), distinctly uttered, **854,** 71.

Fact, evil deed, crime, **791,** 335.
Factor, agent, representative, **8,** 78.
Fainty, faint, sickly, languid.
Falsify, render useless, spoil, **653,** 1095; v. Dryden's note, p. **715¹.**
Fame, rumor, common talk, **553,** 147.
Fanatic, religious enthusiast (in Dryden's time used especially by the Nonconformists).
Farmost, farthest off, **795,** 264.
Fatal, decreed by fate, destined.
Fated, made proof by spells, charmed, **634,** 711.
Fauchion, falchion.
Favor, appearance, look, **125¹,** 30.
Fearful, timid, timorous, **788,** 107.
Featly, with graceful agility, nimbly, **875, 216.**
Fescue, pointer, stick or pin used for pointing, **279,** 38.
Firm, strengthen, confirm, **615,** 356.
Firmamental waters. N. E. D. explains these words, in **49,** 1122, as " liquid as pure as the firmament." But a different explanation is suggested by Genesis i, 7: " And God made the firmament, and divided the waters which were under the firmament from the waters which were above the firmament." Cf. N. E. D., under *Firmamentary*.
Fix, determine: v. n. **897,** 557.
Flaggy, hanging down limply, drooping, **476,** 40.
Flat, flatten.
Flaw, crack, fissure, **204,** 31; sudden uproar or tumult. In **647,** 722 apparently used in the first meaning, but with a tinge of the second as well.
Flitting, shifting, unstable; fleeting, transitory.
Flix, fur (by Dryden used only of the hare, **38,** 526).
Fogue, fougue, fury, ardor, **9,** 203.
Foin (*vb.*), thrust with pointed weapon, lunge, **762,** 196.
Fond (*sb. Fr.*), stock, store, **180²,** 37.
Fond (*adj.*), foolish, trivial, over-affectionate.

Fond (*vb.*), fondle, **534,** 962.
Forbear, have patience with, tolerate, **110,** 37.
Forefend, forfend, forbid, prevent.
Forelay, waylay, **645,** 537.
Foreseize, seize beforehand, **150,** 976 (Tate).
Foreslow, forslow, delay, hinder.
Former, earlier, **302¹,** 32.
Forthright, directly forward, straight on.
Fraischeur (*Fr.*), freshness, **14,** 102.
Fraught (*sb.*), freight, cargo, **208,** 398.
Fraught (*adj.*), laden.
Free, admitted to the privileges of (a corporation or the like), **438,** 43; allowed the use or enjoyment of a place, **251,** 2539.
Frequent, crowded, full, **235,** 1319.
Fright, frighten.
Frightful, timid, alarmed, **561,** 780.
Frize, frieze, sort of coarse woolen cloth, **379,** 107.
Frontless, unblushing, shameless.
Fry, burn (*trans.*), **423,** 14; burn (*intrans.*), **199²,** 33; **553,** 196; boil, seethe, foam, **580,** 186.
Fulminate, strike with the *thunderbolts* of ecclesiastical censure, denounce, **233,** 1156.
Fulsome, nauseating, loathsome, repulsive, **221,** 221.
Fumetery, fumitory, *fumaria officinalis*.

Gage (*sb.*), pledge, security, **29,** 79.
Galbanean, pertaining to galbanum.
Galbanum, a gum resin obtained from certain Persian plants.
Galenical, pertaining to the school of the physician Galen; v. n. **488²,** 41.
Gall'd, chafed, frayed, **39,** 589.
Gallimaufry, hodge-podge, medley, **417¹,** 19.
Gap-tooth'd, with gaps between the teeth.
Garbidge, garbage.
Gaudry, gaudery, showy decoration.
Ga'zette, news-sheet, periodical publication giving record of current events, **87¹,** 5.
Gears, doings, goings on, **128,** 60.
Gem, bud, **845,** 13.
Generous, of good breed or stock, **466,** 119; spirited, **774,** 443.
Genial, natural, **250,** 2441; *genial bed,* marriage bed, **336,** 76.
Geniture. v. n. **12,** 104.
George. v. **Brown george.**
Gibbous, rounded, protuberant, **629,** 308.
Gig, move to and fro (?), **341,** 433. In **261²,** 21, " the verb seems literally to denote the action of some kind of *gig* or whipping top of peculiar construction, having inside it a smaller *gig* of the same shape, which was thrown out by the effect of rapid rotation." N. E. D.
Give on, make an assault, **49,** 1120, n.
Go, walk, **682,** 858.
God-smith, god-maker.
Grabble, feel with the hands, handle rudely or roughly.
Gradual, steps of an altar, **393,** 506 (the only instance of the word in this sense cited by N. E. D.).
Graff. graft.
Grateful, pleasant, agreeable, **199²,** 22; cf. n. **728,** 799.
Grave, engrave.

Graver, engraver.

Gridelin, name of a color, pale purple, or gray violet; sometimes a pale red, **850,** 343.

Grief, physical pain, **697,** 614.

Griesly, Grisly, horrible, ghastly, of forbidding appearance.

Gross, main body of an army or fleet, **42,** 728; large body, mass, **45, 929;** *in gross,* in a general way, without going into particulars, **166,** 322.

Grossly, without discrimination, stupidly, **106¹,** 17.

Grout, sediment, dregs, **479,** 239.

Grutch. v. n. **146,** 661.

Guard, *out of guard,* off guard, by surprise, **204,** 17.

Guilty of their vows. v. n. **582,** 307.

Guttle, eat voraciously, gormandize, **378,** 51.

Habit. v. n. **861,** 578.

Haggard. Often spelled *hagger'd* by Dryden, and probably felt by him as a participle.

Halcyon, kingfisher, **7,** 144; cf. n. **845,** 495.

Hand, the whole arm (apparently), **649,** 853.

Hardly, with difficulty, **779,** 772; vigorously, **649,** 828.

Har'pon, harpoon.

Haste (*vb. trans.*), make move more quickly, hurry.

Hateful, full of hate, cherishing hatred, **754,** 214.

Hatter'd out, worn out, exhausted.

Haulser, hawser.

Haunt, associate with habitually, **567,** 270.

Hawk, hunt on the wing, **698,** 693.

Heap, *on a heap,* together, into one mass, **837,** 312.

Heapy, full or consisting of heaps.

Hear, obey, **750,** 59.

Hearse, bier, coffin, tomb, grave, **791,** 325; for another meaning, v. n. **120,** 858.

Heir, inherit.

Herd, herdsman, pastor, **223,** 391.

High-flying, aiming high, lofty pretension, **125¹,** 6; but cf. note on line.

Hight, was called, **135,** 67; called, **86,** 24.

His, its, **797,** 405 (but in this line there is perhaps a personification).

Hit, *to look to one's hits,* to look to one's chances, **411¹,** 29.

Hobby, a small species of falcon, formerly flown at larks and other small birds.

Hold, refrain, forbear, **207,** 274.

Holland, Holland linen, **43,** 824.

Hollow, hollo, cry out.

Honest, decent, respectable, **195,** 17; fair, comely (v. n. **460,** 540).

Hope, expect, anticipate, **762,** 182.

Horrid, bristling, shaggy, **645,** 519; causing horror, terrible, dreadful, **685,** 1036.

Hostry, hostelry, inn.

Houss, housing, covering attached to a saddle so as to cover the back and flanks of a horse.

Hout, hoot.

Hovel, stack of grain, **266²,** 2 (*Harvest Song*).

Huffing, blustering, swaggering, bullying, **351,** 257.

Hugy, huge.

Husband, husbandman, one who tills the soil, **448,** 351.

Huswife (*vb.*), housewife, economize, manage thriftily, **822,** 9.

Imbrown, embrown, make brown, make dusky.

Imp, to engraft feathers into the wing of a bird, so as to make good deficiencies and improve the power of flight, **39,** 570; *imp'd with wings,* provided with wings, **482,** 439.

Impair, grow worse, deteriorate, **778,** 749.

Impassibility, incapability of suffering, insusceptibility to injury, **509²,** 45.

Impassible, not subject to pain, invulnerable, **855,** 126; incapable of suffering injury or detriment, **219,** 95.

Impassive, not susceptible of physical injury, **599,** 409.

Impor'tune.

Impotent, unrestrained, headlong, passionate, **895,** 366.

Impregnant, impregnated, pregnant, **389,** 203.

Impulse'.

Inartificial, inartistic, clumsy, **787** (*Arg.*).

Inbibe. v. n. **820,** 634.

Inch, move by inches.

Increase, growth, **221.** 268; multiplication of a family, propagation, **134,** 8; offspring, **256,** 208; what breeds in or is produced by any region, **251,** 2542 (spelled *encrease* in this line).

Incubus, lewd evil spirit.

Incumbent, pressing upon, **696,** 543.

Induce, introduce, begin, **362** (*Arg.*).

Induction, the action of formally introducing a clergyman into possession of the church to which he has been presented and instituted, **417²,** 13 (*Epil.*).

Indulge, favor (*fig.*), **468,** 320; let in (*nonce-use*), **842,** 300.

Informing (*adj.* and *sb.*), vitalizing, inspiring, animating, **221,** 251; **381¹,** 22.

Infus'd, poured in, **174,** 74.

Ingenious, talented, possessed of genius, **709¹,** 3.

Ingenuous, befitting a free-born person, high-class, **307²,** 19.

Innocency, innocence.

Innovate upon (on), bring in for the first time, introduce as new.

Inspire, blow upon, **750,** 47; take in by breathing, **631,** 515.

Instance, cite an instance, adduce an example, **518²,** 25.

Instinct' (*sb.*).

Instop, stop, close up, **39,** 586.

Insult' (*sb.*), act of leaping upon, **465,** 99.

Insult (*vb.*), exult proudly or contemptuously, **304²,** 53; assault, assail, **387,** 39.

Insurancer, one who insures or makes sure, **206,** 186.

Interess, interest, cause to be concerned, **289¹,** 54.

Interested, interested, concerned.

Interlope. v. n. **128,** 41.

Intitle, entitle, give a claim to, **293¹, 14.**

Irremeable, irretraceable, admitting of no return.

Issue, place of egress, gate, **621,** 843.

Jack, a leathern jug or tankard.

Jackal'.

Jambeux, armor for the legs.

Joy, rejoice **37,** 467; make rejoice, **36,** 440; congratulate, **783,** 1099; salute with expressions of joy, **360,** 142.

Judgment, competent critic, judge, **52,** 45.

Juppon, jupon, close fitting tunic worn by knights under the hauberk, **768,** 28 (Chaucer).

Just, joust, run at tilt with lances on horseback, **774,** 431.

Justs, jousts, tournament.

Kemb (*vb.*), comb, **371,** 90.

Ken (*sb.*), power of vision, look, gaze, **36,** 443.

Ken (*vb.*), descry, catch sight of.

Kern, Irish peasant.

Kerve, carve, cut.

Key, quay, **45,** 921.

Kid, small child, **411**[1], 19.

Kilderkin, small cask, of the size of half a barrel, holding 16 or 18 gallons.

Kimbo, resembling an arm akimbo, **426,** 67.

Kind, nature, **458,** 326; *by kind*, by nature, naturally, **851,** 496.

King at Arms (more correctly *King of Arms*), the title of the three chief heralds of the College of Arms in England; applied also to similar officers in other countries. (Used by Dryden loosely, without regard to the strict sense, **848,** 240.)

Knare, knar, knot in a tree.

Known, well known, familiar, **369**[2], 1.

Labor, belabor, ply with blows, **473,** 639.

Lade (*vb.*), load (used of persons or trees), **47,** 1008; **404,** 72.

Lag, laggard, hindmost person in a race, **80,** 43.

Lard, fat bacon or pork, **803,** 107.

Lares (*Lat., pl.*), household gods.

Large, generous, **255,** 86.

Largely, freely, loosely, inaccurately, **322**[2], 37.

Latter, later, of a subsequent period, **587,** 690.

Launch, pierce, cut, lance, **473,** 691; hurl, **541,** 361; to be launched, pass into the water, **640,** 140. (*Lanch* is the regular spelling of the early editions.)

Laund, open space among woods, glade, **762,** 235.

Laveer, beat to windward, tack.

Lawn, same as **Laund, 833,** 74.

Laxative, laxative, **778,** 765.

Lazar, poor and diseased person, especially a leper, **26**[2], 6.

Lead, marry, **857,** 267.

Lease, glean, **170,** 72.

Leave, abandon, leave off, **484,** 647; cease, **137,** 205.

Leavy, leafy, **849,** 316.

Lecture, reading matter, thing read, **359,** 63.

Lee, lees, sediment of wine or other liquids, **796,** 317.

Leech, physician.

Legator, testator, one who bequeaths.

Letted of, hindered from, **45,** 885.

Levée, Levee, morning reception.

Ley, lea, arable land under grass, pasture land, **425,** 15.

Like, please, **241,** 1771.

Liking. v. n. **205,** 153.

Limbec, alembic, distilling apparatus.

Limbo, a region on the borders of hell, the abode of the just who died before Christ's coming; used figuratively in **139,** 94 (Tate).

Linstock, staff carrying a match used to fire a cannon.

Liquorish, lustful, wanton.

Lively, vividly, to the life, **889,** 104.

Loader, doublet (in dicing), **335**[1], 27.

Loll, stretch out (the tongue).

Lote, nettle tree, *celtis australis*.

Lubber, big, clumsy, stupid fellow, especially one who lives in idleness, **242,** 1844.

Lubric, lascivious, wanton; in **212,** 63 the original meaning of the word, *smooth and slippery*, is also felt.

Lug, pull (by the hair, etc.), **361,** 272; bait, worry, **899**[1], 4; *lug forth, lug out*, draw one's sword, **154,** 31; **172,** 62.

Luggage, what has to be lugged about, inconveniently heavy baggage, **249,** 2327.

Luxury, lust, lasciviousness, **222,** 362.

Macedon, Macedonian, **751,** 133.

Machine' (**Ma'chine?** 84[1], 10), a contrivance for the sake of effect in a play or other literary work; especially the use of supernatural agencies or persons, **288**[2], 43.

Machining, appearing as a god brought in by a *machine*, or piece of theatrical machinery, **719,** 120; serving the function of a poetic *machine*, **491**[2], 16.

Maidenhead, maidenhood, virginity (used also of men), **443**[1], 14.

Make, do, **875,** 229; proceed, advance, **539,** 281.

Malecontent, malcontent, **244,** 1956.

Manage, Menage, use sparingly, husband; in **41,** 674 used in the sense of *conduct, carry on*, but probably also with a mixture of the preceding meaning.

Manifest of, evidently guilty of, **112,** 204.

Manumize, manumit, set free.

Manure, till, cultivate.

Many, company, crowd, **732,** 107; meiny, retinue, following, **545,** n.

Marling, marline, small line used for winding ropes.

Martlet, martin, swallow, swift.

Mary-bones, marrowbones; but, as used jocularly of the knees (**874,** 192), the word may be popularly connected with Mary, as if devoted to prayer to the Virgin.

Mate, equal, rival, vie with.

Mazer, bowl, originally one of maple wood, **420**[1], 41.

Med'cinable, medicinal, having healing properties, **801,** 707.

Melfoil, milfoil, yarrow.

Menage. v. **Manage.**

Menager, one who *menages*, or *manages;* economizer, **89**², 45.

Metemsu'chosis, metempsychosis, **2,** 72. (Dryden uses an affected form, apparently imitating the Greek spelling and accent; cf. n. **162,** 43.)

Metheglin, a spiced or medicated variety of mead.

Mew, molt, cast or shed the horns, **810,** 320.

Millenary, of the Millennium, **750,** 81.

Mingle, mixture, **53**², 31.

Mischief, worker of mischief, harmful person, **800,** 613; *at mischief,* at a disadvantage, **775, 516** (Chaucer).

Miss, kept mistress.

Miss of, fail to secure, **251, 2483.**

Missioner, missionary, **233,** 1137, n.

Missive, missile, **898, 624.**

Mold, earth regarded as the material of the human body, **221,** 247; structural type or model of a ship, **33,** 287; distinctive nature, or (possibly) plastic material, **50,** 1170; character, native constitution, **797,** 424; body, bodily form, **219,** 81.

Mole, sacrificial cake, **436,** 115.

Molted, deprived of feathers by molting, **39,** 570.

Mon'sieur.

Monster, prodigy, marvel, **640,** 155.

Moppet. In **123,** 36, apparently used in the sense of *rag doll;* the word was also a pet name for children, and was applied contemptuously to men.

Morion, sort of helmet, without beaver or visor.

Motion, inward prompting or impulse, **900**¹, 25 (used by Puritans in a religious sense, and by Dryden, sarcastically, in quite a different one).

Moun'sire, Monsieur, **6,** 90.

Muck. v. n. **251, 2482.**

Mum, a sort of strong ale.

Mungril, mongrel.

Murrey-color'd, of a mulberry (dark red) color, **344,** 669.

Museful, thoughtful, **558,** 572.

Musket, sparrow hawk, inferior sort of hawk, **250,** 2413.

Muss (*sb.*), scramble, as for objects thrown on the ground, **83,** 20.

Næve, spot, blemish, **2,** 55.

Name, used with implication of individual denoted by the *name,* **766,** 504.

Nard, an aromatic plant.

Native. v. n. **831,** 686.

Nature. v. n. **251, 2537.**

Need (*vb.*), be necessary, be needed.

Nephew, grandson, descendant, **845,** 499.

Nerve, sinew, tendon; penis.

Nervous, sinewy, muscular.

Nice, delicately discriminating, **176**², 41; critical, full of danger or uncertainty, **815,** 296; delicate, needing tactful handling, **182**¹, 5 (*prose*).

Niceness, reserve, coyness, **95,** 16.

Nick, criticise, censure, **52,** 57.

Nobless, noblesse, nobility, **24**¹, 12.

Noint, anoint, **727,** 746.

Noiseful, noisy.

Nose, find out, detect, as if by means of a keen scent, **173,** 28.

Notch'd. v. n. **103**¹, 21.

Note, stigma, visible token of reproach, **244, 1986.**

Novel. v. n. **487**², 11.

Now (*sb.*), a present point or moment of time, **204,** 28.

Numerous, harmonious, musical.

Numerousness, rhythmic quality, harmony.

Nuncio, messenger, **289**¹, 23 (perhaps selected by Dryden because of its more frequent use in the sense of a permanent official representative of the Roman See at a foreign court).

Nuntius, 234, 1234. v. **Nuncio.**

Oaf, booby, simpleton.

Obligement, obligation (moral or legal), **223,** 437.

Obnoxious, exposed to (harm).

Obscene, repulsive, loathsome, **233,** 1167.

Obtend, put forward as a reason, allege, **814,** 161; hold out, present in opposition, **655,** 126.

Obtest, entreat, implore.

Offend, wound, hurt, injure, **222,** 323.

Officious, obliging, kind, dutiful.

Oint, anoint.

Once, at some future time, **204,** 32.

Open (of hounds), give tongue, begin to cry when in pursuit on a scent.

Or, ere, before, **474,** 742.

Oraisons, orisons, prayers.

Orb, orbit, **489**¹, 6.

Ore, shore, coast, **255,** 97.

Orient, brilliant, lustrous, **823,** 52.

Ostent, portent, wonder, prodigy; v. **854,** 24, n.

Out (*vb.*), oust, eject.

Overlay, smother by lying on, **767,** 590.

Overlook, oversee, look after, **247,** 2213.

Overpoise, that which outweighs another thing, preponderant weight.

Oversee, overlook, pass over, disregard, **798,** 490.

O'erseen, deceived, deluded, imprudent, **51,** 12.

Overwatch'd, wearied with too much watching or keeping awake, **843,** 344.

Owe, own, possess, **124**², 16.

Owing, indebted, **511**¹, 27.

Pad (*sb.*), saddle (?), **317**¹, 20.

Pad (*vb.*), rob on the highway (not necessarily on foot), **124**², 29.

Padder, footpad, highwayman.

Pain (*sb.*), trouble, difficulty, **30,** 127; *on pain of life,* on pain of forfeiting life, **763,** 253.

Pain (*vb.*), exert, strain, **830,** 627 (Chaucer); used reflexively, **830,** 669.

Painful, troublesome, difficult, **518**¹, 26; laborious, painstaking, **482,** 464.

Painture, painting.

Palliard, debauchee.

Panacee, panace, a fabulous herb to which was ascribed the power of healing all diseases, **697,** 617.

Pardelis (*Lat.*, properly *pardalis*), panther.

Parlous, dangerously cunning, keen, shrewd, **874,** 168.

Paronomasia. v. n. **25**¹, 47.

Pasquin, the Roman Pasquino (man or statue), on whom lampoons were fathered; jester, lampooner, **215,** 2.

Passive, suffering, unresisting, submissive; cf. n. **617,** 554.

Pastern, used of the human ankle, **873,** 52.

Patient, enduring, endurant of, **704,** 1157.

Pay, smear, cover (with pitch, tar, and the like).

Peaking, sneaking, mean-spirited, **173¹,** 15.

Peel, plunder, strip of possessions, **816,** 343.

Peregrine. v. n. **19¹,** 37.

Perfume' (*sb.*).

Persecute, pursue, chase, hunt, **449,** 416.

Per'spective, an optical instrument for viewing objects (telescope, microscope, etc.), **12,** 77.

Philology, the study of literature in a wide sense, polite learning, **743¹,** 34.

Philosophy, the knowledge or study of nature, science, **289²,** 23.

Phylacte'ry, box containing texts of Scripture, worn by Jews during morning prayer on all days except the Sabbath, **223,** 399.

Picture, the art of painting, **414,** 36.

Piety, filial affection, dutifulness, **114,** 419.

Pile (*Lat.*), heavy javelin, **227,** 733, n.

Plagiary, plagiarist, **26¹,** 54.

Plaister (*vb.*), plaster, **477,** 63.

Plant, colonize, settle, **243,** 1883.

Plastron, leather-covered pad, worn by fencers over the chest, **340,** 349.

Pleasure, give pleasure to, **899¹,** 12.

Plume (*sb.*), quill pen, pen, **65¹,** 10.

Plume (*vb.*), pluck, strip, strip off.

Plump, flock, **437,** 16.

Point, witty or ingenious turn of thought, **360,** 167; cf. **919,** 331–364.

Pointed, appointed, **199¹,** 32.

Poll'd. v. n. **243,** 1925.

Poltron', poltroon, coward, **817,** 413.

Pomp, splendid show, pageant, **112,** 242.

Poppit, poppet, doll, idol, **245,** 2074.

Porket, porker, young pig.

Portent'.

Pory, porous, **483,** 536.

Pounce, claw, talon.

Pounc'd, having pounces or talons, **250,** 2411.

Pounder, something weighing a pound (*fig.*)? **341,** 488.

Pounder pear, pound pear, a large variety of cooking pear, **455,** 127.

Pox, name of disease, used in imprecations, **124²,** 18. (Cf. use of *Plague*.)

Pox'd, infected with the disease *pox*, **131,** 266.

Poynant, poignant, **823,** 21.

Practice, frequent, **120,** 825.

Præscious, prescious, prescient, having foreknowledge, **674,** 242.

Prease, press, throng, **637,** 933.

Precession, procession, n. **530,** 671 (misprint?).

Predicament, category, **118,** 680.

Prefer, bring forward, submit (bill, indictment, etc.), **245,** 2075.

Prejudicate (*adj.*), formed prior to knowledge, preconceived, **315²,** 15.

Prelude' (*vb.*), **851,** 451; **Pre'lude** (*vb.*), **256,** 187.

Preludium, prelude, introduction, **869,** 330.

Prepossess, preoccupy, take previous possession of, **658,** 397.

Presage (*vb. trans.*), foretell, give warning of, **205,** 148; have a presentiment of, forebode, **753,** 118; (*vb. intrans.*), have foreknowledge, **450,** 483.

Presage' (*sb.*), prognostic, omen, **255,** 141; presentiment, prophetic impression, **136,** 131; foreknowledge, prescience, **750,** 41.

Present (*vb. trans.*), give a present to, **501²,** 2; (*vb. intrans.*), appear, **15,** 11.

Presume of, presume upon, rely upon as a reason for boldness, **223,** 388.

Prethee, prithee, I pray thee.

Prevail, avail, **115,** 461.

Prevaricate (*vb. trans.*), pervert, make swerve from the normal application or meaning, **160²,** 21.

Prevent, anticipate, come before, forestall, **6,** 131; **668,** 1133 illustrates the passage from this to the usual modern meaning. A corresponding transfer of meaning is found in the noun **Prevention ;** cf. **233,** 1145.

Prime, spring, **242,** 1830.

Probationer, person on probation, or trial as to his fitness for an office or state, **212,** 21.

Procedure, course of action, conduct, **8,** 88.

Process, course of proceedings in a trial at court, **604,** 837.

Prole, prowl, **240,** 1707.

Proponent, one who lays down a proposition or law, **219,** 121. See note on line.

Propriety, right of possession, **500²,** 38.

Pro'spective, telescope, **260²,** 3; cf. **Per'spective.**

Protend, stretch out, thrust forward, **788,** 104.

Protract, delay, defer, **240,** 1677.

Protractive, delaying, of putting off, **249,** 2397.

Prove, make trial of, test, **618,** 610.

Provoke (*vb. trans.*), challenge, **596,** 252; call forth, arouse, awake, **897,** 539; propose (health of some one), **464,** 771; (*vb. intrans.*), appeal, **166,** 346.

Pruce, Prussia, **768,** 31 (Chaucer).

Prune up, of birds, dress the feathers with the bill; used figuratively, **81,** 13.

Ptisan, a mild, harmless drink, or one slightly medicinal, as barley water or herb tea, **210,** 16.

Punk, prostitute, strumpet.

Pupil, ward, person under the care of a guardian.

Purchase (*vb.*), acquire otherwise than by inheritance, **357,** n. 7.

Purchase (*sb.*), that which is acquired otherwise than by inheritance, **8,** 86.

Purfle, border, decorate richly on the edge, **847,** 163 (suggested by Dryden's original).

Pursevant, pursuivant, one of the third and lowest order of heraldic officers, **848,** 250.

Puss, 411¹, 32; cf. **Cat.**

Quaint, skilled in the use of fine language, clever, smart, **680,** 698.

Quarry, bird flown at by a hawk, **219,** 104; animal pursued by hounds, **225,** 593 (opposed to *vermin* or ignoble prey).

Quartil aspect, position of two heavenly bodies distant 90° from each other (an unfriendly aspect), **758,** 500.

Queasy, of the stomach, easily upset, unable to

digest strong food; of conscience, tender, scrupulous, **260**[1], 16.

Quinquina. v. n. **489**[2], 25.

Rack (*sb.*), mass of clouds driven before the wind in the upper air, **696**, 544.

Rack (*vb. intrans.*), drive before the wind (of clouds), **133**[1], 33; (*vb. trans.*), strain as on the rack, give a forced interpretation to, **130**, 156.

Radii (*Lat. pl.*), sort of olive tree, **455**, 124.

Rage, madness, insanity, **545**, 710.

Rampire, rampart (*fig.*), **817**, 401.

Ranch, tear, cut.

Rap (*vb. ; pret.* **Rapt**), carry off, seize, **2**, 52; *rap and rend*, seize and take away violently, **172**, 54.

Rash, cut, slash, **653**, 1094.

Rathe (*adv.*), quickly, early, **455**, 134.

Raven, have a gluttonous desire for, **248**, 2258.

Rebate, blunt, make dull, **775**, 502.

Recepta'cle, place into which persons retire, **846**, 61.

Recess, retiring, withdrawal, **588**, 772.

Rechless, reckless, heedless, **783**, 1074.

Record' (*sb.*), **761**, 115.

Recover (*vb. trans.*), cure, heal, **923**, 778 (Soame).

Reek, rick, stack of hay or grain, **787**, 35.

Re'fectory, eating room, especially of a convent, **242**, 1824.

Refer, bring back, reproduce, represent, **886**, 550.

Reflective, reflected, **47**, 1012.

Refuge, afford a refuge to, shelter, protect, **574**, 779.

Refuse, outcast portion of some class of persons, leavings, **634**, 726. (See note on line.)

Regalio, regalo, present of choice food or drink, elegant repast, **53**[2], 12.

Regorge, swallow back, **794**, 186.

Reject, throw back, put away into a place, **520**[2], 10.

Relation, relationship, kinship, **127**[2], 45.

Release, relax, moderate, **536**, 32.

Relict, relic, **144**, 544 (Tate ?).

Remainders, remnants, **243**, 1896.

Remark, observation, **8**, 82.

Remember, remind, **500**[2], 19.

Remorse, pity, compassion, **663**, 743.

Rend, tear in pieces, **764**, 347; *rap and rend*, v. **Rap.**

Render, give back, restore, **813**, 146; give up, surrender, **474**, 744.

Renegado, renegade.

Renounce. v. n. **125**[1], 34.

Renown, make famous, celebrate, **163**, 75.

Repair (*sb.*), haunt, usual abode, **44**, 886.

Repeat, seek again, return to, **47**, 1028; repeat itself, occur again, **275**, 290.

Repose, place or leave in the control of another, **206**, 238.

Represent, present a second time, give back; v. n. **25**[2], 40.

Reprise, reprisal, act of taking something by way of retaliation.

Republic (*adj.*), republican, pertaining to a republic, **132**, 301.

Require, ask for, demand, **897**, 559; seek after, search for, **466**, 160.

Resolve (*vb. trans.*), melt, dissolve, **223**, 446; (*vb. intrans.*), dissolve, change into, **274**, 229.

Rest, remainder, remnant, **236**, 1379.

Restiff, restive, inactive, declining to go forward, **209**, 472; intractable, refractory, **817**, 416.

Restore, give back (*fig.*), **410**, 194; bring back to mental calm, **485**, 671.

Resty, sluggish, lazy, **170**, 76.

Reti'nue.

Retire (*vb. trans.*), withdraw, remove, take away, **47**, 995.

Revenge, punishment, chastisement, **485**, 660; *in revenge*, in compensation, **385**[2], 46.

Reve'nue.

Review, see again, **546**, 787.

Ridgeling, Ridgil ; half castrated male animal.

Rivel'd, shrivel'd, wrinkled.

Rock, distaff, staff or frame used to hold wool or flax for spinning.

Rondeau, form of lyric poetry characterized by repetition of a refrain, and by a limited number of rhymes. The stanza on p. 263 is not in the strict *rondeau* form.

Rope, be drawn into a thread (of some glutinous element), drop stickily, **458**, 333.

Rout, throng, mob, rabble, **831**, 742.

Rovers. *Shoot at rovers.* v. n. **284**[2], 25.

Ruelle. v. n. **490**[1], 7.

Rummer, large and tall drinking glass, used particularly for Rhenish wine, **215**, 45.

Sacred, devoted to destruction, accursed, **552**, 80 (*Latinism*).

Sagacious, keen-scented, **225**, 577.

Saint. Sarcastically of a Puritan, **832**, 796.

Sallow, willow, **803**, 78.

Salve, soothe as with a salve, redeem, **206**, 243.

Salvo, reservation, excuse, saving clause, **226**, 606.

Saplin, sapling, **834**, 129.

Sarcenet, a fine thin silken fabric, **340**, 364.

Satiate, satiated, glutted, **661**, 574.

Saver. v. n. **239**, 1638.

Savory, savorily, with a relish, **264**[2], 2.

Sawtry, psaltery, stringed instrument somewhat resembling the harp, **850**, 358.

Scabrous, rough, harsh, unmusical, **304**[2], 3.

Scandal, throw scandal upon, traduce, **853**, 607.

Scape (*sb.*), escape, **152**, 1095 (Tate).

Scape (*vb.*), escape.

Schilling, Dutch coin, **376**, 281.

Scour (*vb. trans.*), run over and disperse, **103**, 39; (*vb. intrans.*), roam streets at night, **332**, 440.

Scouring (*sb.*), **74**[2], 19; cf. **Scour.**

Scout (*sb.*), act of scouting or spying, **695**, 528.

Sculler, skiff, boat rowed by one man with sculls, **486**, 735.

Seal, mark as with a seal, bear witness to the genuineness of.

Seam (*sb.*), grease, tallow, lard, **621**, 867.

Search, search for, seek, **500**[2], 23.

Searcloth, cover with searcloth (cerecloth, cloth smeared with wax or similar substance), **39**, 590.

Secure, sure, certain, **800**, 626; *secure of*, safe

from, **855,** 125; (by an ellipsis) safe from finding, **336,** 90.

Securely, without risk or danger, confidently, without fear; in **450, 469** the sense is apparently " without inspiring fear, harmlessly."

Sem, Shem, son of Noah.

Sennight, week.

Sensible, capable of receiving impressions, appreciative, **670,** 1230; *sensible of,* sensitive to, **500[1],** 29.

Sentence, maxim; short saying, usually containing moral instruction, **309[2],** 18.

Sequacious, following, inclined to follow, **253,** 50.

Seraphims, seraphs, **927[1],** 8.

Set, wager, lay a stake, **52,** 54.

Settle, bench, especially one with a high back, to accommodate two or more persons, **802,** 44.

Severely, harshly, mercilessly, **604,** 779.

Shard, leaves or leafstalks of the artichoke and some other vegetables, blanched for table use, **201,** 82; dung, ordure, **222,** 321.

Share, cut, cleave, **652,** 1019.

Sheer (*vb.*), shear, cut; v. n. **34,** 311.

Shelf, sand bank, reef, shoal, **229,** 829.

Shent, injured, destroyed, ruined.

Sherd, shard, fragment of pottery, **803,** 86.

Sheriff. v. n. **153,** 42.

Shipwrack, Shipwrack'd, shipwreck, shipwrecked.

Shog (*sb.*), jog, shock, **78[2],** 28.

Shole, shoal, throng of people, **332,** 395.

Shore, sewer; *common shore,* public sewer, **232,** 1130.

Show, appear, **16,** 137.

Shrewdly, sharply, severely, **236,** 1427.

Shrieve, sheriff, **156[2],** 3.

Sice, six-spot (at dice), **367,** 93.

Sigil. v. n. **853,** 606.

Silly, guileless, helpless, weak, **565,** *l36.*

Simagre, grimace, **404,** 31.

Simar, long robe or light covering worn by women (used loosely, without precise meaning), **850,** 341; **891,** 100.

Sincere, unmixed, unalloyed, **891,** 48; unhurt, uninjured, **855,** 133.

Sincerely, unmixedly, absolutely, **110,** 43.

Sinis'ter.

Skinker, tapster, server of drink, **822,** 803.

Slaver, drivel, suffer spittle to run from the mouth, **892,** 179.

Slidder, slide clumsily or timorously, **546,** 749.

Slight, sleight, cunning trick, **244,** 2004.

Smother, that which smothers, thick dust, **547,** 827.

Snag, rough branch of a tree, **671,** 10.

Snip, shred, small scrap, **900[1],** 14.

Sophisticate, corrupt, adulterated, not genuine, **17,** 6.

Sort, flock, collection, **247,** 2240.

Sot, fool, booby, **186,** 151.

Sound (*vb.*), swoon, **752,** 56.

Souse, swoop down (hawking term), **637,** 931.

South, move towards the south, **484,** 577.

Sovereign, all-powerful, royal, potent.

Spawl, saliva ejected, **364,** 63.

Speaker. v. n. **873,** 84.

Species, sensible presentation, visible image, **625,** 36.

Spet, spit.

Spettle, spittle.

Spire, spiral, curl, **731,** 29.

Spirit, breeze, **459,** 447 (*Latinism*); in **84[1],** 30 apparently pronounced as one syllable (cf. **Sprite**).

Spirit'ual, 232, 1097.

Spoom, sail before a strong wind, **236,** 1390.

Springal, active young man, youth, **353,** 479.

Springe, noose or snare attached to an elastic bough or other object, and, when released, catching the game by flying into the air.

Sprite, spirit, **234,** 1225; cf. **Spirit.**

Spurn, kick, **828,** 435.

Squander (*vb. trans.*), scatter, disperse (of troops or ships), **543,** 571.

Squeasy, queasy, squeamish, **169[1],** 26.

Squintifego, squinting, **376,** 271.

Staff, stanza, **517[2],** 6.

Startle (*vb. intrans.*), move suddenly, as with fright, **778,** 701.

Starve, die, pine away, **757,** 441.

State, commonwealth, republic, **110,** 66; cf. n. **71,** 22.

Stead, frame of a bed, **803,** 78.

Steep, abrupt ascent, steep height, **272,** 91.

Steepy, steep, precipitous.

Steerage, apparatus for steering or directing a course, **843,** 351.

Stench. v. n. **5,** 48.

Sterve, same as **Starve.**

Stew'd. v. n. **79[1],** 24. Christie explains *stew'd,* if it be correct, as " made meager by stewing."

Stickle, separate combatants by intervening, **289[1],** 31; quarrel pertinaciously on slight grounds, **172,** 63.

Stickler. v. n. **5,** 41, and cf. **Stickle.**

Stigmatize, mark with a stigma or brand of disgrace, **223,** 401.

Still (*adv.*), uniformly, always, **778,** 698.

Still (*vb. trans.*), drop, **722,** 323.

Straighten'd, straitened, cramped, **10,** 245.

Strain, embrace, **485,** 726.

Strict, tight, close, **578,** 48.

Stridor, harsh, shrill noise, **705,** 1258.

Stub, stump, end of fallen tree remaining in the ground, **766,** 535.

Stum. v. n. **131,** 270.

Style (*sb.*). v. n. **760,** 34.

Style (*vb.*), write, describe, **151,** 1051 (Tate).

Submit, lower, **16,** 139; v. n. **10,** 249.

Suborn, procure secretly or unlawfully, **801,** 718.

Suburbian, suburban, **135,** 83.

Succeed (*vb. trans.*), give prosperity to, cause to succeed, **50,** 1168; take the place of, **544,** 617; (*vb. intrans.*), approach, cleave to, **474,** 758; descend, **429,** 7.

Success, outcome, result, **510[2],** 12.

Successive, by succession, hereditary, **113,** 301.

Suc'cessor, 852, 556.

Succors, succor, troops serving as aid or assistance, **922[2]** (*Connection*).

Suffice, supply adequately, **820,** 653.

Suffis'd, satisfied, sated, **225,** 554, n.

Suffragating, voting, having right of suffrage, **106**[1], 31.

Suiting, suitable, suited, **793**, 44.

Sumner, summoner, an officer whose duty was to summon persons to appear in court, **746**[1], 28 (Chaucer).

Superfice, surface, **457**, 316.

Surcoat, loose robe worn by knights over the armor, **754**, 148.

Swabber, person who uses a swab, or cleaning mop, on board ship, **376**, 215.

Swage, assuage, soothe, **148**, 781 (Tate).

Sweepy, moving with a sweeping motion, **622**, 937.

Swerve, climb by winding or turning, **544**, 604.

Swill, drink greedily or to excess, **236**, 1418.

Swinge, whip, chastise, punish, **52**[1], 2.

Swizzer, Swiss, native of Switzerland.

Swound (*sb.*), swoon, **781**, 982.

Table. v. n. **751**, 130.

Take, betake one's self, **485**, 662.

Tale, numbering, count, **479**, 212.

Tally, duplicate, counterpart, **274**, 256.

Tarpauling, tarpaulin, canvas made waterproof with tar.

Tawny, tan color, buff.

Tax, accuse, censure, reproach, **238**, 1521.

Tear, rage, rant, bluster, **124**[2], 14.

Teemless, unfruitful, barren, **221**, 228.

Teint, tint, color, **415**, 178.

Tell, count, **298**[1], 24.

Temper, middle course, **251**, 2525.

Tetter, a skin disease of animals, **473**, 672.

That, so that, **851**, 428.

Theologue, theologian, divine, **250**, 2441.

Thick, rapidly, fast, **37**, 478.

Threat, threaten.

Thrid (*sb.* and *vb.*), thread.

Throughly, thoroughly, completely, **211**[1], 14.

Tiller, till, drawer, **340**, 384.

Timely, betimes, in good season, **9**, 190.

Tine, tind, kindle, set fire to, **820**, 635.

Tinkle, ring (of the ears)?, **834**, 94. (C. D. explains as *tingle ;* Webster, as *hear, or resound with, a small, sharp sound.*)

Tire, tier or row of cannon, battery, **239**, 1611.

Tit, girl (used in contempt), **401**, 14.

Tony (abbreviation for *Antony*), simpleton, **80**[2], 15.

Too too, altogether too, excessively, **8**, 111.

Top, excel, do one's utmost, **136**, 167.

Towardly, ready to learn, docile, promising.

Trade, implements of any occupation, **471**, 535.

Traditive, based on tradition, traditional.

Traduction, derivation by descent, inheritance, **212**, 23.

Tralineate, deviate, stray, **877**, 396.

Translate, transfer, transplant, **458**, 361.

Travail, Travel. These two verbs (*labor,* and *make a journey*) are of identical origin, and were not differentiated in Dryden's time. (This is true also of the corresponding nouns.) In some cases, as **240**, 1705, it is hard to tell which sense is the more prominent. The present text preserves the spelling of the original editions.

Travelour, traveler.

Traverse, deny formally, oppose, **784**, 12.

Treas'nous, treasonable.

Trim away, waste by attempting to hold a middle course, waste by vacillation, **241**, 1795.

Trine (*sb.*). v. n. **50**, 1165:

Trin'd, joined in the aspect of a *trine,* **773**, 389.

Triumph' (*vb.*), **696**, 565.

Trivet, three-legged stool or stand; *trivet table,* three-legged table, **803**, 84.

Trumpet, trumpeter, **848**, 228.

Tumbril, tumbrel, dung cart, **825**, 251.

Tun, large cask, specifically one holding 252 wine-gallons.

Turbant, turban.

Turmoil', disturb, agitate, trouble, **526**, 381.

Turney, tourney, tournament.

Tuzz, tuft of hair.

Twillet, twilt (?), quilt, **172**, 50. (Christie, however, emends the text to *toilet,* which may be correct, in the sense of "toilet-service, articles used in making the toilet;" or, less probably, in that of "cloth to be thrown over the shoulders during hair-dressing.")

Two-handed, extra-sized, strapping, powerful.

Tympany, inflation of the belly, bombast, turgidness, **136**, 194.

Unaware, *at unaware,* unexpectedly, by surprise, **758**, 492.

Uncouth, unknown, strange, uncanny, mysterious, **771**, 200.

Uncumber'd, unencumbered, **784**, 18.

Undertake, affirm, guarantee, **828**, 476 (Chaucer).

Undeserving, not meriting. who did not deserve it, **789**, 190.

Undiscern'd, undistinguished, unseparated, **588**, 767.

Unequal, not equal to one's task, incompetent, **121**, 910.

Unfletch'd, unfledged, immature, **53**[1], 14.

Ungodded, not provided with a god, disbelieving in God, atheistical, **245**, 2036.

Unhop'd, unexpected, not looked for, **862**, 657.

Unkemm'd, uncombed, unkempt, **328**, 121.

Unknowing, not knowing how, ignorant, **35**, 384.

Unlade, empty, unload, **50**, 1200.

Unready, not ready, not prepared, **47**, 1016.

Unresisted, resistless, irresistible, **188**, 4.

Unrooted, uprooted, torn up by the roots.

Unruffle, become smooth, cease to be agitated, **524**, 212.

Unsatiate, insatiate, insatiable, **122**, 987.

Unsincere, **44**, 833; opposite of **Sincere.**

Unspell, disenchant, **139**, 117.

Unteach, cause to be forgotten, destroy the teaching of, **257**, 284.

Unthrift, unthrifty person, prodigal, **239**, 1590.

Untune, make inharmonious, **518**[2], 12; v. n. **253**, 63.

Use, accustom, **444**, 63.

Utmost, outmost, farthest, last, **933**, 389.

Vail, profit, tip, money given to a servant by a visitor, **331**, 311.

Vallancy wig, large wig that shades the face, **74²**, 8.

Value, esteem, regard, **737²**, 8.

Van, wing, **863**, 750.

Vare, wand or staff of authority, **117**, 595.

Various, diversified, opposite of monotonous, **802²**, 50; many-colored, variegated, **638**, 2.

Vegetive, vegetative, vegetable, **783**, 1076.

Vehicle, a substance in which medicine is taken, **124¹**, 19.

Vent (vb.), snort, scent (of a hound). **619**, 667.

Verjuice, the juice of crab apples, unripe grapes, and the like; an acid liquor made from such juice, **371**, 73.

Vernish, varnish, **803**, 105.

Vest (sb.). v. n. **53²**, 44; garment, robe, **614**, 340.

Vest (vb.), clothe.

View (sb.), look, gaze, **561**, 780.

Vile, low, mean, of small value, worthless, **461**, 602.

Villanize, debase, degrade, **877**, 405.

Vindicative, vindictive, **89¹**, 4.

Virago, strong, robust woman (without bad sense), **193**, 39.

Virelay, old French form of poem, in short lines, running on two rhymes, with refrain, **850**, 365.

Vizard, Vizard-mask, mask concealing face, person wearing such a mask (a cant term for a courtesan), **62¹**, 13; **67¹**, 4.

Volume, coil, convolution, **579**, 113.

Votress, votaress, female votary, **771**, 225.

Vouch, call to witness, **230**, 951.

Vulgar, common, well-known, **362**, n. 15.

Wait, accompany, escort, attend with respect, **225**, 557.

Wallow. v. n. **78²**, 22.

Want (vb. trans.), be without, lack, **112**, 197; (vb. intrans.), be absent, be lacking, **797**, 372.

Wanting, needy, poor, **48**, 1093.

Ward, defense, protection, **531**, 691.

Warn, admonish, summon, **669**, 1197.

Warp (vb. intrans.), bend, turn, swerve, **585**, 584.

Weazon, weasand, wind pipe.

Weigh, raise, lift up, undertake, **611**, 67.

Well-breath'd, long-breathed, having strong lungs, **117**, 631.

Well-manag'd, well-trained, **670**, 1226.

Wex, wax, increase (of the moon), **901²**, 30.

When (int.), used as an exclamation of impatience, **366**, 12.

Whirlbat, Whorlbat, cestus, sort of boxing glove used by Greeks and Romans, **749¹**, 23, **464**, 30.

Wilder, lead astray, bewilder, **234**, 1254.

Wilding, a wild plant or its fruit; especially a wild crab apple, **388**, 135.

Wilful, voluntary, **235**, 1287.

Wimble, gimlet, **371**, 68.

Winch, wince, **236**, 1427.

Winking, closed (of the eyes), **832**, 800 (Chaucer).

Wit, intellect, intelligence, judgment, sense, **25¹**, 28; person of intellect, genius, **605**, 899.

Witness, testimony, evidence, **218**, 62.

Wittol, contented cuckold, man who knows his wife's infidelity and submits to it, **169**, 48.

Woe (adj.), woful, sorrowful, wretched, **873**, 108 (really a noun, used as subject of was).

Wonderful, wonderfully, **745²**, 38.

Woodbind, woodbine.

Wreathe (vb. trans.), twist, **663**, 745.

Writ of ease. v. **Ease, Writ of.**

Writhe, twist, whirl, **659**, 448.

Writhen, twisted, whirled, **604**, 802.

Yet, in addition, **767**, 576.

Zambra, "Moorish festival or feast, attended with dancing and music" (Velasquez, *Spanish Dictionary*), **63¹**.

INDEX OF FIRST LINES

INDEX OF TITLES